PSYCHOLOGY

SECOND EUROPEAN EDITION

DANIEL SCHACTER

DANIEL GILBERT

DANIEL WEGNER

BRUCE HOOD

palgrave

First published 2016 by
PALGRAVE

Palgrave in the UK is an imprint of Macmillan Publishers Limited, registered in England, company number 785998, of 4 Crinan Street, London, N1 9XW.

Palgrave Macmillan in the US is a division of St Martin's Press LLC, 175 Fifth Avenue, New York, NY 10010.

Palgrave is a global imprint of the above companies and is represented throughout the world.

Palgrave® and Macmillan® are registered trademarks in the United States, the United Kingdom, Europe and other countries.

ISBN 978–1–137–40674–3

This book is printed on paper suitable for recycling and made from fully managed and sustained forest sources. Logging, pulping and manufacturing processes are expected to conform to the environmental regulations of the country of origin.

A catalogue record for this book is available from the British Library.

A catalog record for this book is available from the Library of Congress.

Printed in China

To my girls, Kim, Martha and Esmé

Bruce Hood

We dedicate this edition to the memory of Dan Wegner, our co-author, colleague and deeply missed friend

Daniel Schacter and Daniel Gilbert

About the authors

DANIEL SCHACTER is William R. Kenan, Jr Professor of Psychology at Harvard University. Dan received his BA from the University of North Carolina at Chapel Hill. He subsequently developed a keen interest in amnesiac disorders associated with various kinds of brain damage. He continued his research and education at the University of Toronto, where he received his PhD in 1981. He taught at the faculty at Toronto for the next six years before joining the psychology department at the University of Arizona in 1987. In 1991, he joined the faculty at Harvard University. His research explores the relation between conscious and unconscious forms of memory, the nature of distortions and errors in remembering, and the ways in which we use memory to imagine future events. Many of Schacter's studies are summarized in his 1996 book, *Searching for Memory: The Brain, The Mind, and The Past*, and his 2001 book, *The Seven Sins of Memory: How the Mind Forgets and Remembers*, both winners of the American Psychological Association's William James Book Award. Schacter has also received a number of awards for teaching and research, including the Harvard-Radcliffe Phi Beta Kappa Teaching Prize, the Warren Medal from the Society of Experimental Psychologists, and the Award for Distinguished Scientific Contributions from the American Psychological Association. In 2013, he was elected to the National Academy of Sciences.

DANIEL GILBERT is Edward Pierce Professor of Psychology at Harvard University. Dan received his BA from the University of Colorado at Denver and his PhD from Princeton University. From 1985 to 1996, he taught at the University of Texas, Austin, and in 1996, he joined the faculty of Harvard University. He has received the American Psychological Association's Distinguished Scientific Award for an Early Career Contribution to Psychology, the Diener Award for Outstanding Contributions to Social Psychology, and has won teaching awards that include the Phi Beta Kappa Teaching Prize and the Harvard College Professorship. His research focuses on how and how well people think about their emotional reactions to future events. He is the author of the international bestseller *Stumbling on Happiness*, which won the Royal Society's General Prize for best popular science book of 2007, and he is the co-writer and host of the PBS television series *This Emotional Life*.

DANIEL WEGNER was the John Lindsley Professor of Psychology in Memory of William James at Harvard University. He received his BS in 1970 and PhD in 1974, both from Michigan State University. He began his teaching career at Trinity University in San Antonio, Texas, before his appointments at the University of Virginia in 1990 and then Harvard University in 2000. He was a Fellow of the American Academy of Arts and Sciences and also recipient of the William James Award from the Association for Psychological Science, the Award for Distinguished Scientific Contributions from the American Psychological Association, and the Distinguished Scientist Award from the Society of Experimental Social Psychology. His research focused on thought suppression and mental control, transactive memory in relationships and groups, and the experience of conscious will. His work on thought suppression and consciousness served as the basis of two popular books, *White Bears and Other Unwanted Thoughts* and *The Illusion of Conscious Will*, both of which were named *Choice* Outstanding Academic Titles. He died in 2013.

BRUCE HOOD is Professor of Developmental Psychology in Society at the University of Bristol and Director of the Bristol Cognitive Development Centre. He received his MA and MPhil in psychology from the University of Dundee and his PhD in developmental cognitive neuroscience from the University of Cambridge. He was a research fellow at Hughes Hall, Cambridge, a lecturer at University College London, a visiting scientist at MIT and a faculty professor at Harvard. He has been awarded an Alfred P. Sloan Research Fellowship in Neuroscience, the Young Investigator Award from the International Society of Infancy Researchers and the Robert L. Fantz Memorial Award. He is a Fellow of the Society of American Psychological Science, the British Psychological Society, the Royal Society of Biology and the Royal Institution of Great Britain. He is also President of the British Science Association Psychology Section. He has a wide range of research interests with a developmental and neuroscience perspective. He is the author of three popular science books, *SuperSense: From Superstition to Religion – the Brain Science of Belief*, *The Self Illusion: Why There is No 'You' Inside Your Head*, and *The Domesticated Brain*. In 2011 he was invited to deliver the prestigious Royal Institution Christmas Lectures 'Meet Your Brain', which were broadcast on the BBC. He is founder of the world's largest academic speakers' website, speakezee.org.

Brief contents

Long contents

List of figures

List of tables

Preface

For most of our adult lives, we have been studying the human mind and teaching our students what we and other psychologists have learned about it. We've each written articles in professional journals to convey our findings and ideas to our colleagues, and we've each published popular nonfiction titles to communicate with the general public. For each of us, though, something important has been missing: a text written specifically for students. Reading a textbook should be just as engaging as reading a popular book, and we've worked hard to make sure that happens in *Psychology*.

Talking about psychology from a new perspective

As we wrote this textbook, we found ourselves confronting a question: Why were we attracted to psychology in the first place? Although we each have different interests in psychology that cover a broad range of the field – from cognitive psychology to social psychology to developmental psychology and neuroscience – we all share a common fascination with the errors, illusions, biases and other mental mistakes that reveal how the mind works.

We believe psychology is interesting in large part because it offers insights into the errors of human thought and action. Some of these errors are familiar and amusing (why do we forget jokes the moment we've heard them?), and others are exceptional and tragic (what causes a pilot to fail to deploy his landing gear on approach?). But all of them cry out for explanation. Indeed, if our thoughts, feelings and actions were error free, our lives would be orderly, predictable and dull – and there would be few mysteries for psychology to illuminate.

But human behaviour is endlessly surprising, and its surprises are what motivate us to understand the psychological complexities that produce them. Why is memory so prone to error, and what can be done to improve it? How can people discriminate against others even when they're trying hard not to? How can mobs make normal people behave like monsters? What allows a child with an IQ of 50 to compose a symphony? How can newborn babies know about kinetics and occlusion when they can't even find their own fingers? Psychology offers the possibility of answering such questions from a scientific perspective, and it is this possibility that drew us to the field.

Explaining the 'mindbugs' approach

Every rambunctious child knows that you can learn how a toy works by breaking it. If you want to understand things so that you can eventually fix them and even build new ones, knowing how they break is invaluable. When things break, we learn about the pieces and processes that normally work together. Breakdown and error are not just about destruction and failure – they are paths to knowledge. Psychology has long followed these paths. The 'bugs' of the human mind reveal a great deal about its function, structure and design. For example:

- Freud and other pioneers studied psychological disorders not only to alleviate human misery, but because the disordered mind provides a window through which to view normal psychological functioning
- The social blunders of people with autism teach us how human beings usually manage to have such seamless interactions
- Depression teaches us how most people deal so effectively with the losses and heartbreaks of everyday life
- Visual illusions teach us how the eye and brain normally generate visual experiences that correspond so faithfully to the realities they represent.

These and other examples of mindbugs are integrated throughout the chapters:

- Phantom limb syndrome, in which amputees can feel their missing limbs moving and even feel pain in their absent limbs, sheds light on plasticity in the brain (Chapter 3, p. 111)
- The experience of synaesthesia, where certain musical notes can evoke visual sensations of certain colours or certain sounds can produce an experience of specific tastes, provides clues about how perception works (Chapter 4, pp. 132–3)
- The 'seven sins' of memory are aspects of forgetting and distortion that show how people reconstruct their pasts and also reveal the adaptive functions of memory (Chapter 5, pp. 220–1)
- Savants, such as an English boy named Christopher who was fluent in 16 languages yet lacked the cognitive capacities to live on his own, provide striking evidence that cognition is composed of distinct abilities (Chapter 7, p. 267)
- Stereotyping teaches us how people use categories to make predictions about objects and events they have never seen before (Chapter 14, pp. 596–601)
- Placebo treatments such as sugar pills or therapies with no 'active ingredients' can still sometimes be effective and so show how susceptible we are to psychological influences on our health (Chapter 17, pp. 696–8).

Our experience as teachers suggests that students are every bit as fascinated by these mental oddities as we are. So we've incorporated these inherently interesting examples of human behaviour throughout the text. Derived from the idea of 'computer bugs', we refer to these examples as 'mindbugs'. Mindbugs are useful in illuminating the mechanisms of human psychology: they relate seemingly different topics to one another and highlight the strengths of the human mind as well as its vulnerabilities. We have used these errors, mistakes and behavioural oddities as a thematic focus in each of the domains traditionally covered by introductory textbooks.

This approach has at least two benefits:

1. It provides a conceptual linkage between chapters on normal psychological functions (such as memory, perception and emotion) and chapters on pathology (such as psychological disorders and mental health).
2. Psychologists know that most errors occur when normally adaptive mechanisms temporarily misbehave. For example, the tendency to stereotype others is not merely a bad habit acquired from ignorant parents but a misuse of the normally adaptive tendency to categorize objects and then use what one knows about the category to prejudge the object itself. A focus on mindbugs invites students to think of the mind as an adaptive solution to the problems that human beings face in the real world.

The brain and the classic issues in psychology

Just as psychologists come to understand the mind by observing the instances in which it fails and considering the problems it has adapted to solve, they also understand the mind by examining the brain. Traditionally, psychologists have relied on nature's occasional and inexact experiments to teach them about the function of the brain, and the study of brain-damaged patients continues to be an important source of new information. In the past two decades, emerging neuroimaging technologies, such as functional magnetic resonance imaging (fMRI) and positron emission tomography (PET), have allowed psychologists to peer deep into the healthy, living brain as well. These two methods have led to the birth of a new field called 'cognitive neuroscience', and the findings from this field are already shedding light on some interesting and familiar problems. Consider these examples:

- When people have hallucinations, do they actually see pink elephants and hear the voice of God? Neuroimaging studies have shown that visual and auditory hallucinations are accompanied by increased activity in the regions of the brain normally activated by real visual and auditory experience. This suggests that people really are seeing and hearing during hallucinatory episodes.
- When people claim to remember satanic rituals and childhood sexual abuse, are they really remembering? Neuroimaging studies have revealed that false memories are accompanied by activity in the regions of the brain normally associated with true memories, suggesting that people who claim to remember such events are, in fact, having a memorial experience.
- When people cannot describe how they got somewhere but drove there 'on autopilot', have they really learned the route? Studies of amnesiac patients have revealed that when the patients practise a task, they generally show improvements similar to those of healthy volunteers, despite the fact that they cannot remember ever having performed the task.

Cases such as these provide a natural entry to discussions of fundamental issues in perception, memory and motivation. The brain is the basis of all psychological phenomena, and imaging technologies reveal how the brain creates the miracle of the mind. Our decision to integrate neuroscience in this way reflects the current direction in which the field of psychology is moving. The brain is no longer just the province of specialists – the widespread use of imaging techniques has allowed a whole generation of researchers who study cognition, development, personality, emotion and social psychology to become excited about the possibility of learning how the brain and the mind are interrelated. We have attempted to bring this excitement and new knowledge to introductory students through vivid case illustrations, brain images and nontechnical explanations.

Written to inspire, teach and respect students' intelligence

An introduction to psychology should focus on what is most important and what is most compelling. It should not be a rehashing of all things psychological. To ensure that *Psychology* offers the very best of psychological science, we formed our contributing consultants board and expert reviewer panel in areas outside our own areas of expertise. They advised us on early drafts and throughout the writing process, explaining what is important, what is true, and how to think about the issues and data in their respective fields. Taking this information, we have addressed topics in each subfield of psychology in the greater context of that field as a whole. Each chapter has a narrative arc that tells the story of that field of psychology and provides a thematic context that will hook students from the start. In writing *Psychology*, we have made informed choices about our topic coverage, weighing classic studies and current research to produce a contemporary perspective on the field. We believe that our approach engages students, teaches students, entertains students and, above all, inspires them as we are inspired by psychology.

An additional note for lecturers on the European Edition

Psychology: First European Edition, published in 2012 and based on the original US text *Psychology* by Daniel Schacter, Daniel Gilbert and Daniel Wegner, was thoroughly revised and updated by Bruce Hood to meet the needs of students across Europe, the

UK and beyond. He added a broad range of international research, as well as amusing and interesting cultural references from across the globe.

Drawing on the feedback from a large panel of specialists, every chapter was revised for an international audience and to bring it in line with BPS guidelines for British students. Substantial revisions were made to:

- Chapter 2 **The methods of psychology**: This was adapted and expanded to include more coverage of statistics, such as inferential statistics, t-tests, probability/statistical significance, chi-square, contingency and correlation coefficients. A new section was added on qualitative methods.
- Chapter 5 **Memory**: This was revised to provide a balance between British and global approaches in relation to memory, while also discussing Daniel Schacter's 'seven sins of memory' approach. More emphasis was placed on working memory, flashbulb memory and metamemory.
- Chapter 9 **Intelligence**: This was reworked with a European audience in mind in conjunction with Ian Deary from the University of Edinburgh – one of the world authorities in the field. New sections on emotional intelligence and creativity, and the cognitive basis of intelligence were added.
- Chapter 11 **Development**: This was rewritten and divided into two chapters – Chapter 11 **Cognitive development** and Chapter 12 **Social development.** Coverage of new international research and theories was included, making the chapters at the cutting edge of developmental psychology. There is a strong and distinctive cognitive neuroscience flavour to the new Chapter 11.
- Chapter 16 **Psychological disorders**: The symptom-oriented approach advocated by Bentall was a noteworthy addition to this chapter and is very much a departure from traditional psychiatric diagnosis models. A new section on the difference between DSM and ICD classification systems was added, as well as more discussion of Kraepelin, and a new section on the symptom-oriented approach to diagnosis and on post-traumatic stress disorder (PTSD).

All these additions and changes are maintained in the second edition, and we outline what is new in this textbook below.

New to the second edition

Psychology: Second European Edition has been thoroughly updated with new research and hot topics throughout. Some notable additions are:

- **Two new chapters on social psychology**: the first edition's chapter on social psychology has been hugely expanded and divided into two separate chapters. Chapter 14 **Social relationships** discusses the evolutionary approach, nonverbal communication, reproduction, relationships and loneliness. Chapter 15 **Social groups** examines identifying with groups, stereotyping, social acceptance and attitudes.
- **Brand new *psychomythology* boxes**: these tackle misconceptions about psychology held by the general public, dispelling myths with the use of scientific evidence and logic, and encouraging critical thinking. Examples include:
  - With two choices, it's not always 50:50 (p. 82)
  - You only use 10% of your brain (p. 126)
  - You can learn in your sleep (p. 263)
  - When unsure, it's best to stick to your first hunch (p. 307)
  - People can be hypnotized to kill (p. 352)
  - Money makes you happier (p. 424)
  - Your handwriting can reveal your personality (p. 551)
  - Schizophrenics have a Jekyll and Hyde split personality (p. 666)
- **Brand new *Psychology and me* videos**: these video interviews and associated text boxes feature psychology graduates talking about their current roles as teachers, researchers and practitioners, highlighting what they enjoyed most and found most challenging about their undergraduate degrees and providing nuggets of advice for

students just starting their course. They demonstrate the wide range of careers available to students after they leave university and also the exciting applications of psychological research. See p. xxxii for a list of interviewees.

- **Increased coverage of research methods and statistics:** the second edition has more on qualitative methods and new sections on deduction, induction, Hume and Popper, effect sizes and the problems with significance and probability. **Brand new *stats facts* boxes,** which deal with thorny issues in statistics, are peppered throughout. Examples include:
  - Are women better at multitasking? First ask a Bayesian (p. 139)
  - The dark origins of the Likert scale (p. 602)
  - 'Ch-ch-changes': problems of detecting significant change (p. 440)
- **New *hot science* boxes throughout:** there is at least one new hot science box in every chapter, bringing the second edition right up to date with cutting-edge research and neuroscience. Examples include:
  - Brain soup (p. 88)
  - Wishful seeing (p. 161)
  - Forgive and forget (p. 195)
  - Of mice and men: learning to become fearful (p. 238)
  - 'Far out' thinking (p. 302)
  - Waking the brain (p. 343)
  - Were the Victorians smarter than us? (p. 384)
  - Are you looking for a fight? (p. 398)
  - Darkness makes us shadier characters (p. 608)
  - Fear of holes (p. 642)
  - Ancient wisdom, modern mindfulness (p. 687)
- **New *the real world* boxes, humorous margin anecdotes, and opening vignettes** in selected chapters, for example Alan Turing in Chapter 1, Nelson Mandela in Chapter 14 and narcolepsy in Chapter 8.

The second edition also offers new sections in all chapters, as follows:

Chapter 1 **Psychology: the evolution of a science**

- Epistemology: continental rationalists and British empiricists.
- Early European women pioneers
- Practising psychology in Europe

Chapter 2 **The methods of psychology**

- Deduction, induction and Hume and Popper
- Effect size
- The problems with significance and probability

Chapter 3 **Neuroscience and behaviour**

- Executive functions
- Epigenetics

Chapter 4 **Sensation and perception**

- Study on binding in chicks
- The importance of illusions

Chapter 5 **Memory**

- Childhood reminiscing
- Survival-related encoding
- Computerized working memory training

Chapter 6 **Learning**

- More on Little Albert
- Contingency and blocking

Chapter 7 **Language and thought**

- New study on segmentation in gesture
- Thinking fast and slow

Chapter 8 **Consciousness**

- Halloween study of self-consciousness
- The dreaming brain

Chapter 9 **Intelligence**

- Replication of Shih et al. 1999 Asian priming study
- More on creativity

Chapter 10 **Emotion and motivation**

- Botox and mimicking emotional expression
- More on Capgras syndrome and the function of emotion
- Yerkes-Dodson law
- Self-determination and internalization
- Daydreaming and ego depletion
- Unpredictability and emotion

Chapter 11 **Cognitive development**

- More on motor development
- Affordances on visual cliff
- Motor behaviour predicts school achievement
- More on causality
- Executive function and intelligence

Chapter 12 **Social development**

- Overimitation
- Self-esteem and inflated praise
- Trust and marshmallow test
- Gender bias in motor development
- Empathy, ownership and sharing

Chapter 13 **Personality**

- Peer influence

Chapter 16 **Psychological disorders**

- Introduction and critique of new DSM-5
- Problems of biopsychosocial model
- R. D. Laing
- Critique of classic Rosenhan experiment
- New approaches to understanding multiple levels of causation
- Winter-over syndrome and polar T3 syndrome
- Cultural differences in hearing voices

Chapter 17 **Mental health**

- Recent ECT imaging study
- More on stress response in the HPA
- Loneliness and illness
- The placebo effect

Author's acknowledgements

I would like to thank the Dans for their support. It was an honour to be asked to adapt *Psychology* into the First European Edition, and to come on board as an author of the Second European Edition. As you will see, the style is very accessible without losing any of the importance of the science covered. During work on this second edition, Dan Wegner passed away, which was a tremendous loss not only to his family and friends but also the field. Part of who we are lives on in our children but also in the minds of others who we shape with our ideas. Dan Wegner shaped many minds and this textbook will continue to pass on his legacy.

I would also like to thank the team at Palgrave, especially Amy Grant and Paul Stevens who guided me along the way.

Psychology: Second European Edition has been improved by the comments and suggestions of colleagues and anonymous reviewers. I have endeavoured to incorporate their criticisms and insights to bring this edition fully up to date and make it the most engaging and comprehensive textbook available for students across the UK and Europe. I would like to thank Richard Rowe and Brendan Gough for their work on Chapter 2, The methods of psychology; David Lieberman for his contribution to Chapter 6, Learning; and I am particularly indebted to Ian Deary for his source material which was the basis for much of Chapter 9, Intelligence. Thanks also to Ian for contributing a photograph of his relation, Richard Deary, for the chapter.

I am indebted to the University of Bristol, which has provided a wonderfully supportive environment.

I would also like to thank our advisory panel for their valuable input on the previous edition and the new edition draft manuscript:

- Jason Bohan, University of Glasgow, UK
- Zoltan Dienes, University of Sussex, UK
- Paul Dockree, Trinity College, Dublin, Ireland
- Natalie Donaldson, Rhodes University, South Africa
- Roger Donaldson, Karlstad University, Sweden
- Karen Douglas, University of Kent, UK
- Eddie Edgerton, University of the West of Scotland, UK
- Graeme Fairchild, University of Southampton, UK
- Simon Goodman, Coventry University, UK
- Geoff Hall, University of York, UK
- Kim Berg Johannessen, Aarhus University, Denmark
- Tim Jones, University of Worcester, UK
- Fay Julal, University of Southampton, UK
- Minna Lyons, University of Liverpool, UK
- Paul Reavey, London South Bank University, UK
- Tone Roald, University of Copenhagen, Denmark
- Richard Shillcock, University of Edinburgh, UK
- John Song, De Montfort University, UK

- Andrew Stevenson, Manchester Metropolitan University, UK
- Lesley Tranter, University of Reading, UK
- Brady Wagoner, Aalborg University, Denmark

And finally, many thanks to those who gave up their time to appear in a video for the new *Psychology and me* feature:

- Kylie Pascua Leones
- David Crundall
- Sue Sherman
- Tone Roald
- Richard Keegan
- Tanya Byron
- Sharon Buckland
- Angel Chater

Bruce M. Hood

The publisher and authors are grateful to all those who have provided third-party material for this book. All credit lines appear on the page next to the material in question.

Tour of the book

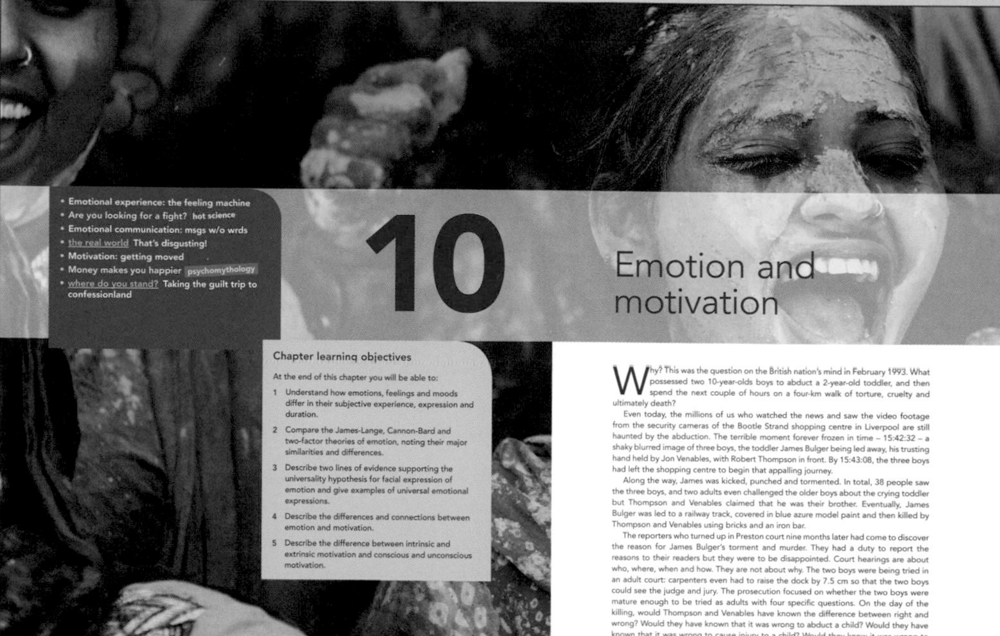

- Emotional experience: the feeling machine
- Are you looking for a fight? hot science
- Emotional communication: msgs w/o wrds
- the real world That's disgusting!
- Motivation: getting moved
- Money makes you happier psychomythology
- where do you stand? Taking the guilt trip to confessionland

10

Emotion and motivation

Chapter learning objectives

At the end of this chapter you will be able to:

1 Understand how emotions, feelings and moods differ in their subjective experience, expression and duration.

2 Compare the James-Lange, Cannon-Bard and two-factor theories of emotion, noting their major similarities and differences.

3 Describe two lines of evidence supporting the universality hypothesis for facial expression of emotion and give examples of universal emotional expressions.

4 Describe the differences and connections between emotion and motivation.

5 Describe the difference between intrinsic and extrinsic motivation and conscious and unconscious motivation.

Why? This was the question on the British nation's mind in February 1993. What possessed two 10-year-olds boys to abduct a 2-year-old toddler, and then spend the next couple of hours on a four-km walk of torture, cruelty and ultimately death?

Even today, the millions of us who watched the news and saw the video footage from the security cameras of the Bootle Strand shopping centre in Liverpool are still haunted by the abduction. The terrible moment forever frozen in time – 15:42:32 – a shaky blurred image of three boys, the toddler James Bulger being led away, his trusting hand held by Jon Venables, with Robert Thompson in front. By 15:43:08, the three boys had left the shopping centre to begin that appalling journey.

Along the way, James was kicked, punched and tormented. In total, 38 people saw the three boys, and two adults even challenged the older boys about the crying toddler but Thompson and Venables claimed that he was their brother. Eventually, James Bulger was led to a railway track, covered in blue azure model paint and then killed by Thompson and Venables using bricks and an iron bar.

The reporters who turned up in Preston court nine months later had come to discover the reason for James Bulger's torment and murder. They had a duty to report the reasons to their readers but they were to be disappointed. Court hearings are about who, where, when and how. They are not about why. The two boys were being tried in an adult court: carpenters even had to raise the dock by 7.5 cm so that the two boys could see the judge and jury. The prosecution focused on whether the two boys were mature enough to be tried as adults with four specific questions. On the day of the killing, would Thompson and Venables have known the difference between right and wrong? Would they have known that it was wrong to abduct a child? Would they have known that it was wrong to cause injury to a child? Would they know it was wrong to

Chapter opening vignette
Stories from everyday life or case studies to capture students' attention and preview the topics covered in the chapter.

Chapter learning objectives
Set out what students should have learned by the end of each chapter and link to central topics in psychology.

The real world
Applies chapter content to real-world phenomena to emphasize that psychology is about everyday experiences.

hot science

Control of learning: from the laboratory to the classroom

It's the night before the final exam in your introductory psychology course. You've put in a lot of time reviewing your course notes and the material in this textbook, and you feel that you have learned most of it pretty well. You are coming down the home stretch with little time left, and you've got to decide whether to devote those precious remaining minutes to studying psychological disorders or social psychology. How do you make that decision? What are its potential consequences? Recent research in cognitive psychology has shown that people's judgements about what they have learned play a critical role in guiding further study and learning (Metcalfe, 2009).

An important part of learning involves assessing how well we know something and how much more time we need to devote to studying it. Experimental evidence reveals that these subjective assessments, which psychologists refer to as *judgements of*

were higher at the end of trial 2 in the 3-1 condition than the 1-3 condition. This illusion occurred because JOLs were influenced by the fact that participants recalled more items in the initial test in the 3-1condition than in the 1-3 condition (remember, the initial test followed three exposures to the list in the 3-1 condition versus only one exposure to the list in the 1-3 condition).

This manipulation then allowed the experimenters to examine whether JOLs influenced how much time people devoted to each pair when the pairs in the two conditions were learned equally well, even though participants didn't think that they were. Critically, Metcalfe and Finn found evidence for a causal effect: the participants chose to devote more time to studying pairs from the 1-3 condition, which they thought were less well learned, than pairs from the 3-1 condition, which they thought were better learned.

The fact that JOLs have a causal effect on how people study is especially important because – as illustrated by the experiment we just considered – JOLs are sometimes inaccurate. For example, after reading and rereading a chapter or article in preparation for

Hot science
Provides insights into cutting-edge research on the chapter's main topics to show that psychology still has many unchartered territories.

the real world

Brain plasticity and sensations in phantom limbs

Long after a limb is amputated, many patients continue to experience sensations where the missing limb would be, a phenomenon called *phantom limb syndrome*. Patients can feel their missing limbs moving, even in coordinated gestures such as shaking hands. Some even report feeling pain in their phantom limbs. Why does this happen? Some evidence suggests that phantom limb syndrome may arise in part because of plasticity in the brain.

Researchers stimulated the skin surface in various regions around the face, torso and arms while monitoring brain activity in amputees and non-amputated volunteers (Ramachandran and Blakeslee, 1998; Ramachandran et al., 1992). Brain-imaging techniques displayed the somatosensory cortical areas activated when the skin was stimulated. This allowed the researchers to map how touch is represented in the somatosensory cortex for different areas of the body. For example, when the face was touched, the researchers could determine which areas in the somatosensory cortex were most active, and when the torso was stimulated, they could see which areas responded, and so on.

Brain scans of the amputees revealed that stimulating areas of the face and upper arm activated an area in the somatosensory cortex that previously would have been activated by a now-missin hand. The face and arm were represented in the somatosensory cortex in an area adjacent to where the person's hand – now amputated – would have been represented. Stimulating the face c arm produced phantom limb sensations in the amputees; they reported 'feeling' a sensation in their missing limbs.

Brain plasticity can explain these results (Pascual-Leone et al., 2005). The cortical representations for the face and the upper arm normally lie on either side of the representation for the hand. The somatosensory areas for the face and upper arm were larger in amputees and had taken over the part of the cortex normally representing the hand. Indeed, the new face and arm

Psychomythology

This brand new feature demonstrates the scientific nature of psychology by dispelling common myths and misconceptions about the discipline, encouraging inquisitive exploration of widely held beliefs.

psychomythology

You only use 10% of your brain

How often have you heard or read that we only use 10% of our brain? Maybe it was an advert for a self-improvement book, or someone claiming to be able to stimulate the untapped resources of the mind. It is so pervasive in society that 30% of US psychology university students (Higbee and Clay, 1998) and 59% of university-educated Brazilian adults have been reported to agree with this claim (Herculano-Houzel, 2002). A recent study of 250 UK schoolchildren found that 70% also thought that you only use this small percentage of your brain (Gjersoe and Hood, 2013).

location in the brain where memories were discovered that if you removed large parts were still capable of solving puzzles, sugge one special location. The implication was th all their brain tissue to solve puzzles, it stoc were not using all of it.

In this chapter you have learned good re 10% myth. First, brain tissue is metabolicall weighs around 2% of the overall body but r average 2,000 calories we need to consume humans evolve a brain that was so expensiv

Psychology and me

Kylie Pascua Leones, Assistant Psychologist, University College London Hospitals (UCLH)

Kylie Pascua Leones is an Assistant Psychologist at UCLH specializing in neuropsychology. Visit www.palgrave.com/schacter to watch Kylie talking about

Psychology and me
A range of exciting and inspiring video interviews with working psychologists. Summarized on the page, full videos are available on the companion website.

stats facts

The dead fish study

A full-length Atlanta salmon lay in the scanner and was asked to determine which emotions people might be experiencing in different social settings shown on the screen. The salmon did not respond because it was a fish after all, and second it was quite dead. Nevertheless, fMRI images of the salmon's head revealed clear activity in the brain region. The purpose of this bizarre study by neuroscientist Craig Bennett and his colleagues (2009) was not simply a joke, but a critical review of the way some fMRI studies might be producing spurious findings based on

Stats facts
Consider challenges of statistical investigation and offer helpful advice for interpreting quantitative and qualitative data.

e of this species' predispositions. This research also helps to explain why some pho- that humans suffer from, such as a fear of heights (acrophobia) or enclosed spaces strophobia), are so common, even in people who have never had unpleasant experi- in these contexts (Mineka and Öhman, 2002). The fears may emerge not from fic conditioning experiences but from observing and learning from the reactions of s.

bservational learning may involve a neural component as well. As you read in ter 3, *mirror neurons* are a type of cell found in the brains of primates (including ns). Mirror neurons fire when an animal performs an action, such as when a mon- eaches for a food item. More importantly, however, mirror neurons also fire when an al watches someone *else* perform the same specific task (Rizzolatti and Craighero,). Although this 'someone else' is usually a fellow member of the same species, some

If only we could model this domestic behaviour at home

Judy, a female chimpanzee, escaped from a US zoo. Before she was recaptured, she was observed entering a bathroom, grabbing a brush and cleaning a toilet. She also wrung out a sponge and cleaned off a refrigerator, according to an Associated Press report. Prior to coming to the zoo, Judy had been a home-reared animal.

Funny-but-true accounts of oddities in human behaviour relating to chapter content.

Where do you stand?
Encourages critical thinking by asking students to respond to a topic and questions, use their own experiences, and generate defensible arguments and cogent opinions.

where do you stand?

Should horse riding be made illegal?

In 2009, Professor David Nutt, the UK government's chief drug adviser, wrote a provocative editorial for a scientific journal entitled 'Equasy: An overlooked addiction with implications for the current debate on drug harms'. In the article, he highlighted the illogical nature of government drug policy in the UK by comparing the harm of drugs to the risks posed by horse riding in an addiction he called 'equasy', short for 'equine addiction syndrome', a condition characterized by gaining pleasure from horses and being prepared to take the risk of falling off/under the horse.

The UK classifies drugs as A, B, C on the basis of their harmfulness. Ecstasy – a class A drug in the same category as heroin and cocaine – kills around 10–30 individuals each year. However, when you compare the risks between horse riding and taking ecstasy, there is not much difference. You are more likely to come to

horse riding and many more su There are also about 100 traffic Making riding illegal would con would, in practice, be easy to d

What about other legal drug are treated as regulated foods, adults aged 35 and over were (HSCIC, 2014), and there were UK in 2013 (ONS, 2015). Comp which account for less than 2,0

If potential harm is the basis alcohol and tobacco become c re-classified into the least harm shouldn't horse riding be made legislate against harmful activit questions posed by Professor N questions the government wan fired the same year. What do yo

Recommended reading

Enns, J. T. (2004) *The Thinking Eye, The Seeing Brain.* New York: Norton. A tour through the visual system, focusing on sensations in the eye and perception in the brain. A fine summary of the key points mentioned in this chapter and a good starting point for branching out to other topics in the science of vision.

Goodale, M. and Milner, D. (2004) *Sight Unseen.* Oxford: OUP. This intriguing book explores conscious and unconscious vision. The authors' arguments from studies of brain damage and neuroscience lead to the proposal of dual systems in visual perception.

Ward. J. (2008) *The Frog Who Croaked Blue: Synaesthesia and the Mixing of the Senses.* Hove: Routledge. Written by one of the world's leading experts on synaesthesia, provides a comprehensive and yet accessible state-of-the-art survey of this phenomenon, with a deft mixture of neuroscience and first-person accounts.

Recommended reading
Identifies key texts for further research and includes accessible trade books, classic texts and modern bestsellers.

Online ancillaries

Psychology and me video interviews

These brand new video interviews feature an international range of lecturers, researchers and practitioners talking about their educational and professional experiences in the dynamic field of psychology. Interviewees share their motivations for wanting to study psychology, as well as the areas of the subject they found most enjoyable and most challenging as a student. They also shine a light on the various fascinating career options open to psychology graduates. Researchers offer insights into the hottest studies taking place in the field, while practitioners provide examples of the many exciting applications of a psychology degree. The useful advice and experiences showcased in these videos make them an excellent resource for any student in their current studies and in their future careers as budding psychologists.

We're delighted to feature a diverse group of psychologists, working in different areas, and across the world. All the videos interviews are available on the companion website, www.palgrave.com/schacter, with accompanying features in relevant chapters, as listed below.

To get started, watch **Bruce Hood**, Professor of Psychology, University of Bristol, and co-author of this book, explaining the idea behind this feature and his own experiences of psychology.

KYLIE PASCUA LEONES, Assistant Psychologist at University College London Hospitals (Chapter 3, Neuroscience and behaviour)

DAVID CRUNDALL, Professor of Psychology at Nottingham Trent University, specializing in hazard perception (Chapter 4, Sensation and perception)

SUE SHERMAN, Senior Lecturer in Psychology at Keele University (Chapter 5, Memory)

TONE ROALD, Assistant Professor at the University of Copenhagen, Denmark, specializing in consciousness and aesthetic experience (Chapter 8, Consciousness)

RICHARD KEEGAN, Assistant Professor of Sport Psychology at the University of Canberra, Australia (Chapter 10, Emotion and motivation)

TANYA BYRON, clinician, author, journalist and broadcaster, best known for *Little Angels* and *The House of Tiny Tearaways* (Chapter 12, Social development)

SHARON BUCKLAND, rehabilitation coordinator at Headway, a charity for the rehabilitation of people who have suffered from brain injuries (Chapter 16, Psychological disorders)

ANGEL CHATER, Lecturer in Behavioural Medicine at University College London (Chapter 17, Mental health)

Companion website

www.palgrave.com/schacter

The fully updated website for the second edition includes a comprehensive suite of learning and teaching materials to aid students and lecturers in completing and delivering psychology courses.

Learning resources

Students will find a wealth of resources to help check their understanding of the contents of the book and further expand their learning.

Resources include:

- **Psychology and me videos:** a collection of videos filmed specifically for the second edition featuring psychology graduates talking about their current roles as teachers, researchers and practitioners.
- **Access to PsychSim 5.0:** an activity program that places students in simulated research or provides them with dynamic demonstrations illustrating fundamental psychological principles. Students will gain a much deeper understanding of core psychological concepts by engaging in the discipline's classic experiments. The program includes a large number of activities, current research into core concepts, illustrations, animations and video, and dynamic interactive simulations that involve students in the practice of psychological research by having them play the role of experimenter or subject.

- **Interactive multiple choice questions** for each chapter.
- **Video and web assignments:** links to relevant clips and websites along with background information and questions.
- **Discussion topics** to spark debate and further thought.
- **Weblinks** and further reading suggestions to widen knowledge and research.
- **Additional information** on studying psychology, how to use a psychology degree, and careers in the discipline for Scandinavian students.

Teaching resources

A selection of resources has been carefully commissioned to help lecturers plan and deliver their courses.

These include:

- PowerPoint slides including all the figures and tables from the book.
- An extensive lecturer manual containing:
  - A guide on how to use the media available with the book in lectures and seminars
  - Lecture suggestions
  - Class exercises
  - Essay questions and guideline answers
  - A lecturer testbank containing true/false, multiple choice and essay questions for every chapter.
- Matrices that map chapters onto the BPS and the EFPA syllabus requirements.
- Video clips of classic and more recent experiments and research, linked to each chapter, for use in your teaching.

1

Chapter learning objectives

At the end of this chapter you will be able to:

1 Explain what is meant by a 'mindbug' and why is it so important to understanding normal psychological functioning.

2 Describe the difference between nativism and philosophical empiricism.

3 Describe how Darwin's theory of natural selection influenced psychology.

4 List the main principles of the behaviourist approach to psychology.

5 Explain how Second World War events influenced psychology in the latter half of the 20th century.

Psychology: the evolution of a science

Alan Turing (1912–54) was one of the most influential mathematicians and scientists of the 20th century, who famously helped crack the code of the Nazi's naval indicator system, Enigma, at Bletchley Park, enabling the Allies to intercept enemy communications, which contributed to their success in the Second World War. He was also one of the founders of computer science, developing the concept of machine intelligence by using mathematical formulae with algorithms to perform computations that could mimic human thought processes. Turing reasoned that the brain was essentially a biological computational device and that eventually we would be able to build intelligent machines that were indistinguishable from humans. Such a machine would have to pass what has become known as the 'Turing test'.

There are only a few individuals whose work has not only changed the world in their own lifetime, but also changed the future of our species. In the case of Alan Turing, his ideas played a crucial part in establishing the foundations of the digital revolution that we are still undergoing 60 years after his death. Every computer, every smartphone and even the internet rely on computations and algorithms. In effect, just about every aspect of modern human life owes a debt to Turing. It therefore befits a textbook on psychology to begin by acknowledging his contribution. Psychologists would like to claim him as one of ours because of his influence on how we understand the mind. However, the events of Turing's life also reveal why we are more than just complicated biological machines. In 1945, he was awarded the OBE by King George VI for his wartime services and made a Fellow of the Royal Society in 1951. Sadly, he was convicted of homosexuality the following year, which was illegal at the time and considered to be a mental illness, and lost his status and security clearance. He underwent chemical 'treatment' consisting of oestrogen injections and eventually died in 1954 through cyanide poisoning, which was ruled by the coroner to be an act of suicide.

Darwin's theories of evolution, adaptation and natural selection have provided insight into why brains and minds work the way they do.

Psychology is not just about computations in the brain. Humans live in complex interdependent groups and share experiences, knowledge and emotions. Our brains are responsible not only for processing the physical nature of the world, but also all the non-physical aspects that are important to our species. Psychology is about people. It is about societies. It is about what is considered 'normal'. It is about feelings. It is about what motivates people to do the things they do. It is even about what would compel one of the 20th-century's most brilliant individuals to take their own life.

A century before Alan Turing, another brilliant thinker had been considering the nature of the human mind. It was no less an intellectual giant than Charles Darwin (1809–82), who predicted in his *On the Origin of Species* (1859, p. 402) that: 'Psychology will be securely based on the foundation ... of the necessary acquirement of each mental power and capacity by gradation. Much light will be thrown on the origin of man and his history.' Darwin's theory of natural selection explained how the diversity of life on earth could arise by the gradual accumulation of features that varied in the population, which were better suited to changing environments. Individuals with these variations were better adapted and so more likely to survive and pass these advantages onto their offspring. Darwin could see no reason to draw a distinction between mechanisms that selected for attributes and behaviours in the animal kingdom and those responsible for the mental faculties found in man.

Darwin's theory of evolution was controversial as it situated humans firmly within the animal kingdom – something that was an affront to most at the time. However, the mid-19th century was a time of turbulent change in the European scientific community. All the major material sciences were witnessing extraordinary upheaval, with new discoveries leading to the development of technologies that would produce a revolution in industry never seen before. Rising among this upheaval was a new science – a science with an origin that could be traced back to the beginnings of human civilization, and yet had remained devoid of data or any notable theory; a science with no obvious technological or industrial associations, whose main focus of inquiry was, instead, central to the notion of what it is to be human. This new science was labelled *psychology* (from a combination of the Greek *psyche*, which means 'soul', and *logos*, which means 'to study'). The word 'psychology' first appeared in the English press in 1853, although psychological issues had preoccupied the earliest thinkers as far back as the classical Greeks. However, psychology could not be considered a 'science' prior to the 19th century because no systematic attempt had been made to pursue or generate the testable hypotheses that were necessary for a field of interest to become a science. Philosophers had pontificated about the nature of the mind but psychology was not yet a science to measure it.

It is not clear why psychology took so long to get started relative to the other sciences. Maybe it was the unobservable workings of the human mind or the lack of suitable methods to measure it, but one major factor was that the inquiry into the nature of what it is to be human bordered dangerously into territory that was deemed to be the prerogative of religion. However, by the 1850s, this territory was increasingly being encroached by scientists searching for ways of measuring and describing the natural world – and the human mind was opened to investigation.

With Darwin's advocacy of psychology, the new science had arrived. But even then, there were many highly educated individuals who resisted the idea that human psychology could be explained and predicted by measureable, lawful processes. Even Alfred Russel Wallace (1823–1913), co-discoverer of natural selection, could not fully commit to the idea as an explanation for all man's faculties. Like Darwin, he agreed that the human body had evolved but that *Homo sapiens* has 'something which he has not derived from his animal progenitors – a spiritual essence or nature … [that] can only find an explanation in the unseen universe of Spirit'. Wallace could not accept that the complexity of the modern human mind could emerge in the same way as any other evolved biological system, and turned towards spiritualism and notions of the soul. When Wallace published his views in 1869, Darwin wrote to him: 'I differ grievously from you; I can see no necessity for calling in an additional and proximate cause [a supernatural force] in regard to Man ... I hope you have not murdered too completely your own and my child.'

The child Darwin was referring to was the theory of natural selection and it would become the stimulus for the growth of psychology as a new science.

Psychology today

Shortly after *On the Origin of Species*, Darwin wrote two books that dealt with psychology, *The Descent of Man* (1871) and *The Expression of the Emotions in Man and Animals* ([1872]1998), although despite these books' apparent emphasis on the human, he remained at heart a natural biologist reporting observations. For psychology to really get going as a science, it needed new techniques, measurements and experiments to test hypotheses regarding the mind and behaviour. It was others who followed soon after who picked up Darwin's gauntlet to forge the new science. All across Europe, scientists began to appear with an interest in experimenting on the mind and behaviour. In Germany, there was a strong tradition in experiments to test the responses of the human body to stimulation that would lead to the development of new techniques to measure unconscious processes. In France, there was interest in the faculties of the mind and the effects of certain types of brain damage. In Britain, the measurement of intelligence and individual differences flourished. This spread of psychological inquiry throughout Europe was strong but the scientific study of psychology really took off in the US over the next 150 years. This is reflected in the fact that most psychological research today is still conducted in the US, with an estimated 64% of the world's 56,000 research psychologists operating there (Rosenzweig, 1992). However, an analysis of the top 100 most eminent psychologists of the 20th century reveals that just under 20% are still European (Haggbloom et al., 2002) and we will be covering much of their contribution throughout this textbook.

As a profession in Europe, psychology continues to grow in strength. According to the European Federation of Psychologists' Associations (EFPA), 46% of all psychologists practise in Europe, with the 36 member associations of the EFPA representing over 300,000 psychologists in 2014. It is also worth noting that there have been some major divisions between US and European psychology, but they are now becoming more aligned, as evidenced by the recent move to bring diagnostic criteria for clinical disorders in the US more in line with those in the rest of the world. We discuss this in more detail in Chapter 16.

The dominance of psychology in the US is largely due to a handful of pioneers who took the new science to America from Europe. Most prominent of these was William James (1842–1910), who originally studied medicine at Harvard but was so impressed by the new science of psychology he found in Europe that on his return to the US, he finished off his medical degree and changed direction to become the first professor of psychology at Harvard University. *The Principles of Psychology* (James, 1890), his landmark book based on his lectures, was more descriptive than scientific, but in it, James addressed big questions with brilliant insight, which is why it is still widely read and remains one of the most influential books ever written on the subject.

If William James were alive today, he would be amazed by the intellectual advances that have taken place in the science he helped create. Indeed, the sophistication and diversity of modern psychology are nothing short of staggering: psychologists today are exploring perception, memory, creativity, consciousness, love, anxiety, addictions and more. They use state-of-the-art technologies to examine what happens in the brain when people feel anger, recall a past experience, undergo hypnosis, or take an intelligence test. They examine the impact of culture on individuals, the origins and uses of language, the ways in which groups form and dissolve, and the similarities and differences between people from different backgrounds. Their research advances the frontiers of basic knowledge and has practical applications as well – from new treatments for depression and anxiety to new systems that allow organizations to function more effectively.

FPG/STAFF/ARCHIVE PHOTOS/GETTY IMAGES

William James (1842–1910) was excited by the new field of psychology, which allowed him to apply a scientific approach to age-old questions about the nature of human beings.

Fields of psychological inquiry

Psychology is *the scientific study of mind and behaviour.* The **mind** refers to *our private inner experience*, the ever-flowing stream of consciousness that is made up *of perceptions, thoughts, memories and feelings*. **Behaviour** refers to *observable actions of human beings*

PSYCHOLOGY The scientific study of mind and behaviour.

MIND Our private inner experience of perceptions, thoughts, memories and feelings.

BEHAVIOUR Observable actions of human beings and nonhuman animals.

and nonhuman animals, the things we do in the world, by ourselves or with others. As you will see in the chapters to come, psychology is an attempt to use scientific methods to address fundamental questions about mind and behaviour that have puzzled people for millennia. The range of research and teaching in psychology today is extensive in a field that is divided broadly into the following areas, which can operate with different methodologies and perspectives:

- *Biological psychology*, sometimes known as 'biopsychology', is the study of how biology interacts with psychological processes. It deals with how our bodies influence and respond to events. For example, what happens in our brain when we are experiencing something or how do drugs change thoughts and behaviours?
- *Cognitive psychology* is the study of mental processes. 'Cognition' refers to thinking and problem solving. How do we do it? What are the different stages that must be operating when we interpret the world and plan our response to it?
- *Developmental psychology* is the study of how psychological processes change over the life span. As we move through infancy, childhood, adolescence, adulthood and finally become elderly, our bodies obviously change but so do our behaviours and minds. What causes these changes?
- *Individual differences* is the study of how psychological processes vary from one person to the next. How do we measure these differences and why do people differ from each other?
- *Social psychology* is the study of the psychological processes that operate when we interact with others and how we behave in groups. For example, what are the effects of groups on our own individual behaviour and thoughts? How do groups form and what keeps people together?

In order to investigate these key areas, psychologists also need to learn about research methods and design, including skills such as statistical analysis. In this chapter, we will also look at the conceptual issues as well as the historical background to the field. This is because conceptual and historical issues are important to understanding how a field of science emerges and develops. For example, how we conceptualize the nature of human psychology shapes the way we go about investigating it, and as you will discover, there have been different schools of thought about human psychology that have had major impacts on the types of research and theories that have been pursued. Of course, science takes place in context and this is why it is also important to understand the historical events that have helped to shape the field, from the invention of different technologies such as computers to world events such as wars. In each of the chapters of this textbook, we consider how such issues have shaped the field.

The five areas described above represent the major approaches to pursuing psychological issues today. It is best to think about these fields as approaches with overlapping points of interest and content rather than discretely packaged areas as you might find in a warehouse store such as IKEA, where furniture, kitchen, bathroom and bedroom sections are all separately displayed. Rather, the psychological phenomena described in these chapters may be relevant to and explained by more than one approach. For example, memory is often considered a central feature of cognitive psychology but:

- Research into how memory is implemented in the brain is relevant to biological psychology
- The study of how memory changes in children is a developmental issue
- Investigations of the relationship between memory and intelligence address individual differences.

So, core areas of interest can be found in a number of different fields. Similarly, a single finding may be relevant to more than one field. For example, consider the effects of frontal brain damage that we introduce in Chapter 3, where we discuss how patients can become disinhibited and impulsive. This has clear relevance to biological psychology because of the brain structures involved, but it is also relevant to developmental psychology because planning and controlling impulsiveness are important for learning. Some people are naturally more disinhibited and impulsive than others, so the role of the frontal lobes is also relevant to the psychology of individual differences as well as mental health. Thus, different fields of psychology overlap significantly in terms of the phenomena they describe, but they may come at the same issue from different perspectives. This may seem confusing, but that's because humans are complicated, and psychology has multiple ways of approaching and interpreting the same complex behaviours.

To illustrate these multiple approaches, let us consider a common event such as a fight breaking out in a school playground. Why did one child hit the other? Psychologists coming from different perspectives will focus on different aspects:

- A psychologist with a biological perspective might be interested in the physiology of the event in terms of arousal, impulsiveness or possibly the role of genes and to what extent a child might have inherited a violent disposition from their parents.
- A psychologist interested in individual differences might want to know whether this aggressive behaviour is a stable feature of the child's personality and whether it is related to other aspects.
- A cognitive psychologist might focus on what the children were thinking. Did one perceive the other as a threat or an easy target?
- A developmental psychologist might to want to know where this aggressive behaviour came from and how it can be controlled.
- A social psychologist might want to know something about the group influences and effects of aggressive behaviour.

STOCKBYTE

Why does this child want to hit the other? Different psychological perspectives provide different ways to interpret everyday events such as this.

In principle, each of these perspectives could have something to say about fights in the playground, but most students new to psychology want to know which of them is the 'correct' approach. However, all the above are relevant and no one approach is more correct than another. To a new student, this is probably one of the most perplexing aspects of psychology – particularly in comparison to other material sciences such as physics, chemistry or biology, which (at least at first) seem to have much more defined approaches and analysis. It may be frustrating, but the human mind is extraordinarily complex. From the mundane act of tying our shoelaces to the marvel of looking at (or even painting) the *Mona Lisa*, it is psychology that can make headway into discovering why we are what we are and do what we do. Importantly, psychologists also want to understand why the mind occasionally functions so *in*effectively in the world, causing us to make errors in reasoning and mistakes in judgement or to experience illusions in perception and gaps in memory.

To get a sense of the kinds of questions psychology is interested in, let's consider a few key questions:

- *What are the bases of perceptions, thoughts, memories and feelings, or our subjective sense of self?* For thousands of years, philosophers tried to understand how the objective, physical world of the body was related to the subjective, psychological world of the mind. How could the immaterial mind connect with the material body? Today, psychologists know that there is no magical connection, and no need for one, because all our subjective experiences arise from the electrical and chemical activities of our brains. This is why Darwin believed that natural selection would also explain the evolution of mental faculties: he viewed them simply as a product of the material brain. Our mental lives are nothing more or less than 'how it feels to be a brain'. (Of course, this is a bit like saying that becoming wealthy involves nothing more or less than making money: it makes something sound simple that isn't.)

As you will see throughout this book, some of the most exciting developments in psychological research focus on how our perceptions, thoughts, memories and feelings are related to activity in the brain. Psychologists and neuroscientists now have the capability, using new technologies, to explore this relationship in ways that seek to unravel the link between functions (what the brain does) and structure (how these functions are implemented in the brain's architecture). One technique known as *functional magnetic resonance imaging* (fMRI) allows scientists to 'scan' a brain and see which parts are active when a person reads a word, sees a face, learns a new skill, or remembers a personal

stats facts

Of mice and men

One lab has recently published the entire map of the neuronal connections, known as a 'connectome', in the mouse brain (Oh et al., 2014). Although the mouse brain is much smaller than the human brain, its connectome map is 1.8 petabytes of data – enough to fill an HD film that would take 24 years of continuous viewing to watch in its entirety.

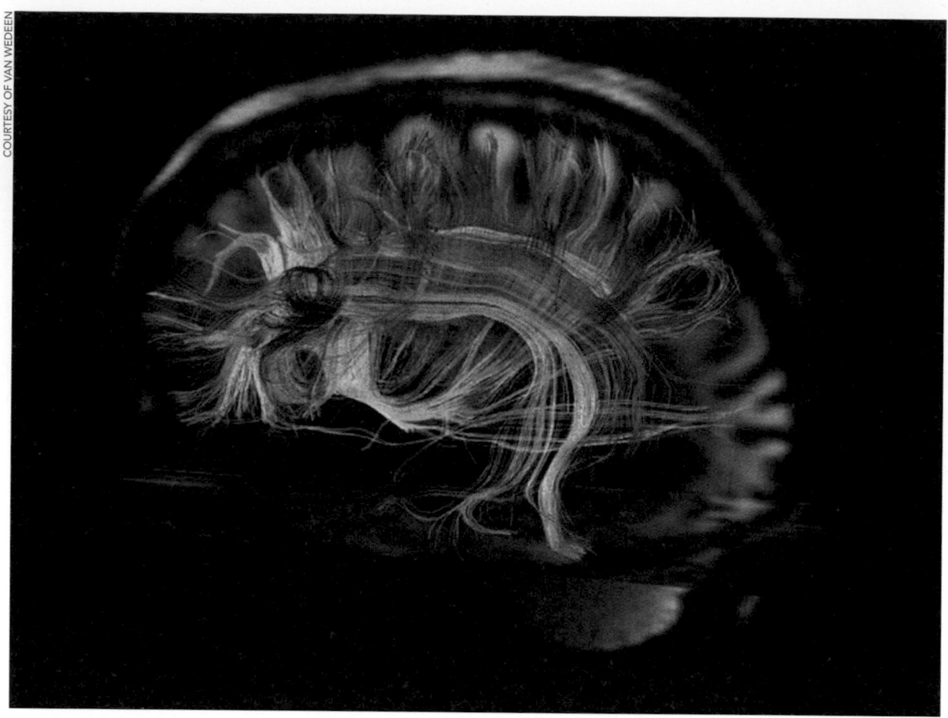
COURTESY OF VAN WEDEEN

Some of the major neural pathways revealed by diffusion tensor imaging (DTI).

experience. *Diffusion tensor imaging* (DTI) enables us to visualize the connections between different brain regions.

In the context of a burgeoning field of new types of neuroimaging, a five-year research programme known as the Human Connectome Project was launched in 2010. This was set up to integrate neuroscience research across 11 institutions based in the US and Europe in order to share the vast amounts of data that imaging studies generate. These new technologies sometimes allow us to answer old psychological questions. In the 19th century, William James was interested in how people acquire complex skills such as the ability to play the violin, and he wondered how the brain enabled great musicians to produce virtuoso performances. What James could only ponder, modern psychologists can discover. For example, the brains of professional and novice pianists were scanned as they made the complex finger movements involved in piano playing, and the results showed that professional pianists have *less* activity than novices in those parts of the brain that guide these finger movements (Krings et al., 2000). This result suggests that extensive practice at the piano changes the brains of professional pianists and the regions controlling finger movements operate more efficiently than they do in novices.

BANANASTOCK

The brains of novice pianists are more active than professional pianists. Despite how much you might despise doing your scales, extensive practice trains your brain to be more efficient.

While the new imaging advances promise to deliver an increasingly accurate picture of the brain's microarchitecture, we must remember that having a good wiring diagram is not enough. Imagine opening up a complex machine to take a picture of the internal circuitry. It does not matter how strong your resolution is, you have to know something about what the different components do and how they work together. The same is true of the brain. In the coming chapters, you will learn how imaging studies and related techniques are beginning to transform our understanding of the brain, but that understanding has to be guided by good psychological models so we know what to look for.

- *How does the mind usually allow us to function effectively in the world?* Scientists sometimes say that form follows function, that is, if we want to understand *how* something works, for example an engine or a thermometer, we need to know what it is working *for*, for example powering vehicles or measuring temperature. As James often noted, 'Thinking is for doing': the function of the mind is to help us do those things that sophisticated animals have to do in order to prosper, such as acquiring food, shelter and mates. Psychological processes are said to be *adaptive,* which means that they promote the welfare and reproduction of organisms that engage in those processes.

For instance, perception allows us to recognize our families, see predators before they see us, and avoid stumbling into oncoming traffic. Language allows us to organize our thoughts and communicate them to others, which enables us to form social groups and cooperate. Memory allows us to avoid solving the same problems over again every time we encounter them and to keep in mind what we are doing and why. Emotions allow us to react quickly to events that have 'life or death' significance, and they enable us to form strong social bonds. The list goes on and on, and as far as anyone can tell, there is no psychological equivalent of the body's appendix, that is, there's no thoroughly useless mental process that we'd all be better off without.

Given the adaptiveness of psychological processes, it is not surprising that those people with deficiencies in these processes often have a pretty tough time. Neurologist Antonio Damasio (1994) described the case of Elliot, a middle-aged husband and father with a good job, whose life was forever changed when surgeons discovered a tumour in the middle of his brain. The surgeons were able to remove the tumour and save his life, and for a while Elliot seemed just fine. But then odd things began to happen. At first, Elliot seemed more likely than usual to make bad decisions, when he could make decisions at all, and as time went on, his bad decisions became truly dreadful ones. He couldn't prioritize tasks at work because he couldn't decide what to do first, and when he did, he got it wrong. Eventually he was fired, and so he pursued a series of risky business ventures, all of which failed, and he lost his life's savings. His wife divorced him, he married again, and his second wife divorced him too.

So what ruined Elliot's life? The neurologists who tested Elliot were unable to detect any decrease in his cognitive functioning. His intelligence was intact, and his ability to speak, think and solve logical problems was every bit as sharp as it ever was. But as they probed further, they made a startling discovery: Elliot was no longer able to experience emotions. For example, Elliot didn't experience anxiety when he poured his entire bank account into a foolish business venture, he didn't experience any sorrow when his wives packed up and left him, and he didn't experience any regret or anger when his boss showed him the door. Most of us have wished from time to time that we could be as stoic and unflappable as that, after all, who needs anxiety, sorrow, regret and anger? The answer is that we all do. Emotions are adaptive because they function as signals that tell us when we are putting ourselves in harm's way. If you felt no anxiety when you thought about an upcoming exam or about borrowing your friend's car without permission, you would probably make a string of poor decisions that would leave you without a degree and without a friend, except perhaps for your cellmate. Elliot didn't have those feelings, and he paid a big price for it. The ability of a basic psychological process, that is, the experience of emotion, to perform its normally adaptive function was missing in poor Elliot's life.

BRAND X PICTURES

What use are emotions? Sometimes they just entertain us at the cinema, but often they are adaptive and guide us to do what's good for us.

- *Why does the mind occasionally function so ineffectively in the world?* The mind is an amazing machine that can do a great many things quickly. We can drive a car while talking to a passenger while recognizing the street address while remembering the name of the song that just came on the radio. But like all machines, the mind often trades accuracy for speed and versatility. This can produce 'bugs' in the system, such as when a computer program starts generating unexpected output or gets caught in a loop. Our mental life is just as susceptible to *mindbugs*, occasional malfunctions in our otherwise efficient mental processing. One of the most fascinating aspects of psychology is that we are *all* prone to a variety of errors and illusions. As we will see in later chapters, especially those containing work on perceptual and cognitive illusions, mindbugs reveal that our minds are constrained to process information and generate solutions in particular ways. Indeed, mindbugs offer a window into the internal workings of the mental machinery to reveal the underlying way it may be organized and the limitations under which it can operate. For example, try answering the following question: 'If a bat costs £1 more than a ball and the combined cost of a bat and a ball is £1.10, how much does the bat cost and how much does the ball cost?' Why do most people get this simple sum wrong? The answer is that there is something about the way we reason that gets in the way of us coming up with the correct solution (the answer is £1.05 and 5p). Mindbugs are not necessarily failings in the mental machinery – rather, they are 'set' ways of going about finding a solution which, overall, might actually be more adaptive as a general approach (Gigerenzer, 1991) even if in individual circumstances things can sometimes go awry.

If thoughts, feelings and actions were error free, then human behaviour would be orderly, predictable and dull, which it clearly is not. Rather, it is endlessly surprising, and its surprises often derive from our ability to do precisely the wrong thing at the wrong time. For example, in two British airline crashes during the 1950s, pilots mistakenly shut down an engine that was operating perfectly normally after they became aware that another engine was failing (Reason and Mycielska, 1982). Although the reasons for such catastrophic mental lapses are not well understood, they resemble far more mundane slips that we all make in our day-to-day lives. Consider two examples from the diaries of people who took part in a study concerning mindbugs in everyday life (Reason and Mycielska, 1982, pp. 70–3):

- I put some money into a machine to get a stamp. When the stamp appeared, I took it and said, 'Thank you'.
- On leaving the room to go to the kitchen, I turned the light off, although several people were there.

If these lapses seem amusing, it is because they are. But they are also potentially important as clues to human nature. For example, notice that the person who bought a stamp said 'Thank you' to the machine and not, 'How do I find the Underground?' In other words, the person did not just do *any* wrong thing; rather, he did something that would have been perfectly right in a real social interaction. As these examples suggest, people often operate on 'autopilot', or behave automatically, relying on well-learned habits they execute without really thinking. When we are not actively focused on what we are saying or doing, these habits may be triggered inappropriately. William James thought that the influence of habit could help explain the seemingly bizarre actions of 'absentminded' people. In *The Principles of Psychology* (1890), he wrote: 'Very absent-minded persons on going into their bedroom to dress for dinner have been known to take off one garment after another and finally get into bed.'

James understood that the mind's mistakes are as instructive as they are intriguing, and modern psychology has found it quite useful to study such mindbugs. Things that are whole and unbroken hum along nicely and do their jobs while leaving no clue about how they do them. Cars speeding down the motorway might as well be working by magic as long as they are working properly, because we have no idea what is moving them along. It is usually only when a car breaks down that we learn about its cylinders, valves, radiators and other fine pieces and processes that normally work together to produce an assembly line. Breakdowns and errors are not just about destruction and failure – they are pathways to knowledge. In the same way, understanding the lapses, errors and mistakes of human behaviour provides a vantage point for understanding normal functioning. The story of Elliot, who broke down after he had brain surgery, is an example that highlights the role that emotions play in guiding normal judgement processes.

Psychology is exciting because it addresses fundamental questions about human experience and behaviour, and the three questions we've just considered are merely the tip of the iceberg. Think of this book as a guide to exploring the rest of the iceberg. But before we don our parkas and grab our pickaxes, we need to understand how the iceberg got here in the first place. To understand psychology in the 21st century, we need to become a bit more familiar with the psychology of the past.

Psychology's roots: the path to a science of mind

When the young William James interrupted his medical studies to travel to Europe during the late 1860s, he wanted to learn about human nature. But he confronted a very different situation than a similarly curious student would confront today, largely because psychology did not yet exist as an independent field of study. As James cheekily wrote: 'The first lecture in psychology that I ever heard was the first I ever gave.' Of course, that doesn't mean no one had ever thought about human nature before. For over 2,000 years, thinkers had pondered the nature of human behaviour and the mind, and in fact, modern psychology acknowledges its deep roots in philosophy. We will begin by examining those roots and then describe some of the early attempts to develop a scientific approach to psychology by relating the mind to the brain. Next we'll see how psychologists divided into different camps or 'schools of thought': *structuralists*, who tried to analyse the mind by breaking it down into its basic components, and *functionalists*, who focused on how mental abilities allow people to adapt to their environments.

Psychology's ancestors: the great philosophers

The desire to understand ourselves is not new. Greek thinkers such as Plato (428–347 BC) and Aristotle (384–322 BC) were among the first to struggle with fundamental questions about how the mind works (Robinson, 1995). Greek philosophers debated many of the questions that psychologists continue to debate today. For example, are cognitive abilities and knowledge inborn, or are they acquired only through experience? Plato argued in favour of **nativism**, which maintains that *certain kinds of knowledge are innate or inborn*. Children in every culture work out early on that sounds can have meanings that can be arranged into words, which then can be arranged into sentences. Before a child is out of nappies, they have already mastered the fundamentals of language without any formal instruction. Is the propensity to learn language 'hardwired', that is, is it something that children are born with? Or does the ability to learn language depend on the child's experience? Aristotle believed that the child's mind was a *tabula rasa* (blank slate) on which experiences were written, and he argued for **philosophical empiricism**, which holds that *all knowledge is acquired through experience.*

NATIVISM The philosophical view that certain kinds of knowledge are innate or inborn.

PHILOSOPHICAL EMPIRICISM The philosophical view that all knowledge is acquired through experience.

Although few modern psychologists believe that nativism or empiricism are entirely correct, the issue of just how much 'nature' and 'nurture' explain any given behaviour is still a matter of controversy. In some ways, it is quite amazing that ancient philosophers were able to articulate so many of the important questions in psychology and offer many excellent insights into their answers without any access to scientific evidence. Their ideas came from personal observations, intuition and speculation. Although they were quite good at arguing with one another, they usually found it impossible to settle their disputes because their approach provided no means of testing their theories. As you will see in Chapter 2, the ability to test a theory is the cornerstone of the scientific approach and the basis for reaching conclusions in modern psychology.

Many current ideas in psychology can be traced to the theories of two Greek philosophers from the 4th century BC: Plato (left) who believed in nativism, and Aristotle (right), who was Plato's student and believed in empiricism.

Epistemology: continental rationalists and British empiricists

EPISTEMOLOGY The study of how knowledge is acquired.

Following from the Greeks, the next major period of philosophical inquiry into the origins of the mind took place during the Enlightenment in the 17th and 18th centuries in Western Europe. In particular, the topic of **epistemology** – *the study of how knowledge is acquired* – was a major interest of the Enlightenment philosophers. When it comes to epistemology, it is standard practice to distinguish between the continental rationalism of René Descartes (France: 1596–1650), Benedict Spinoza (the Netherlands: 1632–77) and Gottfried Leibniz (Germany: 1646–1716) who argued for innate knowledge in opposition to the British empiricism of John Locke (England: 1632–1704), George Berkeley (Ireland: 1685–1753) and David Hume (Scotland: 1711–76) who argued that all knowledge was derived from experience. Within each camp there were differences of opinion and indeed members of each group often shared ideas, but, in general, the distinction is a valid division of the major difference between rationalist a priori knowledge structures (nativism) as opposed to extrinsic experiences guiding epistemology (empiricism).

METAPHYSICS A branch of philosophy that examines the nature of reality.

The types of philosophical questions that the rationalist/empiricist dispute in epistemology covered include **metaphysics** – *a branch of philosophy that examines the nature of reality* – whether God exists, whether humans have free will, and the relation between the mind and body. We all know that the brain and the body are physical objects that we can see and touch and that the subjective contents of our minds – our perceptions, thoughts and feelings – are not. Inner experience seems perfectly real, but where in the world is it?

Descartes argued that body and mind are fundamentally different things – the body is made of a material substance, whereas the mind (or soul) is made of an immaterial or spiritual substance. But if the mind and the body are different things made of different substances, how do they interact? How does the mind tell the body to put its foot forward, and when the body steps on a rusty nail, why does the mind say 'Ouch'? This is the problem of *dualism*, or how mental activity can be reconciled and coordinated with physical behaviour.

PHRENOLOGY A psychological theory which held that specific characteristics are localized in specific regions of the brain.

From the brain to the mind: the French connection

Descartes suggested that the mind influences the body through a tiny structure near the bottom of the brain known as the 'pineal gland'. Unfortunately, he was largely alone in this view, as other philosophers at the time either rejected his explanation or offered alternative ideas. For example, British philosopher Thomas Hobbes (1588–1679) argued that the mind and body are not different things at all; rather, the mind *is* what the brain *does*. From Hobbes' perspective, looking for a place in the brain where the mind meets the body is like looking for the place in a television where the picture meets the flat panel display. As we will see in Chapter 8 on consciousness, most scientists today also reject the mind–body dualism of Descartes.

French doctor Franz Joseph Gall (1758–1828) also thought that brains and minds were linked, but by size rather than by glands. He examined the brains of animals and of people who had died of disease, or as healthy adults, or as children, and observed that mental ability often increases with larger brain size and decreases with damage to the brain. These aspects of Gall's findings were generally accepted (and the part about brain damage still is today). But Gall went far beyond his evidence to develop a psychological theory known as **phrenology**, which held that *specific mental abilities and characteristics, ranging from memory to the capacity for happiness, are localized in specific regions of the brain* (**FIGURE 1.1**). The idea that different parts of the brain are specialized for specific psychological functions turned out to be right; as you'll learn later in the book, a part of the brain called the 'hippocampus' is intimately involved in memory, just as a structure called the 'amygdala' is intimately involved in fear. But phrenology took this idea to an absurd extreme. Gall asserted that the size of bumps or indentations on the skull reflected the size of the brain regions beneath them and that by feeling those bumps, one could tell whether a person was friendly, cautious, assertive, idealistic and so on.

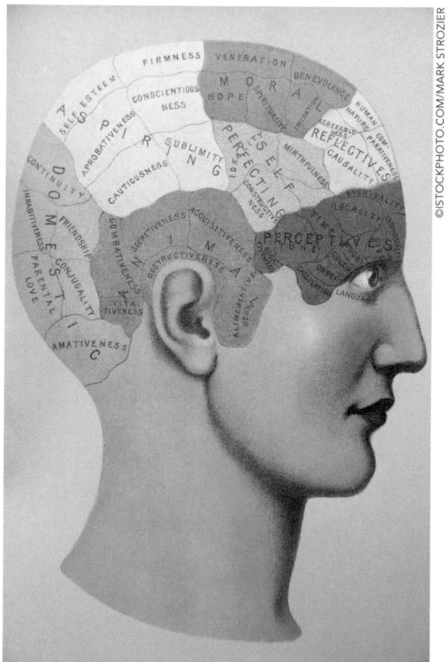

FIGURE **1.1 Phrenology** Francis Gall (1758–1828) developed a theory called phrenology, which suggested that psychological capacities, such as the capacity for friendship, and traits, such as cautiousness and mirth, were located in particular parts of the brain. The more of these capacities and traits a person had, the larger the corresponding bumps on the skull.

Gall's phrenological approach was based entirely on anecdotes and casual observations (Fancher, 1979). For example, Gall recalled that someone he knew had a good memory and large protruding eyes, and thus he suggested that the part of the brain behind the eyes must play a special role in memory. Phrenology made for a nice parlour game but in the end it amounted to a series of strong claims based on weak evidence. Not surprisingly, his critics were galled (so to speak), and they ridiculed many of his proposals. Despite an initially large following, phrenology was quickly discredited (Fancher, 1979).

While Gall was busy playing bumpologist, other French scientists were beginning to link the brain and the mind in a more convincing manner. Biologist Pierre Flourens (1794–1867) was appalled by Gall's far-reaching claims and sloppy methods, and he conducted experiments in which he surgically removed specific parts of the brain from dogs, birds and other animals and found (not surprisingly) that their actions and movements differed from those of animals with intact brains.

Surgeon Paul Broca (1825–80) worked with a patient who had suffered damage to a small part of the left side of the brain (now known as 'Broca's area'). The patient, Monsieur Leborgne, was virtually unable to speak and could utter only the single syllable 'tan'. Yet, the patient understood everything that was said to him and was able to communicate using gestures. Broca had the crucial insight that damage to a specific part of the brain impaired a specific mental function, clearly demonstrating that the brain and mind are closely linked. This was important in the 19th century because at that time, many people accepted Descartes' idea that the mind is separate from, but interacts with, the brain and the body. Broca and Flourens, then, were the first to demonstrate that the mind is grounded in a material substance, namely the brain. Their work jump-started the scientific investigation of mental processes.

From physiology to psychology: a new science is born in Germany

In the middle of the 19th century, psychology benefited from the work of German scientists who were trained in the field of **physiology** – *the study of biological processes, especially in the human body.* Physiologists had developed methods that allowed them to measure such things as the speed of nerve impulses, and some of them had begun to use these methods to measure mental abilities. William James was drawn to the work of two such physiologists: Hermann von Helmholtz (1821–94) and Wilhelm Wundt (1832–1920). During his visit to Berlin in 1867, James wrote: 'It seems to me that perhaps the time has come for psychology to begin to be a science. Helmholtz and a man called Wundt at Heidelberg are working at it.' What attracted James to the work of these two scientists?

PHYSIOLOGY The study of biological processes, especially in the human body.

Helmholtz measures the speed of responses

A brilliant experimenter with a background in physiology and physics, Helmholtz had developed a method for measuring the speed of nerve impulses in a frog's leg, which he then adapted to the study of human beings. Helmholtz trained participants to respond when he applied a **stimulus** – *sensory input from the environment* – to different parts of the leg. He recorded his participants' **reaction time**, *the amount of time taken to respond to a specific stimulus*, after applying the stimulus. Helmholtz found that people generally took longer to respond when their toe was stimulated than when their thigh was stimulated, and the difference between these reaction times allowed him to estimate how long it took a nerve impulse to travel to the brain. These results were astonishing to 19th-century scientists because at that time, just about everyone thought that mental processes occurred instantaneously. When you move your hands in front of your eyes, you don't feel your hands move a fraction of a second before you see them. The real world doesn't appear like one of those late-night films in which the video and the audio are off by just a fraction of a second. Scientists assumed that the neurological processes underlying mental events *must* be instantaneous for everything to be so nicely synchronized, but Helmholtz showed that this wasn't true. In so doing, he also demonstrated that reaction time could be a useful way to study the mind and the brain.

STIMULUS Sensory input from the environment.

REACTION TIME The amount of time taken to respond to a specific stimulus.

Wundt and the development of structuralism

Although Helmholtz's contributions were important, historians generally credit the official emergence of psychology to Wilhelm Wundt, Helmholtz's research assistant

SENSORY PERCEPTION The way that we interpret and process signals received via our senses.

CONSCIOUSNESS A person's subjective experience of the world and the mind.

STRUCTURALISM The analysis of the basic elements that constitute the mind.

INTROSPECTION The subjective observation of one's own experience.

(Rieber, 1980). Wundt published two books outlining his vision of a scientific approach to psychology and describing experiments on **sensory perception**, *the way that we interpret and process signals received via our senses*, which he had conducted in a makeshift laboratory in his home (Schultz and Schultz, 1987). In 1867, Wundt taught what was probably the first course in physiological psychology at the University of Heidelberg, and this course led to the publication of his book *Principles of Physiological Psychology* in 1874. Wundt called the book 'an attempt to mark out [psychology] as a new domain of science' (Fancher, 1979, p. 126). In 1879, at the University of Leipzig, Wundt opened the first laboratory ever to be exclusively devoted to psychological studies, an event that marked the official birth of psychology as an independent field of study. The new lab was full of graduate students carrying out research on topics assigned by Wundt, and it soon attracted young scholars from all over the world who were eager to learn about the new science that Wundt had developed.

Wundt believed that scientific psychology should focus on analysing **consciousness** – *a person's subjective experience of the world and the mind*. Consciousness encompasses a broad range of subjective experiences. We may be conscious of sights, sounds, tastes, smells, bodily sensations, thoughts or feelings. As Wundt tried to work out a way to study consciousness scientifically, he noted that chemists try to understand the structure of matter by breaking down natural substances into basic elements. So he and his students adopted an approach called **structuralism** – *the analysis of the basic elements that constitute the mind*. This approach involved breaking consciousness down into elemental sensations and feelings, and you can do a bit of structuralism right now without leaving your chair.

Consider the contents of your own consciousness. At this very moment you may be aware of the meaning of these words, the visual appearance of the letters on the page, the key ring pressing uncomfortably against your thigh, your feelings of excitement or boredom (probably excitement), the smell of curried chicken, or the nagging question of whether or not to upgrade your smartphone. At any given moment, all sorts of things are swimming in the stream of consciousness, and Wundt tried to analyse them in a systematic way using the method of **introspection** – *the subjective observation of one's own experience*. In a typical experiment, observers (usually students) would be presented with a stimulus (usually a colour or a sound) and then be asked to report their introspections. The observers would describe the brightness of a colour or the loudness of a tone. They were asked to report on their 'raw' sensory experience rather than their interpretations of that experience. For example, an observer presented with this page would not report seeing words on the page, which counts as an interpretation of the experience, but instead might describe a series of black marks, some straight and others curved, against a bright white background. Wundt also attempted to carefully describe the feelings associated with elementary perceptions. For example, when Wundt listened to the clicks produced by a metronome, some of the patterns of sounds were more pleasant than others. By analysing the relation between feelings and perceptual sensations, Wundt and his students hoped to uncover the basic structure of conscious experience.

Wundt tried to provide objective measurements of conscious processes by using reaction time techniques similar to those first developed by Helmholtz. Wundt used reaction times to examine a distinction between the perception and interpretation of a stimulus. His research participants were instructed to press a button as soon as a tone sounded. Some participants were told to concentrate on perceiving the tone before pressing the button, whereas others were told to concentrate only on pressing the button. Those people who concentrated on the tone responded about one-tenth of a second more slowly than those told to concentrate only on pressing the button. Wundt reasoned that both fast and slow participants had to register the tone in consciousness (perception), but only the slower participants also had to interpret the significance of the tone and press the button. The faster research participants, focusing only on the response they were to make, could respond automatically to the tone because they didn't have to engage in the additional step of interpretation (Fancher, 1979). This type of experimentation broke new ground by showing that psychologists could use scientific techniques to disentangle even subtle conscious processes. In fact, as you'll see in later chapters, reaction time procedures have proven extremely useful in modern research.

Exporting European psychology

Although the seeds of the modern science of psychology were sown in Europe, the discipline also took root and flourished in the US. During the late 19th and early 20th century, different aspects of psychology developed and dominated on both sides of the Atlantic. Today, many of those differences have largely disappeared as scientific communication and communities have become more global. The US has the largest number of psychologists and yet there still remain different approaches that reflect the various traditions of psychology that emerged independently.

What does this cloud look like to you? Your response might be different from those of others, and this conflicting experience of the world makes introspection an unreliable means of psychological experimentation.

Titchener and the structuralist approach

The pioneering efforts of Wundt's laboratory launched psychology as an independent science and profoundly influenced the field for the remainder of the 19th century. Many European and US psychologists journeyed to Leipzig to study with Wundt. Among the most eminent was British-born Edward Titchener (1867–1927), who studied with Wundt for two years in the early 1890s. Titchener brought some parts of Wundt's approach when he moved to America, but he also made some changes (Brock, 1993; Rieber, 1980). For instance, whereas Wundt emphasized the relationship between elements of consciousness, Titchener focused on identifying the basic elements themselves. He trained his students to provide detailed descriptions of their conscious images and sensations – a demanding process that Titchener called 'hard introspective labor'. In his textbook *An Outline of Psychology* (1896), Titchener put forward a list of more than 44,000 elemental qualities of conscious experience, most of them visual (32,820) or auditory (11,600) (Schultz and Schultz, 1987).

The influence of the structuralist approach gradually faded, due mostly to the introspective method. Science requires replicable observations – we could never determine the structure of DNA or the life span of a dust mite if every scientist who looked through a microscope saw something different. Alas, even trained observers provided conflicting introspections about their conscious experiences – 'I see a cloud that looks like a duck', 'No, *I* think that cloud looks like a horse' – thus making it difficult for different psychologists to agree on the basic elements of conscious experience. Indeed, some psychologists had doubts about whether it was even possible to identify such elements through introspection alone. One of the most prominent sceptics was someone you've already met – a young man with a bad attitude and a useless medical degree named William James.

James and the functional approach

After finishing his medical degree, William James sank into a deep depression but pulled out of his downward spiral in the early 1870s, when he became inspired by the idea of approaching psychological issues from a scientific perspective. He received a teaching appointment at Harvard (primarily because the president of the university was a neighbour and family friend) and in 1875 offered a course called 'The Relations between Physiology and Psychology'. More importantly, his position at Harvard enabled him to purchase laboratory equipment for classroom experiments, making his the first course at a US university to draw on the new experimental psychology developed by Wundt and his German followers (Schultz and Schultz, 1987). These courses and experiments led James to write his masterpiece, *The Principles of Psychology* (James, 1890).

James agreed with Wundt on some points, including the importance of focusing on immediate experience and the usefulness of introspection as a technique (Bjork, 1983), but he disagreed with Wundt's claim that consciousness could be broken down into separate elements. James believed that trying to isolate and analyse a particular moment of consciousness (as the structuralists did) distorted the essential nature of consciousness. Consciousness, he argued, was more like a flowing stream than a bundle of separate elements. So James decided to approach psychology from a different perspective entirely,

FUNCTIONALISM The study of the purpose mental processes serve in enabling people to adapt to their environment.

NATURAL SELECTION Charles Darwin's theory that the features of an organism that help it survive and reproduce are more likely than other features to be passed on to subsequent generations.

and he developed an approach known as **functionalism** – *the study of the purpose mental processes serve in enabling people to adapt to their environment.* In contrast to structuralism, which examined the structure of mental processes, functionalism set out to understand the functions those mental processes served. (See *the real world* box for some strategies to enhance one of those functions – learning.)

James's thinking was inspired by Charles Darwin's theory of **natural selection** – *the features of an organism that help it survive and reproduce are more likely than other features to be passed on to subsequent generations.* From this perspective, James reasoned, mental abilities must have evolved because they were adaptive, that is, because they helped people solve problems and increased their chances of survival. Like other animals, people have always needed to avoid predators, locate food, build shelters and attract mates. Applying Darwin's principle of natural selection, James (1890) reasoned that consciousness must serve an important biological function and the task for psychologists was to understand what those functions are. Wundt and the other structuralists worked in laboratories, and James felt that such work was limited in its ability to tell us how consciousness functioned in the natural environment. Wundt, in turn, felt that James did not focus enough on new findings from the laboratory that he and the structuralists had begun to produce. Commenting on *The Principles of Psychology*, Wundt conceded that James was a first-rate writer but disapproved of his approach: 'It is literature, it is beautiful, but it is not psychology' (Bjork, 1983, p. 12).

The rest of the world did not agree, and James's functionalist psychology quickly gained followers, especially in the US, where Darwin's ideas were influencing many thinkers. G. Stanley Hall (1844–1924), who studied with Wundt and James, set up the first psychology research laboratory in the US at Johns Hopkins University in 1881. Hall's work focused on development and education and was strongly influenced by evolutionary thinking (Schultz and Schultz, 1987).

The efforts of James and Hall set the stage for functionalism to develop as a major school of psychological thought in the US. Psychology departments that embraced a functionalist approach started to spring up at many major US universities, and in a struggle for survival that would have made Darwin proud, functionalism became more influential than structuralism had ever been. By the time Wundt and Titchener died in the 1920s, functionalism was the dominant approach in Western psychology.

In summary, philosophers have pondered and debated ideas about human nature for millennia, but, given the nature of their approach, they did not provide empirical evidence to support their claims. Some of the earliest successful efforts to develop a science linking mind and behaviour came from Europe, especially Germany. Hermann von Helmholtz furthered the science of the mind by developing methods for measuring reaction time. Wilhelm Wundt, credited with the founding of psychology as a scientific discipline, created the first psychological laboratory and taught the first course in physiological psychology. His structuralist approach focused on analysing the basic elements of consciousness. These two schools of European psychology were exported to the US, where Edward Titchener supported structuralism but William James emphasized the functions of consciousness by applying Darwin's theory of natural selection to the study of the mind, thus helping to establish functionalism and its focus on adaptive processes as the main characteristic of scientific psychology in the US.

the real world

Improving study skills

By reading this book and taking this introductory course, you will learn a great deal about psychology and what many of us take for granted, namely the complexity of processes that generate the simplest human action or thought. Psychology can also offer some practical advice. Unlike other disciplines, psychology can provide a kind of insight that is applicable to everyday life: psychology can help you to learn about psychology.

Psychologists have progressed a great deal in understanding how we remember and learn. We'll explore the science of memory and learning in Chapters 5 and 6, but here we focus on the practical implications of psychological research for everyday life: how you can use psychology to improve your study skills. Such knowledge should help you to perform your best on this course and others, but perhaps more importantly, it can help to prepare you for challenges you will face after graduation. With the rapid pace of technological change in our society, learning and memory skills are more important than ever. Experts estimate that the knowledge and skills required for success in a job will change completely every three to seven years during an individual's career (Hermann et al., 2002). Enhancing your learning and memory skills now should pay off for you later in life in ways we can't yet predict.

Psychologists have focused on mental strategies that can enhance your ability to *acquire* information, to *retain* it over time, and to *retrieve* what you have acquired and retained. Let's begin with the process of acquiring information, that is, transforming what you see and hear into an enduring memory. Our minds don't work like video cameras, passively recording everything that happens around us. To acquire information effectively, you need to actively manipulate it. One easy type of active manipulation is *rehearsal:* repeating to-be-learned information to yourself. You've probably tried this strategy already, but psychologists have found that some types of rehearsal are better than others. A particularly effective strategy is called *spaced rehearsal*, where you repeat information to yourself at increasingly long intervals. For example, suppose that you want to learn the name of a person you've just met named Eric. Repeat the name to yourself right away, wait a few seconds and think of it again, wait for a bit longer (maybe 30 seconds) and bring the name to mind once more, then rehearse the name again after a minute and once more after two or three minutes. Studies show that this type of rehearsal improves long-term learning more than rehearsing the name without any spacing between rehearsals (Landauer and Bjork, 1978). You can apply this technique to names, dates, definitions and many other kinds of information, including concepts presented in this textbook.

Simple rehearsal can be beneficial, but one of the most important lessons from psychological research is that we acquire information most effectively when we think about its meaning and reflect on its significance. In fact, we don't even have to try to remember something if we think deeply enough about what we want to remember; the act of reflection itself will virtually guarantee good memory. For example, suppose that you want to remember why Alan Turing was so important to modern living: How did his understanding of the brain as a computational device lead to the development of machine intelligence? How has Turing's work on machine intelligence affected your life in terms of the everyday technologies you use? Consider whether Turing is correct that we could build robots that were indistinguishable from humans. Could a robot ever be conscious? In attempting to answer such questions, you will need to think about philosophical issues related to the mind and the way psychology and neuroscience approach the mind–body problem. It is much easier to remember new information when you can relate it to something you already know or have considered as a fascinating problem.

You'll also learn later in this book about techniques for visualizing information, first developed by the ancient Greeks, which modern psychological research has proved to be effective memory aids (Paivio, 1969). One such technique, known as the *method of loci*, involves 'mentally depositing' information you wish to remember into familiar locations and then later searching through those locations to recall the information. For example, suppose you want to remember the major contributions of Wundt, Freud and Skinner to the development of psychology. You could use your current or former home as the location and imagine Wundt's reaction time apparatus lying on your bed, Freud's psychoanalysis couch sitting in your living room, and Skinner's rats running around your bathroom. Then, when you need this information, you can 'pull up' an image of your home and take a mental tour through it in order to see what's there. You can use this basic approach with a variety of familiar locations – a school building you know well, a shopping mall and so on – in order to remember many different kinds of information.

You can use each of the mental manipulations discussed here to help you remember and learn the material in this textbook and prepare for your exams:

- Think about and review the information you have acquired at your lecture, seminar or tutorial on a regular basis. Begin soon after the lecture, and then try to timetable regular 'booster' sessions.
- Don't wait until the last second to cram your review into one sitting; research shows that spacing out review and repetition leads to longer lasting recall. Don't just look at your notes or this textbook; test yourself on the material as often as you can. Research also shows that actively retrieving information you've acquired helps you to later remember that information more than just looking at it again.
- Take some of the load off your memory by developing effective note-taking and outlining skills. Students often scribble down vague and fragmentary notes during lectures, thinking that the notes will be good enough to jog memory later. But when the time comes to study, they've forgotten so much that their notes are no longer clear. Realize that you can't write down everything a lecturer says, and try to focus on making detailed notes about the main ideas, facts and people mentioned in the lecture.
- Organize your notes into an outline that clearly highlights the major concepts. The act of organizing an outline will force you to reflect on the information in a way that promotes retention and will also provide you with a helpful study guide to promote self-testing and review.

To follow up on these suggestions and find much more detailed information on learning and study techniques, see Hermann et al. (2002) in the *Recommended reading* section at the end of the chapter.

Errors and illusions reveal psychology

At about the same time that some psychologists were developing structuralism and functionalism, other psychologists were beginning to think about how illusions and disorders might illuminate psychological functioning. They began to realize that one can often understand how something works by examining how it breaks. Let's look first at the illusion that launched a new movement known as Gestalt psychology and then consider how observations of mental disorders influenced the development of psychology. In each case, a careful examination of some mindbugs led to a clearer understanding of human mental functioning.

Illusions of movement and the birth of Gestalt psychology

ILLUSIONS Errors of perception, memory or judgement in which subjective experience differs from objective reality.

Magicians and artists could not earn a living unless people were susceptible to **illusions** – *errors of perception, memory or judgement in which subjective experience differs from*

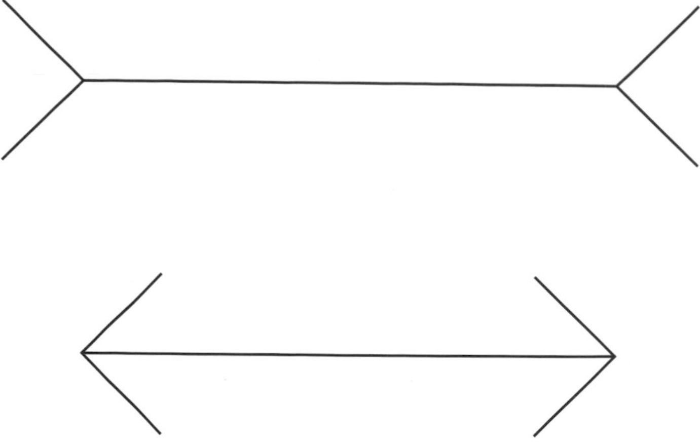

FIGURE **1.2 The Müller-Lyer line illusion** Although they do not appear to be, these two horizontal lines are actually the same length. Gestalt psychologists used illusions like this to show how the perception of a whole object or scene can influence judgements about its individual elements.

objective reality. For example, if you measure the dark horizontal lines shown in **FIGURE 1.2** with a ruler, you'll see that they are of equal length. And yet, for most of us, the top line appears longer than the bottom one. As you'll learn in Chapter 4, this is because the surrounding oblique lines are perceived as corners that influence your perception of the horizontal lines. A similar visual illusion fired the imagination of German psychologist Max Wertheimer (1880–1943), who was enjoying a train ride during his holidays when he had a sudden insight into the nature of visual perception. Wertheimer was so excited by his idea that he went to a shop as soon as he got off the train and purchased equipment for an experiment (Benjamin, 1988). In Wertheimer's experiment, a person was shown two lights that flashed quickly on a screen, one after the other. One light was flashed through a vertical slit, the other through a diagonal slit. When the time between two flashes was relatively long (one-fifth of a second or more), an observer would see that it was just two lights flashing in alternation. But when Wertheimer reduced the time between flashes to around one-twentieth of a second, observers saw a single flash of light moving back and forth (Fancher, 1979; Sarris, 1989).

Creating the illusion of motion was not new. Turn-of-the-century filmmakers already understood that quickly flashing a series of still images, one after the other, could fool people into perceiving motion where none actually existed. But Wertheimer's *interpretation* of this illusion, conceived during his train ride, was the novel element that contributed to the growth of psychology (Benjamin, 1988; Steinman et al., 2000). He reasoned that the perceived motion could not be explained in terms of the separate elements that cause the illusion (the two flashing lights) but instead that the moving flash of light is perceived as a *whole* rather than the sum of its two parts. This unified whole, which in German is called *Gestalt*, makes up the perceptual experience. Wertheimer's interpretation of the illusion led to the development of **Gestalt psychology** – *a psychological approach that emphasizes that we often perceive the whole rather than the sum of the parts.* In other words, the mind imposes organization on what it perceives, so people don't see what the experimenter actually shows them (two separate lights), instead they see the elements as a unified whole (one moving light). This analysis provides an excellent illustration of how illusions can offer clues about the basic principles of the mind.

GESTALT PSYCHOLOGY A psychological approach that emphasizes that we often perceive the whole rather than the sum of the parts.

The Gestaltists' claim was diametrically opposed to the structuralists' claim that experience can be broken down into separate elements. Wertheimer and later Gestalt psychologists such as Kurt Koffka (1886–1941) and Wolfgang Kohler (1887–1967) developed the theory further and came up with additional demonstrations and illusions that strengthened their contention that the mind perceives the whole rather than the sum of its parts. Although Gestalt psychology no longer exists today as a distinct school of thought, its basic claims have influenced the modern study of object perception (as you'll see in Chapter 4) as well as social perception (as you'll see in Chapter 14). Indeed, the notion that the mind imposes structure and organization was a central claim of philosopher Immanuel Kant (1724–1824), and it remains one of modern psychology's most widely accepted principles.

Mental disorders and multiple selves

Just as Gestalt psychologists were discovering that illusions in visual perception can help us understand how the eye and the brain normally work so well, other psychologists were discovering how the bizarre behaviours of patients with psychological disorders could shed light on the workings of the ordinary mind. For example, in 1876, a startling report in a French medical journal described a woman called Felida X (Azam, 1876). Felida was normally shy and quiet, but sometimes she would suddenly become much bolder and more outgoing. Then, without warning, she would just as suddenly return to her usual shy and reserved state. Stranger still, the shy Felida had no memory of what the outgoing Felida had done. Once, while travelling in a carriage, Felida suddenly switched from outgoing to shy and seemed to completely forget that she had just been to the funeral of a close friend. The barrier between the two states was so strong that the shy Felida forgot that she had become pregnant while in her outgoing state.

Felida X was an early example of an unusual condition now called 'dissociative identity disorder' (see Chapter 16), which involves the occurrence of two or more distinct identities within the same individual. French doctors Jean-Martin Charcot (1825–93) and Pierre Janet (1859–1947) reported similar observations when they interviewed patients who had developed a condition known then as **hysteria** – a *temporary loss of cognitive or motor functions, usually as a result of emotionally upsetting experiences.* Hysterical patients became blind, paralysed or lost their memories, even though there was no known physical cause of their problems. However, when the patients were put into a trancelike state through the use of hypnosis (an altered state of consciousness characterized by suggestibility), their symptoms disappeared: blind patients could see, paralysed patients could walk and forgetful patients could remember. After coming out of the hypnotic trance, however, the patients forgot what had happened under hypnosis and again showed their symptoms. Like Felida X, the patients behaved like two different people in the waking versus hypnotic states.

HYSTERIA A temporary loss of cognitive or motor functions, usually as a result of emotionally upsetting experiences.

These peculiar disorders were ignored by Wundt, Titchener and other laboratory scientists, who did not consider them a proper subject for scientific psychology (Bjork, 1983). But William James believed they had important implications for understanding the nature of the mind (Taylor, 2001). He discerned an important mindbug at work, capitalizing on these mental disruptions as a way of understanding the normal operation of the mind. During our ordinary conscious experience, we are only aware of a single 'self', but the aberrations described by Charcot, Janet and others suggested that the brain could create many conscious selves that are not aware of each other's existence (James, 1890). These striking observations also fuelled the imagination of a young doctor from Vienna, Austria, who studied with Charcot in Paris in 1885. His name was Sigmund Freud (1856–1939).

AUTHENTICATED NEWS/ARCHIVE PHOTOS/GETTY IMAGES

In this photograph, Sigmund Freud (1856–1939) sits in his office in Vienna, which was filled with antiquities from all over the world, including artwork related to his ideas about unconscious motives. The couch reserved for his patients placed them in a reclining position, and Freud conducted the psychoanalysis sitting in a position behind their view.

Freud and psychoanalytic theory

After his visit to Charcot's clinic in Paris, Freud returned to Vienna, where he continued his work with hysteric patients. (The word *hysteria* comes from the Latin word *hyster*, which means 'womb'. It was once thought that only women suffered from hysteria, which was thought to be caused by a 'wandering womb'.) Working with the doctor Joseph Breuer (1842–1925), Freud began to make his own observations of hysterics and develop theories to explain their strange behaviours and symptoms. Freud theorized that many of the patients' problems could be traced to the effects of painful childhood experiences that the person could not remember, and he suggested that the powerful influence of these seemingly lost memories revealed the presence of an unconscious mind. According to Freud, the **unconscious** is *the part of the mind that operates outside conscious awareness but influences conscious thoughts, feelings and actions.* This idea led Freud to develop **psychoanalytic theory** – *an approach that emphasizes the importance of unconscious mental processes in shaping feelings, thoughts and behaviours.* From a psychoanalytic perspective, it is important to uncover a person's early experiences and illuminate a person's unconscious anxieties, conflicts and desires (see Chapters 13 and 17). Psychoanalytic theory formed the basis for a therapy that Freud called **psychoanalysis**, which focuses on *bringing unconscious material into conscious awareness to better understand psychological disorders.* During psychoanalysis, patients recalled past experiences ('When I was a toddler, I was frightened by a masked man on a black horse') and related their dreams and fantasies ('Sometimes I close my eyes and imagine not having to pay for this session'). Psychoanalysts used Freud's theoretical approach to interpret what their patients said.

UNCONSCIOUS The part of the mind that operates outside conscious awareness but influences conscious thoughts, feelings and actions.

PSYCHOANALYTIC THEORY Sigmund Freud's approach to understanding human behaviour that emphasizes the importance of unconscious mental processes in shaping feelings, thoughts and behaviours.

PSYCHOANALYSIS A therapeutic approach that focuses on bringing unconscious material into conscious awareness to better understand psychological disorders.

In the early 1900s, Freud and a growing number of followers formed a psychoanalytic movement. Carl Gustav Jung (1875–1961) and Alfred Adler (1870–1937) were prominent in the movement, but both were independent thinkers, and Freud apparently had little tolerance for individuals who challenged his ideas. Soon, Freud broke off his relationships with both men so that he could shape the psychoanalytic movement himself (Sulloway, 1992). Many psychoanalysts were Jewish intellectuals who were forced to flee following the rise of Nazism. As a result, the movement fragmented further: in the US, where many psychoanalysts ended up, it flourished during the war and postwar years. In contrast, it was almost nonexistent in Europe, with the exception of Britain, where Freud and his daughter Anna had found refuge in 1938. The US embraced the 'talking cure', which became familiar in US culture (Kurzweil, 1989) but never really enjoyed the same popularity in Britain, where psychoanalysis remained generally London based and restricted to those who could afford the expensive course of therapy.

Psychoanalytic theory had also become quite controversial because it suggested that understanding a person's thoughts, feelings and behaviour required a thorough exploration of the person's early sexual experiences and unconscious sexual desires. In those days these topics were still taboo. But the heart of the criticism of psychoanalysis was that it lacked scientific rigour, because it was largely based on interpretation of retrospective reports (as we will see in Chapter 17, there was also concern that psychoanalysis was of no therapeutic benefit). It lacked the precision of the early experimentalists who had struggled to make psychology a legitimate science.

Most of Freud's followers, like Freud himself, were trained as doctors and did not conduct psychological experiments in the laboratory, although early in his career, Freud did do some nice laboratory work on the sexual organs of eels. By and large, psychoanalysts did not hold positions in universities and developed their ideas in isolation from the research-based approaches of Wundt, Titchener, James, Hall and others. One of the few times that Freud met the leading academic psychologists was at a conference G. Stanley Hall organized at Clark University in 1909. It was there that William James and Sigmund Freud met for the first time. Although James worked in an academic setting and Freud worked with clinical patients, both men believed that mental aberrations provide important clues into the nature of mind. Each thinker, in his own way, recognized the value of pursuing mindbugs as a clue to human functioning.

Influence of psychoanalysis and the humanistic response

Most historians consider Freud to be one of the two or three most influential thinkers of the 20th century, and the psychoanalytic movement influenced everything from literature and history to politics and art. Within psychology, psychoanalysis had its greatest impact on clinical practice, but over the past 40 years that influence has been considerably diminished.

This is partly because Freud's vision of human nature was a dark one, emphasizing limitations and problems rather than possibilities and potentials. He saw people as hostages to their forgotten childhood experiences and primitive sexual impulses, and the inherent pessimism of his perspective frustrated those psychologists who had a more optimistic view of human nature. The postwar years were positive, invigorating and upbeat: poverty and disease were being conquered by technology, the standard of living was on a sharp rise, and people were landing on the moon. The era was characterized by the accomplishments and not the foibles of the human mind, and Freud's viewpoint was out of step with the spirit of the times.

Freud's ideas were also difficult to test, and a theory that can't be tested is of limited use in psychology or other sciences. Although Freud's emphasis on unconscious processes has had an enduring impact on psychology, psychologists began to have serious misgivings about many aspects of Freud's theory.

It was in these times that psychologists such as Abraham Maslow (1908–70) and Carl Rogers (1902–87) pioneered a new movement called **humanistic psychology** – *an approach to understanding human nature that emphasizes the positive potential of human beings.* Humanistic psychologists focused on the highest aspirations that people had for

HUMANISTIC PSYCHOLOGY An approach to understanding human nature that emphasizes the positive potential of human beings.

themselves. Rather than viewing people as prisoners of events in their remote pasts, humanistic psychologists viewed people as free agents who have an inherent need to develop, grow and reach their full potential. This movement reached its peak in the 1960s when a generation of 'flower children' found it easy to see psychological life as a kind of blossoming of the spirit. Humanistic therapists sought to help people to realize their full potential; in fact, they called them 'clients' rather than 'patients'. In this relationship, the therapist and the client (unlike the psychoanalyst and the patient) were on equal footing.

In summary, psychologists have often focused on mindbugs as a way of understanding human behaviour. The errors, illusions and foibles of mental functioning offer a glimpse into the normal operations of the mind. Max Wertheimer founded Gestalt psychology by examining the illusion that causes us to see the whole instead of its parts. Clinicians such as Jean-Martin Charcot and Pierre Janet studied unusual cases in which patients acted like different people while under hypnosis, raising the possibility that each of us has more than one self. Through his work with hysteric patients, Sigmund Freud developed psychoanalysis, which emphasized the importance of unconscious influences and childhood experiences in shaping thoughts, feelings and behaviour. But happily, humanistic psychologists offered a more optimistic view of the human condition, suggesting that people are inherently disposed towards growth and can usually reach their full potential with a little help from their friends.

Psychology in the 20th century: behaviourism takes centre stage

The schools of psychological thought that had developed by the early 20th century – structuralism, functionalism, psychoanalysis, Gestalt psychology and humanism – differed substantially from one another. But they shared an important similarity: each tried to understand the inner workings of the mind by examining conscious perceptions, thoughts, memories and feelings or by trying to elicit previously unconscious material, all of which were reported by participants in experiments or by patients in a clinical setting. In each case it proved difficult to establish with much certainty just what was going on in people's minds, due to the unreliable nature of the methodology. As the 20th century unfolded, a new approach developed as psychologists challenged the idea that psychology should focus on mental life at all. This new approach was called **behaviourism**, which *advocated that psychologists should restrict themselves to the scientific study of objectively observable behaviour*. Behaviourism represented a dramatic departure from previous schools of thought.

BEHAVIOURISM An approach that advocates that psychologists should restrict themselves to the scientific study of objectively observable behaviour.

Watson and the emergence of behaviourism

John Broadus Watson (1878–1958) received his PhD in 1904 from the University of Chicago (the first psychology PhD ever awarded there), where he was strongly influenced by James Angell (1869–1949), who had worked within the functionalist tradition. But Watson believed that private experience was too idiosyncratic and vague to be an object of scientific inquiry. Science required replicable, objective measurements of phenomena that were accessible to all observers, and the introspective methods used by structuralists and functionalists were far too subjective for that. So, instead of describing conscious experiences, Watson proposed that psychologists focus entirely on the study of behaviour – what people *do*, rather than what people *experience* – because behaviour can be observed by anyone and it can be measured objectively. Watson thought that a focus on behaviour would put a stop to the endless philosophical debates in which psychologists were currently entangled, and it would encourage them to develop practical applications in such areas as business, medicine, law and education. According to Watson, the goal of scientific psychology should be to predict and control behaviour in ways that benefit society.

Why would someone want to throw the 'mind' out of psychology? This may seem excessive, until you notice that Watson studied the behaviour of animals such as rats and birds. In such studies, inferring a mind is a matter of some debate. Shall we say that dogs have minds, for instance, but leave out pigeons? And if we include pigeons, what about worms? Animal behaviour specialists staked out claims in this area. In 1908, Margaret Floy Washburn published *The Animal Mind*, in which she reviewed what was then known about perception, learning and memory in different animal species. She argued that nonhuman animals, much like human animals, have conscious mental experiences (Scarborough and Furumoto, 1987). Watson reacted to this claim with venom. Because we cannot ask pigeons about their private, inner experiences (well, we can *ask*, but they never tell us), Watson decided that the only way to understand how animals learn and adapt was to focus solely on their behaviour, and he suggested that the study of human beings should proceed on the same basis.

Watson was influenced by the work of Russian physiologist Ivan Pavlov (1849–1936), who carried out pioneering research on the physiology of digestion. In the course of this work, Pavlov noticed something interesting about the dogs he was studying (Fancher, 1979). Not only did the dogs salivate at the sight of food, they also salivated at the sight of the person who fed them. The feeders were not food, so why should the mere sight of them trigger a basic digestive response in the dogs? To answer this question, Pavlov developed a procedure in which he sounded a tone every time he fed the dogs, and after a while he observed that the dogs would salivate when they heard the tone alone. In Pavlov's experiments, the sound of the tone was a stimulus that influenced the salivation of the dogs, which was a **response** – *an action or physiological change elicited by a stimulus.* Watson and other behaviourists made these two notions the building blocks of their theories, which is why behaviourism is sometimes called 'stimulus-response' or 'S-R' psychology.

RESPONSE An action or physiological change elicited by a stimulus.

Watson applied Pavlov's techniques to human infants. In a well-known and controversial study, Watson and his research assistant Rosalie Rayner taught an infant known as 'Little Albert' to have a strong fear of a harmless white rat (and other white furry animals and toys) that he had previously not feared. Why would they do such a thing? You'll learn more about this study in Chapter 6, but the short answer is this: Watson believed that human behaviour is powerfully influenced by the environment, and the experiments with Little Albert provided a chance to demonstrate such influence at the earliest stage of life. Neither Watson nor later behaviourists believed that the environment was the *only* influence on behaviour (Todd and Morris, 1992), but they did think it was the most important one. Consistent with that view, Watson became romantically involved with someone prominent in his environment: Rosalie Rayner. He refused to end the affair when confronted by colleagues, and the resulting scandal forced Watson to leave his position at Johns Hopkins University. He found work in a New York advertising agency, where he applied behaviourist principles to marketing and advertising, which certainly involves manipulating the environment to influence behaviour. Watson also wrote popular books that exposed a broad general audience to the behaviourist approach (Watson, 1924a, 1928). The result of all these developments – Pavlov's work in the laboratory, Watson and Rayner's applications to humans, and Watson's practical applications to daily life – was that by the 1920s, behaviourism had become a dominant force in scientific psychology.

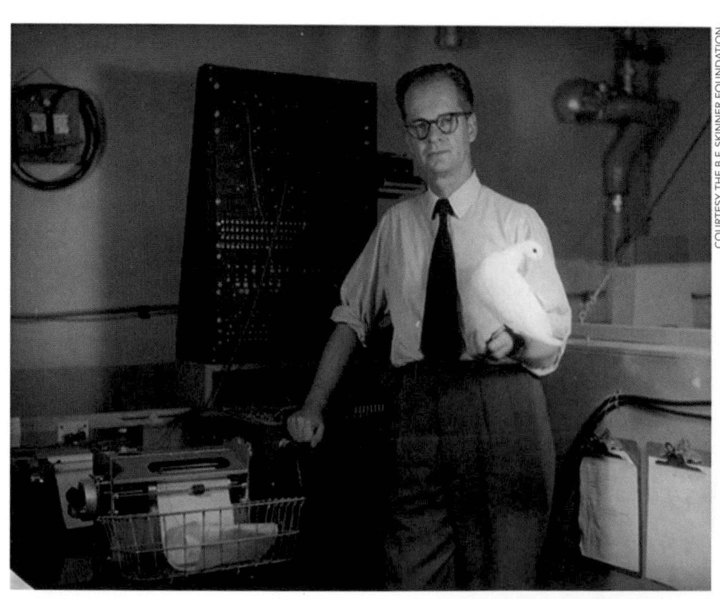

COURTESY THE B.F. SKINNER FOUNDATION

Inspired by Watson's behaviourism, B. F. Skinner (1904–90) investigated the way an animal learns by interacting with its environment.

B. F. Skinner and the development of behaviourism

In 1926, Burrhus Frederic Skinner (1904–90) graduated from Hamilton College in upstate New York. Like William James, Skinner was a young man who couldn't decide what to do with his life. He aspired to become a writer, and his interest in literature led him indirectly to psychology. Skinner wondered whether a novelist could portray a character without understanding why the character behaved as they did, and when he came across Watson's books, he felt he had the answer. Skinner completed his PhD studies in psychology at Harvard (Wiener, 1996) and began to develop a new kind of behaviourism. In Pavlov's experiments, the dogs had been passive participants that stood around, listened to tones and drooled. Skinner recognized that in everyday life, animals don't just stand there – they do something. Animals *act* on their environments in order to find shelter, food or mates, and Skinner wondered if he could develop behaviourist principles that would explain how they *learned* to act in those situations.

Skinner's well-publicized questioning of such cherished notions as free will led to a rumour that he had raised his own daughter in a Skinner box. This urban myth probably originated from the special thermostatically controlled cot he had designed for infants so that they did not have to wear baby clothes. Skinner marketed the cot as a labour-saving invention that simplified a young mother's life and improved baby welfare under various names, including the 'air-crib' and the 'heir conditioner', but it failed to catch on with parents.

Urban myths get out of hand

The rumour was that following a childhood of conditioning by her father, Deborah Skinner Buzan had grown up psychotic and committed suicide by blowing her brains out in a bowling alley in Billings, Montana, back in the 1970s. Following the publication of a book about famous psychological experiments in 2004, Deborah wrote a response in *The Guardian* newspaper. She said that the rumour was a lie – she had never been to Billings, Montana.

Skinner built what he called an 'operant conditioning chamber' but what the rest of the world would forever call a 'Skinner box'. The box has a lever and a food tray, and a hungry rat could get food delivered to the tray by pressing the lever. Skinner observed that when a rat was put in the box, it would wander around, sniffing and exploring, and would usually press the bar by accident, at which point a food pellet would drop into the tray. After that happened, the rate of bar pressing would increase dramatically and remain high until the rat was no longer hungry. Skinner saw evidence for what he called the principle of **reinforcement**, which states that *the consequences of a behaviour determine whether it will be more or less likely to occur again*. The concept of reinforcement became the foundation for Skinner's new approach to behaviourism (see Chapter 6), which he formulated in a landmark book, *The Behaviour of Organisms* (Skinner, 1938).

REINFORCEMENT The consequences of a behaviour determine whether it will be more or less likely to occur again.

Skinner set out to use his ideas about reinforcement to help improve the quality of everyday life. Skinner often worked with pigeons, and he wanted to see whether he could use reinforcement to teach pigeons to do something they did not do naturally. Careful scientific observation revealed that pigeons in the wild almost never take up table tennis, so Skinner decided to use the principle of reinforcement to teach some pigeons to play the game. He first broke the task down into small parts and used the principle of reinforcement to teach the pigeons each of the parts – reinforcing them when they made the right move, for example turning their bats towards the ball, but not when they made the wrong one, for example cooing at the referee. Soon, the pigeons were able to bat the ball back and forth in a relatively entertaining display of athletic prowess.

A full page of letters from readers in an issue of *New Scientist* magazine reported sightings by London Underground passengers of pigeons boarding and disembarking from tube carriages in 'purposeful' ways that suggested they have worked out where they are going.

Skinner was visiting his nine-year-old daughter's class when he realized that he might be able to improve classroom instruction by breaking a complicated task into small bits and then using the principle of reinforcement to teach children each bit (Bjork, 1993). He developed automatic devices known as 'teaching machines' that did exactly that (Skinner, 1958). The teaching machine asked a series of increasingly difficult questions that built on the students' answers to the simpler ones. To learn a complicated mathematics problem, for instance, students would first be asked an easy question about the simplest part of the problem. They would then be told whether the answer was right or wrong, and if a correct response was made, the machine would move on to a more difficult question. Skinner thought that the satisfaction of knowing they were correct would be reinforcing and help students learn.

If young children and pigeons could be successfully trained, why stop there? In the controversial books *Beyond Freedom and Dignity* (1971) and *Walden II* ([1948]1986), Skinner laid out his vision of a utopian society in which behaviour was controlled by the judicious application of the principle of reinforcement. In these books, he put forth the simple but stunning claim that our subjective sense of **free will**, *the ability to choose or decide what to do*, is an illusion and that when we think we are exercising free will, we are actually responding to present and past patterns of reinforcement. We do things in the present that have been rewarding in the past, and our sense of 'choosing' to do them is nothing more than an illusion. In this, Skinner echoed the sentiments of Dutch philosopher Benedict Spinoza ([1677]1982, p. 86), who several centuries earlier had noted that:

FREE WILL The ability to choose or decide what to do.

> men are deceived in thinking themselves free, a belief that consists only in this, that they are conscious of their actions and ignorant of the causes by which they are determined. As to their saying that human actions depend on the will, these are mere words without any corresponding idea.

Skinner argued that his insights could be used to increase human wellbeing and solve social problems. Not surprisingly, that claim sparked an outcry from critics who believed that Skinner was giving away one of our most cherished attributes – free will – and calling for a repressive society that manipulated people for its own ends. Skinner even featured in a popular magazine of the day that called his ideas 'the taming of mankind through a system of dog obedience schools for all' (Bjork, 1993, p. 201). Given the nature of Skinner's ideas, the critics' attacks were understandable – he had seriously underestimated how much people cherish the idea of free will – but in the sober light of hindsight, they were clearly overblown. Skinner did not want to turn society into a 'dog obedience school' or strip people of their personal freedoms. Rather, he argued that an understanding of the principles by which behaviour is generated could be used to increase social welfare, which is precisely what happens when a government launches advertisements to encourage citizens to drink milk or quit smoking. The result of all the controversy, however, was that Skinner's fame reached a level rarely attained by psychologists. One magazine even ranked Skinner just 39 points below Jesus Christ in a poll of 100 most important people who ever lived (Herrnstein, 1977).

NATURAL BEHAVIOURS Instinctual responses that were not learned.

ETHOLOGY The scientific study of animal behaviour in the natural habitat.

Although US behaviourism had its roots in Pavlovian conditioning, in Europe there was a greater interest in the patterns of **natural behaviours** – *instinctual responses that were not learned*. As we will see in Chapter 6 on learning, the problem with Skinner's behaviourism is that it did not take into account the natural predisposition of animals to engage in some complex behaviours that were a consequence of Darwinian natural selection. This was the field of **ethology** – *the scientific study of animal behaviour in the natural habitat* – co-founded by Austrian Konrad Lorenz (1903–89) and Dutchman Niko Tinbergen (1907–88) in the 1930s. The two were initially friends but this relationship was tested when Lorenz joined the Nazi Party in 1938 and Tinbergen ended up a prisoner of war of the Nazis. Some years later they were reconciled and in 1973, Lorenz and Tinbergen shared the only Nobel Prize ever awarded for research in animal behaviour with Karl von Frisch, another Austrian who worked out communication between bees. Ethology is concerned with nonhuman animals, but the implications for our species in terms of evolutionary psychology remain important. Skinner may have dominated US behaviourism and enjoyed celebrity status, but the Nobel Prize was one accolade that eluded him.

In summary, behaviourism advocated the study of observable actions and responses and held that inner mental processes were private events that could not be studied scientifically. Ivan Pavlov and John B. Watson studied the association between stimulus and response and emphasized the importance of the environment in shaping behaviour. Influenced by Watson's behaviourism, B. F. Skinner developed the concept of reinforcement using a 'Skinner box'. He demonstrated that animals and humans repeat behaviours that generate pleasant results and avoid performing those that generate unpleasant results. Skinner extended Watson's contentions about the importance of the environment in shaping behaviour by suggesting that free will is an illusion and that the principle of reinforcement can be used to benefit society.

Beyond behaviourism: psychology expands

Although behaviourism was the dominant approach in US psychology from the 1930s to the 1950s, and hence the most powerful on the world stage where the US was the largest player, it wouldn't dominate the field for much longer, especially as the alternative schools of thought that had coexisted at the same time in Europe started to emerge. In Europe, psychologists were, and had always been, interested in the mind. But why was behaviourism eventually replaced? Although behaviourism allowed psychologists to measure, predict and control behaviour, it did this by ignoring some important things. First, it ignored the mental processes that had fascinated psychologists such as Wundt and James and, in so doing, found itself unable to explain some very important phenomena, such as how children learn language. Second, it ignored the evolutionary history of the organisms it studied and was thus unable to explain why, for example, a rat can learn to associate nausea with food much more quickly than it can learn to associate nausea with a tone or a light, as we examine further later in this chapter and in Chapter 6. Next, we consider how the approaches that ultimately replaced behaviourism met these kinds of problems head-on.

The emergence of cognitive psychology

For almost two decades, psychologists dismissed the problem of the mind as an intractable fairy tale that could not be studied scientifically. There were some exceptions to this rule – including most clinical and social psychologists, who remained deeply committed to the scientific study of mental processes – but, by and large, psychologists happily ignored mental processes until the 1950s, when something important happened: the computer. The advent of computers had an enormous practical impact, of course, but it also had an enormous conceptual impact on psychology. Computers are information-processing systems, and the flow of information through their circuits is clearly no fairy tale. If psychologists could think of mental events – such as remembering, attending, thinking, believing, evaluating, feeling and assessing – as the flow of information through the mind, then they might be able to study the mind scientifically after all. The emergence of the computer led to a re-emergence of interest in mental processes across the discipline of psychology, and it spawned a new approach called **cognitive psychology** – *the scientific study of mental processes, including perception, thought, memory and reasoning.*

COGNITIVE PSYCHOLOGY The scientific study of mental processes, including perception, thought, memory and reasoning.

Early European cognitive pioneers

Even at the height of behaviourist domination in the US, there were a few quiet revolutionaries whose research and writings were focused on mental processes. Much of this originated from Europe where behaviourism had less of a hold in psychology. The German school of Gestalt psychology formed in the 19th century was still strong, and new theories about mental processes were emerging in other countries. For example, Sir Frederic Bartlett (1886–1969) was a British psychologist interested in memory. He was dissatisfied with existing research, especially that of German psychologist Hermann Ebbinghaus (1850–1909), who had performed groundbreaking experiments on memory in 1885 that we'll discuss in Chapter 5. Serving as his own research subject, Ebbinghaus had tried to discover how quickly and how well he could memorize and recall meaningless information, such as the three-letter nonsense syllables *dap*, *kir* and *sul*. Bartlett (1932), however, believed that it was more important to examine memory for the kinds of information people actually encounter in everyday life, so he gave people stories to remember and carefully observed the kinds of errors they made when they tried to recall them some time later. Bartlett discovered many interesting things that Ebbinghaus could never have learned with his nonsense syllables. For example, he found that research participants often remembered what *should* have happened or what they *expected* to happen rather than what actually *did* happen. These and other errors led Bartlett to suggest that memory is not a photographic reproduction of past experience and that our attempts to recall the past are powerfully influenced by our knowledge, beliefs, hopes, aspirations and desires.

Swiss psychologist Jean Piaget (1896–1980) studied children's errors of reasoning on simple games and questions in order to gain insight into the nature and development of the human mind. He appreciated the value of studying mindbugs as a way into understanding the child's mind. For example, in one of his tasks, Piaget would give a three-year-old child a large and a small mound of clay and tell the child to make the two mounds equal. Then Piaget would break one of the clay mounds into smaller pieces and ask the child which mound now had more clay. Although the amount of clay remained the same, of course, three-year-old children usually said that the mound that was broken into smaller pieces was bigger, but by the age of six or seven, they no longer made this error. As you'll see in Chapter 11, Piaget theorized that younger children lack a particular cognitive ability that allows older children to appreciate the fact that the mass of an object remains constant even when it is divided. For Piaget, mindbugs such as these provided key insights into the mental world of the child (Piaget and Inhelder, 1969).

One way that Piaget studied the cognitive ability of children was to give them simple games involving clay.

PHOTO12/UIG/GETTY IMAGES

Jean-Martin Charcot (1825–93) demonstrating hypnosis in one of his early clinics. Like many sciences, psychology started off being largely dominated by white middle-class males.

German psychologist Kurt Lewin (1890–1947) was also a pioneer in the study of thought at a time when thought had been banished from psychology. Lewin (1936) argued that one could best predict a person's behaviour in the world by understanding the person's subjective experience of the world. A television soap opera is a meaningless series of unrelated physical movements unless one thinks about the characters' experiences – how Lucas feels about Steph, what Peggy was planning to say to Archie, and whether Linda's sister, Nancy, will always hate their mother for meddling in the marriage. Lewin realized that it was not the stimulus, but rather the person's interpretation of the stimulus, that determined the person's subsequent behaviour. A pinch on the cheek can be pleasant or unpleasant depending on who administers it, under what circumstances, and to which set of cheeks. Lewin used a special kind of mathematics called *topology* to model the person's subjective experience, and although his topological theories were not particularly influential, his attempts to model mental life and his insistence that psychologists study how people construe their worlds would have a lasting impact on psychology.

Early European women pioneers

Men with bushy beards and smelly cigars dominated these early days of psychology but although women were largely prevented from becoming scientists, there are some notable 19th-century European females who played an important role in the birth of our field. The first British woman to obtain a doctorate in psychology was Beatrice Edgell (1871–1948) who had trained at Würzburg under the influence of the German approach to studying the mind. She pioneered research on time perception, became head of department at Bedford College, London and was elected the first female president of the British Psychological Society in 1930. In developmental psychology, we now recognize that one of the best ways to educate children is to use practices that enable them to learn through discovery – a principle first championed by the Italian psychologist Maria Montessori (1870–1952). Although she was originally trained as a doctor, her **pedagogical approach** – *the scaffolding of learning by instruction* (see Chapter 11) – predates two more famous male developmental psychologists, Jean Piaget and Lev Vygotsky, who, by coincidence, were both born in 1896. Finally, in the field of mental illness, which we cover later in Chapter 17, Melanie Klein (1882–1960), an Austrian-born British psychoanalyst, challenged one of the most dominant psychologists of the last century, Sigmund Freud, who is instantly recognizable as the man with the bushy beard and cigar. Klein was the first psychoanalyst to openly challenge Freud's account by positing a different structure of child development based on her innovative analyses of child's play – something that Freud never bothered to check even though he theorized about children.

PEDAGOGICAL APPROACH The scaffolding of learning by instruction.

© CROWN COPYRIGHT 2016

This navy radar operator must focus his attention for long stretches of time, while making quick, important decisions. The mental processes involved in such tasks are studied by cognitive psychologists.

Technology and the development of cognitive psychology

The contributions of psychologists such as Bartlett, Piaget and Lewin provided early alternatives to behaviourism, but they did not depose it. That job required war. During the Second World War, some of the UK's most brilliant minds, such as Kenneth Craik (1914–45) at the Applied Psychology Unit in Cambridge, were tasked with developing better operator systems for flying planes, guiding missiles and paying attention to radar screens to make the man–machine interface more efficient. Radar operators had to pay close attention to their screens for long periods while trying to decide whether blips were friendly aircraft, enemy aircraft, or flocks of wild geese in need of a good chasing (Ashcraft, 1998; Lachman et al., 1979). How could radar operators be trained to make quicker and more accurate decisions? The answer to this question clearly required more than the swift delivery of pellets to the radar operator's food tray. It required those who designed the equipment to think about and talk about cognitive processes, such as perception, attention, identification, memory and decision making. Behaviourism solved the problem by denying it, and thus some psychologists decided to deny behaviourism and forge ahead with a new approach that would become the cognitive revolution.

British psychologist Donald Broadbent (1926–93) was among the first to study what happens when people try to pay attention to several things at once. For instance, Broadbent observed that pilots can't attend to many different instruments at once and must actively move the focus of their attention from one to another (Best, 1992). Broadbent (1958) showed that the limited capacity to handle incoming information is a fundamental feature of human cognition and that this limit could explain many of the errors that pilots (and other people) made. At about the same time, US psychologist George Miller (1956) pointed out a striking consistency in our capacity limitations across a variety of situations – we can pay attention to, and briefly hold in memory, about seven (give or take two) pieces of information. Cognitive psychologists began conducting experiments and devising theories to better understand the mind's limited capacity, a problem that behaviourists had ignored.

As you have already read, the invention of the computer in the 1950s had a profound impact on psychologists' thinking. People and computers differ in many ways, but both seem to register, store and retrieve information, leading psychologists to wonder whether the computer might be used as a model for the human mind. A computer is made of hardware, for example chips and disk drives today, magnetic tapes and vacuum tubes a half-century ago, and software, stored on optical disks today and on punch cards a half-century ago. If the brain is roughly analogous to the computer's hardware, then perhaps the mind was roughly analogous to a software program. This line of thinking led cognitive psychologists to begin writing computer programs to see what kinds of software could be made to mimic human speech and behaviour (Newell et al., 1958). Another important figure from this period was British mathematician Alan Turing, who we encountered at the start of this chapter.

With all these developments during the 1950s, the field of psychology was turning away from behaviourism towards cognitive psychology. Ironically, this emergence of cognitive psychology was energized by the appearance of a book by B. F. Skinner called *Verbal Behavior* (1957), which offered a behaviourist analysis of language. Noam Chomsky (1928–), a linguist at the Massachusetts Institute of Technology (MIT), published a devastating critique of the book in which he argued that Skinner's insistence on observable behaviour had caused him to miss some of the most important features of language. According to Chomsky, language relies on mental rules that allow people to understand and produce novel words and sentences. The ability of even the youngest child to generate new sentences that they had never heard before flew in the face of the behaviourist claim that children learn to use language by reinforcement. As you will learn in Chapter 7, Chomsky (1959) provided a clever, detailed and thoroughly cognitive account of language that could explain many of the phenomena that the behaviourist account could not.

These developments during the 1950s set the stage for an explosion of cognitive studies during the 1960s. Cognitive psychologists did not return to the old introspective procedures used during the 19th century, but instead developed new and ingenious methods that allowed them to study cognitive processes. The excitement of the new approach was summarized in *Cognitive Psychology,* Ulric Neisser's (1967) landmark book, which provided a foundation for the development of cognitive psychology, which grew and thrived in the years that followed.

The brain meets the mind: the rise of cognitive neuroscience

If cognitive psychologists studied the software of the mind, they had little to say about the hardware of the brain. And yet, as any computer scientist knows, the relationship between software and hardware is crucial: each element needs the other to get the job done. Our mental activities often seem so natural and effortless – noticing the shape of an object, using words in speech or writing, recognizing a face as familiar – that we fail to appreciate the fact that they depend on intricate operations carried out by the brain. This dependence is revealed by dramatic cases in which damage to a particular part of the brain causes a person to lose a specific cognitive ability. Recall that in the 19th century, French doctor Paul Broca described a patient who, after damage to a limited area in the left side of the brain, could not produce words, although he could understand them perfectly well. As you'll see later in the book, damage to other parts of the brain can also result in syndromes that are characterized by the loss of specific mental abilities, for example prosopagnosia, in which the person cannot recognize human faces, or by the emergence of bizarre behaviour or beliefs, for example Capgras syndrome, in which the person believes that a close family member has been replaced by an imposter. These striking – sometimes startling – cases remind us that even the simplest cognitive processes depend on the brain. The high level of interest psychologists now have in the link between brain and mind is rooted in the achievements of pioneering researchers working in the middle of the 20th century.

Karl Lashley (1890–1958), a psychologist who studied with John B. Watson, took an approach similar to the one Pierre Flourens used a century earlier. By training rats to run mazes, surgically removing parts of their brains, and then measuring how well they could run the maze again, Lashley (1960) hoped to find the precise spot in the brain where *learning* occurred. Alas, no one spot seemed to uniquely and reliably eliminate learning. Every area seemed **equipotential** – *equally responsible for enabling learning to occur*. Instead, Lashley simply found that the more of the rat's brain he removed, the more poorly the rat ran the maze, an effect he called the **law of mass action**, where *performance is determined by the quantity of nervous tissue removed and is independent of any particular area*. Lashley was frustrated by his inability to identify a specific site of learning, but his efforts inspired other scientists to take up the challenge. They developed a research area called physiological psychology. Today, this area has grown into **behavioural neuroscience**, which *links psychological processes to activities in the nervous system and other bodily processes*. To learn about the relationship between brain and behaviour, behavioural neuroscientists observe animals' responses as they perform specially constructed tasks, such as running through a maze to obtain food rewards. Neuroscientists can record electrical or chemical responses in the brain as the task is being performed or later remove specific parts of the brain to see how performance is affected (see **FIGURE 1.3**). Of course, experimental brain surgery cannot ethically be performed on human beings, and thus psychologists who want to study the human brain have often had to rely on nature's cruel and inexact experiments. Birth defects, accidents and illnesses often cause damage to particular brain regions, and if this damage disrupts a particular ability, then psychologists deduce that the

EQUIPOTENTIAL Equally responsible for enabling learning to occur.

LAW OF MASS ACTION Performance is determined by the quantity of nervous tissue removed and is independent of any particular area.

BEHAVIOURAL NEUROSCIENCE An approach to psychology that links psychological processes to activities in the nervous system and other bodily processes.

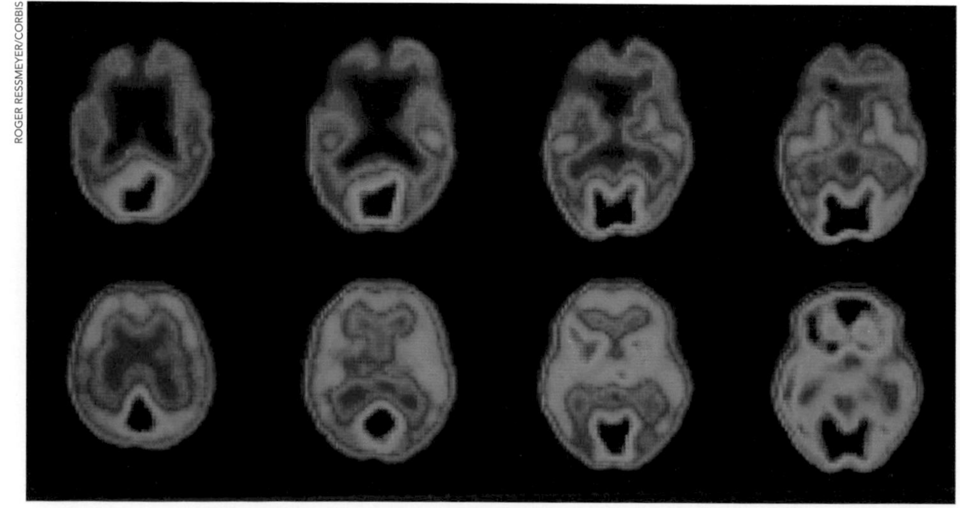

ROGER RESSMEYER/CORBIS

FIGURE 1.3 PET scans of healthy and Alzheimer's brains PET (positron emission tomography) scans are one of a variety of brain-imaging technologies that psychologists use to observe the living brain. The four brain images in the top row come from a person suffering from Alzheimer's disease; the four in the bottom row come from a healthy person of similar age. The red and green areas reflect higher levels of brain activity compared to the blue areas, which reflect lower levels of activity. In each image, the front of the brain is at the top and the back of the brain is at the bottom. You can see that the patient with Alzheimer's disease, compared with the healthy person, shows more extensive areas of lowered activity towards the front of the brain.

region is involved in producing that ability. It turns out that the equipotentiality and law of mass action that Lashley had discovered in rats did not apply to humans, who showed much more localized learning function than rodents. For example, in Chapter 5 you'll learn about a patient whose memory was virtually wiped out by damage to a specific part of the brain, and you'll see how this tragedy provided scientists with remarkable clues about how memories are stored (Scoville and Milner, 1957). But in the late 1980s, technological breakthroughs led to the development of noninvasive 'brain-scanning' techniques that made it possible for psychologists to watch what happens inside a human brain as a person performs a task such as reading, imagining, listening and remembering. Brain scanning is an invaluable tool because it allows us to observe the brain in action and see which parts are involved in which operations (see Chapter 3).

For example, researchers used scanning technology to identify the parts of the brain in the left hemisphere that are involved in specific aspects of language, such as understanding or producing words (Peterson et al., 1989). Later scanning studies showed that people who are deaf from birth but who learn to communicate using sign language rely on regions in the right hemisphere (as well as the left) when signing. In contrast, people with normal hearing who learned sign language after puberty seemed to rely only on the left hemisphere when signing (Newman et al., 2002). These findings suggest that although both spoken and signed language usually rely on the left hemisphere, the right hemisphere can also become involved – but only for a limited period (perhaps until puberty). The findings also provide a neat example of how psychologists can now use scanning techniques to observe people with various kinds of cognitive capacities and use their observations to unravel the mysteries of the mind and the brain (see **FIGURE 1.4**). In fact, there's a name for this area of research. **Cognitive neuroscience** is the *field that attempts to understand the links between cognitive processes and brain activity* (Gazzaniga, 2000).

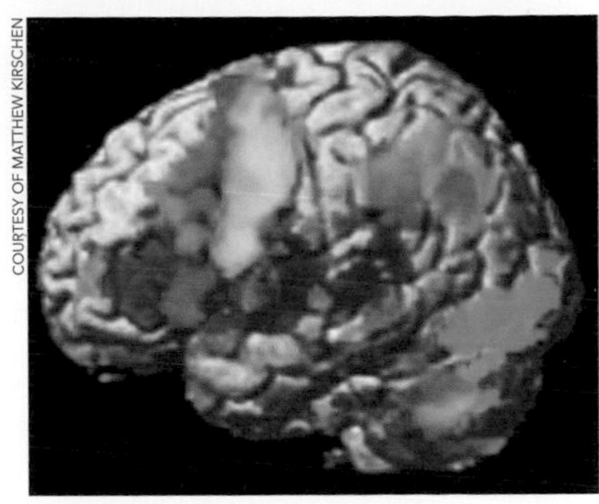

COURTESY OF MATTHEW KIRSCHEN

FIGURE 1.4 More ways to scan a brain fMRI scanners produce more precise images than PET scans, allowing researchers to more accurately localize brain activity. fMRIs are also quicker at capturing images, allowing researchers to measure brain activity over briefer periods. Here, green areas of the brain were active when research participants remembered information presented visually, and red areas were active when they remembered information presented aurally. Yellow areas were active during both types of presentations.

COGNITIVE NEUROSCIENCE A field that attempts to understand the links between cognitive processes and brain activity.

hot science

What makes a scientist?

Over the past decade, a new field has been emerging called the *psychology of science*. It sets out to empirically investigate the full range of psychological processes behind scientific behaviour, interest, talent and creativity (Feist, 2013). Most assume that science is entirely objective and deals only with hard evidence, but of course, thinking up novel experiments, collecting data, analysing it, interpreting and then drawing conclusions all involve psychological processes. Even those of us who are not professional scientists can think scientifically from the very beginning, as we shall encounter in Chapter 11 when we examine Piaget's theory of scientific reasoning in babies and small children.

Scientific thought, as opposed to gut reactions and intuition, is the explicit, logical analysis that is sometimes referred to as 'System 2' thinking that we consider in Chapter 7 (Kahneman, 2012). It is slow and ponderous, whereas the rapid, intuition-based reasoning known as 'System 1' thinking is fast and unconscious. Sometimes, the two come into conflict, which is one of the reasons you get mindbugs that are System 1 operations. For example, we assume that events that receive considerable media attention such as air crashes or child murders are more likely because they seem so familiar when, in fact, they are very rare – a phenomenon we examine in Chapter 7 known as the 'availability bias'. When learning new facts about the trajectories of falling objects, subjects have to resolve scientific and intuitive reasoning that arrive at different answers to a problem by recruiting the activity of frontal brain regions involved in suppressing thoughts (Dunbar et al., 2007). These are believed to inhibit the rapid System 1 tendency to give the intuitive response in order to allow the newly acquired System 2 answer to work.

Indeed, in many ways, science is often counterintuitive; fighting against early and deeply held beliefs about the nature of the world. For example, Darwin's theory of evolution by natural selection is one of the most misunderstood concepts in science that can be traced to the way children naturally think of different species as being essentially distinct and not sharing common ancestors (Kelemen et al., 2014). Even many adults who accept evolution by natural selection as the scientific explanation for the diversity of life still fail to understand the actual mechanism (Gregory, 2009). This is because intuitive theories, those that are spontaneous and not taught, are part of normal cognitive development and can interfere with science education (see Chapter 11). As Susan Carey (2000) pointed out: 'Now we understand that the main barrier to learning the curricular materials we so painstakingly developed is not what the student lacks, but what the student has, namely, alternative conceptual frameworks for understanding the phenomena covered by the theories we are trying to teach.'

The psychology of science also reveals that people (including scientists) are not always objective but seek out and pay more attention to evidence that confirms their hypothesis rather than disconfirming it (Fuselgang and Dunbar, 2005). Scientists from different disciplines also use different ways to think about problems. For example, applied scientists such as meteorologists are more likely to use spatial rotation and mental imaginary to think through a problem compared to astronomers and physicists who are more likely to run through a conceptual simulation using a 'what if' strategy (Trickett et al., 2009). Psychology also operates in the way the experiments are run, especially when biases can operate. Experimenter bias covers a range of problems that can arise when people are involved in the experimental process. Participants may change their behaviour depending on their age, gender and expectations about what they believe the experiment is about (Rosenthal, 1994). The productivity of the research group is also influenced by the personality of the team leaders. Then there is the cultural myth about the link between psychopathology and creativity – the mad genius as it were. Newton, Darwin, Tesla and Faraday are all believed to have suffered some form of psychological disorder. Somehow, the contradiction between mental brilliance and mental dysfunction seems to have captured the public's imagination. However, recent research from over 1 million Swedish creative individuals, including scientists and artists, reveals that they are not more prone to mental illness (Kyaga et al., 2013). One thing that all good scientists have is curiosity. As the science fiction writer Isaac Asimov noted: 'The most exciting phrase to hear in science, the one that heralds new discoveries, is not Eureka! (I found it!) but rather, "hmm ... that's funny ... ".'

The adaptive mind: the emergence of evolutionary psychology

Psychology's renewed interest in mental processes and its growing interest in the brain were two developments that led psychologists away from behaviourism. A third development also pointed them in a different direction – backwards to the beginning of the science in the mid-19th century. Recall that one of behaviourism's key claims was that organisms are blank slates on which experience writes its lessons, and hence any one lesson should be as easily written as another. But European ethologists such as Lorenz and Tinbergen had described all manner of complex animal behaviours that could not have been learned, suggesting natural selection had endowed animals with built-in patterns of responses. In experiments conducted during the 1960s and 70s, psychologist John Garcia and colleagues showed that rats can learn to associate nausea with the smell of food much more quickly than they can learn to associate nausea with a flashing light (Garcia, 1981). Why should this be? In the real world of forests, sewers and rubbish cans, nausea is usually caused by spoiled food and not by lightning, and although these particular rats had been born in a laboratory and had never left their cages, millions of years of evolution had 'prepared' their brains to learn the natural association more quickly than the artificial one. In other words, it was not only the rats' learning history but the rats' *ancestors'* learning histories that determined their ability to learn. That fact was at odds with the behaviourist doctrine, and it became the credo for a new kind of psychology.

EVOLUTIONARY PSYCHOLOGY A psychological approach that explains mind and behaviour in terms of natural selection, where minor variations in the way we think and behave mean that some individuals are more suited to their environments.

Evolutionary psychology *explains mind and behaviour in terms of natural selection, where minor variations in the way we think and behave mean that some individuals are more suited to their environments.* These individuals are said to be better adapted and so are more likely to pass on the genes responsible for these variations to the next generation. Evolutionary psychology was anticipated by Charles Darwin but it would take another 150 years for psychologists to get excited again by the implications of the theory of natural selection. It is only since the publication in 1975 of *Sociobiology*, by biologist E. O. Wilson, that evolutionary thinking has been steadily increasing (Buss, 1999; Pinker, 1997a; Tooby and Cosmides, 2000). Evolutionary psychologists think of the mind as a collection of specialized 'modules' that are designed to solve the human problems our ancestors faced as they attempted to eat, mate and reproduce over millions of years. According to evolutionary psychology, the brain is not an all-purpose computer that can do or learn one thing just as easily as it can do or learn another; rather, it is a computer that was built to do a few things well and everything else not at all. It is a computer that comes with a small suite of built-in applications that are designed to do the things that previous versions of that computer needed to have done.

Consider, for example, how evolutionary psychology treats the emotion of jealousy. All of us who have been in romantic relationships have been jealous, if only because we noticed our partner noticing someone else. Jealousy can be a powerful, overwhelming emotion that we might wish to avoid, but according to evolutionary psychology, it exists today because it once served an adaptive function. If some of our hominid ancestors experienced jealousy and others did not, then the ones who experienced it might have been more likely to guard their mates and act aggressively against their rivals and thus may have been more likely to reproduce their 'selfish genes' (Dawkins, 1976).

Critics of the evolutionary approach point out that many current traits of people and other animals probably evolved to serve different functions than those they currently serve. For example, biologists believe that the feathers of birds probably evolved initially to perform such functions as regulating body temperature or capturing prey and only later served the entirely different function of flight. Likewise, people are reasonably adept at learning to drive a car, but nobody would argue that such an ability is the result of natural selection; the learning abilities that allow us to become skilled car drivers must have evolved for purposes other than driving cars.

Complications like these have led the critics to wonder how evolutionary hypotheses can ever be tested (Coyne, 2000; Sterelny and Griffiths, 1999). We don't have a record of our ancestors' thoughts, feelings and actions, and fossils won't provide much information about the evolution of mind and behaviour. Testing ideas about the evolutionary origins of psychological phenomena is indeed a challenging task, but not an impossible one (Buss et al., 1998; Pinker, 1997b). Evolutionary psychologists hold that behaviours or traits that occur universally in all cultures are good candidates for evolutionary adaptations. For example, physical attractiveness is widely valued by men and women in many cultures, and people from different cultures tend to agree in their judgements of facial attractiveness (Cunningham et al., 1995). As you will learn in Chapter 14, several aspects of facial attractiveness, such as symmetrical facial features, have been linked with enhanced physical and mental health, also suggesting the possibility that it is an evolutionary adaptation (Shackelford and Larsen, 1999).

Evolutionary adaptations should also increase reproductive success. So, if a specific trait or feature has been favoured by natural selection, it should be possible to find some evidence of this in the numbers of offspring produced by the trait's bearers. Consider, for instance, the hypothesis that men tend to be tall because women prefer to mate with tall men. To investigate this hypothesis, researchers conducted a study in which they compared the numbers of offspring from short and tall men. They did their best to equate other factors that might affect the results, such as the level of education attained by short and tall men. Consistent with the evolutionary hypothesis, they found that tall men do indeed bear more offspring than short men (Pawlowski et al., 2000). This kind of study provides evidence that allows evolutionary psychologists to test their ideas. Not every evolutionary hypothesis can be tested, of course, but evolutionary psychologists are becoming increasingly inventive in their attempts.

In summary, psychologists such as Frederic Bartlett, Jean Piaget and Kurt Lewin defied the behaviourist doctrine and studied the inner workings of the mind. Their efforts, as well as those of later pioneers such as Donald Broadbent, paved the way for cognitive psychology to focus on inner mental processes such as perception, attention, memory and reasoning. The field of cognitive psychology developed as a result of the invention of the computer, psychologists' efforts to improve the performance of the military, and Noam Chomsky's theories about language. Cognitive neuroscience attempts to link the brain with the mind through studies of both brain-damaged and healthy people. The recent theoretical emphasis of evolutionary psychology on the adaptive function that minds and brains serve harks back to Darwin's original prediction that natural selection will also explain psychological processes.

Beyond the individual: social and cultural perspectives

The picture we have painted so far may vaguely suggest a scene from some 1950s sci-fi film, in which the protagonist is a living brain that thinks, feels, hopes and worries while suspended in a vat of pink jelly in a basement laboratory. Although psychologists often do focus on the brain and the mind of the individual, they have not lost sight of the fact that human beings are fundamentally social animals who are part of a vast network of family, friends, teachers and co-workers. Trying to understand people in the absence of that fact is a bit like trying to understand an ant or a bee without considering the function and influence of the colony or hive. People are the most important and most complex objects that we ever encounter, and thus it is not surprising that our behaviour is strongly influenced by their presence – or their absence. The two areas of psychology that most strongly emphasize these facts are social and cultural psychology.

The development of social psychology

SOCIAL PSYCHOLOGY A subfield of psychology that studies the causes and consequences of interpersonal behaviour.

Social psychology is the *study of the causes and consequences of interpersonal behaviour.* This broad definition allows social psychologists to address a remarkable variety of topics. Historians trace the birth of social psychology to an experiment conducted in 1895 by psychologist and bicycle enthusiast Norman Triplett, who noticed that cyclists seemed to ride faster when they rode with others, a phenomenon we cover in Chapter 15. Intrigued by this observation, he conducted an experiment that showed that children reeled in a fishing line faster when tested in the presence of other children than when tested alone. Triplett was not trying to improve the fishing abilities of children, of course, but rather was trying to show that the mere presence of other people can influence performance on even the most mundane kinds of tasks.

Social psychology's development began in earnest in the 1930s and was driven by several historical events. The rise of Nazism led many of Germany's most talented scientists to emigrate to America, and among them were psychologists such as Solomon Asch (1907–96) and Kurt Lewin. These psychologists had been strongly influenced by Gestalt psychology, which you'll recall held that 'the whole is greater than the sum of its parts', and although the Gestaltists had been talking about the visual perception of objects, these psychologists felt that the phrase also captured a basic truth about the relationship between social groups and the individuals who constitute them. Philosophers had speculated about the nature of sociality for thousands of years, and political scientists, economists, anthropologists and sociologists had been studying social life scientifically for some time. But these German refugees were the first to generate theories of social behaviour that resembled the theories generated by natural scientists, and more importantly, they were the first to conduct experiments to test their social theories. For example, Lewin (1936) adopted the language of mid-century physics to develop a 'field theory' that viewed social behaviour as the product of 'internal forces', such as personality, goals and beliefs, and 'external forces', such as social pressure and culture, while Asch (1946) performed laboratory experiments to examine the 'mental chemistry' that allows people to combine small bits of information about another person into a full impression of that person's personality.

YOUN JAE-WOOK/STRINGER/AFP/GETTY IMAGES

Social psychology studies how the thoughts, feelings and behaviours of individuals can be influenced by the presence of others. Members of Reverend Sun Myung Moon's Unification Church are often married to one another in ceremonies of 10,000 people or more; in some cases, couples don't know each other before the wedding begins. Social movements such as this have the power to sway individuals.

Other historical events also shaped social psychology in its early years. For example, the Holocaust brought the problems of conformity and obedience into sharp focus, leading psychologists such as Asch (1956) and others to examine the conditions under which people can influence each other to think and act in inhuman or irrational ways. During the Second World War, Henri Tajfel (1919–82) fought for the French but was captured and held as a prisoner of war, never letting his German captors know that he was in fact a Polish Jew. By pretending to be member of another ethnic group, he survived, but after the war, he discovered that all his relatives had perished in the death camps. This experience must have contributed to his work on theories of how groups form that we will encounter in more detail in Chapter 15. Tajfel emigrated to the UK to take up the Chair of Social Psychology at Bristol University and became one of the central figures who shaped the development of postwar European social psychology. Social psychologists today study a wider variety of topics (from social memory to social relationships) and use a wider variety of techniques (from opinion polls to neuroimaging) than did their forebears, but this field of psychology remains dedicated to understanding the brain as a social organ, the mind as a social adaptation, and the individual as a social creature.

The emergence of cultural psychology

Americans and Western Europeans are sometimes surprised to realize that most of the people on the planet are members of neither culture. Although we are all more alike than we are different, there is nonetheless considerable diversity within the human species in social practices, customs and ways of living. Culture refers to the values, traditions and beliefs that are shared by a particular group of people. Although we usually think of culture in terms of nationality and ethnic groups, cultures can also be defined by age (youth culture), sexual orientation (gay culture), religion (Jewish culture), or occupation (academic culture). **Cultural psychology** is *the study of how cultures reflect and shape the psychological processes of their members* (Shweder and Sullivan, 1993). Cultural psychologists study a wide range of phenomena, ranging from visual perception to social interaction, as they seek to understand which of these phenomena are universal and which vary from place to place and time to time.

CULTURAL PSYCHOLOGY The study of how cultures reflect and shape the psychological processes of their members.

Perhaps surprisingly, one of the first psychologists to pay attention to the influence of culture was someone recognized today for pioneering the development of experimental psychology: Wilhelm Wundt. He believed that a complete psychology would have to combine a laboratory approach with a broader cultural perspective. Wundt wrote extensively about cultural and social influences on the mind, producing a 10-volume work on culture and psychology, in which he covered a vast range of topics, such as how people gesture in different cultures or the origins of various myths and religions (Wundt, 1900–20). But Wundt's ideas failed to spark much interest from other psychologists, who had their hands full trying to make sense of results from laboratory experiments and formulating general laws of human behaviour. Outside psychology, anthropologists such as Margaret Mead (1901–78) and Gregory Bateson (1904–80) attempted to understand the workings of culture by travelling to far-flung regions of the world and carefully observing child-rearing patterns, rituals, religious ceremonies and the like. Such studies revealed practices – some bizarre from a 'Western' perspective – that served important functions in a culture, such as the painful ritual of violent body mutilation and bloodletting in mountain tribes of New Guinea, which initiates young boys into training to become warriors (Mead, [1935]1968; Read, 1965). Yet at the time, most anthropologists paid as little attention to psychology as psychologists did to anthropology.

© LIFESIZEIMAGES – ISTOCKPHOTO.COM

BANANASTOCK

Two families, one Japanese, one European, sit down for dinner. Cultural psychology studies the similarities and differences in psychological processes that arise between people living in different cultures.

Cultural psychology only began to emerge as a strong force during the 1980s and 90s, when psychologists and anthropologists began to communicate with each other about their ideas and methods (Stigler et al., 1990). It was then that psychologists rediscovered Wundt as an intellectual ancestor of this area of the field (Jahoda, 1993).

Physicists assume that $e = mc^2$ whether the m is located in Scotland, Outer Mongolia or the Orion Nebula. Chemists assume that water is made of hydrogen and oxygen and that it was made of hydrogen and oxygen in 1609 as well. The laws of physics and chemistry are assumed to be universal, and for much of psychology's history, the same assumption was made about the principles that govern human behaviour (Shweder, 1991). *Absolutism* holds that culture makes little or no difference for most psychological phenomena – that 'honesty is honesty and depression is depression, no matter where one observes it' (Segall et al., 1998, p. 1103). And yet, as any world traveller knows, cultures differ in exciting, delicious and frightening ways, and things that are true of people in one culture are not necessarily true of people in another. *Relativism* holds that psychological phenomena are likely to vary considerably across cultures and should be viewed only in the context of a specific culture (Berry et al., 1992). Although depression is observed in nearly every culture, the symptoms associated with it vary dramatically from one place to another. For example, in Western cultures, depressed people tend to undervalue themselves, whereas depressed people in Eastern cultures do not (Draguns, 1980).

Today, most cultural psychologists fall somewhere between these two extremes. Most psychological phenomena can be influenced by culture, some are completely determined by it, and others seem to be entirely unaffected. For example, the age of a person's earliest memory differs dramatically across cultures (MacDonald et al., 2000), whereas judgements of facial attractiveness do not (Cunningham et al., 1995). As noted when we discussed evolutionary psychology, it seems likely that the most universal phenomena are those that are closely associated with the basic biology that all human beings share. Conversely, the least universal phenomena are those rooted in the varied socialization practices that different cultures evolve. Of course, the only way to determine whether a phenomenon is variable or constant across cultures is to design research to investigate these possibilities, and cultural psychologists do just that (Cole, 1996; Segall et al., 1998).

In summary, social psychology recognizes that people exist as part of a network of other people and examines how individuals influence and interact with one another. Social psychology was pioneered by Germans such as Kurt Lewin, who were motivated by a desire to address social issues and problems. Cultural psychology is concerned with the effects of the broader culture on individuals and similarities and differences among people in different cultures. Within this perspective, absolutists hold that culture has little impact on most psychological phenomena, whereas relativists believe that culture has a powerful effect. Together, social and cultural psychology help expand the discipline's horizons beyond just an examination of individuals. These areas of psychology examine behaviour within the broader context of human interaction.

The profession of psychology: it's not just common sense

Despite its scientific and historical inheritance, there is still a public perception that much of psychology is really just 'common sense' (Eysenck, 2004). This attitude stems partly from the fact that every human engages psychological processes on a daily basis that do not seem particularly remarkable, and partly from the fact that psychology is often portrayed in the media in a fairly trivial and somewhat populist manner in comparison to other sciences. That most of us find daily tasks so simple is a testament to the marvel of evolution, and yet many of these apparently mundane tasks that humans can perform so effortlessly represent some of the hardest problems that engineers are still mostly at a loss to replicate mechanically (Pinker, 1997a). It is our personal experience of what it is to be human – as compared with, say, our complete unfamiliarity with particle physics – that makes the former seem so obvious and intuitive, and the latter so much more difficult and 'scientific'. It has nothing to do with the actual complexity of the systems involved. But try getting the most advanced computer to watch a reality show and predict which contestant is most likely to be voted off next. The outcome might make for trivial television entertainment that every teenager can solve, but the computational processes involved in perceiving, analysing and predicting another's behaviour is immensely complicated. Moreover, we often have little or no insight into the complexity of how we operate. We readily make decisions or have experiences but often cannot actually describe the underlying processes that create them. Finally, common sense is often not that accurate in explaining or predicting human behaviour (Eysenck, 2004). For example, most of us have the commonsense feeling that we make reasoned choices and have free will. When asked to consider the likelihood of their own actions, most people do not believe that they would administer a shock to kill someone if they were ordered to do so, but we know from real life and experimental studies (Milgram, 1974), discussed in Chapter 15, that we do not always think and act as common sense would predict. Psychology is not that obvious.

Now that you've been briefly acquainted with psychology's past and its various theoretical approaches and core domains, let's consider its present by looking at psychology as a profession. We'll look first at the origins of psychology's professional organizations, then at the contexts in which psychologists tend to work, and finally at the kinds of training required to become a psychologist.

Psychologists band together

In many countries across the world, psychologists have chosen to group together to form societies and associations for the advancement of knowledge. In the UK, for example, the Psychological Society (renamed the British Psychological Society (BPS) in 1906) was formed in 1901 in University College London with the aim to 'advance scientific psychological research and to further the cooperation of investigators in the various branches of Psychology'. The society's membership remained relatively small until 1987, when it introduced a Register of Chartered Psychologists, which led to increased membership that currently stands at over 45,000. If a professional is chartered, it is a mark of experience, competence and reputation for anyone looking to employ, consult or learn from a psychologist.

In Australia, psychologists broke away from the BPS where they had been a branch to form the Australian Psychological Society (APS) in 1966, which now has over 17,500 members. New Zealand has its own small but unique organization, the New Zealand Psychological Society (NZPsS), which enjoys reciprocal working arrangements with the neighbouring APS. In the US, the American Psychological Association (APA) has over 150,000 members. The International Union of Psychological Science (IUPsyS) currently has 70 national members from Albania to Zimbabwe, with estimates of well over 500,000 psychologists currently worldwide. That's the size of a large city – imagine spending a day there!

What psychologists do: careers

Psychology can be applied in any area where the scientific principles established in the study of the human mind and behaviour can be used to solve problems or improve performance. When most people think of a professional psychologist, they usually assume that they solve problems related to mental health issues such as depression and anxiety. However, psychologists also operate as counsellors helping people to adjust to negative life events such as bereavement, divorce or unemployment. They often work alongside the medical profession in evaluating patients recovering from head injury, rape or trauma. Psychology is also at the heart of education, playing an important role in identifying children at risk for poor academic achievement and developing strategies and techniques to help them learn. Psychologists operate in the police, courts and prison service and can be found working in human resources departments in most major companies. Psychologists also design better work environments, assess risks in the community and study human behaviour in all its applied forms. More specifically, the main fields of professional psychology are outlined below:

- *Clinical psychology* aims to reduce the psychological distress from difficulties arising in mental health, relationships, learning and any events that can affect the psychological wellbeing across the population. Clinical psychologists typically conduct assessment and evaluation that leads to therapy, counselling or advice. They work largely in health and social care settings.
- *Counselling psychology* is similar to clinical psychology in terms of addressing mental health issues and the factors that contribute to them, but is more concerned with therapeutic practice and requires high levels of interpersonal skills in relating to others in a therapeutic context. Counselling psychologists work in a variety of settings, including health and social care, industry, commerce, the prison service and all levels of education.
- *Educational psychology* is mainly concerned with applying psychological techniques and approaches to help children and young people with difficulties in learning and

social adjustment. Educational psychologists carry out a wide range of tasks aimed at assessing, evaluating and enhancing learning as well as making teachers aware of factors affecting teaching and learning.

- *Forensic psychology* addresses psychological aspects of the legal process including criminal investigations, criminal behaviour and the treatment of criminals. Forensic psychologists may also be consulted to provide a psychological perspective on an investigation and advise on techniques for hostage negotiation. Typical work for a forensic psychologist includes implementing treatment and behaviour modification programmes for criminals, addressing psychological issues of staff and inmates in prisons, advising parole and mental health boards and giving evidence in court. They play an important role in prison life, for example in the UK the largest employer of forensic psychologists is HM Prison Service.
- *Health psychology* is a relatively new field that applies psychological research and methods to promote good health and prevent illness. It tackles potentially harmful behaviours such as alcohol and drug abuse as well as issues related to diet and routine health checks. Health psychologists work in a variety of settings such as hospitals, health authorities and various organizations that take an interest in the wellbeing of their employees.
- *Neuropsychology* deals with the psychological consequences of brain damage arising from disease, disorder or trauma. Work typically involves the assessment, evaluation and implementation of rehabilitation programmes. Neuropsychologists may also be required to give expert witness evidence in court. They mostly work in hospital settings in acute units dealing with brain injury, in rehabilitation centres and in the community.
- *Occupational psychology* aims to improve job satisfaction and productivity of the workforce by the application of psychological principles and techniques. This includes advising on increasing motivation, devising incentives, recruitment, career progression and even coping with redundancy.
- *Sports and exercise psychology*, as the name suggests, applies psychological techniques to sport at the individual and team level to improve performance in training and competition. Most sports psychologists work as consultants but full-time posts are becoming more prevalent.

How do I become a professional psychologist?

So what should you do if you want to become a psychologist? Well to begin with, you usually require a university degree. That's why most of you are reading this book after all. In 2014, 106,000 students applied to study psychology at a British university, which makes it the most popular university degree after nursing (www.ucas.com). For example, in the UK, over 70,000 students took this subject at all levels in 2004/05. Around 80% of students were female, 47% were mature students and 14.5% were ethnic minorities (QAA, 2007). In 2000, the Quality Assurance Agency (QAA), the government body for overseeing higher education in the UK, stated that 'the quality of teaching was high' and that there were 'high progression and completion rates' (QAA, 2007).

One of the key factors in choosing a course is whether it includes a professional accreditation from the country in which you intend to practise – in the UK, for example, courses are accredited by the BPS, as mentioned above. You will need this if you wish to go on to become a chartered psychologist. Becoming chartered is important for establishing professional credibility. In New Zealand and Australia, there is a similar process called registration that entitles you to practise in either country as well as offering support in potential malpractice cases. Through such accreditation schemes, psychological associations take responsibility for training the psychologists of the future to appropriate standards and ensuring that they are fit to practise. For example, according to its website (www.bps.org.uk), the BPS takes responsibility for 'the development, promotion and application of pure and applied psychology for the public good' and 'promotes the efficiency and usefulness of its members by maintaining a high standard of professional education and knowledge'. This is partly achieved through its register of chartered psychologists. Those who the BPS has deemed eligible to do so are entitled to use the designation 'chartered psychologist' and the abbreviation CPsychol after their name. To become chartered, a psychologist must be a member of the BPS and have a first degree in psychology recognized by the society, undertaken society accredited postgraduate qualifications and training and agree to follow the BPS ethical conduct code. But if your degree does not include the relevant accreditation, don't panic! There are usually conversion courses available – in the UK, for example, the Graduate Basis for Chartered Membership (GBC) performs this function.

An undergraduate degree (or conversion course) alone is, however, usually not enough to become a professional psychologist recognized by employers. Typically, students finish an undergraduate university degree and go on to take a graduate degree. This can be a Masters degree on a taught course specializing in an area of interest. A more advanced path is to study for a PhD, which is usually a programme of research focused in one area, for example social, cognitive or developmental psychology. This usually consists of independent research supervised by a faculty member.

Practising psychology in Europe

The European Federation of Psychologists' Associations (EFPA), mentioned at the start of this chapter, is a federation of 36 European national psychological associations, including all 28 EU member states and 8 other European countries. It is of major importance to EFPA members that psychological services are provided by psychologists who are fully qualified, adhering to clear principles of professional ethics.

The EFPA endorses the European Certification in Psychology (EuroPsy), which complies with the standards of education, training and professional practice that are adapted in member states. The EuroPsy enables the mobility of psychologists and the access of clients to high-quality psychological services across Europe. It presents a benchmark or a set of European standards for psychology that serve as the basis for evaluating the academic education and professional training of psychologists across the different countries of the EU, and other countries within EFPA. The EuroPsy comes in two forms, one for basic psychologists and another for specialist psychologists.

EuroPsy for basic psychologists requires them to have:

- received at least five years' academic education in psychology
- done at least one year of practice under the supervision of a qualified supervisor
- provided evidence of current professional competence
- subscribed to a statement on ethical conduct
- engaged in continued professional education.

EuroPsy for specialist psychologists requires them to have:

- met the requirements of the basic EuroPsy
- completed a postgraduate study of at least 400 hours
- gathered at least three years postgraduate experience and training
- done at least 500 hours of specialized practice under supervision of a qualified supervisor, with at least 150 contact hours with the supervisor
- provided evidence of current specialized professional competence.

There is a great deal of variation in the practice and training of psychotherapists in different European countries. In many countries, the field of psychotherapy was partly created outside the university context, which has proven difficult to standardize. At the very least, most countries require postgraduate degrees (Masters and PhDs) before one can practise. One organization, the European Association for Psychotherapy (EAP) has established a European Certificate for Psychotherapy (ECP), whose target goal is mutual recognition and consistent conduct of psychotherapy in Europe. It requires a psychotherapist to fulfil a set of criteria concerning the level of training, supervision and practice, which includes no less than 3,200 hours of training spread over a minimum of seven years, with the first three years being the equivalent of a university degree and the later four years in a training specific to psychotherapy. The EAP represents 128 organizations from 41 European countries including Russia. It has developed ethical guidelines for the protection of patients, which are obligatory for its members, and it publishes the *International Journal of Psychotherapy*.

Where do I go from here?

Job prospects for students with a psychology degree are generally good. Career destinations of psychology graduates are diverse and span a range of industries. Using the UK as an example to illustrate this (QAA, 2007, p. 2):

> a third of graduates who go into permanent employment as psychologists enter public services (such as the healthcare service, education, the Civil Service, and the Armed Forces) ... a third go into industry or commerce, e.g. market research and personnel management ... around one-tenth teach and research in schools, colleges and universities ... 15 to 20 per cent end up working as professional psychologists.

In the UK, psychologists working within the healthcare profession are regulated by the Health and Care Professions Council (HCPC), which covers 16 different professions, including the category of 'practitioner psychologists' who work in one of the main fields described above. Although the remainder of students do not end up working as psychologists, the skills learned during a psychology degree course have wide application in the workplace. These include communication, numeracy, teamwork, critical thinking, computing and independent learning, all of which are highly valued by employers.

So, what are you waiting for? You have the opportunity to study issues that have inspired some of the greatest minds for over 2,000 years. You can learn about new techniques and methods to ask questions that could never before be addressed. You have an opportunity to gain an education that will make you desirable to employers. And best of all, you have the chance to learn something important about the most fascinating thing on the planet – you!

In summary, membership of psychological associations, such as the BPS, APA and APS, has grown dramatically. Psychologists work in clinical, academic and applied settings. Psychologists prepare for research careers through graduate and postdoctoral training and work in a variety of applied settings, including schools, clinics and industry. Psychology is one of the most popular undergraduate degrees with good job prospects providing a wide range of training in skills that are highly favoured by prospective employers.

psychomythology

Psychology is for girls

Take a look at the students around you in your class. Psychology is now the fourth most popular A-level in the UK after English, mathematics and biology. When it was first introduced in 1972, there were only 275 candidates. Just over forty years later there were over 56,000 students in 2013. One might consider this a resounding success in the field except that there is a major problem (Smith, 2011). There is a huge gender imbalance in the students who take psychology, with female psychology students outnumbering male students at a ratio of roughly 4:1.

In Europe, females account for more than 75% of graduates in education and training, around 75% in health and welfare, 70% in humanities and arts, and 60% in social sciences, business and law. In Romania, Estonia, Croatia and Italy (within the EU), more than 90% of graduates in education and training are women (who mainly become teachers). On the other hand, men accounted for more than 80% of graduates in engineering, manufacturing and construction in Germany, Ireland, the Netherlands and Austria (within the EU) and Switzerland, the US and Japan (outside the EU).

Why do boys, overall, choose not to study psychology? An analysis of teachers' opinions and general attitudes indicates that one key issue is the perception that psychology is a female pursuit (Rowley and Delgarno, 2010). Although A-level psychology has been classified as a science since 2008, a large proportion of teachers and pupils did not regard it as being as scientific as chemistry, physics, biology and geology. In part, this was because of the public perception of what science is and in part because a large number of psychology teachers didn't have a science degree. Added to this, the majority of teachers who taught psychology were female. If there is a perception that psychology isn't particularly scientific and is really a topic best suited to females, this reinforces the more general stereotype that males are better suited to science, technology, engineering and mathematics (STEM) subjects.

It is true that there are many more male scientists in physics and engineering today, but then a generation ago there were many more men in biology and medicine, which are now predominantly female pursuits. A large body of research shows that individuals choose pathways they believe they are more suited to, reflecting prevailing cultural stereotypes and opportunities for equality (Dweck, 2008). One final twist is that individuals who are both mathematically gifted and verbally competent are less likely to pursue STEM careers compared to those who are mathematically gifted but with only moderate language skills. Individuals who are good at both tend to be female (Wang et al., 2013).

Males and females are different but we must be cautious in treating them as categorically different, like apples and oranges. Many of the gender differences we ascribe to one or the other are dimensional rather than categorical, more like oranges and lemons (Reis and Carothers, 2014). This distinction between categories versus dimensions is a recurrent theme in psychology that you will encounter throughout this textbook, from the basic perception processing we cover in Chapter 4 to the way we think about psychological disorders in Chapter 16. Rather than assuming that men are from Mars and women are from Venus when it comes to the academic choices they make, it is more prudent to look at the cultural pressures to conform to the expectation of parents, teachers and fellow students. And for those who think psychology is easier than other sciences, remind them that the percentage of students achieving the top grades of A*/A at A-level in the UK in 2013 was only 4%/13% compared to biology (8%/20%), chemistry (8%/25%), physics (9%/22%) and mathematics (16%/26%) (www.jcq.org.uk).

where do you stand?

The perils of procrastination

As you've read in this chapter, the human mind and behaviour are fascinating in part because they are not error free. Mindbugs interest us primarily as paths to achieving a better understanding of mental activity and behaviour, but they also have practical consequences. Let's consider a mindbug that can have significant consequences in your own life: procrastination.

At one time or another, most of us have avoided carrying out a task or put it off to a later time. The task may be unpleasant, difficult or just less entertaining than other things we could be doing at the moment. For university students, procrastination can affect a range of academic activities, such as writing an essay or preparing for a exam. Academic procrastination is not uncommon: over 70% of university students report that they engage in some form of procrastination (Schouwenburg, 1995). Procrastination can be thought of as a mindbug because it prevents the completion of tasks in a timely manner. Although it's fun to go out with your friends tonight, it's not so much fun to worry for three days about your impending history exam or try to study at 4am on the morning of the exam. Studying now, or at least a little bit each day, robs the procrastination mindbug of its power over you.

Some procrastinators defend the practice by claiming that they tend to work best under pressure or by noting that as long as a task gets done, it doesn't matter all that much if it is completed just before the deadline. Is there any merit to such claims, or are they just feeble excuses for counterproductive behaviour?

A study of 60 undergraduate psychology students provides some intriguing answers (Tice and Baumeister, 1997). At the beginning of the semester, the lecturer announced a due date for the term paper and told students that if they could not meet the date, they would receive an extension to a later date. About a month later, students completed a scale that measures tendencies towards procrastination. At that same time, and then again during the last week of class, students recorded health symptoms they had experienced during the past week, the amount of stress they had experienced during that week, and the number of visits they had made to a healthcare centre during the previous month.

Students who scored high on the procrastination scale tended to turn in their papers late. One month into the semester, these procrastinators reported less stress and fewer symptoms of physical illness than did nonprocrastinators. But at the end of the semester, the procrastinators reported *more* stress and *more* health symptoms than did the nonprocrastinators and also reported more visits to the health centre. The procrastinators also received lower grades on their papers and on course exams.

This study shows, then, that procrastination did have some benefits: procrastinators tended to feel better early on, while they were procrastinating and their deadline was far in the future. But they paid a significant cost for this immediate relief: procrastinators not only suffered more stress and health problems as they scrambled to complete their work near the deadline, but also reported more stress and health symptoms across the entire semester. There was also no evidence to support the idea that procrastinators do their 'best work under pressure', since their academic performance was worse than that of nonprocrastinators. Therefore, in addition to making use of the tips provided in *the real world* box on increasing study skills, it would seem wise to avoid procrastination on this module and others.

Where do you stand on procrastination? Calculate your procrastination score by rating the statements below on a scale of 1–5, where 1 = not at all; 2 = incidentally; 3 = sometimes; 4 = most of the time; 5 = always.

How frequently last week did you engage in the following behaviours or thoughts?

1 Drifted off into daydreams while studying
2 Studied the subject matter that you had planned to do
3 Had no energy to study
4 Prepared to study at some point but did not get any further
5 Gave up when studying was not going well
6 Gave up studying early in order to do more pleasant things
7 Put off the completion of a task
8 Allowed yourself to be distracted from your work
9 Experienced concentration problems when studying
10 Interrupted studying for a while in order to do other things
11 Forgot to prepare things for studying
12 Did so many other things that there was insufficient time left for studying
13 Thought that you had enough time left, so that there was really no need to start studying.

So, how did you score? In the original study, they found all students scored between 18 and 63, with the average score being 42.7. You can probably guess that the higher your score, the bigger your procrastination problem!

Chapter review

Psychology today

- Psychology is the scientific study of mind and behaviour. Behaviour is usually adaptive because it helps us meet the challenges of daily living; similarly, the brain and mind usually function effectively and efficiently. Disruptions to the mind and behaviour, in the form of mindbugs, allow us to better understand the normal functions of the mind and behaviour.
- Although most of today's psychologists operate in the US, the scientific origin of our discipline has its roots in 19th-century Europe where the first systematic studies of human behaviour and the mind began.
- Today, psychology has developed into a wide field of inquiry and application, with different domains of interest, methodological approaches and types of explanation.
- Psychologists are also interested in the failures of human thought and behaviour as a way of understanding how these are constrained in the sorts of problems humans have evolved to solve.

Psychology's roots: the path to a science of mind

- Early efforts to develop a science of mind were pioneered by French scientists Pierre Flourens and Paul Broca, who observed the effects of brain damage on the mental abilities of people and animals, and by German scientists such as Hermann von Helmholtz and Wilhelm Wundt, who applied methods from physiology to the study of psychology.

Exporting European psychology

- Following his experience in Wilhelm Wundt's laboratory in Leipzig, Germany, Edward Titchener returned to the US where he developed a school of thought called 'structuralism', which focused on analysing the basic elements of consciousness.
- At Harvard, William James pioneered the school of functionalism, which emphasized the functions of consciousness, and applied Darwin's theory of natural selection to the mind. G. Stanley Hall, at Johns Hopkins, helped organize psychology with the formation of the first professional laboratory, organization and journal in the field.

Errors and illusions reveal psychology

- Max Wertheimer founded Gestalt psychology based on the interpretation of an illusion of apparent motion, in which people perceive flashing lights as a moving whole instead of the sum of its parts.
- Clinicians such as Jean-Martin Charcot and Pierre Janet studied unusual cases in which patients acted like different people while under hypnosis, raising the possibility of more than one conscious self.
- Based on his own observations of clinical patients, Sigmund Freud developed the theory of psychoanalysis, which emphasized the importance of unconscious influences and childhood experiences in shaping thoughts, feelings and behaviour. A more optimistic view of the human condition, espoused by humanistic psychologists such as Abraham Maslow and Carl Rogers, held that people need to grow and reach their full potential.

Psychology in the 20th century: behaviourism takes centre stage

- Behaviourism studies observable actions and responses and holds that inner mental processes are private events that cannot be studied scientifically.
- John Watson launched behaviourism in 1913, studied the association between a stimulus and a response, and emphasized the importance of the environment over genetics in shaping behaviour.
- B. F. Skinner developed the concept of reinforcement, demonstrating that animals and humans will repeat behaviours that generate positive outcomes and avoid those that are associated with unpleasant results.
- In Europe, Skinner's behaviourism was less dominant as ethologists were more interested in the behaviours of animals in their natural habitats.

Beyond behaviourism: psychology expands

- Cognitive psychology is concerned with inner mental processes such as perception, attention, memory and reasoning.
- Much of the emphasis on mental processes was spurred by the war effort to develop more efficient man–machine interactions.
- Cognitive psychology developed as a field due to psychologists' efforts to improve cognitive performance, the invention of the computer, and Noam Chomsky's ideas concerning the development of language.
- Cognitive neuroscience attempts to link the brain with the mind through studies of brain-damaged and healthy patients using neuroimaging techniques that allow glimpses of the brain in action.
- Evolutionary psychology focuses on the adaptive value of the mind and behaviour and seeks to understand current psychological processes in terms of the abilities and traits preserved by natural selection.

Beyond the individual: social and cultural perspectives

- Social psychology recognizes that people exist in a network of other people and examines how individuals influence and interact with one another.
- Cultural psychology is concerned with the effects of the broader culture on individuals and the similarities and differences among people in different cultures.

The profession of psychology: it's not just common sense

- Despite a public perception that much of psychology is just common sense, in truth it addresses some of the most complex questions related to how the mind and behaviour operate.
- To work as a psychologist usually requires at least university degree-level qualifications, often with additional graduate training in specific areas.

- Many countries have professional organizations that represent the interests of working psychologists and accredit degree courses. In Europe, the EFPA is an organization that seeks to standardize training so that individuals can work in different member states.
- Psychologists prepare for research careers through graduate and postdoctoral training and also work in a variety of applied settings, including schools, clinics and industry.

Key terms

behaviour (p. 5)
behavioural neuroscience (p. 28)
behaviourism (p. 21)
cognitive neuroscience (p. 29)
cognitive psychology (p. 25)
consciousness (p. 14)
cultural psychology (p. 33)
epistemology (p. 12)
equipotential (p. 28)
ethology (p. 24)
evolutionary psychology (p. 30)
free will (p. 23)
functionalism (p. 16)
Gestalt psychology (p. 18)
humanistic psychology (p. 20)
hysteria (p. 19)
illusions (p. 17)
introspection (p. 14)
law of mass action (p. 28)
metaphysics (p. 12)
mind (p. 5)
nativism (p. 11)
natural behaviours (p. 24)
natural selection (p. 16)
pedagogical approach (p. 26)
philosophical empiricism (p. 11)
phrenology (p. 12)
physiology (p. 13)
psychoanalysis (p. 19)
psychoanalytic theory (p. 19)
psychology (p. 5)
reaction time (p. 13)
reinforcement (p. 23)
response (p. 22)
sensory perception (p. 14)
social psychology (p. 32)
stimulus (p. 13)
structuralism (p. 14)
unconscious (p. 19)

Recommended reading

Dawkins, R. (1976) *The Selfish Gene.* Oxford: OUP. Probably one of the most influential science books written for a general audience, which inspired at least one of the authors to become a scientist. In the same way that Skinner's behaviourism challenged the notion of free will, the selfish gene view of human evolution shows how we are shaped to respond to the pressure to replicate by engaging in adaptive patterns of behaviour.

Fancher, R. E. (1979) *Pioneers of Psychology.* New York: Norton. Engaging book that examines the history of psychology by painting portraits of the field's pioneers, including many of the psychologists featured in this chapter. A great way to learn more about the history of psychology is by becoming familiar with the lives of its founders.

Gardiner, H. (1987) *The Mind's New Science.* New York: Basic Books. Comprehensive yet accessible account of the cognitive revolution that led to the emergence of the integrative field of cognitive science, combining various disciplines of psychology, philosophy, ethology, artificial intelligence, language and neuroscience.

Hermann, D., Raybeck, D. and Gruneberg, M. (2002) *Improving Memory and Study Skills.* Seattle: Hogrefe & Huber. Excellent book offering a neat introduction to many aspects of cognitive psychology. More importantly, it offers several practical suggestions for improving memory and study habits, and mastering material you are trying to learn.

James, W. ([1890]1999) *The Principles of Psychology.* New York: Holt. Considered by many psychologists to be the 'bible' of psychology, this masterpiece is still exciting to read over a century after it was published. If you do have a chance to read it, you will understand why thousands of psychologists are thankful James bypassed a career in medicine for one in psychology.

Mind Shapers series. Basingstoke: Palgrave Macmillan. Series of brief, accessible introductions to key thinkers in psychology including Skinner and Freud, who you met in this chapter. As you progress through your psychology course, you may also want to explore other psychologists covered by the series, such as Milgram, Fromm and Erikson.

2

- Empiricism: how to know things
- Observation: discovering what people do
- the real world Taking a chance
- Explanation: discovering why people do what they do
- Establishing causality in the brain hot science
- Qualitative research: forget the size, feel the quality
- The ethics of science: first, do no harm
- With two choices, it's not always 50:50 psychomythology
- where do you stand? The morality of immoral experiments

Chapter learning objectives

At the end of this chapter you will be able to:

1 Understand that psychology is an empirical science.

2 Describe the steps in conducting a quantitative piece of psychological research.

3 Appreciate the role of descriptive and inferential statistics in research.

4 Understand qualitative approaches to research.

5 Describe some ethical issues involved in a range of methodological approaches.

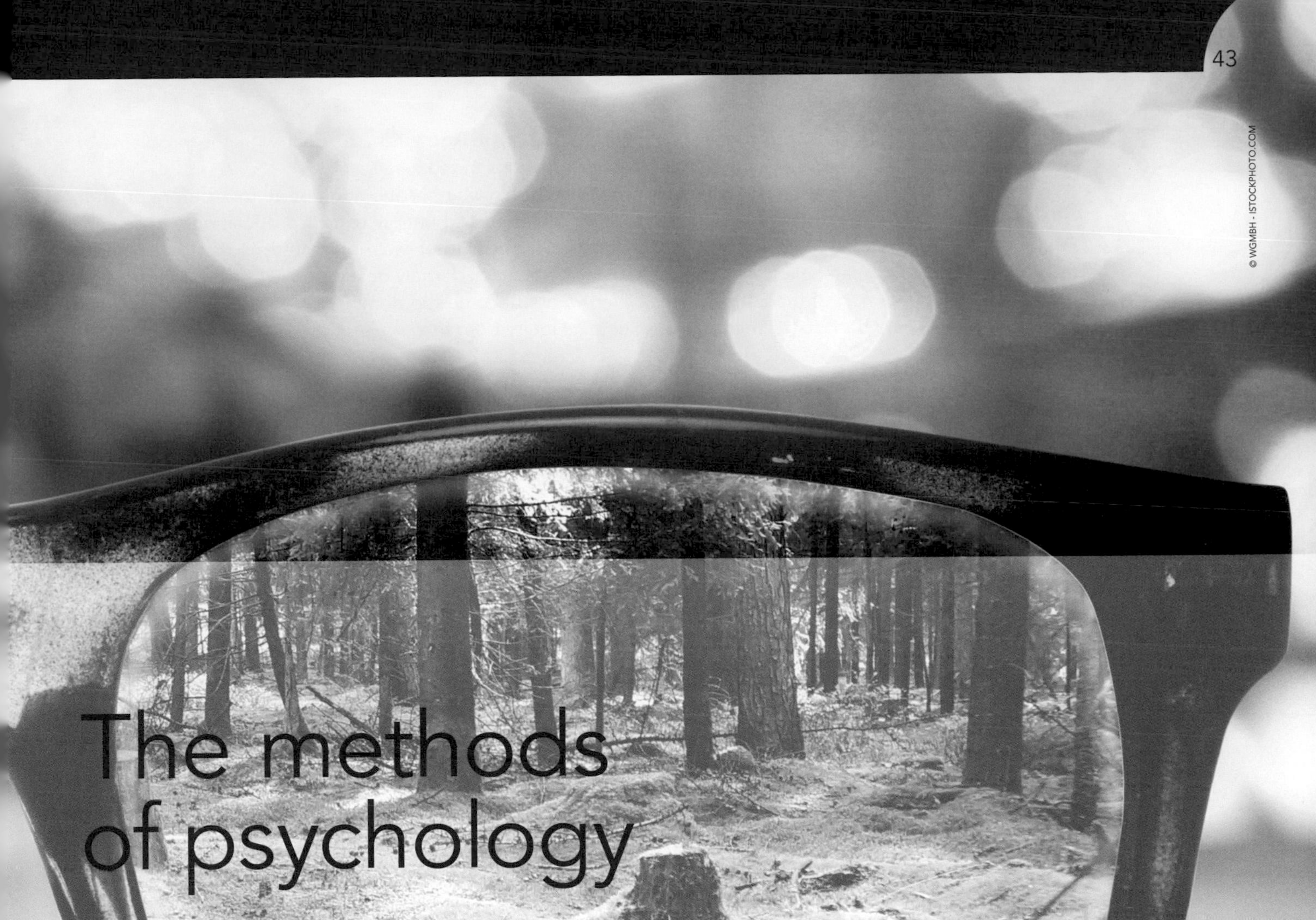

The methods of psychology

When you make a cup of tea, do you pour in the milk first or last? Why is such a trivial domestic question remotely interesting? In the late 1920s, a group of academics and their wives were having afternoon tea in a Cambridge garden, when one lady insisted that the beverage tasted different if the milk was added before or after the tea. According to the story retold by David Salsburg (2002) in his fascinating book *The Lady Tasting Tea: How Statistics Revolutionized Science in the Twentieth Century*, one of the Cambridge academics who was present at the event told him that the men in the group initially scoffed. All except one, that is. A thin, short man with thick glasses and a pointed greying beard excitedly exclaimed: 'Let us test the proposition.' He set about outlining how an experiment should be conducted. Soon the other men joined in with suggestions and within a few minutes they began to test whether the lady could indeed tell the difference by presenting her with cup after cup of tea, as the thin man with the beard noted down her responses. This man was Ronald Aylmer Fisher (1890–1962), a mathematical genius, who would later be knighted for his contribution to statistics – the field of applied mathematical inquiry that would transform scientific research throughout the 20th century.

A major problem that faced 20th-century science was that the world was not as mathematically precise and predictable as the 17th-century clockwork model of the universe had indicated. Even predicting the movements of planets had margins of error. It was thought that if there were errors in scientific predictions, it was because the measurements were imprecise and that with better measuring equipment, scientists would become more accurate. But as Salsburg (2002) points out, the reverse became true – as measurements became more accurate, they detected more and more variation that made scientific predictions more imprecise. This was because complex systems studied in science have a multitude of factors that can influence an outcome. In order

©ISTOCKPHOTO.COM/MARK WRAGG

to answer scientific questions, one had to know how to deal with the problems of measurement and that could include cups of tea.

Sir Ronald Fisher was not interested in whether the addition of milk before or after tea tasted different. Rather, he was interested in how to test propositions in a meaningful way in order to draw conclusions. Fisher was interested in the new field of mathematical modelling known as 'statistics', largely developed in Europe over the first half of the 20th century, which would become the dominant means of inquiry and the basis for all methods of scientific inquiry from then on.

Empiricism: how to know things

When ancient Greeks sprained their ankles, caught the flu or accidentally set their togas on fire, they had to choose between two kinds of doctors: dogmatists (from *dogmatikos*, meaning 'belief'), who thought that the best way to understand illness was to develop theories about the body's functions, and empiricists (from *empeirikos*, meaning 'experience'), who thought that the best way to understand illness was to observe sick people. The rivalry between these two schools of medicine didn't last long, however, because the people who chose to see dogmatists tended to die, which wasn't very good for business. It is little wonder that today we use the word *dogmatism* to describe the tendency for people to cling to their assumptions and the word **empiricism** to describe *the belief that accurate knowledge of the world requires observation of it.* The fact that we can answer questions about the world by observation may seem obvious to you, but this obvious fact is actually a relatively new discovery. Throughout most of human history, people have trusted authority to answer important questions about the world, and it is only in the last millennium (and especially the past three centuries) that people have begun to trust their eyes and ears more than their elders.

EMPIRICISM Originally a Greek school of medicine that stressed the importance of observation, and now generally used to describe any attempt to acquire knowledge by observing objects or events.

The scientific method

Empiricism is the essential element of the **scientific method** – *a set of rules and techniques that allow researchers to avoid the illusions, mistakes and erroneous conclusions that simple observation can produce.* In essence, the scientific method suggests that when we have an idea about the world – about how bats navigate, where the moon came from, or why people can't forget traumatic events – we should gather empirical evidence relevant to that idea and then modify the idea to fit with the evidence. Scientists usually refer to an idea of this kind as a **theory** – *a hypothetical explanation of how and why a phenomenon occurs, usually in the form of a statement about the causal relationship between two or more properties.* We might theorize that bats navigate by making sounds and then listening for the echo, that the moon was formed when a small planet collided with the earth, or that the brain responds to traumatic events by producing chemicals that facilitate memory. Each of these theories is an explanation of how something in the natural world works.

SCIENTIFIC METHOD A set of rules and techniques that allow researchers to avoid the illusions, mistakes and erroneous conclusions that simple observation can produce.

THEORY A hypothetical account of how and why a phenomenon occurs, usually in the form of a statement about the causal relationship between two or more properties.

When scientists set out to develop a theory, they start with the simplest one, and they refer to this as *the rule of parsimony*, which comes from the Latin word *parcere*, meaning 'to spare'. The rule of parsimony is often credited to William Ockham, 14th-century logician, who wrote: 'Plurality should only be posited when necessary', which is essentially the way people in the Middle Ages said: 'Keep it simple, stupid.' Ockham wasn't arguing that nature is simple or that complex theories are wrong. He was merely suggesting that it makes sense to *start* with the simplest theory possible and *then* make the theory more complicated only if we must. Part of what makes $E = mc^2$ such a good theory is that it has exactly three letters and one number.

Theories are ideas about how and why things work the way they do. So how do we decide if a theory is right? Most theories make predictions about what we should and should not be able to observe in the world. For example, if bats really do navigate by making sounds and then listening for echoes, we should observe that deaf bats can't navigate. That 'should statement' is technically known as a **hypothesis** – *a falsifiable prediction made by a theory.* The word *falsifiable* is a critical part of that definition. Why is it important to prove that something can be wrong rather than just plain right? This question

HYPOTHESIS A specific and testable prediction that is usually derived from a theory.

seems absurd, as something should either be right or wrong. In other words, it should be **verifiable** – *something that can be checked by objective measures*. Most of us seek truth in the world, so why the focus on things that could be false? The problem is that some ideas – such as 'God created the universe' – do not specify what we should or should not observe if they are true, and thus no observations can falsify them. Because such ideas do not give rise to hypotheses, they cannot be the subject of scientific investigation. That doesn't mean they're wrong. It just means that we can't judge them by using the scientific method.

VERIFIABLE Something that can be checked by objective measures.

DEDUCTION Drawing inferences where the conclusion must be true if the premises are true.

INDUCTION The process of establishing general truths based on a limited set of observations.

But there is also a fundamental problem about establishing truth based on observation. For example, it is easy to determine whether Sam the swan is white. You simply have to look at him – although some philosophers might argue that direct observation does not prove anything (as we'll see below). Let's assume that your observation is true, but is Sam the exception or does he represent a truth about the universe that swans are white? Remember, scientists want to discover things that are not one-offs but general truths so that they can make statements about the world and win the Nobel Prize. It's a problem because no one can feasibly observe and measure everything and so we have to use reason to establish verification.

BRAND X

Just because this swan is white, does it mean that all swans are white?

One way to reason is to use **deduction** – *drawing inferences where the conclusion must be true if the premises are true* – such as:

Premise: All swans are white
Premise: Sam is a swan
Conclusion: Therefore, Sam is white.

We can deduce that the conclusion is true based on the premises. However, we cannot observe all swans in the world to establish the truth of the first premise and so we must use **induction** – *the process of establishing general truths based on a limited set of observations*. So, by induction, we have:

Premise: Sam the swan is white
Premise: Gertrude the swan is white
Premise: Cynthia the swan is white
... and so on
Conclusion: Therefore, all swans are white.

This conclusion by induction is neither logically true nor is it actually true. As Dienes (2008) points out in this particular example, *everyone* in Europe did believe white swans were a truth of Nature until the Dutch explorer Willem de Vlamingh discovered black swans in Australia in 1697.

The more observations we can make, the more certain we can be we have arrived at a truth, but as noted by the Scottish philosopher David Hume, who we encountered in Chapter 1, the problem with induction is that one can never be certain because there may always be exceptions not yet encountered. So, induction presents a problem for establishing truth beyond reasonable doubt. It is not simply swans but any observations we care to make are problematic.

©ISTOCKPHOTO.COM/STEVEN WYNN

The astronomer Galileo Galilei (1564–1642) was excommunicated and sentenced to prison for sticking to his own observations of the solar system rather than accepting the teachings of the church. In 1597, he wrote to his friend and fellow astronomer Johannes Kepler: 'What would you say of the learned here, who, replete with the pertinacity of the asp, have steadfastly refused to cast a glance through the telescope? What shall we make of this? Shall we laugh, or shall we cry?' As it turned out, the correct answer was *cry*.

Hume went as far as to say that induction can never prove a truth and simply increasing the number of observations does not make a statement any more true. Your car may start every day but that does not mean that it will always start and we know that eventually it will never start – so the number of observations does not make the assumption any more true.

When stated like this it seems that there is a crisis in truth. We can neither measure everything nor rely on past experiences. What are scientists to do? Luckily for us, much of this philosophical conundrum was considered by the Austrian philosopher Karl Popper (1902–94). Popper accepted Hume's original objection to induction and during his lifetime he witnessed how the irrefutable laws of Newtonian physics, which had been based on centuries of observation, were overturned by Einstein's theory of relativity and quantum physics. For Popper, the conclusion was inescapable; you can never establish the truth of theories. This logic led Popper to a radical new way of reasoning about theories. You cannot sensibly prove they are true but you can prove they are false!

We must look for exceptions to disprove the rule, or, in layman's terms, one swallow does not make a summer.

For Popper, scientists must generate and pursue theories not with the emphasis on proving them true with more and more observations, but with the view to falsification. If a theory is falsifiable in principle, then it is a scientific theory, but it can never be proven. In contrast, a theory that is not falsifiable is not a scientific theory but rather pseudoscience and not worthy of pursuit. Only by seeking falsification can science truly progress, which is why scientists spend all their time trying to prove each other wrong. When evidence is consistent with a theory, it increases our confidence in it, but it never makes us completely certain. As Albert Einstein wisely pointed out: 'No amount of experimentation can ever prove me right, but a single experiment can prove me wrong.'

The scientific method suggests that the best way to learn the truth about the world is to develop theories, derive hypotheses from them, test those hypotheses by gathering evidence, and then use that evidence to modify the theories. But what exactly does 'gathering evidence' entail?

The art of looking

EMPIRICAL METHOD A set of rules and techniques for observation.

Most of us hold pet theories about all manner of things: women are worse drivers than men; when a piece of toast falls, it is most likely to land butter-side down; tea tastes better when the milk is added last. Whatever our pet theories may be, they are often simply hunches based on our observations. To change a hunch into a theory, we need to gather evidence to test the claims under consideration. Empiricism is the right approach, but to do it properly requires an **empirical method** – *a set of rules and techniques for observation*. In many sciences, the word *method* refers primarily to technologies that enhance the powers of the senses. Biologists use microscopes and astronomers use telescopes because the phenomena they seek to explain are invisible to the naked eye. Human behaviour, on the other hand, is relatively easy to observe, so you might expect psychology's methods to be relatively simple. In fact, the empirical challenges facing psychologists are among the most daunting in all of modern science, thus psychology's empirical methods are among the most sophisticated in all of modern science. Three things make people especially difficult to study:

- *Complexity:* No galaxy, particle, molecule or machine is as complicated as the human brain. Scientists can describe the birth of a star or the death of a cell in exquisite detail, but they can barely begin to say how the 500 million interconnected neurons that constitute the brain give rise to the thoughts, feelings and actions that are psychology's core concerns.
- *Variability:* In almost all the ways that matter, one *E. coli* bacterium is pretty much like another. But people are as varied as their fingerprints. No two individuals ever do, say, think or feel exactly the same thing under exactly the same circumstances, which means that when you've seen one, you've most definitely not seen them all.
- *Reactivity:* An atom of caesium-133 oscillates 9,192,631,770 times per second regardless of whether anyone is watching. But people often think, feel and act one way when they are being observed and a different way when they are not. When people know they are being studied, they don't always behave as they otherwise would.

In short, human beings are tremendously complex, endlessly variable and uniquely reactive, and these attributes present a major challenge to the scientific study of their behaviour. As you'll see, psychologists have developed a variety of methods that are designed to meet these challenges head-on.

Observation: discovering what people do

There is no escaping the fact that you have to observe *what* people do before you can try to explain *why* they do it. To *observe* something means to use your senses to learn about its properties. For example, when you observe a round, red apple, your brain is using the pattern of light that is falling on your eyes to draw an inference about the apple's identity, shape and colour (as we discuss in Chapter 4). That kind of informal observation is fine for buying fruit but not for doing science. Why? First, casual observations are notoriously unstable. The same apple may appear red in the daylight and crimson at night or spherical to one person and elliptical to another. Second, casual observations can't tell us about many of the properties in which we might be interested. No matter how long and hard you look, you will never be able to discern an apple's crunchiness or pectin content simply by watching it. If you want to know about those properties, you must do more than observe. You must *measure*.

Measurement

For most of human history, people had no idea how old they were because there was no simple way to keep track of time – or weight, volume, density, temperature or anything else for that matter. Today we live in a world of tape measures and rulers, clocks and calendars, milometers, thermometers and mass spectrometers. Measurement is not just the basis of science, it is the basis of modern life. All these measurements have two things in common. Whether we want to measure the intensity of an earthquake, the distance between molecules, or the attitude of a registered voter, we must first *define* the property we wish to measure and then find a way to *detect* it.

Defining and detecting

You probably think you know what *length* is. But if you try to define it without using the word *long*, you get tongue-tied pretty quickly. We use words such as *weight*, *speed* and *length* all the time in ordinary conversation, without realizing that each of these terms has an **operational definition** – *a description of an abstract property in terms of a concrete condition that can be measured.* For example, the operational definition of the property we casually refer to as *length* is 'the change in the location of light over time'. That's right. When we say that a bookshelf is 'a metre long', we are actually saying how long it takes a particle of light to travel from one end of the shelf to the other. (In case you're interested, the answer is 1/299,792,458th of a second. In case you're not interested, that's still the answer.) According to this operational definition, the more time it takes for a photon to travel from one end of a bookshelf to the other, the more 'length' that bookshelf has. Operational definitions specify the concrete events that count as instances of an abstract property. The first step in making any measurement is to define the property we want to measure in concrete terms.

OPERATIONAL DEFINITION A description of an abstract property in terms of a concrete condition that can be measured.

The second step is to find a way to detect the concrete terms that our definition describes. To do this we must use a **measure** – *a device that can detect the events to which an operational definition refers.* For example, length is the change in the location of light over time, and we can detect such changes by using a photon detector, which tells us the location of a particle of light, and a clock, which tells us how long it took the particle of light to travel from one location to another. Once we have determined just how far a photon travels in 1/299,792,458th of a second, we can make our next measurement a lot less expensive by marking that distance on a piece of wood and calling it a ruler. Keep in mind that measures, such as clocks and photon detectors, detect the concrete conditions described by our operational definitions (such as 'change in the location of light over time'), but *they do not detect the property itself* (such as length). Indeed, properties such as shape, colour, length or duration are best thought of as abstract ideas that can never be measured directly. **FIGURE 2.1** shows a variety of old and new measures used by psychologists.

MEASURE A device that can detect the measurable events to which an operational definition refers.

Defining and *detecting* are the two tasks that allow us to measure physical properties, and these same two tasks allow us to measure psychological properties as well. If we wanted to measure happiness, for example, our first task would be to develop an operational definition of that property, that is, to specify some concrete, measurable event that will count as an instance of happiness. For example, we might define happiness as the simultaneous contraction of the *zygomatic major*, the muscle that makes your mouth turn up when you smile, and the *orbicularis oculi*, the muscle that makes your eyes crinkle when you smile. After defining happiness as a specific set of muscular contractions, we would then need to measure those contractions, and the **electromyograph (EMG)**,

ELECTROMYOGRAPH (EMG) A device that measures muscle contractions under the surface of a person's skin.

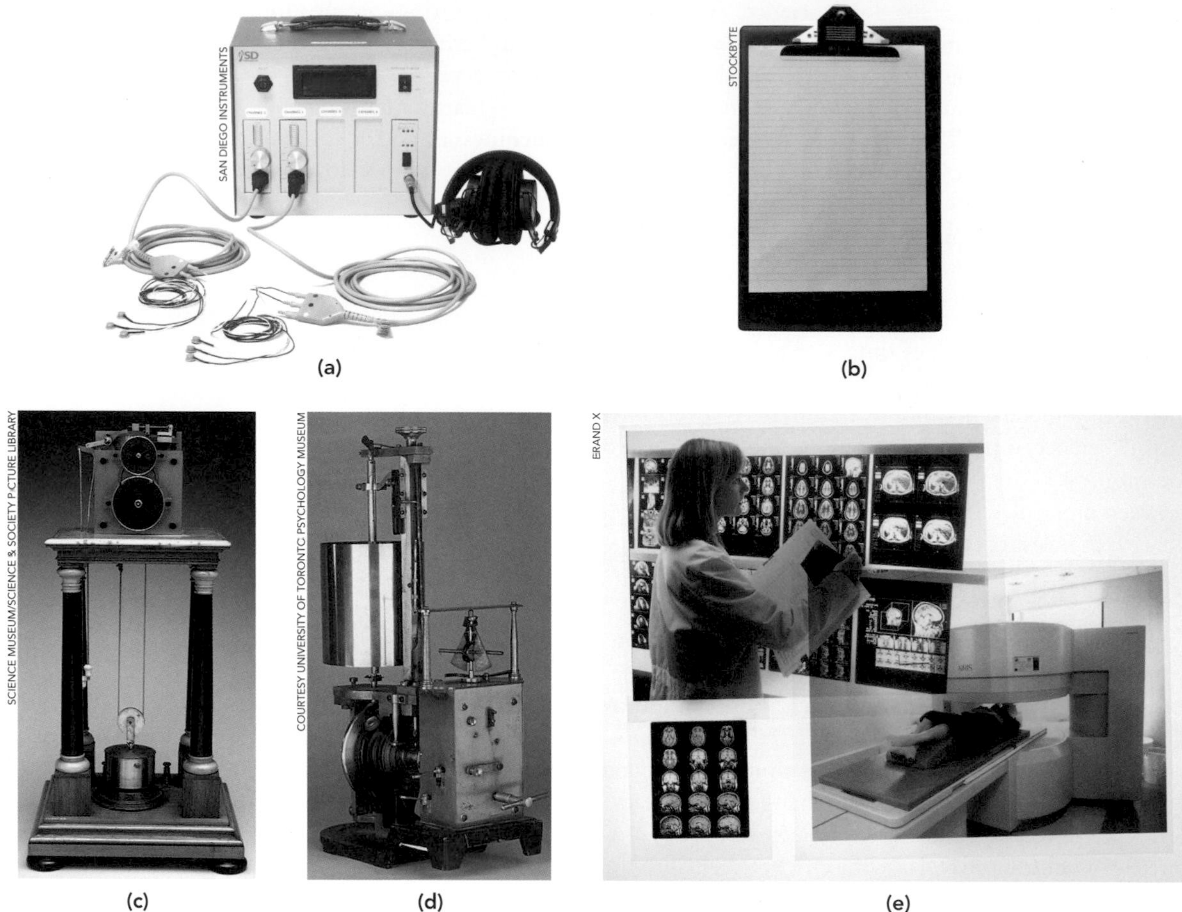

FIGURE 2.1 Some psychological measures Psychological measures may take a variety of forms: (a) a modern electromyograph (EMG) measures the electrical activity of muscles in the face; (b) a questionnaire measures preferences, attitudes and opinions; (c) an 1890 Hipp chronoscope measures reaction times; (d) a 1907 kymograph measures hand movements; and (e) a functional magnetic resonance imaging (fMRI) chamber measures blood flow in the brain.

a device that measures muscle contractions under the surface of a person's skin, would do splendidly. The SR-HLAB EMG system (pictured in Figure 2.1a) features two response modules with two sets of electrodes, allowing measurement of both the zygomatic major and the orbicularis oculi at the same time. Once we have defined happiness and found a way to detect the concrete events that our definition supplies, we are in a position to measure it.

But is this the *right* way to measure happiness? That's hard to say. There are many ways to define the same property and many ways to detect the events that this definition supplies. For instance, we could detect the muscular contractions involved in smiling by using an EMG, or we could detect them by asking a human observer to watch a participant's face and tell us how often the participant smiled. We could define happiness in terms of muscular contractions, or we could define it as a person's self-assessment of their own emotional state, in which case we could measure it by asking people how happy they feel and recording their answers. With so many options for defining and detecting happiness, how are we to choose among them? As you are about to see, there are many ways to define and detect, but some are much better than others.

VALIDITY The characteristic of an observation that allows one to draw accurate inferences from it.

Property (happiness)

Measure (EMG)

Define

Operational definition (muscle contractions)

Detect

FIGURE 2.2 Sources of invalidity The process of *defining* links properties to operational definitions, and the process of *detecting* links operational definitions to measures. Invalidity can result from problems in either of these links.

Validity

Measurement consists of two tasks: *defining*, the process by which properties are linked to operational definitions, and *detecting*, the process by which operational definitions are linked to measures. If we do either of these tasks badly, then any measurement we make will lack validity – *the characteristic of an observation that allows one to draw accurate inferences from it.* Because measurement involves precisely two tasks, there are precisely two ways for a measurement to be invalid (see **FIGURE 2.2**). First, a measurement will be invalid when the operational definition does not adequately define the property, and second, a measurement will be invalid when the measure cannot adequately detect the conditions that the operational definition describes. Let's consider each of these sources of invalidity more closely.

Problems of defining

You can measure a lot of things with a ruler, but happiness isn't one of them because 'change in the location of light over time' is not meaningfully related to the emotional experience we call 'happiness'. We all have some sense of what happiness means, and the distance that a photon travels just isn't it. A good operational definition must have **construct validity** – *the tendency for an operational definition and a property to share meaning*. It makes sense to define *wealth* as the amount of money a person has in savings, investments and property because the concrete object we call *money* is meaningfully related to the abstract concept we call *wealth*. It makes no sense to define *wealth* as the number of tennis balls a person can carry in one hand because this ability (as admirable as it may be) has nothing to do with what we mean by the word *wealth*. Some operational definitions are clearly related to their properties, and some are clearly not.

CONSTRUCT VALIDITY The tendency for an operational definition and a property to have a clear conceptual relation.

The interesting cases fall between these two extremes. For example, is smiling a valid way to define happiness? Well, this definition certainly has construct validity: we all know from experience that smiling and happiness go together like money and wealth do. But if smiling is a valid definition of happiness, then it should also have **predictive validity** – *the tendency for an operational definition to be related to other operational definitions of the same property*. If an operational definition such as smiling is linked to a property such as happiness, then it should also be linked to other operational definitions of happiness. For example, it should be linked to electrical activity in the part of the brain known as the 'right frontal lobe' or to the person's own report of their emotional state. If we could demonstrate that people whose right frontal lobes are active and who say 'I feel really happy right now' also tend to smile, then we could be even more certain that smiling is a valid definition of happiness. Predictive validity gets its name from the fact that knowledge of the conditions specified by one operational definition, for example knowing whether a person is smiling, should enable us to predict the conditions specified by another operational definition, for example whether the person's right frontal lobe is active or whether the person is claiming to be happy. In short, if we do a good job of defining a property, then our measurement of that property will have validity. **FIGURE 2.3** illustrates the relationship between predictive validity and construct validity.

PREDICTIVE VALIDITY The tendency for an operational definition to be related to other operational definitions of the same property.

RF activity

fMRI

COURTESY TAPERT ET AL 2001

Happiness

Construct validity

Predictive validity

Smile

EMG

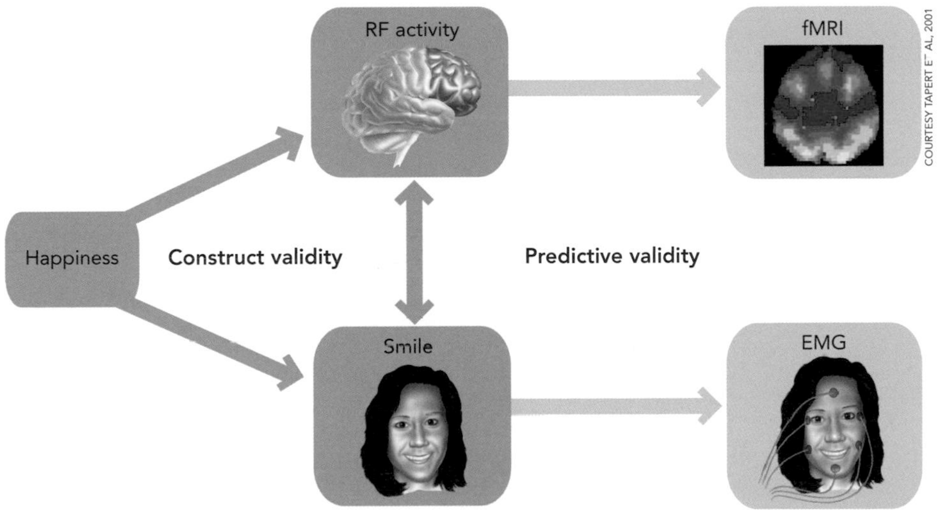

FIGURE **2.3 Kinds of validity** Construct validity (purple) refers to the conceptual relationship between a property and a measure. Predictive validity (green) refers to the relationship between different measures. In this example, the property called 'happiness' is operationally defined as right frontal lobe (RF) activity, which is measured by fMRI, and also as smiling, which is measured by facial EMG.

Problems of detecting

Rulers made of jelly have historically been commercial failures. The stiffness of a yardstick is critical because it means that when we repeatedly use the ruler to measure an object, we repeatedly get the same result. What's more, anyone else who uses the same

RELIABILITY The tendency for a measure to produce the same result whenever it is used to measure the same thing.

POWER The tendency for a measure to produce different results when it is used to measure different things.

yardstick to measure the same object will get the same result we did. **Reliability** is *the tendency for a measure to produce the same result whenever it is used to measure the same thing*, and any measure that lacks this tendency is about as useful as a ruler made of jelly. For example, if a person's zygomatic muscle did not move for 10 minutes, we would expect the EMG to produce the same reading for 10 minutes. If the EMG produced different readings from one minute to the next, then it would be an unreliable measure that was detecting differences that weren't really there. A good measure must be reliable. Another component of reliability is **power** – *the tendency for a measure to produce different results when it is used to measure different things.* If a person's zygomatic muscle moved continuously for 10 minutes, we would expect the EMG to produce different readings in those 10 minutes. If instead the EMG produced the same reading from one minute to the next, then it would be a weak or powerless measure that was failing to detect differences that were really there. Reliable and powerful measures are those that detect the conditions specified by an operational definition when they happen and *only* when they happen.

Validity, reliability and power are prerequisites for accurate measurement. But once you've got a good ruler in hand, the next step is to find something to measure with it. Psychologists have developed techniques for doing that too.

Samples

CASE METHOD A method of gathering scientific knowledge by studying a single individual.

If a pig flew over the Houses of Parliament, it wouldn't matter whether other pigs could do the same trick. The fact that just one pig did it once would challenge our most cherished assumptions about animal physiology, aerodynamics and national security and would thus be an observation well worth making. Similarly, individuals sometimes do remarkable things that deserve close study, and when psychologists study them closely, they are using the **case method** – *a method of gathering scientific knowledge by studying a single individual.* For example, physician Oliver Sacks (1985) described his observations of a brain-damaged patient in a book titled *The Man Who Mistook His Wife for a Hat, and Other Clinical Tales*, and those observations were worth making because this is a rather unusual mistake for a man to make. As you saw in Chapter 1, people with unusual abilities, unusual experiences or unusual deficits often provide important insights about human psychology.

But exceptional cases are the exception, and more often than not, psychologists are in the business of observing *un*exceptional people and trying to explain why they think, feel and act as they do. When psychologists observe ordinary people, they typically observe *many* of them and then try to explain the *average* of those observations rather than explaining each individual observation itself. This simple technique of averaging many observations is one of psychology's most powerful methodological tools.

The law of large numbers

POPULATION The complete collection of people, objects or events that can possibly be measured.

SAMPLE The partial collection of people, objects or events that are measured in a study.

LAW OF LARGE NUMBERS A statistical law stating that as sample size increases, the attributes of a sample will more closely reflect the attributes of the population from which the sample was drawn.

If you sat down and started picking cards from a deck, you would expect to pick as many red cards as black cards over the long run. But *only* over the long run. You would not be surprised if you picked just 2 cards and they both turned out to be red, but you *would* be surprised if you picked 20 cards and they all turned out to be red. You would be surprised by 20 red cards and not by 2 red cards because your intuition tells you that when the number of cards you pick is small, you really can't expect your hand to have the same proportion of red and black cards as does the full deck.

Your intuition is exactly right. A **population** is *the complete collection of people, objects or events that might be measured*, and a **sample** is *the partial collection of people, objects or events that are measured in a study.* In this case, the full deck is a population, and the cards in your hand are a sample of that population. Your intuition about the cards is captured by the **law of large numbers**, *a statistical law stating that as sample size increases, the attributes of the sample will more closely reflect the attributes of the population from which the sample was drawn.* The law of large numbers suggests that as the size of a sample, that is, the number cards in your hand, increases, the ratio of black to red cards in the sample will more closely approximate the ratio of black to red cards in the population.

In plain English, the more cards you pick, the more likely it is that half the cards in your hand will be red and half will be black.

Precisely the same logic informs the methods of psychology. For example, if we wanted to know how happy people are in Oslo, we would begin with an operational definition of happiness. For the sake of simplicity, we might define happiness as a person's belief about their own emotional state. Then we'd develop a way to measure that belief, for example by asking the person to mark a point on a 10-point rating scale where 1 means very unhappy and 10 means very happy. This type of measure that quantifies behavioural measures with numerical values is known as a 'Likert scale', one of the most commonly used in behavioural science despite its sinister origins (see stats facts in Chapter 15).

If we used this measure to measure the happiness of just one Oslo resident, our single observation would tell us little about the happiness of the 624,000 people who actually live in the city. On the other hand, if we were to measure the happiness of 100 or even 1,000 Oslo residents, the average of our measurements would begin to approximate the average happiness of all people in the city. The law of large numbers suggests that as the size of our sample increases, the average happiness of the people in our sample becomes a better approximation of the average happiness of the people in the population. You can prove this to yourself by considering what would happen if you measured the largest possible sample, namely, every person who lives in Oslo. In that case, the average happiness of your sample and the average happiness of the population would be identical (see *the real world* box).

the real world

Taking a chance

Gallup polls are telephone-based interviews where members of the general public are randomly selected to gauge opinions. In the case of extrasensory perception (ESP), they consistently report that nearly three out of every five adults believe in such paranormal abilities. Very few psychologists share this belief, and you might wonder why they tend to be such a sceptical lot. As you have seen, psychology's methods often rely on the laws of probability. Some of these laws, such as the law of large numbers, are intuitively obvious, but others are not, and ignorance of the less obvious laws often leads people to 'know what isn't so' (Gilovich, 1991).

Consider the case of the amazing coincidence. One night you dream that a panda is piloting an airplane over the Indian Ocean, and the next day you tell a friend, who says, 'Wow, I had exactly the same dream last week!' One morning you are humming an old Beatles tune in the shower, and when you get into your car an hour later, the very same song is on the radio. You and your flatmate are wondering what kind of pizza to order when suddenly you both open your mouths and say 'pepperoni and onions' in perfect unison. Coincidences like these feel truly supernatural when they happen. How can we possibly explain them as anything other than instances of precognition (knowing the future before it happens) or telepathy (reading another person's thoughts)?

The same question occurred to Nobel Prize-winning physicist Luis Alverez one day when he was reading the newspaper. A particular story got him thinking about an old university friend he hadn't seen in years. A few minutes later, he turned the page and was shocked to see the very same friend's obituary. Was this a case of precognition (he 'saw' two minutes into his own future) or telepathy (he read the thoughts of someone who was reading the obituary two minutes before he did)? Before jumping to such extraordinary conclusions, Alvarez decided to use probability theory to determine just how amazing this coincidence really was.

First, he estimated the number of friends the average person has, and then he estimated how often the average person thinks about each of those friends. With these estimates in hand, Alvarez did a few simple calculations and determined the likelihood that someone would think about a friend five minutes before learning about that friend's death. The odds, it turned out, were astonishingly high. In a country the size of the US, for example, this amazing coincidence should happen to 10 people every day (Alvarez, 1965). If this seems surprising to you, then know you are not alone. Research has shown that people routinely underestimate the likelihood of coincidences (Diaconis and Mosteller, 1989; Falk and McGregor, 1983; Hintzman et al., 1978). If you want to profit from this fact, you can bet in any group of 24 or more people that at least 2 of them share the same birthday. The odds are in your favour, and the bigger the group, the better the odds. In fact, in a group of 35, the odds are 85%.

So when *should* we be impressed by an amazing coincidence? When it happens more often than we would expect by chance alone. The problem is that we cannot easily calculate the likelihood that a flying panda, a Beatles tune, or a pepperoni and onion pizza will come to mind by chance alone. Science deals with events whose chance occurrence can be estimated, and scientists use this estimate to determine when an event really is or is not surprising. In the real world, we often can't make these estimates with any degree of certainty, which is why we can rarely draw legitimate conclusions about the likelihood of everyday coincidences.

Averaging

Under the right circumstances, the average of a sample can tell us about the average of a population. But it cannot tell us about the individuals in that population. For example, when psychologists claim that women have better fine motor skills than men (and they do), that men have better spatial ability than women (and they do), that children are more suggestible than adults (and they are), or that Londoners care more about sex than algebra (well, it seems likely), their claims are not true – and are not *meant* to be true – of every individual in these populations. Rather, when psychologists say that women have better fine motor skills than men, they mean that when the fine motor skills of a large sample of women and men are measured, the average of the women's measurements is reliably higher than the average of the men's.

FREQUENCY DISTRIBUTION A graphic representation of the measurements of a sample that are arranged by the number of times each measurement was observed.

NORMAL DISTRIBUTION A frequency distribution in which most measurements are concentrated around the mean and fall off towards the tails, and the two sides of the distribution are symmetrical.

FIGURE 2.4 illustrates this point with hypothetical observations that are arranged in a pair of frequency distributions – *graphic representations of the measurements of a sample that are arranged by the number of times each measurement was observed.* These frequency distributions display every possible score on a fine motor skills test on the horizontal axis and display the number of times (or the frequency with which) each score was observed among a sample of men and women on the vertical axis. A frequency distribution can have any shape, but it commonly takes the shape known as a normal distribution (sometimes also called a bell curve). A normal distribution is *a frequency distribution in which most measurements are concentrated around the mean and fall off towards the tails, and the two sides of the distribution are symmetrical.* As you can see in Figure 2.4, normal distributions are *symmetrical,* that is, the left half is a mirror image of the right half, have a peak in the middle, and trail off at the ends. Most scores can be found towards the centre of a normal distribution, with fewer scores at the extremes. In fact, the point at the very centre of a normal distribution is where you'll find the average.

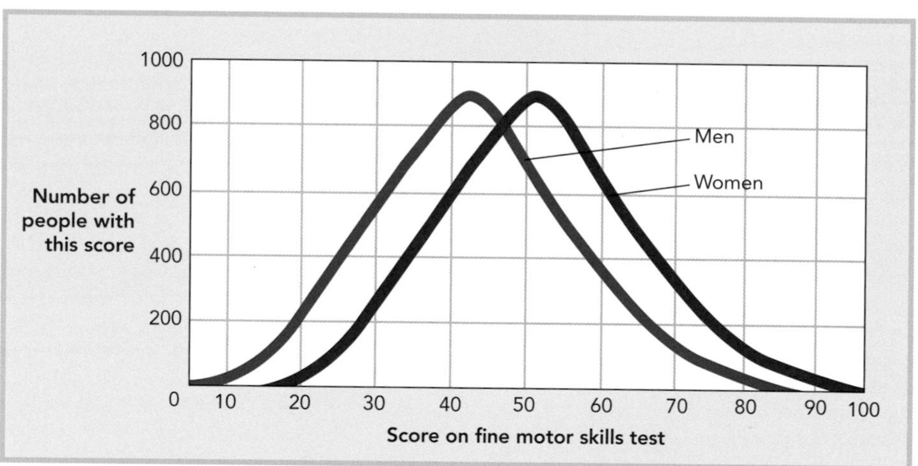

FIGURE 2.4 Frequency distributions This graph shows the hypothetical scores of a sample of men and women who took a test of fine motor skills. The scores are represented along the horizontal axis, and the frequency of each score is represented along the vertical axis. As you can see, the average score of women is a bit higher than the average score of men. Both distributions are examples of normal distributions.

A frequency distribution depicts every measurement in a sample and thus provides a full and complete picture of that sample. But like most full and complete pictures, it is a terribly cumbersome way to communicate information. When we ask a friend how she's been, we don't want her to show us a graph depicting her happiness on each day of the previous six months. Rather, we want a brief summary statement that captures the essential information that such a graph would provide, for example 'I'm doing pretty well', or, 'I've been having some ups and downs lately.' In psychology, brief summary statements that capture the essential information from a frequency distribution are called *descriptive statistics*, of which there are two different kinds:

- *Descriptions of central tendency* are summary statements about the value of the observations that lie near the centre or midpoint of a frequency distribution. When a friend says that she has been 'doing pretty well', she is describing the central tendency (or approximate location of the midpoint) of the frequency distribution of her happiness measurements. The three most common descriptions of central tendency are:
  - the mode – *the value of the most frequently observed observation*
  - the mean – *the average value of the observation, calculated as the sum of all the observations divided by the number of observations*
  - the median – *the value that is greater than or equal to the values of half the observations and less than or equal to half the values of the observations.*

MODE The value of the most frequently observed observation.

MEAN The average value of the observation, calculated as the sum of all the observations divided by the number of observations.

MEDIAN The value that is greater than or equal to the values of half the observations and less than or equal to half the values of the observations.

FIGURE 2.5 shows how each of these descriptive statistics is calculated.

- *Descriptions of variability* are statements about the extent to which the observations in a frequency distribution differ from each other. When a friend says that she has been having some 'ups and downs' lately, she is offering a brief summary statement that describes how the measurements in the frequency distribution of her happiness scores over the past six months tend to differ from one another. A simple description of variability is the range – *the numerical difference between the smallest and largest measurements in a frequency distribution.* There are several other common descriptions of variability. The standard deviation is a measure that *estimates the average difference between each observation and the mean in the population* (see details of the full calculation in the box below).

RANGE The numerical difference between the smallest and largest measurements in a frequency distribution.

STANDARD DEVIATION An estimate of the average difference between each observation and the mean in the population distribution.

- Mode = 3 because there are five 3s and only three 2s, two 1s, two 4s, one 5, one 6, and one 7
- Mean = 3.27 because (1 + 1 + 2 + 2 + 2 + 3 + 3 + 3 + 3 + 3 + 4 + 4 + 5 + 6 + 7)/15 = 3.27
- Median = 3 because 10 scores are ≥ 3 and 10 scores are ≤ 3
- Range = 6 because 7 – 1 = 6

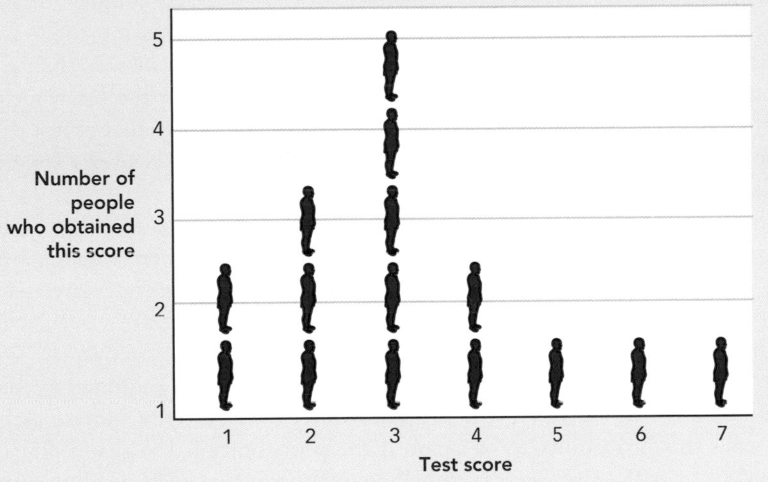

Number of people who obtained this score

Test score

FIGURE 2.5 Some descriptive statistics This frequency distribution shows the scores of 15 individuals on a seven-point test. Descriptive statistics include measures of central tendency (such as the mean, median and mode) and measures of variability (such as the range, variance and standard deviation).

Variance and the standard deviation

Essentially, calculating the standard deviation involves totalling up the differences between each observation and the mean and then dividing by the number of observations. In practice, it is a little more complicated. To start off the calculation, we could subtract the mean from each observation. This would tell us how far each differs from the mean and we could total these differences up. Some of the observations will be bigger than the mean, producing a positive difference and some of the observations will be below the mean, producing a negative difference. This gives us a problem. When we add the differences up, the positive and negative numbers will cancel each other out and total to exactly 0. We don't want this to happen!

Fortunately, there is an easy solution; when you square a number, it always becomes positive. Therefore, if we square the differences before we add them up, the positive differences will remain positive and the negative differences will become positive. Now we can total these squared differences without the problem of positive and negative numbers. This is the *sums of squares*, a calculation that underlies a lot of statistics commonly used in psychology. The next step is to divide by the number of observations. If you were working with the population, this would be straightforward. You would simply divide the sums of squares by the number of observations in the population. Psychologists rarely work with a whole population, however. Instead, we usually take a sample and use it to estimate the characteristics of the larger population. We get a better estimate of the population variance if we divide the sums of squares by the number of observations minus 1. We take one away to compensate mathematically for the fact that we are working with estimates.

At this stage, we have calculated the variance – *the average deviation of each observation from the mean.* This is what we set out to measure and the variance is a well-known statistic in its own right. The problem, though, is that we squared the differences in the calculation and

VARIANCE The average deviation of each observation from the mean.

this squaring has not gone away. So we now have an estimate of the average deviation in squared units. It is much more intuitive to think about the original units (would you prefer a ruler that measured in centimetres or squared centimetres?). The standard deviation converts the variance back to the original metric, simply by taking the square root. An example calculation is shown in Figure 2.5.

As Figure 2.4, shows, the central tendency and the variability of a frequency distribution jointly determine the kinds of conclusions we can draw from it. The mean of the women's scores is higher than the mean of the men's scores, which suggests that women have better fine motor skills than men *on average*. But can we be confident this is a real difference? A male chauvinist might say 'all you have here is a sample of men and a sample of women. Whenever you take two samples from a population, their estimate of the mean are going to differ a bit due to *sampling error*. I don't think women really are better than men at fine motor skills (or anything else).' A debate with the apparently well-educated male chauvinist might well descend into a pantomime, with us saying 'oh yes they are different' and others saying 'oh no they're not'. This debate could go on for eternity if we did not have a second class of statistics – called *inferential statistics* – that can help us settle this sort of debate. In this case, the appropriate inferential statistic is calculated using the *t-test*. It can't give us a definite answer on whether the mean for men is different from the mean for women, but it can allow us to assert whether or not there is a difference while keeping the probability of making an error small over a long run of such decisions.

Probability scores range from 0 to 1. A probability of 0 means something is definitely not going to happen, a probability of 1 means it definitely will happen. Values in between represent differing degrees of uncertainty. A probability of 0.5 indicates there is a 50% chance of something happening. With a little maths (see the box below on the t-test for a full example), we can generate the probability that we make an error over the long run when the two means do not differ, that is, when they are simply estimating the same overall population mean. In order to assert that women have better fine motor skills than men, we want this probability to be small. If the probability is less than 0.05 (usually abbreviated to $p<0.05$), then we can conclude (although not with absolute certainty) that men and women come from a single distribution and accept that women have better fine motor skills than men. When the probability level is less than 0.05, we say that the difference is **statistically significant** – *the observed effect is not due to chance* – that is, when there is really no effect, we will make an error less than 5% of the time. In the context of inferential statistics, 'significance' has a very narrow meaning referring to whether a p value is less than 0.05. Statistical significance does not imply that the result is important, for example in terms of selecting people to be brain surgeons. As you develop as psychologists, we suggest you only use the word 'significant' in this narrow statistical sense.

STATISTICALLY SIGNIFICANT The observed effect is not due to chance.

stats facts

Significant effects are not always significant

One problem with the experimental method is that it may produce findings that are not actually significant in real life. This is because, in most experiments, one attempts to control and reduce the influence of many variables in order to investigate the mechanism of interest. However, this means that by stripping away the influence of other variables, one may produce a distorted view of the phenomenon one is trying to understand. For example, hundreds of studies have shown that unconscious factors influence how we think and act. French psychologists have shown that pleasant smells such as perfume or the smell of pastries are linked to prosocial behaviour such as helping a pedestrian who drops a glove (Guéguen, 2012). And, when choosing someone for a job, we are more likely to favour applicants whose CVs are presented on heavy clipboards (Ackerman et al., 2010). These studies have produced significant effects but it would be wrong to assume that they are significant in the real world. That is because not all things are equal in the real world. It is not like a laboratory where all the potential variables are carefully controlled. There are many other variables that are more likely to influence whether we help someone or offer them a job. This is why effect size plays an important role when considering which variables are the most important. Two variables can both be statistically significant but the one with the larger effect size contributes more to the phenomenon under consideration.

Effect size

EFFECT SIZE An objective and standardized measure of the magnitude of an observed effect.

As noted in the stats facts box above, significance alone should not be the most important consideration when predicting the world around us. The **effect size** – *an objective and standardized measure of the magnitude of an observed effect* (Field, 2005) – gives an indication of the strength of the variables under consideration. As the measure is standardized, this means that effect sizes can be compared across different studies, using different variables with different sample sizes, which is why it is used in meta-analysis where the results of multiple studies are averaged (see Chapter 14 on meta-analysis). Effect size indicates either the strength of associations or the magnitude of differences. A common effect size is the correlation coefficient measure of association between variables (see below). Another, known as Cohen's d, is the effect size for the differences between group means and is simply the difference in the two groups' means divided by the average of standard deviations. For example, on a t-test (see box below), if we see a d of 1, we know that the two groups' means differ by one standard deviation; a d of 0.5 tells us that the two groups' means differ by half a standard deviation and so on. Cohen suggested that $d = 0.2$ be considered a 'small' effect size, 0.5 represents a 'medium' effect size and 0.8 a 'large' effect size. Effect sizes can be more practical than the concept of significance to the extent that some researchers advocate reporting effect sizes and abandoning the pursuit of significance testing (Schmidt and Hunter, 2002).

The problems with significance and probability

One common and potentially dangerous misconception is that a significant result means that something is absolutely true and a non-significant result means something is absolutely false. Most of us want to know what is true – what is certain. The problem, as noted earlier with Popper's criticisms, is that we are limited in what we can measure and be certain of. Therefore, scientists generate hypotheses about what they believe is true. In order to support their hypotheses, they need to test the probability of their observations to determine whether they are significant or due to chance.

Although Ronald Fisher initially introduced the concept of significance, it was Polish mathematician Jerzy Neyman (1894–1981) and British statistician Egon Pearson (1885–1980) who developed hypothesis-testing measures to calculate probabilities and significance, which have become common statistical tools used in research up to this day. Scientists conduct experiments to obtain results that they can interpret. However, there are two potential ways for them to come to the wrong conclusion. The first is called a 'Type I error', where you think you found something when it was not really there. The second is called a 'Type II error', when you think you found nothing, when in fact there is a real effect. Probabilities provide a measure of the likelihood that you have made these types of errors but, in reality, most scientists have been more concerned with Type I errors. In other words, when there is no effect and nothing going on, they don't want to say there is something there.

The measure of significance provides an estimate of the probability of making these errors in the long run. However, when the significance of those results from an experiment is applied to the real world, errors can be potentially dangerous. For example, if you believe a drug cures when it does not (Type I error) or believe that a drug does not cure when it does (Type II error), you will needlessly prescribe treatments because the decisions were based on statistical inferences conducted on a limited sample that failed to detect the real effects in much larger groups.

Aside from the practical dangers of making errors, there are also fundamental misconceptions about probability and significance that many scientists fail to appreciate (Dienes, 2008). Consider how probabilities are calculated. Probabilities are not based on single events but rather on the frequency of outcomes over multiple observations (von Mises, 1957). Imagine a situation where you have to decide whether or not a coin is biased to come up heads more often than tails. One toss of the coin would not tell you. If you tossed it 10 times and it came up heads 7 times, would you be correct in talking about the coin having a probability of 0.7 for heads? That seems obviously wrong because you may get a different number if you toss it another 10 times. Would you be right to believe that it was a crooked coin? No, because it is equally likely that a fair coin could also come up heads 7 out of 10 times. So how many times would the coin have to come up heads before you were convinced the coin was biased? When would a set of results be significant? Twenty heads in a row seems suspiciously significant. It may well be, but if you were to flip a fair coin 1,000 times, there will be sequences when it comes up 20 heads in a row but that does not mean that the coin is weighted. Significance really only applies to the observations under consideration – not for the whole population of potential outcomes. This is why hypothesis-testing should be limited to situations where you specify the study parameters in advance: what sort of effect you are looking for and how big the sample should be in order to find it. Otherwise, there is the danger of making Type I and Type II errors, or fishing for significance by repeatedly testing until your hypothesis has been confirmed by finding an effect that satisfies the $p<0.05$ criterion, sometimes known as 'p-hacking' (Simmons et al., 2013).

These sorts of considerations are often forgotten when we talk about probabilities and are why it is critically important to understand that working with probabilities depends on certain rules and assumptions. The most important consideration is that probabilities do not measure the true state of the world in an error-free way. They simply provide a mathematical estimate based on the data collected but that calculation assumes that sample parameters have been specified in advance.

The t-test

The t-test is used to compare the means of two samples. One version of the t-test is used where you have different people in each sample, for example when comparing men and women, or left- and right-handers. This is called the 'unrelated t-test' because the observations in each sample are unrelated to each other. Just to confuse you, it is also known as the 'independent t-test', for obvious reasons, and perhaps less obviously, the 'between-participants t-test'. Statisticians often have several names for the same thing. Apparently they think statistics would be too easy without this sort of helpfulness.

An alternative form of the t-test is used when the same people are in each sample. This might happen, for example, if you wanted to compare average smoking before and after a smoking reduction course. This form of t-test is known as the 'related t-test', the 'dependent t-test' and the 'within-participants t-test'. The mathematics behind these two t-tests are different, but conceptually they are exactly the same.

A full discussion of the maths underlying the t-test is beyond the scope of this book. There are plenty of readable accounts available already, including the book by Dancey and Reidy (2007) suggested in *Recommended reading* at the end of the chapter. Here, let's briefly look at how the unrelated t-test works. We have simulated some observations that might have been made when looking for differences between men and women in fine motor skills. We have only simulated data for five men and five women in this example. This breaks the rule of large numbers that we discussed earlier, but it keeps the calculation simple.

	Men	Women
1	28	78
2	27	29
3	63	56
4	52	68
5	55	53
Mean	45.0	56.8
Variance	271.5	340.7
Standard deviation	18.5	16.5

As we've seen before, the female mean is higher than the male. However, could we conclude that females in the entire population have better fine motor skills than males, on average, on the basis of this small sample of data? The t-test helps us decide by calculating the probability that the sample means could be this different if they are both estimating the same population mean. It uses the variance in the data to answer the question. There are two types of variance here. First, there is variance within the columns. Look at the numbers. Man number 1 scored 28 on the test of fine motor skills, whereas man number 3 scored 63. The other men also scored differently as well. In the women's column, there is equally wide variation. In the table, this variation is summarized by the standard deviation. There are many possible reasons for this variation. Maybe some men are better than others on the test because they have inherited good genes for fine motor control. Maybe other men scored particularly badly because the researcher inadvertently nudged them when they were performing the test and made them slip up. There are many other similar factors that may cause variation within the columns of the table. We are not interested in the effect of these factors when we are comparing men and women, so we may think of them as nuisances, contributing error variance.

The second source of variation in the table is between the columns. This is best expressed as the difference between the column means. The same sorts of things that cause variance within the columns will also contribute to differences between them. For example, if one man has particularly good genes for fine motor control, this will make his score look high compared to the other men in the column. It will also influence the mean of the column, raising it a little bit. If we took two samples of five men, we would not expect their fine motor control means to be exactly the same. In this case, it would be the error variance contributing to the difference in sample means; the sampling error.

So the error variance contributes to both the variance within the columns and the variance between the columns. There is one factor, though, that contributes only to variance between the columns and not to variance within. It is the factor that *defines* the columns. In this case it is gender. The column means may vary because males or females are better at fine motor control. The variance within the columns cannot be due to gender differences, however, because gender does not vary within the columns. One column is all male. The other is all female.

So we can calculate two variance estimates from the table. The estimate based on within-column variance includes only error variance. The estimate based on differences between the columns contains error variance *and* the effect of gender. The extent to which gender is important can therefore be inferred from the ratio of the within- and between-columns variance. If there is no effect of gender, then these variance estimates should be approximately equal. Conversely, if the effect of gender is large, then the between-columns variance estimate will be much bigger than the within-columns estimate. The t-test is based on these variance estimates and calculates their ratio. Actually, to see the ratio you need to square the t value and this turns it into an F-ratio, but this is a small detail.

For the example data above, the t-value is 1.06, which equates to a variance (F-) ratio of 1.14. Next, we need to calculate the probability of obtaining a t-value of this size by chance, if there wasn't a real difference between the men and women. Fortunately, this is a lot easier than it sounds. The probabilities of obtaining all possible t-values by chance can easily be calculated by any statistical program in milliseconds. A minor complication is that the distribution varies according to the number of observations included in the study. To be precise, it is the *degrees of freedom* that are important but, with regard to the t-test, these are closely related to the number of observations. Explaining degrees of freedom is beyond the scope of this book. We only mention them here because it is conventional to include the degrees of freedom when writing up a t-test.

In our example, the degrees of freedom are 8 (the number of observations – 2). Our t-value was 1.06. With 8 degrees of freedom, the probability of observing a t-value of 1.06 or greater by chance is 0.32. This is quite large, meaning there is a good chance of observing a gender difference this large when there are really no differences between men and women. Formally, our cutoff of interest is $p<0.05$. As 0.32 is bigger than 0.05, we must conclude there is no significant sex difference on the basis of these data.

A good way to write this result up would be:

> An independent t-test showed that fine motor skills did not differ significantly between men (mean = 45.0, standard deviation = 7.4) and women (mean = 56.8, standard deviation = 8.3), $t(8) = 1.06$, $p = 0.32$.

So why don't we get an effect here? A very probable reason is that we have broken the law of large numbers. Sampling five participants from each gender is too few unless there really is an enormous difference between the fine motor skills of men and women in the general population.

©ISTOCKPHOTO.COM/DARREN HUBLEY

On average, men have more upper-body strength than women, but there are still many women with more upper-body strength than many men.

In the box above, our t-test example did not show a significant difference between men and women. This was largely to do with the use of a small sample. Figure 2.4 indicates that there is a significant difference between men and women's fine motor skills. So, let's assume that we have a bigger sample size now, perhaps 75 men and 75 women. We run a t-test regarding the difference between men and women in fine motor skills. This time it gives us a probability value below 0.05, a statistically significant effect. From this we conclude that women have better fine motor skills than men *on average*. But both frequency distributions also have considerable variability, that is, plenty of men scored higher than plenty of women. Indeed, what is true about people on average is almost never true in every case. As you read about studies in other chapters of this book, you will undoubtedly find yourself thinking of exceptions to the conclusions the researchers have drawn. But wait a minute, you may think, the book says that women have better fine motor skills than men, but Dad is a surgeon and Mum can't even thread a needle. So how can that be right? If you have this thought, feel free to go back and look at Figure 2.4, which should remind you that a conclusion can be true on average and still allow for exceptions. One *E. coli* bacterium may be pretty much like the next, but no two people are exactly alike, and because people differ, there is almost nothing interesting that is absolutely true of every one of them at all times. Some Londoners probably do like algebra better than sex, but this does not change the fact that *on average* they prefer thinking about lovemaking to the quadratic equation. Psychology's empirical methods allow us to observe the differences between individuals, explain those differences and, if we wish, look beyond those differences to see underlying patterns of similarity.

Now you understand *why* psychologists measure samples that are drawn from populations and know something about how samples can be used to make inferences about the population. Now let's look at *how* samples are measured in everyday life.

Bias

DEMAND CHARACTERISTICS Those aspects of an observational setting that cause people to behave as they think an observer wants or expects them to behave.

People pick their noses, exceed the speed limit, read each other's post, and skip over major sections of *War and Peace*, and they are especially likely to do these things when they think no one is looking. It is only natural for people to behave a bit differently when they are in the spotlight of each other's attention, but this fact makes people rather difficult to study because while psychologists are trying to discover how people really *do* behave, people are often trying to behave as they think they *should* behave. **Demand characteristics** are *those aspects of an observational setting that cause people to behave as they think an observer wants or expects them to behave*. They are called demand characteristics because they seem to 'demand' or require that people say and do things that they normally might not. If you have ever been asked the question, 'Do you think these jeans make me look fat?', you have experienced a demand characteristic. Demand characteristics hinder our attempts to measure behaviour as it normally unfolds, and psychologists have developed a variety of ways to avoid them.

Avoiding demand characteristics

NATURALISTIC OBSERVATION A method of gathering scientific knowledge by unobtrusively observing people in their natural environments.

People often behave as they think observers want or expect them to behave, and one way to avoid this problem is to observe people without their knowledge. **Naturalistic observation** is *a technique for gathering scientific knowledge by unobtrusively observing people in their natural environments*. For example, naturalistic observation reveals that the biggest groups tend to leave the smallest tips in restaurants (Freeman et al., 1975), hungry shoppers buy the most impulse items at the supermarket (Gilbert et al., 2002a), and Olympic athletes smile more when they win the bronze rather than the silver medal (Medvec et al., 1995). All these conclusions are the result of measurements made by psychologists who observed people who didn't know they were being observed. It is unlikely that any of these things would have happened in exactly the same way if the diners, shoppers and athletes had known they were being scrutinized.

Unfortunately, there are two reasons why naturalistic observation cannot by itself solve the problem of demand characteristics. First, some of the things psychologists want to observe simply don't occur naturally. For example, if we wanted to know whether people who have undergone sensory deprivation perform poorly on motor tasks, we would have to hang around the shopping centre for a very long time before a few dozen blindfolded people with earplugs just happened to wander by and start typing. Second, some of the things that psychologists want to observe can only be gathered from direct interaction with a person, for example by administering a survey, giving tests, conducting an interview, or hooking someone up to an electroencephalogram (EEG). If we wanted to know how often someone worried about dying, how accurately they could remember their first kiss, how quickly they could solve a logic puzzle, or how much electrical activity their brain produced when they felt happy, simply observing them would not do the trick.

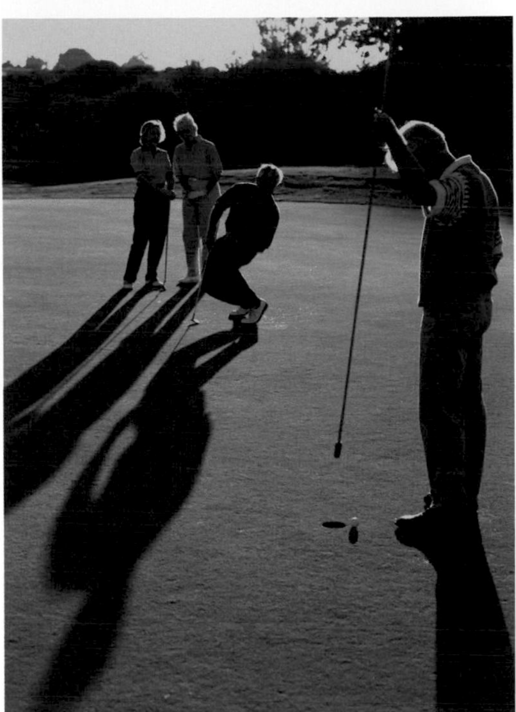

If these golfers knew that they were being observed, would they play by the rules? Erffmeyer (1984) found that golfers are most likely to cheat when they play several opponents at once.

When psychologists cannot avoid demand characteristics by hiding in the bushes, they often avoid them by hiding other things instead. For instance, people are less likely to be influenced by demand characteristics when they cannot be identified as the originators of their actions. Psychologists often take advantage of this fact by allowing people to respond privately, for example by having them complete questionnaires when they are alone, or anonymously, for example by failing to collect personal information, such as the person's name or address. Another technique that psychologists use to avoid demand characteristics is to measure behaviours that are not susceptible to demand. For instance, behaviours can't be influenced by demand characteristics if they are not under voluntary control. You may not want a psychologist to know that you are feeling excited, but you can't prevent your pupils from dilating when you feel aroused. Behaviours are also unlikely to be influenced by demand characteristics when people don't know that the demand and the behaviour are related. You may want a psychologist to believe that you are concentrating on a task, but you probably don't know that your blink rate slows when you are concentrating and thus you won't deliberately blink slowly.

All these tricks of the trade are useful, of course, but the very best way to avoid demand characteristics is to keep the people who are being observed (known as *participants*) from knowing the true purpose of the observation. When participants are kept 'blind' to the observer's expectations, that is, when they do not know what the observer expects them to do, they cannot strive to meet those expectations. If you did not know that a psychologist was studying the effects of baroque music on mood, you would not feel compelled to smile when the psychologist played Bach's Air on the G String. This is why psychologists often do not reveal the true purpose of a study to the participants until the study is over.

Of course, people are clever and curious, and when psychologists don't tell them the purpose of their observations, participants generally try to work it out for themselves ('I wonder why the psychologist is playing the violin and watching me'). That's why psychologists sometimes use *cover stories*, or misleading explanations that are meant to keep participants from discerning the true purpose of an observation. For example, if a psychologist wanted to know how baroque music influenced your mood, they might tell you that the purpose of the study was to determine how quickly people can do logic puzzles while music plays in the background. (We discuss the ethical implications of deceiving people later in this chapter.) In addition, the psychologist might use *filler items*, or pointless measures that are meant to mask the true purpose of the observation. So, for example, they might ask you a few questions that are relevant to the study ('How happy are you right now?') and a few that are not ('Do you like cats more or less than dogs?'), which would make it difficult for you to guess the purpose of the study from the nature of the questions you were asked. These are just a few of the techniques that psychologists use to avoid demand characteristics.

The blind observer

Observers are human beings, and like all human beings, they tend to see what they expect to see. This fact was demonstrated in a classic study in which a group of psychology students were asked to measure the speed with which a rat learned to run through a maze (Rosenthal and Fode, 1963). Some students were told that their rat had been specially bred to be 'maze dull', that is, slow to learn a maze, and others were told that their rat had been specially bred to be 'maze bright', that is, quick to learn a maze. Although all the rats were actually the same breed, the students who *thought* they were measuring the speed of a dull rat reported that their rats took longer to learn the maze than the students who *thought* they were measuring the speed of a bright rat. In other words, the rats seemed to do just what the students who observed them expected them to do.

Why did this happen? There are two reasons:

1 *Expectations can influence observations.* It is easy to make errors when measuring the speed of a rat, and expectations often determine the kinds of errors people make. Does putting one paw over the finish line count as 'learning the maze'? If the rat falls asleep, should the stopwatch be left running or should the rat be awakened and given a second chance? If a rat runs a maze in 18.5 seconds, should that number be rounded up or rounded down before it is recorded? The answers to these questions may depend on whether one thinks the rat is bright or dull. The students who timed the rats probably tried to be honest, vigilant, fair and objective, but their expectations influenced their observations in subtle ways that they could neither detect nor control.

2 *Expectations can influence reality.* Students who expected their rats to learn quickly may have unknowingly done things to help that learning along, for example by muttering 'Oh no!' when the bright rat turned the wrong way in the maze or by petting the bright rat more affectionately than the dull rat and so on.

DOUBLE-BLIND OBSERVATION An observation whose true purpose is hidden from the researcher and the participant.

Observers' expectations, then, can have a powerful influence on both their observations and the behaviour of those they observe. Psychologists use many techniques to avoid these influences, and one of the most common is the double-blind observation – *an observation whose true purpose is hidden from the researcher and the participant.* For example, if the students had not been told which rats were bright and which were dull, they would not have had any expectations about their rats. It is common practice in psychology to keep the observers as blind as the participants and considered the gold standard for studies designed to test the clinical effectiveness of treatments (see Chapter 17). For example, measurements are often made by research assistants who do not know what a particular participant is expected to say or do and who only learn about the nature of the study when it is concluded. Indeed, many modern studies are carried out by the world's blindest experimenter, a computer, which presents information to participants and measures their responses without any expectations whatsoever.

In summary, measurement is a scientific means of observation that involves defining an abstract property in terms of some concrete condition, called an 'operational definition', and then constructing a device, or a measure, that can detect the conditions that the operational definition specifies. A good operational definition shares meaning with the property (construct validity) and is related to other operational definitions (predictive validity). A good measure detects the conditions specified by the operational definition when those conditions occur (power) and not when they don't (reliability). Establishing truth in science is not always as straightforward as it would seem. It turns out that proving a hypothesis is problematic and it is logically more coherent to try to disprove or falsify a hypothesis. Moreover, establishing truth based on analysis of experiments can be misleading as results may give a false picture of the strength and reliability of the effect under consideration.

Psychologists sometimes use the case method to study single, exceptional individuals, but more often they use samples of many people drawn from a population. The law of large numbers suggests that these samples should be relatively large if they are to reflect accurately the properties of the population from which they were drawn. From samples, psychologists draw conclusions about people on average rather than about individuals. Measurements of a sample can be arranged in a frequency distribution, and descriptive statistics can be used to describe some features of that distribution, such as its central tendency (described by the mean, median and mode) and its variability (described by the range, variance and standard deviation). The t-test may be used to identify whether two samples are drawn from the same or different populations.

When people know they are being observed, they may behave as they think they should. Demand characteristics are features of a setting that suggest to people that they should behave in a particular way. Psychologists try to reduce or eliminate demand characteristics by observing participants in their natural habitats or by hiding their expectations from the participant. In double-blind observations, they also hide their expectations from the observer, which ensures that observers are not merely seeing what they expect to see and are not inadvertently causing participants to behave as they expect them to behave.

Explanation: discovering why people do what they do

The techniques discussed so far allow us to construct valid, reliable, powerful and unbiased measures of properties such as happiness, to use those instruments to measure the happiness of a sample without demand characteristics, and to draw conclusions about the happiness of a population. Although scientific research always begins with the careful measurement of properties, its ultimate goal is typically the discovery of *causal relationships between properties.* We may want to know if happy people are more altruistic than unhappy people, but what we really want to know is whether their happiness is the *cause* of their altruism. We may want to know if children who are smacked are more likely to become depressed than children who aren't, but what we really want to know is whether being smacked *caused* their depression. These are the kinds of questions that even the most careful measurements cannot answer. Measurements can tell us how *much* happiness, altruism, smacking and depression occur in a particular sample, but they cannot tell us whether these properties are related and whether their relationship is causal. As you will see, scientists have developed some clever ways of using measurement to answer these questions.

Correlation

If you insult someone, they probably won't give you the time of day. If you have any doubt about this, you can demonstrate it by standing on a street corner, insulting a few people as they walk by ('Hello, you stupid ugly freak ...'), not insulting others ('Hello ...'), and then asking everyone for the time of day ('Could you please tell me what time it is?'). If you did this, you would probably find that many of the people you insulted refused to tell you the time. A few might tell you the time despite the insult. Maybe they thought you were joking or didn't understand what you were saying. Some might even tell you the time and then follow it up with some abuse of their own. Of the people you didn't insult, many more would probably tell you the time. Some may not, however. Some may not know the time and perhaps a few others will refuse because they have the manners of baboons. Imagine you tried this out on a street corner in Aberdeen, setting up a formal study of the relationship. You ask 40 people for the time, insulting half of them in a random order.

In a study of this sort, we can learn about the relationships between objects and events by comparing the *patterns of variation in a series of measurements.* Consider what actually happened when you performed your hypothetical study of insults and requests:

1. You carefully measured a pair of **variables** – *properties whose values can vary across individuals or over time.* You measured one variable whose value could vary from *not insulted* to *insulted*, and you measured a second variable whose value could vary from *refused* to *agreed.* These are categorical variables as they can only take on a fixed set of values and the ordering of the categories is arbitrary.
2. You did this again. And then again. And then again. That is, you made a *series* of measurements rather than making just one.
3. Finally, you will need to discern a pattern in your series of measurements, to determine whether insults and refusals are associated.

VARIABLE A property whose value can vary or change.

The results observed might be as shown in the top half of **TABLE 2.1**, which is called a 'contingency table'. The frequency with which people fall into each combination of insult and agreement are shown here. Each person only appears in one box, referred to as a 'cell'. Table 2.1 shows that 30% of those who were insulted gave them the time of day, whereas 80% of those who were not insulted agreed.

An alternative view is that people in Aberdeen are thick-skinned and equally likely to tell you the time, whether or not you insult them before asking. If so, there should be no association between insult and refusal. How would we expect our contingency table to look in this case? Well, you might think the expected frequency for each cell might be 10, if you thought it was calculated by the number of observations (40) divided by the

TABLE **2.1** **Hypothetical data of the relationship between insults and time-giving**

	Condition	Response		
Observed		**Agreed**	**Refused**	**Total**
	Insulted	6	14	20
	Not insulted	16	4	20
	Total	22	18	40
Expected	Insulted	11	9	20
	Not insulted	11	9	20
	Total	22	18	40

χ^2 calculation
χ^2 = (6 – 11)2/11 + (14 – 9)2/9 + (16 – 11)2/11 + (4 – 9)2/9
= 2.27 + 2.78 + 2.27 + 2.78
= 10.10

number of cells (4). This approach would work if we had equal numbers in the row and column totals. We do regarding the insult rows – you insulted 20 and did not insult 20. We do not regarding the response columns: 22 people told us the time and 18 refused. Instead, we can calculate the expected frequencies in each cell as row total multiplied by column total divided by the total number of observations. This equation works however unbalanced the row and column totals are. For the insulted refused cell this is (20 × 18) / 40 = 9. The rest of the expected frequencies are shown in the bottom half of **TABLE 2.1**.

We can see that our observed frequencies look different from the frequencies expected by chance. So, it looks like there is a genuine association between insult and response. Remember, you only have a small sample here, 40 people out of an Aberdeen population of around 220,000. The key question is: 'How likely is it we could observe such big differences between observed and expected frequencies due to sampling error?' Fortunately, we can answer this question with an inferential statistical test that calculates the Pearson χ^2 statistic – χ^2 may be written chi-square and is pronounced 'kye square'. The calculation is equally easy. For each cell, the expected frequency is subtracted from the observed frequency, squared, and then divided by the expected frequency. The Pearson χ^2 value is the sum of these calculations for each cell, 10.10 in our example. The full computation is shown in Table 2.1. As with the t-test, we need to know the probability of observing a χ^2 statistic of this size by chance. Again, the probability depends in part on the degrees of freedom. These are calculated as the number of rows minus one multiplied by the number of columns minus one. In our example, and for all 2 × 2 tables, this is 1. The probability of observing a χ^2 value of 10.1 with one degree of freedom is about 1 in 1,000, which is very small. This is much less than our criterion value of 0.05. So we can conclude that the observed pattern of frequencies is significantly different from the expected values. Put another way, it means that people are less likely to give you the time of day if you insult them before asking.

A good way to write the results of this statistical test up formally would be:

> A Pearson χ^2 test showed that there was a significant association between giving the time of day and prior insult (χ^2 (1) = 10.10, p = 0.001). Participants were less likely to give the time if they had just been insulted (30%) than if an insult was not given (80%).

In our example, the χ^2 test showed that there was an association between insult and response. The results for five of the participants in this hypothetical study are shown in **TABLE 2.2**. Look at the condition column. As you read down there is variation between insulted and not insulted. In the response column, there is variation, too, between agreed and refused. If you compare the pattern of variation in each column, you will see that there is a degree of synchrony. This synchrony is known as a *pattern of covariation* or a correlation (as in 'co-relation'). Two variables are said to 'covary' or 'be correlated' *when variations in the value of one variable are synchronized with variations in the value of the other.* As Table 2.2 shows, when the value in the condition column varies from *not*

CORRELATION The 'co-relationship' or pattern of covariation between two variables occurs when variations in the value of one variable are synchronized with variations in the value of the other.

insulted to *insulted,* the value in the response column usually varies from *agreed* to *refused.* The χ^2 test told us that there was more synchrony here than chance would predict.

TABLE **2.2** Example of a hypothetical study on whether insults affect participant responses		
Participant	**Condition**	**Response**
1	Not insulted	Gave time
2	Insulted	Refused
3	Not insulted	Refused
4	Not insulted	Gave time
5	Insulted	Refused

By looking for synchronized patterns of variation, we can use measurement to discover the relationships between variables. Indeed, this is the only way anyone has *ever* discovered the relationship between variables, which is why most of the facts you know about the world can be thought of as correlations. For example, you know that adults are generally taller than children, but this is just a shorthand way of saying that as the value of *age* varies from *young* to *old,* the value of *height* varies from *short* to *tall.* You know that people who eat half a kilo of spinach every day generally live longer than people who eat half a kilo of bacon every day, but this is just a shorthand way of saying that as the value of *daily food intake* varies from *spinach* to *bacon,* the value of *longevity* varies from *high* to *low.* We could rephrase our earlier example to say that as *gender* varies from *male* to *female, fine motor control* varies from *low* to *high*. As these statements suggest, correlations are the fundamental building blocks of knowledge.

IMAGESOURCE

When children line up by age, they also tend to line up by height. The pattern of variation in age (from youngest to oldest) is synchronized with the pattern of variation in height (from shortest to tallest).

But correlations do more than just describe the past. They also allow us to predict the future. How long will Susan live if she eats half a kilo of bacon every day? Probably not as long as she would have lived if she'd eaten half a kilo of spinach instead every day. How tall will Walter be on his next birthday? Probably taller if he is turning 21 than if he is turning 2. Both of these are questions about events that have not yet happened, and their answers are predictions based on correlations. When two variables are correlated, knowledge of the value of one variable (daily food intake or age) allows us to make predictions about the value of the other variable (longevity or height). Indeed, every time we suspect something ('I think it's going to rain soon'), worry about something ('The statistics exam will probably be tough'), or feel excited about something ('The freshers ball should be awesome'), we are using the value of one variable to predict the value of another variable with which it is correlated.

Every correlation can be described in two equally reasonable ways. A positive correlation describes a relationship between two variables in 'more-more' or 'less-less' terms. When we say that *more spinach* is associated with *more longevity* or that *less spinach* is associated with *less longevity*, we are describing a positive correlation. A negative correlation describes a relationship between two variables in 'more-less' or 'less-more' terms. When we say that *more bacon* is associated with *less longevity* or that *less bacon* is associated with *more longevity*, we are describing a negative correlation.

Measuring correlation

Occasionally, variables may be perfectly correlated. This means that a particular change in one variable is always associated with a particular change in the other variable. Perfect correlations are rare in everyday life. There is a correlation between age and height that allows us to predict that a child will be shorter than an adult, and this prediction will be right more often than it is wrong. But it *will* be wrong in some instances because there are *some* tall children and *some* short adults.

We used the Pearson χ^2 statistic to test the association between two categorical variables above. In our example, each could take on only two possible values (insulted or not insulted and agreed or refused). Contingency table analysis, where the cells of the table are limited to a small number of categories, is easily extended to variables that can take on three or more levels. However, when the variables of interest are measured on a continuous scale, Karl Pearson developed another statistical test for measuring their association. The Pearson correlation coefficient is *a statistical measure of the direction and strength of a correlation, symbolized by the letter* r (as in 'relationship'). Like most measures, the correlation coefficient has a limited range. What does that mean? Well, if you were to measure the number of hours of sunshine per day in your home town, that measure would have a range of 24 because it could only have a value from 0 to 24. Numbers such as –7 and 36.8 would be meaningless. Similarly, the value of *r* can range from –1 to 1, and numbers outside that range are meaningless. What, then, do the numbers *inside* that range mean (see **FIGURE 2.6**)?

CORRELATION COEFFICIENT A statistical measure of the direction and strength of a correlation, symbolized by the letter *r*.

- When $r = 1$, the relationship between the variables is called a *perfect positive correlation*, which means that every time the value of one variable increases by a certain amount, the value of the second variable also increases by a certain amount, and this happens without exception. If every increase in age of *X* units were associated with an increase in height of *Y* units, then age and height would be perfectly positively correlated (**FIGURE 2.6a**).
- When $r = -1$, the relationship between the variables is called a *perfect negative correlation*, which means that as the value of one variable increases by a certain amount, the value of the second variable *decreases* by a certain amount, and this happens without exception. If every increase in age of *X* units were associated with a decrease in height of *Y* units, then age and height would be perfectly negatively correlated (**FIGURE 2.6b**).
- When $r = 0$, there is no systematic relationship between the variables, which are said to be *uncorrelated*. This means that the pattern of variation of one variable is not synchronized in any way with the pattern of variation of the other. As the value of one variable increases by a certain amount, the value of the second variable may sometimes increase, sometimes decrease, and sometimes do neither. If increases in age of *X* units were sometimes associated with changes in height of *Y* units and sometimes associated with a change in height of *Z* units, then age and height would be uncorrelated (**FIGURE 2.6c**).

The correlations shown in **FIGURES 2.6a** and **b** are perfect correlations, that is, they show patterns of variation that are perfectly synchronized and without exceptions. Such correlations are extremely rare in real life. It may be true that the more bacon you eat, the fewer years you will live, but it's not as though longevity decreases by exactly 1.23 days for every 100 kilos of bacon you put away annually. Bacon eating and longevity are *negatively* correlated, that is, as one increases, the other decreases, but they are also *imperfectly* correlated, and thus *r* will lie somewhere between 0 and –1. But where? That depends on how many exceptions there are to the '*X* more kilos of bacon = *Y* fewer years of life' rule. If there are just a few exceptions, then *r* will be much closer to –1 than to 0. But as the number of exceptions increases, then the value of *r* will begin to move towards 0 and look like the distribution in **FIGURE 2.6c**.

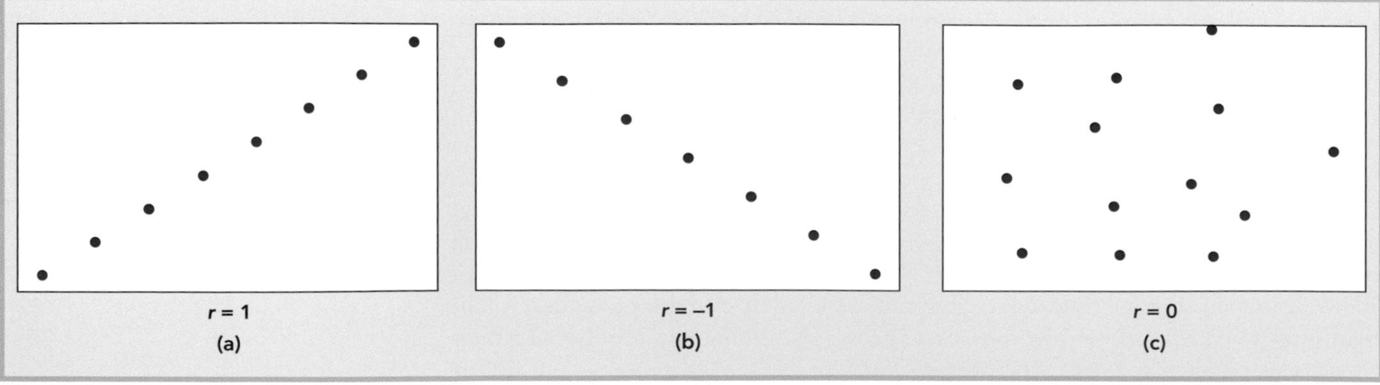

FIGURE 2.6 Three kinds of correlations This figure illustrates pairs of variables that have (a) a perfect positive correlation ($r = 1$), (b) a perfect negative correlation ($r = -1$), and (c) no correlation ($r = 0$).

FIGURE 2.7 shows four cases in which two variables are positively correlated but have different numbers of exceptions, and as you can see, the number of exceptions changes the value of r quite dramatically. Two variables can have a perfect correlation ($r = 1$), a strong correlation, for example $r = 0.80$, a moderate correlation, for example $r = 0.60$, or a weak correlation, for example $r = 0.20$. The correlation coefficient, then, is a measure of both the *direction* and *strength* of the relationship between two variables. The sign of r (plus or minus) tells us the direction of the relationship, and the absolute value of r (between 0 and 1) tells us about the number of exceptions and hence about how confident we can be when using the correlation to make predictions. How is r calculated? This is explained in the box below.

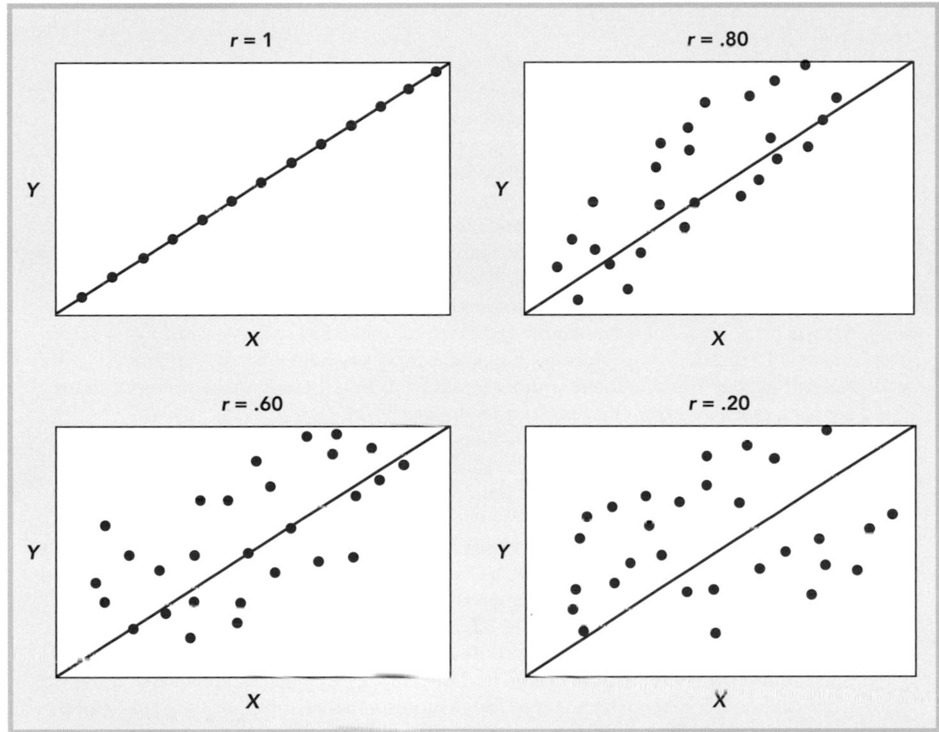

FIGURE **2.7 Positive correlations of different strengths** These graphs represent different degrees of positive correlation between two variables. Scores that are on the line adhere strictly to the rule $X = Y$. The more exceptions there are to this rule, the weaker the correlation.

Calculating *r*: the standardized association between two continuous variables

The Pearson correlation statistic, *r*, measures the extent to which two variables vary together, or covary. The calculation of covariance is similar to the variance calculation we saw earlier. As we saw, the sums of squares is important to the calculation of the variance. We calculated this as the total of the squared difference between each observation and the mean. Squaring simply means we multiply a number by itself, as in $2^2 = 2 \times 2 = 4$. So you could think of the variance calculation as involving multiplying the difference between each observation and the mean by the difference between each observation and the mean. If you think about the variance this way, then what you are doing is close to the calculation of covariance.

Calculating covariance differs from variance in that there are two variables, not one. Let's call them variable *a* and variable *b*. We could calculate the variances of each variable as follows:

$$\text{Variance of } a = \frac{\sum (a - \text{mean of } a) \times (a - \text{mean of } a)}{N - 1}$$

The $\sum$ simply means add up across all the observations in our dataset. N is the number of observations. So for variable *b*, the variance could be calculated as:

$$\text{Variance of } b = \frac{\sum (b - \text{mean of } b) \times (b - \text{mean of } b)}{N - 1}$$

The covariance of *a* and *b* is calculated as:

$$\text{Covariance of } a \text{ and } b = \frac{\sum (a - \text{mean of } a) \times (b - \text{mean of } b)}{N - 1}$$

As you can see, this formula looks very like the variance formula. In fact, you could think of the variance as measuring the extent a variable covaries with itself.

COVARIANCE A measure of how much two variables change together.

The covariance is *a measure of how much two variables change together*. Specifically, it measures the extent to which variation in variable *a* scores, as measured by distance from the mean, is synchronized with variation in *b* scores. An observation where both *a* and *b* are a long way above their respective means will increase the variance by a lot. If *a* is a long way above the mean and *b* is a long way below, this will contribute negatively to the covariance. By dividing by the number of observations minus 1, we are essentially calculating the average similarity of variable *a* and *b*, in terms of their distances from their respective means.

So, that is the covariance and it is a useful statistic in its own right. A major weakness, though, is that the covariance depends on the measurement scale used. Perhaps a researcher in the UK wants to know the relationship between male aggression and car speed and measures aggression in the amount of swearing and speed in miles per hour (mph). They can then calculate the covariance between these measures. If a researcher in Belgium wanted to do the same project, they might also measure the amount of aggression by swearing but speed in kilometres per hour (kph) and use this as the basis of their covariance calculation. The covariances calculated in the two studies could not be immediately compared.

To solve this problem, the unit of measurement needs to be standardized. One could force the metric or English measurement system to be universally adopted but this would probably lead to global rioting. Anyway, it would not be any help when researchers studying links between driving behaviour and aggression used different assessment scales because there is no standard approach that could be enforced here.

What would be ideal is a method by which every single measure you can think of can be transformed onto the same scale. This ideal is realized in the form of z scores. *Z scores* measure variables in terms of standard deviation units. Each observation is scored in terms of how many standard deviations they fall above or below the mean. For example, IQ test scores usually have a mean of 100 and a standard deviation of 15. Therefore, someone who scores 130 on an IQ test has a z score of 2, because they scored two standard deviations above the mean. Somebody who scores 85 would have a z score of –1 and someone who scored 92 of –0.53. Calculating z scores are easy. You simply subtract the mean from an observation and then divide by the standard deviation. When you do this across a whole sample, using the observed mean and standard deviation, the mean becomes 0 and the standard deviation becomes 1. This is true for all measurements, whether they are height measured in feet and inches or metres, heart rate measured in beats per minute, or expenses paid to Members of Parliament measured in pounds down the drain.

So, we have a method of measuring all variables on a standard scale, whatever they are measuring and whatever unit they were originally measured in. Now all we have to do is calculate our covariances based on these standard measurements. When we do this, we calculate the Pearson correlation coefficient. Of course, you do not have to do all the conversion yourself. There is an equation for *r* that works straight from the original measurements. If you use a statistical analysis package on a computer (and who wouldn't?), you don't even have to work the equation out.

The correlation coefficient describes the strength and direction of a relationship. As with other inferential statistics, the correlation is calculated in a sample and we want to make inferences about the population. A normal step is to test whether the observed correlation is sufficiently strong to conclude that the correlation in the population is not 0. To do this, we calculate the probability of observing the sample correlation if the population correlation was 0. If this probability is very small (less than 0.05), we can conclude that there is a significant association between the variables in the population. The larger the sample, the smaller the value of *r* that can be distinguished from 0. Once again, it is strictly the degrees of freedom rather than the sample size that is important here. When assessing *r* values, the degrees of freedom are calculated as the number of observations minus 2. If you have 20 degrees of freedom, then your sample correlation would need to be above 0.42 (or below –0.42) for you to report that a difference had been detected in the sample that achieved a significance level of 0.05. If you had 100 degrees of freedom, however, you could accept a correlation of above 0.20 (or below –0.20) as statistically significant.

Causation

If you watched a cartoon in which a moving block collided with a stationary block, which then went careening off the screen, your brain would instantly make a reasonable assumption, namely that the moving block was the *cause* of the stationary block's motion (Heider and Simmel, 1944; Michotte, 1963). In fact, studies show that infants make such assumptions long before they have had a chance to learn anything about cartoons, blocks, collisions or causality (Oakes and Cohen, 1990). For human beings, detecting causes and effects is as natural as sucking, sleeping and crying, which is what led philosopher Immanuel Kant ([1781]1965) to suggest that people come into the world with cause detectors built into their brains.

Of course, even the best cause detector doesn't work perfectly every time. Perhaps you've had the experience of putting some coins in an arcade game, happily shooting helicopters or dodging vampires for a minute or so, and then suddenly realizing that you never actually pressed start and that the shooting and dodging you saw on the screen had nothing to do with your nimble handling of the joystick. Mistakes like this happen all the time (Wegner and Wheatley, 1999). In fact, our brains are so eager to connect causes with effects that they often make connections that aren't really there, which is why astrology continues to be such a popular diversion (Glick et al., 1989). Conversely, our brains sometimes fail to detect causal relationships that actually do exist. Only in the past century or so have surgeons made it a practice to wash their hands before operating because before that, no one seemed to notice that dirty fingernails were causally related to postsurgical infections. The causal relationships between smoking and lung cancer and between cholesterol and heart disease went undetected for centuries despite the fact that people were smoking tobacco, eating lard and keeling over with some regularity. The point here is that if we want to discover the causal relationships between variables, we need more than mere empiricism. What we need is a method for discovering causal relationships. As you're about to see, we've got one.

©ISTOCKPHOTO.COM/DUNCAN WALKER

Although people have smoked tobacco for centuries, the causal relationship between cigarette smoking and heart and lung disease has only recently been detected.

The third-variable problem

We observe correlations all the time – between cars and pollution, between bacon and heart attacks, between sex and pregnancy. **Natural correlations** are *the correlations observed between naturally occurring variables*, and although such observations can tell us *whether* two variables have a relationship, they cannot tell us what *kind* of relationship these variables have. If you saw two people chatting in a pub, you could be sure that they had some kind of relationship, but you would be hard-pressed to say what it was. They could be spouses, classmates or siblings, and you would need more information, for example matching wedding rings, matching textbooks or matching parents, to work out which. Having a relationship does not automatically make them spouses because while all spouses have relationships, not all people who have relationships are spouses. By the same logic, *all variables that are causally related are correlated, but not all variables that are correlated are causally related.* For example, height and weight are positively correlated, but height does not cause weight and weight does not cause height. Hunger is correlated with thirst, coughing is correlated with sneezing, and a woman's age is correlated with the number of children she has borne. But none of these variables is the cause of the other. Causality is just one of the many relationships that correlated variables may have. The fact that two variables are correlated does not tell us whether they are causally related as well.

NATURAL CORRELATION A correlation observed between naturally occurring variables.

What kinds of relationships can correlated variables have? Consider an example. Many studies of children have found a positive correlation between the amount of

How can third-variable correlation explain the fact that the more tattoos a person has, the more likely they are to be involved in a motorcycle accident?

THIRD-VARIABLE CORRELATION Two variables are correlated only because each is causally related to a third variable.

violence the child sees on television (variable *X*) and the aggressiveness of the child's behaviour (variable *Y*) (Huesmann et al., 2003). The more televised violence a child watches, the more aggressive that child is likely to be. These two variables have a relationship, but exactly what kind of relationship is it? There are precisely three possibilities – two simple ones and one not-so-simple one:

- *X* → *Y*. One simple possibility is that watching televised violence (*X*) causes aggressiveness (*Y*). For example, watching televised violence may teach children that aggression is a reasonable way to vent anger and solve problems.
- *Y* → *X*. Another simple possibility is that aggressiveness (*Y*) causes children to watch televised violence (*X*). For example, children who are naturally aggressive may enjoy televised violence more and may seek opportunities to watch it.
- *Z* → *X and Y*. A final and not-so-simple possibility is that *a third variable* (*Z*) causes children to be both aggressive (*Y*) and watch televised violence (*X*), neither of which is causally related to the other. For example, lack of adult supervision (*Z*) may allow children to get away with bullying others and to get away with watching television shows that adults would normally not allow. If so, then watching televised violence (*X*) and behaving aggressively (*Y*) may not be causally related to each other at all and may instead be the independent effects of a lack of adult supervision (*Z*), just as sneezing and coughing may be independent effects of viral infection, height and weight may be independent effects of nutrition and so on. In other words, the relation between aggressiveness and watching televised violence may be a case of third-variable correlation – *two variables are correlated only because each is causally related to a third variable.*

FIGURE 2.8 shows the three possible causes of any correlation. How can we determine by simple observation which of these three possibilities best describes the relationship between televised violence and aggressiveness? We can't. When we observe a natural correlation, *the possibility of third-variable correlation can never be dismissed.* Don't take this claim on faith. Let's try to dismiss the possibility of third-variable correlation and you'll see why such efforts are always doomed to fail.

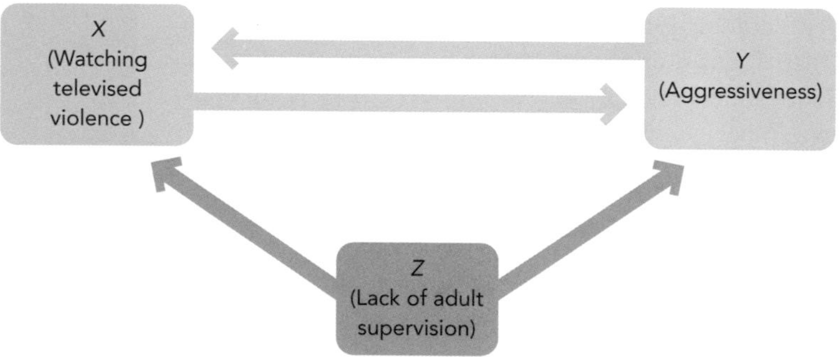

FIGURE 2.8 Causes of correlation If *X* (watching televised violence) and *Y* (aggressiveness) are correlated, then there are exactly three possible explanations: *X* causes *Y*, *Y* causes *X*, or *Z* (some other factor, such as lack of adult supervision) causes both *Y* and *X*, neither of which causes the other.

The most straightforward way to dismiss the possibility that a third variable such as lack of adult supervision (*Z*) caused children to watch televised violence (*X*) and behave aggressively (*Y*) would be to eliminate differences in adult supervision among a group of children and see if the correlation between televised violence and aggressiveness remained. For example, we could observe children in matched samples – *a technique whereby the participants in two samples are identical in terms of a third variable.* For instance, we could observe only children who are supervised by an adult exactly 87% of the time, thus ensuring that every child who watched a lot of televised violence had exactly the same amount of adult supervision as every child who did not watch a lot of televised violence. Alternatively, we could observe children in matched pairs – *a technique whereby each participant in one sample is identical to one other participant in another sample in terms of a third variable.* For instance, we could observe children who experience different amounts of adult supervision, but we could make sure that for every child we observe who watches a lot of televised violence and is supervised 24% of the time, we also observe a child who doesn't watch a lot of televised violence and is supervised 24%

MATCHED SAMPLES An observational technique that involves matching the average of the participants in the experimental and control groups in order to eliminate the possibility that a third variable (and not the independent variable) caused changes in the dependent variable.

MATCHED PAIRS An observational technique that involves matching each participant in the experimental group with a specific participant in the control group in order to eliminate the possibility that a third variable (and not the independent variable) caused changes in the dependent variable.

of the time, thus ensuring that the children who do and do not watch a lot of televised violence have the same amount of adult supervision *on average*. Regardless of which technique we used, we would know that the children who do and don't watch televised violence have equal amounts of adult supervision on average, and thus if those who watch televised violence are more aggressive on average than those who don't, lack of adult supervision cannot be the cause.

Although both techniques can be useful, neither allows us to dismiss the possibility of third-variable correlation. Why? Because even if we use matched samples or matched pairs to dismiss a *particular* third variable (such as lack of adult supervision), we would not be able to dismiss *all* third variables. For example, as soon as we finished making these observations, it might suddenly occur to us that emotionally unstable children may gravitate towards violent TV programmes and may behave aggressively. In other words, 'emotional instability' would be a new third variable that we would have to design new observations to dismiss. Clearly, we could dream up new third variables all day long, and every time we dreamed one up, we would have to rush out and make a whole new set of observations using matched samples or matched pairs to determine whether *this* third variable was the cause of watching televised violence and behaving aggressively.

The problem, then, is that there are an infinite number of third variables out there and thus an infinite number of reasons why X and Y might be correlated. Because most of us don't have the time to perform an infinite number of studies with matched samples or matched pairs, we can never be sure that the natural correlation between *X* and *Y* is evidence of a causal relationship between them. This problem is so troubling and pervasive that it has its own name (and one that's easy to remember). The **third-variable problem** refers to the fact that *a causal relationship between two variables cannot be inferred from the natural correlation between them because of the ever-present possibility of third-variable correlation*. In other words, if we care about causality, natural correlations can never tell us what we really want to know.

THIRD-VARIABLE PROBLEM A causal relationship between two variables cannot be inferred from the correlation between them because of the ever-present possibility of third-variable correlation.

Experimentation

The third-variable problem prevents us from using natural correlations to learn about causal relationships, and so we have to find another method that will. Let's start by considering once again the source of our trouble. We cannot conclude that watching televised violence causes children to behave aggressively because there is some chance that both behaviours are caused by a third variable, such as lack of adult supervision or emotional instability, and there are so many third variables in the world that we could never do enough studies to dismiss them all. Another way of saying this is that children who do watch and don't watch televised violence differ in countless ways, and any one of these countless differences could be the real cause of their different levels of aggressiveness. This suggests that if we could somehow eliminate *all* these countless differences at once – somehow find a sample of children who are perfect clones, with identical amounts of adult supervision, identical amounts of emotional stability, identical histories, identical physiologies, identical neighbourhoods, siblings, toys, schools, teeth, dreams and so on – then the natural correlation between watching televised violence and aggressiveness *would* be evidence of a causal relationship. If we could somehow accomplish this amazing feat, we would have a sample of children, some of whom watch televised violence and some of whom don't, but all of whom are identical in terms of *every possible* third variable. If we found that the children in this sample who watched televised violence were more aggressive than those who did not, then watching televised violence would *have to be* the cause of their different levels of aggressiveness because, after all, watching televised violence would be the *only* thing that distinguished the most aggressive children from the least aggressive children.

Finding a sample of clones is, of course, not very realistic. But as it turns out, scientists have another way to eliminate all the countless differences between the people in a sample. An **experiment** is *a technique for establishing the causal relationship between variables*. The best way to understand how experiments accomplish this amazing feat is by examining their two key features: manipulation and randomization.

EXPERIMENT A technique for establishing the causal relationship between variables.

Manipulation

The most important thing to know about experiments is that you already know the most important thing about experiments because you've been doing them all your life. Imagine, for instance, what you would do if you were watching TV one day when suddenly the picture went fuzzy for 10 minutes, then cleared up, then went fuzzy for a few minutes again and so on. You might suspect that another electronic device, such as your flatmate's new cordless phone, was interfering with the TV reception. Your first step would be to observe and measure carefully, noting the clarity of the TV picture when your flatmate was and was not using their phone. But even if you observed a natural correlation between TV clarity and phone use, the third-variable problem would prevent you from drawing a causal conclusion. After all, if your flatmate was afraid of storms and tended to rush to the phone and call their mum whenever a cloud passed over the house, then clouds (*Z*) could be the cause of the phone calls (*X*) and the TV interference (*Y*).

Because you could not draw a causal conclusion from this natural correlation, you would probably try to create an artificial correlation by standing in front of the TV with the phone in hand, switching it on and off and observing the clarity of the TV picture. If you observed that the artificial pattern of variation you created in the phone (on for one second, off for three seconds, on for eight seconds, off for two seconds) was nicely synchronized with the pattern of variation in the TV (fuzzy for one second, fine for three seconds, fuzzy for eight seconds, fine for two seconds), then you would instantly conclude that the phone was the cause of the interference. Standing in front of the TV and turning the phone on and off may seem to show little common sense, but in doing this, you have discovered and used science's most powerful technique for establishing causal relationships: the experiment. Your actions qualify as an experiment because you used **manipulation** – *systematically altering a variable in order to determine its causal relationship to an outcome of interest.*

MANIPULATION A characteristic of experimentation in which the researcher artificially creates a pattern of variation in an independent variable in order to determine its causal powers. Manipulation usually results in the creation of an experimental group and a control group.

Manipulation is one of the critical ingredients of an experiment. Up to now, we have approached science like polite dinner guests, taking what we were offered and making the best of it. Nature offered us children who differed in how much televised violence they watched and how aggressively they behaved, and we dutifully measured the natural patterns of variation in these two variables and computed their correlations. The problem with this approach is that when all was said and done, we still didn't know what we really wanted to know, namely whether these variables had a causal relationship. No matter how many matched samples or matched pairs we observed, there was always another third variable that we hadn't yet dismissed. Experiments solve this problem. Rather than *measuring* how much televised violence a child watches, *measuring* the child's aggressiveness, and then computing the correlation between these two naturally occurring variables, experiments require that we *manipulate* how much televised violence a child watches in the same way that you manipulated the phone. In essence, we need to systematically switch the watching of televised violence on and off in a sample of children and then see if aggressiveness goes on and off too.

We might do this by asking some children to participate in an experiment and exposing half of them to two hours of televised violence every day for a month while making sure that the other half saw no televised violence at all (see **FIGURE 2.9**). At the end of a month, we could measure the aggressiveness of the children and compare the measurements across the two groups. When we compared these measurements, we would be computing the correlation between a variable we measured (aggressiveness) and a variable we manipulated (televised violence). Instead of looking for synchrony in the patterns of variation that nature offered us, we would have caused a pattern of variation in one variable, observed a pattern of variation in another, and looked for synchrony between them. In so doing, we would have solved the third-variable problem. After all, if we *manipulated* rather than *measured* a child's exposure to televised violence, then we would never have to ask whether a third variable (such as lack of adult supervision) might have caused it. Why? Because we already *know* what caused the child to watch or not watch televised violence. *We* were the cause.

Televised violence	Aggressiveness
Watch	High
Watch	High
Watch	High
Watch	High

Televised violence	Aggressiveness
No watch	Low
No watch	Low
No watch	Low
No watch	Low

FIGURE **2.9 Manipulation** The independent variable is televised violence and the dependent variable is aggressiveness. Manipulation of the independent variable results in an experimental group and a control group. When we compare the behaviour of participants in these two groups, we are actually computing the correlation between the independent variable and the dependent variable.

Doing an experiment, then, involves three critical steps (and several technical terms):

1 We perform a manipulation. We call *the variable that is manipulated* the independent variable because it is under our control, and thus it is 'independent' of what the participant says or does. When we manipulate an independent variable, such as watching televised violence, we create at least two groups of participants: an experimental group, *the group of people who are exposed to an experimental condition under investigation*, such as watching televised violence, and a control group, *the group of people who are similar to the experimental group but not exposed to the same condition under investigation*, such as watching cartoons.

2 Having created a pattern of variation in one variable (televised violence), we now measure the pattern of variation in another variable (aggressiveness). We call *the variable that is measured* the dependent variable because its value 'depends' on what the participant says or does.

3 We check to see whether the patterns of variation in the dependent and independent variables are synchronized.

When we have manipulated an independent variable, measured a dependent variable, and looked to see whether their patterns of variation are synchronized, we've done one of the two things that experimentation requires. Now let's talk about the second.

INDEPENDENT VARIABLE The variable that is manipulated in an experiment.

EXPERIMENTAL GROUP The group of people who are exposed to an experimental condition under investigation.

CONTROL GROUP The group of people matched to an experimental group but not exposed to the condition under investigation.

DEPENDENT VARIABLE The variable that is measured in a study.

Randomization ensures that the participants in the experimental and control groups are, on average, identical in every way except one: the value of the independent variable.

Randomization

Manipulation is one of the two critical features of experimentation that allow us to overcome the third-variable problem and establish a causal relationship between an independent and a dependent variable. The second feature is a bit less intuitive but equally important. Imagine that we did the televised violence experiment by finding a sample of children and asking each child whether they would like to be in the experimental group or

Self-selection is a problem in experimentation. For example, we could never draw conclusions about the effects of military service by comparing those who joined to those who didn't because those who do and don't join differ in so many ways.

SELF-SELECTION The problem that occurs when a participant's inclusion in the experimental or control group is determined by the participant.

RANDOMIZATION A procedure using random assignment to ensure that a participant's inclusion in the experimental or control group is not determined by a third variable.

the control group. Imagine that, conveniently enough, half of the children volunteered to watch two hours of televised violence every day for a month, and the other half volunteered not to. Imagine that we did as each of the children requested, measured their aggressiveness a month later, and found that the children who watched televised violence were more aggressive than those who did not. Would this experiment allow us to conclude that watching televised violence causes aggressiveness? Definitely not – but *why* not? After all, we switched televised violence on and off and watched to see whether aggressiveness went on and off too. So where did we go wrong?

We went wrong when we let the children decide for themselves how much TV they would watch. Many things probably distinguish children who volunteer to watch televised violence from those who don't. For instance, those who volunteer may be older, or stronger or cleverer. Or younger, or weaker or more stupid. Or less often supervised or more emotionally unstable. The list of possible differences goes on and on. The whole point of doing an experiment was to divide children into two groups that differed *in just one way*, namely, in terms of how much televised violence they watched. The moment we allowed the children to select their own groups, the two groups differed in countless ways, and any of those countless differences could have been responsible for differences in their aggressiveness. **Self-selection** is *a problem that occurs when a participant's inclusion in the experimental or control group is determined by the participant.* Just as we cannot allow nature to decide which of the children in our study watches televised violence, we cannot allow the children to decide either. So who decides?

The answer to this question may be a bit surprising: *no one decides*. If we want to be sure that there is one and only one difference between the children who do and do not watch televised violence, then their inclusion in these groups must be *randomly determined*. Most of us use the word *random* to mean 'without a cause' (as in: 'Bill was angry with me today for no reason at all. It was totally random'). This is precisely how the word should be used. If you tossed a coin and a friend asked what had *caused* it to land heads up, you would correctly say that *nothing* had. This is what it means for the outcome of a coin toss to be random. Because the outcome of a coin toss is random, we can put coin flips to work for us to solve the problem that self-selection creates. If we want to be sure that a child's inclusion in the experimental group or the control group was not caused by nature, was not caused by the child, and was not caused by *any* of the infinite number of third variables we could name if we only had the time, then all we have to do is let it be caused by the outcome of a coin toss – which itself has no cause. For example, we could walk up to each child in our experiment, toss a coin, and, if the coin lands heads up, assign the child to watch two hours of televised violence every day for a month. If the coin lands heads down, then we could assign the child to watch no television. **Randomization** is *a procedure that uses random events to ensure that a participant's assignment to the experimental or control group is not determined by a third variable.*

What would happen if we assigned children to groups with a coin toss? As **FIGURE 2.10** shows, the first thing we would expect is that about half the children would be assigned to watch televised violence and about half would not. That would be convenient. But second – and *much* more importantly – we could expect the experimental group and the control group to have roughly equal numbers of supervised children and unsupervised children, roughly equal numbers of emotionally stable and unstable children, roughly equal numbers of big and small children, active and inactive children, short and tall children, funny children and children with blue hair named Larry McSweeny. Indeed, we could expect the two groups to have equal numbers of children who are anything-you-can-ever-name-and-everything-you-can't! Because the two groups will be the same on average in terms of height, weight, emotional stability, adult supervision and every other variable in the known universe except the one

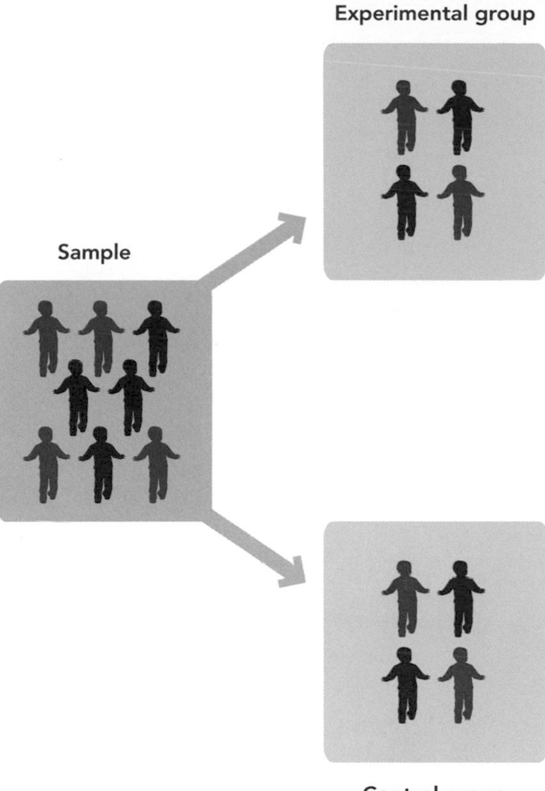

Televised violence	Adult supervision	Aggressiveness
Watch	Yes	High
Watch	No	High
Watch	Yes	High
Watch	No	High

Televised violence	Adult supervision	Aggressiveness
No watch	Yes	Low
No watch	No	Low
No watch	Yes	Low
No watch	No	Low

FIGURE **2.10 Randomization** Children with adult supervision are shown in plum and children without adult supervision are shown in blue. The independent variable is televised violence and the dependent variable is aggressiveness. Randomization ensures that participants in the experimental and control groups are equal on average in terms of all possible third variables. In essence, it ensures that there is no correlation between a third variable and the dependent variable.

we manipulated, we can be more certain that the variable we manipulated (televised violence) caused changes in the variable we measured (aggressiveness). Watching televised violence was the only difference between the two groups of children when we started the experiment, and thus it *probably* is the cause of the differences in aggressiveness we observed a month later (remember certainty and sole causes are rare in complex behavioural sciences when so many factors can play a role, which is why scientists should restrict their conclusions to probabilities).

hot science

Establishing causality in the brain

Sometimes, the best way to learn about something is to see what happens when it breaks, and the human brain is no exception. Scientists have studied the effects of brain damage for centuries, and those studies reveal a lot about how the brain normally works so well. As you read in Chapter 1, in the middle of the 19th century, French surgeon Paul Broca observed that people who had lost their ability to speak often had damage in a particular spot on the left side of their brains. Broca suggested that this region might control speech production but not other functions such as the ability to understand speech. As it turned out, he was right, which is why this brain region is now known as Broca's area.

Scientists have learned a lot about the brain by studying the behaviour of people whose brains are defective or have been damaged by accidents. But the problem with studying brain-damaged patients, of course, is the problem with studying any naturally occurring variable: brain damage may be related to particular patterns of behaviour, but that relationship may or may not be causal. Experimentation is the premier method for establishing causal relationships between variables, but scientists cannot ethically cause brain damage in human beings, and thus they have not been able to establish causal relationships between particular kinds of brain damage and particular patterns of behaviour.

Until now. Scientists have recently discovered a way to mimic brain damage with a benign technique called *transcranial magnetic stimulation* (TMS) (Barker et al., 1985; Hallett, 2000). If you've ever held a magnet under a piece of paper and used it to drag a pin across the paper's surface, you know that magnetic fields can pass through insulating material. The human skull is no exception. TMS delivers a magnetic pulse that passes through the skull and deactivates neurons in the cerebral cortex for a short period. Researchers can direct TMS pulses to particular brain regions – essentially turning them 'off' – and then measure temporary changes in the way a person moves, sees, thinks, remembers, speaks or feels. By manipulating the state of the brain, scientists can perform experiments that establish causal relationships. For example, scientists have recently discovered that magnetic stimulation of the visual cortex temporarily impairs a person's ability to detect the motion of an object without impairing the person's ability to recognize that object (Beckers and Zeki, 1995). This intriguing discovery suggests that motion perception and object recognition are accomplished by different parts of the brain, but moreover, it establishes that the activity of these brain regions *causes* motion perception and object recognition.

For the first time in human history, the causal relationships between particular brain regions and particular behaviours have been unequivocally established. Rather than relying on observational studies of brain-damaged patients or the snapshots provided by magnetic resonance imaging (MRI) or PET scans, researchers can now manipulate brain activity and measure its effects. Studies suggest that TMS has no harmful side effects (Pascual-Leone et al., 1993), and this new tool promises to revolutionize the study of how our brains create our thoughts, feelings and actions. It may also have clinical application as TMS is currently being used in the treatment of depression, although its effectiveness is still in question (see Chapter 17).

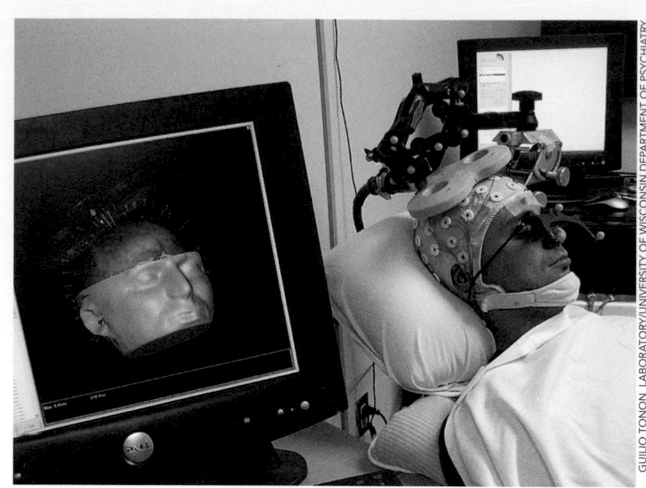
GUILIO TONON LABORATORY/UNIVERSITY OF WISCONSIN DEPARTMENT OF PSYCHIATRY

Transcranial magnetic stimulation activates and deactivates regions of the brain with a magnetic pulse, temporarily mimicking brain damage.

Drawing conclusions

Bearing in mind Popper's concerns about the problems of proof that we encountered earlier, it is important to remember what scientific accounts of the world really are and why non-scientists often misunderstand the conclusions scientists arrive at. Scientists often seem overly cautious and elusive when explaining their findings to the general public who want to know the facts. In reality, good scientists are usually explaining their findings in the context of the studies they have conducted, knowing full well that these are approximations to the real world that have potential weaknesses. In this section, we consider some of the limitations of the experimental method, including what we measure and the population we measure from.

INTERNAL VALIDITY The characteristic of an experiment that allows one to draw accurate inferences about the causal relationship between an independent and dependent variable.

If we were to apply all the techniques we have discussed so far, we could design an experiment that has internal validity – *the characteristic of an experiment that allows one to draw accurate inferences about the causal relationship between an independent and dependent variable.* When we say that an experiment is internally valid, we mean that everything *inside* the experiment is working exactly as it must in order for us to draw conclusions about causal relationships. Specifically, an experiment is internally valid when:

- An independent variable has been effectively manipulated.
- Participants have been randomly assigned to the groups this manipulation created.
- A dependent variable has been measured in an unbiased way with a valid, powerful and reliable measure.
- A correlation has been observed between the pattern of variation created in the independent variable and the pattern of variation measured in the dependent variable.

This final point could be tested with a t-test, assuming we measured aggression with a continuous scale. We would want to know whether the mean aggression score of the violent television group was significantly higher than the mean aggression score in the no violent television group. If we measured aggression on a categorical scale, then a contingency table analysis using the χ^2 statistic would be more appropriate. For example, aggression might be measured categorically as whether the participants punched the experimenter when leaving the laboratory or not.

If we do these things, then we may conclude that manipulated changes in the independent variable caused measured changes in the dependent variable. But we may *not* conclude that one abstract property caused another. For example, even the most well-designed and well-executed study on televised violence and aggressiveness would *not* allow us to conclude that watching televised violence causes aggressiveness. Rather, it would allow us to draw the much more limited conclusion that televised violence *as we defined it* caused aggressiveness *as we defined it* in the *people we studied*. The phrases 'as we defined it' and 'people we studied' represent important restrictions on the kinds of conclusions that scientists may draw, so let's consider each of them in turn.

Representative variables

When we say that we have established a causal relationship between televised violence and aggressiveness *as we have defined them*, we are acknowledging the fact that operational definitions are never perfectly linked to their properties. You will recall that we can never measure an abstract property such as *aggressiveness* but rather can only measure operational definitions of that property, such as *the number of times a child initiates forceful physical contact with other children in the playground during break-time*. Because we cannot measure properties, experiments can never be used to make legitimate claims about them. Experiments allow us to draw conclusions about the causal relationship between the particular operational definitions we manipulated and measured but not about the abstract properties these particular operational definitions represent.

In practice, this is one of those rules to which few people pay serious attention. Consider, for example, the current controversy over the effects of violent video games on children. Some people believe that playing violent video games leads children to behave aggressively, others do not, and both claim that scientific experiments support their arguments (Reichhardt, 2003). So who's right? Nobody is, because experiments do not allow us to draw conclusions about abstractions such as *violent video games* and *aggressive behaviour*. Rather, they allow us to draw very particular conclusions about how *playing Candy Crush for two minutes* or *playing Call of Duty for 10 hours* influences *the tendency to interrupt when others are speaking* or *the tendency to pummel others with blunt objects*. Not surprisingly, experiments on video games and aggression can produce very different results depending on how the independent and dependent variables are operationally defined. Long exposure to a truly violent game will probably produce more aggressive behaviour than brief exposure to a moderately violent game, and exposure to any kind of violent game will probably influence rudeness more easily than it will influence physical aggression.

What, then, is the right way to operationalize such variables? One obvious answer is that experiments should strive for **external validity** – *a property of an experiment in which variables have been operationally defined in a normal, typical or realistic way*. It seems fairly clear that *interrupting* and *pummelling* are not the kinds of aggressive behaviours with which teachers and parents are normally concerned and that most instances of aggression among children lie somewhere between an insult and a chain saw massacre. If the goal of an experiment is to determine whether the kinds of video games that children typically play cause the kinds of aggression in which children typically engage, then external validity is essential.

EXTERNAL VALIDITY A characteristic of an experiment in which the independent and dependent variables are operationally defined in a normal, typical or realistic way.

Indeed, external validity seems like such a good idea that students are often surprised to learn that most psychology experiments are externally *in*valid – and that most psychologists don't mind. The reason for this is that psychologists are rarely trying to learn about the real world by creating tiny replicas of it in their laboratories. Rather, they are usually trying to learn about the real world by using experiments to test theories and hypotheses (Mook, 1983). For example, physicists have a theory stating that heat is the result of the rapid movement of molecules. This theory suggests a hypothesis, namely that if the molecules that constitute an object are slowed, the object should become cooler. Now imagine that a physicist tested this hypothesis by performing an experiment in which a laser was used to slow the movement of the molecules in a rubber ball, whose temperature was then measured. Would we criticize this experiment by saying, 'Sorry, but your experiment teaches us nothing about the real world because in the real world, no one actually uses lasers to slow the movement of the molecules in rubber balls'? Let's hope not. The physicist's theory (molecular motion causes heat) led to a hypothesis about what would happen in the laboratory (slowing the molecules in a rubber ball should cool it), and thus the events that the physicist manipulated and measured in the laboratory served to test the theory.

Similarly, a good theory about the causal relationship between video games and aggression should lead to hypotheses about how people will behave when playing *Call of Duty* for many hours. As such, even these unrepresentative forms of video game playing can serve to test the theory. In short, theories allow us to generate hypotheses about what *can* happen, or what *must* happen or what *will* happen under particular circumstances, and experiments are typically meant to create these circumstances, test the hypotheses and thereby provide evidence for or against the theories that generated them. Experiments are not meant to be miniature versions of everyday life, and thus external invalidity is not necessarily a problem.

Representative samples

RANDOM SAMPLING A technique for choosing participants that ensures that every member of a population has an equal chance of being included in the sample.

You will recall that the law of large numbers advises us to measure many people rather than just one or two so that the average behaviour of the people in our sample will closely approximate the average behaviour of people in the population. But how do we actually *find* the people in our sample? The best way to do this is to use random sampling – *a technique for choosing participants that ensures that every member of a population has an equal chance of being included in the sample.* When we randomly sample participants from a population, we earn the right to *generalize* from the behaviour of the sample to the behaviour of the population, that is, to conclude that what we observed in our experiment would also have been observed if we had measured the entire population. You already have good intuitions about the importance of random sampling. For example, if you stopped at a fruit farm to buy a bag of cherries and the farmer offered to let you taste a few he had specially handpicked from the bag, you'd be reluctant to generalize from that nonrandom sample to the population of cherries in the bag. But if the farmer invited you to pull a few cherries from the bag without looking, you'd probably be willing to take those cherries as reasonably representative of the cherry population.

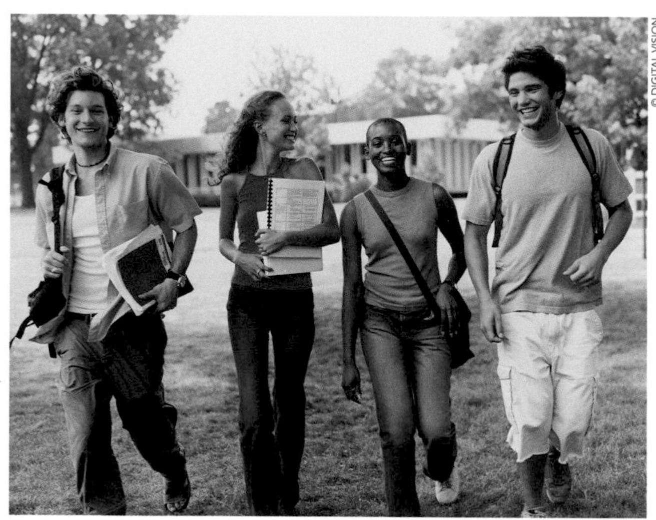

In practice, random sampling is almost impossible to achieve. Therefore, the results from a psychology experiment involving this sample of university students might not be generalizable to the whole population.

Given the importance of random sampling, you may be surprised to learn that psychologists almost never do it. Indeed, virtually every participant in every psychology experiment you will ever read about was a volunteer, and most were university students who were significantly younger, smarter, healthier and wealthier than the average earthling. Psychologists sample their participants the 'wrong way' (by nonrandom sampling) because it is just about impossible to do it the 'right way' (by random sampling). Even if there were an alphabetized list of all the world's human inhabitants from which we could randomly choose our research participants, the likelihood that we could actually perform experiments on those we sampled would be depressingly slim. After all, how would we find the 72-year-old Bedouin woman whose family roams the desert so that we could measure the electrical activity in her brain while she watched cartoons? How would we convince the three-week-old infant in New Delhi to complete a lengthy questionnaire about his political beliefs? Most psychology experiments are conducted by academics (and their students) at universities in the West. As much as they might like to randomly sample the population of the planet, the practical truth is that they are pretty much stuck studying the people who volunteer for their studies.

Random sampling is always impractical and usually impossible. And yet, if we don't randomly sample, then we can't automatically generalize from our sample to the population from which it was drawn. So how can we learn *anything* from psychology experiments? Isn't the failure to randomly sample a fatal flaw? No, it's not. Although we can't automatically generalize from nonrandom samples, there are three reasons why this is not a lethal problem for the science of psychology:

1 *Sometimes generality does not matter*. One flying pig utterly disproves most people's theories of porcine locomotion. Similarly, in psychology, it often doesn't matter if *everyone* does something as long as *someone* does it. If playing a violent video game for one hour caused a nonrandomly selected group of children to start shoving in the lunch queue, this fact would be sufficient evidence against every theory that claimed

that video games cannot cause aggression, and it might even provide important clues about when aggression will and won't occur. An experimental result can be illuminating even when its generality is severely limited.

2 *Sometimes generality can be determined.* When the generality of an experimental result *is* important, psychologists often perform a new experiment that uses the same procedures on a different sample. For example, if we were to measure how some US children behaved after playing *Call of Duty* for two hours, we could then replicate the experiment with Japanese children, or with teenagers or with adults. In essence, we could treat the attributes of our sample, such as culture and age, as independent variables and do experiments to determine whether these attributes influenced our dependent variable. If the results of our study were replicated in numerous nonrandom samples, we could be more confident, although never completely confident, that the results would generalize to the population at large.

3 *Sometimes generality can be assumed.* Instead of asking, 'Is there a compelling reason to generalize from a nonrandom sample?', we might just as easily ask, 'Is there a compelling reason not to?' For example, few of us would be willing to take an experimental drug that could potentially make us smarter and happier if a nonrandom sample of seven participants took the drug and died a slow, painful death. Indeed, we would probably refuse the drug even if the seven subjects were mice. Although the study used a nonrandom sample of participants who are different from us in many ways, we are willing to generalize from their experience to ours because we know that even mice share enough of our basic biology to make it a good bet that what harms them can harm us too. By this same reasoning, if a psychology experiment demonstrated that some US children behaved violently after playing *Call of Duty* for one hour, we might ask whether there is a compelling reason to suspect that Ecuadorian university students or middle-aged Australians would behave any differently. If we had a reason to suspect they would, then the experimental method would provide a way for us to investigate that possibility.

In summary, to determine whether two variables are causally related, we must first determine whether they are related at all. This can be done by measuring each variable many times and then comparing the patterns of variation within each series of measurements. If the patterns covary, then the variables are correlated. Depending on the types of variable (categorical and continuous), different types of inferential statistical tests are helpful in deciding if variables are related. We have seen t-tests are useful when testing whether two means are significantly different. The χ^2 statistic can be used to test associations between two categorical variables (each taking on as many values as you please). When testing associations between two continuous variables, the Pearson correlation coefficient (*r*) is appropriate. These statistical tests barely scratch the surface of the array of sophisticated techniques available to psychologists today.

Even when we observe a correlation between two variables, we can't conclude that they are causally related because there are an infinite number of 'third variables' that might be causing them both. Experiments solve this third-variable problem by manipulating an independent variable, randomly assigning participants to experimental and control groups that this manipulation creates, and measuring a dependent variable. These measurements are then compared across groups using inferential statistics.

An internally valid experiment establishes a causal relationship between variables as they were operationally defined and among the participants whom they included. When an experiment mimics the real world, that is, when it is externally valid and its participants are randomly sampled, we may generalize from its results. If we find a consistent effect in our experiments that predicts what people do in real-world situations, we have discovered something that is both reliable and valid and not something that has been artificially induced in the lab.

Qualitative research: forget the size, feel the quality

So far in this chapter, we have seen how experimental researchers emphasize measurement, prediction, control and objectivity. Overall, this approach to psychological research can be defined as quantitative research, which *uses systematic, scientific investigation in order to measure and quantify phenomena.* However, there is another way of approaching the research process, known as qualitative research, which is more *interested in gaining an in-depth understanding of the human experience and behaviour.* Instead of focusing on objectivity, predictability and numerical measurability,

QUANTITATIVE RESEARCH Uses systematic, scientific investigation in order to measure and quantify phenomena.

QUALITATIVE RESEARCH Interested in gaining an in-depth understanding of the human experience and behaviour.

qualitative researchers seek to investigate the complexity, nuance and richness of human thoughts, feelings and interactions, using things like interviews, newspaper articles and transcripts from TV programmes to explore themes and follow up ideas. These are measures that do not fit neatly into the simple scales and metrics that define quantitative research. The strength of qualitative research is that it captures aspects of psychology that are not easily reduced to numbers. In other words, 'Never mind the width, feel the quality.'

Although the majority of psychological research carried out is quantitative in nature, qualitative research methods are used by small but increasing numbers of psychologists, especially in social, clinical and health psychology, who are situated in the UK, Australasia and parts of Europe, for example Scandinavia. In the past 20 years or so, a growing number of research articles, textbooks, specialist journals and conferences have featured qualitative research methods.

What are qualitative research methods?

Qualitative researchers take a range of different approaches to carrying out their research and there are sometimes sharp differences and disagreements between them (see Madill and Gough, 2008).

For example, some researchers prefer to *collect* original data through conducting and recording interviews and focus group discussions, while others prefer to work with pre-existing data, such as newspaper articles and internet forum material, or to record naturally occurring interactions, such as family arguments or therapy sessions. You can read more about the various forms of qualitative data collection in **TABLE 2.3.** Similarly, when it comes to *analysing* the data they have collected, there are also varying approaches. Some researchers prefer to focus on individual experience, feelings and concerns, for example 'how does it feel to be a victim of crime?', while others favour questions about how people use words to do things, for example 'how do those suffering from "chronic fatigue syndrome" convince others that their "illness" is "legitimate"?' As tends to happen in the world of academia, these different approaches have acquired their own names and acronyms, which you will find summarized in **TABLE 2.4.**

TABLE 2.3 Some important methods of qualitative data collection

Method	Brief description
Interviews	Semi-structured interviews are the most popular interview format and allow participants to introduce issues and topics not anticipated by the researcher. In this way, the interviewer can ask questions important to them while the interviewee has some freedom to talk about what's important to them
Focus group discussions	In focus group discussions, the idea is that participants with something in common talk to each other about the topic in question while the researcher acts as a facilitator. Such discussions can offer insights into social interaction and group identity as well as the topic under investigation
Naturally occurring data	Social psychologists especially may be interested in public or cultural attitudes about the topic in question, for example race relations, and may turn to media representations, newspapers, magazines, advertisements, internet materials, for data to analyse. Psychologists interested in social interaction may transcribe and analyse recordings of everyday talk, for example doctor–patient interactions, telephone helpline talk, family mealtime interactions
Participant observation	Here the researcher joins an existing group or community in order to observe behaviour from within. Such an 'insider' perspective can yield fascinating insights about social practices, norms and taboos
Structured methods	Structured methods are task focused, so research participants may be invited to generate a range of statements about a topic for later discussion (Q-sorts), respond to a researcher-generated story (vignette) or write about their experiences, views and feelings (open-ended questionnaire)

TABLE **2.4 Some important methods of qualitative data analysis**

Method	Brief description
Thematic analysis (TA)	A user-friendly pragmatic approach to managing and analysing qualitative data. Themes are concepts that explain, structure or characterize the data in question. For example, researchers may be interested in the individual experience of rape victims. Initial interviews may highlight aspects or patterns of the experience such as guilt, anger or public perceptions that then become the themes for further investigation. These are not necessarily shared with all victims and so are pursued as individual themes
Grounded theory (GT)	Grounded theory can be thought of as a qualitative approach derived from everyday experiences. Here, data are analysed systematically in order to produce a 'theory' or set of themes that explain the data, in other words, generate a theory. GT also encompasses a flexible approach to data collection called 'theoretical sampling' to test the validity of the theory
Interpretative phenomenological analysis (IPA)	IPA is concerned with understanding individual experiences. It normally encompasses in-depth analysis of semi-structured interviews, and emphasizes identity issues
Narrative analysis (NA)	Narrative approaches invite participants to talk about or write their life story, or some aspect of it. NA attempts to link significant life events and identify core themes
Discourse analysis (DA)	DA researchers are interested in social interaction and how people use language to perform actions, for example blaming, self-promotion, defending one's actions. There is a preference for working with recordings of people talking to each other
Conversation analysis (CA)	CA researchers pay close attention to talk sequences, for example question-answer, and how these move forward and accomplish particular tasks

What can qualitative research methods offer to psychologists?

Methods such as interviews can produce *first-hand, insider accounts* of whatever is being studied, and this can lead to in-depth insight and understanding. For example, we can learn what it feels like to live with prostate cancer via in-depth interviews with male patients, and how this experience may be shaped at least partly by issues of masculine identity (see Broom, 2004).

Importantly too, qualitative analysis can be based on participants' own words and meaning, giving it a 'real-world' resonance. From a psychological viewpoint, this enables us to learn about how individuals experience events in their own terms, and from a social psychological viewpoint, we can also appreciate how the contexts in which individuals live may help shape their experiences. So, for example, interviewees talking about parenthood may point to personal feelings, preferences and struggles while also referring to wider factors, such as gender, work and marital issues.

Traditional, hypothesis-driven quantitative research usually begins with a theory, which is tested through experiments. In contrast, qualitative research projects often begin *without* a theory, instead, they generate theoretical understanding through detailed, systematic analysis of their source material. This approach is perhaps best embodied by the grounded theory approach (Glaser and Strauss, 1967) (see Table 2.4 above) which, as the name suggests, aims to *ground* its theoretical conclusions in participants' terminology.

Another feature of qualitative research is its *flexibility*. This is particularly true of qualitative interviews, where dialogue can often extend well beyond pre-planned questions, participants can cover topics without being prompted, and the interviewer can follow up new lines of inquiry within the interview as and when they arise. For example, if a study on women and childlessness highlights the role of male partners in the decision to reject parenthood, then interviews may be arranged with childless men. In contrast, experimental research is usually tightly designed, with clear hypotheses to be tested on a specified sample.

A third – and perhaps more controversial – feature of qualitative research is the *involvement of the researcher*. In conventional psychological research, the experimenter remains fairly detached from the research participants in order to avoid introducing any bias. So, we can say that quantitative research aspires to the goal of objectivity. Qualitative research does not. Partly this is because bias is more difficult to avoid in qualitative research, because (as we have seen above) the researcher plays a more active role in data collection. But more than this, qualitative researchers argue that objectivity is not really desirable in any case: interviews, for example, work best when a good rapport has been established between interviewer and interviewee.

The obvious problem that comes along with this is that the qualitative researcher's involvement and subjectivity can be seen as undermining the validity of their findings. In order to avoid allegations of bias, qualitative researchers believe that their involvement – and its effects – should be documented and discussed through critical self-reflection within the research process (see Finlay and Gough, 2003). The term 'reflexivity' has been used to convey this idea. In this way, qualitative research hopes to avoid being dismissed as merely biased or subjective, since the researcher's personal influence is itself audited and evaluated as part of the process.

Issues with qualitative research

As you may have guessed from the paragraphs above, mainstream psychologists tend to have concerns about the reliability and validity of qualitative research, as well as the extent to which its findings can be generalized and applied to scenarios beyond the one studied in a particular research project. What have qualitative researchers done to counteract these objections? First, they have taken the reflexive approach mentioned above. Beyond this, they argue that, for them, it makes little sense to speak of reliability or replication, because all qualitative data collection sessions (interviews, focus group discussions, diaries and so on) are to some extent unique and could not be re-created exactly.

Instead, qualitative researchers have developed alternative means of safeguarding the reliability and validity of their research. For example, *data triangulation* involves verifying one account with another – an interview may be verified against a written report, or multiple researchers might analyse the same qualitative data and then agree on significant themes. Qualitative research can sit alongside experiments and questionnaire studies and, in recent years, there has been a trend towards 'mixed methods' research, that is, research that combines qualitative and quantitative methods, in psychology, especially in applied, problem-focused research. For example, a qualitative study may initially identify relevant constructs in an area and a quantitative tool, such as a questionnaire, could then be developed to measure those constructs. Yet, qualitative researchers maintain that there can never be complete correspondence between two or more accounts or interpretations since each person or encounter will bring something different to the table. Also, given the variety of approaches within the qualitative research family, researchers are starting to tailor quality criteria to fit the particular methodology or research project in question (see Parker, 2004).

Within the qualitative research community itself, debates continue over several key issues, ranging from the nature and purpose of qualitative research to the merits and shortcomings of specific methods, making this a lively – if still contentious – field of psychological science.

The ethics of science: first, do no harm

Somewhere along the way, someone probably told you that it isn't nice to treat people like objects. And yet, it may seem that psychologists do just that – creating situations that cause people to feel fearful or sad, to do things that are embarrassing or immoral, and to learn things about themselves that they might not really want to know. Why do psychologists treat people so shabbily? In fact, psychologists go to great lengths to ensure the safety and wellbeing of their research participants, and they are bound by detailed ethical principles as set out by organizations such as the British Psychological Society and the European Federation of Psychologists' Associations. Here are a few of the most important ones regarding research with human participants:

INFORMED CONSENT An agreement to participate in a study made by an adult who has been informed of all the risks that participation may entail.

- *Informed consent:* Participants may not take part in a psychological study unless they have given **informed consent** – *an agreement to participate in a study made by an* *adult who has been informed of all the risks that participation may entail.* This doesn't mean that the person must know everything about the study (the hypothesis), but it does mean that the person must know about anything that might potentially be harmful, painful, embarrassing or unpleasant. If people cannot give informed consent (perhaps because they are children or are mentally incapable), then informed consent must be obtained from their legal guardians. All participants have the right to withdraw consent during or after participation and have their data removed from the study.

- *Freedom from coercion:* Psychologists may not force participation. Coercion not only means physical and psychological coercion but monetary coercion as well. It is unethical to offer people large amounts of money to persuade them to do something they might otherwise decline to do. University students may be invited to participate in studies as part of their training in psychology, but they are ordinarily offered an alternative learning activity if they do not want to participate in research.
- *Protection from harm:* Psychologists must take every possible precaution to protect their research participants from physical or psychological harm. If there are two equally effective ways to study something, the psychologist must use the safer method. If no safe method is available, the psychologist may not perform the study.
- *Debriefing:* Although psychologists need not divulge everything about a study before a person participates, they must divulge it after the person participates. If a participant is deceived in any way before or during a study, the psychologist must provide a debriefing – *a verbal description of the true nature and purpose of a study.* If the participant was changed in any way, for example made to feel sad, the psychologist must attempt to undo that change, for example ask the person to do a task that will make them happy, and restore the participant to the state they were in before the study.

DEBRIEFING A verbal description of the true nature and purpose of a study that psychologists provide to people after they have participated in the study.

These rules require that psychologists show extraordinary concern for their participants' welfare, but how are they enforced? Most psychological research is conducted within universities and universities have ethics committees that review study proposals before they commence. A psychologist may conduct a study only after the relevant ethics committee has reviewed and approved it. As you can imagine, the code of ethics and the procedure for approval are so strict that many studies simply cannot be performed anywhere, by anyone, at any time. For example, psychologists have long wondered how growing up without exposure to language affects a person's subsequent ability to speak and think, but they cannot ethically manipulate such a variable in an experiment. As such, they must be content to study the natural correlations between variables such as language exposure and speaking ability, and they must forever forgo the possibility of firmly establishing causal relationships between these variables. There are many questions that psychologists will never be able to answer definitively because doing so would require unethical experimentation. This is an unavoidable consequence of studying creatures who have fundamental human rights.

In 1924, Carney Landis, a young University of Minnesota psychology graduate student, conducted one the most infamous studies as far as ethics is concerned. He was researching the universality of facial expressions and emotions. A reasonable enough question but what was unquestionable was his methods. He photographed fellow students as they were made to smell ammonia, look at pornography and put their hands into buckets of live frogs. For the coup de grâce, they were made to cut the head off a live rat. His results were inconclusive but he did demonstrate that two out of three people will do what you tell them to decades before Stanley Milgram's research on obedience (see Chapter 15).

Of course, not all research participants have human rights because not all research participants are human. Some are chimpanzees, rats, pigeons or other nonhuman animals. How do the ethical principles of the psychologist apply to nonhuman participants? The question of 'animal rights' is one of the most hotly debated issues of our time, and people on opposite sides of the debate rarely have much good to say about each other. And yet, consider three points on which every reasonable person would agree:

- A very small percentage of psychological experiments are performed on nonhuman animals, and a very small percentage of these experiments cause discomfort or death.
- Nonhuman animals deserve good care, should never be subjected to more discomfort than is absolutely necessary, and should be protected by legislation and ethical principles. In the UK, some relevant legal issues are addressed by the Animals (Scientific Procedures) Act 1986. With regard to psychological research, the British Psychological Society again provides explicit ethical guidelines.
- Some experiments on nonhuman animals have had tremendous benefits for human beings, and many have not.

Although the use of nonhuman participants is rare in psychology, their involvement brings interesting ethical and moral questions into play.

None of these points is in dispute among thoughtful advocates of the different positions, so what exactly is the controversy? The controversy lies in the answer to a single question: Is it morally acceptable to force nonhuman animals to pay certain costs so that human animals can reap uncertain benefits? Our society allows people to eat animals, which is to say that many people believe it is morally acceptable to profit at the expense of a nonhuman animal. A small but significant minority of people disagree. Although there are compelling arguments to be made on both sides of this moral dilemma, it is clearly just that – a *moral* dilemma and not a scientific controversy one can hope to answer with evidence and facts. Anyone who has ever loved a pet can empathize with the plight of the nonhuman animal that is being forced to participate in an experiment, feel pain or even die when it would prefer not to. Anyone who has ever loved a person with a debilitating illness can understand the desire of researchers to develop drugs and medical procedures by doing to nonhuman animals the same things that farmers and animal trainers do every day. Do animals have rights, and if so, do they ever outweigh the rights of people? This is a difficult question with which individuals and societies are currently wrestling. For now, at least, there is no easy answer.

CONDITIONAL PROBABILITY A likelihood that is dependent on other factors.

In summary, psychologists are acutely aware of the responsibilities that come with conducting research with human and nonhuman animals. Care and consideration are taken to make sure that human research participants give their informed and voluntary consent to participate in studies that pose minimal or no risk. Similar principles guide the humane treatment of nonhuman research subjects. Enforcement of these principles by legal, institutional and professional governing bodies ensures that the research process is a meaningful one that can lead to significant increases in knowledge.

psychomythology

With two choices, it's not always 50:50

Not strictly a myth but one of the most common misunderstandings in psychology has to do with reasoning about probability or chance. Here are two examples you can use to test yourself and others, both of which deal with what appears to be simple two-choice, 50:50 decisions. You might even win a bet or two:

1 Mr and Mrs Brown have two children. If we know one of them is a daughter, what is the probability that the other is also a girl?
Answer: Most people will say that the answer must be 50:50 but that would be wrong. The correct answer is one in three or 33%.

2 Consider the famous Monty Hall problem. You are a contestant on a game show and have to choose a fabulous prize (such as a Ferrari, if you like that kind of thing) that is behind one of three doors. Behind the other two doors is a booby prize. Say you choose the middle door B. The host, Monty Hall, says to you, 'Well, you have chosen door B, but first, let me show you what is behind door C.' He opens door C to show you one of the booby prizes. Now that you know what is behind door C, should you stick with door B or switch to door A?
Answer: Most people say the chances are 50:50 and that they will stick (people are less likely to switch after they have made a decision). They should in fact switch because they will be doubling their chances from 33% to 67%.

To understand why the obvious answers are incorrect, you have to be aware of conditional probability – *a likelihood that is dependent on other factors.* In the Mr and Mrs Brown problem, we did not say which child was the daughter; only that one of them was. When you consider every combination of child A and B, you have four possible permutations:

Child A – boy   Child B – boy
Child A – boy   Child B – girl
Child A – girl   Child B – boy
Child A – girl   Child B – girl

We know it cannot be the first combination, which means that the probability of Mr and Mrs Brown having two children who are both daughters is one in three.

In the Monty Hall problem, remember Monty only shows you a booby prize door after you have made your choice (he is obviously not going to show the prize door). When you made your original choice, it was one in three. By switching to the other door, you are selecting a door that is two out of three. Now imagine that instead of just three doors, there are 1,000 doors. Let's say you choose door 429. What is the likelihood that you chose the right door? One in a thousand would be the right answer. Now Monty opens 998 doors except for door 617. Would you swap now?

where do you stand?

The morality of immoral experiments

Is it wrong to benefit from someone else's wrongdoing? Although this may seem like an abstract question for moral philosophers, it is a very real question that scientists must ask when they consider the results of unethical experiments. During the Second World War, Nazi doctors conducted barbaric medical studies on prisoners in concentration camps. They placed prisoners in decompression chambers and then dissected their living brains in order to determine how altitude affects pilots. They irradiated and chemically mutilated the reproductive organs of men and women in order to find inexpensive methods for the mass sterilization of 'racially inferior' people. They infected prisoners with streptococcus and tetanus in order to devise treatments for soldiers who had been exposed to these bacteria. And in one of the most horrible experiments, prisoners were immersed in tanks of ice water so that the doctors could discover how long pilots would survive if they bailed out over the North Sea. The prisoners were frozen, thawed and frozen again until they died. During these experiments, the doctors carefully recorded the prisoners' physiological responses.

These experiments were crimes, hideous beyond all imagining. But the records of these experiments remain, and in some cases they provide valuable information that could never be obtained ethically. For example, because researchers cannot perform controlled studies that would expose volunteers to dangerously cold temperatures, there is still controversy among doctors about the best treatment for hypothermia. In 1988, Dr Robert Pozos, physiologist at the University of Minnesota Medical School, who had spent a lifetime studying hypothermia, came across an unpublished report written in 1945 titled 'The treatment of shock from prolonged exposure to cold, especially in water'. The report described the results of the horrible freezing experiments performed on prisoners at the Dachau concentration camp, and it suggested that contrary to conventional medical wisdom, rapid rewarming (rather than slow rewarming) might be the best way to treat hypothermia.

Should the Nazi medical studies have been published so that modern doctors might more effectively treat hypothermia? Many scientists and ethicists thought they should. 'The prevention of a death outweighs the protection of a memory. The victims' dignity was irrevocably lost in vats of freezing liquid forty years ago. Nothing can change that', argued bioethicist Arthur Caplan. Others disagreed. 'I don't see how any credence can be given to the work of unethical investigators', wrote Dr Arnold Relman, editor of the *New England Journal of Medicine*. 'It goes to legitimising the evil done', added Abraham Foxman, national director of the Anti-Defamation League (Siegel, 1988). The debate about this issue rages on (Caplan, 1992). If we use data that were obtained unethically, are we rewarding those who collected it and legitimizing their actions? Or can we condemn such investigations but still learn from them? Where do you stand?

Chapter review

Empiricism: how to know things

- Empiricism is an important component of the scientific method, which is a set of principles about how to support ideas with evidence.
- While evidence is critical to establishing truth, it is never possible to actually prove a hypothesis, which is why scientists concentrate on falsification as the appropriate way to advance knowledge.
- Statistical analysis enables us to draw inferences about data but interpreting significance can be problematic because of the way the evidence has been sampled.
- Many scientists consider effect sizes to be more meaningful in interpreting data and applying the results to the real world.
- Because casual observation is prone to error, sciences have methods for observation. These methods are unusually sophisticated in psychology because people are unusually complex, variable and reactive.

Observation: discovering what people do

- Observation begins with measurement. Researchers generate operational definitions of the properties they wish to measure and develop measures to detect the conditions that those definitions specify.
- Measures must be valid, reliable and powerful. Validity refers to the relationship between the operational definition and the property (construct validity) and between the operational definition and other operational definitions (predictive validity). Reliability refers to the consistency of a measure, and power refers to the measure's ability to detect differences that do exist and not to detect differences that don't exist.
- Although interesting individuals provide useful information, most measurement is performed on large samples of participants. Larger samples better reflect the characteristics of the population.
- Measurements taken from a sample can be depicted in a frequency distribution, which can be described by various descriptive statistics such as the mean, median, mode and standard deviation.
- Researchers use cover stories and filler items to avoid creating demand characteristics that influence the behaviour of participants. They also use double-blind procedures so that the experimenter's expectations do not influence participants' behaviour or the measurement thereof.

Explanation: discovering why people do what they do

- Psychologists are interested in observing and explaining relationships between variables.
- Correlation refers to a relationship signified by synchronization in the patterns of variation of two variables. The correlation coefficient (r) is a statistic that describes the strength and direction of the relationship between two continuous variables. When one is looking for a relationship between two categorical variables, a contingency table analysis using the χ^2 statistic is appropriate. A t-test may be used when investigating the difference between the means of two groups or conditions.

- Two variables can be correlated for any one of three reasons: $X \rightarrow Y$, $Y \rightarrow X$, or $Z \rightarrow X$ and Y.
- Experimentation can determine for which of these three reasons a pair of variables is correlated. It involves the manipulation of an independent variable, which results in an experimental group and a control group, and the measurement of a dependent variable. It requires that participants be randomly assigned to groups.
- Experiments allow one to test whether changes in an independent variable cause changes in a dependent variable if the experiment is internally valid.
- Because psychologists rarely sample their participants randomly, most psychology experiments lack external validity. This is rarely a problem because experiments are meant to test theories and not to mimic real-world events.

Qualitative research: forget the size, feel the quality

- Qualitative research differs from quantitative approaches in that it is less concerned with measurement and analysis and more focused on individual experiences.
- One of the main advantages of qualitative research is that it addresses issues of experience that are not easily reducible to numbers and takes a more holistic personal approach to the complexity of situations.
- The main datasets are interviews and first-hand reports, which provide rich descriptions that can better inform researchers as to the real-world nature of the experiences under investigation.
- Qualitative research is flexible, allowing researchers to pursue previously unexpected paths of inquiry. However, one caveat is the role of the researcher as a participant in the interview, which can compromise objectivity.
- Concerns about the reliability of qualitative research have been addressed in recent years, with a trend towards mixed method research programmes where qualitative and quantitative approaches are combined.

The ethics of science: first, do no harm

- Psychologists adhere to a strict code of ethics. People must give their informed consent to participate in any study, they must do so free of coercion, they must be protected from physical and psychological harm and participants must be debriefed at the conclusion of the research.
- Ethics committees must approve all research before it is conducted.
- The treatment of animals is governed by strict rules developed by professional organizations, governmental bodies and university committees.

Key terms

case method (p. 50)
conditional probability (p. 82)
construct validity (p. 49)
control group (p. 71)
correlation (p. 62)
correlation coefficient (p. 64)
covariance (p. 66)
debriefing (p. 81)
deduction (p. 45)
demand characteristics (p. 58)
dependent variable (p. 71)
double-blind observation (p. 60)
effect size (p. 55)
electromyograph (EMG) (p. 47)
empirical method (p. 46)
empiricism (p. 44)
experiment (p. 69)
experimental group (p. 71)
external validity (p. 75)
frequency distribution (p. 52)
hypothesis (p. 44)
independent variable (p. 71)
induction (p. 45)
informed consent (p. 80)
internal validity (p. 74)
law of large numbers (p. 50)
manipulation (p. 70)
matched pairs (p. 68)
matched samples (p. 68)
mean (p. 52)
measure (p. 47)
median (p. 52)
mode (p. 52)
natural correlation (p. 67)
naturalistic observation (p. 58)
normal distribution (p. 52)
operational definition (p. 47)
population (p. 50)
power (p. 50)
predictive validity (p. 49)
qualitative research (p. 77)
quantitative research (p. 77)
randomization (p. 72)
random sampling (p. 76)
range (p. 53)
reliability (p. 50)
sample (p. 50)
scientific method (p. 44)
self-selection (p. 72)
standard deviation (p. 53)
statistically significant (p. 54)
theory (p. 44)
third-variable correlation (p. 68)
third-variable problem (p. 69)
validity (p. 48)
variable (p. 61)
variance (p. 53)
verifiable (p. 45)

Recommended reading

Dancey, C. P. and Reidy, J. (2007) *Statistics without Maths for Psychology*. Harlow: Pearson. Well-written and highly accessible introduction to quantitative methods in psychology.

Dienes, Z. (2008) *Understanding Psychology as a Science: An Introduction to Scientific and Statistical Inference.* Basingstoke: Palgrave Macmillan. Thoroughly brilliant read tackling the philosophical and methodological issues raised in psychology.

Salsburg, D. (2002) *The Lady Tasting Tea: How Statistics Revolutionized Science in the Twentieth Century.* New York: W.H. Freeman/Owl Books. Engaging and accessible account of the birth of modern statistical analysis and how it came to dominate all aspects of health, science and technology.

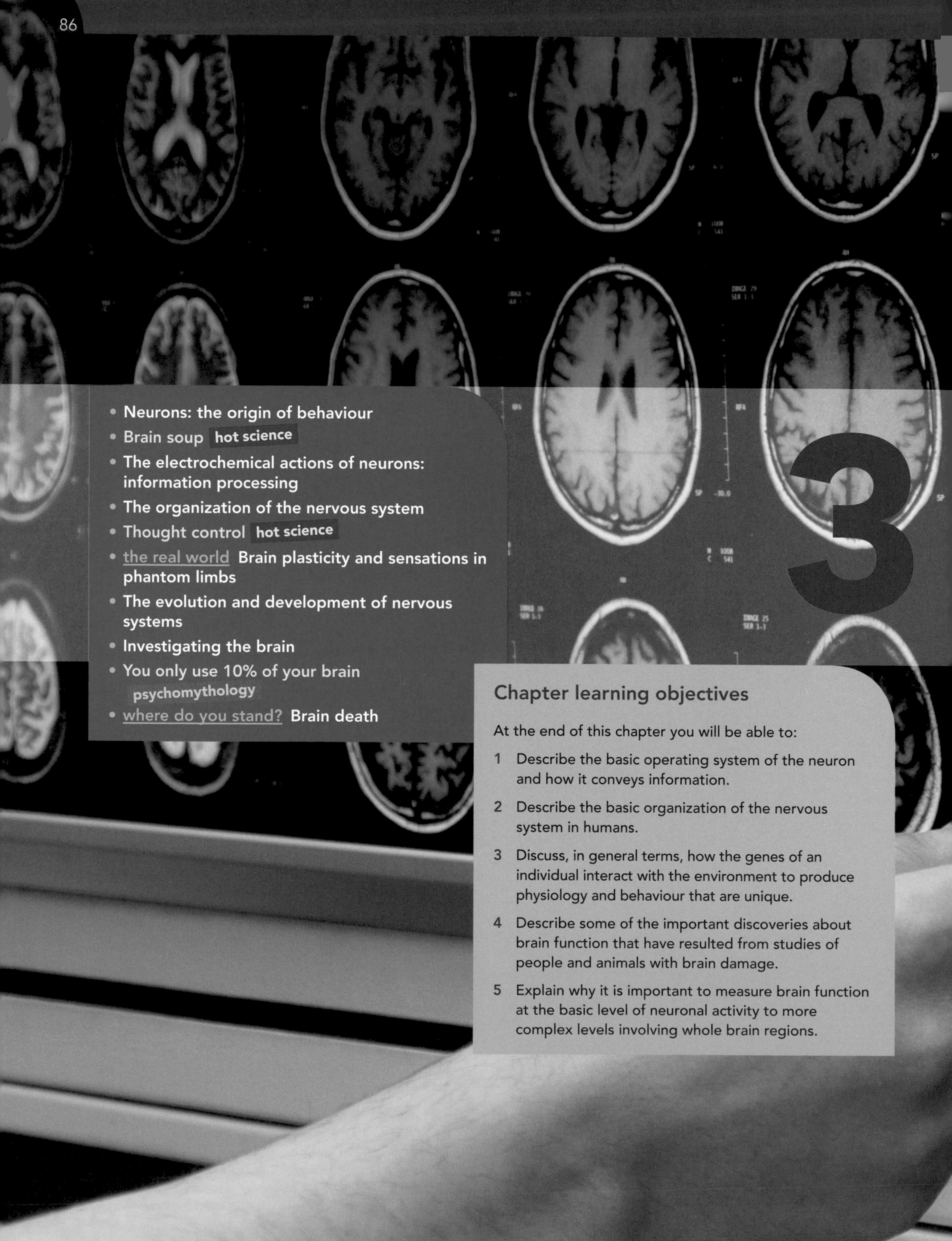

3

Chapter learning objectives

At the end of this chapter you will be able to:

1. Describe the basic operating system of the neuron and how it conveys information.
2. Describe the basic organization of the nervous system in humans.
3. Discuss, in general terms, how the genes of an individual interact with the environment to produce physiology and behaviour that are unique.
4. Describe some of the important discoveries about brain function that have resulted from studies of people and animals with brain damage.
5. Explain why it is important to measure brain function at the basic level of neuronal activity to more complex levels involving whole brain regions.

Neuroscience and behaviour

Have you ever looked in the mirror and had that odd experience where you fail to recognize yourself? You know it must be you but for one moment you are not you. For patient FE, an 87-year-old Australian man, this was not a fleeting impression but rather the source of persistent delusion. He believed that his own reflection was another person, a stranger who was following him around, not only in his home, but anywhere there was a reflecting surface. He had tried talking to this stranger but never got a response. His family tried to reason with him but although it was clear that FE fully understood mirrors, this did not shake his conviction that his reflection was another man that looked just like him. This delusion remained stable over the next two years, and then FE started to have problems recognizing his wife's reflection too. He would later explain: 'I have met the stranger's wife, seen her. I don't think she talks either' (Breen et al., 2001).

The Australian gentleman had mirrored-self misidentification syndrome resulting from a focal dementia that had disrupted the representation in his brain of his own self-identity based on his reflection. Many of us without brain damage can also experience a momentary feeling of unfamiliarity when we look at ourselves in mirrors or photographs (Caputo, 2010), but this disconnection was permanent for FE.

What this extreme case of mirror misidentification reminds us is that if the workings of our brain are altered through disease, damage or drugs, then our mind is correspondingly affected. Our ability to perceive the world around us and recognize familiar things is based not only on information we take in through our senses, but, perhaps more importantly, on the interpretation of this information performed by the brain.

In this chapter, we'll consider how the brain works, what happens when it doesn't, and how both states of affairs determine behaviour. First, we'll introduce you to the basic

© ISTOCKPHOTO.COM/HALFPOINT

unit of information processing in the brain, the neuron. The electrical and chemical activities of neurons are the starting point of all behaviour, thought and emotion. Next, we'll consider the anatomy of the brain, including its overall organization, key structures that perform different functions, and the brain's evolutionary development. Finally, we'll discuss methods that allow us to study the brain and clarify our understanding of how it works. These include methods that examine the damaged brain and methods for scanning the living and healthy brain.

Neurons: the origin of behaviour

Social networking sites are really popular at the moment, with over one in seven of the world's population signed up to Facebook. That's more than 1 billion people communicating with each other. But there's a much bigger number of individuals communicating with each other inside your skull right now, helping you make sense of these big numbers you're reading about. There are approximately *170 billion* cells in your brain that perform a variety of tasks to allow you to function as a human being (see the hot science box).

Humans have thoughts, feelings and behaviours that are often accompanied by visible signals. For example, anticipating seeing a friend waiting up the street for you in the queue for a nightclub may elicit a range of behaviours. An observer might see a smile on your face or notice how fast you are walking; internally, you might mentally rehearse what you'll say to your friend and feel a surge of happiness as you approach them. But all these visible and experiential signs are produced by an underlying invisible physical component coordinated by the activity of your brain cells. The anticipation you have, the happiness you feel and the speed of your feet are the result of information processing in your brain. In a way, all your thoughts, feelings and behaviours spring from cells in the brain that take in information and produce some kind of output.

The 170 billion cells that perform this function trillions of times a day are broadly divided into two classes of cell, the neurons and glia. Neurons are *cells in the nervous system that communicate with one another to perform information-processing tasks*. Glia are *cells that support the functionality of neurons by providing physical support, supplying nutrients and enhancing neuronal communication*. Originally, glia were thought to be nothing more than 'glue' for holding the neurons in place, but they are critically important for normal brain function. Estimates vary, but there are thought to be equal numbers of neurons and glia in the human brain, at around 85 billion each, although the relative proportion of each depends on which part of the brain is under consideration. In this section, we'll look at how these different cells were discovered, what their components are, and how they are specialized for different types of information processing.

NEURONS Cells in the nervous system that communicate with one another to perform information-processing tasks.

GLIA Cells that support the functionality of neurons by providing physical support, supplying nutrients and enhancing neuronal communication.

hot science

Brain soup

How many brain cells are there? How many neuronal and how many glial cells? How would you even begin to count them? If you look through older textbooks, you will encounter the commonly stated facts that the human brain contains 100 billion neurons and that there are 10–50 times more glial cells. However, these estimates turn out to be unsubstantiated by reliable anatomical evidence and may, in fact, have been based on mistaken reports that have been perpetuated to become myths. One of the problems is that it is difficult to count brain cells and there is wide variation not only between different species but also between different parts of the brain. Early estimates were often based on species other than primates, or they examined only one region of the human brain where the density of neurons is different to that in other regions. For example, there are many more neurons in the cerebellum than the cerebral cortex.

Remarkably, there is a new technique to count brain cells by turning them into a kind of soup. Suzana Herculano-Houzel, Brazilian neurophysiologist, has developed a method that isolates the individual cell nuclei that contain the DNA. First, she takes brain slices and mashes them in a mortar and pestle into a paste to which she adds detergent. This destroys the cell bodies leaving the cell nuclei behind in a solution. She then adds a fluorescent marker that makes the nuclei glow blue under ultraviolet (UV) light and counts their number. Herculano-Houzel then measures the density of these glowing nuclei and multiplies that number by the solution's volume to determine the total number of nuclei, which should correspond to the total number of cells in that brain region. She then adds a protein that binds only to the neuronal nuclei and then another fluorescent marker that makes these glow green. By subtracting the number of green from the number of blue, she has calculated the density of neuronal and glial cells in varying species and different brain regions.

Using this technique, Herculano-Houzel found that the human brain contains about 170.68 billion cells, 86.1 billion of which are neurons and 84.6 billion of which are glial cells. Overall, the ratio of neurons to glia is roughly 1:1. However, ratios differ from one region to the next. The number of neurons in the cerebral cortex is around 16 billion, with the majority (approx. 80%) found in the cerebellum. This means that the cortex is mostly made up of connections supported by glial cells with fewer neuronal bodies, whereas the opposite pattern is found in the cerebellum.

There is some mystery as to the origins of the myth that the human brain contains 100 billion neurons. So far, Herculano-Houzel has the best up-to-date peer-reviewed evidence for the numbers reported here. You might wonder why knowing the number of different types of cells in different brain regions, in different species and at different points of development is important. This sort of information may not in itself explain how the brain works but it helps to build theories about what the function of the different cellular architectures might be.

Discovery of how neurons function

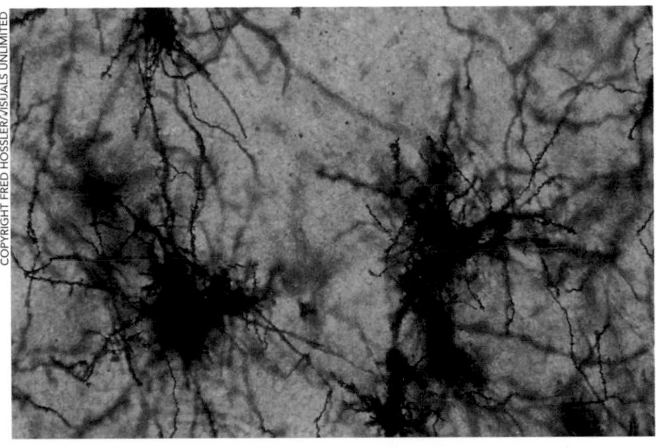

FIGURE 3.1 Golgi-stained neurons Santiago Ramón y Cajal used a Golgi stain to highlight the appearance of neurons. These are Purkinje cells from the cerebellum, known for the elaborate branching of their dendrites.

During the 1800s, scientists began to turn their attention from studying the mechanics of limbs, lungs and livers to studying the harder-to-observe workings of the brain. Philosophers wrote poetically about an 'enchanted loom' that mysteriously wove a tapestry of behaviour, and many scientists confirmed the metaphor (Corsi, 1991). To those scientists, the brain looked as though it were composed of a continuously connected lattice of fine threads, leading to the conclusion that it was one big woven web of material. In 1873, Italian physician Camillo Golgi (1843–1926) discovered a chemical reaction that allowed him to examine brain tissue in much greater detail than ever before. This stain method revealed to Golgi that nervous tissue was not continuous, but rather made up of cell bodies which he believed were interwoven by connections. These were neurons.

However, in the late 1880s, Spanish doctor Santiago Ramón y Cajal (1852–1934) improved on Golgi's technique for staining neurons in the brain and discovered that they came in different shapes and sizes (see **FIGURE 3.1**). Using this technique, Cajal was the first to see that each neuron was composed of a body with many threads extending outwards towards other neurons. Surprisingly, he also saw that the threads of each neuron did not actually touch other neurons. Contrary to Golgi's interpretation of what he saw, Cajal noted that the long slender fibres emerging from cell bodies did not fuse into one mesh. Cajal believed that neurons are the information-processing units of the brain and that even though he saw gaps between neurons, they had to communicate in some way (Rapport, 2005). Until fairly recently, glial cells, which did not show up in these early staining studies, have been considered secondary to the function of neurons because they were believed to play only a supporting role. However, glial cells are equally important, and involved in many more processes than neurons, although neurons get all the limelight because their communicating activity is more conspicuous (see the hot science box). Although glial cells do not send nerve impulses like neurons, they do change in responsiveness to neuronal activity to facilitate communication, indicating that they play an active role in sending and receiving signals in the brain (Fields, 2010).

Components of the neuron

Cajal discovered that neurons are complex structures composed of three basic parts: the cell body, the dendrites and the axon (see **FIGURE 3.2**). Like cells in all organs of the body, neurons have a cell body (also called the *soma*), the largest component of the neuron that *coordinates the information-processing tasks and keeps the cell alive*. Functions such as protein synthesis, energy production and metabolism take place here. The cell body contains a *nucleus*, which houses chromosomes that contain your DNA, or the genetic

CELL BODY The part of a neuron that coordinates information-processing tasks and keeps the cell alive.

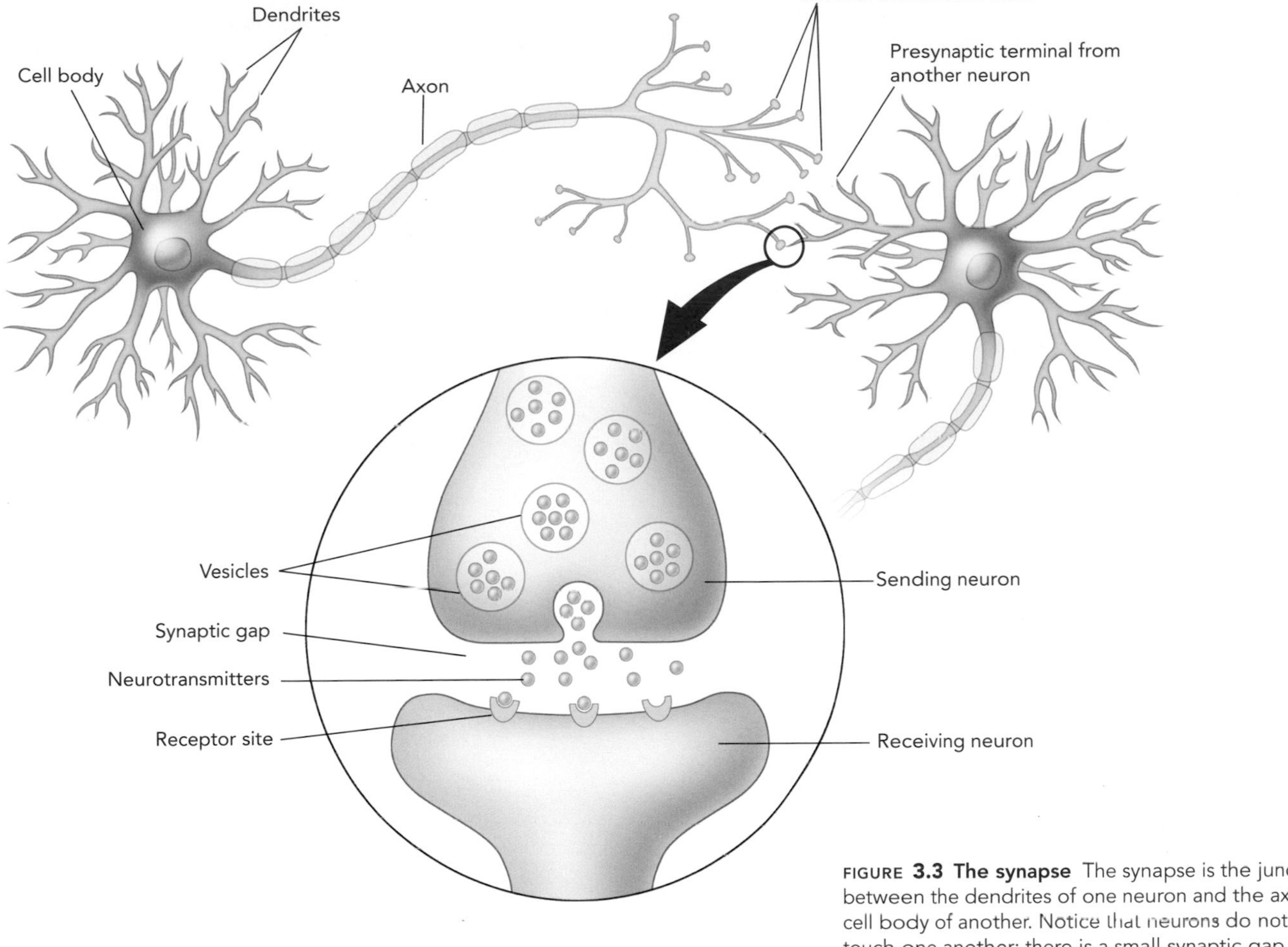

FIGURE 3.3 The synapse The synapse is the junction between the dendrites of one neuron and the axon or cell body of another. Notice that neurons do not actually touch one another: there is a small synaptic gap between them across which information is transmitted.

neurons have specialized endings on their dendrites that receive signals for light, sound, touch, taste and smell. For example, in our eyes, sensory neurons' endings are sensitive to light. Motor neurons *carry signals from the spinal cord to the muscles to produce movement.* These neurons often have long axons that can stretch to muscles at our extremities. However, most of the nervous system is composed of the third type of neuron, interneurons, which *connect sensory neurons, motor neurons or other interneurons.* Some interneurons carry information from sensory neurons into the nervous system, others carry information from the nervous system to motor neurons, and still others perform a variety of information-processing functions within the nervous system. Interneurons work together in small circuits to perform simple tasks, such as identifying the location of a sensory signal, and much more complicated ones, such as recognizing a familiar face.

MOTOR NEURONS Neurons that carry signals from the spinal cord to the muscles to produce movement.

INTERNEURONS Neurons that connect sensory neurons, motor neurons or other interneurons.

Neurons specialized by location

Besides specialization for sensory, motor or connective functions, neurons are also somewhat specialized depending on their location (see **FIGURE 3.4**). For example, *Purkinje cells* are a type of interneuron that carries information from the cerebellum to the rest of the brain and spinal cord. These neurons have dense, elaborate dendrites that resemble bushes (**FIGURE 3.4a**). *Pyramidal cells,* found in the cerebral cortex, have a triangular cell body and a single long dendrite among many smaller dendrites (**FIGURE 3.4b**). *Bipolar cells,* a type of sensory neuron found in the retinas of the eye (see Chapter 4), have a single axon and a few dendrites (**FIGURE 3.4c**). The brain processes different types of information, so a substantial amount of specialization at the cellular level has evolved to handle these tasks.

FIGURE **3.4** **Types of neurons** Neurons have a cell body, an axon and at least one dendrite. The size and shape of neurons vary considerably, however. (a) The Purkinje cell has an elaborate treelike assemblage of dendrites. (b) Pyramidal cells have a triangular cell body and a single, long dendrite with many smaller dendrites. (c) Bipolar cells have a few dendrites and a single axon.

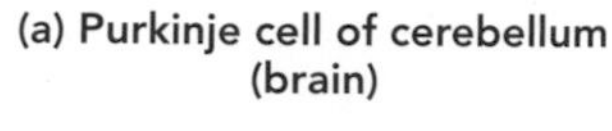

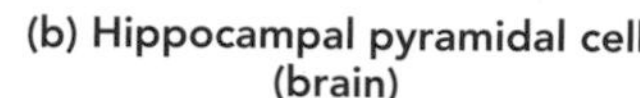

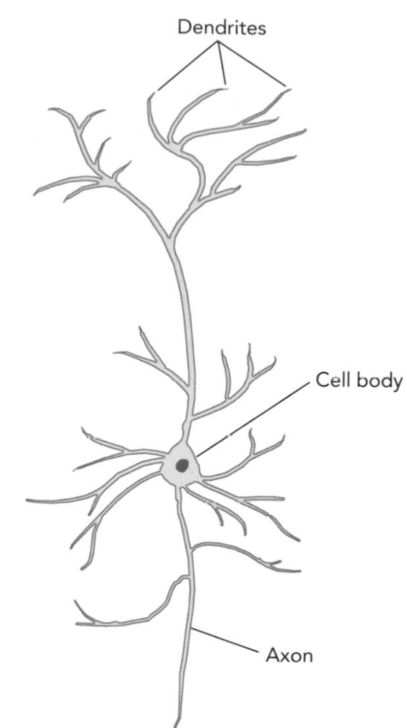

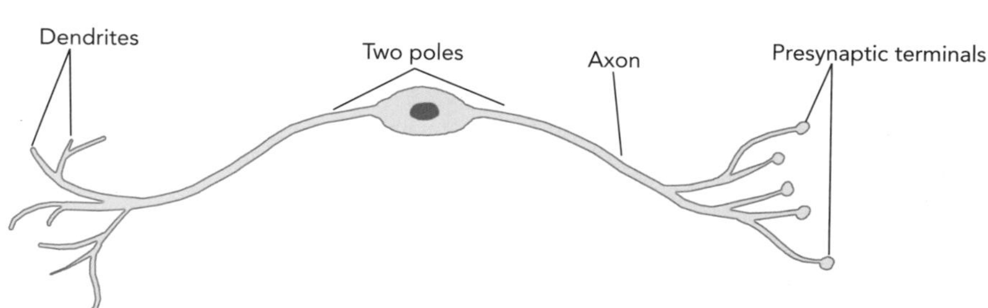

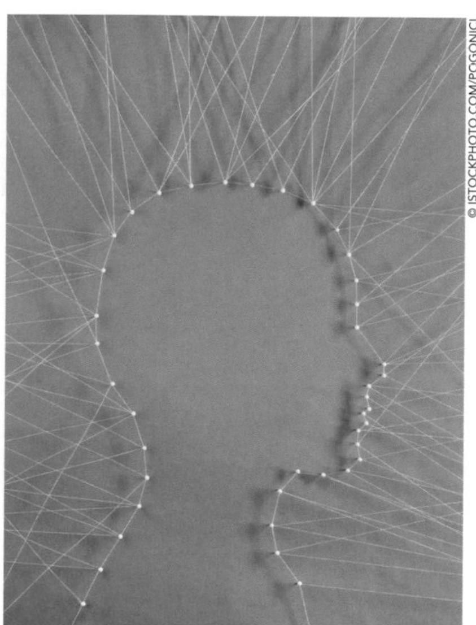

If you had a complete wiring diagram of the human nervous system, why would you still not be able to explain or predict behaviour?

In summary, neurons are the building blocks of the nervous system. They process information received from the outside world, they communicate with one another, and they send messages to the body's muscles and organs. Neurons are composed of three major parts: the cell body, dendrites and the axon. The cell body contains the nucleus, which houses the organism's genetic material. Dendrites receive sensory signals from other neurons and transmit this information to the cell body. Each neuron has only one axon, which carries signals from the cell body to other neurons or to muscles and organs in the body. Neurons don't actually touch: they are separated by a small gap, the synapse across which signals are transmitted from one neuron to another. Glial cells play a crucial role in brain function, facilitating the communicative activity of neurons by forming the myelin sheath, which coats the axon to improve the transmission of nerve impulses. In demyelinating diseases, the myelin sheath deteriorates. Neurons are differentiated according to the functions they perform. The three major types of neurons include sensory neurons, motor neurons and interneurons. Examples of sensory neurons and interneurons are, respectively, bipolar neurons and Purkinje and pyramidal cells.

The electrochemical actions of neurons: information processing

Our thoughts, feelings and actions depend on neural communication, but how does it happen? The communication of information within and between neurons proceeds in two stages – *conduction* and *transmission*. The first stage is the conduction of an electric signal over relatively long distances within neurons, from the dendrites to the cell body, then throughout the axon. The second stage is the transmission of electric signals between neurons over the synapse. Together, these stages are what scientists generally refer to as the *electrochemical action* of neurons.

Electric signalling: conducting information within a neuron

As you'll recall, the neuron's cell membrane is porous: it allows small electrically charged molecules, called *ions,* to flow in and out of the cell. If you imagine using a strainer while you're preparing spaghetti, you'll get the idea. The mesh of the strainer cradles your yummy dinner, but water can still seep in and out of it. Just as the flow of water out of a strainer enhances the quality of pasta, the flow of molecules across a cell membrane enhances the transmission of information in the nervous system.

The resting potential: the origin of the neuron's electrical properties

RESTING POTENTIAL The difference in electric charge between the inside and outside of a neuron's cell membrane.

Neurons have a natural electric charge called the resting potential – *the difference in electric charge between the inside and outside of a neuron's cell membrane* (Kandel, 2000). The resting potential is similar to the difference between the '+' and '–' poles of a battery. Biologists discovered the resting potential in the 1930s while studying marine invertebrates – sea creatures that lack a spine, such as squid and lobsters (Stevens, 1971). They found that large squid have giant axons that connect the brain to muscles in the tail. These axons have a very large diameter, about 100 times bigger than the largest axons in humans, making it easier to explore their electrical properties. In the summer of 1939, British biologists Alan Hodgkin and Andrew Huxley inserted a thin wire into the squid axon so that it touched the jellylike fluid inside. Then they placed another wire just outside the axon in the watery fluid that surrounds it. They found a substantial difference between the electric charges inside and outside the axon, which they called the resting potential. They measured the resting potential at about –70 millivolts, or roughly 1/200th of the charge of an AA battery.

The resting potential arises from the difference in concentrations of ions inside and outside the neuron's cell membrane. Ions can carry a positive (+) or a negative (–) charge. In the resting state, there is a high concentration of a positively charged ion, potassium (K^+), inside the neuron, compared to the relatively low concentration of K^+ outside the neuron. Raising the concentration of K^+ in the fluid outside the neuron to match the concentration of K^+ inside the neuron causes the resting potential to disappear. This simple test confirms that differences in K^+ concentration are the basis of the resting potential (Dowling, 1992).

The concentration of K^+ inside and outside an axon is controlled by channels in the axon membrane that allow molecules to flow in and out of the neuron. In the resting state, the channels that allow K^+ molecules to flow freely across the cell membrane are open, while channels that allow the flow of other molecules are generally closed. There is a naturally higher concentration of K^+ molecules *inside* the neuron, so some K^+ molecules move out of the neuron through the open channels, leaving the inside of the neuron with a charge of about –70 millivolts relative to the outside (see **FIGURE 3.5**).

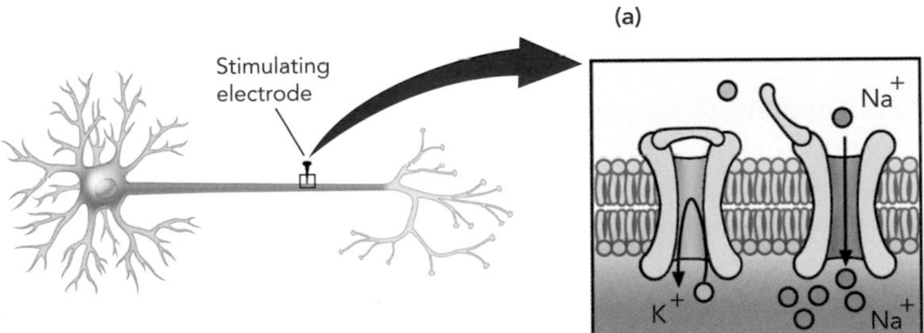

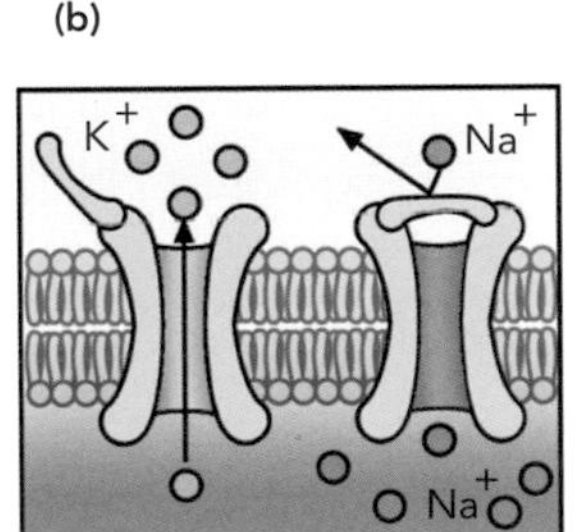

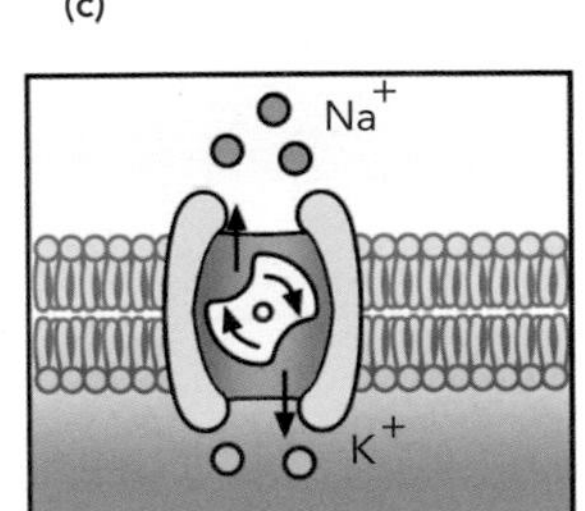

FIGURE 3.5 The action potential (a) Electric stimulation of the neuron shuts down the K^+ channels and opens the Na^+ channels, allowing Na^+ to enter the axon. The increase of Na^+ inside the neuron results in an action potential. (b) In the refractory period after the action potential, the channels return to their original state, allowing K^+ to flow out of the axon. This leaves an abundance of K^+ outside and Na^+ inside the cell. (c) A chemical pump then reverses the ion balance of ions by moving Na^+ out of the axon and K^+ into the axon. The neuron can now generate another action potential.

As an example of this process, imagine a field trip to the zoo. Many zoos have turnstiles that allow only one person at a time to enter. The most eager children rush through the turnstiles to see the lions, tigers and bears, while parents hover outside, deciding where to meet later and who's got the keys to the car. With many children on one side of the turnstile, a greater concentration of parents is left on the opposite side. This is like the many small K^+ ions that move outside the neuron, leaving some large negatively charged molecules inside the neuron, which produces a resting potential across the cell membrane.

The action potential: sending signals across the neuron

ACTION POTENTIAL An electric signal that is conducted along the length of a neuron's axon to a synapse.

The neuron maintains its resting potential most of the time. However, the biologists working with the squid's giant axon noticed that they could produce a signal by stimulating the axon with a brief electric shock, which resulted in the conduction of a large electric impulse down the length of the axon (Hausser, 2000; Hodgkin and Huxley, 1939). This electric impulse is called an action potential – *an electric signal that is conducted along the length of a neuron's axon to the synapse* (see Figure 3.5). The action potential occurs only when the electric shock reaches a certain level, or *threshold*. When the shock was below this threshold, the researchers recorded only tiny signals, which dissipated rapidly. When the shock reached the threshold, a much larger signal, the action potential, was observed. Interestingly, increases in the electric shock above the threshold did *not* increase the strength of the action potential. The action potential is *all or none*: electric stimulation below the threshold fails to produce an action potential, whereas electric stimulation at or above the threshold always produces the action potential. The action potential always occurs with exactly the same characteristics and at the same magnitude regardless of whether the stimulus is at or above the threshold.

Imagine a long line of dominoes waiting to be pushed over. As soon as one topples, it triggers the same response in the next domino and so on. In the same way, an action potential can propagate throughout a neural network without losing any strength of signal.

The biologists working with the giant squid axon observed another surprising property of the action potential: they measured it at a charge of about +40 millivolts, which is well above zero. This suggests that the mechanism driving the action potential could not simply be the loss of the –70 millivolt resting potential because this would have only brought the charge back to zero. So why does the action potential reach a value above zero?

The action potential occurs when there is a change in the state of the axon's membrane channels. Remember, during the resting potential, only the K^+ channels are open. However, when an electric charge is raised to the threshold value, the K^+ channels briefly shut down, and other channels that allow the flow of a *positively* charged ion, sodium (Na^+), are opened. Na^+ is typically much more concentrated outside the axon than inside. When the Na^+ channels open, those positively charged ions flow inside, increasing the positive charge inside the axon relative to that outside. This flow of Na^+ into the axon pushes the action potential to its maximum value of +40 millivolts.

REFRACTORY PERIOD The time following an action potential during which a new action potential cannot be initiated.

After the action potential reaches its maximum, the membrane channels return to their original state, and K^+ flows out until the axon returns to its resting potential. This leaves a lot of extra Na^+ ions inside the axon and a lot of extra K^+ ions outside the axon. During this period where the ions are imbalanced, the neuron cannot initiate another action potential, so it is said to be in a refractory period – *the time following an action potential during which a new action potential cannot be initiated.* Returning to our domino metaphor, the refractory period could be compared to the time taken to stand the individual dominoes back up again in order to repeat the process. (Thankfully for the nervous system, this period is much faster for neurons than dominoes!) The imbalance in ions is eventually reversed by an active chemical 'pump' in the cell membrane that moves Na^+ outside the axon and moves K^+ inside the axon.

Earlier, we described how the action potential occurs at one point in the neuron. But how does this electric charge move down the axon? When an action potential is generated at the beginning of the axon, it spreads a short distance, which generates an action potential at a nearby location on the axon (see Figure 3.5). That action potential also spreads, initiating an action potential at another nearby location and so on, thus transmitting the charge down the length of the axon. This simple mechanism ensures that the action potential travels the full length of the axon and achieves its full intensity at each step, regardless of the distance travelled.

The myelin sheath, which is made up of glial cells that coat and insulate the axon, facilitates the transmission of the action potential. Myelin doesn't cover the entire axon; rather, it clumps around the axon with little breakpoints between clumps, looking like a string of sausages. These breakpoints are called the *nodes of Ranvier*, after French pathologist Louis-Antoine Ranvier, who discovered them (see **FIGURE 3.6**). When an electric current passes down the length of a myelinated axon, the charge 'jumps' from node to node rather than having to traverse the entire axon. This jumping is called *saltatory conduction*, and it helps speed the flow of information down the axon.

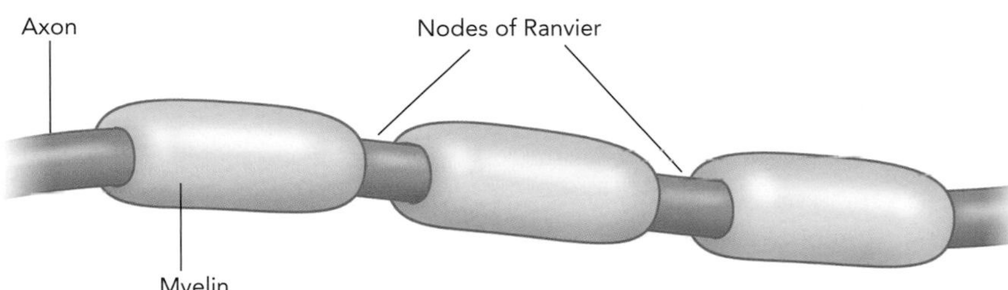

FIGURE 3.6 Myelin and nodes of Ranvier Myelin is formed by a type of glial cell, and it wraps around a neuron's axon to speed the transmission of the action potential along the length of the axon. Breaks in the myelin sheath are called the nodes of Ranvier. The electric impulse jumps from node to node, thereby speeding the conduction of information down the axon.

In summary, the neuron's resting potential is due to differences in the K^+ concentrations inside and outside the cell membrane. If electric signals reach a threshold, this initiates an action potential, an all-or-none signal that moves down the entire length of the axon. The action potential occurs when sodium channels in the axon membrane open and potassium channels close, allowing the Na^+ ions to flow inside the axon. After the action potential has reached its maximum, the sodium channels close and the potassium channels open, allowing K^+ to flow out of the axon, returning the neuron to its resting potential. For a brief refractory period, the action potential cannot be reinitiated. Once it is initiated, the action potential spreads down the axon, jumping across the nodes of Ranvier to the synapse.

Chemical signalling: transmission between neurons

When the action potential reaches the end of an axon, you might think that it stops there. After all, the synaptic space between neurons means that the axon of one neuron and the neighbouring neuron's dendrites do not actually touch one another. However, the electric charge of the action potential takes a form that can cross the relatively small synaptic gap by relying on a bit of chemistry. We'll look at that process of information transmission between neurons in this section.

Axons usually end in terminal buttons – *knoblike structures that branch out from an axon.* A terminal button is filled with tiny *vesicles*, or 'bags', that contain neurotransmitters – *chemicals that transmit information across the synapse to a receiving neuron's dendrites.* The dendrites of the receiving neuron contain receptors – *parts of the cell membrane that receive neurotransmitters and initiate a new electric signal.*

As K^+ and Na^+ flow across a cell membrane, they move the sending neuron, or *presynaptic neuron*, from a resting potential to an action potential. The action potential travels down the length of the axon to the terminal buttons, where it stimulates the release of neurotransmitters from vesicles into the synapse. These neurotransmitters float across the synapse and bind to receptor sites on a nearby dendrite of the receiving neuron, or *postsynaptic neuron*. A new electric potential is initiated in that neuron, and the process continues down that neuron's axon to the next synapse and the next neuron. This electrochemical action, called *synaptic transmission*, allows neurons to communicate with one another and ultimately underlies your thoughts, emotions and behaviour (see **FIGURE 3.7**).

Now that you understand the basic process of how information moves from one neuron to another, let's refine things a bit. You'll recall that a given neuron may make a

TERMINAL BUTTONS Knoblike structures that branch out from an axon.

NEUROTRANSMITTERS Chemicals that transmit information across the synapse to a receiving neuron's dendrites.

RECEPTORS Parts of the cell membrane that receive neurotransmitters and initiate a new electric signal.

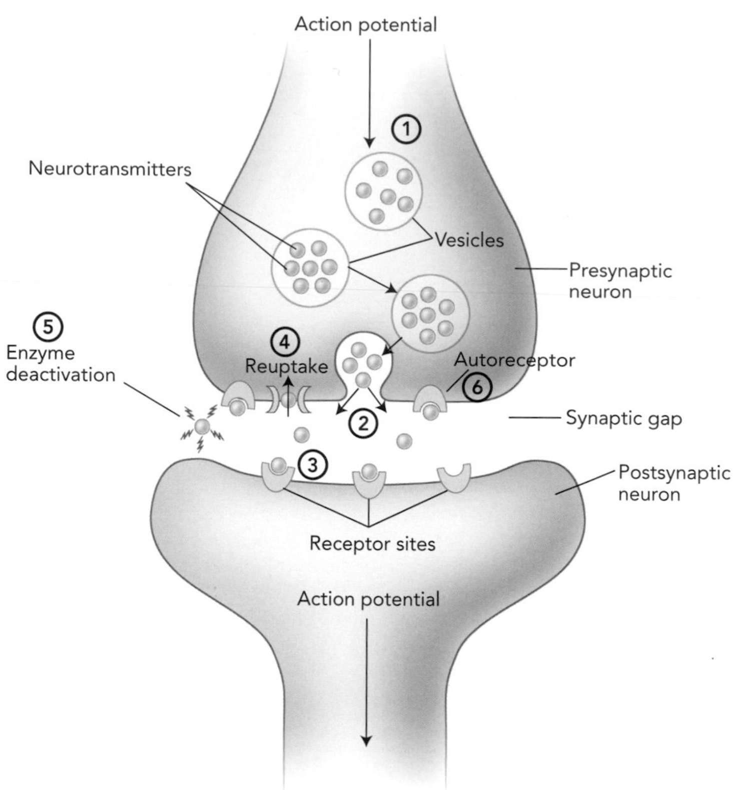

FIGURE **3.7 Synaptic transmission** (1) The action potential travels down the axon and (2) stimulates the release of neurotransmitters from vesicles. (3) Neurotransmitters are released into the synapse, where they float to bind with receptor sites on a dendrite of a postsynaptic neuron, initiating a new action potential. The neurotransmitters are cleared out of the synapse by (4) reuptake into the sending neuron, (5) being broken down by enzymes in the synapse, or (6) binding to autoreceptors on the sending neuron.

few thousand synaptic connections with other neurons, so how would the dendrites know which of the neurotransmitters flooding into the synapse to receive and which to ignore? One answer is that neurons tend to form pathways in the brain that are characterized by specific types of neurotransmitters; one neurotransmitter might be prevalent in one part of the brain, whereas a different neurotransmitter might be prevalent in a different part of the brain.

A second answer is that neurotransmitters and receptor sites act like a lock-and-key system. Just as a particular key will only fit in a particular lock, so some neurotransmitters bind to specific receptor sites on a dendrite. The molecular structure of the neurotransmitter must 'fit' the molecular structure of the receptor site.

Another question is what happens to the neurotransmitters left in the synapse after the chemical message is relayed to the postsynaptic neuron? Something must make neurotransmitters stop acting on neurons, otherwise there'd be no end to the signals they send. Neurotransmitters leave the synapse through three processes (Figure 3.7):

1 *Reuptake* occurs when neurotransmitters are reabsorbed by the terminal buttons of the presynaptic neuron's axon.
2 Neurotransmitters can be destroyed by enzymes in the synapse in a process called *enzyme deactivation*, where specific enzymes break down specific neurotransmitters.
3 Neurotransmitters can bind to the receptor sites called *autoreceptors* on the presynaptic neurons. Autoreceptors detect how much of a neurotransmitter has been released into a synapse and signal the neuron to stop releasing the neurotransmitter when an excess is present.

Types and functions of neurotransmitters

Given that different kinds of neurotransmitters can activate different kinds of receptors, like a lock and key, you might wonder how many types of neurotransmitters are floating across synapses in your brain right now. Today we know that some 60 chemicals play a role in transmitting information throughout the brain and body and that they differentially affect thought, feeling and behaviour, but a few major classes seem particularly important (see **TABLE 3.1**). We'll summarize these here, and you'll meet some of these neurotransmitters again, in later chapters:

ACETYLCHOLINE (ACH) A neurotransmitter involved in a number of functions, including voluntary motor control.

- Acetylcholine (ACh), *a neurotransmitter involved in a number of functions, including voluntary motor control,* was one of the first neurotransmitters discovered. Acetylcholine is found in neurons of the brain and in the synapses where axons connect to muscles and body organs, such as the heart. Acetylcholine activates muscles to initiate motor behaviour, but it also contributes to the regulation of attention, learning, sleeping, dreaming and memory (Gais and Born, 2004; Hasselmo, 2006; Wrenn et al., 2006). These are rather broad effects on a variety of important behaviours, but here are some specific examples. Alzheimer's disease, a medical condition involving severe memory impairments, is associated with the deterioration of ACh-producing neurons. As another example, nicotine excites ACh receptors in the brain, which helps explain why people who wear a nicotine patch often report vivid dreams and why recent ex-smokers often have difficulty thinking or concentrating. Like ACh, other neurotransmitters in the brain affect a range of behaviours.

- Dopamine is *a neurotransmitter that regulates motor behaviour, motivation, pleasure and emotional arousal*. Because of its role in basic motivated behaviours, such as seeking pleasure or associating actions with rewards, dopamine plays a role in drug addiction (Baler and Volkow, 2006). High levels of dopamine have been linked to schizophrenia (Winterer and Weinberger, 2004), while low levels have been linked to Parkinson's.
- Glutamate is *a major excitatory neurotransmitter involved in information transmission throughout the brain*. This means that glutamate enhances the transmission of information. Too much glutamate can overstimulate the brain, causing seizures.
- Gamma-aminobutyric acid (GABA), in contrast, is *the primary inhibitory neurotransmitter in the brain*. Inhibitory neurotransmitters stop the firing of neurons, an activity that also contributes to the function of the organism. Too little GABA, just like too much glutamate, can cause neurons to become overactive.
- Noradrenaline, *a neurotransmitter that influences mood and arousal*, is particularly involved in states of vigilance, or a heightened awareness of dangers in the environment (Ressler and Nemeroff, 1999). Similarly, serotonin is *involved in the regulation of sleep and wakefulness, eating and aggressive behaviour* (Dayan and Huys, 2009; Kroeze and Roth, 1998). Because both neurotransmitters affect mood and arousal, low levels of each have been implicated in mood disorders (Tamminga et al., 2002).
- Endorphins are *chemicals that act within the pain pathways and emotion centres of the brain* (Keefe et al., 2001). The word 'endorphin' is a contraction of endogenous morphine, and that's a pretty apt description. Morphine is a synthetic drug that has a calming and pleasurable effect; an endorphin is an internally produced substance that has similar properties, such as dulling the experience of pain and elevating moods. The 'runner's high' experienced by many athletes as they push their bodies to painful limits of endurance can be explained by the release of endorphins in the brain (Boecker et al., 2008).

DOPAMINE A neurotransmitter that regulates motor behaviour, motivation, pleasure and emotional arousal.

GLUTAMATE A major excitatory neurotransmitter involved in information transmission throughout the brain.

GAMMA-AMINOBUTYRIC ACID (GABA) The primary inhibitory neurotransmitter in the brain.

NORADRENALINE A neurotransmitter that influences mood and arousal.

SEROTONIN A neurotransmitter involved in the regulation of sleep and wakefulness, eating and aggressive behaviour.

ENDORPHINS Chemicals that act within the pain pathways and emotion centres of the brain.

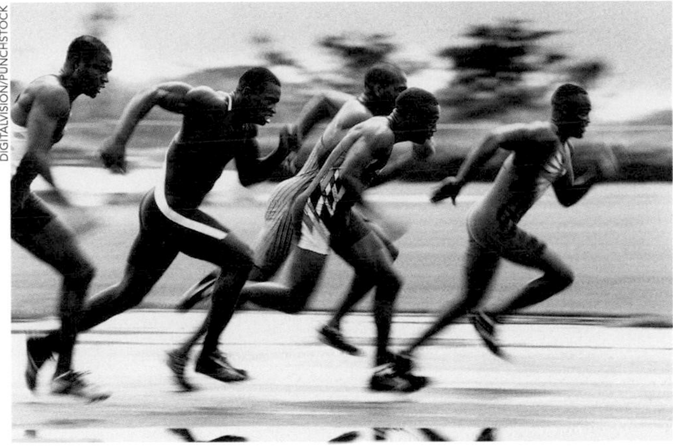
DIGITALVISION/PUNCHSTOCK

When athletes push themselves to the limits of endurance, they may experience subjective highs that result from the release of endorphins – chemical messengers acting in emotion and pain centres that elevate mood and dull the experience of pain.

TABLE 3.1 Neurotransmitters and their functions

Neurotransmitter	Function	Examples of malfunctions
Acetylcholine (ACh)	Regulates motor control, but also contributes to attention, learning, memory, sleeping and dreaming	With Alzheimer's disease, ACh-producing neurons deteriorate
Dopamine	Influences movement, motivation, emotional pleasure and arousal	High levels of dopamine are linked to schizophrenia. Lower levels of dopamine produce the tremors and decreased mobility of Parkinson's
Glutamate	A major excitatory neurotransmitter involved in learning and memory	Oversupply can overstimulate the brain, producing migraines or seizures
Gamma-aminobutyric acid (GABA)	The primary inhibitory neurotransmitter	Undersupply is linked to seizures, tremors and insomnia
Noradrenaline	Helps control mood and arousal	Undersupply can depress mood
Serotonin	Regulates hunger, sleep, arousal and aggressive behaviour	Undersupply linked to depression; Prozac and some other antidepressant drugs raise serotonin levels
Endorphins	Act within the pain pathways and emotion centres of the brain	Lack of endorphins could lower pain threshold or reduce the ability to self-soothe

Each of these neurotransmitters affects thoughts, feelings and behaviour in different ways, so normal functioning involves a delicate balance of each. Even a slight imbalance – too much of one neurotransmitter or not enough of another – can dramatically affect behaviour. These imbalances sometimes occur naturally; for example, the brain doesn't produce enough serotonin, which contributes to depressed or anxious moods. At other times, a person may actively seek to cause imbalances. People who smoke, drink alcohol or take drugs, legal or not, are altering the balance of neurotransmitters in their brains. The drug LSD, for example, is structurally similar to serotonin, so it binds easily with serotonin receptors in the brain, producing similar effects on thoughts, feelings and behaviour. In the next section, we'll look at how some drugs are able to 'trick' receptor sites in just this way.

How drugs mimic neurotransmitters

AGONISTS Drugs that increase the action of a neurotransmitter.

ANTAGONISTS Drugs that block the function of a neurotransmitter.

Many drugs that affect the nervous system operate by increasing, interfering with, or mimicking the manufacture or function of neurotransmitters (Cooper et al., 2003; Sarter, 2006). Agonists are *drugs that increase the action of a neurotransmitter*. Antagonists are *drugs that block the function of a neurotransmitter*. Some drugs alter a step in the production or release of the neurotransmitter, whereas others have a chemical structure so similar to a neurotransmitter that the drug is able to bind to that neuron's receptor. If, by binding to a receptor, a drug activates the neurotransmitter, it is an agonist; if it blocks the action of the neurotransmitter, it is an antagonist (see **FIGURE 3.8**).

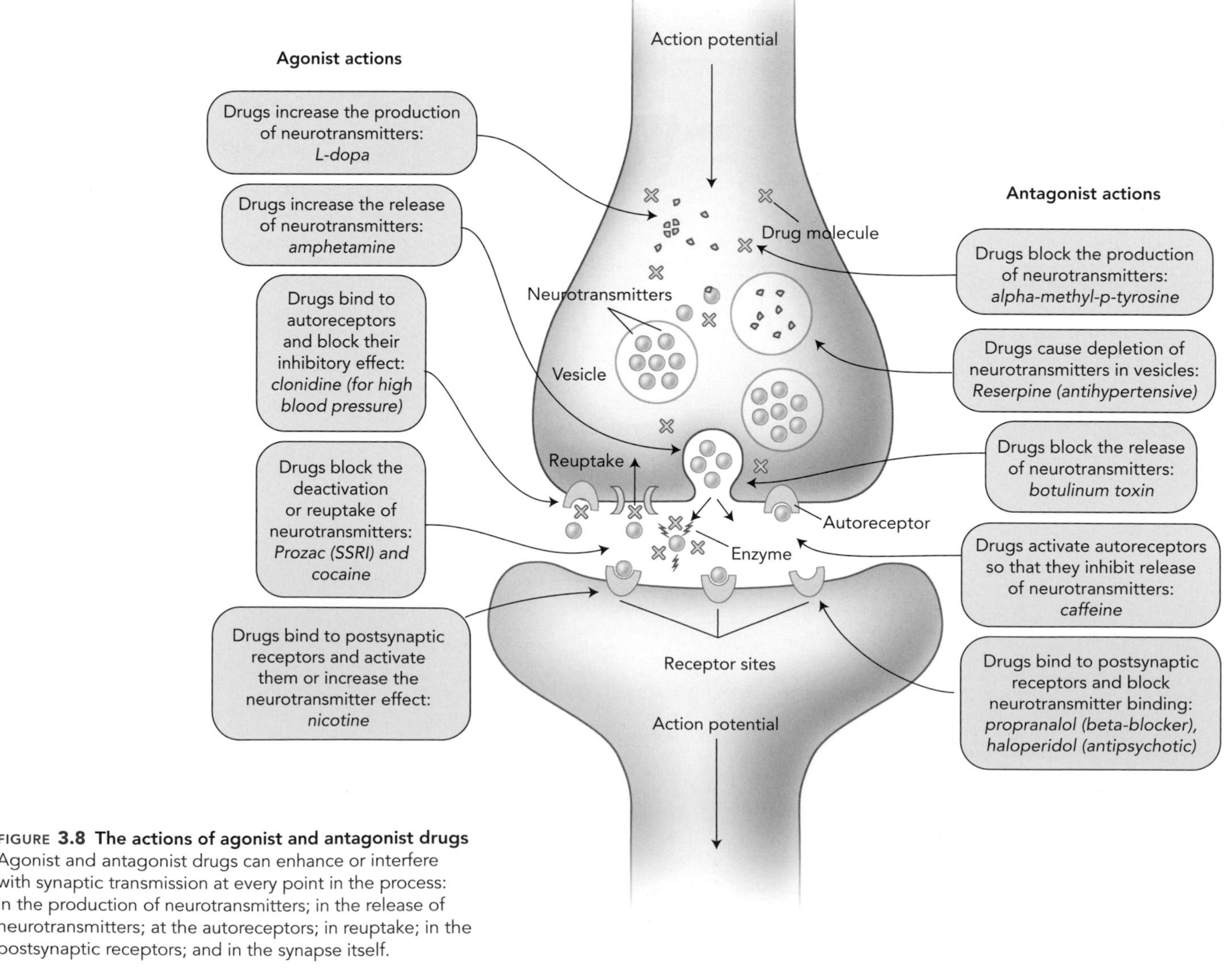

FIGURE 3.8 The actions of agonist and antagonist drugs Agonist and antagonist drugs can enhance or interfere with synaptic transmission at every point in the process: in the production of neurotransmitters; in the release of neurotransmitters; at the autoreceptors; in reuptake; in the postsynaptic receptors; and in the synapse itself.

For example, a drug called L-dopa has been developed to treat Parkinson's, a movement disorder characterized by tremors and difficulty initiating movement and caused by the loss of neurons that use the neurotransmitter dopamine. Dopamine is created in neurons by a modification of a common molecule called L-dopa. Ingesting L-dopa will elevate the amount of L-dopa in the brain and spur the surviving neurons to produce more dopamine. In other words, L-dopa acts as an agonist for dopamine. The use of L-dopa has been reasonably successful in the alleviation of the symptoms of Parkinson's (Muenter and Tyce, 1971; Schapira et al., 2009). However, the effectiveness of L-dopa typically decreases when used over a long period of time, so that many longtime users experience some symptoms of the disease. Actor Michael J. Fox, who was diagnosed with Parkinson's in 1991 and takes L-dopa, describes in his memoir the simple act of trying to brush his teeth (Fox, 2009, pp. 2–3):

> Grasping the toothpaste is nothing compared to the effort it takes to coordinate the two-handed task of wrangling the toothbrush and strangling out a line of paste onto the bristles. By now, my right hand has started up again, rotating at the wrist in a circular motion, perfect for what I'm about to do. My left hand guides my right hand up to my mouth, and once the back of the Oral-B touches the inside of my upper lip, I let go. It's like releasing the tension on a slingshot and compares favorably to the most powerful state-of-the-art electric toothbrush on the market. With no off switch, stopping means seizing my right wrist with my left hand, forcing it down to the sink basin, and shaking the brush loose as though disarming a knife-wielding attacker.

Some unexpected evidence also highlights the central role of dopamine in regulating movement and motor performance. In 1982, six people ranging in age from 25 to 45 from the San Francisco Bay area were admitted to emergency rooms with a bizarre set of symptoms: paralysis, drooling and an inability to speak (Langston, 1995). A diagnosis of advanced Parkinson's was made, as these symptoms are consistent with the later stages of this degenerative disease. It was unusual for six fairly young people to come down with advanced Parkinson's at the same time in the same geographical area. Indeed, none of the patients had Parkinson's, but they were all heroin addicts. These patients thought they were ingesting a synthetic form of heroin (called MPPP), but instead they ingested a close derivative called MPTP, which unfortunately had the effect of destroying dopamine-producing neurons in an area of the brain crucial for motor performance. Hence, these 'frozen addicts' exhibited paralysis and masklike expressions. The patients experienced a remarkable recovery after they were given L-dopa. In fact, it was later discovered that chemists who had worked with MPTP early in their careers later developed Parkinson's. Just as L-dopa acts as an agonist by enhancing the production of dopamine, drugs such as MPTP act as antagonists by destroying dopamine-producing neurons.

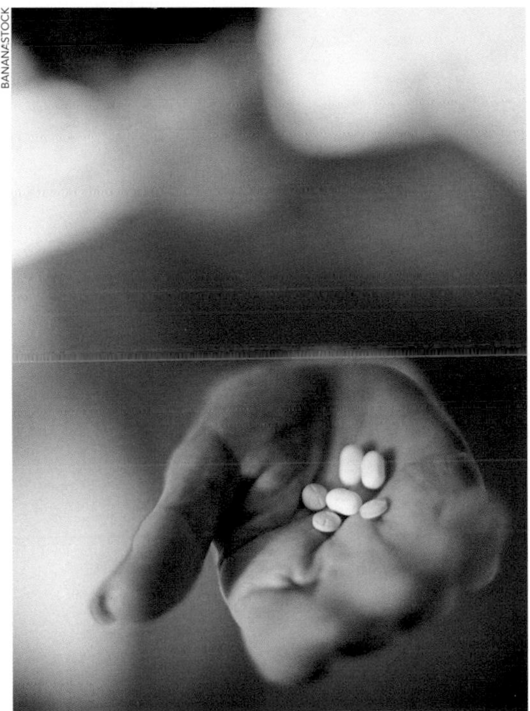
BANANASTOCK

As we saw with Descartes in Chapter 1, most people think that their mind is somehow independent of their brain. Do you think that people would be less likely to take drugs if they knew that they were altering their own brain chemistry?

Like MPTP, other recreational drugs can alter neurotransmitter function. Amphetamine, for example, is a popular drug that stimulates the release of noradrenaline and dopamine. In addition, both amphetamine and cocaine prevent the reuptake of noradrenaline and dopamine. The combination of increased release of noradrenaline and dopamine and prevention of their reuptake floods the synapse with those neurotransmitters, resulting in increased activation of their receptors. Both these drugs are therefore strong agonists, although their psychological effects differ somewhat because of subtle distinctions in where and how they act on the brain. Noradrenaline and dopamine play a critical role in mood control, such that increases in either neurotransmitter result in euphoria, wakefulness and a burst of energy. However, noradrenaline also increases heart rate. An overdose of amphetamine or cocaine can cause the heart to contract so rapidly that heartbeats do not last long enough to pump blood effectively, leading to fainting and sometimes to death.

Prozac, a drug commonly used to treat depression, as you will see in Chapter 17, is another example of a neurotransmitter agonist. Prozac blocks the reuptake of the neurotransmitter serotonin, making it part of a category of drugs called *selective serotonin reuptake inhibitors* (SSRIs) (Wong et al., 1995). Patients suffering from clinical depression typically have reduced levels of serotonin in their brains. By blocking reuptake, more of the neurotransmitter remains in the synapse longer and produces greater activation of serotonin receptors. Serotonin elevates mood, which can help relieve depression.

An antagonist with important medical implications is a class of drugs called *beta-blockers* that obstruct a receptor site for noradrenaline in the heart. Because noradrenaline cannot bind to these receptors, heart rate slows down, which is helpful for disorders in which the heart beats too fast or irregularly. Beta-blockers are also prescribed to reduce the agitation, racing heart and nervousness associated with stage fright (Mills and Dimsdale, 1991).

As you've read, many drugs alter the actions of neurotransmitters. The actions of methamphetamine involve a complex interaction at the neuron's synapses – it affects the pathways for dopamine, serotonin and noradrenaline – making it difficult to interpret exactly how it works. But the combination of its agonist and antagonist effects alters the functions of neurotransmitters that help us perceive and interpret visual images.

In summary, the action potential triggers synaptic transmission through the release of neurotransmitters from the terminal buttons of the sending neuron's axon. Neurotransmitters travel across the synapse to bind with receptors in the receiving neuron's dendrite, completing the transmission of the message. Neurotransmitters bind to dendrites based on existing pathways in the brain and specific receptor sites for neurotransmitters. Neurotransmitters leave the synapse through reuptake, enzyme deactivation, and by binding to autoreceptors. Some of the major neurotransmitters are acetylcholine, dopamine, glutamate, GABA, noradrenaline, serotonin and endorphins. Drugs can affect behaviour by acting as agonists, that is, facilitating or increasing the actions of neurotransmitters, or as antagonists by blocking the action of neurotransmitters.

The organization of the nervous system

Our glimpse into the microscopic world of neurons reveals a lot about their structure and how they communicate with one another. It's quite impressive that billions of tiny engines cause our thoughts, feelings and behaviours. Nonetheless, billions of anything working in isolation suggests a lot of potential but not much direction. Neurons work by forming circuits and pathways in the brain, which in turn influence circuits and pathways in other areas of the body. Without this kind of organization and delegation, neurons would be churning away with little purpose. Neurons are the building blocks that form *nerves*, bundles of axons that are regulated by glial cells that form the insulating myelin sheaths and change in responsiveness to neuronal activity. The nervous system is *an interacting network of neurons that conveys electrochemical information throughout the body*. In this section, we'll look at the major divisions of the nervous system, focusing particularly on structures in the brain and their specific functions.

NERVOUS SYSTEM An interacting network of neurons that conveys electrochemical information throughout the body.

Divisions of the nervous system

There are two major divisions of the nervous system: the central nervous system and the peripheral nervous system (see **FIGURE 3.9**). The central nervous system (CNS) is *composed of the brain and spinal cord*. The CNS receives sensory information from the external world, processes and coordinates this information, and sends commands to the skeletal and muscular systems for action. At the top of the CNS rests the brain, which contains structures that support the most complex perceptual, motor, emotional and cognitive functions of the nervous system. The spinal cord branches down from the brain; nerves that process sensory information and relay commands to the body connect to the spinal cord.

CENTRAL NERVOUS SYSTEM (CNS) The part of the nervous system that is composed of the brain and spinal cord.

The peripheral nervous system (PNS) *connects the central nervous system to the body's organs and muscles*. The peripheral nervous system is itself composed of two major subdivisions, the somatic nervous system and the autonomic nervous system. The somatic nervous system is *a set of nerves that convey information into and out of the central nervous system*. Humans have conscious control over this system and use it to perceive, think and coordinate their behaviours. (However, see Chapter 8 for evidence that conscious

PERIPHERAL NERVOUS SYSTEM (PNS) The part of the nervous system that connects the central nervous system to the body's organs and muscles.

SOMATIC NERVOUS SYSTEM A set of nerves that convey information into and out of the central nervous system.

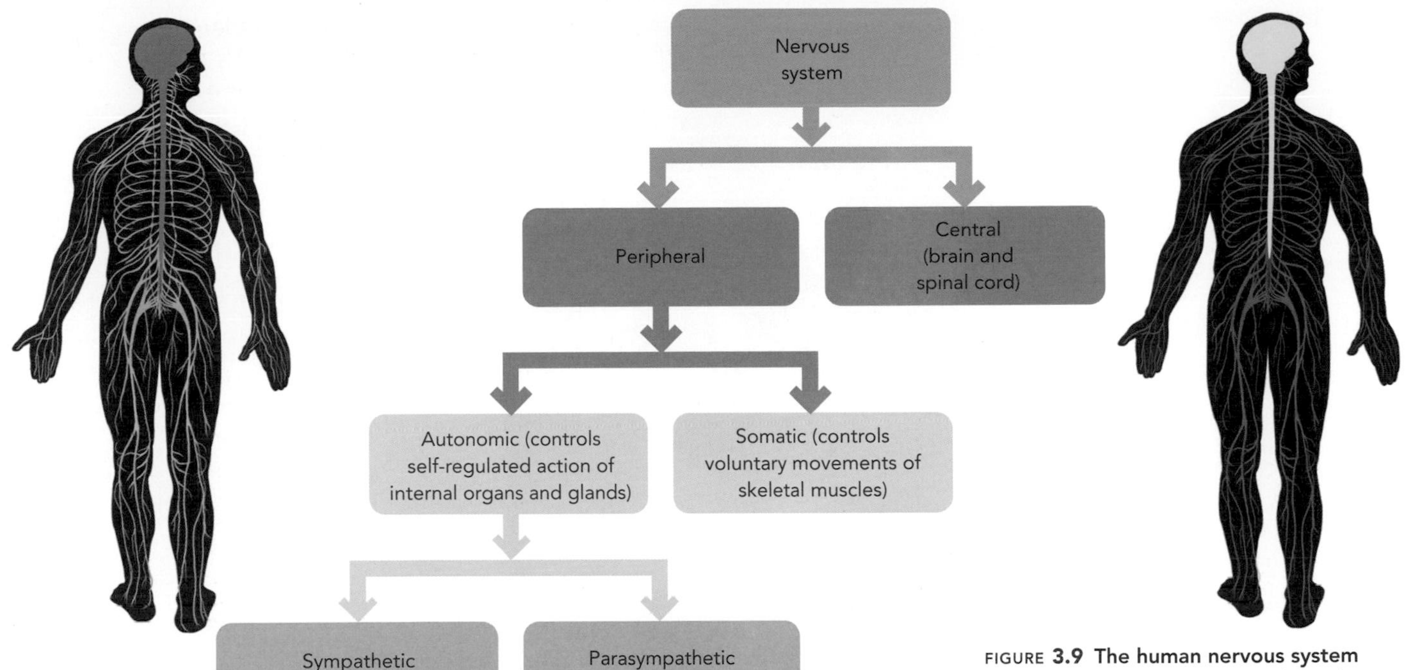

FIGURE **3.9 The human nervous system** The nervous system is organized into the peripheral and central nervous systems. The peripheral nervous system is further divided into the automatic and somatic nervous systems.

control may involve a bit of an illusion.) For example, directing your hand to reach out and pick up a coffee cup involves the elegantly orchestrated activities of the somatic nervous system: information from the receptors in your eyes travels to your brain, registering that a cup is on the table; signals from your brain travel to the muscles in your arm and hand; feedback from those muscles tells your brain that the cup has been grasped; and so on. The somatic nervous system is kind of an 'information superhighway', linking the external world of experience with the internal world of the central nervous system.

In contrast, the autonomic nervous system (ANS) is *a set of nerves that carry involuntary and automatic commands that control blood vessels, body organs and glands*. As suggested by its name, this system works on its own to regulate bodily systems, largely outside conscious control. The ANS has two major subdivisions, the sympathetic nervous system and the parasympathetic nervous system. Each exerts a different type of control on the body. The sympathetic nervous system is *a set of nerves that prepare the body for action in threatening situations*. The nerves in the sympathetic nervous system emanate from the top and bottom of the spinal cord and connect to a variety of organs, such as the eyes, salivary glands, heart and lungs, digestive organs and sex organs (see **FIGURE 3.10**). The sympathetic nervous system coordinates the control of these organs so that the body can take action by fleeing the threatening situation or preparing to face it and fight.

AUTONOMIC NERVOUS SYSTEM (ANS) A set of nerves that carry involuntary and automatic commands that control blood vessels, body organs and glands.

SYMPATHETIC NERVOUS SYSTEM A set of nerves that prepare the body for action in threatening situations.

For example, imagine that you hear footsteps behind you in a dark alley. You feel frightened and turn to see someone approaching you from behind. Your sympathetic nervous system kicks into action at this point: it dilates your pupils to let in more light, increases your heart rate and respiration to pump more oxygen to muscles, diverts blood flow to your brain and muscles, and activates sweat glands to cool your body. To conserve energy, the sympathetic nervous system inhibits salivation and bowel movements, suppresses the body's immune responses, and suppresses responses to pain and injury. The sum total of these fast, automatic responses is that they increase the likelihood that you can deal with the potential threat by standing your ground and fighting or making good your escape, a phenomenon known as the *fight-or-flight response* (see Chapter 17).

The parasympathetic nervous system *helps the body return to a normal resting state*. When you're far away from your would-be attacker, your body doesn't need to remain on red alert. Now the parasympathetic nervous system kicks in to reverse the effects of the sympathetic nervous system and return your body to its normal state. The

PARASYMPATHETIC NERVOUS SYSTEM A set of nerves that help the body return to a normal resting state.

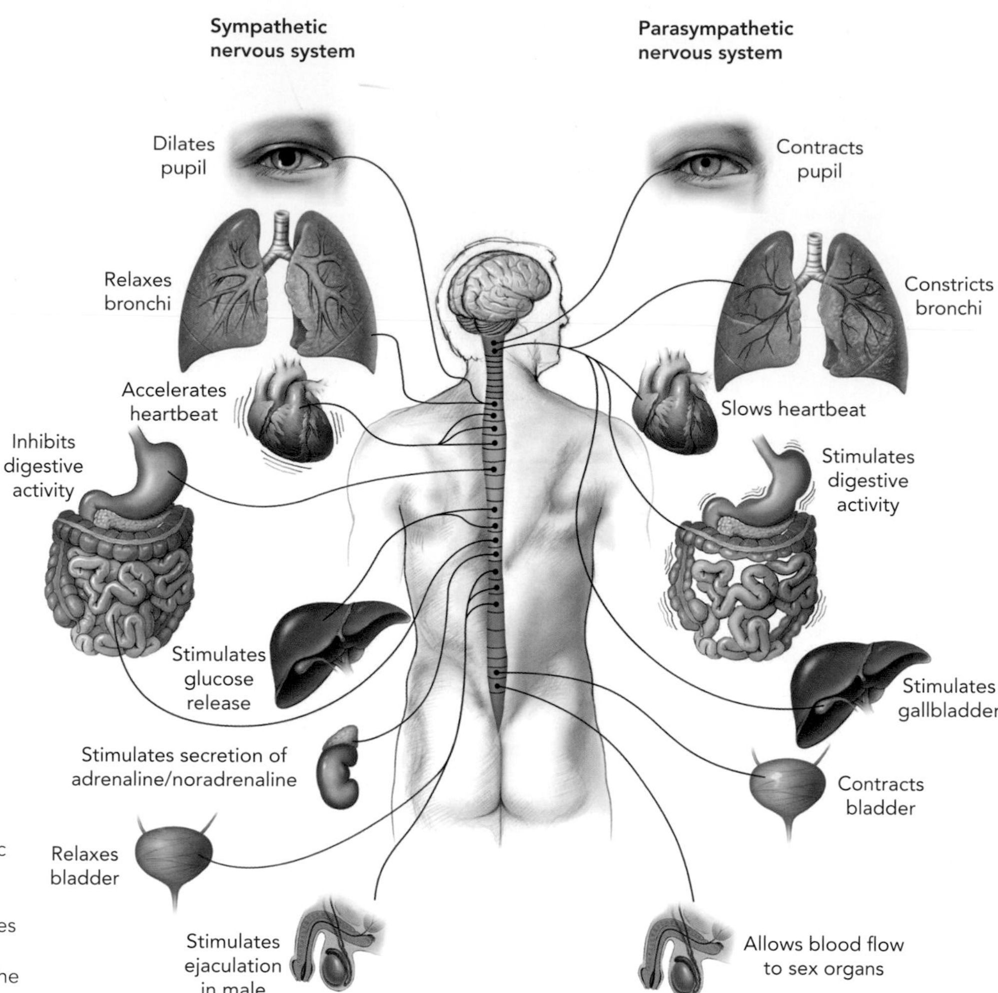

FIGURE **3.10 Sympathetic and parasympathetic systems** The autonomic nervous system is composed of two subsystems that complement each other. Activation of the sympathetic system serves several aspects of arousal, whereas the parasympathetic nervous system returns the body to its normal resting state.

parasympathetic nervous system generally mirrors the connections of the sympathetic nervous system. For example, the parasympathetic nervous system constricts your pupils, slows your heart rate and respiration, diverts blood flow to your digestive system, and decreases activity in your sweat glands (Figure 3.10).

As you might imagine, the sympathetic and parasympathetic nervous systems coordinate to control many bodily functions. One example is sexual behaviour. In men, the parasympathetic nervous system engorges the blood vessels of the penis to produce an erection, but the sympathetic nervous system is responsible for ejaculation. In women, the parasympathetic nervous system produces vaginal lubrication, but the sympathetic nervous system underlies orgasm. In men and women, a successful sexual experience depends on a delicate balance of these two systems; in fact, anxiety about sexual performance can disrupt this balance. For example, sympathetic nervous system activation caused by anxiety can lead to premature ejaculation in males and lack of lubrication in females.

Let's return briefly to an earlier point. Without some kind of coordinated effort, billions and billions of neurons would simply produce trillions and trillions of independent processes. The nervous system has evolved so that the sympathetic and parasympathetic nervous systems work in harmony, which in turn allows the autonomic nervous system to function effortlessly and, in coordination with the somatic nervous system, allows information to be gathered from the external world. This information travels through the peripheral nervous system and is eventually sent to the brain via the spinal cord, where it can be sorted, interpreted, processed and acted on. Like the organizational chart of a complex corporation, the organization of the human nervous system is a triumph of delegation of responsibilities.

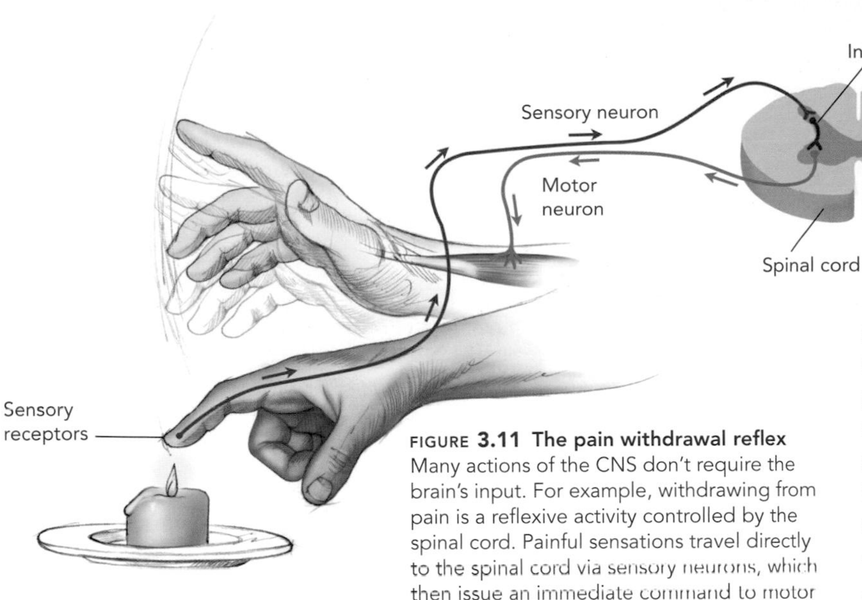

FIGURE 3.11 The pain withdrawal reflex Many actions of the CNS don't require the brain's input. For example, withdrawing from pain is a reflexive activity controlled by the spinal cord. Painful sensations travel directly to the spinal cord via sensory neurons, which then issue an immediate command to motor neurons to retract the hand.

Components of the central nervous system

Compared to the many divisions of the peripheral nervous system, the central nervous system may seem simple. After all, it has only two elements: the brain and the spinal cord. But those two elements are ultimately responsible for most of what we do as humans.

The spinal cord often seems like the brain's poor relation: the brain gets all the glory and the spinal cord just hangs around, doing relatively simple tasks. These tasks, however, are pretty important: keeping you breathing, responding to pain, moving your muscles, allowing you to walk. What's more, without the spinal cord, the brain would not be able to put any of its higher processing into action.

Do you need your brain to tell you to pull your hand away from a flame? For some basic behaviours, the spinal cord doesn't need input from the brain at all. Connections between the sensory inputs and motor neurons in the spinal cord mediate spinal reflexes – *simple pathways in the nervous system that rapidly generate muscle contractions*. For example, if you touch a candle flame, the sensory neurons that register pain send inputs directly into the spinal cord (see **FIGURE 3.11**). Through just a few synaptic connections within the spinal cord, interneurons relay these sensory inputs to motor neurons that connect to your arm muscles and direct you to quickly retract your hand.

More elaborate tasks require the collaboration of the spinal cord and the brain. The peripheral nervous system communicates with the central nervous system through nerves that conduct sensory information into the brain, carry commands out of the brain, or both. The brain sends commands for voluntary movement through the spinal cord to motor neurons, whose axons project out to skeletal muscles and send the message to contract. (See the hot science box for a description of a novel type of movement control.) Damage to the spinal cord severs the connection from the brain to the sensory and motor neurons that are essential to sensory perception and movement. The location of the spinal injury often determines the extent of the abilities that are lost. As you can see in **FIGURE 3.12**, different regions of the spinal cord control different systems of the body. Patients with damage at a particular level of the spinal cord lose sensation of touch and pain in body parts below the level of the injury as well as a loss of motor control of the muscles in the same areas. A spinal injury higher up the cord usually predicts a much poorer prognosis, such as quadriplegia (the loss of sensation and motor control over all limbs), breathing through a respirator, and lifelong immobility.

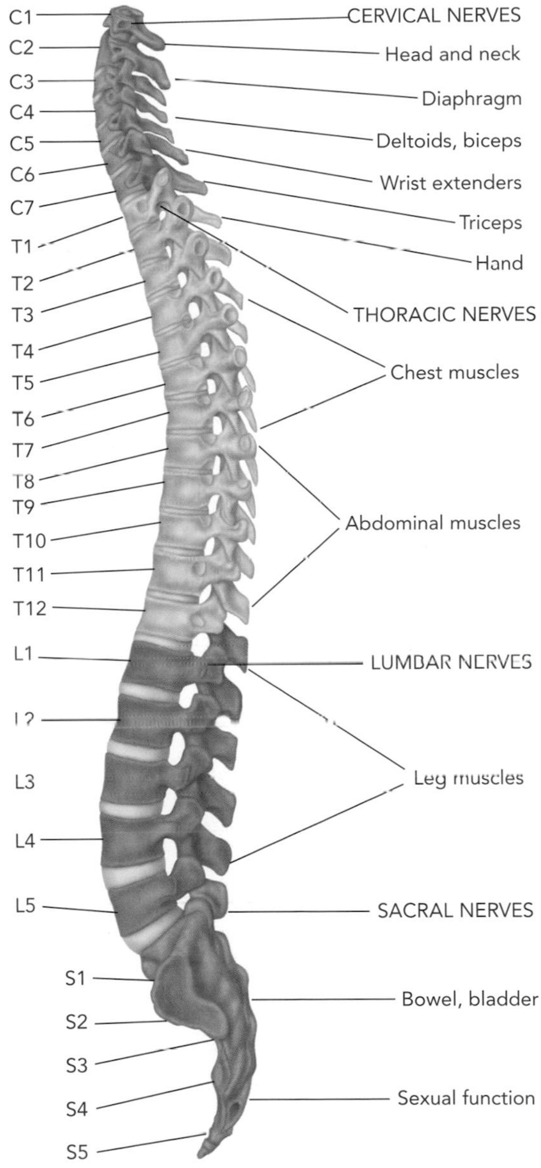

FIGURE 3.12 Regions of the spinal cord The spinal cord is divided into four main sections, each of which controls different parts of the body. Damage higher up the spinal cord usually portends greater impairment.

SPINAL REFLEXES Simple pathways in the nervous system that rapidly generate muscle contractions.

hot science

Thought control

The British sci-fi writer Arthur C. Clarke wrote: 'Any sufficiently advanced technology is indistinguishable from magic.' What could be more magical or in the realm of the paranormal than the ability to control machines with the power of thought alone? During the 1970s, when there was a great interest in paranormal abilities, some people claimed to possess such psychokinetic capabilities, or 'telekinesis', where they could move objects without touching them, but all turned out to be either deluded or fraudsters.

Recently, however, scientists have been bringing that fantasy closer to reality. In 2013, the biomedical engineer Bin He and his team at the University of Minnesota demonstrated that humans could control a robotic quadcopter by thought alone. Five subjects were first asked to imagine moving their left or right hand to guide a cursor on a computer screen. They were also asked to imagine moving the cursor up and down. During these training procedures, the subjects wore a cap that contained electrodes connected to an EEG machine, which recorded the minute fluctuations of electrical brain activity, as discussed at the end of this chapter. These signals were fed into a computer and translated into characteristic patterns that reflected the different control movements, which were then sent via WiFi to the quadcopter to update the direction in which it moved. The quadcopter simultaneously acquired video using onboard cameras to give the subjects feedback.

This brain-computer interface (BCI) technology promises to enable some of the most interactive gaming experiences or the opportunity to amaze your friends with your telekinetic powers, but the real value to society is the potential to restore critical functions to people who are severely disabled by a wide variety of neuromuscular disorders, paralysis or damage.

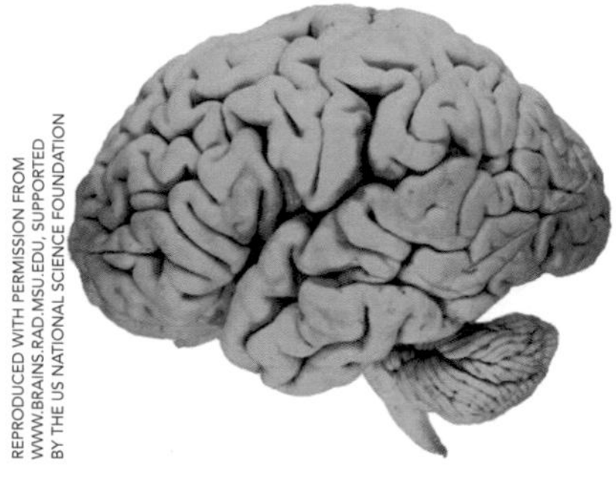

The human brain weighs around 1.3–1.4 kg and isn't much to look at, but its accomplishments are staggering.

Actor Christopher Reeve, who starred as Superman in four Superman films, damaged his spinal cord in a horse-riding accident in 1995, resulting in loss of sensation and motor control in all his body parts below the neck. Despite great efforts over several years, Reeve made only modest gains in his motor control and sensation, highlighting the extent to which we depend on communication from the brain through the spinal cord to the body, and showing how difficult it is to compensate for the loss of these connections (Edgerton et al., 2004). Sadly, Christopher Reeve died in 2004, aged 52, from complications due to his paralysis.

Structure of the brain

The human brain, weighing around 1.3–1.4 kg, is not much to look at. You already know that the neurons and glial cells that make up that jellylike mass are busy humming away, giving you consciousness, feelings and potentially brilliant ideas. But to find out which neurons in which parts of the brain control which functions, scientists first had to divide and conquer, that is, find a way of describing the brain that allows researchers to communicate with one another.

There are several ways that neuroscientists divide up the brain. It can be helpful to talk about areas of the brain from 'bottom to top', noting how the different regions are specialized for different kinds of tasks. In general, simpler functions are performed at the 'lower levels' of the brain, whereas more complex functions are performed at successively 'higher' levels (see **FIGURE 3.13**). As you'll see shortly, the brain can also be approached in a 'side-by-side' fashion: although each side of the brain is roughly analogous, one half of the brain specializes in some tasks that the other half doesn't. Although these divisions make it easier to understand areas of the brain and their functions, keep in mind that none of these structures or areas in the brain can act alone: they are all part of one big, interacting, interdependent whole.

Let's look first at the divisions of the brain and the responsibilities of each part, moving from the bottom to the top. Using this view, we can divide the brain into three parts: the hindbrain, the midbrain and the forebrain (see Figure 3.13).

Forebrain
Midbrain
Hindbrain

FIGURE **3.13 The major divisions of the brain** The brain can be organized into three parts, moving from the bottom to the top, from simpler functions to the more complex: the hindbrain, the midbrain and the forebrain.

The hindbrain

If you follow the spinal cord from your tailbone to where it enters your skull, you'll find it difficult to determine where your spinal cord ends and your brain begins. That's because the spinal cord is continuous with the hindbrain – *an area of the brain that coordinates information coming into and out of the spinal cord*. The hindbrain is sometimes called the *brainstem*; indeed, it looks like a stalk on which the rest of the brain sits. The hindbrain controls the most basic functions of life: respiration, alertness and motor skills. There are three anatomical structures that make up the hindbrain: the medulla, the cerebellum and the pons (see **FIGURE 3.14**).

HINDBRAIN An area of the brain that coordinates information coming into and out of the spinal cord.

MEDULLA An extension of the spinal cord into the skull that coordinates heart rate, circulation and respiration.

RETICULAR FORMATION A brain structure that regulates sleep, wakefulness and levels of arousal.

CEREBELLUM A large structure of the hindbrain that controls fine motor skills.

The medulla is *an extension of the spinal cord into the skull that coordinates heart rate, circulation and respiration*. Inside the medulla is a small cluster of neurons called the reticular formation, which *regulates sleep, wakefulness and levels of arousal*. Damage to this tiny area of the brain can produce dramatically large consequences for behaviour. In one early experiment, for example, researchers stimulated the reticular formation of a sleeping cat. This caused the animal to awaken almost instantaneously and remain alert. Conversely, severing the connections between the reticular formation and the rest of the brain caused the animal to lapse into an irreversible coma (Moruzzi and Magoun, 1949). The reticular formation maintains the same delicate balance between alertness and unconsciousness in humans. In fact, many general anaesthetics work by reducing activity in the reticular formation, rendering the patient unconscious.

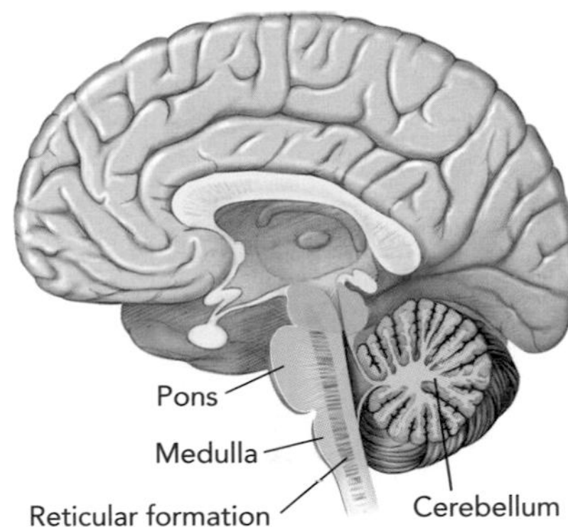

FIGURE 3.14 The hindbrain The hindbrain coordinates information coming into and out of the spinal cord and controls the basic functions of life. It includes the medulla, the reticular formation, the cerebellum and the pons.

Behind the medulla is the cerebellum – *a large structure of the hindbrain that controls fine motor skills*. *Cerebellum* is Latin for 'little brain', and the structure does look like a small replica of the brain. The cerebellum orchestrates the proper sequence of movements when we ride a bike, play the piano or maintain balance while walking and running. The cerebellum contains a layer of Purkinje cells, the elaborate, treelike neurons you read about earlier in the chapter. Purkinje cells are some of the largest neurons in the brain, and they are the sole output for motor coordination originating in the cerebellum and spreading to the rest of the brain.

Damage to the cerebellum produces impairments in coordination and balance, although not the paralysis or immobility you might think would be associated with a motor control centre. This highlights an important role for the cerebellum: it contributes to the 'fine-tuning' of behaviour, smoothing our actions to allow their graceful execution rather than initiating the actions (Smetacek, 2002). The initiation of behaviour involves other areas of the brain; as you'll recall, different brain systems interact and are interdependent with one another.

The last major area of the hindbrain is the pons – *a structure that relays information from the cerebellum to the rest of the brain*. *Pons* means 'bridge' in Latin. Although the detailed functions of the pons remain poorly understood, it essentially acts as a 'relay station' or bridge between the cerebellum and other structures in the brain.

PONS A brain structure that relays information from the cerebellum to the rest of the brain.

The midbrain

Sitting on top of the hindbrain is the *midbrain*, which is relatively small in humans. As you can see in **FIGURE 3.15**, the midbrain contains two main structures: the tectum and the tegmentum. The tectum *orients an organism in the environment*. The tectum receives stimulus input from the eyes, ears and skin and moves the organism in a coordinated way towards the stimulus. For example, when you're studying in a quiet room and you hear a *click* behind and to the right of you, your body will swivel and orient to the direction of the sound: this is your tectum in action.

TECTUM A part of the midbrain that orients an organism in the environment.

The tegmentum is *involved in movement and arousal*, and also helps to orient an organism towards sensory stimuli. However, parts of the tegmentum are involved in pleasure seeking and motivation. It makes sense, then, that an abundance of dopamine-producing neurons is found in this midbrain structure. One region in this area that is so densely packed with dopamine neurons that it appears darker is the *substantia nigra*. You recall that dopamine contributes to motor behaviour, motivation and pleasure: all are tasks that the tegmentum coordinates. Serotonin, a neurotransmitter that contributes to mood and arousal, is also plentiful in the midbrain. The midbrain may be relatively small, but it is a central location of neurotransmitters involved in arousal, mood and motivation and the brain structures that rely on them (White, 1996).

TEGMENTUM A part of the midbrain that is involved in movement and arousal.

You could survive if you had only a hindbrain and a midbrain. The structures in the hindbrain would take care of all the bodily functions necessary to sustain life, and the

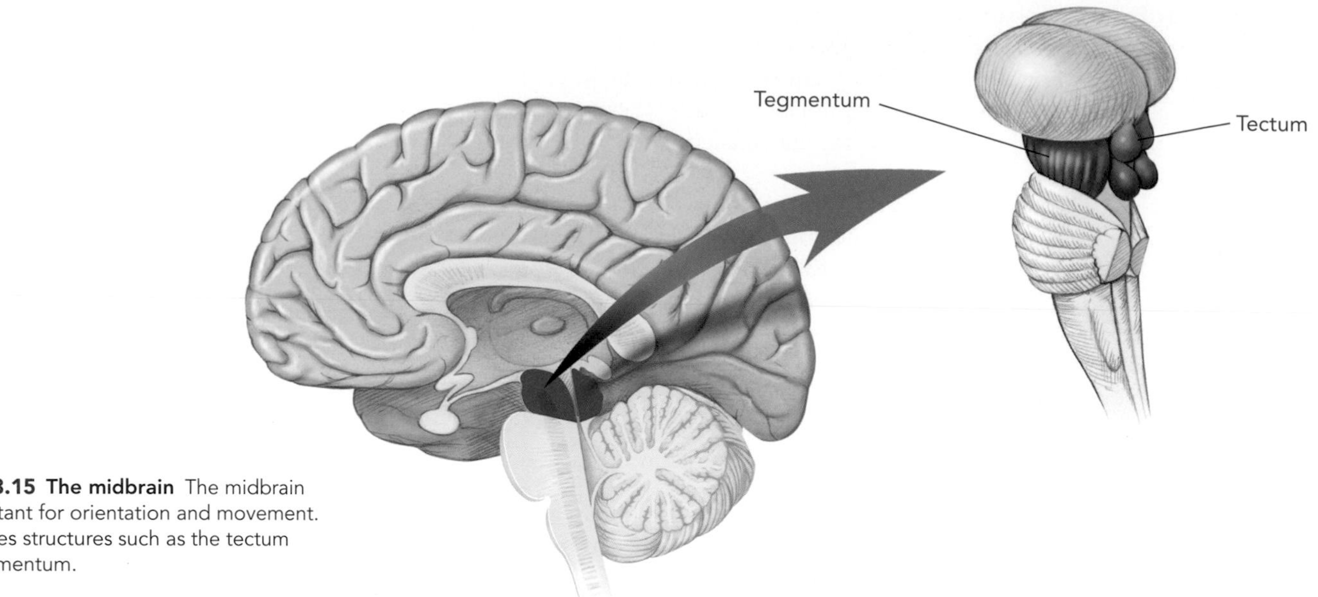

FIGURE 3.15 The midbrain The midbrain is important for orientation and movement. It includes structures such as the tectum and tegmentum.

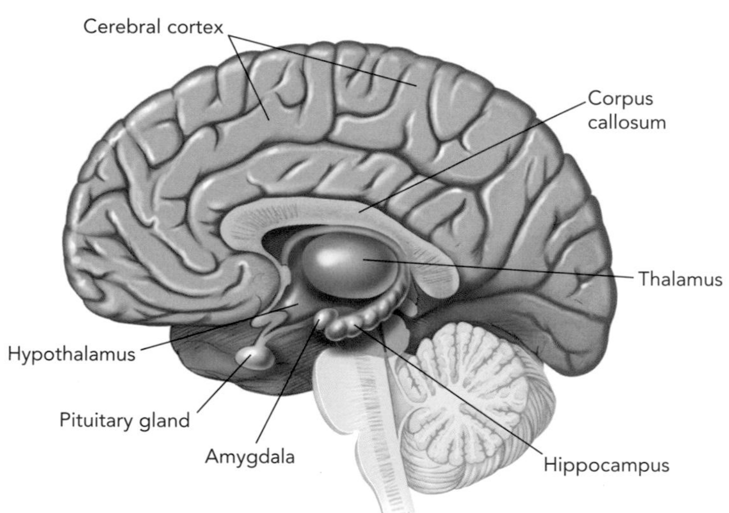

FIGURE 3.16 The forebrain The forebrain is the highest level of the brain and is critical for complex cognitive, emotional, sensory and motor functions. The forebrain is divided into two parts: the cerebral cortex and the underlying subcortical structures. These include the thalamus, hypothalamus, pituitary gland, amygdala and hippocampus. The corpus callosum connects the two hemispheres of the brain.

structures in the midbrain would orient you towards or away from pleasurable or threatening stimuli in the environment. But this wouldn't be much of a life. To understand where the abilities that make us fully human come from, we need to consider the last division of the brain.

The forebrain

When you appreciate the beauty of a poem, detect the sarcasm in a friend's remark, plan to go skiing next winter, or notice the faint glimmer of sadness on a loved one's face, you are enlisting the forebrain. The *forebrain* is the highest level of the brain – literally and figuratively – and controls complex cognitive, emotional, sensory and motor functions (see **FIGURE 3.16**). The forebrain itself is divided into two main sections: the cerebral cortex and the subcortical structures.

The cerebral cortex is *the outermost layer of the brain, visible to the naked eye and divided into two hemispheres.* The subcortical structures are *areas of the forebrain housed under the cerebral cortex near the very centre of the brain.*

We'll have much more to say about the two hemispheres of the cerebral cortex and the functions they serve in the next section, fittingly saving the highest level of the brain for last. First, we'll examine the subcortical structures.

Subcortical structures

The subcortical structures are nestled deep inside the brain, where they are quite protected. If you imagine sticking an index finger in each of your ears and pushing inwards until they touch, that's about where you'd find the thalamus, hypothalamus, pituitary gland, limbic system and basal ganglia (see **FIGURE 3.17**). Each of these subcortical structures plays an important role in relaying information throughout the brain, as well as performing specific tasks that allow us to think, feel and behave as humans.

The thalamus *relays and filters information from the senses and transmits the information to the cerebral cortex.* The thalamus receives inputs from all the major senses except smell, which has direct connections to the cerebral cortex. The thalamus acts as a kind of computer server in a networked system, taking in multiple inputs and relaying them to a variety of locations (Guillery and Sherman, 2002). However, unlike the mechanical

CEREBRAL CORTEX The outermost layer of the brain, visible to the naked eye and divided into two hemispheres.

SUBCORTICAL STRUCTURES Areas of the forebrain housed under the cerebral cortex near the very centre of the brain.

THALAMUS A subcortical structure that relays and filters information from the senses and transmits the information to the cerebral cortex.

operations of a computer – 'send input A to location B' – the thalamus actively filters sensory information, giving more weight to some inputs and less weight to others. The thalamus also closes the pathways of incoming sensations during sleep, providing a valuable function in *not* allowing information to pass to the rest of the brain.

The hypothalamus, located below the thalamus (*hypo* is Greek for 'under'), *regulates body temperature, hunger, thirst and sexual behaviour*. Although the hypothalamus is a tiny area of the brain, clusters of neurons in the hypothalamus oversee a wide range of basic behaviours. For example, the hypothalamus makes sure that body temperature, blood sugar levels and metabolism are kept within an optimal range for normal human functioning. Lesions to some areas of the hypothalamus result in overeating, whereas lesions to other areas leave an animal with no desire for food at all. Also, when you think about sex, messages from your cerebral cortex are sent to the hypothalamus to trigger the release of hormones. Finally, electric stimulation of the hypothalamus in cats can produce hissing and biting, whereas stimulation of other areas in the hypothalamus can produce what appears to be intense pleasure for an animal (Siegel et al., 1999). Researchers James Olds and Peter Milner (1954) found that a small electric current delivered to a certain region of a rat's hypothalamus was extremely rewarding for the animal. In fact, when allowed to press a bar attached to the electrode to initiate their own stimulation, rats would do so several thousand times an hour, often to the point of exhaustion. It's been suggested, then, that the hypothalamus is in charge of the 'four Fs' of behaviour: fighting, fleeing, feeding and mating!

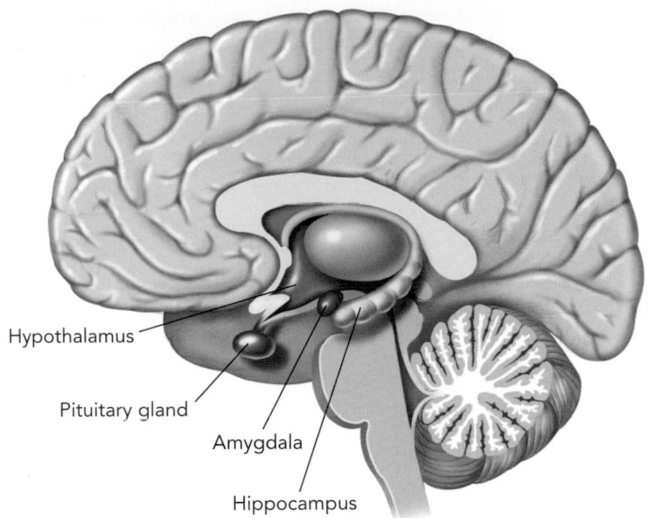

FIGURE 3.17 The limbic system The limbic system is a group of forebrain structures, which includes the hippocampus, the amygdala and the hypothalamus. These structures are involved in motivation, emotion, learning and memory.

HYPOTHALAMUS A subcortical structure that regulates body temperature, hunger, thirst and sexual behaviour.

PITUITARY GLAND The 'master gland' of the body's hormone-producing system, which releases hormones that direct the functions of many other glands in the body.

Located below the hypothalamus is the pituitary gland – *the 'master gland' of the body's hormone-producing system, which releases hormones that direct the functions of many other glands in the body*. The hypothalamus sends hormonal signals to the pituitary gland, which in turn sends hormonal signals to other glands to control stress, digestive activities and reproductive processes. For example, when a baby suckles its mother's breast, sensory neurons in her breast send signals to her hypothalamus, which then signals her pituitary gland to release a hormone called *oxytocin* into the bloodstream (McNeilly et al., 1983). Oxytocin, in turn, stimulates the release of milk from reservoirs in the breast. The pituitary gland is also involved in the response to stress. When we sense a threat, sensory neurons send signals to the hypothalamus, which stimulates the release of adrenocorticotropic hormone (ACTH) from the pituitary gland. ACTH, in turn, stimulates the adrenal glands (above the kidneys) to release hormones that activate the sympathetic nervous system (Selye and Fortier, 1950). As you read earlier in this chapter, the sympathetic nervous system prepares the body to either meet the threat head-on or flee from the situation.

The thalamus, hypothalamus and pituitary gland, located in the centre of the brain, make possible close interaction with several other brain structures: they receive information, process it, and send it back out again. The hypothalamus is part of the limbic system, *a group of forebrain structures, which also include the amygdala and the hippocampus, which are involved in motivation, emotion, learning and memory* (Maclean, 1970; Papez, 1937). The limbic system (from the Latin for 'edge' or 'border') forms a doughnut-shaped boundary where the subcortical structures meet the cerebral cortex (see Figure 3.17). The two remaining structures of the limbic system are the hippocampus (from the Latin for 'sea horse', due to its shape) and the amygdala (from the Latin for 'almond', also due to its shape).

LIMBIC SYSTEM A group of forebrain structures, which include the hypothalamus, the amygdala and the hippocampus, which are involved in motivation, emotion, learning and memory.

The hippocampus is *critical for creating new memories and integrating them into a network of knowledge so that they can be stored indefinitely in other parts of the cerebral cortex*. Patients with damage to the hippocampus can acquire new information and keep it in awareness for a few seconds, but as soon as they are distracted, they forget the information and the experience that produced it (Scoville and Milner, 1957). This kind of disruption is limited to everyday memory for facts and events that we can bring to consciousness; memory of learned habitual routines or emotional reactions remains

HIPPOCAMPUS A structure critical for creating new memories and integrating them into a network of knowledge so that they can be stored indefinitely in other parts of the cerebral cortex.

intact (Squire et al., 1993). As an example, people with damage to the hippocampus can remember how to drive and talk, but they cannot recall where they have recently driven or a conversation they have just had. You will read more about the hippocampus and its role in creating, storing and combining memories in Chapter 5.

AMYGDALA A part of the limbic system, located at the tip of each horn of the hippocampus, that plays a central role in many emotional processes, particularly the formation of emotional memories.

The amygdala, *located at the tip of each horn of the hippocampus, plays a central role in many emotional processes, particularly the formation of emotional memories* (Aggleton, 1992). The amygdala attaches significance to previously neutral events that are associated with fear, punishment or reward (LeDoux, 1992). As an example, think of the last time something scary or unpleasant happened to you: a car came speeding towards you as you began to cross a road or a ferocious dog leapt out of an alley as you passed by. Those stimuli – a car or a dog – are fairly neutral; you don't have a panic attack every time you walk past a used car showroom. The emotional significance attached to events involving those stimuli is the work of the amygdala. When we are in emotionally arousing situations, the amygdala stimulates the hippocampus to remember many details surrounding the situation (Kensinger and Schacter, 2005). For example, after the terrorist attacks of 11 September 2001, most people recalled much more than the fact that planes crashed into the World Trade Center in New York City, the Pentagon in Washington, DC and a field in western Pennsylvania. People who lived through the attacks remember vivid details about where they were, what they were doing, and how they felt when they heard the news, even years later. In particular, the amygdala seems to be especially involved in encoding events as *fearful* (Adolphs et al., 1995). We'll have more to say about the amygdala's role in memory in Chapter 5 and its job in evaluating situations in Chapter 10. For now, keep in mind that a group of neurons the size of a bean buried deep in your brain help you to laugh, weep or shriek in fright when the circumstances call for it and appears to make you remember these events more clearly.

BASAL GANGLIA A set of subcortical structures that direct intentional movements.

There are several other structures in the subcortical area, but we'll consider just one more. The basal ganglia are *a set of subcortical structures that direct intentional movements*. The basal ganglia are located near the thalamus and hypothalamus; they receive input from the cerebral cortex and send outputs to the motor centres in the brainstem (see **FIGURE 3.18**). One part of the basal ganglia, the *striatum*, is involved in the control of posture and movement. Patients who suffer from Parkinson's typically show symptoms of uncontrollable shaking and sudden jerks of the limbs and are unable to initiate a sequence of movements to achieve a specific goal. This happens because the dopamine-producing neurons in the substantia nigra (found in the tegmentum of the midbrain) have become damaged (Dauer and Przedborski, 2003). The undersupply of dopamine then affects the striatum in the basal ganglia, which in turn leads to the visible behavioural symptoms of Parkinson's.

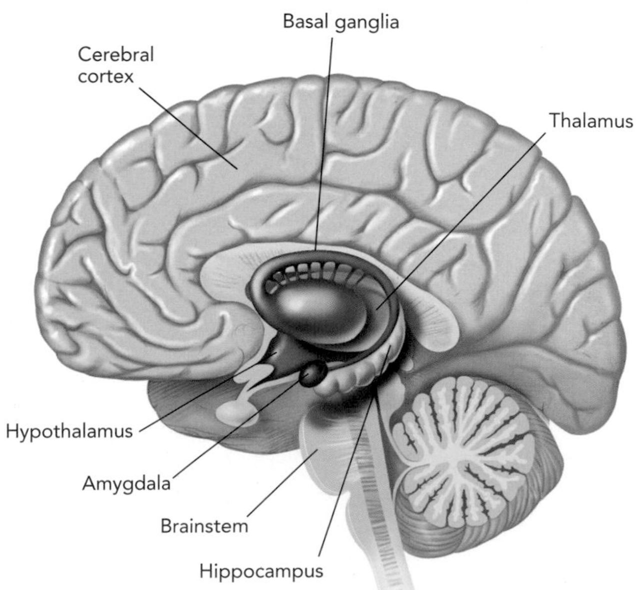

FIGURE **3.18 The basal ganglia** The basal ganglia are a group of subcortical brain structures that direct intentional movement. They receive input from the cerebral cortex and send output to the motor centres in the brainstem.

So, what's the problem in Parkinson's – the jerky movements, the ineffectiveness of the striatum in directing behaviour, the botched interplay of the substantia nigra and the striatum, or the underproduction of dopamine at the neuronal level? The answer is 'all of the above'. This unfortunate disease provides a striking illustration of two themes regarding the brain and behaviour. First, invisible actions at the level of neurons in the brain can produce substantial effects at the level of behaviour. Second, the interaction of hindbrain, midbrain and forebrain structures shows how the various regions are interdependent.

The cerebral cortex

Our tour of the brain has taken us from the very small (neurons) to the somewhat bigger (major divisions of the brain) to the very large: the cerebral cortex. The cortex is the highest level of the brain, and it is responsible for the most complex aspects of perception, emotion, movement and thought (Fuster, 2003). It sits over the rest of the brain, like a mushroom cap shielding the underside and stem, and it is the wrinkled surface you see when looking at the brain with the naked eye.

The smooth surfaces of the cortex – the raised part – are called *gyri* (*gyrus* if just one), and the indentations or fissures are called *sulci* (*sulcus* when singular). Sulci and gyri represent a triumph of evolution. The cerebral cortex occupies about 2,500 cm^3 of space, or roughly the area of a newspaper page. Fitting that much cortex into a human skull is a tough task. But if you crumple a sheet of newspaper, you'll see that the same surface area now fits compactly into a much smaller space. The cortex, with its wrinkles and folds, holds a lot of brainpower in a relatively small package that fits comfortably inside the human skull (see **FIGURE 3.19**).

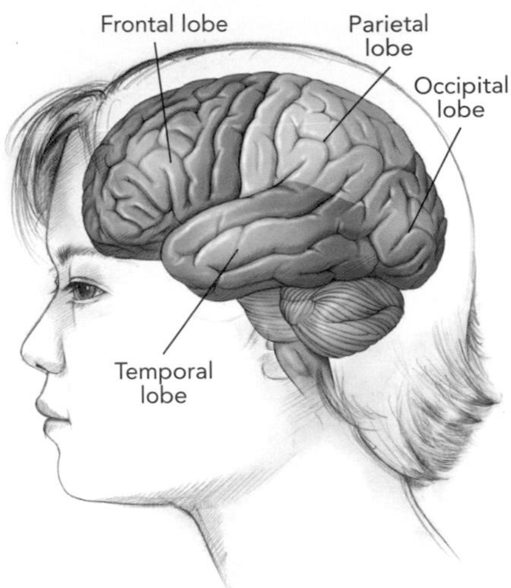

FIGURE 3.19 Cerebral cortex and lobes The four major lobes of the cerebral cortex are the occipital lobe, the parietal lobe, the temporal lobe and the frontal lobe.

The functions of the cerebral cortex can be understood at three levels: the separation of the cortex into two hemispheres; the functions of each hemisphere; and the role of specific cortical areas. The first level of organization divides the cortex into the left and right hemispheres. The two hemispheres are more or less symmetrical in their appearance and, to some extent, in their functions. However, each hemisphere controls the functions of the opposite side of the body. This is called *contralateral control*, meaning that your right cerebral hemisphere perceives stimuli from and controls movements on the left side of your body, whereas your left cerebral hemisphere perceives stimuli from and controls movement on the right side of your body.

The cerebral hemispheres are connected to each other by *commissures*, bundles of axons that make communication possible between parallel areas of the cortex in each half. The largest of these commissures is the corpus callosum – *a thick band of nerve fibres that connects large areas of the cerebral cortex on each side of the brain and supports communication of information across the hemispheres*. This means that information received in the right hemisphere, for example, can pass across the corpus callosum and be registered, virtually instantaneously, in the left hemisphere.

CORPUS CALLOSUM A thick band of nerve fibres that connects large areas of the cerebral cortex on each side of the brain and supports communication of information across the hemispheres.

OCCIPITAL LOBE A region of the cerebral cortex that processes visual information.

PARIETAL LOBE A region of the cerebral cortex whose functions include processing information about touch.

SOMATOSENSORY CORTEX The outermost layer of the parietal lobe area containing a representation of the body map.

The second level of organization in the cerebral cortex distinguishes the functions of the different regions within each hemisphere of the brain. Each hemisphere of the cerebral cortex is divided into four areas or *lobes*: from back to front, these are the occipital lobe, the parietal lobe, the temporal lobe and the frontal lobe, as shown in **FIGURE 3.19**. We'll examine the functions of these lobes in more detail later, noting how scientists have used a variety of techniques to understand the operations of the brain. For now, here's a brief overview of the main functions of each lobe.

The occipital lobe, located at the back of the cerebral cortex, *processes visual information*. Sensory receptors in the eyes send information to the thalamus, which in turn sends information to the primary areas of the occipital lobe, where simple features of the stimulus are extracted. These features are then processed into a more complex 'map' of the stimulus onto the occipital cortex, leading to comprehension of what's being seen. As you might imagine, damage to the primary visual areas of the occipital lobe can leave a person with partial or complete blindness. Information still enters the eyes, which are functioning as normal. But without the ability to process and make sense of the information at the level of the cerebral cortex, the information is as good as lost (Zeki, 2001).

The parietal lobe, located in front of the occipital lobe, carries out functions that include *processing information about touch*. The parietal lobe contains the somatosensory cortex – *the outermost layer of the parietal lobe area containing a representation of the body map* (see **FIGURE 3.20**). Within each hemisphere, the somatosensory cortex represents the skin areas on the contralateral surface of the body. Each part of the somatosensory cortex maps onto a particular part of the body. If a body area is more sensitive, a larger part of the somatosensory cortex is devoted to it. For example, the part of the somatosensory cortex that corresponds to the lips and tongue is larger than the area corresponding to the feet. The somatosensory cortex can be illustrated as a distorted figure, called a *homunculus* ('little man'), in which the body parts are rendered according to how much of the somatosensory cortex is devoted to them (Penfield and Rasmussen, 1950). Directly in front of the somatosensory cortex, in the frontal lobe, is a parallel strip of brain tissue called the *motor cortex*. Like the somatosensory cortex, different parts of the motor cortex correspond to different body parts. The motor cortex initiates voluntary movements and sends messages to the basal ganglia, cerebellum and spinal cord. The motor and somatosensory cortices, then, are like sending and receiving areas of the cerebral cortex, taking in information and sending out commands as the case might be. One

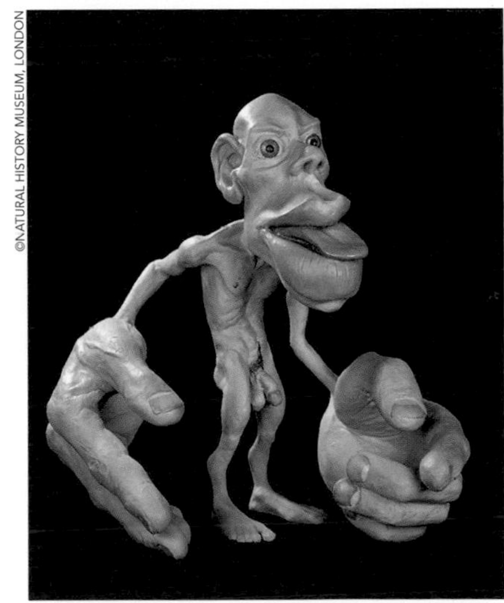

The homunculus is a rendering of the body in which each part is shown in proportion to how much of the somatosensory cortex is devoted to it.

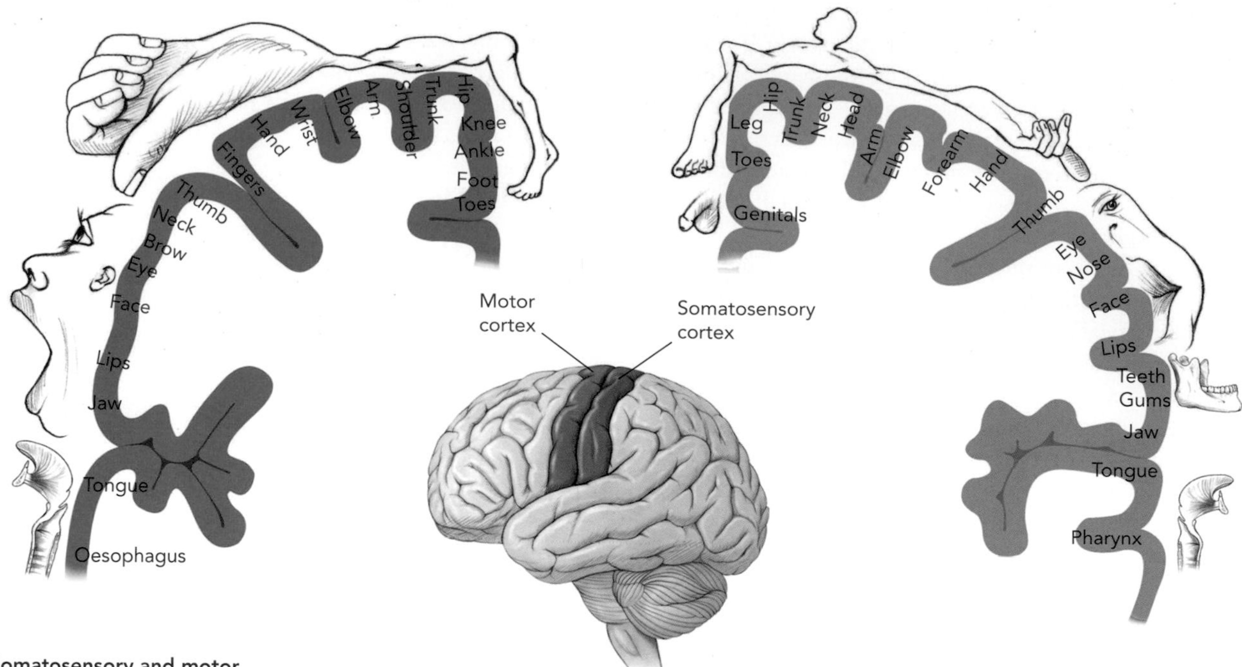

FIGURE **3.20 Somatosensory and motor cortices** The motor cortex, a strip of brain tissue in the frontal lobe, represents and controls different skin and body areas on the contralateral side of the body. Directly behind the motor cortex, in the parietal lobe, lies the somatosensory cortex. Like the motor cortex, the somatosensory cortex represents skin areas of particular parts on the contralateral side of the body.

type of premotor neuron seems to be capable of more socially relevant coordination that has implications for communication. Around one in ten neurons in the motor cortex have been classified as mirror neurons – *cells that are active when performing an action oneself or when observing the same action performed by another*. The discovery of mirror neurons (Gallese et al., 1996) was greeted with much excitement as they might provide a neural basis for how we imitate and copy each other – important social skills that we discuss later in Chapter 12 on social development.

MIRROR NEURONS Cells that are active when performing an action oneself or when observing the same action performed by another.

TEMPORAL LOBE A region of the cerebral cortex responsible for hearing and language.

The temporal lobe, located on the lower side of each hemisphere, is *responsible for hearing and language*. The *primary auditory cortex* in the temporal lobe is analogous to the somatosensory cortex in the parietal lobe and the primary visual areas of the occipital lobe – it receives sensory information from the ears based on the frequencies of sounds. Secondary areas of the temporal lobe then process the information into meaningful units, such as speech and words. The temporal lobe also houses the visual association areas that interpret the meaning of visual stimuli and help us recognize common objects in the environment (Martin, 2007).

FRONTAL LOBE A region of the cerebral cortex that has specialized areas for movement, abstract thinking, planning, memory and judgement.

The frontal lobe, which sits behind the forehead, *has specialized areas for movement, abstract thinking, planning, memory and judgement*. As you just read, it contains the motor cortex, which coordinates movements of muscle groups throughout the body. Other areas in the frontal lobe coordinate thought processes that help us manipulate information and retrieve memories, which we can use to plan our behaviours and interact socially with others. In short, the frontal cortex allows us to do the kind of thinking, imagining, planning and anticipating that sets humans apart from most other species (Stuss and Benson, 1986).

ASSOCIATION AREAS Areas of the cerebral cortex that are composed of neurons that help provide sense and meaning to information registered in the cortex.

PRIMARY VISUAL CORTEX The outermost layer of the occipital lobe area where visual information is processed.

The third level of organization in the cerebral cortex involves the representation of information within specific lobes in the cortex. There is a hierarchy of processing stages from primary areas that handle fine details of information all the way up to association areas, which are *composed of neurons that help provide sense and meaning to information registered in the cortex*. For example, neurons in the primary visual cortex, *the outermost layer of the occipital lobe area where visual information is processed*, are highly specialized – some detect features of the environment that are in a horizontal orientation, others detect movement, and still others process information about human versus nonhuman forms. The association areas of the occipital lobe interpret the information extracted by these primary areas – shape, motion and so on – to make sense of what's being perceived: in this case, perhaps a large cat leaping towards your face. Similarly, neurons in the primary auditory cortex, *the outermost layer of the temporal lobe area where auditory information is processed*, register sound frequencies, but it's the association areas of the temporal lobe that allow you to turn those noises into the meaning of your friend screaming, 'Look out for the cat!' Association areas, then, help stitch together the threads of information in the various parts of the cortex to produce a meaningful understanding of what's being registered in the brain. Neurons in the association areas are usually less specialized and more flexible than neurons in the primary areas. As such, they can be shaped by learning and experience to do their job more effectively. This kind of shaping of neurons by environmental forces allows the brain flexibility, or 'plasticity', our next topic.

PRIMARY AUDITORY CORTEX The outermost layer of the temporal lobe area where auditory information is processed.

Brain plasticity

The cerebral cortex may seem like a fixed structure, one big sheet of neurons designed to help us make sense of our external world. Remarkably, though, sensory cortices are not fixed. They can adapt to changes in sensory inputs, a quality researchers call *plasticity*, that is, the ability to be moulded. As an example, if you lose your middle finger in an accident, the part of the somatosensory area that represents that finger is initially unresponsive (Kaas, 1991). After all, there's no longer any sensory input going from that location to that part of the brain. You might expect the 'left middle finger neurons' of the somatosensory cortex to wither away. However, over time, that area in the somatosensory cortex becomes responsive to stimulation of the fingers *adjacent* to the missing finger. The brain is plastic: functions that were assigned to certain areas of the brain may be capable of being reassigned to other areas of the brain to accommodate changing input from the environment. This suggests that sensory inputs 'compete' for representation in each cortical area. (See *the real world* box for a striking illustration of 'phantom limbs'.)

the real world

Brain plasticity and sensations in phantom limbs

Long after a limb is amputated, many patients continue to experience sensations where the missing limb would be, a phenomenon called *phantom limb syndrome*. Patients can feel their missing limbs moving, even in coordinated gestures such as shaking hands. Some even report feeling pain in their phantom limbs. Why does this happen? Some evidence suggests that phantom limb syndrome may arise in part because of plasticity in the brain.

Researchers stimulated the skin surface in various regions around the face, torso and arms while monitoring brain activity in amputees and non-amputated volunteers (Ramachandran and Blakeslee, 1998; Ramachandran et al., 1992). Brain-imaging techniques displayed the somatosensory cortical areas activated when the skin was stimulated. This allowed the researchers to map how touch is represented in the somatosensory cortex for different areas of the body. For example, when the face was touched, the researchers could determine which areas in the somatosensory cortex were most active, and when the torso was stimulated, they could see which areas responded, and so on.

Brain scans of the amputees revealed that stimulating areas of the face and upper arm activated an area in the somatosensory cortex that previously would have been activated by a now-missing hand. The face and arm were represented in the somatosensory cortex in an area adjacent to where the person's hand now amputated – would have been represented. Stimulating the face or arm produced phantom limb sensations in the amputees; they reported 'feeling' a sensation in their missing limbs.

Brain plasticity can explain these results (Pascual-Leone et al., 2005). The cortical representations for the face and the upper arm normally lie on either side of the representation for the hand. The somatosensory areas for the face and upper arm were larger in amputees and had taken over the part of the cortex normally representing the hand. Indeed, the new face and arm representations were now adjacent to each other, filling in the space occupied by the hand representation. Some of these new mappings were quite concise. For example, in some amputees, when specific areas of the facial skin were activated, the patient reported sensations in just *one finger* of the phantom hand.

This and related research suggest one explanation for a previously poorly understood phenomenon. How can a person 'feel' something that isn't there? Brain plasticity, an adaptive process through which the brain reorganizes itself, offers an answer (Flor et al., 2006). The brain established new mappings that led to novel sensations.

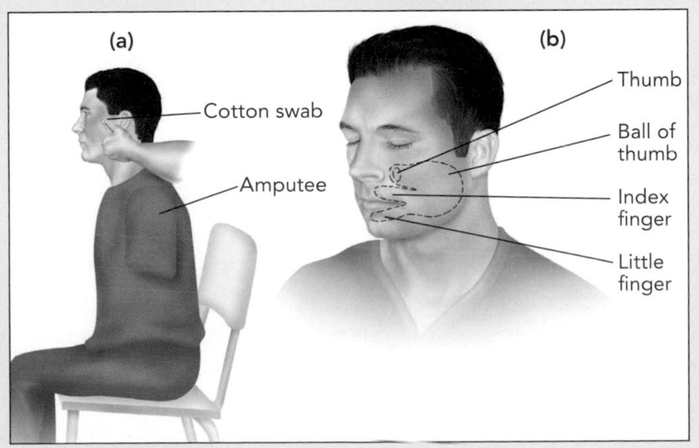

Mapping sensations in phantom limbs (a) Researchers lightly touch an amputee's face with a cotton swab, eliciting sensations in the 'missing' hand. (b) Touching different parts of the cheek can even result in sensations in particular fingers or the thumb of the missing hand.

Plasticity doesn't only occur to compensate for missing digits or limbs, however. An extraordinary amount of stimulation of one finger can result in that finger 'taking over' the representation of the part of the cortex that usually represents other, adjacent fingers (Merzenich et al., 1990). For example, right-handed violinists have an asymmetry in their motor and somatosensory cortex, with greater activity for the region that represents the left hand, which is more dexterous than the right hand (Schwenkreis et al., 2007).

This asymmetry is absent in non-musicians and appears to be related to the finger movements. Similar findings have been obtained with quilt-makers, who may have highly developed areas for the thumb and forefinger, which are critical to their profession, and London taxi drivers, who have overdeveloped brain areas in the hippocampus that are used during spatial navigation (Maguire et al., 2006). If you are not driving a taxi but rather running around London, then there is a good chance that you will be increasing the connectivity in your brain. Studies of rats and other nonhuman animals indicate that exercise such as this increases the number of synapses and promotes the development of new neurons in the hippocampus (Hillman et al., 2008; van Praag, 2009).

This would also appear to be true for humans who undertake cardiovascular exercise (Colcombe et al., 2006). A meta-analysis of 18 intervention studies indicates that the most robust effects were on executive functions, which we discuss later (Colcombe and Kramer, 2003). Some researchers believe this activity-dependent brain plasticity is relevant to treating spinal cord injuries to maximize rehabilitation (Dunlop, 2008).

You will read much more on plasticity in Chapter 11 when we consider the developing mind and the role of action. However, whether it is plasticity in response to brain injury in adults or changing connections in developing brains of young children, both appear to reflect a general principle in neuroscience known as 'use it or lose it'. In other words, for neuronal connections to form and be maintained, they require appropriate stimulation from other neurons or they die off (Shors et al., 2012).

In summary, neurons make up nerves, which in turn form the human nervous system. The nervous system is divided into the peripheral and the central nervous system. The peripheral nervous system connects the central nervous system with the rest of the body, and is itself divided into the somatic nervous system and the autonomic nervous system. The somatic nervous system, which conveys information into and out of the central nervous system, controls voluntary muscles, whereas the autonomic nervous system automatically controls the body's organs. The autonomic nervous system is further divided into the sympathetic and parasympathetic nervous systems, which complement each other in their effects on the body. The sympathetic nervous system prepares the body for action in threatening situations, and the parasympathetic nervous system returns it to its normal state.

The central nervous system is composed of the spinal cord and the brain. The spinal cord can mediate some basic behaviours such as spinal reflexes without input from the brain. The brain can be divided into the hindbrain, midbrain and forebrain. The hindbrain generally coordinates information coming into and out of the spinal cord with structures such as the medulla, the reticular formation, the cerebellum and the pons. These structures respectively coordinate breathing and heart rate, regulate sleep and arousal levels, coordinate fine motor skills, and communicate this information to the cortex. The midbrain, with the help of structures such as the tectum and tegmentum, generally coordinates functions such as orientation to the environment and movement and arousal towards sensory stimuli. The forebrain generally coordinates higher level functions, such as perceiving, feeling and thinking. The forebrain houses subcortical structures, such as the thalamus, hypothalamus, limbic system (including the hippocampus and amygdala) and basal ganglia; all these structures perform a variety of functions related to motivation and emotion. The cerebral cortex, composed of two hemispheres with four lobes each (occipital, parietal, temporal and frontal), performs tasks that help make us fully human: thinking, planning, judging, perceiving and behaving purposefully and voluntarily. Finally, neurons in the brain can be shaped by experience and the environment, making the human brain amazingly plastic.

The evolution and development of nervous systems

One other way to understand the organization of the human nervous system is to consider how it has evolved and adapted from those of other species. This approach helps us to understand how the human brain came to be the way it is, which is surprisingly imperfect. Far from being a single, elegant machine – the 'enchanted loom' philosophers wrote so poetically about – the human brain is instead a system composed of many distinct components that have been added at different times during the course of evolution. The human species has retained what worked best in earlier versions of the brain, then added bits and pieces to get us to our present state through evolution. In this section, we'll look at that process of evolution, and its effect on the development of the human brain and nervous system. Then, we'll look at how genetics and the environment affect the development of the nervous system.

Evolutionary development of the central nervous system

The central nervous system evolved from the very simple one found in simple animals to the elaborate nervous system in humans today. Even the simplest animals have sensory neurons and motor neurons for responding to the environment (Shepherd, 1988). For example, single-celled protozoa have molecules in their cell membrane that are sensitive to food in the water. These molecules trigger the movement of tiny threads called *cilia*, which help propel the protozoa towards the food source. The first neurons appeared in simple invertebrates, such as jellyfish; the sensory neurons in the jellyfish's tentacles can feel the touch of a potentially dangerous predator, which prompts the jellyfish to swim to safety. If you're a jellyfish, this simple neural system is sufficient to keep you alive.

The first central nervous system worthy of the name, though, appeared in flatworms. The flatworm has a collection of neurons in the head – a simple kind of brain – that includes sensory neurons for vision and taste and motor neurons that control feeding behaviour. Emerging from the brain are a pair of tracts that form a spinal cord. They are connected by *commissures*, neural fibres that cross between the left and right side of the nervous system to allow communication between neurons at symmetrical positions on either side of the body. The tracts are also connected by smaller collections of neurons called *ganglia*, which integrate information and coordinate motor behaviour in the body region near each ganglion.

During the course of evolution, a major split in the organization of the nervous system occurred between invertebrate animals (those without a spinal column) and vertebrate animals (those with a spinal column). The central nervous system of invertebrates continued along the 'flatworm plan', but the nervous system in vertebrates changed dramatically.

In all vertebrates, the central nervous system is a single tubular structure, and the brain is a series of expansions of the tube that forms in the embryo. Also, the central nervous system in vertebrates separates sensory and motor processing. Sensory processing occurs mainly in the back of the brain and spinal cord, whereas motor coordination is controlled by the front of the brain and spinal cord, although as you have already seen, there is considerable communication between the sensory and motor areas. Furthermore, the central nervous system is organized into a hierarchy: the lower levels of the brain and spinal cord execute simpler functions, while the higher levels of the nervous system perform more complex functions. As you saw earlier, in humans, reflexes are accomplished in the spinal cord. At the next level, the midbrain executes the more complex task of orienting towards an important stimulus in the environment. Finally, a more complex task, such as imagining what your life will be like 20 years from now, is performed in the forebrain (Addis et al., 2007; Szpunar et al., 2007).

The forebrain undergoes further evolutionary advances in vertebrates. In lower vertebrate species such as amphibians (frogs and newts), the forebrain consists only of small clusters of neurons. In higher vertebrates, including reptiles, birds and mammals, the forebrain is much larger, and it evolves in two different patterns. In reptiles and birds, large groups of neurons form the *striatum*, which controls their most complex behaviours. Birds, in particular, have almost no cerebral cortex, but their striatum is developed enough to control complex behavioural patterns, including learning, song production, social behaviour and reproductive behaviour (Farries, 2004). The striatum is also fairly well developed in mammals, but even more impressive is the cerebral cortex, which develops multiple areas that serve a broad range of higher mental functions. This forebrain development has reached its peak – so far – in humans.

The human brain, then, is not so much one remarkable thing, rather, it is a succession of extensions from a quite serviceable foundation. Like other species, humans have a hindbrain, and like those species, it performs important tasks to keep us alive. For some species, that's sufficient. All flatworms need to do to ensure their species' survival is eat, reproduce and stay alive a reasonable length of time. But as the human brain evolved, structures in the midbrain and forebrain developed to handle the increasingly complex demands of the environment. The forebrain of a frog is about as differentiated as it needs to be to survive in a frog's world. The human forebrain, however, shows substantial refinement, which allows for some remarkable, uniquely human abilities: self-awareness, sophisticated language use, social interaction, abstract reasoning, imagining and empathy, among others.

There is intriguing evidence that the human brain evolved more quickly than the brains of other species (Dorus et al., 2004). Researchers compared the sequences of 200 brain-related genes in mice, rats, monkeys and humans and discovered a collection of genes that evolved more rapidly among primates. What's more, they found that this evolutionary process was more rapid along the lineage that led to humans, that is, primate brains evolved quickly compared to those of other species, but the brains of the primates who eventually became humans evolved even more rapidly. These results suggest that in addition to the normal adaptations that occur over the process of evolution, the genes for human brains took particular advantage of a variety of mutations (changes in a gene's DNA) along the evolutionary pathway. These results also suggest that the human brain is still evolving – becoming bigger and more adapted to the demands of the environment (Evans et al., 2005; Mekel-Bobrov et al., 2005).

Genes may direct the development of the brain on a large, evolutionary scale, but they also guide the development of an individual and, generally, the development of a species. Let's take a brief look at how genes and the environment contribute to the biological bases of behaviour.

Genes and the environment

In Chapter 1 we encountered 'nature versus nurture', as though these twin influences grapple with each other for supremacy in directing a person's behaviour. This suggests that either genetics ('nature') or the environment ('nurture') played a major role in producing particular behaviours, personality traits, psychological disorders, or pretty much any other thing that a human does. The emerging picture from current research is that both nature *and* nurture play a role in directing behaviour, and the focus has shifted to examining the relative contributions of each influence rather than the absolute contributions of either influence alone. In short, it's the interaction of genes and environmental influences that determines what humans do (Gottesman and Hanson, 2005; Rutter and Silberg, 2002). We return to this issue in much greater depth in Chapter 11, but for the moment let us consider the basics of genetic transmission.

What are genes?

Genes are chemical molecules of deoxyribonucleic acid (DNA) encoded within each living cell that carry information about how to build bodies. The gene is *the unit of hereditary transmission* that instructs the cell what to become. They do this by building proteins from amino acids, which in turn are made from combinations of atoms of carbon, hydrogen, oxygen and nitrogen. Every cell in the body has thousands of proteins and DNA determines what type a cell is and how it operates by regulating the production of proteins. Genes are like books in a library that contain information that needs to be read or transcribed in order to build the proteins. The proteins instruct the cell to become anything from hair follicles while others can turn them into neurons. This is a simplistic account and there is considerably more to the story of the mechanism of genes but it is sufficient to know that genes are like sequences of computer code within the cell that control its operation.

> **GENE** The unit of hereditary transmission.

Genes are built from strands of DNA and are organized into large threads called chromosomes – *strands of DNA wound around each other in a double-helix configuration* (see **FIGURE 3.21**). Chromosomes come in pairs, and humans have 23 pairs each. These pairs of chromosomes are similar but not identical: you inherit one of each pair from your father and one from your mother. There's a twist, however: the selection of *which* of each pair is given to you is random.

> **CHROMOSOMES** Strands of DNA wound around each other in a double-helix configuration.

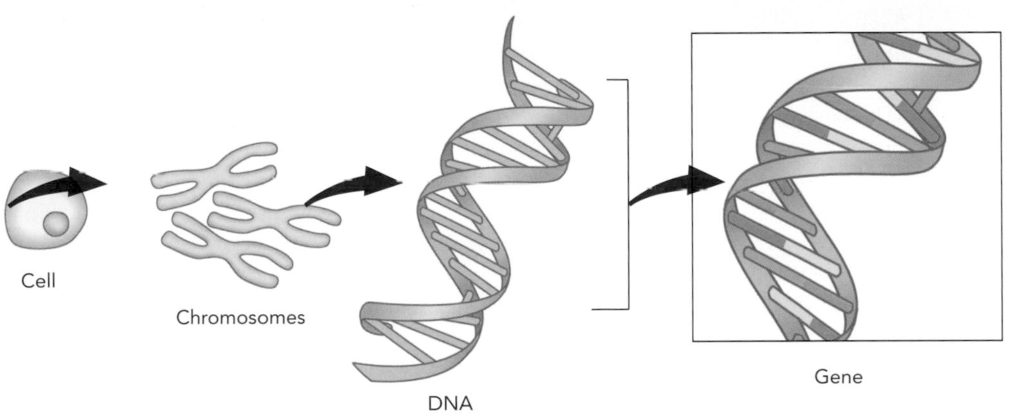

FIGURE 3.21 Genes, chromosomes and their recombination The cell nucleus houses chromosomes, which are made up of double-helix strands of DNA. Every cell in our bodies has 23 pairs of chromosomes. Genes are segments on a strand of DNA with codes that make us who we are.

Perhaps the most striking example of this random distribution is the determination of sex. The chromosomes that determine sex are the X and Y chromosomes; females have two X chromosomes, whereas males have one X and one Y chromosome. You inherited an X chromosome from your mother since she has only X chromosomes to give. Your biological sex, therefore, was determined by whether you received an additional X chromosome or Y chromosome from your father.

There is considerable variability in the genes that individual offspring receive. Nonetheless, children share a higher proportion of their genes with their parents than with more distant relatives or non-relatives. Children share half their genes with each parent, a quarter of their genes with their grandparents, an eighth of their genes with cousins and so on. The probability of sharing genes is called *degree of relatedness*. The most genetically related people are *monozygotic twins* (*identical twins*), who develop from the splitting of a single fertilized egg and therefore share 100% of their genes. *Dizygotic twins* (*fraternal twins*) develop from two separate fertilized eggs and share 50% of their genes, the same as any two siblings born separately.

Many researchers have tried to determine the relative influence of genetics on behaviour. One way to do this is to compare a trait shown by monozygotic twins with that same trait among dizygotic twins. This type of research usually enlists twins who were raised in the same household, so that the impact of their environment – their socioeconomic status, access to education, parental child-rearing practices, environmental stressors – remains relatively constant. Finding that monozygotic twins have a higher prevalence of a specific trait suggests a genetic influence (Boomsma et al., 2002).

As an example, the likelihood that the dizygotic twin of a person who has schizophrenia (a mental disorder we'll discuss in greater detail in Chapter 16) will *also* develop schizophrenia is 27%. However, this statistic rises to 50% for monozygotic twins. This observation suggests a substantial genetic influence on the likelihood of developing schizophrenia. Monozygotic twins share 100% of their genes, and if one assumes environmental influences are relatively consistent for both members of the twin pair, the 50% likelihood can be traced to genetic factors. That sounds scarily high, until you realize that the remaining 50% probability must be due to environmental influences. In short, genetics can contribute to the development, likelihood or onset of a variety of traits. But a more complete picture of genetic influences on behaviour must always take the environmental context into consideration. Genes express themselves within an environment, not in isolation.

Monozygotic siblings share 100% of their genes in common. Studies of monozygotic and dizygotic twins (or polyzygotic in the case of these triplets) help researchers estimate the relative contributions of genes and environmental influences on behaviour.

Epigenetics

There is a buzzword in science today called epigenetics – *the mechanisms of interaction between the environment and genes* – the way nature and nurture work together. Epigenetics provides answers to the sorts of common questions we all ask ourselves. Are we born mad, bad or sad, or is our personality determined by events in our lives? Why are our children so different when we try to treat them equally? Throughout this textbook, we talk about the role of our biology in the environment and epigenetic processes are the mechanism by which gene and experiences interact.

EPIGENETICS The mechanisms of interaction between the environment and genes.

Genes build humans and humans are very complex animals. Each body is made up of trillions of cells and the initial speculation was that humans must have a considerable number of genes to code for all the different arrangements of cells in our bodies. In 1990, scientists working on the human genome project began to map the entire sequence of genes for our species using sophisticated technology that enabled computers to read off the sequences as strings of code. Very soon, it appeared that initial estimates of over 100,000 genes had been way off. Although the project is still continuing, at the last count it would appear that humans have only 20,500 different genes. That may still sound like quite a few but when you consider that the humble fruit fly, *Drosophila melanogaster*, has 15,000 genes, humans look decidedly puny in the genetic endowment department.

The reason scientists initially overestimated the number of genes for humans was because the role of epigenetics was not yet fully appreciated. Moreover, it turns out that there is more information encoded in the few genes we have than is ever actually used. Only 2% of genes appear to be related to building proteins. This information is only activated when the gene becomes expressed and geneticists now understand that only a fraction of genes are expressed. In fact, gene expression is the exception and not the rule. The reason is that genes act like segments of computer code where there is an if-then instruction that is activated by experience. These experiences operate through a number of mechanisms but genetic methylation is typically one that *silences a gene and is believed to play a major role in long-term changes that shape our development*. If you think about genes like books in a library and the library is the full genome, then each gene can be read to build proteins. Methylation acts a bit like moving a book out of reach so the information to build proteins cannot be read or blocking access to it by placing some furniture in front of the book. The trigger to regulate genes by methylation can be any environmental input such as temperature, toxins and even others around us (see Chapter 11 on development and Chapter 17 on the effects of loneliness).

GENETIC METHYLATION A mechanism that silences a gene and is believed to play a major role in long-term changes that shape our development.

The role of environmental factors

Genes set the range of possibilities that can be observed in a population, but the characteristics of any individual within that range are determined by environmental factors and experience. Genetically, it's possible for humans to live comfortably 3,700 m above sea level. The residents of La Paz, Bolivia have done so for centuries. But chances are *you* wouldn't enjoy gasping for breath on a daily basis. Your environmental experiences have made it unlikely for you to live that way, just as the experience and environment of the citizens of La Paz have made living at high altitude quite acceptable. Genetically, you and the Bolivians come from the same species, but the range of genetic capabilities you share is not expressed in the same way. What's more, neither you nor a Bolivian can breathe underwater in Lake Titicaca, which is also 3,700 m above sea level. The genetic capabilities that another species might enjoy, such as breathing underwater, are outside the range of *your* possibilities, no matter how much you might desire them.

With these parameters in mind, behavioural geneticists use calculations based on relatedness to compute the heritability of behaviours (Plomin et al., 2001a, 2001b). Heritability is *a measure of the variability of behavioural traits among individuals that can be accounted for by genetic factors*. Heritability is calculated as a proportion, and its numerical value (index) ranges from 0 to 1.00. A heritability of 0 means that genes do not contribute to individual differences in the behavioural trait, while a heritability of 1.00 means that genes are the *only* reason for the individual differences. As you might guess, scores of 0 or 1.00 occur so infrequently that they serve more as theoretical limits than realistic values; almost nothing in human behaviour is completely due to the environment or owed *completely* to genetic inheritance. Scores between 0 and 1.00, then, indicate that individual differences are caused by varying degrees of genetic and environmental contributions – a little stronger influence of genetics here, a little stronger influence of the environment there, but each always within the context of the other.

HERITABILITY A measure of the variability of behavioural traits among individuals that can be accounted for by genetic factors.

For human behaviour, almost all estimates of heritability are in the moderate range, between 0.30 and 0.60. For example, a heritability index of 0.50 for intelligence indicates that half of the variability in intelligence test scores is attributable to genetic influences and the remaining half is due to environmental influences. Smart parents often (but not always) produce smart children: genetics certainly plays a role. But smart and not-so-smart children attend good or not-so-good schools, practise their piano lessons with more or less regularity, study or do not study as hard as they might, have good and not-so-good teachers and role models and so on. Genetics is only half the story in intelligence. Environmental influences also play a significant role in predicting the basis of intelligence (see Chapter 9).

Heritability has proved to be a theoretically useful and statistically sound concept in helping scientists understand the relative genetic and environmental influences on behaviour. However, there are four important points about heritability to bear in mind:

GETTY IMAGES/ISTOCKPHOTO THINKSTOCK IMAGES/TRILOK SINGH BANGARI

Heritability is calculated within a certain environmental context. Factors such as socioeconomic class, quality of schooling and social setting play an important part in determining intelligence, as well as genes.

1 Remember that *heritability is an abstract concept:* It tells us nothing about the *specific* genes that contribute to a trait. A heritability index of 0.40 gives us a reasonable approximation of the extent to which genes influence a behaviour, but it says nothing about *which* genes are responsible. Flipping that around also illustrates the point. Heritability of 0.40 means that there's also an 'environmentality' of 0.60 in predicting the behaviour in question. Most people would find it extremely difficult, however, to pinpoint what *one exact factor* in the environment contributed to that estimate. With further decoding of the human genome and a greater understanding of each gene's specific roles, scientists someday may be able to isolate the exact genes that contribute to a specific behaviour, but they have not yet attained that degree of precision.
2 *Heritability is a population concept:* It tells us nothing about an individual. For example, a 0.50 heritability of intelligence means that, on average, about 50% of the differences in intellectual performance are attributable to genetic differences among individuals in the population. It does *not* mean that 50% of any given person's intelligence is due to their genetic makeup. Heritability provides guidance for understanding differences across individuals in a population rather than abilities within an individual.
3 *Heritability is dependent on the environment:* Just as behaviour occurs within certain contexts, so do genetic influences. For example, intelligence isn't an unchanging quality: people are intelligent within a particular learning context, a social setting, a family environment, a socioeconomic class and so on. Heritability, therefore, is meaningful only for the environmental conditions in which it was computed, and heritability estimates may change dramatically under other environmental conditions. At present, heritability estimates for intelligence, to stick with our example, are computed across a range of environments and have a fair amount of stability. But if all the earth's population suddenly had access to better nutrition, higher quality schooling and good healthcare, that change in the environmental context would necessitate a recalculation of heritability within those contexts.
4 *Heritability is not fate:* It tells us nothing about the degree to which interventions can change a behavioural trait. Heritability is useful for identifying behavioural traits that are influenced by genes, but it is not useful for determining how individuals will respond to particular environmental conditions or treatments.

In summary, nervous systems evolved from simple collections of sensory and motor neurons in simple animals, such as flatworms, to elaborate centralized nervous systems found in mammals. The evolution of the human nervous system can be thought of as a process of refining, elaborating and expanding structures present in other species. In reptiles and birds, the highest processing area is the striatum, and in mammals, the highest processing area is the cerebral cortex. The human brain appears to have evolved more quickly compared to other species to become adapted to a more complex environment.

The gene, or the unit of hereditary transmission, is built from strands of DNA in a double-helix formation that is organized into chromosomes. Humans have 23 pairs of chromosomes – half come from each parent. A child shares 50% of their genes with each parent. Monozygotic twins share 100% of their genes, while dizygotic twins share 50%, the same as any other siblings. Because of their genetic relatedness, twins are often participants in genetic research.

The study of genetics indicates that genes and the environment work together to influence behaviour. Genes set the range of variation in populations within a given environment, but they do not predict individual characteristics; experience and other environmental factors play a crucial role as well.

Psychology and me

Kylie Pascua Leones, Assistant Psychologist, University College London Hospitals (UCLH)

Kylie Pascua Leones is an Assistant Psychologist at UCLH specializing in neuropsychology. Visit www.palgrave.com/schacter to watch Kylie talking about her work with children and adolescents living with chronic illness, administering neuropsychology assessments and co-facilitating therapeutic groups with professional psychologists. She also discusses how she overcame the challenges presented by her undergraduate psychology degree, and provides invaluable advice on obtaining voluntary positions and getting on to the career ladder.

Investigating the brain

So far, you've read a great deal about the nervous system: how it's organized, how it works, what its components are, and what those components do. But one question remains largely unanswered – *how* do we know all this? Anatomists can dissect a human brain and identify its structures, but they cannot determine which structures play a role in producing which behaviours by dissecting a nonliving brain. In this section, we'll look at some of the methods psychologists and neuroscientists have developed for linking brain structures with the thoughts, feelings and behaviours they direct.

Scientists use a variety of methods to understand how the brain affects behaviour. Let's consider three of the main ones: testing people with brain damage and observing their deficits; studying electrical activity in the brain during behaviour; and conducting brain scans while people perform various tasks. Studying people with brain damage highlights one of the central themes of this book: to better understand the normal operation of a process, it is instructive to understand what happens when that process fails. Observing the behavioural mindbugs that result from damage to certain areas of the brain enables researchers to identify the functions of those areas. The second approach, studying the brain's electrical activity, has a long history and has produced a wealth of information about which neurons fire when behaviour is enacted. The modern extensions of that technique are the various ways that the brain can be scanned, mapped and coded using a variety of sophisticated instruments, which is the third approach we'll consider. Let's examine each of these ways of investigating the brain.

Learning about brain organization by studying the damaged brain

Remember the Australian man at the beginning of the chapter who suddenly acquired problems recognizing himself in the mirror? Much research in neuroscience correlates the loss of specific perceptual, motor, emotional or cognitive functions with specific areas of brain damage (Andrewes, 2001; Kolb and Whishaw, 2003). By studying these mindbugs, neuroscientists can theorize about the functions those brain areas normally perform. The modern history of neuroscience can be dated to the work of Paul Broca (see Chapter 1). In 1861, Broca described a patient who had lost the capacity to produce spoken language, but not the ability to understand language, due to damage in a small area in the left frontal lobe. In 1874, Carl Wernicke (1848–1905) described a patient with an impairment in language comprehension, but not the ability to produce speech, associated with damage to an area in the upper-left temporal lobe. These areas were named, respectively, *Broca's area* and *Wernicke's area*, and they provided the earliest evidence that the brain locations for speech production and speech comprehension are separate and that for most people, the left hemisphere is critical to producing and understanding language (Young, 1990).

The emotional functions of the frontal lobes

Alexander Laing, 31, a modern-day Phineas Gage, had a bright future ahead of him in the British Army before he had a skiing accident that damaged his frontal lobes. Initially, he was paralysed by the accident and unable to speak but he made a rapid recovery. Although he was no longer paralysed and without language, he was left with brain damage that left him extremely disinhibited. His personality was changed and he became obsessed with sex and unable to control his impulses. Alexander was one of the subjects of a 2006 TV documentary series sensitively entitled *Mindshock: Sex on the Brain.*

As you've already seen, the human frontal lobes are a remarkable evolutionary achievement. However, psychology's first glimpse at some functions of the frontal lobes came from a rather unremarkable fellow, so unremarkable, in fact, that a single event in his life defined his place in the annals of psychology's history (Macmillan, 2000). Phineas Gage was a muscular 25-year-old boss of the Rutland & Burlington Railroad excavating crew. On 13 September 1848, in Vermont in the US, he was packing an explosive charge into a crevice in a rock when disaster struck. Here is an account of the event in the words of John M. Harlow (1848), the doctor who examined him:

> The powder and fuse had been adjusted in the hole, and he was in the act of 'tamping it in,' as it is called ... While doing this, his attention was attracted by his men in the pit behind him. Averting his head and looking over his right shoulder, at the same instant

> dropping the iron upon the charge, it struck fire upon the rock, and the explosion followed, which projected the iron obliquely upwards ... passing completely through his head, and high into the air, falling to the ground several [metres] behind him, where it was afterwards picked up by his men, smeared with blood and brain.

In short, Phineas Gage had a metre-long, 6-kg iron rod propelled through his head at high speed. As **FIGURE 3.22** shows, the rod entered through his lower left jaw and exited through the middle top of his head. The most remarkable part of this story is that Gage lived to tell the tale. After the accident, Gage sat up, climbed in the back of a wagon and journeyed to town to seek medical treatment. He lived for another 12 years, residing in various parts of the US and abroad, even joining P. T. Barnum's museum of oddities for a brief stint. He died in 1860 after a series of seizures, whereupon his skull and the iron rod were donated to the Warren Anatomical Museum, Harvard Medical School, where they are still displayed today. Before the accident, Gage had been mild-mannered, quiet, conscientious, and a hard worker. After the accident, however, Gage's personality underwent a significant change. He became irritable, irresponsible, indecisive and given to profanity. The sad decline of Gage's personality and emotional life nonetheless provided an unexpected benefit to psychology. His case study was the first to allow researchers to investigate the hypothesis that the frontal lobe is involved in emotion regulation, planning and decision making. Furthermore, because the connections between the frontal lobe and the subcortical structures of the limbic system were affected, scientists were able to better understand how the amygdala, hippocampus and related brain structures interacted with the cerebral cortex (Damasio, 2005). Although the facts concerning Cage's pre- and post-injury behaviours have been called into question (Macmillan, 2008), his case still represents one of the most influential in the history of neuropsychology.

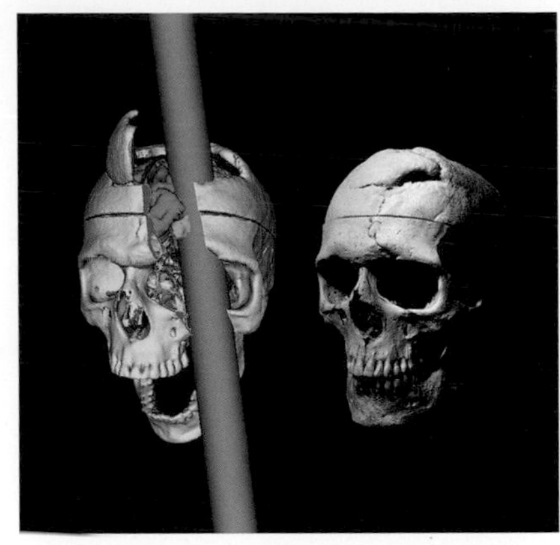

FIGURE 3.22 Phineas Gage Phineas Gage's traumatic accident allowed researchers to investigate the functions of the frontal lobe and its connections with emotion centres in the subcortical structures. The likely path of the metal rod through Gage's skull is reconstructed here.

The organizing functions of the frontal lobes: executive functions

Complex behaviours require different functions for planning, coordination and control – tasks that enlist the activity of the frontal lobes (Baddeley, 2002; Miyake et al., 2000). Rather than being localized in the frontal lobes, complex activities are integrated throughout this region like a neural junction box (Hebb, 1977). One way to think about the frontal lobes is to imagine their role like a senior executive management team overseeing a large company. To be successful, a company must operate economically without wasting too much time and resources. The company needs to be able to take stock of the market, estimate demands, monitor current resources and set into action a planned strategy. The company will need to anticipate economic changes and plan for the future. Although there may be subdivisions in the company that compete for more resources than others, they have to be regulated so that the company as a whole can be more successful. This is why we need executives to manage the various operations that make the business run more efficiently as well as competitively. These executive functions monitor, coordinate, regulate and plan our thoughts and actions. Planning, memory, inhibition and attention are four executive functions (EFs) that operate from within a region that sits back from the front part of the brain known as the *prefrontal cortex*. A prototypical executive function task is the Stroop task (Stroop, 1935), in which one needs to inhibit or override the tendency to produce a more dominant or automatic response (to name the colour word; see below) and has been linked to the frontal lobe function (see Jahanshahi et al., 1998; Kiefer et al., 1998).

The following Stroop task is a test of inhibitory control. Name the colour of ink each word is printed in as quickly as possible:

RED GREEN BLUE GREEN RED BLUE

No doubt you found that fairly easy but try naming the colours again:

RED GREEN BLUE GREEN RED BLUE

When the word and the colour of ink conflict there is interference, which makes it much harder to respond quickly because of the tendency to automatically read the word.

One useful distinction that has been made when considering the role of the prefrontal cortex is the difference between 'hot' and 'cool' EFs (Zelazo and Carlson, 2012). Hot EFs include those impulses and urges that are biological imperatives or emotionally charged drives that threaten to take over control of our thoughts and actions, whereas cool EFs are the logical choices one has to make when presented with a problem to solve that requires rationality. We use cool EFs when we have to remember a telephone number or a list of things to buy from the store. Most of us will repeat the information over and over to keep it fresh in our minds before we forget. If the list of items is too long, then we forget the beginning before we get to the end. The task is even harder if we have to remember two numbers or, worse still, someone starts talking to us when we are trying to concentrate. Cool EFs enable us to keep focus on the problem. In contrast, hot EFs interrupt ongoing events and make us switch priorities. When the danger signs are detected, the hot EFs swing into action to protect us.

The distinct roles of the left and right hemispheres

You'll recall that the cerebral cortex is divided into two hemispheres, although typically the two hemispheres act as one integrated unit. Sometimes, though, disorders can threaten the ability of the brain to function, and the only way to stop them is with radical methods. This is sometimes the case with patients who suffer from severe, intractable epilepsy. Seizures that begin in one hemisphere cross the corpus callosum (the thick band of nerve fibres that allows the two hemispheres to communicate) to the opposite hemisphere and start a feedback loop that results in a kind of firestorm in the brain.

To alleviate the severity of the seizures, surgeons can sever the corpus callosum in a procedure called a *split-brain operation* (technically known as a 'commisuratomy'). This meant that a seizure that starts in one hemisphere is isolated in that hemisphere since there is no longer a connection to the other side. This procedure helps patients with epilepsy but also produces some unusual, if not unpredictable, behaviours.

Nobel laureate Roger Sperry (1913–94) and his colleagues designed several experiments that investigated the behaviours of split-brain patients and in the process revealed a great deal about the independent functions of the left and right hemispheres (Sperry, 1964). Normally, any information that initially enters the left hemisphere is also registered in the right hemisphere and vice versa: the information comes in and travels across the corpus callosum, and both hemispheres understand what's going on. But in a split-brain patient, information entering one hemisphere stays there. Without an intact corpus callosum, there's no way for that information to reach the other hemisphere. Sperry and his colleagues used this understanding of lateralized perception in a series of experiments. For example, they had patients look at a spot in the centre of a screen and then projected a stimulus on one side of the screen, isolating the stimulus to one hemisphere.

The hemispheres themselves are specialized for different kinds of tasks. You just learned about Broca and Wernicke's areas, which revealed that language processing is a left-hemisphere activity. So, imagine that some information came into the left hemisphere of a split-brain patient, and she was asked to verbally describe what it was. This shouldn't be a problem: the left hemisphere has the information, it's the 'speaking' hemisphere, so the patient should be able to verbally describe what she saw. But suppose the patient was asked to reach behind a screen with her left hand and pick up the object she just saw. Remember that the hemispheres exert contralateral control over the body, meaning that the left hand is controlled by the right hemisphere. But this patient's right hemisphere has no clue what the object was because that information was received in the left hemisphere and was unable to travel to the right hemisphere. So, even though the split-brain patient saw the object and could verbally describe it, she would be unable to use the right hemisphere to perform other tasks regarding that object, such as correctly selecting it from a group with her left hand (see **FIGURE 3.23**).

Of course, information presented to the right hemisphere would produce complementary deficits. In this case, a patient might be presented with a familiar object in her left hand (such as a key), be able to demonstrate that she knew what it was (by twisting and turning the key in midair), yet be unable to verbally describe what she was holding. In this case, the information in the right hemisphere is unable to travel to the left hemisphere, which controls the production of speech.

Furthermore, suppose a split-brain person was shown the unusual face in **FIGURE 3.24**. This is called a *chimeric face*, and it is assembled from half-face components of the full faces also shown in the figure. When asked to indicate which face was presented, a split-brain person would indicate that she saw *both* faces because information about the face on the left is recorded in the right hemisphere and information about the face on the right is recorded in the left hemisphere (Levy et al., 1972).

These split-brain studies reveal that the two hemispheres perform different functions and can work together seamlessly as long as the corpus callosum is intact. Without a way to transmit information from one hemisphere to the other, information gets 'stuck' in the hemisphere it initially entered and we become acutely aware of the different functions of each hemisphere. Of course, a split-brain patient can adapt to this by simply moving her eyes a little so that the same information independently enters both hemispheres. Split-brain studies have continued over the past few decades and continue to play an important role in shaping our understanding of how the brain works (Gazzaniga, 2006).

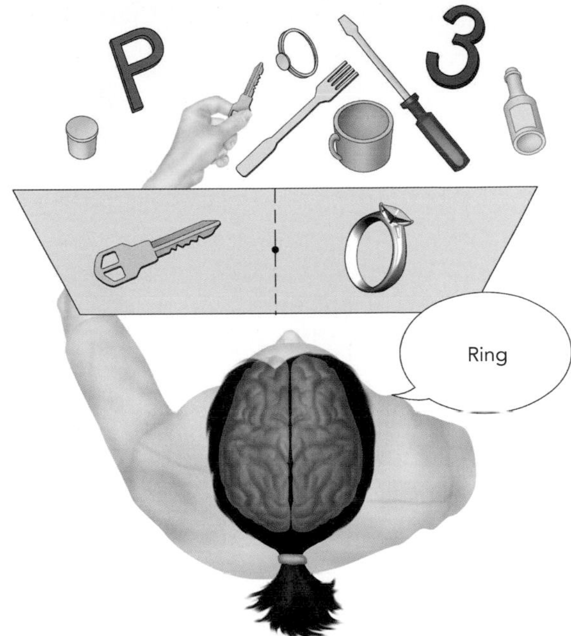

FIGURE 3.23 Split-brain experiment When a split-brain patient is presented with the picture of a ring on the right and a key on the left side of a screen, she can verbalize *ring*, but not *key* because the left hemisphere 'sees' the ring and language is usually located in the left hemisphere. This patient would be able to choose a key with her left hand from a set of objects behind a screen. She would not, however, be able to pick out a ring with her right hand since what the left hemisphere 'sees' is not communicated to the right side of her body.

Listening to the brain: single neurons and the EEG

A second approach to studying the link between brain structures and behaviour involves recording the pattern of electrical activity of neurons. An **electroencephalogram (EEG)** is *a device used to record electrical activity in the brain*. Typically, electrodes are placed on the outside of the head, and even though the source of electrical activity in synapses and action potentials is far removed from these wires, the electric signals can be amplified several thousand times by the EEG. This provides a visual record of the underlying electrical activity, as shown in **FIGURE 3.25**. Using this technique, researchers can determine the amount of brain activity during different states of consciousness. For example, as you'll read in Chapter 8, the brain shows distinctive patterns of electrical activity when awake versus asleep; in fact, there are even different brain-wave patterns associated with different stages of sleep. EEG recordings allow researchers to make these fundamental discoveries about the nature of sleep and wakefulness (Dement, 1974). The EEG can also be used to examine the brain's electrical activity when awake individuals engage in a variety of psychological functions, such as perceiving, learning and remembering.

ELECTROENCEPHALOGRAM (EEG) A device used to record electrical activity in the brain.

A different approach to recording electrical activity resulted in a more refined understanding of the brain's division of responsibilities, even at a cellular level. Nobel laureates David Hubel and Torsten Wiesel (1962) used a technique that inserted electrodes into the occipital lobes of anaesthetized cats and observed the patterns of action potentials of individual neurons. Hubel and Wiesel amplified the action potential signals through a loudspeaker so that the signals could be heard as clicks as well as seen on an oscilloscope. While flashing lights in front of the animal's eye, they recorded the resulting activity of neurons in the occipital cortex. What they discovered was not much of anything: most of the neurons did not respond to this kind of general stimulation.

Nearing the end of what seemed like a failed set of experiments, Hubel and Wiesel projected a glass slide that contained a shadow (caused by the edge of the slide) to show an image in front of the cat's eyes, reasoning that the flaw wouldn't make much

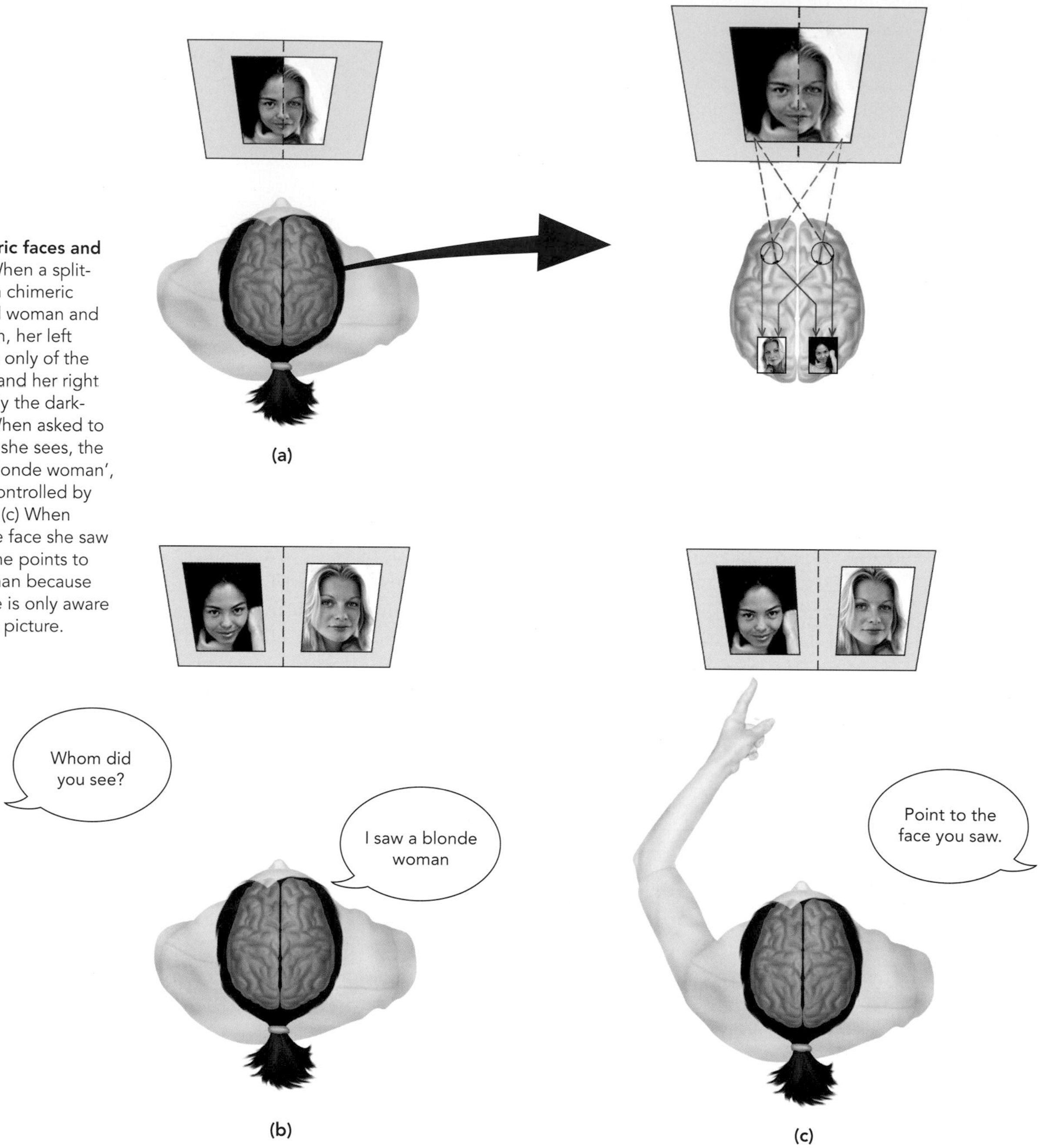

(a)

Whom did you see?

I saw a blonde woman

(b)

Point to the face you saw.

(c)

FIGURE 3.24 Chimeric faces and the split brain (a) When a split-brain patient views a chimeric face of a dark-haired woman and a light-haired woman, her left hemisphere is aware only of the light-haired woman and her right hemisphere sees only the dark-haired woman. (b) When asked to describe the person she sees, the patient answers 'a blonde woman', because speech is controlled by the left hemisphere. (c) When asked to point to the face she saw with her left hand, she points to the dark-haired woman because her right hemisphere is only aware of the left half of the picture.

BANANASTOCK/PUNCHSTOCK

GETTY IMAGES/ISTOCKPHOTO THINKSTOCK IMAGES/LATSALOMAO

FIGURE 3.25 The EEG The EEG records electrical activity in the brain. Many states of consciousness, such as wakefulness and stages of sleep, are characterized by particular types of brain waves.

difference to the already unimpressive experimental outcomes. Instead, they heard a brisk flurry of clicks as the neurons in the cat's occipital lobe fired away. They discovered that neurons in the primary visual cortex are activated whenever a contrast between light and dark occurs in part of the visual field, seen particularly well when the visual stimulus was a thick line of light against a dark background. In this case, the shadow caused by the edge of the slide provided the kind of contrast that prompted particular neurons to respond. They then found that each neuron responded vigorously only when presented with a contrasting edge at a particular orientation. Since then, many studies have shown that neurons in the primary visual cortex represent particular features of visual stimuli, such as contrast, shape and colour (Zeki, 1993).

These neurons in the visual cortex are known as *feature detectors* because they selectively respond to certain aspects of a visual image. For example, some neurons fire only when detecting a vertical line in the middle of the visual field, other neurons fire when a line at a 45^0 angle is perceived, and still others in response to wider lines, horizontal lines, lines in the periphery of the visual field and so on (Livingstone and Hubel, 1988). The discovery of this specialized function for neurons was a huge leap forward in our understanding of how the visual cortex works. Feature detectors identify basic dimensions of a stimulus ('slanted line ... other slanted line ... horizontal line'); those dimensions are then combined during a later stage of visual processing to allow recognition and perception of a stimulus ('oh, it's a letter A').

Other studies have identified a variety of features that are detected by sensory neurons. For example, some visual processing neurons in the temporal lobe are activated only when detecting faces (Kanwisher, 2000; Perrett et al., 1982). When neurons in this region are damaged, the patient may lose the ability to perceive faces, producing a condition known as *prosopagnosia*, which means 'without knowledge of faces' (Kleinschmidt and Cohen, 2006). When the visual processing of the input is intact but the patient fails to recognize what it is they are looking at, they have symptoms of *agnosia*, a term that means 'without knowledge'. These observations – showing that the type of function that is lost or altered when a brain area is damaged corresponds to the kind of information processed by neurons in that cortical area – provide the most compelling evidence linking the brain to the different components that make up our mental life. They prove that the mind–body dualism proposed by Descartes that we encountered in Chapter 1 must be wrong even though most of us naturally think of our mind as separate to our brain and body (Bloom, 2004).

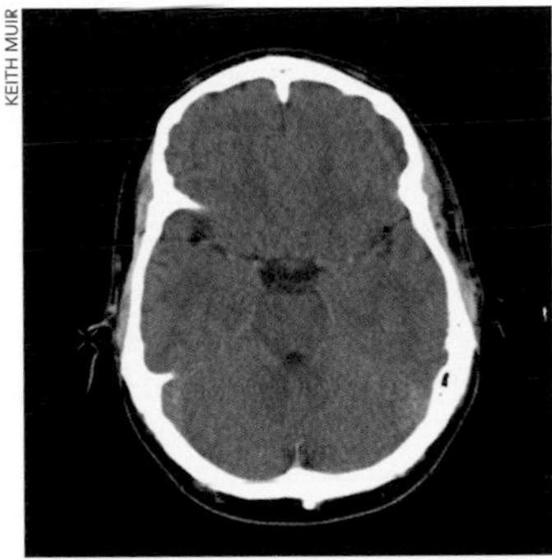
KEITH MUIR

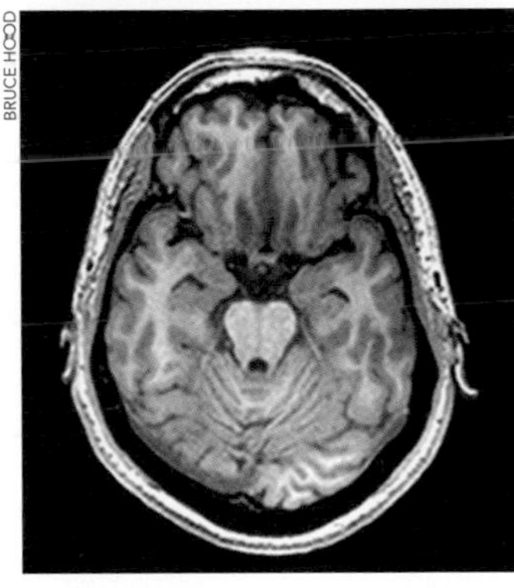
BRUCE HOOD

FIGURE 3.26 Structural imaging techniques (CT and MRI) CT (above) and MRI (below) scans are used to provide information about the structure of the brain and can help to spot tumours and other kinds of damage. Each scan shown here provides a snapshot of a single slice in the brain. Note that the MRI scan provides a clearer, higher resolution image than the CT scan. The MRI image is of Bruce Hood's brain, just to confirm that he has one despite what his colleagues might say!

Brain imaging: from visualizing structure to watching the brain in action

The third major way that neuroscientists can peer into the workings of the human brain has only become possible within the past few decades. EEG readouts give an overall picture of a person's level of consciousness, and single-cell recordings shed light on the actions of particular clumps of neurons. The ideal of neuroscience, however, has been the ability to see the brain in operation while behaviour is being enacted. This goal has been steadily achieved thanks to a wide range of *neuroimaging techniques* that use advanced technology to create images of the living, healthy brain (Posner and Raichle, 1994; Raichle and Mintun, 2006).

Structural brain imaging

One of the first neuroimaging techniques developed was the computerized axial tomography (CT) scan – *a technique that recombines multiple X-ray photographs into a single image*. In a CT scan, a scanner rotates a device around a person's head and takes a series of X-ray photographs from different angles. Computer programs then combine these images to provide views from any angle. CT scans show different densities of tissue in the brain. For example, the higher density skull looks white on a CT scan, the cortex shows up as grey, and the least dense fissures and ventricles in the brain look dark (see FIGURE 3.26). CT scans are used to locate lesions or tumours, which typically appear darker since they are less dense than the cortex.

COMPUTERIZED AXIAL TOMOGRAPHY (CT) A technique that recombines multiple X-ray photographs into a single image.

stats facts

The dead fish study

A full-length Atlanta salmon lay in the scanner and was asked to determine which emotions people might be experiencing in different social settings shown on the screen. The salmon did not respond because it was a fish after all, and second it was quite dead. Nevertheless, fMRI images of the salmon's head revealed clear activity in the brain region. The purpose of this bizarre study by neuroscientist Craig Bennett and his colleagues (2009) was not simply a joke, but a critical review of the way some fMRI studies might be producing spurious findings based on inadequate methodologies. A typical fMRI scan produces thousands of data points for comparison that will generate many false-positive signals (see Type 1 errors in Chapter 2) unless corrected for using statistical procedures, which is why the dead salmon's brain appeared to be active. This report is important because it reminds us that brain scans are not actually pictures of the brain but rather simulations of the activity based on statistical analysis that can be subject to distortions and random effects. The image of different brain areas lighting up is one that is generated because it is easier to visualize the activity rather than interpreting millions of data points.

Magnetic resonance imaging (MRI) is *a technique that uses a powerful magnet to cause charged molecules in soft tissue to realign to produce measureable field distortions*. For very short periods, these brief but powerful magnetic pulses cause molecules in the brain tissue to twist slightly and then relax, which releases a small amount of energy. Differently charged molecules respond differently to the magnetic pulses, so the energy signals reveal brain structures with different molecular compositions. MRI produces pictures of soft tissue at a better resolution than a CT scan, as you can see in **FIGURE 3.26**. These techniques give psychologists a clearer picture of the structure of the brain and can help localize brain damage, as when someone suffers a stroke, but they reveal nothing about the functions of the brain.

Functional brain imaging

Two newer techniques show researchers much more than just the structure of the brain. *Functional brain-imaging* techniques allow us to actually watch the brain in action. These techniques rely on the fact that activated brain areas demand more energy for their neurons to work. This energy is supplied through increased blood flow to the activated areas. Functional imaging techniques can detect such changes in blood flow. Positron emission tomography (PET) is *a technique that uses radioactive markers to measure blood flow in the brain*. A harmless radioactive substance is injected into a person's bloodstream and then the brain is scanned by radiation detectors as the person performs perceptual or cognitive tasks, such as reading or speaking. Areas of the brain that are activated during these tasks demand more energy and greater blood flow, resulting in a higher amount of the radioactivity in that region. The radiation detectors record the level of radioactivity in each region, producing a computerized image of the activated areas (see **FIGURE 3.27**). Note that PET scans differ from CT scans and MRIs, in that the image produced shows activity in the brain while the person performs certain tasks. So, for example, a PET scan of a person speaking would show activation in Broca's area in the left frontal lobe.

For psychologists, the most widely used functional brain-imaging technique nowadays is functional magnetic resonance imaging (fMRI) – *a technique that uses a powerful magnet to cause haemoglobin molecules to realign to measure blood flow in the brain*. Haemoglobin is the molecule in the blood that carries oxygen to our tissues, including the brain. When active neurons demand more energy and blood flow, oxygenated haemoglobin concentrates in the active areas, fMRI detects the oxygenated haemoglobin and provides a picture of the level of activation in each brain area (see **FIGURE 3.27**). Just as MRI was a major advance over CT scans, *functional* MRI represents a similar leap in our ability to record the brain's activity during behaviour. Both fMRI and PET allow researchers to accurately localize changes in the brain. However, fMRI has a couple of advantages over PET. First, fMRI does not require any exposure to a radioactive substance. Second, fMRI can localize changes in brain activity across briefer periods than PET, which makes it more useful for analysing psychological processes that occur extremely quickly, such as reading a word or recognizing a face. With PET, researchers often have to use experimental designs different from those they would use in the psychological laboratory in order to adapt to the limitations of PET technology. With fMRI, researchers can design experiments that more closely resemble the ones they carry out in the psychological laboratory.

Insights from functional imaging

PET and fMRI provide remarkable insights into the types of information processing that take place in specific areas of the brain. For example, when a person performs a simple perceptual task, such as looking at a chessboard, the primary visual areas are activated. When the chessboard is presented to the left visual field, the right visual cortex shows activation, and when the chessboard is presented to the right visual field, the left visual cortex shows activation (Fox et al., 1986). Similarly, when people look at faces, fMRI reveals strong activity in a region in the visual association cortex called the *fusiform gyrus* (Kanwisher et al., 1997). When this structure is damaged, people experience problems with recognizing faces, as we saw in the opening vignette. Finally, when people perform a task that engages emotional processing, for example looking at sad pictures, researchers

MAGNETIC RESONANCE IMAGING (MRI) A technique that uses a powerful magnet to cause charged molecules in soft tissue to realign to produce measureable field distortions.

POSITRON EMISSION TOMOGRAPHY (PET) A technique that uses radioactive markers to measure blood flow in the brain.

FUNCTIONAL MAGNETIC RESONANCE IMAGING (FMRI) A technique that uses a powerful magnet to cause haemoglobin molecules to realign to measure blood flow in the brain.

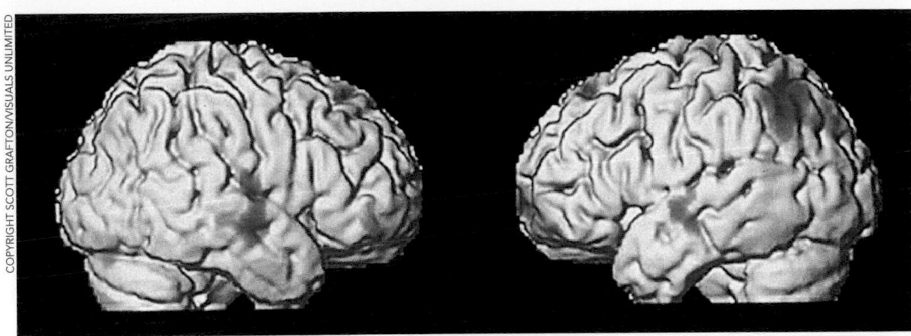

(a) Gesture preparation

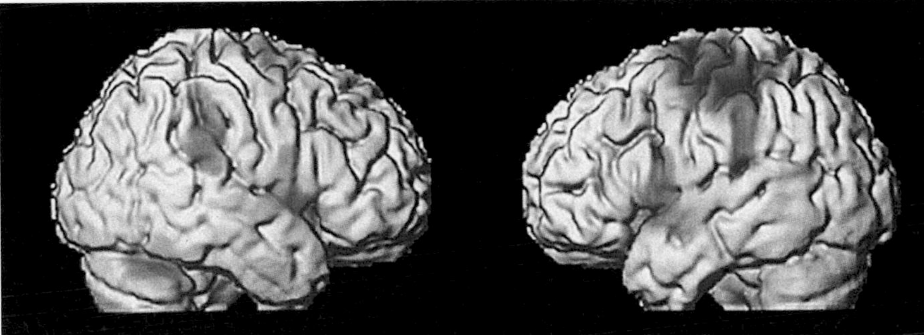

(b) Gesture production

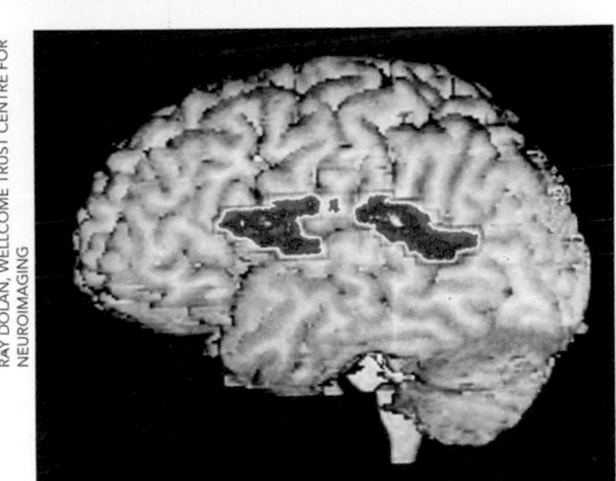

FIGURE 3.27 Functional imaging techniques (PET and fMRI) PET and fMRI scans provide information about the functions of the brain by revealing which brain areas become more or less active in different conditions. The PET scan (directly above) shows areas in the left hemisphere (left, Broca's area; right, lower parietal-upper temporal area) that become active when people hold in mind a string of letters for a few seconds. The fMRI scans (all views to the left) show several different regions in both hemispheres that become active when someone is thinking about a gesture (a) and when performing a gesture (b).

observe significant activation in the amygdala, which you learned earlier is linked with emotional arousal (Phelps, 2006). There is also increased activation in parts of the frontal lobe that are involved in emotional regulation, in fact, in the same areas that were most probably damaged in the case of Phineas Gage (Wang et al., 2005).

As you may have noticed, then, the most modern brain-imaging techniques confirm what studies of brain damage from over 100 years ago suspected. When Broca and Wernicke reached their conclusions about language production and language comprehension, they had little more to go on than some isolated cases and good hunches. PET scans have since confirmed that different areas of the brain are activated when a person is listening to spoken language, reading words on a screen, saying words out loud or thinking of related words. This suggests that different parts of the brain are activated during these related but distinct functions. Similarly, it was pretty clear to the doctor who examined Phineas Gage that the location of Gage's injuries played a major role in his drastic change in personality and emotionality. fMRI scans have since confirmed that the frontal lobe plays a central role in regulating emotion. It's always nice when independent methods – in these instances, very old case studies and very recent technology – arrive at the same conclusions. As you'll also see at various points in the text, brain-imaging techniques such as fMRI are also revealing new and surprising findings, such as the insights described in the where do you stand? box. Although the human brain still holds many mysteries, researchers are developing increasingly sophisticated ways of unravelling them.

In summary, there are three major approaches to studying the link between the brain and behaviour. Neuroscientists observe how perceptual, motor, intellectual and emotional capacities are affected following brain damage. By carefully relating specific psychological and behavioural disruptions to damage in particular areas of the brain, researchers can better understand how the brain area normally plays a role in producing those behaviours. A second approach looks at global electrical activity in the brain and the activity patterns of single neurons. The patterns of electrical activity in large brain areas can be examined from outside the skull using an electroencephalograph (EEG). Single-cell recordings taken from specific neurons can be linked to specific perceptual or behavioural events, suggesting that those neurons represent particular kinds of stimuli or control particular aspects of behaviour. With brain imaging, the third major approach, researchers can scan the brain as people perform different perceptual or intellectual tasks. Correlating energy consumption in particular brain areas with specific cognitive and behavioural events suggests that those brain areas are involved in specific types of perceptual, motor, cognitive or emotional processing.

psychomythology

You only use 10% of your brain

How often have you heard or read that we only use 10% of our brain? Maybe it was an advert for a self-improvement book, or someone claiming to be able to stimulate the untapped resources of the mind. It is so pervasive in society that 30% of US psychology university students (Higbee and Clay, 1998) and 59% of university-educated Brazilian adults have been reported to agree with this claim (Herculano-Houzel, 2002). A recent study of 250 UK schoolchildren found that 70% also thought that you only use this small percentage of your brain (Gjersoe and Hood, 2013).

The origin of the 10% myth is not certain. One candidate is William James, who wrote in 1907: 'We are making use of only a small part of our possible mental and physical resources' (p. 12). James is not talking about the brain, and it is not clear that he is talking about dormant abilities, but the implication is that there is room for improvement. Other sources of support for the 10% myth come from Freud's psychoanalytic theory of the unconscious (see Chapter 13). Freud thought that much of the workings of the mind was obscured or hidden – an idea that fits with the notion of untapped abilities. There is also support from the more physiologically grounded research of Karl Lashley on the principles of equipotentiality and mass action in rats (see Chapter 1). Lashley (1960) was in search of the 'engram', the location in the brain where memories were stored, but he discovered that if you removed large parts of the rat brain, they were still capable of solving puzzles, suggesting that there was no one special location. The implication was that if rats did not need all their brain tissue to solve puzzles, it stood to reason that they were not using all of it.

In this chapter you have learned good reasons to reject the 10% myth. First, brain tissue is metabolically hungry. The brain weighs around 2% of the overall body but requires 20–25% of the average 2,000 calories we need to consume each day. Why would humans evolve a brain that was so expensive to run if we did not use all of it? Second, brain plasticity reveals that neurons are constantly in need of stimulation and that without feedback or interaction with other neurons, they degenerate in the 'use them or lose them' principle. Third, brain damage does disrupt mental function, although it may be more subtle and integrated, making it less obvious to detect. The fact that brain plasticity can compensate for damage suggests an integrated neural system of activation rather than most of the brain being inactive. Finally, both fMRI and PET do not support the 10% myth. Imaging studies reveal that even when we are unconscious there is brain activity, indicating that 90% cannot be inactive. So, the next time someone tells you that you only use 10% of brain, you can tell them: 'Speak for yourself, I use all of mine!'

where do you stand?

Brain death

A story shrouded in mystery is associated with Belgian doctor Andreas Vesalius (1514–64), regarded as one of the founders of modern anatomy. According to the story, Vesalius conducted an autopsy in 1564 in front of a large crowd in Madrid, Spain. When the cadaver's chest was opened, the audience saw that the man's heart was still beating. The possibility that the patient was still alive created a scandal that forced Vesalius to leave Spain, where he was serving as the imperial doctor at the time. He died during his exodus in a shipwreck, on a pilgrimage to Jerusalem under the pressures of the Spanish Inquisition.

We may never know whether this story is accurate. However, it raises a question related to the brain and behaviour that is still fiercely debated today. In Vesalius's time, if a patient didn't appear to be breathing, was generally unresponsive, or gave no strong evidence of a heartbeat, the person could safely be considered dead (despite the occasional misdiagnosis). Modern resuscitative techniques can keep the heart, lungs and other organs functioning for days, months or even years, so doctors have identified measures of brain function that allow them to decide more definitively when someone is dead.

In 1981, the President's Commission for the Study of Ethical Problems in Medicine and Biomedical and Behavioural Research in the US defined brain death as the *irreversible loss of all functions of the brain.* Contrary to what you may think, brain death is not the same as being in a coma or being unresponsive to stimulation. Indeed, even a flat-line EEG does not indicate that all brain functions have stopped; the reticular formation in the hindbrain, which generates spontaneous respiration and heartbeat, may still be active.

Brain death came to the forefront of national attention during March 2005 in the case of Terri Schiavo, a woman who had been kept alive on a respirator for nearly 15 years in a Florida nursing home. She died on 31 March 2005, after the feeding tube that sustained her was removed. A person like Schiavo is commonly referred to as 'brain dead', but such an individual is more accurately described as being in a *persistent vegetative state.* In fact, people in a persistent vegetative state are still considered to be alive by some. Respiration is controlled by structures in the hindbrain, such as the medulla, and will continue as long as this area is intact. A heartbeat does not require input from any area of the brain, so the heart will continue to beat as long it continues to receive oxygen, either by intact respiration or if the patient is artificially ventilated. Also, a patient who is brain dead may continue to have muscle spasms, twitches or even sit up. This so-called *Lazarus reflex* is coordinated solely by the spinal cord.

Terri Schiavo's parents thought she had a substantial level of voluntary consciousness; they felt that she appeared to smile, cry and turn towards the source of a voice. Terri's parents hired doctors who claimed that she had a primitive type of consciousness. However, neurologists who specialize in these cases emphasized that these responses could be automatic reflexes supported by circuits in the thalamus and midbrain. These neurologists considered Schiavo to be in a persistent vegetative state; they failed to see conclusive evidence of consciousness or voluntary behaviour.

Michael, Terri's husband, agreed with the neurologists and asked the courts to remove the feeding tube that kept her alive, a decision a Florida court accepted. Nonetheless, Florida governor Jeb Bush decreed in 2003 that doctors retain Terri's feeding tube and continue to provide medical care. Eventually, the court again ordered her feeding tube removed, and this time it was not replaced, resulting in her death.

Where do you stand on this issue? Should Terri Schiavo have been kept alive indefinitely? The definition of brain death includes the term 'irreversible', suggesting that as long as *any* component of the brain can still function – with or without the aid of a machine –

the person should be considered alive. But does a persistent vegetative state qualify as 'life'? Is a simple consensus of qualified professionals – doctors, nurses, social workers, specialists – sufficient to decide whether someone is 'still living' or at least 'still living enough' to maintain whatever treatments may be in place? How should the wishes of family members be considered? For that matter, should the wishes of lawmakers and politicians play a role at all? What is your position on these questions of the brain and the ultimate behaviour: staying alive?

After you've considered your answers to these questions, consider this. A recent study found evidence that a person diagnosed as being in a vegetative state showed intentional mental activity (Owen et al., 2006). Researchers used fMRI to observe the patterns of brain activity in a 25-year-old woman with severe brain injuries as the result of a traffic accident. When the researchers spoke ambiguous sentences ('The creak came from a beam in the ceiling') and unambiguous sentences ('There was milk and sugar in his coffee'), fMRI revealed that the activated areas in the woman's brain were comparable to those areas activated in the brains of normal volunteers. What's more, when the woman was instructed to imagine playing a game of tennis and then imagine walking through the rooms of her house, the areas of her brain that showed activity were again indistinguishable from those brain areas in normal, healthy volunteers.

The researchers suggest that these findings are evidence for, at least, conscious understanding of spoken commands and, at best, a degree of intentionality in an otherwise vegetative person. The patient's brain activity while 'playing tennis' and 'walking through her house' revealed that she could both understand the researchers' instructions and wilfully complete them. Unfortunately, it's too early to tell how these and other research findings may impact decisions regarding the brain and when life ends (Laureys et al., 2006).

Chapter review

Neurons: the origin of behaviour

- Brain cells are generally divided in the neuronal and glial cells.
- Neurons are the information-processing elements of the nervous system. They are composed of three main elements: the cell body, dendrites and the axon. The cell body contains the nucleus and the machinery necessary for cell metabolism. Multiple dendrites receive signals from other neurons, whereas axons conduct a signal to the synapse.
- The synapse is a junction between neurons. Electrochemical 'messages' cross the synapse to allow neurons to communicate with one another.
- In recent years, it has been shown that glial cells support a number of important functions in the nervous system. As one example, glial cells form a myelin sheath, which is insulating material that speeds the transmission of information down an axon.
- There are three main types of neurons. Sensory neurons receive information from the external world and convey this information to the brain via the spinal cord. Motor neurons carry signals from the spinal cord to the muscles to produce movement. Interneurons connect sensory neurons, motor neurons or other interneurons.

The electrochemical actions of neurons: information processing

- Neurons have a resting potential that is created by the balance of electrical forces on charged molecules that can pass through the cell membrane. In particular, there is a high concentration of potassium ions inside the neuron, relative to outside the neuron.
- At the start of an axon, electric potentials build to produce a depolarization that is above threshold, which is called an action potential. Action potentials fire in a consistent 'all-or-none' fashion and are conducted down the entire length of the axon. In myelinated axons, the electric signal 'jumps' from breakpoint to breakpoint in the myelin sheath.
- When an action potential arrives at the end of an axon, it stimulates the release of neurotransmitters, which are stored in terminal buttons in the axon. The neurotransmitter enters the synapse and then attaches to the dendrite of the receiving cell.
- Neurotransmitters and receptor sites operate in a lock-and-key fashion; only certain neurotransmitters can be taken up by certain receptors.
- An overflow of neurotransmitters in the synapse can be dealt with in one of three ways: reuptake, enzyme deactivation or the action of autoreceptors.
- Some of the major neurotransmitters are acetylcholine, noradrenaline, serotonin, dopamine, glutamate and GABA.
- Many drugs work by facilitating or interfering with a step in the cycle of a neurotransmitter. Drugs that enhance or mimic neurotransmitters are called agonists, whereas those that block neurotransmitters are called antagonists.

The organization of the nervous system

- The nervous system is divided into the central nervous system, composed of the brain and spinal cord, and the peripheral nervous system, composed of the somatic nervous system and the autonomic nervous system. The somatic nervous system receives sensory information and controls the contractions of voluntary muscles. The autonomic nervous system controls the body's organs.
- The autonomic nervous system is divided further into the sympathetic nervous system that prepares the body for action in threatening circumstances and the parasympathetic nervous system that helps return the body to its normal resting state.
- The spinal cord controls basic reflexes and helps transmit information to and from the brain. Injuries to the spinal cord often result in varying degrees of paralysis or other incapacities.
- The brain can be conceptually divided into three main sections: the hindbrain, the midbrain and the forebrain.
- The hindbrain is responsible for life-sustaining functions, such as respiration and consciousness, and contains the medulla, pons and cerebellum. The midbrain contains the tectum and the tegmentum, which help to orient an organism in the environment.

- The forebrain is divided into the cerebral cortex and subcortical structures. The subcortical structures include the thalamus, hypothalamus, pituitary gland, hippocampus, amygdala and basal ganglia. The motivational and emotional functions of some of the subcortical structures are interrelated, suggesting they could be grouped into an overall organization called the limbic system.
- The cerebral cortex is divided into two hemispheres that exert contralateral control over the body. The cortex can also be divided into lobes: occipital, temporal, parietal and frontal. Each lobe coordinates different kinds of behaviours.
- Association areas are parts of the cortex that perform higher level operations. There is also evidence of brain plasticity – the ability of the brain to reassign functions to other brain areas.

The evolution and development of nervous systems

- From an evolutionary perspective, the human brain represents successive developments from previous models. In reptiles and birds, the highest processing area of the brain is the striatum. In mammals, the highest processing area is the cerebral cortex. The structures and functions of the hindbrain and midbrain seen in other species are retained in humans. There is also some evidence that the human forebrain evolved at a comparatively faster rate compared to other mammals.
- Both genes and environmental factors exert influence on people's behaviours. Genes set the range of possible behaviours within a given environment, but they do not predict individual characteristics.
- Heritability is a measure of the variability in behavioural traits that can be accounted for by genetic variation. Despite its utility, there are several cautions to interpreting heritability.

Investigating the brain

- The field of neuroscience investigates the links between the brain and behaviour. Three main approaches to this topic are studies of brain damage, electrical recording of brain activity, and imaging techniques of the brain in action.
- Careful case studies of people with brain damage allow researchers to piece together the normal functioning of the brain. When an area is damaged and a specific deficit results, investigators can work backwards to discover the likely responsibilities of that brain area. Functions such as speech, language use, emotionality, decision making and the independent nature of the cerebral hemispheres benefited from this approach. An electroencephalograph (EEG) lets researchers measure the overall electrical activity of the brain. However, more recent techniques such as CT scans, MRI, PET and fMRI provide an increasingly sophisticated way of observing how the brain responds when a variety of tasks are performed.

Key terms

Recommended reading

Damasio, A. (2005) *Descartes' Error: Emotion, Reason, and the Human Brain.* New York: Penguin. Emotion and reason seem like competing forces in directing our behaviour – one force wants to feel good, while the other wants to think things through. Antonio Damasio, distinguished neuroscientist, considers how emotion and reason relate to each other and how both cooperate to allow the brain to function efficiently.

Frith, C. D. (2007) *Making up the Mind: How the Brain Creates our Mental World* Oxford: Blackwell. British neuroscientist Chris Frith is one of the world's leading experts on the brain and mind and has written probably the best and most accessible account of experimental studies showing how the brain creates our mental world. It is a joy to read.

Jarrett, C. (2015) *Great Myths of the Brain.* Oxford: Wiley-Blackwell. Critical look at many common misconceptions about the brain, including the 10% myth, male/female brain differences and the problem with the 'brain as a computer' metaphor.

Johnson, S. (2004) *Mind Wide Open: Your Brain and the Neuroscience of Everyday Life.* New York: Scribner. Steven Johnson is a science writer who synthesizes scholarly research for a popular audience. In this book, he explores a range of findings related to neuroscience, including techniques for studying the brain (such as MRI), the purposes and functions of brain structures (such as the amygdala), and the meaning behind what the brain does and why it does it.

4

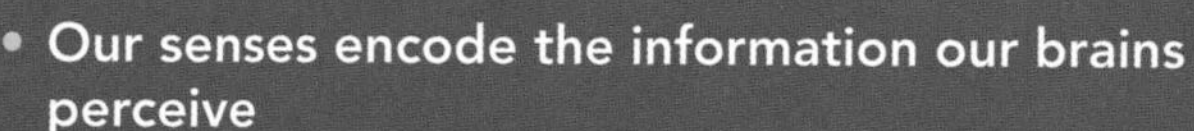

Chapter learning objectives

At the end of this chapter you will be able to:

1. Distinguish between sensation and perception.
2. Describe the principles of signal detection theory.
3. Understand the basic structures of the sensory systems.
4. Give examples and understand the importance of illusions.
5. Understand how sensory information is encoded and transformed into perception.

Sensation and perception

N is sort of ... rubbery ... smooth, L is sort of the consistency of watery paint ... Letters also have vague personalities, but not as strongly as numerals do. (Julieta)

I hear a note by one of the fellows in the band and it's one color. I hear the same note played by someone else and it's a different color. When I hear sustained musical tones, I see just about the same colors that you do, but I see them in textures. (jazz musician Duke Ellington, quoted in George, 1981, p. 226)

Friday is dark maroon, a type of sienna, and Saturday is definitely white. Monday is a cool blue ... Since I was seven, when I first learnt counting, numbers had specific colours. (Geoffrey Rush, actor)

I see the colours inside my head when I think of numbers. I thought everyone had that experience. (Kim)

These comments are not from a recent meeting of the Slightly Odd Society. They're the remarks of otherwise perfectly normal people describing what seem to be perfectly bizarre experiences to everyone except them – they think these experiences are quite commonplace and genuine. Duke Ellington, Stevie Wonder, Tori Amos, Richard Feynman, take your pick, because these and many other notable people have at least one thing in common: their perceptual worlds seem to be quite different from most of ours. All these people have fairly well-documented experiences of synaesthesia, the experience of one sense that is evoked by a different sense. In fact, the last comment above is from the spouse of one of the authors who is a senior medical doctor and certainly not crazy. Until preparing this chapter, the author had been completely unaware for decades that his wife experienced the sensation of colour when thinking about numbers.

DAVID REDFERN/REDFERNS/GETTY IMAGES

Maybe creative types really do have different brains. Successful musicians, actors and artists are common in the list of individuals who report well-documented experiences of synaesthesia. Or maybe it is much more common in the general public than previously thought and we simply hear about it because we are fascinated by the private lives of celebrities. Jazz musician and composer Duke Ellington (1899–1974) perceived timbre as colour while performing on stage.

These unusual perceptual events are varieties of synaesthesia – *the perceptual experience of one sense that is evoked by another sense* (Hubbard and Ramachandran, 2003). For some synaesthetes, musical notes evoke the visual sensation of colour. Other people with synaesthesia see printed letters (see **FIGURE 4.1**) or numbers in specific, consistent colours, for example always seeing the digit 2 as pink and 3 as green. Still others experience specific tastes when certain sounds are heard.

A B C D E

(a) Usual appearance

A B C D E

(b) Appearance to a person with synaesthesia

FIGURE 4.1 Synaesthesia Most of us see letters printed in black as they appear in (a). Some people with synaesthesia link their perceptions of letters with certain colours and perceive letters as printed in different colours, as shown in (b). In synaesthesia, brain regions for different sensory modalities cross-activate one another.

For those of us who don't experience synaesthesia, the prospect of tasting sounds or hearing colours may seem unbelievable or the product of some hallucinogenic experience. Indeed, for many years scientists dismissed synaesthesia either as a rare curiosity or a case of outright faking. But recent research indicates that synaesthesia is far more common than previously believed. British neuroscientist Jamie Ward (2008) estimates that everyone will be closely acquainted with at least six or seven synaesthetes without necessarily knowing who they are. As noted above, this was true for one of the authors who only discovered his wife had always had synaesthesia after telling her about the phenomenon.

Recent research has documented the psychological and neurobiological reality of synaesthesia. For example, a synaesthete who sees the digits 2 and 4 as pink and 3 as green will find it easier to pick out a 2 from a bunch of 3s than from a bunch of 4s, whereas a nonsynaesthete will perform these two tasks equally well (Palmieri et al., 2002). This indicates that people's subjective reports map onto their perceptual experience. Moreover, brain-imaging studies also show that in some synaesthetes, areas of the brain involved in processing colours are more active when they hear words that evoke colour than when they hear tones that don't evoke colour; no such differences are seen among people in a control group (Nunn et al., 2002).

SYNAESTHESIA The perceptual experience of one sense that is evoked by another sense.

MODALITIES Sensory brain regions that process different components of the perceptual world.

So, synaesthesia is neither an isolated curiosity nor the result of faking. In fact, it may indicate that in some people, the brain is 'wired' differently than in most, so that brain regions for different sensory modalities cross-activate one another. Indian-born neurologist Vilayanur 'Rama' Ramachandran's hypothesis (Ramachandran and Hubbard, 2003) is that synaesthesia arises because the separate modalities, *sensory brain regions that process different components of the perceptual world*, are initially all interconnected during the early postnatal months as part of the spurt of typical brain growth that takes place during the first year of life. This explosion of interconnectivity is followed by a period when the brain streamlines these connections that are reinforced though real-world experience (see Chapter 11 for further details). According to Ramachandran, whereas most of us lose interconnections between different modalities, for some reason, synaesthetes maintain many, which is why they experience cross-talk between modalities.

One hypothesis is that synaesthesia is an inherited ability that facilitates creativity (Ramachandran and Hubbard, 2003, p. 29):

> If some genetic factor were to cause excess connections between different brain maps, then depending on where and how widely in the brain the trait was expressed, it could lead to both synesthesia and to a propensity towards linking seemingly unrelated concepts and ideas.

© ISTOCKPHOTO.COM/PEDERK

A study of synaesthetes found that 24% were employed in artistic professions compared to the national average of 2% (Rich et al., 2005).

This proposal is supported by an Australian study of 192 synaesthetes, which found that 24% were employed in artistic professions compared to the national average of 2% (Rich et al., 2005). Another intriguing possibility is that synaesthesia enhances memory. Synaesthetes typically report that they have better memory for learning lists when they can engage their synaesthesia to enrich the learning experience – a claim borne out in experiments that compare them with control subjects (Yaro and Ward, 2007). Whatever the ultimate explanations for this fascinating phenomenon, the recent wave of research shows that synaesthesia is a mindbug that can shed new light on how the brain is organized and how we sense and perceive the world.

In this chapter we'll explore key insights into the nature of sensation and perception. These experiences are basic for survival and reproduction; we wouldn't last long without the ability to accurately make sense of the world around us. Indeed, research on sensation and perception is the basis for much of psychology, a pathway towards understanding more complex cognition and behaviour such as memory, emotion, motivation or decision making. Yet sensation and perception also sometimes reveal mindbugs, ranging from the complexities of synaesthesia to various kinds of perceptual illusions that you might see at a science fair or in a novelty shop. These mindbugs are reminders that the act of perceiving the world is not as simple or straightforward as it might seem. This is because there are multiple stages of sensory processing that must take place before we become consciously aware of the world around us. Our sensory organs may provide us with the raw data but these data have to be number crunched and interpreted to provide meaningful experience.

We'll look at how physical energy in the world around us is encoded by our senses, sent to the brain and enters conscious awareness. Vision is predominant among our senses; correspondingly, we'll devote a fair amount of space to understanding how the visual system works. Then we'll discuss how we perceive sound waves as words or music or noise, followed by the body senses, emphasizing touch, pain and balance. We'll end with the chemical senses of smell and taste, which together allow you to savour the foods you eat. But before doing any of that, we will provide a foundation for examining all the sensory systems by reviewing how psychologists measure sensation and perception in the first place.

Our senses encode the information our brains perceive

From the vantage point of our own consciousness, sensation and perception appear to be one seamless event. Information comes in from the outside world, gets registered and interpreted and triggers some kind of action: no breaks, no balks, just one continuous process. However, psychologists have known for some time now that sensation and perception are two separate activities. This was one of the first discoveries made by Hermann von Helmholtz, German pioneer of experimental psychology, who we read about in Chapter 1. He systematically studied the limits and nature of our sensory capacities and realized that additional processing was undertaken by the brain after the signals had been registered in the central nervous system. So, sensation is the *simple awareness due to the stimulation of a sense organ*. It is the basic registration of light, sound, pressure, odour or taste as parts of your body interact with the physical world. After a sensation registers in your central nervous system, perception, *the organization, identification and interpretation of a sensation in order to form a mental representation,* takes place at the level of your brain.

As an example, your eyes are coursing across these sentences right now. The sensory receptors in your eyeballs are registering different patterns of light reflecting off the page. Your brain, however, is integrating and processing that light information into the meaningful perception of words, such as 'meaningful', 'perception' and 'words'. Your eyes – the sensory organ – aren't really seeing words, they're simply encoding different shapes and patterns of ink on a page. Your brain – the perceptual organ – is transforming those shapes into a coherent mental representation of words and concepts.

If all this sounds a little peculiar, it's because from the vantage point of your conscious experience, it *seems* as if you're reading words directly; again, sensation and perception feel like one single event. If you think of the discussion of brain damage in Chapter 3,

SENSATION Simple awareness due to the stimulation of a sense organ.

PERCEPTION The organization, identification and interpretation of a sensation in order to form a mental representation.

however, you'll recall that sometimes a person's eyes can work just fine, yet the individual is still 'blind' to faces they have seen for many years. Damage to the visual processing centres in the brain can interfere with the interpretation of information coming from the eyes: the senses are intact, but perceptual ability is compromised. Sensation and perception are related – but separate – events.

We all know that sensory events involve vision, hearing, touch, taste and smell. Arguably, we possess several more senses besides these five. Touch, for example, encompasses distinct body senses, including sensitivity to pain and temperature, joint position and balance, and even the state of the gut – perhaps to sense nausea via the autonomic nervous system. Despite the variety of our senses, they all depend on the process of transduction, which occurs *when many sensors in the body convert physical signals from the environment into neural signals sent to the central nervous system.*

TRANSDUCTION What takes place when many sensors in the body convert physical signals from the environment into neural signals sent to the central nervous system.

In vision, light reflected from surfaces provides the eyes with information about the shape, colour and position of objects. In audition, vibrations (from vocal chords or a guitar string, perhaps) cause changes in air pressure that propagate through space to a listener's ears. In touch, the pressure of a surface against the skin signals its shape, texture and temperature. In taste and smell, molecules dispersed in the air or dissolved in saliva reveal the identity of substances that we may or may not want to eat. In each case, physical energy from the world is converted to neural energy inside the central nervous system. We've already seen that synaesthetes experience a mixing of these perceptions; however, even during synaesthesia, the processes of transduction that begin those perceptions are the same. Despite 'hearing colours', your eyes simply can't transduce sound waves, no matter how long you stare at your stereo speakers!

Psychophysics

It's intriguing to consider the possibility that our basic perceptions of sights or sounds might differ fundamentally from those of other people. One reason we find synaesthetes fascinating is because their perceptual experiences are so different from most of ours. But we won't get very far in understanding such differences by simply relying on casual self-reports. As you learned in Chapter 2, to understand a behaviour researchers must first *operationalize* it, and that involves finding a reliable way to measure it.

Any type of scientific investigation requires objective measurements. Measuring the physical energy of a stimulus, such as the colour and brightness of a light, is easy enough: you can probably buy the necessary instruments online to do that yourself. But how do you quantify a person's private, subjective *perception* of that light? It's one thing to know that a torch produces '100 candelas' or gives off '8,000 lumens', but it's another matter entirely to measure a person's psychological experience of that light energy.

GETTY IMAGES/ISTOCKPHOTO THINKSTOCK IMAGES

Two people might both describe this sunset as 'beautiful' and 'orange', but each individual's perception of the moment will be different, based on a cocktail of emotions and memories evoked in the instant.

The structuralists, led by Wilhelm Wundt and Edward Titchener, tried using introspection to measure perceptual experiences (see Chapter 1). They failed miserably at this task. After all, you can describe your experience to another person in words, but that person cannot know directly what you perceive when you look at a sunset. You both may call the sunset 'orange' and 'beautiful', but neither of you can directly perceive the other's experience of the same event. Evoked memories and emotions intertwine with what you are hearing, seeing and smelling, making your perception of an event – and therefore your experience of that event – unique. We return to this fascinating issue in Chapter 8 when we talk about consciousness and why it is impossible to know what it would be like to be a different animal such as bat.

Given that perception is different for each of us, how could we ever hope to measure it? This question was answered in the mid-1800s by German scientist and philosopher Gustav Fechner (1801–87). Fechner was originally trained as a physicist but developed strong interests in philosophy and psychology, especially the study of perception. He began conducting informal studies of visual perception on himself during the 1830s. However, he got a bit carried away with his research and temporarily blinded himself while staring at the sun for a prolonged time. Fechner's eyes became so sensitive to light that he had to bandage them before leaving the house, and they bothered him for the rest of his life. Limited in his abilities, Fechner took on extra work to help support his family, such as translating works from French to German and even writing much of an encyclopedia of household knowledge (Watson, 1978). His workload and eye problems resulted in a psychological breakdown and severe depression, leading him to resign his professorship at the University of Leipzig and go into seclusion.

Although this was a difficult period in his life, it was of great importance to psychology. In his isolation, Fechner was free to think deeply about the issues that interested him the most, especially how it might be possible to link psychology and physics. His efforts led him to develop an approach to measuring sensation and perception called psychophysics – *methods that measure the strength of a stimulus and the observer's sensitivity to that stimulus* (Fechner, [1860]1966). In a typical psychophysics experiment, researchers ask people to make a simple judgement – whether or not they saw a flash of light, for example. The psychophysicist then relates the measured stimulus, such as the brightness of the light flash, to each observer's yes-or-no response.

PSYCHOPHYSICS Methods that measure the strength of a stimulus and the observer's sensitivity to that stimulus.

Measuring thresholds

Psychophysicists begin the measurement process with a single sensory signal to determine precisely how much physical energy is required to evoke a sensation in an observer.

Absolute threshold

The simplest quantitative measurement in psychophysics is the absolute threshold – *the minimal intensity needed to just barely detect a stimulus*. A *threshold* is a boundary. The doorway that separates the inside from the outside of a house is a threshold, as is the boundary between two psychological states, for example 'awareness' and 'unawareness'. In finding the absolute threshold for sensation, the two states in question are *sensing* and *not sensing* some stimulus. **TABLE 4.1** lists the approximate sensory thresholds for each of the five senses.

ABSOLUTE THRESHOLD The minimal intensity needed to just barely detect a stimulus.

TABLE 4.1 Approximate sensory thresholds

Sense	Absolute threshold
Vision	A candle flame 50 km away on a clear, dark night
Hearing	A clock's tick 6 m away when all is quiet
Touch	A fly's wing touching the cheek from 1 cm away
Smell	A single drop of perfume diffused through an area equivalent to the volume of six rooms
Taste	A teaspoon of sugar dissolved in 7.56 L of water

Source: Based on Galanter, 1962

To measure the absolute threshold for detecting a sound, for example, an observer sits in a soundproof room wearing headphones linked to a computer. The experimenter presents a pure tone (the sort of sound made by striking a tuning fork) using the computer to vary the loudness or the length of time each tone lasts and recording how often the observer reports hearing that tone under each condition. The outcome of such an experiment is graphed in **FIGURE 4.2**. Notice from the shape of the curve that the transition from *not hearing* to *hearing* is gradual rather than abrupt. Investigators typically define the absolute threshold as the loudness required for the listener to say they have heard the tone on 50% of the trials.

If we repeat this experiment for many different tones, we can observe and record the thresholds for tones ranging from very low pitch to very high. It turns out that people tend to be most sensitive to the range of tones corresponding to human conversation. If the tone is low enough, such as the lowest note on a pipe organ, most humans cannot hear it at all, we can only feel it. If the tone is high enough, we cannot hear it, but dogs and many other animals can.

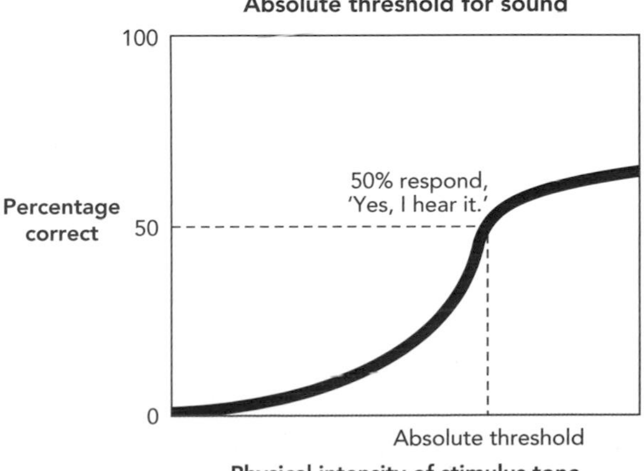

FIGURE 4.2 Absolute threshold Some of us are more sensitive than others, and we may even detect sensory stimulation below our own absolute threshold. Absolute threshold is graphed here as the point where the increasing intensity of the stimulus enables an observer to detect it in 50% of the trials. As its intensity gradually increases, we detect the stimulation more frequently.

Difference thresholds

The absolute threshold is useful for assessing how sensitive we are to faint stimuli, but most everyday perception involves detecting differences among stimuli that are well above the absolute threshold. Most people are pretty adept at noticing that a sofa is red, but they're likely to want to know if the sofa is redder than the curtains they're considering. Similarly, parents can usually detect their own infant's cry from the cries of other babies, but it's probably more useful to be able to differentiate the 'I'm hungry' cry from the 'I'm cranky' cry from the 'something is biting my toes' cry. In short, the human perceptual system excels at detecting *changes* in stimulation rather than the simple onset or offset of stimulation.

JUST NOTICEABLE DIFFERENCE (JND) The minimal change in a stimulus that can just barely be detected.

As a way of measuring this difference threshold, Fechner proposed the just noticeable difference (JND) – *the minimal change in a stimulus that can just barely be detected.* The JND is not a fixed quantity; rather, it depends on how intense the stimuli being measured are and the particular sense being measured. Consider measuring the JND for a bright light. An observer in a dark room is shown a light of fixed intensity, called the *standard* (S), next to a comparison light that is slightly brighter or dimmer than the standard. When S is very dim, observers can see even a very small difference in brightness between the two lights: the JND is small. But if S is bright, a much larger increment is needed to detect the difference: the JND is larger.

In fact, the JND can be calculated for each sense. It is roughly proportional to the magnitude of the standard stimulus. This relationship was first noticed in 1834 by Ernst Weber, a German physiologist who taught at the University of Leipzig around the time that Fechner was a student there and probably influenced Fechner's thinking (Watson, 1978). Fechner applied Weber's insight directly to psychophysics, resulting in a formal relationship called Weber's law, which states that *the just noticeable difference of a stimulus is a constant proportion despite variations in intensity*.

WEBER'S LAW The just noticeable difference of a stimulus is a constant proportion despite variations in intensity.

As an example, the JND for weight is about 2%. If you picked up a 25-g envelope, then a 50-g envelope, you'd probably notice the difference between them. But if you picked up a 2.27-kg package, then a 2.30-kg package, you'd probably detect no difference at all between them. In fact, you'd probably need about a 2.60-kg package to detect a JND. When calculating a difference threshold, it is the proportion between stimuli that is important; the measured size of the difference, whether in brightness, loudness or weight, is irrelevant.

Signal detection

Measuring absolute and difference thresholds requires a critical assumption: that a threshold exists. But much of what scientists know about biology suggests that such a discrete, all-or-none change in the brain is unlikely. Humans don't suddenly and rapidly switch between perceiving and not perceiving; in fact, recall that the transition from *not sensing* to *sensing* is gradual (see Figure 4.2). The same physical stimulus, such as a dim light or a quiet tone, presented on several different occasions may be perceived by the same person on some occasions but not on others. Remember, an absolute threshold is operationalized as perceiving the stimulus 50% of the time, which means that the other 50% of the time it might go undetected.

Cluttered environments such as this music festival present our visual system with a challenging signal detection task.

Our accurate perception of a sensory stimulus, then, can be somewhat haphazard. Whether in the psychophysics lab or out in the world, sensory signals face a lot of competition, or *noise*, which refers to all the other stimuli coming from the internal and external environment. Memories, moods and motives intertwine with what you are seeing, hearing and smelling at any given time. This internal 'noise' competes with your ability to detect a stimulus with perfect, focused attention. Other sights, sounds and smells in the world at large also compete for attention; you rarely have the luxury of attending to just one stimulus apart from everything else. As a consequence of noise, you may not perceive everything that you sense, and you may even perceive things that you haven't sensed.

To see how these mismatches might happen, imagine measuring the electrical activity of a single neuron sending signals from the eye to the brain. As a dim spot of light is flashed onto an observer's eye, the number of subsequent action potentials fluctuates from one presentation to the next even when the light is exactly the same brightness each time. Occasionally, the neuron might fire even if no light is presented – a *spontaneous action potential* has occurred. Sensory systems are noisy; when the signals are very small, dim or quiet, the senses provide only a 'fuzzy' indicator of the state of the world.

This variability among neural responses helps explain why Figure 4.2 shows a gradual rise in the likelihood of hearing a tone. For a fixed tone intensity, the evoked neural response varies a little from one presentation to the next. On some presentations, the auditory neurons' responses will be a bit greater than average, and the listener will be more likely to detect the tone. On other presentations, the neural response will, by chance, be a bit less than average, and the listener will be less likely to detect the tone. On still other occasions, the neurons might produce spontaneous action potentials, leading the observer to claim that a tone was heard when none was presented.

Given the variability in neural responses, observers are faced with a decision. If they say 'Yes, I heard a tone' anytime there is any activity in the auditory system, they will often respond 'yes' when no tone is presented. So observers might adopt a more conservative response criterion, deciding to say 'Yes, I heard a tone' only when the sensory experience is quite obvious. The problem now is that an observer will often miss fainter tones that were actually presented. Think of the last time you had a hearing test. You no doubt missed some of the quiet beeps that were presented, but you also probably said you heard beeps that weren't really there.

An approach to psychophysics called signal detection theory holds that *the response to a stimulus depends on a person's sensitivity to the stimulus in the presence of noise and on a person's response criterion*. That is, observers consider the sensory evidence evoked by the stimulus and compare it to an internal decision criterion (Green and Swets, 1966; Macmillan and Creelman, 2005). If the sensory evidence exceeds the criterion, the observer responds by saying 'Yes, I detected the stimulus', and if it falls short of the criterion, the observer responds by saying 'No, I did not detect the stimulus.'

SIGNAL DETECTION THEORY An observation that the response to a stimulus depends on a person's sensitivity to the stimulus in the presence of noise and on a person's response criterion.

Signal detection theory allows researchers to quantify an observer's response in the presence of noise. In a signal detection experiment, a stimulus, such as a dim light, is randomly presented or not (see **FIGURE 4.3**). If you've ever taken an eye test that checks your peripheral vision, you have an idea about this kind of setup: lights of varying intensity are flashed at various places in the visual field, and your task is to respond anytime you see one. Observers in a signal detection experiment must decide whether they saw the light or not, leading to the four possible outcomes shown in **FIGURE 4.3a**. If the light is presented and the observer correctly responds 'Yes', the outcome is a *hit*. If the light is presented and the observer says 'No', the result is a *miss*. However, if the light is *not* presented and the observer nonetheless says it was, a *false alarm* has occurred. Finally, if the light is *not* presented and the observer responds 'No', a *correct rejection* has occurred: the observer accurately detected the absence of the stimulus.

Observers can adopt a very liberal response criterion, saying 'Yes' at the slightest hint of evidence for the stimulus (see **FIGURE 4.3b**). Notice that this strategy will produce a lot of hits but also a lot of false alarms. Conversely, adopting a very conservative criterion – saying 'Yes' only when the stimulus is clear, strong and unambiguous – should minimize the rate of false alarms but increase the proportion of misses (see **FIGURE 4.3c**).

Signal detection theory is a more sophisticated approach than was used in the early days of establishing absolute thresholds. Back then, it might have been assumed that everyone (or at least a majority of observers) heard a tone or saw a flickering candle

FIGURE 4.3 Signal detection criteria Sensation depends not only on our sensitivity to stimulation but also on how we make decisions. Of the four possible outcomes on the grid, in (a), we may correctly report the presence (a hit) or absence (correct rejection) of a stimulus, fail to detect it (a miss), or say we detect it when it's not there (false alarm). People may be equally sensitive to stimulation but adopt very different decision criteria. Those who tend to say they detect a signal produce many false alarms as well as many hits (b). Those who tend to say they detect no signal minimize false alarms but often miss the stimulus (c). Decision criteria have wide application in areas as diverse as drug trials and dating.

	Yes	No
Light presented	Hit	Miss
Light not presented	False alarm	Correct rejection

(a) Possible outcomes on each trial

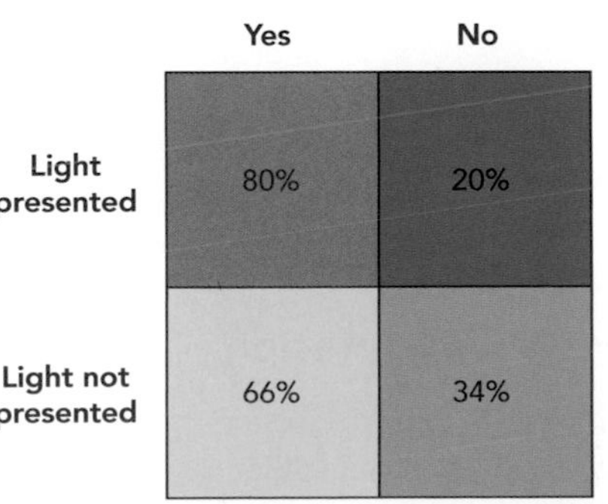

(b) Purely liberal criterion response

	Yes	No
Light presented	35%	65%
Light not presented	20%	80%

(c) Purely conservative criterion response

flame with equal facility. Signal detection theory, in contrast, explicitly takes into account observers' response tendencies, such as liberally saying 'Yes' or reserving identifications only for obvious instances of the stimulus. For example, some events are likely to lead to more variability in responses because they are less discernible, such as whether or not you briefly saw a camouflaged mouse in the forest. Others are going to be more obvious and should lead to greater certainty, such as whether or not there is a stuffed elephant in the corner of the room. Describing these events can be expressed in a measure known as d-prime (d') – *a statistic that gives a relatively pure measure of the observer's sensitivity or ability to detect signals* based on the relative proportion of hits to misses and the group variability in detecting the phenomenon under consideration. If an event has a high d' value, people are more certain when it is present or absent. It's interesting, then, to learn that the ideas behind signal detection theory were developed first by none other than Fechner ([1860]1966). It's not clear why such important ideas were not grasped by later psychologists who appreciated other aspects of Fechner's work, but it's possible that most of those researchers lacked the mathematical training required to appreciate Fechner's insights (Link, 1994). In short, Fechner anticipated long ago that both the characteristics of the stimulus *and* the characteristics of the observer need to be taken into account, producing a better understanding of the perceptual process.

D-PRIME (D') A statistic that gives a relatively pure measure of the observer's sensitivity or ability to detect signals.

Signal detection theory proposes a way to measure *perceptual sensitivity* – how effectively the perceptual system represents sensory events – separately from the observer's decision-making strategy. Two observers with opposite decision criteria and correspondingly distinct hit rates and false alarm rates may exhibit similar levels of sensitivity. In other words, even though one person says 'Yes' much more often than another, both may be equally accurate in distinguishing between the presence or absence of a stimulus. Although the purely conservative and liberal strategies represent two poles on a long continuum of possible decision criteria, signal detection theory has practical applications at home, school, work and even while driving.

For example, a radiologist may have to decide whether a mammogram shows that a patient has breast cancer. The radiologist knows that certain features, such as a mass of a particular size and shape, are associated with the presence of cancer. But noncancerous features can have a very similar appearance to cancerous ones. The radiologist may decide on a strictly liberal criterion and check every possible case of cancer with a biopsy. As shown in Figure 4.3, this decision strategy minimizes the possibility of missing a true cancer but leads to many false alarms. A strictly conservative criterion will cut down on false alarms but will miss some treatable cancers (see Figure 4.3c).

GETTY

Organisms adapt to conditions with continued exposure. The sharp iciness of the water will fade as this diver keeps swimming.

As another example, imagine that the police are on the lookout for a suspected criminal who they have reason to believe will be at a crowded football match. Although the police provided a fairly good description – 1.82-m tall, sandy brown hair, beard, glasses – there are still thousands of people to scan. Rounding up all men between 1.65 m and 1.95 m would probably produce a hit (the criminal is caught) but at the expense of an extraordinary number of false alarms (many innocent people are detained and questioned).

These different types of errors have to be weighed against one another in setting the decision criterion. Signal detection theory offers a practical way to choose among criteria that permit decision makers to take into account the consequences of hits, misses, false alarms and correct rejections (McFall and Treat, 1999; Swets et al., 2000). (For an example of a common everyday task that can interfere with signal detection, see *the real world* box.)

Sensory adaptation

When you walk into a bakery, the aroma of freshly baked bread overwhelms you, but after a few minutes, the smell fades. When you wake up in the middle of the night for a drink of water, the bathroom light blinds you, but after a few minutes, you no longer squint.

These are all examples of sensory adaptation, the observation that *sensitivity to prolonged stimulation tends to decline over time as an organism adapts to current conditions.* Imagine that while you are studying in a quiet room, your neighbour in the flat next door turns on the stereo. That gets your attention, but after a few minutes, the sounds fade from your awareness as you continue your studies. But remember that our perceptual systems emphasize *change* in responding to sensory events: when the music stops, you notice.

SENSORY ADAPTATION Sensitivity to prolonged stimulation tends to decline over time as an organism adapts to current conditions.

the real world

Multitasking

By one estimate, using a mobile phone while driving makes having an accident four times more likely (McEvoy et al., 2005). In response to road safety experts and statistics such as this, some countries are passing laws that restrict, and sometimes ban, using mobile phones while driving. You might think that's a good idea … for everyone else on the road. But surely *you* can manage to punch in a number on a phone, carry on a conversation, or maybe even send a text message while simultaneously driving in a safe and courteous manner. Right?

In a word, *wrong*. The issue here is *selective attention*, perceiving only what's currently relevant to you. Try this. Without moving a muscle, think about the pressure of your skin against your chair right now. Effortlessly, you shifted your attention to allow a sensory signal to enter your awareness. This simple shift shows that your perception of the world depends both on what sensory signals are present and your choice of which signals to attend to and which to ignore. Perception is an active, moment-to-moment exploration for relevant or interesting information, not a passive receptacle for whatever happens to come along.

Talking on a mobile phone while driving demands that you juggle two independent sources of sensory input – vision and audition – at the same time. Normally, this kind of *multitasking* works rather well. It's only when you need to react suddenly that your driving performance may suffer. Researchers have tested experienced drivers in a highly realistic driving simulator, measuring their response times to brake lights and stop signs while they listened to the radio or carried on phone conversations about a political issue, among other tasks (Strayer et al., 2003).

These experienced drivers reacted significantly slower during phone conversations than during the other tasks. This is because a phone conversation requires memory retrieval, deliberation and planning what to say and often carries an emotional stake in the conversation topic. Tasks such as listening to the radio require far less attention or none at all.

The tested drivers became so engaged in their conversations that their minds no longer seemed to be in the car. Their slower braking response translated into an increased stopping distance that, depending on the driver's speed, would have resulted in a rear-end collision. Whether the phone was handheld or hands-free made little difference. This suggests that laws requiring drivers to use hands-free phones may have little effect on reducing accidents.

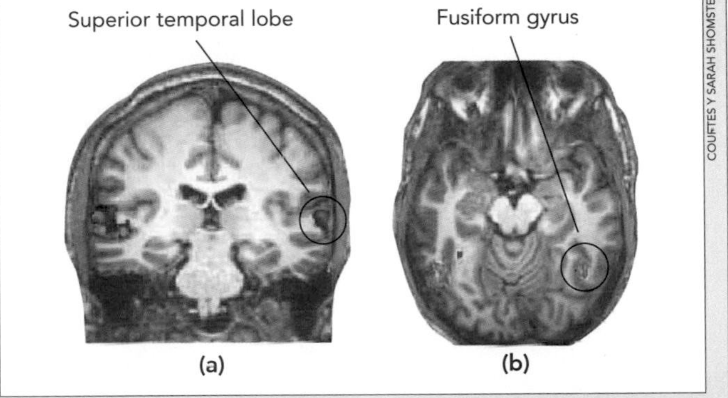

Shifting attention Participants received fMRI scans as they performed tasks that required them to shift their attention between visual and auditory information. (a) When focusing on auditory information, a region in the superior (upper) temporal lobe involved in auditory processing showed increased activity (yellow/orange). (b) In striking contrast, a visual region, the fusiform gyrus, showed decreased activity when participants focused on auditory information (blue).

Other researchers have measured brain activity using fMRI while people were shifting attention between visual and auditory information. The strength of visual and auditory brain activity was affected. When attention was directed to audition, activity in visual areas decreased compared to when attention was directed to vision (Shomstein and Yantis, 2004). It was as if the participants could adjust a mental 'volume knob' to regulate the flow of incoming information according to which task they were attending to at the moment.

So how well do we multitask in several thousand kilograms of metal hurtling down the road? Experienced drivers can handle divided attention to a degree, yet most of us have to acknowledge that we have had close calls due to driving while distracted. Unless you have two heads with one brain each – one to talk and one to concentrate on driving – you might do well to keep your eyes on the road and not on the phone.

stats facts

Are women better at multitasking? First ask a Bayesian

How often have you heard that women are better than men at multitasking? Before you accept any folk wisdom, one needs to consider the evidence. One recent Swedish study reported that men were in fact better than women in an experiment where they had to perform two tasks simultaneously (Mäntylä, 2013). However, critics pointed out that there was little statistical evidence from real-world examples, such as driving and answering a telephone, for gender differences, so why would one expect or indeed look for one in a lab (Strayer et al., 2013)? This is the Bayesian approach to accepting or rejecting significant findings by establishing the prevalence or incidence of the phenomenon under consideration in the general population. The two sets of scientists disagree about the importance of the difference found in the lab but it does raise the interesting question about the relevance of interpreting findings obtained under experimental conditions in a limited situation and extrapolating to the real world.

The fact that the perceptual system is attuned to change is no coincidence. Remember that the central nervous system has evolved to respond to the environment and so the significant events in the world that are most likely going to require some response involve something changing. It makes sense (literally) to have our senses looking for changes rather than trying to estimate absolute levels. However, the flip side is that we have to be able to adapt to changes otherwise we would be in a continual state of alert.

This is why sensory adaptation is a useful process for most organisms. Imagine what your sensory and perceptual world would be like without it. When you put on your jeans in the morning, the feeling of rough cloth against your bare skin would be as noticeable hours later as it was in the first few minutes. The stink of rubbish in your flat when you first walk in would never dissipate. If you had to constantly be aware of how your tongue feels while it is resting in your mouth, you'd be driven to distraction. Our perceptual systems respond more strongly to changes in stimulation rather than to constant stimulation. A stimulus that doesn't change usually doesn't require any action; your car probably emits a certain hum all the time that you've got used to. But a change in stimulation often signals a need for action. If your car starts making different kinds of noises, you're not only more likely to notice them, but you're also more likely to do something about it.

VISUAL ACUITY The ability to see fine detail.

In summary, sensation and perception are critical to survival. Sensation is the simple awareness that results from stimulation of a sense organ, whereas perception organizes, identifies and interprets sensation at the level of the brain. All sensory modalities depend on the process of transduction, which converts physical signals from the environment into neural signals carried by sensory neurons into the central nervous system. In the 19th century, German researchers developed psychophysics, an approach to studying perception that measures the strength of a stimulus and an observer's sensitivity to that stimulus. Psychophysicists have developed procedures for measuring an observer's absolute threshold, the smallest intensity needed to just barely detect a stimulus, and the just noticeable difference (JND), the smallest change in a stimulus that can just barely be detected. Signal detection theory allows researchers to distinguish between an observer's perceptual sensitivity to a stimulus and criteria for making decisions about the stimulus. Sensory adaptation occurs because sensitivity to lengthy stimulation tends to decline over time.

Vision: more than meets the eye

You might be proud of your 20/20 vision, even if it is corrected by glasses or contact lenses. Here, *20/20* refers to a measurement associated with a Snellen chart, named after Hermann Snellen (1834–1908), the Dutch ophthalmologist who developed it as a means of assessing visual acuity, *the ability to see fine detail*, which is the smallest line of letters that a typical person can read from a distance of 20 ft (the metric equivalent is 6/6 vision where the distance is 6 m). But if you dropped into the birds of prey ophthalmologic office, your visual pride would wither. Hawks, eagles, owls and other raptors have much greater visual acuity than humans; in many cases, about eight times greater, or the equivalent of 20/2 vision. That's handy if you want to spot a mouse from a couple of kilometres away, but if you simply need to see where your flatmate left the box of chocolates, you can probably live with the fact that no one ever calls you 'Ol' Eagle Eye'.

Although you won't win any I Spy contests against a hawk, your sophisticated visual system has evolved to transduce visual energy in the world into neural signals in the brain. Humans have sensory receptors in their eyes that respond to wavelengths of light energy. When we look at people, places and things, patterns of light and colour give us information about where one surface stops and another begins. The array of light reflected from those surfaces preserves their shapes and enables us to form a mental representation of a scene (Rodieck, 1998). Understanding vision, then, starts with understanding light.

The Snellen chart is commonly used to measure visual acuity. Chances are you've seen one yourself on more than one occasion.

Sensing light

Visible light is simply the portion of the electromagnetic spectrum that we can see, and it is an extremely small slice. You can think about light as waves of energy. Like ocean waves, light waves vary in height and in the distance between their peaks, or *wavelengths*, as **TABLE 4.2** shows.

TABLE 4.2 Properties of light waves

Physical dimension	Psychological dimension
Length	Hue or what we perceive as colour
Amplitude	Brightness
Purity	Saturation or richness of colour

There are three properties of light waves, each of which has a physical dimension that produces a corresponding psychological dimension:

1 The *length* of a light wave determines its hue, or what humans perceive as colour.
2 The intensity or *amplitude* of a light wave – how high the peaks are – determines what we perceive as the brightness of light.
3 *Purity* is the number of wavelengths that make up the light, which corresponds to what humans perceive as saturation, or the richness of colours (see **FIGURE 4.4**).

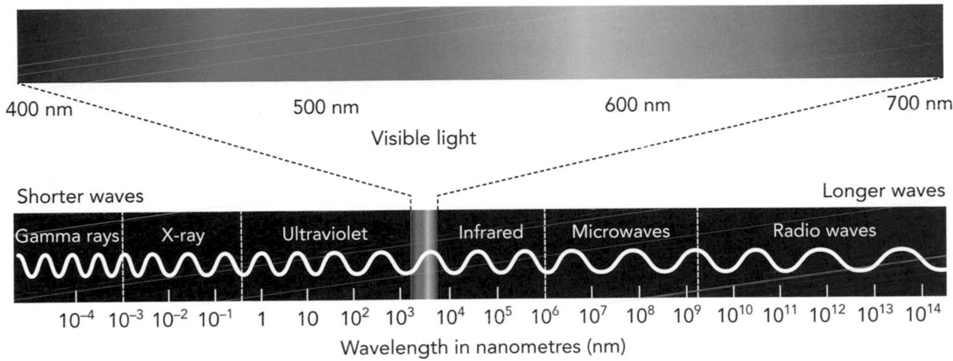

FIGURE 4.4 Electromagnetic spectrum The sliver of light waves visible to humans as a rainbow of colours from violet to red is bounded on the short end by ultraviolet rays, which honeybees can see, and on the long end by infrared waves, on which night-vision equipment operates. Someone wearing night-vision goggles, for example, can detect another person's body heat in complete darkness. Light waves are minute, but the scale along the bottom of this chart offers a glimpse of their varying lengths, measured in nanometres (nm; 1 nm = 1 billionth of a metre).

In other words, light doesn't need a human to have the properties it does: length, amplitude and purity are properties of the light waves themselves. What humans perceive from those properties are colour, brightness and saturation.

To understand how the properties of waves affect how we sense light, it's helpful to understand how our eyes detect light in the first place.

The human eye

FIGURE 4.5 shows the human eye in cross-section. Light that reaches the eyes passes first through a clear, smooth outer tissue called the *cornea*, which bends the light wave and sends it through the *pupil*, a hole in the coloured part of the eye. This coloured part is the *iris*, which is a translucent, doughnut-shaped muscle that controls the size of the pupil and hence the amount of light that can enter the eye.

When you move from the dim illumination of a cinema into the bright sunshine outside, your irises contract, reducing the size of the pupils and the amount of light passing through them. You may still have to shade your eyes until their light-sensitive cells adapt to the brighter light level. This process is a type of sensory adaptation called *light adaptation*.

Immediately behind the iris, muscles inside the eye control the shape of the *lens* to bend the light again and focus it onto the retina – *light-sensitive tissue lining the back of the eyeball*. The muscles change the shape of the lens to focus objects at different distances, making the lens flatter for objects that are far away or rounder for nearby objects. This is called accommodation – *the process by which the eye maintains a clear image on the retina*. **FIGURE 4.6** shows how accommodation works.

RETINA Light-sensitive tissue lining the back of the eyeball.

ACCOMMODATION The process by which the eye maintains a clear image on the retina.

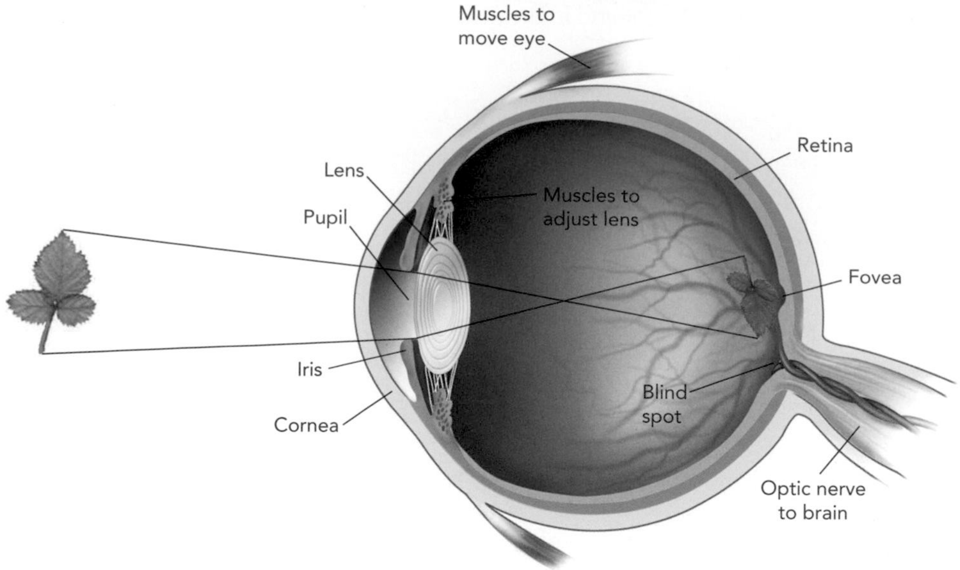

FIGURE 4.5 Anatomy of the human eye Light reflected from a surface enters the eye via the transparent cornea, bending to pass through the pupil at the centre of the coloured iris. Behind the iris, the thickness and shape of the lens adjust to focus the light on the retina, where the image appears upside down and backwards. Basically, this is how a camera lens works. Light-sensitive receptor cells in the retinal surface, excited or inhibited by spots of light, influence the specialized neurons that convey nerve impulses to the brain's visual centres through their axons, which make up the optic nerve.

CONES Photoreceptors that detect colour, operate under normal daylight conditions, and allow us to focus on fine detail.

RODS Photoreceptors that become active only under low light conditions for night vision.

FIGURE 4.6a shows normal vision. However, if your eyeballs are a little too long or a little too short, the lens will not focus images properly on the retina. If the eyeball is too long, images are focused in front of the retina, leading to nearsightedness (myopia), shown in **FIGURE 4.6b**. If the eyeball is too short, images are focused behind the retina, and the result is farsightedness (hyperopia), as shown in **FIGURE 4.6c**. Glasses (spectacles), contact lenses and surgical procedures can correct either condition. For example, glasses and contacts both provide an additional lens to help focus light more appropriately, and procedures such as laser treatment physically reshape the eye's existing lens. For many of us, the natural ageing process means that the mechanisms for bending and focusing light onto the retina need a helping hand as we get older.

Phototransduction in the retina

The retina is the interface between the world of light outside the body and the world of vision inside the central nervous system. Two types of photo*receptor cells* in the retina contain light-sensitive pigments that transduce light into neural impulses. **Cones** *detect colour, operate under normal daylight conditions, and allow us to focus on fine detail.* **Rods** *become active only under low light conditions for night vision* (see **FIGURE 4.7**).

Rods are much more sensitive photoreceptors than cones, but this sensitivity comes at a cost. Because all rods contain the same photopigment, they provide no information about colour and sense only shades of grey. Think about this the next time you wake up in the middle of the night and make your way to the bathroom for a drink of water. Using only the moonlight from the window to light your way, do you see the room in colour or in shades of grey?

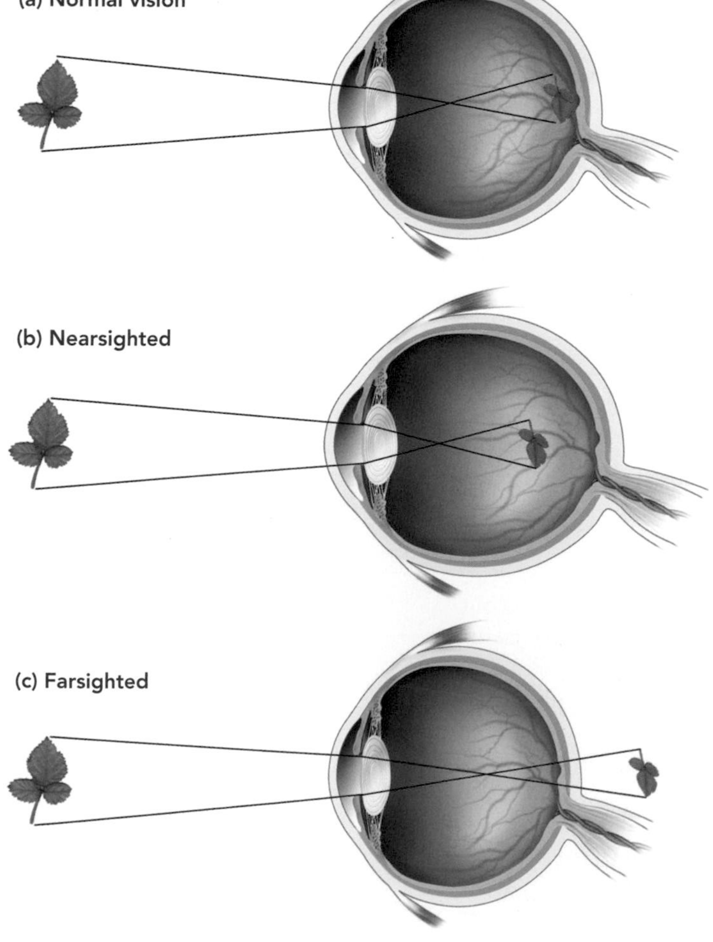

FIGURE 4.6 Accommodation Inside the eye, the lens changes shape to focus nearby or faraway objects on the retina. (a) People with normal vision focus the image on the retina at the back of the eye, both for near and far objects. (b) Nearsighted people see clearly what's nearby, but distant objects are blurry because light from them is focused in front of the retina, a condition called myopia. (c) Farsighted people have the opposite problem: distant objects are clear, but those nearby are blurry because their point of focus falls beyond the surface of the retina, a condition called hyperopia.

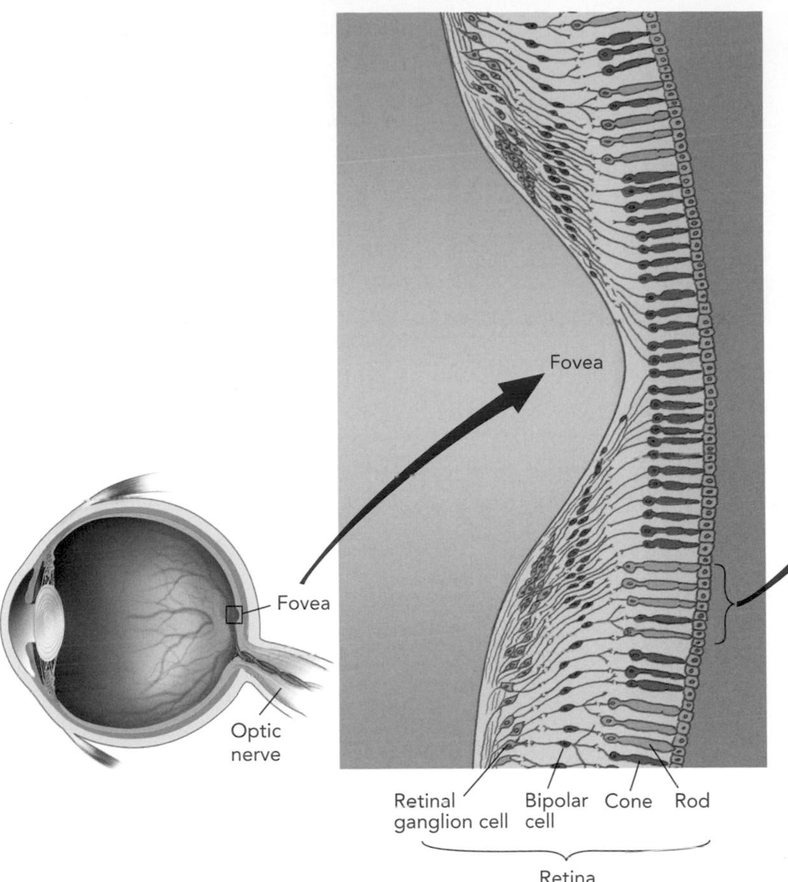

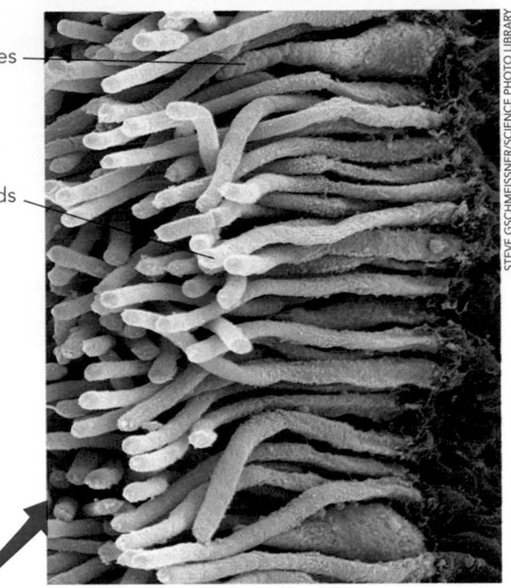

FIGURE 4.7 Close-up of the retina The surface of the retina is composed of photoreceptor cells, the rods and cones, beneath a layer of transparent neurons, the bipolar and retinal ganglion cells, connected in sequence. Viewed close up in this cross-sectional diagram is the area of greatest visual acuity, the fovea, where most colour-sensitive cones are concentrated, allowing us to see fine detail as well as colour. Rods, the predominant photoreceptors activated in low light conditions, are distributed everywhere else on the retina.

Rods and cones differ in several other ways as well, most notably in their numbers. About 120 million rods are distributed more or less evenly around each retina except in the very centre, the **fovea** – *an area of the retina where vision is the clearest and there are no rods at all.* The absence of rods in the fovea decreases the sharpness of vision in reduced light, but it can be overcome. For example, when amateur astronomers view dim stars through their telescopes at night, they know to look a little off to the side of the target so that the image will fall not on the rod-free fovea but on some other part of the retina that contains many highly sensitive rods.

FOVEA An area of the retina where vision is the clearest and there are no rods at all.

In contrast to rods, each retina contains only about 6 million cones, which are densely packed in the fovea and much more sparsely distributed over the rest of the retina, as you can see in Figure 4.7. The high concentration of cones in the fovea directly affects visual acuity and explains why objects off to the side, in your *peripheral vision*, aren't so clear. The light reflecting from those peripheral objects has a difficult time landing in the fovea, making the resulting image less clear. The more fine detail encoded and represented in the visual system, the clearer the perceived image. The process is analogous to the quality of photographs taken with a six-megapixel digital camera versus a two-megapixel camera.

Rods and cones also differ in the way their sensitivity changes when the overall light level changes. Remember that the pupil constricts when you move from dim to bright

The full-colour image on the left is what you'd see when your rods and cones were fully at work. The greyscale image on the right is what you'd see if only your rods were functioning.

FIGURE **4.8 Blind spot demonstration** To find your blind spot, close your left eye and stare at the cross with your right eye. Hold the book 15–30 cm away from your eyes and move it slowly towards and away from you until the dot disappears. The dot is now in your blind spot and so is not visible. At this point, the vertical lines may appear as one continuous line because the visual system fills in the area occupied by the missing dot. To test your left-eye blind spot, turn the book upside down and repeat with your right eye closed.

BLIND SPOT An area of the retina that contains neither rods nor cones and therefore has no mechanism to sense light.

RECEPTIVE FIELD The region of the sensory surface that, when stimulated, causes a change in the firing rate of that neuron.

illumination. Now consider the reverse. When you enter a dark cinema after being outside on a sunny day, your pupil enlarges to let in more light, but at first you will be almost blind to the seating layout. Gradually, however, your vision adapts. This form of sensory adaptation is called *dark adaptation* (Hecht and Mandelbaum, 1938). Cones adapt to the dark within about 8 minutes but aren't too sensitive at low light levels. Rods require about 30 minutes to completely adapt to the dark, but they provide much better sensitivity in dim light, at the cost of colour vision.

The retina is thick with cells. Among the different neuron types that occupy the retina's three distinct layers, the photoreceptor cells (rods and cones) form the innermost layer. The middle layer contains *bipolar cells*, which collect neural signals from the rods and cones and transmit them to the outermost layer of the retina, where neurons called *retinal ganglion cells* (RGCs) organize the signals and send them to the brain. In fact, the wiring of the eye is back to front, with the photoreceptors furthest away from the incoming light that has to pass through the tangle of blood vessels that supply the retina.

The axons and dendrites of photoreceptors and bipolar cells are relatively short (just a few microns long, or millionths of a metre), whereas the axons of the retinal ganglion cells span several centimetres. RGCs are the sensory neurons that connect the retina to various centres within the brain. The bundled RGC axons – about 1.5 million per eye – form the *optic nerve*, which leaves the eye through a hole in the retina called the blind spot, which *contains neither rods nor cones and therefore has no mechanism to sense light*. Try the demonstration in FIGURE **4.8** to find the blind spot in each of your own eyes.

Receptive fields and lateral inhibition

Each axon in the optic nerve originates in an individual retinal ganglion cell, as shown at the bottom of FIGURE **4.9**. Most RGCs respond to input not from a single retinal cone or rod but from an entire patch of adjacent photoreceptors lying side by side, or laterally, in the retina. A particular RGC will respond to light falling anywhere within that small patch, which is called its receptive field – *the region of the sensory surface that, when stimulated, causes a change in the firing rate of that neuron*. Although we'll focus on vision here, the general concept of receptive fields applies to all sensory systems. For example, the cells that connect to the touch centres of the brain have receptive fields, which are the part of the skin that, when stimulated, causes that cell's response to change in some way.

Within a receptive field, neighbouring photoreceptors respond to stimulation differently: some cells are excited, whereas some are inhibited. These opposing responses interact, which means that the signals they send through the bipolar cells to the RGC are based on differing levels of receptor activation, a process called *lateral inhibition*. Moving from top to bottom in Figure 4.9, a spot of light that covers any or all of

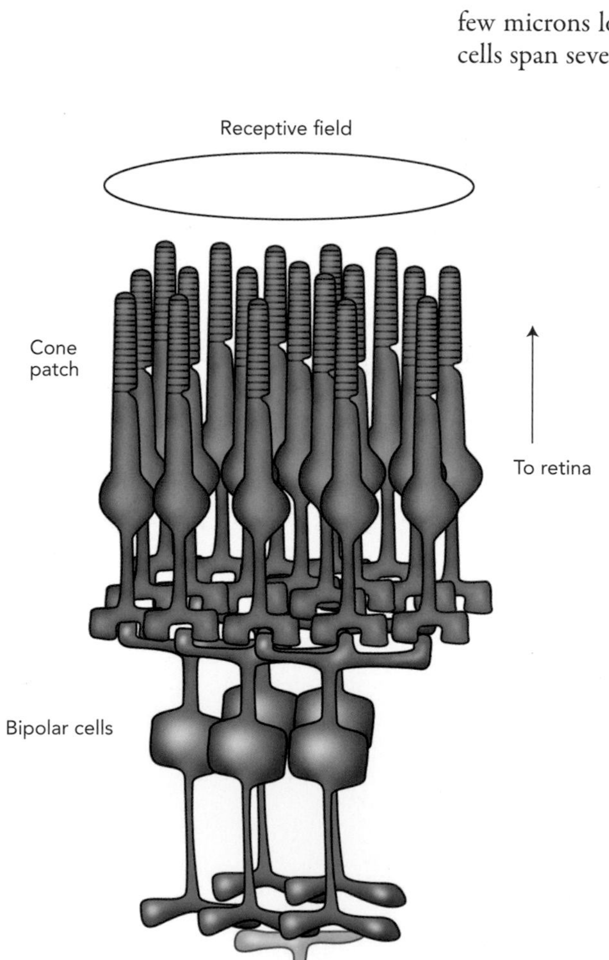

FIGURE **4.9 Receptive field of a retinal ganglion cell** The axon of a retinal ganglion cell, shown at the bottom of the figure, joins with all other RGC axons to form the optic nerve. Moving back towards the surface of the retina in this side view, each RGC connects to a cluster of five or six bipolar cells. The responses conveyed to the ganglion cell by each bipolar cell depend on the combination of excitatory or inhibitory signals transduced by the larger group of photoreceptors connected to that bipolar cell. The entire grouping, from photoreceptors to RGC, forms a receptive field, shown at the top of the figure. The RGC responds to a spot of light falling on any or all of the photoreceptors within its receptive field as a result of lateral inhibition.

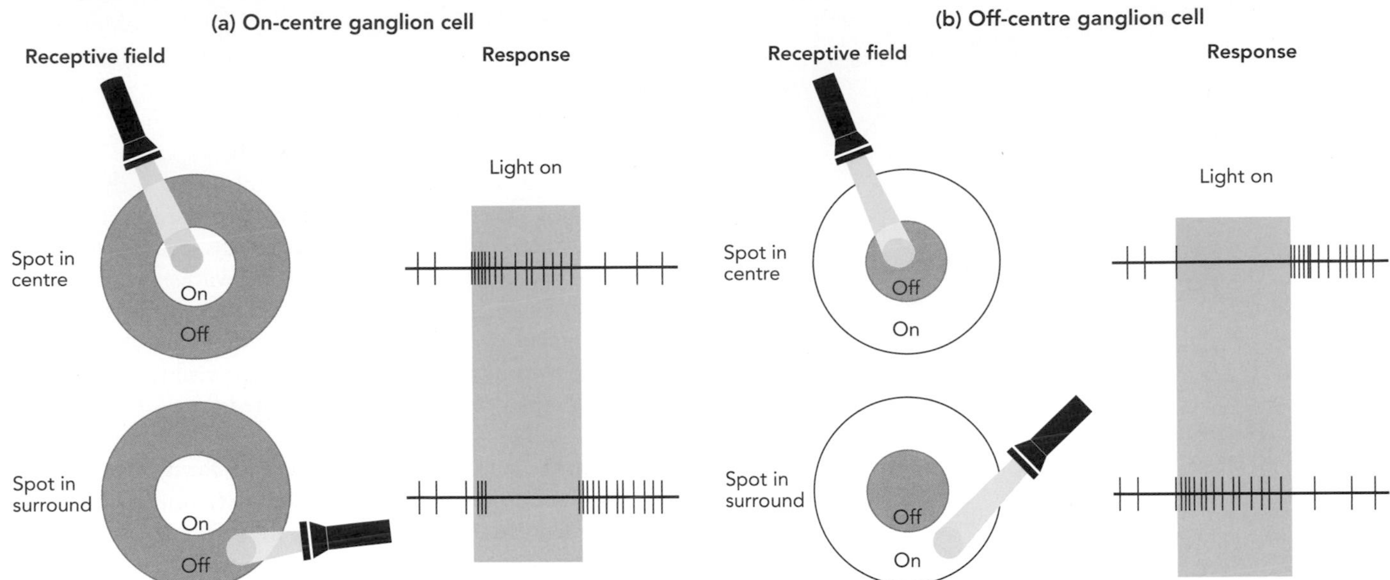

FIGURE 4.10 RGC receptive fields viewed end-on Imagine that you're looking down on the receptive field represented at the top of Figure 4.9. (a) An on-centre ganglion cell increases its firing rate when the receptive field is stimulated by light in the central area, but decreases its firing rate when the light strikes the surrounding area. Both neural response levels are shown in the right column. (b) The off-centre ganglion cell decreases its firing rate when its receptive field is stimulated by light in the central area, but increases its firing rate when the light strikes the surrounding area. Both responses are shown at the right.

the cones will activate one or more bipolar cells, which in turn causes the ganglion cell to change the rate at which it sends action potentials.

A given RGC responds to a spot of light projected anywhere within a small, roughly circular patch of retina (Kuffler, 1953). Most receptive fields contain either a central excitatory zone surrounded by a doughnut-shaped inhibitory zone, which is called an *on-centre cell*, or a central inhibitory zone surrounded by an excitatory zone, which is called an *off-centre cell* (see **FIGURE 4.10**). The doughnut-shaped regions represent patches of retina, as if the top of the diagram in Figure 4.9 were tilted forwards so we could look at the cones end-on.

Think about the response of an on-centre RGC when its receptive field is stimulated with spots of light of different sizes (**FIGURE 4.10a**). A small spot shining on the central excitatory zone increases the RGC's firing rate. When the spot exactly fills the excitatory zone, it elicits the strongest response, whereas light falling on the surrounding inhibitory zone elicits the weakest response or none at all. The response of an off-centre cell, shown in **FIGURE 4.10b**, is just the opposite. A small spot shining on the central inhibitory zone elicits a weak response, and a spot shining on the surrounding excitatory zone elicits a strong response in the RGC.

If a spot of light 'spills over' into the inhibitory zone of either receptive field type, the cell's response decreases somewhat, and if the entire receptive field is stimulated, excitatory and inhibitory activations cancel out due to lateral inhibition and the RGC's response will look similar to its response in the dark. Why would the RGC respond the same way to a uniformly bright field as to a uniformly dark field? The answer is related to a central notion that we keep coming back to, namely that the central nervous system has evolved to detect and process difference thresholds. The visual system encodes *differences* in brightness or colour. In other words, the RGC is a kind of 'spot detector', recording the relative changes in excitation and inhibition of receptive fields.

Lateral inhibition reveals how the visual system begins to encode the spatial structure of a scene and not merely the point-by-point light intensity sensed at each location in the retina. The retina is organized in this way to detect edges – abrupt transitions from light to dark or vice versa. Edges are of supreme importance in vision. They define the shape of objects, and anything that highlights such boundaries improves our ability to see an object's shape, particularly in low light situations.

Perceiving colour

We thrill to the burst of colours during a fireworks display, 'ooh' and 'aah' at nature's palette during sunset, and marvel at the vibrant hues of a peacock's tail feathers. Colour indeed adds zest to the visual world, but it also offers fundamental clues to an object's

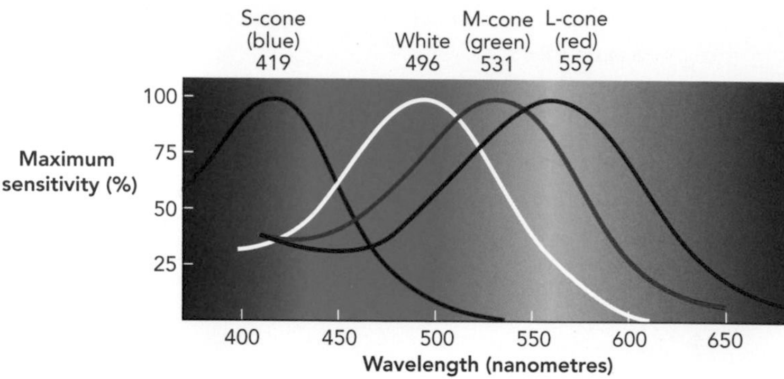

FIGURE 4.11 Seeing in colour We perceive a spectrum of colour because objects selectively absorb some wavelengths of light and reflect others. Colour perception corresponds to the summed activity of the three types of cones. Each type is most sensitive to a narrow range of wavelengths in the visible spectrum – S-cones process short (bluish) light, M-cones process medium (greenish) light and L-cones process long (reddish) light. Rods, represented by the white curve, are most sensitive to the medium wavelengths of visible light but do not contribute to colour perception.

identity. A black banana or blue lips are colour-coded calls to action – to avoid or sound the alarm, as the case might be.

Seeing colour

Sir Isaac Newton pointed out around 1670 that colour is not something 'in' light. In fact, colour is nothing but our perception of light's wavelengths (see **FIGURE 4.11**). We perceive the shortest visible wavelengths as deep purple. As wavelengths increase, the colour perceived changes gradually and continuously to blue, then green, yellow, orange, and, with the longest visible wavelengths, red. This rainbow of hues and accompanying wavelengths is called the *visible spectrum*, illustrated in Figure 4.11.

You'll recall that all rods contain the same photopigment, which makes them ideal for low light vision but bad at distinguishing colours. Cones, by contrast, contain any one of three types of pigment. Each cone absorbs light over a range of wavelengths, but its pigment type is especially sensitive to visible wavelengths that correspond to red (long-wavelength), green (medium-wavelength) or blue (short-wavelength) light. Red, green and blue are the primary colours of light, and the idea that colour perception relies on three components in the retina dates to the 19th century, when it was first proposed by English scientist Thomas Young (1773–1829). Young produced staggering accomplishments – he was a practising doctor and a distinguished physicist, and in his spare time he contributed to solving the mystery of the Rosetta Stone (a tablet that allowed archaeologists to translate ancient languages). He knew so much about so many topics that a recent biographer called him 'the last man who knew everything' (Robinson, 2006). Happily for psychology, Young had some pretty good ideas about how colour vision works. But it was von Helmholtz who more fully developed Young's idea that colour perception results from different combinations of the three basic elements in the retina that respond to the wavelengths corresponding to the three primary colours of light. This insight has several implications and applications.

In one of his early experiments in the darkened room of his study at Trinity College, Cambridge, Newton discovered that white light is made up of all the visible colours of the spectrum. He demonstrated that if one holds a prism into a beam of natural daylight streaming through a shuttered window, it can be decomposed into the full colour spectrum projected on the back wall, as illustrated in **FIGURE 4.12**. This demonstrates that a white surface is reflecting all the visible wavelengths of light. Lighting designers have since used this principle to create colours by combing various amounts of primary colours in a process called *additive colour mixing*.

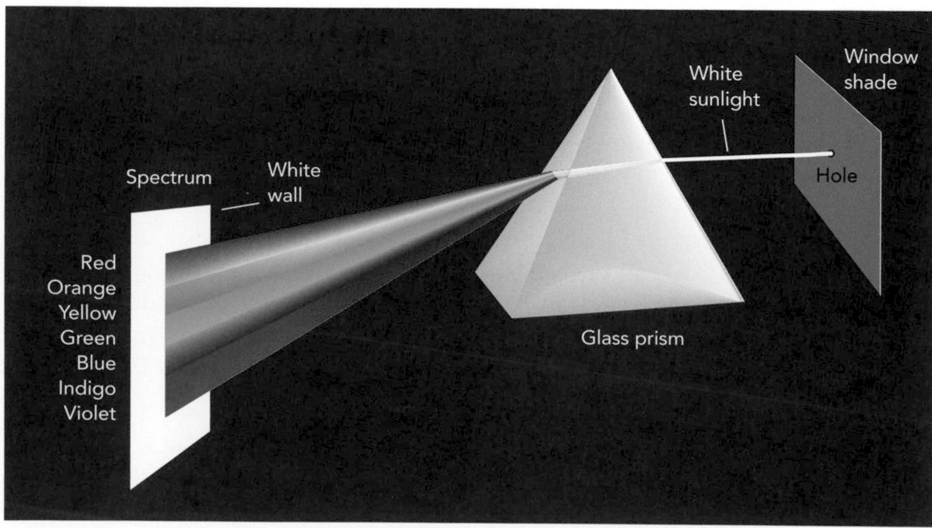

FIGURE 4.12 The colour spectrum In his early experiments with prisms, Sir Isaac Newton demonstrated that natural white light is made up of different wavelengths of light that correspond to the full spectrum of visible colours.

Centuries before Newton first experimented with light, Renaissance painters in Italy had learned that they could re-create any colour found in nature simply by mixing only three colours: red, blue and yellow. You may have discovered this process for yourself by mixing paints. Mixing paint works in the opposite way to mixing light as these pigments absorb different colours from the visible spectrum. This *subtractive colour mixing* works by removing light from the mix, such as when you combine all the different coloured paints in the right proportion, you end up with black. The darker the colour, the less light it contains, which is why black surfaces reflect no light.

When you perceive colour, then, the cone receptors in your retina encode the wavelengths of light reflected from a surface. But colour processing in the human visual system occurs in two stages. The first stage – encoding – occurs in the retina, whereas the second stage – processing – requires the brain (Gegenfurtner and Kiper, 2003).

TRICHROMATIC COLOUR REPRESENTATION The pattern of responding across the three types of cones that provides a unique code for each colour.

FIXTAL

Many people inherit conditions in which either the red or the green photoreceptors do not transduce light properly. Such people have difficulty distinguishing hues that to typical individuals appear as red or green. Unfortunately, in many countries, traffic signals use red and green lights to indicate whether cars should stop or continue at a junction. Why do drivers with red-green blindness not risk accidents every time they approach a junction?

Trichromatic colour representation in the cones

Light striking the retina causes a specific pattern of response in the three cone types (Schnapf et al., 1987). One type responds best to short-wavelength (bluish) light, the second type to medium-wavelength (greenish) light, and the third type to long-wavelength (reddish) light. Researchers refer to them as S-cones, M-cones and L-cones, respectively (see Figure 4.11).

This trichromatic colour representation means that the pattern of responding across the three types of cones provides a unique *code for each colour*. Researchers can 'read out' the wavelength of the light entering the eye by working backwards from the relative firing rates of the three types of cones. A genetic disorder in which one of the cone types is missing – and, in some rare cases, two or all three – causes a *colour deficiency*. Around 4% of the population of Western Europe and the US have a congenital colour deficiency (Jacobs, 1997). This trait is sex-linked, affecting men much more often than women.

Colour deficiency is often referred to as *colour blindness*, but in fact, in the most common form of the condition, people missing only one type of cone can still distinguish many colours, just not as many as someone who has the full complement of three cone types. Like synaesthetes, people whose vision is colour deficient often do not realize that they experience colour differently from others. Colour blindness is usually linked to the X chromosome, which accounts for why it is found in approximately 8% of males and less than 1% of females.

Trichromatic colour representation is well established as the first step of encoding colour in the visual system (Abromov and Gordon, 1994). Sensory adaptation helps to explain the second step.

Colour blindness has implications for which jobs people can hold. One of the first examples of this was a Swedish train crash in 1875, which was attributed to the colour blindness of the driver who could not distinguish signals. However, there are still many individuals who are unaware that they are colour blind. In 2010, Robert Law lost his job after 36 years as a driver of freight trains when it was discovered that he had trouble distinguishing colours. He was responsible for transporting hazardous goods to a Scottish nuclear plant.

Colour-opponent representation into the brain

Recall that sensory adaptation occurs because our sensitivity to prolonged stimulation tends to decline over time. Just like the rest of your body, cones need an occasional break too. Staring too long at one colour fatigues the cones that respond to that colour, producing a form of sensory adaptation called *colour afterimage*. To demonstrate this effect for yourself, follow these instructions for **FIGURE 4.13**:

- Stare at the small cross between the two colour patches for about one minute. Try to keep your eyes as still as possible.
- After a minute, look at the lower cross. You should see a vivid colour aftereffect that lasts for a minute or more. Pay particular attention to the colours in the afterimage.

Were you puzzled that the red patch produces a green afterimage and the green patch produces a red afterimage? This result may seem like nothing more than a curious mind-bug, but in fact it reveals something important about colour perception. The explanation stems from the second stage of colour representation, the colour-opponent system, where *pairs of visual neurons work in opposition* – red-sensitive against green-sensitive cells (as in Figure 4.13) and blue-sensitive against yellow-sensitive cells (Hurvich and

COLOUR-OPPONENT SYSTEM Pairs of visual neurons that work in opposition.

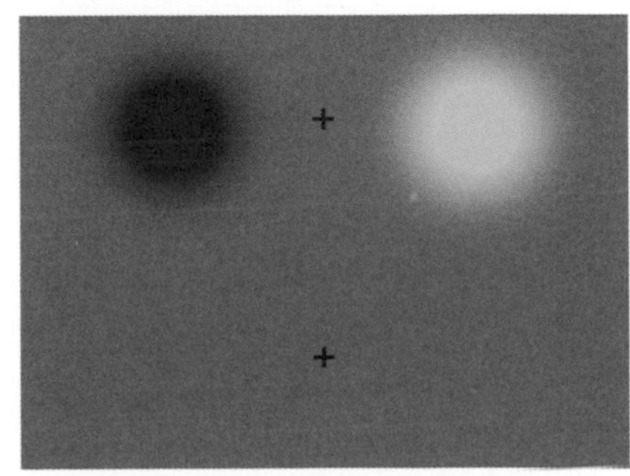

FIGURE **4.13 Colour afterimage demonstration** Follow the accompanying instructions in the text, and sensory adaptation will do the rest. When the afterimage fades, you can get back to reading the chapter.

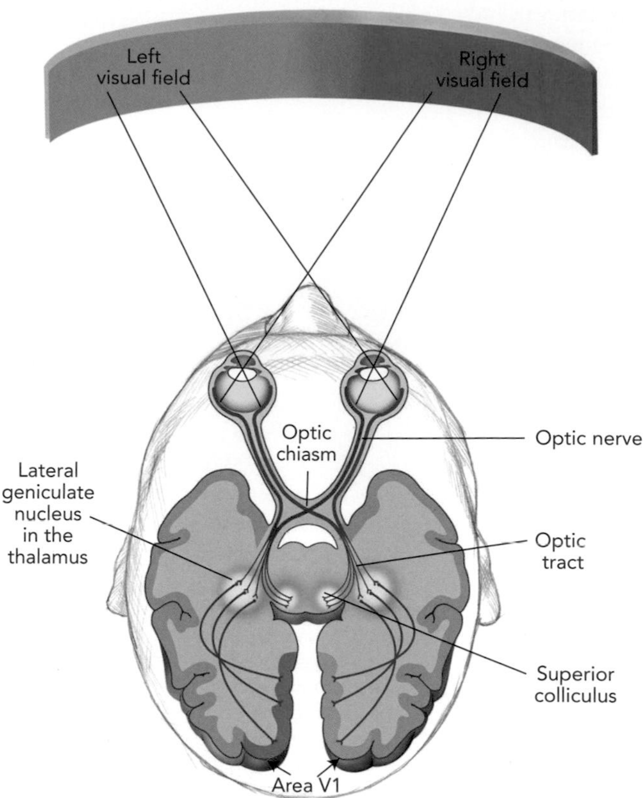

FIGURE **4.14 Visual pathway from eye through brain** Objects in the right visual field stimulate the left half of each retina, and objects in the left visual field stimulate the right half of each retina. The optic nerves, one exiting each eye, are formed by the axons of RGCs emerging from the retina. Just before they enter the brain at the optic chiasm, about half the nerve fibres from each eye cross. The left half of each optic nerve, representing the *right* visual field, runs through the brain's left hemisphere via the thalamus, and the right halves, representing the *left* visual field, travel this route through the right hemisphere. So, information from the right visual field ends up in the left hemisphere and information from the left visual field ends up in the right hemisphere.

AREA V1 The initial processing region of the primary visual cortex.

TOPOGRAPHIC VISUAL ORGANIZATION Adjacent neurons process adjacent portions of the visual field.

Jameson, 1957). How do opponent pairs of *four* colours make sense if we have just *three* cone types?

It may be that opponent pairs evolved to enhance colour perception by taking advantage of excitatory and inhibitory stimulation. Red-green cells are excited (they increase their firing rates) in response to wavelengths corresponding to red and inhibited (they decrease their firing rates) in response to wavelengths corresponding to green. Blue-yellow cells increase their firing rate in response to blue wavelengths (excitatory) and decrease their firing rate in response to yellow wavelengths (inhibitory). The colour pairs are linked to each other as opposites.

The colour-opponent system explains colour aftereffects. When you view a colour, let's say, green, the cones that respond most strongly to green become fatigued over time. Fatigue leads to an imbalance in the inputs to the red-green colour-opponent neurons, beginning with the RGCs: the weakened signal from the green-responsive cones leads to an overall response that emphasizes red. A similar explanation can be made for other colour aftereffects; find a bright blue circle of colour and get ready to make your flatmate see yellow spots!

Working together, the trichromatic and colour-opponent systems begin the process of colour perception. S-, M- and L-cones connect to colour-opponent RGCs with excitatory and/or inhibitory connections that produce the colour-opponent response. Colour-opponent, excitatory-inhibitory processes then continue down the visual pathways to the brain, first to neurons in the thalamus and then to the occipital cortex, as mapped in **FIGURE 4.14** (de Valois et al., 1966).

The visual brain

A great deal of visual processing takes place within the retina itself, including the encoding of simple features such as spots of light, edges and colour. More complex aspects of vision, however, require more powerful processing, and that enlists the brain.

Streams of action potentials containing information encoded by the retina travel to the brain along the optic nerve. Half of the axons in the optic nerve that leave each eye come from RGCs that code information in the right visual field, whereas the other half code information in the left visual field. These two nerve bundles link to the left and right hemispheres of the brain, respectively (see Figure 4.14). The optic nerve travels from each eye to the lateral geniculate nucleus, located in the thalamus. As you will recall from Chapter 3, the thalamus receives inputs from all the senses except smell. From there, the visual signal travels to the back of the brain, to the primary visual cortex, the rear part of the occipital lobe, which is about the size of a credit card in humans. Here, the information is systematically mapped into a representation of the visual scene. The *initial processing region* is known as area V1 and has a topographic visual organization, which means that *adjacent neurons process adjacent portions of the visual field*. In fact, the topographical organization is somewhat distorted as the central portion of the visual field which corresponds to the input from foveal cells is greatly enlarged in area V1, which is exactly what you would expect, given the number and densely packed photoreceptors in this part of the retina. After area V1, there are thought to be about 30–50 additional brain areas specialized for vision, located mainly in the occipital lobe at the back of the brain and in the temporal lobes on the sides of the brain (Orban et al., 2004; van Essen et al., 1992).

Neural systems for perceiving shape

One of the most important functions of vision involves perceiving the shapes of objects; our day-to-day lives would be a mess if we couldn't distinguish individual shapes from one another. Imagine not being able to reliably differentiate between a warm doughnut with glazed icing and a straight stalk of celery and you'll get the idea; breakfast could become a traumatic experience if you couldn't distinguish shapes. Perceiving shape depends on the location and orientation of an object's edges. It is not surprising, then, that area V1 is specialized for encoding edge orientation.

As you read in Chapter 3, neurons in the visual cortex selectively respond to bars and edges in specific orientations in space (Hubel and Wiesel, 1962, 1998). In effect, area V1 contains populations of neurons, each 'tuned' to respond to edges oriented at each position in the visual field. This means that some neurons fire when an object in a vertical orientation is perceived, other neurons fire when an object in a horizontal orientation is perceived, still other neurons fire when objects in a diagonal orientation of 45° are perceived and so on (see **FIGURE 4.15**). By combining the output from this population of neurons, the resultant pattern of activation can code for the varying features of objects and distinguish where a doughnut ends and celery begins.

Pathways for what, where and how

In Chapter 2, you learned how brain researchers have used transcranial magnetic stimulation (TMS) to demonstrate that a person who can recognize what an object is may not be able to perceive that the object is moving. This observation implies that one brain system identifies people and things and another tracks their movements, or guides our movements in relation to them. Two functionally distinct pathways, or *visual streams*, project from the occipital cortex to visual areas in other parts of the brain (see **FIGURE 4.16**):

1 The *ventral* ('below') *stream* travels across the occipital lobe into the lower levels of the temporal lobes and includes brain areas that represent an object's shape and identity, in other words, what it is.
2 The *dorsal* ('above') *stream* travels up from the occipital lobe to the parietal lobes (including some of the middle and upper levels of the temporal lobes), connecting with brain areas that identify the location and motion of an object, in other words, where it is. Because the dorsal stream allows us to perceive spatial relations, researchers originally dubbed it the 'where pathway' (Ungerleider and Mishkin, 1982). More recently, neuroscientists have argued that because the dorsal stream is crucial for guiding movements, such as aiming, reaching or tracking with the eyes, the 'where pathway' should more appropriately be called the 'how pathway' (Milner and Goodale, 1995).

Some of the most dramatic evidence for two distinct visual streams comes from studying the mindbugs that result from brain injury. A patient known as D. F. suffered permanent brain damage following exposure to toxic levels of carbon monoxide (Goodale et al.,

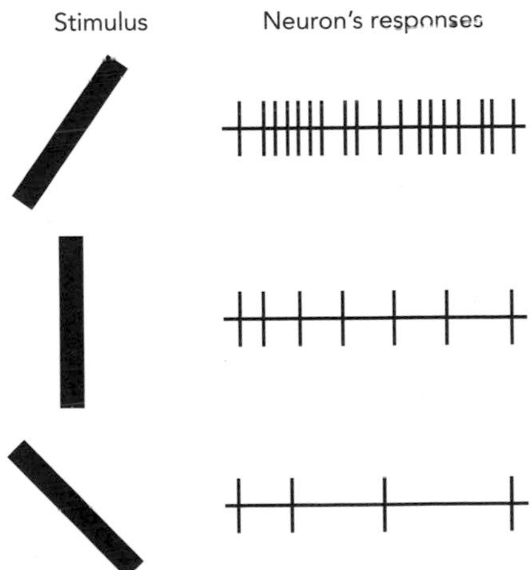

FIGURE 4.15 Single neuron feature detectors Area V1 contains neurons that respond to specific orientations of edges. Here, the responses of a single neuron are recorded as the bars are viewed at different orientations. The response rate on the right reveals that this particular neuron fires continuously when the bar is pointing to the right at 45°, less often when it is vertical, and not at all when it is pointing to the left at 45°.

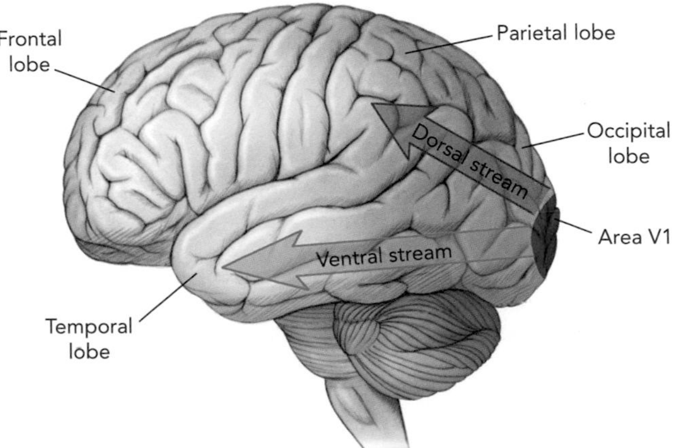

FIGURE 4.16 Visual streaming One interconnected visual system forms a pathway that courses from the occipital visual regions into the lower temporal lobe. This ventral pathway enables us to identify what we see. Another interconnected pathway travels from the occipital lobe through the upper regions of the temporal lobe into the parietal regions. This dorsal pathway allows us to locate objects, track their movements and move in relation to them.

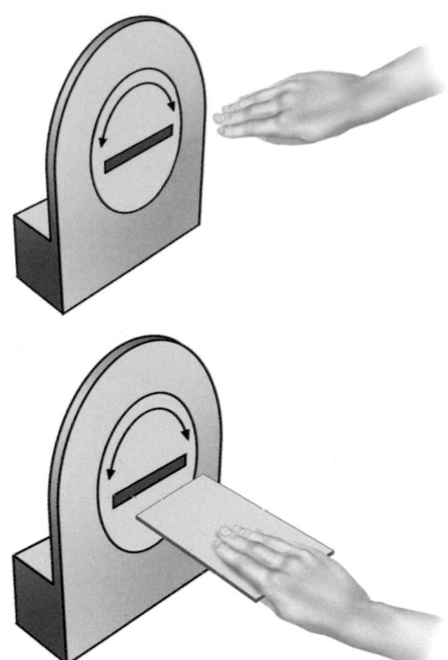

FIGURE 4.17 Testing visual form agnosia When researchers asked patient D. F. to orient her hand to match the angle of the slot in the testing apparatus, as shown at the top, she was unable to comply. Asked to insert a card into the slot at various angles, as shown at the bottom, D. F. accomplished the task virtually to perfection.

VISUAL FORM AGNOSIA The inability to recognize objects by sight.

1991). A large region of the lateral occipital cortex was destroyed, an area in the ventral stream that is very active when people recognize objects. D. F.'s ability to recognize objects by sight was greatly impaired, although her ability to recognize objects by touch was normal. This suggests that the *visual representation* of objects, and not D. F.'s *memory* for objects, was damaged. D. F.'s brain damage belongs to a category called visual form agnosia – *the inability to recognize objects by sight* (Goodale and Milner, 1992, 2004).

Oddly, although D. F. could not recognize objects visually, she could accurately *guide* her actions by sight. D. F. was shown a display board with a slot in it, as in **FIGURE 4.17.** The researchers could adjust the orientation of the slot. In one version of the task, shown at the top in the figure, they asked D. F. to report the orientation of the slot by holding her hand up at the same angle as the slot. D. F. performed very poorly at this task, almost randomly, suggesting that she did not have a reliable representation of visual orientation.

In another version of the task, shown at the bottom in Figure 4.17, D. F. was asked to insert a flat block into the slot, as if she were posting a letter into a letter box. Now, she performed the task almost perfectly. The paradox is that D. F.'s explicit or conscious understanding of what she was seeing was greatly impaired, but her ability to use this same information nonconsciously to guide her movements remained intact. When D. F. was scanned with fMRI, researchers found that she showed normal activation of regions within the dorsal stream during guided movement (James et al., 2003).

Other patients with brain damage to the parietal section of the dorsal stream have difficulty using vision to guide their reaching and grasping movements, a condition termed *optic ataxia* (Perenin and Vighetto, 1988). However, these patients' ventral streams are intact, meaning they recognize what objects are. We can conclude from these two patterns of impairment that the ventral and dorsal visual streams are functionally distinct; it is possible to damage one while leaving the other intact.

Researchers are starting to examine how the two streams must work together during visual perception in order to integrate 'what' and 'where'. One intriguing possibility is suggested by recent fMRI research indicating that some regions within the dorsal stream are sensitive to properties of an object's identity, responding differently, for example, to line drawings of the same object in different sizes or viewed from different vantage points (Konen and Kastner, 2008). The sensitivity of some regions within the dorsal stream to aspects of object identity may allow the dorsal and ventral streams to exchange information and thus promote integration of 'what' and 'where' (Farivar, 2009; Konen and Kastner, 2008).

In summary, light initially passes through several layers in the eye, with the retina linking the world of light outside and the world of visual perception inside the central nervous system. Two types of photoreceptor cells in the retina transduce light into neural impulses: cones, which operate under normal daylight conditions and sense colour, and rods, which are active only under low light conditions for night vision.

The retina contains several layers, and the outermost consists of retinal ganglion cells (RGCs) that collect and send signals to the brain. A particular RGC will respond to light falling anywhere within a small patch that constitutes its receptive field. Light striking the retina causes a specific pattern of response in each of three cone types that are critical to colour perception: short-wavelength (bluish) light, medium-wavelength (greenish) light, and long-wavelength (reddish) light. The overall pattern of response across the three cone types results in a unique code for each colour, known as its trichromatic colour representation. Information encoded by the retina travels to the brain along the optic nerve, which connects to the lateral geniculate nucleus in the thalamus and then to the primary visual cortex, area V1, in the occipital lobe.

Two functionally distinct pathways project from the occipital lobe to visual areas in other parts of the brain. The ventral stream travels into the lower levels of the temporal lobes and includes brain areas that represent an object's shape and identity. The dorsal stream goes from the occipital lobes to the parietal lobes, connecting with brain areas that identify the location and motion of an object.

Integrating visual features

As we've seen, specialized feature detectors in different parts of the visual system analyse each of the multiple features of a visible object – orientation, colour, size, shape and so on. But how are different features combined into single, unified objects? What allows us to perceive so easily and correctly that the girl with the blue bucket in the photo is wearing a red top and the girl with the blue top is not holding a blue bucket? Why don't we see free-floating patches of blue and red, or even incorrect combinations, such as each girl wearing different tops? These questions refer to what researchers call the binding problem in perception, which concerns *how features are linked together so that we see unified objects in our visual world rather than free-floating or miscombined features* (Treisman, 1998, 2006). Recent research indicates that the visual system (in birds at least) may already be set up to bind shape and colour together from the very beginning (Wood, 2014). Specifically, newly hatched chicks presented with a virtual object were able to build an integrated representation of it, binding its colour and shape features into integrated colour-shape representations in memory. For example, they reliably distinguished an object defined by a purple circle and yellow triangle from an object defined by a purple triangle and yellow circle.

Illusory conjunctions: perceptual mistakes

In everyday life, we correctly combine features into unified objects so automatically and effortlessly that it may be difficult to appreciate that binding is ever a problem at all. However, researchers have discovered errors in binding that reveal important clues about how the process works. One such error is known as an illusory conjunction – *a perceptual mistake where features from multiple objects are incorrectly combined*. In a pioneering study of illusory conjunctions, Treisman and Schmidt (1982) briefly showed study participants visual displays in which black digits flanked coloured letters, then instructed them to first report the black digits and second to describe the coloured letters. Participants frequently reported illusory conjunctions, claiming to have seen, for example, a green A or a purple X instead of the purple A and the green X that had actually been shown (see **FIGURE 4.18**). These illusory conjunctions were not just the result of guessing; they occurred more frequently than other kinds of errors, such as reporting a letter or colour that was not present in the display (Figure 4.18). Illusory conjunctions look real to the participants, who were just as confident they had seen them as they were about the actual coloured letters they perceived correctly.

Why do illusory conjunctions occur? Treisman and her colleagues have tried to explain them by proposing a feature integration theory (Treisman, 1998, 2006; Treisman and Gelade, 1980; Treisman and Schmidt, 1982), which *proposes that attention binds individual features together to comprise a composite stimulus*. From this perspective, attention provides the 'glue' necessary to bind features together, and illusory conjunctions occur when it is difficult for participants to pay full attention to the features that need to be glued together. For example, in the experiments we just considered, participants were required to process the digits that flank the coloured letters, thereby reducing attention to the letters and allowing illusory conjunctions to occur. When experimental conditions are changed so that participants can pay full attention to the coloured letters, and they are able to correctly bind their features together, illusory conjunctions disappear (Treisman, 1998; Treisman and Schmidt, 1982).

Feature integration theory also helps to explain some striking effects observed when people search for targets in displays containing many items. When searching through a display containing green Xs and Os (see **FIGURE 4.19**), it does not require much focused attention to spot a target item defined by a unique feature such as a purple X. The purple X seems to simply 'pop out' of the display, and people can find it just as quickly when there are many other nontarget items in the display as when there are only a few nontarget items in the display. But when searching through a display of green Xs and purple Os, a target purple X is no longer defined by a unique feature in relation to the nontarget items; instead, it contains a conjunction of two features, 'X' like the green Xs and 'purple' like the purple Os. Now, the purple X requires focused attention to pick out, and it takes more time to find when the display contains many nontargets than when it contains few nontargets (Treisman, 1998; Treisman and Gelade, 1980) (Figure 4.19).

The role of the parietal lobe

The binding process makes use of feature information processed by structures within the ventral visual stream, the 'what pathway' (Seymour et al., 2010) (see Figure 4.16, above). But because binding involves linking together features processed in distinct parts of the

BINDING PROBLEM How features are linked together so that we see unified objects in our visual world rather than free-floating or miscombined features.

ILLUSORY CONJUNCTION A perceptual mistake where features from multiple objects are incorrectly combined.

FEATURE INTEGRATION THEORY A theory that proposes that attention binds individual features together to comprise a composite stimulus.

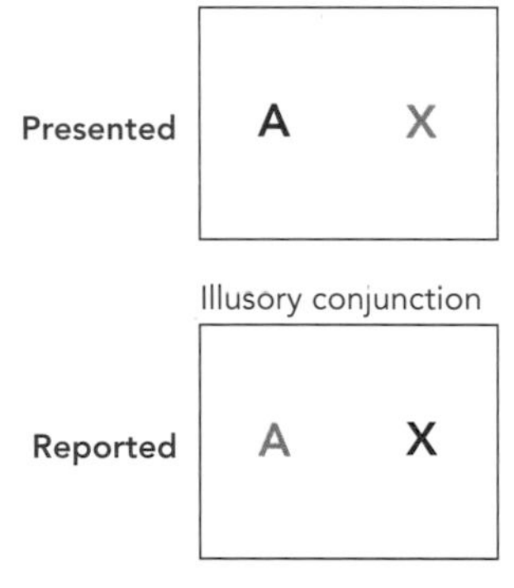

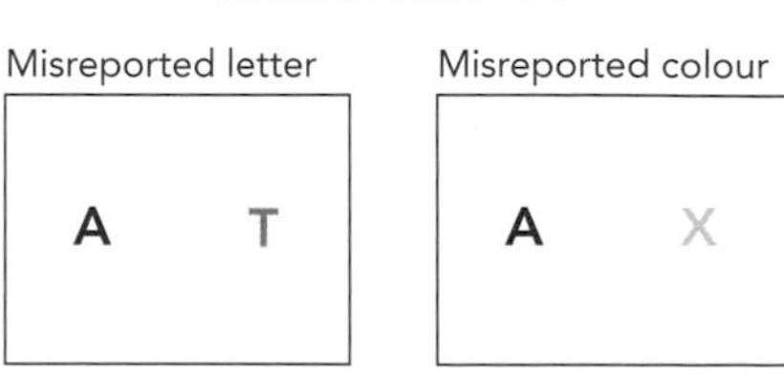

FIGURE 4.18 Illusory conjunctions Illusory conjunctions occur when features such as colour and shape are combined incorrectly. For example, when participants are shown a purple A and green X, they sometimes report seeing a green A and purple X. Other kinds of errors, such as a misreported letter (reporting 'T' when no T was presented) or misreported colour (reporting 'yellow' when no yellow was presented), occur rarely, indicating that illusory conjunctions are not the result of guessing (based on Robertson, 2003).

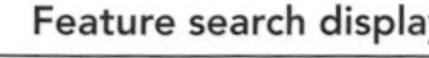

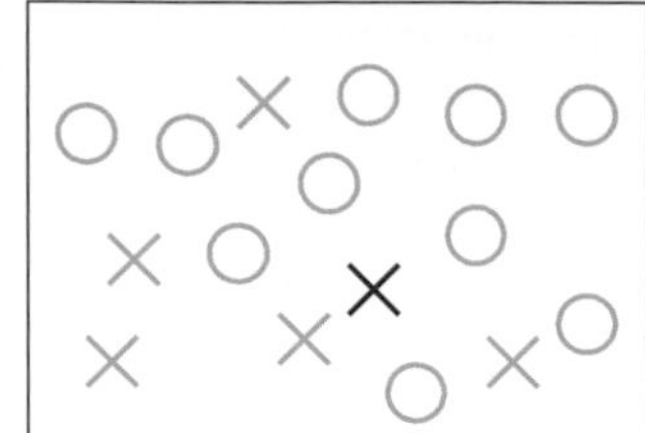

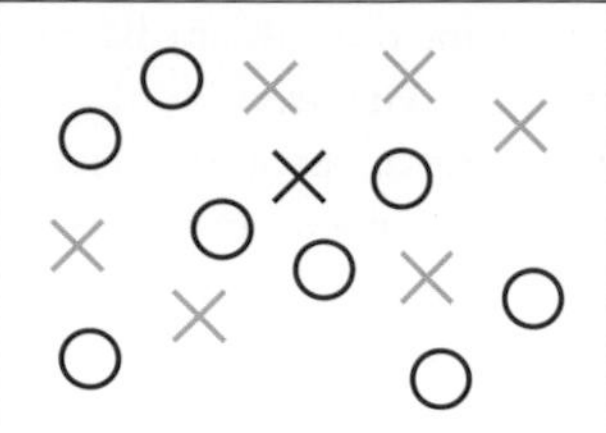

FIGURE 4.19 Visual search If you are asked to try to find the purple X in these displays, it is easy to find when the purple X differs from the surrounding items in either colour or shape (feature search); the target just pops out at you. It is harder to find the purple X when it is surrounded by both purple Os and green Xs (conjunction search), because focused attention is now required to spot the target (based on Robertson, 2003).

ventral stream at a particular spatial location, it also depends critically on the parietal lobe in the dorsal stream, the 'where pathway' (Robertson, 1999). For example, Treisman and others studied a patient, R. M., who had suffered strokes that destroyed his left and right parietal lobes. Although many aspects of his visual function were intact, he had severe problems attending to spatially distinct objects. When presented with stimuli such as those in Figure 4.18, R. M. perceived an abnormally large number of illusory conjunctions, even when he was given as long as 10 seconds to look at the displays (Friedman-Hill et al., 1995; Robertson, 2003). More recent studies of similar patients suggest that damage to the upper and posterior portions of the parietal lobe is likely to produce problems with focused attention, resulting in binding problems and increased illusory conjunctions (Braet and Humphreys, 2009; McCrea et al., 2006). Neuroimaging studies indicate that these same parietal regions are activated in healthy individuals when they perform the kind of visual feature binding that patients with parietal lobe damage are unable to perform (Shafritz et al., 2002), as well as when they search for conjunction features (Corbetta et al., 1995; Donner et al., 2002).

These findings fit neatly with recent TMS studies in which researchers attempted to temporarily 'turn off' the posterior parietal lobe while participants performed a feature binding task involving colours and letters (Braet and Humphreys, 2009). Applying TMS to the posterior parietal lobe during the task resulted in an increased number of illusory conjunctions but not in other kinds of perceptual errors. When TMS was applied to the occipital lobe, it had no effect on illusory conjunctions. Interestingly, the effects of parietal TMS on illusory conjunctions were seen mainly when TMS was applied after presentation of the target item, suggesting that the attentional process supported by the parietal region serves to 'lock in' or consolidate perceived features. These findings help to refine the original suggestion from feature integration theory that feature binding depends critically on attentional processes (Treisman, 1998).

Binding and attention in synaesthesia

The findings and ideas we've just considered turn out to be highly relevant to synaesthesia. We considered examples of synaesthesia at the outset of this chapter, such as consistently perceiving particular letters in a particular colour (see Figure 4.1). Some researchers have characterized synaesthesia as an instance of atypical feature binding. Normal binding of colours and letters, for example, is a response to actual features of the external stimulus, but in synaesthesia, the colour feature is not present in the external stimulus.

Surprisingly, recent research shows that some of the same processes involved in normal feature binding also occur in synaesthesia. fMRI studies of synaesthetic individuals have revealed that the parietal lobe regions are implicated in the normal binding of colour and shape and become active during the experience of letter colour synaesthesia (Weiss et al., 2005). Further, applying TMS to these parietal regions interferes with synaesthetic perceptions (Esterman et al., 2006; Muggleton et al., 2007). Consistent with the idea that parietal activity is related to attentional processes needed for binding, other experiments have shown that synaesthetic bindings, such as seeing a particular digit in a particular colour, depend on attention (Mattingly, 2009; Robertson, 2003; Sagiv et al., 2006). For instance, when dots are quickly presented to a synaesthetic individual together with digits, for example '7', that induce a synaesthetic perception of green, the synaesthete names the colour of the dots more quickly when they are green than when they are orange, that is, when the dot colour matches the colour of the synaesthetic perception. But when

> According to a 2013 report from the British Security Industry Association, there are up to 5.9 million CCTV cameras in the UK. That's one camera for every 11 people. When a culprit has been captured clearly on a CCTV recording and the identity is in question, juries in the UK (and Australia) can be invited to compare the recorded images with the defendant in court. In 2009, 95% of Scotland Yard murder cases used CCTV footage as evidence. However, experimental studies show that approximately 1 in 5 adults misidentify the culprit when asked to make this comparison (Davis and Valentine, 2009). We may have specialized areas for processing faces, but humans are not infallible when it comes to matching recordings with real people.

synaesthetes are instructed to ignore the numbers, there is little difference in the amount of time taken to name the colour of the green and orange dots, suggesting that attention is required to bind the synaesthetic colour to the digit (Robertson, 2003; Sagiv et al., 2006). Although our perceptual experiences differ substantially from those of synaesthetes, they rely on the same basic mechanisms of feature binding.

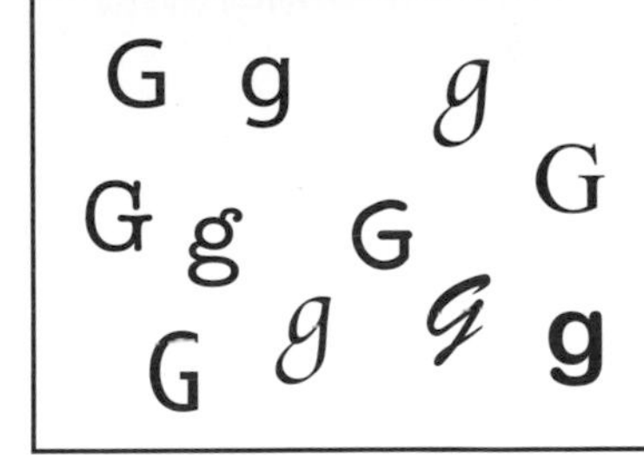

A quick glance and you recognize all these letters as G, but their varying sizes, shapes, angles and orientations ought to make this recognition task difficult. What is it about the process of object recognition that allows us to perform this task effortlessly?

Recognizing objects by sight

Take a quick look at the letters in the accompanying illustration. Even though they're quite different from one another, you probably effortlessly recognized them as all being examples of the letter G. Now consider the same kind of demonstration using your best friend's face. Your friend might have long hair, but one day she decides to get it cut dramatically short. Although your friend now looks strikingly different, you still recognize that person with ease. Add glasses, a dye job, producing reddish hair. Maybe your friend uses coloured contact lenses, or gets piercings to accommodate a nose ring. Any or all of these elements have the effect of producing a distinctly different looking face, yet just like the variability in Gs, you are somehow able to extract the underlying features of the face that allow you to accurately identify your friend.

This thought exercise may seem trivial, but it's no small perceptual feat. If the visual system were somehow stumped each time a minor variation occurred in an object being perceived, the inefficiency of it all would be overwhelming. We'd have to effortfully process information just to perceive our friend as the same person from one meeting to another, not to mention labouring through the process of knowing when a G is really a G. In general, though, object recognition proceeds fairly smoothly, in large part due to the operation of the feature detectors we discussed earlier.

How do feature detectors help the visual system get from a spatial array of light hitting the eye to the accurate perception of an object, such as your friend's face? Some researchers argue for a *modular view*: that specialized brain areas, or modules, detect and represent faces or houses or even body parts. Using fMRI to examine visual processing in healthy young adults, researchers found a subregion in the temporal lobe that responds selectively to faces compared to just about any other object category, while a nearby area responds selectively to buildings and landscapes (Kanwisher et al., 1997). This view suggests that we not only have feature detectors to aid in visual perception but also 'face detectors', 'building detectors' and possibly other types of neurons specialized for particular types of object perception (Kanwisher and Yovel, 2006). How this modularization, *the process of relatively encapsulated function*, comes about is still a matter of controversy. For example, some perceptual categories such as faces may have a degree of pre-specified organization in the brain – nature has wired regions to expect facelike patterns and seek these out. As we will examine in Chapter 12, some theorists argue that we have built-in perceptual templates for recognizing faces, which is why newborn babies prefer to look at faces shortly after birth (Johnson and Morton, 1991). Others argue that modularization emerges as a consequence of exposure and expertise (Elman et al., 1997). As you will discover, the answer appears to be a combination of both built-in propensity and experience.

MODULARIZATION The process of relatively encapsulated function.

Psychologists and researchers who argue for a more *distributed representation* of object categories challenge the modular view. Researchers have shown that although a subregion in the temporal lobes does respond more to faces than to any other category, parts of the brain outside this area may also be involved in face recognition. In this view, it is the pattern of activity across multiple brain regions that identifies any viewed object, including faces (Haxby et al., 2001). Each of these views explains some data better than others, and researchers continue to debate their relative merits.

Representing objects and faces in the brain

Investigations of how the brain responds to complex objects and to faces began in the 1980s with experiments using primates as research subjects. Researchers recorded from single cells in the temporal lobes of macaque monkeys and found that different neurons respond selectively to different object shapes (Tanaka, 1996). Other investigators found neurons that respond best to other monkey faces or to human faces.

In the mid-1990s, neuroscientists began using fMRI to investigate whether specialized neurons like these operate in the human brain. They showed healthy participants photographs of faces, houses and other object categories, for example shoes, tools or dogs. During the past decade, fMRI studies have revealed that some brain regions in the occipital and temporal lobes do respond selectively to specific object categories (Downing et al., 2006).

Another perspective on this issue is provided by experiments designed to measure precisely where seizures originate; these experiments have provided insights on how single neurons in the human brain respond to objects and faces (Quiroga et al., 2005). Electrodes were placed on the temporal lobes of people who suffer from epilepsy. Then the volunteers were shown photographs of faces and objects as the researchers recorded their neural responses. The researchers found that neurons in the temporal lobe respond to specific objects viewed from multiple angles and to people wearing different clothing and facial expressions and photographed from various angles. In some cases, the neurons also respond to the words for the objects they prefer. For example, a neuron that responded to photographs of the Sydney Opera House also responded when the words Sydney Opera were displayed but not when the words Eiffel Tower were displayed (Quiroga et al., 2005).

PERCEPTUAL CONSTANCY A perceptual principle stating that even as aspects of sensory signals change, perception remains consistent.

Taken together, these experiments demonstrate the principle of perceptual constancy – *even as aspects of sensory signals change, perception remains consistent*. Think back once again to our discussion of difference thresholds early in this chapter. Our perceptual systems are sensitive to relative differences in changing stimulation and make allowances for varying sensory input. This general principle helps explain why you still recognize your friend despite changes in hair colour or style or the addition of facial jewellery. It's not as though your visual perceptual system responds to a change with, 'Here's a new and unfamiliar face to perceive.' Rather, it's as though it responds with, 'Interesting, here's a deviation from the way this face usually looks.' Perception is sensitive to changes in stimuli, but perceptual constancies allow us to notice the differences in the first place.

Our visual system allows us to identify people as the same individual even when they change features such as their hairstyle, hair colour, facial hair or jewellery.

Principles of perceptual organization

Before object recognition can even kick in, the visual system must perform another important task: to group the image regions that belong together into a representation of an object. The idea that we tend to perceive a unified, whole object rather than a collection of separate parts is the foundation of Gestalt psychology, which you read about in Chapter 1. Gestalt principles characterize many aspects of human perception. Among the foremost are the Gestalt *perceptual grouping rules* (see **FIGURE 4.20**), which govern how the features and regions of things fit together (Koffka, 1935). Here's a sample:

- *Simplicity:* A basic rule in science is that the simplest explanation is usually the best. This is the idea behind the Gestalt grouping rule of *Pragnanz*, which translates as 'good form'. When confronted with two or more possible interpretations of an object's shape, the visual system tends to select the simplest or most likely interpretation (**FIGURE 4.20a**).
- *Closure:* We tend to fill in missing elements of a visual scene, allowing us to perceive edges that are separated by gaps as belonging to complete objects (**FIGURE 4.20b**).
- *Continuity:* Edges or contours that have the same orientation have what the Gestaltists called 'good continuation', and we tend to group them together perceptually (**FIGURE 4.20c**).
- *Similarity:* Regions that are similar in colour, lightness, shape or texture are perceived as belonging to the same object (**FIGURE 4.20d**).
- *Proximity:* Objects that are close together tend to be grouped together (**FIGURE 4.20e**).
- *Common fate:* Elements of a visual image that move together are perceived as parts of a single moving object (**FIGURE 4.20f**).

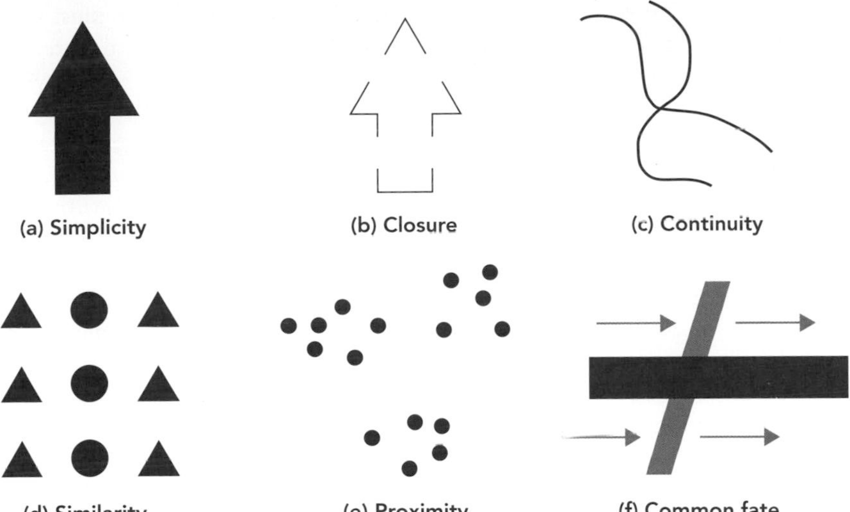

FIGURE 4.20 Perceptual grouping rules Principles first identified by Gestalt psychologists and now supported by experimental evidence demonstrate that the brain is predisposed to impose order on incoming sensations. One neural strategy for perception involves responding to patterns among stimuli and grouping like patterns together.

Separating figure from ground

Perceptual grouping is a powerful aid to our ability to recognize objects by sight. Grouping involves visually separating an object from its surroundings. In Gestalt terms, this means identifying a *figure* apart from the (back)*ground* in which it resides. For example, the words on this page are perceived as figural: they stand out from the ground of the sheet of paper on which they're printed. Similarly, your lecturer is perceived as the figure against the backdrop of all the other elements in the lecture hall. You certainly can perceive these elements differently, of course: the words *and* the paper are all part of a thing called 'a page', and your lecturer *and* the lecture hall can all be perceived as 'your learning environment'. Typically, though, our perceptual systems focus attention on some objects as distinct from their environments.

Size provides one clue to what's figure and what's ground: smaller regions are likely to be figures, such as tiny letters on a big paper. Movement also helps: your lecturer is (we hope) a dynamic lecturer, moving around in a static environment. Another critical step towards object recognition is *edge assignment*. Given an edge, or boundary, between figure and ground, which region does that edge belong to? If the edge belongs to the figure, it helps define the object's shape, and the background continues behind the edge. Sometimes, though, it's not easy to tell which is which.

Danish psychologist Edgar Rubin (1886–1951) capitalized on this ambiguity in developing a famous illusion called the *Rubin vase* or, more generally, a *reversible figure–ground relationship*. You can view this 'face–vase' illusion in **FIGURE 4.21** in two ways, either as a vase on a black background or as a pair of silhouettes facing each other. Your visual system settles on one or the other interpretation and fluctuates between them every few seconds. This happens because the edge that would normally separate figure from ground is really part of neither: it equally defines the contours of the vase as it does the contours of the faces. Evidence from fMRIs shows, quite neatly, that when people are seeing the Rubin image as a face, there is greater activity in the face-selective region of the temporal lobe we discussed earlier than when they are seeing it as a vase (Hasson et al., 2001).

FIGURE 4.21 Ambiguous edges Here's how Rubin's classic reversible figure–ground illusion works. Fix your eyes on the centre of the image, and your perception will alternate between a vase and facing silhouettes, even as the sensory stimulation remains constant.

Theories of object recognition

Researchers have proposed two broad explanations of object recognition, one based on the object as a whole and the other on its parts. Each set of theories has strengths and weaknesses, making object recognition an active area of study in psychology.

According to *image-based object recognition* theories, an object you have seen before is stored in memory as a **template** – *a mental representation that can be directly compared to a viewed shape in the retinal image* (Tarr and Vuong, 2002). Shape templates are stored along with name, category and other associations to that object. Your memory compares

TEMPLATE A mental representation that can be directly compared to a viewed shape in the retinal image.

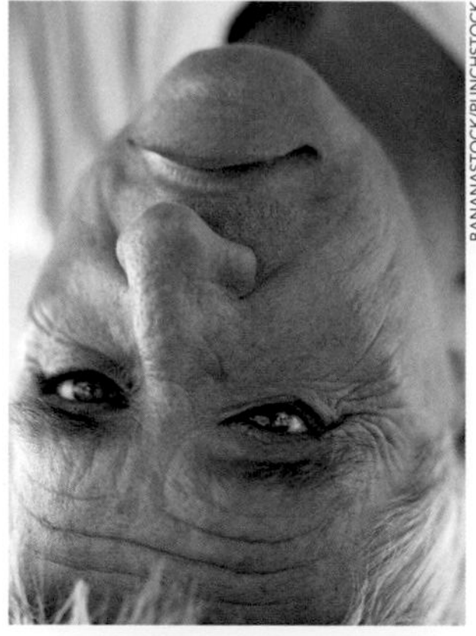

Most people can recognize an image of a face that's been rotated upside down, and they still can even when it's been altered in major ways. In particular, a distortion known as the Thatcher effect or illusion is a phenomenon that often goes unnoticed. It's where the face is upside down but the eyes and the mouth are changed to remain the right way up (see the top photo). If the image is then rotated into the normal position, you're in for a shock, as the face suddenly looks grotesque (see the bottom photo). The illusion is named after Margaret Thatcher, former British prime minister, on whose photograph the effect has been most famously demonstrated. This was originally created by Peter Thompson, a professor at the University of York, England.

its templates to the current retinal image and selects the template that most closely matches the current image. For example, supermarket scanners use a form of template matching to identify the barcodes on labels.

Image-based theories are widely accepted, yet they do not explain everything about object recognition. For one thing, the time it takes to recognize a familiar object does not depend on its current orientation relative to the object's standard orientation: you can quickly recognize that a cup is a cup even when it is tilted on its side. Correctly matching images to templates suggests that you'd have to have one template for cups in a normal orientation, another template for cups on their side, another for cups upside down and so on. This makes for an unwieldy and inefficient system and therefore one that is unlikely to be effective, yet seeing a cup on its side rarely perplexes anyone for long. Another limitation is that image-based theories cannot account for objects you have never seen before. How can you correctly identify an object by matching it to a template if you don't have a template because you've never seen the object before? This roundabout reasoning suggests that people would be mystified when encountering unfamiliar objects, yet actually we make sense of even unfamiliar objects quite readily.

Parts-based object recognition theories propose instead that the brain deconstructs viewed objects into a collection of parts (Marr and Nishihara, 1978). One important parts-based theory contends that objects are stored in memory as structural descriptions: mental inventories of object parts along with the spatial relations among those parts (Biederman, 1987). The parts' inventories act as a sort of 'alphabet' of geometric elements called *geons* that can be combined to make objects, just as letters are combined to form words (see **FIGURE 4.22**). For example, elements such as *curved, cylindrical* or *pointy* might be indexed in an inventory, along with their relations to each other. In parts-based theories, object recognition constructs an image into its visible parts, notes the spatial relations among these parts, and then compares this structural description to inventories stored in memory (see Figure 4.22).

Like image-based theories, parts-based object recognition has major limitations. Most importantly, it allows for object recognition only at the level of categories and not at the level of the individual object. Parts-based theories offer an explanation for recognizing an object such as a face, for example, but are less effective at explaining how you distinguish between your best friend's face and a stranger's face.

As you can see, there are strengths and weaknesses of image-based and parts-based explanations of object recognition. Researchers are developing hybrid theories that attempt to exploit the strengths of each approach (Peissig and Tarr, 2007).

Theories of face recognition

Faces are a special category of object. In comparison to most other objects, faces are more alike than different and yet we are capable of recognizing thousands of individual faces. In other words, how can we be so good at distinguishing individual faces when all faces

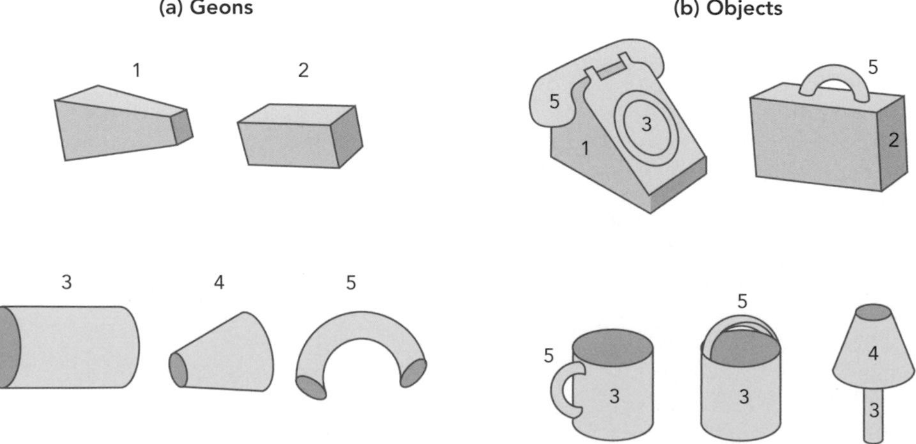

FIGURE 4.22 An alphabet of geometric elements Parts-based theory holds that objects such as those shown in (b) are made up of simpler three-dimensional components called geons, shown in (a), much as letters combine to form different words.

are so similar? Part of the answer is that we have dedicated brain regions for processing faces. We have already discussed in Chapter 3 and above, how the fusiform gyrus is particularly active during face processing. But brain activity does not, in itself, tell us how we process faces. Also, faces are not just objects, they are individual people and so each face tells a story, for example who someone is, how old they are, what race they are. Somehow, all this information is processed when recognizing faces.

To understand how face recognition works, or any complex ability for that matter, you need a theory or model that considers the separate operations that must be involved. For example, the Bruce and Young model of face recognition (Bruce and Young, 1986; Burton and Bruce, 1993) takes into consideration many of the different components that must be active during face recognition. At the most basic level, you need to work out that a pattern is a face so you have to be sensitive to features – hopefully two eyes, a nose and a mouth – in that quantity. If not, why not? Are they facing sideways so only one eye is visible? Are they wearing an eye patch? Having decided that these features are present, you then need to look at how they are arranged or configured in terms of spacing. These two operations are part of the structural encoding – *how the pattern is represented*. The output from structural encoding feeds into additional processing stages that deal with identifying emotional expressions, dynamics of any facial movements, specific identifying features such as hairy moles and, of course, the face recognition stage. If the face is someone you recognize, then you are able to identify them as familiar and hopefully remember their name. This kind of multistage model explains why people recognize faces at all, can fail to recognize familiar faces, or, like most of us, recognize faces but not know their name.

STRUCTURAL ENCODING How the pattern is represented.

Perceiving depth and size

You've probably never appreciated the mundane benefits of knowing where you are at any given time. If you've ever been in an unfamiliar environment, though, the benefits of knowing what's around you become readily apparent. Think of being in a house of mirrors: is the exit to your left or your right, or are you completely turned around? Imagine being in a new shopping centre: was H&M the clothing store on the top floor of the west wing, or was that a Topshop? Are those your friends over there at the food court or just some people who look like them? Knowing what's around you is important. Knowing where each object is located is important too. Whether one object is above, below or to the left or right of another is first encoded in the retinal image.

Objects in the world are arranged in three dimensions – length, width and depth – but the retinal image contains only two dimensions, length and width. How does the brain process a flat, two-dimensional retinal image so that we perceive the depth of an object and how far away it is? The answer lies in a collection of *depth cues* that change as you move through space. Monocular, binocular and motion-based depth cues all help visual perception (Howard, 2002).

Monocular depth cues

If you had to wear an eye patch for a few hours each day, you might predict that you'd have a difficult time perceiving things. After all, there must be a good reason for having two eyes! Actually, unless you are a batsman or a pilot, you can get by quite well with just one eye. That's because we can perceive depth with monocular depth cues – *aspects of a scene that yield information about depth when viewed with only one eye.* These cues rely on the relationship between distance and size. Even with one eye closed, the retinal image of an object you're focused on grows smaller as that object moves farther away and larger as it moves closer. Our brains routinely use these differences in retinal image size, or *relative size,* to perceive distance.

MONOCULAR DEPTH CUES Aspects of a scene that yield information about depth when viewed with only one eye.

This works particularly well in a monocular depth cue called *familiar size.* Most adults, for example, fall within a familiar range of heights (perhaps 1.52–1.98 m), so retinal image size alone is usually a reliable cue to how far away they are. Our visual system automatically corrects for size differences and attributes them to differences in distance. **FIGURE 4.23** demonstrates how strong this mental correction for familiar size is.

FIGURE 4.23 Familiar size and relative size When you view images of people, such as the women in the left-hand photo, or things you know well, the object you perceive as smaller appears farther away. With a little image manipulation, you can see in the right-hand photo that the relative size difference projected on your retinas is far greater than you perceive. The image of the woman in the navy blue jumper is exactly the same size in both photos.

Monocular cues are often called *pictorial depth cues* because they are present even in two-dimensional paintings, photographs and videos where the third dimension of depth is not really there. In addition to relative size and familiar size, there are several more monocular depth cues, such as:

- *Linear perspective*, which describes the phenomenon that parallel lines seem to converge as they recede into the distance (**FIGURE 4.24a**).
- *Texture gradient*, which arises when you view a more or less uniformly patterned surface because the size of the pattern elements, as well as the distance between them, grows smaller as the surface recedes from the observer (**FIGURE 4.24b**).
- *Interposition*, which occurs when one object partly blocks another (**FIGURE 4.24c**). You can infer that the block*ing* object is closer than the block*ed* object. However, interposition by itself cannot provide information about how far apart the two objects are.
- *Relative height in the image* depends on your field of vision (**FIGURE 4.24d**). Objects that are closer to you are lower in your visual field, while faraway objects are higher.

(a) Linear perspective

(b) Texture gradient

(c) Interposition

(d) Relative height

FIGURE 4.24 Pictorial depth cues Visual artists rely on a variety of monocular cues to make their work come to life. You can rely on cues such as (a) linear perspective, (b) texture gradient, (c) interposition, and (d) relative height in an image to infer distance, depth and position, even if you're wearing an eye patch.

Binocular depth cues

Two eyes are better than one, especially when it comes to depth perception. Binocular *depth cues* exist because we have stereoscopic vision: having space between our eyes means that each eye registers a slightly different view of the world.

Hold your right index finger up about 60 cm in front of your face, close one eye, and look at your finger. Now alternate, opening and closing each eye rapidly. Your finger appears to jump back and forth as you do this.

The difference in these two views provides direct and compelling information about depth. The closer the object you're looking at, the greater the binocular disparity – *the difference in the retinal images of the two eyes that provides information about depth*. Your brain computes the disparity between the two retinal images to perceive how far away objects are, as shown in **FIGURE 4.25**. Viewed from above in the figure, the images of the more distant square and the closer circle each fall at different points on each retina.

Binocular disparity as a cue to depth perception was first discussed by Sir Charles Wheatstone in 1838. Wheatstone went on to invent the stereoscope, essentially a holder for a pair of photographs or drawings taken from two horizontally displaced locations (Wheatstone did not lack for original ideas – he also invented the accordion and an early telegraph and coined the term *microphone*). When viewed, one by each eye, the pairs of images evoked a vivid sense of depth. The View-Master toy is the modern successor to Wheatstone's invention, and 3-D films are based on this same idea.

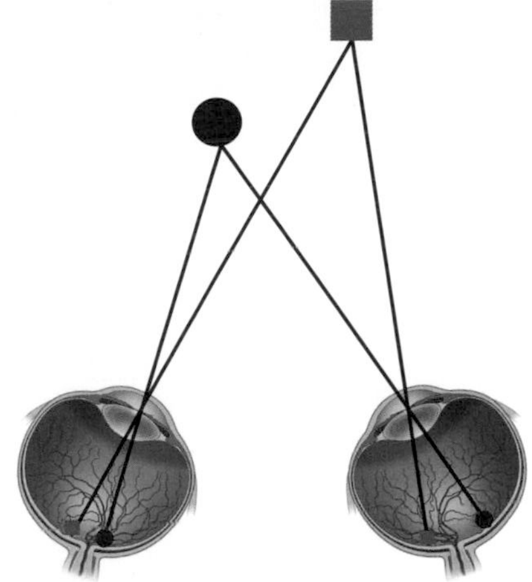

FIGURE 4.25 Binocular disparity We see the world in three dimensions because our eyes are a distance apart and the image of an object falls on the retina of each eye at a slightly different place. In this two-object scene, the images of the square and the circle fall on different points of the retina in each eye. The disparity in the positions of the circle's retinal images provides a compelling cue to depth.

BINOCULAR DISPARITY The difference in the retinal images of the two eyes that provides information about depth.

MOTION PARALLAX A depth cue based on the movement of the head over time.

Motion-based depth cues

When you're riding in a car, bus or train, the scene changes systematically and continuously. Nearby objects appear to zip by quickly, but faraway objects appear to move slowly or not at all. This phenomenon is called motion parallax – *a depth cue based on the movement of the head over time*. The speed and direction of the images on your retina depend on where you are looking and on how far away the objects you see are.

The depth perception you experience from motion parallax is essentially the same as that provided by binocular disparity. Both involve mentally comparing retinal image information from multiple viewpoints. In the case of binocular disparity, two slightly different viewpoints are sampled simultaneously by the two eyes. In motion parallax, the two viewpoints are sampled in succession, over time.

As you move forward through a scene, the motion cues to depth behave a little differently. As objects get closer, their image sizes on the retina increase, and their contours move outwards on the retina, towards the side. *Optic flow*, the pattern of motion that accompanies an observer's forward movement through a scene, is a form of motion parallax. At any given point, the scene ahead moves outwards from the point towards which the observer is moving. This kind of motion parallax is therefore useful for navigation while walking, driving or landing an aeroplane.

If you have ever watched an old episode of *Star Trek*, you will recognize as optic flow the visual effect on the view screen when the spaceship jumps to warp speed. Trails of starlight out ahead expand outwards from a central point. Back on earth, you can see this effect when you look through the windscreen as you drive through a snowstorm at night. As your headlights illuminate the onrushing snowflakes, the flakes at the centre are farthest away (near the horizon) and the flakes on the periphery are closest to you.

Illusions of depth and size

We all are vulnerable to *illusions*, which, as you'll remember from Chapter 1, are errors of perception, memory or judgement in which subjective experience differs from objective reality (Wade, 2005). These mindbugs inspired the Gestalt psychologists, whose contributions continue to influence research on object perception. Recall the Müller-Lyer illusion from Chapter 1 (see Figure 1.2). Even though the horizontal lines in that figure are exactly the same length, the top horizontal line looks longer than the bottom one. That's because you don't perceive the horizontal lines in isolation: your perception of them is related to and influenced by the surrounding oblique lines.

The relation between size and distance has been used to create elaborate illusions that depend on fooling the visual system about how far away objects are. All these illusions

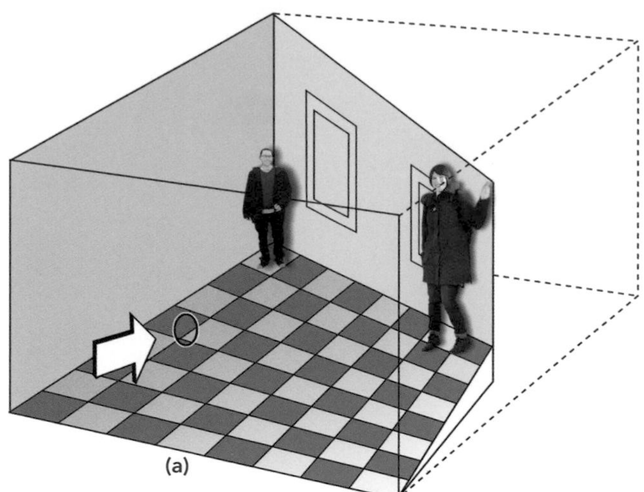

FIGURE 4.26 The amazing Ames room (a) A diagram showing the actual proportions of the Ames room reveals its secrets. The sides of the room form a trapezoid with parallel sides but a back wall that's way off square. The uneven floor makes the room's height in the far back corner shorter than the other. Add misleading cues such as specially designed windows and flooring and position the room's occupants in each far corner and you're ready to lure an unsuspecting observer. (b) Looking into the Ames room through the viewing port with only one eye, the observer infers a normal size–distance relationship – that the man and the woman are the same distance away. But the different image sizes they project on the retina lead the viewer to conclude, based on the monocular cue of familiar size, that the man is very small and the woman is very large.

depend on the same principle: when you view two objects that project the same retinal image size, the object you perceive as farther away will be perceived as larger.

One of the most famous illusions is the *Ames room* (see **FIGURE 4.26**), constructed by US ophthalmologist Adelbert Ames in 1946. The room is trapezoidal in shape rather than square: only two sides are parallel (**FIGURE 4.26a**). A person standing in one corner of an Ames room is physically twice as far away from the viewer as a person standing in the other corner. But when viewed with one eye through the small peephole placed in one wall, the Ames room looks square because the shapes of the windows and the flooring tiles are carefully crafted to *look* square from the viewing port (Ittelson, 1952). The visual system perceives the far wall as perpendicular to the line of sight, so that people standing at different positions along that wall appear to be at the same distance, and the viewer's judgements of their sizes are based directly on retinal image size. As a result, a person standing in the right corner appears to be much larger than a person standing in the left corner (**FIGURE 4.26b**).

The *moon illusion* is another case where incorrectly perceived distance affects the perception of size (Hershenson, 1989). The full moon often appears much larger when it is near the horizon than when it is directly overhead. In fact, the moon projects identical retinal image sizes in both positions. What accounts for this compelling mindbug? When the moon is near the horizon, it appears closer and hence larger because many features – hills, trees, buildings – intervene between the viewer and the moon. Nothing intervenes when the moon is directly overhead, so it appears smaller.

The moon appears to be much larger at the horizon than when it is high in the sky. This illusion happens because of visual cues at the horizon such as buildings and trees.

The importance of illusions

British psychologist Richard Gregory (1966) advocated that illusions were more than just fun, quirky mindbugs but revealed how the brain makes sense of the world by building models of it. These models, or hypotheses as Gregory likened them, lead to expectations that can be violated, creating the experience that things are not what they seem – the basis for all illusions. There are different classes of illusions. Some illusions are purely sensory, such as motion aftereffects where the activity of the movement-sensitive neurons has been modified. It explains why, after staring out the back of a moving vehicle, the scene appears to be still moving in the opposite direction when the vehicle comes to a stop (see the explanation of the waterfall illusion below). Others are more perceptual, such as the depth and size illusions that depend on expectations. Illusions can be found in every modality. Irrespective of what type of illusion one is dealing with, if it is systematic, then it indicates the way the brain is interpreting the world by applying models. But illusions are not all in the mind. Some

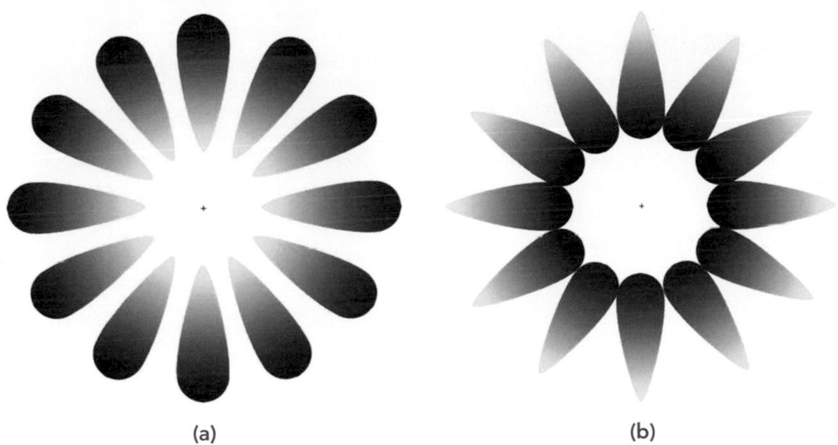

FIGURE 4.27 Brightness illusions Although the centre of the pattern in image (a) looks much brighter than the centre of the pattern in (b), they are identical. You can check by covering up the petals.

illusions can change the way we behave. For example, we have a pupillary reflex that constricts when we enter a bright environment to reduce the amount of light entering the eye. Remarkably, Norwegian psychologists found brightness illusions, such as the one illustrated in **FIGURE 4.27**, also cause the pupils to constrict even though the brightness is entirely illusory (Laeng and Endestad, 2012). What should be a purely reflexive motor behaviour determined by absolute luminance levels turns out to triggered by an illusion.

In a recent follow-up study, researchers measured pupil dilation while participants imagined stimuli of varying brightness such as sunny days, night skies, cloudy skies and dark rooms. Remarkably, even though these were entirely mental images, participants' pupils constricted when thinking about bright environments, indicating that the representations we hold in memory include action-based adjustments that are normally beyond voluntary control (Laeng and Sulutvedt, 2014).

hot science

Wishful seeing

Why does the road always look longer and the hill steeper when you are tired? On the other hand, when they are young, fit and motivated to cross the finish line, runners perceive obstacles such as distances and hills as less long and steep (Bhalla and Proffitt, 1999). Thirsty people see glasses of water as larger and closer (Balcetis and Dunning, 2010; Veltkamp et al., 2008) and even coins seem larger and more within reach when your poor (Balcetis and Dunning, 2010; Dubois et al., 2010). It would seem that objects that can help people fulfil a wish or achieve a goal seem more attainable to those in need. These examples of perceptual distortions are known as *wishful seeing* and reveal that when we perceive the world, we apply a filter of goal-directed expectations to how we interpret it. But is wishful thinking a conscious bias to just pay attention to things that interest us or is it more unconscious than this?

Emily Balcetis, a psychologist at New York University, has designed some ingenious studies to investigate the role of conscious and unconscious processes operating during wishful thinking. In one study, participants were asked to report what they saw on a computer screen that depicted an ambiguous line drawing that could either be seen as a seal or a donkey.

They were told that if the drawing on the screen was a marine animal, they would be forced to sing in an embarrassing karaoke competition in front of judges. If the computer had selected a farm animal, they would be picked to act as one of the judges. This pairing was swapped over for half the subjects. The computer then displayed the ambiguous image for one second. If they had been told that the seal was the embarrassing outcome, almost all (97%) said they saw a donkey. If they participants had been hoping to see the seal to get the less embarrassing outcome, they were less likely to see the donkey. This study tested wishful seeing that was generally out of conscious awareness, but a second study confirms the role of rapid processes that are out of conscious control.

Due to binocular disparity, each eye produces a slightly different retinal image that is used to generate binocular vision. To avoid the problem of 'double vision', the brain suppresses the image from one eye with the image from the other (usually more dominant) eye in a competitive process known as *binocular rivalry*. Binocular rivalry is so powerful that if two different images were presented simultaneously, individuals would only be aware of one.

To capitalize on this quirk of the visual brain, Balcetis and her colleagues (2012) asked participants to wear red-green goggles so that red and green images were filtered selectively to each eye. For example, the letter 'A' written in red would be invisible to the eye wearing the red lens and the number '6' written in green ink would be invisible to the eye with the green lens. This enabled the experimenter to present two different images separately to each eye and test which image would be suppressed by binocular rivalry. Participants were told that they had to accurately report whether they saw a letter or a number that was either presented in red or green, which would correspond either to a gain or a loss in a game to earn money. They were further instructed not to make errors that would cost them a forfeit. Although the presentation was extremely short, only 300 ms, when they wished for numbers (or letters, depending on the reward scheme), they saw the target 64% of the time, which was significantly above chance even though the processes were rapid and not under conscious control. Wishful seeing can be considered a bias that enables individuals to achieve their goals by spurring people on and altering their perceptions.

I know it's around here somewhere

A 44-year-old man was arrested for driving under the influence in Australia's Northern Territory after he asked a police officer how to get to the hard-to-miss Uluru (Ayers Rock, the huge, 348 m-high rock formation that appears red in sunlight), which was about 90 m in front of him, illuminated in his headlights.

Psychology and me

David Crundall, Professor of Psychology, Nottingham Trent University

David Crundall is an applied cognitive psychologist based at Nottingham Trent University in the UK. Visit www.palgrave.com/schacter to watch David talking about his current research into traffic and transport psychology, including the process of learning to drive, why novice drivers are more prone to collision, the effect of using mobile phones while driving, and hazard perception tests. He also provides advice for students on how they can work towards a career in applied psychology.

Perceiving motion

You should now have a good sense of how we see what and where objects are, a process made substantially easier when the objects stay in one place. But real life, of course, is full of moving targets; objects change position over time. To sense motion, the visual system must encode information about both space and time. The simplest case to consider is an observer who does not move trying to perceive an object that does.

As an object moves across an observer's stationary visual field, it first stimulates one location on the retina, and then a little later it stimulates another location on the retina. Neural circuits in the brain can detect this change in position over time and respond to specific speeds and directions of motion (Emerson et al., 1992). A region in the middle of the temporal lobe referred to as *MT* is specialized for the visual perception of motion (Born and Bradley, 2005; Newsome and Paré, 1988), and brain damage in this area leads to a deficit in normal motion perception (Zihl et al., 1983).

Of course, in the real world, rarely are you a stationary observer. As you move around, your head and eyes move all the time, and motion perception is not as simple. The motion perception system must take into account the position and movement of your eyes, and ultimately your head and body, in order to perceive the motions of objects correctly and allow you to approach or avoid them. The brain accomplishes this by monitoring your eye and head movements and 'subtracting' them from the motion in the retinal image.

Motion perception, like colour perception, operates in part on opponent processes and is subject to sensory adaptation. A motion aftereffect called the *waterfall illusion* is analogous to colour aftereffects. If you stare at the downwards rush of a waterfall for several seconds, you'll experience an upwards motion aftereffect when you then look at stationary objects near the waterfall such as trees or rocks. Probably one of the most observed motion aftereffects takes place several week nights in the UK as millions of viewers sit down to watch the spiralling opening credits to the nation's favourite soap opera, *EastEnders*. When the sequence finally comes to a stop, the viewing nation should all experience their TV screens start to rotate in the opposite direction. What's going on here?

The process is similar to seeing green after staring at a patch of red. Motion-sensitive neurons are connected to motion detector cells in the brain that encode motion in opposite directions. A sense of motion comes from the difference in the strength of these two opposing sensors. If one set of motion detector cells is fatigued through adaptation to motion in one direction, then the opposing sensor will take over. The net result is that motion is perceived in the opposite direction. Evidence from fMRIs indicates that when people experience the waterfall illusion while viewing a stationary stimulus, there is increased activity in region MT, which plays a key role in motion perception (Tootell et al., 1995).

The movement of objects in the world is not the only event that can evoke the perception of motion. Neon signs with successively flashing lights can evoke a strong sense of motion, exactly the sort of illusion that inspired Max Wertheimer who we met in Chapter 1. These illusions where the brain integrates successive images or flashes of light into a single moving object are known as *phi phenomenon*. Recall, too, the Gestalt grouping rule of *common fate*: people perceive a series of flashing lights as a whole, moving object (see Figure 4.20f). This *perception of movement as a result of alternating signals appearing in rapid succession in different locations* is called apparent motion.

APPARENT MOTION The perception of movement as a result of alternating signals appearing in rapid succession in different locations.

Video technology and animation depend on apparent motion. A sequence of still images sample the continuous motion in the original scene. In the case of films, the sampling rate (depending on which country you are in) can be 25 or 30 frames per second. A slower sampling rate would produce a much choppier sense of motion, while a faster sampling rate would be a waste of resources because we would not perceive the motion as any smoother than it appears at these rates.

In summary, some regions in the occipital and temporal lobes respond selectively to specific object categories, supporting the modular view that specialized brain areas represent particular classes of objects. The principle of perceptual constancy holds that even as sensory signals change, perception remains consistent. Gestalt principles of perceptual grouping, such as simplicity, closure and continuity, govern how the features and regions of things fit together. Depth perception depends on monocular cues, such as familiar size and linear perspective; binocular cues, such as retinal disparity; and motion-based cues, such as motion parallax, which is based on the movement of the head over time. We experience a sense of motion through the differences in the strengths of output from motion-sensitive neurons. These processes can give rise to illusions such as apparent motion. Illusions are important because they reveal the way the brain operates to build useful models of the world.

Audition: more than meets the ear

Vision is based on the spatial pattern of light waves on the retina. The sense of hearing, by contrast, is all about *sound waves* – changes in air pressure unfolding over time. Plenty of things produce sound waves: the collision of a tree hitting the forest floor, the impact of two hands clapping, the vibration of vocal chords during a stirring speech, the resonance of a bass guitar string during a thrash metal concert. Except for synaesthetes who 'hear colours', understanding most people's auditory experience requires understanding how we transform changes in air pressure into perceived sounds.

Sensing sound

Plucking a guitar string or striking a tuning fork produces a *pure tone*, a simple sound wave that first increases air pressure and then creates a relative vacuum. This cycle repeats hundreds or thousands of times per second as sound waves propagate outwards in all directions from the source.

Just as there are three dimensions of light waves corresponding to three dimensions of visual perception, so there are three physical dimensions of a sound wave. Frequency, amplitude and complexity determine what we hear as the pitch, loudness and quality of a sound (see **TABLE 4.3**).

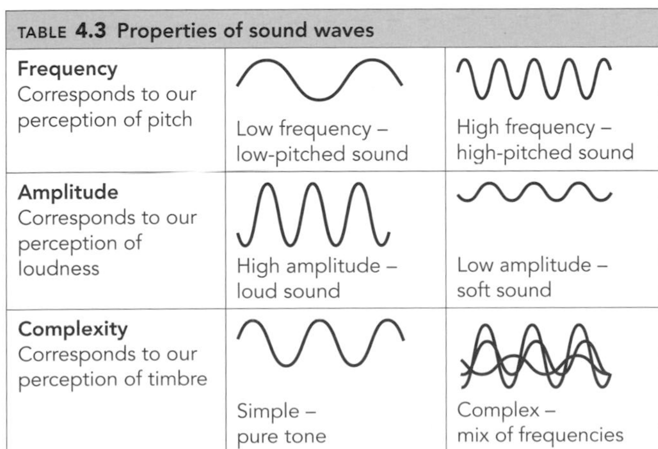

TABLE **4.3 Properties of sound waves**

Frequency Corresponds to our perception of pitch	Low frequency – low-pitched sound	High frequency – high-pitched sound
Amplitude Corresponds to our perception of loudness	High amplitude – loud sound	Low amplitude – soft sound
Complexity Corresponds to our perception of timbre	Simple – pure tone	Complex – mix of frequencies

- The *frequency* of the sound wave, or its wavelength, depends on how often the peak in air pressure passes the ear or a microphone, measured in cycles per second, or hertz (Hz). Changes in the physical frequency of a sound wave are perceived by humans as changes in pitch – *how high or low a sound is*.

PITCH How high or low a sound is.

LOUDNESS A sound's intensity.

- The *amplitude* of a sound wave refers to its height, relative to the threshold for human hearing (which is set at zero decibels, or dB). Amplitude corresponds to loudness – *a sound's intensity*. To give you an idea of amplitude and intensity, the rustling of leaves in a soft breeze is about 20 dB, normal conversation is measured at about 40 dB, shouting produces 70 dB, a Slayer concert is about 130 dB, and the sound of the space shuttle taking off a couple of kilometres away registers at 160 dB or more. That's loud enough to cause permanent damage to the auditory system and is well above the pain threshold; in fact, any sounds above 85 dB can be enough to cause hearing damage, depending on the length and type of exposure.
- Differences in the *complexity* of sound waves, or their mix of frequencies, correspond to timbre – *a listener's experience of sound quality or resonance*. Timbre offers us information about the nature of sound. The same note played at the same loudness produces a perceptually different experience depending on whether it was played on a flute or a trumpet, a phenomenon due entirely to timbre. Many 'natural' sounds also illustrate the complexity of wavelengths, such as the sound of bees buzzing, the tonalities of speech, or the babbling of a brook. Unlike the purity of a tuning fork's hum, the drone of cicadas is a clamour of overlapping sound frequencies.

TIMBRE A listener's experience of sound quality or resonance.

Of the three dimensions of sound waves, frequency provides most of the information we need to identify sounds. Amplitude and complexity contribute texture to our auditory perceptions, but it is frequency that carries their meaning. Sound wave frequencies blend together to create countless sounds, just as different wavelengths of light blend to create the richly coloured world we see.

Moreover, sound wave frequency is as important for audition as spatial perception is for vision. Changes in frequency over time allow us to identify the location of sounds, an ability that can be crucial to survival, and also allow us to understand speech and appreciate music, skills that are valuable to our cultural survival. The focus in our discussion of hearing, then, is on how the auditory system encodes and represents sound wave frequency (Kubovy, 1981).

The human ear

How does the auditory system convert sound waves into neural signals? The process is very different from the visual system, which is not surprising, given that light is a form of electromagnetic radiation, whereas sound is a physical change in air pressure over time: different forms of energy suggest different processes of transduction. The human ear is divided into three distinct parts, as shown in **FIGURE 4.28**. The outer ear collects sound waves and funnels them towards the *middle ear*, which transmits the vibrations to the *inner ear*, embedded in the skull, where they are transduced into neural impulses.

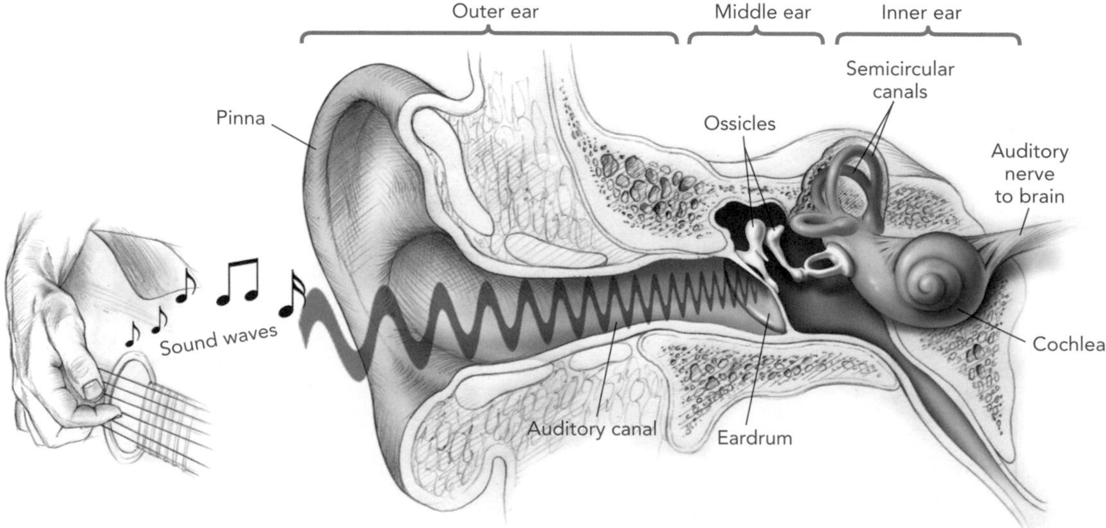

FIGURE 4.28 Anatomy of the human ear The pinna funnels sound waves into the auditory canal to vibrate the eardrum at a rate that corresponds to the sound's frequency. In the middle ear, the ossicles pick up the eardrum vibrations, amplify them, and pass them along by vibrating a membrane at the surface of the fluid-filled cochlea in the inner ear. Here, fluid carries the wave energy to the auditory receptors that transduce it into electrochemical activity, exciting the neurons that form the auditory nerve, leading to the brain.

The outer ear consists of the visible part on the outside of the head (the *pinna*), the auditory canal and the eardrum, an airtight flap of skin that vibrates in response to sound waves gathered by the pinna and channelled into the canal. The middle ear, a tiny, air-filled chamber behind the eardrum, contains the three smallest bones in the body, the *ossicles*. Named for their appearance as hammer, anvil and stirrup, the ossicles fit together into a lever that mechanically transmits and intensifies vibrations from the eardrum to the inner ear.

The inner ear contains the spiral-shaped cochlea (Latin for 'snail') – *a fluid-filled tube that is the organ of auditory transduction*. The cochlea is divided along its length by the basilar membrane – *a structure in the inner ear that undulates when vibrations from the ossicles reach the cochlear fluid* (see **FIGURE 4.29**). Its wavelike movement stimulates thousands of tiny hair cells – *specialized auditory receptor neurons embedded in the basilar membrane*. The hair cells then release neurotransmitter molecules, initiating a neural signal in the auditory nerve that travels to the brain. You might not want to think that the whispered 'I love you' that sends chills up your spine got a kick-start from lots of little hair cells wiggling around, but the mechanics of hearing are what they are!

COCHLEA A fluid-filled tube that is the organ of auditory transduction.

BASILAR MEMBRANE A structure in the inner ear that undulates when vibrations from the ossicles reach the cochlear fluid.

HAIR CELLS Specialized auditory receptor neurons embedded in the basilar membrane.

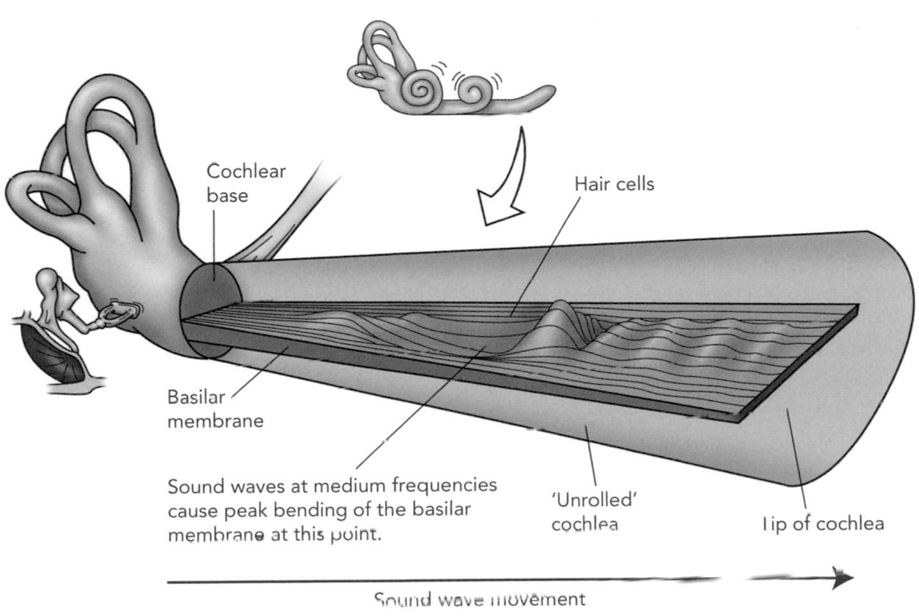

FIGURE 4.29 Auditory transduction Inside the cochlea, shown here as though it were uncoiling, the basilar membrane undulates in response to wave energy in the cochlear fluid. Waves of differing frequencies ripple varying locations along the membrane, from low frequencies at its tip to high frequencies at the base, and bend the embedded hair cell receptors at those locations. The hair cell motion generates impulses in the auditory neurons, whose axons form the auditory nerve that emerges from the cochlea.

Perceiving pitch

From the inner ear, action potentials in the auditory nerve travel to the thalamus and ultimately to the contralateral ('opposite side'; see Chapter 3) hemisphere of the cerebral cortex. This is called area A1 – *a portion of the temporal lobe that contains the primary auditory cortex* (see **FIGURE 4.30**). For most of us, the auditory areas in the left hemisphere analyse sounds related to language and those in the right hemisphere specialize in rhythmic sounds and music.

AREA A1 A portion of the temporal lobe that contains the primary auditory cortex.

Neurons in area A1 respond well to simple tones, and successive auditory areas in the brain process sounds of increasing complexity (Schreiner et al., 2000). Like area V1 in the visual cortex where adjacent areas of the visual field trigger adjacent neurons in a topographic map, area A1 has a tonotopic organization where similar frequencies activate neurons in adjacent locations (see **FIGURE 4.30**, inset). A young adult with normal hearing ideally can detect sounds between about 20 and 20,000 Hz, although the ability to hear at the upper range decreases with age; an upper limit of about 16,000 Hz may be more realistic. The human ear is most sensitive to frequencies around 1,000 to 3,500 Hz. But how is the frequency of a sound wave encoded in a neural signal?

Our ears have evolved two mechanisms to encode sound wave frequency, one for high frequencies and one for low frequencies. The place code, used mainly for high frequencies, is active when *the cochlea encodes different frequencies at different locations along the basilar membrane*. In a series of experiments carried out from the 1930s to the 1950s,

PLACE CODE The cochlea encodes different frequencies at different locations along the basilar membrane.

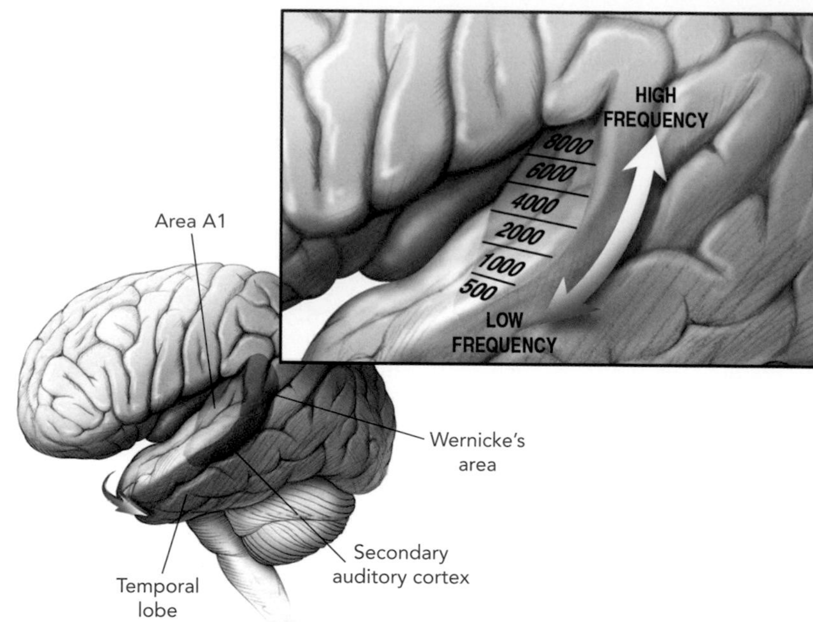

FIGURE 4.30 Primary auditory cortex Area A1 is folded into the temporal lobe beneath the lateral fissure in each hemisphere. The left hemisphere auditory areas govern speech in most people. (inset) The A1 cortex has a tonotopic organization, with lower frequencies mapping towards the front of the brain and higher frequencies towards the back, mirroring the organization of the basilar membrane along the cochlea (see Figure 4.29).

Nobel laureate Georg von Békésy (1899–1972) used a microscope to observe the basilar membrane in the inner ear of cadavers that had been donated for medical research (Békésy, 1960). Békésy found that the movement of the basilar membrane resembles a travelling wave (see Figure 4.29). The wave's shape depends on the frequency of the stimulating pitch. When the frequency is low, the wide, floppy tip (*apex*) of the basilar membrane moves the most, and when the frequency is high, the narrow, stiff end (*base*) of the membrane moves the most.

The movement of the basilar membrane causes hair cells to bend, initiating a neural signal in the auditory nerve. Axons fire the strongest in the hair cells along the area of the basilar membrane that moves the most, in other words, the place of activation on the basilar membrane contributes to the perception of sound. The place code works best for relatively high frequencies that resonate at the basilar membrane's base and less well for low frequencies that resonate at the tip, because low frequencies produce a broad travelling wave and therefore an imprecise frequency code.

TEMPORAL CODE The cochlea registers low frequencies via the firing rate of action potentials entering the auditory nerve.

A complementary process handles lower frequencies. A **temporal code** *registers low frequencies via the firing rate of action potentials entering the auditory nerve*. Action potentials from the hair cells are synchronized in time with the peaks of the incoming sound waves (Johnson, 1980). If you imagine the rhythmic *boom-boom-boom* of a bass drum, you can probably also imagine the *fire-fire-fire* of action potentials corresponding to the beats. This process provides the brain with precise information about pitch that supplements the information provided by the place code.

However, individual neurons can produce action potentials at a maximum rate of only about 1,000 spikes per second, so the temporal code does not work as well as the place code for high frequencies. (Imagine if the action potential has to fire in time with the *rat-a-tat-a-tat-a-tat* of a snare drum roll.) Like trichromatic representation and opponent processes in colour processing, the place code and the temporal code work together to cover the entire range of pitches that people can hear.

Localizing sound sources

Just as the differing positions of our eyes give us stereoscopic vision, the placement of our ears on opposite sides of the head give us stereophonic hearing. The sound arriving at the ear closer to the sound source is louder than the sound in the farther ear, mainly because the listener's head partially blocks sound energy. This loudness difference decreases as the sound source moves from a position directly to one side (maximal difference) to straight ahead (no difference).

Another cue to a sound's location arises from timing: sound waves arrive a little sooner at the near ear than at the far ear. The timing difference can be as brief as a few microseconds, but together with the intensity difference, it is sufficient to allow us to perceive the location of a sound. When the sound source is ambiguous, you may find yourself turning your head from side to side to localize it. By doing this, you are changing the relative intensity and timing of sound waves arriving in your ears and collecting better information about the likely source of the sound. We usually localize sounds by combining our efforts to hear where the source is coming from with our ability to move our eyes to the same location. This behaviour is called visual orienting, *a behavioural response to move the eyes towards a target* that might signal a potential prey or predator. Visual orienting, which gives animals the ability to hunt or avoid being hunted, is a basic form of integration between the senses that we discuss next.

VISUAL ORIENTING A behavioural response to move the eyes towards a target.

Multisensory integration

We began this chapter with the bizarre phenomenon of synaesthesia, but we all have mappings between the senses – just not the weird ones that synaesthetes experience. Up until now, we have been considering sight and sound as two independent sensory modalities but much of the world is full of objects that stimulate more than one sense at the same time. For example, if we drop a priceless Ming dynasty vase, we expect the sound of shattering antique porcelain to occur at the same time as we see it hit the floor, followed shortly after by the shriek of the antique dealer. The sight and the sound are synchronized. It is not only sights and sounds that usually go together. For example, we have certain expectations that if some unseen object feels sharp and jagged in the hand, then it should also look sharp and jagged when we bring it into view. This kind of perceptual expectancy is called multisensory integration – *the perceptual representation of events from more than one sensory modality.*

MULTISENSORY INTEGRATION The perceptual representation of events from more than one sensory modality.

Multisensory integration reflects the reliable sensory properties of the world. For example, we expect certain sights and sounds to be integrated, that is, processed simultaneously to produce a multisensory experience. If we see a drum being beaten with a stick, we expect the sound of the beat to come from the same place as the drum and at the same time. On the other hand, when synchrony between sight and sound is lost, we immediately notice, as in the case of a badly dubbed foreign film where the movements of the actors' mouths and voices are not synchronized (Driver, 1996). You can even create illusions by applying this principle. Ventriloquists typically 'throw' their voice by minimizing the movements of their own mouth and accentuating the movements of the dummy, leading to the compelling impression that the dummy is talking. In such instances, vision is the dominant cue that produces an intersensory mindbug known as the 'ventriloquist effect' (Howard and Templeton, 1966).

Multisensory integration is achieved by neurons in the brain that receive input from more than one sensory modality (Stein and Meredith, 1993). These neurons are sensitive to the source of the signals in terms of location and timing, as in the case of beating a drum. When multisensory neurons receive synchronized activity from the visual and auditory channels, they produce an enhanced response that represents the combined activity of the different senses (Stein et al., 1989). When they are not synchronized, the multisensory neurons are not activated. As we read later in Chapter 11, there is evidence that the basic integration of different senses is present in babies before the first six months. As we shall read a bit later on in the section on taste, even taste experiences seem to be sensitive to multisensory integration.

In summary, perceiving sound depends on three physical dimensions of a sound wave: the frequency of the sound wave determines the pitch; the amplitude determines the loudness; and differences in the complexity, or mix, of frequencies determine the sound quality or timbre. Auditory perception begins in the ear, which consists of an outer ear that funnels sound waves towards the middle ear, which in turn sends the vibrations to the inner ear, which contains the cochlea. Action potentials from the inner ear travel along an auditory pathway through the thalamus to the contralateral primary auditory cortex, area A1, in the temporal lobe. Auditory perception depends on a place code and a temporal code, which together cover the full range of pitches that people can hear. Our ability to localize sound sources depends critically on the placement of our ears on opposite sides of the head. Intersensory integration, where different senses are combined to produce a multisensory experience, is achieved by neurons that receive input from more than one sensory modality.

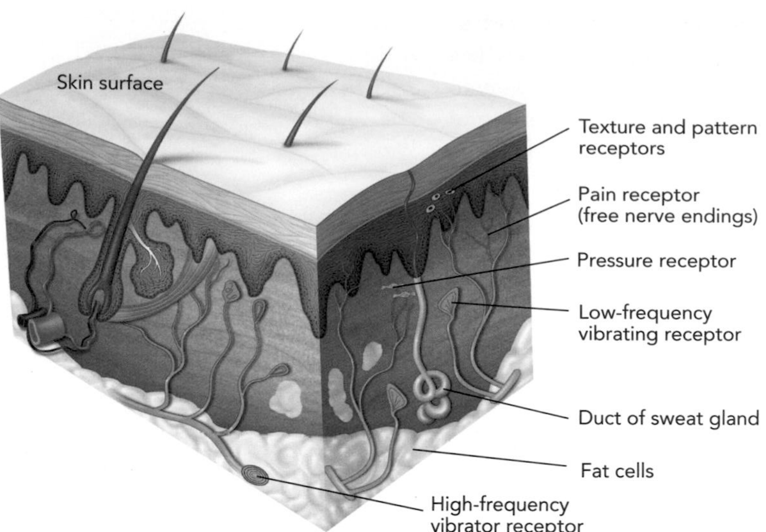

FIGURE **4.31 Touch receptors** Specialized sensory neurons form distinct groups of haptic receptors that detect pressure, temperature and vibrations against the skin. Touch receptors respond to stimulation within their receptive fields, and their long axons enter the brain via the spinal or cranial nerves. Pain receptors populate all body tissues that feel pain. They are distributed around bones and within muscles and internal organs as well as under the skin's surface. Both types of pain receptors – the fibres that transmit immediate, sharp pain sensations quickly and those that signal slow, dull pain that lasts and lasts – are free nerve endings.

HAPTIC PERCEPTION The active exploration of the environment by touching and grasping objects with our hands.

The body senses: more than skin deep

Vision and audition provide information about the world at a distance. By responding to light and sound energy in the environment, these 'distance' senses allow us to identify and locate the objects and people around us. In comparison, the body senses, also called *somatosenses* (*soma* from the Greek for 'body'), are up close and personal. Haptic perception results from our *active exploration of the environment by touching and grasping objects with our hands*. We use sensory receptors in our muscles, tendons and joints as well as a variety of receptors in our skin to get a feel for the world around us (see FIGURE **4.31**).

Touch

Four types of receptor located under the skin's surface enable us to sense pressure, texture, pattern or vibration against the skin (see Figure 4.31). The receptive fields of these specialized cells work together to provide a rich 'tactile' (from Latin 'to touch') experience when you explore an object by feeling it or attempt to grasp it. In addition, *thermoreceptors*, nerve fibres that sense cold and warmth, respond when your skin temperature changes. All these sensations blend seamlessly together in perception, but detailed physiological studies have successfully isolated the parts of the touch system (Johnson, 2002).

Touch begins with the transduction of skin sensations into neural signals. Like cells in the retina of each eye, touch receptors have receptive fields with central excitatory zones surrounded by doughnut-shaped inhibitory zones that, when stimulated, cause that cell's response to change. The representation of touch in the brain follows a topographic scheme, much as vision and hearing do. Think back to the homunculus you read about in Chapter 3; you'll recall that different locations on the body project sensory signals to different locations in the somatosensory cortex in the parietal lobe.

There are two important principles regarding the neural representation of the body's surface. First, there is contralateral organization: the left half of the body is represented in the right half of the brain and vice versa. Second, just as more of the visual brain is devoted to foveal vision where acuity is greatest, more of the tactile brain is devoted to parts of the skin surface that have greater spatial resolution. Regions such as the fingertips and lips are very good at discriminating fine spatial detail, whereas areas such as the lower back are quite poor at that task. These perceptual abilities are a natural consequence of the fact that the fingertips and lips have a relatively dense arrangement of touch receptors and a large topographical representation in the somatosensory cortex, while, comparatively, the lower back, hips and calves have a relatively small representation (Penfield and Rasmussen, 1950).

Pain

Although pain is arguably the least pleasant of sensations, this aspect of touch is among the most important for survival, as pain indicates damage or potential damage to the body. The possibility of a life free from pain might seem appealing, but without the ability to feel pain, we might ignore infections, broken bones or serious burns. Congenital insensitivity to pain, a rare inherited disorder that specifically impairs pain perception, is more of a curse than a blessing. Children who experience this disorder often mutilate themselves, for example biting into their tongues or gouging their skin while scratching, and are at increased risk of dying during childhood (Nagasako et al., 2003).

Tissue damage is transduced by pain receptors, the free nerve endings shown in Figure 4.31. Researchers have distinguished between fast-acting *A-delta fibres*, which transmit the initial sharp pain one might feel right away from a sudden injury, and slower *C fibres*, which transmit the longer lasting, duller pain that persists after the initial injury. If you were running barefoot outside and stubbed your toe against a rock, you would first feel a sudden stinging pain transmitted by A-delta fibres that would die down quickly, only to be replaced by the throbbing but longer lasting pain carried by C fibres. Both the A-delta and C fibres are impaired in cases of congenital insensitivity to pain, which is one reason why the disorder can be life-threatening.

As you'll remember from Chapter 3, the pain withdrawal reflex is coordinated by the spinal cord. No brainpower is required when you touch a hot stove; you retract your hand almost instantaneously. But neural signals for pain – such as wrenching your elbow as you brace yourself from falling – travel to two distinct areas in the brain and evoke two distinct psychological experiences (Treede et al., 1999). One pain pathway sends signals to the somatosensory cortex, identifying where the pain is occurring and what sort of pain it is (sharp, burning, dull). The second pain pathway sends signals to the motivational and emotional centres of the brain, such as the hypothalamus and amygdala, and to the frontal lobe. This is the aspect of pain that is unpleasant and motivates us to escape from or relieve the pain.

MATT CARR/GETTY IMAGES ENTERTAINMENT/GETTY IMAGES

In 2003, Aron Ralston was hiking in a remote canyon in Utah when tragedy struck. A 450-kg boulder pinned him in a 0.9-m wide space for five days, eventually leaving him with no choice but to amputate his own arm with a pocketknife. He then applied a tourniquet, rappelled down the canyon, and hiked out to safety. These and similar stories illustrate that the extent of an injury is not perfectly correlated with the amount of pain felt. Although self-amputation is undoubtedly excruciating, luckily in this case it was not debilitating. The incident is documented in Ralston's 2004 autobiography *Between a Rock and a Hard Place*, and is the subject of Danny Boyle's 2010 film *127 Hours*.

Pain typically feels as if it comes from the site of the tissue damage that caused it. However, the sensation of pain is generated in your brain, which is why amputees can still feel phantom pain in their missing limb (Chapter 3). If you burn your finger, you will perceive the pain as originating there. When you take an opiate painkiller such as morphine, it relieves the sensation of pain at the site of injury but is, in fact, operating on neurotransmitter receptors in your brain. We also have pain receptors in many areas besides the skin – around bones and within muscles and internal organs as well. When pain originates internally, in a body organ for example, we actually feel it on the surface of the body. This kind of referred pain occurs when *sensory information from internal and external areas converge on the same nerve cells in the spinal cord*. One common example is a heart attack: victims often feel pain radiating from the left arm rather than from inside the chest.

REFERRED PAIN Feeling of pain when sensory information from internal and external areas converge on the same nerve cells in the spinal cord.

Pain intensity cannot always be predicted solely from the extent of the injury that causes the pain (Keefe et al., 2005). For example, *turf toe* sounds like the mildest of ailments; it is pain at the base of the big toe as a result of bending or pushing off repeatedly, as a runner might do during a sporting event. This small-sounding injury in a small area of the body can nonetheless put an athlete out of competition for a month with considerable pain. On the other hand, you've probably heard a story or two about someone treading bone-chilling water for hours on end, or dragging their shattered legs a kilometre down a country road to seek help after a tractor accident, or performing some other incredible feat despite searing pain and extensive tissue damage. Pain type and pain intensity show a less-than-perfect correlation, a fact that intrigues researchers.

Some recent evidence indicates that subjective pain intensity may differ among ethnic groups (Campbell and Edwards, 2012). A study that examined responses to various kinds of experimentally induced pain, including heat pain and cold pain, found that compared to young white adults, young black adults had a lower tolerance for several kinds of pain and rated the same pain stimuli as more intense and unpleasant (Campbell et al., 2005).

How do psychologists account for this puzzling variability in pain perception? According to gate-control theory, *signals arriving from pain receptors in the body can be stopped, or gated, by interneurons in the spinal cord via feedback from two directions* (Melzack and Wall, 1965). Pain can be gated by the skin receptors, for example by rubbing the affected area. Rubbing your stubbed toe activates neurons that 'close the gate' to stop pain signals from travelling to the brain. Pain can also be gated from the brain by modulating the activity of pain-transmission neurons. This neural feedback is elicited not by the pain itself, but by activity deep within the thalamus.

GATE-CONTROL THEORY A theory of pain perception based on the idea that signals arriving from pain receptors in the body can be stopped, or gated, by interneurons in the spinal cord via feedback from two directions.

The neural feedback comes from a region in the midbrain called the *periaqueductal grey* (PAG). Under extreme conditions, such as high stress, naturally occurring endorphins can activate the PAG to send inhibitory signals to neurons in the spinal cord that then suppress pain signals to the brain, thereby modulating the experience of pain. The PAG is also activated through the action of opiate drugs, such as morphine.

A different kind of feedback signal can *increase* the sensation of pain. This system is activated by events such as infection and learned danger signals. When we are quite ill, what might otherwise be experienced as mild discomfort can feel quite painful. This pain facilitation signal presumably evolved to motivate people who are ill to rest and avoid strenuous activity, allowing their energy to be devoted to healing.

Gate-control theory offers strong evidence that perception is a two-way street. The senses feed information, such as pain sensations, to the brain, a pattern termed *bottom-up control* by perceptual psychologists. The brain processes these sensory data into perceptual information at successive levels to support movement, object recognition, and eventually more complex cognitive tasks, such as memory and planning. But there is ample evidence that the brain exerts plenty of control over what we sense as well. Visual illusions and the Gestalt principles of filling in, shaping up and rounding out what isn't really there provide some examples. This kind of *top-down control* also explains the descending pain pathway initiated in the midbrain.

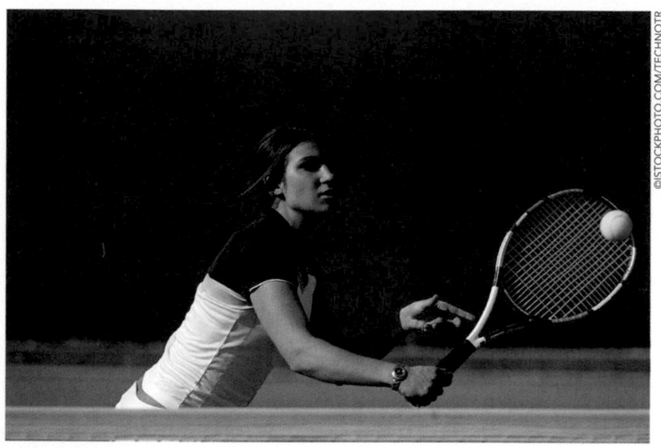

Hitting a ball with a racquet provides feedback as to where your arms and body are in space as well as how the resistance of these objects affects your movement and balance. Successful athletes have particularly well-developed body senses.

Body position, movement and balance

It may sound odd, but one aspect of sensation and perception is knowing where parts of your body are at any given moment. It's not as though your arm sneaks out of the bedroom window at night to meet some friends. Your body needs some way to sense its position in physical space other than moving your eyes to constantly visually check the location of your limbs. Sensations related to position, movement and balance depend on stimulation produced within our bodies. Receptors in the muscles, tendons and joints signal the position of the body in space, whereas information about balance and head movement originates in the inner ear.

Sensory receptors provide the information we need to perceive the position and movement of our limbs, head and body. These receptors also provide feedback about whether we are performing a desired movement correctly and how resistance from held objects may be influencing the movement. For example, when you swing a tennis racquet, the weight of it affects how your muscles move your arm as well as the change in sensation when the racquet hits the ball. Muscle, joint and tendon feedback about how your arms actually moved can be used to improve performance through learning.

VESTIBULAR SYSTEM The three fluid-filled semicircular canals and adjacent organs located next to the cochlea in each inner ear.

Maintaining balance depends primarily on the vestibular system – *the three fluid-filled semicircular canals and adjacent organs located next to the cochlea in each inner ear* (see Figure 4.28 above). The semicircular canals are arranged in three perpendicular orientations and studded with hair cells that detect movement of the fluid when the head moves or accelerates. This detected motion enables us to maintain our balance, or the position of our bodies relative to gravity. The movements of the hair cells encode these somatic sensations (Lackner and DiZio, 2005).

Vision also helps us keep our balance. If you see that you are swaying relative to a vertical orientation, such as the contours of a room, you move your legs and feet to keep from falling over. Psychologists have experimented with this visual aspect of balance by placing people in rooms that can be tilted forwards and backwards (Bertenthal et al., 1997; Lee and Aronson, 1974). If the room tilts enough – particularly when small children are tested – people will topple over as they try to compensate for what their visual system is telling them. When a mismatch between the information provided by visual cues and vestibular feedback occurs, motion sickness can result. Remember this discrepancy the next time you try reading in the back seat of a moving car!

In summary, touch is represented in the brain according to a topographic scheme in which locations on the body project sensory signals to locations in the somatosensory cortex, a part of the parietal lobe. The experience of pain depends on signals that travel along two distinct pathways. One sends signals to the somatosensory cortex to indicate the location and type of pain, and another sends signals to the emotional centres of the brain that result in unpleasant feelings that we wish to escape. The experience of pain varies across individuals, which is explained by bottom-up and top-down aspects of gate-control theory. Balance and acceleration depend primarily on the vestibular system but are also influenced by vision.

The chemical senses: adding flavour

Somatosensation is all about physical changes in or on the body. Vision and audition sense energetic states of the world – light and sound waves – and touch is activated by physical changes in or on the body surface. The last set of senses we'll consider share a chemical basis to combine aspects of distance and proximity. The chemical senses of *olfaction* (smell) and *gustation* (taste) respond to the molecular structure of substances floating into the nasal cavity as you inhale or dissolving in saliva. Smell and taste combine to produce the perceptual experience we call *flavour*.

Smell

Olfaction is the least understood sense and the only one directly connected to the forebrain, with pathways into the frontal lobe, amygdala and other forebrain structures (recall from Chapter 3 that the other senses connect first to the thalamus). This mapping indicates that smell has a close relationship with areas involved in emotional and social behaviour. Smell seems to have evolved in animals as a signalling sense for the familiar – a friendly creature, an edible food, or a sexually receptive mate.

Countless substances release odours into the air, and some of their *odourant molecules* make their way into our noses, drifting in on the air we breathe. Situated along the top of the nasal cavity, shown in **FIGURE 4.32**, is a mucous membrane called the *olfactory*

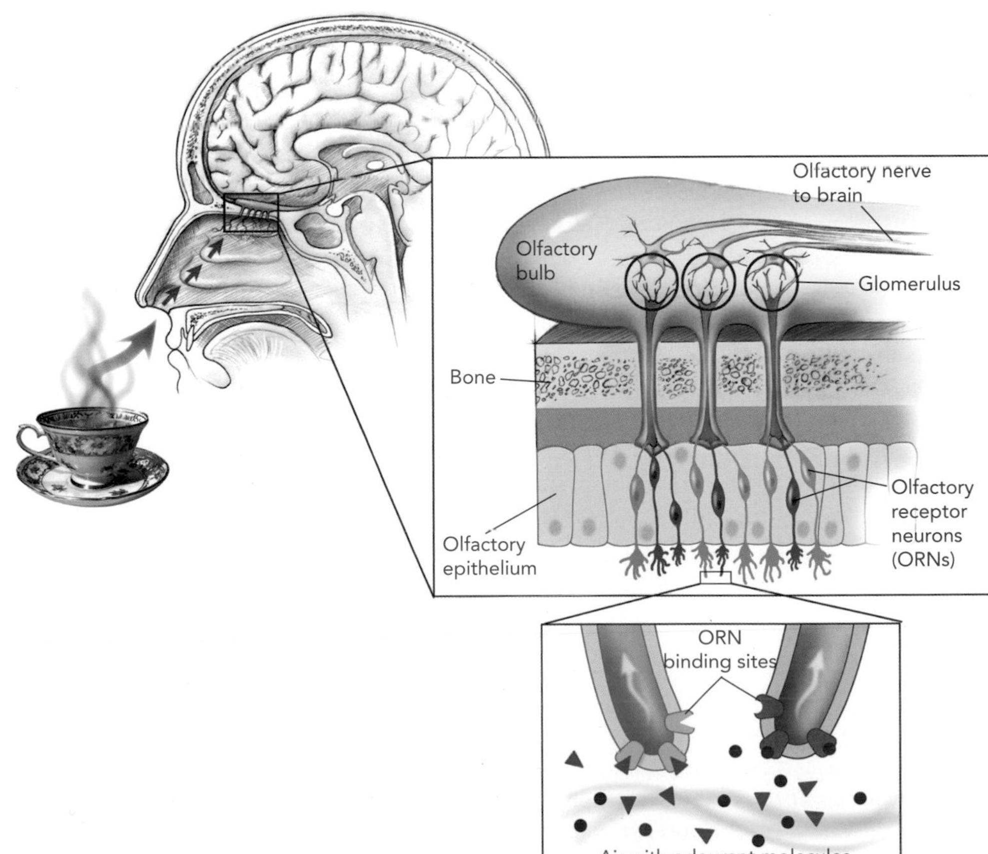

FIGURE **4.32 Anatomy of smell** Along the roof of the nasal cavity, odourant molecules dissolve in the mucous membrane that forms the olfactory epithelium. Odourants may then bind to olfactory receptor neurons (ORNs) embedded in the epithelium. ORNs respond to a range of odours and, once activated, relay action potentials to their associated glomeruli in the olfactory bulb, located just beneath the frontal lobes. The glomeruli synapse on neurons whose axons form the olfactory nerve, which projects directly into the forebrain.

OLFACTORY RECEPTOR NEURONS (ORNS) Receptor cells that initiate the sense of smell.

OLFACTORY BULB A brain structure located above the nasal cavity beneath the frontal lobes.

PHEROMONES Biochemical odourants emitted by other members of their species that can affect an animal's behaviour or physiology.

epithelium, which contains about 10 million olfactory receptor neurons (ORNs) – *receptor cells that initiate the sense of smell.* Odourant molecules bind to sites on these specialized receptors, and if enough bindings occur, the ORNs send action potentials into the olfactory nerve (Dalton, 2003).

Each olfactory neuron has receptors that bind to some odourants but not to others, as if the receptor is a lock and the odourant is the key (see Figure 4.32). Groups of ORNs send their axons from the olfactory epithelium into the olfactory bulb – *a brain structure located above the nasal cavity beneath the frontal lobes.* Humans possess about 350 different ORN types that permit us to discriminate among some 10,000 different odourants through the unique patterns of neural activity each odourant evokes. This setup is similar to our ability to see a vast range of colours based on only a small number of retinal cell types or to feel a range of skin sensations based on only a handful of touch receptor cell types.

The axons of all ORNs of a particular type converge at a site called a *glomerulus* within the olfactory bulb; thus, humans have about 350 glomeruli. Different odourant molecules produce varied patterns of activity (Rubin and Katz, 1999). A given odourant may strongly activate some glomeruli, moderately activate others, and have little effect on still others. The genetic basis for this olfactory coding was worked out in large part by Linda Buck and Richard Axel (1991), who were awarded the Nobel Prize in 2004 for their efforts.

Some dogs have as many as 100 times more ORNs than humans do, producing a correspondingly sharpened ability to detect and discriminate among millions of odours. Nevertheless, humans are sensitive to the smells of some substances in extremely small concentrations. For example, a chemical compound that is added to natural gas to help detect gas leaks can be sensed at a concentration of just 0.0003 parts per million. By contrast, acetone (nail polish remover), something most people regard as pungent, can be detected only if its concentration is 15 parts per million or greater.

The olfactory bulb sends outputs to various centres in the brain, including the parts that are responsible for controlling basic drives, emotions and memories. This explains why smells can have immediate, strongly positive or negative effects on us. If the slightest whiff of an apple pie baking brings back fond memories of childhood or the unexpected sniff of vomit mentally returns you to a particularly bad party you once attended, you've got the idea. Thankfully, sensory adaptation is at work when it comes to smell, just as it is with the other senses. Whether the associations are good or bad, after just a few minutes the smell fades. Smell adaptation makes sense; it allows us to detect new odours that may require us to act, but after that initial evaluation has occurred, it may be best to reduce our sensitivity to allow us to detect other smells. Evidence from fMRIs indicates that experience of a smell can modify odour perception by changing how specific parts of the brain involved in olfaction respond to that smell (Li et al., 2006).

Smell may also play a role in social behaviour. Humans and other animals can detect odours from pheromones – *biochemical odourants emitted by other members of their species that can affect the animal's behaviour or physiology.* Parents can distinguish the smell of their own children from other people's children. An infant can identify the smell of its mother's breast from the smell of other mothers. Even though the recognition of these smells occurs outside conscious awareness, it nonetheless influences behaviour: parents pick up their own children rather than strangers' children, and breast-feeding becomes a personal connection between mother and child. Pheromones also play a role in reproductive behaviour in insects and several mammalian species, including mice, dogs and primates (Brennan and Zufall, 2006). Can the same thing be said of human reproductive behaviour?

Studies of people's preference for the odours of individuals of the opposite sex have produced mixed results, with no consistent tendency for people to prefer them over other pleasant odours. Recent research, however, has provided a link between sexual orientation and responses to odours that may constitute human pheromones. Researchers used positron emission tomography (PET) scans to study the brain's response to two odours, one related to testosterone, which is produced in men's sweat, and the other related to oestrogen, which is found in women's urine. The testosterone-based odour activated the hypothalamus (a part of the brain that controls sexual behaviour; see Chapter 3) in heterosexual women but not heterosexual men, whereas the oestrogen-based odour activated the hypothalamus in heterosexual men but not women. Strikingly, homosexual men responded to the two chemicals in the same way as women did: the hypothalamus was activated by the testosterone- but not oestrogen-based odour (Savic et al., 2005) (see **FIGURE 4.33**). Other common odours unrelated to sexual arousal were processed similarly by all three groups. A follow-up study with lesbian women showed that their responses to the testosterone- and oestrogen-based odours were largely similar to those of heterosexual men (Berglund et al., 2006). Taken together, the two studies suggest that some human pheromones are related to sexual orientation.

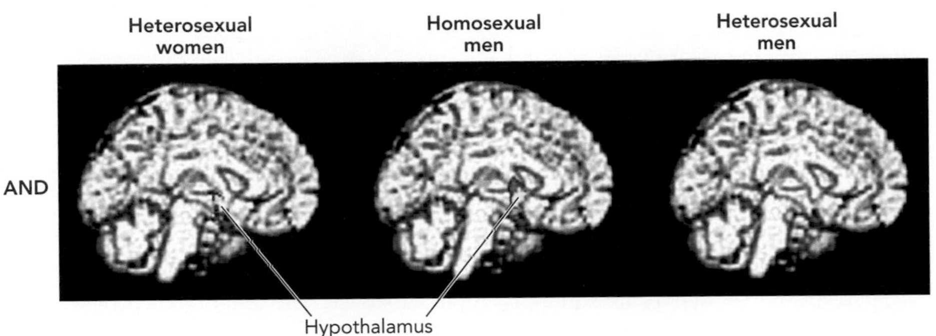

FIGURE 4.33 Smell and social behaviour In a PET study, heterosexual women, homosexual men and heterosexual men were scanned as they were presented with each of several odours. During the presentation of a testosterone-based odour (referred to in the figure as AND), there was significant activation in the hypothalamus for heterosexual women (left) and homosexual men (centre) but not for heterosexual men (right) (Savic et al., 2005).

Other evidence also indicates that pheromones can affect human physiology. Women who live in close proximity for extended periods, flatmates at university for example, tend to synchronize menstrual periods. To test the hypothesis that this synchrony might be mediated by pheromones, a group of women wore cotton pads in their armpits to collect sweat (McClintock, 1971). The secretions were transferred to the upper lip (under the nose) of women with whom they had no other contact. This procedure did indeed cause the menstrual cycles of the pairs to synchronize over time, although the mechanism remains a mystery. It does not appear to involve any conscious awareness of the smell: the recipient women in these studies reported that they could not discriminate between the smell of the pads worn by the donor women from pads that had not been treated. Nonetheless, the introduction of these pheromones contributed to the regulation of the women's bodily states.

Taste

One of the primary responsibilities of the chemical sense of taste is identifying things that are bad for you, as in 'poisonous and lethal'. Many poisons are bitter, and we avoid eating things that nauseate us for good reason, so taste aversions have a clear adaptive significance. Some aspects of taste perception are genetic, such as an aversion to extreme bitterness, and some are learned, such as an aversion to a particular food that once caused nausea (see the sauce Béarnaise phenomenon in Chapter 6). In either case, the direct contact between a tongue and possible foods allows us to anticipate whether something will be harmful or palatable.

The tongue is covered with thousands of small bumps, called *papillae*, which are easily visible to the naked eye. Within each papilla are hundreds of taste buds – *the organ of taste transduction* (see **FIGURE 4.34**). Most of our mouths contain 5,000–10,000 taste buds fairly evenly distributed over the tongue, roof of the mouth and upper throat (Bartoshuk and Beauchamp, 1994; Halpern, 2002). Each taste bud contains 50–100 taste receptor cells. Taste perception fades with age, and, on average, people lose half their taste receptors by the time they turn 20 (Methven et al., 2012). This may help to explain why young children seem to be 'fussy eaters', since their greater number of taste buds brings with it a greater range of taste sensations. (For a striking example of extreme taste sensitivity, see *the real world* box.)

TASTE BUDS The organ of taste transduction.

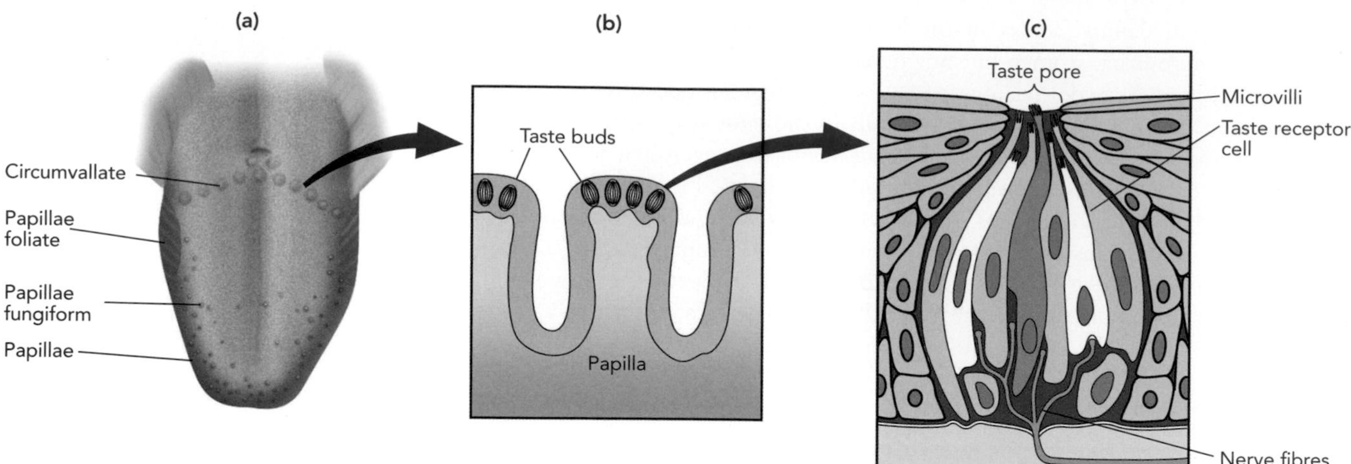

FIGURE **4.34 A taste bud** (a) Taste buds stud the bumps (papillae) on your tongue, shown here, as well as the back, sides and roof of the mouth. (b) Each taste bud contains a range of receptor cells that respond to varying chemical components of foods called tastants. Tastant molecules dissolve in saliva and stimulate the microvilli that form the tips of the taste receptor cells. (c) Each taste bud contacts the branch of a cranial nerve at its base.

The human eye contains millions of rods and cones, the human nose contains some 350 different types of olfactory receptors, but the taste system contains just five main types of taste receptors, corresponding to five primary taste sensations: salt, sour, bitter, sweet and umami (savoury). The first four are quite familiar, but *umami* may not be. In fact, perception researchers are still debating its existence. The umami receptor was discovered by Japanese scientists who attributed it to the tastes evoked by foods containing a high concentration of protein, such as meats and cheeses (Yamaguchi, 1998). If you're a meat eater and you savour the feel of a steak topped with butter or a cheeseburger as it sits in your mouth, you've got an idea of the umami sensation.

Each taste bud contains several types of taste receptor cells whose tips, called *microvilli*, react with *tastant molecules* in food. Salt taste receptors are most strongly activated by sodium chloride – table salt. Sour receptor cells respond to acids, such as vinegar or lime juice. Bitter and sweet taste receptors are more complex. Some 50–80 distinct binding sites in bitter receptors are activated by an equal number of different bitter-tasting chemicals. Sweet receptor cells can also be activated by a wide range of substances in addition to sugars.

Although umami receptor cells are the least well understood, researchers are honing in on their key features (Chandrashekar et al., 2006). They respond most strongly to glutamate, an amino acid in many protein-containing foods. Recall from Chapter 3, glutamate acts as a neurotransmitter; in fact, it's a major excitatory neurotransmitter. The food additive *monosodium glutamate* (MSG), which is often used to flavour Asian foods, particularly activates umami receptors. Some people develop headaches or allergic reactions after eating foods containing MSG.

the real world

Supertasters

We all know fussy eaters. Children who don't like to eat their vegetables quickly come to mind. Even some adults shun dark green vegetables such as Brussels sprouts, kale and broccoli throughout their lifetimes. If you enjoy these vegetables, such taste preferences may seem a little irrational.

But what if different people actually experience the taste of broccoli differently, not like the lie your parents told you – 'It tastes like ice cream' – but in a qualitatively different way from other folks? About 50% of people report a mildly bitter taste in caffeine, saccharine, certain green vegetables and other substances, while roughly 25% report no bitter taste. Members of the first group are called *tasters* and members of the second group are called *nontasters*. The remaining 25% of people are *supertasters*, who report that such substances, especially dark green vegetables, are extremely bitter, to the point of being inedible.

There's an evolutionary rationale for this. Aversion to bitter tastes is present at birth, which is not too surprising, since bitter-tasting substances are often poisons. However, many foods that taste bitter – those dark green veggies included – are beneficial in promoting health and protecting us from disease. Ironically, the very evolutionary mechanism that may keep you from poisoning yourself may also keep you from ingesting some of the healthiest food available.

There are substantial individual differences in taste preference as well. For example, not everyone has taste receptors for bitter sensations, based on their genetics (Bartoshuk et al., 1994). As another example, people from Asia, Africa and South America are more likely to be supertasters than others. Women's sensitivity to bitter tastes tends to intensify during pregnancy but diminish after menopause. Children start out as tasters or supertasters, which could help explain their early tendency towards fussiness in food preference. However, some children grow up to become nontasters.

Supertasters also experience other flavours differently from nontasters. Supertasters get more 'burn' from chillies and more creaminess from fats and thickeners in food than others do. They also experience oral pain more intensely than nontasters (Bartoshuk, 2000). Because supertasters tend to avoid fruits and vegetables that contain tastes they experience as extremely bitter, they may be at increased health risk for diseases such as colon cancer. On the other hand, because they also tend to avoid fatty, creamy foods, they tend to be thinner and may have decreased risk of cardiovascular disease (Bartoshuk, 2000).

The difference between the experiences of nontasters and supertasters can be compared to the difference in experiences among people with normal colour vision and those with genetic colour deficiencies, where at least one of the three cone types is missing. In each case, personal perceptual experiences differ in ways that may be impossible for others to grasp. A colour-deficient supertaster, in fact, has probably learned to avoid the grey broccoli.

Fussy eater or just too many taste buds? Our taste perception declines with age: we lose about half of our taste receptors by the time we're 20 years old. That can make childhood either a time of savoury delight or a sensory overload of taste.

Of course, the variety of taste experiences greatly exceeds the five basic receptors discussed here. Any food molecules dissolved in saliva evoke specific, combined patterns of activity in the five taste receptor types. Although we often think of taste as the primary source for flavour, in fact, taste and smell collaborate to produce this complex perception.

As any wine connoisseur will attest, the full experience of a wine's flavour cannot be appreciated without a finely trained sense of smell. Odourants from substances outside your mouth enter the nasal cavity via the nostrils, and odourants in the mouth enter through the back of the throat. This is why wine aficionados are taught to pull air in over wine held in the mouth: it allows the wine's odourant molecules to enter the nasal cavity through this 'back door'.

You can easily demonstrate the contribution of smell to flavour by tasting a few different foods while holding your nose, preventing the olfactory system from detecting their odours. If you have a head cold, you probably already know how this turns out. Your favourite spicy curry or zesty pasta probably tastes as bland as can be.

But it is not only smell that is important to taste. In the same way that the multisensory integration we discussed earlier reveals expectations about the world, multiple senses can contribute to flavour. For example, wine experts are notoriously easy to fool if you artificially change the colour of the wine (Morrot et al., 2001) (see margin box). The idea that taste is a multisensory experience is one of the principles that guides the culinary expertise of chef Heston Blumenthal. In addition to inventing weird combinations such as snail porridge or cauliflower risotto with chocolate, Heston Blumenthal has been applying neuroscience to enhance the dining experience at his world-famous, three Michelin star restaurant The Fat Duck in Bray, Berkshire. For example, he uses iPods to play a recording of waves breaking on the shoreline to heighten the flavours in his 'Sound of the sea' dish of seafood and edible seaweed on a bed of sand-like tapioca. Even humble crisps taste better if you eat them while listening to loud crunching sounds (Zampini and Spence, 2005). In other dishes, Blumenthal manipulates colour and textures to shift the diner's expectations. According to Jamie Ward (2008), it is precisely this lack of multisensory experience that makes dining at London's Dans le Noir? such a disappointment. On his visit to this restaurant, which serves guests their meals in pitch darkness so that they can focus on flavours alone, Jamie found the food tasted much blander, while much

Red red wine goes to my head

Many wine experts are not as expert as they think. When French graduate student Frédéric Brochet served two identical glasses of white wine, with one coloured red by food colouring, experts described the 'red' wine as tasting like normal red wine and different from the white. Neuroscientist Chuck Spence of Oxford University attributes this wine colour effect to the likelihood of the influence of past experience and that red signals the ripeness of fruits in nature, triggering a shift in taste perception. Try serving white wine in a dark glass at your next party. It is surprisingly hard not to think it tastes like red wine.

of the dining room conversation he heard concerned arguments between a couple about what they thought they were eating.

In summary, our experience of smell, or olfaction, is associated with odourant molecules binding to sites on specialized olfactory receptors, which converge at the glomerulus within the olfactory bulb. The olfactory bulb in turn sends signals to parts of the brain that control drives, emotions and memories, which helps to explain why smells can have immediate and powerful effects on us. Smell is also involved in social behaviour, as illustrated by pheromones, which are related to reproductive behaviour and sexual responses in several species. Sensations of taste depend on taste buds, which are distributed across the tongue, roof of the mouth and upper throat, and on taste receptors that correspond to the five primary taste sensations of salt, sour, bitter, sweet and umami. However, taste is also influenced by other modalities such as vision and even sound.

psychomythology

You can tell when you are being stared at from behind

Have you ever had that strange experience that you are being watched from behind, turned round and discovered that someone is staring at you? It is such a common experience that most individuals believe that they can tell when they are being stared at from behind, even though there is no way they could detect the person doing the staring using normal perception. Edward Titchener (1898), one of the early pioneers in our field of study, reported that his psychology students consistently believed they could detect unseen gaze. Subsequent studies by Coover (1913) found that 68–86% of psychology students reported having had the feeling of being stared at. More recently, Cottrell and colleagues (Cottrell et al., 1996) reported that over 90% of adults believed they could feel the unseen stares of another.

Aside from paranormal explanations (see Sheldrake, 2003), the origins, prevalence and persistence of this particular myth may be attributable to a combination of natural phenomena working together to substantiate this notion in the minds of most people.

Historically, ancient theories of vision, held most notably by Plato and Euclid (*c.* 300 BCE), proposed that vision worked by energy emanating from the eyes. This extramission theory of vision persisted for centuries until Alhazen (965–1040), the great Arab scientist, invented the camera obscura and proved that vision works by intromission, with light entering the eye. Nevertheless, this discovery has done little to shift the intuition that vision works by something leaving the eyes. It is the natural assumption of young children, as evidenced by the way they often draw rays coming out of the eyes when asked to explain how we see (Cottrell and Winner, 1994), and around 60% of adults still think vision is extramission even after they have been given a lecture on perception (Gregg et al., 2001). Why is this and why do people think they can detect the line of sight?

Vision appears to exit the eyes because we move our eyes to fixate on the world. We adjust our eyes to align them to objects of interest, which can be under voluntary control, creating the impression that the observer is the origin and source of the visual process. This intuition is supported by cultural endorsement. The Italian Renaissance writer Francesco Petrarca (1304–74) described the look of love (*innamoramento*) as the transfer of particles from the lover's eyes into the eyes of the beloved that then work their way towards the heart. Many cultures believe in the malevolent Evil Eye, where a curse can be cast by a malevolent glance, and today's comic book heroes, such as Cyclops from the X-men and Superman, have powerful rays that leave the eyes.

Titchner (1898) proposed probably the most compelling explanation for why people believe that they can tell when they are being watched. It is a misinterpreted response bias. Faces are really important to us. When someone turns to look at us, we instinctively turn to face them in order to address the potential interaction. So, if you are in a crowded environment such as a theatre and sense that you are being stared at, you may turn round to see who is looking at you. In doing so, people behind are likely to look at you turning around. This creates the false attribution that you turned around because you felt others staring at you when, in fact, the others are staring because you turn to look at them. Simple, isn't it, and yet we can all feel those eyes burning in to our backs.

where do you stand?

Perception and persuasion

In the 1950s, cinema owners experimented with a new and controversial marketing technique: subliminal advertising. They screened films into which studios had spliced single frames containing photographs of popcorn and soda or word images such as *I'm thirsty*. At normal projection speed, these images were too brief for the audience to perceive consciously, but cinema owners hoped that projecting the messages would register with the audience and thus increase concession sales during intermissions. However, scientific evidence for this kind of subliminal persuasion has been mixed at best.

These days, marketers advocate a more subtle form of advertising known as *sensory branding* (Lindstrom, 2005). The idea is to exploit all the senses to promote a product or a brand. We're used to seeing advertisements that feature exciting, provocative or sexual images to sell products. In TV commercials, these images are accompanied by popular music that advertisers hope will evoke an overall mood favourable to the product. The notion is that the sight and sound of exciting things will become associated with what might be an otherwise drab product.

But sensory branding goes beyond sight and sound by enlisting smell, taste and touch as well as vision and hearing. You probably recognize the distinctive aroma of a newly opened can of Play-Doh or a fresh box of Crayola crayons. Their scents are unmistakable, but they're also somewhat inadvertent. Play-Doh was first sold in 1956 and Crayola crayons appeared in 1903, long before there was any thought given to marketing as a total sensory experience.

Sensory branding is a much more intentional approach to marketing. That new-car smell you anticipate while you take a test drive? Actually, it's a manufactured fragrance sprayed into the car, carefully tested to evoke positive feelings among potential buyers. Bang & Olufsen, the Danish high-end stereo manufacturer, carefully designed its remote control units to have a certain distinctive 'feel' in a user's hand. Singapore Airlines, which has consistently been rated 'the world's best airline', has actually patented the smell of its aeroplane cabins (it's called Stefan Floridian Waters).

Another form of advertising that has grown dramatically in recent years is product placement: companies pay to have their products appear prominently in films and television productions. Do you notice when the star of a film drinks a can of a well-known beverage or drives a particular vehicle model in a car chase? Although viewers may not notice or even be aware of the product, advertisers believe that product placement benefits their bottom lines.

Is there any harm in marketing that bombards the senses or even sneaks through to perception undetected? Advertising is a business, and like any business it is fuelled by innovation in search of a profit. Perhaps these recent trends are simply the next clever step to get potential buyers to pay attention to a product message. On the other hand, is there a point when 'enough is enough'? Do you want to live in a world where every sensory event is trademarked, patented or test-marketed before reaching your perceptual system? Does the phrase, 'Today's sunset was brought to you by the makers of ...' cause you alarm? Where do you stand?

Chapter review

Our senses encode the information our brains perceive

- Sensation and perception are separate events that, from the vantage point of the perceiver, feel like one single process. Sensation is simple awareness due to the stimulation of a sense organ, whereas perception is a brain activity that organizes, identifies and interprets a sensation in order to form a mental representation.
- Transduction is the process that converts physical energy in the world into neural signals in the central nervous system. All senses rely on transduction, although the types of energy being sensed differ, for example light waves for vision, sound waves for audition.
- Psychophysics was a field of study during the mid to late 1800s that sought to understand the link between properties of a physical stimulus and people's psychological reactions to them.
- Psychophysics researchers developed the idea of an absolute threshold, the minimal intensity needed to just barely detect a stimulus, and the difference threshold, the minimal change in a stimulus that can just barely be detected. The difference threshold is also referred to as the just noticeable difference (JND). Signal detection theory represents a refinement of these basic approaches and takes into account perceived hit, miss, false alarm and correct rejection rates.
- Sensory adaptation occurs when sensitivity to prolonged stimulation tends to decline over time as an organism adapts to current conditions. This adaptive process illustrates that the perceptual system is more sensitive to changes in stimulation than to constant levels of stimulation.

Vision: more than meets the eye

- Vision takes place when light waves are transduced by cells in the eye. Light waves have the properties of length, amplitude and purity. These physical properties are perceived as colour, brightness and saturation, respectively.
- Light enters the eye through the cornea and pupil, landing on the retina, tissue that lines the back of each eyeball. The retina is composed of three layers of cells: photoreceptors, bipolar cells and retinal ganglion cells (RGCs). Photoreceptors take the form of rods and cones; rods are specialized for low light vision, whereas cones are specialized for colour vision.
- The optic nerve is composed of bundled axons from the RGCs; it leaves the eye via the blind spot at the back of each eyeball. Retinal ganglion cells have a receptive field that responds to light falling anywhere in it; some responses are excitatory, whereas others are inhibitory.
- Cones specialized to sense red, green or blue wavelengths begin the process of colour vision. Combinations of these cones firing produce the spectrum of colours we can see. Cones also operate in red-green and blue yellow opponent combinations to contribute to colour vision. Additive and subtractive colour mixing determine how shades of colour can be produced.
- The optic nerve makes its way through various parts of the brain to terminate in area V1, the primary visual cortex, located in the occipital lobe. There specialized neurons respond to the sensation of bars and edges in different orientations. The ventral stream leaves the occipital cortex to provide a 'what' visual pathway to other parts of the brain, while the dorsal stream provides a 'where' and 'how' pathway.
- Illusory conjunctions occur when features from separate objects are mistakenly combined. According to feature integration theory, attention provides the 'glue' necessary to bind features together. The parietal lobe is important for this process of feature binding in normal and synaesthetic perception.
- The modular view and the distributed representation view offer explanations of how we perceive and recognize objects in the world. At a minimum, humans show a great deal of perceptual constancy. Even as aspects of sensory signals change, perception remains consistent. We are rarely misled to think that distant objects are actually tiny, that the moon increases in physical size as it rises, or that a friend who grew a moustache is a totally different person.
- Gestalt psychologists delineated basic perceptual principles long ago, such as simplicity, closure, continuity and proximity. Gestalt

psychologists also observed that we tend to perceive figures set against some kind of background. Many visual illusions capitalize on perceptual ambiguities related to these principles.

- Template matching and parts-based explanations of object recognition have strengths and weaknesses. Neither account fully captures how humans correctly and efficiently perceive objects in their environment.
- Monocular, binocular and motion-based cues all enable us to perceive size and depth, although we sometimes fall prey to visual illusions. Humans are also quite adept at perceiving motion through a variety of mechanisms.

Audition: more than meets the ear

- Hearing takes place when sound waves are transduced by receptors in the ear. Sound waves have the properties of frequency, amplitude and complexity. These physical properties are perceived as pitch, loudness and timbre.
- There are three parts of the human ear: the outer ear, the middle ear and the inner ear. The outer ear channels sound waves towards the middle ear, where tiny bones (called ossicles) mechanically transmit and intensify vibrations from the eardrum to the inner ear.
- The inner ear contains the cochlea, which is divided along its length by the basilar membrane. The undulation of the basilar membrane stimulates thousands of tiny hair cells, specialized auditory receptor neurons embedded in the basilar membrane. The hair cells then release neurotransmitter molecules, initiating a neural signal in the auditory nerve.
- A place code and a temporal code are involved in transducing sound frequencies. A place code is used for high-frequency sounds, whereas a temporal code is used for low-frequency sounds. Auditory signals travel to area A1, the primary auditory cortex in the temporal lobe.
- The placement of the ears on the head enables us to localize sounds in the environment.

The body senses: more than skin deep

- Haptic perception involves the active exploration of the environment through touching and grasping. Four types of specialized receptor cells are located under the surface of the skin to transduce pressure, texture, pattern or vibration. There are also receptor cells for sensing temperature and pain.
- The somatosensory strip is organized like a homunculus; areas of the body that are more sensitive occupy a greater area in the somatosensory strip. For example, fingertips have a greater representation than do the calves of the legs.
- Pain is a useful body sense, as without it, we might quickly succumb to the effects of unnoticed wounds. A-delta fibres and C fibres are two types of pathways by which pain signals reach the brain.
- Gate-control theory proposes a bottom-up and a top-down way of controlling pain signals in the body. This helps to account for individual differences in the experience of pain.
- Body position and movement are regulated by receptors located in the muscles, joints and tendons. Balance is regulated by the semicircular canals in the inner ear and to some extent by visual cues.

The chemical senses: adding flavour

- Smell and taste are chemical senses; smell occurs when molecules enter the nose, and taste occurs when molecules are dissolved in saliva. Smell and taste combine to produce the experience of flavour.
- The olfactory epithelium, located at the top of the nasal cavity, contains about 10 million olfactory receptor neurons (ORNs). Each olfactory neuron has receptors that operate like a lock and key with odourant molecules. Groups of ORNs send their axons to a glomerulus within the olfactory bulb.
- Pheromones are biochemical odourants that affect behaviour and physiology. There is mixed evidence that pheromones affect some aspects of human sexual behaviour.
- The tongue is covered with papillae, which contain taste buds, the organs of taste transduction. Each taste bud contains taste receptor cells that respond to either salty, sweet, bitter, sour or umami taste sensations. Umami refers to the savouriness of foods.
- Taste and smell contribute to the perception of flavour. Odourants from food enter the nasal cavity through the nose and the back of the mouth. Plugging your nose while you eat can make palatable foods taste bland or make unpalatable foods taste acceptable.

Key terms

temporal code (p. 166)
timbre (p. 164)
topographic visual organization (p. 148)
transduction (p. 134)
trichromatic colour representation (p. 147)
vestibular system (p. 170)
visual acuity (p. 140)
visual form agnosia (p. 150)
visual orienting (p. 167)
Weber's law (p. 136)

Recommended reading

Enns, J. T. (2004) *The Thinking Eye, The Seeing Brain.* New York: Norton. A tour through the visual system, focusing on sensations in the eye and perception in the brain. A fine summary of the key points mentioned in this chapter and a good starting point for branching out to other topics in the science of vision.

Goodale, M. and Milner, D. (2004) *Sight Unseen.* Oxford: OUP. This intriguing book explores conscious and unconscious vision. The authors' arguments from studies of brain damage and neuroscience lead to the proposal of dual systems in visual perception.

Ward. J. (2008) *The Frog Who Croaked Blue: Synaesthesia and the Mixing of the Senses.* Hove: Routledge. Written by one of the world's leading experts on synaesthesia, provides a comprehensive and yet accessible state-of-the-art survey of this phenomenon, with a deft mixture of neuroscience and first-person accounts.

5

Chapter learning objectives

At the end of this chapter you will be able to:

1. Describe the different hypothesized memory structures.
2. Describe the different stages of memory processing.
3. Describe the different types of memory and how they are encoded.
4. Understand how to improve memory.
5. Explain why we forget.

Memory

Imagine what it must be like to experience every moment of consciousness as if you have just woken up, without any memory for things that happened only a few minutes ago. Imagine constantly living in the present without any past. In her 2005 memoir *Forever Today*, Deborah Wearing describes her husband Clive's tormented existence (pp. 202–3):

> *It was as if every waking moment was the first waking moment. Clive was under the constant impression that he had just emerged from unconsciousness because he had no evidence in his own mind of ever being awake before … 'I haven't heard anything, seen anything, touched anything, smelled anything,' he would say. 'It's like being dead.'*

In 1985, Clive Wearing, an eminent musicologist at Cambridge University with a glittering future ahead of him, was struck down with an infection of the brain, herpes simplex encephalitis, which destroyed his capacity to store any new memories. He remembers many skills, such as how to write and play the piano, and also what his wife Deborah looks like, but he cannot remember anything new that has happened to him since his illness. Clive has profound anterograde amnesia. Anything he experiences is lost within minutes. His memory can even be limited to seconds. He wrote a diary to keep track of his 'never-ending agony', as Deborah described it. The entries make painful reading: '2.00pm – I am awake for the very first time. 2.14pm – I am now conscious. 2.19pm – have just woken for the first time.' Each previous entry is crossed out as he asserts that he has only just become conscious.

Deborah describes how one day she found Clive holding a chocolate in one hand and repeatedly covering and uncovering it with the other hand as if practising a magic

Clive Wearing, eminent Cambridge professor, conductor and pianist, suffered severe amnesia as a result of a brain infection. The infection destroyed his capacity to store any new memories. He remembers how to play the piano but he cannot remember anything new that has happened to him since his illness.

MEMORY The ability to store and retrieve information over time.

trick (Wearing, 2005). Each time he removed his hand he was amazed by the appearance of the chocolate. But this memory loss is also a personal loss. Every time Deborah walks into the room, it's as if she has returned like some long-lost lover and Clive races to embrace her, filled with joy. Clive has also lost many of his older memories, so to compound his misery he has retrograde amnesia. What could be worse than to be trapped forever in the moment, with distant memories fading and not being able to remember anything new?

Memory is *the ability to store and retrieve information over time*, and as Clive's story suggests, it is more than just a handy device that allows us to find our car keys and schedule our dental appointments. In a very real way, our memories define us. Each of us has a unique identity that is intricately tied to the things we have thought, felt, done and experienced. Memories are the residue of those events, the enduring changes that experience makes in our brains and leaves behind when it passes. If an experience passes without leaving a trace, it might just as well not have happened: 'Without memory, our awareness would be confined to an eternal present and our lives would be virtually devoid of meaning' (Schacter and Scarry, 2000, p. 1). For Clive, the past 25 years of his life have come and gone without a trace, leaving him constantly lost and confused. As Deborah put it (Wearing, 2005, pp. 202–3):

> Clive was constantly surrounded by strangers in a strange place, with no knowledge of where he was or what had happened to him. To catch sight of me was always a massive relief – to know that he was not alone, that I still cared, that I loved him, that I was there. Clive was terrified all the time. But I was his life, I was his lifeline. Every time he saw me, he would run to me, fall on me, sobbing, clinging.

Those of us who *can* remember what we did yesterday often fail to appreciate just how complex that act of remembering is because it seems to occur easily. But just consider the role memory plays in the simplest act, such as arranging to meet a friend at the cinema. You must recall your friend's name and telephone number and how to make a call. You must remember what their voice sounds like so that you'll recognize who answers the phone, and you need to remember how to talk to them and how to make sense of the things they say. You need to remember which films are currently playing, as well as the types of films you and your friend enjoy. To find a convenient day and time, you need to remember everything else that is happening in your life as well. Eventually, you will need to remember how to get to the cinema, how to drive your car, and what your friend looks like so you can find one another among the people standing in front of the cinema. And finally, you'll have to remember which film you just saw so that you don't accidentally do this all again tomorrow. These are ordinary tasks – tasks so simple that you never give them a second thought. But the fact is that the most sophisticated computer could not even begin to accomplish them as efficiently as any average human.

Because memory is so remarkably complex, it is also remarkably fragile (Schacter, 1996). Every one of us has had the experience of forgetting something we desperately wanted to remember or remembering something that never really happened. Why does memory serve us so well in some situations and play such cruel tricks on us in other cases? When can we trust our memories and when should we view them sceptically? Is there just one kind of memory, or are there many? These are among the questions that psychologists have asked and answered. In this chapter we will look at memory not as a single, unified process, but as a system made up of different subcomponents. We begin by considering the structure and processes of memory. We will then move on to the nature of enduring memories, how they are created, the brain mechanisms that support them – and why we forget. Finally, we consider the role of memory in our self-awareness, and Schacter's (2001a) seven sins of memory as a useful framework for considering the costs and the benefits of an imperfect memory system.

The structure of memory

When most people talk about memory, they are usually referring to a 'store' of information and experiences they hold about the world. How does information enter this store, and what is it like? An early popular hypothesis concerning the structure of memory is the 'modal' model by Atkinson and Shiffrin (1968), who proposed that memory consists of a flow of information that passes through three stages: sensory memory, a short-term memory and a long-term memory (see **FIGURE 5.1**):

1 First, information enters a temporary **sensory memory** – *a place where sensory information is kept for a few seconds or less.*
2 The information is processed into a nonsensory format and, if relevant, it enters the next stage, a **short-term memory,** *a place where nonsensory information is kept for more than a few seconds but less than a minute*, where it is processed further but usually discarded unless the individual puts in effort to keep the memory active.
3 Finally, this information can enter into **long-term memory** – *a place where information is stored for hours, days, weeks or years.* It is long-term memory that most people are familiar with as, this is the repository for all the information we encounter in a lifetime and the one that fails most conspicuously when we forget.

SENSORY MEMORY A place where sensory information is kept for a few seconds or less.

SHORT-TERM MEMORY A place where nonsensory information is kept for more than a few seconds but less than a minute.

LONG-TERM MEMORY A place where information can be kept for hours, days, weeks or years.

Since its inception, the modal model has proved a useful framework for memory researchers, and although there are still controversies about the exact details of how it works, it's worth taking a look at each of the three stages in more detail.

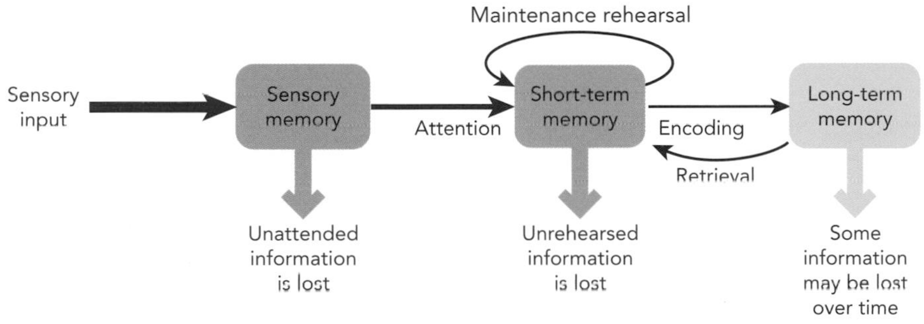

Maintenance rehearsal
Sensory input
Sensory memory
Attention
Short-term memory
Encoding
Retrieval
Long-term memory
Unattended information is lost
Unrehearsed information is lost
Some information may be lost over time

FIGURE 5.1 The flow of information through the memory system Information moves through several stages of memory as it is encoded, stored and made available for later retrieval.

Sensory memory

Sensory memory is the first stage of memory formation. In a series of classic experiments aimed at finding out how sensory memory worked, research participants were asked to remember rows of letters (Sperling, 1960). In one version of the procedure, participants viewed three rows of four letters each, as shown in **FIGURE 5.2**. The researcher flashed the letters on a screen for just 1/20th of a second. When asked to remember all 12 letters they had just seen, participants recalled fewer than half of them (Sperling, 1960). There were two possible explanations for this: either people simply couldn't encode all the letters in such a brief period of time, or they had encoded the letters, but had forgotten some of them during the process of trying recall everything they had seen.

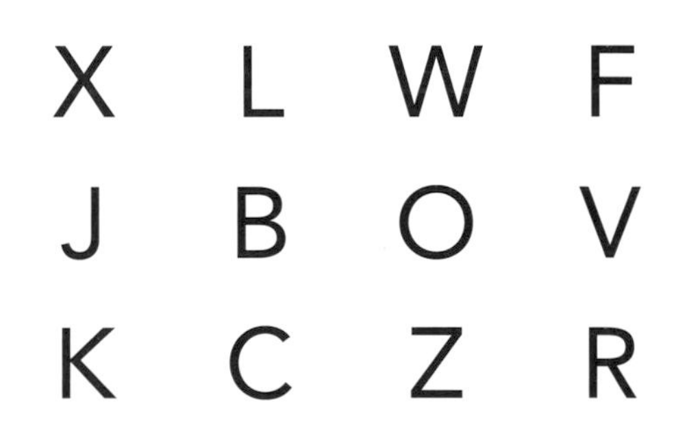

FIGURE 5.2 Iconic memory test When a grid of letters is flashed on a screen for only 1/20th of a second, it is difficult to recall individual letters. But if prompted to remember a particular row immediately after the grid is shown, research participants will do so with high accuracy. Sperling (1960) used this procedure to demonstrate that although iconic memory stores the whole grid, the information fades away too quickly for a person to recall everything.

To test the two ideas, the researchers relied on a clever trick. Just after the letters disappeared from the screen, a tone was sounded to instruct participants to report the letters in a particular row. A *high tone* instructed participants to report the contents of the top row, a *medium* tone instructed participants to report the contents of the middle row, and a *low* tone instructed participants to report the contents of the bottom row. When asked to report only a single row, people recalled almost all the letters in that row. Because the tone sounded *after* the letters disappeared from the screen, the researchers concluded that people could have recalled the same number of letters from *any* of the rows had they been asked to. Participants had no way of knowing which of the three rows would be cued, so the researchers inferred that virtually all the letters had been encoded. Interestingly, they also found that if the tone was substantially delayed, participants couldn't perform the task; the information had slipped away from their sensory memories. Like the afterimage of a torch, the 12 letters flashed on a screen are visual icons, a lingering trace stored in memory for a very short period.

ICONIC MEMORY A fast-decaying store of visual information.

ECHOIC MEMORY A fast-decaying store of auditory information.

Because we have more than one sense, we have more than one kind of sensory memory. **Iconic memory** is a fast-decaying store of visual information. A similar storage area serves as a temporary warehouse for sounds. **Echoic memory** is *a fast-decaying store of auditory information*. When you have difficulty understanding what someone has just said, you probably find yourself replaying the last few words – listening to them echo in your 'mind's ear', so to speak. When you do that, you are accessing information that is being held in your echoic memory store. The hallmark of the iconic and echoic memory stores is that they hold information for a very short time. Iconic memories usually decay in about a second or less, and echoic memories usually decay in about five seconds (Darwin et al., 1972).

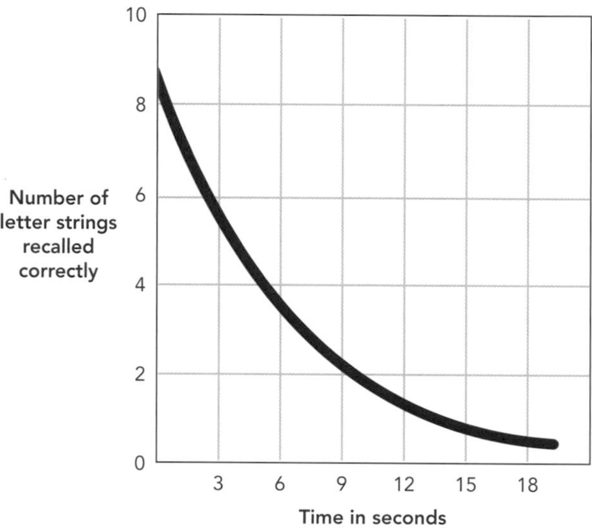

FIGURE **5.3 The decline of short-term memory** A 1959 experiment showed how quickly short-term memory fades without rehearsal. On a test for memory of three-letter strings, research participants were highly accurate when tested a few seconds after exposure to each string, but if the test was delayed another 15 seconds, people barely recalled the strings at all (Peterson and Peterson, 1959).

Short-term memory

The next stage of memory is the short-term memory, where nonsensory information is processed and stored but easily forgotten if not rehearsed. For example, if someone tells you a telephone number, you can usually wait a few seconds and repeat it back with ease. But if you wait too long, you can't. How long is too long? In a study that examined how long people can hold information in short-term memory, research participants were given consonant strings to remember, such as DBX and HLM. After seeing each string, participants were asked to count backwards from 100 by threes for varying amounts of time and were then asked to recall the strings (Peterson and Peterson, 1959). As shown in **FIGURE 5.3**, memory for the consonant strings declined rapidly, from approximately 80% after a 3-second delay to less than 20% after a 20-second delay.

These results suggest that information can be held in the short-term memory for about 15–20 seconds, but for most of us, that's not nearly long enough. So we use a trick that allows us to get around the natural limitations of our short-term memories. If someone gives us a telephone number and we don't have a pencil, we say it over and over again to ourselves until we find one. **Rehearsal** is *the process of keeping information in short-term memory by mentally repeating it*. Why does rehearsal work so well? Because each time you repeat the number, you are putting it back or 're-entering' it into short-term memory, thus giving it another 15–20 seconds of shelf life.

REHEARSAL The process of keeping information in short-term memory by mentally repeating it.

CHUNKING Combining small pieces of information into larger clusters or chunks that are more easily held in short-term memory.

Short-term memory is naturally limited in how *long* it can hold information, but it is also naturally limited in how *much* information it can hold. Experiments suggest that most people can keep approximately seven numbers in short-term memory, and if they put more new numbers in, then old numbers begin to fall out (Miller, 1956). It is no accident that telephone numbers in most countries consist of no more than six or seven digits (plus an area prefix, which is committed to the long-term memory). But there is something puzzling here. If we can keep only seven numbers in short-term memory, how is it that we can also keep seven words? After all, seven words could easily involve more than 50 letters. The answer is that short-term memory can hold about seven *meaningful items*, and therefore one way to circumvent its natural limitations is to group several letters into a single meaningful item. **Chunking** involves *combining small pieces of information into larger clusters or chunks that are more easily held in short-term memory*. Short-term memory can hold about seven chunks of information, and although a word may contain more than 10 letters, it is still considered a single chunk (Miller, 1956).

Working memory

WORKING MEMORY Active maintenance and manipulation of information in short-term storage.

The traditional view is that short-term memory is simply a place to 'hold' information. However, one influential theory suggests that the short-term memory is made up of *operations* and *processes* we use to work with information, collectively known as the **working memory** – *active maintenance and manipulation of information in short-term storage* (Baddeley and Hitch, 1974). In effect, working memory is an 'online' process whereby daily tasks are undertaken by integrating new information from the task with old information stored in memory.

As shown in FIGURE 5.4, working memory includes subsystems that store and manipulate information. The **visuospatial sketchpad** *briefly stores visual and spatial information*. For example, if you wanted to keep the arrangement of pieces on a chessboard in mind as you contemplated your next move, you'd be relying on the visuospatial sketchpad. The **phonological loop** *briefly encodes mental representations of sounds and is made up of a short-term store and an articulatory rehearsal system*. It is active when you are listening to speech or trying to remember a phrase. *Articulatory rehearsal* enables you to remember information by saying it back to yourself so as to keep the memory active. The visuospatial sketchpad and the phonological loop can be simultaneously active; for example, rehearsing someone's telephone number can activate a spoken rehearsal and visual memory. Both systems are considered 'slave systems' to the **central executive** – *an attentional system that coordinates and controls plans of action and output*. The fourth component is the **episodic buffer** – *a temporary storage space where information from long-term memory can be integrated into working memory*.

VISUOSPATIAL SKETCHPAD Briefly stores visual and spatial information.

PHONOLOGICAL LOOP Briefly encodes mental representations of sounds and is made up of a short-term store and an articulatory rehearsal system.

CENTRAL EXECUTIVE An attentional system that coordinates and controls plans of action and output.

EPISODIC BUFFER A temporary storage space where information from long-term memory can be integrated into working memory.

This is all very well in theory, but how might it work in practice? Consider how the subsystems of working memory might coordinate themselves in a daily task such as a bit of mental arithmetic. After reading or hearing 'What is the sum of 25, 17 and 2?', your phonological loop and visuospatial sketchpad would generate representations of numbers in both sight and sound – but in order to do the computation, you would have to remember the rules of addition and how to carry over the units into the tens. This requires mental manipulation of symbols by the central executive based on arithmetic rules that are entered into the episodic buffer retrieved from long-term storage.

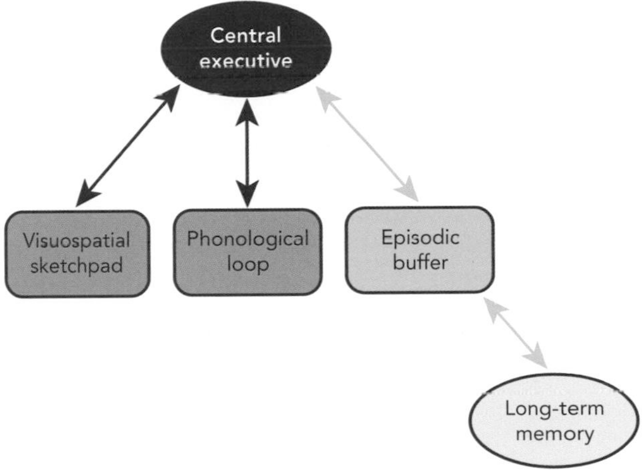

FIGURE 5.4 Schematic of Baddeley's (2000) model of working memory
Working memory consists of the visuospatial sketchpad and phonological loop subsystems that process visual and auditory information, which can be temporarily stored in the episodic buffer via the coordination of the central executive system before passing into long-term memory. The central executive is an attentional system for coordinating activity and output of the subsystems.

ADAPTED FROM BADDELEY (2000). IMAGE ORIGINALLY PUBLISHED IN *TRENDS IN COGNITIVE SCIENCE*, 4, BADDELEY, A.D., THE EPISODIC BUFFER: A NEW COMPONENT OF WORKING MEMORY, 417-23, COPYRIGHT ELSEVIER (2000)

The strongest evidence for the existence of the working memory's subsystems comes from studies that look at what happens when two tasks are completed simultaneously (known as 'dual task' studies). These reveal that performance in the tasks can either be impaired *or* remain unaffected, depending on whether just one subsystem is activated, or whether two different subsystems are being used. The idea is that if two simultaneous tasks use the *same* subsystem, then overall performance should be impaired, because of **interference** – *the drop in accuracy and response time performance when two tasks tap into the same system*. For example, trying to remember verbal information such as someone's name and what they do at a party is hard if you have to simultaneously rehearse other verbal information (Gathercole, 1997). Likewise, trying to trace a route on a map is disrupted by similar simultaneous visuospatial tasks, but unaffected by a simultaneous verbal task (Baddeley and Andrade, 2000). Findings like this suggest that in addition to limited storage capacity, the ability to ignore and selectively attend to information is also one of the key constraints on working memory (Lustig et al., 2001).

INTERFERENCE The drop in accuracy and response time performance when two tasks tap into the same system.

These findings have practical implications – even for students. For example, Salamé and Baddeley (1989) demonstrated that students are better at remembering information when they listen to instrumental music compared with when they listen to music with lyrics, because the lyrics interfere with their phonological loops. Others have also demonstrated the importance of task difficulty over the amount of information that can be remembered. For example, Saito and Miyake (2004) had adults complete the word span task (Daneman and Carpenter, 1980), where the participant has to read aloud sentences of varying length and remember highlighted words from each sentence. The longer the sentences, the more difficult the task, because reading aloud requires resources. The participants were tested on two conditions; one where the delay between learning target words and recalling them was held constant but the task difficulty (sentence length) was varied, and one where the task difficulty was held constant but the retention interval for holding the remembered target words was varied. In both situations, it was the task difficulty that determined memory recall. If working memory is so closely tied to processing efficiency, this explains why working memory functioning is strongly related to performance in intelligence tests, which we look at more closely in Chapter 9.

Help! I've eaten and I can't get home!

In Oslo, Norway, Jermund Skogstad, 50, was moving into his new flat when he took a break to get something to eat. He went to a nearby café but forgot to take his wallet, which contained his new address. He was unable to find his way home. 'This is embarrassing', he told a newspaper a *month* later, hoping that word of his plight would reach his new landlady, to whom he had paid a month's rent in advance.

Recently, working memory has become a hot topic in the so-called brain-training debate (Shipstead et al., 2012a). Commercially available programs such as Cogmed use computerized training to enhance working memory, which is claimed to improve students' scholastic achievement (Shipstead et al., 2012b). However, meta-analysis (see the stats facts in Chapter 15) has shown that these claims may not be fully substantiated (Melby-Lervåg and Hulme, 2012). There are short-term improvements on measures of working memory but the effects are not sustained over months (Hulme and Melby-Lervåg, 2012). One recent study found improvement on the working memory task that participants trained on but did not show the necessary transfer of performance over to other tasks, which is usually considered the gold standard for demonstrating general cognitive improvement (Redick et al., 2013). Others have argued that computerized training works for particular groups of children, especially those who already have poor working memory (Holmes et al., 2009) and that transfer is more meaningful when applied to real-life situations that demand working memory rather than comparing performance on other computerized tasks (Gathercole et al., 2012).

Long-term memory

©FRANCO MAGNANI

SUSAN SCHWARTZENBERG, ©EXPLORATORIUM, WWW.EXPLORATORIUM.EDU

Even years after leaving home in Pontito, Italy, painter Franco Magnani was able to create a near-perfect reproduction of what he'd seen there. Magnani's painting (left), based on a memory of a place he hadn't seen for years, is remarkably similar to the photograph Susan Schwartzenberg took of the actual scene (right).

Artist Franco Magnani was born in Pontito, Italy in 1934. In 1958, he left his village to see the rest of the world, and he settled in San Francisco in the 1960s. Soon after arriving, Magnani began to suffer from a strange illness. Every night he experienced feverish dreams of Pontito, in which he recalled the village in vivid detail. The dreams soon penetrated his waking life in the form of overpowering recollections, and Magnani decided that the only way to rid himself of these images was to capture them on canvas. For the next 20 years, he devoted much of his time to painting in exquisite detail his memories of his beloved village. Many years later, photographer Susan Schwartzenberg went to Pontito, armed with a collection of Magnani's paintings, and photographed each scene from the perspective of the paintings. As you can see, the correspondence between the paintings and the photographs was striking (Sacks, 1995; Schacter, 1996).

Many years intervened between Magnani's visual perception and artistic reconstruction of the village, suggesting that detailed information can sometimes be stored for a very long time. Long-term memory is distinct from short-term memory in two important ways: duration and capacity. Whereas the memory duration of the short-term store is only about a minute, people can recall items from long-term memory even if they haven't recalled them for years. For example, researchers in the US have found that even 50 years after leaving school, people can accurately recognize about 90% of their classmates from yearbook photographs (Bahrick, 2000). Although Franco Magnani's memories are impressive, we are all capable of quite remarkable feats of long-term memory.

It is common practice when reporting case studies to refer to patients only by their initials to protect their identity. Following his death in 2008 at the age of 82, the identity of H. M. was revealed as Henry Gustav Molaison. The following year, his brain was dissected by anatomists at the University of California, San Diego in a 53-hour long procedure that was broadcast live on the internet. Although anonymous in life, Henry became famous in death.

In comparison to short-term memory, long-term memory has no known capacity limits. For example, most people can recall 10,000–15,000 words in their native language, tens of thousands of facts ('The Battle of Hastings was 1066' and '3 × 3 = 9'), and an untold number of personal experiences. Just think of all the song lyrics you can recite by heart, and you'll understand that you've got a lot of information tucked away in long-term memory.

Although there has been some controversy about whether the long-term memory store is separate to the short-term memory store, the profile of memory loss from amnesiac patients like Clive Wearing (who we met at the start of the chapter) supports this division. Clive can retrieve memories from years back, but he can't remember what happened minutes ago. Another well-known patient suffered a similar catastrophic amnesiac disorder. In 1953, a 27-year-old man, known for most of his life simply by his initials H. M., suffered from intractable epilepsy (Scoville and Milner, 1957). To prevent further spread of epileptic tissue, H. M. had parts of his temporal lobes removed, including the hippocampus and some surrounding regions (see **FIGURE 5.5**). (As we discuss in the next section, these regions plays a critical role in remembering.) After the operation, H. M. could converse easily, use and understand language, and perform well in intelligence tests. Indeed, the only thing H. M. could *not* do was remember things that happened to him *after* the operation. For example, he would often forget that he had just eaten a meal or fail to recognize the hospital staff who helped him on a daily basis.

The cases of Clive Wearing and H. M. strongly imply that the short-term and long-term memory stores are separate: memories held in temporary short-term memory are lost if they don't make it into the more permanent storage of long-term memory – but Clive and H. M. have lost the ability to transfer their memories in this manner. This transferring of memories is known as **consolidation** – *the process whereby information must pass from short-term memory into long-term memory in order for it to be remembered* (Craik and Lockhart, 1972). As we will see in the next section, however, consolidation is not guaranteed to happen flawlessly, and it is not just amnesiacs who fail to transfer new memories into the long-term store.

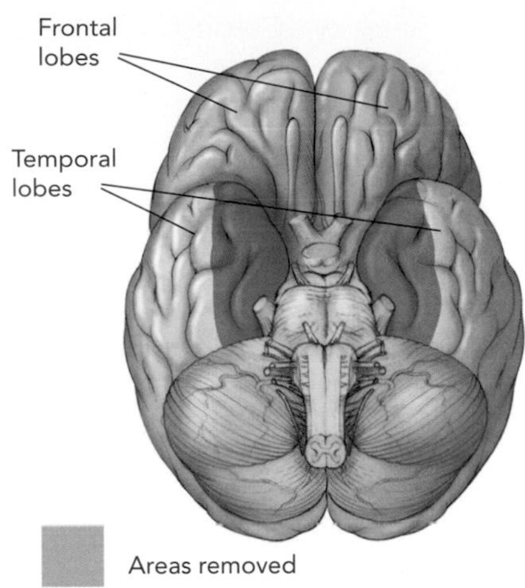

FIGURE 5.5 The hippocampus patient H. M. had his hippocampus and adjacent structures of the medial temporal lobe (indicated by the shaded area) surgically removed to stop his epileptic seizures. As a result, he could not remember things that happened after the surgery.

CONSOLIDATION The process whereby information must pass from short-term memory into long-term memory in order for it to be remembered.

In summary, human memory is thought to comprise multiple systems. Contemporary theories of memory distinguish between different structures that address different types of information for different periods of time. The modal model of memory is the standard division of memory into sensory, short-term and long-term memory. Sensory memory registers information from the senses briefly. Short-term memory holds information coming in from sensory memory for less than a minute (unless it is rehearsed), and has limited capacity. Working memory is a model of short-term memory, which suggests that two subsystems deal separately with phonological and visuospatial information. These subsystems are managed by the central executive, and can be integrated with information from long-term memory via a temporary episodic buffer, in order to perform mental operations. Information from short-term memory feeds into long-term memory, which is the familiar repository of information and experiences that constitute the personal history of the individual, and does not seem to have a finite capacity. Patterns of forgetting support the idea that there are different memory stores for transitory and more long-term information.

Remembering

It may seem obvious but the primary purpose of memory is, of course, to remember. In order to achieve this, however, three important processes must be successfully executed:

- **encoding** – *the process by which we transform what we perceive, think or feel into an enduring memory*
- **storage** – *the process of maintaining information in memory over time*
- **retrieval** – *the process of bringing to mind information that has been previously encoded and stored.*

Different aspects of memory can be recovered depending on how the retrieval is structured, with some memories more elaborated than others. Each of these processes can break down or fail, compromising our ability to remember. As you've seen in other chapters, the mind's errors and misfires provide key insights into its fundamental nature, and there is no better illustration of these mindbugs than in the realm of memory. Although often fascinating and sometimes frustrating, the mindbugs of memory teach us much about how we remember our pasts.

ENCODING The process by which we transform what we perceive, think or feel into an enduring memory.

STORAGE The process of maintaining information in memory over time.

RETRIEVAL The process of bringing to mind information that has been previously encoded and stored.

Encoding: transforming perceptions into memories

For at least 2,000 years, people have thought of memory as a recording device, like some sort of video camera that makes exact copies of information that comes in through our senses and then stores these copies for later use like a recording. This idea is simple and intuitive, but is, in fact, thoroughly and completely incorrect.

In 1932, British psychologist Sir Frederic Bartlett (1886–1969), one of the few psychologists ever to the knighted for his work, demonstrated that memories are not exact copies of past events, rather, they are reconstructed, like stories. In order to demonstrate this, he asked participants to read a brief Native American folktale that had odd imagery and unfamiliar plots in it, and then recount it as best they could after 15 minutes (and sometimes after longer periods). The readers made interesting but understandable errors, often eliminating details that didn't make sense to them or adding elements to make the story more coherent. As the specifics of the story slipped away, the general meaning of the events stayed in memory – but usually with elaborations and embellishments that were consistent with the readers' worldview. Because the story was unfamiliar to the readers, they raided their stores of general information and patched together a reasonable recollection of what *probably* happened. According to Bartlett, this is because participants encode and reconstruct memories via **schemas** – *mental models of the world that contain knowledge that helps us to encode new information into a meaningful context*. The trouble is that sometimes these schemas distort the actual memory to fit with what seems to make sense. For example, in a passage from *The War of Ghosts* (one of the Native American folktales Bartlett used in his experiment), something black comes out of the mouth of one of the Native Americans. However, participants in his experiment remembered reading that the man frothed at the mouth, which seemed more familiar and fitted into their schemas.

SCHEMAS Mental models of the world that contain knowledge that helps us to encode new information into a meaningful context.

So, based on Barlett's findings, we can say that memories are made by *combining* information we already have in our brains with new information that comes in through our senses. In this way, memory is much less like photography and much more like cooking: it's as though we start with a recipe, but we improvise along the way, using old information from previous cooking experiences and combining it with new information, mixing, shaking, baking – and out pops a memory. Memories are *constructed*, not recorded, and encoding is the process by which we transform what we perceive, think or feel into an enduring memory. We will encounter Bartlett's schema theory later in the chapter when we consider why we forget. For the moment, let's look in more detail at the three types of encoding processes: elaborative encoding, visual imagery encoding, and organizational encoding.

Elaborative encoding

Memories are a combination of old and new information, so the nature of any particular memory depends as much on the old information already in our memories as it does on the new information coming in through our senses. In other words, how we remember something depends on how we think about it at the time. In one study, researchers presented participants with a series of words and asked them to make one of three types of judgements (Craik and Tulving, 1975):

1 *Semantic judgements* required the participants to think about the meaning of the words – 'Is *hat* a type of clothing?'
2 *Rhyme judgements* required the participants to think about the sound of the words – 'Does *hat* rhyme with *cat*?'
3 *Visual judgements* required the participants to think about the appearance of the words – 'Is *HAT* written uppercase or lowercase?'

The type of judgement task influenced how participants thought about each word – what old information they combined with the new – and thus had a powerful impact on their memories (see **FIGURE 5.6**). Those participants who made semantic judgements, that is, had thought about the meaning of the words, had much better memory for the words than participants who had thought about how the word looked or sounded. The results of these and many other studies have shown that long-term retention is greatly enhanced by **elaborative encoding**, which involves *actively relating new information to knowledge that is*

ELABORATIVE ENCODING The process of actively relating new information to knowledge that is already in memory.

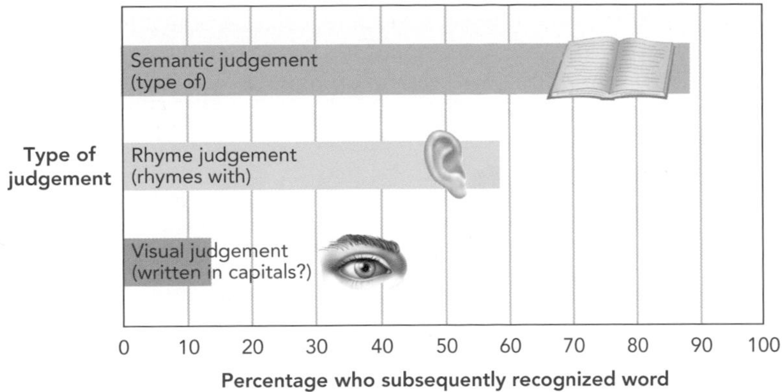

FIGURE **5.6 Levels of processing** Elaborative encoding enhances subsequent retention. Thinking about a word's meaning (making a *semantic judgement*) results in deeper processing – and better memory for the word later – than merely attending to its sound (*rhyme judgement*) or shape (*visual judgement*) (Craik and Tulving, 1975).

already in memory (Brown and Craik, 2000). If you have ever wondered why you can remember 20 experiences (your last summer holiday, your 18th birthday, your first day at university) but not 20 random numbers, then elaborative encoding is the answer. Most of the time we think of the meaning *behind* our experiences, and so we elaboratively encode them without even trying to (Craik and Tulving, 1975). Your 18th birthday party, for example, was probably not just an occasion for cake, but signalled a transition to being able to vote, buy an alcoholic drink, or buy that electric guitar you never really played after a few months because it was hard to learn. The significance and deeper meaning attached to the experience of your birthday allowed you to encode that event more readily, and thereby commit it to your long-term memory.

So where does this elaborative encoding take place? What's going on in the brain when this type of information processing occurs? Studies reveal that elaborative encoding is uniquely associated with increased activity in the inner part of the left temporal lobe and the lower left part of the frontal lobe (see **FIGURE 5.7a**) (Demb et al., 1995; Kapur et al., 1994; Wagner et al., 1998). In fact, the amount of activity in each of these two regions during encoding is directly related to whether people later remember an item. The more activity there is in these areas, the more likely the person will remember the information.

Lower left frontal lobe

(a)

FROM WAGNER, A. D., SCHACTER, D. L., ROTTE, M. ET AL. (1998) REMEMBERING AND FORGETTING OF VERBAL EXPERIENCES AS PREDICTED BY BRAIN ACTIVITY. SCIENCE, 281, 1188–90. REPRINTED WITH PERMISSION FROM AAAS

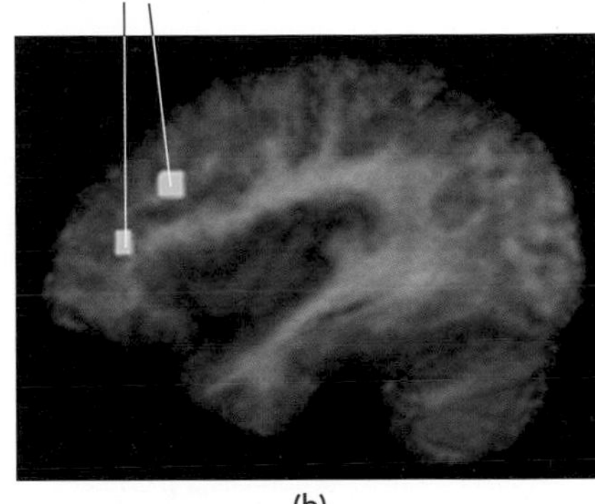

(b)

COURTESY OF C. R. SAVAGE

Occipital lobe

(c)

FIGURE **5.7 Brain activity during different types of judgements** fMRI studies reveal that different parts of the brain are active during different types of judgements. (a) During semantic judgements, the lower left frontal lobe is active; (b) during organizational judgements, the upper left frontal lobe is active; and (c) during visual judgements, the occipital lobe is active.

FROM KOSSLYN, S. M., PASCUAL-LEONE, A., FELICIAN, O. ET AL. (1999) THE ROLE OF AREA 17 IN VISUAL IMAGERY: CONVERGENT EVIDENCE FROM PET AND RTMS. SCIENCE, 284, 167–70. REPRINTED WITH PERMISSION FROM AAAS AND COURTESY OF STEPHEN M. KOSSLYN

Visual imagery encoding

At a banquet in Athens in 477 BC, the Greek poet Simonides regaled his audience with some stand-up poetry. Moments after the compere announced 'Simonides has left the building!' (or something along those lines), the banquet hall collapsed and killed all the people inside. Talk about bringing down the house! Simonides was able to name every one of the dead simply by visualizing each chair around the banquet table and recalling the person who had been sitting there. Simonides wasn't the first, but he was among the most proficient, to use this type of **visual imagery encoding**, which involves *storing new information by converting it into mental pictures* (see **FIGURE 5.8**).

If you wanted to use Simonides' method to create an enduring memory, you could simply convert the information you wanted to remember into a visual image and then 'store it' in a familiar location. This technique is also known as the **method of loci** – *a memory aid that associates information with mental images of locations* (*loci* is Latin for 'places'). For instance, if you were going to the supermarket and wanted to remember to buy milk, crisps and hummus, you could use the rooms in your house as locations and imagine your living room flooded in milk, your bedroom pillows stuffed with crisps, and your bath as a sticky pond of hummus. When you arrived at the supermarket, you could then take a 'mental walk' around your house and 'look' into each room to

VISUAL IMAGERY ENCODING The process of storing new information by converting it into mental pictures.

METHOD OF LOCI A memory aid that associates information with mental images of locations.

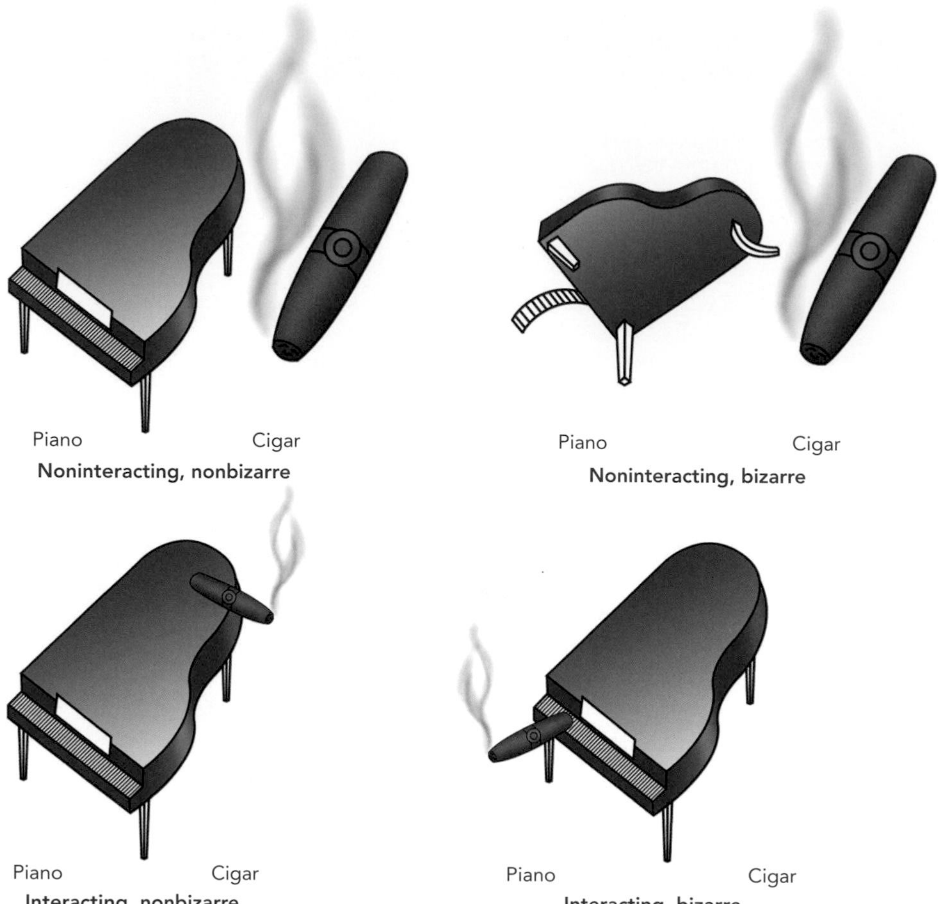

FIGURE **5.8** **Visual imagery** One way to better remember something is by relating it to something else using visual imagery. Here, it is easier to remember a piano and a cigar when they are interacting than as individual items. This strategy works well, whether the images are bizarre or not (Wollen et al., 1972).

remember the items you needed to purchase. (While you're at the supermarket, you might also want to buy a mop to clean up the mess at home!)

Numerous experiments have shown that visual imagery encoding can substantially improve memory. In one experiment, participants who studied lists of words by creating visual images of them later recalled twice as many items as participants who just mentally repeated the words (Schnorr and Atkinson, 1969). Another experiment found similar results for people who studied lists composed of concrete words that are easily visualized, such as *tree*, *battleship* or *sun*, compared to abstract words, such as *idea*, *democracy* or *will* (Paivio, 1969).

DIGITAL VISION

Visual imagery encoding may mean that if you were ever so unlucky as to receive a parking ticket, miserable connotations of this are evoked whenever you see a parked car.

Why does visual imagery encoding work so well? First, visual imagery encoding does some of the same things that elaborative encoding does. When you create a visual image, you relate incoming information to knowledge already in memory. For example, a visual image of a parked car might help you create a link to your memory of your first kiss or (less enticingly) that time when you returned to your car to find a parking ticket slapped on the windscreen. Second, when you use visual imagery to encode words and other verbal information, you end up with two different mental 'placeholders' for the items – a visual one and a verbal one – which gives you more ways to remember them than just a verbal placeholder alone (Paivio, 1971, 1986). How do we know these multiple placeholders are created? As you just read, elaborative encoding seems to activate the frontal and temporal lobes of the brain, but visual imagery encoding activates regions in the occipital lobe (see **FIGURE 5.7c**) (Kosslyn et al., 1993), which as you'll recall from Chapter 3, is the centre of visual processing. This finding suggests that people indeed enlist the visual system when forming memories based on mental images.

Organizational encoding

Have you ever ordered dinner with a group of friends and watched in amazement as your waiter or waitress took the order without writing anything down? To find out how this is done, one researcher spent three months working in a restaurant (Stevens, 1988). The researcher wired each waiter and waitress with a microphone and asked them to think aloud, that is, to say what they were thinking as they walked around all day doing their jobs. The researcher found that as soon as they left a customer's table, the waiters and waitresses immediately began *grouping* or *categorizing* the orders into hot drinks, cold drinks, hot foods and cold foods. The staff also grouped the items into a sequence that matched the layout of the kitchen, first placing drink orders, then hot food orders and finally cold food orders. These processes represent examples of **organizational encoding** – *the act of categorizing information by noticing the relationships between a series of items*.

ORGANIZATIONAL ENCODING The act of categorizing information by noticing the relationships between a series of items.

For example, how easily do you think you could memorize the words *peach, cow, chair, apple, table, cherry, lion, couch, horse, desk*? If you are like most people, this doesn't seem like a particularly easy list to remember. But if you organized the items into three categories – *peach, apple* and *cherry, cow, lion* and *horse, chair, couch* and *desk* – you would probably have no problems. Studies have shown that instructing people to sort items into categories like this is an effective way to enhance their subsequent recall of those items (Mandler, 1967). Even more complex organizational schemes have been used, such as the hierarchy in **FIGURE 5.9** (Bower et al., 1969). As you can see, people improved their recall of individual items by organizing them into multiple-level categories, all the way from a general category such as *animals*, through intermediate categories such as *birds* and *songbirds*, down to specific examples such as *wren* and *sparrow*.

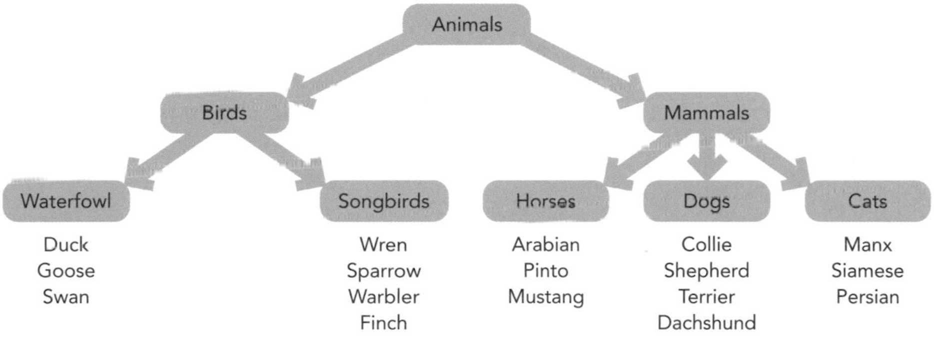

FIGURE 5.9 Organizing words into a hierarchy Organizing words into conceptual groups and relating them to one another, as in this example of a hierarchy, makes it easier to reconstruct the items from memory later (Bower et al., 1969). Keeping track of the 17 items in this example can be facilitated by remembering the hierarchical groupings they fall under.

Organizing by categories encourages you to focus on the similarities between items. But organizational encoding can also take advantage of the differences between items (Hunt and McDaniel, 1993). Look at the following items for a couple of seconds each, and then try to recall them: VRZ, BGR, HPL, WQM, 247, SWY, RNB, PLB. In this list, '247' is the oddball item, and because it stands out from the others, you will probably tend to remember it best – better, in fact, than if it appeared in a list with other numbers (von Restorff, 1933). The relationships between things – how they fit together and how they differ – can help us remember them. Organizational encoding is a type of **mnemonic** – *a device for reorganizing information into more meaningful patterns to remember*. This is why it is much easier to remember the sentence 'Richard Of York Gave Battle In Vain', rather than red, orange, yellow, green, blue, indigo and violet as the colours of rainbow in order. Mnemonics provide an overarching structure that makes it easier to reconstruct the constituent parts.

MNEMONIC A device for reorganizing information into more meaningful patterns to remember.

Just as elaborative and visual imagery encoding activate distinct regions of the brain, so too does organizational encoding. As you can see in **FIGURE 5.7b** above, organizational encoding activates the upper surface of the left frontal lobe (Fletcher et al., 1998;

Savage et al., 2001). Different types of encoding strategies appear to rely on different areas of brain activation.

Encoding of survival-related information

Encoding new information is critical to many aspects of everyday life – the prospects for attaining your degree would be pretty slim without this ability – and the survival of our ancestors probably depended on encoding and later remembering such things as the source of food and water or where a predator appeared (Nairne and Pandeirada, 2008; Sherry and Schacter, 1987). Recent experiments have addressed these ideas by examining the encoding of survival-related information. The experiments were motivated by an evolutionary perspective based on Darwin's principle of natural selection – the features of an organism that help it survive and reproduce are more likely than other features to be passed on to subsequent generations (see Chapter 1). Therefore, memory mechanisms that help us to survive and reproduce should be preserved by natural selection, and our memory systems should be built in a way that allows us to remember especially well-encoded information that is relevant to our survival.

To test this idea, the researchers gave participants three different encoding tasks (Nairne et al., 2007):

1 In the *survival encoding* condition, participants were asked to imagine that they were stranded in the grasslands of a foreign land without any survival materials and that over the next few months they would need supplies of food and water and also need to protect themselves from predators. The researchers then showed participants randomly chosen words, for example *stone*, *meadow*, *chair*, and asked them to rate on a 1–5 scale how relevant each item would be to survival in the hypothetical situation.
2 In the *moving encoding* condition, a second group of participants were asked to imagine that they were planning to move to a new home in a foreign land, and to rate on a 1–5 scale how useful each item might be in helping them to set up a new home. This task is similar in many respects to the survival encoding task, except that it does not involve thinking about survival.
3 In the *pleasantness encoding* condition, a third group were shown the same words and asked to rate on a 1–5 scale the pleasantness of each word. They used a pleasantness encoding task taken from previous research that was proven to involve deep, elaborative encoding of the kind we have already seen is beneficial to later retention.

The findings, displayed in **FIGURE 5.10**, show that participants recalled more words after the survival encoding task than after either the moving or pleasantness tasks. In later studies, the researchers found that survival encoding resulted in higher levels of recall than several other non-survival encoding tasks involving either elaborative encoding, imagery encoding or organizational encoding (Nairne et al., 2008). Exactly what is it about survival encoding that produces such high levels of memory? Survival encoding draws on elements of elaborative, imagery and organizational encoding, which may give it an advantage over any one of the other three. Alternatively, perhaps thinking about information with regard to its survival value is more interesting or emotionally arousing than other kinds of encoding.

FIGURE **5.10 Survival encoding enhances later recall** What does an angry lion that may threaten our survival have to do with recall? Nairne and colleagues (2008) showed that when people encode information with respect to its survival value, later recall is significantly enhanced compared with other conditions in which people encode the same information by judging its usefulness with respect to an upcoming move or by judging its pleasantness (a). Ratings of how relevant the words are to each task were highest for the pleasantness condition and did not differ between survival and moving conditions (b); response times for encoding judgements did not differ for survival and moving conditions, but were slightly faster in the pleasantness condition (c). The point of these latter two findings is that the survival recall advantage cannot be attributed to differences in relevance or response time.

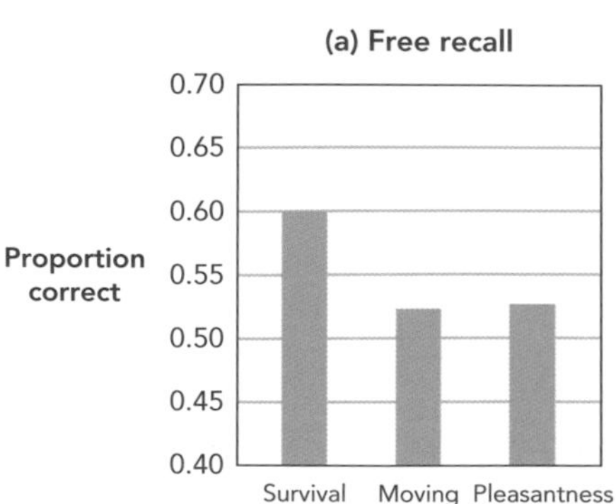

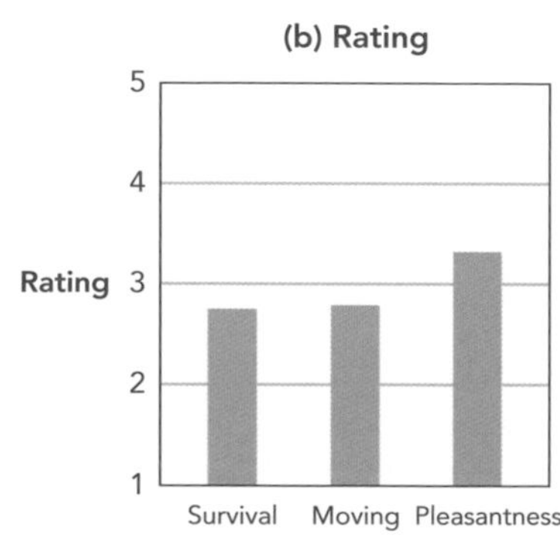

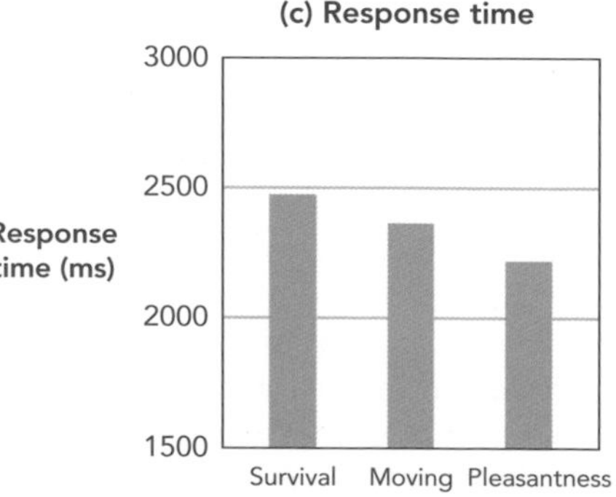

Recent research suggests that survival often requires individuals to engage in future planning (Klein et al., 2011). For example, when participants are asked to imagine different survival scenarios and then asked to encode words with respect to their survival relevance, survival strategies that involve planning, for example building a shelter, produce superior memory recall compared to scenarios that do not involve planning, such as fighting off an immediate attack. Critically, superior recall is also observed for scenarios that involve planning but not survival, such as organizing a dinner party. There again, for some people, executing the perfect dinner party can sometimes be a matter of life or death.

Storage: maintaining different types of memory over time

Encoding is the process of turning perceptions into memories. But one of the hallmarks of a memory is that you can bring it to mind on Tuesday, not on Wednesday, and then bring it to mind again on Thursday. So where are our memories when we aren't using them? Clearly, those memories are *stored* somewhere in your brain. **Memory storage** is *the process of maintaining information in memory over time.* However, not all information stored in memory is of the same type.

MEMORY STORAGE The process of maintaining information in memory over time.

Memories in the brain

We have seen in the previous section that repetition – of short- and long-term memories – can lead to improved recall. Intuitively, this seems to make sense but recent progress in our understanding of the biological makeup of the brain has allowed us to gain an understanding of the biological processes that underpin this. In fact, one of the most exciting developments on the horizon for the memory field is a greater understanding and application of neurochemistry to enhance memory (Marshall, 2004).

Researchers are beginning to understand how memories are encoded in the brain. If you could shrink yourself down to the size of a cell and go wandering around inside someone's brain, where exactly would you look for their memories? You'd probably be tempted to look at their neurons; after all, at the level of the cell, there's really nothing *but* neurons to look at. But that isn't where you'd find them. Research suggests that the best place to look for memories is in the *spaces between* neurons. You'll recall from Chapter 3 that a *synapse* is the small space between the axon of one neuron and the dendrite of another, and neurons communicate by sending neurotransmitters across these synapses. As it turns out, sending a neurotransmitter across a synapse isn't like sending a text message to someone, because the act of sending actually *changes* the connectivity of the communicating neurons. You could text the same message thousands of times and there would be no change between the sender and receiver (except maybe excessive boredom or a restraining order for harassment). However, when neurons send messages to each other, the synapses that connect them change as a function of the communication. Specifically, it strengthens the connection between the two neurons, making it easier for them to transmit to each other the next time. This is why researchers sometimes say 'Cells that fire together wire together' (Hebb, 1949).

The idea that the connections between neurons are strengthened by their communication, thus making communication easier the next time, provides the neurological basis for long-term memory, and much of what we know about this comes from Nobel Prize-winner Eric Kandel and his work on the tiny sea slug *Aplysia californica*. Having an extremely simple nervous system consisting of only 20,000 neurons (compared to roughly 100 billion in the human brain), *Aplysia* has been attractive to Kandel and his colleagues because it is relatively uncomplicated. When an experimenter stimulates *Aplysia*'s tail with a mild electric shock, the slug immediately withdraws its gill, and if the experimenter does it again a moment later, *Aplysia* withdraws its gill even more quickly. If the experimenter comes back an hour later and shocks *Aplysia*, the withdrawal of the gill happens as slowly as it did the first time, as if *Aplysia* can't 'remember' what happened an hour earlier (Abel et al., 1995). But if the experimenter shocks *Aplysia* over and over again, it does develop an enduring 'memory' that can last for days or even weeks. Research suggests that this long-term storage involves the growth of new synaptic connections

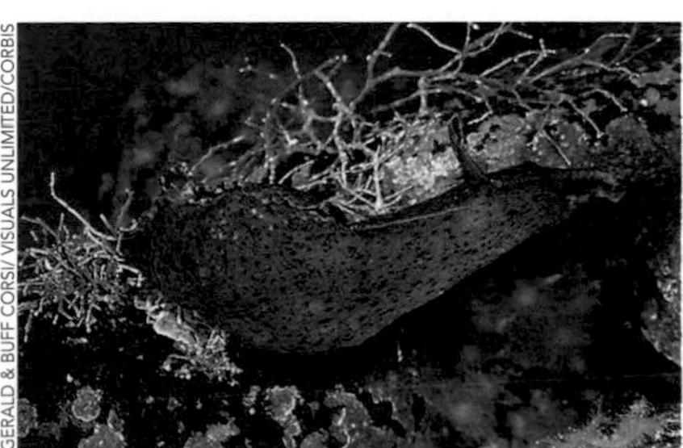

The sea slug *Aplysia californica* is useful to researchers because it has an extremely simple nervous system that can be used to investigate the mechanisms of short- and long-term memory.

between neurons (Abel et al., 1995; Squire and Kandel, 1999). So, learning in *Aplysia* is based on changes involving the synapses for short-term storage (enhanced neurotransmitter release) and long-term storage (growth of new synapses). Any experience that results in memory produces physical changes in the nervous system – even if you're a slug.

If you're something more complex than a slug – say, a mammal – a similar process of synaptic strengthening happens in the hippocampus, which, as we discussed in Chapter 3, is an area crucial for storing new long-term memories. In the early 1970s, researchers applied a brief electrical stimulus to a neural pathway in a rat's hippocampus (Bliss and Lømo, 1973). They found that the electrical current produced a stronger connection between synapses that lay along the pathway and the strengthening lasted for hours or even weeks. They called this **long-term potentiation (LTP)** – *enhanced neural processing that results from the strengthening of synaptic connections.* Long-term potentiation has a number of properties that indicate to researchers that it plays an important role in long-term memory storage:

LONG-TERM POTENTIATION (LTP) Enhanced neural processing that results from the strengthening of synaptic connections.

- It occurs in several pathways within the hippocampus (which we discuss next)
- It can be induced rapidly
- It can last for a long time.

In fact, drugs that block LTP can turn rats into rodent amnesiacs: the animals have great difficulty remembering where they've been recently and easily become lost in a maze (Bliss, 1999; Morris et al., 1986).

So how does LTP take place? What's going on in the neurons in the hippocampus to produce these stronger synaptic connections? The primary agent is a neural receptor site called N-methyl-d-aspartate (NMDA). The **NMDA receptor** *influences the flow of information from one neuron to another across the synapse by controlling the initiation of LTP in most hippocampal pathways* (Bliss, 1999). Here's how it works. The hippocampus contains an abundance of NMDA receptors, more than other areas of the brain. This is not surprising because the hippocampus is intimately involved in the formation of long-term memories. But for these NMDA receptors to become activated, two things must happen at roughly the same time. First, the presynaptic, or 'sending', neuron releases a neurotransmitter called *glutamate* (a major excitatory neurotransmitter in the brain), which attaches to the NMDA receptor site on the postsynaptic, or 'receiving', neuron. Second, excitation takes place in the postsynaptic neuron. Together, these two events initiate LTP, which in turn increases synaptic connections by allowing neurons that fire together to wire together (see **FIGURE 5.11**).

NMDA RECEPTOR A hippocampal receptor site that influences the flow of information from one neuron to another across the synapse by controlling the initiation of long-term potentiation.

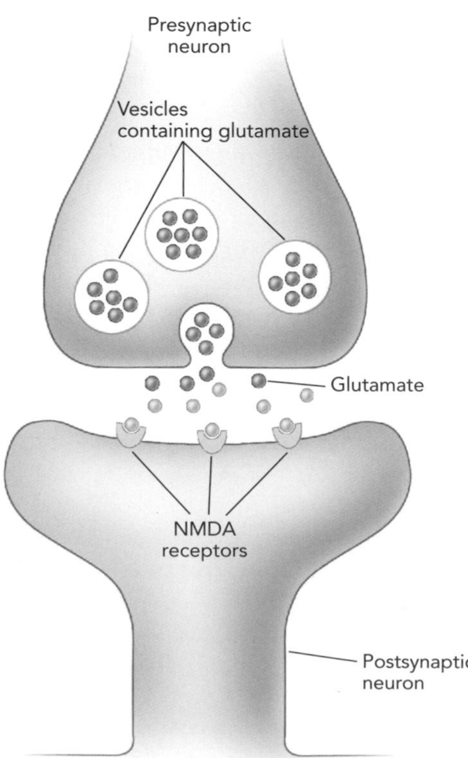

FIGURE **5.11 Long-term potentiation in the hippocampus** The presynaptic neuron (top of figure) releases the neurotransmitter glutamate into the synapse. Glutamate then binds to the NMDA receptor sites on the postsynaptic neuron (bottom). At about the same time, excitation in the postsynaptic neuron takes place. The combined effect of these two processes initiates long-term potentiation and the formation of long-term memories.

Don't get lost wandering around all these neurons; in fact, unshrink yourself from the size of a cell and look at the big picture for a minute. It's easy to say that humans and other animals can form long-term memories. We can tell from a person's behaviour that information has been stored and is able to be called up again and acted on. But it's another matter to understand *how* and *why* long-term memories are formed. The neural research on LTP and NMDA receptors helps us link an observable mental phenomenon ('Look! The squirrel remembered where the nuts were. She went back to the right tree.') with the biological underpinnings that produce it.

Some of the most exciting memory research has built on findings linking LTP and memory to identify a gene that improves memory in mice (Tang et al., 1999). The gene makes a protein that assists the NMDA receptor, which plays an important role in long-term memory by helping to initiate LTP. Mice bred to have extra copies of this gene showed more activity in their NMDA receptors, more LTP and improved performance on several different memory tasks – learning a spatial layout, recognizing familiar objects and recalling a fear-inducing shock (Tang et al., 1999). One strain of these brainy mice have been called 'Doogie mice' after a popular television character Doogie Howser, who is a precocious child medical doctor (Tsien, 2000). More work remains to be done in this area to show conclusively how LTP leads to the formation of long-term memories, but the implications of this line of research are considerable. After all, the average human brain has more neuronal connections than there are stars in our galaxy (Kandel et al., 1995).

Hippocampus: the memory sea horse in the brain

Memory researchers work at different levels in the brain. Beyond the receptors, researchers are interested in particular brain structures. The hippocampus (named after the Greek for 'sea horse' – now that's a visual image you should not forget) is a structure in each temporal lobe that is critically responsible for memory consolidation. As we saw in the discussion of H. M., patients with hippocampal damage are unable to form new long-term memories (Corkin, 2002). The hippocampus is also not fully mature at birth, which may be one of the reasons that children are unable to remember events from their time as infants (Liston and Kagan, 2002), which we will discuss in childhood amnesia shortly.

Animal studies have shown that the hippocampi (there are two) are particularly important in learning tasks that measure route finding and navigation. For example, rats are good swimmers but don't like to swim, so if you place them in a big tank of milky water, they will swim around frantically until they find a submerged platform they can stand on (Morris et al., 1982). Each time they are placed in this 'water maze', they get faster at relocating the platform they cannot see, which means they are using a **spatial memory** – *representation that encodes where something is*. However, hippocampal lesions obliterate this memory, indicating that this area of the brain is specialized for mapping spatial information (O'Keefe and Nadel, 1978).

SPATIAL MEMORY Representation that encodes where something is.

hot science

Forgive and forget

Are you someone who holds a grudge? In doing so, you may actually be impairing your ability to move on to more productive things because you cannot forget the details that are ruminating in your head. Recently, a group of Scottish researchers have shown that you must forgive in order to forget and that even after you have forgiven, you should give the incident no further thought (Noreen et al., 2014).

In an initial session, 30 participants imagined that they were the victim in a series of hypothetical incidents and indicated whether or not they would forgive the transgressor. These incidents included infidelity, slander and theft. These scenarios were matched for word length and contained information relating to the offence, the consequence of the offence, and what the transgressor did to make amends. For each scenario, the transgressor was depicted as a friend, parent, partner, supervisor, work colleague or boss. For example:

> The offence is that your professor does not believe you when you tell them you have not plagiarized your work. The consequence is that you are expelled from the university. Later, your professor realizes you were telling the truth and tries to make amends by attempting to get you reinstated.

After reading each scenario, the participants were asked whether or not they would forgive the transgressor and how confident there were that they would do so. No participants indicated having experienced similar incidents to any of the hypothetical scenarios depicted (either as a victim or an offender). The researchers were able to select 12 forgiven and 12 unforgiven scenarios for each participant (we all differ in what we find acceptable and unacceptable). A week later, participants took part in a second session that had four separate phases:

1. *Learning phase:* Participants saw each of their selected scenarios again, paired with an unrelated neutral cue word and were told to remember the pairing and as much detail of the scenario as possible.
2. *Initial recall phase:* Participants were tested immediately after memorizing the scenarios where only the cue words were presented.
3. *Think/no-think phase:* Participants were told that, depending on the colour of the cue word, they were either to briefly summarize the associated offence, not to think about the event at all, or were given no instruction (which was a baseline condition).
4. *Final recall phase:* Participants saw all the cue words originally presented and were asked to recall details of the scenarios associated with each cue.

As indicated in the graph, participants recalled significantly more details for forgiven scenarios in the think condition (78% recall) compared with the baseline condition, in which no instructions to forget or remember had been given. Participants

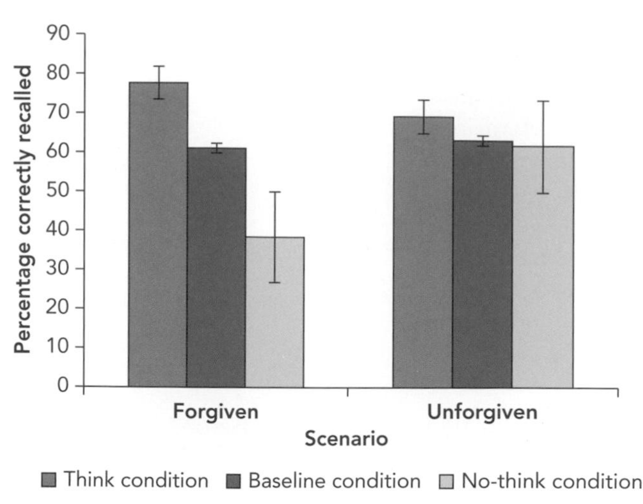

NOREEN, BIERMAN & MACLEOD (2014). FORGIVING YOU IS HARD, BUT FORGETTING SEEMS EASY CAN FORGIVENESS FACILITATE FORGETTING? *PSYCHOLOGICAL SCIENCE*, 25: 1295-302, COPYRIGHT © 2014 BY (SAGE PUBLICATIONS). REPRINTED BY PERMISSION OF SAGE PUBLICATIONS

also recalled more details accurately for forgiven scenarios in the think condition than in the no-think condition (38% recall). Most importantly, the instruction to not think about the event (motivated forgetting) produced significantly less recall than the baseline when no instruction was given. In the unforgiven scenarios, there was no difference between instructions on recall.

These findings indicate that when individuals have already forgiven a transgressor, memories related to the forgiven offence become more susceptible to subsequent motivated forgetting. When individuals have not forgiven the transgressor, however, participants are less successful in suppressing details related to unforgiven incidents. There was also no evidence that unforgiven events produced better memory recall, which runs counter to the common wisdom that people who are unforgiving will remember every little detail.

Once an individual has forgiven a transgressor, the forgiver becomes more successful at suppressing the details concerned with the offence. The ability to forget such upsetting memories may, in turn, provide an effective coping strategy that ultimately enables people to move on with their lives.

PIXTAL

London cab drivers have to pass a test called 'the knowledge' before they get a licence to drive one of the city's famous black cabs. In order to pass, they have to learn 320 standard routes around the city centre, including any landmarks and places of interest along the way, which makes them good candidates for studying spatial knowledge.

What about humans? As noted in Chapter 3 in the section on brain plasticity, London 'cabbies' do not swim around in water tanks, but are famously good at remembering their way around the UK's capital city. In fact, they have to pass a test called 'the knowledge' before they get a licence to operate a taxi, which makes them good candidates for studying spatial knowledge. When asked to think about routes between famous landmarks, PET imaging revealed selective activation of their right hippocampus, whereas when they were asked to think about the landmarks in isolation, this area was not so active (Maguire et al., 2006). This knowledge had increased the processing activity of their brains. So, acquiring knowledge changes the activation of brains, which should not be too surprising to you by now. After all, where else could the knowledge be stored? Next we consider how knowledge that is not studied deliberately comes to be remembered.

Retrieval: bringing memories to mind

There is something fiendishly frustrating about piggy banks. You can put money in them, you can shake them around to assure yourself that the money is there, but you can't easily get the money out, which is why no one carries a piggy bank instead of a wallet. If memory were like a piggy bank, it would be similarly useless. We could make memories, we could store them, and we could even shake our heads around and listen for the telltale jingle. But if we couldn't bring our memories out of storage and use them, what would be the point of saving them in the first place? Retrieval, the bringing to mind of previously encoded and stored information, is perhaps the most important of all memorial processes (Roediger, 2000; Schacter, 2001b).

Retrieval can occur in two ways. First, individuals can use **recall** – *the capacity to spontaneously retrieve information from memory*. If someone remembers the answer to a question such as 'What is the name of the song that won the Eurovision Song Contest in 1974?' without further prompting, they are using free recall. The other form of retrieval is known as **recognition** – *the capacity to correctly match information presented with the contents of memory*. So, if the opening chords of 'Waterloo' were to strike up, a person may be able name the song easily, even if they previously couldn't answer the question 'What is the name of the song that won the Eurovision Song Contest in 1974?', because they recognize the beginning of the tune. This might then prompt them to think 'Ah yes, I seem to remember "Waterloo" won the Eurovision Song

RECALL The capacity to spontaneously retrieve information from memory.

RECOGNITION The capacity to correctly match information presented with the contents of memory.

Contest in 1974.' So, their ability to match the music they heard to their memory of how 'Waterloo' sounds enabled them to access a memory that previously seemed inaccessible.

However, the problem for recall and recognition memory is that very often we are not sure whether the information we retrieve is really a true memory. For example, was the ABBA Eurovision winning song 'Waterloo', or then again, was it 'Mama Mia'? Have we only given 'Waterloo' as the answer to that question in the pub quiz because 'Waterloo' was playing in the background? As we will see later in the chapter when we consider the difference between remembering and knowing, people vary in their certainty that a memory is accurate and this can have real-world consequences. One way to try to improve the reliability of memory is to look for additional information or retrieval cues.

Perhaps bakers get up a bit too early

Burglars broke into the safe in the Wonder Hostess Bakery Outlet in Davenport, Iowa. Police said the burglars had an easy time because the bakery employees could not remember the safe's combination, so they had written it out and posted it on the nearby bulletin board.

Retrieval cues: give us a clue

One of the best ways to retrieve information from *inside* your head is to encounter information *outside* your head that is somehow connected to it. The information outside your head is called a **retrieval cue** – *external information that is associated with stored information and helps bring it to mind*. If you failed to remember 'Waterloo', then mentioning a Swedish supergroup might just jog your memory.

RETRIEVAL CUE External information that is associated with stored information and helps bring it to mind.

Retrieval cues can be incredibly effective. In one experiment, undergraduates studied lists of words, such as *table, peach, bed, apple, chair, grape* and *desk* (Tulving and Pearlstone, 1966). Later, the students took a test in which they were asked to write down all the words from the list they could remember. The students remembered and wrote and remembered some more, and when they were absolutely sure that they had emptied their memory stores of every last word that was in them, they took another test. This time the experimenter asked them to remember the words on the list, but he provided them with retrieval cues, such as 'furniture' or 'fruit'. The students who were sure that they had done all the remembering they possibly could were suddenly able to remember more words (Tulving and Pearlstone, 1966). These results suggest that information is sometimes *available* in memory even when it is momentarily *inaccessible*, and that retrieval cues help us bring inaccessible information to mind.

Although hints are a form of retrieval cue, not all retrieval cues come in the form of hints. The **encoding specificity principle** states that *a retrieval cue can serve as an effective reminder when it helps re-create the specific way in which information was initially encoded* (Tulving and Thomson, 1973). In other words, the thoughts or feelings we had at the time we encoded the information are associated with the information we encoded, and so those thoughts and feelings can also help us retrieve it. This why police re-enact crimes to try to re-create the events that may trigger thoughts and feelings. **State-dependent retrieval** is an example of the encoding specificity principle in action, and is defined as *the tendency for information to be better recalled when the person is in the same state during encoding and retrieval.* State-dependent retrieval has been documented with alcohol and marijuana (Eich, 1980; Weissenborn, 2000). For example, you may come in from a night out on the town and mislay your phone. In the morning, you wake up with a hangover and forget where you put it. However, when you have a few more drinks, you might remember where you put it – as well as all the embarrassing things you did on the previous evening that led to you deciding to hide it in your friend's bedroom. Why should that be? Because a person's physiological or psychological state at the time of encoding is associated with the information being encoded. If the person's state at the time of retrieval matches the person's state at the time of encoding, the state itself serves as a retrieval cue – a bridge that connects the moment at which we experience something to the moment at which we remember it. Similar effects occur with natural (as opposed to drug-induced) states. For example, retrieving information when you are in a sad or happy mood increases the likelihood that you will retrieve sad or happy episodes (Eich, 1995), which is part of the reason it is so hard to 'look on the bright side' when you're feeling low.

ENCODING SPECIFICITY PRINCIPLE The idea that a retrieval cue can serve as an effective reminder when it helps re-create the specific way in which information was initially encoded.

STATE-DEPENDENT RETRIEVAL The tendency for information to be better recalled when the person is in the same state during encoding and retrieval.

Increasing the similarity between the context in which an item is encoded and the context in which it is retrieved can serve as a retrieval cue. For example, in one study,

A whole environment can serve as a retrieval cue. This diver is more likely to remember words she learned underwater than if she had learned them on land.

divers learned some words on land and some other words underwater; they recalled the words best when they were tested in the same dry or wet environment in which they had initially learned them because the environment itself served as a retrieval cue (Godden and Baddeley, 1975). Recovering alcoholics often experience a renewed urge to drink when visiting places in which they once drank because these places serve as retrieval cues. There may even be some wisdom to finding a seat in a classroom, sitting in it every day, and then sitting in it again when you take an exam, because the feel of the chair and the sights you see may help you remember the information you learned while you sat there. Retrieval cues need not be inner states and they need not be external environments – they can even be thoughts themselves, as when one thought calls to mind another, related thought (Anderson et al., 1976).

Consider just one more unusual consequence of the encoding specificity principle. You learned earlier that making semantic judgements about a word, for example 'What does *orange* mean?', usually produces more durable memory for the word than making rhyme judgements, for example 'What rhymes with *orange*?' So, if you were asked to think of a word that rhymes with *brain* and your friend was asked to think about what *brain* means, we would expect your friend to remember the word better the next day than if we simply asked you both 'Hey, what was that word you saw yesterday?' However, if instead of asking that question, we asked you both 'What was that word that rhymed with *train*?', we would expect you to remember it better than your friend did (Fisher and Craik, 1977). This is a fairly astounding finding. Semantic judgements almost always yield better memory than rhyme judgements. But in this case, the typical finding is turned upside down because the retrieval cue matched your encoding context better than it matched your friend's. The principle of **transfer-appropriate processing** states that *memory is likely to transfer from one situation to another when we process information in a way that is appropriate to the retrieval cues that will be available later* (Morris et al., 1977; Roediger et al., 1989) (see **FIGURE 5.12**).

TRANSFER-APPROPRIATE PROCESSING
The idea that memory is likely to transfer from one situation to another when we process information in a way that is appropriate to the retrieval cues that will be available later.

High recall minus baseline

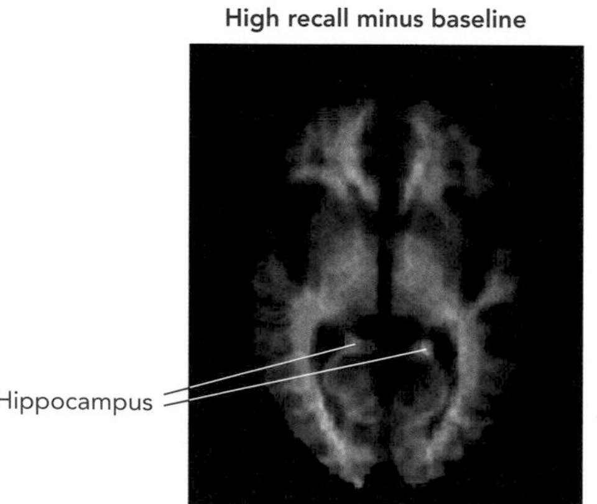

Low recall minus baseline

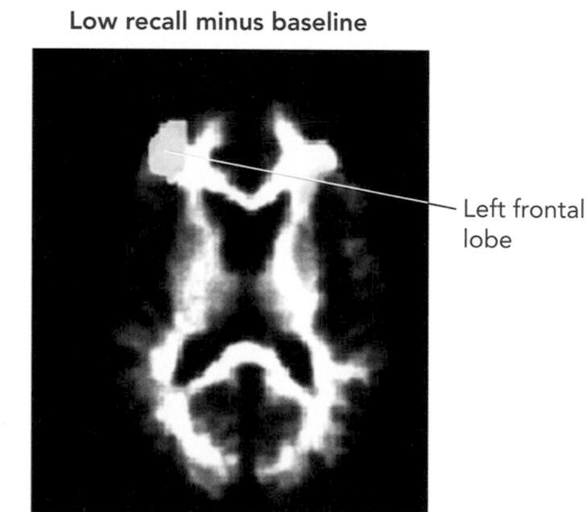

FIGURE **5.12 PET scans of successful and unsuccessful recall** When people successfully remembered words they saw earlier in an experiment, achieving high levels of recall on a test, the hippocampus showed increased activity. When people tried but failed to recall words they had seen earlier, achieving low levels of recall on a test, the left frontal lobe showed increased activity (Schacter et al., 1996a).

There is reason to believe that *trying* to recall an incident and *actually* recalling one are fundamentally different processes that occur in different parts of the brain (Moscovitch, 1994; Schacter, 1996). For example, regions within the right frontal lobe show heightened activity when people retrieve information that was presented to them earlier (Shallice et al., 1994; Squire et al., 1992; Tulving et al., 1994), and many psychologists believe that this activity reflects the mental effort that people put forth when they struggle to dredge up the past event (Lepage et al., 2000). However, successfully remembering a past experience tends to be accompanied by activity in the hippocampal region and also in parts of the brain that play a role in processing the sensory features of an experience (Eldridge et al., 2000; Nyberg et al., 1996; Schacter et al., 1996a). For instance, recall of previously heard sounds is accompanied by activity in the auditory cortex (the upper part of the temporal lobe), whereas recall of previously seen pictures is accompanied by activity in the visual cortex (in the occipital lobe) (Wheeler et al., 2000). Although retrieval may seem like a single process, brain studies suggest that separately identifiable processes are at work.

Implicit and explicit memory

Although Clive Wearing is forever stranded in the present and unable to make new memories, some of the new things that happen to him do seem to leave a mark. For example, Clive knows the layout of the house where he now stays. He can easily find the toilet, kitchen and dining room, which he must have learned since his illness. If he needs to go to the toilet, he can find it – but if you ask him where it is, he cannot tell you (Sacks, 2007). Similarly, H. M. could not make new memories after his surgery, but if he played a game in which he had to track a moving target, his performance gradually improved with each round (Milner, 1962). Clive could not tell you where the mugs, milk, teabags and kettle are in his kitchen, yet through repetition, he seems to have unconsciously 'learned' their location, so that in practice he can make himself a cup of tea. Research suggests that this is not unusual. For example, when patients with amnesia practise a task, they generally show improvements similar to those of healthy volunteers, despite the fact that they cannot remember ever having performed the task.

nebulous sauerkraut vagueness

For instance, to work out the identities of the mirror-inverted words above, you have to mentally manipulate the spatial positions of the letters until you 'see' the word. With practice, most people can read the inverted words faster and faster. But so can people who have amnesia, despite the fact that such patients generally cannot remember having ever seen the words (Cohen and Squire, 1980). Amnesiac patients have even proved capable of learning how to program computers despite having no conscious recollection of their training (Glisky et al., 1986).

The fact that people can be changed by past experiences without having any awareness of those experiences suggests that there must be at least two different kinds of memory (see FIGURE 5.13). **Explicit memory** occurs *when people consciously or intentionally retrieve past experiences*. Recalling last summer's holiday, incidents from a novel you just read, or facts you studied for a test all involve explicit memory. Indeed, whenever you start a sentence with 'I remember ...', you are talking about an explicit memory. **Implicit memory** occurs when *past experiences influence later behaviour and performance, even though people are not trying to recollect them and are not aware that they are remembering them* (Graf and Schacter, 1985; Schacter, 1987). Implicit memories are not consciously recalled, but their presence is 'implied' by our actions. Clive's ability to know his way around his new home even though he has no conscious knowledge of its layout is an example of implicit memory.

EXPLICIT MEMORY The act of consciously or intentionally retrieving past experiences.

IMPLICIT MEMORY The influence of past experiences on later behaviour and performance, even though people are not trying to recollect them and are not aware that they are remembering them.

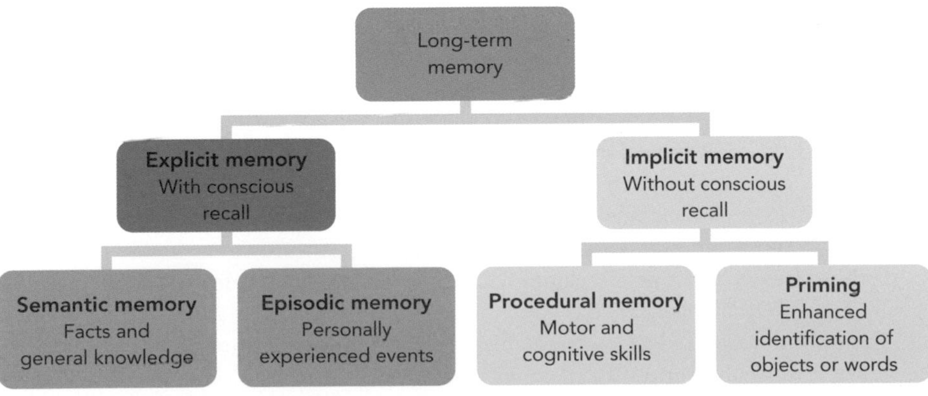

FIGURE **5.13 Multiple forms of memory** Explicit and implicit memories are distinct from each other. Thus, a person with amnesia may lose explicit memory yet display implicit memory for material they cannot consciously recall learning.

PROCEDURAL MEMORY The gradual acquisition of skills as a result of practice, or 'knowing how' to do things.

The examples we've used so far might make implicit memory sound mysterious and strange, but really we all have implicit memories that we use constantly. For example, how do you balance on a two-wheeled bicycle? You might be tempted to say, 'Erm, I don't know', but if you don't know, why can you do it so easily? Your knowledge of how to balance on a bicycle is an example of a particular kind of implicit memory called **procedural memory** – *the gradual acquisition of skills as a result of practice, or 'knowing how' to do things*. One of the hallmarks of procedural memory is that the things you remember, for example how to change gears in a car, how to play a G chord on the guitar, are automatically translated into actions. All you have to do is will the action and it happens, but it happens because you have implicit memories of how to make it happen. Sometimes you can explain how it is done ('Put one finger on the third fret of the E string, one finger ...') and sometimes you can't ('Get on the bike and ... well, uh ... just balance').

The fact that people who have amnesia can acquire new procedural memories suggests that the hippocampal structures that are usually damaged in these patients may be necessary for explicit memory, but they aren't needed for implicit procedural memory. In fact, it appears that brain regions outside the hippocampal area (including areas in the motor cortex) are involved in procedural memory. Chapter 6, on learning, discusses this evidence further, where you will also see that procedural memory is crucial for learning various kinds of motor, perceptual and cognitive skills.

PRIMING An enhanced ability to think of a stimulus, such as a word or object, as a result of a recent exposure to the stimulus.

Not all implicit memories are 'how to' memories. For example, in one study, participants were asked to memorize a list of words, and for some people, that list included the word moon (Nisbett and Wilson, 1977). Later, they were asked to name their favourite brands of several grocery items, including laundry detergent. The results showed that those participants who had earlier memorized the word *moon* were more likely to say that their favourite detergent was a brand known as 'Tide', but none of them were aware that the memorization task had influenced their answer. This is an example of **priming** – *an enhanced ability to think of a stimulus, such as a word or object, as a result of a recent exposure to the stimulus* (Tulving and Schacter, 1990). Just as priming a pump makes water flow more easily, priming the memory system makes some information more accessible.

In one experiment, students were asked to study a long list of words, including items such as *avocado*, *mystery*, *climate*, *octopus* and *assassin* (Tulving et al., 1982). Later, explicit memory was tested by showing participants some of these words along with new ones they hadn't seen and asking them which words were on the list. To test for priming, participants received word fragments and were asked them to come up with a word that fitted the fragment. Try the test yourself:

an––––pe   o–t–p––   ––b–el––   –l–m–te

You probably had difficulty coming up with the answers for the first and third fragments (*antelope*, *umbrella*) but had little problem coming up with answers for the second and fourth (*octopus*, *climate*). Seeing *octopus* and *climate* on the original list primed your ability to generate them on the fragment completion test. In the experiment, people showed priming for studied words even when they failed to consciously remember that they had seen them earlier.

In a sense, the healthy participants in this study behaved like patients with amnesia. Many experiments have shown that amnesiac patients can show substantial priming effects – often as large as healthy, nonamnesiac people – even though they have no explicit memory for the items they studied. In one study, researchers showed patients with amnesia and healthy volunteers in the control group a list of words, including *table* and *hotel*, and then gave them two different types of tests (Graf et al., 1984). One of these tested their explicit memory by providing them with the first three letters of a word, for example *tab...*, and asking them to remember a word from the list that began with those letters. On this test, amnesiac patients remembered fewer words than the healthy volunteers.

The second test was identical to the first, except that people were given the first three letters of a word and simply asked to write down any word that came to mind. In this test, the people who had amnesia produced words from the study list just as often as the healthy volunteers did. As you can see, the two tests were the same, but in one case the participants were asked to produce words from the list, which requires explicit memory, and in the other they were asked to produce any word at all, which requires implicit memory. These and other similar results suggest that priming, like procedural memory, does not require the hippocampal structures that are damaged in cases of amnesia (Schacter and Curran, 2000).

If the hippocampal region isn't required for procedural memory and priming, what parts of the brain *are* involved? Experiments have revealed that priming is associated with *reduced* activity in various regions of the cortex that are activated when people perform an unprimed task. For instance, when research participants are shown the word stem *hot* or *tab* and are asked to provide the first word that comes to mind, parts of the occipital lobe involved in visual processing and parts of the frontal lobe involved in word retrieval become active. But if people perform the same task after being primed by seeing *hotel* and *table*, there's less activity in these same regions (Buckner et al., 1995; Schacter et al., 2004; Wiggs and Martin, 1998). Something similar happens when people see pictures of everyday objects on two different occasions. On the second exposure to a picture, there's less activity in parts of the visual cortex that were activated by seeing the picture initially. Priming seems to make it easier for parts of the cortex that are involved in perceiving a word or object to identify the item after recent exposure to it. This suggests that the brain 'saves' a bit of processing time after priming (see **FIGURE 5.14**).

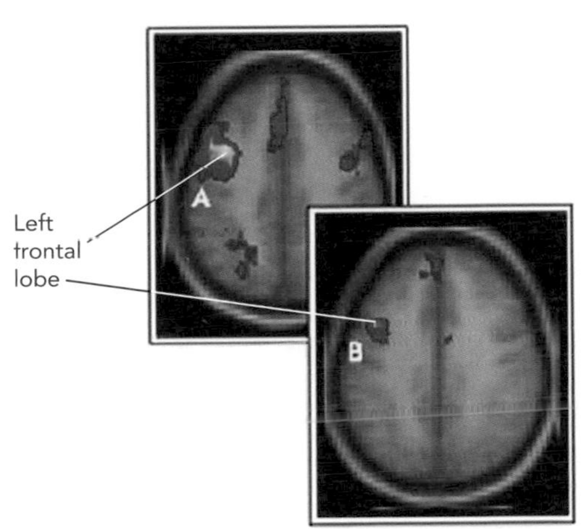

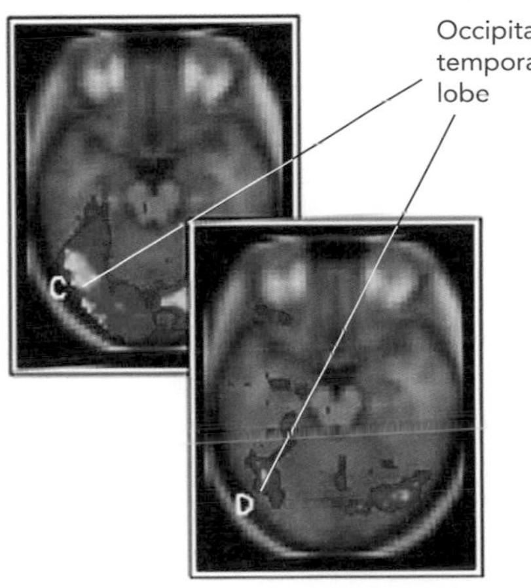

FIGURE **5.14 Primed and unprimed processing of stimuli** Priming is associated with reduced levels of activation in the cortex on a number of different tasks. In each pair of fMRIs, the images on the upper left (A, C) show brain regions in the frontal lobe (A) and occipital/temporal lobe (C) that are active during an unprimed task, in this case, providing a word response to a visual word cue. The images on the lower right within each pair (B, D) show reduced activity in the same regions during the primed version of the same task (Schacter and Buckner, 1998).

Semantic and episodic memory

Consider these two questions: Why do we celebrate on the 25th of December? What is the most spectacular celebration you've ever seen? Irrespective of their religion, most Westerners can come up with an answer to the first question, but we all have our own answers to the second. For instance, *you* might remember the time your neighbour got stuck on his roof trying to put up the most garish Christmas lights, only to be rescued by the fire brigade who had been called out by his distraught wife. However, it is unlikely that anyone else (other than the neighbour, the wife and the fire bridge) has precisely that same memory. Although both questions required you to search your long-term memory and explicitly retrieve information that was stored there, one required you to revisit a particular time and place – or episode – from your personal past, and one required you to dredge up a fact that everyone knows and that is not part of your personal autobiography. These memories are called *episodic* and *semantic* memories, respectively (Tulving, 1972, 1983, 1998).

The time when your neighbour got stuck on his roof trying to put up Christmas lights is a personal experience that forms part of your episodic memory.

SEMANTIC MEMORY A network of associated facts and concepts that make up our general knowledge of the world.

EPISODIC MEMORY The collection of past personal experiences that occurred at a particular time and place.

AUTOBIOGRAPHICAL MEMORY The personal record of significant events of one's life.

FLASHBULB MEMORIES Detailed recollections of when and where we heard about shocking events.

Semantic memory is *a network of associated facts and concepts that make up our general knowledge of the world*, whereas **episodic memory** is *the collection of past personal experiences that occurred at a particular time and place*.

Episodic memory is special because it is the only form of memory that allows us to engage in 'mental time travel', projecting ourselves into the past and revisiting events that have happened to us. This ability allows us to connect our pasts and our presents and construct a cohesive story of our lives. So, it should be no surprise that most people remember important life events such as the births of their children, weddings and funerals. For every individual, such events form the **autobiographical memory**, *the personal record of significant events of one's life*, and not surprisingly, these memories are associated with strong emotions (Conway and Rubin, 1993).

One particular type of autobiographical memory is so vivid, it is almost as if someone took a snapshot of the moment in time. For example, where were you when you saw the pictures of the Twin Towers burning and falling on 11 September 2001? Most of us can recall with great accuracy and detail events surrounding this terrorist attack, almost as though it had happened just yesterday. **Flashbulb memories** are *detailed recollections of when and where we heard about shocking events*. It is as if a mental flashbulb has gone off and recorded the event. Flashbulb memories seem to occur only when an event is emotionally shocking and has some consequence for the individual. For example, almost one year after the surprise resignation of the UK Prime Minister Margaret Thatcher in 1990, 86% of UK participants reported flashbulb memories, compared to only 29% of non-UK participants (Conway et al., 1994). Clearly, this was much more likely to be a flashbulb moment if you were a UK citizen and therefore interested in and affected by the event.

Enhanced retention of flashbulb memories can partly be explained by the emotional arousal caused by the shock of events, which has been shown to increase memory for detail (Kensinger and Schacter, 2005), as we discussed in Chapter 3, and partly by the fact that we tend to talk and think a lot about these experiences, so they are frequently recalled and thereby reinforced. Remember, too, that elaborative encoding enhances memory: when we talk about flashbulb experiences, we elaborate on them and thus further increase their memorability (but may also decrease their accuracy). In fact, several studies have shown that flashbulb memories are not always entirely accurate. For example, many people reported flashbulb memories related to the death of Princess Diana in a car crash in 1997, but 44% of participants in a memory study also remembered seeing video footage showing the crash take place. No such videotape exists but participants were confident they had seen it on TV (Ost et al., 2002).

People who have amnesia can have autobiographical memories of events before they became amnesiac, but they are unable to revisit episodes that happened later. But can people with amnesia create new semantic memories? At London's Institute of Child Health, researchers studied three young adults who suffered damage to the hippocampus during birth as a result of difficult deliveries that interrupted the oxygen supply to their brains (the hippocampus is especially sensitive to the lack of oxygen) (Vargha-Khadem et al., 1997). Their parents noticed that the children could not recall what happened during a typical day, had to be constantly reminded of appointments, and often became lost and disoriented. Beth (14 years old), Jon (19 years old) and Kate (22 years old) all showed clear evidence of episodic memory problems in laboratory tests. In view of their hippocampal damage, you might also expect that all three would perform poorly in school and might even be classified as learning disabled. Remarkably, however, all three learned to read, write and spell, developed normal vocabularies and acquired other kinds of semantic knowledge that allowed them to perform well at school. Based on this evidence, researchers have concluded that the hippocampus is not necessary for acquiring new *semantic* memories.

Episodic memory and imagining the future

We've already seen that episodic memory allows us to travel backwards in time, but it turns out that episodic memory also plays a role in allowing to us to travel forwards in time. An amnesiac patient known by the initials K. C. provided an early clue. K. C. could not recollect any specific episodes from his past, and when asked to imagine a future episode – such as what he might do tomorrow – he reported a complete 'blank' (Tulving, 1985). Consistent with this observation, more recent findings from hippocampal amnesiacs reveal that they have difficulty imagining new experiences, such as sunbathing on a sandy beach (Hassabis et al., 2007). Something similar happens with ageing. When asked either to recall episodes that actually occurred in their pasts or to imagine new episodes that might occur in their futures, elderly adults provided fewer details about what happened, or what might happen, than did university students (Addis et al., 2007). Consistent with these findings, neuroimaging studies reveal that a network of brain regions known to be involved in episodic memory – including the hippocampus – shows similarly increased activity when people remember the past and imagine the future (Addis et al., 2007; Okuda et al., 2003; Szpunar et al., 2007) (see **FIGURE 5.15**).

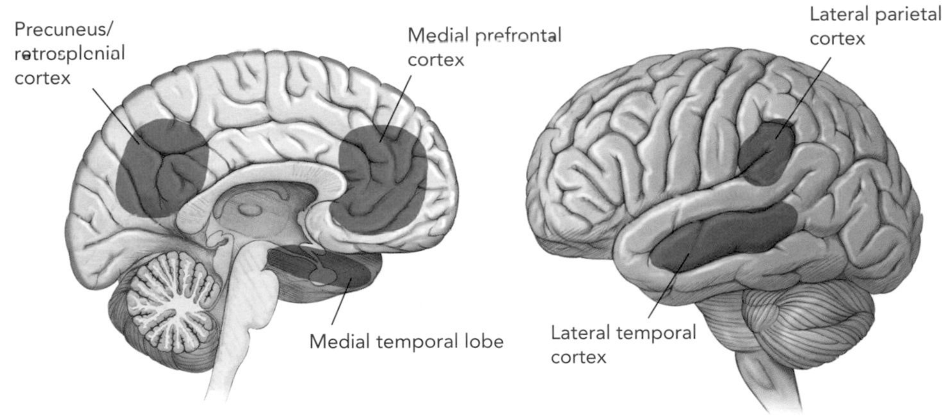

FIGURE **5.15 Remembering the past and imagining the future depend on a common network of brain regions** A common brain network is activated when people remember episodes that actually occurred in their personal pasts and when they imagine episodes that might occur in their personal futures. This network includes the hippocampus, a part of the medial temporal lobe long known to play an important role in episodic memory (Schacter et al., 2007).

Taken together, these observations strongly suggest that we rely heavily on episodic memory to envision the future (Schacter et al., 2008). Episodic memory is well suited to the task, because it is a flexible system that allows us to recombine elements of past experience in new ways, so that we can mentally 'try out' different versions of what might happen (Schacter and Addis, 2007; Suddendorf and Corballis, 2007). For example, when you imagine having a difficult conversation with a friend that will take place in a couple of days, you can draw on past experiences to envisage different ways in which the conversation might unfold, and hopefully avoid saying things that, based on past experience, are likely to make the situation worse.

In summary, remembering is dependent on three processes: encoding, storage and retrieval. Most instances of spectacular memory performance reflect the skilful use of encoding strategies. Elaborative encoding, visual imagery encoding and organizational encoding all enhance recall by using different brain regions to substantiate memories. Encoding information with respect to its survival value is a particularly effective method for increasing subsequent recall, perhaps because our memory systems have evolved in a way that allows us to remember especially well information that is relevant to our survival.

The hippocampus and nearby structures play an important role in long-term memory storage, as shown by the severe amnesia of patients. Memory storage depends on changes in synapses, and long-term potentiation (LTP) increases synaptic connections. Retrieval cues are effective when they help reinstate how we encoded an experience. Moods and inner states can serve as retrieval cues. Retrieval can be separated into the effort we make while trying to remember what happened in the past and the successful recovery of stored information. Explicit memory is the conscious retrieval of content from past experiences, whereas implicit memory refers to the unconscious influences of past experiences on later behaviour and performance. Episodic memory is the collection of personal experiences from a particular time and place, which allows us to recollect the past and imagine the future. Semantic memory is a networked, general, impersonal knowledge of facts, associations and concepts. Autobiographical memories are personal memories of life events that are significant to the individual. Likewise, flashbulb memories are particularly vivid recollections of extreme events and both seem to be dependent on amygdala activation.

Forgetting

You probably haven't given much thought to breathing today, and the reason is that from the moment you woke up, you've been doing it effortlessly and well. But the moment breathing fails, you are reminded of just how important it is. Memory is like that. Every time we see, think, notice, imagine or wonder, we are drawing on our ability to use information stored in our brains, but it isn't until this ability fails that we become acutely aware of just how much we should treasure it. The other problem with memory is not just the loss of information but also the failure to recognize when our memories are not accurate. People like to believe that their memories are good accounts of what actually occurred in their past but the truth is that memories are pieced together and susceptible to all the flaws that go along with reconstructing events after the fact. Also, it's not just the past we forget: we can also forget the future. How often do you set off to the shop to buy something and then end up not buying it? In this section we look at memory as a basis for how we conduct our lives and how things can go so wrong when we forget.

Transience: memories that fade away

TRANSIENCE Forgetting what occurs with the passage of time.

As we saw earlier, memory is considered to be structured into different 'stores' with different capacities and processes. Memory failures can result whenever these capacities or processes are overstretched. However, for most people, memory loss concerns forgetting information that was once stored in long-term memory and is no longer accessible. This process of forgetting appears to be gradual as time passes and more and more detail is lost – as if information seems to fade away with time. This is known as **transience** – *forgetting what occurs with the passage of time*. Transience occurs during the storage phase of memory, after an experience has been encoded and before it is retrieved. You've already seen the workings of transience – rapid forgetting – in sensory storage and short-term storage. Transience also occurs in long-term storage, as illustrated dramatically by amnesiac patients such as Clive and H. M. But transience affects all our memories to some extent. To understand transience, we need to address some key questions: How quickly do our memories fade over time? What kinds of information are we most likely to forget as time passes?

The psychological study of transience dates back to the late 1870s, when a young German philosopher named Hermann Ebbinghaus (1850–1909), the first researcher to study memory, measured his own memory for lists of nonsense syllables at different delays after studying them (Ebbinghaus, [1885]1964). By stripping the to-be-remembered information of all meaning, the *process* of remembering and forgetting could be examined, uncontaminated by any meaning associated with the information itself. Ebbinghaus charted his recall of nonsense syllables over time, creating the forgetting curve shown in FIGURE 5.16. He noted a rapid drop-off in retention during the first few tests, followed by a slower rate of forgetting on later tests – a general pattern confirmed by many subsequent memory researchers (Wixted and Ebbesen, 1991). This consistent finding shows that memories don't fade at a constant rate as time passes; most forgetting happens soon after an event occurs, with increasingly less forgetting as more time passes.

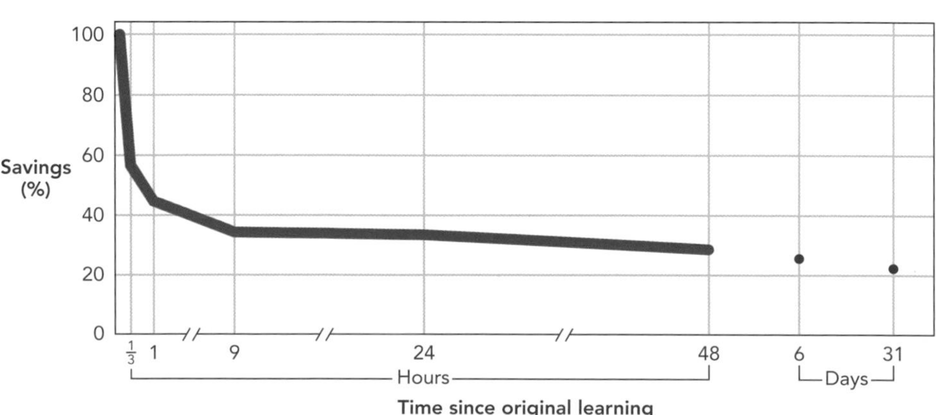

FIGURE **5.16 The curve of forgetting** Hermann Ebbinghaus measured his retention at various delay intervals after he studied lists of nonsense syllables. Retention was measured in percentage savings, that is, the percentage of time needed to relearn the list compared to the time needed to learn it initially.

Memory doesn't just erode with the passage of time: the quality of our memories also changes. At early time points on the forgetting curve – minutes, hours and days – memory preserves a relatively detailed record, allowing us to reproduce the past with reasonable if not perfect accuracy. But with the passing of time, we increasingly rely on our general memories for what usually happens and attempt to reconstruct the details by inference and even sheer guesswork. Transience involves a gradual switch from specific to more general memories (Brewer, 1996; Eldridge et al., 1994; Thompson et al., 1996).

Why does transience happen? Do details of experience simply disappear or decay as time passes? In a study of memory for Spanish vocabulary acquired by English speakers during secondary school or university courses, participants were tested for retention of Spanish at different times (ranging from 1 year to 50 years) after the students stopped taking Spanish courses (Bahrick, 1984, 2000). There was a rapid drop-off in memory for the Spanish vocabulary during the first three years after the students' last class, followed by tiny losses in later years. But research suggests that the decay caused by the mere passage of time is not nearly as important as *what* happens as time passes (see **FIGURE 5.17**). As time goes by, new experiences occur and new memories are created, and these new memories can interfere with our retrieval of old ones. For example, items presented early or late in a word list that participants have to memorize are remembered better that those in the middle, as shown in **FIGURE 5.18** (Glanzer and Cunitz, 1966).

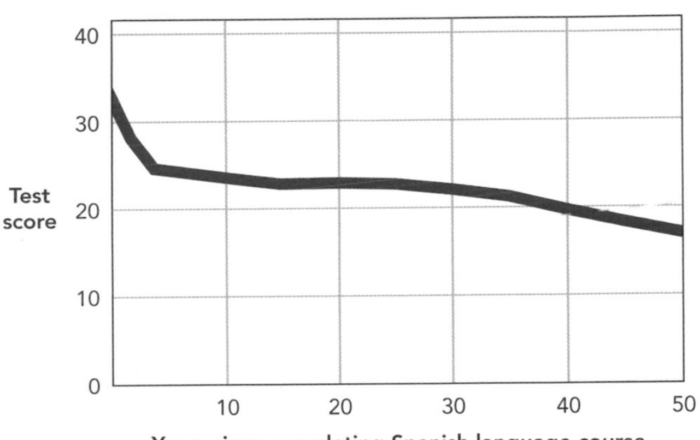

FIGURE 5.17 The decline of Spanish language skills Language skills (measured here as scores on a language exam) decay rapidly for the first few years after instruction ends, followed by a much slower decline over the next few decades. Like many other memories, the knowledge of Spanish is transient unless it is rehearsed or actively used (Bahrick, 1984, 2000).

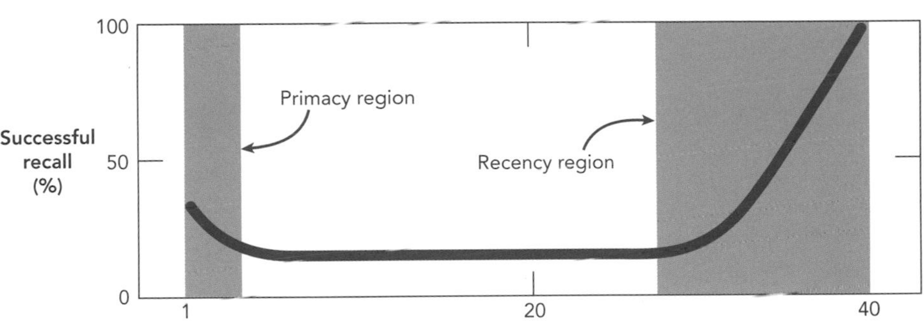

FIGURE 5.18 Serial position curve Example of recall for a list of words demonstrating the primacy and recency effects of better recall for words at the beginning and end of the learning period (Glanzer and Cunitz, 1966).

This is known as the **serial position effect**, *the enhanced memory for events presented at the beginning and end of a learning episode*, and actually involves two separate processes:

- The *primacy effect* for items remembered better at the beginning
- The *recency effect* for items remembered better at the end.

SERIAL POSITION EFFECT The enhanced memory for events presented at the beginning and end of a learning episode.

One explanation for the serial order effect is that items are better encoded into long-term memory when learning begins, because all processing resources are initially available. In the middle of the task, processing is fully occupied and there is more potential for interference. At the end of learning episode, items are less vulnerable to interference as they are still active in memory.

There are two forms of interference. **Retroactive interference** occurs when *later learning impairs memory for information acquired earlier* (Postman and Underwood, 1973). If you carry out similar activities at work each day, by the time Friday rolls around, it may be difficult to remember what you did on Tuesday or Wednesday because later activities blend in with earlier ones. **Proactive interference**, in contrast, refers to *situations in which earlier learning impairs memory for information acquired later.* If you use the same car park each day at work or university, you've probably gone out to find your car and then stood there confused by the memories of having parked it on previous days.

RETROACTIVE INTERFERENCE Situations in which later learning impairs memory for information acquired earlier.

PROACTIVE INTERFERENCE Situations in which earlier learning impairs memory for information acquired later.

The serial order effect is a robust phenomenon and you should bear that in mind if you ever get the chance to choose your slot for a job interview or an audition – it is probably best to go either first or last as you will be more memorable to the selection panel. That's why Bartlett's (1932) schema theory that we encountered earlier (do you remember it?) was such an important contribution to the idea that memory was not simply the laying down of a trace. Rather, memories are *actively* processed and incorporated with existing memories and subsequent experiences.

Money to burn

Chef Albert Grabham of the New House Hotel in Wales hid the restaurant's New Year's Eve earnings in the oven. He failed to remember that when he lit the same oven to prepare the New Year's Day lunch.

Blocking

TIP-OF-THE-TONGUE EXPERIENCE The temporary inability to retrieve information that is stored in memory, accompanied by the feeling that you are on the verge of recovering the information.

BLOCKING A failure to retrieve information that is available in memory even though you are trying to produce it.

One of the most common pleas you will hear if you ever play the popular quiz board game Trivial Pursuit (or anything similar) is 'Don't tell me, don't tell me!' Very often players know that they know the answer to specific questions, but they are agonizingly thwarted in their attempts to retrieve it from their memories. When remembering seems imminent, it is known as a **tip-of-the-tongue experience** – *the temporary inability to retrieve information that is stored in memory, accompanied by the feeling that you are on the verge of recovering the information.*

Look at the definitions in **TABLE 5.1** and try to think of the correct word for each one. Chances are that you will recall some of the words and not others. Some of the unrecalled words will cause you to draw a complete blank, but others will feel as though they are 'on the tip of your tongue'. For example, you may remember the first letter or two of the word and feel certain that it is rolling around in your head *somewhere* but that you just can't retrieve it at the moment. This problem is called **blocking** – *a failure to retrieve information that is available in the memory even though you are trying to produce it.* The sought-after information has been encoded and stored, and a cue is available that would ordinarily trigger recall of it. The information has not faded from memory, and you aren't forgetting to retrieve it. Rather, you are experiencing a full-blown retrieval failure, which makes this memory mindbug especially frustrating. It seems absolutely clear that you should be able to produce the information you seek, but the fact of the matter is that you can't. How can you know you know something but not know what it is?

TABLE 5.1 Inducing a tip-of-the-tongue experience

Instructions
Below are the definitions of 10 uncommon words. Look at each definition and try to think of the word it defines. If you can't think of the word but it seems like it's on the 'tip of your tongue', then try to guess the first letter of the word, or to think of one or two words that sound similar to the one you're trying to find. The answers are given below. No cheating!

Definitions

1 A blood feud in which members of the family of a murdered person try to kill the murderer or members of his family
2 A protecting charm to ward off spirits
3 A dark, hard, glassy volcanic rock
4 A person who makes maps
5 A man whose wife has proved unfaithful
6 The sacred beetle of the ancient Egyptians
7 The staff of Hermes, a medical symbol
8 The capital city of Latvia
9 A home for care of the terminally ill, or a house of rest for strangers; often kept by a religious order
10 Something out of keeping with the times in which it exists

Answers: 1. Vendetta 2. Amulet 3. Obsidian 4. Cartographer 5. Cuckold 6. Scarab 7. Caduceus 8. Riga, 9. Hospice 10. Anachronism

The tip-of-the-tongue state has been described as 'a mild torment, something like [being] on the brink of a sneeze' (Brown and McNeil, 1966, p. 326). Researchers have found that when people are in tip-of-the-tongue states, they often know something about the item they can't recall. For example, when trying to remember a word, people frequently know the first letter of the word, less frequently know the final letter, and even less often know the middle letters. During tip-of-the-tongue states, people also frequently come up with words that are related in sound or meaning to the sought-after item. If you blocked on any of the items in Table 5.1, you might have thought of a word that was similar to the one you were seeking even though you were sure that it was not the blocked word itself.

Blocking and tip-of-the-tongue states occur especially often for the names of people and places (Cohen, 1990; Valentine et al., 1996). Why? Because their links to related concepts and knowledge are weaker than for common names. That somebody's last name is Baker doesn't tell us much about the person, but saying that he *is* a baker does. To illustrate this point, researchers showed people pictures of cartoon and comic strip characters, some with descriptive names that highlighted key features of the character, for example Grumpy, Snow White, Scrooge, and others with arbitrary names, for example Aladdin, Mary Poppins, Pinocchio (Brédart and Valentine, 1998). Even though the two types of names were equally familiar to participants in the experiment, they blocked less often on the descriptive names than on the arbitrary names.

Although it's frustrating when it occurs, blocking is a relatively infrequent event for most of us. However, it occurs more often as we grow older, and it is a common complaint among people in their sixties and seventies (Burke et al., 1991). Even more strikingly, some brain-damaged patients live in an almost perpetual tip-of-the-tongue state. One patient could recall the names of only 2 of 40 famous people when she saw their photographs, compared to 25 out of 40 for healthy volunteers in the control group (Semenza and Zettin, 1989). Yet, she could still recall correctly the occupations of 32 of these people – the same number as healthy people could recall – indicating that she did know who they were after all. This case and similar ones have given researchers important clues about what parts of the brain are involved in retrieving proper names. Name blocking usually results from damage to parts of the left temporal lobe on the surface of the cortex, most often as a result of a stroke. In fact, studies that show strong activation of regions within the temporal lobe when people recall proper names support this idea (Damasio et al., 1996; Tempini et al., 1998).

Absentmindedness

In 2008, Robert Napier took his 17th-century Italian violin to London to be valued. He was pleasantly surprised to hear that it was worth £180,000 – but it would not be the only surprise that day. On disemabarking from the train at his home town in Wiltshire, he realized that he had left the valuable instrument on the luggage rack above where he had been sitting. He never saw it again, despite a frantic effort and offer of a £10,000 reward. How on earth could he have forgotten to pick up something so important and valuable that had been the whole purpose of his trip to London?

When Robert got off the train, he forgot to remember to collect his violin from the luggage rack. This was an expensive example of **absentmindedness** – *a lapse in attention that results in memory failure.* But what is absentmindedness? Attention plays a vital role in encoding information into long-term memory and, crucially, a phenomenon called **divided attention** – *situations where individuals have to simultaneously monitor more than one source of information.* In studies of divided attention, research participants are given materials to remember, such as a list of words, a story or a series of pictures. At the same time, they are required to perform an additional task that draws their attention away from the material. For example, in one study, participants listened to lists of 15 words for a later memory test (Craik et al., 1996). They were allowed to pay full attention to some of the lists, but while they heard other lists, they simultaneously viewed a visual display containing four boxes and pressed different keys to indicate where an asterisk was appearing and disappearing. On a later test, participants recalled far fewer words from the list they had heard while their attention was divided.

ABSENTMINDEDNESS A lapse in attention that results in memory failure.

DIVIDED ATTENTION Situations where individuals have to simultaneously monitor more than one source of information.

Many everyday instances of absentmindedness probably result from a kind of divided attention that occurs frequently in our daily lives. Mentally consumed with planning for a psychology exam the next day, you might place your keys in an unusual spot as you are reading over your notes. Because your attention was focused on the exam and not your keys, you do not encode where you put the keys. So, you later have no memory of the incident and must frantically search before finding the keys. At least Robert Napier knew where he had left his violin but attentional lapses can also produce total amnesia for events. For example, attentional lapses that lead to absentminded forgetting are particularly common during routine activities, such as driving or typing, that do not require elaborative encoding. When you first learn to drive a car, you pay careful attention to every step of the activity. As your skill increases with practice, you rely more and more on procedural memory, and less and less attention is required to perform the same tasks (Anderson and Fincham, 1994; Logan, 1988). Most experienced drivers, for example, are familiar with the unsettling experience of cruising along at 112 km per hour on a motorway and suddenly realizing that they have no recollection of the road for the past 8 km. Experienced drivers rely on the well-learned skills that allow them to drive safely even when on 'autopilot'. Absorbed with other concerns, they remember nothing of it – until they face the prosecution in court.

What happens in the brain when attention is divided? In one study, volunteers tried to learn a list of word pairs while researchers scanned their brains with positron emission tomography (PET) (Shallice et al., 1994). Some people simultaneously performed a task that took little attention (they moved a bar the same way over and over again), whereas other people simultaneously performed a task that took a great deal of attention (they repeatedly moved a bar but in a novel, unpredictable way each time). The researchers observed less activity in the participants' lower left frontal lobe when their attention was divided. As you saw earlier, greater activity in the lower left frontal region during encoding is associated with better memory. Dividing attention, then, prevents the lower left frontal lobe from playing its normal role in elaborative encoding, and the result is absentminded forgetting.

Neuroimaging evidence also links the lower left frontal lobe with automatic behaviour. Researchers performed PET scans while they showed volunteers a series of common nouns and asked them to generate related verbs (Raichle et al., 1994). For example, when shown the noun *dog*, participants might generate the verb *bark* or *walk*. When the volunteers first performed this task, it was associated with extensive activity in the lower left frontal lobe (and many other parts of the brain). This activity probably reflected a kind of elaborative encoding related to thinking about the properties of dogs and the kinds of actions they perform. Remembering dog facts requires a bit of mental work. But as the volunteers practised the task repeatedly with the same nouns and generated the verbs more quickly and automatically, activity in the lower left frontal lobe gradually decreased. This suggests that automatic behaviours, which are the cause of many absent-minded errors, are associated with low levels of left prefrontal activity, which reflects more shallow as opposed to elaborative encoding.

Avoiding these mindbugs often requires having a cue available at the moment you need to remember to carry out an action. For example, air traffic controllers must sometimes postpone an action but remember to carry it out later, such as when they cannot immediately grant a pilot's request to change altitude. In a simulated air traffic control experiment, researchers provided controllers with electronic signals to remind them to carry out a deferred request one minute later. The reminders were made available either during the one-minute waiting period, at the time the controller needed to act on the deferred request, or both. Compared with a condition in which no reminder was provided, controllers' memory for the deferred action improved only when the reminder was available at the time needed for retrieval. Providing the reminder during the waiting period did not help (Vortac et al., 1995). An early reminder, then, is no reminder at all.

Prospective memory: forgetting the future

Absentmindedness is the most common memory failure complaint because our daily lives depend on executing planned goals (Mäntylä, 2003). So far we have been considering forgetting as a loss of **retrospective memory** – *information learned in the past.* However, we also make plans for the future that we intend to act out. If we forget to carry these out, this is a failure in **prospective memory** – *remembering to do things in the future* (Einstein and McDaniel, 1990). On any given day, you need to remember the times and places of your lectures and seminars, you need to remember with whom and where you are having lunch, you need to remember which grocery items to pick up for dinner, and you need to remember which page of this book you were on when you fell asleep. Forgetting these things would leave you uneducated, friendless, hungry and with an unsettling desire to start reading this book from the beginning.

RETROSPECTIVE MEMORY Information learned in the past.

PROSPECTIVE MEMORY Remembering to do things in the future.

There are a number of important differences between retrospective and prospective memory. First, prospective memory tends to be crucially concerned with *when* something should be remembered, whereas retrospective memory is primarily concerned with *what* should be remembered (Baddeley, 1990). Unlike retrospective memory that deals with the past, prospective memory has two components: remembering what to do in the future, and remembering to do it. The first component is similar to a retrospective memory ('What do I normally do?') but the second component is unique to prospective memory. This requires the capacity to self-monitor, so it is not simply a memory exercise, but also requires conscious awareness and attention. As we learned in Chapter 3, these are functions that are supported by the frontal lobes and so patients with damage to these regions may have impaired prospective memory but unaffected retrospective memory (Radvansky, 2006).

There are two types of prospective memory: event based and time based. Event-based memories require an action when an event occurs, such as remembering to post a letter when you pass a letter box. Time-based events require an action when a certain time or interval is reached, such as remembering to call your friend after an exam. In general, time-based prospective memories are harder to remember because they usually require monitoring the passage of time, which can be difficult. In contrast, event-based memories are more likely to be triggered by an external cue, such as the sight of a letter box (Einstein et al., 1995). That said, both forms of prospective memory require attention. When Robert Napier got off the train, it is most probable that his attention was not on his valuable violin, and this supposition is borne out by Robert's own account of the events leading up to his failure to pick it up: 'It was the first time I had been on one of the new, fast trains to Bedwyn and as I got off I was just thinking about the train and whether it would fit on the platform. I just wasn't thinking about the violin' (*London Evening Standard*, 15 April 2008).

Amnesia

As we read at the beginning of this chapter, amnesiac patients like Clive Wearing and H. M. suffer from a condition known as **anterograde amnesia** – *the inability to transfer new information from the short-term store into the long-term store*. Some amnesiac patients also suffer from **retrograde amnesia** – *the inability to retrieve information that was acquired before a particular date, usually the date of an injury or operation*. Although H. M. could not store new memories, he was generally able to recall knowledge acquired during adolescence and childhood and could also recall some of his youthful experiences, although his early personal memories lacked detail (Corkin, 2002). We know that H. M. had the hippocampus regions of both lobes surgically removed and the fact that he had much worse anterograde than retrograde amnesia suggests that the hippocampal region is *not* the site of the long-term memory store; indeed, research has shown that different aspects of a single memory are stored in different places in the cortex (Damasio, 1989; Schacter, 1996; Squire and Kandel, 1999). Consider, for example, your memory of a live event, a concert or a football match, that you attended. Memories of the performers' appearance are probably stored in your visual cortex, perhaps in the occipital lobe or inferior temporal lobe (see Chapters 3 and 4). Memories of the music or the crowd roaring are probably stored in your auditory cortex.

If different parts of a memory are stored in different parts of the brain, why does hippocampal damage cause any kind of amnesia at all? Think about it: if bits and pieces of experience are scattered throughout the cortex, then *something* has to gather them together in order for us to have a single, integrated memory. Psychologists now believe that the hippocampal region serves this function, acting as a kind of 'index' that links together all these otherwise separate bits and pieces so that we remember them as one (Schacter, 1996; Squire, 1992; Teyler and DiScenna, 1986). If you were making a pie, the recipe would serve as an index – it would tell you to retrieve butter from the refrigerator, flour and sugar from the cupboard and rhubarb from the garden and then to mix them all together to produce the pie. But if the hippocampus is a memory index, then why was H. M. able to recall scenes from his childhood? Good question! It

ANTEROGRADE AMNESIA The inability to transfer new information from the short-term store into the long-term store.

RETROGRADE AMNESIA The inability to retrieve information that was acquired before a particular date, usually the date of an injury or operation.

Piano man gets into a fugue

In 2005, a young man was washed up on a beach on the Kent coast. Police found him wandering the streets in a soaked suit with no identification on him. He did not speak a word and was taken to the psychiatric unit of the local hospital. A rumour soon spread that the mystery man was in a fugue state of memory loss and that he was a European virtuoso pianist, after a member of staff reported hearing him playing Tchaikovsky on a piano. This story had all the makings of a Hollywood film until it was disclosed some months later that the man was actually 20-year-old Andreas Grassl from Germany who had jumped off the Eurostar ferry in a failed suicide attempt. Moreover, he had spoken to staff at the hospital and was unable to play a single note on the piano. Such stories highlight the media's tendency to speculate about and elaborate on items well beyond the facts.

appears that when people recall experiences over and over again, the bits and pieces start to become integrated, and they no longer need the hippocampal index to tie them together. If you made rhubarb pies every day, you wouldn't need a recipe after only a week or so. When the sugar came out, so would the flour. Scientists are still debating the extent to which the hippocampal regions helps us to remember details of our old memories (Bayley et al., 2005; Moscovitch et al., 2006), but the notion of the hippocampus as an index explains why people like H. M. *cannot* make new memories and why they *can* remember old ones.

Temporary amnesia

CONCUSSION A loss of consciousness that can range from moments to weeks.

Some individuals may suffer a temporary memory loss either as a result of an acquired head injury or an extreme psychological state. A serious blow to the head can cause **concussion**, *a loss of consciousness that can range from moments to weeks*, which is often associated with memory loss. Trevor Rees-Jones, Princess Diana's bodyguard, who was involved in the fatal car crash that killed her, suffered concussion that left him with no memory of the incident. He was later able to recall getting into the car but not the chase leading up to the crash. This is fairly typical for memory loss associated with concussion: there is a retrograde amnesia for events just prior to the injury, which suggests that memory of the events is only held in a temporary store and does not become encoded into long-term memory.

FUGUE STATE An amnesia of one's previous life and identity.

A more bizarre and controversial temporary amnesia is known as a **fugue state** – *an amnesia of one's previous life and identity* (Schacter et al., 1982). On 23 July 2003, Doug Bruce found himself on a New York subway train with no idea of why he was on the train, no memory of who he was and no memory of either his family or life. When he looked at a video of himself and his friends taken some years previously, for instance, he could identify himself as the man in the video but no longer felt any relationship either to that man, that is, himself, or to his lifelong friends. It was if he was watching someone else's life. Unlike concussion, which is more transient and tied to a specific head injury event, fugue states are better viewed as a response to, or as a means of coping with, the effects of distressing life crises such as bereavement, divorce or criminal prosecution (Schacter et al., 1982). For whatever reason, individuals appear to lose, or want to lose, their sense of self-identity.

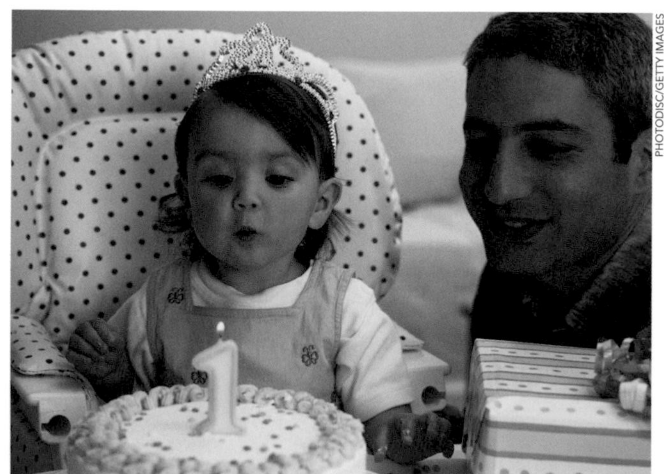
PHOTODISC/GETTY IMAGES

Can you remember your first birthday? If not, you are probably suffering from childhood amnesia.

Ageing and memory

What's the earliest memory you have? There are always the odd few, and they are indeed odd, who say they can remember being born. But if you are like the majority of normal people, you probably have no memory of yourself before your second birthday and even then, the memories from around that time are fragmented and unconnected. For most of us, first memories date from three to five years of age. People generally cannot remember incidents that occurred before they were two years old, probably because the brain regions necessary for episodic memory are not yet fully mature (Nadel and Zola-Morgan, 1984; Schacter and Moscovitch, 1984). In one study, researchers asked individuals aged between 4 and 20 years old to recall as much as they could about the birth of a younger sibling (Sheingold and Tenney, 1982). Participants who were at least three years old at the time of the birth remembered it in considerable detail, whereas participants who were younger than three years old at the time of the birth remembered little or nothing. This failure to remember is not due to transience: 70-year-olds generally remember many events from 50 years earlier, but 20-year-olds almost never remember anything from 18 or 19 years before (Eacott, 1999).

CHILDHOOD AMNESIA An inability to remember events from the early years of life.

As you will read in Chapter 11 on cognitive development, we know that infants can remember events, so why is it that most of us have **childhood amnesia** – *an inability to remember events from the early years of life?* One hypothesis is that early memories are procedural, and that autobiographical memories depend on maturation of the hippocampus and neocortical regions of the brain, which takes place around the second year (Nelson, 2002). Other possible explanations address the role of language and knowledge to form schemas that make sense of experiences and help to encode memories (Simcock and Hayne, 2002).

Over the course of childhood and early adulthood, there is a general development in memory. As children learn more about the world, their semantic memory increases (Chi and Koeske, 1983) and they become more skilled at organizing, storing and retrieving information as well as using strategies to remember (Radvansky, 2006). One way to facilitate this process is parent–child reminiscing, where adults talk to their children about the day's events. The typical two- to three-year-old barrier for childhood amnesia can be pushed back to a younger age if parents provide a narrative framework of interpretation to help children make sense of their experiences and form better memories (Nelson and Fivush, 2004). This may also explain cultural differences in childhood amnesia. Western parents typically use child-centred narratives focusing on achievements ('How well did you do today – were you awesome?') compared to Eastern parents who use an integrative approach, where the day's events are discussed in relation to communal activities and play down strong emotions that might segregate them from the group ('What was the class activity today?') (Wang, 2006). As a result, it is argued that children from Western cultures have typically earlier, more detailed and more emotionally elaborated memories than children from Eastern cultures (Han et al., 1998) – a pattern that persists through to adulthood (Pillemer, 1998).

Another factor is cognitive efficiency. Working memory consistently improves and this largely reflects increased speed of processing (Kail, 1991). In addition, children become better at blocking out irrelevant information. For example, in a 'directed forgetting' task, children were asked to learn one list of words and then instructed to forget them so that a new list could be learned. Results showed that they become increasingly skilled at ignoring the first list of words as they get older, and by 10 years of age, they are as good as young adults (Harnishfeger and Pope, 1996).

As most of us are all too aware, things start to go wrong in the memory department as we become older: being forgetful is one of the major complaints of old age. Some of the most dramatic changes in age-related forgetting may be caused by the same phenomena as forgetting in young children. For example, just as the speed of general processing increased during childhood, so it slows down with age (Perfect, 1994): some theorists view this decline in processing speed as the major cause of memory failure (Salthouse, 1996b). However, as we are reminded in Chapter 2 about the relationship between variables, we must be careful about attributing all memory failure to processing speed, which remains a correlational and not necessarily a causal factor (Baddeley, 2007).

Another ability that is thought to decline in old age is inhibition. Inhibition is linked to the dorsolateral prefrontal cortex (DLPC), which also declines with age (MacPherson et al., 2002). Older adults perform similarly to younger adults with DLPC damage (Stuss et al., 1996) and, when trying to remember, they experience more difficulty in inhibiting irrelevant information (Dempster, 1992). Paradoxically, these older adults have a memory problem because they are remembering too much rather than too little.

In summary, we all forget information that we once held in memory, but for different reasons. Transience is reflected by a rapid decline in memory followed by more gradual forgetting. With the passing of time, memory switches from detailed to general. Both decay and interference contribute to transience. Blocking occurs when stored information is temporarily inaccessible, as when information is on the tip of the tongue. Absentmindedness results from failures of attention, shallow encoding and the influence of automatic behaviours, and is often associated with forgetting to do things in the future. Amnesia can be either permanent following significant brain damage or temporary as a consequence of concussion or psychological stress. We tend to forget our early years, but as we develop through childhood, we show steady improvement in memory. In later adulthood and old age, memory declines again, mostly as a result of a change in processing efficiency and inhibition.

Metamemory

METAMEMORY The subjective awareness of one's own memory.

The first thing to remember about memory is that it is very personal. Memory is so central to our experience of self that, for many of us, it is impossible to dissociate the two. Fugue states reflect the intimate relationship between our memories and identity. Our thoughts and actions are dependent on our memories, which is why it is important that there is a pretty good match between our memories and the reality of the world. For example, if you think that you turned off the iron before leaving the house, then it is important that your memory serves you well. But what if you falsely remember turning off the iron? You might end up burning down your house. **Metamemory**, *the subjective awareness of one's own memory*, is how we know that our memories are correct. This is the important difference between *remembering* you turned off your iron and *knowing* that you did so.

Knowing that you know

FEELING OF KNOWING (FOK) The subjective awareness of information that cannot be retrieved from memory.

When you remember, you have a vivid recollection of encoding the information and can access that information in consciousness. When you know something, you do not necessarily remember how and where you learned the information. For example, we may know what the capital of Spain is, but we do not necessarily remember where and when we learned this fact. This can lead to those situations where we know that we know something and still we are unable to remember it, yet we are certain that if we heard it or saw it, we would recognize it. For example, most of us know the names of Snow White's seven dwarves but we may not be able to remember them all. However, we know that we know them and are sure that 'Snitchy' is not one of them and we would be able to recognize the correct names if we were told. If we are very nearly able to access the names, we might experience the tip-of-the-tongue phenomenon we encountered earlier. Much of the time, however, we aren't quite so close to successful retrieval, we simply have the **feeling of knowing (FOK)** – *the subjective awareness of information that cannot be retrieved from memory*. FOK judgements are theoretically interesting because they reveal that individuals are aware of the contents of their memory even though the information is not explicit. For example, after failing to recall an answer, individuals can accurately predict whether they will identify information if it is subsequently shown (Hart, 1965). This is also why contestants on speed-response quiz shows such as *University Challenge* often 'buzz in' before they can actually remember the answer: they are aware that they know before they have actually retrieved the information (Reder, 1987).

Strong FOK judgements, where there is a strong subjective sense of knowing the answer, are related to increasing amounts of partial information (Koriat, 1993), which is why questions on quiz shows such as *University Challenge* are often phrased to reveal progressively more information to trigger recall ('Who was a leading 20th-century US playwright, who died in 2005, was married to Marilyn Monroe and wrote *Death of a Salesman*? Answer: Arthur Miller). Partial information also predicts whether the individual experiences a sense of remembering or simply knowing (Hicks and Marsh, 2002). As partial information mounts up, individuals switch from initially knowing to remembering (Koriat and Levy-Sadot, 2001). When we 'remember' as opposed to 'know' something, different memory processes are operating. In terms of the distinction we encountered earlier, remembering is associated with episodic memory, whereas knowing is semantic memory.

The distinction between remembering and knowing is also relevant to the difference between the memories reported by experts and novices in a given subject area. Experts almost always recall more information accurately than novices, but there is no difference in recognition tests, such as 'Is Snitchy one of the Snow White's seven dwarves?' We recognize that this is not a name we have encountered before. For example, in a study of sci-fi nerdiness, students read stories based on the TV series *Star Trek*. On a subsequent recognition test, there was no difference between students who were 'Trekkies' compared to normal students who were not familiar with the show. However, the Trekkies reported more often that they remembered reading the information, which indicates that their prior knowledge (an obsession with *Star Trek*) affected the memory experience (Long and Prat, 2002). This is because their background knowledge of *Star Trek* helps to elaborate the memory trace they were forming while reading the stories by providing more points of reference and context.

Source monitoring and misattributions

If we are sure that we remember as opposed to simply know, this indicates that we can identify the point in time when the memory was formed. Therefore, an important component of memory is attributing where our memories came from. This is known as **source monitoring** – *recall of when, where and how information was acquired* (Johnson et al., 1993; Schacter et al., 1984). People sometimes correctly recall a fact they learned earlier or accurately recognize a person or object they have seen before, but misattribute the source of this knowledge. **Memory misattributions** – *assigning a recollection or an idea to the wrong source* – can contribute to the formation of false memories. Experiments have shown, for instance, that people can remember perfectly well that they saw a previously presented face yet misremember the time or place they saw it (Davies, 1988), as happened to the rape victim in the Donald Thomson incident (see the vignette in the margin).

SOURCE MONITORING Recall of when, where and how information was acquired.

MEMORY MISATTRIBUTION Assigning a recollection or an idea to the wrong source.

Memory researcher Donald Thomson was accused of rape based on the victim's detailed recollection of his face, but he was eventually cleared when it was revealed he had a watertight alibi. Ironically, at the time of the rape, Thomson was giving a live TV interview on the subject of distorted memories. The victim had been watching the show just before she was assaulted and, in an awful turn of events, consequently misattributed her memory of Thomson's face to the rapist (Schacter, 1996; Thomson, 1988).

There are three basic types of source monitoring: internal, external and reality (Johnson et al., 1993):

1 *Internal source monitoring* involves distinguishing between events that an individual thought about doing versus events they actually did – 'Did I turn off the iron or just think I did?' Here, perceptual details, such as remembering seeing the switch flick off, are critical for establishing the validity of the memory.
2 *External source monitoring* involves distinguishing between two external sources – 'Was it Jane or Sarah who told me?' Here, contextual information, such as the fact that you only tend to gossip with Jane, helps to decide the likely source of the memory.
3 *Reality source monitoring* involves distinguishing between an actual event and an imagined one – 'Did I actually see the video footage of Princess Diana's car crash, or do I just think I did?' Here, reality can usually be checked against corroborating evidence, such as the presence of other witnesses, and the existence or otherwise of such a video, although there is still considerable scope for groups of individuals to falsely remember an event.

Misattribution might explain the extremely bizarre but very common memory phenomenon of the **déjà vu experience** – *where you suddenly feel that you have been in a situation before even though you can't recall any details.* A present situation that is similar to a past experience may trigger a general sense of familiarity that is mistakenly attributed to having been in the exact situation previously (Reed, 1988). When the experience is particularly intense and the person cannot tell that a situation is new, they may believe that they are really reliving a familiar experience: this phenomenon is called **déjà vécu** – *a confabulated memory where the individual is certain that the new experience is old.* One theory as to the cause of déjà vu and déjà vécu is that the 'familiar' associated recollections from long-term memory are normally inhibited, but when déjà vu or déjà vécu occurs, this inhibition partly fails, meaning that you experience the 'familiarity' signal but not the associated memory (Moulin et al., 2005).

DÉJÀ VU EXPERIENCE Where you suddenly feel that you have been in a situation before even though you can't recall any details.

DÉJÀ VÉCU A confabulated memory where the individual is certain that the new experience is old.

Patients with damage to the frontal lobes are especially prone to source monitoring errors (Schacter et al., 1984; Shimamura and Squire, 1987). This is probably because the frontal lobes play a significant role in effortful retrieval processes, which are required to dredge up the correct source of a memory. These patients sometimes produce bizarre misattributions. In 1991, a British photographer in his mid-forties known as M. R. was overcome with feelings of familiarity about people he didn't know. He kept asking his wife whether each new passing stranger was 'somebody' – a film star, TV newsperson or local celebrity. M. R.'s feelings were so intense that he often could not resist approaching strangers and asking whether they were indeed famous celebrities. When given formal

Psychology and me

Sue Sherman, Senior Lecturer in Psychology, Keele University

Sue Sherman is Senior Lecturer in Psychology at Keele University in the UK. Visit www.palgrave.com/schacter to watch Sue talking about her research into false memory for words, brand names and music, and the intersection of psychology and linguistics. She also talks about how she came to study psychology and what she found most challenging.

FALSE MEMORIES Recollection of events that never happened.

tests, M. R. recognized the faces of actual celebrities as accurately as did healthy volunteers in the control group. But M. R. also 'recognized' more than 75% of unfamiliar faces, whereas healthy controls hardly ever did. Neurological examinations revealed that M. R. suffered from multiple sclerosis, which had caused damage to his frontal lobes (Ward et al., 1999).

False memories

In 2005, shortly after the London bombings, a young Brazilian man Jean Charles de Menezes entered Stockwell tube station, used his travel card to pay the fare, calmly walked through the barriers and slowly descended the escalator. He then ran across the platform to board the newly arrived train as most commuters do. Menezes boarded the train and found one of the first available seats. Moments later he was shot dead by police officers hunting for suspect suicide bombers. It was a tragic case of misidentification. Menezes was totally innocent. What was remarkable was the reports based on eyewitness testimony that followed. Witnesses stated that up to 20 police officers in plain clothes pursued a fleeing Menezes into Stockwell station, that he jumped over the ticket barrier, ran down an escalator and tried to jump on to a train. However, CCTV recordings showed Menezes passing through the barriers normally. In all likelihood, it was a police officer pursuing Menezes who vaulted the barrier. Source monitoring errors contribute to **false memories**, *recollection of events that never happened*, and yet people are convinced that they really did experience the event they report.

Research on false memories is probably one of the most studied and most controversial areas of applied psychology because of the implications that eyewitness testimony have for convictions. However, as we have seen throughout this chapter, memories are reconstructed rather than replayed, which makes them susceptible to all manner of distortions. A simple way to study false memories is to use the rather lengthily named Deese-Roediger-McDermott (DRM) paradigm (Deese, 1959; Roediger and McDermott, 1995, 2000), where participants have to remember lists of words. Take the following test and there is a good chance you will experience false memories for yourself. First study the two lists of words presented in TABLE 5.2 by reading each word for about one second. When you are done, return to the paragraph you were reading for more instructions, but don't look back at the table.

TABLE 5.2 False recognition

Sour	Thread
Ice cream	Pin
Sugar	Eye
Bitter	Sewing
Good	Sharp
Taste	Point
Tooth	Prick
Nice	Thimble
Honey	Haystack
Soda	Pain
Chocolate	Hurt
Heart	Injection
Cake	Syringe
Tart	Cloth
Pie	Knitting

Now take a recognition test by indicating which of these words – *taste*, *bread*, *needle*, *king*, *sweet*, *thread* – appeared on the lists you just studied. If you think that *taste* and *thread* were on the lists you studied, you're right. And if you think that *bread* and *king* weren't on those lists, you're also right. But if you think that *needle* or *sweet* appeared on the lists, you're dead wrong.

Most people make exactly the same mistake, claiming with confidence that they saw *needle* and *sweet* on the list. This is an example of **false recognition** – *a feeling of familiarity about something that hasn't been encountered before.* Experiments have shown that undergraduates claim to recognize *needle* and *sweet* about as often (84%) as they claim to recognize words that were on the list (86%). Undergraduates claimed to recognize unrelated words such as *bread* or *king* only 20% of the time. This type of false recognition occurs because all the words in the lists are associated with *needle* or *sweet*. Seeing each word in the study list activates related words. Because *needle* and *sweet* are related to all the associates, they become more activated than other words – so highly activated that only minutes later, people swear that they actually studied the words. This is the same problem we encountered in Chapter 4 when discussing signal detection thresholds and being certain about whether information is a hit, miss, false alarm or a correct rejection. Just as signal detection theory predicts that similarity will lead to confusion in perception, so false recognition shows that the same is true for memory.

FALSE RECOGNITION A feeling of familiarity about something that hasn't been encountered before.

The DRM paradigm reveals how easy it is for participants to mistake a powerful feeling of familiarity for actually having seen (or heard) something. Brain-scanning studies using PET and fMRI have shown one reason why people are so easily fooled into 'remembering' words such as *needle* and *sweet*: many of the same brain regions are active during false recognition and true recognition, including the hippocampus (Cabeza et al., 2001; Schacter et al., 1996b; Slotnick and Schacter, 2004). However, there are some differences in brain activity. For example, a PET experiment revealed that a part of the auditory cortex (on the surface of the temporal lobe) showed greater activity for words that had actually been heard earlier in the experiment than for associated words such as *needle* or *sweet*, which had not been heard previously (Schacter et al., 1996b). A later fMRI study showed that true recognition of previously studied visual shapes produced more activity in parts of the visual cortex than false recognition of new shapes that looked similar to those previously studied (Slotnick and Schacter, 2004) (see **FIGURE 5.19**).

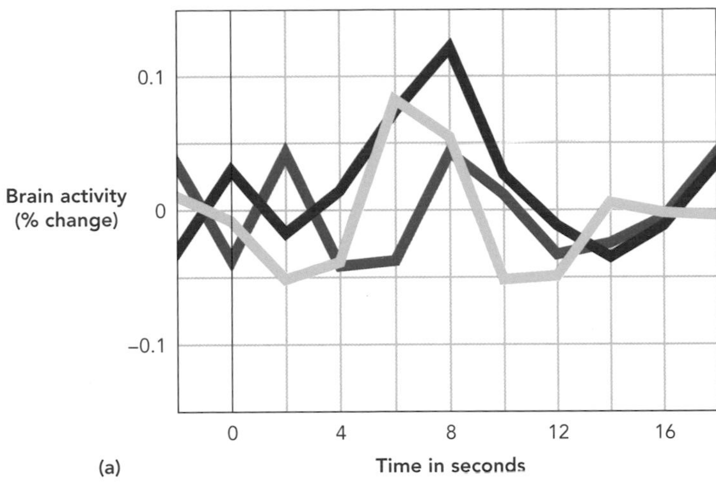

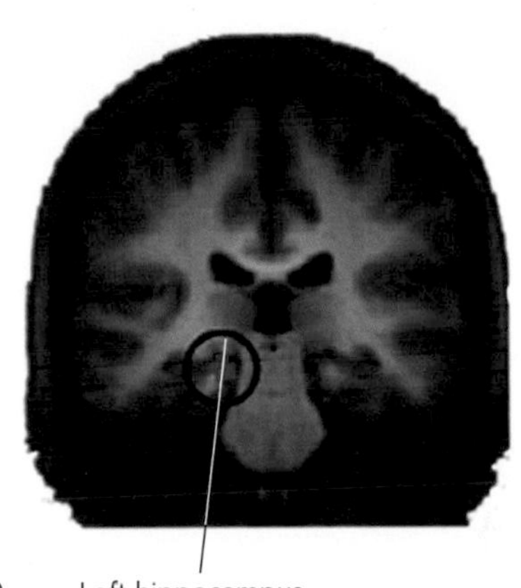

FIGURE 5.19 Hippocampal activity during true and false recognition Many brain regions show similar activation during true and false recognition, including the hippocampus. The figure shows results from an fMRI study of true and false recognition of visual shapes (Slotnick and Schacter, 2004). (a) A graph showing the activity level in the strength of the fMRI signal from the hippocampus over time. This shows that after a few seconds, there is comparable activation for true recognition of previously studied shapes (blue line) and false recognition of similar shapes that were not presented (yellow line). Both true and false recognition show increased hippocampal activity compared with correctly classifying unrelated shapes as new (green line). (b) A region of the left hippocampus.

It is possible to reduce or avoid false memories by presenting distinctive information (such as a picture of *thread*), and encouraging participants to require specific recollections of seeing the picture before they say 'yes' on a recognition test (Schacter et al., 1999). Unfortunately, we do not always demand specific recollections before we say that we encountered a word in an experiment or – more importantly – make a positive identification of a suspect. When people experience a strong sense of familiarity about a person, object or event but lack specific recollections, a potentially dangerous recipe for memory misattribution is in place. Understanding this point may be a key to reducing the dangerous consequences of misattribution in eyewitness testimony (see *the real world* box).

Biases

Signal detection theory tells us that the extent to which signals can be discriminated from background noise will determine the extent to which individuals are certain that a signal is present. The same is true for information used to identify correct memories and reject false ones. If people are uncertain about a memory, they can easily be confused, leading to false memories. However, in addition to discriminability, individuals operate with a set of thought processes that interpret information in a particular way, which influences the degree to which they are willing to accept what they remember as new or old. This is the problem of **bias** – *the distorting influences of present knowledge, beliefs and feelings on recollection of previous experiences*. Sometimes, what people remember from their pasts says less about what actually happened than about what they think, feel or believe now. Witnesses remembered seeing Menezes fleeing from the police in the London Underground because this was consistent with the initial news reports. Other researchers have also found that our current moods can bias our recall of past experiences (Bower, 1981; Eich, 1995). So, in addition to helping you recall actual sad memories (as you saw earlier in this chapter), a sad mood can also bias your recollections of experiences that may not have been so sad. Bias can influence memory in three ways:

1 By altering the past to fit the present – *consistency bias*
2 By exaggerating differences between past and present – *change bias*
3 By distorting the past to make us look better – *egocentric bias*.

BIAS The distorting influences of present knowledge, beliefs and feelings on recollection of previous experiences.

The way each member of this happy couple recalls earlier feelings towards the other depends on how each currently views their relationship.

In addition to moods, current knowledge and beliefs can produce biasing effects. Several researchers have described a *consistency bias*, in which people reconstruct the past to fit what they presently know or believe. One US researcher asked people in 1973 to rate their attitudes towards a variety of 'controversial' social issues, including the legalization of marijuana, women's rights and aid to minorities (Marcus, 1986). They were asked to make the same rating again in 1982 and also to indicate what their attitudes had been in 1973. Researchers found that participants' recollections of their 1973 attitudes in 1982 were more closely related to what they believed in 1982 than to what they had actually said in 1973.

The consistency bias is often quite striking in romantically involved couples. In a study of dating couples, participants were asked to evaluate themselves, their dating partner and their relationship twice – first in an initial session and then again two months later (McFarland and Ross, 1987). During the second session, participants were also asked to recall their earlier evaluations. Researchers found that participants whose relationships had soured over time recalled their initial evaluations as more negative than they really were. However, when participants reported a positive or deeper relationship in the present, they also recalled having felt more liking or loving in the past.

the real world

Deadly misattributions

Eyewitness testimony is not only unreliable but is also given undue weight in cases where there is evidence for innocence. For example, in 1969, Laszlo Virag was convicted of stealing from parking meters and wounding a police officer with a gun while escaping in a car chase in Liverpool. Despite his alibi and other contradictions to indicate he was innocent, for example he did not drive a car, Virag was identified by eight witnesses as the man who committed the crime. It was only after he had served 5 years of a 10-year prison sentence that the real culprit was apprehended and Virag was pardoned. He was later offered £17,500 compensation.

This emphasis on eyewitness testimony and failure to consider contradictory evidence was studied experimentally by US memory researcher Elizabeth Loftus (1974), who conducted a study where groups of adults were asked to play the role of jurors. They were told about a robbery and murder in a shop where the robber was seen running into a block of flats where the 'defendant' lived. They were also told that there was money found in the defendant's flat and there was some chemical residue on his clothes that could have come from the scene of the crime. The defendant denied the crime, explained where the money came from and how residue ended up on his clothes. On this information alone, 18% of the jury judged the defendant to be guilty. However, when eyewitness testimony from a shop worker was added in another condition, the guilty decision rose to 72% of the jury. In a third condition, the eyewitness testimony of the shop worker was discredited by showing that they had not worn their glasses, had poor vision and could not have seen the face of the defendant. Despite such discrediting information, 68% of the jury still found the defendant guilty.

In 1974, a UK committee under the chairmanship of the well-known criminal lawyer Lord Devlin was formed to investigate the reliability and use of eyewitness testimony. The committee examined all 2,116 identification parades held in England and Wales for the year 1973 and discovered that a suspect was picked out of 45% of parades. After identification, 82% (850 individuals) were prosecuted, of which 347 were prosecuted on the basis of eyewitness testimony alone and 256 were convicted.

Based on the outstanding work of memory researchers such as Loftus and the miscarriages of justice identified by its investigations, the committee produced the Devlin Report in 1976, which recommended that a trial judge be required to instruct the jury that it is not safe to convict on a single eyewitness testimony alone except in exceptional circumstances, for example the witness is a close friend or relative, or when there is substantial corroborative evidence.

You might expect memory experts like Elizabeth Loftus to be less susceptible to false memories and yet she describes how, when she was in her thirties, her uncle reminded her of the time, when she was 14 years old, she discovered her own mother drowned in the family swimming pool. This brought back vivid memories of this terrible discovery, except that these memories were false. It was not the young Elizabeth who had discovered her mother's body but her aunt. Later, Loftus said (quoted in Neimark, 1996): 'The most horrifying idea is that what we believe with all our hearts is not necessarily the truth.'

Just as we sometimes exaggerate the similarity of the past and the present, we sometimes exaggerate the *difference* between what we feel or believe now and what we felt or believed in the past. In other words, *change biases* also occur. For example, most of us would like to believe that our romantic attachments grow stronger over time. In one study, dating couples were asked, once a year for four years, to assess the present quality of their relationships and to recall how they felt in past years

(Sprecher, 1999). Couples who stayed together for the four years recalled that the strength of their love had increased since they last reported on it. Yet their actual ratings at the time did not show any increases in love and attachment. Objectively, the couples did not love each other more today than yesterday. But they did from the subjective perspective of memory.

Sometimes we exaggerate the change between present and past in order make ourselves look good in retrospect, thus revealing a self-enhancing or *egocentric bias*. For example, students sometimes remember feeling more anxious before taking an exam than they actually reported at the time (Keuler and Safer, 1998), and blood donors sometimes recall being more nervous about giving blood than they actually were (Breckler, 1994). In both cases, change biases colour memory and make people feel that they behaved more bravely or courageously than they actually did. Our memories for the grades we achieved in school also reflect an egocentric bias. Can you recall your grades from secondary school courses? Do you remember how many As and Ds appeared on your report card? Chances are that you will recall more of the good grades than the bad ones. When university students tried to remember secondary school grades and their memories were checked against actual transcripts, they were highly accurate for grades of A (89% correct) and extremely inaccurate for grades of D (29% correct) (Bahrick et al., 1996). The students were remembering the past as they wanted it to be rather than the way it was.

Suggestibility and intrusion errors

On 4 October 1992, an El Al cargo plane crashed into a block of flats in a southern suburb of Amsterdam, killing 39 residents and all 4 members of the airline crew. The disaster dominated news in the Netherlands for days, as people viewed footage of the crash scene and read about the catastrophe. Ten months later, Dutch psychologists asked a simple question of university students: 'Did you see the television film of the moment the plane hit the apartment building?' Fifty-five per cent answered 'yes'. In a follow-up study, 66% responded affirmatively (Crombag et al., 1996). The students also recalled details concerning the speed and angle of the plane when it hit the building and what happened to the body of the plane after the collision. All of this might seem perfectly normal except for one key fact: there was no TV film of the moment when the plane actually crashed. The researchers had asked a suggestive question that implied that TV film of the crash had been shown. Respondents may have viewed TV film of the post-crash scene, and they may have read, imagined or talked about what might have happened when the plane hit the building, but they most definitely did not see it. The suggestive question led participants to misattribute information from these or other sources to a film that did not exist. **Suggestibility** is the *tendency to incorporate misleading information from external sources into personal recollections*. Suggestibility is closely related to memory misattribution, in the sense that converting suggestions into inaccurate memories must involve misattribution. Unlike suggestibility, however, memory misattribution often occurs in the absence of specific suggestions.

SUGGESTIBILITY The tendency to incorporate misleading information from external sources into personal recollections.

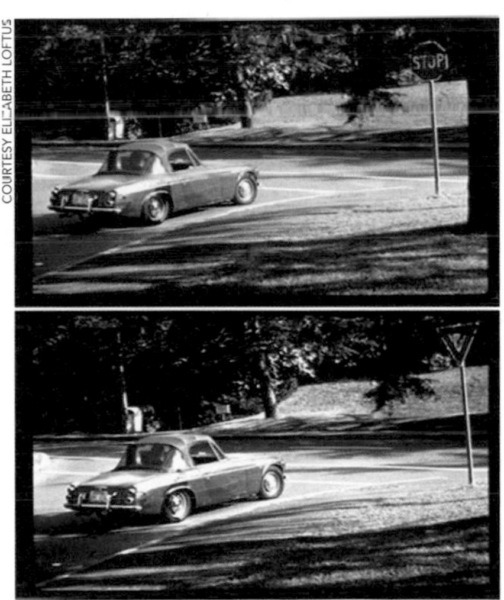

COURTESY ELIZABETH LOFTUS

In a classic experiment by Elizabeth Loftus, people were shown a video of a car at a stop sign. Those who later received a misleading suggestion that the car had stopped at a give way sign often claimed they had seen the car at a give way sign (Loftus et al., 1978).

There's plenty of research evidence of suggestibility. For example, in one study, Elizabeth Loftus and her colleagues showed participants a videotape of an accident involving a white sports car (Loftus, 1975; Loftus et al., 1978). Some participants were then asked how fast the car was going when it passed the barn. Nearly 20% of these individuals later recalled seeing a barn in the videotape – even though there was no barn – while participants who weren't asked about a barn almost never recalled seeing one. In later experiments, Loftus showed that people who received a misleading suggestion that they had earlier seen a car stop at a 'give way' sign (they had actually seen the car at a 'stop sign') often claimed later to remember seeing a give way sign. Misleading suggestions do not eliminate the original memory (Berkerian and Bowers, 1983; McCloskey and Zaragoza, 1985). Instead, they cause participants to make **source memory**, *recall of when, where and how information was acquired*, errors, that is, they have difficulty recollecting whether they actually saw a give way sign or only learned about it later.

SOURCE MEMORY Recall of when, where and how information was acquired.

If misleading details can be implanted in people's memories, is it also possible to suggest entire episodes that never occurred? Could you be convinced, for example, that you had once been lost in a shopping centre as a child or spilled a bowl of punch at a wedding, even though these events never actually happened? The answer seems to be 'yes' (Loftus, 1993, 2003). In one study, the research participant, a teenager named Chris, was asked by his older brother, Jim, to try to remember the time Chris had been lost in a shopping centre at age five. He initially recalled nothing, but after several days, Chris produced a detailed recollection of the event. He recalled that he 'felt so scared I would never see my family again' and remembered that a kindly old man wearing a flannel shirt found him crying (Loftus, 1993, p. 532). But according to Jim and other family members, Chris was never lost in a shopping centre. Of 24 participants in a larger study on implanted memories, approximately 25% falsely remembered being lost as a child in a shopping centre or a similar public place (Loftus and Pickrell, 1995).

Other researchers have also successfully implanted false memories of childhood experiences in a significant minority of participants (Hyman and Billings, 1998; Hyman and Pentland, 1996). In one study, students were asked about several childhood events that, according to their parents, actually happened. But they were also asked about an event that never happened. For instance, the students were asked if they remembered a wedding reception they attended when they were five, running around with some other children and bumping into a table, spilling the punch bowl on the parents of the bride. Students remembered nearly all the true events and initially reported no memory for the false events. However, with repeated probing, 20–40% of the participants in different experimental conditions eventually came to describe some memory of the false event.

People develop false memories in response to suggestions for some of the same reasons that memory misattribution occurs. We do not store all the details of our experiences in memory, making us vulnerable to accepting suggestions about what might have happened or should have happened. In addition, visual imagery plays an important role in constructing false memories (Goff and Roediger, 1998). Asking people to imagine an event like spilling punch all over the bride's parents at a wedding increases the likelihood that they will develop a false memory of it (Hyman and Pentland, 1996).

Persistence: failing to forget

What is the most embarrassing moment you can remember? Was it something from your childhood? Sometimes, we simply want to forget embarrassing moments, but most of us can live with them. For others, memories can become nightmares that refuse to go away.

Artist Melinda Stickney-Gibson awoke in her Chicago apartment to the smell of smoke. She jumped out of bed and saw black plumes rising through cracks in the floor. Melinda tried to call the fire department, but the phone lines had already burned out. Raging flames had engulfed the entire building, and there was no chance to escape except by jumping from her third-floor window. Shortly after she crashed to the ground, the building exploded into a brilliant fireball. She lost all her possessions and her beloved dog, but she saved her own life. Alas, that life was never the same again. Melinda became overwhelmed by memories of the fire and frequently could think of little else. Her paintings, which were previously bright, colourful abstractions, became dark meditations that included only black, orange and ochre – the colours of the fire. When Melinda sat down in front of a blank canvas to start a new painting, her memories of that awful night intruded. She remembered the incident vividly for years, even after she had recovered physically from the injuries suffered in her fall (Schacter, 1996).

PERSISTENCE The intrusive recollection of events that we wish we could forget.

Melinda Stickney-Gibson's experiences illustrate **persistence** – *the intrusive recollection of events that we wish we could forget*. Melinda's experience is far from unique: persistence frequently occurs after disturbing or traumatic incidents, such as the fire that destroyed her home. Although being able to quickly call up memories is usually considered a good thing, in the case of persistence, that ability mutates into a bedevilling mindbug.

Controlled laboratory studies have revealed that emotional experiences tend to be better remembered than unemotional ones. For instance, memory for unpleasant pictures, such as mutilated bodies, or pleasant ones, such as attractive men and women, is more accurate than for emotionally neutral pictures, such as household objects (Ochsner, 2000). Emotional arousal seems to focus our attention on the central features of an event. In one experiment, people who viewed an emotionally arousing sequence of slides involving a bloody car accident remembered more of the central themes and fewer peripheral details than people who viewed an unemotional sequence (Christianson and Loftus, 1987). Intrusive memories are undesirable consequences of the fact that emotional experiences generally lead to more vivid and enduring recollections than unemotional experiences do.

Why do our brains succumb to persistence? Like the vivid flashbulb memories we encountered earlier, these memories are associated with strong emotions. A key player in the brain's response to emotional events is the amygdala (see Chapter 3). Buried deep in the inner regions of the temporal lobe (as shown in **FIGURE 5.20**), the amygdala is located next to the hippocampus but performs different functions. Damage to the amygdala does not result in a general memory deficit. Patients with amygdala damage, however, do not remember emotional events any better than unemotional events (Cahill and McGaugh, 1998).

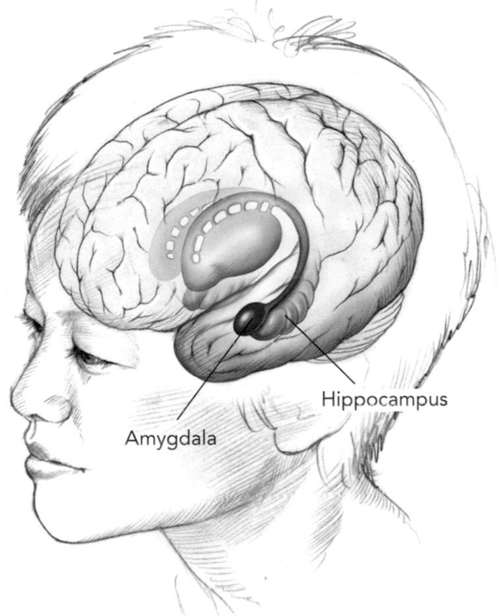

FIGURE **5.20 The amygdala's influence on memory** The amygdala, located next to the hippocampus, responds strongly to emotional events. Patients with amygdala damage are unable to remember emotional events any better than unemotional ones (Cahill and McGaugh, 1998).

For example, consider what happened when people viewed a series of photographic slides that began with a mother walking her child to school and later included an emotionally arousing event: the child being hit by a car. When tested later, the research participants remembered the arousing event better than the mundane ones. But patients with amygdala damage remembered the mundane and emotionally arousing events equally well (Cahill and McGaugh, 1998). PET and fMRI scans show that when healthy people view a slide sequence that includes an emotionally arousing event, the level of activity in their amygdalas at the time they see it is a good predictor of their subsequent memory for the slide. When there is heightened activity in the amygdala as people watch emotional events, there's a better chance that they will recall those events on a later test (Cahill et al., 1996; Kensinger and Schacter, 2005).

The amygdala influences hormonal systems that kick into high gear when we experience an arousing event. The release of stress-related hormones, such as adrenaline and cortisol, mobilizes the brain and the body in the face of threat or other sources of stress. These hormones also enhance memory for the experience. For instance, administering stress-related hormones heightens a rat's memory for an electrical shock or for places in a maze that it has visited recently (LeDoux, 1996). When the amygdala is damaged, it no longer releases the stress-related hormones that enhance memory. When people are given a drug that interferes with the release of stress-related hormones, their memory for the emotional sections of a slide sequence is no better than their memory for the mundane sections. It seems, then, that the amygdala influences memory storage by turning on the hormones that allow us to respond to and vividly remember emotionally arousing events.

In summary, memory forms much of the basis for self-identity. Without memories, we would not be ourselves. When we remember, it is like a personal recollection of an event and can be facilitated with partial information that helps to retrieve the memory. On the other hand, we can know things without remembering how or where we encoded the memory. Determining the origin and source of memories is critically important for self-identity and failures of such metamemory can lead to the creation of distorted or false memories. Sometimes, false memories arise because we are suggestible to misleading information from external sources. Persistence refers to memories that cannot be easily forgotten and are associated with traumatic events.

Memory failures: Schacter's seven sins of memory

We've seen in other contexts how an understanding of mindbugs – those foibles and errors of human thought and action – can reveal the normal operation of various behaviours. In this final section, we bring together all the work on memory failures and distortions in a framework that not only helps to make sense of the field, but also provides a good way of remembering memory mindbugs, as the 'seven sins' of memory. These 'sins' are:

1. *transience* – forgetting over time
2. *absentmindedness* – lapses in attention that result in forgetting
3. *blocking* – temporary inability to retrieve information
4. *memory misattribution* – confusing the source of a memory
5. *suggestibility* – incorporating misleading information into a memory
6. *bias* – the influence of present knowledge, beliefs and feelings on recollections of the past
7. *persistence* – recalling unwanted memories we would prefer to forget.

Some sins (transience, blocking, persistence and absentmindedness) are classified as forgetting errors, whereas others (misattribution, suggestibility and bias) represent distortions, as shown in **TABLE 5.3** (Schacter, 1999, 2001a).

TABLE 5.3 Seven sins of memory

Error	Type	Description	Example
Transience	Forgetting	Reduced memory over time	Forgetting the plot to a book
Blocking	Forgetting	Inability to remember needed information	Forgetting someone's name
Absentmindedness	Forgetting	Reduced memory due to failing to pay attention	Leaving your umbrella on a train
Misattribution	Distortion	Assigning memory to the wrong source	Thinking that Jane told you a rumour when in fact it was Sarah
Suggestibility	Distortion	Altering a memory because of misleading information	Developing a false memory such as remembering someone leaping over a barrier after reading newspaper reports
Bias	Distortion	Influence of current knowledge on our memory for past events	Thinking that you knew the answer to a question after being told
Persistence	Forgetting	The resurgence of unwanted or disturbing memories that we would like to forget	Ruminating over an argument where you said something hurtful to someone you care about

You may have concluded that evolution burdened us with an extremely inefficient memory system, which is so prone to error that it often jeopardizes our wellbeing. Not so. The seven sins are the price we pay for the many benefits that memory provides (Schacter, 2001a). These mindbugs are the occasional result of the normally efficient operation of the human memory system.

Consider the seemingly annoying nature of transience, for example. Wouldn't it be great to remember all the details of every incident in your life, no matter how much time had passed? Not necessarily. It is helpful and sometimes important to forget information that isn't current, like an old phone number. If we didn't gradually forget information over time, our minds would be cluttered with details we no longer needed (Bjork and Bjork, 1988). Information that is used infrequently is less likely to be needed in the future than information that is used more frequently over the same period (Anderson and Schooler, 1991, 2000). Memory, in essence, makes a bet that when we haven't used information recently, we probably won't need it in the future. We win this bet more often than we lose it, making transience an adaptive property of memory. But we are acutely aware of the losses – the frustrations of forgetting – and are never aware of the wins. That's why people are often quick to complain about their memories: the drawbacks of forgetting are painfully evident, but the benefits of forgetting are hidden.

Similarly, although blocking is such a frustrating experience that we are often tempted to bite the tips of our tongues clean off, it has adaptive features (Bjork and Bjork, 1988). As with transience, people generally block information that has not been used recently because the odds are that such information will not be needed in the future. In general, blocking helps the memory system to run smoothly and efficiently but occasionally causes embarrassing incidents of retrieval failure.

Absentmindedness can also be irritating, but we would be even more irritated without it. Absentminded errors happen in part because events that receive little attention and elaboration when they occur are difficult to recall later. But if all events were registered in elaborate detail, our minds would be cluttered with useless information. This is just what happened in the unusual case of journalist Solomon Shereshevskii (Luria, 1968). He formed and retained highly detailed memories of almost everything that happened to him, important or not. Because Shereshevskii's mind was always populated with trivia, he was unable to generalize or function at an abstract level. The struggle to forget plagued him throughout his life, and he used elaborate rituals to try to rid himself of the mass of information competing for space in his mind. The details of past experiences that left Shereshevskii overwhelmed by information are best denied entry to memory in the first place.

Memory misattribution and suggestibility both occur because we often fail to recall the details of exactly when and where we saw a face or learned a fact. This is because memory is adapted to retain information that is most likely to be needed in the environment in which it operates. As Shereshevskii's experience illustrates, we seldom need to remember all the precise contextual details of every experience. Our memories carefully record such details only when we think they may be needed later, and most of the time we are better off for it. We pay the price, however, when we are required to recollect specific information about an experience that did not elicit any special effort to encode details about its source.

Bias is also a problem, skewing our memories so that we depict ourselves in an overly favourable light. This mindbug may seem self-serving and unduly optimistic, but it can produce the benefit of contributing to our overall sense of contentment. Holding positive illusions about ourselves can lead to greater psychological wellbeing (Taylor, 1989).

Finally, persistence has both a dark and light side. Although it can cause us to be haunted by traumas that we'd be better off forgetting, overall, it is probably adaptive to remember threatening or traumatic events that could pose a threat to survival. If you could conveniently forget being burned on a hot stove, you might fail to avoid stoves in the future.

In summary, memory's mindbugs can be classified into seven 'sins'. Although each of the seven sins can cause trouble in our lives, they have an adaptive side as well. You can think of the seven sins as costs we pay for benefits that allow memory to work as well as it does most of the time.

psychomythology

Memory myths

Rather than focusing on just one myth, Dan Simons and Chris Chabris (2011) set out to investigate six of the most common memory myths in a sample of 1,500 demographically representative members of the US public. Prior to their study, only one large-scale study had been conducted on prospective jurors about their beliefs concerning eyewitness testimony (Schmechel et al., 2006), so Simons and Chabris wanted to test the public understanding about memory more generally and compare that to opinions from a panel of 16 memory experts. From the most to least misconceived were the following:

1 *Amnesia:* 82.7% of respondents agreed that 'people suffering from amnesia typically cannot recall their own name or identity' (0% of experts agreed).

2 *Unexpected events:* 77.5% agreed that 'people generally notice when something unexpected enters their field of view, even when they're paying attention to something else' (three experts did not know/unclear; the rest disagreed).
3 *Video memory:* 63.0% agreed that 'human memory works like a video camera, accurately recording the events we see and hear so that we can review and inspect them later' (0% of experts agreed).
4 *Hypnosis:* 55.4% agreed that 'hypnosis is useful in helping witnesses accurately recall details of crimes' (two experts did not know/unclear; the rest disagreed).
5 *Permanent memory:* 47.6% agreed that 'once you have experienced an event and formed a memory of it, that memory does not change' (one expert did not know/unclear; the rest disagreed).
6 *Confident testimony:* 37.1% agreed that 'in my opinion, the testimony of one confident eyewitness should be enough evidence to convict a defendant of a crime' (0% of experts agreed).

Although there were a few minority instances of uncertainty in the experts on three beliefs, there were no instances where they agreed with the public misconception. Therefore, each of these misconceptions runs counter to expert scientific consensus and reflects a fundamental misunderstanding of the way memory works. This discrepancy between science and popular beliefs confirms the danger of relying on intuition or common sense when evaluating claims about psychology and the mind.

where do you stand?

Recovered memories and childhood abuse

Few crimes can be as hideous as child abuse, but what about adults who suddenly develop memories of childhood events that happened many years ago? How accurate are their recollections? This question was at the centre of a controversy that arose during the 1980s and 90s concerning the accuracy of childhood memories that people recall during psychotherapy. Suggestibility played an important role in the controversy. Diana Halbrooks was a happily married woman from Texas who started psychotherapy in the late 1980s. As her treatment progressed, she began recalling disturbing incidents from her childhood, for example that her mother had tried to kill her and her father had abused her sexually. Although her parents denied that these events had ever occurred, her therapist encouraged her to believe in the reality of her memories. Had Halbrooks retrieved terrible memories of events that had actually occurred, or were the memories inaccurate, perhaps the result of suggestive probing during psychotherapy?

In the early 1990s, more and more families found themselves coping with similar stories. Educated middle-class women (and some men) entered psychotherapy for depression or related problems, only to emerge with recovered memories of previously forgotten childhood sexual abuse, typically perpetrated by fathers and sometimes by mothers. Families and psychologists were split by these controversies. Patients believed their memories were real, and many therapists supported those beliefs, but accused parents contended that the alleged abuses had never happened and that they were instead the products of false memories. A number of prominent memory researchers, as well as some therapists, raised doubts about the accuracy of recovered memories, noting that memory is susceptible to suggestion and distortion (Lindsay and Read, 1994; Loftus, 1993). But others questioned whether people would ever falsely recall such a traumatic event as childhood sexual abuse (Freyd, 1996; Herman, 1992).

In 2010, an international group of eminent psychologists and psychiatrists wrote to the Archbishop of Canterbury urging the Church to withdraw support for a self-help book aimed at victims of child sexual abuse, claiming it contained misleading and potentially harmful information about the reliability of childhood memories of sexual abuse. This issue had become prominent following the revelation of extensive paedophilia activity by priests. The authors of the book asserted that: 'If you are unable to remember any specific instances ... but still have a feeling that something abusive happened to you, it probably did' (Bass and Davis, 1988, p. 21). Of greater concern was the opinion of the church advisers who had recommended the book that there was no such thing as false memories – a claim refuted by the international group of experts. In an attempt to address the scandals of child abuse by priests, the Church of England had ignored scientific evidence that false memories were real.

However, several lines of evidence suggest that many recovered memories are inaccurate. First, some people have recovered highly implausible memories of being abused repeatedly during bizarre practices in satanic cults, and yet there is no proof of these practices or even that the cults exist (Pendergrast, 1995; Wright, 1994). Second, a number of the techniques used by psychotherapists to try to pull up forgotten childhood memories are clearly suggestive. A survey of 145 therapists in the US revealed that approximately 1 in 3 tried to help patients remember childhood sexual abuse by using hypnosis or encouraging them to imagine incidents that might or might not have actually happened (Poole et al., 1995). Yet imagining past events and hypnosis can help create false memories (Garry et al., 1996; Hyman and Pentland, 1996; McConkey et al., 1998).

The reports of recovered memories of child abuse in the US directly contributed to a generalized hysteria relating to alleged satanic child abuse on the remote Scottish island of South Ronaldsay, Orkney in 1991, where children were removed from their families and taken into care by social workers, who had been strongly influenced by the recovered abuse 'memories' coming to light in the US. When the case against the abusers came to court, it was dismissed after a single day, the social workers' handling of the situation being judged to be 'fundamentally flawed'. By the end of the 1990s, the number of new cases of disputed recovered memories of childhood sexual abuse had slowed to a trickle (McHugh et al., 2004). This probably occurred, at least in part, because some of the therapists who had been using suggestive procedures stopped doing so (McNally, 2003).

But where do you stand on the need to protect the child from abuse by adults? Child abuse is still a major problem in today's society, as evidenced by recent high-profile deaths. Should we accept the validity of child abuse claims until proven otherwise? Clearly, the possibility for false recovered memories is very real but can we afford to ignore the few reports that are genuine?

Instructions

Please label each of the events listed as a personal 'recollection' or as an event that you 'know' happened but that is not a personal memory. If you neither 'recollect' nor 'know' the event (perhaps because you never experienced it), please label it as 'don't know'. For each event you 'recollect' or 'know', indicate your age at the time the event occurred, as best as you can determine, with the year followed by month (for example, 4.0 is four years old exactly, 4.6 is four and a half years old, 4.9 is four and three-quarters and so on).

Event	Recollect	Know	Age	Don't know
You read your first book with chapters	☐	☐	☐	☐
You went to your first sleepover	☐	☐	☐	☐
You saw your first film in a cinema	☐	☐	☐	☐
You took your first swimming lesson	☐	☐	☐	☐
You joined your first organized sports team	☐	☐	☐	☐
You learned to write in cursive	☐	☐	☐	☐
You stopped taking naps	☐	☐	☐	☐
You learned to spell your name	☐	☐	☐	☐
You went to an amusement park for the first time	☐	☐	☐	☐
You were toilet trained	☐	☐	☐	☐
Your first permanent tooth came in	☐	☐	☐	☐
You learned to ride a bicycle (two wheels, no stabilizers)	☐	☐	☐	☐
You slept in a bed instead of a cot	☐	☐	☐	☐

Multhaup, K. S., Johnson, M. D. and Tetirick, J. C. (2005) The wane of childhood amnesia for autobiographical and public event memories. Memory, 13, 161–73. Items sampled from experiments 1 and 2, p. 172, reprinted by permission of the publisher (Taylor & Francis Ltd, www.tandfonline.com)

Chapter review

The structure of memory

- Memory is not a unitary system but one that is composed of different subsystems. One of the most common models of understanding memory is the three-stage modal model that divides it into sensory memory, short-term memory and long-term memory.
- The major forms of memory storage hold information for different amounts of time: sensory memory (a second or two), short-term or working memory (less than a minute), and long-term memory (minutes, hours, weeks and years).

Remembering

- Memories are not passive recordings of the world but instead result from combining incoming information with previous experiences. Encoding is the process of linking new and old information.
- Elaborative encoding (actively linking incoming information to existing associations and knowledge), visual imagery encoding (converting incoming information into mental pictures) and organizational encoding (noticing relationships among items you want to encode) all benefit memory.
- Different regions within the frontal lobe play important roles in elaborative encoding and organizational encoding, whereas the visual cortex (occipital lobe) appears to be important for visual imagery encoding.
- The nature of stored memories can be broadly divided into explicit memory, involving conscious, intentional retrieval of previous experiences, and implicit memory, which is a nonconscious, unintentional form of memory.
- Priming (an enhanced ability to think of a stimulus as a result of recent exposure to the stimulus) and procedural memory (learning skills from practice) both draw on implicit memory.
- Episodic memory (recollection of specific personal experiences) and semantic memory (general knowledge of the world) involve explicit recall of information.
- Autobiographical memories are personal memories usually associated with significant life events, whereas flashbulb memories are usually vivid recollections associated with unexpected dramatic events.
- The hippocampus puts information into long-term storage so that it can later be consciously remembered. Amnesiac patients with damage to the hippocampal region have little ability to remember their recent experiences.
- Memories are most likely stored in the synapses that connect neurons to one another.
- Recall of past experiences depends critically on retrieval cues, which trigger recall by reinstating what we thought or how we felt during the encoding of an experience.
- Information or experiences we can't recall on our own are sometimes only temporarily inaccessible and can be brought to mind with appropriate retrieval cues.

- Different parts of the brain seem to be activated when we put forth the mental effort to try to call up a past experience and when we actually remember the experience.

Forgetting

- We can forget for a variety of different reasons. Transience refers to the decay of a memory trace over time or because of interference with other memory traces. Blocking occurs when we know we have the memory but are unable to retrieve it.
- Absentmindedness is a failure to remember to do something and is critically dependent on lapses of attention. This may also occur for prospective memory where we forget to perform some action in the future.
- Amnesia can result from permanent or transient brain injury and can produce a loss of previous memory as well as a failure to store new memories.
- Memory loss is commonly found in the ageing population, although it may be more to do with the speed of processing rather than storage failure.

Metamemory

- Our sense of self and identity is critically dependent on being aware and having access to our own memories as well as appreciating the difference between actually remembering or just knowing.
- Metamemory is subject to distortions and biases, which produce false memories that are misperceived as being accurate representations of the past.
- Some individuals suffer from memories associated with some traumatic life event that they cannot forget.

Memory failures: Schacter's seven sins of memory

- One useful framework for considering memory failures is Schacter's 'seven sins of memory'. Each of the seven sins has adaptive features. The sins are the price we pay for benefits in memory that generally serve us well. Understanding these memory mindbugs helps researchers to better understand the normal operations of memory.

Key terms

Recommended reading

Brainerd, C. J. and Reyna, V. F. (2005) *The Science of False Memory*. New York: OUP. Written by two of the leading researchers into the nature of false memories, provides a readable summary of what we know about false memories and how they differ from true memories.

Fernyhough, C. (2013) *Pieces of Light: The New Science of Memory*. London: Profile. Drawing on case studies, personal experience and the latest research, delves into the memories of the very young and very old, and explores how amnesia and trauma can affect how we view the past. Exquisitely written and meticulously researched, it blends science and literature, the ordinary and the extraordinary, to illuminate the way we remember and forget.

Schacter, D. L. (2001) *The Seven Sins of Memory*. Boston: Houghton Mifflin. Provides a more in-depth treatment of memory's seven sins than that provided in this chapter, including many more examples of how the seven sins affect us in everyday life.

Wearing, D. (2005) *Forever Today*. London: Doubleday. Clive Wearing is a gifted musician who also has the dubious distinction of having one of the most severe cases of amnesia ever documented. His memory lasts for about seven seconds, making every experience seem new to him. His wife, Deborah, wrote this book about their relationship and the challenges associated with coping with this kind of brain damage.

6

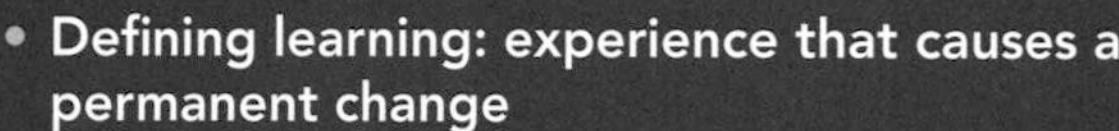

- Defining learning: experience that causes a permanent change
- Classical conditioning: one thing leads to another
- the real world Understanding drug overdoses
- Of mice and men: learning to become fearful hot science
- Operant conditioning: reinforcements from the environment
- Control of learning: from the laboratory to the classroom hot science
- Observational learning: look at me
- Implicit learning: under the wires
- the real world What's the best way to learn?
- You can learn in your sleep psychomythology
- where do you stand? Learning for rewards or for its own sake?

Chapter learning objectives

At the end of this chapter you will be able to:

1 Define learning and discuss how it can take various forms.

2 Distinguish between different mechanisms that increase or decrease behaviour.

3 Understand how shaping works and provide examples.

4 Explain how different schedules of reinforcement produce different patterns of behaviour.

5 Understand the limits of behavioural theories to explaining all human activities.

GETTY IMAGES/ISTOCKPHOTO/THINKSTOCK IMAGES

Learning

On 22 July 2011, Anders Breivik, dressed as a police officer, landed on the tiny Norwegian island of Utøya which was hosting 564 people, mostly youths, attending a political summer camp. On his arrival, he said he was there for security reasons following a car bomb that he had detonated in the capital, Oslo, a few hours earlier. Breivik had planted that bomb but was now on a rampage killing spree. For over 80 minutes, Breivik hunted down and killed 69 individuals, 33 under the age of 18. It was a terrifying atrocity. The youths were isolated on this small island with no possibility of escape other than swimming to the mainland across the cold fjord, with the risk of drowning. Breivik was brutal, often shooting the victims several times, thus leaving many youths having witnessed horrifying sights. Many of the youths knew each other. One particular terrifying feature was that many victims were lured out of their safe hiding places because they thought Breivik, dressed as a policeman, was there to save them. The youths did not know who to trust anymore and it would take extra effort for the eventual rescuers to convince them that they were now safe.

Many of the 495 survivors have been left traumatized by the Norwegian massacre and are suffering from post-traumatic stress disorder (PTSD). One of the symptoms of PTSD is that everyday sights and sounds, such as a door slamming loudly, can set off flashbacks and trigger precisely the same cascade of emotions in the brain as did the original traumatic experience. Some victims have been left constantly vigilant for situations that were associated with the initial trauma. Whenever she finds herself in unfamiliar rooms, Marte Fevang Smith, an 18-year-old from Tønsberg, says she's always looking for an escape route. She can't imagine getting on a crowded bus because it's 'a situation I absolutely can't control'. One day after she had mustered the strength to return to school, she was attending a birthday party when a balloon popped, which sent her fleeing out of the room as it reminded her of gunshot. Others have tried to unlearn

This photo shows Anders Breivik sitting handcuffed, moments after his arrest, still dressed in the police uniform that lured victims out of their hiding places and into danger.

associations formed during the massacre. Caroline Winge, a 19-year-old from Trondheim, asked to visit a police shooting range so she could get used to the sound of gunfire and being around police officers. The Norwegian massacre had left many of its victims with a legacy of learned association that they needed to lose.

The Norwegian government funds a unique mass programme of therapy for all connected with the Utøya massacre, including survivors, family members, members of the rescue services and countless volunteers who helped. Part of this therapy includes return trips to the island, which are intended to help individuals reconcile their memories of the atrocity and learn more positive associations to replace them by the shared experience. In other words, to learn to let go. In this chapter, we'll consider this type of associative learning as well as other ways that knowledge is acquired and stored.

Defining learning: experience that causes a permanent change

LEARNING A relatively permanent change in the state of the learner due to experience.

Learning is shorthand for a collection of different techniques, procedures and outcomes that produce changes in an organism's behaviour. Learning psychologists have identified and studied as many as 40 different kinds of learning. However, there is a basic principle at the core of all of them: learning involves *some experience that results in a relatively permanent change in the state of the learner.* This definition emphasizes several key ideas: learning is based on experience; learning produces changes in the organism; and these changes can be relatively permanent. Think of the balloon popping that terrified Marte; the association she learned could last for years.

Learning can also be conscious and deliberate or unconscious. For example, memorizing the names of all the capital cities in the world is a conscious and deliberate activity, with an explicit awareness of the learning process as it is taking place. In comparison, the kind of learning that associated the sound of a balloon popping with images of horror is much more implicit. Some other forms of learning start out explicitly but become more implicit over time. When you first learned to drive a car, for example, you probably devoted a lot of attention to the many movements and sequences that needed to be carried out simultaneously ('step lightly on the accelerator while you flick the indicator and look in the rear-view mirror while you turn the steering wheel'). That complex interplay of motions is now probably quite effortless and automatic for you. Explicit learning has become implicit over time.

These distinctions in learning might remind you of similar distinctions in memory, and for good reason. In Chapter 5, you read about the differences between implicit and explicit memories as well as procedural, semantic and episodic memories. Do different forms of learning mirror different types of memory? It's not that simple, but it is true that learning and memory are inextricably linked. Learning produces memories, and conversely, the existence of memories implies that knowledge was acquired, that experience was registered and recorded in the brain, or that learning has taken place.

The case of habituation

Let's consider some of the simplest forms of learning. If you've ever lived under the flight path of an airport, near railway tracks or by a busy motorway, you probably noticed the deafening roar as a Boeing 737 made its way towards the landing strip, the clatter of a train speeding down the track or the sound of traffic when you first moved in. You probably also noticed that after a while, the roar wasn't quite so deafening anymore and that eventually you ignored the sounds of the planes, trains or cars in your vicinity.

HABITUATION A general process in which repeated or prolonged exposure to a stimulus results in a gradual reduction in responding.

Habituation is *a general process in which repeated or prolonged exposure to a stimulus results in a gradual reduction in responding.* For example, imagine you are enjoying a leisurely walk in the countryside when suddenly you hear the sound of a shotgun nearby. This will produce a startle response: you'll stop, your eyes will widen, your muscles will tense, and your body will experience an increase in sweating, blood pressure and alertness. If you hear another gunshot moments later, you may show another startle response, but it will be less dramatic and subside more quickly. If a third shot should occur, you will likely not respond at all. You will have become *habituated* to the sound of the gunshot.

Habituation is a simple form of learning. An experience results in a change in the state of the learner: in the preceding example, you begin by reacting one way to a stimulus and, with experience, your reactions change. However, this kind of change usually isn't permanent. In most cases of habituation, a person will exhibit the original reaction if enough time has gone by. To continue our example, if you hear a gunshot a week later, you will almost certainly have a full-blown startle response again.

A simple experiment explored the question of just how robust habituation to a loud sound could be (Leaton, 1976). One group of rats was exposed to several hundred loud tones within a five-minute span. Another group was exposed to one loud tone each day over an 11-day period. The researchers found that the two groups reacted quite differently. The rats in the first group showed the expected startle response at first, but it quickly gave way to a rather indifferent attitude towards the tones. However, this reaction didn't last. When the tone was presented 24 hours later, the rats showed a full-blown startle response. The rats in the other group, however, showed a slow, continuous decline in the startle response over the entire 11 days of the experiment. The second outcome reflects the basic principle underlying most types of learning – that change in behaviour has some permanence to it.

DIGITAL VISION

Living near a busy train line can be unpleasant. Most people who live near major train lines become habituated to the sound of trains going past.

Learning and behaviourism

As you'll recall from Chapter 1, a sizable chunk of psychology's history was devoted to a single dominant viewpoint. Behaviourism, with its insistence on measuring only observable, quantifiable behaviour and its dismissal of mental activity as unobservable, was the major outlook of most psychologists working from the 1930s to the 1950s. This was also the period during which much fundamental work on learning theory took place.

You might find the intersection of behaviourism and learning theory a bit surprising. After all, at one level, learning seems abstract: something intangible happens to you, and you think or behave differently thereafter. It seems that you'd need to explain that transformation in terms of a change in mental outlook, the development of a new way of thinking, or any of several other phrases that evoke mental processes that behaviourists do not employ in trying to explain behaviour. In fact, most behaviourists argued that the 'permanent change in experience' that resulted from learning could be demonstrated equally well in almost any organism: rats, dogs, pigeons, mice, pigs or humans. From this perspective, behaviourists viewed learning as a purely behavioural, eminently observable activity. Insofar as learning involves conscious mental processes, behaviourists argued that these mental processes cannot be observed reliably, and thus cannot help us to understand behaviour.

As you'll see shortly, in many ways the behaviourists were right. Much of what we know about how organisms learn comes directly from the behaviourists' observations of behaviours. However, the behaviourists also overstated their case. There are some important cognitive considerations, that is, elements of mental activity, that need to be addressed in order to understand the learning process.

Classical conditioning: one thing leads to another

You'll recall from Chapter 1 that John B. Watson kick-started the behaviourist movement, arguing that psychologists should 'never use the terms *consciousness, mental states, mind, content, introspectively verifiable, imagery*, and the like' (Watson, 1913, p. 166). Watson's firebrand stance was fuelled in large part by the work of Russian physiologist Ivan Pavlov.

Pavlov was awarded the Nobel Prize in Physiology in 1904 for his work on the salivation of dogs. Pavlov studied the digestive processes of laboratory animals by surgically implanting test tubes into the cheeks of dogs to measure their salivary responses to different kinds of foods. Serendipitously, however, his explorations into spit and drool revealed the mechanics of one form of learning, which came to be called classical conditioning. **Classical conditioning** occurs *when a stimulus evokes a response because of being paired with a stimulus that naturally evokes a response.* In his classic experiments, Pavlov showed that dogs learned to salivate to neutral stimuli such as a bell or a tone after that stimulus had been associated with another stimulus that naturally evokes salivation, such as food.

CLASSICAL CONDITIONING When a stimulus evokes a response because of being paired with a stimulus that naturally evokes a response.

Pavlov's experiments on classical conditioning

Pavlov's basic experimental setup involved cradling dogs in a harness to administer the foods and measure the salivary response, as shown in **FIGURE 6.1**. He noticed that dogs that previously had been in the experiment began to produce a kind of 'anticipatory' salivary response as soon as they were put in the harness, before any food was presented. Pavlov and his colleagues regarded these responses as annoyances at first because they interfered with collecting naturally occurring salivary secretions. In reality, the dogs were behaving in line with the four basic elements of classical conditioning.

FIGURE 6.1 Pavlov's apparatus for studying classical conditioning Pavlov presented auditory stimuli to the animals using a buzzer. Visual stimuli could be presented on the screen. The inset shows a close-up of the tube inserted in the dog's salivary gland for collecting saliva.

When the dogs were initially presented with a plate of food, they began to salivate. No surprise here – placing food in front of most animals will launch the salivary process. Pavlov called the presentation of food an **unconditioned stimulus (US)** – *something that reliably produces a naturally occurring reaction in an organism.* He called the dogs' salivation an **unconditioned response (UR)** – *a reflexive reaction that is reliably elicited by an unconditioned stimulus.* The whole thing is quite natural and sensible: food makes animals salivate.

UNCONDITIONED STIMULUS (US) Something that reliably produces a naturally occurring reaction in an organism.

UNCONDITIONED RESPONSE (UR) A reflexive reaction that is reliably elicited by an unconditioned stimulus.

Pavlov soon discovered that he could make the dogs salivate to stimuli that don't usually make animals salivate, such as the sound of a buzzer. In various experiments, Pavlov paired the presentation of food with the sound of a buzzer, the ticking of a metronome, the humming of a tuning fork or the flash of a light (Pavlov, 1927). Sure enough, he found that the dogs salivated to the sound of a buzzer, the ticking of a metronome, the humming of a tuning fork or the flash of a light, each of which had become a **conditioned stimulus (CS)** – *a stimulus that at first does not produce the response that is eventually conditioned; its capacity to do so depends (is conditional) on pairing with the unconditioned stimulus* (see **FIGURE 6.2**). When dogs hear the sound of a buzzer in the wild, they're not known to salivate: there's nothing natural or predictable about the sound of a buzzer producing a particular kind of behaviour in a dog.

CONDITIONED STIMULUS (CS) A stimulus that at first does not produce the response that is eventually conditioned by pairing with an unconditioned stimulus.

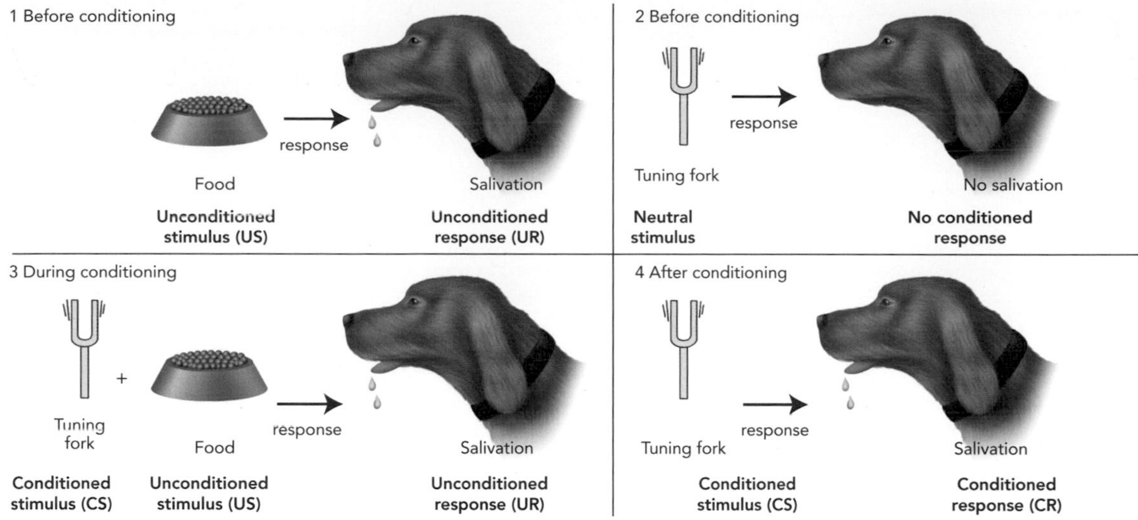

FIGURE **6.2 The elements of classical conditioning** In classical conditioning, a previously neutral stimulus (such as the sound of a buzzer or bell) is paired with an unconditioned stimulus (such as the presentation of food). After several trials associating the two, the conditioned stimulus (the sound) alone can produce a conditioned response.

However, when the conditioned stimulus (CS), in this case the sound of a buzzer, is paired over time with the unconditioned stimulus (US), or the food, the animal will learn to associate food with the sound and eventually the CS is sufficient to produce a response, or salivation. Pavlov called this a conditioned response (CR) – *a response produced by a conditioned stimulus because of its association with an unconditioned stimulus*. The conditioned response is usually similar to the unconditioned response. In this example, the dogs' salivation (CR) was eventually prompted by the sound of the buzzer (CS) alone because the sound of the buzzer and the food (US) had been associated so often in the past.

CONDITIONED RESPONSE (CR) A reaction to a conditioned stimulus produced by pairing it with an unconditioned stimulus.

Conditioned and unconditioned responses are usually similar – in our example, the dog salivates to both buzzer and food – but this is not always the case. If a rat receives an electric shock to its paws, for example, its unconditioned response will be to jump and run. If the shock is always preceded by a buzzer, however, then eventually the rat will begin to freeze as soon as it hears the buzzer. The conditioned response of freezing is clearly very different from the unconditioned response of running, but both can be understood as attempts to cope with danger. If you're a rat and suddenly experience intense pain in your paw, it makes sense to run in order to escape from a dangerous situation. If you have a warning that danger is imminent, however – perhaps you've heard a predator approaching – then your chances of survival are better if you freeze, as freezing reduces the chances of detection. So, while conditioned and unconditioned responses are usually similar, we also need to recognize that they sometimes differ. As we will see later, evolution has honed conditioning so as to select conditioned responses that will be most effective in helping us to prepare for an imminent unconditioned stimulus.

The basic principles of classical conditioning

When Pavlov's findings first appeared in the scientific and popular literature (Pavlov, 1923a, 1923b), they produced a flurry of excitement because psychologists now had demonstrable evidence of how conditioning produced learned behaviours. This was the kind of behaviourist psychology John B. Watson was proposing: an organism experiences events or stimuli that are observable and measurable, and changes in that organism can be directly observed and measured. Dogs learned to salivate to the sound of a buzzer, and there was no need to resort to explanations about why it had happened, what the dog wanted, or how the animal thought about the situation. In other words, there was no need to consider the mind in this classical conditioning paradigm, which appealed to Watson and the behaviourists. Pavlov also appreciated the significance of his discovery and embarked on a systematic investigation of the mechanisms of classical conditioning. Let's take a closer look at some of these principles. (As *the real world* box shows, these principles help explain how drug overdoses occur.)

the real world

Understanding drug overdoses

All too often, police are confronted with a perplexing problem: the sudden death of addicts from a drug overdose. These deaths are puzzling for at least three reasons. The victims are often experienced drug users, the dose taken is usually not larger than what they usually take, and the deaths tend to occur in unusual settings. Experienced drug users are just that: experienced! You'd think that if a heroin addict or crack cocaine user were ingesting a typical amount of a substance they'd used many times before, the chances of an overdose would be *lower* than usual.

Classical conditioning provides some insight into how these deaths occur. First, when classical conditioning takes place, the conditioned stimulus (CS) is more than a simple tone: it also includes the overall *context* within which the conditioning takes place. Indeed, Pavlov's dogs often began to salivate even as they approached the experimental apparatus. Second, many conditioned responses (CRs) are compensatory reactions to the unconditioned stimulus (US). In some of Pavlov's early experiments, he used a very mild acid solution as the US because it produces large amounts of saliva that dilute the acid in the dog's mouth. When that salivary response is eventually conditioned to the sound of a tone, in a way it represents the remnants of the body's natural reaction to the presentation of the US.

These two finer points of classical conditioning help explain what happens when someone takes a drug such as heroin (Siegel, 1984). When the drug is injected, the entire setting (the drug paraphernalia, the room, the lighting, the addict's usual companions) functions as the CS, and the addict's brain reacts to the heroin by secreting neurotransmitters that counteract its effects. Over time, this protective physiological response becomes part of the CR, and like all CRs, it occurs in the presence of the CS but prior to the actual administration of the drug. These compensatory physiological reactions are also what make drug abusers take increasingly larger doses to achieve the same effect; ultimately, these reactions produce *drug tolerance* – a form of physiological habituation discussed above.

Based on these principles of classical conditioning, taking drugs in a new environment can be fatal for a longtime drug user. If an addict injects the usual dose in a setting that is sufficiently novel or where heroin has never been taken before, the CS is now altered. What's more, the physiological compensatory CR either does not occur or is substantially decreased. As a result, the addict's usual dose becomes an overdose and death often results. This effect has also been shown experimentally: rats that have had extensive experience with morphine in one setting were much more likely to survive dose increases in that same setting than in a novel one (Siegel, 1976).

In this way, the basic principles of classical conditioning help to explain this real-world tragedy of drug overdose. Intuitively, addicts may stick with the crack houses, opium dens or 'shooting galleries' with which they're familiar for this very reason. Although drug dens and crack houses may be considered a blight, it is often safer for addicts to use drugs there. The environment becomes part of the addict's CS, so, ironically, busting crack houses may contribute to more deaths from drug overdose when addicts are pushed to use drugs in new situations.

A drug den/crack house.

Acquisition

ACQUISITION The phase of classical conditioning when the CS and the US are presented together.

If you have a dog, cast your mind back to when you first got it. Chances are it didn't seem too smart, especially the way it stared at you vacantly as you went into the kitchen, not anticipating that food was on the way. That's because learning through classical conditioning requires some period of association between the CS and US. This period is called acquisition – *the phase of classical conditioning when the CS and the US are presented together*. During the initial phase of classical conditioning, typically there is a gradual increase in learning: it starts low, rises rapidly and then slowly tapers off, as shown on the left side of **FIGURE 6.3**. Pavlov's dogs gradually increased their amount of salivation over several trials of pairing a tone with the presentation of food, and similarly, your dog eventually learned to associate your kitchen preparations with the subsequent appearance of food. After learning has been established, the CS by itself will reliably elicit the CR.

Second-order conditioning

SECOND-ORDER CONDITIONING Conditioning where the US is a stimulus that acquired its ability to produce learning from an earlier procedure in which it was used as a CS.

After conditioning has been established, a phenomenon called second-order conditioning can be demonstrated – *conditioning where the US is a stimulus that acquired its ability to produce learning from an earlier procedure in which it was used as a CS*. For example, in an early study, Pavlov repeatedly paired a new CS, a black square, with the now-reliable tone. After a number of training trials, his dogs produced a salivary response to the black

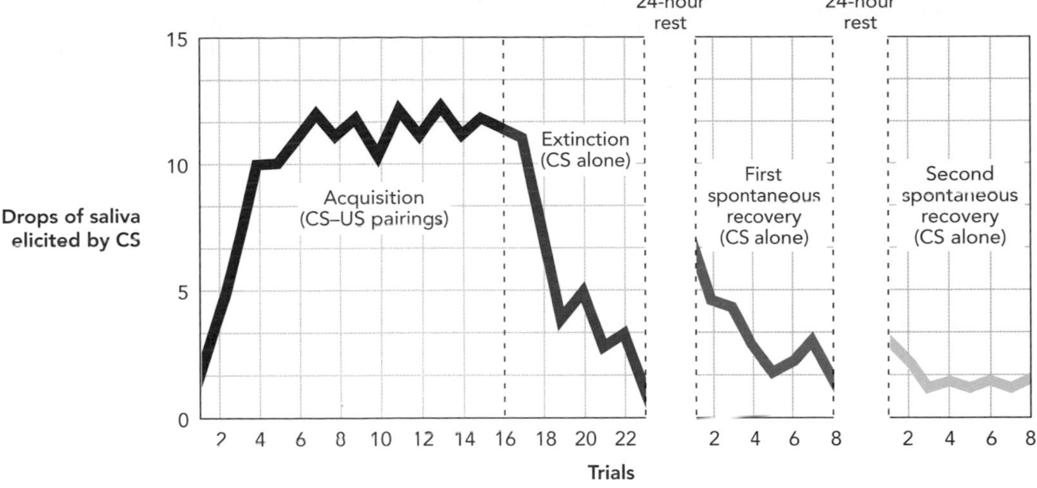

FIGURE 6.3 Acquisition, extinction and spontaneous recovery In classical conditioning, the CS is originally neutral and produces no specific response. After several trials pairing the CS with the US, the CS alone comes to elicit the salivary response (the CR). Learning tends to take place fairly rapidly and then levels off as stable responding develops. In extinction, the CR diminishes quickly until it no longer occurs. A rest period, however, is typically followed by spontaneous recovery of the CR. In fact, a well-learned CR may show spontaneous recovery after more than one rest period even though there have been no additional learning trials.

square even though the square itself had never been directly associated with the food. You could do the same thing with your own dog. After she has learned the association between your kitchen noises and the presentation of food, you might try humming a particular tune each time you walk into the kitchen for any reason. After a while, you should find that humming the tune by itself causes your dog to drool.

Psychologists quickly appreciated the applications of second-order conditioning to daily life. For example, it can help explain why some people desire money to the point that they hoard it and value it even more than the objects it can be used to purchase. Money is initially used to purchase objects that produce gratifying outcomes, such as expensive cars or flat-screen TVs. Although money is not directly associated with the thrill of a high-speed drive in a new sports car or the amazing clarity of a high-definition TV, through second-order conditioning, money can become linked with these desirable qualities.

Extinction

After Pavlov and his colleagues had explored the process of acquisition extensively, they turned to the next logical question: What would happen if they continued to present the CS (tone) but stopped presenting the US (food)? Repeatedly presenting the CS without the US produces exactly the result you might imagine. As shown on the right side of the first panel in Figure 6.3, behaviour declines abruptly and continues to drop until eventually the dog ceases to salivate to the sound of the tone. This process is called extinction – *the gradual elimination of a learned response that occurs when the CS is no longer followed by the US.* The term was introduced because the conditioned response is 'extinguished' and no longer observed. If you make noises in the kitchen without subsequently presenting a meaty plate of dog food, eventually your dog will stop salivating or even getting aroused every time you walk into the kitchen.

EXTINCTION The gradual elimination of a learned response that occurs when the CS is no longer followed by the US.

Spontaneous recovery

Having established that he could produce learning through conditioning and then extinguish it, Pavlov wondered if this elimination of conditioned behaviour was permanent. Is a single session of extinction sufficient to knock out the CR completely, or is there some residual change in the dog's behaviour so that the CR might reappear?

To explore this question, Pavlov extinguished the classically conditioned salivation response and then allowed the dogs to have a short rest period. When they were brought back to the lab and presented with the CS again, they displayed spontaneous recovery – *the tendency of a learned behaviour to recover from extinction after a rest period.* This phenomenon is shown in the middle panel in Figure 6.3. Notice that this recovery takes place even though there have not been any additional associations between the CS and US. Some spontaneous recovery of the conditioned response even takes place in what is essentially a second extinction session after another period of rest (see the right-hand

SPONTANEOUS RECOVERY The tendency of a learned behaviour to recover from extinction after a rest period.

panel in Figure 6.3). Clearly, extinction had not completely wiped out the learning that had been acquired. The ability of the CS to elicit the CR was weakened, but it was not eliminated.

The discovery that responses spontaneously recover following extinction is interesting in itself, but it also raised potentially awkward questions about the nature of extinction. The simplest way to explain extinction is to assume that when a CS is presented on its own, without the US following, the association between them is weakened. Each new extinction trial would produce a further weakening, until the connection eventually disappears. But if the connection between the CS and the US is abolished, how is it possible for the CS to again produce a response when it is presented 24 hours later? The fact that the CS still produces a response is compelling evidence that some sort of connection between the CS and the US still exists. But that poses a new problem. If the CS–US association is intact, why did the dog stop salivating during the previous extinction session?

EXCITATORY ASSOCIATION A process that increases the likelihood of a response.

INHIBITORY ASSOCIATION A process that decreases the likelihood of a response.

To explain this, Pavlov proposed that learning involves two fundamentally different kinds of association, **excitatory association**, *a process that increases the likelihood of a response*, and **inhibitory association**, *a process that decreases the likelihood of a response*. His analysis started with the assumption that every stimulus activates its own, unique area or set of neurons within the brain, which he called a 'centre'. When a buzzer is sounded, for example, one brain centre will be activated; when food is presented, a different centre will be activated. These centres can be thought of as cortical representations of the stimulus; whenever a certain stimulus is presented, it will always activate the same cortical representation.

Up to this point, Pavlov's analysis was consistent with what was then known about how the brain worked, but he now added a new, critically important assumption. *Whenever activity in one centre of the brain is closely followed by activity in another*, he said, *the neural connection between the two centres will be strengthened*. In our buzzer example, the fact that the buzzer is followed by food would mean that activity in the buzzer centre would be followed by activity in the food centre, and thus the neural connection between them would be strengthened. The next time the buzzer was presented, therefore, activity in the buzzer centre would spread to the food centre. Moreover, Pavlov's research on digestion had convinced him that there is an innate connection between the food centre and the salivary glands, so that activity in the food centre automatically triggers salivation. Putting all this together, Pavlov proposed that presentation of the buzzer would activate the buzzer centre, which would activate the food centre, which, finally, would activate the salivary glands. In other words, when the dog heard the buzzer, it should begin to salivate, which, of course, is exactly what Pavlov had observed.

What, then, of extinction? Why does presenting the CS on its own lead to a weakening of the previously learned response? The answer, according to Pavlov, was not that the CS–US association was weakened; he believed that once this association was formed, it would remain intact. However, during extinction, a *new* connection would be formed, an *inhibitory* connection where activity in the first centre led to a *reduction* in activity in the second centre. In our salivary conditioning example, presentation of the buzzer on its own during extinction would result in the formation of a new, inhibitory connection between the buzzer and food centres. The next time the buzzer was presented, activity would still be transmitted to the food centre via the excitatory connection, leading to a tendency to salivate. However, an electrical signal would also be sent via the new inhibitory connection, and this would act to reduce or inhibit activity in the food centre. As a result, there would be less salivation on this trial. As extinction trials continued, the inhibitory connection would become progressively stronger, until eventually its strength would match that of the excitatory connection, and the two impulses would effectively cancel each other out. At this point, the dog would no longer salivate when it heard the buzzer, and extinction would be complete.

By assuming the existence of excitatory and inhibitory connections in the brain, Pavlov was able to account for conditioning and extinction. Why, though, does responding spontaneously recover after extinction is complete? If the excitatory and inhibitory connections are equally strong at the completion of extinction, why should the mere passage of time result in the reappearance of salivation? Pavlov's explanation was that the inhibitory connection is more fragile, and thus more easily disrupted by the passage of time.

Subsequent research has not supported this part of his analysis, and learning theorists have proposed other explanations for spontaneous recovery (see, for example, Bouton, 2002). The assumptions at the heart of Pavlov's account, however – the existence of excitatory and inhibitory processes that oppose each other – have been repeatedly confirmed.

Generalization

Imagine you've been struggling with a useless tin-opener for years, and eventually you decide to buy a new one. Let's say the new one makes a slightly different sound. Did you consider your dog at any point in this decision making? After all, Fido had associated the sound of the old tin-opener with the onset of food, and now you've gone and changed things. Do you think your dog will be stumped, unable to anticipate the presentation of her food? Will a whole new round of conditioning need to be established with this modified CS?

Probably not. It wouldn't be very adaptive for an organism if each little change in the CS–US pairing required an extensive regimen of new learning. Rather, the phenomenon of **generalization** tends to take place, in which there is *an increase in responding to a stimulus because of its similarity to a CS that was paired with a US.* As this definition implies, the less the new stimulus resembles the CS, the less conditioned responding is observed. If you replaced the tin-opener with an electric tin-opener, your dog would probably show a much weaker conditioned response (Pearce, 1987; Rescorla, 2006).

GENERALIZATION An increase in responding to a stimulus because of its similarity to a CS that was paired with a US.

As an illustrative case, consider a hypothetical generalization study where a 1,000-hertz (Hz) tone is the CS during the acquisition phase. The test stimuli are tones of higher or lower pitches. As you might expect, an animal gives the maximum response to the original stimulus of 1,000 Hz, with a systematic drop-off as the pitch of the replacement stimulus is farther away from the original tone of 1,000 Hz, regardless of whether the tone was higher or lower. Interestingly, when the stimulus is one of the octaves of the original stimulus (octaves in music are tones that are direct multiples of each other), either 500 Hz or 2,000 Hz, there is a slight increase in responding. In these cases, the rate of responding is lower than that of the original CS but higher than it is in other cases of dissimilar tones. The animals clearly show that they detect octaves just like we do, and in this case, responding has generalized to those octaves (see **FIGURE 6.4**).

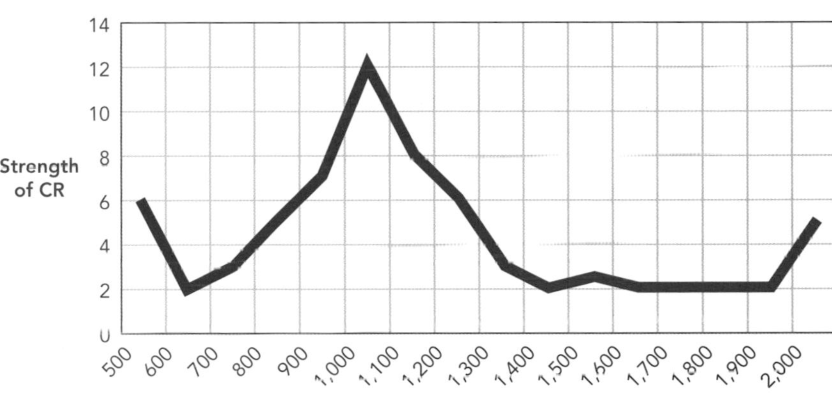

FIGURE **6.4 Stimulus generalization** In this experiment, an animal was conditioned using a 1,000-Hz tone (the CS) and tested with a variety of tones of higher and lower pitches. As the pitches move further away from the original CS, the strength of the CR drops off systematically. However, when the tone is an octave of the original, either 500 or 2,000 Hz, there is an increase in the CR.

Discrimination

When a response generalizes to a new stimulus, two things are happening. First, by responding to the new stimulus used during generalization testing, the organism demonstrates that it recognizes the similarity between the original CS and the new stimulus. Second, by displaying *diminished* responding to that new stimulus, it also tells us that it notices a difference between the two stimuli. In the second case, the organism shows **discrimination** – *the capacity to distinguish between similar but distinct stimuli.* Conceptually, generalization and discrimination are two sides of the same coin. The more organisms show one, the less they show the other, and training can modify the balance between the two.

DISCRIMINATION The capacity to distinguish between similar but distinct stimuli.

Conditioned emotional responses: the case of Little Albert

Before you conclude that classical conditioning is merely a sophisticated way to train your dog, let's revisit the larger principles of Pavlov's work. Classical conditioning demonstrates that durable, substantial changes in behaviour can be achieved simply by setting up the proper conditions. By skilfully associating a naturally occurring US with an appropriate CS, an organism can learn to perform a variety of behaviours, often after relatively few acquisition trials. There is no reference to an organism's *wanting* to learn the behaviour, *willingness* to do it, *thinking* about the situation, or *reasoning* through the available options. We don't need to consider internal and cognitive explanations to demonstrate the effects of classical conditioning: the stimuli, the eliciting circumstances and the resulting behaviour are there to be observed by one and all.

It was this kind of simplicity that appealed to behaviourists such as John B. Watson. His rallying cry for a behaviourist psychology was based, in large part, on his dissatisfaction with what he saw as mysterious, philosophical and unverifiable internal explanations for behaviour that were being offered by Wundt, Freud and others during the early days of psychology (see Chapter 1). In fact, Watson thought that it was possible to develop general explanations of pretty much *any* behaviour of *any* organism based on classical conditioning principles.

As a step in that direction, Watson embarked on a controversial study with his research assistant Rosalie Rayner (Watson and Rayner, 1920). To support his contention that even complex behaviours were the result of conditioning, Watson enlisted the assistance of nine-month-old 'Little Albert'. Albert was a healthy, well-developed child, and, by Watson's assessment, 'stolid and unemotional' (Watson and Rayner, 1920, p. 1). Watson wanted to see if such a child could be classically conditioned to experience a strong emotional reaction – namely fear.

John Watson and Rosalie Raynor show Little Albert an unusual bunny mask. Why doesn't the mere presence of these experimenters serve as a conditioned stimulus in itself?

Watson presented Little Albert with a variety of stimuli: a white rat, a dog, a rabbit, various masks and a burning newspaper. Albert's reactions in most cases were curiosity or indifference, and he showed no fear of any of the items. Watson also established that something *could* make him afraid. While Albert was watching Rayner, Watson unexpectedly struck a large steel bar with a hammer, producing a loud noise. Predictably, this caused Albert to cry, tremble and be generally displeased.

Watson and Rayner then led Little Albert through the acquisition phase of classical conditioning. Albert was presented with a white rat. As soon as he reached out to touch it, the steel bar was struck. This pairing occurred again and again over several trials. Eventually, the sight of the rat alone caused Albert to recoil in terror, crying and clamouring to get away from it. In this situation, a US (the loud sound) was paired with a CS (the presence of the rat) such that the CS by itself was sufficient to produce the CR (a fearful reaction). Little Albert also showed stimulus generalization. The sight of a white rabbit, a seal fur coat and a Santa Claus mask produced the same kinds of fear reactions in the infant.

What was Watson's goal in all this?

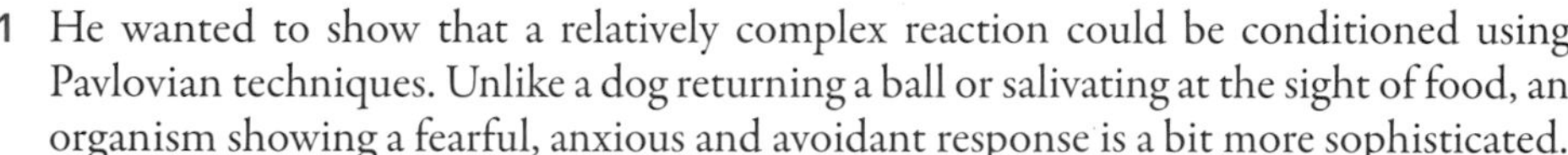

1. He wanted to show that a relatively complex reaction could be conditioned using Pavlovian techniques. Unlike a dog returning a ball or salivating at the sight of food, an organism showing a fearful, anxious and avoidant response is a bit more sophisticated.
2. He wanted to show that emotional responses such as fear and anxiety could be produced by classical conditioning and therefore need not be the product of deeper unconscious processes or early life experiences, as Freud and his followers had argued (see Chapter 1). Instead, Watson proposed that fears could be learned, just like any other behaviour.
3. Watson wanted to confirm that conditioning could be applied to humans as well as to other animals. Work with dogs, rats, birds and other species had shown the utility of classical conditioning as a form of learning, but an application to humans demonstrated the universality of the principles. This bolstered Watson's view that psychology was the study of behaviour and that it didn't matter if that behaviour was enacted by a dog, a rat or a little boy.

This study was controversial in its cavalier treatment of a young child, especially given that Watson and Rayner did not follow up with Albert or his mother during the ensuing years (Harris, 1979). Like many classic studies, a number of the claims about the Little Albert study have become distorted in the retelling, even in academic textbooks (Jarrett,

2008). For example, authors have invented stimuli that Albert was never tested on, including a cat, a man's beard, a white furry glove, his aunt, a teddy bear, as well as the oft-cited claim that he became fearful of all 'furry animals'. In general, it is the claims for widespread generalization of fear conditioning to other stimuli that is the basis for the most serious misrepresentation. Modern ethical guidelines that govern the treatment of research participants ensure that this kind of study could not be conducted today. At the time, however, it was consistent with a behaviourist view of psychology. As Watson (1930, p. 104) summarized his position several years later:

> Give me a dozen healthy infants, well-formed, and my own specified world to bring them up in and I'll guarantee to take any one at random and train him to become any type of specialist I might select – doctor, lawyer, artist, merchant-chief and, yes, even beggar-man and thief, regardless of his talents, penchants, tendencies, abilities, vocations, and race of his ancestors.

In the very next sentence, Watson (1930, p. 104) added: 'I am going beyond my facts and I admit it, but so have the advocates of the contrary and they have been doing it for many thousands of years.' In short, Watson was promoting a staunch view that learning and the environment were responsible for determining behaviour, more so than genetics or personality, as 'advocates to the contrary' might have believed at the time. Watson intended his statements to be extreme in order to shake up the young discipline of psychology and highlight the importance of acquired experiences in shaping behaviour.

A deeper understanding of classical conditioning

As a form of learning, classical conditioning could be reliably produced, it had a simple set of principles, and it had applications to real-life situations. In short, classical conditioning offered a good deal of utility for psychologists who sought to understand the mechanisms underlying learning, and it continues to do so today.

Like a lot of strong starters, though, classical conditioning has been subjected to deeper scrutiny in order to understand exactly how, when and why it works. Let's examine three areas that give us a closer look at the mechanisms of classical conditioning.

The neural elements of classical conditioning

Pavlov saw his research as providing insights into how the brain works. After all, he was trained in medicine, not psychology, and was a bit surprised when psychologists became excited by his findings. Recent research has clarified some of what Pavlov hoped to understand about conditioning and the brain.

The case of Little Albert and the earlier discussion of Anders Brievik's victims share a common theme: they are both examples of fear conditioning. In Chapter 3, you saw that the amygdala plays an important role in the experience of emotion, including fear and anxiety. So, it should come as no surprise that the amygdala, particularly an area known as the *central nucleus*, is also critical for emotional conditioning.

Consider a rat that is conditioned to a series of CS–US pairings, where the CS is a tone and the US is a mild electric shock. When rats experience sudden painful stimuli in nature, they show a defensive reaction, known as *freezing*, where they crouch down and sit motionless. In addition, their autonomic nervous systems go to work: heart rate and blood pressure increase, and various hormones associated with stress are released. When fear conditioning takes place, these two components – one behavioural and one physiological – occur, except that now they are elicited by the CS.

The central nucleus of the amygdala plays a role in producing both these outcomes through two distinct connections with other parts of the brain. If connections linking the amygdala to the lateral part of the hypothalamus (a particular part of the midbrain) are disrupted or severed, the rat does not exhibit the behavioural freezing response, and the autonomic responses associated with fear cease (LeDoux et al., 1988). Hence, the action of the amygdala is an essential element in fear conditioning, and its links with other areas of the brain are responsible for producing specific features of conditioning. The amygdala is involved in fear conditioning in people as well as rats and other animals (Phelps and LeDoux, 2005).

hot science

Of mice and men: learning to become fearful

What we worry about changes as we age. Many children are frightened of strangers and the dark. Teenagers are frightened of being rejected by their peers. Adults are frightened of losing their jobs and being unable to support their families. Conditioning models of learning fear have to consider the different challenges and threats we face at different times in our lives as well as how we respond.

Using Pavlovian fear conditioning, researchers investigated the ability to regulate fear through extinction learning, once the threat had been removed, in both mice and humans (Pattwell et al., 2012). The humans were children, adolescents and adults and for comparison in mouse years, the mice were 23, 29 and 70 days old. To establish a fear response, multiple pairings of an unpleasant stimulus (electric shock or aversive noise) with a neutral stimulus (a tone or a light) formed a learned association (conditioned fear response), where the neutral stimulus signalled the impending unpleasant stimulus. In humans, this conditioned fear response is characterized by changes in autonomic arousal associated with the fight-or-flight response (see Chapter 3). In mice, the conditioned fear response is a characteristic 'freezing' behaviour where they do not move. In both mice and humans, the fear response involves activation of the amygdala, as noted in the text.

Once the conditioned fear response was established, they estimated its strength by measuring extinction rates, which involved presenting the conditioned stimulus in the absence of the unpleasant stimulus. Extinction learning, which is not to be confused with forgetting, is an inhibitory process where the formed association is mediated by the prefrontal cortex in rodents and humans (Milard and Quirk, 2012). In both mice and humans, the surprising result was that the adolescent group showed less fear as measured by galvanic skin response in humans and freezing behaviour in mice, compared to the younger and older groups.

One important factor that plays a major role in learning fear is the context. Simply returning to a location where fear conditioning took place is sufficient to produce the conditioned fear response (Pattwell et al., 2011). This contextual effect reflects the role of the hippocampus in signalling the relevance of cues from the environment that one is in danger. To explore the role of context in fear across development, the pre-adolescent, adolescent and adult mice were tested in a further set of experiments where, after 24 hours, they were simply returned to the environment where the fear response had been conditioned but without the presentation of the conditioned stimulus. Again, in comparison to the younger and older groups, the adolescent mice were less fearful.

Why might adolescent mice and humans be less fearful? One suggestion is that being afraid is counterproductive to being brave enough to venture out and explore new environments. If they never left, these teenagers would just eat their parents out of house and home, and without the prospect of mating, be unlikely to pass on their genes.

These findings have potentially important implications for clinical practice. One of the most common forms of therapy for anxiety disorders is exposure-based cognitive behavioural therapy (see Chapter 16). This treatment consists of identifying the cues that trigger the anxiety, followed by desensitization of the patient, whereby the associated fear is extinguished by repeated exposure. However, if extinction learning is attenuated in adolescence, then exposure-based techniques may be less effective (Pattwell et al., 2013).

The cognitive elements of classical conditioning

Pavlov's work was a behaviourist's dream come true. In this view, conditioning is something that *happens to* a dog, a rat or a person, apart from what the organism thinks about the conditioning situation. However, an early experiment by Zener (1937) provided some of the earliest evidence that classical conditioning might not just be a simple process in which a CS elicits a response automatically, without thought. Zener's procedure was almost identical to that used by Pavlov – he strapped dogs into a harness and exposed them to pairings of a CS and food – but he observed his dogs very carefully as conditioning progressed. Like Pavlov, he observed an increase in salivation, but he also found that when the CS was presented, the dogs began to turn towards the tray where the food was delivered, as if they were *expecting* the food. Indeed, if released from the harness, they would approach the tray and wait there. Maybe classical conditioning isn't such an unthinking, mechanical process as behaviourists had originally assumed (Rescorla, 1966, 1988).

Results like this suggest that dogs in conditioning experiments do not just salivate automatically when they hear the CS, they seem to realize that it signals food (see also Colwill and Motzkin, 1994). One possible interpretation is that conditioning is essentially a cognitive process – Pavlov's dogs formed an expectation that the buzzer was going to be followed by food, and it was this expectation that led them to salivate. This prediction is called **contingency** – *the organism has an expectation about how well the CS signals the appearance of the US* (Rescorla and Wagner, 1972). In a classic experiment, two groups of rats were conditioned to pair a tone with an electric shock (Rescorla, 1968). For one group, the tone always preceded the shock so that the tone became a CS that elicited fear. In the other group, the rats received the same number of tones and electric shock pairings but there were also trials when the tone was presented without the

CONTINGENCY The organism has an expectation about how well the CS signals the appearance of the US.

subsequent shock. According to Pavlov's classical conditioning, both groups should have formed an association between the tone and the shock but this was not true for the second group because the tone did not reliably predict the shock. This expectancy explains another phenomenon observed in conditioning known as *blocking* (Kamin, 1969). When a stimulus (a tone) has been paired with a shock to produce a conditioned fear response, this experience blocks the capacity to learn other associations when the tone is present. For example, rats who were initially conditioned to fear a tone and a shock, and who were then presented with a tone and light followed by the shock, did not learn to associate the light with the shock. Rats without this prior experience of the tone learned to associate the light with the shock. In short, organisms take into consideration expectations when learning new associations, which makes a lot of sense. There are so many potential stimuli in a complex world that could be associated with learning that it is important to take note of those that are most likely based on past experiences.

Other evidence, however, suggests that the situation is not quite as simple as this, as it appears that conditioning can occur even in the absence of expectations. In a study by Öhman and Soares (1998), participants were repeatedly shown pictures of a snake and a spider, with one of these stimuli followed by a mild electric shock. For example, some participants received a shock whenever the snake was presented, but not following the spider. Similar procedures have been used in other experiments on conditioning – the procedure is called *discrimination training* – and the typical result is that people learn to respond only to the stimulus that signals the US. The unusual feature of Öhman and Soares' study, however, was that the pictures were presented in such a way that participants were not consciously aware of what they were seeing. They were subliminally presented very briefly, for three one-hundreths of a second, and each presentation was immediately followed by a meaningless jumble of dark and light shapes. Previous research had shown that masking stimuli presented in this way effectively removes the opportunity for people to have time to become consciously aware of them (Marcel, 1983). The experimenters confirmed that this was the case by asking participants on each trial which picture had been presented: the percentage of correct responses was almost exactly at chance (50.5%), confirming that participants were not confident which picture had been presented. And yet, despite having no explicit awareness of the pictures, they showed clear signs of conditioning, as levels of fear were much higher on trials where the stimulus that had been paired with shock was presented. The picture of the snake was eliciting fear even though participants did not see it; the process was entirely unconscious.

In Öhman and Soares' study, a picture of a snake was used to elicit fear conditioning in participants even when they were entirely unaware.

The evidence of the role of cognition in conditioning is thus somewhat confusing. In some experiments, people do seem to be aware of the relationship between the CS and US, but in others, conditioning seems to occur at an unconscious level. There is as yet no consensus among learning psychologists as to how best to interpret this conflicting evidence, but one possibility is that both views are correct. Perhaps early in the course of evolution, an essentially simple form of conditioning evolved, one in which a CS elicits the appropriate response automatically, without thought, but that over time, as the brain evolved and became more sophisticated, cognitive processes came to play a greater role. (For one presentation of this view, see Lieberman, 2004.) If so, conditioning may usually involve awareness of the relationship between the CS and the US, but it may also be possible for us to be conditioned without our knowing it.

The evolutionary elements of classical conditioning

In addition to this possible cognitive component in conditioning, evolutionary mechanisms also play an important role. As you learned in Chapter 1, evolution and natural selection go hand in hand with adaptiveness: behaviours that are adaptive allow an organism to survive and thrive in its environment. In the case of classical conditioning, psychologists began to appreciate how this type of learning could have adaptive value.

Even psychologists who know how conditioning operates can still develop food aversions. When Martin Seligman fell violently ill with flu after eating steak Béarnaise, he could no longer face eating this dish that he once enjoyed.

Research exploring this adaptiveness has focused on three main areas: conditioned food aversions, conditioned food preferences, and biological preparedness.

Food aversions can occur for quite sensible reasons, as when Aunt Dolly offers you her famous oxtail and kidney pie and you politely decline. Food aversions can also be classically conditioned. There is even one famous episode that has been entitled the 'sauce Béarnaise' phenomenon. Psychologist Martin Seligman recounts how he developed an aversion to sauce Béarnaise one evening after dining with his wife:

> Sauce bearnaise is an egg-thickened, tarragon flavoured concoction, and it used to be my favourite sauce. It now tastes awful to me. This happened several years ago, when I felt the effects of the stomach flu about 6 hours after eating filet mignon with sauce béarnaise. I became violently ill and spent most of the night vomiting. The next time I had sauce bearnaise, I couldn't bear the taste of it. (Seligman and Hager, 1972, p. 8)

Why would one bad incident taint food preferences in such a lasting way? On the face of it, this looks like a case of classical conditioning. The sauce Béarnaise was the CS, its apparent toxicity was the US, and the resulting gastric distress was the UR. The UR (the nausea) became linked to the once-neutral CS (the sauce Béarnaise) and became a CR (an aversion to sauce Béarnaise). However, Seligman noted that if it was classical conditioning, it violated several Pavlovian laws. First, the time between the meal and the distress was at least six hours; usually a response follows a stimulus fairly quickly. Second, it was only the sauce and not any other stimulus that became the source of the aversion. Most baffling, this aversion was cemented with a single acquisition trial. Usually, it takes several pairings of a CS and US to establish learning. Finally, knowledge of the actual cause of the illness had no effect on the aversion. Seligman's wife had the same meal and did not get sick. He later discovered that his close colleague had also been struck down with stomach flu, proving that it was not related to the sauce Béarnaise: 'Yet in spite of this knowledge, I could not inhibit my aversion' (Seligman and Hager, 1972, p. 8).

These peculiarities are not so peculiar from an evolutionary perspective. What seems like a mindbug is actually the manifestation of an adaptive process. Any species that forages or consumes a variety of foods needs to develop a mechanism by which it can learn to avoid any food that once made it ill. To have adaptive value, this mechanism should have several properties:

1 There should be rapid learning that occurs in perhaps one or two trials. If learning takes more trials than this, the animal could die from eating a toxic substance repeatedly.
2 Conditioning should be able to take place over long intervals, perhaps up to several hours. Toxic substances often don't cause illness immediately, so the organism would need to form an association between food and the illness over a longer term.
3 The organism should develop the aversion to the smell or taste of the food rather than its ingestion. It's more adaptive to reject a potentially toxic substance based on smell alone than it is to ingest it.
4 Learned aversions should occur more often with novel foods than familiar ones. It is not adaptive for an animal to develop an aversion to everything it has eaten on the particular day it got sick. In fact, rats have been shown to have a bias to acquire an aversion to novel tasting substances, suggesting that the learning system takes into account familiarity of stimuli in the environment (Kalat, 1974).

Researchers illustrated the adaptiveness of classical conditioning in a series of studies with rats (Garcia and Koelling, 1966). They used a variety of CSs (visual, auditory, tactile, taste and smell) and several different USs (injection of a toxic substance, radiation) that caused nausea and vomiting hours later. The researchers found weak or no conditioning when the CS was a visual, auditory or tactile stimulus, but a strong food aversion developed with stimuli that have a distinct taste and smell. In one experiment, they presented water accompanied by bright lights and tinkling sounds as the CS, and little or no conditioned aversion was observed. However, if the CS was water laced with a harmless but distinctly flavoured novel substance (such as strawberry), the researchers found a strong aversion to the smell and taste of strawberries. Moreover, if the CS was a familiar food that the animal had eaten before, the aversion was much less likely to develop. Other researchers have shown that these food aversions can be acquired even when the organism is unconscious. Rats that were administered a toxic substance while under total anaesthesia developed a taste aversion to foods they had eaten earlier when awake (Rabin and Rabin, 1984).

This research had an interesting application. It led to the development of a technique for dealing with an unanticipated side effect of radiation and chemotherapy. Cancer patients who experience nausea with their treatments often develop aversions to foods they ate before the therapy. Broberg and Bernstein (1987) reasoned that, if the findings with rats generalized to humans, a simple technique should minimize the negative consequences of this effect. They gave their patients an unusual food (coconut- or cola-flavoured confectionary) at the end of the last meal before undergoing treatment. Sure enough, the conditioned food aversions that the patients developed were overwhelmingly for one of the unusual flavours and not for any of the other foods in the meal. Patients were spared developing aversions to more common foods that they are more likely to eat. So, understanding the basis of mindbugs can have practical as well as theoretical value.

Other research has revealed a parallel mechanism, one that allows organisms to learn to *prefer* particular substances over others (Sclafani, 1995). In one study, rats were given flavoured water, for example cherry. As they drank, a nutritive substance, such as sucrose, was delivered directly into their stomachs. On other occasions, another flavour, for example orange, was used, but it was paired with the delivery of water to their stomachs. After only a few trials, the rats developed a strong preference for the flavour paired with sucrose over that paired with water. The effect also occurs with substances other than sucrose: recent work shows that conditioned food preferences can be produced by sources of fat, such as corn oil and safflower oil (Ackroff et al., 2005).

Studies such as these suggest that evolution has provided each species with a kind of **biological preparedness**, *a propensity for learning particular kinds of associations over others*, so that some behaviours are relatively easy to condition in some species but not others. For example, the taste and smell stimuli that produce food aversions in rats do not work with most species of birds. Birds depend primarily on visual cues for finding food and are relatively insensitive to taste and smell. However, as you might guess, it is relatively easy to produce a food aversion in birds using an unfamiliar visual stimulus as the CS, such as a brightly coloured food (Wilcoxon et al., 1971). Indeed, most researchers agree that conditioning works best with stimuli that are biologically relevant to the organism (Domjan, 2005)

BIOLOGICAL PREPAREDNESS A propensity for learning particular kinds of associations over others.

Humans also have biological predispositions for conditioning, as in the case of phobias. As you'll see in Chapter 16, phobias are strong, irrational, emotional reactions to some stimulus or situation. Early behaviourists, such as Watson, viewed them as the result of simple classical conditioning: a CS is paired with a threatening US. However, research on learned aversions and preferences suggests that his perspective may have been a bit naive. Humans do indeed suffer from a variety of phobias, but not all phobias occur with the same frequency. Some phobias are common, whereas others are quite rare, and some are relatively mild, whereas others can be debilitating. Virtually everyone has cut themselves with a kitchen knife, yet phobias associated with knives are so rare that they are almost nonexistent. But fear of the dark and fear of heights are common and often show up in individuals who have never had any particularly unpleasant experiences associated with the dark or with heights.

Humans have a biological preparedness to develop phobias of situations that, in our evolutionary past, were potentially dangerous to survival (Öhman and Mineka, 2001). A species that is relatively physically vulnerable and has poor night vision needs to be wary of predators that lurk in the night. A species that spends a good bit of time in trees will live longer if it develops a healthy appreciation of the dangers of falling. All manner of spiders, snakes and creepy crawly things are commonly the source of phobias, even when they are not that common or are even absent in the environment, such as Ireland and New Zealand. Hence, we are biologically prepared for easy classical conditioning to fear circumstances, such as darkness, heights, snakes or insects, which, ironically, are no longer as life-threatening as they were for our ancestors – well, certainly not that often in the modern world.

In summary, classical conditioning is a form of learning involving the pairing of a neutral stimulus with a meaningful event or stimulus. Ivan Pavlov's initial work paired a neutral tone (a conditioned stimulus, CS) with a meaningful act: the presentation of food to a hungry animal (an unconditioned stimulus, US). As he and others demonstrated, the pairing of a CS and a US during the acquisition phase of classical conditioning eventually allows the CS by itself to elicit a response called a conditioned response (CR).

Classical conditioning was embraced by behaviourists such as John B. Watson, who viewed it as providing a foundation for a model of human behaviour. Watson believed that no higher level functions, such as thinking or awareness, needed to be invoked to understand behaviour. As later researchers showed, however, the underlying mechanism of classical conditioning turned out to be more complex (and more interesting) than the simple association between a CS and a US. As Pavlov assumed, the brain is involved in many types of conditioning, as in the case of fear conditioning and the action of the amygdala. Researchers discovered that many species form expectations, suggesting that classical conditioning involves some degree of cognition. The evolutionary aspects of classical conditioning show that each species is biologically predisposed to acquire particular CS–US associations based on its evolutionary history. In short, classical conditioning is not an arbitrary mechanism that merely forms associations. Rather, it is a sophisticated mechanism that evolved precisely because it has adaptive value.

Operant conditioning: reinforcements from the environment

The learned behaviours you've seen so far share a common feature: they all occurred beyond the voluntary control of the organism. Most animals don't voluntarily salivate, feel nauseous or experience spasms of anxiety; rather, these animals exhibit these responses involuntarily during the conditioning process. In fact, these reflex-like behaviours make up only a small portion of our behavioural repertoires. The remainder are behaviours we voluntarily perform, behaviours that modify and change the environment around us. The study of classical conditioning is the study of behaviours that are *reactive.* We turn now to a different form of learning: **operant conditioning** – *a type of learning in which the consequences of an organism's behaviour determine whether it will be repeated in the future.* The study of operant conditioning is the exploration of behaviours that are *active.*

OPERANT CONDITIONING A type of learning in which the consequences of an organism's behaviour determine whether it will be repeated in the future.

The early days: the law of effect

The study of how active behaviour affects the environment began at about the same time as classical conditioning. In fact, Edward L. Thorndike (1874–1949) first examined active behaviours back in the 1890s, before Pavlov published his findings. Thorndike's research focused on *instrumental behaviours*, that is, behaviour that required an organism to *do* something, solve a problem or otherwise manipulate elements of its environment (Thorndike, 1898). For example, Thorndike completed several experiments using a puzzle box, which was a wooden crate with a door that would open when a concealed lever was moved in the right way (see **FIGURE 6.5**). A hungry cat placed in a puzzle box would try various behaviours to get out – scratching at the door, meowing loudly, sniffing the inside of the box, putting its paw through the openings – but only one behaviour opened the door and led to food: tripping the lever in just the right way. After this happened, Thorndike placed the cat back in the box for another round. Don't get the wrong idea. Thorndike probably really liked cats. Far from teasing them, he was after an important behavioural principle.

FIGURE 6.5 Thorndike's puzzle box In Thorndike's original experiments, food was placed just outside the door of the puzzle box, where the cat could see it. If the cat triggered the appropriate lever, it would open the door and let the cat out.

As illustrated in **FIGURE 6.6**, over successive trials, the cats learned to escape from the box more quickly, although this learning proved much more gradual than might have been expected, with rapid escapes on some trials followed by much longer escape times on subsequent trials. The gradual and uneven nature of this progress suggested to Thorndike that the cats were not solving the problem through insight or understanding. Instead, he argued, the correct response was being automatically strengthened by the food that followed it. Just as Pavlov had attributed classical conditioning to the formation of an association between two stimuli,

Thorndike suggested that the cats were learning an association between the stimulus of the box and the response of pressing the latch. The presentation of food was gradually 'stamping in' an association between the stimulus and response, so that the stimulus of the box would eventually elicit the response of pressing the latch automatically.

Let's examine this idea in a bit more detail. When a cat was first placed in the box, it would have performed any number of likely, but ultimately ineffective behaviours, but only one would have led to freedom and food. That behaviour was *instrumental* for the cat in achieving the desired outcome: escape from the box and access to food. Over time, the ineffective behaviours become less and less frequent, and the one instrumental behaviour (going right for the latch) becomes more frequent. From these observations, Thorndike developed the **law of effect**, which states that *behaviours that are followed by a 'satisfying state of affairs' tend to be repeated and those that produce an 'unpleasant state of affairs' are less likely to be repeated.*

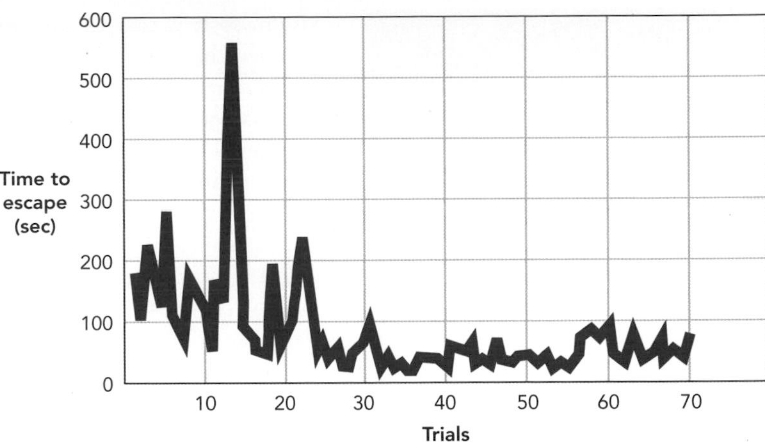

FIGURE 6.6 The law of effect Thorndike's cats displayed trial-and-error behaviour when trying to escape from the puzzle box. At first, they made lots of irrelevant movements and actions but, gradually, they began to escape from the box more quickly.

LAW OF EFFECT The principle that behaviours that are followed by a 'satisfying state of affairs' tend to be repeated and those that produce an 'unpleasant state of affairs' are less likely to be repeated.

The circumstances that Thorndike used to study learning were very different from those in studies of classical conditioning. Remember that in classical conditioning experiments, the US occurred on every training trial, no matter what the animal did. Pavlov delivered food to the dog whether it salivated or not. But in Thorndike's work, the behaviour of the animal determined what happened next. If the behaviour was 'correct', that is, the latch was triggered, the animal was rewarded with food. Incorrect behaviours produced no results and the animal was stuck in the box until it performed the correct behaviour. Although different from classical conditioning, Thorndike's work resonated with most behaviourists at the time. It was still observable, quantifiable and free from explanations involving the mind (Galef, 1998).

Oddly, John B. Watson, the founder of behaviourism, originally rejected Thorndike's ideas about the potential of rewards to influence behaviour. Watson thought this was some kind of magic, possibly akin to some cognitive explanation of 'wanting' or 'willingness' to perform a behaviour, almost as if rewards had some goal stored inside them, waiting to trigger a behaviour. It took a different kind of behaviourist promoting a different kind of behaviourism to develop Thorndike's ideas into a unified explanation of learning.

Reinforcement, punishment and the development of operant conditioning

Several decades after Thorndike's work, B. F. Skinner (who we met in Chapter 1) coined the term **operant behaviour** to refer to *behaviour that an organism produces that has some impact on the environment, which in turn changes because of that impact.* In Skinner's system, all these emitted behaviours 'operated' on the environment in some manner, in the sense that they produced some form of change in that environment. In some cases, these environmental changes strengthened the behaviours that produced them, that is, they *reinforced* them; in others, they made them less likely to occur, that is, they *punished* them. Skinner's elegantly simple observation was that most organisms do *not* behave like a dog in a harness, passively waiting to receive food, no matter what the circumstances. Rather, most organisms are like cats in a box, actively engaging the environment in which they find themselves to reap rewards (Skinner, 1938, 1953).

OPERANT BEHAVIOUR Behaviour that has some impact on the environment and changes because of that impact.

In order to study operant behaviour scientifically, Skinner developed a variation on Thorndike's puzzle box. The *operant conditioning chamber*, or *Skinner box* as it is commonly called, shown in **FIGURE 6.7**, allows a researcher to study the behaviour of small organisms in a controlled environment. In his early experiments, Skinner preferred using rats, but he quickly shifted to using pigeons. Pigeons turned out to be easily trained; they display remarkable persistence, they need relatively little sleep, and they have excellent

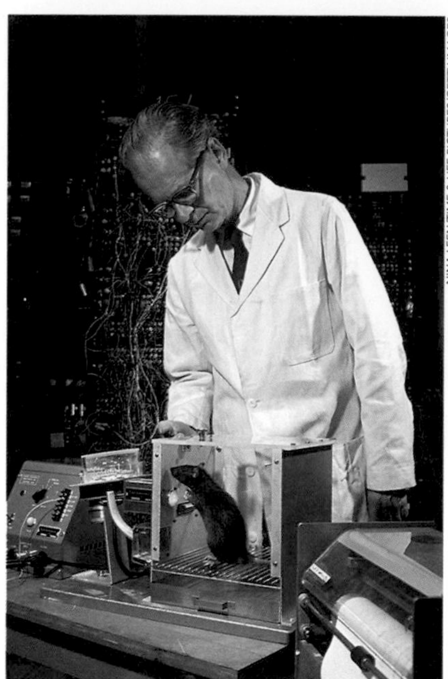

FIGURE **6.7 Skinner box** The photograph shows B. F. Skinner with a Skinner box, or operant conditioning chamber. In a typical Skinner box, a rat, pigeon or other suitably sized animal is placed in this environment and observed during learning trials that use operant conditioning principles.

REINFORCER Any stimulus or event that functions to increase the likelihood of the behaviour that led to it.

PUNISHER Any stimulus or event that functions to decrease the likelihood of the behaviour that led to it.

vision, so it is easy to present them with a wide range of stimuli. Moreover, Skinner believed that the fundamental laws of learning are the same across most vertebrate species, so that studying learning in one organism would shed light on learning in others. With a focus on behaviour and no recourse for mental processes to get in the way, Skinner could easily conduct research with participants that were readily available and easy to manage.

Skinner's approach to the study of learning focused on *reinforcement* and *punishment*. These terms, which have commonsense connotations, turned out to be rather difficult to define. For example, some people love roller coasters, whereas others find them horrifying; the chance to go on one will be reinforcing for one group but punishing for another. Dogs can be trained with praise and a good belly rub – procedures that are nearly useless for most cats. Skinner settled on a 'neutral' definition that would characterize each term by its effect on behaviour. Therefore, a reinforcer is *any stimulus or event that functions to increase the likelihood of the behaviour that led to it*, whereas a punisher is *any stimulus or event that functions to decrease the likelihood of the behaviour that led to it.*

Stimuli may be in the form of either *presenting* something or *removing* it, but whether or not the effect is reinforcing or punishing depends on exactly *what* is being presented or removed. For example, presenting food is usually reinforcing, producing an increase in the behaviour that led to it; whereas removing food is often punishing, leading to a decrease in the behaviour. Conversely, turning on (presenting) an electric shock is typically punishing – reducing the behaviour that led to it; while turning it off (removing) is rewarding – increasing the behaviour that led to it.

To keep these possibilities distinct, Skinner used the term *positive* for situations in which a stimulus was presented and *negative* for situations in which it was removed. Consequently, there is *positive reinforcement*, where something desirable, like food, is presented, and *negative reinforcement*, where something undesirable, like an electric shock, is removed, as well as *positive punishment*, where something unpleasant is administered, and *negative punishment*, where something desirable is removed. Here, the words *positive* and *negative* mean, respectively, something that is *added* or something that is *taken away*. As you can see from TABLE **6.1**, positive and negative reinforcement increase the likelihood of the behaviour and positive and negative punishment decrease the likelihood of the behaviour.

TABLE **6.1 Reinforcement and punishment**

	Increases the likelihood of behaviour	Decreases the likelihood of behaviour
Stimulus is presented	Positive reinforcement	Positive punishment
Stimulus is removed	Negative reinforcement	Negative punishment

These distinctions can be confusing at first; after all, 'negative reinforcement' and 'punishment' both sound like they should be 'bad' and produce the same type of behaviour. There are a couple of ways to keep track of these distinctions. First, remember that *positive* and *negative* simply mean *presentation* or *removal*, and the terms don't necessarily mean 'good' or 'bad', as they do in everyday speech. Negative reinforcement, for example, involves something pleasant; it's the *removal* of something unpleasant, like a shock, and the absence of a shock is indeed pleasant.

Second, bear in mind that reinforcement is generally more effective than punishment in promoting learning. There are many reasons for this (Gershoff, 2002), but one is that punishment signals that an unacceptable behaviour has occurred, but it doesn't specify what should be done instead. Spanking a young child for starting to run into a busy street certainly stops the behaviour, which, in this case, is probably a good idea. But it doesn't promote any kind of learning about the *desired* behaviour. Should the child never venture into a street, wait for an adult, hold someone's hand, walk slowly into the busy street, or what? A more effective strategy would be to skilfully administer reinforcement for desired behaviours. Each time the child waits for an adult and holds that person's hand, for example, reinforcement would be given, perhaps in the form of verbal praise ('That's the right thing to do!'), a warm smile, a big hug, or the presentation of some other stimulus that the child finds desirable. Remember the law of effect – the intended behaviour of waiting for an adult should become more frequent, and unwanted behaviours such as running into the street should decrease.

Primary and secondary reinforcement and punishment

Reinforcers and punishers often gain their functions from basic biological mechanisms. A pigeon that pecks at a target in a Skinner box is usually reinforced with food pellets, just as an animal that learns to escape a mild electric shock has avoided the punishment of tingly paws. Food, comfort, shelter or warmth are examples of *primary reinforcers*, reinforcers that are effective from birth for all members of a species. They do not need to be learned, as all members need them to survive and will behave accordingly to gain access to them.

Some reinforcers, however, are not effective from birth, but are *learned*. Indeed, the rewards that probably influence us the most in our daily lives – an encouraging grin from a friend or colleague, a bronze trophy, money – are all learned, to at least some degree. Imagine giving a six-month-old infant money to try to reward its behaviour – it probably doesn't require a formal experiment to confirm that it wouldn't work. Reinforcers like money are not innately effective, but acquire their effectiveness through experience, so they are called *secondary reinforcers*.

Secondary reinforcers typically acquire their effectiveness through pairing with primary reinforcers, in a process resembling classical conditioning. In our example of money, it starts out as a neutral CS that, through its association with primary USs like acquiring food or shelter, takes on a conditioned emotional element. Flashing lights, originally a neutral CS, acquire powerful negative elements through association with a speeding ticket and a fine. Under normal circumstances, as long as the CS–US link is maintained, the secondary reinforcers and punishers can be used to modify and control behaviour. If the links are broken, that is, an extinction procedure is introduced, they typically lose these functions. Money that is no longer backed by a solvent financial system quickly loses its reinforcing capacity and becomes worth no more than the paper it is printed on.

Secondary reinforcers often aren't valuable in themselves. After all, money is just pieces of paper, as illustrated by this virtually worthless 10 million mark note, which was used during the German hyperinflation of 1923. The reinforcing quality of secondary reinforcers derives from their association with primary reinforcers.

The neutrality of reinforcers

Some reinforcers are more effective than others, but this is not always easy to discern. However, as David Premack (1962) pointed out, there is a simple and practical way to check. The *Premack principle* states that discerning which of two activities someone would rather engage in means that the preferred activity can be used to reinforce a nonpreferred one. For example, most children, given a free choice, would rather spend time watching TV than doing homework. As many parents have discovered, the preferred activity can be a useful reinforcer for the performance of the nonpreferred activity – no TV until the homework's done! Of course, this reinforcement will not work for all children. There are some who prefer doing their homework to watching TV; for these children, the effectiveness of the reinforcers will be reversed. In short, it's important to establish a hierarchy of behaviours for an individual in order to determine which kinds of events might be maximally reinforcing.

The Premack principle makes it clear why Skinner's neutral definitions of reinforcement and punishment make sense. A stimulus or event will be *relatively* reinforcing based on a host of factors, many of which are specific to the individual. What's more, the effectiveness of particular stimuli can be manipulated. For example, it seems pretty obvious that water can be used to reinforce a thirsty rat for running in an exercise wheel. However, the relationship between these two activities can be reversed. Depriving a rat of exercise for several days but allowing it free access to water creates a situation in which the rat will now drink in order to be given the opportunity to spend time running in the wheel.

Some limiting conditions of reinforcement

Any card-carrying behaviourist from the 1930s to the 1960s would tell you that providing rewards for performing a behaviour should make that behaviour more likely to occur again in the future. Unfortunately, this isn't always the case, and sometimes the presentation of rewards can cause the exact opposite effect: a decrease in performing the behaviour. This mindbug occurs because extrinsic reinforcement – rewards that come from external sources – sometimes undermines the reasons why people engage in behaviour in the first place. People often engage in activities for intrinsic rewards, such as the pure pleasure of simply doing the behaviour. In such cases, providing an extrinsic reward can have the paradoxical effect of reducing interest.

In one early demonstration, nursery school children were given coloured pens and paper and asked to draw whatever they wanted (Lepper and Greene, 1978). For a young child, this is a pretty satisfying event, as the pleasures of drawing and creative expression are rewarding by themselves. Some children, though, received a Good Player Award for their efforts at artwork, whereas other children did not. As you may have guessed, the good players spent more time at the task than the other children. As you may not have guessed, when the experimenters stopped handing out the Good Player Awards to the first group, the amount of time the children spent drawing dropped significantly below that of the group that never received any external reinforcements.

©ISTOCKPHOTO.COM/VANESSA MOROSINI

Drawing pictures is fun. Drawing pictures for external rewards might, oddly enough, make drawing pictures seem like much less fun.

It seems strange that a reward should weaken a response rather than strengthen it, and several possible explanations have been proposed. One is that the children initially engaged in drawing simply because they enjoyed it. When the reward was introduced, their motivation changed: they were no longer producing drawings because it was fun, but in order to obtain the attractive Good Player Award. But if the purpose in drawing was to obtain a reward, then drawing wasn't fun, it was a chore that had to be done in order to obtain the reward. The reward, in this view, was undermining the children's original intrinsic interest. Results like this are sometimes described as demonstrating the overjustification effect, in which *external rewards undermine the intrinsic satisfaction of performing a behaviour*.

> **OVERJUSTIFICATION EFFECT**
> Circumstances when external rewards can undermine the intrinsic satisfaction of performing a behaviour.

The overjustification effect is important – it tells us that in some situations, rewards can be harmful – but it is equally important not to misinterpret it. It is not the case that rewards are *always* harmful. If a child doesn't like cleaning their room, praising them when they do a good job is hardly going to reduce their interest, as there is no interest to be reduced. Moreover, subsequent research has shown that even where there is intrinsic interest, a reward is not necessarily harmful; it depends very much on what the reward is and how it is used. If the reward is praise, for example, the effect may be to increase interest, as when a child praised for playing the piano well develops a sense of pride – 'Hey, I'm good at this!' – and begins to really enjoy playing. If the reinforcer is a material reward such as money, on the other hand, the danger of undermining seems to be greater (see Cameron and Pierce, 1996; Deci et al., 1999). The issues are complex, and we will discuss them further at the end of the chapter, in the where do you stand? box. For now, the important point is that while rewards can be effective in changing behaviour, we also need to recognize that there are limits to this effectiveness.

The basic principles of operant conditioning

After establishing how reinforcement and punishment produced learned behaviour, Skinner and other scientists began to expand the parameters of operant conditioning. This took the form of investigating some phenomena that were well known in classical conditioning, such as discrimination, generalization and extinction, as well as some practical applications, such as how best to administer reinforcement or how to produce complex learned behaviours in an organism. Let's look at some of these basic principles of operant conditioning.

Discrimination, generalization and the importance of context

Here are some things you probably haven't given much thought to: we all take off our clothes at least once a day, but not usually in public; we scream at rock concerts but not in libraries. Although these observations may seem like nothing more than common sense, Thorndike was the first to recognize the underlying message: learning takes place *in contexts*, not in the free range of any plausible situation. As Skinner rephrased it later, most behaviour is under *stimulus control*, which develops when a particular response only occurs when the appropriate stimulus is present.

It's easy to demonstrate this simple truth. If a pigeon is reinforced for pecking a key whenever a particular tone is sounded but never reinforced if the tone is absent, that tone will quickly become a *discriminative stimulus*, or a stimulus that is associated with reinforcement for key pecking in that situation. Pigeons, reinforced under these conditions, will quickly learn to engage in vigorous key pressing whenever the tone sounds but cease if it is turned off. The tone sets the occasion for the pigeon to emit the operant response, much like being at a rock concert sets the occasion for your loud, raucous behaviour.

Stimulus control, perhaps not surprisingly, shows both discrimination and generalization effects similar to those we saw with classical conditioning. To demonstrate this, researchers used either a painting by French Impressionist Claude Monet or one of Pablo Picasso's paintings from his Cubist period for the discriminative stimulus (Watanabe et al., 1995). Participants in the experiment were only reinforced if they responded when the appropriate painting was present. After training, the participants discriminated appropriately; those trained with the Monet painting responded when other paintings by Monet were presented and those trained with a Picasso painting reacted when other Cubist paintings by Picasso were shown. And as you might expect, Monet-trained participants did not react to Picassos and Picasso-trained participants did not respond to Monets. What's more, the research participants showed that they could generalize *across* painters as long as they were from the same artistic tradition. Those trained with Monet responded appropriately when shown paintings by Auguste Renoir (another French Impressionist), and the Picasso-trained participants responded to artwork by Cubist painter Henri Matisse, despite never having seen these paintings before. If these results don't seem particularly startling to you, it might help to know that the research participants were pigeons that were trained to key peck to these various works of art. Stimulus control, and its ability to foster stimulus discrimination and stimulus generalization, is effective even if the stimulus has no meaning to the respondent.

Extinction

As in classical conditioning, operant behaviour undergoes extinction when the reinforcements stop. Pigeons cease pecking at a key if food is no longer presented following the behaviour. You wouldn't put more money into a vending machine if it failed to give you its promised chocolate, and warm smiles that are greeted with scowls and frowns will quickly disappear. On the surface, extinction of operant behaviour looks like that of classical conditioning: the response rate drops off fairly rapidly and, if a rest period is provided, spontaneous recovery is typically seen.

However, there is an important difference. In a typical experiment on classical conditioning, the US occurs on every trial, no matter what the organism does. In operant conditioning, the reinforcements only occur when the proper response has been made, and they don't always occur even then. Not every trip into the forest produces nuts for a squirrel, car salespeople don't sell to everyone who takes a test drive, and researchers run many experiments that do not work out and never get published. Yet these behaviours don't weaken and gradually extinguish. In fact, they typically become stronger and more resilient. The effect of reinforcement thus depends on how often a behaviour is reinforced; this principle is an important cornerstone of operant conditioning that we'll examine next.

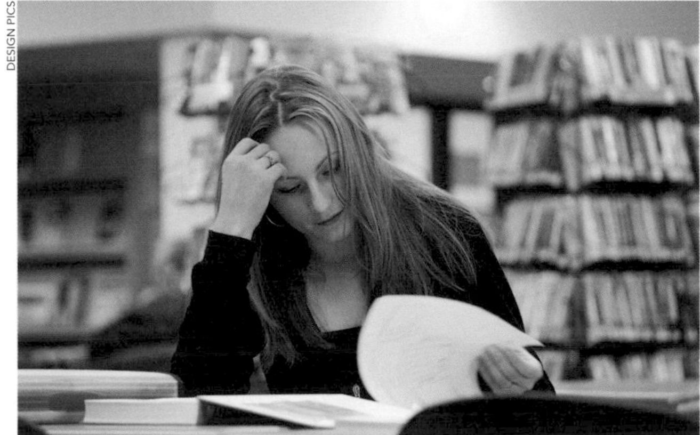

Students cramming for an exam often show the same kind of behaviour as pigeons being reinforced under a fixed interval (FI) schedule.

Schedules of reinforcement

Skinner was intrigued by the apparent paradox surrounding extinction and he described how he began studying it in his autobiography (Skinner, 1979). He was laboriously rolling ground rat meal and water to make food pellets to reinforce the rats in his early experiments. It occurred to him that perhaps he could save time and effort by not giving his rats a pellet for every bar press but instead delivering food on some intermittent schedule. The results of this hunch were dramatic. Not only did the rats continue bar pressing but they also shifted the rate and pattern of bar pressing depending on the timing and frequency of the presentation of the reinforcers. Unlike classical conditioning, where the sheer *number* of learning trials was important, in operant conditioning, the *pattern* with which reinforcements appeared was crucial.

Skinner explored dozens of what came to be known as *schedules of reinforcement* (Ferster and Skinner, 1957) (see **FIGURE 6.8**). The two most important are *interval schedules*, in which reinforcement is based on how much *time* has elapsed since the previous reinforcement, and *ratio schedules*, in which reinforcement is based on *how many responses* have been made. The term 'ratio' is used because there is a specified ratio of responses to reinforcers.

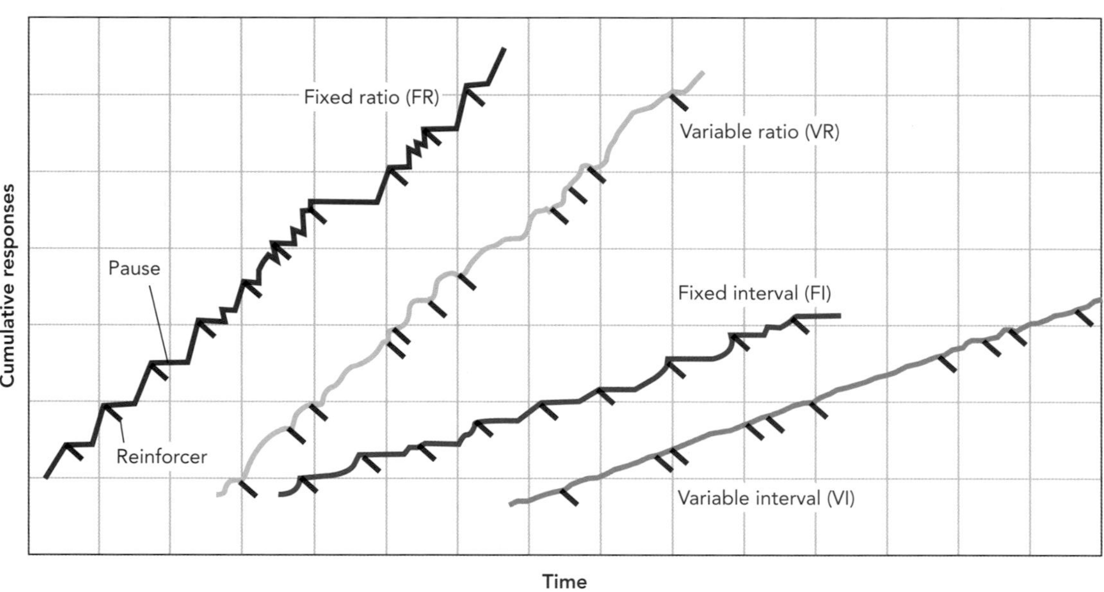

FIGURE 6.8 Reinforcement schedules Different schedules of reinforcement produce different rates of responding. The coloured lines represent how many responses have been made under each type of reinforcement. The black slash marks indicate when reinforcement was administered. Notice that ratio schedules tend to produce higher rates of responding than interval schedules, as shown by the steeper lines for fixed ratio and variable ratio reinforcement.

> **FIXED INTERVAL (FI) SCHEDULE** Reinforcement will become available when a fixed time period has elapsed following the previous reinforcement. The first response after this interval will produce the reinforcer.

Under a fixed interval (FI) schedule, *reinforcement will become available when a fixed time period has elapsed following the previous reinforcement. The first response after this interval will produce the reinforcer.* For example, on a two-minute FI schedule, a response will be reinforced only after two minutes have expired since the last reinforcement. Note that in an FI schedule, reinforcement is not necessarily delivered when the fixed time has elapsed; reinforcement becomes *available* at that time, but it will be delivered only when a response is made. If a rat didn't respond until three minutes had elapsed, or three hours, it would not obtain food until that moment, which would then trigger the timing of a new interval.

Rats and pigeons in Skinner boxes produce predictable patterns of behaviour under these schedules. They show little responding right after the presentation of reinforcement, but as the next time interval draws to a close, they show a burst of responding. This pattern of accelerating responding is known as an *FI scallop*, because of its scallop shell-like appearance when graphed in figures like Figure 6.8. If this pattern seems odd to you, consider that virtually every undergraduate has behaved exactly like this. They do relatively little work until just before the exam, then engage in a burst of reading and studying.

> **VARIABLE INTERVAL (VI) SCHEDULE** Reinforcement will become available when a time period has elapsed following the previous reinforcement, but unlike the FI schedule, the length of the waiting period varies from one reinforcer to the next.

Under a variable interval (VI) schedule, *reinforcement will become available when a time period has elapsed following the previous reinforcement, but unlike the FI schedule, the length of the waiting period varies from one reinforcer to the next.* For example, on a two-minute VI schedule, responses will be reinforced every two minutes *on average* but not after each two-minute period. Sometimes the first response after 20 seconds will be reinforced, sometimes the first response after 90 seconds and so on. VI schedules typically produce steady, consistent responding because the time until the next reinforcement is less predictable.

©ISTOCKPHOTO.COM/LISA KYLE YOUNG

Radio station promotions and giveaways often follow a variable interval (VI) schedule of reinforcement.

Under a fixed ratio (FR) schedule, *reinforcement will be delivered after a specific number of responses have been made.* One schedule might present reinforcement after every fourth response, while a different schedule might present reinforcement after every 20 responses. The special case of presenting reinforcement after *each* response is called *continuous reinforcement*, which is what drove Skinner to investigate these schedules in the first place. Notice that in each example, the ratio of reinforcements to responses, once set, remains fixed.

There are many situations in which people, sometimes unknowingly, find themselves being reinforced on an FR schedule: book clubs often give you a 'freebie' after a set number of regular purchases; pieceworkers get paid after making a fixed number of products; and some credit card companies return a percentage of the amount charged to their customers. When an FR schedule is operating, it is possible, in principle, to know exactly when the next reinforcer is due. A laundry pieceworker on a 10-response FR schedule who has just washed and ironed the ninth shirt knows that payment is coming after the next shirt is done.

FIXED RATIO (FR) SCHEDULE Reinforcement will be delivered after a specific number of responses have been made.

Under a variable ratio (VR) schedule, *reinforcement will be delivered after a specified average number of responses have been made.* For example, if a laundry worker was following a 10-response VR schedule instead of an FR schedule, they would still be paid, on average, for every 10 shirts washed and ironed but not for *each* 10th shirt. Most people who work in sales find themselves operating under VR schedules. Estate agents won't sell every house they show but will establish an average ratio of houses shown to houses sold. Fruit machines in a modern casino pay out on VR schedules that are determined by the random number generator that controls the play of the machines. A casino might advertise that it pays out on 'every 100 pulls on average', which could be true. However, one player might hit a jackpot after 3 pulls on a fruit machine, whereas another player might not hit until after 80 pulls. The ratio of responses to reinforcements is variable, which probably helps casinos stay in business.

VARIABLE RATIO (VR) SCHEDULE Reinforcement will be delivered after a specified average number of responses have been made.

All ratio schedules encourage high and consistent rates of responding because the number of rewards received is directly related to the number of responses made. Unlike a rat following an FI schedule, where food is delivered at a specified time regardless of the number of responses, rats following a ratio schedule should respond quickly and often. Both schedules provide intermittent reinforcement – *only some of the responses made are followed by reinforcement.* They all produce behaviour that is much more resistant to extinction than a continuous reinforcement schedule. One way to think about this effect is to recognize that the more irregular and intermittent a schedule is, the more difficult it becomes for an organism to detect when it has actually been placed on extinction.

INTERMITTENT REINFORCEMENT An operant conditioning relationship in which only some of the responses made are followed by reinforcement.

For example, if you've just put a coin into a drinks machine that, unbeknown to you, is broken, no can comes out. Because you're used to getting your can of drink on a continuous reinforcement schedule – money produces can – this abrupt change in the environment is easily noticed and you are unlikely to put additional coins into the machine: you'd quickly show extinction. However, if you've put your money into a fruit machine that, unbeknown to you, is broken, do you stop after one or two plays? Almost certainly not. If you're a regular player, you're used to going for many plays in a row without winning anything, so it's difficult to tell that anything is out of the ordinary. Under conditions of intermittent reinforcement, all organisms will show considerable resistance to extinction and continue for many trials before they stop responding. The effect has even been observed in infants (Weir et al., 2005).

INTERMITTENT REINFORCEMENT EFFECT Operant behaviours that are maintained under intermittent reinforcement schedules resist extinction better than those maintained under continuous reinforcement.

This relationship between intermittent reinforcement schedules and the robustness of the behaviour they produce is called the **intermittent reinforcement effect** – *operant behaviours that are maintained under intermittent reinforcement schedules resist extinction better than those maintained under continuous reinforcement.* In one extreme case, Skinner gradually extended a VR schedule until he managed to get a pigeon to make an astonishing 10,000 pecks at an illuminated key for one food reinforcer. Behaviour maintained under a schedule like this is virtually immune to extinction.

Shaping through successive approximations

Have you ever been to a sea life centre and wondered how the dolphins learn to jump up in the air, twist around, splash back down, do a somersault, and then jump through a hoop, all in one smooth motion? Well, they don't. Wait – of course they do, you've seen them. It's just that they don't learn to do all those complex aquabatics in *one* smooth motion. Rather, elements of their behaviour are shaped over time until the final product looks like one smooth motion.

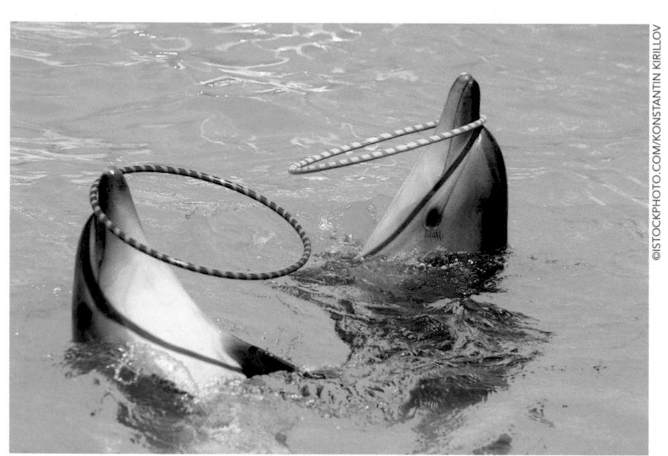
©ISTOCKPHOTO.COM/KONSTANTIN KIRILLOV

Training animals by shaping their behaviour through successive approximation can result in some extraordinary feats as demonstrated by these dolphins.

Skinner noted that the trial-by-trial experiments of Pavlov and Thorndike were rather artificial. Behaviour rarely occurs in fixed frameworks where a stimulus is presented and then an organism has to engage in some activity or another. We are continuously acting and behaving, and the world around us reacts in response to our actions. Most of our behaviours, then, are the result of **shaping** – *learning that results from the reinforcement of successive approximations to a final desired behaviour.* For example, Skinner noted that if you put a rat in a Skinner box and wait for it to press the bar, you could end up waiting a long time: bar pressing just isn't very high on a rat's natural hierarchy of responses. However, it is relatively easy to 'shape' bar pressing. Watch the rat closely: if it turns in the direction of the bar, deliver a food reward. This will reinforce turning towards the bar, making such a movement more likely. Now wait for the rat to take a step towards the bar before delivering food, which will reinforce moving towards the bar. After the rat walks closer to the bar, wait until it touches the bar before presenting the food. Notice that none of these behaviours is the final desired behaviour – reliably pressing the bar. Rather, each behaviour is a *successive approximation* to the final product, or a behaviour that gets incrementally closer to the overall desired behaviour. In the dolphin example – and, indeed, in many instances of animal training in which relatively simple animals seem to perform astoundingly complex behaviours – you can think through how each smaller behaviour is reinforced until the overall sequence of behaviour is performed reliably.

SHAPING Learning that results from the reinforcement of successive approximations to a final desired behaviour.

Superstitious behaviour

Everything we've discussed so far suggests that one of the keys to establishing reliable operant behaviour is the correlation between an organism's response and the occurrence of reinforcement. In the case of continuous reinforcement, when every response is followed by the presentation of a reinforcer, there is a one-to-one, or perfect, correlation. In the case of intermittent reinforcement, the correlation is weaker, that is, not every response is met with the delivery of reinforcement, but it's not zero. As you read in Chapter 2, however, just because two things are correlated, that is, they tend to occur together in time and space, doesn't imply that there is causality, that is, the presence of one reliably causes the other to occur.

Skinner (1948) designed an experiment that illustrates this distinction. He put several pigeons in Skinner boxes, set the food dispenser to deliver food every 15 seconds, and left the birds to their own devices. Later he returned and found the birds engaging in odd, idiosyncratic behaviours, such as pecking aimlessly in a corner or turning in circles. He referred to these behaviours as 'superstitious' and offered a behaviourist analysis of their occurrence. The pigeons, he argued, were simply repeating behaviours that had been accidentally reinforced. A pigeon that just happened to have pecked randomly in the corner when the food showed up had connected the delivery of food to that behaviour. Because this pecking behaviour was 'reinforced' by the delivery of food, the pigeon was likely to repeat it. Now, pecking in the corner was more likely to occur, and it was more likely to be reinforced 15 seconds later when the food appeared again.

For each pigeon, the behaviour reinforced would most probably be whatever the pigeon happened to be doing when the food was first delivered. Skinner's pigeons acted as though there was a causal relationship between their behaviours and the appearance of food, when it was merely an accidental correlation. While Skinner's account makes for a plausible explanation of the pigeons' behaviour, it is not without criticism. For example, later researchers showed that there were a variety of behaviours that appeared early on in the training and that most pigeons ended up with same behaviour of pecking at the dispenser just before food delivery (Staddon and Simmelhag, 1971). Moreover, bird experts argued that the other behaviours that seemed superstitious were not accidental acts but were all examples food-searching behaviour in pigeons (Timberlake and Lucas, 1985).

While conditioned superstitious behaviour is controversial in pigeons, it does appear to be robust in at least some humans (Ono, 1987). Football players who score a goal on a day when they happened not to have showered are likely to continue that tradition, labouring under the belief that the accidental correlation between poor personal hygiene and a good day on the pitch is somehow causal. This 'stench causes goals' hypothesis is just one of many examples of human superstitions (Gilbert et al., 2000; Radford and Radford, 1949). Even the most highly educated and powerful among us such as President Barack Obama are susceptible to superstitious rituals, as reflected by the fact that he played basketball for good luck on the morning of every primary election leading up to his presidential election. Former Prime Minister Tony Blair always wore the same pair of lucky shoes for Prime Minister's Questions in the House of Commons where he would have to respond to criticism and answer difficult questions. It would seem that in situations where outcomes are important, there may be a natural disposition to form superstitious beliefs and behaviours, which could be part of what makes us human (Hood, 2009).

Sporting rituals

People believe in many different superstitions and engage in all kinds of superstitious behaviours. This is particularly true for sportspeople, leading to all manner of strange rituals. Tennis players are famously superstitious. John McEnroe would not stand on the white service line, Serena Williams always wears the same pair of socks throughout the tournament and Andy Murray will not hold a trophy he has not yet won, although that last one is increasingly less of a problem for Murray.

A deeper understanding of operant conditioning

Like classical conditioning, operant conditioning quickly proved powerful. It's difficult to argue this fact when a rat learns to perform relatively complex behaviours after only 20 minutes of practice, prompted by little more than the skilful presentation of rat food. The results are evident: 'learning' in its most fundamental sense is a change in behaviour brought about by experience. In this case, the rat didn't perform the task at first, and then, after a little training, it learned to perform the task very well indeed. Case closed.

Well, not quite. Although we could simply note that the rat's behaviour has changed and leave it at that, there are other ways of viewing learning that can considerably enrich our understanding. We'll look at three: the neural, cognitive and evolutionary perspectives on operant conditioning.

The neural elements of operant conditioning

Soon after psychologists came to appreciate the range and variety of things that could function as reinforcers, they began looking for underlying brain mechanisms that might account for these effects. The first hint of how specific brain structures might contribute to the process of reinforcement came from the discovery of what came to be called *pleasure centres.* James Olds (1956) inserted tiny electrodes into different parts of a rat's brain and allowed the animal to control electric stimulation of its own brain by pressing a bar. He discovered that some brain areas, particularly those in the limbic system (see Chapter 3), produced what appeared to be intensely positive experiences: rats would press the bar repeatedly to stimulate these structures. These rats would ignore food, water and other life-sustaining necessities for hours on end simply to receive stimulation directly in the brain. Olds then called these parts of the brain 'pleasure centres' (see **FIGURE 6.9**).

Based on this research, researchers implanted stimulating electrodes into the brains of patients who suffered from disorders such as intractable epilepsy in the hope that they could be used to develop new therapeutic techniques. In a number of cases, these patients

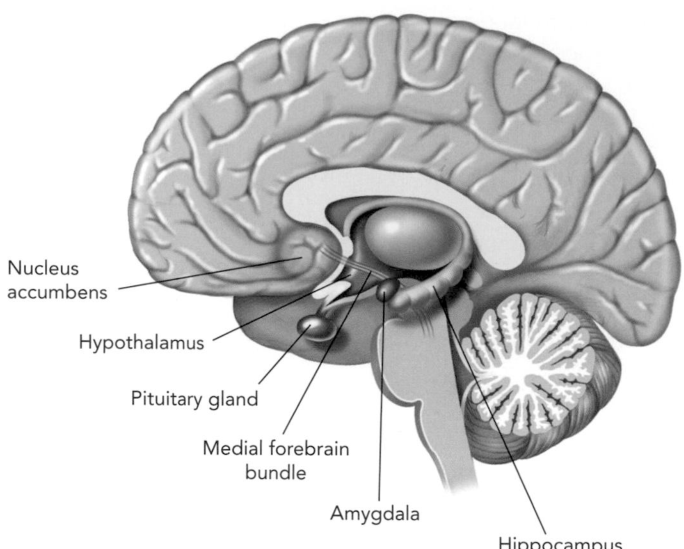

FIGURE 6.9 Pleasure centres in the brain The nucleus accumbens, medial forebrain bundle and hypothalamus are all major pleasure centres in the brain.

did indeed experience a distinct sense of pleasure, most often when the electrodes were placed in limbic areas. Some patients reported feelings that were sexual in nature, but most merely responded that they 'felt good' in some vague sense. These studies have been abandoned for various reasons, ranging from questions about their ethics to failures to find any particularly useful therapeutic applications (Valenstein, 1973, 1986).

In the years since these early studies, researchers have identified a number of structures and pathways in the brain that deliver rewards through stimulation (Wise, 1989, 2005). The neurons in the *medial forebrain bundle*, a pathway that meanders its way from the midbrain through the *hypothalamus* into the *nucleus accumbens*, are the most susceptible to stimulation that produces pleasure. This is not surprising, as psychologists have identified this bundle of cells as crucial to behaviours that clearly involve pleasure, such as eating, drinking and engaging in sexual activity. Also, the neurons along this pathway and especially those in the nucleus accumbens itself are all *dopaminergic*, that is, they secrete the neurotransmitter *dopamine*. Remember from Chapter 3 that higher levels of dopamine in the brain are usually associated with positive emotions.

Researchers have found good support for this 'reward centre':

1 As you've just seen, rats will work to stimulate this pathway at the expense of other basic needs (Olds and Fobes, 1981). However, if drugs that block the action of dopamine are administered to the rats, they cease stimulating the pleasure centres (Stellar et al., 1983).
2 Drugs such as cocaine, amphetamine and opiates activate these pathways and centres (Moghaddam and Bunney, 1989), but dopamine-blocking drugs dramatically diminish their reinforcing effects (White and Milner, 1992).
3 fMRI studies (see Chapter 3) show increased activity in the nucleus accumbens in heterosexual men looking at pictures of attractive women (Aharon et al., 2001) and in individuals who believe they are about to receive money (Knutson et al., 2001).
4 Rats that are given primary reinforcers such as food or water or are allowed to engage in sexual activity show increased dopamine secretion in the nucleus accumbens – but only if the rats are hungry, thirsty or sexually aroused (Damsma et al., 1992).

This last finding is exactly what we might expect, given our earlier discussion of the complexities of reinforcement. After all, food tastes a lot better when we are hungry and sexual activity is more pleasurable when we are aroused. These biological structures underlying rewards and reinforcements probably evolved to ensure that species engaged in activities that helped survival and reproduction.

The cognitive elements of operant conditioning

In Skinner's day, most operant conditioning researchers argued for a strict behaviourist interpretation of learning. The central tenet of this approach is that behaviour should be explained in terms of the environmental conditions that give rise to it, not in terms of internal mental states. To explain why someone is eating, for example, a behaviourist would be more likely to focus on the fact that they haven't eaten for 12 hours, or that eating at noon has become a habit for them, rather than by appealing to internal feelings of hunger. There are, however, different versions of behaviourism, with somewhat different attitudes to mental states. As we have seen, Watson believed that psychologists should ignore mental states, and even at some points denied their existence. Skinner (1950), on the other hand, never doubted the reality of mental states such as thinking or dreaming. However, like Watson, he believed that there were serious problems in observing such states accurately, and he argued that psychology would progress much more rapidly if it focused on external causes that could be measured objectively – in our example of eating, how many hours had elapsed since a previous meal, rather than how hungry someone felt. Similarly, if Skinner had wanted to understand the causes of crime, he would have examined the role of observable factors such as economic conditions and children's upbringing, not criminals' conscious or unconscious feelings. If we wanted to change behaviour, he said, then ultimately we must understand the environmental variables that control it, so why not study these variables in the first place?

Skinner's emphasis on observable causes of behaviour was to prove enormously powerful, as he and his followers went on to develop many effective techniques for changing behaviour – shaping and schedules are just two examples. However, his views were increasingly challenged by cognitive psychologists, who believed that mental states play a critical role in determining behaviour, and thus it would be foolish to ignore them. Several lines of research suggest that considering the role of cognition can enhance our understanding of operant conditioning.

Edward Chace Tolman (1886–1959) was the strongest early advocate of a cognitive approach to operant learning. Tolman was dissatisfied with the simple stimulus-response (S-R) approach to understanding learning, arguing that there was more to learning than just knowing the circumstances in the environment (the properties of the stimulus) and being able to observe a particular outcome (the reinforced response). Instead, Tolman proposed that an animal established a means–ends relationship, that is, the conditioning experience produced knowledge or a belief that, in this particular situation, a specific reward (the end state) will appear if a specific response (the means to that end) is made. In this view, the stimulus does not directly evoke a response; rather, it establishes an internal cognitive state, which then produces the behaviour. These cognitive theories of learning focus less on the S-R connection and more on what happens in the organism's mind when faced with the stimulus. In contrast to staunch S-R behaviourists, cognitively oriented psychologists such as Tolman are more concerned with what goes on between the S and the R.

LATENT LEARNING A condition in which something is learned but it is not manifested as a behavioural change until sometime in the future.

Early studies with rats and mazes supported the influence of cognition on operant conditioning. Rats that had learned to run through a maze for a small reward ran much faster when they were switched to a larger reward; in fact, they ran faster than a comparable group that had always had the large reward (Crespi, 1942). Similarly, rats that were switched from the large reward to the small one ran slower than those who always had the smaller rewards. In both cases, the rats acted as though they had a pretty good idea of what to expect at the end of the maze. Their behaviour revealed a cognitive element: the rats appeared to be either excited or annoyed about changes in the reward and seemed to make corresponding changes in their behaviour.

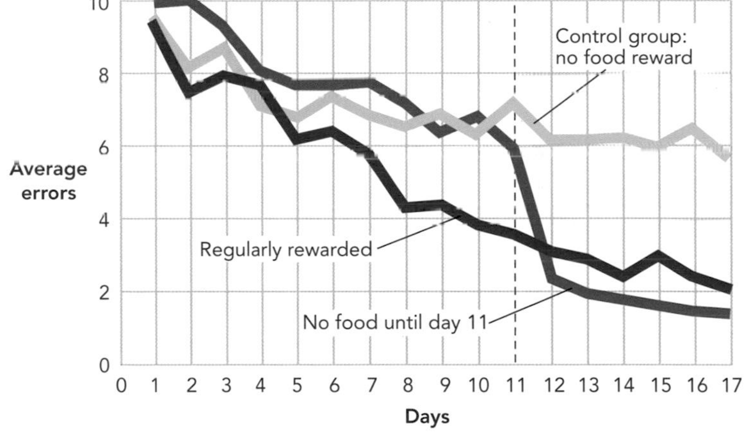

FIGURE 6.10 Latent learning Rats in a control group that never received any reinforcement (in green) improved at finding their way through the maze over 17 days but not by much. Rats that received regular reinforcements (in blue) showed fairly clear learning; their error rate decreased steadily over time. Rats in the latent learning group (in purple) were treated exactly like the control group rats for the first 10 days and then like the regularly rewarded group for the last 7 days. Their dramatic improvement on day 12 shows that these rats had learned a lot about the maze and the location of the goal box even though they had never received reinforcements. Notice also that on the last 7 days, these latent learners actually seem to make *fewer* errors than their regularly rewarded counterparts.

During the 1930s and 40s, Tolman and his students conducted studies that focused on *latent learning* and *cognitive maps*, two phenomena that suggested that simple stimulus-response interpretations of operant learning behaviour are inadequate. In latent learning, *something is learned but it is not manifested as a behavioural change until sometime in the future.* Latent learning can easily be established in rats and occurs without any obvious reinforcement, a finding that posed a direct challenge to the then-dominant behaviourist position that all learning required some form of reinforcement (Tolman and Honzik, 1930a).

Tolman gave three groups of rats access to a complex maze every day for over two weeks. The control group never received any reinforcement for navigating the maze. They were simply allowed to run around until they reached the goal box at the end of the maze. In **FIGURE 6.10**, you can see that over the two weeks of the study, this group (in green) got a little better at finding their way through the maze but not by much. A second group of rats received regular reinforcements; when they reached the goal box, they found a small food reward there. Not surprisingly, these rats showed clear learning, as can be seen in blue in Figure 6.10. A third group was treated exactly like the control group for the first 10 days and then rewarded for the last 7 days. This group's behaviour (in purple) was quite striking. For the first 10 days, they behaved like the rats in the control group. However, during the final 7 days, they behaved a lot like the rats in the second group that had been reinforced every day. Clearly, the rats in this third group had learned a lot about the maze and the location of the goal box during those first 10 days, even though they had not received any reinforcements for their behaviour. In other words, they showed evidence of latent learning.

These results suggested to Tolman that beyond simply learning 'start here, end here', his rats had developed a sophisticated mental picture of the maze. Tolman called this a **cognitive map** – *a mental representation of the physical features of the environment.* Beyond simply learning 'start here, end here', Tolman thought that the rats had developed a mental picture of the maze, more along the lines of 'make two lefts, then a right, then a quick left at the corner'. He devised several experiments to test this idea (Tolman and Honzik, 1930b; Tolman et al., 1946), but we'll focus on a later study by Vander Wall (1982). In Vander Wall's study, the subjects were birds called Clark's nutcrackers, a species possessing an apparently quite remarkable memory. They live in alpine regions where food is hard to find in winter, so they harvest seeds in the autumn and then store them underground in hiding places called *caches*. Because each cache contains an average of only four seeds, a bird needs to recover a minimum of 2,500 caches each winter in order to survive. One possible explanation of how the birds achieve this feat is that they actually remember the location of all 2,500 caches – a phenomenal memory load. Another possibility, however, is that they search for distinguishing locations, for example signs of disturbance in the soil, to identify where the seeds have been hidden.

COGNITIVE MAP A mental representation of the physical features of the environment.

To test these hypotheses, Vander Wall allowed two birds to hide seeds in a fenced-in enclosure containing landmarks such as rocks and shrubs. Several days later, he again released the birds into the enclosure, but this time also released two other birds – a control group – that had not hidden seeds there. If the birds relied on cues such as signs of disturbance, both groups should have been equally successful at locating the seeds, but that wasn't the case. The birds searched by probing the soil with their beaks; for the control group, only 10% of the probes were successful, whereas the birds that had hidden the seeds were successful on 70% of their probes. Vander Wall was also able to show that the birds were using the landmarks in the enclosure to guide their searches. If he moved the landmarks 30 cm to the right before releasing the birds for the test, they would search almost exactly 30 cm to the right of where they had hidden the seeds. These results suggest that the birds were not just searching at random, they were using landmarks to remember where they had hidden the seeds and then went there with almost unerring accuracy. If success rates in the wild are similar, it would imply that these birds form extraordinarily detailed cognitive maps of their environments, containing the locations of thousands of caches in relation to the landmarks that define them.

We should note that the question of whether animals can form cognitive maps has been controversial. Many of the experiments that at first seemed to support the existence of such maps eventually proved to be explicable in terms of simpler mechanisms (for example, Pearce, 2008). On the other hand, taken together with the evidence for cognitive skills such as language in animals, operant conditioning does seem to be a considerably more sophisticated process than Thorndike's studies first suggested.

The evolutionary elements of operant conditioning

As you'll recall, classical conditioning has an adaptive value that has been fine-tuned by evolution. Not surprisingly, we can also view operant conditioning from an evolutionary perspective. This viewpoint grew out of a set of curious observations from the early days of conditioning experiments. Several behaviourists who were using simple T mazes, like the one shown in **FIGURE 6.11**, to study learning in rats discovered that if a rat found food in one arm of the maze on the first trial of the day, it typically ran down the *other* arm on the very next trial. A staunch behaviourist wouldn't expect the rats to behave this way. After all, the rats in these experiments were hungry and they had just been reinforced for turning in a particular direction. According to operant conditioning, this should *increase* the likelihood of turning in that same direction, not reduce it. With additional trials, the rats eventually learned to go to the arm with the food, but they had to learn to overcome this initial tendency to go 'the wrong way'. How can we explain this mindbug?

What was puzzling from a behaviourist perspective makes sense when viewed from an evolutionary perspective. Rats are foragers, and like all foraging species, they have evolved a highly adaptive strategy for survival. They move around in their environment looking for food. If they find it somewhere, they eat it (or store it) and then look somewhere else for more. If they do not find food, they forage in another part of the environment. So, if the rat just found food in the *right* arm of a T maze, the obvious place to look next time is the *left* arm. The rat knows that there isn't any more food in the right arm because it just ate the food it found there. Indeed, foraging animals such as rats have well-developed **spatial representations**, *the capacity to encode, process and store information about the shape and layout of the physical environment*, that allow them to construct cognitive maps. These maps enable them to search their environment efficiently. If given the opportunity to explore a complex environment like the multiple T maze shown in **FIGURE 6.12**, rats will systematically go from arm to arm collecting food, rarely returning to an arm they have previously visited (Olton and Samuelson, 1976). So, in this case, it's not the rat who is the victim of a mindbug, it's the behaviourist theorist!

Keller Breland and Marian Breland, two of Skinner's former students, were among the first researchers to discover that it wasn't just rats in T mazes that presented a problem for behaviourists (Breland and Breland, 1961).

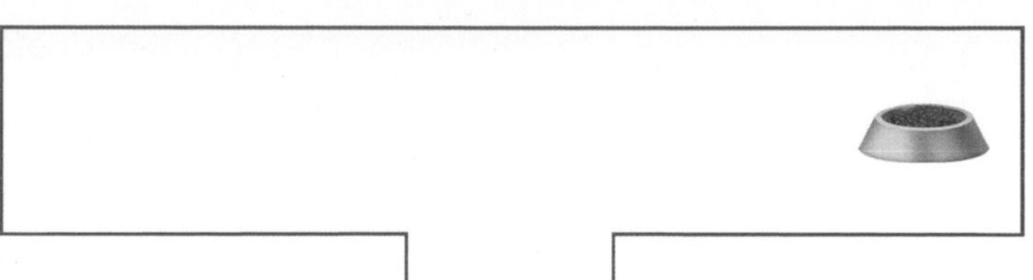

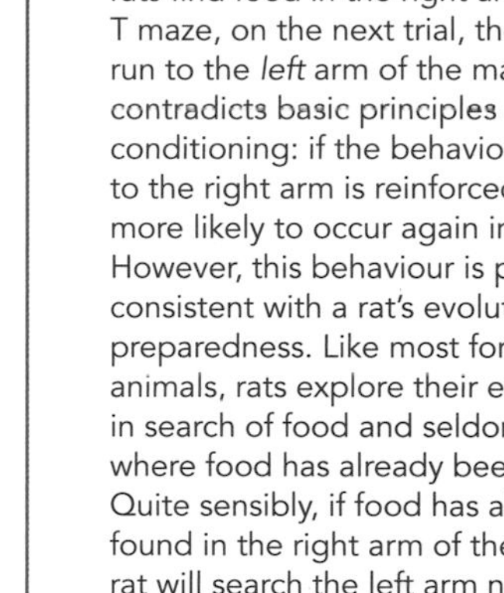

FIGURE 6.11 A simple T maze When rats find food in the right arm of a typical T maze, on the next trial, they will often run to the *left* arm of the maze. This contradicts basic principles of operant conditioning: if the behaviour of running to the right arm is reinforced, it should be more likely to occur again in the future. However, this behaviour is perfectly consistent with a rat's evolutionary preparedness. Like most foraging animals, rats explore their environments in search of food and seldom return to where food has already been found. Quite sensibly, if food has already been found in the right arm of the T maze, the rat will search the left arm next to see if *more* food is there.

SPATIAL REPRESENTATION The capacity to encode, process and store information about the shape and layout of the physical environment.

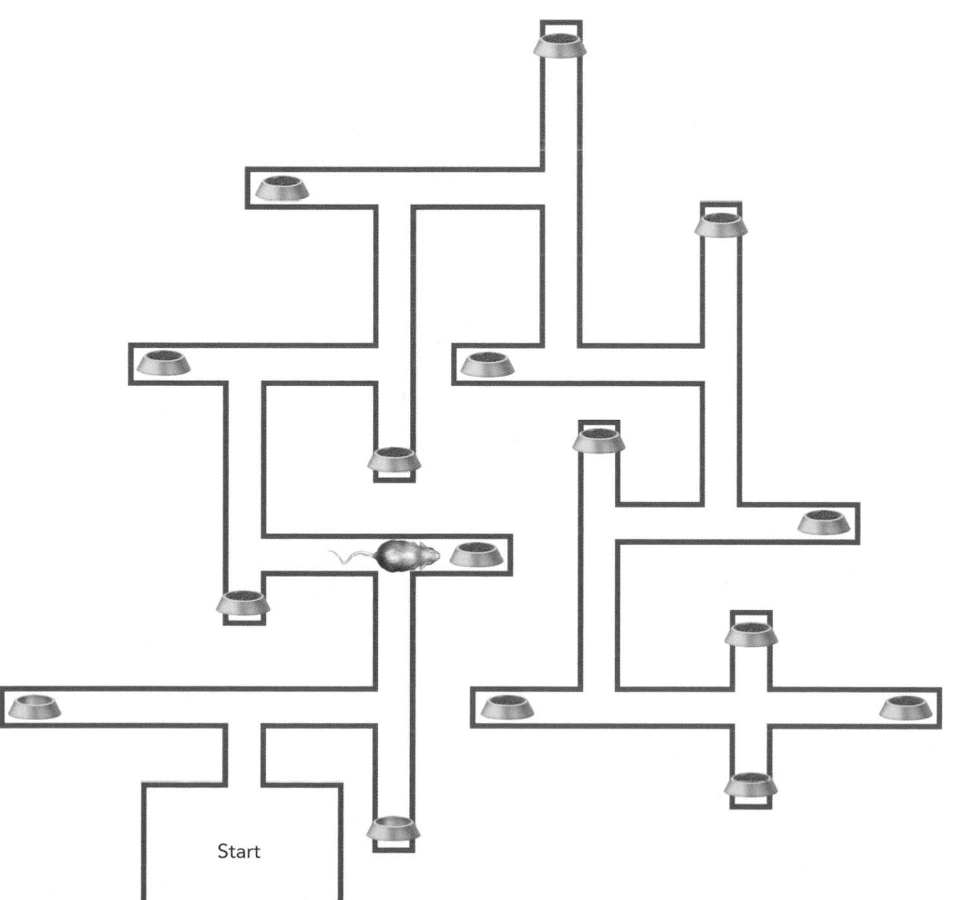

FIGURE 6.12 A multiple T maze Like many other foraging species, rats placed in a multiple T maze such as this one show evidence of their evolutionary preparedness. These rats will systematically travel from arm to arm in search of food, never returning to arms they have already visited.

The misbehaviour of organisms. Pigs are biologically predisposed to root out their food, just as raccoons are predisposed to wash their food. Trying to train either species to behave differently can prove to be an exercise in futility.

The Brelands pointed out that psychologists and the organisms they study often seemed to 'disagree' on what the organisms should be doing. Their argument was simple. When this kind of dispute develops, the animals are always right, and the psychologists had better rethink their theories.

The Brelands, who made a career out of training animals for commercials and films, often used pigs, because pigs are surprisingly good at learning all sorts of tricks. However, they discovered that it was extremely difficult to teach a pig the simple task of dropping coins in a box. Instead of depositing the coins, the pigs persisted in rooting with them as if they were digging them up in soil, tossing them in the air with their snouts and pushing them around. The Brelands tried to train raccoons at the same task, with different but equally dismal results. The raccoons spent their time rubbing the coins between their paws instead of dropping them in the box.

Having learned the association between the coins and food through conditioning, the animals began to treat the coins as stand-ins for food. But because pigs are biologically predisposed to root out their food, and raccoons have evolved to clean their food by rubbing it with their paws, this is exactly what each species of animal did with the coins. For example, the raccoons failed to follow the simple route to obtaining food by dropping the coins in the box; 'nature' took over and they wasted time rubbing the coins together.

The Brelands' work shows that each species, including humans, is biologically predisposed to learn some things more readily than others and to respond to stimuli in ways that are consistent with its evolutionary history (Gallistel, 2000). Such adaptive behaviours, however, evolved over extraordinarily long periods and in particular environmental contexts. If those circumstances change, some of the behavioural mechanisms that support learning can lead an organism astray. The point is that although much of every organism's behaviour results from predispositions sharpened by evolutionary mechanisms, these mechanisms can sometimes have ironic consequences.

A clever series of studies showed how evolved predispositions to learn can backfire on an animal (Thomas, 1981). Rats were placed in a Skinner box and the timer was set to deliver food every 20 seconds, no matter what the rats did. In fact, if they just lay around doing absolutely nothing, they were guaranteed to get 3 food pellets every minute. However, the feeding mechanism was rigged so that if a rat did press the bar before the full 20 seconds was up, it would immediately receive the pellet scheduled for the end of that interval. However, this response would also *cancel* the pellet scheduled for the end of the following 20-second interval. In other words, a rat that pressed the bar regularly would lose out on every other reinforcement. It could only get a food pellet half the time, and its overall rations would be cut in half, reduced from 3 pellets every minute to an average of only 1.5 pellets. Yet, the association between the bar press and the immediate delivery of food was sufficiently strong that the rats still showed systematic increases in bar pressing, some of them averaging over 25 bar presses a minute.

These rats showed the perils of impatience. By opting for immediate rewards, they ended up losing out in the long run. What seems to be a perverse mindbug is a consequence of the usually adaptive tendency to interpret responses that are immediately followed by food as having produced that food. In this case, acting too readily on the association between bar pressing and food delivery backfired as a long-term adaptive strategy.

In summary, operant conditioning, as developed by B. F. Skinner, is a process by which behaviours are reinforced and therefore become more likely to occur, complex behaviours are shaped through reinforcement, and the contingencies between actions and outcomes are critical in determining how an organism's behaviours will be displayed. It deals with the interlocking of actions and outcomes as a predictable chain of events. It demonstrates that simple laws of cause and effect can explain how the complexity of actions can emerge as well as the seemingly irrational behaviour of superstitious rituals. Like Watson, Skinner tried to explain behaviour without considering cognitive or evolutionary mechanisms. However, as with classical conditioning, this approach turned out to have serious shortcomings. Operant conditioning has clear cognitive components. Organisms behave as though they have expectations about the outcomes of their actions and adjust their actions accordingly. Moreover, the associative mechanisms that underlie operant conditioning have their roots in evolutionary biology. Some things are relatively easily learned and others are difficult; the history of the species is usually the best clue as to which will be which.

hot science

Control of learning: from the laboratory to the classroom

It's the night before the final exam in your introductory psychology course. You've put in a lot of time reviewing your course notes and the material in this textbook, and you feel that you have learned most of it pretty well. You are coming down the home stretch with little time left, and you've got to decide whether to devote those precious remaining minutes to studying psychological disorders or social psychology. How do you make that decision? What are its potential consequences? Recent research in cognitive psychology has shown that people's judgements about what they have learned play a critical role in guiding further study and learning (Metcalfe, 2009).

An important part of learning involves assessing how well we know something and how much more time we need to devote to studying it. Experimental evidence reveals that these subjective assessments, which psychologists refer to as *judgements of learning* (JOLs), are related to learning. People typically devote more time to studying items that they judge they have not learned well (Son and Metcalfe, 2000). However, this relationship might simply reflect the fact that items that are difficult to learn require more study time than easier items, rather than showing that JOLs have a causal effect on how people approach the learning task.

Metcalfe and Finn (2008) provided evidence for a causal effect by taking advantage of an illusion that influences JOLs. The illusion occurs when people are given lists of word pairs. Some pairs are studied three times in trial 1, given an initial test, and then studied one more time in trial 2 before a final test (3-1 condition); other pairs are studied once in trial 1, given an initial test, and then studied three times in trial 2 before a final test (1-3 condition).

You should not be surprised to find out that on the final test, people recalled the same number of pairs from the 3-1 and 1-3 conditions; after all, they studied all the word pairs the same number of times. Thus, the items in the two conditions were learned equally well. Further, participants made their JOLs about each word pair in the final study presentation of trial 2 – at a time when items from the 3-1 and 1-3 conditions should have been equally well learned. Strikingly, though, the participants' JOLs were higher at the end of trial 2 in the 3-1 condition than the 1-3 condition. This illusion occurred because JOLs were influenced by the fact that participants recalled more items in the initial test in the 3-1condition than in the 1-3 condition (remember, the initial test followed three exposures to the list in the 3-1 condition versus only one exposure to the list in the 1-3 condition).

This manipulation then allowed the experimenters to examine whether JOLs influenced how much time people devoted to each pair when the pairs in the two conditions were learned equally well, even though participants didn't think that they were. Critically, Metcalfe and Finn found evidence for a causal effect: the participants chose to devote more time to studying pairs from the 1-3 condition, which they thought were less well learned, than pairs from the 3-1 condition, which they thought were better learned.

The fact that JOLs have a causal effect on how people study is especially important because – as illustrated by the experiment we just considered – JOLs are sometimes inaccurate. For example, after reading and rereading a chapter or article in preparation for an exam, the material will probably feel quite familiar, and that feeling may convince you that you've learned the material well enough that you don't need to study it further. However, the feeling of familiarity can be misleading: although we think it reflects a deep understanding of the material, it may instead be a manifestation of a low-level process such as perceptual priming (see Chapter 5), which may not reflect either comprehension or the kind of learning that will be required to perform well on an exam (Bjork and Bjork, 2011). One way to avoid being fooled by such misleading subjective impressions is to test yourself from time to time when studying for an exam under conditions similar to those that will occur during the exam. As we saw in Chapter 5, testing oneself improves later learning of the target material more than simply restudying it.

So, if you are preparing for the final exam in this course and need to decide whether to devote more time to studying psychological disorders or social psychology, try to exert control over learning by testing yourself on material from the two chapters; you can use the results of those tests to help you decide which chapter requires further work. We can exert control over learning, but we also need to be aware of the possible pitfalls in attempting to exercise that control.

Observational learning: look at me

The guiding principle of operant conditioning is that reinforcement determines future behaviour. That tenet fits well with behaviourism's insistence on observable action as the appropriate level of explanation and behaviourists' reluctance to consider what was going on in the mind. As we've already seen, however, cognition helps explain why operant conditioning doesn't always happen as behaviourists would expect. The next section looks at learning by keeping one's eyes and ears open to the surrounding environment and further chips away at the strict behaviourist doctrine.

Learning without direct experience

Consider this story about four-year-old Rodney and his two-year-old sister Hannah. Their parents had always told them to keep away from the cooker, and that's good advice for any child and many an adult. Being a mischievous imp, however, Rodney decided one day to turn on a burner, place his hand over it, and slowly press down ... until the singeing of his flesh led him to recoil, shrieking in pain. Rodney was just fine – more scared than hurt – and no one hearing this story doubts that he learned something important that day. But no one doubts that little Hannah, who stood by watching these events unfold, *also* learned the same lesson. Rodney's story is a behaviourist's textbook example: the administration of punishment led to a learned change in his behaviour. But how can we explain Hannah's learning? She received neither punishment nor reinforcement – indeed, she didn't even have direct experience with the wicked appliance – yet it's arguable that she's just as likely to keep her hands away from cookers in the future as Rodney is.

OBSERVATIONAL LEARNING Learning takes place by watching the actions of others.

Hannah's is a case of **observational learning**, in which *learning takes place by watching the actions of others.* Observational learning challenges behaviourism's reinforcement-based explanations of classical and operant conditioning, but there is no doubt that this type of learning produces changes in behaviour. In all societies, appropriate social behaviour is passed on from generation to generation largely through observation (Bandura, 1965). The rituals and behaviours that are a part of our culture are acquired by each new generation, not only through deliberate training of the young but also through young people observing the patterns of behaviours of their elders. Tasks such as using chopsticks or learning to operate a TV's remote control are more easily acquired if we watch them being carried out before we try ourselves. Even complex motor tasks, such as performing surgery, are learned in part through extensive observation and imitation of models. And anyone who is about to undergo surgery is grateful for observational learning. Just the thought of a generation of surgeons acquiring their surgical techniques using the trial-and-error techniques studied by Thorndike or the shaping of successive approximations that captivated Skinner would make any of us nervous.

IMAGE SOURCE

Observational learning plays an important role in many sports and activities. In this yoga class, students learn through watching their teacher and classmates.

In Chapter 12, we take a more in-depth look at observational learning in humans, but in this chapter, as an introduction, we will look at its operation in animals.

Observational learning in animals

Humans aren't the only creatures capable of learning through observing. A wide variety of species learn by observing. In one study, for example, pigeons watched other pigeons get reinforced for either pecking at the feeder or stepping on a bar. When placed in the box later, the pigeons tended to use whatever technique they had observed other pigeons using earlier (Zentall et al., 1996).

In an interesting series of studies, researchers showed that laboratory-raised rhesus monkeys that had never seen a snake would develop a fear of snakes simply by observing the fear reactions of other monkeys (Cook and Mineka, 1990; Mineka and Cook, 1988). In fact, the fear reactions of these lab-raised monkeys were so authentic and pronounced that they could function as models for still *other* lab-raised monkeys, creating a kind of observational learning 'chain'. These results also support our earlier discussion of how each species has evolved particular biological predispositions for specific behaviours. Virtually every rhesus monkey raised in the wild has a fear of snakes, which strongly suggests that such a fear is one of this species' predispositions. This research also helps to explain why some phobias that humans suffer from, such as a fear of heights (acrophobia) or enclosed spaces (claustrophobia), are so common, even in people who have never had unpleasant experiences in these contexts (Mineka and Öhman, 2002). The fears may emerge not from specific conditioning experiences but from observing and learning from the reactions of others.

Observational learning may involve a neural component as well. As you read in Chapter 3, *mirror neurons* are a type of cell found in the brains of primates (including humans). Mirror neurons fire when an animal performs an action, such as when a monkey reaches for a food item. More importantly, however, mirror neurons also fire when an animal watches someone *else* perform the same specific task (Rizzolatti and Craighero, 2004). Although this 'someone else' is usually a fellow member of the same species, some research suggests that mirror neurons in monkeys also fire when they observe humans performing an action (Fogassi et al., 2005). For example, monkeys' mirror neurons fired when they observed humans grasping for a piece of food, either to eat it or put it in a container.

Mirror neurons, then, may play a critical role in the imitation of behaviour as well as the prediction of future behaviour (Rizzolatti, 2004). If the neurons fire when another organism is seen performing an action, it could indicate an awareness of intentionality, or that the animal is anticipating a likely course of future actions. Both of these elements – rote imitation of well-understood behaviours and an awareness of how behaviour is likely to unfold – contribute to observational learning.

Observational learning is an important process by which species gather information about the world around them. Shaping by successive approximations can be slow and tedious, and trial-and-error learning often results in many errors before learning is complete. However, when one organism patterns its actions on another organism's successful behaviours, learning is speeded up and potentially dangerous errors are prevented.

If only we could model this domestic behaviour at home

Judy, a female chimpanzee, escaped from a US zoo. Before she was recaptured, she was observed entering a bathroom, grabbing a brush and cleaning a toilet. She also wrung out a sponge and cleaned off a refrigerator, according to an Associated Press report. Prior to coming to the zoo, Judy had been a home-reared animal.

In summary, classical and operant conditioning are forms of learning that are best understood as having cognitive and functional components that are the result of evolutionary processes. The same is true for observational learning. The cognitive component is fairly clear but observational learning also has roots in evolutionary biology and for the most basic of reasons: it has survival value. Learning by observing another individual to successfully negotiate a dangerous environment, deciding not to eat a food that has made others ill, or avoiding conflicts with those who have been seen to vanquish all their opponents are all behavioural advantages that can save an organism considerable pain or even its life.

Implicit learning: under the wires

So far, we have covered a lot of what is known about learning with only the briefest consideration of *awareness* in the learning process. You may remember we distinguished between explicit learning and implicit learning at the beginning of the chapter. People often know that they are learning, are aware of what they're learning, and can describe what they know about a topic. If you have learned something concrete, such as doing arithmetic or typing on a computer keyboard, you know that you know it and you know *what* it is you know.

But did Pavlov's dogs *know* that they had been conditioned to salivate to a buzzer? In the case of the sauce Béarnaise phenomenon, we may form associations based on false assumptions (that it is the food and not flu that caused our illness). It certainly makes sense to ask whether these basic learning processes in humans require an awareness on the part of the learner. Perhaps some permanent changes in experience can be acquired without the benefit of awareness.

Researchers began to investigate how children learned such complex behaviours as language and social conduct (Reber, 1967). Most children, by the time they are six or seven years old, are linguistically and socially fairly sophisticated. Yet, most children reach this state with very little explicit awareness that they have learned something and with equally little awareness of what it is they have actually learned. This simple observation poses theoretical challenges to traditional learning theories. As you'll recall from Chapter 1, linguist Noam Chomsky (1959) challenged behaviourist explanations of complex processes such as language acquisition and socialization. Learning to speak and understand English, for example, involves more than acquiring a series of stimulus-response associations or reinforcing successive approximations to grammatical sentences. Using a language is a creative process. Virtually every sentence we speak, hear, write or read is new. You understand this sentence that you are reading now, although this is almost certainly the first time you have encountered these words in this particular order. In fact, virtually every one of the sentences in this textbook is new to you, yet you understand them with little difficulty. Behaviourism cannot account for this kind of abstract process, so how can we tackle this problem?

For starters, it's safe to assume that people are sensitive to the patterns of events that occur in the world around them. Most people don't stumble through life thoroughly unaware of what's going on. (Okay, maybe some people you know might seem to!) But people usually are attuned to linguistic, social, emotional or sensorimotor events in the world around them so much so that they gradually build up internal representations of those patterns that were acquired without explicit awareness. This process is often called **implicit learning** – *learning that takes place largely independent of awareness of the process and the products of information acquisition.* As an example, although children are often given explicit rules of social conduct ('Don't chew with your mouth open'), they learn how to behave in a civilized way through experience. They're probably not aware of when or how they learned a particular course of action and may not even be able to state the general principle underlying their behaviour. Yet, most kids have learned not to eat with their feet, to listen when they are spoken to, and not to kick the dog. Implicit learning is knowledge that sneaks in 'under the wires'.

IMPLICIT LEARNING Learning that takes place largely independent of awareness of the process and the products of information acquisition.

Ways to study implicit learning

Early studies of implicit learning showed research participants 15 or 20 letter strings and asked them to memorize them. The letter strings, which at first glance look like nonsense syllables, were actually formed using a complex set of rules called an *artificial grammar* (see **FIGURE 6.13**). Participants were not told anything about the rules, but with experience, they gradually developed a vague, intuitive sense of the 'correctness' of particular letter groupings. These letter groups became familiar to the participants, and they processed these letter groupings more rapidly and efficiently than the 'incorrect' letter groupings (Reber, 1967, 1996).

Take a look at the letter strings shown in Figure 6.13. The ones on the left are 'correct' and follow the rules of the artificial grammar, while the ones on the right all violated the rules. The differences are pretty subtle, and if you haven't been through the learning phase of the experiment, both sets look a lot alike. In fact, each nongrammatical string only has a single letter violation. Research participants are asked to classify new letter strings based on whether they follow the rules of the grammar. People turn out to be quite good at this task (usually they get 60–70% correct), but they are unable to provide much in the way of explicit awareness of the rules and regularities they are using. The experience is like when you come across a sentence with a grammatical error – you are immediately aware that something is wrong and you can certainly make the sentence grammatical. But unless you are a trained linguist, you'll probably find it difficult to articulate which rules of English grammar were violated or which rules you used to repair the sentence.

Grammatical strings	Nongrammatical strings
VXJJ	VXTJJ
XXVT	XVTVVJ
VJTVXJ	VJTTVTV
VJTVTV	VJTXXVJ
XXXXVX	XXXVTJJ

FIGURE **6.13 Artificial grammar and implicit learning** These are examples of letter strings formed by an artificial grammar. Research participants are exposed to the rules of the grammar and are later tested on new letter strings. Participants show reliable accuracy at distinguishing the valid, grammatical strings from the invalid, nongrammatical strings even though they usually can't explicitly state the rule they are following when making such judgements. Using an artificial grammar is one way of studying implicit learning (Reber, 1996).

Other studies of implicit learning have used a *serial reaction time* task (Nissen and Bullemer, 1987). Here, research participants are presented with five small boxes on a computer screen. Each box lights up briefly, and when it does, the person is asked to press the button that is just underneath that box as quickly as possible. Immediately after the button is pressed, a different box lights up, the person has to press the corresponding button and so on. As with the artificial grammar task, the sequence of lights appears to be random, but in fact it follows a pattern. Research participants eventually get faster with practice as they learn to anticipate which box is most likely to light up next. If the sequence is changed or the patterns are modified, people's reaction times slow down, indicating that they were actually learning the sequence and not simply learning to press buttons quickly.

In these experiments, people are not looking for rules or patterns; they are 'blind' to the goals of the experiments. The participants' learning takes place outside their awareness. These studies establish implicit learning as a distinct form of learning (Stadler and Frensch, 1998).

Implicit learning has some characteristics that distinguish it from explicit learning. For example, when asked to carry out implicit tasks, people differ relatively little from one another, but on explicit tasks, such as conscious problem solving, they show large individual-to-individual differences (Reber et al., 1991). Implicit learning also seems to be unrelated to IQ: people with high scores on standard intelligence tests are no better at implicit learning tasks, on average, than those whose scores are more modest (Reber and Allen, 2000). Implicit learning changes little across the life span. Researchers discovered well-developed implicit learning of complex, rule-governed auditory patterns in eight-month-old infants (Saffran et al., 1996). Infants heard streams of speech that contained experimenter-defined nonsense words. For example, the infants might hear a sequence such as 'bidakupadotigolabubidaku', which contains the nonsense word *bida*. The infants weren't given any explicit clues as to which sounds were 'words' and which were not, but after several repetitions, the infants showed signs that they had learned the novel words. Infants tend to prefer novel information that had not been presented earlier rather than the nonsense words such as *bida* that had been presented. This was established by the amount of time infants spent attending to a speaker on one side playing each sound. Remarkably, the infants in this study were as good at learning these sequences as university students. At the other end of the life span, researchers have found that implicit learning abilities extend well into old age and they decline more slowly than explicit learning abilities (Howard and Howard, 1997).

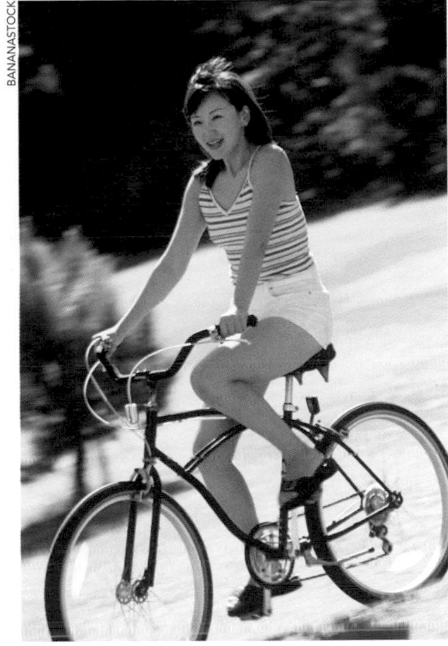

BANANASTOCK

Implicit learning, which is involved in acquiring and retaining the skills needed to ride a bicycle, tends to be less affected by age than explicit learning.

Implicit learning is remarkably resistant to various disorders that are known to affect explicit learning. A group of patients suffering from various psychoses were so severely impaired that they could not solve simple problems that university students had little difficulty with. Yet, these patients were able to solve an artificial grammar learning task about as well as university students (Abrams and Reber, 1988). Other studies have found that profoundly amnesiac patients not only show normal implicit memories but also display virtually normal implicit learning of artificial grammar (Knowlton et al., 1992). In fact, these patients made accurate judgements about novel letter strings even though they had essentially no explicit memory of having been in the learning phase of the experiment.

Implicit and explicit learning use distinct neural pathways

The fact that patients suffering from psychoses or amnesia show implicit learning strongly suggests that the brain structures that underlie implicit leaning are distinct from those that underlie explicit learning. What's more, it appears that distinct regions of the brain may be activated, depending on how people approach a task.

Researchers found that distinct parts of the brain are activated when people approach a learning task in either an implicit or an explicit manner (Reber et al., 2003). Participants completed a simple pattern perception procedure. During the initial phase of the study, everyone saw a series of dot patterns, each of which looked like an array of stars in the night sky. In fact, all the stimuli were constructed to conform to an underlying prototypical dot pattern. The dots, however, varied so much that it was virtually impossible for a viewer to guess that they all had this common structure. Before the experiment began, half of the participants were told about the existence of the prototype; in other words, they were given instructions that encouraged explicit processing. The others were given standard implicit learning instructions: they were told nothing other than to pay attention to the dot patterns. The participants were then scanned as they made decisions about new dot patterns, attempting to categorize them into those that conformed to the prototype and those that did not. Interestingly, both groups performed equally well on this task, correctly classifying about 65% of the new dot patterns. However, the brain scans revealed that the two groups were making these decisions using very different parts of their brains (see **FIGURE 6.14**). Participants who were given the explicit instructions showed *increased* brain activity in the prefrontal cortex, parietal cortex, hippocampus and a variety of other areas known to be associated with the processing of explicit memories. Those given the implicit instructions showed *decreased* brain activation primarily in the occipital region, which is involved in visual processing. This finding suggests that participants recruited distinct brain structures in different ways depending on whether they were approaching the task using explicit or implicit learning.

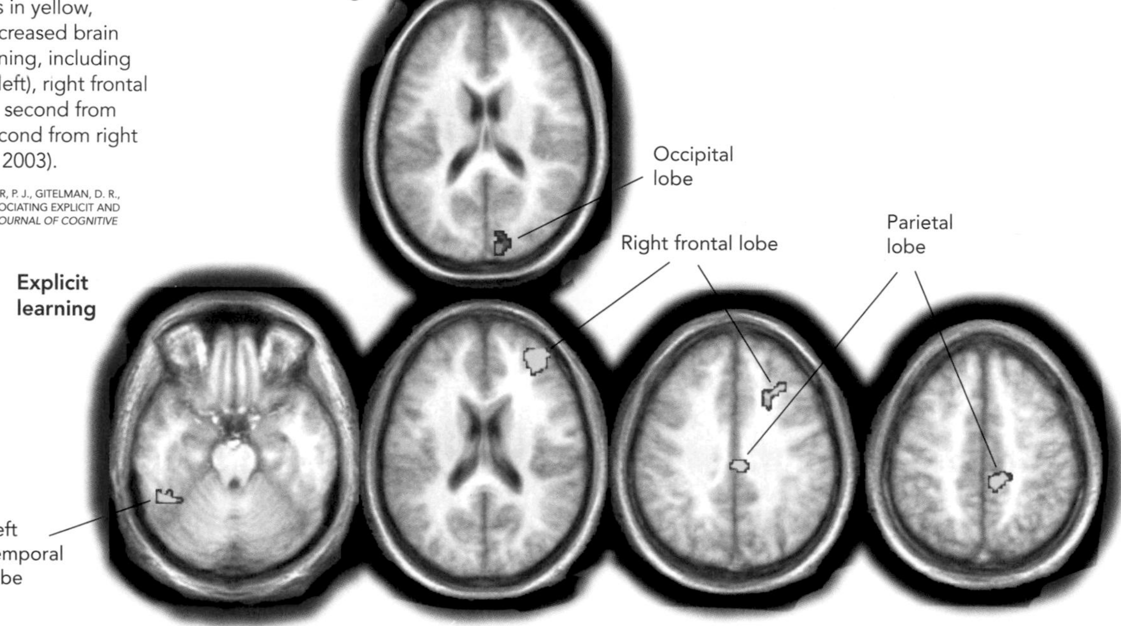

FIGURE 6.14 Implicit and explicit learning activate different brain areas Research participants were scanned with fMRI while engaged in either implicit or explicit learning about the categorization of dot patterns. The occipital region (in blue) showed decreased brain activity after implicit learning. The areas in yellow, orange and red showed increased brain activity during explicit learning, including the left temporal lobe (far left), right frontal lobe (second from left and second from right) and parietal lobe (second from right and far right) (Reber et al., 2003).

the real world

What's the best way to learn?

With decades of research on animal learning, you might think that we should know how best to educate human students. This is not always the case. Unfortunately, without the luxury of resources such as time, much education is conducted in a way that is not optimal for learning. For example, as we have already discovered, learning spaced out over a period of time is more likely to be retained for longer than information that is crammed into one session in an all-nighter. Practice also leads to more robust and durable learning than massed practice (Cepeda et al., 2006; Carpenter et al., 2009). Like throwing wet mud against a wall, you can get a large gloop to hold momentarily but it you want the information to stick, you have to throw smaller handfuls over time for it to build up. Unfortunately, that is not really how the education and evaluation systems work in most countries. Most operate with a method whereby students are taught on a course and then assessed on what they can remember at the end. This leads to a situation where students have to revise and focus on what they have just been taught rather than return to previous material that may also be related but not under examination. Although optimal in terms of students' short-term goals, this strategy is costly for the long-term aim of maintaining accessibility of knowledge and skills. For example, medical students forget roughly 25–35% of basic science knowledge after 1 year, more than 50% by the next year and 80–85% after 25 years (Custers and ten Cate, 2011). This does raise some serious concerns about what education is for and who is best suited to do well in the current system of rapid turnover and evaluation.

One recent study has shown that in the case of year 8 students (in their second year at senior school) learning a second language, different reviewing strategies produced significantly different learning outcomes (Lindsey et al., 2014). Students had 10 chapters of Spanish translation to learn over ten weeks and were entered into a web-based revision programme that produced three different strategies for revising for 30 minutes a week. In the *massed* strategy, students reviewed the current week's material – a strategy that is typically used by most schools. In the *generic spaced* strategy, students learned material that was selected based on previous students' performance, which gave an indication of the difficulty of the material to be learned. Finally, one group were given a *personalized spaced* strategy that took into consideration the student's own previous attempts at learning material, so that each student was, in effect, acting as their own guideline. For example, if they spent more time on material in the past, and made the correct translation, then there was no need to spend further time trying to remember.

When tested for Spanish translation at the end of the semester and then one month later, the best strategy was the personalized spaced strategy, followed by the generic spaced strategy and then lastly the massed. The most likely explanation is that individuals are the best source to consult when evaluating the difficulty they will have in learning new material, followed next by the group consensus, with simple block learning failing to take into consideration the difference in the nature of the material to be learned.

Consistent with the adaptive-scheduling literature (Metzler-Baddeley and Baddeley, 2009), this study shows that a one-size-fits-all variety of revision is significantly less effective than personalized strategies. However, the difficulty remains in trying to implement personalized strategies in an education system under pressure to demonstrate that short-term goals have been met at the cost of achieving long-terms aims.

In summary, implicit learning is a process that detects, learns and stores patterns without the application of explicit awareness on the part of the learner. Complex behaviours, such as language use or socialization, can be learned through this implicit process. Tasks that have been used to document implicit learning include artificial grammar and serial reaction time tasks. Implicit and explicit learning differ from each other in a number of ways. There are fewer individual differences in implicit than explicit learning, psychotic and amnesiac patients with explicit learning problems can exhibit intact implicit learning, and neuroimaging studies indicate that implicit and explicit learning recruit distinct brain structures, sometimes in different ways.

psychomythology

You can learn in your sleep

In a 1992 episode of *The Simpsons*, Homer decides to lose weight by sending off for a sleep-learning tape to induce weight loss. However, the mail-order company sends him vocabulary builder tapes instead, so that Homer continues to put on weight but unexpectedly becomes an extraordinarily eloquent speaker. Proponents of sleep-assisted learning or *hypnopaedia* have claimed that, like Homer, you can also learn foreign languages, pass exams, stop smoking, reduce stress and even become a better lover simply by listening to subliminal messages in your sleep. The invention of sleep learning can be traced to Alois B. Saliger, a New York fraudster, who, in 1927, invented the 'Psycho-Phone' with ads that claimed that 'this automatic suggestion machine enables you to direct the vast powers of your unconscious mind during sleep'. Sound familiar? (See Chapter 3's psychomythology – You only use 10% of your brain.) The myth of sleep learning has become so pervasive that it pops up in popular culture in the likes of cult films such as *A Clockwork Orange*, and the hit sitcom, *Friends*. A survey of undergraduate students revealed that 68% believed that people can learn in their sleep (Brown, 1983).

Part of the myth has some basis in truth. It has been shown that we can incorporate external stimulation into our dreams. Have you ever dreamed about a fire emergency only to discover that it is the sound of your alarm clock as you awake? Classic research by Dement and Wolpert (1958) showed that if you squirt water on the face of a sleeping participant, they report they dreamed of a leaking roof. Somewhere between 10–50% of us will incorporate external stimuli such as bells, red lights and voices into our dreams (Berger, 1963; Bradley and Meddis, 1974; Conduit and Coleman, 1998).

Also, as you learned in Chapter 5, experiences that become part of our permanent memories are those that undergo a variety of neurological modifications, and there are good reasons for believing that many of these changes take place during sleep. For example, researchers asked participants to complete a task that involved learning a series of digits presented as stimulus-response sequences but didn't tell them that the series of digits followed a complex rule. Participants exhibited implicit learning – they got faster as they practised the task – but only about 25% of them showed awareness of the rule. However, after a night's sleep, nearly 60% of the participants discovered the rule. It wasn't just the passage of time that caused this dramatic increase in learning and insight. Participants in the control group, who stayed awake for the same eight hours after learning, showed a rate of insight comparable to that shown by the original data, that is, only about 25% of them discovered the rule. It also didn't matter what time of day these events took place. Eight hours awake during the day produced the same outcomes as eight hours awake during the night (Wagner et al., 2004). These striking results suggest that sleep can promote the restructuring of knowledge, providing the backdrop for what later appears as sudden and spontaneous insights.

However, there is no evidence that sleeping individuals can acquire skills that require conscious attention. When subjects' brain waves are monitored to ensure that they are truly unconscious, there is little or no evidence for sleep-assisted learning (Logie and Della Sala, 1999). Rather than trying to cram for your exams by listening to sleep tapes, it is probably better to get a good night's rest!

where do you stand?

Learning for rewards or for its own sake?

The principles of operant conditioning and the merits of reinforcement have more than found their way into mainstream culture. The least psychology-savvy parent intuitively understands that rewarding a child's good behaviour should make that behaviour more likely to occur in the future; the 'law of effect' may mean nothing to this parent, but the principle and the outcome are readily appreciated nonetheless. And what parent wouldn't want the best for their child? If reward shapes good behaviour, then more reward must be the pathway to exemplary behaviour, often in the form of good grades, high test scores and overall clean living. So, bring on the rewards!

Maybe, maybe not. As you learned earlier in this chapter, the *overjustification effect* predicts that too much external reinforcement for performing an intrinsically rewarding task can sometimes undermine future performance. Rewarding a child for getting good marks might backfire: the child may come to see the behaviour as directed towards the attainment of rewards rather than for its own satisfying outcomes. In short, learning should be fun for its own sake, not because new toys, new clothes or cash are riding on a set of straight As.

Many parents – and some schools – seem to think differently. For example, at your primary school, were gold stars ever handed out as a reward for particularly good work? And do you have friends whose parents shower them with gifts each time they get good exam results? (In fact, you may have experienced this yourself.) Nobody objects to a little recognition now and then, and it's nice to know that others appreciate your hard work. But where is the line? Does it make a difference how much money is being offered?

Also, as you will discover in Chapter 11, sometimes praise can be counterproductive for a child. If a child is praised too much for being clever, they may come to believe that all their successes come down to their natural ability so that when they are faced with a difficult challenge, they are more likely to give up because they think it is beyond their capability (Cain and Dweck, 1995).

Is this much ado about nothing or too much of a good thing? Some proponents of rewarding good academic performance argue that it mirrors the real world that, presumably, academic performance is preparing students to enter. After all, in most jobs, better performance is reinforced with better salaries, so why not model that in the school system? Even without the promise of financial reward from one's parents, doesn't the prospect of winning a place at the university of your choice represent an extrinsic reward in its own right? How is that different from hard cash? On the other hand, shouldn't the search for knowledge be reward enough? Is the subtle shift away from wanting to learn for its own sake to wanting to learn for a reward harmful in the long run? Where do you stand on this issue?

Chapter review

Defining learning: experience that causes a permanent change

- Learning refers to any of several processes that produce relatively permanent changes in an organism's behaviour.
- Habituation is a process by which an organism changes the way it reacts to external stimuli as a result of repeated or prolonged exposure. Short-term habituation is distinguished from learning because the changes are not long lasting. Long-term habituation is generally regarded as learning.

Classical conditioning: one thing leads to another

- Classical conditioning is a kind of learning in which a conditioned stimulus (CS) begins to elicit a conditioned response (CR) as a result of pairing with an unconditioned stimulus (US); an unconditioned stimulus is one that innately elicits a reflex-like behaviour (UR).
- Stimulus generalization occurs if a CS that is similar to the one used in the original training is introduced. Stimulus discrimination is the flip side of generalization.
- Extinction of a learned response will occur if the CS is presented repeatedly without being followed by the US. Spontaneous recovery occurs if an organism is allowed a rest period following extinction.
- Classical conditioning was originally viewed as an automatic and mechanical process. However, it was soon discovered that neural, cognitive and evolutionary elements were involved in the process.

Operant conditioning: reinforcements from the environment

- Operant conditioning is a kind of learning in which behaviours are shaped by their consequences.
- Whereas classical conditioning involves reflex-like behaviours elicited from an organism, operant conditioning deals with overt, controlled and emitted behaviours.
- Reinforcement is any operation that functions to increase the likelihood of the behaviour that led to it. Punishment functions to decrease the likelihood of the behaviour.
- Like classical conditioning, operant conditioning shows acquisition, generalization, discrimination and extinction. The schedule with which reinforcements are delivered has a dramatic effect on how well an operant behaviour is learned and how resistant it is to extinction.
- Like classical conditioning, operant conditioning is better understood by taking into account underlying neural, cognitive and evolutionary components.
- Latent learning and the development of cognitive maps in animals clearly implicate cognitive factors underlying operant learning. The evolutionary histories of individual species promote different patterns of operant learning.

Observational learning: look at me

- Learning can take place through the observation of others and does not necessarily require that the acquired behaviours be performed and reinforced.
- Observational learning occurs in various animal species, including pigeons and monkeys. At a neural level, mirror cells are implicated in the imitation and expectation of behaviour.

Implicit learning: under the wires

- Implicit learning takes place largely in the absence of awareness of either the actual learning or the knowledge of what was learned. Infants show intact implicit learning long before they develop conscious awareness. Various patient populations, such as psychotics and those with severe neurological disorders, show virtually normal implicit learning.
- Implicit learning is mediated by areas in the brain that are distinct from those activated during explicit learning. The brain structures that regulate the implicit learning system evolved much earlier than those that regulate explicit processing.

Key terms

acquisition (p. 232)
biological preparedness (p. 241)
classical conditioning (p. 230)
cognitive map (p. 254)
conditioned response (CR) (p. 231)
conditioned stimulus (CS) (p. 230)
contingency (p. 238)
discrimination (p. 235)
excitatory association (p. 234)
extinction (p. 233)
fixed interval (FI) schedule (p. 248)
fixed ratio (FR) schedule (p. 249)
generalization (p. 235)
habituation (p. 228)
implicit learning (p. 260)
inhibitory association (p. 234)
intermittent reinforcement (p. 249)
intermittent reinforcement effect (p. 250)
latent learning (p. 253)
law of effect (p. 243)
learning (p. 228)
observational learning (p. 258)
operant behaviour (p. 243)
operant conditioning (p. 242)
overjustification effect (p. 246)
punisher (p. 244)
reinforcer (p. 244)
second-order conditioning (p. 232)
shaping (p. 250)
spatial representation (p. 255)
spontaneous recovery (p. 233)
unconditioned response (UR) (p. 230)
unconditioned stimulus (US) (p. 230)
variable interval (VI) schedule (p. 248)
variable ratio (VR) schedule (p. 249)

Recommended reading

Buckley, K. W. (1989) *Mechanical Man: John Broadus Watson and the Beginnings of Behaviourism.* New York: Guilford Press. There are many biographies of Watson available, but this is one of the best. Kerry Buckley is a historian specializing in the history of psychology, and has published numerous scholarly works on Watson's life and ideas.

Hood, B. (2009) *Supersense: From Superstition to Religion – The Brain Science of Belief.* London: Constable & Robinson. Popular science book that expounds the theory that humans are naturally inclined to form superstitious rituals and hold supernatural beliefs as a consequence of the way our brains have evolved to seek out patterns and infer hidden mechanisms.

Skinner, B. F. (1971) *Beyond Freedom and Dignity.* New York: Bantam Books. This book, reprinted by Hackett Publishing in 2002, is largely considered Skinner's definitive statement on humankind and its behaviour. Skinner argues that most of society's problems can be better addressed by reshaping the environment following the principles of operant conditioning. Outmoded concepts such as 'freedom' and 'human dignity' should be abandoned in favour of developing more effective cultural practices. A controversial book when it first appeared, it remains so today.

Todes, D. P. (2000) *Pavlov: Exploring the Animal Machine.* New York: OUP. This overview of Pavlov's life and work is part of the Oxford Portraits in Science series, a set of titles that provide easy access to information about key scientists in all disciplines. This title should provide a bit more background about Pavlov's discoveries and the events in his life that helped shape his work.

7

Chapter learning objectives

At the end of this chapter you will be able to:

1. Describe the basic goals and building blocks of language.
2. Compare the behaviourist, nativist and interactionist explanations of language development.
3. State the linguistic determinism hypothesis and give evidence for and against it.
4. Describe and explain how concepts constrain cognition.
5. Describe and explain the range of different mindbugs that influence reasoning and decision making.

Language and thought

An English boy named Christopher showed an amazing talent for languages. By the age of six, he had learned French from his sister's schoolbooks, and he acquired Greek from a textbook in only three months. His talent was so prodigious that when he was an adult, Christopher could converse fluently in 16 languages. When tested on English–French translations, he scored as well as a native French speaker. Presented with a made-up language, he figured out the complex rules easily, even though advanced language students found them virtually impossible to decipher (Smith and Tsimpli, 1995).

If you've concluded that Christopher is extremely intelligent, perhaps even a genius, you're wrong. Instead, he's a savant with highly limited cognitive abilities. His scores on standard intelligence tests are far below normal. He fails simple cognitive tests that four-year-old children pass with ease, and he cannot even learn the rules for simple games like noughts and crosses. Despite his dazzling talent, Christopher lives in a halfway house because he does not have the cognitive capacity to make decisions, reason or solve problems in a way that would allow him to live independently.

Christopher's strengths and weaknesses offer compelling evidence that cognition is composed of distinct abilities. People who learn languages with lightning speed are not necessarily gifted at decision making or problem solving. People who excel at reasoning may have no special ability to master languages. In this chapter, you will learn about several higher cognitive functions that distinguish us as humans: acquiring and using language, forming concepts and categories, making decisions, solving problems, and reasoning. We excel at these skills compared with other animals, and they help define who we are as a species.

LANGUAGE A system for communicating with others using signals that convey meaning and are combined according to rules of grammar.

Bees communicate with each other about the location of food by doing a waggle dance that indicates the direction and distance of food from the hive.

Language and communication: nothing's more personal

Language is *a system for communicating with others using signals that convey meaning and are combined according to rules of grammar.* Language allows individuals to exchange information about the world, coordinate group action, and form strong social bonds. Most social species have systems of communication that allow them to transmit messages to each other. Bees communicate the location of food sources by means of a 'waggle dance' that indicates the direction and distance of the food source from the hive (Kirchner and Towne, 1994; von Frisch, 1974). Vervet monkeys have three different warning calls that uniquely signal the presence of their main predators – a leopard, an eagle and a snake (Cheney and Seyfarth, 1990). A leopard call provokes them to climb higher into a tree, while an eagle call makes them look up into the sky. Each different warning call conveys a particular meaning and functions like a word in a simple language.

In this section, we'll examine the elements of human language that contribute to its complex structure, the ease with which we acquire language despite this complexity, and how biological and environmental influences shape language acquisition and use. We'll also look at startling disorders that reveal how language is organized in the brain and at researchers' attempts to teach apes human language. Finally, we'll consider the long-standing puzzle of how language and thought are related.

The complex structure of human language

Human language may have evolved from signalling systems used by other species. However, three striking differences distinguish human language from vervet monkey yelps:

1 The complex structure of human language distinguishes it from simpler signalling systems. Most humans can express a wider range of ideas and concepts than are found in the communications of other species.
2 Humans use words to refer to intangible things, such as *unicorn* or *democracy*. These words could not have originated as simple alarm calls.
3 We use language to name, categorize and describe things to ourselves when we think, which influences how knowledge is organized in our brains. It's doubtful that bees consciously think, 'I'll fly north today to find more honey so the queen will be impressed!'

Compared with other forms of communication, human language is a relatively recent evolutionary phenomenon, emerging as a spoken system no more than 1–3 million years ago and as a written system as little as 6,000 years ago. There are approximately 4,000 human languages, which linguists have grouped into about 50 language families (Nadasdy, 1995). Despite their differences, all these languages share a basic structure involving a set of sounds and rules for combining those sounds to produce meanings.

Generating language

The building blocks of language are sounds that form words, which are usually arranged into phrases to generate sentences. According to Levelt (1989), the act of speech involves at least three separate processes:

1 *Conceptualization:* the speaker plans the content of the message to be communicated – 'What do you want to say?'
2 *Formulation:* the speaker transforms the message into a sentences in terms of its constituent parts – 'How do you want to say it in a meaningful way that others will understand?'
3 *Articulation:* the speaker executes the process of delivering the message – 'How to speak the message you want to communicate.'

Conceptualization operates at the thought level and reflects the message to be conveyed within the context of the situation (Clark and Carlson, 1981). This planning is based on who is present, what has to be said and the circumstances under which the communication takes place. For example, conversations between lovers are different to those between bosses and employees (or at least they should be!). When there is no time pressure, speakers fully plan in advance what they want to say (Ferreira and Swets, 2002). However, messages change if you want someone else to respond quickly, as in 'Look out!'

Formulation is like the blueprint of what you want to say in terms of the actual words to be used and how they are ordered. This requires lexicalization – *the process whereby the thoughts underlying the words are turned into sounds.* In Chapter 5, we encountered that familiar and frustrating 'tip-of-the-tongue' feeling – when you just cannot quite seem to find the right word (usually something slightly obscure or unusual). For example, what is the word that means to formally give up the throne? You may know that you know it, but be unable to say what the answer is. Such episodes reveal that there is a problem of retrieving the word from memory but that the conceptualization stage has occurred although the formulation process has not (Brown and McNeill, 1966).

LEXICALIZATION The process whereby the thoughts underlying the words are turned into sounds.

Articulation addresses how words physically are uttered in speech. The larynx (voice box), tongue and mouth are all involved in this process, shaping the flow of air to produce different sounds. Interestingly, although modern humans and Neanderthals shared many physical similarities, it has been suggested that Neanderthals would not have been able to articulate as clearly as we do, because they could not control their tongues as well (Harley, 2008).

Basic characteristics

The smallest unit of sound, for example 'ba' and 'pa', that is recognizable as speech rather than as random noise is the phoneme. These building blocks of spoken language differ in how they are produced. For example, when you say *ba*, your vocal cords start to vibrate as soon as you begin the sound, but when you say *pa*, there is a 60-millisecond lag between the time you start the *p* sound and the time your vocal cords start to vibrate. *B* and *p* are classified as separate phonemes in English because they differ in the way they are produced by the human speaker.

PHONEME The smallest unit of sound, for example 'ba' or 'pa', that is recognizable as speech rather than as random noise.

Different languages use between 12 and 85 phonemes; English has about 40 (Miller, 1994). What makes something a phoneme rather than noise depends on its use as a speech signal, not on its physical properties. For example, the language spoken by the !Kung people of Namibia, Botswana and Angola includes a clicking sound, a phoneme that does not appear in English.

Every language has phonological rules that *indicate how phonemes can be combined to produce speech sounds, for example '-ed' to signify the past tense of a verb.* The phonological rules of different languages specify whether particular speech sounds are used to form words within that particular language. For example, the initial sound *ts* is acceptable in German but not in English. As you'll see in a little while, infants are born with the ability to distinguish between phonemes, and learning the rules for combining them occurs automatically as long as infants hear language spoken around them.

PHONOLOGICAL RULES A set of rules that indicate how phonemes can be combined to produce speech sounds, for example '-ed' to signify the past tense of a verb.

Phonemes are combined to make morphemes – *the smallest meaningful units of language, for example 'cats' contains two, cat + plural s* (see FIGURE **7.1**). For example, your brain recognizes the *pe* sound you make at the beginning of *pat* as a speech *sound*, but it carries no particular meaning. The morpheme *pat*, on the other hand, is recognized as an element of speech that carries meaning.

MORPHEMES The smallest meaningful units of language, for example 'cats' contains two, cat + plural s.

All languages have a grammar – *a set of rules that specify how the units of language can be combined to produce meaningful messages.* These rules generally fall into two categories: rules of morphology and rules of syntax. Morphological rules *indicate how morphemes can be combined to form words.* Some morphemes – content morphemes and function morphemes – can stand alone as words. *Content morphemes* refer to things and events (for example 'cat', 'dog', 'take'). *Function morphemes* serve grammatical functions, such as tying sentences together ('and', 'or', 'but') or indicating time ('when'). About half the morphemes in human languages are function morphemes, and it is the function morphemes that make human language grammatically complex enough to permit us to express abstract ideas rather than simply to verbally point to real objects in the here and now.

GRAMMAR A set of rules that specify how the units of language can be combined to produce meaningful messages.

MORPHOLOGICAL RULES A set of rules that indicate how morphemes can be combined to form words.

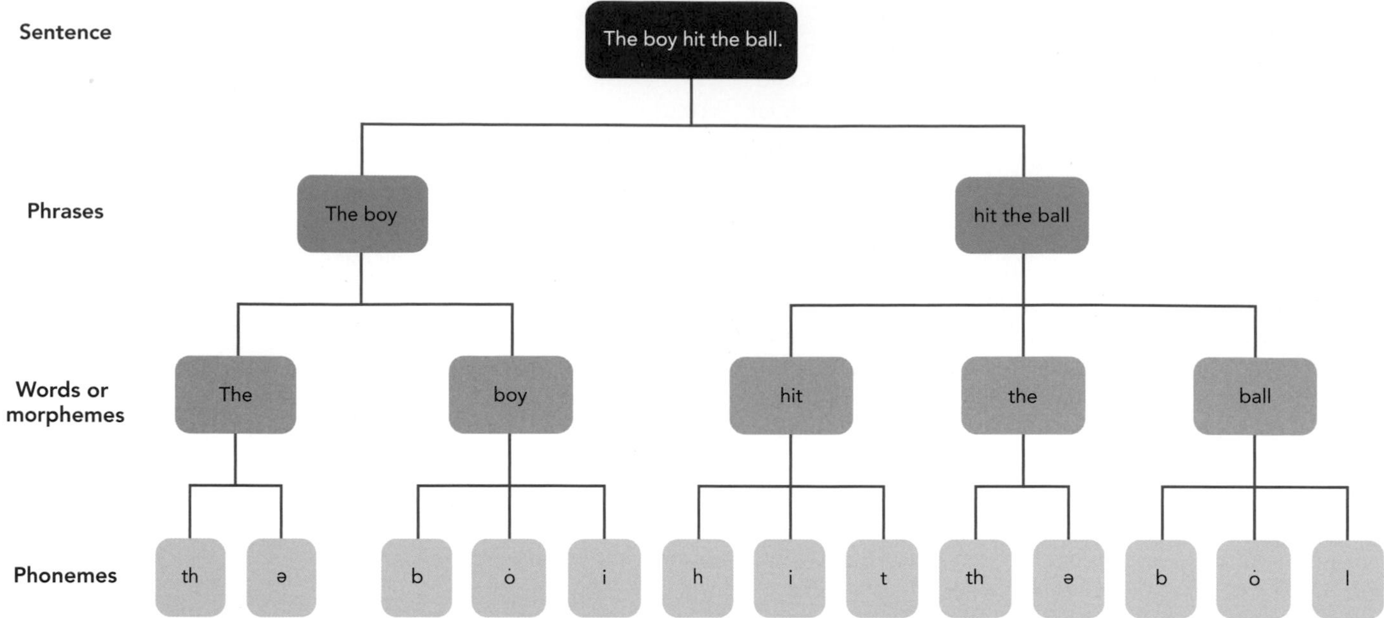

FIGURE **7.1** **Units of language** A sentence – the largest unit of language – can be broken down into progressively smaller units: phrases, morphemes and phonemes. In all languages, phonemes and morphemes form words, which can be combined into phrases and ultimately into sentences.

SYNTACTICAL RULES A set of rules that indicate how words can be combined to form phrases and sentences.

Content and function morphemes can be combined and recombined to form an infinite number of new sentences, which are governed by syntax. Syntactical rules *indicate how words can be combined to form phrases and sentences.* A simple syntactical rule in English is that every sentence must contain one or more nouns, which may be combined with adjectives or articles to create noun phrases (see FIGURE **7.2**). A sentence also must contain one or more verbs, which may be combined with adverbs or articles to create verb phrases. The utterance 'dogs bark' is a full sentence because it contains both a noun phrase and a verb phrase. The utterance 'the big grey dog over by the building' is not a sentence because there is no verb phrase, only a very long noun phrase. If someone uttered that phrase to you, you'd find yourself wondering, 'Yes, well, what about the dog?', that is, you'd be waiting for a verb phrase.

Chatterboxes: conversation

Talking and listening to others is an important human preoccupation. Conversation is a collaborative effort that allows information to be communicated. Every time we communicate, we perform a speech act, that is, we try to get things done with language (Austin, 1976; Searle, 1969). According to Searle (1969), every speech act falls into five communicative categories:

1 *Representative:* Asserting a fact or conveying a belief that a statement is true –'I am a psychology student.'
2 *Directive:* Trying to get the audience to do something such as answer a question – 'Are you a psychology student too?'
3 *Commissive:* An assertion of a future goal – 'I want to graduate with a first-class honours degree.'
4 *Expressive:* Revealing an internal psychological state – 'I am not so sure that I have done enough revision to get a first.'
5 *Declarative:* Announcing a new or previously unattended state of affairs – 'This is the first time I have told anyone about my concerns.'

ALIGNMENT The process whereby speakers share a reciprocal arrangement to exchange information.

But there is more to conversation than simply making speech acts. Pickering and Garrod (2004) proposed that the success of a conversation depends on the alignment of speakers and listeners. Alignment *is the process whereby speakers share a reciprocal arrangement to exchange information.* This is achieved largely by four automatic mechanisms of priming, inference, the use of routine expressions, and the monitoring and repair of language:

1 Priming, which we encountered in Chapter 5, is the enhanced ability to think of a stimulus, such as a word or object, as a result of a recent exposure to the stimulus.

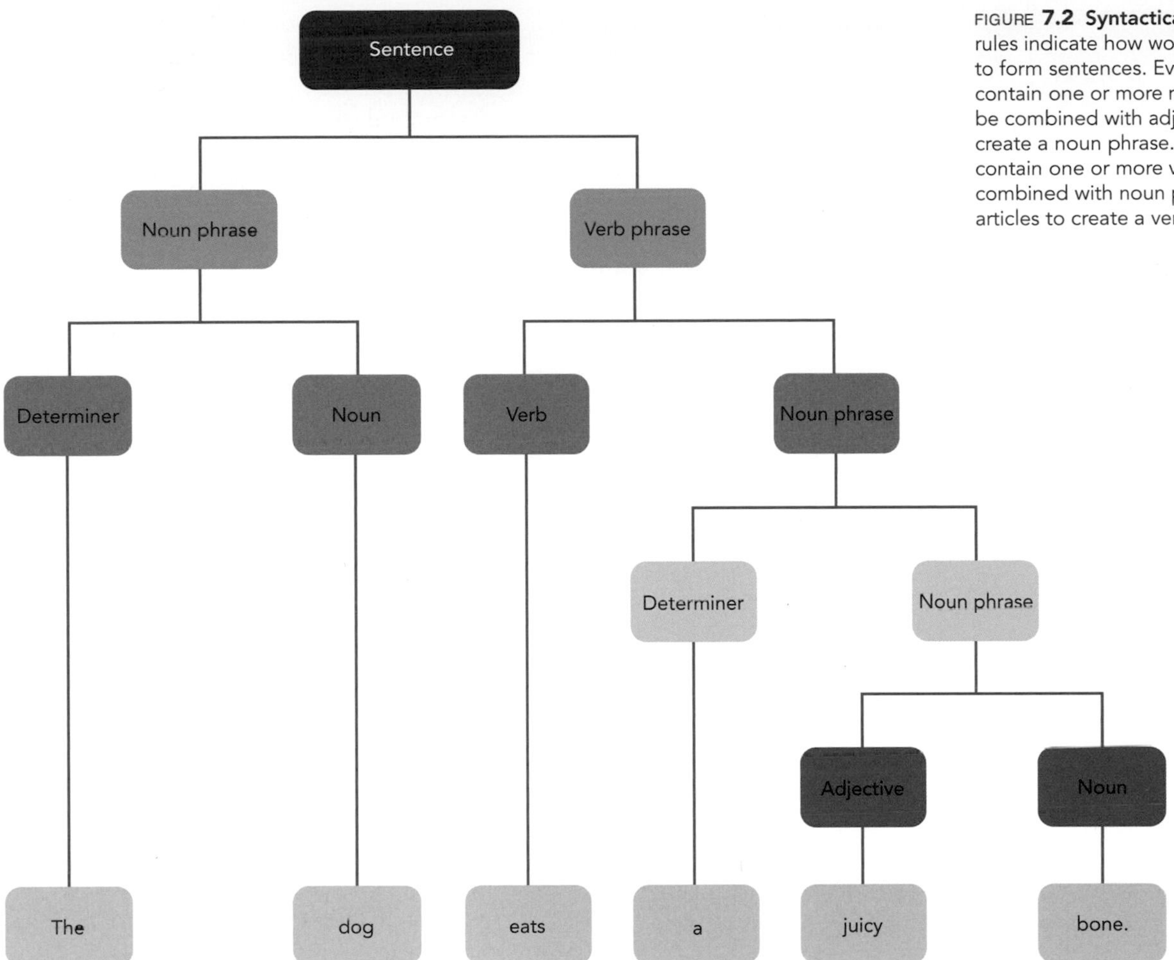

FIGURE **7.2 Syntactical rules** Syntactical rules indicate how words can be combined to form sentences. Every sentence must contain one or more nouns, which may be combined with adjectives or articles to create a noun phrase. A sentence also must contain one or more verbs, which may be combined with noun phrases, adverbs or articles to create a verb phrase.

2 Inference is where *speakers generate deeper conceptual understanding based on what has been said.*
3 Routine expressions are *unambiguous conventions that facilitate language*, such as 'As I said before ...'.
4 Speech monitoring and repair of language occurs when *speakers interact to understand what others are saying by seeking clarification*, such as 'So what you are really saying is ...'.

Clearly, successful conversation requires smooth turn-taking, which is signalled by the structure of the language, the nature of the information being exchanged, the intonation and phrasing of the speaker, and the nonverbal signals such as gaze that instruct each speaker and listener when to exchange roles (Sacks et al., 1974). As you are probably well aware, some of us are much better at conversation than others, and it is a skill that takes time to develop.

INFERENCE Speakers generate deeper conceptual understanding based on what has been said.

ROUTINE EXPRESSIONS Unambiguous conventions that facilitate language.

SPEECH MONITORING AND REPAIR Speakers interact to understand what others are saying by seeking clarification.

Language development

Language is a complex cognitive skill, yet we learn to speak and understand with little effort. We can carry on complex conversations with playmates and family before we begin school. Let's look at how children master the complexity of language despite having very little formal training.

Three characteristics of language development are worth bearing in mind:

1 Children learn language at an astonishingly rapid rate. The average one-year-old has a vocabulary of 10 words. This expands to over 10,000 words in the next four years, requiring the child to learn, on average, 6–7 new words every day.

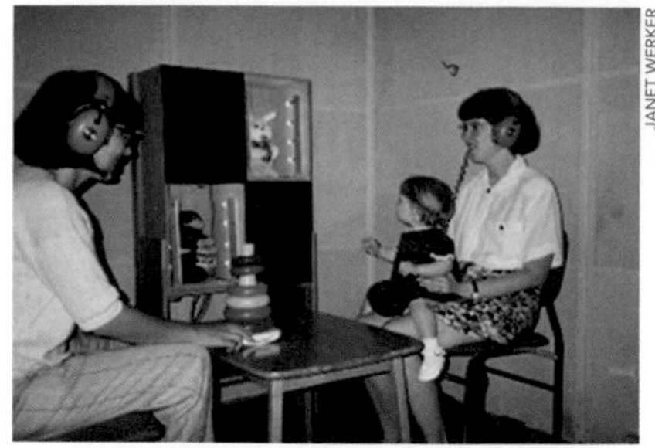

In this test, the baby watches an animated toy animal while a single speech sound is repeated. After a few repetitions, the sound changes and then the display changes, and then they both change again. If the baby switches their attention when the sound changes, they are anticipating the new display, which demonstrates that they can discriminate between the sounds.

For Japanese speakers, English words that have *l* and *r* sounds are often confused, which can lead to comical miscommunication. Steven Pinker (1994) wrote about his visit to Japan in *The Language Instinct* where he described how the Japanese linguist Masaaki Yamanashi greeted him with a twinkle and said: 'In Japan, we have been very interested in Clinton's erection.' This was several years before the US president would face impeachment in 1998 following the revelations of his extramarital affairs.

2 Children make few errors while learning to speak, and the errors they do make usually respect grammatical rules. This is an extraordinary feat. There are over 3 million ways to rearrange the words in any 10-word sentence, but only a few of these arrangements will be both grammatically correct and meaningful (Bickerton, 1990).
3 Children's *passive mastery* of language develops faster than their *active mastery.* At every stage of language development, children understand language better than they speak.

Distinguishing speech sounds

At birth, infants can distinguish between all the contrasting sounds that occur in all human languages. Within the first six months of life, they lose this ability, and, like their parents, can only distinguish between the contrasting sounds in the language they hear being spoken around them. For example, two distinct sounds in English are the *l* sound and the *r* sound, as in *lead* and *read.* These sounds are not distinguished in Japanese, where the *l* and *r* sounds fall within the same phoneme. Japanese adults cannot hear the difference between these two phonemes, but English-speaking adults can distinguish between them easily, and so can Japanese infants.

In one study, researchers constructed a tape of a voice saying 'la-la-la' or 'ra-ra-ra' repeatedly (Eimas et al., 1971). They rigged a dummy so that whenever an infant sucked on it, a tape player that broadcasted the 'la-la' tape was activated. When the *la-la* sound began playing in response to their sucking, the babies were delighted and kept sucking on the dummy to keep the *la-la* sound playing. After a while, they began to lose interest, and sucking frequency declined to about half its initial rate. At this point, the experimenters switched the tape so that the voice now said 'ra-ra-ra' repeatedly. The Japanese infants began sucking again with vigour, indicating that they could hear the difference between the old, boring *la* sound and the new, interesting *ra* sound.

These kinds of studies help explain why it is so difficult to learn a second language as an adult. You might not even be able to *hear* some of the speech sounds that carry crucial information in the language you want to learn, much less pronounce them properly. In a very real sense, your brain has become too specialized for your native language! That's not to say that if you've been exposed to a second language at an early stage in your life, you lose all trace of the linguistic skills you obtained as a child. For example, British children who spent their early years in India or South Africa and heard some Hindi or Zulu, but who grew up into adults isolated from these foreign languages, were able to distinguish differences between phonemes in these languages better than adults who were never exposed (Bowers et al., 2009). This shows that early exposure to a language as a child can leave some residual memory for its phonetic structures.

Infants can distinguish between speech sounds, but they cannot produce them reliably, relying mostly on cooing, cries, laughs and other vocalizations to communicate. Between the ages of about four and six months, they begin to babble speech sounds. Regardless of the language they hear spoken, all infants go through the same babbling sequence. For example, *d* and *t* appear in infant babbling before *m* and *n.* Even deaf babies babble sounds they've never heard, and produce the same patterns of sounds as hearing babies do (Ollers and Eilers, 1988). This is evidence that babies aren't simply imitating the sounds they hear and suggests that babbling is a natural part of the language development process. Deaf babies don't babble as much, however, and their babbling is delayed relative to hearing babies (eleven months rather than six).

In order for vocal babbling to continue, babies must be able to hear themselves. In fact, delayed babbling or the cessation of babbling merits testing for possible hearing difficulties. However, babbling is not an early version of language, as the repertoire is very limited. Rather, it may reflect how infants practise at gaining control over the motor mechanisms that are used for articulation (Clark and Clark, 1977). This may explain why deaf infants whose parents communicate using sign language begin to babble with their hands at the same age that hearing children begin to babble vocally – between four and six months (Petitto and Marentette, 1991). Their manual babbling consists of movements that eventually form some of the symbols that become fundamental components of sign languages.

Language milestones

At about 10–12 months of age, babies begin to utter (or sign) their first words. By 18 months, they can say about 50 words and can understand several times more than that. Toddlers generally learn nouns before verbs, and the nouns they learn first are names for everyday, concrete objects, for example chair, table, milk (see TABLE **7.1**). At about this time, their vocabularies undergo explosive growth. By the time the average child begins school, a vocabulary of 10,000 words is not unusual. At the start of secondary school, the average child knows the meanings of 40,000 words. By university, the average student's vocabulary is about 200,000 words. Fast mapping, in which *children map a word onto an underlying concept after only a single exposure*, enables them to learn at this rapid pace (Mervis and Bertrand, 1994).

FAST MAPPING Children map a word onto an underlying concept after only a single exposure.

TABLE **7.1 Language milestones**

Average age	Language milestones
0–4 months	Can tell the difference between speech sounds (phonemes). Cooing, especially in response to speech
4–6 months	Babbles consonants
6–10 months	Understands some words and simple requests
10–12 months	Begins to use single words
12–18 months	Vocabulary of 30–50 words – simple nouns, adjectives and action words
18–24 months	Two-word phrases ordered according to syntactic rules. Vocabulary of 50–200 words. Understands rules
24–36 months	Vocabulary of about 1,000 words. Production of phrases and incomplete sentences
36–60 months	Vocabulary grows to more than 10,000 words. Production of full sentences. Mastery of grammatical morphemes, such as *-ed* for past tense, and function words, such as *the, and, but*. Can form questions and negations

How does this happen? Researchers have suggested a number of constraints that limit how words are learned (Markman, 1990). For example, children assume that the word applies to the whole object rather than one part of it. If they hear the word 'car', children map the label to the whole vehicle and not just the wheels or the windscreen. Initially, children apply words to refer to the whole category, so that the child will use 'car' to refer to any vehicle that resembles a car – including trucks and vans. With experience, the child learns to apply the word exclusively so that a car is just a 'car' and not also a 'taxi' or a 'tractor'. As we will see in Chapter 12, children also learn to label an object with a word by interacting socially with adults who help to shape the rapid learning by drawing the child's attention to the object and naming it. This mapping process is astonishingly easy for young children, and contrasts dramatically with the effort required later to learn other concepts and skills, such as arithmetic or writing.

Around 24 months, children begin to form two-word sentences, such as 'more milk' or 'throw ball'. Such sentences are referred to as telegraphic speech because they are *devoid of function morphemes and consist mostly of content words.* Yet, despite the absence of function words, such as prepositions or articles, these two-word sentences tend to be grammatical; the words are ordered in a manner consistent with the syntactical rules of the language children are learning to speak. So, for example, toddlers will say 'throw ball' rather than 'ball throw' when they want you to throw the ball to them, and 'more milk' rather than 'milk more' when they want you to give them more milk. With these seemingly primitive expressions, two-year-olds show that they have already acquired an appreciation of the syntactical rules of the language they are learning.

TELEGRAPHIC SPEECH Speech that is devoid of function morphemes and consists mostly of content words.

The emergence of grammatical rules

Evidence of the ease with which children acquire grammatical rules comes from some interesting developmental mindbugs: errors that children make while forming sentences. If you listen to average two- or three-year-old children speaking, you may notice that they use the correct past tense versions of common verbs, as in the expressions 'I ran' and 'You ate'. By the age of four or five, the same children will be using incorrect forms of these verbs, saying such things as 'I runned' or 'You eated' – forms most children are unlikely to have ever heard (Prasada and Pinker, 1993). The reason is that very young children memorize the particular sounds, that is, words, that express what they want to communicate. But as children acquire the grammatical rules of their language, they tend to *overgeneralize*. For example, if a child overgeneralizes the rule that past tense is indicated by *-ed*, then *run* becomes *runned* or even *ranned* instead of *ran*.

These errors show that language acquisition is not simply a matter of imitating adult speech. Instead, children acquire grammatical rules by listening to the speech around them and using the rules to create verbal forms they've never heard. They manage this without explicit awareness of the grammatical rules they've learned. In fact, few children or adults can articulate the grammatical rules of their native language, yet the speech they produce obeys these rules.

By about three years of age, children begin to generate complete simple sentences that include function words, for example 'Give me *the* ball' and 'That belongs *to* me'. The sentences increase in complexity over the next two years. By four to five years of age, many aspects of the language acquisition process are complete. As children continue to mature, their language skills become more refined, with added appreciation of the subtler communicative uses of language, such as humour, sarcasm and irony.

Language development and cognitive development

Language development typically unfolds as a sequence of steps in which one milestone is achieved before moving on to the next. Nearly all infants begin with one-word utterances before moving on to telegraphic speech and then to simple sentences that include function morphemes. It's hard to find solid evidence of infants launching immediately into speaking in sentences, although you may occasionally hear reports of such feats from proud parents, including possibly your own! This orderly progression could result from general cognitive development that is unrelated to experience with a specific language (Shore, 1986; Wexler, 1999). For example, perhaps infants begin with one- and then two-word utterances because their short-term memories are so limited that initially they can only hold in mind a word or two; additional cognitive development might be necessary before they have the capacity to put together a simple sentence. By contrast, the orderly progression might depend on experience with a specific language, reflecting a child's emerging knowledge of that language (Bates and Goodman, 1997; Gillette et al., 1999).

These two possibilities are difficult to tease apart, but recent research has begun to do so using a novel strategy: examining the acquisition of English by internationally adopted children who did not know any English prior to adoption (Snedeker et al., 2007). While most adoptees to Western countries are infants or toddlers, a significant proportion are preschoolers. Studying the acquisition of English in a slightly older population provides a unique opportunity to explore the relationship between language development and cognitive development. If the orderly sequence of milestones that characterizes the acquisition of English by infants is a by-product of general cognitive development, then different patterns should be observed in older internationally adopted children, who are more advanced cognitively than infants. However, if the milestones of language development are critically dependent on experience with a specific language – English – then language learning in older adopted children should show the same orderly progression as seen in infants.

The researchers examined preschoolers ranging from two and a half to five and a half years old, 3–18 months after they were adopted from China (Snedeker et al., 2007). They did so by posting materials to parents, who periodically recorded language samples in their homes and also completed questionnaires concerning specific features of language observed in their children. These data were compared to similar data obtained from monolingual infants. The main result was clear-cut: language acquisition in preschool adopted children showed the same orderly progression of milestones that characterizes infants. These children began with one-word utterances before moving on to

hot science

Bedtime stories are best repeated

Shared storybook reading helps preschool children learn words (Hargrave and Sénéchal, 2000; Reese et al., 2010) and promotes later academic success (Rimm-Kaufman and Pianta, 2000; Whitehurst et al., 1988). But as every parent who reads to their child knows, they often want to hear the same story over and over again, such as *Goodnight Moon* or *The Very Hungry Caterpillar*. This may seem pointless as it would make more sense to hear lots of different stories to increase the vocabulary size but it turns out that repetition is a good strategy for remembering the words. Studies of three-year-olds found that those children who heard the same stories repeatedly over the course of a week performed very well on immediate recall and retention tasks. In contrast, children who heard different stories were only accurate on immediate recall during the last two sessions and failed to learn any of the new words (Horst et al., 2011). Better still is to read to the child before a nap. Preschool children were either read the same story repeatedly or different stories, and either napped after the stories or remained awake. They were then tested 2.5 hours later, 24 hours later and 7 days later to see how many words they could remember. The best memory for words came from those children who heard repeated readings and were allowed to nap immediately afterwards. A key finding is that children who read different stories before napping learned words as well as children who had the advantage of hearing the same story. In contrast, children who read different stories and remained awake never caught up to their peers on later word learning tests (Williams and Horst, 2014). So, while learning the same material over and over again helps you to remember, it is more important that you get a good night's rest so that you can consolidate the memory, as described in Chapter 5.

IMAGE SOURCE

Hearing the same story multiple times helps the recall and retention skills of young children.

simple word combinations. Further, their vocabulary, just like that of infants, was initially dominated by nouns and they produced few function morphemes. These results indicate that some of the key milestones of language development depend on experience with English. However, the adopted children did add new words to their vocabularies more quickly than infants did, perhaps reflecting an influence of general cognitive development. Overall, though, the main message from this study is that observed shifts in early language development reflect specific characteristics of language learning rather than general limitations of cognitive development.

Theories of language development

We know a good deal about how language develops, but the underlying acquisition processes have been the subject of considerable controversy and (at times) angry exchanges among theoreticians. The study of language and cognition underwent an enormous change in the 1950s, when linguist Noam Chomsky (1959) published a blistering reply to B. F. Skinner's behaviourist explanation of language learning. As you learned in Chapter 1, Skinner used principles of reinforcement to argue that we learn language the way he thought we learn everything – through imitation, instruction and trial-and-error learning. According to Chomsky, however, language learning capacities are built into the brain, which is specialized to rapidly acquire language through simple exposure to speech. Let's look at each theory and then examine more recent accounts of language development.

Behaviourist explanations

According to behaviourists, children acquire language through simple principles of operant conditioning (Skinner, 1957), which you learned about in Chapter 6. As infants mature, they begin to vocalize. Those vocalizations that are not reinforced gradually diminish, and those that are reinforced remain in the developing child's repertoire. So, for example, when an infant gurgles 'prah', most parents are pretty indifferent. However, a sound that even remotely resembles 'da-da' is likely to be reinforced with smiles, whoops and cackles of 'Goooood baaaaaby!' by doting parents. Maturing children also imitate the speech patterns they hear. Then parents or other adults shape those speech patterns by reinforcing those that are grammatical and ignoring or punishing those that are ungrammatical. 'I no want milk' is likely to be squelched by parental clucks and titters, whereas 'No milk for me, thanks' will probably be reinforced. According to Skinner, then, we learn to talk in the same way we learn any other skill: through reinforcement, shaping, extinction and the other basic principles of operant conditioning.

The behavioural explanation is attractive because it offers a simple account of language development, but the theory cannot account for many fundamental characteristics of language development (Chomsky, 1986; Pinker, 1994; Pinker and Bloom, 1990):

1 Parents don't spend much time teaching their children to speak grammatically. In one well-documented study, researchers found that parents typically respond more to the truth content of their children's statements than to the grammar (Brown and Hanlon, 1970). So, for example, when a child expresses a sentiment such as 'Nobody like me', their mother will respond with something like 'Why do you think that?' or 'I like you!', rather than 'Now, listen carefully and repeat after me: nobody like*s* me.'
2 Children generate many more grammatical sentences than they ever hear. A behaviourist account would require that children repeat sentences they have heard before and learned. Instead, it is much more likely that children simply acquire the ability to generate grammatical sentences. This shows that children don't just imitate; they learn the rules for generating new sentences.
3 As you read earlier in this chapter, the errors children make when learning to speak tend to be overgeneralizations of grammatical rules. The behaviourist explanation would not predict these overgeneralizations if children were learning through trial and error or simply imitating what they hear. In other words, it would be difficult to overgeneralize if language development consisted solely of reinforced individual sentences or phrases.

NATIVIST THEORY The view that language development is best explained as an innate, biological capacity.

LANGUAGE ACQUISITION DEVICE (LAD) A collection of processes that facilitate language learning.

GENETIC DYSPHASIA A syndrome characterized by an inability to learn the grammatical structure of language despite having otherwise normal intelligence.

Nativist explanations

Contrary to Skinner's behaviourist theory of language acquisition, Chomsky and others have argued that humans have a particular ability for language that is separate from general intelligence. This nativist theory holds that *language development is best explained as an innate, biological capacity.* According to Chomsky, the human brain is equipped with a language acquisition device (LAD) – *a collection of processes that facilitate language learning.* Language processes naturally emerge as the infant matures, provided the infant receives adequate input to maintain the acquisition process.

Christopher's story in our opening vignette is consistent with the nativist view of language development – his genius for language acquisition, despite his low overall intelligence, indicates that language capacity can be distinct from other mental capacities. Other individuals show the opposite pattern: people with normal or near-normal intelligence can find certain aspects of human language difficult or impossible to learn. This condition is known genetic dysphasia – *a syndrome characterized by an inability to learn the grammatical structure of language despite having otherwise normal intelligence.* Genetic dysphasia tends to run in families, and a single dominant gene has been implicated in its transmission (Gopnik, 1990a, 1990b). Consider some sentences generated by children with the disorder:

> She remembered when she hurts herself the other day.
> Carol is cry in the church.

Notice that the ideas these children are trying to communicate are intelligent. The problem lies in their inability to grasp syntactical rules (see Figure 7.2). Individuals with the disorder cannot correctly complete the following simple sentences, which require a rudimentary grasp of past tense and pluralization rules:

> Here is a 'wug'. Here are two of them. There are two ...
> Here is a man who likes to 'rick'. Yesterday he did the same thing. Yesterday he ...

Average four-year-old children can successfully complete these sentences, yet adults with genetic dysphasia may find them difficult or impossible (see FIGURE **7.3**). Their problems with grammatical rules persist even if they receive special language training. When asked

This is a wug.

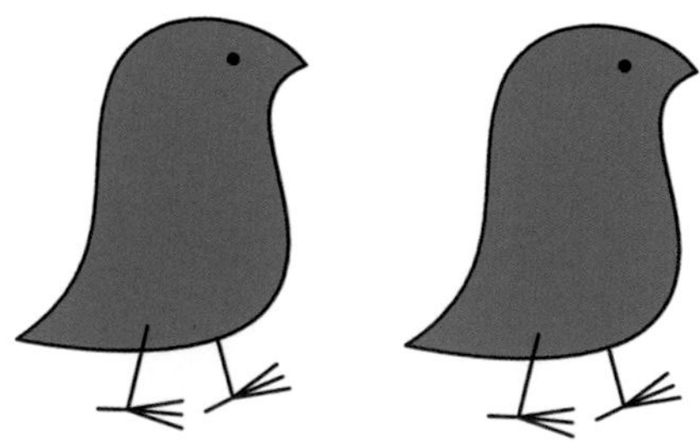

Now there is another one.
There are two of them.
There are two ______.

FIGURE **7.3 An item from the wug test** The test was designed as a way to explore whether children can utilize rules for forming plurals and past tense in words they've never heard.

to describe what she did over the weekend, one child wrote: 'On Saturday I watch TV.' Her teacher corrected the sentence to 'On Saturday, I watch*ed* TV', drawing attention to the *-ed* rule for describing past events. The following week, the child was asked to write another account of what she did over the weekend. She wrote: 'On Saturday I wash myself and I watched TV and I went to bed.' Notice that although she had memorized the past tense forms *watched* and *went*, she could not generalize the rule to form the past tense of another word (*washed*).

As predicted by the nativist view, studies of people with genetic dysphasia suggest that normal children learn the grammatical rules of human language with ease in part because they are 'wired' to do so. This biological predisposition to acquire language explains why newborn infants can make contrasts between phonemes that occur in all human languages – even phonemes they've never heard spoken. If we learned language through imitation, as behaviourists theorized, infants would only distinguish the phonemes they'd actually heard. The nativist theory also explains why deaf babies babble speech sounds they have never heard and why the pattern of language development is similar in children throughout the world. These characteristics of language development are just what would be expected if our biological heritage provided us with the broad mechanics of human language.

In 1493, James IV of Scotland reputedly sent two infants to Inchkeith, an island in the Firth of Forth, to be raised by a mute woman, because he wanted to know what language the children would end up speaking if they never heard an adult talk. According to the diarist Robert Lindsay of Pitscottie, who reported the incident some years later, 'Sum says they spak goode Hebrew.'

Also consistent with the nativist view is evidence that language can be acquired only during a restricted period of development, as has been observed with songbirds. If young songbirds are prevented from hearing adult birds sing during a particular period in their early lives, they do not learn to sing. A similar mechanism seems to affect human language learning, as illustrated by the tragic case of Genie (Curtiss, 1977). At the age of 20 months, Genie was tied to a chair by her parents and kept in virtual isolation. Her father forbade Genie's mother and brother to speak to her, and he himself only growled and barked at her. She remained in this brutal state until the age of 13, when her partially blind mother left home with her following an argument with Genie's father. Genie's life improved substantially, and she received years of language instruction. But it was too late. Her language skills remained extremely primitive. She developed a basic vocabulary and could communicate her ideas, but she could not grasp the grammatical rules of English. In contrast, Isabelle – a child who also suffered social isolation and silence but only until the age of 6 – required a year of language training to learn to speak normally (Brown, 1958; Davis, 1947). Similar cases have been reported, with a common theme: once puberty is reached, acquiring language becomes extremely difficult (Brown, 1958).

However, in looking at cases where children have been raised in deprived environments, we must consider the role of other factors that might contribute to impaired development. For example, was Genie brain-damaged before the isolation? What about the emotional deprivation she must have suffered? We re-examine these issues in Chapter 12, when we consider the cases of children raised in abnormal social environments. Nevertheless, despite the implications of additional factors, data from studies of second language learning in otherwise normal immigrants support the idea that exposure to language before puberty is critical. In one US study, researchers found that the proficiency with which immigrants spoke English depended not on how long they'd lived in the US, but on their age at immigration (Johnson and Newport, 1989). Those who arrived as children were the most proficient, whereas among those who immigrated after puberty, proficiency showed a significant decline regardless of the number of years in their new country. Given these data, it is unfortunate that many schools in the US and UK do not offer other languages until pupils reach the age of 11 or 12. In contrast, European children are exposed to and taught several languages at a much earlier age, with half of EU children learning at least one foreign language in primary school. This probably reflects the fact that most European countries are more multilingual because of the close proximity, integration and migration of peoples from different countries.

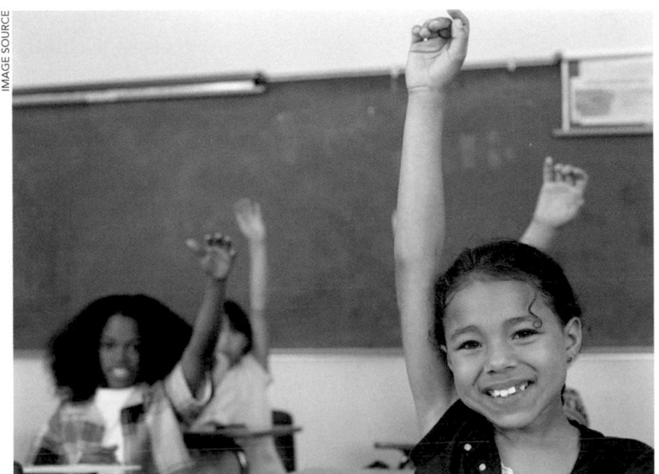
IMAGE SOURCE

Immigrants who learn English as a second language are more proficient if they start to learn English before puberty rather than after.

Interactionist explanations

Nativist theories are often criticized because they do not explain *how* language develops, they merely explain *why*. A complete theory of language acquisition requires an explanation of the processes by which the innate, biological capacity for language combines with environmental experience. This is just what interactionist accounts of language acquisition do. Interactionists point out that parents tailor their verbal interactions with children in ways that simplify the language acquisition process. They speak slowly, enunciate clearly, and use simpler sentences than they do when speaking with adults (Bruner, 1983; Farrar, 1990). This observation supports the interactionist notion that although infants are born with an innate ability to acquire language, social interactions play a crucial role in language.

We know that simple exposure is not enough. This is illustrated by the case of Jim, who was a hearing child born to deaf parents who only used sign language in the household but let him listen to the radio and watch TV (Sachs et al., 1981). By age three years and nine months, Jim had a little language, plus a few words from TV jingles. Although he had heard a great deal of spoken language, it was not directed towards him. However, after interacting with speaking adults, his language developed rapidly. Jim's case implies that passive exposure to language on the TV is not enough for language development, even when programmes are designed specially for children. That's why Dutch children watching a popular children's show that was broadcast in German did not learn any German (Snow et al., 1976). According to interactionist accounts of language, biological and cognitive mechanisms of language are necessary but are not sufficient, as language development must occur in the context of meaningful social interactions (Harley, 2008). In Chapter 12, we examine some of these mechanisms of social interaction that make language acquisition possible.

Further evidence of the interaction of biology and experience comes from a fascinating study of deaf children's creation of a new language (Senghas et al., 2004). Prior to about 1980, deaf children in Nicaragua stayed at home and usually had little contact with other deaf individuals. In 1981, some deaf children began to attend a new vocational school. At first, the school did not teach a formal sign language, and none of the children had learned to sign at home, but once they started to meet regularly in school, they began to communicate using systematic hand signals that they invented and developed jointly.

Over the past 25 years, their sign language has developed considerably, and researchers have studied this new language for the telltale characteristics of languages that have evolved over much longer periods. For instance, mature languages typically break down experience into separate components. When we describe something in motion, such as a rock rolling down a hill, two simultaneous aspects of the event – the type of movement (rolling) and the direction of movement (down) – are expressed by a sequence of two words. If we simply made a gesture, however, we would use a single continuous downward movement to indicate the type and direction of movement simultaneously. This is exactly what the first children to develop the Nicaraguan sign language did. But younger groups of children, who have developed the sign language further, use separate signs to describe the direction and type of movement – a defining characteristic of mature languages. The fact that the younger children did not merely copy the signs from the older users suggests that a predisposition exists to use language to dissect our experiences. Thus, their acts of creation neatly illustrate the interplay of nativism (the predisposition to use language) and experience (growing up in a community of deaf children). This segmentation of motion and direction when gesturing is not restricted to sign language used by deaf people, but has recently been observed in the gestures of typical four-year-olds asked to communicate with an adult without using words. This indicates that young children spontaneously bring fundamental properties of language into their communication system (Clay et al., 2014).

The neurological specialization that allows language to develop

As the brain matures, specific neurological structures become specialized for different functions. In the case of language, two areas, sometimes referred to as the 'language centres' of the brain, develop. We came across these two areas in Chapter 3. Broca's area is located in the left frontal cortex and is involved in the production of the sequential patterns in vocal and sign languages (see FIGURE 7.4). Wernicke's area, located in the left temporal cortex, is involved in language comprehension, whether spoken or signed. As the brain matures, these areas become increasingly specialized for language, so much so that damage to them results in a serious condition called aphasia – *difficulty in producing or comprehending language.*

As you saw in Chapter 1, Broca's area is named after French doctor Paul Broca, who first reported on speech problems resulting from damage to a specific area of the left frontal cortex (Broca, 1861, 1863). Patients with this damage understand language relatively well, although they have increasing comprehension difficulty as grammatical structures get more complex. But their real struggle is with speech production. Typically, they speak in short, staccato phrases that consist mostly of content morphemes, for example *cat, dog*. Function morphemes, for example *and, but*, are usually missing and grammatical structure is impaired. A person with *Broca's aphasia* might say something like: 'Ah, Monday, uh, Casey park. Two, uh, friends, and, uh, 30 minutes.'

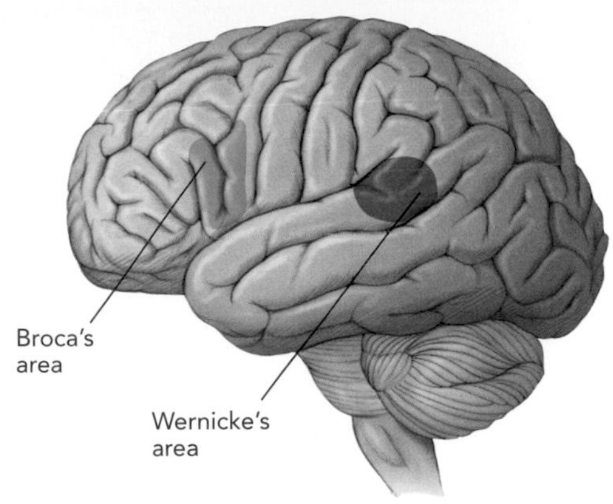

FIGURE **7.4 Broca's and Wernicke's areas** Neuroscientists study people with brain damage in order to better understand how the brain normally operates. When Broca's area is damaged, patients have a hard time producing sentences. When Wernicke's area is damaged, patients can produce sentences, but they tend to be meaningless.

APHASIA Difficulty in producing or comprehending language.

German neurologist Carl Wernicke (1874) first described the area that bears his name after observing speech difficulty in patients who had sustained damage to the left posterior temporal cortex. Patients with *Wernicke's aphasia* differ from those with Broca's aphasia in two ways. They can produce grammatical speech, but it tends to be meaningless, and they have considerable difficulty comprehending language. A patient suffering from Wernicke's aphasia might say something like: 'Feel very well. In other words, I used to be able to work cigarettes. I don't know how. Things I couldn't hear from are here.'

In normal language processing, Wernicke's area is highly active when we make judgements about word meaning, and damage to this area impairs comprehension of spoken and signed language, although the ability to identify nonlanguage sounds is unimpaired. For example, Japanese can be written using symbols that, like the English alphabet, represent speech sounds, or by using pictographs that, like Chinese pictographs, represent ideas. Japanese patients who suffer from Wernicke's aphasia encounter difficulties in writing and understanding the symbols that represent speech sounds but not pictographs.

In normal language development, Broca's area and Wernicke's area become specialized for processing and producing language as long as the developing child is exposed to spoken or signed language. As the cases of Genie and Isabelle show, there is a critical period during which this specialization occurs, and if the developing brain does not receive adequate language input, this process can be permanently disrupted.

Can other species learn human language?

The human vocal tract and the extremely nimble human hand are better suited to human language than the throats and paws of other species. Nonetheless, attempts have been made to teach nonhuman animals, particularly apes, to communicate using human language.

Early attempts to teach apes to speak failed dismally because their vocal tracts cannot accommodate the sounds used in human languages (Hayes and Hayes, 1951). Later attempts to teach apes human language have met with more success, including teaching them to use sign language and computer-monitored keyboards that display geometric symbols that represent words. Allen and Beatrix Gardner were the first to use sign language with apes (Gardner and Gardner, 1969). The Gardners worked with a young female chimpanzee named Washoe as though she were a deaf child, signing to her regularly, rewarding her correct efforts at signing, and assisting her acquisition of signs by manipulating her hands in a process referred to as 'moulding'. In four years, Washoe learned approximately 160 words and could construct simple sentences, such as 'More fruit'. She also formed novel word constructions such as 'water bird' for 'duck'. After a fight with a rhesus monkey, she signed 'dirty monkey!' This constituted a creative use of the term because she had only been taught the use of 'dirty' to refer to soiled objects.

Other chimpanzees were immersed in sign language in a similar fashion, and Washoe and her companions were soon signing to each other, creating a learning environment conducive to language acquisition. One of Washoe's cohorts, a chimpanzee named Lucy, learned to sign 'drink fruit' for watermelon. When Washoe's second infant died, her caretakers arranged for her to adopt an infant chimpanzee named Loulis. In a few months, young Loulis, who was not exposed to human signers, learned 68 signs simply by watching Washoe communicate with the other chimpanzees. People who have observed these interactions and are themselves fluent in sign language report little difficulty in following the conversations (Fouts and Bodamer, 1987). One such observer, a *New York Times* reporter who spent some time with Washoe, reported: 'Suddenly I realized I was conversing with a member of another species in my native tongue.'

To give you some idea of what chimp communication is like, take a look at the three sets of sentences shown in FIGURE **7.5**, read the caption, think about it, then continue reading the text.

The first set consists of the two-word sentences of a normal toddler. Washoe produced the second set and 13-year-old Genie the third set. All are grammatical; they follow the rules of English, and so we can easily understand what is being communicated. What is striking – particularly in the case of 13-year-old Genie – is the lack of grammatical complexity in the sentences. Rather than saying 'At school, I washed my face', or 'Mike is painting', Genie's expressions lack function morphemes (like *-ed* in the past tense), determiners and so on. The ability to produce grammatically complex sentences appears to depend on having particular neural circuitry. This circuitry seems to be lacking in chimps, takes time to develop in humans, and can be disrupted by extreme environmental deprivation during critical periods (Maynard-Smith and Szathmary, 1995).

Set 1	Set 2	Set 3
Big train; Red book.	Drink red; Comb black.	Want milk.
Walk street; Go store.	Clothes Mrs G; You hat.	Mike paint.
Put book; Hit ball.	Go in; Look out.	At school, wash face.

FIGURE **7.5 Differing language skills** These sets of sentences were produced by: 13-year-old Genie, who was deprived of social contact during her upbringing; a normal 2-year-old toddler; and a chimpanzee who was taught sign language. Can you guess which speaker produced which set of sentences? Make your guesses before continuing to read the text.

Other researchers have taught bonobo chimpanzees to communicate using a geometric keyboard system (Savage-Rumbaugh et al., 1998). Their star pupil, Kanzi, learned the keyboard system by watching researchers try to teach his mother. Like Loulis, young Kanzi picked up the language relatively easily (his mother never did learn the system), suggesting that, like humans, birds and other species, apes experience a critical period for acquiring communicative systems.

Kanzi has learned hundreds of words and has combined them to form thousands of word combinations. Also like human children, his passive mastery of language appears to exceed his ability to produce language. In one study, researchers tested nine-year-old Kanzi's understanding of 660 spoken sentences. The grammatically complex sentences asked him to perform simple actions, such as 'Go get the balloon that's in the microwave' and 'Pour the Perrier into the Coke'. Some sentences were also potentially misleading, such as 'Get the pine needles that are in the refrigerator', when there were pine needles in clear view on the floor. Impressively, Kanzi correctly carried out 72% of the 660 requests (Savage-Rumbaugh and Lewin, 1996).

APE COGNITION AND CONSERVATION INITIATIVE

Kanzi, a young male chimpanzee, learned hundreds of words and word combinations through a keyboard system as he watched researchers try to teach his mother.

These results indicate that apes can acquire sizable vocabularies, string words together to form short sentences, and process sentences that are grammatically complex. Their skills are especially impressive because human language is hardly their normal means of communication. Research with apes also suggests that the neurological 'wiring' that allows us to learn language overlaps to some degree with theirs, and perhaps with other species.

Equally informative are the limitations that apes exhibit when learning, comprehending and using human language:

1 The first limitation is the size of the vocabularies they acquire. As mentioned, Washoe's and Kanzi's vocabularies number in the hundreds, but an average four-year-old human child has a vocabulary of approximately 10,000 words.
2 The second limitation is the type of words they can master, primarily names for concrete objects and simple actions. Apes (and several other species) have the ability to map arbitrary sounds or symbols onto objects and actions, but learning, say, the

meaning of the word *economics* would be difficult for Washoe or Kanzi. In other words, apes can learn signs for concepts they understand, but their conceptual repertoire is smaller and simpler than humans.

3 The third and perhaps most important limitation is the complexity of grammar that apes can use and comprehend. Apes can string signs together, but their constructions rarely exceed three or four words, and when they do, they are rarely grammatical. For example, the gorilla Koko once signed 'Stomach me you orange juice' out of concern for her caretaker, who was complaining of a stomach ache. Koko apparently thought giving her orange juice would help. This communication shows compassion and intelligence on Koko's part but difficulty with the grammatical complexity of American Sign Language. Comparing the grammatical structures produced by apes with those produced by human children highlights the complexity of human language as well as the ease and speed with which we generate and comprehend it.

Reading and writing

Just consider for one moment how amazing it is that you have never read this sentence before, and yet you are able to understand what it means. Even though someone you have never met wrote it some time ago, many miles away, you are nevertheless transported in time and space to a point where the writer wanted to get you to consider how amazing writing was. This is why reading and writing are arguably humankind's greatest inventions.

Until fairly recently in civilization, most humans were unable to use reading or writing to communicate. According to a United Nations report (UNDP, 2009), Estonia, Latvia and Cuba have the highest literacy rates in the world (at 99.8%), whereas countries like Mali and Chad are at the bottom of the scale, with only one in four able to read or write. Unlike spoken language, which is acquired spontaneously by most children in a normal environment, reading and writing are skills that require learning through education.

LEXICON Our mental dictionary.

GRAPHEME Unit of written language that corresponds to a phoneme.

DUAL-ROUTE MODELS Propose that there are essentially two pathways to the lexicon.

DIRECT LEXICAL ROUTE One where the grapheme maps directly onto the phoneme.

INDIRECT SUBLEXICAL ROUTE One that does not involve the lexicon at all but maps the grapheme directly onto the pronunciation.

Reading and writing were invented some 5,000 years ago independently in the Middle East, East and Southeast Asia and Mesoamerica. Early scholars discovered that a system of symbols could be used to convey information (Harley, 2008) through a process of decoding the symbols into words and meaning. The full store of words and their meaning is called the lexicon – *our mental dictionary*. Accessing the lexicon requires translating the symbols or graphemes, *units of written language that correspond to phonemes*, to re-create the words. For example, the word 'steak' has four graphemes: s-t-ea-k. This mapping is the spelling-to-sound correspondence where each grapheme has a typical sound that also enables the reader to decode completely new words (Harley, 2008). For example, you can read and pronounce a made-up word such as 'decatify' (as 'de-ca-ti-fy') because it has a *regular* grapheme-to-phoneme mapping. You may even conclude that it might mean 'to remove cats', based on your lexicon of similarly structured real words such as 'demystify' which means to make less mystifying.

However, not all words are regular, especially in English. For example, the common word 'have' has an *irregular* grapheme-to-phoneme correspondence. It is not pronounced in the same way as 'rave', 'save' and 'wave'. Reading therefore requires a system that can cope with regular *and* irregular words. Dual-route models of reading *propose that there are essentially two pathways to the lexicon*, as illustrated in FIGURE **7.6**.

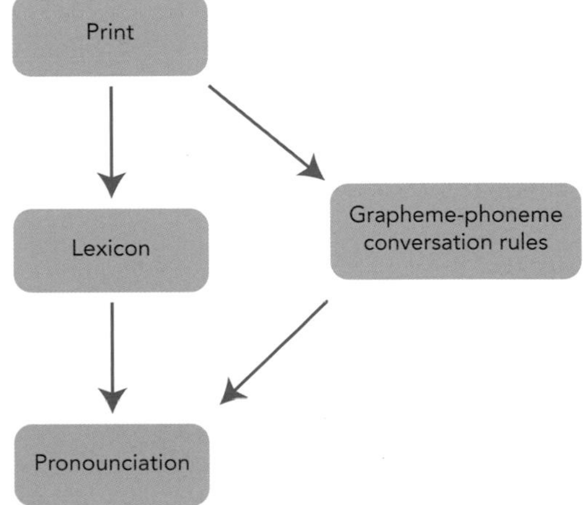

FIGURE **7.6 Dual-route model of reading** The dual-route model of reading has two routes for turning words into sounds – a direct access or lexical route, which is needed for irregular words, and a grapheme-to-phoneme conversion or indirect route, which is needed for non-words.

For irregular words, there is direct lexical route – *one where the grapheme maps directly onto the phoneme* based on the information stored in the lexicon. Pronunciation of words such as 'yacht' or 'aisle' are simply learned and stored in the lexicon. There is no need to work out the mapping between grapheme and phoneme. However, we can also read novel words or non-words such as 'nate' or 'smeak' that do not have a lexicon entry, so pronunciation is accessed via an indirect sublexical route – *one that does not involve the lexicon at all, but maps the grapheme directly onto the pronunciation*. This explains why learners often mispronounce irregular words, as they have not yet learned the exceptions to the general rule, and are relying on the direct lexical route only.

DYSLEXIA A disorder involving difficulty with reading and writing.

SURFACE DYSLEXIA People are unable to read irregular words.

PHONOLOGICAL DYSLEXIA People are unable to read pronounceable non-words.

Dual-route models help to understand different forms of **dyslexia** – *a disorder involving difficulty with reading and writing*. Dyslexia can be a developmental disorder that emerges during childhood, or it can be acquired through brain damage or disease. People with **surface dyslexia** are *unable to read irregular words*. They often make the error of applying the rules for regular words when reading irregular words; for example, they might pronounce 'have' in the same way as 'save', but have no problem with regular words and non-words. In terms of the dual-route model, they are impaired on the direct lexical route. In contrast, people with **phonological dyslexia** are *unable to read pronounceable non-words*, which indicates that they can only use the direct lexical pathway and are impaired on the indirect sublexical route (Shallice and Warrington, 1975). For example, they cannot read the non-word 'slamp' but can read an equally difficult real word, 'slump'.

SEMANTICS Meaning of a word.

SEMANTIC PRIMING The meaning of a word influences the processing of other words that are conceptually related.

DEEP DYSLEXIA Readers cannot retrieve the meaning of words.

While dual-route models account well for the dissociation between surface and phonological dyslexia, they are too simplistic to account for other features of reading that suggest more complicated designs (Harley, 2008). For example, there is good evidence that the **semantics**, *meaning of a word*, is accessed in parallel with the attempt to read it. If we read the word 'doctor', this makes it easier and quicker to read subsequent related words such as 'nurse' or 'ambulance'. This effect is known as **semantic priming** – *the meaning of a word influences the processing of other words that are conceptually related* (McNamara, 2005). Other forms of reading disorders, such as **deep dyslexia**, where *readers cannot retrieve the meaning of words*, suggest that simple grapheme-to-phoneme mapping is only part of the process. For example, a deep dyslexic might see the word 'daughter' and say 'sister'. This shows that conceptual knowledge is also required for reading. How we think determines how we read language – and some would argue that the reverse is also true, language determines how we think.

Language and thought: How are they related?

LINGUISTIC DETERMINISM HYPOTHESIS Language shapes the nature of thought.

Language is such a dominant feature of our mental world that it is tempting to equate language with thought. Some theorists have even argued that language is simply a means of expressing thought. The **linguistic determinism hypothesis** maintains that *language shapes the nature of thought*. This idea was championed by Benjamin Whorf (1956), an engineer who studied language in his spare time and was especially interested in Native American languages. The most frequently cited example of linguistic determinism comes from the Inuit in Canada. Their language was thought to have many different terms for frozen white flakes of precipitation, for which we use the word *snow*. Whorf believed that because they have so many terms for snow, the Inuit perceive and think about snow differently than English speakers.

Whorf has been criticized for the anecdotal nature of his observations (Pinker, 1994). To begin, his assertion that Inuits have many different words for snow is simply not true (Harley, 2008). Indeed, English may have more words for snow that describe different states, such as powder, drifted, caked, hardpack, slush, sleet, snowstorm, flurry, blizzard and so on. So Whorf's assumption of a limited range in English is wrong. Also, some controlled research has cast doubt on Whorf's hypothesis. Eleanor Rosch (1973) studied the Dani, an isolated agricultural tribe living in New Guinea. They have only two terms for colours that roughly refer to 'dark' and 'light'. If Whorf's hypothesis were correct, you would expect the Dani to have problems perceiving and learning different shades of colour. But in Rosch's experiments, they learned shades of colour just as well as people who have many more colour terms in their first language.

The Inuit in Canada use many different terms for snow, leading Benjamin Whorf to propose that they think about snow differently than English speakers.

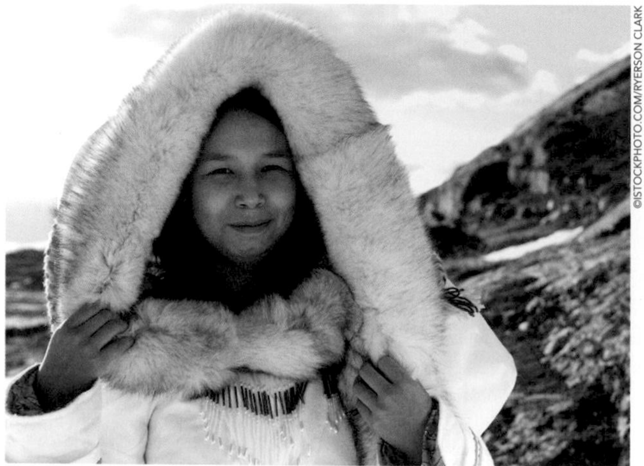

However, more recent evidence shows that language may influence colour processing (Roberson et al., 2004). Researchers compared English children with African children from a cattle-herding tribe in Namibia known as the Himba. The English have 11 basic colour terms, but the Himba, who are largely isolated from the outside world, have only 5. For example, they use the term *serandu* to refer to what English speakers would call red, pink or orange. Researchers showed a series of coloured tiles to each child and then asked the child to choose that colour from an array of 22 different colours. The youngest children, both English and Himba, who knew few or no colour names, tended to confuse similar colours. But as the children grew and acquired more names for colours, their choices increasingly reflected the colour terms they had learned. English children made fewer errors matching tiles that had English colour names, while Himba children made fewer errors for tiles with colour names in Himba. These results support the linguistic relativity hypothesis – *language may influence the way we think and perceive.*

LINGUISTIC RELATIVITY HYPOTHESIS The proposal that language may influence the way we think and perceive.

In another study supporting Whorf's hypothesis, researchers looked at the way people think about time. In English, we often use spatial terms; for example we look *forward* to a promising future or move a meeting *back* to fit our schedule. We also use these terms to describe horizontal spatial relations, such as taking three steps *forward* or two steps *back* (Boroditsky, 2001). In contrast, speakers of Mandarin (Chinese) often describe time using terms that refer to a vertical spatial dimension; for example earlier events are referred to as 'up' and later events as 'down'. To test the effect of this difference, researchers showed English speakers and Mandarin speakers either a horizontal or vertical display of objects and then asked them to make a judgement involving time, such as whether March comes before April (Boroditsky, 2001). English speakers were faster to make the time judgements after seeing a horizontal display, whereas for Mandarin speakers, the opposite was true. When English speakers learned to use Mandarin spatial terms, their time judgements were also faster after seeing the vertical display. This result neatly shows a direct influence of language on thought.

Benjamin Whorf was, in fact, a fire prevention inspector for an insurance company, who noted that language sometimes misled people. For example, people behaved cautiously near what they categorized as 'full petrol drums' but carelessly near 'empty petrol drums', with devastating consequences. Empty petrol drums are full of petrol vapour, which is much more explosive than liquid petrol.

Current research into the relationship between language and numerical cognition (our understanding of numbers) provides another opportunity to test Whorf's hypothesis. Number systems vary among different languages. English has a complex system with 13 primitive terms (0–12), then 7 'teens' (13–19), followed by more rule-based terms from 20–100. In contrast, Chinese only has 11 primitive terms (0–10) and then three special terms for 100, 1,000, 10,000. For example, 11 is simply 'ten plus one' in Chinese. The differing complexities of these two systems explains why English-speaking children take longer to learn numbers from 0–20 compared to Chinese children (Miller and Stigler, 1987). Take another example. The Welsh language is notoriously difficult to learn because of its vowel combinations. Welsh number words may have the same number of syllables as English number words, but they are harder to pronounce, which explains why bilinguals take longer to do mental arithmetic in Welsh (Ellis and Hennelly, 1980). However, both these examples are really addressing issues of *performance*, rather than the question of whether language restricts *thought processes* about numbers. For example, Australian Aboriginal languages such as Warlpiri have a very limited number system, which only includes three generic types of number words: one, two and greater than two. However, when Aboriginal children who speak Warlpiri were compared to English children on tasks that require counting, no significant differences were found in their performance (Butterworth et al., 2008).

It seems safe to conclude that there is some limited support for the Whorfian hypothesis and that while language may help on performance tasks where there is a need to discriminate different categories, the idea of equating thought with language seems a leap too far. Bear in mind also that thought abilities can be severely impaired while language abilities are relatively spared (and vice versa), as illustrated by the dramatic case of Christopher you read earlier.

In summary, human language is characterized by a complex organization, from phonemes to morphemes to phrases and finally sentences. Each of these levels of human language is constructed and understood according to grammatical rules, none of which are ever taught explicitly. Instead, children appear to be biologically predisposed to process language in ways that allow them to extract grammatical rules from the language they hear, a predisposition that takes the form of neurological specialization. Our abilities to produce and comprehend language depend on distinct regions of the brain, with Broca's area critical for language production and Wernicke's area critical for comprehension. Nonhuman primates can learn new vocabulary and construct simple sentences, but there are significant limitations on the size of their vocabularies and the grammatical complexity they can handle. Unlike speech, reading and writing were invented by humans and must be learned through education. Disorders of reading reveal different processes through which the written symbol is translated into meaningful words. Recent studies on colour processing, time judgements and numerical cognition point to a limited influence of language on thought. However, it is also clear that language and thought are to some extent separate.

Concepts and categories: how we think

CONCEPT A mental representation that groups or categorizes shared features of related objects, events or other stimuli.

Concept refers to a *mental representation that groups or categorizes shared features of related objects, events or other stimuli.* A concept is an abstract representation, description or definition that serves to designate a class or category of things. For example, your concept of a chair might include such features as sturdiness, relative flatness, an object you can sit on. That set of attributes defines a category of objects in the world – desk chairs, sunloungers, flat rocks, bar stools and so on – that can all be described in that way.

Concepts are fundamental to our ability to think and make sense of the world. As with other aspects of cognition, we can gain insight into how concepts are organized by looking at some instances in which they are rather disorganized. We'll encounter some mindbugs in the form of unusual disorders that help us understand how concepts are organized in the brain. We'll also compare various theories that explain the organization of concepts and then consider studies of children that demonstrate how we acquire concepts.

The organization of concepts and category-specific deficits

CATEGORY-SPECIFIC DEFICIT A neurological syndrome characterized by an inability to recognize objects that belong to a particular category while leaving the ability to recognize objects outside the category undisturbed.

Over 20 years ago, two neuropsychologists described a mindbug resulting from brain injury that had major implications for understanding how concepts are organized (Warrington and McCarthy, 1983). Their patient could not recognize a variety of human-made objects or retrieve any information about them, but his knowledge of living things and foods was perfectly normal. In the following year, two neuropsychologists reported four patients who exhibited the reverse pattern: they could recognize information about human-made objects, but their ability to recognize information about living things and foods was severely impaired (Warrington and Shallice, 1984). Since the publication of these pioneering studies, many more cases have been reported (Martin and Caramazza, 2003). The syndrome is called category-specific deficit – *an inability to recognize objects that belong to a particular category while leaving the ability to recognize objects outside the category undisturbed.*

Category-specific deficits like these have been observed even when the brain trauma that produces them occurs shortly after birth. Two researchers reported the case of Adam, a 16-year-old boy who suffered a stroke the day after he was born (Farah and Rabinowitz, 2003). Adam has severe difficulty recognizing faces and other biological objects. When shown a picture of a cherry, he identified it as 'a Chinese yo-yo', and when shown a picture of a mouse, he identified it as an owl. He made errors like these on 79% of the animal pictures and 54% of the plant pictures he was shown. In contrast, he made only 15% errors when identifying pictures of nonliving things, such as spatulas, brooms and cigars. The fact that 16-year-old Adam exhibited category-specific deficits despite suffering his stroke when he was only one day old strongly suggests that the brain is 'prewired' to organize perceptual and sensory inputs into broad-based categories, such as living and nonliving things.

The type of category-specific deficit suffered depends on where the brain is damaged. Deficits usually result when an individual suffers a stroke or other trauma to areas in the left hemisphere of the cerebral cortex (Martin and Caramazza, 2003). Damage to the front part of the left temporal lobe results in difficulty identifying humans, damage to the lower left temporal lobe results in difficulty identifying animals, and damage to the region where the temporal lobe meets the occipital and parietal lobes impairs the ability to retrieve names of tools (Damasio et al., 1996). Similarly, when healthy people undertake the same task, imaging studies have demonstrated that the same regions of the brain are more active during the naming of tools than animals and vice versa, as shown in FIGURE 7.7 (Martin and Chao, 2001).

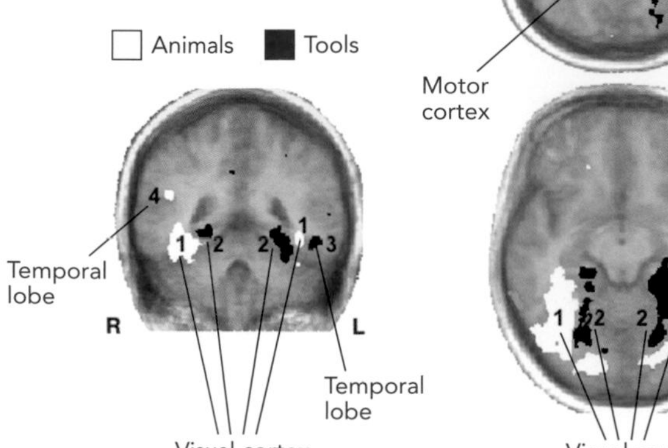

FIGURE **7.7 Brain areas involved in category-specific processing** Participants were asked to silently name pictures of animals and tools while they were scanned with fMRI. The fMRIs revealed greater activity in the areas in white when participants named animals, and areas in black showed greater activity when participants named tools. Specific regions indicated by numbers include areas within the visual cortex (1, 2), parts of the temporal lobe (3, 4), and the motor cortex (5). Note that the images are left/right reversed (Martin and Chao, 2001).

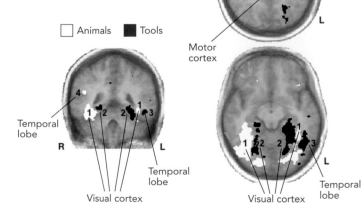

Cases of category-specific deficit provide new insights into how the brain organizes our concepts about the world, classifying them into categories based on shared similarities. Our category for 'dog' may be something like 'small, four-footed animal with fur that wags its tail and barks'. Our category for 'bird' may be something like 'small, winged, beaked creature that flies'. We form these categories in large part by noticing similarities among objects and events that we experience in everyday life. A stroke or trauma that damaged the particular place in your brain that stores your 'dog' category would wipe out your ability to recognize dogs or remember anything about them.

Psychological theories of concepts and categories

Psychologists have investigated the nature of human concepts, how they are acquired, and how they are used to make decisions and guide actions. Early psychological theories described concepts as rules that specify the necessary and sufficient conditions for membership in a particular category. A necessary condition is something that must be true of the object in order for it to belong to the category. A sufficient condition is something that, if it is true of the object, proves that it belongs to the category. For example, suppose you came upon an unfamiliar animal and you were trying to determine whether it was a dog. It is necessary that the creature be a mammal, otherwise it doesn't belong to the category 'dog' because all dogs are mammals. 'Mammal' is therefore a necessary condition for membership in the category 'dog'. Suppose someone told you that the creature was a German shepherd and you know that a German shepherd is a type of dog. 'German shepherd' is a sufficient condition for membership in the category 'dog'. If you know that the creature is a German shepherd, this is sufficient to categorize it as a dog.

©ISTOCKPHOTO.COM/DIGITALSKILLET

There is family resemblance between family members despite the fact that there is no defining feature they all have in common. Instead, there are shared common features. Someone who also shares some of those features may be categorized as belonging to the family.

Most natural categories, however, cannot be so easily defined in terms of this classical approach of necessary and sufficient conditions. For example, what is your definition of 'dog'? Can you come up with a rule of 'dogship' that includes all dogs and excludes all nondogs? Most people can't, but they still use the term *dog* intelligently, easily classifying objects as dogs or nondogs. Several theories seek to explain how people perform these acts of categorization.

Family resemblance theory

Eleanor Rosch put aside necessity and sufficiency to develop a theory of concepts based on family resemblance – where *members of a category have features that appear to be characteristic of category members but may not be possessed by every member* (Rosch, 1973, 1975; Rosch and Mervis, 1975; Wittgenstein, [1953]1999). For example, you and your brother may have your mother's eyes, although you and your sister may have your father's high cheekbones. There is a strong family resemblance between you, your parents and your siblings despite the fact that there isn't one necessarily defining feature that you all have in common. Similarly, many members of the 'bird' category have feathers and wings, so these are the characteristic features. Anything that has these features is likely to be classified as a bird because of this 'family resemblance' to other members of the bird category. FIGURE **7.8** illustrates family resemblance theory.

FAMILY RESEMBLANCE THEORY Members of a category have features that appear to be characteristic of category members but may not be possessed by every member.

Prototype theory

Building on the idea of family resemblance, Rosch also proposed prototype theory – *our psychological categorization is organized around the properties of the most typical member of the category*. A prototype possesses most (or all) of the most characteristic features of the category. If you lived in Europe or the US, the prototype of the bird category might be something like a wren: a small animal with feathers and wings that flies through the air, lays eggs and sings (see FIGURE **7.9**). If you lived in Antarctica, your prototype of a bird might be a penguin: a small animal that has flippers, swims and lays eggs.

PROTOTYPE THEORY Our psychological categorization is organized around the properties of the most typical member of the category.

According to prototype theory, if your prototypical bird is a robin, then a canary would be considered a better example of a bird than an ostrich, because a canary has more features in common with a robin than an ostrich does. People make category

FIGURE **7.8 Family resemblance theory** The family resemblance here is unmistakable, even though no two Smith brothers share all the family features. The prototype is brother 9. He has it all: brown hair, large ears, large nose, moustache and glasses.

Properties	Generic bird	Wren	Blue heron	Golden eagle	Domestic goose	Penguin
Flies regularly	✓	✓	✓	✓		
Sings	✓	✓	✓			
Lays eggs	✓	✓	✓	✓	✓	✓
Is small	✓	✓				
Nests in trees	✓	✓				

FIGURE **7.9 Critical features of a category** We tend to think of a generic bird as possessing a number of critical features, but not every bird possesses all those features. In Europe, a wren is a 'better example' of a bird than a penguin or an ostrich.

judgements by comparing new instances to the category's prototype. This contrasts with the classical approach to concepts, in which something either is or is not an example of a concept, that is, it either does or does not belong in the category 'dog' or 'bird'.

Several lines of research support prototype theory. In one set of studies, researchers asked people to list the attributes of several category members (Rosch and Mervis, 1975) (see FIGURE **7.10**). For example, 'apple', 'coconut' and 'orange' are members of the category 'fruit'. Attributes are characteristic features, such as green, round and juicy for 'apple', brown, round and hairy for 'coconut', and orange, round and juicy for 'orange'.

The researchers then calculated a family resemblance score for each category member, which reflected the number of attributes a member had that were shared by other members of the category. In our example, 'apple' and 'orange' have two attributes that are shared by other members of the category (round and juicy), so they would each receive a family resemblance score of 2. 'Coconut', on the other hand, has only one attribute in common with the other members (round), so it would receive a family resemblance score of 1.

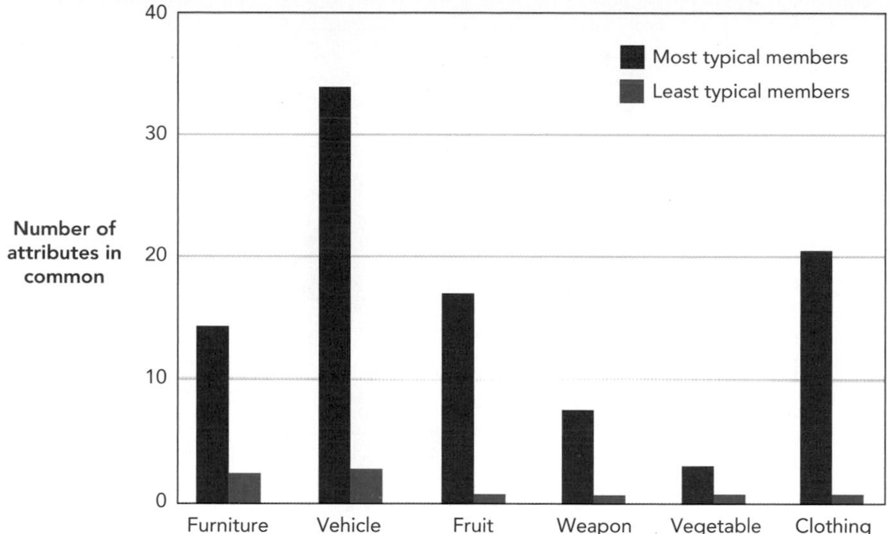

FIGURE **7.10** **Prototype theory** Category members that have many features in common with other members are rated as more typical of the category than are members that share few common features (Rosch and Mervis, 1975).

Another group of people were then asked to rate how typical of the category each member was on a scale of 1–7, with higher scores representing greater typicality. These ratings were highly correlated with family resemblance scores. The items that were rated as highly typical had many attributes in common with other members of the category, whereas items that were rated as atypical had few. For example, 'apple' and 'peach' were rated as typical members of the category 'fruit', whereas 'coconut' and 'fig' were rated as atypical. Similarly, 'robin' and 'bluebird' received high typicality ratings for the category 'bird', whereas 'chicken' and 'ostrich' were rated as atypical.

According to prototype theory, results such as these show that our concepts are organized in terms of typicality and shared features and not simply in terms of rules defining necessary and sufficient conditions. Participants in these studies knew that, for example, chickens and robins are both birds, but their mental concept 'bird' is organized according to shared features, not according to a purely logical definition.

Exemplar theory

In contrast to prototype theory, exemplar theory holds that *we make category judgements by comparing a new instance with stored memories of other instances of the category* (Medin and Schaffer, 1978). Imagine that you're out walking in the woods, and out of the corner of your eye you spot a four-legged animal that might be a wolf or a coyote but reminds you of your cousin's German shepherd. You figure it must be a dog and continue to enjoy your walk rather than fleeing in a panic. You probably categorized this new animal as a dog because it bore a striking resemblance to other dogs you've encountered; in other words, it was a good example (or an *exemplar*) of the category 'dog'. Exemplar theory does a better job than prototype theory in accounting for certain aspects of categorization, especially in that we recall not only what a *prototypical* dog looks like but also what *specific* dogs look like. FIGURE **7.11** illustrates the difference between prototype theory and exemplar theory.

EXEMPLAR THEORY A theory of categorization that argues that we make category judgements by comparing a new instance with stored memories of other instances of the category.

Researchers using neuroimaging techniques have concluded that we use prototypes and exemplars when forming concepts and categories. The visual cortex is involved in forming prototypes, whereas the prefrontal cortex and basal ganglia are involved in learning exemplars (Ashby and Ell, 2001). This evidence suggests that exemplar-based learning involves analysis and decision making (prefrontal cortex), whereas prototype formation is a more holistic process involving image processing (visual cortex).

In one set of studies (Marsolek, 1995), participants classified prototypes faster when the stimuli were presented to the right visual field, meaning that the left hemisphere received the input first (see Chapter 3 for a discussion of how the two hemispheres

FIGURE **7.11 Prototype theory and exemplar theory** According to prototype theory, we classify new objects by comparing them to the 'prototype' (or most typical) member of a category. According to exemplar theory, we classify new objects by comparing them to all category members.

receive input from the outside world). In contrast, participants classified previously seen exemplars faster when images were presented to the left visual field (meaning that the right hemisphere received the input first). These results suggest that the left hemisphere is primarily involved in forming prototypes and the right hemisphere is mainly active in recognizing exemplars.

In summary, we organize knowledge about objects, events or other stimuli by creating concepts, prototypes and exemplars. Studies of people with cognitive deficits have shown that the brain organizes concepts into distinct categories, such as living things and human-made things. We acquire concepts using three theories. Family resemblance theory, which states that items in the same category share certain features, if not all; prototype theory, which uses the most 'typical' member of a category to assess new items; and exemplar theory, which states that we compare new items with stored memories of other members of the category. Finally, studies have shown that prototypes and exemplars are processed in different parts of the brain.

Judging, valuing and deciding: sometimes we're logical, sometimes not

We use categories and concepts to guide the hundreds of decisions and judgements we make during the course of an average day. Some decisions are easy – what to wear, what to eat for breakfast, and whether to walk, catch the bus or ride a bicycle to lectures – and some are more difficult – which car to buy, which flat to rent, who to hang out with on Friday night, and even which job to take after graduation.

Decision making, like other cognitive activities, is vulnerable to mindbugs – many of little consequence. Had you really thought through your decision to go out with

Mary, you might have called Emily instead, who's a lot more fun, but all in all, your decision about the evening was okay. The same kinds of slips in the decision-making process can have tragic results, however. Consider the actual case of a well-meaning surgeon who advised many of his female patients to undergo a mastectomy in order to avoid developing breast cancer. A newspaper article described his 'pioneering' approach (Dawes, 1986). During a two-year period, this doctor convinced 90 'high-risk' women without cancer to sacrifice their breasts 'in a heroic exchange for the certainty of saving their lives and protecting their loved ones from suffering and loss' (Gigerenzer, 2002, p. 82). Unfortunately, the doctor did not interpret the statistical data on breast cancer properly. If he had, he would have found that the vast majority of these women (85 out of 90, to be exact) were not expected to develop breast cancer at all (see *the real world* example).

Although extreme, this case is not unusual. In one experiment, 100 doctors were asked to predict the incidence of breast cancer among women whose mammogram screening tests showed possible evidence of breast cancer. The doctors were told to take into consideration the rarity of breast cancer (1% of the population at the time the study was done) and radiologists' record in diagnosing the condition – correctly recognized only 79% of the time and falsely diagnosed almost 10% of the time. Of the 100 doctors, 95 estimated the probability that cancer was present to be about 75%. The correct answer was 8%. The doctors apparently experienced difficulty taking so much information into account when making their decision (Eddy, 1982). Similar dismal results have been reported with a number of medical screening tests (Hoffrage and Gigerenzer, 1996; Windeler and Kobberling, 1986).

Before you conclude that humans are poorly equipped to make important decisions, note that our success rate often depends on the nature of the task. We excel at some cognitive tasks, such as estimating *frequency*, or simply the number of times something will happen. In contrast, we perform poorly on tasks that require us to think in terms of *probabilities*, or the likelihood that something will happen, as in the medical examples just discussed. Even with probabilities, however, performance varies depending on how the problem is described. Let's find out why this is so.

Kylie Minogue was diagnosed with early-stage breast cancer in 2005, after seeking a second opinion because she was initially told she had nothing to worry about. However, diagnosis of breast cancer can be tricky. A group of 100 doctors were asked to predict the incidence of breast cancer among women who test positive for breast cancer on mammogram screening tests. Ninety-five of the 100 doctors estimated the probability of breast cancer after a positive mammogram to be about 75%. The correct answer was 8% (Eddy, 1982).

BASE RATES The actual likelihood of events occurring.

the real world

Using Bayes to make life or death decisions

If we want to understand the probability and significance of events among the general population, we need to take into account the real incidence of events in the world. For example, screening tests used regularly in medicine present real problems of understanding probability. Rarely are they 100% accurate, which means that they can give positive or negative results that may not reflect reality. What you want to know is whether a positive result is representative of the presence of a disease (true positive) or is an error (false positive). But you also want to know whether a negative result means that you are not ill (true negative) or, in fact, the test has missed the presence of the disease (false negative).

Consider the following scenario. Approximately 1% of women aged 40 who participate in routine breast screening programmes have breast cancer; 80% of women with breast cancer will give a true positive result on mammography, and around 9.6% of women without breast cancer will give a false positive result. This means the test says they have cancer when in fact they do not. Imagine you are a woman in this age group and you undergo mammography only to find that it comes back positive. What is the likelihood that you actually have breast cancer?

Most people estimate the wrong answer. Surprisingly and even more worryingly, around 85% of doctors also give the wrong answer (Gigerenzer, 2002). Most think that it must be somewhere around four out of five times based on the true positive estimate of 80%. In fact, the true estimate is only 7.8%, less than one out of ten times (see table below).

Prevalence of breast cancer in 1,000 women aged 40	Test gives positive result
Disease present in 1% = 10 women	80% (10) = 8 women
Disease absent in 99% = 990 women	9.6% (990) = 95 women Therefore, 8 + 95 women give a positive result but only 8 actually have cancer (8/103) = 7.8%

How can this be? Remember that the true incidence of breast cancer in this population is only 1%. The problem is a bit easier when you consider larger numbers. If we looked at 1,000 women, only 10 on average would have breast cancer. But if the test has a false positive rate of 9.6%, then correcting for false negatives, one can soon understand that the positive test result you received is much more likely to be an error. You are much more likely to be one of those 95 women who give a false positive result when you do not have cancer.

These sorts of probability problems require an understanding of Bayesian statistics that take into consideration base rates – *the actual likelihood of events occurring* – rather than the one-off situation. Imagine that you have a coin toss. You assume that the choice is 50:50 heads or tails. But if you discover that the coin is weighted in some way to come up tails more often, you would know that the odds were stacked. However, in order to know which was likely, you would need to know what the prior likelihood of the incidence of tails versus heads was based on past throws (see the psychomythology example at the end of this chapter).

Bayesian statistics is critical to understanding patterns in and incidence of events in the population, which is why it is so important to medical issues in epidemiology (the study of patterns, causes and effects of health and disease conditions in populations), such as vaccination programmes. As individuals, we are generally not aware of the overall base rates for the group we belong to, but focus on our own scenarios instead. There may be 'lies, damned lies and statistics', but if they are calculated correctly, they may save your life.

Decision making: rational, optimal and otherwise

RATIONAL CHOICE THEORY The classical view that we make decisions by determining how likely something is to happen, judging the value of the outcome, and then multiplying the two.

Economists contend that if we are rational and are free to make our own decisions, we will behave as predicted by rational choice theory – *we make decisions by determining how likely something is to happen, judging the value of the outcome, and then multiplying the two* (Edwards, 1955). This means that our judgements will vary depending on the value we assign to the possible outcomes. Suppose, for example, you were asked to choose between a 10% opportunity to gain £500 and a 20% chance of gaining £2,000. The rational person would choose the second alternative because the expected payoff is £400 (£2,000 × 20%), whereas the first offers an expected gain of only £50 (£500 × 10%). Selecting the option with the highest expected value seems so straightforward that many economists accepted the basic ideas in rational choice theory. But how well does this theory describe decision making in our everyday lives? In many cases, the answer is 'not very well'.

©ISTOCKPHOTO.COM/DAVID CROCKETT

People don't always make rational choices. When a lottery jackpot is larger than usual, more people will buy lottery tickets, thinking that they might 'win big'. However, more people buying lottery tickets reduces the probability of any one person winning the lottery. Ironically, people have a better chance of winning a lottery with a relatively small jackpot.

As you learned earlier in the chapter, humans easily recognize recurring patterns, group events and objects into categories based on similarity, and classify new events and objects by deciding how similar they are to categories that have already been learned. However, these strengths of human decision making can turn into weaknesses when certain tasks inadvertently activate these skills. In other words, the same principles that allow cognition to occur easily and accurately can pop up as mindbugs to bedevil our decision making.

Judging frequencies and probabilities

Consider the following list of words:

> block table block pen telephone block disk glass table block telephone block watch table chocolate

You probably noticed that the words *block* and *table* occurred more frequently than the other words. In fact, studies have shown that people are quite good at estimating the frequency with which things occur. How many times did the word *block* occur in the above list? Chances are, you guessed the correct answer of five, or something pretty close to five. You probably also remember *block* and *table* better than the other words, as more frequently presented items are generally easier to remember than less frequently presented ones. Adults judge frequency accurately and nearly automatically, and young children perform just as well on similar tasks. All this suggests that this type of processing is 'natural' and easy for most humans to accomplish (Barsalou and Ross, 1986; Gallistel and Gelman, 1992; Hasher and Zacks, 1984).

This skill matters quite a bit when it comes to decision making. As you'll remember from *the real world* example, doctors performed dismally when they were asked to estimate the true probability of breast cancer among women who showed possible evidence of the disease. However, dramatically different results were obtained when the study was repeated using *frequency* information instead of *probability* information. Stating the problem as '10 out of every 1,000 women actually have breast cancer', instead of '1% of women actually have breast cancer', led 46% of the doctors to derive the right answer, compared to only 8% who came up with right answer when the problem was presented using probabilities (Hoffrage and Gigerenzer, 1998). This finding suggests that, at a minimum, when seeking advice – even from a highly skilled decision maker – make sure that your problem is described using frequencies rather than probabilities.

Now, let me calculate how likely it is we'll walk away from this

Some of the 286 survivors (out of 340) of a Dutch charter plane that crashed in a freak wind in the resort town of Faro, Portugal gathered to tell their stories to reporters. Wim Kodman, 27, who is a botanist, said he was trying to calm a friend during the wind turbulence by appealing to logic. Said Kodman: 'I told him, "I'm a scientist; we're objective." I told him a crash was improbable. I was trying to remember the exact probability when we smashed into the ground.'

Availability bias

Take a look at the list of names in FIGURE 7.12. Now look away from the book and estimate the number of male names and female names in the figure. Did you notice that some of the women on the list are famous and none of the men are? Was your estimate off because you thought the list contained more women's than men's names (Tversky and Kahneman, 1973, 1974)? The reverse would have been true if you had looked at a list with the names of famous men and unknown women, because people typically fall prey to a mindbug called the availability bias, in which *items that are more readily available in memory are judged as having occurred more frequently.*

The availability bias affects our estimates because memory strength and frequency of occurrence are directly related. Frequently occurring items are remembered more easily than *in*frequently occurring items, so you naturally conclude that items for which you have better memory must also have been more frequent. Unfortunately, better memory in this case was not due to greater *frequency,* but to greater *familiarity.*

Shortcuts such as the availability bias are sometimes referred to as heuristics – *fast and efficient strategies that may facilitate decision making but do not guarantee that a solution will be reached.* Heuristics are mental shortcuts, or 'rules of thumb', that are often – but not always – effective when approaching a problem (Swinkels, 2003). In contrast, an algorithm is *a well-defined sequence of procedures or rules that guarantees a solution to a problem.* Consider, for example, two approaches to finding a misplaced object. You try to remember the last time the object was in your possession; or you follow a set of directions that identify its location, for example your flatmate sheepishly telling you to walk over to the bookcase near the door and look in the yellow coffee cup, where she put your car keys when tidying up the room. The first procedure is an intelligent heuristic that may be successful, but you could continue searching your memory until you finally run out of time or patience. The second strategy is a series of well-defined steps that, if properly executed, will guarantee a solution.

Jennifer Aniston	Robert Kingston
Judy Smith	Gilbert Chapman
Frank Carson	Gwyneth Paltrow
Elizabeth Taylor	Martin Mitchell
Daniel Hunt	Thomas Hughes
Henry Vaughan	Michael Drayton
Agatha Christie	Julia Roberts
Arthur Hutchinson	Hillary Clinton
Jennifer Lopez	Jack Lindsay
Allan Nevins	Richard Gilder
Jane Austen	George Nathan
Joseph Litton	Britney Spears

FIGURE 7.12 **Availability bias** Look at this list of names, then look away and estimate the number of women's and men's names.

AVAILABILITY BIAS Items that are more readily available in memory are judged as having occurred more frequently.

HEURISTICS Fast and efficient strategies that may facilitate decision making but do not guarantee that a solution will be reached.

ALGORITHM A well-defined sequence of procedures or rules that guarantees a solution to a problem.

The conjunction fallacy

The availability bias illustrates a potential source of error in human cognition. Unfortunately, it's not the only one. Consider the following description:

> Linda is 31 years old, single, outspoken and very bright. At university, she studied philosophy. As a student, she was deeply concerned with issues of discrimination and social justice and also participated in antinuclear demonstrations. Which state of affairs is more probable?
>
> 1 Linda is a bank clerk.
>
> 2 Linda is a bank clerk and is active in the feminist movement.

In one study, 89% of participants rated option 2 as more probable than option 1 (Tversky and Kahneman, 1983), although that's logically impossible. Let's say there's a 20% chance that Linda is a bank clerk; after all, there are plenty of occupations she might hold. Independently, let's say there's also a 20% chance that she's active in the feminist movement, and she probably has lots of interests. The joint probability that *both* things are true simultaneously is the product of their separate probabilities. In other words, the 20% chance that she's a clerk multiplied by the 20% chance that she's in the feminist movement produces a 4% chance that both things are true at the same time ($0.20 \times 0.20 = 0.04$, or 4%). The combined probability of events is always less than the independent probability of each event; therefore, it's always *more* probable that any one state of affairs is true than is a set of events simultaneously.

This mindbug is called the conjunction fallacy because *people think that two events are more likely to occur together than either individual event.* The fallacy is that with more and more pieces of information, people think there's a higher probability that all are true. Actually, the probability diminishes rapidly. Based on her description, do you also think Linda is liberal rather than conservative in her political opinions? Do you think she also writes poetry? Do you think she's also signed her name to fair-housing petitions? With each additional bit of information, you probably think you're getting a better and better

CONJUNCTION FALLACY People think that two events are more likely to occur together than either individual event.

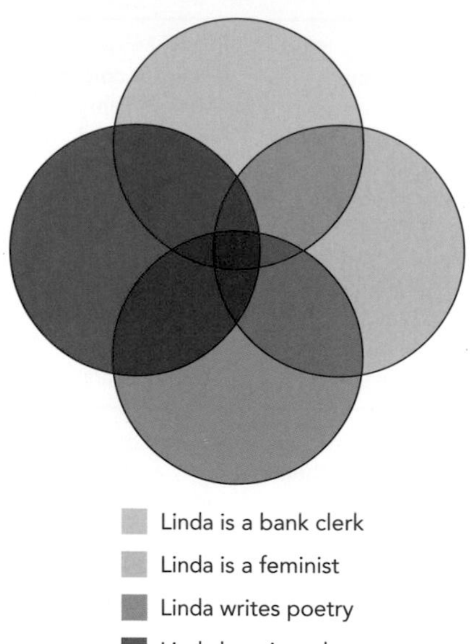
Linda is a bank clerk
Linda is a feminist
Linda writes poetry
Linda has signed a fair-housing petition

FIGURE **7.13 The conjunction fallacy** People often think that with each additional bit of information, the probability that all the facts are simultaneously true of a person increases. In fact, the probability decreases dramatically. Notice how the intersection of all these possibilities is much smaller than the area of any one possibility alone.

description of Linda, but as you can see in FIGURE **7.13**, the likelihood of all those events being true *at the same time* is very small.

Representativeness heuristic

Think about the following situation:

> A panel of psychologists wrote 100 descriptions based on interviews with engineers and lawyers. *The descriptions came from 70 engineers and 30 lawyers.* You will be shown a random selection of these descriptions. Read each and then pause and decide if it is more likely that the person is an engineer or a lawyer. Note your decision and read on.
>
> 1 Jack enjoys reading books on social and political issues. During the interview, he displayed particular skill at argument.
>
> 2 Tom is a loner who enjoys working on mathematical puzzles during his spare time. During the interview, his speech remained fairly abstract and his emotions were well controlled.
>
> 3 Harry is a bright man and an avid squash player. During the interview, he asked many insightful questions and was very well spoken.

Research participants were shown a series of descriptions like these and asked after each one to judge the likelihood that the person described was a lawyer or an engineer (Kahneman and Tversky, 1973). Remember, of the descriptions, 70 were engineers and 30 were lawyers. If participants took this proportion into consideration, their judgements should have reflected the fact that there were more than twice as many engineers as lawyers. But a mindbug was operating: researchers found that people didn't use this information and based their judgements solely on how closely the description matched their concepts of lawyers and engineers. So, the majority of participants thought descriptions such as 1 were more likely to be lawyers, those like 2 were more likely to be engineers, and those like 3 could be either.

Consider participants' judgements about Harry. His description doesn't sound like a lawyer's or an engineer's, so most people said he was *equally likely* to hold either occupation. But the pool contains more than twice as many engineers as lawyers, so it is far *more* likely that he is an engineer. People again seem to ignore information about base rate, forming their judgements on similarities to categories (see real world example). Researchers call this the representativeness heuristic – *a mental shortcut that involves making a probability judgement by comparing an object or event to a prototype of the object or event* (Kahneman and Tversky, 1973). Thus, the probability judgements were skewed towards the participants' prototypes of lawyer and engineer. The greater the similarity, the more likely they were judged to be members of that category despite the existence of much more useful base rates.

REPRESENTATIVENESS HEURISTIC A mental shortcut that involves making a probability judgement by comparing an object or event to a prototype of the object or event.

Mindbugs such as availability, representativeness or the conjunction fallacy highlight the strengths and weakness of the way we think. We are very good at forming categories based on prototypes and making classification judgements on the basis of similarity to prototypes. Judging probabilities is not our strong suit. As we saw earlier in this chapter, the human brain easily processes frequency information and decision-making performance can usually be improved if probability problems are reframed using frequencies.

Framing effects

You've seen that according to rational choice theory, our judgements will vary depending on the value we place on the expected outcome. So, how effective are we at assigning value to our choices? Not surprisingly, a mindbug can affect this situation. Studies show that framing effects, which occur when *people give different answers to the same problem depending on how the problem is phrased (or framed)*, can influence the assignment of value.

FRAMING EFFECTS People give different answers to the same problem depending on how the problem is phrased (or framed).

For example, if people are told that a particular drug has a 70% effectiveness rate, they're usually pretty impressed: 70% of the time the drug cures what ails you sounds like a good deal. Tell them instead that a drug has a 30% failure rate – 30% of the time it does no good – and they typically perceive it as risky, potentially harmful, something to be avoided. Notice that the information is the same: a 70% effectiveness rate means that 30% of the time it's ineffective. The way the information is framed, however, leads to substantially different conclusions (Tversky and Kahneman, 1981).

One of the most striking framing effects is the sunk-cost fallacy, which occurs when *people make decisions about a current situation based on what they have previously invested in the situation.* Imagine waiting in a queue for three hours, paying £60 for a ticket to see your favourite band, and waking on the day of the outdoor concert to find that it's bitterly cold and rainy. If you go, you'll feel miserable. But you go anyway, reasoning that the £60 you paid for the ticket and the time you spent queueing will have been wasted if you stay home. Notice that you have two choices: spend £60 and stay comfortably at home, or spend £60 and endure many uncomfortable hours in the rain. Either way, the £60 is gone, it's a sunk cost, irretrievable at the moment of your decision. But the way you framed the problem created a mindbug: because you invested time and money, you feel obliged to follow through, even though it's something you no longer want. If you can turn off the mindbug and ask 'Would I rather spend £60 to be comfortable or spend it to be miserable?', the clever choice is clear: stay home and listen to the podcast!

SUNK-COST FALLACY A framing effect in which people make decisions about a current situation based on what they have previously invested in the situation.

WWW.JUPITERIMAGES.COM

The fact that this concert-goer has already invested in buying a ticket influences their decision making. The sunk-cost fallacy mindbug makes them more likely to go to the concert even though they would be happier (and drier) staying at home!

Even governments are guilty of making decisions based on the sunk-cost fallacy. During the 1960s, the British and French governments collaborated on building Concorde, the first supersonic passenger plane. Even though development costs escalated to a point where the plane was no longer financially worth building, both governments continued to plough money into the venture because too much had been invested to quit (Arkes and Ayton, 1999). Mindbugs can be costly!

Why do we make decision-making errors?

As you have seen, everyday decision making seems riddled with errors and shortcomings. Our decisions vary wildly depending on how a problem is presented, for example frequencies versus probabilities, or framed in terms of losses rather than savings, and we seem to be prone to fallacies, such as the sunk-cost fallacy or the conjunction fallacy. Psychologists have developed several explanations for why everyday decision making suffers from these failings. We'll review two of the most influential theories – prospect theory and the frequency format hypothesis.

Prospect theory

According to a totally rational model of inference, people should make decisions that maximize value; in other words, they should seek to increase what psychologists and economists call *expected utility.* We face decisions like this every day. If you are making a decision that involves money and money is what you value, you should choose the outcome that is likely to bring you the most money. When deciding which of two flats to rent, you'd compare the monthly expenses for each and choose the one that leaves more money in your pocket.

As you have seen, however, people often make decisions that are inconsistent with this simple principle. The question is, why? To explain these effects, Amos Tversky and Daniel Kahneman (1992) developed prospect theory, which *proposes that people choose to take on risk when evaluating potential losses and avoid risks when evaluating potential gains.* These decision processes take place in two phases:

PROSPECT THEORY Proposes that people choose to take on risk when evaluating potential losses and avoid risks when evaluating potential gains.

1 People simplify the available information. So, in a task like choosing a flat, they tend to ignore a lot of potentially useful information because flats differ in so many ways – the closeness of restaurants, the presence of a garden, the colour of the carpet and so on. Comparing each flat on each factor is simply too much work, whereas focusing on only differences that matter is more efficient.

2 In the second phase, people choose the prospect they believe offers the best value. This value is personal and may differ from an objective measure of 'best value'. For example, you might choose the flat with the higher rent because you can walk to eight great bars and restaurants.

Prospect theory makes other assumptions that account for people's choice patterns. One assumption, called the *certainty effect*, suggests that when making decisions, people give greater weight to outcomes that are a sure thing. When deciding between playing a lottery with an 80% chance of winning £4,000 or receiving £3,000 outright, most people choose the £3,000, even though the expected value of the first choice is £200 more (£4,000 × 80% = £3,200). Apparently, people weigh certainty much more heavily than expected payoffs when making choices.

Prospect theory also assumes that in evaluating choices, people compare them to a reference point. For example, suppose you're still torn between two flats. The £400 monthly rent for flat A is reduced by £10 if you pay before the fifth of the month. A £10 surcharge is tacked onto the £390 per month rent for flat B if you pay after the fifth of the month. Although the flats are objectively identical in terms of cost, different reference points may make flat A seem psychologically more appealing than B. The reference point for flat A is £400, and the offer describes a change in terms of a potential gain (money saved), whereas the reference point for B is £390, and the change involves a potential loss (money penalized).

Prospect theory also assumes that people are more willing to take risks to avoid losses than to achieve gains. Given a choice between a definite £300 rebate on your first month's rent or spinning a wheel that offers an 80% chance of getting a £400 rebate, you'll probably choose the lower sure payoff over the higher potential payoff (£400 × 80% = £320). However, given a choice between a sure fine of £300 for damaging a flat or a spinning of a wheel that has an 80% chance of a £400 fine, most people will choose the higher potential loss over the sure loss. This asymmetry in risk preferences shows that we are willing to take on risk if we think it will ward off a loss, but we're risk averse if we expect to lose some benefits.

Frequency format hypothesis

FREQUENCY FORMAT HYPOTHESIS The proposal that our minds evolved to notice how frequently things occur, not how likely they are to occur.

According to the frequency format hypothesis, *our minds evolved to notice how frequently things occur, not how likely they are to occur* (Gigerenzer, 1996; Gigerenzer and Hoffrage, 1995). Thus, we interpret, process and manipulate information about frequency with comparative ease because that's the way quantitative information usually occurs in natural circumstances. For example, the 20 men, 15 women, 5 dogs, 13 cars and 2 bicycle accidents you encountered on the way to lectures came in the form of frequencies, not probabilities or percentages. Probabilities and percentages are, evolutionarily speaking, recent developments, emerging in the mid-17th century (Hacking, 1975). Millennia passed before humans developed these cultural notions, and years of schooling are needed to competently use them as everyday cognitive tools. Thus, our susceptibility to mindbugs when dealing with probabilities is not surprising.

In contrast, people can track frequencies virtually effortlessly and flawlessly (Hasher and Zacks, 1984). We are also remarkably good at recognizing how often two events occur together (Mandel and Lehman, 1998; Spellman, 1996; Waldmann, 2000). Infants as young as six months of age can tell the difference between displays that differ in the number of items present (Starkey et al., 1983, 1990). Frequency monitoring is a basic biological capacity rather than a skill learned through formal instruction. According to the frequency format hypothesis, presenting statistical information in frequency format rather than probability format results in improved performance because it capitalizes on our evolutionary strengths (Gigerenzer and Hoffrage, 1995; Hertwig and Gigerenzer, 1999).

Thinking fast and slow

As one of the few psychologists ever to win a Nobel Prize, Daniel Kahneman is one of the most important thinkers in the discipline alive today. Many of the biases and effects described in this chapter discovered by Kahneman and his colleagues have been summarized in his bestseller, *Thinking, Fast and Slow* (Kahneman, 2012). In this book, Kahneman outlines how most human decision making is either rapid and intuitive or slow and calculated. For example, if you look at the face of the man in the photo, you can tell almost immediately that the person is angry and about to say something unpleasant, possibly in an aggressive manner, directed at you. These decisions are almost effortless (unless you have some form of social perception processing problem).

DIGITAL VISION/GETTY IMAGES

In contrast, now decide whether the following is correct: 7 × 19 = 143. For most of us (mathematicians excluded), this decision process is much harder, much slower and requires effortful mental calculation. This difference in decision making is captured by the division in reasoning known as System 1 and System 2 (Stanovich and West, 2000). System 1 *operates automatically and quickly, with little or no effort and no sense of voluntary control*; System 2 *allocates attention to more taxing and mental activities and is often associated with a subjective experience of making choices*. System 1 includes innate skills, many of them shared with animals, which are present early in development (see Chapters 11 and 12), and well-rehearsed knowledge that requires minimal effort to retrieve (for example, the capital of France). Acquired expertise can become System 1, such as learning to ride a bike. In contrast, System 2 requires logic, analysis and concentration to solve task demands.

SYSTEM 1 Operates automatically and quickly, with little or no effort and no sense of voluntary control; SYSTEM 2 Allocates attention to more taxing and mental activities and is often associated with a subjective experience of making choices.

One of the main differences between System 1 and System 2 is the interference effect from competing tasks. When you have to divert attention, System 1 reasoning is much less disrupted compared to System 2. For example, solving the 7 × 19 problem is much harder if you have to concentrate on overtaking a truck on a narrow road. On the other hand, if the truck driver is the man in the picture above, then you know almost immediately that there may be a bit of road rage going on. We encountered this type of dual task interference in Chapter 5 when discussing the role of executive functions and working memory. This is because System 2 reasoning is dependent on executive functions. System 1 may be more automatic but it also means that it can make errors when intuitions fail us. For example, if a 50-kg cannonball and a 1-kg bowling ball of equal size and wind resistance are dropped from a tower, which lands first? Our intuition is to say the cannonball, when in fact they should hit the ground at the same time (Champagne et al., 1980). As we see in Chapter 11, intuitive theories can generate incorrect decisions that just seem right. Indeed, many of the other mindbugs described throughout this textbook are examples of System 1 processes.

Decision making and the brain

A patient identified as 'Elliot' (who you met in Chapter 1) was a successful businessman, husband and father prior to developing a brain tumour. After surgery, his intellectual abilities seemed intact, but he was unable to differentiate between important and unimportant activities and would spend hours at mundane tasks. He lost his job and got involved in several risky financial ventures that bankrupted him. He had no difficulty discussing what had happened, but his descriptions were so detached and dispassionate that it seemed as though his abstract intellectual functions had become dissociated from his social and emotional abilities.

Research confirms that this interpretation of Elliot's downfall is correct. In one study, researchers looked at how healthy volunteers differed from people with prefrontal lobe damage on a risky decision-making task (Bechara et al., 1994, 1997). Four decks of cards were placed face down, and participants were required to make 100 selections of cards that specified an amount of play money they could win or lose. Two of the decks usually provided large payoffs or large losses, whereas the other two provided smaller payoffs and losses. While playing the game, participants' galvanic skin responses (GSRs) were recorded to measure heightened emotional reactions.

The performance of players with prefrontal lobe damage mirrored Elliot's real-life problems. They selected cards equally from the riskier and the safer decks, leading most to eventually go bankrupt. At first, the healthy volunteers also selected from each deck equally, but they gradually shifted to choosing primarily from the safer decks. This difference in strategy occurred even though both groups showed strong emotional reactions to big gains and losses, as measured by their comparable GSR scores.

The two groups differed in one important way. As the game progressed, the healthy participants began to show anticipatory emotional reactions when they even *considered* choosing a card from the risky deck. Their GSR scores jumped dramatically even before they were able to say that some decks were riskier than others (Bechara et al., 1997). The patients with prefrontal damage didn't show these anticipatory feelings when they were thinking about selecting a card from the risky deck. Apparently, their emotional reactions did not guide their thinking, and so they continued to make risky decisions, as shown in FIGURE **7.14**.

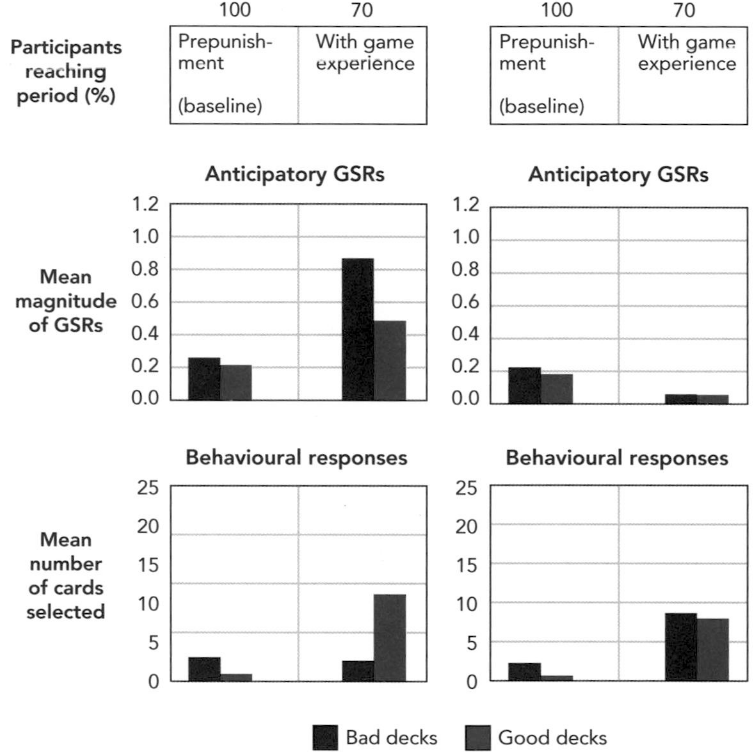

FIGURE **7.14 The neuroscience of risky decision making** In a study of risky decision making, researchers compared healthy controls' choices to those made by people with damage to the prefrontal cortex. Participants played a game in which they selected a card from one of four decks. Two of the decks were made up of riskier cards – those with large payoffs or large losses. The other two contained 'safer' cards – those with much smaller payoffs and losses. At the beginning of the game, both groups chose cards from the two decks with equal frequency. Over the course of the game, the healthy controls avoided the bad decks and showed large emotional responses (GSRs) when they even considered choosing a card from a 'risky' deck. Patients with prefrontal brain damage, on the other hand, continued to choose cards from the two decks with equal frequency and showed no evidence of emotional learning. These participants eventually went bankrupt (Bechara et al., 1997).

Further studies of these patients suggest that their risky decision making grows out of insensitivity to the future consequences of their behaviour. Unable to think beyond immediate consequences, they could not shift their choices in response to a rising rate of losses or a declining rate of rewards (Bechara et al., 2000). Interestingly, substance-dependent individuals, such as alcoholics and cocaine addicts, act the same way. Most perform as poorly on the gambling task as patients with prefrontal damage. In fact, their scores can be predicted on the basis of a combination of factors, such as years of substance abuse, duration of current abstinence, and number of relapses and times in treatment (Bechara et al., 2001). More recent work has extended these impairments on the gambling task across cultures to Chinese adolescents (Johnson et al., 2008).

Neuroimaging studies of healthy individuals have provided evidence that fits well with the earlier studies of patients with damage to the prefrontal cortex. When performing the gambling task, an area in the prefrontal cortex is activated when participants need to make risky decisions as compared to safe decisions (Fukui et al., 2005; Lawrence et al., 2009). Indeed, the activated region is in the part of the prefrontal cortex that is typically damaged in patients who perform poorly on the gambling task, and greater activation in this region is correlated with better task performance in healthy individuals (Fukui et al., 2005; Lawrence et al., 2009). Taken together, the neuroimaging and lesion studies show that aspects of risky decision making depend critically on the contributions of the prefrontal cortex.

In summary, human decision making often departs from a completely rational process, and the mindbugs that accompany this departure tell us a lot about how the human mind works. The values we place on outcomes weigh so heavily in our judgements that they sometimes overshadow objective evidence. When people are asked to make probability judgements, they will turn the problem into something they know how to solve, such as judging memory strength, judging similarity to prototypes, or estimating frequencies. This can lead to errors of judgement. When a problem fits their mental algorithms, people show considerable skill at making appropriate judgements. In making a judgement about the probability of an event, performance can vary dramatically. Because we feel that avoiding losses is more important than achieving gains, framing effects can affect our choices. Emotional information also strongly influences our decision making, even when we are not aware of it. Although this mindbug can lead us astray, it is often crucial for making decisions in everyday life.

Problem solving: working it out

You have a problem when you find yourself in a place where you don't want to be. In such circumstances, you try to find a way to change the situation so that you end up in a situation you *do* want. Let's say that it's the night before an exam, and you are trying to study but just can't settle down and focus on the material. This is a situation you don't want. So, you try to think of ways to help yourself focus. You might begin with the material that most interests you or provide yourself with rewards, such as a music break or trip to the refrigerator. If these activities enable you to get down to work, your problem is solved.

Two major types of problems complicate our daily lives. The first and most frequent is the *ill-defined problem*, one that does not have a clear goal or well-defined solution paths. Your study block is an ill-defined problem: your goal isn't clearly defined, that is, 'somehow get focused', and the solution path for achieving the goal is even less clear, that is, there are many ways to gain focus. Most everyday problems – being a 'better person', finding that 'special someone', achieving 'success' – are ill defined. In contrast, a *well-defined problem* is one with clearly specified goals and clearly defined solution paths. Examples include following a clear set of directions to get to a lecture, solving simple algebra problems, or assembling a Lego model with the help of instructions.

CORBIS

Although it may not be easy to put together a Lego model, having instructions for assembly makes it a well-defined problem.

Means-ends analysis

In 1945, German psychologist Karl Duncker reported some important studies of the problem-solving process. He presented people with ill-defined problems and asked them to 'think aloud' while solving them. Based on what people said about how they solve problems, Duncker (1945) described problem solving in terms of means-ends analysis – *a process of searching for the means or steps to reduce the differences between the current situation and the desired goal.* This process usually took the following steps:

MEANS-ENDS ANALYSIS A process of searching for the means or steps to reduce the differences between the current situation and the desired goal.

1 Analyse the goal state, that is, the desired outcome you want to attain.
2 Analyse the current state, that is, your starting point, or the current situation.
3 List the differences between the current state and the goal state.
4 Reduce the list of differences by:
   - direct means – a procedure that solves the problem without intermediate steps
   - generating a subgoal – an intermediate step on the way to solving the problem
   - finding a similar problem that has a known solution.

Consider, for example, one of Duncker's problems:

> A patient has an inoperable tumour in his abdomen. The tumour is inoperable because it is surrounded by healthy but fragile tissue that would be severely damaged during surgery. How can the patient be saved?

The *goal state* is a patient without the tumour and with undamaged surrounding tissue. The *current state* is a patient with an inoperable tumour surrounded by fragile tissue. The *difference* between these two states is the tumour. A *direct means solution* would be to destroy the tumour with X-rays (radiation therapy), but the required X-ray dose would destroy the fragile surrounding tissue and possibly kill the patient.

A *subgoal* would be to modify the X-ray machine to deliver a weaker dose. After this subgoal is achieved, a direct means solution could be to deliver the weaker dose to the patient's abdomen. But this solution won't work either. The weaker dose wouldn't damage the healthy tissue but also wouldn't destroy the tumour. So, what to do? We find a similar problem that has a known solution. Let's see how this can be done.

Analogical problem solving

ANALOGICAL PROBLEM SOLVING Solving a problem by finding a similar problem with a known solution and applying that solution to the current problem.

When we engage in analogical problem solving, we attempt to *solve a problem by finding a similar problem with a known solution and applying that solution to the current problem.* Consider the following story:

> An island surrounded by bridges is the site of an enemy fortress. The massive fortification is so strongly defended that only a very large army could take it. Unfortunately, the bridges would collapse under the weight of such a huge force. So, a clever general divides the army into several smaller units and sends the units over different bridges, timing the crossings so that the many streams of soldiers converge on the fortress at the same time and the fortress is taken.

Does this story suggest a solution to the tumour problem? It should. Removing a tumour and attacking a fortress are different problems, but the two problems are analogous because they share a common structure. The *goal state* is a conquered fortress with undamaged surrounding bridges. The *current state* is an occupied fortress surrounded by fragile bridges. The *difference* between the two states is the occupying enemy. The *solution* is to divide the required force into smaller units that are light enough to spare the fragile bridges and send them down the bridges simultaneously so that they converge on the fortress. The combined units will form an army strong enough to take the fortress (see FIGURE **7.15**).

This analogous problem of the island fortress suggests the following direct means solution to the tumour problem:

> Surround the patient with X-ray machines and simultaneously send weaker doses that converge on the tumour. The combined strength of the weaker X-ray doses will be sufficient to destroy the tumour, but the individual doses will be weak enough to spare the surrounding healthy tissue.

Did this solution occur to you after reading the fortress story? In studies that have used the tumour problem, only 10% of participants spontaneously generated the

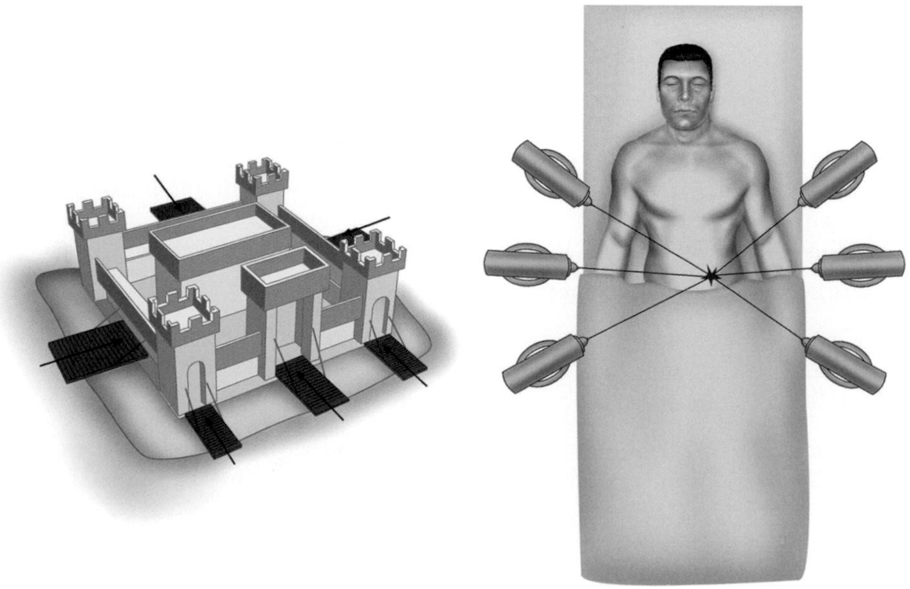

FIGURE **7.15 Analogical problem solving** Just as smaller, lighter battalions can reach the fortress without damaging the bridges, so can many small X-ray doses get to the tumour without harming the delicate surrounding tissue. In both cases, the additive strength achieves the objective.

correct solution. This percentage rose to 30% if participants read the island fortress problem or other analogous story. However, the success climbed dramatically to 75% among participants who had a chance to read more than one analogous problem or were given a deliberate hint to use the solution to the fortress story (Gick and Holyoak, 1980).

Why was the fortress problem so ineffective by itself? Apparently, problem solving among novices is strongly affected by superficial similarities between problems, and the analogy between the tumour and fortress problems lies deep in their structure (Catrambone, 2002). In a set of studies demonstrating this mindbug, a researcher used examples to demonstrate solutions to mathematics problems. When participants tried to solve new problems, they often spontaneously reminded themselves of instructional examples that had the same cover story as the problem they were trying to solve – regardless of whether the mathematical structures were the same. For example, they made remarks such as 'Oh, yeah, another pizza problem', rather than 'Oh, yeah, another convergence problem' (Ross, 1984).

Creativity and insight

Analogical problem solving shows us that successfully solving a problem often depends on learning the principles underlying a particular type of problem and also that solving lots of problems improves our ability to recognize certain problem types and generate effective solutions. Some problem solving, however, seems to involve brilliant flashes of insight and creative solutions that have never before been tried. Creative and insightful solutions often rely on restructuring a problem so that it turns into a problem you already know how to solve.

Genius and insight

Consider the exceptional mind of mathematician Friedrich Gauss (1777–1855). One day, Gauss's primary school teacher asked the class to add up the numbers 1 to 10. While his classmates laboriously worked out their sums, Gauss had a flash of insight that caused the answer to occur to him immediately.

Gauss imagined the numbers 1 to 10 as weights lined up on a balance beam, as shown in FIGURE **7.16**. Starting at the left, each 'weight' increases by 1. In order for the beam to balance, each weight on the left must be paired with a weight on the right. You can see this by starting at the middle and noticing that 5 + 6 = 11, then moving outwards, 4 + 7 = 11, 3 + 8 = 11 and so on. This produces five number pairs that add up to 11. Now the problem is easy – multiply. Gauss's genius lay in restructuring the problem in a way that

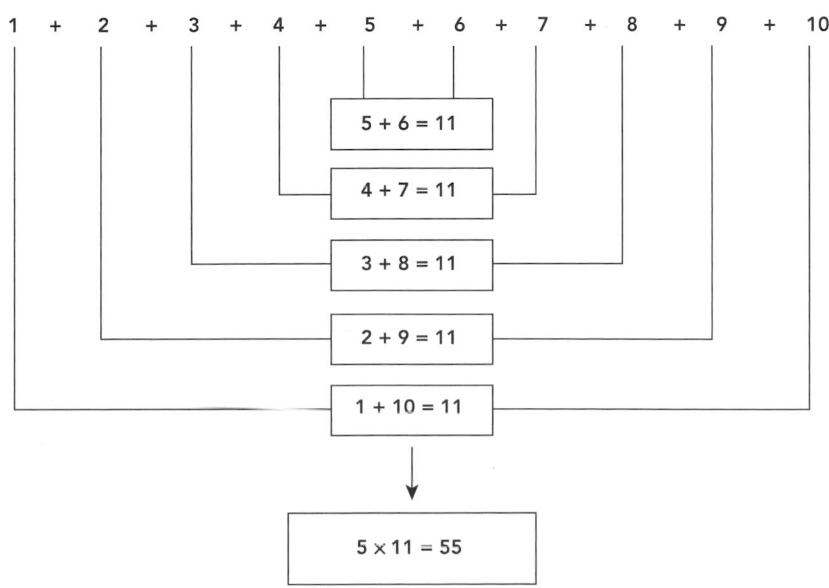

FIGURE **7.16 Genius and insight** Young Friedrich Gauss imagined the scheme shown here and quickly reduced a laborious addition problem to an easy multiplication task. Gauss's early insight led him to later realize an intriguing truth: this simple solution generalizes to number series of any length (after Wertheimer, [1945]1982).

allowed him to notice a simple and elegant solution to an otherwise tedious task – a procedure, by the way, that generalizes to series of any length.

According to Gestalt psychologists, insights such as these reflect a spontaneous restructuring of a problem. A sudden flash of insight contrasts with incremental problem-solving procedures in which one gradually gets closer and closer to a solution. Early researchers studying insight found that people were more likely to solve a non-insight problem if they felt they were gradually getting 'warmer' (incrementally closer to the solution). But whether someone felt 'warm' did not predict the likelihood of their solving an insight problem (Metcalfe and Wiebe, 1987). The solution for an insight problem seemed to appear out of the blue, regardless of what the participant felt.

Analogical reasoning is responsible for one of the most useful inventions of the 20th century. When George de Mestral looked at burdock seeds under a microscope, he saw that they were barbed and hook-like and had meshed with the looped fibres in his clothes. At the time, conventional zip fasteners were constantly jamming and he realized that he could develop a more simple attachment system. Today, Velcro is everywhere, including NASA where it was used on the Space Shuttle. George de Mestral made a fortune after selling his patent, but continued to work on inventions including the invaluable asparagus peeler.

Later research, however, suggests that sudden insightful solutions may actually result from unconscious incremental processes (Bowers et al., 1990). In one study, research participants were shown paired, three-word series, such as those in FIGURE **7.17**, and asked to find a fourth word that was associated with the three words in each series. However, only one series in each pair had a common associate. Solvable series were termed *coherent*, whereas those with no solution were called *incoherent*. Even if participants couldn't find a solution, they could reliably decide, more than by chance alone, which of the pairs was coherent. However, if insightful solutions actually occur in a sudden, all-or-nothing manner, their performance should have been no better than chance. Thus, the findings suggest that even insightful problem solving is an incremental process – one that occurs outside conscious awareness. The process works something like this. The pattern of clues that constitute a problem unconsciously activates relevant information in memory. Activation then spreads through the memory network, recruiting additional relevant information (Bowers et al., 1990). When sufficient information has been activated, it crosses the threshold of awareness and we experience a sudden flash of insight into the problem's solution.

Coherent	Incoherent
Playing Credit Report	Still Pages Music
Blank White Lines	Light Folk Head
Ticket Shop Broker	Town Root Car
Magic Plush Floor	House Lion Butter
Base Snow Dance	Swan Army Mask
Gold Stool Tender	Noise Foam Shade

Solutions: Card, paper, pawn, carpet, ball, bar

FIGURE **7.17 Insightful solutions are really incremental** Participants were asked to find a fourth word that was associated with the other three words in each series. Even if they couldn't find a solution, they could reliably choose which series of three words were solvable and which were not. Try to solve these (after Bowers et al., 1990).

Finding a connection between the words *strawberry* and *traffic* might take some time, even for someone motivated to work out how they are related. But if the word *strawberry* activates *jam* in long-term memory (see Chapter 5) and the activation spreads from *strawberry* to *traffic*, the solution to the puzzle may suddenly spring into awareness without the thinker knowing how it got there. What would seem like an all-or-nothing, sudden insight would result from an incremental process that consists of activation spreading through memory, adding new information as more knowledge is activated.

The 'Aha!' moment that accompanies a sudden flash of insight is a compelling experience, one that highlights that solving a problem based on insight *feels* radically different from solving it through step-by-step analysis or trial and error. This difference in subjective experience suggests that something different is going on in the brain when we solve a problem using insight instead of analytic strategies. Imaging studies using EEG and fMRI have provided evidence that this is so, and have also revealed clues as to why some people rely more on insight than others (Kounios and Beeman, 2009).

To examine brain activity associated with insight, researchers used a procedure called the *compound remote associates test*. Participants were required to solve tasks to find the correct word associated with three others. For example, the correct solution for *crab, pine* and *sauce* would be *apple*. Participants used analytical strategies to work out the answer but sometimes they had a sudden insight. One-third of a second before participants came up with the solution through insight, there was a sudden and dramatic burst of high-frequency electrical activity (40 cycles per second or Hz) (Jung-Beeman et al., 2004). This activity was centred over the front part of the right temporal lobe, slightly above the right ear. The researchers then performed a similar study using fMRI to measure brain activity, and found that this right temporal area was the only region in the entire brain that showed greater activity for insight solutions compared with solutions based on analytic strategies.

While these findings demonstrate that brain activity differs for each type of problem-solving approach, they leave open a critical question: why do people solve some problems with insight and others with analytic strategies? The great French scientist Louis Pasteur once stated that: 'Chance favours only the prepared mind.' Inspired by this observation, the researchers asked whether brain activity occurring just before the presentation of a problem influenced whether that problem was solved via insight or analytic strategies (Kounios et al., 2006). It did. In the moments before a problem was solved with an insight solution, there was increased activity deep in the frontal lobes, in a part of the brain known as the 'anterior cingulate', which controls cognitive processes such as the ability to switch attention from one thing to another. The researchers suggested that this increased activity in the anterior cingulate allowed participants to attend to and detect associations that were only weakly activated, perhaps at a subconscious level, and that facilitate sudden insight.

A related study using the compound remote associates task revealed that when people were in a positive mood, they solved more problems with insight than people who were in a less positive mood (Subramaniam et al., 2009). Moreover, positive mood was associated with heightened activity in the anterior cingulate during the moments before a problem was presented, suggesting that being in a positive mood helps to prepare the brain for sudden insight by 'turning on' that part of the brain and thereby increasing one's ability to detect associations that aid problem solution.

The same research team also asked whether brain activity prior to problem solving provides clues about which individuals are more likely to rely on insight over analytic strategies to solve compound remote associates problems (Kounios et al., 2008). Using EEG to measure resting brain activity, they found that insight problem solvers showed more resting activity in the right cerebral hemisphere than analytic problem solvers, which is consistent with other research linking creativity with right-hemisphere activity (Folley and Park, 2005; Howard-Jones et al., 2005).

The results of these studies suggest that the familiar image of a light bulb going off in your head when you experience an 'Aha!' moment is on the mark: those moments are indeed accompanied by something like an electrical power surge in the brain, and are preceded by specific types of electrical activity patterns. It seems likely that future research will tell us much more about how to turn on the mental light bulb and keep it burning bright.

hot science

'Far out' thinking

Solve this analogy: *forest* is to *tree* as *army* is to ...? If your analogical reasoning is working fine, you should have readily answered *soldier*, but what else do we use analogical thinking for other than solving brain teasers, and how do we do it? Analogical reasoning is a general human capacity involved in most domains, although perhaps notably in creative problem-solving areas such as science, design, art and engineering (Christensen and Schunn, 2007). One of the most famous examples of the result of analogical thinking is Velcro, invented in 1948 by the Swiss engineer George de Mestral who, after taking his dog for walk, noticed how the seeds of the burdock plant had attached themselves to his socks and the dog's fur (see the vignette above).

Some analogies are more creative than others, and some are not very creative at all. The creative insight from analogy depends on the extent to which the items being mapped are relatively close or relatively distant with respect to their superficial semantic features (Green et al., 2010; Holyoak and Thagard, 1995). The more distant the mappings are, the less obvious the link between them, and so they tend to be more novel (Dunbar and Blanchette, 2001; Holyoak and Thagard, 1995).

One recent study has shown that generating verbal analogies using semantic items that were distantly related is more effective in promoting relational creative thinking in a subsequent visual task than generating analogies that were more closely similar (Vendetti et al., 2014). Participants were presented with analogy problems each consisting of four words in an A:B:C:D format. Analogies were either distantly related semantically or closely related. For example if the A:B pair was *nose:scent*, then the distantly related C:D pair was *antenna:signal;* whereas the closely related C:D pair was *tongue:taste.* One group of participants presented with close and distant analogies on a computer screen had to decide whether the match was valid or not as quickly as possible. For example, an invalid close C:D pair for the A:B pair *nose:scent* would be *tongue:hearing* and an invalid distant C:D pair would be *antenna:expensive.* Another group of participants were presented with only valid analogies and had to use their creative insight to generate the correct C:D solution to either close or distant A:B analogies. After completing the verbal analogy task, both groups were then tested on a relational mapping picture task to test whether there was any transfer of creativity into another domain (Markman and Gentner, 1993).

Participants were shown scenes such as those illustrated opposite at the same time. After 10 seconds, one of the objects in the top scene was highlighted (for example, the umbrella), and participants had to indicate which object in the bottom scene 'goes with' the highlighted object in the top scene. For each pair of scenes, the bottom picture included both a potential featural match (for example, the umbrella over the coffee stand) and a potential relational match (for example, the newspaper the woman is holding over her head, which performs a function similar to the umbrella in the top scene).

Analysis of performance revealed that there was no difference in detecting the relational matches in the picture task for the group of participants who simply decided whether close and distant analogies were correct or not. However, participants in the generation task who had to come up with solutions to the analogies detected more relational matches if they had been tested on the distant analogies as opposed to the close ones. This effect was present even when fluid intelligence (see Chapter 9), overall accuracy and response time had been taken into consideration.

How do we solve such tasks? Imaging studies and work with patients with head injuries support the role of the most anterior lateral portion of the prefrontal cortex, generally termed the frontopolar or rostrolateral, which is activated by tasks that require integration of multiple relations, processing relatively abstract concepts, or negotiating hierarchical goal structures (for a review, see Knowlton and Holyoak, 2009). For example, imaging studies reveal that brain activity in this region during analogy tasks covaries directly with the semantic relationship between solutions generated even after task difficulty has been taken into consideration (Green at al., 2012). There is increased recruitment of the frontopolar prefrontal cortex as a mechanism for integrating semantically distant information to generate solutions in creative analogical reasoning.

If the same neural activation is associated with complex analogical reasoning (Bunge et al., 2005; Cho et al., 2010), creativity (Ellamil et al., 2012; Green et al., 2012) and abstract thought (Christoff et al., 2009), this suggests that using cross-domain analogies, compared with staying within a superficially similar domain, is more likely to lead to creative and innovative outcomes when generating ideas. In other words, 'far out' thinking not only makes you more creative but can help you to solve complex problems as well.

Functional fixedness

If insight is a simple incremental process, why isn't its occurrence more frequent? In the research discussed previously, participants produced insightful solutions only 25% of the time. Insight is rare because problem solving (like decision making) suffers from framing effects. In problem solving, framing tends to limit the types of solutions that occur to us.

Functional fixedness, *the tendency to perceive the functions of objects as fixed*, is a mindbug that constricts our thinking. Look at FIGURES **7.18** and **7.19** and see if you can solve the problems before reading on. In Figure 7.18, your task is to use these objects – a box of matches, some drawing pins and a candle – to mount the candle on the wall to illuminate a dark room. In Figure 7.19, you're holding a string hanging from the ceiling and using the items on the table, but without letting go of the string, you're expected to reach another string too far away to grasp. (The solutions are shown in FIGURES **7.21** and **7.22**.)

FIGURE **7.18 Functional fixedness and the candle problem** How can you use these objects – a box of matches, some drawing pins and a candle – to mount the candle on the wall so that it illuminates the room? Give this problem some thought before you check the answer in Figure 7.21.

FUNCTIONAL FIXEDNESS The tendency to perceive the functions of objects as fixed.

Difficulty solving these problems derives from our tendency to think of the objects only in terms of their normal, typical or 'fixed' functions. We don't think to use the matchbox for a candleholder because boxes typically hold matches, not candles. Similarly, using the hammer as a pendulum weight doesn't spring to mind because hammers are typically used to pound things. Did functional fixedness prevent you from solving these problems?

Sometimes framing limits our ability to generate a solution. Before reading on, look at FIGURE **7.20**. Without lifting your pencil from the page, try to connect all nine dots with only four straight lines.

To solve this problem, you must allow the lines you draw to extend outside the imaginary box that surrounds the dots (see FIGURE **7.23**). This constraint does not reside in the problem but in the mind of the problem solver. Despite the apparent sudden flash of insight that seems to yield a solution to problems of this type, research indicates that the thought processes people use when solving even this type of insight problem are best described as an incremental, means-ends analysis (MacGregor et al., 2001).

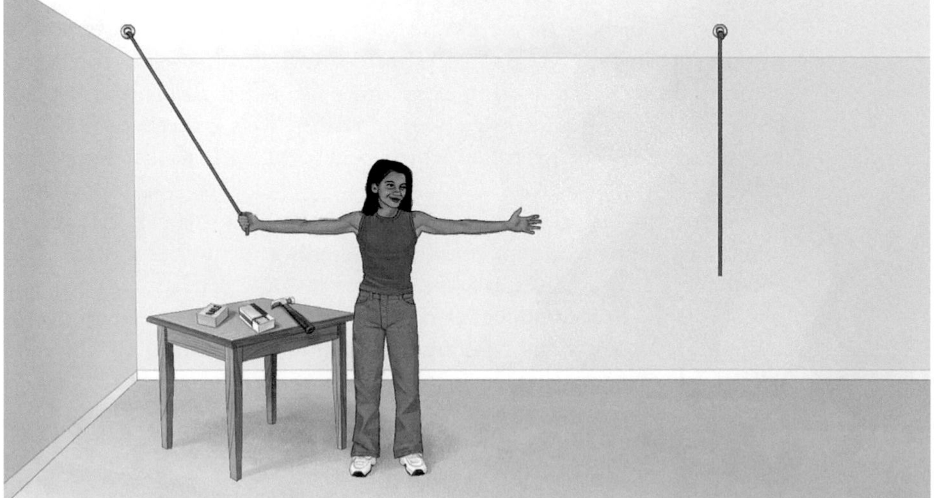

FIGURE **7.19 Functional fixedness and the string problem** The strings hung from hooks on the ceiling are long enough to be tied together, but they are too far apart to reach one while holding onto the other. Using the tools shown on the table, how can you accomplish the task? Compare your answer to that in Figure 7.22.

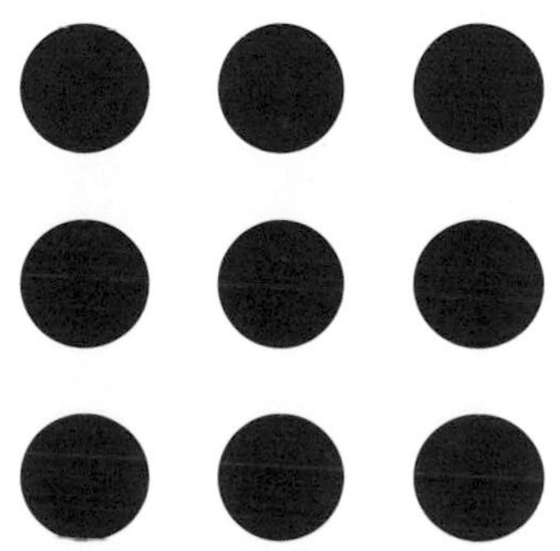

FIGURE **7.20 The nine dot problem** Connect all nine dots with four straight lines without lifting your pencil from the paper. Compare your answer to those in Figure 7.23, p. 305.

In summary, like concept formation and decision making, problem solving is a process in which new inputs (in this case, problems) are interpreted in terms of old knowledge. Problems may be ill defined or well defined, leading to more or less obvious solutions. The solutions we generate depend as much on the organization of our knowledge as on the objective characteristics of the problems. Means-end analysis and analogical problem solving offer pathways to effective solutions, although we often frame things in terms of what we already know and understand. Sometimes, as in the case of functional fixedness, that knowledge can restrict our problem-solving processes, making it difficult to find solutions that should be easy to find.

Transforming information: how we reach conclusions

REASONING A mental activity that consists of organizing information or beliefs into a series of steps to reach conclusions.

Reasoning is *a mental activity that consists of organizing information or beliefs into a series of steps to reach conclusions*. Sometimes our reasoning seems sensible and straightforward, and at other times it seems a little off. Consider some reasons offered by people who filed actual car insurance claims (www.swapmeetdave.com):

- 'I left for work this morning at 7am as usual when I collided straight into a bus. The bus was five minutes early.'
- 'Coming home, I drove into the wrong house and collided with a tree I don't have.'
- 'My car was legally parked as it backed into another vehicle.'
- 'The indirect cause of the accident was a little guy in a small car with a big mouth.'
- 'Windshield broke. Cause unknown. Probably voodoo.'

PRACTICAL REASONING Working out what to do, or reasoning directed towards action.

THEORETICAL REASONING Reasoning directed towards arriving at a belief.

When people like these hapless drivers argue with you in a way that seems inconsistent or poorly thought out, you may accuse them of being 'illogical'. Logic is a system of rules that specifies which conclusions follow from a set of statements. To put it another way, if you know that a given set of statements is true, logic will tell you which other statements *must* also be true. If the statement 'Jack and Jill went up the hill' is true, then according to the rules of logic, the statement 'Jill went up the hill' must also be true. To accept the truth of the first statement while denying the truth of the second statement would be a contradiction. Logic is a tool for evaluating reasoning, but it should not be confused with the process of reasoning itself. Equating logic and reasoning would be like equating carpenter's tools (logic) with building a house (reasoning).

Earlier in the chapter, we discussed decision making, which often depends on reasoning with probabilities. Practical reasoning and theoretical reasoning also allow us to make decisions (Walton, 1990). Practical reasoning is *working out what to do, or reasoning directed towards action*. Means-ends analysis is one kind of practical reasoning. An example is working out how to get to a concert across town if you don't have a car. In contrast, theoretical reasoning (sometimes also called *discursive reasoning*) is *reasoning directed towards arriving at a belief*. We use theoretical reasoning when we try to determine which beliefs follow logically from other beliefs.

Suppose you asked your friend Bruce to take you to a concert, and he said his car wasn't working. You'd undoubtedly find another way to get to the concert. If you then spied him driving into the concert car park, you might reason: 'Bruce told me his car wasn't working. He just drove into the car park. If his car wasn't working, he couldn't drive it here. So, either he suddenly fixed it, or he was lying to me. If he was lying to me, he's not much of a friend.' Notice the absence of an action-oriented goal. Theoretical reasoning is just a series of inferences concluding in a belief – in this case, about your so-called friend's unfriendliness!

FIGURE **7.21 The solution to the candle problem** What makes this problem difficult is that the usual function of the box (to hold matches) interferes with recognizing that it can be tacked onto the wall to serve as a candleholder.

If you concluded from these examples that we are equally adept at both types of reasoning, experimental evidence suggests you're wrong. People generally find working out what to do easier than deciding which beliefs follow logically from other beliefs. In cross-cultural studies, this tendency to respond practically when theoretical reasoning is sought has been demonstrated in individuals without schooling. Consider,

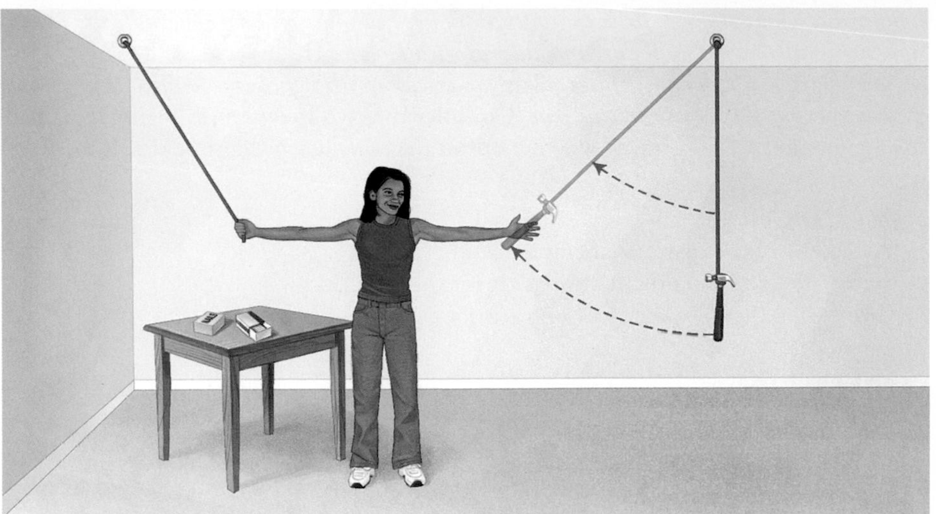

FIGURE **7.22 The solution to the string problem** The usual function of the hammer (to pound things) interferes with recognizing that it can also serve as a weighted pendulum to swing the string into the person's grasp.

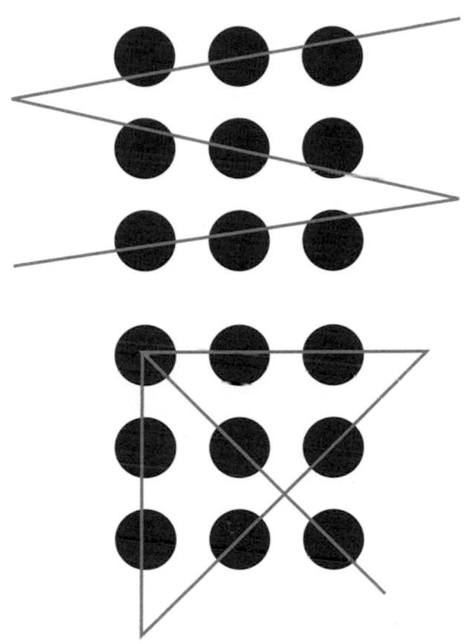

FIGURE **7.23 Two solutions to the nine dot problem** Solving this problem requires thinking 'outside the box', that is, going outside the imaginary box implied by the dot arrangement. The limiting box isn't really there, it's imposed by the problem solver's perceptual set.

for example, this dialogue between a Nigerian rice farmer, a member of the preliterate Kpelle people, and an American researcher (Scribner, 1975, p. 155):

Experimenter:	All Kpelle men are rice farmers. Mr. Smith (this is a Western name) is not a rice farmer. Is he a Kpelle man?
Participant:	I don't know the man in person. I have not laid eyes on the man himself.
Experimenter:	Just think about the statement.
Participant:	If I know him in person, I can answer that question, but since I do not know him in person, I cannot answer that question.
Experimenter:	Try and answer from your Kpelle sense.
Participant:	If you know a person, if a question comes up about him, you are able to answer. But if you do not know a person, if a question comes up about him, it's hard for you to answer it.

As this excerpt shows, the participant does not seem to understand that the problem can be resolved with theoretical reasoning. Instead, he is concerned with retrieving and verifying facts, a strategy that does not work for this type of task.

A very different picture emerges when members of preliterate cultures are given tasks that require practical reasoning. One well-known study of rural Kenyans illustrates a typical result (Harkness et al., 1981). The problem describes a dilemma in which a boy must decide whether to obey his father and give the family some of the money he has earned, even though his father previously promised that the boy could keep it all. After hearing the dilemma, the participants were asked what the boy should do. Here is a typical response from a villager:

> A child has to give you what you ask for just in the same way as when he asks for anything you give it to him. Why then should he be selfish with what he has? A parent loves his child and maybe the son refused without knowing the need of helping his father ... By showing respect to one another, friendship between us is assured, and as a result this will increase the prosperity of our family.

This preliterate individual had little difficulty understanding this practical problem. His response is intelligent, insightful and well reasoned. A principal finding from this kind of cross-cultural research is that the appearance of competency on reasoning tests depends more on whether the task makes sense to participants than on their problem-solving ability.

Educated individuals in industrial societies are prone to similar failures in reasoning. Psychological studies have identified a mindbug called the **belief bias**, in which *people's*

BELIEF BIAS People's judgements about whether to accept conclusions depend more on how believable the conclusions are than on whether the arguments are logically valid.

SYLLOGISTIC REASONING Determining whether a conclusion follows from two statements that are assumed to be true.

judgements about whether to accept conclusions depend more on how believable the conclusions are than on whether the arguments are logically valid (Evans et al., 1983).

For example, in **syllogistic reasoning**, we assess *whether a conclusion follows from two statements that are assumed to be true.* Consider the two following syllogisms, evaluate the argument, and ask yourself whether or not the conclusions must be true if the statements are true:

Syllogism 1

Statement 1: No cigarettes are inexpensive.
Statement 2: Some addictive things are inexpensive.
Conclusion: Some addictive things are not cigarettes.

Syllogism 2

Statement 1: No addictive things are inexpensive.
Statement 2: Some cigarettes are inexpensive.
Conclusion: Some cigarettes are not addictive.

If you're like most people, you probably concluded that the reasoning is valid in syllogism 1 but flawed in syllogism 2. Indeed, researchers found that nearly 100% of participants accepted the first conclusion as valid, but fewer than half accepted the second (Evans et al., 1983). But notice that the syllogisms are in exactly the same form. This form of syllogism is valid, so both conclusions are valid. Evidently, the believability of the conclusions influences people's judgements.

Research using fMRI provides novel insights into belief biases on reasoning tasks. In *belief-laden* trials, participants were scanned while they reasoned about syllogisms that could be influenced by knowledge affecting the believability of the conclusions. In *belief-neutral* trials, syllogisms contained obscure terms whose meaning was unknown to participants, as in the following example:

Syllogism 3

Statement 1: No codes are highly complex.
Statement 2: Some quipu are highly complex.
Conclusion: No quipu are codes.

Belief-neutral reasoning activated different brain regions than did belief-laden reasoning (as shown in FIGURE **7.24**). Activity in a part of the left temporal lobe involved in retrieving and selecting facts from long-term memory increased during belief-laden reasoning. In contrast, that part of the brain showed little activity and parts of the parietal lobe involved in mathematical reasoning and spatial representation showed greater activity during belief-neutral reasoning (Goel and Dolan, 2003). This evidence suggests that participants took different approaches to the two types of reasoning tasks, relying on previously encoded memories in belief-laden reasoning and on more abstract thought processes in belief-neutral reasoning.

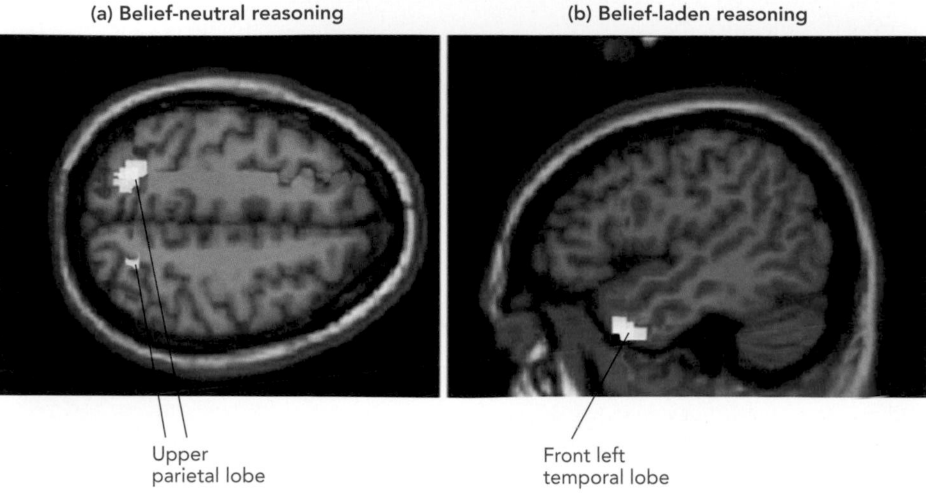

FIGURE **7.24 Active brain regions in reasoning** These images from an fMRI study show that different types of reasoning activate different brain regions. (a) Areas within the parietal lobe were especially active during logical reasoning that is not influenced by prior beliefs (belief-neutral reasoning), whereas (b) an area within the left temporal lobe showed enhanced activity during reasoning that was influenced by prior beliefs (belief-laden reasoning). This suggests that people approach each type of reasoning problem in a different way (Goel and Dolan, 2003).

In summary, the success of human reasoning depends on the content of the argument or scenario under consideration. People seem to excel at practical reasoning, while stumbling when theoretical reasoning requires evaluation of the truth of a set of arguments. Belief bias describes a mindbug that distorts judgements about conclusions of arguments, causing people to focus on the believability of the conclusions rather than the logical connections between the premises. Neuroimaging provides evidence that different brain regions are associated with different types of reasoning. We can see here and elsewhere in the chapter that some of the same strategies that earlier helped us to understand perception, memory and learning – carefully examining mindbugs and trying to integrate information about the brain into our psychological analyses – are equally helpful in understanding thought and language.

psychomythology

When unsure, it's best to stick to your first hunch

Many of you will be familiar with multiple-choice question (MCQ) tests. Indeed, the online material that accompanies this textbook provides lecturers with banks of MCQs based on its content. Your lecturer or other students may also have told you that if you are unsure about a particular question, the best thing to do is to stick with the answer you chose first. This is known as the *first instinct fallacy* and around three-quarters of students believe it to be true (Benjamin et al., 1984). The notion that one should rely on first hunches was made popular in Malcolm Gladwell's bestseller *Blink* and many companies, such as the doomed bank Lehman Brothers, whose collapse in 2008 triggered the subsequent global economic recession, bought into the idea that going on gut instincts was good for business. However, analysis of actual MCQ performance indicates that when students do change their answers, they are more than twice as likely to change an incorrect answer to a correct one than vice versa. So, if you have reason to doubt your first answer, you should always change it. There are two qualifications to this. First, you should not change your answers if you are guessing. Changing your answer only works when there is reason to think that the first answer may be wrong (Shatz and Best, 1987). Second, students who normally do badly on MCQs may benefit less from changing their answer (Best, 1979). Why do so many people believe the first instinct fallacy? Possibly because beliefs about how to do well on examinations have a particular strength that makes them propagate easily, especially if lecturers endorse the belief. Also, as noted in this chapter, there are a number of cognitive biases operating in these situations. People do not like changing their minds when there is a possibility that they will make an error. They are also more likely to remember instances when they did change a correct to an incorrect answer, which will loom more strongly in their memory. Intuition does have its uses, but it should not be exalted above analysis. As the astronomer Carl Sagan once said when pressed by a taxi driver to give his gut feelings about the possibility of extraterrestrial life: 'I try not to think with my gut!'

where do you stand?

Choosing a mate

Perhaps the most important decision we make as adults is who to marry. Your spouse is a partner in all your most valued and intimate human activities: bearing and raising children, acquiring and sharing wealth, and providing emotional sustenance. If divorce rates are considered, however, it appears that we are not very good at making this type of decision. According to the Office for National Statistics (ONS, 2012), divorce rates in England and Wales in 2011 indicated that approximately 42% of marriages ended in divorce with approximately 13 divorces every hour. One in three divorces occurred before couples reached their twentieth anniversary. The percentage of marriages ending in divorce increased more rapidly in the first 10 years of marriage than the 10 years after that.

The UK divorce rate is at the top end of European divorce rates, but across the EU, the average is still around one in three marriages ending in divorce. Why is choosing a mate such a difficult decision? It may be that mate choice constitutes the ultimate 'ill-defined' problem. There are no clearly specified decision-making procedures that will ensure a satisfactory outcome. The desired goal itself (the 'spouse' or 'perfect marriage') may be difficult to specify precisely, may change as a function of age, and, perhaps most importantly, may be defined differently by the two parties involved. A large body of research indicates that men and women value different characteristics in prospective mates. Research by more than 50 scientists studying more than 10,000 individuals inhabiting 33 countries shows that women prefer male mates who possess good financial prospects, favourable social status and ambition, while men prefer female mates who possess physical attractiveness and good health (Buss, 1994; Buss et al., 1990).

The most frequent explanation for this virtually universal sex-linked difference is that men and women, with respect to reproductive success, have confronted different adaptive problems over evolutionary history (Buss, 1994; Buss and Schmitt, 1993). The different adaptive problems between the genders concern parental investment, which researchers define as any investment of time, energy or risk that an animal makes to enhance the survival and eventual reproduction of an offspring (Krebs and Davies, 1991; Trivers, 1972a). Among mammals, females typically invest more in childbearing and child-rearing than males do. Females carry the offspring within their bodies, undergo the risks of childbirth, nurse the infant, and care for their offspring until they are old enough to care for themselves. The reproductive cost for females is therefore greater than for males. This means that reproductive success in females is limited by access to resources, while reproductive success in males is limited by access to potential mates.

Where do you stand on the issue of choosing a mate? Do you think that we should take this type of evolutionary analysis seriously? If so, does this mean that we are 'prisoners of biology'? We don't think so – while we are affected by our evolutionary history, we are not constrained by it. For example, one study found that Hungarian women did not seek mates with resources as frequently as females in other nations (Bereczkei et al., 1997). Since the collapse of communism in Hungary, there are still relatively few men with an income sufficient enough to maintain a family. The researchers speculated that, because of this, females in this culture have shifted their attention to cues other than those referring to resources when seeking mates, such as physical attractiveness or compatibility of values (Bereczkei et al., 1997). Understanding mating decisions clearly requires us to take into account social and cultural factors as well as cognitive and evolutionary ones.

Chapter review

Language and communication: nothing's more personal

- Human language is characterized by a complex organization, from phonemes to morphemes to phrases and finally to sentences. Each level of human language is constructed and understood according to grammatical rules, none of which are taught explicitly.
- Children appear to be biologically predisposed to process language in ways that allow them to extract grammatical rules from the language they hear. This language acquisition device emerges as a child matures.
- Some areas of the human brain are specialized for language processing. For example, Broca's area is specialized for language production and Wernicke's area is specialized for language comprehension.
- Apes can learn new vocabulary and construct simple sentences but compared with humans are limited in terms of vocabulary and grammatical complexity.
- According to the linguistic relativity hypothesis, language may influence thought. Research also reveals that thought influences language.

Concepts and categories: how we think

- We store our knowledge in three main ways – our experiences in terms of individual memories, generalizations that take the form of prototypes, and factual information that is codified in terms of rules.
- The brain organizes concepts into distinct categories, such as living things and human-made things. We rely on family resemblance, prototypes and exemplars to categorize and keep track of our knowledge about the world.
- We use concepts and categories to solve problems, make inferences and guide judgements.

Judging, valuing and deciding: sometimes we're logical, sometimes not

- Human decision making often departs from a strictly rational model of inference. Numerous processes interject themselves to make decision making less than perfect.
- We excel at estimating frequencies, defining categories and making similarity judgements, but we do not make probability judgements very well. The frequency format hypothesis suggests that evolution might have played a role in our superior frequency estimates.
- Human decision-making performance varies dramatically depending on whether or not the task is presented in a format that fits our mental algorithms.
- Many decision-making tasks require evaluating the probability of events as well as their value to us. Evaluating value is crucial for making the kinds of decisions we normally encounter in everyday life, but is also vulnerable to errors.
- Errors in decision making often take the form of biases and heuristic reasoning. For example, the availability bias, the conjunction fallacy and the representativeness heuristic all illustrate potential pitfalls in judgement.
- Decision making can vary depending on how the decision is framed. For example, framing influences our feelings towards avoiding losses versus achieving gains. Prospect theory was developed in part to account for these tendencies.
- Emotional information strongly influences our decision making even when we are not aware of it.

Problem solving: working it out

- Problem solving is a process in which new information is interpreted in terms of old knowledge. The solutions we generate often depend on the organization of our knowledge as well as the objective characteristics of the problems. Problems can be either ill defined or well defined.
- There are several effective approaches to problem solving. Means-ends analysis is a process of moving a current state more in line with a desired end state. In analogical problem solving, we attempt to solve a problem by finding a similar problem with a known solution and applying that solution to the current problem.
- Creative and insightful solutions often involve 'restructuring' a problem so that it turns into a problem for which a solution procedure is already known.

Transforming information: how we reach conclusions

- The success of human reasoning depends on the content of the argument or scenario under consideration.
- Our reasoning performance varies as a function of the kinds of tasks we are required to do. We perform better on tasks that require practical reasoning than we do on tasks that require theoretical reasoning.

Key terms

linguistic determinism hypothesis (p. 282)
linguistic relativity hypothesis (p. 283)
means-ends analysis (p. 297)
morphemes (p. 269)
morphological rules (p. 269)
nativist theory (p. 276)
phoneme (p. 269)
phonological dyslexia (p. 282)
phonological rules (p. 269)
practical reasoning (p. 304)
prospect theory (p. 293)
prototype theory (p. 285)
rational choice theory (p. 290)
reasoning (p. 304)
representativeness heuristic (p. 292)
routine expressions (p. 271)
semantic priming (p. 282)
semantics (p. 282)
speech monitoring and repair (p. 271)
sunk-cost fallacy (p. 293)
surface dyslexia (p. 282)
syllogistic reasoning (p. 306)
syntactical rules (p. 270)
System 1 and System 2 (p. 295)
telegraphic speech (p. 273)
theoretical reasoning (p. 304)

Recommended reading

Harley, T. (2008) *The Psychology of Language: From Data to Theory* (3rd edn). Hove: Psychology Press. Probably the best and most accessible undergraduate textbook on language.

Kahneman, D. (2012) *Thinking, Fast and Slow*. London: Penguin. Bestseller written by one of the most important psychologists, summarizes the vast literature on how we reason and the biases that operate in the human mind.

Leighton, J. P. and Sternberg, R. J. (eds) (2003) *The Nature of Reasoning*. Cambridge, MA: CUP. Handy collection of current theory and research on the psychology of reasoning, presents the state of the science and also charts new directions. Comprehensive account of what is known about reasoning in psychology and cognitive science.

Pinker, S. (1994) *The Language Instinct*. New York: Morrow. Provocative, entertaining and skilfully written book on language and language development by a professor who specializes in language research.

Thaler, R. H. and Sunstein, C. R. (2009) *Nudge: Improving Decisions about Health, Wealth and Happiness*. London: Penguin. Provides a different perspective on how we can influence people and how we think about choice.

8

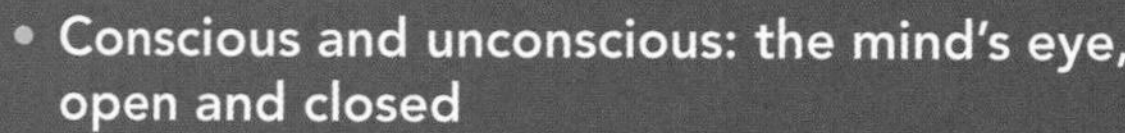

Chapter learning objectives

At the end of this chapter you will be able to:

1 Describe four characteristics of consciousness and some of the major problems of studying it.

2 Explain the relevance of key notions including the Cartesian theatre, the homunculus, the philosopher's zombie and animal consciousness.

3 Briefly evaluate the evidence for unconscious processes.

4 Describe different models of attention with supporting experimental evidence.

5 Compare and contrast different states of consciousness including sleep, dreaming, drug intoxication and hypnosis.

PISKUNOV ISTOCKPHOTO.COM

Consciousness

As every parent soon discovers, teenagers like their sleep. In that sense, Chloe Glasson, a 15-year-old from Kirkcaldy in Fife, Scotland, seems like every other normal teenager. The difference is that Chloe falls asleep dozens of times a day at school, on buses and out with friends. According to Chloe:

> *It can happen at any time. I've really been lucky that I've not hurt myself falling asleep while standing up and I ask myself every day how I've managed. At school I'll be sitting at my desk and this wave of tiredness takes over. Then my eyes start to roll and droop and that's when I know what's about to happen. I just go out.*

Chloe also lapses into an 'automatic behaviour state', which leaves her acting like a robot. As a result, she can't be left alone in a bath or trusted to take public transport herself.

Chloe is not a typical teenager. She has narcolepsy, a rare, long-term brain disorder that causes a person to suddenly fall asleep at inappropriate times and affects 0.5% of the population. Although narcolepsy has been linked to specific genes, in Chloe's case she probably developed the disorder as a side effect of the Pandemrix vaccine administered to combat the H1N1 influenza (more commonly known as 'swine flu') pandemic in Europe in 2009. Other countries including Sweden and Finland also reported an increase in the incidence of narcolepsy associated with the Pandemrix vaccine.

Around two-thirds of narcoleptic patients also have cataplexy attacks, which involve a temporary involuntary muscle weakness in response to emotions or the anticipation of emotion. Positive emotions such as laughter are the most potent triggers, although anger, fear, embarrassment and surprise may also provoke attacks. Dr Claire Allen, a 40-year-old research scientist with narcolepsy from Cambridge, loses strength in her hands and nods forward for a few seconds and blacks out around 100 times during the day whenever she laughs.

The Nightmare, painted in 1781 by the Anglo-Swiss artist Henry Fuseli (1741–1825), depicts a night demon known as an 'incubus' that was believed to sit on the sleeper's chest, pinning them down in order to take sexual advantage of them.

Another symptom of narcolepsy is sleep paralysis, where one is fully conscious while drifting off to sleep or on awakening but is unable to move because the muscles are paralysed. This is also quite a common experience in individuals without narcolepsy, and in the past was often attributed to malevolent demons visiting the victims in their beds, as dramatically depicted by Henry Fuseli in his 1781 painting, *The Nightmare*.

Most of the time, of course, consciousness is something we cherish. How else could we experience a favourite work of art, the latest hit record on the radio, the taste of a sweet, juicy peach, or the touch of a loved one's hand? Consciousness is, as you recall from Chapter 1, a person's subjective experience of the world and the mind. Although you might think of consciousness as simply 'being awake', the defining feature of consciousness is *experience*, which you have when you're not awake but experiencing a vivid dream. Conscious experience is essential to what it means to be human. It also makes us unique because it is impossible for one person to experience another's consciousness. Your consciousness is utterly private, a world of personal experience that only you can know.

How can this private world be studied? One way to explore consciousness is to examine it directly, trying to understand what it is like, how it seems to be created, how it works, and how it compares with the mind's *un*conscious processes. We'll begin with this direct approach, looking at the mysteries of consciousness and its known properties. Another way to explore consciousness is to examine its altered states, in other words, the cases in which the experience of being human departs from normal, everyday waking. We will probe these changes, beginning with the major alterations that happen during sleep, when waking consciousness steals away only to be replaced by the surreal form of consciousness experienced in dreams. Then we'll look into how we alter our consciousness through intoxication with alcohol and other drugs, and other changes in consciousness that occur during hypnosis and meditation. Like the traveller who learns the meaning of *home* by roaming far away, we can learn the meaning of consciousness by exploring its exotic variations.

Conscious and unconscious: the mind's eye, open and closed

What does it feel like to be you right now? It probably feels as though you are somewhere inside your head, looking out at the world through your eyes. You can feel your hands on this book, perhaps, and notice the position of your body or the sounds in the room when you turn towards them. If you shut your eyes, you may be able to imagine things in your mind, even though thoughts and feelings come and go all the while, passing through your imagination. Philosopher Daniel Dennett (1991) called this 'place in your head' where 'you' are the Cartesian theatre (after philosopher René Descartes) – *a mental screen or stage on which things appear to be presented for viewing by your mind's eye.* The Cartesian theatre, unfortunately, isn't available on DVD, making it impossible to share exactly what's on your mental screen with anyone else. They can't get inside your head to watch the same show. The private, personal nature of consciousness means that although we can tell others what we are thinking, they can never truly share our actual experience. As you'll recall from Chapter 1, Wilhelm Wundt encountered similar problems when studying consciousness and trying to measure personal experience. Even today, while we may be able to record the physiological changes in brain activity with modern scanning techniques, researchers cannot measure the actual conscious experience. When you tell someone you are studying psychology, they may often think that you want to 'get inside their head' or 'read their minds'. Nothing could be more difficult when it comes to consciousness. We'll look at the difficulty of studying consciousness directly but also examine the nature of consciousness (what it is that can be seen in this mental theatre) and then explore the unconscious mind (what is *not* visible to the mind's eye).

CARTESIAN THEATRE (after philosopher René Descartes) A mental screen or stage on which things appear to be presented for viewing by the mind's eye.

Mysteries of consciousness

Other sciences, such as physics, chemistry and biology, have the great luxury of studying *objects*, things we all can see. Psychology studies objects too, looking at people and their brains and behaviours, but it has the unique challenge of also trying to make sense of the *subjective experience* we all have as conscious individuals and how this is generated by the brain. This is sometimes called the hard problem of consciousness – *the difficulty of explaining how subjective experience could ever arise* (Chalmers, 1996). A physicist is not concerned with what it is like to be a neutron, a biologist does not explain what it must be like to be a plant, but psychologists hope to understand what it is like to be a human, that is, grasping the subjective perspectives of the people they study. So, psychologists hope to include an understanding of phenomenology, *how things seem to the conscious person, in terms of the quality of experience*, in their understanding of mind and behaviour. After all, consciousness is an extraordinary human property that could well be unique to us. But including phenomenology in psychology brings up mysteries pondered by great thinkers almost since the beginning of thinking. Let's consider some of the more vexing mysteries of consciousness: the homunculus problem, the problem of other minds and the mind–body problem.

HARD PROBLEM OF CONSCIOUSNESS The difficulty of explaining how subjective experience could ever arise.

PHENOMENOLOGY How things actually seem in the state of consciousness in terms of the quality of experience.

Who's in control?

For most of us, our daily experience of consciousness feels as if we exist inside our heads, somewhere behind our eyes, experiencing and acting on the world. We are like some driver of a complicated machine, making decisions, controlling actions and feeling what it is like to be us. However, if our personal experience of the Cartesian theatre is an illusion, then this sense that we exist inside our heads looking out on the world needs careful consideration. First, the idea of someone inside the head is an example of the homunculus problem – *the difficulty of explaining the experience of consciousness by advocating another internal self.* We encountered the homunculus in Chapter 3 as the distorted representation of the body's somatosensory cortex – the freaky ghoul who looks like he may have come out of Tim Burton's *The Nightmare Before Christmas*. In this context, a homunculus is like having a 'mini-me' inside your head making decisions. The homunculus is a problem because if there really was a 'mini-me' inside your head, then who is *inside* the head of the homunculus and so on and so on? This would become an infinite regress leading to no end.

HOMUNCULUS PROBLEM Difficulty of explaining the experience of consciousness by advocating another internal self.

If the homunculus does not exist, then who is in control? This question raises the issue of Spinoza's free will we encountered in Chapter 1. Free will is the common assumption that individuals are in control of the decisions they make and have the choice to do one thing versus another. However, remember that behaviourists such as Skinner claimed that personal free will was an illusion because behaviour and thoughts could be shaped by reinforcement or punishment from the environment. While cognitive psychology has shown that behaviourism is limited in explaining all human behaviour, research described throughout this textbook continues to reveal how unconscious mechanisms play a role in our decision making. In short, science undermines the reality of free will as a force of personal choice.

The trouble is we are so used to our conscious experience of free will that to reject it is something most of us find difficult to accept. Also, without the notion of free will, fundamental principles of how we treat others begin to look shaky. For example, in law we hold people responsible as individuals for the decisions they take, but if the individual is simply responding to circumstances out of their control, then are they truly responsible? To many of us, the morality of rewards for good deeds and punishment for evil acts seems unwarranted without the concept of free will. Maybe this is why we experience a sense of free will as a useful mechanism that confers social responsibility?

While the case for the *existence* of free will being responsible for decisions may be scientifically weak, the personal *experience* of free will is extremely strong. Most of us feel the experience of conscious free will as we go about our daily basis of making choices: 'We think we did it.' Why is this? It has been suggested that the *we think we did it* experience could be a useful way of keeping track of our decisions and actions (Wegner, 2002).

This is because the unconscious influences and processes that lead to these choices are too complicated to monitor, but we can keep track of the outcome as a feeling that we have made the decision. For example, when we laugh at a joke, there are many influences and processes that determine that bizarre bodily convulsion, but the loud guffaw reminds us that we find something funny. In the same way, having a sense of free will over our thoughts and actions binds us to these as the author of these decisions even when that is not the case. In this way, a sense of free will could help us keep track of what we have done, what we have not done, and what we may, or may not, do in the future. After all, it is useful to know who is responsible.

The problem of other minds

PROBLEM OF OTHER MINDS The fundamental difficulty we have in perceiving the consciousness of others.

QUALIA Subjective experiences we have as part of our mental life.

One great barrier to getting inside someone else's head is called the problem of other minds – *the fundamental difficulty we have in perceiving the consciousness of others.* How do you know that anyone else is conscious? They tell you they are conscious, of course, and are often willing to describe in depth how they feel, how they think, what they are experiencing, and how good or bad it all is. These mental states, or qualia, are the *subjective experiences we have as part of our mental life.* There is a personal quality to qualia – the bitterness of lemon juice, the redness of the colour red or the pain of rejection – that cannot be directly accessed by others, no matter how well you describe the experience.

The problem of other minds also means that there is no way you can tell if another person's experience of anything is at all like yours. Although you know what the colour red looks like to you, for instance, you cannot know whether it looks the same to other people. Maybe they're seeing what you see as blue and just *calling* it red in a consistent way. If their inner experience 'looks' blue, but they say it looks hot and is the colour of a tomato, you'll never be able to tell that their experience differs from yours. Of course, most people have come to trust each other in describing their inner lives, reaching the general assumption that other human minds are very much like their own. But they don't know this for a fact, and they can't know it directly. As we saw in Chapter 4, before synaesthesia was recognized as a real phenomena, individuals with this condition were unaware that most other people did not have the same qualia of experience.

Others can tell us about their qualia, but perhaps they are just *saying* these things. There is no clear way to distinguish a conscious person from someone who might do and say all the same things as a conscious person but who is *not* conscious. Philosophers have called this hypothetical nonconscious person a 'zombie', in reference to the living-yet-dead creatures of horror films (Chalmers, 1996). A philosopher's zombie could talk about experiences ('The lights are so bright!') and even seem to react to them (wincing and turning away) but might not be having any inner experience at all. The possibility of a nonconscious zombie is often used as an argument against the idea that consciousness is simply something that emerges out of the brain. If a zombie with a dead brain is indistinguishable from a conscious human with a living brain, then the argument runs that there must be some additional property independent of brains responsible for consciousness. However, Dennett (1991) argues that the philosopher's zombie is not possible and we are falling victim to the illogical error that there must be some additional non-material property to explain mental life. He argues that if a zombie is indistinguishable from a human down to the very cells that make up the brain, then it would be conscious. If the brain were dead, there would be no consciousness.

MATERIALISM Philosophical position that mental states are a product of physical processes alone.

Most neuroscientists also reject these philosophical arguments about hypothetical zombies because research shows that altering brain activity through damage, disease, drugs or direct stimulation alters conscious experience. In other words, 'the mind is what the brain does' (Minsky, 1986, p. 287). This exclusively physical interpretation of mental life is known as materialism – *the philosophical position that mental states are a product of physical systems alone.* Materialism dispenses with any need to explain consciousness in terms of some additional property that resides in the brain. This is an idea that most of us find unsettling, because it suggests that our experience of our own mental life, consciousness and free will is the product of a complicated 'meat machine' (Minsky, quoted in Turkle, 1997, p. 7) and that is a very dehumanized vision of ourselves.

Even if consciousness is solely a product of the physical brain, there are still many questions. How does the brain generate consciousness? Do other animals with different brains have conscious experience, and if so, what is it like? In an essay entitled 'What is it like to be a bat?', philosopher Thomas Nagel (1974) wondered what it's like flying around in a dark cave, sensing the walls through the echoes made by your ultrasonic screeches. Would your experience of the cave include visual images, sounds, or something else entirely? It's difficult to imagine, as we're not bats. And if we had the mind of a bat, we would not have the mind of a human, so how could we possibly ever know what it is like to be bat? If bat consciousness is hard to imagine, what about all the other animals? When a puppy looks up at you with those warm brown eyes, seemingly saying 'I love you and everything you stand for', you can't really know what it's like in there – so your appreciation of the puppy's mind reflects what's going on in *your* head more than in the puppy's. This is a feature of anthropomorphism – *the tendency to attribute human qualities to nonhuman things*. In considering others as having minds, we all too readily assume that they exhibit the same mental life we ourselves experience. It is much easier to interact with animals and even babies by assuming that they share the same conscious awareness (Dennett, 1991), but what grounds do we have for inferring consciousness in others? What is the mental life of an infant or animal like?

This leads to the more general question: How do people perceive other minds? Researchers conducting a large online survey asked people to compare the minds of 13 different targets, such as a baby, chimp, robot, man and woman, on 18 different mental capacities, such as feeling pain, pleasure, hunger and consciousness (see **FIGURE 8.1**) (Gray et al., 2007). Respondents who were judging the mental capacity to feel pain, for example, compared pairs of targets: Is a frog or a dog more able to feel pain? Is a baby or a robot more able to feel pain? Is a seven-week-old fetus or a man in a persistent vegetative state more able to feel pain? When the researchers examined all the comparisons on the different mental capacities with the computational technique of factor analysis (see Chapter 9), they found two dimensions of mind perception. People judge minds according to the capacity for *experience*, such as the ability to feel pain, pleasure, hunger, consciousness, anger or fear, and the capacity for *agency*, such as the ability for self control, planning, memory or thought. As shown in Figure 8.1, respondents rated some targets as having little experience or agency (the dead person), others as having experiences but little agency (the baby), and yet others as having both experience and agency (adult humans). Still others were perceived to have agency without experiences (the robot, God). The perception of minds, then, involves more than just whether something has a mind. People appreciate that minds have experiences and act as agents that perform actions. We return to this issue in Chapter 12 when we examine the evidence that children develop this capacity to see others as having minds.

We have a fundamental problem in perceiving the consciousness of others. This child will anthropomorphically attribute human qualities to the puppy, assuming that animals exhibit the same mental life we do.

ANTHROPOMORPHISM The tendency to attribute human qualities to nonhuman things.

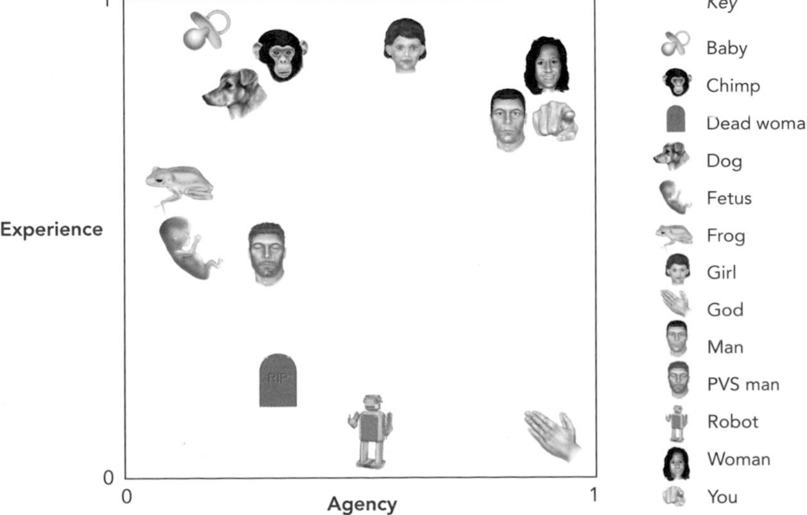

FIGURE 8.1 Dimensions of mind perception When participants judged the mental capacities of 13 targets, two dimensions of mind perception were discovered (Gray et al., 2007). Participants perceived minds as varying in the capacity for experience, such as abilities to feel pain or pleasure, and in the capacity for agency, such as abilities to plan or exert self-control. They perceived normal adult humans (male, female or 'you', the respondent) to have minds on both dimensions, whereas other targets were perceived to have reduced experience or agency. The man in a persistent vegetative state ('PVS man'), for example, was judged to have only some experience and very little agency.

Ultimately, the problem of other minds is a problem for psychological science. As you'll remember from Chapter 2, the scientific method requires that any observation made by one scientist should, in principle, be available for observation by any other scientist. But if other minds aren't observable, how can consciousness be a topic of scientific study? One radical solution is to eliminate consciousness from psychology entirely and follow the other sciences into total objectivity by renouncing the study of *anything* mental. This was the solution offered by behaviourism, and it turned out to have its own shortcomings, as you saw in Chapter 1. Despite the problem of other minds, modern psychology has embraced the study of consciousness. What was once regarded as mysterious and never open to understanding has, in fact, stimulated debate that questions the way we think about what it is to be human.

The mind–body problem

MIND–BODY PROBLEM The issue of how the mind is related to the brain and body.

Another mystery of consciousness is the mind–body problem – *the issue of how the mind is related to the brain and body.* French philosopher and mathematician René Descartes is famous for proposing, among other things, that mind and body are made of different substances. As you read in Chapter 1, Descartes believed that the human body is a machine made of physical matter but that the human mind or soul is a separate entity made of a 'thinking substance'. He proposed that the mind has its effects on the brain and body through the pineal gland, a small pine-shaped structure located near the centre of the brain. It appears to be unitary, whereas the rest of the brain is split into right and left halves. Descartes reasoned that because it was a unitary structure, this made it the most likely site for the interaction between the body and soul. In fact, the pineal gland is divisible and is not even a nerve structure but an endocrine gland quite poorly equipped to integrate the activity of the neuronal networks of the brain that must be responsible for generating human consciousness. Even if the pineal gland was the site for the conjunction of body and soul, the hard problem remains. How does something like the mind, which has no physical property, emerge from or interact with the physical structures of the body?

Most psychologists assume that mental events are intimately tied to brain events, such that every thought, perception or feeling is associated with a particular pattern of activation of neurons in the brain (see Chapter 3). Thinking about a particular duck, for instance, occurs with a unique array of neural connections and activations. If the neurons repeat that pattern, you must be thinking of the duck; conversely, if you think of the duck, the brain activity occurs in that pattern. Studies of the brain structures associated with conscious thinking in particular (as opposed to all the other mental efforts that go on in the background of the mind) suggest that conscious thought is supported widely in the brain by many different structures (Koch, 2004).

However, consciousness does not feel like the product of some meat machine that is our body. That is because each of us experiences mental life as something separate to our bodies. When we look in the mirror, we can see how our outward appearance may change but we do not feel that the observer is different. We may change our opinions and thoughts over time, but we still feel like the same 'person' having those thoughts and opinions. Also, our daily, phenomenological experience of body and mind is that the mind is in control of the body. We feel that we exist somewhere behind our eyes, like a ship's captain of the body issuing commands and making decisions. We feel the authorship of our actions.

One telling set of studies, however, suggests that the brain's activities *precede* the activities of the conscious mind. The electrical activity in volunteers' brains was measured using sensors placed on their scalps as they repeatedly decided when to move a hand (Libet, 1985) (see **FIGURE 8.2**). Participants were also asked to indicate exactly when they consciously chose to move by reporting the position of a dot moving rapidly around the face of a clock just at the point of the decision (**FIGURE 8.2a**). As a rule, the brain begins to show electrical activity around half a second before a voluntary action (535 milliseconds (ms) to be exact). This makes sense since brain activity certainly seems to be necessary to get an action started.

What this experiment revealed, though, was that the brain also started to show electrical activity before the person's conscious decision to move. As shown in **FIGURE 8.2b**, these studies found that the brain becomes active more than 300 ms before participants report

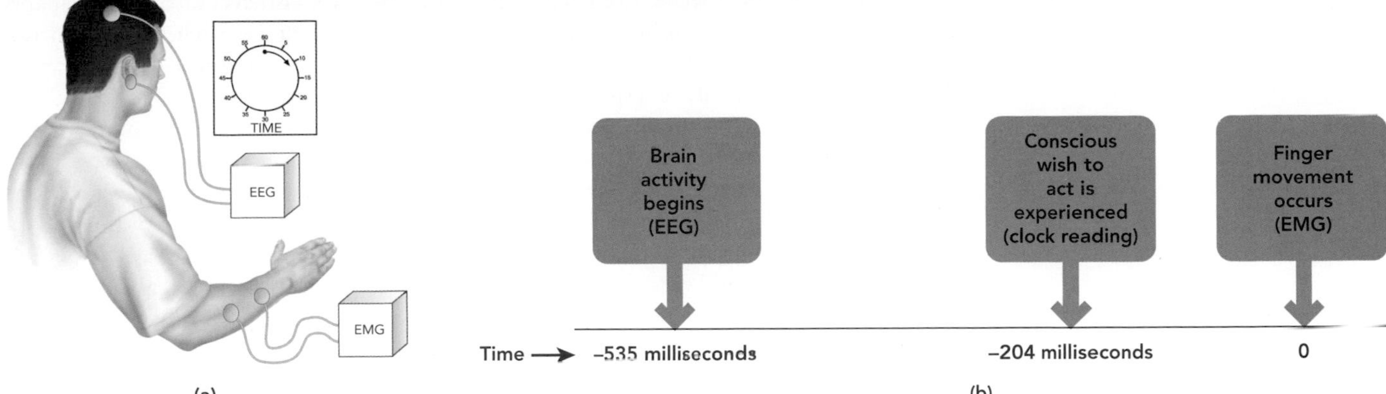

FIGURE 8.2 The timing of conscious will (a) In Benjamin Libet's experiments, the participant was asked to move fingers at will while simultaneously watching a dot move around the face of a clock to mark the moment at which the action was consciously willed. Meanwhile, EEG sensors timed the onset of brain activation and EMG sensors timed the muscle movement. (b) The experiment showed that brain activity (EEG) precedes the willed movement of the finger (EMG), but that the reported time of consciously willing the finger to move follows the brain activity.

that they are consciously trying to move. The feeling that you are consciously willing your actions, it seems, may be a result rather than a cause of your brain activity. Although your personal intuition is that you *think* of an action and *then* do it, these experiments suggest that your brain is getting started before *either* the thinking or the doing, preparing the way for both thought and action. More recently, researchers using fMRI demonstrated that brain activity seven seconds before a participant felt they had made the conscious decision to choose a button predicted which of the two buttons they would subsequently press (Soon et al., 2008). Quite simply, it may appear to us that our minds are leading our brains and bodies, but the order of events may be the other way around (Wegner, 2002). To most of us, our personal experience of consciousness feels like someone is in charge of decision making, but in fact, consciousness may simply be making sense of our thoughts and actions after they have already been activated by unconscious processes. This after-the-fact interpretive role of consciousness explains a surprising demonstration of choice blindness – *when people are unaware of their decision-making processes and justify a choice as if it were already decided*. Adults were asked to choose which of two female faces was more attractive, as shown in **FIGURE 8.3**. On some trials, immediately after making their choice, participants were asked to explain why they had selected a particular face. However, by use of sleight of hand, they were sometimes handed the card with the

CHOICE BLINDNESS When people are unaware of their decision making processes and justify a choice as if it were already decided.

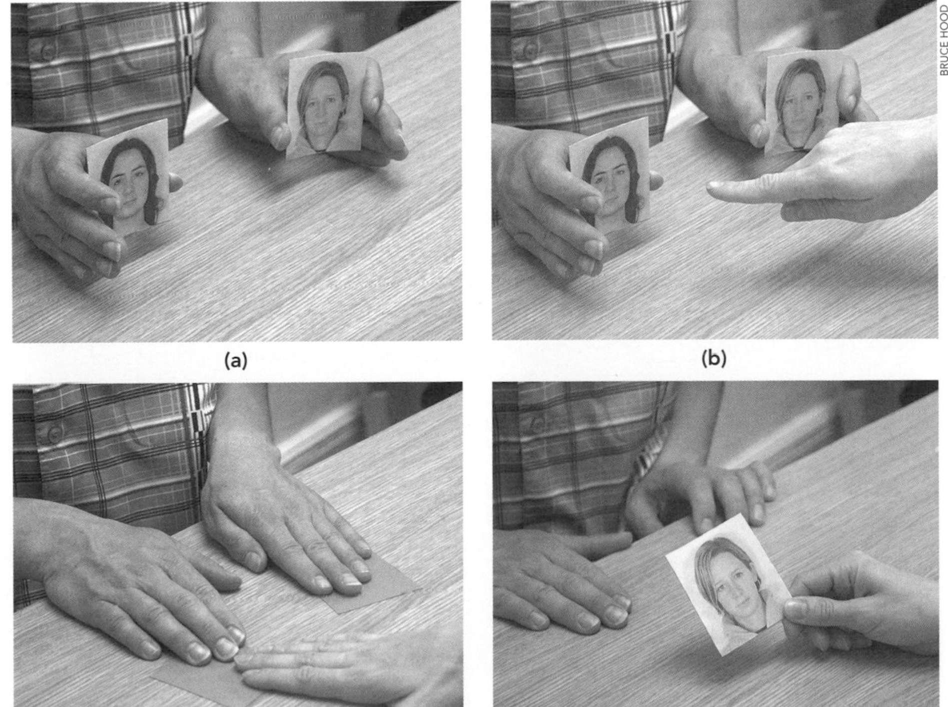

FIGURE 8.3 Choice blindness Participants were shown two female faces (a) and asked to choose which female was more attractive (b) and then justify why they picked one face over another. Every so often the faces were cleverly switched by sleight of hand (c). Most adults did not notice the switch and then explained why the face they had just rejected (d) was the more attractive one (Johansson et al., 2005).

face they had just rejected. Not only were most switches undetected but participants went on to give explanations for preferring the switched face even when they had not chosen it (Johansson et al., 2005). As Steven Pinker (2003, p. 43) put it: 'The conscious mind – the self or soul – is a spin doctor, not the commander-in-chief.'

Consciousness gives us this sense of a coherent self, resident within our bodies, having experiences and making decisions. It is an appealing intuition that most of us have about our mental lives, but philosophers and psychologists reveal that many of these intuitions can be easily deconstructed and may even be illusions. It explains many of the unconscious influences in our decision making and why, for example, we may say that we are not racist or sexist and yet implicit association tests, considered at the end of Chapter 15, reveal that these sorts of prejudicial biases are not under conscious control.

The way we think about consciousness may be wrong but it is still a component of mental life, just one that is not amenable to measurement, which makes it difficult to study. Although researchers may not be able to see the consciousness of others or know exactly how consciousness arises from the brain, this does not prevent them from collecting people's reports of conscious experiences and learning how these reports reveal the nature of consciousness. We'll consider that topic next.

The nature of consciousness

How would you describe your own consciousness? Researchers examining people's descriptions suggest that consciousness has four basic properties – intentionality, unity, selectivity and transience – that it occurs on different levels, and includes a range of different contents. Let's examine each of these points in turn.

Four basic properties

Consciousness is often *about* something. Philosophers call this first property the *intentionality of consciousness*, the quality of being directed towards an object, which is not to be confused with the more familiar sense of intention as characterizing something done on purpose. Psychologists, in turn, have tried to measure the relationship between consciousness and its objects as a process of actively selecting something to attend to, examining the size and duration of the relationship. How long can consciousness be directed towards an object, and how many objects can it take on at one time? Researchers have found that conscious attention is limited and that without it, objects can often fail to reach conscious awareness even when they are staring you in the face (see **FIGURE 8.4**). The phenomenon known as change blindness, *unawareness of significant events changing in full view*, reveals that, without attention, we miss much of what is happening in the world (Rensink et al., 1997). It's another example of a mindbug that reflects a feature of the way our minds work. Moreover, we may actually 'fill in' the missing portions of experience by making assumptions in much the same way that we perceptually fill the visual blind spot (see Chapter 4). Despite all the lush detail you see in your mind's eye, the kaleidoscope of sights and sounds and feelings and thoughts, the object of your consciousness at any one moment is just a small part of all this. To describe how this limitation works, psychologists refer to three other properties of consciousness: unity, selectivity and transience.

CHANGE BLINDNESS When people are unaware of significant event changes that happen in full view.

BRUCE HOOD

FIGURE 8.4 Spot the difference Study the first photograph carefully and see if you can tell what is different from the second photograph. This is made all the more difficult if each photograph is flashed up, one after the other, with a brief (80 ms) blank screen in between. This difficulty in spotting the difference is known as 'change blindness' (Rensick et al., 1997) and demonstrates that attention is necessary for becoming consciously aware of the world around us.

The *unity of consciousness* is its resistance to division. This property becomes clear when you try to attend to more than one thing at a time. You may wishfully think that you can study and watch TV simultaneously, for example, but research suggests not. One study had research participants divide their attention by reacting to two games superimposed on a TV screen. They had to push one button when one person slapped another's hands in the first game and push another button when a ball was passed in the second game. The participants were easily able to follow one game at a time, but their performance took a nosedive when they tried to follow both simultaneously. Their error rate when attending to the two tasks was eight times greater than when attending to either task alone (Neisser and Becklen, 1975). In other words, your attempts to study could seriously interfere with a full appreciation of your TV show! In another classic demonstration of the importance of attention for awareness, adults were asked to count the number of times that players wearing white T-shirts passed a basketball to each other. The task was hard because there was another team of players wearing black T-shirts that had to be ignored (see **FIGURE 8.5**). Adults could easily keep track of the number of passes by concentrating on the white team. However, what half the adults failed to notice was a man wearing a gorilla suit strolling among the players, beating his chest and then strolling off again (Simons and Chabris, 1999). The scope of our consciousness is limited and this has implications for what we notice in the world. Maintaining a coherent unity of consciousness makes it difficult for us to divide attention among differing events.

DICHOTIC LISTENING A task in which people wearing headphones hear different messages presented to each ear.

COCKTAIL PARTY PHENOMENON People tune in to one message even while they filter out others nearby.

FIGURE 8.5 Gorillas in our midst Participants have to count the number of times the ball is passed between players wearing the white T-shirts. Around 50% of adults fail to notice the gorilla walk on in the middle of the game, beat its chest and then walk off again (Simons and Chabris, 1999).

FIGURE PROVIDED BY DANIEL SIMONS WWW.DANSIMONS.COM WWW.THEINVISIBLEGORILLA.COM

The *selectivity of consciousness* is its capacity to include some objects and not others. This property is shown through studies of dichotic listening, *in which people wearing headphones are presented with different messages in each ear.* Research participants were instructed to repeat aloud the words they heard in one ear while a different message was presented to the other ear (Cherry, 1953). As a result of focusing on the words they were supposed to repeat, participants noticed little of the second message, often not even realizing that at some point it changed from one language to another (English to German). So, consciousness *filters out* some information including irrelevant messages or even men in gorilla suits. At the same time, participants did notice when the voice in the unattended ear changed from a male to a female voice, suggesting that the selectivity of consciousness can also work to *tune in* other information.

How does consciousness decide what to filter in and what to tune out? The conscious system is most inclined to select information of special interest to the person, in what has come to be known as the cocktail party phenomenon – *people tune in to one message even while they filter out others nearby.* In the dichotic listening situation, for example, research participants are especially likely to notice if their own name is spoken into the unattended ear (Moray, 1959). Perhaps you too have noticed how abruptly your attention is diverted from whatever conversation you are having when someone else within earshot at the party mentions your name. Selectivity is not only a property of waking consciousness, however; the mind works this way in other states. People are more sensitive to their own name than other names, for example, even during sleep (Oswald et al., 1960).

© STOCKDISC ROYALTY FREE PHOTOS

Participants in a dichotic listening experiment hear different messages played to the right and left ear and may be asked to 'shadow' one of the messages by repeating it aloud.

The final basic property is the *transience of consciousness*, or its tendency to change. Consciousness wiggles and fidgets like an impatient toddler. The mind wanders, not just sometimes but incessantly, from one 'right now' to the next 'right now' and then on to the next (Wegner, 1997). This is why, when we are distracted, our ability to concentrate is impaired. William James (1890, p. 239), whom you met in Chapter 1, famously described consciousness as a stream:

> Consciousness ... does not appear to itself chopped up in bits. Such words as 'chain' or 'train' do not describe it ... It is nothing jointed; it flows. A 'river' or a 'stream' are the metaphors by which it is most naturally described.

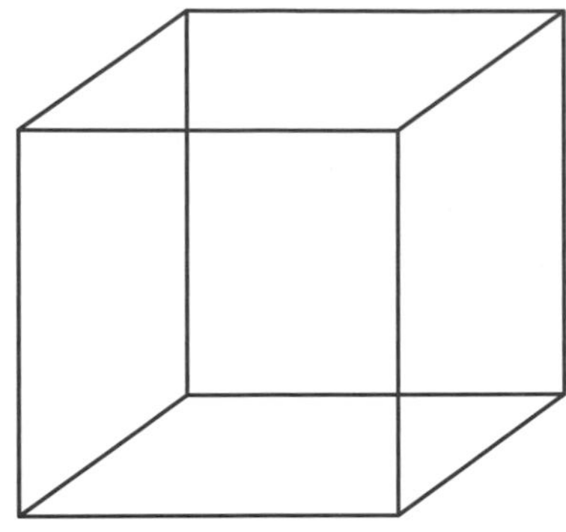

FIGURE 8.6 The Necker cube This cube has the property of reversible perspective, in that you can bring one or the other of its two square faces to the front in your mind's eye. Although it may take a while to reverse the figure at first, once people have learned to do it, they can reverse it regularly, about once every three seconds (Gomez et al., 1995). The stream of consciousness flows even when the target is a constant object.

However, if consciousness can be considered as a stream, it is a turbulent one, with many eddies and diversions.

The stream of consciousness may flow in this way partly because of the limited capacity of working memory. Remember from Chapter 5 that you can hold only so much information in your mind, so when more information is selected, some of what is currently there must disappear. As a result, your focus of attention keeps changing. The Necker cube (see **FIGURE 8.6**) is the visual counterpart to stream of consciousness writing. Although the cube is a constant object, the stream of consciousness flows, reversing the figure. Moreover, the fact that you cannot simultaneously see both versions of the cube reflects the unity of consciousness described earlier.

The basic properties of consciousness are reminiscent of the 'bouncing ball' that moves from word to word when the lyrics of a sing-along tune are shown on a karaoke machine. The ball always bounces on something (intentionality), there is only one ball (unity), the ball selects one target and not others (selectivity), and the ball keeps bouncing all the time (transience).

Levels of consciousness

Consciousness can also be understood as having levels, ranging from minimal consciousness to full consciousness to self-consciousness. The levels of consciousness that psychologists distinguish are not a matter of degree of overall brain activity but instead involve different qualities of awareness of the world and of the self.

In its minimal form, consciousness is just a connection between the person and the world. When you sense the sun coming in through the window, for example, you might turn towards the light. Such minimal consciousness is *a low level of awareness that occurs when the mind inputs sensations and may output behaviour* (Armstrong, 1980). This level of consciousness is a kind of sensory awareness and responsiveness, something that could even happen when someone pokes you during sleep and you turn over. Something seems to register in your mind, at least in the sense that you experience it, but you may not think at all about having had the experience. It could be that animals or even plants, for that matter, can have this minimal level of consciousness. In Chapter 5, we learned about the sea slug that learns to withdraw its breathing gill after it is prodded. Does it have any awareness of this event? But, because of the problem of other minds and the notorious reluctance of animals and plants to talk to us, we can't know for sure that they *experience* the things that make them respond. At least in the case of humans, we can safely assume that there is something it 'feels like' to be them and when they're awake, they are at least minimally conscious.

MINIMAL CONSCIOUSNESS A low level of awareness that occurs when the mind inputs sensations and may output behaviour.

Human consciousness is often more than this, of course, but what exactly gets added? Consider the glorious feeling of waking up on a spring morning as rays of sun stream across your pillow. It's not just that you are having this experience; being fully conscious means that you are also *aware* that you are having this experience. The critical ingredient that accompanies full consciousness is that *you know and are able to report your mental state.* That's a subtle distinction; being fully conscious means that you are aware of having a mental state while you are experiencing the mental state itself. When you have a hurt leg and mindlessly rub it, for instance, your pain may be minimally conscious. After all, you seem to be experiencing pain

FULL CONSCIOUSNESS Consciousness in which you know and are able to report your mental state.

because you are indeed rubbing your leg. It is only when you realize that it hurts, though, that the pain becomes fully conscious. Full consciousness involves not only thinking about things but also thinking about the fact that you are thinking about things (Jaynes, 1976).

Full consciousness fluctuates over time, coming and going throughout the day. You've no doubt had experiences of reading and suddenly realizing that you have 'zoned out' and are not processing what you read. When people are asked to report each time they zone out during reading, they report doing this every few minutes. Even then, when an experimenter asks these people at other random points in their reading whether they are zoned out at that moment, they are sometimes caught in the state of having 'zoned out' even before they've noticed it (Schooler et al., 2001). It's at just this point – when you are zoned out but don't know it – that you seem to be unaware of your own mental state. You are minimally conscious of wherever your mind has wandered to, and you return with a jolt into the full consciousness that your mind had drifted away from. Thinking about thinking allows you to realize that you weren't thinking about what you wanted to be thinking about.

Self-consciousness is a curse and a blessing. Looking in the mirror can make people evaluate themselves on deeper attributes such as honesty as well as superficial ones such as looks.

Full consciousness involves a certain consciousness of oneself; the person notices the self in a particular mental state ('Here I am, reading this sentence'). However, this is not quite the same thing as *self*-consciousness. Sometimes, consciousness is entirely flooded with the self ('Gosh, I'm such a good reader!'), focusing on the self to the exclusion of almost everything else. James (1890) and other theorists have suggested that self-consciousness is yet another *distinct level of consciousness in which the person's attention is drawn to the self as an object.* Most people report experiencing such self-consciousness when they are embarrassed, when they find themselves the focus of attention in a group, when someone focuses a camera on them, or when they are deeply introspective about their thoughts, feelings or personal qualities.

SELF-CONSCIOUSNESS A distinct level of consciousness in which the person's attention is drawn to the self as an object.

Self-consciousness brings with it a tendency to evaluate yourself and notice your shortcomings. Looking in a mirror, for example, is all it takes to make people evaluate themselves – thinking not just about their looks but also about whether they are good or bad in other ways. People go out of their way to avoid mirrors when they've done something they are ashamed of (Duval and Wicklund, 1972).

Self-consciousness can certainly spoil a good mood, so much so that a tendency to be chronically self-conscious is associated with depression (Pyszczynski et al., 1987). However, because it makes people self-critical, the self-consciousness that results when people see their own mirror images can make them briefly more helpful, more cooperative and less aggressive (Gibbons, 1990). In one classic study conducted on Halloween night in Canada, researchers found that children were less likely to be greedy by helping themselves to more sweets even though they had been instructed to take only one if there was a large mirror in the room compared to when no mirror was present (Beaman et al., 1979). Most undergraduate students (71%) were also found to cheat on an anagram test compared to only 7% who cheated when there was a mirror in the exam room (Diener and Wallbom, 1976). Perhaps everyone would be a bit more civilized if mirrors were held up for them to see themselves as objects of their own scrutiny.

Most animals can't follow this path to civilization. The typical dog, cat or bird seems mystified by a mirror, ignoring it or acting as though there is some other creature in there. However, chimpanzees that have spent time with mirrors sometimes behave in ways that suggest they recognize themselves in a mirror. To examine this, researchers painted an odourless red dye over the eyebrow of an anaesthetized chimp and then watched when the awakened chimp was presented with a mirror (Gallup, 1970). If the chimp interpreted the mirror image as a representation of some other chimp with an unusual approach to cosmetics, we would expect it just to look at the mirror or perhaps reach towards it. But the chimp reached towards its *own eye* as it looked into the mirror – not the mirror image – suggesting that it recognized the image as a reflection of itself.

Researchers are now also conducting mirror self-recognition experiments on non-mammalian species, such as this magpie.

Versions of this experiment, known as 'the rouge test', have now been repeated with many different animals (Gallup, 1977), and it turns out that, like humans, animals such as chimpanzees and orangutans, possibly dolphins (Reiss and Marino, 2001) and maybe even elephants (Plotnik et al., 2006) recognize their own mirror images. Dogs, cats, birds, monkeys and gorillas have been tested and don't seem to know they are looking at themselves. Even humans don't have self-recognition right away. Infants don't recognize themselves in mirrors until they've reached about 18 months of age (Lewis and Brooks-Gunn, 1979). The experience of self-consciousness, as measured by self-recognition in mirrors, is limited to a few animals and to humans only after a certain stage of development.

Conscious contents

What's on your mind? For that matter, what's on everybody's mind? The contents of consciousness are, of course, as rich and varied as human experience itself. But there are some common themes in the topics that occupy consciousness and the form that consciousness seems to take as different contents come to mind.

One way to learn what is on people's minds is to ask them, and much research has called on people simply to *think aloud.* A more systematic approach is the *experience sampling technique*, in which people are asked to report their conscious experiences at particular times. Equipped with electronic beepers, for example, participants are asked to record their current thoughts when beeped at random times throughout the day (Csikszentmihalyi and Larson, 1987). Experience sampling studies show that consciousness is dominated by the immediate environment – what is seen, felt, heard, tasted and smelled, all are at the forefront of the mind. Much of consciousness beyond this orientation to the environment turns to the person's *current concerns*, or what the person is thinking about repeatedly (Klinger, 1975). **TABLE 8.1** shows the results of a Minnesota study where 175 university students were asked to report their current concerns (Goetzman et al., 1994). The researchers sorted the concerns into the categories shown in Table 8.1. Keep in mind that these concerns are ones the students didn't mind reporting to psychologists; their private preoccupations may have been different and probably far more interesting.

TABLE 8.1 What's on your mind? University students' current concerns

Current concern category	Example	Frequency of students who mentioned the concern
Family	Gain better relations with immediate family	40%
Flatmate	Change attitude or behaviour of flatmate	29%
Household	Clean room	52%
Friends	Make new friends	42%
Dating	Desire to date a certain person	24%
Sexual intimacy	Abstaining from sex	16%
Health	Diet and exercises	85%
Employment	Get a summer job	33%
Education	Go to graduate school	43%
Social activities	Gain acceptance into a campus organization	34%
Religious	Attend church more	51%
Financial	Pay rent or bills	8%
Government	Change government policy	14%

Think for a moment about your own current concerns. What topics have been on your mind the most in the past day or two? Your mental 'to do' list may include things you want to get, keep, avoid, work on, remember and so on (Little, 1993). Items on the list often pop into mind, sometimes even with an emotional punch ('The test in this tutorial group is tomorrow!'). People in one study had their GSR (galvanic skin response) measured to assess their emotional responses (Nikula et al., 1993). GSR sensors attached to their fingers indicated when their skin became moist – a good indication that they were thinking about something distressing. Once in a while, GSR would rise spontaneously, and at these times, the researchers quizzed the participants about their conscious thoughts. These emotional moments, compared to those when GSR was normal, often corresponded with a current concern popping into mind. Thoughts that are not themselves emotional can still come to mind with an emotional bang when they are topics of our current concern.

Current concerns do not seem all that concerning, however, during daydreaming – *a state of consciousness in which a seemingly purposeless flow of thoughts comes to mind.* When thoughts drift along in this way, it may seem as if you are just wasting time. However, psychologists have long suspected that daydreams reflect the mind's attempts to deal with difficult projects and problems. A computer program designed to simulate daydreams works on the basis of this assumption to produce passages that resemble human daydreams (Mueller, 1990). The program draws on the idea that people learn from past experiences by 'replaying' them in daydreams, that they discover creative approaches to the future by imaging fanciful scenarios, and that all this helps them to control and channel their emotions.

DAYDREAMING A state of consciousness in which a seemingly purposeless flow of thoughts comes to mind.

In one case, the Daydreamer program was given the information that it had been turned down for a date by a famous actress and was then allowed to 'daydream' in response. In a daydream, it imagined that going out with the actress would have been a hassle because of the reporters; this daydream helped to rationalize the failure and make it less disappointing. Another daydream by the program envisioned a new way of asking her out, one that would have secured her phone number so she could have been approached again later on; this response created new information that would be helpful in similar situations in the future. Human daydreams and fantasies, like these computer-simulated versions, may be more useful than they appear at first glance.

The current concerns that populate consciousness can sometimes gain the upper hand, transforming daydreams or everyday thoughts into rumination and worry. Thoughts that return again and again, or problem-solving attempts that never seem to succeed, can come to dominate consciousness. When this happens, people may exert mental control – *the attempt to change conscious states of mind.* For example, someone troubled by a recurring worry about the future ('What if I can't get a decent job when I graduate?') might choose to try not to think about this because it causes too much anxiety and uncertainty. Whenever this thought comes to mind, the person engages in thought suppression – *the conscious avoidance of a thought.* This may seem like a perfectly sensible strategy because it eliminates the worry and allows the person to move on to think about something else.

MENTAL CONTROL The attempt to change conscious states of mind

THOUGHT SUPPRESSION The conscious avoidance of a thought.

Or does it? Fyodor Dostoevsky (1821–81), the great Russian novelist, remarked on the difficulty of thought suppression: 'Try to pose for yourself this task: not to think of a polar bear, and you will see that the cursed thing will come to mind every minute.' Inspired by this observation, Daniel Wegner and his colleagues (1987) gave people this exact task in the lab. Participants were asked to try not to think about a white bear for five minutes while they recorded all their thoughts aloud into a tape recorder. In addition, they were asked to ring a bell if the thought of a white bear came to mind. On average, they mentioned the white bear or rang the bell (indicating the thought) more than once per minute. Thought suppression simply didn't work and instead produced a flurry of returns of the unwanted thought. What's more, when some research participants later were specifically asked to change tasks and deliberately *think* about a white bear, they became oddly preoccupied with it. A graph of their bell rings in **FIGURE 8.7** shows that these participants had the white bear come to mind far more often than people who had only been asked to think about the bear from the outset, with no prior suppression. This rebound effect of thought suppression, *the tendency of a thought to return to consciousness with greater frequency following suppression*, suggests that attempts at mental control may indeed be difficult. The act of trying to suppress a thought may itself cause that thought to return to consciousness in a robust way.

REBOUND EFFECT OF THOUGHT SUPPRESSION The tendency of a thought to return to consciousness with greater frequency following suppression.

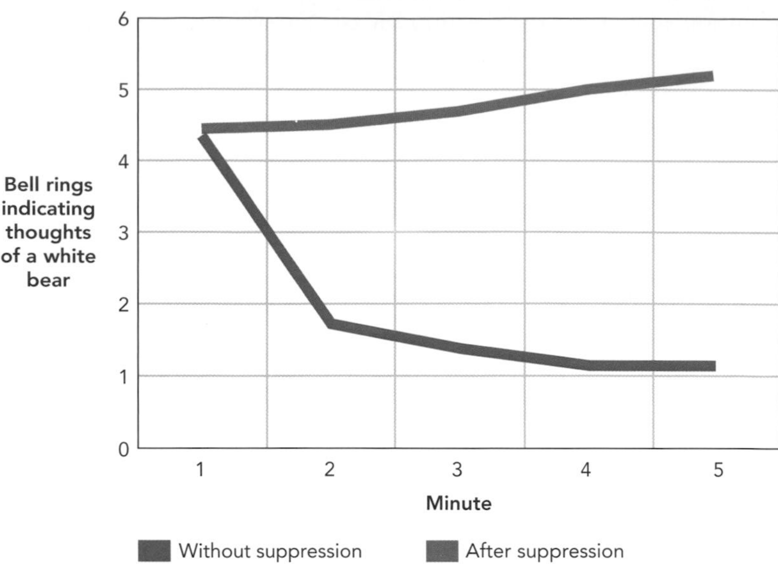

FIGURE 8.7 Rebound effect Research participants were first asked to try not to think about a white bear, and then they were asked to think about it and to ring a bell whenever it came to mind. Compared to those who were simply asked to think about a bear without prior suppression, those people who *first* suppressed the thought showed a rebound of increased thinking (Wegner et al., 1987).

As with thought suppression, other attempts to 'steer' consciousness in any direction can result in mental states that are precisely the opposite of those desired. How ironic: trying to consciously achieve one task may produce precisely the opposite outcome! These ironic effects seem most likely to occur when the person is distracted or under stress. People who are distracted while they are trying to get into a good mood, for example, tend to become sad (Wegner et al., 1993), and those who are distracted while trying to relax actually become more anxious than those who are not trying to relax (Wegner, 1989). Likewise, an attempt not to overshoot a golf putt, undertaken during distraction, often yields the unwanted overshot (Wegner et al., 1998). The theory of ironic processes of mental control proposes that *ironic errors occur because the mental process that monitors errors can itself produce them* (Wegner, 1994a, 1994b). In the attempt not to think of a white bear, for instance, a small part of the mind is ironically *searching* for the white bear.

IRONIC PROCESSES OF MENTAL CONTROL Mental processes that can produce ironic errors because monitoring for errors can itself produce them.

This ironic-monitoring process is *not* present in consciousness. After all, trying not to think of something would be useless if monitoring the progress of suppression required keeping that target in consciousness. For example, if trying not to think of a white bear meant that you consciously kept repeating to yourself, 'No white bear! No white bear!', you've failed before you've begun: that thought is present in consciousness even as you strive to eliminate it. Rather, the ironic monitor is a process of the mind that works *outside* consciousness, making us sensitive to all the things we do not want to think, feel or do, so that we can notice and consciously take steps to regain control if these things come back to mind. The person trying not to think about a white bear, for example, would unconsciously monitor any signs of the thought and so be prompted to try consciously to think of something else if it returns. As this unconscious monitoring whirs along in the background, it unfortunately increases the person's sensitivity to the very thought that is unwanted. Ironic processes are mental functions that are needed for effective mental control – they help in the process of banishing a thought from consciousness – but they can sometimes yield the very failure they seem designed to overcome. Ironic processes of mental control are among the mindbugs that the study of psychology holds up for examination. And because ironic processes occur outside consciousness, they also remind us that much of the mind's machinery may be hidden from our view, lying outside the fringes of our experience.

Go ahead, look away from the book for a minute and try not to think about a white bear.

The unconscious mind

Conscious experience is so central to the human condition that it is easy to see why psychologists want to understand it. Ever since Descartes recognized conscious thought as the foundation for proving the existence of oneself, thinkers have had a very conscious-centric view of the mind. Descartes famously questioned the nature of existence by a process of deductive reasoning. He realized that there were many experiences in life that one could not necessarily be certain of. For example, as we saw in Chapter 4, perceptual illusions often fool the observer even when they are aware that things are not what they seem. Descartes began to question everything he had previously held to be true and realized that nothing about personal experience was logically certain. In his 1641 treatise on the subject, *Meditations on First Philosophy*, Descartes wrote: 'I have found by experience that the senses sometimes deceive, and it is prudent never to trust completely those that have deceived us even once.' He went on to argue that even statements such as 'I am sitting here by the fire' may be false since one could be dreaming or hallucinating. In short, the only certainty of existence one could logically hold to be true was that being consciously aware of one's own thinking was proof of existence, hence his now-famous dictum: 'Cogito ergo sum' (I think, therefore I am).

However, this emphasis on the conscious mind may be misguided. Many mental processes are unconscious, in the sense that they occur without our experience of them. When we speak, for instance:

> We are not really conscious either of the search for words, or of putting the words together into phrases, or of putting the phrases into sentences ... [The] actual process of thinking ... is not conscious at all ... only its preparation, its materials, and its end result are consciously perceived. (Jaynes, 1976, p. 40)

Just to put the role of consciousness in perspective, think for a moment about the mental processes involved in simple addition. What happens in consciousness between hearing a problem (What's 4 plus 5?) and thinking of the answer (9)? Probably nothing – the answer just appears in the mind. But this is a piece of calculation that must take at least a bit of thinking. After all, at a very young age, you may have had to solve such problems by counting on your fingers. Now that you don't have to do that anymore, the answer seems to pop into your head automatically, by virtue of a process that doesn't require you to be aware of any underlying steps, and, for that matter, doesn't even *allow* you to be aware of the steps. The answer just suddenly appears.

In the early part of the 20th century, when structuralist psychologists, such as Wundt, believed that introspection was the best method of research (see Chapter 1), research volunteers trained in describing their thoughts tried to discern what happens in these cases – when a simple problem brings to mind a simple answer (for example, Watt, 1905). They drew the same blank you probably did. Nothing conscious seems to bridge this gap, but the answer comes from somewhere, and this emptiness points to the unconscious mind. To explore these hidden recesses, we can look at the classical theory of the unconscious introduced by Sigmund Freud and then at the modern cognitive psychology of unconscious mental processes.

Freudian unconscious

The true champion of the unconscious mind was Sigmund Freud. As you read in Chapter 1, Freud's psychoanalytic theory viewed conscious thought as the surface of a much deeper mind made up of unconscious processes. Far more than just a collection of hidden processes, Freud described a dynamic unconscious – *an active system encompassing a lifetime of hidden memories, the person's deepest instincts and desires, and the person's inner struggle to control these forces.* The dynamic unconscious might contain hidden sexual thoughts about one's parents, or destructive urges aimed at a helpless infant – the kinds of thoughts people keep secret from others and may not even acknowledge to themselves. According to Freud's theory, the unconscious is a force to be held in check by repression – *a mental process that removes unacceptable thoughts and memories from consciousness and keeps them in the unconscious.* Without repression, a person might think, do or say every unconscious impulse or animal urge, no matter how selfish or immoral. With repression, these desires are held in the recesses of the dynamic unconscious.

DYNAMIC UNCONSCIOUS An active system encompassing a lifetime of hidden memories, the person's deepest instincts and desires, and the person's inner struggle to control these forces.

REPRESSION A mental process that removes unacceptable thoughts and memories from consciousness and keeps them in the unconscious.

Freud looked for evidence of the unconscious mind in speech errors and lapses of consciousness, what are now commonly called 'Freudian slips'. Forgetting the name of someone you dislike, for example, is a mindbug that seems to have special meaning.

Freud believed that errors are not random and instead have some surplus meaning that may appear to have been created by an intelligent unconscious mind, even though the person consciously disavows them. In many instances, these slips reveal taboo urges related to sex and swearing. For example, on BBC Radio 4's *Today* programme, presenter James Naughtie interviewed Jeremy Hunt, the culture minister. Unfortunately, the veteran BBC presenter slipped up and substituted the obscene four-letter 'c' word into his question before quickly correcting himself.

One experiment revealed that slips of speech can indeed be prompted by a person's pressing concerns (Motley and Baars, 1979). Research participants in one group were told they might receive minor electric shocks, whereas those in another group heard no mention of this. Each person was then asked to read quickly through a series of word pairs, including *shad bock*. Those in the group warned about the shocks slipped up more often when pronouncing this pair, blurting out *bad shock*.

Unlike errors created in experiments such as this one, many of the meaningful errors Freud attributed to the dynamic unconscious were not predicted in advance and so seem to depend on clever after-the-fact interpretations. That's not so good. Suggesting a pattern to a series of random events is quite clever, but it's not the same as scientifically predicting and explaining when and why an event should happen. Anyone can offer a reasonable, compelling explanation for an event after it has already happened, but the true work of science is to offer testable hypotheses that are evaluated based on reliable evidence. Freud's type of interpretation is sometimes called the 'sharpshooter fallacy', based on the story of a Texan who fires several shots into the side of a barn and then draws a bull's-eye around them, claiming to be an expert shot. Such post-hoc ('after-the-fact') analysis was typical of Freud's approach; hence his theory was criticized as being unscientific because of its lack of predictive power (see Chapter 1). Freud's book *The Psychopathology of Everyday Life* (Freud, [1901]1938) suggests not so much that the dynamic unconscious produces errors but that Freud himself was a master at finding meaning in errors that might otherwise have seemed random.

Cognitive unconscious

Although heavily criticized, many modern psychologists share Freud's interest in the impact of unconscious mental processes on consciousness and behaviour. However, rather than Freud's vision of the unconscious as a teeming menagerie of animal urges and repressed thoughts, the current study of the unconscious mind views it as the factory that builds the products of conscious thought and behaviour (Kihlstrom, 1987; Wilson, 2002). The cognitive unconscious includes *all the mental processes that are not experienced by the person but give rise to the person's thoughts, choices, emotions and behaviour.*

> COGNITIVE UNCONSCIOUS The mental processes that are not experienced by the person but give rise to the person's thoughts, choices, emotions and behaviour.
>
> SUBLIMINAL PERCEPTION A thought or behaviour that is influenced by stimuli that a person cannot consciously report perceiving.

One indication of the cognitive unconscious at work is when the person's thought or behaviour is changed by exposure to information outside consciousness. This happens in subliminal perception, *a thought or behaviour that is influenced by stimuli that a person cannot consciously report perceiving*, which we encountered in the discussion of covert advertising in Chapter 4. Worries about the potential of subliminal influence were first provoked in 1957, when James Vicary, a marketer, claimed that he had increased concession sales at a New Jersey theatre by flashing the words 'Eat Popcorn' and 'Drink Coke' briefly on the screen during films. It turns out his story was a hoax, and many attempts to increase sales using similar methods have failed. But the idea of influencing behaviour outside consciousness created a wave of alarm about insidious 'subliminal persuasion' that still concerns people (Epley et al., 1999; Pratkanis, 1992).

Subliminal perception does occur (Kihlstrom, 1987), but the degree of influence it has on behaviour is not very large (Dijksterhuis et al., 2005). One set of studies examined whether beverage choices could be influenced by brief visual exposures to thirst-related words (Strahan et al., 2002). Research volunteers were asked to perform a computer task that involved deciding whether each of 26 letter strings was a word or not. This ensured that they would be looking intently at the screen when, just before each letter string appeared, a target was shown that could not be consciously perceived: a word was flashed for 16 ms just off the centre of the screen, followed by a row of Xs in that spot to mask any visual memory of the word. For half the participants, this subliminal word was thirst related (such as *thirst* and *dry*) and for the other half it was unrelated (such as *pirate* and *won*). Afterwards, when the volunteers were given a choice of free coupons towards the purchase of possible new sports beverages Super-Quencher ('the best thirst-quenching beverage ever developed') and PowerPro ('the best electrolyte-restoring beverage ever developed'), those who had been subliminally exposed to thirst words more often chose Super-Quencher (see **FIGURE 8.8**).

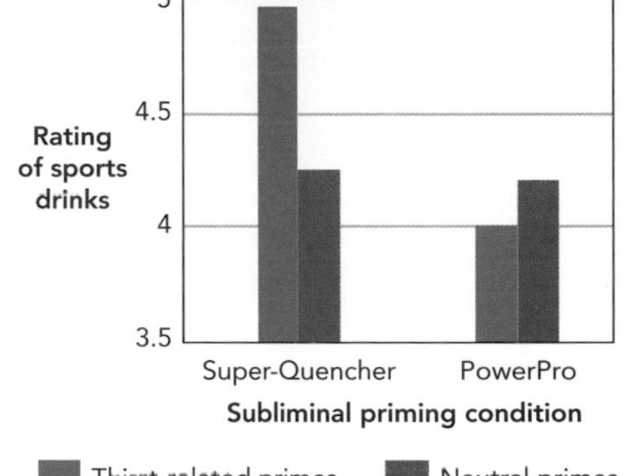

FIGURE 8.8 Subliminal influence Among people subliminally primed with thirst words, preference for the thirst-quenching beverage Super-Quencher increased relative to another sports drink PowerPro (Strahan et al., 2002).

There are two important footnotes to this research. First, the influence of the subliminal persuasion was primarily found for people who reported already being thirsty when the experiment started. The subliminal exposure to thirst words had little effect on people who didn't feel thirsty, suggesting that Vicary's 'Drink Coke' campaign, even if it had actually happened, would not have drawn people out to the lobby unless they were already inclined to go. Second, the researchers also conducted a study in which other participants were shown the target words at a slower speed (300 ms) so the words could be seen and consciously recognized. Their conscious perception of the thirst words had effects just like subliminal perception. Subliminal influences might be worrisome because they can change behaviour without our conscious awareness but not because they are more powerful in comparison to conscious influences.

However, some believe that the research into and interpretation of subliminal perception are unwarranted (Bargh and Morsella, 2008). By definition, subliminal perception is too weak or brief to enter conscious awareness. In addition, the subliminal research agenda was motivated by marketing and mistakenly equated unconscious processes with unintentional ones. The failure to find consistent subliminal effects should not have been interpreted as evidence that the unconscious was not very bright.

In some cases, however, the unconscious mind can make better decisions than the conscious mind. Dutch psychologist Ap Dijksterhuis argues that the processing capacity of conscious thinking is too limited to integrate this information because people are not able to concentrate consciously on more than one different thing simultaneously. In one of his studies, participants were given information about three potential flatmates and asked to choose which of them they would prefer to share with (Dijksterhuis, 2004). Each flatmate was described with 12 attributes that were either positive (such as 'has fun friends') or negative (such as 'has annoying friends'). The research participants weren't told that the information was rigged to make one flatmate a good choice, one intermediate and the last one a real nightmare. One group of participants were given four minutes to make a conscious decision, another group where asked to make an immediate decision and the last group were given a problem-solving task, which also took four minutes so that they could reach an unconscious decision. The unconscious decision group showed a stronger preference for the good flatmate than the immediate decision or conscious decision groups. Dijksterhuis would argue that it is better not to think about some problems and let unconscious processes do all the work.

In some cases, consciousness can even hinder us by drawing attention to idiosyncratic ideas and taking attention away from your 'gut feeling' (Wilson and Schooler, 1991). This may be why you sometimes end up more satisfied with decisions you make after just 'letting it happen' than with the decisions you consciously agonize over.

Should all decisions be made unconsciously? It is important to remember that even gut feelings can be wrong. As we saw in the psychomythology example on decision making in Chapter 7, there are many biases and fallacies operating that seem intuitively correct but are, in fact, wrong, such as always sticking with your first answer on multiple-choice question tests. On balance, this new research on the apparent intelligence of unconscious decisions suggests that simply devoting more time and thought to a decision is no guarantee that the best choice will be made.

In summary, consciousness is a mystery of psychology because other people's minds cannot be perceived directly and the relationship between mind and body is perplexing. Nonetheless, people's reports of their consciousness can be studied, and these reveal basic properties such as intentionality, unity, selectivity and transience. Consciousness can also be understood in terms of levels – minimal consciousness, full consciousness and self-consciousness – and can be investigated for contents such as current concerns, daydreams and unwanted thoughts. There are mental processes that are not conscious, and there are two main interpretations of these. Unconscious processes are sometimes understood as expressions of the Freudian dynamic unconscious but are more commonly viewed as processes of the cognitive unconscious that create and influence our conscious thoughts and behaviours. The cognitive unconscious is at work when subliminal perception influences a person's thoughts or behaviour without the person's awareness.

Attention

SELECTIVE ATTENTION The process whereby we focus mental processing on a limited range of events.

'Pay attention!' How often did we hear that phrase when growing up? We pay attention when we concentrate – but how much does paying attention cost? Selective attention is *the process whereby we focus mental processing on a limited range of events*. As James (1890, p. 403) wrote: 'Everyone knows what attention is. It is the taking possession by the mind, in clear and vivid forms, of one out of what seems several simultaneously possible objects or streams of thought.' Without selective attention, we would not be consciously 'aware'. In the basketball example described earlier, if your selective attention is occupied by counting passes, you fail to become consciously aware of the gorilla.

Why do we need selective attention? Consider for a moment all the sensory input you could potentially attend to as you read this book. Can you hear cars outside in the street? Can you smell the mustiness of the library books? Can you feel the warmth of the radiator? Can you feel the pressure of the chair on your buttocks? Without selective attention, we would be swamped with sensory overload and unable to concentrate.

Early versus late selection

INFORMATION BOTTLENECK When the channel of information processing has a limited capacity.

We are consciously aware of only a small fraction of all the potential experiences that could impinge on our sensory system and without some form of filtering we could become overwhelmed. This is sometimes known as an information bottleneck – *where the channel of information processing has a limited capacity* because the volume of data is too much. Donald Broadbent (1958) argued that this is because the information-processing capacity of our minds is limited and therefore only the important messages should be allowed to get through. Broadbent was motivated by his wartime experiences of radar operators trying to communicate with several pilots at the same time as their voices were relayed over a single speaker. In his landmark book on attention, he proposed that selective attention is a filtering mechanism that operates early in the stream of processing, allowing only crucial information through. That's why, for example, you pick out your name in a crowded room, when you are not consciously listening to everyone else's conversations simultaneously.

EARLY FILTER MODEL Selective attention model that proposes that information is discarded early in the stream of processing.

ATTENUATION MODEL Selective attention model that proposes that information is not entirely discarded in the stream of processing but is suppressed relative to other important signals.

The problem with Broadbent's early filter model, *which advocates an early selection of information in the sequence of processing*, is that information *not* selected for attention is still processed. For example, in the dichotic listening task described earlier, you are still aware of various properties of the unattended message, even though it has not been selected for attention. This led Treisman (1964) to propose a variation on Broadbent's filter account called the attenuation model – *where information was still processed in the sequence but unattended messages were attenuated or dampened relative to the target message*. Treisman showed that target detection in a dichotic listening task was very poor for the unattended ear compared to targets presented to the attended ear (Treisman and Geffen, 1967). However, early selection models of attention cannot explain how all the information is processed and prioritized without causing a bottleneck. In order to make a choice on what to attenuate, you must be aware of the alternatives, so, for selection to occur, there must be some evaluation of *all* the messages potentially competing for conscious awareness.

RESPONSE SELECTION MODEL Selective attention model that proposes that selection occurs late in the stream of processing before a response has been made.

If all messages are evaluated to some extent, selection must occur late in the stream of processing when there are decisions to be made. Deutsch and Deutsch's (1963) response selection model argued that there was indeed an information bottleneck but the *limited capacity occurred after the signals were processed but before a response could be made.* Therefore, Treisman's effects on the target detection task occurred because there was competition for responding to two potential sources of information. According to Deutsch and Deutsch's response selection model, all signals were still getting through the information bottleneck, but not necessarily consciously experienced. This claim was substantiated in a remarkable study where a stress response was conditioned in adults by associating target words with an electric shock. In the same way Watson conditioned a fear response in Little Albert (see Chapter 6), adults were conditioned to expect an electric shock after hearing certain words. After establishing a conditioned fear response as measured by GSR, participants were asked to selectively attend to messages in one ear in a dichotic listening task similar to Treisman's study. Whenever target words were presented in the unattended ear, participants failed to consciously report them as Treisman had found, but participants showed a GSR, indicating that the target words were still unconsciously processed (Corteen and Dunn, 1974). Moreover, a subsequent study showed that participants produced a GSR for unattended synonyms of conditioned words (von Wright et al., 1975). So, if you had been conditioned to the word 'vehicle', you would still show a fear response if the word 'car' was presented in the unattended channel. Early selection models could not account for such findings. Synonyms are conceptually similar words that are generated and understood at a high level in the language system. The fact that the unattended word 'car' triggered a fear response originally conditioned to 'vehicle' proved that unattended signals were not only registered, but processed late in the stream of information evaluation.

There appears to be evidence for early and late selection, which is not a satisfying state of affairs when it comes to explaining how attention operates. One possible solution to this apparent contradiction has been offered by Nilli Lavie's (1995) load model – *where task difficulty determines whether selection is early or late*. She demonstrated that when studies report evidence of early selection, the task is typically difficult in terms of 'perceptual load', for example a demanding task with lots of possible targets, whereas studies that report late selection are comparatively lighter in terms of load, for example a simple task with a single target. The implication of this would seem to be that we can moderate the nature of our selective attention to deal with the task demands – making it early when tasks are complex, and late when tasks are simple. Expertise also plays a role in how we allocate or focus attention. As we saw in Chapter 5, when you first learn to drive a car, this ability requires 'multitasking' – you have to coordinate the need to control the car and pay attention to the traffic around you. Learner drivers need to concentrate because these are new skills that demand attention. They are unlikely to listen to the car radio or engage the passenger in conversation. However, experienced drivers can easily control the car, monitor traffic, listen out for a favourite record on the radio and hold a conversation at the same time. But even experienced drivers can have their attention automatically drawn to something not relevant to driving. For example, the problem of using a mobile phone during driving is less to do with holding a phone and more to do with misallocating attention to the conversation when the driver should be concentrating on the road (Strayer et al., 2003). This is why drivers using hands-free phones still cause fatal accidents.

LOAD MODEL Attentional model that explains early and late selection as a consequence of the task difficulty.

It is not the act of holding a mobile phone while driving that has the potential to cause an accident, but the misallocation of attention, as you focus on the conversation and not on the road.

Shifting attention

So far we have been talking about selective attention as a receptive process where one sits back and tries to make sense of the cacophony of incoming signals. But we are not couch potatoes waiting for the world to come to us. We actively engage the world looking for information. Usually, when we want to attend to something, we align or orient towards the source. In the case of visual targets, for example, we shift our gaze. Under these circumstances, our attention shift is *overt*, as the direction of gaze and attention coincide. However, Helmholtz ([1866]1970) first reported that it is possible to look in one direction but pay attention to another location. James (1890) later described a similar process of *covert* attention shifting, which he thought was particularly well developed in female schoolteachers – no doubt a skill that enabled them to detect the naughty children misbehaving even though they were reading from a book or facing in another direction.

Over 100 years later, Michael Posner (1980) developed an experimental cueing task to confirm Helmholtz's original report. Participants performed a simple reaction time task where they had to press a button whenever a light appeared at any one of several locations on a computer screen. Prior to the onset of the light, a cue was presented that provided information about the likely location of the target (see **FIGURE 8.9**). When the cue was valid, there was a benefit of faster response times compared to either a no cue condition or an invalid cue trial where the participant was directed to the wrong location. Like James's schoolteachers who could keep their eyes on the blackboard and pay attention to the children, even though participants in the experiments did not move their eyes, their attention was automatically being drawn to events around them.

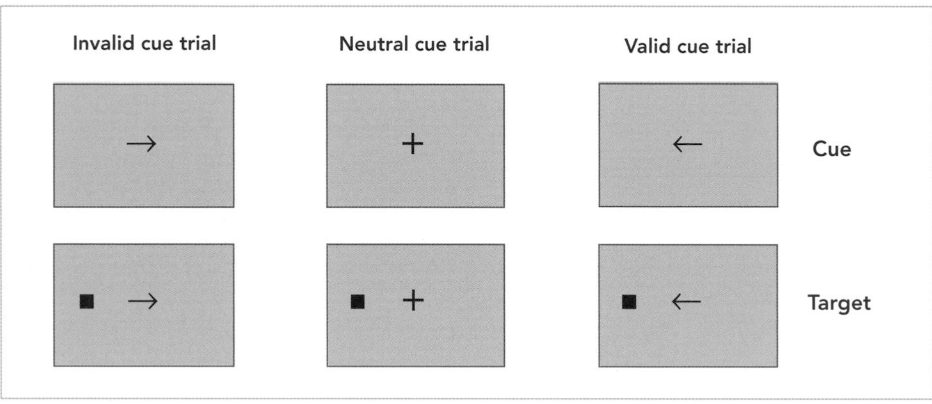

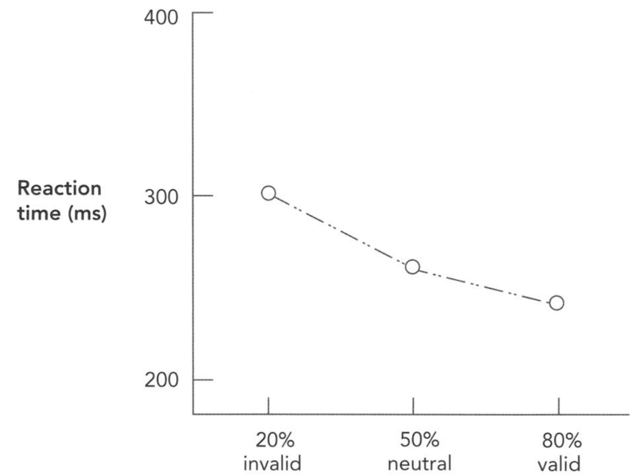

FIGURE 8.9 Posner cueing paradigm The upper panel shows the display sequence for the three trial types. The target is preceded by a cue that indicates the probable location of the target, this cue can be invalid, valid or no cue can be present (so-called neutral cue). The cue is followed by a target that the participant is required to respond to as quickly and accurately as possible. The lower panel shows a graph of typical results from this type of experiment. Participants are both faster than the neutral condition for valid trials and slower than the neutral condition for invalid trials (Findlay and Gilchrist, 2003).

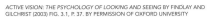

ACTIVE VISION: THE PSYCHOLOGY OF LOOKING AND SEEING BY FINDLAY AND GILCHRIST (2003) FIG. 3.1, P. 37. BY PERMISSION OF OXFORD UNIVERSITY

Posner likened visual attention to a spotlight that could be directed at portions of the visual field to illuminate targets in its beam. The spotlight of attention could be guided by voluntary internal processes when we want to find something, or reflexively triggered by external events that make us respond. For example, we can voluntarily control our attention when searching for a book on the shelf but a brief flash of light or a sudden sound automatically captures our attention and is difficult to ignore. The spotlight metaphor is useful but limited in a number of important ways (Humphreys and Bruce, 1989). For example, what or who controls the spotlight? There cannot be a single process in control because that evokes the problem of our old friend the homunculus again. There must be multiple influences competing to control a spotlight. Also, a spotlight suggests that events outside the beam are not detected, but we know from the work on selection models described earlier that information is not necessarily discarded if it is not attended to. However, as we will discover next, this may happen when certain brain regions are damaged that result in bizarre attentional failures.

Disorders of attention following brain damage

As we saw in Chapter 3, neuroscience is the study of the relationship between neural activity and mental functions. One way to investigate this is through the effects of brain damage. In Europe, partly as a consequence of both world wars in the first half of the 20th century, there has been a long tradition in the field of neuropsychology of looking at the effects of brain damage and in particular local lesions. Lesions are areas of brain damage that can result from a direct injury such as a blow to the head or a bullet, but also more commonly from an infarct or stroke where disrupted blood supply causes tissue to die. When this happens, there can be a corresponding loss of mental function previously supported by this region. Some lesions cause specific disruptions of mental function, which is why neuropsychologists regard the brain as responsible for our consciousness. One mental function that can be disrupted by brain lesions is attention and different lesions produce different attentional disorders.

Unilateral visual neglect

Damage to the dorsal pathway including the parietal lobe described in Chapter 4 can produce a bizarre condition known as unilateral visual neglect – *where patients fail to notice or attend to stimuli that appear on the side of space opposite the site of a hemispheric lesion.* This disorder is most typically found in patients with lesions of the right parietal lobe, which produces a loss of attention to events and objects in their left visual field. For example, they may eat food only off the right side of the plate, fail to notice someone standing on their left side or ignore words on the left side of the page. The condition is not due to blindness, which can result from lesions involving the visual cortex we described in Chapter 4, because patients with unilateral visual neglect (or 'neglect patients') notice objects in the affected side of space if their attention is drawn towards them. Neglect is most pronounced when the patient is presented simultaneously with two visual stimuli, one in each field. Clinicians can easily test this by presenting one or both index fingers in the left and right visual field of the neglect patient (see **FIGURE 8.10**). When only one finger is presented, the patient will readily detect it in either field (**FIGURE 8.10a**). However, if both fingers are presented simultaneously to a patient with left neglect, the finger in the left field is not reported (**FIGURE 8.10b**) – it seems to be 'extinguished' by the finger in the right field (de Renzi, 1982). This is thought to be caused by a failure to disengage attention from the target in the 'good', right-hand field. Neglect patients cued to the good side on a Posner cueing task also fail to notice the target appearing in the contralesional (opposite side to lesion) field, or take a long time to detect it (Posner et al., 1984).

UNILATERAL VISUAL NEGLECT A condition where patients fail to notice or attend to stimuli that appear on the side of space opposite the site of a hemispheric lesion.

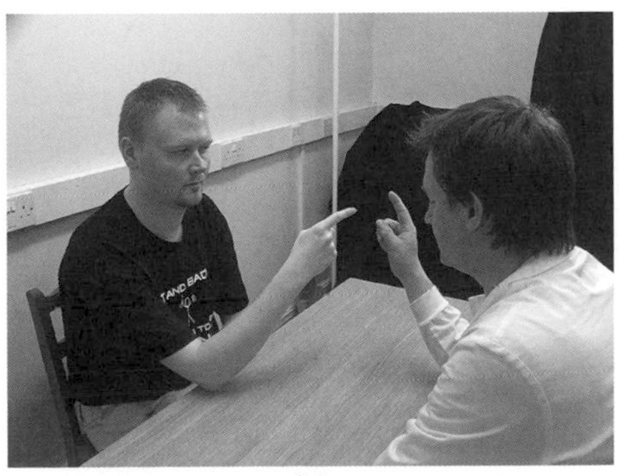

(a)

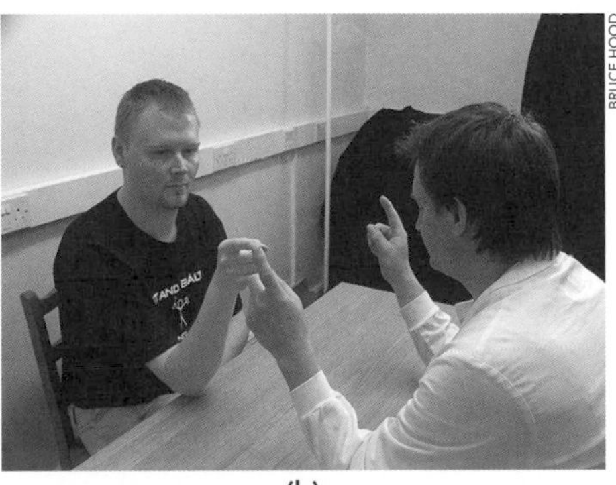

(b)

BRUCE HOOD

FIGURE 8.10 Extinction in a patient with unilateral neglect When two targets are presented simultaneously in each visual field, the patient neglects the target in the field opposite the sight of their lesion (b). However, they can attend to this target when it is presented alone in the affected field (a).

Another remarkable feature of unilateral visual neglect is that it also affects mental imagery. As we saw in Chapter 5, we can form visual mental images to help us create memories. For example, if you are asked to visualize your bedroom, you can form a mental picture of it. You can report various objects in the layout on both sides of the room. However, neglect patients fail to report objects on the contralesional side of their mental

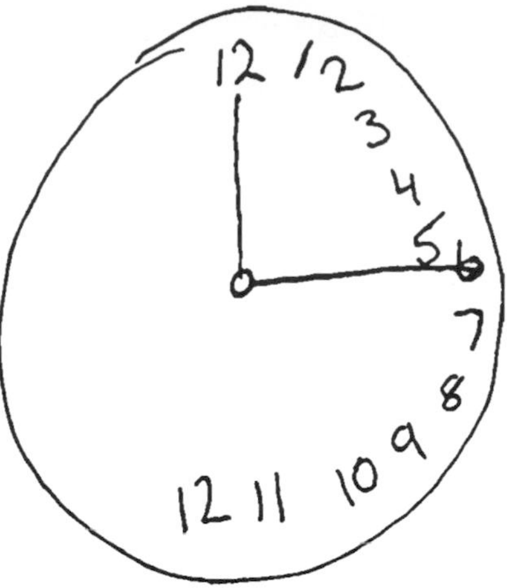

FIGURE 8.11 Visual neglect in a drawing task When asked to draw the face of a clock, some visual neglect patients miss out the numerals on the side of the clock opposite the lesion or bunch all the numbers up on one side as if the affected side did not exist (Smith et al., 2007).

image. For example, when Italian neglect patients were asked to visualize a famous square in Milan and report what they saw standing from the steps of the cathedral, they reported all the shops lining the right side of the square. They were then asked to imagine walking to the opposite side of the square to turn round and face the cathedral. This time they reported all the remaining shops that had previously been on the left side but were now on the right (Bisiach and Luzzati, 1978). In the same way that we navigate around mental images as if we are really there (Kosslyn, 1973), neglect patients fail to navigate into the contralesional side of their imagined world.

As well as failing to register the contralesional aspects of the world, neglect patients also produce distorted representations of it. For example, neglect patients typically produce lopsided or incomplete drawings of objects that have two sides (see **FIGURE 8.11**). When asked to draw a clock face, they may either ignore the digits 7 to 12 or try to squeeze all 12 digits into the right side of the clock (Smith et al., 2007). The most common measure of neglect studied is the 'line bisection task' (Albert, 1973). In this task, the patient is presented with a straight line and simply has to draw a mark to bisect the line in the middle. Left neglect patients usually place the mark much closer to the right side, as if they have failed to notice the extent of the line into the left visual field. If lines of different lengths are presented, the amount of error towards the right side is proportional to the length of each line. This reveals something important and paradoxical about unilateral visual neglect. In order to make an error that is proportional to the length of each line, the patient must be aware *at some level* of the total length of the line. Left neglect patients shown two drawings of a house that were identical except that one had flames coming out of a left-side window said that they would prefer to live in the other house, despite never reporting the fire (Marshall and Halligan, 1988). This is where findings help with our study of conscious and unconscious thought, because, at some level, they were aware that one house was on fire, although they were not consciously aware of it. Perhaps this also explains why neglect patients who make bisection errors on the line task perform much better when they make a speedy response to pick up a rod of similar length in the middle (Robertson et al., 1995). Presumably, the rapid act of picking up the rod is under less conscious guidance than the standard line bisection drawing. So, we must conclude that, for some reason, information from the neglected side of space is processed but not made available to consciousness.

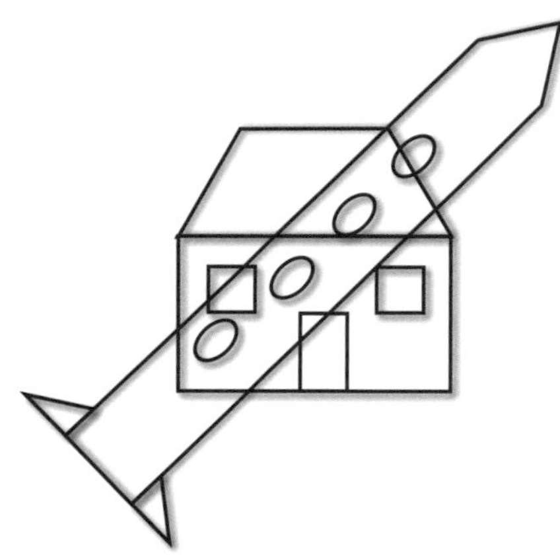

FIGURE 8.12 Attention and overlapping figures Patients with disorders of attention such as Balint's syndrome have difficulty shifting attention when there is competition from different potential targets. They have difficulty seeing the different patterns in overlapping figures.

BALINT'S SYNDROME An attentional disorder where the patient loses the ability to voluntarily shift visual attention to new locations, which is associated with damage to both sides of the brain.

Balint's syndrome, identified by Austro-Hungarian neurologist Rezso Balint in 1909, *an attentional disorder where the patient loses the ability to voluntarily shift visual attention to new locations, which is associated with damage to both sides of the brain*, is much rarer than unilateral visual neglect but in many ways is related because it appears to be a generalized, rather than one-sided disorder of visual neglect. Balint's patients fail to notice objects outside their attentional spotlight even when they are staring them straight in the face. For example, they have great difficulty distinguishing overlapping figures (see **FIGURE 8.12**) as this requires the ability to shift attention between the two figures. Like the Necker cube we encountered earlier, attention allows us to selectively appreciate competing experiences to the exclusion of others. In Balint's syndrome, this ability to voluntarily shift attention is compromised and, as it usually involves damage to both parietal regions, it could be regarded as bilateral neglect disorder.

Blindsight

During the First World War, George Riddoch, a young Scottish army medical officer, described soldiers who were blinded following gunshot injuries to the primary visual cortex (Riddoch, 1917). Damage to area V1 of the primary visual cortex produces cortical blindness and usually the patient reports seeing nothing in the affected field, yet these soldiers seemed to notice the 'vague and shadowy' movement of objects in the blind field (Riddoch, 1917). This phenomenon, known as blindsight, *residual vision in the absence of cortical processing* (Weiskrantz, 1986), was first studied by Nick Humphrey in the 1960s, who worked with a monkey called Helen (Humphrey and Wieskrantz, 1967). Helen had had her entire visual cortex surgically removed and everyone assumed the monkey was blind, but Humphrey noticed that Helen responded to movement and over the course of several years trained her to 'see' again. After seven years, Helen could pick crumbs off the floor and catch a fly. In fact, she was indistinguishable from a sighted monkey. Was she conscious of seeing? The answer is probably not. We know this because of findings with a separate patient – human this time. Patient D. B. was an adult who had also had part of his visual cortex removed to treat a tumour. He was blind in the corresponding portion of the visual field. However, when he was forced to guess, D. B. could accurately detect a target presented in the affected region even though he was unable to be describe it. Although he could detect targets, D. B. reported being blind and consciously unaware of what he seemed to be 'seeing' (Weiskrantz, 1986). Blindsight proves that there are multiple visual processing areas in addition to area V1 that could support unconscious vision.

BLINDSIGHT Residual visual capability supported by subcortical mechanisms following removal or damage to cortical visual areas.

However, unconscious vision is limited. Although Helen the monkey managed to develop a new way of 'seeing' the world, human blindsight patients have not shown the same level of recovery. We know this from a study of two babies who had an entire hemisphere of their brains surgically removed to alleviate intractable epilepsy (Braddick et al., 1992). Following the operation, these babies were blind in the visual field opposite the side of the removed hemisphere and, yet, when presented with a single target, they moved their eyes and head to orient towards it. They had blindsight. However, if two targets were presented in each field simultaneously, they did not look to the target in the blind field. In a world of competing visual targets, we need the capacity to shift our attention in order for us to become consciously aware of them.

Consciousness: What's it for?

It seems absurd to ask the question: Why do we have consciousness? We literally could not imagine life without it! That was Descartes' brilliant deduction for the proof of existence. All the qualia that make up our experiences, all the thoughts and concepts that occupy our minds, all the desires and beliefs that motivate our behaviour would be absent without consciousness. And, yet, as we have seen in this chapter, much of what our minds are up to is not made available to consciousness. This is Descartes' error. The mind is a product of the brain and consciousness appears to be the least informed about what is going on. So why have it? It is not enough to answer that we need it to be us. This only restates the question why do we need it? It is a tough question to answer but there are a number of intriguing speculations that are worth considering. One possibility is that our brains generate the experience of consciousness to keep track of the outcome of all the unconscious processes by giving us a sense of ownership over them – even if they happen before we are aware of them (Wegner, 2002). In this interpretation, consciousness provides a rich contextual framework in which we interlace multiple unconscious processes for future reference. In this way, consciousness generates the personal experience that is stored as an episodic memory, which we encountered in Chapter 5.

Another possibility related to attention is that we have evolved consciousness as an interface between the parallel world of multiple mental processes and the sequential demands of the world, so that our experience *seems* to be linear (Bargh, 1997). We would probably be overwhelmed by possibilities unless we were able to act in this serial manner. Such answers are functional, in that they provide a reason for consciousness in terms of design. However, the answer to the question of how such a design feature could have emerged through natural selection in the first place is still up for grabs.

Psychology and me

Tone Roald, Assistant Professor of Psychology, University of Copenhagen

Tone Roald is an Assistant Professor of Psychology at the University of Copenhagen in Denmark. Visit www.palgrave.com/schacter to watch Tone talking about her research in consciousness studies, particularly people's aesthetic experiences and how they react to paintings, and how infants develop meaning through use of their own bodies. She also talks about why she wanted to study psychology and what she found most challenging.

In summary, a remarkable picture is emerging about the nature of the conscious mind. Clearly, much of what we consciously report is only a fraction of what we are constantly processing and this appears to be related to what we are attending to. There is a whole unconscious mind at work feeding information to the conscious mind to form awareness. However, we would be completely overwhelmed and paralysed with indecision if we became consciously aware of everything we process simultaneously. So, attention plays a crucial role in filtering the information and determining what gets through to our conscious awareness and what remains unconscious. The processes that control attention combine the need to respond to the world with the need to sample experiences voluntarily, and this seems to require a coordinated system of shifting and engaging attentional resources between competing potential sources. When the brain regions that support these attentional networks are disrupted, so too is the conscious picture of the world we experience.

Sleep and dreaming: good night, mind

So far we have focused on the activities of the waking mind and what these can tell us about consciousness, but the world we experience radically alters every night when we fall asleep and this too has important relevance for the idea of consciousness. Sleep can produce a state of unconsciousness in which the mind and brain apparently turn off the functions that create experience: the Cartesian theatre is closed. But this is an oversimplification because the theatre actually seems to reopen during the night for special shows of bizarre cult films – in other words, dreams. Dream consciousness involves a transformation of experience that is so radical it is commonly considered an altered state of consciousness – *a form of experience that departs significantly from the normal subjective experience of the world and the mind.* Such altered states can be accompanied by changes in thinking, disturbances in the sense of time, feelings of a loss of control, changes in emotional expression, alterations in body image and sense of self, perceptual distortions, and changes in meaning or significance (Ludwig, 1966). The world of sleep and dreams, then, provides two unique perspectives on consciousness: a view of the mind without consciousness and a view of consciousness in an altered state.

ALTERED STATES OF CONSCIOUSNESS Forms of experience that depart from the normal subjective experience of the world and the mind.

Sleep

Consider a typical night. As you begin to fall asleep, the busy, task-oriented thoughts of the waking mind are replaced by wandering thoughts and images, odd juxtapositions, some of them almost dreamlike. This presleep consciousness is called the *hypnagogic state.* On some rare nights you might experience a *hypnic jerk*, a sudden quiver or sensation of dropping, as though missing a step on a staircase. (No one is quite sure why these happen, but there is no truth to the theory that you are actually levitating and then fall.) Eventually, your presence of mind goes away entirely. Time and experience stop, you are unconscious, and there seems to be no 'you' there to have experiences. But then come dreams, whole vistas of a vivid and surrealistic consciousness you just don't get during the day, a set of experiences that occur, with the odd prerequisite that there is nothing 'out there' you are actually experiencing. Also, the 'you' of your dream world is very different to that of your waking world. Isn't it strange that when you are dreaming, all your experiences are directed to the content of your dream, with very little self-reflective thought that is so characteristic of the waking state of consciousness (Hobson, 2002). More patches of unconsciousness may occur, with more dreams here and there. And finally, the glimmerings of waking consciousness return again in a foggy and imprecise form as you enter postsleep consciousness (the *hypnopompic state*) and then awake, often with bad hair.

Sleep cycle

The sequence of events that occurs during a night of sleep is part of one of the major rhythms of human life, the cycle of sleep and waking. This circadian rhythm is *a naturally occurring 24-hour cycle* – from the Latin *circa*, 'about', and *dies*, 'day'. Even people who are sequestered in underground buildings without clocks ('time-free environments') and are allowed to sleep when they want to tend to have a rest-activity cycle of about 25.1 hours (Aschoff, 1965). This slight deviation from 24 hours is not easily explained (Lavie, 2001), but it seems to underlie the tendency many people have to

CIRCADIAN RHYTHM A naturally occurring 24-hour cycle.

want to stay up a little later each night and wake up a little later each day. We're 25.1-hour people living in a 24-hour world.

The sleep cycle is far more than a simple on/off routine, however, as many bodily and psychological processes ebb and flow in this rhythm. In 1929, researchers made EEG (electroencephalograph) recordings of the human brain for the first time (Berger, 1929; see Chapter 3). Before this, many people had offered descriptions of their night-time experiences, and researchers knew that there were deeper and lighter periods of sleep, as well as dream periods. But no one had been able to measure much of anything about sleep without waking up the sleeper and ruining it. The EEG recordings revealed a regular pattern of changes in electrical activity in the brain accompanying the circadian cycle. During waking, these changes involve alternation between high-frequency activity (called *beta waves*) during alertness and lower frequency activity (*alpha waves*) during relaxation.

The largest changes in EEG occur during sleep. These changes show a regular pattern over the course of the night that allowed sleep researchers to identify five sleep stages (see **FIGURE 8.13**). In stage 1, the EEG moves to frequency patterns even lower than alpha waves (*theta waves*). In stage 2, these patterns are interrupted by short bursts of activity called *sleep spindles* and *K complexes*, and the sleeper becomes somewhat more difficult to awaken. Stages 3 and 4 are the deepest stages of sleep, known as slow-wave sleep, in which the EEG patterns show activity called *delta waves*.

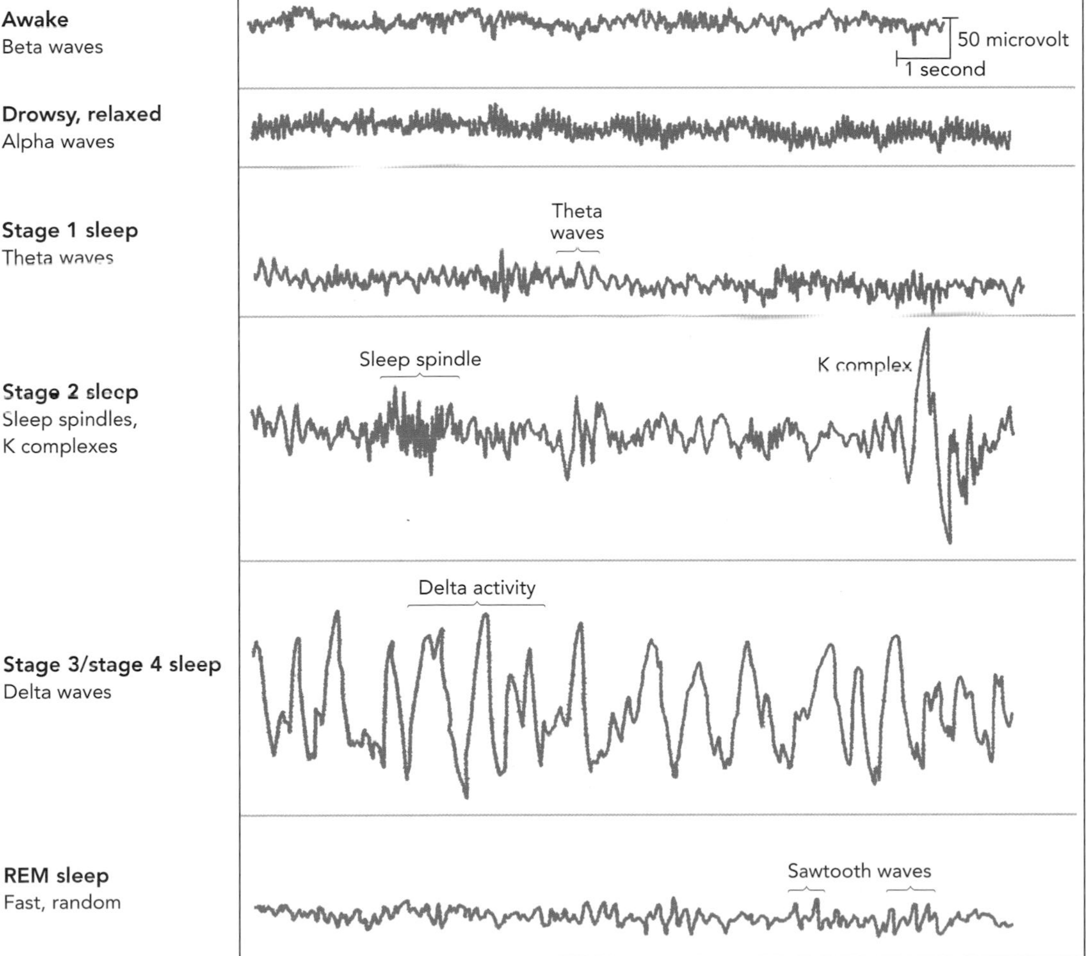

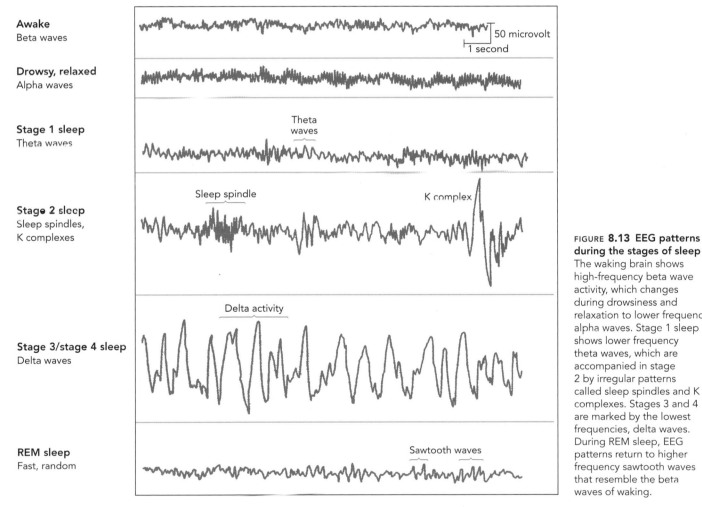

FIGURE 8.13 EEG patterns during the stages of sleep The waking brain shows high-frequency beta wave activity, which changes during drowsiness and relaxation to lower frequency alpha waves. Stage 1 sleep shows lower frequency theta waves, which are accompanied in stage 2 by irregular patterns called sleep spindles and K complexes. Stages 3 and 4 are marked by the lowest frequencies, delta waves. During REM sleep, EEG patterns return to higher frequency sawtooth waves that resemble the beta waves of waking.

During REM (rapid eye movement) sleep, *a stage of sleep characterized by rapid eye movements and a high level of brain activity*, EEG patterns become high-frequency sawtooth waves, similar to beta waves, suggesting that the mind at this time is as active as it is during waking (see Figure 8.13). This is sometimes referred to as *paradoxical sleep* as the

REM (RAPID EYE MOVEMENT) SLEEP A stage of sleep characterized by rapid eye movements and a high level of brain activity. Sometimes known as paradoxical sleep.

ELECTROOCULOGRAPH (EOG) A device that measures eye movements.

mind appears as active in this state as when we are fully awake. Using an **electrooculograph** (EOG), *a device that measures eye movements*, during sleep, researchers found that sleepers wakened during REM periods reported having dreams much more often than those wakened during non-REM periods (Aserinsky and Kleitman, 1953). During REM sleep, the pulse quickens, blood pressure rises, and there are telltale signs of sexual arousal. At the same time, measurements of muscle movements indicate that the sleeper is very still, except for a rapid side-to-side movement of the eyes. (Watch someone sleeping and you may be able to see the REMs through their closed eyelids. Be careful doing this with strangers on a train.)

Although many people believe that they don't dream much (if at all), some 95% of people awakened during REM sleep report dreams. If you've ever wondered whether dreams actually take place in an instant or whether they take as long to happen as the events they portray might take, the analysis of REM sleep offers an answer. Sleep researchers William Dement and Nathaniel Kleitman (1957) woke volunteers either 5 minutes or 15 minutes after the onset of REM sleep and asked them to judge, on the basis of the events in the remembered dream, how long they had been dreaming. The majority of sleepers were correct, suggesting that dreaming occurs in 'real time'. The discovery of REM sleep has offered many insights into dreaming, but not all dreams occur in REM periods. Some dreams are also reported in other sleep stages (non-REM sleep, also called *NREM sleep*) but not as many, and the dreams that occur at these times are described as less wild than REM dreams and more like normal thinking.

Putting EEG and REM data together produces a picture of how a typical night's sleep progresses through cycles of sleep stages (see **FIGURE 8.14**). In the first hour of the night, you fall all the way from waking to the fourth and deepest stage of sleep, the stage marked by delta waves. These slow waves indicate a general synchronization of neural firing, as though the brain is doing one thing at this time rather than many – the neuronal equivalent of 'the wave' moving through the crowd at a stadium, as lots of individuals move together in synchrony. You then return to lighter sleep stages, eventually reaching REM and dreamland. Note that although REM sleep is lighter than that of lower stages, it is deep enough that you may be difficult to awaken. You then continue to cycle between REM and slow-wave sleep stages every 90 minutes or so throughout the night. Periods of REM last longer as the night goes on, and lighter sleep stages predominate between these periods, with the deeper slow-wave stages 3 and 4 disappearing halfway through the night. Although you're either unconscious or dream-conscious at the time, your brain and mind cycle through a remarkable array of different states each time you have a night's sleep.

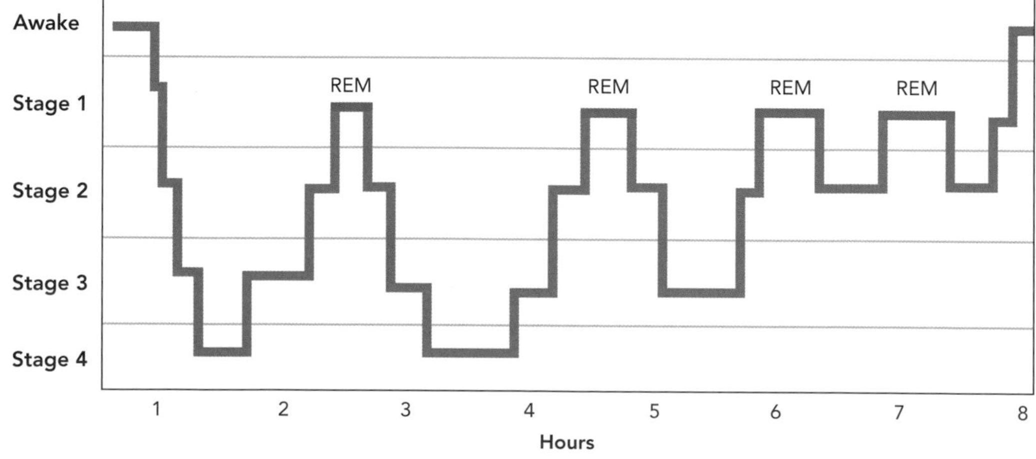

FIGURE 8.14 Stages of sleep during the night Over the course of the typical night, sleep cycles into deeper stages early on and then more shallow stages later. REM periods become longer in later cycles, and the deeper slow-wave sleep of stages 3 and 4 disappears halfway through the night.

Sleep needs and deprivation

How much do people sleep? The answer depends on the age of the sleeper (Dement, 1999). Newborns will sleep six to eight times in 24 hours, often totalling more than 16 hours. Their napping cycle gets consolidated into 'sleeping through the night', usually sometime between 9 and 18 months, but sometimes even later. The typical six-year-old child might need 11–12 hours of sleep, and the progression to less sleep then continues into adulthood, when the average is 7–7.5 hours per night. With ageing, people can get along with even less sleep than that. Over a whole lifetime, we get about one hour of sleep for every two hours we are awake.

This is a lot of sleeping, and you might wonder whether less than this might be tolerable. Rather than sleeping our lives away, perhaps we can stay awake and enjoy life. The world record for staying awake belongs to Randy Gardner, who, at age 17, stayed up for 264 hours and 12 minutes in 1965 for a science project. Randy was followed around for much of the 11 days and nights by sleep researchers, who noted that he seemed remarkably chipper and easy to keep awake during the day – but that he struggled mightily at night, when fighting drowsiness required heroic measures. Along with the researchers, he spent the last night in a penny arcade playing hundreds of games on a baseball machine. He won easily, suggesting that even extreme sleep deprivation is not entirely debilitating or that sleep researchers are lousy at arcade games. The main symptom of his deprivation was sleepiness, along with a couple of minor hallucinatory experiences. When Randy finally did go to sleep, he slept only 14 hours and 40 minutes and awakened essentially recovered (Dement, 1978).

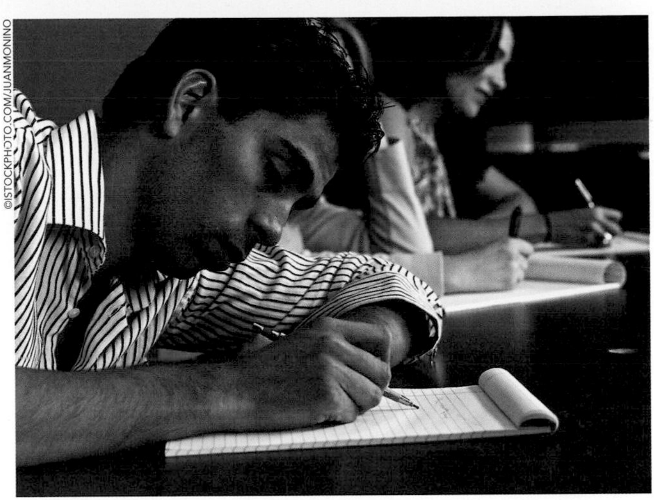

Sleep deprivation can often be diagnosed without the help of any psychologists or brain-scanning equipment.

Feats like this one suggest that sleep might be expendable. This is the theory behind the classic 'all-nighter' that you may have tried on the way to a rough exam. But it turns out that this theory is mistaken. Robert Stickgold and his colleagues (2000a) found that when people learning a difficult perceptual task are kept up all night after they finished practising the task, their learning of the task is wiped out. Even after two nights of catch-up sleep, they show little indication of their initial training on the task. Sleep following learning appears to be essential for memory consolidation (see Chapter 5). It is as though memories normally deteriorate unless sleep occurs to help keep them in place. Studying all night may help you cram for the exam, but it won't make the material stick, which pretty much defeats the whole point.

Sleep turns out to be a necessity rather than a luxury in other ways as well. At the extreme, sleep loss can be fatal. When rats are forced to break Randy Gardner's human waking record and stay awake even longer, they have trouble regulating their body temperature and lose weight although they eat much more than normal. Their bodily systems break down and they die, on average, in 21 days (Rechsthaffen et al., 1983). Shakespeare called sleep 'nature's soft nurse', and it is clear that even for healthy young humans, a few hours of sleep deprivation each night can have a cumulative detrimental effect: reducing mental acuity and reaction time, increasing irritability and depression, and increasing the risk of accidents and injury (Coren, 1997).

Some studies have deprived people of different sleep stages selectively by waking them whenever certain stages are detected. Studies of REM sleep deprivation indicate that this part of sleep is important psychologically, as memory problems and excessive aggression are observed in humans and rats after only a few days of being wakened whenever REM activity starts (Ellman et al., 1991). The brain must value something about REM sleep because REM deprivation causes a rebound of more REM sleep the next night (Brunner et al., 1990). Deprivation from slow-wave sleep (in stages 3 and 4), in turn, has more physical effects, with just a few nights of deprivation leaving people feeling tired, fatigued and hypersensitive to muscle and bone pain (Lentz et al., 1999).

It's clearly dangerous to neglect the need for sleep. But why would we have such a need in the first place? Insects don't seem to sleep, but most 'higher' animals do, including fish and birds. Giraffes sleep less than 2 hours daily, whereas brown bats snooze for almost 20 hours. These variations in sleep needs, and the very existence of a need, are hard to explain. Is the restoration that happens during the unconsciousness of sleep something that simply can't be achieved during consciousness? Sleep is, after all, potentially costly in the course of evolution. Why would natural selection produce in all mammals a state of unconsciousness that puts the animal at risk by making them temporarily paralysed and relatively unaware of their surroundings? There must be a really good reason for this seemingly dangerous behaviour. The sleep deprivation studies with rats described earlier indicate that sleep is necessary for at least three vital bodily functions, thermoregulation, immune system and metabolism (Rechtschaffen et al., 1983):

THERMOREGULATION Biological processes that maintain optimal body heat during different states of wakefulness.

1 Thermoregulation is the *biological thermostatic process that maintains optimal body temperature during different states of wakefulness.* Without sleep, rats cannot regulate their body temperature, which has serious consequences for brain functioning. If we become either overheated or underheated, our brains do not work well, in fact they go to sleep. That's why the pace of life is so much slower in tropical countries and people dying from hypothermia in extreme cold go to sleep. Apparently, the mountaineer's mnemonic for the onset of hypothermia is: 'First you mumble, then you fumble, and then you stumble and finally you tumble!'
2 The immune system is the *body's defence mechanism for combating potential disease from both internal and external invaders.*
3 Metabolism is the *process whereby our bodies convert stored resources into energy.* Normally, this process can speed up or slow down to adjust to the body's energy demands. However, by the end of three to four weeks, the sleep-deprived rats were metabolically starved and died despite the presence of abundant food (Rechtschaffen et al., 1983).

IMMUNE SYSTEM Biological defence system for combating potential disease from both internal and external invaders.

METABOLISM Biological processes that convert stored resources into energy.

Sleep deprivation appears to affect the immune system by disabling the initial response to disease (Palma et al., 2006). The longer the sleep deprivation, the greater the disruption to the body's restorative processes.

Sleep disorders

In answer to the question 'Did you sleep well?', comedian Stephen Wright said: 'No, I made a couple of mistakes.' Sleeping well is something everyone would love to do, but for many people, sleep disorders are mindbugs that can get in the way. Disorders that plague sleep include insomnia, sleep apnea, somnambulism, narcolepsy, sleep paralysis, nightmares and night terrors. Perhaps the most common sleep disorder is insomnia – *difficulty in falling asleep or staying asleep.* About 15% of adults complain of severe or frequent insomnia, and another 15% report having mild or occasional insomnia (Bootzin et al., 1993). Although people often overestimate their insomnia, the distress caused even by the perception of insomnia can be significant. There are many causes of insomnia, including anxiety associated with stressful life events, so insomnia may sometimes be a sign of other emotional difficulties.

INSOMNIA Difficulty in falling asleep or staying asleep.

Insomnia can be exacerbated by worry about insomnia (Borkevec, 1982). No doubt you've experienced some nights on which sleeping was a high priority, such as before a presentation or an important interview, and you've found that you were unable to fall asleep and may have even stayed up later than usual. In this situation, sleeping seems to be an emergency, and every wish to sleep takes you further from that goal. The desire to sleep initiates an ironic process of mental control – a heightened sensitivity to signs of sleeplessness – and this sensitivity interferes with sleep. In fact, participants in an experiment who were instructed to go to sleep quickly became hypersensitive and had more difficulty sleeping than those who were not instructed to hurry (Ansfield et al., 1996). The paradoxical solution for insomnia in some cases, then, may be to give up the pursuit of sleep and instead find something else to do.

Giving up on trying so hard to sleep is probably better than another common remedy – the use of sleeping pills. Although sedatives can be useful for brief sleep problems associated with emotional events, their long-term use is not effective. To begin with, sleeping pills, which are usually some form of benzodiazepine (see Chapter 17), are addictive. People become dependent on the pills to sleep and may need to increase the dose over time to achieve the same effect. Even in short-term use, sedatives can interfere with the normal sleep cycle. Although they promote sleep, they reduce the proportion of time spent in REM and slow-wave sleep (Nishino et al., 1995), robbing people of dreams and their deepest sleep stages. As a result, the quality of sleep achieved with pills may not be as high as without, and there may be side effects such as grogginess and irritability during the day. Finally, stopping the treatment suddenly can produce insomnia that is worse than before.

Sleep apnea is *a disorder in which the person stops breathing for brief periods while asleep.* A person with apnea usually snores, as apnea involves an involuntary obstruction of the breathing passage. When episodes of apnea occur for over 10 seconds at a time and recur many times during the night, they may cause many awakenings and sleep loss or insomnia. Apnea occurs most often in middle-aged, overweight men (Partinen, 1994) and may go undiagnosed because it is not easy for the sleeper to notice. Bed partners may be the ones who finally get tired of the snoring and noisy gasping for air when the sleeper's breathing restarts, or the sleeper may eventually seek treatment because of excessive sleepiness during the day. Therapies involving weight loss, drugs or surgery may solve the problem.

SLEEP APNEA A disorder in which the person stops breathing for brief periods while asleep.

Another sleep disorder is somnambulism, commonly called sleepwalking, which *occurs when a person arises and walks around while asleep.* Sleepwalking is more common in children, peaking around the age of 11 or 12, with as many as 25% of children experiencing at least one episode (Empson, 1984). Sleepwalking tends to happen early in the night, usually in slow-wave sleep, and sleepwalkers may awaken during their walk or return to bed without waking, in which case they will probably not remember the episode in the morning. The sleepwalker's eyes are usually open in a glassy stare, although walking with hands outstretched is uncommon except in cartoons. Sleepwalking is not usually linked to any additional problems and is only problematic in that sleepwalkers can hurt themselves. People who walk while they are sleeping do not tend to be very coordinated and can trip over furniture or fall down stairs. Contrary to popular belief, it is safe to wake sleepwalkers or lead them back to bed.

Sleepdriving

In 2014, a 10-year-old girl from Toledo, Ohio woke up in the middle of the night, picked up her dad's car keys and set off down the road at the wheel of the family car until she ran into four parked cars, came to a stop, and finally woke up. Luckily for her, she was unhurt but she was cited with failure to control, not wearing a seatbelt, and operating a vehicle without a licence. This might seem a bit harsh as she had had an episode of somnambulism, but the police explained it was standard procedure to cite in a situation like this, so the victims could get help from their insurance companies with repairs.

There are other sleep disorders that are less common:

- Narcolepsy is *a disorder in which sudden sleep attacks occur in the middle of waking activities.* Narcolepsy involves the intrusion of a dreaming state of sleep (with REM) into waking and is often accompanied by unrelenting excessive sleepiness and uncontrollable sleep attacks lasting from 30 seconds to 30 minutes. This disorder appears to have a genetic basis, as it runs in families, and can be treated effectively with medication.
- Sleep paralysis is *the experience of waking up unable to move* and is sometimes associated with narcolepsy. This eerie experience usually lasts only a few moments, happens in hypnagogic or hypnopompic sleep, and may occur with an experience of pressure on the chest (Hishakawa, 1976).
- Night terrors (or sleep terrors) are *abrupt awakenings with panic and intense emotional arousal.* These terrors, which occur mainly in boys aged three to seven, happen most often in NREM sleep early in the sleep cycle and do not usually have dream content the sleeper can report.

SOMNAMBULISM (sleepwalking) Occurs when the person arises and walks around while asleep.

NARCOLEPSY A disorder in which sudden sleep attacks occur in the middle of waking activities.

SLEEP PARALYSIS The experience of waking up unable to move.

NIGHT TERRORS (or sleep terrors) Abrupt awakenings with panic and intense emotional arousal.

To sum up, there is a lot going on when we close our eyes for the night. Humans follow a pretty regular sleep cycle, going through five stages of NREM and REM sleep during the night. Disruptions to that cycle, either from sleep deprivation or sleep disorders, can produce consequences for waking consciousness. But something else happens during a night's sleep that affects our consciousness, both while asleep and when we wake up. It's dreaming, and we'll look at what psychologists know about dreams next.

Dreams

Pioneering sleep researcher William C. Dement (1959) said: 'Dreaming permits each and every one of us to be quietly and safely insane every night of our lives.' Indeed, dreams do seem to have a touch of insanity about them. We experience crazy things in dreams, but even more bizarre is the fact that we are the writers, producers and directors of the crazy things we experience. Just what are these experiences and how can they be explained?

Dream consciousness

Dreams depart dramatically from reality. You may dream of being naked in public, falling from a great height, sleeping through an important appointment, your teeth being loose and falling out, being chased, or even flying (Holloway, 2001). These things don't happen much in reality unless you have a very bad life.

The quality of consciousness in dreaming is also altered significantly from waking consciousness. There are five major characteristics of dream consciousness that distinguish it from the waking state (Hobson, 1988):

1 We feel *emotion* intensely, whether it is bliss or terror, love or awe.
2 Dream *thought* is illogical: the continuities of time, place and person don't apply. You may find you are in one place and then another, without any travel in between, or people may change identity from one dream scene to the next.
3 *Sensation* is fully formed and meaningful: visual sensation is predominant, and you may also deeply experience sound, touch and movement, although pain is uncommon.
4 We experience *uncritical acceptance*, as though the images and events were perfectly normal rather than bizarre.
5 A final feature of dreaming is the *difficulty of remembering* the dream after it is over. People often remember dreams only if they are awakened during the dream and even then may lose recall for the dream within just a few minutes of waking. If waking memory were this bad, you'd be standing around half-naked in the street much of the time, having forgotten your destination, clothes and probably your bus fare.

Some of the most memorable dreams are nightmares, as these frightening dreams often wake up the dreamer. One set of daily dream logs from university undergraduates suggested that the average student has about 24 nightmares per year (Wood and Bootzin, 1990), although some people may have them as often as every night. Children have more nightmares than adults, and people who have experienced traumatic events are inclined to have nightmares that relive those events. Following the 1989 earthquake in the San Francisco Bay area, for example, students who had experienced the quake reported more nightmares than those who had not and often reported that the dreams were about the quake (Wood et al., 1992). This effect of trauma may not only produce dreams of the traumatic event. When police officers experience 'critical incidents' of conflict and danger, they tend to have more nightmares in general (Neylan et al., 2002).

Not all our dreams are fantastic and surreal, however. We also dream about mundane topics that reflect prior waking experiences or 'day residue'. Current conscious concerns pop up (Nikles et al., 1998), along with images from the recent past. A dream may even incorporate sensations experienced during sleep, as when sleepers in one study were led to dream of water when drops were sprayed on their faces during REM sleep (Dement and Wolpert, 1958). The day residue does not usually include episodic memories, that is, complete daytime events replayed in the mind. Rather, dreams that reflect the day's experience tend to single out sensory experiences or objects from waking life. After watching a badminton tournament one evening, for example, you might dream about shuttlecocks darting through the air. Rats trained to learn a spatial maze exhibited patterns of activity in their hippocampus while they were asleep that were identical to those triggered during the actual learning when they were awake (Skaggs and McNaughton, 1996). It was as if they were replaying the day's events over and over in their heads. One study had research participants play the computer game Tetris and found that participants often reported dreaming about the Tetris geometrical figures falling down, even though they seldom reported dreams about being in the experiment or playing the game (Stickgold et al., 2001). Even severely amnesiac patients who couldn't recall playing the game at all reported Tetris-like images appearing in their dreams (Stickgold et al., 2000b). The content of dreams takes snapshots from the day rather than retelling stories of what you have done or seen. This means that dreams often come without clear plots or storylines, and so they may not make a lot of sense.

Dream theories

Dreams are puzzles that cry out to be solved. How could you *not* want to make sense out of these experiences? Although dreams are fantastic and confusing, they are emotionally riveting, filled with vivid images from your own life, and they seem very real. The search for dream meaning goes all the way back to biblical figures, who interpreted dreams and looked for prophecies in them. In the Old Testament, the prophet Daniel curried favour with King Nebuchadnezzar of Babylon by interpreting the king's dream. The question of what dreams mean has been burning since antiquity, mainly because the meaning of dreams is usually far from obvious.

In the first psychological theory of dreams, Freud ([1900]1965) proposed that dreams are confusing and obscure because the dynamic unconscious creates them precisely *to be* confusing and obscure. According to Freud's theory, dreams represent wishes, and some of these wishes are so unacceptable, taboo and anxiety producing that the mind can only express them in disguised form. Freud believed that many of the most unacceptable wishes are sexual, so he interpreted a dream of a train going into a tunnel as symbolic of sexual intercourse. According to Freud, the **manifest content** of a dream, *a dream's apparent topic or superficial meaning*, is a smokescreen for its **latent content**, *a dream's true underlying meaning.* For example, a dream about a tree burning down in the park across the street from where a friend once lived (the manifest content) might represent a camouflaged wish for the death of the friend (the latent content). In this case, wishing for the death of a friend is unacceptable, so it is disguised as a tree on fire. The problem with this approach is that there are an infinite number of potential interpretations of any dream and finding the correct one is a matter of guesswork – and of convincing the dreamer that one interpretation is superior to the others.

MANIFEST CONTENT A dream's apparent topic or superficial meaning.

LATENT CONTENT A dream's true underlying meaning.

Although dreams may not represent elaborately hidden wishes, there is evidence that they do feature the return of suppressed thoughts. Researchers asked volunteers to think of a personal acquaintance and then to spend five minutes before going to bed writing down whatever came to mind (Wegner et al., 2004). Some participants were asked to suppress thoughts of this person as they wrote, others were asked to focus on thoughts of the person, and yet others were asked just to write freely about anything. The next morning, participants wrote dream reports. Overall, all participants mentioned dreaming more about the person they had named than about other people. But they most often dreamed of the person they named if they were in the group that had been assigned to suppress thoughts of the person the night before. This finding suggests that Freud was right to suspect that dreams harbour unwanted thoughts. Perhaps this is why actors dream of forgetting their lines, travellers dream of getting lost and football players dream of fumbling the ball. However, there is a huge leap of logic to get from underlying anxiety manifest in dreams to complex psychosexual tension as proposed by Freud.

Another key theory of dreaming is the activation-synthesis model (Hobson and McCarley, 1977). The **activation-synthesis model** proposes that *dreams are produced when the mind attempts to make sense of random neural activity that occurs in the brain during sleep.* During waking consciousness, the mind is devoted to interpreting lots of information that arrives through the senses. For example, you work out that the odd noise you're hearing during a lecture is your mobile phone vibrating, or you realize that the strange smell in the hall outside your room must be from burned popcorn. In the dream state, the mind doesn't have access to external sensations, but it keeps on doing what it usually does: interpreting information. Because that information now comes from neural activations that occur without the continuity provided by the perception of reality, the brain's interpretive mechanisms can run free. This might be why, for example, a person in a dream can sometimes change into someone else. There is no actual person being perceived to help the mind keep a stable view. In the mind's effort to perceive and give meaning to brain activation, the person you view in a dream about a corner shop might seem to be a shop assistant but then change to be your favourite lecturer when the dream scene moves to your university. The great interest people have in interpreting their dreams the next morning may be an extension of the interpretive activity they've been doing all night.

ACTIVATION-SYNTHESIS MODEL The theory that dreams are produced when the brain attempts to make sense of neural activations that occur randomly during sleep.

The dreaming brain

What happens in the brain when we dream? Several studies have made fMRI scans of people's brains during sleep, focusing on the areas of the brain that show changes in activation during REM periods. These studies show that the brain changes that occur during

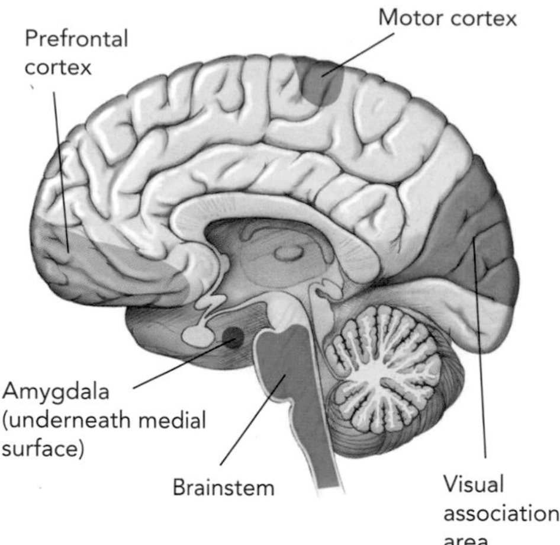

(a) Medial view

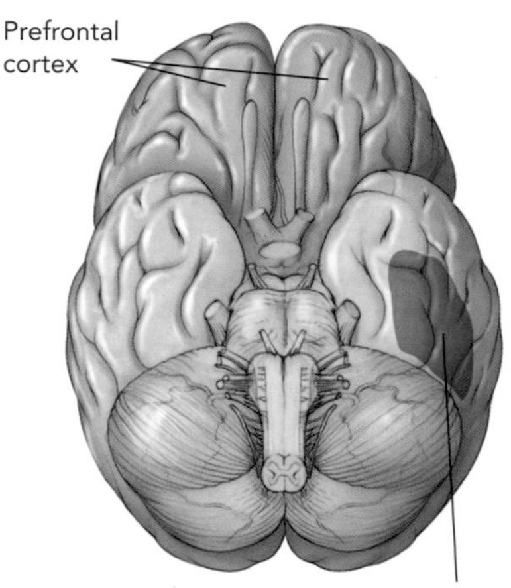

(b) Ventral view

FIGURE **8.15 Brain activation and deactivation during REM sleep** Brain areas shaded red are activated during REM sleep, and those shaded blue are deactivated. (a) The medial view shows the activation of the amygdala, the visual association area, the motor cortex and the brainstem, and the deactivation of the prefrontal cortex. (b) The ventral view shows the activation of other visual association areas and the deactivation of the prefrontal cortex (Schwartz and Maquet, 2002).

REM sleep correspond with certain alterations of consciousness that occur in dreaming. **FIGURE 8.15** shows some of the patterns of activation and deactivation found in the dreaming brain (Schwartz and Maquet, 2002).

One notable feature that distinguishes dreams from waking consciousness, for instance, is their scariness. By definition, nightmares are terrifying, but even your common, run-of-the-mill dream is often populated with anxiety-producing images (Neilson et al., 1991). There are heights to look down from, dangerous people lurking, the occasional monster, lots of minor worries, and at least once in a while that major exam you've forgotten about until your friend reminds you. These thoughts suggest that the brain areas responsible for fear or emotion somehow work overtime in dreams, and it turns out that this is visible in fMRI scans. The amygdala is involved in responses to threatening or stressful events, and the amygdala is indeed quite active during REM sleep.

The typical dream is also a visual wonderland, with visual events present in almost all dreams. However, there are fewer auditory sensations, even fewer tactile sensations, and almost no smells or tastes. This dream 'picture show' doesn't involve actual perception, just the imagination of visual events. It turns out that the areas of the brain responsible for visual perception are *not* activated during dreaming, whereas the visual association areas in the occipital lobe that are responsible for visual imagery *do* show activation (Braun et al., 1998), as shown in **FIGURE 8.15**. Your brain is clever enough to realize that it's not really seeing bizarre images but acts instead as though it's imagining bizarre images.

During REM, the prefrontal cortex shows relatively less arousal than it usually does during waking consciousness. What does this mean for the dreamer? As a rule, the prefrontal areas are associated with planning and executing actions, and often dreams seem to be unplanned and rambling. Perhaps this is why dreams often don't have sensible storylines – they've been scripted by an author whose ability to plan is inactive.

Another odd fact of dreaming is that while the eyes are moving rapidly, the body is otherwise still. During REM sleep, the motor cortex is activated, but spinal neurons running through the brainstem inhibit the expression of this motor activation (Lai and Siegal, 1999). This turns out to be a useful property of brain activation in dreaming; otherwise, you might get up and act out every dream! In fact, when this inhibitory area is lesioned in cats, they become highly active during REM sleep (Jouvet and Mounier, 1961). People who are thrashing around during sleep are probably not dreaming. If they were dreaming, they'd be very still. The brain specifically inhibits movement during dreams, perhaps to keep us from hurting ourselves.

One day brain scans may also help to solve the intriguing question of whether people can be aware that they are dreaming. Some people claim that they only become aware they have been dreaming when they wake up and realize 'it was all a dream'. In this case, the dream state seems to be like the waking state of minimal consciousness, in that the person is not aware of being in the mental state. Other individuals, however, report that they sometimes know they are dreaming while the dream is ongoing – they experience the dream equivalent to full consciousness. Such *lucid dreaming*, the awareness of dreaming during the dream, has often been described (LaBerge and Rheingold, 1990) but is still a matter of controversy because evidence of such dreams comes only from these descriptions reported by the dreamers. One goal of brain-imaging research is to examine how the brain may be involved in the creation of such elusive states of mind. Researchers have not yet established whether there are differences in brain activation between minimal consciousness and full consciousness during waking, but perhaps if they do, brain research can corroborate the reports of lucid dreamers.

At present, studies of the activities of the dreaming brain yield a picture of dreaming as a unique state of mind. The brain's activities in dreaming underlie extensive visual activity, reductions of other sensations, increased sensitivity to emotions such as fear, lessened capacities for planning, and the prevention of movement.

A dream answer

Are there answers to be found in dreams? The Freudian theory and the activation-synthesis theory differ in the significance they place on the meaning of dreams. In Freud's theory, dreams begin with meaning, whereas in the activation-synthesis theory, dreams begin randomly, but meaning can be added as the mind lends interpretations in the process of dreaming. Which account best describes the role of dreams? According to dream researcher Bob Stickgold: 'Freud was 50 per cent right and 100 per cent wrong.' Unconscious processes feed into the content of dreams but they are not organized plots of latent content, certainly not content that can be reliably investigated. The problem with psychoanalytic dream analysis is that it does not make testable predictions and anything goes in dream interpretation. Any psychoanalytic interpretation can be given for a dream. But by their nature dreams are neither coherent nor reliable. For example, dream transcripts were taken from 20 participants and half of these were edited so that the various segments were spliced at points of discontinuity to form new transcripts. Expert psychoanalysts and non-experts performed equally badly at spotting the originals from the spliced dream accounts (Stickgold et al., 1994). As is so often reported in this textbook, the human mind cannot help but interpret and see connections where there are none. However, unconscious processes can influence the content of our dreams, with surprising results. As we saw in Chapter 5 in the case of the tip-of-the-tongue phenomenon, effortful thought mediated by frontal activity can sometimes impair our ability to retrieve a nugget of information from memory. When we stop thinking about the problem, the answer often pops into mind. Likewise, when the frontal regions of our analytical thought shut down during dreaming, the associative thinking of dreams allows us to think imaginatively and come up with answers upon awakening. German chemist Kekulé reputedly dreamt of a snake swallowing its own tail, which gave him a critical insight into the circular structure of the benzene molecule. One of the most successful Beatles tunes, 'Yesterday', came to Paul McCartney in a dream: 'I woke up with a lovely tune in my head. I thought, "That's great, I wonder what that is?"' Mary Shelley, the creator of *Frankenstein*, conceived the story in a dream. Even the golfer Jack Nicklaus dreamt about a new golf swing that he successfully applied the following day. Freed from the tyranny of conscious effortful control, we sleep perchance to dream.

VEGETATIVE STATE A state of wakefulness without awareness and overt communication.

hot science

Waking the brain

Brain damage can produce a number of disorders of consciousness. A blow to the head can render an individual unconscious in a coma for varying lengths of time, depending the extent of the injury. However, individuals coming out of a coma can enter a vegetative state – *a state of wakefulness without awareness and overt communication.* In this condition, patients can open their eyelids occasionally and demonstrate sleep-wake cycles, but until fairly recently were thought to completely lack cognitive function. That was until Adrian Owen, a former Cambridge neuroscientist now based in Canada, working with his Belgian colleagues at the University of Liège, used fMRI technology to communicate with patients in a vegetative state (Monti et al., 2010).

Owen knew that when healthy, conscious adults imagine playing tennis, they show activation in a region of the motor cortex called the supplementary motor area, and when they think about navigating through a house, they generate activity in the parahippocampal gyrus, right in the centre of the brain. Some years earlier, Owen had found a 23-year-old female patient in a vegetative state who showed the same differential activation when asked to imagine playing tennis compared to walking around her house (Owen et al., 2006). This gave him the ingenious idea to use the differential brain activity to answer either yes or no to questions, in much the same way we can signal one tap for 'yes' and two taps for 'no'.

The experimenters could not know whether the patients understood what was being said to them, but they placed them in the fMRI scanner and asked them to perform two imagery tasks. They instructed patients to imagine two scenarios. In the motor imagery task, they were instructed to imagine standing still on a tennis court and then swinging an arm to 'hit the ball' back and forth to an imagined instructor. In the spatial imagery task, the patients were instructed to imagine navigating the streets of a familiar city or walking from room to room in their home and visualizing all they would 'see' if they were there.

Of the 54 patients enrolled in the study, five were able to wilfully modulate their brain activity and one in particular, patient 23, was able to answer questions. Although he showed no overt signs of communication and awareness in bedside tests, patient 23, a young male car accident victim, was able to answer questions inside the scanner. For example, in response to the question 'Is your father's name Alexander?', patient 23 responded 'yes' (correctly) with activity that matched that observed on the motor imagery localizer scan. In response to the question 'Is your father's name Thomas?', the patient responded 'no' (also correctly) with activity that matched that observed in the spatial imagery localizer scan.

Not surprisingly, these studies created a media storm because it showed that for at least some patients in a vegetative state, they were conscious. Can you imagine such a terrible situation – awake and aware but not able to move or communicate? Some disagree with this horrific conclusion. We cannot know for certain that patient 23 was conscious because, as we have seen in this chapter, consciousness is not an all-or-nothing state, but has different levels. We can process information implicitly without it ever entering consciousness. But what if these patients are conscious and can communicate? Do we dare ask them the ultimate question about whether they want their medical life support to be withdrawn?

In summary, sleep and dreaming present a view of the mind with an altered state of consciousness. EEG and EOG measures have revealed that during a night's sleep, the brain passes through a five-stage sleep cycle, moving in and out of lighter sleep stages, from slow-wave sleep stages to the REM sleep stage, in which most dreaming occurs. Sleep needs decrease over the life span, but deprivation from sleep and dreams has psychological and physical costs. Sleep can be disrupted through disorders that include insomnia, sleep apnea, somnambulism, narcolepsy, sleep paralysis and night terrors. Dreaming is an altered state of consciousness in which the dreamer uncritically accepts changes in emotion, thought and sensation but poorly remembers the dream on awakening. Dream consciousness is paralleled by changes in brain activation, and theories of dreaming include Freud's psychoanalytic theory and more current views such as the activation-synthesis model.

Drugs and consciousness: artificial inspiration

Aldous Huxley, author of the anti-utopian novel *Brave New World*, once wrote of his experiences with the drug mescaline in *The Doors of Perception*, which described the intense experience that accompanied his departure from normal consciousness. Huxley (1954, p. 5) described

> a world where everything shone with the Inner Light, and was infinite in its significance. The legs, for example, of that chair – how miraculous their tubularity, how supernatural their polished smoothness! I spent several minutes – or was it several centuries? – not merely gazing at those bamboo legs, but actually *being* them.

PSYCHOACTIVE DRUG A chemical that influences consciousness or behaviour by altering the brain's chemical message system.

Being the legs of a chair? This is better than being a seat cushion, but it still sounds like an odd experience. Still, many people seek out such experiences, often through using drugs. Psychoactive drugs are *chemicals that influence consciousness or behaviour by altering the brain's chemical message system.* As you read in Chapter 3, information is communicated in the brain through neurotransmitters that convey neural impulses to neighbouring neurons. Some of the most common neurotransmitters are serotonin, dopamine, gamma-aminobutyric acid (GABA) and acetylcholine. Drugs alter these neural connections by preventing the bonding of neurotransmitters to sites in the postsynaptic neuron or by inhibiting the reuptake or enhancing the bonding and transmission of neurotransmitters. Different drugs can intensify or dull transmission patterns, creating changes in brain electrical activity that mimic the natural operations of the brain. For example, a drug such as Valium (a benzodiazepine) induces sleep but prevents dreaming and so creates a state similar to slow-wave sleep, that is, what the brain naturally develops several times each night. Other drugs prompt patterns of brain activity that do not occur naturally, however, and their influence on consciousness can be dramatic. Like Huxley experiencing himself becoming the legs of a chair, people using drugs can have experiences unlike any they might find in normal waking consciousness or even in dreams. To understand these altered states, let's explore how people use and abuse drugs, and examine the major categories of psychoactive drugs.

Why do children enjoy spinning around until they get so dizzy they fall down? Even from a young age, there seems to be something enjoyable about altering states of consciousness.

Drug use and abuse

There is something strangely attractive about states of consciousness that depart from the norm, and people throughout history have sought out these altered states by dancing, fasting, chanting, meditating and ingesting a bizarre assortment of chemicals to intoxicate themselves (Tart, 1969). People pursue altered consciousness even when there are costs, from the nausea that accompanies dizziness to the life-wrecking obsession with a drug that can come with addiction. In this regard, the pursuit of altered consciousness can be a malicious mindbug.

Often, drug-induced changes in consciousness begin as pleasant and spark an initial attraction. Researchers have measured the attractiveness of psychoactive drugs by seeing how much laboratory animals will work to get them. In one study, researchers allowed rats to intravenously administer cocaine to themselves by pressing a lever (Bozarth and Wise, 1985). Rats given free access to cocaine increased their use over the course of the 30-day study. They not only continued to self-administer at a high rate but also occasionally binged to the point of giving themselves convulsions. They stopped grooming themselves and eating until they lost on average almost a third of their body weight. About 90% of the rats died by the end of the study.

Rats are not tiny humans, of course, so such research is not a firm basis for understanding human responses to cocaine. But these results do make it clear that cocaine is addictive and that the results of such addiction can be dire. Studies of the self-administration of drugs in laboratory animals show that animals will work to obtain not only cocaine but also alcohol, amphetamines, barbiturates, caffeine, opiates (such as morphine and heroin), nicotine, phencyclidine (PCP, known as angel dust), MDMA (known as ecstasy) and THC (tetrahydrocannabinol, the active ingredient in marijuana). There are some psychoactive drugs that animals won't work for, such as mescaline or the antipsychotic drug phenothiazine, suggesting that these drugs have less potential for causing addiction (Bozarth, 1987).

HARM REDUCTION APPROACH A response to high-risk behaviours that focuses on reducing the harm such behaviours have on people's lives.

the real world

Drugs and the regulation of consciousness

Why does everyone have an opinion about drug use? Given that it's not possible to perceive what happens in anyone else's mind (that problematic 'other minds' mystery of consciousness), why does it matter so much to us what people do to their own consciousness? Is consciousness something that governments should be able to legislate for – or should people be free to choose their own conscious states (McWilliams, 1993)? After all, how can a 'free society' justify regulating what people do inside their own heads?

Individuals and governments alike answer these questions by pointing to the costs of drug addiction, to the addict and the society that must 'carry' unproductive people, pay for their welfare, and often even take care of their children. Drug users appear to be troublemakers and criminals, the culprits behind all those 'drug-related' shootings, knifings, robberies and petty thefts you see in the news day after day. Just about all large cities across the world have drug-related crime problems but in the US in the early 1970s, many cities had areas that had become combat zones for drug gangs. If people did not buy drugs, the gangs and violence would disappear. You might even be able to understand the frustration that led Darryl Gates, then chief of the Los Angeles Police Department, to remark to the US Senate Judiciary Committee in 1990 that 'casual drug users should be taken out and shot'. Although most government officials were more compassionate than this, widespread anger about the drug problem surfaced in the form of the 'War on Drugs', a US government programme that focused on drug use as a criminal offence and attempted to stop drug use through the imprisonment of users.

In the UK, various drug czars have tried to address the problem but there does not appear to be prohibitive legislation that works. Maybe it is time to consider legalization to take the profit out of the drugs trade or at least direct it back into society. This is what has happened with alcohol.

Social commentators such as economist Milton Friedman and psychiatrist Thomas Szasz believe that the War on Drugs is much like the era of Prohibition, the American government's 1920–33 ban on alcohol (Trebach and Zeese, 1992). This famous experiment failed because the harm produced by the policy outweighed the damage produced by legal alcohol consumption. Illegal alcohol became wildly expensive, and the promise of large profits led to the rapid growth of organized criminal suppliers, an entire criminal subculture complete with gang killings and turf wars over distribution rights. With the huge jump in organized crime came a parallel wave of crime by 'users' – illegal alcohol was so expensive that people who were dependent on it begged, stole or sold anything to get money to buy it. In many ways, it mirrors what is happening with today's illegal drug trade.

The War on Drugs led to the same buildup of criminal supply systems, along with an increase in crimes committed by users to get drug money – and an unprecedented increase in the incarceration of drug offenders. From 1990 to 2007, for example, the number of drug offenders in US state and federal prisons increased from 179,070 to 348,736 – a jump of 94% (Bureau of Justice Statistics, 2008) – not because of a measurable increase in drug use, but because of the increased use of imprisonment for drug offences. Many people who were being prevented from ruining their lives with drugs were instead having their lives ruined by prison. These observations bring up the question of whether it is the drug use that causes social problems or the *prohibition* of drug use that causes these problems.

What should be done? One possibility is the harm reduction approach – *a response to high-risk behaviours that focuses on reducing the harm such behaviours have on people's lives* (Marlatt, 1998). This approach, which originated in the Netherlands and England, focuses on reducing drug harm rather than reducing drug use. Harm reduction involves tactics such as providing intravenous drug users with sterile syringes to help them avoid contracting HIV and other infections from shared needles. Harm reduction may even involve providing drugs for addicts to reduce the risks of poisoning and overdose they face when they buy impure drugs of unknown dosage from criminal suppliers. In turn, a harm reduction idea for alcoholics is to allow moderate drinking; the demand to be cold sober may keep many alcoholics on the street and away from any treatment at all (Marlatt et al., 1993). Harm reduction strategies do not always find public support because they challenge the popular idea that the solution to drug and alcohol problems must always be prohibition: stopping use entirely.

The mistaken belief in prohibition is fuelled, in part, by the worry that drug use turns people into criminals and causes psychological disorders. A key study that followed 101 children as they grew from age 3 to 18 did not confirm this theory (Shedler and Block, 1990). Personality assessments given to participants showed that those who were frequent drug users at 18 were indeed the most irresponsible, inconsiderate, irritable, rebellious, suffered low self-esteem and so on. However, the adjustment problems of the frequent users were *already present* in early childhood, long before they started using drugs. Some other factor (a poor family environment as a child, perhaps) caused their adjustment problems *and* their frequent drug use. As you read in Chapter 2, in this case, a third variable was at work in producing a correlation. It may be that allowing some limited forms of drug use and focusing greater attention on reducing harm would not create the problems we fear.

Harm reduction seems to be working in the Netherlands. The Netherlands Ministry of Justice (1999) reported that the decriminalization of marijuana there in 1979 has not led to increased use and that the use of other drugs remains at a level far below that of other European countries and the US. Conversely, in the US, the War on Drugs seems to have had little real impact. A comparison of drug users in Amsterdam and San Francisco revealed that the city in which marijuana is criminalized – San Francisco – had higher rates of drug use for marijuana and other drugs (Reinarman et al., 2004). Separating the markets in which people buy marijuana and alcohol from those in which they get 'hard' drugs such as heroin, cocaine or methamphetamine may create a social barrier that reduces interest in the hard drugs. There may be solutions that involve reasonable responses to drugs, a middle ground between prohibition and deregulation, as a way of reducing harm. Since 1996, 18 US states and the District of Columbia have enacted laws to legalize the use of marijuana for medical purposes. And in 2012 Colorado and Washington became the first two states to legalize marijuana for purely recreational purposes. Perhaps we can eliminate some casualties in the War on Drugs by fighting drug harm rather than heaping further harm on drug users. Regulating consciousness may be less important for society than reducing the harm that is caused when individuals try to regulate their own consciousness through drug use.

In the Netherlands, marijuana use is not prosecuted. The drug is sold in 'coffee shops' to those over 18.

Hallucinogens

HALLUCINOGENS Drugs that alter sensation and perception and often cause visual and auditory hallucinations.

The drugs that produce the most extreme alterations of consciousness are the hallucinogens – *drugs that alter sensation and perception, often causing hallucinations*. These include LSD (lysergic acid diethylamide, commonly known as 'acid'), mescaline, psilocybin, PCP and ketamine (an animal anaesthetic). Some of these drugs are derived from plants (mescaline from the peyote cactus, psilocybin from so-called 'magic mushrooms') and have been used by people since ancient times. For example, the ingestion of peyote plays a prominent role in some Native American religious practices. The other hallucinogens are largely synthetic. LSD was first made by chemist Albert Hofmann in 1938, leading to a rash of experimentation that influenced popular culture in the 1960s. Timothy Leary, at the time a Harvard psychology professor, championed the use of LSD to 'turn on, tune in, and drop out'; the Beatles sang of *L*ucy in the *s*ky with *d*iamonds (denying, of course, that this might be a reference to LSD); and the wave of interest led many people to experiment with hallucinogens.

The experiment was not a great success. These drugs produce profound changes in perception. Sensations may seem unusually intense, objects may seem to move or change, patterns or colours may appear, and these perceptions may be accompanied by exaggerated emotions ranging from blissful transcendence to abject terror. These are the 'I've-become-the-legs-of-a-chair!' drugs. But the effects of hallucinogens are dramatic and unpredictable, creating a psychological roller-coaster ride that some people find intriguing but others find deeply disturbing. Hallucinogens are the main class of drugs that animals *won't* work to self-administer, so it is not surprising that in humans these drugs are unlikely to be addictive. Hallucinogens do not induce significant tolerance or dependence, and overdose deaths are rare. Although hallucinogens still enjoy a marginal popularity with people interested in experimenting with their perceptions, they have been more a cultural trend than a dangerous attraction.

CANNABIS Drug derived from the hemp plant.

The *leaves, buds and resin of the hemp plant* contain THC, the active ingredient in cannabis. When smoked or eaten, either as is or in concentrated form as *hashish*, this drug produces an intoxication that is mildly hallucinogenic. Users describe the experience as euphoric, with heightened senses of sight and sound and the perception of a rush of ideas. Cannabis affects judgement and short-term memory and impairs motor skills and coordination – making driving a car or operating heavy equipment a poor choice during its use ('Where did I leave the darn bulldozer?'). Researchers have found that receptors in the brain that respond to THC (Stephens, 1999) are normally activated by a neurotransmitter called *anandamide* that is naturally produced in the brain (Wiley, 1999). Anandamide is involved in the regulation of mood, memory, appetite and pain perception and has been found to temporarily stimulate overeating in laboratory animals, much as cannabis does in humans (Williams and Kirkham, 1999). Some chemicals found in dark chocolate also mimic anandamide, although very weakly, perhaps accounting for the wellbeing some people claim they enjoy after a 'dose' of chocolate.

The addiction potential of cannabis is not strong, as tolerance does not seem to develop, and physical withdrawal symptoms are minimal. Psychological dependence is possible, however, and some people do become chronic users. Cannabis use has been widespread throughout the world for recorded history, as a medicine for pain and/or nausea and as a recreational drug, but its use remains controversial. Queen Victoria was fond of the occasional 'toke' to relieve her menstrual pain and today cannabis is known to alleviate the symptoms of a number of medical conditions such multiple sclerosis. Cannabis was reclassified as a class B drug in 2009 in the UK, because of the increased toxicity of recently modified varieties of the plant (see where do you stand? box).

In summary, psychoactive drugs influence consciousness by altering the brain's chemical messaging system and intensifying or dulling the effects of neurotransmitters. The altered consciousness brought about by drug use is attractive to many people, but in many cases drugs cause serious harm. Each of the major classes of psychoactive drugs was developed for medical, social or religious reasons, but each has different effects and presents a different array of dangers.

Hypnosis: open to suggestion

You may have never been hypnotized, but you have probably heard or read about it. Its wonders are often described with an air of amazement, and demonstrations of stage hypnosis make it seem powerful and mysterious. When you think of hypnosis, you may envision people down on all fours acting like farm animals or perhaps 'regressing' to early childhood and talking in childlike voices. Some of what you might think is true, but many of the common beliefs about hypnosis are false. Hypnosis *is a social interaction in which one person (the hypnotist) makes suggestions that lead to a change in another person's (the subject's) subjective experience of the world* (Kirsch et al., 2011). During hypnosis, people follow instructions readily and feel that their actions are things that are happening to them rather than things they are doing (Lynn et al., 1990). In this way, hypnopsis is an extreme form of behavioural compliance, *doing what you are told or expected to do*, in which case it does not really represent a loss of control as such ('you are under my control') but rather a willingness to conform and believe that you are no longer responsible for your actions (Wagstaff, 1981).

HYPNOSIS A social interaction in which one person (the hypnotist) makes suggestions that lead to a change in another person's (the subject's) subjective experience of the world.

BEHAVIOURAL COMPLIANCE Doing what you are told or expected to do.

Induction and susceptibility

How are people hypnotized? An early form of hypnotic induction is credited to Franz Anton Mesmer (1734–1815), a doctor working in Paris. He attempted to cure people of illness through contact with what he called 'animal magnetism'. He introduced patients to his theory that a force could be generated from water and iron to rejuvenate their health and then proceeded to involve them in several curious rituals. Patients held on to iron rods immersed in a large water tub, sometimes with their waists loosely tied to the tub with rope, and were asked to sit quietly while Mesmer passed his hands lightly over their bodies (Gauld, 1992). These theatrical gestures led many patients to believe that their ailments were cured. Some patients reported miraculous cures of chronic stomach problems, headaches, paralysis and even blindness, and those whose cures were less

The theatrical gestures involved in Mesmer's water tubs led people to believe their ailments were cured.

dramatic still often agreed that they too felt better for all this. *Mesmerism* became a major sensation. Although Mesmer's theory was eventually discredited and he was dismissed as a charlatan (it turned out that none of the water tubs or paraphernalia were even needed for the effect), his technique of influencing people developed into what is now called 'hypnosis'.

The essence of Mesmer's technique was persuading people that his actions would influence them. In a modern hypnotic induction, many people already know enough about hypnosis to suspect that something the hypnotist does might indeed have an effect on them. To induce hypnosis, then, a hypnotist may ask the person to be hypnotized to sit quietly and focus on some item (such as a spot on the wall) and then suggest to the person what effects hypnosis will have, for example 'Your eyelids are slowly closing' or 'Your arms are getting heavy'. Modern hypnosis shares a common theme with mesmerism: in both cases, the hypnotist and participant engage in a social interaction in which the participants are led to expect that certain things will happen to them that are outside their conscious will (Wegner, 2002).

The induction of hypnosis usually involves a number of different 'suggestions', ideas the hypnotist mentions to the volunteer about what the volunteer will do. Some of these ideas seem to cause the actions – just thinking about their eyelids slowly closing, for instance, may make many people shut their eyes briefly or at least blink. Just as you may find yawning contagious when you think about someone else yawning, many different behaviours can be made more common just by concentrating on them. In hypnosis, a series of behaviour suggestions can induce in some people a state of mind that makes them susceptible to even very unusual suggestions, such as getting down on all fours and sniffing in the corner.

Not everyone is equally hypnotizable. Susceptibility varies greatly, such that some hypnotic 'virtuosos' are strongly influenced, most people are only moderately influenced, and some people are entirely unaffected. Susceptibility is not easily predicted by a person's personality traits, so tests of hypnotic susceptibility are made up of a series of suggestions in a standard hypnotic induction. One of the best indicators of a person's susceptibility is the person's own judgement. So, if you think you might be hypnotizable, you may well be (Hilgard, 1965). People with active, vivid imaginations, or who are easily absorbed in activities such as watching a movie, are also somewhat more prone to be good candidates for hypnosis (Sheehan, 1979; Tellegen and Atkinson, 1974).

Hypnotic effects

From watching stage hypnotism, you might think that the major effect of hypnosis is making people do peculiar things. In fact, there are some impressive demonstrations. At the 1849 festivities for Prince Albert's birthday, for example, a hypnotized guest was asked to ignore any loud noises and then didn't even flinch when a pistol was fired near his face. The real effects of hypnosis are often clouded, however, by extravagant claims, for example that hypnotized people can perform extraordinary physical stunts, or can remember things they have forgotten in normal consciousness.

Hypnosis has been touted as a cure for lost memory. The claim that hypnosis helps people to unearth memories they are not able to retrieve in normal consciousness seems to have surfaced because hypnotized people often make up memories to satisfy the hypnotist's suggestions. For example, in the 1980s in the US, Paul Ingram, a sheriff's deputy accused of sexual abuse by his daughters, was asked by interrogators in session after session to relax and imagine having committed the crimes. He emerged from these sessions having confessed to dozens of horrendous acts of 'satanic ritual abuse'. These confessions were called into question, however, when independent investigator Richard Ofshe (1992) used the same technique to ask Ingram about a crime that Ofshe had simply made up out of thin air, something of which Ingram had never been accused. Ingram produced a three-page handwritten confession, complete with dialogue. Still, prosecutors in the case accepted Ingram's guilty plea, and he was only released in 2003 after a public outcry and years of work on his defence. After a person claims to remember something, even under hypnosis, it is difficult to convince others that the memory was false (Loftus and Ketchum, 1994).

Hypnosis can also undermine memory. People susceptible to hypnosis can be led to experience posthypnotic amnesia – *the failure to retrieve memories following hypnotic suggestions to forget.* Ernest Hilgard (1986) taught a hypnotized person the populations of some remote cities, for example, and then suggested that he forget the study session. The person was quite surprised after the session at being able to give the census figures correctly. (Asked how he knew the answers, the individual decided he might have learned them from a TV programme.) Such amnesia can then be reversed in subsequent hypnosis.

POSTHYPNOTIC AMNESIA The failure to retrieve memories following hypnotic suggestions to forget.

However, research does *not* find that people can retrieve through hypnosis memories that were not originally lost through hypnosis. Instead, hypnotized people try to report memories in line with the hypnotist's questioning. In one study, 27 hypnotizable research volunteers were given suggestions during hypnosis that they had been awakened by loud noises in the night a week before. After hypnosis, 13 of them – roughly 50% – reported that they had been awakened by loud noises (Laurence and Perry, 1983). Hypnosis does not enhance the accuracy of memory, it only increases the person's *confidence* in false memory reports (Kihlstrom, 1985).

Although all the preceding claims for hypnosis are somewhat debatable, one well-established effect is hypnotic analgesia – *the reduction of pain through hypnosis in people who are hypnotically susceptible.* For example, one study (see **FIGURE 8.16**) found that for pain induced in volunteers in the laboratory, hypnosis was more effective than morphine, diazepam (Valium), aspirin, acupuncture or placebos (Stern et al., 1977). For people who are hypnotically susceptible, hypnosis can be used to control pain in surgeries and dental procedures, in some cases more effectively than any form of anaesthesia (Druckman and Bjork, 1994; Kihlstrom, 1985). Evidence for pain control supports the idea that hypnosis is a different state of consciousness and not entirely a matter of skilful role-playing on the part of highly motivated people.

HYPNOTIC ANALGESIA The reduction of pain through hypnosis in people who are susceptible to hypnosis.

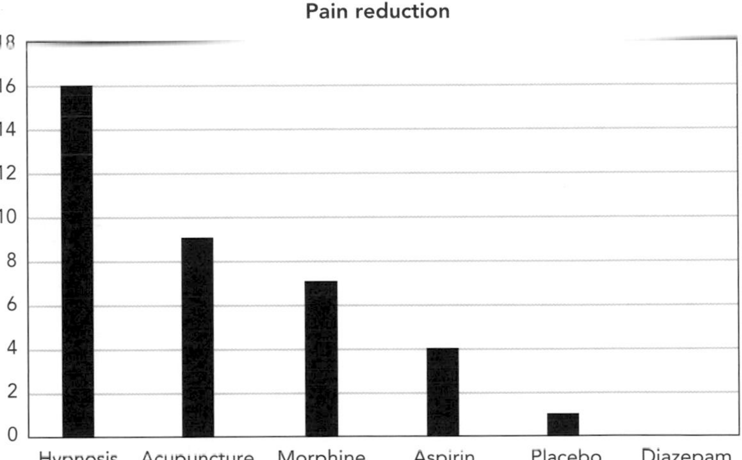

FIGURE 8.16 Hypnotic analgesia The degree of pain reduction reported by people using different techniques for the treatment of laboratory-induced pain. Hypnosis wins (Stern et al., 1977).

The conscious state of hypnosis is accompanied by unique patterns of brain activation. In one study, researchers prescreened highly hypnotizable people for their ability to hallucinate during hypnosis (Szechtman et al., 1998). After a standard hypnotic induction, these participants were tested in a PET (positron emission tomography) scanner while performing each of three tasks: perception, imagination and hypnotic hallucination. For the perception task, participants heard a recording of the sentence 'The man did not speak often, but when he did, it was worth hearing what he had to say.' For the imagination task, they were asked to imagine hearing this line again. For the hypnotic hallucination task, they listened as the hypnotist suggested that the tape was playing once more (although it was not). The researchers expected this last suggestion to prompt an auditory hallucination of the line, and participants indeed reported thinking they heard it.

The PET scan revealed that the right anterior cingulate cortex, an area involved in the regulation of attention, was just as active while the participants were hallucinating as when they were actually hearing the line. However, there was less activation in this brain area when participants were merely imagining the sentence. **FIGURE 8.17** shows where the right anterior cingulate area was activated in the hypnotizable participants during hearing and hallucinating. This pattern of activation was not found in people who were not highly hypnotizable. The researchers concluded that hypnosis stimulated the brain to register the hallucinated voice as real rather than as imagined.

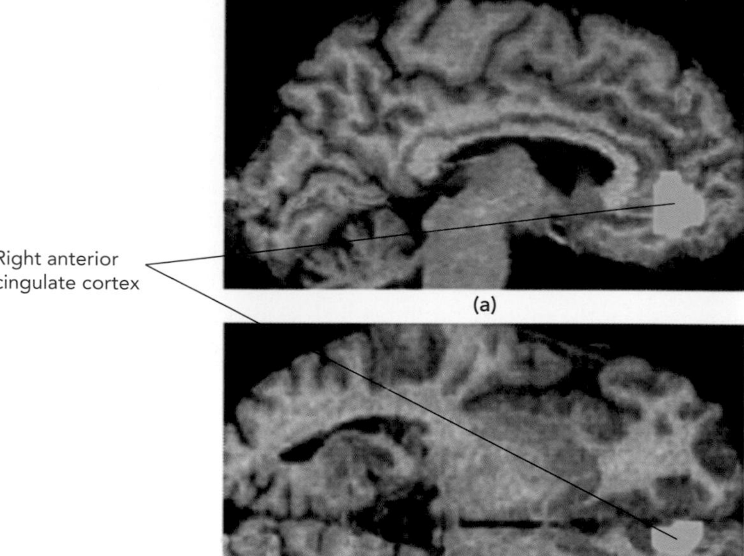

FIGURE 8.17 Brain activity during hypnosis Researchers found right anterior cingulate cortex activation in hypnotized research participants both when they were hearing a target sentence and when they were following the suggestion to hallucinate the sentence. The right anterior cingulate cortex is involved in the regulation of attention. The brain is viewed here in two cross-sectional scans: (a) upright and (b) horizontal.

In summary, although there are many claims for hypnosis that overstate its effects, this phenomenon characterized by suggestibility does have a range of real effects on individuals who are susceptible. Inductions of hypnosis can create the experience that one's actions are occurring involuntarily, influence memory reports, lead people to experience posthypnotic amnesia, and even induce analgesia during surgical procedures.

hot science

Out-of-body experiences: watch your back

We not only create models of the external world that may be illusory, but we also generate models of our own bodies based on the different senses that can be illusory. One of the most famous demonstrations of a body illusion is where participants experience that a rubber hand that occupies a position where their normal hand should be can 'feel' sensations (Botvinick and Cohen, 1998). To induce the 'rubber hand' illusion, a standing screen is positioned between the participant's right hand on a table and an artificial hand (see figure). The participant is instructed to focus on the artificial hand while the experimenter with two paintbrushes simultaneously lightly strokes their real right hand and the rubber hand. This is done to produce touch sensation on their out-of-view real hand while the participant watches the movements of the brush on the rubber hand. After about 10 minutes, around 70% of participants report that the sensation of touch appears to come from the location of the rubber hand. This phenomenon suggests that we can experience relocation of our sensation of touch because our brain uses the visual information to specify the location of our limbs.

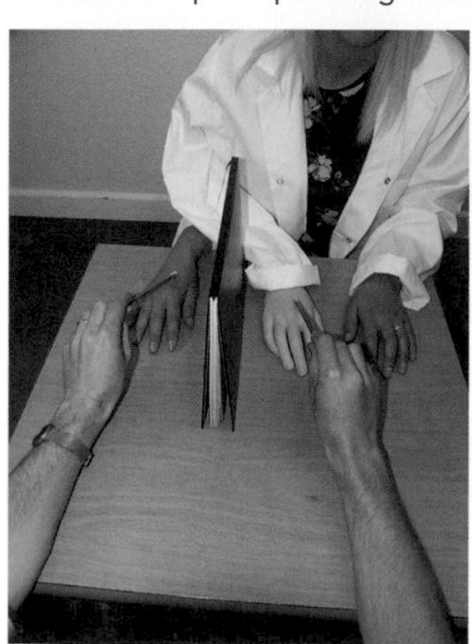

If the sense of our own physical body in space can be distorted when vision and touch are scrambled, could this have something to do with the bizarre phenomenon of out-of-body experiences (OBEs)? An OBE is typically an experience where an individual feels that their consciousness has left their body and they can see themselves from a distance. This phenomenon has been around for thousands of years and, unsurprisingly, is interpreted by many as evidence for a non-material soul. People in all cultures report OBEs (Alcock and Otis, 1980) and about 25% of university students and 10% of the general public have reported at least one OBE (Alvardo, 2000). Although folklore is that OBEs are typically associated with near-death experiences such as drowning or heart attack, most occur when people are relaxed, asleep, dreaming, medicated, using psychedelic drugs, anesthetized, experiencing seizures or migraines (Blackmore, 1984).

Swedish neuroscientist Henrik Ehrsson wanted to know whether the power of vision to relocate our sense of body could be used to produce an OBE. To investigate, he had participants wear goggles that displayed the view from a camera pointed at their back (Ehrsson, 2007). With the aid of video technology, they were able to literally watch their own backs, which appeared to be in front of them visually! Then, using the same induction technique as the rubber hand illusion, Ehrsson tapped the participant's chest with a rod while prodding a second rod at the camera aimed at their back. Around 80% of participants have an OBE where they experience themselves as behind their bodies taking the perspective of the camera looking at the stranger in front of them, which is, of course, really them!

Not only can you convince individuals that they are dislocated from their bodies, you can make them think that their bodies are larger or smaller using the same video trickery combined with the rubber hand induction technique. In a recent study, Preston and Ehrsson (2014) showed participants the head-mounted view looking at the stomach of either a slimmer or wider bodied mannequin (see figure).

Again, by stroking the mannequin at the same time as the unseen real body, participants readily experienced an ownership of the mannequin body. What is remarkable is that illusory ownership of a slimmer body resulted in participants perceiving their actual body as slimmer and giving higher ratings of body satisfaction, demonstrating a direct link between perception and how individuals feel about their own bodies (Preston and Ehrsson, 2014).

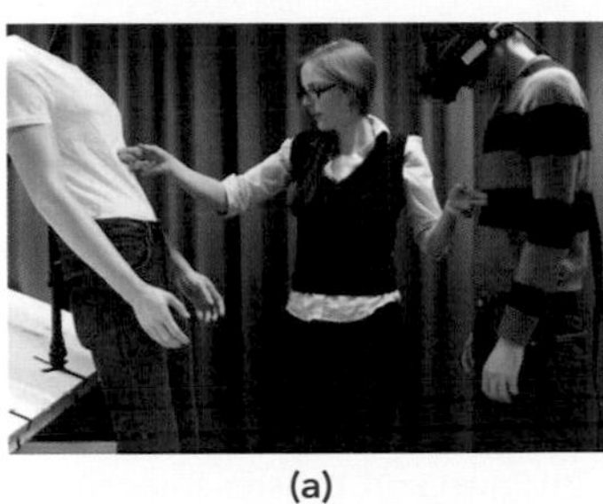
(a)

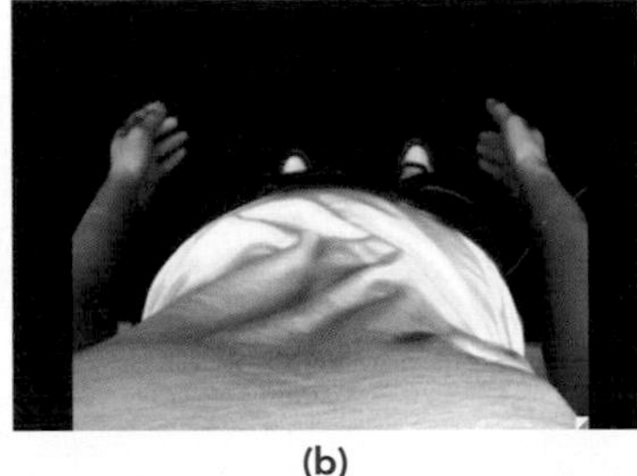
(b)

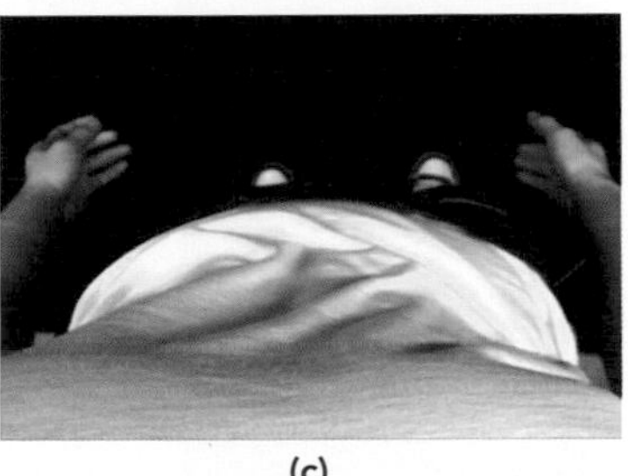
(c)

Experimental setup. (a) The illusion was induced by synchronously stroking the mannequin body and the corresponding part of the participant's body. (b) Participant view through the head-mounted display of the male mannequin in the small and large (c) body conditions.

Meditation and religious experiences: higher consciousness

Some altered states of consciousness occur without hypnosis, without drugs and without other external aids. In fact, the altered states of consciousness that occur naturally or through special practices such as meditation can provide some of the best moments in life. Abraham Maslow (1962) described these 'peak experiences' as special states of mind in which you feel fully alive and glad to be human. Sometimes, these come from simple pleasures – a breathtaking sunset or a magical moment of personal creativity – and other times they can arise through meditative or religious experiences.

Evil avatars

Researchers have found that sometimes we get so immersed in virtual experiences that we take on the personality of the avatars (Yoon and Vargas, 2014). Participants who played the evil character 'Voldemort' in a video game dished out more unpleasant chilli sauce to an unknown future participant compared to those whose avatar was the heroic character 'Superman', who gave out more pleasant chocolate sauce.

Meditation

Meditation is *the practice of intentional contemplation*. Techniques of meditation are associated with a variety of religious traditions and are also practised outside religious contexts. The techniques vary widely. Some forms of meditation call for attempts to clear the mind of thought, others involve focusing on a single thought, for example thinking about a candle flame, and still others involve concentration on breathing or on a mantra, a repetitive sound such as *om*. At a minimum, the techniques have in common a period of quiet.

MEDITATION The practice of intentional contemplation.

Why would someone meditate? The time spent meditating can be restful and revitalizing, and according to meditation enthusiasts, the repeated practice of meditation can enhance psychological wellbeing. The evidence for such long-term positive effects of meditation is controversial (Druckman and Bjork, 1994), but meditation does produce temporarily altered patterns of brain activation. Meditation influences EEG recordings of brain waves, usually producing patterns known as *alpha waves* that are associated with relaxation (Dillbeck and Orme-Johnson, 1987). A brain-scanning study of Buddhist practitioners during meditation found especially low levels of activation in the posterior superior parietal lobe (Newberg et al., 2001). This area is normally associated with judging physical space and orienting oneself in space – knowing angles, distances and the physical landscape and distinguishing between the self and other objects in space. When this area is deactivated during meditation, its normal function of locating the self in space may subside to yield an experience of immersion and a loss of self.

©ISTOCKPHOTO.COM/KAREN MOLLER

In Cairo, a whirling dervish of the Sufi tradition performs the Sema, a spiritual ceremony that aids the quest for divine illumination.

Ecstatic religious experiences

In some religious traditions, people describe personal experiences of altered consciousness – feelings of ecstasy, rapture, conversion or mystical union. Members of a religious group may 'speak in tongues', or the celebrants may go into trances, report seeing visions or feel as though they are possessed by spirits. These altered states may happen during prayer or worship or without any special religious activity. Over 40% of one sample of Americans reported having a profound experience of this kind at least once in their lives (Greeley, 1975), and altered states of consciousness of one sort or another are associated with religious practices around the world (Bourguignon, 1968).

Like meditation, certain brain activation patterns are associated with ecstatic religious experiences. Some people who experience religious fervour show the same type of brain activation that occurs in some cases of epilepsy. Several prophets, saints and founders of religions have been documented as having epilepsy; for example, Joan of Arc had symptoms of epilepsy accompanying the religious visions that inspired her and her followers (Saver and Rabin, 1997). People asked to describe what it is like to have a seizure, in turn, sometimes report feeling what they call a religious 'aura'. One patient described his seizures as consisting of feelings of incredible contentment, detachment and fulfilment, accompanied by the visualization of a bright light and soft music; sometimes he also saw a bearded man he assumed was Jesus Christ (Morgan, 1990). Surgery to remove a tumour in the patient's right anterior temporal lobe eliminated the seizures but also stopped his religious ecstasies. Cases such as this suggest that the right anterior temporal lobe might be involved when people without epilepsy experience profound religious feelings. The special moments of connection that people feel with God or the universe may depend on the way in which brain activation promotes a religious state of consciousness.

The states of religious ecstasy and meditation are just two of the intriguing varieties of experience that consciousness makes available to us. Our consciousness ranges from the normal everyday awareness of walking, thinking or gazing at a picture to an array of states that are far from normal or everyday – sleep, dreams, drug intoxication, hypnosis and beyond. These states of mind stand as a reminder that the human mind is not just something that students of psychology can look at and study. The mind is something each of us looks *through* at the world and at ourselves.

In summary, meditation and religious ecstasy can be understood as altered states of consciousness. Meditation involves contemplation that may focus on a specific thought, sound or action (such as breathing) or may be an attempt to avoid any focus. The practice of meditation promotes relaxation in the short term, but the long-term benefits claimed by enthusiasts have not been established. Ecstatic religious experiences may have a basis in the same brain region – the right anterior temporal lobe – associated with some forms of epilepsy.

psychomythology

People can be hypnotized to kill

Derren Brown is a famous TV performer and magician in the UK who uses the allure of psychology to create spectacular shows. In 'The Assassin', the first episode of his 2011 TV series called *Derren Brown: The Experiments*, he claimed to have hypnotized an audience member to shoot the celebrity comedian Stephen Fry during a public performance. It was all great entertainment but can you really put someone into a trance state where they have no control over their actions?

Hypnotists often claim that their volunteers can perform great feats not possible when the volunteers are fully conscious. One of the claims for superhuman strength involves asking a hypnotized person to become 'stiff as a board' and lie unsupported with shoulders on one chair and feet on another. However, many people can do this without hypnosis. Similarly, the claim that people will perform extreme actions when hypnotized fails to take into account that people will also perform these actions when they are simply under a lot of social pressure. Some early studies reported, for instance, that hypnotized people could be led to throw what they thought was a flask of acid in an experimenter's face (Rowland, 1939; Young, 1948). However, in further examinations of this phenomenon, participants who were not hypnotized were asked to *simulate* being hypnotized (Orne and Evans, 1965). They were instructed to be so convincing in faking their hypnosis that they would fool the experimenter. These people, just like the hypnotized participants, threw what they thought was acid in the experimenter's face. Clearly, hypnotic induction was not a necessary requirement to produce this behaviour in the research participants.

Did Derren Brown create an assassin through the power of hypnosis? The short answer is 'No', and you cannot hypnotize someone to do something they are not already willing to do (Lynn et al., 1990). Audience members go to see stage hypnotists for entertainment and that includes being willing to go up on stage and do strange things, but they are not acting unwillingly. Indeed, most people who undergo hypnosis later report that they were not in a trance. Derren Brown's assassin probably knew all along that his participation was for the purposes of entertainment or maybe he really doesn't like Stephen Fry!

where do you stand?

Should horse riding be made illegal?

In 2009, Professor David Nutt, the UK government's chief drug adviser, wrote a provocative editorial for a scientific journal entitled 'Equasy: An overlooked addiction with implications for the current debate on drug harms'. In the article, he highlighted the illogical nature of government drug policy in the UK by comparing the harm of drugs to the risks posed by horse riding in an addiction he called 'equasy', short for 'equine addiction syndrome', a condition characterized by gaining pleasure from horses and being prepared to take the risk of falling off/under the horse.

The UK classifies drugs as A, B, C on the basis of their harmfulness. Ecstasy – a class A drug in the same category as heroin and cocaine – kills around 10–30 individuals each year. However, when you compare the risks between horse riding and taking ecstasy, there is not much difference. You are more likely to come to some form of harm riding a horse (1 in 350 episodes) than taking ecstasy (1 in 10,000 episodes). About 10 people a year are killed horse riding and many more suffer permanent neurological damage. There are also about 100 traffic accidents caused by horse riding. Making riding illegal would completely prevent all these harms and would, in practice, be easy to do.

What about other legal drugs such as alcohol and tobacco? They are treated as regulated foods, and yet 17% (79,700) of all deaths of adults aged 35 and over were estimated to be caused by smoking (HSCIC, 2014), and there were 8,416 alcohol-related deaths in the UK in 2013 (ONS, 2015). Compare these figures to illegal drugs, which account for less than 2,000 UK deaths per year.

If potential harm is the basis for classifying drugs, then shouldn't alcohol and tobacco become class A drugs? Shouldn't ecstasy be reclassified into the least harmful category class C and if not, shouldn't horse riding be made illegal if governments are trying to legislate against harmful activities? These were all legitimate questions posed by Professor Nutt, but apparently not the sort of questions the government wanted to address, which is why he was fired the same year. What do you think? Has the UK got its drug policies based on harmfulness all wrong?

Chapter review

Conscious and unconscious: the mind's eye, open and closed

- Consciousness is a mystery of psychology because other people's minds cannot be perceived directly and the relationship between mind and body is perplexing.
- Consciousness is intentional, unified, selective and transient, and can be viewed as having levels of minimal consciousness, full consciousness and self-consciousness. The contents of the stream of consciousness include current concerns, daydreams and unwanted thoughts.
- Unconscious processes are sometimes understood as expressions of the Freudian dynamic unconscious, but are more commonly seen as processes of the cognitive unconscious that create and influence conscious thoughts and behaviours.

Attention

- Attention is the process whereby we selectively process information. It is linked to consciousness because we are not aware of what we are not attending to.
- Attention can operate at a number of different levels in the stream of processing, occurring either early or late, depending on the nature of the task.
- Selective attention refers to the way our focus of attention can be directed by either internal states or external events.
- Selective attention can be disrupted by damage and disease in different brain regions, which can produce bizarre distortions of conscious experience.

Sleep and dreaming: good night, mind

- The sleep cycle involves a regular pattern of sleep and dreaming that creates altered states of consciousness. Humans progress through stages of NREM and REM sleep throughout the night.
- There are several sleep disorders that influence the quality of sleep and dreams, including insomnia, sleep apnea, somnambulism, narcolepsy, sleep paralysis, nightmares and night terrors.
- Sleep deprivation and dream deprivation are detrimental to psychological effectiveness and physical health.
- The contents of dreams are related to waking life and can be understood by examining the areas of the brain that are activated when people dream. Different theories about why dreams occur and their potential meanings have been proposed. Older views focus on symbolism and the unconscious, whereas more recent accounts approach dreaming as an aspect of normal brain activity.

Drugs and consciousness: artificial inspiration

- Psychoactive drugs influence consciousness and sometimes produce addiction.
- Specific effects on consciousness and behaviour occur with different classes of psychoactive drugs. These classes include depressants, stimulants, narcotics, hallucinogens and marijuana.
- Hallucinogens produce altered sensations and perceptions. Examples include LSD, psilocybin, mescaline, PCP and ketamine.
- Marijuana, the leaves and buds of the hemp plant, produces heightened sensations but impairs memory and motor skills.

Hypnosis: open to suggestion

- Inductions of hypnosis in susceptible people can make them feel that their actions are occurring involuntarily and leading them to follow the hypnotist's suggestions.
- Hypnosis can cause amnesia and lead people to make up memories, but is useful as an analgesic for pain.

Meditation and religious experiences: higher consciousness

- Changes in consciousness away from the normal state may be attained through meditation, yielding short-term relaxation but no measured long-term effects.
- Religious experiences are sometimes associated with brain regions that are also affected by epilepsy.

Key terms

activation-synthesis model (p. 341)
altered states of consciousness (p. 334)
anthropomorphism (p. 315)
attenuation model (p. 328)
Balint's syndrome (p. 332)
behavioural compliance (p. 347)
blindsight (p. 333)
cannabis (p. 346)
Cartesian theatre (p. 312)
change blindness (p. 318)
choice blindness (p. 317)
circadian rhythm (p. 334)
cocktail party phenomenon (p. 319)
cognitive unconscious (p. 326)
daydreaming (p. 323)
dichotic listening (p. 319)
dynamic unconscious (p. 325)
early filter model (p. 328)
electrooculograph (EOG) (p. 336)
full consciousness (p. 320)
hallucinogens (p. 346)
hard problem of consciousness (p. 313)
harm reduction approach (p. 345)
homunculus problem (p. 313)
hypnosis (p. 347)
hypnotic analgesia (p. 349)
immune system (p. 338)
information bottleneck (p. 328)
insomnia (p. 338)
ironic processes of mental control (p. 324)
latent content (p. 341)
load model (p. 329)
manifest content (p. 341)
materialism (p. 314)
meditation (p. 351)
mental control (p. 323)
metabolism (p. 338)
mind–body problem (p. 316)
minimal consciousness (p. 320)
narcolepsy (p. 339)
night terrors (p. 339)
phenomenology (p. 313)
posthypnotic amnesia (p. 349)
problem of other minds (p. 314)
psychoactive drug (p. 344)
qualia (p. 314)
rebound effect of thought suppression (p. 323)
REM (rapid eye movement) sleep (p. 335)
repression (p. 325)
response selection model (p. 328)
selective attention (p. 328)
self-consciousness (p. 321)
sleep apnea (p. 339)
sleep paralysis (p. 339)
somnambulism (p. 339)
subliminal perception (p. 326)
thermoregulation (p. 338)
thought suppression (p. 323)
unilateral visual neglect (p. 331)
vegetative state (p. 343)

Recommended reading

Blackmore, S. (2004) *Consciousness: An Introduction.* New York: Oxford University Press. Blends philosophy, psychology and neuroscience in a clear, enjoyable and colourfully written introduction to the field of consciousness.

Frith, C. (2007) *Making Up the Mind: How the Brain Creates Our Mental World.* Oxford: Blackwell. Frith is one the leading brain-imaging experts who has done more than most to apply this technique to the fascinating conundrum of mental life.

Hobson, A. (1988) *The Dreaming Brain: How the Brain Creates Both the Sense and the Nonsense of Dreams.* New York: Basic Books. Hobson examines the history of dream theories, including psychoanalytic theory, and then provides his own 'activation-synthesis' hypothesis – that dreaming is the brain's way of making sense of its own night-time activations.

Wegner, D. M. (2002) *The Illusion of Conscious Will.* Cambridge, MA: MIT Press. Describes how it is that we come to believe that we consciously will our own actions; along the way examining such anomalies as phantom limbs, Ouija board spelling, spirit possession and hypnosis.

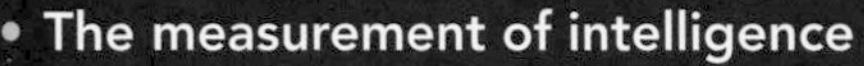

9

Chapter learning objectives

At the end of this chapter you will be able to:

1. Explain the origins of the development of intelligence testing, how it is used and what relationship it has with an individual's outcomes in life.
2. Understand the different models used to conceptualize the structure of intelligence.
3. Understand factors that produce group differences in intelligence.
4. Understand the cognitive processes that are necessary for intelligence.
5. Explain why intelligence is stable over time but absolute intelligence typically changes over the course of a lifetime.

Intelligence

In Scotland, on Wednesday morning, 1 June 1932, 11-year-old Richard D sat at his school desk. He was given a mental test booklet by his teacher. He tried some example questions. The teachers throughout the Scottish nation read out exactly the same instructions to 87,497 other children. Simultaneously, 87,498 children then started answering the questions in an IQ-type examination called the Moray House Test. And, 45 minutes later, a whole nation had been tested, the first and only country ever to do so. This was the Scottish Mental Survey of 1932 (SMS1932).

The questions Richard D answered involved things like reasoning, following instructions, cracking codes, understanding sayings, working with numbers, knowing what words meant, thinking about shapes and so on. There was a mixture of mental tasks, different from his everyday school lessons and school examinations.

Then Richard D and 87,497 other children born in 1921 went back to their normal lessons and got on with the rest of their lives. Richard's family, two parents and six children, lived in a one-bedroom miners' terraced cottage. He left school three years later, at the earliest possible leaving age of 14, to become a miner like his father and brothers. None of the family had any education beyond the most basic. He and the other children in the SMS1932 never knew their IQ scores. They were not used for any educational selection. The data were sent back to Edinburgh and summarized in long-forgotten reports. Richard D, despite his poor background, had an IQ of 120. Such a score might have taken him to university, or even to become a professor.

Sixty-five years later, Ian Deary, psychology professor at Edinburgh University, was working with his friend Professor Lawrence Whalley on a question about the relationship between cardiovascular disease and the decline in mental functions. Professor Whalley wanted to know whether Scottish adults with heart disease were also more likely to experience a decline in cognitive ability. However, to answer that question, Professor

IAN DEARY

Richard Deary, aged 21, who was killed in action in 1942 when his submarine struck a mine in the Mediterranean Sea.

Deary told him he needed the individuals' cognitive performance scores prior to any illness to correct for any later differences. By chance, while thinking over this problem, Professor Deary learned that such data existed in the form of the SMS1932, but for the whole of Scotland. Together, they set out to discover this treasure trove of information in a locked basement room in Edinburgh. Inside each book, they saw neat, copperplate-written lists of the names and IQ test scores of almost every Scottish child born in 1921: the SMS1932. The people whose names they saw would now be in their late seventies if they were still alive. More than half were dead, men more than women. Many men had died fighting in the Second World War. Richard D is thought to have died when his submarine struck a mine in the Mediterranean Sea in 1942. Richard Deary never became a university professor. That fate would fall on the shoulders of his nephew, Ian.

The two professors wondered whether a single number, the score on a test that took place when people were 11 years old, could affect the rest of their lives. They began research programmes to trace people from the SMS1932, alive and dead. They found that the score on the Moray House Test, the summary of the 11-year-olds' efficiency in thinking over those 45 minutes in 1932, had astonishing properties (Deary et al., 2004). When they tested the same people again at almost 80 years old, the rank order of scores was similar: people at the bottom, middle and top still tended to be there. The test score was associated with how long people lived, whether they developed lung cancer, a psychiatric illness or dementia. People who had different scores on the test at age 11 went on to live different lives, as they described in their book, *A Lifetime of Intelligence* (Deary et al., 2009).

William Wordsworth, 19th-century English poet, wrote 'The child is father of the man' to convey the notion that how we are when we are young shapes how we will develop into an adult. It would seem that findings from the 1932 Scottish survey and follow-up six decades later indicate that Wordsworth was correct. But how can performance on a test as a child predict the life someone will lead over the next 65 years? One answer is that by 11 years of age, we are already in possession of a brain that generates thinking and understanding to influence how we will reason for the rest of our lives. Circumstances and life events may vary, but the way we interpret and deal with different experiences may already be largely constrained by the way we think.

Cognitive psychology attempts to discover the architecture of human cognition, describing and explaining what thinking processes we share as a species – what makes humans intelligent. But individuals vary. Some individuals are cleverer than others. Whereas cognitive psychology addresses the intelligence of the human mind, an **individual differences approach**, *the assessment and evaluation of individual psychological abilities*, studies variance among people's minds and why people differ in intelligence. To assess these differences in human mental ability, scientists adopt the statistical methodology of **psychometrics** – *the science of measuring mental capacities and processes*. The study of psychometric intelligence differences addresses the following topics:

- It asks about the nature and number of abilities on which humans show differences.
- It composes tests to measure cognitive differences.
- It seeks the origins of mental ability differences, including social, cognitive and biological causes.
- It studies whether cognitive ability tests predict differences in real-life attainments.

This chapter is about individual differences in cognitive abilities as measured by psychometric tests, but it is not about the tests per se. It is about the nature of people's differences in mental capabilities. It is about what causes these differences and whether they matter.

INDIVIDUAL DIFFERENCES APPROACH The assessment and evaluation of individual psychological abilities.

PSYCHOMETRICS The science of measuring mental capacities and processes.

The measurement of intelligence

People recognized that humans were different in their thinking powers before psychometric tests were invented to measure them. Plato (*c.* 428–347 BC) wrote in *The Republic*, in the form of a legend, that: those whose natures were fashioned of gold were made to rule; those of silver were made to be auxiliaries; and those formed from brass or iron were made to be husbandmen and craftsmen. He suggested that prospective rulers should be tried by many tests for their fitness to rule. Today, we have techniques to measure these individual differences.

In this section, we describe some of the pioneers who studied differences in human ability and developed a new science to measure them. We describe the two major developments from which all of today's research into mental ability differences arose. The first is the discovery that people who are good at one mental skill tend to be good at others too, and the century of debate it caused. The second is the invention of the first psychometric intelligence test, and the worldwide industry it spawned.

The study of mental ability differences begins

The scientific study of human cognitive ability differences began late in the 19th century with the emergence of psychology as a new discipline, as we saw in Chapter 1. The measurement of mental function gained credibility following the developments in experimental and statistical approaches and soon researchers were looking at individual differences in intelligence.

Galton and Spearman: the discovery of '*g*'

Sir Francis Galton (1822–1911), a half-cousin of Charles Darwin, was an English gentleman with a large private income, who contributed to the theory, testing and statistical analysis of mental abilities. Although he is widely acknowledged to have contributed much to this area, his intellectual biography devoted only 18 out of 350 pages to his studies in psychology (Gillham, 2001). This is because Galton contributed to so many areas of science. In his early career, he was a medical student, an African explorer, a travel writer and an influential and leading geographer. He also contributed to the field of meteorology, pioneering the popular weather map (still published in newspapers today) and documenting anticyclonic weather systems for the first time. In his later career, he turned to the biological sciences, especially genetics. He made basic contributions to modern **biometrics** – *the application of statistics to biological phenomena*. He devised the correlation coefficient (discussed in Chapter 2). He made contributions to the science of fingerprinting. His psychological contributions included the study of memory, devising the self-report questionnaire, and suggesting the twin study to examine genetic influences.

GAVAN TREDOUX HTTP://GALTON.ORG

Sir Francis Galton (1822–1911) studied the physical and psychological traits that appeared to run in families. In his book *Hereditary Genius*, he concluded that intelligence was largely inherited.

Galton's studies of mental ability included family-based studies of eminence, most notably men who had achieved success in society, published in his book *Hereditary Genius* (1869). He conceptualized general mental ability as a largely heritable trait with, like some physical traits, a normal distribution (discussed in Chapter 2) in the population. With no tests of mental ability then available, Galton relied on the human pedigrees of eminence including university and military examination results. Almost 20 years later he gathered some ability data himself (Gillham, 2001). He did careful genealogical studies of eminent families, and he collected measurements that ranged from head size to the ability to discriminate tones from over 12,000 people. Many years after Galton's death, these data were still being analysed (Johnson et al., 1985).

BIOMETRICS The application of statistics to biological phenomena.

Galton was a prolific and disparate genius, providing many ideas for those who would later collect data on human ability. In his writings, there is an emphasis on two aspects of mental ability differences: their origins, and their applications (Galton, 1883). These separate issues are important, because they define the contributions of those who would follow in his footsteps to pursue the science of mental ability differences.

Most notable to follow Galton was Charles Spearman (1863–1945), an English army officer who left the Royal Engineers aged 34 to take his PhD with Wundt in Germany. He made three major contributions to the study of cognitive ability differences:

1 He invented a technique known as **factor analysis** – *a statistical technique that explains a large number of correlations in terms of a small number of underlying factors* (Bartholomew, 1995).
2 He provided evidence that differences in the ability to make fine sensory discriminations are part of the foundation of differences in higher cognitive functions.
3 He proposed that intelligence had a core general component shared by all tasks with specific aptitudes on different measures.

FACTOR ANALYSIS A statistical technique that explains a large number of correlations in terms of a small number of underlying factors.

Spearman's two-factor theory proposed that intelligence was generated by a *general cognitive factor*, which he called '*g*' and specific factors he called '*s*'. His discovery of general intelligence, or the *g* factor, occurred in 1904 after assessing groups of school children on tests of sensory acuity (visual, auditory and tactile) and related these to their scores on school subjects and teachers' estimates of their intellectual ability. **TABLE 9.1** illustrates the pattern for school children's scores in classroom tests. He described this pattern of association as a 'positive manifold' because all the measures were positively related to each other. Note that the correlations decrease as they progress down the columns and from left to right along the rows: this indicated to Spearman (1904) that a single factor underlies individual differences in performance.

TABLE 9.1 Spearman's 'positive manifold' of correlations among school subjects

	Classics	French	English	Maths	Pitch	Music
Classics	–					
French	0.83	–				
English	0.78	0.67	–			
Maths	0.70	0.67	0.64	–		
Pitch	0.66	0.65	0.54	0.45	–	
Music	0.63	0.57	0.51	0.51	0.40	–

Spearman's research revealed two things:

1. He found most of these measures were indeed *positively* correlated. Children who scored high on one measure, for example distinguishing the musical note C sharp from D, tended to score high on the other measures, for example solving algebraic equations. Some psychologists have called this finding 'the most replicated result in all of psychology' (Deary, 2000, p. 6).
2. Although different measures were positively correlated, they were not *perfectly* correlated. The child who had the highest score on one measure didn't necessarily have the highest score on *every* measure.

TWO-FACTOR THEORY OF INTELLIGENCE Spearman's theory suggesting that every task requires a combination of a general ability (*g*) and skills that are specific to the task (s) and shared with no other.

Spearman combined these two facts into a **two-factor theory of intelligence**, which purposed that *every task requires a combination of a general ability* (g) *and skills that are specific to the task* (s) *and shared with no other* (see **FIGURE 9.1**). In Spearman's own words:

> Under certain conditions the score of a person at a mental test can be divided into two factors, one of which is always the same in all tests, whereas the other varies from one test to another; the former is called the general factor or G, while the other is called the specific factor. This then is what the G term means, a score-factor and nothing more. (Deary et al., 2008, p. 163)

Spearman reckoned that the number of these specific abilities was very large. It is not correct to associate Spearman with an emphasis solely on general ability (*g*), because he also thought that there were individual differences in these more specific mental abilities. However, it is Spearman's *g* that has proved among the most durable and controversial discoveries in psychology. It still attracts much attention and affirmation a century after it was first conceived (Sternberg and Grigorenko, 2002).

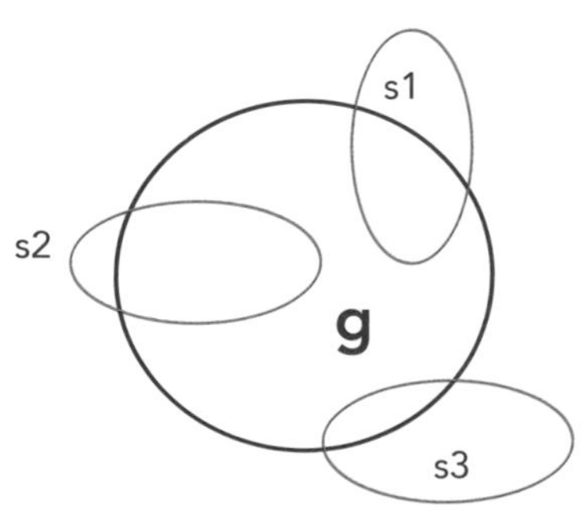

FIGURE 9.1 Spearman's two-factor theory of intelligence The ovals are examples of three hypothetical mental tests. Note how each test draws upon *g* (some more than others) and a specific ability. The number of specific abilities is potentially very large.

Binet and the first intelligence test

Around the end of the 19th century, other European pioneers of individual differences began to appear. France had instituted a sweeping set of education reforms that made a primary school education available to children of every social class, and suddenly French classrooms were filled with a heterogeneous mix of children who differed dramatically in their readiness to learn. The French government called on Alfred Binet and Theodore Simon to develop a test that would allow educators to develop remedial programmes for those children who lagged behind their peers. Binet (1909) wrote: 'Before these children could be educated, they had to be selected. How could this be done?'

Binet and Simon worried that if teachers were allowed to do the selecting, the remedial classrooms would be filled with poor children, and if parents were allowed to do the selecting, the remedial classrooms would be empty. So they set out to develop an objective test that would provide an unbiased measure of a child's ability. They began, sensibly enough, by looking for tasks that the best students in a class could perform and the worst students could not – in other words, tasks that could distinguish the best and worst students in a current class and could be used to predict a future child's success in school. The tasks they tried included solving logic problems, remembering words, copying pictures, distinguishing edible and inedible foods, making rhymes, and answering questions such as: 'When anyone has offended you and asks you to excuse him, what ought you to do?' Binet and Simon settled on 30 of these tasks and assembled them into a test they claimed could measure a child's 'natural intelligence'. What did they mean by that phrase?

> We here separate natural intelligence and instruction ... by disregarding, insofar as possible, the degree of instruction which the subject possesses ... We give him nothing to read, nothing to write, and submit him to no test in which he might succeed by means of rote learning. In fact, we do not even notice his inability to read if a case occurs. It is simply the level of his natural intelligence that is taken into account. (Binet, 1905, p. 42)

Binet and Simon designed their test to measure a child's *aptitude* for learning independent of the child's prior educational *achievement*, and it was in this sense that they called theirs a test of 'natural intelligence'. They suggested that teachers could use their test to estimate a child's 'mental level' simply by computing the average test score of children in different age groups and then finding the age group whose average test score was most like that of the child's. For example, a child who was 10 years old but whose score was about the same as the score of the average 8-year-old was considered to have the mental level of an 8-year-old and thus in need of remedial education.

German psychologist William Stern (1914) suggested that this mental level could be thought of as a child's *mental age* and that the best way to determine whether a child was developing normally was to examine the ratio of the child's mental age to the child's physical age. American psychologist Lewis Terman (1916) formalized this comparison with the intelligence quotient or **ratio IQ** – *a statistic obtained by dividing a person's mental age by the person's physical age and then multiplying the quotient by 100.* Thus, a 10-year-old child whose test score was about the same as the average 10-year-old child's test score would have a ratio IQ of 100 because (10/10) × 100 = 100. But a 10-year-old child whose test score was about the same as the average 8-year-old child's test score would have a ratio IQ of 80 because (8/10) × 100 = 80.

RATIO IQ A statistic obtained by dividing a person's mental age by the person's physical age and then multiplying the quotient by 100 (see deviation IQ).

The ratio of a person's mental and physical ages seems like a handy way to talk about their intelligence, until you stop and think about it. For example, a 6-year-old who performs like the average 12-year-old will have a ratio IQ of 200. That makes a certain amount of sense because a 6-year-old who can do algebra is pretty darn smart. But a 30-year-old who performs like the average 60-year-old will also have a ratio IQ of 200. That doesn't make much sense because it means that a perfectly ordinary 30-year-old need only maintain their mental abilities for a few decades to be labelled a genius.

As a result of anomalies such as this, researchers devised a new measure called the **deviation IQ** – *a statistic obtained by dividing a person's test score by the average test score of people in the same age group and then multiplying the quotient by 100.* According to this formula, a person who scored the same as the average person their age would have a deviation IQ of 100. The good thing about the deviation IQ is that a 30-year-old cannot become a genius simply by getting older. The bad thing about the deviation IQ is that it does not allow comparisons between people of different ages. A 5-year-old and a 65-year-old might both have a deviation IQ of 120 because they both outscored their peers, but this does not mean that they are equally intelligent. To solve this problem, modern researchers compute the ratio IQ for children and the deviation IQ for adults. **FIGURE 9.2** shows the percentage of people who typically score at each level of IQ on a standard intelligence test.

DEVIATION IQ A statistic obtained by dividing a person's test score by the average test score of people in the same age group and then multiplying the quotient by 100 (see ratio IQ).

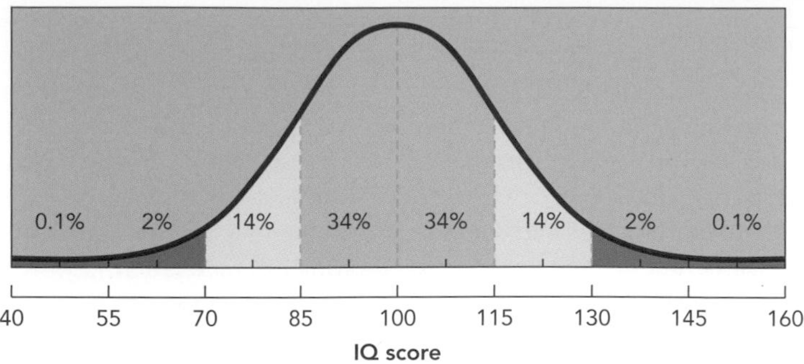

FIGURE **9.2 The normal curve of intelligence** Deviation IQ scores produce a normal bell curve. This chart shows the percentage of people who score in each range of IQ.

The growth of an industry

Few things are more dangerous than a man with a mission. In the 1920s, US psychologist Henry Goddard took Binet's test from Continental Europe, and had it and Binet's papers translated (Zenderland, 1998). Goddard evangelized about the intelligence tests, and administered them to arriving immigrants at Ellis Island, concluding that the overwhelming majority of Jews, Hungarians, Italians and Russians were 'feebleminded'. Goddard also used his tests to identify feebleminded American families, who, he claimed, were largely responsible for the nation's social problems, and suggested that the government should segregate them in isolated colonies and 'take away from these people the power of procreation' (Goddard, 1913, p. 107). The US subsequently passed laws restricting the immigration of people from Southern and Eastern Europe, and 27 states passed laws requiring the sterilization of 'defectives'. In 1917, a committee that included Goddard, Robert Yerkes and Louis Terman developed multiple-choice mental tests to examine US army recruits during the First World War (Fancher, 1987). By 1919, they had tested over 1.7 million people, and about 2.5 million were tested eventually.

The failure of practical intelligence

In 1993, police charged Vernon Edsel Brooks of Raleigh, North Carolina with robbing a Radio Shack. Although Brooks had been smart enough to take the surveillance camera with him when he fled, he neglected to take the recorder to which it was attached.

From Goddard's day to our own, intelligence tests have been used to rationalize prejudice and legitimate discrimination against people of different races, religions and nationalities, and while intelligence testing has achieved many notable successes, its history is marred by more than its fair share of fraud and disgrace (Chorover, 1980; Lewontin et al., 1984). The fact that intelligence tests have occasionally been used to further detestable ends is especially ironic because they were originally developed to help the poorest school children prosper, learn and grow.

The psychometric mental testing that started with Binet and Simon's attempt to help identify at-risk French children back in 1905 has blossomed into a whole psychometric industry that exists today to test infants, children, adults, older people, people with learning difficulties and special clinical groups. Some tests are interview based, others are given in groups, some are paper and pencil and many are now computerized. They are used by the military, clinicians and educators, and most large companies invest in a human resource department that will evaluate their workforce and potential employees using psychometric measures. You will have probably taken at least one psychometric measure yourself.

Is a Rubik's cube an intelligence test? Intelligence is a hypothetical property that makes possible consequential behaviour such as school achievement and job performance, and people who can perform such behaviours can often solve puzzles like this one.

The logic of intelligence testing

Binet and Simon's test did a good job of predicting a child's performance in school, and intelligence is almost certainly one of the factors that contributes to that performance. But surely there are others. Affability, motivation, intact hearing, doting parents – all seem likely to influence a child's scholastic performance. Binet and Simon's test identified students who were likely to perform poorly in school, but was it a test of intelligence?

As you learned in Chapter 2, psychological research typically involves generating an operational definition of a hypothetical property that one wishes to measure. For instance, if we wanted to study aggressiveness in children, we might operationally define it as 'shoving others'. We might then measure aggressiveness by following a small group of children around for a week and noting how many times they shoved. Of course, that kind of measurement takes such a long time that it wouldn't be practical to do with a large group of children, so instead we might develop a set of questions ('Do you believe that most people need a good kick in the shins from time to time?') or a set of tasks ('How quickly can you decapitate this doll?') that are easy to administer and the answers to which are known to be highly correlated with shoving.

We could then easily give this set of questions and tasks – which we could call a *test* – to a large group of children. But would it be an 'aggressiveness test'? Strictly speaking, no. It would be a measure of *responses* ('Yes, I think most people do need a good kick in the shins from time to time') that are known to be correlated with *consequential behaviours* (shoving) that are thought to be correlated with a *hypothetical property* (aggressiveness). Our test would be quite useful for identifying bullies before they started shoving their peers, but it would not be a test of aggressiveness, because the correlation between the responses and the consequential behaviours would be imperfect, for example some children will say that others need a good kick in the shins but then not actually do it, and the correlation between the consequential behaviours and the property would be imperfect too, for example some children may shove because they are nearsighted or clumsy.

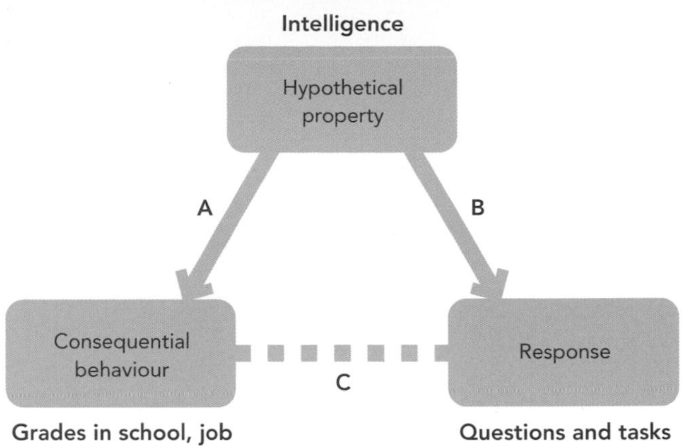

FIGURE 9.3 The logic of intelligence testing An intelligence test is a set of questions and tasks that elicit responses. These responses are correlated with numerous consequential behaviours (path C), presumably because the hypothetical property called 'intelligence' causes the responses (path B) and the consequential behaviours (path A).

What's true of aggressiveness tests is also true of intelligence tests. **FIGURE 9.3** illustrates the distinction between *responses*, *consequential behaviours* and *hypothetical properties* and shows how an intelligence test is built. We begin with the assumption that a hypothetical property called 'intelligence' enables people to perform a wide variety of consequential behaviours such as getting good grades in school, becoming a group leader, earning a large income, finding the best route to the gym, or inventing a greaseless kebab. Measuring how well people perform each of these consequential behaviours would, of course, be highly impractical, so instead we devise an easily administered set of tasks, for example a geometric puzzle, and questions, for example '*Butterfly* is to *caterpillar* as *woman* is to ...', whose performance is known to be correlated with those behaviours. Now, instead of measuring the consequential behaviours, which is difficult to do, we can simply give people our test, which is easy to do. We could certainly call this 'an intelligence test', as long as we understood that what we mean by that phrase is 'a measurement of responses that are imperfectly correlated with consequential behaviours that are imperfectly correlated with intelligence'. In other words, intelligence tests do not 'measure' intelligence in the same way that thermometers measure temperature. Rather, they measure the ability to answer questions and perform tasks that are highly correlated with the ability to get good grades, solve real-world problems and so on.

Finding such questions and tasks isn't easy, and since Binet and Simon's day, psychologists have worked hard to construct intelligence tests that can predict a person's ability to perform the consequential behaviours that intelligence should make possible. Today, the most widely used intelligence tests are the *Stanford-Binet* (a test based on Binet and Simon's original test but modified and updated many times, most notably by Lewis Terman and his colleagues at Stanford University) and the *WAIS* (the Wechsler Adult Intelligence Scale). Both tests require respondents to answer a variety of questions and solve a variety of problems. For example, the WAIS's 13 subtests involve seeing similarities and differences, drawing inferences, working out and applying rules, remembering and manipulating material, constructing shapes, articulating the meaning of words, recalling general knowledge, explaining practical actions in everyday life, working with numbers, attending to details and so on. Only 3 of the 13 tests require the examinee to write anything down, and none requires writing words. Some sample problems are shown in **TABLE 9.2**.

SCIENCE MUSEUM/SSPL

A 1937 version of an intelligence testing kit used to carry out the Stanford-Binet intelligence test, including flash cards and props.

The consequences of intelligence testing

Psychometric intelligence tests were a near-instant, worldwide success after their invention, because they were perceived as being useful. They had predictive validity (discussed in Chapter 2). Specifically, psychometric intelligence test scores have been found to predict education, work and health outcomes.

TABLE 9.2 **The Wechsler Adult Intelligence Scale III**

WAIS-III subtest	Mental activity assessed
Vocabulary	The test taker is asked to tell the examiner what certain words mean. For example, chair (easy), hesitant (medium), presumptuous (hard). There are 33 words in all
Similarities	The test taker says what two words have in common. For example: In what way are an apple and a pear alike? In what way are a painting and a symphony alike? There are 19 such questions
Information	There are 28 general knowledge questions. These cover people, places and events. For example: How many days are in a week? What is the capital of France? Name three oceans. Who wrote *The Inferno?*
Comprehension	These are questions about everyday life problems, aspects of society, and proverbs. For example: Tell me some reasons why we put food in a refrigerator. Why do people require driving licences? What does it mean to say 'a bird in the hand is worth two in the bush'?
Picture completion	The test taker is asked to spot the missing element in a series of more than 20 colour drawings. For example: spokes might be missing from one wheel in a picture of a bicycle; in a picture of a person, the person's jacket could be missing a buttonhole
Block design	The test taker is shown two-dimensional patterns made up of red and white squares and triangles. They have to reproduce these patterns using cubes with red and white faces
Matrix reasoning	The test taker is asked to add a missing element to a pattern so that it progresses logically
Picture arrangement	The test taker is given a series of cartoon drawings and asked to put them in an order that tells a logical story
Arithmetic	The test taker attempts to solve 20 mental arithmetic problems, progressing from easy to difficult ones
Digit span	The test taker repeats a sequence of numbers to the examiner. Sequences run from two to nine numbers in length. In the second part of this test, the sequences must be repeated in reverse order. An easy example is to repeat 3-7-4. A harder one is 3-9-1-7-4-5-3-9
Letter-number sequencing	The examiner reads a series of alternate letters and numbers. The test taker is asked to repeat them, putting the numbers first and in numerical order, followed by the letters in alphabetical order. For example, they would repeat W-4-G-8-L-3 as 3-4-8-G-L-W
Digit symbol coding	The test taker writes down the number that corresponds to a code for a given symbol, for example a cross, a circle and an upside-down T, and does as many as they can in 90 seconds
Symbol search	The test taker indicates whether one of a pair of abstract symbols is contained in a list of abstract symbols. There are many of these lists, and the test taker does as many as they can in two minutes

Psychometric intelligence and education

Binet and Simon would be pleased to know that intelligence tests predict school performance better than they predict just about anything else. The correlation between a person's score on a standard intelligence test and their academic performance is roughly $r = 0.5$ across a wide range of people and situations.

An especially large and representative study of mental ability and educational outcomes was conducted in the UK (Smith et al., 2001). About 24,000 students in 176 schools sat the Cognitive Abilities Test (CAT), mostly on entry to secondary school at age 11–12 years. Four years later, the students' scores on the General Certificate of Secondary Education (GCSE) national public examinations were recorded. There were 16 different academic subjects, each with an eight-point scale. The correlation between the CAT total score (measuring *g*) and the total GCSE performance score (an overall record of academic achievement) was 0.74. Even the more practical subjects, such as art and design, creative arts and physical education, had correlations around or above 0.5 with *g* (CAT total) scores recorded four years earlier.

Psychometric intelligence and work

An intelligence test score is also the best predictor of the number of years of education an individual will receive, which is, in part, why these scores also predict a person's occupational status and income. For example, a person's score on an intelligence test taken in early adulthood correlates about $r = 0.4$ with the person's later occupational status (Jencks, 1979). One study of brothers found that the brother who exceeded his sibling by 15 IQ points had, on average, about 17% greater annual earnings. FIGURE 9.4 shows the average weekly income of people who have equal amounts of education but different intelligence test scores. There is also a strong correlation between the average intelligence score of a nation and its overall economic status (Lynn and Vanhanen, 2002). Clearly, it pays to be clever.

In the US where psychometric measures such as the Scholastic Aptitude Test (SAT) or the Graduate Record Exam (GRE) are routinely used as part of the university entrance requirement, some psychologists have pointed out that prestigious occupations with high salaries typically require university degrees and that universities typically use test scores as one of their criteria for admission, which means that intelligence test scores may *predict* occupational success in part because they *influence* it. Although this is probably true, it is also true that intelligence test scores predict outcomes they cannot possibly influence, such as how likely teenagers are to commit crimes and how long adults will live, neither of which is determined by an admissions committee (Gottfredson and Deary, 2004; Whalley and Deary, 2001).

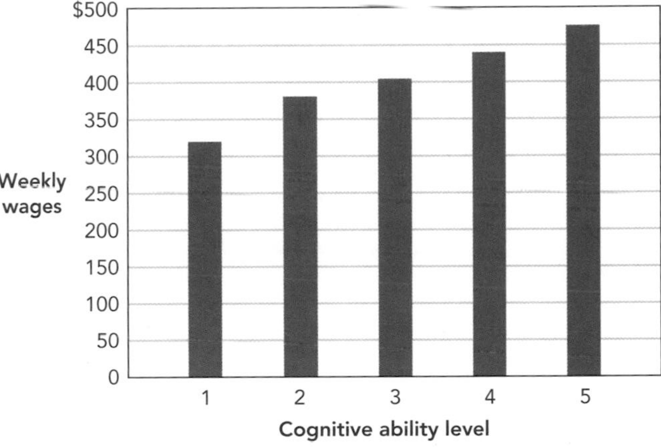

FIGURE **9.4 Income and intelligence** When the amount of education is held constant, people's cognitive abilities still predict their incomes (Ceci and Williams, 1997).

Indeed, a reanalysis of the data from thousands of studies revealed that intelligence test scores are among the best predictors of how well employees perform in their jobs (Hunter and Hunter, 1984), and job performance correlates more highly with intelligence ($r = 0.53$) than with factors such as performance during a job interview ($r = 0.14$) or education ($r = 0.10$). The conclusion to be drawn from almost a century of research on the topic is that 'for hiring employees without previous experience in the job, the most valid measure of future performance and learning is general mental ability' (Schmidt and Hunter, 1998, p. 252). In the US where these tests are such good predictors of job performance, the cost of *not* using them would equal total corporate profits, or 20% of the federal budget (Hunter and Hunter, 1984). With such financial incentives and a globalizing economy, it is ironic that the intelligence testing industry is spreading back from over the Atlantic to its birthplace in Europe.

Intelligence scores also do a reasonably good job of predicting a wide variety of behaviours that most of us think of as 'clever' (see *the real world* box). One study identified 320 people with extremely high intelligence test scores at age 13 and followed them for 10 years (Lubinski et al., 2001). Not only were they 50 times more likely than the general population to gain graduate degrees and 500 times more likely than the general population to obtain a perfect GRE score, but also, at a time when fewer than a quarter of their peers had completed an undergraduate degree, they had already published scientific studies in peer-reviewed journals and stories in leading literary magazines, obtained prestigious scholastic fellowships, written operas, developed successful commercial products and obtained patents.

Psychometric intelligence and health

But intelligence scores don't just predict success in academia and work. When those two professors were rooting around in that Edinburgh basement looking for the SMS1932 data, they were pursuing a question in **epidemiology** – *the scientific examination of factors that contribute to disease.* Epidemiologists have repeatedly demonstrated that a variety of diseases are linked to social class and education, which in turn are related to intelligence. Different levels of intelligence represent degrees of risk. As we saw in the 1932 Scottish study at the beginning of this chapter, cognitive ability measured at age 11 was a strong predictor of whether the individual would be alive at 76 years of age. The

EPIDEMIOLOGY The scientific examination of factors that contribute to disease.

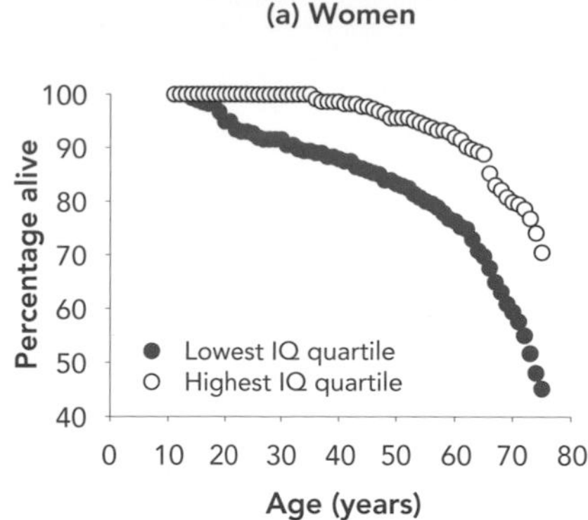

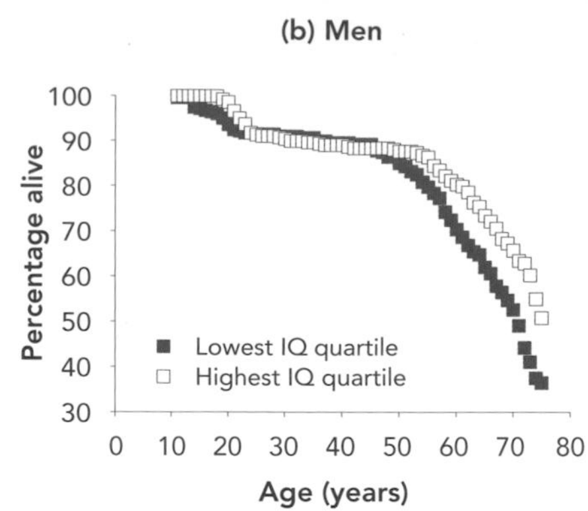

FIGURE 9.5 Longevity of women and men tested in the 1932 Scottish Mental Survey The percentage of people alive at different ages with respect to their score on the Moray House Test at age 11 as tested in the Scottish Mental Survey of 1932. (a) Note how, from early in life, women in the top quarter of IQ scores survive in greater proportions than women in the lower quarter of IQ scores. (b) Note the different pattern from women. During the years of the Second World War, men in the top quarter of IQ scores die in greater numbers than low IQ men. However, by age 60 or so, men in the top quarter of IQ scores are surviving in greater numbers.

mean chances of being alive when the IQ score was 15 points (1 standard deviation) below the group average was 71% for women and 83% for men (see **FIGURE 9.5**). The lesser effect of mental ability on longevity for men was because, during the Second World War, the men killed in military service had higher mean IQs than the general population. Further follow-up studies with the Scottish Mental Survey's participants found that lower IQ at age 11 was related to an increased chance of developing and dying from lung cancer (Deary et al., 2003) and cardiovascular diseases (Hart et al., 2005), and suffering psychiatric illness (Walker et al., 2002); associations that do not appear to be substantially caused by the confounding influence of social class (Hart et al., 2005).

Intelligence scores predict consequential outcomes in education, work and health and this is reflected in many of the behaviours that we would expect intelligent people to perform throughout their lives (see **FIGURE 9.6**). Unfortunately, those with the lower intelligence test scores are disproportionately represented in the underclass of poverty and unemployment. However, these consequential outcomes are in themselves arguably part of a self-fulfilling prophecy. What is the causal link between performance on psychometric tests and life outcomes? As we shall see, genes and the environment contribute to intelligence but understanding the causal mechanism and whether it can be manipulated by intervention is still a major controversial issue.

Moreover, there is evidence that intelligence test scores predict basic responses that cannot possibly be influenced by the scores themselves. For instance, when people are briefly exposed to a pair of vertical lines and are asked to determine which is longer,

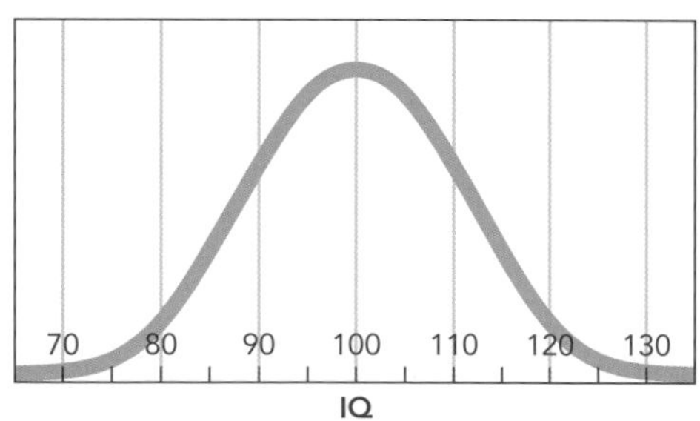

Population percentages

Total population distribution	5	20	50	20	5
Out of labour force more than one month out of year (men)	22	19	15	14	10
Unemployed more than one month out of year (men)	12	10	7	7	2
Divorced in five years	21	22	23	15	9
Had children outside marriage (women)	32	17	8	4	2
Lives in poverty	30	16	6	3	2
Ever incarcerated (men)	7	7	3	1	0
Chronic welfare recipient (mothers)	31	17	8	2	0
Secondary school dropout	55	35	6	0.4	0

FIGURE 9.6 Life outcomes and intelligence People with lower intelligence test scores typically have poorer life outcomes. This chart shows the percentage of people at different levels of IQ who experience the negative life outcomes listed on the left.

people with high intelligence test scores have considerably shorter 'inspection times', which is defined as the minimum duration of exposure necessary to get the answer right (Deary and Stough, 1996; Grudnick and Kranzler, 2001; Nettleback and Lally, 1976). The same is true when people attempt to distinguish between colours or between tones (Acton and Schroeder, 2001). People with high intelligence test scores also have faster and less variable reaction times to almost any kind of stimulus (Deary et al., 2001).

In summary, early intelligence tests were originally designed to predict a child's scholastic performance but were eventually used to calculate an intelligence quotient, either as a ratio of the person's mental to physical age, or as a deviation of the person's test score from the average score of their peers. Intelligence is a hypothetical property that cannot be directly measured, so intelligence tests measure responses (to questions and on tasks) that are known to be correlated with consequential behaviours that are thought to be made possible by intelligence. These consequential behaviours include academic performance, job performance, health and wealth, all of which are enhanced by intelligence.

the real world

Look smart

Your interview is in 30 minutes. You've checked your hair twice, eaten your weight in breath mints, combed your CV for typos, and rehearsed your answers to all the standard questions. Now you have to dazzle them with your intelligence, whether you've got it or not. Because intelligence is one of the most valued of all human traits, we are often in the business of trying to make others think we're smart regardless of whether that's true. So we make clever jokes and drop the names of some of the longer books we've read in the hope that prospective employers, prospective dates, prospective customers and prospective in-laws will be appropriately impressed.

But are we doing the right things, and if so, are we getting the credit we deserve? Research shows that ordinary people are, in fact, reasonably good judges of other people's intelligence (Borkenau and Liebler, 1995). For example, observers can look at a pair of photographs and reliably determine which of the two people in them is smarter (Zebrowitz et al., 2002). When observers watch one-minute videos of different people engaged in social interactions, they can accurately estimate which person has the highest IQ, even if they see the videos without sound (Murphy et al., 2003b).

People base their judgements of intelligence on a wide range of cues, from physical features (being tall and attractive) to dress (being well groomed and wearing glasses) to behaviour (walking and talking quickly). Yet none of these cues is a reliable indicator of a person's intelligence. The reason why people are such good judges of intelligence is that in addition to all these useless cues, they also take into account one very useful cue: eye gaze. As it turns out, intelligent people hold the gaze of their conversation partners when they are speaking and when they are listening, and observers know this, which is what enables them to accurately estimate a person's intelligence despite their mythical beliefs about the informational value of spectacles and ties (Murphy et al., 2003b). All this is especially true when the observers are women, who tend to be better judges of intelligence, and the people being observed are men, whose intelligence tends to be easier to judge.

The bottom line? Breath mints are fine and a little gel on the cowlick certainly can't hurt, but when you get to the interview, don't forget to stare.

The nature of intelligence: general or specific?

Are intelligent people generally good at all things or are they more likely to have specific abilities? This question is at the heart of cognitive psychology. What is the architecture of the mind? Is it best characterized as one big problem solver or is it best thought of as a collection of specialized abilities? The science of intelligence has grappled with this question for more than 100 years. We all know that each of us excel at some abilities and not others, so the answer might seem trivially obvious. But as we have seen, IQ test scores do predict consequential behaviours that hint at the existence of a hypothetical property called 'intelligence'. But is there really such a property, or is intelligence just a meaningless abstraction?

The architecture of intelligence

Spearman's discovery of the general factor in human mental abilities was the spur for many researchers who suggested theories of mental ability differences that either denied *g*'s existence or tried to elaborate on it in some way. For example, Louis Thurstone (1938) noticed that while scores on most tests were indeed positively correlated, scores on verbal tests were more highly correlated with scores on other verbal tests than they were with scores on perceptual tests. **TABLE 9.3** illustrates this issue with modern data, using four subtests from the standardization sample of a recent version of the WAIS. All the correlations are positive and relatively strong. Note the higher correlations between tests of the same mental ability domain.

In contrast to Spearman, Louis Thurstone (1887–1955) believed that people had several primary mental abilities and not a single ability called general intelligence.

COURTESY THE L. L. THURSTONE PSYCHOMETRIC LABORATORY, UNIVERSITY OF NORTH CAROLINA AT CHAPEL HILL

TABLE 9.3 Correlations among WAIS subtests, illustrating group factors in human ability differences

	Information (verbal)	Vocabulary (verbal)	Block design (spatial)	Object assembly (spatial)
Information (verbal)	–			
Vocabulary (verbal)	0.83	–		
Block design (spatial)	0.47	0.47	–	
Object assembly (spatial)	0.49	0.49	0.69	–

However, if Spearman's strict hierarchy of correlations was correct, it should be possible to arrange the matrix such that the correlations formed a specific pattern: they should be able to be arranged so that they decrease in size as they go down the columns and across the rows from left to right. Instead, there are strong correlations between the two verbal tests and the two spatial tests. They cannot be arranged in Spearman's strict hierarchy. This accords with common sense. We are aware of a pattern of cognitive strengths and relative weaknesses in individuals. Some of us are good at crosswords and word games, while others are better at mental arithmetic and jigsaw puzzles.

Thurstone took this 'clustering of correlations' to mean that there was actually no such thing as *g*, instead there were a few stable and independent mental abilities such as perceptual ability, verbal ability and numerical ability, which he called the *primary mental abilities*. These primary mental abilities were neither general like *g*, for example a person might have strong verbal abilities and weak numerical abilities, nor specific like Spearman's concept of *s*, for example a person who had strong verbal abilities tended to speak and read well. In essence, Thurstone argued that just as we have games called football and rugby but no game called sport, so we have abilities such as verbal ability and perceptual ability but no general ability called intelligence. **TABLE 9.4** shows the primary mental abilities that Thurstone identified.

TABLE 9.4 Thurstone's primary mental abilities

Primary mental ability	Description
Word fluency	Ability to solve anagrams and to find rhymes, etc.
Verbal comprehension	Ability to understand words and sentences
Number	Ability to make mental and other numerical computations
Space	Ability to visualize a complex shape in various orientations
Memory	Ability to recall verbal material, learn pairs of unrelated words, etc.
Perceptual speed	Ability to detect visual details quickly
Reasoning	Ability to induce a general rule from a few instances

The debate among Spearman, Thurstone and other mathematical giants continued throughout most of the 20th century as psychologists hotly argued about the existence of *g*. But in the 1980s, a new mathematical technique called *confirmatory factor analysis* brought the debate to a quiet close by revealing that Spearman and Thurstone had both been right in their own way. Specifically, this new technique showed that the correlations between scores on different mental ability tests are best described by a three-level hierarchy (see **FIGURE 9.7**), with a *general factor* (like Spearman's *g*) at the top, *specific factors* (like Spearman's *s*) at the bottom, and a set of factors called *group factors* (like Thurstone's *primary mental abilities*) in the middle (Gustafsson, 1984). A reanalysis of massive amounts of data collected over 60 years from more than 130,000 healthy adults, school children, infants, university students, people with learning disabilities and people with mental and physical illnesses has shown that almost every study done over the past half-century results in a three-level hierarchy of this kind (Carroll, 1993). This hierarchy suggests that people have a general ability called intelligence, which is made up of a small set of independent subabilities, which are made up of a large set of specific abilities that are unique to particular tasks. Although this resolution to 100 years of disagreement is not particularly exciting, it has the compensatory benefit of being true.

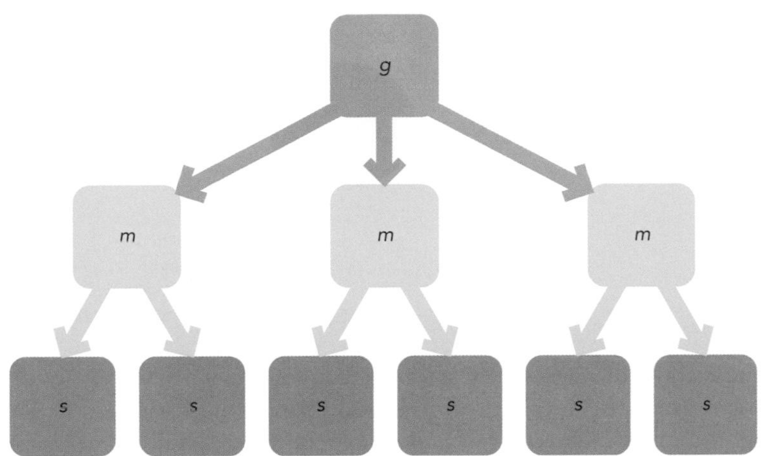

FIGURE **9.7** **A three-level hierarchy** Most intelligence test data are best described by a three-level hierarchy, with general intelligence (*g*) at the top, specific abilities (*s*) at the bottom, and a small number of middle-level abilities (*m*) (sometimes called group factors) in the middle.

The middle-level abilities

Most psychologists agree that there are specific mental abilities as well as a general mental ability and that one of the important challenges is to describe the broad domains of ability that lie between them. Some psychologists have taken a *bottom-up approach* to this problem by starting with people's responses on intelligence tests and then looking to see what kinds of independent clusters these responses form. Other psychologists have taken a *top-down approach* to this problem by starting with a broad survey of human abilities and then looking to see which of these abilities intelligence tests measure – or fail to measure. These approaches have led to rather different suggestions about the best way to describe the middle-level abilities that constitute intelligence.

The bottom-up approach

One way to determine the nature of the middle-level abilities is to start with the data and work our way up. Just as Spearman and Thurstone did, we could compute the correlations between the performances of a large number of people on a large number of tests and then see how those correlations cluster. For example, imagine that we tested how quickly and well a large group of people could balance teacups, understand Shakespeare, swat flies, and add up the whole numbers between one and a thousand (see FIGURE **9.8**). Now imagine that we computed the correlation between scores on each of these tests and observed a pattern of correlations, as shown in FIGURE **9.8a**. What would this pattern tell us? This pattern suggests that a person who can swat flies well can also balance teacups well and that a person who can understand Shakespeare well can also add up numbers well, but that a person who can swat flies well and balance teacups well may or may not be able to add up numbers or understand Shakespeare well. From this pattern, we could conclude that there are two middle-level abilities (shown in FIGURE **9.8b**), which we might call 'physical coordination', the ability that allows people to swat flies and balance teacups well, and 'academic skill', the ability that allows people to understand Shakespeare and add up numbers well. This pattern suggests that different specific abilities such as fly swatting and teacup balancing are made possible by a single middle-level ability and that this middle-level ability is unrelated to the other middle-level ability, which makes possible adding up numbers and understanding Shakespeare. As this

©ISTOCKPHOTO.COM/ANNE DE HAAS

Fluid and crystallized intelligence may have different neural substrates, which may explain why Alzheimer's disease impairs fluid intelligence more strongly than crystalized intelligence.

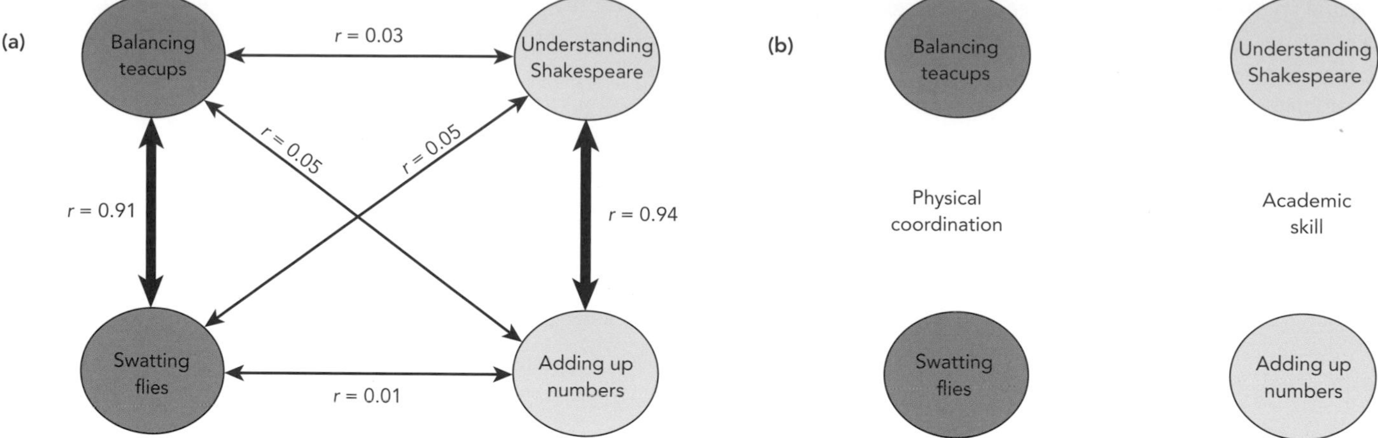

FIGURE **9.8 Patterns of correlation can reveal middle-level abilities** The pattern of correlations shown in (a) suggests that these four specific abilities can be thought of as instances of the two middle-level abilities – physical coordination and academic skill – shown in (b).

example reveals, simply by examining the pattern of correlations between different tests, we can divine the nature and number of the middle-level abilities.

In the real world, of course, there are more than four tests. So what kinds of patterns do we observe when we calculate the correlations between the tests of mental ability that psychologists use? This is precisely what psychologist John Carroll (1993) set out to discover in his landmark analysis of intelligence test scores from nearly 500 studies conducted over a half-century. Carroll found that the pattern of correlations among these tests suggested the existence of eight independent middle-level abilities: *memory and learning, visual perception, auditory perception, retrieval ability, cognitive speediness, processing speed, fluid intelligence* and *crystallized intelligence.* Although most of the abilities on this list are self-explanatory, the last two are not. **Fluid intelligence** is *the biologically limited capacity for processing information*, and **crystallized intelligence** is *the accuracy and amount of information available for processing* (Horn and Cattell, 1966). If we think of the brain as a machine that uses old information ('Some spiders don't spin webs' and 'All spiders eat insects') as raw material to produce new information ('That means some spiders must stalk their prey rather than trapping them'), then fluid intelligence refers to the way the machine runs and crystallized intelligence refers to the information it uses and produces (Salthouse, 2000). Whereas crystallized intelligence is generally assessed by tests of vocabulary, factual information and so on, fluid intelligence is generally assessed by tests that pose novel, abstract problems that must be solved under time pressure, such as the Raven's Progressive Matrices Test, shown in **FIGURE 9.9**.

FLUID INTELLIGENCE The biologically limited capacity for processing information (see crystallized intelligence).

CRYSTALLIZED INTELLIGENCE The accuracy and amount of information available for processing (see fluid intelligence).

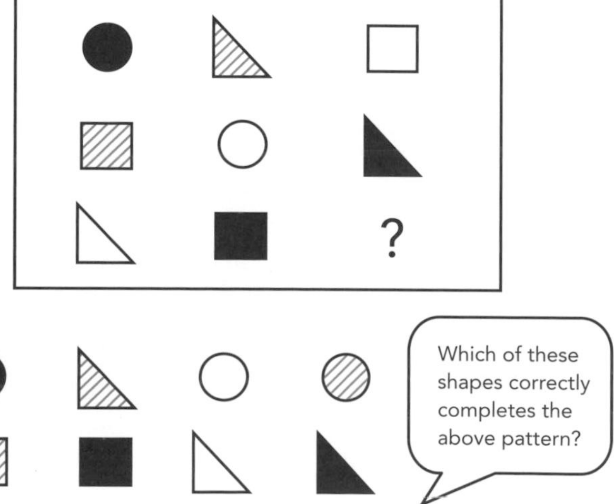

FIGURE **9.9 Raven's Progressive Matrices Test** This item from the Raven's Progressive Matrices Test measures nonverbal reasoning abilities and is unlikely to be culturally biased.

The top-down approach

The bottom-up approach attempts to discover the middle-level abilities by analysing people's responses to questions on intelligence tests. The good thing about this approach is that its conclusions are based on hard evidence. But the bad thing about this approach is that it is incapable of discovering any middle-level ability that intelligence tests fail to measure. For example, no intelligence test asks people to find three new uses for an origami bird or answer the question: 'What is the question you thought you'd be asked but weren't?' As a result, the scores from these tests may be incapable of revealing a middle-level ability such as creativity. Are there middle-level abilities to which the bottom-up approach is blind? Psychologist Robert Sternberg believes there are. He suggests that there are three kinds of intelligence:

1 *Analytical intelligence:* the ability to identify and define problems and to find strategies for solving them.
2 *Creative intelligence:* the ability to generate novel solutions.
3 *Practical intelligence:* the ability to apply and implement these solutions in everyday settings.

Sternberg (1999) sought to place his theory between what he viewed as two extremes in this area of research: those who emphasize the *g* factor, are limited to using standard psychometric tests, and employ factor analysis; and those who emphasize newer, multiple intelligences, but have collected few data to support them.

According to Sternberg (1999), standard intelligence tests typically confront people with clearly defined problems that have one right answer and then supply all the information needed to solve them. These kinds of problems require (and thus serve to measure) analytic intelligence. But everyday life confronts people with situations in which they must formulate the problem, find the information needed to solve it, and then choose among multiple acceptable solutions. **Tacit knowledge** is the *information that people have about specific, everyday life situations*, but practical intelligence is the ability to apply that knowledge in an adaptive way. Some studies suggest that these different kinds of intelligence are independent. For example, workers at milk-processing plants develop complex strategies for efficiently combining partially filled cases of milk, and not only do they outperform highly educated white-collar workers, but their performance is also unrelated to their scores on intelligence tests, suggesting that practical and analytic intelligence are not the same thing (Scribner, 1984). Sternberg has argued that tests of practical intelligence are better than tests of analytic intelligence at predicting a person's job performance, although such claims have been severely criticized (Brody, 2003; Gottfredson, 2003).

TACIT KNOWLEDGE The information that people have about specific, everyday life situations.

Psychologist Howard Gardner (1983) also believes that standard intelligence tests fail to measure some important human abilities. His observations of ordinary people, people with brain damage, **prodigies**, *people of normal intelligence who have an extraordinary ability*, and **savants**, *people of low intelligence who have an extraordinary ability*, led him to conclude that there are eight distinct kinds of intelligence: *linguistic*, *logical-mathematical*, *spatial*, *musical*, *bodily-kinesthetic*, *interpersonal*, *intrapersonal* and *naturalistic*.

PRODIGY A person of normal intelligence who has an extraordinary ability.

SAVANT A person of low intelligence who has an extraordinary ability.

Gardner's theory highlights aspects of human accomplishment and skill often omitted in psychometric studies. The focus on prodigies and savants emphasizes some aspects of ability differences that are outside the realm of the general factor. However, there are limitations too (Brody, 1992; Sternberg, 1999). Gardener has yet to operationalize the intelligences in the form of validated assessments and conduct adequate empirical research. Although there are few data to confirm the existence or independence of these eight abilities, Gardner's suggestions are intriguing. Moreover, he argues that standard intelligence tests measure only the first three of these abilities because they are most valued by Western culture, but that other cultures may conceive of intelligence differently. For instance, the Confucian tradition emphasizes the ability to behave properly, the Taoist tradition emphasizes humility and self-knowledge, and the Buddhist tradition emphasizes determination and mental effort (Yang and Sternberg, 1997). Westerners regard people as intelligent when they speak quickly and often, but Africans regard

The five-year-old who drew the picture on the left is a savant, a 'low-functioning' autistic child with a mental age of about three years. The picture on the right was drawn by a normal four-year-old child.

people as intelligent when they are deliberate and quiet (Irvine, 1978). Unlike Western societies, many African and Asian societies conceive of intelligence as including social responsibility and cooperativeness (Azuma and Kashiwagi, 1987; Serpell, 1974; White and Kirkpatrick, 1985), and the word for *intelligence* in Zimbabwe, *ngware*, means to be wise in social relationships.

Definitions of intelligence may even differ within a culture. Californians of Latino ancestry are more likely to equate intelligence with social competence, while Californians of Asian ancestry are more likely to equate it with cognitive skill (Okagaki and Sternberg, 1993). Some researchers take all this to mean that different cultures have radically different conceptualizations of intelligence, but others are convinced that what appear to be differences in the conceptualization of intelligence are really just differences in language. They argue that every culture values the ability to solve important problems and what really distinguishes cultures is the *kinds* of problems considered to be important.

Where does all this leave us? About 18 years ago, 52 experts on the topic came together to see if they could put an end to this century-long debate by agreeing on a standard definition of intelligence (Gottfredson, 1997, p. 13). They concluded that intelligence is

> a very general mental capability that, among other things, involves the ability to reason, plan, solve problems, think abstractly, comprehend complex ideas, learn quickly, and learn from experience. It is not merely book learning, a narrow academic skill, or test-taking smarts. Rather, it reflects a broader and deeper capability for comprehending our surroundings – 'catching on,' 'making sense' of things, or 'figuring out' what to do.

INTELLIGENCE A hypothetical mental ability that enables people to direct their thinking, adapt to their circumstances, and learn from their experiences.

We may then (at long last) define **intelligence** as *a hypothetical mental ability that enables people to direct their thinking, adapt to their circumstances, and learn from their experiences.* Although this definition is not particularly crisp, it does seem to capture the basic themes that characterize the scientist's and the layperson's conception of intelligence.

What intelligence tests omit

Intelligence tests assess individual differences in various cognitive functions. They do not assess many other aspects of the human mind, and there will always be situations where personal aspects other than cognitive ability are the key factors. Some of these will be non-cognitive, for example personality traits are important predictors for some aspects of humans' social and emotional lives (Matthews and Deary, 1998). Intelligence tests also omit commonsense aspects of human thinking, such as emotional intelligence, creativity and wisdom.

Emotional intelligence: reading others' emotional states

How often have you heard descriptions that someone is a 'people person'? This description reflects a popular concept among the general public that some individuals have an enhanced **emotional intelligence** – *the ability to empathize and evaluate others' emotions.* Some people seem to be especially skilled in social situations and more sensitive to the feelings of others or adept at getting on with them. Although popularized by Goleman (1995), emotional intelligence shares aspects of two of Gardner's (1983) constructs of interpersonal and intrapersonal intelligence. One measure developed to assess emotional intelligence, the Multi-Factorial Emotional Intelligence Scale (Mayer et al., 1999), has four main substrates: identification of emotion in oneself, using emotion to facilitate thoughts and actions, understanding and reasoning about emotions, and being able to regulate emotion in oneself and others.

EMOTIONAL INTELLIGENCE The ability to empathize and evaluate others' emotions.

Emotional intelligence as a construct seems plausible because we assume from personal experience that the most popular people seem to get further in life, and there is some research evidence that social skills contribute to success at work (Ferris et al., 2001) but only if the individual is already competent at their job. Less obvious is that this ability to get on with others reflects a separate aspect of human intelligence that is solely related to emotion. As we will see in Chapter 10, emotion is itself a difficult thing to evaluate, so emotional intelligence has been treated with some scepticism by the scientific community. Its problems of conceptualization, measurement and validity led the major scientific review on the topic to conclude that most of the claims made for emotional intelligence were unsubstantiated (Matthews et al., 2003). While emotional intelligence refers to a collection of social skills, its structure is elusive and difficult to quantify. Instead, emotional intelligence may be simply a convenient way of redescribing a collection of traits that psychologists can already measure in other ways. As one group of researchers concluded: 'It remains uncertain whether there is anything about emotional intelligence that psychologists working within the fields of personality, intelligence, and applied psychological research do not already know' (Roberts et al., 2001, p. 200). Yet it seems likely that emotional intelligence will remain a popular description for those who appear more socially skilled.

Creativity: thinking outside the box

'Oh, he's so creative!' Just about every parent trots that line out when describing their child. Companies want employees who think 'outside the box' and there are hundreds of management books that promise to stimulate your creative powers, but what exactly is creativity? In Chapter 7, we encountered creativity as an aspect of human thought. Here, we consider creativity as a type of intelligence. One definition of **creativity** is *the ability to generate ideas or alternatives that may be useful in solving problems, communicating and entertaining ourselves* (Franken, 1998). Creative thinking involves the realization of a problem, determining the causes of the problem, formulating a plan to address it, and executing the correct solution (Feldhusen, 1993). Sternberg (2001) describes creative people as individuals who do not follow the crowd but generate unusual and sometimes counterintuitive ideas that open up a new way of seeing the world.

CREATIVITY The ability to generate ideas or alternatives that may be useful in solving problems, communicating and entertaining ourselves.

According to British psychologist Hans Eysenck (1995), creative individuals possess personality traits (most notably psychoticism that we encounter in Chapter 13) that promote novel behaviour and thoughts. They think in analogical ways, are highly intelligent, love hard work, dislike the traditional and are self-confident. Creativity is also linked to natural curiosity (Kashdan, 2009). Other descriptions of creativity are more to do with the production of something novel that is appreciated for its aesthetic value. We talk about creativity all the time in everyday language and admire 'creative geniuses' such as artists, musicians and writers but the term remains elusive and even more difficult to evaluate. The main research problem with creativity is that it is difficult to test in a valid way. Descriptions of creative geniuses are interesting, but they do not provide a way of reliably testing for it (Gardner, 1983). And you can hardly ask someone to come into a laboratory and write a novel, compose a symphony or paint a masterpiece.

IMAGE SOURCE

We often talk about creativity in relation to the production of objects of aesthetic beauty. But this is difficult to test objectively.

Typically, the link between creativity and intelligence is not particularly strong. According to meta-analytic evidence, the average correlation between manifest indicators of these two traits is rather modest (r = 0.17) (Kim, 2005). However, a stronger relationship is found at lower compared to higher levels of IQ in a phenomenon known as the *threshold effect* (Karwowski, and Gralewski, 2013). According to the threshold effect hypothesis, intelligence represents a necessary (but not sufficient) precondition of creativity that is relevant up to a certain intelligence level, then further increases of intelligence beyond that threshold become less important. Austrian researchers have shown that the threshold effect holds for some measures of creativity, such as being able to think up new ideas, and not others, such as aptitude in music, literature or the theatre (Jauk et al., 2013). They have also shown a link between fluid intelligence, creativity and the executive functions of working memory, selective attention and inhibition, encountered in Chapter 3. In line with previous meta-analysis that revealed an average correlation of 0.48 between intelligence and working memory (Ackerman et al., 2005), fluid intelligence was strongly predicted by working memory but not selective attention or inhibition. In contrast, creativity was predicted by working memory and inhibition but not selective attention (Benedek et al., 2014). In other words, being smart depends on being able to hold something in mind, whereas being creative also requires the ability to suppress thoughts and actions that can interfere with performance.

Wisdom comes with age

Wisdom is another valued human concept that traditional mental tests are not well suited to assessing. It is also a concept that defies easy validation. Some researchers have used scenario-based reasoning about life – its problems, planning, management and review – to assess individual differences in wisdom (Baltes and Staudinger, 2000). In this definition, **wisdom** is *an expert knowledge system concerning the fundamental pragmatics of life*. The target material and process of assessment are not unlike Sternberg's practical intelligence. Wisdom is related to individual differences in mental ability, but involves more. It is one aspect of human cognition in which old people perform as well as able young adults (Baltes et al., 1995), and in which adolescents perform less well (Pasupathi et al., 2001). In a sense, wisdom seems to be something that comes with age and experience.

WISDOM An expert knowledge system concerning the fundamental pragmatics of life.

In summary, a person's score on one test of mental ability is likely to be highly (but not perfectly) correlated with their score on another. This led Charles Spearman to suggest that performances require both *g* (general intelligence) and *s* (specific abilities). Modern research reveals that between *g* and *s* are several middle-level abilities. The bottom-up approach suggests that there are eight of them, but the top-down approach suggests that there may be other middle-level abilities such as creativity and wisdom that intelligence tests don't measure. Cultures may disagree about what constitutes intelligence, but Western scientists agree that it involves reasoning, planning, solving problems, thinking abstractly, comprehending complex ideas and learning quickly from experience.

The origins of intelligence: from DNA to SES

Stanford professor Lewis Terman improved on Binet and Simon's work and produced the intelligence test now known as the *Stanford-Binet*. Among the things this test revealed was that whites performed much better than non-whites: 'Are the inferior races really inferior, or are they merely unfortunate in their lack of opportunity to learn?' he asked, and then answered unequivocally: 'Their dullness seems to be racial, or at least inherent in the family stocks from which they come.' He went on to suggest that 'children of this group should be segregated into separate classes ... [because] they cannot master abstractions but they can often be made into efficient workers' (Terman, 1916, p. 91).

A century later, these sentences make us cringe, and it is difficult to decide which of Terman's suggestions is the most repugnant:

- Is it the suggestion that a person's intelligence is a product of their genes?
- Is it the suggestion that members of some racial groups score better than others on intelligence tests?

- Or is it the suggestion that the groups that score best do so because they are genetically superior?

If all these suggestions seem abhorrent to you, you may be surprised to learn that the first and second suggestions are now widely accepted as facts by most scientists. Intelligence *is* influenced by genes and some groups *do* perform better than others on intelligence tests. However, the last of Terman's suggestions – that genes *cause* some groups to outperform others – is not a fact. Indeed, it is a highly provocative claim that has been the subject of passionate and acrimonious debate. Let's examine all three suggestions and see what the facts really are.

Intelligence and genes

If you ask a professor why their children are clever, they will probably say that they inherited good genes! Ask them why their students are clever, and they will probably tell you that they have a good professor teaching them! This joke highlights the attitudes we have towards inherited intelligence and the role of the environment, which we first encountered in Chapter 1 and has cropped up since as the tension between nature and nurture. Intelligence is a function of how and how well the brain works, and given that brains are designed by genes, it would be rather remarkable if genes *didn't* play a role in determining a person's intelligence.

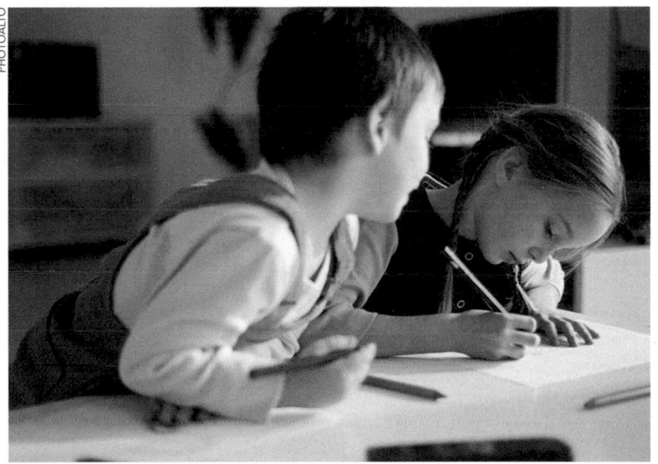
PHOTOALTO

How intelligent is this little boy compared to his sister? How far is their similarity in intelligence related to genetic or environmental factors?

The importance of genes is easy to see when we compare the intelligence test scores of people who do and do not share genes. For example, brothers and sisters share genes, and thus we should expect the intelligence test scores of siblings to be much more similar than the intelligence test scores of unrelated people. And they are – by a country mile. But there is a problem with this kind of comparison, which is that siblings share many things other than genes. For instance, siblings typically grow up in the same house, go to the same schools, read many of the same books and have many of the same friends. Thus, the similarity of their intelligence test scores may reflect the similarity of their genes or it may reflect the similarity of their experiences. To solve this problem, psychologists have studied the similarity of the intelligence test scores of people who share genes but not experiences, who share experiences but not genes, or who share both.

IDENTICAL TWINS (monozygotic twins) Twins who develop from the splitting of a single egg that was fertilized by a single sperm (see fraternal twins).

FRATERNAL TWINS (dizygotic twins) Twins who develop from two different eggs that were fertilized by two different sperm (see identical twins).

Identical twins (or monozygotic twins) are *twins who develop from the splitting of a single egg that was fertilized by a single sperm*, and **fraternal twins** (or dizygotic twins) are *twins who develop from two different eggs that were fertilized by two different sperm.* Identical twins are genetic copies of each other, whereas fraternal twins are merely siblings who happened to have spent nine months together in their mother's womb. Identical twins share 100% of their genes, and fraternal twins (like all siblings who have the same biological mother and father) share on average 50% of their genes. Studies show that the intelligence test scores of identical twins are correlated about $r = 0.86$ when the twins are raised in the same household and about $r = 0.78$ when they are raised in different households, for example when they are adopted by different families. As you'll notice from **TABLE 9.5**, identical twins who are raised apart have more similar intelligence test scores than fraternal twins who are raised together.

In other words, people who share all their genes have extremely similar intelligence test scores regardless of whether they share experiences. Indeed, the correlation between the intelligence test scores of identical twins who have never met is about the same as the correlation between the intelligence test scores of a single person who has taken the test twice. By comparison, the intelligence test scores of unrelated people raised in the same household, for example two siblings, one or both of whom were adopted, are correlated about $r = 0.32$ (Bouchard and McGue, 1981). These patterns of correlation suggest that genes play an important role in determining intelligence. Of course, Table 9.5 shows that shared environments play a role too. Genetic influence can be seen by noting that identical twins raised apart are more similar than fraternal twins raised together, but

TABLE **9.5 Intelligence test correlations between people with different relationships**

Relationship	Shared home?	% shared genes	Correlation between intelligence test scores (r)
Twins			
Identical twins (n = 4,672)	Yes	100%	0.86
Identical twins (n = 93)	No	100%	0.78
Fraternal twins (n = 5,533)	Yes	50%	0.60
Parents and children			
Parent-biological child (n = 8,433)	Yes	50%	0.42
Parent-biological child (n = 720)	No	50%	0.24
Nonbiological parent-adopted child (n = 1,491)	Yes	0%	0.19
Siblings			
Biological siblings (2 parents in common) (n = 26,473)	Yes	50%	0.47
Nonbiological siblings (no parents in common) (n = 714)	Yes	0%	0.32
Biological siblings (2 parents in common) (n = 203)	No	50%	0.24

Source: Plomin et al., 2001a, p. 168

environmental influence can be seen by noting that unrelated siblings raised together are more similar than related siblings raised apart.

HERITABILITY COEFFICIENT A statistic (commonly denoted as h^2) that describes the proportion of the difference between people's scores that can be explained by differences in their genetic makeup.

Exactly how powerful is the effect of genes on intelligence? The **heritability coefficient** is *a statistic (commonly denoted as* h^2*) that describes the proportion of the difference between people's scores that can be explained by differences in their genetic makeup.* When the data from numerous studies of children and adults are analysed together, the heritability of intelligence is roughly 0.5, which is to say that about 50% of the difference between people's intelligence test scores is due to genetic differences between them (Plomin and Spinath, 2004). This fact may tempt you to conclude that half your intelligence is due to your genes and half is due to your experiences, but that's not right. To understand why, consider the rectangles in FIGURE 9.10.

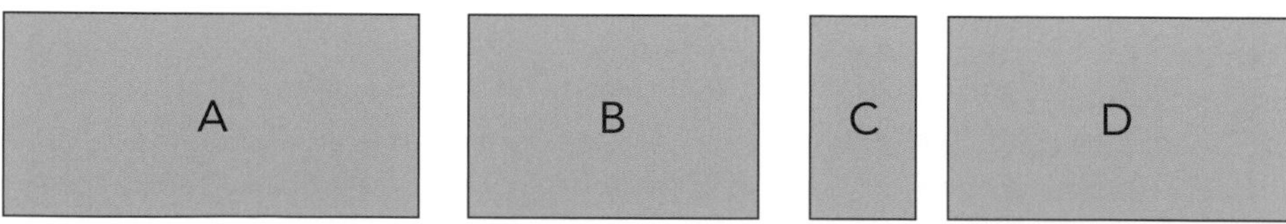

FIGURE **9.10 How to ask a stupid question** These four rectangles differ in size. How much of the difference in their sizes is due to differences in their widths and how much is due to differences in their heights? Answer: 100% and 0%, respectively. Now, how much of rectangle A's size is due to width and how much is due to height? Answer: that's a stupid question.

These rectangles clearly differ in size. If you were asked to say what percentage of the difference in their sizes is due to differences in their heights and what percentage is due to differences in their widths, you would quickly and correctly say that 100% of the difference in their sizes is due to differences in their widths and 0% is due to differences in their heights, which are, after all, identical. Good answer. Now, if you were asked to say how much of the size of rectangle A was due to its height and how much was due to its width, you would quickly and correctly say: 'That's a stupid question.' And it is a stupid question because the size of a single rectangle cannot be due more (or less) to height than to width. Only the *differences* in the sizes of rectangles can.

Similarly, if you measured the intelligence of all the people in your psychology tutorial group and were then asked to say what percentage of the difference in their intelligences was due to differences in their genes and what percentage was due to differences in their experiences, you would quickly and correctly say that about half was due to each. That's what the heritability coefficient of 0.5 suggests. If you were next asked to say how much of a particular fellow student's intelligence is due to their genes and how much is due to their experiences, you would (we hope) quickly and correctly say: 'That's a stupid question.' It is a stupid question because the intelligence of a single person cannot be due more (or less) to genes than to experience.

A river separates one of the richest and one of the poorest neighbourhoods in Mumbai, India. Research suggests that intelligence is more heritable in wealthy than poor neighbourhoods.

The heritability coefficient tells us why people in a particular group differ from one another, thus its value can change depending on the particular group of people we measure. For example, the heritability of intelligence among wealthy children is about 0.72 and among poor children about 0.10 (Turkheimer et al., 2003). How can that be? Well, if we assume that wealthy children have fairly similar environments, that is, if they all have nice homes with books, plenty of free time, ample nutrition and so on, then all the differences in their intelligence must be due to the one and only factor that distinguishes them from each other, namely their genes. Conversely, if we assume that poor children have fairly different environments, that is, some have books and free time and ample nutrition while others have some or none of these, then the difference in their intelligences may be due to either of the factors that distinguish them, namely their genes and their environments. The heritability coefficient can also depend on the age of the people being measured and is typically larger among adults than among children (see **FIGURE 9.11**), which suggests that the environments of any pair of 65-year-olds tend to be more similar than the environments of any pair of 3-year-olds. In short, when people have identical experiences, then the difference in their intelligences must be due to the difference in their genes, and when people have identical genes, then the difference in their intelligences must be due to the difference in their experiences. It may seem paradoxical, but in a sci-fi world of perfect clones, the heritability of intelligence (and of everything else) would be zero.

Does this imply that in a sci-fi world of individuals who lived in exactly the same kinds of houses and received exactly the same kinds of meals, educations, parental care and so on, the heritability coefficient would be 1? Not likely. Two unrelated people who live in the same household will have *some* but not *all* of their experiences in common.

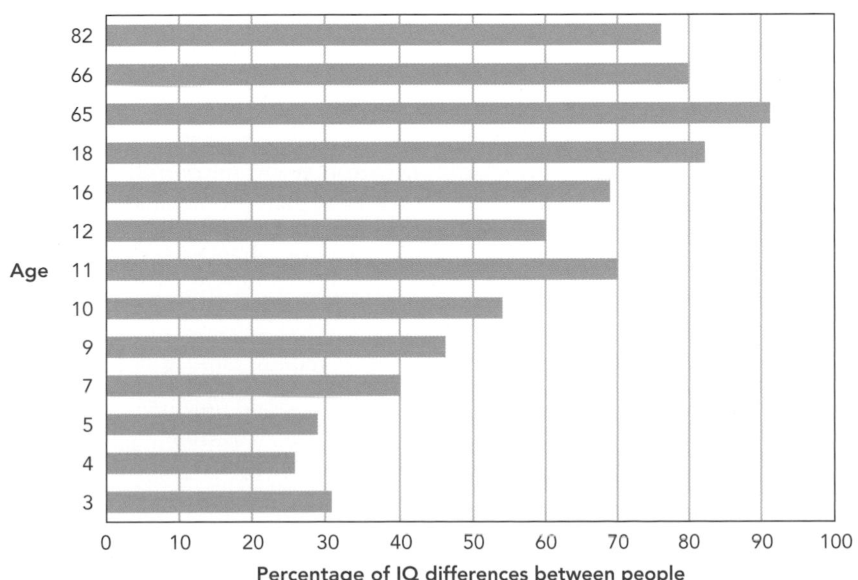

FIGURE **9.11 Age and heritability of intelligence** The heritability of intelligence generally increases with the age of the sample measured.

SHARED ENVIRONMENT Those environmental factors that are experienced by all relevant members of a household (see nonshared environment).

NONSHARED ENVIRONMENT Those environmental factors that are not experienced by all relevant members of a household (see shared environment).

The **shared environment** refers to *those environmental factors that are experienced by all relevant members of a household.* For example, siblings raised in the same household have about the same level of affluence, the same number and type of books, the same diet and so on. The **nonshared environment** refers to *those environmental factors that are not experienced by all relevant members of a household.* Siblings raised in the same household may have very different friends and teachers and may contract different illnesses. Being raised in the same household is only a rough measure of the similarity of two people's experiences (Turkheimer and Waldron, 2000). As psychologist Eric Turkheimer (2000, p. 162) notes:

> The appropriate conclusion [to draw from twin studies] is not so much that the family environment does not matter for development, but rather that the part of the family environment that is shared by siblings does not matter. What does matter is the individual environments of children, their peers, and the aspects of their parenting that they do not share.

Heritability coefficients give us some sense of how large a role genes play in explaining differences in intelligence. But whether large or small, exactly *how* do genes play their role? It is tempting to imagine an 'intelligence gene' that directly determines a person's brainpower at birth in the same way that, say, the haemoglobin beta gene found on chromosome 11p15.4 directly determines whether a person will be anaemic. But a gene that influences intelligence is not necessarily an 'intelligence gene' (Posthuma and de Geus, 2006). For instance, a gene that caused someone to enjoy the smell of library dust or to interact successfully with other people would almost surely make that person smarter, but it would be strange to call either of these an 'intelligence gene'. Although it is tempting to think of genes as the direct cause of traits, they may actually exert some of their most powerful influences by determining the nature of the social, physical and intellectual environments in which people live their lives (Plomin et al., 2001a). This fact suggests that the distinction between genes and environments – between nature and nurture – is not just simple, but simple-minded. Genes and environments interact in complex ways to make us who we are, and although psychologists do not yet know enough to say exactly how these interactions unfold, they do know enough to say that Terman's first suggestion was right: intelligence is influenced by genes. We re-examine this issue in Chapter 11 when we consider cognitive development.

Intelligence and groups

But what of Terman's second suggestion? Are some groups of people more intelligent than others? We should all hope so. If atomic scientists and neurosurgeons aren't a little bit smarter than other people, then those of us who live near nuclear power plants or need spinal cord surgery have a lot to worry about. Between-group differences in intelligence are not inherently troubling. No one is troubled by the possibility that Nobel laureates are on average more intelligent than shoe salespeople, and that includes the shoe salespeople. But most of us are extremely troubled by the possibility that people of one gender, race or nationality are more intelligent than people of another, because intelligence is a valuable commodity and it doesn't seem fair for a few groups to corner the market by accident of birth or geography. But fair or not, some groups do routinely outscore others on intelligence tests. For example, Asians routinely outscore whites, who routinely outscore Latinos, who routinely outscore blacks (Neisser et al., 1996; Rushton, 1995). Women routinely outscore men on tests that require rapid access to and use of semantic information, production and comprehension of complex prose, fine motor skills, and perceptual speed of verbal intelligence, but men routinely outscore women on tests that require transformations in visual or spatial memory, certain motor skills, spatiotemporal responding, and fluid reasoning in abstract mathematical and scientific domains (Halpern, 1997). Indeed, group differences in performance on intelligence tests 'are among the most thoroughly documented findings in psychology' (Suzuki and Valencia, 1997, p. 1104). Although the average difference between groups is considerably less than the average difference within groups, Terman's second suggestion was right.

Some groups really do perform better than others on intelligence tests. The important questions that follow from this fact are: Do group differences in intelligence test scores reflect group differences in actual intelligence? If so, what causes these group differences?

Group differences in scores

As mentioned earlier, intelligence tests are imperfect measures of the hypothetical property called intelligence. Do those imperfections create an advantage for one group over another? There is little doubt that the earliest intelligence tests were culturally biased, that is, they asked questions whose answers were more likely to be known by members of one culture (usually white Europeans) than another. When Binet and Simon asked students: 'When anyone has offended you and asks you to excuse him, what ought you to do?', they were looking for answers such as: 'Accept the apology graciously.' The answer 'Demand three goats' would have been counted as wrong. But intelligence tests have come a long way in a century, and one would have to look hard to find questions on a modern intelligence test that have a clear cultural bias (Suzuki and Valencia, 1997). Moreover, group differences emerge even on those portions of intelligence tests that measure nonverbal skills, such as the Raven's Progressive Matrices Test (see Figure 9.9 above). In short, culturally biased tests are unlikely to explain group differences in intelligence test scores.

But even when test *questions* are unbiased, testing *situations* may not be. For example, African American students perform more poorly on tests if they are asked to report their race at the top of the answer sheet, because doing so causes them to feel anxious about confirming racial stereotypes and this anxiety naturally interferes with their test performance (Steele and Aronson, 1995). European American students do not show the same effect when asked to report their race. When Asian American women are reminded of their gender, they perform unusually poorly on tests of mathematical skill, presumably because they are aware of stereotypes suggesting that women can't do mathematics. But when the same women are reminded of their ethnicity, they perform unusually well on the same tests, presumably because they are aware of stereotypes suggesting that Asians are especially good at mathematics (Shih et al., 1999). Indeed, a large replication study found that when women are unaware of the race or gender stereotype, the effect disappears (Gibson et al., 2014). Even simply reading an essay suggesting that mathematical ability is strongly influenced by genes causes women to perform more poorly on subsequent tests of mathematical skill (Dar-Nimrod and Heine, 2006). Findings such as these remind us that the situation in which intelligence tests are administered can affect members of different groups differently and may cause group differences in performance that do not reflect group differences in intelligence.

Can anxiety over racial and gender stereotypes affect individual student performance? Studies show that if these students are asked to list their ethnicities prior to taking the exam, the African American students will score poorly and the Asian American students will score higher than if neither group was asked to list their ethnicity. Interestingly, if Asian American women are asked to list their gender instead of their race, the opposite occurs and the women will perform more poorly than expected on maths tests. What can these studies teach us about standardized testing?

Group differences in intelligence

Situational biases may explain some of the between-group difference in intelligence test scores but surely not all. If we assume that some of these differences reflect real differences in the abilities that intelligence tests measure, then what could account for these ability differences? The obvious candidates are genes and experiences. Although scientists do not yet know enough about the complex interaction of these two candidates to say which is the more important determinant of between-group differences, this much is clear: different groups *may* have different genes that influence intelligence, but they *definitely* have different experiences that influence intelligence. For example, in Western societies, the average black child has lower socioeconomic status (SES) than the average white child. Black children come from families with less income, attend worse schools, and have lower birth weights, poorer diets, higher rates of chronic illness, lower rates of treatment and so on (Acevedo-Garcia et al., 2007; National Center for Health Statistics, 2004). All these factors can affect intelligence. Indeed, for almost a century, socioeconomic status has proved to be a better predictor than ethnicity of a child's intelligence test performance. As one researcher wrote in 1921: 'There is more likeness between children of the same social status but different race than children of the same race but of different social status' (Arlitt, 1921, p. 183). Everyone agrees that *some* percentage of the between-group difference in intelligence is accounted for by experiential differences, and the only question is whether *any* of the between-group difference in intelligence is accounted for by genetic differences.

Some scientists believe that the answer to this question is yes, and others believe the answer is no. Perhaps because the question is so technically difficult to answer or perhaps because the answer has such important social and political repercussions, there is as yet no consensus among those who have carefully studied the data. To draw firm conclusions about genetic causes of between-group differences will require the identification of a gene or gene complex whose presence is strongly correlated with performance on intelligence tests, and the demonstration that this gene or gene complex is more prevalent in one group than another. Such findings are critical to establishing the role of genes in producing between-group differences.

For example, scientists know that Eastern European Jews are more likely than others to carry a mutant gene that produces Tay-Sachs disease. Evidence shows that between-group differences in susceptibility to Tay-Sachs are genetic in origin, and it is the kind of evidence that is currently lacking in the debate on genetic causes of between-group differences in intelligence. So far, investigators have explored only a small portion of the human genome and have found no replicable, significant associations between particular genes and intelligence (Plomin et al., 2001b). The molecular genetic investigation of intelligence has just begun, but until such evidence is found or found lacking, we can expect the debate about genetic causes of between-group differences in intelligence to continue without a convincing resolution. When the American Psychological Association appointed a special task force to summarize what is known about the cause of the difference between the intelligence test scores of black and white Americans, it concluded (Neisser et al., 1996, p. 97):

> Culturally based explanations of the Black/White IQ differential have been proposed; some are plausible, but so far none has been conclusively supported. There is even less empirical support for a genetic interpretation. In short, no adequate explanation of the differential between the IQ means of Blacks and Whites is presently available.

Such is the state of the art.

In summary, genes exert a significant influence on intelligence. The heritability coefficient (h^2) tells us what percentage of the difference between the intelligence scores of different people is attributable to differences in their genes, and this statistic changes depending on the socioeconomic level and age of the people being measured. Genes may directly influence intelligence, but they may also influence it by determining the environments to which people are drawn and by which they are shaped. Some groups of people have lower average intelligence test scores than others. Part of the difference between groups is clearly attributable to environmental factors, and it is not yet known whether some of the difference is also attributable to genetic factors.

Cognitive bases of intelligence differences

Genes build brains that generate cognition to solve problems. We started out this chapter by describing how cognitive psychology was concerned with describing and explaining the thought processes humans share. One approach to understanding intelligence has been to look at it in terms of the underlying cognitive information-processing mechanisms. If we consider the analogy of the brain to a computer, then the efficiency of problem solving will be partly dependent on the limits of memory storage and speed of processing. Here, we consider how researchers have attempted to derive a better understanding of intelligence by looking at these components.

Working memory: keeping it in mind

In Chapter 5 we encountered a particular short-term memory system known as 'working memory', which has a limited capacity to temporarily store and process information (Baddeley, 1986). Research on the possible cognitive foundations of psychometric intelligence differences has emphasized the contribution of working memory (Conway et al., 2002). There are a number of ways to assess working memory differences, and all of these point towards the concept of working memory being closely related to Spearman's *g*. Some ways of assessing working memory involve the careful manipulation of the working memory loads of well-structured mental test items (Embretson, 1995; Embretson and Schmidt-McCollam, 2000). Others are simpler, such as the reading span, where participants read a series of sentences and recall the final word. Using such techniques, Conway and colleagues (2002) found a strong correlation between working memory capacity and fluid intelligence and concluded that both were dependent on controlled processes and attention.

Kyllonen and Christal (1990) argued that general fluid intelligence and working memory both reflect 'the ability to keep a representation active, particularly in the face of interference and distraction'. Other researchers used different tests of working memory and also found high correlations with psychometric intelligence (Engle et al., 1999). Some researchers take these results to mean that working memory is basic to intelligence differences (Miyake et al., 2001). A slight caution is that tests of 'working memory' are similar in format and content to standard psychometric tests, leading some researchers to suggest that it is *g* differences that cause so-called 'working memory differences' (Stauffer et al., 1996). In other words, the relationship between working memory and *g* is simply a case of renaming the same ability with two labels.

Reaction time: Is intelligence simply faster responding?

As you will recall from Chapter 1, one of the first mental abilities to be systematically measured by Helmholtz in the 19th century was reaction time. With the introduction of psychometric intelligence tests, researchers discovered that differences were significantly correlated with processing speed: people who did better on cognitive tests had faster reaction times (Beck, 1933). However, there was little follow up of this result until the later years of the 20th century, with the coming of information-processing models of reaction times (Hunt, 1980).

Hick's law

The most widely applied procedure in psychometric intelligence research is the Hick reaction time test (Jensen, 1987). This involves measuring people's choice reaction times in conditions with various numbers of choices (see **FIGURE 9.12**). Examine the top half of **FIGURE 9.12a**. It shows a reaction time box. There is a central 'home' button on which the subject rests a finger. There are eight response buttons surrounding it. When one of these lights up, the subject must move from the home button and press it as quickly as possible. The bottom half of the figure shows that the process may be repeated with four, two and one stimuli. If we plot the person's response time, as shown in **FIGURE 9.12b**, into the logarithm of the number of choices (lights), there is a straight-line association known as *Hick's law* (Hick, 1952).

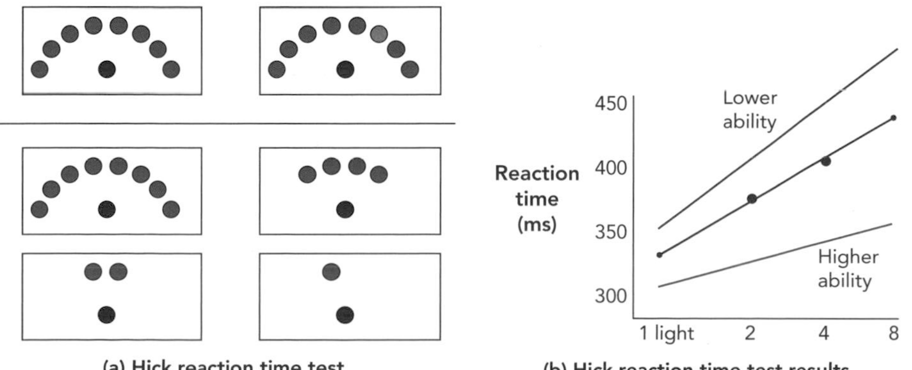

FIGURE 9.12 The Hick reaction time test and results (a) Above the horizontal line, a light comes on and the subject must lift their finger from the 'home' button and press the light as fast as possible. Below the line, the reaction time may take place with four, two and one stimuli. In the case of one, there is no choice. (b) Reaction time becomes slower as the number of choices increases. The hypothesis is that people with high psychometric intelligence have flatter slopes than people with lower ability, that is, they have a better 'rate of gain of information'.

The slope of this line was thought to assess the efficiency of a property of the person's mental processing called the 'rate of gain of information'. The hypothesis was that the slope would be steeper in people with lower psychometric intelligence, because they coped less well with complex information. However, the slope of the Hick's function has only a weak association with mental ability differences (Jensen, 1987; Deary, 2000). More interestingly, it turned out that performance on the speed response task produced differing degrees of variable performance between individuals and it was this variation that correlated with intelligence. Being steady is important! It is now well established that people who score better on mental tests have less variable reaction times. It is not yet understood why. Some have suggested that this might be caused by higher ability people adopting complex cognitive strategies, but the evidence points towards an explanation involving some basic processing advantages in people with higher psychometric intelligence (Neubauer, 1997).

The correlations between the relatively high-level abilities tested in psychometric intelligence tests and the much simpler reaction time speed and variability are now well established. Although the effect size is modest, the association between two such diverse mental domains does tell us that performance in complex thinking might be underpinned by advantages in simpler cognitive processes, such as the quickness and reliability of responding to simple stimuli. Some have suggested that the genetic influences on so-called 'elementary cognitive tasks' might be the basis for the heritability of the general mental ability factor (Plomin and Spinath, 2002). To use a metaphor, if you consider these elementary components as the bricks and mortar on a building site, then you can appreciate how the building materials can support a complex construct like intelligence.

In summary, there are correlations between psychometric intelligence test scores and more basic information-processing levels. At the higher level, there are strong correlations between working memory and *g*. Therefore, research on working memory might help to understand the meaning of *g* differences. At the experimental psychology level, there are significant correlations between reaction time speed and variability and psychometric intelligence differences. The link between these simpler cognitive skills and mental test scores can help to provide a more mechanistic understanding of mental ability differences.

The future of intelligence: wising up

Even after 100 years, the issue of measuring intelligence is still controversial. Unlike other attributes of human ability, intelligence comes with a whole baggage of prejudices and biases. Measuring intelligence has moral and political implications about how we should treat those with less cognitive ability and what policies should be put in place to eliminate discrimination and promote equality.

It would seem that everyone has an opinion (not necessarily well informed) about intelligence. When we hear about genetic influences on intelligence, most laypersons mistakenly believe that our genes are our destinies – that 'genetic' is a synonym for 'unchangeable'. In fact, traits that are influenced by genes are almost always modifiable. For example, the Dutch were renowned for being short in the 19th century but are now the second-tallest people in the world, and most scientists attribute their dramatic and rapid change in height to changes in diet. Yes, height is a highly heritable trait. But genes do not dictate a person's precise height so much as they dictate the range of heights that a person may achieve (Scarr and McCartney, 1983). 'Genes do not fix behaviour, rather they establish a range of possible reactions to the range of possible experiences that environments can provide' (Weinberg, 1989, p. 101).

Changing intelligence

So, is intelligence like height in this regard? Alfred Binet (1909, p. 107) thought so:

> A few modern philosophers ... assert that an individual's intelligence is a fixed quantity that cannot be increased. We must protest and react against this brutal pessimism ... With practice, training, and above all method, we manage to increase our attention, our memory, our judgment, and literally to become more intelligent than we were before.

Was Binet right? Can intelligence change? Yes, it can and it does. For example, **TABLE 9.6** shows the results of six longitudinal studies in which the same people were given intelligence tests many years apart.

TABLE 9.6 The stability of intelligence test scores over time

Study	Mean initial age (years)	Mean follow-up age (years)	Correlation (r)
1	2	9	0.56
2	14	42	0.68
3	19	61	0.78
4	25	65	0.78
5	30	43	0.64–.79
6	50	70	0.90

Source: Deary et al., 2000

The relatively large correlations between the pairs of tests tell us that the people who got the best (or worst) scores when the test was administered the first time tended to get the best (or worst) scores when it was administered the second time. In other words, an individual's *relative intelligence* is likely to be stable over time, and the people who are the most intelligent at age 11 are likely to be the most intelligent at age 90 (Deary et al., 2000, 2004, 2006, 2013). On the other hand, an individual's *absolute intelligence* typically changes over the course of their lifetime (Owens, 1966; Schaie, 1996, 2005; Schwartzman et al., 1987). How can a person's relative intelligence remain stable if their absolute intelligence changes? Well, the shortest person in your year 1 primary school class was probably not the tallest person in your year 13 secondary school class, which is to say that the relative heights of your classmates probably stayed about the same as they aged. On the other hand, everyone got taller (we hope) between year 1 and year 13, which is to say that everyone's absolute height changed. Intelligence is like that. Not only does it change over the life span but it also changes in some domains more than others. For example, on tests that measure vocabulary, general information and verbal reasoning, people show little change from the ages of 18–70, but on tests that are timed, have abstract material, involve making new memories, or require reasoning about spatial relationships, most people show marked declines in performance as they age (Avolio and Waldman, 1994; Lindenberger and Baltes, 1997; Salthouse, 2001). Furthermore, there is increasing evidence of an age-related decline in general intelligence (Salthouse, 1996a, 2000), which may be due to a slowing of the brain's processing speed (Salthouse, 1996b; Zimprich and Martin, 2002).

Perhaps it is some consolation that while intelligence tends to decrease across the life span, it tends to increase across generations. The *Flynn effect* refers to the accidental discovery by political scientist James Flynn that the average intelligence test score has been rising by about 0.3% every year, which is to say that the average person today scores about 15 IQ points higher than the average person did 50 years ago (Dickens and Flynn, 2001; Flynn, 1984). Researchers have attributed the effect to better nutrition, better parenting, better schooling, better test-taking ability, and the visual and spatial demands of TV and video games (Neisser, 1998). But other researchers (and that includes James Flynn) are not convinced that the statistical trend represents a real change in intelligence (Holloway, 1999) (See the hot science box.)

There's something fishy in Durham

Following a controversial report that increasing omega-3 oils in the diet improves children's intelligence (Richardson and Montgomery, 2005), Durham County Council, where the original studies were conducted, embarked on a programme of giving school children omega-3 supplement pills at a cost that exceeded the amount spent on school meals, which, if balanced correctly in the first place, would have contained sufficient omega-3 anyway (Goldacre, 2008). Such is the lure of simple solutions to increase intelligence.

Improving intelligence

Intelligence waxes and wanes naturally. But what about intentional efforts to improve it? Modern education is an attempt to do just that on a mass scale, and the correlation between the amount of formal education a person receives and their intelligence is quite high – somewhere in the range of $r = 0.55–0.90$ (Ceci, 1991; Neisser et al., 1996). But is this correlation so high because clever people tend to stay in school or because school makes people clever? The answer, it seems, is both. More intelligent people are indeed more likely to stay on at school and go on to university, but it also appears that staying in school can itself increase IQ (Ceci and Williams, 1997). Although psychologists cannot ethically perform experiments to determine whether education increases intelligence, because doing so would entail depriving some people of education, there are naturally occurring data that support this claim.

For instance, the intelligence of school children declines during the summer, and these declines are most pronounced for children whose summers are spent on the least academically oriented activities (Hayes and Grether, 1983; Heyns, 1978). Furthermore, children born in the first nine months of a calendar year typically start school an entire year earlier than those born in the last three months of the same year, and sure enough, students with late birthdays tend to have lower intelligence test scores than students with early birthdays (Baltes and Reinert, 1969). (By the way, three of the authors of this book who were born in

IMAGE SOURCE

Despite what children may want to believe, going to school does make them cleverer. IQ levels of children actually drop during the summer holidays when they are removed from an academic environment and are out playing in the sunshine.

February and March find this much easier to believe than the author born in November, but perhaps that's because he's not as clever as they are!) Does this mean that anyone can be a genius with enough education? Unfortunately not. Educational programmes can reliably increase intelligence, but studies suggest that such programmes usually have only a minor impact, tend to enhance test-taking ability more than cognitive ability, and have effects that dwindle and vanish within a few years (Perkins and Grotzer, 1997). In other words, educational programmes appear to produce increases in intelligence that are smaller, narrower and shorter lived than we might wish.

hot science

Were the Victorians smarter than us?

Since the end of the Second World War, IQ scores have been going up in what is referred to as the Flynn effect (Flynn, 1987), and on average the worldwide increase in IQ scores is approximately 3 points per decade (Flynn, 2009). These gains are thought to be almost entirely due to improved environmental conditions including better health, nutrition and education (Neisser, 1998). Improvements in living conditions and educational opportunities have been shown to positively affect intelligence (Flynn, 1987; Lynn, 1998; Rönnlund et al., 2013; Sundet et al., 2008), which indicates that the Flynn effect is attributable to an increase in intelligence of individuals rather than a general improvement of the populations as a whole (Lynn, 2011).

The problem with the Flynn effect is that since Queen Victoria came to the throne in 1837, the smartest people have been having fewer children and those who are less intelligent have been having more, in a process known as *dysgenic fertility*. If intelligence is largely heritable, then why is the population IQ as a whole rising? Our inherited intelligence must be going down over the generations but our acquired intelligence is going up. In other words, each generation must be born with slightly less capable brains than our parents but this decline is masked because later generations are born into a world that increasingly boosts our intelligence. If this is true, is there any evidence that the Victorians were smarter than us?

The Victorian polymath Francis Galton was the first to suggest that reaction time (the speed with which a person can respond to a stimulus) is a basic indicator of mental ability, and his suggestion has been confirmed by modern-day research (Deary et al., 2001).

We don't know enough about experimental conditions, such as those in Galton's 19th-century laboratory to reliably compare results on reaction time.

Recently, a group of Swedish, Dutch and Irish researchers (Woodley et al., 2013) went back and analysed all the data on human reaction time collected between 1884 and 2004 (including data collected by Galton himself) from populations sampled from the US, the UK, Canada, Australia and Finland. What they found was striking. The average reaction time has got slower since the Victorian era. The figure below shows the average reaction time of people in different studies conducted in different years.

The graph shows the average reaction time plotted against the year it was measured. The size of the bubbles is categorically determined by sample size, with small bubbles representing studies with *N* values <50 and large bubbles representing *N* values ≥50.

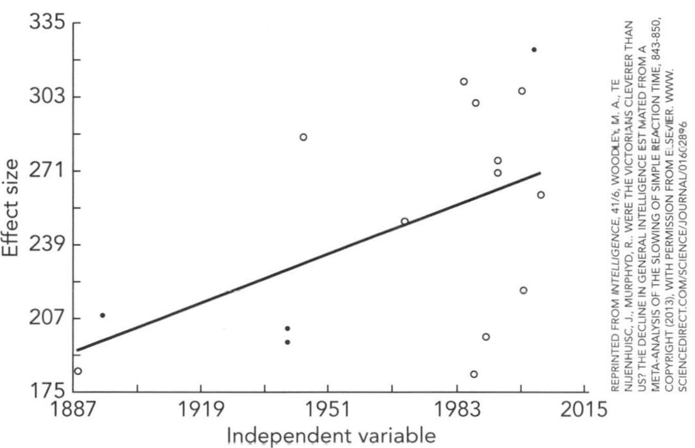

According to this meta-analysis of 16 studies since 1887, IQ has been declining by −1.16 points per decade. Does this mean that we are getting dumber and this fact is being obscured by the big IQ boost from environmental factors? Possibly, but there are many potential methodological problems, discussed in Chapter 2. Were there sampling biases in the older data? Were these predominantly male participants? What about experimenter expectations? How accurate was the equipment in the 19th century?

The study has proved provocative and generated considerable controversy and criticism from other prominent intelligence researchers (Woodley et al., 2014). However, without a time machine, we can't go back and check what Galton did in his 19th-century laboratory in order to produce a precise replication. We *do* know that his apparatus consisted of a pendulum suspended by a thread that was stretched by two elastic bands and we know that participants were only given one trial to detect its movement in a early pre-computer-era reaction time test (Johnson et al., 1985). But we do *not* know whether the ready signal was a pat on the back or a verbal command, Go! There are so many possible inconsistencies between how these early studies were put together and how reaction times are measured now that it is difficult to compare the data they produced.

The Victorian era was an astonishing period of innovation but it seems speculative that this was a result of fast reaction times. On the other hand, the hypothesis that *g* intelligence as reflected by reaction time changes through dysgenic fertility is a perfectly testable area of hot science.

the real world

Putting brain training to the test

Brain training is a multi-million pound industry that claims that individuals can enhance their overall intelligence and halt decline in mental ability through the repeated use of computerized games and tests. There are studies that show that elderly people can benefit from such computerized games training (Papp et al., 2009) as well as young preschool children (Thorell et al., 2009), but the evidence that such training translates to overall cognitive performance in the real world is sparse.

Neuroscientist Adrian Owen and his colleagues set out to test the claim that commercially available computerized brain-training programs improve general cognitive function in the wider population (Owen et al., 2010). Their question was whether playing computerized brain-training games would improve performance on cognitive tests and generalize to other untrained tasks. Their experiment was conducted on a sample of over 11,430 participants who took part in a six-week study coordinated by the popular BBC programme *Bang Goes the Theory* in 2010.

Participants logged on to a BBC website and undertook a benchmark set of tasks that measured a broad range of cognitive abilities. They were then assigned to one of two experimental groups, with a third assigned to a control group. The first group undertook training tasks that addressed reasoning, planning and problem solving. The second experimental group undertook tasks that addressed short-term memory, attention, mathematics and visuospatial skills. The third control group answered obscure questions. After six weeks, each group was reassessed on the benchmark test of general performance. Although every group showed a significant improvement on the specific tasks they were trained on, there was no significant improvement on benchmark tasks compared to the control group. Thus, individuals got better on the training tasks because practice makes perfect, but this did not generalize to other tasks.

Education is a moderately effective way to increase intelligence, but it is also expensive and time-consuming. Not surprisingly, then, scientists are looking for cheaper, quicker and more effective ways to boost IQ. This is especially obvious in the US where intelligence testing is more prevalent than in Europe. *Cognitive enhancers* are drugs that produce improvements in the psychological processes that underlie intelligent behaviour, such as memory, attention and executive function. For example, conventional stimulants such as methylphenidate (Ritalin) can enhance cognitive performance, which is why there has been an alarming increase in their abuse by healthy US students over the past few years (Elliott et al., 1997; Halliday et al., 1994; McKetin et al., 1999). Cognitive performance can also be enhanced by a new class of drugs called ampakines, which boost the activity of the neurotransmitter glutamate (Ingvar et al., 1997). For example, modafinil is a dopamine reuptake inhibitor that has been shown to improve short-term memory and planning abilities in healthy young volunteers (Turner et al., 2003).

As we read in Chapter 5, scientists have also successfully manipulated the genes that guide hippocampal development and created a strain of 'smart mice' that have extraordinary memory and learning abilities, leading researchers to conclude that the 'genetic enhancement of mental and cognitive attributes such as intelligence and memory in mammals is feasible' (Tang et al., 1999, p. 64). Although no one has yet developed a safe and powerful 'smart pill', many experts believe that this is likely to happen in the next few years (Farah et al., 2004; Rose, 2002; Turner and Sahakian, 2006). Clearly, we are about to enter a brave new world.

What kind of world will it be? Because people who are above average in intelligence tend to have better health, longer lives, better jobs and higher incomes than those who are below average, we may be tempted to conclude that the more intelligence we have, the better off we are. In general, this is probably true, but there are some reasons to be cautious. For example, although moderately gifted children (those with IQs of 130–150) are as well adjusted as their less intelligent peers, profoundly gifted children (with IQs of 180 or more) have a rate of social and emotional problems that is twice that of an average child (Winner, 1997). This is not all that surprising when you consider how out of step such children are with their peers. Moreover, the gifts of childhood do not necessarily ripen into the fruits of adulthood. Profoundly gifted children are no more likely than moderately intelligent children to become major contributors to the fields in which they work (Richert, 1997; Terman and Oden, 1959). No one knows why this is. Perhaps there is a natural limit on how much intelligence can influence life outcomes, or perhaps the educational system fails to help profoundly gifted children make the best use of their talents (Robinson and Clinkenbeard, 1998).

It is interesting to note that gifted children are rarely gifted in all departments. Instead, they tend to have specialized gifts. For example, more than 95% of gifted children show a sharp disparity between their mathematical and verbal abilities (Achter et al., 1996), suggesting that those who are exceptionally talented in one domain are not quite so talented in the other. Indeed, as the study of savants shows, children can be profoundly gifted in one area and severely challenged in another (Fiering and Taft, 1985; Reis et al., 1995; Richert, 1997; Yewchuk, 1985). Some research suggests that what really distinguishes gifted children is the sheer amount of time they spend engaged in their domain of excellence (Ericsson and Charness, 1999). The essence of nature's 'gift' may be the capacity for passionate devotion to a single activity.

In summary, intelligence tends to decrease over the life span and increase across generations. Education increases intelligence, but its impact is smaller, narrower and shorter lived than we might wish. Cognitive enhancers can also increase intelligence, although it is not clear by how much. People who are extremely intelligent are not necessarily happier, and their gifts tend to be highly specialized.

psychomythology

Male brains are better suited for STEM than female brains

One of the most pernicious myths circulating in our society is that females are not as good as males at science, technology, engineering and maths (STEM). As noted in Chapter 1, females far outnumber males in the study of psychology but not in the study of STEM subjects. Those who are numerically skilled tend to take STEM subjects and, given this, there has been a long and controversial debate about why there are more males represented in these fields. Some people think that males possess some intrinsic aptitude, but this idea is unfounded and cost Lawrence Summers, president of Harvard University, his job when he espoused this belief in public in 2005.

Male and female brains are not the same and there are some well-established differences in, for example, size, grey matter and white matter volumes and asymmetries between the two hemispheres, which may be responsible for regional specialization that supports different thinking styles and aptitudes for spatial reasoning, but the effects sizes (see Chapter 2) are too small to account for the gender gap observed. The imbalances typically observed in Western societies are not universal so are unlikely to represent biological differences in the brain. When gender differences have been found, such as in maths ability, the effects sizes favouring males are smaller than international differences, again indicating that biology plays a lesser role than culture. Also, gender differences in maths and science ability are smaller in countries with higher gender equality, indicating that cognitive gender differences are decreasing as a function of increased gender equality (Else-Quest et al., 2010; Guiso et al., 2008).

Recently, a group of European researchers predicted that if environmental factors play such an important role, then women who have historically been disadvantaged because of gender inequalities will show much greater improvement on IQ measures in countries experiencing better environmental conditions through economic growth (Weber et al., 2014). Data on measures of episodic memory, numeracy and category fluency from 17,000 males and 14,000 females were grouped into three geographical European regions: Northern Europe (Denmark, Sweden), Central Europe (Austria, Belgium, Czech Republic, France, Germany, the Netherlands, Poland, Switzerland) and Southern Europe (Greece, Italy, Spain). Using regional development as a measure of economic status, they found that improved living conditions and less gender-restricted educational opportunities were associated with increased gender differences *favouring* women on episodic memory, category fluency and a *decrease* or *elimination* of the well-established gender difference on numeracy. In other words, these changes took place as a result of women gaining more than men from societal improvements over time, thereby increasing their general cognitive ability more than that of men.

So why are more male students applying for STEM subjects at university? As we noted in Chapter 1, there are strong cultural stereotypes operating even among teachers. Another possibility is a systematic bias. As a whole, the differences between all males and all females is small but the variation in male performance is much greater so that there are many more at the lower and upper ends of the distribution. Therefore, at the more competitive end of the spectrum when applying to further education, the males who sit the entrance exams will already be those at the upper end of the distribution. That is not the same as saying males have better aptitude than females for STEM subjects.

In 2007, an expert panel, which historically disagreed over the issue of gender differences in cognition, produced a report concluding that there was no single factor to blame for the discrepancy but the most likely explanation was that cultural stereotypes bias males and females to study different topics (Halpern et al., 2007) and that these kick in when students are considering the different types of careers they want to pursue (Ferriman et al., 2009).

IMAGE100

Are biological, cultural or environmental differences the cause of gender disparity in the areas of science, technology, engineering and maths?

where do you stand?

Should we ban the use of smart drugs?

Athletes are regularly tested for the presence of banned substances that are known to enhance their performance. Although some of these drugs may be safe (others are definitely not), they provide an unfair advantage and if discovered the athlete is usually disqualified. But what about other competitions such as exams? If we had a drug that could enhance intelligence by improving cognition and did so by a neurobiological process that was safe, how would you feel about using such a drug?

Many of us take vitamins and supplements to maintain a healthy body, but what about substances that make our brains more efficient? Most of us would like to be smarter and very few want to be dumber. As we noted in the chapter, high IQ comes with a whole range of benefits, which is why there has been considerable interest in the use of so-called 'smart drugs' or cognition enhancers (CEs) from the UK public and in the media. A 2011 thriller, *Limitless*, explored the topic by telling the story of an author with writer's block (played by Bradley Cooper) who takes a miraculous CE that gives him superhuman powers of cognition that enable him to write a bestseller in a day, make a killing on the stock market and, of course, outmanoeuvre deadly assassins trying to retrieve the drug.

Such a pill is still science fiction but there are drugs known to enhance our cognition, which include amphetamine (Adderall), methylphenidate (Ritalin) and modafinil. Adderall and Ritalin are only available legally on prescription, and the buying or selling of these drugs through online pharmacies is illegal. Modafinil is a controlled drug available only in the US, and although online purchase is legal, online sale is not.

In a recent special edition of the journal *Neuropharmacology* dedicated to discussing CEs, evidence was presented to support the case for better performance after taking CEs. For example, Cambridge researchers have shown that modafinil improves performance on measures of executive functions (Müller et al., 2013). It seems to operate by increasing the participant's motivation so that tasks become more pleasurable and satisfying; this fits with the general report from users who say that the drug improves concentration and enhances the ability to work for longer periods (Sahakian and Morein-Zamir, 2011). While the number of individuals using CEs in Europe is quite small, and the current crop of CEs may not set the world alight, as depicted in *Limitless*, there is no reason why they could not become more powerful and more prevalent in society (Ragan et al., 2013).

Would they raise the same kinds of issues that we're seeing in sports when people use enhancers? How would you feel for example if you knew other students were using CEs to study throughout the term and not under exam conditions? Isn't the question really about fair access to CEs so that no one has an advantage? In which case, we should all be taking them. Finally, if we are happy to enhance our minds artificially, why do we insist that athletes win on natural ability? Where do you stand?

Chapter review

The measurement of intelligence

- Francis Galton was the first to show that people had correlated measures of mental and physical attributes. Charles Spearman later discovered that a person's score on one test of mental ability is likely to be highly (but not perfectly) correlated with their score on another. This led Spearman to suggest that performances require *g* (general intelligence) and *s* (specific abilities).
- Early intelligence tests devised by Binet and Simon in France were designed to predict a child's scholastic performance but were eventually used to calculate an intelligence quotient (IQ), either as a ratio of the person's mental to physical age or as a deviation of the person's test score from the average score of their peers.
- Intelligence is a hypothetical property that cannot be directly measured, so intelligence tests measure responses (to questions and on tasks) that are known to be correlated with consequential behaviours that are thought to be made possible by intelligence.
- These consequential behaviours include academic performance, job performance, health and wealth, all of which are enhanced by intelligence.

The nature of intelligence: general or specific?

- Modern research reveals that between *g* and *s* are several middle-level abilities. The bottom-up approach suggests that there are eight of them, but the top-down approach suggests that there may be other middle-level abilities that intelligence tests don't measure.
- Cultures may disagree about what constitutes intelligence, but Western scientists agree that it involves reasoning, planning, solving problems, thinking abstractly, comprehending complex ideas, and learning quickly from experience.
- Although the concept of emotional intelligence has widespread popular appeal, it remains controversial as a genuine, independently validated measure.

The origins of intelligence: from DNA to SES

- Genes exert a significant influence on intelligence. The heritability coefficient (h^2) tells us what percentage of the difference between the intelligence scores of different people is attributable to differences in their genes, and this statistic changes depending on the socioeconomic level and age of the people being measured.
- Genes may directly influence intelligence, but they may also influence it by determining the environments to which people are drawn and by which they are shaped.
- Some groups of people have lower average intelligence test scores than others. Part of the difference between groups is clearly attributable to environmental factors, but it is not yet known whether some of the difference is also attributable to genetic factors.

Cognitive bases of intelligence differences

- All information must be processed by the brain, which means that the information-processing capacity will necessarily have a limiting factor on intelligence.
- Two major aspects of information-processing capacity are working memory and information-processing speed.
- Studies show that working memory is correlated with '*g*' but may be confounded by the shared similarity of task demands.
- Surprisingly, information-processing speed as measured by fast reaction times has minimal correlation with general intelligence. However, consistent rather than variable performance on speed reaction time tasks is a good predictor of intelligence for reasons unknown at the moment.

The future of intelligence: wising up

- Intelligence tends to decrease over the life span and increase across generations.
- Education increases intelligence, but its impact is smaller, narrower and shorter lived than we might wish.
- Cognitive enhancers can also increase intelligence, although it is not clear by how much.
- People who are extremely intelligent are not necessarily happier, and their gifts tend to be highly specialized.

Key terms

biometrics (p. 359)
creativity (p. 373)
crystallized intelligence (p. 370)
deviation IQ (p. 361)
emotional intelligence (p. 373)
epidemiology (p. 365)
factor analysis (p. 359)
fluid intelligence (p. 370)
fraternal twins (p. 375)
heritability coefficient (p. 376)
identical twins (p. 375)
individual differences approach (p. 358)
intelligence (p. 372)
nonshared environment (p. 378)
prodigy (p. 371)
psychometrics (p. 358)
ratio IQ (p. 361)
savant (p. 371)
shared environment (p. 378)
tacit knowledge (p. 371)
two-factor theory of intelligence (p. 360)
wisdom (p. 374)

Recommended reading

Deary, I. J. (2001) *Intelligence: A Very Short Introduction.* Oxford: OUP. Short, accessible and lively introduction to many of the important issues in the study of intelligence by one of the leading scientists in the area. Each chapter deals with a different topic, such as whether there are several different types of intelligence, whether intelligence differences are caused by genes or the environment, the biological basis of intelligence differences, and whether intelligence declines or increases as we grow older.

Herrnstein, R. J. and Murray, C. (1994) *The Bell Curve.* New York: Free Press. *National Review* wrote: 'Our intellectual landscape has been disrupted by the equivalent of an earthquake.' And it was true. *The Bell Curve* was one of the most controversial books of the second half of the 20th century. It examined the influence of intelligence on life outcomes and discussed the stratification of US society on the basis of intelligence differences. But what made it so controversial was its claim that group differences in intelligence are largely genetic. Find out for yourself what the debate was about.

Hurley, D. (2014) *Smarter: The New Science of Building Brain Power.* New York: Viking. A journalist sets out on a task to boost his intelligence, evaluating the evidence on interventions such as brain training, meditation, smart drugs and the latest neuroscience research in the field. Enjoyable and balanced read.

Mackintosh, N. J. (1998) *IQ and Human Intelligence.* Oxford: OUP. Provides an authoritative overview of the main issues surrounding the modern development of IQ tests, the heritability of intelligence, theories of intelligence, environmental effects on IQ, factor analysis, relationship of cognitive psychology to measuring IQ, and intelligence in the social context. The clear, accessible style and numerous explanatory boxes make this an ideal text for advanced undergraduate and graduate students in psychology.

10

Chapter learning objectives

At the end of this chapter you will be able to:

1 Understand how emotions, feelings and moods differ in their subjective experience, expression and duration.

2 Compare the James-Lange, Cannon-Bard and two-factor theories of emotion, noting their major similarities and differences.

3 Describe two lines of evidence supporting the universality hypothesis for facial expression of emotion and give examples of universal emotional expressions.

4 Describe the differences and connections between emotion and motivation.

5 Describe the difference between intrinsic and extrinsic motivation and conscious and unconscious motivation.

Emotion and motivation

Why? This was the question on the British nation's mind in February 1993. What possessed two 10-year-olds boys to abduct a 2-year-old toddler, and then spend the next couple of hours on a four-km walk of torture, cruelty and ultimately death?

Even today, the millions of us who watched the news and saw the video footage from the security cameras of the Bootle Strand shopping centre in Liverpool are still haunted by the abduction. The terrible moment forever frozen in time – 15:42:32 – a shaky blurred image of three boys, the toddler James Bulger being led away, his trusting hand held by Jon Venables, with Robert Thompson in front. By 15:43:08, the three boys had left the shopping centre to begin that appalling journey.

Along the way, James was kicked, punched and tormented. In total, 38 people saw the three boys, and two adults even challenged the older boys about the crying toddler but Thompson and Venables claimed that he was their brother. Eventually, James Bulger was led to a railway track, covered in blue azure model paint and then killed by Thompson and Venables using bricks and an iron bar.

The reporters who turned up in Preston court nine months later had come to discover the reason for James Bulger's torment and murder. They had a duty to report the reasons to their readers but they were to be disappointed. Court hearings are about who, where, when and how. They are not about why. The two boys were being tried in an adult court: carpenters even had to raise the dock by 7.5 cm so that the two boys could see the judge and jury. The prosecution focused on whether the two boys were mature enough to be tried as adults with four specific questions. On the day of the killing, would Thompson and Venables have known the difference between right and wrong? Would they have known that it was wrong to abduct a child? Would they have known that it was wrong to cause injury to a child? Would they know it was wrong to

CCTV GETTY IMAGES

leave an injured child on a railway track? 'Why?' was not a question for the court.

The court heard about the background of the two boys, who grew up in a deprived area of Liverpool where unemployment was high and neither one of their parents had a job. They learned that the boys were held back for a year because they were failing at school. The list of items the two boys had shoplifted during the day at the shopping centre was read out and included the blue azure model paint that would be poured over the head of James before he was killed. And they heard the testimony of the two boys accusing each other for being responsible for the crime. According to Robert, Jon had said: 'Let's get a kid, I haven't hit one for ages.' According to Jon, Robert said: 'Let's get this kid lost, let's get him lost outside so when he goes in the road he'll get knocked over.' But what the court did not hear was 'why'.

In his harrowing account of the James Bulger murder trial, writer Blake Morrison (1997), who covered the case, keeps coming back to the question of 'why?' Thompson and Venables did not carry weapons and seemed to have killed James when they got to the end of the journey with whatever was available at the railway track – bricks and an iron bar. Even if the murder was not premeditated, why did Thompson and Venables set out to abduct a small child? How could Thompson and Venables not have felt sadness, remorse or disgust? What emotions did they have on that railway track as they battered a weeping toddler to death? In summing up, the judge called the killing of James Bulger 'an act of unparalleled evil and barbarity'. And yet Morrison's account of Thompson and Venables suggests that they were not that unusual. There was nothing in their backgrounds to suggest that they would become murderers. Brutal, unprovoked, callous attacks are mercifully rare in our society, but questions about why people do the things they do are not. When we ask why people feel and act as they do, we are asking questions about their emotions and motivations. As you will see, emotions and motivations are intimately connected, and understanding their connection allows us to answer the 'Why?' question everyone is asking.

Emotional experience: the feeling machine

Trying to describe love to someone who had never experienced it would be a bit like trying to describe green to someone who was born blind. You could tell them about its sources ('It's that feeling you get when you see your boyfriend across the room') and you could describe its physiological correlates ('It makes your pupils dilate'), but in the end, your descriptions would largely miss the point because the essential feature of love – like the essential feature of all emotions – is the *experience.* It *feels* like something to love, and what it feels like is love's defining attribute (Heavey et al., 2012).

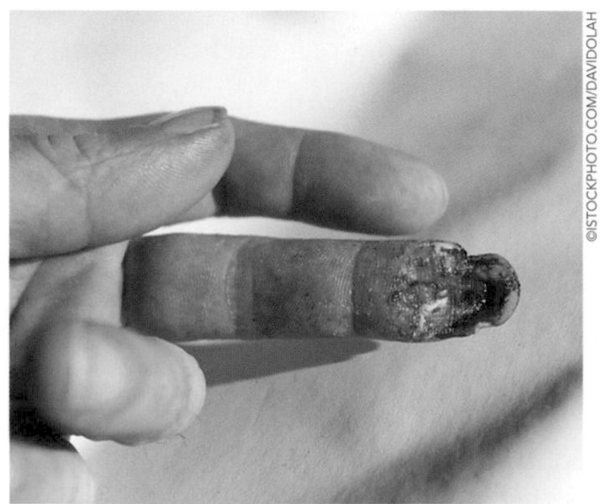
©ISTOCKPHOTO.COM/DAVIDOLAH

©ISTOCKPHOTO.COM/MICHELLEGIBSON

For most people, these pictures evoke emotional experiences. Having these experiences is easy, but describing them is difficult.

What is emotion?

Emotion (or *affect*) is a term that covers a complex variety of related phenomena. However, because of the subjective, personal nature of emotional states, it is often difficult for an individual to accurately describe the intensity and nature of the affect they are experiencing. Fox (2008) has drawn a useful distinction between emotions, feelings and moods, each of which has subtle differences in duration, intensity and our conscious experience of them. Understanding this distinction helps us to appreciate the different approaches researchers have used when describing emotional states. In their basic form, emotions are specific and consistent responses to a significant internal or external event that are brief in duration and consist of a particular pattern of physiological responses. Most researchers think there are a limited number of universal core emotions that have their basis in biological inheritance (Izard, 1977). Emotions are also object oriented, in that they are generated by discrete events and have typically been studied in experiments designed to elicit a particular emotional response. For example, fear and happiness can be suddenly triggered by a threat or a reward. On the other hand, feelings are more subjective and reflect the internal, experienced representation of emotions. In other words, while emotions are public affairs, the **feelings** associated with these emotions are the *private conscious thoughts* that the individual has during the episode. For example, if you see your ex-partner with someone else, you might *feel* jealous, without necessarily displaying any obvious emotion on the outside (although it doesn't always work!). Finally, **moods** are *generalized, diffuse states or dispositions that are less intense but last longer than emotional responses.* Unlike emotions, moods are not necessarily object oriented, and may instead reflect a general disposition over a period of time, although they may have been triggered initially by an emotional event. In comparison to basic emotions, feelings and moods are more generalized and based on self-report questionnaires. This distinction between the various types of emotional experience is necessary, but for the remainder of the chapter we will use the all-inclusive term 'emotion', as it conveniently conveys the notion of an affective state. As such, **emotion** can be defined as *a positive or negative experience that is associated with a particular pattern of physiological activity.*

FEELINGS Private conscious thoughts that accompany emotions.

MOODS Generalized, diffuse states or dispositions that are less intense but last longer than emotional responses.

EMOTIONS Positive or negative experiences that are associated with a particular pattern of physiological activity.

All emotions generate states of body and mind that produce physiological, behavioural and cognitive changes. Most researchers agree that emotions have an evolutionary origin, in that they function to motivate adaptive behaviours that would have been critical for survival, including, for example, finding food and shelter, finding sexual partners, nurturing and protecting offspring, and avoiding or escaping from dangerous situations (Tooby and Cosmides, 1990). However, this list is incomplete when one considers the various demands and activities that make up the complexity of modern life and one has therefore to question whether all emotions are biologically determined. While core emotional responses may be evolved, their expression can be shaped by culture and learning. For example, **disgust**, *an intense negative response that triggers feelings of nausea*, is generally considered a core emotional state found in every culture (Levenson et al., 1992). Some stimuli are universally disgusting (such as the smell of decaying flesh) – they automatically trigger nausea in humans and do not have to be learned. Other stimuli are much more dependent on what is considered revolting in the culture (see *the real world* box). Or consider emotional responses that seem to be unique to one culture, such as *amae* in Japan, which is the pleasant feeling one gets when accepted by another person or group (Fox, 2008). While such an emotional experience is not entirely alien to Western culture, it doesn't constitute a core emotional response as it does in Japan where conformity and group acceptance are highly valued.

DISGUST An intense negative response that triggers feelings of nausea.

As emotions are often accompanied by subjective thoughts (see 'feelings' above), some researchers think that such thoughts are unobservable and should be ignored in the scientific study of emotion in favour of more measurable responses (LeDoux, 1996). Undaunted, psychologists have developed a technique that capitalizes on the fact that, while people can't always say what an emotional experience feels like ('Love is ... um ... uh ...'), they can usually say how similar it is to another ('Love is more like happiness than anger'). By asking people to rate the similarity of dozens of emotional experiences, psychologists have been able to map these experiences using a sophisticated technique known as *multidimensional scaling*. The maths behind this technique is complex, but the logic is simple. If you listed the distances between a dozen European cities and then handed the list to a friend and challenged him to draw a map on which every city was the listed distance from every other, your friend would be forced to draw a map of Europe because there is no other map that allows every city to appear at precisely the right distance from every other. Yes, there are lots of ways to draw a map so that London is 494 km from Amsterdam, but there is only one way to draw a map so that London is 494 km from Amsterdam *and* 656 km from Edinburgh *and* 1,196 km from Copenhagen and so on. The point is that a map of the physical landscape can be generated from nothing but a list of distances between cities.

The same logic can be used to generate a map of the emotional landscape. If you listed the similarity of a dozen emotional experiences – giving smaller numbers to those that were conceptually 'close' to each other and larger numbers to those that are conceptually 'far away' from each other – and then challenged a friend to draw a map on which every experience was the listed 'distance' from every other, your friend would draw a map like the one shown in **FIGURE 10.1**. This is the unique map that allows every emotional experience to be precisely the right 'distance' from every other. What good is this map?

As it turns out, maps don't just show how close things are to each other, they also reveal the *dimensions* on which those things vary. For example, a map reveals that cities differ on two dimensions called longitude and latitude, and thus every city can be described by its unique coordinates in this two-dimensional space. Similarly, an emotion map reveals that emotional experiences differ on two dimensions that are called *valence* (how positive or negative the experience is) and *arousal* (how active or passive the experience is), and every emotional experience can be described by its unique coordinates in this two-dimensional space (Russell, 1980; Watson and Tellegen, 1985).

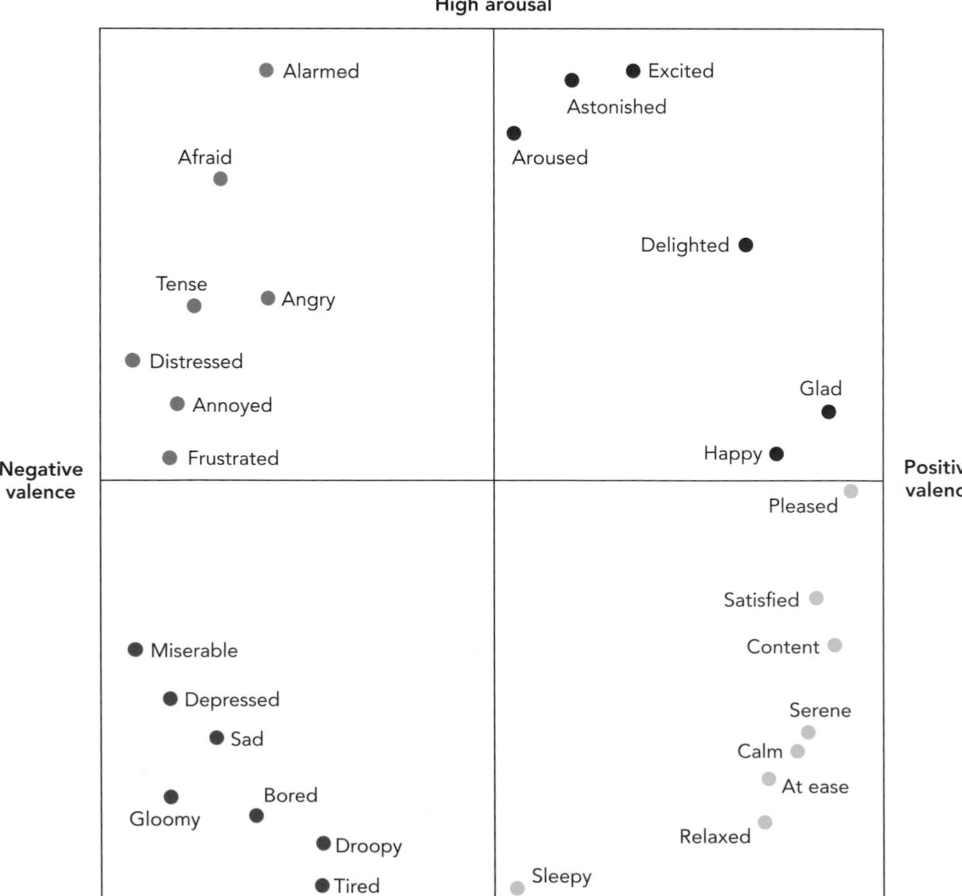

FIGURE 10.1 Two dimensions of emotional experiences Just as cities can be mapped by their longitude and latitude, emotions can be mapped by their arousal and valence.

This map of emotional experience suggests that any definition of emotion must include two things. First, the fact that emotional experiences are always good or bad, and second, the fact that these experiences are associated with characteristic levels of bodily arousal. If we extend the metaphor of emotional experience as a feeling machine, then consider it like a car. Arousal is the power of the engine driving the car, whereas emotions are the different directions the car is steered towards in response to the different experiences that elicit a response. So, emotions are determined by the combination of the experience and the physiological response. As you are about to see, the first step in understanding emotion involves understanding how experience and physiological activity are related.

The emotional body

You probably think that if you walked into your kitchen right now and saw a bear nosing through the cupboards, you would feel fear, your heart would start to pound, and the muscles in your legs would prepare you for running. You'd also be wondering what a bear was doing on the loose if you didn't live in bear country! But William James and Carl Lange used the example of running away from bears to argue that events generate responses that trigger emotions and not the other way round (Lange and James, 1922). The James-Lange theory of emotion asserts that *stimuli trigger activity in the autonomic nervous system, which in turn produces an emotional experience in the brain.* In other words, first you see the bear, then your heart starts pounding and your leg muscles contract, and *then* you experience fear, which is simply your experience of your body's activity. As James (1884, pp. 189–90) wrote: 'Bodily changes follow directly the perception of the exciting fact ... And feeling of the same changes as they occur *is* the emotion.' For James, each unique emotional experience was associated with a unique pattern of 'bodily reverberation', and he suggested that without all the heart pounding and muscle clenching, there would be no experience of emotion at all. In short, James saw emotional experience as the consequence – and not the cause – of our physiological reactions to objects and events in the world.

JAMES-LANGE THEORY A theory about the relationship between emotional experience and physiological activity suggesting that stimuli trigger activity in the autonomic nervous system, which in turn produces an emotional experience in the brain.

But Walter Cannon, James's former student, disagreed, and together with *his* student, Philip Bard, Cannon proposed an alternative to James's theory. The Cannon-Bard theory of emotion suggests that *a stimulus simultaneously triggers activity in the autonomic nervous system and emotional experience in the brain* (Bard, 1934; Cannon, 1927). Cannon favoured his own theory over the James-Lange theory for several reasons:

CANNON-BARD THEORY A theory about the relationship between emotional experience and physiological activity suggesting that a stimulus simultaneously triggers activity in the autonomic nervous system and emotional experience in the brain.

1. The autonomic nervous system reacts too slowly to account for the rapid onset of emotional experience. For example, a blush is an autonomic response to embarrassment that takes 15–30 seconds to occur, and yet one can feel embarrassed long before that, so how could the blush be the cause of the feeling?
2. People often have difficulty accurately detecting changes in their own autonomic activity, such as their heart rates. If people cannot detect increases in their heart rates, how can they experience those increases as an emotion?
3. If nonemotional stimuli – such as temperature – can cause the same pattern of autonomic activity that emotional stimuli do, then why don't people feel afraid when they get a fever?
4. Cannon argued that there simply weren't enough unique patterns of autonomic activity to account for all the unique emotional experiences people have. If many different emotional experiences are associated with the same pattern of autonomic activity, how could that pattern of activity be the sole determinant of the emotional experience?

These are all good questions, and about 30 years after Cannon asked them, psychologists Stanley Schachter and Jerome Singer (1962) supplied some answers. James and Lange were right, they claimed, to equate emotion with the perception of one's bodily reactions. Cannon and Bard were also right, they claimed, to note that there are not nearly enough distinct bodily reactions to account for the wide variety of emotions that human beings can experience. Whereas James and Lange had suggested that different emotions are *different experiences* of *different patterns* of bodily activity, Schachter and Singer claimed that different emotions are merely *different interpretations* of *a single pattern* of bodily activity, which they called 'undifferentiated physiological arousal' (see **FIGURE 10.2**).

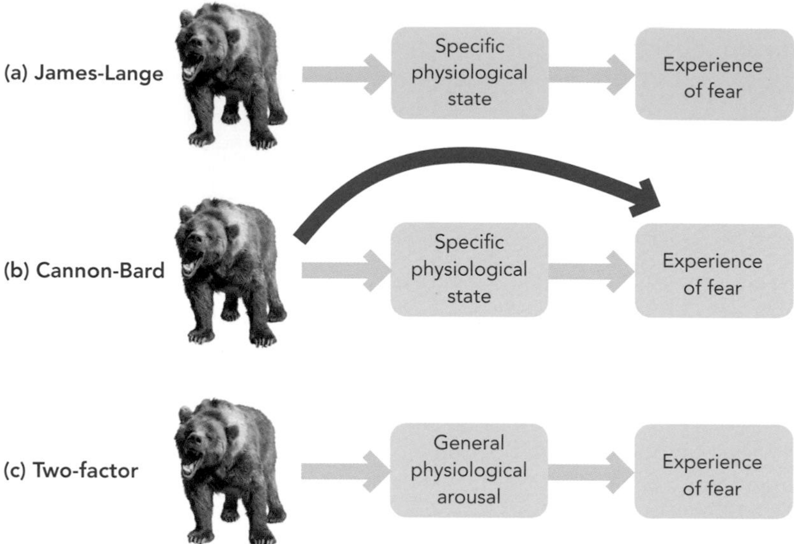

FIGURE 10.2 Classic theories of emotion Classic theories make different claims about the origins of emotion. (a) The James-Lange theory suggests that stimuli trigger specific physiological states, which are then experienced as emotions. (b) The Cannon-Bard theory suggests that stimuli trigger specific physiological states and emotional experiences independently. (c) The two-factor theory suggests that stimuli trigger general physiological arousal whose cause the brain interprets, and this interpretation leads to emotional experience.

TWO-FACTOR THEORY A theory about the relationship between emotional experience and physiological activity suggesting that emotions are inferences about the causes of undifferentiated physiological arousal.

Schachter and Singer's two-factor theory of emotion claims that *emotions are inferences about the causes of undifferentiated physiological arousal.* When you see a bear in your kitchen, your heart begins to pound. Your brain quickly scans the environment, looking for a reasonable explanation for all that pounding, and it finds, of all things, a bear. Having noticed both a bear and a pounding heart, your brain then does what brains do so well: it puts two and two together, makes a logical inference, and interprets your arousal as fear. In other words, when people are physiologically aroused in the presence of something they think should scare them, they label their arousal as *fear.* But if they have precisely the same bodily response in the presence of something they think should delight them, they may label that arousal as *excitement.* According to Schachter and Singer, people have the same physiological reaction to all emotional stimuli, but they interpret that reaction differently on different occasions.

To demonstrate their claim, Schachter and Singer (1962) gave participants in an experiment an injection of adrenaline, a hormone and neurotransmitter that mimics the action of the sympathetic nervous system (see Chapter 3), causing increases in blood pressure, heart rate, blood flow to the brain, blood sugar levels and respiration. Some participants were correctly informed that the side effects of the injection would include trembling hands, a flushed face and an increased heart rate. Other participants were incorrectly informed that the side effects of the injection would include numb feet, an itching sensation all over the body and a slight headache. Next, participants were given the opportunity to interact with one of two people who, unbeknown to them, were confederates of the experimenter. In one condition of the experiment, the confederate acted giddy, doodling on some paper, crumbling it into a makeshift basketball, constructing paper aeroplanes, and swinging some hula hoops they found. In the other condition, the confederate acted surly, spending their time grousing and harrumphing their way through a questionnaire before finally ripping up the paper and storming out of the room. Schachter and Singer predicted that participants who were correctly informed about the side effects would correctly interpret their arousal ('I'm feeling a little revved up because of the shot'), but participants who were not correctly informed about the side effects would seek an explanation for their arousal – and the confederate's behaviour would supply it. Specifically, they predicted that when the confederate acted playfully, the misinformed participants would conclude that they were feeling *happy*, but when the confederate acted nasty, they would conclude that they were feeling *angry.* And that's just what happened.

How has the two-factor model fared in the last half-century? In one sense, it has fared quite well. Research has shown that when people are aroused, say, by having them ride an exercise bike in the laboratory, they subsequently find attractive people more attractive, annoying people more annoying and funny cartoons funnier – as if they were interpreting their exercise-induced arousal as attraction, annoyance and delight, respectively (Byrne et al., 1975; Dutton and Aron, 1974; Zillmann et al., 1972). Indeed, these effects occur even when people merely *think* they're aroused, for example when they hear an audiotape of a rapidly beating heart and are led to believe that the heartbeat they're hearing is their own (Valins, 1966). These and other studies suggest that people can indeed misattribute their arousal to other stimuli in their environments and the inferences people draw about the causes of their arousal can influence their emotional experience.

On the other hand, one of the model's central claims is that all emotional experiences derive from the same pattern of bodily activity, namely undifferentiated physiological arousal. Research has not been so kind to this part of the theory. Paul Ekman and colleagues (1983) measured participants' physiological reactions as they experienced six different emotions, and found that anger, fear and sadness each produced a higher heart rate than disgust, fear and disgust produced higher galvanic skin responses (GSRs, the measure of arousal) than sadness or anger, and anger produced a larger increase in GSR than fear (see **FIGURE 10.3**).

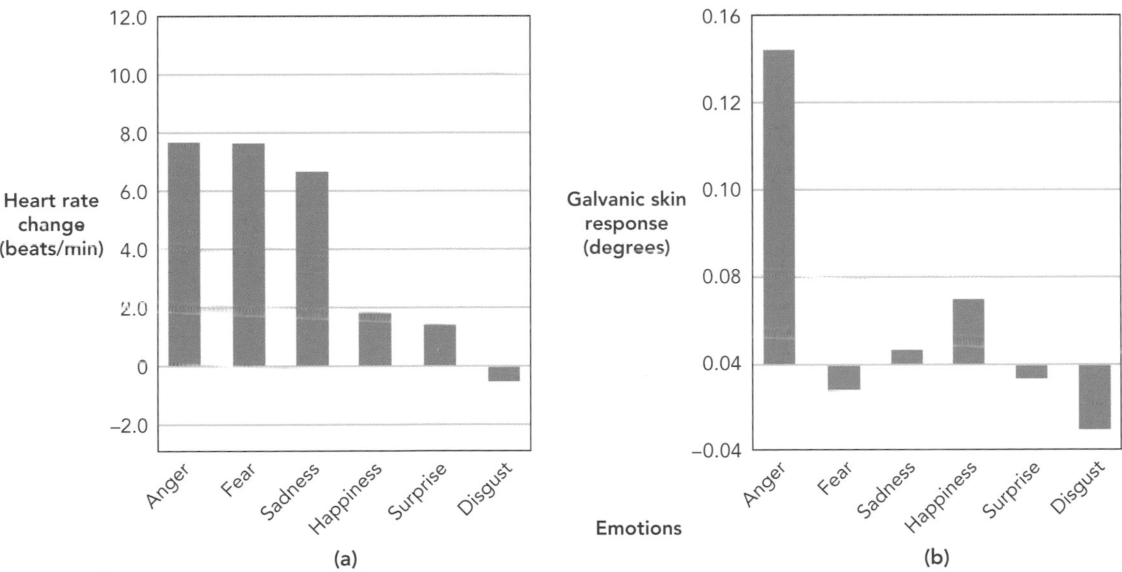

FIGURE 10.3 Different physiological patterns of emotion Contrary to the claims of the two-factor theory, different emotions do seem to have different underlying patterns of physiological arousal. (a) Anger, fear and sadness all produce higher heart rates compared to happiness, surprise and disgust. (b) Anger produces a much larger increase in GSR than any other emotion.

This general pattern has been replicated across different age groups, professions, genders and cultures (Levenson et al., 1990, 1991, 1992). In fact, some physiological responses seem unique to specific emotions. For example, a blush is the result of increased blood volume in the subcutaneous capillaries in the face, neck and chest, and research suggests that people blush when they feel embarrassment but not when they feel any other emotion (Leary et al., 1992). Similarly, certain patterns of activity in the parasympathetic branch of the autonomic nervous system, which is responsible for slowing and calming rather than speeding and exciting, seem uniquely related to prosocial emotions such as compassion (Oately et al., 2006).

It now appears that James and Lange were right when they suggested that patterns of physiological response are not the same for all emotions. But it appears that Cannon and Bard were right when they suggested that people are not perfectly sensitive to these patterns of response, which is why people must sometimes make inferences about what they are feeling. Our bodily activity and our mental activity are both the causes and the consequences of our emotional experience. The precise nature of their interplay is not yet fully understood, but as you are about to see, much progress has been made over past few decades by following the trail of emotion from the beating heart to the living brain.

hot science

Are you looking for a fight?

Hopefully, you may never have a hostile encounter with an aggressor but if you ever have to square up to another, it is important to recognize a 'fight face'. The trouble with many aggressive individuals is that they tend to treat ambiguous expressions as hostile, which means they are likely to make a pre-emptive violent assault (Dodge, 1993). Aggressive individuals with conduct disorder and antisocial behaviour are also impaired in perception of emotional expression, which contributes towards their bias to perceive ambiguous faces as antagonistic (Fairchild et al., 2009). The problem is that by acting aggressively towards another, that person may, in turn, respond with aggression, which creates a self-fulfilling prophecy.

One way to break this chain of aggressive behaviour is to induce a bias to see others as nonaggressive using a false feedback training paradigm. Perceptual biases, such as the difficulty of distinguishing between faces from different races, can be modified through training (Lebrecht et al., 2009). With this in mind, researchers conducted a study to shift the perceptual hostility bias in delinquent teenagers, most of whom already had criminal convictions and were attending a programme for high-risk repeat offenders (Penton-Voak et al., 2013). First, they generated prototypical happy and angry composite images from individual male faces showing a happy and an angry facial expression. These prototypical images were used as end points to generate a linear morph sequence that consisted of 15 images for each face, which changed incrementally from unambiguously happy to unambiguously angry, with emotionally ambiguous images in the middle. The faces were presented randomly and participants were asked to decide whether each face was happy or angry, which produced an individual baseline bias.

Once a baseline preference had established where in the sequence individuals began to see faces as being more aggressive, the experimental group of teenagers were given a training sequence with false feedback to make them think that faces they initially saw as aggressive were actually nonaggressive. For example, if they saw the middle face in the figure as aggressive in baseline, they were told that it was, in fact, happy. The control group received accurate feedback. After the training sessions, teenagers in the experimental group were much more likely to rate ambiguous faces towards the nonaggressive end of the scale compared to the controls.

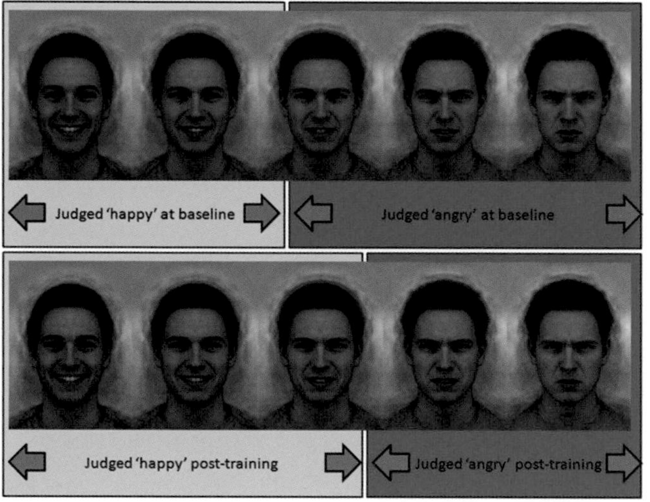

This is an interesting example of training a perceptual bias, but does it have any relevance to the real world? Remember, these were troubled youths with a history of violence. Remarkably, the effect of the study was long-lasting and altered their behaviour in general. The teenagers kept diaries and were evaluated by staff who were unaware of which condition each teenager had been in. After only two weeks, those teenagers who had their anger bias shifted to being more positive were happier, less aggressive and involved in less conflict incidents as rated by the staff.

The emotional brain

German-American psychologist Heinrich Klüver was curious: Why do monkeys smack their lips after being given hallucinogenic drugs? So, on the afternoon of 7 December 1936, he and Paul Bucy removed the temporal lobe of a particularly aggressive rhesus monkey named Aurora and ultimately learned nothing whatsoever about lip smacking. They did, however, produce what Klüver (1951, p. 151) would later call 'the most striking behaviour changes ever produced by a brain operation in animals'. Their surgical experiments revealed that monkeys whose temporal lobes had been removed would eat just about anything and have sex with just about anyone or anything, as though they could no longer distinguish between good and bad food or good and bad mates. But the most striking thing about these monkeys was their extraordinary lack of fear. They were eerily calm when being handled by experimenters or being confronted by snakes, both of which rhesus monkeys typically find alarming (Klüver and Bucy, 1937, 1939). This constellation of behaviours became known as 'temporal lobe syndrome' or 'Klüver-Bucy syndrome', although it was later pointed out that the syndrome had been described in 1888 by Brown and Schafer.

What explained this surgical taming? As it turned out, when Klüver and Bucy lesioned the monkey's temporal lobe, they also damaged her limbic system (Weiskrantz, 1956), which is a set of cortical and subcortical structures that include, among others, the amygdala and the nucleus accumbens (see Chapter 3). Scientists had long suspected that the limbic system played an important role in the generation of emotions (Papez, 1937), and these experiments confirmed that speculation in the case of fear. A few decades later, psychologists James Olds and Peter Milner (1954) implanted electrodes in the brains of rats to see how the rats would respond to direct electrical stimulation of their brains. When Olds and Milner stimulated the rat's limbic system, they found that it quickly returned to whatever part of the cage it had just been in, as though the rat were trying to re-create the circumstances that had led to the electric stimulation. When they allowed the rat to stimulate its own brain by pressing a lever, the rat did so for hours on end, often choosing electric stimulation over food. These studies suggested that the limbic system was also implicated in the experience of emotions such as pleasure.

More recent research has demonstrated that a particular limbic structure – the amygdala – plays a key role in the production of emotion. William James (1884, p. 189) claimed that 'bodily changes follow directly the perception of the exciting fact', which means that some part of the brain decides which facts are exciting. Between the moment that information about an approaching bear enters our eyes and the moment our heart starts pounding, our brain has to decide that a bear is something to be afraid of. That decision is called an appraisal – *an evaluation of the emotion-relevant aspects of a stimulus* (Arnold, 1960; Lazarus, 1984; Roseman, 1984; Roseman and Smith, 2001; Scherer, 1999, 2001), and research suggests that making appraisals is the amygdala's primary job (see **FIGURE 10.4**). Interestingly, although people with amygdala damage don't feel fear when they see a threat, they do feel fear when they experience a threat. For example, if you breathe a mixture of oxygen that contains 35% CO_2, this automatically induces panic attacks as one feels that one is suffocating (Colasanti et al., 2008). Three patients with bilateral amygdala damage administered with the CO_2 inhalation experienced fear and panic attacks (Feinstein et al., 2013).

APPRAISAL An evaluation of the emotion-relevant aspects of a stimulus that is performed by the amygdala.

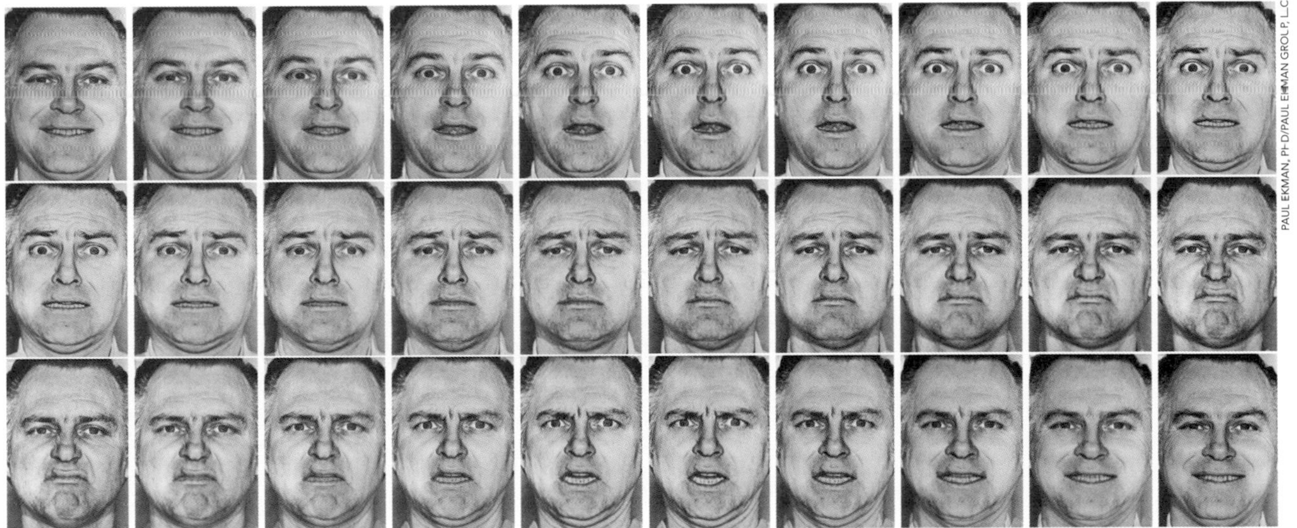

FIGURE 10.4 Emotion recognition and the amygdala Facial expressions of emotion were morphed into a continuum that ran from happiness to surprise to fear to sadness to disgust to anger and back to happiness. This sequence was shown to a patient with bilateral amygdala damage and to a group of 10 people without brain damage. Although the patient's recognition of happiness, sadness and surprise was generally in line with that of the undamaged group, her recognition of anger, disgust and fear was impaired (Calder et al., 1996).

For example, in one study, researchers performed an operation on monkeys so that information entering the monkey's left eye could be transmitted to the amygdala but information entering the monkey's right eye could not (Downer, 1961). When these monkeys were allowed to see a threatening stimulus with only their left eye, they responded with fear and alarm, but when they were allowed to see the threatening stimulus with only their right eye, they were calm and unruffled. These results suggest that if visual information doesn't reach the amygdala, its emotional significance cannot be assessed. Klüver and Bucy's monkeys were calm in the presence of a snake

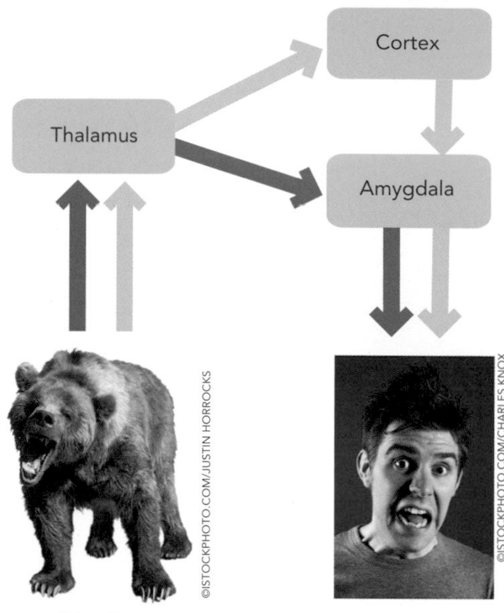

FIGURE 10.5 The fast and slow pathways of fear According to Joseph LeDoux, information about a stimulus takes two routes simultaneously: the 'fast pathway' (shown in purple), which goes from the thalamus directly to the amygdala, and the 'slow pathway' (shown in green), which goes from the thalamus to the cortex and then to the amygdala. Because the amygdala receives information from the thalamus before it receives information from the cortex, people can be afraid of something before they know what it is.

because their amygdalae had been damaged, so the sight of a snake was no longer coded as threatening. Research on human beings has reached a similar conclusion. For example, normal people have superior memory for emotionally evocative words such as *death* or *faeces*, but people whose amygdalae are damaged (LaBar and Phelps, 1998) or who take drugs that temporarily impair neurotransmission in the amygdala (van Stegeren et al., 1998) do not.

The amygdala's job is to make a rapid appraisal of a stimulus, thus it does not require much information (Zajonc, 1980, 1984). When people are shown fearful faces at speeds so fast they are unaware of having seen them, their amygdalae show increased activity (Whalen et al., 1998). Psychologist Joseph LeDoux (2000) mapped the route that information about a stimulus takes through the brain and found that it is transmitted simultaneously along two distinct routes: the 'fast pathway', which goes from the thalamus directly to the amygdala, and the 'slow pathway', which goes from the thalamus to the cortex and *then* to the amygdala (see **FIGURE 10.5**).

This means that while the cortex is slowly using the information to conduct a full-scale investigation of the stimulus's identity and importance ('This seems to be an animal ... probably a mammal ... perhaps a member of the genus *Ursus*'), the amygdala has already received the information directly from the thalamus and is making one fast and simple decision: 'Is this bad for me?' If the amygdala's answer to that question is 'yes', it initiates the neural processes that ultimately produce the bodily reactions and conscious experience we call 'fear'.

When the cortex finally finishes processing the information, it sends a signal to the amygdala telling it to maintain fear ('We've now analysed all the data up here, and sure enough, that thing is a bear – and bears bite!') or decrease it ('Relax, it's just some guy in a bear costume'). When people are asked to *experience* emotions such as happiness, sadness, fear and anger, they show increased activity in the limbic system and decreased activity in the cortex (Damasio et al., 2000), but when people are asked to *inhibit* these emotions, they show increased cortical activity and decreased limbic activity (Ochsner et al., 2002). Going back to our emotional car metaphor, in a sense, the amygdala presses the emotional accelerator pedal and the cortex then hits the brakes. That's why adults with cortical damage and children (whose cortices are not well developed) have difficulty inhibiting their emotions (Stuss and Benson, 1986).

Studies of the brain confirm what psychologists have long suspected. Emotion is a primitive system that prepares us to react rapidly and on the basis of little information to things that are relevant to our survival and wellbeing. While our newly acquired cortex identifies a stimulus, considers what it knows about it, and carefully plans a response, our ancient limbic system does what it has done so well for all those millennia before the cortex evolved: it makes a split-second decision about the significance of the objects and events in our environment and, when necessary, prepares our hearts and our legs to get away as quickly as possible.

The regulation of emotion

EMOTION REGULATION The use of cognitive and behavioural strategies to influence one's emotional experience.

No one is agnostic about their own emotional experience. We may not care whether we have cereal or eggs for breakfast, whether we play cricket or cards this afternoon, or whether we spend a few minutes thinking about hedgehogs, earwax or the Second World War. But we always care whether we are feeling happy or fearful, angry or relaxed, joyful or disgusted. Because we care so much about our emotional experiences, we take an active role in determining which ones we will have. **Emotion regulation** refers to *the cognitive and behavioural strategies people use to influence their own emotional experience.* Although emotion regulation is typically an attempt to turn negative emotions into positive ones, there are times when people feel a bit too chipper for their own good and seek ways to 'cheer down' (Erber et al., 1996; Parrott, 1993). A patient who is feeling depressed may whistle a silly song while waiting for their doctor, and a doctor who is feeling silly may think a few depressing thoughts before entering the room to give the patient bad news. Both are regulating their emotional experience.

Nine out of ten people report that they attempt to regulate their emotional experience at least once a day (Gross, 1998), and they describe more than a thousand different strategies for doing so (Parkinson and Totterdell, 1999). Some of these are behavioural strategies, for example avoiding situations that trigger unwanted emotions, doing distracting activities, or taking drugs, and some are cognitive strategies, for example trying not to think about the cause of the unwanted emotion, or recruiting memories that trigger the desired emotion. Arguably, controlling emotions is an important part of socialization and in Chapter 12, we investigate ways in which young children express emotions and how these are regulated by the social environment and parental influence. Research suggests that one of the most effective strategies for emotion regulation is **reappraisal**, which involves *changing one's emotional experience by changing the meaning of the emotion-eliciting stimulus.* How people think about an event can determine how they feel about it. For example, participants who watched a circumcision that was described as a joyous religious ritual had slower heart rates, lower skin conductance levels, and reported less distress than participants who watched the circumcision but did not hear the same description (Lazarus and Alfert, 1964). Everyone knows that the phrase 'Don't forget your umbrella' elicits annoyance when construed as nagging and gratitude when construed as caring, and we can regulate our emotional experience by construing it in one of these ways rather than the other.

More than two millennia ago, Roman emperor Marcus Aurelius wrote: 'If you are distressed by anything external, the pain is not due to the thing itself, but to your estimate of it; and this you have the power to revoke at any moment.' But is that true? Do we have the power to change how we think about events in order to change our emotional experiences? Research suggests that to some extent we do. In one study, participants' brains were scanned as they saw photos that induced negative emotions, such as a photo of a woman crying during a funeral. Some participants were then asked to reappraise the picture by imagining that the woman in the photo was at a wedding rather than a funeral. The results showed that when participants initially saw the photo, their amygdalae became active. But as they reappraised the picture, several key areas of the cortex became active, and moments later, their amygdalae were deactivated (Ochsner et al., 2002). In other words, participants consciously and wilfully turned down the activity of their own amygdalae simply by thinking about the photo in a different way.

Studies such as these demonstrate at the neural level what psychologists have observed for centuries at the behavioural level. Because emotions are reactions to the appraisals of an event and not the event itself, changes in appraisal bring about changes in emotional experience. Some of us are better at appraisal than others (Malooly et al., 2013), and as you will learn in Chapter 16, therapists often attempt to alleviate depression and distress by helping people find new ways to think about the events that happen to them (Jamieson et al., 2013). Indeed, reappraisal appears to be important for mental and physical health (Davidson et al., 2000), and the inability to reappraise events lies at the heart of psychiatric disorders such as depression (Gross and Munoz, 1995).

However, one must be careful not to make the mistake of assuming that all emotions recruit the activity of single, specific brain areas. Rather, emotions activate integrated networks of neuronal connections between the cortical regions and the limbic system. In some instances, such as in the case of happiness and sadness, different emotions are currently indistinguishable at the neuronal level using functional imaging techniques (Murphy et al., 2003a). This may suggest that some brain areas may play a more general role in experiencing some emotions, such as happiness and sadness, whereas others appear to be relatively more specific, for discrete emotions such as fear, anger and disgust (Fox, 2008).

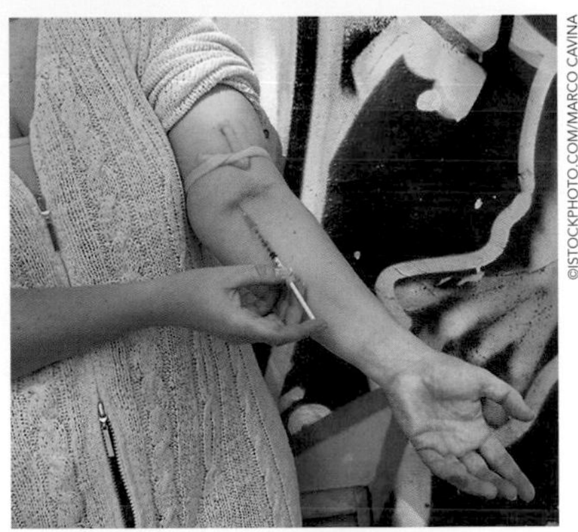

Taking heroin and singing karaoke would seem to have little in common, but both can be forms of emotion regulation.

REAPPRAISAL A strategy that involves changing one's emotional experience by changing the meaning of the emotion-eliciting stimulus.

Who enforces the emotion regulation?

In 1991, the mayor of Sund, Norway proposed a resolution to the town council that banned crankiness and required people to be happy and think positively. The resolution contained an exemption for those who had a good reason to be unhappy.

In summary, emotional experiences are difficult to describe, but a useful distinction to draw is between emotions, feelings and moods, each of which differs in its duration, intensity and cognitive appraisal. Another useful way to consider such states is in terms of two underlying dimensions: arousal and valence. Psychologists have spent more than a century trying to understand how emotional experience and physiological activity are related. The James-Lange theory suggests that a stimulus causes a physiological reaction, which leads to an emotional experience; the Cannon-Bard theory suggests that a stimulus causes an emotional experience and a physiological reaction simultaneously; and Schachter and Singer's two-factor theory suggests that a stimulus causes undifferentiated physiological arousal about which people draw inferences. None of these theories is entirely right, but each has elements that are supported by research.

Emotions are produced by the complex interaction of limbic and cortical structures. Information about a stimulus is sent simultaneously to the amygdala, which makes a quick appraisal of the stimulus's goodness or badness, and the cortex, which does a slower and more comprehensive analysis of the stimulus. In some instances, the amygdala will trigger an emotional experience that the cortex later inhibits. People care about their emotional experiences and use many strategies to regulate them. Reappraisal involves changing the way one thinks about an object or event, and is one of the most effective strategies for emotion regulation.

Emotional communication: msgs w/o wrds

EMOTIONAL EXPRESSION Any observable sign of an emotional state.

As we discussed earlier, feelings that accompany emotions may be private events, but the 'bodily reactions' that emotions produce are not. An emotional expression is *any observable sign of an emotional state*, and human beings exhibit many such signs. For example, blushing and sweating are clear physiological responses. Others are more subtle. People's emotional states influence the way they talk – from intonation and inflection to loudness and duration – and research shows that listeners can infer a speaker's emotional state from vocal cues alone with better-than-chance accuracy, although vocal signs of anger, happiness and sadness are somewhat easier to recognize than vocal signs of fear and disgust (Banse and Scherer, 1996; Frick, 1985). The voice is not the only clue to a person's emotional state. In fact, observers can often estimate a person's emotional state from the direction of the person's gaze, their gait and posture, and even from a person's touch (Dittrich et al., 1996; Keltner and Shiota, 2003; Wallbott, 1998). In some sense, we are walking, talking advertisements for what's going on inside us.

No part of the body is more exquisitely designed for communicating emotion than the face. Underneath every face lie 43 muscles capable of creating more than 10,000 unique configurations, which enable a face to convey information about its owner's emotional state with an astonishing degree of subtlety and specificity (Ekman, 1965). Psychologists Paul Ekman and Wallace Friesen (1978) spent years cataloguing the muscle movements of which the human face is capable. They isolated 46 unique movements, which they called *action units*, and they gave each one a number and a memorable name, such as 'cheek puffer', 'dimpler' and 'nasolabial deepener'. Research has shown that combinations of these action units are reliably related to specific emotional states (Davidson et al., 1990). For example, when someone feels happy, the movements of the *zygomatic major* (a muscle that pulls the lip corners up) and the *obicularis oculi* (a muscle that crinkles the outside edges of the eyes) produce a unique facial expression that psychologists describe as 'action units 6 and 12' and that the rest of us simply call smiling (Ekman and Friesen, 1982; Frank et al., 1993; Steiner, 1986).

Communicative expression

Why are our emotions written all over our faces? In 1872, Charles Darwin published *The Expression of the Emotions in Man and Animals*, in which he speculated about the evolutionary significance of emotional expression (Darwin, [1872]1998). Darwin noticed that people and animals seem to share certain facial and postural expressions, and he suggested that these expressions are a means by which organisms communicate information about their internal states to each other. If a dominant animal can bare its teeth and communicate the message 'I am angry with you' and if a subordinate animal can lower its head and communicate the message 'I am afraid of you', then the two may be able to establish a pecking order without actually spilling blood. Emotional expressions are a convenient way for one animal to let another animal know how it is feeling and hence how it is prepared to act. In this sense, emotional expressions are a bit like the words or phrases of a nonverbal language.

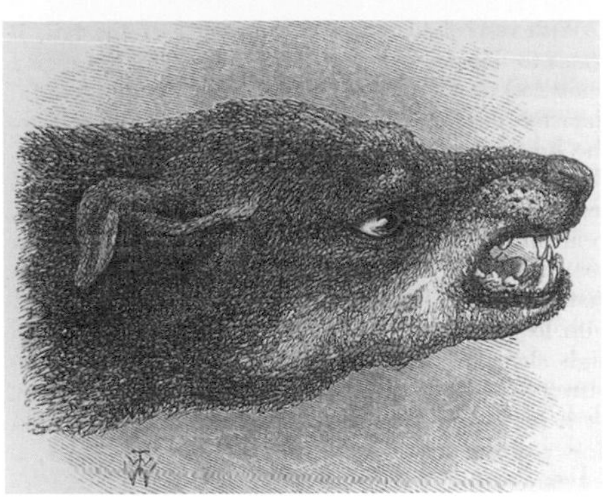

Some animals looking soothed, angry and sulky, according to Charles Darwin.

The universality of expression

Of course, a language only works if everybody speaks the same one, and that fact led Darwin to develop the **universality hypothesis**, which suggests that *emotional expressions have the same meaning for everyone.* In other words, everyone expresses happiness with a smile and everyone understands that a smile signifies happiness. Two lines of evidence suggest that Darwin was largely correct. First, people are quite accurate at judging the emotional expressions of members of other cultures (Boucher and Carlson, 1980; Ekman and Friesen, 1971; Ekman et al., 1987; Elfenbein and Ambady, 2002; Frank and Stennet, 2001; Haidt and Keltner, 1999; Izard, 1971; McAndrew, 1986; Shimoda et al., 1978). Not only do Argentinians, Alaskans, Algerians and Afghans all recognize a smile as a sign of happiness and a frown as a sign of sadness, but so do members of preliterate cultures where there is no written word to describe these emotions. In the 1950s, researchers showed photographs of people expressing anger, disgust, fear, happiness, sadness and surprise to members of the South Fore, a people who lived a Stone Age existence in the highlands of Papua New Guinea and who had had little contact with the outside world. The researchers discovered that the Fore could recognize the emotional expressions of Americans about as accurately as Americans could and vice versa. The one striking exception to this rule was that the Fore had trouble distinguishing expressions of surprise from expressions of fear, perhaps because for people who live in the wild, surprises are rarely pleasant.

UNIVERSALITY HYPOTHESIS The hypothesis that emotional expressions have the same meaning for everyone.

The second line of evidence in favour of the universality hypothesis is that people who have never seen a human face make the same facial expressions as those who have. For instance, congenitally blind people make all the facial expressions associated with the basic emotions, and although their expressions are not quite as recognizable as those made by sighted individuals, the underlying action of the facial muscles is quite similar (Galati et al., 1997). Two-day-old infants, who have had virtually no exposure to human faces, react to sweet tastes with a smile and to bitter tastes with an expression of disgust (Steiner, 1973, 1979). It's an automatic response triggered by taste and different to the social smiling seen some months later in response to other people (see Chapter 12). In short, a good deal of evidence suggests that the facial displays of at least six emotions – anger, disgust, fear, happiness, sadness and surprise – are universal. Recent evidence suggests that some other emotions, such as embarrassment, amusement, guilt or shame, may have a universal pattern of facial expression as well (Keltner, 1995; Keltner and Buswell, 1996; Keltner and Haidt, 1999; Keltner and Harker, 1998).

On 19 September 1982, Scott Fahlman posted a message to an internet user's group that read: 'I propose the following character sequence for joke markers: :-) Read it sideways.' And so the emoticon was born. Fahlman's smile is a sign of happiness, whereas his emoticon is a symbol.

The cause and effect of expression

Why do so many people seem to express so many emotions in the same ways? After all, people in different cultures don't speak the same languages, so why do they smile the same smiles and frown the same frowns? The answer is that words are *symbols* and facial expressions are *signs.* Symbols are arbitrary designations that have no causal relationship with the things they symbolize. We English speakers use the word *cat* to indicate a particular animal, but there is nothing about felines that actually causes this particular sound to pop out of our mouths, and we aren't surprised when other human beings make different sounds – such as the Hawaiian word *popoki* or the Italian *gatto* – to indicate the same thing. Facial expressions, on the other hand, are not arbitrary symbols of emotion. They are signs of emotion, and signs are *caused* by the things they signify. The feeling of happiness *causes* the contraction of the zygomatic major and thus its contraction is a sign of that feeling, in the same way a footprint in the snow is a sign that someone walked there.

FACIAL FEEDBACK HYPOTHESIS The hypothesis that emotional expressions can cause the emotional experiences they signify.

Although emotional experiences cause emotional expressions, there are instances in which the causal path runs in the other direction. The **facial feedback hypothesis** (Adelmann and Zajonc, 1989; Izard, 1971; Tomkins, 1981) suggests that *emotional expressions can cause the emotional experiences they signify*. For instance, people feel happier when they are asked to make the sound of a long *e* or hold a pencil in their teeth (both of which cause contraction of the zygomatic major) than when they are asked to make the sound of a long *u* or hold a pencil in their lips (Strack et al., 1988a; Zajonc, 1989) (see **FIGURE 10.6**). Also, when we mimic someone else's expression with our own muscles, we can readily access the same emotion usually responsible for generating that expression. This may be why people who have their own facial muscles temporarily paralysed following a Botox injection to remove wrinkles are not as good at reading other people's emotional expressions because they are unable to copy them (Neal and Chatrand, 2011). This also may explain why, compared to those receiving different cosmetic treatments, Botox patients report less negative emotions such as depression and anxiety (Davis et al., 2010).

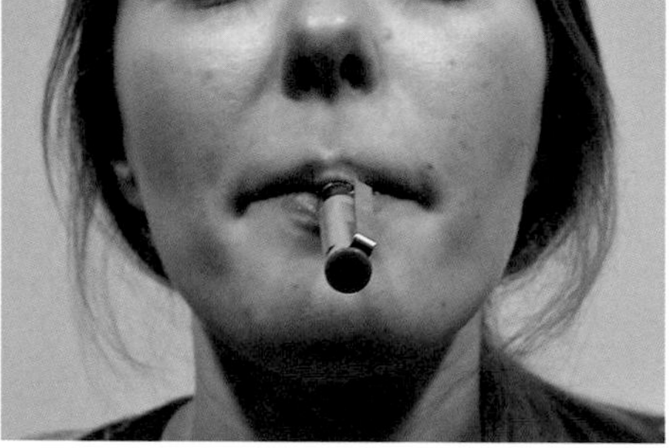

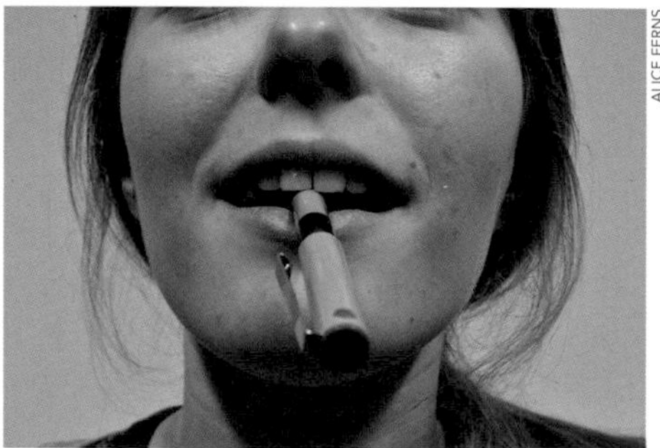

ALICE FERNS

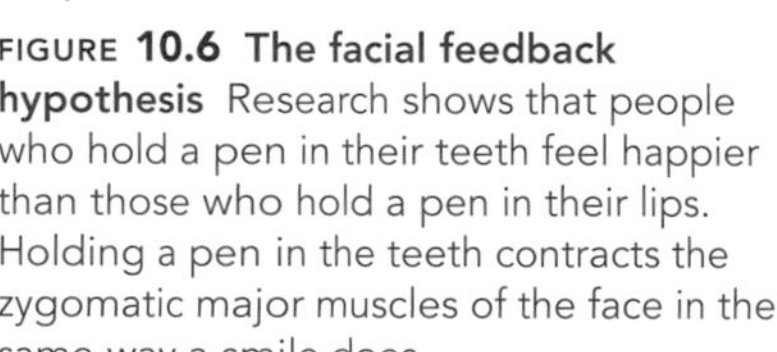

FIGURE 10.6 The facial feedback hypothesis Research shows that people who hold a pen in their teeth feel happier than those who hold a pen in their lips. Holding a pen in the teeth contracts the zygomatic major muscles of the face in the same way a smile does.

The sausage poison

Botox is a strain of botulinum toxin, one of the most lethal toxins known to be responsible for botulism, a serious life-threatening bacterial infection caused by improperly prepared meat products that leads to death in approximately 5–10% of cases. The German physician (and poet) Justinus Kerner (1786–1862) described botulinum toxin as a 'sausage poison' after the Latin for sausage, *botulus*.

Some researchers believe that this happens because the muscle contractions of a smile change the temperature of the brain, which in turn brings about a pleasant affective state (Zajonc, 1989). Others believe that the smile and the feeling of happiness become so strongly associated through experience that one always brings about the other, in the way we saw, in Chapter 6, that reflexive behaviours could be conditioned. Although no one is sure why it happens, smiling does seem to be a cheap cure for feeling miserable.

The fact that emotional expressions can cause the emotional experiences they signify may help to explain why people are generally so good at recognizing the emotional expressions of others. Some studies suggest that observers unconsciously mimic the body postures and facial expressions of the people they are watching (Chartrand and Bargh, 1999; Dimberg, 1982). When we see someone lean forward and smile, we lean very slightly and slightly contract our zygomatic major. What purpose does this subtle mimicry serve? If making a facial expression brings about the feeling it signifies, then one can tell what others are feeling simply by imitating their expressions and thereby experiencing their feelings oneself (Lipps, 1907). If this is actually what happens, we would expect people who have trouble experiencing emotions to have trouble recognizing the emotional expressions of others. In fact, people with amygdala damage are typically quite poor at recognizing facial expressions of fear and anger (Adolphs et al., 1999), and this is especially true if their brain damage was sustained early in life (Adolphs et al., 1997).

Similarly, people who are low in empathy find it difficult to know what others are feeling, and research shows that they are less likely to mimic the facial expressions of those with whom they interact (Sonnby-Borgstrom et al., 2003). All this suggests that our emotional expressions play an important role in sending and receiving information (see *the real world* box).

Deceptive expression

Given how important emotional expressions are, it's no wonder that people have learned to use them to their advantage. Because you can control most of the muscles in your face, you don't have to display the emotion you are actually feeling or actually feel the emotion you are displaying. When your flatmate makes a sarcastic remark about your haircut, you may make the facial expression for contempt (accompanied, perhaps, by a reinforcing hand gesture), but when your boss makes the same remark, you probably swallow hard and display a pained smile. Your expressions are moderated by your knowledge that it is permissible to show contempt for your peers but not for your superiors. Display rules are *norms for the control of emotional expression* (Ekman, 1972; Ekman and Friesen, 1968), and following them requires using several techniques:

DISPLAY RULES Norms for the control of emotional expression.

- *Intensification:* exaggerating the expression of one's emotion, as when a person pretends to be more surprised by a gift than they really are.

the real world

That's disgusting!

If you want to feel one of the most powerful, most irrational and most poorly understood of all emotions, just spit in a glass of water. Then drink it. Despite the fact that the spit is yours and it was in your mouth just a moment ago, you will probably experience disgust.

Psychologist Paul Rozin has spent a lifetime disgusting people in order to understand the nature of this emotion, which is produced by the prospect of incorporating an offensive substance into one's body (Rozin and Fallon, 1987). Disgust is characterized by feelings of nausea, a facial expression marked by distinct actions of the nose and mouth, and an etymology meaning 'bad taste' (Rozin et al., 1999). In this sense, disgust is a kind of defensive response that ensures that improper substances do not enter our bodies through our mouths, noses or other orifices. For Westerners, these improper substances include certain animals, such as rats and cockroaches, certain body products, such as vomit, faeces or blood, and certain foods, such as dog meat. The thought of eating a sumptuous meal of stewed monkey brains or biting into an apple teeming with maggots may make most of us feel nauseous, despite the fact that people in many other countries find both dishes quite palatable. Things that remind us of our animal nature, such as poor hygiene (body odour), inappropriate sex (that is, with animals or family members), body boundary violations (open sores, amputated limbs), or contact with death (touching a corpse, watching an autopsy) also elicit disgust (Rozin and Fallon, 1987; Rozin et al., 1999). We like to distance ourselves from the rest of the animal kingdom, so reminders of our own animal origins, from belching to blood to barbarity, are tagged as disgusting.

Disgust plays an important role, but it can be quite irrational, and its irrationality seems to follow two rules. The first is the rule of *contagion*, which suggests that any two things that were once in contact will continue to share their properties. So, for example, would you be willing to lick raisins off a fly swatter? Of course not. The fly swatter may have invisible traces of cockroach legs and fly guts on it, and those things can make you sick. Okay, then, what if the fly swatter were washed in alcohol, heated to within a degree of melting, and cooled to within a degree of breaking, making it the most sterile and hygienic thing in your entire house? Would you lick raisins off it then? Most people still say no (Rozin et al., 1986b). And the reason is that the swatter once touched an insect and thus it will forever have a disgusting 'insectness' that cannot be cleaned away.

FON HIPSCHMAN, © EXPLORATORIUM, WWW.EXPLORATORIUM.EDU

San Francisco's Exploratorium features an exhibit on disgust that invites visitors to drink clean water from a toilet.

The second irrational rule is the rule of *similarity*, which suggests that things that share appearances also share properties. If someone whipped up a batch of fudge that was shaped to look convincingly like dog poo, chances are you'd turn down the opportunity to sample it. Fudge is fudge, of course, and its shape shouldn't matter, but most people still balk at this proposition (Rozin et al., 1986b) – most people, that is, except children. Children under two years of age will readily put any number of disgusting things in their mouths, which suggests that disgust (unlike many emotions) develops late in life (Rozin et al., 1986a). A 4-year-old will avoid eating human hair because it doesn't taste very good, but a 10-year-old child will avoid eating it because … well, it's haaaaaaaaair – and that's disgusting!

If you want to observe the irrationality of disgust for yourself, just offer your friends some guacamole in a disposable nappy or some lemonade in a potty. And make sure you stir it with a comb!

- *Deintensification:* muting the expression of one's emotion, as when the loser of a contest tries to look less distressed than they really are.
- *Masking:* expressing one emotion while feeling another, as when a poker player tries to look distressed rather than delighted as they examine a hand with four aces.
- *Neutralizing:* feeling an emotion but displaying no expression, as when judges try not to betray their leanings while lawyers make their arguments.

Although people in different cultures all use the same techniques, they use them in the service of different display rules. For example, in one study, Japanese and American university students watched an unpleasant film of car accidents and amputations (Ekman, 1972; Friesen, 1972). When the students didn't know that the experimenters were observing them, Japanese and American students made similar expressions of disgust, but when they realized that they were being observed, the Japanese students, but not the American students, masked their disgust with pleasant expressions. In many Asian societies, there is a strong cultural norm against displaying negative emotions in the presence of a respected person, and people in these societies may mask or neutralize their expressions. The fact that different cultures have different display rules may also help to explain the fact that people are better at recognizing the facial expressions of people from their own cultures (Elfenbein and Ambady, 2002).

Our attempts to obey our culture's display rules don't always work out so well. Darwin ([1872]1998, p. 79) noted that 'those muscles of the face which are least obedient to the will, will sometimes alone betray a slight and passing emotion'. Despite our best attempts to smile bravely when we receive a poor mark on an exam or appear concerned when a friend receives the same, our voices, bodies and faces are 'leaky' instruments that may betray our emotional states even when we don't want them to. Four sets of features can allow a careful observer to tell whether our emotional expression is sincere (Ekman, 2003):

1. *Morphology:* Certain facial muscles tend to resist conscious control, and for a trained observer, these so-called *reliable muscles* are quite revealing. For example, the zygomatic major raises the corners of the mouth, and this happens when people smile spontaneously or when they force themselves to smile. But only a genuine, spontaneous smile engages the obicularis oculi, which crinkles the corners of the eyes (see FIGURE 10.7).
2. *Symmetry:* Sincere expressions are a bit more symmetrical than insincere expressions. A slightly lopsided smile is less likely to be genuine than a perfectly even one.
3. *Duration:* Sincere expressions tend to last between half a second and five seconds, and expressions that last for shorter or longer periods are more likely to be insincere.
4. *Temporal patterning:* Sincere expressions appear and disappear smoothly over a few seconds, whereas insincere expressions tend to have more abrupt onsets and offsets.

PAUL EKMAN, PHD/PAUL EKMAN GROUP, LLC

FIGURE 10.7 Genuine and fake smiles
Both spontaneous smiles (left) and voluntary smiles (right) raise the corners of the mouth, but only a spontaneous smile crinkles the corners of the eye.

Our emotions don't just leak on our faces, they leak all over the place. Research has shown that many aspects of our verbal and nonverbal behaviour are altered when we tell a lie (DePaulo et al., 2003). For example, liars speak more slowly, take longer to respond to questions, and respond in less detail than those who are telling the truth. Liars are also less fluent, less engaging, more uncertain, more tense, and less pleasant than truth tellers. Oddly enough, one of the telltale signs of a liar is that their performances tend to be just a bit too good. Liars' speech lacks the imperfections of truthful speech, such as superfluous details ('I noticed the robber was wearing the same shoes I saw on sale last week at Schuh and I found myself wondering what he paid for them'), spontaneous corrections ('He was 1.80 m tall ... well, no, actually more like 1.87'), and expressions of self-doubt ('I think he had blue eyes, but I'm really not sure'). Liars are also less likely to refer to themselves in the use of 'I' in comparison to people telling the truth (Wiseman, 2007).

Given the reliable differences between sincere and insincere expressions, you might think that people would be quite good at telling one from the other. In fact, studies show that human lie detection ability is fairly awful. In studies in which a score of 100% represents perfect accuracy and a score of 50% represents pure chance, some trained professionals can attain scores of 80% (Ekman and O'Sullivan, 1991; Ekman et al., 1999). But under most conditions, most people score barely better than chance (Ekman, 1992; Zuckerman and Driver, 1985). One reason for this is that people have a strong bias towards believing that others are sincere. In everyday life, most people are sincere most of the time, so it makes sense that we are predisposed to believe what we see and hear. This may explain why people tend to mistake liars for truth tellers but not the other way around (Gilbert, 1991). A second reason why people are such poor lie detectors is that they don't seem to know which pieces of information to attend to and which to ignore. People seem to think that certain things – such as whether a person speaks quickly or averts their gaze – are associated with lying when, in fact, they are not, and people seem to think that certain other things – such as talking too little or repeating words – are not associated with lying when, in fact, they are. These instances of myth and ignorance may explain why the correlation between a person's ability to detect lies and their confidence in that ability is essentially zero (DePaulo et al., 1997).

When people can't do something well, for example adding up numbers or picking up heavy rocks, they typically turn the job over to machines (see **FIGURE 10.8**). Can machines detect lies better than we can? It depends on who you ask. The most widely used lie detection machine is the *polygraph*, which measures a variety of physiological responses associated with stress, which people often feel when they are afraid of being caught

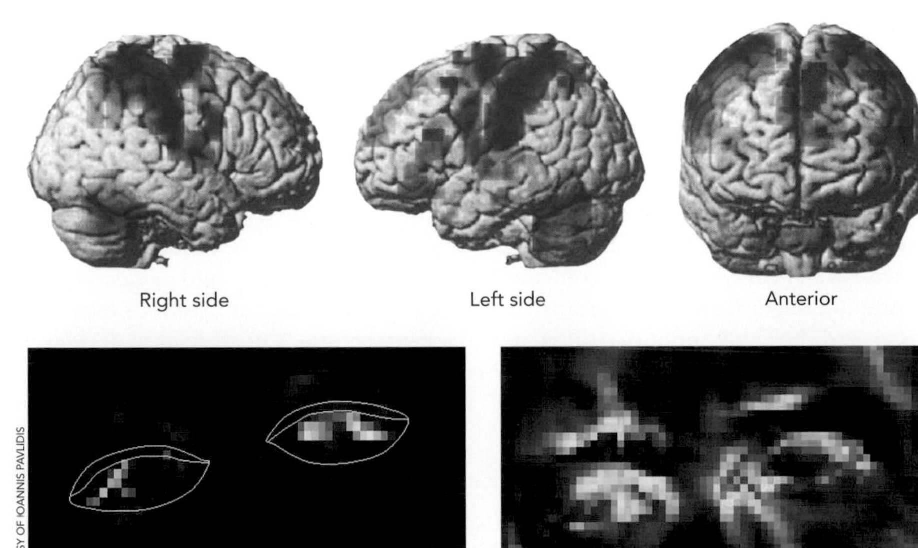

FIGURE 10.8 Lie detection machines Some researchers hope to replace the polygraph with more accurate machines, such as those that measure changes in blood flow in the brain and the face. As the top panel shows, some areas of the brain are more active when people tell lies than when they tell the truth (shown in red), and some are more active when people tell the truth than when they tell lies (shown in blue) (Langleben et al., 2005). The bottom panel shows images taken by a thermal camera that detects the heat caused by blood flow to different parts of the face. The images show a person's face before (left) and after (right) telling a lie (Pavlidis et al., 2002). Although neither of these new techniques is extremely accurate, that could soon change.

TOP PANEL: FIGURE COURTESY DANIEL LANGLEBEN AND KOSHA RUPAREL, UNIVERSITY OF PENNSYLVANIA. LANGLEBEN, D. D., LOUGHEAD, J. W., BILKER, W. B. ET AL. (2005) TELLING TRUTH FROM LIE IN INDIVIDUAL SUBJECTS WITH FAST EVENT-RELATED FMRI. *HUMAN BRAIN MAPPING*, 26, 262–72 in a lie. (One such response we have encountered frequently in this textbook is the GSR measure of autonomic arousal, discussed in Chapter 8.) In fact, the polygraph is so widely used by the US government and businesses that the US National Research Council recently met to consider all the scientific evidence on its validity. After much study, it concluded that the polygraph can indeed detect lies at a rate significantly better than chance. However, it also concluded that 'almost a century of research in scientific psychology and physiology provides little basis for the expectation that a polygraph test could have extremely high accuracy' ((National Research Council, 2003, p. 212).

The council went on to note the dangers of using a test that has the polygraph's error rate. Imagine, for example, that in a group of 10,000 people, 10 are terrorists, and when hooked up to a polygraph, all 10,000 people proclaim their innocence. Given the machine's error rate, a polygraph operator who caught 8 of the 10 terrorists would also 'catch' 1,598 innocent people. If the operator were willing to use more stringent criteria for guilt, they could reduce the number of innocent people they caught to 39, but then they'd only catch 2 of the 10 terrorists. Furthermore, these numbers assume that the terrorists don't know how to fool the polygraph, which is something that people can, in fact, be trained to do. The National Research Council (2003, p. 6) warned:

> Given its level of accuracy, achieving a high probability of identifying individuals who pose major security risks in a population with a very low proportion of such individuals would require setting the test to be so sensitive that hundreds, or even thousands, of innocent individuals would be implicated for every major security violator correctly identified.

However, not all countries consider the polygraph reliable. In the UK, the use of the polygraph is not admissible in a court of law. The British Psychological Society (2004, p. 30) published a report, which concluded that: 'the polygraph ... has inherent weaknesses. Error rates in polygraphic deception detection can be high ... Polygraph deception detection procedures should not be ascribed a special status.' In short, neither people nor machines are particularly good at lie detection, which is why lying continues to be a staple of human social interaction (see where do you stand? box).

In summary, the voice, the body and the face all communicate information about a person's emotional state. Darwin suggested that these emotional expressions are the same for all people and are universally understood, and research suggests that this is generally true. Emotional expressions are caused by the emotions they signify, but they can also cause those emotions. Emotional mimicry allows people to experience and hence identify the emotions of others.

Not all emotional expressions are sincere because people use display rules to help them decide which emotions to express. Cultures have different display rules, but people obey them by using the same set of techniques. There are reliable differences between sincere and insincere emotional expressions, just as there are reliable differences between truthful and untruthful utterances, but people are generally poor at determining when an expression or an utterance is sincere. Although machines such as the polygraph can make this determination with better-than-chance accuracy, its error rates are dangerously high.

Motivation: getting moved

MOTIVATION The purpose for or cause of an action.

You now know something about how emotions are produced, experienced and communicated. But what in the world are they *for*? Emotions have several functions, and one of the most important is that they motivate behaviour. Motivation refers to *the purpose for or cause of an action,* and it is no coincidence that the words *emotion* and *motivation* share a common linguistic root that means 'to move'. We act because our emotions move us to do so, and they move us in two different ways. First, emotions provide us with *information* about the world, and second, emotions are the *objectives* towards which we strive. Let's examine each of these in turn.

The function of emotion

In the middle of the night, Ian Robertson, a neuropsychologist working at Trinity College, Dublin, got a phone call from his elderly mother asking him to speak to his father. She said he was confused and believed that he was living in the wrong house and she wanted Ian to reason with him. When his father came on the phone, Ian tried using logic to get him to realize that it must be his house. He asked his father to acknowledge various unique features of the home and even pointed out the tree in the garden they planted together when he was a young boy. Ian eventually persuaded his father to stay until he could visit. A few days later, his father let slip during a conversation something about 'the real mum'. This is when Ian understood that his father believed that not only was the house not his, but his own wife was an imposter. She may have looked like her but she was not his real wife. It was only much later that Ian realized that his father also thought he was not the real son, which explained the interpersonal distance that had grown between them in their conversations. Ian's father had Capgras syndrome following a stroke (see **FIGURE 10.9**). People who suffer from this syndrome typically believe that one or more of their family members are imposters. Ian's father had sustained damage to the neural connections between his temporal lobe (where representations of familiar stimuli like faces and homes are stored) and his limbic system (where emotions are generated). As a result, when he looked around the family home and saw his wife's face, he could easily recognize them, but because this information was not transmitted to his limbic system, he didn't feel the warm emotions that these familiar sights once produced. His wife 'looked right' but didn't 'feel right', and so he concluded that she must be an imposter.

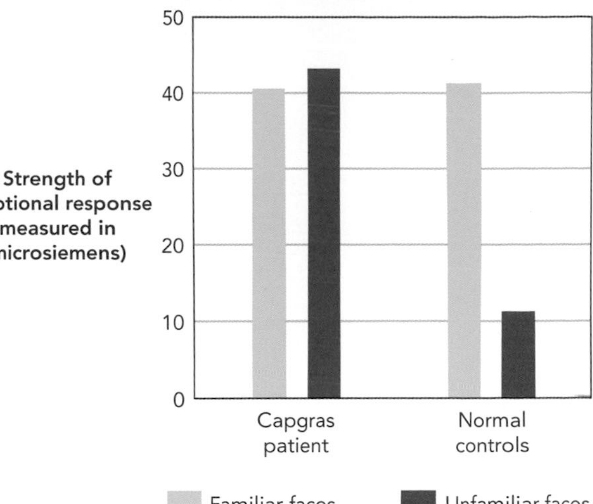

FIGURE 10.9 Capgras syndrome This graph shows the emotional responses (as measured by GSR) of a patient with Capgras syndrome and a group of control participants to a set of familiar and unfamiliar faces. Although the controls have stronger emotional responses to the familiar than the unfamiliar faces, the Capgras patient has similar emotional responses to both (Hirstein and Ramachandran, 1997).

> **A dangerous delusion**
>
> Capgras syndrome is very rare, which is just as well, as sufferers have been known to kill 'imposters'. In one extreme case, a sufferer who thought his father had been replaced by a robot decapitated him, looking for the batteries and microfilm inside the head.

His father's conclusions were wrong, of course, but his logic was sound. He had used his emotional experience as information about the world, and studies show that most of us do the same thing. For example, people report being more satisfied with their lives in general when they are asked the question on a sunny day rather than a rainy day. Why? Because people feel happier on sunny days, and they use their happiness as information about the quality of their lives (Schwarz and Clore, 1983). People who are in good moods believe that they have a higher probability of winning a lottery than people who are in bad moods. Why? Because people use their moods as information about the likelihood of succeeding at a task (Isen and Patrick, 1983). We all know that satisfying lives and bright futures make us feel good, so when we feel good, we naturally conclude that our lives must be satisfying and our futures must be bright. Because the world influences our emotions, our emotions provide information about the world (Schwarz et al., 1988).

Indeed, without this information, we wouldn't know what to do next. When neurologist Antonio Damasio was asked to examine a patient with an unusual form of brain damage, he asked the patient to choose between two dates for an appointment. As Damasio (1994, p. 193) later noted:

> For the better part of a half-hour, the patient enumerated reasons for and against each of the two dates: Previous engagements, proximity to other engagements, possible meteorological conditions, virtually anything that one could reasonably think about concerning a simple date ... He was walking us through a tiresome cost-benefit analysis, an endless outlining and fruitless comparison of options and possible consequences.

This patient's inability to make a simple decision was not due to any impairment of his ability to think or reason. On the contrary, he could think and reason all too well. What he couldn't do was feel. The patient's injury had left him unable to experience emotion, and thus when he entertained one option ('If I come next Tuesday, I'll have to cancel my lunch with Fred'), he didn't feel any better or any worse than when he entertained another ('If I come next Wednesday, I'll have to get up early to catch the bus'). And because he *felt* nothing when he thought about an option, he couldn't decide which was better. Studies show that when patients with this particular kind of brain damage are given the opportunity to gamble, they make a lot of reckless bets because they don't feel the twinge of anxiety that most of us would feel and would take to mean we're about to do something stupid. It's only fair to note that under certain circumstances, these patients are superior investors, precisely because they are willing to take risks that others will not (Shiv et al., 2005).

Emotions motivate us by providing information about the world, but they also motivate us more directly. People strongly prefer to experience positive rather than negative emotions, and the emotional experiences that we call happiness, satisfaction, pleasure and joy are often the goals, the ends, the objectives that our behaviour is meant to accomplish. The **hedonic principle** is *the notion that all people are motivated to experience pleasure and avoid pain*, and some clever people have argued that this single principle can explain all human behaviour. For example, Aristotle (1998) observed that if one traces any human motivation to its source, one will always find the desire for pleasure, or what he called 'happiness'. According to Aristotle, the pursuit of pleasure and the avoidance of pain 'is a first principle, for it is for the sake of this that we all do all that we do'.

HEDONIC PRINCIPLE The notion that all people are motivated to experience pleasure and avoid pain.

This may sound a bit extreme, but it isn't hard to convince yourself that Aristotle was on to something. If a friend asked you why you went to the shopping centre, you might explain that you wanted to buy a new pair of gloves. If your friend then asked why you wanted to buy a new pair of gloves, you might explain that you wanted to keep your hands warm. If your friend then asked why you wanted to keep your hands warm, you might explain that warm hands are a pleasure and cold hands are a pain. Each of these motivations rests on another, and thus each of your answers would make sense.

But if your friend then asked you why you wanted to experience pleasure instead of pain, you'd find yourself tongue-tied. There is no answer to this question because there is no other motivation on which the desire for pleasure rests. The desire for pleasure is at the bottom of the pile – it holds everything else up and nothing lies beneath it. We want many other things, of course, from peace and prosperity to health and security, but the reason we want these things is that they (like new gloves) help us to experience pleasure and avoid pain. Plato (1956), Aristotle's teacher, asked about all the many things that human beings call *good:* 'Are these things good for any other reason except that they end in pleasure, and get rid of and avert pain? Are you looking to any other standard but pleasure and pain when you call them good?' Plato was suggesting that pleasure doesn't just matter to us – it is what *mattering* means.

Many people voluntarily do things that cause them pain. According to the hedonic principle, people would not visit the dentist unless the pain of having dental work was ultimately outweighed by the pleasure of having had it done.

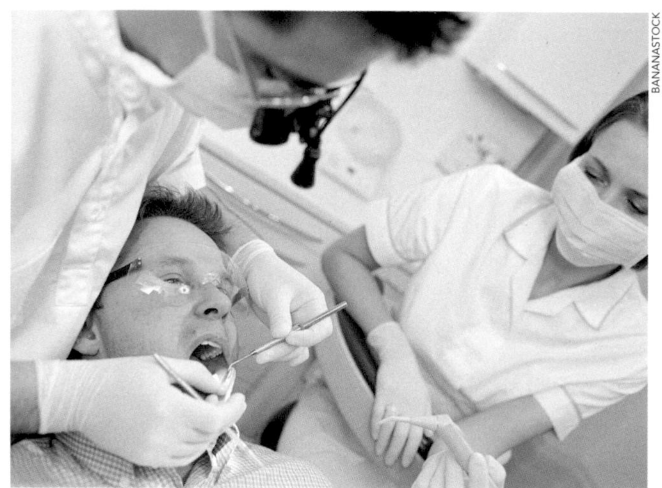
BANANASTOCK

According to the hedonic principle, then, our emotional experience can be thought of as a gauge that ranges from bad to good, and our primary motivation – perhaps even our *sole* motivation – is to keep the needle on the gauge as close to *g* as possible. Even when we voluntarily do things that tilt the needle in the opposite direction, such as letting the dentist drill our teeth or waking up early for a boring lecture, we are doing these things because we believe that they will nudge the needle towards *g* in the future and keep it there longer.

The conceptualization of motivation

The hedonic principle sets the stage for an understanding of motivation but leaves many questions unanswered. For example, if our primary motivation is to keep the needle on *g*, so to speak, then which things push the needle in that direction and which things push it away? And where do these things get the power to push our needle around, and exactly how do they do the pushing? The answers to such questions lie in two concepts that have played an unusually important role in the history of psychology: *instincts* and *drives.*

Instincts

When a newborn baby is given a drop of sugar water, it smiles, but when it is given a check for £10,000, it acts like it couldn't care less. By the time the baby gets into university, these responses pretty much reverse. It seems clear that nature endows us with certain motivations and that experience endows us with others. Over a century ago, William McDougall ([1908]2003, p. 458) argued that:

> observation of animals of any one species shows that all members of the species seek and strive toward a limited number of goals of certain types ... and all members of the

> species seek these goals independently of example and of prior experience of attainment of them ... We are justified, then, in inferring that each member of the species inherits the tendencies of the species to seek goals of these several types.

William James (1890, p. 383) called the inherited tendency to seek a particular goal an *instinct*, which he defined as 'the faculty of acting in such a way as to produce certain ends, without foresight of the ends, and without previous education in the performance'. According to both McDougall and James, nature hardwired penguins, parrots, puppies and people to want certain things without training and execute the behaviours that produced these things without thinking. They and other psychologists of their time tried to make a list of what those things were.

Unfortunately, they were quite successful, and in just a few decades the list of instincts they generated had grown preposterously long, including some rather exotic entries such as 'the instinct to be secretive' and 'the instinct to grind one's teeth' (both contributed by James himself). In his 1924 survey of the burgeoning literature on instinct, sociologist Luther Bernard (1924, p. 21) counted 5,759 instincts and concluded that after three decades of list making, the term seemed to be suffering from 'a great variety of usage and the almost universal lack of critical standards'. Furthermore, explaining the fact that people befriend each other by claiming that people have an 'affiliation instinct' didn't seem like much of an explanation at all. When Aristotle explained the downhill movement of water and the upward movement of fire by claiming that the former had 'gravity' and the latter had 'levity', it didn't take long for his fellow philosophers to catch on to the fact that Aristotle had merely named these tendencies and not really explained them. Psychologists worried that instincts were explanatory tautologies of Aristotelian proportion (Ayres, 1921; Dunlap, 1919; Field, 1921).

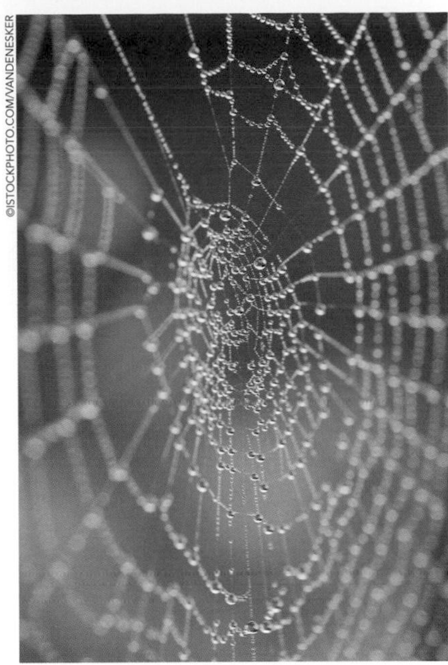

All animals are born with the motivation and the ability to perform certain complex behaviours. Spiders don't teach their offspring how to build elaborate webs, but their offspring build them nonetheless.

By 1930, the concept of instinct had taken 'a sharp turn toward obscurity' (Herrnstein, 1972, p. 23). Yes, the concept was somewhat vague and vacuous, but that wasn't its real problem. Its real problem was that it flew in the face of US psychology's newest and most unstoppable force: behaviourism. Behaviourists rejected the concept of instinct on two grounds:

1. They believed that behaviour could be best explained by the external stimuli that evoke it and not by reference to the hypothetical internal states on which it depends. John Watson (1913, p. 163) had written that 'the time seems to have come when psychology must discard all reference to consciousness', and behaviourists saw instincts as just the sort of unnecessary 'internal talk' that Watson dismissed.
2. Behaviourists were not concerned with the notion of inherited behaviour because for them all complex behaviour was learned. Because instincts were inherited tendencies that resided inside the organism, behaviourists considered them less worthy of experimental investigation.

Drives

But within a few decades, some of Watson's younger followers began to realize that without addressing internal states, certain phenomena were difficult to explain. For example, if all behaviour is a response to an external stimulus, why does a rat that is sitting still in its cage at 9am start wandering around and looking for food by noon? Nothing in the cage has changed, so why has the rat's behaviour changed? What visible, measurable external stimulus is the wandering rat responding to? The obvious answer (obvious, at least, to any ordinary person) is that the rat is responding to something inside itself, which meant that one should look inside the rat if one wanted to explain its wandering. Because the right answer obviously had something to do with internal states and because Watson had forbidden behaviourists to talk about internal states, his young followers – the 'new behaviourists' – had to use code words. The code word chosen by their leader B. F. Skinner (1932a, 1932b) was *drive*.

The new behaviourists began by noting that bodies are like thermostats. When thermostats detect that the room is too cold, they send signals that initiate corrective actions such as turning on a boiler. Similarly, when bodies detect that they are underfed, they send signals that initiate corrective actions such as eating. **Homeostasis** is *the tendency for*

HOMEOSTASIS The tendency for a system to take action to keep itself in a particular state.

DRIVE An internal state generated by departures from physiological optimality.

INCENTIVES External rewards that act to motivate behaviours.

a system to take action to keep itself in a particular state, and two of the new behaviourists, Clark Hull and Kenneth Spence, suggested that rats, people and thermostats are all homeostatic mechanisms. To survive, an organism needs to maintain precise levels of nutrition, warmth and so on, and when these levels depart from an optimal point, the organism receives a signal to take corrective action. That signal is called a **drive** – *an internal state generated to redress an imbalance in vitally important functions.* According to Hull and Spence, it isn't food per se that organisms find rewarding, it is the reduction of the drive for food. Hunger is a drive, a drive is an internal state, and when organisms eat, they are attempting to change their internal state. It is important to understand that behaviourists had to use a great many words in order to avoid using the forbidden ones that might suggest an internal state was involved!

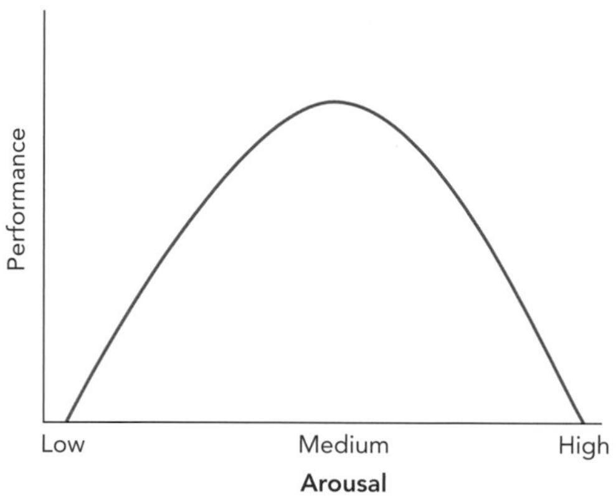

FIGURE **10.10 The Yerkes-Dodson law** Performance increases with arousal until it reaches an optimal level, after which it declines as arousal interferes with performance.

In his classic 1943 book, *Principles of Behavior*, Hull proposed that drives create physiological arousal, which activates behaviours until performing them reduces the drive. If a behaviour consistently reduces a drive, then over time it becomes a habit, which explains many idiosyncratic behaviours that people can develop. For example, many of our daily routines started out to satisfy some drive such as always stopping at the same shop to buy a snack, which reduces the hunger drive. However, this can develop into a habit that becomes self-reinforcing even when you are not so hungry. One problem with Hull's drive theory was that it failed to account for behaviours that did not appear to satisfy any biological need. For example, why are you reading this book? Why do students study? These behaviours are not simply due to some internal biological state, but are elicited by **incentives** – *external rewards that act to motivate behaviours.* Many of the things we do in life are motivated by incentives such as prestige and money, and these are determined, to a large extent, by what culture regards as valuable. Arguably, however, they are a means to an end to satisfy other drives such as reproduction.

Arousal and performance

If drives motivate behaviour, then you might assume the stronger the arousal, the better the performance. That is true up to a certain point, but as Robert Yerkes and John Dodson (1908) observed when using electric shocks to train rats to run mazes, if the shock is too much, the poor animals become overly aroused and scamper in random directions, thus failing to solve the maze. This led them to propose the Yerkes-Dodson law that there is an inverted 'U' relationship between levels of arousal and performance (see **FIGURE 10.10**).

The Yerkes-Dodson law explains why exam performance is poor when you are drowsy (underaroused) and when you anxious (overaroused). It also explains why actors and athletes can 'choke' in public when their performance is disrupted by too much arousal (see Chapter 15).

Psychology and me

Richard Keegan, Assistant Professor in Sport and Exercise Sciences, University of Canberra

Richard Keegan is a sport psychologist based at the University of Canberra in Australia. Visit www.palgrave.com/schacter to watch Richard talking about the research he conducted for his PhD into how the people around an athlete affect their motivation at different age levels, and his current research into mental fatigue and its impact on performance and its applications. He also offers some advice for students just starting their undergraduate psychology degrees.

Eating and mating

The words *instinct* and *drive* are no longer widely used in psychology, but the concepts remain part of the modern conception of motivation. The concept of instinct reminds us that nature endows organisms with a tendency to seek certain things, and the concept of drive reminds us that this seeking is initiated by an internal state. Psychologist William McDougall (1930) called the study of motivation *hormic psychology*, a term derived from the Greek word for 'urge', and people clearly have urges – some of which they acquire through experience and some of which they do not – that motivate them to take action. What kinds of urges do we have, and what kinds of actions do we take to satisfy them?

Abraham Maslow (1954) attempted to organize the list of human urges – or, as he called them, *needs* – in a meaningful way (see **FIGURE 10.11**). He noted that some needs, such as the need to eat, must be satisfied before others, such as the need to mate, and he built a hierarchy of needs that had the strongest and most immediate needs at the bottom and the weakest and most deferrable needs at the top. Maslow suggested that, as a rule, people will not experience a need until all the needs below it are met. So, when people are hungry, thirsty or exhausted, they will not seek intellectual fulfilment or

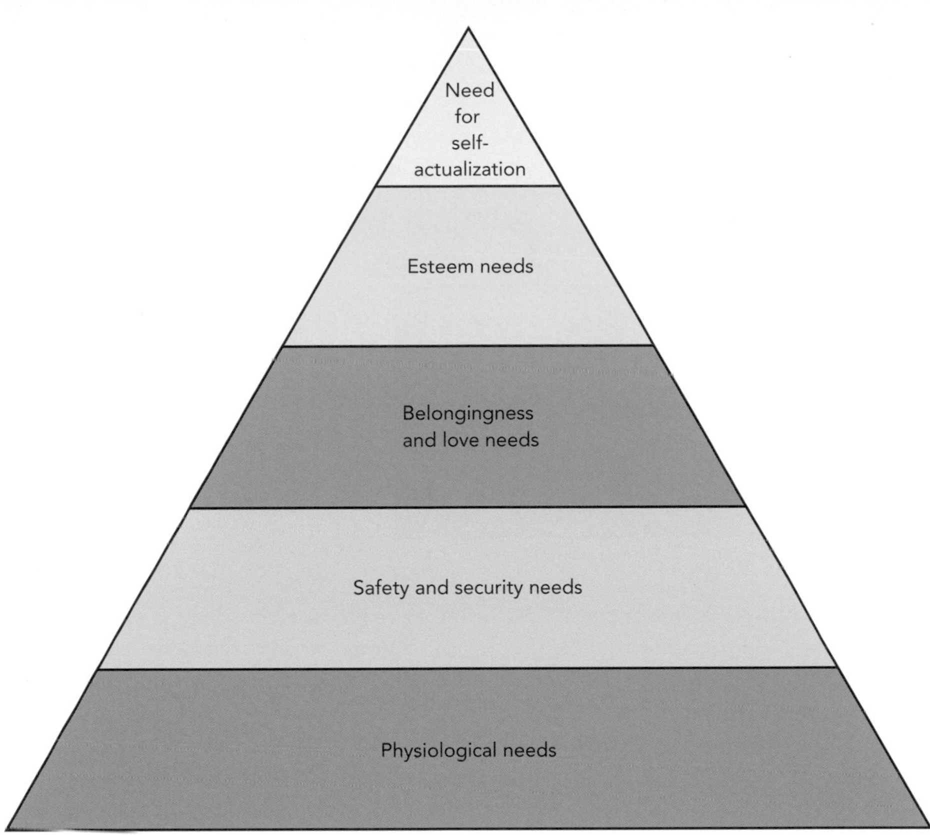

FIGURE **10.11 Maslow's hierarchy of needs** Humans are motivated to satisfy a variety of needs. Psychologist Abraham Maslow thought these needs formed a hierarchy, with lower order needs forming a base and self-actualization needs forming a pinnacle. He suggested that people don't experience higher needs until the needs below them have been met.

moral clarity, which is to say that philosophy is a luxury of the well fed. Although many aspects of Maslow's theory failed to win empirical support, for example a person on a hunger strike may value their principles more than their physical needs (see Wahba and Bridwell, 1976), the idea that some needs take precedence over others is clearly right. And although there are exceptions, those that typically take precedence are those we share with other mammals and are related to our common biology. Two of these needs – the need to eat and the need to mate – are among the most powerful and well studied, so let's see how they work.

The hunger signal

Hunger tells an organism to eat. But how does hunger arise? At every moment, your body is sending signals to your brain about its current energy state. If your body needs energy, it sends an *orexigenic* (increasing or stimulating the appetite) signal to tell your brain to switch hunger on, and if your body has sufficient energy, it sends an *anorexigenic* (suppressing the appetite) signal to tell your brain to switch hunger off (Gropp et al., 2005). No one knows precisely what these signals are or how they are sent and received, but research has identified a variety of candidates. For example, *leptin* is a chemical secreted by fat cells, and it appears to be an anorexigenic signal that tells the brain to switch hunger off. *Ghrelin* is a chemical produced in the stomach, and it appears to be an orexigenic signal that tells the brain to switch hunger on (Inui, 2001; Nakazato et al., 2001). Blood concentrations of ghrelin increase just before eating and decrease as eating proceeds (Cummings et al., 2001), and when people are injected with ghrelin, they become intensely hungry and eat about 30% more than usual (Wren et al., 2001). These are just two of the chemical messengers that tell the brain when to switch hunger on or off. Some researchers believe that there is no general state called 'hunger', rather there are many different hungers, each of which is a response to a unique nutritional deficit and is switched on by a unique chemical messenger (Rozin and Kalat, 1971). For example, rats that are deprived of protein will turn down fats and carbohydrates and specifically seek proteins, suggesting that they are experiencing a specific 'protein hunger' and not a general hunger (Rozin, 1968).

The experience of hunger is caused by chemical signals sent by your body to your brain.

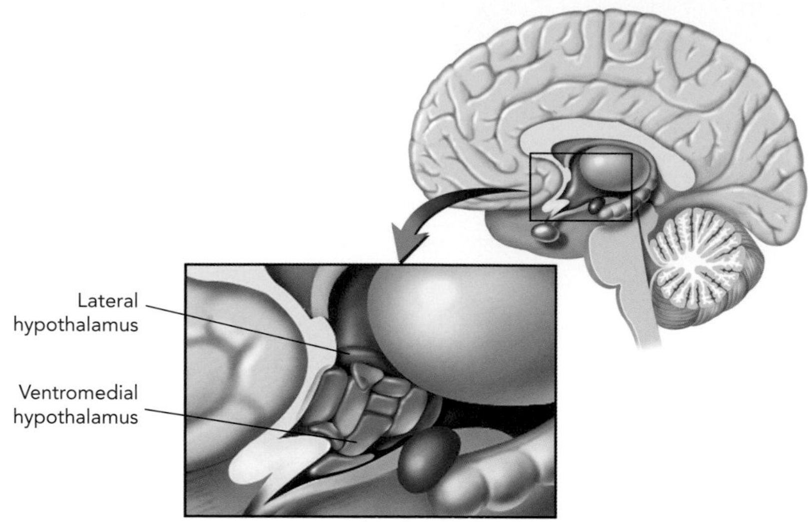

FIGURE 10.12 Hunger, satiety and the hypothalamus The hypothalamus comprises many parts. In general, the lateral hypothalamus receives the signals that turn hunger on and the ventromedial hypothalamus receives the signals that turn hunger off.

Whether hunger is one signal or many, the primary receiver of these signals is the hypothalamus. Different parts of the hypothalamus receive different signals (see FIGURE 10.12). The *lateral hypothalamus* receives orexigenic signals, and when it is destroyed, animals sitting in a cage full of food will starve themselves to death. The *ventromedial hypothalamus* receives anorexigenic signals, and when it is destroyed, animals will gorge themselves to the point of illness and obesity (Miller, 1960; Steinbaum and Miller, 1965). These two structures were once thought to be the 'hunger centre' and 'satiety centre' of the brain, but recent research has shown that this view is far too simple. For example, some studies suggest that damage to the ventromedial hypothalamus causes animals to eat because it increases insulin production, which causes a larger percentage of the animal's meal to be turned into fat. This means that a smaller percentage of the animal's meal is available to meet its immediate energy needs, thus the animal must eat more to compensate (Woods et al., 1998). It is tempting to think of different brain areas as hunger and satiety centres, but as psychologist Douglas Mook (1996, p. 98) noted:

> A map of the brain will not look like a map of Europe: Spain for satiety, France for feeding, Denmark for drinking. It will look more like a map of the Los Angeles freeway system, with routes diverging, converging, and crossing over, and many different destinations even for those all traveling the same route at the moment.

Hypothalamic structures play an important role in turning hunger on and off, but the way they execute these functions is complex and poorly understood (Stellar and Stellar, 1985).

Eating problems

Maslow's model helps to explain what goes wrong in clinical disorders when the motivational hierarchy is distorted. For example, one of the basic physiological needs that should be a primary foundation for all behaviour is to maintain optimal food intake. This should be a straightforward act, as feelings of hunger tell us when to eat and when to stop. But, according to the World Health Organization (WHO, 2015), in 2014 more than 1.9 billion adults did not know when to stop. One in four of us were overweight and 11% of males and 15% of women were obese. More worryingly, we are placing this burden on the next generation. Around 42 million children under the age of five were overweight or obese in 2013. Obesity is defined as having a body mass index (BMI) of 30 or greater, while being overweight is a BMI greater than or equal to 25. FIGURE 10.13 allows you to compute your BMI, and the odds are that you won't like what you learn. Recent figures from England show that the trend is increasing. Between 1993 and 2013, the proportion of adults who were obese increased from 15% to 25% (Public Health England, n.d.). A UK government report predicts that by 2050, 60% of men, 50% of women and 25% of children in the UK will be obese (Foresight, 2007).

FIGURE **10.13 Body mass index**

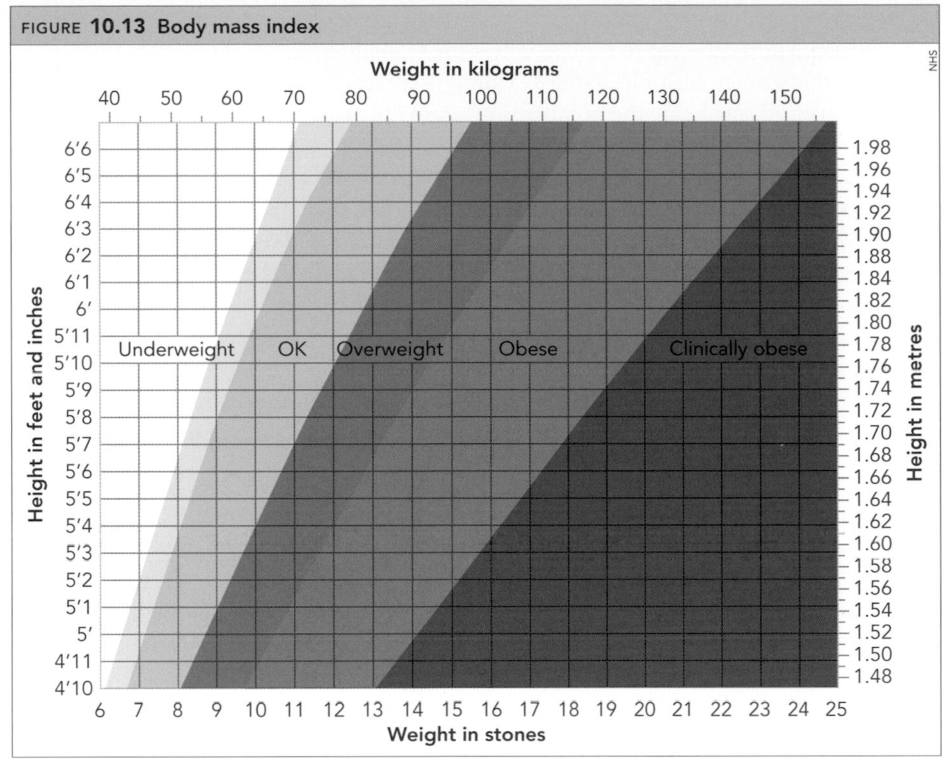

Overweight and obesity are leading risks for deaths worldwide. According to the WHO (n.d.), an estimated 56 million people died worldwide in 2012. The majority of these deaths (68%) were due to noncommunicable diseases that are all, to some extent, related to obesity, including cardiovascular disease, diabetes and different forms of cancer. Obesity not only increases the risk of death but obese people are viewed negatively by others, have lower self-esteem, and a lower quality of life (Hebl and Heatherton, 1997; Kolotkin et al., 2001). Indeed, the stigma of obesity is so powerful that average-weight people are viewed negatively if they even have a relationship with someone who is obese (Hebl and Mannix, 2003).

Obesity can result from biochemical abnormalities, and it seems to have a strong genetic component, but overeating is often a part of its cause. If the brain has a complex system of on and off switches that regulate hunger, why does anyone overeat? Hunger is just one of the reasons why people eat, and not always the most important one. For example, whether a person eats depends on their knowledge of when they last ate, which is why amnesiacs will happily eat a second lunch shortly after finishing an unremembered first one (Rozin et al., 1998). People often eat when they are emotionally unsettled but sometimes simply out of habit ('It's noon') or obligation ('Everyone else is ordering lunch'), all of which can cause people to eat more than they should.

Moreover, nature seems to have designed us for overeating. For most of our evolutionary history, the kinds and amounts of food available to people made it unlikely that anyone would eat too much, and the main food-related problem facing our ancestors was starvation. Their brains and bodies evolved two strategies to avoid it:

1 They developed a strong attraction to foods that provided large amounts of energy per bite, in other words, foods that were calorifically rich, which is why most of us prefer burgers and milkshakes to celery and water.
2 They developed an ability to store excess food energy in the form of fat, which enabled them to eat more than they needed when food was plentiful and then live off their reserves when food was scarce.

We are beautifully engineered for a world in which food is generally low in calories and scarce, but the problem is we don't live in that world anymore. Instead, most of us live in a world in which the calorie-laden miracles of modern technology – from chocolate cupcakes to sausage pizzas – are inexpensive and readily available.

Does eating chocolate make you feel better? Shrewd marketers would have you believe so, and it seems that we, and particularly women, buy into that theory. It's certainly not for its nutritional value.

But it's not just our biological heritage that contributes to obesity, and a look at common food cravings can help to explain why. One Canadian survey showed that nearly all (97%) young women and most (68%) young men report a strong urge to eat certain foods, with chocolate being the number one target (Benton et al., 1998). Apart from the high sugar and fat content, new discoveries about the pharmacological properties of the different chemicals contained in chocolate are often touted as the reason people crave it but the reality is that these substances are not present in sufficient quantities to have any effect (Benton, 2001). And in any case, if chocolate craving did serve an adaptive function, why is it so much more pronounced in women? In reality, the craving for chocolate, particularly among women, is attributable to the psychological responses generated by eating chocolate, and this in turn is probably more to do with cultural expectations and effective marketing (Hetherington, 2001).

For all the reasons outlined above, it is all too easy to overeat and become overweight or obese, and it is all too difficult to reverse course. The human body resists weight loss in two ways:

1 When we gain weight, we experience an increase in the size and number of fat cells in our bodies, usually in our abdomens if we are male and in our thighs and buttocks if we are female. But when we lose weight, we experience a decrease in the size of our fat cells but no decrease in their number. Once our bodies have added a fat cell, that cell is pretty much there to stay. It may become thinner when we diet, but it is unlikely to die.
2 Our bodies respond to dieting by decreasing our metabolism, the rate at which energy is used by the body. When our bodies sense that we are living through a famine, which is what they conclude when we refuse to feed them, they find more efficient ways to turn food into fat – a great trick for our ancestors but a real nuisance for us. Indeed, when rats are overfed, then put on diets, then overfed again and put on diets again, they gain weight faster and lose it more slowly the second time around, which suggests that with each round of dieting, their bodies become increasingly efficient at converting food to fat (Brownell et al., 1986). The bottom line is that avoiding obesity is much easier than overcoming it.

BULIMIA NERVOSA An eating disorder characterized by binge eating followed by activities intended to compensate for the food intake.

Less prevalent, but in many ways more attention grabbing are eating disorders where individuals deliberately starve or purge themselves, sometimes to the point of starvation – something that seems perverse to most of us. For instance, **bulimia nervosa** is *a disorder characterized by binge eating followed by activities intended to compensate for the food intake.* Bulimics typically ingest large quantities of food in a relatively short period and then take laxatives or induce vomiting to purge the food from their bodies. They may also crash diet, have enemas, take diuretics or other medications, or engage in excessive exercise to offset the food intake. Bulimics are caught in a cycle. They eat to ameliorate negative emotions such as sadness and anxiety, but then concern about weight gain leads them to experience negative emotions such as guilt and self-loathing, and these emotions then lead them to behaviours to lose weight.

ANOREXIA NERVOSA An eating disorder characterized by an intense fear of being fat and severe restriction of food intake.

Anorexia nervosa is *a disorder characterized by an intense fear of being fat and severe restriction of food intake.* Anorexics tend to have a distorted body image that leads them to believe they are fat when they are actually emaciated, and they tend to be high-achieving perfectionists who see their severe control of eating as a triumph of will over impulse. Contrary to what you might expect, anorexics have extremely *high* levels of ghrelin in their blood, which suggests that their bodies are trying desperately to switch hunger on, but that hunger's call is being suppressed, ignored or overridden (Ariyasu et al., 2001).

Eating disorders are more prevalent in women than men. A 2012 survey by the Royal College of Psychiatrists in the UK estimated that lifetime prevalence rates for anorexia nervosa in the general population ranged from 0.9 to 4.3% for females (Hudson et al., 2007; Wade and Bulik, 2007), and 4–7% for bulimia nervosa (Favaro et al., 2004). The lifetime prevalence of binge eating disorder was 3.5% in women and 2.0% in men (Hudson et al., 2007), but the incidence of eating disorders was highest for girls aged 15–19 and boys aged 10–14 (Micali et al., 2013).

Anorexics believe that thinness equals beauty, and it isn't hard to understand why. For example, in the US, the average woman is 1.62 m tall and weighs 63 kg, but the average

US fashion model is 1.80 m tall and weighs 53 kg. Indeed, most university-age women want to be thinner than they are, and nearly one in five reports being *embarrassed* to buy a chocolate bar (Rozin et al., 2003).

Sexual interest

Reproduction is another biological need in Maslow's hierarchical model but as essayist Florence King (1990) once remarked: 'I've had sex and I've had food, and I'd rather eat.' Indeed, food motivates us more strongly than sex because food is essential to our survival. But sex is essential to our DNA's survival, and thus evolution has ensured that a healthy desire for sex is wired deep into the brain of every mammal. In some ways, that wiring scheme is simple. Glands secrete hormones, which travel through the blood to the brain and stimulate sexual desire. But which hormones, which parts of the brain, and what triggers the launch in the first place?

A hormone called dehydroepiandrosterone (DHEA) seems to be involved in the initial onset of sexual desire. Males and females begin producing this slow-acting hormone at about age 6, which may explain why boys and girls both experience their initial sexual interest at about age 10, despite the fact that boys reach puberty much later than girls. Two other hormones have more gender-specific effects. Both males and females produce testosterone and oestrogen, but males produce more of the former and females produce more of the latter. As you will learn in Chapter 11, these two hormones are largely responsible for the physical and psychological changes that characterize puberty. But are they also responsible for the waxing and waning of sexual desire in adults? The answer appears to be yes – as long as those adults are rats. Testosterone increases the sexual desire of male rats by acting on a particular area of the hypothalamus, and oestrogen increases the sexual desire of female rats by acting on a different area of the hypothalamus. Lesions to these areas reduce sexual motivation in the respective genders, and when testosterone or oestrogen is applied to these areas, sexual motivation increases. In short, testosterone regulates sexual desire in male rats and oestrogen regulates sexual desire and fertility in female rats.

The story for human beings is far more interesting. The females of most mammalian species, for example dogs, cats and rats, have little or no interest in sex except when their oestrogen levels are high, which happens when they are ovulating, that is, when they are 'in oestrus' or 'in heat'. In other words, oestrogen regulates ovulation and sexual interest in these mammals. But female human beings – like female monkeys and apes – can be interested in sex at any point in their monthly cycles. Although the level of oestrogen in a woman's body changes dramatically over the course of her monthly menstrual cycle, studies suggest that sexual desire changes little if at all. Somewhere in the course of our evolution, it seems, women's sexual interest became independent of their ovulation. Some theorists have speculated that the advantage of this independence was that it made it more difficult for males to know whether a female was in the fertile phase of her monthly cycle. Male mammals often guard their mates jealously when their mates are ovulating but go off in search of other females when their mates are not. If a male cannot use his mate's sexual receptivity to tell when she is ovulating, he has no choice but to stay around and guard her all the time. For females who are trying to keep their mates at home so that they will contribute to the rearing of children, sexual interest that is continuous and independent of fertility may be an excellent strategy.

If oestrogen is not the hormonal basis of women's sex drives, what is? Two pieces of evidence suggests that the answer is testosterone – the same hormone that drives male sexuality. First, when women are given testosterone, their sex drives increase. Second, men naturally have more testosterone than women, and they have a stronger sex drive. Men are more likely than women to think about sex, have sexual fantasies, seek sex and sexual variety (whether positions or partners), masturbate, want sex at an early point in a relationship, sacrifice other things for sex, have permissive attitudes towards sex, and complain about low sex drive in their partners. Indeed, a group of researchers summarized decades of research on sex drive by concluding that 'by all measures, men have a stronger sex drive than women ... there were no measures that showed women having stronger sex drives than men' (Baumeister et al., 2001, p. 263). All this suggests that testosterone may be the hormonal basis of sex drive in men and women.

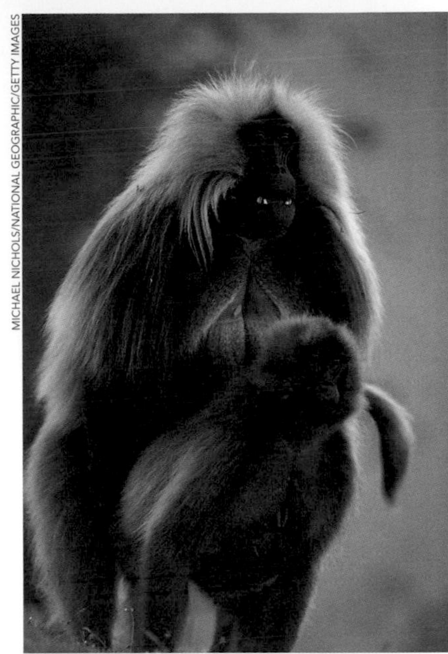

The red colouration on the female gelada's chest indicates she is in oestrus and thus amenable to sex. The sexual interest of female human beings is not limited to a particular time in their monthly cycle, and they do not clearly advertise their fertility.

Sexual activity

Men and women may have different levels of sexual drive, but their physiological responses during sex are fairly similar. Prior to the 1960s, data on human sexual behaviour consisted primarily of people's answers to questions about their sex lives, and you may have noticed that this is a topic about which people don't always tell the truth. William Masters and Virginia Johnson (1966) changed all that by conducting groundbreaking studies in which they actually measured the physical responses of many hundreds of volunteers as they masturbated or had sex in the laboratory. Their work led to many discoveries, including a better understanding of the human sexual response cycle – *the stages of physiological arousal during sexual activity* (see **FIGURE 10.14**).

HUMAN SEXUAL RESPONSE CYCLE The stages of physiological arousal during sexual activity.

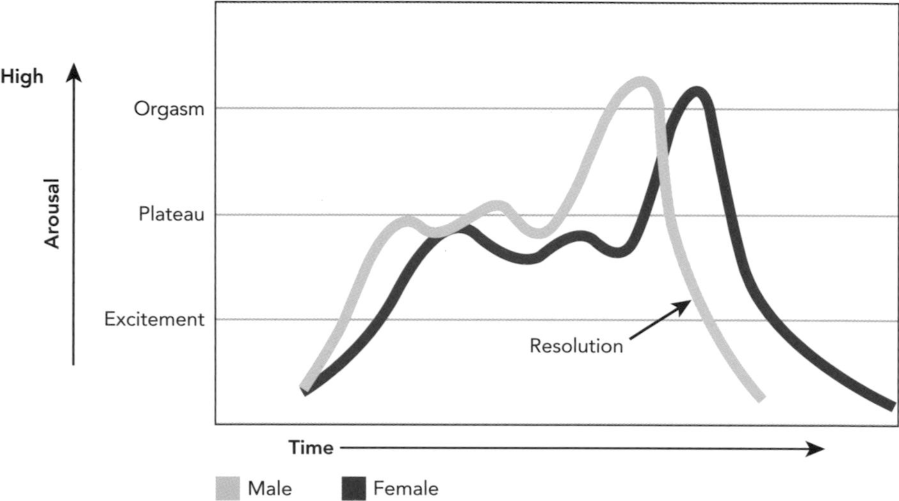

FIGURE **10.14 The human sexual response cycle** The pattern of the sexual response cycle is quite similar for men and for women. Both men and women go through the excitement, plateau, orgasm and resolutions phases, although the timing of their response may differ.

Human sexual response has four phases:

1 During the *excitement phase*, muscle tension and blood flow increase in and around the sexual organs, heart and respiration rates increase, and blood pressure rises. Men and women may experience erect nipples and a 'sex flush' on the skin of the upper body and face. A man's penis typically becomes erect or partially erect and his testicles draw upwards, while a woman's vagina typically becomes lubricated and her clitoris becomes swollen.

2 During the *plateau phase*, heart rate and muscle tension increase further. A man's urinary bladder closes to prevent urine from mixing with semen, and muscles at the base of his penis begin a steady rhythmic contraction. A man's Cowper gland may secrete a small amount of lubricating fluid, which often contains enough sperm to cause pregnancy. A woman's clitoris may withdraw slightly, and her vagina may become more lubricated. Her outer vagina may swell, and her muscles may tighten and reduce the diameter of the opening of the vagina.

3 During the *orgasm phase*, breathing becomes extremely rapid and the pelvic muscles begin a series of rhythmic contractions. Both men and women experience quick cycles of muscle contraction of the anus and lower pelvic muscles, and women often experience uterine and vaginal contractions as well. During this phase, men ejaculate about 2–5 ml of semen, depending on how long it has been since their last orgasm and how long they were aroused prior to ejaculation. Around 95% of heterosexual men and 69% of heterosexual women reported having an orgasm during their last sexual encounter (Richters et al., 2006), although it is worth noting that roughly 15% of women never experience orgasm, less than half experience orgasm from intercourse alone, and roughly half report having 'faked' an orgasm at least once (Wiederman, 1997). The frequency with which women have orgasms seems to have a relatively large genetic component (Dawood et al., 2005). When men and women do have orgasms, they typically experience them as intensely pleasurable, and although many

of us assume that these pleasurable experiences are different for men and women, studies suggest that they are similar (Mah and Binik, 2002). Indeed, when gynaecologists, psychologists and medical students read people's descriptions of their orgasmic experiences, they cannot reliably tell whether those descriptions were written by men or women (Vance and Wagner, 1976).

4 During the *resolution phase*, muscles relax, blood pressure drops, and the body returns to its resting state. Most men and women experience a *refractory period*, during which further stimulation does not produce excitement. This period may last from minutes to days and is typically longer for men than for women.

Men and women are similar in their responses during sexual activity, and they are also similar in their reasons for engaging in sexual activity in the first place. Sex is necessary for reproduction, of course, but the vast majority of sexual acts are performed for other reasons, which include experiencing pleasure, coping with negative emotions, increasing emotional intimacy between partners, pleasing one's partner, impressing one's friends, and reassuring oneself of one's own attractiveness (Cooper et al., 1998). Women and men report that their primary motivation for having sex is to create intimacy with their partners. Women are less likely than men to have sex to impress their friends, and men become less likely to have sex for this reason as they get older. Interestingly, as they age, men and women are more likely to have sex for pleasure but no less likely to have sex to reassure themselves of their attractiveness. It is worth noting that not all sex is motivated by one of these reasons. About half of women and a quarter of men report having unwanted sexual activity in a dating relationship as young adults (O'Sullivan and Allegeier, 1998). We will have much more to say about sexual attraction and relationships in Chapter 14.

Kinds of motivation

We have seen that eating and mating are two things that human beings are strongly motivated to do, but what are the others, and how do they relate to each other? Alas, there is no widely accepted taxonomy of human motivations, which has made it difficult for psychologists to develop theories about where motivations come from and how they operate. Nonetheless, psychologists have made initial progress by identifying several of the dimensions on which motivations differ.

Intrinsic versus extrinsic motivation

Taking a psychology exam is not like eating a plate of chips. One makes you tired and the other makes you fat, one requires that you move your lips and one requires that you don't and so on. But the key difference between these activities is that one is a means to an end and one is an end in itself. An extrinsic motivation is *a motivation to take actions that are not themselves rewarding but lead to reward.* When we brush our teeth and gargle with mouthwash so we can avoid gum disease, fillings and bad breath (and get dates), when we work hard for money so we can pay our rent (and get dates), and when we take an exam so we can get a university degree (and get money to get dates), we are extrinsically motivated. None of these things directly brings pleasure, but all may lead to pleasure in the long run. An intrinsic motivation is *a motivation to take actions that are themselves rewarding.* When we eat chips because they taste good, exercise because it feels good, or listen to music because it sounds good, we are intrinsically motivated. These activities don't have to *have* a payoff because they *are* a payoff.

EXTRINSIC MOTIVATION A motivation to take actions that are not themselves rewarding but lead to reward.

INTRINSIC MOTIVATION A motivation to take actions that are themselves rewarding.

Extrinsic motivation sometimes gets a bad press. As young adults, we tend to believe that people should 'follow their hearts' and 'do what they love', and we feel sorry for or disdainful of students who choose courses just to please their parents and parents who choose jobs just to earn a lot of money. But the fact is that our ability to engage in behaviours that are unrewarding in the present because we believe they will bring greater rewards in the future is one of our species' most significant talents, and no other species can do it quite as well as we can (Gilbert, 2006). In research on the ability to delay gratification, people are typically faced with a choice between getting something they want now, for example a scoop of ice cream, or waiting and getting more of what they want

The torment of waiting for ice cream is an extrinsic motivation, as you know the rewards will be greater in the end. Could you resist?

later, for example two scoops of ice cream. Waiting for ice cream is a lot like taking an exam or brushing teeth: it isn't much fun, but you do it because you know you will reap greater rewards in the end. In Chapter 12, we will examine how four-year-old children who can delay gratification are judged to be more intelligent and socially competent 10 years later and have higher academic scores when they enter university (Mischel et al., 1989). In fact, the ability to delay gratification is a better predictor of a child's results in school than the child's IQ (Duckworth and Seligman, 2005). Apparently, there is something to be said for extrinsic motivation.

There is a lot to be said for intrinsic motivation too. People work harder when they are intrinsically motivated, they enjoy what they do more, and they do it more creatively. Both kinds of motivation have advantages, which is why many of us try to build lives in which we are intrinsically and extrinsically motivated by the same activity – lives in which we are paid big money for doing exactly what we like to do best. Who hasn't fantasized about becoming a professional artist, a professional athlete or a professional chocolatier? Alas, research suggests that it is difficult to have your chocolate and eat it, because extrinsic rewards can undermine intrinsic rewards (Deci et al., 1999; Henderlong and Lepper, 2002). We discussed this overjustification effect in Chapter 6, where rewards actually undermine motivation. For example, in one study, students who were intrinsically interested in a puzzle were either paid to complete it or completed it for free, and those who were paid were less likely to play with the puzzle later on (Deci, 1971). It appears that under some circumstances, people take rewards to indicate that an activity isn't inherently pleasurable ('If they had to pay me to do that puzzle, it couldn't have been a very fun one'), thus rewards can cause people to lose their intrinsic motivation.

Just as rewards can undermine intrinsic motivation, punishments can create it. In one study, children who had no intrinsic interest in playing with a toy suddenly gained an interest when the experimenter threatened to punish them if they touched it (Aronson, 1963). Students who had no intrinsic motivation to cheat on a test were more likely to do so if the experimenter explicitly warned against it (Wilson and Lassiter, 1982). Threats can suggest that a forbidden activity is desirable, and so they can have the paradoxical consequence of promoting the very behaviours they are meant to discourage. For example, when a group of childcare centres got fed up with parents who arrived late to pick up their children, some of them instituted a financial penalty for tardiness. As **FIGURE 10.15** shows, the financial penalty caused an *increase* in late arrivals (Gneezy and Rustichini, 2000). Why? Because parents are intrinsically motivated to fetch their kids and they generally do their best to be on time. But when the childcare centres imposed a fine for late arrival, the parents became extrinsically motivated to fetch their children, and because the fine wasn't particularly large, they decided to pay a small financial penalty in order to leave their children for an extra hour. When threats and rewards change intrinsic motivation into extrinsic motivation, unexpected consequences can follow.

People are be motivated by intrinsic and extrinsic factors and it is these considerations that are taken into account when considering why people do the things they do. One

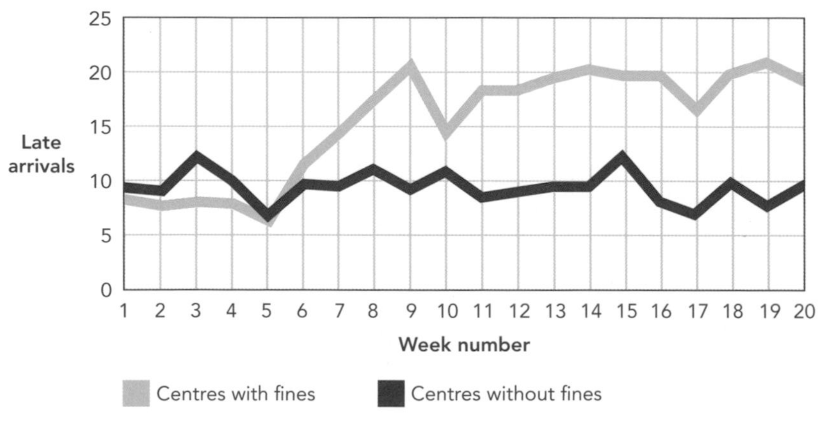

FIGURE 10.15 When threats backfire Threats can cause behaviours that were once intrinsically motivated to become extrinsically motivated. Childcare centres that instituted fines for late-arriving parents saw an increase in the number of parents who arrived late.

framework that integrates intrinsic and extrinsic motivation is self-determination theory – which *emphasizes the need to understand human motivation in terms of competence, autonomy and relatedness* (Ryan and Deci, 2000). Individuals are motivated when they feel competent, which, in turn, is influenced by feedback, often in the form of positive comments from others (Deci, 1975). That competence also depends on the person feeling autonomous, namely that they are responsible for the success. However, self-determination theory argues that, for most of us, goals are only worth pursuing if others, to whom we feel related, also think they are worthwhile. Critical to self-determination theory is the process of internalization – *where extrinsic influences are incorporated into intrinsic motivations*. Internalization is part of socialization that takes place largely during development when children learn to adopt the motivations that society generally promotes. However, as we will discover in Chapter 15, adults often internalize group attitudes and preferences in order to be accepted by others.

SELF-DETERMINATION THEORY Emphasizes the need to understand human motivation in terms of competence, autonomy and relatedness.

INTERNALIZATION Where extrinsic influences are incorporated into intrinsic motivations.

Conscious versus unconscious motivation

When prizewinning artists or scientists are asked to explain their achievements, they typically say things like 'I wanted to liberate colour from form' or 'I wanted to cure diabetes'. They almost never say: 'I wanted to exceed my father's accomplishments, thereby proving to my mother that I was worthy of her love.' A conscious motivation is *a motivation of which one is aware*, and an unconscious motivation is *a motivation of which one is not aware*. Freud believed that people have unconscious motivations, but do they? In one sense, this is a trivial question. As you learned in Chapter 8, people often can't identify the reasons for or causes of their own behaviour, and in this sense, people have motivations of which they are unaware. We may avoid films that star a particular actor without also knowing that the reason why we can't stand his face is that he resembles a maths teacher who we loathed at school.

CONSCIOUS MOTIVATION A motivation of which one is aware.

UNCONSCIOUS MOTIVATION A motivation of which one is not aware.

But some psychologists have suggested that people have unconscious motivations that are anything but trivial. For example, David McClelland and colleagues argued that people vary in their need for achievement – *the motivation to solve worthwhile problems* (McClelland et al., 1953). They argued that this basic motivation is unconscious and thus must be measured with special techniques such as the inkblot test, where people have to say what images they can see in a splodge of ink. The amount of 'achievement-related imagery' in the person's story ostensibly reveals the person's unconscious need for achievement. (You'll learn more about these sorts of tests in Chapter 13.) Although there has been much controversy about the validity and reliability of measures such as these (Lilienfeld et al., 2000; Tuerlinckx et al., 2002), research shows that a person's responses on this test reliably predict the person's behaviour in certain circumstances. For example, they can predict a child's results in school (Khalid, 1991). Research also suggests that this motivation can be 'primed' in much the same way that thoughts and feelings can be primed. For example, when words such as *achievement* are presented briefly, those people will work especially hard to solve a puzzle (Bargh et al., 2001) and will feel especially unhappy if they fail (Chartrand et al, 2006).

NEED FOR ACHIEVEMENT The motivation to solve worthwhile problems.

Some of our motivations are conscious and some are not. So which are which? Someone who is shopping for gloves may be simultaneously motivated to increase their happiness, keep their hands warm and find the right aisle in the shop. Which of these motives will they be aware of? You'll notice that some of them are quite general (increasing happiness) and some are quite specific (looking for the glove department). Robin Vallacher and Daniel Wegner (1985, 1987) have suggested that people tend to be aware of their general motivations unless the complexities of executing an action force them to become aware of their specific motivations. For example, if a person is changing a light bulb and is asked about their motivation, they may say something like 'I'm helping my dad out'. But the moment the light bulb gets stuck, their answer will change to 'I'm trying to get these threads aligned'. The person has both motivations, but is conscious of the more general motivation when the action is easy and the more specific motivation when the action is difficult. In one experiment, participants drank coffee from either a normal mug or a mug that had a heavy weight attached to the bottom, which made the mug difficult to manipulate. When asked what they were doing, those who were drinking from the normal mug explained that they were 'satisfying my needs', whereas those who were drinking from the weighted mug explained that they were 'swallowing' (Wegner et al., 1984). As we saw in Chapter 8 when we described consciousness as 'a spin doctor' of experience, we readily modify the reasons for our motivation depending on changing circumstances.

Daydreaming and ego depletion

Were you ever told off for daydreaming in class as a child? Even as adults, many of us find our minds wandering during the day; often in the middle of a tedious task, which reflects a lack of concentration. However, daydreaming can be a useful offline activity that enables us to mentally process goals and develop plans even though its components are spontaneous and fragmentary (Klinger, 2013). The absence of directed active thought when our minds wander also facilitates creative problem solving. Individuals given the opportunity to daydream are better at coming up with solutions after an undemanding task that allows for mind-wandering compared to one that requires concentration (Baird et al. 2012). We also make better decisions after a bit of daydreaming. For example, participants given the choice of receiving €10 immediately or a larger reward (up to €50) later are more likely to delay immediate reward after an undemanding task that allows for mind-wandering (Smallwood, 2013).

An alternative explanation for the benefits of mind-wandering are the negative consequences of concentration related to another motivation phenomenon known as *ego depletion* (Baumeister, 2002). Whenever we exert willpower such as concentrating on a hard task, it comes at a cost – a cost that makes us more susceptible to temptation later. Ego depletion explains willpower like a mental muscle that can be fatigued. There is only so much willpower you can exert and when it becomes depleted, you become vulnerable to the temptations and drives of impulsive thoughts and behaviours.

Ego depletion explains why so many of us give into behaviours that are potentially self-defeating. All sorts of experiences can deplete our ego strength from enduring bad smells, tackling difficult puzzles, putting up with others in crowded situations or simply being electrocuted with an unpredictable mild shock. Baumeister and Tiernay (2012) have demonstrated that after enduring these taxing experiences, many of us go on to drink too much, eat too much or engage in activities we would prefer to avoid or at best limit. We encounter willpower again in Chapter 12 when we discuss the development of self-control.

Approach versus avoidance motivation

Poet James Thurber (1956) wrote: 'All men should strive to learn before they die/what they are running from, and to, and why.' The hedonic principle describes two conceptually distinct motivations: a motivation to 'run to' pleasure and a motivation to 'run from' pain. These correspond to what psychologists call an approach motivation, *a motivation to experience a positive outcome*, and an avoidance motivation, *a motivation not to experience a negative outcome.* Although pleasure and pain seem like two sides of the same coin, they are independent phenomena that occur in different parts of the brain (Davidson et al., 1990), so it's not surprising that the motivation to experience positive emotions and the motivation not to experience negative emotions behave a bit differently.

APPROACH MOTIVATION A motivation to experience positive outcomes.

AVOIDANCE MOTIVATION A motivation not to experience negative outcomes.

For example, research suggests that, all things being equal, avoidance motivations tend to be more powerful than approach motivations. Most people will turn down a chance to bet on a coin toss that would pay them €10 if it came up heads but would require them to pay €8 if it came up tails, because they believe that the pain of losing €8 will be more intense than the pleasure of winning €10 (Kahneman and Tversky, 1979). Because people expect losses to have more powerful emotional consequences than equal-size gains, they will take more risks to avoid a loss than to achieve a gain. When participants are told that a disease is expected to kill 600 people and that one vaccine will definitely save 400 people, whereas another has a one-third chance of saving 600 people and a two-thirds chance of saving no one, they typically say that the government should play it safe and use the first vaccine. But when people are told that one vaccine will definitely allow 200 people to die, whereas the other has a one-third chance of letting no one die and a two-thirds chance of letting 600 people die, they say that the government should gamble and use the second vaccine (Tversky and Kahneman, 1981). If you whip out your calculator, you will quickly see that these are two ways of describing the same thing, yet when the vaccines are described in terms of the number of lives lost instead of the number of lives gained, most people are ready to take a big risk in order to avoid the horrible loss of 600 human lives.

Although avoidance motivation tends to be stronger than approach motivation overall, there are people for whom this is more or less true. For instance, people with a high need for achievement tend to be somewhat more motivated by their hope for success, whereas people with a low need for achievement tend to be somewhat more motivated by their fear of failure. This causes the 'highs' to set reasonable goals that maximize their chances of achieving a worthwhile, meaningful success, and it causes 'lows' to set goals that are either too easy, which ensures their success, or too difficult, which provides an excuse for their failure. When participants in one study were invited to play a game in which they had to toss a ring onto a pole and were allowed to stand as close to the pole as they wished, participants with a high need for achievement tended to stand an intermediate distance from the pole – close enough to make success a good possibility, but far enough to make success worthwhile. Participants with a low need for achievement, on the other hand, were more likely to stand close to the pole or far from it (Atkinson and Litwin, 1960).

In a US study, participants were given an anagram task. Some were told that they would be paid $4 for the experiment, but they could earn an extra dollar by finding 90% or more of all the possible words. Others were told that they would be paid $5 for the experiment, but they could avoid losing a dollar by not missing more than 10% of all the possible words. (As with the example above, you'll realize that both alternatives represent the same thing.) People who had a 'promotion focus', a tendency to think in terms of achieving gains, performed better in the first case than in the second. But people who had a 'prevention focus', a tendency to think in terms of avoiding losses, performed better in the second case than in the first (Shah et al., 1998).

Finally, we must remember that some individuals deliberately seek out challenges the rest of us avoid. How else can we explain those who test their endurance on physically demanding tasks like marathon running or engage in risky behaviours unless it provided them with a motivation? For some of us, setting and achieving personal goals that others may avoid is an important motivation in life. Others are thrill seekers who enjoy taking risks. *Sensation seeking* is a personality trait defined by the search for experiences and feelings that are 'varied, novel, complex and intense', and the readiness to 'take physical, social, legal, and financial risks for the sake of such experiences' (Zuckerman, 2009). Here, the normal hedonic principle that most of us exercise in avoiding negative outcomes is outweighed by the pleasurable sensation when the risk is overcome.

Unpredictability and emotion

Most of us are motivated to achieve future goals in the pursuit of happiness but, remarkably, many of us are not that good at predicting how satisfied we will be when we do so. Consider these unlikely scenarios: would you rather win the lottery or become permanently disabled? You probably think that's the easiest question you've ever been asked. After all, isn't it *obvious* that one of these events would make you deliriously happy for years to come and the other would make you hopelessly depressed? Obvious, yes, but not necessarily true. Research shows that just a year after the event, lottery winners and paraplegics are about equally happy (Brickman et al., 1978). If you find that hard to believe, then you're not alone. Timothy Wilson and Daniel Gilbert have studied affective forecasting, *the process by which people predict their emotional reactions to future events*, and they've found that people are not particularly good at predicting how they will feel after experiencing positive or negative events (Gilbert et al., 2002; Wilson and Gilbert, 2003). People routinely overestimate the joy of falling in love and the pain of falling out of it, the thrill of winning a football game and the agony of losing one, the delight of getting promoted and the distress of getting fired – and many other good and bad events (Gilbert et al., 1998; Wilson et al., 2000a). The fact is that you could know exactly what your future will hold and still not know how much you're going to like it when you get there.

AFFECTIVE FORECASTING The process by which people predict their emotional reactions to future events.

Why are we so poor at forecasting our emotional reactions to future events? One reason is that most of us have a poor understanding of how our own emotions work. One of the basic laws of emotion is that people have stronger emotional reactions to events whose causes they don't understand ('Yikes! What was that thumping noise?') than to events whose causes they do understand ('The washing machine is making that thumping noise again'). This has implications for happiness. For example, unexpected windfalls of cash generate more happiness than when the same amount of money is received expectedly (Wilson et al., 2005). Which is unfortunate, as people typically *prefer* to have an explanation rather than remain in the dark, thus they may choose things that undermine their own happiness.

In one study, the participants were university students who were linked to an internet chat room where they had conversations with several other students (Wilson et al., 2005). After a while, the experimenter asked everyone in the chat room to send a private email to the person whom they liked best, explaining why they liked that person so much. What participants didn't know was that all the 'other students' with whom they were chatting were actually confederates of the experimenter. As soon as the participants sent off their emails, they received emails from *every one* of the 'other students' explaining why the other student had chosen the participant as the person they liked most. In one condition of the study, every email was clearly identified so that the participant could tell which of the other students had sent it. In another condition, the emails were anonymous so that the participant couldn't tell which student had sent which message. The results revealed two things. First, participants were happier when they could *not* identify the sender of the messages than when they could. Because unexplained events produce more intense and enduring emotions, the students who were 'in the dark' about this happy event were happier for longer. Second, when a new group of participants were asked whether they would prefer to be able to identify the sender of each email or be kept in the dark, every one of them said they would prefer to know the sender's identity. It's a bit like receiving an unexpected Valentine rather than the usual one your mum sends you.

Studies such as these suggest that most people don't know enough about the nature of their own emotions to predict how happy they will be in different situations or choose the situations that will make them happiest. Our emotional blind spots, it seems, can make us strangers to ourselves (Gilbert, 2006; Wilson, 2002).

In summary, emotions motivate us indirectly by providing information about the world, but they also motivate us directly. The hedonic principle suggests that people approach pleasure and avoid pain and that this basic motivation underlies all others. All organisms are born with some motivations and acquire others through experience.

When the body experiences a deficit, we experience a drive to remedy it. Biological drives such as eating and mating generally take precedence over others. Hunger is the result of a complex system of physiological processes, and problems with this system can lead to eating disorders and obesity, both of which are difficult to overcome. With regard to sexual drives, men and women tend to be more similar than different. Both genders experience the same sequence of physiological arousal, engage in sex for most of the same reasons, and have sex drives that are regulated by testosterone.

People have many motivations that can be classified in many ways. Intrinsic motivations can be undermined by extrinsic rewards and punishments. People tend to be aware of their more general motivations unless difficulty with the production of action forces them to be aware of their more specific motivations. Avoidance motivations are generally more powerful than approach motivations, but this is truer for some people than for others.

People are motivated to pursue future goals with the expectation that they will be happy when they achieve them but they are remarkably poor at predicting future emotional states. In general, people prefer predictable events but unpredictable ones generate stronger emotional responses.

psychomythology

Money makes you happier

The sassy American comedienne Mae West once said: 'I've been rich and I've been poor. Believe me rich is better.' The belief that wealth is associated with happiness is common but mostly illusory. Wealthier people are relatively satisfied with their lives but are barely happier than others in moment-to-moment experiences. They also tend to be more tense, and do not spend more time in particularly enjoyable activities. Moreover, the effect of income on life satisfaction seems to be transient, as discussed earlier when there is a sudden windfall such as winning the lottery.

Daniel Kahneman, Nobel Prize-winning psychologist, found that people tend to exaggerate how much happiness wealth will bring them because they focus on the wrong things (Kahneman et al., 2006). When people consider the impact of any single factor on their wellbeing, they are prone to exaggerate its importance. For example, if you ask students 'How happy are you with your life in general?' and ' How many dates did you have last month?', the correlation between the answers to these questions was found to be –0.012 (not statistically different from 0). However, if you reverse the order of the questions, the correlation was found to rise to 0.66 with another sample of students (Strack et al., 1988b). By focusing first on dates, this causes that aspect of life to become salient and its importance to be exaggerated when the respondents are then asked the more general question about happiness. The initial anchoring of the question to romantic relationships means that students can then calculate a measure of happiness tied to this factor. In short, people do not know how happy they are in absolute terms (in comparison to knowing how old or how tall they are) but rely on estimates by comparison. The problem when considering how happy you are, is what do you draw a comparison with?

It turns out that so long as we are not in abject poverty, most of us are happy. However, richer people are happier because they are more likely to consider their happiness in terms of how they compare to what others have achieved. In industrialized societies, relative wealth becomes more important that absolute wealth, which creates a constant arms race of consumption and happiness (Firebaugh and Schroeder, 2009). If you get richer than your peers, you may feel you're better off than they are. But soon you'll make richer new friends, so your relative wealth won't be greater than it was before. This creates a pattern whereby individuals spend more time chasing wealth even when they do not really need to, but in doing so, they rarely achieve greater levels of happiness.

where do you stand?

Taking the guilt trip to confessionland

The use of polygraph testing is highly controversial and is neither uniformly dismissed nor accepted across the different legal systems of Europe. For example, it is used regularly in Belgium but has never been used in Spain. In Germany, it has been banned from penal procedures, whereas the Netherlands is undecided about the admissibility of polygraph evidence. The use of the polygraph in Nordic countries is mixed, with Finland the greatest proponent of the technique, Norway and Sweden much less so and it is not used at all in Denmark. In Switzerland, the polygraph is considered an infringement of the European Convention on Human Rights and so is outlawed (Meijer and van Koppen, 2008).

In the UK, evidence based on polygraph measures is inadmissible in a court of law, but the polygraph is used in the post-conviction management of sex offenders. This is because reoffending rates in sex criminals are high (Hanson et al., 2003), and one of the best methods of reducing reoffending has been found to be getting individuals to confess. This can be difficult in individuals who have a long history of concealment and lying (English et al., 2003), but the polygraph increases the likelihood that convicted sex offenders will comply with treatment protocols and disclose information about previous offences, victims and behaviours that contribute to recidivism (Grubin et al., 2004).

In Belgium, where the polygraph was adopted in the 1990s, there was a significant breakthrough in solving major criminal cases not because the technique disclosed new information, but because suspects were more likely to confess either during the polygraph testing session or afterwards. As far as the Belgian police are concerned, the dubious nature of the evidence obtained via the polygraph is irrelevant but the effect it has on confessions is not (Meijer and van Koppen, 2008).

It would appear that the experience of taking a polygraph test triggers confessions possibly because suspects believe that the technique works, or the need to own up to a crime when confronted with the details under examination is compelling. In other words, taking the test triggers guilt-motivated confession. But should a civilized society use a technique that has questionable validity as a means of extracting information? If polygraphy is flawed, is it still right to condone the deception and pretence that the technique works if it produces the desired outcome? Does the end justify the means? What about the use of the polygraph for the treatment of sex offenders? Is this an exceptional situation that justifies the use of the technique? What do you think?

Chapter review

Emotional experience: the feeling machine

- Emotions, feeling and moods all relate to affective states of varying intensity and duration. Emotional experiences are difficult to describe, but psychologists have identified their two underlying dimensions: arousal and valence.
- Psychologists have spent more than a century trying to understand how emotional experience and physiological activity are related. The James-Lange theory suggests that a stimulus causes a physiological reaction, which leads to an emotional experience; the Cannon-Bard theory suggests that a stimulus causes an emotional experience and a physiological reaction simultaneously; and Schachter and Singer's two-factor theory suggests that a stimulus causes undifferentiated physiological arousal about which people draw inferences.
- Emotions are produced by the complex interaction of limbic and cortical structures. Information about a stimulus is sent simultaneously to the amygdala, which makes a quick appraisal of the stimulus's goodness or badness, and the cortex, which does a slower and more comprehensive analysis of the stimulus. In some instances, the amygdala will trigger an emotional experience that the cortex later inhibits.
- People care about their emotional experiences and use many strategies to regulate them. Reappraisal involves changing the way one thinks about an object or event, and is one of the most effective strategies for emotion regulation.

Emotional communication: msgs w/o wrds

- Darwin suggested that emotional expressions are the same for all people and are universally understood, and research suggests that this is generally true.
- Emotional expressions are caused by the emotions they signify, but they can also cause those emotions.
- Emotional mimicry allows people to experience and hence identify the emotions of others.
- Not all emotional expressions are sincere because people use display rules to help them decide which emotions to express. Cultures have different display rules, but people obey them by using the same set of techniques.
- There are reliable differences between sincere and insincere emotional expressions, just as there are reliable differences between truthful and untruthful utterances, but people are generally poor at determining when an expression or an utterance is sincere. Although machines such as the polygraph can make this determination with better-than-chance accuracy, their error rates are dangerously high.

Motivation: getting moved

- Emotions motivate us indirectly by providing information about the world, but they also motivate us directly. The hedonic principle suggests that people approach pleasure and avoid pain and this basic motivation underlies all others.
- All organisms are born with some motivations and acquire others through experience.
- When the body experiences a deficit, we experience a drive to remedy it. Biological drives such as eating and mating generally take precedence over others.
- Hunger is the result of a complex system of physiological processes, and problems with this system can lead to eating disorders and obesity, both of which are difficult to overcome.
- With regard to sexual drives, men and women tend to be more similar than different. Both genders experience the same sequence of physiological arousal, engage in sex for most of the same reasons, and have sex drives that are regulated by testosterone.
- Intrinsic motivations such as immediate gratification can be undermined by extrinsic rewards and punishments where there are some additional stages before payback.
- According to self-determination theory, people reconcile intrinsic and extrinsic motivations based on perceptions of competence, autonomy and relatedness to others that become internalized motivations.
- People tend to be aware of their more general motivations unless difficulty with the production of action forces them to be aware of their more specific motivations.
- Undirected thought processes such as daydreaming and mind-wandering enable unconscious processing of goal-related activities during undemanding tasks. In contrast, concentration in difficult situations can deplete willpower, which makes individuals to vulnerable to impulsive drives and behaviours.
- Avoidance motivations such as pain are generally more powerful than approach motivations such as pleasure, but this is more true for some people than for others.

Key terms

affective forecasting (p. 423)
anorexia nervosa (p. 416)
appraisal (p. 399)
approach motivation (p. 422)
avoidance motivation (p. 422)
bulimia nervosa (p. 416)
Cannon-Bard theory (p. 395)
conscious motivation (p. 421)
disgust (p. 393)
display rules (p. 405)
drive (p. 412)
emotional expression (p. 402)
emotion regulation (p. 400)
emotions (p. 393)
extrinsic motivation (p. 419)
facial feedback hypothesis (p. 404)
feelings (p. 393)
hedonic principle (p. 410)
homeostasis (p. 411)
human sexual response cycle (p. 418)
incentives (p. 412)
internalization (p. 421)
intrinsic motivation (p. 419)
James-Lange theory (p. 395)
moods (p. 393)
motivation (p. 408)
need for achievement (p. 421)
reappraisal (p. 401)
self-determination theory (p. 421)
two-factor theory (p. 396)
unconscious motivation (p. 421)
universality hypothesis (p. 403)

Recommended reading

Ekman, P. (2003) *Emotions Revealed: Recognizing Faces and Feelings to Improve Communication and Emotional Life.* New York: Times Books. Psychologist Paul Ekman explains the roots of our emotions and their expressions and answers questions such as: How does our body signal to others whether we are slightly sad or anguished, peeved or enraged? Can we learn to distinguish between a polite smile and the genuine thing? Can we ever truly control our emotions? Fascinating, fun book, packed with unique exercises and photographs.

Fox, E. (2008) *Emotion Science: Cognitive and Neuroscientific Approaches to Understanding Human Emotions.* Basingstoke: Palgrave Macmillan. Psychologist Elaine Fox draws on a wide array of research to present an integrated picture of normal and disordered emotions, with a particular emphasis of drawing the distinction between emotions, moods and feelings.

Gilbert, D. T. (2006) *Stumbling on Happiness.* New York: Knopf. In this award-winning international bestseller, psychologist Daniel Gilbert examines our uniquely human ability to imagine the future and predict how much we will like it when we get there. *New Scientist* described it as 'a witty, insightful and superbly entertaining trek through the foibles of human imagination'.

11

Chapter learning objectives

At the end of this chapter you will be able to:

1. Understand why the nature versus nurture question is naive.
2. Understand the methodologies to test young infants and children.
3. Describe the basic sensory and perceptual mechanisms operating in infants.
4. Describe the different theories of cognitive development.
5. Explain the major changes in cognition after childhood.

Cognitive development

Over the past 30 years, there has been a growing appreciation of two important points about child development. First, from a very early age, children are actively interpreting the world around them, and second, these early experiences can have long-term consequences for how they turn out as adults in later life. This has led to the creation of a whole industry of babycare products that claim to promote infant cognitive development. However, the following shocking report, published in 1997, cast doubt on these practices:

> *Los Angeles – A surprising new study released on Monday by UCLA's Institute for Child Development revealed that human babies, long thought by psychologists to be highly inquisitive and adaptable, are actually extraordinarily stupid. The study, an 18-month battery of intelligence tests administered to over 3,500 babies, concluded categorically that babies are 'so stupid, it's not even funny.' According to Institute president Molly Bentley, in an effort to determine infant survival instincts when attacked, the babies were prodded in an aggressive manner with a broken broom handle. Over 90 per cent of them, when poked, failed to make even rudimentary attempts to defend themselves. The remaining 10 per cent responded by vacating their bowels. 'It is unlikely that the presence of the babies' fecal matter, however foul-smelling, would have a measurable defensive effect against an attacker in a real-world situation,' Bentley said.*

The report went on to reveal that in comparison to dogs, chickens and even worms, babies also performed the least adaptively when left on a mound of dirt in a torrential downpour. While the other creatures sought cover, the babies just lay there gurgling.

©ISTOCKPHOTO.COM/JO UNRUH

This is, of course, a spoof article – from the satirical publication *The Onion* – lampooning a previous cover feature in *Life* magazine (July 1993) entitled 'Babies are Smarter than you Think', which reported that infants can count, understand words before they speak and have amazing powers of memory. As you will discover in this chapter, claims for such early, sophisticated abilities are true to some extent, but it is easy to understand why babies seem so helpless when you first look at them (see **FIGURE 11.1**). Their limited communication and motor skills do not reflect their amazing knowledge and learning capacity.

However, in the 20th century, psychologists made some remarkable discoveries about what we seem to know at birth, what we must learn along the way, and what we never seem to get quite right. It has even revealed some surprising delights of old age.

NICK ROMANENKO

FIGURE **11.1 Infant development** On the couch from left to right are infants aged 18, 15, 12, 9, 6, 3 and 2 months old. Notice how the two babies below 6 months of age lack sufficient motor skills to sit unsupported.

From birth to infancy, from childhood to adolescence, from young adulthood to old age, one of the most obvious facts about human beings is that they change over time. We even call humans different names depending on how old they are:

- Newborns are just that – *newly born babies* from the point where they pop out, to when there are sent home with mum.
- Infancy comes from the Latin *ins fari*, which translates as 'unable to speak', and usually covers *the period from birth up to around about the second year of life*, when children begin to produce syntactically correct utterances, as we discovered in Chapter 7.
- The long period following infancy is called childhood – *the stage of development that begins at about 18–24 months and lasts until adolescence.*
- Adolescence is *the period of development that begins with the onset of sexual maturity (about 11–14 years of age) and lasts until the beginning of adulthood (18–21).*

After that, people generally do not want to be reminded of, or labelled by, their age. Developmental psychology is *the study of continuity and change across the life span*, and it has two prime objectives. The first is to accurately describe the significant psychological transitions between states of stability that occur over a lifetime. The second is to explain the nature of those changes in terms of mechanisms. Our development includes dramatic transformations and striking consistencies in the way we look, think, feel and act. In this chapter we focus on cognitive development and the various processes that feed into that ability. We will examine how information is gathered by the senses, interpreted by perceptual processes into organized, meaningful patterns that then form the basis for thinking and reasoning we call 'cognition'. We will look at special techniques and methods used to study young children, and finally we will consider some of the theories that make sense of cognitive development in terms of the underlying mechanisms.

Cognition is what makes us smart but much of what we think about is other people. In Chapter 12, we turn our attention to social development because not only do humans excel at learning from others, but we are also dependent on the emotional social bonds that form between individuals to become well-adjusted members of our species.

NEWBORNS Newly born infants.

INFANCY The period from birth up to around about the second year of life.

CHILDHOOD The stage of development that begins at about 18–24 months and lasts until adolescence.

ADOLESCENCE The period of development that begins with the onset of sexual maturity (about 11–14 years of age) and lasts until the beginning of adulthood (18–21).

DEVELOPMENTAL PSYCHOLOGY The study of continuity and change across the life span.

Nature versus nurture: an unnatural division

What makes us who we are? Pick up any tabloid newspaper today and you will read journalists writing about the causes of human behaviour (from aggression to having a sense of humour) in terms of the nature versus nurture debate – *the naive distinction about whether development is genetically determined or dependent on the environment*. Are individuals born aggressive (nature) or do they become that way through experiences (nurture)? Are some people natural comedians or do they become the class clown as a result of their experiences? Are men different from women because of their brains or because society treats men and women differently? As we saw in Chapter 1, the origins of this debate can be traced back to the Greek philosophical arguments between Plato, who favoured the 'nature' position of nativism, and his student Aristotle, who advocated the 'nurture' position of philosophical empiricism.

NATURE VERSUS NURTURE The naive distinction about whether development is genetically determined or dependent on the environment.

For centuries after, people questioned how nature and nurture influenced child development and in particular how the mind is formed in early childhood. Philosopher John Locke (1632–1704) argued that the mind was a blank sheet of paper on which experience formed lasting impressions to shape the emerging mind (Locke, [1690] 1947, p. 2):

> Let us then suppose the mind to be, as we say, white paper void of all characters without any ideas. How comes it to be furnished? Whence comes it by that vast store which the busy and boundless fancy of man has painted on it with an almost endless variety? Whence has it all the materials of reason and knowledge? To this I answer, in one word, from EXPERIENCE.

Such empiricism later formed the foundation of the behaviourism movement, which we encountered in Chapter 6, with John B. Watson's claim that he could take any child and shape the course of their development into any outcome he wanted. In contrast, others argued that much of the child's development was built in from the beginning. Today, we recognize these influences in terms of the genetic disposition we inherit from our parents.

The epigenetic landscape

Today, no credible theorist would argue that all complex human behaviours and functions can be understood either as driven entirely by nature or entirely by nurture. We now understand that the genes that influence development also depend on the environment to determine how they are expressed. In fact, that environment comprises not only the outside world, but also the mother's womb. These days, it is inconceivable that one could talk about development in the absence of any environmental influence.

There is another good reason why we must acknowledge the role of the environment. One of the remarkable discoveries of the human genome project, *where scientists set out to identify all the human genes*, was how few genes there appeared to be in comparison to the complexity of humans. This supports the contention that the environment has a significant role in causing various influences of genes to be switched on and off by experiences.

HUMAN GENOME PROJECT Where scientists set out to identify all the human genes.

There are two primary forces that control development. The first force is contained within the genetic instructions encoded in our DNA, which tell molecules how to form and organize themselves to build our bodies. These instructions reflect the evolutionary history of humans as a species and the relatively strong contribution from our most recent ancestors. However, these instructions unfold within an environment that is constantly changing and so all development also has to have some external component – the second primary force. For example, the African butterfly *Bicyclus anynana* comes in two different varieties, either colourful or drab, depending on whether the larvae hatch in the wet or dry season. The genes don't know in advance so are simply switched on by the environment (Marcus, 2004). Or consider animal sex – not the act but rather how it is determined. It turns out that a number of species have their sex controlled by the environment. For example, the temperature of the nest where alligator eggs incubate determines the sex of the hatchlings (Ferguson and Joanen, 1982). Too cold (below 30°C) and you get all females, too hot (above 34°C) and they are all born males. More remarkable are clownfish that can change sex during their own lifetime. What Pixar's

©ISTOCKPHOTO.COM/JODI JACOBSON

For all animals, including humans, development is the product of instructions encoded in our DNA working in an ever-changing environment. In the case of the clownfish, the effect of the environment can have a significant impact on development. When the dominant female in a school of clownfish dies, the most dominant male changes into a female and takes over her role (Buston et al., 2004).

film *Finding Nemo* did not tell the audience is that clownfish are transsexual. When the dominant female in a school of clownfish dies, the most dominant male changes into a female and takes over (Buston et al., 2004). So, when tabloid newspapers focus on nature versus nurture as an either/or question, they are being naive, because genetic instructions *always* require an environment in which to operate. This is especially true in certain dispositions towards disease, as illustrated in *the real world* example of phenylketonuria (PKU).

the real world

Phenylketonuria: A disorder of nature or nurture?

Phenylketonuria (PKU) is a genetic disorder of chromosome 12, which, if left untreated, inevitably leads to severe brain damage, including mental retardation. This is because individuals with PKU lack an enzyme that breaks down the amino acid phenylalanine in the brain that builds up over time to become neurotoxic.

Phenylalanine is present in a number of foodstuffs but particularly in artificial sweeteners such as aspartame (E951), which are used in many products, from soft drinks to yoghurts. In order to prevent the effects of excessive levels of phenylalanine, children with PKU have to be put on a strict diet, avoiding food that contains phenylalanine for the rest of their lives.

PKU is a good case study for considering the nature–nurture issue. PKU is caused by a recessive gene and does not adversely affect development because more often the presence of a dominant gene cancels the negative influence of recessive effects. However, if both parents possess the recessive gene, the child will be born with PKU and may therefore suffer brain damage. One could argue that mental retardation caused by PKU is genetically determined by nature. But the effects of PKU can be avoided if the child is kept on a special diet, indicating that the course of development is dependent on the environment. Indeed, one could argue that it is phenylalanine in the environment that is responsible for the brain damage. So where is the disorder? Is it in the genes or the environment? The answer is that it is in both. In the same way that PKU can only be understood as an interaction between nature and nurture, developmental theories should seek to understand the interaction of genes within the environment and the relative contribution of both.

As we noted in Chapter 3, epigenesis is the idea that explains development as the interaction between genes and environment through various regulating processes such as genetic methylation. There is a further misconception that genetic instructions are rigid or deterministic, that is, indicating no influence from the environment. However, we know that epigenesis, especially that related to developing behaviour and cognition, is genetically specified in terms of probabilities rather than absolute certainty.

CANALIZATION The idea of development as constrained epigenesis.

One way to consider probabilistic development is Waddington's (1942) notion of canalization – *the idea of development as constrained epigenesis* (see **FIGURE 11.2**). If one considers the course of development to be like a ball rolling down an epigenetic landscape made up of valleys and troughs of different depths, some parts of the journey are going to be well specified. Other phases of development are more easily perturbed

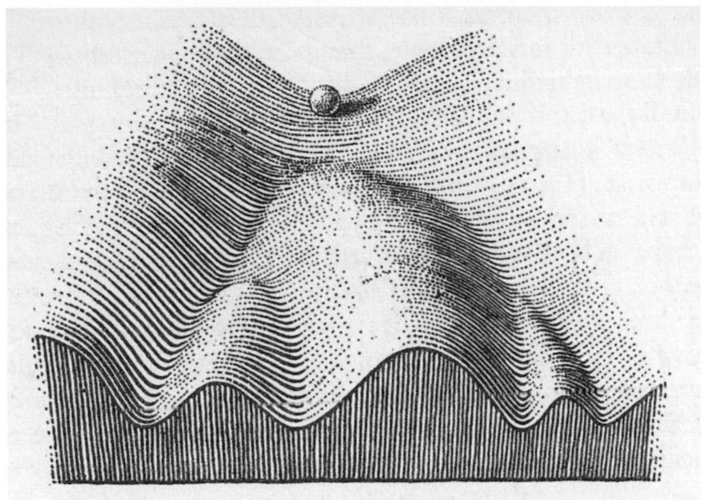

FIGURE 11.2 Waddington's development paths Waddington proposed that developmental paths varied in the extent to which they could be easily perturbed by a change in the environment, or remained relatively unchanged because the path was deeply canalized.

because the course is less well specified. In the same way, there are some developmental changes that are highly probable, such as eye colour or height (assuming you feed the child and nothing unusual happens during growth), whereas others, such as musical ability or interest in butterflies, are less predictable because the contributing factors are less well specified. Developmental psychology attempts to understand the factors that control the course of change as we age.

Prenatality: a womb with a view

You probably calculate your age by counting your birthdays, but the fact is that when you were born, you were already nine months old. The prenatal stage of development *ends with birth*, but it begins nine months earlier when about 200 million sperm begin a hazardous journey from a woman's vagina, through her uterus and on to her Fallopian tubes. Many of these sperm have defects that prevent them from swimming vigorously enough to make progress, and others get stuck in the spermatazoidal equivalent of a traffic jam in which too many sperm are on the same road, headed in the same direction at the same time. Of those that manage to make their way through the uterus, many take a wrong turn and end up in the Fallopian tube that does not contain an egg. A mere 200 or so (0.0001%) of the original 200 million sperm manage to find the right Fallopian tube and get close enough to an egg to release digestive enzymes that erode the egg's protective outer layer. As soon as one of these sperm manages to penetrate the coating, the egg quickly releases a chemical that seals the coating and keeps all the remaining sperm from entering. (Think of them as silver medalists.) After triumphing over massive odds, the one successful sperm sheds its tail and fertilizes the egg. In about 12 hours, the nuclei of the sperm and the egg merge, and the prenatal development of a unique human being begins. Next, we will consider some of the major changes to take place following conception, including structural changes in the egg, development of the brain and the importance of the womb environment.

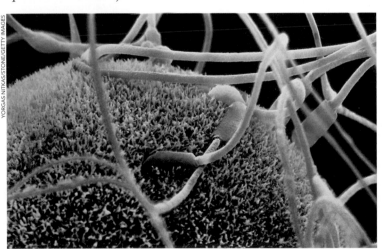

PRENATAL STAGE Ends with birth, but it begins at conception.

This electron micrograph shows a false colour image of several human sperm, one of which is fertilizing an egg.

Prenatal development

The fertilized egg is called a zygote – *a single cell that contains chromosomes from both a sperm and an egg*. From the first moment of its existence, a zygote has one thing in

ZYGOTE A single cell that contains chromosomes from both a sperm and an egg.

common with the person it will ultimately become: sex. Each human sperm cell and each human egg cell contains 23 *chromosomes* that contain *genes*, which provide the blueprint for all biological development. Some sperm carry an X chromosome, and others carry a Y chromosome. If the egg is fertilized by a sperm that carries a Y chromosome, the zygote is male; if the egg is fertilized by a sperm that carries an X chromosome, the zygote is female.

GERMINAL STAGE The two-week period that begins at conception.

The two-week period that begins at conception is known as the germinal stage, and it is during this stage that the one-celled zygote begins to divide – into two cells that divide into four, which divide into eight and so on. By the time of birth, the zygote has divided into trillions of cells, each of which contains exactly one set of 23 chromosomes from the sperm and one set of 23 chromosomes from the egg. During the germinal stage, the zygote migrates back down the Fallopian tube and implants itself in the wall of the uterus. This is a difficult journey, and about half of all zygotes do not complete it, either because they are defective or they implant themselves in an inhospitable part of the uterus. Male zygotes are especially unlikely to complete this journey, and no one understands why.

EMBRYONIC STAGE Period that lasts from the second week until about the eighth week.

BLASTOCYST Cluster ball of embryonic cells.

EMBRYONIC DISK Three-layered flattened structure that emerges from the blastocyst.

ENDODERM Embryonic disk layer that goes on to form the internal organs.

MESODERM Embryonic disk layer that goes on to form the skeletal muscles.

ECTODERM Embryonic disk layer that goes on to form the skin and nervous system.

When the zygote implants itself on the uterine wall, a new stage of development begins. The embryonic stage is *a period that lasts from the second week until about the eighth week* (see **FIGURE 11.3**). During this stage, the zygote continues to divide and its cells begin to differentiate, eventually *forming a ball of cells* known as a blastocyst, which *flattens out to become the three-layered* embryonic disk, which comprises the endoderm, *which will go on to form the internal organs*, the mesoderm, *which becomes the skeletal muscles*, and the ectoderm, *which becomes the skin and nervous system*. This embryo is just 2.5 cm long, but already has a beating heart and other body parts, such as arms and legs.

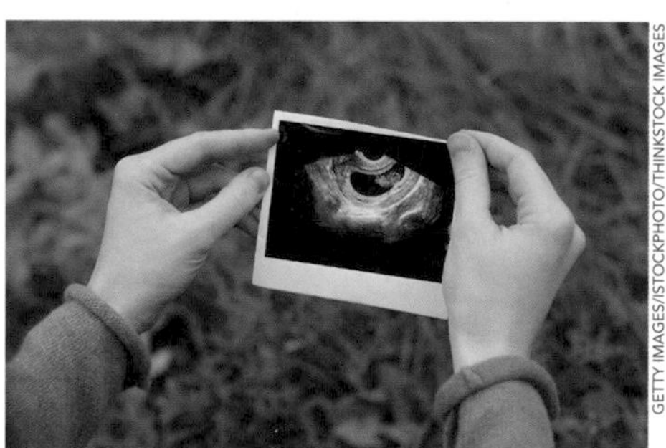

GETTY IMAGES/ISTOCKPHOTO/THINKSTOCK IMAGES

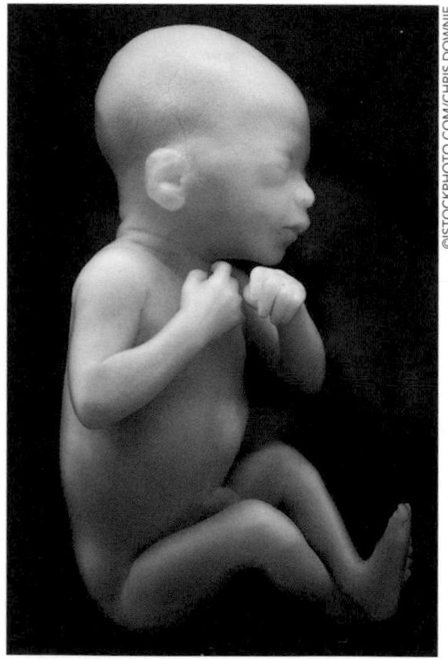

©ISTOCKPHOTO.COM/CHRIS DOWNIE

FIGURE 11.3 Prenatal development Human beings undergo amazing development in the nine months of prenatal development.

Embryos that have one X chromosome and one Y chromosome begin to produce a hormone called testosterone, which masculinizes their reproductive organs, whereas embryos that have two X chromosomes do not. For alligators, it's temperature, but for humans, it's testosterone that determines sex. Without testosterone, the embryo continues developing as a female. In a sense, then, males are a specialized form of females. This biological fact must come as somewhat of a shock to those who hold the literal biblical view that Eve was created from Adam's rib – at one point, we were all Eves as embryos!

FETAL STAGE The period that lasts from the ninth week until birth.

The fetal stage is *the period that lasts from the ninth week until birth*. The embryo at this stage is known as a *fetus*, and it has a skeleton and muscles that make it capable of movement. During the last three months of the fetal stage, the size of the fetus increases rapidly. It develops a layer of insulating fat beneath its skin, and its digestive and respiratory systems mature.

Building a brain

The brain begins to form early on as a portion of the ectoderm folds over to become the neural tube, *the cylindrical structure of the embryonic central nervous system*, from which the forebrain and midbrain emerge at one end, while the other end becomes the spinal cord. Around the third and fourth week of life, cells within the neural tube begin dividing to produce neural cells that are generated at a peak rate of 250,000 per minute (Cowan, 1979). This process, known as neurogenesis, *the formation of neural cells*, continues until almost all the 100 billion neurons that typically make up the human brain are generated by around 18 weeks after conception (Rakic, 1995). From within the neural tube, these neural cells migrate to their final position in the central nervous system. As described in Chapter 3, around half are glial cells, with the remainder becoming different types of neurons, made up of a cell body and varying axon configurations. Those cells that are formed and reach their final destination last end up in the cortical regions of the brain. Humans have a relatively large cortical area in comparison to other animals, giving us greater processing capacity. In fact, one of the reasons that the brain surface is covered in creases is that this cortical area is so large in humans that it has to fold into crevices or convolutions in order to fit as much of it as possible inside the skull. In addition to cortical regions on the outside, the forebrain also has underlying subcortical structures, deeper inside the brain. Many of these subcortical structures, especially those related to sensory functioning, are more mature around the time of birth in comparison to the cortical structures, which continue to develop postnatally.

NEURAL TUBE The cylindrical structure of the embryonic central nervous system.

NEUROGENESIS The formation of neural cells.

Prenatal environment

The brain is the most complex organ in the body and the most sensitive structure to develop in the womb, subject to all manner of insults from the prenatal environment. It is natural to assume that genes influence development from the moment of conception and the environment influences development from the moment of birth. But that's not so. The womb is an environment that influences development in a multitude of ways. For example, the *placenta* is the organ that physically links the bloodstreams of the mother and the developing embryo or fetus and permits the exchange of materials. As such, the foods a woman eats during pregnancy can affect fetal development. Towards the end of the Second World War, the Nazis imposed a food embargo on large Dutch cities and many pregnant women suffered severe food deprivation. Subsequent research on their children's development demonstrated that food deprivation during the first six months of pregnancy caused the children to have physical problems (Stein et al., 1975) and psychological problems, most notably an increased likelihood of schizophrenia and antisocial personality disorder (Neugebauer et al., 1999; Susser et al., 1999).

These effects are not unique to food. Almost anything that a woman eats, drinks, inhales, injects or otherwise comes into contact with can pass through the placenta and affect the development of her fetus. *Agents that damage the process of development* are called teratogens, which literally means 'monster makers'. Teratogens include environmental poisons, such as lead in the water, paint dust in the air, or mercury in fish, but they also include common substances such as tobacco and alcohol. For example, fetal alcohol syndrome is *a developmental disorder that stems from heavy alcohol use by the mother during pregnancy*, and it increases the risk of birth defects, especially with respect to the shape and size of the head and the structure of the brain. Children with fetal alcohol syndrome frequently exhibit impaired cognitive development and have more problems with academic achievement than other children (Carmichael Olson et al., 1997; Streissguth et al., 1999). Similarly, babies whose mothers smoke tobacco have lower birth weights (Horta et al., 1997) and are more likely to have perceptual and attentional problems in childhood (Fried and Watkinson, 2000). Even secondhand smoke can lead to reduced birth weight and deficits in attention and learning (Makin et al., 1991; Windham et al., 1999). The effect of teratogens generally depends on the developmental stage at which they are encountered. The embryo is more vulnerable to teratogens than the fetus, but structures such as the central nervous system are vulnerable throughout the entire prenatal period.

How do you measure up?

Levels of circulating fetal testosterone during weeks 8–14 of gestation predict the length of fingers. In most human males, the ring finger is longer than the index finger and the ratio of this finger difference is related to masculine behaviours. In most women, both fingers are about the same length. However, females with masculine digit ratios have more masculine behaviours, whereas males with female ratios exhibit more typically feminine behaviours.

TERATOGENS Agents that damage the process of development.

FETAL ALCOHOL SYNDROME A developmental disorder that stems from heavy alcohol use by the mother during pregnancy.

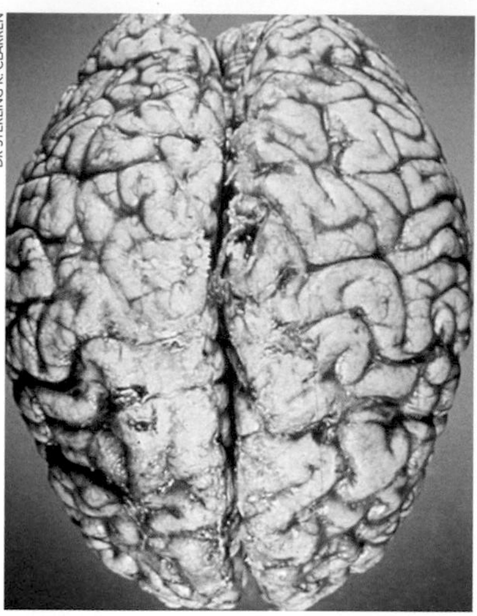

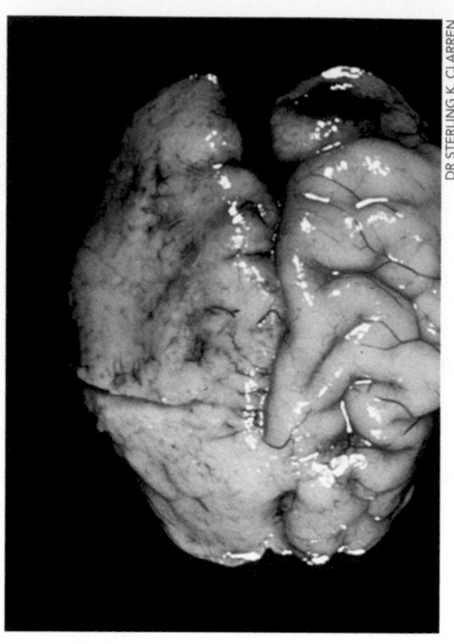

The photo on the left shows the brain of a normal six-week-old child and the image on the right shows the brain of a six-week-old child born with fetal alcohol syndrome.

In Northern Ireland, when tested postnatally using the familiarity for preference technique, babies whose mothers had tuned in regularly for their daily dose of the Australian TV soap opera *Neighbours* during their pregnancy remembered the show's theme tune, but did not respond to *Coronation Street or Eastenders* (Hepper, 1988).

The prenatal environment is rich with chemicals, but it is also rich with information. Unlike a car, which operates only after it has been fully assembled, the human brain functions even as it is being built, and research shows that the developing fetus can sense stimulation – and can learn. Wombs are dark because only the brightest light can filter through the mother's abdomen, but they are not quiet. High-frequency sounds tend to be muffled, but low-frequency sounds penetrate the mother's abdomen. The fetus can hear its mother's heartbeat and the gastrointestinal sounds associated with her digestion, but most importantly, it can hear its mother's voice. Newborns who are just two hours old will suck a nipple more vigorously when they hear the sound of their mother's voice than when they hear the voice of a female stranger (Querleu et al., 1984), which suggests that they became familiar with their mother's voice while they were developing inside her. Experiments confirm this. In one study, researchers arranged for some women to read aloud a short passage from *The Cat in the Hat* repeatedly during the last six weeks of pregnancy. Once the babies were born, the researchers tested their reactions to passages from *The Cat in the Hat* as well as other stories. Babies whose mothers had read aloud reacted differently to the passage from *The Cat in the Hat* than they did to an unfamiliar passage, whereas infants whose mothers had not read aloud reacted to both passages similarly (DeCasper and Spence, 1986). They could not hear the individual words (it must be like listening to conversation under water), but they picked up on *the rhythm of speech* or prosody as it is known. Clearly, the unborn fetus is already immersed in a world of sound. When two pregnant women are having a conversation, there are at least four individuals listening.

PROSODY The rhythm of speech.

Postnatal life: wiring and firing

In Chapter 3, we learned about brain plasticity in adults who had lost limbs and how their brains managed to rewire themselves to compensate for the loss. Here, we look at the normal developing brain after birth and the processes designed to encode information from the environment outside the womb as patterns of activation. Most of us are born around 40 weeks' gestation, but the brain still has considerable development to undergo as it wires itself up to respond to the early postnatal environment.

Brain development after birth

Cortical development is usually related to increased connectivity between the neurons in different regions of the brain as cells start to wire up and 'talk' to each other. Cortical cells start connecting up through three major generative processes, *those that lead to the formation of new structures* that continue through early childhood:

1 Arborization – a *process where the cell axon lengthens and grows increasing dendritic branches* (arborization comes from the Latin for trees).

GENERATIVE PROCESSES Those that lead to the formation of new structures.

ARBORIZATION Process where the cell axon lengthens and grows increasing dendritic branches.

2 Synaptogenesis – *the increase in the number of synaptic junctions where cells communicate through the activity of neurotransmitters.*
3 Myelination – *the formation of a fatty sheath around the axons of a brain cell.* Just as plastic sheathing insulates an electrical wire, myelin insulates the brain cell axon and improves the communication between neurons.

SYNAPTOGENESIS The increase in the number of synaptic junctions where cells communicate through the activity of neurotransmitters.

MYELINATION The formation of a fatty sheath around the axons of a brain cell.

All these processes of growth do not occur at the same time throughout the brain. For example, the spinal cord and the brainstem have more myelin than the cerebral cortex itself, and the myelination of the cortex continues into adulthood. In the cortex, these generative processes lead to an exuberant overproduction of neuronal connections that form mostly after birth. However, approximately 40% of this synaptic connectivity is eliminated in a fourth process known as synaptic pruning – *the mechanism whereby synaptic connections die off.* During peak 'pruning' periods, it has been estimated that as many as 100,000 synapses may be eliminated per second (Kolb, 1995). Why would brain development include such a self-destructive process? One answer is that discarding those connections that are not active makes the brain more efficient. In this way, the brain tunes into the environment by streamlining its processing. For example, as we learned in Chapter 7, every infant has the ability to discriminate any language phoneme before six months of age, but this flexibility is increasingly lost as the child grows up within a particular language environment. Brain development has the potential to encode different sounds because each sound activates a different pattern of neurons in the auditory cortex. This is why there is an initial overproduction of connectivity in the first place. However, if specific patterns are not activated by input from the environment, then the unused connections are lost. In other words, as noted in Chapter 3, one of the major principles of shaping neuronal connectivity is to either 'Use it or lose it!'

SYNAPTIC PRUNING The process whereby synaptic connections die off.

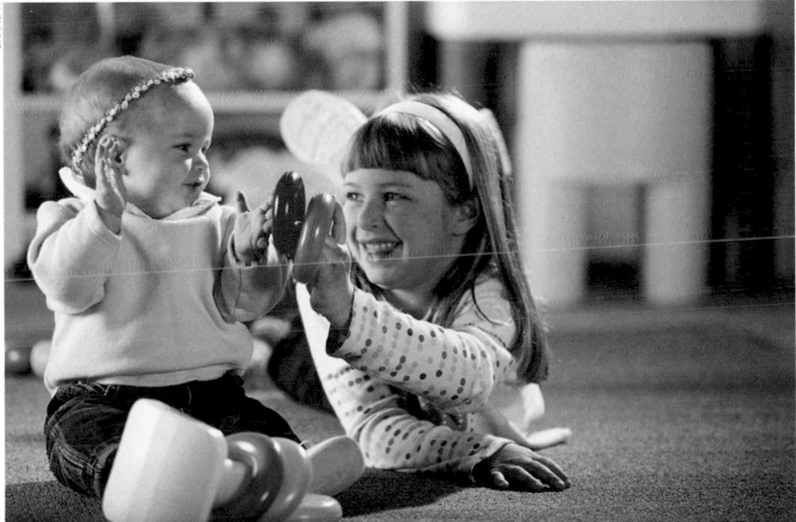

BRAND X

No other animal on the planet has the same capacity as humans to learn from others around them. The fact that our underdeveloped brains are specifically shaped by the unique social and physical environment into which we are born allows us to be exceptionally adaptable.

Brain putty

In comparison with other mammals, humans have the most protracted period of childhood and brain development. Indeed, recent research indicates that the brain is still developing well into adolescence (Burnett and Blakemore, 2009). Whereas a newborn chimp's brain is nearly 60% of its adult size, a newborn human's brain is only 25% of its adult size, which is to say that 75% of the brain's growth occurs outside the womb. Why are human beings born with such underdeveloped brains when other primates are not? There are at least three reasons:

1 The human brain has nearly tripled in size in just 2 million years of evolution, and bigger brains require bigger heads to house them. If a newborn's head were closer to its adult size, the baby could not pass through its mother's birth canal.
2 One of our species' greatest talents is its ability to adapt to a wide range of novel environments such as different climates, terrains or social structures. Rather than arriving in the world with a fully developed brain that may or may not meet the requirements of its environment, human beings arrive with brains that do much of their developing *within* the very environments in which they will function.
3 Probably most importantly, no other animal on the planet has the same capacity as humans to learn from others around them. As we will read in Chapter 12, we are particularly social animals that spend much of our lives learning from others. This capacity to learn requires flexibility in a brain that has to encode new information. The fact that our underdeveloped brains are specifically shaped by the unique social and physical environment into which we are born allows us to be exceptionally adaptable. This *capacity for the brain to be moulded by experience* is known as plasticity.

PLASTICITY The capacity for the brain to be moulded by experience.

EXPERIENCE-EXPECTANT PLASTICITY Much of the neural organization is largely pre-specified, waiting for input from the environment.

EXPERIENCE-DEPENDENT PLASTICITY Much of the neural organization is not pre-specified and depends on input from the environment.

SENSITIVE PERIODS OF DEVELOPMENT Relatively specific times when appropriate environmental input is expected.

We encountered plasticity in adults in Chapter 3 but here we look at it in the developing brain.

There are two different types of plasticity – experience-expectant and experience-dependent (Greenough and Black, 1992). In experience-expectant plasticity, *much of the neural organization is largely pre-specified, waiting for input from the environment.* In experience-dependent plasticity, *much of the neural organization is not pre-specified and depends on input from the environment.* These two processes reflect an evolutionary strategy for brain development. Experience-expectant plasticity encodes features of the environment that have not changed over millions of years. They simply *expect* certain information from the environment that is recurrent from one generation to the next. Experience-dependent plasticity is more flexible in adapting to circumstances that may emerge within a generation.

Experience-expectant plasticity typically operates within sensitive periods of development – *relatively specific times when appropriate environmental input is expected.* Sensitive periods are like windows of opportunity where environmental input can influence how certain neuronal networks wire together. It's like having a special offer that is only valid for a limited time. When external input occurs outside the sensitive period, it does not have as much lasting impact on the neuronal wiring, if any. For example, the development of the visual system depends on the infant receiving appropriate visual stimulation within the first six months to activate the visual-processing areas that are expecting such environmental input (Hubel, 1988). If the child is deprived of critical visual input during this sensitive period, their ability to develop appropriate visual function is increasingly lost (Atkinson, 2000). Hence, it is difficult to restore normal vision to children who have been deprived of normal visual stimulation during the sensitive period. Although these deprived children may be given extra visual stimulation later in life, the cortical regions that were expecting input have ceased to remain plastic: their window of opportunity has closed.

However, humans also have a boundless capacity to learn new experiences and encode these as memories. This relies on experience-dependent plasticity and should not be constrained by *when* the environment provides stimulation. For example, Donald Hebb (1949) demonstrated that rats raised in complex environments that provide lots of experiences and stimulation have greater cortical connectivity in their brains than rats raised in isolated environments with little stimulation. Musicians who train for years also have greater connectivity and activation of those regions of the brain that control their finger movements (Elbert et al., 1995). Experience-dependent plasticity explains how London taxi drivers get around the capital by storing 'the knowledge' in their hippocampus, briefly mentioned in Chapter 3 (Maguire et al., 2000).

In summary, development is governed by genes working within the environment. Thus, nature and nurture are always intertwined, although the relative contribution of each depends on whether experiences are expected or dependent for development to unfold. Moreover, outcomes are not always predictably cast in stone because there are many potential factors that can play a role. So, developmental processes are more probabilistic (might happen) than deterministic (definitely will happen). During these early stages, the emerging brain rapidly develops through generative processes that increase connectivity between neurons. After birth, some of these connections are lost as the brain moulds to specific information from the environment. Brain plasticity means that the infant is sensitive to various influences from the environment, including those teratogens that are potentially harmful in the long term. Although the fetus cannot see much in the womb, it can hear sounds and become familiar with those it hears often, such as its mother's voice.

The science of studying change

Have you ever tried to tell a joke to an infant or discuss politics with a toddler? You would be wasting your time. Unlike most other areas, developmental psychology presents considerable methodological challenges to the researcher because children are just so different from adults. Also, change can happen so fast. One minute your children are in nappies, the next you are negotiating how much pocket money they can have. In this section, we will look at the unique practical difficulties that face developmental researchers and how they go about measuring change.

Changing patterns

Developmental change can follow a number of different patterns that reveal important aspects about the underlying processes. If you imagine a graph with time on the horizontal X-axis and the measure of behaviour on the vertical Y-axis, you can see examples of different plots of development. A distinction is often drawn between two types of change: quantitative, *the amount or quantity of change*, and qualitative, *the type or quality of change*. For example, an increase in the number of words an infant can say would be a quantitative change, but the emergence of their ability to produce new sentences would be a qualitative change, reflecting the emergence of a new stage of language production. Whenever there is a significant transition in development, scientists get excited. This is because qualitative changes suggest that significantly different mechanisms are operating, whereas gradual increases on a regular basis suggest that the same mechanisms are simply being used more efficiently.

QUANTITATIVE CHANGE The amount or quantity of change.

QUALITATIVE CHANGE The type or quality of change.

Developmental change is rarely smooth or linear but undergoes periods of stability and instability. These periods of change can be graphed in different ways, as shown in FIGURE 11.4. A continuous developmental function indicates a steadily increasing ability or quantity, as in FIGURE 11.4a. Some aspects of physical change such as weight and height gain have such periods of steady continuous change during childhood. Other developmental functions show the opposite pattern as there is a declining loss of function, as illustrated in FIGURE 11.4b. These examples reflect the decline of a developmental ability that is no longer required. For example, losing the ability to discriminate phonemes in a foreign language might show a progressive downward trend. Discontinuous or step functions (FIGURE 11.4c) are common developmental patterns that reflect the combination of periods of stability and change. Most aspects of development follow such patterns as development shows qualitative and quantitative change. Whenever the transitions are significant and universal, in that all children progress through the same phase, this point of change is called a milestone – *an important demarcating event on the path of development*. Developmental milestones are found in many aspects of life change. The significance of such discontinuities is addressed by stage theories – *those that advocate development as a fundamental reorganization of the*

MILESTONE An important demarcating event on the path of development.

STAGE THEORIES Theories that advocate development as a fundamental reorganization of the underlying mechanisms.

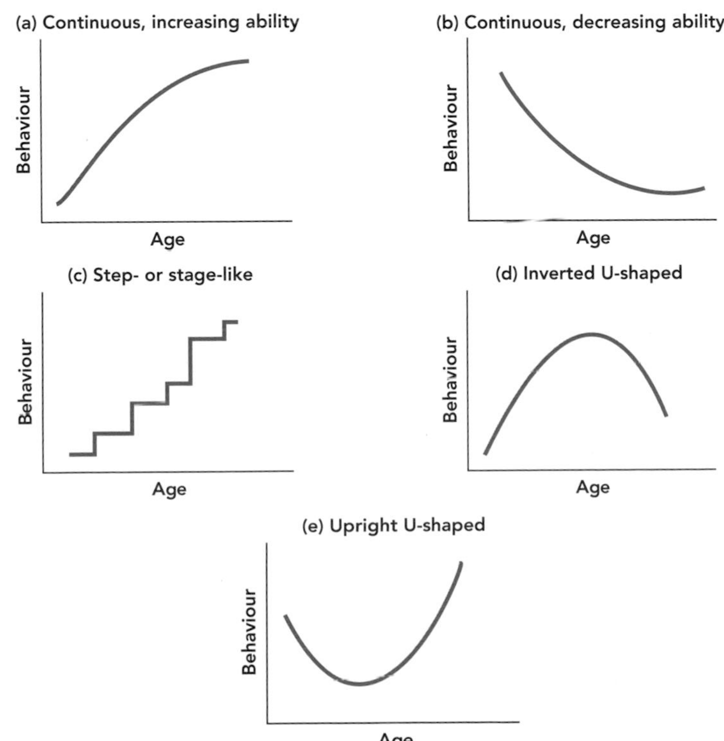

FIGURE **11.4 Common developmental functions** Graphs (a) to (e) show five of the most common developmental functions, indicating the way people typically develop, change or grow with age. Usually, as here, time is represented on the X-axis and measure of behaviour, or changes in behaviour, is represented on the Y-axis (Muir, 1999).

stats facts

'Ch-ch-changes': problems of detecting significant change

Developmental change is usually studied by comparing performance in cross-sectional time slices of distinct individuals or repeated longitudinal testing of the same individuals over lengthy periods of time. In either case, the study of change has relied on group data and this methodological constraint has served to generate theories of groups rather than individuals. The problem is that we cannot derive valid generalizations about the course of change in individuals from the course of change in a group average (Greenwald, 2011). There is no such thing as a group brain. For example, there is a common belief in the 'word spurt', where there is a significant increase in the child's vocabulary around 18 months of age. While it is fair to say that there is a qualitative change in their ability to produce two-word utterances that have syntax, there is no evidence of an explosion of word learning. The word spurt is probably spurious because it is based on vocabulary size of groups of children of different ages rather than the rate of word acquisition of individual children (Bloom, 2000). Even if one were to track the individual word acquisition of a single child, there are instances where there will be dips in performance such as weeks when the child may be ill. There are qualitative changes in cognitive development but one has to be sure that these changes are neither obscured nor generated by the problems of sampling individuals versus groups over various time frames.

underlying mechanisms. Another significant pattern of developmental change is the 'U'-shaped function that can be either inverted as in **FIGURE 11.4d** or upright as in **FIGURE 11.4e**. Examples of inverted 'U'-shaped developmental changes are functions that steadily increase over time to reach a peak and then begin a decline. Many psychological functions such as attention, memory and speed of processing steadily improve from childhood through to adulthood and then decline in old age. Upright 'U'-shaped developmental changes are more unusual and reflect a decline in some function that re-emerges later on. For example, the infant has a stepping reflex that is present at birth but then drops out after a few months to re-emerge as part of mature walking. Many infantile reflexes similarly appear to vanish but are in fact incorporated into more complex behaviours later in development.

Developmental designs

Researchers must be certain that the patterns they find reflect real developmental changes rather than errors due to the way the data have been collected. As developmental change happens over time, researchers typically measure those changes using one of two types of research design – either longitudinal research, *based on a representative sample of children who are then studied repeatedly over time*, or cross-sectional research, *based on groups of children who represent a cross-section of the population*. Both have strengths and weaknesses.

Longitudinal studies employ a powerful design tool known as the repeated measure, where *several data points are collected from the same individual*, which controls for individual variation. Individual variation is always a problem in measuring change because individuals start off so different from one another. Without repeated measures, small studies are more prone to distortions in the measurements that reflect the variation that already exists between individuals. For example, if a researcher predicts that different types of schooling will produce different levels of academic achievement, they need to control for the individual academic ability of each child that exists at the beginning of the study. Otherwise, one might incorrectly conclude that one type of schooling was better when, in fact, children entering one school were already academically more gifted than children entering another school.

However, there are some considerable problems with longitudinal designs. Researchers do not always have the luxury of time, effort and money to conduct longitudinal studies where the question of interest extends over a long period. Longitudinal studies also represent a considerable commitment on behalf of the participant to remain in the study and they may choose to drop out. For example, in our hypothetical school comparison study, children may move to a different school because the parents are unhappy with the level of teaching. Another problem for repeated measures testing is that the data collected are influenced by the fact that the participant has been tested more than once. For example, the children in our imaginary school study might improve on tasks simply through the repeated practice of taking tests.

Cross-sectional designs are the most commonly used technique for measuring developmental change. Here, researchers study groups of children who represent a cross-section of the population. For example, if you think there is a significant change in working memory over middle childhood, then you would probably study samples of 6-, 8- and 10-year-olds to look for significant group differences. This technique is much less expensive and time-consuming in comparison with longitudinal designs and does not suffer the drawbacks of repeated measures and participant drop-out. However, cross-sectional studies have the potential for a cohort bias – *anomalies that are predominant in one group that distort comparison between groups*. For example, in a hypothetical study of social networking sites, we might conclude that the internet works best for adolescents compared to older adults because of their different social worlds. However, any effect may be more to do with adolescents' expertise in using computers in contrast with less computer-savvy adults.

LONGITUDINAL RESEARCH Experimental designs based on a representative sample of children who are then studied repeatedly over time.

CROSS-SECTIONAL RESEARCH Experimental designs based on groups of children who represent a cross-section of the population.

REPEATED MEASURE Several data points are collected from the same individual.

COHORT BIAS Anomalies that are predominant in one group that distort comparison between groups.

How to study young children

The majority of experimental psychology has been based on studies involving two populations, laboratory rats and undergraduate students – both are available in large numbers and will readily work for rewards of food pellets or course credits. However, one of the most challenging aspects of developmental psychology is how to actually study young children, who have no interest in food or money as rewards. The second major problem of studying young children is obvious from Figure 11.1. Young children are very different from adults. Consider the obstacles that developmental psychologists face. Communication and comprehension is limited. Motor responses may be much slower, disorganized or even absent. Finally, there are considerable ethical considerations when conducting experiments with children who may not be capable of giving fully informed consent to take part in studies. Faced with these challenges, developmental psychologists have had to devise methodologies that tap into the natural responses that exist within the child's own repertoire of behaviours.

The simplest noninvasive way to study children is to watch their behaviour in their natural environment. It is no surprise that biologist Charles Darwin (1877) was one of the first to apply this naturalistic observational technique to his son 'Doddy'. However, Darwin undertook no further investigation of the behaviours he recorded. As with many of the animals he described on his voyages, Darwin produced extended lists of information on the behaviour of his son, but without any real interpretation. It was Jean Piaget (1896–1980), Swiss developmental psychologist, who refined the naturalistic observation method into a clinical method of studying children – *manipulating the situation to see how the child's behaviour changes in a reliable manner*. This method combines observation with a 'hunch', that is, what Piaget thought was going on in the mind of the child. For example, in describing his seven-month-old daughter Lucienne's inability to understand that objects continue to exist when out of sight, Piaget (1954a, p. 15) reported:

CLINICAL METHOD OF STUDYING CHILDREN
Manipulating the situation to see how the child's behaviour changes in a reliable manner.

> OBS 7. At 0:7 Lucienne grasps a small doll which I present to her for the first time. She examines it with great interest, then lets it go (not intentionally); she immediately looks for it in front of her but does not see it right away. When she has found it, I take it from her and place a coverlet over it before her eyes (Lucienne is seated); no reaction.

Piaget wanted to know how Lucienne would respond to him hiding the doll with a cover. His observation of her apparent memory loss for the toy lead Piaget to conclude that, for infants of this age, objects that were 'out of sight' were also 'out of mind'. The infant had no memory or enduring representation of the unseen object. As we will see later, the interpretation of this seemingly simple observation was incorrect. Nevertheless, Piaget was the first to use experimental manipulation to produce scientific studies of young children that enabled others to repeat and test his observations many decades later.

Following Piaget's lead, most modern developmental studies of young children employ some elements of his experimental approach, but with the benefit of advances in methods and techniques. Today's developmental psychologists have an arsenal of experimental methodologies and techniques used to answer questions about young children who otherwise have limited communication skills. Much of this has been due to technological advances and in particular the development of low-cost, high-quality video recording. Imagine how laborious it must have been to document subtle behaviours in the pre-video era, as Darwin and Piaget did. Video recording enables the researcher to look out for subtle developmental changes that might otherwise be missed. Videos also allow you to take more accurate objective measures of behaviour such as response times. Due to the difficult nature of testing children, researchers generally have to use noninvasive measures that capture as much as possible of the child's natural abilities. Thankfully, one of the best and easiest methods relies on our human disposition to attend to things we like, get bored easily and show renewed interest whenever we encounter something different from what we expected.

Jean Piaget (1896–1980) is widely considered to be the father of modern developmental psychology.

Habituation: preference for novelty

One of the first infant experiments to use a timing measure of attention was a visual preferences study conducted by Robert Fantz (1961). Fantz placed young babies on their backs and presented them with various visual patterns to look at and simply recorded the amount of time they spent looking at each pattern. He discovered that the infants preferred to look at certain patterns compared with others. The visual preference paradigm is a *technique that uses difference in duration of looking to infer pattern discrimination*, but is rather limited because there has to be a sufficient level of difference and interest in discriminating patterns. However, the technique is more powerful when investigating the infant's preference for new experiences or a preference for novelty.

VISUAL PREFERENCE PARADIGM Technique that uses difference in duration of looking to infer pattern discrimination.

As we saw in Chapter 6, the simplest example of learning occurs when an organism initially responds to some form of stimulation but, with repeated exposure, this response declines through the process of habituation. This simplicity is one reason why habituation is the most common experimental method used with very young children. Initially, infants are presented with some stimulus event repeatedly until their interest declines or habituates. When a new stimulus is introduced that is sufficiently different from the habituated stimulus, there is an initial recovery of attention as the child recognizes and begins processing the new situation. The most common form of response measured in human infants is the amount of visual attention they direct towards a source of interest, in other words, how long they stare at an event. This allows researchers to look for a preference for novelty, *following habituation, organisms prefer to attend to novel stimulation*, by habituating the infant to one type of stimulus until they get bored and then introducing a novel stimulus. If there is a significant recovery of interest, then the researcher can assume that the infant can distinguish between the two events. The infant must have noticed the difference if they prefer the novel event.

PREFERENCE FOR NOVELTY PARADIGM Following habituation, organisms prefer to attend to novel stimulation.

Although simple, this preference for novelty technique is extremely powerful as it enables the researcher to test how well the infant differentiates aspects of the world. It can be used to investigate simple perceptual discrimination of sights and sounds right through to investigating complicated event sequences that vary in their conceptual complexity. Even you and I would eventually get bored watching reruns of the same complex thriller over and over again. The power of repeated exposure is that if a core important question can be stripped down to its bare essentials so that any change in it is qualitatively different, then it can be investigated using the preference for novelty paradigm. For example, Woodward (1998) wanted to know if infants understood that people's actions were usually goal directed. In other words, are actions purposeful? That's a big question about other people's mental states that we address in Chapter 14. There are many complicated actions and goals that people can have, such as becoming an astronaut or gaining a psychology degree. However, a much simpler one is reaching (action) for a toy (goal). Woodward discovered that infants can infer goals and intentions when watching someone reach for an object because they show longer looking when the adult appears to change goals. In fact, many researchers refer to this as the violation of expectancy (VOE) paradigm – *where the anticipated outcome is deliberately contravened*. Researchers who advocate the VOE paradigm emphasize the interpretation that the infant is not simply passively sitting back and watching the world go by but is actively trying to work out what should happen next (Baillargeon, 1994). In this way, researchers have been able to investigate infants' knowledge without them having to show us what they know from their actions, which, as we have already established, are pretty limited.

VIOLATION OF EXPECTANCY (VOE) PARADIGM Where the anticipated outcome is deliberately contravened.

Other behavioural techniques

Behavioural techniques can include all measurable actions. Once an infant has gained some degree of motor control, they can act on the world in a purposeful way. Sometimes, experimenters have to be creative in tapping into behaviours they can measure. For example, some researchers measure the amount of sucking an infant does when presented with an event. A novel event causes the infant to pause in their sucking and then resume after they have paid enough attention. Once they habituate to this event, they begin sucking again at a higher rate. If you give a baby a dummy to suck while they are presented with old and new events and this dummy is connected by a tube to a pressure transducer, the change in their sucking behaviour can be measured by computers and used to control presentations (Juscyzk, 1985).

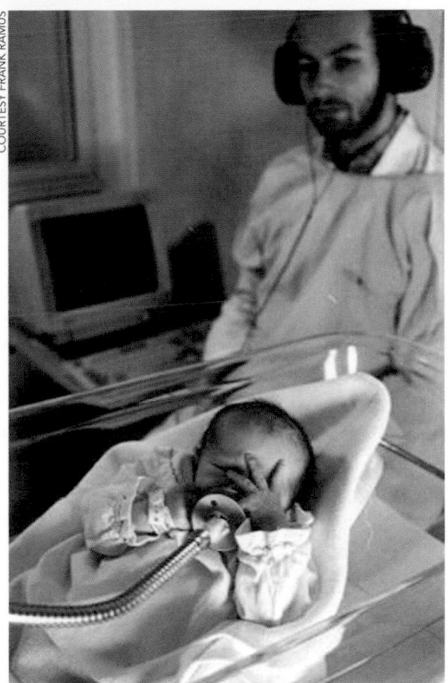
COURTESY FRANK RAMUS

This newborn is controlling the presentation of sounds by the amount of sucking that is registered by a computer.

Technological advances in the infant lab

More recent technological advances, most notably in computer programming, have enabled researchers to collect more fine-grained measures of young children's abilities. For example, noninvasive eye trackers allow researchers to record exactly where a child is looking during a particular presentation, and are now in fairly common use in developmental research. These systems generally work by recording reflected infrared light created by shining a harmless invisible beam into the infant's eye that is reflected back in much the same way that cats' eyes reflect light. Another technique that has made considerable progress in recent years is EEG recording, using the same principles as those described in Chapter 3 but adapted especially for young children. This allows researchers to study localized brain activity without having to put the child into a noisy brain scanner. The baby in **FIGURE 11.5** is wearing a *geodesic sensor net*, a network of sensitive electrodes that detects tiny changes in the electrical voltage at the scalp surface, reflecting the underlying activity of neurons in the brain. With enough electrodes on the net, researchers can measure the relative activity between different areas as the baby performs tasks.

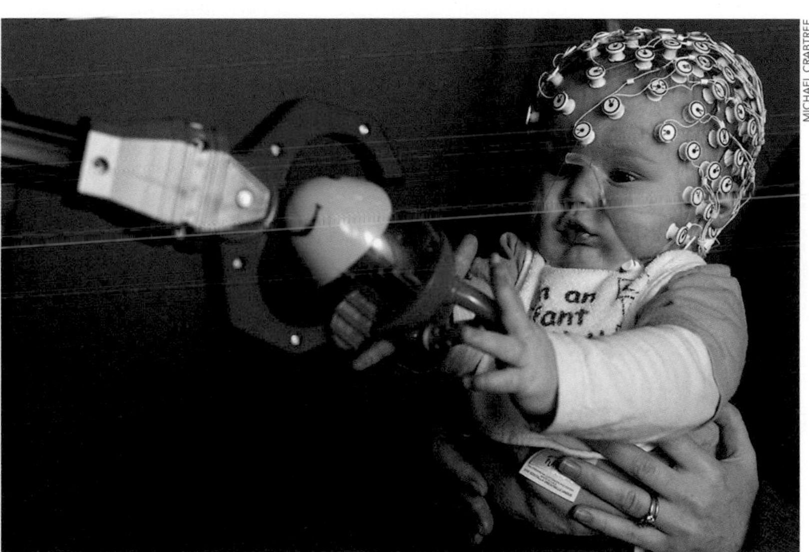
MICHAEL CRABTREE

FIGURE 11.5 Measuring brain activity in infants The baby is wearing a geodesic sensor net, a network of sensitive electrodes that detects tiny changes in the electrical voltage at the scalp surface, reflecting the underlying activity of neurons in the brain. Researchers can use this device to measure the relative activity between different areas as the baby performs tasks, for example reaching for a toy, as shown here.

Interview technique

Once a child is capable of language, they represent a completely different experimental animal as far as the researcher is concerned. They can be asked what they think and understand through a structured interview – *a consistent set of questions about a topic under consideration*. This approach was first applied by Piaget, working as Binet's assistant in Paris when they were developing the intelligence tests we encountered in Chapter 9. One of Piaget's greatest insights and contributions to developmental psychology was the realization that children's errors were often more revealing about the way their minds work in comparison to the answers they got right. By focusing on errors, you could say that Piaget was the first developmental psychologist to study children's mindbugs.

STRUCTURED INTERVIEW A consistent set of questions about a topic under consideration.

However, there are several experimental problems with language to keep in mind. The first is that language depends on comprehension and this may not be fully developed in the children being studied. Researchers must check that children not only understand what any question means, but also that they have sufficient language skills to express what they are thinking. For example, before the age of three years, children have a bias to respond 'Yes' to any question (Fritzley and Lee, 2003) that makes structured interviews problematic.

In summary, development consists of quantitative and qualitative changes that reflect different linear and nonlinear processes. Nonlinear change is especially interesting to psychologists, as it suggests a fundamental reorganization of underlying mechanisms. Change is measured using different designs with a variety of techniques that work best, given the limitations of testing young children. Some of the most common techniques are those that do not depend on language, which can be limited in children. Piaget was the first developmental psychologist to systematically study young children and was particularly interested in evidence for early mindbugs.

Beyond the blooming, buzzing confusion

Try to imagine what it must be like to be born – to leave the intimate, warm cocoon of the human womb and enter the sterile, bleached cacophony of a hospital delivery suite, a room flooded with bright light, tubes, cold metal objects, large moving bodies, agitated voices and machines that go *ping*. What does the newborn make of all this fuss? It's enough to make you want to cry.

When American philosopher William James (1890, p. 488) considered the world of the newborn, he concluded that it must be like one 'great blooming buzzing confusion'. However, James was wrong in his assumption. The newborn's world is not as chaotic as he predicted. What we understand about infants depends on our methods of investigation. We now know that their worlds are more organized than originally assumed. In this section we examine how recent methodological advances have revealed early sensory processing and how the information from the senses is organized into perceptions that support motor behaviour.

Making sense of the world: sensation

Vision

Of all the senses, humans are predominantly dependent on vision, with a large proportion of sensory cortical processing dedicated to this function, as discussed in Chapter 4. But the visual cortex is relatively immature at birth; so until recently, psychologists assumed that newborns had little visual capacity and that the vision they did have must be supported by subcortical processes (Bronson, 1974). However, recent evidence of perceptual abilities indicates that newborns have at least some rudimentary cortical function. So how much can a young child actually see?

ACUITY The level of finest visual detail that can be resolved.

VISUAL SCANNING The ability to selectively move one's eyes around the environment.

VISUAL CONTRAST Areas of greatest brightness relative to darkness.

New parents like to stand around the cot and make silly faces at their baby because they think the baby will be amused. In fact, newborns have a rather limited range of vision. Their visual acuity – *the level of finest visual detail that can be perceived* – would qualify them as being legally blind (Banks and Salapatek, 1983). What they can see at a distance of 6 m is roughly equivalent to the level of detail that an adult can see at 180 m (not that they would look that far anyway). Young infants have poor accommodation, the ability to focus over a range of distances, and tend to remain focused on objects within about a 90-cm radius (Braddick and Atkinson, 1979). They also have reduced visual scanning – *the ability to selectively move their eyes around the environment* – which suggests that they cannot selectively attend to multiple visual targets at an early age. This is why infants below the age of two months often display a 'sticky fixation' behaviour, where they appear to lock their gaze on highly visible objects from which they cannot easily disengage (Hood et al., 1998).

If you measure where young infants look when they are presented with visual patterns, their scan patterns are restricted and often focused on areas of most visual contrast – the *areas of greatest brightness relative to darkness*. For example, when presented with a face to look at, the visual scanning of a one-month-old is restricted to a localized feature of highest contrast such as the hairline, yet despite this poor quality, the newborn's level of vision is still sufficient for making out enough detail to distinguish faces, a skill that has particular significance and relevance during this early period, which we discuss in Chapter 12.

By two months, an infant has more control over where they look (Salapatek, 1975). This increase in scanning is dependent on maturing cortical visual mechanisms that enable flexible control over eye movements. In fact, the visual cortex matures so rapidly that by the age of around six months, a child's vision is comparable to that of an adult (Atkinson, 2000), and includes the higher order visual functions described in Chapter 4, such as colour discrimination, motion detection and depth perception.

Audition

Newborns have already experienced an auditory environment within their mother's womb and so they have relatively well-developed hearing at birth. They still have some way to go though: the faintest sound they respond to is around four times louder than the quietest sound that an adult can detect, and will not reach adult levels until around five to eight years (Maurer and Maurer, 1988). Newborns also visually orient to sounds by turning towards the source, suggesting that the visual and auditory systems are already coordinated to seek out multisensory events that stimulate more than one sensory system, as described in the Multisensory integration section of Chapter 4. This is because the world is made up of sights and sounds that correspond. If you hear a sound, you turn in expectation to see what caused it. In this way, the human brain is beginning to perceive the world through organizing sensory input into reliable patterns.

Taste and smell

In addition to sights and sounds, infants also learn about tastes and smells. However, we know a lot less about the development of these senses because, frankly, there has been less research on them. What is known is that these senses are operating early on and also show evidence of learning through exposure. For example, in the uterus, the fetus swallows amniotic fluids and appears to have a preference for sweetness. We know this from a study where a physician injected saccharine into the amniotic fluid of a pregnant mother and recorded an increased consumption of amniotic fluid by the fetus (Gandelman, 1992). Newborns maintain this preference for sweetness and, like adults, will smile in response to sweet substances (Lipsitt, 1977).

Amniotic fluid can also take on flavours from the food eaten by the mother and this can translate into food preferences once the child is born. For example, Mennella and colleagues (2001) found preferences for carrot-flavoured food in infants whose mothers drank carrot juice during the last trimester of pregnancy. Newborns also prefer the smell of their own mothers (and vice versa). An infant will turn towards the breast that is lactating, and prefers the smell of its own mother's milk to that of another mother (Macfarlane, 1975). It is worth noting that infants do not habituate to their mothers, suggesting that different mechanisms are operating compared to ones used for learning, when there is generally a decrease in the infant's response. Could all these early examples of taste and smell biases also explain early cultural preferences for certain types of food?

IMAGE SOURCE

Do you have a sweet tooth? It could be that your mother's eating habits during pregnancy have affected your own food preferences.

Touch

Initially, the infant's ability to act on the world is limited – it is unable to reach or grasp, and will not be able to do so until the cortical systems reach a greater level of maturity. However, young infants thrive on touch from others. That's why mothers instinctively cradle and cuddle their infants to soothe them. In fact, touch can play an important role in babies born prematurely. Around 1 in 10 babies in the West are born prematurely, with associated low birth weight that can lead to developmental complications. However, these babies have a significant (31–47%) increase in weight following a daily regime of baby massage over two weeks compared with control babies who receive no intervention (Field et al., 2004). One possible explanation based on animal studies is that stimulation by touch activates the release of hormones in the brain that regulate metabolism and growth. For example, mother rats lick their young pups to stimulate the release of growth hormones (Schanberg and Field, 1987). Without such stimulation, the pups are stunted in size.

Sorting out the world: perception

The world assaults our senses with information overload – James's 'blooming buzzing confusion'. For example, consider vision and take a look around you for a moment. The visual world is a complex environment that needs organizing and interpreting. As an adult, you can readily do this as you immediately recognize objects and backgrounds, even when they are cluttered or partly obscured. Experience enables you to do this seemingly simple task, but how does a developing infant interpret the world? How do they begin to sort everything out into different types of objects with different properties? How do they make sense of the confusion? Perceptual development is the process that begins to unscramble this mess by detecting patterns and filling in missing information. It is a process that starts within the womb.

MENTAL REPRESENTATIONS Patterns of neuronal activity that refer to aspects of the external world.

We already know that the infant has been learning in the womb and that much of the mental machinery for processing the world is already in place through the process of experience-expectant organization described earlier. The brain is just waiting for the right environmental experiences to start wiring up the networks of cells that form the contents of our minds. These patterns of brain activation are the basis for mental representations – *patterns of neuronal activity that initially refer to aspects of the external world.* We can also mentally represent all manner of things not in the external world but such imagination is likely to take time to develop. Representations or 're-presentations' are what the brain generates and stores – copies of world experiences that are in a format that allow us to think about them further. For example, consider some possible representations of a pencil we may have in our brains. It has physical representations (for example, what shape, size, colour and weight is it?), functional representations (what can it be used for?) and semantic representations (what else does the thought of a pencil bring to mind?). It may even have a symbolic representation as a phallic object if you are a Freudian psychoanalyst. The point (pun!) is that representations are one of the major things brains compute. From sensation through to cognition, representations are the outputs that feed into each next level of computation in the central nervous system (see FIGURE 11.6). To begin, sensory representations feed into the perceptual processes that organize the input into meaningful patterns. From here, perceptual representations form the basis for cognition – the processes that allow us to think about and interpret the world. That is why representations are the fundamental building blocks for all higher mental processes. Our brain 're-presents' reality as a pattern of activation that can be used to understand and predict the world so that we formulate actions to deal with it. The flow of information is also bidirectional. Not only do bottom-up processes feed into higher levels of representation, but this top-down knowledge can influence how we process and interpret information at lower levels.

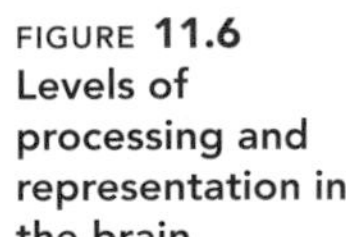
FIGURE 11.6 Levels of processing and representation in the brain

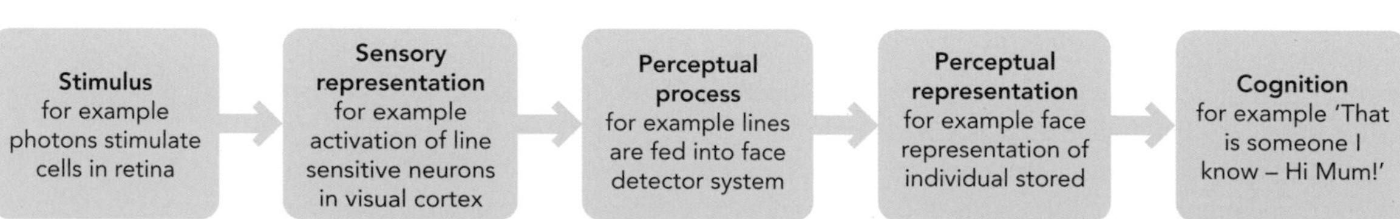

As soon as the infant encounters patterns of sensory stimulation, they begin to organize this information into representations. When the fetus is learning the pattern of their mother's voice or a particular soap theme tune, the sound is organized into representations that can be stored. This organizational process is powerful because it has to contend with the fact that information may be ambiguous or missing. Again, take another look around the room you are reading this book in. How many of the objects are fully visible and how many of them are partially occluded? Where does the wall begin and the floor end? We take for granted the complexity of our perceptual processes because they operate so effortlessly that we are not aware of the difficult task that perception solves. Luckily, nature has built some rules for learning into the system that help the newborn start to make sense of their sensations. These are the perceptual processes we employ to segment the world into experiences.

Using the habituation technique described earlier, British infancy researcher Alan Slater has shown greater levels of perceptual organization than previously attributed to the newborn, suggesting a kind of perceptual 'hardwiring'. For example, newborns represent perceptual constancies, compensatory processes that adjust for perceived physical changes of size and shape, which enable them to recognize that as an object moves (and thus the visual image projected on to the retina changes), it still remains the same object (Slater et al., 1990). This was tested by presenting objects at different distances or orientations and seeing if the newborns were aware of the constant size and shape of the objects in the outside world despite the changes that occur on the retina when objects move. An example of a newborn infant size constancy experiment is shown in FIGURE 11.7.

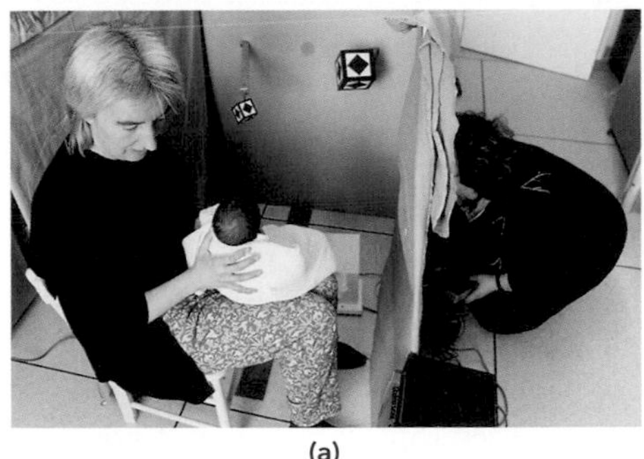

(a)

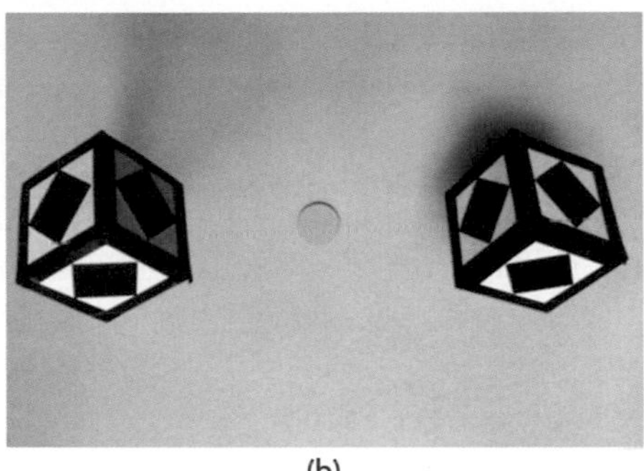

(b)

FIGURE **11.7 Testing for perceptual constancy** In their size constancy experiment, Slater et al. (1990) familiarized newborn infants to either a large or a small cube, which, over trials, was presented at different distances from the eyes. On subsequent test trials, the infants looked more at a different-sized cube than at the same-sized one, despite the fact that the paired stimuli were at different distances in order to make their retinal size the same. (a) An infant being tested, and (b), the sizes of the two cubes from the infant's viewing point (Slater et al., 1990).

Newborns can also distinguish the angles of lines, which, as we read in Chapter 3 on detecting line orientation, is a rudimentary basis of shape perception and evidence for early cortical activity (Atkinson et al., 1988). As shown in FIGURE 11.8, newborns were first familiarized to a set of lines that either formed an acute or obtuse angle (Slater et al., 1991). Following habituation, the newborn was presented with two new test stimuli – one with a new and one with the old angle. Newborns looked longer at the new angle, indicating that they must have extracted the angle from repeated exposure to new sets of lines.

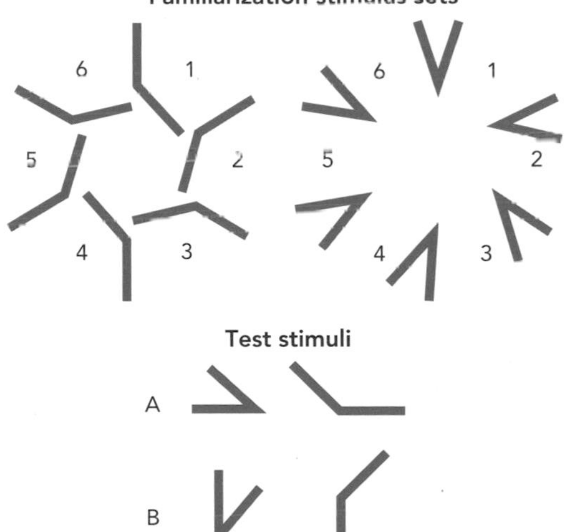

FIGURE **11.8 Angle discrimination in newborns** Newborns were first familiarized to a set of lines that either formed an acute or obtuse angle (Slater et al., 1991). Following habituation, the newborn was presented with two new test stimuli – one with a new and one with the old angle. Newborns looked longer at the new angle, indicating that they must have extracted the angle from repeated exposure to new sets of lines.

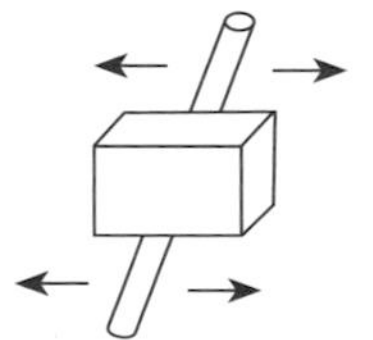

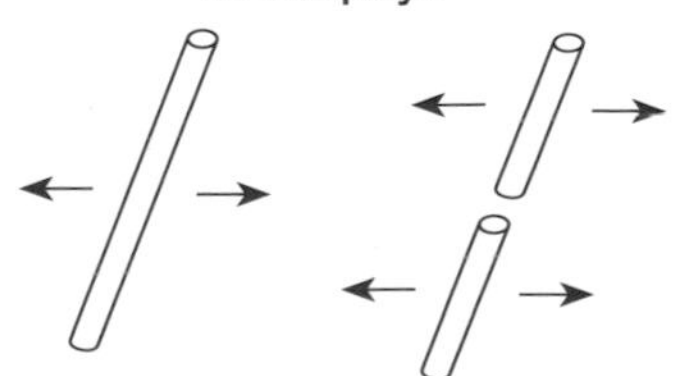

FIGURE **11.9 Filling in the gaps** Infants were habituated to the rod moving to and fro behind the block. In the test, they looked longer at the broken rod moving even though it was more similar to the display they saw during habituation (Kellman and Spelke, 1983).

Newborns can even fill in missing information. Imagine watching your lecturer move to and fro behind a table. Although you cannot see the middle portion of their body, you assume their torso is connected to their legs. You do not need to know about bodies to make this assumption. This is because when two objects move together at exactly the same speed and in the same direction, the perceptual system is inclined to see them as part of the same object. After all, what is the likelihood of two objects doing this in tandem if they are not connected in some way? This was tested in a study where four-month-olds were habituated to a display where a rod appeared to be moving to and fro behind a block (see FIGURE 11.9). Infants were then shown two test displays – either a complete or broken rod undergoing the same movement. Despite the fact that the broken rod was visually more similar to the habituation display, infants looked longer at this compared to the solid rod, suggesting that the infants had perceptually filled in the hidden segment. You might say that babies were 'joining up the dots' and 'filling in the blanks'.

Crossmodal perception

CROSSMODAL PERCEPTION The capacity to detect correspondences of different features in the world from different sensory modalities.

Crossmodal perception is defined as *the capacity to detect correspondences of different features in the world from different sensory modalities.* It requires combining representations from different sensory events. For example, if you slam a book down onto the table (visual event), you expect to hear the loud thud (auditory event) at the same time. This is a crossmodal event of vision and sound. If you have ever seen a badly dubbed film where the soundtrack is not in time with what's happening on screen, you'll know how excruciating it can be to watch, because we *expect* certain sensory information from different sources to be coordinated, especially in the case of watching faces and hearing voices. Crossmodal perception depends on the integration of information from the visual and auditory processing regions of the brain and is present from at least four months of age. To establish this, researchers presented infants with two films of toys bouncing up and down, but with only one soundtrack playing from a speaker between the two screens. This single soundtrack was synchronized to one of the films but not the other, and the infants preferred to watch the film that was synchronized (Spelke, 1976). It is not clear whether newborns are also sensitive to such crossmodal synchronization but they can learn to associate one sight with a particular sound. Using a habituation paradigm, newborns were presented with different toy–sound pairings and later showed recognition when these pairings where changed (Morrongiello et al., 1994).

hot science

Infant boubas and kikis: Evidence for early synaesthesia?

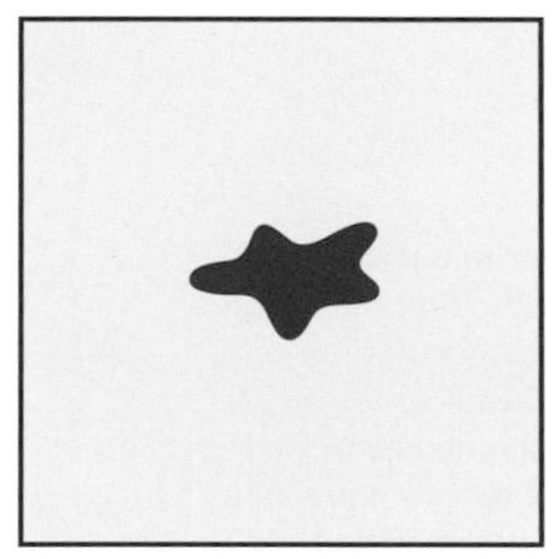

Take a look at these two shapes. One is called a 'bouba' and the other is a 'kiki'. Which do you think is which? Almost all adults (95–98%) think that the smooth bulbous object will be the bouba and the jagged one is the kiki (Ramachandran and Hubbard, 2001), as do many toddlers (Maurer et al., 2006). Although these shapes and names are totally made up, people assume there is a correspondence between the statistical properties of shapes and sounds, which is a form of crossmodal matching. In Chapter 4, we discussed cases of adults who experience bizarre crossmodal matching in synaesthesia where sensation in one modality induces perception normally associated with a different modality. However, Daphne Maurer, Canadian infant psychologist, thinks that rather than synaesthesia being a bizarre form of crossmodal perception, it may be the natural state of the perceptual world of the newborn (Maurer and Mondloch, 2006). Maurer (1997) argues that newborns do not have to learn how the different senses go together because they are already all mapped up. Reminiscent of James's 'blooming buzzing confusion', Maurer and Maurer (1988, p. 51) write:

> The newborn does not keep his sensations separate from one another. He mixes sights, sounds, feelings and smells into a sensual bouillabaisse. Sights have sounds, feelings have tastes, and smells can make him dizzy. The wildest of the 1960's psychedelia could not begin to compare with the everyday experience of a baby's entry into the world.

In support of this position, a study (Walker et al., 2010) presented three- to four-month-old infants with two crossmodal matching experiments. In the first experiment, they examined the correspondence between auditory pitch and visuospatial height of an animated ball moving up and down the screen. Normally, we associate rising height with rising pitch (Rofler and Butler, 1967). To test for this correspondence in infants, the researchers played a tone that either started low and rose in tone or changed in the opposite direction. Three out of four babies looked longer when the pitch rising in tone was paired with the congruent animation of the ball rising in height, rather than reverse incongruent pairing.

In the second experiment, infants watched as a shape that began in the form of a pointy kiki morphed into the shape of a bouba accompanied by a tone that went from either a congruent high pitch to a low pitch or the reverse. The expectation was that low-pitched noises were more like the bouba sound and should be paired with the smooth shape, whereas high-pitched sounds are more akin to the jagged shape (Walker and Smith, 1985). Again, most babies (75%) looked significantly longer overall at the pairing of the congruent match (high pitch and kiki/low pitch and bouba) than the incongruent match (high pitch and bouba/low pitch and kiki). These findings indicated that young infants were sensitive to synaesthetic crossmodality correspondences and this was unlikely to be learned, as both the sounds and the images are novel and the babies were preverbal.

This was a remarkable pair of findings that spurred other researchers to test the claims. In one recent critical replication, Lewkowicz and Minar (2014) argued that the problem with the original stimulus was that it was confounded because changing pitch is also associated with changing loudness. When the ball was paired with the low pitch at the bottom of the screen, it was louder and therefore more likely to attract the infant's attention. They tried a different auditory tone to control for the confounding variable and failed to find a replication. This is a plausible alternative account except that it does not explain the infant preference found in the original second experiment where the morphing shape always began as the pointy kiki that was either paired with the congruent high-pitch tone that lowered, or paired with the tone that rose in pitch (Walker et al., 2014). More substantially, other researchers testing Dutch babies replicated the height/high-pitch preference and also found a similar preference for correspondences between high pitch and thinness and low pitch and thickness (Dolscheid et al., 2014).

These recent studies support and do not change the original interpretation, so why tell you about them? As we noted in the hot science feature in Chapter 2, important findings require replication and all attempts to reproduce findings should be reported when evaluating claims. This is a good case example where an important report has not simply been taken on face value but also replicated in a different culture, with a conceptually related prediction that makes it a more robust finding.

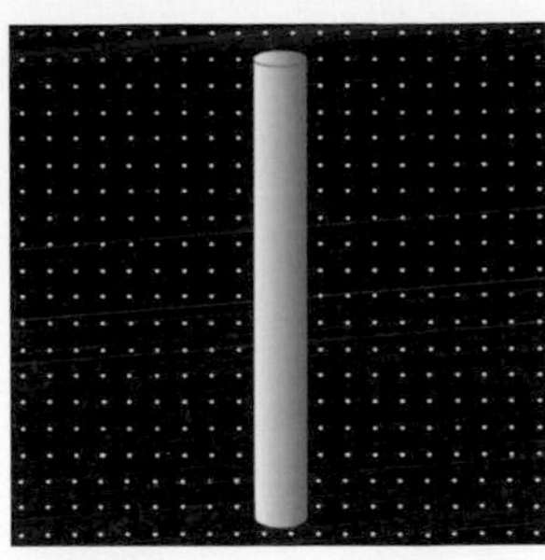

Stimuli for the thinness/thickness study in Dutch babies.

It would appear that young infants appreciate the correspondence between the nature of sounds and sights. This supports the hypothesis (not entirely proven) that rather than learning to make bizarre correspondences, adult synaesthetes may have brains that have failed to lose the sensory correspondences that the rest of us have lost, possibly because theirs were not pruned back with experience. The bouba/kiki effect could be a remnant of those innate correspondences from when they were infants.

Acting on the world: motor

MOTOR DEVELOPMENT The emergence of the ability to execute physical actions such as reaching, grasping, crawling and walking.

REFLEXES Specific patterns of motor response that are triggered by specific patterns of sensory stimulation.

Sensing and perceiving the world is all very well, but in evolution, it would appear that the primary reason for a living organism to develop a brain is so that it can move around at will and act on its environment. Living organisms such as plants and moulds do not need to move around and so don't have brains. Or consider the example of the sea squirt (*Ascidiacea*). To begin with, it has a simple central nervous system that it uses to navigate around on the ocean floor until it finds a suitable location where it can attach itself to a rock. Having found a permanent position, the sea squirt undergoes a *metamorphosis*; as it no longer needs to negotiate the hazards of the environment, it proceeds to digest its own nervous system. (Maybe the same thing can be said to happen to humans when they retire or get a permanent job where there is no prospect of moving on!) We need brains to get around and act on the world.

Motor development is *the emergence of the ability to execute physical actions such as reaching, grasping, crawling and walking*, and it undergoes significant improvement during infancy. Initially, infants are born with a limited set of innate, unlearned motor responses known as reflexes – *specific patterns of motor response that are triggered by specific patterns of sensory stimulation*. For example, the 'rooting reflex' is the tendency for infants to move their mouths towards any object that touches their cheek, and the 'sucking reflex' is the tendency to suck any object that enters their mouths. These two reflexes allow newborns to find their mother's nipple and begin feeding – a behaviour so vitally important that nature took no chances and hard-wired it into every one of us. These actions are not dependent on the newborn's still-developing cortex, but are mostly supported by subcortical brain mechanisms. Interestingly, many reflexes that are present at birth seem to disappear in the first few months as an

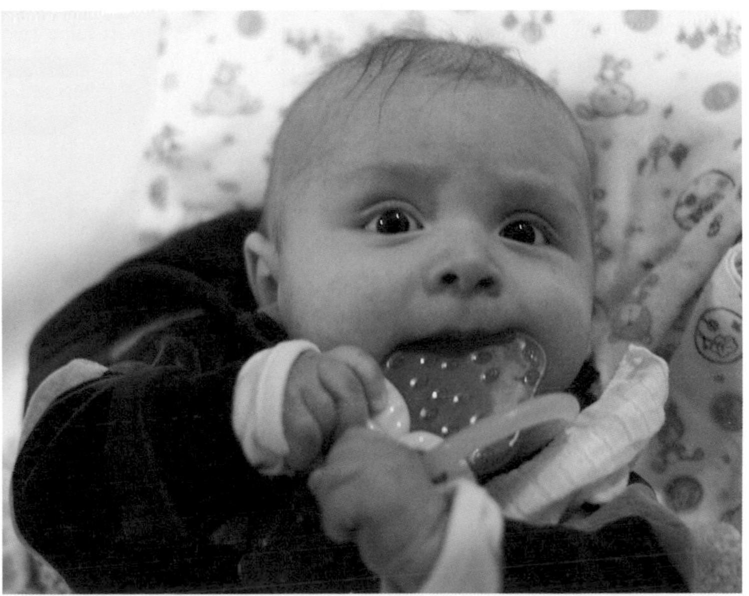

Infants are born with a 'sucking reflex', which is linked to the rooting reflex and breastfeeding, and is a tendency to suck any object that enters their mouths.

Newborns have a grasp reflex, so any suitable object placed in their hands will be firmly grasped.

Some children develop motor skills earlier than others.

infant's cortex develops and plays an increasing role in more sophisticated motor behaviour. For example, newborns have a grasp reflex so any suitable object placed in their hands will be firmly grasped. In fact, the grasp reflex is so strong that you can pick an infant off the ground simply by the strength of them grasping onto your fingers. Eventually, however, the grasping action becomes integrated with the reaching action, which is not a reflex, but instead comes increasingly under the voluntary control of the infant (von Hofsten, 1979).

The development of control over their movements comes about as a result of intrinsic ('nature') and extrinsic ('nurture') influences. On the one hand, the cortex is maturing (the nature factor), but on the other, it requires appropriate environmental factors to stimulate it (the nurture factor). As shown in **FIGURE 11.10**, motor skills generally emerge in an orderly sequence, but they do not emerge to a strict timetable. Rather, the timing of these skills is influenced by many factors, such as the baby's incentive for reaching, body weight, muscular development and general level of activity. In one study, for example, babies who had visually stimulating mobiles hanging above their cots began reaching for objects six weeks earlier than babies who did not (White and Held, 1966).

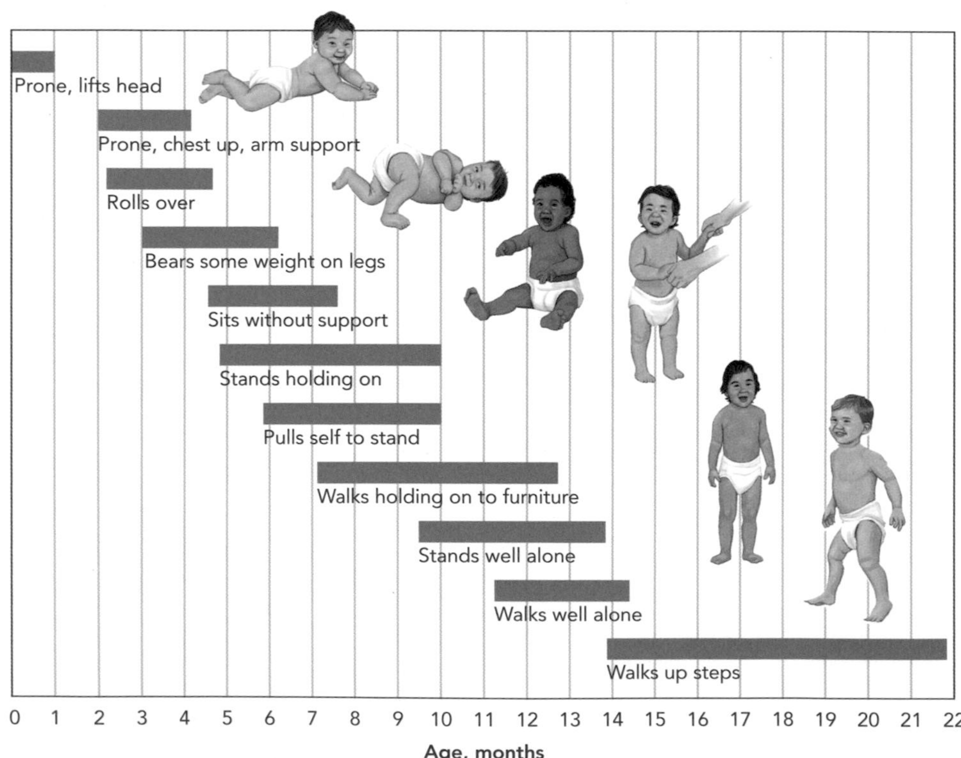

FIGURE **11.10 Motor development** Infants learn to control their bodies from head to feet and from centre to periphery. These skills emerge in a strict sequence.

The input from environment comes not only from the physical world but also the social one. For example, three-month-old babies can anticipate when their mother is about to pick them up, based on her outstretched arms, and will adjust their own posture to make it easier (Reddy et al., 2013). This is not simply a learned behaviour, rather this ability requires understanding that others have intentions, which is why some postural adjustment is absent in babies who are later diagnosed with autism (Saint-Georges et al., 2011) (see also autism and theory of mind in Chapter 12).

The rapidly developing cortex of the human infant enables babies to expand their repertoire of representations as they explore and discover new aspects of the world and this happens right down to the basic sensory features they can detect. For example, because we have two eyes, the visual system receives two slightly different images of the world that can be recombined to produce stereopsis – *the perception of depth by combining the images from each eye*. In much the same way that 3-D films work by presenting two slightly different images to each eye with those special glasses, the brain recombines the disparate signals from each to give the impression of depth. However, this process relies on cortical mechanisms and for this reason stereopsis has not been found in infants younger than three months, because their visual cortex has not yet sufficiently matured (Held et al., 1980). Nevertheless, as we saw in Chapter 4, there are other monocular cues to depth that babies can use.

Even if infants can detect depth using monocular cues, it is not clear that they really appreciate the consequences of depth until they are capable of acting on the world and moving about. We know this from one of the well-known perception studies by Eleanor Gibson and Richard Walk (1960), who built a visual cliff, *a platform with a shallow drop on one side and a steep cliff on the other*, to test depth perception in infants (see **FIGURE 11.11**). Don't worry, it wasn't a test to see if babies bounce. Across both sides was a thick plate of glass so that the infant could not fall. As soon as infants were able to crawl, from around the age of six months, they would cross over the shallow side when beckoned by their mother, but refuse to cross over the side with the visual cliff. However, if a six-week-old infant was lowered onto the glass over the cliff side, their heart rate decelerated – a measure of interest and attention – indicating that they noticed the drop but were not obviously scared, which usually produces increased heart rate, as we described in Chapter 3 (Campos et al., 1970). Indeed, it is not clear that infants are that scared of the deep side of the visual cliff (Adolph et al., 2014). On a version of the visual cliff where the drop is adjustable until it simply becomes a step, infants who are more experienced at crawling and walking will attempt to cross compared to infants who are still novices (Kretch and Adolph, 2013). Infants may avoid crossing over the deep side but that is because they perceive affordances – *potentials for possible actions by agents acting on the environment*. For example, a door handle offers an affordance for how it must be gripped by the hand. In the same way, different surfaces offer affordances for locomotion – the relations between bodies and the relevant properties of the environment that make an action such as descent possible or impossible. Infants explore their environment looking for affordances to discover what is possible.

Probably the most theoretically important aspects of these studies is the idea that perceptual motor experience improves the way we are able to understand and explore the world around us, that is, movement has implications about how we think about the world. This idea is captured in J. J. Gibson's (1979) dictum: 'We must perceive in order to move, but we must also move in order to perceive.' In other words, action and perception are coordinated systems that feedback information from experience to generate representations of the world. Indeed, one recent 14-year longitudinal study has shown that infant motor-exploratory competence assessed at five months predicts academic achievement at adolescence, supporting the idea that exploring and understanding the physical world lays the foundation for intellectual development (Bornstein et al., 2013). As we will see next, this idea formed the basis of Piaget's most ambitious theory of cognitive development.

Go naked

Studies of babies wearing nappies reveal that they are delayed in their development of walking, making more missteps and falling over more often compared to naked babies (Cole et al., 2012). Cloth nappies were worse than disposable ones, but not as bad as parenting practices in northern China where babies are kept in fine sandbags that absorb waste but severely restrict the movement of their legs, thus delaying sitting and walking (Mei, 1994).

STEREOPSIS The perception of depth by combining the images from each eye.

VISUAL CLIFF A platform with a shallow drop on one side and a steep cliff on the other.

AFFORDANCES Potentials for possible actions by agents acting on the environment.

FIGURE 11.11 The visual cliff Consisting of a platform with a shallow drop on one side and steep cliff on the other, and a thick plate of glass on both sides so that the infant cannot fall, a visual cliff can be used to test the depth perception of infants and their fear responses to a steep drop in height.

In summary, newborns enter the world equipped with simple sensory, perceptual and motor skills that undergo rapid development as their cortical brain mechanisms mature and they are exposed to appropriate environmental experience. Sensory and perceptual processes achieve almost adult levels by the end of infancy, with later differences more to do with strategies for interpreting. Motor skills, initially limited to reflexes in the newborn, rapidly improve, enabling infants to explore their environment, which, in turn, stimulates development.

Understanding the world: cognition

Perception allows you to detect the patterns in the world, while cognition is the interpretation of those patterns into meaningful events that enable you to understand and predict the world. Cognition is what makes us clever, by combining experience with reasoning. As we learned in Chapter 1, philosophers have pondered the origins and nature of human cognition for millennia, but it has only been in the past 100 years or so that scientists have set out to investigate the development of these issues with systematic observations and experiments with children. In this section, we look at cognitive development, starting with Piaget's influential and still relevant approach. Then we will turn to more recent accounts that emerged partially as a reaction to Piagetian theory, and partly as a result of improved research methods and our better understanding of cognitive science. Finally, we acknowledge the contribution of Vygotsky's sociocultural approach, which forms part of the basis for social development that is covered in Chapter 12.

Piaget's theory of cognitive development

The father of cognitive development studies is generally acknowledged to be Jean Piaget, whom we met earlier in the chapter as he studied his daughter Lucienne. Piaget himself was an exceptional child, publishing his first scientific paper at the age of 10 on an albino sparrow he observed at his local park. Talk about an overachiever! His early interest in biology would later influence his theory about cognitive development in humans, which began during his stint with Binet working on children's intelligence.

Piaget expected children to make mistakes when confronted with difficult problems, but what surprised him was that children in the same age group typically made the same mistakes, which virtually disappeared when these children graduated to the next age group. This led Piaget to conclude that there were underlying mechanisms that limited a child's understanding of the world. As these mechanisms reorganized themselves, they would produce qualitative changes, causing the child to develop through a sequence of 'stages' in cognitive development, hence Piaget's theory is a stage theory.

Piaget proposed that children pass through four sequential stages, which he called the *sensorimotor* stage, the *preoperational* stage, the *concrete operational* stage, and the *formal operational* stage. According to his stage theory, children reason in a completely dissimilar way from one stage to the next. The stages are universal, *every child in every culture goes through the same stages*, and invariant, *every child goes through the same sequence in the same order at roughly the same time*. Piaget thought that maturation, *biologically constrained change*, combined with the child's own experiences and activities in their worlds to produce cognitive development (Piaget, 1954a) (see **TABLE 11.1**).

UNIVERSAL Every child in every culture goes through the same stages.

INVARIANT Every child goes through the same sequence in the same order at roughly the same time.

MATURATION Biologically constrained change.

TABLE **11.1 Piaget's four stages of cognitive development**

Stage	Characteristics
Sensorimotor (birth–2 years)	Infant experiences world through movement and senses, develops schemas, begins to act intentionally, and shows evidence of understanding object permanence
Preoperational (2–6 years)	Child acquires motor skills but does not understand conservation of physical properties. Child begins this stage by thinking egocentrically but ends with a basic understanding of other minds
Concrete operational (6–11 years)	Child can think logically about physical objects and events and understands conservation of physical properties
Formal operational (11 years and up)	Child can think logically about abstract propositions and hypotheticals

The first of Piaget's four stages is the sensorimotor stage – *a stage of development that begins at birth and lasts through infancy*. As the word *sensorimotor* suggests, infants at this stage use their ability to *sense* (perceptual development) and their ability to *move* (motor development) to acquire information about the world in which they live (cognitive development). By actively exploring their environments with their eyes, mouths and fingers, infants begin to construct schemas, which can be thought of as theories about or models of the way the world works.

SENSORIMOTOR STAGE A stage of development that begins at birth and lasts through infancy.

As every scientist knows, the key advantage of having a theory is that one can use it to predict and control what will happen in novel situations. If an infant learns that tugging at a stuffed animal causes the toy to come closer, that observation is incorporated into the infant's theory about how physical objects behave, and the infant can later use that theory when they want a different object to come closer, such as a rattle or a ball. Piaget called this process assimilation, which occurs when *infants apply their schemas in novel situations*. Of course, if the infant tugs the tail of the family cat, the cat is likely to sprint in the opposite direction. Infants' theories about the world ('Things come closer if I pull them') are occasionally contradicted, and thus infants must occasionally adjust their schemas in light of their new experiences ('Aha! *Inanimate* things come closer when I pull them'). Piaget called this process accommodation, which occurs when *infants revise their schemas in light of new information*. Piaget believed that cognitive development was an ongoing process in which infants develop, apply and adjust their schemas as they build an understanding of the world.

ASSIMILATION When infants apply their schemas in novel situations.

ACCOMMODATION When infants revise their schemas in light of new information.

OBJECT PERMANENCE The idea that objects continue to exist even when they are not visible.

What kinds of schemas do infants develop, apply and adjust? Piaget suggested that infants do not have – and hence must acquire – some basic understandings about the physical world. For example, when you put a pair of socks away, you know that the socks exist even after you close the drawer, and you would be quite surprised if you opened the drawer a moment later and found it empty. But according to Piaget, this would not surprise an infant because infants do not have the concept of object permanence – *the idea that objects continue to exist even when they are not visible*. Piaget noted that in the first few months of life, infants act as though objects stop existing the moment they are out of sight. It's like Clive Wearing's extreme form of amnesia we described in Chapter 5 where he immediately forgets where things are if they are covered. For instance, as noted earlier in Piaget's observation of his daughter Lucienne, infants below the age of around eight months do not search for objects if they are hidden under a cloth. As far as Piaget was concerned, without basic object permanence, 'out of sight was out of mind'. Even when infants do begin to search for hidden objects after eight months, they still do not have a mature sense of object permanence. For example, Piaget noted in his classic observation that an infant who successfully retrieves an object from hiding location *A* will frequently return to search there even when they have seen the object hidden at a new location *B*. Piaget interpreted this '*A not B error*' as an indication that the infant still did not have a representation of the object as something that exists independently of their own sensorimotor actions.

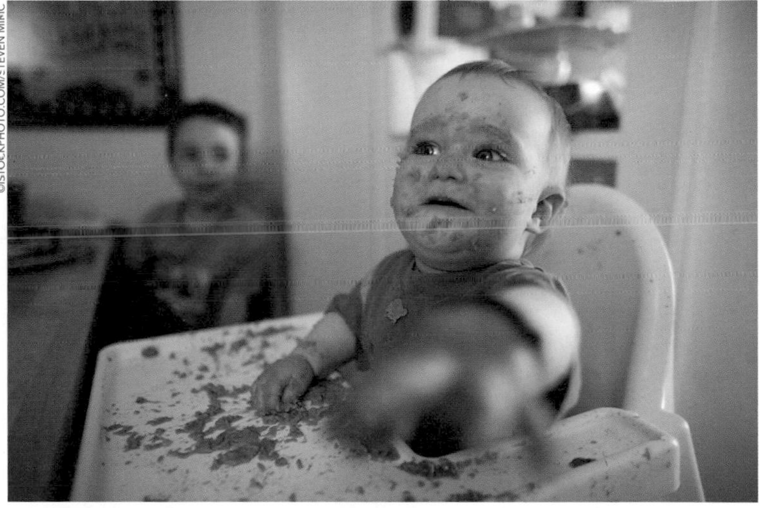
©ISTOCKPHOTO.COM/STEVEN MIRIC

During the sensorimotor stage, infants explore with their hands and mouths, learning important lessons about the physical world such as, 'if you whack your dinner hard enough, you can use it as a face mask'.

Some problems for Piagetian search failure

Was Piaget right? One of the main problems in his theory was that it was largely based on the child's inability to pass tasks that were set up in a specific way. However, there is more than one way to fail at a task, so you have to ask whether failure is due to limited competence, *an inability to understand what needs to be done to solve the task*, or limited performance, *an inability to execute the necessary actions to solve the task*. Piaget thought search failure was due to limited competence but maybe the task was too demanding. For example, infant object search requires not only a representation of the missing object

LIMITED COMPETENCE An inability to understand what needs to be done to solve the task.

LIMITED PERFORMANCE An inability to execute the necessary actions to solve the task.

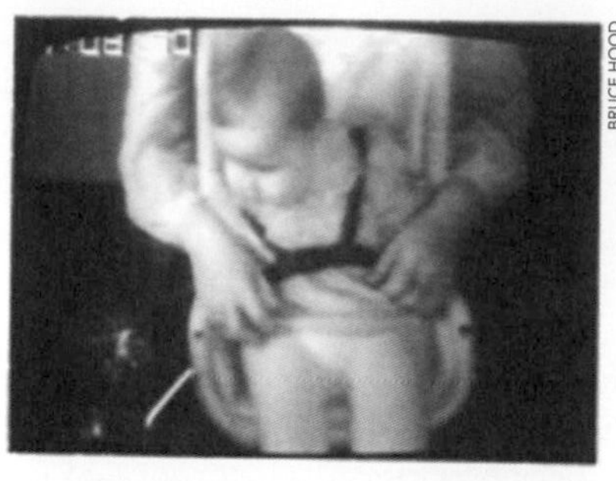

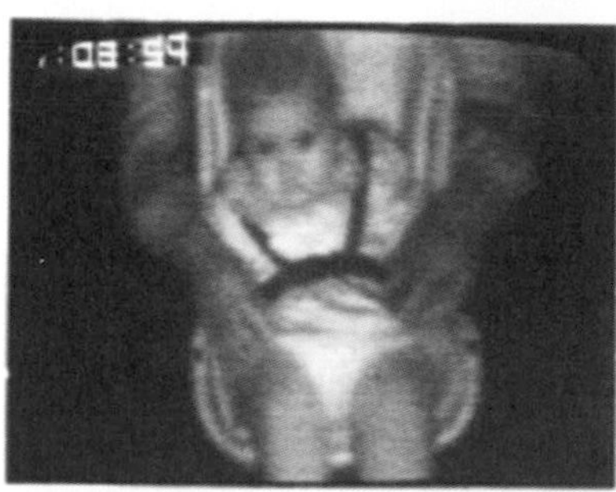

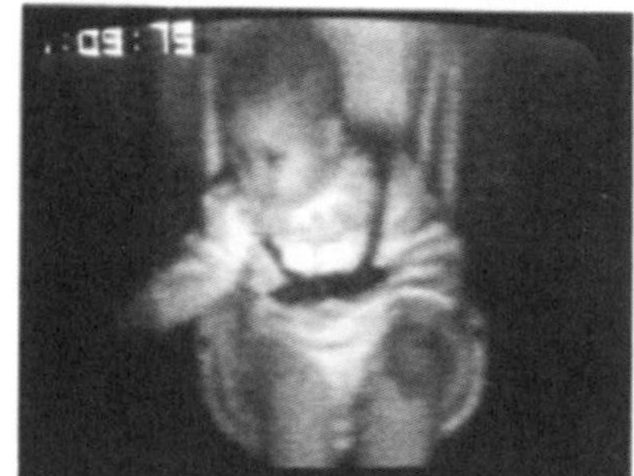

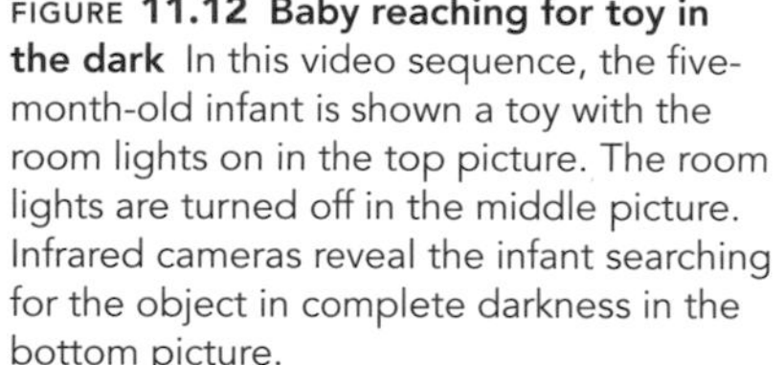

FIGURE 11.12 Baby reaching for toy in the dark In this video sequence, the five-month-old infant is shown a toy with the room lights on in the top picture. The room lights are turned off in the middle picture. Infrared cameras reveal the infant searching for the object in complete darkness in the bottom picture.

but also a retrieval plan and prerequisite motor skills. Removing cloths to search underneath for toys is too difficult at seven months. However, if you turn the room lights out so that a toy is no longer visible, even five-month-olds will reach out to search for it, suggesting that they do appreciate that objects continue to exist when out of sight (Hood and Willatts, 1986) (see **FIGURE 11.12**).

Recent research using the VOE (violation of expectancy) paradigm described earlier has also shown that young infants not only understand that unseen objects continue to exist, but also that they have properties that lead to predictable outcomes. For instance, in one study, infants were shown a miniature drawbridge that flipped up and down. Once the babies got used to this, they watched as a box was placed behind the drawbridge – in its path but out of their sight. Some infants then saw a *possible* event: the drawbridge began to flip and then suddenly stopped, as if impeded by the box the infants could not see. Other infants saw an *impossible* event: the drawbridge began to flip and then continued, as if unimpeded by the box (see **FIGURE 11.13**). What did infants do? Four-month-old infants stared longer at the impossible event than at the possible event, suggesting that they noted that something was amiss (Baillargeon et al., 1985). The only thing that made the event impossible, of course, was the presence of an unseen box. The fact that the infants looked longer at the impossible event suggests that they knew the box existed even when they could not see it.

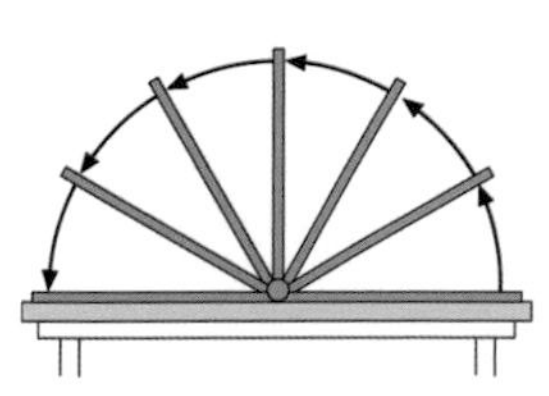

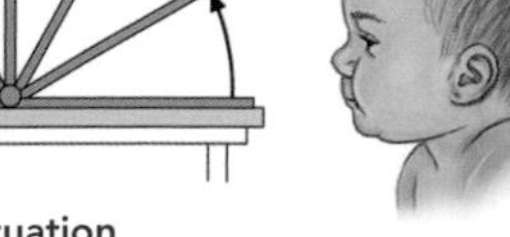

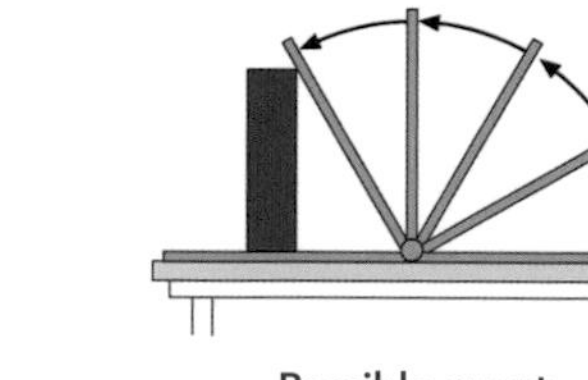

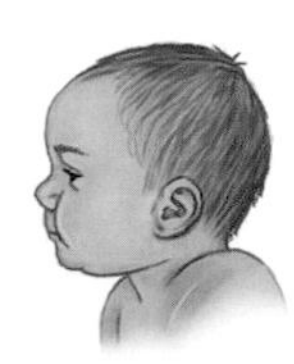

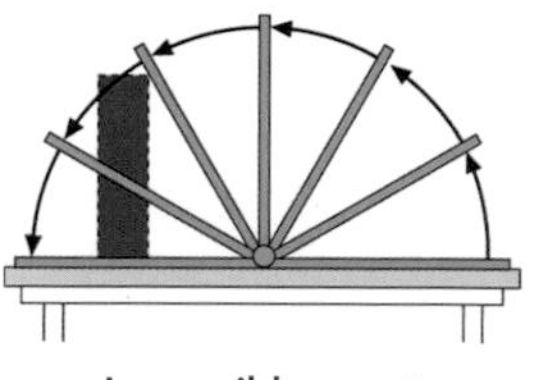

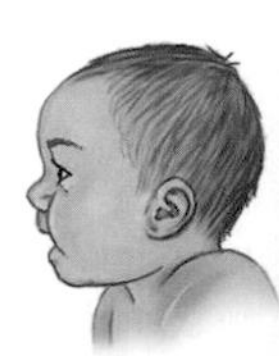

(a)

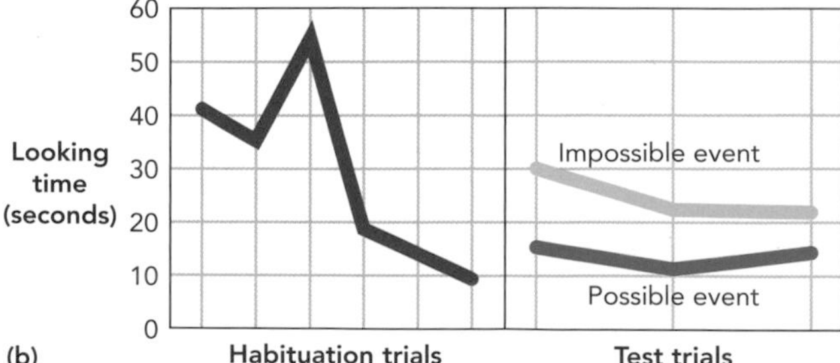

FIGURE 11.13 The possible and the impossible event (a) In the habituation trials, infants watched a drawbridge flip back and forth with nothing in its path until they grew bored. Then a box was placed behind the drawbridge and the infants were shown one of two events. In the possible event, the box kept the drawbridge from flipping all the water over, while in the impossible event, it did not. (b) The graph shows the infants' 'looking time' during the habituation and the test trials. During the test trials, their interest was reawakened by the impossible event but not by the possible event (Baillargeon et al., 1985).

This capacity to keep track of unseen objects also forms the basis of early counting. In her infant studies of addition/subtraction, Karen Wynn (1992) showed five-month-old infants a Mickey Mouse doll placed on a stage. A screen then came up to hide the doll. Next, infants watched as an experimenter holding another doll placed her hand behind the screen and then withdrew her empty hand a moment later. How many Mickey Mouses (or should that be Mice?) were behind the screen? The VOE technique revealed that infants expected two dolls and looked longer at only one (see **FIGURE 11.14**). In another version of the experiment, Wynn started off by showing the infants two dolls and then removed one of the dolls from behind the screen. Again, they looked longer when the outcome did not match the expected subtraction. Is this the same as counting that older children use? No, because infants can only keep track of small numbers (up to a maximum of about four). To count larger numbers, children have to acquire a second number system that maps number terms against quantities (Carey, 2009).

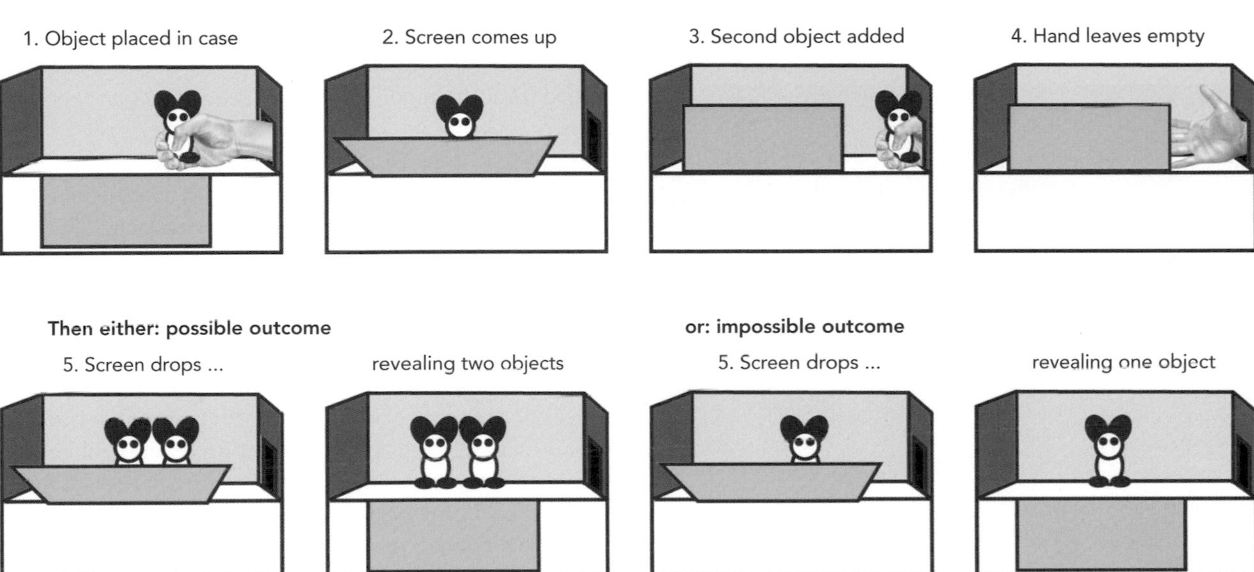

FIGURE 11.14 The Mickey Mouse task This experiment suggests that the capacity to keep track of unseen objects forms the basis of early counting in infants (Wynn, 1992). Infants witnessed two mouse dolls being placed behind a screen and when the screen was removed, subjects who were shown one doll sitting on the stage (the impossible event) stared longer than those who were shown two dolls (the possible event). This suggests that the infants were keeping track of the number of mouse dolls that were – or at least should have been – behind the screen.

Before we leave criticisms of Piaget based on looking time, we must consider one potential problem for interpreting findings based on the VOE technique. Although all these experiments suggest that infants have a better understanding of the physical world than Piaget originally claimed, it is still not clear whether they are consciously aware of, or understand, knowledge they appear to reveal by looking longer at unexpected events. For example, an adult may think that someone familiar seems different on a particular day, and consequently look longer at them, without noticing that they have had a haircut until they are told. At some level we know the person is different, but not necessarily why. In the same way, infants may possess cognitive mechanisms that notice anomalous events in the environment that cause the infant to look longer ('Something's not right here'), but it does not mean that the infant knows what is wrong about the event.

Cognitive development after infancy

After infancy, one of the most important things children learn how to do is what Piaget called 'concrete operations'. What does this mean? When you first learned to do arithmetic, you began by learning about *things* called numbers, and then you learned how to *operate* on those things by adding, dividing, subtracting and multiplying them. Piaget suggested that cognitive development during childhood is a bit like that. Infants learn about physical *things*, then children learn how those things can be *operated* on or transformed. For example, we all know that ice melts into water, which evaporates as steam; that a red apple can look grey in low light; and that the weight of a pizza remains the same no matter how many slices we cut it into. But we all know these things because we are adults. Studies suggest that young children don't share our understanding and that older children do.

PREOPERATIONAL STAGE Stage of development that begins at about 2 years and ends at about 6 years.

CONCRETE OPERATIONAL STAGE Stage of development that begins at about 6 years and ends at about 11 years.

CONSERVATION The notion that the quantitative properties of an object are invariant despite changes in the object's appearance.

In terms of Piaget's theory, early childhood is divided in two stages. The first is a preoperational stage, *the stage of development that begins at about 2 years and ends at about 6 years*, during which the child cannot perform concrete operations. The second is the concrete operational stage, *the stage of development that begins at about 6 years and ends at about 11 years*, during which the child can perform concrete operations. In one study, Piaget showed children a row of cups and asked them to place an egg in each. Preoperational children were able to do this, and afterwards they readily agreed that there were just as many eggs as there were cups. Then Piaget removed the eggs and spread them out in a long line that extended beyond the row of cups. Preoperational children incorrectly claimed that there were now more eggs than cups, pointing out that the row of eggs was longer than the row of cups and hence there must be more of them. Concrete operational children, on the other hand, correctly reported that the number of eggs did not change when they were spread out in a longer line. They understood that *quantity* is a property of a set of objects that does not change when an operation such as *spreading out* alters the set's appearance (Piaget, 1954b). Piaget called this insight conservation – *the notion that the quantitative properties of an object are invariant despite changes in the object's appearance.*

BRUCE HOOD

When preoperational children are shown two equal-size glasses filled with equal amounts of liquid, they correctly say that neither glass 'has more'. But when the contents of one glass are poured into a taller, thinner glass, they incorrectly say that the taller glass 'has more'. Concrete operational children don't make this mistake because they recognize that operations such as pouring change the appearance of the liquid but not its actual volume.

Concrete operational children can understand that when a ball of clay is rolled, stretched or flattened, it is still the same amount of clay despite the fact that it looks larger in one form than another. They can understand that when water is poured from a short, wide beaker into a tall, thin cylinder, it is still the same amount of water despite the fact that the water level in the cylinder is higher. They can understand that when a sponge is painted grey to look like a rock, it is still a sponge despite its mineral appearance. Once children can make a distinction between objects and their mental representation of objects, between an object's properties and an object's appearance, they can begin to understand that some operations change what an object *looks* like without changing what the object *is* like.

Why don't preoperational children seem to grasp the notion of conservation? Piaget suggested that children have several tendencies that explain their mistakes. For instance, *centration* is the tendency to focus on just one property of an object to the exclusion of all others. Whereas adults can consider several properties at once, children focus on the length of the line of eggs without simultaneously considering the amount of space between each egg. Piaget also suggested that children fail to think about *reversibility.* That is, they do not consider the fact that the operation that made the line of eggs longer could be reversed, that the eggs could be repositioned more closely together and the line would become shorter. But errors such as these may be manifestations of a more basic problem. One reason why preoperational children do not fully grasp the notion of conservation is that they do not fully grasp the fact that they have *minds* and that these minds contain *mental representations* of the world.

APPEARANCE–REALITY DISTINCTION The appreciation that looks can be deceiving.

As adults, we all grasp this fact, which is why we distinguish between the subjective and the objective, between appearances and realities, between things in the mind and things in the world. Young children have trouble understanding the appearance–reality distinction – *the appreciation that looks can be deceiving*. For example, Flavell and colleagues (1983) presented three-, four- and five-year-olds with deceptive toys, such as sponges that looked like rocks. After playing with the objects, the children were asked what the objects 'really, really were'. While most four- and five-year-olds could easily answer the question (a sponge), three-year-olds said that not only did the sponge look like a rock but that it *was* a rock. Once children understand that brains represent – and hence can misrepresent – objects in the world, they are in a better position to solve a variety of problems that require them to ignore an object's subjective appearance while attempting to understand its objective properties. Around the same time, between three and four years of age, most children also start to get really good at appreciating that others can have misrepresentations about the world – a social skill we explore further in Chapter 12.

Children at the concrete operational stage can solve a variety of physical problems. But it isn't until they move on to the formal operational stage, *the stage of development that begins around the age of 11 and lasts through adulthood*, that they can solve nonphysical problems with similar ease. Childhood ends when formal operations begin, and people who move on to this stage (and Piaget believed that some people never did) are able to reason systematically about abstract concepts such as *liberty* and *love* and about events that *will* happen, that *might have* happened, and that *never* happened. At the concrete operational stage, children realize that their minds contain mental representations that *refer* to things in the world, but at the formal operational stage, they realize that some of their mental representations have no physical referents at all. There are no tangible objects in the world to which words such as *freedom* or *mortality* refer, and yet people at the formal operational stage can think and reason about such concepts in a systematic way. The ability to generate, consider, reason about or otherwise operate on these nonreferential abstractions is the hallmark of formal operations.

FORMAL OPERATIONAL STAGE The stage of development that begins around the age of 11 and lasts through adulthood.

This is also the age when young adolescents are capable of *hypothetico-deductive reasoning*. This occurs where they are faced with a problem, apply a general solution, and then deduce which factors are most important in generating the correct answer. For example, in Piaget's famous pendulum task, he asked adolescents to determine what influenced the speed at which a pendulum swings through its arc. Typically, formal operational adolescents come up with four possible factors: length of the string, weight of the object hung on it, how high the object is before it is released, and the force applied to the object. By varying one factor at a time, they then discover that only the length of the string matters. Individuals who reach this point in cognitive development should possess the necessarily skills for critical, scientific thinking.

Cognitive development – from the sensorimotor stage to formal operations – is a complex journey, and Piaget's ideas about it were nothing less than groundbreaking, noting many mindbugs along the way. Although many of his ideas have held up quite well, in the past few decades, psychologists have discovered two important ways in which his claims must be qualified:

1 Piaget specified the ages at which transitions between stages occurred, but modern experiments reveal that children generally acquire many of the abilities that Piaget described much *earlier* than he realized. For example, Piaget believed infants had no object representation because they did not actively search for objects that were moved from their sight. However, every year, researchers using the VOE technique reveal more instances where babies demonstrate their ability to perform sophisticated cognitive tasks.
2 Piaget thought that children graduated from one stage to another in the same way that they move from preschool to year 1: a child is either in preschool *or* year 1 and never in both, that is, there is a particular moment of transition to which everyone can point. However, modern psychologists see development as a more continuous and less step-like progression. Children who are transitioning between stages may perform more mature behaviours one day and less mature behaviours the next. So, cognitive development is more like the changing of the seasons than graduation: the days get colder as summer turns to autumn, but there are always a few cool days in August (sadly) and a few warm days in October (thank goodness).

Information-processing approaches

We have seen that Piaget considered cognitive development as a discontinuous process consisting of different stepped stages, and that recent research has produced observations that contradict this. But why? How do we explain the continuous transition between different phases? One approach that seeks to address this is modern information-processing theories that are very much influenced by the analogy of the mind to a computer: children are able to use more efficient strategies, increased capacity to process and store information, and faster mental operations to solve ever more complicated problems.

Strategies

According to Siegler's (1996) overlapping waves theory, children have the ability to approach a single problem in different ways, enabling them to develop new strategies to tackle new situations. For example, imagine trying to balance different weights on a beam. How does the child go about solving this puzzle? A child who fixates only on weight will fail to take into consideration the distance on the beam. That's why a very light child who sits at the end of a seesaw can balance with a heavier adult who sits closer to the middle. Weight and distance must both be considered and manipulated in order to solve the task. Siegler argues that children learn through experience that applying only one strategy is ineffectual and different strategies must be considered. By adopting a variable strategies approach, children learn to modify strategies to deal with general classes of problems and identify selective strategies for specific problems. For example, when children first learn to tell the time, they do so by counting the number of minutes forward from the hour. However, with increasing ability to count backwards, they can suddenly switch to the hour minus minutes answer. Counting backwards produces a new time-telling strategy (Siegler and McGilly, 1989).

Executive functions

EXECUTIVE FUNCTIONS Mental operations that enable us to coordinate our thoughts and behaviours.

Executive functions refer to *mental operations that enable us to coordinate our thoughts and behaviours* using the processes of planning, working memory and response inhibition. In Chapter 5 we learned that working memory is the temporary buffer store that we use to keep a representation in mind when we need it to solve a problem. For example, to solve a search task like the ones typically set by Piaget, an infant must keep in their working memory the last place where they saw a toy hidden. If they can't keep this location in mind, they soon forget where the toy was placed. They also have to plan their actions and remember to execute actions in the correct order (Willatts, 1997). But planning and memory alone are not enough, as most tasks have many distractions that have to be ignored. For example, to successfully reach for one particular toy, you have to avoid the distraction of other toys nearby – you have to focus on the one you want. That's where inhibition – *the ability to suppress intrusive thoughts and behaviours* – comes in. Without inhibition to avoid unwanted actions, an individual would be constantly distracted by other things in the world. To act smart, you need to plan, remember where stuff is and focus!

INHIBITION The ability to suppress intrusive thoughts and behaviours.

Together, planning, working memory and response inhibition are a powerful combination that enable us to solve tasks (Diamond, 1991). These executive functions are supported by circuitry in the prefrontal cortex: as the brain in this area matures, children's ability to solve tasks improves (Baird et al., 2002). Lesions of the frontal cortex are accompanied with executive dysfunction so that the ability to solve tasks deteriorates (Diamond and Goldman-Rakic, 1989). This brain-based explanation fits with the competence–performance distinction we described earlier. For example, in the classic Piagetian search task, maybe young infants who fail can form representations of hidden toys but they lack the planning to execute a retrieval sequence and the inhibition to avoid being distracted by other things in the room.

Executive function assessed in young children predicts later school achievement in several areas, including mathematical reasoning (Bull et al., 2008), analytical reasoning (Richland and Burchinal, 2013) and fluid intelligence (Duncan, 2005), which was described in Chapter 9 as the processing capacity to think and reason. It increases with age, plateaus in early adulthood and then shows significant decline in old age, particularly after age 55 (Nettelbeck and Burns, 2009), in line with other cognitive functions, which we consider next.

Memory

Remember that in Chapter 5 we learned how childhood amnesia appears to limit the earliest memories up to around two years of age (don't say you have forgotten already).

Childhood amnesia (sometimes called infantile amnesia) is not simply due to the passage of time and forgetting. For example, 70-year-olds can remember many more events from 50 years earlier than 20-year-olds who have forgotten what it was like being a baby only 18 years previously (Eacott, 1999). Rather, there is something qualitatively different about memory in young children. Childhood amnesia is a fascinating phenomenon because it raises a number of issues related to different types of memory and how these develop independently.

We know that the fetus learns in the womb, so babies clearly form memories from a very early stage. Early learning also depends on the ability to form long-term memory. For example, three-month-old infants can learn to recognize a particular mobile hung over their cot using an operant conditioning paradigm where a ribbon is tied from the mobile to their leg (Rovee and Rovee, 1969). Babies will kick vigorously to make the mobile jiggle, which is pleasing for them to watch but eventually they habituate to this excitement and kick less. If you then introduce a new mobile some weeks later, they kick more vigorously again, showing that they remember the old mobile and have noticed that the new one is different (Rovee-Collier, 1999). However, these examples of long-term memory may be limited to procedural or implicit knowledge – the infant does not need to consciously reflect on their experiences. For example, we may not be able to describe how to ride a bike but, somehow, we can remember what to do when we sit on one after many years.

Another example of long-term memory is the deferred imitation paradigm – *where the infant imitates an event demonstrated some time earlier*. For example, the infant observes an adult doing something unusual, remembers this event, and then repeats the action a week later (Meltzoff, 1988a). In one study, after watching an experimenter activate a light box by bending over and touching the switch with their head, 14-month-old infants could remember and repeat this unusual action. This could not simply be explained by the principles of conditioned learning as the infant only observed the experimenter's actions and there was no reinforcement at the time to shape the behaviour (Meltzoff, 1988b).

DEFERRED IMITATION PARADIGM Where the infant imitates an event demonstrated some time earlier.

So, it would appear that long-term memories for actions and events can form during infancy and yet we retain very few autobiographical memories from this period. One possible explanation for this is that the memories we carry through to adulthood are in some way linked to our ability to speak and use language, so infants who cannot yet speak are unable to encode memories in a way that enables them to be retained in the long term (Simcock and Hayne, 2002). Between the ages of one and three, language dramatically improves, and as we discussed in Chapter 5, language supports schemas that help the child to remember events (Bauer, 1995). For example, children in their third year talk quite well and can remember a trip to McDonald's a year earlier (Nelson, 1986) and remember more if prompted by the parent (Nelson and Fivush, 2004). However, these memories appear to be relatively limited and do not survive into adulthood, so language cannot be the only explanation.

In Chapter 5 we learned that meaningful sequences are easier to recall than disorganized events. Another possible explanation of how memory increases and changes in quality with age is a change in the child's ability to understand events and encode them in a meaningful way. Children forget because they lack the frameworks for recounting and storing events, which is why memories are fragmented and piecemeal (Fivush and Hammond, 1990). This logic may also influence source monitoring (described in Chapter 5), where we accurately attribute memories to the correct origin. In one study, Drummey and Newcombe (2002) presented children of four, six and eight years of age with 10 novel facts told by an experimenter, a puppet, a teacher or a parent. One week later, they were asked to recall what they had learned and who told them. There was a steady, quantitative improvement with age in the number of facts children recalled but, most importantly, a significant improvement in the ability to remember who gave the information between four and six years of age, indicating a qualitative shift in source memory monitoring.

One framework to make sense of these diverse findings is that all these different types of memory are dependent on different neural circuits, each of which matures at a different speed (Nelson, 2002). This would explain why implicit and procedural knowledge, which are less dependent on frontal cortical structures, appear much earlier than autobiographical, explicit and source memory, which require these structures (Squire and Knowlton, 2000). However, a simple brain storage explanation only solves one part of the puzzle of why we cannot remember much before our second birthday. Any explanation must also include aspects of how we process and interpret the events that make up our lives. This might explain why children whose parents talk to them more frequently about the past have much better early childhood memories as adolescents because these conversations help to organize the early memories into meaningful events (Jack et al., 2009).

Causal reasoning

CAUSAL REASONING When we infer that events happening close together in time and space are linked in some causal way.

Another way of making sense of the world is causal reasoning, which happens *when we infer that events happening close together in time and space are linked in some causal way* (Hume, [1748]1999). For example, when we see a white snooker ball hit a red one that moves off, we infer that the white ball caused the movement of the red one. The timing of the event is crucial for perceiving a causal collision and if the timing is wrong, then no causal collision is perceived. However, this is only an inference, as we cannot directly observe the transfer of energy between the balls. To take things a step further, imagine watching an *animation* of snooker balls colliding with one another: although there is no actual transfer of energy between the balls (just pixels on a screen), watching the animation still produces exactly the same inference of force in our minds. Babies also make these causal inferences. If you visually habituate them to a red ball launching a white ball, they will look longer when this event is reversed because now the white ball is launching the red ball. However, if there is a delay after the collision and before the red snooker ball moves off, they, like adults, do *not* treat this interaction between the balls as causal and so do not look longer when the sequence is reversed (Leslie and Keeble, 1987).

DIGITAL VISION

We infer the white ball causes the red ball to move when it strikes it.

By 16–24 months, infants quickly learn the causal properties of particular objects in the *blicket detector* paradigm, where a novel object placed on a machine activates an interesting noise that they find rewarding (Gopnik and Sobel, 2000). They also become sensitive to the causal relationship *between* objects to produce outcomes (Walker and Gopnick, 2014). For example, 18- to 30-month-olds can learn to activate a novel toy that plays music by placing a pair of identical blocks on it and not non-identical pairs or single blocks alone. In other conditions, the rule was changed so that only pairs of non-identical blocks worked. While human children can understand which causal rules to apply based on the relationship of objects in just a few trials, such higher order relational reasoning is much more difficult for primates, who take hundreds of trials before they learn (Premack, 1988).

Goswami (1998) argues that causal reasoning continues to operate throughout development as children use their experience of events to infer unobservable sequences and predict future outcomes. For example, three-year-old children who see a jumbled sequence of pictures of apple segments, a whole apple and a knife cutting an apple can reorder them so that they follow a logical causal sequence (Gelman et al., 1980). They understand that a cause must precede an effect and use this principle to work out which events are most likely to be responsible for producing outcomes. Older children are more sophisticated in the types of knowledge and experience they draw on to decide causality. For example, if we see a box with two levers, one that is heavy and one that is delicate, and we then hear a loud noise or a gentle sound, we are much more likely to infer that the heavy lever is associated with the loud noise and the delicate lever causes the gentle sound (Goswami, 2008).

When judging causality, older children give greater consideration to the *similarity* of preceding events and outcomes than to their *timing* (Shultz and Ravinsky, 1977). Thus, armed with a simple set of causal principles, children have the mental tools to work out why things happen in the world.

Core knowledge theories

In the last section we considered how information-processing accounts of cognition focus on the developing brain to explain limits of and changes in children's reasoning. Another approach is to consider the development of the brain over evolutionary history. As you have no doubt already deduced, the brain did not fall out of the sky, ready packaged to deal with the world (Cosmides and Tooby, 1994). Instead, the brain evolved as a system of mechanisms to solve the same recurrent problems that would have faced our ancestors. Core knowledge theories differ from Piagetian and information-processing theories because they argue that the child is born with a certain hardwired understanding about the world, rather than just the general tools to acquire that understanding. These are like innate theories that have evolved as a product of natural selection, and enable us to develop some of the most complex and uniquely human skills, such as speech and language. In contrast to Piagetian and information-processing theories that advocate primarily general learning abilities, core knowledge theories propose that children enter the world with both these general learning mechanisms plus specialized mechanisms for solving specific problems such as how to acquire language.

One metaphor that captures the principles of core knowledge is the Swiss army knife (Hirschfeld and Gelman, 1994). A Swiss army knife is made up of a general all-purpose blade that performs a variety of operations – from peeling an apple to whittling a stick. In addition, it has a number of specialized tools for removing stones from hooves, uncorking bottles and even tweezers for plucking hairs. In the same way, core knowledge theories say that the mental machinery of the mind combines general and specific mechanisms. The general abilities are the same as those identified by the information-processing theories, that is, strategy formation, executive functions, inhibitory control and memory. These general tools can be applied to help solve a variety of different problems. In contrast, core knowledge theorists argue that some skills, such as language learning, cannot be achieved using general learning mechanisms alone, but require built-in, domain-specific mechanisms. It is this specific built-in mechanism that enables any child, raised in any culture, to learn a language at roughly the same time and with little instruction from parents, which we discussed in Chapter 7 (Chomsky, 1998).

The core knowledge approach to cognitive development argues that there are core principles that guide learning in a variety of different domains besides language. Other examples of core domains are those for estimating small numbers (Carey, 2009) and even an appreciation of navigation and spatial layout of the environment (Wang and Spelke, 2002) – skills that our earlier ancestors would have found handy. Therefore, core knowledge principles are universal, do not change over a lifetime of experience, and do not have to be learned (Spelke, 2000). That's not to say that core knowledge concepts cannot contain variations, only that the fundamental properties or principles remain relatively unchanged. For example, a core knowledge principle might be that 'all objects have a degree of solidity, meaning that they will stop the movement of another object when they collide'. However, there are varying *degrees* of solidity among objects, and these have to be discovered through experience, leading to an increasingly sophisticated understanding of the differences between objects and nonobjects (Baillargeon, 1994).

Core knowledge theorists argue that our brains are equipped to solve specific, recurrent problems through conceptual reasoning (Carey, 2009). Concepts are units of thought that form the basis for beliefs and theories that have some reliable relationship with reality. Some concepts are universal and have existed since the origins of modern man, for example concepts related to objects, number and space, the sorts of concepts that have been found in infants using VOE techniques. Acquiring these concepts early would have conferred a great evolutionary advantage in prehistoric times. In contrast, other concepts are products of culture, such as poker, etiquette and even marriage. These are not hardwired from birth, but are learned from others around us. This division reflects the experience-expectant and experience-dependent types of information that can be encountered over the course of development.

INTUITIVE THEORIES Rudimentary frameworks that are not explicitly taught and explain related aspects of the world.

Core knowledge theorists believe that young children are equipped with innate mechanisms that enable the child to organize their conceptual frameworks into intuitive theories – *rudimentary frameworks that are not explicitly taught and explain related aspects of the world* (Carey, 2009). Intuitive theories are not innate, but the mechanisms for generating them are innate. They work like general 'rules of thumb' that children generate through causal reasoning (see above), which they can apply when they encounter novel yet familiar problems. Young children may not even be consciously aware of what they are thinking at first, and only later can they come to reflect on the content of their theories (Karmiloff-Smith, 1992). In this sense, intuitive theories are different from the formal scientific theories generated by adults to explain events in the world using explicit lawful rules. However, one property that intuitive theories share with scientific theories is that they can be difficult to change. For example, just like pre-Galileo adults in the Middle Ages in Europe who believed in the scientific theory that the earth was the centre of the universe and would not accept Galileo's evidence that the sun was in fact the centre of the universe, children caught in the grip of an intuitive theory also show a degree of resistance to evidence that may appear to contradict their theories (Hood, 1995). For example, between the ages of four and eight, children develop an intuitive theory about balance (Karmiloff-Smith and Inhelder, 1975). When asked to balance a series of wooden rods on a fulcrum, six- and eight-year-olds immediately balanced the rod in the middle. Four-year-olds eventually discovered this solution with a bit of trial and error. However, when children were given rods that were secretly weighted at one end so that they could not balance in the middle, a 'U'-shaped function of behavioural change was found. Eight-year-olds initially placed the rod in the middle and, seeing that it did not balance, adjusted the position until it did. Four-year-olds also showed flexibility and correctly learned to balance the uneven rod. However, six-year-olds were inflexible and repeatedly placed the rod in the middle even when it continued to tip over. Eventually, many six-year-olds got frustrated and gave up, saying that the task was impossible. This is evidence of theory-like reasoning. Initially, four-year-olds had no theory and simply approached the problem in a trial-and-error manner. Both six- and eight-year-olds had a theory that symmetrical objects balance in the middle but only the older children had the flexibility to learn that there are sometimes exceptions to this rule. In contrast, six-year-olds in the grip of their theory were unable to be flexible. Another compelling example of an intuitive theory at work is the reluctance of preschoolers to stop searching for a ball dropped in a curved tube in the box directly below (Hood, 1995) (see **FIGURE 11.15**).

FIGURE 11.15 Hood's tubes In this search task, preschoolers have to find a ball dropped down a chimney into a tube that feeds into a nonaligned cup below. Before four years of age, children repeatedly search in the cup directly below.

It is not only children who have intuitive theories. Many adults hold such theories even though they may be unaware of them (McCloskey, 1983). For example, physics students tend to predict that the heavier of two objects will fall faster because of the weight difference, although they have had a formal education in Newtonian mechanics and should therefore know that they will fall at the same rate (Champagne et al., 1980). Thus, it would appear that answers based on intuitive reasoning are more accessible than those derived from formal education (Kozhevnikov and Hegarty, 2001). This is supported by neuroimaging studies that show that when adults are learning counterintuitive Newtonian mechanics, brain regions associated with executive functions are activated (Dunbar and Fugelsang, 2005) and intuitive theories are never entirely abandoned (Petitto and Dunbar, 2004). These findings suggest that executive functions such as inhibition may be necessary to overcome intuitions and early education might benefit from taking into consideration the naive theories that children spontaneously bring into the classroom (Carey, 1985).

Intuitive theories operate within three broad domains that capture most of human experience: the physical world, the living world and the psychological world (Wellman and Gelman, 1992). In short, young children are little physicists, biologists and psychologists. Their reasoning in each of these areas develops at different rates across childhood, but all show evidence of early built-in mechanisms operating before the first birthday. Again, we know this from experiments using the VOE paradigm. For example, in the physics domain, infants understand that inanimate objects do not go in and out of existence but have permanence, solidity, remain bounded, move on continuous paths and do not move by themselves (Spelke et al., 1992). In the biology domain, infants predict that living things can move by themselves in unpredictable paths and distinguish people as a special class of living thing (Poulin-Dubois, 1999). They are surprised when a toy moves by itself, which is why clockwork toys sometimes frighten babies. In the psychology domain, they expect people to be intentional and behave in a goal-directed manner. For example, six-month-old infants are surprised when a hand reaching for a particular toy suddenly starts to reach for a different object instead, but they are not surprised when a mechanical arm behaves in the same way. This indicates that they see human reaching as a goal-directed, intentional act (Woodward, 1998).

Beyond infancy, children continue to refine their intuitive theories to account for more encounters and experiences in the world. For example, as children increasingly learn to categorize the world into different types of things, they draw a distinction between natural and man-made items through a process known as 'psychological essentialism' (Gelman, 2003). Psychological essentialism is *the belief that things in nature and in particular living things are what they are because of some inner property or essence.* Preschoolers appreciate that all dogs have a kind of essence of 'dogginess' that makes them different from cats, which have a 'cattiness' essence instead. Five-year-olds understand that a puppy raised in a litter of kittens would still grow up into a dog with all the doggy qualities (Johnson and Solomon, 1996). Likewise, if an evil scientist changed the outward appearance of an animal such as a fox into a badger by surgery, they would appreciate that the animal was still a fox despite what it looked like (Keil, 1989). In contrast, children do not hold such essentialism to artificial objects – they willingly accept that a teapot could be made into a bird feeder. Thus, young children are guided by intuitive processes to spontaneously generate naive theories to explain the world around them.

PSYCHOLOGICAL ESSENTIALISM The belief that things in nature and in particular living things are what they are because of some inner property or essence.

©ISTOCKPHOTO.COM/DAVID GUNN

Five-year-olds understand that a puppy raised in a litter of kittens would still grow up into a dog with all the doggy qualities (Johnson and Solomon, 1996).

How many theories are there? It all depends on how sophisticated you become. As we develop, we have a lot of world experience, enabling us to generate a large number of domain-specific theories, for example how to balance objects, when is something alive, or what makes the best wine? However, where we lack relevant knowledge, we are just like children, and must rely on domain-general principles of causal reasoning through trial and error to establish new theories (Brown and DeLoache, 1978).

Sociocultural theories

Before ending our discussion of early cognitive development, we have to say something about social development and the role it plays in thinking. Of all the primates, humans have the most protracted period of childhood. While many aspects of the developing mind may be hardwired, or at least appear early in development, most of the period of childhood is taken up with learning from others. Chapter 12 is dedicated to examining the importance of social development as a fundamental human attribute in itself, but we also consider social factors in this chapter on cognition, because of all the animals on the planet, humans are clearly dependent on learning and exchanging knowledge with others.

Piaget largely neglected the role of society and culture in formulating and stimulating cognitive development. He thought that children were born curious and their cognitive development unfolded as a result of their interaction with objects in the world, such as eggs, clay, sponges and cats. He saw the child as a lone scientist who made observations, developed theories and then revised those theories in light of new observations. Yet very few scientists start from scratch. What usually happens is that they receive training from more experienced scientists and inherit the theories and methods of their disciplines. According to Russian psychologist Lev Vygotsky (1896–1934), children do much the same thing. Vygotsky was born in the same year as Piaget, but unlike Piaget, he believed that cognitive development was largely the result of the child's interaction with members of their own culture rather than their interaction with objects. Vygotsky noted that *cultural tools*, such as language and counting systems, exert a strong influence on cognitive development. Language systems and counting systems are not merely ways for children to *express* their thoughts, they are ways for children to *have* thoughts, which is why children can perform certain tasks only if they are allowed to talk to themselves.

For example, in English, the numbers beyond 20 are named by a decade (twenty) that is followed by a digit (one) and their names follow a logical pattern (twenty-one, twenty-two, twenty-three and so on). In Chinese, the numbers from 11 to 19 are similarly constructed (ten-one, ten-two, ten-three ...). But in English, the names of the numbers between 11 and 19 either reverse the order of the decade and the digit (sixteen, seventeen) or are more arbitrary (eleven, twelve). The difference in the regularity of these two systems makes a big difference to the children who must learn them. It is obvious to a Chinese child that 12 – which is called 'ten-two' – can be decomposed into 10 and 2, but it is not so obvious to a Western child, who calls the number 'twelve' (see **FIGURE 11.16**). In one study, children from many countries were asked to hand an experimenter a certain number of bricks. Some of the bricks were single, and some were glued together in strips of 10. When Asian children were asked to hand the experimenter 26 bricks, they tended to hand over two strips of 10 plus 6 singles. Non-Asian children tended to use the clumsier strategy of counting out 26 single bricks (Miura et al., 1994). Results such as these suggest that the regularity of the counting system that children inherit can promote or discourage their discovery of the fact that two-digit numbers can be decomposed.

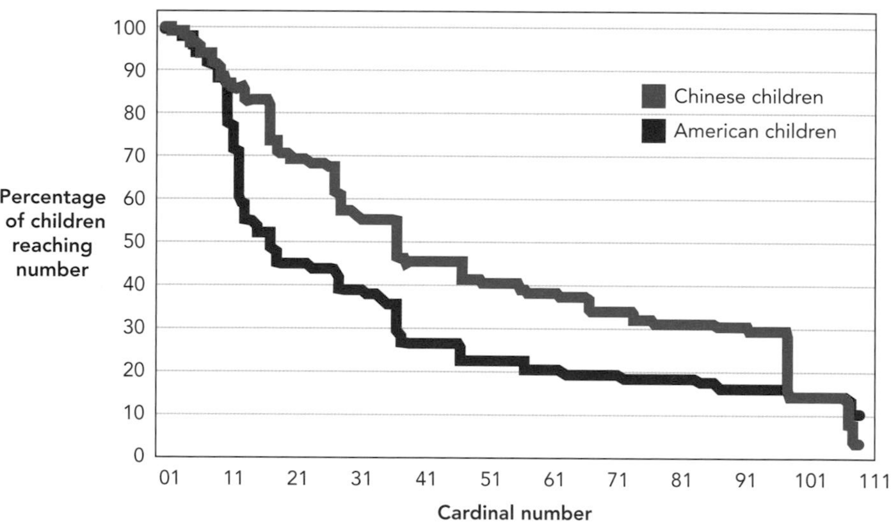

FIGURE 11.16 Twelve or two-teen As this graph shows, the percentage of American children who can count through the cardinal numbers drops off suddenly when they hit the number 11, whereas the percentage of Chinese children shows a more gradual decline.

Vygotsky believed that at any age, a child was capable of acquiring a wide – but nonetheless bounded – range of skills, which he called the child's *zone of proximal development.* He suggested that children who interacted with adults or more knowledgeable peers tended to acquire skills towards the top of this range, whereas children who did not tended to acquire skills towards the bottom. Parents seem to have a natural understanding of the zone of proximal development. They tend to direct their instruction towards the upper end of a child's range of skills, and as the child becomes more competent, they encourage the child to think about problems at higher levels. Of course, the ability to learn from others requires fundamental communicative skills that take time to develop. These emerging tendencies prepare the infant to learn from more skilled members of its species (see Chapter 12).

The real world

Must try harder

Does our understanding of cognitive development translate into the classroom? This depends on the teacher and school but surprisingly, psychological research conducted on children over the decades has had less influence on formal education than one would imagine. Many believe that this is because education has become focused on obtaining good scores for pupils and schools, so the emphasis is on performance achievement rather than how to educate.

The problem is that children are very different on many important factors such as their aptitudes, personalities, rates of learning and attitudes towards schoolwork. For example, consider two children struggling to solve a maths problem. One might consider it a challenge and be motivated to find the correct solution, whereas the other might feel that there is no point because they are not capable of solving it. According to Carol Dweck (1999), the first child has a *mastery orientation* and enjoys rising to the challenge, whereas the other child has a *helpless orientation* and is not motivated to complete the task and may regard the exercise as pointless. Children with a helpless orientation tend to base their competence on how they think they are doing relative to others and so are dependent on praise, which is why they fear failure more than children with a mastery orientation who are less influenced by the opinion of others but want to push themselves.

Children also differ in their beliefs about the source of ability. Many children (and adults!) operate with an *entity theory* of intelligence, where they believe that success or failure is fixed by natural ability and is unchanging, which is why they consider themselves either smart or stupid. Other children hold an *incremental theory* of intelligence, where they attribute intelligence to effort and experience, which is why they are more likely to persevere with difficult problems (Cain and Dweck, 1995; Dweck and Leggett, 1988).

With these differences in beliefs about ability, there will be different consequences for different types of teacher feedback. If you always praise ('Good job') or criticize ('Your maths is not up to standard') based on outcomes, this will have a greater influence on the helpless-oriented child who believes in fixed intelligence compared to the mastery-oriented one. In contrast, praising the effort ('Well deserved') or criticizing lack of application ('I think you could have tried harder') will be more influential with the child who holds an incremental perspective compared to the child who holds an entity view of intelligence.

Teachers also hold differing views about the nature of intelligence, which can affect school achievement. In one study, 10-year-old children were told that their performance on a test was either due to their natural intelligence or their ability to work hard (Mueller and Dweck, 1998). Both sets were then given a difficult second task that was well beyond their capability, which no one could complete. However, in a third test, the children who thought their initial successes on the first task were due to their intelligence also gave up more easily because they attributed their failure to their limited natural ability, which made them less likely to persevere on the last task. In contrast, children who thought their performance was all down to hard work not only stuck longer on the unsolvable task, but also enjoyed it more. Although such findings fit into sociocultural theories such as Vygotsky's, where what others do and say influence cognitive development, this type of work is also consistent with the formation of our self-identity, which we discuss in Chapter 12.

In summary, different theories of cognitive development emphasize varying degrees of internal processes combined with external experiences to produce mental representations. Piaget's theory was the first to explain cognitive development as a universal, stage-like process where the child increasingly discovers that the world is full of objects that have properties independent of their own perceptions. By incorporating these discoveries into mental representations, the child develops more sophisticated and flexible ways of thinking about the world. However, Piaget focused on performance errors and underestimated much of the true competence that children possess. In recent years, new techniques have revealed that young children possess sophisticated representations but may lack the ability to act on them appropriately because of limited performance skills. These early abilities motivated evolutionary based accounts of cognitive development such as core theory that proposes more innate organization. Information-processing theories consider development to be achieved by the combination of emerging skills, which rely on integrating developing brain systems. Many modern approaches emphasize development as consisting of specific domains of ability rather than general, across-the-board change. Finally, Vygotsky's sociocultural theory emphasizes the role of adults to scaffold cognitive development by adapting the learning environment to fit best with individual children's abilities.

Later cognitive development and decline

For many of you reading this textbook, you are, believe it or not, very close to your best. The early twenties are the peak years for health, stamina, vigour and prowess, and because our psychology is so closely tied to our biology, these are also the years during which most of our cognitive abilities are at their sharpest. At this very moment, you see further, hear better, remember more and weigh less than you ever will again. Enjoy it. This glorious moment at life's summit will last for a few more years, and then, somewhere between the ages of 26 and 30, you will begin the slow and steady decline that does not end until you do. In this final section, we briefly consider cognitive development after childhood and how it changes over the later years.

Adolescence: minding the gap

Between childhood and adulthood is the extended developmental stage of adolescence that may not qualify for a 'hood' of its own, but is clearly distinct from the stages that come before and after. The transition to adolescence is sudden and clearly marked. In just three or four years, the average adolescent gains about 18 kg and grows about 25 cm. Girls' growth rates begin to accelerate around the age of 10, and they reach their full heights at around 15–16. Boys experience an equivalent growth spurt about two years later and reach their full heights at around 17–18. This growth spurt signals the onset of puberty – *bodily changes associated with sexual maturity.* These changes involve primary sex characteristics – *bodily structures that are directly involved in reproduction* – for example the onset of menstruation in girls and the enlargement of the testes, scrotum and penis and the emergence of the capacity for ejaculation in boys. They also involve secondary sex characteristics – *bodily structures that change dramatically with sexual maturity but are not directly involved in reproduction* – for example the enlargement of the breasts and the widening of the hips in girls, and the appearance of facial hair, pubic hair, underarm hair, and the lowering of the voice in both sexes. This pattern of changes is caused by increased production of sex-specific hormones: oestrogen in girls and testosterone in boys.

PUBERTY Bodily changes associated with sexual maturity.

PRIMARY SEX CHARACTERISTICS Bodily structures that are directly involved in reproduction.

SECONDARY SEX CHARACTERISTICS Bodily structures that change dramatically with sexual maturity but are not directly involved in reproduction.

Just as the body changes during adolescence, so too does the brain. For example, there is a marked increase in the growth rate of tissue connecting different regions of the brain just before puberty (Thompson et al., 2000). Between the ages of 6 and 13, the connections between the temporal lobe (the brain region specialized for language) and the parietal lobe (the brain region specialized for understanding spatial relations) multiply rapidly and then stop – just about the time that the critical period for learning a language ends (see **FIGURE 11.17**). But the most intriguing set of changes associated with adolescence occur in the prefrontal cortex. As we noted earlier, early brain development includes the generation of neural connections and the destruction of some of these connections through synaptic pruning; recent evidence suggests that the prefrontal cortex undergoes a wave of synaptic proliferation just before puberty and a second round of synaptic pruning during adolescence (Giedd et al., 1999). Clearly, the adolescent brain is a work in progress.

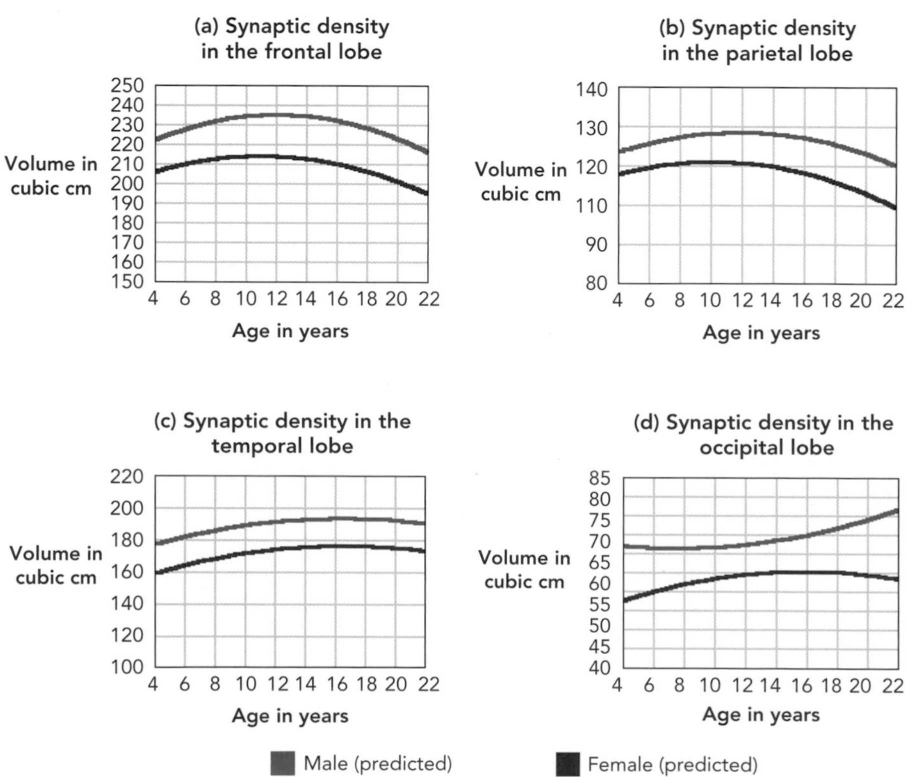

FIGURE 11.17 Your brain during puberty The development of neurons peaks in the frontal and parietal lobes at about age 12 (a, b), in the temporal lobe at about age 16 (c), and continues to increase in the occipital lobe through to age 20 (d).

Adulthood: the short happy future

It takes fewer than 7,000 days for a single-celled zygote to become a registered voter. The speed with which this radical transformation happens is astonishing, which is why, when we see our baby cousin or teenage nephew at the annual family reunion, we feel compelled to say things like 'My, how you've grown!' On the other hand, middle-aged uncles usually elicit remarks along the lines of 'You haven't changed a bit!' Indeed, the rate of observable physical change slows considerably in adulthood – *the stage of development that begins around 18–21 years and ends at death*. This is all the more remarkable when you consider that adulthood lasts about three times longer than all the previous stages combined. Because observable change slows from a gallop to a crawl, we sometimes have the sense that adulthood is a destination to which development delivers us and once we've arrived, our journey is complete. But that's not so. Although they are more gradual and less noticeable, many physical, cognitive and emotional changes take place between our first legal beer and our last breath.

ADULTHOOD The stage of development that begins around 18–21 years and ends at death.

Changing abilities

The physical transformations that take place during adulthood can be characterized succinctly: things quickly get worse slowly. In other words, our physical decline begins painfully early but is mercifully gradual. A mere 10–15 years after puberty, your body will begin to deteriorate in almost every way. Your muscles will be replaced by fat, your skin will become less elastic, your hair will thin and your bones will weaken, your sensory abilities will become less acute, and your brain cells will die at an accelerated rate. If you are a woman, your ovaries will stop producing eggs and you will become infertile; if you are a man, your erections will be fewer and further apart. Indeed, other than being more resistant to colds and less sensitive to pain, older bodies just don't work as well as younger ones.

Although these physical changes happen slowly, as they accumulate, they begin to have measurable psychological consequences (see **FIGURE 11.18**). For instance, as your brain ages, your prefrontal cortex and its associated subcortical connections will deteriorate more quickly than the other areas of your brain (Raz, 2000). As you already know, the prefrontal cortex is responsible for executive functions, which means that you will experience the most noticeable cognitive decline on tasks that require effort, initiative or strategy. We all know that memory worsens with age, but not all memory worsens at the same rate. Older adults show a much more pronounced decline in tests of working memory (the ability to hold information 'in mind') than tests of long term memory (the ability to retrieve information), a much more pronounced decline in tests of episodic memory (the ability to remember particular past events) than tests of semantic memory (the ability to remember general information such as the meanings of words), and a much more pronounced decline in tests of retrieval (the ability to 'go find' information in memory) than tests of recognition (the ability to decide whether information was encountered before).

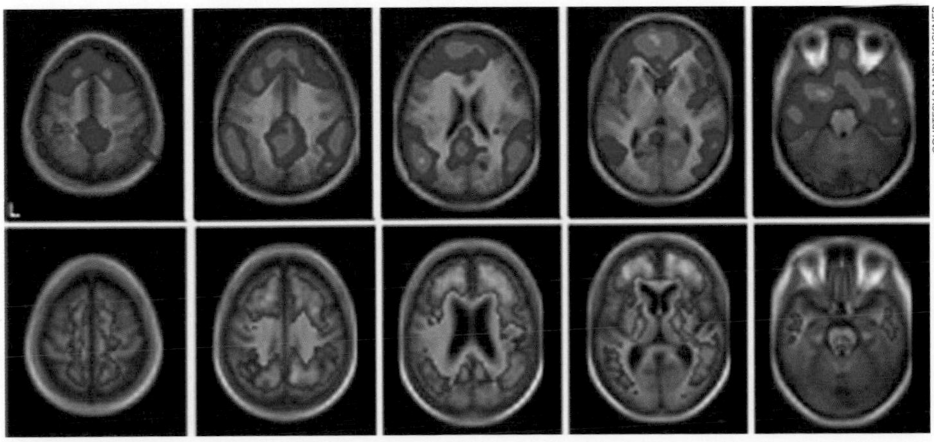

COURTESY RANDY BUCKNER

FIGURE 11.18 Alzheimer's and daydreaming In Europe, Alzheimer's disease affects 5% of the over-65 population and more than 20% of those over 85, who suffer severe impairments of language, thought and memory. The disease is characterized by the formation of abnormal clumps of material called 'amyloid plaques'. Interestingly, these plaques seem to develop in the very regions of the brain that are active when healthy people are musing, daydreaming or letting their minds wander. The lower panel shows brain activity among healthy young adults who are daydreaming. The upper panel shows the location of amyloid plaques in older adults who have Alzheimer's disease. The regions include the medial and lateral posterior parietal regions, posterior cingulate, retrosplenial cortex and frontal cortex along the midline. This fact has led some scientists to suggest that Alzheimer's disease may be the result of high metabolic activity over the course of a lifetime; in a sense, the everyday wear and tear caused by daydreaming (Buckner et al., 2005).

And yet, while the cognitive machinery gets rustier with age, research suggests that the operators of that machinery often compensate by using it more skilfully. Although older chess players *remember* chess positions more poorly than younger players do, they *play* as well as younger players because they search the board more efficiently (Charness, 1981). Although older typists *react* more slowly than younger typists do, they *type* as quickly and accurately as younger typists because they are better at anticipating the next word (Salthouse, 1984). Years of experience often allow people to develop strategies in their special domains of expertise that can compensate for cognitive decline (Bäckman and Dixon, 1992; Salthouse, 1987). Older airline pilots are considerably worse than younger pilots when it comes to keeping a list of words in short-term memory, but this age difference disappears when those words are the 'heading commands' that pilots receive from the control tower every day (Morrow et al., 1994). This pattern of errors suggests that older adults are somehow compensating for age-related declines in memory and attention.

How do older adults implement these compensatory strategies? When a younger person tries to keep verbal information in working memory, their left prefrontal cortex is more strongly activated than the right, and when they try to keep spatial information in working memory, their right prefrontal cortex is more strongly activated than the left (Smith and Jonides, 1997). But this *bilateral asymmetry* is not seen among older adults, and some scientists take this to mean that older brains compensate for the declining abilities of one neural structure by calling on other neural structures to help out (Cabeza, 2002) (see **FIGURE 11.19**). The young brain can be characterized as a group of specialists, but as these specialists become older and less able, they begin to work together on tasks that each once handled independently. In short, the machinery of body and brain does break down with age, but a seasoned driver in an old car can often hold his own against a younger person in a souped-up one.

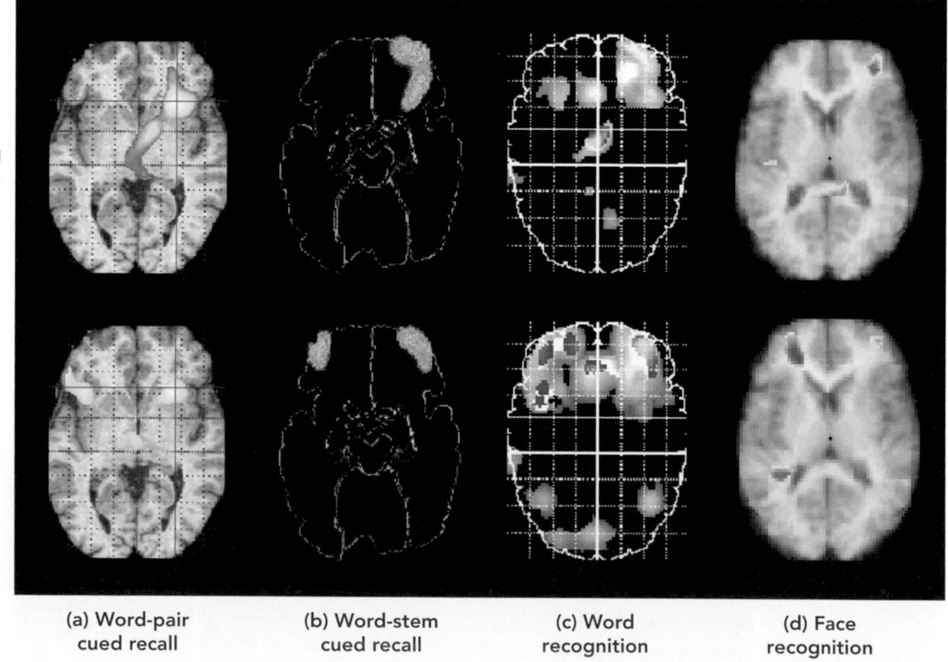

FIGURE 11.19 Bilaterality in older and younger brains Across a variety of tasks, older adult brains show bilateral activation and young adult brains show unilateral activation. One possible explanation for this is that older brains compensate for the declining abilities of one neural structure by calling on other neural structures for help (Cabeza, 2002).

Changing orientations

One reason why grandad can't find his car keys is that his prefrontal cortex doesn't function like it used to. Executive functions of working memory, planning and inhibition become increasingly compromised with old age (Graham et al., 1997). But another reason is that the location of car keys just isn't the sort of thing that grandads spend their precious time memorizing. According to *socioemotional selectivity theory* (Carstensen and Turk-Charles, 1994), younger adults are generally oriented towards the acquisition of information that will be useful to them in the future, for example reading the newspaper, whereas older adults are generally oriented towards information that brings emotional satisfaction in the present, for example reading novels. Because young people have such long futures, they *invest* their time attending to, thinking about and remembering potentially *useful information* that may serve them well in the many days to come. But older people have shorter futures and so they *spend* their time attending to, thinking about and remembering *positive information* that serves them well in the moment (see **FIGURE 11.20**). As people age, they spend less time thinking about the future, but contrary to our stereotypes of the elderly, they do not spend more time thinking about the past (Carstensen et al., 1999). Rather, they spend more time thinking about the present. Research suggests that the shortening of the future is indeed the cause of this basic change in our orientation towards information, which also occurs among younger people who learn that they have a terminal illness (Carstensen and Fredrickson, 1998).

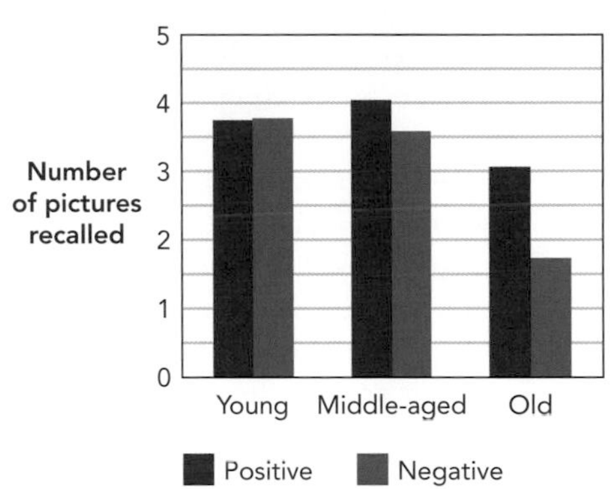

FIGURE 11.20 Memory for pictures Memory declines with age in general, but the ability to remember negative information, such as unpleasant pictures, declines much more quickly than the ability to remember positive information (Carstensen et al., 2000).

Some of the declines in the cognitive performance of older adults may have less to do with changes in their brains and more to do with changes in their orientation (Hess, 2005). For example, older people do considerably worse than younger people when they are asked to remember a series of unpleasant faces, but they do only slightly worse when they are asked to remember a series of pleasant faces (Mather and Carstensen, 2003). Apparently, older adults find it difficult to attend to information that doesn't make them happy, and so they perform poorly on many standard memory tasks, which rarely include photos of their grandchildren. Perhaps it is not surprising, then, that people remember their lives more positively as they age (Kennedy et al., 2004).

This change in orientation towards information influences much more than memory. Not only are older adults less likely than younger adults to attend to or remember negative information, but they are also less likely to be emotionally influenced by it. Whereas younger adults show activation of the amygdala when they see pleasant and unpleasant pictures, older adults show greater activation when they see pleasant pictures than when they see unpleasant pictures (Mather et al., 2004). Studies also reveal that as people age, they tend to experience far fewer negative emotions (Carstensen et al., 2000; Charles et al., 2001; Mroczek and Spiro, 2005) (see **FIGURE 11.21**). What's more, older people seem better able than younger people to sustain their positive emotional experiences and curtail their negative ones (Lawton et al., 1992).

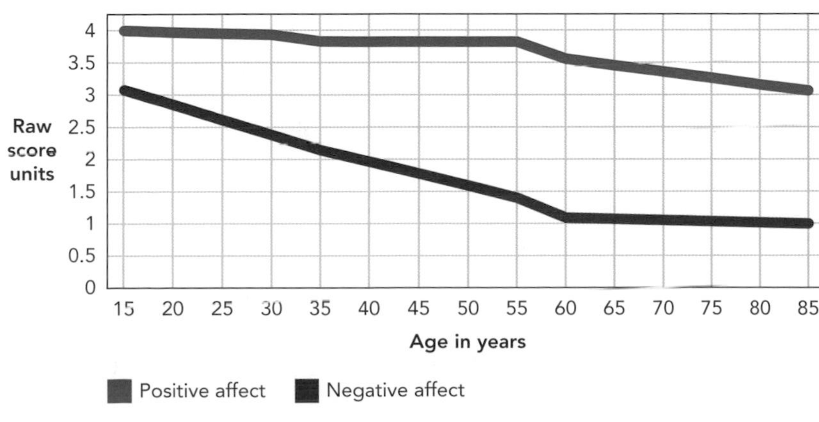

FIGURE 11.21 Happiness and age Despite what our youth-oriented culture would have us believe, people's overall happiness generally increases with age. As this graph shows, people experience a small decrease in positive affect beginning around age 55, but this is more than compensated for by the large decrease in negative affect that begins around age 15 and continues through middle age (Charles et al., 2001).

The change in our orientation towards information also influences our activities. Psychologists have long known that social networks get smaller as people age, and they have assumed that this happens because friends die at an accelerating rate. Some of this shrinkage is indeed due to loss, but it now appears that much of it is a matter of choice. Because a shortened future orients people towards emotionally satisfying rather than intellectually profitable information, older adults become more selective about who they interact with, choosing to spend time with family and a few close friends rather than with a large circle of acquaintances. One study followed a group of people from the 1930s to the 1990s and found that their rate of interaction with acquaintances declined from early to middle adulthood, but their rate of interaction with spouses, parents and siblings stayed stable or increased (Carstensen, 1992). A study of older adults who ranged in age from 69 to 104 found that the oldest adults had fewer peripheral social partners than the younger adults, but just as many emotionally close partners who they identified as members of their 'inner circle' (Lang and Carstensen, 1994). Apparently, 'Let's go and meet some new people' just isn't something that most 60-year-olds tend to say. In a 1997 survey, 38% of people over 65 described themselves as very happy, but only 28% of 18- to 29-year-olds said the same (Pew Research Center for the People and the Press, 1997). Although in the West, we tend to be obsessed with staying young, research suggests that one of the best ways to increase one's share of happiness in life is simply to get older. People focus more on emotional and rewarding goals as they near the end of life. The machinery may not work as well, but the passengers seem to enjoy the ride more.

In summary, older adults show declines in working memory, episodic memory and retrieval tasks, but they often develop strategies to compensate. Gradual physical decline begins early in adulthood and has clear psychological consequences, some of which are offset by increases in skill and expertise. Older people are more oriented towards emotionally satisfying information, which influences their basic cognitive performance, the size and structure of their social networks, and their general happiness.

psychomythology

Babies' intelligence can be 'hothoused' with smart media

While it is true that infant brain plasticity is shaped by early experiences and deprivation can impair development during critical periods, it does not follow that extra stimulation will boost development over and beyond the normal course that can be expected from a sufficient environment. *Hothousing*, a term borrowed from horticulture when young plants are raised in conditions to stimulate growth, refers to interventions intended to significantly advance babies' abilities, especially in relation to intelligence, and it is big business. 'Baby Einstein', a range of products sold by Disney, is intended to stimulate infant brain development through exposure to music, images, languages and even numbers. Although the company is cautious in its claims, the name 'Einstein' is meant to imply a link with a recognized intellectual genius. While such multimedia products sell well, their educational claims are dubious. In 2007, University of Washington researchers reported that each hour per day of viewing baby DVDs/videos in infants aged 8–16 months, which had been marketed to parents as tools to facilitate language development, was found to be associated with a significant decrement in language learning (Zimmerman et al., 2007). This study was cited as one of the reasons that the American Academy of Pediatrics (AAP, 2011) recommended that children below two years of age should not be exposed to such multimedia products. In fairness to the originator of the Baby Einstein concept, it was argued that these products were never intended to replace but rather supplement normal parent–child interaction. Furthermore, a recent reanalysis of the original University of Washington data concluded that exposure to baby videos could be construed as positive, neutral or negative depending on the statistical analysis (Ferguson and Donnellan, 2014). However, they also concluded that effect sizes were trivial, undermining any claims that these products can boost child development.

where do you stand?

Parental licensing

It is clear that early experiences and environments shape the developing brain and can leave a lasting impression on the growing child. For example, mothers who take drugs during pregnancy and parents who smoke around their young children are placing them at risk. As we will see in Chapter 12, children raised in abusive households are more likely to suffer emotional problems later in life, which can lead to a vicious cycle of domestic violence that can be directed towards others. In contrast, parents who interact with their children by reading to them on a regular basis or discussing how their day has been are likely to optimize their child's cognitive development. Given the impact parents' actions can have on the physical and psychological wellbeing of their children, should adults always have the right to bear children?

Most citizens of democratic countries agree that individuals should have the right to make their own life choices, but what of the rights of young children? What about parents who are simply not fit to look after their children? Does the state have the right to take them away from their parents, and should the rest of society be expected to support and raise them? Should prospective parents prove they are capable of raising children, in other words, pass an exam to obtain a licence? After all, if we demand that people meet certain standards before they are allowed to *adopt* children, why should we not demand that they meet the same standards before being allowed to *bear* children? Are our biological children worth less than our adopted ones?

Every one of us pays the price when parents abuse, neglect or fail to educate their children. Bad parents impose significant socioeconomic burdens on the rest of society, not to mention on their own children. Society has a clear interest in *preventing* (and not just punishing) abusive and negligent parenting. Bad parenting can have devastating consequences for children and society, and we should all be concerned about it, but is parental licensing the right solution, or is it a bad answer to a good question? Where do you stand?

Chapter review

Nature versus nurture: an unnatural division

- Developmental psychology is the study of change throughout the human life span. The mechanisms responsible for producing that change are usually distinguished as caused either by 'nature' or 'nurture'. However, epigenesis reveals that these mechanisms interact in a probabilistic manner.

Prenatality: a womb with a view

- Life begins when a sperm and egg produce a zygote. The zygote develops into an embryo and then a fetus, and all are impacted by the environment of the womb. Brain development is characterized by periods of rapid interconnectivity between cortical neurons that operate within sensitive periods.

The science of studying change

- Different developmental patterns of change are interpreted to reflect underlying mechanisms but have to be carefully evaluated in light of statistical problems of measurement. Longitudinal research measures change repeatedly within the same individuals over time, but is a costly process. Cross-sectional research samples across different ages, but is subject to cohort bias.
- Conducting research on young children presents considerable difficulties as they lack mature communication and comprehension skills. Techniques such as habituation or search bypass these problems by measuring nonverbal behaviour.

Beyond the blooming, buzzing confusion

- The newborn infant is equipped with sensory and perceptual mechanisms to interpret the external world, and has already begun that learning process in utero. Vision, hearing, taste, touch and smell are all operating, although some are more dependent on brain maturation than others. Nevertheless, the newborn has the capacity to turn sensory input into meaningful patterns through perceptual processes that generate mental representations.
- Motor development rapidly enables the infant to play an increasingly explorative role in discovering the nature of the world around them. Cognition is the mental 'model building' that the child generates to understand the world and make predictions about how it operates.

Understanding the world: cognition

- Jean Piaget believed that cognitive development takes place in four stages: sensorimotor, preoperational, concrete operational and formal operational. Among the things infants learn in these stages are that objects continue to exist even when they are out of sight, that objects have enduring properties that are not changed by superficial transformations, and that their minds represent objects.
- More recent approaches to understanding cognitive development have moved away from Piaget's stage model, and focused on more specific domains of knowledge and the role of information-processing mechanisms. Executive functions of memory and inhibition can explain many performance limitations on children's ability to solve problems.
- Intuitive theories are spontaneous models that children generate to explain aspects of the world. These can be superseded by other models obtained through education but may reside even in adults. Vygostky emphasized the role of social interaction and communication in stimulating cognitive development.

Later cognitive development and decline

- Adolescence marks the beginning of sexual maturity, the intensification of sexual interest and, for some, the onset of sexual activity.
- Biology plays an important role in determining whether adolescents are attracted to members of the same or the opposite sex.
- As people age, they show physical and psychological declines that may be offset by compensatory strategies. They also tend to concentrate on people and things that make them happy.

Key terms

accommodation (p. 453)
acuity (p. 444)
adolescence (p. 430)
adulthood (p. 467)
affordances (p. 451)
appearance–reality distinction (p. 456)
arborization (p. 436)
assimilation (p. 453)
blastocyst (p. 434)
canalization (p. 432)
causal reasoning (p. 460)
childhood (p. 430)
clinical method of studying children (p. 441)
cohort bias (p. 440)
concrete operational stage (p. 456)
conservation (p. 456)
cross-sectional research (p. 440)
crossmodal perception (p. 448)
deferred imitation paradigm (p. 459)
developmental psychology (p. 430)
ectoderm (p. 434)
embryonic disk (p. 434)
embryonic stage (p. 434)
endoderm (p. 434)
executive functions (p. 458)
experience-dependent plasticity (p. 438)
experience-expectant plasticity (p. 438)
fetal alcohol syndrome (p. 435)
fetal stage (p. 434)
formal operational stage (p. 457)
generative processes (p. 436)
germinal stage (p. 434)
human genome project (p. 431)
infancy (p. 430)
inhibition (p. 458)
intuitive theories (p. 462)
invariant (p. 452)
limited competence (p. 453)
limited performance (p. 453)
longitudinal research (p. 440)
maturation (p. 452)
mental representations (p. 446)
mesoderm (p. 434)
milestone (p. 439)
motor development (p. 449)
myelination (p. 437)
nature versus nurture (p. 431)
neural tube (p. 435)
neurogenesis (p. 435)
newborns (p. 430)
object permanence (p. 453)
plasticity (p. 437)
preference for novelty paradigm (p. 442)
prenatal stage (p. 433)
preoperational stage (p. 456)
primary sex characteristics (p. 466)
prosody (p. 436)
psychological essentialism (p. 463)
puberty (p. 466)
qualitative change (p. 439)
quantitative change (p. 439)
reflexes (p. 449)
repeated measure (p. 440)
secondary sex characteristics (p. 466)
sensitive periods of development (p. 438)
sensorimotor stage (p. 453)
stage theories (p. 439)
stereopsis (p. 451)
structured interview (p. 443)
synaptic pruning (p. 437)
synaptogenesis (p. 437)
teratogens (p. 435)
universal (p. 452)
violation of expectancy (VOE) paradigm (p. 442)
visual cliff (p. 451)
visual contrast (p. 444)
visual preference paradigm (p. 442)
visual scanning (p. 444)
zygote (p. 433)

Recommended reading

Galinsky, E. (2010) *Mind in the Making: The Seven Essential Life Skills Every Child Needs*. New York: Harper Collins. Although written in the style of a parenting manual, takes many of the findings from developmental research and provides an easily accessible account of how different cognitive skills observed in the laboratory translate into real-life examples for parents to consider.

Gopnik, A., Meltzoff, A. and Kuhl, P. (1999) *The Scientist in the Crib: What Early Learning Tells Us About the Mind*. New York: HarperCollins. These developmental scientists present decades of research on cognitive development that reveal what infants know and how they learn about people, objects and language. They suggest that babies are born knowing a lot more than previously thought by psychologists such as Piaget, and they describe their own and other developmentalists' research in this accessible book.

Marcus, G. (2004) *The Birth of the Mind: How a Tiny Number of Genes Creates the Complexities of Human Thought*. New York: Basic Books. One of the more accessible popular science books to unravel the complexities of the gene–environment interaction, written for the general public by a developmental psychologist.

Chapter learning objectives

At the end of this chapter you will be able to:

1. Describe the behaviours and mechanisms that facilitate early social bonding.
2. Understand what having a theory of mind entails and how to test for it.
3. Describe theories of attachment and alternative explanations for the different patterns of attachment observed in the strange situation.
4. Evaluate the different factors that contribute to self-identity.
5. Evaluate the different theories of moral development.

© ARTISTICCAPTURES/ISTOCKPHOTO.COM

Social development

Towards the end of the 18th century, a naked boy approximately 11–12 years of age was captured in woods in the Aveyron region of southwest France. Victor, as he would later be named, was probably one of the many children abandoned as toddlers during these harsh times. Somehow, he had survived the elements for many years, living in total social isolation.

Victor was brought back to civilization just as France was recovering from the social upheaval of the French Revolution. At that time, French philosopher Jean Jacques Rousseau, writing about the ills and injustices of society, had argued that man was born inherently good but that society corrupted the 'noble savage' within all of us. So when news of Victor, 'the wild boy of Aveyron', reached Paris, the intelligentsia were eager to meet him. As a child uncorrupted by society, he could be the living embodiment of Rousseau's noble savage.

However, Victor was far from the idealized notion of moral purity. He lacked any social skills whatsoever and was only interested in food. He made animal noises and defecated indiscriminately. At first it was thought that he might be deaf and mute, so he initially spent time at the National Institute for the Deaf and Dumb, but it soon became apparent that Victor's problems were more profound than lack of communication. Itard, the young doctor who had been treating children at the institute, described Victor in his memoirs (1802, p. 17):

> *a disgusting, slovenly boy, affected with spasmodic, and frequently with convulsive motions, continually balancing himself like some of the animals in the menagerie, biting and scratching those who contradicted him, expressing no kind of affection for those who attended upon him; and, in short, indifferent to every body, and paying no regard to any thing.*

Undaunted by this challenging scenario, Itard attempted to rehabilitate Victor. He believed that with patient training, Victor could be taught to communicate and then be integrated back into society. At first, progress looked promising as Victor started to understand spoken commands. However, his ability to communicate did not develop further, and the only word he mastered was *lait* (milk) spelled out with wooden letters. Although there was an improvement in his social skills (Victor learned to wear clothes), the fact that he never learned to speak was a major disappointment to Itard. After five years of intensive training, Itard abandoned his attempt to reintegrate Victor into society and he remained in the care of Itard's housekeeper until his death in 1828.

FERAL CHILDREN Children raised in isolation from society.

Cases of feral children, *children raised in isolation from society*, promise to teach us much about the effects of social deprivation on normal development. But without knowing something about the state of a child *before* abandonment, it is difficult to judge which effects are caused by the child's isolation and which may have been caused by other factors. For example, reviewing the case of Victor, child development expert Uta Frith observes that he displayed many of the characteristics of severe autism. We also do not know whether and to what extent early malnourishment may have contributed to potential brain damage, which may have constrained the amount of rehabilitation possible. The case of Victor and Itard's failed attempt to rehabilitate him raises a whole series of questions about the importance of social interaction, the mechanisms by which it operates and how different environments can influence the social development of the individual. In this chapter, we will examine how far we have come in understanding these issues.

Homo psychologicus

In comparison with every other primate and mammal, humans spend the longest proportion of their lives being reared as children. Why is this? One explanation is that we have evolved to learn from others and our extended childhood reflects this process of socialization (Meltzoff et al., 2009). However, for that we need a brain equipped for social interactions. In this chapter, we will examine how the pattern of social interaction develops over the life span. Initially, our first social relationship is directed to our primary carer (usually our mother). During infancy, a strong bond and intimacy usually becomes established between the infant and mother, supported by mechanisms in both that operate to consolidate this early relationship. Over this period, the infant becomes increasingly aware of themselves as distinct from others. Following infancy, the child begins to interact with others of the same age, which requires additional socialization mechanisms. Entering society means conforming to the social norms and moral principles that operate in that particular group. At the end of childhood, most individuals seek to establish an intimate bond with another in a relationship in which to have children and begin the whole cycle again. Without social skills, this reproductive cycle would be disrupted. So, although modern man is known as *Homo sapiens* (wise man), psychologist Nick Humphrey (1984) has suggested an alternative title, *Homo psychologicus* (psychological man), to reflect the fact that we are an extremely social species and we appear to have evolved considerable social skills to interact with others. In this section, we will look at the early stages of social development, investigating how a lack of social contact can have devastating long-term effects, and how, to some extent, babies and adults appear programmed to pay attention to and interact with one another.

Feral and institutionalized children

We do not know for certain the circumstances surrounding Victor's background, but studies of children raised in institutions during the Second World War by French psychoanalyst René Spitz (1949) reveal that, despite receiving adequate nourishment and healthcare, infants still developed psychological problems because of the lack of social interaction. This discovery ran counter to the views of many childcare experts of the day, who did not appreciate that infants could be so emotionally dependent (Emde, 1992).

The importance of early social interaction was confirmed experimentally in studies by Harry Harlow (1958; Harlow and Harlow, 1965), who discovered that baby rhesus monkeys that were well fed and reared in warm, safe environments but with no social contact for the first six months of their lives still developed a variety of pathologies. For example, they compulsively rocked back and forth while biting themselves, and when they were finally introduced to other monkeys, they avoided them entirely. In comparison, monkeys who were isolated after the first six months did not develop abnormal behaviour, indicating that the first six months was a particularly sensitive period for socialization. Monkeys who were reared in isolation from birth turned out to be incapable of communicating with or learning from others of their kind. When the females from this group reached maturity, they were artificially inseminated to become mothers, but they ignored, rejected and sometimes even killed their own offspring.

HARLOW PRIMATE LAB

GETTY IMAGES/ISTOCKPHOTO/THINKSTOCK IMAGES

The top image shows one of Harlow's monkeys being raised using an artificial terry towelling mother. Monkeys who were reared in isolation from birth turned out to be incapable of communicating with or learning from others of their kind, unlike those reared with their natural mothers (bottom image).

Recovering from social isolation

It is clear that early social isolation can have profound effects on later development, but are these effects irreversible? In the rhesus monkey studies, Harlow found that animals isolated from birth could be rehabilitated after six months if they were paired with younger, normally reared animals who seemed intent on trying to form a social connection with these deprived animals. At first, the isolated animals avoided these enthusiastic 'therapist' monkeys but, after a few weeks, started displaying typical social behaviour and were indistinguishable from the normal monkeys by the end of their first year (Soumi and Harlow, 1972).

Can deprived children also be rehabilitated? One early study of orphans moved to a more socially enriched environment found that they fared better as adults on educational attainment compared with those orphans left behind, who fell below national standards (Skeels, 1966). However, this study did not have proper matched controls, where the children moved to the enriched environment were compared to a group of children left behind who closely resembled them. In fact, those left behind had much lower intelligence scores, so it is no surprise that they did not fare as well as those removed from the orphanage (Longstreth, 1981).

In the early 1990s, scientists had the opportunity to study the effects of social isolation and rehabilitation in greater detail, as the plight of a large number of Romanian orphans came to light. Marxist leader Nicolae Ceausescu had outlawed birth control and ordered women to bear more children in an attempt to increase the country's population. In an already poor economy, many of the resulting children were simply abandoned at birth by their parents and instead reared in large orphanages. Children at these institutions were not only malnourished, they had virtually no interaction with their so-called 'carers'. Some babies had been left lying on their backs for so long that their heads had flattened abnormally.

To investigate the long-term effects of such extreme social deprivation, the physical, cognitive and social development of around 150 children up to the age of six were studied in comparison with a similar age-matched sample of British children (O'Connor et al., 2000; Rutter et al., 2004). When the children arrived in the UK, most of them were severely underweight and undersized; they were also behind British children of the same age in terms of their ability to solve problems, and were socially impaired. What kind of outcome could be expected from such a poor start? In general, improvement in physical, cognitive and social development followed a similar pattern: children adopted before the age of six months showed the greatest recovery, but those adopted after the age of six months remained increasingly delayed despite the nurturing environments provided by their adoptive families. So, the longer a child had been kept in the orphanage after the age of six months, the more compromised their development. This finding can be linked back to the idea of plasticity and experience-expectant development we encountered in Chapter 11, suggesting that in addition to physical and cognitive growth, nature has also built in mechanisms to seek out social stimulation. As part of our evolutionary legacy, human development depends on social interaction and without this early exposure, it becomes increasingly difficult to compensate for this early loss.

Early social interaction

The first significant social relationship we have in our lives is almost always with our mother. As helpless infants, we are dependent on our mothers for milk and, as a parent, most adults will instinctively attend to and protect the infant. That's why babies don't need to fend off the attack with a broom handle, as parodied in the Chapter 11 opening vignette. However, babies are also born tuned in to their mother, as shown by their preference for their own mother's voice and smell. Austrian animal expert Konrad Lorenz (1903–89) identified a corresponding biological imperative in the bird world (1943), where he found that the offspring of some birds exhibited imprinting – *a process where the hatchlings bond to their mother at first sight and then follow her about everywhere.* When Lorenz was a child, he wanted to be a goose. As he explained in his Nobel Prize acceptance speech in 1973:

IMPRINTING A process where the hatchlings bond to their mother at first sight and then follow her about everywhere.

> I yearned to become a wild goose and, on realizing that this was impossible, I desperately wanted to *have* one and, when this also proved impossible, I settled for having domestic ducks ... From a neighbour, I got a one day old duckling and found, to my intense joy, that it transferred its following response to my person.

Most mothers will instinctively defend their offspring. During a routine security check at Boston airport, the wife of one the authors of this book threatened to overpower an armed guard and smash through the glass barrier to retrieve her newborn, carried by the nanny who had accidentally been separated from them while she searched for the passports. The guard, recognizing the maternal rage, immediately let her through. This is why most animal experts caution against approaching young offspring when the mother is about.

Every farmer knows that a baby duck or goose will normally follow its mother everywhere she goes, but what Lorenz discovered as a child (and proved scientifically as an adult) is that a newly hatched gosling will faithfully follow the first moving object to which it is exposed. If that object is a human being or a tennis ball, the hatchling will ignore its mother and follow the object instead. Lorenz (1952) theorized that the first moving object a hatchling saw was somehow imprinted on its bird brain as 'the thing I must always stay near'.

Newborn face preferences

Lorenz's work on imprinting inspired psychologist Mark Johnson to investigate whether similar behaviour existed in human newborns. He gave newborns a choice of two patterns to look at, one of which resembled a face, and one of which was equivalent, but did not (see **FIGURE 12.1**). He found that newborns preferred to look at the face-like patterns (Johnson et al., 1991).

Based largely on studies of imprinting in birds (Horn, 1985), John Morton and Mark Johnson (1991) proposed that human newborns were born with Conspec – *a system that orients the infant towards face-like structures and is supported by mature subcortical brain mechanisms, present at birth.* As the visual and cortical systems mature, newborns become more efficient at learning to encode specific faces and, in particular, the unique features that we use to tell faces apart. Johnson and Morton called this acquired ability Conlearn – *a system largely supported by maturing cortical brain mechanisms that learns about specific faces.*

CONSPEC A system that orients the infant towards face-like structures and is supported by mature subcortical brain mechanisms, present at birth.

CONLEARN A system largely supported by maturing cortical brain mechanisms that learns about specific faces.

In one study using social isolation (Sugita, 2008), infant monkeys were separated from their mother from birth and reared with no exposure to faces for 6–24 months. Before being allowed to see a face, the monkeys showed a preference for human and monkey faces in photographs, and they discriminated human faces as well as monkey

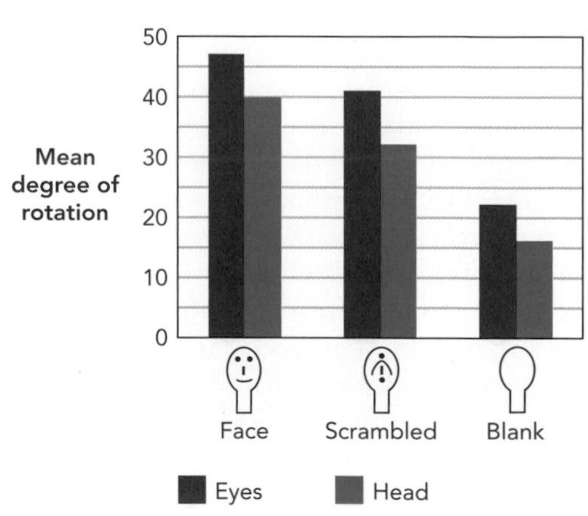

FIGURE 12.1 Newborn face recognition The graph shows the degree of following with eyes and head turning to each stimulus. Newborn infants prefer to pay more attention to the face-like pattern compared to the scrambled face, even though they effectively contain the same amount of pattern. They are least attentive when there is no pattern.

faces. After the period of isolation, they were exposed to either human or monkey faces for one month and showed a marked inability to discriminate faces they had not been exposed to. This shows that there is a built-in preference for faces and experience shapes face processing to become more selective.

The newborn preference for faces is reciprocated – most adults are attracted to babies. For most of us, babies are cute, especially if you are a parent or someone beyond the age of puberty. They simply look so attractive because of babyness – *a term coined by Lorenz (1943) to describe the relative attractiveness of big eyes and big heads.* Babyness also explains why we like puppies, kittens, rabbits and other animals that have relatively large eyes in large heads. These physical attributes tend to evoke a positive response in adults. For example, in one study, researchers asked children ranging from 7 years old to adolescence which of two pictures they preferred, either the adult or the baby of a variety of species (Fullard and Reiling, 1976). Up to 12 years of age, children preferred the picture of the adult, but there was a significant switch in girls between 12 and 14 years and in boys between 14 and 16 years to prefer the picture of the baby. This coincides with puberty, suggesting that there is a biological basis for this preference.

Babyness, or the physical attributes of relatively large eyes in a large head, can be advantageous in both the human and animal worlds, as it tends to evoke a caring response from adults (Lorenz, 1943).

Newborns don't merely look longer at faces, they respond to them in other surprising ways. Researchers in one study stood close to some newborns while sticking out their tongues and stood close to other newborns while pursing their lips. Newborns in the first group stuck out their own tongues more often than those in the second group, and newborns in the second group pursed their lips more often than those in the first group (Meltzoff and Moore, 1977). The newborns were imitating the facial expression of the adults even though they had never seen their own face, suggesting an early mapping of the infant's representation of their own face with that of another human. In fact, newborns have since been found to mimic facial expressions in their very first *hour* of life (Reissland, 1988). Should this be interpreted as an early attempt to communicate? Probably not, because the response has a limited repertoire and is difficult to elicit. But what these studies show is that the potential for mimicry is there, and (crucially) that parents reciprocate anyway *as if* the baby is trying to communicate.

BABYNESS A term coined by Lorenz (1943) to describe the relative attractiveness of big eyes and big heads.

JOINT ATTENTION The capacity to coordinate the social interaction with attention direction towards objects of mutual interest.

SOCIAL SMILING Smiles directed towards people.

CONTINGENT BEHAVIOUR Synchronized responding.

Joint attention

As they approach their first birthday, infants exhibit an increased ability to interact with adults and share attention directed towards objects of interest (Dunham and Moore, 1995). This *capacity to coordinate the social interaction with attention direction towards objects of mutual interest* is known as joint attention. The most obvious form of joint attention is when individuals follow each other's gaze. However, the foundations for joint attention can be found in much younger infants when that gaze is directed at each other. From around two months, the baby begins making its first deliberate attempts at social interaction in the form of social smiling – *smiles directed towards people* (White, 1985). This a momentous event for any parent, signifying a new stage of development recognized around the world in different cultures. For example, when visitors come to visit a Navaho family with a new baby, it is polite to inquire: 'Has the baby laughed yet?' If the answer is 'yes', this is treated as an occasion for rejoicing and ceremony (Leighton and Kluckhohn, [1947]1969, p. 29).

Initially, babies smile at many things, but mostly they smile at humans. They are, however, indiscriminate at whom they smile, and become distressed if the recipient does not respond but maintains a still face (Ellsworth et al., 1993). Social smiling may be a hardwired behaviour but is also dependent on social reinforcement from the adult. For example, congenitally blind infants also smile at around the same time as sighted infants, but if their smiles are not reinforced by reciprocal social interaction (such as jiggling or bouncing), the smiles disappear (Fraiberg, 1974). This provides a good illustration of the importance of contingent behaviour – *synchronized responding from an adult.* It provides a powerful social cue for

Social smiling is a natural response from babies, but it requires interaction and reciprocation from a partner to be maintained.

interaction. For example, a five-month-old placed in a baby walker is more likely to approach a stranger who has responded contingently than one who maintained a close distance to the infant but did not respond to attempts to interact (Roedell and Slaby, 1977). That's why 'peek-a-boo' (where the adult interacts and responds contingently to the infant) is more than just a game – it's a way for infants to identify adults who are interested in them (Morgan and Ricciuti, 1969).

It is worth noting that this early social exchange shared by infants and mothers also depends on the nature of the relationship. For example, mothers who suffer from postnatal depression have a qualitatively different social experience with their infants at two months of age, with either too much or too little interaction (Murray et al., 1996). Either they exaggerate the normal type of interaction or they have flat emotional affects, which have both been found to be predictive of poorer cognitive outcome at 18 months. So, it is not just any interaction that is essential for healthy development, but only those that seem to be optimally linked to synchronizing infant and mother.

Gaze following

DYADIC RELATIONSHIP Where the focus of interest is between two individuals.

TRIADIC RELATIONSHIP Where attention is directed between two individuals and a third potential source.

When an infant and an adult stare at one another ('mutual gaze'), their relationship is referred to as dyadic. A dyadic relationship is one *where the focus of interest is between two individuals.* When a mother interacts with her baby, they spend about 70% of the time looking at one another when the baby is aged around six weeks (Kaye and Fogel, 1980). By six months, however, infants spend about 33% of playtime staring at their mother, and in the remaining time, start to switch their attention to objects, much as Piaget described in Chapter 11. At this stage, the infant begins to understand that another person's direction of gaze might signal interest in other things in the world. In this triadic relationship, *where attention is directed between two individuals and a third potential source*, we can signal to the other individual that there is something worth looking at by simply shifting our gaze. (To test this, try standing in a busy street staring up at the sky, and watch how many people stare up as well!) Humans find it difficult to ignore another person's direction of gaze. Even three-month-old infants will sometimes follow an adult's direction of gaze (Hood et al., 1998), although this behaviour emerges reliably at around nine months, when an infant will turn to see what appears to be capturing an adult's attention if they suddenly look away (Scaife and Bruner, 1975) (see FIGURE 12.2).

This is all very interesting, but what purpose does it serve? In fact, joint attention facilitates language learning, because when an adult labels an object with a new word,

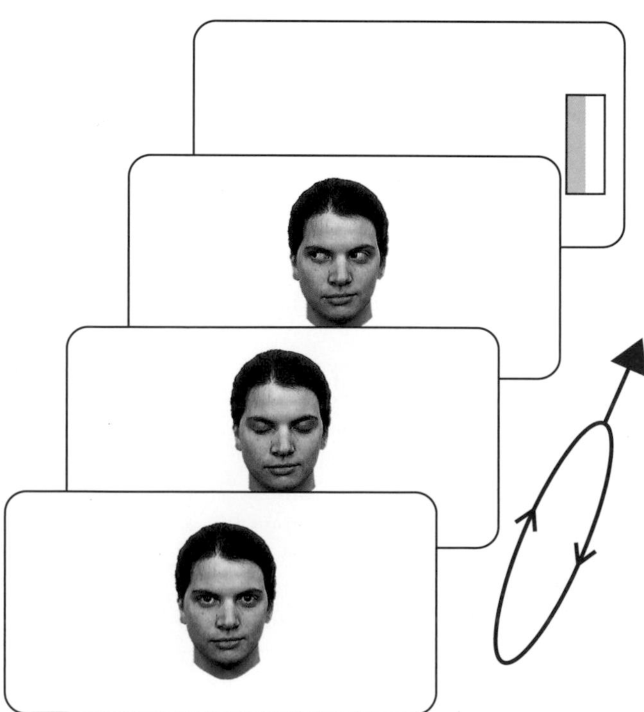

FIGURE **12.2 Gaze following** Computerized displays reveal that young infants pay attention to direction of eye gaze because they are slower to look at the black and white target if it is preceded by an adult who looks in the opposite direction, compared to looking in the same direction as the target location.

they usually look at or point to the object at the same time (Baldwin, 1991). The link between joint attention and language is aptly illustrated by the fact that the younger the age at which an infant demonstrates proficient joint attention, the faster their subsequent language acquisition (Carpenter et al., 1998).

At about the same time as they learn to follow a line of gaze, infants also begin social referencing – *looking at carers to gauge their reactions in unfamiliar or threatening circumstances* (Campos and Stenberg, 1981). If the carer looks concerned, infants hesitate and are wary, whereas if the carer smiles, they are much more relaxed (Walden and Baxter, 1989). For example, infants' reactions to unexpected events (like a jack-in-the-box toy) are strongly influenced by how their mothers respond (Hornik et al., 1987).

SOCIAL REFERENCING Looking at carers to gauge their reactions in unfamiliar or threatening circumstances.

By four years of age, children can reliably read another's direction of gaze not only as an indicator of where their attention is focused, but also as an indicator of what they are thinking. For example, children shown a picture of a cartoon character called Charlie looking at one of four potential sweets can tell which one he wants based on the direction of his gaze (Baron-Cohen et al., 1995). At this age, they can also take into consideration the amount of time Charlie spends looking at one target in comparison to others as a measure of which target he prefers (Einav and Hood, 2006).

Pointing

Another way in which the infant can establish joint attention is through pointing, which becomes prevalent around the end of the first year (Carpenter et al., 1998). Two types of pointing have been distinguished: protoimperative, *to direct another's attention to obtain a particular goal*, and protodeclarative, *to direct another's attention to an object or event of interest*. If the infant sees something they want that is out of reach, they point to it protoimperatively until the adult works out what they want and retrieves it for them.

PROTOIMPERATIVE POINTING To direct another's attention to obtain a particular goal.

PROTODECLARATIVE POINTING To direct another's attention to an object or event of interest.

A variety of primates will make protoimperative gestures (Maestripieri, 2005), although pointing with the index finger is uniquely human because of the structure of the human hand (Butterworth, 1998). However, protodeclarative pointing is uniquely human: only children seem to want to share interesting sights with others, suggesting that this type of pointing is truly a communicative act (Bates et al., 1975). To test this idea, Liszkowski and colleagues (2004) examined the relationship between joint attention and protodeclarative pointing in one-year-olds. First, an infant was placed facing a curtain. An adult came in and sat next to the infant, but facing to the side, so they could see the curtain if they turned 90° to the side. A hand puppet then appeared from behind the curtain, and the infant pointed to this exciting event. The experiment was carried out under four conditions:

1 In the *joint attention* condition, the adult turned to look at the puppet and back to the child, talking excitedly about the event.
2 In the *face* condition, the adult kept their attention on the infant and spoke excitedly about the child, 'You are in a good mood aren't you?'
3 In the *event* condition, the adult simply turned and looked at the puppet but not back at the infant.
4 In the *ignore* condition, the adult ignored the puppet and the infant.

Liszkowski and colleagues measured the frequency and duration of the infants' pointing over 10 separate trials, and found that it was more prevalent during the joint attention condition (75% of trials). Sharing interest in the novel event was the adult reaction that seemed most likely to increase infants' motivation to point. However, in the other conditions, infants showed more bouts of agitated pointing within a given trial – trying to direct the adult's attention as if to say, 'Look, it's behind you, dummy!' In short, pointing is a declarative act dependent on the context and how the adult responds.

Infants can establish joint attention through pointing.

In summary, humans are exquisitely tuned to social interaction from the very beginning, with adults and infants equipped with biases and preferences to attend to each other. In addition to nourishment and safety, infants need social interaction within the first six months to develop normally. If infants are raised in an impoverished social environment, long-term abnormal social and cognitive development is likely. Early social interaction is usually dyadic between the infant and mother, but increasingly becomes more sophisticated as the infant uses gaze following and pointing to increase joint attention to objects of mutual interest. In this way, social interaction facilitates cognitive development.

Attachment

ATTACHMENT An emotional bond.

Social development is more than just watching, learning and anticipating what others might do next. Typically, developing children also have a strong emotional need that shows itself as attachment – *an emotional bond* – with a primary carer. Attachment has three key features:

1 *Proximity seeking:* the attached child will stay close to the primary carer.
2 *Secure base:* the primary carer provides a secure base from which the attached child can explore the world as if tied by invisible elastic.
3 *Separation protest:* attached children will be distressed and cry if separated from the primary carer.

In this section, we examine why children form these strong emotional bonds and also the factors that contribute to different strengths and styles of attachment.

Bowlby's theory

Following on from the work of René Spitz who we encountered earlier, after the Second World War, British psychiatrist John Bowlby (1907–90) studied institutionalized children who had been separated from their families during the London Blitz. He found increased depression, emotional disturbance and delinquent behaviour, leading him to conclude that the early social environment was critically important to normal socialization. These were not feral children like Victor left in the wilds to survive by themselves. Rather they were normal children raised in foster homes that lacked some important social dimension that was present in their home environment. In short, young children needed love as much as nourishment (Bowlby, 1953).

©ISTOCKPHOTO.COM/SERGEY IVANOV

©ISTOCKPHOTO.COM/BENLIN

Like goslings, human babies need to stay close to their mothers to survive. Unlike goslings, human babies know how to get their mothers to come to them rather than the other way around.

Bowlby believed that infants were motivated by biological drives such as warmth, hunger and thirst that they sought to appease. Pleasure was experienced when the needs were satisfied. The mother was simply a means to an end to satisfying these drives. However, such drive-reduction accounts did not explain why Harlow's monkeys who were given adequate sustenance and institutionalized children given good care still developed abnormally. Rather, Bowlby thought that attachment to the carer was the innate primary drive. He was influenced by Lorenz's imprinting studies and sought to understand whether similar biological mechanisms might explain how human infants form attachments to their carers (Bowlby, 1969, 1973, 1980).

Bowlby began by noting that from the moment they are born, goslings waddle after their mothers and monkeys cling to their mothers' furry chests because the newborns of both species must stay close to their carers to survive. Human babies, he suggested, have a similar need, but they are much less physically developed than goslings or monkeys and hence cannot waddle or cling. As they cannot stay close to their carers, human babies pursue a different strategy – they do things that cause their carers to stay close to them. When a baby cries, gurgles, coos, makes eye contact or smiles, most adults reflexively move towards the baby, and Bowlby (1958, p. 364) claimed that this is *why* the baby emits these 'come hither' signals:

> there matures in the early months of life of the human infant a complex and nicely balanced equipment of instinctual responses, the function of which is to ensure that he obtains parental care sufficient for his survival. To this end the equipment includes responses which promote his close proximity to a parent and ... evoke parental activity.

Bowlby proposed that attachment developed in three distinct phases. During the initial pre-attachment phase (up to two months), babies begin by sending these signals to anyone within range to receive them, but during the next four months, they begin to keep a mental tally of who responds most often and most promptly, and they soon begin to target their signals to the primary carer. This person quickly becomes the emotional centre of the infant's universe. Infants feel secure in the primary carer's presence and will happily crawl around, exploring their environments with their eyes, ears, fingers and mouths. But if their primary carer goes too far away, infants begin to feel insecure, and like the imprinted gosling, they take action to decrease the distance between themselves and their primary carer, perhaps by crawling towards their carer or crying until their carer moves towards them. Indeed, anything that threatens the infant's sense of security, for example the sudden appearance of a stranger in the room, will often induce stranger anxiety – *a fearful response associated with crying and attempts to cling or move closer to the carer*. Stranger anxiety clearly marks the second phase of attachment at around seven months. The final phase of attachment around the end of the infancy period at two years is characterized by a goal-directed partnership between the child and carer, where the child increasingly becomes more confident at exploratory forays further away from the adult who is seen as a secure base. In Bowlby's view, children are a bit like batsmen in a game of rounders or cricket: they feel secure when they are touching the bases or while behind their creases but become increasingly anxious and insecure as they step farther and farther away from them. Bowlby believed that all this happens because evolution has equipped human infants with a social drive that is every bit as basic as the physical drives for nutrition that cause infants to suck during breastfeeding.

STRANGER ANXIETY A fearful response associated with crying and attempts to cling or move closer to the carer.

STRANGE SITUATION A behavioural test used to determine a child's attachment style.

Separation behaviour: the strange situation of Dr Ainsworth

One problem with Bowlby's theory was that it failed to take into account individual differences in attachment 'styles' discovered by his colleague Mary Ainsworth (1913–99). After training with Bowlby in London, Ainsworth worked first in Uganda and then later in the US, and in her observations of mother–infant interactions, she noted that there were different patterns of attachment style (1967).

Taking stranger anxiety as a basis, Ainsworth (Ainsworth et al., 1978) developed what has come to be known as the strange situation – *a behavioural test used to determine a child's attachment style*. The test, usually undertaken between one and two years of age, involves bringing a child and their primary carer – usually the child's mother – to a laboratory room where there are two chairs. A series of events are then staged that range from abandonment (in which the primary carer briefly leaves the room) to reunion (in which the primary carer returns) as well as several interactions with a stranger, both in the absence and presence of the primary carer. For example, a strange situation might proceed as follows:

1 Mother and infant introduced into room
2 Mother and infant alone, infant free to explore (three mins)
3 Enter female stranger who sits down and talks to mother, and then tries to engage the infant in play (three mins)
4 Mother leaves infant and stranger alone (three mins*)
5 First reunion. Mother returns and stranger leaves. Mother attempts to settle infant if necessary and then withdraws to her chair (three mins)
6 Mother leaves infant alone (three mins*)
7 Stranger returns and tries to settle infant if necessary and then withdraws to her chair (three mins*)

Psychology and me

Tanya Byron, clinician, journalist, author and broadcaster

Tanya Byron is a Chartered Clinical Psychologist specializing in working with children and adolescents, and has been working in this field, both in the NHS and privately, for 20 years. She is also a Professor in the Public Understanding of Science, and as a clinician, journalist, author and broadcaster she works with and writes about a variety of psychological and emotional issues as well as mental health difficulties that affect people of all ages. Visit www.palgrave.com/schacter to read more about Tanya's work, what she wished she'd known when she was doing her undergraduate psychology degree, and what advice she has for students about their future careers.

8 Second reunion. Mother returns and stranger leaves. Mother settles infant if necessary and then withdraws to her chair (three mins).

(*episodes are terminated if the mother feels that her child is becomingly overly upset.) Impartial observers watch the infant (usually via a hidden camera) and code their reactions during the two reunion episodes according to four indices:

- *proximity seeking:* where the infant seeks to be close to the mother
- *contact maintenance:* where the infant clings to the mother
- *resistance:* where the infant refuses to settle and is petulant
- *avoidance:* where the infant does not seek out the mother and appears indifferent.

These infants' reactions tend to fit one of four main attachment styles: *secure, avoidant, ambivalent* or *disorganized:*

1. Roughly 60% of infants display a *secure* attachment style. If these infants are distressed when their carer leaves the room, they go to her promptly when she returns and are quickly calmed by her proximity. If they are not distressed when their carer leaves the room, they acknowledge her return with a glance or a greeting. These infants seem to regard their carer as a *secure base* from which to explore their environments (Waters and Cummings, 2000).
2. Roughly 20% of infants display an *avoidant* attachment style (sometimes called an *insecure-avoidant* style). These infants are generally not distressed when their carer leaves the room, and they generally do not acknowledge her when she returns.
3. Roughly 15% of infants display an *ambivalent* attachment style (sometimes called an *insecure-resistant* style). These infants are almost always distressed when their carer leaves the room, and they go to her promptly when she returns. But then they rebuff their carer's attempt to calm them, arching their backs and squirming to get away when their carer tries to comfort them.
4. Roughly 5% or fewer of infants display a *disorganized* attachment style. These infants show no consistent pattern of responses. They may or may not be distressed when their carer leaves, they may or may not go to her when she returns, and their reactions are often contradictory. For example, they may look fearful as they approach their carer, they may be calm when she leaves and then suddenly become angry, or they may simply freeze and appear confused or disoriented (Main and Solomon, 1986).

If the attachment relationship is seen as a balance between exploratory behaviour of the environment and safety provided by the primary carer (as originally proposed by Bowlby), then securely attached children have got the correct balance (see FIGURE 12.3). They protest at separation and seek to quickly re-establish the relationship on reunion and thus settle more easily. Ambivalent children are too clingy to the mother, reluctant to explore the environment and indignant that she would ever leave. Avoidant children could not care less about the mother and are in danger of wandering off. Disorganized children cannot make their minds up about how to react.

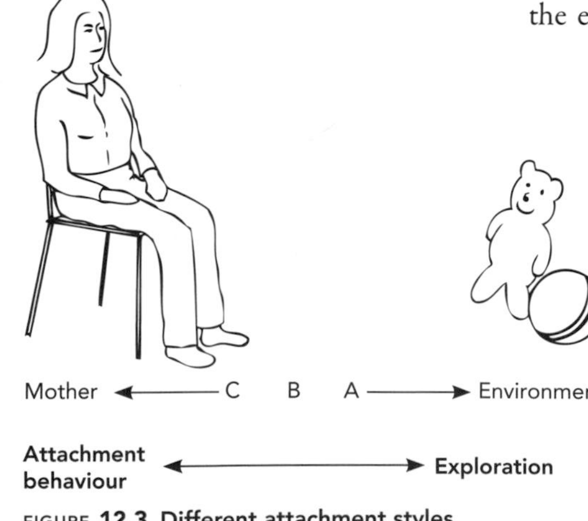

FIGURE 12.3 Different attachment styles The different attachment styles can be represented as the relative relationship between maintaining proximity to the mother and exploration of the environment. Ambivalent children (C) are too attached to the mother, while avoidant children (A) are too independent. Securely attached children (B) have the correct balance between attachment to mother and exploration.

Cultural variations in attachment style

If attachment is an evolutionary mechanism as Bowlby proposed, then there should be universal patterns of attachment that remain consistent from one environment to the next. However, one of the problems of attachment theory is that there appears to be a degree of variation in attachment styles depending on where you raise the child. In other words, the environment plays an important role in the strange situation.

Research has shown that a child's behaviour in the strange situation correlates fairly well with their behaviour at home (Solomon and George, 1999) and in the lab (see FIGURE 12.4). Nonetheless, as with any classification system of stable personality traits (see Chapter 13), this one should be interpreted cautiously. For instance, it is not unusual for a child's attachment style to change over time (Lamb et al., 1992). Infants will also form attachment to the father towards the end of the first year, and the nature of the interaction may be qualitatively different, with fathers more likely to provide playful physical stimulation. So, attachment is not exclusively directed to the mother and it can

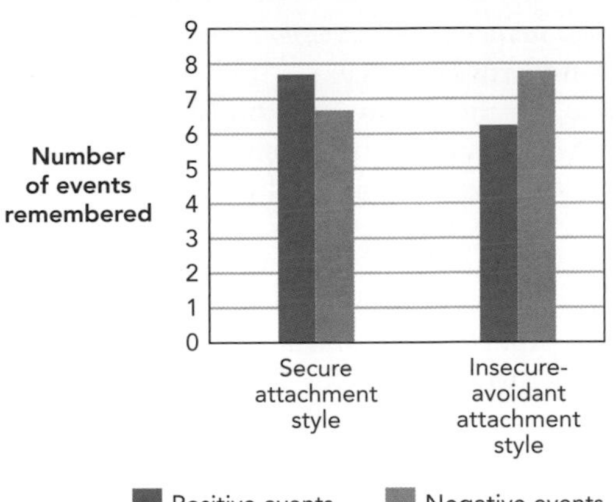

FIGURE **12.4 Attachment style and memory** We often remember best those events that fit with our view of the world. Researchers assessed one-year-old children's attachment styles with the strange situation test. Two years later, the same group of children were shown a puppet show in which some happy events (the puppet got a present) or unhappy events (the puppet spilled his juice) occurred. Securely attached children later remembered more of the happy events than the unhappy ones, but insecurely attached children showed the opposite pattern (Belsky et al., 1996).

take on different styles with others. Although most infants prefer their mother's company when upset or frightened, they tend to prefer their fathers as playmates (Lamb, 1997).

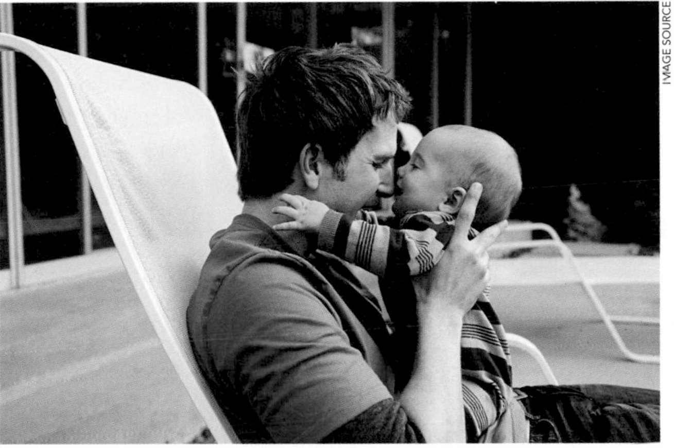
IMAGE SOURCE

Playtime! Dads are more fun, or so babies tend to think.

Importantly, too, while some aspects of attachment style appear to be stable across cultures – secure attachment is the most common style in just about every country that has ever been studied (van IJzendoorn and Sagi, 1999) – other aspects of attachment style vary across cultures (van IJzendoorn and Kroonenberg, 1988). For example, German children are more likely to have avoidant rather than ambivalent attachment styles (Grossmann et al., 1985), whereas Japanese children are more likely to have ambivalent and often no avoidant attachment styles (Miyake et al., 1985). One explanation for this is that parenting styles and attitudes play an important role in determining attachment styles. For example, German mothers are more likely to foster independence in their children (leading to a greater representation of avoidant attachment in their children), whereas Japanese mothers traditionally stay at home, spending a considerable amount of time with their often only child (meaning that the strange situation is very unusual and upsetting for Japanese children). This also explains why Japanese children show less exploratory behaviour in the strange situation, because they are unfamiliar with the scenario (Rothbaum et al., 2000). This explanation is supported by studies of Japanese career women who have adopted childcare practices more similar to those used in, say, Germany, when their children then exhibit behaviour similar to the attachment styles found in the West (Durrett et al., 1984).

So, we can see that the culture in which a child is raised can affect their attachment style and this cultural 'relativity' challenges the validity of using attachment style for cross-cultural comparisons. Clearly, attachment styles should not be viewed either as sharply defined categories or immutable characteristics of the child (Takahashi, 1986). Such differences in cultural parenting style may also explain why attachment objects, *blankets and soft toys that children are emotionally attached to and use for reassurance*, are much more common in Europe and the US (Passman, 1987), where the child is separated from the mother during sleep, and relatively unusual in Japan, where high maternal contact during sleep is favoured (Hobara, 2003). Attachment objects acquire sentimental value, often making them irreplaceable. When offered an identical copy as a replacement attachment object, children were more likely to refuse to accept the copy (Hood and Bloom, 2008), which fits in with theories that these objects operate as surrogates for the mother (Bowlby, 1969; Winnicott, 1953).

ATTACHMENT OBJECTS Blankets and soft toys that children are emotionally attached to and use for reassurance.

Working models of attachment

Why do different infants have different attachment styles? The need to form attachment may be innate, but the quality of that attachment is influenced by the child, the primary carer and how they interact. For example, attachment theorists argue that

BRAND X

Cultural attitudes affect attachment. Traditionally, Japanese infants would not need soft toys for comfort as they sleep with their mothers, while European mothers favour independence and encourage children to sleep alone.

parental sensitivity – *consistent attentiveness to the infant's emotional wellbeing* – is the key to establishing secure attachment (Ainsworth et al., 1978). Studies of insecurely attached mothers and their infants indicate that those who are inconsistent or anxious about attending to their infants tend to have children with an ambivalent attachment style, whereas those mothers who are less attentive or concerned have infants with a more avoidant attachment style (Isabella, 1993).

Infants seem to keep track of the parental sensitivity of their primary carer and use this information to create an internal working model of attachment – *a set of expectations about how the primary carer will respond when the child feels insecure.* Infants with different attachment styles appear to have different working models. For example, securely attached infants tend to have parents with secure working models of attachment (see FIGURE 12.5). Studies have shown that mothers of securely attached infants tend to be especially sensitive to signs of their child's emotional state, especially good at detecting their infant's 'request' for reassurance, and especially responsive to that request (Ainsworth et al., 1978; de Wolff and van IJzendoorn, 1997). Mothers of infants with an ambivalent attachment style tend to respond inconsistently, only sometimes attending to their infants when they show signs of distress. Mothers of infants with an avoidant attachment style are typically indifferent to their child's need for reassurance and may even reject their attempts at physical closeness (Isabella, 1993). In short, infants with a secure attachment style seem to be certain that their primary carer will respond, infants with an avoidant attachment style seem to be certain that their primary carer will not respond, and infants with an ambivalent attachment style seem to be uncertain about whether their primary carer will respond. Infants with a disorganized attachment style seem to be confused about their carers, which has led some psychologists to speculate that this style primarily characterizes children who have been abused (Carolson, 1998; Cicchetti and Toth, 1998). However, such speculation needs to be treated with extreme caution when considering the variability of human personality and the consequences of false accusations.

PARENTAL SENSITIVITY Consistent attentiveness to the infant's emotional wellbeing.

INTERNAL WORKING MODEL A set of expectations about how the primary carer will respond when the child feels insecure.

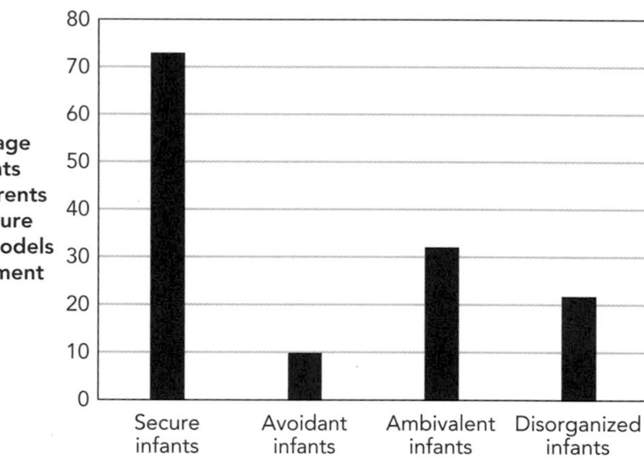

FIGURE 12.5 Parents' attachment styles affect their children's attachment styles Studies suggest that securely attached infants tend to have parents who have secure working models of attachment (van IJzendoorn, 1995).

hot science

Being licked is better than being ignored

What could be worse than being licked by a rat? Well, if you are a baby rat pup, this is a good thing as female rats have a strong maternal instinct. When mothers are rearing their pups in the nest, they will invest time licking and grooming their brood. Some female rats are much more conscientious, with very high rates of licking, whereas others are less so – a trait these mothers share with all their sisters (Champagne et al., 2003). What is remarkable is that if you take female pups from a low-licking mother and raise them in the litter of a high-licking mother, they will acquire this attentive trait. Likewise, if you cross-foster in the opposite direction, you get the opposite effect (Francis et al., 1999). Is this rat example simply a case of learning how to raise your pups? There is more to it than that. Grooming and licking appear to regulate the baby rats' response to stress. Those mothers with a high-licking rate produce offspring who cope much better with stress than those from a low-licking mother. They also grow up into more resilient adult rats and, if female, pass this behavioural trait on to the next generation (Meaney, 2001).

Grooming and licking release the 'feel good' neurotransmitter serotonin that regulates the genes that operate in the hippocampus to activate the stress response (see Chapter 17). This process is epigenetic, as the environment regulates gene activity by DNA methylation, as we discussed in Chapter 3. In contrast, these genes are switched off in the understimulated pups, whereas it is almost never methylated in the pups of high-licking mothers. Even though DNA methylation patterns tend to be stable, if you cross-foster the pups of high- and low-licking mothers during the critical period, you can reverse the methylation of the genes in the hippocampus. In short, the early grooming experience is turning the genes on or off to deal with life's stressful events (McGowan et al., 2011).

This may be all well and good for rats, but what of humans? Children raised in abusive households suffer not only from episodes of violence and harm but also from the unpredictability of when the next abuse will happen. Unpredictability is corrosive to coping, as we are not able to relax but must maintain our stress response in a state of high alert (see Chapter 17 on stress and coping). This will produce long-term disruption of the capacity to deal with stress, which can have consequences many years later. In a study reminiscent of Bowlby's original work on refugee children, Finnish scientists followed up 282 children evacuated during the Second World War to test the effects of separation from parents on their stress responses decades later. Those separated from their parents during the war as young children had higher reactivity to stress tests 60 years after the early separation, indicating that their brain physiology had been altered permanently by this experience (Pesonen et al., 2010). The older the child was at the time of the evacuation, the more resilient they were and the less disruption to their ability to cope with stress as adults.

In a recent study of teenagers whose parents had reported stress during their child's upbringing, methylation of environmental stressor genes was investigated (Essex et al., 2013). The effects of the mother's stress were only evident if it had occurred when the child was still an infant. Fathers also produced methylation in stress-related genes but only when the child was older, during preschool years. It has been reported for some time that absent or deadbeat fathers have an influence on psychological adjustment (Boyce et al., 2005), but this study is some of the growing evidence to point the finger of suspicion at epigenetic processes (described in Chapter 11, when environmental events trigger genetic regulatory mechanisms).

Temperament

If different internal working models cause infants to have different attachment styles, what causes infants to have different working models? Attachment is an interaction between two people, and thus both of them – the primary carer and the child – play a role in determining the nature of the child's working model. We'll look first at the role of the child, specifically their temperament, in this process, before moving on to consider how the primary carer can influence attachment style.

A child's temperament, *a characteristic pattern of emotional reactivity*, plays an important role in determining attachment style. Very young children vary in their tendency towards fearfulness, irritability, activity, positive affect and other emotional traits (Rothbart and Bates, 1998). This variability can be measured by parental reports or by using physiological measures, such as heart rate or blood flow to the brain. Some infants are more emotionally reactive and intensely irritated by unexpected events than others. These infants thrash and cry when shown a new toy or a new person; they grow into children who tend to avoid novel people, objects and situations; and they ultimately become quiet, cautious and sometimes shy adults (Schwartz et al., 2003). Harvard psychologist Jerome Kagan (1994) estimates that around 15% of infants have this 'inhibited' temperament, which is attributed to a highly reactive limbic system (see Chapter 3) that is easily startled and fails to habituate quickly to novelty. At the other end of this spectrum of behavioural inhibition, *the tendency towards shyness and fear of novelty*, are 'uninhibited' children (around 10%) who are eager to jump into a new situation and not fearful of strangers, with the remaining 75% of children falling somewhere in between these two extreme positions.

TEMPERAMENT A characteristic pattern of emotional reactivity.

BEHAVIOURAL INHIBITION The tendency towards shyness and fear of novelty.

These differences have been reported to be stable over time. For example, infants at 4 months who react fearfully to novel stimuli – such as sudden movements, loud sounds or unfamiliar people – tend to be more subdued, less social and less positive at 21 months, taking longer to settle in new environments and clinging to their mothers (Fox et al., 2001). By contrast, uninhibited toddlers will interact with strangers and enjoy all manner of new experiences and maintain this behaviour at follow-up assessments at five and seven years of age. Children who were inhibited infants remained fearful of strangers and unwilling to try a novel task such as balancing on a beam. Of the children who maintained the same temperament over the first seven years, over half of them kept this profile well into adolescence, suggesting that it constitutes a fairly stable aspect of personality.

Temperament is largely to do with the genes, as the correlation between inhibition scores of identical twins has been found to be around +0.5 to +0.6 in identical twins

(Buss and Plomin, 1984) and one study found a correlation as high as +0.82 for identical twins compared with +0.47 for non-identical twins (DiLalla et al., 1994). These relatively high correlations suggest that from the earliest moments of life, some infants are biologically predisposed to respond to novel situations in a characteristic manner. This partly explains why, in Ainsworth's strange situation, inhibited children feel insecure when their primary carer leaves a room and are inconsolable when they return.

Goodness of fit

While temperament might be an important component of social development, it is a predisposition, not a determinant. For example, longitudinal studies have found that inhibited children do not necessarily grow up into dysfunctional adults (Chess and Thomas, 1982; Thomas and Chess, 1989). This is because (as with so many aspects of development) the environment can play a role in shaping attachment. In particular, the way parents respond to their child – with patience or indifference and so on – is a key influence. This is what Thomas and Chess call a goodness of fit – *the extent to which the child's environment is compatible with their temperament*. When children have difficult temperaments and grow up with parents who cannot control their child's behaviour, they are more likely to grow up into adolescents with serious problems (Maziade et al., 1990). However, parents who adapt to their child's temperament with patience, by allowing their child more time to adjust to change, produce children who grow up into better adjusted adults. By contrast, parents who are either impatient or, at the other extreme, overprotective tend to produce children who never learn to control their own behaviour in order to adapt to stressful situations. In short, it is best for parents of inhibited children to recognize this disposition in their child, prepare their child for potential stressful situations, and then patiently adjust and provide support as their child deals with the situation (Kagan, 1994).

GOODNESS OF FIT The extent to which the child's environment is compatible with their temperament.

Research suggests that differences in how carers respond are probably due in large measure to differences in their ability to read their infant's emotional state. Mothers who are highly sensitive to these signs are almost twice as likely to have a securely attached child as mothers who are less sensitive (van IJzendoorn and Sagi, 1999). Although such data only indicate a *correlation* between sensitivity and secure attachment, there is reason to suspect that a mother's sensitivity and responsiveness *cause* the infant's attachment style. Researchers in the Netherlands studied a group of young mothers whose babies were particularly irritable or difficult. When the babies were about 6 months old, half the mothers participated in a training programme designed to sensitize them to their babies' emotional signals and encourage them to be more responsive. The results showed that when the children were 18 months, 24 months and 36 months old, those whose mothers had received the training were more likely to have a secure attachment style than those whose mothers did not (van den Boon, 1994, 1995). Another study found that when mothers think of their babies as unique individuals with emotional lives and not just as creatures with urgent physical needs, their infants end up more securely attached (Meins, 2003; Meins et al., 2001).

Does a baby's attachment style have any influence on their subsequent development? The jury is still out on that question. Children who are securely attached as infants do better than children who are not securely attached on a wide variety of measures, from the quality of their social relationships (Schneider et al., 2001; Steele et al., 1999; Vondra et al., 2001) to their academic achievement (Jacobson and Hoffman, 1997). Bretherton (1985) proposed that this is because children apply the working models they developed as infants to their later relationships with teachers and friends, which is to say that attachment style causes securely attached infants to become more successful children and adults (Sroufe et al., 1990). One US study showed that at age 10, children who were securely attached infants were more sociable at summer camp, formed more friends, and were more self-confident and less dependent on others, according to other campers and camp counsellors. Five years later at a reunion camp, they were still the more sociable (Sroufe et al., 1999). But other psychologists argue that attachment style is correlated with later success only because both are caused by the same environment, which is to say that sensitive and responsive carers are causes of the infant's attachment style and the child's subsequent success (Lamb et al., 1985). Others find no evidence that infant attachment styles predict adult profiles (Lewis, 1997). Because the data on the long-term consequences of infant attachment styles are mostly correlational (apart from the Dutch studies mentioned above), this debate will not be easily resolved. But it is not unreasonable to suspect that both arguments are right to some extent.

In concluding this section, the decades of research on attachment demonstrate that there are many factors that can potentially play a role in attachment style, including the temperaments of infant and mother, environmental circumstances and cultural influences. This complexity of factors suggests that attachment is and should be shaped by the environment. Natural selection should allow sufficient flexibility to adapt rather than specify one particular style and set of circumstances to produce different forms of attachment. This point was made by British ethologist Robert Hinde (1982, p. 71) in his summary on the field of human attachment research:

> We must accept that individuals differ and societies are complex, and that mothers and babies will be programmed not simply to form one sort of relationship but a range of possible relationships according to circumstances. So we must be concerned not with normal mothers and deviant mothers but with a range of styles and a capacity to select appropriately between them ... *Natural selection must surely have operated to produce conditional maternal strategies, not stereotypy.*

In summary, infants are programmed to form significant emotional attachments to their primary carers, although the nature of that attachment is influenced by a variety of factors. Some theorists believe that attachment styles remain consistent across the life span and different infant styles affect later adult sociability. Others emphasize the role of environmental differences found in culture in shaping attachment. Another set consider the role of the temperament of the child and how parents react to this as the main influence in social adjustment.

Development of social cognition

In many ways, the human brain can be considered a social brain, because many of the problems we encounter and solve are to do with thinking about other people and predicting what they will do next. In particular, we can understand others as goal-directed agents. Here, agent is not some employee of the secret service, but rather *a being that operates purposefully with intention to achieve outcomes in the world.* These intentions are the mental states of desires and beliefs – wanting something and expecting states of the world to be true. For example, an intentional agent may want a banana to eat (desire) and go to the fridge where they expect there should be some bananas that were put there yesterday (belief). This capacity to infer mental states enables humans to understand and predict the actions of others as goal directed. This is extremely adaptive, as understanding and predicting others enables us to interact with them socially. Imagine how difficult it would be to interact with someone who was unpredictable. In this section, we look at the emergence of social cognition, *the processes by which people come to understand others*, as a combination of skills including understanding others in terms of their goals and different perspectives and also the fact that sometimes others are mistaken in their beliefs.

AGENT A being that operates purposefully with intention to achieve outcomes in the world.

SOCIAL COGNITION The processes by which people come to understand others.

Discovering others as intentional agents

They say that imitation is the sincerest form of flattery, which may be one reason why young infants imitate adult facial expressions. Imitation is also an efficient way of learning from others and this capacity to copy becomes well established during the second half of the first year. Around the age of six to nine months, infants will copy novel actions of an adult, such as trying to operate a new object they have never seen before after a delay of 24 hours (Bauer, 2002) and as much as one week later (Meltzoff, 1988b).

Infants also increasingly understand others as motivated by intentions and goals. In other words, they see behaviour as being logical and so they are surprised when adults act erratically. In one study, infants saw two stuffed animals, one of which was a kitten. The experimenter stared at the kitten and said: 'Ooh, look at the kitty.' A screen was lowered and then raised again to reveal the experimenter holding either the kitten or the other toy. If the experimenter was holding the other toy, one-year-olds looked longer – indicating that infants appreciate that people's desires guide actions (Phillips et al., 2002).

This appreciation of intentionality is also important even when goals are thwarted. In one study, 18-month-old infants observed an adult trying to pull one end off a dumbbell toy, without success because their hand kept slipping off. Another group of infants observed a machine with pincers trying to pull the end off the same dumbbell toy and again failing. When handed the same toy, only the infants who observed the *human* pulled the end off the toy themselves, indicating that they had attributed intentionality to the person but not the machine (Meltzoff, 1995).

Moreover, infants do not simply copy what they see. In a clever study shown in **FIGURE 12.6**, 14-month-old infants watched as an experimenter activated the light box by bending over and touching the switch with her head (Gergely et al., 2002). This experiment was carried out under various conditions: sometimes the experimenter's hands were restricted by a blanket wrapped around her body, and sometimes they were not – and some infants saw her carry out the operation with *and* without the restrictive blanket, while others saw only the blanket-restricted version. When infants were brought back a week later, those who saw the experimenter switch on the light with her head *even though her hands were free* used their own heads to activate the switch. In contrast, those who had *only* seen the blanket-restricted version of the operation simply switched the light on with their hands.

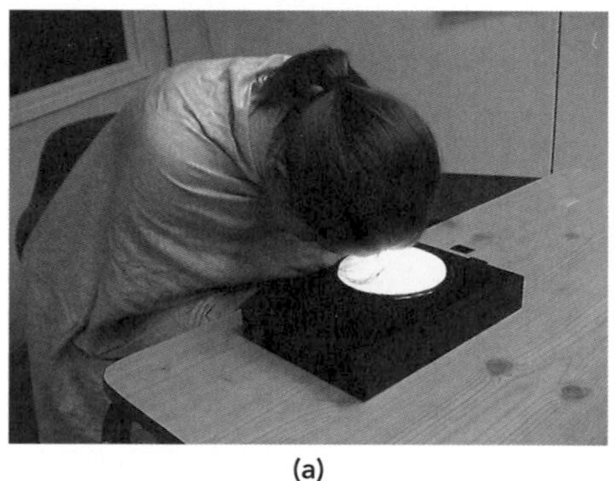

(a)

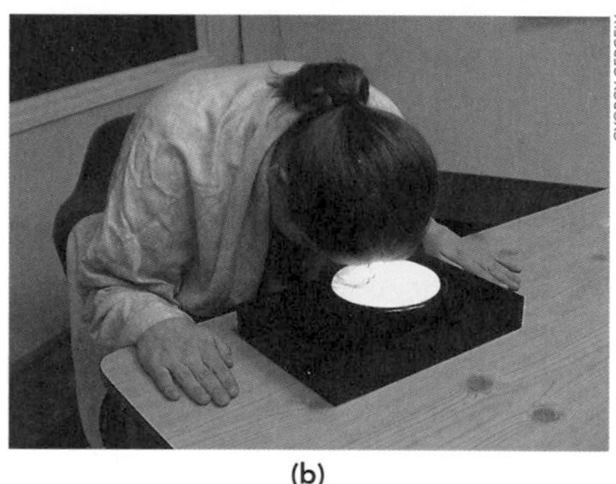

(b)

GYORGY GERGELY

FIGURE 12.6 Light box experiment Infants watched an adult activate a light switch with their forehead either with her hands bound (a) or free (b). Only in condition (b) did the infants activate the switch with their own forehead.

What does this tell us about what was going on in the infants' minds? Well, those who had seen the restricted *and* the non-restricted version of the experiment assumed that the head action was *necessary* to work the light box, otherwise, why wouldn't the experimenter just have used her hands when they were free? However, infants who had seen the experimenter *only* while restricted by the blanket assumed that the experimenter had to use her head because her hands weren't available. In other words, the infants in both experiments were not copying the experimenter's actions per se, but rather seeing them as directed towards achieving an intentional goal that required evaluating the constraints of the situation.

Older children will copy adults' actions even when the children know the actions are pointless. In one study, preschoolers watched an adult open a clear plastic box to retrieve a toy (Horner and Whiten, 2005). Some actions were necessary such as opening a door on the front of the box, whereas other actions were irrelevant such as lifting a rod that lay on top. When presented with these sorts of sequences, children copied the relevant *and* irrelevant actions, whereas chimpanzees copied only those actions that were necessary to solve a task. The apes behaved in a way that was directed towards the goal of retrieving the reward, whereas for children, the goal was to faithfully copy the adult. Why would children overimitate a pointless action? For the simple reason that children are more interested in fitting in socially with the adult than learning how to solve the task in the best possible way (Lyons et al., 2007). Developmental psychologist Cristine Legare thinks that such blind imitation in children is the precursor of later adult rituals – activities with symbolic significance that demonstrate that members of a group have shared values that bind them together (Legare and Hermann, 2013).

Sometimes, however, we mistakenly attribute intentionality to nonhuman objects when they display behaviours that seem humanlike. (As we saw in Chapter 8, this attribution is known as 'anthropomorphism'.) For example, in a study of joint attention, 12- and 15-month-olds were presented with a faceless, furry box that was remotely controlled by experimenters to respond either contingently (in a synchronized way) or noncontingently to their behaviour. The robotic box then rotated in a certain direction, as if to look at something, and the experimenters observed whether or not the infants followed its gaze. If the box had responded contingently to the infants' behaviour, they were significantly more likely to turn in the same direction when it turned than if the box had responded noncontingently (Johnson et al., 1998). In this way, contingent behaviour from the box had generated joint attention! Robots that behave contingently with infants by simply looking at them are also treated as if they have minds and will be imitated (Itakura et al., 2008). So, while the dumbbell experiment shows that infants understand human beings as motivated by intentions, the robot studies show that so long as objects engage with the infant in a way that could be considered social, they are treated as if they have minds.

Early social interaction as pedagogy

Hungarian infant psychologists Gergely Csibra and György Gergely have argued that the repertoire of infants' early social interaction is best understood from a perspective of pedagogy – *the transfer of knowledge primarily for the purpose of teaching*. As the world is complex, natural selection has favoured behaviours that increase the likelihood that infants will pick up relevant information from adults who know more. This is a two-way process, requiring attentive infants but also receptive adults who can direct the infant to relevant information. For example, adults often adopt ostentatious behaviours with exaggerated movements, expressions and sounds to attract the infant's attention, such as motherese – *that high-pitched, musical voice that adults make when communicating with infants* (Fernald, 1991). Infants are much more likely to attend to motherese even when spoken in a foreign language they have never heard before (Werker et al., 1994). Likewise, infants are much more likely to imitate when adults capture the infant's attention initially. For example, in the light switch imitation study described above (Gergely et al., 2002), if the adult did not engage the infants' attention by looking at them first, then the infants did not imitate the adult's behaviour. From the infants' point of view, activating light switches with the head was clearly not an important thing for them to learn. Pedagogy provides a useful framework when considering what behaviours are best adapted for early social interaction (Csibra and Gergely, 2006).

PEDAGOGY The transfer of knowledge primarily for the purpose of teaching.

MOTHERESE That high-pitched, musical voice that adults make when communicating with infants.

Discovering other minds

By the end of their second year, children grasp that people not only have desires, but that these may differ from their own. For example, two-year-olds understand that characters in stories may have different preferences from their own, so in a story, a character may want to play with a doll, even if the child themselves prefers to play with a truck (or vice versa) (Gopnik and Slaughter, 1991). Children can even infer preferences from nonverbal responses. For example, when 18-month-olds see an adult express disgust while eating a food they themselves enjoy, they hand the adult a different food, as if they understand that different people have different tastes (Repacholi and Gopnik, 1997).

While two-year-old children may appreciate that others have individual desires that motivate their behaviour, they have trouble understanding that others have mental states or beliefs. For example, children were told a story about a character 'Sam', who believed that there were bananas in the cupboard but none in the fridge. Children were then told that, in fact, there were bananas in the cupboard and the fridge, yet they were not surprised when Sam looked in the fridge for bananas (Wellman and Woolley, 1990). So, it seems that two-year-olds are not able to recognize that others have beliefs that are mental representations about the world, which should guide their behaviour.

©ISTOCKPHOTO/KHALUS IVAN

Children involved in 'pretend play' must be able to have multiple representations of different objects. For example, the child in this photo knows that the banana is *really* a banana but understands that for himself and others it can *also* be a telephone. Pretend play is an important step in developing the capacity to think about other people's thoughts.

Although imitation, joint attention and even understanding someone's food preferences are abilities that seem to tap into thinking about thoughts, you could still do these things without fully understanding what was on someone else's mind. Before they can reach the stage of understanding others as guided by independent thoughts, children have to develop the capacity for metarepresentation – *thinking about thoughts*. Scottish psychologist Alan Leslie (1987) argues that before children can really appreciate and understand the thoughts of others, they must first be able to think about their own thoughts. For Leslie, the development of 'pretend' play, that is, play that involves pretending something is actually something else, is an important stage in this process, as it depends on the ability to have flexible metarepresentations. For example, a banana can be used in pretend play as a telephone if it is held up to the head and you speak into it as if having a conversation. When a child pretends the banana is a telephone, they and the others around them understand what the banana *really* is, and what the child *intends* it to be. To do this, the child must suspend or 'quarantine' the representation of the banana as a fruit in order to represent it as a household appliance instead. So, children involved in 'pretending' games must have *multiple* representations of a single object, allowing them to entertain make-believe worlds. As we will see next, this flexibility of thought requires the ability to take a different perspective.

METAREPRESENTATION Thinking about thoughts.

MENTAL PERSPECTIVE TAKING Thinking about what goes on in other people's mind.

Egocentrism

One of the problems of appreciating another's mental state is that it requires you to ignore your own. Piaget argued that preoperational children don't fully grasp the fact that other people have minds that may represent the same objects in different ways from their own. In other words, young children have problems in mental perspective taking – *understanding someone else's point of view*. For example, Piaget and Inhelder (1956) showed young children a model of three mountains of different sizes with distinct landmarks and asked them to have a good look at it. Once they had done this, they were seated and a doll was placed on the opposite side of the model to the child. The child was then asked to identify a photograph of what the doll on the opposite side of the table was seeing. Children of three to four years of age typically chose a picture taken from their own perspective. Hence, they generally expect others to see the world as they do. In later studies, children who typically fail the three mountains task can successfully hide a doll from the view of a 'policeman' doll, suggesting that it is not that three- and four-year-olds are incapable of taking another's perspective, but they are inclined to their own view if the task is too difficult (Donaldson, 1978). This egocentrism – *the tendency to adopt a self-centred viewpoint* – does not mean that children are being inconsiderate, they simply find it difficult to represent another person's perspective. The experiment with the mountains investigates the ability to view physical, spatial things from another's perspective, but it is not only spatial perspective taking that is egocentric. Communication can also seem self-centred. Preschool children typically talk past each other:

EGOCENTRISM The tendency to adopt a self-centred viewpoint.

'I have a tricycle'
'So what ... I am going to grow up to be a policeman'
'It is blue'
'I want to be just like my dad'

PHOTODISC/GETTY IMAGES

Because children are egocentric, they think that others see what they see. When small children are told to hide, they sometimes cover their eyes. Because they cannot see themselves, they think others can't see them either.

Between the ages of four and seven, speech does become less egocentric but communication is still very one-sided. Imagine trying to describe an array of different objects over a telephone to someone who has to choose the same objects but can't see where you are looking. This is very hard for four- and five-year-olds, who are unable to consider another's perspective when communicating instructions (Yule, 1997). When children listen, they also fail to ask for additional information in order to solve such tasks. Difficulties persist until the end of early childhood and only by around nine years can children convey and ask for additional instructions to successfully complete this kind of communication task (Lloyd et al., 1998). (Arguably, of course, some of us never develop these kinds of abilities, and grow up in adulthood with a similar stubborn egocentric outlook on life, never asking for directions!)

Mind reading: theory of mind

You don't need to be psychic to read minds – you simply have to be a typically developed human who can easily interpret and infer what others are thinking based on their behaviour. We do it all the time when we try to understand and predict why people do the things they do and what they may do next. This includes appreciating that people may entertain a false belief – *a mental state of presumed truth that turns out to be incorrect.* For example, I may believe that my bananas are in the fridge even though someone moved then to the cupboard without telling me. As I hold a false belief, I should behave accordingly and look in the fridge when I want a banana. Understanding false beliefs is important for social development because it allows for a true appreciation of *intersubjectivity*, where one must be capable of understanding that others can hold beliefs they think are true but which are, in fact, false. We can easily anticipate someone else's behaviour based on true beliefs in a situation by simply predicting what the correct course of action should be. However, to comprehend why someone would do something incorrect, assuming they are not insane or unable to do the right thing, we understand that they must hold a false belief (Dennett, 1978).

FALSE BELIEF A mental state of presumed truth that turns out to be incorrect.

When children understand that people are intentional agents motivated by mental states, they are said to have acquired a theory of mind – *the understanding that human behaviour is guided by beliefs that may or may not be true.* This is a fundamental skill for *Homo psychologicus*, because when you can understand that others operate with desires and beliefs, you can anticipate what they will do next. A theory of mind enables us to outwit our opponents. We can rob our neighbour or steal their partner because they wrongly believe these things are safe. However, the same appreciation also applies to our own beliefs. We need to understand that sometimes we may be wrong.

THEORY OF MIND The understanding that human behaviour is guided by beliefs that may or may not be true.

Researchers have investigated these mental representations by interrogating children about their beliefs before and after states of the world have changed. For example, in one study, they showed young children a 'Smarties' tube (a popular British confectionary) and then opened it, revealing that it contained pencils instead of sweets. Then the researchers closed the tube and asked: 'When I first showed you the tube all closed up like this, what did you think was inside?' Most five-year-olds were initially amused by the trick, said 'Smarties' and then predicted that other children who had not looked in the tube would make the same mistake (Gopnik and Astington, 1988). In contrast, most three-year-olds said 'pencils' and claimed they knew there were pencils in the tube all along and predicted that other children would also know that the tube contained pencils and not sweets. Three-year-old children are so egocentric that they assume everybody has the same knowledge state as they themselves have in the present moment: even their own past selves are like other people – they cannot imagine having been in a different state, and so they believe that their past self must always have known what they know now. An alternative explanation is that the child has the 'curse of knowledge' (Birch and Bloom, 2007) and is unable to ignore the current true state of the world.

Probably the most well-known and also one of the most studied experiments in the theory of mind research is the false belief task (Wimmer and Perner, 1983). Here, children observe a scenario typically acted out with two dolls ('Sally' and 'Anne') and narrated by the experimenter (see **FIGURE 12.7**). To begin with, they see Sally place her chocolate in a chest and then leave the room. Anne arrives a moment later, finds the chocolate, and then moves it to the sink cupboard. The children are then asked where Sally will look for the chocolate when she returns – in the chest where she had initially put it or in the sink cupboard where the children know it is currently. Most five-year-olds realize that Sally would search the chest first because, after all, Sally had not seen the chocolate being moved. But three-year-olds typically claim that Sally would look in the

FIGURE 12.7 The Sally-Anne false belief task Children are told that Sally and Anne live together (a) and that one day, Sally puts her chocolate in one location (b, the chest) and leaves. While Sally is out, Anne moves Sally's chocolate to a new location (c, the sink cupboard). The child is asked 'Where will Sally look for her chocolate when she returns?' (d).

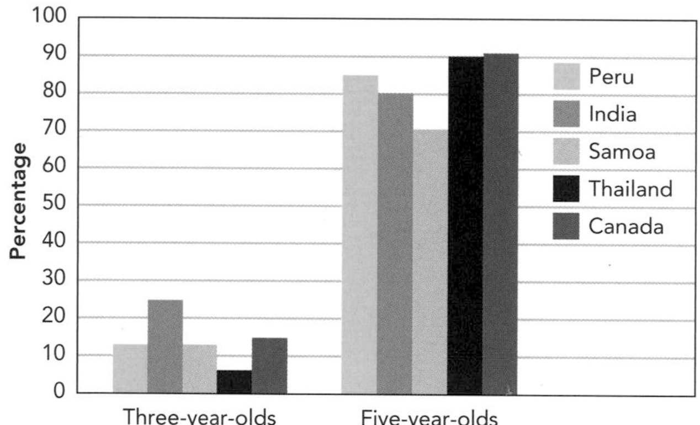

FIGURE 12.8 The false belief task across cultures A small percentage of three-year-olds and a large percentage of five-year-olds give the correct response in the false belief task. Research shows that this transition happens at about the same time in a wide variety of cultures.

T. CALLAGHAN, P. ROCHAT, A. LILLARD ET AL. (2005) SYNCHRONY IN THE ONSET OF MENTAL-STATE REASONING: EVIDENCE FROM FIVE CULTURES, *PSYCHOLOGICAL SCIENCE*, MAY 2005 16: 378-84, © 2005 BY (SAGE PUBLICATIONS). REPRINTED BY PERMISSION OF SAGE PUBLICATIONS.

sink cupboard because, after all, *they* know that's where the chocolate really is. Children all over the world pass and fail the false belief task at about the same age (Callaghan et al., 2005) (see **FIGURE 12.8**).

The false belief task is controversial as it gives rise to at least three differing interpretations. One interpretation is that the child lacks the competence to generate the necessary representations of minds that are central to solving the task (Astington and Gopnik, 1991; Perner, 1991). Other investigators claim that three-year-olds possess the prerequisite mental machinery to generate false belief representation but fail because the task demands competence in verbal skills and conversational conventions (Lewis et al., 1994; Siegal and Peterson, 1994). Finally, yet other researchers argue that the task places excessive demands on executive functions (see Chapter 11), such that children find it difficult to inhibit the tendency to say what they know to be true, namely where the chocolate is now (Carlson and Moses, 2001; Russell, 1996).

Many factors influence children's performance on the false belief test. A meta-analysis of 178 separate studies revealed five main factors (Wellman et al., 2001):

1 Children perform better if they are told the motive for Anne moving the chocolate, for example she may have been planning to trick Sally.
2 Children are more likely to pass if they themselves perform the action of moving the chocolate.
3 Children perform better if Sally's belief is explicitly stated: 'Sally thinks her chocolate is in the chest.'
4 Children perform better if the time frame of the events is emphasized: 'When Sally comes back, where will she look *first* for her chocolate?'
5 Children are much better on the task if the chocolate is eaten in the story, thereby removing it as a focus of attention.

As with many tasks that seem to bamboozle children, changing the way you ask the question or perform the task can affect performance. In many ways, the work on the false belief task echoes the same arguments that were raised about the performance–competence distinction for reasoning about objects in Chapter 11. Remember, Piaget argued that infants who failed to search for hidden objects had not yet developed the concept of object permanence, but subsequent experiments, for example the magic trick with the drawbridge, revealed that, in fact, they did appreciate the permanence of objects because they looked longer at impossible outcomes. Interestingly, 15-month-old infants also look longer at a violation of expectancy version of the Sally-Anne task when an adult does not behave in accordance with a false belief (Onishi and Baillargeon, 2005). Infants look longer when an adult goes to search in a new location even though they did not see the object move from the old location. It is not an impossible event as such, just not expected if the adult did not know the object had moved.

Piaget would have been amazed at children's performances on the false belief task, as he would have predicted that they were still egocentric at this age. Perner (1991) thinks that children do not yet possess the capacity to represent what others are thinking until somewhere between three and four years of age. How, then, do we interpret infants' performance on violation of expectancy versions of the experiment? Leslie (1994) would argue that, in fact, infants already possess built-in mechanisms for attributing mental states to others and that failure on the false belief task was simply a performance limitation similar to the distinction between competence and performance we encountered with search failures in Chapter 11.

One approach to investigate this performance limitation has been to use a 'false photograph' task, which has the same 'competing representations' issue as the Sally-Anne task, but does not require the child to think about mental states or beliefs. Zaitchik (1990) used two popular US TV characters, 'Bert' and 'Ernie' from *Sesame Street*, and got them to take photographs of their favourite rubber duck at various locations with an instamatic Polaroid camera. After photographing the rubber duck on the bed, Ernie moved the duck to a new location before the film developed. The child was then asked: 'In the picture, where is the rubber duck?' Zaitchik found that three- and four-year-olds performed at chance on this task, not knowing for certain what the correct answer was. From this, she concluded that it is not the failure to represent mental states *in others* that causes children to struggle with the false belief task. Instead, the findings of her experiment seem to suggest that children struggle with *any* competing representations. In other words, any situation where the state of affairs has changed sets up possible alternative answers that confuse young children.

However, the rubber duck study compared different children of different ages. Within-subject design studies that compare the same child on both tasks reveal that three-year-olds still find the false belief task harder, with 76% passing the false photograph task compared to 32% on the false belief task (Slaughter, 1998). One possibility is that mental representations as compared to pictorial representations are just that much harder for young children. This is supported by the discovery that language seems to be the most important factor in determining performance on theory of mind tasks (Astington and Baird, 2005). The way that carers talk to children is a good predictor of their success at these tests. Children whose carers frequently talk about thoughts and feelings tend to be good at understanding beliefs and belief-based emotions. Some psychologists speculate that children benefit from hearing psychological words such as *want*, *think*, *know* and *sad*; others suggest that children benefit from the grammatically complex sentences that typically contain these psychological words; and some believe that carers who use psychological words are also more effective in getting children to reflect on mental states. This is one reason why children with autism who are language impaired are believed to perform poorly on theory of mind tasks (see *the real world* box). Children's language skills are an excellent predictor of how well they perform on false belief tests, such as the one in which Sally looks for her chocolate, and for normal and autistic children, the likelihood of correctly completing this test increases with verbal ability (Happé, 1995).

This emphasis on language and social cognition would also explain why deaf children, who are born to hearing parents who do not know sign language, also seem to lag behind their peers in acquiring a theory of mind. These children are slow to learn to communicate because they do not have ready access to any form of conventional language, and this restriction seems to slow the development of their understanding of false beliefs even at 5 or 6 years of age (DeVilliers, 2005; Peterson and Siegal, 1998). Deaf children aged

the real world

Autism: mindblindness

In this chapter we have considered how typical children develop into *Homo psychologicus* by paying special attention to others, interacting with them, forming relationships, interpreting their goals, and ultimately understanding others as individuals who have their own minds. This leads to the typical development of a socially independent individual capable of negotiating the hazards of the complex social world.

However, not all children achieve this level of social competence. At least 1 in 2,500 children (and possibly even higher with recent studies) develop autism – *a complex neurodevelopmental disorder characterized by three primary features:*

1. *abnormalities in verbal and nonverbal communication*, such as delay or total lack of spoken language with no attempt to communicate through gestures
2. *repetitive or stereotyped activities*, such as preoccupation with restricted interests and often with ritualistic routines
3. *profound difficulties in reciprocal social interaction*, such as a lack of social interaction and an inability to read eye gaze, facial expressions and other nonverbal indicators of mental states.

Cambridge psychologist Simon Baron-Cohen (1995) calls this lack of social competence 'mindblindness', following from the title of Alison Gopnik's (1993, p. 5) terrifying vision of what it must be like to have autism at a dinner party:

> Around me bags of skin are draped over chairs, and stuffed into pieces of cloth, they shift and protrude in unexpected ways … Two dark spots near the top of them swivel restlessly back and forth. A hole beneath the spots fills with food and from it comes a stream of noises. Imagine that the noisy skin-bags suddenly moved towards you, and their noises grew loud, and you had no idea why, no way of explaining them or predicting what they would do next.

Without the capacity to understand and read others as intentional agents, the social world must be confusing and scary, which may be why autistic individuals refrain from social encounters they find frightening. Baron-Cohen argues that autism is caused by an impaired theory of mind. In particular, those with autism do not seem to understand that other people can have false beliefs (Baron-Cohen et al., 1985), belief-based emotions (Baron-Cohen, 1991a), or self-conscious emotions such as embarrassment and shame (Heerey et al., 2003). They also do not engage in normal joint attention or point declaratively (Baron-Cohen, 1991b). While the profile of social impairment fits with a deficit theory of mind, the main problem with this account is that it does not explain many stereotyped and repetitive behaviours that form one significant component of the disorder.

In contrast to their social impairments, individuals with autism can have relatively good memory, visuospatial skills, musical and artistic ability and in some rare instances are savants – individuals who excel well beyond most typical levels of performance (Frith, 2003). However, for most individuals with autism, the prognosis is not good.

A milder form of autism is Asperger's syndrome, in which individuals may have the social impairment found with autism, but not the language and cognitive impairment. Together, both come under the heading of *autism spectrum disorder* (ASD) – a term used to indicate wide variation in IQ, language and behavioural symptoms. ASD is present in 1 in every 100 births in the UK (Baird et al., 2006). Autism is usually diagnosed around three to four years of age, whereas Asperger's syndrome is diagnosed somewhat later, around seven to eight years. Autism and ASD are more common in boys compared to girls, and the fact that the rates are higher in identical compared to non-identical twins is evidence for a genetic component (Bailey et al., 1995), but, as yet, the main causes for both disorders remain unknown.

The first diagnosis of autism occurs at a time when many children are being immunized in preparation for schooling. In what is now regarded as a medical scandal, a study published in 1998 reported a link between autism and the administration of the triple vaccine for mumps, measles and rubella (the 'MMR' jab) in 12 children. This sparked a media frenzy and panic about the MMR vaccine that led to many parents refusing to have their children vaccinated or opting for the supposedly less dangerous single dose approach, where each vaccine was administered individually. This scare was compounded by Prime Minister Tony Blair's refusal to say at the time whether his new son Leo had been given the triple vaccine. The original study reporting the link has subsequently been discredited and refuted by larger epidemiological studies that show no increased risk of autism with the triple vaccine (Madsen et al., 2002). However, according to the most recent report from Public Health England, there continues to be a significant rise in the incidence of measles and mumps as a result of a generation of unvaccinated children (PHE, 2014).

AUTISM A complex neurodevelopmental disorder characterized by three primary features: abnormal communication, stereotyped behaviours and impaired social interaction.

5–11 years given the false photograph task and the standard false belief task had no difficulty with the photograph task but performed significantly worse on the false belief task just like 3-year-olds (Peterson and Siegal, 1998). However, deaf children of deaf parents raised in a household where they are taught sign language early on develop a theory of mind at roughly the same time as typical children (Woolfe et al., 2002). This indicates that communication – and especially communication about thoughts and feelings – is an important tool for helping children to make sense of their own and others' minds (Harris et al., 2005).

In summarizing the vast amount of research on the false belief task, Flavell and Miller (1998, p. 874) reached the following moderate position on the topic:

> Many young 3-year-olds probably do have some beginning understanding, but this understanding is severely limited in several respects. It is fragile, with its expression easily impeded by information processing, and other limitations … It is probably rarely accessed spontaneously in the child's everyday, extra-laboratory life … Finally, the understanding itself may be different from what the older child possesses – more implicit, more procedural, less accessible to reflection and verbal expression.

It could be added that there is more to acquiring a theory of mind than passing the false belief task and there is more to passing a false belief task than a theory of mind (Bloom and German, 2000). Only when a child understands the concept of mental representation can they understand that different people – including themselves at different times – sometimes have different beliefs. Although most of us ultimately achieve this insight, research suggests that even adults sometimes have trouble believing that others see the world differently than they do (Gilovich et al., 1999; Royzman et al., 2003). It seems that egocentrism goes away, but that it doesn't go very far.

In summary, preschool children start to appreciate people as intentional agents, motivated by the internal mental states of desires and beliefs. However, they are still very limited in fully appreciating that others may have different perspectives from their own and that people can have false beliefs. Developing such a theory of mind is dependent on a number of factors, but familiarity with talking about mental states and reduced egocentrism are two important developmental changes that lead towards it.

Who am I?

When we think about ourselves, we have a collection of self-concepts – *thoughts we have about our bodies, our personality, our relationships and our beliefs*. The development of this idea of our 'self' is at the core of who we think we are and influences the way we live our lives and how much enjoyment and wellbeing we experience. We have seen that as children develop, they discover their own minds and the minds of others. But in many ways, we shape our sense of self by how we think we are perceived by others. As James Mark Baldwin (1897, p. 30) observed:

SELF-CONCEPTS Thoughts we have about our bodies, our personality, our relationships and our beliefs.

> The development of the child's personality could not go on at all without the constant modification of sense of himself by suggestions from others. So he himself, at every stage, is really in part someone else, even in his own thought of himself.

In this section we will consider the development of some of the components that contribute to the sense of self, including self-recognition, self-esteem, self-control, gender development, and the role of friendship.

Self-recognition

Initially, infants acquire a rudimentary sense of self as they begin to interact with and control actions in the world. Remember from Chapter 11 how Piaget regarded this discovery as a stage-like progression of understanding of the physical world of objects as separate and composed of independent entities. Initially, infants' sense of self appears to emerge as a consequence of predicting the movements of their own bodies. For example, by three to five months, infants have expectations about their own limb movements because they look longer at videos of their own leg movement as seen from a different perspective than their own, which may reflect surprise at seeing their left and right legs reversed (Rochat and Striano, 2002). Over the first six months, infants discover properties of their physical selves as distinct from those objects and people around them. They learn what they can control and influence, and what they should respond to (Thompson, 1998). For example, newborns will turn towards someone stroking their cheek. However, if the stroking is done with their own hand, they will not turn towards it – indicating that they can distinguish between self and external stimulation (Rochat and Hespos, 1997). Over the first year, they increasingly learn about the consequences of their own actions as a distinct individual acting in the world (Rochat, 2009).

BRUCE HOOD
This child has just passed the rouge test.

As we noted in Chapter 8, most infants don't recognize themselves in mirrors until around 18 months (Lewis and Brooks-Gunn, 1979). It's not that they don't understand mirrors because at 10 months they can turn round to look at objects lowered behind them when viewing the event in a mirror (Bertenthal and Fischer, 1978). Some 15-month-olds recognize themselves but only around 18 months do infants pass the 'rouge test', described in Chapter 8 (Asendorpf et al., 1996). The rouge test may not be so much a measure of self-recognition but when children become self-conscious about how they look to others. Developmental psychologist Philippe Rochat (2009) reasons that at 18 months, infants are not bothered about what they look like to others and so are not particularly concerned if they have a red smudge on their nose. Somewhere around the second year, children are more concerned with their appearance and how they present to others, which is why much older children in rural Kenyan villages fail the rouge test. They know they have something on their face, they are just not sure whether to remove it in front of the Western scientist visiting their village.

By the age of two, children can tell us about their emerging sense of self and begin using the personal pronouns, 'I, me, my and mine', when referring to themselves and 'you' when talking about others (Stipek et al., 1990). However, the preschool child's self-concept is still fairly restricted – 'I am two, I have a teddy, I am hungry' – and rarely concerns psychological traits or other mental states (Livesley and Bromley, 1973). At this point, the child is still very self-centred, with a limited sense of others around them.

Schooling and interaction with other children gradually help the child to redefine themselves in terms of the different social units to which they may belong, so that by around age eight, their self-concept may involve statements such as 'I am a cub scout' or 'I am a Manchester United fan'. This is when children start to form a sense of group or social identity where they see themselves as members of groups – a process we will consider in more depth in Chapter 14. Now the child has a much richer repertoire of self-descriptions, such as 'I am funny' or 'I am curious'. They are also much more competitive now and see their achievements in comparison to others around them (Pomerantz et al., 1995).

SELF-ESTEEM The sense of self-worth.

The emergence of a self-concept is strongly related to the development of self-esteem – *the sense of self-worth*. Harter (1999) has found that preschool children distinguish only two broad aspects of self-esteem: how good they are at solving problems or physical tasks, and how well liked they are. However, by around 11–14 years, self-esteem has become multidimensional, with overall self-worth evaluated by five dimensions:

1 scholastic achievement – doing well in school
2 social acceptance – being popular
3 behavioural conduct – not getting into trouble
4 athletic competence – being sporty
5 physical appearance – being good looking.

From the age of eight years, children increasingly become more accurate and realistic about where they rank in these different dimensions, but alongside this awareness, they also develop aspirations or ideals of where they would *like* to be. This can create a gap between the real and ideal self that creates problems of expectation (Harter, 1999). This problem can be compounded by the effects of social feedback from peers, parents and teachers. Those with high self-esteem tend to come from family backgrounds that are supportive and encouraging, which helps the child to think positively about themselves (Doyle et al., 2000).

In Western societies, we often lavish our children with compliments such as 'That's an incredibly beautiful drawing' or 'You are awesome!' Anyone observing US parenting cannot fail to notice the exuberant praise children often receive. This is because most parents (around 87%) believe that inflated praise raises the child's self-esteem (Brummelman et al., 2014a). However, Dutch researchers have shown that inflated praise works well with 8- to 12-year-olds who already have high self-esteem, but in children with low self-esteem it is counterproductive (Brummelman et al., 2014b). Children with low self-esteem given inflated praise on one set of problems subsequently avoid difficult tasks. One possible reason is that when children receive positive inflated praise, they prefer to avoid more challenging tasks that induce a fear of failure (see real world feature in Chapter 11).

Self-control

In order to integrate successfully into society, we have to be able to regulate our own behaviour. Very often social interaction results in a conflict of interest and will between individuals that must somehow be resolved. These coordinating abilities depend on self-control – *the general capacity to regulate thoughts and behaviours in the face of conflict*. As we read in Chapter 11, self-control develops significantly over the preschool years as reflected by increased executive functions that help to plan, organize and inhibit thoughts and behaviours. Individual differences in executive functions not only account for performance on various cognitive tasks, but also contribute to the child's social development. This is because one of the major hurdles in becoming sociable is exercising self-control and learning to be less egocentric. To be a member of a social group, you have to withhold desires and impulses to strategically negotiate with others. For example, if you are so self-centred as to ignore others, you will find it difficult to share resources such as information or even take the time to understand what someone else thinks. Without self-control, individuals would be in constant conflict fighting over resources.

SELF-CONTROL The general capacity to regulate thoughts and behaviours in the face of conflict.

At the core of self-control is the ability to inhibit thoughts and behaviours. Maccoby (1980) identifies four kinds of inhibition:

1. *Inhibition of movement:* small children find it difficult to stop actions once they have been triggered. So, almost unstoppable actions can be triggered by, for example, verbal commands, which is why children are so bad at 'Simon says' games.
2. *Inhibition of emotion:* children find it difficult to curtail their emotional outbursts, but they must learn to do so, particularly in social contexts when their outbursts might be deemed inappropriate.
3. *Inhibition of conclusion:* young children are prone to answer quickly before fully considering problems. (Note this is similar to the problems generated by intuitive theories raised in Chapter 11 where children respond with the bias before considering the alternatives.)
4. *Inhibition of choice:* young children find it difficult to delay immediate gratification in order to receive a better reward later (Mischel, 1968).

The delay of gratification task (Mischel, 1981) is a particularly revealing measure of self-control that also predicts how well a child will get on later in life (see **FIGURE 12.9**). Preschool children were presented with a tray on which was placed two delicious

(a) (b) (c) (d)

BRUCE HOOD

FIGURE **12.9 The delay of gratification task** The child is told that they can have one marshmallow now or wait until the experimenter returns when they can have two. The delay of gratification is how long the child can tolerate the absence of the experimenter before giving into temptation.

marshmallows. They were told by the experimenter as they left the room that they could have one now, but if they waited until the experimenter came back, then they could have two. The most impulsive children simply gobbled up the marshmallows without waiting, whereas those that could wait the longest managed to engage in other activities to distract themselves from the treat. Not only did these long delayers receive a better reward, but they were also found to be more sociable and clever than the impulsive children years later. Remarkably, length of delay of gratification at 4 years of age also predicted school performance at 14 years (Rodriguez et al., 1989) and later achievement at around 27 years (Shoda et al., 1990). Drug taking was also less prevalent in men who had demonstrated greater self-control as toddlers (Mischel and Ayduk, 2004). Even after 40 years, individuals who could not resist the tempting marshmallow as a toddler still have less self-control on a simple reaction time task where they had to suppress the urge to respond (Casey et al., 2011). Clearly, the capacity to exercise self-control is a valuable personal attribute that can be observed early in childhood and can predict one's future self.

Is self-control immune to social influence? Bandura and Mischel (1965) tested this in the classic delay of gratification study with a twist. First, they identified children who were impulsive and those with more self-control on the marshmallow test. Then they showed the children adults demonstrating the opposite response profile, that is, impulsive children watched the adult exert self-control and vice versa. What happened when the children were put in a choice situation again? Most simply copied the adults' behaviour, indicating that they take their cue on how to behave from adults.

Correlational studies also reveal that children's self-control is influenced by how their parents behave, but with one exception. Children from families with strict parents usually exhibit less self-control (Donovan et al., 2000). By being too controlling, parents are not allowing their children to internalize control (Kochanska et al., 2001). To foster self-control, parents must relinquish control and allow children more independence (Silverman and Ragusa, 1990). So, for independence to develop, parents and children must learn to detach their emotional dependence on one another. Attachment may influence the nature of the relationships children form, but they must also learn to stand on their own two feet and self-control is part of the package of skills necessary to negotiate an unpredictable social jungle.

Finally, the issue of trust must be considered when interpreting the marshmallow experiment. If a child is raised in an unpredictable environment where there is poor supervision and others who might steal their possessions or food, then the only guaranteed treats are the ones you have already swallowed (Kidd et al., 2013). If an adult promises but fails to give a sticker to four-year-olds in a drawing task, these children are less likely to delay gratification on a subsequent marshmallow task. So, the link between failure of self-control as a child and later delinquency and criminality as an adult may also include the lack of trust experienced at an early age as much as the biological factors that enable us to delay gratification (Michaelson et al., 2013). Children from broken, impoverished homes do not trust as much as those raised in more supportive environments. No wonder they will take what they can get because, for them, the metaphorical bird in the hand is worth more than two in the bush.

Gender development: boys will be boys

GENDER The set of characteristics that distinguish between males and females.

When describing ourselves, one of the first things we talk about is whether we are male or female. Our gender, *the set of characteristics that distinguish between males and females*, conveys a large volume of presumed information about who we are – whether we like it or not. However, no man (or woman for that matter) is an island. As a social animal, we have to fit in with those around us and that includes conforming to gender stereotypes in our culture. 'Sex' differences refer to the biological factors that divide males and females, whereas 'gender' differences refer to those differences that are the product of biological and cultural experiences. For example, boys are more likely to fight than girls, but this is due to a combination of biological predisposition and the fact that male aggression is generally more 'acceptable' in society (Munroe et al., 2000).

It has not always been the case that the fashion was to dress boys in blue and girls in pink. Up until the early 1900s, pink was considered a strong colour and blue was thought to be more delicate and feminine. In 1927, *Time* magazine wrote: 'In Belgium, Princess Astrid gave birth a fortnight ago to a 7-lb daughter. The cradle … had been optimistically outfitted in pink, the color for boys, that for a girl being blue.'

Children have an awareness of their own gender from around two years of age: we know this because at the age of two, three-quarters of children will identify themselves with corresponding pictures of other boys and girls (Thompson, 1975). By the age of four years, they appreciate that gender is usually stable across the life span and that outward appearances (such as clothing and length of hair) can be deceptive. Preschool children also attribute gender stereotypes to male and female, for example agreeing that girl dolls talk a lot, never hit, often need help, like to play with other dolls, and like to help mummy with the housework. Boy dolls like to play with cars, help their dads and act aggressively (Kuhn et al., 1978). By the time children reach six years of age, they think men are better mechanics and pilots, whereas women are better designers and secretaries (Levy et al., 2000).

In fact, gender stereotypes increase in rigidity between four and six years and then show a decline from six to nine years (Banerjee and Lintern, 2000). Why is this so? In Chapter 11, we saw that children operate with intuitive theories that are initially rigid and resistant to counterevidence. The same may hold true for naive theories about gender, in that children initially formulate an absolute rule about gender and possibly exaggerate it in order to clarify the distinction (Maccoby, 2002). Once children have established their own gender identity, they have a good idea of what it is to be a male or a female. This then allows them to accommodate more flexibility and exceptions because they recognize that they, like others, may possess exceptions to the general gender profiles, for example some girls like football (Signorella et al., 1993).

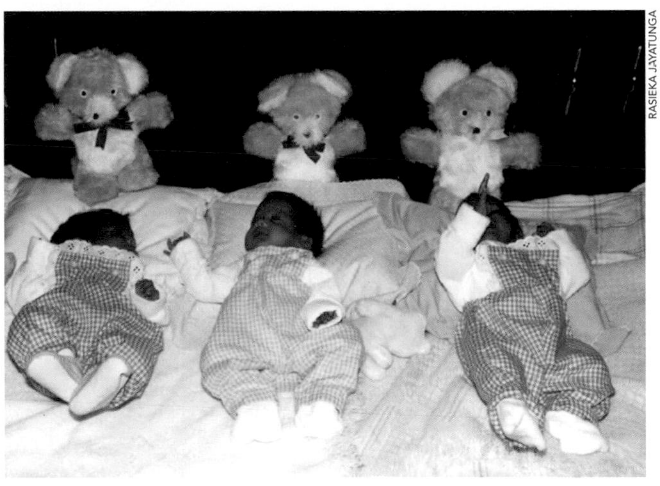

RASIEKA JAYATUNGA

Some gender stereotypes are universal while other attitudes are more specific, but all cultures have gender stereotypes that operate early in the home and are perpetuated during development. In the West, parents typically dress female infants in pink and males in blue.

Gender socialization

Some gender stereotypes are universal. For example, most cultures regard mothers as primarily responsible for childcare and preparing food (Rossi, 1997). Other attitudes are more specific, but all cultures have gender stereotypes that operate early in the home and are perpetuated during development. For example, in the West, parents typically dress female infants in pink and males in blue. (It has to be said that this is a reasonable strategy as it is difficult to tell the difference between male and female infants.) They prepare the bedrooms of their young children to conform to gender stereotypes (girls' rooms pink, boys' rooms blue) (Pomerleau et al., 1990) and buy them gender-stereotyped toys (dolls for girls and trucks for boys) (Fisher-Thompson, 1993). When they are old enough to be able to help out around the house, boys are expected to help wash the car or mow the lawn, while girls are expected to help prepare meals or look after younger siblings (Grusec et al., 1996). At 18 months, mothers tend to talk about emotional problems more often with their daughters than with their sons (Dunn et al., 1987) and on a visit to a science museum, parents were three times more likely to explain displays to boys than girls (Crowley et al., 2001).

Even something normally considered as non-social such as motor development can be influenced by parental biases. Boys outshine girls in a range of motor skills, but there are no reported gender differences in motor performance during infancy. However, when asked to estimate the angle of slope that their 11-month-old babies were capable of crawling down, mothers of girls underestimated and mothers of boys overestimated what their babies were capable of (Mondschein et al., 2000). Moreover, when asked to predict what their babies would attempt, mothers of boys predicted that they were more adventurous, indicating that parental gender biases can influence the sorts of expectations and circumstances that will influence motor experiences.

Even the way parents talk about boys and girls differ. Recall in Chapter 11 that essentialism is the psychological belief that there are inherent invisible properties that define the true nature of something. The same goes for language about, and related to, gender. Parents are often guilty of making gender essentialist statements that are generalized for the group as a whole. For example, 'Boys play football' and 'Girls take ballet' imply that these are essential qualities for the group. When reading stories to their toddlers, nearly all (96%) mothers were found to use such gender-stereotyped essentialist language, rather than 'Some boys play football' or 'Some girls take ballet' (Gelman et al., 2004).

You might think that the school classroom provides a more balanced environment, but even here, gender differences are reinforced. In mixed classes, boys are more likely to volunteer answers, receive more attention from teachers, and earn more praise for correct answers (Sadker and Sadker, 1994). Is it any wonder, then, that by 11–14 years, girls' academic self-esteem is significantly lower than boys (Kling et al., 1999)? And yet, according to the UK Office for National Statistics (ONS, 2007), girls outperform boys at all levels of education from primary school right through to university.

Gender differences

Despite common misconceptions, boys and girls are equivalent on most aspects of intelligence and cognitive function, sharing almost identical scores on IQ tests (Halpern, 2004) (see Chapter 9 for more about IQ tests). There are, however, differences in the developmental path for certain abilities. For example, girls are more fluent in language than boys as preschoolers but this difference disappears by age six (Bornstein et al., 2004). Boys, on the other hand, score higher on measures of spatial reasoning, a difference that appears during the preschool years and becomes more substantial during adolescence (Halpern, 2004). However, this difference is only found in some spatial tasks such as navigation (Kimura, 1999) and not others (Blakemore et al., 2009). Another common assumption is that males are better than females at mathematical reasoning, a belief that cost Lawrence Summers, president of Harvard University, his job in 2005 for publicly stating that women have less innate ability for science and maths than men. However, a meta-analysis reveals that the differences are, in fact, small (Hyde et al., 1990), with some studies showing greater mathematical ability in females during middle childhood (Willingham and Cole, 1997).

Baron-Cohen (2003) argues that there are real group differences between males and females due to biological factors related to levels of the hormone testosterone operating in fetal brain growth. Remember from Chapter 11 how the release of testosterone has a masculizing effect on fetal development. Baron-Cohen argues that male brains are more inclined towards activities that require systemizing, *analysing tasks in term of systems and patterns* governed by underlying rules, compared to female brains that are specialized for activities that require empathizing, *identifying another person's emotions and thoughts* and responding with appropriate social interaction. Evidence for his theory comes from studies that show that levels of prenatal testosterone predict male patterns of behaviour at four years (Knickmeyer et al., 2005). Also, girls with adrenal hyperplasia, which results in increased testosterone activity, are more likely to exhibit more 'tomboy' behaviour (Hines, 2004).

SYSTEMIZING Analysing tasks in term of systems and patterns.

EMPATHIZING Identifying another person's emotions and thoughts.

However, female empathizing may also be culturally reinforced from the very start as we interact with male and female babies in different ways. For example, one study found female infants engaged in more mutual gaze than males at three to four months, but no difference when they were newborns (Leeb and Rejskind, 2004). One intriguing possibility is that mothers tend to hold females infants in a face-to-face position, whereas male infants are held facing out towards the world (Malatesta et al., 1989). When adults think they are interacting with a male infant who is in fact a female and vice versa, they engage in more gender-specific activities (Will et al., 1976). Clearly, there is more to wearing pink and blue than fashion. As soon as we assign gender to a child, we start shaping our attitudes and behaviour to fit with the stereotypes that, in turn, perpetuate the gender myths.

On the other hand, it is also unlikely that all gender biases are entirely the result of cultural influences. For example, it is not just little girls who prefer to play with dolls. A 14-year study in Uganda's Kibale National Park found that female chimps play with sticks as if they were dolls compared to males chimps who treated them differently, suggesting that biological differences for nurturing behaviour that emerge first as play exist in other species (Kahlenberg and Wrangham, 2010). However, as we saw in the discussion on epigenesis (Chapter 11), complex behaviours often emerge as the interaction between biology and environment.

What are friends for?

For young children, including this little gang, sociodramatic play is an important part of friendship in early childhood.

Harlow's isolate-reared monkeys that we read about at the beginning of this chapter did eventually rehabilitate if they were reintroduced to others that attempted to socially engage. This finding suggests that peers can contribute to the social development of the individual even after an abnormal start (Suomi and Harlow, 1972).

Peers provide a unique social context, different from the parental framework, where individuals of similar age can develop a sense of identity as well as hone their social skills (Sullivan, 1953). When these relationships are positive, intimate and sustained, they become friendships. Friendships begin in late infancy after the first birthday (Howes, 1983) but typically being to flourish from around two years of age (Ross and Lollis, 1989). Here, we see the emergence of cooperative activities best revealed during play. As we saw with Leslie's work on metarepresentation, pretend play is a fundamental component of a shared perspective, as participants must suspend reality and engage in sociodramatic play – *games involving fantasy role-playing* ('I'll be the prince and you can be the dragon').

SOCIODRAMATIC PLAY Games involving fantasy role-playing.

Sociodramatic play requires reciprocity, coordination of roles and agreeing on rules, which, while present in young preschoolers, develops dramatically between three and five years of age (Rubin et al., 1999). In particular, it provides a forum for children to express emotions and discuss mental states. Children who discuss emotions with their friends develop a better understanding of others' mental and emotional states compared with children who do not share these intimate friendships (Hughes and Dunn, 1998). Some have argued that the mutual understanding and communication fostered by sociodramatic play is a crucial component in constructing the sense of self-identity (Singer and Singer, 2006).

In 2003, Cornwall couple David Pollard and Amy Taylor met in Second Life, a virtual world inhabited by millions of internet users. They even shared a virtual wedding before becoming hitched in real life. Online, Pollard was a sharp-suited, long-haired muscleman and Taylor was a slim, dark-haired young woman with a penchant for cowboy outfits. The trouble was that real life was simply not as satisfying as the virtual world, especially when Amy caught David's avatar enjoying an online affair with another virtual character in 2008. They divorced in real life shortly afterwards.

Even when children do not have playmates available, they can still have an imaginary friend or companion they can talk to or play with (Taylor, 1999). For many parents, imaginary companions seem so bizarre that there has been concern that such behaviour may be indicative of some emotional disturbance. In contrast, research shows that imaginary companions are extremely common. Marjorie Taylor has interviewed hundreds of children and found that 63% of children between three and four years of age have imaginary companions that were still reported when she interviewed the children later at seven to eight years of age (Taylor et al., 2004). There were no obvious personality differences between children who had imaginary companions and those who did not (Taylor, 1999). Furthermore, children with imaginary companions were not more withdrawn or socially delayed. In contrast, children who created imaginary companions were more likely to be firstborns or only children, watch relatively little TV, be more verbally skilful, and more advanced on theory of mind (Taylor and Carlson, 1997). All these factors make sense if the child has a lot of free time on their own without the distraction of TV and having the verbal abilities combined with a theory of mind to invent another persona. (The daughter of one of the authors used this ability to her advantage by always blaming her imaginary companion 'Donald' for any broken household items or missing biscuits.)

Sociodramatic play and imaginary companions may be common throughout childhood but both disappear around 10 years. Why? One suggestion is that children simply become more sophisticated as adolescents, seeking fantasy in books, TV and computer games (Thornton, 2008). Some adults even go as far as to continue pretend play by joining historical societies where they get to dress up in uniforms and re-enact battle scenes at the weekend. Other adults do this behind closed doors.

Finding myself: adolescent self-identity

'Who am I?' is a question asked by amnesiacs and adolescents, but they ask it for different reasons. Adolescents can typically remember their names and email addresses, but they are much less sure about what they want, what they believe, and what they *should* want and believe. The child's view of themselves and their world is tightly tied to the views of their parents, but puberty creates a new set of needs that begin to snip away at these bonds by orienting the adolescent towards peers rather than parents. Psychologist Erik Erikson (1959) characterized each stage of life by the major task confronting the individual at that stage, and he suggested that the major 'task' of adolescence was the development of an adult identity (see **TABLE 12.1**). Whereas children define themselves almost entirely in terms of their relationships with parents and siblings, adolescence marks a shift in emphasis from family relations to peer relations.

TABLE **12.1 Erikson's stages of human development**

Stage	Ages	Crisis	Key event	Positive resolution
1 Oral-sensory	Birth to 12–18 months	Trust vs. mistrust	Feeding	Child develops a belief that the environment can be counted on to meet their basic physiological and social needs
2 Muscular-anal	18 months to 3 years	Autonomy vs. shame/doubt	Toilet training	Child learns what they can control and develops a sense of free will and corresponding sense of regret and sorrow for inappropriate use of self-control
3 Locomotor	3–6 years	Initiative vs. guilt	Independence	Child learns to begin action, to explore, to imagine, and to feel remorse for actions
4 Latency	6–12 years	Industry vs. inferiority	School	Child learns to do things well or correctly in comparison to a standard or to others
5 Adolescence	12–18 years	Identity vs. role confusion	Peer relationships	Adolescent develops a sense of self in relationship to others and to own internal thoughts and desires
6 Young adulthood	19–40 years	Intimacy vs. isolation	Love relationships	Person develops the ability to give and receive love; begins to make long-term commitment to relationships
7 Middle adulthood	40–65 years	Generativity vs. stagnation	Parenting	Person develops interest in guiding the development of the next generation
8 Maturity	65 to death	Ego integrity vs. despair	Reflection on and acceptance of one's life	Person develops a sense of acceptance of life as it was lived and the importance of the people and relationships that individual developed over the life span

Two things can make this shift difficult. First, children cannot choose their parents, but adolescents can choose their peers. As such, adolescents have the power to shape themselves by joining groups that will lead them to develop new values, attitudes, beliefs and perspectives. In Chapter 14 we return to this idea that membership of groups is partly how we define ourselves in terms of identity. In a sense, the adolescent has the opportunity to invent the adult they will soon become, and the responsibility this opportunity entails can be overwhelming. Second, as adolescents strive for greater autonomy, their parents naturally rebel. For instance, parents and adolescents tend to disagree about the age at which certain adult behaviours, such as staying out late or having sex, become permissible, and you don't need a psychologist to tell you which position each party tends to hold (Holmbeck and O'Donnell, 1991). Because adolescents and parents often have different ideas about who should control the adolescent's behaviour, their relationships may become more confrontational and less close and their interactions briefer and less frequent (Larson and Richards, 1991).

But these conflicts and tensions are not as dramatic, pervasive and inevitable as many seem to believe. For example, adolescents tend to have aspirations and values that are quite similar to those of their parents (Elder and Conger, 2000), and familial bickering tends to be about much smaller issues, such as dress and language, which explains why teenagers argue more with their mothers (who are typically in charge of such issues) than with their fathers (Caspi et al., 1993). Furthermore, in cultures that emphasize the importance of duty and obligation, parents and adolescents may show few if any signs of tension and conflict (Greenfield et al., 2003).

As adolescents pull away from their parents, they move towards their peers. Studies show that across a wide variety of cultures, historical epochs and even species, peer relations evolve in a similar way (Dunphy, 1963; Weisfeld, 1999). Young adolescents initially form groups or 'cliques' with others of their gender, many of whom were friends during childhood (Brown et al., 1994). Next, male cliques and female cliques begin to meet in public places, such as town squares or shopping centres, and they begin to interact, but only in groups and only in public. After a few years, the older members of these single-sex cliques 'peel off' and form smaller, mixed-sex cliques, which may assemble in private as well as in public but usually as a group. Finally, couples (typically a male and a female) 'peel off' from the small mixed-sex clique and begin romantic relationships.

The celebrity culture where individuals spend so much time and effort trying to be liked and recognized by others has even infiltrated our schools. In 2008, the UK Association of Teachers and Lecturers reported that two-thirds of pupils aspired to be famous with no discernible talent.

Studies show that throughout adolescence, people spend increasing amounts of time with opposite-sex peers while maintaining the amount of time they spend with same-sex peers (Richards et al., 1998), and they accomplish this by spending less time with their parents (Larson and Richards, 1991). Although peers exert considerable influence on the adolescent's beliefs and behaviours – for better and for worse – this influence generally occurs because adolescents respect, admire and like their peers and not because their peers pressure them (Susman et al., 1994). Acceptance by peers is tremendously important to adolescents, and those who are rejected by their peers tend to be withdrawn, lonely and depressed (Pope and Bierman, 1999). Fortunately for those of us who were 13-year-old nerds, individuals who are unpopular in early adolescence can become popular in later adolescence as their peers become less rigid and more tolerant (Kinney, 1993).

Although we all ask the question 'Who am I?' at some point in growing up, or at least if we do not ask the question, we consider who we think we are from time to time, the answer appears to be one that does not just come from within, but can be found by looking at those around us. The sense of self is one that has been largely constructed by those around us, which explains why most of us care so much about what others think. This is because we are defined by others and are preoccupied with the fear of rejection by the group. Maybe that's why Philippe Rochat (2009, p. 224) recently commented: 'To be ignored and rejected by others is indeed the worst punishment and the worst suffering of all. It is psychological death.'

In summary, children develop a sense of self that emerges as they become more integrated and socialized with those around them. Initially, children use parents as role models to aspire to, with an increasing sense of independence as they grow older. Self-esteem is a critically important component of the self-concept and is particularly sensitive to external validation from others. Society is also influential in perpetuating stereotypes that the child assimilates. When formed, children initially have strong gender stereotypes that weaken later. During adolescence, self-identity is increasingly seen in the context of peers; however, adolescent and parental differences are not as intractable as generally perceived, with both parties sharing many common attitudes.

Moral development

Human society is founded on the principles of morality – *the rules that govern the right and wrong of how we should behave and treat others*. Not only do these rules form the basis of the laws that govern society, but they also influence how we feel about breaking them. Stealing is not only morally wrong but it makes you feel bad as well. This is the conscience that most (but not all) of us experience when we act immorally. Where does the sense of right and wrong come from and how does it develop in the child? In this final section of the chapter, we look first at the early emergence of behaviours in the child that are directed towards helping others as well as the different theories that explain how

MORALITY The rules that govern the right and wrong of how we should behave and treat others.

children develop a sense of morality. It would seem obvious that rules must be handed down from the law-makers in society and that we learn to be moral from observing how others behave. However, we also consider whether some aspects of morality may be *un*learned and we look at some remarkable new evidence that suggests that even babies can be sensitive to morality.

Prosocial behaviour: doing what's right

From the moment of birth, human beings can make one distinction quickly and well, and that's the distinction between pleasure and pain. Before babies hit their very first nappies, they can tell when something feels good, they can tell when something feels bad, and they strongly prefer the former to the latter. But as they mature, they begin to notice that their pleasures ('Throwing food is fun') are often someone else's pains ('Throwing food makes Mummy cross'), which means that doing what they please doesn't always please others. This is a problem. Human beings need each other to survive and thrive, and when people make others feel bad, then others tend to avoid them, exclude them or retaliate against them. To get on with others, we have to be prosocial.

PROSOCIAL BEHAVIOURS Voluntary acts that are intended to help others, such as giving, sharing, cooperating and protecting, which may have some potential benefit to the prosocial individual.

ALTRUISM A specific prosocial behaviour that helps others but without any necessary expectation of reciprocal benefit.

Prosocial behaviours are *voluntary acts that are intended to help others, such as giving, sharing, cooperating and protecting, which may have some potential benefit to the prosocial individual.* Altruism is *a specific prosocial behaviour that helps others but without any necessary expectation of reciprocal benefit.* Infants exhibit prosocial behaviour from around 8–12 months by offering to share objects with parents and peers (Hay et al., 1991). Arguably, this is an example of reciprocal play, where the infant expects others to return the favour. However, infants will even act altruistically to help others to attain their goals when there is no immediate benefit. In one study, an adult staggered into the room laden down with heavy books in both hands and headed over to a closed cabinet. Infants aged 18 months immediately recognized that this adult needed help and went over to the open the cabinet door without any instruction or coaxing (Warneken and Tomasello, 2006). They would also pick up an accidentally dropped marker pen for an adult. Even very young children are keen to help others.

Of course, these are overt acts of kindness but recent looking time experiments have revealed that even younger babies may know the difference between right and wrong. In one set of studies, infants were shown a cartoon where a geometric red sphere appears to want to climb up a steep hill (Kuhlmeier et al., 2003). At one point, a green pyramid shape comes along and pushes the sphere up the slope until it reaches the top. To most of us, this seems to be a case where the pyramid has helped the sphere up the slope. In a second scene, the red sphere is again trying to climb up the hill but this time, along comes a yellow cube that blocks the path and then pushes the sphere down the slope. The cube has hindered the sphere. Although these are simple animations of geometric shapes, we readily see them as intentional agents either helping or hindering. Just like you or me, the one-year-olds watching these sequences also judge the nature of each shape as good or bad based on the way it behaves. We know this because infants look longer when one of the objects switches 'behaviour' from being helpful to hindering. This is not just a simple visual preference for seeing something new, either. When later offered a replica toy of the helper or hinderer to play with, almost all babies choose the helper doll (Hamlin et al., 2007). Babies prefer to play with the Good Samaritan. These biases to be helpful and prosocial can become compromised as infants grow up into toddlers who have to compete for attention and resources, often outside the family home.

One might conclude on the basis of these early helping behaviours that children are naturally inclined to be kind to everyone but the emerging picture is much more sophisticated (Bloom, 2013). First, early prosociality is not indiscriminate. By 12 months, infants are exhibiting in-group and out-group biases or 'us and them' preferences (Mahajan and Wynn, 2012). Although, as noted above, infants will help adults, these examples may be more strategic as the adults are seen as potential allies (Bloom, 2014). Babies also respond positively to social approval. They may be motivated to help by the expectation of emotional reward and attention from others (Wynn, 2009). Of course, this interpretation applies to motivation in general, as adults will behave prosocially even in the absence of immediate reward through the internalization of societal norms by associative learning processes (Mead, 1934). Aside from spontaneous helping, children's earliest cooperation, comforting and sharing behaviours depend on adult communication before two years of age (Svetlova et al., 2013).

It is not until their second year that most infants display instrumental prosocial behaviours such as helping, sharing or comforting (Zahn-Waxler and Radke-Yarrow, 1990) and even then, this is directed mostly at known individuals. Children rarely spontaneously share or exhibit acts of kindness towards strangers until four to five years of age. Like infants, toddlers continue to demonstrate in-group biases and out-group prejudices. For example, three-year-olds regard others with shared toy preferences, food preferences or hair colour as more desirable playmates than those with different preferences (Fawcett and Markson, 2010). Even arbitrary differences such as the colour of a T-shirt can lead to discrimination, with a bias towards those wearing the same and against those with a different colour (Patterson and Bigler, 2006).

Developing self-identity is a prerequisite for prosociality towards others. It is notable that it is around three to four years of age when children begin to demonstrate a clear awareness that others have independent thoughts and attitudes, and children begin to become self-conscious, as indicated by the emergence of blushing, embarrassment, shame and guilt – all behaviours and states of mind that reflect a concern and awareness of other's social approval (Lewis, 1992). Toddlers with greater advanced self–other understanding exhibit more prosocial behaviour even when controlled for age (Brownell et al., 2013a). Two-year-olds who can represent their own versus others' actions in pretend play are better at coordinating and cooperating as well as taking an adult's perspective and understanding internal states of motivation and goals (Brownell and Carriger, 1990; Brownell et al., 2006). This perception of others is linked to developing theory of mind competence, as discussed above. Furthermore, toddlers who understand object ownership as part of self-identity are also more likely to spontaneously share without adult prompting (Brownell et al., 2013b).

Ownership

About 75% of young children's conflicts with peers concern possessions (Shantz, 1987). As soon as a toy comes into possession of another child, other preschoolers want it (Hay and Ross, 1982). When we take possession of objects, they become 'mine' – 'my' coffee cup, or 'my' phone. Possessions serve an important function as ostensive markers for self-identity and status, and the degree to which we respect ownership reflects our cultural and moral values.

In Western society, understanding and conforming to ownership rules is an important moral skill that can be traced to early childhood. Children as young as 14 months can name owners and their possessions (Rodgon and Rashman, 1976) and soon after, the emerging sense of self is accompanied by increased use of personal pronouns and ownership expressions related to objects (Levine, 1983). At first, children only enforce property rights for their own possessions, so that two-year-olds will protest if their stuff is taken away (Ross et al., 2011). By three years of age, children will intervene on behalf of another by telling a puppet to 'stop' if it tries to steal someone else's hat (Rassano et al., 2011).

What makes this interesting from a psychological perspective is that ownership has to be constructed from nonobvious properties (Gelman et al., 2012). After all, a stolen apple doesn't look any different from any other apple. So, the allocation of ownership has to be inferred based on various conventions. For most adults, the common convention today is to consider the default principle that objects are the property of *someone.* However, ownership can transfer through some form of transaction such as gifting, barter or sale. One important way to determine ownership is to consider an object's history. For example, children and adults attribute ownership of an object to the first person they see possessing it (Friedman et al., 2013). However, young children aged two to five years can understand that ownership is not wholly reducible to current possession (Eisenberg-Berg et al., 1981) and four-year-olds appreciate the concept of temporary custody (Meroni et al., 2007).

Another aspect of history that is important is the extent to which an object becomes owned through the expenditure of effort through creation or labour. When it comes to the trade-off between materials and creativity, preschoolers are more likely to attribute ownership to the one who did all the work and came up with the idea, whereas adults take into consideration who owned the original source material (Kanngiesser et al., 2010). Later, children start to understand the notion of intellectual property. In one study children were asked to make up a story and then an experimenter retold it to another, either acknowledging that it was the child's idea or taking the credit themselves. As early as age five, children disliked those who took credit after stealing their ideas (Olson and Shaw, 2011). Ownership must be reconciled with the need to fit in with others. Children have to learn to share and be reasonable about possessions because one cannot live a purely selfish life without running the risk of being rejected by the group.

Sharing

Young children are notoriously selfish. Although they spontaneously empathize with others' emotions, preschoolers will not willingly share their own food at lunchtime unless they have been specifically asked (Birch and Billman, 1986). They do understand that they cannot keep objects that belong to others but left to their own devices, young children tend not to share with other children (Gummerum et al., 2010). As many parents know, they have to be told to share (see hot science box).

hot science

A problem shared

As many parents know, toddlers often have to be told to share. However, when forced to cooperate, toddlers seem to understand the point of sharing. Pairs of three-year-old children were faced with a problem where both individuals had to jointly pull on two ropes to dislodge a barrier that released desirable marbles (Hamann et al., 2011). The clever trick was that the mechanism was rigged to give one individual a greater reward than the other, despite their joint effort. When this happened, the child who received the greater reward shared their winnings with the other child. If they had not worked together and the apparatus simply delivered an unexpected reward to one child, they did not share. In this cooperative situation, young children were willing to share just like older children. In contrast, chimpanzees hardly ever share. Faced with the same barrier problem but working for food instead of marbles, chimpanzees kept the reward for themselves, irrespective of whether they had help or not from another chimpanzee.

Whether we are inclined to share with others also depends on external circumstances. For example, in one remarkable study, children who had witnessed a devastating earthquake in the Sichuan province of China in 2008 were evaluated before and after the natural disaster on how altruistic they were (Li et al., 2013). By chance, the researchers had been collecting data in this region before the earthquake and noted that there were few differences between the six- and nine-year-olds on a variety of measures of altruism. However, the disaster threw these children into dire circumstances. After the earthquake, 95% were homeless, 37% had one parent who was unemployed because of the disaster, 8% had an injured member of the family, and 2% had a member of the family killed. To assess altruism, children were given a number of stickers in a sealed envelope and told they could donate some of their stickers to an anonymous classmate (Benenson et al., 2007). One month after the disaster, nine-year-olds were more altruistic compared to before the event, whereas six-year-olds were more selfish. After three years had passed, both age groups returned to their pre-earthquake levels of altruism. The authors propose that stress and negative events induce self-focused thinking in younger children, whereas older children become more empathetic (Decety, 2010), which is why they acted more prosocially.

It would appear that when young children work together, they share the fruits of their labour (see hot science box). Yet, only when they are older than five years will they spontaneously begin to share treats from a sudden windfall. With more socialization, children become increasingly sensitive to the inequalities that life sometimes brings and act more altruistically (Blake and Rand, 2010). This would be the noble interpretation. On the other hand, it may be that with experience, children learn that the social norm is to share because in all likelihood this will be reciprocated in future encounters. An even darker, more Machiavellian explanation is that people share or are generous in order to enhance their reputation in the eyes of others by appearing to be kind. Support for this ulterior motive comes from observations that adults are less financially generous when there is no audience to witness their donations or the amount they donate remains anonymous (Reinstein and Riener, 2012). It would seem that noble acts of generosity are intended to help ourselves more than help others. This is also true of children. When five-year-olds were presented with the opportunity to share stickers, they were decidedly ungenerous unless the recipient was present and the amount they shared was transparent (Leimgruber et al., 2012). Although there may be examples of prosociality in young children in experimental studies on sharing (see Chernyak and Kushnir, 2013), it is not clear that these examples are true altruism or rather sensitivity of what is expected when adults are present.

Some toddlers, on the other hand, seem defiantly antisocial. Four-year-olds who engaged in violent pretend play ('I've got some swords and you're dead!') were unresponsive to another child's distress during play and less likely to be empathic at age six when questioned about bullying (Dunn and Hughes, 2001). Aggression shows greater continuity across childhood and adolescence than any other facet of social development, which suggests that unlike prosocial behaviours, aggression may be comparatively resistant to the influence of others (Loeber and Stouthamer-Loeber, 1998). One intriguing line of research is the relationship between the executive function of inhibitory control and prosociality. Inhibitory control enables self-regulation, which is important for prosociality where it is necessary to forego or inhibit one's own goals in order to comply with the competing goals of others (Kochanska et al., 1997). However, parental influence in terms of discipline will modulate prosocial behaviour (Kochanska, 1997). As noted above, antisocial and aggressive behaviour in boys may be a combination of biology and cultural stereotypes, which points to the role of social learning that we consider next.

Social learning theory

The old saying 'spare the rod, spoil the child' reflects the common belief that discipline is critical to social development. Behaviourists argue that moral development progresses by reinforced learning, in that reward and punishment are used to shape the child's behaviour (Watson, 1930). However, for behaviour to be either reinforced or extinguished, it needs to first appear in the child. To address this, social learning theorists argue that children imitate and copy behaviour they observe from others in a process called 'observational learning' or modelling, which was described briefly in Chapter 6 (Bandura, 1977).

In a series of studies that have become landmarks in psychology, Albert Bandura and his colleagues (1961) investigated the parameters of *observational learning* – learning that occurs when one person observes another person being rewarded or punished. The researchers escorted individual preschoolers into a play area, where they found a number of desirable toys they could play with, stickers, ink stamps, crayons, all things four-year-olds typically like. An adult *model*, someone whose behaviour might serve as a guide for others, was then led into the room and seated in the opposite corner, where there were several adult toys. There were toy cars, a small mallet and a Bobo doll, a large inflatable plastic toy with a weighted bottom that allows it to bounce back upright when knocked down. The adult played quietly for a bit but then started behaving aggressively towards the Bobo doll, knocking it down, jumping on it, hitting it with the mallet, kicking it around the room, and yelling 'Pow!' and 'Kick him!' When the children who observed these actions were later allowed to play with a variety of toys, including a child-size Bobo doll, they were more than twice as likely to interact with it in an aggressive manner than a group of children who hadn't observed the aggressive model.

So what? Kids like to break stuff, and after all, Bobo dolls are made to be punched. Although that's true, as **FIGURE 12.10** shows, the degree of imitation that the children showed was startling. In fact, the adult model purposely used novel behaviours such as hitting the doll with a mallet or throwing it up in the air so that the researchers could distinguish aggressive acts that were clearly the result of observational learning. The children in these studies also showed that they were sensitive to the consequences of the actions they observed. When the children observed a model being rewarded and praised for aggressive behaviour, they displayed an increase in aggression (Bandura et al., 1963). However, if they saw that the adult model was later punished for the aggression, they did not reproduce the behaviour. This response inhibition is due to vicarious punishment – *the tendency not to repeat behaviours that we observe others being punished for performing.*

VICARIOUS PUNISHMENT The tendency not to repeat behaviours that we observe others being punished for performing.

FIGURE 12.10 Beating up Bobo Children who were exposed to an adult model who behaved aggressively towards a Bobo doll were likely to behave aggressively themselves. This behaviour occurred in the absence of any direct reinforcement. Observational learning was responsible for producing the children's behaviours.

So, the teacher who publicly disciplines the child in class is hoping that the others will learn by observation the consequences of similar behaviour (Bandura, 1965).

However, children are selective in who and what they model. First, they are more likely to model older, more competent individuals. Preschoolers are more likely to model the behaviours of adults who display prosocial behaviour compared to adults who are cold and distant (Yarrow et al., 1973). Models are most influential during the preschool years and children are more likely to behave prosocially if they were raised in a household with a consistent exposure to caring adults, presumably because they have internalized prosocial rules from repeated observation (Mussen and Eisenberg-Berg, 1977). There is some evidence of a correlation between the prosocial behaviour of fathers and their children but, surprisingly, no link with the behaviour of the mother (Eisenberg et al., 1992). This suggests that social learning includes a process of evaluation of who the other person is and the relevance of the observed behaviour based on expectations. In other words, children also think about the actions they see modelled. These sorts of findings led Bandura (1986) to refine his theory into a 'social cognitive theory', whereby observational learning increasingly depends on the basic cognitive processes of *attending* to others, *encoding* what is observed, *storing* that information in memory and *retrieving* it at a later date.

The observational learning seen in Bandura's studies has implications for social learning, the cultural transmission of norms and values, and psychotherapy, as well as moral and ethical issues (Bandura, 1977, 1994). Social learning theory also explains much of the gender socialization described earlier. For example, children pay more attention to same-sex adult models, imitate them more, and consequently remember better what they saw them do (Bussey and Bandura, 1992). A recent review of the literature on the effects of viewing violence on subsequent behaviour concluded that viewing media violence has immediate and long-term effects in increasing the likelihood of aggressive and violent behaviour among young people (Anderson et al., 2003). The American Psychological Association (APA) even issued a press release in 2005 stating that watching violent video games increased aggressive behaviour, thoughts, feelings and reduced prosocial behaviour. While these conclusions are consistent with Bandura's work, the findings are controversial, with many psychologists disagreeing with the APA statement. In 2013, an open letter signed by 228 scholars urged the APA to retract the statement on a number of grounds, including that the evidence was weak, unreasonably extrapolated from laboratory to real-life situations and inconsistent, with no consensus among researchers.

Piaget's position on knowing what's right

As a cognitive theorist, Piaget would have been less inclined to behaviourist accounts of moral development because he looked towards the mental operations that children must employ when reasoning about right and wrong. He spent time playing marbles with children and quizzing them about how they came to know the rules of the game and what they thought should happen to children who broke them. By listening carefully to what children said, Piaget ([1932]1965) noticed that their moral thinking changed systematically over time in three important ways:

1. Piaget noticed that children's moral thinking tends to shift *from realism to relativism.* Very young children regard moral rules as real, inviolable truths about the world that (like most truths) are communicated to them by authorities such as teachers and parents. For the young child, right and wrong are like day and night – they exist in the world and do not depend on what people think or say. That's why young children generally don't believe that a bad action, such as hitting someone, can be good even if everyone agreed to allow it. As they mature, children begin to realize that some moral rules (for example, wives should obey their husbands) are inventions and not discoveries and that groups of people can therefore agree to adopt them, change them or abandon them entirely.
2. Piaget noticed that children's moral thinking tends to shift *from prescriptions to principles.* In general, before they reach secondary school, young children think of moral rules as guidelines for specific actions in specific situations ('Children should take turns playing marbles'). As they mature, children come to see that rules are expressions of more general principles, such as fairness and equity, which means that rules can be abandoned or modified when they fail to serve the general principle ('If a child missed his turn, then it would be fair to give him two turns').
3. Piaget noticed that children's moral thinking tends to shift *from consequences to intentions.* For the younger child, an unintentional action that causes great harm seems 'more wrong' than an intentional action that causes slight harm because young children tend to judge the morality of an action by its consequences rather than by what the actor intended (cf. Yuill and Perner, 1988). As they mature, children begin to see that the morality of an action is critically dependent on the actor's state of mind, so an accidental wrong begins to seem less 'wrong' than a intentional one, even if the consequences are worse.

Piaget thought of moral reasoning as a skill, and he believed that its development was closely tied to other cognitive skills, such as the ability to think abstractly, to take another's perspective and so on.

Kohlberg's stage theory

Psychologist Lawrence Kohlberg (1927–87) picked up where Piaget left off and offered a more detailed theory of the development of moral reasoning. According to Kohlberg (1963, 1986), moral reasoning proceeds through three main stages. Kohlberg based his theory on people's responses to a series of moral dilemmas such as this one:

> In a country where citizens have to pay for healthcare, a woman was near death from a special kind of cancer. There was one drug that the doctors thought might save her. It was a form of radium that a pharmacist in the same town had recently discovered. The drug was expensive to make, but the pharmacist was charging ten times what the drug cost him to make. He paid $200 for the radium and charged $2,000 for a small dose of the drug. The sick woman's husband, Heinz, went to everyone he knew to borrow the money, but he could only get together about $1,000, half of what it cost. He told the pharmacist that his wife was dying and asked him to sell it cheaper or let him pay later.

> But the pharmacist said: 'No, I discovered the drug and I'm going to make money from it.' So Heinz got desperate and broke into the man's store to steal the drug for his wife. Should the husband have done that?

PRECONVENTIONAL STAGE A stage of moral development in which the morality of an action is primarily determined by its consequences for the actor.

CONVENTIONAL STAGE A stage of moral development in which the morality of an action is primarily determined by the extent to which it conforms to social rules.

POSTCONVENTIONAL STAGE A stage of moral development at which the morality of an action is determined by a set of general principles that reflect core values.

On the basis of their responses, Kohlberg concluded that most children were initially at the preconventional stage – *a stage of moral development in which the morality of an action is primarily determined by its consequences for the actor.* Immoral actions are those for which one is punished, and the appropriate resolution to any moral dilemma is to choose the behaviour with the least likelihood of punishment. For example, children at this stage often base their moral judgement of Heinz on the relative costs of one decision ('It would be bad if he got blamed for his wife's death') and another ('It would be bad if he went to jail for stealing').

Kohlberg argued that at about the time of adolescence, children move to the conventional stage – *a stage of moral development in which the morality of an action is primarily determined by the extent to which it conforms to social rules.* Children at this stage believe that everyone should uphold the generally accepted norms of their cultures, obey the laws of society, and fulfil their civic duties and familial obligations. They believe that Heinz must weigh the dishonour he will bring upon himself and his family by stealing (that is, breaking a law) against the guilt he will feel if he allows his wife to die (that is, failing to fulfil a duty). Children at this stage are concerned not just about punishments and prison sentences but also about the approval and opprobrium of others. Immoral actions are those for which one is condemned.

Finally, Kohlberg believed that some adults move to the postconventional stage, *a stage of moral development at which the morality of an action is determined by a set of general principles that reflect core values*, such as the right to life, liberty and the pursuit of happiness. When a behaviour violates these principles, it is immoral, and if a law requires these principles to be violated, then it should be disobeyed. For a person who has reached the postconventional stage, a woman's life is always more important than a shopkeeper's profits and so stealing the drug is not only a moral behaviour, it is a moral obligation. Kohlberg believed that people must go through these stages in this order because each requires a more sophisticated set of cognitive skills than the one before it. He also believed that different people take different amounts of time to move through them and that many people never reach the last one.

Research supports Kohlberg's general claim that moral reasoning shifts from an emphasis on punishment to an emphasis on social rules and finally to an emphasis on ethical principles (Walker, 1988). But research also suggests that these stages are not quite as discrete as Kohlberg thought. For instance, a single person may use preconventional, conventional and postconventional thinking in different circumstances, which suggests that the developing person does not 'reach a stage' so much as 'acquires a skill' that he may or may not use on a particular occasion.

The use of the male pronoun here is intentional. Because Kohlberg developed his theory by studying a sample of US boys, some critics have suggested that it does not describe the development of moral thinking in girls (Gilligan, 1982). Carol Gilligan argues that men tend to see morality in terms of justice based on abstract rules, whereas women are more inclined to reason on the basis of human compassion. If men are more rule based and women are more empathetic, then many women may not reach the third stage of postconventional morality. However, there is very little consistent evidence that men score higher than females on moral reasoning. One should also be cautious of gender differences based on studies that often invoke cultural stereotypes where men and women conform to expectations (Fine, 2010).

Kohlberg's claim that his stages of moral development are universal and shared by all children is more problematic (Simpson, 1974). Some non-Western societies value obedience and community over liberty and individuality, and thus the moral reasoning of people in those societies may appear to reflect a conventional devotion to social norms, when it actually reflects a postconventional consideration of ethical principles. For example, Indian children are more likely to regard helping others as a moral obligation rather than a personal choice, which probably reflects the difference between the

Western emphasis on individuality compared to an Indian emphasis on communal responsibility and sacrifice for others (Killen and Turiel, 1998).

Other critics have noted that while a child's level of moral reasoning is generally correlated with their own moral behaviour (Blasi, 1980), that correlation is not particularly strong. This is particularly true when the moral behaviour involves doing a good deed rather than refraining from doing a bad deed (Haidt, 2001; Thoma et al., 1999). For example, the child's ability to reason what's right (sharing their lunch with friends) does not necessarily predict that they will sometimes do something wrong (shoplifting). These critics suggest that how people reason about morality may be interesting in the abstract, but it has little to do with how people actually behave in their everyday lives. So, if moral reasoning doesn't determine moral behaviour, what does?

Moral intuition: feeling what's right

Research on moral reasoning portrays children as little jurists who use rational analysis – sometimes simple and sometimes sophisticated – to distinguish between right and wrong. But moral dilemmas don't just make us think, they also make us *feel.* Consider two scenarios:

> You are standing on a bridge. Below you can see a runaway tram hurtling down the track towards five people who will be killed if it remains on its present course. You are sure that you can save these people by flipping a lever that will switch the tram onto a different track, where it will kill just one person instead of five. Is it morally permissible to divert the tram and prevent five deaths at the cost of one?

Now consider a slightly different version of this problem:

> You and a large man are standing on a bridge. Below you can see a runaway tram hurtling down the track towards five people who will be killed if it remains on its present course. You are sure that you can save these people by pushing the large man onto the track, where his body will be caught up in the tram's wheels and stop it before it kills the five people. Is it morally permissible to push the large man and thus prevent five deaths at the cost of one?

If you are like most people, you believe that it is morally permissible to sacrifice one person for the sake of five in the first case but not in the second case (see **FIGURE 12.11**). And if you are like most people, you can't say why. Indeed, you probably didn't reach this conclusion by moral reasoning at all. Rather, you had a negative emotional reaction to the mere thought of pushing another human being into the path of an oncoming tram, and that reaction was sufficient to convince you that pushing him would be wrong. You may have come up with a few good arguments to support this position, but those arguments probably followed rather than preceded your conclusion (Greene et al., 2001).

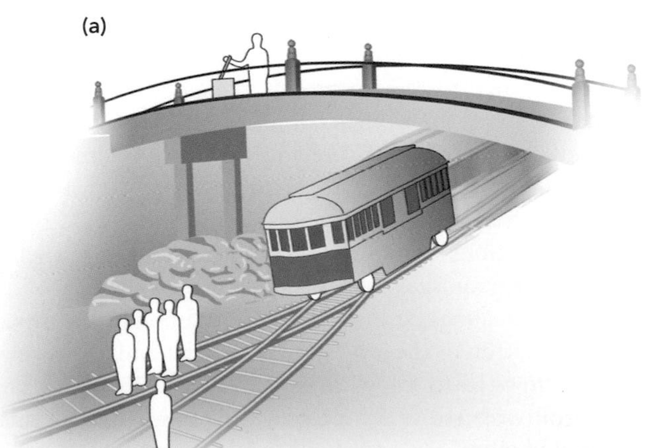

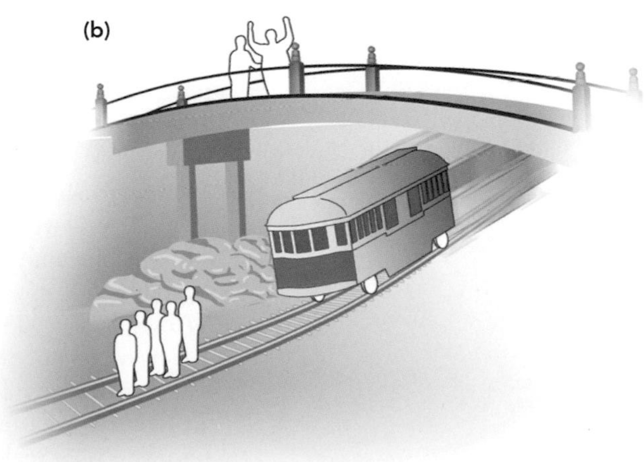

FIGURE **12.11 The tram problem** Why does it seem permissible to trade one life for five lives by pulling a switch (a) but not by pushing a man from a bridge (b)? Research suggests that the scenario shown in (a) and this emotional response may be the basis for our moral intuitions.

The way people respond to cases such as these has convinced some psychologists that moral judgements are the consequences – and not the causes – of emotional reactions (Haidt, 2001). According to this *moral intuitionist* perspective, we have evolved to react emotionally to a small family of events that are particularly relevant to reproduction and survival, and we have developed the distinction between right and wrong as a way of labelling and explaining these emotional reactions. For instance, most of us think that incest disgusts us because we consider it wrong. But another possibility is that we consider it wrong because it disgusts us. Incest is a poor method for producing genetically viable offspring, and thus nature may have selected for people who are disgusted by it. Our reasoning about the immorality of incest may follow from that disgust rather than cause it. Some research supports the moral intuitionist perspective. In one experiment, participants were hypnotized and told that whenever they heard the word *take*, they would experience 'a brief pang of disgust ... a sickening feeling in your stomach'. After they came out of the hypnotic state, the participants were asked to rate the morality of several actions, ranging from incest to bribery. When the description of the action contained the word *take*, participants rated the action as less moral, suggesting that their feelings were guiding – rather than being guided by – their moral reasoning (Wheatley and Haidt, 2005).

According to the moral intuitionist perspective, the reason most people consider it permissible to stop a tram by pulling a switch but not by pushing someone onto the tracks is that people have negative emotional reactions to other people's physical pain (Greene et al., 2001). In the pushing scenario, this pain is a *direct* consequence of action, whereas in the switch scenario, it is an *indirect* consequence although it is equally as causal (see Hauser, 2006 for a fuller discussion of this intriguing conundrum). This aversion to others' suffering begins early in childhood. When adults in one study pretended to hit their thumbs with a hammer, even very young children seemed alarmed and attempted to comfort them (Zahn-Waxler et al., 1992). These efforts are occasionally clumsy or inappropriate – for example a toddler may offer a distressed adult a teddy bear – but they suggest that children are moved by other people's pain. Indeed, even very young children distinguish between actions that are wrong because they violate a social rule and actions that are wrong because they cause suffering. When asked whether it would be okay to leave toys on the floor in a school that allowed such behaviour, young children tend to say it would. But when asked whether it would be okay to hit another child in a school that allowed such behaviour, young children tend to say it would not (Smetana, 1981; Smetana and Braeges, 1990). Indeed, young children up to age 10 say that hitting is wrong even if an adult instructs someone to do it (Laupa and Turiel, 1986).

Children clearly think about transgressions that cause others to be observably distressed (for example, hitting) differently from transgressions that do not (for example, eating with one's fingers). Why might that be? One possibility is that observing distress automatically triggers an empathic reaction in the brain of the observer. Recent research has shown that some of the brain regions that are activated when people experience an unpleasant emotion are also activated when people see someone else experience that emotion (Carr et al., 2003). (See the discussion of mirror neurons in Chapter 3.) In one study, women received a shock or watched their romantic partners receive a shock on different parts of their bodies. The regions of the women's brains that processed information about the physical location of the shock were activated only when the women experienced the shock themselves, but the regions that processed emotional information were activated whether the women received the shock or observed it (Singer et al., 2004). Similarly, the emotion-relevant brain regions that are activated when a person smells a foul odour are also activated when the person sees someone else smelling the foul odour (Wicker et al., 2003). Studies such as these suggest that our brains respond to other people's *expressions* of distress by creating within us the *experience* of distress, and this mechanism may have evolved because it allows us to know instantly what others are feeling. The fact that we can actually *feel* another person's distress may explain why even a small child who is incapable of sophisticated moral reasoning still considers it wrong to inflict distress on others.

In summary, as a social species, each child has to integrate into the rest of society by, first, developing a sense of their own self-identity and what is expected of them and, second, by establishing the moral guidelines for the group. While it might seem that these processes are entirely shaped by the environment, there is intriguing evidence for self-identity and moral reasoning that there are built-in processes that operate universally. Young children will spontaneously help others even when there is no obvious immediate benefit, suggesting that even in social development, nature and nurture work hand in hand. However, as they enter into complex social environments, they increasingly show evidence of biases towards those they identify with and prejudices against others. Some of these moral codes may reflect deep-seated prosocial mechanisms based on empathy but, in general, children become more sophisticated and strategic about those they help as they learn to encode the various cultural rules and norms of acceptable behaviour.

psychomythology

Teenagers take risks because their brains are immature

Adolescence is often portrayed as a time of raging hormones and temporary insanity. On the plus side, crushes will never be better and thrills will not be quite the same in adulthood. If you have read recent tabloid stories, then you might be tempted to conclude that teenagers are out of control because they have no frontal lobes to put a stop to impulsive behaviour. It is true that teenagers are twice as likely to be killed by taking unnecessary risks compared to when they were children (Dahl, 2001) and also that significant developments take place in brain circuitry during adolescence (Blakemore, 2012). However, the relationship between these findings is not likely to be straightforward (Casey and Caudle, 2013). What we do know is that teenagers take risks not because they cannot recognize the dangers or lack self-control, but to impress others. If you test them on computer driving games, there are no differences between 14-year-olds, 19-year-olds and 37-year-olds when tested alone (Gardner and Steinberg, 2005). However, when there is a group of their peers in the testing room, 14-year-olds demonstrate behaviour that is twice as risky, travelling at faster speeds and having a larger number of crashes. There is also a 50% increase in the risky behaviour of 19-year-olds. In contrast, adults showed no difference in behaviour when tested alone or with friends. Another reason why teenagers take risks is that thrills register with greater sensitivity in the reward centres of the brain, making it more likely that they will seek out more dangerous but reinforcing opportunities (Galván, 2013). Much of this reinforcement comes from one's friends rather than family, which is one reason why teenagers want to spend more time with mates and often behave very differently when out of the house. So, showing off is not so much a brain immaturity but a strategy teenagers adopt to win friends that gives them a greater buzz.

where do you stand?

Should unhappy parents divorce or stay together?

In virtually all societies, young adults leave home, get married and have children of their own. They may stay at home until the day of their wedding or they may live on their own for years, but by and large, most human beings eventually leave one family and start another. While parenthood is a genetic imperative to reproduce, marriage is a cultural invention.

But do marriage and children really make us happy? Research has consistently shown that married people live longer, have more frequent sex (and enjoy that sex more), and earn more money than unmarried people (Waite, 1995). Given these differences, it is no surprise that married people consistently report being happier than unmarried people, whether those unmarried people are single, widowed, divorced or cohabiting (Johnson and Wu, 2002). That's why many researchers consider marriage one of the best investments a person can make in their own happiness. But other researchers suggest that married people may be happier because happy people may be more likely to get married – so marriage may be the consequence, and not the cause, of happiness (Lucas et al., 2003). The general consensus among scientists seems to be that both positions are right. Even before marriage, people who end up married tend to be happier than those who never marry, but marriage does seem to confer further benefits.

Children are another story. In general, research suggests that children decrease rather than increase their parents' happiness (DiTella et al., 2003). For example, parents typically report lower marital satisfaction than nonparents, and the more children they have, the less satisfaction they report (Twenge et al., 2003). Studies of marital satisfaction at different points in the life span reveal an interesting pattern of peaks and valleys. Marital satisfaction starts out high, plummets at about the time the children are preschoolers, begins to recover, plummets again when the children are in adolescence, and returns to its premarital levels only when children leave home.

But around 40% of marriages in Europe end in divorce, according to 2002 statistics (Thornton, 2008). Although many children of divorced parents cope with the situation, others do less well at school, have psychological problems, lower self-esteem, and they themselves are more likely to get divorced as adults (Hetherington et al., 1998). Children who were between two and six years of age when their parents divorced grow up into adults who engage in more unsafe sex, alcohol and drug abuse, and a succession of unstable romantic relationships (Wallerstein and Lewis, 1998).

With these sorts of outcomes, one might immediately think that divorce is a bad thing. So, should governments legislate to make divorce more difficult? What do you think is more damaging – divorce or being stuck in an unhappy marriage for the sake of the children? What might the material and practical consequences of divorce mean for the child? Where do you stand?

Chapter review

Homo psychologicus

- Humans are particularly social animals, with an extended period of child rearing that appears to be tailored to learning from others and forming socioemotional bonds. These bonds are vulnerable to the effects of social isolation in the first year of birth but progressively less with age.
- Human newborns are attuned to others from the start and will preferentially seek out faces to interact with over the early months through social smiling and imitation.
- Early social interaction is mutual (dyadic) between infants and carers, but begins to expand to take in objects of interest for shared attention (triadic), thereby establishing social communication about the world. Infants also interpret other people's behaviour and actions as intentional and develop perspectives other than their own.

Attachment

- Around six months of age, infants show an increased emotional attachment to the primary carer and a corresponding wariness of strangers. Bowlby's theory of attachment advocates that this is an evolved mechanism that operates to maintain proximity between the infant and carer.
- Children have different styles of attachment, as revealed by the way they respond to Ainsworth's strange situation. These differences of responses reflect a combination of parenting style, cultural norms and the individual differences that are due to reactivity and temperament.
- Self-control exhibited at four years of age in the delay of gratification test predicts sociability, academic performance and adult adjustment many years later.

Development of social cognition

- From very early on, infants will imitate the actions of others, but, with development, increasingly infer these actions as driven by others' intentional goals.
- Much of this early social interaction can be considered pedagogical where the goal is to transfer knowledge through teaching.
- Although young children are initially egocentric, they increasingly understand that others have mental states of desires and beliefs that may differ from their own.
- Theory of mind refers to those skills for inferring mental states and beliefs that are the building blocks for metarepresentation (thinking about thoughts). Theory of mind may be a uniquely human ability and is conspicuously impaired in children with autism.
- Performance on theory of mind tasks is enhanced among children who are competent with language and familiar with discussing thoughts and feelings. It is impaired in children with poor executive control, suggesting that no one single factor explains what changes on these tasks between three and four years.

Who am I?

- Social development includes an awareness of self-identity, which is partly a reflection of how we see ourselves in relation to others. First we must learn to recognize ourselves as distinct, which probably occurs somewhere during the second year.
- Notions of self-esteem are initially very limited in preschoolers but become multidimensional by middle childhood.
- Gender identity results from a combination of physiology and environment, operating to reinforce cultural stereotypes at home and in the classroom. Cognitive differences between males and females may be more spurious than real, and are amplified by cultural expectations that widen the performance gap between boys and girls on stereotyped activities as they mature into adults.
- Friendships offer a special environment for children to interact and develop roles independently of adults. Games involving cooperation and coordination help to develop the social skills to understand another's point of view.
- Puberty and adolescence are marked by an increasing distance between the child and the parent in an attempt to define a unique identity, and an increasing reliance on peers.

Moral development

- Although spontaneous prosocial behaviour (where young children will help an adult) is evident during the second year of life, children are also influenced by watching and copying the behaviour of others.
- Cognitive theories of moral development identify different stages of reasoning about right and wrong that progressively shift from rigid rules at an early age towards more flexible decisions based on mitigating circumstances.
- Evolutionary psychology accounts of morality highlight the power of intuitive mechanisms for evaluating important dilemmas even though the individual cannot necessarily articulate the basis for the decision they arrive at.

Key terms

agent (p. 489)
altruism (p. 506)
attachment (p. 482)
attachment objects (p. 485)
autism (p. 496)
babyness (p. 479)
behavioural inhibition (p. 487)
Conlearn (p. 478)
Conspec (p. 478)
contingent behaviour (p. 479)
conventional stage (p. 512)
dyadic relationship (p. 480)
egocentrism (p. 492)
empathizing (p. 502)
false belief (p. 493)
feral children (p. 476)
gender (p. 500)
goodness of fit (p. 488)
imprinting (p. 478)
internal working model (p. 486)
joint attention (p. 479)
mental perspective taking (p. 492)
metarepresentation (p. 492)
morality (p. 505)

motherese (p. 491)
parental sensitivity (p. 486)
pedagogy (p. 491)
postconventional stage (p. 512)
preconventional stage (p. 512)
prosocial behaviours (p. 506)
protodeclarative pointing (p. 481)
protoimperative pointing (p. 481)
self-concepts (p. 497)
self-control (p. 499)
self-esteem (p. 498)
social cognition (p. 489)
social referencing (p. 481)
social smiling (p. 479)
sociodramatic play (p. 503)
stranger anxiety (p. 483)
strange situation (p. 483)
systemizing (p. 502)
temperament (p. 487)
theory of mind (p. 493)
triadic relationship (p. 480)
vicarious punishment (p. 509)

Recommended reading

Bloom, P. (2013) *Just Babies: The Origins of Good and Evil.* New York: Crown. Bloom is one of the most entertaining and yet authoritative psychologists writing books accessible for a general audience.

DeLoache, J. S. and Gottlieb, A. (2000) *A World of Babies: Imagined Childcare Guides for Seven Societies.* Cambridge: CUP. Explores cultural differences in child-rearing practices in seven cultures. Written as a series of fictional childcare manuals in the style of *Dr Spock's Baby and Child Care,* the authors use factual information from real sources as well as research by psychologists, anthropologists and historians.

Fernyhough, C. (2008) *The Baby in the Mirror.* London: Granta Books. Charles Fernyhough is a developmental psychologist of the Vygotsky tradition who also happens to be a talented essayist. He documents in detail his own daughter's early development with the eye of scientist but written with the compassion of a father.

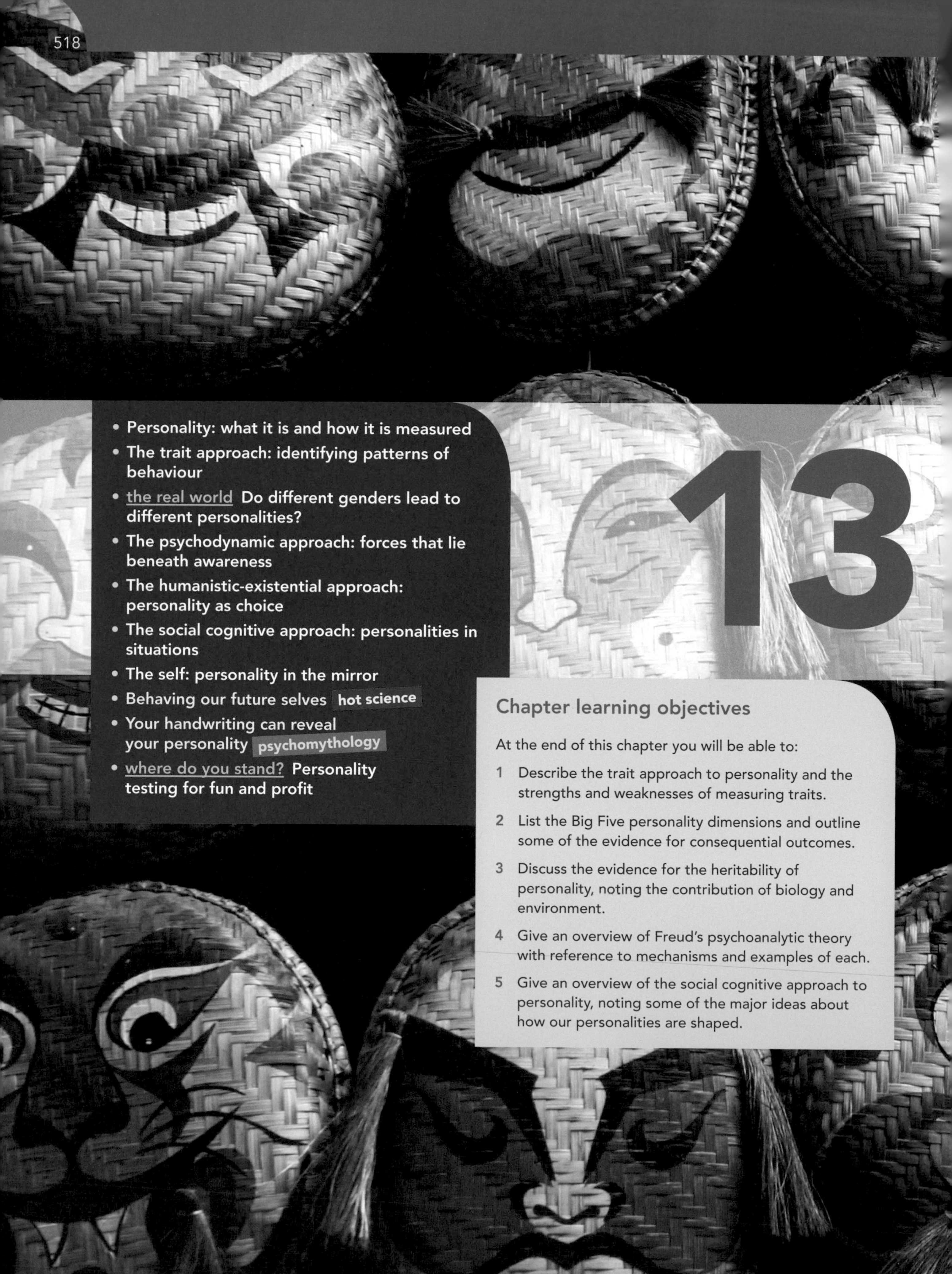

13

Chapter learning objectives

At the end of this chapter you will be able to:

1. Describe the trait approach to personality and the strengths and weaknesses of measuring traits.
2. List the Big Five personality dimensions and outline some of the evidence for consequential outcomes.
3. Discuss the evidence for the heritability of personality, noting the contribution of biology and environment.
4. Give an overview of Freud's psychoanalytic theory with reference to mechanisms and examples of each.
5. Give an overview of the social cognitive approach to personality, noting some of the major ideas about how our personalities are shaped.

Personality

Edith Piaf (1915–63), a cabaret star with a haunting voice, was the top French singer during the 1940s and 50s. Her songs ached with desolation and lost love, echoing her own life – a tragic story of addictions and fleeting relationships. She became close to many men, but each new love was undone by her compulsive promiscuity. Her only child, fathered by a delivery boy she met at age 16, died in infancy. Her lovers included a brutal pimp, a nightclub owner who contributed the stage name *Piaf* (Parisian slang for 'sparrow'), and, as her fame grew, a succession of would-be singers who hoped to gain by association with her. She fell into alcoholism and, after a car accident, became addicted to morphine – once even stepping offstage during a show to inject herself through her skirt. Her legendary vulnerability and diminutive 142-cm stature clashed with the great strength of her stage presence and the raw emotional power of her music. Her songs 'La vie en rose', 'Milord' and 'Non, je ne regrette rien' (No regrets) became anthems of Paris and France.

How can we account for this unique personality? What could make someone so magnetic and yet so self-destructive – so strong and yet so weak? We could look to her parents. Edith's mother was an alcoholic street singer known for prostitution at carnivals and circuses. She neglected her infant daughter and after two months abandoned her to the father, a Parisian street acrobat. Edith's father was more loving but also failed her, sending her to be raised by his mother, who ran a brothel in Normandy. Life at the brothel was not especially wholesome and inspirational either. Three-year-old Edith briefly became blind, and when her sight returned, she surely saw much that shaped her personality. In her autobiography, she wrote: 'This upbringing had not made me very sentimental … I thought that when a boy signaled to a girl, the girl should never refuse. I thought women should behave like that' (Piaf, 2004, p. 62).

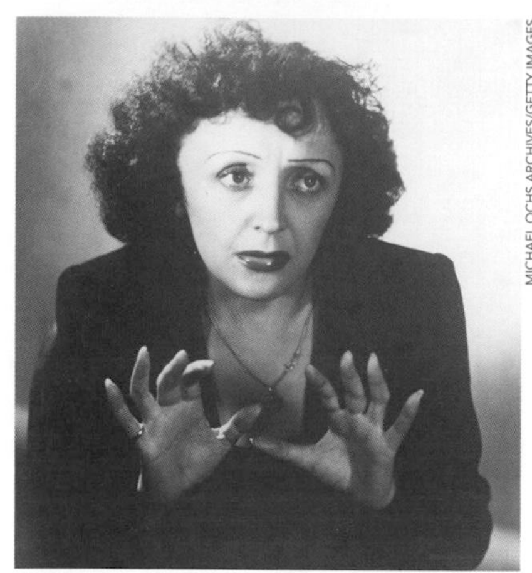
MICHAEL OCHS ARCHIVES/GETTY IMAGES

Still regarded as one of France's greatest popular singers, Edith Piaf's strength was in the passionate power of her voice. The complexities of her tragic life offer avenues for exploring the nature of personality.

The forces that create any one personality are always something of a mystery. Your personality is different from anyone else's and expresses itself pretty consistently across settings – at home, at lectures and elsewhere. You pay attention to others' personality differences when you choose your friends and when dealing with difficult people. But how and why do people differ psychologically? By studying many unique individuals, psychologists seek to gather enough information to scientifically answer these central questions of personality psychology. Edith Piaf, always one for a quirky quote, once observed: 'Your whole personality is in your nose' (Piaf, 2004, p. 66). There's more to it than that.

Personality is *an individual's characteristic style of behaving, thinking and feeling.* Piaf's addictions to alcohol and morphine, her belief that sex should be undertaken with almost anyone who asked for it, and her melodramatic style of song and life were all parts of her personality. In this chapter, we will explore personality, first by looking at what it is and how it is measured and then by focusing on four main approaches to understanding personality – trait, psychodynamic, humanistic-existential, and social cognitive. (Psychologists have personalities too, so their different approaches, even to the topic of personality, shouldn't be that surprising.) At the end of the chapter, we will discuss the psychology of self to see how our views of what we are like can shape and define our personality.

PERSONALITY An individual's characteristic style of behaving, thinking and feeling.

Personality: what it is and how it is measured

Greek scholar Theophrastus (*c.* 371–287 BC) was probably the first personality theorist. He was fascinated by the fact that his fellow Athenians generally shared the same upbringing but were so different in the way they behaved and thought. Theophrastus studied people as they went about their daily lives and noted that certain styles of behaviour and thinking seemed to cluster together, which led him to conclude that there were character types or personalities. In his great work *The Characters* (1929), Theophrastus identified 29 different personalities, many of which would be recognizable in today's society. For example, he coined the term 'superstitious', whose main features involved religiosity in excess of the usual. According to Theophrastus (1929, p. 79), such a person:

> would seem to be a sort of coward with respect to the divine; and your Superstitious man such as will not sally forth for the day till he have washed his hands and sprinkled himself in the Nine Springs, and put a bit of bay-leaf from a temple in his mouth. And if a cat cross his path he will not proceed on his way till someone else gone by, or he have cast three stones across the street.

Although written over 2,000 years ago, the description does sound remarkably similar to an overly anxious individual with excessive ritualistic behaviour, symptomatic of obsessive-compulsive disorder (discussed in Chapter 16). Modern personality theorists continue with Theophrastus' general approach that behaviours are not randomly distributed but form characteristic patterns or types. Researchers may still ask Theophrastus' question 'How do people differ?', but armed with modern experimental, statistical and biological measures, they go beyond simple description and ask: Why do people's personalities differ? How can personality be assessed?

Describing and explaining personality

Like early biology studies, the descriptive aspect of personality psychology is taxonomic in approach. The first biologists earnestly attempted to classify all plants and animals – whether lichens or ants or fossilized skunks. Similarly, personality psychologists began by labelling and describing different personalities. And just as biology came of age with Darwin's theory of evolution, which *explained* how differences among species arose, the maturing study of personality has also developed explanations of the basis for psychological differences among people.

What people are like

Most personality psychologists focus on specific, psychologically meaningful individual differences – characteristics such as honesty, anxiousness or moodiness. Still, personality is often in the eye of the beholder. When, for example, one person describes another as 'a loser', you may wonder whether you have just learned more about the describer or the person being described. Interestingly, studies that ask acquaintances to describe each other find a high degree of similarity among any one individual's descriptions of many different people ('John thinks Bob is considerate, Jeff is kind, and Gina is nice to others'). In contrast, resemblance is quite low when many people describe one person ('Bob thinks John is smart, Jeff thinks he is competitive, and Gina thinks he has a good sense of humour') (Dornbusch et al., 1965). As you will see, theorists also differ in their views on the characteristics of personality worth describing.

Why people are the way they are

What drove Edith Piaf to embrace men, alcohol and morphine? What made the 'sparrow' fly from nest to nest? In general, explanations of personality differences are concerned with *prior events* that can shape an individual's personality, or *anticipated events* that might motivate the person to reveal particular personality characteristics. In a biological and chemical prior event, Edith received genes from her parents that may have led her to a life of addiction and broken loves. Researchers interested in events that happen prior to our behaviour delve into our subconscious and our circumstances and interpersonal surroundings as well as studying our biology and brains.

Edith expected that she would find love through sexual relationships and happiness in drugs and alcohol, and those motives also might explain her behaviour. The consideration of anticipated events emphasizes the person's own perspective and often seems intimate and personal in its reflection of the person's inner life – hopes, fears and aspirations. Of course, our understanding of the puzzle that was Edith Piaf's life – or the life of any ordinary woman or man – also depends on insights into the interaction between the past and future. We need to know how her history may have shaped her motivations. If we were to ask Edith why she so often found herself desiring immediate sexual liaisons without wondering about the future of her relationships, she might have offered motivational explanations, pointing to what she wanted and what she loved to do. But she was also aware of the forces that prompted these desires and would often admit that her behaviour seemed to be the product of forces beyond her control. Personality psychologists study questions of how our personalities are determined by the forces in our minds and our personal history of heredity and environment and by the choices we make and the goals we seek.

Measuring personality

Of all the things psychologists have set out to measure, personality must be one of the toughest. How do you capture the uniqueness of a person? Do people fit neatly into the pigeonholes of personality that can be easily labelled? Different traditions have tended to favour different measurement techniques. The general personality measures can be classified broadly into personality inventories and projective techniques.

Personality inventories

To learn about an individual's personality, you could follow the person around and, clipboard in hand, record every single thing the person does, says, thinks and feels – including how long this goes on before the person calls the police. Some observations might involve your own impressions ('Day 5: seems to be getting irritable'); others would involve objectively observable events that anyone could verify ('Day 7: grabbed my pencil and broke it in half, then bit my hand').

Psychologists have worked out ways to obtain objective data on personality without driving their subjects to distraction. The most popular technique is the **self-report** – *a series of answers to a questionnaire that asks people to indicate the extent to which sets of statements or adjectives accurately describe their own behaviour or mental state.*

SELF-REPORT A series of answers to a questionnaire that asks people to indicate the extent to which sets of statements or adjectives accurately describe their own behaviour or mental state.

TABLE 13.1 Sensation-seeking scale		
Circle one		**Sample items**
T	F	I enjoy getting into new situations where you can't predict how things will turn out
T	F	I'll try anything once
T	F	I sometimes do 'crazy' things just for fun
T	F	I like to explore a strange city or section of town by myself, even if it means getting lost

MINNESOTA MULTIPHASIC PERSONALITY INVENTORY (MMPI) A well-researched, clinical questionnaire used to assess personality and psychological problems.

The respondent typically produces a self-description by circling a number on a scale or indicating whether an item is true or false. The researcher then combines the answers to get a general sense of the individual's personality with respect to a particular domain. **TABLE 13.1** shows several items from a self-report test of sensation seeking, the tendency to seek out new and exciting sensations (Zuckerman et al., 1964). In this case, the respondent is asked to indicate whether each statement is true (T) or false (F). A person with high levels of sensation seeking would mark most of these statements 'true'.

Perhaps the best-known self-report measure is the **Minnesota Multiphasic Personality Inventory (MMPI)** – *a well-researched, clinical questionnaire used to assess personality and psychological problems.* The MMPI consists of more than 500 descriptive statements, for example 'I often feel like breaking things', 'I think the world is a dangerous place' and 'I'm good at socializing', to which the respondent answers 'true', 'false' or 'cannot say', depending on whether or not the item applies to them. Its 10 main subscales measure different personality characteristics, which are thought to represent personality difficulties when demonstrated to an extreme degree (Hathaway and McKinley, 1951). Like many early psychological tests, the original items were generated by studying how specific groups of people as compared to the general population completed a variety of items and then creating the scales from the items these groups answered differently.

In addition to assessing tendencies towards clinical problems, for example depression, hypochondria, anxiety, paranoia and unconventional ideas or bizarre thoughts and beliefs, the MMPI measures some relatively general personality characteristics, such as degree of masculine and feminine gender role identification, sociability versus social inhibition, and impulsivity. The MMPI also includes *validity scales* that assess a person's attitudes towards test taking and any tendency to try to distort the results by faking answers.

Personality inventories such as the MMPI are easy to administer, you just give someone a pencil and away they go. The person's scores can be calculated by a computer and compared with the average ratings of thousands of other test takers. Because no interpretation of the responses is needed, biases are minimized. Of course, an accurate reading of personality will only occur if people provide honest responses, especially about characteristics that might be unflattering, and if they don't always agree or always disagree – a phenomenon known as *response style.* The validity scales help to detect these problems but cannot take them away altogether.

Another drawback is related to the actual characteristics being measured. Certain personality factors may function largely outside consciousness, and so asking people to tell us about them makes little sense. For example, would someone know if they were conceited? A truly self-centred person would probably not even know it. Despite potential drawbacks, however, personality inventories remain an efficient and effective means of testing, classifying and researching a wide range of personality characteristics.

Projective techniques

PROJECTIVE TECHNIQUES A standard series of ambiguous stimuli designed to elicit unique responses that reveal inner aspects of an individual's personality.

The second major class of tools for evaluating personality is the **projective techniques** – *a standard series of ambiguous stimuli designed to elicit unique responses that reveal inner aspects of an individual's personality.* The developers of projective tests assumed that people will project personality factors that are out of awareness – wishes, concerns, impulses and ways of seeing the world – onto ambiguous stimuli and will not censor these responses. As an example of such projection, consider the game of cloud watching. If you and a friend were looking at the sky one day and they suddenly became seriously upset because one cloud looked like a flesh-eating monster, this response would reveal a lot more about their inner conflicts than their explicit answer to a direct question about the kinds of things that frighten them.

RORSCHACH INKBLOT TEST A projective personality test in which individual interpretations of the meaning of a set of unstructured inkblots are analysed to identify a respondent's inner feelings and interpret their personality structure.

Probably the best-known and mostly widely used technique is the **Rorschach inkblot test** – *a projective personality test in which individual interpretations of the meaning of a set of unstructured inkblots are analysed to identify a respondent's inner feelings and interpret their personality structure.* Swiss psychiatrist Hermann Rorschach devised the test in 1918 by pouring ink on paper and folding the pages in half (Ellenberger, 1954). The Rorschach responses are scored according to complicated systems (derived in part from research with patients) that classify *what* is seen (content), *where* it is seen (location), and *why* it is seen that way (determinants). For example, a person who never makes use of the colour in some of the blots may be thought to have a restricted and inhibited emotional style (Klopfer and Kelley, 1942). Someone who is unable to see obvious items (such as the birds or people that most people see when they look at an image similar to the one in FIGURE 13.1) when they respond to a blot may be described as having difficulty perceiving the world as others do and as seeing things according to their unique perspective (Exner, 1993; Rapaport, 1946).

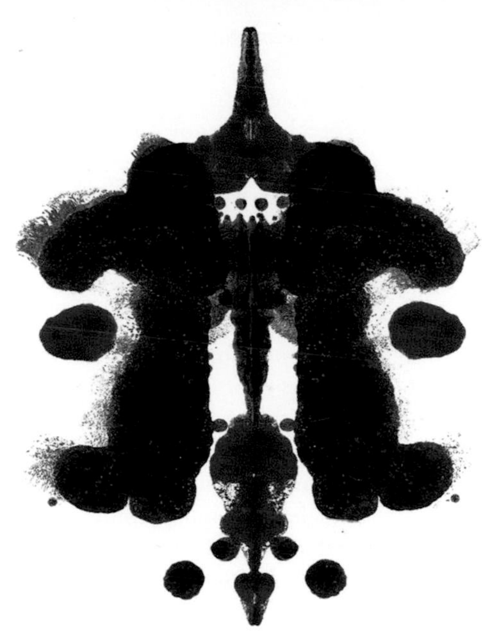

FIGURE 13.1 **Sample Rorschach inkblot** Test takers are shown a card such as this and asked, 'What might this be?' What they perceive, where they see it, and why it looks that way are assumed to reflect unconscious aspects of their personality (Zulliger, 1941).

Can psychologists using the Rorschach test discover aspects of personality that are usually hidden, even from the person taking the test? Critics argue that although the Rorschach test captures some of the more complex and private aspects of personality, it is open to the subjective interpretation and theoretical biases of the examiner. In fact, to have value, a test of personality should permit prediction of a person's behaviour, but evidence is sparse that Rorschach test scores have such predictive value (Dawes, 1994; Fowler, 1985; Wood et al., 1996, 2003). Many psychologists still use the technique, but it is losing its popularity (Garb, 1999; Widiger, 2001).

Projective tests remain controversial in psychology. Despite the rich picture of personality and the insights into an individual's motives that these tests offer, they should be understood primarily as a way in which the psychologist can get to know someone personally and intuitively (McClelland et al., 1953). When measured by rigorous scientific criteria, projective tests like the Rorschach have not been found to be reliable or valid in predicting behaviour (Lilienfeld et al., 2003).

Rorschach test with tomato sauce?

In March 1991, motorists in Stone Mountain, Georgia reported seeing the image of Christ in a forkful of spaghetti on a Pizza Hut hoarding. One woman said the image caused her to abandon plans to quit her church choir.

In summary, a person's characteristic style of behaving, thinking and feeling is what psychologists call 'personality'. Among the key questions for personality psychologists are the following: How best to describe personality? How best to explain how personalities come about? And how do we measure personality? Psychologists have developed a number of measurement instruments to assess personality. Two general classes of personality tests are personality inventories, such as the MMPI, and projective techniques, such as the Rorschach inkblot test.

The trait approach: identifying patterns of behaviour

Imagine writing a story about the people you know. To capture their special qualities, you might describe their traits: Emma is *friendly*, *aggressive* and *domineering*, while Bob is *flaky*, *humorous* and *superficial*. With a dictionary and a free afternoon, you might even be able to describe Amy as *perspicacious* and *flagitious*, that's 'discerning' and 'wicked' in plain English. The trait approach to personality uses such trait terms to characterize differences among individuals. In attempting to create manageable and meaningful sets of descriptors, trait theorists face two significant challenges: narrowing down the almost infinite set of adjectives, and answering the more basic question of why people have particular traits – whether they arise from biological or hereditary foundations.

Traits as behavioural dispositions and motives

Gordon Allport (1937), one of the first trait theorists, proposed that personality can best be understood as a combination of traits. A **trait** is *a relatively stable disposition to*

TRAIT A relatively stable disposition to behave in a particular and consistent way.

A wardrobe isn't just a place for clothes. In some cases, it's a personality test.

behave in a particular and consistent way. For example, a person who keeps their books organized alphabetically on bookshelves, hangs their clothing neatly in the wardrobe, knows the timetable for the local bus, keeps a clear agenda in a daily planner, and lists birthdays of friends and family on their calendar can be said to have the trait of *orderliness.* This trait consistently manifests itself in a variety of settings. Some psychologists can even make a fairly accurate personality assessment based on an analysis of the objects and the way we lay out our bedrooms or office space (Gosling et al., 2002).

The 'orderliness' trait describes a person but doesn't explain their behaviour. *Why* does the person behave in this way? There are two basic ways in which a trait might serve as an explanation – the trait may be a pre-existing disposition of the person that causes the person's behaviour, or it may be a motivation that guides the person's behaviour. Allport saw traits as pre-existing dispositions, causes of behaviour that reliably trigger the behaviour. The person's orderliness, for example, is an inner property of the person that will cause the person to straighten things up and be tidy in a wide array of situations. US psychologist Henry Murray's interest in motivation led him to suggest that traits reflect needs or desires. Just as a hunger motive might explain someone's many trips to the corner shop, a need for orderliness might explain the neat wardrobe, organized calendar and familiarity with the bus schedule (Murray and Kluckhohn, 1953). As a rule, researchers examining traits as causes have used personality inventories to measure them, whereas those examining traits as motives have more often used projective tests.

What kinds of personality traits have been studied? Among the hundreds of traits that researchers have described and measured is right-wing *authoritarianism*, or the tendency towards political conservatism, obedience to authority, and conformity. In the 1940s, this characteristic drew the attention of researchers who were trying to understand what made people support the rise of Nazi Germany and fascism after the First World War (Adorno et al., 1950). Although research on the personality traits that lead to political conservatism continues (Jost et al., 2003), the topic became less focal for researchers once the Second World War receded into history. However, as you will read in Chapter 15, authoritarianism is relevant to social psychology and turns out to be related to prejudice directed towards others (Altemeyer, 1998). It is also still considered in relation to the Big Five personality traits that we consider shortly (Perry and Sibley, 2012). Examples of other traits that have come into vogue over the years include cognitive complexity as a measure of processing style, defensiveness, hypnotizability, sensation seeking and optimism. As with TV shows and hairstyles, fashions in trait dimensions come and go over time.

The search for core traits

Picking a fashionable trait and studying it in depth doesn't get us very far in the search for the core of human character – the basic set of traits that define how humans differ from one another. How have researchers tried to discover such core traits?

Classification using language

The study of core traits began with an exploration of how personality is represented in the store of wisdom we call 'language'. Generation after generation, people have described people with words, so early psychologists proposed that core traits could be discerned by finding the main themes in all the adjectives used to describe personality. In one such analysis, a painstaking count of relevant words in an English dictionary resulted in a list of over 18,000 potential traits (Allport and Odbert, 1936).

Although narrowing down such a list isn't too difficult because so many words are synonyms, for example *giving, generous* and *bighearted* all mean more or less the same thing, the process is still too subjective to permit development of a true set of core of traits. Just looking at trait-like words that seemed to represent motives, for example, led Murray (1938) to propose over 40 basic motivations in addition to the need for orderliness. Further, similarity in meaning may not be the only basis for relationships among traits. Adjectives that describe certain behaviours tend to be associated with one another even though they do not mean the same thing; for example, it's hard to imagine a *calm*

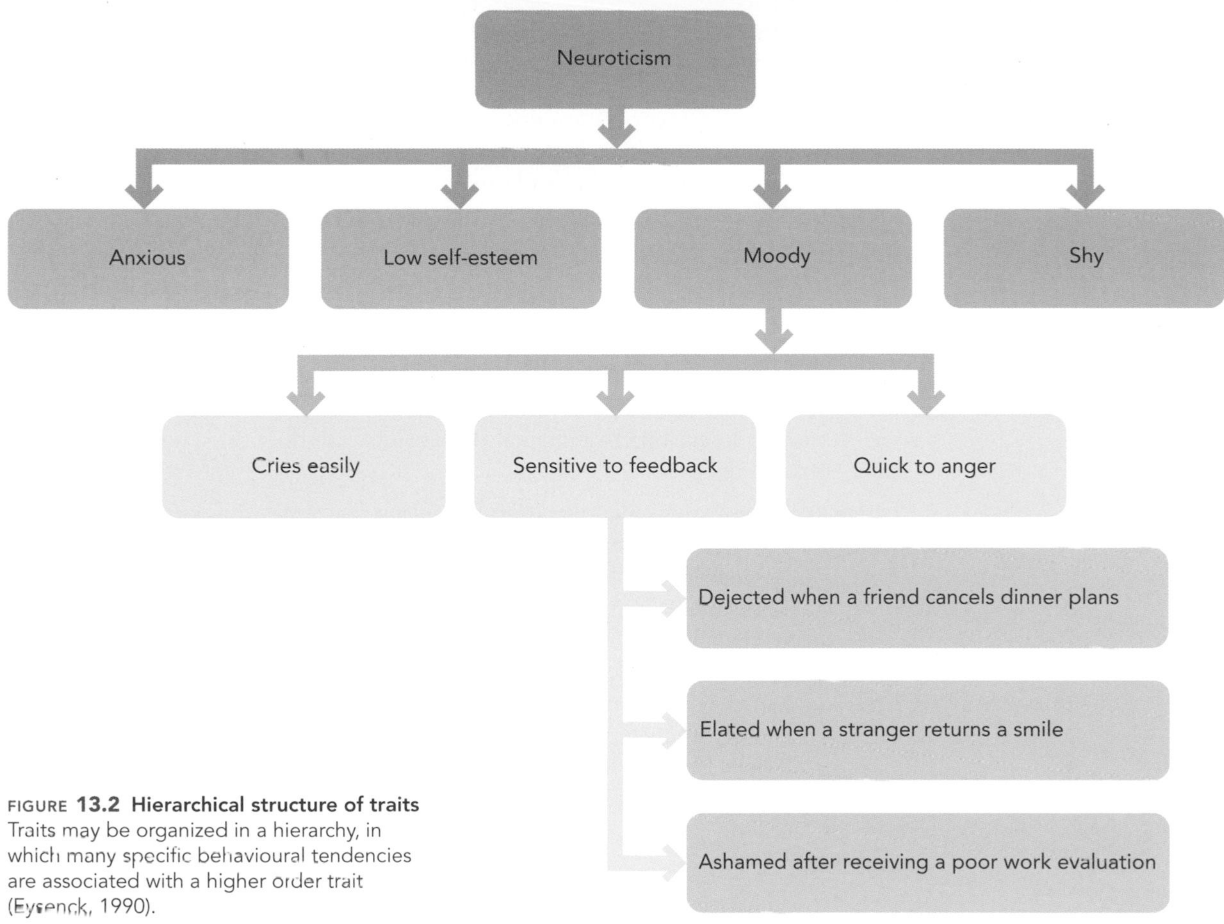

FIGURE **13.2 Hierarchical structure of traits** Traits may be organized in a hierarchy, in which many specific behavioural tendencies are associated with a higher order trait (Eysenck, 1990).

person who is not also *even-tempered*, although the words describe different personality characteristics. As you can see in **FIGURE 13.2**, behavioural tendencies might be related in a hierarchical pattern.

Factor analysis

In many ways, the study of personality has the same problems as those facing the study of intelligence: How many different dimensions do these constructs have? To answer this, researchers have used the same computational procedure called *factor analysis*, described in Chapter 9, which sorts trait terms into a small number of underlying dimensions, or 'factors', based on how people use the traits to rate themselves. In a typical study using factor analysis, hundreds of people rate themselves on hundreds of adjectives, indicating how accurately each one describes their personality. The researcher then calculates the patterns to determine similarities in the raters' usage of descriptions of personality. Aspects of personality that typically go together are known as **oblique factors**, *items that correlate with each other*, such as 'responsible' and 'careful'. Factor analysis can also reveal which adjectives are unrelated. For example, if people who describe themselves as *responsible* are neither more nor less likely to describe themselves as *creative* or *innovative*, the factor analysis would reveal that responsibility and creativity/innovation represent different factors. When they don't go together, they are known as **orthogonal factors**, *items that are uncorrelated*, such as 'responsible' and 'careless'. Each factor is typically presented as a continuum, ranging from one extreme trait, such as responsible, to its opposite, in this case, careless.

OBLIQUE FACTORS Items that correlate with each other.

ORTHOGONAL FACTORS Items that are uncorrelated.

Factor analysis has three major limitations:

1. You only get out what you put in. In other words, if the descriptions entered into the analysis do not include aspects of 'pride', for example, this can never come out in the analysis as an aspect of personality.

2 It is only a statistical technique that reveals correlations. When factors are highly correlated, there is the temptation to think that one causes the other. To take our example above, one might conclude that high responsibility leads to greater care. However, as we saw in Chapter 2, correlation does not mean cause because of the third-variable problem. Two items could be highly correlated because of some unknown third variable. For example, responsibility and care might both be related to obsessional thinking, but that's just an educated guess.
3 The structure of personality depends on whether you think it is important to look for oblique or orthogonal factors. This is why different factor analysis techniques have yielded different views of personality structure. Raymond Cattell (1950) concentrated on oblique factors and ended up with a 16-factor theory of personality, whereas others have found his scheme too complex and have argued for theories with far fewer basic dimensions. Hans Eysenck (1967) took the opposite tack of looking for orthogonal factors and developed a model of personality with only two (later expanded to three) major traits.

Eysenck's factor analysis identified one dimension that distinguished people who are sociable and active (extroverts) from those who are relatively introspective and quiet (introverts). His analysis also identified a second dimension ranging from the tendency to be very neurotic or emotionally unstable to the tendency to be more emotionally stable. He believed that many behavioural tendencies could be understood in terms of their relation to these core traits. FIGURE 13.3 suggests that these two dimensions may not be an oversimplified view, as the two central dimensions seem to capture and characterize a much larger number of specific traits.

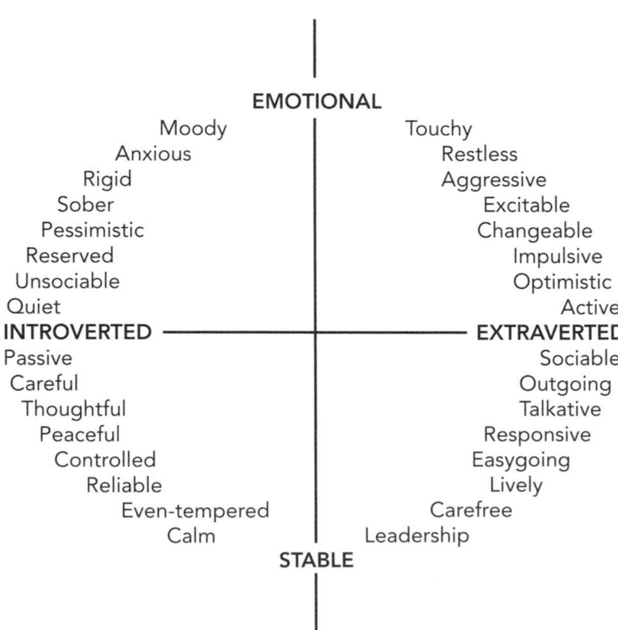

FIGURE **13.3 Eysenck's depiction of trait dimensions** The trait dimensions shown here can be combined to describe a great deal of the variability in human personality. If you look at the adjectives between any two of the four possible points on the grid, you'll see an interesting range of possible surface characteristics (Eysenck and Eysenck, 1985).

The Big Five dimensions of personality: 'OCEAN'

BIG FIVE The traits of the five-factor model: openness to experience, conscientiousness, extroversion, agreeableness and neuroticism.

Today, many factor analysis researchers agree that personality is best captured by 5 factors rather than 2, 3, 16, 40 or 18,000 (John and Srivastava, 1999; McCrae and Costa, 1999). The **Big Five**, as they are affectionately called, are *the traits of the five-factor model: openness to experience, conscientiousness, extroversion, agreeableness and neuroticism*, or OCEAN for convenience (see TABLE 13.2). The five-factor model, which overlaps with the pioneering work of Cattell and Eysenck, is now widely preferred for several reasons:

1 Modern factor analysis techniques confirm that this set of five factors strikes the right balance between accounting for as much variation in personality as possible while avoiding overlapping traits.

2 In a large number of studies using different kinds of data – people's descriptions of their own personalities, other people's descriptions of their personalities, interviewer checklists and behavioural observation – the same five factors have emerged. For example, spouses' ratings for each other on the Big Five reveal moderately high correlations of +0.59 for openness, +0.57 for conscientiousness, +0.53 for extroversion, +0.59 for agreeableness and +0.53 for neuroticism (McCrae and Costa, 1990).

3 Perhaps most important, the basic five-factor structure seems to show up across a wide range of participants, including children, adults in other cultures, and even among those who use other languages, suggesting that the Big Five may be universal (John and Srivastava, 1999).

TABLE **13.2 The Big Five factor model**

Openness to experience	imaginative . . . . . . down-to-earth variety . . . . routine independent . . . . conforming
Conscientiousness	organized . . . . disorganized careful . . . . careless self-disciplined . . . . . . weak-willed
Extraversion	social . . . . retiring fun loving . . . . sober affectionate . . . . reserved
Agreeableness	softhearted . . . . ruthless trusting . . . . suspicious helpful . . . . uncooperative
Neuroticism	worried . . . . calm insecure . . . . secure self-pitying . . . . self-satisfied

Source: McCrae and Costa, 1990, 1999

In fact, the Big Five dimensions are so 'universal' that they show up even when people are asked to evaluate the traits of complete strangers (Passini and Norman, 1966). This finding suggests that these personality dimensions might reside 'in the eye of the beholder' – categories that people use to evaluate others regardless of how well they know them. However, it's not all perception. The reality of these traits has been clearly established in research showing that self-reports on the Big Five are associated with predictable patterns of behaviour and social outcomes, which we examine next.

Personality traits and consequential outcomes

Research on the Big Five has shown that people's personalities tend to remain stable throughout their lifetime, with scores at one time in life correlating strongly with scores at later dates, even later decades (Caspi et al., 2005). Some variability is typical in childhood, with less in adolescence and then greater stability in adulthood. So, if these measures are stable, one of the major questions about personality assessments like the Big Five is whether they have any real-world value in terms of consequential outcomes. One recent survey of the research literature on the Big Five has revealed that there are indeed consequences of personality on several important outcomes, including individual wellbeing, health, longevity, partnerships, jobs and criminal activity (Ozer and Benet-Martínez, 2006).

Individual outcomes

Subjective wellbeing (SWB) is *an individual's evaluation of their own lives in terms of how satisfied they are and how they feel about their life.* SWB is strongly predicted by personality traits that are largely a function of temperament, that is, extroversion and neuroticism. This is probably because individuals with high extroversion and low neuroticism scores have high self-esteem, which we discuss later in this chapter. They see events in a more positive light and are less responsive to negative feedback. However, the relationship between extroversion, neuroticism and SWB is moderated by culture. In individualistic Western cultures where pleasure and positive mood are highly prized and emphasized, high extroversion and low neuroticism are a strong predictor of SWB. This is less so in Eastern cultures where individualism is less valued (Schimmack et al., 2002).

SUBJECTIVE WELLBEING (SWB) An individual's evaluation of their own lives in terms of how satisfied they are and how they feel about their life.

Our physical health and mortality are also related to personality. With regards to longevity, high extroversion and conscientiousness predict longer lives (Danner et al., 2001; Friedman et al., 1995), whereas low agreeableness predicts poorer physical health and earlier death (Miller et al., 1996). High extroversion might operate because those who are more outgoing have more extensive social networks and support, which are associated with better health outcomes (Berkman et al., 2000). People who have high conscientiousness are also more careful about exercise and diet, and less likely to smoke and have unhealthy habits (Bogg and Roberts, 2004).

Interpersonal outcomes

Social adjustment in terms of peers and family relationships have mostly been studied in children and adolescents largely because, as William James (1890, p. 121) put it: 'It is well for the world that in most of us, by the age of thirty, the character has set like plaster, and will never soften again.' Of the Big Five, agreeableness and extroversion are the best predictors of those who have friends (Jensen-Campbell et al., 2002). Children who are less agreeable and less extroverted are more argumentative and withdrawn and, unsurprisingly, have fewer friends (Newcomb et al., 1993). Children who have high neuroticism, low conscientiousness and low extroversion also have poorer relationships with their parents (Belsky et al., 2003). However, German researchers have recently demonstrated that peer contexts account for individual differences in personality development *well after* childhood (Reitz et al., 2014). For instance, recent longitudinal studies showed that life experiences involving different peer contexts, such as graduation (Bleidorn, 2012), military service (Jackson et al., 2012) or occupation (Denissen et al., 2014; Wille and De Fruyt, 2014), influence personality development beyond adolescence. For example, even five years after the end of military training in the German army, individuals had lower levels of agreeableness (Jackson et al., 2012).

In terms of forming stable romantic relationships, those who have low agreeableness and high neuroticism tend to have higher dissatisfaction with their partners, experience more conflict and abuse and ultimately higher rates of separation and divorce (Karney and Bradbury, 1995). This is understandable when one considers that there are always going to be sources of tension and conflict in a relationship that must be resolved for the partnership to endure. All the Big Five have been related to attachment styles (Shaver and Brennan, 1992), which we learned about in Chapter 12 and discuss again in Chapter 14, because adult attachment styles predict the success of romantic relationships.

Occupational outcomes

Many of today's organizations and employers use personality assessment in the recruitment of their staff, so it is unsurprising that different employers seek different qualities in their workforce (see where do you stand? box at end of chapter). Two large meta-analyses (Barrick et al., 2003; Larson et al., 2002) found that, in general, employees with high extroversion and high agreeableness tended to work in jobs that require good social skills and teamwork. Those with high openness tended to be in jobs that require more artistic and creative effort. Neuroticism was not reliably related to any occupation. Across all types of work, high conscientiousness was predictive of job performance.

Low conscientiousness seems to be consistently associated with various aspects of criminality and antisocial behaviour (Shiner et al., 2002). It is related to behaviour problems in adolescent boys (Ge and Conger, 1999), antisocial behaviour (Shiner et al., 2002), deviance and even suicide attempts (Verona et al., 2001), and along with low agreeableness, low conscientiousness predicts those most likely to abuse drink and drugs (John and Srivastava, 1999; Walton and Roberts, 2004).

Traits as biological building blocks

Can we explain *why* a person has a stable set of personality traits? Many trait theorists have argued that immutable brain and biological processes produce the remarkable stability of traits over the life span. Allport viewed traits as characteristics of the brain that influence the way people respond to their environment. And, as you will see, Eysenck searched for a connection between his trait dimensions and specific individual differences in the workings of the brain.

Brain damage certainly can produce personality change, as the classic case of Phineas Gage so vividly demonstrates (see Chapter 3). You may recall that after the blasting accident that blew a steel rod through his frontal lobes, Gage showed a dramatic loss of social appropriateness and conscientiousness (Damasio, 1994). In fact, when someone experiences a profound change in personality, testing often reveals the presence of brain pathologies such as Alzheimer's disease, stroke or brain tumour (Feinberg, 2001). The administration of antidepressant medication and other pharmaceutical treatments that change brain chemistry can also trigger personality changes, for example making people somewhat more extroverted and less neurotic (Bagby et al., 1999; Knutson et al., 1998).

Genes, traits and personality

Some of the most compelling evidence for the importance of biological factors in personality comes from the domain of behavioural genetics. Like researchers studying genetic influences on intelligence (see Chapter 9), personality psychologists have looked at correlations between the traits in identical (monozygotic) twins who share the same genes and fraternal (dizygotic) twins, who, on average, share only half of their genes. The evidence has been generally consistent. In one review of studies involving over 24,000 twin pairs, identical twins proved markedly more similar to each other in personality than fraternal twins (Loehlin, 1992).

Simply put, the more genes you have in common with someone, the more similar your personalities are likely to be. Genetics seems to influence most personality traits, and current estimates place the average genetic component of personality in the range of 0.40–0.60. These heritability coefficients, as you learned in Chapter 9, indicate that roughly half the variability among individuals results from genetic factors (Bouchard and Loehlin, 2001). Genetic factors do not account for everything – the remaining half of the variability in personality can be explained by differences in life experiences and other factors – but they appear to be remarkably influential (see *the real world* box). Studies of twins suggest that the extent to which the Big Five traits derive from genetic differences ranges from 0.35 to 0.49 (see **TABLE 13.3**).

TABLE 13.3 Heritability estimates for the Big Five personality traits

Trait dimension	Heritability
Openness	0.45
Conscientiousness	0.38
Extraversion	0.49
Agreeableness	0.35
Neuroticism	0.41

Source: Loehlin, 1992

the real world

Do different genders lead to different personalities?

©ISTOCKPHOTO/TROELS GRAUGAARD

Does a person's gender tell us anything meaningful about how they think, feel and respond? Personality psychologists have struggled with such questions for decades. Do you think there is a typical 'female' personality or a typical 'male' personality?

Researchers have found some reliable differences between men and women with respect to their self-reported traits, attitudes and behaviours (Feingold, 1994). Some of these findings conform to Western stereotypes of 'masculine' and 'feminine'. For example, researchers have found women to be more verbally expressive, more sensitive to nonverbal cues, and more nurturing than men. And although men are more physically aggressive than women, women appear to engage in more social relationship aggression (for example ignoring someone) than men (Eagly and Steffen, 1986). Other gender differences include more assertiveness, slightly higher self-esteem, a more casual approach to sex, and greater sensation seeking in men compared with women. On the Big Five, women have been found to be higher on agreeableness and neuroticism than men, but the genders do not differ in openness to experience. On a variety of other personality characteristics, including helpfulness and sexual desire, men and women on average show no reliable differences.

What do gender differences actually mean? Keep in mind that even statistically significant differences reflect *average group* differences. Men and women are far more alike than they are different, and on an individual level, knowledge of group differences may have little value in predicting whether, for example, your girlfriend will be agreeable and nurturing or your boyfriend will be a sensation seeker. If you base your assessment of people on stereotypes of men's and women's personalities rather than learning about each individual, you will frequently be incorrect.

As we discussed in Chapter 12, the debate about the origins of gender differences in personality often involves contrasting an evolutionary biological perspective with a social cognitive perspective known as *social learning theory*. The evolutionary perspective holds that men and women have evolved different personality characteristics in part because their reproductive success depends on different behaviours. For instance, aggressiveness in men may have an adaptive value in intimidating sexual rivals; women who are agreeable and nurturing may have evolved to protect and ensure the survival of their offspring (Campbell, 1999) as well as to secure a reliable mate and provider (Buss, 1989).

According to social role theory, personality characteristics and behavioural differences between men and women result from cultural standards and expectations that assign them socially permissible jobs, activities and family positions (Eagly and Wood, 1999). Because of their physical size and their freedom from childbearing, men historically took roles of greater power – roles that in postindustrial society don't necessarily require physical strength. These differences then snowball, with men generally taking roles that require assertiveness and aggression, for example manager, school headteacher, surgeon, and women pursuing roles that emphasize greater supportiveness and nurturance, for example nurse, nursery worker, teacher.

Regardless of the source of gender differences in personality, the degree to which people identify personally with masculine and feminine stereotypes may tell us about important personality differences between individuals. Sandra Bem (1974) designed a scale, the Bem Sex Role Inventory, which assesses the degree of identification with stereotypically masculine and feminine traits. Bem suggested that psychologically *androgynous* people – those who adopt the 'best of both worlds', identifying with positive feminine traits (such as kindness) and positive masculine traits (such as assertiveness) – might be better adjusted than people who identify strongly with only one sex role. Research shows that this is particularly true for women, perhaps because many of the traits stereotypically associated with masculinity (such as assertiveness and achievement) are related to psychological health (Cook, 1985).

Bem Sex Role Inventory sample items

Respondents taking the Bem Sex Role Inventory (1974) rate themselves on each of the 60 items on a 1–7 scale without seeing the gender categorization. Then the scale is scored for masculinity – use of stereotypically masculine items, femininity – use of stereotypically feminine items, and androgyny – use of stereotypically masculine and feminine adjectives to describe oneself.

Masculine items:	Feminine items:
Self-reliant	Yielding
Defends own beliefs	Affectionate
Independent	Flatterable
Assertive	Sympathetic
Forceful	Sensitive to the needs of others

There seems to be a closer link to genetics in influencing personality than environmental factors. These twins in cute matching outfits might share similar personality characteristics, but so would twins raised apart in separate families.

As in the study of intelligence, potential confounding factors must be ruled out to ensure that effects are truly due to genetics and not environmental experiences. Are identical twins treated more similarly and do they have a greater *shared environment* than fraternal twins? As children, were they dressed in the same snappy outfits and did they go to the same birthday parties and could this somehow have produced similarities in their personalities? Studies of identical twins reared far apart in adoptive families – an experience that pretty much eliminates the potential effect of shared environmental factors – suggest that shared environments have little impact. Reared-apart identical twins end up at least as similar in personality as those who grow up together (McGue and Bouchard, 1998; Tellegen et al., 1988).

Indeed, one provocative, related finding is that shared environmental factors such as parental divorce or parenting style may have little direct impact on personality (Plomin and Caspi, 1999). According to these researchers, simply growing up in the same family does not make people very similar: in fact, when two siblings are similar, this is thought to be primarily due to genetic similarities.

Researchers have also assessed specific behavioural and attitude similarities in twins, and the evidence for heritability in these studies is often striking. When 3,000 pairs of US identical and fraternal twins were asked their opinions on political and social issues, such as the death penalty, censorship and nudist camps, significantly high heritability estimates were obtained for these and many other attitudes; for example, the score for views on the death penalty was approximately 0.50 (Martin et al., 1986). A specific gene directly responsible for attitudes on the death penalty or any other specific behaviour or attitude is extremely unlikely. Rather, a set of genes – or, more likely, many sets of genes interacting – may produce a specific physiological characteristic such as a tendency to have a strong fear reaction in anticipation of punishment. This biological factor may then shape the person's belief about a range of social issues, perhaps including whether the fear of punishment is effective in deterring criminal behaviour (Tesser, 1993).

Do animals have personalities?

Another source of evidence for the biological basis of human personality comes from the study of nonhuman animals. Any dog owner, zookeeper or cattle farmer can tell you that individual animals have characteristic patterns of behaviour. One Missouri woman who reportedly enjoyed raising chickens in her suburban home said that 'the best part' was 'knowing them as individuals' (Tucker, 2003). As far as we know, this pet owner did not give her feathered companions a personality test, although researcher Sam Gosling (1998) used this approach in a study of a group of spotted hyenas. Well, not exactly. He recruited four human observers to use personality scales to rate the different hyenas in the group. When he examined ratings on the scales, he found five dimensions, of which three closely resembled the Big Five traits of neuroticism, that is, fearfulness and emotional reactivity, openness to experience, that is, curiosity, and agreeableness, that is, absence of aggression.

In similar studies of guppies and octopi, individual differences in traits resembling extroversion and neuroticism were reliably observed (Gosling and John, 1999). In each study, researchers identified particular behaviours they felt reflected each trait based on their observation of the animals' normal repertoire of activities. Octopi, for example, seldom get invited out to parties, so they cannot be assessed for their socializing tendencies ('He was all hands!'), but they do vary in terms of whether they prefer to eat in the safety of their den or are willing to venture out at feeding time, thus a behaviour that corresponds to extroversion can reasonably be assessed (Gosling and John, 1999). Because different observers seem to agree on where an animal falls on a given dimension, the findings do not simply reflect a particular observer's imagination or tendency to *anthropomorphize*, that is, to attribute human characteristics to nonhuman animals. Such findings of cross-species commonality in behavioural styles help to support the idea that there are biological mechanisms that underlie personality traits shared by many species.

From an evolutionary perspective, differences in personality reflect alternative adaptations that species – human and nonhuman – have evolved to deal with the challenges of survival and reproduction. For example, if you were to hang around a bar for an evening or two, you would soon see that humans have evolved more than one way to attract and keep a mate. People who are extroverted would probably show off to attract attention, whereas you'd be likely to see people high in agreeableness displaying affection and nurturance (Buss, 1996). Both approaches might work well to attract mates and reproduce successfully – depending on the environment. Through this process of natural selection, those characteristics that have proved successful in our evolutionary struggle for survival have been passed on to future generations.

Traits in the brain

But what neurophysiological mechanisms influence the development of personality traits? Let's look at some of the current thinking on this topic, focusing on the extroversion/introversion dimension. In his personality model, Eysenck (1967) speculated that extroversion and introversion might arise from individual differences in alertness. Extroverts may need to seek out social interaction, parties and even mayhem in an attempt to achieve full mental stimulation, whereas introverts may avoid these situations because they are so sensitive that such stimulation is unpleasant.

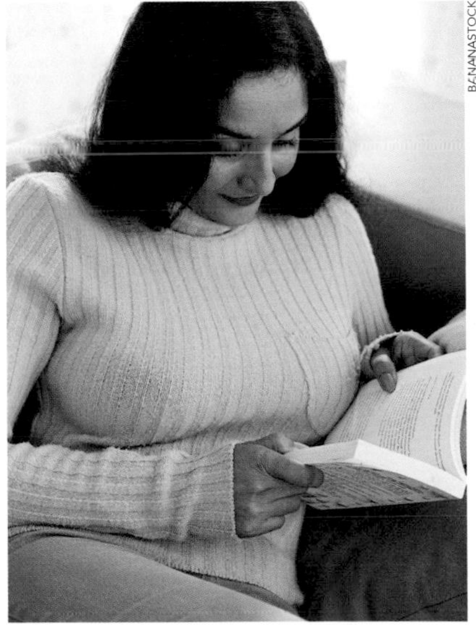

BANANASTOCK

Do you think that people who are introverted prefer to be less sociable or are they less sociable because they are introverted?

Eysenck argued that differences in levels of cortical arousal underlie differences between extroverts and introverts. Extroverts pursue stimulation because their *reticular formation* – the part of the brain that regulates arousal, or alertness (as described in Chapter 3) – is not easily stimulated. To achieve greater cortical arousal and feel fully alert, Eysenck argued, extroverts are drawn to activities such as listening to loud music and having a lot of social contact. In contrast, introverts may prefer reading or quiet activities because their cortex is easily stimulated to a higher than optimal point.

Later, Eysenck (1978) added a third dimension that he called *psychoticism* – individuals who score high on this factor were 'egocentric, aggressive, impulsive, impersonal, cold, lacking in empathy and concern for others, and generally unconcerned about the rights and welfare of others' (Eysenck, 1982, p. 11). These three factors of neuroticism, extraversion and psychoticism were assessed using Eysenck's Personality Questionnaire and found to be almost uncorrelated, indicating that they were indeed independent dimensions of personality.

Behavioural and physiological research generally supports Eysenck's view. When introverts and extroverts are presented with a range of intense stimuli, introverts respond more strongly, including salivating more when a drop of lemon juice is placed on their tongues and reacting more negatively to electric shocks or loud noises (Bartol and Costello, 1976; Stelmack, 1990). This reactivity has an impact on the ability to concentrate. Extroverts tend to perform well at tasks that are done in a noisy, arousing context – such as bartending or teaching – whereas introverts are better at tasks that require concentration in tranquil contexts – such as the work of a librarian or night-time security guard (Geen, 1984; Lieberman and Rosenthal, 2001; Matthews and Gilliland, 1999).

In a refined version of Eysenck's ideas about arousability, Jeffrey Gray (1970) proposed that the dimensions of extroversion/introversion and neuroticism reflect two basic brain systems. The *behavioural activation system* (BAS), essentially a 'go' system, activates approach behaviour in response to the anticipation of reward. The *behavioural inhibition system* (BIS), a 'stop' system, inhibits behaviour in response to stimuli signalling punishment. According to Gray, individual differences in the reactivity of these systems may underlie Eysenck's two personality dimensions. People with a highly reactive BAS may actively engage the environment, seeking social reinforcement in a highly extroverted manner. People with a highly reactive BIS, on the other hand, might tend towards neuroticism and emotional instability, anxiously focusing on the possibility of negative outcomes and perceiving the world as threatening. In Gray's analysis, each person might have some combination of these two tendencies, so each person's level of extroversion and neuroticism is produced by the activity of specific brain systems.

In summary, the trait approach tries to identify personality dimensions that can be used to characterize individuals' behaviour. Researchers have attempted to boil down the potentially huge array of things people do, think and feel into some core personality dimensions. Many personality psychologists currently focus on the Big Five personality factors: openness to experience, conscientiousness, extroversion, agreeableness and neuroticism (OCEAN). The emphasis in these theories is on broad personality dispositions that are relatively consistent across situations. The Big Five factors have been shown to have consequential outcomes related to individual wellbeing, health, relationships, job satisfaction and criminality. To address the question of explanation, trait theorists often adopt a biological perspective, construing personality as largely the result of brain mechanisms and processes that are inborn.

The psychodynamic approach: forces that lie beneath awareness

If you have ever posted an unsigned cheque or letter, locked yourself out of the house, or called someone by the wrong name, you probably dismissed your error as a mere annoyance – maybe the result of distraction or insufficient sleep. Sigmund Freud did not ignore such subtle errors, what he called the 'psychopathologies of everyday life'; instead, he built a theory on them.

Rather than trying to understand personality in terms of broad theories for describing individual differences, Freud looked for personality in the details – the meanings and insights revealed by careful analysis of the tiniest blemishes in a person's thoughts and behaviour. Working with patients who came to him with disorders that did not seem to have any physical basis, he began by interpreting the origins of their common mindbugs, errors that have come to be called 'Freudian slips'. To understand this perennially controversial theory, let's explore how Freud and his followers viewed unconscious motivation, the structure of the mind, psychological defences, and personality development.

Unconscious motives

Freud used the term *psychoanalysis* to refer to his theory of personality and method of treating patients. Freud's ideas were the first of many theories building on his basic notion that personality is a mystery to the person who 'owns' it because we can't know our own deepest motives. The theories of Freud and his followers, such as Carl Jung, Alfred Adler and Karen Horney (discussed in Chapter 17), are referred to as the 'psychodynamic approach'. According to the **psychodynamic approach**, *personality is formed by needs, strivings and desires, largely operating outside awareness – motives that can produce emotional disorders.*

PSYCHODYNAMIC APPROACH An approach that regards personality as formed by needs, strivings and desires, largely operating outside awareness – motives that can also produce emotional disorders.

Mindbugs offer glimpses into these hidden motives. Imagine if you forget your best friend's birthday. Her complaint about your slip – 'You don't care enough to remember!' – might offer you real insight into the current state of your relationship. Psychodynamic explanations assume that the motives that guide even the smallest nuances of our behaviour develop in our early relationships and conflicts with carers. Thus, a psychodynamic interpretation of Edith Piaf's tangled path through life might attribute her problems to her tragic abandonment in childhood and her early experiences in a brothel, which shaped her basic desires in ways that were beyond her awareness.

As you'll recall from Chapter 8, Freud made a strong distinction between the conscious and unconscious mind. He distinguished three different levels of mental life: conscious, preconscious and unconscious. *Conscious* aspects of mental life are those in awareness at any given moment, but there are a range of *preconscious* mental contents as well – aspects of mental life that are outside awareness but could easily enter consciousness. The tune of your national anthem, for example, may not have been running through your mind just now, but you probably can bring it to mind easily. Although psychologists today might call such items unconscious – because they are, after all, not currently being experienced – Freud reserved the term *unconscious* for the special part of the mind that has great psychological significance. In fact, he spoke of '*the* unconscious' as though it were an agent or a force. Psychologists call this construct the *dynamic unconscious*, which refers to an active system encompassing a lifetime of hidden memories, the person's deepest instincts and desires, and the person's inner struggle to control these forces, which we first encountered in Chapter 8. The dynamic unconscious, unlike the national anthem, is not something you can easily bring to mind; nevertheless, proponents of the theory believe it is the level that most strongly influences personality.

The power of the unconscious comes from its early origins – experiences that shaped the mind before a person could even put thoughts and feelings into words – and from its contents, which are embarrassing, unspeakable and even frightening because they operate without any control by consciousness. Imagine having violent competitive feelings towards your father ('I wish I could beat the old man at something, or just beat him up') or a death wish towards a sibling ('It would be so great if my snotty sister just got run over'). Whew! Impulses like that are assumed to remain in the unconscious because such powerful forces would be too much for consciousness to bear.

Cigar, pencil, hammer, skyscraper … gherkin? Freud believed that the id represents its wishes in terms of symbols. He would probably have been delighted with the symbols to be found in the London skyline.

GETTY IMAGES/ISTOCKPHOTO THINKSTOCK IMAGES

In Freud's psychoanalytic psychotherapy, the process of revealing the unconscious is the main focus of therapy. Freud assumed that insight into the unconscious can never be gained directly, however, because conscious self-reports could never tap the cloaked and censored depths of the unconscious. Psychologists who adopt the psychodynamic approach use projective tests such as the Rorschach inkblot test in the hope of discerning unconscious themes and issues that can be examined in therapy. As you will see in Chapter 17, psychodynamic psychotherapy makes use of a number of indirect techniques, such as dream interpretation and word association, as a means of undressing – er, *assessing* – the workings of the unconscious mind.

The structure of the mind: id, ego and superego

To explain the emotional difficulties that beset his patients, Freud proposed that the mind consists of three independent, interacting and often conflicting systems – the id, the ego and the superego:

- The most basic system, the **id**, is *the part of the mind containing the drives present at birth; it is the source of our bodily needs, wants, desires and impulses, particularly our sexual and aggressive drives.* Freud believed that the id reflects our 'true psychic reality' before the impact of the outside world with all its restraints. The id operates according to the **pleasure principle** – *the psychic force that motivates the tendency to seek immediate gratification of any impulse.* If governed by the id alone, you would never be able to tolerate the build-up of hunger while waiting to be served at a restaurant but would simply grab food from nearby tables.

ID The part of the mind containing the drives present at birth; it is the source of our bodily needs, wants, desires and impulses, particularly our sexual and aggressive drives.

PLEASURE PRINCIPLE The psychic force that motivates the tendency to seek immediate gratification of any impulse.

EGO The component of personality, developed through contact with the external world, that enables us to deal with life's practical demands.

REALITY PRINCIPLE The regulating mechanism that enables the individual to delay gratifying immediate needs and function effectively in the real world.

SUPEREGO The mental system that reflects the internalization of cultural rules, mainly learned as parents exercise their authority.

- All that the id can do is wish. To deal with reality, a second system emerges from the id during the first six to eight months of life. The **ego** is *the component of personality, developed through contact with the external world, that enables us to deal with life's practical demands.* The ego operates according to the **reality principle** – *the regulating mechanism that enables the individual to delay gratifying immediate needs and function effectively in the real world.* The ego can be thought of as the 'self', with functions such as logical thought, problem solving, creativity, attention and decision making. The ego helps you to resist the impulse to snatch others' food and also finds the restaurant and pays the bill. In doing this work, however, it serves the id. The excellent meal in the company of friends is a pleasure that gratifies its desires.
- The final system of the mind to emerge (between the ages of three and six) is the **superego** – *the mental system that reflects the internalization of cultural rules, mainly learned as parents exercise their authority.* The superego consists of a set of guidelines, internal standards and other codes of conduct that regulate and control our behaviours, thoughts and fantasies. It acts as a kind of conscience, punishing us when it finds we are doing or thinking something wrong (by producing guilt or other painful feelings) and rewarding us (with feelings of pride or self-congratulation) for living up to ideal standards. Like the id, the superego's hold on reality is tenuous. It is not equipped to differentiate between a thought or fantasy and actual behaviour in the real world and will punish or reward regardless of whether we actually do something (bad or good) or merely think about it. For the superego, simply coveting your dinner partner's cheesecake is the equivalent of having grabbed it and wolfed it down. A really strict superego might dole out an appropriate punishment for such imagined gluttony – a wave of guilt or even a stomach ache.

Dealing with inner conflict

According to Freud, the relative strength of the interactions among the three systems of mind – that is, which system is usually dominant – determines an individual's basic personality structure. The id force of personal needs, the superego force of social pressures to quell those needs, and the ego force of reality's demands together create constant controversy, almost like a puppet show or a bad play.

Imagine how these inner agents might have fought for their own interests in Edith Piaf's mind. Her autobiography (2004) reveals an id that was working overtime to generate desires – to take many lovers and follow every wish to indulge in alcohol and morphine. Her superego was weak and unable to resist these impulses ('All I've ever done all my life is disobey') and instead could only generate feelings of worthlessness following her transgressions: 'I am stupid. I always told you I was. I hate myself, and I have no confidence in myself whatsoever.' For a woman whose famous songs include one called 'No regrets', she appeared to have many. Her ego, saddled with the job of dealing with reality while her superego lost battle after battle to her id, must have been worried about what would become of her. In her words: 'God, am I scared! I don't know why, but I'm terrified. I know something's going to happen to me. I don't know what, but I feel it will be something awful, something irreparable.'

Anxiety as a driving force

According to Freud, the dynamics between the id, ego and superego are largely governed by *anxiety*, an unpleasant feeling that arises when unwanted thoughts or feelings occur, such as when the id seeks a gratification that the ego thinks will lead to real-world dangers or the superego sees as eliciting punishment. He considered anxiety to be a primary emotional reaction that, from an evolutionary standpoint, has adaptive value as a signal that something is wrong. In contrast to the fear that can be created by specific threats in the outside world (say, a cement truck thundering towards you), anxiety more often arises when the threats are ambiguous or even the product of imagination. A person who thinks about making a nasty remark to a flatmate, for example, might feel anxiety about angering the flatmate or guilt about hurting the flatmate's feelings, all without an actual external threat in sight.

The degree to which the ego anticipates danger depends on the person's early childhood experiences with the id's basic drive states. For example, someone who was harshly punished for shows of anger or aggression as a child might feel anxious over any upsurge of aggression in adulthood, even if that aggression is appropriate and understandable. Without any actual looming cement truck in sight, inner struggles can create profound anxiety.

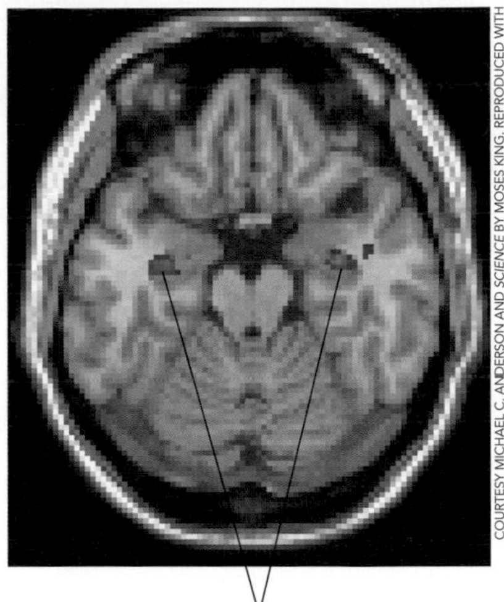

FIGURE **13.4 Decreased hippocampal activity during memory suppression** fMRI scans of people intentionally trying to forget a list of words reveal reduced activation (shown in blue) in the left and right hippocampal areas (Anderson et al., 2004).

Defence mechanisms

When the ego receives an 'alert signal' in the form of anxiety, it launches into a defensive position in an attempt to ward off the anxiety. According to Freud, it first tries *repression*, which, as you read in Chapter 8, is a mental process that removes painful experiences and unacceptable impulses from the conscious mind. Repression is sometimes referred to as 'motivated forgetting'. Indeed, neuroscientific evidence on the repression of memories reveals that this form of mental control may involve decreased activation of the hippocampus, a region (as discussed in Chapter 5) central to memory (Anderson et al., 2004) (see **FIGURE 13.4**).

Repression may not be adequate to keep unacceptable drives from entering consciousness. When such material begins to surface, the ego can employ other means of self-deception, called **defence mechanisms** – *unconscious coping mechanisms that reduce anxiety generated by threats from unacceptable impulses.* Anna Freud (1936), Freud's daughter and a psychodynamic theorist, identified a number of defence mechanisms and detailed how they operate. Let's look at a few of the most common:

DEFENCE MECHANISMS Unconscious coping mechanisms that reduce anxiety generated by threats from unacceptable impulses.

RATIONALIZATION A defence mechanism that involves supplying a reasonable-sounding explanation for unacceptable feelings and behaviour to conceal (mostly from oneself) one's underlying motives or feelings.

REACTION FORMATION A defence mechanism that involves unconsciously replacing threatening inner wishes and fantasies with an exaggerated version of their opposite.

PROJECTION A defence mechanism that involves attributing one's own threatening feelings, motives or impulses to another person or group.

1. **Rationalization** – *a defence mechanism that involves supplying a reasonable-sounding explanation for unacceptable feelings and behaviour to conceal (mostly from oneself) one's underlying motives or feelings.* For example, someone who drops a class after having failed an exam might tell themselves that they are quitting because poor ventilation in the classroom made it impossible to concentrate. In rationalization, we tell ourselves a 'likely story' to explain our behaviour instead of facing its real but less comfortable meaning.
2. **Reaction formation** – *a defence mechanism that involves unconsciously replacing threatening inner wishes and fantasies with an exaggerated version of their opposite.* Examples include being excessively nice to someone you dislike, finding yourself worried and protective about a person you have thoughts of hurting, or being cold and indifferent towards someone to whom you are strongly attracted. As with all defences, reaction formation doesn't always do a good job at concealing the underlying intention from others. For instance, a child with strong ambivalent feelings towards her new brother may literally try to smother him with hugs and cuddles, loving him almost to death!

   A revealing example of reaction formation was discovered in research on men who report *homophobia* – the dread of gay men and lesbians (Adams et al., 1996). Homophobic participants, heterosexual men who agreed with statements such as 'I would feel nervous being with a group of homosexuals', and a comparison group of non-homophobic men were shown videos of sexual activity, including heterosexual, gay male and lesbian segments. Each man's sexual arousal was then assessed by means of a device that measures penile tumescence. Curiously, the homophobic men showed greater arousal to the male homosexual images than men in the control group. The psychoanalytic interpretation seems clear. Men troubled by their own homosexual arousal formed opposite reactions to this unacceptable feeling, turning their unwanted attraction into 'dread'.
3. **Projection** – *a defence mechanism that involves attributing one's own threatening feelings, motives or impulses to another person or group.* In one study, people were asked to try to suppress thoughts about recent feedback suggesting that they had undesirable personal traits (such as rigidity or dishonesty). When they were later asked to judge others' personality characteristics, their ratings were more negative than those of a comparison group who had not been asked to suppress thoughts of their faults

Through reaction formation, a person defends against underlying feelings, such as covering hostility with an exaggerated display of affection. Maybe there's more to this sibling squeeze than love?

REGRESSION A defence mechanism in which the ego deals with internal conflict and perceived threat by reverting to an immature behaviour or earlier stage of development.

DISPLACEMENT A defence mechanism that involves shifting unacceptable wishes or drives to a neutral or less threatening alternative.

IDENTIFICATION A defence mechanism that helps deal with feelings of threat and anxiety by enabling us unconsciously to take on the characteristics of another person who seems more powerful or better able to cope.

SUBLIMATION A defence mechanism that involves channelling unacceptable sexual or aggressive drives into socially acceptable and culturally enhancing activities.

(Newman et al., 1995). Projection offers comfort: it's not so bad to have unacceptable qualities if someone else has them too!

4 **Regression** – *a defence mechanism in which the ego deals with internal conflict and perceived threat by reverting to an immature behaviour or earlier stage of development*, a time when things felt safer and more secure. Examples of regression include the use of baby talk or whining in a child (or adult) who has already mastered appropriate speech or a return to thumb sucking, teddy bear cuddling, or watching cartoons in response to something distressing.

5 **Displacement** – *a defence mechanism that involves shifting unacceptable wishes or drives to a neutral or less threatening alternative.* Displacement should be familiar to you if you've ever slammed a door, or thrown a textbook across a room, or yelled at your flatmate or your cat when you were really angry at your boss.

6 **Identification** – *a defence mechanism that helps deal with feelings of threat and anxiety by enabling us unconsciously to take on the characteristics of another person who seems more powerful or better able to cope.* This sometimes involves the phenomenon known as *identification with the aggressor*, in which anxiety is reduced by becoming like the person posing the threat. A child whose parent bullies or severely punishes them may later take on the characteristics of that parent and begin bullying others.

7 **Sublimation** – *a defence mechanism that involves channelling unacceptable sexual or aggressive drives into socially acceptable and culturally enhancing activities.* Freud considered sublimation crucial to the development and maintenance of civilization and culture. Football, rugby and other contact sports, for example, may be construed as culturally sanctioned and valued activities that channel our aggressive drives. Art, music, poetry and dance may also be considered vehicles that transform and channel id impulses – sexual and aggressive – into valued activities of benefit to society. Indeed, according to Freud, one of the beauties of sublimation is that, at some level, the drive is satisfied and discharged while not being too threatening for the ego or superego.

Defence mechanisms are useful mindbugs. They help us to overcome anxiety and engage effectively with the outside world. The ego's capacity to use defence mechanisms in a healthy and flexible fashion may depend on the nature of early experiences with carers, the defence mechanisms they used, and possibly some biological and temperamental factors as well (McWilliams, 1994). Our characteristic style of defence becomes our signature in dealing with the world, and an essential aspect of our personality.

Regression to a simpler time

In November 1994, Lance Binkowski, 20, was charged with reckless endangerment in Brookfield, Wisconsin, when he ran from police. Officers had been called after Binkowski had pounded on the back door of a nursery while dressed in a large sleepsuit with built-in feet, with a dummy in his mouth and clutching a teddy bear and a nappy bag. According to the police chief, Binkowski intended no harm to the children but 'had his own personal reasons' for being there.

Psychosexual stages and the development of personality

Freud had a great talent for coming up with troubling, highly controversial ideas. People in Victorian society did not openly discuss how much fun it is to suck on things, the frustrations of their own toilet training, or their childhood sexual desire for their mother. Today, some people dismiss this aspect of psychoanalytic theory as just plain rude, but like others who have encountered these ideas, you may find yourself wondering whether your own strong reaction is a signal of how important Freud's observations may be. Many consider his views on personality development to be fanciful, and they are no longer widely held because little research evidence supports them; nevertheless, people find this part of his legacy oddly fascinating.

PSYCHOSEXUAL STAGES Distinct early life stages through which personality is formed as children experience sexual pleasures from specific body areas and carers redirect or interfere with those pleasures.

Freud believed that a person's basic personality is formed before the age of six, during a series of sensitive periods, or life stages, when experiences influence all that will follow. Freud called them **psychosexual stages** – *distinct early life stages through which personality is formed as children experience sexual pleasures from specific body areas and carers redirect or interfere with those pleasures.* He argued that as a result of adult interference with pleasure-seeking energies, the child experiences conflict. At each stage, a different bodily region, or *erotogenic* zone, dominates the child's subjective experience; for example, during the oral stage, pleasure centres on the mouth. Each region represents a battleground between the child's id impulses and the adult external world. **TABLE 13.4** provides a summary of the psychosexual stages.

TABLE **13.4 The psychosexual stages**

Stage	Oral	Anal	Phallic	Latency	Genital
Age	0–18 months	2–3 years	3–5 years	5–13 years	Adulthood
Erotogenic zone	Mouth	Anus/urethra	Penis/clitoris	–	Penis/vagina
Areas of conflict with carer	Feeding, weaning	Toileting	Masturbation (Oedipus conflict)	–	Adult responsibilities
Associated personality features	Talkative, dependent, addictive, needy	Orderly, controlling, disorganized, sloppy	Flirtatious, vain, jealous, competitive	–	Authentic investments in love and work; capacity for healthy adult relationships

Freud believed that problems and conflicts encountered at any psychosexual stage will influence personality in adulthood. Conflict resulting from a person's being deprived or, paradoxically, overindulged at a given stage could result in a phenomenon Freud called **fixation** – *a person's pleasure-seeking drives become stuck, or arrested, at that psychosexual stage.* Freud described particular personality traits as being derived from fixations at the different psychosexual stages:

FIXATION A phenomenon in which a person's pleasure-seeking drives become psychologically stuck, or arrested, at a particular psychosexual stage.

ORAL STAGE The first psychosexual stage, in which experience centres on the pleasures and frustrations associated with the mouth, sucking and being fed.

1 In the first year and a half of life, the infant is in the **oral stage**, *during which experience centres on the pleasures and frustrations associated with the mouth, sucking and being fed.* Infants who are deprived of pleasurable feeding or indulgently overfed may develop an oral personality, that is, their lives will centre on issues related to fullness and emptiness and what they can 'take in' from others and the environment. When angry, such people may express themselves with 'biting' sarcasm and 'mouth off' at others – referred to as *oral aggression.* Personality traits associated with the oral stage include depression, lack of trust, envy and being demanding.

ANAL STAGE The second psychosexual stage, which is dominated by the pleasures and frustrations associated with the anus, retention and expulsion of faeces and urine, and toilet training.

2 Between two and three years of age, the child moves on to the **anal stage**, *during which experience is dominated by the pleasures and frustrations associated with the anus, retention and expulsion of faeces and urine, and toilet training.* From the toddler's perspective, the soiling of one's nappies is a wonderful convenience that can feel pretty good. But sooner or later carers begin to disagree, and their opinions are voiced more strongly as the child gets older. Individuals who have had difficulty negotiating this conflict may develop a rigid personality and remain preoccupied with issues of control of others and of themselves and their emotions. They may be preoccupied with their possessions, money, issues of submission and rebellion, and concerns about cleanliness versus messiness.

PHALLIC STAGE The third psychosexual stage, during which experience is dominated by the pleasure, conflict and frustration associated with the phallic-genital region as well as coping with powerful incestuous feelings of love, hate, jealousy and conflict.

OEDIPUS CONFLICT A developmental experience in which a child's conflicting feelings towards the opposite-sex parent are (usually) resolved by identifying with the same-sex parent.

3 Between the ages of three and five years, the child is in the **phallic stage**, *during which experience is dominated by the pleasure, conflict and frustration associated with the phallic-genital region as well as coping with powerful incestuous feelings of love, hate, jealousy and conflict.* In part, parental concerns about the child's developing awareness of the genital region set off the conflict. The child may touch their genitals in public or explore masturbation and may be curious about the parent's genitals.

During the phallic stage, boys are said to struggle with a tumultuous emotional experience that Freud called the Oedipus conflict. According to Freud, the **Oedipus conflict** is *a developmental experience in which a child's conflicting feelings towards the opposite-sex parent are (usually) resolved by identifying with the same-sex parent.* The name for this conflict is derived from the ancient Greek myth of Oedipus (as recounted in the play *Oedipus Rex*, by Sophocles), a young man who unknowingly kills his father and ends up marrying his mother. Oedipus eventually learns the nature of his transgressions, is overcome with such shame and guilt that he blinds himself, and then is exiled from his home. Freud alludes to this myth as a metaphor for the

According to the psychodynamic approach, at four or five years of age, children are in the throes of the Oedipus conflict. At this time, children experience intense feelings of love, hate, jealousy and anxiety related to their longings towards their parents and the wish for an exclusive love relationship with their fathers or mothers.

LATENCY STAGE The fourth psychosexual stage, in which the primary focus is on the further development of intellectual, creative, interpersonal and athletic skills.

GENITAL STAGE The final psychosexual stage, a time for the coming together of the mature adult personality with a capacity to love, work and relate to others in a mutually satisfying and reciprocal manner.

painful struggles children go through as they experience both loving and hostile feelings towards their parents during development.

Freud viewed growing up with a mother and father as a passionate experience through which we try to secure our place in relation with others, develop autonomy, and learn the most basic rules of social life. As children reach the age of four or five, they start to wonder about their love affair with Mummy, noticing she has positive feelings for someone else (Daddy). In dealing with this love triangle and balancing the wish for an exclusive loving relationship with one parent against the possibility of jeopardizing the relationship with the other, the child comes to realize that they are the odd one out. Although boys and girls experience and resolve this conflict differently, Freud believed that both must give up their oedipal desires if they are to be able to move on and build a life with a partner in the future. The anxiety engendered by this conflict, he believed, is controlled through repression (of the sexual longings) and identification (with the same-sex parent), and this marks the final development of the superego – the internal representation of parental authority.

The personality styles that can arise from fixation at this stage involve morality and sex-role identity. Individuals who get stuck in the phallic period and are unable to resolve the Oedipus conflict tend to be unusually preoccupied with issues of seduction, jealousy, competition, power and authority. For men, this may include issues of competitiveness, being macho and powerful, and overvaluing success and potency. In women, Freud thought, difficulties at this stage may result in exaggerated expressions of femininity: seductiveness, flirtatiousness and jealousy.

4 A more relaxed period in which children are no longer struggling with the power of their sexual and aggressive drives follows the intensity of the Oedipus conflict. Between the ages of 5 and 13 children experience the **latency stage**, *in which the primary focus is on the further development of intellectual, creative, interpersonal and athletic skills.* Because Freud believed that the most significant aspects of personality development occur during the first three psychosexual stages (before the age of 5 years), psychodynamic psychologists do not speak of fixation at the latency period. Simply making it to the latency period relatively undisturbed by conflicts of the earlier stages is a sign of healthy personality development.

5 At puberty and thereafter, the fifth and final stage of personality development occurs. This, the **genital stage**, is *the time for the coming together of the mature adult personality with a capacity to love, work and relate to others in a mutually satisfying and reciprocal manner.* The degree to which the individual is encumbered by unresolved conflicts at the earlier stages will impact whether they will be able to achieve a genital level of development. Freud believed that people who are fixated in a prior stage fail in developing healthy adult sexuality and a well-adjusted adult personality.

What should we make of all this? On the one hand, the psychoanalytic theory of psychosexual stages offers an intriguing picture of early family relationships and the extent to which they allow the child to satisfy basic needs and wishes. The theory picks up on themes that seem to ring true in many cases: you may very well know people who seem to be 'oral' or 'anal', for example, or who have issues about sexuality that seem to have had a great influence on their personalities. The idea that people must negotiate a way to experience the pleasures of the body in a social world does seem wise. This observation has been a key focus of the many psychodynamic theories that have been offered since Freud's death (for example Adler, 1927; Erikson, 1959; Horney, 1937; Sullivan, 1953) and even now continues to provide a rich model of personality (Andersen and Berk, 1998; Westen, 1991).

Critics argue, however, that psychodynamic explanations are too complex and tend to focus on after-the-fact interpretation rather than testable prediction. Describing a person fixated at the oral stage as 'biting', for example, seems just so much wordplay, not the basis of a scientific theory. And the control issues that preoccupy an adult with a so-called 'anal' character might reflect an inborn headstrong and controlling temperament and have nothing to do with a parental style of toilet training. The psychosexual stage theory offers a compelling set of story plots for interpreting lives once they have unfolded but has not generated the kinds of clear-cut predictions that inspire research.

In summary, Freud believed that personality results from a complex interplay of biology and environmental experience that creates the person's unconscious motives. The psychodynamic approach sees the mind as consisting of the interacting systems of id, ego and superego, which are aimed at satisfying our drives while dealing with reality and our internalized standards of conduct. He explained personality in terms of the sexual and aggressive forces that drive us, our characteristic ways of using defence mechanisms to deal with anxiety, and the degree to which we are able to move through a series of developmental psychosexual stages relatively unhindered.

The humanistic-existential approach: personality as choice

In the 1950s and 60s, psychologists began to try to understand personality from a viewpoint quite different from trait theory's biological determinism and Freud's focus on unconscious drives from unresolved child experiences. These new humanistic and existential theorists turned their attention to how humans make *healthy choices* that create their personalities.

Proponents of the new approach argued that the ability to consider the future is a core aspect of the human experience that elevates us above our animal nature, giving us the freedom to choose our actions through the exercise of will. Humanistic psychologists emphasized a positive, optimistic view of human nature that highlights people's inherent goodness and their potential for personal growth. Existentialist psychologists focused on the individual as a responsible agent who is free to create and live their life while negotiating the issue of meaning and the reality of death. The humanistic-existential approach integrates these insights with a focus on how a personality can become optimal.

Human needs and self-actualization

SELF-ACTUALIZING TENDENCY The human motive towards realizing our inner potential.

Humanists see the **self-actualizing tendency** – *the human motive towards realizing our inner potential* – as a major factor in personality. The pursuit of knowledge, the expression of one's creativity, the quest for spiritual enlightenment, and the desire to give to society are all examples of self-actualization. Abraham Maslow (1970), a noted humanistic theorist, outlined the steps that people take as they move towards self-actualization. As you saw in Chapter 10, Maslow proposed a *hierarchy of needs*, a model of essential human needs arranged according to their priority, in which basic physiological and safety needs must be satisfied before a person can afford to focus on higher level psychological needs. Only when these basic needs are satisfied can you pursue higher needs, culminating in *self-actualization* – the need to be good, to be fully alive and to find meaning in life.

Maslow observed that when people are fully engaged in self-actualizing activities, they occasionally have *peak experiences*. As discussed in Chapter 8, such experiences are altered states of consciousness in which the person loses sense of time and feels in touch with a higher aspect of human existence. Mihaly Csikszentmihalyi (1990) found that engagement in tasks that exactly match one's abilities creates a mental state of energized focus that he called *flow* (see **FIGURE 13.5**). Tasks that are below our abilities cause boredom, those that are too challenging cause anxiety, and those that are 'just right' lead to the experience of flow. If you

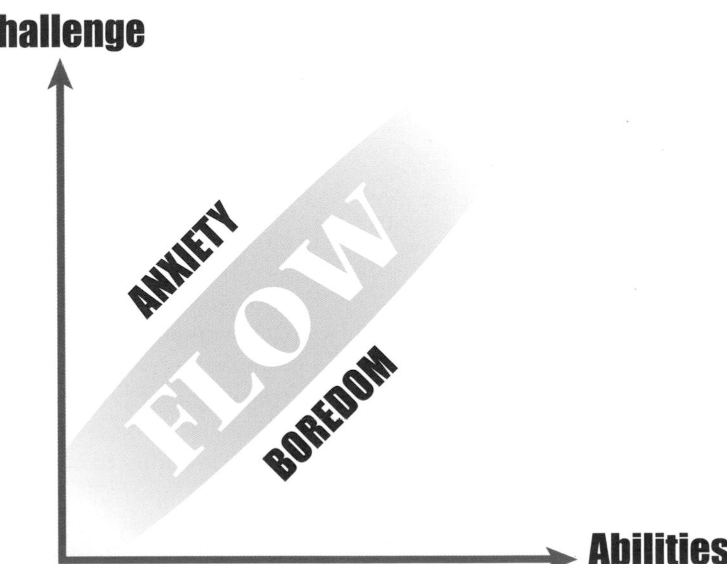

FIGURE **13.5 Flow experience** It feels good to do things that challenge your abilities but not too much. Csikszentmihalyi (1990) described this feeling between boredom and anxiety as the 'flow experience'.

know how to play the piano, for example, and are playing a Chopin prelude that you know well enough that it just matches your abilities, you are likely to experience this optimal state. In the same way that we saw how Vygotsky theorized a zone of proximal development for cognitive development in children (Chapter 11), adults also seem to enjoy tasks that tax their abilities just a little but not too much. People report being happier at these times than at any other times. Humanists believe that such peak experiences, or states of flow, reflect the realization of one's human potential and represent the height of personality development.

Conditions for growth

Humanist psychologists explain individual personality differences as arising from the various ways that the environment facilitates – or blocks – attempts to satisfy psychological needs. Like a wilting plant deprived of water, sunshine and nutrients, an individual growing up in an arid social environment can fail to develop their unique potential. For example, someone with the inherent potential to be a great scientist, artist, parent or teacher might never realize these talents if their energies and resources are instead directed towards meeting basic needs of security, belongingness and so on.

UNCONDITIONAL POSITIVE REGARD An attitude of nonjudgmental acceptance towards another person.

Noted humanist psychotherapist Carl Rogers (1951) believed that healthy personality development requires **unconditional positive regard** – *an attitude of nonjudgmental acceptance towards another person*. In particular, he argued, children must be shown that they are loved and valued and that this positive regard will not be withdrawn, no matter how the child behaves (even if the behaviour itself is not accepted or valued). He believed that unconditional positive regard is necessary for people to experience the fullness of their being and their inherent goodness and to develop their potential and accept what they cannot become. In particular, positive regard is crucial for the development of an authentic self that can be in genuine contact with others. However, this may lead to a false sense of achievement and expectation. Research indicates that when people shape their lives around goals that do not match their true nature and capabilities, they are less likely to be happy than those whose lives and goals do match (Ryan and Deci, 2000).

Personality as existence

Existentialists agree with humanists about many of the features of personality but focus on challenges to the human condition that are more profound than the lack of a nurturing environment. Rollo May (1983) and Victor Frankl (2000) argued that specific aspects of the human condition, such as awareness of our own existence and the ability to make choices about how to behave, have a double-edged quality. They bring an extraordinary richness and dignity to human life, but they also force us to confront realities that are difficult to face, such as the prospect of our own death. The **existential approach** *regards personality as governed by an individual's ongoing choices and decisions in the context of the realities of life and death.*

EXISTENTIAL APPROACH A school of thought that regards personality as governed by an individual's ongoing choices and decisions in the context of the realities of life and death.

According to the existential perspective, the difficulties we face in finding meaning in life and accepting the responsibility of making free choices provoke a type of anxiety existentialists call *angst* (the anxiety of fully being). You may have experienced angst if you've ever contemplated the way even a small decision can alter your life course. Deciding what to study, when to move to a new city, or whether to cross the street at a particular moment can forever change your whole life path – and your personality. The human ability to consider limitless numbers of goals and actions is exhilarating, but it can also open the door to profound questions such as: Why am I here? What is the meaning of my life?

Thinking about the meaning of existence can also evoke an awareness of its opposite – the potential for nonexistence and death. According to the existentialists, as we think about the inevitability of death, the resulting angst, terror and fear (or *dread*) can lead us to experience the heaviness of any given moment. What, then, should we do with each moment? What is the purpose of living if life as we know it will end one day, perhaps even today? Alternatively, does life have more meaning, given that it is so temporary?

The existentialists believe that we inevitably ask these questions when we are truly in touch with our human experience. Jean-Paul Sartre, existential philosopher, said: 'Everything has been figured out except how to live.'

Existential theorists do not suggest that people consider these profound existential issues on a day-to-day and moment-to-moment basis. Rather than ruminate about death and meaning, people typically pursue superficial answers that help them deal with the angst and dread they experience, and the defences they construct form the basis of their personalities (Binswanger, 1958; May, 1983).

Unfortunately, security-providing defence mechanisms can be self-defeating and stifle the potential for personal growth. The pursuit of superficial relationships can make possible the avoidance of real intimacy. A fortress of consumer goods can provide a false sense of security. Immersion in drugs or addictive behaviours such as compulsive web browsing, video gaming or TV watching can numb the mind to existential realities. More commonly, people find security from existential dread by devoting themselves to upholding the values and standards of their culture or families, seldom questioning whether these values fit with their own views. Studies of *mortality salience* have shown that people defend themselves in this way when they have been guided to think even briefly about their own death (Pyszczynski et al., 2003). As compared with people who are merely thinking about an unpleasant experience such as dental pain, those for whom mortality is salient become unusually protective of their family, culture, country and religion. Mortality salience has been found to prompt people to condemn critics of their government, recommend tougher sentences for lawbreakers, disparage members of other religious faiths, express prejudice towards other races and ethnicities, and become defensive of their own worldviews. Perhaps this phenomenon explains why millions of Americans responded to the terror of the 9/11 attacks by rushing to buy and display their own American flag.

JOSHUA ZIMMERMAN

Expressions of patriotism blossomed for months after the terrorist attacks of 11 September 2001.

If defences are so thin and pointless, how do you deal with existence? For existentialists, the solution is to face the issues square on and learn to accept and tolerate the pain of existence. Indeed, being fully human means confronting existential realities rather than denying them or embracing comforting illusions. This requires the courage to accept the inherent anxiety and the dread of nonbeing that is part of being alive. Such courage may be facilitated by developing supportive relationships with others who can supply unconditional positive regard. There's something about being loved that helps take away the angst.

In summary, the humanistic-existential approach to personality grew out of philosophical traditions that are very much at odds with most of the assumptions of the trait and psychoanalytic approaches. The humanists see personality as directed by an inherent striving towards self-actualization and the development of our unique human potential. They see people as basically good and, if provided with unconditional positive regard, naturally predisposed towards seeking self-actualization. Existentialists focus on angst and dread and the defensive response people often have to these very human experiences.

The social cognitive approach: personalities in situations

What is it like to be a person? The social cognitive approach to personality explores what it is like to be the person who tries to understand what to do in life's many encounters with people, events and situations. The **social cognitive approach** *views personality in terms of how the person thinks about the situations encountered in daily life and behaves in response to them.* Bringing together insights from social psychology, cognitive psychology and learning theory, this approach emphasizes how the person experiences and construes situations (Bandura, 1986; Mischel and Shoda, 1999; Ross and Nisbett, 1991; Wegner and Gilbert, 2000).

SOCIAL COGNITIVE APPROACH Views personality in terms of how the person thinks about the situations encountered in daily life and behaves in response to them.

The idea that situations cause behaviour became clear in basic studies of learning. Consider how the late B. F. Skinner, strict behaviourist and observer of rats and pigeons (see Chapter 6), would explain your behaviour right now. If you have been reinforced in the past by getting good results when studying only the night before an exam, he would have predicted that you are in fact reading these words for the first time the night before an exam! If you have been reinforced for studying well in advance, he would have predicted that you are reading this chapter with plenty of time to spare. For a behaviourist, then, differences in behaviour patterns reflect differences in how the behaviours have been rewarded in past situations.

Researchers in social cognition agree that the situation and learning history are key determinants of behaviour, but they go much further than Skinner would have in looking inside the psychological 'black box' of the mind to examine the thoughts and feelings that come between the situation and the person's response to it. Because human 'situations' and 'reinforcements' are radically open to interpretation, social cognitive psychologists focus on how people *perceive* their environments. People think about their goals, the consequences of their behaviour, and how they might achieve certain things in different situations (Lewin, 1951). The social cognitive approach looks at how personality and situation interact to cause behaviour, how personality contributes to the way people construct situations in their own minds, and how people's goals and expectancies influence their responses to situations.

Consistency of personality across situations

Although social cognitive psychologists attribute behaviour to the individual's personality and their situation, situation can often trump personality. For example, a person would have to be pretty strange to act exactly the same way at a funeral service and a fancy dress party. In their belief that the strong push and pull of situations can influence almost everyone, social cognitive psychologists are somewhat at odds with the basic assumptions of classic personality psychology, that is, that personality characteristics (such as traits, needs, unconscious drives) cause people to behave in the same way across situations and over time. At the core of the social cognitive approach is a natural puzzle, the person–situation controversy, which focuses on *the question of whether behaviour is caused more by personality or situational factors.*

PERSON–SITUATION CONTROVERSY The question of whether behaviour is caused more by personality or situational factors.

This controversy began in earnest when Walter Mischel (1968) argued that measured personality traits often do a poor job of predicting individuals' behaviour. Mischel reviewed decades of research that compared scores on standard personality tests with actual behaviour, looking at evidence from studies asking questions such as: 'Does a person with a high score on a test of introversion actually spend more time alone than someone with a low score?' Mischel's disturbing conclusion was that the average correlation between trait and behaviour is only about 0.30. This is certainly better than zero (that is, chance) but not very good when you remember that a perfect prediction is represented by a correlation of 1.0.

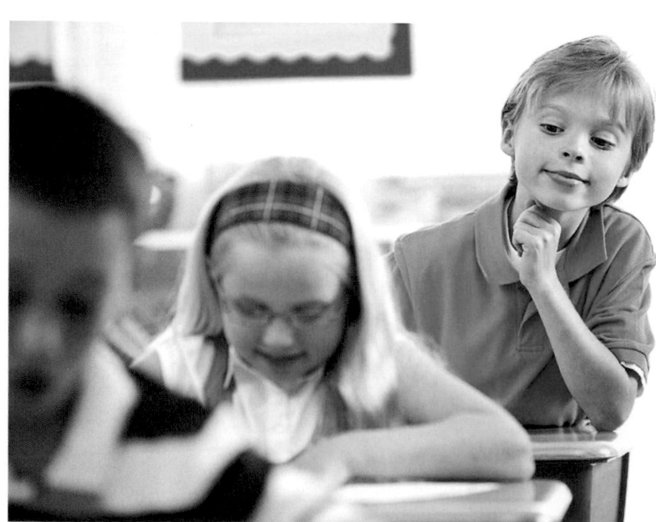

Is this student, cheating on a test, more likely than others to steal sweets or lie to his grandmother? Social cognitive research indicates that behaviour in one situation does not necessarily predict behaviour in a different situation.

Mischel also noted that knowing how a person will behave in one situation is not particularly helpful in predicting the person's behaviour in another situation. For example, in some now classic studies, Hartshorne and May (1928) assessed children's honesty by examining their willingness to cheat on a test and found that such dishonesty was not consistent from one situation to another. The assessment of a child's trait of honesty in a cheating situation was of almost no use in predicting whether the child would act honestly in a different situation, such as when given the opportunity to steal money. Mischel proposed that measured traits do not predict behaviours very well because behaviours are determined more by situational factors than personality theorists were willing to acknowledge.

Is there no personality, then? Do we all just do what situations require? The person–situation controversy has inspired many studies in the years since Mischel's critique, and it turns out that information about personality and situation are necessary to predict behaviour. Although people may not necessarily act the same way across situations, they often do act in a similar manner within the same type of situation (Mischel and Shoda, 1999). A person who is outgoing at parties but withdrawn at the office would be difficult to characterize as an extrovert or an introvert, but if they are *always* outgoing at parties and *always* withdrawn at the office, personality consistency within situations has been demonstrated. They may be the 'office bore' from nine to five, but at night they become a 'party animal'.

Among the children in Hartshorne and May's studies (1928), cheating versus not cheating on a test was actually a fairly good predictor of cheating on a test later, as long as the situation was similar. Personality consistency, then, appears to be a matter of when and where a certain kind of behaviour tends to be shown. Social cognitive theorists believe that these patterns of personality consistency in response to situations arise from the way different people construe situations and the ways different people pursue goals within situations.

Personal constructs

How can we understand differences in the way situations are interpreted? Recall our notion of personality often existing in the eye of the beholder. Situations may also exist in the eye of the beholder. One person's gold mine may be another person's hole in the dirt. George Kelly (1955) realized that these differences in perspective could be used to understand the *perceiver's* personality. He suggested that people view the social world from differing perspectives and that these different views arise through the application of **personal constructs** – *dimensions people use in making sense of their experiences.* Consider, for example, different individuals' personal constructs of a clown. One person may see him as a source of fun, another as a tragic figure, and yet another as so frightening that the circus is off limits.

PERSONAL CONSTRUCTS Dimensions people use in making sense of their experiences.

Here's how Kelly assessed personal constructs about social relationships. He'd ask people to:

1 list the people in their life
2 consider three of the people and state a way in which two of them were similar to each other and different from the third
3 repeat this for other triads of people to produce a list of the dimensions used to classify friends and family.

One respondent might focus on the degree to which people (self included) are lazy or hardworking, for example, while someone else might attend to the degree to which people are sociable or unfriendly.

Kelly proposed that different personal constructs (*construals*) are the key to personality differences, that is, that different construals lead to disparate behaviours. Taking a long break from work for a leisurely lunch might seem lazy to you. To your friend, the break might seem an ideal opportunity for catching up with friends, so they will wonder why you always choose to eat at your desk. Social cognitive theory explains different responses to situations with the idea that people see things in different ways.

Are two of these people taller and one shorter? Are two wearing black while one is wearing red? Or are two the parents and one the son? George Kelly held that the personal constructs we use to distinguish among people in our lives are basic elements of our own personalities.

Personal goals and expectancies

Social cognitive theories also recognize that a person's unique perspective on situations is reflected in their personal goals, which are often conscious. In fact, people can usually tell you their goals, whether they are to 'find a date for this weekend', 'get a good mark in psychology', 'establish a fulfilling career', or just 'get this packet of sweets open'. These goals often reflect the tasks that are appropriate to the person's situation and in a larger sense fit the person's role and stage of life (Cantor, 1990; Klinger, 1977; Little, 1983; Vallacher and Wegner, 1985). For instance, common goals for adolescents include being popular, achieving greater independence from parents and family, and getting into their first-choice university. Common goals for adults include developing a meaningful career, finding a mate, securing financial stability, and starting a family.

OUTCOME EXPECTANCIES A person's assumptions about the likely consequences of a future behaviour.

People translate goals into behaviour in part through **outcome expectancies** – *a person's assumptions about the likely consequences of a future behaviour.* Just as a lab rat learns that pressing a bar releases a food pellet, we learn that 'if I am friendly towards people, they will be friendly in return', or 'if I ask people to pull my finger, they will withdraw from me'. So we learn to perform behaviours that we expect will have the outcome of moving us closer to our goals. Outcome expectancies are learned through direct experience, bitter and sweet, and observing other people's actions and their consequences.

Outcome expectancies combine with a person's goals to produce the person's characteristic style of behaviour. An individual with the goal of making friends and the expectancy that being kind will produce warmth in return is likely to behave very differently from an individual whose goal is to achieve fame at any cost and who believes that shameless self-promotion is the route to fame. We do not all want the same things from life, and our personalities largely reflect the goals we pursue and the expectancies we have about the best ways to pursue them.

LOCUS OF CONTROL A person's tendency to perceive the control of rewards as internal to the self or external in the environment.

People differ in their generalized expectancy for achieving goals. Some people seem to feel that they are fully in control of what happens to them in life, whereas others feel that the world doles out rewards and punishments to them irrespective of their actions. Julian Rotter (1966) developed a questionnaire (see **TABLE 13.5**) to measure a disposition he called **locus of control** – *a person's tendency to perceive the control of rewards as internal to the self or external in the environment*. People whose answers suggest that they believe they control their own destiny are said to have an *internal* locus of control, whereas those who believe that outcomes are random, determined by luck or controlled by other people are described as having an *external* locus of control. These beliefs translate into individual differences in emotion and behaviour. For example, people with an internal locus of control tend to be less anxious, achieve more and cope better with stress than people with an external orientation (Lefcourt, 1982). To get a sense of your standing on this trait dimension, choose one of the options for each of the sample items from the locus of control scale in Table 13.5. For each pair of items, choose the option that most closely reflects your personal belief. Your answers will tell you if you have more of an internal or external locus of control.

TABLE 13.5 Rotter's locus of control scale

For each pair of items, choose the option that most closely reflects your personal belief. Then look at the answer to see if you have more of an internal or external locus of control.
1a Many of the unhappy things in people's lives are partly due to bad luck 1b People's misfortunes result from the mistakes they make
2a I have often found that what is going to happen will happen 2b Trusting to fate has never turned out as well for me as making a decision to take a definite course of action
3a Becoming a success is a matter of hard work; luck has little or nothing to do with it 3b Getting a good job depends mainly on being in the right place at the right time
4a When I make plans, I am almost certain that I can make them work 4b It is not always wise to plan too far ahead because many things turn out to be a matter of good or bad fortune anyhow
Answer: A more internal locus of control would be reflected in choosing options 1b, 2b, 3a and 4a

Source: Rotter, 1966

In summary, the social cognitive approach focuses on personality as arising from individuals' behaviour in situations. Rather than assuming that people have broad dispositions that are consistent across situations, the social cognitive approach describes the consistency of behaviour observed in particular situations. Situations and persons mean different things to different people, as suggested by Kelly's personal construct theory, and people may also differ in the conscious goals they seek and expectations they have about how their behaviour can enable them to reach their goals in different situations. In taking the perspective of the individual who is trying to negotiate the complexities of the world, the social cognitive approach to personality emphasizes how the person sees things and what the person wants in each situation.

The self: personality in the mirror

Imagine that you wake up tomorrow morning, drag yourself into the bathroom, look into the mirror, and don't recognize the face looking back at you. This was the plight of a patient studied by neurologist Todd Feinberg (2001). One day, the woman, married for 30 years and the mother of two grown children, began to respond to her mirror image as if it were a different person. She talked to and challenged the person in the mirror. When there was no response, she tried to attack it as if it were an intruder. Her husband, shaken by this bizarre behaviour, took her to the neurologist, who was gradually able to convince her that the image in the mirror was in fact herself.

Most of us are pretty familiar with the face that looks back at us from every mirror. We developed the ability to recognize ourselves in mirrors by 18 months of age (as discussed in Chapters 8 and 12), and we share this skill with chimps and other apes who have been raised in the presence of mirrors. Self-recognition in mirrors signals our amazing capacity for reflexive thinking, for directing attention to our own thoughts, feelings and actions – an ability that enables us to construct ideas about our own personality. Unlike a cow, which will never know that it has a poor sense of humour, or a cat, which will never know that it is awfully friendly (for a cat), humans have rich and detailed self-knowledge.

Admittedly, none of us know all there is to know about our own personality, but we do have enough self-knowledge to reliably respond to personality inventories and report on our traits and behaviours. In Chapter 12, we learned about the developing sense of self in the child and the influences that contribute to this emerging aspect of human nature. Here, we return to the issues of how we think about ourselves – our *self-concept* – and how we feel about ourselves – our *self-esteem*. This is because self-concept and self-esteem are critically important facets of personality, not just because they reveal how people see their own personalities, but because they also guide how people think others will see them.

Self-concept

In his renowned psychology textbook, William James (1890) included a theory of self in which he pointed to the self's two facets, the *I* and the *Me*. The *I* is the self that thinks, experiences and acts in the world – it is the self as a *knower*. The *Me* is the self that is an object in the world – it is the self that is *known*. The *I* is much like consciousness, then, a perspective on all of experience (see Chapter 8), but the *Me* is less mysterious, it is just a concept of a person.

If asked to describe your *Me*, you might mention your physical characteristics (male or female, tall or short, dark-skinned or light), your activities (listening to reggae, alternative rock, jazz, or classical music), your personality traits (extroverted or introverted, agreeable or independent), or your social roles (student, son or daughter, member of a hiking club, manager of a football club). These features make up the self-concept we encountered in Chapter 12, which are the thoughts we have about our bodies, our personality, our relationships and our beliefs that develop from social experiences and affect our behaviour throughout life. A person's self-concept is an organized body of knowledge that develops from social experiences and has a profound effect on a person's behaviour throughout life.

Self-concept organization

Almost everyone has a place for memorabilia, a drawer or box somewhere that holds all those sentimental keepsakes – photos, cards and letters, maybe that scrap of the old security blanket – all memories of 'life as *Me*'. Perhaps you've wanted to organize these things sometime but haven't got around to it. Fortunately, the knowledge of ourselves that we store in our *autobiographical memory* seems to be organized naturally in two ways – as narratives about episodes in our lives and in terms of traits (as would be suggested by the distinction between episodic and semantic memory discussed in Chapter 5).

The aspect of the self-concept that is a *self-narrative* – a story we tell about ourselves – can be brief or lengthy. Your life story could start with your birth and upbringing, describe

PHOTODISC/GETTY IMAGES

A key element in personality involves the stories, myths and fairy tales we tell ourselves about our lives. Are you living the story of the prince or princess in a castle, or are you the troll in the woods?

a series of defining moments, and end where you are today. You could select specific events and experiences, goals and life tasks, and memories of places and people that have influenced you. Self-narrative organizes the highlights (and lows) of your life into a story in which you are the leading character and binds them together into your self-concept. Narrative psychologists argue that we construct a story or myth (because it is not always true) about ourselves that weaves together all the different experiences, feelings and attitudes that shape our lives. For example, Dan McAdams (1993) gives a case study of Margaret, a 45-year-old mother who volunteered to tell her life story as part of his research project. We learn bizarre details about how she drove over 2,000 miles with her teenage daughter to her former Catholic boarding school so that she could desecrate the chapel. How she had refused to give up her baby daughter for adoption. How she had never had a stable relationship because that required a foundation she had never had. How she had to look after her sickly mother who died in her arms. How she sees her daughter as the only stable thing in her life. All these details may be true but McAdams proposes that they represent a script or a story, engaging as any soap opera. Maybe this is one of the reasons why soap operas are so popular because they resonate with people's own lives. In Margaret's case, her story seems to be one of a tragic victim and indeed she may have been. However, McAdams argues that someone else could have taken the same details and constructed a story of personal triumph over adversity. Like all stories, the overall feel depends on how the events are depicted and that is why it is a personal myth – it may have little bearing on the actual truth. However, once constructed, the personal myth influences the way we see our own identity and how we portray ourselves to the world. Likewise, psychodynamic and humanistic-existential psychologists suggest that people's self-narratives reflect their fantasies and thoughts about core motives and approaches to existence.

Self-concept is also organized in a more abstract way, in terms of personality traits. Just as you can judge an object on its attributes ('Is this apple green?'), you are able to judge yourself on any number of traits – whether you are considerate, clever, lazy, active or, for that matter, green – and do so quite reliably, making the same rating on multiple occasions. Hazel Markus (1977) observed that each person finds certain unique personality traits particularly important for conceptualizing the self. One person might define themself as independent, for example, whereas another might not care much about their level of independence but instead emphasize their sense of style. Markus called the traits people use to define themselves *self-schemas*, emphasizing that they draw information about the self into a coherent scheme. In one study, Markus (1977) asked people to indicate whether they had a trait by pressing response buttons marked 'me' or 'not me'. She found that participants' judgement reaction times were faster for self-schemas than for other traits. It's as though some facets of the self-concept have almost a 'knee-jerk' quality – letting us tell quickly who we are and who we are not.

Medial prefrontal cortex

COURTESY WILLIAM KELLEY

FIGURE 13.6 Self-concept in the brain fMRI scans reveal that the medial prefrontal cortex is activated (shown here in red and yellow) when people make judgements of whether they possess certain personality traits compared to judging whether the traits apply to someone else (Kelley et al., 2002).

Research also shows that the traits people use to judge the self tend to stick in memory. When people make judgements of themselves on traits, they later recall the traits better than when they judge other people on the same traits (Rogers et al., 1977). For example, answering a question such as 'Are you generous?' – no matter what your answer – is likely to enhance your memory for the trait generous. In studies of this effect of *self-relevance* on memory, researchers using imaging technologies have found that the simple activity of making judgements about the trait self-concept is accompanied by activation of the medial prefrontal cortex – a brain area involved in understanding people (Mitchell et al., 2002). This activation is stronger, however, when people are judging their own standing on traits (see **FIGURE 13.6**) than when they are judging the standing of someone else (Kelley et al., 2002). Such stronger activation, then, is linked with better memory for the traits being judged (Macrae et al., 2004). Studies have not been entirely conclusive about which brain areas are most involved in the processing of self-information (Morin, 2002), but they do show that memory for traits is strengthened when the medial prefrontal cortex is activated during self-judgements.

How do our behaviour self-narratives and trait self-concepts compare? These two methods of self-conceptualization don't always match up. You may think of yourself as an honest person, for example, but also recall that time you nabbed a handful of change from your parents' dresser and conveniently forgot to replace it. The traits we use to describe ourselves are generalizations, and not every episode in our life stories may fit. In fact, research suggests that the stores of knowledge about our behaviours and traits are not very well integrated (Kihlstrom and Klein, 1994). In people who develop amnesia, for example, memory for behaviours can be lost even though the trait self-concept remains stable (Klein, 2004). People can have a pretty strong sense of who they are even though they may not remember a single example of when they acted that way.

Causes and effects of self-concept

How do self-concepts arise, and how do they affect us? In some sense, you learn more about yourself every day. People tell you that you were an idiot last night, for instance, or that you're looking good today. Although we can gain self-knowledge in private moments of insight, we more often arrive at our self-concepts through interacting with others. As we saw in Chapter 12, young children in particular receive plenty of feedback from their parents, teachers, siblings and friends about their characteristics, and this helps them to form an idea of who they are. Even adults would find it difficult to hold a view of the self as 'kind' or 'clever' if no one else ever shared this impression. The sense of self, then, is largely developed and maintained in relationships with others.

Over the course of a lifetime, however, we become less and less impressed with what others have to say about us. Social theorist George Herbert Mead (1934) observed that all the things people have said about us accumulate after a while into what we see as a kind of consensus held by the 'generalized other'. We typically adopt this general view of ourselves that is as stable as our concept of anything and hold on to it stubbornly. As a result, the person who says you're a fool may upset you momentarily, but you bounce back, secure in the knowledge that you're not truly a fool. And just as we might argue vehemently with someone who tried to tell us that a refrigerator is a pair of underpants or that up is actually down and to the left, we are likely to defend our self-concept against anyone whose view of us departs from our own.

Because it is so stable, a major effect of the self-concept is to promote consistency in behaviour across situations (Lecky, 1945). As existential theorists emphasize, people derive a comforting sense of familiarity and stability from knowing who they are. We tend to engage in what William Swann (1983) called **self-verification**, *the tendency to seek evidence to confirm the self-concept*, and we find it disconcerting if someone sees us differently from the way we see ourselves. In one study, Swann (1983) gave people who considered themselves submissive feedback that they seemed very dominant and forceful. Rather than accepting this discrepant information, they went out of their way to act in an extremely submissive manner. Our tendency to project onto the world our concept of the self contributes to personality coherence. This talent for self-reflection enables the personality to become self-sustaining.

SELF-VERIFICATION The tendency to seek evidence to confirm the self-concept.

Self-esteem

When you think about yourself, do you feel good and worthy? Do you like yourself, or do you feel bad and have negative, self-critical thoughts? As we saw in Chapter 12, we defined self-esteem as the sense of self-worth. It is the extent to which an individual likes, values and accepts the self and this evaluation begins in childhood. The way children are encouraged to think about themselves and their achievements by others forms the basis of self-esteem (Keltikangas-Järvinen et al., 2003), although as we saw, there are also individual differences based on temperament. Anxious children tend to grow up into anxious adults concerned about how others evaluate them, which in turn affects self-esteem.

Thousands of studies have examined differences between people with high self-esteem (who generally like themselves) and those with relatively low self-esteem (who are less keen on, and may actively dislike, themselves). Researchers who study self-esteem typically ask participants to fill out a self-esteem questionnaire, such as one shown in **TABLE 13.6** (Rosenberg, 1965). This widely used measure of self-esteem asks people to evaluate themselves in terms of each statement. People who strongly agree with the positive statements about themselves and strongly disagree with the negative statements are considered to have high self-esteem.

TABLE 13.6 Rosenberg self-esteem scale				
Consider each statement and circle SA for strongly agree, A for agree, D for disagree, and SD for strongly disagree. Then work out your score, as shown below.				
1 On the whole, I am satisfied with myself	SA	A	D	SD
2 At times, I think I am no good at all	SA	A	D	SD
3 I feel that I have a number of good qualities	SA	A	D	SD
4 I am able to do things as well as most other people	SA	A	D	SD
5 I feel I do not have much to be proud of	SA	A	D	SD
6 I certainly feel useless at times	SA	A	D	SD
7 I feel that I'm a person of worth, at least on an equal plane with others	SA	A	D	SD
8 I wish I could have more respect for myself	SA	A	D	SD
9 All in all, I am inclined to feel that I am a failure	SA	A	D	SD
10 I take a positive attitude toward myself	SA	A	D	SD
Scoring: For items 1, 3, 4, 7 and 10, SA = 3, A = 2, D = 1, SD = 0; for items 2, 5, 6, 8 and 9, the scoring is reversed, with SA = 0, A = 1, D = 2, SD = 3. The higher the total score, the higher one's self-esteem				

Source: Rosenberg, 1965

Although some personality psychologists have argued that self-esteem determines virtually everything about a person's life – from the tendency to engage in criminal activity and violence to professional success – evidence has accumulated that the benefits of high self-esteem are less striking and all-encompassing but still significant. In general, compared with people with low self-esteem, those with high self-esteem tend to live happier and healthier lives, cope better with stress, and are more likely to persist at difficult tasks. In contrast, individuals with low self-esteem are more likely, for example, to perceive rejection in ambiguous feedback from others and develop eating disorders than those with high self-esteem (Baumeister et al., 2003). How does this aspect of personality develop, and why does everyone – whether high or low in self-esteem – seem to *want* high self-esteem?

Sources of self-esteem

Some psychologists contend that high self-esteem arises primarily from being accepted and valued by significant others (Brown, 1993). In Chapter 15 we will examine how group membership is critical to our self-esteem. Others focus on the influence of specific self-evaluations, judgements about one's value or competence in specific domains such as appearance, athletics or scholastics. People's overall self-esteem is probably the result of a combination of these factors, including the security of feeling accepted and the satisfaction of positive self-regard. But these sources of self-esteem do not directly influence how we evaluate ourselves. Instead, feedback we receive about ourselves differs in its impact depending on who we choose for comparisons, the unconscious perspectives we take on ourselves, and our personal belief in whether the feedback actually matters for who we are.

Consider first how comparisons can influence self-esteem. As an example, James (1890) noted that an accomplished athlete who is the second best in the world should feel pretty proud, but this athlete might not if the standard of comparison involves being best in the world. In fact, athletes in the 1992 Olympics who had won silver medals looked less happy during the medal ceremony than those who had won bronze (Medvec et al., 1995). Following pioneering work by Carl Rogers (1957), researchers have investigated the way people compare themselves to standards and how that makes them feel. If the actual self is seen as falling short of the ideal self – the person they would like to be – people tend to feel sad or dejected; when they become aware that the actual self is inconsistent with the self they have a duty to be, they are likely to feel anxious or agitated (Higgins, 1987).

The unconscious perspectives we take on feedback can also affect our sense of self-worth. In one study, researchers looked at the effect of an authority figure's disapproval on self-esteem. They examined the self-esteem of young, Catholic, female participants who had read an article in *Cosmopolitan* that described a woman's sexual dream (in page 3 language) and who had either seen a photo of a disapproving-looking pope or a photo of an unfamiliar disapproving person. The photos were shown subliminally, that is, in such brief flashes that the women could not consciously recognize who they had seen. In self-ratings made afterwards, the women in the disapproving-pope group showed a marked reduction in self-esteem compared with the other women. They rated themselves as less competent, more anxious and less moral. In the words of the researchers, self-esteem can be influenced when an important authority figure is 'watching you from the back of your mind' (Baldwin et al., 1989, p. 435).

Feedback can have different effects on self-esteem depending on its connection to the self-concept. Not surprisingly, overall self-esteem has been found to be affected most by self-evaluations in domains we consider most important. One person's self-worth might be entirely contingent on, for example, how well they do in school, whereas another's self-worth might be based on their physical attractiveness (Crocker and Wolfe, 2001; Pelham, 1985). To fully understand the impact of feedback on any individual, however, we also need to know whether their self-worth is *entirely* contingent on domain-specific self-evaluations and so fluctuates in response to evaluative feedback and performance outcomes, or if the person has a core sense of self-acceptance that gives a feeling of worth even in the face of significant failures (Kernis, 2003; Ryan and Deci, 2000). Overall, then, the comparisons we make, the unconscious perspectives we take, and the ways in which we attach our self-esteem to specific features of our self-concept can influence the impact on self-esteem of social feedback and success or failure in life tasks.

hot science

Behaving our future selves

Many of us look back over our lives and wonder if we would have made different choices if we knew then what we know now. In addition to inventing Facebook and buying shares in Apple, some of us would probably like to have avoided the mistakes that landed us in trouble.

Individuals who are inclined towards delinquency are often said to be living in the here and now, seeking instant gratification from sex, drugs and rock 'n' roll without taking into consideration the long term consequences (Gottfredson and Hirschi, 1990; Hirschi 2004). People who live for the moment tend to respond to tangible goals in the environment more than intangible future goals, and lack the capacity to delay gratification (Nagin and Pogarsky, 2003; see also Chapter 12 on the development of self-control). Individuals in general tend to think about their current selves and future selves as different people (Wakslak et al., 2008), so are more ready to identify with their future self in three months of being asked than with their future self 20 years down the road (Herschfeld, 2011). Oxford philosopher Derek Parfit (1986) explained: 'when we imagine plans in the further future, we imagine them less vividly, or believe confusedly that they will somehow be less real or less painful'.

How can we stop this? One way is to write a letter to ourselves in the future. In one experiment, participants were asked to write a letter to themselves either 3 months or 20 years later (van Gelder et al., 2013). They were told to 'Think about who you will be in (3 months or 20 years), and write about the person you are now, which topics are important and dear to you, and how you see your life'. They were then asked to fill out a questionnaire that assessed attitudes to delinquency, including petty theft, insurance fraud, illegal downloading and receiving stolen goods. Analysis revealed that the group that had been asked to contemplate themselves in 20 years' time scored significantly lower on the delinquency measure than those who were asked to write a letter to themselves only 3 months into the future.

In a second study, the experimenters created an age-progressed computerized version of each participant that was projected through a virtual reality system so that they saw their 'older' selves in a virtual environment. The control group were shown an avatar that matched their current age. Wearing virtual reality goggles, participants were asked to cross the virtual room and look in the mirror. Imagine what a shock that must have been to see your face looking much older! After the virtual experience, they took the goggles off and entered another room where they were then asked to rate the experience and complete a hard general knowledge quiz for a cash reward that was rigged to allow them cheat by looking at the answers. Both the control and experimental participants rated the avatar experience as realistic. However, those who saw a rendition of their face that matched their current age were four times more likely to cheat (24%) compared to those whose avatar was made to look much older (6%) on the quiz to gain extra money (van Gelder et al., 2013).

The desire for self-esteem

What's so great about self-esteem? Why do people want to see themselves in a positive light and avoid seeing themselves negatively? The key theories on the benefits of self-esteem focus on status, belonging and security.

Does self-esteem feel good because it reflects our degree of social dominance or status? People with high self-esteem seem to carry themselves in a way that is similar to

High self-esteem in humans may reflect the same sort of social status and respect that dominant male gorillas enjoy.

high-status animals of other social species. Dominant male gorillas, for example, appear confident and comfortable and not anxious or withdrawn. Perhaps high self-esteem in humans reflects high social status or suggests that the person is worthy of respect, and this perception triggers natural affective responses (Barkow, 1980; Maslow, 1937).

Could the desire for self-esteem come from a basic need to belong or be related to others? Evolutionary theory holds that early humans who managed to survive to pass on their genes were those able to maintain good relations with others rather than being cast out to fend for themselves. Clearly, belonging to groups is adaptive, as is knowing whether you are accepted and we return to this again in Chapter 15 when we consider group psychology. Thus, self-esteem could be a kind of *sociometer*, an inner gauge of how much a person feels included by others at any given moment (Leary and Baumeister, 2000). According to evolutionary theory, then, we seek higher self-esteem because we have evolved to seek out belongingness in our families, work groups and culture, and higher self-esteem indicates that we are being accepted.

The idea that self-esteem is a matter of security is consistent with the existential and psychodynamic approaches to personality. The studies of mortality salience discussed earlier suggest that the source of distress underlying negative self-esteem is ultimately the fear of death (Solomon et al., 1991). In this view, humans find it anxiety provoking, in fact terrifying, to contemplate their own mortality, and so they try to defend against this awareness by immersing themselves in activities (such as earning money or dressing up to appear attractive) that their culture defines as meaningful and valuable. The desire for self-esteem is a need to find value in ourselves as a way of escaping the anxiety associated with recognizing our mortality. The higher our self-esteem, the less anxious we feel with the knowledge that someday we will no longer exist.

Whatever the reason that low self-esteem feels so bad and high self-esteem feels so good, people are generally motivated to see themselves positively. In fact, we often process information in a biased manner in order to feel good about the self. Research on the **self-serving bias** shows that *people tend to take credit for their successes but downplay responsibility for their failures.* You may have noticed this tendency in yourself, particularly in terms of the attributions you make about exams when you get a good result ('I studied really intensely, and I'm good at that subject') or a bad one ('It was ridiculously tricky and the professor is an idiot').

SELF-SERVING BIAS People's tendency to take credit for their successes but downplay responsibility for their failures.

On the whole, most people satisfy the desire for high self-esteem and maintain a reasonably positive view of self by engaging in the self-serving bias. In fact, if people are asked to rate themselves across a range of characteristics, they tend to see themselves as better than the average person in most domains (Alicke et al., 1995). For example, 90% of drivers describe their driving skills as better than average, and 86% of workers rate their performance on the job as above average. Even among university professors, 94% feel they are above average in teaching ability compared with other professors (Cross, 1977). These kinds of judgements simply cannot be accurate, statistically speaking, since the average of a group of people has to be the average, not better than average. This mindbug may be adaptive, however. We return to this issue in Chapter 16 when we examine how people who do not engage in this self-serving bias to boost their self-esteem tend to be more at risk for depression, anxiety and related health problems (Taylor and Brown, 1988).

On the other hand, a few people take positive self-esteem to the extreme. Unfortunately, seeing yourself as much, much better than average – a trait called **narcissism**, *a grandiose view of the self combined with a tendency to seek admiration from and exploit others* – brings some costs. In fact, at its extreme, narcissism is considered a personality disorder (see Chapter 16). Research has documented disadvantages of an overinflated view of self, most of which arise from the need to defend that grandiose view at all costs. For example, when highly narcissistic individuals in one study were given feedback that someone thought poorly of them, their aggressiveness increased as

NARCISSISM A trait that reflects a grandiose view of the self combined with a tendency to seek admiration from and exploit others.

did their willingness to deliver loud blasts of noise to punish the person who had insulted them (Bushman and Baumeister, 1998).

The self is that part of the personality that the person knows and can report about. Some of the personality measures we have seen in this chapter – such as personality inventories based on self-reports – are really no different from measures of self-concept. Both depend on the person's perceptions and memories of the self's behaviour and traits. But personality runs deeper than this. The unconscious forces identified in psychodynamic approaches provide themes for behaviour, and sources of mental disorder, that are not accessible for self-report. The humanistic and existential approaches remind us of the profound concerns we humans face and the difficulties we may have in understanding all the forces that shape our self-views. Finally, in emphasizing how personality shapes our perceptions of social life, the social cognitive approach brings the self back to centre stage. The self, after all, is the hub of each person's social world.

Special, so very special

In 2003, furious at a rush-hour accident that blocked traffic in the Boston suburb of Weymouth, Anna Gitlin, 25, motorist (and software engineer) went ballistic at a police officer and then allegedly bumped him with her car, screaming: 'I don't care who [expletive deleted by the *Boston Globe*] died. I'm more important.'

In summary, the self-concept is a person's knowledge of their behaviours, traits and other characteristics. The content of the self-concept ranges from episodic memories of behaviour and larger self-narratives to specific beliefs about personality traits. The self-concept incorporates important dimensions called 'self-schemas', and neurological evidence suggests that the processing of information about one's self-concept activates the medial prefrontal cortex. People's self-concept develops through social feedback, and they often act to try to verify these views, which promotes consistency in behaviour across different situations.

Self-esteem is a person's evaluation of self and is correlated with other indicators of wellbeing. Sources of self-esteem include secure acceptance from others as well as evaluations of the self derived from comparing against standards. Several theories have been proposed to explain the positive feelings associated with positive self-evaluations, including locating these feelings in perceptions of status, belonging, or of being symbolically protected against mortality. People often cling to positive self-evaluations by engaging in the self-serving bias to boost their self-esteem.

The trait of narcissism involves defensively clinging to an overly positive view of self, which can sometimes produce negative social behaviour.

psychomythology

Your handwriting can reveal your personality

There is a common belief that your handwriting can reveal aspects of your personality. Maybe small, neat handwriting is typical of introverts, whereas bold, strident strokes of the pen are typical of extroverts. Indeed, there are professional graphologists who provide businesses and organizations with personality assessments based on anonymous samples of handwriting. According to the British Academy of Graphology (www.graphology.co.uk):

> Graphology is the analysis of the psychological structure of the human subject through his or her handwriting. The central nervous system provides a direct and undistorted link to the deeper self. Every human mind comprises a unique and immensely complex blend of character and accumulated experiences of life. Handwriting reflects this by evolving constantly. No two samples are the same. Our graphologists study psychology and psychoanalysis. This, combined with the acquired skills of detailed analysis of the formation of writing, enables the detection and assessment of key personality elements such as ambition, energy, sociability, adaptability, sensitivity, etc.

The academy offers training for a diploma and there are various graphology organizations throughout Europe. Getting information about who actually uses graphology in recruitment is not easy, but does it actually work? Unfortunately, the available scientific analysis of graphology does not support claims that it can reliably assess different personality traits nor is it a good predictor of job placement. First, the relationship between writing characteristics and personal characteristics does not seem to stand up. A recent Polish study of 260 participants found no evidence that writing characteristics as assessed by a panel of forensic experts were specific to the Big Five personality traits (Gawda, 2014).

Maybe forensic experts who specialize in looking for forged signatures and handwriting are not as skilled as graphologists who can tap into the 'deeper self'. However, a meta-analysis (see the strengths of meta-analysis in Chapter 14) of 17 studies investigating the performance of 63 graphologists and 51 nongraphologists (psychologists and laypersons) who evaluated 1,223 scripts suggests otherwise (Neter and Ben-Shakhar, 1989). First, all the personality variables from the different studies were summarized into three dimensions: work proficiency, social-psychological attributes, and a general evaluation. Correlations were then calculated between the different types of people who judged the scripts and the different personality dimensions. The meta-analysis was disappointing. The correlations between the inferences made by all judges (graphologists and nongraphologists) was low, at between 0.136 and 0.206 for the three dimensions. Graphologists alone were no better at agreeing with each other than nongraphologists, with correlations between 0.153 and 0.177. In fact, graphologists were less successful in predicting future behaviour from handwriting analysis than psychologists in almost all the dimensions.

What should you use to vet job applicants, then? A meta-analysis based on 85 years of studying different methods of personnel selection showed that graphology was the least valid method, producing an effect size r of 0.02 (see Chapter 2 on effect size). The best predictor was an assessment of general intelligence with an effect size of 0.51 (Schmidt and Hunter, 1998). So, if you want to hire someone to screen your candidates, choose a certified psychologist who can administer and interpret IQ tests; and if not, they could check out the handwriting and still be better than a graphologist!

where do you stand?

Personality testing for fun and profit

Many people enjoy filling out personality tests. In fact, dozens of websites, magazine articles and popular books offer personality tests to complete as well as handy summaries of test scores. Google *personality test* and you'll see. Unfortunately, many personality tests are no more than a collection of questions someone has put together to offer entertainment to test takers. These tests yield a sense of self-insight that is no more valid than what you might get from the random 'wisdom' of a fortune cookie or your daily horoscope.

The personality tests discussed in this chapter are more valid, of course. They have been developed and refined to offer reliable predictions of a person's tendencies. Still, the validity of many personality tests, particularly the projective tests, remains controversial, and critics question whether personality tests should be used for serious purposes.

Would one or more personality tests help you decide what career path to follow after university? Research findings have demonstrated correlations between personality dimensions and certain work-related indicators. In research on the Big Five, for example, people who are high in extroversion have been found to do well in sales and management positions. And, as you might expect, people scoring high in conscientiousness tend to get better job performance ratings, while people high in agreeableness and low in neuroticism do well in jobs that require working in groups (John and Srivastava, 1999).

In fact, business, government and the military often use personality tests in hiring. And vocational counsellors use the Myers-Briggs Type Indicator personality test (which primarily assesses the individual's standing on the extroversion/introversion personality dimension) to direct people towards occupations that match their strengths. Although such tests have been criticized for their flimsy theoretical and research foundations (Paul, 2004), businesses have not abandoned them. The possibility also exists that such tests might someday be used to predict whether criminals behind bars have been rehabilitated or might return to crime if released. If tests could be developed that would predict with certainty whether a person would be likely to commit a violent crime or become a terrorist or a sexual predator, do you think such tests should be used to make decisions about people's lives?

Before you answer, why not take a quick personality test yourself? Usually, personality tests have hundreds of questions to establish scores on different traits, but psychologist Sam Gosling has produced a brief version of the Big Five (Gosling et al., 2003). If you would like to know your brief Big Five scores, write a value next to each statement to indicate the extent to which you agree or disagree with that statement.

Use the following scale: 1 = disagree strongly, 2 = disagree moderately, 3 = disagree a little, 4 = neither agree nor disagree, 5 = agree a little, 6 = agree moderately, 7 = agree strongly.

I see myself as:

1 Extroverted, enthusiastic
2 Critical, quarrelsome
3 Dependable, self-disciplined
4 Anxious, easily upset
5 Open to new experiences, complex
6 Reserved, quiet
7 Sympathetic, warm
8 Disorganized, careless
9 Calm, emotionally stable
10 Conventional, uncreative

To work out your Big Five scores, perform the following conversions:

Openness	=	(8 – your score on item 10) + your score on item 5
Conscientiousness	=	(8 – your score on item 8) + your score on item 3
Extroversion	=	(8 – your score on item 6) + your score on item 1
Agreeableness	=	(8 – your score on item 2) + your score on item 7
Neuroticism	=	(8 – your score on item 9) + your score on item 4

For comparison, here are the mean scores for thousands of males and females reported by Gosling (2009).

Big Five domain	Females	Males
Openness	10.8	10.7
Conscientiousness	11.0	10.4
Extroversion	9.1	8.5
Agreeableness	10.6	10.1
Neuroticism	6.7	5.7

Chart 2.3 from Gosling, S. D. (2009) Snoop: *What Your Stuff Says About You*, p. 38. Reproduced with permission of Profile Books

Now that you have a rough idea of your personality profile and how it relates to others, what do you think about their use in today's society? Think of all you have learned about the different approaches to personality, the strengths and weaknesses of different kinds of tests, the person–situation controversy, and the fact that personality measures do correlate significantly (although not perfectly) with a person's behaviours. Are personality tests useful for making decisions about people now? If such tests were perfected, should they be used in the future? Where do you stand?

Chapter review

Personality: what it is and how it is measured

- Personality psychologists seek ways to describe and also explain individuals' styles of behaving, thinking and feeling.
- Personality inventories, such as the MMPI and other self-report questionnaires, can be used to assess people's views of themselves and their own personality characteristics.
- Projective techniques, such as the Rorschach inkblot test, can be used to assess aspects of people's personalities of which they may be unaware and that are difficult to access through self-report.

The trait approach: identifying patterns of behaviour

- Most contemporary trait psychologists are interested in the study of the Big Five: openness, conscientiousness, extroversion, agreeableness and neuroticism (OCEAN).
- Trait psychologists often look to biological factors to explain the existence of traits.
- Behavioural genetic research and studies of animal behaviour generally support the biological underpinning of traits.

- Traits are thought to arise from neuropsychological factors such as the arousability of the cortex.

The psychodynamic approach: forces that lie beneath awareness

- Psychodynamic theories hold that behaviour is shaped by motivations operating outside consciousness.
- Freud's model of the structure of the mind includes the id, ego and superego.
- People use a variety of defence mechanisms to deal with anxiety and mental conflict.
- People can become fixated at a specific developmental stage, which then shapes their adult personality.
- Early childhood experiences play a significant role in the formation of personality.

The humanistic-existential approach: personality as choice

- Human behaviour is motivated by the tendency to actualize our inherent potentials.
- Humans have a hierarchically organized set of basic psychological needs.
- People require unconditional positive regard for optimal personality development and growth.
- Human existence includes feelings of angst and dread, which people often defend against by restricting the range of their experience.
- Authentic existence involves facing the realities of life, and the accompanying angst and dread, with courage.

The social cognitive approach: personalities in situations

- Behaviour is determined not only by personality but also by how people respond to the situations they encounter.
- Different people make sense of their experiences in different ways, and this shapes their personalities.
- Core elements of personality involve goals and expectancies about the likelihood of goal attainment.

The self: personality in the mirror

- The human capacity for self-reflection allows people to form a self-concept and develop a characteristic level of self-esteem.
- The self-concept includes self-narratives that represent behaviour and self-schemas that represent personality traits.
- The medial prefrontal cortex is implicated in memory for the trait self-concept.
- People's feelings of self-esteem are influenced by feedback about the self that is filtered by processes of self-evaluation.
- Most people tend to see themselves as better than average.
- Narcissism is the trait of excessive high self-esteem.

Key terms

anal stage (p. 537)
Big Five (p. 526)
defence mechanisms (p. 535)
displacement (p. 536)
ego (p. 534)
existential approach (p. 540)
fixation (p. 537)
genital stage (p. 538)
id (p. 533)
identification (p. 536)
latency stage (p. 538)
locus of control (p. 544)
Minnesota Multiphasic Personality Inventory (MMPI) (p. 522)
narcissism (p. 550)
oblique factors (p. 525)
Oedipus conflict (p. 537)
oral stage (p. 537)
orthogonal factors (p. 525)
outcome expectancies (p. 544)
personal constructs (p. 543)
personality (p. 520)
person–situation controversy (p. 542)
phallic stage (p. 537)
pleasure principle (p. 533)
projection (p. 535)
projective techniques (p. 522)
psychodynamic approach (p. 532)
psychosexual stages (p. 536)
rationalization (p. 535)
reaction formation (p. 535)
reality principle (p. 534)
regression (p. 536)
Rorschach inkblot test (p. 522)
self-actualizing tendency (p. 539)
self-report (p. 521)
self-serving bias (p. 550)
self-verification (p. 547)
social cognitive approach (p. 541)
subjective wellbeing (SWB) (p. 527)
sublimation (p. 536)
superego (p. 534)
trait (p. 523)
unconditional positive regard (p. 540)

Recommended reading

Freud, S. (1952) *A General Introduction to Psychoanalysis.* New York: Pocket Books. Sigmund Freud's own introduction to psychoanalytic theory. This version is among the most readable and concise, with a wide array of examples.

Gosling, S. (2009) *Snoop: What Your Stuff Says About You.* London: Profile Books. Hugely enjoyable introduction to personality assessment in the context of what our bedrooms and office space reveal about our personality.

Hood, B. (2012) *The Self Illusion: Why There is No 'You' Inside Your Head.* London: Constable & Robinson. Provocative thesis that the integrated sense of self we experience on a daily basis is an illusion constructed by the brain to provide a coherent narrative in order to make sense of the multitude of conscious and unconscious influences arising from internal and external sources. In short, how the brain weaves a sense of self.

Paul, A. M. (2004) *The Cult of Personality Testing.* New York: Free Press. Critique of personality testing, examines how tests can be unreliable and invalid and asks whether employers, therapists or courts should trust personality test results.

14

Chapter learning objectives

At the end of this chapter you will be able to:

1. Understand that human interactions are primarily for the purpose of survival.
2. Appreciate that helping and hurting are opposite forms of behaviour that arise in situations where resources are scarce.
3. Recognize that humans have a rich repertoire of behaviour communication that does not involve language.
4. Identify the biological, situational, physical, individual and psychological factors that contribute to aggression, attraction and altruism.
5. Understand that humans need the companionship of others.

Social relationships

> *I was locked up for 23 hours a day with 30 minutes of exercise in the morning and again in the afternoon. I had never been in isolation before, and every hour seemed like a year. There was no natural light in my cell; a single bulb burned overhead 24 hours a day. I did not have a wristwatch and I often thought it was the middle of the night when it was only late afternoon. I had nothing to read, nothing to write on or with, no one to talk to. The mind begins to turn in on itself, and one desperately wants something outside oneself on which to fix one's attention. I have known men who took half-a-dozen lashes in preference to being locked up alone. After a time in solitary I relished the company even of the insects in my cell, and found myself on the verge of initiating conversations with a cockroach … Nothing is more dehumanizing than the absence of human companionship.* (Mandela, 1995, pp. 396–7)

Like Nelson Mandela, another person who experienced the pain of isolation is Shane Bauer, one of three American hikers who were arrested for alleged espionage in Iran in 2009. Shane was sentenced to eight years' imprisonment and wrote that the worst time of the 26 months he spent in gaol was time he spent in solitary confinement. This experience in a foreign land would leave a profound effect on Shane and his attitude towards imprisonment. One might be tempted to regard Iran's punishment as typical of oppressive regimes but the shocking truth is that the US has an estimated 25,000 prisoners currently in solitary confinement. On his return to the US, Bauer (2012) wrote an article for the magazine *Mother Jones*, where he said: 'Solitary in Iran nearly broke me. I never thought I'd see worse in American prisons.' He was determined to reveal the horrors of his homeland's use of solitary confinement as a form of legalized torture. On a visit to a Californian prison, an officer asked him about his time in an Iranian prison. Shane explained: 'No part of my experience – not the uncertainty of when I would be

© ISTOCKPHOTO.COM/RUVANBOSHOFF

free again, not the tortured screams of other prisoners – was worse than the four months I spent in solitary confinement. What would he say if I told him I needed human contact so badly that I woke every morning hoping to be interrogated?'

Social behaviour: interacting with people

Human beings are social animals, and social psychology studies the causes and consequences of their social interactions. In this chapter, we consider social interactions in relation to individuals and in Chapter 15, social interactions in relation to groups. As noted in Chapter 1, Darwin talked about understanding the human mind 'as the necessary acquirement of each mental power and capacity by gradation', and throughout this textbook we have considered psychology from this evolutionary perspective. Those who are better adapted to fit with the changing environment pass on their genes to the next generation, and one of most powerful adaptations of our species is our capacity for social interaction. When humans began to settle down in large groups at the end of the ice age around 20,000 years ago, complex societies emerged that began to increasingly regulate how we behaved (Hood, 2014). It was this new social environment and how well we interacted with others that determined whether or not we survived.

We all need others to survive if not simply to pass on our genes. Every so often, many of us like to spend time alone to escape the 'rat race' but very few of us are true hermits preferring to shun the company of others for long periods. This is because we are social animals that have evolved to live and thrive in groups. Some of the most rewarding experiences we can have as members of the human species occur in the company of others. Relationships, ceremonies, sports, concerts and just about every pleasurable facet of human existence depend on our interactions with others. We are motivated to spend time in the company of others for a variety of different reasons, but much of our social interaction revolves around the two fundamental tasks of *survival* and *reproduction*.

Survival: the struggle for resources

For most animals, survival is a struggle because the resources that life requires – food, water and shelter – are scarce. Human beings engage in social interactions that range from hurting each other to helping each other. However, what is considered acceptable behaviour now depends on what our societies permit. The primeval struggle for survival that shaped our earliest behaviours had to adapt to the new competition to live together in group harmony; nevertheless, we still carry a legacy from our evolutionary past that plays a role in our modern behaviours. Consider hurting and helping, two ways of interacting with others that produce different outcomes. *Hurting* and *helping* are antonyms, so you might expect them to have little in common. But as you will see, these opposite forms of social behaviour are often different solutions to the same problem of scarce resources.

Aggression

AGGRESSION Behaviour whose purpose is to harm another.

The simplest way to solve the problem of scarce resources is to take what you want and use whatever force you can against anyone who tries to stop you. **Aggression** is *behaviour whose purpose is to harm another*, and a quick glance at the front page of the newspaper reveals that human beings are as capable of aggression as any other animal and better at it than most (Anderson and Bushman, 2002; Geen, 1998). The 17th-century English philosopher Thomas Hobbes thought that aggression was part of human nature; an opinion echoed by author William Golding, who wrote about the descent of children marooned on a desert island into violent savagery and anarchy when there was no society to guide them in *Lord of the Flies* (1954). Golding had been influenced by his experiences of the Second World War, and in his 1983 acceptance speech for the Nobel Prize in literature, said: 'I must say that anyone who moved through those years without understanding that man produces evil as a bee produces honey, must have been blind or wrong in the head.' These nativist views reflect an evolutionary perspective on the origins of aggression championed by another Nobel Laureate, the ethologist Konrad Lorenz, who researched social development and who we encountered in Chapter 12. Lorenz argued that aggression was an instinct shaped by natural selection as much as the drive for food and drink. He wrote that it is 'always favourable for the species if the stronger of two rivals takes possession of the territory or of the female' (Lorenz, 1966, p. 26).

An important key concept of Lorenz's comparison of aggression to the drives of hunger and thirst was that unless the need to aggress was satiated, it would build up in strength until a breaking point was reached. For Lorenz, not only was aggression an instinct, but it was one that had to be expressed. If there was no legitimate target for aggression, it was likely to be exorcised in a process known as catharsis – *purging or releasing pent-up emotions through activities that redirect the focus onto other sources*. In the case of aggression, this would be anger; thus, the idea is that if you get angry, you should take out your aggressive energy on a punch bag or other strenuous activities so that it will eventually dissipate.

CATHARSIS Purging or releasing pent-up emotions through activities that redirect the focus onto other sources.

Catharsis seems to be an intuitively plausible release mechanism. After all, we often talk about being 'under pressure', but the evidence that it actually alleviates aggression is weak. Cathartic techniques such as redirecting aggressive energy through sport or vigorous physical exercise (Frinter and Rubinson, 1993) do not seem to reduce the likelihood of aggression (Bushman et al., 2001). If anything, they may even be reinforcing, because those who believe that cathartic acts help them to 'let off steam', by playing sport for example, tend to be the individuals who seek out the most aggressive forms (Wann et al., 1999). If catharsis by physical activity alleviated pent-up aggressive emotions, then players of the most violent contact sports should be the mildest off the pitch. However, the best prediction of aggression on the sports field is also aggression off the field (Maxwell and Visek, 2009).

This fighter pilot employs aggression in a focused, deliberate manner to accomplish a precise goal: to help his nation win a war.

Clearly, humans fight over many more things than the basic needs for sustenance and the ability to pass on their genes. People will fight over reputation, respect and other intangible psychological concepts that are considered worth defending. Aggression can also be expressed in different forms. A useful distinction is sometimes drawn between instrumental and hostile aggression (Krahé, 2008). *Instrumental aggression* is *premeditated*, which occurs when people consciously decide to use aggression to achieve their goals. The bank robber who threatens a cashier wants to be wealthier and the zealot who assassinates a politician wants the government to change its policies. Each of these individuals has a goal, and each inflicts harm in order to achieve it.

But the newspaper stories that make us shake our heads in disbelief are those that describe *hostile aggression,* which occurs when people aggress spontaneously and without premeditation. Hostile aggression is impulsive and rarely about scarce resources. When celebrities suddenly lash out at the paparazzi, it is often not in their best interest to be photographed brawling with the press, yet something snaps in their cool demeanour and control. Studies of violent crime suggest that about a third of all murders begin with a quarrel over a trivial matter (Daly and Wilson, 1988), and the stabbings, beatings, lootings and shootings that make headlines are not calculated attempts to achieve a goal. Rather, hostile aggression is a response to an unpleasant internal state, such as frustration, anger or pain (Berkowitz, 1990). Frustration that cannot be expressed in the form of aggressive retaliation against the original source is *displaced* – directed to an innocent target or person who is more easily accessible or less threatening and is captured by the frustration-aggression principle, which suggests that *people aggress when their goals are thwarted* (Berkowitz, 1989; Dollard et al., 1939). The robber's goal of having money is thwarted by the clerk who is standing in front of the cash register, and so the robber aggresses in order to eliminate that obstacle. When a lab rat is given a painful electric shock, it will attack anything in its cage, including other animals, stuffed dolls, or even tennis balls (Berkowitz, 1993). Injecting a rat with stress hormones can lead it to attack as well (Kruk et al., 2004). In the natural environment, the source of an animal's pain is often nearby, such as a predator or a bush full of prickly thorns, and thus impulsive aggression may have evolved as a way to eliminate sources of pain.

FRUSTRATION-AGGRESSION PRINCIPLE A principle stating that people aggress when their goals are thwarted.

Factors in aggression

The complexity of human social interactions requires much more refined levels of analysis to understand what makes someone aggressive. Some of us are more prone to aggress, so a multitude of factors are likely to play a role. Who are more likely to aggress, when is it more likely, and why does it happen? To answer these questions we need to consider the biological, individual and situational factors that contribute to aggressive behaviour.

Biological factors

In *On the Origin of Species*, Darwin (1859) wrote about how humans had domesticated wild animals to make them tame and to shape desirable characteristics. For example, all dogs have been selectively bred from wolves over the past 15,000 years to become man's (and woman's) best friend. However, some dogs such as pit bull terriers have been bred to be more aggressive than others such as the Labrador. Domestication demonstrates that aggression and tameness can be shaped by selective breeding, which must involve inheriting dispositions through the genes. One possible mechanism is the selection for genes that control the regulatory systems associated with aggression. To test this idea, Russian geneticist Dmitri Belyaev began a programme of research in the 1950s to see if he could domesticate the Siberian silver fox, which had previously never been tamed. He did this by selecting only those foxes that were less aggressive and less likely to run away when approached by the experimenter. These were then bred together and within a dozen or so generations of selective breeding, the offspring were markedly more docile. As the animals were all reared in the same environment, selecting for tameness meant choosing those individuals with genetic variation in the systems that govern the body's physiological mechanisms that control aggression. These genes were then more likely to be passed on to subsequent generations (Trut et al., 2009).

EUGENICS Selective breeding in humans to increase the prevalence of desired characteristics in the population.

Selective breeding in humans is a highly controversial topic as it is the basis for eugenics – *selective breeding in humans to increase the prevalence of desired characteristics in the population*. Eugenics was a central tenet of the Nazi's programme of genocide of groups they believed weakened the genetic pool. Although eugenics has been discredited and largely reviled in civilized society as morally and ethically deplorable, forms of selective breeding still operate through various societal mechanisms such as marriage restrictions within certain groups that constrain who mates with whom. The role of genes can be studied in a more naturalistic way by comparing identical with non-identical twins brought up in the same and separate environments (described in Chapter 3). A number of these twin studies have established that levels of aggression are more similar in identical twins than non-identical twins (Miles and Carey, 1997), but identical twins are also more similar in physical appearance, which may play a role in how they are treated by others (see physical attraction later in the chapter).

The single best biological predictor of impulsive aggression is gender (Wrangham and Peterson, 1997). Crimes such as assault, battery and murder are almost exclusively perpetrated by men – especially young men – who were responsible for 97% of same-sex murders in the US, Britain and Canada (Archer, 1994). Victims are also far more likely to be other males than females (see **TABLE 14.1**). In an analysis of murders over a 34-year period, this gender gap was found in 18 countries with the exception of Denmark, where the trend was reversed (Gartner et al., 1990).

Many studies show that aggression is strongly correlated with levels of the neurotransmitter serotonin and the hormone testosterone. We encountered serotonin in Chapter 3 as one the brain's neurotransmitters that regulates various drive behaviours including aggression. Across a variety of species, low serotonin levels have been linked to aggression and dominance behaviour, while elevated levels have been connected with affiliation and prosocial behaviour such as trust (Crockett, 2009). However, the relationship is not straightforward. Drugs that increase serotonin activity have no effect on individuals with no history of aggression but significantly reduce retaliation in those with a history of violence who would normally aggress when provoked (Berman et al., 2009).

Testosterone has long been associated with aggression and dominance behaviour and is typically higher in men than women (see Chapter 11), in younger men than older men, and in violent criminals than nonviolent criminals (Dabbs et al., 1995). The hormone doesn't cause aggression directly, but it does seem to prepare men for aggressing by making them feel extremely powerful and overconfident in their ability to prevail in a fight. Male chimpanzees with high testosterone tend to stand tall and hold their chins high

TABLE **14.1 Descriptive statistics on female and male homicide victimization rates, 18 nations, 1951–84**

	Female victimization rate (per 100,000 females) – mean (SD)	Male victimization rate (per 100,000 males) – mean (SD)
United States	3.2 (0.85)	11.17 (3.79)
Finland	1.54 (0.34)	3.95 (0.74)
Canada	1.24 (0.37)	2.29 (0.82)
Australia	1.24 (0.21)	2.04 (0.32)
Japan	1.09 (0.24)	1.96 (0.63)
Austria	1.04 (0.25)	1.44 (0.35)
West Germany	0.92 (0.15)	1.41 (0.17)
Belgium	0.86 (0.26)	1.07 (0.42)
New Zealand	0.85 (0.38)	1.3 (0.46)
Switzerland	0.83 (0.24)	0.94 (0.32)
Denmark	0.82 (0.27)	0.71 (0.34)
Sweden	0.76 (0.17)	1.09 (0.38)
Italy	0.66 (0.13)	2.20 (0.8)
France	0.64 (0.13)	1.15 (0.69)
England and Wales	0.62 (0.18)	0.89 0.21)
Norway	0.48 (0.22)	0.81 (0.38)
Netherlands	0.36 (0.16)	0.79 (0.39)
Ireland	0.31 (0.28)	0.75 (0.44)

R. Gartner, K. Baker, F. C. Pampel, Gender Stratification and the Gender Gap in Homicide Victimization, *Social Problems* (1990) 37(4): 593-612, Table 1. By permission of Oxford University Press and the authors

(Muller and Wrangham, 2004), and human beings with high testosterone walk more purposefully, focus more directly on the people they are talking to, and speak in a more forward and independent manner (Dabbs et al., 2001). Not only does testosterone cause men to feel confident and powerful but it also leaves them feeling easily irritated and frustrated (Dabbs et al., 1997). A journalist who took a testosterone injection described an incident that began when he gave his wayward dog a swat on the hindquarters:

> 'Don't smack your dog!' yelled a burly guy a few yards away. What I found myself yelling back at him is not printable in this magazine, but I have never used that language in public before, let alone bellowed it at the top of my voice. He shouted back, and within seconds I was actually close to hitting him. He backed down and slunk off. I strutted home, chest puffed up, contrite beagle dragged sheepishly behind me. It wasn't until half an hour later that I realized I had been a complete jerk and had nearly gotten into the first public brawl of my life. (Sullivan, 2000, p. 46)

Although women can be just as aggressive as men, their aggression tends to be more premeditated than impulsive. Women are *much* less likely than men to aggress without provocation or to aggress in ways that cause physical injury, but they are only *slightly* less likely than men to aggress when provoked or to aggress in ways that cause psychological injury (Bettencourt and Miller, 1996; Eagly and Steffen, 1986). Indeed, women may even be *more* likely than men to aggress by causing social harm, for example by ostracizing others or spreading malicious rumours about them (Crick and Grotpeter, 1995). Women may be less likely to punch but the social isolation they can inflict can be even more hurtful.

Individual factors

It is all very well to say that one gender is more aggressive than another (at least in terms of impulsive aggression), but such sweeping statements fail to explain individual differences that are equally important when trying to understand social interactions.

When men aggress, it is often in response to perceived challenges or threats – not to their lives or their resources, but to their dominance and their status. For example, when there is no competitive threat or confrontation, testosterone may, in fact, promote prosocial behaviour when maintaining high status and reputation are best served by positive behaviour (Boksem et al., 2013). Indeed, three-quarters of all murders can be classified as 'status competitions' or 'contests to save face' (Daly and Wilson, 1988).

What determines an individual's perception of challenge? In Chapter 13 we introduced the self-concept, the view we have of who we think we are as individuals. The self is a complicated, multifaceted and multilayered concept, which may be largely constructed by our social interactions (Hood, 2012), but, in general, we try to maintain a coherent story about who we are by maintaining our sense of worth or self-esteem. As noted in Chapter 13, individuals defined as narcissistic, who seek out the approval and admiration of others to maintain high self-esteem, tend to be more aggressive against those who threaten their self-esteem. When given feedback that someone thought poorly of them, their aggressiveness increased, as did their willingness to deliver loud blasts of noise to punish the person who had insulted them (Bushman and Baumeister, 1998). This was also found to be true when their aggression was directed against an innocent third party even before they had been given the poor grade (Reidy et al., 2010). Even apparent threats to their self-image through negative evaluation can trigger aggression in individuals for whom image is paramount, irrespective of whether others are responsible or not. However, the relationship between self-esteem and aggression is not straightforward, as schoolchildren with very low and very high self-esteem based on their academic performance can be more prone to violence (Taylor et al., 2007).

Situational factors

Some human aggression is also a response to an unpleasant internal state. For instance, the rate of violent crime is strongly associated with a city's average daytime temperature (Anderson, 1989). It has been calculated that with the predicted increase in temperature due to global warming, there will be an estimated extra 100,000 serious assaults per year in the US by 2050 (Anderson et al., 1997). When people feel hot and bothered, they tend to behave aggressively. But other events that upset the body's status quo such as smelling unpleasant odours, immersing your hand in painfully cold water, and even seeing a disgusting scene can lead to unpleasant internal states and hence trigger aggressive behaviour (Berkowitz, 1990). What's notable about these instances of hostile aggression is that they are often directed towards people who are not responsible for the unpleasant state and, as such, have little chance of alleviating it. Like a shocked rat that attacks the tennis ball in its cage, people who feel frustrated, hurt or angry often aggress against others simply because they are nearby.

Perhaps William James (1911, p. 272) was right when he wrote: 'our ancestors have bred pugnacity into our bone and marrow and thousands of years of peace won't breed it out of us'. But just because aggression may be part of our evolutionary past and implemented in the neurochemistry of our brains, it doesn't mean that it has to be part of our future. Cultures can effectively encourage or discourage aggression, which is why violent crime rates vary so much between otherwise similar countries, such as the US and Canada. Both nations have a similar number of guns per capita, yet the murder rate is three times higher south of the Canadian border (UNODC, 2011). Are Canadians nicer people? Possibly, but a much more likely factor is the social inequality at every population level, which is significantly greater in the US (Daly et al., 2001); a conclusion also reached in Michael Moore's (2002) Oscar-winning documentary film on US gun violence, *Bowling for Columbine*.

PRESS ASSOCIATION IMAGES

Culture has a strong influence on violence. In Iraq, where murder is a part of everyday life, young boys stage a mock execution.

With so much focus on murder and gun violence in the US, especially through the medium of press and film, one might be tempted to believe that living there is very dangerous, but in 2011 Estonia and Lithuania, two member states of the EU, had higher murder rates. Even within a country, aggression has a distinct cultural geography. For example, violent crime in the US is much more prevalent in the South, where men are taught to react aggressively when they feel their status has been challenged (Nisbett and Cohen, 1996). This phenomenon is known as a culture of honour – *aggression linked to one's reputation for toughness, machismo and willingness to avenge a wrong or an insult*. In one set of experiments, researchers insulted volunteers from northern and southern states and found that the southerners were more likely to feel that their status had been diminished by the insult (Cohen et al., 1996). The southerners also experienced a greater increase in testosterone than the northerners, and they were physically more assertive when a 6-foot 3-inch, 250-pound man got in their way as they left the experimental room.

CULTURE OF HONOUR Aggression linked to one's reputation for toughness, machismo and willingness to avenge a wrong or an insult.

Social psychologists Robbie Sutton and Karen Douglas (2013) ask us to imagine one group in British society brutalizing another by murdering hundreds of its people, severely beating and raping thousands every year – a horrifying thought, but a reality if one considers the disproportionate amount of domestic violence directed at females compared to males. Around the world, one of the leading causes of female death in their reproductive years is murder by a current or former partner and has been estimated to be as high as cancer (Garcia-Moreno et al., 2005). Although domestic violence is between two individuals, it can be considered an intergroup phenomenon and may reflect cultural norms of what is considered acceptable violence, as in the extreme case of so-called 'honour killings', where daughters are murdered for bringing shame and disrepute on the family.

People learn by example, and when cultures exemplify violence, violence increases measurably. Despite what the film and game industries may claim, studies show that watching violent TV shows and playing violent video games make people more aggressive (Anderson and Bushman, 2001) and less cooperative (Sheese and Graziano, 2005). In summarizing an analysis of over 300 studies, Anderson and colleagues (2003, p. 81) concluded: 'Research on violent television and films, electronic games, and music reveals unequivocal evidence that media violence increases the likelihood of aggressive and violent behaviour in both immediate and long-term contexts.' As we saw in Bandura's (1977) model of observational learning based on his social learning theory (Chapter 12), humans are inclined from a very early age to copy behaviour from others and aggression is learned by observing others' violence.

In 2013, a graphic video of the beheading of a woman by a Mexican drug gang was posted on Facebook. With over 1 billion subscribers, it is likely that the video has been viewed by thousands of children. The social network had introduced a temporary ban on such material earlier in the year, but later decided that it was in the public interest to make the video available. It was only after public pressure and criticism from politicians that the video was removed. Ironically, images of breastfeeding have never been allowed on Facebook. It would appear that as far as censorship is concerned, the violent end of a life is more acceptable to view than the nurturing beginning of one.

On the other hand, when cultures exemplify peaceful behaviour or conflict resolution, aggression is less prevalent. For example, the Inuit of the Canadian Artic traditionally avoided interpersonal aggression (Briggs, 2000). When conflict was unavoidable, they would settle the issue with song contests where the victor was the one who delivered the most effective verbal put-down of the opponent – a practice made popular in US hip-hop culture where *battle rapping* is a form of competitive performance. In nonhuman groups, the removal of aggression can shape the culture. For example, in the mid-1980s, an unusual disease killed the aggressive males in a particular troop of wild baboons in Kenya, leaving only the less aggressive males to reproduce. A decade later, researchers discovered that a new 'culture' had emerged among the descendants of the peaceful males. This new generation of male baboons were less aggressive, groomed and affiliated with females, were more tolerant of low-ranking males, and showed fewer signs of physiological stress (Sapolsky and Share, 2004). If baboons can learn to get along, surely people can too.

An ecological model of aggression

One way to consider the relevant roles of different factors that contribute to aggression is shown in the World Health Organization ecological model (WHO, 2002) on the multifaceted nature of violence (FIGURE 14.1). The model is divided into four levels. The first level identifies biological and personal history factors that influence how individuals behave and their propensity to aggress. These include genetic dispositions, effects of early environments, age and history of substance abuse. The second level considers close relationships including friends and family. For example, as discussed in the psychomythology example in Chapter 12, peer groups have

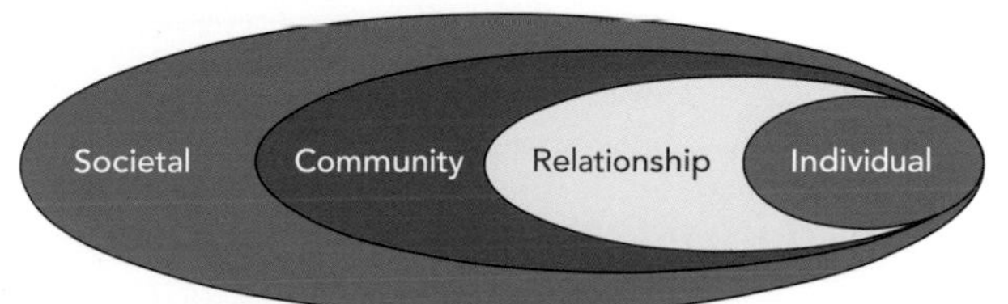

FIGURE **14.1 The WHO ecological model** This shows the embedded nature of different factors that contribute to violence

WORLD HEALTH ORGANIZATION, VIOLENCE PREVENTION ALLIANCE WWW.WHO.INT/VIOLENCEPREVENTION/APPROACH/ECOLOGY/EN/

a particularly strong influence on teenage risk taking. The third level considers the community variables such as the economic environment and population density. The fourth level addresses the broader context of society that fosters aggression such as cultural norms, political instability and availability of guns. The levels are overlapping to illustrate how factors at each level at strengthened or modified by factors at another. No single factor is sufficient to explain why an individual aggresses, which further indicates that prevention must also operate at multiple levels.

Cooperation: deal or no deal

COOPERATION Behaviour by two or more individuals that leads to mutual benefit.

Aggression may enable individuals to win conflicts over resources, but when individuals work together, they can often attain more resources for themselves than either could have attained alone. Cooperation – *behaviour by two or more individuals that leads to mutual benefit* (Deutsch, 1949; Pruitt, 1998) – is one of our species' greatest achievements, right up there with language, fire and opposable thumbs (Axelrod, 1984; Axelrod and Hamilton, 1981). Every road and supermarket, every TV and MP3 player, every ballet and surgery is the result of cooperation, and it is difficult to think of an important human achievement that could have occurred without it. As we read in Chapter 12 on social development, cooperation is a behaviour that develops as children learn to share. They initially cooperate only when the situation requires coordination and only later do they begin to spontaneously cooperate as a reflection of a growing sense of fair play.

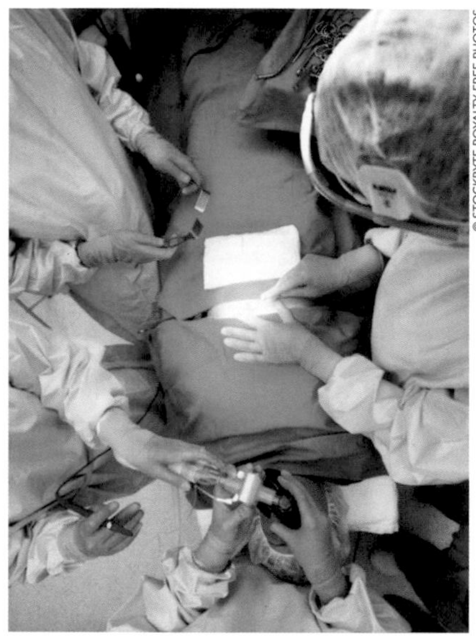

A surgery involves the careful orchestration and coordination of many pairs of hands: multiple surgeons, nurses and anaesthetists must all work together.

If the benefits of cooperation are plentiful and clear, why don't people cooperate all the time? The answer is that cooperation sometimes requires decisions that sacrifice the individual's interests for the sake of the group. In team sports, individual players have to sometimes pass on opportunities for personal triumph to others in order for the team to win. Rubbish recycling can be an inconvenience for each householder but it benefits wider society. Wars could not be waged unless individual soldiers were willing to make the ultimate sacrifice. Even on the battlefield, soldiers at war with each other have found moments of cooperation, as in the Second World War, when British and German soldiers came out of their trenches to celebrate Christmas by singing carols and playing a friendly game of football in no man's land (Hastings, 2013).

Cooperation does not always come at a personal cost but it can be risky, as a simple game called *the prisoner's dilemma* illustrates. Imagine that you and your friend have been arrested for bank robbery and are being interrogated separately. The detectives tell you that if you betray your friend and give evidence against them, they will get 30 years in prison but you will walk free. If you both say nothing, you'll each get 1 year for wasting police time. But if you and your friend both blame each other, you'll each get 10 years in prison. What should you do? If you study **FIGURE 14.2**, you'll see that you and your friend would be wise to cooperate. If you trust your friend and refuse to blame your friend and if your friend trusts you and does the same, you will both get a light sentence. But if you refuse to implicate your friend and they betray you, then your friend gets to go home while you rot away in prison. Princeton mathematician John Nash (the subject of *A Beautiful Mind*, the Hollywood blockbuster) studied the prisoner's dilemma using mathematics to determine the optimal strategies, which led him to conclude that noncooperation was the best policy (Nash, 1951). However, mathematics fails to take into consideration psychology. If prisoners are allowed to communicate, cooperation rather than being selfish wins out as the most successful strategy (Adami and Hintze, 2013). This is also true of real life. Individuals use gossip to transmit information about others' reputations in order to establish cooperative allegiances and ostracize those who are willing to exploit the trust of the group (Feinberg et al., 2014). Also, the framing of the situation is critical. When Stanford students played a money version of the prisoner's dilemma called the 'Wall Street' game, they were significantly less willing to cooperate than students who played the same version called the 'Community' game (Liberman et al., 2002).

	Cooperation B does not confess	**Noncooperation** B confesses
Cooperation A does not confess	A gets 1 year B gets 1 year	A gets 30 years B gets 0 years
Noncooperation A confesses	A gets 0 years B gets 30 years	A gets 10 years B gets 10 years

FIGURE 14.2 The prisoner's dilemma game This game illustrates the benefits and costs of cooperation. Players A and B receive benefits whose size depends on whether they independently decide to cooperate. Mutual cooperation leads to a relatively moderate benefit to both players, but if only one player cooperates, the cooperator gets no benefit and the noncooperator gets a large benefit.

The prisoner's dilemma is interesting because it mirrors the risks and benefits of cooperation in everyday life. It is sometimes described as a **public goods dilemma** – *a situation where individuals are better off if they do not contribute but the group as a whole is worse off.* For example, in most European countries, taxes are used to pay for the main social support structures of health, education and unemployment benefit. If everyone pays their taxes, everyone enjoys the benefits of a society that is not fragmented by inequality. If no one pays taxes, the social support structures start to collapse. There is a *moderate* benefit to everyone if everyone pays taxes, but there is a *huge* benefit to the few noncooperators who don't pay taxes because they get to enjoy the social benefits made possible without contributing to the cost. This public goods dilemma presents a problem and people have to decide whether to pay taxes and risk supporting the freeloaders or to cheat and risk having society collapse. If you are like most people, you would be perfectly willing to cooperate in this sort of dilemma but you worry that others won't do the same. So, what can you do to minimize your risks?

PUBLIC GOODS DILEMMA A situation where individuals are better off if they do not contribute but the group as a whole is worse off.

First, there are compulsory legal mechanisms that operate to remove the individual's decision about whether or not to contribute to society. These are the explicit laws drawn up by the various authorities that govern us. However, in the absence of explicit laws, what may surprise you is that most of us also have an ability to detect cheaters at a personal level, which may be part of an intuitive mechanism for identifying the potential freeloaders in our midst. For example, in the Wason card selection task (**FIGURE 14.3**), participants are asked to turn over two cards to test for violations of an abstract rule of the form 'If P, then Q'. Logic dictates that best way to test for violations in this case is to turn over the cards marked P and Not Q. But because people have a mindbug called the *hypothesis confirming bias*, only about 25% of the participants turn over the correct cards, and most turn over the cards marked P and Q. People find this abstract logical exercise quite difficult. But when participants are asked to determine whether a *cheater* is violating a social rule that has precisely the same form – for example, 'If the man is drinking beer (P), then he is over the legal age (Q)' – the number of participants who turn over the correct cards nearly triples (Cosmides, 1989). There is some controversy about why this happens (Cheng and Holyoak, 1989; Fodor, 2000; Gigerenzer and Hug, 1992), but one explanation is that human beings have a uniquely powerful capacity to detect cheaters that surpasses their capacity for logical reasoning in general.

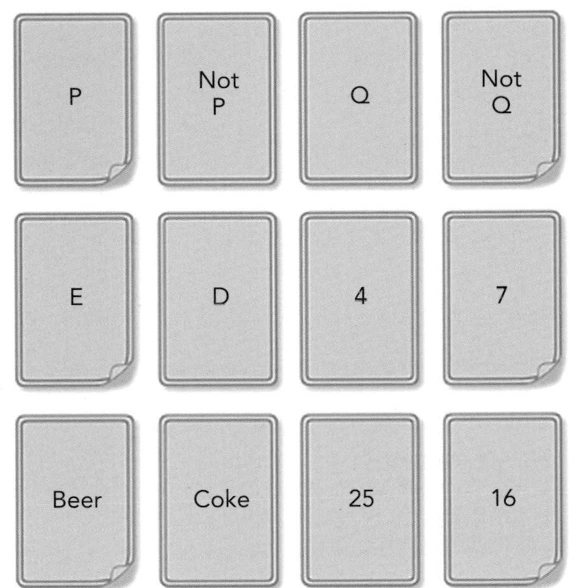

FIGURE **14.3 The Wason card selection task** Participants are asked to turn over two cards to test the rule, 'If there is a "P" on one side, there must also be a "Q" on the other side'. Logic dictates that participants should turn over the 'P' and 'Not Q' cards in the top row. Few pick the correct cards and choose 'P' and 'Q'. Likewise, if the task is to test the rule, 'If there is a vowel on one side, then there must be a number on the other', again participants tend to turn over the 'E' and '4' cards in the middle row. However, if the task, shown in the last row, is a more familiar social rule about underage drinking, 'If you are drinking alcohol, you must be over the age of 18', participants do much better by selecting the 'Beer' and '16' cards as they realize that being 25 means you do not have to be drinking alcohol.

People not only detect cheaters but also have a powerful reaction to them. Imagine that I offered you £10, no strings attached. I am sure you would gladly accept the offer. Now imagine a different scenario where I offered £100 to another person who was allowed to keep some of it only if they shared it with you. Whether or not they got to keep any money depended on your decision. What if they offered you £10 and kept £90 for themselves? Chances are you would refuse the offer so that you both end up empty-handed. The *ultimatum game* requires one player (the divider) to divide a monetary prize into two parts and offer one of the parts to a second player (the decider), who can either accept or reject the offer. If the decider rejects the offer, then both players get nothing and the game is over. Studies show that deciders typically reject offers they consider unfair because they'd rather get nothing than be cheated (Fehr and Gaechter, 2002; Thaler, 1988). Most people think it is unfair to be offered anything below 20% and rather than accept something for nothing, they would prefer that the other person did not get anything at all (Guth et al., 1982). There is also evidence that we become more prosocial and willing to cooperate as levels of neurotransmitters fluctuate. In line with the prosocial role of some neurotransmitters, rejection is greater if serotonin levels are low. Participants in the ultimatum game who had been given a drug that depletes serotonin levels rejected a greater proportion of unfair, but not fair offers (Crockett et al., 2008). Again, behaviour can be modulated by our biology.

Friendly fish

If you want to someone to trust you, you could try to ensure that they eat a lot of fish, soybeans, eggs and spinach as these are all natural sources of the essential amino acid tryptophan, a precursor to serotonin, that has been shown to increase cooperation in the ultimatum game (Colzato et al., 2013).

Deception

LIES Deliberate attempts to generate a false belief to manipulate situations.

When individuals cooperate, they operate under the assumption of mutual trust and honesty, which is why lying is not tolerated in mutually beneficial relationships. Nobody likes to be lied to, yet just about everybody tells lies – *deliberate attempts to generate a false belief to manipulate situations*. We can either withhold important information or implant false information through deception so as to control the thoughts and behaviours of others. Lying includes not only generating falsehoods, but also not fully disclosing relevant information in situations where that information is important. If someone says they do not lie, then they don't know what a lie is, they don't have anyone to lie to, or they're lying.

Diary studies kept for a week reveal that less than one in ten of us say that they did not lie at all during the period (DePaulo and Kashy, 1998). The five most common lies are about our feelings and opinions, our actions, plans and whereabouts, our knowledge, achievements and failings, our explanations for behaviours, and facts and personal possessions (DePaulo, 2004). In some situations it is morally preferably to lie. If a murderer turns up at our house asking where their intended victim is hiding, clearly we should lie if we know the answer. Sometimes we lie to avoid upsetting someone else's feelings, which we call 'white lies'. However, most lies we tell are about ourselves (DePaulo et al., 1996). People tell lies to enhance their self-esteem, to get others to like them or to gain respect. They also lie to avoid punishment. Such lying is done to conceal our true feelings, motives, plans and actions because we believe that others will judge us more negatively if we reveal the truth.

SELF-DECEPTION A capacity to convince ourselves that a falsehood is true.

Not only do we tell lies about ourselves to improve our standing with others, but we also lie to ourselves. Self-deception – *a capacity to convince ourselves that a falsehood is true* – occurs when individuals display biases to ignore, underrepresent, forget or misinterpret to favour welcome over unwelcome information (von Hippel and Trivers, 2011). It presents an interesting challenge to evolutionary accounts of human reasoning where one might assume that it is always preferable to be fully cognizant of critical information. However, sociobiologist Robert Trivers (2011) argues that we have developed the capacity for self-deception so that we may deceive others more easily by not emitting cues that reveal we are lying. When people are forced to maintain the truth and a lie simultaneously, this places demands on their executive functions to ensure that they tell a consistent story that does not contradict itself. However, by deceiving ourselves that the lie is true, there is no conflict, so we can better deceive others.

Altruism

In the early hours of the morning of 13 March 1964, the screams of a woman could be heard resonating around the Kew Gardens neighbourhood of Queens, New York City. Kitty Genovese had been stabbed in the chest by an assailant and was screaming out for help. Lights went on in the surrounding apartments, and from the seventh floor one neighbour yelled 'Let that girl alone!' As the assailant was initially scared away, Kitty tried to make her way to the stairwell of her apartment, continuing to scream for help. However, the attacker returned 10 minutes later and continued to stab Kitty before sexually assaulting her. Police received their first call around 3:50am, a good half hour before the screams had initially woken up the neighbourhood but, by that point, Kitty was dead. What makes this murder so notable is not the brutality of the attack, but the apparent apathy of the dozens of neighbours who heard Kitty's screams.

BYSTANDER EFFECT When numerous people fail to help strangers in an emergency situation.

The Kitty Genovese murder is still shocking today because most of us would like to believe that we would go to the aid of someone in need of help. It is the most famous example of the bystander effect – *when numerous people fail to help strangers in an emergency situation.* Spurred by the Kitty Genovese case, in a classic set of studies, psychologists John Darley and Bibb Latané staged emergency situations with Columbia students to investigate the factors that affect the likelihood of individuals acting to help others. In one study (Darley and Latané, 1968), two, three or six students were seated in separate cubicles discussing the problems of living in the city over an intercom system. In fact, there was only one true participant. The others were all in on the study and instructed to behave in a controlled way. One individual was a young graduate, Richard Nisbett, who went on to become a famous social psychologist interested in culture that we talk about at the beginning of Chapter 15. He was the experimental confederate who faked a seizure, asked for help and then apparently began to choke. One might assume that with more potential helpers in an emergency situation, there should be a greater likelihood for bystander intervention, whereas the opposite pattern was found. As **FIGURE 14.4** illustrates, the real participants' likeliness to come to the aid of the 'victim' in terms of giving assistance and the time it took them to respond was inversely related to the number of bystanders.

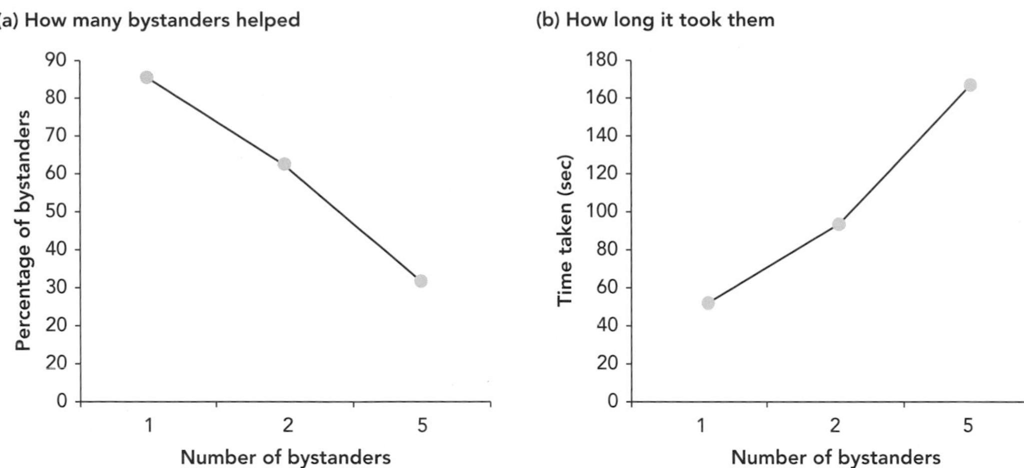

FIGURE 14.4 Bystander intervention depends on the number of bystanders The number of bystanders who helped in Darley and Latané's (1968) experiment (a), and how long it took them to begin helping (b), as a function of the number of bystanders (including themselves) they believed were witnessing the emergency.

In another emergency study (Latané and Darley, 1968), smoke was pumped into a room in which participants were filling out questionnaires. On their own, 75% of participants reported the smoke, whereas only 38% raised alarm when the room contained three individuals.

Although the Kitty Genovese murder details are undisputed, the lack of responsiveness from the neighbours has been called into question. The newspapers at the time blamed urban apathy but later investigation by three British psychologists revealed that the report was more myth than factual (Manning et al., 2007). There were fewer witnesses than originally reported and it is not clear that they recognized the crisis. However, numerous other cases show that the bystander effect is a real phenomenon. For example, on 18 April 2010, 32-year old Hugo Alfredo Tale-Yax was stabbed in New York City while coming to the aid of a woman being attacked by a knife-wielding assailant. Tale-Yax bled to death on the pavement for almost an hour and a half before medical personnel from the fire department appeared at the scene. Surveillance footage captured the whole incident and showed that 25 people passed him by as he lay dying. One even took a picture with his mobile phone, while another lifted him up, saw the blood, then walked away. It is not clear what was going through the minds of these bystanders who failed to save the dying man, but nearly 50 years of research suggests that we should not always assume that people will immediately help others even though they can.

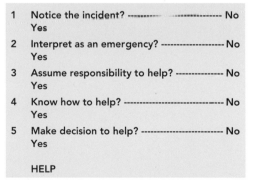

1 Notice the incident? ---------------------------- No
Yes
2 Interpret as an emergency? ------------------- No
Yes
3 Assume responsibility to help? -------------- No
Yes
4 Know how to help? ------------------------------ No
Yes
5 Make decision to help? ------------------------ No
Yes

HELP

FIGURE 14.5 Five-step model of bystander effect

Why is it that individuals are less likely to help when there are more people around? Why should more be less in emergency situations? To explain the bystander effect, Latané and Darley (1970) proposed a five-step model, illustrated in **FIGURE 14.5**. Steps 1 and 2 are all to do with perception of the situation. Clearly, if you do not notice the incident or do not interpret it as an emergency, there is no need to respond. In the Kitty Genovese case, neighbours may have misinterpreted the noise as high-spirited youths or maybe as a couple having a quarrel. The interesting question is why do people fail to intervene when they recognize there is an emergency? This is where numbers count in Step 3. If you are the only witness, there is no one else to shoulder the responsibility, so individuals take charge because they reason 'If I don't help, then no one will'. However, as soon as there are others present, there is a diffusion of responsibility – *individuals feel diminished responsibility for their actions because they are surrounded by others who are acting in the same way*. This is one reason why actions taken by a group can be less

DIFFUSION OF RESPONSIBILITY Individuals feel diminished responsibility for their actions because they are surrounded by others who are acting in the same way.

PLURALISTIC IGNORANCE Where people fail to accurately evaluate others' behaviour.

We tend to assume that other people are having more fun, getting more dates and drinking much more than we are. However, individuals are notoriously bad at accurately evaluating other people's normative behaviour – a phenomenon known as 'pluralistic ignorance'. For example, university students assume that other students drink much more than they do on average and are happier with the drinking culture on campus (Prentice and Miller, 1993). This is because students tend to remember extreme examples of intoxication from nursing sick flatmates and hearing about serious injury or death related to drinking. The trouble with pluralistic ignorance is that individuals may change their own behaviours to fit in with what they think is normal. Don't feel obliged to follow the crowd.

effective, as we will discuss in Chapter 15 when we consider group decision making. A second reason, as illustrated by the smoke room experiment, is pluralistic ignorance – *where people fail to accurately evaluate others' behaviour.* In this situation, they wrongly assume, based on the inactivity of others, that action is not required. In other words, 'If no one else is responding, then the situation must be safe'. At Step 4 in the model, having decided that there is an emergency that needs a response, a bystander may fail to act if they do not possess the requisite skills to assist. This is why first aiding courses, such as those offered by the Red Cross or St John's Ambulance in the UK, are so important because, very often, lives can be saved with simple basic knowledge and skills. Finally, in Step 5, even if a bystander recognizes the emergency and is in a position to help, they may still decide not to intervene. These situations are the most perplexing and constitute the most disturbing examples of non-altruistic behaviour. Why would anyone refuse to help another in an emergency when they are capable of doing so?

While the bystander effect is shocking, it is not necessarily what most people would do. Manning and colleagues (Manning et al., 2007) argue that the misinterpretation and mistelling of the Kitty Genovese murder case biases us to conclude that people's natural disposition is not to help others when, in fact, the opposite may be true. In some cases, groups increase the likelihood of intervening (Levine and Crowther, 2008). For example, if individuals all know each other, then larger groups are more likely to help, whereas the opposite is true if they are all strangers. Likewise, bystanders are more likely to intervene if the victim is identified as a member of their group – something we consider further in Chapter 15.

For most of us, our decision to help does not always require an immediate emergency. Help can take the form of contributing to a long-term campaign raising awareness, undertaking voluntary work with disadvantaged children, assisting someone weighed down with luggage or simply stopping to give someone directions. When we selflessly help others, we are engaging in altruism, that is, behaviour that benefits another without benefiting oneself. Being helpful is generally in our nature and we are more likely to note when someone is not helpful, which is why the failure of bystander intervention is so shocking.

Although William Golding thought that the atrocities of war were clear evidence that man was inherently evil, wars also produce many examples of individuals placing themselves in potential danger in order to help others. For example, it has been estimated that during the Holocaust, somewhere between 50,000 to 500,000 non-Jewish people risked their own lives in Nazi-occupied Europe to shelter Jewish people from the death camps, with many more helping indirectly by providing food and communication (Oliner and Oliner, 1988). Immediately after the 7/7 terrorist bombings in London in 2005, ordinary citizens demonstrated extreme acts of bravery by returning to help the victims caught in the blast. Tim Coulson, a teacher from Henley-on-Thames, battered through a plate glass window dividing his train's carriage from the one in front, which was devastated by the suicide bomber. He said: 'The first few moments were about fear for my own life, but following that there was the reality that I was not dead while others were in agony. It was like a trigger that I must do something to help' (Foggo, 2007). Indeed, heroism may be uncommon but it is not unheard of, which is to say that human beings are clearly capable of genuine altruism. Some studies even suggest that we tend to underestimate just how altruistic most people are (Miller and Ratner, 1998).

The capacity for altruism seems to be characteristically human. Examples of animal altruism exist but they are rare and restricted to those species that exhibit strong co-dependence such as marmosets (Burkart et al., 2007). In these cases, it is strategically in their interests to be help others to increase their likelihood of breeding. No other animal on the planet behaves as altruistically as humans do. Of course, there are some species such as worker ants and bees that spend their lives caring for the offspring of the queen rather than bearing offspring of their own. They will even make the ultimate sacrifice for the good of the nest or the hive when it comes under attack. Birds and squirrels give 'alarm calls' when they see a predator, which puts them at increased risk of being eaten but allows their fellow birds and squirrels to escape. Although such behaviours may appear to be altruistic, they are actually self-interested because individuals who promote the survival of their relatives are promoting the survival of their own genes (Hamilton, 1964). Evolution has programmed their behaviour to be self-sacrificial. Research shows that animals are much more 'altruistic' towards their own kin, known as kin selection – *the process by which evolution selects for genes that cause individuals to provide benefits to their relatives.* The squirrels that give alarm calls are those that are most closely related to the other squirrels with which they live (Maynard-Smith, 1965). Honeybees may raise the queen offspring, but as it turns out, an odd genetic quirk makes honeybees more closely related to the queen's offspring than they would be to their own. In short, nonhuman animals cooperate with relatives, but cooperating with relatives is not necessarily altruistic.

KIN SELECTION The process by which evolution selects for genes that cause individuals to provide benefits to their relatives.

Not all nonhuman cooperation takes place between closely related individuals. For example, male baboons will risk injury to help an unrelated baboon win a fight, and monkeys will spend time grooming unrelated monkeys when they could be looking out for themselves. Such behaviours may appear to be instances of noble generosity, but careful studies of primates have revealed that the individuals who perform such favours tend to receive favours in return. Reciprocal altruism is *behaviour that benefits another with the expectation that those benefits will be returned in the future*, and despite the second word in its name, it isn't very altruistic at all (Trivers, 1972b). Indeed, reciprocal altruism is merely cooperation extended over long periods of time.

RECIPROCAL ALTRUISM Behaviour that benefits another with the expectation that those benefits will be returned in the future.

So what about people? Like other animals, people are generally willing to contribute to the benefit of others in direct proportion to their degree of relatedness (Burnstein et al., 1994). Unlike other animals, however, human beings are also willing to provide benefits to complete strangers who will never be able to return the favour (Batson, 2002).

Who gets help?

We help our children because they are dependent on us but as we age and become increasingly independent, we are less likely to seek and be given help (Shell and Eisenberg, 1992). Males are also less likely to seek or be given assistance than females (Pearce, 1980), which may reflect gender stereotypes that they are the 'weaker sex'. Attractive people receive more help than unattractive people (Wilson and Dovidio, 1985) even when there is no possibility of forming a future relationship (Benson et al., 1976). We are also more likely to help those who we identify with. For example, the identifiable victim effect (IVE) – *the tendency to offer greater assistance to an individual rather than a group* – is thought to reflect our bias to empathize with individuals rather than large numbers of victims (Karen et al., 1997). This is one reason why charities use the poster child strategy to focus a campaign around an individual rather than a group (Slovac, 2007). News media also exploit the IVE to maximize the impact of a story by providing a face and identity to tug at our emotional heart strings.

IDENTIFIABLE VICTIM EFFECT (IVE) The tendency to offer greater assistance to an individual rather than a group.

Factors in altruism

In the same way that there are different factors associated with aggression, there are also a multitude of factors associated with altruism on the flip side of the coin of human interaction.

Biological factors

If it is not kin selection or reciprocal altruism, why are humans so altruistic? As Abraham Lincoln said: 'When I do good, I feel good. When I do bad, I feel bad. That's my religion.' The kindness of strangers reminds us that humans are an altruistic species willing to help others even when there is no obvious payoff. The simple reason for much of human altruism is that we feel better about ourselves when we help and worse when we do not. For example, when we help others through charitable donations, we get a 'warm glow' – an experience that registers in the pleasure centres of our brain (described in Chapter 6), which includes the nucleus accumbens (Harbargh et al., 2007). Arguably, such self-serving emotional pleasure undermines noble selfless interpretations of altruistic acts.

This poster is designed to play on our emotional sympathies, giving us an individual face to identify with and playing on our biological instinct to protect young children.

As in aggression, a relationship has been found between altruism and gender. Men tend to display more acts of helping than women in situations where heroism and bravery are involved, such as running into a burning building to save someone, and this gender difference has been observed across cultures (Johnson et al., 1989). In contrast, females are more likely to help in long-term care and volunteering (Becker and Eagly, 2004). These differences have been interpreted from an evolutionary perspective, where females prefer males who demonstrate acts of bravery over those who display cowardice, and males prefer females who are more nurturing and invested in long-term support (Kelly and Dunbar, 2001). However, such generalizations may equally reflect societal norms and gender stereotypes without necessarily being influenced by biology.

Individual factors

MACHIAVELLIANISM A personality trait of willingness to exploit and manipulate others.

EMPATHIC CONCERN The disposition to take the perspective of others and resonate with their emotions.

A number of individual factors have been linked to altruistic behaviour. For example, Machiavellianism, *a personality trait of willingness to exploit and manipulate others* – named after the medieval Italian scholar who wrote about how to govern through cunning and strategy – is, unsurprisingly, negatively correlated with helping (McHoskey, 1999). In contrast, empathic concern – *the disposition to take the perspective of others and resonate with their emotions* – is reflected in altruistic behaviour (Bierhof et al., 1991), such as donating to charity (Davis, 1983) and even volunteering to stand in for someone else's suffering (Carlo et al., 1991). The fact that empathic concern is evidenced early in development (see Chapter 12) suggests that it may have a genetic basis (Knight et al., 1994).

EXTENSIVITY The obligation individuals feel towards others beyond their immediate friends and family.

Feelings of responsibility towards others, which are reflected in our group identity (discussed in Chapter 15), also predict altruism. Specifically, extensivity – *the obligation individuals feel towards others beyond their immediate friends and family* – predicts charitable behaviour and willingness to volunteer (Einolf, 2010). Such values are also enshrined and encouraged in different religions (see the Good Samaritan below), and those who describe themselves as religious spend more time volunteering (Hansen et al., 1995). However, religious fundamentalists are more selective in their altruism, preferring to help those they feel are deserving rather than those whose behaviour (such as homosexuality) conflicts with their religious teachings (Batson et al., 1999).

JUST WORLD HYPOTHESIS The belief that people get what they deserve and deserve what they get.

Other personal worldviews influence our likelihood of helping others. The just world hypothesis – *the belief that people get what they deserve and deserve what they get* – explains why some people hold the controversial view that rape victims (Abrams et al., 2003) and victims of domestic abuse (Summers and Feldman, 1984) are responsible for their fate. This perverse derogation of the victim may reflect a bias to assume that everything happens for a reason and the world operates in a predictable, causal way (Lerner, 1980). People need to believe that the world is fair so that they can maintain feelings of control over their own eventual fate. Remarkably, rather than ignoring the plight of others, those who hold just worldviews may help others more in the belief that their actions will be rewarded through a 'what goes around, comes around' type of reasoning, which is why generous acts by students are more common prior to examinations (Zuckerman, 1975).

GETTY/ PHOTODISC

If someone else had already volunteered to help this young woman, we would be 10 times more likely to offer additional assistance.

Situational factors

We are much more likely to be altruistic if we witness others around us being helpful. We are 10 times more likely to stop to help a woman with a flat tyre if we saw someone else helping out in a similar situation (Bryan and Test, 1967). Arguably it is the presence of positive, helpful role models during childhood that facilitates the development of an altruistic disposition later in life (Schroeder et al., 1995), although this may be moderated by the culture at large. Levine and colleagues (Levine et al., 2001) examined the likelihood of people helping a blind person cross the road, picking up a pen after someone had dropped it, and assisting an injured person to pick up a magazine and discovered considerable variation across 23 different countries. The most helpful countries were Brazil, Costa Rica, Malawi and India, followed closely by three European countries, Austria, Spain and Denmark. Close to the bottom were the US, Singapore and Malaysia. Although there must be a multitude of influences operating on such a gross measure of national altruism, it may be the case that those cultures that foster notions of individuality and self-sufficiency (discussed at length in Chapter 15) are the least likely to display altruistic help towards strangers (Miller and Bersoff, 1994).

Another situational factor operating in altruism is our tendency to identify with individuals, similar to the IVE discussed above. For example, people are more likely to help others who dress like us, are the same nationality and share the same attitudes (Dovidio and Morris, 1975). Manchester United football fans are more likely to help another in distress wearing the same team colours than someone wearing the Liverpool colours (Levine et al., 2005).

Similar to the just world hypothesis, where a belief in fate seems to be in operation, guilty feelings can also make us more altruistic to third parties. For example, female shoppers who were led to believe that they had broken someone else's camera were three times more likely to come to the assistance of someone with a split shopping bag than women who broke the camera and were told it was not their fault (Regan et al., 1972). Perhaps they believed they could 'cancel out' their perceived mistakes by doing a good deed.

Moreover, our willingness to help is often a calculation based on the perceived costs to ourselves, which is why people are less likely to help when physical intervention is required and there is a possibility they may be injured (Fischer et al., 2011). But sometimes the cost is simply time. Consider the biblical story of the Good Samaritan about a man who was robbed, stripped and left in a ditch. As the parable goes, two religious individuals initially pass the man by, but do not help. The third man to pass is from Samaria, an outcast group, but still he helps the victim. In a classic re-creation of this scenario, Darley and Batson (1973) contrived an experimental version where they asked Princeton theology graduate students to give a talk on the Good Samaritan to undergraduates in a building across the campus. In one condition, students were told that there was ample time to reach the building. In another condition, the seminary students were told that they were already late and needed to get to the lecture as soon as possible. On route to the building, each student encountered a confederate in a doorway who was slumped over, groaning and complaining that he was having trouble breathing. Who would help this man who was clearly in distress? The seminary students who were not in a hurry were six times more likely to give assistance than the students in hurry. Only one in ten of those students in a hurry offered help, even though they were supposed to be giving a talk about altruism and the Good Samaritan!

Meta-analysis of the bystander effect

In reviewing the literature on the bystander effect in a meta-analysis of studies published between the 1960s and 2010 with over 7,700 participants, Fischer and colleagues (Fischer et al., 2011) obtained an overall effect size of –0.35, which is moderate (see effect size in Chapter 2). In other words, the bystander effect is not a trivial phenomenon but is by no means inevitable. Their analysis revealed that the factors most likely to reduce the bystander effect were dangerous (as opposed to safe) situations, a requirement for physical intervention (people were more likely to get involved if they had to actually do something) and the presence of perpetrators (signalling a causal reason for the situation). This pattern of findings is consistent with an arousal-cost-reward analysis, which proposes that dangerous emergencies are recognized faster and more clearly as real emergencies, thereby inducing higher levels of arousal and hence more physical responsiveness (Fischer et al., 2011).

Many studies on altruism are fairly old but do you recognize examples from your own personal history where guilt has made you go out and do something good? Have you ever offered to help a fellow student who was having a bad time at home because your situation was much better? Have you turned down the offer to go to a party because your friend was not invited? It is also probably correct to say that most of us have found ourselves in situations where we have had the potential to help others but we did not.

stats facts

Strength in numbers

Situational and cultural factors change over time, which calls into question whether the bystander effect seen in the Kitty Genovese case would be operating in today's society where values and expectations are different. One way to answer this type of question is to perform a statistical procedure called a 'meta-analysis' where the findings of groups of studies are combined to produce an overall test of an effect. For example, imagine that you consider 100 studies on whether the bystander effect is in operation and discover 50 which reveal that people offer less help when there are a group of witnesses compared to individuals, and 50 which reveal the opposite (Dienes, 2008). You might be tempted to conclude that the bystander effect is thrown into doubt. If the null hypothesis that there is no relationship between the presence or absence of groups and the likelihood of helping was true, one would expect to find 5 studies to be significant by chance alone. That is what the 5% significance level means (see Chapter 2 for a full discussion of statistical significance). However, one would not expect to find 50 studies all showing a significant effect in the same direction by chance alone. Meta-analysis allows you to combine studies and consider the overall patterns. It also allows you to calculate an average effect size because effect sizes are independent of the different methodologies used (again see Chapter 2 on effect size). It is an essential statistical approach for evaluating effects based on large numbers, which can be a useful way of investigating complex phenomena that are often found in social psychology studies. Look out for them, as they are generally considered to be a more reliable and valid assessment of human behaviour than individual studies, which are subject to more artefacts and biases.

Attribution: drawing inferences from actions

When we interact with others, we need to know why people do the things they do. In Chapter 12 we talked about the importance of operating with a theory of mind, but we still have to work out what is on another person's mind. Interacting with other individuals means judging them by their own words and deeds. This is more difficult than it sounds because the relationship between what a person *is* and what a person *says* or *does* is not always straightforward. An honest person may lie to save a friend from embarrassment, and a dishonest person may tell the truth to bolster her credibility. Happy people have some rotten days, polite people can be rude in traffic, and people who despise us can be flattering when they need a favour. In short, a person's behaviour *sometimes* tells us about the kind of person they are, but sometimes it simply tells us about the kind of situation they happen to be in.

To judge a person accurately, we need to know not only *what* they did but also *why* they did it. Is the footballer who scored a goal a talented player, or was the wind blowing in just the right direction? Is the politician who gave the pro-life speech really opposed to abortion, or were they just trying to win the conservative vote? When we answer questions such as these, we are making attributions – *inferences about the causes of people's behaviours* (Gilbert, 1998; Heider, 1958; Jones and Davis, 1965; Kelley, 1967). We make *situational attributions* when we decide that a person's behaviour was caused by some temporary aspect of the situation in which it happened ('They were lucky the wind carried the ball into the goal'), and we make *dispositional attributions* when we decide that a person's behaviour was caused by their relatively enduring tendency to think, feel or act in a particular way ('They have a great eye and a powerful right foot').

ATTRIBUTION An inference about the cause of a person's behaviour.

How do we know whether to make a dispositional or a situational attribution? According to Harold Kelley's *covariation model* (Kelley, 1967), we use three kinds of information: consistency, distinctiveness and consensus. For example, imagine that you wanted to know why your neighbour didn't mow their lawn last weekend. Are they lazy, or did bad weather keep them indoors? According to the covariation model, we should consider information about:

- the *regularity* of their action: consistency information
- the *generality* of their action: distinctiveness information
- the *typicality* of their action: consensus information.

If your neighbour rarely mows their lawn ('not mowing' is consistent over time), if they avoided every other form of work last weekend (lawn mowing is not distinctive), and if everyone else on the block mowed their lawns last weekend (your neighbour's action is not consensual with the actions of others), then you should probably make a dispositional attribution, such as 'My neighbour is lazy'. On the other hand, if your neighbour usually mows their lawn at the weekend (their current action of 'not mowing' is inconsistent over time), if they fixed the back door and painted the kitchen last weekend (their action is distinctive), and if no one else on the block mowed their lawns last weekend (your neighbour's action is consensual with the actions of others), then you should probably make a situational attribution, such as 'It must have been raining'. As **FIGURE 14.6** shows, patterns of consistency, distinctiveness and consensus provide useful information about the cause of a person's behaviour.

CORRESPONDENCE BIAS The tendency to make a dispositional attribution even when a person's behaviour was caused by the situation.

Research suggests that people don't always use this information as they should. Psychologist Edward E. Jones discovered the correspondence bias – *the tendency to make a dispositional attribution even when a person's behaviour was caused by the*

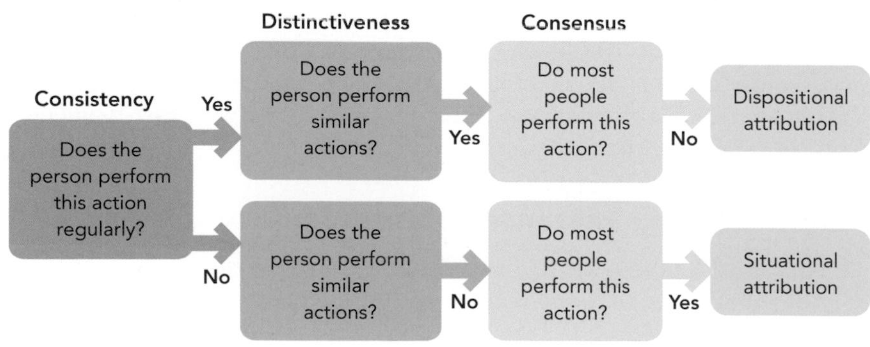

FIGURE **14.6 The covariation model of attribution** Harold Kelley's covariation model tells us how to use information to make an attribution for another person's action, such as their failure to mow the lawn last week. If the person's action is consistent (they often fail to mow the lawn) but not distinctive (they avoid other kinds of work) and not consensual (other people did mow their lawns last week), then the model tells us to make a dispositional attribution. If the person's action is not consistent (they usually mow their lawn) but is distinctive (they don't avoid other kinds of work) and consensual (other people didn't mow their lawns last week), the model tells us to make a situational attribution.

situation (Gilbert and Malone, 1995; Jones and Harris, 1967; Ross, 1977). This bias is one of the most commonly observed mindbugs, which is why psychologist Lee Ross has called it the *fundamental attribution error*. For example, volunteers in one experiment played a trivia game in which one participant acted as the 'quizmaster' and made up a list of unusual questions, another participant acted as the 'contestant' and tried to answer those questions, and a third participant acted as the 'observer' and simply watched the game. The quizmasters tended to ask tricky questions based on their own idiosyncratic knowledge, and contestants were generally unable to answer them. After watching the game, the observers were asked to decide how knowledgeable the quizmaster and the contestant were. Although the quizmasters had asked good questions and the contestants had given bad answers, it should have been clear to the observers that all this asking and answering was a product of the roles they had been assigned to play and the contestant would have asked equally good questions and the quizmaster would have given equally bad answers had their roles been reversed. Yet observers tended to rate the quizmaster as more knowledgeable than the contestant (Ross et al., 1977) and were more likely to choose the quizmaster as their own partner in an upcoming game (Quattrone, 1982). Even when we know that a successful athlete had a home advantage or a successful entrepreneur had family connections, we tend to attribute their success to talent and tenacity.

The tendency towards correspondence bias varies from person to person (D'Agostino and Fincher-Kiefer, 1992), situation to situation (Fein et al., 1990), and culture to culture (Choi et al., 1999), but research suggests that, as a general rule, people tend to make dispositional attributions even when other people's actions were clearly caused by the situations in which they happened. Indeed, people often make dispositional attributions even when *they themselves* have caused the other person's actions (which is why 'Tell me you love me' remains such a popular request) (Gilbert and Jones, 1986). Why do we make dispositional attributions even when we shouldn't?

First, the situational causes of behaviour are often invisible (Ichheiser, 1949). For example, lecturers tend to assume that fawning students really do admire them in spite of the strong incentive for students to suck up to those who control their grades. The problem is that lecturers can *see* the student laughing at witless jokes and applauding after boring lectures, but they cannot *see* 'control over marks'. Situations are not as tangible or visible as behaviours, so it is all too easy to ignore them (Taylor and Fiske, 1978). Second, even when situations are too obvious to ignore, we find it difficult to *use* the information we have about them. For example, when participants in one study were asked to perform a mentally taxing task (such as keeping a seven-digit number in mind) while making attributions, they had no difficulty making dispositional attributions, but they found it quite difficult to make situational attributions (Gilbert et al., 1988; Winter and Uleman, 1984). Situational attributions tend to be more complex and require more time and attention, which means that they are less likely to be made in the busy world of everyday life. Information about situations is hard to get and hard to use, thus we are prone to believe that others' actions are caused by their dispositions.

We are more prone to correspondence bias when judging others than when judging ourselves. The **actor-observer effect** is *the tendency to make situational attributions for our own behaviours while making dispositional attributions for the identical behaviour of others* (Jones and Nisbett, 1972). When university students were asked to explain why they and their friends had chosen their particular topics of study, they tended to explain their own choices in terms of situations ('I chose economics because my parents told me I have to support myself as soon as I've finished university') but tended to explain their friends' choices in terms of dispositions ('Norma chose economics because she's materialistic') (Nisbett et al., 1973). The actor-observer effect occurs because people typically have *more information* about the situations that caused their own behaviour than about the situations that caused other people's behaviour. We can remember getting the please-study-something-practical lecture from our parents, but we weren't at Norma's house to see her get the same lecture. As observers, we are focused on another person's behaviour, but as actors, we are focused – quite literally – on the situations in which our behaviour

ACTOR-OBSERVER EFFECT The tendency to make situational attributions for our own behaviours while making dispositional attributions for the identical behaviour of others.

occurs. In fact, when conversationalists are shown a videotape of their conversation that allows them to see it from their partner's point of view, they tend to make dispositional attributions for their own behaviour and situational attributions for their partner's (Storms, 1973; Taylor and Fiske, 1975).

In summary, competition is a ubiquitous feature in natural selection where resources are scarce, and the two best ways to acquiring sought-after resources are through aggression and cooperation. Human aggression is a complex phenomenon that can be acted out in a number of ways and is dependent on at least four sets of factors, including individual predispositions, dysfunctional relationships, impoverished community environments and societal or cultural expectations.

Cooperation is a characteristically human attribute that underpins our species' capacity to build more complex societies and technologies. We cooperate not only because it is a successful strategy to share benefits, but also because it makes us feel good. However, we are not slavish drones that automatically bend over backwards to help anyone; we are always on the lookout for those who are trying to cheat the systems of reciprocity. We are inclined to lend a hand but we will seek retaliation if we believe we have been wronged. In order to make these sorts of decisions, we have to have brains that are sophisticated enough to interpret others in terms of their motives and goals.

We make inferences about people based on their behaviours, assuming that others act as they do because of the situations in which they find themselves or because of their own dispositions. However, we tend to attribute actions to dispositions even when we should not. We are less prone to this error when making attributions for our own behaviour.

Nonverbal communication

Without communication, interactions with others would be severely limited. We use language to communicate information, express goals and coordinate our interactions. We covered verbal language in Chapter 7 but in addition to the spoken and written word, humans possess another system of communication that is nonverbal. Imagine that you find yourself in a foreign land and unable to speak the language. Even without verbal information you can still understand much about other people through nonverbal communication, principally by interpreting other people's behaviour. Nonverbal communication refers to *the sending and receiving of thoughts and feelings without using language*.

NONVERBAL COMMUNICATION The sending and receiving of thoughts and feelings without using language.

Logically, in the evolution of our species, early hominids must have possessed the capability to communicate nonverbally before language emerged. Social psychologist Nalini Ambady argues that nonverbal communication is the speediest, most effortless, and historically developed means for adapting to the social world and forms the foundation of social perception, cognition, interaction and behaviour (Ambady and Weisbuch, 2010). Well before we understand words, infants are producing and interpreting nonverbal communication (see Chapter 12).

As a social animal, we needed to communicate goals and intentions in a way others could interpret before we evolved the capability to verbalize – a communication skill we continue to share with other social animals today (Preston and de Waal, 2002). Not only do we communicate intent but we also use nonverbal communication to signal status. For example, two functions that rely on nonverbal communication that are consistently found in social animals are dominance and affiliation – where individual animals are in the social hierarchy of groups and the allegiances they have formed (de Waal, 1982). Humans are no different. The way we walk, the way we talk, and how we stand and look at each other all reveal how dominant we regard ourselves and who we like (Hall et al., 2005).

Although the nature of specific social interactions among humans is complex and subject to a multitude of different factors, nonverbal communication is thought to serve at least five basic functions (Patterson, 1983):

1 Expressing intimacy with others: touch, gaze, facial expressions and distance
2 Establishing dominance and status: gestures and posture
3 Providing information about inner mental states: facial expressions
4 Regulating verbal conversation: gestures and mutual gaze
5 Directing others' behaviour: through gestures such as pointing and gaze.

In many ways, nonverbal communication can provide supplementary information to the spoken word, but it can sometimes conflict with what is being said. This contradiction in messages is referred to as 'nonverbal leakage' and refers to the generally accepted position we explored in Chapter 10 that nonverbal behaviour reveals emotions (Ekman and Frisen, 1969). Whereas producing and processing verbal messages is cognitively demanding (Gilbert et al., 1987), much of nonverbal communication is automatic and difficult to control. This explains why we may unintentionally reveal what we really think in social situations where we are expected to suppress our true feelings, which could be bad for social harmony. We can control our nonverbal communication but it taxes our capacity on subsequent tests of executive function. For example, Richeson and Shelton (2003) demonstrated that white people who held negative implicit associations towards black people suppressed nonverbal behaviour (reducing limb, bodily and eye movement) during an interaction with a black person but subsequently exhibited heightened interference on Stroop tasks (see Chapter 3), which suggests that they were exerting attentional control not to reveal their underlying prejudice through the different channels of nonverbal communication.

Channels of interaction

As we saw in the list above, nonverbal communication includes social touching, subtle facial expressions, gaze and interpersonal distance, as well as the extent to which behaviours are mirrored or copied by individuals. One useful distinction to draw is the difference between micro- and macro-levels of nonverbal behaviours. Micro-level nonverbal behaviours are individual behaviours, sometimes referred to as 'cues', such as smiles, eyebrow raises, and other emotional expressions (see Chapter 10). Macro-level nonverbal behaviours generally refer to constellations of behaviour that are imbued with broader psychological meaning, such as displays of warmth, dominance or immediacy, which in many ways are more likely to generalize across people, cultures and time (Ambady et al., 2000). They represent the acknowledged social norms for signalling nonverbal information within different communities, in other words, the right way to behave towards different members of the group.

Physical contact

Physical contact is a very personal form of nonverbal communication whose meaning is dependent on who is involved in the act. As we saw in Chapter 12, touch is essential in forming normal social relationships in human and nonhuman primates during rearing, and it continues to play an important role in strengthening and maintaining close bonds in intimate relationships later in life. This critical role also highlights when touch is inappropriate between two individuals who are not in an established intimate relationship. Touch can also be used to signal dominance or induce compliance in others (Burgoon et al., 1989). There are also gender and cultural differences. In general, individuals tend to touch the opposite sex and men are much more likely to touch women than the reverse (Henley, 1973). Women do not like the touch of a strange man, which is likely to be interpreted as a sexual advance, whereas men are more indifferent to physical contact from a woman (Heslin and Alper, 1983). British, US and Asian cultures prefer much less physical contact than Mediterranean, Middle Eastern and South American countries (Argyle, 1990). These sensitivities to touch are also reflected by differences in interpersonal space – *preferred distance maintained by individuals* (Hall, 1966). Anthropologist Edward T. Hall (1966) identified four zones of interpersonal space, which determine whether the nature of the social relationship between individuals is being violated:

INTERPERSONAL SPACE Preferred distance maintained by individuals.

- *intimate:* up to 0.5 m – suitable for intimate relationships and physical contact
- *personal:* 0.5–1 m – suitable for minimal touch but not close enough for smell
- *social:* 1–4 m – suitable for communication without physical contact
- *public:* over 4 m – suitable for presentations to groups.

When an individual is said to be invading another's personal space, they are violating the acceptable proximity based on the relationship they have with the other person. When we say someone is 'standoffish', we are interpreting their maintenance of greater interpersonal space as a signal that they do not regard themselves as intimate in relationships.

Facial expressions

Darwin (1872) believed that specific facial expressions were directly caused by specific emotions and that this relationship was universal. In a meta-analysis of over 162 samples of facial emotions from countries ranging from New Guinea to Malaysia and Germany to Ethiopia, only 3% of these cross-cultural samples demonstrated even a *single emotion* being recognized at rates below chance (Elfenbein and Ambady, 2002). However, the face can signal confusion, interest and boredom, which are states of cognitive engagement rather than primary emotions. Social interaction with someone who is expressionless as result of facial paralysis from disorders such Möbius syndrome (Bogart and Matsumoto, 2010), Bell's palsy (Coulson et al., 2004) or, more commonly, Parkinson's disease (Hemmesch et al., 2009) can be very impaired, indicating the important role expressions play in communication. As we noted in Chapter 10, the ability to generate an expression is an important component of experiencing emotions but we are surprisingly poor at reading our own facial expressions and other nonverbal signals. Studies show that people are moderately accurate in estimating how much they smile but are not good at estimating how much they nod, gesture, self-touch and gaze towards others (Hall et al., 2002, 2007). Even when we are told to monitor our own facial expressions, we typically overestimate them in comparison to others watching us (Gilovich et al., 1998).

Gaze

As we tend to look at what interests us, gaze, as signalled by the direction of the head and the eyes, is an important channel of nonverbal communication because it reveals when and where someone's attention is focused. In Chapter 12, we saw that mutual gaze is present early in development and that infants follow direction of gaze as a way to maintain joint attention. Gaze behaviour is also a precursor to communication, which is why we try to catch someone's eye before we strike up a conversation. In face-to-face conversation, the person listening spends roughly about twice the amount of time looking at the speaker, who will periodically glance at the listener, especially when they are making an important point or expecting a response (Argyle and Dean, 1965). We can gauge how much interest or boredom they are expressing and whether they have been registering the important messages by watching their gaze behaviour.

Not only do we seek out the gaze of others but it can be difficult to ignore, especially if they are staring at us. Another person's gaze can be so powerful that when they shift their eyes to look elsewhere, we automatically shift our own attention to align with theirs (Driver et al., 1999). Direct staring, especially if prolonged, triggers the emotional centres of the brain we discussed in Chapter 10, including the amygdala (Adams et al, 2003). If the other person is someone you like, the experience can be pleasing, but it is distressing if they are strangers. As with interpersonal space, there are cultural differences. In many Mediterranean countries it is considered normal to stare, which makes some foreign tourists feel uncomfortable at being gawked at when on holiday (Argyle and Cook, 1976). Direct eye contact, especially between someone of lower status with someone of higher status such as a student and teacher in Japanese culture, is not considered polite. Japanese people perceive direct gaze as angrier, unapproachable and more unpleasant (Akechi et al., 2013), whereas in the West, we tend to regard someone who does not look you in the eye during a conversation as being shifty and deceitful, which is, in fact, not true (see the psychomythology box).

DEAGOSTINI/G. DAGLI ORTI/GETTY IMAGES

The Cheat with the Ace of Diamonds (1635), Georges de La Tour's famous painting, is a perfect example of the power of gaze.

Take a moment to look over the picture *The Cheat with the Ace of Diamonds* until you have worked out what is going on. In all likelihood, your eyes were instinctively drawn to the lady card player at the centre of the picture and from there, you probably followed her line of gaze to the waitress and then to the faces of the two other players. Studies of the eye movements of adults looking at pictures of individuals in social settings produce predictable paths of scrutiny that reveal how we seek out others' gaze and attention when interpreting complex social interactions (Yarbus, 1967). The eyes may be the windows to the soul, but they are also useful in inferring what's on another's mind (see psychomythology box at end of chapter).

Behavioural mimicry

Once we identify with others in our group, we are more likely to copy their nonverbal behaviour. This change to match others around us is known as the chameleon effect – *the mimicking of postures, expressions, gestures and patterns of behaviour such as speech or moods* – named after the exotic lizard that can change its skin colour to blend in with its surroundings (Chartrand and Bargh, 1999). These are acts of affiliation signalling our allegiances. We want to be seen to be like others in the group in order to consolidate our position and we do so by copying them. We copy those people we like, who, in turn, like us more, thereby increasing the likelihood that they will copy us (van Baaren et al., 2003a).

CHAMELEON EFFECT The mimicking of postures, expressions, gestures and patterns of behaviour such as speech or moods.

Not only do we like people who mimic us more but we are willing to help them out if they request favours from us (van Baaren et al., 2004a). We even feel like a better human being after we have been copied and it can last long after the encounter. In one study, after being mimicked, participants donated twice as much money to a charity box as they left the experiment compared to those who had not been copied, even though the donations were anonymous (van Baaren et al., 2004b). We even tip waitresses more when they mimic us (van Baaren et al., 2003b). However, if someone from an out-group copies us, we interpret this mimicry as mockery – an act of provocation (Stel et al., 2010).

Emotional contagion

We tend to like those who copy our behaviour but we also copy each other's emotions, even unintentionally (Hatfield et al., 1993). Emotional contagion is *the tendency to automatically mimic and synchronize expressions, vocalizations, postures and movements with those of another person and, consequently, to converge emotionally* (Fischer et al., 1990). One possible mechanism for emotional contagion is the mirror neuron system we introduced in Chapter 3, whereby we are able to mimic the motor responses of others that, in turn, could trigger the experience of emotions through the facial feedback hypothesis described in Chapter 10. This is supported by a Swedish study of students who had the activity of their face muscles measured as they looked at people displaying either happy or angry facial expressions (Dimberg, 1982). Recordings of their own face muscles showed increased muscular activity over the zygomaticus major (cheek) muscle region for happy expressions, whereas angry faces produced greater frowning over the corrugator supercilii (brow) muscle region.

EMOTIONAL CONTAGION The tendency to automatically mimic and synchronize expressions, vocalizations, postures and movements with those of another person and, consequently, to converge emotionally.

It is not only visual mimicry that can induce emotional contagion. Have you ever found yourself laughing at a joke more heartily when you hear others laughing? This is why TV comedies are often accompanied with a laughter track synchronized to when a joke has been made. In one of the first experimental studies of 'canned laughter', students listened to jokes when they thought they were alone or when they were with four others who could also hear them (Nosanchuk and Lightstone, 1974). They were substantially more likely to laugh when they thought they could be heard than when they thought they were alone. However, this may have been simply an example of social compliance we described above.

Does a joke seem funnier when there are other people laughing along? Is this a sign of emotional contagion or social compliance?

Robert Provine, an expert on the biology of laughing, thinks that laughing along with other emotions provides a powerful mechanism for signalling social allegiance. He has demonstrated that even the sound of laughter from a novelty box will trigger similar laughing in around 50% of students and smiling in over 90% (Provine, 1992). However, with repeated exposure this artificial laughter declines significantly as the joke wears a bit thin. The efficacy of laughter alone to elicit laughter

In 1962, there was an outbreak of contagious laughter in a girls' boarding school in Tanzania. The first symptoms appeared on 30 January, when three girls got the giggles and couldn't stop laughing. The symptoms quickly spread to 95 students, forcing the school to close on 18 March. Soon, related outbreaks were reported in other schools in Central Africa and the laughter epidemic spread like wildfire, ceasing two-and-a-half years later and afflicting nearly 1,000 people.

raises the intriguing possibility that human beings have auditory 'feature detectors' – neural circuits that respond exclusively to this species-typical vocalization – but social context is also important (Provine, 1996).

Decoding nonverbal communication

It is not enough to send out a communication unless others can read it. Surprisingly, nonverbal communication can be rapidly and richly interpreted with only the briefest amount of information. Thin slicing – *our capacity to accurately interpret social information from brief observations of behaviour* – is a reliable phenomenon that many of us can do (Ambady and Rosenthal, 1992). It is the ultimate of first impressions as we can make complex social judgements from as little as 6 seconds of video footage that is completely nonverbal (Winerman, 2005). In one study by Ambady and Rosenthal (1993), 13 graduate teaching fellows were videoed as they taught their classes. Three random 10-second clips from each recording were combined into one 30-second silent clip and showed to students who did not know the teachers. The student judges rated the teachers on variables such as 'accepting', 'active', 'competent' and 'confident', which were combined to produce an overall approval rating. It later transpired that this approval rating correlated at 0.76 with actual end of term class ratings from students who had taken the class, which is a strong relationship. It turns out that we can discern sexual orientation, sexual promiscuity, racial bias and status dominance from thin slices of nonverbal behaviour (Ambady and Weisbuch, 2010).

THIN SLICING Our capacity to accurately interpret social information from brief observations of behaviour.

People's capacity to decode nonverbal behaviour generally improves with age and experience (Buck, 1984; DePaulo and Rosenthal, 1982). Also, in line with the cultural stereotype of 'female intuition', females from at least school age do appear to be more accurate at interpreting nonverbal communication (Rosip and Hall, 2004). Although the difference is not great, it is consistent (Knapp et al., 2013). While females are more sensitive to reading emotions in faces (Hampson et al., 2006), there is some evidence to indicate that males have an advantage in detecting nonverbal signals of aggression in other males (Wagner et al., 1986).

In summary, language is a primary channel for communication. However, in addition to verbal communication, humans possess sophisticated nonverbal communication skills that use facial expressions, gaze processing, mirrored behaviour and copied emotions. They are used to convey additional information and signal allegiances and affiliation with others. Most individuals are unaware of their own nonverbal signals, which can be rapidly transmitted and decoded by others even when there is very little content.

Reproduction

Reading others in terms of their intentions is important for survival. Do they want to fight you or befriend you? Ultimately, we evolved to pass on our genes, so survival is a prerequisite for reproduction. A vehicle for genes must stay alive in order to build the next vehicle, so it is unsurprising that our urge to reproduce – which involves everything from having sex to raising children – is every bit as strong as our urge to stay alive. Indeed, a great deal of our social behaviour can be understood in terms of our basic reproductive drive (Buss and Kenrick, 1998). However, the biological imperative has been superseded by other drives that can trump the need to reproduce. Many individuals enjoy sexual relationships where there is no expectation to reproduce or they take active measures to prevent conception. Likewise, same-sex relationships prove that attraction is not always directed to a biologically opposite partner and homosexual couples may or may not decide to raise children. Therefore, the biological imperative to reproduce cannot be the sole determinant of our social behaviour. In this section we discuss mechanisms whereby males and females are attracted towards each other for the purposes of reproduction, but acknowledge that humans are complex beings who do not neatly fit into one category versus another, with much diversity in between.

PHOTODISC

Same-sex couples show that the biological urge to reproduce is not the only governing motivation in our relationships with others.

Selectivity

Survival is the first step on the road to reproduction, but the second step involves finding someone of the opposite sex who has taken the first step too. You need only look around whatever room you are in to know that not just anyone will do. People *select* their reproductive and sexual partners, and perhaps the most striking fact about this selection is that women are more selective than men (Feingold, 1992a). In one study, an attractive person (who was working for the experimenters) approached an opposite-sex stranger on a college campus and asked one of two questions: 'Would you go out tonight?' or, 'Would you go to bed with me?' About half of the men and women who were approached agreed to go out with the attractive person. Although *none* of the women agreed to go to bed with the person, *three-quarters* of the men did (Clark and Hatfield, 1989).

What makes women the choosier sex? One explanation focuses on differences in male and female reproductive biology (Buss and Schmitt, 1993; Trivers, 1972a). One can consider the problem as a simple cost–benefit analysis. As men produce billions of sperm in their lifetimes, their ability to conceive a child tomorrow is not inhibited by having conceived one today, and conception has no significant physical costs. On the other hand, women produce a small number of eggs in their lifetimes, conception eliminates their ability to conceive for at least nine more months, and pregnancy produces physical changes that increase their nutritional requirements and put them at risk of illness and death. Therefore, if a man makes an 'evolutionary mistake' by mating with a woman whose genes do not produce healthy offspring, the cost in biological terms is minimal. But if a woman makes the same mistake by mating with a man whose genes do not produce healthy offspring, she has lost a precious egg, borne the costs of pregnancy, risked her life in childbirth, and missed at least nine months of other reproductive opportunities. Women are naturally more selective because reproduction is much more costly for women than for men.

Although reproductive biology makes sex a more expensive proposition for women than for men, it is important to note two things. First, women are more selective than men *on average*, but there is still tremendous variability *among* men and *among* women (Gangestad and Simpson, 2000). We've described the typical reproductive strategies of *most* women and men but certainly not the strategy of any particular woman or man. Second, like biology, social norms can also make sex differentially expensive for women and men and can thereby increase or decrease gender differences in selectivity (Eagly and Wood, 1999). For example, in cultures that glorify promiscuous men as *playboys* and disparage promiscuous women as *sluts,* women are likely to be much more selective than men because the reputational costs of sex are much higher. When cultures lower the costs of sex for women by providing access to effective birth control, promoting the financial independence of women, or adopting communal styles of child rearing, women do indeed become less selective (Kasser and Sharma, 1999). Similarly, when sex is expensive for men, for example when they are choosing a long-term mate for a monogamous relationship rather than a short-term mate for a weekend, they can be every bit as selective as women (Kenrick et al., 1990). Our basic biology generally makes sex a more expensive proposition for women than for men, but social forces can exaggerate, equalize or reverse those costs. The higher the costs, the greater the selectivity.

Attraction

For most of us, there are a small number of people with whom we are willing to have sex, an even smaller number of people with whom we are willing to have children, and a staggeringly large number of people with whom we are unwilling to have either. So, when we meet someone new, how do we decide which of these categories they belong in? Many things go into choosing a date, a lover, or a partner for life, but perhaps none is more important than the simple feeling we call *attraction* (Berscheid and Reiss, 1998). Sonnets and symphonies have been written about this feeling, wars have been waged and kingdoms have been lost over it. It may be difficult to describe the feeling with precision, but one thing about it is perfectly clear: some people cause us to experience it and others do not. Research suggests that attraction is caused by a wide range of factors that can be roughly divided into the situational, the physical and the psychological.

Situational factors

MERE EXPOSURE EFFECT The tendency for liking to increase with the frequency of exposure.

One of the best predictors of any kind of interpersonal relationship is the physical proximity of the people involved (Nahemow and Lawton, 1975). For example, in one study, students who had been randomly assigned to university housing were asked to name their three closest friends, and nearly half named their next-door neighbour (Festinger et al., 1950). We tend to think that we select our friends and romantic partners on the basis of their personalities, appearances and so on – and we do – but we only get to select from the pool of people whom we have met, and the likelihood of meeting a potential partner naturally increases with proximity. Before you ever start auditioning and ruling out potential mates, geography has already ruled out 99.999% of the world's population for you. As William Kephart (1961, p. 269) quipped: 'Cherished notions about romantic love notwithstanding, the chances are about 50-50 that the "one and only" lives within walking distance.'

BANANASTOCK

This man probably prefers the bottom picture, but his wife probably prefers the top picture. Why? Because like most of us, he is used to seeing himself in the mirror. The mere exposure effect explains why people prefer mirror reversed images of themselves and why their friends and families prefer normal images of them (Mita et al., 1977).

Proximity not only provides the opportunity for attraction but it also provides the motivation. People naturally work hard to like those with whom they expect to have social interactions (Darley and Berscheid, 1967). When new neighbours move into the house next door, you know your day-to-day existence will be better if you like them than if you detest them, and so you make every effort to like them. In fact, the closer they live, the more effort you make.

Proximity provides something else as well. Every time we encounter a person, that person becomes a bit more familiar to us, and people – like other animals – generally prefer familiar to novel stimuli. *The tendency for liking to increase with the frequency of exposure* is called the mere exposure effect (Bornstein, 1989; Zajonc, 1968), and it is so powerful that it even occurs when we don't know we've been exposed to it. For instance, in some experiments, geometric shapes, faces or alphabetical characters were flashed onto a computer screen so quickly that participants were unaware of having seen them. These participants were then shown some of the 'old' stimuli that had been flashed across the screen as well as some 'new' stimuli that had not. Although they could not reliably tell which stimuli were old and which were new, participants tended to *like* the old stimuli better than the new ones (Monahan et al., 2000). In other words, the mere act of being exposed to some things (rather than others) in the environment led to increased liking for those things.

Proximity exposes us to certain people on a regular basis, and being exposed causes those people to feel familiar to us and hence increases our liking of them (Brockner and Swap, 1976). This effect can have some unusual consequences. In one study, police trainees who lined up alphabetically at the start of each class ended up being most attracted to other trainees whose surnames began with letters that were the same as (or close to) the first letters of their own surnames (Segal, 1974). We might like to think that attraction is determined solely by the qualities of the people involved, but research demonstrates that it is often the result of geographical accidents that put people in the same place at the same time.

Of course, some places and times are better than others. What kinds of situations promote attraction? You may recall from Chapter 10 that people can misinterpret physiological arousal as a sign of attraction (Byrne et al., 1975; Schachter and Singer, 1962). In one study, experimenters observed men as they crossed a swaying suspension bridge. A young woman who was actually working for the experimenters approached the men either when they were in the middle of the bridge or after they had finished crossing it. The woman asked the men to complete a survey, and after they did so, she gave each man her telephone number and offered to explain her project in greater detail if he called. The men who had met the woman in the middle of the swaying bridge were much more likely to call than the men who had met the woman only after they had crossed the bridge (Dutton and Aron, 1974). Why? The men experienced more physiological arousal when they completed the questionnaire on the suspension bridge, and some of those men mistook that arousal for attraction. Apparently, a sheer blouse and a sheer drop have similar effects on men, who easily confuse the two.

Another situational factor related to proximity is similarity. People tend to like others who are similar to themselves (Berschied and Reis, 1998; Caspi and Herbener, 1990; Ptacek and Dodge, 1995). In one study, 1,000 engaged couples were assessed on 88 characteristics and their concordance rates – *degree of statistical similarity based on co-occurrence* – were compared to 'couples' who were generated by randomly pairing individual members of one couple to those from another (Burgess and Wallin, 1953). Real couples were more alike on 66 of the 88 measures and on no measure were real couples more dissimilar to their partner than one would expect by chance.

CONCORDANCE RATES Degree of statistical similarity based on co-occurrence.

Biological factors

Once people are in the same place at the same time, they can begin to learn about each other's personal qualities, and in most cases, the first quality they learn about is the other person's appearance. You know from experience that a person's appearance influences your attraction towards them, but research suggests that this influence is stronger than most of us might suspect. In one study, Elaine Walster and her colleagues arranged a dance for first-year university students and randomly assigned each student to an opposite-sex partner. Midway through the dance, the students confidentially reported how much they liked their partner, how attractive they thought their partner was, and how much they would like to see their partner again. The researchers measured many of the students' attributes – from their attitudes to their personalities – and they found that the partner's physical appearance was the *only* attribute that influenced the students' feelings of attraction (Walster et al., 1966). Field studies have revealed the same thing. For instance, one study found that a man's height and a woman's weight were among the best predictors of how many responses a personal ad received (Lynn and Shurgot, 1984), and another study found that physical attractiveness was the *only* factor that predicted the online dating choices of women and men (Green et al., 1984).

Physical beauty is important in just about every interpersonal context (Etcoff, 1999; Langlois et al., 2000). Beautiful people have more friends, more dates, more sex and more fun than the rest of us (Curran and Lippold, 1975), and they can even expect to earn 10% more money over the course of their lives (Hamermesh and Biddle, 1994). People tend to believe that beautiful people have superior personal qualities (Dion et al., 1972; Eagly et al., 1991), and in some cases they do. For instance, because beautiful people have more friends and more opportunities for social interaction, they tend to have better social skills than less beautiful people (Feingold, 1992b). Beauty is so powerful that it even influences how mothers treat their own children: mothers of attractive children are more affectionate and playful with their children compared to mothers of less attractive children (Langlois et al., 1995). It is interesting to note that although men and women are equally influenced by the beauty of their potential partners, men are more likely than women to acknowledge this fact (Feingold, 1990).

In 2010, Melissa Nelson, a 33-year-old dental assistant in Fort Dodge, Iowa was fired by her boss for being too good-looking. He argued that he had grown too attracted to her and was worried he would try to start an affair. Ms Nelson sued for unfair dismissal but lost the initial case as well as the later appeal in 2013. Clarifying the rationale for its earlier ruling, the all-male court found that bosses can fire employees who they and their spouses see as threats to their marriages.

So, it pays to be beautiful. But what exactly constitutes beauty? Those of us who are less than perfect like to think that beauty is in the eye of the beholder. Although standards of beauty do indeed vary from person to person and culture to culture, many aspects of physical appearance seem to be universally appreciated or disdained (Cunningham et al., 1995). For example:

- Male bodies are considered most attractive when they approximate an inverted triangle, that is, broad shoulders with a narrow waist and hips, and female bodies are considered most attractive when they approximate an hourglass, that is, broad shoulders and hips with a narrow waist. In fact, the most attractive female body across many cultures seems to be the 'perfect hourglass' in which the waist is precisely 70% the size of the hips (Singh, 1993).
- Human faces and human bodies are generally considered more attractive when they are *bilaterally symmetrical*, that is, when the left half is a mirror image of the right (Perrett et al., 1999).

© ISTOCKPHOTO.COM/JOEYGIL

Sumo wrestlers are considered sex symbols in Japan.

- Characteristics such as large eyes, high eyebrows and a small chin make people look immature or 'baby-faced' (Berry and McArthur, 1985). This is Lorenz's (1943) 'babyness' factor we described in Chapter 12. As a general rule, female faces are considered more attractive when they have immature features, but male faces are considered more attractive when they have mature features (Cunningham et al., 1990; Zebrowitz and Montepare, 1992).

Is there any rhyme or reason to this list of scenic attractions? The evolutionary perspective suggests that we should be attracted to people who have the *genes* and the propensity for *parental behaviour* that will enable our children to grow, prosper and become parents themselves. In other words, the things we find attractive in others should be reasonably reliable indicators of their genetic qualities and parental tendencies. Are they?

- Testosterone causes male bodies to become 'inverted triangles' just as oestrogen causes female bodies to become 'hourglasses'. Men who are high in testosterone tend to be socially dominant and therefore have more resources to devote to their offspring, whereas women who are high in oestrogen tend to be especially fertile and potentially have more offspring to make use of those resources. In other words, body shape is an indicator of male dominance and female fertility. In fact, women who have the 'perfect hourglass' figure tend to bear healthier children than women with other waist-to-hip ratios (Singh, 1993).
- Asymmetrical features can be signs of genetic mutation, prenatal exposure to pathogens, or susceptibility to disease (Jones et al., 2001; Thornhill and Gangestad, 1993), so physical symmetry is an indicator of overall health. People not only *prefer* symmetrical features, but they are expert at detecting them. For instance, women can discriminate symmetrical and asymmetrical men *by smell*, and their preference for symmetrical men is more pronounced when they are ovulating (Thornhill and Gangestad, 1999a).
- Faces are considered more attractive when they are closer to the average norm of faces for the population. By using computer-generated faces that average the features from many faces, as shown in **FIGURE 14.7**, researchers were able to demonstrate that we find average Joe and plain Jane the most attractive (Langlois and Roggman, 1990; see also Perrett, 2010, for an extensive review).
- Younger women are generally more fertile than older women, whereas older men generally have more resources than younger men. Thus, a youthful appearance is a signal of a woman's ability to bear children, just as a mature appearance is a signal of a man's ability to raise them. Studies have shown that women prefer older men and men prefer younger women across a wide variety of human cultures (Buss, 1989).

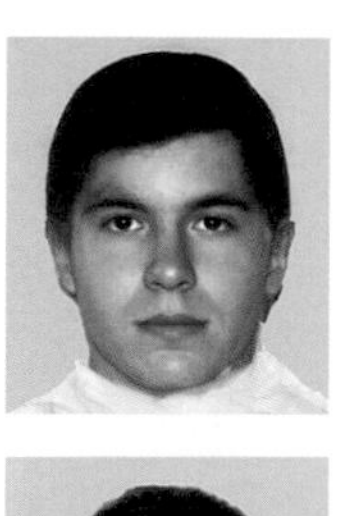

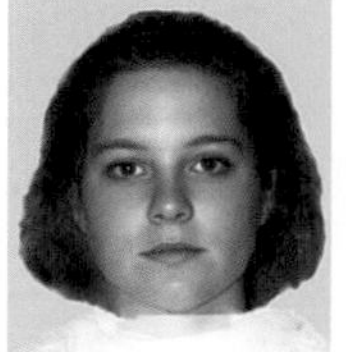
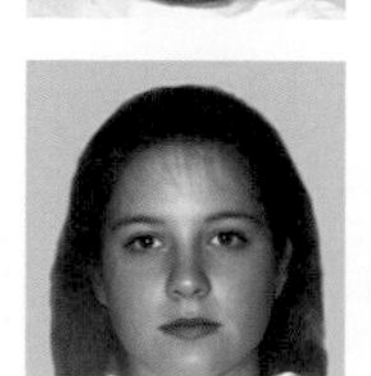
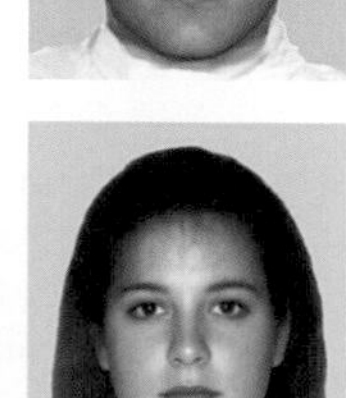
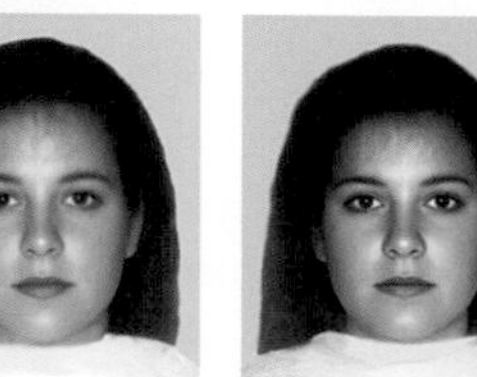
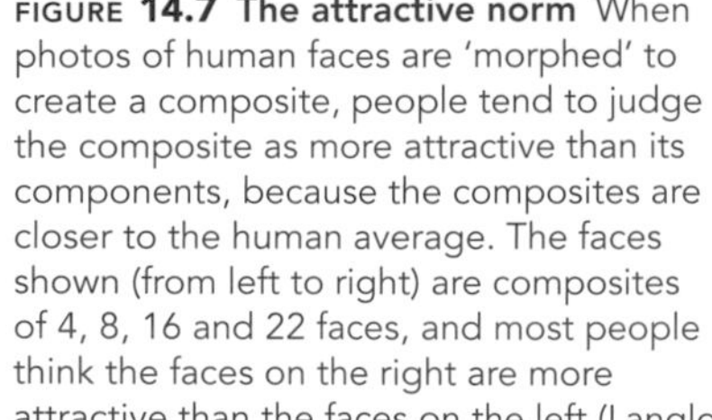

COURTESY JUDITH LANGLOIS

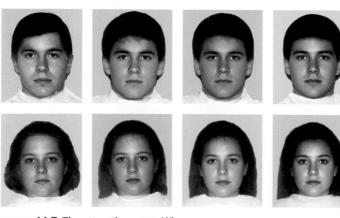

FIGURE 14.7 The attractive norm When photos of human faces are 'morphed' to create a composite, people tend to judge the composite as more attractive than its components, because the composites are closer to the human average. The faces shown (from left to right) are composites of 4, 8, 16 and 22 faces, and most people think the faces on the right are more attractive than the faces on the left (Langlois and Roggman, 1990).

The evolutionary perspective suggests that the feeling we call *attraction* is simply our genes' way of telling us that we are in the presence of a person who has the genes and the propensity towards parental behaviour to make those genes immortal. Physical attractiveness is a cue to health (Thornhill and Gangestad, 1999b), which explains why we also pay particular attention to those with disfigurements or blemishes because we are on the lookout for those who may be harbouring potential disease (Park et al., 2003). In many ways, our attraction towards physical beauty and aversion towards those who are considered ugly represents a *behavioural immune system* that biases us towards good genes (Schaller and Park, 2011).

Although we like those who are beautiful, we also think those whom we like are beautiful (Kniffin and Wilson, 2004); for example, once in a loving relationship, we think our partners are more attractive than others who rate them (Murray et al., 1996a; Murray and Holmes, 1997). This lends support to the old saying 'beauty is in the eye of the beholder'. Remarkably, people's perceptions of attractiveness can changed by group consensus. In one study, men initially rated photographs of 180 women for attractiveness (Zaki et al., 2011). They were then placed in an fMRI scanner and asked to rate all the faces again, but this time they were provided with information about how each one had apparently been rated by a group of peers. In fact, the group ratings were not from peers but completely random. If the group said 'hot' but the participant had originally rated the face as 'not', the participant shifted his rating higher and there was an increase in activation in two areas associated with evaluating rewards, the nucleus accumbens and the orbitofrontal cortex. Both areas light up when viewing sexually attractive faces. When the group rated a face the participant had originally decided was beautiful as less attractive, there was a corresponding downward shift in his rating and brain activity in the target regions. As we will see in Chapter 15, what others think can affect our own personal decisions.

hot science

Hot MPs at the ballot box

Immunological responses form a biological defence system that responds to threats from pathogens by mobilizing responses to deal with infection. It also includes mechanisms for recognizing potential threats. For example, T lymphocytes, also called killer T cells, directly attack other cells carrying certain foreign or abnormal molecules on their surfaces. In the same way that our bodies recognize potential infection, our minds also respond to the risk of infection by engaging behaviours that reduce this threat by avoidance in what is called the 'behavioural immune system' (Schaller and Park, 2011). For example, we avoid and are disgusted by things that pose an infection risk (such as a pile of faeces, putrid meat) or others who appear to be infected (have wounds or smell badly). It seems obvious that such encounters are unpleasant but the extent to which you engage in avoidance is predicted by how strong your biological immune system is operating (Schaller and Park, 2011). Indeed, regardless of an individual's actual immunity strength, people who perceive themselves to be more vulnerable to infection exhibit greater behavioural avoidance (Ackerman et al., 2009). Moreover, because true pathogens are not visible to the naked eye, the behavioural immune system operates on the default assumption that they are present and looks for any imperfection or difference that marks individuals out as deviant, which explains much of the prejudice against individuals with blemishes or disfigurements (Schaller and Park, 2011).

The behavioural immune system also influences the extent to which other kinds of traits are valued. As noted, many studies have shown that we value individuals who are considered attractive. Even beautiful politicians fare better. In lab experiments and examinations of real voting behaviour, people are more likely to vote for physically attractive candidates (see Banducci et al., 2008; Berggren et al., 2010; Budesheim and DePaola, 1994). This has usually been attributed to the 'halo effect' (Thorndike, 1920), where attractiveness is believed to be a proxy for a variety of positive personality traits.

A recent study published in *Psychological Science* offers an alternative interpretation based on the behavioural immune system (White et al., 2013). First, in a naturalistic study, photographs of genuine candidates in a US election were rated for attractiveness and then checked against the outcome of the election. The analysis also included a correction for political affiliation, incumbent status and whether they represented an area associated with poor health, which could also influence decisions. Analysis supported the prediction that physical attractiveness affected voting behaviour. In a second experimental study, potential voters read one of three different stories. One story primed the threat of infection about a person volunteering at a geriatric ward who encountered a number of disgusting events – being sneezed on by a sickly person, seeing a person with an open wound, and finding a hair in their lunch. Another story primed a non-biological threat about a person, home alone during a stormy night, who realizes there is an intruder in their house. A third story was a control story about a person organizing their office. They were then asked to rate personal qualities out of 17 characteristics they felt were important in selecting a political leader. Those who read the biological threat story rated physical attractiveness relative to other threats to be more important in a leader.

Finally, in a third experiment combining findings from the first two, 156 US individuals again read three stories that either triggered a biological, a non-biological or no threat mindset and were asked to choose between six of the most attractive and six of the least attractive British MPs as rated by the British public on a website (sexymp.co.uk). The Sexy MP website displays randomly paired official photos of British MPs and allows the public to choose which member of each pair they would prefer to have sex with, which generates an overall ranking of the attractiveness of all members. After reading stories of biological threats that triggered their biological immune system, participants voted more often for the physically more attractive MPs. It is no surprise, then, that many politicians rely on image consultants when trying to get elected. However, if the biological immune system is operating, maybe they should just try to remain squeaky clean.

Psychological factors

If attraction is all about big biceps and high cheekbones, then why don't we just skip the small talk and pick our mates from photographs? Because attraction is about much more than physical signals of fertility and resources. Physical attributes may determine who draws our attention and quickens our pulse, but after people begin interacting, they quickly go beyond appearances (Cramer et al., 1996; Regan, 1998). People's *inner qualities* – personalities, points of view, attitudes, beliefs, values, ambitions and abilities – play an important role in determining their sustained interest in each other, and there isn't much mystery about the kinds of inner qualities people find most attractive. For example, intelligence, sense of humour, sensitivity and ambition are high on just about everybody's list (Daniel et al., 1985).

IMAGNO/HULTON ARCHIVE/GETTY IMAGES

PETER WILLI/SUPERSTOCK/GETTY IMAGES

THE THREE GRACES, C. 1885/SIR EDWARD BURNE-JONES/ THE BRIDGEMAN ART LIBRARY/GETTY IMAGES

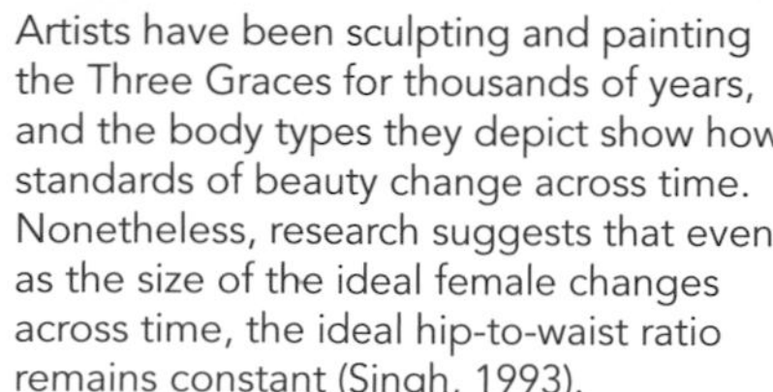

Artists have been sculpting and painting the Three Graces for thousands of years, and the body types they depict show how standards of beauty change across time. Nonetheless, research suggests that even as the size of the ideal female changes across time, the ideal hip-to-waist ratio remains constant (Singh, 1993).

Although we may be attracted to the person with the quickest wit and the highest IQ, research suggests that we typically interact with people whose standing on these dimensions is roughly *similar* to our own (Byrne et al., 1970; Byrne and Nelson, 1965; Hatfield and Rapson, 1992; Neimeyer and Mitchell, 1988). We marry people with similar levels of education, religious background, ethnicity, socioeconomic status and personality (Botwin et al., 1997; Buss, 1985; Caspi and Herbener, 1990), and some research even suggests that we are unusually likely to marry someone whose surname starts with the same letter of the alphabet as ours (Jones et al., 2004).

Why is similarity so attractive?

1 It's easy to interact with people who are similar to us because we can instantly agree on a wide range of issues, such as what to eat, where to live, how to raise children, and how to spend our money.
2 When someone shares our attitudes and beliefs, we feel a bit more confident that those attitudes and beliefs are correct (Byrne and Clore, 1970). Indeed, research shows that when the accuracy of a person's attitudes and beliefs is challenged, similarity becomes an even more important determinant of their attraction to others (Greenberg et al., 1990; Hirschberger et al., 2002).
3 If we like people who share our attitudes and beliefs, we can reasonably expect them to like us for the same reason, and *being* liked is a powerful source of attraction (Aronson and Worchel, 1966; Backman and Secord, 1959; Condon and Crano, 1988).

It is worth noting that our desire for similarity goes beyond attitudes and beliefs. For example, we may admire extraordinary skill in athletes and actors, but when it comes to friends and lovers, extraordinary people can threaten our self-esteem and make us feel a bit nervous about our own competence (Tesser, 1991). As such, we are generally attracted to competent people who, just like us, have small pockets of incompetence. Why? It seems that people who are annoyingly perfect are perfectly annoying. Having a flaw or two 'humanizes' people and makes them seem more accessible – and similar – to us (Aronson et al., 1966).

Long-term relationships

Selecting an attractive mate is the beginning of the reproductive process, but the real work consists of bearing and raising children. For human beings, that work is ordinarily done in the context of committed, long-term, romantic relationships such as a marriage. Only a few animals have relationships of this kind, so why are we among them? As we saw in Chapter 12, humans are fairly unique animals that have one of the most protracted periods of child development and rearing in comparison to any other species. Whereas other species are up and running soon after birth, humans spend years before they are capable of being self-sufficient or reproducing. As such, human infants need a great deal of care, often more than one parent can provide. If human infants were more like tadpoles – ready at birth to swim, find food and escape predators – then their parents might not need to form and maintain relationships. But human infants are remarkably helpless creatures who require years of intense care before they can fend for themselves, so human adults do almost all of their reproducing in the context of committed, long-term relationships. (By the way, some baby birds also require more food than one adult carer can provide, and the adults of those species also tend to form long-term relationships.)

©ISTOCKPHOTO.COM/RUSLAN DASHINSKY

©ISTOCKPHOTO.COM/JAMES BREY

Although humans and birds are different in so many ways, we do share one characteristic with songbirds. Their young are also helpless at birth and thus require significant parental care.

Love

If a committed, long-term relationship hasn't happened to you yet, there is a good chance that it may. In 2010, there were 2.2 million marriages in the EU. The figures vary from country to country but it is still a common practice. According to the Office of National Statistics, during 2011, there was one marriage every two minutes in the UK, with around half the adult population currently married (ONS, 2012). How do we decide whom to marry? The evolutionary perspective suggests that marriage is all about making and raising babies, but if you're like most people, *you* think that marriage is all about love. Indeed, about 85% of American adults say that they would not marry without love (Kephart, 1967; Simpson et al., 1986), the vast majority say they would sacrifice their other life goals to attain it (Hammersla and Frease-McMahan, 1990), and most list love as one of the two most important sources of happiness in life (Freedman, 1978). The fact that marriage is all about love seems so obvious that people are often surprised to learn that this so-called 'fact' is a rather recent invention (Brehm, 1992; Fisher, 1993; Hunt, 1959). Throughout history and across cultures, marriage has traditionally served a variety of economic (and decidedly unromantic) functions, ranging from cementing agreements between clans to paying back debts. Ancient Greeks and Romans married, but they considered love a form of madness. Twelfth-century Europeans married but thought of love as a game to be played by knights and ladies of the court (who happened to be married, but not to the knights). Indeed, it wasn't until the 17th century that Westerners began seriously considering the possibility that love might actually be a *reason* to get married.

But is it? Most people who get married expect to stay married, and in this respect, many people are wrong. The 2011 divorce statistics for England and Wales estimate that 42% of marriages ended in divorce (ONS, 2012). Although there are many reasons for this (Gottman, 1994; Karney and Bradbury, 1995), one is that couples don't always have a clear understanding of what love is. Indeed, a language that uses the same word to describe the deepest forms of intimacy ('I love Emily') and the most shallow forms of satisfaction ('I love ketchup') is bound to confuse the people who speak it, which is why people debate endlessly the question of whether they are really 'in love'. Psychologists try to sidestep this confusion by distinguishing between two basic kinds of love: passionate love, which is *an experience involving feelings of euphoria, intimacy, and intense sexual attraction*, and companionate love, which is *an experience involving affection, trust, and concern for a partner's wellbeing* (Hatfield, 1988; Rubin, 1973; Sternberg, 1986).

PASSIONATE LOVE An experience involving feelings of euphoria, intimacy and intense sexual attraction.

COMPANIONATE LOVE An experience involving affection, trust, and concern for a partner's wellbeing.

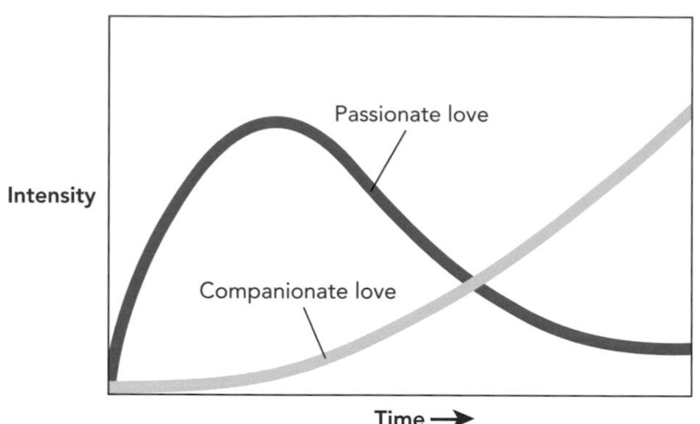

FIGURE 14.8 Passionate and companionate love Passionate and companionate love have different time courses and trajectories. Passionate love begins to within just a few months, but companionate love can grow slowly and steadily over the years.

The ideal romantic relationship gives rise to both types of love, but the speeds, trajectories and durations of the two experiences are markedly different (FIGURE 14.8).

Passionate love has a rapid onset, reaches its peak quickly, and begins to diminish within just a few months. Companionate love, on the other hand, takes some time to get started, grows slowly, and need never stop. As such, the love we feel early in a relationship is not the same love we feel later. When people marry for passionate love, they may not choose a partner with whom they can easily develop companionate love, and if they don't understand how quickly passionate love cools, they may blame their partners when it does. In many cultures, parents try to keep children from making these mistakes by choosing their marriage partners for them. Some studies suggest that arranged marriages yield greater satisfaction over the long term than 'love matches' (Yelsma and Athappilly, 1988), but other studies suggest just the opposite (Xiaohe and Whyte, 1990). If there are any benefits to arranged marriage, they may derive from the fact that parents are less likely to pick partners on the basis of passionate love and more likely to pick partners who have a high potential for companionate love (Haidt, 2006).

IMAGE SOURCE

Although companionate love lacks the ardent initial intensity of passionate love, it grows over time, built on the foundations of trust and affection.

As we saw above, people in love often view their partners as more beautiful than others view them. They also tend to see them as more intelligent and more desirable than others might think realistic, to the extent that they experience illusions and biases (Murray et al., 1996a; Gagné and Lydon, 2004). When couples rate each other on virtuous traits (for example, patience, understanding) as well as faults (for example, how often they complain, moodiness), individuals rated their partners more positively than they saw themselves (Murray et al., 1996b). Individuals were happier in their relationships when they idealized their partners and their partners idealized them, suggesting that a certain degree of mutual illusion may be a critical feature of satisfying relationships. Remarkably, this mutual admiration applies to physical attraction as well. When individuals were asked to select a photograph of their partner that had been altered either to be less attractive, an accurate representation, or enhanced to be more attractive, those in a happy relationship selected the most flattering image, whereas individuals dissatisfied with their relationship showed the opposite pattern (Penton-Voak et al., 2007). However, the pattern was only significant for the women, which raises the possibility that the mechanism serves to consolidate the relationship for females who have an evolutionary bias to maintain relationships (Haselton and Funder, 2006).

Failure of long-term relationships

We've examined some of the factors that draw people into intimate relationships and keep them together, but what determines when people will be drawn out? Although feelings of love, happiness and satisfaction may lead us to marriage, the lack of those feelings doesn't seem to lead us to divorce. Marital satisfaction is only weakly correlated with marital stability (Karney and Bradbury, 1995), suggesting that relationships break up or remain intact for reasons other than the satisfaction of those involved (Drigotas and Rusbult, 1992; Rusbult and van Lange, 2003). Relationships offer benefits, such as love, sex and financial security, but they exact costs, such as increased responsibility, increased conflict and loss of freedom. Social exchange is *the hypothesis that people remain in relationships only as long as they perceive a favourable ratio of costs to benefits* (Homans, 1961; Thibaut and Kelley, 1959). For example, a relationship that provides an acceptable level of benefits at a reasonable cost would probably be maintained. Research suggests that this hypothesis is generally true with three important additions:

> SOCIAL EXCHANGE The hypothesis that people remain in relationships only as long as they perceive a favourable ratio of costs to benefits.

> COMPARISON LEVEL The cost–benefit ratio that people believe they deserve or could attain in another relationship.

1 People calculate their cost–benefit ratios by comparing them to alternatives. A person's comparison level refers to *the cost–benefit ratio that people believe they deserve or could attain in another relationship* (Rusbult et al., 1991; Thibaut and Kelley, 1959).

A cost–benefit ratio that is acceptable to two people who are stranded on a desert island might not be acceptable to the same two people if they were living in a large city where each had access to other potential partners. A cost–benefit ratio seems favourable when we feel that it is the best we can or should do.

2 People may hope to maximize their cost–benefit ratios, but they do not want them to be markedly different from their partner's. Most people seek **equity** – *a state of affairs in which the cost–benefit ratios of two partners are roughly equal* (Messick and Cook, 1983; Walster et al., 1978). For example, spouses are more distressed when their respective cost–benefit ratios are *different* than when their cost–benefit ratios are *unfavourable*, and this is true even when their cost–benefit ratio is *more* favourable than their partner's (Schafer and Keith, 1980).

EQUITY A state of affairs in which the cost–benefit ratios of two partners are roughly equal.

3 Relationships can be thought of as investments into which people pour resources such as time, money and affection, and research suggests that after people have poured significant resources into their relationships, they are more willing to settle for less favourable cost–benefit ratios (Kelley, 1983; Rusbult, 1983). This is one of the reasons why people are much more likely to end new marriages than old ones (Bramlett and Mosher, 2002; Cherlin, 1992).

Remarkably, one predictor of long-term relationships is our experience of parental attachment as a child. In Chapter 12, we learned about different infant attachment styles as a measure of the emotional bond that exists between mothers and their offspring. As attachment styles are believed to be stable attributes of personality because they generate internal working models of how to cope socially (Bowlby, 1969), researchers have investigated whether adult attachment styles influence relationships (Hazan and Shaver, 1987). The evidence seems to support this position. For example, individuals with a secure attachment style compared to those with an insecure attachment style (see **TABLE 14.2**) are less likely to be jealous (Buunk, 1997), seek support more often (Simpson et al., 1992) and are less afraid of being abandoned (Davis et al., 2003). Securely attached adults are also more trusting of their partners (Mikulincer, 1998), enjoy a more stable and satisfying relationship (Simpson, 1990) and report higher levels of commitment, intimacy and passion (Buunk and Dijkstra, 2008). As you remember from Chapter 12, different infant attachment styles reflect the environment to some extent and while some may regard attachment as a stable component of personality, it is worth noting that the nature of the parental relationship with the child may, in turn, influence the child's own parenting style when they grow up to have children of their own.

TABLE **14.2 Measures of adult attachment style**
Question: Which of the following best describes your feelings?
Secure: I find it relatively easy to get close to others and am comfortable depending on them and having them depend on me. I don't often worry about being abandoned or about someone getting too close to me.
Avoidant: I am somewhat uncomfortable being close to others; I find it difficult to trust them completely, difficult to allow myself to depend on them. I am nervous when anyone gets too close, and often feel partners want to be more intimate than I am comfortable with.
Anxious/ambivalent: I find that others are reluctant to get as close as I would like. I often worry that my partner doesn't really love me or won't want to stay with me. I want to merge completely with another person, and this desire sometimes scares people away.

Source: Hazan and Shaver, 1987

Loneliness

We opened this chapter with autobiographical accounts of what it is like to be in solitary confinement. Even those who voluntarily seek out isolation can suffer. Forty years ago, French scientist Michel Siffre conducted a series of studies to investigate the rhythms of the body when isolated from external measures of time such as natural sunlight. He spent months in caves without any clocks or calendars. Even though he was in constant communication with his assistants above ground, his mental health began to deteriorate. In his last study conducted in a cave in Texas, he began to lose his sanity. He became so lonely that he tried to capture a mouse he had named Mus that occasionally rummaged through his supplies. Siffre (1975) wrote in his diary:

> My patience prevails. After much hesitation, Mus edges up to the jam. I admire his little shining eyes, his sleek coat. I slam down the dish. He is captured! At last I will have a companion in my solitude. My heart pounds with excitement. For the first time since entering the cave, I feel a surge of joy. Carefully I inch up the casserole. I hear small squeaks of distress. Mus lies on his side. The edge of the descending dish apparently caught him on the head. I stare at him with swelling grief. The whispers die away. He is still. Desolation overwhelms me.

Arguably, humans are one of the most socially dependent animals on the planet. We have proportionally the longest period of child rearing of any species where we depend on assistance from adults, and when we grow up, it has been estimated that the average adults spend about 80% of their waking hours in the company of others, and time with others is preferred to the time spent alone (Emler, 1994; Kahneman et al., 2004).

For many, the worst thing in the world is loneliness. Not only can it cause emotional pain but it can also have serious consequences for physical health. Loneliness impacts on the immune system (Cole et al., 2007), making individuals more prone to illness and, in general, is linked to a multitude of problems including cardiovascular risk, obesity, alcoholism, depression, suicide and premature death (Cacioppo et al., 2003; Pressman et al., 2005).

Avoiding loneliness has become one of the major issues in our society. According to the Office for National Statistics (ONS, 2014), 7.1 million people in the UK were living alone in 2011. Most of these (6 million, which is 78%) are over the age of 45 and with increasing life expectancy, the problem is likely to worsen. Everyone has experienced loneliness but few of us will ever own up to it – certainly not to strangers – and we are more likely to talk about our medical problems. It has such a social stigma, that to say one is lonely is to reveal that one is inadequate (Rokach, 2013). After all, if someone is lonely, they must have problems making friends or forming relationships. Analysis of large social networks reveals that we tend to shun those who are already lonely, which compounds the problem (Cacioppo et al, 2009). Yet, we can all experience isolation and loneliness whether we like it or not. It is a sad reality that even in our modern society of instant communication and social networking, many of us still live, and will end our lives, alone.

Ostracism

OSTRACISM Active rejection by other group members.

More painful than involuntary loneliness is ostracism – *active rejection by other group members*. Kicked out, cut off, defriended, or blocked – it doesn't matter how it is done. In some species, ostracism leads to death (Gruter and Masters, 1986) and for humans it can be psychologically traumatizing. This is something that Kip Williams from Purdue University knows from experience. One day while walking his dog, he was accidentally hit in the back with a Frisbee. In good humour, he flipped it back to the two players who began tossing it back to Kip. After about a minute, they returned their attention to each other. When it became apparent that he had been excluded from the game, the psychology professor was surprised at how upset he was. He felt humiliated but it gave him a great idea to develop a computer simulation called *Cyberball,* where participants play a game in which a ball is tossed back and forth on a screen between two other virtual players. Just as in the Frisbee experience, the computer included the player for varying amounts of time and then unexpectedly excluded them (Williams et al., 2000).

Even when naive participants played Cyberball for only a couple of minutes and were told that it was only a computer simulation, they still felt rejected. Not only that, but they felt physically hurt. Indeed, imaging studies reveal that being excluded from a group activates areas of the brain that are normally activated by physical pain (Eisenberger et al., 2003). This has led to the *social pain hypothesis*, which proposes that being socially ostracized or rejected triggers the dorsal anterior cingulate, a brain region that is normally activated during painful physical experiences and is associated with unpleasant emotions rather than the sensation of pain itself (Eisenberger and Leiberman, 2004). Their feelings were really hurt. But it also hurts to hurt others. Using the same paradigm, studies reveal that being forced to ostracize others is upsetting too (Legate et al., 2013). People who were instructed to ignore others who they had just been playing with felt bad.

Research with Cyberball reveals how easy it is to induce social pain, but why should social exclusion be painful? As we learned in Chapter 4, pain reactions warn us that damage has taken place or is about to take place. If ostracism is so potentially harmful, then Williams argues that we have evolved mechanisms to register when we are in danger of being ostracized (Williams and Nida, 2011). This registers as pain to trigger a set of coping mechanisms that help to reinstate ourselves in the social situation that threatens to expel us. As soon as it becomes clear that we are in danger of being ostracized, we activate social ingratiating strategies (Williams, 2009). We become extra helpful, going out of our way to curry favour with individuals within the group. We can become obsequious, agreeing and sucking up to others even when they are in the wrong.

If these ingratiating strategies fail, ostracized individuals can become less helpful and more aggressive to those who have rejected them. In one study based on Milgram's conditioned learning paradigm, ostracized individuals sought revenge by punishing those who had rejected them with more painful blasts of loud noise. If the participant did not perceive the others as a group, they administered lower painful bursts (Gaertner et al., 2008). Sometimes, it does not matter whether or not the others are the perpetrators of the ostracism when individuals act out of spite. For example, in a Cyberball study, ostracized individuals gave an innocent bystander five times the amount of hot chilli sauce as a punishment even when they knew the victim hated the sauce (Warbuton et al., 2006).

This spiteful nature of revenge has led to the view that many of the tragic cases of school shootings and murderous rampages were perpetrated by individuals who felt socially rejected. An analysis of the diaries of school shooters found that in 13 of the 15 cases examined, the perpetrators had been targets of ostracism (Leary et al., 2003). Clearly, not everyone who has been ostracized goes on a shooting rampage, but if the ostracism persists, then excluded individuals eventually experience alienation and worthlessness. They often withdraw from society and become profoundly depressed and contemplate suicide. As humans, we all need to belong.

In summary, organisms survive to reproduce, and reproduction requires choosing the right mate. Biology and culture tend to make the costs of reproduction higher for women than for men, so women tend to be choosier when selecting potential mates. Attraction is a feeling that draws us closer to a potential mate, and it has situational and personal determinants. Physical appearance plays an unusually important role, but psychological determinants are also important, and people seem to be most attracted to those who are similar to them on a wide variety of dimensions. Reproduction is usually accomplished within the context of a long-term, committed relationship. People weigh the costs and benefits of their relationships and tend to dissolve them when they think they can or should do better, when they and their partners have very different cost–benefit ratios, or when they have little invested in the relationship. Adult attachment style may be a legacy of the early mother–child social interaction but it does appear to predict the satisfaction and stability of adult relationships.

Most of us will probably not escape loneliness in our old age because of the way modern Western society has increasingly made living alone more common. The worst thing you can do to most people is to forcibly isolate them. Deliberate ostracism is an aversive state that triggers attempts to reintegrate back into the group, which, if unsuccessful, can cause retaliatory behaviour.

psychomythology

'The truth is written all over the face'

Sometimes, nonverbal communication contradicts the verbal content of a message, for example when someone is lying, which has led to the widely held beliefs that 'the truth is written all over the face' and that it is easy to detect a lie. There was even a popular US crime show, *Lie to Me*, starring British actor Tim Roth as an expert who claimed to use nonverbal cues to identify lies. However, a meta-analysis of 206 studies involving a total of 24,000 judgements of truths and lies revealed that the mean accuracy was just 54% – not much better than tossing a coin (Bond and DePaulo, 2006). In one 'megalab' study using over 41,000 members of the UK general public, Sir Robin Day, a well-known British political commentator, was interviewed twice about his favourite films. He lied in one of the interviews and transcripts of each were printed in a newspaper, broadcast on the radio and shown on TV (Wiseman, 1995). Radio listeners detected lies 73.4% of the time compared to only 51.8% of those who watched the same segment on TV, and those who read the interview in the newspaper were correct 64.2% of the time. It turns out that the best predictor of when someone is lying is not their nonverbal behaviour but the number of times they refer to themselves with first person singular pronouns. When people are lying, they are less likely to use 'I', 'me' or 'my' (Newman et al.,

2003). James Pennebaker, at the University of Texas at Austin, developed a text analysis programme that analyses written or spoken samples on a word-by-word basis, which predicts the personality and health of the communicator and whether or not they are lying (Pennebaker et al., 2001). When people want to hide some aspect of themselves from others, they typically use fewer self-references in order to dissociate themselves from what they are saying (Knapp et al., 1974). Likewise, individuals who respond defensively when discussing personal topics distance themselves from their accounts (Barrett et al., 2002). Although liars have some control over the content of their stories, their underlying state of mind may leak out through the style of language used to tell the story. We are more sensitive to that information when we only have the verbal content to process. So, the best way to detect a liar is to listen to what they are saying and not watch their face.

where do you stand?

The model employee

When you have looked through fashion magazines, you may have noticed that the models for the clothes are very beautiful. Beauty sells and so employers argue that physical attractiveness is good for business, but is this discrimination fair? Beautiful people enjoy better lives and more opportunities than those of us who are less attractive. They are more likely to get jobs (Cash and Kilcullen, 1985), earn larger salaries (French, 2002; Frieze et al., 1991), are more likely to get elected (Berggren et al., 2010; White et al., 2013), and get lighter prison sentences if they ever get convicted (Downs and Lyons, 1991). It seems unfair that we should have to look at them every day as well. Some employers, such as hospitality businesses, model agencies and airlines, actively recruit workers who are pleasing on the eye. Arguably, the fashion industry controls what is considered attractive by promoting the images deemed appropriate for the public to see, even modifying images of well-known celebrities to make them more attractive. However, there is a backlash especially from top female stars, including Lady Gaga, Beyoncé, Kate Winslet and Keira Knightley, who have spoken out or refused photographers permission to digitally modify or enhance their published images. In an industry that is blatantly biased against women who age or put on weight, these manipulations are perpetuating stereotypes of beauty. Employers cannot discriminate on the basis of race or religion, so why can they discriminate on the basis of physical beauty? Should businesses be required to disregard a person's physical attractiveness when hiring or do they have the right to give customers what they want? Where do you stand?

Chapter review

Social behaviour: interacting with people

- Human beings are social animals, and social psychology is the study of the causes and consequences of their social interaction. Like all animals, human beings are designed to survive and reproduce.
- Survival requires scarce resources, and two primary ways to get them are aggression and cooperation. Impulsive aggression is a reaction to a negative internal state, and males are particularly prone to use aggression to ensure their status. The primary risk of cooperation is that others may take benefits without bearing costs.
- Humans have an extraordinary capacity for altruism where they selflessly help others without necessarily expecting help in return. Although altruism is observed in other animals, it is primarily found in those species that are more closely genetically related. In contrast, human altruism is much more common and reflects more complex factors related to cultural norms and morality.
- Deception involves either lying or neglecting to fully disclose in order to maintain an advantage and is most easily achieved when we convince ourselves that we are not deceiving.

Nonverbal communication

- Nonverbal communication provides additional information that may not be available or readily conveyed in language. It can also facilitate interactions between individuals by signalling affinity. Contrary to common assumption, it is not always a better indicator of truthfulness in those who deliberately deceive.

Reproduction

- Reproduction requires choosing the right mate. Because biology and culture make the costs of reproduction so much higher for women than for men, women tend to be choosier.
- Attraction is a feeling that draws us closer to a potential mate, and it has situational and personal determinants. Of the personal determinants, physical appearance plays an unusually important role because it can provide indicators of a person's genetic endowment and their willingness and ability to provide for offspring. Psychological determinants are also important, and people seem to be most attracted to those who are similar to them on a wide variety of dimensions.
- Reproduction is usually accomplished within the context of a long-term romantic relationship that is initially characterized by feelings of intense attraction and later by feelings of friendship. People weigh the costs and benefits of their relationships and tend to dissolve them when they think they can or should do better, when they and their partners have very different cost–benefit ratios, or when they have little invested in the relationship.
- Loneliness is an increasingly common situation in the modern era that presents considerable challenges to mental and physical well-being as it is associated with a multitude of negative outcomes. Enforced isolation in the form of ostracism can trigger extreme emotional distress, with corresponding psychological malaise and attempts at retaliation.

Key terms

actor-observer effect (p. 571)
aggression (p. 556)
attribution (p. 570)
bystander effect (p. 564)
catharsis (p. 557)
chameleon effect (p. 575)
companionate love (p. 583)
comparison level (p. 584)
concordance rates (p. 579)
cooperation (p. 562)
correspondence bias (p. 570)
culture of honour (p. 561)
diffusion of responsibility (p. 565)
emotional contagion (p. 575)
empathic concern (p. 568)
equity (p. 585)
eugenics (p. 558)
extensivity (p. 568)
frustration-aggression principle (p. 557)
identifiable victim effect (IVE) (p. 567)
interpersonal space (p. 573)
just world hypothesis (p. 568)
kin selection (p. 567)
lies (p. 564)
Machiavellianism (p. 568)
mere exposure effect (p. 578)
nonverbal communication (p. 572)
ostracism (p. 586)
passionate love (p. 583)
pluralistic ignorance (p. 566)
public goods dilemma (p. 563)
reciprocal altruism (p. 567)
self-deception (p. 564)
social exchange (p. 584)
thin slicing (p. 576)

Recommended reading

Baumeister, R. F. (1999) *Evil: Inside Human Violence and Cruelty.* New York: Freeman. A leading social psychologist presents a discussion of the psychological roots of human aggression and violence. Challenges much of the conventional wisdom regarding where violence comes from.

Buss, D. M. (2003) *The Evolution of Desire: Strategies of Human Mating* (2nd edn). New York: Basic Books. Surveys research on intimate relationships from the evolutionary perspective. The adaptive significance of behaviours related to love and relationships receives special attention.

Knapp, M. L., Hall, J. A. and Horgan, T. G. (2013) *Nonverbal Communication in Human Interaction* (8th edn). Belmont, CA: Wadsworth. Comprehensive and readable compendium of research and theory on nonverbal communication written by a communication scholar and two social psychologists.

Sutton, R. and Douglas, K. (2013) *Social Psychology*. Basingstoke: Palgrave Macmillan. One of the best undergraduate textbooks covering the European perspective on social psychology.

15

Chapter learning objectives

At the end of this chapter you will be able to:

1. Understand that individuals can belong to and identify with more than one group.
2. Appreciate how easily groups can be formed.
3. Recognize that individuals behave differently in groups than they would when alone.
4. Understand the difference between persuasion, conformity and obedience, and describe classic experiments that illustrate them.
5. Explain in-groups and out-groups and how these function to generate self-esteem and identity.

Social groups

Over four hot summer days in August 2011, Britain's inner cities exploded in a wave of violent public unrest. At its conclusion, five lives were lost, stores were looted and swathes of England's urban landscape were reduced to devastated wasteland. It began with a peaceful protest in Tottenham, London on Saturday afternoon, 6 August, when friends and family of Mark Duggan, a suspected criminal who had been shot dead by armed police during an arrest, marched on the police station demanding an explanation. What happened over the next few hours is subject to debate, but what is clear is that tensions gradually escalated, as police made only limited attempts to talk to the demonstrators. Rumours began to circulate and soon there were exaggerated reports of the shooting, claiming it was an execution. The crowd violence was said to be ignited when a 16-year-old girl stepped forward to confront the police and was attacked with shields and batons. By nightfall, a full-scale riot was underway in North London, with looting, arson and attacks on buses and cars. Soon, the violence had engulfed much of London and over the next few days spread to cities and towns outside the capital as far apart as Birmingham, Liverpool, Manchester and Nottingham. Commentators were quick to look for culprit causes – social class, education, ethnic group, poor parenting, unemployment, boredom and so on. The British prime minister talked about a 'sick society' dominated by gangs of thugs. However, it soon became apparent that there was not just one type of rioter but a variety from different backgrounds and of different ages. Many were disaffected youths from deprived backgrounds but there was an Oxford law graduate, a primary school teacher, an organic chef, children of a pastor and other unlikely 'criminals'. In attempting to categorize the typical looter, the authorities had failed to understand that coherent groups can consist of very different individuals. In this chapter, we look at the psychology of groups as a dynamic property that emerges out of a collection of individuals and the circumstances they find themselves in.

© ISTOCKPHOTO.COM/JOHNNY GREIG

Living in groups

In Chapter 14 we looked at individual relationships in terms of helping and hurting others, communicating through our behaviours, physical attraction, and the way long-term partnerships change over time. Here, we look at individuals as members of groups, and how groups influence us even in situations when we do not know the other members individually. On any given day, most of us interact with a wide variety of people, such as friends, co-workers, family members and strangers, in a variety of contexts, such as work, school, commerce and recreation. Some of the most productive, satisfying and enjoyable pastimes can be spent in the company of others. In fact, one of the best predictors of a person's general happiness and life satisfaction is the quality and extent of their group memberships (Myers and Diener, 1995). As a social animal, humans have evolved to collaborate, cooperate and coexist in groups – *collections of two or more people who believe they have something in common*. Groups are a way to lower the risks of cooperation and increase the odds of survival that we addressed in Chapter 14, but they are more than that. We are not merely *in* our groups: We *are* our groups.

GROUP A collection of two or more people who believe they have something in common.

We're all related to Charlemagne

Many of us would like to claim a famous ancestor, but few of us can trace our family tree back to a historical character. However, genetics proves that we are all related to famous people in the past. Analysis of DNA segments of 2,257 individuals across Europe shows that the extent of shared gene sequences can only be explained by the fact that anyone alive today must be related to any individual who was alive 1,000 years ago. Therefore, anyone alive 1,000 years ago who left any descendants will be an ancestor of every European, which is why all Europeans are descendents of Charlemagne (Ralph and Coop, 2013).

The role of culture in social psychology

One of the challenges facing psychologists who wish to understand social psychology is to find a single framework within which all the many forms of social behaviour can be organized and understood. Throughout this textbook we have been advocating evolution by natural selection to provide such a framework (Dawkins, 1976). As you learned in Chapter 3, parents pass along some of their genes to their children, who in turn pass along some of *their* genetic material to their children and so on. Individual humans disappear after 80 years or so, but their genetic material may be transmitted across generations into all the descendents. It's convenient to think of ourselves as people who happen to have genes inside them, but the evolutionary perspective suggests that we are really genes that happen to have people around them.

This 'gene's eye view' of evolution is the premise behind biologist Richard Dawkins' (1976) bestseller *The Selfish Gene*, in which he argues that we are *vehicles* for our genes, and our genes are the *designers* of and *passengers* in these vehicles. Genes are designers because they determine how the vehicles are constructed and thereby influence how the vehicles operate. Your genes help determine your size and shape, traits and tastes, and capabilities and limitations, rendering some of us finely tuned Ferraris and some of us more reliable family cars. And genes are passengers because they can potentially ride around forever if they can just get their old vehicles to build new vehicles before the old vehicles wear out. After 3.5 billion years of practice, genes have become pretty good at designing vehicles of this kind, and the latest model on the showroom floor is you.

In Chapter 14, we considered different types of individuals' social behaviour such as aggression, attraction and cooperation as adaptations from the evolutionary perspective. However, this emphasis on the gene's eye view for shaping indivuduals' social behaviour fails to consider the role of cultures, which increasingly began to shape human behaviour as we settled down to live in large groups at the end of the last ice age. Much social psychology concerns group phenomena where others influence the individual, which cannot be predicted at the gene level. If genes determined all social behaviours, we would expect to find identical social behaviours in every culture. While there are universal components of social behaviour (which may or may not be encoded in our genes), there is also considerable variation from one society to the next. For example, as we saw in Chapter 12, most humans exhibit moral behaviour but moral reasoning differs between cultures that are more individualistic, such as Western societies, compared to those that are more collectivistic, such as those found in the East and Southeast Asia (Killen and Turiel, 1998). It is more likely that genes and environment combine to generate socially adaptive behaviours tailored for different cultures so that the individual is ultimately successful in reproducing. The evolutionary perspective must be correct, in that those who succeed will breed, but historical and local events will produce different social environments requiring different strategies. So, a combined approach of genes operating in environments allows for human universals and local group variation to play a role in what is acceptable social behaviour for that community.

The other problem with ignoring the cultural perspective is that by focusing on individuals and their cognitive processes, social psychology is really not that 'social' at all (Ross et al., 2010; Sutton and Douglas, 2013). The experimental method may be fine for drilling down into a phenomenon by controlling for all the potential variables that may play some role, but in doing so, you produce an artificial situation that does not reflect what would have happen in real life (see discussion of problems of experimental method in Chapter 2).

Finally, as we noted in Chapter 1, the bulk of psychological research has been conducted on individuals from Western, industrialized nations, with the findings then extrapolated to apply to all humans. However, cultures play an important role in the way individuals think and behave and as we learned in Chapter 12, much of the influence is transferred during our long social development and the way children are raised. Although the human brain is built by genes to produce the same system for processing the world, culture can shape those mechanisms. In his 2005 book, *The Geography of Thought*, Richard Nisbett (who we read about in Chapter 14) documents many studies showing that people from the East perceive and think differently from Westerners. For example, in one study (Masuda and Nisbett, 2001), Japanese and US adults were shown eight coloured underwater vignettes with shoals of fish lasting 20 secs, similar to the one depicted in the still in **FIGURE 15.1**. The scenes were all characterized by having one or more 'focal' fish that were larger, brighter and faster moving than the others. The scene also contained background details related to colour of water, rocks, plants and so on. After watching the vignettes, US and Japanese participants equally recalled details about the focal fish but the Japanese participants recalled 60% more references to the background elements.

With their historical bias of living in relatively collectivist groups where individualism is frowned on, the Japanese pay more attention to relative context than US participants who live in Western individualist societies (Triandis, 1995). Remarkably, this attentional bias operates when looking at complex visual scenes. For example, eye movement recordings of Eastern and Western adults viewing natural images reveal that Westerners fixate longer and more often on the focal object in a complex scene compared to Easterners who also fixate on the background more (Chua et al., 2005). One potential origin of this perceptual bias are the cultural influences operating during the developmental formation of the self-concept (discussed in Chapters 12 and 13). Whereas the individualist perspective is emphasized from toddlerhood, young Eastern children are spoken to, constantly reminded and expected to always relate to others in an interdependent way (Nisbett, 2005).

While these issues about culture may seem to undermine the evolutionary approach to deriving a general understanding about humans in living in large groups, it does not contradict the biological perspective. Rather, it should serve to remind us that the human brain is a social brain sufficiently evolved to adapt to different environments, including the different social environments that emerge over time as cultures.

FIGURE 15.1 Cultural differences in the way complex scenes are processed

Identifying with groups

How do communities ever get started in the first place? After all, cooperation requires that someone take an initial risk to benefit an individual who has not yet benefited them and then *trust* that that individual will someday repay the favour. Some groups seem more sociobiological where there is some adaptive value in coming and staying together, as in the case of families or, millions of years ago, hunting parties where having two or more individuals cooperating was an advantage. Other groups seem more utilitarian and may arise from cultural practices or situations where it is beneficial to share resources, such as clubs or neighbourhoods. However, as we noted in Chapter 14, in order to survive, there is a human predisposition for the need to belong – *a universal and innate tendency for humans to form and maintain stable, strong and positive relationship with others* (Baumeister and Leary, 1995).

NEED TO BELONG A universal and innate tendency for humans to form and maintain stable, strong and positive relationship with others.

Every one of us is a member of many groups. Smaller groups include families and teams, whereas larger ones can be religions and nations. One useful way of defining groups (but less easy to say) is to consider their degree of entitativity – *the extent to which a group of individuals are perceived to be cohesive, interconnected, similar, interactive and sharing common goals* (Campbell, 1958). This is a fairly old term that is experiencing a resurgence of interest, as it is possible to divide a wide range of groups into four basic subtypes of increasing entitativity, as shown in **TABLE 15.1** (Lickel et al., 2000).

ENTITATIVITY The extent to which a group of individuals are perceived to be cohesive, interconnected, similar, interactive and sharing common goals.

TABLE **15.1 Different levels of entitativity**

	Type of group	Examples
1	Intimacy groups (most entitativity)	Family, romantic partners, friends
2	Task groups	Colleagues, committees, work groups
3	Social categories	Women, Muslim, British
4	Loose associations (least entitativity)	Neighbours, rock music fans

Although there are profound differences between such groups, they all seem to have one thing in common: the people in them tend to display discrimination – *positive or negative behaviour towards another person based on their group membership*. Specifically, people tend to be positively biased towards members of their own groups, tend to discriminate in favour of their own groups, and tend to expect that their fellow group members will do the same for them in the future (see also prejudice below). Because people favour members of their own groups, group membership allows people to know in advance who is most and least likely to repay their efforts to cooperate, and this knowledge reduces the risks of cooperation.

DISCRIMINATION Positive or negative behaviour towards another person based on their group membership.

Why do we form these beliefs about members of our groups compared to non-members? One of the most significant contributions to understanding the psychology of groups was *social identity theory* proposed by Henri Tajfel (1978). As we read in Chapter 1, Tajfel was acutely aware of the power of group identity that he witnessed first hand as a Jewish prisoner of war of the Germans during the First World War. Wars are waged for a variety of reasons but there can be few scenarios more extreme than war where social identity is given as the primary reason to enter into such conflict. According to Tajfel (1981, p. 255), social identity is 'part of the individual's self-concept which derives from their knowledge of their membership of a social group (or groups) together with the value and emotional significance of that membership'. This idea of self-identity was later extended and developed by his co-worker John Turner, who proposed *self-categorization theory* (Turner et al., 1987), where individuals form a hierarchy of identities based on the ever-increasing level of inclusion, as shown in **FIGURE 15.2.**

We humans
We Europeans
They, the Australians
We British
They, the French
I, me
Others

FIGURE **15.2 Turner's levels of self-categorization and identity** Individuals can hold multilayered hierarchical notions of self-identity depending on how they view their group membership.

ADAPTED FROM *REDISCOVERING THE SOCIAL GROUP: SELF-CATEGORIZATION THEORY*, TURNER, J. C. REPRODUCED WITH PERMISSION OF BLACKWELL PUBLISHING, INC VIA COPYRIGHT CLEARANCE CENTER

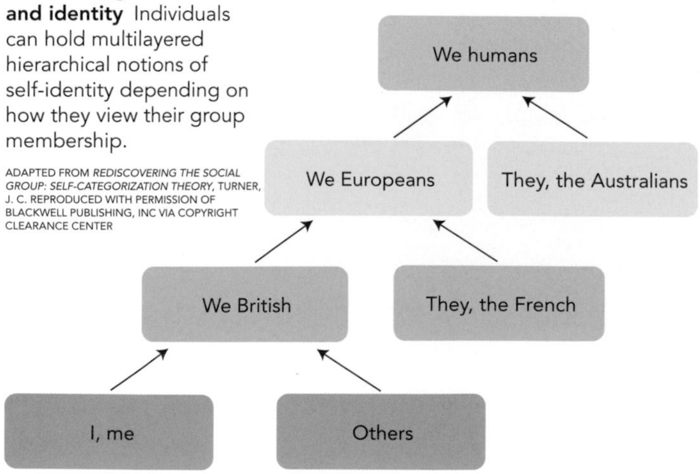

According to the theory of self-categorization, individuals can hold multilayered notions of self-identity depending on

how they view their group membership. For example, at the basic level there is the individual who is different from others. If one applies a national identity framework, as illustrated in Figure 15.2, one can consider identity in increasingly inclusive groups. Problems occur when there is a conflict between different self-categorizations as in the case between nationality and religion. For example, this issue has become relevant in the current political climate where British Muslims are being asked to identify whether they are primarily British or Muslim. Clearly, there are many personal factors that will contribute to this decision. Readiness to adopt an identity will depend on the strength of one's need to feel that they should belong to one group or another (Brewer, 1991). Thus, social identity and self-categorization explain why conflicts occur because individuals primarily feel threatened as a group and respond accordingly as a collective.

Groups require cohesion and part of that requires members to share an enhanced group identity. Research shows that people do indeed favour members of the in-group, *a human category of which a person is a member*, more than they favour members of the out-group, *a human category of which a person is not a member* (Sumner, 1906), and that it doesn't take much to create this kind of favouritism. In one set of studies, participants were shown abstract paintings by two artists and were then divided into two groups based on their preference for one artist or the other (Tajfel, 1970; Tajfel et al., 1971). When participants were subsequently asked to allocate money to other participants, they consistently allocated more money to those in their group (Brewer, 1979).

IN-GROUP A human category of which a person is a member.

OUT-GROUP A human category of which a person is not a member.

Indeed, participants show positive discrimination even when they are randomly assigned to completely meaningless groups such as 'group X' and 'group Y' (Hodson and Sorrentino, 2001; Locksley et al., 1980). In other words, just knowing that 'I'm one of *us* and not one of *them*' seems sufficient to produce this kind of favouritism (see also Robbers Cave study below). Just as people feel positively about and act positively towards members of their own groups, they think negatively about and act negatively towards members of other groups (Hewstone et al., 2002), and this happens even when group membership is determined by nothing more meaningful than a coin flip (Locksley et al., 1980).

Cultural variations in social group identity

As noted earlier, there are different cultural profiles when it comes to attitudes to group identity. In the West and most notably in the US, society is characterized as individualistic – *where success and responsibility are focused on individual achievement* – as opposed to many Eastern cultures, such as Indian and Japanese, that are more collectivistic – *where success and responsibility are seen as a reflection of group effort* (Triandis, 1995). In the US, 'the squeaky wheel gets the grease', but in Japan, 'the nail that stands out gets pounded down'. Or consider how a North American company intent on increasing productivity may ask its workforce to begin the day with self-empowerment exercises such as looking into the mirror each morning and saying, 'I am productive' 100 times, whereas a similar Japanese company may instruct its workforce to begin the day by telling a fellow employee how productive they are. Such anecdotes capture major cultural variations between nations (Markus and Kitayama, 1991). These characterizations may be somewhat simplistic as there are many social subgroups within nations. Nevertheless, there have been suggestions of cultural differences when it comes to group identity formation (Kashima et al., 2001). For example, individualistic cultures promote an independent self-construal, whereas collectivistic cultures are more associated with an interdependent notion of the self. Independent individuals see themselves as autonomous entities defined predominantly in terms of abstract, internal attributes like traits, abilities and attitudes. In contrast, interdependent individuals see themselves as socially embedded and defined predominantly in terms of relationships with others, group membership and social roles (Simon and Trötschel, 2008).

INDIVIDUALISTIC Where success and responsibility are focused on individual achievement.

COLLECTIVISTIC Where success and responsibility are seen as a reflection of group effort.

You would think that differing attitudes must be a result of development within a culture as children learn to adopt the prevalent social norms, but one study demonstrated how different independent and interdependent attitudes could be manipulated within individuals from the same culture. Experimenters primed North American students with either independence or interdependence values by circling either independent pronouns

('I' or 'mine') or interdependent pronouns ('we' or 'ours'). Participants primed with independent pronouns gave higher endorsements to individualistic statements, whereas those primed with interdependence gave higher endorsements to collectivistic values (Gardener et al., 1999). Such manipulations reveal that we are much more malleable to conforming to group norms rather than holding deep-seated notions about group and self-identity.

In summary, we grow up and live in groups that are defined by varying degrees of relatedness. Families are the first and smallest group that most of us belong to, whereas cultures represent the largest group (other than the human species). In between are a variety of groups we identify with that represent the different categories of interest and activities we belong to. Cultures differ in two basic ways. Traditional Eastern cultures promote an interdependent or collectivist perspective, whereas Western cultures prefer the independent or individualistic view. These differences influence the way individuals perceive the world and how they behave in groups.

Thinking about others

As you are probably already well aware, the term 'psychologist' evokes many misconceptions in your family and friends who do not know much about the field. Have you had anyone mock you for 'trying to read their minds' yet? If not, you will. But you do not have to be a psychologist to read minds. The truth is that humans read minds naturally. Not literally, of course, that would be telepathy, which is not the stuff of science, but each of us has a brain that has evolved to process other people and try to interpret and anticipate their thoughts and behaviours. This enables us to understand and predict others. As we saw in Chapter 12, without this ability we would be exhibiting one of the diagnostic features of autism and incapable of understanding why people do and think the things they do. This skill is not mindreading but social cognition, and most of us specialize in precisely the same subject.

Indeed, the human brain itself seems specialized for social cognition. For example, the medial prefrontal cortex is activated when people think about the attributes of other people but not about the attributes of inanimate objects such as houses or tools (Mitchell et al., 2002). Although most brain areas show diminished activity when a person is at rest, the medial prefrontal cortex remains active all the time (Gusnard and Raichle, 2001). Some of us are not only pretty good at reading others, but also derive great pleasure from social interaction. When placed in a brain scanner, these 'people persons' were found to have structurally larger regions of the medial prefrontal cortex and the ventral striatum – a brain region associated with reward from basic drives like food and sex (Lebreton et al., 2009). Why should the brain have specific areas that are dedicated to processing information about just *one* of the millions of objects it might encounter, and why should those areas remain active day and night? Because of the millions of objects a person might encounter, another person is the single most important one. We all specialize in drawing inferences about other people – about their thoughts and feelings, their beliefs and desires, their abilities and aspirations, their intentions, needs, and characters – because other people can provide us with the greatest benefits and exact from us the greatest costs.

As it turns out, the inferences we draw about other people are based on the categories to which they belong and the things they say and do. The trouble is that we tend to use these categories before we have even had the chance to find out who somebody really is.

Stereotyping

CATEGORIZATION The process by which people identify a stimulus as a member of a class of related stimuli.

STEREOTYPING The process by which people draw inferences about others based on their knowledge of the categories to which others belong.

One of the potential problems of being associated with a group is that people jump to conclusions about what you are like as an individual. You'll recall from Chapter 7 that categorization is *the process by which people identify a stimulus as a member of a class of related stimuli*. Once we have identified a novel stimulus as a member of a category ('That's a textbook'), we can then use our knowledge of the category to make educated guesses about the properties of the novel stimulus ('It's probably expensive') and act accordingly ('I think I'll borrow it from the library'). The same is true of people. Stereotyping is *the process by which people draw inferences about others based on their knowledge of the categories to which others belong*. As we saw in Chapter 12, stereotyping operates from early childhood in the way adults treat children and how they respond. The moment we categorize a person as an adult, a male, a footballer and a Russian, we can use our knowledge of those categories to make some educated guesses about him; for example, he shaves his face but not his legs, he understands the offside rule, and he knows more about Chekhov than we do. When we offer children sweets instead of alcohol or ask service station attendants for directions instead of dating advice, we are making inferences about people we have never met before based solely on their category membership. As these examples suggest, stereotyping is a useful process (Allport, 1954). Imagine if you could not categorize people. You would spend a lot of time and effort with each new encounter, which would make life difficult to conduct efficiently. Yet, ever since the word 'stereotype' was coined in 1936, it has had a distasteful connotation. Why? Because stereotyping is a useful process that can often produce harmful results, and it does so because stereotypes can be inaccurate, overused, self-perpetuating and automatic.

Stereotypes can be inaccurate

The inferences we draw about individuals are only as accurate as our stereotypes about the categories to which they belong. There is no evidence to indicate that Jews are especially materialistic or that black people are especially lazy, yet surveys show that most US university students, the majority of whom are white Caucasians, have held such beliefs for most of the past century (Gilbert, 1951; Karlins et al., 1969; Katz and Braly, 1933). We aren't born holding these beliefs, so how do we acquire them? There are only two ways to acquire a belief about anything: to see for yourself or to take somebody else's word for it. In fact, most of what we know about the members of human categories is hearsay – stuff we picked up from friends and uncles, novels and newspapers, jokes and films and late-night TV. Many of the people who believe that Jews are materialistic and black people are lazy have never actually met someone who is Jewish or black, and their beliefs are a result of listening too closely to what others told them. In the process of inheriting the wisdom of our culture, it is inevitable we also inherit its ignorance.

But even direct observation can produce inaccurate stereotypes. For example, research participants in one study were shown a long series of positive and negative behaviours and were told that each behaviour had been performed by a member of one of two groups: group A or group B (FIGURE 15.3). There were more positive than negative behaviours in the series, and there were more members of group A than group B. In other words, negative behaviours were rarer than positive behaviours, and group B members were rarer than group A members. The series of behaviours was carefully arranged so that each group behaved negatively exactly one-third of the time. After seeing the series, participants correctly remembered that group A had behaved negatively one-third of the time. However, they incorrectly remembered that group B had behaved negatively *more than half* the time (Hamilton and Gifford, 1976).

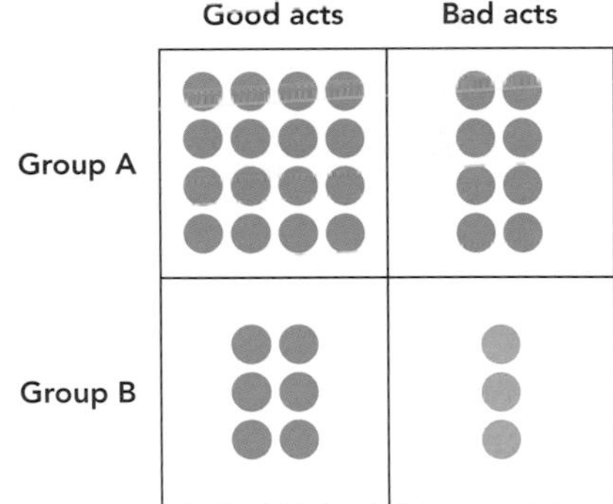

FIGURE **15.3 Illusory correlation** Group A and group B each perform two-thirds good acts and one-third bad acts. However, 'group B' and 'bad acts' are both rare, leading people to notice and remember their co-occurrence, which leads them to perceive a correlation between group membership and behaviour that isn't really there.

Why did this happen? Bad behaviour was rare and being a member of group B was rare; thus, participants were especially likely to notice when the two co-occurred ('Aha! There's one of those unusual group B people doing an unusually awful thing again'). This is an example of an *illusory correlation,* or seeing a strong pattern of relationship between two things when little or no relationship exists. These findings help explain why members of majority groups tend to overestimate the number of crimes (which are relatively rare events) committed by members of minority groups (who are relatively rare people, that's why they're in the minority). Even when we directly observe people, we can end up with inaccurate beliefs about the groups to which they belong. This mindbug has the potential to create disastrous consequences for societies and social relationships.

Stereotypes can be overused

Human categories are so variable that our stereotypes may offer only the vaguest of clues about the individuals who populate those categories. You probably believe that men have greater upper body strength than women, and this belief is right *on average*. But the upper body strength of individuals *within* each of these categories is so varied that you cannot easily predict how much weight a particular person can lift simply by knowing

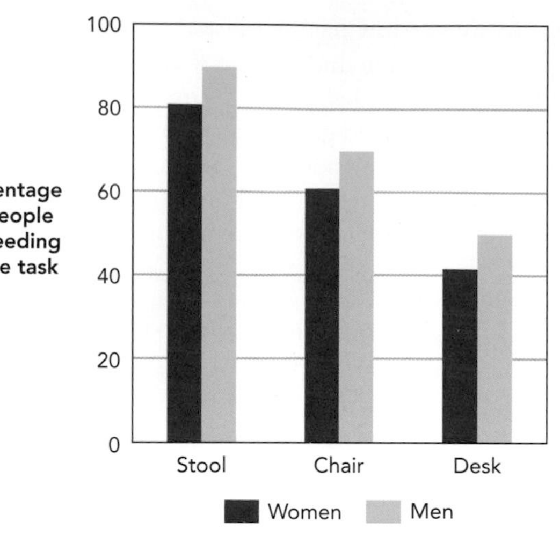

FIGURE **15.4 Intracategory and intercategory variability** As these hypothetical data show, when people are asked to lift a stool, a chair or a desk above their heads, a larger percentage of men than women succeed at each task. But notice that although men seem to have greater upper body strength on average, there are still plenty of women who can lift a desk and plenty of men who can't lift a stool. In other words, because individuals *within* each of these gender categories differ so much, it is difficult to predict how much weight a person can lift simply by knowing their gender.

that person's gender (FIGURE **15.4**). The inherent variability of human categories makes stereotypes much less useful than they might otherwise be. In our quest to define the forest, we often miss the uniqueness of each tree.

Alas, we don't always recognize this because the mere act of categorizing a stimulus tends to warp our perceptions of that category's variability. For instance, participants in some studies were shown a series of lines of different lengths (FIGURE **15.5**) (McGarty and Turner, 1992; Tajfel and Wilkes, 1963). For one group of participants, the longest lines were labelled A and the shortest lines were labelled B, as they are on the right side of Figure 15.5. For the second group of participants, the lines were shown without these category labels, as they are on the left side of Figure 15.5. Interestingly, those participants who saw the category labels *overestimated* the similarity of the lines that shared a label and *underestimated* the similarity of lines that did not.

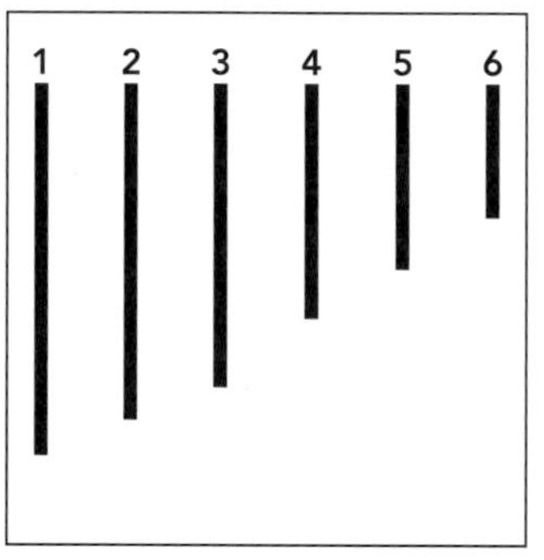

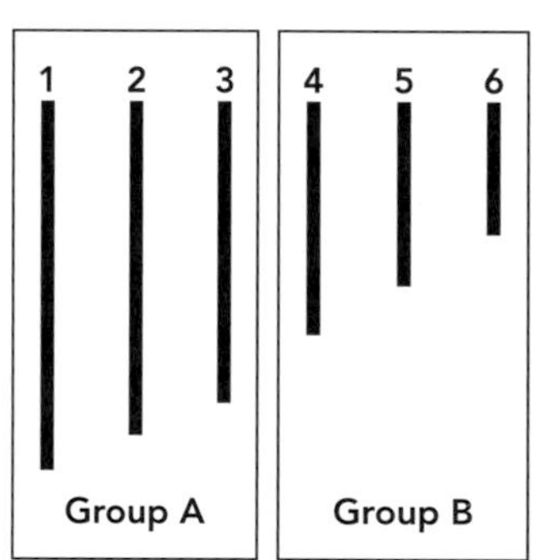

FIGURE **15.5 Assimilation and contrast** People who see the lines on the right tend to *overestimate the similarity* of lines 1 and 3 and *underestimate the similarity* of lines 3 and 4. Simply labelling lines 1–3 'group A' and lines 4–6 'group B' causes the lines within a group to seem more similar to each other than they really are and the lines in different groups to seem more different from each other than they really are.

You've probably experienced this phenomenon yourself. For instance, we all identify colours as members of categories such as *blue* or *green,* and this leads us to overestimate the similarity of colours that share a category label and to underestimate the similarity of colours that do not. This is why we see discrete *bands* of colour when we look at rainbows, which are actually a smooth continuum of colours. This is also why we tend to underestimate the distance between cities in the same country, such as Blackpool and London, and overestimate the distance between cities in different countries, such as Geneva and Milan (Burris and Branscombe, 2005). What's true of colours and distances is true of people as well. The mere act of categorizing people as black or white, Jew or Arab, artists or accountants can cause us to underestimate the variability within those categories ('All artists are wacky') and overestimate the variability between them ('They're much wackier than accountants'). When we underestimate the variability of a human category, we feel justified in using our stereotypes.

The tendency to underestimate variability is especially likely when the person we are judging is a member of an out-group rather than a member of our in-group. In one study, Princeton students were shown a video of a person choosing to listen to a particular kind of music, such as jazz rather than classical (Quattrone and Jones, 1980). When the participants were told that the person in the video was a fellow Princeton student, they were reluctant to conclude that 'the average Princeton student' preferred jazz to classical because *these* Princeton students in the study recognized how distinctive and unique each Princeton student is. But when these Princeton students were told that the person in the video was a Rutgers student, they readily concluded that the average Rutgers student preferred jazz to classical. After all, Rutgers students are all pretty much alike! Yet, when the same study was performed with Rutgers students as participants, the Rutgers students were reluctant to draw conclusions about the average Rutgers student but were quick to draw conclusions about the average Princeton student. Of course, as European students reading about these studies of Princeton and Rutgers students, we do not draw a distinction but group them together as typical North American students obsessed with the opposite sex, drinking and pranks, based on nothing more than the countless Hollywood films where they are portrayed as such.

In 2012, the mayor of a Triberg, a small town in Germany, announced the opening of a new car park that had provision of 12 'woman-only' spaces that were extra-large, well lit and near the exits. The public reaction was one of accusations of sexism but the defiant Mayor Gallus Strobel told German news magazine *Der Spiegel*: 'Women can come here and prove me wrong, and while they're at it, they can see the town's attractions.' However, they needn't have bothered to make the trip to prove him wrong. A study of surveillance tapes by the car park firm NCP, which employed a team of researchers to observe 2,500 drivers across its 700 car parks in Britain over a one month period, found that women may have taken longer to park than men but they were much better at it.

Stereotypes can be self-perpetuating

When we meet a man who likes ballet more than football or a senior citizen who likes hip-hop more than easy-listening, why don't we recognize that our stereotypes are inaccurate? Stereotypes are a bit like viruses, and once they take up residence inside us, they perpetuate themselves and resist even our most concerted efforts to eradicate them. Stereotypes are self-perpetuating because we see what we expect to see, we cause others to behave as we expect them to behave, and we tend to modify our stereotypes rather than abandon them. Each of these mindbugs contributes to the maintenance of stereotypic thinking. Let's look at them in turn:

- Perceptual confirmation is *the tendency for observers to perceive what they expect to perceive*. You may recall the study described in Chapter 2 in which students who were falsely told that a particular rat was bred to be stupid tended to underestimate that rat's performance in a maze. The same thing can happen with people. In one study, participants listened to a basketball game and were asked to evaluate the performance of one of the players. Although all participants heard the same prerecorded game, some were led to believe the player was black and others were led to believe the player was white. Participants' stereotypes led them to expect different performances from athletes of different ethnic origins. In fact, the participants perceived just what they expected. Those who believed the player was black thought he had exhibited greater athletic ability but less intelligence than did those who thought he was white (Stone et al., 1997). Although people are especially inclined to notice and remember behaviours that are clearly at odds with their stereotypes, for example a skinhead reciting Shakespearean sonnets or a celebrity robbing a shop, most ordinary behaviours are ambiguous, thus we tend to see them as confirming rather than disconfirming our stereotypes (Stangor and McMillan, 1992). Stereotypes perpetuate themselves in part by biasing our perception of individuals, leading us to believe that those individuals have confirmed our stereotypes when, in fact, they have not (Fiske, 1998).

PERCEPTUAL CONFIRMATION The tendency for observers to perceive what they expect to perceive.

SELF-FULFILLING PROPHECY A phenomenon whereby observers bring about what they expect to perceive.

- Stereotypes influence perception, but they also influence reality. A self-fulfilling prophecy is *a phenomenon whereby observers bring about what they expect to perceive*. When people know that observers have a negative stereotype about them, they may experience *stereotype threat* – fear of confirming an observer's stereotype. Ironically, this fear can cause people to behave in precisely the way the stereotype predicts. In one study, students of African or European ancestry were given a test, and half the students in each group were asked to list their race at the top of the exam. Students who were not asked to list their race performed as well as their entrance exam scores suggested they should (Steele and Aronson, 1995). But when students were asked to list their races, students of African ancestry performed more poorly than their entrance exam scores suggested they should (FIGURE 15.6). Other measures confirmed that the students of African descent who had been asked to list their race were worried about confirming a stereotype about their group, and this worry impaired their performance. The same effect also holds true for female stereotypes. Women performed worse on a difficult task when they were told in advance that it was diagnostic of maths intelligence compared to women not given this information (Martens et al., 2006).

Perceptual confirmation led participants to believe that a basketball player who was black would exhibit greater athleticism but less intelligence than a white player.

- Stereotype threat is just one of many ways in which observers may cause others to confirm a stereotype. For example, observers tend to behave unpleasantly towards people about whom they hold negative stereotypes, which, in turn, leads those people to behave unpleasantly, thus confirming the observer's initial belief that 'those kinds

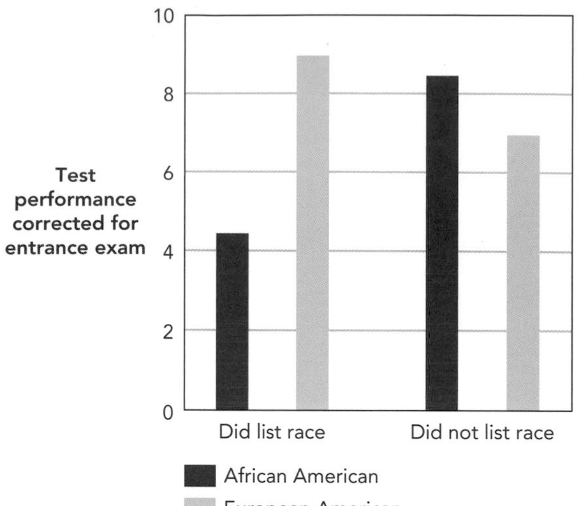

FIGURE 15.6 Stereotype threat and test performance When asked to indicate their race before starting a test, African American students perform more poorly than their entrance exam scores suggest they should.

of people' just aren't very nice (Harris and Rosenthal, 1985). Similarly, observers tend to seek information that confirms rather than disconfirms their stereotypes (Snyder and Swann, 1978). When a man asks a woman, 'Do you like cooking more than sewing?', he is giving her very little opportunity to explain that she actually prefers sumo wrestling to both. Stereotypes perpetuate themselves in part by causing the stereotyped individual to behave in ways that confirm the stereotype.

- When a person clearly disconfirms an observer's stereotype, the observer may find ways to modify, and therefore retain, the stereotype (Weber and Crocker, 1983). For example, people tend to believe that public relations agents are sociable. In one study, participants learned about a PR agent who was *slightly* unsociable, and the results showed that their stereotypes about PR agents shifted a bit to accommodate this new information. But when participants learned about a PR agent who was *extremely* unsociable, their stereotypes did not change at all (Kunda and Oleson, 1997). Why? Because when participants encountered an *extremely* unsociable PR agent ('Rick, a PR agent from Edinburgh who works primarily with divorce lawyers, just can't stand the company of other people'), they engaged in *subtyping*. Rather than changing their stereotypes of PR agents ('I guess they aren't such a sociable bunch'), they created a new, highly specialized subcategory of PR agents ('PR agents from Scotland who work for small law firms are very unsociable'), which allowed them to think of the extremely unsociable PR agent as 'an exception to the rule' and thereby preserve their stereotypes about PR agents in general. Subtyping is a powerful method for preserving our stereotypes in the face of contradictory evidence.

Many of us think that nuns are traditional and proper. Does this photo of a hula-hooping nun change your stereotype, or are you tempted to subtype them instead?

SCOTT GRIESSEL/DREAMSTIME.COM

Stereotyping can be automatic

If stereotypes are inaccurate and self-perpetuating, why don't we just stop using them? Over a number of years, social psychologist Louise Pendry has instructed her undergraduate lab class to read the following passage:

> A father and his son were involved in a car accident in which the father was killed and the son was seriously injured. The father was pronounced dead at the scene of the accident and his body was taken to a local morgue. The son was taken by ambulance to a nearby hospital and was immediately wheeled into an emergency operating theatre. A surgeon was called. Upon arrival, and seeing the patient, the attending surgeon exclaimed, 'Oh my God, it's my son!'

When asked to explain the scenario, often more than 40% of the class are unable to explain it (Pendry, 2008, p. 69). Why is it the case that many students do not immediately realize that the surgeon is female and must be his mother? One reason is that when we think about people, we have two modes of thinking. One is fast and automatic that occurs without intention or effort. The other is a more controlled process that is intentional, under volitional control and effortful. This is the System 1 and System 2 thinking (Kahneman, 2012) we encountered in Chapter 7. The reason that students fail to recognize the female surgeon in the road traffic accident scenario is that their automatic thinking generates a common stereotype of a male surgeon.

Stereotyping can happen *unconsciously* (we don't always know we are doing it) and *automatically* (we often cannot avoid doing it even when we try). For example, in one study, photos of black or white men holding guns or cameras were flashed on a computer screen for less than one second each. Participants earned money by pressing a button labelled 'shoot' whenever the man on the screen was holding a gun but lost money if they shot a man holding a camera. The participants made some mistakes, of course, but two kinds of mistakes they made were quite disturbing: they tended to shoot black men holding cameras and were less likely to shoot white men holding guns (Correll et al., 2002). Although the photos appeared on the screen so quickly that participants did not have enough time to consciously consult their stereotypes, those stereotypes worked unconsciously, causing them to mistake a camera for a gun when it was in the hands of a black man and a gun for a camera when it was in the hands of a white man. Interestingly, black participants were just as likely to make this pattern of errors as white participants.

Stereotypes are made up from all the information we have absorbed over the years about members of different human categories, for better or worse, and we can't *decide* not to use that information any more than we can *decide* not to see the colour green, not to remember our high school graduation, or not to enjoy the smell of lavender in bloom. In fact, trying not to use stereotypes can make matters worse instead of better. Participants in one study were shown a photograph of a tough-looking male 'skinhead' and were asked to write an essay describing a typical day in his life. Some of the participants were told that they should not allow their stereotypes about skinheads to influence their essays and others were given no such instructions. Next, the experimenter brought each participant to a room with eight empty chairs. The first chair had a jacket draped over it, and the experimenter explained that it belonged to the person in the photograph, who had gone to the toilet. Where did participants choose to sit? Participants who had been told not to let their stereotypes influence their essays sat farther away from the skinhead's jacket than participants who had been given no instructions (Macrae et al., 1994).

BRANDX

Although the idea of a female surgeon is not a new one, automatic thinking led many students to revert to traditional gender norms.

Why did this happen? As you learned in Chapter 8, attempts to suppress a thought can increase the likelihood that people will experience the very thought they are trying to suppress (Wegner et al., 1987). Stereotypical thoughts are no exception. Although stereotyping is often unconscious and automatic, it is not inevitable (Blair, 2002). We cannot stop using stereotypes with the flick of a mental switch, but research shows that stereotyping effects can be reduced (and sometimes eliminated) by a variety of factors, ranging from educational programmes (Kawakami et al., 2000; Rudman et al., 2001) to damage to the prefrontal cortex (Milne and Grafman, 2001). Education is probably the better social policy.

Prejudice

Stereotyping entails a degree of discrimination against out-group members in the form of prejudice – *a negative evaluation of, and attitude towards, individuals based on negative group stereotypes.* Although stereotyping, discrimination and prejudice are often related, they need not necessarily always operate together. Individuals can discriminate without necessarily being prejudiced, as in interfaith marriages. Or one can be prejudiced but prevented from discrimination by legisilation aimed at equality. There are laws against racism and homophobia in many countries to protect minority groups but prejudice need not be restricted to the few. Around half the population regularly experience prejudice, in the form of sexism against females, and whether you like it or not, most of us in Westernized society will eventually experience prejudice in the form of ageism. Again, there are laws in many societies to prevent discrimination but even individuals who do not consider themselves to be prejudiced can still hold implicit stereotypes (see where do you stand?).

PREJUDICE A negative evaluation of, and attitude towards, individuals based on negative group stereotypes.

We learned earlier that as soon as groups are formed, individuals develop favourtism to in-group members and negative biases against out-group members, and that mechanisms such as illusory correlations lead us to systematic biases, but why are we prejudiced against others at all? Next, we consider how individual differences and group mechanisms have been used to explain prejudice.

Individual differences associated with prejudice

Prejudice can be the obvious response to others whose values and beliefs differ from our own (Duckitt, 2006). In attempting to interpret the world around us and the social environments we occupy, we seek structure, order and predictability, with a right and wrong way to do things. If others differ from us in their way of doing things, we perceive them as a threat to our own worldview. People who score highly on measures designed to tap into their personal need for structure or the need to avoid ambiguity and preference for certainty are more prejudiced (Neuberg and Newsom, 1993). For example, if you get upset by unpredictable situations, hate plans that have to change at the last minute, prefer a well-ordered life and dislike spontaneity, there is a good chance you will also tend to think stereotypically with a degree of prejudice (for a summary, see Sutton and Douglas, 2013).

Some of us prefer social order and structure and are more willing to yield to authority and agree with harsh punishment for those who defy or threaten the status quo. We often describe such people as being 'close-minded', which makes them prone to prejudice (Kruglanski, 2006). Also, as we saw in Chapter 13, some individuals score highly on measures of right-wing authoritarianism (Altemeyer, 1981), which again makes them prejudiced towards minority groups (Altemeyer, 1998). A related personality concept is social dominance orientation – *a preference for hierarchical relations between groups, with one's own group being the most dominant* (Sidanius and Pratto, 1999) – which again predicts prejudice against minorities but also against policies designed to minimize social injustices and provide universal welfare (Pratto et al., 1994).

SOCIAL DOMINANCE ORIENTATION A preference for hierarchical relations between groups, with one's own group being the most dominant.

The problem with ascribing individual prejudice to personality types is that individuals can easily become prejudiced in different contexts, which suggests that group influences and circumstances must be taken into consideration. For example, following 9/11, there was a significant increase in hostile treatment and violence against Muslims in the Netherlands (EUMC, 2001). In 2005, the Pew Global Project found that 51% of the Dutch participants had unfavourable opinions about Muslims (González et al., 2008). History tells us that whole nations can suddenly become prejudiced at times of threat and conflict. Differences in individual thinking (such as close-mindedness) may be related to prejudice but these are strongly linked to group influences.

stats facts

The dark origins of the Likert scale

The Likert scale is commonly used to measure attitudes in various areas of psychology where researchers want to quantify responses in a standardized way. It usually comprises a question (or set of questions) with a corresponding set of responses that range in terms of the level of agreement to disagreement. A typical five-point scale would range from strongly disagree, disagree, neither agree nor disagree, agree, strongly agree. Variations of the Likert measures include visual analogue scales (a horizontal line), where participants indicate their level of agreement by how far along the scale they believe their attitudes match the statement.

Likert scales are useful for generating numerical data based on opinions that may be difficult to measure in large groups or during open-ended interviews when there is too much variation in individual responses requiring qualitative analysis (see Chapter 2). However, like many sciences that have dark episodes of immoral activity in their past, sush as poison gases (chemistry), germ warfare (biology) and nuclear weapons (physics), psychology is no different. Invented by Rensis Likert, an organizational psychologist based at the US Department of Agriculture between the two world wars, the Likert scale was originally used to assess public opinion, including attitudes towards blacks – whether they should receive education, whether they should be treated as equal to whites, and whether it was acceptable to lynch a black 'who is insolent to a white man'.

Group influences associated with prejudice

In Chapter 14 we described the struggle for survival of individuals to pass on their genes but we have become so co-dependent as a species that competition for survival is arguably now at the group level. *Realistic group conflict theory* (Sherif, 1966; LeVine and Campbell, 1972) predicts that discrimination and prejudice should increase when resources are scarce at the group level. This will be especially true in 'zero-sum' situations where only one group can benefit from resources at the expense of all others. This is supported by historical analysis of times of economic hardship, which have consistently been associated with increased hostility and prejudice. For example, when unemployment rose dramatically in the US during the Great Depression, there was increased hostility towards German immigrants as predicted by the frustration-aggression principle (encountered in Chapter 14) (Dollard, 1938). In the UK, the rise of the UKIP political party during 2014 has been associated with increased concerns over uncontrolled immigration.

Intergroup conflict has also been studied experimentally. In a classic study inspired by William Golding's *Lord of the Flies*, 11-year-old schoolboys were taken to an Oklahoma summer camp called the Robbers Cave and divided into two groups (Sherif et al., 1961). The groups chose their own names (the Rattlers and the Eagles), their insignia, flags and T-shirts. In the first phase of the study, the groups worked independently on tasks to foster group unity such as pitching tents and preparing meals. In the second phase, the Rattlers and the Eagles competed in tournaments including sports games, treasures hunts and cabin inspections to win prizes. At this point, the insults started to be hurled at each other. They soon stole each other's flags and fights broke out. In the final phase, the two groups were brought together in noncompetitive situations to determine whether the hostility demonstrated in phase two had dissipated. However, just simply being together was enough to trigger the name-calling, jeering and food fights. Here, there was no competition and yet group prejudices prevailed. The boys were then told that the water supply to the camp had been disrupted and both groups were needed to pull a broken-down truck out of trouble. It was only after the researchers introduced these superordinate goals – *goals that depend on the collaborative effort of two or more groups* – that the intergroup conflict disappeared. By emphazing a greater group membership (all boys at the Robbers Cave camp), the Eagles and the Rattlers put aside their previous grievances and worked as a superordinate group.

SUPERORDINATE GOALS Goals that depend on the collaborative effort of two or more groups.

However, economic hardship cannot be the only reason for prejudice. Consider the common prejudice against immigrants. In countries like France, Austria and Australia, which have overcome most major economic and security problems, other cultural and political factors have fostered resentment towards immigrants (Deangelis, 2008). Also, an analysis of prejudice in European countries shows that there are paradoxical differences between the most disadvantaged and better off members of a group. Poor economic conditions reduce prejudice against immigrants among disadvantaged groups, but simultaneously increase prejudice in the more advantaged who should be at greater threat (Kunovich, 2004).

Hostility based on competition between groups has intuitive appeal but there are problems with this perspective. As noted earlier, simply identifying as a member of a group is sufficient to trigger in-group biases and out-group prejudice (Tajfel, 1970), and the Robbers Cave study showed that prejudice persisted even when there was no competition. Another problem is that we belong to more than one group and so it is not clear where the battle lines of competition arise. When immigrants threaten to take jobs, the poorest may see themselves as members of the same disadvantaged group in search of opportunities rather than members of a hierarchical society that already favours the most advantaged. This class struggle perspective has more to do with Marx's political ideology than Darwin's theory of natural selection.

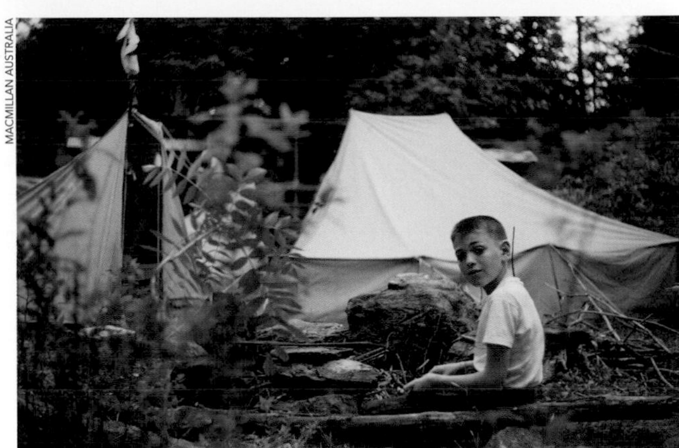

MACMILLAN AUSTRALIA

The Robbers Cave experiment showed that intergroup conflict emerged in competitive and noncompetitive situations, and only dissipated with the introduction of superordinate goals, requiring collective collaboration.

Behaving in groups

Have you ever noticed the frenzy that goes on at feeding time when there is a group of animals? Many species, including rats, dogs, fish, frogs and even armadillos, will scoff down more food in the presence of others (Boice et al., 1974; Harlow, 1932; Platt et al., 1967; Ross and Ross, 1949; Uematsu, 1970). Humans also tend to eat more and faster in the company of others (de Castro, 1994). These are all examples of the effects of groups on individual behaviour. Feeding seems an obvious situation where individual behaviour is modified by the presence of others, as there may be competition for food and one does not want to lose out in the free-for-all. When you are one your own, you can take your time.

But the presence of others can influence other behaviours as well, such as how well we perform in tests. In one of social psychology's first experiments, Norman Triplett (1898, p. 516), an early cycling enthusiast, noticed that racers achieved faster times when they were in competition against other riders compared to racing alone against the clock. He believed that the:

> bodily presence of another rider is a stimulus to the racer in arousing the competitive instinct; that another can thus be the means of releasing or freeing nervous energy for him that he cannot of himself release; and, further, that the sight of movement in that other by perhaps suggesting a higher rate of speed, is also an inspiration to greater effort.

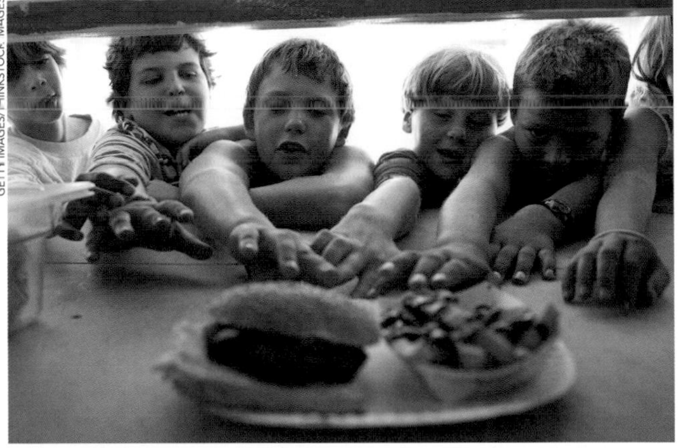

GETTY IMAGES/I-INKSTOCK IMAGES

These hungry beasts make feeding time a free-for-all.

To test his hypothesis, Triplett presented 40 children with a task where they had to reel in fishing lines as fast as they could on blocks of trials where they were either alone or in a group. The findings confirmed his hypothesis; and later studies went on to demonstrate that the effect was not due to competition per se, rather, the mere presence of an audience (Gates, 1924) was sufficient to induce social facilitation – *improved individual performance in the company of others*.

SOCIAL FACILITATION Improved individual performance in the company of others.

Social facilitation is not unique to humans but can be found throughout the animal kingdom. Horses and kangeroos will run faster in the presence of other horses and kangaroos (Pays et al., 2009; van Dierendonck et al., 1995) and even insects like ants and fruit flies (Chen, 1937; Connelly, 1968) show enhanced performance in groups, indicating that social facilitation is a fundamental feature of animal behaviour. The fact that social facilitation can also be found in the unsocial centipede suggests that it does not depend on the animal living in groups to trigger the behaviour (Hosey et al., 1985). It may be that we are more sensitive to our own performance capability when we can

An inconvenient convenience

Most males are probably familiar with social inhibition when standing at the urinals in public toilets. One study showed that men take longer to urinate when someone is standing immediately next to them at a urinal than when they are alone (Middlemast et al., 1976). There is also an unwritten law that it is unacceptable to stand next to another man at the urinals if some distance can be maintained.

SOCIAL INHIBITION Where the presence of others inhibits or impairs performance.

SPOTLIGHT EFFECT People's overestimation of the amount of attention others are paying to them.

DOMINANT RESPONSE The thing you are most inclined to do.

compare and contrast it with that of another like us. In this way, we can 'raise our game' when there is competition around. But even when there is no competition, the mere presence of others can influence your behaviour. An audience can alter your performance. Meta-analysis of the 'home advantage' benefit in athletic competitions indicates that home teams will win approximately 60% of their contests (Jamieson, 2010).

Audiences do not always make us perform better. Even when we are motivated to do the best we can, having others around sometimes impairs us. One of the earliest demonstrations to challenge Triplett's original social facilitation effect was a study of Harvard students' ability to construct philosophical arguments as best they could in a five-minute period (Allport, 1920). Students were found to produce much better arguments when working alone than when another student was present. This detrimental effect of groups on performance has been found on a range of tasks including arithmetic, memory and maze learning, as well as in animal performance (for meta-analysis of social facilitation, see Bond and Titus, 1983). This flipside to the social facilitation of performance is social inhibition – *where the presence of others inhibits or impairs performance*. In the context of competition, this is also known as 'choking', especially in sports when individuals who are normally proficient unexpectedly fail to perform up to expectations with an audience present. Missed penalties in football are the classic example where the pressure of the crowd can turn even the most skilled footballer into one with two left feet.

Social facilitation and social inhibition are exacerbated by focused self-awareness known as the spotlight effect – *people's overestimation of the amount of attention others are paying to them*. Whether it is speaking up in a group discussion, skiing too close to the chairlifts or tripping over in public, we overestimate how much we think others have noticed our behaviour (Epley et al., 2002; Gilovich et al, 2002; Savitsky et al., 2001). In one study, students were asked to wear an embarrassing T-shirt before joining a group (Gilovich et al., 2000). They felt they stood out and estimated that, on average, 46% of the other students would have noticed the T-shirt when, in fact, it was half that (23%). No wonder teenagers hate to wear 'embarrassing' clothing picked out by their mothers!

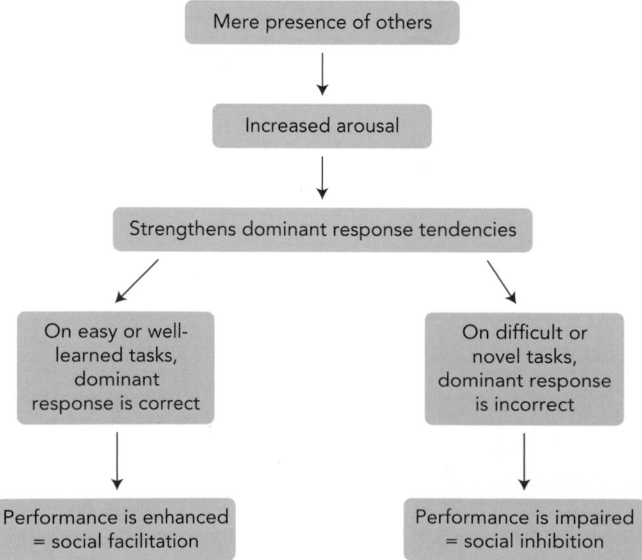

FIGURE 15.7 Zajonc's model of social facilitation The mere presence of others increases arousal and strengthens the dominant response, which in well-learned or easy tasks is the correct behaviour but in new or unlearned tasks, dominant responses are not conducive to successful performance.

To account for the apparently contradictory effects of the influence of groups on performance, Zajonc (1965) proposed a dual route model of social facilitation, as shown in FIGURE 15.7. Zajonc's model was originally based on Hull's learning theory (1943) and has three components derived from other areas of psychology. First, the mere presence of others triggers an increase in autonomic arousal (described in Chapter 3). We know from the Yerkes-Dodson law that raising arousal improves drive and performance so long as the increase does not exceed the optimal level (see Chapter 10). Increased arousal makes a person in Zajonc's model more likely to execute, in the third stage, what he calls the dominant response – *the thing you are most inclined to do*. So, the success of the outcome depends on the circumstances. In the situation of a well-learned or easy task, the dominant response is the most likely and the most appropriate, which is why performance will be enhanced. However, in a novel task or one that is unlearned, the dominant response may be one that is not conducive to success, such as a fight-or-flight reaction where the urge to panic takes over. Here, performance is impaired by counterproductive activities.

Zajonc's (1965) drive theory was revolutionary not only for offering a neat explanation of divergent results, but also for tying social facilitation to arousal (Feinberg and Aiello, 2006). Subsequent studies provided additional validation for the model as well as some support for the hypothesized physiological state changes. A recent meta-analysis of athletic performance confirms that an audience produces moderate improvements (Oviatt and Iso-Ahola, 2008). However, the model predicts that improvement depends on how skilled you are. For example, skilled pool players (defined as those who achieve over 70% of their attempted shots to pot the ball when alone) were shown to achieve an increase in potting success to 80% when others were present. In contrast, poor players (defined as those who average only 40% success of their attempted shots to pot the ball when alone) performed worse, making only 25% of their attempts at sinking the balls when they being watched (Michaels et al., 1982). Heart rate of individuals performing tasks has also been found to be raised in the presence of others, with differing patterns indicating different responses from those who demonstrated social facilitation compared to those who exhibited social inhibition (Blascovich et al., 1999).

Zajonc's original model was soon challenged by alternative accounts of social facilitation. For example, the effect of the mere presence of an audience is probably too simplistic because it depends on how the individual evaluates the group. If the audience is blindfolded or not paying attention, the social facilitation is attenuated (Cottrell et al., 1968), which has led to the proposal that social facilitation depends on evaluation apprehension – *performance is affected by how people think they are being judged.* This explains some of the individual variations in social facilitation. For example, individuals who are particularly concerned by others' opinions are more susceptible to the influence of an audience (Geen, 1983). Competitors perform better when they are pitted against others who they perceive as superior (Muller et al., 2004). However, concerns over negative, but not positive, evaluation have been shown to be important in social facilitation (Geen and Gange, 1977). In other words, it is the fear of failure that seems to be a major factor. Another class of accounts concentrates less on drive explanations and more on cognition, framing the social facilitation/inhibition effects in the context of distraction and attention (Baron et al., 1978). According to these distraction accounts, difficult, but not easy, tasks require attention, which is why they are compromised when in the presence of a distracting audience.

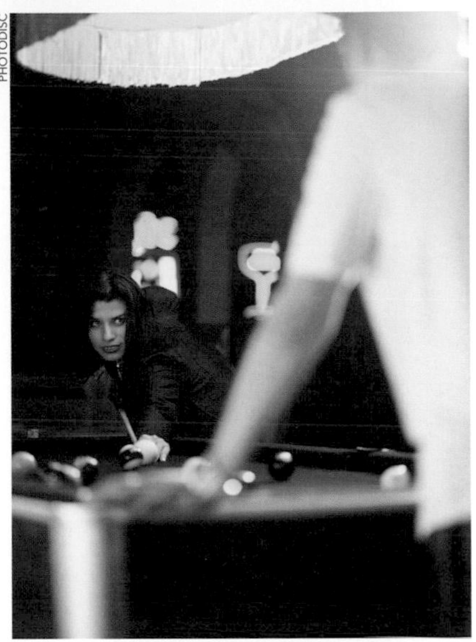

Accomplished players raise their game in the presence of others, while weaker players might crumble under the pressure.

EVALUATION APPREHENSION Performance is affected by how people think they are being judged.

In general, it appears that for humans, there are a multitude of factors that play a role in whether groups generate facilitation, inhibition or no effects at all on performance. Unlike insects running mazes, humans are also motivated by what others think, so most of us are sensitive to exhibiting poor performance that may be negatively evaluated by them. Therefore, it seems fair to conclude that Zajonc's drive theory has general universal application in the animal kingdom but that variations observed in humans in different situations may be a reflection of the importance of the nature of the perceived relationship between the group and the individual.

Group effort: when many hands don't always make light work

Social facilitation explains why, as individuals, we may 'up our game' when we want to be seen in a good light by others, but what happens when we are working with others in a group effort? While social facilitation has been observed for different behaviours among diverse species, the presence of others does not always facilitate behaviours that are in the best interest of the group. As we noted in Chapter 14, studies of the bystander effect reveal that individuals are less likely to step forward and help an innocent person in distress when there are many others present.

In some situations, groups can diminish our sense of personal responsibility for our own actions. For example, social loafing occurs when *people expend less effort when working in a group than when working alone.* In one of the earliest studies of social loafing, Ringelmann (1913) measured how much effort his students exerted in a tug of war test to pull on a rope when there were varying numbers of others. He discovered a linear relationship between the amount of effort individuals exerted and the number of people in the group – as the number increased, effort declined. Maybe there is a problem coordinating larger numbers of people to pull together more effectively. However, a later study using blindfolded subjects who thought they were either pulling alone or in a group also exhibited social loafing (Ingham et al., 1974), indicating that it was the motivation and not the capacity to coordinate many efforts. Likewise, audience members who were asked to applaud as loud as they could while wearing headphones who thought they were either in a group or by themselves exhibited less motivation to act when they thought there were others (Latané et al., 1979).

SOCIAL LOAFING People expend less effort when working in a group than when working alone.

The effect is not restricted to effortful behaviour. When they are in a large compared to a small group, individuals leave worse tips at restaurants (Freeman et al., 1975), donate less money to charitable causes (Wiesenthal et al., 1983), and are less likely to respond when someone says hello (Jones and Foshay, 1984). Whether the group is made up of work colleagues (van Dick et al., 2009), classmates (Jassawalla et al., 2009) or handball teammates (Høigaard et al., 2010), people take a 'free ride' on the efforts of others. It is not that social loafers are individuals who cynically exploit the efforts of others; in fact, they generally believe they are contributing as much as others in the group. Free riders, on the other hand, are fully aware of what they are not doing and regard others as 'mugs' to be taken advantage of.

A meta-analysis of 78 studies found that social loafing was a robust phenomenon occurring in over 80% of the investigations considered (Karau and Williams, 1993). How can we understand the effects of groups that increase our performance in social facilitation in some circumstances and yet reduce our efforts in social loafing? The answer has something to do with whether performance on the task is primarily perceived as a group effort or dependent on the individual. Social loafing occurs because individuals expect their effort to be less likely to be given credit when working collectively than working independently. When they are tested alone, individuals assume that credit will be perceived to be accountable to them alone, whereas there is a diffusion of credit in a group. When people do not feel accountable for performance, they are more likely to expend less effort. However, the meta-analysis also revealed that group characteristics are associated with different levels of social loafing.

When group members are friendly and exhibit strong entitativity (discussed earlier), there is less social loafing (Karau and Williams, 1997; Worchel et al., 1998). Cultural differences in social group identity also emerge in social loafing phenomena. Individualistic societies such as the UK, the US and Australia are more prone to social loafing, whereas collectivist societies such as Japan and China exhibit less social loafing in experimental studies (Karau and Williams, 1993). Although social loafing may be implicit, collectivist societies such as Japan (Kugihara, 1999) and China (Earley, 1989) seem to induce performance contributions by individuals working in groups much more strongly than in the West.

It is also noteworthy that not pulling one's weight is simply not in the mindset of collectivist societies where such behaviour would be considered shameful. Indeed, Eastern societies have often been described as 'shame cultures', where failure to match up to others' expectations is a primary negative emotion, whereas Western societies are more 'guilt cultures', where individuals feel bad because they have not maintained their own self-imposed moral standards (Wong and Tsai, 2007). In other words, while shame has an external group orientation, guilt has an internal self-orientation (Smith et al., 2002).

Gender is also another group category, as social loafing is more prevalent among males compared to females across cultures (Gabrenya et al., 1985). Males tend to loaf more as they grow older, whereas social loafing in females remains constant with age. It is not clear why males are more likely to coast on the efforts of others, but females may be more inclined to collectivist rather than individualistic attitudes when working in groups (Anderson and Blanchard, 1982).

Deindividuation: Do we really get lost in the crowd?

Imagine that you were lucky enough to win tickets to see your favourite performer in concert at Glastonbury. Maybe it's Lady Gaga or David Bowie. No doubt in the sea of thousands of fans you would have a great time singing along and dancing to your favourite tracks. You might even show off some of your best moves or make advances towards another attractive fan. Now imagine that you won a fantastic prize (truly a fantasy) where you can have Lady Gaga or David Bowie perform in your own living room with just you as the audience. Again, this would be an amazing experience but it is unlikely that you would be singing along and dancing in the same way as you did at Glastonbury. Indeed, you may even feel quite self-conscious and embarrassed.

People behave differently when they are in a group as opposed to be alone. In fact, one of the primary reasons that people spend large amounts of time, effort and money to attend arena events such as concerts and sports competitions is precisely because the experience is so different when there are a large number of people. Crowd behaviour is known as an emergent property – *patterns that only arise out of the interaction of many elements*. Emergent properties are found throughout nature – the world's weather systems, the flocking of birds and even the major upheavals in stock markets. In each of these systems, there are interactions that produce outcomes that level out the complexity of the mix. In the case of people, the mix can become an ugly mob.

EMERGENT PROPERTY Patterns that only arise out of the interaction of many elements.

One of the first to provide an analysis of mob behaviour was French sociologist Gustave Le Bon ([1896]1908). He was fascinated by the crowd behaviour during the social unrest in 19th-century Paris and drew parallels with the frenzied behaviour observed in animals during feeding. He believed that reasonable, rational people could behave in animalistic ways because they had lost their sense of personal responsibility by becoming an anonymous member of the crowd.

Le Bon's analysis of crowd violence has operated as a pervasive explanation of antinormative behaviour – *activities that are transgressions of general social norms*. This may be rowdiness, vandalism, looting, provocation, aggression and other aspects of antisocial behaviour. Most of the time, we regard ourselves as individuals responsible for our actions and concerned with the consequences of our behaviour. However, when we join a group, we can experience deindividuation – *a perceived loss of individual identity accompanied by diminished self-regulation*. Le Bon's original analysis of the mob became almost a manifesto for authorities to harness the power of the crowd to serve their aims and, unsurprisingly, deindividuation had a major influence on 20th-century politics, most notably with the dictators Stalin, Hitler and Mussolini, who used rallies to cement their position (Moscovici, 1981). George Orwell's *1984* was a fictional account of how to control the masses by deindividuation but clearly a pastiche of 20th-century dictatorships.

ANTINORMATIVE BEHAVIOUR Activities that are transgressions of general social norms.

DEINDIVIDUATION A perceived loss of individual identity accompanied by diminished self-regulation.

Even today, we still look at atrocities around the world such as the Rwandan genocide in 1994 and try to understand why crowds can be so cruel to their victims. Zimbardo (2007) thinks that many of the worst aspects of human cruelty can be understood by what he calls 'the Lucifer effect', when we are deindividuated under a cloak of anonymity. According to Zimbardo (1970), when we are deindividuated by the crowd, we are less aware of our self, more focused on others and less inhibited, which makes us more likely to engage in impulsive behaviours, especially when crowd activity raises our levels of arousal to a frenzy.

Most of the work on deindividuation has been based on retrospective analysis. For example, a study of lynchings of African Americans between 1899 and 1946 lends support to the relationship between group size and violence (Mullen, 1986). As the size of the group increases, so does the violence (Leader et al., 2007). Suicide baiting is a particularly shameful phenomenon, where individuals who are comtemplating jumping from tall structures are encouraged by onlookers to take their own lives. An analysis of 21 cases of attempted suicide where crowds were present, based on newspaper reports between 1966 and 1979, found that suicide baiting was reported in 10 cases (Mann, 1981). The factors that seemed to link this suicide baiting were larger crowds, the distance between the crowd and the victim, and the cover of night – arguably, all factors that lead to greater anonymity.

When we are made more self-aware by the pictures of staring eyes, we are less likely to make a moral transgression (Bateson et al., 2006). People are also less likely to cheat when they can see themselves in a mirror (Diener and Wallbom, 1976; Vallacher and Solodky, 1979). Children told to take only one sweet when they were out 'trick or treating' in Seattle homes on Halloween were more likely to take handfuls of sweets when in a group compared to individual children (Diener et al., 1976). In these situations, it is argued that deindividuation occurs when attention is naturally drawn to others and *away* from themselves; thus, they are less likely to abide by their own moral values (Mullen, 1986; Mullen et al., 1989; Wegner and Schaefer, 1978). Some experimental studies have provided support for this deindividuation hypothesis. For example, individuals in loud, stimulating environments, such as low-lit rooms with loud rock music playing, experience reduced public self-awareness and become more disinhibited and aggressive in their actions (Prentice-Dunn and Rogers, 1982).

Suicide baiting

In January 2010, a distressed woman on a bridge over the M60 motorway in Manchester, England brought the traffic to a four-hour standstill while the police attempted to talk her down. Steve Penk, a radio DJ, thought it would be amusing to play Van Halen's hit track, 'Jump', for the frustrated drivers caught up in the drama. Moments later, the woman jumped, allegedly after hearing the song on a radio turned up by one of the waiting motorists. Luckily, the woman survived her suicide attempt but Penk was unrepentant about his suicide baiting.

The London riots we opened this chapter with were described in the press as evidence of 'a mob mentality', which has become a cliché, but despite its intuitive appeal and long track record as an explanation for crowd violence, deindividuation is controversial for several reasons. First, not all crowd behaviour is antinormative in a negative way. Indeed, being in a crowd can be liberating when one does not behave as one normally would, as that change in behaviour can be very positive. Religious congregations, political rallies and even the crowds at Glastonbury can all have a good time and very often people are much more prosocial towards each other, which is partly why they are attracted there in the first place. Second, the literature on deindividuation is largely retrospective and based on real-life events so is not easily subject to experimental investigation. By finding examples of crowd violence, proponents are cherry picking the data to support the deindividuation hypothesis that groups lead to negative behaviour. However, where systematic research has been conducted, a meta-analysis of over 60 independent studies found little consistent support for the hypothesis that anonymity, large groups and reduced self-awareness cause antisocial behaviour (Potmes and Spears, 1998).

It is true that large crowds may behave in antinormative ways, but as Steven Reicher (2001, p. 186) has noted: 'Simply by being part of the crowd, individuals lose all sense of self and all sense of responsibility. Yet, at the same time, they gain a sentiment of invincible power due to their numbers.' This power can be used for good, and for every street gang that murders an innocent victim, there are many civic groups that clean up rubbish from a neighbourhood park, and for every bloody riot, there are many peaceful protests. After the 2011 London riots, an army of volunteer citizens armed with brushes set about cleaning up the mess left behind. By focusing only on the negative examples of group behaviour, deindividuation discards the strengths and retains the weaknesses of Le Bon's argument.

Moreover, the antinormative behaviour exhibited by crowds is not necessarily because individuals have become deindividuated. Rather, just like the flock of birds or swarm of insects, crowds take on a new emergent property (mentioned above) acting as a collective. *Emergent norm theory* (Turner and Killian, 1987) proposes that individuals in a group are motivated to behave in ways that reflect the group norms. This process is not totally random nor is it entirely prescripted. If the crowd has gathered to protest, in all likelihood there will be trouble, but it is not inevitable. There is no group mind as such nor is the group unanimous, rather members of the group seek to establish an identity, as described above, which is subject to the presence of internal and external factors. For example, as we learned in Chapter 10 with Schacter and Singer's two-factor theory of emotion, individuals are motivated to make sense of situations and can be influenced by others in the group. If there are agent provocateurs in the crowd who seek to incite violence, this can shift the group dynamic, which is why known hooligans are banned from football matches. Likewise, an analysis of football hooliganism reveals that styles of policing also play a significant role in determining whether violence occurs. Football fans do not become spontaneously violent unless they perceive they have been victimized and feel justified to retaliate against the authorities (Stott et al., 2008).

hot science

Darkness makes us shadier characters

While deindividuation may be a controversial hypothesis, there is some support for the idea that increasing anonymity encourages moral transgressions. Darkness conceals identity and is associated with increased incidence of criminal assaults (Hartley, 1974) and more aggressive behaviour (Page and Moss, 1976). However, the increase in aggression and disinhibited behaviour may not be so much that darkness reduces the likelihood of being identified, but that it creates a sense of illusory anonymity experienced by the perpetrator. In a set of experiments, the effect of darkness on cheating was first established in students who were paid to tidy up a room (Zhong et al., 2010). They were more likely to cheat on the task to earn money when the room was dimly rather than brightly lit. However, in a test of illusory anonymity, students in a second study were asked to play a gambling game online where there was no face-to-face contact with the opponent. In this situation, they were more likely to cheat if they wore dark sunglasses compared to regular spectacles even though there was no one else in the room. They also reported that they felt more anonymous when wearing the sunglasses. The authors concluded that darkness, whether actual or subjective, induces a false sense of concealment, leading people to feel that their identities are hidden, which, in turn, increases the likelihood of moral transgressions. This may also be related to the common association between darkness and doing wrong. Adults asked to reminisce about an ethical or unethical episode from their past differed in their perceived brightness of a room (Banerjee et al., 2012). Those who thought about bad deeds reported that the room seemed darker than those who thought about a good deed. When you think about it, just about every representation in our culture from folklore, paintings, books and films portrays evil as dark and goodness as light. Bad things happen in the dark and good things happen in the light. From heaven and hell to Star Wars, the dark forces or the dark arts are the ones we associated with doing wrong.

Thinking in groups

Just as our behaviour changes in groups, so does the way we think, and in at least two ways that are counterintuitive. First, as the saying goes, 'two heads are better than one', where we assume that groups should be better at problem solving when there are more people to contribute their knowledge and perspectives. Second, when a group is made up of people from diverse experiences and backgrounds, we expect extreme individual views to become moderated by the average opinion of the crowd. In fact, both assumptions are not always correct.

Groupthink

It is generally assumed that larger groups should make better informed collective decisions. After all, there would seem to be much more potential for bias and ignorance with fewer people and larger groups mean more knowledge and perspectives to bring to bear upon the problem. However, history is littered with examples where groups have made poor decisions that have been attributed to faulty decision processes. One explanation for this is groupthink, where *people set aside individual opinions and doubts in favour of achieving a group consensus*, at the cost of ignoring pertinent information or failing to accurately evaluate risks (Janis, 1972). Groupthink has been implicated in a number of disasters, such as the US failure to anticipate the 1941 Japanese attack on Pearl Harbor despite clear warnings and the 1986 *Challenger* Space Shuttle explosion where engineer warnings about faulty fuel systems were ignored (for a review, see Rose, 2011). In these examples, groups failed to adequately evaluate information and consider the options, with a characteristic tendency for individuals not to raise their concerns but rather to go with the emerging group consensus.

GROUPTHINK People set aside individual opinions and doubts in favour of achieving a group consensus.

According to Janis (1982; Janis and Mann, 1977), groupthink emerges when five antecedent conditions are met:

1 the group is cohesive, with members coming from similar backgrounds
2 the group is isolated from outside opinions
3 there is a lack of procedures for information search and appraisal
4 a strong directive leadership is present
5 high stress with a low degree of hope of finding a better solution than the one favoured by the leader or other influence people.

The combination of wanting to be a 'team player' and 'not wanting to upset the apple cart' puts pressure on individuals to follow strong opinions or directives from the most dominant members of the group and not seek alternatives or assess risks. With these incentives in mind, Janis (1982) provided a set of recommendations for management to put in place to prevent groupthink mistakes happening. These have been implanted in a variety of real-life situations (Hart, 1998), but support for the concept of groupthink is equivocal (Turner and Pratkanis, 1998). Like deindividuation, evaluating and predicting groupthink suffers from the same problem of being based on analysis of retrospective reports. They say that everyone with hindsight has 20/20 vision, which means that it is easy to spot when mistakes were made but much harder to predict when they will happen (see the psychomythology box).

Group polarization

Groups are usually made up of like-minded individuals who share common backgrounds, experiences, attitudes and goals. As the saying goes, 'birds of a feather flock

GROUP POLARIZATION Attitudes and decisions tend to become more extreme than those held and made by individuals.

together'. One might assume that this type of consensual thinking should lead individuals to become more moderate in their shared views, when, in fact, they can become more extreme, in a phenomenon known as group polarization – *attitudes and decisions tend to become more extreme than those held and made by individuals*. One might assume that individuals would shift their opinions to reflect the group average but research has shown that people shift their opinion within the range of distribution of the values within the group, in order to occupy more distinct and riskier positions (Jellison and Riskind, 1970). For example, when students gossip about others, negative opinions become even stronger (Brauer et al., 2001). Even within the relative anonymity of social networking sites such as Twitter, debates become more extreme (Yardi and Boyd, 2010).

Group polarization appears to be a robust phenomenon and can be found to be operating early in childhood. As we noted in Chapter 12, when children identify with being either a boy or a girl, they begin to adopt and enforce the gender stereotypes present in society (Miller et al., 2013). Children will self-segregate into all-male and all-female groups, which cements the group identity and provides the right circumstances for polarization (Maccoby, 2002).

One reason we are inclined to shift our position is that it is in our nature to compare ourselves in relation to others (Festinger, 1954). A group opinion has no objective dimensions but if want to identify with the group, we need to be recognized as someone who is representative of that opinion and so we adopt a more readily identifiable position. Sometimes, this urge for such oneupmanship becomes absurd, as in the classic Monty Python sketch where four Yorkshiremen sit around drinking expensive French wine and reminisce about how humble their beginnings were:

First Yorkshireman: I was happier then and I had nothin'. We used to live in this tiny old house with great big holes in the roof.
Second Yorkshireman: House! You were lucky to live in a house! We used to live in one room, all twenty-six of us, no furniture, 'alf the floor was missing, and we were all 'uddled together in one corner for fear of falling.
Third Yorkshireman: Eh, you were lucky to have a room! We used to have to live in t' corridor!
Fourth Yorkshireman: Oh, we used to dream of livin' in a corridor!

Social networking sites

One of the future challenges facing social psychologists is to understand and predict the effects of the phenomenon of the popularity of social networking sites (SNSs), which is changing the social environment for many of us. Currently, more than one in seven of the human population on the planet use SNSs such as Facebook and this figure increases dramatically when considering different countries. In Europe, over 300 million individuals use SNSs, around 40% of the population. Much of the research on social behaviour via the internet has concentrated on the difference between computer-mediated communication compared to real-life interactions and, in general, studies indicate that people communicate in more extreme ways on the internet than they would in real life (Sutton and Douglas, 2013). They reveal more about themselves and are more hostile, which is especially true in situations where the communication is anonymous; consistent with deindividuation described above (for a review, see Douglas, 2007). SNSs also provide a convenient means of manipulating self-esteem where individuals can be electronically 'liked', 'favourited' or have their communications redistributed as a sign of group approval. However, SNSs also enable negative social behaviours such as 'trolling' and 'flaming', where individuals are victimized in a phenomenon known as *cyberbullying*. What is not clear is whether cyberbullying is simply a new way of being cruel to others. Traditional bullying and cyberbullying are closely related: those who are bullied at school are bullied online and those who bully at school bully online (Kowalski and Limber, 2013).

In Chapter 14 we learned about emotional contagion and also noted the automaticity of negative emotions related to exclusion via computer-mediated social behaviours. This also happen on SNSs. In a recent controversial study conducted by Facebook, which was deemed by many to violate ethical standards of full disclosure and the option to opt out, researchers deliberately manipulated the content of their friends' news feed on 689,000 Facebook users' home pages (Kramera et al., 2014). When emotionally positive posts were reduced in the news feeds for one week in 2013, the users themselves posted updates with fewer positive and more negative words. Although the effect size was very small at d = 0.001 (see effect size in Chapter 2), given the scale of Facebook, this would have corresponded to hundreds of thousands of emotion expressions in status updates per day. Also, it is not known whether the emotional contagion observed online translated into offline experiences and moods.

In summary, we make inferences about people based on the groups to which they belong, which is the basis of stereotyping. This method can lead us to misjudge others for four reasons: stereotypes can be inaccurate, overused, perpetuate themselves, and operate unconsciously and automatically, which makes it difficult to avoid using them. Negative stereotypes are the basis for prejudice. While competition between groups seems an intuitive reason for discrimination and prejudice against out-group members, most studies show that simply being a member of a group triggers in-group preferences and out-group prejudices.

Groups influence our own individual behaviour. When we compete in front of others, we either produce enhanced or impaired performance depending on how competent we are at the task and how we think we are being evaluated by the group. When we work in groups, we either contribute positively or put in less effort, depending on whether we consider success on the task at the individual or group level. Individuals often gain a sense of collective identity when they congregate in groups. Group violence has often been attributed to a loss of personal responsibility, but there are also examples where groups act positively. Contrary to popular wisdom, collective reasoning in groups is not always the best strategy for optimal decision making because individuals are motivated to retain membership of the group rather than be outspoken or critical of poor decisions. Groups can even coerce individuals into more extreme positions as individuals adopt more distinct positions that they believe reflect the group consensus. The rise of the social networking phenomenon poses fresh questions about how new technologies will shape our social behaviour in the future.

Influencing others

What would your superpower be if you could have anything? Apart from having amazing powers that defy the laws of nature, such as the ability to fly or breathe underwater, many of us would like to be able to control other people and make them do what we want. To some extent, this is what social psychology gives us – the ability to interact with and influence other people. Most of us strive to become better social beings, to be liked, loved, admired, respected, obeyed and generally treated as special. One of the reasons that the reality TV format has become so popular is that it has allowed relative 'nobodies' to come from obscurity and enjoy the attention of others, to become a 'somebody'. This gives the average viewer hope that they will become significant over and beyond others. Superpowers such as flying would be great but when it comes right down to it, the ability to control other people would probably be more useful. After all, the things we want from life – gourmet food, interesting jobs, big houses, fancy cars – can be given to us by others, and the things we prize above all – loving families, loyal friends, admiring children, appreciative employers – cannot be had in any other way.

Social influence is *the control of one person's behaviour by another*, and those who know how to exert such influence can have and be just about anything they please (Cialdini and Trost, 1998). Human beings are not unique in their exercise of, or susceptibility to, social influence. Indeed, influence is the fundamental force that binds the individual members of any social species together, and without it there could be no groups, no cooperation and no altruism. All social animals exert and yield to social influence, but human beings have raised influence to the status of an art form, developing subtle and complex techniques not observed anywhere else in the natural world.

SOCIAL INFLUENCE The control of one person's behaviour by another.

How does social influence work? There are two primary mechanisms that make individuals susceptible to social influence:

1 A desire to be accepted and to avoid being rejected. This is the driving force behind becoming a member of a group. Without social acceptance, we cannot benefit from group membership and we also suffer the social pain of ostracism (discussed in Chapter 14).
2 A motivation for our behaviours and the need to be justified in our actions. While many of us would like to believe that we are independent thinkers who do not run with the crowd, the truth is that most of us desire to be members of a group that, in turn, shapes our attitudes and ultimately our behaviour.

Social acceptance

We depend on others for safety, sustenance and solidarity, all of which become conspicuous by their absence. Having others like us, accept us and approve of us is a powerful human motive (Baumeister and Leary, 1995; Leary et al., 1995), and because group acceptance is a motive, we succumb to the influence of the group by adopting its perspectives. This influence comes in several different forms.

Normative influence

You probably know that you are supposed to face forwards in a lift and you shouldn't talk to the person next to you even if you were talking to them before you got in the lift, unless you are the only two people in the lift, in which case, it's okay to talk and face sideways but still not backwards. What's so interesting about rules such as these is that they are elaborate and unwritten. No one ever taught you this complicated lift etiquette, nonetheless you managed to pick it up along the way. The unwritten rules that govern social behaviour are called norms – *customary standards for behaviour that are widely shared by members of a culture* (Miller and Prentice, 1996). We learn norms with exceptional ease and we obey them with exceptional fidelity because we know that if we don't, others won't approve of us.

NORMS Customary standards for behaviour that are widely shared by members of a culture.

Our slavish devotion to norms provides a powerful lever for influence. Normative influence occurs when *one person's behaviour is influenced by another person's behaviour because the latter provides information about what is appropriate.* For example, every human culture has a norm of reciprocity – *the unwritten rule that people should benefit those who have benefited them* (Gouldner, 1960). If a stranger helped you jump-start your car when the battery is flat, you would find it difficult to refuse their request to use your mobile phone because you know that those who accept kindness without returning it do not meet with social approval. Similarly, when a friend pays for lunch, you probably feel an immediate urge to repay the favour, perhaps even offering, 'My treat next time', or words to that effect. Indeed, the norm of reciprocity is so strong that when researchers randomly pulled the names of strangers from a telephone directory and sent them all Christmas cards, they received Christmas cards back from most (Kunz and Woolcott, 1976). Some social influence techniques trade on this norm of reciprocity. For example, waiters and waitresses get bigger tips when they give customers a mint along with the bill because customers feel obligated to do 'a little extra' for those who have done 'a little extra' for them (Strohmetz et al., 2002). For the same reason, street sellers may hand you a flower or some 'lucky heather' you didn't really want because they know it will increase the odds that you'll acquiesce to their subsequent request for money.

NORMATIVE INFLUENCE One person's behaviour is influenced by another person's behaviour because the latter provides information about what is appropriate.

NORM OF RECIPROCITY The unwritten rule that people should benefit those who have benefited them.

The norm of reciprocity always involves swapping, but the swapping doesn't always involve favours. The door-in-the-face technique is *a strategy that uses reciprocating concessions to influence behaviour.* Here's how it works. You ask someone for something more valuable than you really want, you wait for that person to refuse (to 'slam the door in your face'), and then you ask the person for what you really want. This technique works like a charm. In one study, researchers asked university students to volunteer to supervise adolescents who were going on a field trip, and only 17% of the students agreed. But when the researchers first asked students to commit to spending two hours per week for two years working at a youth detention centre (to which every one of the students said

DOOR-IN-THE-FACE TECHNIQUE A strategy that uses reciprocating concessions to influence behaviour.

no) and *then* asked them if they'd be willing to supervise the field trip, 50% of the students agreed (Cialdini et al., 1975).

There's a mindbug at work here. People were more likely to endorse the second request *because* they refused the first request, although most people would balk at the second request if they heard it by itself. How does this technique involve the norm of reciprocity? The researchers began by asking for a large favour, which the student firmly refused. They then made a concession by asking for a smaller favour. Because the researchers made a concession, the norm of reciprocity demanded that the student make one too.

Informational influence

Other human beings have pretty much the same sensory apparatus that we do, thus we rely on their reactions to the world to tell us *about* the world. If everyone in a cinema suddenly jumped up and ran screaming for the exit, you'd probably join them, not because you were afraid they'd think less of you if you didn't, but because their behaviour suggests that there was something worth running from. Informational influence occurs when *a person's behaviour is influenced by another person's behaviour because the latter provides information about what is good or true*. You can demonstrate the power of informational influence by standing in the middle of the pavement, tilting your head back, and staring at the top of a tall building. Research shows that within just a few minutes, other people will begin stopping and staring too, believing that you must know something they don't (Milgram et al., 1969).

INFORMATIONAL INFLUENCE A person's behaviour is influenced by another person's behaviour because the latter provides information about what is good or true.

You are the constant target of informational influence. When a salesperson tells you that 'most people buy the deluxe model', they are artfully suggesting that you should consider how others behave and then take that behaviour as information about the quality of the product. Advertisements that refer to soft drinks as 'popular' or books as 'bestsellers' are reminding you that other people are buying these particular drinks and novels, which suggests that they know something you don't and that you'd be wise to follow their example. As we noted in Chapter 14, emotional contagion such as laughing and crying provide strong informational cues about how to behave in the company of others (Hatfield et al., 1994). Bars and nightclubs may waive the cover charge for the first group of patrons because they know that when a club looks full, passersby will assume that others spent money to get into the club and the club must be worth the expense. In short, the world is full of objects and events that we know little about, and we can often cure our ignorance by paying attention to the way in which others are acting towards them. Observing the reactions of other people is a bit like having an extra pair of eyes. Alas, the very thing that makes us open to information leaves us open to manipulation as well.

CONFORMITY The tendency to do what others do simply because others are doing it.

Conformity

People can influence us by invoking familiar norms. But if you've ever found yourself sneaking a peek at the diner next to you, hoping to discover whether the little fork is supposed to be used for the fish or the salad, then you know that other people can also influence us by defining *new* norms in ambiguous, confusing or novel situations. Conformity is *the tendency to do what others do simply because others are doing it,* and it results in part from normative influence.

In a classic study, Solomon Asch (1951, 1956) had participants sit in a room with seven other people who appeared to be ordinary participants but who were actually trained actors. An experimenter explained that the participants would be shown cards with three lines printed on them and that their job was to state which of the three lines matched a 'standard line' printed on another card (**FIGURE 15.8**). The experimenter held up a card and then went around the room, asking each person to answer aloud in turn. The real participant was among the last to be called on. Everything was normal on the first two trials, but on the third trial, something odd happened. The actors all began giving the same wrong answer. What did the real participant do? Results showed that 75% of them conformed and announced

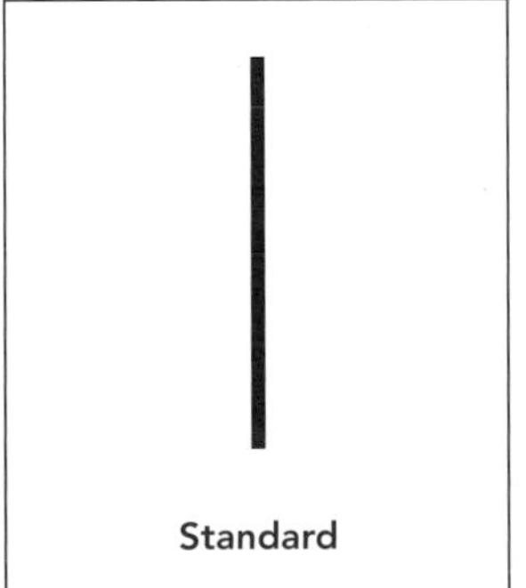

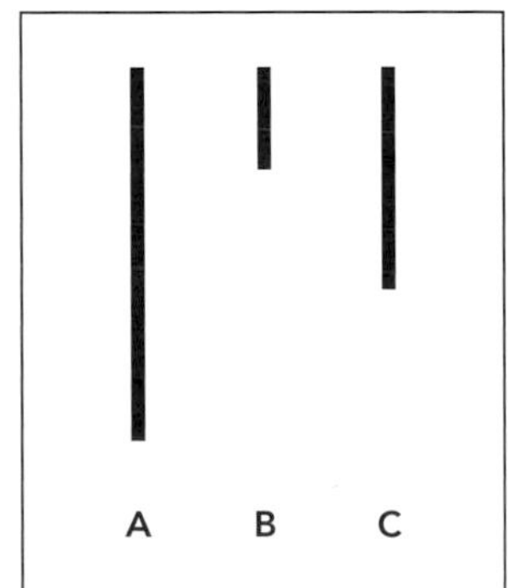

FIGURE **15.8 Asch's conformity study** If you were asked which of the lines on the right – A, B or C – matches the standard line on the left, what would you say? Research on conformity suggests that your answer would depend, in part, on how other people in the room answered the same question.

The perplexed research participant (centre), flanked by confederates who are 'in' on the experiment, is on the verge of conformity in one of Solomon Asch's line judging experiments.

IMAGE BY WILLIAM VANDIVERT. ORIGINALLY APPEARED IN S. E. ASCH, OPINIONS AND SOCIAL PRESSURE, *SCIENTIFIC AMERICAN*, 1955, 193(5): 31–5

the wrong answer on at least one trial. Subsequent research has shown that these participants were indeed succumbing to normative influence. For example, when the number of actors was increased, participants in this situation were even more likely to conform; but if even one actor did not conform, participants were much less likely to do so (Asch, 1955; Nemeth and Chiles, 1988). Participants didn't actually misperceive the length of the lines; that would be pretty difficult for someone with normal vision to do. Rather, they merely said something they didn't believe in to gain social approval.

The behaviour of others can tell us what is proper, appropriate, expected and accepted, in other words, it can define a norm, and once a norm is defined, anyone who cares about social approval will experience tremendous pressure to honour it. When a Holiday Inn in Tempe, Arizona, left a variety of different 'message cards' in their guests' bathrooms in the hopes of convincing those guests to reuse their towels rather than laundering them every day, they discovered that the single most effective message was the one that simply read: 'Seventy five percent of our guests use their towels more than once' (Cialdini, 2005).

Minority social influence

As we noted in our discussion of the tragic life of Alan Turing in Chapter 1, there was a time when it was considered appropriate to persecute and prosecute minority groups such as homosexuals. There was also a time when it was considered perfectly respectable to keep slaves and use young children for dangerous jobs. The youngest child executed in England was John Dean, aged around eight years, who was hanged in Abingdon, Oxfordshire for setting fire to two barns in 1629. We may be appalled by these examples of the injustices by our ancestors but they were only conforming to attitudes and behaviours that were quite acceptable back then. If these were the majority opinions, how did a small group of activists eventually shift the majority opinion?

Asch's conformity study is a measure of majority social influence but history proves that eventually the majority opinion can shift towards a minority position. Conformity to group norms may be powerful, but minorities can influence the majority over time. According to Serge Moscovici (1980), Romanian-born French social psychologist, majority and minority influences operate in different ways. Conformity to the majority activates a social comparison process, whereby individuals conform to the group consensus without attending much to the issue at hand so that any private consideration is minimal or short-lived. The primary goal is to be seen to be a group player, as Asch had demonstrated. In contrast, minority influences trigger a validation process, whereby the individual notes the discrepancy and attempts to understand why the minority consistently holds their position. This evaluation results in a deeper consideration of the issue at hand at the private level and supports divergent thinking and innovation that can eventually lead to a conversion to the minority position. The critical factor for minority influence is that individuals espousing these views must be consistent, so that the others they wish to influence appreciate the unity of their discordant position.

To test the importance of consistency, Moscovici and his colleagues placed two conferderates along with four real participants in a colour perception task (Moscovici et al., 1969). They were shown 36 slides of different shades of green/blue and asked to state the colour of each slide out loud. Some slides were ambiguous but the critical slides were clearly blue and when tested alone real participants said so. However, in one condition, the two confederates answered green for each of the 36 slides. In a second condition, they answered green 24 times and blue 12 times. Real participants were more likely to agree with the confederates that the critical slides were green if they had been in the condition where the confederates were consistent in their responses. Those participants in the condition where the confederates varied between green and blue rarely concurred with the confederates. Maybe those in the first condition simply conformed in public but really thought the blue slides were green – they just didn't want to disagree with the two weirdos who thought everything was green. However, after the study was over, participants in the consistent condition were given another green/blue perception test on their own in private and their perceptual bias shifted towards the green spectrum. The minority influence of those weirdos had shifted their private decisions.

It is unquestionable that majority opinions change by minority influence, but there is much controversy over the mechanisms of change (see Sutton and Douglas, 2013). Meta-analysis also reveals that minority influence is a reliable phenomenon (Wood et al., 1994), but critics have pointed out that conformity studies in general, including those by Asch and Moscovici, are contrived lab experiments with very little ecological validity (Sampson, 1991). Participants are usually college students with little knowledge of each other, whereas real minority groups such as political activists operate in different settings with determined oppositions from majority groups who are motivated by real-world considerations that can be economic, political or religious. As with other areas of experimental psychology, one must remember that in stripping away the complexity of the world in order to drill down to the mechanisms of interest, there is always a danger of missing the bigger picture.

Obedience: the banality of evil

Other people's behaviour can provide information about norms, but in most situations there are a few people whom we all recognize as having special authority to define and enforce the norms. At public events, where marshalls who control the crowds may only be spotty 16-year-olds you would not normally listen to or bother to give the time of day, we nevertheless do what they tell us in the context of the event because they have the authority conferred on them. When told to find our seats, we do so, and if asked to form an orderly queue, we obey, especially if we are English. Obedience is *the tendency to do what authorities tell us to do simply because they tell us to do it.*

OBEDIENCE The tendency to do what authorities tell us to do simply because they tell us to do it.

Why do we obey authorities? Well, okay, sometimes they have guns, but not usually the spotty 16 year olds. Authorities can influence us by threatening punishment and promising reward, but research suggests that much of their influence is *normative* (Tyler, 1990). Stanley Milgram (1963) demonstrated this in one of psychology's most infamous experiments. The participants in this experiment were people of all ages who answered an ad in the local newspaper asking them to take part in a study of learning and memory. When they arrived at the lab, they met a middle-aged man who was introduced as another participant but who was actually a trained actor. An experimenter in a lab coat explained that the participant would play the role of *teacher* and the actor would play the role of *learner*. The teacher and learner would sit in different rooms, the teacher would read words to the learner over a microphone, and the learner would then repeat the words back to the teacher. If the learner made a mistake, the teacher would press a button that delivered an electric shock to the learner. Each time the learner made an error, the teacher would increase the level of shock (**FIGURE 15.9**).

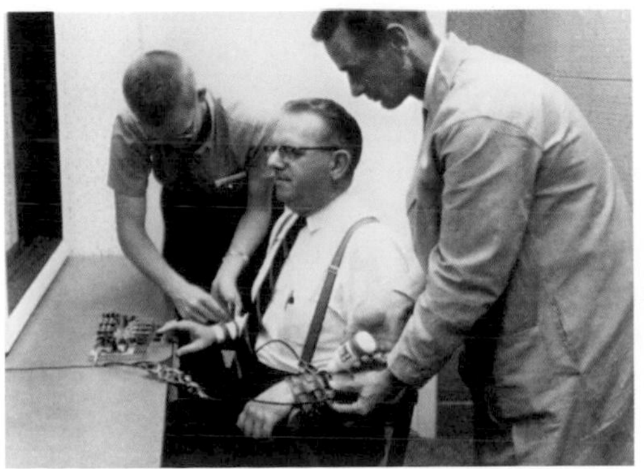

FIGURE **15.9 Milgram's obedience studies** The learner (left) is being hooked up to the shock generator (right) that was used in Stanley Milgram's obedience studies.

The shock-generating machine, which of course wasn't actually hooked up, offered 30 levels of shock, ranging from 15 volts (labelled 'slight shock') to 450 volts (labelled 'Danger: Severe shock').

After the learner was strapped into his chair, the experiment began. When the learner made his first mistake, the participant dutifully delivered a 15-volt shock. As the learner made more mistakes, he received more shocks. When the participant delivered the 75-volt shock, the learner cried out in pain. At 150 volts, the learner screamed, 'Get me out of here. I told you I have heart trouble ... I refuse to go on. Let me out!' With every shock, the learner's screams became more agonized as he pleaded pitifully for his freedom. Then, after receiving the 330-volt shock, the learner stopped responding altogether. Participants were naturally upset by all of this, and they typically asked the experimenter to stop the experiment. But the experimenter simply replied: 'You have no choice; you must go on.' The experimenter never threatened the participant with punishment of any kind. Rather, he just stood there with his clipboard in hand and calmly instructed the participant to continue. What did the participants do? Eighty per cent of the participants continued to shock the learner even after he screamed, complained, pleaded and then fell silent. And 62% went all the way, delivering the highest possible voltage.

Were these people psychopathic sadists? No. Would a normal person electrocute a stranger just because some guy in a lab coat told them to? The answer, it seems, is yes, because being *normal* means being sensitive to and respectful of social norms. The participants in this experiment knew that hurting others is *often* wrong but not *always* wrong. Doctors give painful injections and teachers give painful exams. There are many situations in which it is permissible, and even desirable, to cause someone to suffer in the service of a higher goal. The experimenter's calm demeanor and persistent instruction suggested that he, and not the participant, knew what was appropriate in this particular situation. Indeed, subsequent research confirmed that participants' obedience was due to normative pressure. When the experimenter's authority to define the norm was undermined, for example when a second experimenter appeared to disagree with the first or when a person who wasn't wearing a lab coat gave the instructions, participants rarely did what they were told to do (Milgram, 1974; Miller, 1986).

It is a historical point of interest that Stanley Milgram, a secular Jew, was motivated to undertake his research on obedience because he wanted to know why so many Holocaust victims seemingly went to their deaths without offering any resistance (Blass, 1998). Why did they not fight these monsters? However, as philosopher Hannah Arendt (1963), commenting on Nazi war criminal Adolf Eichmann, pointed out, the trouble with Eichmann and his like was that they were neither perverted nor sadistic but simply, 'terribly and terrifyingly normal'. Seemingly ordinary people had committed extraordinary crimes. In reviewing the impact of his research, Milgram (1974, p. 6) concluded: 'After witnessing hundreds of ordinary people submit to the authority in our own experiments, I must conclude that Arendt's conception of the banality of evil comes closer to the truth than one might imagine.'

Do abusive people seek power or does power lead people to be abusive? In a related line of research, Philip Zimbardo built a simulated prison in the basement of the Stanford psychology department and randomly assigned volunteers to play the role of prisoner or guard. The study had to be abandoned when many of the 'guards' began abusing the 'prisoners'. In a situation where ordinary people were given the power to harm, they used it. The researchers wrote: 'If these reactions had been observed within the confines of an existing penal institution, it is probable that a dispositional hypothesis [or, attribution] would be invoked as an explanation' (Haney et al., 1973). Indeed, more than 30 years later, the prisoner abuse and torture at Abu Ghraib in Iraq was officially denounced as the work of 'a few bad apples'.

These examples seem to suggest that we are all sheep prepared to go with the crowd even when that means behaving in an immoral way. Another interpretation is that we can reinterpret our behaviour as not being bad at all, but rather for the good of the group. In Zimbardo's prison study, some of the 'guards' acted out personas based on films they believed were appropriate for the experiment. Even in Milgram's shocking studies, participants were more likely to comply with the instructions if they were told that it was necessary for the success of the study rather than simply told that they had no choice. It may be that these examples of extreme obedience and compliance are less about people blindly following orders but rather persuading others to believe in the importance of what they are doing. This creates a diffusion of accountability where the individual no longer feels responsible for their actions. British social psychologists Alex Haslam and Steve Reicher (2008, p. 19) repeated Zimbardo's prison study, and noted: 'People do great wrong, not because they are unaware of what they are doing but because they consider it to be right. This is possible because they actively identify with groups whose ideology justifies and condones the oppression and destruction of others.'

Attitudes

We do the things we do because of our attitudes and beliefs. Just about every action relies on an attitude, *a positive or negative evaluation of an object or event,* and a belief, *an assumed knowledge about an object or event that is not proven.* Even the simplest actions are based on attitudes and beliefs. When we are hungry, we open the fridge and grab an apple because our attitudes tell us that apples taste good and our beliefs tell us that those tasty apples are to be found in the fridge. In a sense, attitudes tell us what we should do ('Eat an apple') and beliefs tell us how we should do it ('Start by opening the fridge'). If attitudes or beliefs are inaccurate, that is, if we don't know what is good and we don't know what is true, then our actions are fruitless. Because we rely so heavily on our attitudes and beliefs to guide our actions, it isn't surprising that we want to have the right ones. We are motivated to be accurate, and like any motive, this one leaves us vulnerable to social influence.

ATTITUDE A positive or negative evaluation of an object or event.

BELIEF An assumed knowledge about an object or event that is not proven.

Persuasion

When the next government election rolls around, two things will happen. First, the candidates will say that they intend to win your vote by making arguments that focus on the issues. Second, the candidates will then avoid arguments, ignore issues and attempt to win your vote with a variety of cheap tricks. What the candidates promise to do and what they actually do reflect two basic forms of persuasion – *a person's attitudes or beliefs are influenced by a communication from another person* (Petty and Wegener, 1998). The candidates will promise to persuade you by demonstrating that their positions on the issues are the most practical, intelligent, fair and beneficial. Having made that promise, they will then devote most of their financial resources to persuading you by other means, for example by dressing nicely and smiling a lot, surrounding themselves with famous athletes and film stars, repeatedly pairing their opponent's name with words and images that nobody much cares for and so on. In other words, the candidates will promise to engage in systematic persuasion – *a change in attitudes or beliefs brought about by appeals to reason* – but they will spend most of their time and money engaged in heuristic persuasion – *a change in attitudes or beliefs brought about by appeals to habit or emotion* (Chaiken, 1980; Petty and Cacioppo, 1986).

PERSUASION A person's attitudes or beliefs are influenced by a communication from another person.

SYSTEMATIC PERSUASION A change in attitudes or beliefs brought about by appeals to reason.

HEURISTIC PERSUASION A change in attitudes or beliefs brought about by appeals to habit or emotion.

How do these two forms of persuasion work? *Systematic persuasion* appeals to logic and reason. People should be more persuaded when evidence and arguments are strong rather than weak. Although this is often true, there are many rhetorical devices that can make arguments and evidence seem stronger than they actually are. For example, it is often tempting to ignore one's opponents but research suggests that people are generally more persuaded by communications that refute opposing positions than by communications that ignore them (Hovland and Weiss, 1951). Similarly, research shows that people generally pay more attention to the argument they hear first but remember best the argument they hear last. As such, a candidate may prefer to speak first if the debate is being held one day before the election but may prefer to speak last if the debate is being held one month before the election (Miller and Campbell, 1959).

Heuristic persuasion appeals to habit and emotion. Rather than weighing evidence and analysing arguments, people often use *heuristics* – simple shortcuts or 'rules of thumb' – to help them decide whether to believe a communication (see Chapter 7 on heuristics). For instance, stereotypes can operate as heuristics. If you are evaluating an argument for financing a climbing frame in your local park and are told that the users will be mostly boys, you may believe that inactive boys are more likely to become delinquent and be persuaded by this gender stereotype. Emotions can also function as heuristics. In one study, participants who drank a sweet cola were more persuaded by a speech about comprehensive exams than were participants who drank a bitter tonic (Albarracin and Kumkale, 2003). Rather than evaluating the arguments and evidence, participants seemed to rely on a simple heuristic: 'If I feel good when I hear an argument, it's probably right.' These are only two of the many heuristics people use to decide whether to accept or reject a communication. Other examples, such as 'If everyone else says it, it must be true', or 'Experts know more than I do', are familiar to all of us.

Which of these forms of persuasion is more effective? It depends on how closely the audience is listening. Weighing evidence and analysing arguments is more effortful and time-consuming than using a simple heuristic, and thus people tend to weigh and analyse only when the communication is about something they consider important. For example, in one study, university students heard a speech that contained either strong or weak arguments in favour of instituting comprehensive exams at their school (Petty et al., 1981). Some students were told that the speaker was a university professor, and others were told that the speaker was a secondary school student. Some students were told that their university was considering implementing these exams right away, whereas others were told that their university was considering implementing these exams in 10 years. As **FIGURE 15.10** shows, when students thought the new exams might affect them personally, they were motivated to consider the evidence, and they were systematically persuaded. That is, their attitudes and beliefs were influenced by the strength of the arguments and not by the status of the speaker. But when students thought the new exams would not affect them personally, they were not motivated to consider the evidence, and thus they were heuristically persuaded. That is, their attitudes and beliefs were influenced by the status of the speaker but not by the strength of the arguments (see *the real world* box).

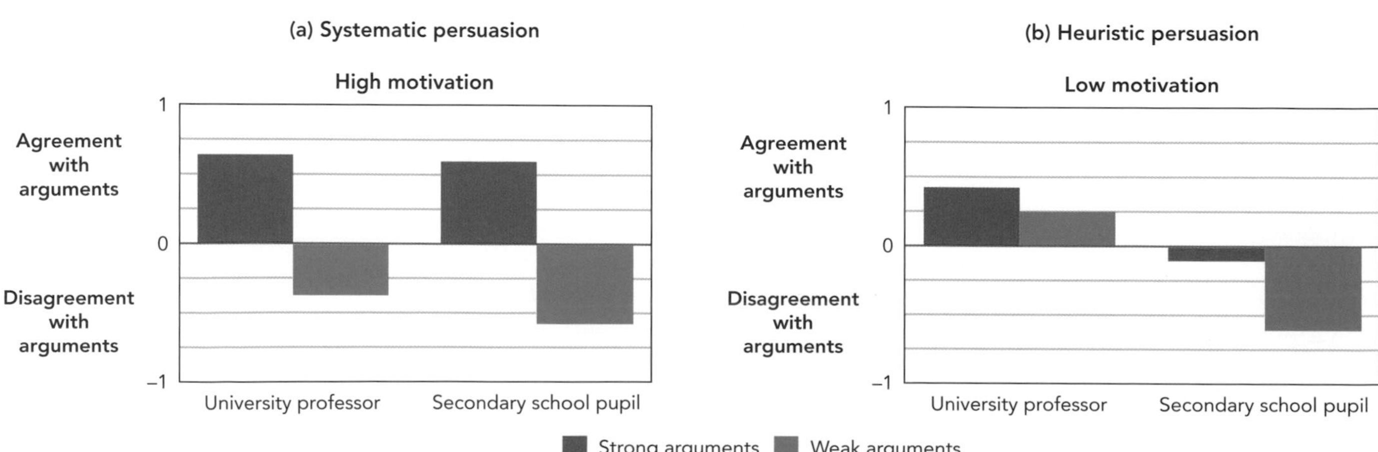

FIGURE 15.10 Systematic and heuristic persuasion (a) When students were motivated to analyse arguments because they would be personally affected by them, their attitudes were influenced by the strength of the arguments (strong arguments were more persuasive than weak arguments) but not by the status of the communicator (the professor was not more persuasive than the pupil). (b) When students were not motivated to analyse arguments because they would not be personally affected by them, their attitudes were influenced by the status of the communicator (the professor was more persuasive than the pupil) but not by the strength of the arguments (strong arguments were no more persuasive than weak arguments) (Petty et al., 1981).

the real world

This just in

Does a university student's choice of degree reveal anything about them? Research suggests that it does. In a recent study of 18,521 university students, researchers found that psychology undergraduates have better social skills and more active social lives than students who take other subjects. Indeed, among final-year students, those taking psychology were the most likely to be involved in a long-term romantic relationship, have a 'warm and trusting' relationship with their parents, and have remained in contact with their school friends. Perhaps the most amazing thing about the results of this survey is that we made them up. That's right. Everything you just read is a lie.

Now, if you had to guess which students really *do* have the best social skills, what would your answer be? If you're like most people who read the preceding paragraph, you would be especially willing to entertain the possibility that the correct answer is *psychology undergraduates*. Although you were explicitly told that the sentences you read were fiction, research provides three reasons to suspect that you will, nonetheless, tend to believe them, at least at first, at least a little, and maybe even a lot later on:

1 *The perseverance effect:* Judges often tell juries to ignore what they've just heard, but this is easier to say than do. For example, participants in one study performed a task and were then told that they had performed very well or very poorly (Ross et al., 1975). After a few minutes, the experimenter confessed that the participant had actually been given success or failure feedback that had nothing whatsoever to do with their actual performance. When participants were then asked to predict how they thought they would *really* perform on the task, those who had received success feedback predicted that they would perform better than those who received failure feedback, despite the fact that they now knew the feedback was false. Subsequent studies have shown that this happened because the participants invented explanations for their success or their failure, and when the performance feedback was later discredited, these explanations remained (Anderson et al., 1980). Because people explain things to themselves, they cannot easily 'undo' the effects of information after they find out it is false.

2 *The unbelieving effect:* When someone tells you something, it *feels* as though you first consider it and then decide whether to believe it or not. But research suggests that this feeling is an illusion and that the human mind actually believes *everything* it hears and then quickly 'unbelieves' some of it. This tendency was remarked on by the great Dutch philosopher Spinoza, who conjectured that the mere comprehension of a statement entails the tacit acceptance of its being true, while rejecting statements as false is harder. For example, participants in one study were told about a robbery and given false information that made the criminal seem unusually cruel ('Kevin threatened to sexually assault the cashier') or unusually kind ('Kevin apologized to the cashier for having to rob the shop') (Gilbert et al., 1993). All participants knew that this information was completely false, but while they were reading the information, some were interrupted with another task. The results showed that interruption prevented these participants from unbelieving the false information they initially believed despite knowing it was false. As such, these participants recommended a longer prison term for the 'cruel criminal' than the 'kind criminal'. It seems that people believe first and ask questions later, which tends to make them a bit more gullible than they should be (Arkes et al., 1991; Gilbert et al., 1990). Recent imaging studies have shown that we find it easier to accept statements as being true, whereas rejecting them as false activates brain regions of the anterior insula associated with negative emotions of disgust (Harris et al., 2008).

3 *The sleeper effect:* You probably remember hearing that eccentric pop star Michael Jackson used to sleep in a hyperbaric chamber. But where did you hear about it? Chances are you read about this from some daily tabloid newspaper that delights in sensationalist news stories. You already know that information in such newspapers deserves to be treated with maximal scepticism, and you probably didn't believe the story when you read it. So why do you believe it now? Research suggests that communications from unreliable sources can have a delayed impact because people tend to forget the source of information before they forget the information itself (Hovland et al., 1949). In one study, participants heard an essay touting a new consumer product and then learned that the essay had been written either by the manufacturer or an independent consumer organization (Pratkanis et al., 1988). Although participants were not initially persuaded by the manufacturer's essay, they *were* persuaded later on; in fact, they were ultimately *just as persuaded* by the essay when it was written by the manufacturer as when it was written by the independent consumer organization. Information that makes us initially sceptical can remain in memory long after our scepticism has evaporated.

The sad part of this story is that there are no data suggesting that psychology undergraduates have better social skills or more active social lives than other students. However, the happy part of this story is that psychology students are much more likely than other students to have a sophisticated understanding of the perseverance effect, the unbelieving effect and the sleeper effect. Of course, knowing about these phenomena doesn't necessarily prevent them from occurring, so the next time you are reading a daily tabloid or flicking through one of the countless celebrity magazines, remember that people tend to believe what they read and maybe you should pick up a good book instead.

Consistency

If a friend told you that rabbits had just staged a coup in Antarctica and were halting all carrot exports, you probably wouldn't turn on the news channel to see if it was true. You'd know right away that your friend was joking because the statement is logically inconsistent with other things you know are true; for example, rabbits rarely instigate revolutions and Antarctica does not export carrots. People evaluate the accuracy of new beliefs by assessing their *consistency* with old beliefs, and although this is not a foolproof method for determining whether something is true, it provides a pretty good approximation. Most people have a desire for accuracy, and because consistency is a rough measure of accuracy, most of us have a desire for consistency as well (Cialdini et al., 1995).

FOOT-IN-THE-DOOR TECHNIQUE A strategy that uses a person's desire for consistency to influence that person's behaviour.

Our desire for consistency can leave us vulnerable to social influence. For example, the foot-in-the-door technique is *a strategy that uses a person's desire for consistency to influence that person's behaviour* (Burger, 1999). In one study, experimenters went to a neighbourhood, knocked on doors, and asked homeowners if they would install in their front gardens a large, unsightly sign that said 'Drive Carefully'. Only 17% of the homeowners agreed to install the sign. The experimenters asked some other homeowners to sign a petition urging the government to promote safe driving, which almost all agreed to do, and *then* asked those homeowners if they would install the unsightly sign. Fifty-five per cent of *these* homeowners agreed to install the sign (Freedman and Fraser, 1966). Why would a homeowner be more likely to grant two requests than one?

Just imagine how the homeowners probably felt. They had just signed a petition stating that safe driving was important to them, and they knew that refusing to install the sign would be inconsistent with that action. As they wrestled with these facts, they probably began to experience a feeling you might call 'squirming' but Leon Festinger called cognitive dissonance – *an unpleasant state that arises when a person recognizes the inconsistency of their actions, attitudes or beliefs* (Festinger, 1957). Festinger made many major contributions to the field of social psychology, one of which started with this simple observation. When people experience the unpleasant state of cognitive dissonance, they naturally try to alleviate it, and one way to alleviate it is to change one's actions, attitudes or beliefs in order to restore consistency among them (Aronson, 1969; Cooper and Fazio, 1984). In other words, if you want to stop squirming, let them plant the sign in your front garden.

COGNITIVE DISSONANCE An unpleasant state that arises when a person recognizes the inconsistency of their actions, attitudes or beliefs.

The fact that we often alleviate cognitive dissonance by changing our actions, attitudes or beliefs can leave us vulnerable to other people's efforts to change them for us. In one study, female university students applied to join a weekly discussion on 'the psychology of sex'. Women in the control group were allowed to join the discussion, but women in the experimental group were allowed to join the discussion only after first passing an embarrassing test that involved reading pornographic fiction to a strange man. Although the carefully staged discussion was as dull as possible, the researchers found that women in the experimental group found it more interesting than women in the control group (Aronson and Mills, 1958). As FIGURE 15.11 shows, women in the experimental group knew that they had paid a steep price to join the group ('I read all that lurid pornography out loud!'), but that belief was inconsistent with the belief that the discussion was worthless ('This discussion isn't interesting at all'). As such, the women experienced cognitive dissonance, which they alleviated by changing their beliefs about the value of the discussion ('You know, this discussion is much more interesting than I first thought'). We normally think that people pay for things because they value them, but as this study shows, people sometimes value things because they've paid for them. It is little wonder that some gangs use initiation rituals to breed loyalty, some religions require their adherents to make large personal or monetary sacrifices, some gourmet restaurants charge outrageous amounts to keep their patrons coming back, or that some men and women play hard to get to maintain their suitors' interest.

Problem: cognitive dissonance
I suffered to join the discussion.
≠
I didn't like the discussion.
Solution: change a cognition
I suffered to join the discussion.
=
I liked the discussion.

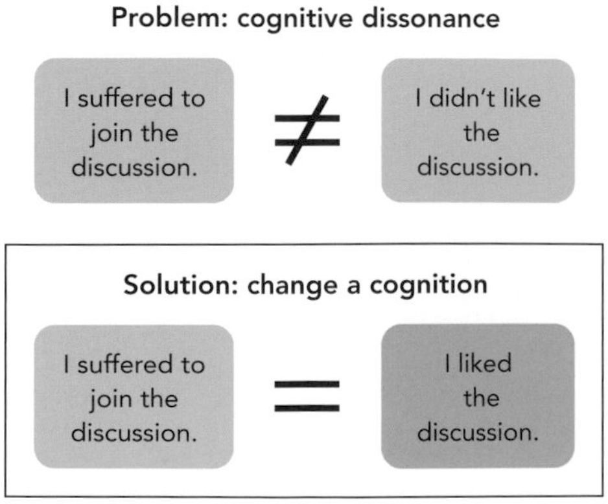

FIGURE 15.11 Effort justification and cognitive dissonance Suffering for something of little value can cause cognitive dissonance. One way to eliminate that dissonance is to change your belief about the value of the thing you suffered for.

We desire consistency, but there are inevitably occasions when we just can't help but be inconsistent, for example when we tell a friend that her new hairstyle is 'unusually trendy' when it actually resembles a drowned rat after an unfortunate encounter with a food blender. Why don't we experience cognitive dissonance under such circumstances and come to believe our own lies? Because telling a friend her hairstyle is trendy is inconsistent with the belief that her hairstyle is hideous, but it is perfectly consistent with the belief that one should be nice to one's friends. When small inconsistencies are *justified* by large consistencies, cognitive dissonance does not occur.

For example, participants in one study were asked to perform a dull task that involved turning knobs one way, then the other, and then back again. After the participants were sufficiently bored, the experimenter explained that he desperately needed a few more people to volunteer for the study, and he asked the participants to go into the hallway, find another person, and tell that person that the knob-turning task was great fun. The experimenter offered some participants $1 to tell this lie, and he offered other participants $20. All participants agreed to tell the lie, and after they did so, they were asked to report their true enjoyment of the knob-turning task. The results showed that participants liked the task *more* when they were paid $1 than $20 to lie about it (Festinger and Carlsmith, 1959). Why? Because the belief that *the knob-turning task was dull* was inconsistent with the belief that *I recommended the task to that person in the hallway,* but the latter belief was perfectly consistent with the belief that *$20 is a lot of money*. For some participants, the large payment justified the lie, so only those people who received the small payment experienced cognitive dissonance. As such, only the participants who received $1 felt the need to restore consistency by changing their beliefs about the enjoyableness of the task (FIGURE 15.12).

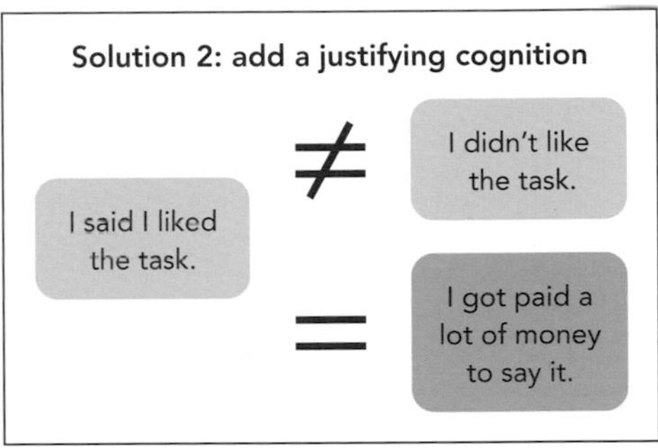

FIGURE 15.12 Reducing cognitive dissonance Behaving in ways that are inconsistent with our attitudes and beliefs can cause cognitive dissonance. One way to eliminate that dissonance is to change your attitude or belief. Another way is to add a justification.

Attitudes and planned behaviour: do what you mean

We generally assume that our attitudes will predict our behaviour. If we hold a negative attitude to overeating, smoking or drinking too much alcohol, then we would like to refrain from these behaviours. Conversely, if we hold positive attitudes towards behaviours, then we say we intend to carry them out. However, we all know that some behaviours are much more difficult to stop than others and sometimes we do not stop doing them despite what we might intend to do.

Is it simply the case that we do not have control over our behaviours no matter what we think we would do? Clearly, there are circumstances that play a role in shaping our attitudes and intentions towards subsequent behaviour. One of the most influential models to account for attitudes and behaviour is the theory of planned behaviour (Ajzen, 1991).

According to the model illustrated in FIGURE 15.13, intentions to act are based on three streams of processing: behavioural beliefs, normative beliefs and control beliefs:

1 *Behavioural beliefs:* the individual's perceived relationship between their belief and behaviour ('I think studying hard will produce better exam results'). This, in turn, determines the attitude towards the behaviour ('I want to do well in my exams so I will study').
2 *Normative beliefs:* the expectations held by important others such as friends and family ('students who study hard will obtain better exam results'). This determines the subjective norm that is the pressure to engage or not in a behaviour ('my family expects me to study hard to get good exam results'). Notice that although both sets of beliefs correspond in the current example, they need not. For example, I may think that practising in my rock band is the way to success, whereas my family may disagree.
3 *Control beliefs:* the factors that facilitate or impede the behaviour ('I want to study hard but I have a part-time job'). In turn, these influence the perceived behavioural control ('I may have a part-time job but I believe I can still do the necessary work').

In what is now a classic study of the relationship between attitudes and behaviour, sociologist Richard LaPierre (1934) travelled around the US with a Chinese couple in 1934 for three months to discover if there would be negative prejudice from restaurants and hotels. Only 1 out of 250 establishments refused to serve the couple despite the widespread prejudice against Asians in the 1930s. However, after the tour, LaPierre contacted the hotels and restaurant to ask if they would be willing to serve Chinese couples and 90% of those that responded said they would not. Clearly, attitudes and behaviours do not necessarily match up.

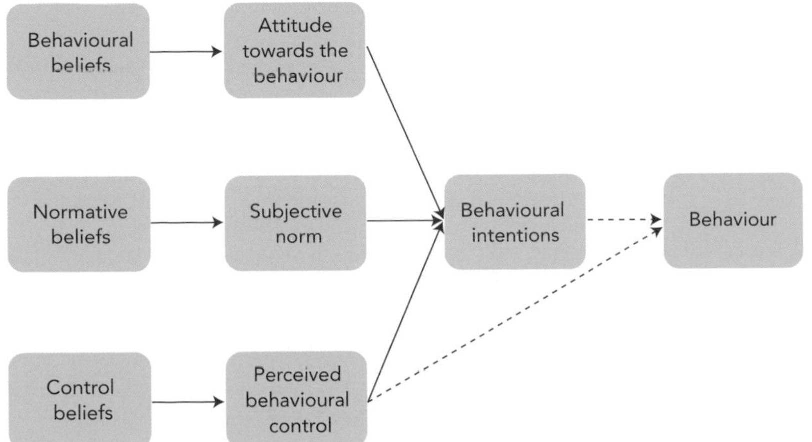

FIGURE 15.13 Ajzen's theory of planned behaviour This theory can be used to calculate the strength of the intention to act based on the beliefs of the individual, the group and the perceived control concerning the situation.

All three streams feed into the intention, which is the individual's readiness to perform a given behaviour. The behaviour is the intended act but note that the model also contains a reality check, which is the actual behavioural control that the individual has ('the time to undertake the necessary studying'). By taking into consideration personal beliefs as well as the attitudes of others, in addition to perceived and actual control, the theory of planned behaviour has been successfully applied to predict all manner of human behaviour, including whether British motorists drive recklessly (Parker et al., 1995), British women use dietary supplements (Conner et al., 2003), Australian females stick to diets (Nejad et al., 2005), and even whether men use condoms (Albarracin et al., 2001). Such approaches are necessary to predict the complex processes and influences that lead to behaviours.

In summary, people want to be accepted by others, so they try not to violate social norms. One particularly strong norm is that people should benefit those who have benefited them, and several influence techniques put people in a position where they must either comply with a request or risk violating that norm. When people look to the behaviour of others as a guide for their own actions, they often end up conforming or obeying, sometimes with disastrous results. However, norms do change over time and while the majority opinion may prevail, minority influences show that individuals are not destined to conform all the time. Finally, people's behaviour is motivated by attitudes and beliefs, and these are influenced in three ways. First, people use communications from others to help them decide what to think, although some of those communications appeal to reason and some appeal to habit or emotion. Second, people's attitudes are shaped by comparing new information to old information. When they recognize inconsistencies among their attitudes, beliefs and actions, they may experience cognitive dissonance. Finally, the theory of planned behaviour combines beliefs from personal attitudes with group norms and perceived ability to act to determine the strength of the intention to act.

psychomythology

Brainstorming

Have you ever been asked to 'brainstorm'? There is a common belief that groups of individuals can come up with many more creative and imaginative new ideas and solutions when they are encouraged to say whatever comes to mind without fear of criticism. The term was coined by US advertising guru Alex Osborn in the 1950s when he wrote that individuals in a group should engage in a 'brainstorm', which means 'using the brain to storm a creative problem – and doing so in commando fashion, with each stormer attacking the same objective' (Osborn, 1953, p. 297). For brainstorming to work, there were four basic rules:

1. Come up with as many ideas as you can
2. Do not criticize one another's ideas
3. Freewheel and share wild ideas
4. Expand and elaborate on existing ideas.

The most critical aspect of brainstorming, which distinguished it from other forms of group decision making, was that there was to be no criticism or negative feedback from other members that would inhibit individuals from offering ideas. While this aspect of brainstorming is consistent with social inhibition and seems plausible, subsequent experimental studies of brainstorming have failed to provide unanimous support for Osborn's contention that free thinking in a group is more effective than individual efforts. Groups are less creative than individuals alone (McGrath, 1984). The first test of brainstorming conducted by Yale psychologists found that individuals working alone generated twice as many more feasible solutions when their efforts were later pooled together than the ideas generated by groups (Taylor et al., 1958). In addition, when participants were told that they would score higher for creativity, they generated fewer ideas than those operating with Osborn's brainstorming rules, but what they came up with were better, more practical ideas. When people are told to be creative, they are, but when they are not given any instructions, they just come up with more suggestions. According to Keith Sawyer, a business psychologist at Washington University and author of *Group Genius: The Creative Power of Collaboration* (2008, p. 60): 'Decades of research have consistently shown that brainstorming groups think of far fewer ideas than the same number of people who work alone and later pool their ideas.'

where do you stand?

Are you prejudiced?

Satirist Ambrose Bierce (1911) defined a *bigot* as 'one who is obstinately and zealously attached to an opinion that you do not entertain'. Indeed, most of us think of prejudice as a bad habit whose defining feature is that other people do it and we don't. Not so fast. Just because you don't sit around thinking evil thoughts about people who don't share your religious or ethnic background doesn't mean you are free of prejudice. Research by psychologists Anthony Greenwald, Mahzarin Banaji and their colleagues using the *implicit association test* (IAT) suggests that even people who think of themselves as egalitarian can harbour unconscious prejudices against members of out-groups.

In one study, white participants were asked to classify a series of words (Greenwald et al., 1998). Some of the words were common nouns such as *tulip* or *aunt*, and some of the words were proper names such as *Greg* or *Jamal*. The common nouns were related to a dislikable category such as *insects* or to a likable category such as *flowers*. The proper names were related to the participant's in-group (whites) or their out-group (blacks). When one of these words appeared on the computer screen, the participant's job was to press a button as quickly as possible to indicate whether it was a flower, an insect, a predominantly white name, or a predominantly black name.

Now comes the interesting part. Although the participants were asked to classify the words as belonging to one of four categories, the experimental apparatus only had two buttons. On the *consistent* trials, participants were told to press the right-hand button if the word was either an insect or a black name and to press the left-hand button if the word was a flower or a white name. On the *inconsistent* trials, participants were told to press the left-hand button if the word was a flower or a black name and to press the right-hand button if the word was an insect or a white name. Why did the experimenters arrange and rearrange the apparatus this way? Because previous research has shown that a classification task of this sort is much easier if the dislikable words (or the likable words) share a single button. Thus, if white participants disliked black names, they should have found the classification task easier when black names and insects shared one button and white names and flowers shared the other. Consistent trials should have been easier than inconsistent trials *only* if participants disliked black names and liked white names. As the results in the figure show, white participants were much faster on the consistent than the inconsistent trials.

Do these results mean that these white participants were a bunch of hate-mongers? Probably not. Psychologists since Freud have recognized that people can consciously think one thing while unconsciously feeling another. White people who honestly believe in tolerance, diversity and racial equality and harbour no conscious prejudice towards black people may still show evidence of unconscious prejudice on the IAT (Greenwald and Nosek, 2001). In fact, black participants also show unconscious prejudice against black people (Lieberman et al., 2005).

How can our conscious and unconscious attitudes be so different? You know from Chapter 6 that if an experimentor repeatedly exposed you to the word *democracy* while administering an electric shock, you would eventually develop a negative association with that word. Yet, if the experimenter explicitly asked you how you felt about democracy, you would probably say you liked it. In other words, you would have a negative unconscious attitude towards democracy based on nothing more than the pairing of the word with an electric shock, and a positive conscious attitude towards democracy based on your knowledge of world politics (Wilson et al., 2000b). Similarly, white people who have positive conscious attitudes towards black people may nonetheless develop negative unconscious attitudes simply by watching films and reading newspapers that pair black names and faces with negative concepts, such as *poverty* and *crime*. In these US studies, because all participants have been exposed to the same media, black people have the same unconscious attitudes towards their own group as white people (Greenwald et al., 2002). Conscious and unconscious attitudes are real, and each influences behaviour under different circumstances (Eberhardt, 2005; Phelps et al., 2000).

This research has potentially profound social, moral, legal and ethical implications. For instance, in most European countries, employers are not allowed to discriminate against applicants on the basis of gender or race (among other things), and they face severe legal repercussions if they are found to have done so. Yet, if people have prejudices they don't know about and can't control – if they consciously believe all the right things but unconsciously believe some of the wrong ones – how can they be held accountable for any ill actions that their prejudices may produce? Before you decide where you stand on this issue, you might want to take the IAT yourself at https://implicit.harvard.edu/implicit/demo.

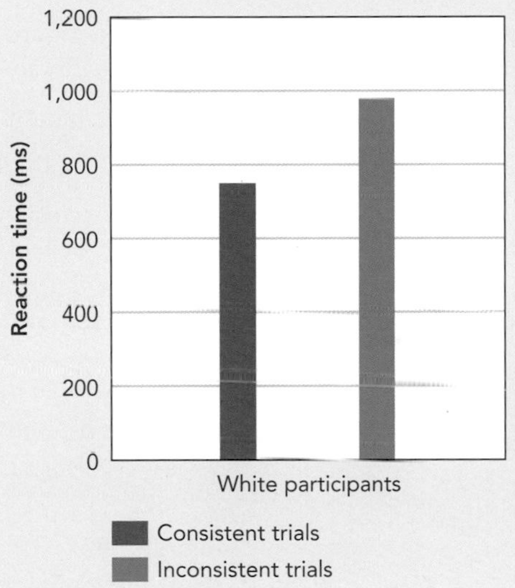

Results of an IAT experiment In this IAT experiment, white participants respond faster on consistent trials when a likable object is paired with a white name. The reaction time on inconsistent trials is considerably slower (Greenwald et al., 1998).

Chapter review

Living with others

- Our species has evolved to live in groups but human society is made up of many different groups that an individual can belong to.
- While an evolutionary perspective helps to understand the emergence of group behaviour from a genetic perspective, cultural psychology emphasizes understanding the role of nongenetic mechanisms.
- Cultural perspectives are particularly important because most theories have been derived from research conducted on Western participants, which may not apply to other cultures
- In order to belong to a group, an individual must identify with the group, which entails adopting the biases and prejudices that operate on the basis of stereotypes and prejudices. Moreover, most of us identify with more than one group, which can present conflicts of interest.

Thinking about others

- We make inferences about people based on the categories to which they belong. This method can lead us to misjudge others for four reasons:
  1. Stereotypes can be inaccurate, either because our cultures have given us misinformation or because we have seen relationships between category membership and behaviour that don't actually exist.
  2. Stereotypes can be overused because the mere act of categorization leads us to see category members as having more in common than they actually do. This is especially likely to happen when we are judging members of categories to which we do not belong.
  3. Stereotypes can perpetuate themselves by causing us to see what we expect to see, to treat others in ways that lead them to

behave as we expected, and to 'explain away' disconfirming evidence.

4 Stereotypes can operate unconsciously and automatically, which makes it difficult to avoid using them.

- Stereotyping is often associated with prejudice. There are individual differences that predict prejudice related to a tendency to prefer order and conformity, as well as group effects that emerge when resources are limited that stimulate intergroup conflicts. Much of these biases can be eliminated when individuals see themselves as part of a superordinate hierarchy. However, competition for resources cannot explain all biases that may arise automatically out of in-group and out-group discrimination.
- We also make inferences about people based on their actions. We assume that other people act as they do because of the situations in which they find themselves or because of their own dispositions.
- When a person's action is low in consistency, high in distinctiveness, and high in consensus, we should attribute the action to the situation. But research shows that we tend to attribute actions to dispositions even when we should not. This happens because situations are difficult to see and because information about situations is difficult to use.
- Sometimes performance is enhanced when we behave in groups but it can also be suboptimal if we do not believe that we are accountable for our effort.

Influencing others

- People want to be accepted by others, thus they try not to violate norms. One particularly strong norm is that people should benefit those who have benefited them, and several influence techniques put people in a position where they must either comply with a request or risk violating that norm.
- When people do not know the norms in a particular situation, they look to the behaviour of others. As such, they often end up doing what others are doing or doing what they are told to do. This kind of conformity and obedience can sometimes lead to shocking outcomes.
- People are motivated to have accurate attitudes and beliefs, and use communications from others to help them decide what is true. Some communications appeal to reason and some appeal to habit or emotion. People also decide what is true by comparing new information to old information. When they recognize inconsistencies among their attitudes, beliefs and actions, they may experience an unpleasant state of cognitive dissonance. To alleviate this state, people may attempt to eliminate the inconsistency or to justify it.
- Intentions to act are determined by a combination of personal attitudes, group norms and the actual abilities to attain the desired goals.
- Individuals behave in groups in way that they would not normally do when alone.
- When groups have to make decisions, the process can be distorted by a lack of careful objectivity. The desire to maintain group inclusion can sometimes trump reasonable individual decisions.
- Social networking is emerging as a dynamic new way of social interaction with rapid communication and transmission of social approval and rejection. It is not clear yet how this will culturally shape group behaviour.

Key terms

antinormative behaviour (p. 607)
attitude (p. 617)
belief (p. 617)
categorization (p. 596)
cognitive dissonance (p. 620)
collectivistic (p. 595)
conformity (p. 613)
deindividuation (p. 607)
discrimination (p. 594)
dominant response (p. 604)
door-in-the-face technique (p. 612)
emergent property (p. 607)
entitativity (p. 594)
evaluation apprehension (p. 605)
foot-in-the-door technique (p. 620)
group (p. 592)
group polarization (p. 610)
groupthink (p. 609)
heuristic persuasion (p. 617)
individualistic (p. 595)
informational influence (p. 613)
in-group (p. 595)
need to belong (p. 594)
normative influence (p. 612)
norm of reciprocity (p. 612)
norms (p. 612)
obedience (p. 615)
out-group (p. 595)
perceptual confirmation (p. 599)
persuasion (p. 617)
prejudice (p. 601)
self-fulfilling prophecy (p. 599)
social dominance orientation (p. 602)
social facilitation (p. 603)
social influence (p. 611)
social inhibition (p. 604)
social loafing (p. 605)
spotlight effect (p. 604)
stereotyping (p. 596)
superordinate goals (p. 602)
systematic persuasion (p. 617)

Recommended reading

Cialdini, R. B. (2000) *Influence: Science and Practice* (4th edn). New York: Morrow. Classic volume presenting an engaging, witty and scientific discussion of techniques for wielding and escaping social influence. Robert Cialdini has conducted a wealth of studies in this area.

Hood, B. (2014) *The Domesticated Brain*. London: Pelican. Humans have lived in groups for a very long time but 20,000 years ago marked a major transition from hunter-gatherer societies to living in large settled communities and the beginnings of civilization. How did this happen and what were the changes in social behaviour that changed the way we developed as a social animal?

Sutton, R. and Douglas, K. (2013) *Social Psychology*. Basingstoke: Palgrave Macmillan. One of the best undergraduate textbooks covering the European perspective on social psychology.

16

- Identifying psychological disorders: What is abnormal?
- the real world Cultural variants of abnormal behaviour
- Anxiety disorders: when fears take over
- Fear of holes hot science
- Dissociative disorders: going to pieces
- Mood disorders: at the mercy of emotions
- the real world Suicide risk and prevention
- Schizophrenia: losing the grasp on reality
- Personality disorders: going to extremes
- Schizophrenics have a Jekyll and Hyde split personality psychomythology
- where do you stand? Normal or abnormal

Chapter learning objectives

At the end of this chapter you will be able to:

1 Explain how an understanding of psychological disorders informs our theories of normal psychology.

2 Describe the difference between the medical model and symptom-oriented approaches to mental disorder.

3 Describe some of the weaknesses of the classification systems for mental disorders.

4 Distinguish between the major divisions of mental disorder and describe the major symptom clusters for each disorder.

5 Evaluate the evidence for psychological, biological and social factors that contribute to different mental disorders.

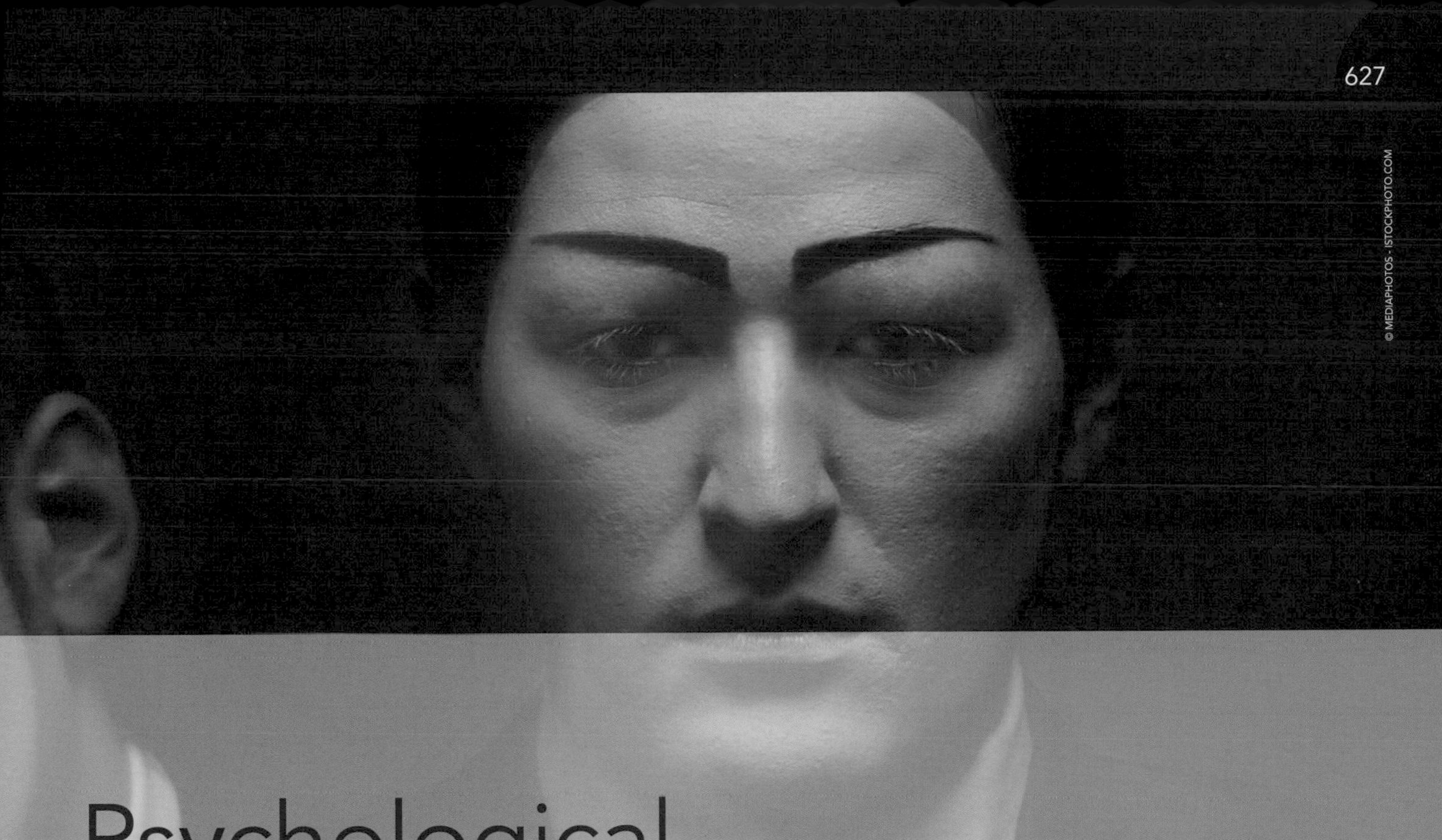

© MEDIAPHOTOS · ISTOCKPHOTO.COM

Psychological disorders

Virginia Woolf (1882–1941) left her walking stick on the bank of the river, put a large stone in the pocket of her coat, and made her way into the water. Her body was found three weeks later. She had written to her husband: 'Dearest, I feel certain I am going mad again … And I shan't recover this time. I begin to hear voices, and I can't concentrate. So I am doing what seems the best thing to do' (Dally, 1999, p. 182). Thus, near Rodmell in Sussex, on 28 March 1941, life ended for the prolific novelist and essayist, central figure of the avant-garde literary salon known as the 'Bloomsbury Group', influential feminist and unfortunate victim of lifelong 'breakdowns', with swings in mood between wretched depression and manic excitement.

The madness afflicting Woolf is now known as bipolar disorder. At one extreme were her episodes of depression – sullen, despondent, her creativity at a halt, she was sometimes bedridden for months by her illness. These periods alternated with mania, when, as her husband Leonard recounted: 'She talked almost without stopping for 2 or 3 days, paying no attention to anyone in the room or anything said to her.' Her language 'became completely incoherent, a mere jumble of dissociated words'. At the height of her spells, birds spoke to her in Greek, her dead mother reappeared and scolded her, and voices commanded her to 'do wild things'. She refused to eat, wrote pages of nonsense, and launched tirades of abuse at her husband and her companions (Dally, 1999, p. 240).

Between these phases, Woolf somehow managed a brilliant literary life. Her Victorian family had seen no reason for a woman to attend university, but the absence of schooling did not prevent her from becoming the extraordinary intellectual figure celebrated in the title of Edward Albee's 1962 play *Who's Afraid of Virginia Woolf?* All told, she produced 9 novels, a play, 5 volumes of essays and more than 14 volumes of diaries and letters. Her novels broke away from the traditions of strict plot and setting to explore the inner lives and musings of her characters, and her observations revealed

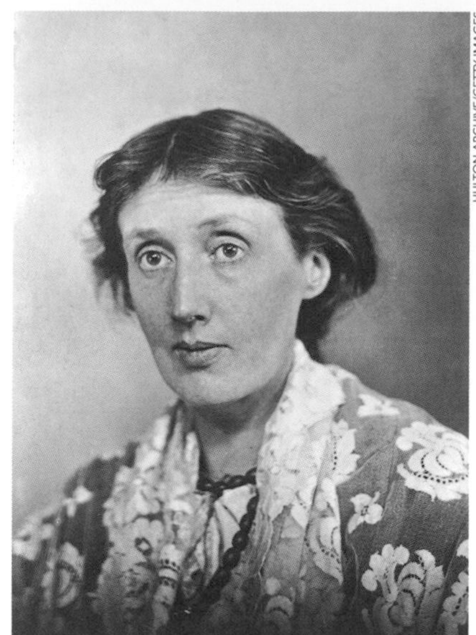

English novelist and critic Virginia Woolf in 1902. Her lifelong affliction with bipolar disorder ended in suicide, but the manic phases of her illness helped to fuel her prolific writing.

a keen appreciation of her own experience of psychological disorder. In a letter to a friend, she remarked: 'As an experience, madness is terrific … and not to be sniffed at, and in its lava I still find most of the things I write about' (Dally, 1999, p. 240). The price Woolf paid for her genius was, of course, a dear one, and her husband and companions shared the burden of dealing with her disorder. Disorders of the mind can create immense pain.

When you break your leg, this causes physical, psychological and even social problems. With our modern healthcare system, doctors can accurately measure the extent of the fracture with various imaging techniques, measure the body's reaction to injury by taking various blood levels and measure the amount of mobility impairment that will impact on your capacity to look after yourself out in society. There are well-established treatments such as immobilizing the injury in a cast, administering antibiotics to combat infection and providing a wheelchair or crunches until the leg is healed. When it comes to breaking your leg, the causal mechanisms of injury, symptoms and treatment are pretty much well understood. But such understanding is almost completely absent when it comes to diagnosing, understanding and treating illnesses of the mind. In this chapter we look at the problems of applying the medical model approach to psychological problems.

Symptoms reflecting problems of the mind, called *psychological*, or *mental, disorders*, are hard to define and explain. Most mental health experts agree that a psychological disorder is not, say, extreme anxiety before a chemistry test or deep sadness at the death of a beloved pet. Nor is an inability to read or do arithmetic a problem of the mind even if they are distressing to the individual. Rather, to qualify as a mental disorder, thoughts, feelings and emotions must be persistent, harmful to the person experiencing them, and uncontrollable in comparison to normal functioning. In Europe, approximately 50% of people will be affected by some type of psychological disorder during the course of their lives – at a substantial cost in health, productivity and happiness (Wittchen et al., 2011). Data compiled by the Global Burden of Disease study reveal that after cardiovascular disease, mental disorders are the second greatest contributor to a loss of years of healthy life in the US (Murray and Lopez, 1996). It is estimated that about 27% (82.7 million) of the adult EU population, 18–65 years of age, were affected by at least one mental disorder in a 12-month period (Wittchen and Jacobi, 2005). Problems of the mind are nearly as great a plague on humanity as problems of the heart.

Psychologists who study mental disorders seek to uncover ways to understand, treat and prevent such human misery. And because they reveal the mind's limits and functions, the study of mental disorders offers insights into the nature of normal mental functioning. The mindbugs, discussed in previous chapters as the errors of human psychology, proliferate in mental disorder. This chapter goes deeper into the study of mindbugs than any other in the book because it is devoted to the psychological problems that are so persistent and intense that they interfere with people's lives. In discovering what goes wrong in psychological disorders, we learn what the mind must do in order to run trouble free. But we also learn that normal and abnormal minds are on a continuum of fluctuating states. As Virginia Woolf's emotional roller coaster makes clear, for example, the normal mind must regulate its moods to maintain emotional stability.

The study of psychological disorders can be unsettling because you may well see yourself mirrored in the various conditions. Like medical students who come to worry about their own symptoms with each new disease they examine, students of abnormal psychology can catch their own version of 'medical students' disease', noticing personal oddities as they read about the peculiarities of others (Woods et al., 1966). Is your late-night frenzy to finish an assignment a kind of mania? Is your fear of snakes a phobia? Does forgetting where you left your keys qualify you for diagnosis with a dissociative disorder? Please relax. You may not always avoid self-diagnosis, but you're not alone. Studying psychological disorders heightens everyone's sensitivity to their own eccentricities. That's because the clinical symptoms of mental disorders are often simply extreme variations of the normal mental function that we all experience. In fact, you would be 'abnormal' if studying psychological disorders *didn't* make you reflect on yourself.

In this chapter, we first consider the question: What is abnormal? Virginia Woolf's bouts of depression and mania and her eventual suicide certainly seem abnormal, but at times, she was fine. The enormously complicated human mind can produce behaviours, thoughts and emotions that change radically from moment to moment. How do psychologists decide that a particular mind is disordered? We will examine the key factors that must be weighed in making such a decision. Our exploration of psychological disorders will then focus on each of several major forms of mental disorder, including anxiety disorders, dissociative disorders, mood disorders, schizophrenia and personality disorders. As we view each of these problems, we will look at how they can influence the person's thoughts and behaviour and what is known about their prevalence and causes.

Identifying psychological disorders: What is abnormal?

The idea of a *psychological disorder* is a relatively recent invention, historically speaking. People who act strangely or report bizarre thoughts or emotions have been known since ancient times, but their difficulties were often understood in the context of religion or the supernatural. In some cultures and religious traditions, madness is still interpreted as possession by animal spirits or demons, enchantment by a witch or shaman, or as God's punishment for wrongdoing. In many societies, including our own, people with mental abnormalities have commonly been treated as criminals – punished, imprisoned or put to death for their 'crime' of deviating from the normal. Madness has been feared and ridiculed, and people with mental disorders have often been victims of grave maltreatment. Over the past 200 years, these ways of looking at psychological abnormalities have largely been replaced in industrialized areas of the world by a medical model – *the conceptualization of psychological abnormalities as diseases that, like biological diseases, have symptoms and causes and possible cures.*

Treating psychological disorders in the same way we treat illness suggests that a first step is to determine the nature of the problem through *diagnosis*. In diagnosis, clinicians seek to determine the nature of the patient's psychological disorder by assessing *symptoms* – behaviours, thoughts and emotions suggestive of an underlying abnormal *syndrome*, a coherent cluster of symptoms usually due to a single cause. So, for example, just as a fever, sniffles and a cough are symptoms of a cold, wild behaviour, refusal to eat, and tirades of abuse may point to an episode of mania.

Medical models of psychological disorder use classification systems developed mostly by psychiatrists – *medical doctors concerned with the treatment of psychological disorders*. In the US, the focus of psychological disorder is on mental disorder that is covered by the DSM-5, *a US classification system* (Diagnostic and Statistical Manual of Mental Disorders, *5th edn*) *that describes the features used to diagnose each recognized mental disorder and indicates how the disorder can be distinguished from other, similar problems*, which was developed by the American Psychiatric Association (APA, 2013). However, Europe and many other countries use the *ICD-10 Classification of Mental and Behavioural Disorders*, developed by the World Health Organization (WHO, 1992), which addresses physical and mental disorders. Both list categories of disorders thought to be distinct types.

The introduction of a diagnostic classification system was not only motivated by the medical model of psychiatric illness but also as a practical way of providing a common framework that different clinicians and researchers could use to describe the variety of conditions they encountered. Also, without a diagnostic system, healthcare providers are limited in their ability to allocate resources and financially plan for services. Patients and their families also want answers as to what's wrong, so there is an added incentive to provide a diagnosis that seems to offer a reassuring explanation for behaviours that seem

Psychology and me

Sharon Buckland, Rehabilitation Worker, Headway

Sharon Buckland is a rehabilitation worker working at Headway Cambridgeshire in the UK. Headway offers specialist services and support to people with an acquired brain injury and other neurological conditions. Visit www.palgrave.com/schacter to watch a video of Sharon talking about why she decided to study psychology, the volunteering work she did while at university and how this led her to where she is now, and the fascinating day-to-day activities she undertakes at Headway.

According to the theory of physiognomy, mental disorders could be diagnosed from facial features. This fanciful theory is now discredited as superstition but was popular from antiquity until the early 20th century.

MEDICAL MODEL The conceptualization of psychological abnormalities as diseases that, like biological diseases, have symptoms and causes and possible cures.

PSYCHIATRISTS Medical doctors concerned with the treatment of mental disorders.

DSM-5 A US classification system (*Diagnostic and Statistical Manual of Mental Disorders*, 5th edn) that describes the features used to diagnose each recognized mental disorder and indicates how the disorder can be distinguished from other, similar problems.

so abnormal. It's not ideal having two systems but for various historical and practical reasons, two systems exist, although there are efforts to harmonize them in the coming years (First, 2009).

As useful as the medical model can be, it should nonetheless be viewed with some scepticism. As you will discover in Chapter 17, some of the most successful treatments for disordered behaviour or thought focus on simply eliminating the behaviour or thought – no effort is made to treat the root 'syndrome'. Not only does the medical model have limitations, it may contribute to the problems that psychological disorders present to the individual and society by incorrectly physicalizing and stigmatizing a condition that is best considered as relative and situational. In other words, psychological disorders are not the same as medical illnesses.

To understand how psychological disorders are defined and diagnosed, we'll first consider definitions of normal and abnormal behaviour. Then we'll look at how psychological disorders are categorized into groups, how the causes and cures of disorders are viewed in the medical model, and what consequences can occur – for better or worse – when such disorders are diagnosed. Finally, we will examine an approach that dispenses with the psychiatric diagnosis altogether in favour of focusing solely on the patient's symptoms.

Defining the boundaries of normality

A major misconception is the idea that a psychological disorder can be defined entirely in terms of deviation from the average, the typical, or 'healthy'. Yes, people who have psychological disorders may behave, think or experience emotions in unusual ways, but simple departure from the norm can't be the whole picture, or we'd be rapidly diagnosing disorders in the most creative and visionary people. Sorry, Einstein, that theory's kind of weird! Ugh, Picasso, those paintings don't seem normal! And if deviation were the only sign of psychological disorder, people who experience events that force them to be deviant, such as extremely stressful or bizarre situations that require unusual responses, would also be diagnosable. If you scream bloody murder and become wildly agitated when someone runs towards you carrying a homemade bomb, does that mean *you* have the psychological disorder?

The North American system

The DSM-5, published in 2013, is the most recent edition of the manual used by clinicians trained in the North American system of mental health care. It is produced by the American Psychiatric Association, which is reflected in its medical focus on the diagnosis of 22 major categories containing more than 200 different disorders. In addition to these major categories of defined disorders, the DSM-5 also describes conditions that may be included as formal disorders subject to future research as well as conditions that are subject to cultural variation.

Critics of the DSM-5, including many professional psychology associations such as the American Psychological Association and the British Psychological Society, believe that the latest version has again lowered diagnostic thresholds across a variety of disorders as well as emphasizing the medicalization of normal psychological adjustment processes. For example, *mild neurocognitive disorder*, cognitive decline that goes beyond the normal ageing process, might be diagnosed in the elderly whose memory decline simply reflects the normal ageing process described in Chapter 5. The general shift in emphasis to the role of development in psychological disorders means that children are increasingly being targeted for medical treatment. For example, the new condition of *disruptive mood dysregulation disorder* (DMDD), where children who have three tantrums week and frequent irritability for a year receive a diagnosis, has been particularly controversial. Not only is DMDD lacking in supporting evidence that it exists as a condition, but Dr Allen Frances, a leading child psychologist and former chair of the committee that produced the previous DSM-IV, also lamented, in relation to temper tantrum disorders, that 'these kids have a disease called "childhood"' (Frances, 2013).

The European system

The ICD-10, *published by the World Health Organization (WHO, 1992), is used throughout much of Europe and other parts of the world. Rather than using the term 'psychological disorder', it refers to mental and behavioural disorders, which are defined as 'the existence of a clinically recognizable set of symptoms or behaviour associated in most cases with distress and interference with personal functions'.* (Like the DSM-5, which was recently updated, the new ICD-11 is due for release in 2017.) It identifies 11 major categories of mental disorder (each has numerous subcategories), as shown in **TABLE 16.1**.

ICD-10 A classification system, published by the World Health Organization (WHO, 1992), used throughout much of Europe and other parts of the world. Rather than using the term 'psychological disorder', it refers to mental and behavioural disorders, which are defined as 'the existence of a clinically recognizable set of symptoms or behaviour associated in most cases with distress and interference with personal functions'.

TABLE **16.1 Main ICD-10 diagnostic categories of mental disorders**

1	*Organic, including symptomatic, mental disorders:* Cognitive impairment due to brain disease or injury, such as Alzheimer's disease, delirium and organic amnesia
2	*Mental and behavioural disorders due to use of psychoactive substances:* Misuse of, and dependence on, psychoactive substances, including alcohol, illegal drugs and prescription medication
3	*Schizophrenia, schizotypal and delusional disorders:* Disorders characterized by distortions of thought and perception and emotions that are inappropriate or blunted. At some phase, delusions and hallucinations usually occur
4	*Mood (affective) disorders:* Disturbances of normal mood; individuals may be extremely depressed, abnormally elated, or may alternate between these two extremes
5	*Neurotic, stress-related and somatoform disorders:* Disorders characterized by excessive anxiety, extreme and persistent reactions to stress, and alterations in consciousness and identity due to emotional problems, and presentation of physical symptoms that have no medical basis
6	*Behavioural syndromes associated with physiological disturbances and physical factors:* Eating disorders, sleep disorders, sexual disorders, and disorders occurring during the postnatal period
7	*Disorders of adult personality and behaviour:* Long-standing patterns of maladaptive behaviour that constitute immature and inappropriate ways of coping with stress or solving problems
8	*Mental retardation:* Arrested or incomplete development of the mind, characterized by impairment of skills which contribute to the overall level of intelligence
9	*Disorders of psychological development:* Disorders with onset in childhood resulting in impairment or delay of language, visual-spatial and motor skills
10	*Behavioural and emotional disorders with onset usually occurring in childhood and adolescence:* Hyperkinetic disorders characterized by an early onset, lack of persistence in activities, and disorganized, ill-regulated and excessive activity
11	*Unspecified mental disorder:* Any disorder which is none of the above

Source: WHO, 2004

There are similarities between the DSM-5 and ICD-10. For example, both share a common categorization for major psychotic disorders such as schizophrenia, schizotypal and delusional states. However, there are also major differences. The ICD-10 is the most frequently used system worldwide for clinical diagnosis, whereas the DSM is the most frequently used system for research (mainly because in the past most of this research has taken place in the US). Whereas the ICD-10 has 11 major categories of mental disorder, the DSM-5 has twice as many. These differences can have major implications. For example, research using the previous version of the DSM revealed that children were more likely to be diagnosed with major depressive disorder/depressive episode and attention deficit hyperactivity disorder/disturbance using the DSM compared to the ICD criterion (Sørensen et al., 2005). Of the 176 criteria sets that exist in both systems, only one, transient tic disorder, is identical. Twenty-one per cent of criteria sets had conceptually based differences and 78% had nonconceptually based differences (First, 2009). One thing that both classification systems share is a lack of predictive validity – neither is particularly good at anticipating how the mental disorder will progress and, as noted earlier, there are no good measures of aeitology – something that mental models assume (see below).

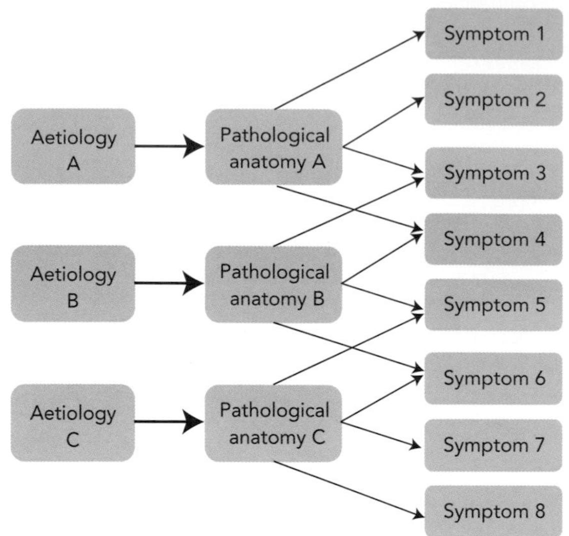

FIGURE 16.1 Kraepelin's model of psychiatric disorder (1887) In Kraepelin's model, each disorder had a typical symptom profile even though different disorders could share the same symptoms (Bentall, 2003).

PATHOLOGY A unique disorder.

AETIOLOGY A causal pathway of circumstances that create a pathology.

Classification of psychological disorders

Classification systems such as the DSM-5 or ICD-10 did not drop out of the sky fully formed, rather they evolved as the fields of psychology and psychiatry have developed, and the revision process continues to this day. One of the pioneers of mental disorder diagnosis was German psychiatrist Emil Kraepelin (1856–1926), who shaped much of the 20th-century's attitude and adoption of the medical model. His approach is illustrated in **FIGURE 16.1**.

According to Kraepelin (1907), mental disorders were illnesses that fell into a relatively small number of types that would eventually be understood by advances in medicine and our understanding of the brain. Each disorder produced a cluster of diagnostic symptoms that reflected a discrete underlying pathology, *a unique disorder*, which, in turn, had a unique aetiology – *causal pathway of circumstances that create the pathology*.

In the early 20th century, and following Kraepelin's influence, European and US clinicians typically divided disorders into two categories: *neurosis*, a condition that involves anxiety but in which the person is still in touch with reality, and *psychosis*, a condition in which the person experiences serious distortions of perception and thought that weaken their grasp on reality. Although many disorders fit these categories, for example obsessive-compulsive disorder as a neurosis, and schizophrenia as a form of psychosis, no consensus existed on the qualities present in the categories. The terms were mainly used to describe relative severity.

In 1952, in recognition of the need to have a consensual diagnostic system for therapists and researchers, the first version of the *Diagnostic and Statistical Manual of Mental Disorders* (DSM) was published, followed by a revision in 1968 (DSM-II). These early versions provided a common language for talking about disorders, but the diagnostic criteria were still often vague and based on tenuous theoretical assumptions. For example, the DSM-II contained a description of *neurosis* that was based only on Freudian psychodynamic theory (discussed in Chapter 13). The definition was clear in specifying that 'anxiety is the chief characteristic of the neuroses'. However, it then went on to say that the anxiety 'may be felt and expressed directly, or it may be controlled unconsciously and automatically by conversion, displacement, and various other psychological mechanisms' (APA, 1968, p. 39). Even for an expert in Freudian theory, this definition is open to many interpretations. It suggests that the anxiety might or might not be felt and could be transformed into just about any sort of physical symptom (through conversion) or psychological symptom (through displacement), and that any of these symptoms would count as neurosis. On the basis of this definition, everyone in the world is neurotic.

Unsurprisingly, early versions of the classification systems led to unreliable diagnoses. As we explained in Chapter 2, unreliability of measurement leads to confusion about what is being measured. Clinicians using this system could come up with wildly different diagnoses of a particular cluster of symptoms, so they still had to use their own judgement in deciding whether treatments were necessary and whether the treatments had helped the person, hurt the person, or had no effect.

To address the problem of reliability and promote better agreement among diagnosticians, developers of succeeding editions of the classification systems have tried to define mental disorders as objectively as possible. Controversial, subjective theoretical concepts have been replaced with behavioural terms that allow clinicians to observe objectively and assess the frequency of disorders. The term *neurosis*, for example, has been replaced by a more concretely described classification called *anxiety disorders*, each of which is defined in terms of observable features such as excessive anxiety in general, excessive anxiety in a particular setting and so on.

The major mental disorders distinguished in the DSM-5 are shown in **TABLE 16.2**. Because the mind can go awry in such a remarkably large number of ways, however, the path to reliable diagnosis remains thorny. In general, the DSM-5 and ICD-10 produce better diagnostic reliability than earlier versions, but critics argue that considerable room

TABLE 16.2 Main DSM-5 categories of mental disorder

1	*Neurodevelopmental disorders:* These are conditions that begin early in development and cause significant impairments in functioning, such as intellectual disability (formerly called 'mental retardation'), autism spectrum, and attention-deficit/hyperactivity disorder
2	*Schizophrenia spectrum and other psychotic disorders:* This is a group of disorders characterized by major disturbances in perception, thought, language, emotion, and behaviour. At least one core positive symptom of delusions, hallucinations or disorganized speech must be present
3	*Bipolar and related disorders:* These disorders include major fluctuations in mood – from mania to depression – and also can include psychotic experiences
4	*Depressive disorders:* These are conditions characterized by extreme and persistent periods of depressed mood. This category now contains a new condition, disruptive mood dysregulation disorder specifically targeted at children who exhibit persistent irritability and frequent episodes of extreme behavioural disruption
5	*Anxiety disorders:* These are disorders characterized by excessive fear and anxiety that are extreme enough to impair a person's functioning, such as panic disorder, generalized anxiety disorder, and specific phobia
6	*Obsessive-compulsive and related disorders:* A new category previously in anxiety disorders that is characterized by the presence of obsessive thinking followed by compulsive behaviour in response to that thinking. Excessive hoarding is recognized as a new diagnosis under this category
7	*Trauma- and stressor-related disorders:* A new category previously in anxiety disorders that develop in response to a traumatic event, such as post-traumatic stress disorder
8	*Dissociative disorders:* These are conditions characterized by disruptions or discontinuity in consciousness, memory, or identity such as dissociative identity disorder (formerly called 'multiple personality disorder')
9	*Somatic symptom and related disorders:* These are conditions in which a person experiences bodily symptoms (e.g. pain, fatigue) associated with significant distress or impairment
10	*Feeding and eating disorders:* These are problems with eating that impair health or functioning such as anorexia nervosa and bulimia nervosa
11	*Elimination disorders:* These involve inappropriate elimination of urine or faeces (e.g. bed-wetting)
12	*Sleep-wake disorders:* These are problems of sleep-wake cycle, such as insomnia, narcolepsy, and sleep apnea
13	*Sexual dysfunction:* These are problems related to unsatisfactory sexual activity, such as erectile disorder and painful intercourse that must persist for at least 6 months
14	*Gender dysphoria:* A new diagnostic class of a single disorder that reflects the incongruence between a person's experienced/expressed gender and assigned gender
15	*Disruptive, impulse-control, and conduct disorders:* These are conditions involving problems controlling emotions and behaviours, such as defiant rebellion, intermittent explosive outbursts, antisocial behaviour and kleptomania
16	*Substance-related and addictive behaviours:* These disorders involve persistent use and abuse of substances that lead to significant problems and also includes behavioural addictions such as gambling
17	*Neurocognitive disorders:* These include disorders of thinking caused by conditions such as Alzheimer's disease or traumatic brain injury
18	*Personality disorders:* These are enduring patterns of thinking, feeling and behaving that lead to significant life problems
19	*Paraphillic disorders:* These are conditions characterized by inappropriate sexual activity that is currently causing distress or harm to the individual or a paraphilia whose satisfaction has entailed personal harm, or risk of harm, to others such as paedophilia
20	*Other mental disorders:* A residual category for conditions that do not fit into one of the other categories but are associated with significant distress or impairment such as an unspecified mental disorder due to a medical condition not previously recognized
21	*Medication-induced movement disorders and other adverse effects of medication:* These are disorders of physical movement such as tremors that are caused by medication
22	*Other conditions that may be the focus of clinical attention:* These include problems related to abuse, neglect, relationships, and other problems

Source: APA, 2013

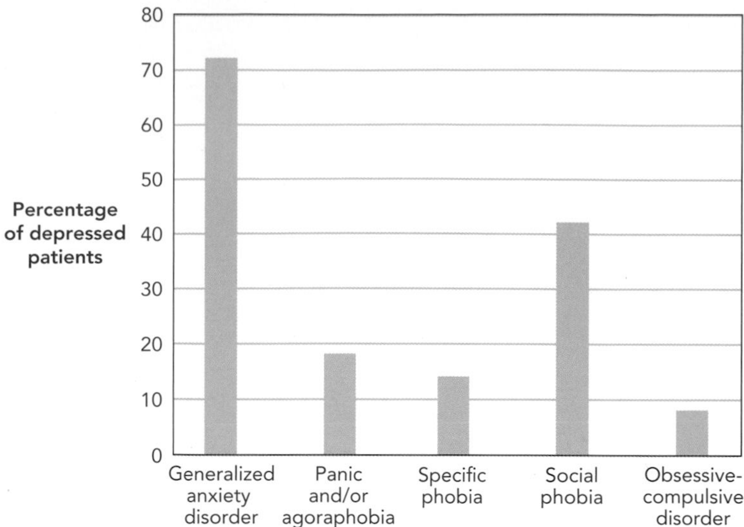

FIGURE 16.2 Comorbidity of depression and anxiety disorders The comorbidity of depression and anxiety disorders is substantial. Of 102 patients whose primary diagnosis was depression (major depressive disorder or dysthymia), large percentages also had a secondary diagnosis of one or more anxiety disorders (Brown et al., 2001).

COMORBIDITY The co-occurrence of two or more disorders in a single individual.

for improvement remains. Numerous diagnostic categories continue to depend on interpretation-based criteria rather than observable behaviour, and diagnosis continues to focus on patient self-reports, which are susceptible to censorship and distortion. Levels of agreement among different diagnosticians can vary depending on the diagnostic category (Bertelsen, 1999; Nathan and Lagenbucher, 1999). Agreement among diagnosticians on, say, whether a patient has schizophrenia may even depend on the clinic setting. Such disagreement may not reflect differences in the prevalence of schizophrenia in various localities but rather in the array of symptoms the clinicians were trained to expect in people with the disorder (Keller et al., 1995).

Diagnostic difficulty is further increased when a person suffers from more than one disorder. As shown in FIGURE 16.2, people with depression (a mood disorder) often have secondary diagnoses of anxiety disorders, for example. *The co-occurrence of two or more disorders in a single individual* is referred to as comorbidity and is relatively common in patients seen within the DSM diagnostic system (Kessler et al., 1994). Comorbidity raises a host of confusing possibilities. A person could be depressed because a phobia makes social situations impossible, or the person could be phobic about showing a despairing mood in public, or the disorders could be unrelated but co-occurring. Diagnosticians try hard to solve the problem of comorbidity because understanding the underlying basis for a person's disorder may suggest methods of treatment.

Classification and causation

The medical model suggests that knowing a person's diagnosis is useful because any given category of mental illness is likely to have a distinctive cause. In other words, just as different viruses, bacteria, types of trauma or genetic weakness cause different physical illnesses, so a specifiable pattern of causes (aetiology) may exist for different mental disorders. The medical model also suggests that each category of mental disorder is likely to have a common prognosis, a typical course over time, and susceptibility to treatment and cure. Unfortunately, as noted earlier, the medical model is usually an oversimplification – it is rarely useful to focus on a single cause that is internal to the person and that suggests a single cure. For example, 'Mad Hatter syndrome', first described in the 1800s in workers who used a mercury compound in making felt hats, was one of those rare single-cause disorders. The symptoms were trembling, loss of memory and coordination, slurred speech, depression, and anxiety. The cause was mercury poisoning. The cure was getting out of the hat business. Things are seldom so simple, however, and a full explanation of all the different ways in which the mind can become disordered needs to take into account multiple levels of causation.

The *biopsychosocial model*, an integrated perspective that incorporates biological, psychological and environmental factors, offers the most comprehensive and useful framework for understanding most mental disorders (Engel, 1977). On the biological side, the focus is on genetic influences, biochemical imbalances and structural abnormalities of the brain. The psychological perspective focuses on maladaptive learning and coping, cognitive biases, dysfunctional attitudes and interpersonal problems. Environmental factors include poor socialization, stressful life circumstances and cultural and social inequities. Unfortunately, the biopsychosocial model is problematic for a number of important reasons that undermine its real usefulness (Cromby et al., 2013). First, it must be true that all three factors are involved to some extent but the model does not really define a working or testable structure. Second, it assumes that the three components are separate when in fact they are interrelated, making it difficult to tease apart the separate contributions. With little current understanding of the reciprocal relationship between biology, psychology and social environment, the chain of causality cannot be established. Some have argued that attempts to frame investigations in a biopsychosocial framework are really biologically dominated exercises that simply tack on culture and mind as contextual afterthoughts (Read, 2005).

The complexity of causation suggests that different individuals can experience a similar mental disorder, for example depression, for different reasons. A person might fall into depression as a result of biological causes, for example genetics or hormones, or psychological causes, for example faulty beliefs, hopelessness or poor strategies for coping with loss, or environmental causes, for example stress or loneliness, or, more probably, as a result of some combination of these factors. And, of course, multiple causes pretty much rule out single cures.

The notion that the causes of disorders are always internal can also lead to another error – that of overlooking external causes. What would be your reaction to a fellow student who appeared one day with a bucket on their head and sat quietly through a lecture except for an occasional mellow, bell-like cough? Pretty weird, you'd probably think. And you'd wonder: A stunt to get attention? A protest? Some kind of demonstration dreamed up by the professor? Do they actually think this is cool? Despite your consideration of external pressures (politics or the professor's request), you'd probably wind up focusing on internal dispositions (a need for attention or a poor sense of style). When trying to understand the behaviour of others, people typically overlook external causes and focus on characteristics internal to the person. Such blindness to external causes is a common mindbug called the *fundamental attribution error* (discussed in Chapter 14).

The Mad Hatter in *Alice's Adventures in Wonderland* was Lewis Carroll's portrayal of a mental disorder common among hatmakers in the 1800s. Hatters could become 'mad as a hatter' because when they processed felt for hats, they unwittingly exposed themselves to a mercury compound that produced serious side effects.

The observation that most disorders have internal and external causes has given rise to a theory known as the diathesis-stress model, which *suggests that a person may be predisposed to a mental disorder that remains unexpressed until triggered by stress.* The diathesis is the internal predisposition and the stress is the external trigger (see Chapter 17). For example, most people were able to cope with their strong emotional reactions to the terrorist attack of 11 September 2001. However, for some who had a predisposition to negative emotions or were already contending with major life stressors, the horror of the events may have overwhelmed their ability to cope, thereby precipitating a mental disorder.

DIATHESIS-STRESS MODEL Suggests that a person may be predisposed to a mental disorder that remains unexpressed until triggered by stress.

A diathesis can be inherited. Like mental abilities (see Chapter 9) and personality traits (see Chapter 13), psychological disorders vary in their *heritability*. However, inherent in the notion that stressful conditions are necessary for the disorder to manifest itself is the assumption that heritability is not destiny. A person who inherits a diathesis may never encounter the precipitating stress, whereas someone with little genetic propensity to a disorder may come to suffer from it, given the right pattern of stress. The relationship between diathesis and stress can snowball, growing over time because an initial vulnerability becomes more severe as the individual reacts to the stress. Imagine Maria, for example, who has a genetic predisposition to be introverted and sensitive to social rejection and who is snubbed at a party by someone she thought was her friend. She might start avoiding this 'friend' and others to prevent another rejection. Over time, Maria gains a reputation as a loner and is shunned again and again. She has the same reaction each time and eventually becomes so withdrawn that depression and anxiety result. Diathesis and stress can work together subtly over time, making it a challenge to pick apart aetiological factors.

The tendency to oversimplify mental disorders by attributing them to single, internal causes is nowhere more evident than in the interpretation of the role of the brain in mental disorders. Brain scans of people with and without disorders can give rise to an unusually strong impression that psychological problems are internal – 'Look, there it is!' – and perhaps also permanent, inevitable and even untreatable. It's as if tracing a disorder to a patient's brain renders them immune from other influences. For example, discovering that the brains of individuals with depression show unique patterns of activation (discussed later in this chapter) may make it difficult to appreciate external causes of this disorder. Falling prey to this kind of mindbug is about as useful as assuming that, having learned about the role of the olfactory area of the brain in perceiving the fragrance of the rose, we no longer need any roses. Brain influences and processes are fundamentally important for knowing the full story of mental disorders but are not the only chapter in that story (see *the real world* box).

GETTY IMAGES/ISTOCKPHOTO/THINKSTOCK IMAGES

This woman might respond well to sleeping tablets, but take care not to assume that biology is at the root of her problems.

Searching for the biological causes of mental disorders in the brain and body also tends to invite a particular error in explanation – the *intervention-causation fallacy.* This fallacy involves the assumption that if a treatment is effective, it must address the cause of the problem. Thus, if a patient responds favourably to drugs or other biological interventions, the cause of the disorder is attributed to biology. Conversely, if a psychological intervention such as psychotherapy alleviates the symptoms, psychological factors are seen as the root of the problem. This may sometimes be true, but it is certainly not a general rule. To get a sense of the error in this logic, imagine that you've spent sleepless night after sleepless night worrying about a loved one who was recently hospitalized with a serious illness. You discover that taking sleeping pills before bed helps you sleep. On the basis of your favourable response, should we conclude that your insomnia was caused by a deficiency of sleeping pills, that a part of your brain needed the chemicals in the pills? Of course not. Your anxiety and sleeplessness were due to your loved one's illness, not the absence of a pill. Be cautious about drawing inferences about causality based on responsiveness to treatment; the cure does not necessarily point to the cause.

The diagnosis and classification of mental disorders provide a useful basis for exploring the causes and cures of psychological problems. At the same time, these tools make it all too easy to assume that the problems arise from single, internal causes that are inherited and involve brain dysfunction and can therefore be dispelled with an intervention that simply eliminates the cause. Psychological problems are usually more challenging and complicated than this ideal model would suggest.

the real world

Cultural variants of psychological disorders

People dress differently in different parts of the world, they eat differently, they speak differently and, it turns out, they can have different psychological disorders as well. Cultural and societal factors can play an important role in the development and expression of psychological disorders. Consider anorexia nervosa, an eating disorder that primarily afflicts young women, which is characterized by intense fear of gaining weight, and often leads to extreme weight loss (discussed in Chapter 10). This disorder is far more prevalent in industrialized societies, where models and film stars who attain unrealistic thinness represent the feminine ideal, than in nonindustrialized countries, where a heavier, more rounded body type is considered beautiful (Hsu, 1990). This cultural difference is even 'catching', as Middle Eastern and Asian women have been found to increase their risk for anorexia when they move to Western countries to live or study (Mumford et al., 1991; Nasser, 1986).

Looking at cross-cultural differences reveals how different socialization practices can foster different psychological problems and how cultural expectations shape our perceptions of those problems. For example, in Western societies, depression and anxiety are frequent reactions to stressful life experiences. However, in China, the effects of stress are more likely to be manifested in physical problems, such as fatigue, weakness and other bodily complaints (Kleinman, 1986, 1988). Such differences suggest that it is a mistake to presume that the diagnostic criteria described in the DSM and ICD manuals are universal across cultures. Psychologists need to tailor their diagnoses to accommodate culture-specific issues that may contribute to clients' problems. Indeed, evidence is mounting that treatment is more effective when therapists are knowledgeable about their clients' cultures (Sue et al., 1991; Tharp, 1991; Yeh et al., 1994).

The DSM-5 has introduced three concepts that make a significant advance over previous versions in understanding cultural variations of psychological disorders. These are:

1. *Cultural syndromes:* 'clusters of symptoms and attributions that tend to co-occur among individuals in specific cultural groups, communities, or contexts … that are recognized locally as coherent patterns of experience'
2. *Cultural idioms of distress:* 'ways of expressing distress that may not involve specific symptoms or syndromes, but that provide collective, shared ways of experiencing and talking about personal or social concerns'
3. *Cultural explanations of distress or perceived causes:* 'labels, attributions, or features of an explanatory model that indicate culturally recognized meaning or etiology for symptoms, illness or distress' (APA, 2013, p. 758).

In addition, the DSM-5 includes a Cultural Formulation Interview (CFI) to aid researchers and therapists in their quest to understand the relevance of cultural factors to mental health. The CFI is a semi-structured interview comprising 16 questions that focus on individual experience and social context, in order to assess cultural factors using a person-centred approach.

The importance of cultural differences can be appreciated in the case of panic attacks, which are an anxiety disorder, described in detail in this chapter. Sufferers experience acute physical symptoms of breathlessness, heart palpitations, sweating and dizziness, which are also indicators of extreme sympathetic nervous activity (described in Chapter 3). These physiological symptoms are accompanied by feelings of panic and dread that may or may not be associated with a particular situation but are often thought to be the beginning of a heart attack. In the West, panic attacks are a syndrome with symptoms and a recognized physiological profile. Now compare panic attack to *khyâl cup* ('wind attack'), a syndrome found among Cambodians, with symptoms including palpitations, dizziness, shortness of breath and neck soreness, the triggers for which might be worry, fright, standing up, riding in a car, or going into a crowded area. The attack also includes catastrophic cognitions related to the symptoms that create pernicious loops (fear of the symptoms amplifies the symptoms and consequently the fear). This sounds similar to the symptoms of panic disorder but the aetiology is believed to be different, which influences how Westerners and Cambodians think and reason about the disorder.

Westerners with panic disorder rarely complain of neck pain, joints soreness, tinnitus and headaches, but for Cambodians, the panic attacks result from *khyâl* (a wind-like substance that flows along with blood throughout the body) that suddenly starts flowing up towards the heart, lungs and neck. Cambodian patients are greatly concerned about sore necks, because they attribute this pain to excessive wind and blood pressure at the neck that they believe will rupture the vessels. They also worry about 'limb blockage' and the 'death of arms and legs', signalled by cold feet and hands (another symptom of sympathetic nervous activity), which Cambodians believe indicate the disruption in the flow of *khyâl* (Hofmann and Hinton, 2014).

Unlike a common cold, which has the same symptoms around the world, psychological disorders can express themselves differently in different cultures. The medical model doesn't seem to tell the whole story about disorders of the mind, because 'diseases' that vary between cultures might not be diseases at all and may instead be socially shared ways of expressing and interpreting symptoms.

Consequences of labelling

What would your life be like if your nickname was 'Crazy'? On hearing your name, people might treat you as if you were odd, and you might find yourself responding by becoming irritated, sullen or even downright strange. In the same way, psychiatric labels can have negative consequences despite mental health workers' good intensions when they use them in diagnosis. The labels carry excess baggage in the form of negative stereotypes, and these can create new problems.

The stigma associated with psychological disorders may help to explain why nearly 70% of people with diagnosable mental disorders do not seek treatment (Kessler et al., 1996; Regier et al., 1993; Sussman et al., 1987). Many people believe that a psychological disorder is a sign of personal weakness or a consequence of wrongdoing (Angermeyer and Matschinger, 1996a). Another widespread belief falsely suggests that psychiatric patients are dangerous (Angermeyer and Matschinger, 1996b; Phelan et al., 2000; Wolff et al., 1996), despite considerable evidence that such people are not violent (Eronen et al., 1998; Steadman et al., 1998; Swanson, 1994; Torrey, 1994). In light of these misconceptions, a watchful concern and even avoidance when in the presence of individuals with mental disorders is not surprising (Link et al., 1999). To steer clear of these difficulties, people with mental disorders often try to keep their problems secret.

Unfortunately, educating people about psychological disorders does not dispel the stigma borne by those with these problems (Phelan et al., 1997). In fact, expectations created by psychiatric labels can sometimes even compromise the judgement of mental health professionals (Garb, 1998; Langer and Abelson, 1974; Temerlin and Trousdale, 1969). In the classic demonstration of this phenomenon, US psychologist David Rosenhan and six associates reported to different mental hospitals complaining of 'hearing voices', a symptom sometimes found in people with schizophrenia. Each was admitted to a hospital as a result of this feigned complaint, and each then promptly reported that the symptom had ceased. Many of their fellow patients soon identified them as normal, but hospital staff were much more reluctant to make this decision. It took an average of 19 days for the false patients to secure their release, with a high of 62 days and a low of 9 days. Even then, they were released with the diagnosis of 'schizophrenia in remission' – a sticky label indeed (Rosenhan, 1973).

If psychiatric labelling conjures biases in the general public and psychiatric hospital staff, does it also adversely affect the self-view of the person who is labelled? At the extreme, some commentators, such as sociologist Thomas Scheff (1984), have claimed that labels for mental disorders actually serve to create the disorders. One of the most outspoken early critics of psychiatric labelling was Scottish psychiatrist R. D. Laing who refused to acknowledge mental disorder as a biomedical clinical problem. He even went so far as to argue that insanity or psychosis was a perfectly rational adjustment to an insane world (Laing, 1960). He rejected the medical interventions used to treat mental disorders; instead, he advocated and practised therapies that were supposed to address emotional, social turmoil brought about by existential crisis. On a visit to a Chicago psychiatric hospital, he was asked to examine a young girl diagnosed as schizophrenic. The girl was locked in a padded cell in a special hospital, and sat there naked rocking to and fro. The doctors asked Laing what he would do about her. Unexpectedly, Laing stripped off and entered her cell, where he sat with her, naked, rocking in time with her. After about twenty minutes, she started speaking, something she had not done for several months. The doctors were amazed. 'Did it never occur to you to do that?', Laing commented to them later.

These radical ideas reflected much of the anti-establishment sentiments of the time and largely went out of favour during the 1970s, but have generated renewed approval in light of the recent trend to overmedicalize mental disorders and the realization that pharmaceutical treatments have limited success (see Chapter 17).

Few believe that the millions of people worldwide who suffer psychological disorders do so merely because they have received diagnoses. Even the interpretation of Rosenhan's famous (1973) study where they faked schizophrenic symptoms is problematic because the clinicians changed the diagnosis to one of 'in remission', which is rare in a psychiatric setting, indicating that the staff recognized that the patients were behaving normally (Spitzer, 1976). If a patient presents at a psychiatric clinic with symptoms of schizophrenia, why would you immediately assume that they were a healthy person all along?

If there is an issue with labelling, it is more likely that the labelled person comes to view the self negatively – not just as psychologically disordered but also as hopeless or worthless. People who think poorly of themselves can develop defeatist attitudes and as a result may fail to work towards their own recovery. In one small step towards counteracting such consequences, clinicians have adopted the important practice of applying labels to the disorder and not to the people who have disorders. For example, a patient might be described as 'a person with schizophrenia' rather than as 'a schizophrenic'. You'll note that we follow this model in the text.

Symptom-oriented approach

In contrast to the medical model first introduced by Kraepelin and subsequently adopted and developed in much of Western psychiatry (especially in the US), there has been a movement in Europe away from the diagnostic approach to one that focuses on symptoms (see Bentall, 2003). Much of this is motivated by a number of shortfalls and weaknesses of the medical model. First, most symptoms of mental disorder are not reliably related to any underlying pathology that can be easily identified (APA, 2000; Keisler, 1999; Persons, 1986). Unlike most medical diseases where objective measures of underlying pathology, such as germs or microorganisms, can be detected, no such evidence exists for most mental disorders. (There are a number of organic disorders such as various dementias listed in the ICD-10 that do have brain pathologies.) Second, the mind is not simply a physical system but a psychological one that reflects an individual's past, as well as their current circumstances, including economic and social status. Therefore, mental disorder is not independent but has to be seen in the context of the individual and their situation. For example, your broken leg is a broken leg wherever you drag it, but a psychological disorder may be a consequence of a particular environment or situation. Most problematic is that symptoms regarded as abnormal are on a sliding scale of normality, which makes defining abnormality a real problem. The diagnostic classification systems we have been discussing here are arguably culturally specific and lack the necessary reliability and validity that one would expect from typical disease models found in medicine.

This has led a number of mental health professionals, especially in Europe, to challenge the psychiatric diagnosis approach to mental disorder and advocate instead a symptom-oriented approach – *individuals are primarily treated on the basis of behaviours and thoughts they find problematic and disturbing*. If one focuses on symptoms alone, there is no need to identify a single underlying pathological disorder, as Kraepelin originally proposed, and which has been so elusive to find. In contrast, the symptom-oriented

SYMPTOM-ORIENTED APPROACH
Individuals are primarily treated on the basis of behaviours and thoughts they find problematic and disturbing.

approach regards the emphasis on a single pathology as misguided and advocates a dimensional characterization rather than categorical diagnosis. This approach allows for multiple causal pathways. It is worth emphasizing that this approach is not antibiological as it also acknowledges the role of brain function as central to understanding complex psychological disorders. In short, understanding and treating mental disorders require more than single aetiologies based on assumed neurological imbalances, but also require psychological and environmental factors to be taken into consideration. The symptom-oriented approach is not without its critics (Mojtabi and Rieder, 1998), but it does appear to be gaining support, especially in Europe (Bentall, 2003).

New approaches to understanding multiple levels of causation

On publication of the DSM-5 in 2013, Thomas Insel, director of the US National Institute of Mental Health (NIMH), noted that although many people describe the DSM as a bible, it is more accurate to think of it as a dictionary that provides labels and definitions: 'People think that everything has to match DSM criteria, but you know what? Biology never read that book' (Insel, quoted in Belluck and Carey, 2013). More damning for the adoption of the DSM-5 is that Insel stated that the manual lacked validity and the NIMH would no longer be funding projects based on DSM diagnosis alone. In order to better understand what actually causes psychological disorders, NIMH researchers introduced a new framework focused not on the currently defined DSM-5 categories of disorders, but on the more basic biological, cognitive and behavioural constructs that are believed to be the basis of psychological orders.

The new system, the *Research Domain Criteria (RDoC) project* – an initiative that aims to guide the classification and understanding of mental disorders by revealing the basic processes that give rise to them – incorporates biological, psychological and social factors that offer a more comprehensive and useful framework for understanding underlying causes. On the biological side, the focus is on genetic influences, biochemical imbalances and structural abnormalities of the brain. The psychological perspective focuses on attention, perception, working memory, language and cognitive control problems. Social factors include relationships, communication, self-awareness and understanding of others. In Europe, a recent new initiative called the Roadmap for Mental Health Research in Europe (ROAMER; Haro et al., 2014) also seeks to adopt a multi-layered approach to addressing psychological disorders.

These symptom-oriented perspectives bring the study of psychological disorders into line with other therapeutic approaches. For example, if you are experiencing chest pain, severe headaches, fatigue and difficulty breathing, it is unlikely you are suffering from four separate disorders (chest pain disorder, headache disorder, fatigue disorder and breathing disorder). Instead, we know it is more likely that these are all symptoms of an underlying disease process of hypertension. Also, just like hypertension, there will be a range from normal to abnormal levels in each of the symptoms and so treatments will be targeted at those that fall out of the normal range. This approach also allows for profiles of symptoms to change as a dynamic interplay shifts between all the factors that contribute to the overall profile of the patient. It remains to be seen whether the RDoC eventually replaces the DSM but the former is primarily aimed at researchers, whereas the latter is a diagnostic labelling system favoured by clinicians who are often under pressure to come up with a name to account for an individual's abnormal thoughts and behaviours.

In summary, researchers and clinicians, especially in the US, have tended to follow a medical model of psychological disorders in which symptoms are understood to indicate the nature of the underlying problem. To diagnose a disorder, mental health professionals use classification systems that define a psychological disorder as occurring when the person experiences disturbances of thought, emotion or behaviour that produce distress or impairment of normal functioning. The US uses the DSM-5, whereas the rest of the world tends to use the ICD-10. These classification systems include a global assessment of functioning and multiple categories of disorders. Comorbidity of disorders is common, and the idea that a disorder has a single, internal cause is often an oversimplification, because many disorders arise from multiple causes or as a result of the interaction of diathesis and stress. It is also an error to assume that the intervention that cures a disorder reflects the cause of the disorder. The classification of disorders brings with it the possibility of a significant stigma that can create its own problems. When a person is given a diagnosis, the label can be difficult to overcome because the label changes how the person is perceived by mental health workers, others, and even the self. More problematic for classification systems based on the medical model is that single aetiologies for psychological disorders have remained elusive, indicating that psychological disorders represent complex problems with multiple causal factors. In light of the problems of relying on the medical model of psychological disorders, European mental health professionals and increasingly those in the US are adopting a symptom-oriented approach rather than medical diagnosis.

Anxiety disorders: when fears take over

ANXIETY DISORDER The class of mental disorder in which anxiety is the predominant feature.

'Okay, we have decided to bring the final exam forward to next week.' If your lecturer had actually said that, you would probably have experienced a wave of anxiety and dread. Your reaction would be appropriate but, no matter how intense the feeling, would not be a sign that you have a mental disorder. In fact, situation-related anxiety is normal and can be adaptive; in this case, perhaps by reminding you to keep up with your revision. When anxiety arises that is out of proportion to real threats and challenges, however, it is maladaptive. It can take hold of people's lives, steal their peace of mind and undermine their ability to function normally. Pathological anxiety is expressed as an anxiety disorder – *the class of mental disorder in which anxiety is the predominant feature.* People commonly experience more than one type of anxiety disorder at a given time, and there is significant comorbidity between anxiety and depression (Brown and Barlow, 2002). Among the anxiety disorders recognized are *generalized anxiety disorder*, *phobic disorders*, *panic disorder* and *obsessive-compulsive disorder.*

Generalized anxiety disorder

Terry, a 31-year-old man, began to experience debilitating anxiety during his first year as a hospital doctor. The 36-hour on-call periods were gruelling, and he became concerned that he and other new doctors were making too many errors and oversights. He worried incessantly for a year and finally resigned his position. However, he continued to be plagued with anxiety about making mistakes – self-doubt that extended to his personal relationships. When he eventually sought treatment, he described himself as 'worthless' and unable to control his debilitating anxiety, and he complained of headaches and constant fatigue (Vitkus, 1996).

GENERALIZED ANXIETY DISORDER (GAD) A disorder characterized by chronic excessive worry accompanied by three or more of the following symptoms: restlessness, fatigue, concentration problems, irritability, muscle tension and sleep disturbance.

Terry's symptoms are typical of generalized anxiety disorder – called *generalized* because the unrelenting worries are not focused on any particular threat; they are, in fact, often exaggerated and irrational. In people suffering from generalized anxiety disorder (GAD), *chronic excessive worry is accompanied by three or more of the following symptoms: restlessness, fatigue, concentration problems, irritability, muscle tension and sleep disturbance.* The uncontrollable worrying produces a sense of loss of control that can so erode self-confidence that simple decisions seem fraught with dire consequences. For example, Terry needed to buy a new suit for a special occasion but began shaking and sweating when he approached a clothes shop because he was afraid of choosing the 'wrong' suit. He became so anxious that he could not even enter the shop.

GAD develops in about 1 in 50 people at some stage in life but usually first appears in the twenties and accounts for about 10% of all mental disorders seen in primary care in Europe (Lieb et al., 2005). GAD occurs more frequently in lower socioeconomic groups than in middle- and upper-income groups (Blazer et al., 1991), and is approximately twice as common in women as in men (Eaton et al., 1994). Research suggests that biological and psychological factors contribute to the risk of GAD. Family studies indicate a mild-to-modest level of heritability (Kendler et al., 1992; Mackinnon and Foley, 1996; Plomin et al., 1997). Although identical twin studies of GAD are rare, some evidence suggests that compared with fraternal twins, identical twins have modestly higher *concordance rates* (the percentage of pairs that share the characteristic) (Hettema et al., 2001). Moreover, teasing out environmental versus personality influences on concordance rates is quite difficult.

Some patients with GAD respond to certain prescription drugs, which suggests that neurotransmitter imbalances may play a role in the disorder. The precise nature of this imbalance is not clear, but *benzodiazepines* – a class of sedative drugs that appear to stimulate the neurotransmitter gamma-aminobutyric acid (GABA) – can sometimes reduce the symptoms of GAD. However, other drugs that do not directly affect GABA levels, for example antidepressants such as Prozac, can also be helpful in the treatment of GAD (Gobert et al., 1999; Michelson et al., 1999; Roy-Byrne and Cowley, 1998). To complicate matters, these different prescription drugs do not help all patients and, in some cases, can produce serious side effects and dependency.

Psychological explanations focus on anxiety-provoking situations in explaining high levels of GAD. The condition is especially prevalent among people who have low incomes, live in large cities, or are trapped in environments rendered unpredictable by political and economic strife. The relatively high rates of GAD among women may also be related to stress because women are more likely than men to live in poverty, experience discrimination, or be subjected to sexual or physical abuse (Koss, 1990; Strickland, 1991). Research shows that unpredictable traumatic experiences in childhood increase the risk of developing GAD, and this evidence also supports the idea that stressful experiences play a role (Torgensen, 1983). Moreover, major life changes (new job, new baby, personal loss, physical illness and so on) often immediately precede the development of GAD (Blazer et al., 1987). Still, many people who might be expected to develop GAD don't, supporting the diathesis-stress notion that personal vulnerability must also be a key factor in this disorder.

Phobic disorders

Unlike the generalized anxiety of GAD, anxiety in a phobic disorder is more specific. The ICD-10 describes phobic disorders *as a group of disorders in which anxiety is evoked only, or predominantly, in certain well-defined situations that are not currently dangerous.* As a result, these situations are characteristically avoided or endured with dread. The patient's concern may be focused on individual symptoms like palpitations or feeling faint and is often associated with secondary fears of dying, losing control or going mad. An individual with a phobic disorder recognizes that the fear is irrational but cannot prevent it from interfering with everyday functioning. Consider Mary, a 47-year-old mother of three, who sought treatment for *claustrophobia* – an intense fear of enclosed spaces. She traced her fear to childhood, when her older siblings would scare her by locking her in cupboards and confining her under blankets. Her own children grown, she wanted to find a job but could not because of a terror of lifts and other confined places that, she felt, shackled her to her home (Carson et al., 2000). Many people feel anxious in enclosed spaces, but Mary's fears were abnormal and dysfunctional because they were wildly disproportional to any actual risk and they imposed unwanted restrictions on her life.

PHOBIC DISORDERS Disorders in which anxiety is evoked only, or predominantly, in certain well-defined situations that are not currently dangerous.

SPECIFIC PHOBIA An irrational fear restricted to highly specific situations.

According to the ICD-10, a specific phobia is *an irrational fear restricted to highly specific situations, such as proximity to particular animals, heights, thunder, darkness, flying, closed spaces, urinating or defecating in public toilets, eating certain foods, dentistry, or the sight of blood or injury.* Specific phobias tend to fall into five categories:

1 animals, for example dogs, cats, rats, snakes, spiders
2 natural environments, for example heights, darkness, water, storms
3 situations, for example bridges, lifts, tunnels, enclosed places
4 blood, injections and injury
5 other phobias, including illness and death.

PRESS ASSOCIATION IMAGES

No fear of heights here. A construction worker relaxes on a steel beam 259 m above ground during the 1932 construction of the Art Deco RCA Building (now the GE Building) of the Rockefeller Center in Manhattan, New York.

Most people expect many more categories because they've heard some of the fanciful Greek or Latin terms invented for specific phobias. One website (www.phobialist.com) lists phobias that include, among others, 'kathisophobia' (a fear of sitting down),

SOCIAL PHOBIA An irrational fear of scrutiny by other people leading to avoidance of social situations.

'homichlophobia' (fear of fog) and 'ephebiphobia' (fear of teenagers). The terms sound technical enough to be included in diagnostic manuals, but you won't find them there. These curious pseudomedical terms obscure the fact that specific phobias share common symptoms and are merely aimed at different objects. Approximately 11% of people in the US will develop a specific phobia during their lives and, for reasons unknown, the risk seems to be increasing in younger generations (Magee et al., 1996). With few exceptions, for example fear of heights, specific phobias are much more common among women than men, with a ratio of about four to one (Kessler et al., 1994, 1996).

Don't look down!

A *Los Angeles Times* story in 1992 on fear of heights featured an interview with the psychotherapist who heads the Anxiety Disorders Association. He reported that one of his patients could cross the 60-m high Chesapeake Bay Bridge in Maryland only if his wife drove the car and locked him in the boot.

Social phobia is defined in the ICD-10 as a disorder that involves *an irrational fear of scrutiny by other people leading to avoidance of social situations.* More pervasive social phobias are usually associated with low self-esteem and fear of criticism. Social phobia can be restricted to situations such as public speaking, eating in public, or urinating in a public lavatory, or generalized to a variety of social situations that involve being observed or interacting with unfamiliar people. Individuals with social phobia try to avoid situations where unfamiliar people might evaluate them, and they experience intense anxiety and distress when public exposure is unavoidable. Social phobia can develop in childhood, but it typically emerges between early adolescence and the age of 25 (Schneier et al., 1992). In Europe, the estimated lifetime prevalence of social phobia is around 6% (Fehm et al., 2005), although twice as many people experience this disorder in the US – about 11% of men and 15% of women qualify for diagnosis at some time in their lives (Kessler et al., 1994). Even higher rates are found among people who are undereducated, have low incomes, or both (Magee et al., 1996).

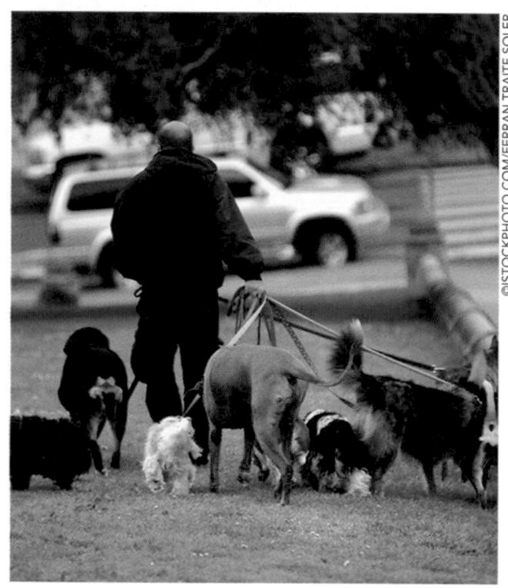

To someone with a phobia of dogs, there are no best friends in this park.

Why are phobias so common? The high rates of specific and social phobias suggest a predisposition to be fearful of certain objects and situations. Indeed, most of the situations and objects of people's phobias could pose a real threat, for example falling from a high place or being attacked by a vicious dog or poisonous snake or spider. Social situations have their own dangers. A roomful of strangers may not attack or bite, but they could form impressions that affect your prospects for friends, jobs or marriage.

PREPAREDNESS THEORY OF PHOBIAS People are instinctively predisposed towards certain fears.

TRYPOPHOBIA The fear of holes.

Observations such as these are the basis for the preparedness theory of phobias – *people are instinctively predisposed towards certain fears* (see hot science box). The preparedness theory, proposed by Martin Seligman (1971), is supported by research showing that humans and monkeys can quickly be conditioned to have a fear response for stimuli such as snakes and spiders but not for neutral stimuli such as flowers or toy rabbits (Cook and Mineka, 1989; Öhman et al., 1985). Similarly, research on facial expressions has shown that people are more easily conditioned to fear angry facial expressions than other types of expressions (Öhman and Dimberg, 1978; Öhman et al., 1985). Phobias are particularly likely to form for objects that evolution has predisposed us to avoid. This idea is also supported by studies of the heritability of phobias. Family studies of specific phobias indicate greater concordance rates for identical than fraternal twins (Kendler et al., 1992, 2002; O'Laughlin and Malle, 2002). Other studies have found that over 30% of first-degree relatives (parents, siblings or children) of patients with specific phobias also have a phobia (Fryer et al., 1990).

hot science

Fear of holes

One the authors of this textbook was alarmed to discover that his teenage daughter had a phobia of holes. She felt nauseous and fearful of images as innocuous as honeycombs, Swiss cheese and even holes in aerated chocolate. This is called trypophobia – *the fear of holes.* Vision researchers at the University of Essex have recently investigated this peculiar phobia and discovered that not only is it quite common, but they have also provided an account of why we may have a natural aversion to images of holes, based on their visual properties associated with noxious stimuli (Cole and Wilkins, 2013).

They began by establishing how common an aversion to holes was by asking 286 adults (91 male and 195 female; age range approximately 18–55 years) to look at a picture of the seed head of the lotus flower. Ten males (11%) and 36 females (18%) reported that the image made them uncomfortable or was repulsive to look at. Another group of individuals who did not report overt trypophobia still regarded images of holes as discomforting.

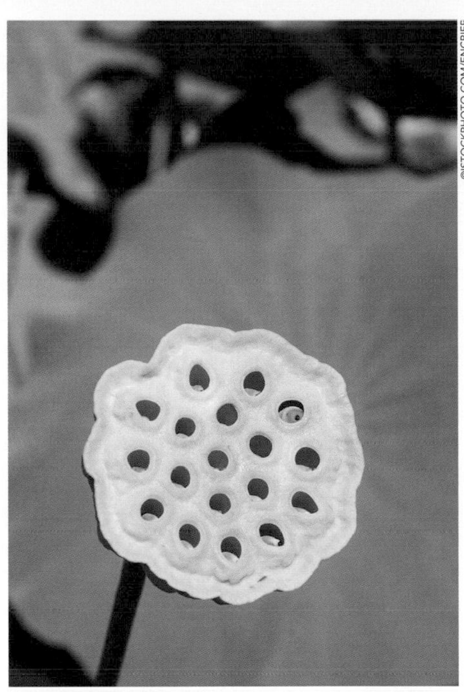

For many years, researchers have been aware of aversion and discomfort caused by the viewing of certain geometric patterns, which are attributable to their spectral properties (Wilkins et al., 1984). Spectral properties tell you about the structure of an image in terms of where the power is based on contrast and spatial frequency (SF). Contrast is a measure of the difference between areas of brightness and darkness in an image and all images are made up of different spatial frequencies. An image with many low spatial frequencies is typically bland with little detail (such as clouds), whereas an image with much high spatial frequency is detailed (see above).

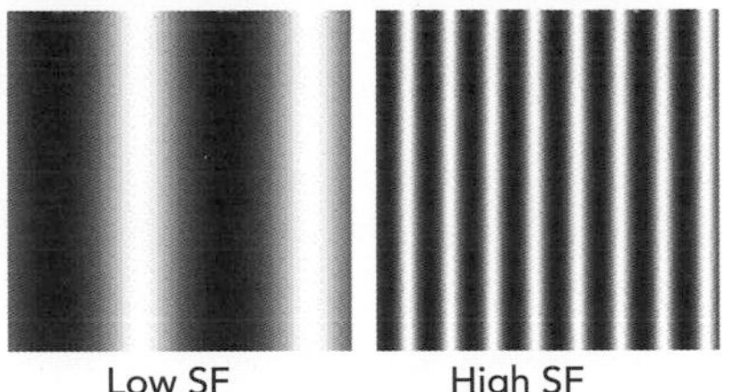

When they ran natural images taken from www.trypophobia.com through a spectral analysis, which gives measures of power based on contrast and spatial frequency, they discovered that the trypophobic images consistently had greater energy at midrange and high spatial frequencies.

The researchers then ran a series of images of poisonous animals, including the blue-ringed octopus, the box jellyfish, the Brazilian wandering spider, the deathstalker scorpion, the inland taipan snake, the king cobra snake, the marbled cone snail, the poison dart frog, the puffer fish and the stonefish. Not only was the spectral power analysis consistent between these diverse poisonous animals but the overall pattern was similar to the trypophobic images. In other words, images of holes have the same visual properties as images of poisonous creatures, indicating that a Darwinian survival mechanism, consistent with the preparedness theory of phobias, may be at the root of this odd phobia.

Temperament (see Chapter 12) may also play a role in vulnerability to phobias. Researchers have found that infants who display excessive shyness and inhibition are at an increased risk for developing a phobic behaviour later in life (Hirschfeld et al., 1992; Morris, 2001; Stein et al., 2001). Neurobiological factors may also play a role. Abnormalities in the neurotransmitters serotonin and dopamine are more common in individuals who report phobias than they are among people who don't (Stein et al., 1998). In addition, individuals with phobias sometimes show abnormally high levels of activity in the amygdala, an area of the brain linked with the development of emotional associations (discussed in Chapter 10; see Hirschfeld et al., 1992; LeDoux, 1998; Morris, 2001; Ninan, 1999; Stein et al., 2001).

This evidence does not rule out the influence of environments and upbringing on the development of phobic overreactions. As learning theorist John Watson (1924b) demonstrated many years ago, phobias can be classically conditioned (see Chapter 6 discussion of Little Albert and the white rat). Similarly, the discomfort of a dog bite could create a conditioned association between dogs and pain, resulting in an irrational fear of all dogs. The idea that phobias are learned from emotional experiences with feared objects, however, is not a complete explanation for their occurrence. Most studies find that people with phobias are no more likely than people without phobias to recall personal experiences with the feared object that could have provided the basis for classical conditioning (Craske, 1999; McNally and Steketee, 1985). Moreover, many people are bitten by dogs, but few develop phobias. Despite its shortcomings, however, the idea that this is a matter of learning provides a useful model for therapy (see Chapter 17).

Panic disorder

If you suddenly found yourself in danger of death, a wave of panic might wash over you. People who suffer panic attacks are frequently overwhelmed by such intense fears and powerful physical symptoms of anxiety – in the absence of actual danger.

Mindy, a 25-year-old art director, had been having panic attacks with increasing frequency, often two or three times a day, when she finally sought help at a clinic. The attacks began with a sudden wave of 'horrible fear' that seemed to come out of nowhere, often accompanied by trembling, nausea and a tightening of the chest. The attacks began when she was at secondary school and had continued intermittently ever since. During an episode, Mindy feared that she would do something crazy (Spitzer et al., 1994).

PANIC DISORDER A disorder characterized by recurrent attacks of severe anxiety (panic), which are not restricted to any particular situation or set of circumstances and are therefore unpredictable.

Mindy's condition, called panic disorder, is defined in the ICD-10 as *a disorder characterized by recurrent attacks of severe anxiety (panic), which are not restricted to any particular situation or set of circumstances and are therefore unpredictable.* The acute symptoms of a panic attack typically last only a few minutes and include shortness of breath, heart palpitations, sweating, dizziness, depersonalization (a feeling of being detached from one's body) or derealization (a feeling that the external world is strange or unreal), and a fear that one is going crazy or about to die. Unsurprisingly, panic attacks often send people rushing to hospitals or their doctors' surgeries for what they believe is either an acute cardiac, respiratory or neurological episode (Hirschfeld, 1996). Unfortunately, because many of the symptoms mimic various medical disorders, a correct diagnosis may take years in spite of costly medical tests that produce normal results (Hirschfeld, 1996; Katon, 1994).

AGORAPHOBIA An extreme fear of leaving home, entering shops, crowds and public places, or travelling alone on trains, buses or planes.

A common complication of panic disorder is agoraphobia, defined by the ICD-10 as *an extreme fear of leaving home, entering shops, crowds and public places, or travelling alone on trains, buses or planes.* Many individuals with agoraphobia are not frightened of public places in themselves; instead, they are afraid of having a panic attack in a public place or around strangers who might view them with disdain or fail to help them. In severe cases, people who have panic disorder with agoraphobia are unable to leave home, sometimes for years on end.

In panic disorder with agoraphobia, the fear of having a panic attack in public may prevent the person from going outside.

Approximately 8–12% of the general population report having an occasional panic attack, typically during a period of intense stress (Norton et al., 1985; Salge et al., 1988; Telch et al., 1989). An occasional episode is not sufficient for a diagnosis of panic disorder, the individual also has to experience significant dread and anxiety about having another attack. When this criterion is applied, approximately 3.5% of people in the US will have diagnosable panic disorder sometime in their lives, and of those, about three out of seven will also develop agoraphobia (Kessler et al., 1994). In a 12-month period, the incidence of panic disorder across 14 European countries was consistent at around 1–2% of the general public, with the first onset during adolescence or early adulthood (Goodwin et al., 2005). Panic disorder is especially prevalent among women, who are twice as likely to be diagnosed with it as men (Goodwin et al., 2005; Weissman et al., 1997). Family studies suggest a modest hereditary component to panic disorder. If one identical twin has the disorder, the likelihood of the other twin having it is about 30% (Crowe, 1990; Kendler et al., 1995; Torgensen, 1983).

In an effort to understand the role that physiological arousal plays in panic attacks, researchers have compared the responses of experimental participants with and without panic disorder to *sodium lactate*, a chemical that produces rapid, shallow breathing and heart palpitations. Those with panic disorder were found to be acutely sensitive to the drug; a few minutes after administration, 60–90% experienced a panic attack. Participants without the disorder rarely responded to the drug with a panic attack (Liebowitz et al., 1985a, 1985b).

The difference in responses to the chemical may be due to differing interpretations of physiological signs of anxiety, that is, people who experience panic attacks may be hypersensitive to physiological signs of anxiety, which they interpret as having disastrous consequences for their wellbeing. Supporting this cognitive explanation is research showing that people who are high in anxiety sensitivity, that is, they believe that bodily arousal and other symptoms of anxiety can have dire consequences, have an elevated risk of experiencing panic attacks (Schmidt et al., 1997; Telch et al., 1989). Thus, panic attacks may be traceable to the fear of fear itself.

Obsessive-compulsive disorder

Although anxiety plays a role in obsessive-compulsive disorder, the primary symptoms are unwanted, recurrent thoughts and actions. You've probably had the experience of having something – say, a silly song – pop into your head and 'play' over and over, or you've started to do something pointless – like counting ceiling tiles during a boring lecture – and found it hard to stop. In some people, such repetitive thoughts and actions become a serious problem.

Karen, a 34-year-old with four children, sought treatment after several months of experiencing intrusive, repetitive thoughts in which she imagined that one or more of her children was having a serious accident. In addition, an extensive series of protective counting rituals hampered her daily routine. For example, when food shopping, Karen had the feeling that if she selected the first item (say, a box of cereal) on a shelf, something terrible would happen to her oldest child. If she selected the second item, some unknown disaster would befall her second child and so on for the four children. The children's ages were also important. The sixth item in a row, for example, was associated with her youngest child, who was six years old. Karen's preoccupation with numbers extended to other activities, most notably the pattern in which she smoked cigarettes and drank coffee. If she had one cigarette, she felt that she had to smoke at least four in a row or one of her children would be harmed in some way. If she drank one cup of coffee, she felt compelled to drink four more to protect her children from harm. She acknowledged that her counting rituals were irrational, but she found that she became extremely anxious when she tried to stop (Oltmanns et al., 1991).

According to the ICD-10, Karen's symptoms are typical of obsessive-compulsive disorder (OCD), which is *characterized by recurrent obsessional thoughts or compulsive acts designed to fend off thoughts that interfere significantly with an individual's functioning.* Obsessional thoughts are ideas, images or impulses that repeatedly enter the patient's mind in a stereotyped form. They are almost invariably distressing and the patient often tries, unsuccessfully, to resist them. They are, however, recognized as their own thoughts, even though they are involuntary and often repugnant. Compulsive acts or rituals are stereotyped behaviours that are repeated again and again. They are not inherently enjoyable, nor do they result in the completion of inherently useful tasks. Their function is to prevent some objectively unlikely event, often involving harm to or caused by the patient, which they fear might otherwise occur. Usually, this behaviour is recognized by the patient as pointless or ineffectual and repeated attempts are made to resist. Anxiety plays a role in this disorder because the obsessive thoughts typically produce anxiety, and the compulsive behaviours are performed to reduce it. It is not uncommon for people to have occasional intrusive thoughts that prompt ritualistic behaviour, for example double or triple checking that the garage door is closed or the oven is off, but the obsessions and compulsions of OCD are intense, frequent and experienced as irrational and excessive. Attempts to cope with the obsessive thoughts by trying to suppress or ignore them are of little or no benefit. In fact, thought suppression can backfire (see Chapter 8), increasing the frequency and intensity of the obsessive thoughts (Wegner, 1994b; Wenzlaff and Wegner, 2000).

Approximately 2.5% of people will develop OCD sometime in their lives, with similar rates across different cultures (Gibbs, 1996; Karno and Golding, 1991; Robins and Regier, 1991). Women tend to be more susceptible than men, but the difference is not large (Karno and Golding, 1991). The World Health Organization ranks OCD as the tenth most disabling illness of any kind, in terms of lost earnings and diminished quality of life. The most common obsessions involve contamination, aggression, death, sex, disease, orderliness and disfigurement (Jenike et al., 1986; Rachman and DeSilva, 1978). Compulsions typically take the form of cleaning, checking, repeating, ordering/arranging and counting (Antony et al., 1998). Although compulsive behaviour is

OBSESSIVE-COMPULSIVE DISORDER (OCD) A disorder characterized by recurrent obsessional thoughts or compulsive acts designed to fend off thoughts that interfere significantly with an individual's functioning.

Becks and his cans of Pepsi

OCD affects as many as 3 in 100 people – from young children to older adults – regardless of gender and social or cultural background. Famous sufferers include Charles Darwin, and more recently, David Beckham explained how the disorder affects his life: 'I have got this disorder where I have to have everything in a straight line or everything has to be in pairs. I'll put my Pepsi cans in the fridge and if there's one too many then I'll put it in another cupboard somewhere.' Maybe that's why he cancelled his lucrative advertising deal with the drinks company in 2008.

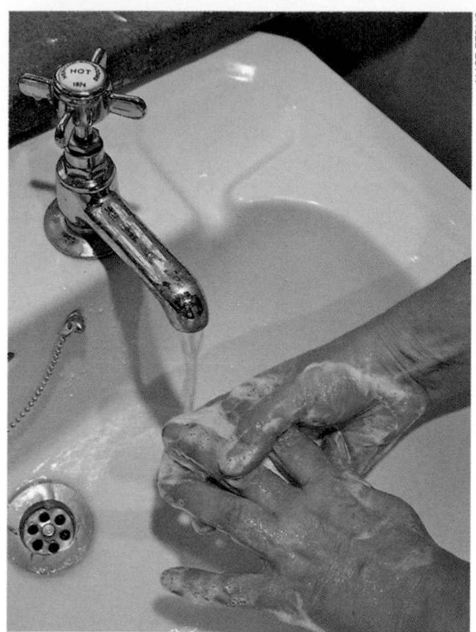
ALICE FERNS

Everyone knows that hand washing is a good idea. But the feeling that one 'must wash one's hands' can come to mind many dozens of times a day in some people with OCD, leading to compulsive washing and even damage to the skin.

always excessive, it can vary considerably in intensity and frequency. For example, fear of contamination may lead to 15 minutes of hand washing in some individuals, while others may need to spend hours with disinfectants and extremely hot water, scrubbing their hands until they bleed.

The obsessions that plague individuals with OCD typically derive from concerns that could pose a real threat (such as contamination, aggression, disease), which supports preparedness theory. After all, thinking repeatedly about whether we've left the oven on when we leave the house makes sense if we want to return to a house that is not 'well done'. The concept of preparedness places OCD in the same evolutionary context as phobias (Marks and Nesse, 1994). However, as with phobias, we need to consider other factors to explain why fears that may have served an evolutionary purpose can become so distorted and maladaptive.

Family studies indicate a moderate genetic heritability for OCD. Identical twins show a higher concordance than fraternal twins. Relatives of individuals with OCD may not have the disorder themselves, but they are at greater risk for other types of anxiety disorders than members of the general public (Billet et al., 1998). Researchers have not determined the biological mechanisms that may contribute to OCD, but some evidence implicates heightened neural activity in the *caudate nucleus* of the brain, a portion of the basal ganglia (discussed in Chapter 3) known to be involved in the initiation of intentional actions (Kronig et al., 1999). Drugs that increase the activity of the neurotransmitter serotonin in the brain can inhibit the activity of the caudate nucleus and relieve some of the symptoms of OCD (Hansen et al., 2002). However, this finding does not indicate that overactivity of the caudate nucleus is the cause of OCD. It could also be an effect of the disorder: patients with OCD often respond favourably to psychotherapy and show a corresponding reduction in activity in the caudate nucleus (Baxter et al., 1992).

Post-traumatic stress disorder

POST-TRAUMATIC STRESS DISORDER (PTSD) An anxiety disorder that can appear some weeks or months after a person lives through an experience so threatening and uncontrollable that they are left with feelings of terror and helplessness.

Post-traumatic stress disorder (PTSD) is *an anxiety disorder that can appear some weeks or months after a person lives through an experience so threatening and uncontrollable that they are left with feelings of terror and helplessness*. PTSD is characterized by recurrent reliving of the trauma as intrusive memories or flashbacks. This can also manifest as dreams or nightmares, occurring against a background of anxiety and depression, detachment from other people, unresponsiveness to surroundings, and avoidance of activities and situations reminiscent of the trauma. The psychological scars left by traumatic events are nowhere more apparent than in war. Many soldiers returning from combat have PTSD symptoms, including flashbacks of battle, exaggerated anxiety and startle reactions, and even medical conditions that do not arise from physical damage (such as paralysis or chronic fatigue). Known as 'shell shock' in the First World War and 'combat fatigue' in the Second World War, the disorder continues to appear in soldiers currently engaged in today's military conflicts.

PTSD symptoms do not quickly subside when service members come home. For example, the US Centers for Disease Control (CDC, 1988) found that even 20 years after the Vietnam War, 15% of veterans who had seen combat continued to report lingering symptoms. Florence Nightingale, the founder of modern nursing, is said to have returned to England from the Crimean War (1853–56) with chronic fatigue that continued for the rest of her life. This long-term psychological response is now recognized not only among the victims, witnesses and perpetrators of war but also among ordinary people who are traumatized by any of life's terrible events. For example, the terrorist attacks in New York, London and Barcelona not only left victims with physical injuries but many with PTSD. One study tracked PTSD symptoms in New York City residents after 11 September 2001 (Galea et al., 2002) (see **FIGURE 16.3**). One to two months after the 9/11 attacks, 7.5% of those interviewed reported multiple PTSD symptoms, such as recurrent intrusive memories or distressing dreams of the event, efforts to suppress thoughts of the event, and unusual nervousness or difficulty falling asleep. Among people in the study who lived in the immediate vicinity of the towers, 20% were diagnosed with PTSD.

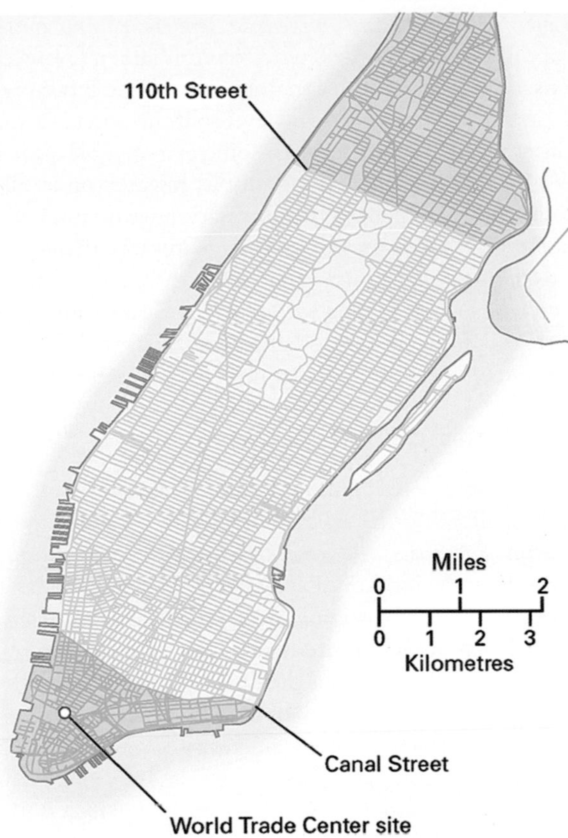

FIGURE **16.3 Manhattan** PTSD symptoms were more pronounced in New York City respondents who were near the twin towers of the World Trade Center at the time of the 11 September attacks. Participants were sampled from the area between 110th Street and Canal Street (yellow) and from the south of Canal Street (orange) – the area nearest the towers.

In summary, people with anxiety disorders have irrational worries and fears that undermine their ability to function normally. The anxiety may be chronic, as in generalized anxiety disorder (GAD), tied to an object or situation, as in the phobic disorders (specific phobia and social phobia), or the result of some traumatic experience, as in post-traumatic stress disorder (PTSD). Phobias typically involve stimuli that humans are evolutionarily prepared to find threatening. People who suffer from panic disorder experience a sudden and intense attack of anxiety that is terrifying and can lead them to become agoraphobic and housebound for fear of public humiliation. People with obsessive-compulsive disorder (OCD) experience recurring, anxiety-provoking thoughts that compel them to engage in ritualistic, irrational behaviour. In general, the anxiety disorders show a moderate level of heritability but appear to be best explained by a combination of biological, psychological and environmental factors.

Dissociative disorders: going to pieces

Can the human mind come apart? Could a person forget who she is one day but remember the next? Mary, a 35-year-old social worker being treated with hypnosis for chronic pain in her forearm, mentioned to her doctor that she often found her car low on fuel in the morning despite her having filled it with petrol the day before. Overnight, the odometer would gain 30–60 km, although she had no memory of driving the car.

During one hypnotic session, Mary suddenly blurted out in a strange voice: 'It's about time you knew about me.' In the new voice, she identified herself as 'Marian' and described the drives she took at night, which were retreats to the nearby hills to 'work out problems'. Mary knew nothing of 'Marian' and her night-time adventures. Marian was as abrupt and hostile as Mary was compliant and caring. In the course of therapy, six other personalities emerged (including one who claimed to be a six-year-old child), and considerable tension and disagreement developed among the personalities. On one occasion, one of the personalities threatened suicide and forbade the therapist from discussing it with the other personalities, noting that it would be 'a violation of doctor-patient confidentiality' (Spitzer et al., 1994).

Mary suffers from a type of dissociative disorder, defined by the ICD-10 as *a condition in which there is a partial or complete loss of the normal integration between memories*

DISSOCIATIVE DISORDER A condition in which there is a partial or complete loss of the normal integration between memories of the past, awareness of identity and immediate sensations, and control of bodily movements that can vary in length up to many years.

of the past, awareness of identity and immediate sensations, and control of bodily movements. All types of dissociative disorders tend to remit after a few weeks or months, particularly if their onset is associated with a traumatic life event, but more chronic disorders, particularly paralyses and anaesthesias, may develop if the onset is associated with insoluble problems or interpersonal difficulties. To some extent, a bit of dissociation, or 'splitting', of cognitive processes is normal. For example, research on implicit memory shows that we often retain and are influenced by information we do not consciously remember (discussed in Chapter 5). Moreover, we can engage in more than one activity or mental process while maintaining only dim awareness of the perceptions and decisions that guide other behaviours (such as talking while driving a car). Our ordinary continuity of memory and awareness of our personal identity contrasts with Mary's profound cognitive fragmentation and blindness to her own mental processes and states.

Dissociative identity disorder

DISSOCIATIVE IDENTITY DISORDER (DID) The presence within an individual of two or more distinct identities that at different times take control of the individual's behaviour.

Dissociative identity disorder (DID), more familiarly known by the ICD-10 classification of multiple personality disorder, is characterized by *the presence within an individual of two or more distinct identities that at different times take control of the individual's behaviour.* The most dramatic form of dissociative disorder, DID has attracted considerable popular attention. When the original personality, or *host personality*, is dominant, the individual is often unaware of the alternate personalities, or *alters* (as in Mary's case). However, the alters typically know about the host personality and about each other. The number of distinct identities can range considerably, with some cases numbering more than 100. Sometimes, alters share certain characteristics, and sometimes they are dissimilar, assuming different vocal patterns, dialects, ages, morals and even gender identities. Multiple personality disorder implies that more than one person is in 'residence', but the disorder is better conceptualized as involving multiple patterns of thought and behaviour, each of which is associated with a different identity.

Prior to 1970, DID was considered rare, with only about 100 cases reported in the professional literature worldwide. However, since that time, the number of reported cases has grown enormously. Recent estimates are that between 0.5% and 1% of the general population suffer from the disorder, with a female to male prevalence of about 9 to 1 (Maldonado and Butler, 1998). Most patients are diagnosed when they are in their twenties or thirties, although the actual age of onset is probably during childhood (Maldonado and Butler, 1998; Putnam et al., 1986).

The strange transition of DID – from a rare disorder to a minor epidemic – has raised concerns that the disorder is a matter of faking or fashion (Spanos, 1994). The most common explanation targets psychotherapists who, although often well meaning, are said to have created the disorder in patients who are vulnerable to their suggestive procedures. Accounts of how therapists treat DID, often using hypnosis, have revealed some cajoling and coaxing of clients into reporting evidence of alternate personalities (Acocella, 1999).

Most patients with DID report a history of severe childhood abuse and trauma (Coons, 1994; Putnam et al., 1986), and that evidence supports a popular explanation rooted in psychodynamic theory. From this viewpoint, the helpless child, confronted with intolerable abuse and trauma, responds with the primitive psychological defence of splitting or dissociating to escape the pain and horror. Because the child cannot escape the situation, they essentially escape from themselves. Once the dissociation takes hold, it can set in motion a psychological process that may lead to the development of multiple identities (Kluft, 1984, 1991).

Critics of the psychodynamic explanation of DID have raised the possibility that individuals who exhibit trauma and DID may be responding to their therapists' expectations that the two are linked (Humphreys and Dennett, 1989; Kluft, 1991; Lalonde et al., 2001). Moreover, in most cases, the determination of childhood trauma is based on self-reported memories, which can be susceptible to errors and distortions (Dorahy, 2001). Curiously, early abuse and trauma are especially prevalent in low-income households, while cases of multiple personality occur almost exclusively among people of middle income (Acocella, 1999). In short, dissociative identity disorder is poorly understood and deep questions exist about what it is, how it arises, and how it can be treated.

Dissociative amnesia and dissociative fugue

Amnesia, *The Bourne Identity*, *Eternal Sunshine of the Spotless Mind*, *50 First Dates*, *Memento* and *The Man Without a Past* are all well-known films that reveal Hollywood's fascination with forms of dissociative disorder involving memory. We described peculiar examples of memory and identity loss in Chapter 5 but here we consider them again as a separate category within dissociative disorders. The memory oddities invented for film don't always correspond to the real disorders, dissociative amnesia and dissociative fugue. These conditions cannot result from normal forgetting or brain injury, drugs or another mental disorder, for example PTSD. Rather:

- Dissociative amnesia is *the sudden loss of memory for significant personal information.* The memory loss is typically for a traumatic specific event or period of time but can involve extended periods (months or years) of a person's life (Kihlstrom, 2005).
- Dissociative fugue involves *the sudden loss of memory for one's personal history, accompanied by an abrupt departure from home and the assumption of a new identity.* The fugue state is usually associated with stressful life circumstances and can be brief or lengthy.

DISSOCIATIVE AMNESIA The sudden loss of memory for significant personal information.

DISSOCIATIVE FUGUE The sudden loss of memory for one's personal history, accompanied by an abrupt departure from home and the assumption of a new identity.

'Burt', a 42-year-old cook in a small town, came to the attention of police when he got into a heated altercation with another man where he worked. When the police took 'Burt' to the hospital, they discovered that he had no identification documents and was clueless about his past. While he was in the hospital, the police matched his description to that of Gene Saunders, a resident of a city 320 km away, who had disappeared a month earlier. When Gene's wife came to identify him, he denied knowing her and his real identity. Before he disappeared, Gene Saunders had been experiencing considerable difficulties at home and at work and had become withdrawn and irritable. Two days before he left, he had a violent argument with his 18-year-old son, who accused him of being a failure (Spitzer et al., 1994).

Dissociative amnesia and dissociative fugue usually emerge in adulthood and rarely occur after the age of 50 (Sackeim and Devanand, 1991). Dissociative fugue states usually end rather abruptly, and victims typically recover their memories and personal identities. Dissociative amnesia may also be temporary. People have lost significant personal memories and then recovered them later (Brenneis, 2000; Schooler et al., 1997).

In summary, the dissociative disorders involve severely disjointed and fragmented cognitive processes reflected in significant disruptions in memory, awareness or personality. People with dissociative identity disorder (DID) shift between two or more identities that are distinctive from each other in terms of personal memories, behavioural characteristics and attitudes. Previously rare, reported cases of DID have been increasing as the disorder has received more widespread media attention, leading some researchers to believe that it may be overdiagnosed or even created in therapy. Psychodynamic theorists speculate that DID arises when a young person uses psychological detachment as a means of coping with trauma, which eventually leads to a splitting or dissociation among normally integrated psychological functions. Dissociative amnesia and dissociative fugue involve significant memory loss that is too extensive to be the result of normal forgetting and cannot be attributed to brain injury, drugs or another mental disorder. Both disorders are believed to be associated with life stresses. In addition to loss of one's personal history, dissociative fugue is accompanied by an abrupt departure from home and the assumption of a new identity.

Mood disorders: at the mercy of emotions

You're probably in a mood right now. Maybe you're happy that it's almost time to get a snack or saddened by something you heard on the radio, or you may feel good or bad without having a clue why. As you learned in Chapter 10, moods are relatively long-lasting, nonspecific emotional states, and *nonspecific* means we often may have no idea what has caused a mood. Changing moods lend variety to our experiences, like different coloured lights shining on the stage as we play out our lives. However, for people like Virginia Woolf and others with mood disorders, moods can become so intense that they are pulled or pushed into life-threatening actions. Mood disorders, *mental disorders that have mood disturbance as their predominant feature*, take two main forms: depression and bipolar disorder.

MOOD DISORDERS Mental disorders that have mood disturbance as their predominant feature.

Depressive disorders

Depression is much more than sadness. The experience of R. A., a 58-year-old man who visited his doctor for treatment of his diabetes, is fairly typical. During the visit, he mentioned difficulties falling asleep and staying asleep that left him chronically fatigued. He complained that over the past six months, he'd stopped exercising and gained 5 kg and had lost interest in socializing. Although nothing he normally enjoyed, including sexual activity, could give him pleasure anymore, he denied feeling particularly sad but did say that he had trouble concentrating and was forgetful, irritable, impatient and frustrated. Although he continued to work, he felt that whatever was happening to him was interfering with his life (Lustman et al., 2002).

Most people occasionally feel depressed, pessimistic and unmotivated. As comic Emo Philips remarked: 'Some mornings, it's just not worth gnawing through the leather straps.' But these periods are relatively short-lived and mild compared with R. A.'s sense of hopelessness and weariness and his lack of normal pleasures. Depression is also different from the sorrow and grief that accompany the death of a loved one – a normal, possibly adaptive response to a tragic situation (Bowlby, 1980). Instead, depressive mood disorders are dysfunctional, chronic and fall outside the range of socially or culturally expected responses.

MAJOR DEPRESSIVE DISORDER A disorder characterized by a severely depressed mood that lasts two weeks or more and is accompanied by feelings of worthlessness and lack of pleasure, lethargy, and sleep and appetite disturbances.

DYSTHYMIA A disorder that involves the same symptoms as depression only less severe, but the symptoms last longer, persisting for at least two years.

RECURRENT DEPRESSIVE DISORDER A moderately depressed mood that persists for at least two years and is punctuated by periods of major depression.

SEASONAL AFFECTIVE DISORDER (SAD) Depression that involves recurrent depressive episodes in a seasonal pattern.

Major depressive disorder, also known as unipolar depression, is characterized by *a severely depressed mood that lasts two weeks or more and is accompanied by feelings of worthlessness and lack of pleasure, lethargy, and sleep and appetite disturbances.* The bodily symptoms in major depression may seem contrary – sleeping too much or sleeping very little, for example, or overeating or failing to eat. Great sadness or despair is not always present, although intrusive thoughts of failure or ending one's life are not uncommon. In a related condition called dysthymia, *the same cognitive and bodily problems as in depression are present, but they are less severe and last longer, persisting for at least two years.* When both types co-occur, the resulting condition is called recurrent depressive disorder and is defined as *a moderately depressed mood that persists for at least two years and is punctuated by periods of major depression.* In the ICD-10, recurrent depressive disorder is further subdivided into categories with and without psychotic episodes and mild, moderate or severe depressive episodes.

Some people experience *recurrent depressive episodes in a seasonal pattern*, commonly known as seasonal affective disorder (SAD). In most cases, the episodes begin in autumn or winter and remit in spring, a pattern that is due to reduced levels of light over the colder seasons (Tam et al., 1995). Recurrent summer depressive episodes are not unknown. A winter-related pattern of depression appears to be more prevalent in higher latitudes. Researchers studying polar workers have identified a *winter-over syndrome,* which includes insomnia, depressed mood, irritability, reduced physical and cognitive tempo, social withdrawal, and fugue-like states (the 20-ft stare in the 10-ft room, referred to as the *Antarctic stare*), as well as psychosomatic symptoms (Roberts, 2011).

©ISTOCKPHOTO.COM/THOMAS KNAUER

A time for seasonal affective disorder. When the sun goes away, sadness can play.

On average, major depression lasts about six months (Beck, 1967; Robins and Guze, 1972). However, without treatment, approximately 80% of individuals will experience at least one recurrence of the disorder (Judd, 1997; Mueller et al., 1999). Compared with people who have a single episode, individuals with recurrent depression have more severe symptoms, higher rates of depression in their families, more suicide attempts, and higher rates of divorce (Merikangas et al., 1994). The median lifetime risk for depression of about 16% seems to be increasing in younger generations (Lavori et al., 1987; Wittchen et al., 1994). For example, a large international study found evidence of a substantial global increase in the risk for depression across the past century (Cross-National Collaborative Research Group, 1992).

This situation is especially dire for women who are diagnosed with depression at a rate twice that of men (Kessler et al., 1996; Lavori et al., 1987; Robins et al., 1984; Wittchen et al., 1994). Socioeconomic standing has been invoked as an explanation for women's heightened risk. Their incomes are lower than those of men, and poverty could cause depression. Sex differences in hormones are another possibility: oestrogen, androgen and progesterone influence depression; and some women experience *postnatal depression* (depression following childbirth) due to changing hormone balances. Susan Nolen-Hoeksema (1987, 1990) has examined the evidence and argues that these causes are not sufficient to explain the size of the sex difference in depression. She believes that the culprit is response style – women's tendency to accept, disclose and ruminate on their negative emotions in contrast with men's tendency to deny negative emotions and engage in self-distraction such as work and drinking alcohol. Perhaps women's higher rates reflect a willingness to face their depression. The search for causes of this disorder in women and men continues and extends to biological and psychological factors.

The worst way to have the best time of your life

Working in the Antarctic is one of the harshest environments on the planet; indeed, it has been compared to the sorts of challenges that might face humans who populate new worlds. However, rates of severe psychiatric disorder are relatively low at around 5%, mainly because individuals are intensely screened for the appropriate personalities, who tend to be introverts or 'professional isolates' (Natani and Shurley, 1974). Working in the Antarctic can also induce profound changes in one's outlook, spirituality and appreciation of nature, especially after successfully overcoming adversity, which produces a *salutogenic effect* – a positive reaction that emerges from managing stress (Antonovsky, 1979). This may explain why many consider the experience life changing and want to return. For some, it is the worst way to have the best time of your life.

Biological factors

Heritability estimates for major depression typically range from 33% to 45% (Plomin et al., 1997; Wallace et al., 2002). However, as with most types of mental disorders, heritability rates vary as a function of severity. For example, a relatively large study of twins found that the concordance rates for severe major depression (defined as three or more episodes) were quite high, with a rate of 59% for identical twins and 30% for fraternal twins (Bertelsen et al., 1977). In contrast, concordance rates for less severe major depression (defined as fewer than three episodes) fell to 33% for identical twins and 14% for fraternal twins. Heritability rates for dysthymia are low and inconsistent (Katz and McGuffin, 1993; Plomin et al., 1997; Roth and Mountjoy, 1997).

Beginning in the 1950s, researchers noticed that drugs that increased levels of the neurotransmitters noradrenaline and serotonin could sometimes reduce depression. This observation suggested that depression might be caused by an absolute or relative depletion of these neurotransmitters and sparked a revolution in the pharmacological treatment of depression (Schildkraut, 1965), leading to the development and widespread use of such popular prescription drugs as Prozac (see Chapter 17). Further research has shown, however, that reduced levels of these neurotransmitters cannot be the whole story. For example, some studies have found *increases* in noradrenaline activity among depressed patients (Thase and Howland, 1995). Moreover, although the antidepressant medications change neurochemical transmission in less than a day, they typically take at least two weeks to relieve depressive symptoms. A biochemical model of depression has yet to be developed that accounts for all the evidence.

Depression may involve diminished activity in the left prefrontal cortex and increased activity in the right prefrontal cortex (see **FIGURE 16.4**), areas of the brain involved in the processing of emotions (Davidson, 2004; Davidson et al., 2002). For example, stroke patients with damage to the left prefrontal cortex often experience higher levels of depression than would otherwise be expected (Robinson and Downhill, 1995). Severely depressed individuals who do not have brain damage often show diminished activity in the anterior (prefrontal) regions of the cerebral hemispheres, especially on the left side (Thase and Howland, 1995). These abnormal activity patterns may be effects of the mood disturbance, or they may cause people to be more susceptible to depression. The possibility that activity in this brain area does cause depression is supported by the findings that similar types of brain abnormalities occur in patients in remission (Henriques and Davidson, 1990) and in children who are at risk for depression (Tomarken et al., 1994).

Another syndrome related to winter-over syndrome associated with living for extended periods in polar climates is *polar T3 syndrome* – a condition where individuals suffer depressive symptomatology and disruption of cognitive performance related to polar living. This may result from altered thyroid hormone function and a significant reduction in serum total triiodothyronine (T3) (Palinkas et al., 1997). Clear or 'frank' levels of hypothyroidism are associated with major mental disorders including severe depression and mania. However, individuals with subclinical hypothyroidism, where physical symptoms are not obvious, often report depression, anxiety and inability to concentrate that respond well to hormone replacement (Monzanil et al., 1993).

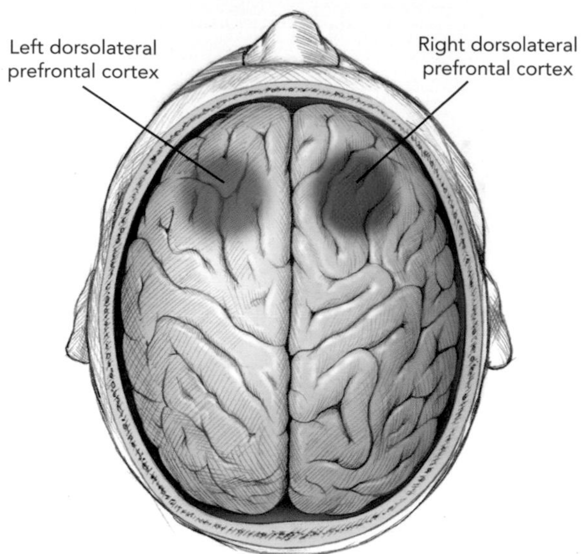

FIGURE **16.4 Brain and depression** Reduced activation in the left dorsolateral prefrontal cortex (blue) and increased activation in the right dorsolateral prefrontal cortex (red) have been found to be linked with depression in several studies.

Psychological factors

If optimists see the world through rose-tinted glasses, depressed individuals seem to view it through lenses that are smudged dark grey. Their negative cognitive style is remarkably consistent and, some argue, begins in childhood with experiences that foster pessimism and low self-worth (Blatt and Homann, 1992; Cutler and Nolen-Hoeksema, 1991; Gibb et al., 2001). Aaron Beck (1967), one of the first theorists to emphasize the role of thought in depression, noted that his depressed patients distorted perceptions of their experiences and embraced dysfunctional attitudes that promoted and maintained negative mood states.

Elaborating on this idea, researchers have proposed a theory of depression that emphasizes the role of people's negative inferences about the causes of their experiences (Abramson et al., 1978). Helplessness theory maintains *that individuals who are prone to depression automatically attribute negative experiences to causes that are internal (their own fault), stable (unlikely to change) and global (widespread).* For example, a student at risk of depression might view a bad exam grade as a sign of low intelligence (internal) that will never change (stable) and will lead to failure in all their future endeavours (global). In contrast, a student without this tendency might have the opposite response, attributing the bad grade to something external (poor teaching), unstable (a missed study session) and/or specific (boring subject).

HELPLESSNESS THEORY The idea that individuals who are prone to depression automatically attribute negative experiences to causes that are internal (their own fault), stable (unlikely to change) and global (widespread).

Supporting the role of thought in depression is a large body of evidence that depressed individuals' judgements, memories and attributions are negatively biased (Abramson et al., 2002; Blatt and Zuroff, 1992; Coyne and Whiffen, 1995; Wenzlaff and Grozier, 1988). However, in these studies, thoughts and judgements were assessed *during* depression, raising the possibility that the biases may be a consequence rather than a cause of the mood disturbance. To demonstrate that negative thoughts contribute to depression, the thoughts must *precede* the development of the disorder. With a few exceptions (Alloy et al., 1999), research has not detected obvious signs of maladaptive thinking prior to the onset of the depressive mood disturbance (Ingram et al., 1998).

Of course, prior negative thoughts may exist in disguised forms as subtle tendencies to attend to negative information or interpret feedback in a negative way. Indeed, numerous studies suggest that people at risk of depression have latent depressive biases that can be activated by negative moods (Ingram et al., 1998). Thus, a gloomy, rainy afternoon could evoke a mood of sadness and isolation, and instead of taking the initiative and calling someone to chat, the person at risk would become dejected. Once activated, these latent biases may contribute to a progressive worsening of mood that can result in depression (see *the real world* box).

the real world

Suicide risk and prevention

Suicide is a leading cause of death in young to middle-aged people, especially men. The World Health Organization reported that in 1996 alone, more than 150,000 people committed suicide in 38 European countries. The annual worldwide death toll from suicide is well over a million (WHO, 2011). Although people have various reasons for taking their own lives, approximately 50% kill themselves during the recovery phase of a depressive episode (Isacsson and Rich, 1997). The lifetime risk of suicide in people with mood disorders is about 4%, compared to a risk of only 0.5% in the general population (Bostwick and Pankratz, 2000). In the US, women attempt suicide about three to four times more often than men. However, because men typically use more lethal methods than women (such as guns versus pills), men are three to four times more likely to actually kill themselves than women (Canetto and Lester, 1995). The tragic effects of suicide extend beyond the loss of life, compounding the grief of families and loved ones who must contend with feelings of abandonment, guilt, shame and futility.

Researchers have identified a variety of motives for suicide, including a profound sense of alienation, intolerable psychological or physical suffering or both, hopelessness, an escape from feelings of worthlessness, and a desperate cry for help (Baumeister and Tice, 1990; Durkheim, 1951; Joiner, 2006). Suicide rates increase with age, and ageing white men are especially at risk (Joiner, 2006; NIMH, 2003). Studies also show an increased risk of suicide among family members with a relative who committed suicide (Kety, 1990; Mann et al., 1999). This elevated risk may be a function of biological factors in depression, or suicide could be contagious, with exposure making it a more salient option during desperate times. Contagious effects are suggested by the occasional clusters of 'copycat' suicides in which several people – usually teenagers – attempt to kill themselves following a highly publicized case (Gould, 1990). Newspaper coverage (Phillips, 1974) and TV news reporting (Stack, 2000) have been found to be linked to cluster suicides and are thought to facilitate the social learning of suicide-related behaviours (Mesoudi, 2009). This may explain the unusually high incidence of teenage suicides in the small South Wales town of Bridgend during 2007–08, where over 20 teenagers killed themselves.

The contagion of suicide has been called the 'Werther effect' after the rash of suicides that followed the 1774 publication of Goethe's tale of a young romantic who shot himself over a lost love. Werther was wearing a blue coat and yellow vest when he took his life, and so many young men were found dead in similar garb that the book was banned in several countries. In fact, suicide in the US has been found to increase after nationally televised news or feature stories about suicide (Phillips and Carstensen, 1986), but imitation is not inevitable. When rock musician Kurt Cobain shot himself in 1994, according to research, the Werther effect was not found in his home town of Seattle (Jobes et al., 1996) or Australia (Martin and Koo, 1997).

How can you tell if someone is at risk of suicide? Unfortunately, definitive prediction is impossible, but a variety of warning signs can suggest an increased risk (Substance Abuse and Mental Health Services Administration, 2005). Any one sign is a cause for concern, and the risk is especially serious when several occur together:

- Talk about suicide. About 90% of people who are suicidal discuss their intentions, so this obvious warning sign should not be dismissed as simply a means of gaining attention. Although most

The Clifton Suspension Bridge in Bristol, England is a well known suicide spot. Each year, approximately four people jump off the bridge despite the barriers and plaques giving The Samaritans' phone number. Only one person has ever survived. Following an argument with her boyfriend, Sarah Ann Henley leapt from the bridge in 1885. Her billowing dress acted like a parachute and she was cushioned by the crinoline petticoats she wore. She was injured but eventually recovered, and died in 1948 at the grand old age of 84.

US suicide rates reveal that men are more likely to commit suicide than women at all ages, men's likelihood of suicide grows in early adulthood, and white men remain most suicide prone throughout life, with a spike in the later years (NIMH, 2003).

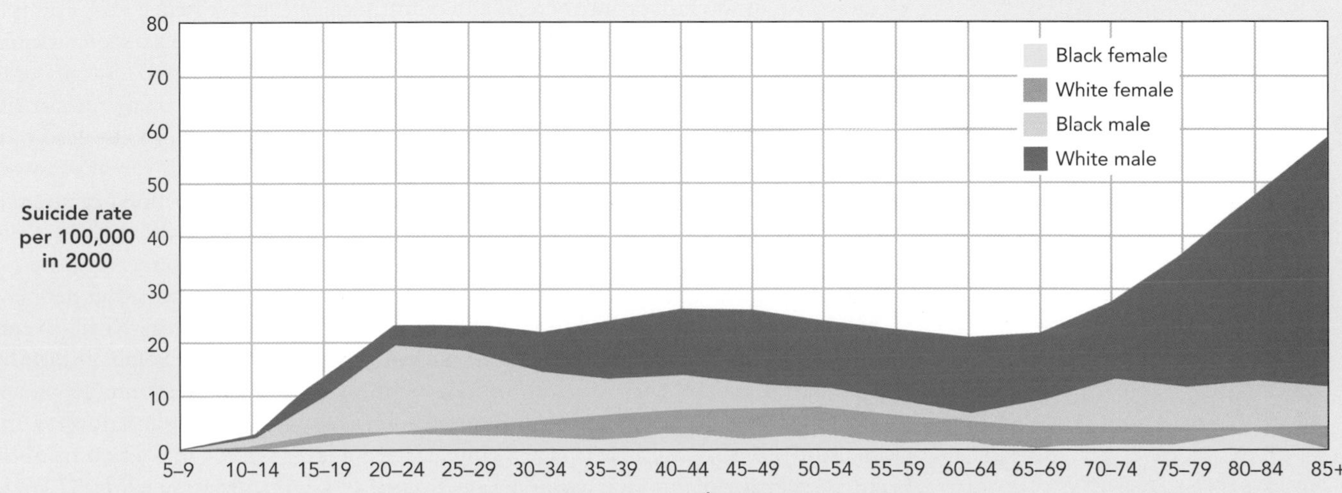

people who threaten suicide do not actually attempt it, they are at greater risk than those who do not talk about it.

- An upturn in mood following a prolonged depressive episode. Surprisingly, suicide risk increases at this point. In fact, a sudden lifting of mood may reflect relief at the prospect that suicide will end the emotional suffering.
- A failed love interest, romantic breakup, or loss of a loved one through separation or death.
- A severe, stressful event that is especially shameful or humiliating.
- A family history of suicide, especially of a parent.
- Unusual reckless or risky behaviour, seemingly carried out without thinking.
- An unexplained decline in school or workplace performance.
- Withdrawal from friends, family and regular activities.
- Expressing feelings of being trapped, as though there's 'no way out'.
- 'Cleaning house' by giving away prized possessions.
- Increased alcohol or drug use. Substance abuse is associated with approximately 25–50% of suicides and is especially associated with adolescent suicides (Conwell et al., 1996; Woods et al., 1997).

Although discussing suicide with someone possibly at risk might seem to increase actual risk, a caring listener can help to put issues in better perspective and reduce feelings of isolation. Anyone who is potentially suicidal should be encouraged to seek professional help. Colleges and universities have student counselling centres, and most cities have suicide prevention centres with 24-hour hotlines and walk-in emergency counselling.

Some have argued that this classic picture of people with depression being negatively biased is incorrect and it is the non-depressed who are, in fact, positively biased (Alloy and Abramson, 1988). As we saw in Chapter 13, people have a self-serving bias to boost their self-esteem. This is supported by studies that reveal that non-depressed individuals tend to take more credit for when things turn out well than people with depression who are more realistic (Lyon et al., 1999). This depressive realism hypothesis proposes that the world is a rather unpleasant place and *that non-depressed individuals insulate themselves against negativity by adopting a positive attributional style, whereas people with depression are more realistic.* Depressives may be sadder, but they are wiser. It seems likely that there may be some truth to this hypothesis in people with moderate depression, but negative attributional style is significantly elevated in the most depressed (Bentall, 2003).

DEPRESSIVE REALISM HYPOTHESIS
Proposes that non-depressed individuals insulate themselves against negativity by adopting a positive attributional style, whereas people with depression are more realistic.

Negative thinking can be hard to detect in individuals at risk of depression because they are struggling to suppress the thoughts that threaten their emotional wellbeing. Thought suppression is an effortful process that can be disrupted when cognitive resources are depleted (see Chapter 8). Unsurprisingly, when cognitive demands arise (time pressures, distraction, stress and so on), individuals who are at risk of depression often display heightened levels of negative thinking (Wenzlaff and Bates, 1998; Wenzlaff and Eisenberg, 2001). They may worry about failures, think that people are avoiding them, or wonder whether anything is worthwhile. This breakdown in mental control may explain why stressful life events such as a prolonged illness or the loss of a loved one often precede a descent into depression (Kessler, 1997). Ironically, thought suppression itself may intensify depressive thoughts and ultimately contribute to relapse (Rude et al., 2002; Wenzlaff, 2005; Wenzlaff and Bates, 1998).

Research suggests that people at risk of depression may inadvertently construct their social worlds in ways that contribute to and confirm their negative beliefs. For example, depressed individuals with low self-esteem have been found to seek social feedback that confirms their negative self-views (Giesler et al., 1996; Joiner et al., 1997; Swann et al., 1992). They seek companions who are likely to criticize or belittle them, almost like wearing a sign that says 'Kick me hard'. Uncertainty about self-worth can also lead individuals at risk of depression to seek excessive reassurance ('Are you really sure it's okay for me to hang out with you guys?'). This behaviour can lead to social rejection because others are likely to view it as inappropriate and demanding (Joiner, 2002; Joiner and Metalsky, 1995; Joiner et al., 1999). Thus, depression can be self-perpetuating if people who are depressed behave in ways that prompt depressing reactions from other people.

Having such a depressive style does not bode well for coping with negative life events, which impact on all of us at some point in our lives (see Chapter 17). Some of these life events are unavoidable such as family bereavement, whereas others are more dependent on individual circumstances and environments such as single parenting and poverty. In a classic study, Brown and Harris (1978) interviewed a large sample of women from the Camberwell area of London using a Life Events and Difficulties Schedule (LEDS), which assesses the impact of stressful life events on mental wellbeing. They found that

61% of those diagnosed with depression had experienced at least one very stressful negative life event in the eight months before the interview compared with 19% of non-depressed women. However, they also found that not all those who experienced negative life events developed depression, indicating that other factors can compensate for this stress, especially integration into the community and social support, which are also assessed by the schedule. This fits with the emerging consensus that loneliness and lack of social contact are important contributing factors in psychological and physical health (see Chapter 17). Research using the LEDS continues to provide supporting evidence for a diathesis-stress model of depression (Farmer and McGuffin, 2003) and has been replicated numerous times in different communities including the Outer Hebrides of Scotland (Brown and Prudo, 1981).

If you commit suicide, I'll kill you

Until fairly recently, suicide has been considered a crime in most Western societies. Christians regarded it a mortal sin and by the 10th century, English law considered it a crime where the perpetrator would forfeit their entire estate. In addition, the corpse would be publicly dragged through the streets and then buried in unconsecrated ground, typically at a crossroads, which is how Tucker's Grave in Somerset got its name. Thankfully, not every suicide attempt is successful, but in 117 AD, Roman Emperor Hadrian declared that attempted suicide by his soldiers was an act of intended desertion and made it punishable by … execution.

Bipolar disorder

If depression is bad, would the opposite be better? Not for Virginia Woolf nor for Julie, a 20-year-old second-year university student. When first seen by a clinician, Julie had gone five days without sleep and, like Woolf, was extremely active and expressing bizarre thoughts and ideas. She proclaimed to friends that she did not menstruate because she was 'of a third sex, a gender above the two human sexes'. She claimed to be a 'superwoman', capable of avoiding human sexuality and yet still able to give birth. Preoccupied with the politics of global disarmament, she felt she had switched souls with a senior politician, had tapped into his thoughts and memories, and could save the world from nuclear destruction. She began to campaign for an elected position in government, even though no elections were scheduled at that time. Worried that she would forget some of her thoughts, she had been leaving hundreds of notes about her ideas and activities everywhere, including on the walls and furniture of her dormitory room (Vitkus, 1999).

In addition to her manic episodes, Julie – like Woolf – had a history of depression. The diagnostic label for their constellation of symptoms is bipolar affective disorder, which according to the ICD-10 is *a disorder characterized by two or more episodes in which the patient's mood and activity levels are significantly disturbed, this disturbance consisting on some occasions of an elevation of mood and increased energy and activity (hypomania or mania) and on others of a lowering of mood and decreased energy and activity (depression).* In about two-thirds of patients, manic episodes immediately precede or immediately follow depressive episodes (Whybrow, 1997). The depressive phase of bipolar disorder is often clinically indistinguishable from major depression (Perris, 1992). In the manic phase, mood can be elevated, expansive or irritable. Other prominent symptoms include grandiosity, decreased need for sleep, talkativeness, racing thoughts, distractibility and reckless behaviour, such as compulsive gambling, sexual indiscretions and unrestrained spending sprees. The ICD-10 further distinguishes between various subtypes of bipolar disorder where psychotic features such as hallucinations (erroneous perceptions) and delusions (erroneous beliefs) may be present, so the disorder can be misdiagnosed as schizophrenia.

BIPOLAR AFFECTIVE DISORDER A disorder characterized by two or more episodes in which the patient's mood and activity levels are significantly disturbed, this disturbance consisting on some occasions of an elevation of mood and increased energy and activity (hypomania or mania) and on others of a lowering of mood and decreased energy and activity (depression).

The lifetime risk for bipolar disorder is about 1.3% for men and women (Wittchen et al., 1994). Bipolar disorder is typically a recurrent condition, with approximately 90% of afflicted people suffering from several episodes over a lifetime (Coryell et al., 1995). About 10% of cases have *rapid cycling bipolar disorder*, characterized by at least four mood episodes (either manic or depressive) every year. Rapid cycling is more common in women than in men and is sometimes precipitated by taking certain kinds of antidepressant drugs (Liebenluft, 1996; Whybrow, 1997). Unfortunately, bipolar disorder tends to be persistent. In one study, 24% of patients had relapsed within six months of recovery from an episode, and 77% had at least one new episode within four years of recovery (Coryell et al., 1995).

A significant minority of people with bipolar disorder are highly creative, artistic or otherwise outstanding in some way. Before the mania becomes too pronounced, the energy, grandiosity and ambition that it supplies may help people achieve great things. In addition to Virginia Woolf, notable individuals thought to have had or still have the disorder include artist Vincent Van Gogh, former British Prime Minister Winston Churchill, polymath Stephen Fry and musician Sting.

Winston Churchill made a pet of his bipolar illness, calling his depression the 'black dog' that followed him around.

Biological factors

Among the various mental disorders, bipolar disorder has the highest rate of heritability, with concordance as high as 80% for identical twins and 16% for fraternal twins (Bertelsen et al., 1977). Despite considerable effort on the part of researchers, specific genes that contribute to bipolar disorder have not yet been identified (Goodwin and Ghaemi, 1998; Plomin et al., 1997). Close relatives of an individual with bipolar disorder are also at heightened risk for unipolar depression (Bertelsen et al., 1977), a finding that raises the possibility that the genetic transmission of bipolar disorder is connected to the genetic transmission of unipolar depression. Thus, bipolar disorder may be *polygenic*, that is, arising from the action of many genes in an additive or interactive fashion.

Biochemical imbalances may be involved in bipolar disorder, but specific neurotransmitters have not been identified. Some researchers have suggested that low levels of serotonin and noradrenaline may contribute to the emotional roller coaster that characterizes bipolar disorder (Whybrow, 1997). This notion is not well substantiated and doesn't explain why lithium, a chemical unrelated to these neurotransmitters, often helps stabilize the depressive and manic symptoms associated with bipolar disorder (see Chapter 16).

Psychological factors

Stressful life experiences often precede manic and depressive episodes (Ellicot et al., 1990; Hammen, 1995). One study found that severely stressed patients took an average of three times longer to recover from an episode than patients not affected by stress (Johnson and Miller, 1997). The stress–disorder relationship is not simple, however. High levels of stress have less impact on patients with extroverted personalities than those who are more introverted (Swednsen et al., 1995). Personality characteristics such as neuroticism and conscientiousness have also been found to predict increases in bipolar symptoms over time (Lozano and Johnson, 2001). Finally, patients living with family members who are hostile towards or critical of the patient are more likely to relapse than patients with supportive families (Miklowitz et al., 1988).

In summary, the mood disorders are mental disorders in which a disturbance in mood is the predominant feature. Depressive disorder (or unipolar depression) is characterized by a severely depressed mood lasting at least two weeks; symptoms include excessive self-criticism, guilt, difficulty concentrating, suicidal thoughts, sleep and appetite disturbances, and lethargy. Dysthymia, a related disorder, involves less severe symptoms that persist for at least two years. For reasons that are not well understood, women are approximately twice as likely as men to suffer from depression. Studies of depression reveal a moderate level of heritability and it may involve neurotransmitter imbalances, although the exact nature of the imbalance remains unclear. Patterns of negative thinking may also contribute to depression by tainting perceptions and judgements. One such pattern is the tendency to explain personal failures by attributing them to internal, stable, global causes. In addition, depression-prone individuals may inadvertently behave in ways that lead to social rejection, thereby contributing to and confirming a sense of low self-worth.

Bipolar disorder is an unstable emotional condition involving extreme mood swings of depression and mania. The manic phase is characterized by periods of abnormally and persistently elevated, expansive or irritable mood, lasting at least one week. Bipolar disorder has a high rate of heritability, although it is unclear which gene or genes may be responsible for the problem. Patients with bipolar disorder often respond favourably to drug therapy (for example lithium), but the precise nature of the drug action is not well understood. Finally, stress and family problems may also contribute to the onset and maintenance of bipolar disorder.

Schizophrenia: losing the grasp on reality

The 2001 film *A Beautiful Mind* tells the story of John Nash, the brilliant, quirky Nobel Prize-winning mathematician, as he gradually develops schizophrenia. The film subtly conveys his passage into psychological disorder, making it difficult for the viewer to realize that he has lost touch with reality until his abnormality suddenly looms. When a colleague asked him how a man devoted to reason and logical proof could believe that extraterrestrials were sending him messages, Nash replied: 'Because the ideas I had about supernatural beings came to me in the same way that my mathematical ideas did, so I took them seriously.' Nash was suffering from schizophrenia, one of the most devastating and mystifying of the mental disorders.

Symptoms and types of schizophrenia

Schizophrenia is characterized by *the profound disruption of basic psychological processes, a distorted perception of reality, altered or blunted emotion, and disturbances in thought, motivation and behaviour.* Traditionally, schizophrenia was regarded primarily as a disturbance of thought and perception, in which the sense of reality becomes severely distorted and confused. However, this condition is now understood to take different forms affecting a wide range of symptoms, including delusion, hallucination, disorganized speech, grossly disorganized behaviour or catatonic behaviour, and negative symptoms. Let's consider each symptom in detail:

SCHIZOPHRENIA A disorder characterized by the profound disruption of basic psychological processes, a distorted perception of reality, altered or blunted emotion, and disturbances in thought, motivation and behaviour.

- Delusion is *a patently false belief system, often bizarre and grandiose, that is maintained in spite of its irrationality.* For example, an individual with schizophrenia may believe that they are Jesus Christ, Napoleon, Joan of Arc or some other famous person. Such delusions of identity have helped foster the misconception that schizophrenia involves multiple personalities. Unlike dissociative identity disorder, however, adopted identities in schizophrenia do not alternate, exhibit amnesia for one another, or otherwise 'split'. Delusions of persecution are also common. The patient's belief that the secret service, demons, extraterrestrials or other malevolent forces are conspiring to harm the patient or control their mind may represent an attempt to make sense of the tormenting delusions (Roberts, 1991). People with schizophrenia have little or no insight into their disordered perceptual and thought processes. Because they cannot understand that they have lost control of their own minds, they may develop unusual beliefs and theories that attribute control to external agents.

DELUSION A patently false belief system, often bizarre and grandiose, that is maintained in spite of its irrationality.

- Hallucination is *a false perceptual experience that has a compelling sense of being real despite the absence of external stimulation.* The perceptual disturbances associated with schizophrenia can include hearing, seeing or smelling things that are not there or having tactile sensations in the absence of relevant sensory stimulation. Schizophrenic hallucinations are often auditory, for example hearing voices that no one else can hear. Among people with schizophrenia, some 65% report hearing voices repeatedly (Frith and Fletcher, 1995). British psychiatrist Henry Maudsley (1886) long ago proposed that these voices are in fact produced in the mind of the schizophrenic individual, and recent research substantiates his idea. In one PET imaging study, auditory hallucinations were accompanied by activation in Broca's area, the part of the brain (as discussed in Chapters 3 and 7) associated with the production of language (McGuire et al., 1993). Unfortunately, the voices heard in schizophrenia seldom sound like the self or a kindly uncle offering advice. They command, scold, suggest bizarre actions or offer snide comments. One patient reported a voice saying: 'He's getting up now. He's going to wash. It's about time' (Frith and Fletcher, 1995). One recent intriguing discovery, based on patients' interviews, is that the nature of the auditory hallucinations depends on the culture (Luhrmann et al., 2014). In the US, the reported voices were harsher, and in Africa and India, more benign. Another striking difference was that while many of the African and Indian patients registered predominantly positive experiences with their voices, not one American did. Participants from the US were more likely to report violent commands than those in India and Ghana, who were more likely than the Americans to report rich relationships with their voices and less likely to describe the voices as the sign of a disturbed mind. One way to interpret this cultural variation is the difference between the focus on independence in the Western self-concept compared to the interdependent perspective in Eastern and non-Westernized societies (described in Chapter 15).

HALLUCINATION A false perceptual experience that has a compelling sense of being real despite the absence of external stimulation.

- Disorganized speech is *a severe disruption of verbal communication in which ideas shift rapidly and incoherently from one to another unrelated topic.* The abnormal speech patterns in schizophrenia reflect difficulties in organizing thoughts and focusing attention. Responses to questions are often irrelevant, ideas are loosely associated, and words are used in peculiar ways. For example, asked by her doctor, 'Can you tell me the name of this place?', one patient with schizophrenia responded: 'I have not been a drinker for 16 years. I am taking a mental rest after a "carter" assignment of "quill." You know, a "penwrap." I had contracts with Warner Brothers Studios and Eugene

DISORGANIZED SPEECH A severe disruption of verbal communication in which ideas shift rapidly and incoherently from one to another unrelated topic.

broke phonograph records but Mike protested. I have been with the police department for 35 years. I am made of flesh and blood – see, Doctor' [pulling up her dress] (Carson et al., 2000, p. 474).

GROSSLY DISORGANIZED BEHAVIOUR Behaviour that is inappropriate for the situation or ineffective in attaining goals, often with specific motor disturbances.

CATATONIC BEHAVIOUR A marked decrease in all movement or an increase in muscular rigidity and overactivity.

- Grossly disorganized behaviour is *behaviour that is inappropriate for the situation or ineffective in attaining goals, often with specific motor disturbances.* A patient might exhibit constant childlike silliness, improper sexual behaviour (such as masturbating in public), dishevelled appearance, or loud shouting or swearing. Specific motor disturbances might include strange movements, rigid posturing, odd mannerisms, bizarre grimacing or hyperactivity. Catatonic behaviour is *a marked decrease in all movement or an increase in muscular rigidity and overactivity.* Patients with *catatonia* may actively resist movement (when someone is trying to move them) or become completely unresponsive and unaware of their surroundings in a *catatonic stupor.* In addition, patients receiving drug therapy may exhibit motor symptoms, such as rigidity or spasm, as a side effect of the medication. Indeed, the DSM-IV has proposed a diagnostic category labelled 'medication-induced movement disorders' that identifies motor disturbances arising from the use of medications of the sort commonly used to treat schizophrenia.

NEGATIVE SYMPTOMS Emotional and social withdrawal, apathy, poverty of speech, and other indications of the absence or insufficiency of normal behaviour, motivation and emotion.

- Negative symptoms include *emotional and social withdrawal, apathy, poverty of speech, and other indications of the absence or insufficiency of normal behaviour, motivation and emotion.* These symptoms refer to things missing in people with schizophrenia, in contrast to the positive symptoms, such as hallucinations, that appear more in people with schizophrenia than in other people. Negative symptoms may rob people of emotion, for example leaving them with flat, deadpan responses. Or their ability to act wilfully may be reduced, their interest in people or events undermined, or their capacity to focus attention impaired.

The various symptoms of schizophrenia do not all occur in every case. Instead, the disorder can take quite different forms. There have been several attempts to categorize schizophrenia into different types. British psychiatrist Tim Crow (1980) suggested a division into type 1 and type 2. Type 1 schizophrenia is primarily thought to be caused by a biochemical imbalance in the brain and is characterized by florid *positive symptoms* – the hallucinations and delusions described above. Type 2 schizophrenia is more chronic and thought to reflect a progressive atrophy of brain regions that results in the negative symptoms described above of apathy and social withdrawal. The current ICD-10 identifies six subtypes of schizophrenia (see **TABLE 16.3**).

TABLE 16.3 Types of schizophrenia defined by the ICD-10

Types	Characteristics
Paranoid	Symptoms dominated by relatively stable, often paranoid delusions, usually accompanied by hallucinations, particularly of the auditory variety, and perceptual disturbances. Disturbances of affect, volition and speech, and catatonic symptoms are either absent or relatively inconspicuous
Catatonic	Often characterized by prominent psychomotor disturbances that may alternate between extremes such as hyperkinesis and stupor, or automatic obedience and negativism. Constrained attitudes and postures may be maintained for long periods. Episodes of violent excitement may be a striking feature of the condition. The catatonic phenomena may be combined with a dreamlike (oneiroid) state with vivid scenic hallucinations
Hebephrenic	A form of schizophrenia in which affective changes are prominent, delusions and hallucinations fleeting and fragmentary, behaviour irresponsible and unpredictable, and mannerisms common. The mood is shallow and inappropriate, thought is disorganized, and speech is incoherent. There is a tendency to social isolation. Usually the prognosis is poor because of the rapid development of 'negative' symptoms, particularly flattening of affect and loss of volition. Hebephrenia is normally diagnosed only in adolescents or young adults
Undifferentiated	Psychotic conditions meeting the general diagnostic criteria for schizophrenia but not conforming to any of the subtypes of paranoid, catatonic or hebephrenic, or exhibiting the features of more than one of them without a clear predominance of a particular set of diagnostic characteristics

Residual	A chronic stage in the development of a schizophrenic illness in which there has been a clear progression from an early stage to a later stage characterized by long-term, although not necessarily irreversible, 'negative' symptoms, for example psychomotor slowing, underactivity, blunting of affect, passivity and lack of initiative, poverty of quantity or content of speech, poor nonverbal communication by facial expression, eye contact, voice modulation and posture, and poor self-care and social performance
Simple	A disorder in which there is an insidious but progressive development of oddities of conduct, inability to meet the demands of society, and decline in total performance. The characteristic negative features of residual schizophrenia, for example blunting of affect and loss of volition, develop without being preceded by any overt psychotic symptoms

Source: WHO, 2004

Three of these types – paranoid, catatonic and hebephrenic – depend primarily on the relative prominence of various symptoms. The *paranoid* type involves preoccupation with delusions and hallucinations; the *catatonic* type involves immobility and stupor or agitated, purposeless motor activity; the *hebephrenic* type is often the most severe, featuring disorganized speech and behaviour and flat or inappropriate emotion. *Undifferentiated* type cases do not neatly fall into these three categories and the *residual* type describes individuals who have had at least one florid schizophrenic episode but still have lingering chronic symptoms. The *simple* type is a gradual decline into negative symptoms without a precipitating psychotic episode. However, the most recent version of the DSM-5 has eliminated schizophrenia subtypes because of their limited diagnostic stability, low reliability and poor validity. In addition, subtypes have not been shown to exhibit distinctive patterns of treatment response or longitudinal course. It remains to be seen whether the forthcoming ICD-11, due in 2015, will retain schizophrenia subtypes or move to a dimensional approach.

Schizophrenia occurs in about 1% of the population and is about equally common in men and women (Gottesman, 1991; Jablensky, 1997). The first episode typically occurs during late adolescence or early adulthood (Gottesman, 1991), although females usually have a later onset than males (Iacono and Beiser, 1992; Marcus et al., 1993). Despite its relatively low frequency, schizophrenia is the primary diagnosis for nearly 40% of all admissions to state and county mental hospitals in the US; it is the second most frequent diagnosis for inpatient psychiatric admission at other types of institutions (Rosenstein et al., 1990). One of the most comprehensive international studies of schizophrenia in Demark, India, Ireland, Nigeria, Russia, Japan, the Czech Republic, the US and the UK revealed that the incidence was comparable (Jablenskey et al., 1992). The disproportionate rate of hospitalization for schizophrenia is a testament to the devastation it causes in people's lives.

Biological factors

Ever since Kraepelin (1899) first remarked that schizophrenia was so severe that it suggested 'organic', or biological, origins, researchers have sought evidence for this position. Over the years, this evidence has been accumulating for the role of biology in schizophrenia from studies of genetic factors, prenatal and perinatal environments, biochemical factors and neuroanatomy.

Genetic factors

Family studies indicate that the closer a person's genetic relatedness to a person with schizophrenia, the greater the likelihood of developing the disorder (Gottesman, 1991). As shown in **FIGURE 16.5**, concordance rates increase dramatically with biological relatedness. The rates are estimates and vary considerably from study to study, but almost every study finds the average concordance rates higher for identical twins (48%) than for fraternal twins (17%), which suggests a genetic component for the disorder (Torrey et al., 1994).

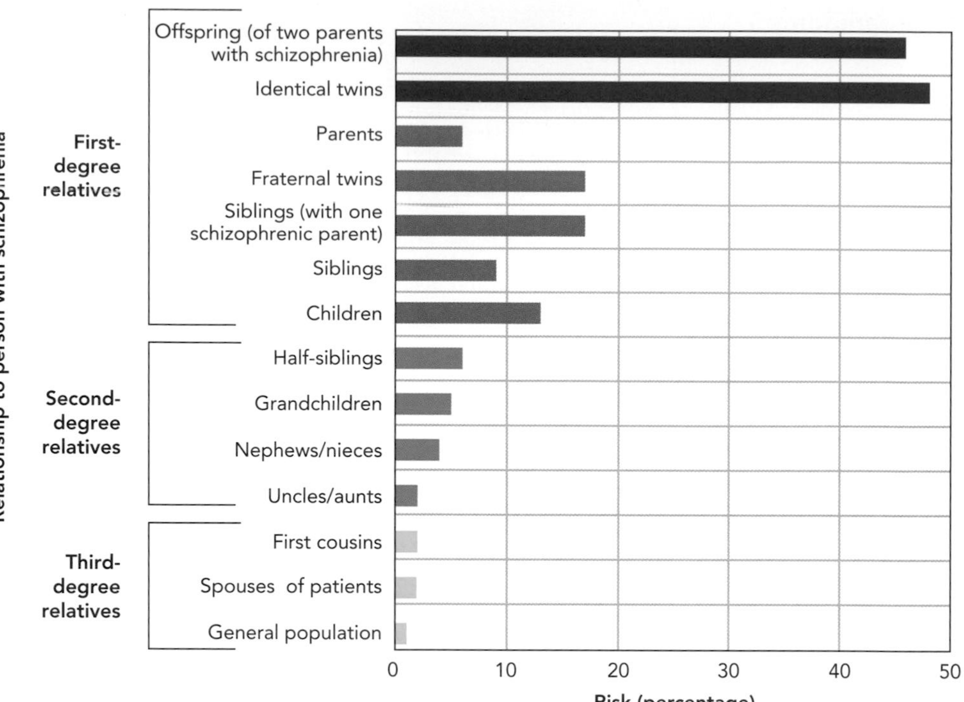

FIGURE **16.5 Average risk of developing schizophrenia** The risk of schizophrenia among biological relatives is greater for those with greater degrees of relatedness. An identical twin of a twin with schizophrenia has a 48% risk of developing schizophrenia, for example, and offspring of two parents with schizophrenia have a 46% risk of developing the disorder (adapted from Gottesman, 1991).

Prenatal and perinatal factors

Although genetics clearly has a strong predisposing role in schizophrenia, considerable evidence suggests that the prenatal and perinatal environments may also affect concordance rates in identical twins (Jurewicz et al., 2001; Thaker, 2002; Torrey et al., 1994). For example, because approximately 70% of identical twins share the same prenatal blood supply, toxins in the mother's blood could contribute to the high concordance rate. When one twin develops schizophrenia and the other twin does not, birth records often show that the afflicted twin is second born and had a lower birth weight (Wahl, 1976). In addition, people with late winter or early spring birth dates have about a 20% greater risk of schizophrenia than those born in late summer or early autumn (DeLisi et al., 1986), raising the possibility that viral exposure during a critical period of brain development may contribute to the risk of schizophrenia (Rothermundt et al., 2001). Further support for this idea comes from studies showing that maternal influenza in the second trimester of pregnancy is associated with an increased risk of schizophrenia (Wright et al., 1995).

Biochemical factors

DOPAMINE HYPOTHESIS The idea that schizophrenia involves an excess of dopamine activity.

During the 1950s, major tranquilizers were discovered that could reduce the symptoms of schizophrenia by lowering levels of the neurotransmitter dopamine. The effectiveness of many drugs in alleviating schizophrenic symptoms is related to their capacity to reduce dopamine in the brain. This finding suggested the dopamine hypothesis – *the idea that schizophrenia involves an excess of dopamine activity.* The hypothesis has been invoked to explain why amphetamines, which increase dopamine levels, often aggravate the symptoms of schizophrenia.

If only things were so simple. Considerable evidence suggests that this hypothesis is inadequate (Csermansky and Grace, 1998; Grace and Moore, 1998). For example, many individuals with schizophrenia do not respond favourably to dopamine-blocking drugs, for example major tranquilizers, and those who do seldom show a complete remission of symptoms. Moreover, the drugs block dopamine receptors very rapidly, yet individuals with schizophrenia typically do not show a beneficial response for weeks. Finally, research has implicated other neurotransmitters in schizophrenia, suggesting that the disorder may involve a complex interaction among a host of different biochemicals (Benes, 1998; Lewis et al., 1999; Sawa and Snyder, 2002). In sum, the precise role of neurotransmitters in schizophrenia has yet to be determined.

Neuroanatomy

When neuroimaging techniques became available, researchers immediately started looking for distinctive anatomical features of the brain in individuals with schizophrenia. The earliest observations revealed enlargement of the *ventricles*, hollow areas filled with cerebrospinal fluid, lying deep within the core of the brain (Johnstone et al., 1976). In some patients, primarily those with chronic, negative symptoms, the ventricles were abnormally enlarged, suggesting a loss of brain tissue mass that could arise from an anomaly in prenatal development (Arnold et al., 1998; Heaton et al., 1994).

Understanding the significance of this brain abnormality for schizophrenia is complicated by several factors, however. First, such enlarged ventricles are found in only a minority of cases of schizophrenia. Second, some individuals who do not have schizophrenia also show evidence of enlarged ventricles. Finally, this type of brain abnormality can be caused by the long-term use of some types of antipsychotic medications commonly prescribed in schizophrenia (Breggin, 1990; Cohen, 1997; Gur et al., 1998).

Recent neuroimaging studies provide evidence of a variety of brain abnormalities in schizophrenia. Paul Thompson and his colleagues (2001b) examined changes in the brains of adolescents whose MRI scans could be traced sequentially from the onset of schizophrenia. By morphing the images onto a standardized brain, the researchers were able to detect progressive tissue loss beginning in the parietal lobe and eventually encompassing much of the brain (see **FIGURE 16.6**). All adolescents lose some grey matter over time in a kind of normal 'pruning' of the brain that we discussed in brain development in Chapter 11, but in the case of those developing schizophrenia, the loss was dramatic enough to seem pathological. A variety of specific brain changes found in other studies suggest a clear relationship between biological changes in the brain and the progression of schizophrenia (Shenton et al., 2001).

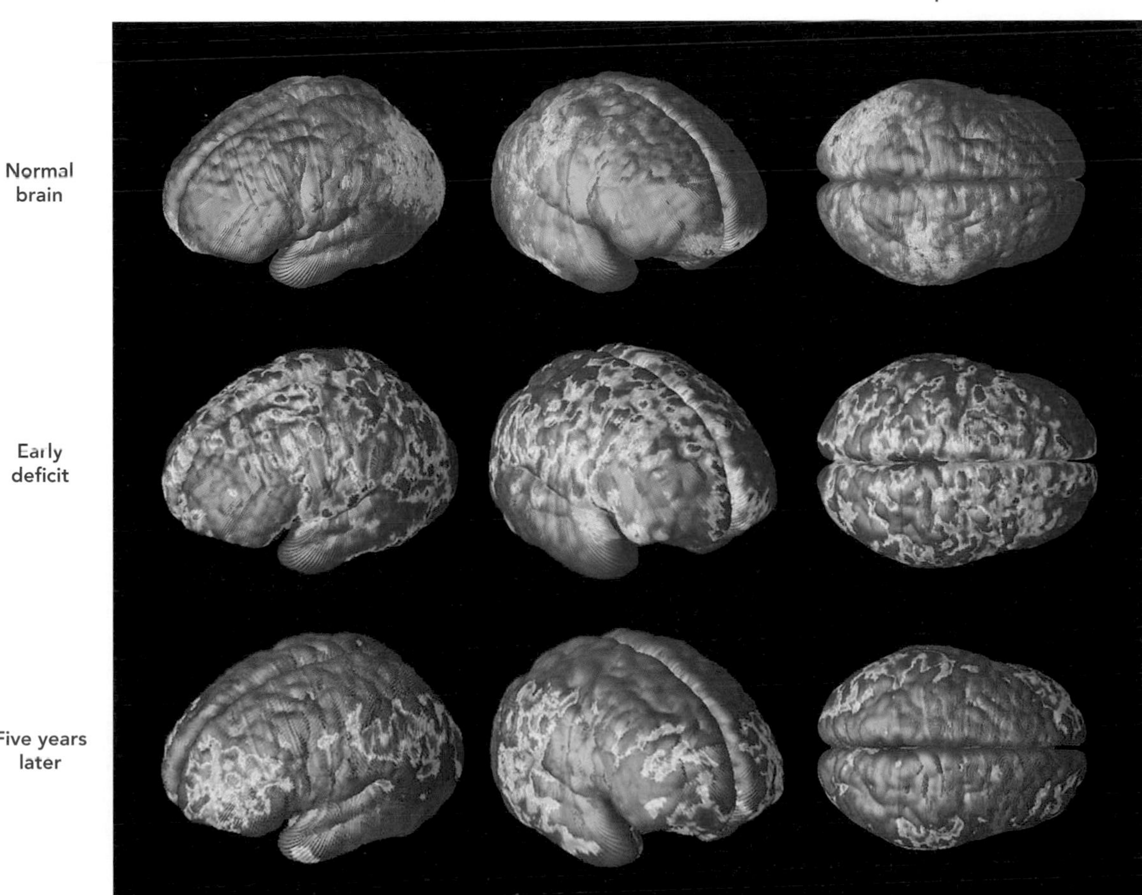

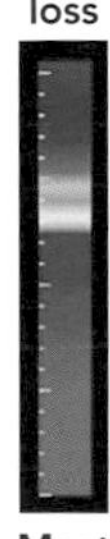

FIGURE **16.6 Brain tissue loss in adolescent schizophrenia** MRI scan composites reveal brain tissue loss in adolescents diagnosed with schizophrenia. Normal brains (top) show minimal loss due to 'pruning'. Early deficit scans (middle) reveal loss in the parietal areas. Patients at this stage may experience symptoms such as hallucinations or bizarre thoughts. Scans five years later (bottom) reveal extensive tissue loss over much of the cortex. Patients at this stage are likely to suffer from delusions, disorganized speech and behaviour, and negative symptoms such as social withdrawal (Thompson et al., 2001b).

Psychological factors

With all these potential biological contributors to schizophrenia, you might think there would be few psychological or social causes of the disorder. However, one of the few unequivocal discoveries in our understanding of schizophrenia is that the development of and recovery from the condition is highly dependent on the family environment. One large-scale study compared the risk of schizophrenia in children adopted into healthy families and those adopted into severely disturbed families (Tienari et al., 2004). (Disturbed families were defined as those with extreme conflict, lack of communication or chaotic relationships.) Among children whose biological mothers had schizophrenia, the disturbed environment increased the likelihood of developing schizophrenia – an outcome that was not found among children who were also reared in disturbed families but whose biological mothers did *not* have schizophrenia. This finding provides support for the diathesis-stress model described earlier.

EXPRESSED EMOTION (EE) Emotional overinvolvement (intrusiveness) and excessive criticism directed towards the former patient by their family.

In a related vein, researchers have found that a certain type of negative communication pattern in families is associated with higher relapse for schizophrenia. The pattern, called expressed emotion (EE), involves *emotional overinvolvement (intrusiveness) and excessive criticism directed towards the former patient by their family.* The mother who says 'I cry when I think about how you used to be before all this started', for example, is not producing a particularly comforting environment for the patient. In fact, having highly critical close relatives was a stronger predictor of negative self-esteem in patients with schizophrenia, which in turn predicted Crow's positive symptoms (Barrowclough et al., 2003). These encounters are also stressful. People with schizophrenia exhibit unusually high levels of autonomic arousal as measured by GSR (Chapter 8) when meeting high EE relatives (Tarrier and Turpin, 1992). Former patients who return to this type of family environment are at a considerably higher risk of relapse than those who return to more adaptive families (Butzlaff and Hooley, 1998; Hooley and Hiller, 1998; Linszen et al., 1997). The extent to which these negative communication patterns contribute to schizophrenia or merely reflect the turmoil of having a family member with schizophrenia is not clear. For example, EE seems to rise and fall depending on the disturbed child's current difficulties in the home (Linszen et al., 1997; Scazufca and Kuipers, 1998). Conclusions about the role of family functioning in the risk of schizophrenia must be tempered by the realization that the studies in this area are correlational and a basic association between characteristics does not indicate that one causes the other (see Chapter 2). Thus, although dysfunction in families may contribute to schizophrenia, the reverse may also be true. High EE parents are more likely to report encounters with their offspring who have schizophrenia as more stressful and a burden that they cope with by ignoring the problem or resorting to alcohol (Kuipers and Raune, 2000). These relatives are also more likely to attribute blame for the condition to the individual rather than external factors, which explains why they are so critical in the first place (Brewin et al., 1991; Barrowclough et al., 1996). But it's not just the family who exacerbate the situation. Psychiatric care staff also exhibit EE and hostels with higher EE have patients who either discharge themselves unwell back into the community much earlier (Ball et al., 1992), or have a poorer quality of life and worse psychiatric symptoms than those in low EE hostels (Snyder et al., 1994).

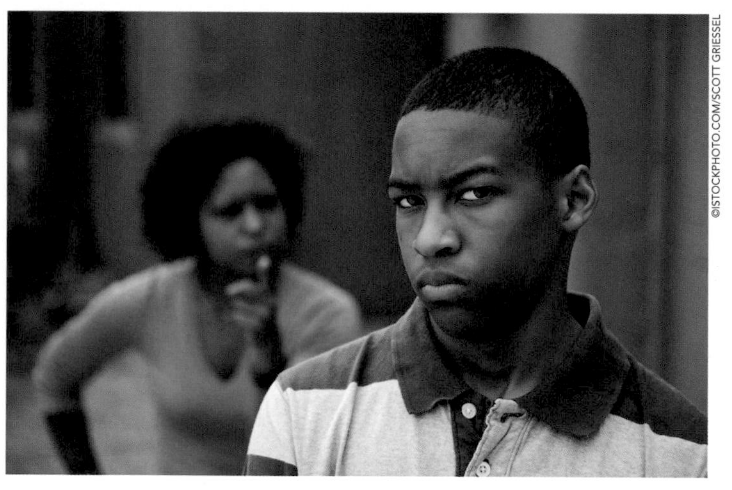

When mothers complain. High levels of expressed emotion in the family predict relapse among patients treated for schizophrenia.

The dysfunctional and bizarre behaviour of a family member with schizophrenia may in itself promote dysfunctional communications and interactions among family members and those who care for them. However, psychosocial approaches to schizophrenia are not only therapeutically necessarily but have to be incorporated into any model that explains the aetiology of the condition.

In summary, schizophrenia is a profound disorder involving hallucinations, disorganized thoughts and behaviour, and emotional and social withdrawal. Different subtypes of schizophrenia have been identified: paranoid, catatonic, hebephrenic, undifferentiated, residual and simple. Schizophrenia affects only 1% of the population, but it accounts for a disproportionate share of psychiatric hospitalizations. Genetic factors play a role in the development of schizophrenia, but they do not provide a complete account. The first drugs that reduced the availability of dopamine sometimes reduced the symptoms of schizophrenia, suggesting that the disorder involved an excess of dopamine activity. However, recent research suggests that schizophrenia may involve a complex interaction among a variety of neurotransmitters. Neuroimaging studies have found brain abnormalities such as enlarged ventricles in some patients and a general tendency for some loss of grey matter as the disorder develops. Finally, the risk of developing schizophrenia and the likelihood of relapse are significantly affected by the quality of family communication patterns and relationships.

Personality disorders: going to extremes

Think for a minute about school acquaintances whose personalities made them stand out – not necessarily in a good way. Was there a space geek, for example, a person who didn't seem to make sense, wore strange outfits, sometimes wouldn't respond in conversation or would respond by bringing up weird things like astrology or mind reading? Or perhaps a drama queen, someone whose theatrics and exaggerated emotions turned everything into a big deal? And don't forget the neat freak, the perfectionist obsessed with control, who had the perfectly organized desk, precisely arranged hair and immaculate clothing. One way to describe such people is to say they simply have *personalities*, the unique patterns of traits we explored in Chapter 12. But sometimes personal traits can become so rigid and confining that they blend over into mental disorders. Personality disorders are *disorders characterized by deeply ingrained, inflexible patterns of thinking, feeling or relating to others, or controlling impulses that cause distress or impaired functioning.* The US and European classification systems identify 10 personality disorders but let's focus on the DSM-5 types of personality disorders and then take a closer look at *antisocial personality disorder.*

PERSONALITY DISORDERS Disorders characterized by deeply ingrained, inflexible patterns of thinking, feeling or relating to others, or controlling impulses that cause distress or impaired functioning.

Types of personality disorders

DSM-5 personality disorders (see **TABLE 16.4**) fall into three clusters – *odd/eccentric, dramatic/erratic* and *anxious/inhibited.* The space geek, for example, could have *schizotypal personality disorder* (odd/eccentric cluster), the drama queen could have *histrionic personality disorder* (dramatic/erratic cluster) and the neat freak could have *obsessive-compulsive personality disorder* (anxious/inhibited cluster). In fact, browsing through the list may awaken other school memories. Don't rush to judgement, however. Most of your former classmates are probably quite healthy and fall far short of qualifying for a diagnosis; after all, school can be a rocky time for everyone. The DSM-5 even notes that early personality problems often do not persist into adulthood. Still, the array of personality disorders suggests that there are multiple ways an individual's gift of a unique personality could become a burden.

Personality disorders are some of the most controversial classifications in mental disorders. First, critics question whether having a problem personality is really a disorder. Given that around 15% of the US population has a personality disorder that fits a DSM-5 category, perhaps it might be better just to admit that a lot of people are difficult and leave it at that. Another question is whether personality problems correspond to 'disorders' in that there are distinct types or whether such problems might be better understood as extreme values on trait dimensions such as the Big Five traits discussed in Chapter 13 (Trull and Durrett, 2005).

Many people with personality disorders won't admit to them, and this adds a further diagnostic complication. Personality measurement depends largely on self-reports – a pointless undertaking when self-insight is the exception rather than the rule. Not incidentally, people with exaggerated personalities create problems for themselves, disturb those around them, and often seem blind to the high impact their personalities can have. It's as if their disorder blinds them to their disorder. In people suffering from

TABLE **16.4 Clusters of personality disorders as defined by the DSM-5**

Cluster	Personality disorder	Characteristics
A Odd/ eccentric	Schizotypal	Peculiar or eccentric manners of speaking or dressing. Strange beliefs. 'Magical thinking' such as belief in ESP or telepathy. Difficulty forming relationships. May react oddly in conversation, not respond, or talk to self. Speech elaborate or difficult to follow. (Possibly a mild form of schizophrenia)
	Paranoid	Distrust in others, suspicion that people have sinister motives. Apt to challenge the loyalties of friends and read hostile intentions into others' actions. Prone to anger and aggressive outbursts but otherwise emotionally cold. Often jealous, guarded, secretive, overly serious
	Schizoid	Extreme introversion and withdrawal from relationships. Prefers to be alone, little interest in others. Humourless, distant, often absorbed with own thoughts and feelings, a daydreamer. Fearful of closeness, with poor social skills, often seen as a 'loner'
B Dramatic/ erratic	Antisocial	Impoverished moral sense or 'conscience'. History of deception, crime, legal problems, impulsive and aggressive or violent behaviour. Little emotional empathy or remorse for hurting others. Manipulative, careless, callous. At high risk for substance abuse and alcoholism
	Borderline	Unstable moods and intense, stormy personal relationships. Frequent mood changes and anger, unpredictable impulses. Self-mutilation or suicidal threats or gestures to get attention or manipulate others. Self-image fluctuation and a tendency to see others as 'all good' or 'all bad'
	Histrionic	Constant attention seeking. Grandiose language, provocative dress, exaggerated illnesses, all to gain attention. Believes that everyone loves them. Emotional, lively, overly dramatic, enthusiastic and excessively flirtatious. Shallow and labile true emotions. 'Onstage'
	Narcissistic	Inflated sense of self-importance, absorbed by fantasies of self and success. Exaggerates own achievement, assumes others will recognize they are superior. Good first impressions but poor longer term relationships. Exploitative of others
C Anxious/ inhibited	Avoidant	Socially anxious and uncomfortable unless they are confident of being liked. In contrast with schizoid person, yearns for social contact. Fears criticism and worries about being embarrassed in front of others. Avoids social situations due to fear of rejection
	Dependent	Submissive, dependent, requiring excessive approval, reassurance and advice. Clings to people and fears losing them. Lacking self-confidence. Uncomfortable when alone. May be devastated by end of close relationship or suicidal if breakup is threatened
	Obsessive-compulsive	Conscientious, orderly, perfectionist. Excessive need to do everything 'right'. Inflexibly high standards and caution can interfere with their productivity. Fear of errors can make them strict and controlling. Poor expression of emotions. (Not the same as obsessive-compulsive disorder)

Source: APA, 2013

paranoid personality disorder, for example, suspicion of anyone who accuses them of paranoia is likely; similarly, people with narcissistic personality disorder are likely to see comments on their personality as mere jealousy. It's difficult to see a troubled personality from the inside.

Although some self-report surveys designed to assess personality disorders have proved useful (Clark, 2007), the lack of insight typical of personality disorders renders most instruments untrustworthy. To solve this problem, researchers have turned to *peer nomination* measures, reports by others who know the person. Just like your school classmates who gossiped about the personality problems of their peers, people in any group seem to develop common conceptions of which members are most troubled or troubling.

Research on peer nominations in university societies and groups of military recruits reveals that groups arrive at remarkably homogeneous assessments of their personality-disordered members (Oltmanns and Turkheimer, 2006). Through gossip or personal experience with the 'square pegs in round holes', everybody seems to know who is paranoid, dependent, avoidant or unusual in some other way. Peer nominations using basic reports of the behaviour of people in a group can predict which members will have further problems, such as dropping out of university or being discharged early from the military (Fiedler et al., 2004).

The common feature of personality disorders is a failure to take other people's perspectives, particularly on the self. People with personality disorders often blame others, society or the universe for their difficulties, distorting their perceptions of the world in a way that makes the personality disorder seem perfectly normal – at least to them. In many of the personality disorders, this blindness perpetuates the disorder and so hurts the person who suffers from it: people with personality disorders are often unhappy or depressed. Antisocial personality disorder, however, is particularly likely to go beyond harm to self and to exact a cost on anyone who knows the person, because the individual with antisocial personality disorder also lacks insight into what it means to hurt others.

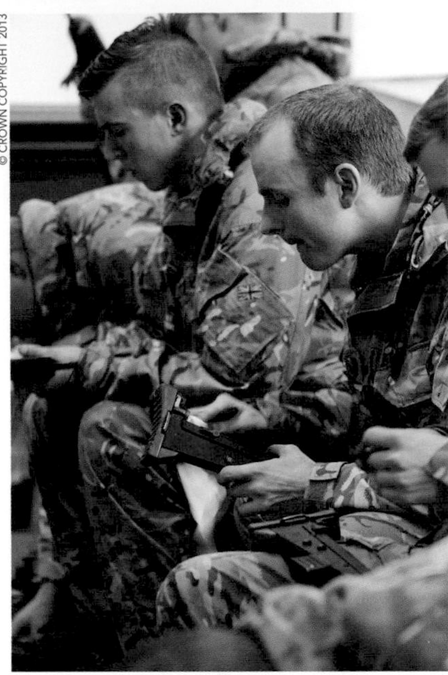

Military recruits going through basic training develop knowledge of one another's personalities. Their judgements of one another at the end of training – peer nominations – produce valid predictions of who will later receive early discharge from the military.

Antisocial personality disorder

Henri Désiré Landru began using the personal columns to attract a woman 'interested in matrimony' in Paris in 1914, and he succeeded in seducing 10 of them. He robbed them of their savings, poisoned them and cremated them in his oven, also disposing of a boy and two dogs along the way. He recorded his murders in a notebook and maintained a marriage and a mistress all the while. The gruesome actions of serial killers such as Landru leave us frightened and wondering how a fellow human being seems indifferent to another's torment and pain. However, indifference to the plight of others can be found in many more common instances such as bullying or even reckless driving which endangers lives. Are these individuals thoughtless or do they simply not care? The DSM-5 suggests that any pattern of extreme disregard for other people should be considered a personality disorder and offers the category antisocial personality disorder (APD), defined as *a pervasive pattern of disregard for and violation of the rights of others that begins in childhood or early adolescence and continues into adulthood.*

ANTISOCIAL PERSONALITY DISORDER (APD) A pervasive pattern of disregard for and violation of the rights of others that begins in childhood or early adolescence and continues into adulthood.

Adults with an APD diagnosis typically have a history of *conduct disorder* before the age of 15 – problems such as aggression, destruction of property, rule violations, and deceitfulness, lying or stealing. Early fire setting and cruelty to animals often predict antisocial tendencies. In adulthood, the diagnosis of APD is given to individuals who show three or more of a set of seven diagnostic signs: illegal behaviour, deception, impulsivity, physical aggression, recklessness, irresponsibility, and a lack of remorse for wrongdoing. About 3.6% of the general population have antisocial personality disorder, and the rate of occurrence in men is three times the rate in women (Grant et al., 2004).

The terms *sociopath* and *psychopath* describe people with APD who are especially cold-hearted, manipulative and ruthless, yet may be glib and charming (Cleckley, 1976; Hare, 1998). Although psychologists usually try to explain the development of abnormal behaviour as a product of childhood experiences or difficult life circumstances, those who work with APD seem less forgiving, often noting the sheer dangerousness of people with this disorder. Many people with APD do commit crimes, and many are caught because of the frequency and flagrancy of their infractions. In one study, among 22,790 prisoners, 47% of the men and 21% of women were diagnosed with APD (Fazel and Danesh, 2002). These proportions are higher than one finds in the general public but do such statistics support the notion of a 'criminal personality', a person born to be wild, or do they simply reflect our societies' tendency to stick all its bad apples in one basket where they are even more likely to become more distanced from others?

The early onset of conduct problems and the lack of success in treatment suggest that career criminality has an internal cause (Lykken, 1995). Evidence of brain abnormalities in people with APD is also accumulating (Blair et al., 2005). One line of investigation has looked at sensitivity to fear in psychopaths and individuals who show no such psychopathology. For example, criminal psychopaths who are shown negative emotional words such as *hate* or *corpse* exhibit less activity in the amygdala and hippocampus than noncriminals (Kiehl et al., 2001). The two brain areas are involved in the process of fear conditioning (Patrick et al., 1994), so their relative inactivity in such studies suggests that psychopaths are less sensitive to fear than other people. Violent psychopaths can target their aggression towards the self as well as others, often behaving in reckless ways that lead to violent ends. It might seem peaceful to go through life 'without fear', but perhaps fear is useful in keeping people from the extremes of antisocial behaviour.

The psychological disorders we have examined in this chapter represent a tragic loss of human potential. The contentment, peace and love that people could be enjoying are crowded out by pain and suffering when the mind goes awry to create disorders. A scientific approach to mental disorders that views them through a medical model is beginning to sort out their symptoms and causes. As we will see in Chapter 17, this approach already offers remarkably effective treatments for some disorders and for other disorders offers hope that pain and suffering can be alleviated in the future.

In summary, personality disorders are deeply ingrained, inflexible patterns of thinking, feeling, relating to others, or controlling impulses that cause distress or impaired functioning. They include three clusters – odd/eccentric, dramatic/erratic, and anxious/inhibited. The classification of these disorders is controversial because they may be no more than extreme examples of normal personality, represent personality dimensions rather than types of disorder, and are often comorbid with other disorders. One unifying feature of personality disorders is patients' lack of insight into their disorders, so self-report measurement of these disorders is ineffective and peer nomination procedures are more successful. Antisocial personality disorder (APD) is associated with a lack of moral emotions and behaviour. Those with APD can be manipulative, dangerous and reckless, often hurting others and sometimes hurting themselves. 'Criminal personalities' are often found in prison populations.

psychomythology

Schizophrenics have a Jekyll and Hyde split personality

Schizophrenia, originally coined by Eugene Bleuler ([1911]1950) from the Greek ('split mind'), is one of the most misconceived conditions in psychology and among the wider general public. Surveys indicate that at least half of us believe that a schizophrenic is someone with a split personality (for a review, see Lilienfeld et al., 2010). Part of the problem stems from the comparison of schizophrenia to Robert Louis Stevenson's 1886 supernatural horror *The Strange Case of Dr Jekyll and Mr Hyde* in which the main character has a split personality, reflecting the author's belief in 'man's dual nature' for good and evil. This was compounded by the fact that pioneer psychologists such as G. Stanley Hall used the metaphor of Jekyll and Hyde when talking about schizophrenia (McNally, 2007). In his original conception of the disorder, Bleuler used the term of split mind to refer to the fractionation of the continuity of mental processes such as feelings and thoughts. For example, if we feel sad at one moment, this is associated with thoughts related to that sadness and there is continuity from one moment to the next until such thoughts and feelings gradually transition to different states. In schizophrenia, feelings and thoughts can be dissociated and make sudden unpredictable transitions that present like a different personality. While the DSM-5 and ICD-10 recognize dissociative identity disorders (DID), where individuals present with what appears to be multiple distinct personalities, DID is still controversial and not characteristic of schizophrenia. For example, DID individuals are more likely to report voices inside their head, whereas schizophrenics who hear voices typically believe that they originate externally. If the Jekyll and Hyde nature of schizophrenia is a myth, it is one that is perpetuated in the media because it seems to provide an explanatory cause for individuals who display divergent thoughts and actions.

where do you stand?

Normal or abnormal

In the course of learning about mental disorders, you may have found yourself thinking about how they relate to your own experience. On the one hand, imagining the experience of those with anxiety disorders or depression is fairly easy because you know what it feels like to be tense or blue. On the other hand, severe disorders may seem more foreign because they involve extreme distortions of reality reflected by hallucinations and bizarre delusions. But just how unusual are these severe symptoms? In the accompanying table, you will find a list of symptoms that are sometimes considered indications of delusional beliefs (Peters et al., 1999). Rate each according to your own judgement of whether the feeling or belief is normal or abnormal.

Some of these symptoms are at least moderately common. In one study of 375 university students, 71% of participants reported hearing brief, occasional hallucinated voices during periods of wakefulness, and 39% had heard their own thoughts spoken aloud (Linszen et al., 1997; Posey and Losch, 1983). A study of 586 university students found that 30–40% had heard voices when no one was present, and of these, almost half heard voices at least once a month (Barrett and Etheridge, 1992). Reports of verbal hallucinations were not associated with measures of overt or incipient psychopathology. Apparently, hallucinatory experiences – at least of an auditory type – may not be as abnormal as you might have guessed. This fact is recognized by the Hearing Voices Network, set up in the UK to raise awareness of voice hearing, visions, tactile sensations and other sensory experiences. Far from being a diagnostic indicator of psychosis, such experiences are extremely common.

What about delusional thinking? If beliefs about scientifically unverified, paranormal experiences are any gauge, many people appear to hold some pretty odd notions. For example, in a survey of 60,000 adults, 50% expressed a belief in thought transference between two people, 25% said they believe in ghosts, and 25% in reincarnation (Cox and Cowling, 1989). Formal diagnostic interviews with a cross-section of ordinary US residents revealed that approximately 8% had delusions that met criteria for paranoia (Eaton et al., 1991). A comparison of the performance on a delusional beliefs questionnaire of healthy individuals and patients with psychotic disorders revealed, not unexpectedly, that the healthy group was less delusional than the psychotic group; however, approximately 10% of the normal group had scores that were higher than the average for the psychotic group (Peters et al., 1999).

So what is normal or abnormal? Each of us may have some personal quirks that others would surely find abnormal, and we can certainly identify some of the things our friends do as pretty peculiar as well. As we have tried to demonstrate in this chapter, however, questions of what is normal or abnormal hinge more on what causes difficulty in people's lives than on simple counts of what behaviours are common or uncommon. Where do you stand?

Instructions Rate each of the following statements from 0 (perfectly normal) to 10 (very abnormal). Don't include what might be normal or abnormal under the influence of drugs – consider only a nonintoxicated state of mind.	
Perfectly normal **Very abnormal** 0 1 2 3 4 5 6 7 8 9 10	
Feeling you are under the control of some force or power other than yourself	0 1 2 3 4 5 6 7 8 9 10
Feeling as if you are a robot or zombie without a will of your own	0 1 2 3 4 5 6 7 8 9 10
Feeling as if you are possessed by someone or something else	0 1 2 3 4 5 6 7 8 9 10
Feeling as if your actions and feelings are not under your control	0 1 2 3 4 5 6 7 8 9 10
Feeling as if someone is playing games with your mind	0 1 2 3 4 5 6 7 8 9 10
Feeling as if people seem to drop hints about you or say things with a double meaning	0 1 2 3 4 5 6 7 8 9 10
Feeling as if things in magazines or on TV were written especially for you	0 1 2 3 4 5 6 7 8 9 10
Thinking that everyone is gossiping about you	0 1 2 3 4 5 6 7 8 9 10
Feeling as if some people are not what they seem to be	0 1 2 3 4 5 6 7 8 9 10
Feeling as if things around you are unreal, as if it was all part of an experiment	0 1 2 3 4 5 6 7 8 9 10
Feeling as if someone is deliberately trying to harm you	0 1 2 3 4 5 6 7 8 9 10
Feeling as if you are being persecuted in some way	0 1 2 3 4 5 6 7 8 9 10
Feeling as if there is a conspiracy against you	0 1 2 3 4 5 6 7 8 9 10
Feeling as if some organization or institution has it in for you	0 1 2 3 4 5 6 7 8 9 10
Feeling as if someone or something is watching you	0 1 2 3 4 5 6 7 8 9 10
Feeling as if you have special abilities or powers	0 1 2 3 4 5 6 7 8 9 10
Feeling as if there is a special mission or purpose to your life	0 1 2 3 4 5 6 7 8 9 10
Feeling as if there is a mysterious power working for the good of the world	0 1 2 3 4 5 6 7 8 9 10
Feeling as if you are destined to be someone very important	0 1 2 3 4 5 6 7 8 9 10
Feeling that you are a very special or unusual person	0 1 2 3 4 5 6 7 8 9 10
Feeling that you are especially close to God	0 1 2 3 4 5 6 7 8 9 10
Thinking that people can communicate telepathically	0 1 2 3 4 5 6 7 8 9 10
Feeling as if electrical devices such as computers can influence the way you think	0 1 2 3 4 5 6 7 8 9 10
Feeling as if there are forces around you that affect you in strange ways	0 1 2 3 4 5 6 7 8 9 10
Feeling as if you have been chosen by God in some way	0 1 2 3 4 5 6 7 8 9 10
Believing in the power of witchcraft, voodoo or the occult	0 1 2 3 4 5 6 7 8 9 10
Worrying that your partner may be unfaithful	0 1 2 3 4 5 6 7 8 9 10
Thinking that you smell very unusual to other people	0 1 2 3 4 5 6 7 8 9 10
Feeling as if your body is changing in a peculiar way	0 1 2 3 4 5 6 7 8 9 10

Thinking that strangers want to have sex with you	0 1 2 3 4 5 6 7 8 9 10
Feeling you have sinned more than the average person	0 1 2 3 4 5 6 7 8 9 10
Feeling that people look at you oddly because of your appearance	0 1 2 3 4 5 6 7 8 9 10
Feeling as if you had no thoughts in your head at all	0 1 2 3 4 5 6 7 8 9 10
Feeling as if your insides might be rotting	0 1 2 3 4 5 6 7 8 9 10
Feeling as if the world is about to end	0 1 2 3 4 5 6 7 8 9 10
Having your thoughts feel alien to you in some way	0 1 2 3 4 5 6 7 8 9 10

Adapted from E. R. Peters, S. A. Joseph & P. A. Garety (1999) Measurement of Delusional Ideation in the Normal Population: Introducing the PDI (Peters et al. Delusions Inventory). *Schizophrenia Bulletin*, 25(3): 553-76, by permission of Oxford University Press

Chapter review

Identifying psychological disorders: What is abnormal?

- The study of abnormal behaviour not only enhances our understanding of the causes and treatments of psychological disorders but also offers insights about normal psychological functioning.
- The reliable identification and classification of psychological disorders are essential to the scientific study and treatment of psychological problems.
- Although imperfect, the classification systems such as the DSM or ICD are noteworthy attempts to identify the key elements of various psychological conditions. Progressive revisions of these classification systems have led to improvements in reliability, but room for improvement remains.
- An alternative approach to diagnostic classification systems is the symptom-oriented approach that dispenses with the single aetiology concept and focuses on symptoms from a dimensional rather that categorical perspective
- Psychological disorders must result from a combination of influences, including biological, psychological and social environmental factors. However, biopsychosocial models are not well defined because the causal relationship between these factors is not well understood. What is clear is that the diagnosis and treatment of psychological disorders cannot be undertaken in the absence of appreciating the critical role of social factors.
- The diathesis-stress model proposes that a person may possess a predisposition to a mental disorder that remains unexpressed until it is triggered by stress.
- The social stigma associated with psychological disorders can lead to labelling effects that may, in some circumstances, undermine objective judgements and perceptions.

Anxiety disorders: when fears take over

- Anxiety disorders involve irrational worries and fears that undermine wellbeing and cause dysfunction.
- The anxiety may be chronic, as in generalized anxiety disorder (GAD), or it may be tied to a specific object or situation, as in the phobic disorders.
- In panic disorder, people experience a sudden and intense attack of anxiety that is terrifying and can lead them to become housebound for fear of public humiliation.
- People with obsessive-compulsive disorder (OCD) experience repetitive, anxiety-provoking thoughts that compel them to engage in ritualistic, irrational behaviour.
- Post-traumatic stress disorder (PTSD) is characterized by recurrent thoughts about some traumatic event that can appear weeks and months later, and is typically found in war veterans and survivors of various form of disaster.

Dissociative disorders: going to pieces

- The dissociative disorders involve severely disjointed and fragmented cognitive processes reflected in significant disruptions in memory, awareness or personality.
- People with dissociative identity disorder (DID) shift between two or more identities that are distinct from each other in personal memories, behavioural characteristics and attitudes. Reported cases of DID have been increasing since the 1970s as the disorder has received more widespread media attention, leading some researchers to believe that it may be overdiagnosed.
- Dissociative amnesia and dissociative fugue involve significant memory loss that is not the result of normal forgetting and cannot be attributed to brain injury, drugs or another mental disorder. The memory loss is often associated with stressful life circumstances. In addition to a memory loss for one's personal history, dissociative fugue is accompanied by an abrupt departure from home and the assumption of a new identity.

Mood disorders: at the mercy of emotions

- Major depression, also known as unipolar depression, is characterized by a severely depressed mood that is associated with excessive self-criticism, guilt, concentration difficulties, suicidal thoughts, sleep and appetite disturbances, and lethargy. Approximately twice as many women are diagnosed with depression as men.
- Dysthymia is a less severe form of depression that persists for several years.
- Depression shows a moderate level of heritability and may involve neurochemical imbalances. Cognitive biases may also contribute to depression by tainting judgements and perceptions. In addition, depression-prone individuals may inadvertently behave in ways that lead to social rejection, thereby contributing to and confirming a sense of low self-worth.
- Bipolar disorder is an unstable emotional condition involving extreme mood swings of depression and mania. The manic phase is characterized by periods of abnormally and persistently elevated, expansive or irritable mood.
- Bipolar disorder has a high rate of heritability, although it is unclear which gene or genes may be responsible for the problem.

Stress and family problems may also contribute to the onset and maintenance of the disorder.

Schizophrenia: losing the grasp on reality

- Schizophrenia is a profound disorder that can bring hallucinations, delusions, disorganized speech, disorganized or catatonic behaviour, and negative symptoms such as motivational deficits. Different subtypes of schizophrenia have been identified: paranoid, catatonic, hebephrenic, undifferentiated, residual and simple. Although schizophrenia affects only 1% of the population, it accounts for a disproportionate share of psychiatric hospitalizations.
- Genetic factors play a role in the development of schizophrenia, but they do not provide a complete account. Neuroimaging studies have found brain abnormalities such as enlarged ventricles in some patients and a general tendency for some loss of grey matter as the disorder develops. Drugs that reduce the availability of dopamine sometimes reduce the symptoms of schizophrenia, but research suggests that schizophrenia may involve a complex interaction among a variety of neurotransmitters. The risk of developing schizophrenia and the likelihood of relapse are significantly affected by the quality of family communication patterns and relationships.

Personality disorders: going to extremes

- Personality disorders are deeply ingrained, inflexible patterns of thinking, feeling, relating to others, or controlling impulses that cause distress or impaired functioning.
- The personality disorders include three clusters – odd/eccentric, dramatic/erratic, and anxious/inhibited. However, the classification of these disorders is controversial because they may be no more than extremes of personality or dimensions rather than types, and they are frequently comorbid with other disorders.
- Patients with personality disorders often lack insight into their disorders. Self-report measurement of these disorders is thus difficult, but peer nomination procedures can be successful.
- Antisocial personality disorder (APD) is associated with a lack of moral emotions and behaviour. People with APD can be manipulative, dangerous and reckless, often hurting others or themselves, and are often found in prison populations.

Key terms

Recommended reading

Bentall, R. P. (2003) *Madness Explained: Psychosis and Human Nature*. London: Allen Lane. Winner of the British Psychological Society book award 2004, this easily accessible account of the origins and pitfalls of medical models of mental disorders is a tour de force against diagnostic approaches. Bentall is a leading voice in the symptom-oriented approach to mental disorder.

Jamison, K. R. (1999) *Night Falls Fast: Understanding Suicide.* New York: Random House. Kay Jamison, author of the national bestseller *An Unquiet Mind* and a researcher on mood disorders, examines the phenomenon of suicide using data and powerful examples. She discusses the biological, psychological and sociocultural factors that contribute to suicide and highlights the remarkable lack of attention given to this common killer that claims thousands of lives each year.

Nasar, S. (1998) *A Beautiful Mind.* New York: Simon & Schuster. Recounts the story of John Nash, a mathematics prodigy who was awarded the 1993 Nobel Prize in Economics for his influential early contributions but whose work was interrupted for more than 20 years by schizophrenia. The story of his life, his accomplishments and his struggle with and recovery from schizophrenia are told in moving detail. The book was the basis for the film of the same name.

Osborn, I. (1998) *Tormenting Thoughts and Secret Rituals: The Hidden Epidemic of Obsessive-Compulsive Disorder.* New York: Dell. Written from the prospective of a clinician who also suffers from OCD, this book is lively, lucid, informative and scholarly.

17

- Treatment: historical perspective
- Medical and biological treatments: healing the mind through the brain
- Psychological therapies: healing the mind through interaction
- the real world Mental health professionals
- Ancient wisdom, modern mindfulness hot science
- Treatment effectiveness: for better or for worse
- Environmental perspective: sources of stress
- Stress reactions: all shook up
- Stress management: dealing with it
- Electroconvulsive shock treatment is shocking psychomythology
- where do you stand? Genetic screening for mental health?

Chapter learning objectives

At the end of this chapter you will be able to:

1 Appreciate early approaches to treating mental disorder and how these have changed in the past 200 years.

2 Describe some of the biological and medical approaches to treating mental disorder.

3 Distinguish and describe different forms of psychotherapy.

4 Evaluate the effectiveness of different forms of treatment for mental disorder.

5 Describe the mechanisms of stress-related illness and techniques that can reduce their negative impact.

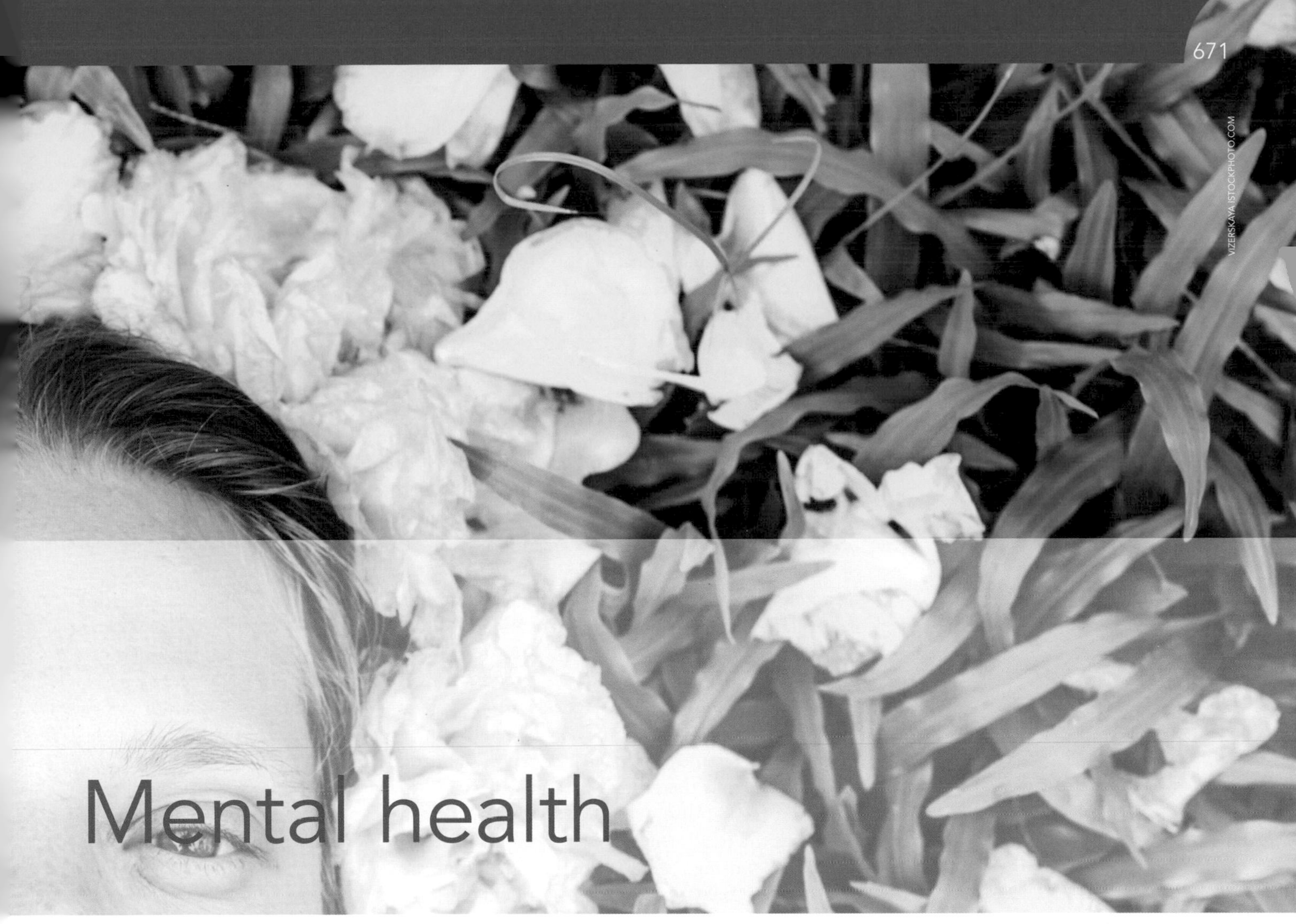

Mental health

At the age of 17, Anneliese Michel, a German girl born in Bavaria in 1952, began suffering from unusual seizures during the night, which involved her body suddenly becoming rigid, the sensation of an enormous weight on her chest, paralysis and an inability to speak. Initially, the doctors diagnosed epilepsy and prescribed anti-epileptic medication but this did not seem to alleviate her symptoms and she developed severe depression. As a devout Catholic, Anneliese became convinced that she was possessed by demons. She reported seeing demonic faces and spoke in strange voices. At the age of 23, she sought help from the Catholic Church who agreed to perform an exorcism of the young girl. From September 1975 for the next year, one or two exorcisms that could last hours were held every week. During these sessions, prayers and incantations to banish her demons were evoked and she had to perform genuflections, where the individual has to drop to their knees as a penance. She refused to eat and apparently intended her death by starvation to 'atone for the wayward youth of the day and the apostate priests of the modern church'. During the last week of her life, Anneliese was too ill to perform the genuflections that had ruptured her kneecaps and so was assisted by her parents. She died on 1 July 1975 from severe malnutrition and dehydration. The two priests who had conducted the exorcism and both parents were later convicted of negligent manslaughter.

Treatment: historical perspective

The history of the treatment of mental disorder is not a particularly pleasant one but even in this modern era, as illustrated by the tragic case of Anneliese Michel, some people still regard psychiatric disorder as some form of supernatural affliction. As you read in Chapter 16, a large proportion of society will suffer from some form of mental disorder at some point in their lives. These disorders have many different symptoms, causes and consequences. It is now widely accepted that biological, psychological and environmental factors are responsible for the onset, course and outcome of mental disorders, so various treatments address these factors to reduce the symptoms that cause distress and problems for the individual. In this chapter, we will examine treatments and approaches from each of these three perspectives, although it is worth emphasizing that the origin and treatment of all mental disorders should be regarded as the interaction of biology, psychology and environment.

Demonic possession

DEMONIC POSSESSION A supernatural account for mental disorder.

TREPANNING Drilling a hole in the skull.

From the beginnings of human civilization, various societies regarded mental disorder as **demonic possession** – *a supernatural account for mental disorder*. This is understandable in that some types of mental disorder, especially psychotic episodes such as those experienced by Anneliese Michel, manifest as bizarre thoughts and behaviours that seem completely out of character. There is anthropological evidence, for example, that thousands of years ago the occasional human was 'treated' for some malady by the practice of **trepanning** – *drilling a hole in the skull* – perhaps in the belief that this would release the evil spirits that people thought were affecting the mind (Alt et al., 1997). Trepanned skulls have been found dating from the late Paleolithic period and the procedure must have worked otherwise the practice would not have persisted in virtually every part of the world. These crude Stone Age operations were done with a piece of flint and the fact that many of these skulls show new bone growth around the edge of the hole indicates that patients often survived such dangerous and undoubtedly painful operations. One possibility is that the crude operation alleviated intracranial pressure that could have produced mental disorders (Gross, 1999). So, while the supernatural explanation was not valid, the treatment may have been effective in some instances. Thousands of years later, when writing developed, early civilizations recorded their explanations for mental disorder. The Babylonians had a specific demon, Idta, responsible for mental disorder, and similar examples of demonic explanation can be found in early Chinese, Egyptian and Hebrew accounts. Treatment therefore consisted of rituals to force the evil spirit to leave the body such as beating, torture and starvation.

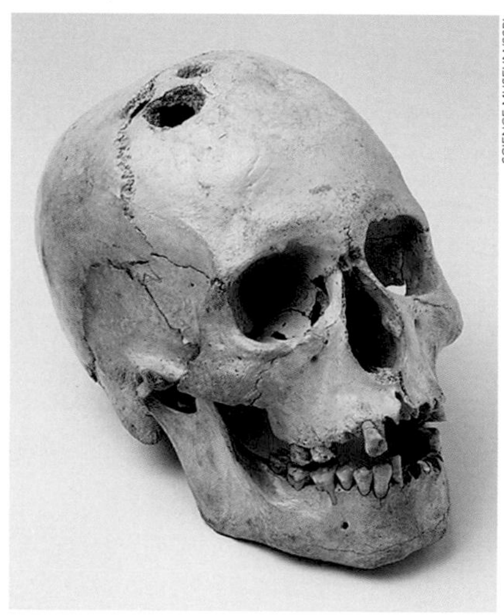

SCIENCE MUSEUM/SSPL

This trepanned skull from the Bronze Age (2200–2000 BC) was excavated in Jericho, Palestine. Four holes were drilled in the skull and the patient lived afterwards, as shown by the regrowth of bone covering the holes. Don't try this at home!

Humoural theories

HUMOURS The humours are blood, black bile, yellow bile and phlegm. These four humours corresponded to the four primary qualities (hot, dry, cold and wet), the four elements (fire, air, earth and water) and four psychological temperaments (sanguine, bilious, melancholic and phlegmatic).

The Greek word for nature is *physis*, which gives us our words physics and physician, although we use the term 'doctor' in Europe, so it is no coincidence that the Greeks thought that the body and mind were linked. Unlike supernatural accounts, the early Greek doctors regarded mental disorders as a natural consequence of some bodily imbalance. Hippocrates, the father of modern medicine (that's why all doctors are expected to take the Hippocratic oath), advocated that a healthy body and mind was achieved by the correct balance of four bodily fluids or **humours** – *blood, black bile, yellow bile and phlegm. These four humours corresponded to the four primary qualities (hot, dry, cold and wet), the four elements (fire, air, earth and water) and four psychological temperaments (sanguine, bilious, melancholic and phlegmatic).* All mental disorders could be explained by an imbalance of the humours, so treatments consisted of redressing this imbalance (Porter, 2003). For example, an excess of blood was believed to be responsible for mood swings and could be treated by avoiding blood-rich foods such as red meat or by bloodletting, a practice that persisted in Europe until the 19th century. Today, many traditional medical approaches still regard understanding illness and treatment as one of imbalance.

After the Greeks

While Greek theories were misguided, at least they did not advocate evil spirits for the causes of mental disorders. However, following the fall of the Roman Empire, Europe entered a period known as the Dark Ages, where superstition and demonology proliferated. Many of the early accounts of demonic possession could have been cases of schizophrenia, which, after all, does sometimes present to the sufferer as hearing voices or some external agent inserting thoughts into their mind. Epilepsy and organic disorders also produce bizarre behaviours that were interpreted as demonic possession. For example, in Salem, New England in 1692, eight girls suddenly developed disordered speech, made strange gestures and had convulsive fits that were attributed to witchcraft. This sparked a witch-hunt and trials that would lead to the hanging of nineteen people and one man crushed to death by a stone. It is unlikely that all the girls developed psychosis by chance at the same time. Rather, there must have been some environmental factor. One intriguing explanation for the origin of the girls' psychotic symptoms is that it was due to poisoning from **ergot** – *a mind-altering fungus* – that had grown on wet rye harvested to make bread (Caporael, 1976). Ergot poisoning produces crawling sensations on the skin, tingling in the fingers, vertigo, vomiting, hallucinations and convulsions. (The whole episode is dramatized in *The Crucible*, a 1953 play by Arthur Miller.)

ERGOT A mind-altering fungus.

Other theories for mental disorder also appealed to supernatural causes. For example, full moons were, and to some extent still are, thought to trigger mental disorder (Rotten and Kelly, 1985), which is where the word 'lunatic' comes from. In some cultures today, demonic possession is still regarded as an explanation for mental disorders, and while modern medicine has been introduced to every known society today, many of the world's population in undeveloped countries still seek out traditional healers to treat mental disorders using supernatural practices.

The emergence of the asylums

Confinement of those with mental disorders began in Europe around the 15th century with the first **asylums** – *workhouses to house beggars and those with mental disorders*. One of the first hospitals that dealt with mental disorder was the Priory of St Mary of Bethlem in London, founded in 1243. It remained in operation for the next 700 years, only closing in 1948, and would become synonymous with the worst aspects of mental asylums. The word 'bedlam', describing a scene of wild uproar and confusion, is a shortened version of Bethlem, which became a major tourist attraction by the 18th century, when visitors would pay to watch the antics of the confined patients. One wonders whether the current viewing public's appetite for dysfunctional characters on reality TV is no less a return to voyeurism of the mentally disordered for entertainment.

ASYLUMS Workhouses to house beggars and those with mental disorders.

Treatment of patients in these asylums was shocking in more ways than one. One of the most common methods employed was confinement and restraint, which also had obvious practical advantages of controlling the patient from harming others and themselves. Benjamin Rush, father of US psychiatry, developed a 'tranquilizing chair' to which the patient was strapped by their arms and feet, with a head restraint that blocked their vision, often for weeks. Other forms of confinement included the 'English coffin', essentially an upright cabinet for restraining the patient. When they were not manacled to the wall or strapped into seats, patients were spun around in devices to 'bring them to their senses'. And when electricity became available in the 19th century, this was put to widespread use in the psychiatric hospitals across Europe as a means of shocking patients (literally) back to normality (Beveridge and Renvoize, 1988).

At the end of the 18th century, Philippe Pinel was put in charge of La Bicêtre, a large Parisian asylum. Possibly as a result of the liberty advocated by the architects of the French Revolution, he released the patients from their chains and allowed them to roam around the asylum grounds. Patients who had been previously unmanageable become calm and easy to handle. The asylum was opened up and well-lit, ventilated rooms replaced the former dungeons. Soon, patients who had been incarcerated for years were eventually discharged and returned to normal life.

Pinel's humane approach to patients with mental disorders was mirrored in other places. Quaker William Tuke was so appalled by the conditions at the York Asylum that he formed the York Retreat in 1796, a country estate outside York that provided (and still provides) a quiet sanctuary for patients to recover. Soon, similar retreats were established in the US. However, for the majority of patients, psychiatric treatment was mainly a pitiful existence in crowded bedlam-type asylums and institutions that have only been closed down in the past few decades in modern Western countries, but remain today in some poorer countries.

In summary, from the very beginning, humans have treated others who may have had some form of mental disorder. Early accounts of mental disorder may have assumed demonic possession and treatments consisted of rituals to exorcise the evil spirits or make the body inhabitable by beatings or starvation. In contrast, Greek doctors regarded mental disorders as a consequence of an imbalance of four bodily fluids, blood, black bile, yellow bile and phlegm. Under this model, treatment included practices designed to restore the balance. The first hospitals for patients with mental disorders were mostly asylums that locked sufferers away from society and often kept them restrained for long periods. Other treatments included attempts to shock the patient back to normality.

Medical and biological treatments: healing the mind through the brain

Ever since someone discovered that a knock to the head can affect the mind, people have suspected that direct brain interventions might hold the keys to a cure for psychological disorders. As we saw earlier, trepanning may have been used for treating mental disorder in the Stone Age. Certainly, such radical surgery was used as a treatment for mental disorder until the 18th century, when it was abandoned for more restraint-based approaches (Gross, 1999). Even now, surgery for psychological disorders is a last resort, and treatments that focus on the brain usually involve interventions that are less dramatic. The use of drugs to influence the brain was also discovered in prehistory, for example alcohol has been around for a long time, and drug treatments have grown in variety and effectiveness to become what is now the most common medical approach in treating psychological disorders.

The fact that the brain can be understood as a biological organ – like the stomach or the elbow – makes it tempting to think of medical and biological treatments as 'magic bullets' for mental health, quick fixes that achieve easily what psychotherapy might take a long time to achieve or might never do. Just as taking an aspirin can reduce the pain of tennis elbow, we might assume that medicating the brain could potentially reduce just about any psychological symptom. Perhaps there is a pill to calm obsessive worries about driving a car into oncoming traffic? Or a pill to neutralize the schizophrenic symptom of hearing voices? A pill to stop nail biting? Current knowledge about the brain usually doesn't allow treatments to be so specific. Instead, biological and medical treatments often have broad effects, such as improving a person's mood or making the person calmer. These treatments can reduce the frequency or severity of some symptoms but may not always succeed as magic bullets.

In this section, we will explore the variety of medical and biological treatments currently in use, looking first at medications that broadly target psychosis, anxiety and depression, and then at other biologically based treatments that influence the brain but do not involve drugs.

Antipsychotic medications

The story of drug treatments for severe psychological disorders starts with a stuffy nose. As you may know, the antihistamines we take for a stuffy nose caused by allergies often have the side effect of inducing drowsiness. French chemist Paul Charpentier synthesized a drug related to antihistamine from coal tar in 1951, and tests on animals revealed that it had a much stronger sedative effect than antihistamine. Even better, this sedative administered to people with schizophrenia often left them euphoric and docile when they had formerly been agitated and incorrigible (Barondes, 2003). The drug was chlorpromazine, the first in a series of **antipsychotic drugs**, which *treat schizophrenia and related psychotic disorders*.

ANTIPSYCHOTIC DRUGS Drugs that treat schizophrenia and related psychotic disorders.

Through the 1950s and 60s, related medications such as thioridazine and haloperidol were introduced and completely changed the way schizophrenia was managed. Before the introduction of antipsychotic drugs, people with schizophrenia often exhibited bizarre symptoms and were sometimes so disruptive and difficult to manage that the only way to protect them (and other people) was to keep them in asylums. In the period following the introduction of these drugs, the number of people in psychiatric hospitals decreased by more than two-thirds. Antipsychotic drugs made possible the deinstitutionalization of hundreds of thousands of people and gave a major boost to the field of **psychopharmacology** – *the study of drug effects on psychological states and symptoms.*

PSYCHOPHARMACOLOGY The study of drug effects on psychological states and symptoms.

These antipsychotic medications are believed to block dopamine receptors in parts of the brain such as the mesolimbic area, an area between the tegmentum (in the midbrain) and the limbic system (see Chapter 3). The medication reduces dopamine activity in these areas. As you read in Chapter 16, the effectiveness of schizophrenia medications led to the 'dopamine hypothesis', suggesting that schizophrenia may be caused by excess dopamine in the synapse. Research has indeed found that dopamine *over*activity in the mesolimbic areas of the brain is related to the more bizarre positive symptoms of schizophrenia, such as hallucinations and delusions (described in Chapter 16) (Marangell et al., 2003).

Although antipsychotic drugs work well for positive symptoms, it turns out that negative symptoms such as emotional numbing and social withdrawal may be related to dopamine *under*activity in the mesocortical areas of the brain (connections between parts of the tegmentum and the cortex). This may help explain why antipsychotic medications do not relieve negative symptoms well. Instead of a medication that blocks dopamine receptors, negative symptoms require a medication that *increases* the amount of dopamine available at the synapse. This is a good example of how medical treatments can have broad psychological effects but cannot target specific psychological symptoms.

©ISTOCKPHOTO.COM/MARKUS DIVIS

People with schizophrenia are two to three times more likely to smoke tobacco than the average person (Kelly and McCreadie, 2000). There are several explanations being tested for this, including the possibility that people with schizophrenia seek out nicotine to reduce their symptoms. If this is true, their 'self-medication' may point the way towards new drug treatments for the disorder that might be more helpful and less harmful than smoking.

After the introduction of antipsychotic medications, there was little change in the available treatments for schizophrenia for more than a quarter of a century. However, in the 1990s, a new class of antipsychotic drugs was introduced. These newer drugs, which include clozapine, risperidone and olanzepine, have become known as *atypical antipsychotics* (the older drugs are now often referred to as *conventional* or *typical* antipsychotics). Unlike the older antipsychotic medications, these newer drugs appear to affect the dopamine and serotonin systems, blocking both types of receptors. The ability to block serotonin receptors appears to be a useful addition, since enhanced serotonin activity in the brain has been implicated in some of the core difficulties in schizophrenia, such as cognitive and perceptual disruptions, as well as mood disturbances. This may explain why atypical antipsychotics work at least as well as older drugs for the positive symptoms of schizophrenia but also work fairly well for negative symptoms (Bradford et al., 2002).

Like most medications, antipsychotic drugs have side effects. The side effects can be sufficiently unpleasant that some people 'go off their meds', preferring their symptoms to the drug. One side effect that often occurs with long-term use is *tardive dyskinesia*, a condition of involuntary movements of the face, mouth and extremities. In fact, patients often need to take another medication to treat the unwanted side effects of the conventional antipsychotic drugs. Side effects of the newer medications tend to be milder than those of the older antipsychotics. For that reason, the atypical antipsychotics are now usually the frontline treatments for schizophrenia (Marangell et al., 2003).

Anti-anxiety medications

Anti-anxiety medications are *drugs that help reduce a person's experience of fear or anxiety.* The most commonly used anti-anxiety medications are the *benzodiazepines*, a type of tranquilizer that works by facilitating the action of the neurotransmitter gamma-aminobutyric acid (GABA; see Chapter 3). GABA inhibits certain neurons in the brain, producing a calming effect for the person. Commonly prescribed benzodiazepines

ANTI-ANXIETY MEDICATIONS Drugs that help reduce a person's experience of fear or anxiety.

include diazepam, lorazepam and temazepam. The benzodiazepines typically take effect in a matter of minutes and are effective for reducing the symptoms of anxiety disorders (Roy-Byrne and Cowley, 2002).

Nonetheless, these days doctors are relatively cautious when prescribing benzodiazepines. They tend to prescribe them at lower dosages and for shorter periods than in the past. One concern is that these drugs have the potential for abuse. They are often associated with the development of **drug tolerance** – *the need for higher dosages of a drug over time to achieve the same effects following long-term use.* Furthermore, after people become tolerant of a drug, they risk significant withdrawal symptoms following discontinuation. Some withdrawal symptoms include increased heart rate, shakiness, insomnia, agitation and anxiety – the very symptoms the drug was taken to eliminate. Therefore, patients who take benzodiazepines for extended periods may have difficulty coming off these drugs and should discontinue their medications gradually to minimize withdrawal symptoms (Schatzberg et al., 2003). Another consideration when prescribing benzodiazepines is their side effects. The most common side effect is drowsiness, although benzodiazepines can also have negative effects on coordination and memory.

DRUG TOLERANCE The need for higher doses of a drug over time to achieve the same effects following long-term use.

Buspirone, a newer drug, has been shown to reduce anxiety among individuals who suffer from generalized anxiety disorder (GAD). Buspirone is not as effective as the benzodiazepines for anxiety disorders other than GAD, but it doesn't produce the drowsiness and withdrawal symptoms associated with them (Roy-Byrne and Cowley, 2002).

Antidepressants and mood stabilizers

Antidepressants are *a class of drugs that help lift people's mood.* Over the past few decades, the three most commonly prescribed antidepressants were the monoamine oxidase inhibitors (MAOIs), tricyclic antidepressants and selective serotonin reuptake inhibitors (SSRIs):

ANTIDEPRESSANTS A class of drugs that help lift people's mood.

- *Monoamine oxidase inhibitors (MAOIs):* Antidepressants were first introduced in the 1950s, when iproniazid, a drug that was used to treat tuberculosis, was found to elevate mood (Selikoff et al., 1952). Iproniazid is an MAOI, a medication that prevents the enzyme monoamine oxidase from breaking down neurotransmitters such as noradrenaline, serotonin and dopamine. However, despite their effectiveness, MAOIs are rarely prescribed anymore. MAOI side effects such as dizziness and loss of sexual interest are often difficult to tolerate, and these drugs interact with many different medications, including over-the-counter cold medicines. They also can cause dangerous increases in blood pressure when taken with foods that contain tyramine, a natural substance formed from the breakdown of protein in certain cheeses, beans, aged meats, soya products and draft beer.
- *Tricyclic antidepressants:* These were also introduced in the 1950s, and include drugs such as imipramine and amitriptyline. These medications block the reuptake of noradrenaline and serotonin, thereby increasing the amount of neurotransmitter in the synaptic space between neurons. The most common side effects of tricyclic antidepressants include dry mouth, constipation, difficulty urinating, blurred vision and racing heart (Marangell et al., 2003). Although these drugs are still prescribed, they are used much less frequently than they were in the past because of these side effects.
- *Selective serotonin reuptake inhibitors (SSRIs):* Among the most commonly used antidepressants today are the SSRIs, which include drugs such as fluoxetine, citalopram and paroxetine. The SSRIs work by blocking the reuptake of serotonin in the brain, which makes more serotonin available in the synaptic space between neurons. The greater availability of serotonin in the synapse gives the neuron a better chance of 'recognizing' and using this neurotransmitter in sending the desired signal. The SSRIs were developed based on hypotheses that low levels of serotonin are a causal factor in depression (see Chapter 16). Supporting this hypothesis, SSRIs are effective for depression, but recent large-scale studies have questioned whether this effectiveness is restricted to the most severe forms of the disorder (see later). SSRIs are called 'selective' because, unlike

the tricyclic antidepressants, which work on the serotonin and noradrenaline systems, SSRIs work more specifically on the serotonin system (see FIGURE 17.1).

- *Serotonin and noradrenaline reuptake inhibitors (SNRIs):* Recently, a number of new antidepressants, the SNRIs, such as duloxetine and venlafaxine, have been introduced. These antidepressants have characteristics that make them unique from the three classes of antidepressants discussed so far and appear to have fewer side effects than the tricyclic antidepressants and MAOIs.

Antidepressants take from a few weeks to more than a month before they start to have an effect. Besides relieving the symptoms of depression, almost all antidepressants effectively treat anxiety disorders, and many of them can resolve other problems, such as eating disorders. In fact, several companies that manufacture SSRIs have recently marketed their drugs as treatments for anxiety disorders rather than for their antidepressant effects. The general improvement in mood and outlook produced by antidepressants is attractive not only to people who are clinically depressed or anxious but also to many others seeking to level out the emotional hills and valleys of everyday life. Prozac, an SSRI, is widely prescribed for people who are not suffering from specific disorders, and there is considerable debate about whether antidepressants should be used in this way to contribute to the wellbeing of people who have not been diagnosed with a psychological disorder (Kramer, 1997).

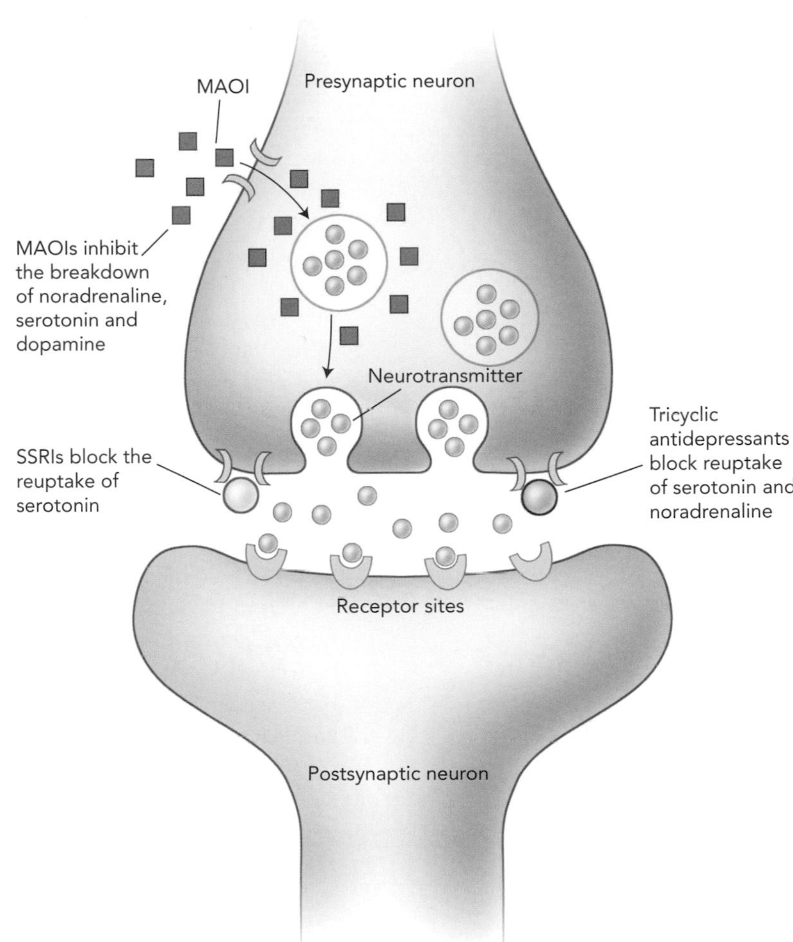

FIGURE **17.1 Antidepressant drug actions** Antidepressant drugs such as SNRIs, SSRIs and tricyclic antidepressants act on the neurotransmitters such as serotonin, dopamine and noradrenaline by inhibiting their breakdown and blocking reuptake. These actions make more of the neurotransmitter available for release and leave more of the neurotransmitter in the synaptic gap to activate the receptor sites on the postsynaptic neuron. These drugs relieve depression and often alleviate anxiety and other disorders.

Although antidepressants are effective in treating unipolar depression, they are not recommended for treating bipolar disorder, which is characterized by manic and depressive episodes (see Chapter 16). Antidepressants are not prescribed because they might trigger a manic episode in a person with bipolar disorder. Instead, bipolar disorder is treated with *mood stabilizers*, which are medications used to suppress the swings between mania and depression. Commonly used mood stabilizers include lithium and valproate. Even in unipolar depression, lithium is sometimes effective when combined with traditional antidepressants in people who do not respond to antidepressants alone.

Lithium has been associated with possible long-term kidney and thyroid problems, so people taking lithium must monitor their blood levels of lithium on a regular basis. Further, lithium has a precise range in which it is useful for each person, another reason it should be closely monitored with blood tests. On the other hand, valproate does not require such careful blood monitoring. In sum, although antidepressants are effective for a wide variety of problems, mood stabilizers may be required when a person's symptoms include extreme swings between highs and lows, such as experienced with bipolar disorder.

Biological treatments beyond medication

Although medication can be an effective biological treatment, for some people medications do not work or the side effects are intolerable. If this group of people don't respond to psychotherapy either, what other options do they have to achieve symptom relief? There are some additional avenues of help, but some are risky or poorly understood. In this section, we review biological treatments that go beyond medication and also look at the controversy surrounding them. These biological treatments include electroconvulsive therapy, neurostimulation, phototherapy and psychosurgery.

Electroconvulsive therapy

When electricity became available in the 19th century, it was put to widespread use in the psychiatric hospitals across Europe as a means of shocking patients (literally) back to normality (Beveridge and Renvoize, 1988). More commonly known as 'shock therapy', **electroconvulsive therapy (ECT)** is *a treatment that involves inducing a mild seizure by delivering an electrical shock to the brain.* The technique was developed in 1938 by two Italian doctors Cerletti and Bini who thought that mental disorder could be treated by inducing epileptic seizures that were thought to somehow reset the brain. The shock is applied to the person's scalp for less than a second. ECT is primarily used to treat severe depression, although it may also be useful for treating mania (Mukherjee et al., 1994). When first introduced, ECT was administered without any muscle relaxants or anaesthetic, so participants often experienced muscle contractions and spasms during the seizure, some of which led to injuries. The procedure was frightening and painful for the recipient. Today, ECT is administered when the patient has been pretreated with muscle relaxants and is under general anaesthetic, so the patient does not have convulsions and is not conscious of the procedure. In the UK, the National Institute of Health and Clinical Excellence has looked in detail at the use of ECT and has said that it should be used only in severe depression, severe mania or catatonia (described in Chapter 16). ECT is most often used for severe depression, usually only when other treatments have failed (see psychomythology box).

ELECTROCONVULSIVE THERAPY (ECT) A treatment that involves inducing a mild seizure by delivering an electrical shock to the brain.

It is still unclear exactly how such a radical treatment can produce therapeutic effects but a recent Scottish study using before and after fMRI on a small sample of patients with severe depression that did not respond to other treatments found that ECT altered the activity of frontal systems by strongly down regulating connectivity in the dorsal lateral prefrontal cortex – part of the circuitry implicated in this mood disorder (Perrin et al., 2012). A recent review of 26 imaging studies of the longitudinal effects of ECT also point to the common finding of decreased frontal activation in terms of metabolism and connectivity (Abbott et al., 2014).

Neurostimulation therapies

Transcranial magnetic stimulation (TMS) is *a treatment that involves placing a powerful pulsed magnet over a person's scalp, which alters neuronal activity in the brain* (George et al., 1999). As a treatment for depression, the magnet is placed just above the right or left eyebrow in an effort to stimulate the right or left prefrontal cortex – areas of the brain implicated in depression. TMS is an exciting development because it is noninvasive and has fewer side effects than ECT. Also, people do not require an anaesthetic for this procedure. Side effects are minimal; they may include mild headache and a small risk of seizure, but TMS has no impact on memory or concentration. Enough studies have shown a positive effect on depression to suggest that TMS is useful (McNamara et al., 2001), even in treating depression that is unresponsive to medication (Fitzgerald et al., 2003; Kauffmann et al., 2004). In fact, a recent study comparing TMS with ECT found that both procedures were effective, with no significant differences between them (Janicak et al., 2002). Other studies have investigated the utility of TMS for problems such as hallucinations, and early results are promising (Hoffman et al., 2003).

TRANSCRANIAL MAGNETIC STIMULATION (TMS) A treatment that involves placing a powerful pulsed magnet over a person's scalp, which alters neuronal activity in the brain.

Vagus nerve stimulation (VNS) is *a relatively new treatment that involves electrically stimulating the vagus nerve, which induces changes in blood flow to the brain.* It was originally discovered after epileptic patients who were treated for their seizures with vagus nerve stimulation often showed improved mood, even though some patients showed no change in their seizure symptoms (Marangell et al., 2004). VNS is particularly useful for treatment-resistant patients with major depression. One suggested mechanism is that VNS changes the blood flow to brain regions implicated in depression in the same way that antidepressants work (Marangell et al., 2007).

VAGUS NERVE STIMULATION (VNS) A relatively new treatment that involves electrically stimulating the vagus nerve, which induces changes in blood flow to the brain.

Phototherapy

Phototherapy, *a therapy that involves repeated exposure to bright light*, may be helpful to people who have a seasonal pattern to their depression. This could include people

PHOTOTHERAPY A therapy that involves repeated exposure to bright light.

suffering with seasonal affective disorder (SAD; see Chapter 16), or those who experience depression only in the winter months due to the lack of light. Typically, the patient is exposed to bright light in the mornings, using a lamp designed for this purpose. Treatments lasting two hours each day for a week seem to be effective, at least in the short term (Terman et al., 1989).

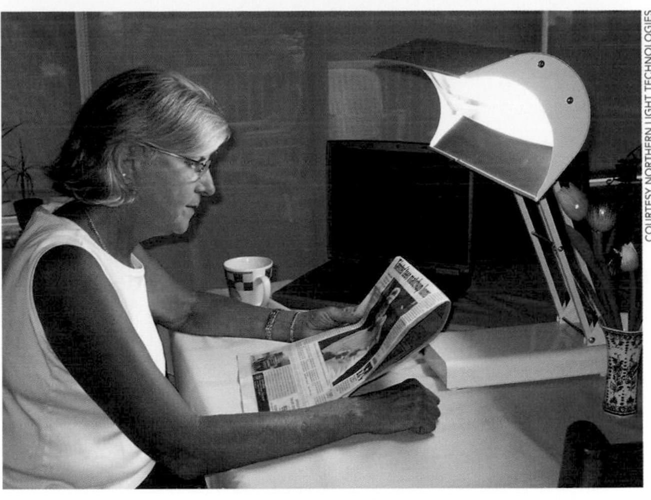

COURTESY NORTHERN LIGHT TECHNOLOGIES

Repeated exposure to bright light has been proved to be useful for treating SAD, a form of depression that occurs only in the winter months, probably in reaction to reduced sunlight.

Psychosurgery

In rare cases, **psychosurgery** – *the surgical destruction of specific brain areas* – is used to treat certain psychological disorders, such as obsessive-compulsive disorder (OCD). Psychosurgery has a controversial history, beginning in the 1930s with the invention of the *lobotomy* by Portuguese doctor Egas Moniz (1874–1955). After discovering that certain surgical procedures on animal brains calmed behaviour, Moniz began to use similar techniques on violent or agitated human patients. Lobotomies involved inserting an instrument into the brain through the patient's eye socket or through holes drilled in the side of the head. The objective was to sever connections between the frontal lobes and inner brain structures such as the thalamus, known to be involved in emotion. Although some lobotomies produced highly successful results and Moniz received the 1949 Nobel Prize for his work, significant side effects such as extreme lethargy or childlike impulsivity detracted from these benefits. Lobotomy was used too widely for years, leaving many people devastated by these permanent side effects, and there is an ongoing movement challenging the award of the Nobel to Moniz. The development of antipsychotic drugs in the 1950s provided a safer way to treat violent patients and brought the practice of lobotomy to an end (Swayze, 1995).

PSYCHOSURGERY The surgical destruction of specific brain areas.

Today, psychosurgeries are far more precise than the lobotomies of the 1930s and 40s in targeting particular brain areas to lesion. This increased precision has produced better results. For example, patients suffering from OCD who fail to respond to treatment (including several trials of medications and cognitive behavioural treatment, which we discuss below) may benefit from specific surgical procedures called *cingulotomy* and *anterior capsulotomy*. Cingulotomy involves destroying part of the cingulate gyrus and corpus callosum (see Chapter 3). Anterior capsulotomy involves creating small lesions to disrupt the pathway between the caudate nucleus and putamen. Long-term follow-up studies suggest that more than a quarter of patients with OCD who do not respond to standard treatments report significant benefit following psychosurgery, with relatively few side effects (Baer et al., 1995; Cumming et al., 1995; Hay et al., 1993). A few case studies suggest that psychosurgery may be useful for some individuals with severe depression or bipolar disorder who don't respond to standard treatments (Bridges et al., 1994). However, due to the intrusive nature of psychosurgery and lack of controlled studies, these procedures are currently reserved for the most severe cases.

In summary, the past 50 years have seen a revolution in the development of biomedical treatments for a wide range of mental illnesses. Medications have been developed to treat schizophrenia and psychotic disorders, depression, bipolar disorder and anxiety disorders. In the case of depression, other biomedical treatments such as electroconvulsive therapy, neurostimulation and phototherapy may provide relief. Psychosurgery in the form of a lobotomy is no longer performed, but some psychosurgical treatments are effective when other forms of treatment have been exhausted.

Psychological therapies: healing the mind through interaction

Psychological therapy, or **psychotherapy**, is *an interaction between a therapist and someone suffering from a psychological problem, with the goal of providing support or relief from the problem.* Although there are similarities among all the psychotherapies, each approach is unique in its goals, aims and methods. Currently, there are over 400 different systems

PSYCHOTHERAPY An interaction between a therapist and someone suffering from a psychological problem, with the goal of providing support or relief from the problem.

of psychotherapy, some of which are well known but many of which are unorthodox and exist on the periphery of treatment (Corsini, 2000). Most therapists will use a variety of techniques depending on the nature of the mental disorder as well as the individual client. In treating mental disorder, psychotherapies are particularly beneficial over and above biomedical approaches by addressing three goals:

1 to provide an insight to the patient to get them to appreciate the origins of their problem
2 to identify and change dysfunctional ways of thinking that contribute to the mental disorder
3 to identify and change behaviour patterns that contribute to the mental disorder.

Different psychotherapies can be used to address these different goals, so there is no 'one size fits all' approach (see *the real world* box). A recent study of 1,000 US psychotherapists revealed that over a third used an eclectic or integrative orientation – the use of a mixture of techniques. **Eclectic psychotherapy** involves *drawing on techniques from different forms of therapy, depending on the client and the problem.* The eclectic therapeutic approach has been found to be more effective in treating mental disorders such as panic disorder than any one therapy alone (Acierno et al., 1993). For example, an eclectic psychotherapist might use behavioural principles to work on a patient's fear of flying, humanistic principles to validate their distress over difficult family interactions, and family therapy techniques to change any dysfunctional patterns within the family that were contributing to the problem. We'll discuss the specifics of behavioural, humanistic, and family systems therapies in more detail a bit later. The point here is that most therapists apply an appropriate theoretical perspective that is suited to the problem at hand rather than adhering to a single theoretical perspective for all clients' problems.

ECLECTIC PSYCHOTHERAPY A therapy that involves drawing on techniques from different forms of therapy, depending on the client and the problem.

We will examine four major psychotherapies – psychodynamic, behavioural, cognitive, and humanistic/existential – and also explore how psychotherapy techniques are used in groups.

Psychodynamic therapy

Psychodynamic psychotherapy has its roots in Freud's psychoanalytically oriented theory of personality (see Chapter 13). **Psychodynamic psychotherapies** *explore childhood events and encourage individuals to use this understanding to develop insight into their psychological problems.* There are a number of different psychodynamic therapies that can vary substantially, but they all share the belief that the path to overcoming psychological problems is to develop insight into the unconscious memories, impulses, wishes and conflicts that are assumed to underlie these problems. Psychodynamic therapies include psychoanalysis and modern psychodynamic therapy, such as interpersonal psychotherapy.

PSYCHODYNAMIC PSYCHOTHERAPIES Therapies that explore childhood events and encourage individuals to use this understanding to develop insight into their psychological problems.

Psychoanalysis

In the late 1800s and early 1900s, Sigmund Freud developed *psychoanalysis,* a form of therapy that emphasizes the role of uncovering unconscious desires to develop insight into psychological problems. As you saw in Chapter 13, psychoanalysis assumes that humans are born with aggressive and sexual urges that are repressed during childhood development through the use of defence mechanisms. According to Freud, neurosis is a consequence of unresolved conflicts between the id, the ego and the superego. Psychoanalysts encourage their clients to bring these repressed conflicts into consciousness so that they can understand them and reduce their unwanted influences. Psychoanalysts focus a great deal on early childhood events because they believe that urges and conflicts were likely to be repressed during this time.

Freud reasoned that unconscious processes can be uncovered and conflicts revealed when the conscious mind is diverted from controlling the client's thinking. The unconscious is deeply hidden, however, so catching the unconscious at work takes special techniques and typically requires a long time. Traditional psychoanalysis takes place over an average of three to six years, with four or five sessions per week (Ursano and Silberman, 2003). During a session, the client reclines on a couch, facing away from the analyst, and

the real world

Mental health professionals

What do you do if you're ready to seek the help of a mental health professional? To whom do you turn? Therapists have widely varying backgrounds and training, which affects the kinds of services they offer. Before you choose a therapist, it is useful to have an understanding of a therapist's background, training and areas of expertise. There are several major 'flavours':

- *Psychologists:* In the UK and many other countries, anyone who has graduated with a degree in psychology accredited by the professional psychology society for that country (see Chapter 1) can call themselves a psychologist. In the field of mental disorder and treatment, there are a number of different types of psychologists who have relative expertise:
  - *Clinical psychologists* have typically undertaken three years of postgraduate training and specialize in assessment and evaluation that leads to therapy, counselling or advice.
  - *Counselling psychologists* are similar to clinical psychologists in terms of addressing mental health issues, but are more concerned with interpersonal skills in a therapeutic context.
  - *Health psychologists* aim to change behaviours and attitudes to promote good health and prevent illness, which can include mental disorder.
- *Psychiatrists:* A psychiatrist is a medical doctor who has completed an undergraduate degree in medicine with specialized postgraduate training in assessing and treating mental disorders. In the UK, psychiatrists are the only mental health professionals who can prescribe medications, although some also practise psychotherapy. GPs can also prescribe medications for mental disorders and often are the first to see people with such disorders because people consult them for a wide range of health problems. However, GPs do not typically receive much training in the diagnosis or treatment of mental disorders, and they do not practise psychotherapy.
- *Social workers:* Social workers have a master's degree in social work and have training in working with people in dire life situations such as poverty, homelessness or family conflict. Clinical or psychiatric social workers also receive special training to help people in these situations who have mental disorders. Social workers often work in government or private social service agencies, and they may also work in hospitals or have a private practice.

In the UK, all the above professionals are regulated and offer treatment for mental disorders available on the NHS but there are also many private alternative therapists or healers who offer treatment but are usually unregulated. If you think you need to speak to someone about seeking treatment and you don't have access to your GP, the best course of action is to make inquiries at your student advisory centre where they have contacts with therapists who are usually experienced in dealing with the student population. They should be more than willing to help.

©ISTOCKPHOTO.COM/REDHELGA

Which one? Finding the right psychotherapist can seem like finding the best watermelon. You won't really know until you've had a taste. Shoppers sometimes thump melons, believing that the sweetest ones sound different, but no one quite knows how a good one will sound. In the case of psychotherapists, fortunately, no thumping is required. You can find out about their qualifications in advance and even talk to several to see which one seems right.

is asked to express whatever thoughts and feelings come to mind. Occasionally, the analyst may comment on some of the information presented by the client, but the analyst does not express their values and judgements. The stereotypical image you might have of psychological therapy – a person lying on a couch talking to a person sitting in a chair – springs from this Freudian approach.

GEORGE DOYLE/STOCKBYTE/GETTY IMAGES

In traditional psychoanalysis, the patient lies on a couch, with the therapist sitting behind, out of the patient's view.

Repression and developing insight

As noted in Chapter 13, a key concept of psychoanalytic theory and therapy is repression, where unpleasant and unresolved conflicts are actively ignored and forced out of conscious awareness. The goal of psychoanalysis is for the client to understand the unconscious in a process Freud called *developing insight*. He noted that patients benefited from understanding why their problems produced such strange thoughts and behaviours because the underlying problem has been repressed. Asking the person to freely associate to an idea is just one way of revealing the repressed problem. Freud's psychoanalytic technique also encourages such insights through dream analysis, interpretation, and the analysis of resistance:

- *Free association:* In **free association**, *the client reports every thought that enters the mind, without censorship or filtering.* This strategy allows the stream of consciousness to flow unimpeded. If the client stops, the therapist prompts further associations ('And what does that make you think of?'). Clients often find the process of

FREE ASSOCIATION A therapeutic technique where the client reports every thought that enters the mind, without censorship or filtering.

RESISTANCE A reluctance to cooperate with treatment for fear of confronting unpleasant unconscious material.

free association difficult due to ingrained defence mechanisms and **resistance** – *a reluctance to cooperate with treatment for fear of confronting unpleasant unconscious material.* For example, you might find that if you simply sit in a room alone and start freely associating out loud, you end up saying some things you'd rather not have come to mind, or at least things you might hesitate to say in public! As a client becomes more trusting and less defended in the context of a good therapeutic relationship, the free association process becomes easier.

- *Dream analysis:* Psychoanalysis treats dreams as metaphors that symbolize unconscious conflicts or wishes. A psychoanalytic therapy session might begin with an invitation for the client to recount a dream, after which they might be asked to participate in the interpretation by freely associating to the dream. A client might report that a dream about school and an angry teacher reminded them a bit of their mother. The psychoanalyst might pursue that link by asking the client for more ideas about what this reminder could mean. Rather than taking a dream at face value (the manifest content), the psychoanalyst would seek out its hidden meaning (the latent content) to examine its importance for the client.
- *Interpretation:* This is the process by which the therapist deciphers the meaning (for example, unconscious impulses or fantasies) underlying what the client says and does. The analyst suggests possible meanings to the client, looking for signs that the correct meaning has been discovered. Unfortunately, a correct interpretation is usually not accompanied by giant flashing neon lights.
- *Analysis of resistance:* In the process of 'trying on' different interpretations of the client's thoughts and actions, the analyst may suggest an interpretation that the client finds particularly unacceptable. For example, the therapist might suggest that the client's problem with obsessive health worries could be traced to a childhood rivalry with her mother for her father's love and attention. The client could find the suggestion insulting ('I'd never think of my father *that way*') and fervently resist the interpretation. Curiously, the analyst might interpret this resistance as a signal not that the interpretation is wrong but that the interpretation is on the right track. The queen in Shakespeare's *Hamlet* indicated that vigorous resistance to an idea might reveal a person's underlying belief in that idea when she said: 'The lady doth protest too much, methinks.'

The process of transference

Over the course of an intensive and lengthy process of analysis, the client and psychoanalyst often develop a close relationship. Freud noticed this relationship developing in his analyses and was at first troubled by it. Clients would develop an unusually strong attachment to him, almost as though they were viewing him as a parent or lover, and he worried that this could interfere with achieving the goal of insight. Over time, however, he came to believe that the development and resolution of this relationship was a key process of psychoanalysis.

TRANSFERENCE When the analyst begins to assume a major significance in the client's life and the client reacts to the analyst based on unconscious childhood fantasies.

Transference occurs *when the analyst begins to assume a major significance in the client's life and the client reacts to the analyst based on unconscious childhood fantasies.* Successful psychoanalysis involves analysing the transference so that the client understands this reaction and why it occurs. In fact, insight, the ultimate goal of psychoanalysis, may be enhanced because interpretations of the client's interaction with the therapist also have implications for the client's past and future relationships (Andersen and Berk, 1998).

Beyond psychoanalysis

Early in the history of psychoanalysis, several of Freud's students broke away from him and developed their own approaches to psychotherapy. Carl Jung (1875–1961) and Alfred Adler (1870–1937) agreed with Freud that insight was a key therapeutic goal but disagreed that insight usually involves unconscious conflicts about sex and aggression (Arlow, 2000). Instead, Jung emphasized what he called the **collective unconscious** – *the culturally determined symbols and myths that are shared among all people.* Jung held that these widely known ideas about kinds of people, situations or stories could serve as a basis for interpretation beyond sex or aggression, and his viewpoint is a rich compilation of such ideas. Alfred Adler believed that emotional conflicts are the result of perceptions

COLLECTIVE UNCONSCIOUS The culturally determined symbols and myths that are shared among all people.

of inferiority and that psychotherapy should help people to overcome problems resulting from inferior social status, sex roles and discrimination.

Another analyst to break with Freud was Melanie Klein (1882–1960), who believed that primitive fantasies of loss and persecution, for example worrying about a parent dying or about being bullied, were important factors underlying mental illness. Throughout the first half of the 20th century, other influential theorists pursued the development of psychodynamic theories to include greater focus on the social foundations of psychology. Karen Horney (1885–1952) disagreed with Freud about the inherent differences in the psychology of men and women and traced such differences to society and culture rather than biology. Harry Stack Sullivan (1892–1949) emphasized the importance of interpersonal relationships in the formation of emotional problems, and Heinz Kohut (1913–81) expanded psychodynamic psychotherapy by focusing on how the individual forms an understanding of self through relationships with others.

Modern psychodynamic psychotherapies differ from classical psychoanalysis in many ways. For starters, the therapist and client typically sit face to face. In addition, therapy is less intensive, with meetings often occurring only once a week and the duration of therapy lasting months rather than years. In contrast to classical psychoanalysis, modern psychodynamic therapists are more likely to see relief from symptoms as a reasonable goal for therapy (in addition to the goal of facilitating insight), and they are more likely to offer support or advice in addition to interpretation (Henry et al., 1994). Therapists are also now less likely to interpret a client's statements as a sign of unconscious sexual or aggressive impulses. However, other concepts, such as transference and fostering insight into unconscious processes, remain features of most psychodynamic therapies. Psychodynamic psychotherapy has had an enormous impact on how emotional problems are treated, influencing most subsequent schools of therapy in some form. Freud's couch cast a long shadow.

Psychology and me

Dr Angel Chater, Lecturer in Behavioural Medicine at University College London

Dr Angel Chater is a health psychologist working in the School of Pharmacy at University College London in the UK. Visit www.palgrave.com/schacter to watch a video of Angel talking about the fascinating practical work she does to enable people to cope with illness, manage their weight and change their eating behaviours, as well her research into behaviour change interventions and the training she provides to pharmacists to enhance their understanding of health behaviour decision making and effective communication skills. She also explains why she decided to study psychology, what she most and least enjoyed during her undergraduate degree, and she gives some advice for students just starting out.

Behavioural and cognitive therapies

Unlike psychodynamic psychotherapy, which emphasizes early developmental processes as the source of psychological dysfunction, cognitive and behavioural treatments emphasize the current factors that contribute to the problem – dysfunctional thoughts and maladaptive behaviours. Cognitive and behavioural therapies have been around for almost half a century, and they continue to increase in popularity. Historically, cognitive and behavioural therapies were considered distinct systems of therapy, and some people continue to follow this distinction, using solely behavioural *or* cognitive techniques. However, many therapists now integrate these approaches into a unified set of procedures known as *cognitive behavioural therapy* (CBT). In this section, we will review the origins and techniques of behavioural and cognitive therapies and explore how these techniques are integrated into CBT.

Behaviour therapy

The idea of focusing treatment on the client's behaviour rather than the client's unconscious was an innovation inspired by behaviourism. As you read in Chapter 1, psychologists' frustration with theories positing 'invisible' mental properties that are difficult to test and impossible to observe launched the behaviourist movement. Behaviourists found psychoanalytic ideas particularly hard to test. How do you know that a person has an unconscious conflict, for example, or that insight has occurred? No wonder psychoanalysis takes so long – it's like looking for a shadow in the dark. Behavioural principles, on the other hand, focused solely on symptoms that could be observed, for example avoidance of a feared object, such as refusing to get on an aeroplane. In the 1950s and 60s, clinical psychologists began to apply learning theory to the treatment of disorders, which set the stage for the growth of behaviour therapy (Eysenck, 1960; Wolpe, 1958). **Behaviour therapy** *assumes that disordered behaviour is learned and that symptom relief is achieved through changing overt maladaptive behaviours into more constructive behaviours.*

BEHAVIOUR THERAPY A therapy that assumes that disordered behaviour is learned and that symptom relief is achieved through changing overt maladaptive behaviours into more constructive behaviours.

B. F. Skinner first used the term *behaviour therapy* to describe how the principles of learning could be used to change problem behaviours in people with schizophrenia

©ISTOCKPHOTO.COM/BRAD KILLER

A behavioural therapist might treat this temper tantrum with an analysis of the antecedents, behaviour and the consequences of the act.

(Lindsley et al., 1953). Since then, a variety of behaviour therapy techniques have been developed for a number of disorders. Many of the learning principles you encountered in Chapter 6 have been applied to treatment, including those based on operant conditioning procedures, which focus on reinforcement and punishment, and those based on classical conditioning procedures, which focus on extinction. Behaviour therapy techniques can eliminate unwanted behaviours, such as stopping a child from throwing temper tantrums, promote desired behaviours, such as leading a withdrawn patient to participate in social interactions, and reduce unwanted emotional responses, such as helping a phobic patient to stop fearing snakes.

Eliminating unwanted behaviours

What would you do if a three-year-old child was in the habit of throwing tantrums at the supermarket? A behaviour therapist might look first at what happens before the tantrum. Is the child hungry, did they miss a nap, or is there something they want? Does the parent usually neglect the child during shopping? The therapist would also investigate what happens after the tantrum. Did the child get chocolate to 'shut them up'? Did the mortified parent whisk them out to the car and beg them to be quiet? The study of operant conditioning shows that behaviour can be predicted by its *antecedents* (the stimuli that occur beforehand) and its *consequences* (the reinforcing or punishing events that follow) and adjusting these might help to change the behaviour.

In fact, a solution might be as easy as A-B-C (antecedent-behaviour-consequence). Giving the child more attention in the supermarket beforehand, for example, might prevent the whole incident. If the child throws a tantrum anyway, making the consequences less reinforcing (no chocolate) and more punishing (a period of time-out in the car while the parent watches from nearby rather than a rush of attention) could eliminate the problem behaviour. For people in danger of developing a poor long-term relationship with their child because of frequent tantrums or other problem behaviours, behaviour therapy can bring welcome relief and a fresh start. Taking the time to understand a problem behaviour in its context can make it less mystifying when it happens, and more open to modification (Tavris, 1989).

AVERSION THERAPY Using positive punishment to reduce the frequency of an undesirable behaviour.

Aversion therapy, another operant technique for reducing problem behaviours, involves *using positive punishment to reduce the frequency of an undesirable behaviour.* Remember from Chapter 6 that 'positive' is not pleasant in this context, but means that the punishment is always administered. For example, alcoholism is sometimes treated with a drug called disulfiram, which increases the patient's sensitivity to alcohol so that drinking even a small amount leads to an intense and unpleasant physical reaction such as nausea or headaches. Although aversive therapies are sometimes useful for controlling an unwanted behaviour over the short term, in many cases they are not particularly useful for long-term change. In other words, the enticement of an addiction can sometimes be so powerful that a person will tolerate discomfort and illness in order to experience whatever positive benefit the addiction provides.

Promoting desired behaviours

TOKEN ECONOMY Giving clients 'tokens' for desired behaviours, which they can later trade for rewards.

In a psychiatric hospital, patients may sometimes become unresponsive and apathetic, withdrawing from social interaction and failing to participate in treatment programmes. A behaviour therapy technique sometimes used in such cases is the **token economy** – *giving clients 'tokens' for desired behaviours, which they can later trade for rewards.* Tokens for behaviours such as cleaning their rooms, taking exercise or helping other patients signal positive reinforcement because they can be exchanged for rewards such as time away from the hospital, TV privileges and special foods. Token economies have proved to be effective while the system of rewards is in place, but the learned behaviours are not usually maintained when the reinforcements are discontinued (Glynn, 1990). Similar systems used in classrooms to encourage positive behaviours may work temporarily in school but can undermine pupils' interest in these behaviours when the reinforcements are no longer available (Lepper and Greene, 1976). A child who is rewarded for controlling their temper in class may become an ogre in the playground when no teacher is present to offer rewards for good behaviour.

Reinforcement techniques can sometimes be highly successful in *skills training* for adults with psychosis who may be less responsive to therapies that rely on insight. In one of the first studies to apply behavioural treatments to psychotic patients, Aylon and Azrin (1968) set aside an entire ward to run a token economy for 45 women with schizophrenia who had been in psychiatric hospitals for an average of 16 years. The women were rewarded with tokens for making beds, brushing teeth and other daily skills that they had neglected as a result of being institutionalized for so many years. It is generally recognized that behavioural reinforcement techniques are an effective means of shaping adaptive behaviour for chronic patients, but they are not in themselves a sufficient treatment.

EXPOSURE THERAPY Confronting an emotion-arousing stimulus directly and repeatedly, ultimately leading to a decrease in the emotional response.

SYSTEMATIC DESENSITIZATION A procedure in which a client relaxes all the muscles of their body while imagining being in increasingly frightening situations.

MODELLING The process by which a person learns behaviour by observing and imitating others.

Reducing unwanted emotional responses

One of the most powerful ways to reduce fear is by gradual exposure to the feared object or situation, a behavioural method originated by psychiatrist Joseph Wolpe (1958). Wolpe's **exposure therapy** involves *confronting an emotion-arousing stimulus directly and repeatedly, ultimately leading to a decrease in the emotional response.* This technique depends on the processes of habituation and response extinction, which were originally discovered in the study of classical conditioning (see Chapter 6). Wolpe called his form of treatment **systematic desensitization** – *a procedure in which a client relaxes all the muscles of their body while imagining being in increasingly frightening situations.* For example, a client who fears snakes might first imagine seeing a photograph of a snake, followed by imagining seeing a snake that is inside an aquarium, followed eventually by imagining holding a large snake, all the while engaging in exercises that relax the muscles of the body. Cognitive behavioural therapists use an exposure hierarchy to expose the client gradually to the feared object or situation. Easier situations are practised first, and as fear decreases, the client progresses to more difficult or frightening situations (see **TABLE 17.1**).

TABLE 17.1 Exposure hierarchy for social phobia

Item	Fear (0–100)
1 Have a party and invite everyone from work	99
2 Go to a party for one hour without drinking	90
3 Invite Cindy to have dinner and see a movie	85
4 Go for a job interview	80
5 Ask boss for a day off work	65
6 Ask questions in a meeting at work	65
7 Eat lunch with co-workers	60
8 Talk to a stranger on the bus	50
9 Talk to cousin on the telephone for 10 minutes	40
10 Ask for directions at the petrol station	35

Source: Ellis, 1991

Systematic desensitization has changed since Wolpe's introduction of the technique (Antony and Swinson, 2000). Exposure is an effective treatment without the relaxation component (Öst et al., 1984), so relaxation is often omitted. Relaxation techniques can be effective by themselves for treating anxiety and managing stress more generally, but they are not essential for desensitization. Wolpe's systematic desensitization also relied strongly on exposure in the imagination, but it is now known that *in vivo exposure,* live exposure, is more effective than imaginary exposure (Emmelkamp and Wessels, 1975; Stern and Marks, 1973). In other words, if a person fears driving, it is better for the person to get behind the wheel of the car and drive than simply to imagine driving. However, imaginary exposure is still recommended in cases where people are so frightened of their thoughts or memories that they can't even bring themselves to attempt live exposure.

Another technique that can be successfully applied in treating fear responses is **modelling** – *the process by which a person learns behaviour by observing and imitating others.* As we saw in Chapter 12, children copy what they see others doing. The same is true for phobic adults watching someone engage with a feared target such as handling a snake. Studies of adults and children watching videos of models enjoying a trip to the dentists or going through various hospital procedures have shown that adults and children can overcome their fears by such observational learning (Thorpe and Olson, 1997).

Virtual reality therapy involves a kind of systematic desensitization to an imagined stimulus. Imagination can be heightened through the use of video and audio simulations, making the entire experience more like a live exposure. Virtual reality programmes can provide exposure for people who fear flying, driving, spiders, snakes, public speaking, heights or thunderstorms. Clients can be treated for post-traumatic stress disorder (see Chapter 16) through exposure to specific stimuli, for example virtual combat in Iraq, or

MACMILLAN AUSTRALIA

Exposure therapy is a powerful treatment for overcoming fear. Up to 90% of individuals with animal phobias are able to overcome their fears in as little as one session lasting two to three hours.

a virtual terrorist attack. One study comparing three sessions of virtual reality exposure to three sessions of live exposure for individuals with a specific phobia of heights found that both treatments were equally effective in reducing participants' fear and that this improvement was maintained when participants were assessed again six months later (Emmelkamp et al., 2002).

Exposure can be adapted for particular types of problems. For example, exposure can be combined with *response prevention*, which involves resisting the urge to engage in a compulsive ritual or some other protective behaviour. Individuals with OCD (see Chapter 16) who wash their hands many times each day for fear of contamination would be encouraged to touch a feared object like a door handle (exposure) while resisting the urge to wash their hands (response prevention). The exposure helps them extinguish the emotional reaction to the thought of contamination over time, and the response prevention keeps them from performing the ritual behaviour that they usually use to neutralize the emotion.

Cognitive therapy

In the 1960s and 70s, a number of psychologists and psychiatrists began to enlist cognitive explanations to understand learning-based phenomena. For example, traditional learning theorists might explain a phobia as the outcome of a classical conditioning experience such as being bitten by a dog, where the dog bite leads to the development of a dog phobia through the simple association of the dog with the experience of pain. Cognitive theorists took this simple learning paradigm a step further and they began to emphasize the *meaning* of the event. It might not be the event itself that caused the fear, but rather the individual's beliefs and assumptions about the event and the feared stimulus. In the case of a dog bite, cognitive theorists might focus on a person's new or strengthened belief that dogs are dangerous to explain the fear. Whereas behaviour therapy doesn't take into account the person's thoughts and feelings and instead focuses only on the behaviour and the situation, cognitive therapy uses the person's reasoning capabilities and rational self-control in the therapy.

Psychiatrist Aaron Beck (1921–) and psychologist Albert Ellis (1913–2007) are most often credited for founding cognitive treatments. Beck and Ellis felt that the best way to alleviate emotional pain was to help a client change the biased or unrealistic thoughts that were at the core of the client's problems. Beck called his brand of treatment **cognitive therapy**, which *focuses on helping a client identify and correct any distorted thinking about self, others or the world* (for example Beck and Weishaar, 2000). Ellis (2000) referred to his treatment as *rational emotive behaviour therapy*, in which the therapist points out errors in thinking that the client is making. Although these therapies share the common belief that psychological problems arise from biased or distorted interpretations of events, they also differ in some ways. Beck's approach is gentler than Ellis's, with the therapist helping the client discover errors in thinking by using pointed questions to guide the client's discovery. Ellis's approach is more direct and forceful, with the therapist actively pointing out flaws in thinking to the client and using humour to identify these flaws.

COGNITIVE THERAPY Therapy that focuses on helping a client identify and correct any distorted thinking about self, others or the world.

Cognitive therapies use a principal technique called **cognitive restructuring**, which *involves teaching clients to question the automatic beliefs, assumptions and predictions that often lead to negative emotions and to replace negative thinking with more realistic and positive beliefs*. Specifically, clients are taught to examine the evidence for and against a particular belief or to be more accepting of outcomes that may be undesirable yet still manageable. For example, a depressed client may believe that they are stupid and will never pass their university courses – all on the basis of one poor exam mark. In this situation, the therapist would work with the client to examine the validity of this belief. The therapist would consider relevant evidence such as marks on previous exams, performance on other coursework, and examples of intelligence outside university. It may be that the client has never failed a course before and has achieved good marks in this particular course in the past. In this case, the therapist would encourage the client to consider all this information in determining whether they are truly 'stupid'.

COGNITIVE RESTRUCTURING This involves teaching clients to question the automatic beliefs, assumptions and predictions that often lead to negative emotions and to replace negative thinking with more realistic and positive beliefs.

The goal of cognitive restructuring is *not* to have a client think positively if there is no reason to think positively. If the client really was having trouble at university, it would not be realistic to think that they will easily pass the course. In cases like this, the therapist may instead help the client decide whether doing poorly in one course constitutes being 'stupid' and whether there is anything the client can do to better prepare for future exams. **TABLE 17.2** shows a variety of potentially irrational ideas – beliefs and convictions that could be true or false – that can unleash unwanted emotions such as anger, depression or anxiety. Any of these irrational beliefs can become a mindbug, bedevilling a person with serious emotional problems if left unchallenged.

TABLE 17.2 Common irrational beliefs and their emotional responses

Belief	Emotional response
I have to get this done immediately. I must be perfect.	Anxiety, stress
Something terrible will happen. Everyone is watching me. I won't be able to make friends.	Embarrassment, social anxiety
People know something is wrong with me. I'm a loser and will always be a loser. Nobody will ever love me.	Sadness, depression
She did that to me on purpose. He is evil and should be punished. Things ought to be different.	Anger, irritability

Source: Ellis, 1991

Some forms of cognitive therapy include techniques for coping with unwanted thoughts and feelings, techniques that resemble meditation (see Chapter 8). Clients may be encouraged to attend to their troubling thoughts or emotions or be given meditative techniques that allow them to gain a new focus. **Mindfulness meditation** *teaches an individual to be fully present in each moment, be aware of their thoughts, feelings and sensations, and detect symptoms before they become a problem.* Researchers have found mindfulness meditation to be helpful for preventing relapse in depression. In one study, people recovering from depression were about half as likely to relapse during a 60-week assessment period if they received mindfulness meditation-based cognitive therapy than if they received treatment as usual (Teasdale et al., 2000) (see the hot science box).

MINDFULNESS MEDITATION A technique that teaches an individual to be fully present in each moment, be aware of their thoughts, feelings and sensations, and detect symptoms before they become a problem.

hot science

Ancient wisdom, modern mindfulness

As we saw in Chapter 8, meditation is an altered state of consciousness induced by contemplation during long periods of silence. For those who follow the teachings of Buddha, meditation forms a core component of their practices, as an exercise and as a way of achieving spiritual enlightenment. Until fairly recently, meditation was considered within the realms of spirituality and a fringe activity, but the practice is currently enjoying a period of popularity backed up by scientific investigation and endorsement from some of the world's leading neuroscientists.

Michael Posner, famous for his work on the neuroscience of attention, and one of the few psychologists to receive the National Medal of Science from President Obama, was initially indifferent to meditation but was approached by Yi-Yuan Tang, a Chinese neuroscientist who wanted to investigate brain activity changes following meditation. Yang persuaded Posner to image the brains of individuals following mindfulness meditation.

Mindfulness meditation instructs the individual to let go of effortful thinking and allow mental experiences to come and go without judgement but rather be considered in a state of restful alertness. It encompasses focusing attention on thoughts, emotions and body sensations, simply observing them as they arise and pass away. The exercises operate to regulate and focus attention on immediate conscious awareness rather than drift into considerations about the past and the future. It seeks to reduce the tendency to evaluate experiences in terms of either negative or positive appraisal.

In comparison to control subjects who only underwent relaxation, Posner and Yang found that other subjects who undertook mindfulness meditation (even as little as 20–30 minutes a day for a month) produced reorganization and connectivity of the white matter in the anterior cingulate cortex, a region located a few inches above and behind the eyebrows that is involved in effortful thinking and self-regulation (Tang et al., 2010, 2012). This is the same region that is changed by hypnosis (see Chapter 8).

This change in brain activity may also be related to health. Mindfulness-based interventions have been shown to be beneficial in the treatment of a number of clinical disorders, including anxiety, depression, substance abuse, eating disorders and chronic pain (for a review, see Hölzel et al., 2011). Even those of us who are relatively healthy can benefit from meditation as it makes us feel better and more relaxed in our thinking. But how does it work? The simple answer is that we simply do not know for sure yet, but it is likely to involve mind management.

A recent review (Hölzel et al., 2011) of the field has proposed four mechanisms operating in mindfulness meditation that have been shown to produce behavioural changes and related activity in differing brain regions:

1 attention regulation
2 body awareness
3 emotion regulation, including reappraisal, exposure, extinction and reconsolidation
4 change in perspective on the self.

These are all changes in the mind but how does such mindfulness influence our bodies? This is one of the recurrent issues in psychology – the mind–body problem we encountered in Chapter 1 and one of the main controversies when it comes to understanding the relationship between neuroscience and psychology. It seems that self-regulation is part of our coping strategy to deal with stress and that simply mentally switching off each day for as little as 20 minutes better prepares us to deal with life's problems.

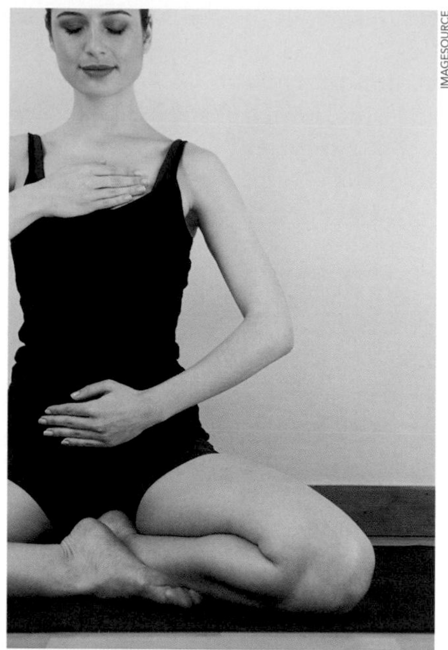
IMAGESOURCE

Now backed by scientific evidence, the practice of mindfulness meditation is growing in popularity. A key teaching is to regulate and focus attention on the present moment, and this has been shown to be a useful treatment method for many clinical disorders.

Cognitive behavioural therapy (CBT)

COGNITIVE BEHAVIOURAL THERAPY (CBT) Therapy that uses a blend of cognitive and behavioural therapeutic strategies.

Today, the extent to which therapists use cognitive versus behavioural techniques depends on the individual therapist and the type of problem being treated. Most therapists working with anxiety and depression use **cognitive behavioural therapy (CBT)** – *a blend of cognitive and behavioural therapeutic strategies*. In a way, this technique acknowledges that there may be behaviours that people cannot control through rational thought but also that there are ways of helping people to think more rationally when thought does play a role. Moving beyond its roots in behaviour therapy and cognitive therapy, however, CBT has developed its own unique features. In addition to focusing on dysfunctional thoughts and maladaptive behaviours, CBT is often described as problem focused and action oriented, structured, transparent and flexible:

- *Problem focused/action oriented:* CBT is undertaken for specific problems, and tries to solve these problems by encouraging the client to act. Typically, the therapist and client will identify specific goals, such as reducing the frequency of panic attacks or returning to work after a bout of depression, and then select specific strategies to help meet those goals, thereby decreasing the client's suffering. The client is expected to *do* things, such as practise relaxation exercises or use a diary to monitor relevant symptoms, for example the severity of a depressed mood, or panic attack symptoms. This is in contrast to psychodynamic or other therapies where goals may not be explicitly discussed or agreed on and the client's only necessary action is to attend the therapy session.
- *Structured:* CBT sessions typically begin with setting an agenda for the meeting and a review of homework from the previous week. For example, the client and therapist may decide at the beginning of the session to discuss a particular incident from the client's week and use this as an example for learning a therapy technique that may be useful, such as keeping a diary. Much of the session focuses on learning new skills or practising particular therapy techniques. In the treatment of anxiety, it is not uncommon for the therapist and client to spend the session confronting the client's feared

situation, which may include learning-oriented activities such as the client giving a presentation in front of the therapist. Often, each session ends with a homework assignment to be completed before the next session. In contrast, in a psychodynamic therapy session, the client may be asked to use free association for much of the session, with no expectations on what content will be covered.

- *Transparent:* CBT also contrasts with psychodynamic approaches in its assumptions about what the client can know. CBT is *transparent,* in that nothing is withheld from the client. By the end of the course of therapy, most clients have a good understanding of the treatment they have received as well as the specific techniques used to make the desired changes. For example, clients with OCD who fear contamination would feel confident in knowing how to confront feared situations such as public toilets and why confronting this situation is helpful. Self-help readings are often used to reinforce what is learned in sessions.
- *Flexible:* Usually, CBT is a fairly brief form of therapy, lasting 10–20 sessions, depending on the problem. It may be conducted individually or with groups of clients. The frequency of sessions varies. For example, CBT has been found to be useful for OCD in a weekly outpatient format over several months, or in a more intensive format, with daily sessions occurring over three weeks. CBT may also be conducted outside the therapist's office. For example, an individual undergoing exposure therapy for a fear of lifts might undergo entire treatment sessions on actual lifts.

©ISTOCKPHOTO.COM/MAX HOMAND

The cognitive behaviour therapy (CBT) client with obsessive-compulsive disorder (OCD) who fears contamination in a public toilet might be given 'homework' to visit three such toilets in a week, not necessarily to touch anything but just to look.

Because CBT is based on learning models, it is not surprising that the practice of CBT resembles school. Therapists take the role of teacher and clients become students. The goal of teaching the client new ways to think and behave is pursued through lessons, homework and, yes, even tests – 'let's try picking up that snake!' In this way, the CBT model of therapy differs from the more mystical relationship between the therapist and client in psychodynamic psychotherapy, in which the therapist serves almost as a kind of spiritual guide urging the client towards insight.

Humanistic and existential therapies

Humanistic and existential therapies emerged in the middle of the 20th century, in part as a reaction to the negative views that psychodynamic psychotherapies hold about human nature. Psychodynamic approaches emphasize unconscious drives towards sex and aggression, as we noted earlier. On the other hand, humanistic and existential therapies assume that human nature is generally positive and emphasize the natural tendency of each individual to strive for personal improvement. There are many different approaches that fall under the category of humanistic and existential therapies. They share the assumption that psychological problems stem from feelings of alienation and loneliness, and that these feelings can be traced to failures to reach one's potential (in the humanistic approach) or from failures to find meaning in life (in the existential approach). Although interest in humanistic and existential therapies peaked in the 1960s and 70s, some therapists continue to use these approaches today. This section describes the two most well-known therapies of this viewpoint – one from a humanistic perspective (person-centred therapy) and one from existential therapy (Gestalt therapy).

Person-centred therapy

Person-centred therapy (also known as *client-centred therapy*) *assumes that all individuals have a tendency towards growth and that this growth can be facilitated by acceptance and genuine reactions from the therapist.* Psychologist Carl Rogers (1902–87) developed person-centred therapy in the 1940s and 50s (Rogers, 1951). Person-centred therapy assumes that each individual is qualified to determine their own goals for therapy, such as

PERSON-CENTRED THERAPY (also known as client-centred therapy) A method of therapy that assumes that all individuals have a tendency towards growth and that this growth can be facilitated by acceptance and genuine reactions from the therapist.

feeling more confident or making a career decision, and even the frequency and length of therapy. In this type of *nondirective* treatment, the therapist tends not to provide advice or suggestions about what the client should be doing. Instead, the therapist paraphrases the client's words, mirroring the client's thoughts and sentiments, for example 'I think I hear you saying ... '. Person-centred therapists believe that with adequate support, the client will recognize the right things to do.

Rogers encouraged person-centred therapists to demonstrate three basic qualities: congruence, empathy and unconditional positive regard:

1 *Congruence:* openness and honesty in the therapeutic relationship, ensuring that the therapist communicates the same message at all levels. For example, the same message must be communicated in the therapist's words, facial expression and body language. Saying 'I think your concerns are valid' while smirking would simply not do.
2 *Empathy:* the continuous process of trying to understand the client by getting inside their way of thinking, feeling and understanding the world. Seeing the world from the client's perspective enables the therapist to better appreciate the client's apprehensions, worries or fears.
3 *Unconditional positive regard:* the therapist shows this by providing a nonjudgemental, warm and accepting environment in which the client can feel safe expressing their thoughts and feelings.

Here is an example of what person-centred therapy might sound like for a client who is dealing with conflicted feelings about her daughter being away at university (Raskin and Rogers, 2000, p. 144):

Client: I'm having a lot of problems dealing with my daughter. She's 20 years old; she's in college; I'm having a lot of trouble letting her go ... And I have a lot of guilt feelings about her; I have a real need to hang on to her.

Therapist: A need to hang on so you can kind of make up for the things you feel guilty about – is that part of it?

C: There's a lot of that ... Also, she's been a real friend to me and filled my life ... And it's very hard ... a lot of empty places now that she's not with me.

T: The old vacuum, sort of, when she's not there.

C: Yes. Yes. I would also like to be the kind of mother that could be strong and say, you know, 'Go and have a good life,' and this is really hard for me to do.

T: It's very hard to give up something that's been so precious in your life but also something that has caused you pain when you mentioned guilt.

C: Yeah, and I'm aware that I have some anger toward her that I don't always get what I want. I have needs that are not met. And, uh, I don't feel I have a right to those needs. You know ... She's a daughter; she's not my mother – though sometimes I feel as if I'd like her to mother me ... It's very difficult for me to ask for that and have a right to it.

T: So it may be unreasonable, but still, when she doesn't meet your needs, it makes you mad.

C: Yeah, I get very, very angry with her.

From this example, you can see that the goal of the exchange was not to uncover repressed conflicts, as in psychodynamic therapy, or to challenge unrealistic thoughts, as in CBT. Instead, the person-centred therapist tried to understand the client's experience and reflect that experience back to her in a supportive way, encouraging the client's natural tendency towards growth. This style of therapy is reminiscent of psychoanalysis in its way of encouraging the client towards the free expression of thoughts and feelings, although humanistic therapies clearly start from a set of assumptions about human nature that differ diametrically from psychodynamic theories.

GESTALT THERAPY Therapy that has the goal of helping the client become aware of their thoughts, behaviours, experiences and feelings and to 'own' or take responsibility for them.

Gestalt therapy

Gestalt therapy was founded by Frederick 'Fritz' Perls (1893–1970) and his colleagues in the 1940s and 50s (Perls et al., 1951). **Gestalt therapy** *has the goal of helping the client become aware of their thoughts, behaviours, experiences and feelings and to 'own' or take* *responsibility for them*. Gestalt therapists are encouraged to be enthusiastic and warm towards their clients, an approach they share with person-centred therapists. To help facilitate the client's awareness, Gestalt therapists also reflect back to the client their impressions of the client.

Gestalt therapy emphasizes the experiences and behaviours that are occurring at that particular moment in the therapy session. For example, if a client is talking about something stressful that occurred during the previous week, the therapist might shift the attention to the client's current experience by asking: 'How do you feel as you describe what happened to you?' This technique is known as *focusing*. Clients are also encouraged to put their feelings into action. One way to do this is the *empty chair technique*, in which the client imagines that another person, for example a spouse, a parent, a co-worker, is sitting in an empty chair, opposite the client. The client then moves from chair to chair, alternating from role-playing what they would say to the other person and what they imagine the other person would respond. In this type of therapy, the goal is to facilitate awareness of the client's thoughts, feelings, behaviours and experiences in the 'here and now'. A variety of techniques are used to facilitate awareness, with the assumption that greater honesty and awareness will clear a path to living more fully and meaningfully.

Groups in therapy

It is natural to think of psychopathology as an illness that affects only the individual. A particular person 'is depressed', for example, or 'has anxiety'. Yet each person lives in a world of other people, and interactions with others may intensify and even create disorders. A depressed person may be lonely after moving away from friends and loved ones, for example, or an anxious person could be worried about pressures from parents. These ideas suggest that people might be able to recover from disorders in the same way they got into them – not just as an individual effort, but through social processes. Indeed, psychotherapy itself is a form of social interaction, an interaction specifically aimed at healing, so therapy conducted in groups of people is just a further development of the basic idea of therapy.

In this section, we'll look at types of psychotherapy for people in groups. We'll begin with therapies that attempt to treat whole groups – couples and family therapies. Then we'll explore treatment options that expand psychotherapy to include multiple individual participants, often with similar problems – group therapies and self-help and support groups.

Couples and family therapy

When a couple are 'having problems', neither individual may be suffering from any psychopathology. Rather, it may be the relationship itself that is disordered. *Couples therapy* is when a married, cohabitating or dating couple are seen together in therapy to work on problems usually arising within the relationship. There are cases when therapy with even larger groups is warranted. An individual may be having a problem – say, an adolescent is abusing alcohol – but the source of the problem is in the individual's relationships with family members; perhaps the mother is herself an alcoholic who subtly encourages the adolescent to drink and the father travels and neglects the family. In this case, it could be useful for the therapist to work with them all in *family therapy* – psychotherapy involving members of a family.

Individual partners who seek couples therapy may not suffer from any psychological disorders themselves, rather it is the health of the relationship between the two of them that needs attention.

The roots of couples and family therapies date back more than 100 years, beginning in the field of social work and related movements (Broderick and Schrader, 1991). Early therapies were educational in nature, often designed to teach individuals (mostly women) about marriage, parenting and family life (Kaslow and Celano, 1995), for example how to take care of domestic responsibilities. These treatments evolved into therapies designed specifically for couples. Today, couples come to therapy for many different reasons, including difficulty communicating, for example frequent arguing or a lack of communication, sexual dysfunction, marital dissatisfaction, domestic violence, or difficulties dealing with a specific problem impacting the relationship, for example when one person in the couple suffers from severe depression.

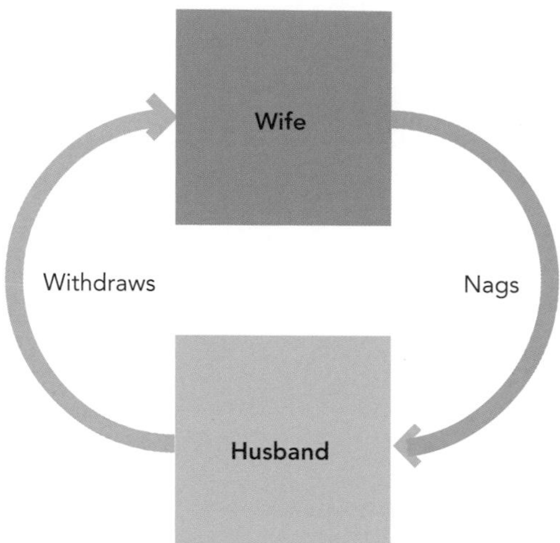

FIGURE **17.2 Self-defeating interaction cycle** A couple can get caught up in a self-defeating interaction cycle when both partners believe they are acting rationally in response to the other's behaviour. There may be no end to the conflict; for example, a husband withdraws from his wife to avoid her nagging and she nags him for withdrawing and then he withdraws to avoid her nagging ... and on and on.

A traditional use of couples therapy might involve a couple seeking help because they are unhappy with their relationship. In this scenario, both of them are expected to attend therapy sessions and the problem is seen as arising from their interaction rather than from the problems of one half of the couple. For example, it might be that the wife nags the husband, and he withdraws into solitary hobbies and watching sports. She is lonely and unhappy, complaining to him whenever she can about how he avoids her. He is deeply dissatisfied, finding every chance he can to escape her bitter complaints by going out to the garden shed. A key part of their misery as a couple, then, might be that each of them sees the problem as something the other person is doing. He sees the problem as her nagging, and she sees the problem as his withdrawal. With both people present, a therapist can gather information from both parties about the nature of the problem as well as observe the couple's actual interactions. In this case, a therapist might be able to help them see the self-defeating cycle of their interaction (see FIGURE **17.2**). Treatment strategies would target changes in *both* parties, focusing on ways to break their repetitive dysfunctional pattern (Watzlawick et al., 1967).

Couples therapy can also be useful when the relationship itself aids individual therapy for one of the partners. For example, a CBT approach for treating panic disorder with agoraphobia (fear of places that are difficult or embarrassing to escape from in case of a panic attack) has been adapted into a couples-based format (Barlow et al., 1984). In this programme, treatment includes the standard CBT techniques, such as exposure and cognitive restructuring, except that spouses join the clients in each therapy session and often participate in homework assignments. Spouses are included to help them better understand the nature of the disorder, train them to be coaches during exposure homework practices, ensure that they are not doing things to undermine the treatment (such as helping the client to avoid feared situations), and improve communication in the couple regarding the panic and agoraphobia symptoms. Treatment for agoraphobia and panic disorder that includes spouses has been found to be more effective than treatment for clients alone (Barlow et al., 1984).

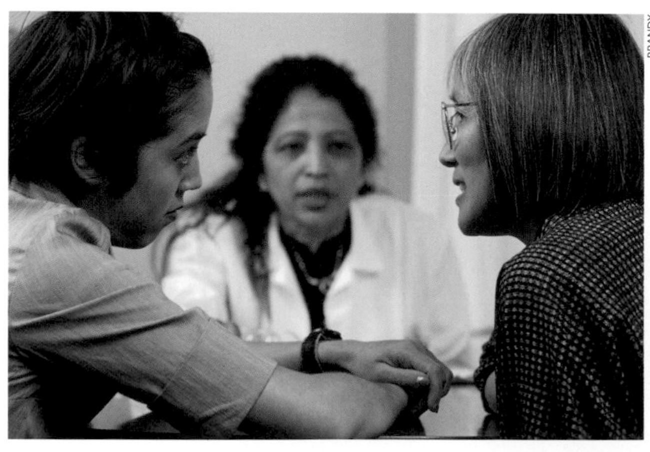

Families enter therapy for many reasons, sometimes to help particular members and at other times because there are problems in one or more of the relationships in the family.

In family therapy, the 'client' is the entire family rather than one person. The family is thought of as a *system*, so one person's symptoms are symptoms of the family system as a whole. Family therapists believe that problem behaviours exhibited by a particular family member are the result of a dysfunctional family system. For example, an adolescent girl suffering from an eating disorder might be treated in therapy with her mother, father and older brother. The therapist would work to understand how the family members relate to one another, how the family is organized, and how it changes over time. In discussions with the family, the therapist might discover that the parents' excessive enthusiasm about her brother's athletic career led the girl to try to gain their approval by controlling her weight to become 'beautiful'. Couples and family therapy involve more than one person attending therapy together, and the problems and solutions are seen as arising from the *interaction* of these individuals rather than simply from any one individual.

Group therapy

If individual clients can benefit from talking with a psychotherapist, perhaps they can also benefit from talking with other clients who are talking with the therapist. This is **group therapy** – *a technique in which multiple participants (who often do not know one another at the outset) work on their individual problems in a group setting*. Many psychotherapies, for example psychodynamic psychotherapy, CBT, humanistic and existential therapies, have been adapted for groups, although traditional psychoanalysis is a problem because the couch gets so crowded. The therapist in group therapy serves more as a discussion leader than a personal therapist, conducting the sessions by talking with individuals and encouraging them to talk with one another. Group therapy is often used for people who have a common problem, such as substance abuse, but it can also be used for those with differing problems. Group therapy can be helpful for many of the problems targeted by individual therapies, such as anxiety, depression, body image issues, substance abuse or coping with divorce.

GROUP THERAPY A technique in which multiple participants (who often do not know one another at the outset) work on their individual problems in a group setting.

Why do people choose group therapy? One advantage is that groups provide a context in which clients can practise relating to others. People in group therapy have a 'built-in' set of peers whom they have to talk to and get along with on a regular basis. This can be especially helpful for clients who are otherwise socially isolated. Second, attending a group with others who have similar problems shows clients that they are not alone in their suffering. Third, group members model appropriate behaviours for one another and share their insights about how to deal with their problems. Beyond these advantages, there is also the practical side. Group treatment is more cost-effective than individual therapy, using less therapist time and allowing more people to participate in treatment. Individuals who might not otherwise be able to afford psychotherapy may be able to manage the cost of group therapy.

There are also disadvantages of group therapy over individual therapy. It may be difficult to assemble a group of individuals who have similar needs. This is particularly an issue with CBT, which tends to focus on specific problems such as depression or panic disorder. Group therapy may become a problem if one or more members undermine the treatment of other group members. This can occur if some group members dominate the discussions, threaten other group members, or make others in the group uncomfortable; for example attempting to date other members. Finally, clients in group therapy get less attention than they might in individual psychotherapy. As a result, those who tend to participate less in the group may not benefit as much as those who participate more.

On balance, group therapy is often a useful format for treating a wide variety of problems, and it has been effectively used with a number of different types of therapy. When group therapy is not available or the person is not ready for this type of intervention, self-help or support groups may be a good alternative.

Self-help and support groups

In countries without a national health service, the costs of healthcare continue to escalate each year, leading to increasing pressure to find creative ways to improve access to treatment. Self-help and support groups provide help at reasonable or sometimes no cost. Typically, self-help and support groups are discussion or internet chat groups that focus on a particular disorder or difficult life experience and are often run by peers who have themselves struggled with the same issues. For example, many self-help groups offer support to cancer survivors or parents of children with autism. There are online support groups for people with mood disorders, eating disorders, substance abuse problems and self-harming disorders – in fact, just about every psychological disorder. In addition to being cost-effective, self-help and support groups allow people to realize that they are not the only ones with a particular problem and give them the opportunity to offer guidance and support to each other based on personal experiences of success.

Considered together, the many social approaches to psychotherapy reveal how important interpersonal relationships are for each of us. It may not always be clear how psychotherapy works, whether one approach is better than another, or what particular theory should be used to understand how problems have developed. What is clear, however, is that social interactions between people – in individual therapy and all the different forms of group therapy – can be useful in treating psychological disorders.

Combining psychotherapy with medication

An eclectic approach to mental disorder also includes considering whether medication is warranted as part of the treatment programme. Many studies have compared medication, psychological treatments and combinations of these approaches for addressing psychological disorders. The results of these studies often depend on the particular problem being considered. For example, in the cases of schizophrenia and bipolar disorder, researchers have found that medication is a necessary part of treatment, and studies have tended to examine whether adding psychotherapeutic treatments such as social skills training or cognitive behavioural treatment can be helpful. For severe disorders, then, medication is usually a critical first step.

In the cases of anxiety disorders and depression, however, questions about treatment often involve deciding whether medication *or* psychotherapy should be used. CBT, medications and their combinations have been found to be about equally effective. One study compared CBT, imipramine, and CBT plus imipramine with a placebo (administration of an inert medication; see below) for the treatment of panic disorder (Barlow et al., 2000). After 12 weeks of treatment, CBT alone and imipramine alone were found to be superior to a placebo (see FIGURE 17.3). For the CBT-plus-imipramine condition, the response rate also exceeded the placebo but was not significantly better than that for either CBT or imipramine alone. In other words, either treatment was better than nothing, but the combination of treatments was not significantly more effective than one or the other.

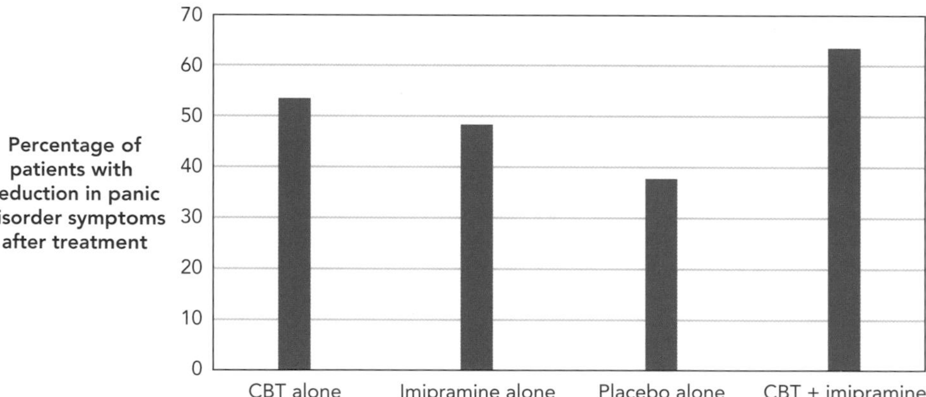

FIGURE **17.3 Effectiveness of medication and psychotherapy for panic disorder** One study of CBT and medication (imipramine) for panic disorder found that the effects of CBT, medication, and treatment that combined CBT and medication were not significantly different over the short term, although all three were superior to the placebo condition (Barlow et al., 2000).

We do know that therapy and medication are effective, so one question is whether they work through similar mechanisms. A recent study of people with social phobia examined patterns of cerebral blood flow following treatment using either citalopram (an SSRI) or CBT (Furmark et al., 2002). Patients in both groups were alerted to the possibility that they would soon have to speak in public. In both groups, those who responded to treatment showed similar reductions in activation in the amygdala, hippocampus and neighbouring cortical areas during this challenge (see FIGURE 17.4). As you'll recall from Chapter 5, the amygdala and hippocampus play significant roles in memory for emotional information. These findings suggest that therapy and medication affect the brain in regions associated with a reaction to threat. Although it might seem that events that influence the brain should be physical – after all, the brain is a physical object – the physical administration of a drug and the psychological application of psychotherapy produce similar influences on the brain.

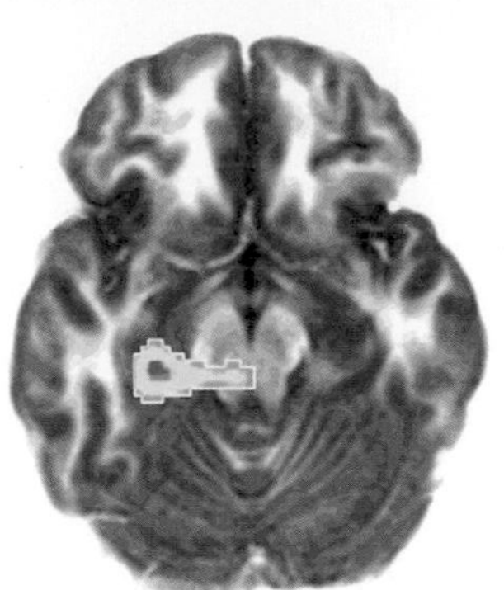
(a) CBT

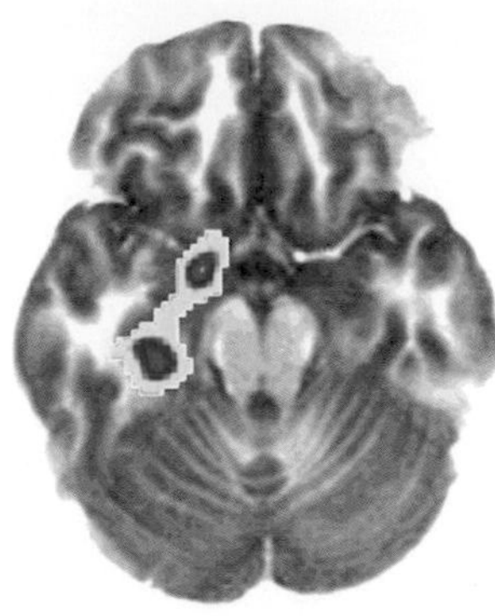
(b) Medication

FIGURE **17.4 Effects of medication and therapy on the brain** PET scans of patients with social phobia showed similar reductions in activation of the amygdala/hippocampus region after they received treatment with CBT (a) and citalopram, an SSRI (b) (Furmark et al., 2002).

COURTESY TOMAS FURMARK

Findings such as these suggest that it is not always necessary to combine medication with psychotherapy; often, one type of treatment or the other will do just fine. There are other cases, however, in which both are helpful, such as when drugs help a person to become calm enough to interact successfully with a therapist or when therapy is used to help the person make cognitive or behavioural changes that will later allow medication to be reduced or eliminated. Also, remember from Chapter 5 that there is an emerging area of cognitive enhancers that seem to improve memory and learning that have been successfully applied in psychotherapy for fear of heights (Ressler et al., 2004). Whatever magic medication can provide must be coordinated with the magic of psychotherapy. In the next section, we will see if these strategies work.

In summary, there are several major forms of psychotherapy. Freud's psychoanalysis was the initial model for all the psychodynamic therapies, which together emphasize helping clients to gain insight into their unconscious conflicts. Behaviour therapy, which applies learning principles to specific behaviour problems, and cognitive therapy, which aims at challenging irrational thoughts, have been merged by many therapists into cognitive behaviour therapy (CBT). Humanistic therapies (such as person-centred therapy) and existential approaches (such as Gestalt therapy) focus on helping people to develop a sense of personal worth. Approaches to psychotherapy can also involve more than one person, targeting either group problems or individual problems by involving couples, families or groups of clients brought together for the purpose of therapy. Many mental health professionals adopt an eclectic approach that means considering multiple strategies for dealing with complex mental disorders. Depending on the nature of the disorder and the individual involved, this may include a combination of medication and psychotherapy.

Treatment effectiveness: for better or for worse

Throughout this chapter, we have explored various biomedical and psychological treatments that may help people with psychological disorders. But do these treatments actually work, and which ones work better than others? To answer these questions, we'll first consider how we can evaluate the effectiveness of treatments. Then we'll turn to the evidence from these evaluations to see when therapy works. With any luck, false noses will not be necessary for anyone.

Evaluating treatments

Treatment can have three possible outcomes: a client's symptoms can improve, stay the same, or worsen. How can we determine which of these has happened as a result of a particular treatment? The main problem in answering this question is the problem faced by researchers generally: deciding whether one event has caused another. Did the treatment cause a cure?

As you learned in Chapter 2, this can be a difficult detective exercise. The detection is made even more difficult because people may approach treatment evaluation unscientifically, often by simply noticing an improvement, no improvement or that dreaded decline, and reaching a conclusion based on that sole observation. Treatment evaluation can be susceptible to illusions – mindbugs in how people process information about treatment effects – and these illusions can only be overcome by scientific evaluation.

Treatment illusions

Imagine you're sick and the doctor says 'Take a pill'. You follow the doctor's orders, and you get better. To what do you attribute your improvement? If you're like most people, you reach the conclusion that the pill cured you. How could this be an illusion? There are at least three ways. Maybe you would have got better anyway; maybe the pill wasn't the active ingredient in your cure; or maybe after you're better, you mistakenly remember having been more ill than you really were. These possibilities point to three potential illusions of treatment – those produced by natural improvement, nonspecific treatment effects, or reconstructive memory.

Natural improvement

Natural improvement is the tendency of symptoms to return to their mean or average level, a process sometimes called *regression to the mean*. The illusion in this case happens when you mistakenly conclude that a treatment has made you better when you would have got better anyway. People typically turn to therapy or medication when their symptoms are at their worst, so they start their personal 'experiment' to see if treatment makes them improve at a time when things couldn't get much worse. When this is the case, the client's symptoms will often improve, regardless of whether there was any treatment at all; when you're at rock bottom, there's nowhere to go but up. In most cases, for example, depression that becomes severe enough to make a person a candidate for treatment will tend to lift in several months. A person who enters therapy for depression may develop an illusion that the therapy works because the therapy coincides with the typical course of the illness and the person's natural return to health.

Nonspecific treatment effects

Another treatment illusion occurs when a client or therapist attributes the client's improvement to a feature of treatment, although that feature wasn't really the active element that caused improvement. Recovery could be produced by *nonspecific treatment effects* that are not related to the specific mechanisms by which treatment is supposed to be working. For example, antidepressant medications are thought to work by changing brain chemistry to increase levels of serotonin, noradrenaline and/or dopamine. However, the doctor prescribing the medication might simply be a pleasant and hopeful individual who gives the client a sense that things will improve. Client and doctor alike might attribute the client's improvement to brain changes, whereas the true active ingredient was the warm relationship with the good doctor.

Nonspecific treatment effects include many factors that might accompany a treatment. The client's decision to seek help, for example, might create a personal commitment, a kind of 'turning over a new leaf', and the resulting behaviour changes could be helpful. Alternatively, staying away from alcohol because of its possible interaction with depression medication might be more useful as a treatment than the medication itself.

The placebo effect

Simply knowing that you are getting a treatment can be a nonspecific treatment effect. These instances include the positive influences that can be produced by a **placebo** – *an inert substance or procedure that has been applied with the expectation that a healing response will be produced*. For example, if you take a sugar pill that does not contain any painkiller for a headache thinking it is aspirin, this pill is a placebo. The classic placebo is the sugar pill, but sticking plasters, injections, heating pads, neck rubs, homeopathic remedies and even kind words can have **placebo effects** – *clinically significant psychological or physiological responses to a therapeutically inert substance or procedure*. For the effect to occur, however, the recipient must know that a treatment is taking place (Stewart-Williams, 2004), but this is also true of active treatments such as morphine injections (Benedetti et al., 2003). We know that the placebo effect is truly a case of mind over body by comparing the effectiveness of different placebos. People hold certain assumptions based on expectations, marketing, intuitive biases as well what they have been told by others (Goldacre, 2008). These expectations can be remarkably specific, mirroring in detail what patients believe about the nature of medicine, for example that two pills

stats facts

Clinical study designs

As we noted in Chapter 2, researchers and participants can have biases that compromise the objectivity of an experiment. This is especially true in clinical trials to evaluate the effectiveness of treatments where the placebo effect operates. One way to evaluate the true clinical effectiveness of a treatment is to use a randomized double-blind design where neither the researcher nor the patients know who has been given the active treatment and who has been given the control nonactive treatment until after the study is conducted. It is randomized because patients are selected for either the active or nonactive control group by chance. This eliminates systematic expectations when everybody knows that there is a real and a sham treatment but not who is receiving which. The randomized double-blind design is the gold standard for evaluating treatments, which is why various authorities around the world insist on this design when evaluating the effectiveness of treatments. The problem is, of course, an ethical one. If you are ill, would you be happy to discover that you were not given the active treatment? It is a difficult call but given that the placebo effect is a real and powerful phenomenon, one has to check that active treatments are more effective than the benefits of positive expectations. Assigning a subject to a placebo group can pose an ethical problem if it violates their right to receive the best available treatment. The Declaration of Helsinki provides guidelines on this issue (www.wma.net/en/30publications/10policies/b3).

PLACEBO An inert substance or procedure that has been applied with the expectation that a healing response will be produced.

PLACEBO EFFECT A clinically significant psychological or physiological response to a therapeutically inert substance or procedure.

work better than one and an injection works better than a pill (de Craen et al., 1999). Even the colour of a placebo pills makes a difference. Patients believe that red, yellow and orange pills are associated with a stimulant effect, while blue and green are related to a tranquilizing effect (de Craen et al., 1996).

How do placebos operate? Do people really feel pain but distort their report of the experience to make it consistent with their beliefs about treatment? Or does the placebo actually reduce the pain a patient experiences? Howard Fields and Jon Levine (1984) discovered that placebos trigger the release of endorphins (or *endogenous opiates*), painkilling chemicals similar to morphine that are produced by the brain (see Chapter 8). In their experiments, they found that an injection of naloxone, an opiate-blocking drug, typically reduces the benefit of an opiate such as morphine and a placebo injection, suggesting that the placebo has its painkilling effects because it triggers the release of endorphins.

The activation of specific brain areas associated with pain is also modulated by a placebo. One set of fMRI studies examined brain activation as volunteers were exposed to electric shock or heat (Wager et al., 2004). In preparation for some exposures to these painful stimuli, a placebo cream was applied to the skin, and the participant was told it was an analgesic that would reduce the pain. Other participants merely experienced the pain. As **FIGURE 17.5** shows, the fMRI scans showed decreased activation during placebo analgesia in the thalamus, anterior cingulate cortex and insula, pain-sensitive brain regions that were activated during untreated pain. These findings suggest that placebos are not leading people to misreport their pain experience, but are reducing brain activity in areas normally active during the pain experience.

Placebos can have profound effects in the case of psychological treatments. Research shows that a large percentage of individuals with anxiety, depression and other emotional problems experience significant improvement after a treatment. One study compared the decrease in symptoms of OCD between adolescents taking an SSRI antidepressant (Prozac) and those taking a placebo over the course of 13 weeks (Geller et al., 2001). Participants receiving medication showed a dramatic decrease in symptoms over time. Those taking a placebo also showed a reduction in symptoms over time, and the difference between the Prozac and placebo groups only became significant in the seventh week of treatment (see **FIGURE 17.6**). In fact, some psychologists estimate that up to 75% of the effects shown by antidepressant medications are due to the placebo effect (Kirsch and Sapirstein, 1998). One recent meta-analysis of the effectiveness of SSRIs concluded that, compared with placebos, these antidepressants did not produce clinically significant improvements in depression in patients who initially have moderate or even severe

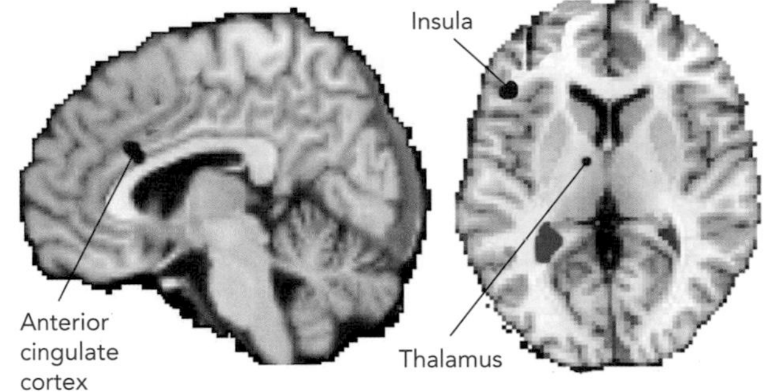

FIGURE 17.5 The brain's response to a placebo fMRI scans reveal that some brain regions normally activated when people report pain in response to shocks are deactivated when these individuals are given a placebo analgesic during the shock. These regions include the anterior cingulated cortex (shown in the left-hand image, a right medial view of the brain) and the insula and thalamus (both shown in the right-hand image, a ventral view of the brain) (Wager et al., 2004).

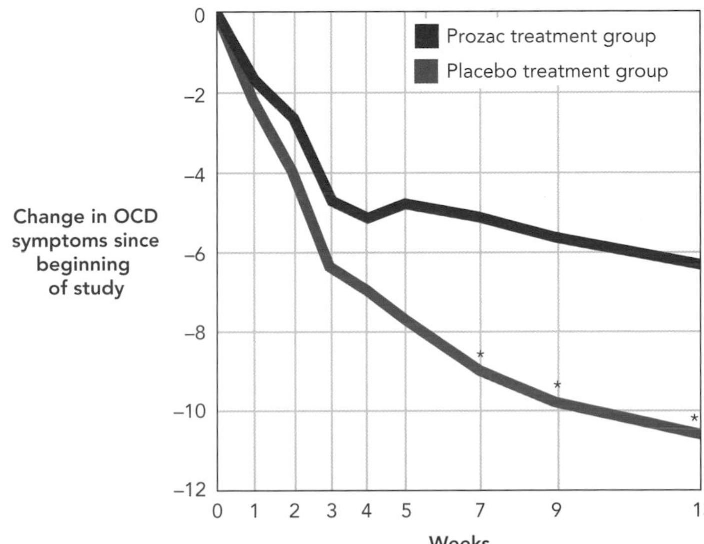

FIGURE 17.6 The placebo effect Two groups of patients were given pills to treat OCD. The first group was given Prozac, an antidepressant, and the second group was given an inert sugar pill, a placebo. Interestingly, both groups showed significant improvement in their depression symptoms until week 7, when the benefits of taking the placebo levelled off. As shown by the asterisks (*), Prozac reduced symptoms significantly more than the placebo pills by weeks 7,9 and 13 (Geller et al., 2001).

The placebo's evil twin

While positive expectations can induce the placebo effect, there is also the opposite outcome where negative expectations induce illness known as the *nocebo effect.* As a poor student, one of the authors used to take part in drug trials research where double-blind procedures were used (see stats facts). In one trial of a new analgesic using 10 student volunteers, he reacted to the drug with nausea and dizziness and had to be withdrawn from the study. Soon after, another student became sick with the same symptoms. The difference was that this other student had been given the inert control substance! He had experienced a nocebo effect.

depression, but only showed significant effects in the most severely depressed patients (Kirsch et al., 2008). Simply knowing that you're taking something for a problem can provide a measure of relief, even though what you're taking has no pharmacologically active ingredient.

Reconstructive memory

A third treatment illusion can come about when the client's motivation to get well causes errors in *reconstructive memory* for the original symptoms. You might think that you've improved because of a treatment when in fact you're simply misremembering that your symptoms before treatment were worse than they actually were. This tendency was first observed in research examining the effectiveness of a study skills class (Conway and Ross, 1984). Some students who wanted to take the class signed up and completed it, whereas others were randomly assigned to a waiting list until the class could be offered again. When their study abilities were measured afterwards, those who took the class were no better at studying than their wait-listed counterparts. However, those who took the class *said* that they had improved. How could this be? Those participants recalled their study skills before the class as being worse than they had been. This motivated reconstruction of the past was dubbed by the researchers 'getting what you want by revising what you had' (Conway and Ross, 1984). A client who forms a strong expectation of success in therapy might conclude later that even a useless treatment had worked wonders – by recalling past symptoms and troubles as worse than they were and thereby making the treatment seem effective.

When you feel you've come a long way, you may remember where you started as farther down than it was. People who feel they have improved from a treatment may reconstruct memories of the past that exaggerate their problems.

A person who enters treatment is often anxious to get well, so may be especially likely to succumb to errors and illusions in assessing the effectiveness of the treatment. Treatments can look as if they have worked when mindbugs lead us to ignore natural improvement, overlook nonspecific treatment effects (such as the placebo effect), and reconstruct our pretreatment history as worse than it was. Such treatment illusions can be overcome by using scientific methods to evaluate treatments, rather than trusting only our potentially faulty personal skills of observation.

Treatment studies

How can treatment be evaluated in a way that allows us to choose treatments that work and not waste time with procedures that may be useless or even harmful? Treatment studies depend generally on the research design concepts covered in Chapter 2 but also depend on some ideas that are unique to the evaluation of psychological treatments.

There are two main types of treatment studies – outcome studies and process studies:

1 *Outcome studies* are designed to evaluate *whether* a particular treatment works, often in relation to some other treatment or a control condition. For example, to study the outcome of treatment for depression, researchers might compare the self-reported moods and symptoms of two groups of people who were initially depressed – those who had received a treatment for six weeks and a control group who had also been selected for the study but had been assigned to a waiting list for later treatment and were simply tested six weeks after their selection. The outcome study could determine whether this treatment had any benefit.

2 *Process studies* are designed to answer questions regarding *why* a treatment works or under what circumstances a treatment works. For example, process researchers might examine whether a treatment for depression is more effective for certain clients than others. Does a particular drug have better effects for women than men? Process studies can also examine whether some parts of the treatment are particularly helpful, whereas others are irrelevant to the treatment's success. For example,

in CBT for depression, is there more improvement if the therapy includes an assignment for the patient to write down each morning a plan of activities for the day? Process studies can refine therapies and target their influence to make them more effective.

Outcome and process studies can be plagued by treatment illusions, so scientists usually design their research to overcome them. Ideally, for example, a treatment should be assessed in a *double-blind experiment*, where neither the patient nor the researcher/therapist know which treatment the patient is receiving (see Chapter 2). In the case of drug studies, this isn't hard to arrange because active drugs and placebos can be made to look alike to patients and researchers during the study. Keeping patients and researchers 'in the dark' is much harder in the study of psychotherapy; in fact, it may even be impossible. The patient and the therapist can easily notice the differences in treatments such as psychoanalysis and behaviour therapy, for example, so there's no way to keep the beliefs and expectations of patient and therapist out of the picture in evaluating psychotherapy effectiveness.

The treatment illusions caused by natural improvement and reconstructive memory happen when people compare their symptoms before treatment to their symptoms after treatment, so treatment researchers typically try to avoid before/after comparisons within a single treatment group. A treatment (or experimental) group and a control group need to be randomly selected from the same population of patients before the study and then compared at the end of treatment. That way, natural improvement or motivated reconstructive memory cannot cause illusions of effective treatment.

But what should happen to the control group during the treatment? If they simply stay home waiting until they can get treatment later (a wait-list control group), they won't receive the nonspecific effects of the treatment that the treatment group enjoys, such as visiting the comforting therapist or taking a medication. The researchers comparing *treatment* to *no treatment* might conclude erroneously that the treatment worked when, in reality, *any* treatment would have worked. For this reason, treatment studies commonly include a placebo treatment condition. In drug studies, the placebos are inactive medications given in the same way as the active medication; in psychotherapy studies, more elaborate activities that are like psychotherapy, for example yoga classes or meditation, are sometimes used to control for the nonspecific effects of psychotherapy. The scientific evaluation of treatment is designed to overcome the mindbugs that might make us jump to the conclusion that a treatment works when, in fact, it does not.

Which treatments work?

There are hundreds of published papers comparing various forms of psychotherapy to one another and to medication treatments. Every once in a while, someone takes a broad look at all this research and expresses the worry that treatment in general is not very effective and psychotherapy in particular is a waste of everyone's time.

Distinguished psychologist Hans Eysenck (1916–97) reviewed the relatively few studies of psychotherapy effectiveness available in 1952 and raised a furore among therapists by concluding that psychotherapy – particularly psychoanalysis – was not only ineffective but seemed to *impede* recovery (Eysenck, 1952). He concluded that 72% of patients recovered spontaneously over a two-year period without any treatment compared to 44% of patients receiving psychoanalysis (Eysenck, 1952). Psychoanalysis was not only ineffectual, it was positively bad for you! However, Eysenck's son Michael, another prominent British psychologist, has shown that his father's analysis was inaccurate and unfair (Eysenck, 2004). For example, other researchers using the same original data as Eysenck reported an 83% success rate for psychoanalytic therapy compared to a 30% spontaneous recovery (Bergin, 1971). One wonders what Freud would have made of this father–son disagreement.

Although critiques of psychotherapy continue to point out weaknesses in how patients are tested, diagnosed and treated (Dawes, 1994), there is strong evidence generally supporting the effectiveness of many treatments. The key question then becomes: Which treatments are effective for which problems (Hunsley and Di Giulio, 2002)?

Comparing treatments

One of the most enduring debates in clinical psychology concerns how the various psychotherapies compare to one another. Some psychologists have argued for years that evidence supports the conclusion that most psychotherapies work about equally well. In this view, it is the nonspecific factors shared by all forms of psychotherapy, such as contact with and empathy from a professional, that contribute to change (Luborsky et al., 2002; Luborsky and Singer, 1975). In contrast, others have argued that there are important differences between therapies and certain treatments are more effective than others, especially for treating particular types of problems (Beutler, 2002; Hunsley and Di Giulio, 2002). After all, you don't go to a foot doctor for a toothache. Different therapies ought to be differentially helpful for different problems. Some of these differences have been articulated in an attempt to compile a list of effective and helpful psychological treatments for particular problems.

In 1995, the American Psychological Association (APA) published one of the first attempts to define criteria for determining whether a particular type of psychotherapy is effective for a particular problem (Task Force on Promotion and Dissemination of Psychological Procedures, 1995). The official criteria for empirically validated treatments defined two levels of empirical support: *well-established treatments*, those with a high level of support, and *probably efficacious treatments*, those with preliminary support. After these criteria were established, a list of empirically supported treatments was published by the APA (Chambless et al., 1998; Woody and Sanderson, 1998). **TABLES 17.3** and **17.4** show examples of each kind of treatment.

There is little doubt that clients should have the opportunity to receive treatments that work, but there is still much disagreement about what the best approaches to treatment are. Some well-known therapies are conspicuously absent in the list of well-established treatments – psychoanalysis, for example – and criticisms of the effectiveness of types of therapy have led their defenders to fault the list of well-established treatments as flawed or incomplete. For example, critics have argued that treatments such as long-term psychodynamic therapy are not easily studied and for this reason may never make the list. Although the list is not perfect, the new emphasis on identifying which treatments are effective for which problems provides valuable information to psychotherapy consumers.

TABLE **17.3 Some well-established psychological treatments**

Type of treatment	Patient's problem
Cognitive behaviour therapy	Panic disorder with and without agoraphobia
Cognitive therapy	Depression
Cognitive therapy	Bulimia
Interpersonal therapy	Depression
Behaviour therapy (exposure and response prevention)	Obsessive-compulsive disorder
Behaviour therapy	Childhood enuresis (bed-wetting)
Behaviour therapy	Marital difficulties

TABLE **17.4 Some probably efficacious psychological treatments**

Type of treatment	Patient's problem
Behaviour therapy	Cocaine abuse
Brief psychodynamic therapy	Opiate dependence
Cognitive behaviour therapy	Opiate dependence
Brief psychodynamic therapy	Depression
Interpersonal therapy	Bulimia
Behaviour therapy	Offensive sexual behaviour

Dangers of treatment: the myth of mental illness

Can psychotherapy or medication do damage? Psychologists who treat mental health problems adhere to the same Hippocratic ideal held by medical workers: 'First, do no harm.' But even the best intentions cannot keep some treatments from causing unintended harm. Psychiatrist Thomas Szasz (1920–2012) was part of a movement in the 1960s that included R. D. Laing, who we encountered in Chapter 16, who held psychiatry and psychology accountable for such effects by making the extreme argument that mental illness is a myth created by those who hope to make money treating it (Szasz, 1960). From this perspective, all treatments are worthless and any harm is too much harm. This cynical view certainly doesn't describe the thousands of mental health workers who devote themselves to improving the lives of people with psychological disorders on a daily basis, but it does make you wonder about the harm psychological treatment might cause.

Some medications for mental disorders are potentially dangerous because of side effects, potential drug interactions and other complications. This is one of the arguments made by the medical community for why doctors should be solely responsible for prescribing drugs. Many drugs used for psychological treatments present the same types of problems as those associated with the recreational use of drugs or alcohol. For example, psychological medications may be addictive, creating long-term dependency with serious withdrawal symptoms. This is the case for Ritalin, often prescribed for attention deficit and hyperactivity disorder in children. Because it is chemically related to amphetamine, it can cause some of the same negative side effects to patients that have led lawmakers to ban amphetamines for the general public. The strongest critics of drug treatments claim that drugs do no more than trade one unwanted symptom for another – trading depression for sexual disinterest, anxiety for intoxication, or agitation for lethargy and dulled emotion (for example, Breggin, 2000). The 'magic bullet' of drug treatments may sometimes amount to shooting ourselves in the foot. Prescribing medication for psychological disorders is a serious step that mental health workers must always take with caution.

Could there be dangers in psychotherapy as well? What could be harmful about sitting in a room talking with a sympathetic psychologist? Any chance the psychologist will bite? The dangers of psychotherapy are more subtle, but one danger is clear enough in some cases that there is a name for it: **iatrogenic illness** is *a disorder or symptom that occurs as a result of a medical or psychotherapeutic treatment itself* (for example, Boisvert and Faust, 2002). Such an illness might arise, for example, when a psychotherapist becomes convinced that a client has a disorder that, in fact, the client does not have. As a result, the therapist works to help the client accept that diagnosis and participate in psychotherapy to treat that disorder. Being treated for a disorder can, under certain conditions, make a person show signs of that very disorder, and so an iatrogenic illness is born.

IATROGENIC ILLNESS A disorder or symptom that occurs as a result of a medical or psychotherapeutic treatment itself.

There are cases of patients who have been influenced through hypnosis and repeated suggestions in therapy to believe that they have dissociative identity disorder (even coming to express multiple personalities) or to believe that they were subjected to traumatic events as a child and 'recover' memories of such events, when investigation reveals no evidence for these problems prior to therapy (Acocella, 1999; McNally, 2003; Ofshe and Watters, 1994). There are people who have entered therapy with a vague sense that something odd has happened to them and who emerge after hypnosis or other imagination-enhancing techniques with the conviction that their therapist's theory was right – they were abducted by space aliens (Clancy, 2005). Needless to say, a therapy that leads patients to develop such bizarre beliefs is doing more harm than good.

A client who enters therapy is often vulnerable, feeling defeated as a result of life problems that have led to the psychotherapist's office. People in this position may be open to a therapist's influence, and this is usually a good thing, if it's the beginning of an interaction that can bring the person back to health. But just as the therapeutic relationship has great power to heal, its abuse can produce problems that would not have existed otherwise. Psychotherapists must be aware of this power and take care to avoid harming those they would help.

In summary, observing improvement during treatment does not necessarily mean that the treatment is effective. The scientific evaluation of treatments is necessary, otherwise people may overlook natural improvement, nonspecific treatment effects, such as the placebo effect, and reconstructive memory processes – illusions that can leave them thinking that treatment was effective when it was not. Treatment studies focus on treatment outcomes and processes, using research methods such as double-blind techniques and placebo control groups that yield clear inferences about treatment effectiveness. Treatments for psychological disorders are generally more effective than no treatment at all, but certain treatments are more effective for certain disorders. Lists of treatments shown by research to be well established, or probably efficacious, are being recommended by psychology organizations to guide healthcare providers and patients. The evaluation of treatments also shows that they are not without drawbacks, and medication and psychotherapy have dangers that ethical practitioners must consider carefully in designing treatments.

Environmental perspective: sources of stress

So far, we have considered the treatment of mental disorder in terms of biology and psychology but, as noted in Chapter 16, there is a third component to mental health – the environment. That environment includes where we live, and how we live our lives. For most of us, life has its **stressors** – *specific events or chronic pressures that place demands on a person or threaten the person's wellbeing.* Although such stressors rarely result in sudden disorder, they do have immediate and cumulative effects that can influence mental and physical health. Stressors are personal events that affect the comfortable pattern of our lives and little annoyances that bug us day after day. Let's look at the life events that can cause stress, the chronic sources of stress, and the relationship between a lack of perceived control and the impact of stressors.

STRESSORS Specific events or chronic pressures that place demands on a person or threaten the person's wellbeing.

Stressful events

People often seem to get sick after major life events. In pioneering work, Thomas Holmes and Richard Rahe (1967) followed up on this observation, proposing that major life changes cause stress and increased stress causes illness. To test their idea, they asked people to rate the magnitude of readjustment required by each of many events found to be associated with the onset of illness (Rahe et al., 1964). The resulting list of life events is remarkably predictive. Simply adding up the degree of life change for a person is a significant indicator of the person's future illness (Miller, 1996). Individuals experiencing more than 300 life change units over a period of one year were more at risk for physical and mental health problems including heart disease, diabetes, asthma, anxiety and depression (Martin, 1989). A person who is divorced and loses a job and has a friend die all in a year, for example, is more likely to get sick than one who escapes the year with only a divorce.

TABLE **17.5 Examples of stressful life events**

Event	Stress rating
Death of spouse	100
Divorce	73
Marriage	50
Retirement	45
Trouble with boss	23
Christmas	12

Reprinted from The Journal of Psychosomatic Research, 11/2, Holmes, T. H. and Rahe, R. H., The social readjustment rating scale, 213–18, Copyright (1967), with permission from Elsevier. www.jpsychores.com

Some examples of stressful life events taken from Holmes and Rahe's (1967) social readjustment rating scale are shown in TABLE 17.5. You may wonder why positive events are included. Stressful life events are unpleasant, right? Why would getting married be stressful? Isn't a wedding supposed to be fun? Research has shown that compared with negative events, positive events produce less psychological distress and fewer physical symptoms (McFarlane et al., 1980), and the happiness can sometimes even counteract the effects of negative events (Fredrickson, 2000). However, positive events often require readjustment and preparedness that many people find extremely stressful (for example, Brown and McGill, 1989), so these events are included in computing life change scores. Also, one weakness of Holmes and Rahe's checklist approach is that people respond to life events in different ways depending on what support they have and how they perceive the event. This is why Brown and Harris (1978) developed the structured interview called the Life Events and Difficulties Schedule (encountered in Chapter 16 when we looked at environmental causes of depression).

Home sweet home

Leaving the stability of home is stressful. Homesickness is the yearning for home, family and friends that most students experience on arrival at university (Fisher, 1989). It is a complex psychological state of disturbance characterized by increased anxiety, depression, obsessional behaviour as well as absent-mindedness. Longitudinal studies of UK university students show that homesickness is particularly common during the first term, with around 60–70% of first-year students experiencing it, and no difference between males and females. The incidence declines from the first to the second, third and fourth term, but there is still around 18–30% in the fourth year (Fisher and Hood, 1987). If you feel like this, you are not alone. Try speaking to a counsellor if these feelings start to disrupt your university life. Be prepared to be homesick.

Chronic stressors

Life would be simpler if an occasional stressful event such as a wedding or a lost job were the only pressure we faced. At least each event would be limited in scope, with a beginning, a middle and, ideally, an end. But unfortunately, life brings with it continued exposure to **chronic stressors** – *sources of stress that occur continuously or repeatedly.* Strained relationships, long queues at the supermarket, nagging relatives, overwork, money troubles – small stressors that may be easy to ignore if they happen only occasionally can accumulate to produce distress and illness. People who report having a lot of daily hassles also report more psychological symptoms (Kanner et al., 1981) and physical symptoms (Delongis et al., 1982), and these effects often have a greater and longer lasting impact than major life events.

CHRONIC STRESSORS Sources of stress that occur continuously or repeatedly.

Of course, some people may simply be complainers – people who have so much to say about their daily hassles and health that they make it *look* as if hassles cause health problems. These same people may also complain about their heating bills and how the government is out to get them. In fact, proneness towards complaints (also called *negative affectivity*) underlies part of the relationship between hassles and health

(Dohrenwend et al., 1984). People who express negative emotions in one area of life tend to do so in other areas, creating an apparent relationship between hassles and health that may not reflect cause and effect. However, the bulk of research shows that even when this tendency is taken into account, life hassles still lead to psychological and physical problems (Critelli and Ee, 1996).

Many chronic stressors are linked to particular environments. For example, features of city life – noise, traffic, crowding, pollution and even the threat of violence – provide particularly insistent sources of chronic stress. Rural areas have their own chronic stressors, of course, especially isolation and lack of access to amenities such as healthcare. The realization that chronic stressors are linked to environments has spawned the subfield *environmental psychology*, the scientific study of environmental effects on behaviour and health. In one study of the influence of noise on children, environmental psychologists looked at the impact of attending schools under the flight path of Los Angeles International Airport. Did the noise of more than 300 jets flying overhead each day have an influence beyond making kids yell to be heard? Compared with children matched for race, economic background and ethnicity who attended nearby schools away from the noise, children whose school was under the flight path had higher blood pressure and gave up more easily when working on difficult problems and puzzles (Cohen et al., 1980).

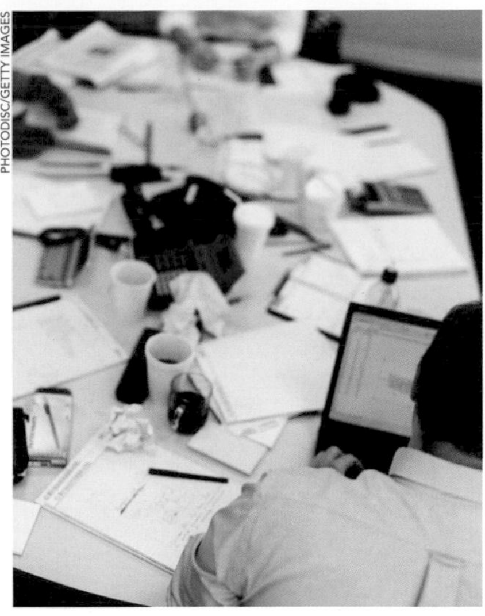
PHOTODISC/GETTY IMAGES

Crazy busy? The daily hassle of more work than time can become a significant stressor, as well as a fire hazard.

Perceived control over stressful events

What do stressful life changes and daily hassles have in common? What could possibly link job loss, weddings and noisy jets? Immediately, of course, their threat to the person or the status quo is easy to see. Stressors challenge you to *do something* – to take some action to eliminate or overcome the stressor.

Paradoxically, events are most stressful when there is *nothing to do* – no way to deal with the challenge. Expecting that you will have control over what happens to you is associated with effectiveness in dealing with stress. Researchers David Glass and Jerome Singer (1972), in classic studies of *perceived control*, looked at the aftereffects of loud noise on people who could or could not control it. Participants were asked to solve puzzles and proofread in a quiet room or in a room filled with noise as loud as that in classrooms under the LA flight path. Glass and Singer found that bursts of such noise hurt people's performance on the tasks after the noise was over. However, this dramatic decline in performance was prevented among participants who were told during the noise period that they could stop the noise just by pushing a button. They didn't actually take this option, but access to the 'panic button' shielded them from the detrimental effects of the noise.

Subsequent studies have found that a lack of perceived control underlies other stressors too. The stressful effects of crowding, for example, appear to stem from the feeling that you can't control getting away from the crowded conditions (Sherrod, 1974). Being jammed into student accommodation may be easier to handle, after all, the moment you learn of the button that opens the trapdoor under your roommate's chair. Or at least believing that you have this control makes it more bearable.

©ISTOCKPHOTO.COM/ENVIROMANTIC

When the flight attendant announces that 'we have a full cabin on this flight', conditions can be stressful, not so much because of the crowding, but because there is no obvious control over the crowding. Taking control, for example by keeping busy or wearing headphones to decrease contact with others or even by talking with people and getting to know them, may help decrease the stress.

In summary, stressors include major life events and minor hassles and can sometimes be traced to particular stressful environments. Stressors seem to add up over time: the more chronic the stressor, the more harmful the effects. Life events, hassles and environmental stressors all produce a threat to the person's mental and physical wellbeing that is perceived as difficult or impossible to control.

Stress reactions: all shook up

An accident at the Three Mile Island nuclear plant near Harrisburg, Pennsylvania, on 28 March 1979, created a near meltdown in the reactor and released radioactivity into the air and the Susquehanna River. The situation was out of control for two days, on the brink of a major disaster that was only averted when plant operators luckily made the right decision to repressurize the coolant system. Local residents learned that their lives were in grave danger, and 140,000 people packed up and fled the area. Most eventually returned when the danger had subsided, but they suffered lasting effects of the stress associated with this potentially deadly event.

A study conducted a year and a half later compared area residents with people from unaffected areas (Fleming et al., 1985). The local group showed physical signs of stress. They had relatively high levels of *catecholamines* (biochemicals indicating the activation of emotional systems) and fewer white blood cells available to fight infection (Schaeffer et al., 1985). The residents also suffered psychological effects, including higher levels of anxiety, depression and alienation compared with people from elsewhere. Even on a simple proofreading task, residents performed more poorly than people from unaffected areas. Because the radiation released was not sufficient to account for any of these effects, they were attributed to the aftermath of stress. In short, stress can produce changes in every system of the body, influencing how people feel and how they act. Let's look at how the process works.

Physical reactions

FIGHT-OR-FLIGHT RESPONSE An emotional and physiological reaction to an emergency that increases readiness for action.

Walter Cannon (1929) coined a phrase to describe the body's response to any threatening stimulus: the **fight-or-flight response** – *an emotional and physiological reaction to an emergency that increases readiness for action.* When the sirens began wailing at Three Mile Island, the area residents no doubt felt rattled in exactly this way. The mind asks: 'Should I stay and battle this somehow, or should I run like mad?' And the body prepares to react. If you're a cat at this time, your hair stands on end. If you're a human, your hair stands on end too, but not as visibly. Cannon recognized this common response across species and suspected that it might be the body's first mobilization to any threat. Research conducted since Cannon's discovery has revealed what is happening in the brain and body during this reaction.

Brain activation in response to threat occurs in the hypothalamus, stimulating the nearby pituitary gland, which in turn releases adrenocorticotropic hormone (ACTH). The ACTH then travels through the bloodstream and stimulates the adrenal glands on top of the kidneys (see **FIGURE 17.7**). In this cascading response of the *hypothalamus-pituitary-adrenal (HPA) axis*, the adrenal glands are then stimulated to release hormones, including the catecholamines mentioned earlier (adrenaline and noradrenaline), which increase sympathetic nervous system activation (and therefore

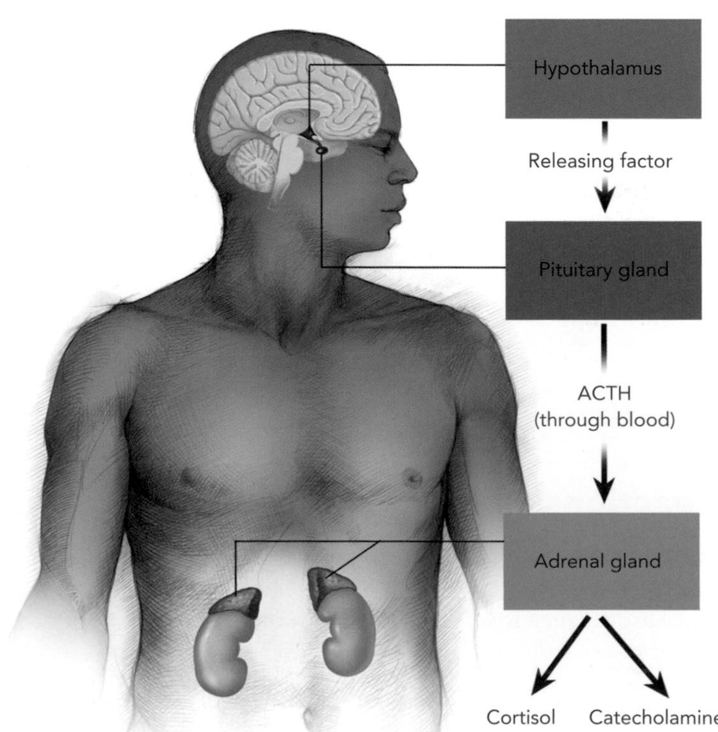

FIGURE 17.7 HPA axis Just a few seconds after a fearful stimulus is perceived, the hypothalamus activates the pituitary gland to release adrenocorticotropic hormone (ACTH). The ACTH then travels through the bloodstream to activate the adrenal glands to release catecholamines and cortisol, which energize the fight-or-flight response.

increase heart rate, blood pressure and respiration rate) and decrease parasympathetic activation (see Chapter 3). The increased respiration and blood pressure make more oxygen available to the muscles to energize attack or initiate escape. The adrenal glands also release *cortisol*, a hormone that increases the concentration of glucose in the blood to make fuel available to the muscles. Everything is prepared for a full-tilt response to the threat.

Stress effects on the immune response

The immune system is a complex response system that protects the body from bacteria, viruses and other foreign substances. Stressful events can compromise the immune responses that fight infection. For example, in one study, medical student volunteers agreed to receive small wounds to the roof of the mouth. Researchers observed that these wounds healed more slowly during exam periods than during summer holidays (Marucha et al., 1998). In another study, a set of selfless, healthy volunteers permitted researchers to swab common cold virus in their noses (Cohen et al., 1998). You might think that a direct application of the virus would be like exposure to a massive full-facial sneeze and that all the participants would catch colds. The researchers observed, though, that some people got colds and others didn't, and stress helped account for the difference. People who had experienced chronic stressors (lasting a month or longer) were more likely to suffer colds as a result of their inoculation than the other people tested. In particular, participants who had lost a job or were going through extended interpersonal problems with family or friends were most susceptible to the virus. Brief stressful life events (those lasting less than a month) had no impact.

Maintaining high levels of stress over long periods leads to a chronic impairment in our ability to cope with life's ups and downs. It is like keeping your foot on the accelerator pedal, and revving the engine until it blows up; it will eventually cause damage to the HPA axis mechanisms and subsequent illness and impairment of your immune system. Chronic stress has also been linked to psychiatric disorders such as depression, with most individuals suffering from major depression having increased HPA activity (Pariante and Miller, 2001). So, to keep body and mind in a healthy state, you need to be able to regulate your stress response. Part of this regulation is provided by the hippocampus, the structure associated with memory (Chapter 3). Within the hippocampus, there are glucocorticoid receptors that monitor levels of glucose and cortisol in the bloodstream. When levels of circulating glucose and cortisol reach a critical level, the hippocampus signals the hypothalamus to shut down the HPA process in the same way that a thermostat on a heater regulates temperature. If a thermostat is faulty, the house freezes or overheats. Likewise, if the HPA is disrupted, either you do not respond adequately to stress or you overreact.

The effect of stress on the immune response may help to explain why social status is related to health. Studies of British civil servants beginning in the 1960s found that mortality varied precisely with civil service grade: the higher the classification, the lower the rates of death, regardless of cause (Marmot et al., 1991). One explanation is that people in lower status jobs more often engage in unhealthy behaviour such as smoking and drinking alcohol, and there is evidence of this. But there is also evidence that the stress of living life at the bottom levels of society increases the risk of infections by weakening the immune system. People who perceive themselves as low in social status are more prone to suffer from respiratory infections, for example, than those who do not bear this social burden – and the same holds true for low-status male monkeys (Cohen, 1999).

One of the most common stressors is loneliness (see Chapter 14). Loneliness has the same impact on health as obesity and inactivity (Holt-Lunstad et al., 2010), which indicates that it is a serious medical problem that goes largely unnoticed. We are always being told to lose weight and take exercise but when did you last time see a government campaign to improve our circle of friends? Loneliness affects health through dysregulation of the immune system caused by stress leading to inflammation (Jaremka et al., 2013), and has been shown to directly influence viral infection from the herpes virus (Dixon et al., 2006), the Epstein-Barr virus (Glaser et al., 1985) and immune system response to the influenza vaccine (Pressman et al., 2005).

The mechanism of influence is likely to be epigenetic (see Chapter 3). An analysis of the DNA in the white blood cells or *leukocytes* of lonely adults reveals different levels of gene expression in comparison to adults who are not lonely (Cole et al., 2007). Specifically, the genes responsible for producing antibodies to infection were downgraded, making their immune response less effective. This may explain why lonely adults are more vulnerable to diseases. What is remarkable is that the different gene expression is only found in those individuals who *feel* they are lonely and is not related to the number of social contacts they have. Even some of the most popular people can still be the loneliest in a crowd because it is how they feel that is more important than their actual social circles.

Psychological reactions

The body's response to stress is intertwined with the mind's responses. Perhaps the first thing the mind does is try to sort things out – to interpret whether an event is threatening or not and, if it is, whether something can be done about it. When faced with stressful events that are perceived as uncontrollable, the mind, like the body, responds in ways that can lead to health problems. Psychological reactions to stress can eventually result in stress disorders, such as post-traumatic stress disorder (PTSD) or the mental breakdown known as 'burnout'.

Stress interpretation

GETTY

Primary appraisal allows you to interpret a roller coaster as a potentially pleasurable experience rather than a fatal one!

The interpretation of a stimulus as stressful or not is called *primary appraisal* (Lazarus and Folkman, 1984). Primary appraisal allows you to realize that a small dark spot on your shirt is a stressor ('spider!') or that a 113-km/h drop from a great height in a small car full of screaming people is not a stressor ('roller coaster!').

In a demonstration of the importance of interpretation, researchers used a gruesome film of a subincision – a kind of genital surgery that is part of some tribal initiation rites – to severely stress volunteer participants (Speisman et al., 1964). Self-reports and participants' autonomic arousal (heart rate and galvanic skin response level) were the measures of stress. Before viewing the film, one group listened to an 'intellectual' introduction that discussed the rite from an anthropologist's point of view, while another heard an introduction that downplayed the pain and emphasized the coming-of-age aspect of the initiation. Both interpretations markedly reduced the film viewers' stress compared with another group, whose viewing was preceded by a lecture accentuating the pain and trauma.

The next step in interpretation is *secondary appraisal* – determining whether the stressor is something you can handle or not, that is, whether you have control over the event (Lazarus and Folkman, 1984). Interestingly, the body responds differently depending on whether the stressor is perceived as a *threat* (a stressor you believe you might *not* be able to overcome) or a *challenge* (a stressor you feel fairly confident you *can* control) (Blascovich and Tomaka, 1996). The same midterm exam could be a challenge if you were well prepared and a threat if you neglected to study.

Although threats and challenges raise heart rate, threats increase vascular reactivity, such as constriction of the blood vessels, which can lead to high blood pressure. In one study, researchers found that an interaction as innocuous as a conversation can produce threat or challenge responses depending on the race of the conversation partner. Asked to talk with another, unfamiliar student, white students showed a challenge reaction when the student was white and a threat reaction when the student was black (Mendes et al., 2002). Similar results were found in studies that looked at other kinds of differences, such as lower socioeconomic status or disfigured facial features (Blascovich et al., 2001). It's as if social unfamiliarity creates the same kind of stress as lack of preparedness for an exam. In fact, doing 'homework' (having previously interacted with members of an unfamiliar group) tempers the threat reaction (Blascovich et al., 2001). The stress management techniques discussed in the next section may be lifesavers for such people.

In summary, the body and the mind both react to stress. The body responds with an initial fight-or-flight reaction that activates the hypothalamus-pituitary-adrenal (HPA) axis. Stressful events can also compromise the immune system that can adversely affect those at risk due to poor social conditions. The psychological costs of stress are to some extent dependent on how situations are appraised and interpreted but, in some cases, can eventually lead to anxiety disorders or depression.

Stress management: dealing with it

Most university students (92%) say they occasionally feel overwhelmed by the tasks they face, and over a third say they have dropped courses or received low grades in response to severe stress (Deuenwald, 2003). No doubt you are among the lucky 8% who are entirely cool and report no stress. But just in case you're not, you may appreciate our exploration of stress management techniques – ways to counteract psychological and physical stress reactions directly by managing your mind and body, and ways to sidestep stress by managing your situation. These techniques resemble some of the forms of CBT, but they are strategies people often exercise on their own, without the help of a therapist.

Mind management

A significant part of stress management is control of the mind. A number of basic strategies are available, including ignoring the stressor, thinking about the stressor, and trying to think about the stressor in a new way. In the language of psychology, these techniques are known as *repressive coping*, *rational coping* and *reframing*.

Repressive coping

Controlling your thoughts isn't easy, but some people do seem to be able to banish unpleasant thoughts from their mind. This style of dealing with stress, called **repressive coping**, is *characterized by avoiding situations or thoughts that are reminders of a stressor and maintaining an artificially positive viewpoint.* On self-report measures of coping style, *repressors* seldom report physical symptoms of anxiety such as sweaty palms, shakiness, a racing heart, or a nervous stomach (Weinberger et al., 1979). They paint an impossibly rosy picture of their lives, reporting, for example, that they are always polite and never lie, and they can't remember many events that made them sad or afraid. Everyone has *some* problems, of course, but repressors are good at deliberately ignoring them (Barnier et al., 2004).

REPRESSIVE COPING A response to stress characterized by avoiding situations or thoughts that are reminders of a stressor and maintaining an artificially positive viewpoint.

However, repressive coping comes with costs. Although it may make sense to try to avoid stressful thoughts and situations when stress is at its peak, research indicates that longer term use of such strategies can be harmful (Suls and Fletcher, 1985; Wegner and Pennebaker, 1993). The avoidance of thoughts and situations makes your world a bit smaller each day; a better approach is to come to grips with fears or problems. This is the basic idea of rational coping.

Rational coping

Rational coping *involves facing the stressor and working to overcome it.* This strategy is the opposite of repressive coping and so may seem to be the most unpleasant and unnerving thing you could do when faced with stress. It requires approaching rather than avoiding a stressor in order to lessen its longer term negative impact (Hayes et al., 1999). Rational coping is a three-step process:

RATIONAL COPING A strategy that involves facing the stressor and working to overcome it.

1 *acceptance:* coming to realize that the stressor exists and cannot be wished away
2 *exposure:* attending to the stressor, thinking about it, and even seeking it out
3 *understanding:* working to find the meaning of the stressor in your life.

When the trauma is particularly intense, rational coping may be difficult to undertake. In rape trauma, for example, even accepting that it happened takes time and effort; the initial impulse is to deny the event and try to live as though it had never occurred. Research on how psychotherapy helps people cope with rape trauma has focused on the exposure step by helping victims to confront and think about what happened. Using a technique called 'prolonged exposure', rape survivors relive the traumatic event in their imagination by recording a verbal account of the event and then listening to the recording daily. In one study, rape survivors were instructed to seek out objectively safe situations that caused them anxiety or that they had avoided. This sounds like bitter medicine indeed, but it is remarkably effective, producing significant reductions in anxiety compared to no therapy and compared to other therapies that promote more gradual and subtle forms of exposure (Foa et al., 1999).

The third element of rational coping involves coming to an understanding of the meaning of the stressful events. A trauma victim may wonder again and again: 'Why me?' 'How did it happen?' Survivors of incest frequently voice the desire to make sense of their trauma (Silver et al., 1983), a process that is difficult, even impossible, during bouts of suppression and avoidance.

REFRAMING A strategy that involves finding a new or creative way to think about a stressor that reduces its threat.

Reframing

Changing the way you think is another way to cope with stressful thoughts. Rather than suppressing the thoughts or coping rationally, people sometimes engage in a strategy of **reframing**, which *involves finding a new or creative way to think about a stressor that reduces its threat*. If you experience anxiety at the thought of public speaking, for example, you might reframe by shifting from thinking of an audience as evaluating you to thinking of yourself as evaluating them, and this might make speech giving easier. Or you could focus on the people in the audience most responsive to your message and even seek them out afterwards to ask what interested them about your speech. This way of reframing the stressor might not work for everyone. To be effective, reframing involves discovering a creative solution that will work for you.

STOCKBYTE

If you're nervous about public speaking, reframing the situation and imagining yourself in the position of power can increase your confidence.

Reframing apparently can take place spontaneously if people are given the opportunity to spend time thinking and writing about stressful events. In an important series of studies, Jamie Pennebaker (1989) found that the physical health of a group of university students improved after they spent a few hours writing about their deepest thoughts and feelings. Compared with students who had written about something else, members of the self-disclosure group were less likely in subsequent months to visit the student health centre; they also used less aspirin and achieved better grades (Pennebaker and Beall, 1986; Pennebaker et al., 1990). In fact, engaging in such expressive writing was found to improve immune function (Pennebaker et al., 1988), while suppressing emotional topics weakened it (Petrie et al., 1998). The positive effect of self-disclosing writing may reflect its usefulness in reframing trauma and reducing stress.

In summary, people often try to manage their minds by trying to suppress stressful thoughts or avoiding situations that produce them. Such repressive coping is not particularly effective for most people, and better alternatives include rationally coping with the stressor and engaging in reframing to see it differently.

psychomythology

Electroconvulsive shock treatment is shocking

Most people believe ECT to be a dangerous, painful procedure that can leave the patient in a vegetative state. One study of 1,737 members of the Swiss general public found that 57% thought the procedure harmful, with only 1% regarding it as helpful (Lauber et al., 2005). Early forms of ECT were dangerous but the modern practice is no more dangerous than receiving a general anaesthetic (Shiwach et al., 2001) and less dangerous than childbirth (Abrams, 1997). The main detrimental side effect of ECT is impaired short-term memory, which usually improves over the first month or two after the end of treatment. In addition, patients undergoing this procedure sometimes report headaches and muscle aches afterwards (Marangell et al., 2003). Despite these side effects, the treatment can be effective as a last resort. About half the individuals who do not respond to medication alone may find ECT helpful in treating their depression (Prudic et al., 1996). In fact, the one group who seem less opposed to ECT are the patients themselves who undergo the treatment, with the majority (98%) saying they would do it again if the severe depression recurred (Pettinati et al., 1994).

The public negative attitude towards ECT probably stems from a fear of electrocution (Kimball, 2007) but much of the blame must be levelled at the media. If you have ever seen *One Flew Over the Cuckoo's Nest* or other portrayals of ECT in films or on TV, then, in all likelihood, you will have seen the procedure being administered by ruthless hospital staff to unwilling patients who react in terror before convulsing as the electric current is applied. It may make for dramatic viewing but it bears little resemblance to the procedure that may be the last resort for the severely depressed.

where do you stand?

Genetic screening for mental health?

Currently, there are a number of genetic tests for disorders that lead to mental health problems, including PKU, fragile X syndrome and Huntingdon's disease. Advances in our understanding of the role of genes in contributing to mental health means that we potentially face a future where it is possible to identify individuals at risk for other mental health illnesses. We may also be able to provide genetic counselling to women in the same way we currently do for Down syndrome and other developmental disorders so that mothers can make the choice to terminate a pregnancy.

The question is: Should we undertake this type of genetic screening for mental health issues? The cost of mental health to society and the individual is enormous but should we try to eliminate the problem by genetic screening? In most instances, mental health problems will be complex and represent the interaction of a variety of environmental and individual factors, so it seems that determining an individual's outcome will rarely be certain. On the other hand, if an individual does have a predisposition to substance abuse, for example, then an early intervention may steer them on a different path.

A more worrying concern is the emergence of a number of commercial companies willing to provide direct-to-customer diagnostic services so that members of the public can access their own genetic information. This new trend of personal genomics will enable an individual to have their own DNA sequenced. But should they able to do so? Already, European countries including the UK have banned direct-to-customer genetic screening services, but the internet means that it will be practically impossible to stop such activities. Also, is it right that we prevent people finding out about their predispositions? After all, it is information concerning their bodies we are talking about. Why should they not be allowed to know? One concern is that providing people with information on their own genetic dispositions, unless interpreted through the medium of a health professional or genetic counsellor, will lead to undue worries or rash healthcare decisions on behalf of the informed person. Arguably, it is preferable for people to remain ignorant about their personal genome than to let the 'genome' out of the bottle.

Even if interventions can be effective, should society intervene in shaping the mental health profile of its citizens? Imagine a world without Van Gogh, Mark Twain or Churchill? Each of these individuals suffered from mental health problems and arguably some of their creativity was as a result of their bipolar disorder. Would you want to know if you, your future partner or your future children were at risk? Where do you stand?

Chapter review

Treatment: historical perspective

- From the very beginning it would appear that humans have treated mental disorder. The first civilizations regarded mental disorder as a consequence of demonic possession and supernatural activity.
- The Greeks were the first to consider mental disorder as a consequence of some physical problem and thought that imbalances in bodily fluids (humours) produced different types of disorder. Treatment consisted of practices believed to change the balance of the four humours.
- During the Dark Ages, a mental disorder was thought to have a supernatural origin and was attributed to witchcraft. The first asylums to house the homeless and mentally disordered appeared towards the end of the medieval period and were appalling institutions where patients were either shackled or treated with procedures thought to shock them back to normality.
- Towards the end of the 18th century, progressive thinkers tried new humane approaches to the treatment of the mentally disordered but this remained a minority perspective, with institutions continuing to operate well into the 20th century.

Medical and biological treatments: healing the mind through the brain

- Biomedical treatments include medications, and other biologically based treatments, such as direct intervention in the brain.
- Medications have undergone significant improvement over the past few decades and can be effective for psychotic symptoms, anxiety, depression and other disorders. However, the side effects of these medications may be unpleasant or annoying for a patient.
- Treatments such as electroconvulsive therapy (ECT), neurostimulation and psychosurgery can be of benefit for serious and intractable disorders, and phototherapy may be helpful for seasonal affective disorder (SAD). Radical techniques, such as the lobotomy, have been largely abandoned in favour of more focused, better defined and better understood procedures.

Psychological therapies: healing the mind through interaction

- There are hundreds of different types of psychological therapies, with the most commonly used being psychodynamic, behavioural, cognitive and humanistic/existential.
- Psychodynamic therapy is based on Freudian psychoanalysis and focuses on helping a client develop insight into their psychological problems. Techniques such as free association, dream analysis, interpretation of a client's statements and behaviours, and the analysis of resistance during treatment provide avenues towards insight.
- There are many varieties of psychodynamic therapies; most were originated by psychologists who studied with Freud but later broke away from his singular viewpoint.

- Behaviour therapy helps clients change maladaptive behaviours to more adaptive ones. Aversion therapy, establishing a token economy, exposure therapy and systematic desensitization are techniques based on traditional principles of learning theory.
- Cognitive therapy teaches clients to challenge maladaptive beliefs. Rational-emotive behaviour therapy, cognitive restructuring and mindfulness meditation are specific examples of this approach.
- Cognitive behaviour therapy (CBT) combines the individual strategies of behaviour therapy and cognitive therapy. CBT is problem focused and action oriented, structured, transparent and flexible.
- Humanistic and existential therapies seek to help clients become more aware of their feelings and concerns in an effort to allow clients to continue on a natural path of growth. Humanistic therapies emphasize congruence, empathy and unconditional positive regard in the therapist's treatment of a client. Gestalt therapy, an existentialist approach, uses methods such as focusing and the empty chair technique.
- Treatment delivered to people in groups includes couples and family therapy as well as group therapy. Group therapy allows multiple clients to work with a therapist and with each other towards overcoming psychological disorders. Self-help groups bring together individuals who can benefit from one another's experiences to deal with their problems.

Treatment effectiveness: for better or for worse

- There is considerable interest in scientifically determining if a therapy is better than nothing, better than a placebo, or better than an alternative treatment. From this research, a number of treatments for particular problems have been shown to be effective.
- There are significant dangers of treatment, including the side effects of drugs and the potential for psychotherapy to create iatrogenic psychological disorders that were not present when the therapy was initiated.

Environmental perspective: sources of stress

- Stressors include major life changes and minor hassles and can sometimes be traced to particular stressful environments.
- Stressors add up over time, with more chronic stressors producing more harmful effects.
- All stressors produce a threat to the person's wellbeing that is perceived as difficult or impossible to control.

Stress reactions: all shook up

- The body responds to stress with an initial 'fight-or-flight' reaction and the activation of the hypothalamus-pituitary-adrenal (HPA) axis.
- The effects of stress are moderated to some extent by the social status of individuals, with those from lower status jobs more at risk.
- The mind's reaction to stress begins with primary and secondary appraisal and can yield disorders such as depression, burnout or post-traumatic stress disorder (PTSD) in which thoughts of the stressor plague the mind.

Stress management: dealing with it

- People manage their stress by controlling the way they think about it.
- Repressive coping is not effective for most people, and better alternatives include rationally coping with the stressor and engaging in reframing to see things differently.

Key terms

anti-anxiety medications (p. 675)
antidepressants (p. 676)
antipsychotic drugs (p. 674)
asylums (p. 673)
aversion therapy (p. 684)
behaviour therapy (p. 683)
chronic stressors (p. 702)
cognitive behavioural therapy (CBT) (p. 688)
cognitive restructuring (p. 686)
cognitive therapy (p. 686)
collective unconscious (p. 682)
demonic possession (p. 672)
drug tolerance (p. 676)
eclectic psychotherapy (p. 680)
electroconvulsive therapy (ECT) (p. 678)
ergot (p. 673)
exposure therapy (p. 685)
fight-or-flight response (p. 704)
free association (p. 681)
Gestalt therapy (p. 690)
group therapy (p. 693)
humours (p. 672)
iatrogenic illness (p. 701)
mindfulness meditation (p. 687)
modelling (p. 685)
person-centred therapy (p. 689)
phototherapy (p. 678)
placebo (p. 696)
placebo effect (p. 696)
psychodynamic psychotherapies (p. 680)
psychopharmacology (p. 675)
psychosurgery (p. 679)
psychotherapy (p. 679)
rational coping (p. 707)
reframing (p. 708)
repressive coping (p. 707)
resistance (p. 682)
stressors (p. 702)
systematic desensitization (p. 685)
token economy (p. 684)
transcranial magnetic stimulation (TMS) (p. 678)
transference (p. 682)
trepanning (p. 672)
vagus nerve stimulation (VNS) (p. 678)

Recommended reading

Byron, T. (2014) *The Skeleton Cupboard: The Making of a Clinical Psychologist*. London: Macmillan. Series of gripping chapters based on case studies encountered during Byron's training as a clinical psychologist.

Sapolsky, R. M. (2004) *Why Zebras Don't Get Ulcers: The Acclaimed Guide to Stress, Stress-related Diseases, and Coping* (3rd edn). San Francisco, CA: Freeman. Covers the technical side of stress in a way that is accessible to the layperson. Masterfully presents a wide range of facts, discoveries and anecdotes on the biology and psychology of stress in humans and other species.

Glossary

absentmindedness A lapse in attention that results in memory failure.
absolute threshold The minimal intensity needed to just barely detect a stimulus.
accommodation The process by which the eye maintains a clear image on the retina.
accommodation When infants revise their schemas in light of new information.
acetylcholine (ACH) A neurotransmitter involved in a number of functions, including voluntary motor control.
acquisition The phase of classical conditioning when the CS and the US are presented together.
action potential An electric signal that is conducted along the length of a neuron's axon to a synapse.
activation-synthesis model The theory that dreams are produced when the brain attempts to make sense of neural activations that occur randomly during sleep.
actor-observer effect The tendency to make situational attributions for our own behaviours while making dispositional attributions for the identical behaviour of others.
acuity The level of finest visual detail that can be resolved.
adolescence The period of development that begins with the onset of sexual maturity (about 11–14 years of age) and lasts until the beginning of adulthood (18–21).
adulthood The stage of development that begins around 18–21 years and ends at death.
aetiology A causal pathway of circumstances that create a pathology.
affective forecasting The process by which people predict their emotional reactions to future events.
affordances Potentials for possible actions by agents acting on the environment.
agent A being that operates purposefully with intention to achieve outcomes in the world.
aggression Behaviour whose purpose is to harm another.
agonists Drugs that increase the action of a neurotransmitter.
agoraphobia An extreme fear of leaving home, entering shops, crowds and public places, or travelling alone on trains, buses or planes.
algorithm A well-defined sequence of procedures or rules that guarantees a solution to a problem.
alignment The process whereby speakers share a reciprocal arrangement to exchange information.
altered states of consciousness Forms of experience that depart from the normal subjective experience of the world and the mind.
altruism A specific prosocial behaviour that helps others but without any necessary expectation of reciprocal benefit.
amygdala A part of the limbic system, located at the tip of each horn of the hippocampus, that plays a central role in many emotional processes, particularly the formation of emotional memories.
analogical problem solving Solving a problem by finding a similar problem with a known solution and applying that solution to the current problem.
anal stage The second psychosexual stage, which is dominated by the pleasures and frustrations associated with the anus, retention and expulsion of faeces and urine, and toilet training.
anorexia nervosa An eating disorder characterized by an intense fear of being fat and severe restriction of food intake.
antagonists Drugs that block the function of a neurotransmitter.
anterograde amnesia The inability to transfer new information from the short-term store into the long-term store.
anthropomorphism The tendency to attribute human qualities to nonhuman things.
anti-anxiety medications Drugs that help reduce a person's experience of fear or anxiety.
antidepressants A class of drugs that help lift people's mood.
antinormative behaviour Activities that are transgressions of general social norms.
antipsychotic drugs Drugs that treat schizophrenia and related psychotic disorders.
antisocial personality disorder (APD) A pervasive pattern of disregard for and violation of the rights of others that begins in childhood or early adolescence and continues into adulthood.
anxiety disorder The class of mental disorder in which anxiety is the predominant feature.
aphasia Difficulty in producing or comprehending language.
apparent motion The perception of movement as a result of alternating signals appearing in rapid succession in different locations.
appearance–reality distinction The appreciation that looks can be deceiving.
appraisal An evaluation of the emotion-relevant aspects of a stimulus that is performed by the amygdala.
approach motivation A motivation to experience positive outcomes.
arborization Process where the cell axon lengthens and grows increasing dendritic branches.
area A1 A portion of the temporal lobe that contains the primary auditory cortex.
area V1 The initial processing region of the primary visual cortex.
assimilation When infants apply their schemas in novel situations.
association areas Areas of the cerebral cortex that are composed of neurons that help provide sense and meaning to information registered in the cortex.
asylums Workhouses to house beggars and those with mental disorders.
attachment An emotional bond.
attachment objects Blankets and soft toys that children are emotionally attached to and use for reassurance.

attenuation model Selective attention model that proposes that information is not entirely discarded in the stream of processing but is suppressed relative to other important signals.
attitude A positive or negative evaluation of an object or event.
attribution An inference about the cause of a person's behaviour.
autism A complex neurodevelopmental disorder characterized by three primary features: abnormal communication, stereotyped behaviours and impaired social interaction.
autobiographical memory The personal record of significant events of one's life.
autonomic nervous system (ANS) A set of nerves that carries involuntary and automatic commands that control blood vessels, body organs and glands.
availability bias Items that are more readily available in memory are judged as having occurred more frequently.
aversion therapy Using positive punishment to reduce the frequency of an undesirable behaviour.
avoidance motivation A motivation not to experience negative outcomes.
axon The part of a neuron that transmits information to other neurons, muscles or glands.
babyness A term coined by Lorenz (1943) to describe the relative attractiveness of big eyes and big heads.
Balint's syndrome An attentional disorder where the patient loses the ability to voluntarily shift visual attention to new locations, which is associated with damage to both sides of the brain.
basal ganglia A set of subcortical structures that direct intentional movements.
base rates The actual likelihood of events occurring.
basilar membrane A structure in the inner ear that undulates when vibrations from the ossicles reach the cochlear fluid.
behaviour Observable actions of human beings and nonhuman animals.
behavioural compliance Doing what you are told or expected to do.
behavioural inhibition The tendency towards shyness and fear of novelty.
behavioural neuroscience An approach to psychology that links psychological processes to activities in the nervous system and other bodily processes.
behaviourism An approach that advocates that psychologists restrict themselves to the scientific study of objectively observable behaviour.
behaviour therapy A therapy that assumes that disordered behaviour is learned and that symptom relief is achieved through changing overt maladaptive behaviours into more constructive behaviours.
belief An assumed piece of knowledge about an object or event that is not proven.
belief bias People's judgements about whether to accept conclusions depend more on how believable the conclusions are than on whether the arguments are logically valid.
bias The distorting influences of present knowledge, beliefs and feelings on recollection of previous experiences.
Big Five The traits of the five-factor model: openness to experience, conscientiousness, extroversion, agreeableness and neuroticism.
binding problem How features are linked together so that we see unified objects in our visual world rather than free-floating or miscombined features.
binocular disparity The difference in the retinal images of the two eyes that provides information about depth.
biological preparedness A propensity for learning particular kinds of associations over others.
biometrics The application of statistics to biological phenomena.
bipolar affective disorder A disorder characterized by two or more episodes in which the patient's mood and activity levels are significantly disturbed, this disturbance consisting on some occasions of an elevation of mood and increased energy and activity (hypomania or mania) and on others of a lowering of mood and decreased energy and activity (depression).
blastocyst Cluster ball of embryonic cells.
blindsight Residual visual capability supported by subcortical mechanisms following removal or damage to cortical visual areas.
blind spot An area of the retina that contains neither rods nor cones and therefore has no mechanism to sense light.
blocking A failure to retrieve information that is available in memory even though you are trying to produce it.
bulimia nervosa An eating disorder characterized by binge eating followed by activities intended to compensate for the food intake.
bystander effect When numerous people fail to help strangers in an emergency situation.
bystander intervention The act of helping strangers in an emergency situation.
canalization The idea of development as constrained epigenesis.
cannabis Drug derived from the hemp plant.
Cannon-Bard theory A theory about the relationship between emotional experience and physiological activity suggesting that a stimulus simultaneously triggers activity in the autonomic nervous system and emotional experience in the brain.
Cartesian theatre (after philosopher René Descartes) A mental screen or stage on which things appear to be presented for viewing by the mind's eye.
case method A method of gathering scientific knowledge by studying a single individual.
catatonic behaviour A marked decrease in all movement or an increase in muscular rigidity and overactivity.
categorization The process by which people identify a stimulus as a member of a class of related stimuli.
category-specific deficit A neurological syndrome characterized by an inability to recognize objects that belong to a particular category while leaving the ability to recognize objects outside the category undisturbed.
catharsis Purging or releasing pent-up emotions through activities that redirect the focus onto other sources.
causal reasoning When we infer that events happening close together in time and space are linked in some causal way.
cell body The part of a neuron that coordinates information processing tasks and keeps the cell alive.
central executive An attentional system that coordinates and controls plans of action and output.
central nervous system (CNS) The part of the nervous system that is composed of the brain and spinal cord.
cerebellum A large structure of the hindbrain that controls fine motor skills.
cerebral cortex The outermost layer of the brain, visible to the naked eye and divided into two hemispheres.
chameleon effect The mimicking of postures, expressions, gestures and patterns of behaviour such as speech or moods.
change blindness When people are unaware of significant event changes that happen in full view.
childhood The stage of development that begins at about 18–24 months and lasts until adolescence.
childhood amnesia An inability to remember events from the early years of life.
choice blindness When people are unaware of their decision-making processes and justify a choice as if it were already decided.
chromosomes Strands of DNA wound around each other in a double-helix configuration.
chronic stressors Sources of stress that occur continuously or repeatedly.
chunking Combining small pieces of information into larger clusters or chunks that are more easily held in short-term memory.
circadian rhythm A naturally occurring 24-hour cycle.
classical conditioning When a stimulus evokes a response because of being paired with a stimulus that naturally evokes a response.

clinical method of studying children Manipulating the situation to see how the child's behaviour changes in a reliable manner.
cochlea A fluid-filled tube that is the organ of auditory transduction.
cocktail party phenomenon People tune in to one message even while they filter out others nearby.
cognitive behavioural therapy (CBT) Therapy that uses a blend of cognitive and behavioural therapeutic strategies.
cognitive dissonance An unpleasant state that arises when a person recognizes the inconsistency of their actions, attitudes or beliefs.
cognitive map A mental representation of the physical features of the environment.
cognitive neuroscience A field that attempts to understand the links between cognitive processes and brain activity.
cognitive psychology The scientific study of mental processes, including perception, thought, memory and reasoning.
cognitive restructuring This involves teaching clients to question the automatic beliefs, assumptions and predictions that often lead to negative emotions and to replace negative thinking with more realistic and positive beliefs.
cognitive therapy Therapy that focuses on helping a client identify and correct any distorted thinking about self, others or the world.
cognitive unconscious The mental processes that are not experienced by the person but give rise to the person's thoughts, choices, emotions and behaviour.
cohort bias Anomalies that are predominant in one group that distort comparison between groups.
collective unconscious The culturally determined symbols and myths that are shared among all people.
collectivistic Where success and responsibility are seen as a reflection of group effort.
colour-opponent system Pairs of visual neurons that work in opposition.
comorbidity The co-occurrence of two or more disorders in a single individual.
companionate love An experience involving affection, trust and concern for a partner's wellbeing.
comparison level The cost–benefit ratio that people believe they deserve or could attain in another relationship.
computerized axial tomography (CT) A technique that recombines multiple X-ray photographs into a single image.
concept A mental representation that groups or categorizes shared features of related objects, events or other stimuli.
concordance rates Degree of statistical similarity based on co-occurrence.
concrete operational stage Stage of development that begins at about 6 years and ends at about 11 years.
concussion A loss of consciousness that can range from moments to weeks.
conditional probability A likelihood that is dependent on other factors.
conditioned response (CR) A reaction to a conditioned stimulus produced by pairing it with an unconditioned stimulus.
conditioned stimulus (CS) A stimulus that at first does not produce the response that is eventually conditioned by pairing with an unconditioned stimulus.
cones Photoreceptors that detect colour, operate under normal daylight conditions, and allow us to focus on fine detail.
conformity The tendency to do what others do simply because others are doing it.
conjunction fallacy People think that two events are more likely to occur together than either individual event.
Conlearn A system largely supported by maturing cortical brain mechanisms that learns about specific faces.
conscious motivation A motivation of which one is aware.
consciousness A person's subjective experience of the world and the mind.
conservation The notion that the quantitative properties of an object are invariant despite changes in the object's appearance.
consolidation The process whereby information must pass from short-term memory into long-term memory in order for it to be remembered.
Conspec A system that orients the infant towards face-like structures and is supported by mature subcortical brain mechanisms, present at birth.
construct validity The tendency for an operational definition and a property to have a clear conceptual relation.
contingency The organism has an expectation about how well the CS signals the appearance of the US.
contingent behaviour Synchronized responding.
control group The group of people matched to an experimental group but not exposed to the condition under investigation.
conventional stage A stage of moral development in which the morality of an action is primarily determined by the extent to which it conforms to social rules.
cooperation Behaviour by two or more individuals that leads to mutual benefit.
corpus callosum A thick band of nerve fibres that connects large areas of the cerebral cortex on each side of the brain and supports communication of information across the hemispheres.
correlation The 'co-relationship' or pattern of covariation between two variables occurs when variations in the value of one variable are synchronized with variations in the value of the other.
correlation coefficient A statistical measure of the direction and strength of a correlation, which is symbolized by the letter r.
correspondence bias The tendency to make a dispositional attribution even when a person's behaviour was caused by the situation.
covariance A measure of how much two variables change together.
creativity The ability to generate ideas or alternatives that may be useful in solving problems, communicating and entertaining ourselves.
crossmodal perception The capacity to detect correspondences of different features in the world from different sensory modalities.
cross-sectional research Experimental designs based on groups of children who represent a cross-section of the population.
crystallized intelligence The accuracy and amount of information available for processing (see fluid intelligence).
cultural psychology The study of how cultures reflect and shape the psychological processes of their members.
culture of honour Aggression linked to one's reputation for toughness, machismo and willingness to avenge a wrong or an insult.
daydreaming A state of consciousness in which a seemingly purposeless flow of thoughts comes to mind.
debriefing A verbal description of the true nature and purpose of a study that psychologists provide to people after they have participated in the study.
deduction Drawing inferences where the conclusion must be true if the premises are true.
deep dyslexia Readers cannot retrieve the meaning of words.
defence mechanisms Unconscious coping mechanisms that reduce anxiety generated by threats from unacceptable impulses.
deferred imitation paradigm Where the infant imitates an event demonstrated some time earlier.
deindividuation A perceived loss of individual identity accompanied by diminished self-regulation.
déjà vécu A confabulated memory where the individual is certain that the new experience is old.
déjà vu experience Where you suddenly feel that you have been in a situation before even though you can't recall any details.
delusion A patently false belief system, often bizarre and grandiose, that is maintained in spite of its irrationality.
demand characteristics Those aspects of an observational setting that cause people to behave as they think an observer wants or expects them to behave.

demonic possession A supernatural account for mental disorder.
dendrites The part of a neuron that receives information from other neurons and relays it to the cell body.
dependent variable The variable that is measured in a study.
depressive realism hypothesis Proposes that non-depressed individuals insulate themselves against negativity by adopting a positive attributional style, whereas people with depression are more realistic.
developmental psychology The study of continuity and change across the life span.
deviation IQ A statistic obtained by dividing a person's test score by the average test score of people in the same age group and then multiplying the quotient by 100 (see ratio IQ).
diathesis-stress model Suggests that a person may be predisposed to a mental disorder that remains unexpressed until triggered by stress.
dichotic listening A task in which people wearing headphones hear different messages presented to each ear.
diffusion of responsibility Individuals feel diminished responsibility for their actions because they are surrounded by others who are acting in the same way.
direct lexical route One where the grapheme maps directly onto the phoneme.
discrimination Positive or negative behaviour towards another person based on their group membership.
discrimination The capacity to distinguish between similar but distinct stimuli.
disgust An intense negative response that triggers feelings of nausea.
disorganized speech A severe disruption of verbal communication in which ideas shift rapidly and incoherently from one to another unrelated topic.
displacement A defence mechanism that involves shifting unacceptable wishes or drives to a neutral or less threatening alternative.
display rules Norms for the control of emotional expression.
dissociative amnesia The sudden loss of memory for significant personal information.
dissociative disorder A condition in which there is a partial or complete loss of the normal integration between memories of the past, awareness of identity and immediate sensations, and control of bodily movements that can vary in length up to many years.
dissociative fugue The sudden loss of memory for one's personal history, accompanied by an abrupt departure from home and the assumption of a new identity.
dissociative identity disorder (DID) The presence within an individual of two or more distinct identities that at different times take control of the individual's behaviour.
divided attention Situations where individuals have to simultaneously monitor more than one source of information.
dominant response The thing you are most inclined to do.
door-in-the-face technique A strategy that uses reciprocating concessions to influence behaviour.
dopamine A neurotransmitter that regulates motor behaviour, motivation, pleasure and emotional arousal.
dopamine hypothesis The idea that schizophrenia involves an excess of dopamine activity.
double-blind observation An observation whose true purpose is hidden from the researcher and the participant.
d-prime (d') A statistic that gives a relatively pure measure of the observer's sensitivity or ability to detect signals.
drive An internal state generated by departures from physiological optimality.
drug tolerance The need for higher doses of a drug over time to achieve the same effects following long-term use.
DSM-5 A US classification system (*Diagnostic and Statistical Manual of Mental Disorders*, 5th edn) that describes the features used to diagnose each recognized mental disorder and indicates how the disorder can be distinguished from other, similar problems.
dual-route models Propose that there are essentially two pathways to the lexicon.
dyadic relationship Where the focus of interest is between two individuals.
dynamic unconscious An active system encompassing a lifetime of hidden memories, the person's deepest instincts and desires, and the person's inner struggle to control these forces.
dyslexia A disorder involving difficulty with reading and writing.
dysthymia A disorder that involves the same symptoms as depression only less severe, but the symptoms last longer, persisting for at least two years.
early filter model Selective attention model that proposes that information is discarded early in the stream of processing.
echoic memory A fast-decaying store of auditory information.
eclectic psychotherapy A therapy that involves drawing on techniques from different forms of therapy, depending on the client and the problem.
ectoderm Embryonic disk layer that goes on to form the skin and nervous system.
ego The component of personality, developed through contact with the external world, that enables us to deal with life's practical demands.
egocentrism The tendency to adopt a self-centred viewpoint.
effect size An objective and standardized measure of the magnitude of an observed effect.
elaborative encoding The process of actively relating new information to knowledge that is already in memory.
electroconvulsive therapy (ECT) A treatment that involves inducing a mild seizure by delivering an electrical shock to the brain.
electroencephalogram (EEG) A device used to record electrical activity in the brain.
electromyograph (EMG) A device that measures muscle contractions under the surface of a person's skin.
electrooculograph (EOG) A device that measures eye movements.
embryonic disk Three-layered flattened structure that emerges from the blastocyst.
embryonic stage Period that lasts from the second week until about the eighth week.
emergent property Patterns that only arise out of the interaction of many elements.
emotional contagion The tendency to automatically mimic and synchronize expressions, vocalizations, postures and movements with those of another person and, consequently, to converge emotionally.
emotional expression Any observable sign of an emotional state.
emotional intelligence The ability to empathize and evaluate others' emotions.
emotion regulation The use of cognitive and behavioural strategies to influence one's emotional experience.
emotions Positive or negative experiences that are associated with a particular pattern of physiological activity.
empathic concern The disposition to take the perspective of others and resonate with their emotions.
empathizing Identifying another person's emotions and thoughts.
empirical method A set of rules and techniques for observation.
empiricism Originally a Greek school of medicine that stressed the importance of observation, and now generally used to describe any attempt to acquire knowledge by observing objects or events.
encoding The process by which we transform what we perceive, think or feel into an enduring memory.
encoding specificity principle The idea that a retrieval cue can serve as an effective reminder when it helps re-create the specific way in which information was initially encoded.
endoderm Embryonic disk layer that goes on to form the internal organs.
endorphins Chemicals that act within the pain pathways and emotion centres of the brain.

entitativity The extent to which a group of individuals are perceived to be cohesive, interconnected, similar, interactive and sharing common goals.
epidemiology The scientific examination of factors that contribute to disease.
epigenetics The mechanisms of interaction between the environment and genes.
episodic buffer A temporary storage space where information from long-term memory can be integrated into working memory.
episodic memory The collection of past personal experiences that occurred at a particular time and place.
epistemology The study of how knowledge is acquired.
equipotential Equally responsible for enabling learning to occur.
equity A state of affairs in which the cost–benefit ratios of two partners are roughly equal.
ergot A mind-altering fungus.
ethology The scientific study of animal behaviour in the natural habitat.
eugenics Selective breeding in humans to increase the prevalence of desired characteristics in the population.
evaluation apprehension Performance is affected by how people think they are being judged.
evolutionary psychology A psychological approach that explains mind and behaviour in terms of the adaptive value of abilities that are preserved over time by natural selection.
excitatory association A process that increases the likelihood of a response.
executive functions Mental operations that enable us to coordinate our thoughts and behaviours.
exemplar theory A theory of categorization that argues that we make category judgements by comparing a new instance with stored memories of other instances of the category.
existential approach A school of thought that regards personality as governed by an individual's ongoing choices and decisions in the context of the realities of life and death.
experience-dependent plasticity Much of the neural organization is not pre-specified and depends on input from the environment.
experience-expectant plasticity Much of the neural organization is largely pre-specified, waiting for input from the environment.
experiment A technique for establishing the causal relationship between variables.
experimental group The group of people who are exposed to an experimental condition under investigation.
explicit memory The act of consciously or intentionally retrieving past experiences.
exposure therapy Confronting an emotion-arousing stimulus directly and repeatedly, ultimately leading to a decrease in the emotional response.
expressed emotion (EE) Emotional overinvolvement (intrusiveness) and excessive criticism directed towards the former patient by their family.
extensivity The obligation individuals feel towards others beyond their immediate friends and family.
external validity A characteristic of an experiment in which the independent and dependent variables are operationally defined in a normal, typical or realistic way.
extinction The gradual elimination of a learned response that occurs when the CS is no longer followed by the US.
extrinsic motivation A motivation to take actions that are not themselves rewarding but lead to reward.
facial feedback hypothesis The hypothesis that emotional expressions can cause the emotional experiences they signify.
factor analysis A statistical technique that explains a large number of correlations in terms of a small number of underlying factors.
false belief A mental state of presumed truth that turns out to be incorrect.
false memories Recollection of events that never happened.
false recognition A feeling of familiarity about something that hasn't been encountered before.
family resemblance theory Members of a category have features that appear to be characteristic of category members but may not be possessed by every member.
fast mapping Children map a word onto an underlying concept after only a single exposure.
feature integration theory A theory that proposes that attention binds individual features together to comprise a composite stimulus.
feeling of knowing (FOK) The subjective awareness of information that cannot be retrieved from memory.
feelings Private conscious thoughts that accompany emotions.
feral children Children raised in isolation from society.
fetal alcohol syndrome A developmental disorder that stems from heavy alcohol use by the mother during pregnancy.
fetal stage The period that lasts from the ninth week until birth.
fight-or-flight response An emotional and physiological reaction to an emergency that increases readiness for action.
fixation A phenomenon in which a person's pleasure-seeking drives become psychologically stuck, or arrested, at a particular psychosexual stage.
fixed interval (FI) schedule Reinforcement will become available when a fixed time period has elapsed following the previous reinforcement. The first response after this interval will produce the reinforcer.
fixed ratio (FR) schedule Reinforcement will be delivered after a specific number of responses have been made.
flashbulb memories Detailed recollections of when and where we heard about shocking events.
fluid intelligence The biologically limited capacity for processing information (see crystallized intelligence).
foot-in-the-door technique A strategy that uses a person's desire for consistency to influence that person's behaviour.
formal operational stage The stage of development that begins around the age of 11 and lasts through adulthood.
fovea An area of the retina where vision is the clearest and there are no rods at all.
framing effects People give different answers to the same problem depending on how the problem is phrased (or framed).
fraternal twins (dizygotic twins) Twins who develop from two different eggs that were fertilized by two different sperm (see identical twins).
free association A therapeutic technique where the client reports every thought that enters the mind, without censorship or filtering.
free will The ability to choose or decide what to do.
frequency distribution A graphic representation of the measurements of a sample that are arranged by the number of times each measurement was observed.
frequency format hypothesis The proposal that our minds evolved to notice how frequently things occur, not how likely they are to occur.
frontal lobe A region of the cerebral cortex that has specialized areas for movement, abstract thinking, planning, memory and judgement.
frustration-aggression principle A principle stating that people aggress when their goals are thwarted.
fugue state An amnesia of one's previous life and identity.
full consciousness Consciousness in which you know and are able to report your mental state.
functional fixedness The tendency to perceive the functions of objects as fixed.
functionalism The study of the purpose mental processes serve in enabling people to adapt to their environment.
functional magnetic resonance imaging (fMRI) A technique that uses a powerful magnet to cause haemoglobin molecules to realign to measure blood flow in the brain.

gamma-aminobutyric acid (GABA) The primary inhibitory neurotransmitter in the brain.
gate-control theory A theory of pain perception based on the idea that signals arriving from pain receptors in the body can be stopped, or gated, by interneurons in the spinal cord via feedback from two directions.
gender The set of characteristics that distinguish between males and females.
gene The unit of hereditary transmission.
generalization An increase in responding to a stimulus because of its similarity to a CS that was paired with a US.
generalized anxiety disorder (GAD) A disorder characterized by chronic excessive worry accompanied by three or more of the following symptoms: restlessness, fatigue, concentration problems, irritability, muscle tension and sleep disturbance.
generative processes Those that lead to the formation of new structures.
genetic dysphasia A syndrome characterized by an inability to learn the grammatical structure of language despite having otherwise normal intelligence.
genetic methylation A mechanism that silences a gene and is believed to play a major role in long-term changes that shape our development.
genital stage The final psychosexual stage, a time for the coming together of the mature adult personality with a capacity to love, work and relate to others in a mutually satisfying and reciprocal manner.
germinal stage The two-week period that begins at conception.
Gestalt psychology A psychological approach that emphasizes that we often perceive the whole rather than the sum of the parts.
Gestalt therapy Therapy that has the goal of helping the client become aware of their thoughts, behaviours, experiences and feelings and to 'own' or take responsibility for them.
glia Cells that support the functionality of neurons by providing physical support, supplying nutrients and enhancing neuronal communication.
glutamate A major excitatory neurotransmitter involved in information transmission throughout the brain.
goodness of fit The extent to which the child's environment is compatible with their temperament.
grammar A set of rules that specify how the units of language can be combined to produce meaningful messages.
grapheme Unit of written language that corresponds to a phoneme.
grossly disorganized behaviour Behaviour that is inappropriate for the situation or ineffective in attaining goals, often with specific motor disturbances.
group A collection of two or more people who believe they have something in common.
group polarization Attitudes and decisions tend to become more extreme than those held and made by individuals.
group therapy A technique in which multiple participants (who often do not know one another at the outset) work on their individual problems in a group setting.
groupthink People set aside individual opinions and doubts in favour of achieving a group consensus.
habituation A general process in which repeated or prolonged exposure to a stimulus results in a gradual reduction in responding.
hair cells Specialized auditory receptor neurons embedded in the basilar membrane.
hallucination A false perceptual experience that has a compelling sense of being real despite the absence of external stimulation.
hallucinogens Drugs that alter sensation and perception and often cause visual and auditory hallucinations.
haptic perception The active exploration of the environment by touching and grasping objects with our hands.
hard problem of consciousness The difficulty of explaining how subjective experience could ever arise.
harm reduction approach A response to high-risk behaviours that focuses on reducing the harm such behaviours have on people's lives.
hedonic principle The notion that all people are motivated to experience pleasure and avoid pain.
helplessness theory The idea that individuals who are prone to depression automatically attribute negative experiences to causes that are internal (their own fault), stable (unlikely to change) and global (widespread).
heritability A measure of the variability of behavioural traits among individuals that can be accounted for by genetic factors.
heritability coefficient A statistic (commonly denoted as h^2) that describes the proportion of the difference between people's scores that can be explained by differences in their genetic makeup.
heuristic persuasion A change in attitudes or beliefs brought about by appeals to habit or emotion.
heuristics Fast and efficient strategies that may facilitate decision making but do not guarantee that a solution will be reached.
hindbrain An area of the brain that coordinates information coming into and out of the spinal cord.
hippocampus A structure critical for creating new memories and integrating them into a network of knowledge so that they can be stored indefinitely in other parts of the cerebral cortex.
homeostasis The tendency for a system to take action to keep itself in a particular state.
homunculus problem Difficulty of explaining the notion of an inner self experiencing consciousness that does not evoke an infinite regress.
human genome project Where scientists set out to identify all the human genes.
humanistic psychology An approach to understanding human nature that emphasizes the positive potential of human beings.
human sexual response cycle The stages of physiological arousal during sexual activity.
humours The humours are blood, black bile, yellow bile and phlegm. These four humours corresponded to the four primary qualities (hot, dry, cold and wet), the four elements (fire, air, earth and water) and four psychological temperaments (sanguine, bilious, melancholic and phlegmatic).
hypnosis An altered state of consciousness characterized by suggestibility and the feeling that one's actions are occurring involuntarily.
hypnotic analgesia The reduction of pain through hypnosis in people who are susceptible to hypnosis.
hypothalamus A subcortical structure that regulates body temperature, hunger, thirst and sexual behaviour.
hypothesis A specific and testable prediction that is usually derived from a theory.
hysteria A temporary loss of cognitive or motor functions, usually as a result of emotionally upsetting experiences.
iatrogenic illness A disorder or symptom that occurs as a result of a medical or psychotherapeutic treatment itself.
ICD-10 A classification system, published by the World Health Organization (WHO, 1992), used throughout much of Europe and other parts of the world. Rather than using the term 'psychological disorder', it refers to mental and behavioural disorders, which are defined as 'the existence of a clinically recognizable set of symptoms or behaviour associated in most cases with distress and interference with personal functions'.
iconic memory A fast-decaying store of visual information.
id The part of the mind containing the drives present at birth; it is the source of our bodily needs, wants, desires and impulses, particularly our sexual and aggressive drives.
identical twins (monozygotic twins) Twins who develop from the splitting of a single egg that was fertilized by a single sperm (see fraternal twins).

identifiable victim effect (IVE) The tendency to offer greater assistance to an individual rather than a group.
identification A defence mechanism that helps deal with feelings of threat and anxiety by enabling us unconsciously to take on the characteristics of another person who seems more powerful or better able to cope.
illusions Errors of perception, memory or judgement in which subjective experience differs from objective reality.
illusory conjunction A perceptual mistake where features from multiple objects are incorrectly combined.
immune system Biological defence system for combating potential disease from both internal and external invaders.
implicit learning Learning that takes place largely independent of awareness of the process and the products of information acquisition.
implicit memory The influence of past experiences on later behaviour and performance, even though people are not trying to recollect them and are not aware that they are remembering them.
imprinting A process where the hatchlings bond to their mother at first sight and then follow her about everywhere.
incentives External rewards that act to motivate behaviours.
independent variable The variable that is manipulated in an experiment.
indirect sublexical route One that does not involve the lexicon at all but maps the grapheme directly onto the pronunciation.
individual differences approach The assessment and evaluation of individual psychological abilities.
individualistic Where success and responsibility are focused on individual achievement.
induction The process of establishing general truths based on a limited set of observations.
infancy The period from birth up to around about the second year of life.
inference Speakers generate deeper conceptual understanding based on what has been said.
informational influence A person's behaviour is influenced by another person's behaviour because the latter provides information about what is good or true.
information bottleneck When the channel of information processing has a limited capacity.
informed consent An agreement to participate in a study made by a person who has been informed of all the risks that participation may entail.
in-group A human category of which a person is a member.
in-group bias The tendency to exhibit favouritism towards one's own group members and hence oneself.
inhibition The ability to suppress intrusive thoughts and behaviours.
inhibitory association A process that decreases the likelihood of a response.
insomnia Difficulty in falling asleep or staying asleep.
intelligence A hypothetical mental ability that enables people to direct their thinking, adapt to their circumstances, and learn from their experiences.
interference The drop in accuracy and response time performance when two tasks tap into the same system.
intergroup differentiation The process of drawing favourable comparisons with other groups.
intermittent reinforcement An operant conditioning relationship in which only some of the responses made are followed by reinforcement.
intermittent reinforcement effect Operant behaviours that are maintained under intermittent reinforcement schedules resist extinction better than those maintained under continuous reinforcement.
internalization Where extrinsic influences are incorporated into intrinsic motivations.
internal validity The characteristic of an experiment that allows one to draw accurate inferences about the causal relationship between an independent and dependent variable.
internal working model A set of expectations about how the primary carer will respond when the child feels insecure.
interneurons Neurons that connect sensory neurons, motor neurons or other interneurons.
interpersonal space Preferred distance maintained by individuals.
intrinsic motivation A motivation to take actions that are themselves rewarding.
introspection The subjective observation of one's own experience.
intuitive theories Rudimentary frameworks that are not explicitly taught and explain related aspects of the world.
invariant Every child goes through the same sequence in the same order at roughly the same time.
ironic processes of mental control Mental processes that can produce ironic errors because monitoring for errors can itself produce them.
James-Lange theory A theory about the relationship between emotional experience and physiological activity suggesting that stimuli trigger activity in the autonomic nervous system, which in turn produces an emotional experience in the brain.
joint attention The capacity to coordinate the social interaction with attention direction towards objects of mutual interest.
just noticeable difference (JND) The minimal change in a stimulus that can just barely be detected.
just world hypothesis The belief that people get what they deserve and deserve what they get.
kin selection The process by which evolution selects for genes that cause individuals to provide benefits to their relatives.
language A system for communicating with others using signals that convey meaning and are combined according to rules of grammar.
language acquisition device (LAD) A collection of processes that facilitate language learning.
latency stage The fourth psychosexual stage, in which the primary focus is on the further development of intellectual, creative, interpersonal and athletic skills.
latent content A dream's true underlying meaning.
latent learning A condition in which something is learned but it is not manifested as a behavioural change until sometime in the future.
law of effect The principle that behaviours that are followed by a 'satisfying state of affairs' tend to be repeated and those that produce an 'unpleasant state of affairs' are less likely to be repeated.
law of large numbers A statistical law stating that as sample size increases, the attributes of a sample will more closely reflect the attributes of the population from which the sample was drawn.
law of mass action Performance is determined by the quantity of nervous tissue removed and is independent of any particular area.
learning A relatively permanent change in the state of the learner due to experience.
lexicalization The process whereby the thoughts underlying the words are turned into sounds.
lexicon Our mental dictionary.
lies Deliberate attempts to generate a false belief to manipulate situations.
limbic system A group of forebrain structures, which include the hypothalamus, the amygdala and the hippocampus, which are involved in motivation, emotion, learning and memory.
limited competence An inability to understand what needs to be done to solve the task.
limited performance An inability to execute the necessary actions to solve the task.
linguistic determinism hypothesis Language shapes the nature of thought.
linguistic relativity hypothesis The proposal that language may influence the way we think and perceive.

load model Attentional model that explains early and late selection as a consequence of the task difficulty.

locus of control A person's tendency to perceive the control of rewards as internal to the self or external in the environment.

longitudinal research Experimental designs based on a representative sample of children who are then studied repeatedly over time.

long-term memory A place where information can be kept for hours, days, weeks or years.

long-term potentiation (LTP) Enhanced neural processing that results from the strengthening of synaptic connections.

loudness A sound's intensity.

Machiavellianism A personality trait of willingness to exploit and manipulate others.

magnetic resonance imaging (MRI) A technique that uses a powerful magnet to cause charged molecules in soft tissue to realign to produce measureable field distortions.

major depressive disorder A disorder characterized by a severely depressed mood that lasts two weeks or more and is accompanied by feelings of worthlessness and lack of pleasure, lethargy, and sleep and appetite disturbances.

manifest content A dream's apparent topic or superficial meaning.

manipulation A characteristic of experimentation in which the researcher artificially creates a pattern of variation in an independent variable in order to determine its causal powers. Manipulation usually results in the creation of an experimental group and a control group.

matched pairs An observational technique that involves matching each participant in the experimental group with a specific participant in the control group in order to eliminate the possibility that a third variable (and not the independent variable) caused changes in the dependent variable.

matched samples An observational technique that involves matching the average of the participants in the experimental and control groups in order to eliminate the possibility that a third variable (and not the independent variable) caused changes in the dependent variable.

materialism Philosophical position that mental states are a product of physical processes alone.

maturation Biologically constrained change.

mean The average value of the observation, calculated as the sum of all the observations divided by the number of observations.

means-ends analysis A process of searching for the means or steps to reduce the differences between the current situation and the desired goal.

measure A device that can detect the measurable events to which an operational definition refers.

median The value that is greater than or equal to the values of half the observations and less than or equal to half the values of the observations.

medical model The conceptualization of psychological abnormalities as diseases that, like biological diseases, have symptoms and causes and possible cures.

meditation The practice of intentional contemplation.

medulla An extension of the spinal cord into the skull that coordinates heart rate, circulation and respiration.

memory The ability to store and retrieve information over time.

memory misattribution Assigning a recollection or an idea to the wrong source.

memory storage The process of maintaining information in memory over time.

mental control The attempt to change conscious states of mind.

mental perspective taking Thinking about what goes on in other people's mind.

mental representations Patterns of neuronal activity that refer to aspects of the external world.

mere exposure effect The tendency for liking to increase with the frequency of exposure.

mesoderm Embryonic disk layer that goes on to form the skeletal muscles.

metabolism Biological processes that convert stored resources into energy.

metamemory The subjective awareness of one's own memory.

metaphysics A branch of philosophy that examines the nature of reality.

metarepresentation Thinking about thoughts.

method of loci A memory aid that associates information with mental images of locations.

milestone An important demarcating event on the path of development.

mind Our private inner experience of perceptions, thoughts, memories and feelings.

mind–body problem The issue of how the mind is related to the brain and body.

mindfulness meditation A technique that teaches an individual to be fully present in each moment, be aware of their thoughts, feelings and sensations, and detect symptoms before they become a problem.

minimal consciousness A low level of awareness that occurs when the mind inputs sensations and may output behaviour.

Minnesota Multiphasic Personality Inventory (MMPI) A well-researched, clinical questionnaire used to assess personality and psychological problems.

mirror neurons Cells that are active when performing an action oneself or when observing the same action performed by another.

mnemonic A device for reorganizing information into more meaningful patterns to remember.

modalities Sensory brain regions that process different components of the perceptual world.

mode The value of the most frequently observed observation.

modelling The process by which a person learns behaviour by observing and imitating others.

modularization The process of relatively encapsulated function.

monocular depth cues Aspects of a scene that yield information about depth when viewed with only one eye.

mood disorders Mental disorders that have mood disturbance as their predominant feature.

moods Generalized, diffuse states or dispositions that are less intense but last longer than emotional responses.

morality The rules that govern the right and wrong of how we should behave and treat others.

morphemes The smallest meaningful units of language, for example 'cats' contains two, cat + plural s.

morphological rules A set of rules that indicate how morphemes can be combined to form words.

motherese That high-pitched, musical voice that adults make when communicating with infants.

motion parallax A depth cue based on the movement of the head over time.

motivation The purpose for or cause of an action.

motor development The emergence of the ability to execute physical actions such as reaching, grasping, crawling and walking.

motor neurons Neurons that carry signals from the spinal cord to the muscles to produce movement.

multisensory integration The perceptual representation of events from more than one sensory modality.

myelination The formation of a fatty sheath around the axons of a brain cell.

myelin sheath An insulating layer of fatty material.

narcissism A trait that reflects a grandiose view of the self combined with a tendency to seek admiration from and exploit others.

narcolepsy A disorder in which sudden sleep attacks occur in the middle of waking activities.

nativism The philosophical view that certain kinds of knowledge are innate or inborn.

nativist theory The view that language development is best explained as an innate, biological capacity.

natural behaviours Instinctual responses that were not learned.

natural correlation A correlation observed between naturally occurring variables.

naturalistic observation A method of gathering scientific knowledge by unobtrusively observing people in their natural environments.

natural selection Charles Darwin's theory that the features of an organism that help it survive and reproduce are more likely than other features to be passed on to subsequent generations.

nature versus nurture The naive distinction about whether development is genetically determined or dependent on the environment.

need for achievement The motivation to solve worthwhile problems.

need to belong A universal and innate tendency for humans to form and maintain stable strong and positive relationship with others.

negative symptoms Emotional and social withdrawal, apathy, poverty of speech, and other indications of the absence or insufficiency of normal behaviour, motivation and emotion.

nervous system An interacting network of neurons that conveys electrochemical information throughout the body.

neural tube The cylindrical structure of the embryonic central nervous system.

neurogenesis The formation of neural cells.

neurons Cells in the nervous system that communicate with one another to perform information-processing tasks.

neurotransmitters Chemicals that transmit information across the synapse to a receiving neuron's dendrites.

newborns Newly born infants.

night terrors (or sleep terrors) Abrupt awakenings with panic and intense emotional arousal.

NMDA receptor A hippocampal receptor site that influences the flow of information from one neuron to another across the synapse by controlling the initiation of long-term potentiation.

nonshared environment Those environmental factors that are not experienced by all relevant members of a household (see shared environment).

nonverbal communication The sending and receiving of thoughts and feelings without using language.

noradrenaline A neurotransmitter that influences mood and arousal.

normal distribution A frequency distribution in which most measurements are concentrated around the mean and fall off towards the tails, and the two sides of the distribution are symmetrical.

normative influence One person's behaviour is influenced by another person's behaviour because the latter provides information about what is appropriate.

norm of reciprocity The unwritten rule that people should benefit those who have benefited them.

norms Customary standards for behaviour that are widely shared by members of a culture.

obedience The tendency to do what authorities tell us to do simply because they tell us to do it.

object permanence The idea that objects continue to exist even when they are not visible.

oblique factors Items that correlate with each other.

observational learning Learning takes place by watching the actions of others.

obsessive-compulsive disorder (OCD) A disorder characterized by recurrent obsessional thoughts or compulsive acts designed to fend off thoughts that interfere significantly with an individual's functioning.

occipital lobe A region of the cerebral cortex that processes visual information.

Oedipus conflict A developmental experience in which a child's conflicting feelings towards the opposite-sex parent are (usually) resolved by identifying with the same-sex parent.

olfactory bulb A brain structure located above the nasal cavity beneath the frontal lobes.

olfactory receptor neurons (ORNS) Receptor cells that initiate the sense of smell.

operant behaviour Behaviour that has some impact on the environment and changes because of that impact.

operant conditioning A type of learning in which the consequences of an organism's behaviour determine whether it will be repeated in the future.

operational definition A description of an abstract property in terms of a concrete condition that can be measured.

oral stage The first psychosexual stage, in which experience centres on the pleasures and frustrations associated with the mouth, sucking and being fed.

organizational encoding The act of categorizing information by noticing the relationships between a series of items.

orthogonal factors Items that are uncorrelated.

ostracism Active rejection by other group members.

outcome expectancies A person's assumptions about the likely consequences of a future behaviour.

out-group A human category of which a person is not a member.

overjustification effect Circumstances when external rewards can undermine the intrinsic satisfaction of performing a behaviour.

panic disorder A disorder characterized by recurrent attacks of severe anxiety (panic), which are not restricted to any particular situation or set of circumstances and are therefore unpredictable.

parasympathetic nervous system A set of nerves that help the body return to a normal resting state.

parental sensitivity Consistent attentiveness to the infant's emotional wellbeing.

parietal lobe A region of the cerebral cortex whose functions include processing information about touch.

passionate love An experience involving feelings of euphoria, intimacy and intense sexual attraction.

pathology A unique disorder.

pedagogical approach The scaffolding of learning by instruction.

pedagogy The transfer of knowledge primarily for the purpose of teaching.

perception The organization, identification and interpretation of a sensation in order to form a mental representation.

perceptual confirmation A phenomenon that occurs when observers perceive what they expect to perceive.

perceptual constancy A perceptual principle stating that even as aspects of sensory signals change, perception remains consistent.

peripheral nervous system (PNS) The part of the nervous system that connects the central nervous system to the body's organs and muscles.

persistence The intrusive recollection of events that we wish we could forget.

personal constructs Dimensions people use in making sense of their experiences.

personality An individual's characteristic style of behaving, thinking and feeling.

personality disorders Disorders characterized by deeply ingrained, inflexible patterns of thinking, feeling or relating to others, or controlling impulses that cause distress or impaired functioning.

person-centred therapy (also known as client-centred therapy) A method of therapy that assumes that all individuals have a tendency towards growth and that this growth can be facilitated by acceptance and genuine reactions from the therapist.

person–situation controversy The question of whether behaviour is caused more by personality or situational factors.

persuasion A person's attitudes or beliefs are influenced by a communication from another person.

phallic stage The third psychosexual stage, during which experience is dominated by the pleasure, conflict and frustration associated with the phallic-genital region as well as coping with powerful incestuous feelings of love, hate, jealousy and conflict.

phenomenology How things actually seem in the state of consciousness in terms of the quality of experience.
pheromones Biochemical odourants emitted by other members of their species that can affect an animal's behaviour or physiology.
philosophical empiricism The philosophical view that all knowledge is acquired through experience.
phobic disorders Disorders in which anxiety is evoked only, or predominantly, in certain well-defined situations that are not currently dangerous.
phoneme The smallest unit of sound, for example 'ba' or 'pa', that is recognizable as speech rather than as random noise.
phonological dyslexia People are unable to read pronounceable non-words.
phonological loop Briefly encodes mental representations of sounds and is made up of a short-term store and an articulatory rehearsal system.
phonological rules A set of rules that indicate how phonemes can be combined to produce speech sounds, for example '-ed' to signify the past tense of a verb.
phototherapy A therapy that involves repeated exposure to bright light.
phrenology A now defunct theory that specific mental abilities and characteristics, ranging from memory to the capacity for happiness, are localized in specific regions of the brain.
physiology The study of biological processes, especially in the human body.
pitch How high or low a sound is.
pituitary gland The 'master gland' of the body's hormone producing system, which releases hormones that direct the functions of many other glands in the body.
placebo An inert substance or procedure that has been applied with the expectation that a healing response will be produced.
placebo effect A clinically significant psychological or physiological response to a therapeutically inert substance or procedure.
place code The cochlea encodes different frequencies at different locations along the basilar membrane.
plasticity The capacity for the brain to be moulded by experience.
pleasure principle The psychic force that motivates the tendency to seek immediate gratification of any impulse.
pluralistic ignorance Where people fail to accurately evaluate others' behaviour.
pons A brain structure that relays information from the cerebellum to the rest of the brain.
population The complete collection of people, objects or events that can possibly be measured.
positron emission tomography (PET) A technique that uses radioactive markers to measure blood flow in the brain.
postconventional stage A stage of moral development at which the morality of an action is determined by a set of general principles that reflect core values.
posthypnotic amnesia The failure to retrieve memories following hypnotic suggestions to forget.
post-traumatic stress disorder (PTSD) An anxiety disorder that can appear some weeks or months after a person lives through an experience so threatening and uncontrollable that they are left with feelings of terror and helplessness.
power The tendency for a measure to produce different results when it is used to measure different things.
practical reasoning Working out what to do, or reasoning directed towards action.
preconventional stage A stage of moral development in which the morality of an action is primarily determined by its consequences for the actor.
predictive validity The tendency for an operational definition to be related to other operational definitions of the same property.
preference for novelty paradigm Following habituation, organisms prefer to attend to novel stimulation.
prejudice A negative evaluation of, and attitude towards, individuals based on negative group stereotypes.
prenatal stage Ends with birth, but it begins at conception.
preoperational stage Stage of development that begins at about 2 years and ends at about 6 years.
preparedness theory of phobias People are instinctively predisposed towards certain fears.
primary auditory cortex The outermost layer of the temporal lobe area where auditory information is processed.
primary sex characteristics Bodily structures that are directly involved in reproduction.
primary visual cortex The outermost layer of the occipital lobe area where visual information is processed.
priming An enhanced ability to think of a stimulus, such as a word or object, as a result of a recent exposure to the stimulus.
proactive interference Situations in which earlier learning impairs memory for information acquired later.
problem of other minds The fundamental difficulty we have in perceiving the consciousness of others.
procedural memory The gradual acquisition of skills as a result of practice, or 'knowing how' to do things.
prodigy A person of normal intelligence who has an extraordinary ability.
projection A defence mechanism that involves attributing one's own threatening feelings, motives or impulses to another person or group.
projective techniques A standard series of ambiguous stimuli designed to elicit unique responses that reveal inner aspects of an individual's personality.
prosocial behaviours Voluntary acts that are intended to help others, such as giving, sharing, cooperating and protecting, which may have some potential benefit to the prosocial individual.
prosody The rhythm of speech.
prospective memory Remembering to do things in the future.
prospect theory Proposes that people choose to take on risk when evaluating potential losses and avoid risks when evaluating potential gains.
protodeclarative pointing To direct another's attention to an object or event of interest.
protoimperative pointing To direct another's attention to obtain a particular goal.
prototype theory Our psychological categorization is organized around the properties of the most typical member of the category.
psychiatrists Medical doctors concerned with the treatment of mental disorders.
psychoactive drug A chemical that influences consciousness or behaviour by altering the brain's chemical message system.
psychoanalysis A therapeutic approach that focuses on bringing unconscious material into conscious awareness to better understand psychological disorders.
psychoanalytic theory Sigmund Freud's approach to understanding human behaviour that emphasizes the importance of unconscious mental processes in shaping feelings, thoughts and behaviours.
psychodynamic approach An approach that regards personality as formed by needs, strivings and desires, largely operating outside awareness – motives that can also produce emotional disorders.
psychodynamic psychotherapies Therapies that explore childhood events and encourage individuals to use this understanding to develop insight into their psychological problems.
psychological essentialism The belief that things in nature and in particular living things are what they are because of some inner property or essence.
psychology The scientific study of mind and behaviour.
psychometrics The science of measuring mental capacities and processes.

psychopharmacology The study of drug effects on psychological states and symptoms.
psychophysics Methods that measure the strength of a stimulus and the observer's sensitivity to that stimulus.
psychosexual stages Distinct early life stages through which personality is formed as children experience sexual pleasures from specific body areas and carers redirect or interfere with those pleasures.
psychosurgery The surgical destruction of specific brain areas.
psychotherapy An interaction between a therapist and someone suffering from a psychological problem, with the goal of providing support or relief from the problem.
puberty Bodily changes associated with sexual maturity.
public goods dilemma A situation where individuals are better off if they do not contribute but the group as a whole is worse off.
punisher Any stimulus or event that functions to decrease the likelihood of the behaviour that led to it.
qualia Subjective experiences we have as part of our mental life.
qualitative change The type or quality of change.
qualitative research Interested in gaining an in-depth understanding of the human experience and behaviour.
quantitative change The amount or quantity of change.
quantitative research Uses systematic, scientific investigation in order to measure and quantify phenomena.
randomization A procedure using random assignment to ensure that a participant's inclusion in the experimental or control group is not determined by a third variable.
random sampling A technique for choosing participants that ensures that every member of a population has an equal chance of being included in the sample.
range The numerical difference between the smallest and largest measurements in a frequency distribution.
ratio IQ A statistic obtained by dividing a person's mental age by the person's physical age and then multiplying the quotient by 100 (see deviation IQ).
rational choice theory The classical view that we make decisions by determining how likely something is to happen, judging the value of the outcome, and then multiplying the two.
rational coping A strategy that involves facing the stressor and working to overcome it.
rationalization A defence mechanism that involves supplying a reasonable-sounding explanation for unacceptable feelings and behaviour to conceal (mostly from oneself) one's underlying motives or feelings.
reaction formation A defence mechanism that involves unconsciously replacing threatening inner wishes and fantasies with an exaggerated version of their opposite.
reaction time The amount of time taken to respond to a specific stimulus.
reality principle The regulating mechanism that enables the individual to delay gratifying immediate needs and function effectively in the real world.
reappraisal A strategy that involves changing one's emotional experience by changing the meaning of the emotion-eliciting stimulus.
reasoning A mental activity that consists of organizing information or beliefs into a series of steps to reach conclusions.
rebound effect of thought suppression The tendency of a thought to return to consciousness with greater frequency following suppression.
recall The capacity to spontaneously retrieve information from memory.
receptive field The region of the sensory surface that, when stimulated, causes a change in the firing rate of that neuron.
receptors Parts of the cell membrane that receive neurotransmitters and initiate a new electric signal.
reciprocal altruism Behaviour that benefits another with the expectation that those benefits will be returned in the future.
recognition The capacity to correctly match information presented with the contents of memory.
recurrent depressive disorder A moderately depressed mood that persists for at least two years and is punctuated by periods of major depression.
referred pain Feeling of pain when sensory information from internal and external areas converge on the same nerve cells in the spinal cord.
reflexes Specific patterns of motor response that are triggered by specific patterns of sensory stimulation.
refractory period The time following an action potential during which a new action potential cannot be initiated.
reframing A strategy that involves finding a new or creative way to think about a stressor that reduces its threat.
regression A defence mechanism in which the ego deals with internal conflict and perceived threat by reverting to an immature behaviour or earlier stage of development.
rehearsal The process of keeping information in short-term memory by mentally repeating it.
reinforcement The consequences of a behaviour determine whether it will be more or less likely to occur again.
reinforcer Any stimulus or event that functions to increase the likelihood of the behaviour that led to it.
reliability The tendency for a measure to produce the same result whenever it is used to measure the same thing.
REM (rapid eye movement) sleep A stage of sleep characterized by rapid eye movements and a high level of brain activity. Sometimes known as paradoxical sleep.
repeated measure Several data points are collected from the same individual.
representativeness heuristic A mental shortcut that involves making a probability judgement by comparing an object or event to a prototype of the object or event.
repression A mental process that removes unacceptable thoughts and memories from consciousness and keeps them in the unconscious.
repressive coping A response to stress characterized by avoiding situations or thoughts that are reminders of a stressor and maintaining an artificially positive viewpoint.
resistance A reluctance to cooperate with treatment for fear of confronting unpleasant unconscious material.
response An action or physiological change elicited by a stimulus.
response selection model Selective attention model that proposes that selection occurs late in the stream of processing before a response has been made.
resting potential The difference in electric charge between the inside and outside of a neuron's cell membrane.
reticular formation A brain structure that regulates sleep, wakefulness and levels of arousal.
retina Light-sensitive tissue lining the back of the eyeball.
retrieval The process of bringing to mind information that has been previously encoded and stored.
retrieval cue External information that is associated with stored information and helps bring it to mind.
retroactive interference Situations in which later learning impairs memory for information acquired earlier.
retrograde amnesia The inability to retrieve information that was acquired before a particular date, usually the date of an injury or operation.
retrospective memory Information learned in the past.
rods Photoreceptors that become active only under low light conditions for night vision.
Rorschach inkblot test A projective personality test in which individual interpretations of the meaning of a set of unstructured inkblots are analysed to identify a respondent's inner feelings and interpret their personality structure.
routine expressions Unambiguous conventions that facilitate language.

sample The partial collection of people, objects or events that are measured in a study.
savant A person of low intelligence who has an extraordinary ability.
schemas Mental models of the world that contain knowledge that helps us to encode new information into a meaningful context.
schizophrenia A disorder characterized by the profound disruption of basic psychological processes, a distorted perception of reality, altered or blunted emotion, and disturbances in thought, motivation and behaviour.
scientific method A set of rules and techniques that allow researchers to avoid the illusions, mistakes and erroneous conclusions that simple observation can produce.
seasonal affective disorder (SAD) Depression that involves recurrent depressive episodes in a seasonal pattern.
secondary sex characteristics Bodily structures that change dramatically with sexual maturity but are not directly involved in reproduction.
second-order conditioning Conditioning where the US is a stimulus that acquired its ability to produce learning from an earlier procedure in which it was used as a CS.
selective attention The process whereby we focus mental processing on a limited range of events.
self-actualizing tendency The human motive towards realizing our inner potential.
self-concept Thoughts we have about our bodies, our personality, our relationships and our beliefs.
self-consciousness A distinct level of consciousness in which the person's attention is drawn to the self as an object.
self-control The general capacity to regulate thoughts and behaviours in the face of conflict.
self-deception A capacity to convince ourselves that a falsehood is true.
self-determination theory Emphasizes the need to understand human motivation in terms of competence, autonomy and relatedness.
self-esteem The sense of self-worth.
self-fulfilling prophecy A phenomenon whereby observers bring about what they expect to perceive.
self-report A series of answers to a questionnaire that asks people to indicate the extent to which sets of statements or adjectives accurately describe their own behaviour or mental state.
self-selection The problem that occurs when a participant's inclusion in the experimental or control group is determined by the participant.
self-serving bias People's tendency to take credit for their successes but downplay responsibility for their failures.
self-verification The tendency to seek evidence to confirm the self-concept.
semantic memory A network of associated facts and concepts that make up our general knowledge of the world.
semantic priming The meaning of a word influences the processing of other words that are conceptually related.
semantics Meaning of a word.
sensation Simple awareness due to the stimulation of a sense organ.
sensitive periods of development Relatively specific times when appropriate environmental input is expected.
sensorimotor stage A stage of development that begins at birth and lasts through infancy.
sensory adaptation Sensitivity to prolonged stimulation tends to decline over time as an organism adapts to current conditions.
sensory memory A place where sensory information is kept for a few seconds or less.
sensory neurons Neurons that receive information from the external world and convey this information to the brain via the spinal cord.
sensory perception The way that we interpret and process signals received via our senses.
serial position effect The enhanced memory for events presented at the beginning and end of a learning episode.
serotonin A neurotransmitter involved in the regulation of sleep and wakefulness, eating and aggressive behaviour.
shaping Learning that results from the reinforcement of successive approximations to a final desired behaviour.
shared environment Those environmental factors that are experienced by all relevant members of a household (see nonshared environment).
short-term memory A place where nonsensory information is kept for more than a few seconds but less than a minute.
signal detection theory An observation that the response to a stimulus depends on a person's sensitivity to the stimulus in the presence of noise and on a person's response criterion.
sleep apnea A disorder in which the person stops breathing for brief periods while asleep.
sleep paralysis The experience of waking up unable to move.
social cognition The processes by which people come to understand others.
social cognitive approach Views personality in terms of how the person thinks about the situations encountered in daily life and behaves in response to them.
social dominance orientation A preference for hierarchical relations between groups, with one's own group being the most dominant.
social exchange The hypothesis that people remain in relationships only as long as they perceive a favourable ratio of costs to benefits.
social facilitation Improved individual performance in the company of others.
social influence The control of one person's behaviour by another.
social inhibition Where the presence of others inhibits or impairs performance.
social loafing People expend less effort when working in a group than when working alone.
social phobia An irrational fear of scrutiny by other people leading to avoidance of social situations.
social psychology A subfield of psychology that studies the causes and consequences of interpersonal behaviour.
social referencing Looking at carers to gauge their reactions in unfamiliar or threatening circumstances.
social smiling Smiles directed towards people.
sociodramatic play Games involving fantasy role-playing.
somatic nervous system A set of nerves that conveys information into and out of the central nervous system.
somatosensory cortex The outermost layer of the parietal lobe area containing a representation of the body map.
somnambulism (sleepwalking) Occurs when the person arises and walks around while asleep.
source memory Recall of when, where and how information was acquired.
source monitoring Recall of when, where and how information was acquired.
spatial memory Representation that encodes where something is.
spatial representation The capacity to encode, process and store information about the shape and layout of the physical environment.
specific phobia An irrational fear restricted to highly specific situations.
speech monitoring and repair Speakers interact to understand what others are saying by seeking clarification.
spinal reflexes Simple pathways in the nervous system that rapidly generate muscle contractions.
spontaneous recovery The tendency of a learned behaviour to recover from extinction after a rest period.
spotlight effect People's overestimation of the amount of attention others are paying to them.
stage theories Theories that advocate development as a fundamental reorganization of the underlying mechanisms.
standard deviation An estimate of the average difference between each observation and the mean in the population distribution.

state-dependent retrieval The tendency for information to be better recalled when the person is in the same state during encoding and retrieval.
statistically significant The observed effect is not due to chance.
stereopsis The perception of depth by combining the images from each eye.
stereotyping The process by which people draw inferences about others based on their knowledge of the categories to which others belong.
stimulus Sensory input from the environment.
storage The process of maintaining information in memory over time.
stranger anxiety A fearful response associated with crying and attempts to cling or move closer to the carer.
strange situation A behavioural test used to determine a child's attachment style.
stressors Specific events or chronic pressures that place demands on a person or threaten the person's wellbeing.
structural encoding How the pattern is represented.
structuralism The analysis of the basic elements that constitute the mind.
structured interview A consistent set of questions about a topic under consideration.
subcortical structures Areas of the forebrain housed under the cerebral cortex near the very centre of the brain.
subjective wellbeing (SWB) An individual's evaluation of their own lives in terms of how satisfied they are and how they feel about their life.
sublimation A defence mechanism that involves channelling unacceptable sexual or aggressive drives into socially acceptable and culturally enhancing activities.
subliminal perception A thought or behaviour that is influenced by stimuli that a person cannot consciously report perceiving.
suggestibility The tendency to incorporate misleading information from external sources into personal recollections.
sunk-cost fallacy A framing effect in which people make decisions about a current situation based on what they have previously invested in the situation.
superego The mental system that reflects the internalization of cultural rules, mainly learned as parents exercise their authority.
superordinate goals Goals that depend on the collaborative effort of two or more groups.
surface dyslexia People are unable to read irregular words.
syllogistic reasoning Determining whether a conclusion follows from two statements that are assumed to be true.
sympathetic nervous system A set of nerves that prepares the body for action in threatening situations.
symptom-oriented approach Individuals are primarily treated on the basis of behaviours and thoughts they find problematic and disturbing.
synaesthesia The perceptual experience of one sense that is evoked by another sense.
synapse The junction or region between the axon of one neuron and the dendrites or cell body of another.
synaptic pruning The process whereby synaptic connections die off.
synaptogenesis The increase in the number of synaptic junctions where cells communicate through the activity of neurotransmitters.
syntactical rules A set of rules that indicate how words can be combined to form phrases and sentences.
System 1 Operates automatically and quickly, with little or no effort and no sense of voluntary control; **System 2** Allocates attention to more taxing and mental activities and is often associated with a subjective experience of making choices.
systematic desensitization A procedure in which a client relaxes all the muscles of their body while imagining being in increasingly frightening situations.
systematic persuasion A change in attitudes or beliefs brought about by appeals to reason.
systemizing Analysing tasks in term of systems and patterns.
tacit knowledge The information that people have about specific, everyday life situations.
taste buds The organ of taste transduction.
tectum A part of the midbrain that orients an organism in the environment.
tegmentum A part of the midbrain that is involved in movement and arousal.
telegraphic speech Speech that is devoid of function morphemes and consists mostly of content words.
temperament A characteristic pattern of emotional reactivity.
template A mental representation that can be directly compared to a viewed shape in the retinal image.
temporal code The cochlea registers low frequencies via the firing rate of action potentials entering the auditory nerve.
temporal lobe A region of the cerebral cortex responsible for hearing and language.
teratogens Agents that damage the process of development.
terminal buttons Knoblike structures that branch out from an axon.
thalamus A subcortical structure that relays and filters information from the senses and transmits the information to the cerebral cortex.
theoretical reasoning Reasoning directed towards arriving at a belief.
theory A hypothetical account of how and why a phenomenon occurs, usually in the form of a statement about the causal relationship between two or more properties.
theory of mind The understanding that human behaviour is guided by beliefs that may or may not be true.
thermoregulation Biological processes that maintain optimal body heat during different states of wakefulness.
thin slicing Our capacity to accurately interpret social information from brief observations of behaviour.
third-variable correlation Two variables are correlated only because each is causally related to a third variable.
third-variable problem A causal relationship between two variables cannot be inferred from the correlation between them because of the ever-present possibility of third variable correlation.
thought suppression The conscious avoidance of a thought.
timbre A listener's experience of sound quality or resonance.
tip-of-the-tongue experience The temporary inability to retrieve information that is stored in memory, accompanied by the feeling that you are on the verge of recovering the information.
token economy Giving clients 'tokens' for desired behaviours, which they can later trade for rewards.
topographic visual organization Adjacent neurons process adjacent portions of the visual field.
trait A relatively stable disposition to behave in a particular and consistent way.
transcranial magnetic stimulation (TMS) A treatment that involves placing a powerful pulsed magnet over a person's scalp, which alters neuronal activity in the brain.
transduction What takes place when many sensors in the body convert physical signals from the environment into neural signals sent to the central nervous system.
transfer-appropriate processing The idea that memory is likely to transfer from one situation to another when we process information in a way that is appropriate to the retrieval cues that will be available later.
transference When the analyst begins to assume a major significance in the client's life and the client reacts to the analyst based on unconscious childhood fantasies.
transience Forgetting what occurs with the passage of time.
trepanning Drilling a hole in the skull.
triadic relationship Where attention is directed between two individuals and a third potential source.

trichromatic colour representation The pattern of responding across the three types of cones that provides a unique code for each colour.
trypophobia The fear of holes.
two-factor theory A theory about the relationship between emotional experience and physiological activity suggesting that emotions are inferences about the causes of undifferentiated physiological arousal.
two-factor theory of intelligence Spearman's theory suggesting that every task requires a combination of a general ability (g) and skills that are specific to the task (s) and shared with no other.
unconditional positive regard An attitude of nonjudgmental acceptance towards another person.
unconditioned response (UR) A reflexive reaction that is reliably elicited by an unconditioned stimulus.
unconditioned stimulus (US) Something that reliably produces a naturally occurring reaction in an organism.
unconscious The part of the mind that operates outside conscious awareness but influences conscious thoughts, feelings and actions.
unconscious motivation A motivation of which one is not aware.
unilateral visual neglect A condition where patients fail to notice or attend to stimuli that appear on the side of space opposite the site of a hemispheric lesion.
universal Every child in every culture goes through the same stages.
universality hypothesis The hypothesis that emotional expressions have the same meaning for everyone.
vagus nerve stimulation (VNS) A relatively new treatment that involves electrically stimulating the vagus nerve, which induces changes in blood flow to the brain.
validity The characteristic of an observation that allows one to draw accurate inferences from it.
variable A property whose value can vary or change.
variable interval (V1) schedule Reinforcement will become available when a time period has elapsed following the previous reinforcement, but unlike the FI schedule, the length of the waiting period varies from one reinforcer to the next.
variable ratio (VR) schedule Reinforcement will be delivered after a specified average number of responses have been made.
variance The average deviation of each observation from the mean.
vegetative state A state of wakefulness without awareness and overt communication.
verifiable Something that can be checked by objective measures.
vestibular system The three fluid-filled semicircular canals and adjacent organs located next to the cochlea in each inner ear.
vicarious punishment The tendency not to repeat behaviours that we observe others being punished for performing.
violation of expectancy (VOE) paradigm Where the anticipated outcome is deliberately contravened.
visual acuity The ability to see fine detail.
visual cliff A platform with a shallow drop on one side and a steep cliff on the other.
visual contrast Areas of greatest brightness relative to darkness.
visual form agnosia The inability to recognize objects by sight.
visual imagery encoding The process of storing new information by converting it into mental pictures.
visual orienting A behavioural response to move the eyes towards a target.
visual preference paradigm Technique that uses difference in duration of looking to infer pattern discrimination.
visual scanning The ability to selectively move one's eyes around the environment.
visuospatial sketchpad Briefly stores visual and spatial information.
Weber's law The just noticeable difference of a stimulus is a constant proportion despite variations in intensity.
wisdom An expert knowledge system concerning the fundamental pragmatics of life.
working memory Active maintenance and manipulation of information in short-term storage.
zygote A single cell that contains chromosomes from both a sperm and an egg.

References

AAP (American Academy of Pediatrics) (2011) Media use by children younger than 2 years. *Pediatrics*, 128, 1040–5.

Abbott, C. C., Gallegos, P., Rediske, N. et al. (2014) A review of longitudinal electroconvulsive therapy neuroimaging investigations. *Journal of Geriatric Psychiatry and Neurology*, 27, 33–46.

Abel, T., Alberini, C., Ghirardi, M. et al. (1995) Steps toward a molecular definition of memory consolidation. In D. L. Schacter (ed.) *Memory Distortion: How Minds, Brains and Societies Reconstruct the Past* (pp. 298–328). Cambridge, MA: Harvard University Press.

Abrams, D., Viki, G. T., Masser, B. and Bohner, G. (2003) Perceptions of stranger and acquaintance rape: The role of benevolent and hostile sexism in victim blame and rape proclivity. *Journal of Personality and Social Psychology*, 84, 111–25.

Abrams, M. and Reber, A. S. (1988) Implicit learning: Robustness in the face of psychiatric disorders. *Journal of Psycholinguistic Research*, 17, 425–39.

Abrams, R. (1997) *Electroconvulsive Therapy* (3rd edn). New York: OUP.

Abramson, L. Y., Alloy, L. B., Hankin, B. L. et al. (2002) Cognitive vulnerability-stress models of depression in a self-regulatory and psychobiological context. In I. H. Gotlib and C. L. Hammen (eds) *Handbook of Depression* (pp. 268–94). New York: Guilford Press.

Abramson, L. Y., Seligman, M. E. and Teasdale, J. D. (1978) Learned helplessness in humans: Critique and reformulation. *Journal of Abnormal Psychology*, 87, 49–74.

Abromov, I. and Gordon, J. (1994) Color appearance: On seeing red – or yellow, or green, or blue. *Annual Review of Psychology*, 45, 451–85.

Acevedo-Garcia, D., McArdle, N., Osypuk, T. L. et al. (2007) *Children Left Behind: How Metropolitan Areas are Failing America's Children.* Boston: Harvard School of Public Health.

Achter, J. A., Lubinski, D. and Benbow, C. P. (1996) Multipotentiality among the intellectually gifted: 'It was never there and already it's vanishing'. *Journal of Counseling Psychology*, 43, 65–76.

Acierno, R. E., Hersen, M. and van Hasselt, V. B. (1993) Interventions for panic disorder: A critical review of the literature. *Clinical Psychology Review*, 18, 561–78.

Ackerman, J. M., Nocera, C. and Bargh, J. (2010) Incidental haptic sensations influence social judgments and decisions. *Science*, 328(5986), 1712–15.

Ackerman, J. M., Becker, D. V., Mortensen, C. R. et al. (2009) A pox on the mind: Disjunction of attention and memory in processing physical disfigurement. *Journal of Experimental Social Psychology*, 45, 478– 85.

Ackerman, P. L., Beier, M. E. and Boyle, M. O. (2005) Working memory and intelligence: The same or different constructs? *Psychological Bulletin*, 131, 30–60.

Ackroff, K., Luxas, F. and Sclafani, A. (2005) Flavor preference conditioning as a function of fat source. *Physiology and Behavior*, 85, 448–60.

Acocella, J. (1999) *Creating Hysteria: Women and Multiple Personality Disorder.* San Francisco: Jossey-Bass.

Acton, G. S. and Schroeder, D. H. (2001) Sensory discrimination as related to general intelligence. *Intelligence*, 29, 263–71.

Adami, C. and Hintze, A. (2013) Evolutionary instability of zero determinant strategies demonstrates that winning is not everything. *Nature Communications*, 4, 2193.

Adams, H. E., Wright, L. W. Jr and Lohr, B. A. (1996) Is homophobia associated with homosexual arousal? *Journal of Abnormal Psychology*, 105, 440–5.

Addis, D. R., Wong, A. T. and Schacter, D. L. (2007) Remembering the past and imagining the future: Common and distinct neural substrates during event construction and elaboration. *Neuropsychologia*, 45, 1363–77.

Adelmann, P. K. and Zajonc, R. B. (1989) Facial efference and the experience of emotion. *Annual Review of Psychology*, 40, 249–80.

Adler, A. (1927) *Understanding Human Nature.* Greenwich, CT: Fawcett.

Adolph, K. E., Kretch, K. S. and and LoBue, V. (2014) Fear of heights in infants? *Current Directions in Psychological Science,* 23, 60–6.

Adolphs, R., Cahil, L., Schul, R. and Babinsky, R. (1997) Impaired declarative memory for emotional material following bilateral amygdala damage in humans. *Learning and Memory*, 4, 291–300.

Adolphs, R., Russell, J. A. and Tranel, D. (1999) A role for the human amygdala in recognizing emotional arousal from unpleasant stimuli. *Psychological Science*, 10, 167–71.

Adolphs, R., Tranel, D., Damasio, H. and Damasio, A. R. (1995) Fear and the human amygdala. *Journal of Neuroscience* 15, 5879–91.

Adorno, T. W., Frenkel-Brunswik, E., Levinson, D. J. and Sanford, R. N. (1950) *The Authoritarian Personality.* New York: Harper & Row.

Aggleton, J. (ed.) (1992) *The Amygdala: Neurobiological Aspects of Emotion, Memory and Mental Dysfunction.* New York: Wiley-Liss.

Aharon, I., Etcoff, N., Ariely, D. et al. (2001) Beautiful faces have variable reward value: fMRI and behavioral evidence. *Neuron*, 32, 537–51.

Ainsworth, M. D. (1967) *Infancy in Uganda: Infant Care and the Growth of Love.* Baltimore: Johns Hopkins University Press.

Ainsworth, M. D., Blehar, M. C., Waters, E. and Wall, S. (1978) *Patterns of Attachment: Assess in the Strange Situation and at Home.* Hillsdale, NJ: Erlbaum.

Ajzen, I. (1991) The theory of planned behaviour. *Organizational Behavior and Human Decision Processes*, 50, 179–211.

Ajzen, I. (2002) Perceived behavioral control, self-efficacy, locus of control, and the theory of planned behavior. *Journal of Applied Social Psychology*, 32, 665–83.

Akechi, H., Senju, A., Uibo, H. et al. (2013) Attention to eye contact in the West and East: Autonomic responses and evaluative ratings. *PLoS ONE*, 8(3), e59312.

Albarracin, D. and Kumkale, G. T. (2003) Affect as information in persuasion: A model of affect identification and discounting. *Journal of Personality & Social Psychology*, 84, 453–69.

Albarracin, D., Johnson, B. T., Fishbein, M. and Muellerieile, P. A. (2001) Theories of reasoned action and planned behavior as models of condom use: Meta-analysis. *Psychological Bulletin*, 127, 142–61.

Albee, E. (1962) *Who's Afraid of Virginia Woolf?* New York: Atheneum.

Albert, M. L. (1973) A simple test of visual neglect. *Neurology*, 23, 658–64.

Alcock, J. and Otis, L. P. (1980) Critical thinking and belief in the paranormal. *Pychological Reports*, 46, 479–82.

Alicke, M. D., Klotz, M. L., Breitenbecher, D. L. et al. (1995) Personal contact, individuation, and the better-than-average effect. *Journal of Personality and Social Psychology*, 68, 804–24.

Alloy, L. B. and Abramson, L. Y. (1988) Depressive realism: Four theoretical perspectives. In L. B. Alloy (ed.) *Cognitive Processes in Depression* (pp. 223–65). New York: Guilford Press.

Alloy, L. B., Jacobson, N. H. and Acocella, J. (1999) *Casebook in Abnormal Psychology* (4th edn). New York: McGraw-Hill.

Allport, F. H. (1920) The influence of the group upon association and thought. *Journal of Experimental Psychology*, 3, 159–82.

Allport, G. W. (1937) *Personality: A Psychological Interpretation.* New York: Holt.

Allport, G. W. (1954) *The Nature of Prejudice.* Cambridge, MA: Addison-Wesley.

Allport, G. W. and Odbert, H. S. (1936) Trait-names: A psycholexical study. *Psychological Monographs*, 47, 592.

Alt, K. W., Jeunesse, C., Buitrago-Téllez, C. H. et al. (1997) Evidence for stone age cranial surgery. *Nature*, 387, 360.

Altemeyer, B. (1981) *Right-wing Authoritarianism.* Winnipeg: University of Manitoba Press.

Altemeyer, B. (1998) The other 'authoritarian personality'. In M. Zanna (ed.) *Advances in Experimental Social Psychology* (vol. 30, pp. 47–92). San Diego, CA: Academic Press.

Alvardo, C. S. (2000) Out-of-body experiences. In E. Cardena, S. J. Lynn and S. Krippner (eds) *The Varieties of Anomalous Experience* (pp. 183–218). Washington, DC: APA.

Alvarez, L. W. (1965) A pseudo experience in parapsychology. *Science*, 148, 1541.

Ambady, N. and Rosenthal, R. (1992) Thin slices of expressive behavior as predictors of interpersonal consequences: A meta-analysis. *Psychological Bulletin*, 111, 256–74.

Ambady, N. and Rosenthal, R. (1993) Half a minute: Predicting teacher evaluations from thin slices of behavior and physical attractiveness. *Journal of Personality and Social Psychology*, 64, 431–41.

Ambady, N. and Weisbuch, M. (2010) Nonverbal behavior. In D. T. Gilbert, S. T. Fiske and G. Lindzey (eds) *Handbook of Social Psychology* (5th edn, pp. 464–97). New York: McGraw-Hill.

Ambady, N., Bernieri, F. J. and Richeson, J. A. (2000) Toward a histology of social behavior: Judgmental accuracy from thin slices of the behavioral stream. In M. Zanna (ed.) *Advances in Experimental Social Psychology* (vol. 32, pp. 201–71). San Diego, CA: Academic Press.

Andersen, S. M. and Berk, J. S. (1998) Transference in everyday experience: Implications of experimental research for relevant clinical phenomena. *Review of General Psychology*, 2, 81–120.

Anderson, C. A. (1989) Temperature and aggression: Ubiquitous effects of heat on occurrence of human violence. *Psychological Bulletin*, 106, 74–96.

Anderson, C. A. and Bushman, B. J. (2001) Effects of violent video games on aggressive behavior, aggressive cognition, aggressive affect, physiological arousal, and prosocial behavior: A meta-analytic review of the scientific literature. *Psychological Science*, 12, 353–9.

Anderson, C. A. and Bushman, B. J. (2002) Human aggression. *Annual Review of Psychology*, 53, 27–51.

Anderson, C. A., Bushman, B. J. and Groom, R. W. (1997) Hot years and serious and deadly assault: Empirical tests of the heat hypothesis. *Journal of Personality and Social Psychology*, 73, 1213–23.

Anderson, C. A., Lepper, M. R. and Ross, L. (1980) Perseverance of social theories: The role of explanation in the persistence of discredited information. *Journal of Personality and Social Psychology*, 39, 1037–49.

Anderson, C. A., Berkowitz, L., Donnerstein, E. et al. (2003) The influence of media violence on youth. *Psychological Science in the Public Interest*, 4, 81–110.

Anderson, J. R. and Fincham, J. M. (1994) Acquisition of procedural skills from examples. *Journal of Experimental Psychology: Learning, Memory, and Cognition*, 20, 1322–40.

Anderson, J. R. and Schooler, L. J. (1991) Reflections of the environment in memory. *Psychological Science*, 2, 396–408.

Anderson, J. R. and Schooler, L. J. (2000) The adaptive nature of memory. In E. Tulving and F. I. Craik (eds) *The Oxford Handbook of Memory* (pp. 557–70). Oxford: OUP.

Anderson, L. R. and Blanchard, P. N. (1982) Sex differences in task and social-emotional behavior. *Basic and Applied Social Psychology*, 3, 109–39.

Anderson, M. C., Ochsner, K. N., Kuhl, B. et al. (2004) Neural systems underlying the suppression of unwanted memories. *Science*, 303, 232–5.

Anderson, R. C., Pichert, J. W., Goetz, E. T. et al. (1976) Instantiation of general terms. *Journal of Verbal Learning and Verbal Behavior*, 15, 667–79.

Andrewes, D. (2001) *Neuropsychology: From Theory to Practice.* Hove: Psychology Press.

Angermeyer, M. C. and Matschinger, H. (1996a) Lay beliefs about the causes of mental disorders: A new methodological approach. *Social Psychiatry & Psychiatric Epidemiology*, 21, 309–15.

Angermeyer, M. C. and Matschinger, H. (1996b) The effect of violent attacks by schizophrenic persons on the attitude of the public towards the mentally ill. *Social Science and Medicine*, 43, 1721–8.

Ansfield, M., Wegner, D. M. and Bowser, R. (1996) Ironic effects of sleep urgency. *Behavior Research and Therapy*, 34, 523–31.

Antonovsky, A. (1979) *Health, Stress and Coping.* San Francisco: Jossey-Bass.

Antony, M. M. and Swinson, R. P. (2000) *Phobic Disorders and Panic in Adults: A Guide to Assessment and Treatment.* Washington, DC: APA.

Antony, M. M., Downie, F. and Swinson, R. (1998) Diagnostic issues and epidemiology in obsessive-compulsive disorder. In R. Swinson, M. Antony, S. Rachman and M. Richter (eds) *Obsessive-compulsive Disorder: Theory, Research, and Treatment* (pp. 3–32). New York: Guilford Press.

APA (American Psychiatric Association) (1968) *Diagnostic and Statistical Manual of Mental Disorders* (DSM-II) (2nd edn). Washington, DC: American Psychiatric Press.

APA (2000) *Diagnostic and Statistical Manual of Mental Disorders: DSM-IV-TR* (4th edn). Washington, DC: American Psychiatric Press.

APA (2013) *Diagnostic and Statistical Manual of Mental Disorders: DSM-5* (5th edn). Washington, DC: American Psychiatric Press.

Archer, J. E. (ed.) (1994) *Male Violence.* London: Routledge.

Arendt, H. (1963) *Eichmann in Jerusalem: A Report on the Banality of Evil.* London: Faber and Faber.

Argyle, M. and Cook, M. (1976) *Gaze and Mutual Gaze.* Cambridge: CUP.

Argyle, M. and Dean, J. (1965) Eye-contact, distance and affiliation. *Sociometry*, 28, 289–304.

Aristotle (1998) *The Nichomachean Ethics* (trans. D. W. Ross). Oxford: OUP.

Ariyasu, H., Takaya, K., Tagami, T. et al. (2001) Stomach is a major source of circulating ghrelin, and feeding state determines plasma ghrelin-like immunoreactivity levels in humans. *Journal of Clinical Endocrinology and Metabolism*, 86, 4753–8.

Arkes, H. R. and Ayton, P. (1999) The sunk cost and Concorde effects: Are humans less rational than lower animals? *Psychological Bulletin*, 125, 591–600.

Arkes, H. R., Boehm, L. E. and Xu, G. (1991) Determinants of judged validity. *Journal of Experimental Social Psychology*, 27, 576–605.

Arlitt, A. H. (1921) On the need for caution in establishing race norms. *Journal of Applied Psychology*, 5, 179–83.

Arlow, J. A. (2000) Psychoanalysis. In R. J. Corsini and D. Wedding (eds) *Current Psychotherapies* (6th edn, pp. 16–53). Itasca, IL: F. E. Peacock.

Armstrong, D. M. (1980) *The Nature of Mind.* Ithaca, NY: Cornell University Press.

Arnold, M. B. (ed.) (1960) *Emotion and Personality: Psychological Aspects*, vol. 1. New York: Columbia University Press.

Arnold, S. E., Trojanowski, J. Q., Gur, R. E. et al. (1998) Absence of neurodegeneration and neural injury in the cerebral cortex in a sample of elderly patients with schizophrenia. *Archives of General Psychiatry*, 55, 225–32.

Aronson, E. (1963) Effect of the severity of threat on the devaluation of forbidden behavior. *Journal of Abnormal and Social Psychology*, 66, 584–8.

Aronson, E. (1969) The theory of cognitive dissonance: A current perspective. In L. Berkowitz (ed.) *Advances in Experimental Social Psychology* (vol. 4, pp. 1–34). New York: Academic Press.

Aronson, E. and Mills, J. (1958) The effect of severity of initiation on liking for a group. *Journal of Abnormal and Social Psychology*, 59, 177–81.

Aronson, E. and Worchel, P. (1966) Similarity versus liking as determinants of interpersonal attractiveness. *Psychonomic Science*, 5, 157–8.

Aronson, E., Willerman, B. and Floyd, J. (1966) The effect of a pratfall on increasing interpersonal attractiveness. *Psychonomic Science*, 4, 227–8.

Asch, S. E. (1946) Forming impressions of personality. *Journal of Abnormal and Social Psychology*, 41, 258–90.

Asch, S. E. (1951) Effects of group pressure on the modification and distortion of judgments. In H. Guetzkow (ed.) *Groups, Leadership, and Men* (pp. 177–90). Pittsburgh: Carnegie Press.

Asch, S. E. (1955) Opinions and social pressure. *Scientific American*, 193, 31–5.

Asch, S. E. (1956) Studies of independence and conformity: 1 A minority of one against a unanimous majority. *Psychological Monographs: General and Applied*, 70, 1–70.

Aschoff, J. (1965) Circadian rhythms in man. *Science*, 148, 1427–32.

Asendorpf, J. B., Warkentin, V. and Baudonnière, P. M. (1996) Self-awareness and other-awareness, 2. Mirror self-recognition, social contingency awareness and synchronic imitation. *Developmental Psychology*, 32, 313–21.

Aserinsky, E. and Kleitman, N. (1953) Regularly occurring periods of eye motility, and concomitant phenomena, during sleep. *Science*, 118, 273–274.

Ashby, F. G. and Ell, S. W. (2001) The neurobiology of human category learning. *Trends in Cognitive Sciences*, 5, 204–10.

Ashcraft, M. H. (1998) *Fundamentals of Cognition.* New York: Longman.

Astington, J. W. and Baird, J. (2005) *Why Language Matters for Theory of Mind.* Oxford: OUP.

Astington, J. W. and Gopnick, A. (1991) Theoretical explanations of children's understanding of the mind. *British Journal of Developmental Psychology*, 9, 7–32.

Atkinson, J. (2000) *The Developing Visual Brain*. Oxford: OUP.

Atkinson, J. W. and Litwin, G. H. (1960) Achievement motive and test anxiety conceived as motive to approach success and motive to avoid failure. *Journal of Abnormal and Social Psychology*, 60, 52–63.

Atkinson, J., Hood, B., Wattam-Bell, J. et al. (1988) Development of orientation discrimination in infancy. *Perception*, 17, 587–95.

Atkinson, R. C. and Shiffrin, R. M. (1968) Human memory: A proposed system and its control processes. *The Psychology of Learning and Motivation*, 2, 89–195.

Austin, J. L. (1976) *How To Do Things With Words* (2nd edn). Oxford: OUP.

Avolio, B. J. and Waldman, D. A. (1994) Variations in cognitive, perceptual, and psychomotor abilities across the working life span: Examining the effects of race, sex, experience, education, and occupational type. *Psychology and Aging*, 9, 430–42.

Axelrod, R. (1984) *The Evolution of Cooperation.* New York: Basic Books.

Axelrod, R. and Hamilton, W. D. (1981) The evolution of cooperation. *Science*, 211, 1390–6.

Ayllon, T. and Azrin, N. H. (1968) Reinforcer sampling: A technique for increasing the behavior of mental patients. *Journal of Applied Behavioral Analysis*, 1, 13–20.

Ayres, C. E. (1921) Instinct and capacity, 1. The instinct of belief-in-instincts. *Journal of Philosophy*, 18, 561–5.

Azam, E. (1876) Dé doublement de la personnalité: Suite de l'histoié de Felida X. *Revue Scientifique*, 6, 265–9.

Azuma, H. and Kashiwagi, K. (1987) Descriptors for an intelligent person: A Japanese study. *Japanese Psychological Research*, 29, 17–26.

Backman, C. W. and Secord, P. F. (1959) The effect of perceived liking on interpersonal attraction. *Human Relations*, 12, 379–84.

Bäckman, L. and Dixon, R. A. (1992) Psychological compensation: A theoretical framework. *Psychological Bulletin*, 112, 259–83.

Baddeley, A. D. (1986) *Working Memory*. Oxford: OUP.

Baddeley, A. D. (1990) *Human Memory: Theory and Practice.* London: Lawrence Erlbaum.

Baddeley, A. D. (2000) The episodic buffer: A new component of working memory. *Trends in Cognitive Science*, 4, 417–23.

Baddeley, A. D. (2002) Fractionating the central executive. In D. Stuss and R. Knight (eds) *Principles of Frontal Lobe Functioning* (pp. 246–60). New York: OUP.

Baddeley, A. D. (2007) *Working Memory, Thought and Action*. Oxford: OUP.

Baddeley, A. D. and Andrade, J. (2000) Working memory and the vividness of imagery. *Journal of Experimental Psychology*, 129, 126–45.

Baddeley, A. D. and Hitch, G. J. (1974) Working memory. In S. Dornic (ed.) *Attention and Performance* (pp. 647–65). Hillsdale, NJ: Erlbaum.

Baer, L., Rauch, S. L., Ballantine, H. T. Jr et al. (1995) Cingulotomy for intractable obsessive-compulsive disorder: Prospective long-term follow-up of 18 patients. *Archives of General Psychiatry*, 52, 384–92.

Bagby, R. M., Levitan, R. D., Kennedy, S. H. et al. (1999) Selective alteration of personality in response to nor adrenergic and serotonergic antidepressant medication in depressed sample: Evidence of non-specificity. *Psychiatry Research*, 86, 211–16.

Bahrick, H. P. (1984) Semantic memory content in permastore: 50 years of memory for Spanish learned in school. *Journal of Experimental Psychology: General*, 113, 1–29.

Bahrick, H. P. (2000) Long-term maintenance of knowledge. In E. Tulving and F. I. Craik (eds) *The Oxford Handbook of Memory* (pp. 347–62). New York: OUP.

Bahrick, H. P., Hall, L. K. and Berger, S. A. (1996) Accuracy and distortion in memory for high school grades. *Psychological Science*, 7, 265–71.

Bailey, A., Le Couteur, A., Gottesman, I. et al. (1995) Autism as a strongly genetic disorder: Evidence from a British twin study. *Psychological Medicine*, 25, 63–77.

Baillargeon, R. (1994) How do infants learn about the physical world. *Current Directions in Psychological Science*, 3, 133–40.

Baillargeon, R., Spelke, E. S. and Wasserman, S. (1985) Object permanence in 5-month-old infants. *Cognition*, 20, 191–208.

Baird, A. A., Kagan, J., Gaudette, T. et al. (2002) Frontal lobe activation during object permanence: Data from near-infrared spectroscopy. *NeuroImage*, 16, 1120–6.

Baird, B., Smallwood, J., Mrazek, M. D. et al. (2012) Inspired by distraction: mind wandering facilitates creative incubation. *Psychological Science*, 23, 1117–22.

Baird, G., Simonoff, E., Pickles, A. et al. (2006) Prevalence of disorders of the autism spectrum in a population cohort of children in South East Thames: The Special Needs and Autism Project. *Lancet*, 368, 210–15.

Balcetis, E. and Dunning, D. (2010) Wishful seeing: Desired objects are seen as closer. *Psychological Science*, 21, 147–52.

Balcetis, E., Dunning, D. and Granot, Y. (2012) Subjective value determines initial dominance in binocular rivalry. *Journal of Experimental Social Psychology*, 48, 122–9.

Baldwin, D. (1991) Infants' contribution to the achievement of joint reference. *Child Development*, 62, 875–90.

Baldwin, J. M. (1897) *Social and Ethical Interpretations in Mental Development: A Study in Social Psychology*. New York: Macmillan.

Baldwin, M. W., Carrell, S. E. and Lopez, D. F. (1989) Priming relationship schemas: My advisor and the Pope are watching me from the back of my mind. *Journal of Experimental Social Psychology*, 26, 435–54.

Baler, R. D. and Volkow, N. D. (2006) Drug addiction: the neurobiology of disrupted self-control. *Trends in Molecular Medicine*, 12, 559–66.

Ball, R. A., Moore, E. and Kuipers, L. (1992) Expressed emotion in community care staff: A comparison of patient outcome in a nine month follow-up of two hostels. *Social Psychiatry and Psychiatric Epidemiology*, 27, 35–9.

Baltes, P. B. and Reinert, G. (1969) Cohort effects in cognitive development of children as revealed by cross-sectional sequences. *Developmental Psychology*, 1, 169–77.

Baltes, P. B. and Staudinger, U. M. (2000) Wisdom: A metaheuristic (pragmatic) to orchestrate mind and virtue toward excellence. *American Psychologist*, 55, 122–36.

Baltes, P. B., Staudinger, U. M., Maercker, A. and Smith, J. (1995) People nominated as wise: A comparative study of wisdom-related knowledge. *Psychology & Aging*, 10, 155–66.

Banducci, S. A., Karp, J. A., Thrasher, M. and Rallings, C. (2008) Ballot photographs as cues in low-information elections. *Political Psychology*, 29, 903–17.

Bandura, A. (1965) Influence of models' reinforcement contingencies on the acquisition of imitative responses. *Journal of Social and Personality Psychology*, 1, 589–95.

Bandura, A. (1977) *Social Learning Theory*. Englewood Cliffs, NJ: Prentice Hall.

Bandura, A. (1986) *Social Foundations of Thought and Action: A Social Cognitive Theory*. Englewood Cliffs, NJ: Prentice Hall.

Bandura, A. (1994) Social cognitive theory of mass communication. In J. Bryant and D. Zillmann (eds) *Media Effects: Advances in Theory and Research* (pp. 61–90). Hillsdale, NJ: Erlbaum.

Bandura, A. and Mischel, W. (1965) Modification of self-imposed delay of reward through exposure to live and symbolic models. *Journal of Personality and Social Psychology*, 2, 698–705.

Bandura, A., Ross, D. and Ross, S. (1961) Transmission of aggression through imitation of adult models. *Journal of Abnormal and Social Psychology*, 63, 575–82.

Bandura, A., Ross, D. and Ross, S. (1963) Vicarious reinforcement and imitative learning. *Journal of Abnormal and Social Psychology*, 67, 601–7.

Banerjee, R. and Lintern, V. (2000) Boys will be boys: The effects of social evaluation concerns on gender-typing. *Social Development*, 9, 397–408.

Banerjee, P., Chaterjee, P. and Sinha, J. (2012) Is it light or dark? Recalling moral behavior changes perception of brightness. *Psychological Science*, 23, 407–9.

Banks, M. S. and Salapatek, P. (1983) Infant visual perception. In M. Haith and J. Campos (eds) *Handbook of Child Psychology: Biology and Infancy*. New York: Wiley.

Banse, R. and Scherer, K. R. (1996) Acoustic profiles in vocal emotion expression. *Journal of Personality and Social Psychology*, 70, 614–36.

Bard, P. (1934) On emotional experience after decortication with some remarks on theoretical views. *Psychological Review*, 41, 309–29.

Bargh, J. A. (1997) The automaticity of everyday life. In R. S. Wyer, Jr (ed.) *The Automaticity of Everyday Life: Advances in Social Cognition* (vol. 10, pp. 1–61). Mahwah, NJ: Erlbaum.

Bargh, J. A. and Morsella, E. (2008) The unconscious mind. *Perspectives on Psychological Science*, 3, 73–89.

Bargh, J. A., Gollwitzer, P. M., Lee-Chai, A. et al. (2001) Bypassing the will: Automatic and controlled self-regulation. *Journal of Personality and Social Psychology*, 81, 1014–27.

Barker, A. T., Jalinous, R. and Freeston, I. L. (1985) Noninvasive magnetic stimulation of the human motor cortex. *Lancet*, 2, 1106–7.

Barkow, J. (1980) Prestige and self-esteem: A biosocial interpretation. In D. R. Omark, F. F. Stayer and D. G. Freedman (eds) *Dominance Relations* (pp. 319–22). New York: Garland.

Barlow, D. H., O'Brien, G. T. and Last, C. G. (1984) Couples treatment of agoraphobia. *Behavior Therapy*, 15, 41–58.

Barlow, D. H., Gorman, J. M., Shear, M. K. and Woods, S. W. (2000) Cognitive-behavioral therapy, imipramine, or their combination for panic disorder: A randomized controlled trial. *Journal of the American Medical Association*, 283(19), 2529–36.

Barnier, A. J., Levin, K. and Maher, A. (2004) Suppressing thoughts of past events: Are repressive copers good suppressors? *Cognition and Emotion*, 18, 457–77.

Baron, R. S., Moore, D. and Sanders, G. S. (1978) Distraction as a source of drive in social facilitation research. *Journal of Personality and Social Psychology*, 36, 816–24.

Baron-Cohen, S. (1991a) Do people with autism understand what causes emotion? *Child Development*, 62, 385–95.

Baron-Cohen, S. (1991b) Precursors to a theory of mind: Understanding attention in others. In A. Whiten (ed.) *Natural Theories of Mind: Evolution, Development and Simulation of Everyday Mindreading* (pp. 233–51). Oxford: Blackwell.

Baron-Cohen, S. (1995) *Mindblindness: An Essay on Autism and Theory of Mind*. Cambridge, MA: MIT Press.

Baron-Cohen, S. (2003) *The Essential Difference: The Truth About the Male and Female Brain*. New York: Basic Books.

Baron-Cohen, S., Leslie, A. and Frith, U. (1985) Does the autistic child have a 'theory of mind'? *Cognition*, 21, 37–46.

Baron-Cohen, S., Campbell, R., Karmiloff-Smith, A. et al. (1995) Are children with autism blind to the mentalistic significance of the eyes? *British Journal of Developmental Psychology*, 13, 379–98.

Barondes, S. (2003) *Better than Prozac*. New York: OUP.

Barrett, L. F., Williams, N. L. and Fong, G. T. (2002) An analysis of defensive verbal behavior. *Personality and Social Psychology Bulletin*, 28, 776–88.

Barrett, T. R. and Etheridge, J. B. (1992) Verbal hallucinations in normals, I: People who hear voices. *Applied Cognitive Psychology*, 6, 379–87.

Barrick, M. R., Mount, M. K. and Gupta, R. (2003) Meta-analysis of the relationship between the Five Factor model of personality and Holland's occupational types. *Personnel Psychology*, 56, 45–74.

Barrowclough, C., Tarrier, N. and Johnston, M. (1996) Distress, expressed emotion and attributions in relatives of schizophrenia patients. *Schizophrenia Bulletin*, 22, 691–702.

Barrowclough, C., Tarrier, N., Humphreys, L. et al. (2003) Self-esteem in schizophrenia: Relationships between self-evaluation, family attitudes, and symptomatology. *Journal of Abnormal Psychology*, 112, 92–9.

Barsalou, L. W. and Ross, B. H. (1986) The roles of automatic and strategic processing in sensitivity to superordinate and property frequency. *Journal of Experimental Psychology: Learning, Memory and Cognition*, 12, 116–34.

Bartholomew, D. J. (1995) Spearman and the origin and development of test theory. *British Journal of Mathematical and Statistical Psychology*, 48, 211–20.

Bartlett, F. C. (1932) *Remembering*. Cambridge: CUP.

Bartol, C. R. and Costello, N. (1976) Extraversion as a function of temporal duration of electric shock: An exploratory study. *Perceptual and Motor Skills*, 42, 1174.

Bartoshuk, L. M. (2000) Comparing sensory experiences across individuals: Recent psychophysical advances illuminate genetic variation in taste perception. *Chemical Senses*, 25, 447–60.

Bartoshuk, L. M. and Beauchamp, G. K. (1994) Chemical senses. *Annual Review of Psychology*, 45, 419–45.

Bartoshuk, L. M., Duffy, V. B. and Miller, I. J. (1994) PTC/PROP tasting: Anatomy, psychophysics, and sex effects. *Physiology and Behavior*, 56, 1165–71.

Bass, E. and Davis, L. (1988) *The Courage to Heal: A Guide for Women Survivors of Child Sexual Abuse*. New York: Harper & Row.

Bates, E. and Goodman, J. C. (1997) On the inseparability of grammar and the lexicon: Evidence from acquisition, aphasia and real-time processing. *Language and Cognitive Processes*, 12, 507–84.

Bates, E., Camaioni, L. and Volterra, V. (1975) The acquisition of performatives prior to speech. *Merrill-Palmer Quarterly*, 21, 205–24.

Bateson, M., Nettle, D. and Roberts, G. (2006) Cues of being watched enhance cooperation in a real-world setting. *Biology Letters*, 2(3), 412–14.

Batson, C. D. (2002) Addressing the altruism question experimentally. In S. G. Post and L. G. Underwood (eds) *Altruism & Altruistic Love: Science, Philosophy and Religion in Dialogue* (pp. 89–105). London: OUP.

Batson, C. D., Floyd, R. B., Meyer, J. M. and Winner, A. L. (1999) 'And who is my neighbor?': Intrinsic religion as a source of universal compassion. *Journal for the Scientific Study of Religion*, 38, 445–57.

Bauer, P. J. (1995) Recalling past events: From infancy to early childhood. *Annals of Child Development*, 11, 25–71.

Bauer, P. J. (2002) Long-term recall memory: Behavioral and neuro-developmental changes in the first 2 years of life. *Current Directions in Psychological Science*, 11, 137–41.

Bauer, S. (2012) Solitary in Iran nearly broke me. Then I went inside America's prisons, www.motherjones.com/politics/2012/10/solitary-confinement-shane-bauer.

Baumeister, R. F. (2002) Ego depletion and self-control failure: An energy model of the self's executive function. *Self and Identity*, 1, 129–36.

Baumeister, R. F. and Leary, M. R. (1995) The need to belong: Desire for interpersonal attachments as a fundamental human motivation. *Psychological Bulletin*, 117, 497–529.

Baumeister, R. F. and Tice, D. M. (1990) Anxiety and social exclusion. *Journal of Social and Clinical Psychology*, 9, 165–95.

Baumeister, R. F. and Tiernay, J. (2012) *Willpower: Why Self-Control is the Secret to Success*. London: Penguin.

Baumeister, R. F., Cantanese, K. R. and Vohs, K. D. (2001) Is there a gender difference in strength of sex drive? Theoretical views, conceptual distinctions, and a review of relevant evidence. *Personality and Social Psychology Review*, 5, 242–73.

Baumeister, R. F., Campbell, J. D., Krueger, J. I. and Vohs, K. D. (2003) Does high self-esteem cause better performance, interpersonal success, happiness, or healthier lifestyles? *Psychological Science in the Public Interest*, 4, 1–44.

Baxter, L. R., Schwartz, J. M., Bergman, K. S. et al. (1992) Caudate glucose metabolic rate changes with both drug behavior therapy for obsessive-compulsive disorder. *Archives of General Psychiatry*, 49, 681–9.

Bayley, P. J., Gold, J. J., Hopkins, R. O. and Squire, L. R. (2005) The neuroanatomy of remote memory. *Neuron*, 46, 799–810.

Beaman, A. L., Diener, E. and Klentz, B. (1979) Self-awareness and transgression in children: Two field studies, *Journal of Personality and Social Psychology*, 37, 1835–46.

Bechara, A., Tranel, D. and Damasio, H. (2000) Characterization of the decision-making deficit of patients with ventromedial prefrontal cortex lesions. *Brain*, 123, 2189–202.

Bechara, A., Damasio, A. R., Damasio, H. and Anderson, S. W. (1994) Insensitivity to future consequences following damage to human prefrontal cortex. *Cognition*, 50, 7–15.

Bechara, A., Damasio, H., Tranel, D. and Damasio, A. R. (1997) Deciding advantageously before knowing the advantageous strategy. *Science*, 275, 1293–5.

Bechara, A., Dolan, S., Denburg, N. et al. (2001) Decision-making deficits, linked to a dysfunctional ventromedial prefrontal cortex, revealed in alcohol and stimulant abusers. *Neuropsychologia*, 39, 376–89.

Beck, A. T. (1967) *Depression: Causes and Treatment*. Philadelphia: University of Pennsylvania Press.

Beck, A. T. and Weishaar, M. (2000) Cognitive therapy. In R. J. Corsini and D. Wedding (eds) *Current Psychotherapies* (6th edn, pp. 241–72). Itasca, IL: F. E. Peacock.

Beck, L. F. (1933) The role of speed in intelligence. *Psychological Bulletin*, 30, 169–78.

Becker, S. W. and Eagly, A. H. (2004) The heroism of women and men. *American Psychologist*, 59, 173–8.

Beckers, G. and Zeki, S. (1995) The consequences of inactivating areas V1 and V5 on visual motion perception. *Brain*, 118, 49–60.

Békésy, G. von (1960) *Experiments in Hearing*. New York: McGraw-Hill.

Belluck, P. and Carey, B. (2013) Psychiatry's guide is out of touch with science, experts say. *The New York Times*, 6 May.

Belsky, J., Spritz, B. and Crnic, K. (1996) Infant attachment security and affective-cognitive information processing at age 3. *Psychological Science*, 7, 111–14.

Belsky, J., Jaffee, S. R., Caspi, A. et al. (2003) Intergenerational relationships in young adulthood and their life course, mental health and personality correlates. *Journal of Family Psychology*, 17, 460–71.

Bem, S. L. (1974) The measure of psychological androgyny. *Journal of Consulting & Clinical Psychology*, 42, 155–62.

Benedek, M., Jauk, E., Sommer, M. et al. (2014) Intelligence, creativity, and cognitive control: The common and differential involvement of executive functions in intelligence and creativity. *Intelligence*, 46, 73–83.

Benedetti, F., Maggi, G. and Lopiano, L. (2003) Open versus hidden medical treatment: The patient's knowledge about a therapy affects the therapy outcome. *Prevention & Treatment*, 6(1), doi: 10.1037/1522-3736.6.0001a.

Benenson, J. F., Pascoe, J. and Radmore, N. (2007) Children's altruistic behaviour in the dictator game. *Evolution & Human Behavior*, 28, 168–75.

Benes, F. M. (1998) Model generation and testing to probe neural circuitry in the cingulated cortex of postmortem schizophrenia brain. *Schizophrenia Bulletin*, 24, 219–30.

Benjamin, L. T. Jr (ed.) (1988) *A History of Psychology: Original Sources and Contemporary Research*. New York: McGraw-Hill.

Benjamin, L. T., Cavell, T. A. and Shallenberger, W. R. (1984) Staying with initial answers on objective tests: Is it a myth? *Teaching of Psychology*, 11, 133–41.

Bennett, C. M., Baird, A. A., Miller, M. B. and Wolford, G. L. (2009) Neural correlates of interspecies perspective taking in the post-mortem Atlantic salmon: An argument for proper multiple comparisons correction. 15th Annual Meeting of the Organization for Human Brain Mapping, San Francisco, CA.

Benson, P. L., Karabenick, S. A. and Lerner, R. M. (1976) Pretty pleases: The effects of attractiveness, race, and sex on receiving help. *Journal of Experimental Social Psychology*, 12, 409–15.

Bentall, R. P. (2003) *Madness Explained: Psychosis and Human Nature.* London: Allen Lane.

Benton, D. (2001) Psychological and pharmacological explanations of chocolate craving. In M. H. Hetherington (ed.) *Food Cravings and Addiction* (pp. 265–93). Leatherhead: Leatherhead Food Research Association.

Benton, D., Greenfield, K. and Morgan, M. (1998) The development of the attitudes to chocolate questionnaire. *Personality and Individual Differences*, 24, 513–20.

Bereczkei, T., Vorgos, S., Gal, A. and Bernath, L. (1997) Resources, attractiveness, family commitment; reproductive decisions in human mate choice. *Journal of Ethology*, 103, 681–99.

Berger, H. (1929) Über das Elektroenkephalogram des Menschen. *Archiv fuer Psychiatrie*, 87, 527–70.

Berger, R. J. (1963) Experimental modification of dream content by meaningful verbal stimuli. *British Journal of Psychiatry*, 109, 722–40.

Berggren, N., Jordahl, H. and Poutvaara, P. (2010) The looks of a winner: Beauty and electoral success. *Journal of Public Economics*, 94, 8–15.

Bergin, A. E. (1971) The evaluation of therapeutic outcomes. In A. E. Bergin and S. L. Garfield (eds) *Handbook of Psychotherapy and Behaviour Change* (pp. 217–70). New York: Wiley.

Berglund, H., Lindstrom, P. and Savic, I. (2006) Brain response to putative pheromones in lesbian women. *Proceedings of the National Academy of Sciences*, 103, 8269–74.

Berkerian, D. A. and Bowers, J. M. (1983) Eyewitness testimony: Were we misled? *Journal of Experimental Psychology: Learning, Memory, and Cognition*, 9, 139–45.

Berkman, L. F., Glass, T., Brissette, I. and Seeman T. E. (2000) From social integration to health. *Social Science Medicine*, 51, 843–57.

Berkowitz, L. (1989) Frustration-aggression hypothesis: Examination and reformulation. *Psychological Bulletin*, 106, 59–73.

Berkowitz, L. (1990) On the formation and regulation of anger and aggression: A cognitive-neoassociationistic analysis. *American Psychologist*, 45, 494–503.

Berkowitz, L. (1993) Pain and aggression: Some findings and implications. *Motivation and Emotion*, 17, 277–93.

Berman, M. E., McCloskey, M. S., Fanning, J. R. et al. (2009) Serotonin augmentation reduces response to attack in aggressive individuals. *Psychological Science*, 20, 714–20.

Bernard, L. L. (1924) *Instinct: A Study in Social Psychology.* New York: Holt.

Berry, D. S. and McArthur, L. Z. (1985) Some components and consequences of a babyface. *Journal of Personality and Social Psychology*, 48, 312–23.

Berry, J. W., Poortinga, Y. H., Segall, M. H. and Dasen, P. R. (1992) *Cross-cultural Psychology: Research and Applications.* New York: CUP.

Berscheid, E. and Reiss, H. T. (1998) Interpersonal attraction and close relationships. In D. T. Gilbert, S. T. Fiske and G. Lindzey (eds) *The Handbook of Social Psychology* (4th edn, vol. 2, pp. 193–281). New York: McGraw-Hill.

Bertelsen, A. (1999) Reflections on the clinical utility of the ICD-10 and DSM-IV classifications and their diagnostic criteria. *Australian and New Zealand Journal of Psychiatry*, 33, 166–73.

Bertelsen, B., Harvald, B. and Hauge, M. (1977) A Danish twin study of manic-depressive disorders. *British Journal of Psychiatry*, 130, 330–51.

Bertenthal, B. I., Rose, J. L. and Bai, D. L. (1997) Perception-action coupling in the development of visual control of posture. *Journal of Experimental Psychology: Human Perception & Performance*, 23, 1631–43.

Berthenthal, I. and Fischer, K. W. (1978) Development of self-recognition in the infant. *Developmental Psychology*, 14, 44–50.

Best, J. B. (1979) Item difficulty and answer changing. *Teaching of Psychology*, 6, 228–30.

Best, J. B. (1992) *Cognitive Psychology* (3rd edn). New York: West Publishing.

Bettencourt, B. A. and Miller, N. (1996) Gender differences in aggression as a function of provocation: A meta-analysis. *Psychological Bulletin*, 119, 422–47.

Beutler, L. E. (2002) The dodo bird is extinct. *Clinical Psychology: Science and Practice*, 9, 30–4.

Beveridge, A. W. and Renvoize, E. B. (1988) Electricity: A history of its use in the treatment of mental illness in Britain during the second half of the 19th century. *British Journal of Psychiatry*, 153, 157–62.

Bhalla, M. and Proffitt, D. R. (1999) Visual-motor recalibration in geographical slant perception. *Journal of Experimental Psychology: Human Perception and Performance*, 25, 1076–96.

Bickerton, D. (1990) *Language and Species.* Chicago: Chicago University Press.

Biederman, I. (1987) Recognition-by-components: A theory of human image understanding. *Psychological Review*, 94, 115–47.

Bierce, A. (1911) *The Devil's Dictionary.* New York: A. & C. Boni.

Bierhof, H. W., Klein, R. and Kramp, P. (1991) Evidence for the altruistic personality from data on accident research. *Journal of Personality*, 59, 263–80.

Billet, E., Richter, J. and Kennedy, J. (1998) Genetics of obsessive-compulsive disorder. In R. Swinson, M. Anthony, S. Rachman and M. Richter (eds) *Obsessive-compulsive Disorder: Theory, Research, and Treatment* (pp. 181–206). New York: Guilford Press.

Binet, A. (1905) New methods for the diagnosis of the intellectual level of subnormals. *L'Année Psychologique*, 12, 191–244.

Binet, A. (1909) *Les idées modernes sur les enfants.* Paris: Flammarion.

Binswanger, L. (1958) The existential analysis school of thought. In R. May (ed.) *Existence: A New Dimension in Psychiatry and Psychology.* New York: Basic Books.

Birch, L. L. and Billman, J. (1986) Preschool children's food sharing with friends and acquaintances. *Child Development*, 57, 387–95.

Birch, S. A. and Bloom, P. (2007) The curse of knowledge in reasoning about false beliefs. *Psychological Science*, 18, 382–6.

Bisiach, E. and Luzzati, C. (1978) Unilateral neglect in representational space. *Cortex*, 14, 129–33.

Bjork, D. W. (1983) *The Compromised Scientist: William James in the Development of American Psychology.* New York: Columbia University Press.

Bjork, D. W. (1993) *B. F. Skinner: A Life.* New York: Basic Books.

Bjork, E. L. and Bjork, R. A. (2011) Making things hard on yourself, but in a good way: Creating desirable difficulties to enhance learning. In M. A. Gernsbacher, R. W. Pewe, L. M. Hough and J. R. Pomerantz (eds) *Psychology and the Real World: Essays Illustrating Fundamental Contributions to Society* (pp. 56–64). New York: Worth.

Bjork, R. A. and Bjork, E. L. (1988) On the adaptive aspects of retrieval failure in autobiographical memory. In M. M. Gruneberg, P. E. Morris and R. N. Sykes (eds) *Practical Aspects of Memory: Current Research and Issues* (pp. 283–8). Chichester: Wiley.

Blackmore, S. (1984) A postal survey of OBEs and other experiences. *Journal of the Society of Psychical Research*, 52, 225–44.

Blair, I. V. (2002) The malleability of automatic stereotypes and prejudice. *Personality and Social Psychology Review*, 6, 242–61.

Blair, J., Peschardt, K. and Mitchell, D. R. (2005) *Psychopath: Emotion and the Brain.* Oxford: Blackwell.

Blake, P. and Rand, D. (2010) Currency value moderates equity preference among young children. *Evolution and Human Behavior*, 31, 210–18.

Blakemore, J. E., Berenbaum, S. A. and Liben, L. S. (2009) *Gender Development*. New York: Taylor and Francis.

Blakemore, S. J. (2012) Imaging brain development: The adolescent brain. *Neuroimage*, 61, 397–406.

Blascovich, J. and Tomaka, J. (1996) The biopsychosocial model of arousal regulation. In M. P. Zanna (ed.) *Advances in Experimental Social Psychology* (vol. 28, pp. 1–51). San Diego, CA: Academic Press.

Blascovich, J., Mendes, W. B., Hunter, S. B. and Salomon, K. (1999) 'Social facilitation' as challenge and threat. *Journal of Personality and Social Psychology*, 77, 68–77.

Blascovich, J., Mendes, W. B., Hunter, S. B. et al. (2001) Perceiver threat in social interactions with stigmatized others. *Journal of Personality and Social Psychology*, 80, 253–67.

Blasi, A. (1980) Bridging moral cognition and moral action: A critical review of the literature. *Psychological Bulletin*, 88, 1–45.

Blass, T. (1998) The roots of Milgram's obedience experiments and their relevance to the Holocaust. *Analyse & Kritik*, 20, 46–53.

Blatt, S. J. and Homann, E. (1992) Parent-child interaction in the etiology of dependent and self-critical depression. *Clinical Psychology Review*, 12, 47–91.

Blatt, S. J. and Zuroff, D. C. (1992) Interpersonal relatedness and self-definition: Two prototypes for depression. *Clinical Psychology Review*, 12, 527–62.

Blazer, D. G., Hughes, D. and George, L. D. (1987) Stressful life events and the onset of a generalized anxiety syndrome. *American Journal of Psychiatry*, 144, 1178–83.

Blazer, D. G., Hughes, D. J., George, L. K. et al. (1991) Generalized anxiety disorder. In L. N. Robins and D. A. Regier (eds) *Psychiatric Disorders in America* (pp. 180–203). New York: Free Press.

Bleidorn, W. (2012) Hitting the road to adulthood: Short-term personality development during a major life transition. *Personality and Social Psychology Bulletin*, 38, 1594–608.

Bleuler, E. ([1911]1950) *Dementia Praecox or the Group of Schizophrenias* (trans. J. Zinkin). New York: International Universities Press.

Bliss, T. V. (1999) Young receptors make smart mice. *Nature*, 401, 25–7.

Bliss, T. V. and Lømo, W. T. (1973) Long-lasting potentiation of synaptic transmission in the dentate area of the anesthetized rabbit following stimulation of the perforant path. *Journal of Physiology*, 232, 331–56.

Bloom, P. (2000) *How Children Learn the Meanings of Words*. Cambridge, MA: MIT Press.

Bloom, P. (2004) *Descartes' Baby: How the Science of Child Development Explains What Makes us Human*. New York: Basic Books.

Bloom, P. (2013) *Just Babies: The Origins of Good and Evil*. New York: Crown.

Bloom, P. (2014) Horrible children: The limits of natural morality. In M. R. Banaji and S. A. Gelman (eds) *Navigating the Social World: What Infants, Children and Other Species Can Teach Us* (pp. 348–51). New York: OUP.

Bloom, P. and German, T. (2000) Two reasons to abandon the false belief as a test of theory of mind. *Cognition*, 77, 25–31.

Boecker, H., Sprenger, T., Spilker, M. E. et al. (2008) The runner's high: Opioidergic mechanisms in the human brain. *Cerebral Cortex*, 18, 2523–31.

Bogart, K. R. and Matsumoto, D. (2010) Living with Moebius Syndrome: Adjustment, social competence, and satisfaction with life. *Cleft Palate–Craniofacial Journal*, 47, 134–42.

Bogg, T. and Roberts, B. W. (2004) Conscientiousness and health behaviours: A meta-analysis. *Psychological Bulletin*, 130, 887–919.

Boice, R., Quanty, C. B. and Williams, R. C. (1974) Competition and possible dominance in turtles, toads and frogs. *Journal of Comparative and Physiological Psychology*, 86, 116–31.

Boisvert, C. M. and Faust, D. (2002) Iatrogenic symptoms in psychotherapy: A theoretical exploration of the potential impact of labels, language, and belief systems. *American Journal of Psychotherapy*, 56, 244–59.

Boksem, M. A., Mehta, P. H., van den Bergh, B. et al. (2013) Testosterone inhibits trust but promotes reciprocity. *Psychological Science*, 24, 2306–14.

Bond, C. and DePaulo, B. (2006) Accuracy of deception judgments. *Personality and Social Psychology Review*, 10, 214–34.

Bond, C. F. and Titus, L. J. (1983) Social facilitation: A meta-analysis of 241 studies. *Psychological Bulletin*, 94, 265–92.

Boomsma, D., Busjahn, A. and Peltonen, L. (2002) Classical twin studies and beyond. *Nature Reviews Genetics*, 3, 872–82.

Bootzin, R. R., Manber, R., Perlis, M. L. et al. (1993) Sleep disorders. In P. B. Sutker and H. E. Adams (eds) *Comprehensive Handbook of Psychopathology* (2nd edn, pp. 531–61). New York: Plenum Press.

Borkenau, P. and Liebler, A. (1995) Observable attributes as manifestations and cues of personality and intelligence. *Journal of Personality*, 63, 1–25.

Borkevec, T. D. (1982) Insomnia. *Journal of Consulting and Clinical Psychology*, 50, 880–95.

Born, R. T. and Bradley, D. C. (2005) Structure and function of visual area MT. *Annual Review of Neuroscience*, 28, 157–89.

Bornstein, M. H., Hahn, C. S. and Haynes, O. M. (2004) Specific and general language performance across early childhood: Stability and gender considerations. *First Language*, 24, 267–304.

Bornstein, M. H., Hahn, C.-S. and Suwalsky, J. T. (2013) Physically developed and exploratory young infants contribute to their own long-term academic achievement. *Psychological Science*, 24, 1906–17.

Bornstein, R. F. (1989) Exposure and affect: Overview and meta-analysis of research, 1968–1987. *Psychological Bulletin*, 106, 265–89.

Boroditsky, L. (2001) Does language shape thought? Mandarin and English speakers' conceptions of time. *Cognitive Psychology*, 43, 1–22.

Bostwick, J. M. and Pankratz, S. (2000) Affective disorders and suicide risk: A reexamination. *American Journal of Psychiatry*, 157, 1925–32.

Botvinick, M. and Cohen, J. (1998) Rubber hands 'feel' touch that eyes see. *Nature*, 391, 576.

Botwin, M. D., Buss, D. M. and Shackelford, T. K. (1997) Personality and mate preferences: Five factors in mate selection and marital satisfaction. *Journal of Personality*, 65, 107–36.

Bouchard, T. J. and Loehlin, J. C. (2001) Genes, evolution, and personality. *Behavioral Genetics*, 31, 243–73.

Bouchard, T. J. and McGue, M. (1981) Familial studies of intelligence: A review. *Science*, 212, 1055–9.

Boucher, J. D. and Carlson, G. E. (1980) Recognition of facial expressions in three cultures. *Journal of Cross-Cultural Psychology*, 11, 263–80.

Bourguignon, E. (1968) World distribution and patterns of possession states. In R. Prince (ed.) *Trance and Possession States* (pp. 3–34). Montreal: R. M. Burke Memorial Society.

Bouton, M. E. (2002) *Learning and Behaviour: A Contemporary Synthesis*. Sunderland, MA: Sinauer.

Bower, G. H. (1981) Mood and memory. *American Psychologist*, 36, 129–48.

Bower, G. H., Clark, M. C., Lesgold, A. M. and Winzenz, D. (1969) Hierarchical retrieval schemes in recall of categorical word lists. *Journal of Verbal Learning and Verbal Behavior*, 8, 323–43.

Bowers, J. S., Mattys, S. L. and Gage, S. H. (2009) Preserved implicit knowledge of a forgotten childhood language. *Psychological Science*, 20, 1064–106.

Bowers, K. S., Regehr, G., Balthazard, C. and Parker, D. (1990) Intuition in the context of discovery. *Cognitive Psychology*, 22, 72–110.

Bowlby, J. (1953) *Child Care and the Growth of Love*. Baltimore: Pelican Books.

Bowlby, J. (1958) The nature of the child's tie to his mother. *International Journal of Psychoanalysis*, 39, 350–73.

Bowlby, J. (1969) *Attachment and Loss*, vol. 1. *Attachment*. New York: Basic Books.

Bowlby, J. (1973) *Attachment and Loss*, vol. 2. *Separation*. New York: Basic Books.

Bowlby, J. (1980) *Attachment and Loss*, vol. 3. *Loss: Sadness and Depression*. New York: Basic Books.

Boyce, W. T., Essex, M. J., Alkon, A. et al. (2005) Early father involvement moderates biobehavioral susceptibility to mental health problems in middle childhood. *Journal of the American Academy of Child and Adolescent Psychiatry*, 45, 1510–20.

Bozarth, M. A. (ed.) (1987) *Methods of Assessing the Reinforcing Properties of Abused Drugs*. New York: Springer-Verlag.

Bozarth, M. A. and Wise, R. A. (1985) Toxicity associated with long-term intravenous heroin and cocaine self-administration in the rat. *Journal of the American Medical Association*, 254, 81–3.

Braddick, O. J. and Atkinson, J. (1979) Accommodation and acuity in the human infant. In R. D. Freeman (ed.) *Developmental Neurobiology of Vision*. New York: Plenum Press.

Braddick, O. J., Atkinson, J., Hood, B. et al. (1992) Possible blindsight in infants lacking one cerebral hemisphere. *Nature*, 360, 461–3.

Bradford, D., Stroup, S. and Lieberman, J. (2002) Pharmacological treatments for schizophrenia. In P. E. Nathan and J. M. Gorman (eds) *A Guide to Treatments that Work* (2nd edn, pp. 169–99). New York: OUP.

Bradley, C. and Meddis, R. (1974) Arousal thresholds in dreaming sleep. *Physiological Psychology*, 2, 109–10.

Braet, W. and Humphreys, G. W. (2009) The role of reentrant processes in feature binding: Evidence from neuropsychology and TMS on late onset illusory conjunctions. *Visual Cognition*, 17, 25–47.

Bramlett, M. D. and Mosher, W. D. (2002) *Cohabitation, Marriage, Divorce, and Remarriage in the United States*. Hyattsville, MD: National Center for Health Statistics.

Brauer, M., Judd, C. M. and Jacquelin, V. (2001) The communication of social stereotypes: The effect of groups discussion and information distribution on stereotypic appraisals. *Journal of Personality and Social Psychology*, 81, 463–75.

Braun, A. R., Balkin, T. J., Wesensten, N. J. et al. (1998) Dissociated pattern of activity in visual cortices and their projections during rapid eye movement sleep. *Science*, 279, 91–5.

Breckler, S. J. (1994) Memory for the experiment of donating blood: Just how bad was it? *Basic and Applied Social Psychology*, 15, 467–88.

Brédart, S. and Valentine, T. (1998) Descriptiveness and proper name retrieval. *Memory*, 6, 199–206.

Breen, N., Caine, D. and Coltheart, M. (2001) Mirrored-self misidentification: Two cases of focal onset dementia. *Neurocase*, 7, 239–54.

Breggin, P. R. (1990) Brain damage, dementia, and persistent cognitive dysfunction associated with neuroleptic drugs: Evidence, etiology, implications. *Journal of Mind and Behavior*, 11, 425–63.

Breggin, P. R. (2000) *Reclaiming Our Children*. Cambridge, MA: Perseus Books.

Brehm, S. S. (1992) *Intimate Relationships* (2nd edn). New York: McGraw-Hill.

Breland, K. and Breland, M. (1961) The misbehavior of organisms. *American Psychologist*, 16, 681–4.

Brennan, P. A. and Zufall, F. (2006) Pheromonal communication in vertebrates. *Nature*, 444, 308–15.

Brenneis, C. B. (2000) Evaluating the evidence: Can we find authenticated recovered memory? *Journal of the American Psychoanalytic Association*, 17, 61–77.

Bretherton, I. (1985) Attachment theory: Retrospect and prospect. *Monographs of the Society for Research in Child Development*, 50(1–2, Serial No. 209).

Brewer, M. B. (1979) In-group bias in the minimal intergroup situation: A cognitive-motivational analysis. *Psychological Bulletin*, 86, 307–24.

Brewer, M. B. (1991) The social self: On being the same and different at the same time. *Personality and Social Psychology Bulletin*, 17, 475–82.

Brewer, W. F. (1996) What is recollective memory? In D. C. Rubin (ed.) *Remembering Our Past: Studies in Autobiographical Memory* (pp. 19–66). New York: CUP.

Brewin, C. R., MacCarthy, B., Duda, K. and Vaughn, C. E. (1991) Attribution and expressed emotion in the relatives of patients with schizophrenia. *Journal of Abnormal Psychology*, 100, 546–54.

Brickman, P., Coates, D. and Janoff-Bulman, R. J. (1978) Lottery winners and accident victims: Is happiness relative? *Journal of Personality and Social Psychology*, 36, 917–27.

Bridges, P. K., Bartlett, J. R., Hale, A. S. et al. (1994) Psychosurgery: stereotactic subcaudate tractomy: An indispensable treatment. *British Journal of Psychiatry*, 165, 599–611.

Briggs, J. L. (2000) Conflict management in a modern Inuit community. In P. Schweitzer, M. Biesele and R. K. Hitchcock (eds) *Hunters and Gatherers in the Modern World: Conflict, Resistance, and Self-Determination* (pp. 110–24). New York: Berghahn Books.

British Psychological Society (2004) *A Review of the Current Scientific Status and Fields of Application of Polygraph Deception Detection*. Leicester: British Psychological Society.

Broadbent, D. E. (1958) *Perception and Communication*. London: Pergamon Press.

Broberg, D. J. and Bernstein, I. L. (1987) Candy as a scapegoat in the prevention of food aversions in children receiving chemotherapy. *Cancer*, 60, 2344–7.

Broca, P. (1861) Remarques sur le siège de la faculté du langage articulé; suivies d'une observation d'aphemie (perte de la parole). *Bulletin de la société anatomique de Paris*, 36, 330–57.

Broca, P. (1863) Localisation des fonction cerebrales: Siège du langage articulé. *Bulletin de la société d'anthropologie de Paris*, 4, 200–2.

Brock, A. (1993) Something old, something new: The 'reappraisal' of Wilhelm Wundt in textbooks. *Theory & Psychology*, 3(2), 235–42.

Brockner, J. and Swap, W. C. (1976) Effects of repeated exposure and attitudinal similarity on self-disclosure and interpersonal attraction. *Journal of Personality and Social Psychology*, 33, 531–40.

Broderick, C. B. and Schrader, S. S. (1991) The history of professional marriage and family therapy. In A. S. Gurman and D. P. Kniskern (eds) *Handbook of Family Therapy* (pp. 3–40). New York: Brunner/Mazel.

Brody, N. (1992) *Intelligence* (2nd edn). New York: Academic.

Brody, N. (2003) Construct validation of the Sternberg Triarchic Abilities Test: Comment and reanalysis. *Intelligence*, 31(4), 319–29.

Bronson, G. (1974) The postnatal growth of visual capacity. *Child Development*, 45, 873–90.

Broom, A. (2004) Prostate cancer and masculinity in Australian society: A case of stolen identity. *International Journal of Men's Health*, 3(2), 73–91.

Brosnan, S. F. and DeWaal, F. B. (2003) Monkeys reject unequal pay. *Nature*, 425, 297–9.

Brown, A. and DeLoache, J. (1978) Skills, plans and self regulation. In R. Siegler (ed.) *Children's Thinking: What Develops?* Hillsdale, NJ: Lawrence Erlbaum.

Brown, B. B., Mory, M. and Kinney, D. (1994) Casting crowds in a relational perspective: Caricature, channel, and context. In G. A. Montemayor and T. Gullotta (eds) *Advances in Adolescent Development: Personal Relationships during Adolescence* (vol. 5, pp. 123–67). Newbury Park, CA: Sage.

Brown, G. W. and Harris, T. (1978) *Social Origins of Depression*. New York: Free Press.

Brown, G. W. and Prudo, R. (1981) Psychiatric disorders in a rural and urban population, I. Aetiology of depression. *Psychological Medicine*, 11, 581–99.

Brown, J. D. (1993) Self-esteem and self-evaluation: Feeling is believing. In J. M. Suls (ed.) *The Self in Social Perspective: Psychological Perspectives on the Self* (vol. 4, pp. 27–58). Hillsdale, NJ: Erlbaum.

Brown, J. D. and McGill, K. L. (1989) The cost of good fortune: When positive life events produce negative health consequences. *Journal of Personality & Social Psychology*, 57, 1103–10.

Brown, L. T. (1983) Some more misconceptions about psychology among introductory psychology students. *Teaching of Psychology*, 10, 207–10.

Brown, R. (1958) *Words and Things*. New York: Free Press.

Brown, R. and Hanlon, C. (1970) Derivational complexity and order of acquisition in child speech. In J. R. Hayes (ed.) *Cognition and the Development of Language* (pp. 11–53). New York: Wiley.

Brown, R. and McNeill, D. (1966) The 'tip of the tongue' phenomenon. *Journal of Verbal Learning and Verbal Behavior*, 5, 325–37.

Brown, S. C. and Craik, F. I. (2000) Encoding and retrieval of information. In E. Tulving and F. I. Craik (eds) *The Oxford Handbook of Memory* (pp. 93–107). New York: OUP.

Brown, T. A. and Barlow, D. H. (2002) Classification of anxiety and mood disorders. In D. H. Barlow (ed.) *Anxiety and its Disorders: The Nature and Treatment of Anxiety and Panic* (2nd edn, pp. 292–327). New York: Guilford Press.

Brown, T. A., Campbell, L. A., Lehman, C. L. et al. (2001) Current and lifetime comorbidity of the DSM-IV anxiety and mood disorders in a large clinical sample. *Journal of Abnormal Psychology*, 110, 585–99.

Brownell, C. A. and Carriger, M. (1990) Changes in cooperation and self-other differentiation during the second year. *Child Development*, 61, 1164–74.

Brownell, C. A., Nichols, S. R. and Svetlova, M. (2013a) Converging developments in prosocial behavior and self-other understanding in the second year of life. In M. R. Banaji and S. A. Gelman (eds) *Navigating the Social World: What Infants, Children and Other Species Can Teach Us* (pp. 385–90). New York: OUP.

Brownell, C. A., Ramani, G. and Zerwas, S. (2006) Becoming a social partner with peers: Cooperation and social understanding in one- and two-year-olds. *Child Development*, 77, 804–21.

Brownell, C. A., Iesue, S., Nichols, S. R. and Svetlova, M. (2013b) Mine or yours? Development of sharing in toddlers in relationship to ownership understanding. *Child Development*, 84, 906–20.

Brownell, K. D., Greenwood, M. R., Stellar, E. and Shrager, E. E. (1986) The effects of repeated cycles of weight loss and regain in rats. *Physiology and Behavior*, 38, 459–64.

Bruce, V. and Young, A. W. (1986) Understanding face recognition. *British Journal of Psychology*, 77, 305–27.

Brummelman, E., Thomaes, S., Overbeck, G. et al. (2014a) On feeding those hungry for praise: Person praise backfires in children with low self-esteem. *Journal of Experimental Psychology: General*, 143, 9–14.

Brummelman, E., Thomaes, S., Overbeck, G. et al. (2014b) 'That's not just beautiful – that's incredibly beautiful!' The adverse impact of inflated praise on children with low self-esteem. *Psychological Science*, 25, 728–35.

Bruner, J. S. (1983) Education as social invention. *Journal of Social Issues*, 39, 129–41.

Brunner, D. P., Dijk, D. J., Tobler, I. and Borbely, A. A. (1990) Effect of partial sleep deprivation on sleep stages and EEG power spectra. *Electroencephalography and Clinical Neurophysiology*, 75, 492–9.

Bryan, J. H. and Test, M. A. (1967) Models and helping: Naturalistic studies in aiding behaviour. *Journal of Personality and Social Psychology*, 6, 400–7.

Buck, L. and Axel, R. (1991) A novel multigene family may encode odorant receptors: A molecular basis for odor recognition. *Cell*, 65, 175–87.

Buck, R. (1984) *The Communication of Emotion*. New York: Guilford Press.

Buckner, R. L., Petersen, S. E., Ojemann, J. G. et al. (1995) Functional anatomical studies of explicit and implicit memory retrieval tasks. *Journal of Neuroscience*, 15, 12–29.

Buckner, R. L., Snyder, A. Z., Shannon, B. J. et al. (2005) Molecular, structural, and functional characterization of Alzheimer's disease: Evidence for a relationship between default activity, amyloid, and memory. *Journal of Neuroscience*, 25, 7709–17.

Budesheim, T. L. and DePaola, S. J. (1994) Beauty or the beast? The effects of appearance, personality, and issue information on evaluations of political candidates. *Personality and Social Psychology Bulletin*, 20, 339–48.

Bull, R., Epsy, K. A. and Wiebe, S. A. (2008) Short-term working memory and executive functioning in preschoolers: Longitudinal predictors of mathematical achievement at age 7 years. *Developmental Neuropsychology*, 33, 205–28.

Bunge, S. A., Wendelken, C., Badre, D. and Wagner, A. D. (2005) Analogical reasoning and prefrontal cortex: Evidence for separable retrieval and integration mechanisms. *Cerebral Cortex*, 15, 239–49.

Bureau of Justice Statistics (2008) *Prisoners in 2007*. Washington, DC: US Department of Justice.

Burger, J. M. (1999) The foot-in-the-door compliance procedure: A multiple-process analysis and review. *Personality and Social Psychology Review*, 3, 303–25.

Burgess, E. W. and Wallin, P. (1953) *Engagement and Marriage*. New York: Lippincott.

Burgoon, J. K., Buller, D. B. and Woodall, W. G. (1989) *Nonverbal Communication: The Unspoken Dialogue*. New York: Harper & Row.

Burkart, J. M., Fehr, E., Efferson, C. and van Schaik, C. P. (2007) Other-regarding preferences in a non-human primate: Common marmosets provision food altruistically. *Proceedings of the National Academy*, 104, 19762–6.

Burke, D., MacKay, D. G., Worthley, J. S. and Wade, E. (1991) On the tip of the tongue: What causes word failure in young and older adults? *Journal of Memory and Language*, 30, 237–46.

Burnett, S. and Blakemore, S. J. (2009) The development of adolescent social cognition. *Annals of the New York Academy of Science*, 1167, 51–6.

Burnstein, E., Crandall, C. and Kitayama, S. (1994) Some neo-Darwinian decision rules for altruism: Weighing cues for inclusive fitness as a function of the biological importance of the decision. *Journal of Personality & Social Psychology*, 67, 773–89.

Burris, C. T. and Branscombe, N. R. (2005) Distorted distance estimation induced by a self-relevant national boundary. *Journal of Experimental Social Psychology*, 41, 305–12.

Burton, A. M. and Bruce, V. (1993) Naming faces and naming names: Exploring an interactive activation model of person recognition. *Memory*, 1, 457–80.

Bushman, B. J. and Baumeister, R. F. (1998) Threatened egotism, narcissism, self-esteem, and direct and displaced aggression: Does self-love or self-hate lead to violence? *Journal of Personality and Social Psychology*, 75, 219–29.

Bushman, B. J., Baumeister, R. F. and Phillips, C. M. (2001) Do people aggress to improve mood? Catharsis beliefs, affect regulation opportunity and aggressive responding. *Journal of Personality and Social Psychology*, 81, 17–32.

Buss, A. H. and Plomin, R. (1984) *Temperament: Early Developing Personality Traits*. Hillsdale, NJ: Erlbaum.

Buss, D. M. (1985) Human mate selection. *American Scientist*, 73, 47–51.

Buss, D. M. (1989) Sex differences in human mate preferences: Evolutionary hypotheses tested in 37 cultures. *Behavioral and Brain Sciences*, 12, 1–49.

Buss, D. M. (1994) *The Evolution of Desire: Strategies of Human Mating*. New York: Basic Books.

Buss, D. M. (1996) Social adaptation and five major factors of personality. In J. S. Wiggins (ed.) *The Five-factor Model of Personality: Theoretical Perspectives* (pp. 180–208). New York: Guilford Press.

Buss, D. M. (1999) *Evolutionary Psychology: The New Science of the Mind*. Boston: Allyn & Bacon.

Buss, D. M. and Kenrick, D. T. (1998) Evolutionary social psychology. In D. T. Gilbert, S. T. Fiske and G. Lindzey (eds) *The Handbook of Social Psychology* (4th edn, pp. 982–1026). New York: McGraw-Hill.

Buss, D. M. and Schmitt, D. P. (1993) Sexual strategies theory: An evolutionary perspective on human mating. *Psychological Review*, 100, 204–32.

Buss, D. M., Abbott, M., Angleitner, A. et al. (1990) International preferences in selecting mates: A study of 37 cultures. *Journal of Cross-Cultural Psychology*, 21, 5–47.

Buss, D. M., Haselton, M. G., Shackelford, T. K. et al. (1998) Adaptations, exaptations, and spandrels. *American Psychologist*, 53, 533–48.

Bussey, K. and Bandura, A. (1992) Self-regulatory mechanisms governing gender development. *Child Development*, 63, 1236–50.

Buston, P. M., Munday, P. L. and Warner, R. R. (2004) Evolutionary biology: Sex change and relative body size in animals. *Nature*, 428(6983), doi: 10.1038/nature02512.

Butterworth, B., Reeve, R., Reynolds, F. and Lloyd, D. (2008) Numerical thought with and without words: Evidence from indigenous Australian children. *Proceedings of the National Academy of Sciences*, 105, 13179–84.

Butterworth, G. E. (1998) What is special about pointing in babies? In F. Simion and G. E. Butterworth (eds) *The Development of Sensory, Motor and Cognitive Processes in Infancy* (pp. 171–90). Hove: Psychology Press.

Butzlaff, R. L. and Hooley, J. M. (1998) Expressed emotion and psychiatric relapse: A meta-analysis. *Archives of General Psychiatry*, 55, 547–52.

Buunk, A. P. (1997) Personality, birth order and attachment styles as related to various types of jealousy. *Personality and Individual Differences*, 23, 997–1006.

Buunk, A. P. and Dijkstra, P. (2008) Affiliation, attraction and close relationships. In M. Hewstone, W. Stroebe and K. Jonas (eds) *Introduction to Social Psychology: A European Perspective*. London: Blackwell.

Byrne, D. and Clore, G. L. (1970) A reinforcement model of evaluative responses. *Personality: An International Journal*, 1, 103–28.

Byrne, D. and Nelson, D. (1965) Attraction as a linear function of proportion of positive reinforcements. *Journal of Personality and Social Psychology*, 1, 659–63.

Byrne, D., Ervin, C. R. and Lamberth, J. (1970) Continuity between the experimental study of attraction and real-life computer dating. *Journal of Personality and Social Psychology*, 16, 157–65.

Byrne, D., Allgeier, A. R., Winslow, L. and Buckman, J. (1975) The situational facilitation of interpersonal attraction: A three-factor hypothesis. *Journal of Applied Social Psychology*, 5, 1–15.

Cabeza, R. (2002) Hemispheric asymmetry reduction in older adults: The HAROLD model. *Psychology and Aging*, 17, 85–100.

Cabeza, R., Rao, S., Wagner, A. D. et al. (2001) Can medial temporal lobe regions distinguish true from false? An event-related fMRI study of veridical and illusory recognition memory. *Proceedings of the National Academy of Sciences*, 98, 4805–10.

Cacioppo, J. T., Fowler, J. H. and Christakis, N. A. (2009) Alone in the crowd: The structure and spread of loneliness in a large social network. *Journal of Personality and Social Psychology*, 97, 977–91.

Cacioppo, J. T., Hawkley, L. C. and Berntson, G. G. (2003) The anatomy of loneliness. *Current Directions in Psychological Science*, 12, 71–4.

Cahill, L. and McGaugh, J. L. (1998) Mechanisms of emotional arousal and lasting declarative memory. *Trends in Neurosciences*, 21, 294–9.

Cahill, L., Haier, R. J., Fallon, J. et al. (1996) Amygdala activity at encoding correlated with long-term, free recall of emotional information. *Proceedings of the National Academy of Sciences*, 93, 8016–21.

Cain, K. M. and Dweck, C .S. (1995) The relation between motivational patterns and achievement cognitions through the elementary years. *Merrill-Palmer Quarterly*, 41, 25–52.

Calder, A. J., Young, A. W., Rowland, D. et al. (1996) Facial emotion recognition after bilateral amygdala damage: Differentially severe impairment of fear. *Cognitive Neuropsychology*, 13, 699–745.

Callaghan, T., Rochat, P., Lillard, A. et al. (2005) Synchrony in the onset of mental-state reasoning: Evidence from five cultures. *Psychological Science*, 16, 378–84.

Cameron, J. and Pierce, W. D. (1996) The debate about rewards and intrinsic motivation: Protests and accusations do not alter the results. *Review of Educational Research*, 66, 39–51.

Campbell, A. (1999) Staying alive: Evolution, culture, and women's intra-sexual aggression. *Behavioral & Brain Sciences*, 22, 203–52.

Campbell, C. M. and Edwards, R. R. (2012) Ethnic differences in pain and pain management. *Pain Management*, 2, 219–30.

Campbell, C. M., Edwards, R. R. and Fillingim, R. B. (2005) Ethnic differences in responses to multiple experimental pain stimuli. *Pain*, 113, 20–6.

Campbell, D. T. (1958) Common fate, similarity and other indices of the status of the aggregates of persons as social entities. *Behavioral Science*, 3, 14–25.

Campos, J. J. and Stenberg, C. R. (1981) Perception, appraisal and emotion: The onset of social referencing. In M. E. Lamb and L. R. Sherrod (eds) *Infant Social Cognition: Empirical and Theoretical Considerations* (pp. 273–314). Hillsdale, NJ: Erlbaum.

Campos, J. J., Langer, A. and Krowitz, A. (1970) Cardiac responses on the visual cliff in prelocomotor human infants. *Science*, 170, 196–7.

Canetto, S. and Lester, D. (1995) Gender and the primary prevention of suicide mortality. *Suicide and Life Threatening Behavior*, 25, 85–9.

Cannon, W. B. (1927) The James-Lange theory of emotion: A critical examination and alternate theory. *American Journal of Psychology*, 39, 106–24.

Cannon, W. B. (1929) *Bodily Changes in Pain, Hunger, Fear, and Rage: An Account of Recent Research into the Function of Emotional Excitement* (2nd edn). New York: Appleton-Century-Crofts.

Cantor, N. (1990) From thought to behavior: 'Having' and 'doing' in the study of personality and cognition. *American Psychologist*, 45, 735–50.

Caplan, A. L. (ed.) (1992) *When Medicine Went Mad: Bioethics and the Holocaust.* Totowa, NJ: Humana Press.

Caporael, L. (1976) Ergotism: The satan loosed in Salem? *Science*, 192, 21–6.

Caputo, G. B. (2010) Strange-face-in-the-mirror illusion. *Perception*, 39, 1007–8.

Carey, S. (1985) *Conceptual Change in Childhood*. Cambridge, MA: MIT Press.

Carey, S. (2000) Science education as conceptual change. *Journal of Applied Developmental Psychology*, 21, 13–19.

Carey, S. (2009) *The Origins of Concepts*. Oxford: OUP.

Carlo, G., Eisenberg, N., Troyer, D. et al. (1991) The altruistic personality: In what contexts is it apparent? *Journal of Personality and Social Psychology*, 61, 450–8.

Carlson, S. M. and Moses, L. J. (2001) Individual differences in inhibitory control and children's theory of mind. *Child Development*, 72, 1032–53.

Carmichael Olson, H., Streissguth, A. P., Sampson, P. D. et al. (1997) Association of prenatal alcohol exposure with behavioral and learning problems in early adolescence. *Journal of the American Academy of Child and Adolescent Psychiatry*, 36, 1187–94.

Carolson, E. A. (1998) A prospective longitudinal study of attachment disorganization/disorientation. *Child Development*, 69, 1107–28.

Carpenter, M., Nagell, K. and Tomasello, M. (1998) Social cognition, joint attention and communicative competence from 9 to 15 months of age. *Monographs of the Society for Research in Child Development*, 63(4, Serial no. 255).

Carpenter, S., Pashler, H. and Cepeda, N. (2009) Using tests to enhance 8th grade students' retention of U.S. history facts. *Applied Cognitive Psychology*, 23, 760–71.

Carr, L., Iacoboni, M., Dubeau, M. et al. (2003) Neural mechanisms of empathy in humans: A relay from neural systems for imitation to limbic areas. *Proceedings of the National Academy of Sciences*, 100, 5497–502.

Carroll, J. B. (1993) *Human Cognitive Abilities.* Cambridge: CUP.

Carson, R. C., Butcher, J. N. and Mineka, S. (2000) *Abnormal Psychology and Modern Life* (11th edn). Boston: Allyn & Bacon.

Carstensen, L. L. (1992) Social and emotional patterns in adulthood: Support for socioemotional selectivity theory. *Psychology and Aging*, 7, 331–8.

Carstensen, L. L. and Fredrickson, B. L. (1998) Influence of HIV status and age on cognitive representations of others. *Health Psychology*, 17, 1–10.

Carstensen, L. L. and Turk-Charles, S. (1994) The salience of emotion across the adult life span. *Psychology and Aging*, 9, 259–64.

Carstensen, L. L., Isaacowitz, D. M. and Charles, S. T. (1999) Taking time seriously: A theory of socioemotional selectivity. *American Psychologist*, 54, 165–81.

Carstensen, L. L., Pasupathi, M., Mayr, U. and Nesselroade, J. R. (2000) Emotional experience in everyday life across the adult life span. *Journal of Personality & Social Psychology*, 79, 644–55.

Casey, B. J. and Caudle, K. (2013) The teenage brain: Self control. *Current Directions in Psychological Science*, 22, 82–7.

Casey, B. J., Somerville, L .H., Gotlib, I. H. et al. (2011) Behavioral and neural correlates of delay of gratification 40 years later. *Proceedings of the National Academy of Sciences,* 108, 14998–15003.

Cash, T. E. and Kilcullen, R. N. (1985). The eye of the beholder: Susceptibility to sexism and beautyism in the evaluation of managerial applicants. *Journal of Applied Social Psychology*, 15, 591–605.

Caspi, A. and Herbener, E. S. (1990) Continuity and change: Assortative marriage and the consistency of personality in adulthood. *Journal of Personality and Social Psychology*, 58, 250–8.

Caspi, A., Roberts, B. W. and Shiner, R. L. (2005) Personality development: Stability and change. *Annual Review of Psychology*, 56, 453–84.

Caspi, A., Lynam, D., Moffitt, T. E. and Silva, P. A. (1993) Unraveling girls' delinquency: Biological, dispositional, and contextual contributions to adolescent misbehavior. *Developmental Psychology*, 29, 19–30.

Catrambone, R. (2002) The effects of surface and structural feature matches on the access of story analogs. *Journal of Experimental Psychology: Learning, Memory and Cognition*, 28, 318–34.

Cattell, R. B. (1950) *Personality: A Systematic, Theoretical, and Factual Study.* New York: McGraw-Hill.

CDC (Centers for Disease Control) (1988) Health status of Vietnam veterans, I. Psychosocial characteristics. *Journal of the American Medical Association*, 259, 2701–8.

Ceci, S. J. (1991) How much does schooling influence general intelligence and its cognitive components? A reassessment of the evidence. *Developmental Psychology*, 27, 703–22.

Ceci, S. J. and Williams, W. M. (1997) Schooling, intelligence, and income. *American Psychologist*, 52, 1051–8.

Cepeda, N., Pashler, H., Vul, E. et al. (2006) Distributed practice in verbal recall tasks: A review and quantitative synthesis. *Psychological Bulletin*, 132, 354–80.

Chaiken, S. (1980) Heuristic versus systematic information processing and the use of source versus message cues in persuasion. *Journal of Personality and Social Psychology*, 39, 752–66.

Chalmers, D. (1996) *The Conscious Mind: In Search of a Fundamental Theory.* New York: OUP.

Chambless, D. L., Baker, M. J., Baucom, D. H. et al. (1998) Update on empirically validated therapies, II. *Clinical Psychologist*, 51(1), 3–14.

Champagne, A. B., Klopfer, L. E. and Anderson, J. H. (1980) Factors influencing the learning of classical mechanics. *American Journal of Physics*, 48, 1074–9.

Champagne, F. A., Francis, D. D., Mar, A. and Meaney, M. J. (2003) Naturally-occurring variations in maternal care in the rat as a mediating influence for the effects of environment on the development of individual differences in stress reactivity. *Physiology & Behavior*, 79, 359–71.

Chandrashekar, J., Hoon, M. A., Ryba, N. J. and Zuker, C. S. (2006) The receptors and cells for human tastes. *Nature*, 444, 288–94.

Charles, S. T., Reynolds, C. A. and Gatz, M. (2001) Age-related differences and change in positive and negative affect over 23 years. *Journal of Personality and Social Psychology*, 80, 136–51.

Charness, N. (1981) Aging and skilled problem solving. *Journal of Experimental Psychology: General*, 110, 21–38.

Chartrand, T. L. and Bargh, J. A. (1999) The chameleon effect: The perception-behavior link and social interaction. *Journal of Personality and Social Psychology*, 76, 893–910.

Chartrand, T. L., van Baaren, R. B. and Bargh, J. A. (2006) Linking automatic evaluation to mood and information processing style: Consequences for experienced affect, impression formation, and stereotyping. *Journal of Experimental Psychology: General,* 135, 70–7.

Chen, S. C. (1937) Social modification of the activity of ants in nest-building. *Physiological Zoology*, 10, 420–36.

Cheney, D. L. and Seyfarth, R. M. (1990) *How Monkeys See the World.* Chicago: University of Chicago Press.

Cheng, P. W. and Holyoak, K. J. (1989) On the natural selection of reasoning theories. *Cognition*, 33, 285–313.

Cherlin, A. J. (ed.) (1992) *Marriage, Divorce, Remarriage* (2nd edn). Cambridge, MA: Harvard University Press.

Chernyak, N. and Kushnir, T. (2013) Giving preschoolers choice increases sharing behaviour. *Psychological Science*, 24, 1971–9.

Cherry, C. (1953) Some experiments on the recognition of speech with one and two ears. *Journal of the Acoustical Society of America*, 25, 275–9.

Chess, S. and Thomas, A. (1982) Infant bonding: Mystique and reality. *American Journal of Orthopsychiatry*, 52, 213–21.

Chi, M. T. and Koeske, R. D. (1983) Network representation of a child's dinosaur knowledge. *Developmental Psychology*, 19, 29–39.

Cho, S., Moody, T. D., Fernandino, L. et al. (2009) Common and dissociable prefrontal loci associated with component mechanisms of analogical reasoning. *Cerebral Cortex*, 20, 524–33.

Choi, I., Nisbett, R. E. and Norenzayan, A. (1999) Causal attribution across cultures: Variation and universality. *Psychological Bulletin*, 125, 47–63.

Chomsky, N. (1959) A review of *Verbal Behavior* by B. F. Skinner. *Language*, 35, 26–58.

Chomsky, N. (1986) *Knowledge of Language: Its Nature, Origin, and Use.* New York: Praeger.

Chomsky, N. (1998) *Language and the Problems of Knowledge.* Cambridge, MA: MIT Press.

Chorover, S. L. (1980) *From Genesis to Genocide: The Meaning of Human Nature and the Power of Behavior Control.* Cambridge, MA: MIT Press.

Christensen, B. T. and Schunn, C. D. (2007) The relationship of analogical distance to analogical function and pre-inventive structure: The case of engineering design. *Memory & Cognition*, 35, 29–38.

Christianson, S.-A. and Loftus, E. F. (1987) Memory for traumatic events. *Applied Cognitive Psychology*, 1, 225–39.

Christoff, K., Keramatian, K., Gordon, A. M. et al. (2009) Prefrontal organization of cognitive control according to levels of abstraction. *Brain Research*, 1286, 94–105.

Chua, H. F., Boland, J. E. and Nisbett, R. E. (2005) Cultural variation in eye movements during scene perception. *Proceedings of the National Academy of Sciences,* 102, 12629–33.

Cialdini, R. B. (2005) Don't throw in the towel: Use social influence research. *American Psychological Society*, 18, 33–4.
Cialdini, R. B. and Trost, M. R. (1998) Social influence: Social norms, conformity, and compliance. In D. T. Gilbert, S. T. Fiske and G. Lindzey (eds) *The Handbook of Social Psychology* (4th edn, vol. 2, pp. 151–92). New York: McGraw-Hill.
Cialdini, R. B., Trost, M. R. and Newsom, J. T. (1995) Preference for consistency: The development of a valid measure and the discovery of surprising behavioral implications. *Journal of Personality and Social Psychology*, 69, 318–28.
Cialdini, R. B., Vincent, J. E., Lewis, S. K. et al. (1975) Reciprocal concessions procedure for inducing compliance: The door-in-the-face technique. *Journal of Personality and Social Psychology*, 31, 206–15.
Cicchetti, D. and Toth, S. L. (1998) Perspectives on research and practice in developmental psychopathology. In I. E. Sigel and K. A. Renninger (eds) *Handbook of Child Psychology*, vol. 4. *Child Psychology in Practice* (5th edn, pp. 479–583). New York: Wiley.
Clancy, S. A. (2005) *Abducted: How People Come to Believe They Were Kidnapped by Aliens.* Cambridge. MA: Harvard University Press.
Clark, H. H. and Carlson, T. B. (1981) Context for comprehension. In J. Long and A. Baddeley (eds) *Attention and Performance IX: Information Processing* (pp. 313–30). Hillsdale, NJ: Lawrence Erlbaum.
Clark, H. H. and Clark, E. V. (1977) *Psychology and Language*. New York: Harcourt Brace Jovanovich.
Clark, L. A. (2007) Assessment and diagnosis of personality disorder: Perennial issues and emerging conceptualization. *Annual Review of Psychology*, 58, 227–57.
Clark, R. D. and Hatfield, E. (1989) Gender differences in receptivity to sexual offers. *Journal of Psychology and Human Sexuality*, 2, 39–55.
Clay, Z., Pople, S., Hood, B. and Kita, S. (2014) Young children make their gestural communication systems more language-like: Segmentation and linearization of semantic elements in motion events. *Psychological Science*, 25(8), 1518–25.
Cleckley, H. M. (1976) *The Mask of Sanity* (5th edn). St Louis: Mosby.
Cohen, D. (1997) A critique of the use of neuroleptic drugs in psychiatry. In S. Fisher and R. P. Greenberg (eds) *From Placebo to Panacea: Putting Psychiatric Drugs to Test* (pp. 173–228). New York: Wiley.
Cohen, D., Nisbett, R. E., Bowdle, B. F. and Schwarz, N. (1996) Insult, aggression, and the southern culture of honor: An 'experimental ethnography'. *Journal of Personality and Social Psychology*, 70, 945–60.
Cohen, G. (1990) Why is it difficult to put names to faces? *British Journal of Psychology*, 81, 287–97.
Cohen, N. J. and Squire, L. R. (1980) Preserved learning and retention of pattern analyzing skill in amnesics: Dissociation of knowing how and knowing that. *Science*, 210, 207–10.
Cohen, S. (1999) Social status and susceptibility to respiratory infections. *New York Academy of Sciences*, 896, 246–53.
Cohen, S., Evans, G. W., Krantz, D. S. and Stokols, D. (1980) Physiological, motivational, and cognitive effects of aircraft noise on children. *American Psychologist*, 35, 231–43.
Cohen, S., Frank, E., Doyle, W. J. et al. (1998) Types of stressors that increase susceptibility to the common cold in healthy adults. *Health Psychology*, 17, 214–23.
Colasanti, A., Salamon, E., Schruers, K. et al. (2008) Carbon dioxide-induced emotion and respiratory symptoms in healthy volunteers. *Neuropsychopharmacology*, 33, 3103–10.
Colcombe, S. J. and Kramer, A. F. (2003) Fitness effects on the cognitive function of older adults: A meta-analysis study. *Psychological Science*, 14, 125–30.
Colcombe, S. J., Erickson, K. I., Scalf, P. E. et al. (2006) Aerobic exercise training increases brain volume in aging humans. *Journal of Gerontology A: Biological Sciences and Medical Sciences*, 11, 1166–70.
Cole, G. G. and Wilkins, A. J. (2013) Fear of holes. *Psychological Science*, 24, 1980–5.
Cole, M. (1996) *Cultural Psychology: A Once and Future Discipline.* Cambridge, MA: Harvard University Press.
Cole, S. W., Hawkley, L. C., Arevalo, J. M. et al. (2007) Social regulation of gene expression in human leukocytes. *Genome Biology*, 8, R189.
Cole, W. G., Lingman, J. M. and Adolph, K. E. (2012) Go naked: Diapers affect infant walking. *Developmental Science*, 15, 783–90.
Colwill, R. M. and Motzkin, D. K. (1994) Encoding of the unconditioned stimulus in Pavlovian conditioning. *Animal Learning and Behaviour,* 22, 384–94.
Colzato, L. S., Steenbergen, L., de Kwaadsteniet, E. W. et al. (2013) Tryptophan promotes interpersonal trust. *Psychological Science*, 24, 2575–7.
Condon, J. W. and Crano, W. D. (1988) Inferred evaluation and the relation between attitude similarity and interpersonal attraction. *Journal of Personality and Social Psychology*, 54, 789–97.
Conduit, R. and Coleman, G. (1998) Conditioned salivation and associated dreams from REM sleep. *Dreaming*, 8, 243–62.
Conner, M., Kirk, S. F., Cade, J. E. and Barrett, J. H. (2003) Environmental influences: Factors influencing a woman's decision to use dietary supplements. *Journal of Nutrition*, 133, 1978–82.
Connolly, K. (1968) The social facilitation of preening behavior of *Drosophilia melanogaster*. *Animal Behavior*, 16, 385–91.
Conway, A. R., Cowan, N., Bunting, M. F. et al. (2002) A latent variable analysis of working memory capacity, short-term memory capacity, processing speed and general fluid intelligence. *Intelligence*, 30, 163–83.
Conway, M. A. and Ross, M. (1984) Getting what you want by revising what you had. *Journal of Personality and Social Psychology*, 47, 738–48.
Conway, M. A. and Rubin, D. C. (1993) The structure of autobiographical memory. In A. F. Collins, S. E. Gathercole, M. A. Conway and P. E. Morris (eds) *Theories of Memory* (pp. 163–188). Hove: Psychology Press.
Conway, M. A., Anderson, S. J., Larsen, S. F. et al. (1994) The formation of flashbulb memories. *Memory and Cognition*, 22, 326–43.
Conwell, Y., Duberstein, P. R., Cox, C. et al. (1996) Relationships of age and axis I diagnoses in victims of completed suicide: A psychological autopsy study. *American Journal of Psychiatry*, 153, 1001–8.
Cook, E. P. (1985) *Psychological Androgyny*. New York: Pergamon Press.
Cook, M. and Mineka, S. (1989) Observational conditioning of fear to fear-relevant versus fear-irrelevant stimuli in rhesus monkeys. *Journal of Abnormal Psychology*, 98, 448–59.
Cook, M. and Mineka, S. (1990) Selective associations in the observational conditioning of fear in rhesus monkeys. *Journal of Experimental Psychology: Animal Behavior Process*, 16, 372–89.
Coons, P. M. (1994) Confirmation of childhood abuse in child and adolescent cases of multiple personality disorder and dissociative disorder not otherwise specified. *Journal of Nervous and Mental Disease*, 182, 461–4.
Cooper, J. and Fazio, R. H. (1984) A new look at dissonance theory. In L. Berkowitz (ed.) *Advances in Experimental Social Psychology* (vol. 17, pp. 229–66). New York: Academic Press.
Cooper, J. R., Bloom, F. E. and Roth, R. H. (2003) *Biochemical Basis of Neuropharmacology*. New York: OUP.
Cooper, M. L., Shapiro, C. M. and Powers, A. M. (1998) Motivations for sex and risky sexual behavior among adolescents and young adults: A functional perspective. *Journal of Personality and Social Psychology*, 75, 1528–58.
Coover, J. E. (1913) The feeling of being stared at – experimental. *American Journal of Psychology*, 24, 570–5.
Corbetta, M., Shulman, G. L., Miezin, F. M. and Petersen, S. E. (1995) Superior parietal cortex activation during spatial attention shifts and visual feature conjunction. *Science*, 270, 802–5.

Coren, S. (1997) *Sleep Thieves.* New York: Free Press.

Corkin, S. (2002) What's new with the amnesic patient HM? *Nature Reviews Neuroscience*, 3, 153–60.

Correll, J., Park, B., Judd, C. M. and Wittenbrink, B. (2002) The police officer's dilemma: Using ethnicity to disambiguate potentially threatening individuals. *Journal of Personality and Social Psychology*, 83, 1314–29.

Corsi, P. (1991) *The Enchanted Loom: Chapters in the History of Neuroscience.* New York: OUP.

Corsini, R. J. (2000) Introduction. In R. J. Corsini and D. Wedding (eds) *Current Psychotherapies* (6th edn, pp. 1–15). Itasca, IL: F. E. Peacock.

Corteen, R. S. and Dunn, D. (1974) Shock-associated words in a nonattended message: A test for momentary awareness. *Journal of Experimental Psychology*, 102, 1143–4.

Coryell, W., Endicott, J., Maser, J. D. et al. (1995) The likelihood of recurrence in bipolar affective disorder: The importance of episode recency. *Journal of Affective Disorders*, 33, 201–6.

Cosmides, L. (1989) The logic of social exchange: Has natural selection shaped how humans reason? Studies with the Wason selection task. *Cognition*, 31, 187–276.

Cosmides, L. and Tooby J. (1994) Origins of domain-specificity: The evolution of functional organization. In L.A. Hirschfeld and S. Gelman (eds) *Mapping the Mind: Domain Specificity in Cognition and Culture* (pp. 85–116). New York: CUP.

Cottrell, J. E. and Winer, G. A. (1994) Development in the understanding of perception: The decline of extramission perception beliefs. *Developmental Psychology*, 30, 218–28.

Cottrell, J. E., Winer, G. A. and Smith, M. C. (1996) Beliefs of children and adults about feeling stares of unseen others. *Developmental Psychology*, 32, 50–61.

Cottrell, N. B., Wack, D. L., Sekerak, G. J. and Rittle, R. H. (1968) Social facilitation of dominant responses by the presence of an audience and the mere presence of others. *Journal of Personality and Social Psychology*, 9, 245–50.

Coulson, S. E., O'Dwyer, N., Adams, R. and Croxson, G. R. (2004) Expression of emotion and quality of life following facial nerve paralysis. *Otology & Neurotology*, 25, 1014–19.

Cowan, W. M. (1979) The development of the human brain. *Scientific American*, 241, 112–33.

Cox, D. and Cowling, P. (1989) *Are You Normal?* London: Tower Press.

Coyne, J. A. (2000) Of vice and men: The laity tales of evolutionary psychology. *The New Republic*, 147, 27–34.

Coyne, J. C. and Whiffen, V. E. (1995) Issues in personality as diathesis for depression: The case of sociotropy-dependency and autonomy self-criticism. *Psychological Bulletin*, 118, 358–78.

Craik, F. I. and Lockhart, R. S. (1972) Levels of processing: A framework for memory research. *Journal of Verbal Learning and Verbal Behavior*, 11, 671–84.

Craik, F. I. and Tulving, E. (1975) Depth of processing and the retention of words in episodic memory. *Journal of Experimental Psychology: General*, 104, 268–94.

Craik, F. I., Govoni, R., Naveh-Benjamin, M. and Anderson, N. D. (1996) The effects of divided attention on encoding and retrieval processes in human memory. *Journal of Experimental Psychology: General*, 125, 159–80.

Cramer, R. E., Schaefer, J. T. and Reid, S. (1996) Identifying the ideal mate: More evidence for male-female convergence. *Current Psychology: Developmental, Learning, Personality, Social*, 15, 157–66.

Craske, M. G. (1999) *Anxiety Disorders: Psychological Approaches to Theory and Treatment.* Boulder, CO: Westview.

Crespi, L. P. (1942) Quantitative variation in incentive and performance in the white rat. *American Journal of Psychology*, 55, 467–517.

Crick, N. R. and Grotpeter, J. K. (1995) Relational aggression, gender, and social-psychological adjustment. *Child Development*, 66, 710–22.

Critelli, J. W. and Ee, J. S. (1996) Stress and physical illness: Development of an integrative model. In T. W. Miller (ed.) *Theory and Assessment of Stressful Life Events* (pp. 139–59). Madison, CT: International Universities Press.

Crocker, J. and Wolfe, C. T. (2001) Contingencies of self-worth. *Psychological Review*, 108(3), 593–623.

Crockett, M. J. (2009) The neurochemistry of fairness. Clarifying the link between serotonin and prosocial behavior. *Annals of the New York Academy of Sciences*, 1167, 76–86.

Crockett, M. J., Clark, L., Tabibnia, G. et al. (2008) Serotonin modulates behavioral reactions to unfairness. *Science*, 320, 1739.

Crombag, H. F., Wagenaar, W. A. and van Koppen, P. J. (1996) Crashing memories and the problem of 'source monitoring'. *Applied Cognitive Psychology*, 10, 95–104.

Cromby, J., Harper, D. and Reavy, P. (2013) *Psychology, Mental Health and Distress.* Basingstoke: Palgrave Macmillan.

Cross, P. (1977) Not can but will college teachers be improved? *New Directions for Higher Education*, 17, 1–15.

Cross-National Collaborative Research Group (1992) The changing rate of major depression: Cross-national comparison. *Journal of the American Medical Association*, 268, 3098–105.

Crow, T. J. (1980) Molecular pathology of schizophrenia: More than one disease process? *British Medical Journal*, 280, 66–8.

Crowe, R. (1990) Panic disorder: Genetic considerations. *Journal of Psychiatric Researchers*, 24, 129–34.

Crowley, K., Callanan, M. A., Tenenbaum, H. R. and Allen, E. (2001) Parents explain more often to boys than to girls during shared scientific thinking. *Psychological Science*, 12, 258–61.

Csermansky, J. G. and Grace, A. A. (1998) New models of the pathophysiology of schizophrenia: Editor's introduction. *Schizophrenia Bulletin*, 24, 185–7.

Csibra, G. and Gergely, G. (2006) Social learning and social cognition: The case of pedagogy. In M. H. Johnson and Y. M. Munakata (eds) *Processes of Change in Brain and Cognitive Development: Attention and Performance* XXI (pp. 249–74). Oxford: OUP.

Csikszentmihalyi, M. (1990) *Flow: The Psychology of Optimal Experience.* New York: Harper & Row.

Csikszentmihalyi, M. and Larson, R. (1987) Validity and reliability of the experience-sampling method. *Journal of Nervous & Mental Disease*, 175, 526–36.

Cumming, S., Hay, P., Lee, T. and Sachdev, P. (1995) Neuropsychological outcome from psychosurgery for obsessive-compulsive disorder. *Australian and New Zealand Journal of Psychiatry*, 29, 293–8.

Cummings, D. E., Purnell, J. Q., Frayo, R. S. et al. (2001) A preprandial rise in plasma ghrelin levels suggests a role in meal initiation in humans. *Diabetes*, 50, 1714–19.

Cunningham, M. R., Barbee, A. P. and Pike, C. L. (1990) What do women want? Facialmetric assessment of multiple motives in the perception of male facial physical attractiveness. *Journal of Personality & Social Psychology*, 59, 61–72.

Cunningham, M. R., Roberts, A. R., Barbee, A. P. et al. (1995) 'Their ideas of beauty are, on the whole, the same as ours': Consistency and variability in the cross-cultural perception of female physical attractiveness. *Journal of Personality and Social Psychology*, 68, 261–79.

Curran, J. P. and Lippold, S. (1975) The effects of physical attraction and attitude similarity on attraction in dating dyads. *Journal of Personality*, 43, 528–39.

Curtiss, S. (1977) *Genie: A Psycholinguistic Study of a Modern-day 'Wild-child'.* New York: Academic Press.

Custers, E. and ten Cate, O. (2011) Very long-term retention of basic science knowledge in doctors after graduation. *Medical Education*, 45, 422–30.

Cutler, S. and Nolen-Hoeksema, S. (1991) Accounting for sex differences in depression through female victimization: Childhood sexual abuse. *Sex Roles*, 24, 425–38.

Dabbs, J. M., Strong, R. and Milun, R. (1997) Exploring the mind of testosterone: A beeper study. *Journal of Research in Personality*, 31, 577–87.

Dabbs, J. M., Carr, T. S., Frady, R. L. and Riad, J. K. (1995) Testosterone, crime, and misbehavior among 692 male prison inmates. *Personality and Individual Differences*, 18, 627–33.

Dabbs, J. M., Bernieri, F. J., Strong, R. K. et al. (2001) Going on stage: Testosterone in greetings and meetings. *Journal of Research in Personality*, 35, 27–40.

D'Agostino, P. R. and Fincher-Kiefer, R. (1992) Need for cognition and correspondence bias. *Social Cognition*, 10, 151–63.

Dahl, R. E. (2001) Affect regulation, brain development, and behavioural/emotional health in adolescence. *CNS Spectrum*, 6, 60–72.

Dally, P. (1999) *The Marriage of Heaven and Hell: Manic Depression and the Life of Virginia Woolf.* New York: St Martin's Griffin.

Dalton, P. (2003) Olfaction. In H. Pashler and S. Yantis (eds) *Stevens' Handbook of Experimental Psychology*, vol. 1. *Sensation and Perception* (3rd edn, pp. 691–746). New York: Wiley.

Daly, M. and Wilson, M. (1988) Evolutionary social psychology and family homicide. *Science*, 242, 519–24.

Daly, M., Wilson, M. and Vasdev, S. (2001) Income inequality and homicide rates in Canada and the United States. *Canadian Journal of Criminology*, 43, 219–36.

Damasio, A. R. (1989) Time-locked multiregional retroactivation: A systems-level proposal for the neural substrates of recall and recognition. *Cognition*, 33, 25–62.

Damasio, A. R. (1994) *Descartes' Error: Emotion, Reason, and the Human Brain.* New York: Putnam.

Damasio, A. R. (2005) *Descartes' Error: Emotion, Reason, and the Human Brain* (2nd edn). New York: Penguin.

Damasio, A. R., Grabowski, T. J., Bechara, A. et al. (2000) Subcortical and cortical brain activity during the feeling of self-generated emotions. *Nature Neuroscience*, 3, 1049–56.

Damasio, H., Grabowski, T. J., Tranel, D. et al. (1996) A neural basis for lexical retrieval. *Nature*, 380, 499–505.

Damsma, G., Pfaus, J. G., Wenkstern, D. et al. (1992) Sexual behavior increases dopamine transmission in the nucleus accumbens and striatum of male rats: Comparison with novelty and locomotion. *Behavioral Neurosciences*, 106, 181–91.

Daneman, M. and Carpenter, P. A. (1980) Individual differences in working memory and reading. *Journal of Verbal Learning and Verbal Behavior*, 19, 450–66.

Daniel, H. J., O'Brien, K. F., McCabe, R. B. and Quinter, V. E. (1985) Values in mate selection: A 1984 campus survey. *College Student Journal*, 19, 44–50.

Danner, D. D., Snowdon, D. A. and Friesen, W. V. (2001) Positive emotions in early life and longevity: Findings from the nun study. *Journal of Personality and Social Psychology*, 80, 804–13.

Darley, J. M. and Batson, C. D. (1973) From Jerusalem to Jericho: A study of situational and dispositional variables in helping behavior. *Journal of Personality and Social Psychology*, 27, 100–8.

Darley, J. M. and Berscheid, E. (1967) Increased liking caused by the anticipation of interpersonal contact. *Human Relations*, 10, 29–40.

Darley, J. M. and Latané, B. (1968) Bystander intervention in emergencies: Diffusion of responsibility. *Journal of Personality and Social Psychology*, 8, 377–83.

Dar-Nimrod, I. and Heine, S. J. (2006) Exposure to scientific theories affects women's math performance. *Science*, 314, 435.

Darwin, C. (1859) *On the Origin of Species by Means of Natural Selection.* London: J. Murray.

Darwin, C. (1871) *The Descent of Man, and Selection in Relation to Sex.* London: J. Murray.

Darwin, C. ([1872]1998) *The Expression of the Emotions in Man and Animals* (ed. P. Ekman). New York: OUP.

Darwin, C. (1877) A biographical sketch of an infant. *Mind: A Quarterly Review of Psychology and Philosophy*, 7, 285–94.

Darwin, C. J., Turvey, M. T. and Crowder, R. G. (1972) An auditory analogue of the Sperling partial report procedure: Evidence for brief auditory storage. *Cognitive Psychology*, 3, 255–67.

Dauer, W. and Przedborski, S. (2003) Parkinson's disease: Mechanisms and models. *Neuron*, 39, 889–909.

Davidson, R. J. (2004) What does the prefrontal cortex 'do' in affect: Perspectives on frontal EEG asymmetry research. *Biological Psychology*, 67, 219–33.

Davidson, R. J., Putnam, K. M. and Larson, C. L. (2000) Dysfunction in the neural circuitry of emotion regulation: A possible prelude to violence. *Science*, 289, 591–4.

Davidson, R. J., Pizzagalli, D., Nitschke, J. B. and Putnam, K. (2002) Depression: Perspectives from affective neuroscience. *Annual Review of Psychology*, 53, 545–74.

Davidson, R. J., Ekman, P., Saron, C. et al. (1990) Emotional expression and brain physiology I: Approach/withdrawal and cerebral asymmetry. *Journal of Personality and Social Psychology*, 58, 330–41.

Davies, G. (1988) Faces and places: Laboratory research on context and face recognition. In G. M. Davies and D. M. Thomson (eds) *Memory in Context: Context in Memory* (pp. 35–53). New York: Wiley.

Davis, D., Shaver, P. R. and Vernon, M. L. (2003) Physical, emotional and behavioural reactions to breaking up: The role of gender, age, emotional involvement and attachment style. *Journal of Personality and Social Psychology*, 29(7), 871–84.

Davis, J. and Valentine, T. (2009) CCTV on trial: Matching video images with the defendant in the dock. *Applied Cognitive Psychology*, 23, 482–505.

Davis, J. I., Senghas, A., Brandt, F. and Oschner, K. N. (2010) The effects of BOTOX injections on emotional experience. *Emotion*, 10, 433–40.

Davis, K. (1947) Final note on a case of extreme social isolation. *American Journal of Sociology*, 52, 432–7.

Davis, M. H. (1983) Measuring individual differences in empathy: Evidence for a multidimensional approach. *Journal of Personality and Social Psychology*, 44, 113–26.

Dawes, R. M. (1986) Representative thinking in clinical judgment. *Clinical Psychology Review*, 6, 425–41.

Dawes, R. M. (1994) *House of Cards: Psychology and Psychotherapy Built on Myth.* New York: Free Press.

Dawkins, R. J. (1976) *The Selfish Gene.* Oxford: OUP.

Dawood, K., Kirk, K. M., Bailey, J. M. et al. (2005) Genetic and environmental influences on the frequency of orgasm in women. *Twin Research*, 8, 27–33.

Dayan, P. and Huys, Q. J. (2009) Serotonin in affective control. *Annual Review of Neuroscience*, 32, 95–126.

Deangelis, R. A. (2008) A rising tide for Jean-Marie, Jörg, and Pauline? Xenophobic populism in comparative perspective. *Australian Journal of Politics & History*, 49, 75–92.

Deary, I. J. (2000) *Looking Down on Human Intelligence: From Psychometrics to the Brain.* New York: OUP.

Deary, I. J. and Stough, C. (1996) Intelligence and inspection time: Achievements, prospects, and problems. *American Psychologist*, 51, 599–608.

Deary, I. J., Der, G. and Ford, G. (2001) Reaction time and intelligence differences: A population based cohort study. *Intelligence*, 29, 389–99.

Deary, I. J., Lawn, M. and Bartholomew, D. J. (2008) A conversation between Charles Spearman, Godfrey Thomson, and Edward L. Thorndike: The International Examinations Inquiry Meetings 1931–1938. *History of Psychology*, 11(3), 163.

Deary, I. J., Pattie, A. and Starr, J. M. (2013) The stability of intelligence from age 11 to age 90 years: The Lothian Birth Cohort of 1921. *Psychological Science*, 24, 2361–8.

Deary, I. J., Whalley, L. J. and Starr, J. M. (2003) IQ at age 11 and longevity. In C. E. Finch, J.-M. Robine and Y. Christen (eds) *Brain and Longevity: Perspectives in Longevity* (pp. 153–64). Berlin: Springer.

Deary, I. J., Whalley, L. J. and Starr, J. M. (2009) *A Lifetime of Intelligence: Follow-up Studies of the Scottish Mental Surveys of 1932 and 1947.* Washington, DC: APA.

Deary, I. J., Whalley, L. J., Batty, G. D. and Starr, J. M. (2006) Physical fitness and lifetime cognitive change. *Neurology*, 67, 1195–200.

Deary, I. J., Whalley, L. J., Lemmon, H. et al. (2000) The stability of individual differences in mental ability from childhood to old age: Follow-up of the 1932 Scottish Mental Survey. *Intelligence*, 28, 49–55.

Deary, I. J., Whiteman, M. C., Starr, J. M. et al. (2004) The impact of childhood intelligence on later life: Following up the Scottish mental surveys of 1932 and 1947. *Journal of Personality and Social Psychology*, 86, 130–47.

DeCasper, A. J. and Spence, M. J. (1986) Prenatal maternal speech influences newborns' perception of speech sounds. *Infant Behavior & Development*, 9, 133–50.

De Castro, J. M. (1994) Family and friends produce greater social facilitation of food intake than other companions. *Physiology and Behavior*, 56, 445–55.

Decety, J. (2010) The neurodevelopment of empathy in humans. *Developmental Neuroscience*, 32, 257–67.

Deci, E. L. (1971) Effects of externally mediated rewards on intrinsic motivation. *Journal of Personality and Social Psychology*, 18, 105–15.

Deci, E. L. (1975) *Intrinsic Motivation*. New York: Plenum.

Deci, E. L., Koestner, R. and Ryan, R. M. (1999) A meta-analytic review of experiments examining the effects of extrinsic rewards on intrinsic motivation. *Psychological Bulletin*, 125, 627–68.

De Craen, A. J., Roos, P. J., de Vries, A. L. and Kleijnen J. (1996) Effect of colour of drugs: systematic review of perceived effect of drugs and of their effectiveness. *British Medical Journal*, 313, 1624–6.

De Craen, A. J., Moerman, D. E., Heisterkamp, S. H. et al. (1999) Placebo effect in the treatment of duodenal ulcer. *British Journal of Clinical Pharmacology*, 48, 853–60.

Deese, J. (1959) On the prediction of occurrence of particular verbal intrusions in immediate recall. *Journal of Experimental Psychology*, 58, 17–22.

DeLisi, L. E., Crow, T. J. and Hirsch, S. R. (1986) The third biannual workshops on schizophrenia. *Archives of General Psychiatry*, 43, 706–11.

Delongis, A., Coyne, J. C., Dakof, G. et al. (1982) Relationship of daily hassles, uplifts, and major life events to health status. *Health Psychology*, 1, 119–36.

Demb, J. B., Desmond, J. E., Wagner, A. D. et al. (1995) Semantic encoding and retrieval in the left inferior prefrontal cortex: A functional MRI study of task difficulty and process specificity. *Journal of Neuroscience*, 15, 5870–8.

Dement, W. C. (1959) Dreams. *Time*, 30 November.

Dement, W. C. (1974) *Some Must Watch While Some Must Sleep*. San Francisco: W. H. Freeman.

Dement, W. C. (1978) *Some Must Watch While Some Must Sleep.* New York: Norton.

Dement, W. C. (1999) *The Promise of Sleep.* New York: Delacorte Press.

Dement, W. C. and Kleitman, N. (1957) The relation of eye movements during sleep to dream activity: An objective method for the study of dreaming. *Journal of Experimental Psychology*, 53, 339–46.

Dement, W. C. and Wolpert, E. (1958) Relation of eye movements, body motility, and external stimuli to dream content. *Journal of Experimental Psychology*, 55, 543–53.

Dempster, F. N. (1992) The rise and fall of the inhibitory mechanism: Toward a unified theory of cognitive development and aging. *Developmental Review*, 12, 454–75.

Denissen, J. A., Ulfers, H., Lüdtke, O. et al. (2014) Longitudinal transactions between personality and occupational roles: A large and heterogeneous study of job beginners stayers and changers. *Developmental Psychology*, 50, 1931–42.

Dennett, D. (1978) Beliefs about beliefs. *Behavioural and Brain Sciences*, 1, 568–70.

Dennett, D. (1991) *Consciousness Explained.* New York: Basic Books.

DePaulo, B. M. (2004) The many faces of lies. In A. G. Miller (ed.) *The Social Psychology of Good and Evil* (pp. 303–26). New York: Guilford Press.

DePaulo, B. M. and Kashy, D. A. (1998) Everyday lies in close and casual relationships. *Journal of Personality and Social Psychology*, 74, 63–79.

DePaulo, B. M. and Rosenthal, R. (1982) Measuring the development of sensitivity to nonverbal communication. In C. E. Izard and P. B. Read (eds) *Measuring Emotions in Infants and Children* (pp. 205–50). New York: CUP.

DePaulo, B. M., Charlton, K., Cooper, H. et al. (1997) The accuracy-confidence correlation in the detection of deception. *Personality and Social Psychology Review*, 1, 346–57.

DePaulo, B. M., Kashy, D. A., Kirkendol, S. E. et al. (1996) Lying in everyday life. *Journal of Personality and Social Psychology*, 70, 979–95.

DePaulo, B. M., Lindsay, J. J., Malone, B. E. et al. (2003) Cues to deception. *Psychological Bulletin*, 129, 74–118.

De Renzi, E. (1982) *Disorders of Space Exploration and Cognition*. Chichester: John Wiley & Sons.

Deuenwald, M. (2003) Students find another staple of campus life: Stress. *New York Times*, 12 June.

Deutsch, J. A. and Deutsch, D. (1963) Attention: Some theoretical considerations. *Psychological Review*, 87, 272–300.

Deutsch, M. (1949) A theory of cooperation and competition. *Human Relations*, 2, 29–152.

De Valois, R. L., Abramov, I. and Jacobs, G. (1966) Analysis of response patterns of LGN cells. *Journal of the Optical Society of America* [A], 56, 966–77.

DeVilliers, P. (2005) The role of language in theory-of-mind development: What deaf children tell us. In J. W. Astington and J. A. Baird (eds) *Why Language Matters for Theory of Mind* (pp. 266–97). Oxford: OUP.

De Waal, F. B. (1982) *Chimpanzee Politics: Power and Sex Among Apes*. Baltimore: Johns Hopkins University Press.

De Wolff, M. and van IJzendoorn, M. H. (1997) Sensitivity and attachment: A meta-analysis on parental antecedents of infant attachment. *Child Development*, 68, 571–91.

Diaconis, P. and Mosteller, F. (1989) Methods for studying coincidences. *Journal of the American Statistical Association*, 84, 853–61.

Diamond, A. (1991) Neuropsychological insights into the meaning of object concept development. In S. Carey and R. Gelman (eds) *The Epigenesis of Mind: Essays on Biology and Cognition* (pp. 67–110). Hillsdale, NJ: Lawrence Erlbaum.

Diamond, A. and Goldman-Rakic, P. S. (1989) Comparison of human infants and infant rhesus monkeys on Piaget's AB task: Evidence for dependence on dorsolateral prefrontal cortex. *Experimental Brain Research*, 74, 24–40.

Dickens, W. T. and Flynn, J. R. (2001) Heritability estimates versus large environmental effects: The IQ paradox resolved. *Psychological Review*, 108, 346–69.

Diener, E. and Wallbom, M. (1976) Effects of self-awareness on antinormative behavior. *Journal of Research in Personality*, 10, 107–11.

Diener, E., Fraser, S. C., Beaman, A. L. and Kelem, R. T. (1976) Effects of deindividuation variables on stealing among Halloween trick-or-treaters. *Journal of Personality and Social Psychology*, 33, 178–83.

Dienes, Z. (2008) *Understanding Psychology as a Science*. Basingstoke: Palgrave Macmillan.

Dijksterhuis, A. (2004) Think different: The merits of unconscious thought in preference development and decision making. *Journal of Personality and Social Psychology*, 87, 586–98.

Dijksterhuis, A., Aarts, H. and Smith, P. K. (2005) The power of the subliminal: On subliminal persuasion and other potential applications. In J. S. Hassin and J. A. Bargh (eds) *The New Unconscious* (pp. 77–106). New York: OUP.

DiLalla, L. F., Kagan, J. and Reznick, S. J. (1994) Genetic etiology of behavioural inhibition among 2-year-old children. *Infant Behaviour and Development*, 17, 405–12.

Dillbeck, M. C. and Orme-Johnson, D. W. (1987) Physiological differences between transcendental meditation and rest. *American Psychologist*, 42, 879–81.

Dimberg, U. (1982) Facial reactions to facial expressions. *Psychophysiology*, 19, 643–7.

Dion, K., Berscheid, E. and Walster, E. (1972) What is beautiful is good. *Journal of Personality and Social Psychology*, 24, 285–90.

DiTella, R., MacCulloch, R. J. and Oswald, A. J. (2003) The macroeconomics of happiness. *Review of Economics and Statistics*, 85, 809–27.

Dittrich, W. H., Troscianko, T., Lea, S. and Morgan, D. (1996) Perception of emotion from dynamic point-light displays represented in dance. *Perception*, 25, 727–38.

Dixon, D., Cruess, S., Kilbourn, K. et al. (2006) Social support mediates loneliness and human herpesvirus type 6 (HHV-6) antibody titers. *Journal of Applied Social Psychology*, 31, 1111–32.

Dodge, K. A. (1993) Social-cognitive mechanisms in the development of conduct disorder and depression. *Annual Review of Psychology*, 44, 559–84.

Dohrenwend, B. S., Dohrenwend, B. P., Dodson, M. and Shrout, P. E. (1984) Symptoms, hassles, social supports, and life events: Problem of confounded measures. *Journal of Abnormal Psychology*, 93, 222–30.

Dollard, J. (1938) Hostility and fear in social life. *Social Forces*, 17, 15–26.

Dollard, J., Doob, L. W., Miller, N. E. et al. (1939) *Frustration and Aggression*. Oxford: Yale University Press.

Dolscheid, S., Hunnius, S., Casasanto, D. and Majid, A. (2014) Prelinguistic infants are sensitive to space-pitch associations found across cultures. *Psychological Science*, 25, 1256–61.

Domjan, M. (2005) Pavlovian conditioning: A functional perspective. *Annual Review of Psychology*, 56, 179–206.

Donaldson, M. (1978) *Children's Minds*. London: Fontana/Croom Helm.

Donner, T. H., Kettermann, A., Diesch, E. et al. (2002) Visual feature and conjunction searches of equal difficulty engage only partially overlapping frontoparietal net-works. *Neuroimage*, 15, 16–25.

Donovan, W. L., Leavitt, L.A. and Walsh, R.O. (2000) Maternal illusory control predicts socialization strategies and toddler compliance. *Developmental Psychology*, 36, 402–11.

Dorahy, M. J. (2001) Dissociative identity disorder and memory dysfunction: The current state of experimental research and its future directions. *Clinical Psychology Review*, 21, 771–95.

Dornbusch, S. M., Hastorf, A. H., Richardson, S. A. et al. (1965) The perceiver and perceived: Their relative influence on categories of interpersonal perception. *Journal of Personality and Social Psychology*, 1, 434–40.

Dorus, S., Vallender, E. J., Evans, P. D. et al. (2004) Accelerated evolution of nervous system genes in the origin of *Homo sapiens*. *Cell*, 119, 1027–40.

Douglas, K. M. (2007) Psychology, discrimination and date groups online. In A. N. Joinson, K. McKenna, T. Postmes and U. Reips (eds) *The Oxford Handbook of Internet Psychology* (pp. 155–64). Oxford: OUP.

Dovidio, J. F. and Morris, W. N. (1975) Effects of stress and commonality of fate on helping behaviour. *Journal of Personality and Social Psychology*, 31, 145–9.

Dowling, J. E. (1992) *Neurons and Networks: An Introduction to Neuroscience*. Cambridge, MA: Harvard University Press.

Downer, J. D. (1961) Changes in visual gnostic function and emotional behavior following unilateral temporal damage in the 'split-brain' monkey. *Nature*, 191, 50–1.

Downing, P. E., Chan, A. W., Peelen, M. V. et al. (2006) Domain specificity in visual cortex. *Cerebral Cortex*, 16, 1453–61.

Downs, A. C. and Lyons, P. M. (1991) Natural observations of the links between attractiveness and initial legal judgements. *Personality and Social Psychology Bulletin*, 17, 541–7.

Doyle, A. B., Markiewicz, D., Brendgen, M. et al. (2000) Child attachment security and self concept: Associations with mother and with father attachment style and marital quality. *Merrill Palmer Quarterly*, 46, 514–39.

Draguns, J. G. (1980) Psychological disorders of clinical severity. In H. C. Triandis and J. G. Draguns (eds) *Handbook of Cross-cultural Psychology* (vol. 6, pp. 99–174). Boston: Allyn & Bacon.

Drigotas, S. M. and Rusbult, C. E. (1992) Should I stay or should I go? A dependence model of breakups. *Journal of Personality and Social Psychology*, 62, 62–87.

Driver, J. (1996) Enhancement of selective listening by illusory mislocation of speech sounds due to lip-reading. *Nature*, 381, 66–8.

Driver, J., Ricciardelli, P., Kidd, P. et al. (1999) Gaze perception triggers visuo-spatial orienting in a reflexive manner. *Visual Cognition*, 6, 509–40.

Druckman, D. and Bjork, R. A. (1994) *Learning, Remembering, Believing: Enhancing Human Performance*. Washington, DC: National Academy Press.

Drummey, A. B. and Newcombe, N. S. (2002) Developmental changes in source memory. *Developmental Science*, 5, 502–13.

Dubois, D., Rucker, D. D. and Galinsky, A. D. (2010) The accentuation bias: Money literally looms larger (and sometimes smaller) to the powerless. *Social Psychological and Personality Science*, 3, 199–205.

Duckitt, J. (2006) Differential effects of right wing authoritarianism and social dominance orientation on outgroup attitudes and their mediation by threat from and competitiveness to outgroups. *Personality and Social Psychology Bulletin*, 32, 684–96.

Duckworth, A. L. and Seligman, M. E. (2005) Self-discipline outdoes IQ in predicting academic performance of adolescents. *Psychological Science*, 16, 939–44.

Dunbar, K. and Blanchette, I. (2001) The in vivo/in vitro approach to cognition: The case of analogy. *Trends in Cognitive Sciences*, 5, 334–9.

Dunbar, K. and Fugelsang, J. (2005) Scientific thinking and reasoning. In K. Holyoak and R. G. Morrison (eds) *Cambridge Handbook of Thinking and Reasoning* (pp. 705–25). Cambridge: CUP.

Dunbar, K. N., Fugelsang, J. A. and Stein, C. (2007) Do naïve theories ever go away? Using brain and behavior to understand changes in concepts. In M. C. Lovett and P. Shah (eds) *Thinking with Data* (pp. 193–205). Mahwah, NJ: Lawrence Erlbaum.

Duncan, J. (2005) Frontal lobe function and general intelligence: Why it matters. *Cortex*, 41, 215–17.

Duncker, K. (1945) On problem-solving. *Psychological Monographs*, 58, no. 5.

Dunham, P. J. and Moore, C. (1995) Current themes in research of joint attention. In C. Moore and P. Dunham (eds) *Joint Attention: Its Origin and Role in Development* (pp. 15–28). Hillsdale, NJ: Lawrence Erlbaum.

Dunlap, K. (1919) Are there any instincts? *Journal of Abnormal Psychology*, 14, 307–11.

Dunlop, S. A. (2008) Activity-dependent plasticity: Implications for recovery after spinal cord injury. *Trends in Neurosciences*, 31, 410–18.

Dunn, J. and Hughes, C. (2001) 'I've got some swords and you're dead!' Violent fantasy, antisocial behaviour, friendship and moral sensibility inn young children. *Child Development*, 72, 491–505.

Dunn, J., Bretherton, I. and Munn, P. (1987) Conversations about feeling states between mothers and their young children. *Developmental Psychology*, 23, 132–9.

Dunphy, D. C. (1963) The social structure of urban adolescent peer groups. *Sociometry*, 26, 230–46.

Durkheim, E. (1951) *Suicide: A Study in Sociology* (trans. G. Simpson). New York: Free Press.

Durrett, M. E., Otaki, M. and Richards, P. (1984) Attachment and mother's perception of support from the father. *Journal of the International Society for the Study of Behavioral Development*, 7, 167–76.

Dutton, D. G. and Aron, A. P. (1974) Some evidence for heightened sexual attraction under conditions of high anxiety. *Journal of Personality and Social Psychology*, 30, 510–17.

Duval, S. and Wicklund, R. A. (1972) *A Theory of Objective Self Awareness.* New York: Academic Press.

Dweck, C. S. (1999) *Self-theories: Their Role in Motivation, Personality, and Development.* Philadelphia, PA: Psychology Press.

Dweck, C. S. (2008) *Mindsets and Math/Science Achievement*. New York: Carnegie Corporation of New York.

Dweck, C. S. and Leggett, E. L. (1988) A social-cognitive approach to motivation and personality. *Psychological Review*, 95, 256–73.

Eacott, M. J. (1999) Memory for the events of early childhood. *Current Directions in Psychological Science*, 8, 46–9.

Eagly, A. H. and Steffen, V. J. (1986) Gender and aggressive behavior: A meta-analytic review of the social psychological literature. *Psychological Bulletin*, 100, 309–30.

Eagly, A. H. and Wood, W. (1999) The origins of sex differences in human behavior: Evolved dispositions versus social roles. *American Psychologist*, 54, 408–23.

Eagly, A. H., Ashmore, R. D., Makhijani, M. G. and Longo, L. C. (1991) What is beautiful is good, but ... : A meta-analytic review of research on the physical attractiveness stereotype. *Psychological Bulletin*, 110, 109–28.

Earley, P. C. (1989) Social loafing and collectivism: A comparison of United States and the People's Republic of China. *Administrative Science Quarterly*, 34, 565–81.

Eaton, W. W., Kessler, R. C., Wittchen, H. U. and McGee, W. J. (1994) Panic and panic disorder in the United States. *American Journal of Psychiatry*, 151, 413–20.

Eaton, W. W., Romanoski, A., Anthony, J. C. and Nestadt, G. (1991) Screening for psychosis in the general population with a self-report interview. *Journal of Nervous and Mental Disease*, 179, 689–93.

Ebbinghaus, H. ([1885]1964) *Memory: A Contribution to Experimental Psychology.* New York: Dover.

Eberhardt, J. L. (2005) Imaging race. *American Psychologist*, 60, 181–90.

Eddy, D. M. (1982) Probabilistic reasoning in clinical medicine: Problems and opportunities. In D. Kahneman, P. Slovic and A. Tversky (eds) *Judgments Under Uncertainty: Heuristics and Biases* (pp. 249–67). Cambridge, MA: CUP.

Edgerton, V. R., Tillakaratne, J. K., Bigbee, A. J. et al. (2004) Plasticity of the spinal neural circuitry after injury. *Annual Review of Neuroscience*, 27, 145–67.

Edwards, W. (1955) The theory of decision making. *Psychological Bulletin*, 51, 201–14.

Ehrsson, H. (2007) The experimental induction of out-of-body experiences. *Science*, 317, 1048.

Eich, J. E. (1980) The cue-dependent nature of state-dependent retention. *Memory & Cognition*, 8, 157–73.

Eich, J. E. (1995) Searching for mood dependent memory. *Psychological Science*, 6, 67–75.

Eimas, P. D., Siqueland, E. R., Jusczyk, P. and Vigorito, J. (1971) Speech perception in infants. *Science*, 171, 303–6.

Einav, S. and Hood, B. M. (2006) Children's use of the temporal dimension of gaze for inferring preference. *Developmental Psychology*, 42, 142–52.

Einolf, C. J. (2010) Does extensivity form part of the altruistic personality? An empirical test of Oliner and Oliner's theory. *Social Science Research*, 39, 142–51.

Einstein, G. O. and McDaniel, M. A. (1990) Normal aging and prospective memory. *Journal of Experimental Psychology: Learning, Memory, and Cognition*, 16, 717–26.

Einstein, G. O., McDaniel, M. A., Richardson, S. L. et al. (1995) Aging and prospective memory: Examining the influences of self-initiated retrieval processes. *Journal of Experimental Psychology: Learning, Memory, and Cognition*, 21, 996–1007.

Eisenberg, N., Fabes, R. A., Carlo, G. et al. (1992) The relations of maternal practices and characteristics to children's vicarious emotional responsiveness. *Child Development*, 63, 583–602.

Eisenberg-Berg, N., Haake, R. J. and Bartlett, K. (1981) The effects of possession and ownership on the sharing and proprietary behaviors of preschool children. *Merrill-Palmer Quarterly*, 27, 61–8.

Eisenberger, N. I. and Lieberman, M. D. (2004) Why rejection hurts: A common neural alarm system for physical and social pain. *Trends in Cognitive Science*, 8, 294–9.

Eisenberger, N. I., Lieberman, M. D. and Williams, K. D. (2003) Does rejection hurt? An fMRI study of social exclusion. *Science*, 302, 290–2.

Ekman, P. (1965) Differential communication of affect by head and body cues. *Journal of Personality and Social Psychology*, 2, 726–35.

Ekman, P. (1972) Universals and cultural differences in facial expressions of emotion. In J. K. Cole (ed.) *Nebraska Symposium on Motivation, 1971* (pp. 207–83). Lincoln: University of Nebraska Press.

Ekman, P. (1992) *Telling Lies.* New York: Norton.

Ekman, P. (2003) Darwin, deception, and facial expression. *Annals of the New York Academy of Science*, 1000, 205–21.

Ekman, P. and Friesen, W. V. (1968) Nonverbal behavior in psychotherapy research. In J. M. Shlien (ed.) *Research in Psychotherapy* (vol. 3, pp. 179–216). Washington, DC: APA.

Ekman, P. and Friesen, W. V. (1969) Nonverbal leakage and clues to deception. *Psychiatry*, 32, 88–105.

Ekman, P. and Friesen, W. V. (1971) Constants across cultures in the face and emotion. *Journal of Personality and Social Psychology*, 17, 124–9.

Ekman, P. and Friesen, W. V. (1978) *The Facial Action Coding System.* Palo Alto, CA: Consulting Psychologists Press.

Ekman, P. and Friesen, W. V. (1982) Felt, false, and miserable smiles. *Journal of Nonverbal Behavior*, 6, 238–52.

Ekman, P. and O'Sullivan, M. (1991) Who can catch a liar? *American Psychologist*, 46(9), 913–20.

Ekman, P., Levenson, R. W. and Friesen, W. V. (1983) Autonomic nervous system activity distinguishes among emotions. *Science*, 221, 1208–10.

Ekman, P., O'Sullivan, M. and Frank, M. G. (1999) A few can catch a liar. *Psychological Science*, 10, 263–6.

Ekman, P., Friesen, W. V., O'Sullivan, M. et al. (1987) Universals and cultural differences in the judgments of facial expressions of emotion. *Journal of Personality and Social Psychology*, 53, 712–17.

Elbert, T., Pantev, C., Wienbruch, C. et al. (1995) Increased cortical representation of the fingers of the left hand in string players. *Science*, 270, 305–7.

Elder, G. H. and Conger, R. D. (2000) *Children of the Land: Adversity and Success in Rural America.* Chicago: University of Chicago Press.

Eldridge, L. L., Knowlton, B. J., Furmanski, C. S. et al. (2000) Remembering episodes: A selective role for the hippocampus during retrieval. *Nature Neuroscience*, 3, 1149–52.

Eldridge, M. A., Barnard, P. J. and Bekerian, D. A. (1994) Autobiographical memory and daily schemas at work. *Memory*, 2, 51–74.

Elfenbein, H. A. and Ambady, N. (2002) On the universality and cultural specificity of emotion recognition: A meta-analysis. *Psychological Bulletin*, 128, 203–35.

Ellamil, M., Dobson, C., Beeman, M. and Christoff, K. (2012) Evaluative and generative modes of thought during the creative process. *NeuroImage*, 59, 1783–94.

Ellenberger, H. F. (1954) The life and work of Hermann Rorschach (1884–1922). *Bulletin of the Menninger Clinic*, 18, 173–213.

Ellicot, A., Hammen, C., Gitlin, M. et al. (1990) Life events and course of bipolar disorder. *American Journal of Psychiatry*, 147, 1194–8.

Elliott, R., Sahakian, B. J., Matthews, K. et al. (1997) Effects of methylphenidate on spatial working memory and planning in healthy young adults. *Psychopharmacology*, 131, 196–206.

Ellis, A. (2000) Rational emotive behavior therapy. In R. J. Corsini and D. Wedding (eds) *Current Psychotherapies* (6th edn, pp. 168–204). Itasca, IL: F. E. Peacock.

Ellis, R. and Hennelly, R. A. (1980) A bilingual word-length effect: Implications for intelligence testing and the relative ease of mental calculations in Welsh and English. *British Journal of Psychology*, 71, 43–52.

Ellman, S. J., Spielman, A. J., Luck, D. et al. (1991) REM deprivation: A review. In S. J. Ellman and J. S. Antrobus (eds) *The Mind in Sleep: Psychology and Psychophysiology* (2nd edn, pp. 329–76). New York: Wiley.

Ellsworth, C., Muir, D. and Hains, S. (1993) Social-competence and person-object differentiation: An analysis of the still-face effect. *Developmental Psychology*, 29, 63–73.

Elman, J. L., Bates, E. A., Johnson, M. H. et al. (1997) *Rethinking Innateness: A Connectionist Perspective on Development*. Cambridge, MA: MIT Press.

Else-Quest, N. M., Hyde, J. S. and Linn, M. C. (2010) Cross-national patterns of gender differences in mathematics: A meta-analysis. *Psychological Bulletin*, 136, 103–27.

Embretson, S. E. (1995) The role of working memory capacity and general control processes in intelligence. *Intelligence*, 20, 169–89.

Embretson, S. E. and Schmidt-McCollam, K. M. (2000) Psychometric approaches to understanding and measuring intelligence. In Sternberg, R. J. (ed.) *Handbook of Intelligence* (pp. 423–44). New York: CUP.

Emde, R. N. (1992) Individual meaning and increasing complexity: Contributions of Sigmund Freud and Rene Spitz to developmental psychology. *Developmental Psychology*, 28, 347–59.

Emerson, R. C., Bergen, J. R. and Adelson, E. H. (1992) Directionally selective complex cells and the computation of motion energy in cat visual cortex. *Vision Research*, 32, 203–18.

Emler N. (1994) Gossip, reputation and adaptation. In R. F. Goodman and A. Ben-Ze'ev (eds) *Good Gossip* (pp. 117–38). Lawrence, KS: University of Kansas Press.

Emmelkamp, P. M. and Wessels, H. (1975) Flooding in imagination vs. flooding in vivo: A comparison with agoraphobics. *Behaviour Research and Therapy*, 13, 7–15.

Emmelkamp, P. M., Krijn, M., Hulsbosch, A. M. et al. (2002) Virtual reality treatment versus exposure in vivo: A comparative evaluation in acrophobia. *Behaviour Research and Therapy*, 40(5), 509–16.

Empson, J. A. (1984) Sleep and its disorders. In R. Stevens (ed.) *Aspects of Consciousness*. New York: Academic Press.

Engel, G. (1977) The new for a new medical model. *Science*, 196, 129–36.

Engle, R. W., Tuholski, S. W., Laughlin, J. E. and Conway, A. R. (1999) Working memory, short-term memory and general fluid intelligence: A latent-variable approach. *Journal of Experimental Psychology: General*, 128, 309–31.

English, K., Jones, L., Patrick, D. and Pasini-Hill, D. (2003) Sexual offender containment: Use of the postconviction polygraph. *Annals of the New York Academy of Sciences*, 989, 411–27.

Epley, N., Savitsky, K. and Gilovich, T. (2002) Empathy neglect: Reconciling the spotlight effect and the correspondence bias. *Journal of Personality and Social Psychology*, 83, 300–12

Epley, N., Savitsky, K. and Kachelski, R. A. (1999) What every skeptic should know about subliminal persuasion. *Skeptical Inquirer*, 23, 40–5, 58.

Erber, R., Wegner, D. M. and Therriault, N. (1996) On being cool and collected: Mood regulation in anticipation of social interaction. *Journal of Personality and Social Psychology*, 70, 757–66.

Erffmeyer, E. S. (1984) Rule-violating behavior on the golf course. *Perceptual and Motor Skills*, 59, 591–6.

Ericsson, K. A. and Charness, N. (1999) Expert performance: Its structure and acquisition. In S. J. Ceci and W. M. Williams (eds) *The Nature-Nurture Debate: The Essential Readings* (pp. 200–56). Oxford: Blackwell.

Erikson, E. (1959) *Identity and the Life Cycle: Selected Papers*. New York: International Universities Press.

Eronen, M., Angermeyer, M. C. and Schulze, B. (1998) The psychiatric epidemiology of violent behavior. *Social Psychiatry & Psychiatric Epidemiology*, 33, 13–23.

Essex, M. J., Boyce, W. T., Hertzman, C. et al. (2013) Epigenetic vestiges of early developmental adversity: Childhood stress exposure and DNA methylation in adolescence. *Child Development*, 84, 58–75.

Esterman, M., Verstynen, T., Ivry, R. B. and Robertson, L. C. (2006) Coming unbound: Disrupting automatic integration of synesthetic color and graphemes by transcranial magnetic stimulation of the right parietal lobe. *Journal of Cognitive Neuroscience*, 18, 1570–6.

Etcoff, N. (1999) *Survival of the Prettiest: The Science of Beauty*. New York: Doubleday.

EUMC (2001) Report to EUMC on 'post September 11th developments'. Dutch Monitoring Centre on Racism and Xenophobia, www.lbr.nl/internationaal/DUMC/publicatie/index.html.

Evans, J. S., Barston, J. L. and Pollard, P. (1983) On the conflict between logic and belief in syllogistic reasoning. *Memory & Cognition*, 11, 295–306.

Evans, P. D., Gilbert, S. L., Mekel-Bobrov, N. et al. (2005) Microcephalin, a gene regulating brain size, continues to evolve adaptively in humans. *Science*, 309, 1717–20.

Exner, J. E. (1993) *The Rorschach: A Comprehensive System*, vol. 1. *Basic Foundations*. New York: Wiley.

Eysenck, H. J. (1952) The effects of psychotherapy: An evaluation. *Journal of Consulting and Clinical Psychology*, 16, 319–24.

Eysenck, H. J. (1960) *Behavior Therapy and the Neuroses*. Oxford: Pergamon Press.

Eysenck, H. J. (1967) *The Biological Basis of Personality*. Springfield, IL: Charles C. Thomas.

Eysenck, H. J. (1978) Superfactors P, E, and N in a comprehensive factor space. *Multivariate Behavioral Research*, 13, 475–82.

Eysenck, H. J. (1982) *Personality, Genetics and Behavior*. New York: Praeger.

Eysenck, H. J. (1990) Biological dimensions of personality. In L. A. Pervin (ed.) *Handbook of Personality: Theory and Research* (pp. 244–76). New York: Guilford Press.

Eysenck, H. J. (1995) *Genius: The Natural History of Creativity*. New York: CUP.

Eysenck, M. (2004) *Psychology: An International Perspective*. Hove: Psychology Press.

Eysenck, S. B. and Eysenck, H. J. (1985) *Personality and Individual Differences: A Natural Science Approach*. New York: Plenum Press.

Fairchild, G., van Goozen, S. H., Calder, A. J. et al. (2009) Deficits in facial expression recognition in male adolescents with early-onset or adolescence-onset conduct disorder. *Journal of Child Psychology and Psychiatry*, 50, 627–36.

Falk, R. and McGregor, D. (1983) The surprisingness of coincidences. In P. Humphreys, O. Svenson and A. Vari (eds) *Analysing and Aiding Decision Processes* (pp. 489–502). New York: North Holland.

Fancher, R. E. (1979) *Pioneers of Psychology*. New York: Norton.

Fancher, R. E. (1987) *The Intelligence Men: Makers of the IQ Controversy*. New York: Norton.

Fantz, R. (1961) The origin of form perception. *Scientific American*, 204, 66–72.

Farah, M. J. and Rabinowitz, C. (2003) Genetic and environmental influences on the organization of semantic memory in the brain: Is 'living things' an innate category? *Cognitive Neuropsychology*, 20, 401–8.

Farah, M. J., Illes, J. Cook-Deegan, R. et al. (2004) Neurocognitive enhancement: What can we do and what should we do? *Nature Reviews Neuroscience*, 5, 421–6.

Farivar, R. (2009) Dorsal-ventral integration in object recognition. *Brain Research Reviews,* 61, 144–53.

Farmer, A. E. and McGuffin, P. (2003) Humiliation, loss and other types of life events and difficulties: A comparison of depressed subjects, healthy controls and their siblings. *Psychological Medicine*, 33, 1169–75.

Farrar, M. J. (1990) Discourse and the acquisition of grammatical morphemes. *Journal of Child Language*, 17, 607–24.

Farries, M. A. (2004) The avian song system in comparative perspective. *Annals of the New York Academy of Sciences*, 1016, 61–76.

Favaro, A., Ferrara, S. and Santonastaso, P. (2004) The spectrum of eating disorders in young women: a prevalence study in a general population sample. *Psychosomatic Medicine*, 65, 701–8.

Fawcett, C. A. and Markson, L. (2010) Children reason about shared preferences. *Developmental Psychology,* 46, 299–309.

Fazel, S. and Danesh, J. (2002) Serious mental disorder in 23,000 prisoners: A review of 62 surveys. *Lancet*, 359, 545–50.

Fechner, G. T. ([1860]1966) *Elements of Psychophysics* (trans. H. E. Alder). New York: Holt, Rinehart & Wilson.

Fehm, L., Pelissolo, A., Furmark, T. and Wittchen, H. (2005) Size and burden of social phobia in Europe. *European Neuropsychopharmacology*, 15, 453–62.

Fehr, E. and Gaechter, S. (2002) Altruistic punishment in humans. *Nature*, 415, 137–40.

Fein, S., Hilton, J. L. and Miller, D. T. (1990) Suspicion of ulterior motivation and the correspondence bias. *Journal of Personality and Social Psychology*, 58, 753–64.

Feinberg, J. M. and Aiello, J. R. (2006) Social facilitation: A test of competing theories. *Journal of Applied Social Psychology*, 36, 1087–109.

Feinberg, M., Willer, R. and Shultz, M. (2014) Gossip and ostracism promote cooperation in groups. *Psychological Science*, 25, 656–64.

Feinberg, T. E. (2001) *Altered Egos: How the Brain Creates the Self.* New York: OUP.

Feingold, A. (1990) Gender differences in effects of physical attractiveness on romantic attraction: A comparison across five research paradigms. *Journal of Personality and Social Psychology*, 59, 981–93.

Feingold, A. (1992a) Gender differences in mate selection preferences: A test of the parental investment model. *Psychological Bulletin*, 112, 125–39.

Feingold, A. (1992b) Good-looking people are not what we think. *Psychological Bulletin*, 111, 304–41.

Feingold, A. (1994) Gender differences in personality: A meta-analysis. *Psychological Bulletin*, 116, 429–56.

Feinstein, J. S., Buzza, C., Hurleman, R. et al. (2013) Fear and panic in humans with bilateral amygdala damage. *Nature Neuroscience*, 16, 270–2.

Feist, G. J. (2013) The psychology of scientific thought and behaviour. *The Psychologist*, 26, 864–7.

Feldhusen, J. F. (1993) A conception of creative thinking and creativity training. In S. G. Isaksen, M. C. Murdoch, R. L. Firestien and D. J. Treffinger (eds) *Nurturing and Developing Creativity: The Emergence of a Discipline* (pp. 31–50). Norwood, NJ: Ablex.

Ferguson, C. J. and Donnellan, M. B. (2014) Is the association between children's baby video viewing and poor language development robust? A reanalysis of Zimmerman, Christakis, and Meltzoff (2007). *Developmental Psychology*, 50, 129–37.

Ferguson, M. W. and Joanen, T. (1982) Temperature of egg incubation determines sex in Alligator mississippiensis. *Nature*, 296, 850–3.

Fernald, A. (1991) Prosody in speech to children: Prelinguistic and linguistic functions. *Annals of Child Development*, 8, 43–80.

Ferreira, F. and Swets, B. (2002) How incremental is language production? Evidence from the production of utterances requiring the computation of arithmetic sums. *Journal of Memory and Language*, 46, 57–84.

Ferriman, K., Lubinski, D. and Benbow, C. P. (2009) Work preferences, life values, and personal views of top math/science graduate students and the profoundly gifted: Developmental changes and gender differences during emerging adulthood and parenthood. *Journal of Personality and Social Psychology*, 97, 517–32.

Ferris, G. R., Witt, L. A. and Hochwater, W. A. (2001) Interaction of social skill and general mental ability on job performance and salary. *Journal of Applied Psychology*, 86, 1075–82.

Ferster, C. B. and Skinner, B. F. (1957) *Schedules of Reinforcement.* New York: Appleton-Century-Crofts.

Festinger, L. (1954) A theory of social comparison processes. *Human Relations*, 7, 117–40.

Festinger, L. (1957) *A Theory of Cognitive Dissonance.* Stanford, CA: Stanford University Press.

Festinger, L. and Carlsmith, J. M. (1959) Cognitive consequences of forced compliance. *Journal of Abnormal and Social Psychology*, 58, 203–10.

Festinger, L., Schachter, S. and Back, K. (1950) *Social Pressures in Informal Groups: A Study of Human Factors in Housing.* Oxford: Harper & Row.

Fiedler, E. R., Oltmanns, T. F. and Turkheimer, E. (2004) Traits associated with personality disorders and adjustment to military life: Predictive validity of self and peer reports. *Military Medicine*, 169, 32–40.

Field, A. (2005) Meta-analysis. In J. Miles and P. Gilbert (eds) *A Handbook of Research Methods in Clinical and Health Psychology* (pp. 295–308). Oxford: OUP.

Field, G. C. (1921) Faculty psychology and instinct psychology. *Mind*, 30, 257–70.

Field, T., Hernandez-Reif, M. and Freedman, J. (2004) Stimulation programs for preterm infants. *Social Policy Report*, 18, 1–19.

Fields, H. L. and Levine, J. D. (1984) Placebo analgesia: A role for endorphins? *Trends in Neurosciences*, 7, 271–3.

Fields, R. D. (2010) Change in the brain's white matter. *Science*, 330, 768–9.

Fiering, C. and Taft, L. (1985) The gifted learning disabled: Not a paradox. *Pediatric Annals*, 14, 729–32.

Findlay, J. M. and Gilchrist, I. D. (2003) *Active Vision: The Psychology of Looking and Seeing*. Oxford: OUP.

Fine, C. (2010) *Delusions of Gender: How Our Minds, Society, and Neurosexism Create Difference.* New York: W.W. Norton.

Fink, M. (2001) Convulsive therapy: A review of the first 55 years. *Journal of Affective Disorders*, 63, 1–15.

Finkel, E. J. and Eastwick, P. W. (2009) Arbitrary social norms influ-ence sex differences in romantic selectivity. *Psychological Science,* 20, 1290–5.

Finlay, L. and Gough. B. (eds) (2003) *Reflexivity: A Practical Guide for Researchers in Health And Social Science*. Oxford: Blackwell.

Firebaugh, G. and Schroeder, M. B. (2009) Does your neighbor's income affect your happiness? *American Journal of Sociology*, 115, 805–31.

First, M. B. (2009) Harmonisation of ICD–11 and DSM–V: Opportunities and challenges. *British Journal of Psychiatry*, 195, 382–90.

Fischer, K. W., Shaver, P. R. and Carnochan, P. (1992) How emotions develop and how they organize development. *Cognition and Emotion*, 4, 81–127.

Fischer, P., Krueger, J. L., Greitemeyer, T. et al. (2011) The bystander-effect: A meta-analytic review on bystander intervention in dangerous and non-dangerous situations. *Psychological Bulletin*, 137, 517–37.

Fisher, H. E. (1993) *Anatomy of Love: The Mysteries of Mating, Marriage, and Why We Stray*. New York: Fawcett.

Fisher, R. P. and Craik, F. I. (1977) The interaction between encoding and retrieval operations in cued recall. *Journal of Experimental Psychology: Human Learning and Perception*, 3, 153–71.

Fisher, S. (1989) *Homesickness, Cognition and Health*. Hove: LEA.

Fisher, S. and Hood, B. (1987) The stress of the transition to university: A longitudinal study of vulnerability to psychological disturbance and homesickness. *British Journal of Psychology*, 78, 425–41.

Fisher-Thompson, D. (1993) Adult toy purchase for children: Factors affecting sex-typed toy selection. *Journal of Applied Developmental Psychology*, 14, 385–406.

Fiske, S. T. (1998) Stereotyping, prejudice, and discrimination. In D. T. Gilbert, S. T. Fiske and G. Lindzey (eds) *The Handbook of Social Psychology* (4th edn, vol. 2, pp. 357–411). New York: McGraw-Hill.

Fitzgerald, P. B., Brown, T. L., Marston, N. A. et al. (2003) Transcranial magnetic stimulation in the treatment of depression: A double-blind, placebo-controlled trial. *Archives of General Psychiatry*, 60, 1002–8.

Fivush, R. and Hammond, N. R. (1990) Autobiographical memory across the preschool years: Toward reconceptualising childhood amnesia. In R. Fivush and J. Hudson (eds) *Knowing and Remembering in Young Children*. New York: CUP.

Flavell, J. H. and Miller, P. H. (1998) Social cognition. In D. Kuhn and R. S. Siegler (eds) *Handbook of Child Psychology*, vol. 2. *Cognition, Perception and Language* (5th edn, pp. 851–98). New York: Wiley.

Flavell, J. H., Flavell, E. R. and Green, F. L. (1983) Development of the appearance reality distinction. *Cognitive Psychology*, 15, 95–120.

Fleming, R., Baum, A., Gisriel, M. M. and Gatchel, R. J. (1985) Mediating influences of social support on stress at Three Mile Island. In A. Monat and R. S. Lazarus (eds) *Stress and Coping: An Anthology* (2nd edn, pp. 95–106). New York: Columbia University Press.

Fletcher, P. C., Shallice, T. and Dolan, R. J. (1998) The functional roles of prefrontal cortex in episodic memory, I. Encoding. *Brain*, 121, 1239–48.

Flor, H., Nikolajsen, L. and Jensen, T. S. (2006) Phantom limb pain: A case of maladaptive CNS plasticity? *Nature Reviews Neuroscience*, 7, 873–81.

Flynn, J. R. (1984) The mean IQ of Americans: Massive gains 1932 to 1978. *Psychological Bulletin*, 95, 29–51.

Flynn, J. R. (1987) Massive IQ gains in 14 nations: What IQ tests really measure. *Psychological Bulletin*, 101, 171–91.

Flynn, J. R. (2009) *What is Intelligence? Beyond the Flynn Effect*. Cambridge: CUP.

Foa, E. B., Dancu, C. V., Hembree, E. A. et al. (1999) A comparison of exposure therapy, stress inoculation training, and their combination for reducing posttraumatic stress disorder in female assault victims. *Journal of Consulting & Clinical Psychology*, 67, 194–200.

Fodor, J. (2000) Why we are so good at catching cheaters. *Cognition*, 75, 2932.

Fogassi, L., Ferrari, P. F., Gesierich, B. et al. (2005) Parietal lobe: From action organization to intention understanding. *Science*, 308, 662–7.

Foggo, D. (2007) Medal snub for civilian 7/7 heroes. *Sunday Times*, 30 December.

Folley, B. S. and Park, S. (2005) Verbal creativity and schizotypal personality in relation to prefrontal hemispheric laterality: A behavioural and near-infrared optical imaging study. *Schizophrenia Research*, 80, 271–82.

Foresight (2007) *Tackling Obesities: Future Choices*, www.gov.uk/government/collections/tackling-obesities-future-choices.

Fouts, R. S. and Bodamer, M. (1987) Preliminary report to the National Geographic Society on 'Chimpanzee intrapersonal signing'. *Friends of Washoe*, 7, 4–12.

Fowler, D. (1985) Landmarks in computer-assisted psychological assessment. *Journal of Consulting and Clinical Psychology*, 53, 748–59.

Fox, E. (2008) *Emotional Science*. Basingstoke: Palgrave Macmillan.

Fox, M. J. (2009) *Always Looking Up: The Adventures of an Incurable Optimist*. New York: Hyperion Books.

Fox, N. A., Henderson, H. A., Rubin, K. H. et al. (2001) Continuity and discontinuity of behavioural inhibition and exuberance: Psychophysiological and behavioural influences across the first four years of life. *Child Development*, 72, 1–21.

Fox, P. T., Mintun, M. A., Raichle, M. E. et al. (1986) Mapping human visual cortex with positron emission tomography. *Nature*, 323, 806–9.

Fraiberg, S. H. (1974) Blind infants and their mothers: An examination of the sign system. In M. Lewis and L. Rosenblum (eds) *The Effect of the Infant on its Caregiver* (pp. 215–32). New York: Wiley.

Frances, A. (2013) A disease called 'childhood'. *New York Post*, 31 March, http://nypost.com/2013/03/31/a-disease-called-childhood.

Francis, D. D., Diorio, J., Liu, D. and Meaney, M. J. (1999) Nongenomic transmission across generations in maternal behavior and stress responses in the rat, *Science*, 286, 1155–8.

Frank, M. G. and Stennet, J. (2001) The forced-choice paradigm and the perception of facial expressions of emotion. *Journal of Personality and Social Psychology*, 80, 75–85.

Frank, M. G., Ekman, P. and Friesen, W. V. (1993) Behavioral markers and recognizability of the smile of enjoyment. *Journal of Personality and Social Psychology*, 64, 83–93.

Franken, R. E. (1998) *Human Motivation* (4th edn). Pacific Grove, CA: Brooks Cole.

Frankl, V. (2000) *Man's Search for Meaning*. New York: Beacon Press.

Fredrickson, B. L. (2000) Cultivating positive emotions to optimize health and well-being. *Prevention and Treatment*, 31, 1–25.

Fredrickson, B. L. (2001) The role of positive emotions in positive psychology: The broaden-and-build theory of positive emotions. *American Psychologist*, 56, 218–26.

Freedman, J. (1978) *Happy People: What Happiness Is, Who Has It, and Why*. New York: Harcourt Brace Jovanovich.

Freedman, J. L. and Fraser, S. C. (1966) Compliance without pressure: The foot-in-the-door technique. *Journal of Personality and Social Psychology*, 4, 195–202.

Freeman, S., Walker, M. R., Borden, R. and Latané, B. (1975) Diffusion of responsibility and restaurant tipping: Cheaper by the bunch. *Personality and Social Psychology Bulletin*, 1, 584–7.

French, M. T. (2002) Physical appearance and earnings: Further evidence. *Applied Economics*, 34, 569–72.

Freud, A. (1936) *The Ego and the Mechanisms of Defense*. New York: International Universities Press.

Freud, S. ([1900]1965) *The Interpretation of Dreams* (trans. J. Strachey). New York: Avon.

Freud, S. ([1901]1938) The psychopathology of everyday life. In A. A. Brill (ed.) *The Basic Writings of Sigmund Freud* (pp. 33–178). New York: Basic Books.

Freyd, J. J. (1996) *Betrayal Trauma: The Logic of Forgetting Childhood Abuse*. Cambridge, MA: Harvard University Press.

Frick, R. W. (1985) Communicating emotion: The role of prosodic features. *Psychological Bulletin*, 97, 412–29.

Fried, P. A. and Watkinson, B. (2000) Visuoperceptual functioning differs in 9- to 12-year-olds prenatally exposed to cigarettes and marijuana. *Neurotoxicology and Teratology*, 22, 11–20.

Friedman, H. S., Tucker, J. S., Schwartz, J. E. et al. (1995) Psychosocial and behavioural predictors of longevity: The aging and death of the 'Termites'. *American Psychologist*, 50, 69–78.

Friedman, O., van de Vondervoort, J. W., Defeyter, M. A. and Neary, K. R. (2013) First possession, history, and young children's ownership judgments. *Child Development*, 84, 1519–25.

Friedman-Hill, S. R., Robertson, L. C. and Treisman, A. (1995) Parietal contributions to visual feature binding: Evidence from a patient with bilateral lesions. *Science,* 269, 853–5.

Friesen, W. V. (1972) Cultural differences in facial expressions in a social situation: An experimental test of the concept of display rules. Unpublished doctoral dissertation, University of California, San Francisco.

Frieze, I. H., Olson, J. E. and Russell, J. (1991) Attractiveness and income for men and women in management. *Journal of Applied Social Psychology*, 21, 1039–57.

Frinter, M. P. and Rubinson, L. (1993) Acquaintance rape: The influence of alcohol, fraternity membership and sports team membership. *Journal of Sex Education and Therapy*, 19, 272–84.

Frith, C. D. and Fletcher, P. (1995) Voices from nowhere. *Critical Quarterly*, 37, 71–83.

Frith, U. (2003) *Autism: Explaining the Enigma* (2nd edn). Oxford: Blackwell.

Fritzley, V. H. and Lee, K. (2003) Do young children always say yes to yes-no questions? A metadevelopmental study of the affirmation bais. *Child Development*, 74, 1278–94.

Fryer, A. J., Mannuzza, S., Gallops, M. S. et al. (1990) Familial transmission of simple phobias and fears: A preliminary report. *Archives of General Psychiatry*, 47, 252–6.

Fugelsang, J. A. and Dunbar, K. N. (2005) Brain-based mechanisms underlying complex causal thinking. *Neuropsychologia*, 43, 1204–13.

Fukui, H., Murai, T., Fukuyama, H. et al. (2005) Functional activity related to risk anticipation during performance of the Iowa gambling task. *Neuroimage,* 24, 253–9.

Fullard, W. and Reiling, A. M. (1976) An investigation of Lorenz's babyness. *Child Development*, 50, 915–22.

Furmark, T., Tillfors, M., Marteinsdottir, I. et al. (2002) Common changes in cerebral blood flow in patients with social phobia treated with citalopram or cognitive-behavioral therapy. *Archives of General Psychiatry*, 59(5), 425–33.

Fuster, J. M. (2003) *Cortex and Mind.* New York: OUP.

Gabrenya, W. K., Wang, Y. E. and Latané, B. (1985) Social loafing on an optimizing task: Cross-cultural differences among Chinese and Americans. *Journal of Cross-Cultural Psychology*, 16, 223–42.

Gaertner, L., Iuzzini, J. and O'Mara, E. M. (2008) When rejection by one fosters aggression against many: Multiple-victim aggression as a consequence of social rejection and perceived groupness. *Journal of Experimental Social Psychology*, 44, 958–70.

Gagné, F. M. and Lydon, J. E. (2004) Bias and accuracy in close relationships: An integrative review. *Personality and Social Psychology Review*, 8(4), 322–38.

Gais, S. and Born, J. (2004) Low acetylcholine during slow-wave sleep is critical for declaratived memory consolidation. *Proceedings of the National Academy of Sciences*, 101, 2140–4.

Galanter, E. (1962) Contemporary psychophysics. In R. Brown, E. Galanter, E. H. Hess and G. Mandler (eds) *New Directions in Psychology* (pp. 87–156). New York: Holt, Rinehart & Winston.

Galati, D., Scherer, K. R. and Ricci-Bitt, P. E. (1997) Voluntary facial expression of emotion: Comparing congenitally blind with normally sighted encoders. *Journal of Personality and Social Psychology*, 73, 1363–79.

Galea, S., Ahern, J., Resnick, H. et al. (2002) Psychological sequelae of the September 11 terrorist attacks in New York City. *New England Journal of Medicine*, 346(13), 982–7.

Galef, B. (1998) Edward Thorndike: Revolutionary psychologist, ambiguous biologist. *American Psychologist*, 53, 1128–34.

Gallese, V., Fadiga, L., Fogassi, L. and Rizzolatti, G. (1996) Action recognition in the premotor cortex. *Brain*, 119, 593–609.

Gallistel, C. R. (2000) The replacement of general-purpose learning models with adaptively specialized learning modules. In M. S. Gazzaniga (ed.) *The New Cognitive Neurosciences* (pp. 1179–91). Cambridge, MA: MIT Press.

Gallistel, C. R. and Gelman, R. (1992) Preverbal and verbal counting and computation. *Cognition*, Special issue: *Numerical Cognition*, 44, 43–74.

Gallup, G. G. (1970) Chimpanzees: self-recognition. *Science*, 167, 86–7.

Gallup, G. G. (1977) Self-recognition in primates: A comparative approach to the bidirectional properties of consciousness. *American Psychologist*, 32, 329–38.

Galton, F. (1869) *Hereditary Genius: An Inquiry into its Laws and Consequences.* London: Macmillan/Fontana.

Galton, F. (1883) *Inquiries into Human Faculty*. London: Dent.

Galván, A. (2013) The teenage brain: Sensitivity to reward. *Current Directions in Psychological Science*, 22, 88–93.

Gandelman, R. (1992) *The Psychobiology of Behavioral Development*. Oxford: OUP.

Gangestad, S. W. and Simpson, J. A. (2000) On the evolutionary psychology of human mating: Trade-offs and strategic pluralism. *Behavioral and Brain Sciences*, 23, 573–87.

Garb, H. N. (1998) *Studying the Clinician: Judgment Research and Psychological Assessment.* Washington, DC: APA.

Garb, H. N. (1999) Call for a moratorium on the use of the Rorschach inkblot test in clinical and forensic settings. *Assessment*, 6, 313–15.

Garcia, J. (1981) Tilting at the windmills of academe. *American Psychologist*, 36, 149–58.

Garcia, J. and Koelling, R. A. (1966) Relation of cue to consequence in avoidance learning. *Psychonomic Science*, 4, 123–4.

Garcia-Moreno, C., Heise, L., Jansen, H. A. et al. (2005) Violence against women. *Science*, 310, 1282–3.

Gardener, W. L., Gabriel, S. and Lee, A. Y. (1999) 'I' value freedom but 'we' value relationships: Self-construal priming mirrors cultural differences in judgment. *Psychological Science*, 10, 321–6.

Gardner, H. (1983) *Frames of Mind: The Theory of Multiple Intelligences*. New York: Basic Books.

Gardner, M. and Steinberg, L. (2005) Peer influence on risk taking, risk preference, and risky decision making in adolescence and adulthood. *Developmental Psychology*, 41, 625–35.

Gardner, R. A. and Gardner, B. T. (1969) Teaching sign language to a chimpanzee. *Science*, 165, 664–72.

Garry, M., Manning, C., Loftus, E. F. and Sherman, S. J. (1996) Imagination inflation: Imagining a childhood event inflates confidence that it occurred. *Psychonomic Bulletin and Review*, 3, 208–14.

Gartner, R., Baker, K. and Pampel, F. C. (1990) Gender stratification and the gender gap in homicide victimization. *Social Problems*, 37(4): 593–612.

Gates, G. S. (1924) The effects of an audience upon performance. *Journal of Abnormal and Social Psychology*, 18, 334–42.

Gathercole, S. (1997) Models of short-term memory. In M. A. Conway (ed.) *Cognitive Models of Memory* (pp. 13–45). Cambridge, MA: MIT Press.

Gathercole, S. E., Dunning, D. L. and Holmes, J. (2012) Cogmed training: Let's be realistic about intervention research. *Journal of Applied Research in Memory and Cognition*, 1(3), 201–3.

Gauld, A. (1992) *The History of Hypnotism.* Cambridge: CUP.

Gawda, B. (2014) Lack of evidence for the assessment of personality traits using handwriting analysis. *Polish Psychological Bulletin*, 45, 73–9.

Gazzaniga, M. S. (ed.) (2000) *The New Cognitive Neurosciences.* Cambridge, MA: MIT Press.

Gazzaniga, M. S. (2006) Forty-five years of split brain research and still going strong. *Nature Reviews Neuroscience*, 6, 653–9.

Ge, X. and Conger, R. D. (1999) Adjustment problems and emerging personality characteristics from early to late adolescence. *American Journal of Community Psychology*, 27, 429–59.

Geen, R. G. (1983) Evaluation apprehension and social facilitation/inhibition of learning. *Motivation and Emotion*, 7, 203–12.

Geen, R. G. (1984) Preferred stimulation levels in introverts and extraverts: Effects on arousal and performance. *Journal of Personality and Social Psychology*, 46, 1303–12.

Geen, R. G. (1998) Aggression and antisocial behavior. In D. T. Gilbert, S. T. Fiske and G. Lindzey (eds) *The Handbook of Social Psychology* (4th edn, vol. 2, pp. 317–56). New York: McGraw-Hill.

Geen, R. G. and Gange, J. J. (1977) Drive theory of social facilitation: Twelve years of theory and research. *Psychological Bulletin*, 84, 1267–88.

Gegenfurtner, K. R. and Kiper, D. C. (2003) Color vision. *Annual Review of Neuroscience*, 26, 181–206.

Geller, D. A., Hoog, S. L., Heiligenstein, J. H. et al. (2001) Fluoxetine treatment for obsessive-compulsive disorder in children and adolescents: A placebo-controlled clinical trial. *Journal of the American Academy of Child and Adolescent Psychiatry*, 40, 773–9.

Gelman, R., Bullock, M. and Meck, E. (1980) Preschooler's understanding of simple object transformations. *Child Development*, 51, 691–9.

Gelman, S. A. (2003) *The Essential Child: Origins of Essentialism in Everyday Thought*. New York: OUP.

Gelman, S. A., Manczak, E. M. and Noles, N. S. (2012) The nonobvious basis of ownership: preschool children trace the history and value of owned objects. *Child Development*, 83, 1732–47.

Gelman, S. A., Taylor, M. G. and Nguyen, S. P. (2004) Mother-child conversations about gender. *Monographs of the Society for Research in Child Development*, 69(1, serial no. 275).

George, D. (1981) *Sweet Man: The Real Duke Ellington*. New York: Putnam.

George, M. S., Lisanby, S. H. and Sackeim, H. A. (1999) Transcranial magnetic stimulation: Applications in neuropsychiatry. *Archives of General Psychiatry*, 56, 300–11.

Gergely, G., Bekkering, H. and Király, I. (2002) Rational imitation in preverbal infants. *Nature*, 415, 755.

Gershoff, E. T. (2002) Corporal punishment by parents and associated child behaviors and experiences: A meta-analytic and theoretical review. *Psychological Bulletin*, 128, 539–79.

Gibb, B. E., Alloy, L. B. and Tierney, S. (2001) History of childhood maltreatment, negative cognitive styles, and episodes of depression in adulthood. *Cognitive Therapy and Research*, 25, 425–46.

Gibbons, F. X. (1990) Self-attention and behavior: A review and theoretical update. In M. P. Zanna (ed.) *Advances in Experimental Social Psychology* (vol. 23, pp. 249–303). San Diego, CA: Academic Press.

Gibbs, N. A. (1996) Nonclinical populations in research on obsessive-compulsive disorder: A critical review. *Clinical Psychology Review*, 16, 729–73.

Gibson, C. E., Losee, J. and Vitiello, C. (2014) A replication attempt of stereotype susceptibility (Shih, Pittinsky and Ambady, 1999). *Social Psychology*, 45, 194–8.

Gibson, E. J. and Walk, R. D. (1960) The 'visual cliff'. *Scientific American*, 202, 67–71.

Gibson, J. J. (1979) *The Ecological Approach to Visual Perception*. Boston, MA: Houghton Mifflin.

Gick, M. L. and Holyoak, K. J. (1980) Analogical problem solving. *Cognitive Psychology*, 12, 306–55.

Giedd, J. N., Blumenthal, J., Jeffries, N. O. et al. (1999) Brain development during childhood and adolescence: A longitudinal MRI study. *Nature Neuroscience*, 2, 861–3.

Giesler, R. B., Josephs, R. A. and Swann, W. B. Jr (1996) Self-verification in clinical depression: The desire for negative evaluation. *Journal of Abnormal Psychology*, 105, 358–68.

Gigerenzer, G. (1991) From tools to theories: A heuristic of discovery in cognitive psychology. *Psychological Review*, 98, 254–67.

Gigerenzer, G. (1996) The psychology of good judgment: Frequency formats and simple algorithms. *Journal of Medical Decision Making*, 16, 273–80.

Gigerenzer, G. (2002) *Calculated Risks: How to Know When Numbers Deceive You*. New York: Simon & Schuster.

Gigerenzer, G. and Hoffrage, U. (1995) How to improve Bayesian reasoning without instruction: Frequency formats. *Psychological Review*, 102, 684–704.

Gigerenzer, G. and Hug, K. (1992) Domain-specific reasoning: Social contracts, cheating, and perspective change. *Cognition*, 43, 127–71.

Gilbert, D. T. (1991) How mental systems believe. *American Psychologist*, 46, 107–19.

Gilbert, D. T. (1998) Ordinary personology. In D. T. Gilbert, S. T. Fiske and G. Lindzey (eds) *The Handbook of Social Psychology* (4th edn, vol. 2, pp. 89–150). New York: McGraw-Hill.

Gilbert, D. T. (2006) *Stumbling on Happiness*. New York: Knopf.

Gilbert, D. T. and Jones, E. E. (1986) Perceiver-induced constraint: Interpretations of self-generated reality. *Journal of Personality and Social Psychology*, 50, 269–80.

Gilbert, D. T. and Malone, P. S. (1995) The correspondence bias. *Psychological Bulletin*, 117, 21–38.

Gilbert, D. T., Gill, M. J. and Wilson, T. D. (2002) The future is now: Temporal correction in affective forecasting. *Organizational Behavior and Human Decision Processes*, 88, 430–44.

Gilbert, D. T., Jones, E. E. and Pelham, B. W. (1987) Influence and inference: What the active perceiver overlooks. *Journal of Personality and Social Psychology*, 52, 861–70.

Gilbert, D. T., Krull, D. S. and Malone, P. S. (1990) Unbelieving the unbelievable: Some problems in the rejection of false information. *Journal of Personality and Social Psychology*, 59, 601–13.

Gilbert, D. T., Pelham, B. W. and Krull, D. S. (1988) On cognitive busyness: When persons perceive meet persons perceived. *Journal of Personality and Social Psychology*, 54, 733–40.

Gilbert, D. T., Tafarodi, R. W. and Malone, P. S. (1993) You can't not believe everything you read. *Journal of Personality and Social Psychology*, 65, 221–33.

Gilbert, D. T., Brown, R. P., Pinel, E. C. and Wilson, T. D. (2000) The illusion of external agency. *Journal of Personality and Social Psychology*, 79, 690–700.

Gilbert, D. T., Pinel, E. C., Wilson, T. D. et al. (1998) Immune neglect: A source of durability bias in affective forecasting. *Journal of Personality and Social Psychology*, 75, 617–38.

Gilbert, G. M. (1951) Stereotype persistence and change among college students. *Journal of Abnormal and Social Psychology*, 46, 245–54.

Gillette, J., Gleitman, H., Gleitman, L. and Lederer, A. (1999) Human simulation of vocabulary learning. *Cognition*, 73, 135–76.

Gillham, N. W. (2001) *A Life of Sir Francis Galton: From African Exploration to the Birth of Eugenics*. Oxford: OUP.

Gilligan, C. (1982) *In a Different Voice: Psychological Theory and Women's Development*. Cambridge, MA: Harvard University Press.

Gilovich, T. (1991) *How We Know What Isn't So: The Fallibility of Human Reason in Everyday Life*. New York: Free Press.

Gilovich, T., Kruger, J. and Medvec, V. H. (2002) The spotlight effect revisited: Overestimating the manifest variability in our actions and appearance. *Journal of Experimental Social Psychology*, 38, 93–9.

Gilovich, T., Kruger, J. and Savitsky, K. (1999) Everyday egocentrism and everyday interpersonal problems. In R. M. Kowalski and M. R. Leary (eds) *The Social Psychology of Emotional and Behavioral Problems: Interfaces of Social and Clinical Psychology* (pp. 69–95). Washington, DC: APA.

Gilovich, T., Medvec, V. H. and Savitsky, K. (2000) The spotlight effect in social judgment: An egocentric bias in estimates of the salience of one's own actions and appearance. *Journal of Personality and Social Psychology*, 79, 211–22.

Gilovich, T., Savitsky, K. and Medvec, V. H. (1998) The illusion of transparency: Biased assessments of others' ability to read one's emotional states. *Journal of Personality and Social Psychology*, 75, 332–46.

Gjersoe, N. L. and Hood, B. (2013) Changing children's understanding of the brain: A longitudinal study of the Royal Institution Christmas lectures as a measure of public engagement. *PLoS ONE*, 8(11), e80928.

Glanzer, M. and Cunitz, A. R. (1966) Two storage mechanisms in free recall. *Journal of Verbal Learning and Verbal Behavior*, 5, 351–60.

Glaser, B. G. and Strauss, A. L. (1967) *The Discovery of Grounded Theory: Strategies for Qualitative Research*. Chicago: Aldine.

Glaser, R., Kiecolt-Glaser, J. K., Speicher, C. E. and Holliday, J. E. (1985) Stress, loneliness and changes in herpesvirus latency. *Journal of Behavioral Medicine*, 8, 249–60.

Glass, D. C. and Singer, J. E. (1972) *Urban Stress: Experiments on Noise and Social Stressors*. New York: Academic Press.

Glick, P., Gottesman, D. and Jolton, J. (1989) The fault is not in the stars: Susceptibility of skeptics and believers in astrology to the Barnum effect. *Personality & Social Psychology Bulletin*, 15, 572–83.

Glisky, E. L., Schacter, D. L. and Tulving, E. (1986) Computer learning by memory-impaired patients: Acquisition and retention of complex knowledge. *Neuropsychologia*, 24, 313–28.

Glynn, S. M. (1990) Token economy approaches for psychiatric patients: Progress and pitfalls over 25 years. *Behavior Modification*, 14, 383–407.

Gneezy, U. and Rustichini, A. (2000) A fine is a price. *Journal of Legal Studies*, 29, 1–17.

Gobert, A., Rivet, J. M., Cistarelli, L. et al. (1999) Buspirone modulates basal and fluoxetine-stimulated dialysate levels of dopamine, noradrenaline, and serotonin in the frontal cortex of freely moving rats: Activation of serotonin 1A receptors and blockade of alpha2-adrenergic receptors underlie its actions. *Neuroscience*, 93, 1251–62.

Goddard, H. H. (1913) *The Kallikak Family: A Study in the Heredity of Feeble-mindedness*. New York: Macmillan.

Godden, D. R. and Baddeley, A. D. (1975) Context-dependent memory in two natural environments: On land and underwater. *British Journal of Psychology*, 66, 325–31.

Goel, V. and Dolan, R. J. (2003) Explaining modulation of reasoning by belief. *Cognition*, 87, 11–22.

Goetzman, E. S., Hughes, T. and Klinger, E. (1994) Current concerns of college students in a midwestern sample. Unpublished report, University of Minnesota.

Goff, L. M. and Roediger, H. L. III (1998) Imagination inflation for action events: Repeated imaginings lead to illusory recollections. *Memory & Cognition*, 26, 20–33.

Goldacre, B. (2008) *Bad Science*. London: Fourth Estate.

Goleman, D. (1995) *Emotional Intelligence*. New York: Bantam Books.

Gomez, C., Argandota, E. D., Solier, R. G. et al. (1995) Timing and competition in networks representing ambiguous figures. *Brain and Cognition*, 29, 103–14.

González, K. V., Verkuyten, M., Weesie, J. and Poppe, E. (2008) Prejudice towards Muslims in The Netherlands: Testing integrated threat theory. *British Journal of Social Psychology*, 47, 667–85.

Goodale, M. A. and Milner, A. D. (1992) Separate visual pathways for perception and action. *Trends in Neurosciences*, 15, 20–5.

Goodale, M. A. and Milner, A. D. (2004) *Sight Unseen*. Oxford: OUP.

Goodale, M. A., Milner, A. D., Jakobson, L. S. and Carey, D. P. (1991) A neurological dissociation between perceiving objects and grasping them. *Nature*, 349, 154–6.

Goodwin, F. K. and Ghaemi, S. N. (1998) Understanding manic-depressive illness. *Archives of General Psychiatry*, 55, 23–5.

Goodwin, R., Faravelli, C., Rosi, S. et al. (2005) The epidemiology of panic disorder and agoraphobia in Europe. *European Neuropsychopharmacology*, 15, 435–43.

Gopnik, A. (1993) Mindblindness. Unpublished essay. University of California, Berkeley.

Gopnik, A. and Astington, J. W. (1988) Children's understanding of representational change and its relation to the understanding of false belief and the appearance reality distinction. *Child Development*, 59, 26–37.

Gopnik, A. and Slaughter, V. (1991) Young children's understanding of changes in their mental states. *Child Development*, 62, 98–110.

Gopnik, A. and Sobel, D. (2000) Detecting blickets: How young children use information about novel causal powers in categorization and induction. *Child Development*, 71, 1205–22.

Gopnik, M. (1990a) Feature-blind grammar and dysphasia. *Nature*, 344, 715.

Gopnik, M. (1990b) Feature blindness: A case study. *Language Acquisition: A Journal of Developmental Linguistics*, 1, 139–64.

Gosling, S. D. (1998) Personality dimensions in spotted hyenas (*Crocuta crocuta*). *Journal of Comparative Psychology*, 112, 107–18.

Gosling, S. D. (2009) *Snoop: What Your Stuff Says About You*. London: Profile Books.

Gosling, S. D. and John, O. P. (1999) Personality dimensions in nonhuman animals: A cross-species review. *Current Directions in Psychological Science*, 8, 69–75.

Gosling, S. D., Ko, S. J., Mannarelli, T. and Morris, M. E. (2002) A room with a cue: Judgements of personality based on offices and bedrooms. *Journal of Personality and Social Psychology*, 82, 379–98.

Gosling, S. D., Rentfrow, P. J. and Swann, W. B. Jr (2003) A very brief measure of the big-five personality domains. *Journal of Research in Personality*, 37, 504–28.

Goswami, U. (1998) *Cognition in Children*. Hove: Psychology Press.

Goswami, U. (2008) *Cognitive Development: The Learning Brain*. Hove: Psychology Press.

Gottesman, I. I. (1991) *Schizophrenia Genesis: The Origins of Madness*. New York: Freeman.

Gottesman, I. I. and Hanson, D. R. (2005) Human development: Biological and genetic processes. *Annual Review of Psychology*, 56, 263–86.

Gottfredson, L. S. (1997) Mainstream science on intelligence: An editorial with 52 signatories, history, and bibliography. *Intelligence*, 24, 13–23.

Gottfredson, L. S. (1998) The general intelligence factor. *Scientific American Presents*, 9, 24–9.

Gottfredson, L. S. (2003) Dissecting practical intelligence theory: Its claims and evidence. *Intelligence*, 31(4), 343–97.

Gottfredson, L. S. and Deary, I. J. (2004) Intelligence predicts health and longevity, but why? *Current Directions in Psychological Science*, 13, 1–4.

Gottfredson, M. R. and Hirschi, T. (1990) *A General Theory of Crime*. Stanford, CA: Stanford University Press.

Gottman, J. M. (1994) *What Predicts Divorce? The Relationship between Marital Processes and Marital Outcomes*. Hillsdale, NJ: Erlbaum.

Gould, M. S. (1990) Suicide clusters and media exposure. In S. J. Blumenthal and D. J. Kupfer (eds) *Suicide Over the Life Cycle: Risk Factors, Assessment, and Treatment of Suicidal Patients* (pp. 517–32). Washington, DC: American Psychiatric Press.

Gouldner, A. W. (1960) The norm of reciprocity. *American Sociological Review*, 25, 161–78.

Grace, A. A. and Moore, H. (1998) Regulation of information flow in the nucleus accumbens: A model for the pathophysiology of schizophrenia. In M. F. Lanzenweger and R. H. Dworkin (eds) *Origins and Development of Schizophrenia* (pp. 123–60). Washington, DC: APA.

Graf, P. and Schacter, D. L. (1985) Implicit and explicit memory for new associations in normal subjects and amnesic patients. *Journal of Experimental Psychology: Learning, Memory, and Cognition*, 11, 501–18.

Graf, P., Squire, L. R. and Mandler, G. (1984) The information that amnesic patients do not forget. *Journal of Experimental Psychology: Learning, Memory, and Cognition*, 10, 164–78.

Graham, J. E., Rockwood, K., Beattie, B. L. et al. (1997) Prevalence and severity of cognitive impairment with and without dementia in an elderly population. *The Lancet*, 349, 1793–6.

Grant, B. F., Hasin, D. S., Stinson, F. S. et al. (2004) Prevalence, correlates, and disability of personality disorders in the U.S.: Results from the National Epidemiologic Survey on Alcohol and Related Conditions. *Journal of Clinical Psychiatry*, 65, 948–58.

Gray, H. M., Gray, K. and Wegner, D. M. (2007) Dimensions of mind perception. *Science*, 315, 619.

Gray, J. A. (1970) The psychophysiological basis of introversion-extraversion. *Behavior Research and Therapy*, 8, 249–66.

Greeley, A. M. (1975) *The Sociology of the Paranormal: A Reconnaissance.* Beverly Hills, CA: Sage.

Green, A. E., Fugelsang, J. A., Kraemer, D. J. et al. (2010) Connecting long distance: Semantic distance in analogical reasoning modulates frontopolar cortex activity. *Cerebral Cortex*, 20, 70–6.

Green, A. E., Fugelsang, J. A., Kraemer, D. J. et al. (2012) Neural correlates of creativity in analogical reasoning. *Journal of Experimental Psychology: Learning, Memory, and Cognition*, 38, 264–72.

Green, D. A. and Swets, J. A. (1966) *Signal Detection Theory and Psychophysics.* New York: Wiley.

Green, S. K., Buchanan, D. R. and Heuer, S. K. (1984) Winners, losers, and choosers: A field investigation of dating initiation. *Personality & Social Psychology Bulletin*, 10, 502–11.

Greenberg, J., Pyszczynski, T., Solomon, S. et al. (1990) Evidence for terror management theory II: The effects of mortality salience on reactions to those who threaten or bolster the cultural worldview. *Journal of Personality and Social Psychology*, 58, 308–18.

Greene, J. D., Sommerville, R. B., Nystrom, L. E. et al. (2001) An fMRI investigation of emotional engagement in moral judgment. *Science*, 293, 2105–8.

Greenfield, P. M., Keller, H., Fuligni, A. and Maynard, A. (2003) Cultural pathways through universal development. *Annual Review of Psychology*, 54, 461–90.

Greenough, W. T. and Black, J. E. (1992) Induction of brain structures by experience: Substrates for cognitive development. In M. Gunnar and C. Nelson (eds) *Minnesota Symposium on Child Psychology*, vol. 24, *Developmental Behavioral Neuroscience* (pp. 155–200). Hillsdale, NJ: Erlbaum.

Greenwald, A. G. (2011) There is nothing so theoretical as a good method. *Perspectives on Psychological Science*, 7, 99–108.

Greenwald, A. G. and Nosek, B. A. (2001) Health of the Implicit Association Test at age 3. *Zeitschrift für Experimentelle Psychologie*, 48, 85–93.

Greenwald, A. G., McGhee, D. E. and Schwartz, J. L. (1998) Measuring individual differences in implicit cognition: The implicit association test. *Journal of Personality & Social Psychology*, 74, 1464–80.

Greenwald, A. G., Banaji, M. R., Rudman, L. A. et al. (2002) A unified theory of implicit attitudes, stereotypes, self-esteem, and self-concept. *Psychological Review*, 109, 3–25.

Gregg, V. R., Winer, G. A., Cottrell, J. E. et al. (2001) The persistence of a misconception about vision after educational interventions. *Psychological Bulletin & Review*, 8, 622–6.

Gregory, R. L. (1966) *Eye and Brain: The Psychology of Seeing*. London: Weidenfeld & Nicolson.

Gregory, T. R. (2009) Understanding natural selection: Essential concepts and common misconceptions. *Evolution: Education & Outreach*, 2, 156–75.

Gropp, E., Shanabrough, M., Borok, E. et al. (2005) Agouti-related peptide-expressing neurons are mandatory for feeding. *Nature Neuroscience*, 8, 1289–91.

Gross, C. (1999) A hole in the head. *The Neuroscientist*, 5, 263–9.

Gross, J. J. (1998) Antecedent- and response-focused emotion regulation: Divergent consequences for experience, expression, and physiology. *Journal of Personality and Social Psychology*, 74, 224–37.

Gross, J. J. and Munoz, R. F. (1995) Emotion regulation and mental health. *Clinical Psychology: Science and Practice*, 2, 151–64.

Grossman, K., Grossman, K. E., Spangler, S. et al. (1985) Maternal sensitivity and newborn orientation responses as related to quality of attachment in northern Germany. In I. Bertherton and E. Waters (eds) Growing points of attachment theory. *Monographs of the Society for Research in Child Development*, 50(209), 233–56.

Grubin, D., Madsen, L., Parsons, S. et al. (2004) A prospective study of the impact of polygraphy on high-risk behaviours in adult sex offenders. *Sexual Abuse: A Journal of Research and Treatment*, 16, 209–22.

Grudnick, J. L. and Kranzler, J. H. (2001) Meta-analysis of the relationship between intelligence and inspection time. *Intelligence*, 29, 523–35.

Grusec, J. E., Goodnow, J. J. and Cohen, L. (1996) Household work and development of concern for others. *Developmental Psychology*, 32, 999–1007.

Gruter, M. and Masters, R. D. (eds) (1986) Ostracism: A social and biological phenomenon. Special issue, *Ethology and Sociobiology*, 7, 149–395.

Guéguen, N. (2012) The sweet smell of ... implicit helping: Effects of pleasant ambient fragrance on spontaneous help in shopping malls. *Journal of Social Psychology*, 152, 397–400.

Guillery, R. W. and Sherman, S. M. (2002) Thalamic relay functions and their role in corticocortical communication: Generalizations from the visual system. *Neuron*, 33, 163–75.

Guiso, L., Monte, F., Sapienza, P. and Zingales, L. (2008) Diversity: Culture, gender, and math. *Science*, 320(5880), 1164–5.

Gummerum, M., Hanoch, Y., Keller, M. et al. (2010) Preschoolers' allocations in the dictator game: The role of moral emotions. *Journal of Economic Psychology*, 31, 25–34.

Gupta, R. K., Best, J. and MacMahon, E. (2005) Mumps and the UK epidemic 2005. *British Medical Journal*, 330, 1132–5.

Gur, R. E., Cowell, P., Turetsky, B. I. et al. (1998) A follow-up magnetic resonance imaging study of schizophrenia: Relationship of neuranatomical changes to clinical and neurobehavioral measures. *Archives of General Psychiatry*, 55, 145–52.

Gusnard, D. A. and Raichle, M. E. (2001) Searching for a baseline: Functional imaging and the resting human brain. *Nature Reviews: Neuroscience*, 2, 685–94.

Gustafsson, J.-E. (1984) A unifying model for the structure of intellectual abilities. *Intelligence*, 8, 179–203.

Guth, W., Schmittberger, R. and Scwarze, B. (1982) An experimental analysis of ultimatum bargaining. *Journal of Economic Behavior & Organization*, 3, 367–88.

Hacking, I. (1975) *The Emergence of Probability.* Cambridge, MA: CUP.

Haggbloom, S. J., Warnick, R., Warnick, J. E. et al. (2002) The 100 most eminent psychologists of the 20th century. *Review of General Psychology*, 6, 139–52.

Haidt, J. (2001) The emotional dog and its rational tail: A social intuitionist approach to moral judgment. *Psychological Review*, 108, 814–34.

Haidt, J. (2006) *The Happiness Hypothesis: Finding Modern Truth in Ancient Wisdom.* New York: Basic Books.

Haidt, J. and Keltner, D. (1999) Culture and facial expression: Open-ended methods find more expressions and a gradient of recognition. *Cognition and Emotion*, 13, 225–66.

Hall, E. T. (1966) *The Hidden Dimension.* New York: Anchor Books.

Hall, J. A., Coats, E. J. and Smith-LeBeau, L. (2005) Nonverbal behavior and the vertical dimension of social relations: A meta-analysis. *Psychological Bulletin*, 131, 898–924.

Hall, J. A., Horgan, T. G. and Carter, J. D. (2002) Assigned and felt status in relation to observer-coded and participant-reported smiling. *Journal of Nonverbal Behavior*, 26, 63–81.

Hall, J. A., Murphy, N. A. and Schmid-Mast, M. (2007) Nonverbal self-accuracy in interpersonal interaction. *Personality and Social Psychology Bulletin*, 33, 1675–85.

Hallett, M. (2000) Transcranial magnetic stimulation and the human brain. *Nature*, 406, 147–50.

Halliday, R., Naylor, H., Brandeis, D. et al. (1994) The effect of D-amphetamine, clonidine, and yohimbine on human information processing. *Psychophysiology*, 31, 331–7.

Halpern, B. (2002) Taste. In H. Pashler and S. Yantis (eds) *Stevens' Handbook of Experimental Psychology*, vol 1. *Sensation and Perception* (3rd edn, pp. 653–90). New York: Wiley.

Halpern, D. F. (1997) Sex differences in intelligence: Implications for education. *American Psychologist*, 52, 1091–102.

Halpern, D. F. (2004) A cognitive-process taxonomy for sex differences in cognitive abilites. *Current Directions in Psychological Science*, 13, 135–9.

Halpern, D. F., Benbow, C. P., Geary, D. C. et al. (2007) The science of sex differences in science and mathematics. *Psychological Science in the Public Interest*, 8, 1–5.

Hamann, K., Warneken, F., Greenberg, J. R. and Tomasello, M. (2011) Collaboration encourages equal sharing in children but not in chimpanzees. *Nature*, 476, 328–31.

Hamermesh, D. S. and Biddle, J. E. (1994) Beauty and the labor market. *American Economic Review*, 84, 1174–95.

Hamilton, D. L. and Gifford, R. K. (1976) Illusory correlation in interpersonal perception: A cognitive basis of stereotypic judgements. *Journal of Experimental Social Psychology*, 12, 392–407.

Hamilton, W. D. (1964) The genetical evolution of social behaviour. *Journal of Theoretical Biology*, 7, 1–16.

Hamlin, J. K., Wynn, K. and Bloom, P. (2007) Social evaluation by preverbal infants. *Nature*, 450, 557–9.

Hammen, C. L. (1995) Stress and the course of unipolar disorders. In C. M. Mazure (ed.) *Does Stress Cause Psychiatric Illness?* (pp. 87–110). Washington, DC: American Psychiatric Press.

Hammersla, J. F. and Frease-McMahan, L. (1990) University students' priorities: Life goals vs. relationships. *Sex Roles*, 23, 1–14.

Hampson, E., van Anders, S. M. and Mullin, L. I. (2006) A female advantage in the recognition of emotional facial expressions: Test of an evolutionary hypothesis. *Evolution and Human Behavior*, 27, 401–16.

Han, J. J., Leichtman, M. D. and Wang, Q. (1998) Autobiographical memory in Korean, Chinese, and American children. *Developmental Psychology*, 34, 701–13.

Haney, C., Banks, C. and Zimbardo, P. G. (1973) Interpersonal dynamics in a simulated prison. *International Journal of Criminology and Penology*, 1, 69–97.

Hansen, D. E., Vandenberg, B. and Patterson, M. L. (1995) The effects of religious orientation on spontaneous and nonspontaneous helping. *Personality and Individual Differences*, 19, 101–4.

Hansen, E. S., Hasselbalch, S., Law, I. and Bolwig, T. G. (2002) The caudate nucleus in obsessive-compulsive disorder. Reduced metabolism following treatment with paroxetine: A PET study. *International Journal of Neuropsychopharmacology*, 5, 1–10.

Hanson, R. K., Morton, K. E. and Harris, A. J. (2003) Sexual offenders recidivism risk: What we know and what we need to know. *Annals of the New York Academy of Sciences*, 989, 154–66.

Happé, F. G. (1995) The role of age and verbal ability in the theory-of-mind performance of subjects with autism. *Child Development*, 66, 843–55.

Harbaugh, W. T., Mayr, U. and Burghart, D. R. (2007) Neural responses to taxation and voluntary giving reveal motives for charitable donations. *Science*, 316, 1622–5.

Hare, R. D. (1998) *Without Conscience: The Disturbing World of the Psychopaths Among Us*. New York: Guilford Press.

Hargrave, A. C. and Sénéchal, M. (2000) A book reading intervention with preschool children who have limited vocabularies: The benefits of regular reading and dialogic reading. *Early Childhood Research Quarterly*, 15, 75–90.

Harkness, S., Edwards, C. P. and Super, C. M. (1981) Social roles and moral reasoning: A case study in a rural African community. *Developmental Psychology*, 17, 595–603.

Harley, T. (2008) *Psychology of Language: From Data to Theory* (3rd edn). Hove: Psychology Press.

Harlow, H. F. (1932) Social facilitation of feeding in the albino rat. *The Pedagogical Seminary and Journal of Genetic Psychology*, 41, 211–21.

Harlow, H. F. (1958) The nature of love. *American Psychologist*, 13, 573–685.

Harlow, H. F. and Harlow, M. L. (1965) The affectional systems. In A. M. Schrier, H. F. Harlow and F. Stollnitz (eds) *Behavior of Nonhuman Primates* (vol. 2, pp. 287–334). New York: Academic Press.

Harlow, J. M. (1848) Passage of an iron rod through the head. *Boston Medical and Surgical Journal*, 39, 389–93.

Harnishfeger, K. K. and Pope, R. S. (1996) Intending to forget: The development of cognitive inhibition in directed forgetting. *Journal of Experimental Child Psychology*, 62, 292–315.

Haro, J. M., Ayso-Mateos, J. L., Bitter, I. et al. (2014) ROAMER: Roadmap for Mental Health in Europe. *International Journal of Methods in Psychiatric Research*, 23, 1–14.

Harris, B. (1979) Whatever happened to Little Albert? *American Psychologist*, 34, 151–60.

Harris, M. J. and Rosenthal, R. (1985) Mediation of interpersonal expectancy effects: 31 meta-analyses. *Psychological Bulletin*, 97, 363–86.

Harris, P. L., de Rosnay, M. and Pons, F. (2005) Language and children's understanding of mental states. *Current Directions in Psychological Science*, 14, 69–73.

Harris, S., Sheth, S. A. and Cohen, M. S. (2008) Functional neuroimaging of belief, disbelief and uncertainty. *Annals of Neurology*, 63, 141–7.

Hart, C. L., Taylor, M. D., Davey Smith, G. et al. (2005) Childhood IQ and all cause mortality before and after age 65: Prospective observational study linking the Scottish Mental Survey 1932 and the Midspan studies. *British Journal of Health Psychology*, 10, 153–65.

Hart, J. T. (1965) Memory and the feeling-of-knowing experience. *Journal of Educational Psychology*, 56, 208–16.

Hart, P. T. (1998) Preventing groupthink revisited: Evaluating and reforming groups in government. *Organizational Behavior and Human Decision Processes*, 73, 306–26.

Harter, S. (1999) *The Construction of the Self: A Developmental Perspective*. New York: Guilford Press.

Hartley, J. E. (1974) *Lighting Reinforces Crime Fight*. Pittsfield, MA: Buttenheim.

Hartshorne, H. and May, M. (1928) *Studies in Deceit*. New York: Macmillan.

Haselton, M. G. and Funder, D. (2006) The evolution of accuracy and bias in social judgment. In M. Schaller, J. A. Simpson and D. T. Kenrick (eds) *Evolution and Social Psychology* (2nd edn, pp. 15–37). New York: Psychology Press.

Hasher, L. and Zacks, R. T. (1984) Automatic processing of fundamental information: The case of frequency of occurrence. *American Psychologist*, 39, 1372–88.

Haslam, A. and Reicher, S. (2008) Questioning the banality of evil. *The Psychologist*, 21, 16–19.

Hassabis, D., Kumaran, D., Vann, S. D. and Maguire, E. A. (2007) Patients with hippocampal amnesia cannot imagine new experiences. *Proceedings of the National Academy of Sciences,* 104, 1726–31.

Hasselmo, M. E. (2006) The role of acetylcholine in learning and memory. *Current Opinion in Neurobiology*, 16, 710–15.

Hasson, U., Hendler, T., Bashat, D. B. and Malach, R. (2001) Vase or face? A neural correlate of shape-selective grouping processes in the human brain. *Journal of Cognitive Neuroscience*, 13, 744–53.

Hastings, M. (2013) *Catastrophe 1914: Europe Goes To War*. London: William Collins.

Hatfield, E. (1988) Passionate and companionate love. In R. J. Sternberg and M. L. Barnes (eds) *The Psychology of Love* (pp. 191–217). New Haven, CT: Yale University Press.

Hatfield, E. and Rapson, R. L. (1992) Similarity and attraction in close relationships. *Communication Monographs*, 59, 209–12.

Hatfield, E., Cacioppo, J. L. and Rapson, R. L. (1993) Emotional contagion. *Current Directions in Psychological Sciences*, 2, 96–9.

Hatfield, E., Cacioppo, J. T. and Rapson, R. L. (1994) *Emotional Contagion*. Cambridge: CUP.

Hathaway, S. R. and McKinley, J. C. (1951) *Minnesota Multiphasic Personality Inventory Manual.* New York: Psychological Corporation.

Hauser, M. D. (2006) *Moral Minds: How Nature Designed our Universal Sense of Right and Wrong*. New York: HarperCollins.

Hausser, M. (2000) The Hodgkin-Huxley theory of the action potential. *Nature Neuroscience*, 3, 1165.

Haxby, J. V., Gobbini, M. I., Furey, M. L. et al. (2001) Distributed and overlapping representations of faces and objects in ventral temporal cortex. *Science*, 293, 2425–30.

Hay, D. F. and Ross, H. S. (1982) The social nature of early conflict. *Child Development*, 53, 105–13.

Hay, D. F., Caplan, M., Castle, J. and Simson, C. A. (1991) Does sharing become increasingly 'rational' in the second year of life? *Developmental Psychology*, 27, 987–93.

Hay, P., Sachdev, P., Cumming, S. et al. (1993) Treatment of obsessive-compulsive disorder by psychosurgery. *Acta Psychiatrica Scandinavica*, 87, 197–207.

Hayes, D. P. and Grether, J. (1983) The school year and vacations: When do students learn? *Cornell Journal of Social Relations*, 17, 56–71.

Hayes, K. and Hayes, C. (1951) The intellectual development of a home-raised chimpanzee. *Proceedings of the American Philosophical Society*, 95, 105–9.

Hayes, S. C., Strosahl, K. and Wilson, K. G. (1999) *Acceptance and Commitment Therapy: An Experiential Approach to Behavior Change.* New York: Guilford Press.

Hazan, C. and Shaver, P. (1987) Romantic love conceptualized as an attachment process. *Journal of Personality and Social Psychology*, 52, 511–24.

Heaton, R., Paulsen, J. S., McAdams, L. A. et al. (1994) Neuropsychological deficits in schizophrenia: Relationship to age, chronicity, and dementia. *Archives of General Psychiatry*, 51, 469–76.

Heavey, C. L., Hurlburt, R. T. and Lefforge, N. L. (2012) Toward a phenomenology of feelings. *Emotion*, 12, 763–77.

Hebb, D. O. (1949) *The Organization of Behavior.* New York: Wiley.

Hebb, D. O. (1977) Wilder Penfield: His legacy to neurology. The frontal lobe. *Canadian Medical Association Journal*, 116(12), 1373–4.

Hebl, M. R. and Heatherton, T. F. (1997) The stigma of obesity in women: The difference is Black and White. *Personality and Social Psychology Bulletin*, 24, 417–26.

Hebl, M. R. and Mannix, L. M. (2003) The weight of obesity in evaluating others: A mere proximity effect. *Personality and Social Psychology Bulletin*, 29, 28–38.

Hecht, S. and Mandelbaum, M. (1938) Rod-cone dark adaptation and vitamin A. *Science*, 88, 219–21.

Heerey, E. A., Keltner, D. and Capps, L. M. (2003) Making sense of self-conscious emotion: Linking theory of mind and emotion in children with autism. *Emotion*, 3, 394–400.

Heider, F. (1958) *The Psychology of Interpersonal Relations.* New York: Wiley.

Heider, F. and Simmel, M. (1944) An experimental study of apparent behavior. *American Journal of Psychology*, 57, 243–59.

Held, R., Birch, E. E. and Gwiazda, J. (1980) Stereoacuity of human infants. *Proceedings of the National Academy of Sciences*, 77, 5572–4.

Helmholtz, H. (1866) *Handbuch der Physiologischen Optik*. Hamburg: L. Voss. English translation in D. L. MacAdam (1970) *Sources of Color Science*. Cambridge MA: MIT Press.

Hemmesch, A. R., Tickle-Degnen, L. and Zebrowitz, L. A. (2009) The influence of facial masking and sex on older adults' impressions of individuals with Parkinson's disease. *Psychology and Aging*, 24, 542–9.

Henderlong, J. and Lepper, M. R. (2002) The effects of praise on children's intrinsic motivation: A review and synthesis. *Psychological Bulletin*, 128, 774–95.

Henley, N. M. (1973) Status and sex: Some touching observations. *Bulletin for the Psychonomic Society*, 2, 91–3.

Henriques, J. B. and Davidson, R. J. (1990) Regional brain electrical asymmetries discriminate between previously depressed and healthy control subjects. *Journal of Abnormal Psychology*, 99, 22–31.

Henry, W. P., Strupp, H. H., Schacht, T. E. and Gaston, L. (1994) Psychodynamic approaches. In A. E. Bergin and S. L. Garfield (eds) *Handbook of Psychotherapy and Behavior Change* (pp. 467–508). New York: Wiley.

Hepper, P. G. (1988) Fetal 'soap' addiction. *The Lancet*, 1, 1347–8.

Herculano-Houzel, S. (2002) Do you know your brain? A survey on public neuroscience literacy at the closing of the decade of the brain. *Neuroscientist*, 8, 98–110.

Herman, J. L. (1992) *Trauma and Recovery.* New York: Basic Books.

Hermann, D. J., Raybeck, D. and Gruneberg, M. (2002) *Improving Memory and Study Skills: Advances in Theory and Practice.* Seattle: Hogrefe & Huber.

Herrnstein, R. J. (1972) Nature as nurture: Behaviorism and the instinct doctrine. *Behaviorism*, 1, 23–52.

Herrnstein, R. J. (1977) The evolution of behaviorism. *American Psychologist*, 32, 593–603.

Herschfeld, H. E. (2011) Future self-continuity: How conceptions of the future self transform intertemporal choice. *Annals of the New York Academy of Sciences*, 1235, 30–43.

Hershenson, M. (ed.) (1989) *The Moon Illusion.* Hillsdale, NJ: Erlbaum.

Hertwig, R. and Gigerenzer, G. (1999) The 'conjunction fallacy' revisited: How intelligent inferences look like reasoning errors. *Journal of Behavioral Decision Making*, 12, 275–305.

Heslin, R. and Alper, T. (1983) Touch: A bonding gesture. In J. M. Wiemann and R. P. Harrison (eds) *Nonverbal Interaction* (pp. 47–75). Beverly Hills, CA: Sage.

Hess, T. M. (2005) Memory and aging in context. *Psychological Bulletin*, 131, 383–406.

Hetherington, E. M., Bridges, M. and Insabella, G. M. (1998) What matters? What does not? Five perspectives on the association between marital transitions and children's adjustment. *American Psychologist*, 53, 167–84.

Hetherington, M. H. (2001) Chocolate: From adoration to addiction. In M. H. Hetherington (ed.) *Food Cravings and Addiction* (pp. 295–319). Leatherhead: Leatherhead Food Research Association.

Hettema, J. M., Neale, M. C. and Kendler, K. S. (2001) A review and meta-analysis of the genetic epidemiology of anxiety disorders. *American Journal of Psychiatry*, 158, 1568–78.

Hewstone, M., Rubin, M. and Willis, H. (2002) Intergroup bias. *Annual Review of Psychology*, 53, 575–604.

Heyns, B. (1978) *Summer Learning and the Effects of Schooling.* New York: Academic Press.

Hick, W. E. (1952) On the rate of gain of information. *Quarterly Journal of Experimental Psychology*, 4, 11–26.
Hicks, J. L. and Marsh, R. L. (2002) On predicting the future states of awareness for recognition of unrecallable items. *Memory and Cognition*, 30, 60–6.
Higbee, K. L. and Clay, S. L. (1998) College students' beliefs in the ten-percent myth. *Journal of Psychology: Interdisciplinary and Applied*, 132, 469–76.
Higgins, E. T. (1987) Self-discrepancy theory: A theory relating self and affect. *Psychological Review*, 94, 319–40.
Hilgard, E. R. (1965) *Hypnotic Susceptibility.* New York: Harcourt, Brace and World.
Hilgard, E. R. (1986) *Divided Consciousness: Multiple Controls in Human Thought and Action.* New York: Wiley-Interscience.
Hillman, C. H., Erickson, K. I. and Kramer, A. F. (2008) Be smart, exercise your heart: Exercise effects on brain and cognition. *Nature Reviews Neuroscience*, 9, 58–65.
Hinde, R. A. (1982) Attachment: Some conceptualand biological issues. In C. Parkes and J. Stevenson-Hinde (eds) *The Place of Attachment in Human Behaviour* (pp. 60–78). New York: Basic Books.
Hines, M. (2004) *Brain Gender.* New York: OUP.
Hintzman, D. L., Asher, S. J. and Stern, L. D. (1978) Incidental retrieval and memory for coincidences. In M. M. Gruneberg, P. E. Morris and R. N. Sykes (eds) *Practical Aspects of Memory* (pp. 61–8). New York: Academic Press.
Hirschberger, G., Florian, V. and Mikulincer, M. (2002) The anxiety buffering function of close relationships: Mortality salience effects on the readiness to compromise mate selection standards. *European Journal of Social Psychology*, 32, 609–25.
Hirschfeld, D. R., Rosenbaum, J. F., Biederman, J. et al. (1992) Stable behavioral inhibition and its association with anxiety disorder. *Journal of the American Academy of Child and Adolescent Psychiatry*, 31, 103–11.
Hirschfeld, L. A. and Gelman, S. A. (eds) (1994) *Mapping the Mind: Domain Specificity in Cognition and Culture.* New York: CUP.
Hirschfeld, R. M. (1996) Panic disorder: Diagnosis, epidemiology, and clinical course. *Journal of Clinical Psychiatry*, 57, 3–8.
Hirschi, T. (2004) Self control and crime. In R. F. Baumeister and K. D. Vohs (eds) *Handbook of Self-regulation: Research, Theory and Applications* (pp. 537–52). New York: Guilford Press.
Hirstein, W. and Ramachandran, V. S. (1997) Capgras syndrome: A novel probe for understanding the neural representation of the identity and familiarity of persons. *Proceedings: Biological Sciences*, 264, 437–44.
Hishakawa, Y. (1976) Sleep paralysis. In C. Guilleminault, W. C. Dement and P. Passouant (eds) *Narcolepsy: Advances in Sleep Research* (vol. 3, pp. 97–124). New York: Spectrum.
Hobara, M. (2003) Prevalence of transitional objects in young children in Tokyo and New York. *Infant Mental Health Journal*, 24, 174–91.
Hobson, J. A. (1988) *The Dreaming Brain.* New York: Basic Books.
Hobson, J. A. (2002) *Dreaming: An Introduction to Sleep Science.* Oxford: OUP.
Hobson, J. A. and McCarley, R. W. (1977) The brain as a dream-state generator: An activation-synthesis hypothesis of the dream process. *American Journal of Psychiatry*, 134, 1335–68.
Hodgkin, A. L. and Huxley, A. F. (1939) Action potential recorded from inside a nerve fibre. *Nature*, 144, 710–12.
Hodson, G. and Sorrentino, R. M. (2001) Just who favors in in-group? Personality differences in reactions to uncertainty in the minimal group paradigm. *Group Dynamics*, 5, 92–101.
Hoffman, R. E., Hawkins, K. A., Gueorguieva, R. et al. (2003) Transcranial magnetic stimulation of left temporoparietal cortex and medication-resistant auditory hallucinations. *Archives of General Psychiatry*, 60, 49–56.
Hoffrage, U. and Gigerenzer, G. (1996) The impact of information representation on Bayesian reasoning. In G. Cottrell (ed.) *Proceedings of the Eighteenth Annual Conference of the Cognitive Science Society* (pp. 126–30). Mahwah, NJ: Erlbaum.
Hoffrage, U. and Gigerenzer, G. (1998) Using natural frequencies to improve diagnostic inferences. *Academic Medicine*, 73, 538–40.
Hofmann, S. G. and Hinton, D. E. (2014) Cross-cultural aspects of anxiety disorders. *Current Psychiatry Reports*, 16, 450–5.
Høigaard, R., Fuglestad, S., Peters, D. M. et al. (2010) Role satisfaction mediates the relation between role ambiguity and social loafing among elite women handball players. *Journal of Applied Sports Psychology*, 22, 408–19.
Hollander, E. P. (1964) *Leaders, Groups, and Influence.* Oxford: OUP.
Holloway, G. (2001) *The Complete Dream Book: What Your Dreams Tell About You and Your Life.* Naperville, IL: Sourcebooks.
Holloway, M. (1999) Flynn's effect. *Scientific American*, 280(1), 37–8.
Holmbeck, G. N. and O'Donnell, K. (1991) Discrepancies between perceptions of decision making and behavioral autonomy. In R. L. Paikoff (ed.) *New Directions for Child Development: Shared Views in the Family During Adolescence* (pp. 1–8). San Francisco, CA: Jossey-Bass.
Holmes, J., Gathercole, S. E. and Dunning, D. L. (2009) Adaptive training leads to sustained enhancement of poor working memory in children. *Developmental Science*, 12, 9–15.
Holmes, T. H. and Rahe, R. H. (1967) The social readjustment rating scale. *Journal of Psychosomatic Research*, 11, 213–318.
Holt-Lunstad, J., Smith, T. B. and Layton, J. B. (2010) Social relationships and mortality risk: A meta-analytic review. *PLoS Med*, 7(7), e1000316.
Holyoak, K. J. and Thagard, P. (1995) *Mental Leaps: Analogy in Creative Thought*. Cambridge, MA: MIT Press.
Hölzel, B. K., Lazar, S. W., Gard, T. et al. (2011) How does mindfulness meditation work? Proposing mechanisms of action from a conceptual and neural perspective. *Perspectives on Psychological Science*, 6, 537–59.
Homans, G. C. (1961) *Social Behavior.* New York: Harcourt, Brace and World.
Hood, B. M. (1995) Gravity rules for two- to four-year-olds? *Cognitive Development*, 10, 577–98.
Hood, B. M. (2009) *SuperSense: From Superstition to Religion – the Brain Science of Belief.* London: Constable & Robinson.
Hood, B. M. (2012) *The Self Illusion: Why There is No 'You' Inside Your Head.* London: Constable & Robinson.
Hood, B. M. (2014) *The Domesticated Brain*. London: Pelican.
Hood, B. M. and Bloom, P. (2008) Children prefer certain individuals over perfect duplicates. *Cognition*, 106, 455–62.
Hood, B. M. and Willatts, P. (1986) Reaching in the dark to an object's remembered position. Evidence for object permanence in 5-month-old infants. *British Journal of Developmental Psychology*, 4, 57–65.
Hood, B. M., Atkinson, J. and Braddick, O. J. (1998) Selection-for-action and the development of visual selective attention. In J. E. Richards (ed.) *Cognitive Neuroscience of Attention: A Developmental Perspective* (pp. 219–49). Hillsdale, NJ: Lawrence Erlbaum.
Hood, B. M., Willen, J. D. and Driver, J. (1998) An eye direction detector triggers shifts of visual attention in human infants. *Psychological Science*, 9, 53–6.
Hooley, J. M. and Hiller, J. B. (1998) Expressed emotion and the pathogenesis of relapse in schizophrenia. In M. F. Lenzenweger and R. H. Dworkin (eds) *Origins and Development of Schizophrenia* (pp. 447–68). Washington, DC: APA.
Horn, G. (1985) *Memory, Imprinting and the Brain: An Inquiry into Mechanisms*. Oxford: Clarendon Press.
Horn, J. L. and Cattell, R. B. (1966) Refinement and test of the theory of fluid and crystallized general intelligences. *Journal of Educational Psychology*, 5, 253–70.

Horner, V. and Whiten, A. (2005) Causal knowledge and imitation/emulation switching in chimpanzees (*Pan troglodytes*) and children (*Homo sapiens*). *Animal Cognition*, 8, 164–81.

Horney, K. (1937) *The Neurotic Personality of Our Time.* New York: Norton.

Hornik, R., Risenhoover, N. and Gunnar, M. (1987) The effects of maternal positive, neutral and negative affective communications on infants' responses to new toys. *Child Development*, 58, 937–44.

Horst, J. S., Parsons, K. L. and Bryan, N. M. (2011) Get the story straight: Contextual repetition promotes word learning from storybooks. *Frontiers in Developmental Psychology*, 4, 1–11.

Horta, B. L., Victoria, C. G., Menezes, A. M. et al. (1997) Low birthweight, preterm births and intrauterine growth retardation in relation to maternal smoking. *Pediatrics and Perinatal Epidemiology*, 11, 140–51.

Hosey, G. R., Wood, M., Thompson, R. J. and Druck, P. L. (1985) Social facilitation in a non-social animal, the centipede, *Lithobius forticatus*. *Behavioral Processes*, 10, 123–30.

Hovland, C. I. and Weiss, W. (1951) The influence of source credibility on communication effectiveness. *Public Opinion Quarterly*, 15, 635–50.

Hovland, C. I., Lumsdaine, A. A. and Sheffield, F. D. (1949) *Experiments on Mass Communications.* Princeton, NJ: Princeton University Press.

Howard, I. P. (2002) Depth perception. In S. Yantis and H. Pashler (eds) *Stevens' Handbook of Experimental Psychology*, vol. 1. *Sensation and Perception* (3rd edn, pp. 77–120). New York: Wiley.

Howard, I. P. and Templeton, W. B. (1966) *Human Spatial Orientation.* London: Wiley.

Howard, J. H. Jr and Howard, D. V. (1997) Age differences in implicit learning of higher order dependencies in serial patterns. *Psychology and Aging*, 12, 634–56.

Howard-Jones, P. A., Blakemore, S.-J., Samuel, E. A. et al. (2005) Semantic divergence and creative story generation: An fMRI investigation. *Cognitive Brain Research*, 25, 240–50.

Howes, C. (1983) Patterns of friendship. *Child Development*, 54, 1041–53.

HSCIC (2014) Statistics on Smoking: England 2014, www.hscic.gov.uk/catalogue/PUB14988/smok-eng-2014-rep.pdf.

Hsu, L. K. (1990) *Eating Disorders.* New York: Guilford Press.

Hubbard, E. M. and Ramachandran, V. S. (2003) Refining the experimental lever. *Journal of Consciousness Studies*, 10, 77–84.

Hubel, D. H. (1988) *Eye, Brain, and Vision.* New York: Freeman.

Hubel, D. H. and Wiesel, T. N. (1962) Receptive fields, binocular interaction and functional architecture in the cat's visual cortex. *Journal of Physiology*, 160, 106–54.

Hubel, D. H. and Wiesel, T. N. (1998) Early exploration of the visual cortex. *Neuron*, 20, 401–12.

Hudson, J. I., Hiripi, E., Pope, H. G. and Kessler, R. C. (2007) The prevalence and correlates of eating disorders in the national comorbidity survey replication. *Biological Psychiatry*, 61(3), 348–58.

Huesmann, L. R., Moise-Titus, J., Podolski, C.-L. and Eron, L. D. (2003) Longitudinal relations between children's exposure to TV violence and their aggressive and violent behavior in young adulthood: 1977–1992. *Developmental Psychology*, 39, 201–21.

Hughes, C. and Dunn, J. (1998) Understanding mind and emotion: Longitudinal associations with mental-state talk between young friends. *Developmental Psychology*, 34, 1026–37.

Hull, C. L. (1943) *Principles of Behavior: An Introduction to Behavior Theory*. Oxford: Appleton-Century-Crofts.

Hulme, C. and Melby-Levårg, M. (2012) Current evidence does not support the claims made for Cogmed working memory training. *Journal of Applied Research in Memory and Cognition*, 1, 197–200.

Hume, D. ([1748]1999) *Enquiry Concerning Human Understanding.* Sections IV–VII (paras 20–61), pp 25–79. Oxford: OUP.

Humphrey, N. (1984) *Consciousness Regained*. Oxford: OUP.

Humphrey, N. and Weiskrantz, L. (1967) Vision in monkeys after removal of the striate cortex. *Nature*, 215, 595–7.

Humphreys, G. W. and Bruce, V. (1989) *Visual Cognition: Computational, Experimental, and Neuropsychological Perspectives.* London: Lawrence Erlbaum.

Humphreys, N. and Dennett, D. C. (1989) Speaking for our selves. *Raritan: A Quarterly Review*, 9, 68–98.

Hunsley, J. and Di Giulio, G. (2002) Dodo bird, phoenix, or urban legend? The question of psychotherapy equivalence. *Scientific Review of Mental Health Practice*, 1, 13–24.

Hunt, E. (1980) Intelligence as an information processing concept. *British Journal of Psychology*, 71, 449–74.

Hunt, M. (1959) *The Natural History of Love.* New York: Knopf.

Hunt, R. R. and McDaniel, M. A. (1993) The enigma of organization and distinctiveness. *Journal of Memory and Language*, 32, 421–45.

Hunter, J. E. and Hunter, R. F. (1984) Validity and utility of alternative predictors of job performance. *Psychological Bulletin*, 96, 72–98.

Hurvich, L. M. and Jameson, D. (1957) An opponent process theory of color vision. *Psychological Review*, 64, 384–404.

Huxley, A. (1954) *The Doors of Perception.* New York: Harper & Row.

Hyde, J. S., Fenneman, E. and Lamon, S. J. (1990) Gender differences in mathematics performance: A meta-analysis. *Psychological Bulletin*, 107, 139–55.

Hyman, I. E. Jr and Billings, F. J. (1998) Individual differences and the creation of false childhood memories. *Memory*, 6, 1–20.

Hyman, I. E. Jr and Pentland, J. (1996) The role of mental imagery in the creation of false childhood memories. *Journal of Memory and Language*, 35, 101–17.

Iacono, W. G. and Beiser, M. (1992) Where are women in first-episode studies of schizophrenia? *Schizophrenia Bulletin*, 18, 471–80.

Ichheiser, G. (1949) Misunderstandings in human relations: A study in false social perceptions. *American Journal of Sociology*, 55(Part 2), 1–70.

Ingham, A. G., Levinger, G., Graves, J. and Peckham, V. (1974) The Ringelmann effect: Studies of group size and group performance. *Journal of Experimental Social Psychology*, 10, 371–84.

Ingram, R. E., Miranda, J. and Segal, Z. V. (1998) *Cognitive Vulnerability to Depression.* New York: Guilford Press.

Ingvar, M., Ambros-Ingerson, J., Davis, M. et al. (1997) Enhancement by an ampakine of memory encoding in humans. *Experimental Neurology*, 146, 553–9.

Inui, A. (2001) Ghrelin: An orexigenic and somatotrophic signal from the stomach. *Nature Reviews Neuroscience*, 2, 551–60.

Irvine, J. T. (1978) Wolof magical thinking: Culture and conservation revisited. *Journal of Cross Cultural Psychology*, 9, 300–10.

Isabella, R. A. (1993) Origins of attachment: Maternal interactive behaviour across the first year. *Child Development*, 64, 605–21.

Isacsson, G. and Rich, C. L. (1997) Depression and antidepressants, and suicide: Pharmacoepidemiological evidence for suicide prevention. In R. W. Maris, M. M. Silverman and S. S. Canetton (eds) *Review of Suicidology* (pp. 168–201). New York: Guilford Press.

Isen, A. M. and Patrick, R. (1983) The effect of positive feelings on risk-taking: When the chips are down. *Organizational Behavior and Human Performance*, 31, 194–202.

Itakura, S., Ishida, H., Kanda, T. et al. (2008) How to build an intentional android: Infants' imitation of a robot's goal-directed actions. *Infancy*, 13, 519–32.

Itard, J. M. (1802) *An Historical Account of the Discovery and Education of a Savage Man or of the First Developments, Physical and Moral of the Young Savage Caught in the Woods near Averyon in the Year 1798.* London: Richard Phillips.

Ittelson, W. H. (1952) *The Ames Demonstrations in Perception.* Princeton, NJ: Princeton University Press.

Izard, C. (1971) *The Face of Emotion.* New York: Appleton-Century-Crofts.

Izard, C. (1977) *Human Emotions*. New York: Plenum Press.

Jablensky, A. (1997) The 100-year epidemiology of schizophrenia. *Schizophrenia Research*, 28, 111–25.

Jablensky, A., Sartorious, N. Ernberg, G. et al. (1992) Schizophrenia: Manifestations, incidence and course in different cultures. A WHO ten country study. *Psychological Medicine Monograph*, Supplement 20, 1–97.

Jack, F., MacDonald, S., Reese, E. and Hayne, H. (2009) Maternal reminiscing style during early childhood predicts the age of adolescents' earliest memories. *Child Development*, 80, 496–505.

Jackson, J. J., Thoemmes, F., Jonkmann, K. et al. (2012) Military training and personality trait development: Does the military make the man, or does the man make the military? *Psychological Science*, 23, 270–7.

Jacobs, G. H. (1997) Color vision polymorphisms in New World monkeys: Implications for the evolution of primate trichomacy. In W. G. Kinzey (ed.) *New World Primates: Ecology, Evolution and Behavior* (pp. 45–74). New York: Aldine de Gruyter.

Jacobson, T. and Hoffman, V. (1997) Children's attachment representations: Longitudinal relations to school behavior and academic competency in middle childhood and adolescence. *Developmental Psychology*, 33, 703–10.

Jahanshahi, M., Profice, P., Brown, R. G. et al. (1998) The effects of transcranial magnetic stimulation over the dorsolateral prefrontal cortex on suppression of habitual counting during random number generation. *Brain*, 121, 1533–44.

Jahoda, G. (1993) *Crossroads Between Culture and Mind*. Cambridge, MA: Harvard University Press.

James, T. W., Culham, J., Humphrey, G. K. et al. (2003) Ventral occipital lesions impair object recognition but not object-directed grasping: An fMRI study. *Brain*, 126, 2463–75.

James, W. (1884) What is an emotion? *Mind*, 9, 188–205.

James, W. (1890) *The Principles of Psychology*. Cambridge, MA: Harvard University Press.

James, W. (1902) *The Varieties of Religious Experience: A Study in Human Nature*. New York: Longman.

James, W. (1907) The energies of men. *Philosophical Review*, 16, 1–20.

James, W. (1911) *Memories and Studies*. New York: Longman.

Jamieson, J. P. (2010) The home field advantage: A meta-analysis. *Journal of Applied Social Psychology*, 40, 1819–48.

Jamieson, J. P., Nock, M. K. and Mendes, W. B. (2013) Changing the conceptualization of stress in social anxiety disorder: Affective and physiological consequences. *Clinical Psychological Science*, 1, 363–74.

Jamison, K. R. (1999) *Night Falls Fast: Understanding Suicide*. New York: Random House.

Janicak, P. G., Dowd, S. M., Martis, B. et al. (2002) Repetitive transcranial magnetic stimulation versus electroconvulsive therapy for major depression: Preliminary results of a randomized trial. *Biological Psychiatry*, 51, 659–67.

Janis, I. L. (1972) *Victims of Groupthink*. Boston, MA: Houghton Mifflin.

Janis, I. L. (1982) *Groupthink: Psychological Studies of Policy Decisions and Fiascoes* (2nd edn). Boston: Houghton Mifflin.

Janis, I. L. and Mann, L. (1977) *Decision Making*. New York: Free Press.

Jaremka, L. M., Fagundes, C. P., Peng, J. et al. (2013) Loneliness promotes inflammation during acute stress. *Psychological Science*, 24, 1089–97.

Jarrett, C. (2008) Foundations of sand? *The Psychologist*, 21, 756–9.

Jassawalla, A., Sashittal, H. and Malshe, A. (2009) Students' perception of social loafing: Its antecedents and consequences in undergraduate business classroom tests. *Academy of Management Learning and Education*, 8, 42–54.

Jauk, E., Benedek, M., Dunst, B. and Neubauer, A. C. (2013) The relationship between intelligence and creativity: New support for the threshold hypothesis by means of empirical breakpoint detection. *Intelligence*, 41, 212–21.

Jaynes, J. (1976) *The Origin of Consciousness in the Breakdown of the Bicameral Mind*. London: Allen Lane.

Jellison, J. M. and Riskind, J. (1970) A social comparison of abilities interpretation of risk-taking behavior. *Journal of Personality and Social Psychology*, 15, 375–90.

Jencks, C. (1979) *Who Gets Ahead? The Determinants of Economic Success in America*. New York: Wiley.

Jenike, M. A., Baer, L. and Minichiello, W. E. (1986) *Obsessive-compulsive Disorders: Theory and Management*. Littleton, MA: PSG Publishing.

Jensen, A. R. (1987) Individual differences in the Hick paradigm. In P. A. Vernon (ed.) *Speed of Information Processing and Intelligence* (pp. 101–75). Norwood, NJ: Ablex.

Jensen-Campbell, L. A., Adams, R., Perry, D. G. et al. (2002) Agreeableness, extraversion and peer relations in early adolescence: Winning friends and deflecting aggression. *Journal of Research in Personality*, 36, 224–51.

Jobes, D. A., Berman, A. L., O'Carroll, P. W. et al. (1996) The Kurt Cobain suicide crisis: Perspectives from research, public health, and the news media. *Suicide and Life-Threatening Behavior*, 26, 269–71.

Johansson, P., Hall, L., Sikström, S. and Olsson, A. (2005) Failure to detect mismatches between intention and outcome in a simple decision task. *Science*, 310, 116–19.

John, O. P. and Srivastava, S. (1999) The Big Five trait taxonomy: History, measurement, and theoretical perspectives. In L. A. Pervin and O. P. John (eds) *Handbook of Personality: Theory and Research* (2nd edn, pp. 102–38). New York: Guilford Press.

Johnson, C. A., Xiao, L., Palmer, P. et al. (2008) Affective decision-making deficits, linked to dysfunctional ventromedial prefrontal cortex, revealed in 10th grade Chinese adolescent binge drinkers. *Neuropsychologia*, 46, 714–26.

Johnson, D. H. (1980) The relationship between spike rate and synchrony in responses of auditory-nerve fibers to single tones. *Journal of the Acoustical Society of America*, 68, 1115–22.

Johnson, D. R. and Wu, J. (2002) An empirical test of crisis, social selection, and role explanations of the relationship between marital disruption and psychological distress: A pooled time-series analysis of four-wave panel data. *Journal of Marriage and the Family*, 64, 211–24.

Johnson, J. S. and Newport, E. L. (1989) Critical period effects in second language learning: The influence of maturational state on the acquisition of English as a second language. *Cognitive Psychology*, 21, 60–99.

Johnson, K. (2002) Neural basis of haptic perception. In H. Pashler and S. Yantis (eds) *Stevens' Handbook of Experimental Psychology*, vol. 1. *Sensation and Perception* (3rd edn, pp. 537–83). New York: Wiley.

Johnson, M. H. and Morton, J. (1991) *Biology and Cognitive Development: The Case of Face Recognition*. Oxford: Blackwell.

Johnson, M. H., Dziurawiec, S., Ellis, H. D. and Morton, J. (1991) Newborns' preferential tracking of face-like stimuli and its subsequent decline. *Cognition*, 40, 1–19.

Johnson, M. K., Hashstroudi, S. and Lindsay, S. (1993) Source monitoring. *Psychological Bulletin*, 114, 3–28.

Johnson, R. C., Danko, G. P., Darvill, T. J. et al. (1989) Cross-cultural assessment of altruism and its correlates. *Personality and Individual Differences*, 10, 855–68.

Johnson, R. C., McClearn, G. E., Yuen, S. et al. (1985) Galton's data a century later. *American Psychologist*, 40, 875–92.

Johnson, S. C. and Solomon, G. E. (1996) Why dogs have puppies and cats have kittens: The role of birth in young children's understanding of biological origins. *Child Development*, 68, 404–19.

Johnson, S. C., Slaughter, V. and Carey, S. (1998) Whose gaze will infants follow? Features that elicit gaze-following in 12-month-olds. *Developmental Science*, 1, 233–8.

Johnson, S. L. and Miller, I. (1997) Negative life events and time to recover from episodes of bipolar disorder. *Journal of Abnormal Psychology*, 106, 449–57.

Johnstone, E. C., Crow, T. J., Frith, C. et al. (1976) Cerebral ventricular size and cognitive impairment in chronic schizophrenia. *Lancet*, 2, 924–6.

Joiner, T. E. Jr (2002) Depression in its interpersonal context. In I. H. Gotlib and C. Hammen (eds) *Handbook of Depression* (pp. 295–313). New York: Guilford Press.

Joiner, T. E. Jr (2006) *Why People Die by Suicide*. Cambridge, MA: Harvard University Press.

Joiner, T. E. Jr and Metalsky, G. I. (1995) A prospective test of an integrative interpersonal theory of depression: A naturalistic study of college roommates. *Journal of Personality and Social Psychology*, 69, 778–88.

Joiner, T. E. Jr, Katz, J. and Lew, A. S. (1997) Self-verification and depression among youth psychiatric inpatients. *Journal of Abnormal Psychology*, 106, 608–18.

Joiner, T. E. Jr, Metalsky, G. I., Katz, J. and Beach, S. R. (1999) Be (re) assured: Excessive reassurance-seeking has (at least) some explanatory power regarding depression. *Psychological Inquiry*, 10, 305–8.

Jones, B. C., Little, A. C., Penton-Voak, I. S. et al. (2001) Facial symmetry and judgements of apparent health: Support for a 'good genes' explanation of the attractiveness-symmetry relationship. *Evolution and Human Behavior*, 22, 417–29.

Jones, E. E. and Davis, K. E. (1965) From acts to dispositions: The attribution process in person perception. In L. Berkowitz (ed.) *Advances in Experimental Social Psychology* (vol. 2, pp. 219–66). New York: Academic Press.

Jones, E. E. and Harris, V. A. (1967) The attribution of attitudes. *Journal of Experimental Social Psychology*, 3, 1–24.

Jones, E. E. and Nisbett, R. E. (1972) The actor and the observer: Divergent perceptions of the causes of behavior. In E. E. Jones, D. E. Kanouse, H. H. Kelley et al. (eds) *Attribution: Perceiving the Causes of Behavior* (pp. 79–94). Morristown, NJ: General Learning Press.

Jones, J. T., Pelham, B. W., Carvallo, M. and Mirenberg, M. C. (2004) How do I love thee? Let me count the Js: Implicit egotism and interpersonal attraction. *Journal of Personality and Social Psychology*, 87, 665–83.

Jones, L. M. and Foshay, N. N. (1984) Diffusion of responsibility in a nonemergency situation: Response to a greeting from a stranger. *Journal of Social Psychology*, 123, 155–8.

Jost, J. T., Glaser, J., Kruglanski, A. W. and Sullaway, F. J. (2003) Political conservatism as motivated social cognition. *Psychological Bulletin*, 129, 339–75.

Jouvet, M. and Mounier, D. (1961) Identification of the neural structures responsible for rapid cortical activity during normal sleep. *Journal de Physiologie*, 53, 379–80.

Judd, L. L. (1997) The clinical course of unipolar major depressive disorders. *Archives of General Psychiatry*, 54, 989–91.

Jung-Beeman, M., Bowden, E. M., Haberman, J. et al. (2004) Neural activity when people solve verbal problems with insight. *PLoS Biology*, 2, 500–10.

Jurewicz, I., Owen, R. J. and O'Donovan, M. C. (2001) Searching for susceptibility genes in schizophrenia. *European Neuropsychopharmacology*, 11, 395–8.

Jusczyk, P. W. (1985) The high-amplitude sucking technique as a methodological tool in speech perception research. In G. Gottlieb and N. A. Krasnegor (eds) *Measurement of Audition and Vision in the First Year of Postnatal Life: A Methodological Overview* (pp. 195–222). Norwood, NJ: Ablex.

Kaas, J. H. (1991) Plasticity of sensory and motor maps in adult mammals. *Annual Review of Neuroscience*, 14, 137–67.

Kagan, J. (1994) *Galen's Prophecy: Temperament in Human Nature*. New York: Basic Books.

Kahlenberg, S. M. and Wrangham, R. W. (2010) Sex differences in chimpanzees' use of sticks as play objects resemble those of children. *Current Biology*, 20, R1067–8.

Kahneman, D. (2012) *Thinking, Fast and Slow*. London: Penguin.

Kahneman, D. and Tversky, A. (1973) On the psychology of prediction. *Psychological Review*, 80, 237–51.

Kahneman, D. and Tversky, A. (1979) Prospect theory: An analysis of decision under risk. *Econometrica*, 47, 263–91.

Kahneman, D., Krueger, A. B., Schkade, D. A. et al. (2004) A survey method for characterizing daily life experience: The day reconstruction method. *Science*, 306(5702), 1776–80.

Kahneman, D., Krueger, A. B., Schkade, D. et al. (2006) Would you be happier if you were richer? A focusing illusion. *Science*, 312(5782), 1908–10.

Kail, R. (1991) Processing time declines exponentially during childhood and adolescence. *Developmental Psychology*, 27, 259–66.

Kalat, J. W. (1974) Taste salience depends on novelty, not concentration, in taste-aversion learning in the rat. *Journal of Comparative and Physiological Psychology*, 86, 47–50.

Kamin, L. J. (1969) Predictability, surprise, attention, and conditioning. In B. A. Campbell and R. M. Church (eds) *Punishment and Aversive Behavior* (pp. 279–96). New York: Appleton-Century-Crofts.

Kandel, E. R. (2000) Nerve cells and behavior. In E. R. Kandel, J. H. Schwartz and T. M. Jessell (eds) *Principles of Neural Science* (pp. 19–35). New York: McGraw-Hill.

Kandel, E. R., Schwartz, J. H. and Jessell, T. M. (1995) *Essentials of Neural Science and Behavior*. Norwalk, CT: Appleton & Lange.

Kanner, A. D., Coyne, J. C., Schaefer, C. and Lazarus, R. S. (1981) Comparison of two modes of stress management: Daily hassles and uplifts versus major life events. *Journal of Behavioral Medicine*, 4, 1–39.

Kanngiesser, P., Gjersoe, N. L. and Hood, B. M. (2010) Transfer of property ownership following creative labour in preschool children and adults. *Psychological Science*, 21, 1236–41.

Kant, I. ([1781]1965) *Critique of Pure Reason* (trans. N. K. Smith). New York: St Martin's Press.

Kanwisher, N. (2000) Domain specificity in face perception. *Nature Neuroscience*, 3, 759–63.

Kanwisher, N. and Yovel, G. (2006) The fusiform face area: A cortical region specialized for the perception of faces. *Philosophical Transactions of the Royal Society (B)*, 361, 2109–28.

Kanwisher, N., McDermott, J. and Chun, M. M. (1997) The fusiform face area: A module in human extrastriate cortex specialized for face perception. *Journal of Neuroscience*, 17, 4302–11.

Kapur, S., Craik, F. I., Tulving, E. et al. (1994) Neuroanatomical correlates of encoding in episodic memory: Levels of processing effects. *Proceedings of the National Academy of Sciences*, 91, 2008–11.

Karau, S. J. and Williams, K. D. (1993) Social loafing: A meta-analytic review and theoretical integration. *Journal of Personality and Social Psychology*, 65, 681–706.

Karau, S. J. and Williams, K. D. (1997) The effects of group cohesiveness on social loafing and social compensation. *Group Dynamics: Theory, Research and Practice*, 1, 156–68.

Karen, E., Jenni, K. E. and Loewenstein, G. (1997) Explaining the 'identifiable victim effect'. *Journal of Risk and Uncertainty*, 14, 235–57.

Karlins, M., Coffman, T. L. and Walters, G. (1969) On the fading of social stereotypes: Studies in three generations of college students. *Journal of Personality and Social Psychology*, 13, 1–16.

Karmiloff-Smith, A. (1992) *Beyond Modularity: A Developmental Perspective on Cognitive Science*. Cambridge, MA: MIT Press.

Karmiloff-Smith, A. and Inhelder, B. (1975) If you want to get ahead, get a theory, *Cognition*, 23, 95–147.

Karney, B. R. and Bradbury, T. N. (1995) The longitudinal course of marital quality and stability: A review of theory, method and research. *Psychological Bulletin*, 118, 3–34.

Karno, M. and Golding, J. M. (1991) Obsessive-compulsive disorder. In L. N. Robins and D. A. Regier (eds) *Psychiatric Disorders in America: The Epidemiologic Catchment Area Study* (pp. 204–19). New York: Free Press.

Karwowski, M. and Gralewski, J. (2013) Threshold hypothesis: Fact or artifact? *Thinking Skills and Creativity*, 8, 25–33.

Kashdan, T. (2009) *Curious: Discover the Missing Ingredient to a Fulfilling Life*. New York: William Morrow.

Kashima, Y., Kashima, E., and Alderidge, J. (2001) Toward cultural dynamics of self-conceptions. In C. Sedikides and M. B. Brewer (eds) *Individual Self, Relational Self, Collective Self* (pp. 277–98). Philadelphia: Psychology Press.

Kaslow, N. J. and Celano, M. P. (1995) The family therapies. In A. S. Gurman and A. S. Messer (eds) *Essential Psychotherapies* (6th edn, pp. 343–402). New York: Guilford Press.

Kasser, T. and Sharma, Y. S. (1999) Reproductive freedom, educational equality, and females' preference for resource-acquisition characteristics in mates. *Psychological Science*, 10, 374–7.

Katon, W. (1994) Primary care–psychiatry panic disorder management. In B. E. Wolfe and J. D. Maser (eds) *Treatment of Panic Disorder: A Consensus Development Conference* (pp. 41–56). Washington, DC: American Psychiatric Press.

Katz, D. and Braly, K. (1933) Racial stereotypes of one hundred college students. *Journal of Abnormal and Social Psychology*, 28, 280–90.

Katz, R. and McGuffin, P. (1993) The genetics of affective disorders. In J. P. Chapman and D. C. Fowles (eds) *Progress in Experimental Personality and Psychopathology Research* (vol. 16, pp. 200–21). New York: Springer.

Kauffmann, C. D., Cheema, M. A. and Miller, B. E. (2004) Slow right prefrontal transcranial magnetic stimulation as a treatment for medication-resistant depression: A double-blind, placebo-controlled study. *Depression and Anxiety*, 19, 59–62.

Kawakami, K., Dovidio, J. F., Moll, J. et al. (2000) Just say no (to stereotyping): Effects of training in the negation of stereotypic associations on stereotype activation. *Journal of Personality and Social Psychology*, 78, 871–88.

Kaye, K. and Fogel, A. (1980) The temporal structure of face-to-face communication between mothers and infants. *Developmental Psychology*, 14, 454–64.

Keefe, F. J., Abernathy, A. P. and Campbell, L. C. (2005) Psychological approaches to understanding and treating disease-related pain. *Annual Review of Psychology*, 56, 601–30.

Keefe, F. J., Lumley, M., Anderson, T. et al. (2001) Pain and emotion: New research directions. *Journal of Clinical Psychology*, 57, 587–607.

Keil, F. (1989) *Concepts, Kinds, and Cognitive Development*. Cambridge, MA: Bradford Books.

Keisler, D. J. (1999) *Beyond the Disease Model of Mental Disorders*. New York: Praeger.

Kelemen, D., Emmons, N. A., Schillaci, R. S. and Ganea, P. A. (2014) Young children can be taught basic natural selection using a picture-storybook intervention. *Psychological Science*, 25, 893–902.

Keller, M. B., Klein, D. N., Hirschfeld, R. M. et al. (1995) Results of the *DSM-IV* mood disorders field trial. *American Journal of Psychiatry*, 152, 843–9.

Kelley, H. H. (1967) Attribution theory in social psychology. In D. Levine (ed.) *Nebraska Symposium on Motivation* (vol. 15, pp. 192–238). Lincoln: University of Nebraska Press.

Kelley, H. H. (1983) Love and commitment. In H. H. Kelley, E. Berscheid, A. Christensen and J. H. Harvey (eds) *Close Relationships* (pp. 265–314). New York: Freeman.

Kelley, W. M., Macrae, C. N., Wyland, C. L. et al. (2002) Finding the self? An event-related fMRI study. *Journal of Cognitive Neuroscience*, 14, 785–94.

Kellman, P. J. and Spelke, E. S. (1983) Perception of partly occluded objects in infancy. *Cognitive Psychology*, 15, 483–524.

Kelly, C. and McCreadie, R. (2000) Cigarette smoking and schizophrenia. *Advances in Psychiatric Treatment*, 6, 327–31.

Kelly, G. (1955) *The Psychology of Personal Constructs*. New York: Norton.

Kelly, S. and Dunbar, R. I. (2001) Who dares wins: Heroism versus altruism in women's mate choice. *Human Nature*, 12, 89–105.

Keltikangas-Järvinen, L., Kivimäki, M. and Keskivaara, P. (2003) Parental practices, self-esteem and adult temperament: 17-year follow-up study of four population-based age cohorts. *Personality and Individual Differences*, 34, 431–47.

Keltner, D. (1995) Signs of appeasement: Evidence for the distinct displays of embarrassment, amusement, and shame. *Journal of Personality and Social Psychology*, 68, 441–4.

Keltner, D. and Buswell, B. N. (1996) Evidence for the distinctness of embarrassment, shame, and guilt: A study of recalled antecedents and facial expressions of emotion. *Cognition and Emotion*, 10, 155–71.

Keltner, D. and Haidt, J. (1999) Social functions of emotions at four levels of analysis. *Cognition and Emotion*, 13, 505–21.

Keltner, D. and Harker, L. A. (1998) The forms and functions of the nonverbal signal of shame. In P. Gilbert and B. Andrews (eds) *Shame: Interpersonal Behavior, Psychopathology, and Culture* (pp. 78–98). New York: OUP.

Keltner, D. and Shiota, M. N. (2003) New displays and new emotions: A commentary on Rozin and Cohen (2003). *Emotion*, 3, 86–91.

Kendler, K. S., Myers, J. and Prescott, C. A. (2002) The etiology of phobias: An evaluation of the stress-diathesis model. *Archives of General Psychiatry*, 59, 242–8.

Kendler, K. S., Neale, M., Kessler, R. C. and Heath, A. (1992) Generalized anxiety disorder in women: A population-based twin study. *Archives of General Psychiatry*, 49, 267–72.

Kendler, K. S., Walters, E. E., Neale, M. C. et al. (1995) The structure of the genetic and environmental risk factors for six major psychiatric disorders in women: Phobia, generalized anxiety disorder, panic disorder, bulimia, major depression, and alcoholism. *Archives of General Psychiatry*, 52, 374–83.

Kennedy, Q., Mather, M. and Carstensen, L. L. (2004) The role of motivation in the age-related positivity effect in autobiographical memory. *Psychological Science*, 15, 208–14.

Kenrick, D. T., Sadalla, E. K., Groth, G. and Trost, M. R. (1990) Evolution, traits, and the stages of human courtship: Qualifying the parental investment model. *Journal of Personality*, 58, 97–116.

Kensinger, E. A. and Schacter, D. L. (2005) Emotional content and reality monitoring ability: fMRI evidence for the influence of encoding processes. *Neuropsychologia*, 43, 1429–43.

Kephart, W. M. (1961) *The Family, Society and the Individual*. Boston: Houghton Mifflin.

Kephart, W. M. (1967) Some correlates of romantic love. *Journal of Marriage and the Family*, 29, 470–4.

Kernis, M. H. (2003) Toward a conceptualization of optimal self-esteem. *Psychological Inquiry*, 14, 1–26.

Kessler, R. C. (1997) The effects of stressful life events on depression. *Annual Review of Psychology*, 48, 191–214.

Kessler, R. C., McGonagle, K. A., Zhao, S. et al. (1994) Lifetime and 12-month prevalence of *DSM-III-R* psychiatric disorders in the United States: Results from the National Comorbidity Study. *Archives of General Psychiatry*, 51, 8–19.

Kessler, R. C., Nelson, C. B., McGonagle, K. A. et al. (1996) Comorbidity of *DSM-III-R* major depressive disorder in the general population: Results from the U.S. national comorbidity survey. *British Journal of Psychiatry*, 168, 17–30.

Kety, S. S. (1990) Genetic factors in suicide: Family, twin, and adoption studies. In S. J. Blumenthal and D. J. Kupfer (eds) *Suicide over the Life Cycle: Risk Factors, Assessment, and Treatment of Suicidal Patients* (pp. 127–33). Washington, DC: American Psychiatric Press.

Keuler, D. J. and Safer, M. A. (1998) Memory bias in the assessment and recall of pre-exam anxiety: How anxious was I? *Applied Cognitive Psychology*, 12, S127–37.

Khalid, R. (1991) Personality and academic achievement: A thematic apperception perspective. *British Journal of Projective Psychology*, 36, 25–34.

Kidd, C., Palmeri, H. and Aslin, R. N. (2013) Rational snacking: Young children's decision-making on the marshmallow task is moderated by beliefs about environmental reliability. *Cognition*, 126, 109–14.

Kiefer, M., Marzinzik, F., Weisbrod, M. et al. (1998) The time course of brain activations during response inhibition: Evidence from event-related potentials in a go/no go task. *NeuroReport*, 9, 765–70.

Kiehl, K. A., Smith, A. M., Hare, R. D. et al. (2001) Limbic abnormalities in affective processing by criminal psychopaths as revealed by functional magnetic resonance imaging. *Biological Psychiatry*, 50, 677–84.

Kihlstrom, J. F. (1985) Hypnosis. *Annual Review of Psychology*, 36, 385–418.

Kihlstrom, J. F. (1987) The cognitive unconscious. *Science*, 237, 1445–52.

Kihlstrom, J. F. (2005) Dissociative disorders. *Annual Review of Clinical Psychology*, 1, 227–53.

Kihlstrom, J. F. and Klein, S. B. (1994) The self as a knowledge structure. In R. S. Wyer and T. K. Srull (eds) *Handbook of Social Cognition* (2nd edn, vol. 1, pp. 153–208). Hillsdale, NJ: Erlbaum.

Killen, M. and Turiel, E. (1998) Adolescents' and young adults' evaluations of helping and sacrificing for others. *Journal for Research on Adolescence*, 8, 355–75.

Kim, K. H. (2005) Can only intelligent people be creative? A meta-analysis. *Journal of Secondary Gifted Education*, 16, 57–66.

Kimball, J. N. (2007) Electroconvulsive therapy: An outdated treatment, or one whose time has come? *Southern Medical Journal*, 100, 462–3.

Kimura, D. (1999) *Sex and Cognition*. Cambridge, MA: MIT Press.

King, F. (1990) *Lump It or Leave It*. New York: St Martin's Press.

Kinney, D. A. (1993) From nerds to normals: The recovery of identity among adolescents from middle school to high school. *Sociology of Education*, 66, 21–40.

Kirchner, W. H. and Towne, W. F. (1994) The sensory basis of the honeybee's dance language. *Scientific American*, 270(6), 74–80.

Kirsch, I. and Sapirstein, G. (1998) Listening to Prozac but hearing placebo: A meta-analysis of antidepressant medication. *Prevention and Treatment*, 1(2).

Kirsch, I., Cardeña, E., Derbyshire, S. et al. (2011) Definitions of hypnosis and hypnotizability and their relation to suggestion and suggestibility: A consensus statement. *Contemporary Hypnosis and Integrative Therapy*, 28(9), 107–15.

Kirsch, I., Deacon, B. J., Huedo-Medina, T. B. et al. (2008) Initial severity and anti-depressant benefits: A meta-analysis of data submitted to the Food and Drug Administration. *PLoS Med*, 5(2), e45, doi: 10.1371/journal.pmed.0050045.

Klein, S. B. (2004) The cognitive neuroscience of knowing one's self. In M. Gazzaniga (ed.) *The Cognitive Neurosciences* (3rd edn, pp. 1007–89). Cambridge, MA: MIT Press.

Klein, S. B., Robertson, T. E. and Delton, A. W. (2011) The future orientation of memory: Planning as a key component mediating the high levels of recall found with survival processing. *Memory*, 19, 121–39.

Kleinman, A. M. (1986) *Social Origins of Distress and Disease: Depression, Neurasthenia and Pain in Modern China*. New Haven, CT: Yale University Press.

Kleinman, A. M. (1988) *Rethinking Psychiatry: From Cultural Category to Personal Experience*. New York: Free Press.

Kleinschmidt, A. and Cohen, L. (2006) The neural bases of prosopagnosia and pure alexia: Recent insights from functional neuroimaging. *Current Opinion in Neurology*, 19, 386–91.

Kling, K. C., Hyde, J. S., Showers, C. J. and Buswell, B. N. (1999) Gender differences in self-esteem: A meta-analysis. *Psychological Bulletin*, 125, 470–500.

Klinger, E. (1975) Consequences of commitment to and disengagement from incentives. *Psychological Review*, 82, 1–25.

Klinger, E. (1977) *Meaning and Void*. Minneapolis: University of Minnesota Press.

Klinger, E. (2013) Goal commitments and the content of thoughts and dreams: Basic principles. *Frontiers in Psychology*, 4, 1–17.

Klopfer, B. and Kelley, D. (1942) *The Rorschach Technique*. Yonkers, NY: World Book.

Kluft, R. P. (1984) Treatment of multiple personality. *Psychiatric Clinics of North America*, 7, 9–29.

Kluft, R. P. (1991) Multiple personality disorder. In A. Tasman and S. M. Goldfinger (eds) *American Psychiatric Press Review of Psychiatry* (vol. 10, pp. 161–88). Washington, DC: American Psychiatric Press.

Klüver, H. (1951) Functional differences between the occipital and temporal lobes with special reference to the interrelations of behavior and extracerebral mechanisms. In L. A. Jeffress (ed.) *Cerebral Mechanisms in Behavior* (pp. 147–99). New York: Wiley.

Klüver, H. and Bucy, P. C. (1937) 'Psychic blindness' and other symptoms following bilateral temporal lobectomy in Rhesus monkeys. *American Journal of Physiology*, 119, 352–3.

Klüver, H. and Bucy, P. C. (1939) Preliminary analysis of functions of the temporal lobes in monkeys. *Archives of Neurology and Psychiatry*, 42, 979–1000.

Knapp, M. L., Hall, J. A. and Horgan, T. G. (2013) *Nonverbal Communication in Human Interaction* (8th edn). Belmont, CA: Wadsworth.

Knapp, M. L., Hart, R. P. and Dennis, H. S. (1974) An exploration of deception as a communication construct. *Human Communication Research*, 1, 15–29.

Knickmeyer, R., Baron-Cohen, S., Reggatt, P. and Taylor, K. (2005) Foetal testosterone, social relationships and restricted interested in children. *Journal of Child Psychology and Psychiatry*, 45, 1–13.

Kniffin, K. M. and Wilson, D. S. (2004) The effect of nonphysical traits on the perception of physical attractiveness: Three naturalistic studies. *Evolution and Human Behavior*, 25, 88–101.

Knight, G. P., Johnson, L. G., Carlo, G. and Eisenberg, N. (1994) A multiplicative model of the dispositional antecedents to prosocial behavior: Predicting more of the people, more of the time. *Journal of Personality and Social Psychology*, 66, 178–83.

Knowlton, B. J. and Holyoak, K. J. (2009) Prefrontal substrate of human relational reasoning. In M. S. Gazzaniga (ed.) *The Cognitive Neurosciences* (4th edn, pp. 1005–17). Cambridge, MA: MIT Press.

Knowlton, B. J., Ramus, S. J. and Squire, L. R. (1992) Intact artificial grammar learning in amnesia: Dissociation of classification learning and explicit memory for specific instances. *Psychological Science*, 3, 173–9.

Knutson, B., Adams, C. M., Fong, G. W. and Hommer, D. (2001) Anticipation of increasing monetary reward selectively recruits nucleus accumbens. *Journal of Neurosciences*, 21, 1–5.

Knutson, B., Wolkowitz, O. M., Cole, S. W. et al. (1998) Selective alteration of personality and social behavior by serotonergic intervention. *American Journal of Psychiatry*, 155, 373–9.

Koch, C. (2004) *The Quest for Consciousness: A Neurobiological Approach*. Englewood, CO: Roberts & Co.

Kochanska, G. (1997) Multiple pathways to conscience for children with different temperaments: From toddlerhood to age 5. *Developmental Psychology*, 33, 228–40.

Kochanska, G., Coy, K. C. and Murray, K. T. (2001) The development of self-regulation in the first four years of life. *Child Development*, 72, 1091–111.

Kochanska, G., Murray, K. and Coy, K. C. (1997) Inhibitory control as a contributor to conscience in childhood: From toddler to early school age. *Child Development*, 68, 263–77.

Koffka, K. (1935) *Principles of Gestalt Psychology*. New York: Harcourt, Brace and World.

Kohlberg, L. (1963) Development of children's orientation towards a moral order (Part I): Sequencing in the development of moral thought. *Vita Humana*, 6, 11–36.

Kohlberg, L. (1986) A current statement on some theoretical issues. In S. Modgil and C. Modgil (eds) *Lawrence Kohlberg: Consensus and Controversy* (pp. 485–546). Philadelphia: Falmer.

Kolb, B. (1995) *Brian Plasticity and Development*. Hillsdale, NJ: Erlbaum.

Kolb, B. and Whishaw, I. Q. (2003) *Fundamentals of Human Neuropsychology* (5th edn). New York: Worth.

Kolotkin, R. L., Meter, K. and Williams, G. R. (2001) Quality of life and obesity. *Obesity Reviews*, 219–29.

Konen, C. S. and Kastner, S. (2008) Two hierarchically organized neural systems for object information in human visual cortex. *Nature Neuroscience*, 11, 224–31.

Koriat, A. (1993) How do we know what we know? The accessibility model of the feeling of knowing. *Psychological Review*, 100, 609–39.

Koriat, A. and Levy-Sadot, R. (2001) The combined contributions of the cue-familiarty and accessibility heuristics to feelings of knowing. *Journal of Experimental Psychology: Learning, Memory and Cognition*, 27, 34–53.

Koss, M. P. (1990) The women's mental health research agenda: Violence against women. *American Psychologist*, 45, 374–80.

Kosslyn, S. M. (1973) Scanning visual images: Some structural implications. *Perception and Psychophysics*, 14, 90–4.

Kosslyn, S. M., Alpert, N. M., Thompson, W. L. et al. (1993) Visual mental imagery activates topographically organized visual cortex: PET investigations. *Journal of Cognitive Neuroscience*, 5, 263–87.

Kounios, J. and Beeman, M. (2009) The Aha! moment. *Current Directions in Psychological Science*, 18, 210–16.

Kounios, J., Fleck, J. L., Green, D. L. et al. (2008) The origins of insight in resting-state brain activity. *Neuropsychologia*, 46, 281–91.

Kounios, J., Frymiare, J. L., Bowden, E. M. et al. (2006) The prepared mind: Neural activity prior to problem presentation predicts subsequent solution by sudden insight. *Psychological Science*, 17, 882–90.

Kowalski, R. M. and Limber, S. P. (2013) Psychological, physical, and academic correlates of cyberbullying and traditional bullying. *Journal of Adolescent Health*, 53, 13–20.

Kozhevnikov, M. and Hegarty, M. (2001) Impetus beliefs as default heurstic: Dissociation between explicit and implicit knowledge about motion. *Psychonomic Bulletin & Review*, 8, 439–53.

Kraepelin, E. (1887) *Die Richlungen der Psychiatrischen Forschung*. Leipzig: Vogel.

Kraepelin, E. (1899) *Psychiatrie*. Leipzig: Barth.

Kraepelin, E. (1907) *Textbook of Psychiatry* (7th edn) (trans. A. R. Diefendorf). London: Macmillan.

Krahé, B. (2008) Aggression. In M. Hewstone, W. Stroebe and K. Jonas (eds) *Introduction to Social Psychology* (pp. 156–75). Oxford: Blackwell.

Kramer, P. D. (1997) *Listening to Prozac* (rev. edn). New York: Penguin.

Kramera, A. D., Guillory, J. E. and Hancock, J. T. (2014) Experimental evidence of massive-scale emotional contagion through social networks. *Proceedings of the National Academy of Sciences*, 111, 8788–90.

Krebs, J. R. and Davies, N. B. (1991) *Behavioural Ecology: An Evolutionary Approach* (3rd edn). Sutherland, MA: Sinauer.

Kretch, K. S. and Adolph, K. E. (2013) Cliff or step? Posture-specific learning at the edge of a drop-off. *Child Development*, 84, 226–40.

Krings, T., Topper, R., Foltys, H. et al. (2000) Cortical activation patterns during complex motor tasks in piano players and control subjects. A functional magnetic resonance imaging study. *Neuroscience Letters*, 278, 189–93.

Kroeze, W. K. and Roth, B. L. (1998) The molecular biology of serotonin receptors: Therapeutic implications for the interface of mood and psychosis. *Biological Psychiatry*, 44, 1128–42.

Kronig, M. H., Apter, J., Asnis, G. et al. (1999) Placebo-controlled multicenter study of sertraline treatment for obsessive-compulsive disorder. *Journal of Clinical Psychopharmacology*, 19, 172–6.

Kruglanski, A. W. (2006) *The Psychology of Close-mindedness*. New York: Psychology Press.

Kruk, M. R., Halasz, J., Meelis, W. and Haller, J. (2004) Fast positive feedback between the adrenocortical stress response and a brain mechanism involved in aggressive behavior. *Behavioral Neuroscience*, 118, 1062–70.

Kubovy, M. (1981) Concurrent-pitch segregation and the theory of indispensable attributes. In M. Kubovy and J. R. Pomerantz (eds) *Perceptual Organization* (pp. 55–96). Hillsdale, NJ: Erlbaum.

Kuffler, S. W. (1953) Discharge patterns and function organization of mammalian retina. *Journal of Neurophysiology*, 16, 37–68.

Kugihara, N. (1999) Gender and social loafing in Japan. *Journal of Social Psychology*, 139, 516–26.

Kuhlmeier, V., Wynn, K. and Bloom, P. (2003) Attribution of dispositional states by 12-month-olds. *Psychological Science*, 14, 402–8.

Kuhn, D., Nash, S. C. and Brucken, L. (1978) Sex-role concepts of two- and three-year-olds. *Child Development*, 49, 445–51.

Kuipers, E. and Raune, D. (2000) The early development of expressed emotion and burdern in the families of first-onset psychosis. In M. Birchwood, D. Fowler and C. Jackson (eds) *Early Intervention in Psychosis* (pp. 128–40). London: Wiley.

Kunda, Z. and Oleson, K. C. (1997) When exceptions prove the rule: How extremity of deviance determines the impact of deviant examples on stereotypes. *Journal of Personality and Social Psychology*, 72, 965–79.

Kunovich, R. M. (2004) Social structural position and prejudice: An exploration of cross-national differences in regression slopes. *Social Science Research*, 33, 20–44.

Kunz, P. R. and Woolcott, M. (1976) Season's greetings: From my status to yours. *Social Science Research*, 5, 269–78.

Kurzweil, E. (1989) *The Freudians: A Comparative Perspective*. New Haven, CT: Yale University Press.

Kutchins, H. and Kirk, S. A. (1997) *Making Us Crazy: DSM: The Psychiatric Bible and the Creation of Mental Disorders*. New York: Free Press.

Kyaga, S., Landén, M., Bomana, M. et al. (2013) Mental illness, suicide and creativity: 40-year prospective total population study. *Journal of Psychiatric Research*, 47, 83–90.

Kyllonen, P. C. and Christal, R. E. (1990) Reasoning ability is (little more than) working memory capacity?! *Intelligence*, 14, 389–433.

LaBar, K. S. and Phelps, E. A. (1998) Arousal-mediated memory consolidation: Role of the medial temporal lobe in humans. *Psychological Science*, 9, 490–3.

LaBerge, S. and Rheingold, H. (1990) *Exploring the World of Lucid Dreaming*. New York: Ballantine.

Lachman, R., Lachman, J. L. and Butterfield, E. C. (1979) *Cognitive Psychology and Information Processing: An Introduction*. Hillsdale, NJ: Erlbaum.

Lackner, J. R. and DiZio, P. (2005) Vestibular, proprioceptive, and haptic contributions to spatial orientation. *Annual Review of Psychology*, 56, 115–47.

Laeng, B. and Endestad, T. (2012) Bright illusions reduce the eye's pupil. *Proceedings of the National Academy of Sciences*, 109, 2162–7.

Laeng, B. and Sulutvedt, U. (2014) The eye pupil adjusts to imaginary light. *Psychological Science*, 25, 188–97.

Lai, Y. and Siegal, J. (1999) Muscle atonia in REM sleep. In B. Mallick and S. Inoue (eds) *Rapid Eye Movement Sleep* (pp. 69–90). New Delhi: Narosa.

Laing, R. D. (1960) *The Divided Self: An Existential Study in Sanity and Madness*. Harmondsworth: Penguin.

Lalonde, J. K., Hudson, J. I., Gigante, R. A. and Pope, H. G. Jr (2001) Canadian and American psychiatrists' attitudes toward dissociative disorders diagnoses. *Canadian Journal of Psychiatry*, 46, 407–12.

Lamb, M. E. (1997) *The Role of Father in Child Development* (3rd edn). New York: Wiley.

Lamb, M. E., Sternberg, K. J. and Prodromidis, M. (1992) Nonmaternal care and the security of infant/mother attachment: A reanalysis of the data. *Infant Behavior & Development*, 15, 71–83.

Lamb, M. E., Thompson, R. A., Gardner, W. and Charnov, E. L. (1985) *Infant-mother Attachment: The Origins and Developmental Significance of Individual Differences in Strange Situation Behavior.* Hillsdale, NJ: Erlbaum.

Lamm, H. and Myers, D. G. (1978) Group-induced polarization of attitudes and behavior. *Advances in Experimental Social Psychology*, 11, 145–95.

Landauer, T. K. and Bjork, R. A. (1978) Optimum rehearsal patterns and name learning. In M. M. Gruneberg, P. E. Morris and R. N. Sykes (eds) *Practical Aspects of Memory* (pp. 625–32). New York: Academic Press.

Lang, F. R. and Carstensen, L. L. (1994) Close emotional relationships in late life: Further support for proactive aging in the social domain. *Psychology and Aging*, 9, 315–24.

Lange, C. G. and James, W. (1922) *The Emotions.* Baltimore: Williams & Wilkins.

Langer, E. J. and Abelson, R. P. (1974) A patient by any other name ... Clinician group difference in labeling bias. *Journal of Consulting & Clinical Psychology*, 42, 4–9.

Langleben, D. D., Loughead, J. W., Bilker, W. B. et al. (2005) Telling truth from lie in individual subjects with fast event-related fMRI. *Human Brain Mapping*, 26, 262–72.

Langlois, J. H. and Roggman, L. A. (1990) Attractive faces are only average. *Psychological Science*, 1, 115–21.

Langlois, J. H., Ritter, J. M., Casey, R. J. and Sawin, D. B. (1995) Infant attractiveness predicts maternal behaviors and attitudes. *Developmental Psychology*, 31, 464–72.

Langlois, J. H., Kalakanis, L., Rubenstein, A. J. et al. (2000) Maxims or myths of beauty? A meta-analytic and theoretical review. *Psychological Bulletin*, 126, 390–423.

Langston, J. W. (1995) *The Case of the Frozen Addicts.* New York: Pantheon.

LaPierre, R. T. (1934) Attitudes vs actions. *Social Forces*, 13, 230–7.

Larson, L. M., Rottinghaus, P. J. and Borgen, F. H. (2002) Meta-analyses of Big Six interests and Big Five personality factors. *Journal of Vocational Behaviour*, 61, 217–39.

Larson, R. and Richards, M. H. (1991) Daily companionship in late childhood and early adolescence – changing developmental contexts. *Child Development*, 62, 284–300.

Lashley, K. S. (1960) In search of the engram. In F. A. Beach, D. O. Hebb, C. T. Morgan and H. W. Nissen (eds) *The Neuropsychology of Lashley* (pp. 454–82). New York: McGraw-Hill.

Latané, B. and Darley, J. M. (1968) Group inhibition of bystander intervention in emergencies. *Journal of Personality and Social Psychology*, 10, 215–21.

Latané, B. and Darley, J. M. (1970) *The Unresponsive Bystander: Why Doesn't He Help?* New York: Appleton-Century-Crofts.

Latané, B., Williams, K. and Harkins, S. (1979) Many hands make light the work: The causes and consequences of social loafing. *Journal of Personality and Social Psychology*, 37, 822–32.

Lauber, C., Nordt, C., Falcato, L. and Rössler, W. (2005) Can a seizure help? The public's attitude toward ECT. *Psychiatry Research*, 134, 205–9.

Laupa, M. and Turiel, E. (1986) Children's conceptions of adult and peer authority. *Child Development*, 57, 405–12.

Laurence, J. and Perry, C. (1983) Hypnotically created memory among high hypnotizable subjects. *Science*, 222, 523–4.

Laureys, S., Giacino, J. T., Schiff, N. D. et al. (2006) How should functional imaging of patients with disorders of consciousness contribute to their clinical rehabilitation needs? *Current Opinion in Neurology*, 19, 520–7.

Lavie, N. (1995) Perceptual load as a major determinant of the locus of selection in visual attention. *Perception and Psychophysics*, 56, 183–97.

Lavie, P. (2001) Sleep-wake as a biological rhythm. *Annual Review of Psychology*, 52, 277–303.

Lavori, P. W., Klerman, G. L., Keller, M. B. et al. (1987) Age-period-cohort analysis of secular trends in onset of major depression: Findings in siblings of patients with major affective disorder. *Journal of Psychiatric Researchers*, 21, 23–5.

Lawrence, N. S., Jollant, F., O'Daly, O. et al. (2009) Distinct roles of prefrontal cortical subregions in the Iowa Gambling Task. *Cerebral Cortex*, 19, 1134–43.

Lawton, M. P., Kleban, M. H., Rajagopal, D. and Dean, J. (1992) The dimensions of affective experience in three age groups. *Psychology and Aging*, 7, 171–84.

Lazarus, R. S. (1984) On the primacy of cognition. *American Psychologist*, 39, 124–9.

Lazarus, R. S. and Alfert, E. (1964) Short-circuiting of threat by experimentally altering cognitive appraisal. *Journal of Abnormal and Social Psychology*, 69, 195–205.

Lazarus, R. S. and Folkman, S. (1984) *Stress, Appraisal, and Coping.* New York: Springer.

Le Bon, G. ([1896]1908) *The Crowd: A Study of the Popular Mind.* London, Unwin.

Leader, T. I., Mullen, B. and Abrams, D. (2007) Without mercy: The immediate impact of size on lynch mob atrocity. *Personality and Social Psychology Bulletin*, 33, 1340–52.

Leary, M. R. (1990) Responses to social exclusion: Social anxiety, jealousy, loneliness, depression, and low self-esteem. *Journal of Social and Clinical Psychology*, 9, 221–9.

Leary, M. R. and Baumeister, R. F. (2000) The nature and function of self-esteem: Sociometer theory. In M. P. Zanna (ed.) *Advances in Experimental Social Psychology* (vol. 32, pp. 1–62). San Diego: Academic Press.

Leary, M. R., Kowalski, R. M. and Smith, L. (2003) Case studies of the school shootings. *Aggressive Behaviour*, 29, 202–14.

Leary, M. R., Britt, T. W., Cutlip, W. D. and Templeton, J. L. (1992) Social blushing. *Psychological Bulletin*, 112, 446–60.

Leary, M. R., Tambor, E. S., Terdal, S. K. and Downs, D. L. (1995) Self-esteem as an interpersonal monitor: The sociometer hypothesis. *Journal of Personality and Social Psychology*, 68, 518–30.

Leaton, R. N. (1976) Long-term retention of the habituation of lick suppression and startle response produced by a single auditory stimulus. *Journal of Experimental Psychology: Animal Behavior Processes*, 2, 248–59.

Lebrecht, S., Pierce, L. J., Tarr, M. J. and Tanaka, J. W. (2009) Perceptual other-race training reduces implicit racial bias. *PLoS ONE*, 4(1), e4215.

Lebreton, M., Barnes, A., Miettunen, J. et al. (2009) The brain structural disposition to social interaction. *European Journal of Neuroscience*, 29, 2247–52.

Lecky, P. (1945) *Self-consistency: A Theory of Personality.* New York: Island Press.

LeDoux, J. E. (1992) Brain mechanisms of emotion and emotional learning. *Current Opinion in Neurobiology*, 2, 191–7.

LeDoux, J. E. (1996) *The Emotional Brain: The Mysterious Underpinnings of Emotional Life.* New York: Simon & Schuster.

LeDoux, J. E. (1998) Fear and the brain: Where have we been, and where are we going? *Biological Psychiatry*, 153, 1229–38.

LeDoux, J. E. (2000) Emotion circuits in the brain. *Annual Review of Neuroscience*, 23, 155–84.

LeDoux, J. E., Iwata, J., Cicchetti, P. and Reis, D. J. (1988) Different projections of the central amygdaloid nucleus mediate autonomic and behavioral correlates of conditioned fear. *Journal of Neuroscience*, 8, 2517–29.

Lee, D. N. and Aronson, E. (1974) Visual proprioceptive control of standing in human infants. *Perception & Psychophysics*, 15, 529–32.

Leeb, R. T. and Rejskind, N. M. (2004) Here's looking at you, kid! A longitudinal study of perceived gender differences in mutual gaze behaviour in young infants. *Sex Roles*, 50, 1–14.

Lefcourt, H. M. (1982) *Locus of Control: Current Trends in Theory and Research* (2nd edn). Hillsdale, NJ: Erlbaum.

Legare, C. H. and Herrmann, P. A. (2013) Cognitive consequences and constraints on reasoning about ritual. *Religion, Brain and Behavior*, 3, 63–5.

Legate, N., DeHaan, C. R., Weinstein, N. and Ryan, R. M. (2013) Hurting you hurts me too: The psychological costs of complying with ostracism. *Psychological Science*, 24, 583–8.

Leighton, D. and Kluckhorn, C. ([1947]1969) *Children of the People: The Navaho Individual and his Development*. Cambridge, MA: Harvard University Press.

Leimgruber, K. L., Shaw, A., Santos, L. R. and Olson, K. R. (2012) Young children are more generous when others are aware of their actions. *PLoS ONE*, 7(10), e48292.

Lentz, M. J., Landis, C. A., Rothermel, J. and Shaver, J. L. (1999) Effects of selective slow wave sleep disruption on musculoskeletal pain and fatigue in middle aged women. *Journal of Rheumatology*, 26, 1586–92.

Lepage, M., Ghaffar, O., Nyberg, L. and Tulving, E. (2000) Prefrontal cortex and episodic memory retrieval mode. *Proceedings of the National Academy of Sciences*, 97, 506–11.

Lepper, M. R. and Greene, D. (1976) *The Hidden Costs of Reward: New Perspectives on the Psychology of Human Motivation*. Hillsdale, NJ: Erlbaum.

Lepper, M. R. and Greene, D. (1978) Overjustification research and beyond: Toward a means-end analysis of intrinsic and extrinsic motivation. In M. R. Lepper and D. Greene (eds) *The Hidden Costs of Reward: New Perspectives on the Psychology of Human Motivation* (pp. 109–48). New York: Wiley.

Lerner, M. J. (1980) *The Belief in a Just World: A Fundamental Delusion*. New York: Plenum.

Leslie, A. M. (1987) Pretense and representation: The origins of 'theory of mind'. *Psychological Review*, 94, 412–26.

Leslie, A. M. (1994) ToMM, ToBY and agency: Core architecture and domain specificity. In L. Hirshfeld and S. Gelman (eds) *Mapping the Mind: Domain Specificity in Cognition and Culture* (pp. 119–48). Cambridge: CUP.

Leslie, A. M. and Keeble, S. (1987) Do six-month-old infants perceive causality? *Cognition*, 25, 265–88.

Levelt, M. F. (1989) *Speaking: From Intention to Articulation*. Cambridge, MA: MIT Press.

Levenson, R. W., Ekman, P. and Friesen, W. V. (1990) Voluntary facial action generates emotion-specific autonomic nervous system activity. *Psychophysiology*, 27, 363–84.

Levenson, R. W., Cartensen, L. L., Friesen, W. V. and Ekman, P. (1991) Emotion physiology, and expression in old age. *Psychology and Aging*, 6, 28–35.

Levenson, R. W., Ekman, P., Heider, K. and Friesen, W. V. (1992) Emotion and automatic nervous system activity in the Minangkabau of West Sumatra. *Journal of Personality and Social Psychology*, 62, 972–88.

Levine, L. E. (1983) Mine: Self-definition in 2-year-old boys. *Developmental Psychology*, 19, 544–9.

Levine, M. and Crowther, S. (2008) The responsive bystander: How social group membership and group size can encourage as well as inhibit bystander intervention. *Journal of Personality and Social Psychology*, 95, 1429–39.

Levine, M., Prosser, A., Evans, D. and Reicher, S. (2005) Identity and emergency intervention: How social group membership and inclusiveness of group boundaries shape helping behavior. *Personality and Social Psychology Bulletin*, 31, 443–53.

LeVine, R. A. and Campbell, D. T. (1972) *Ethnocentrism*. New York: Wiley.

Levine, R. V., Norenzayan, A. and Philbrick, K. (2001) Cross-cultural differences in helping strangers. *Journal of Cross-cultural Psychology*, 32, 543–60.

Levy, G. D., Sadovsky, A. L. and Troseth, G. L. (2000) Aspects of young children's perceptions of gender-types occupations. *Sex Roles*, 36, 1–21.

Levy, J., Trevarthen, C. and Sperry, R. W. (1972) Perception of bilateral chimeric figures following hemispheric disconnection. *Brain*, 95, 61–78.

Lewin, K. (1936) *Principles of Topological Psychology*. New York: McGraw-Hill.

Lewin, K. (1951) Behavior and development as a function of the total situation. In K. Lewin, *Field Theory in Social Science: Selected Theoretical Papers* (pp. 791–843). New York: Harper & Row.

Lewis, C., Freeman, N. H., Hagestadt, E. and Douglas, H. (1994) Narrative access and production in preschooler's false belief reasoning. *Cognitive Development*, 9, 397–424.

Lewis, M. (1992) The self in self-conscious emotions. In D. Stipek, S. Recchia and S. McClintic (eds) Self-evaluation in young children. *Monographs of the Society for Research in Child Development*, 57(1, Serial No. 226).

Lewis, M. (1997) *Altering Fate: Why the Past Does Not Predict the Future*. New York: Guilford Press.

Lewis, M. and Brooks-Gunn, J. (1979) *Social Cognition and the Acquisition of Self*. New York: Plenum Press.

Lewis, R., Kapur, S., Jones, C. et al. (1999) Serotonin 5-HT-sub-2 receptors in schizophrenia: A PET study using [-sup-1-sup-8F] setoperone in neuroleptic-naive patients and normal subjects. *American Journal of Psychiatry*, 156, 72–8.

Lewkowicz, D. J. and Minar N. (2014) Infants are not sensitive to synesthetic cross-modality correspondences: A comment on Walker et al. (2010). *Psychological Science*, 25, 832–4.

Lewontin, R., Rose, S. and Kamin, L. J. (1984) *Not in Our Genes*. New York: Pantheon.

Li, W., Lexenberg, E., Parrish, T. and Gottfried, J. A. (2006) Learning to smell the roses: Experience-dependent neural plasticity in human piriform and orbitofrontal cortices. *Neuron*, 52, 1097–108.

Li, Y., Li, H., Decety, J. and Lee, K. (2013) Experiencing a natural disaster alters children's altruistic giving. *Psychological Science*, 24, 1686–95.

Liberman, V., Samuels, S. M. and Ross, L. (2002). The name of the game: Predictive power of reputation vs. situational labels in the prisoners' dilemma game moves. *Personality and Social Psychology Bulletin*, 30, 1175–85.

Libet, B. (1985) Unconscious cerebral initiative and the role of conscious will in voluntary action. *Behavioral and Brain Sciences*, 8, 529–66.

Lickel, B., Hamilton, D. L., Lewis, A. et al. (2000) Varieties of groups and the perception of group entitativity. *Journal of Personality and Social Psychology*, 78, 223–46.

Lieb, R., Becker, E. and Altamura, C. (2005) The epidemiology of generalized anxiety disorder in Europe. *European Neuropsychopharmacology*, 15, 445–2.

Liebenluft, E. (1996) Women with bipolar illness: Clinical and research issues. *American Journal of Psychiatry*, 153, 163–73.

Lieberman, D. A. (2004) *Learning and Memory: An Integrative Approach*. Belmont, CA: Wadsworth.

Lieberman, M. D. and Rosenthal, R. (2001) Why introverts can't always tell who likes them: Multitasking and nonverbal decoding. *Journal of Personality and Social Psychology*, 80, 294–310.

Lieberman, M. D., Hariri, A., Jarcho, J. M. et al. (2005) An fMRI investigation of race-related amygdala activity in African American and Caucasian-American individuals. *Nature Neuroscience*, 8, 720–2.

Liebowitz, M. R., Fyer, A. J., Gorman, J. M. et al. (1985a) Specificity of lactate infusions in social phobia versus panic disorders. *American Journal of Psychiatry*, 142, 947–50.

Liebowitz, M. R., Gorman, J. M., Fyer, A. J. et al. (1985b) Lactate provocation of panic attacks, II. Biochemical and physiological findings. *Archives of General Psychiatry*, 42, 709–19.

Lilienfeld, S. O., Lynn, S. J. and Lohr, J. M. (eds) (2003) *Science and Pseudoscience in Clinical Psychology*. New York: Guilford Press.

Lilienfeld, S. O., Wood, J. M. and Garb, H. N. (2000) The scientific status of projective techniques. *Psychological Science in the Public Interest*, 1, 27–66.

Lindenberger, U. and Baltes, P. B. (1997) Intellectual functioning in old and very old age: Cross-sectional results from the Berling aging study. *Psychology and Aging*, 12, 410–32.

Lindsay, D. S. and Read, J. D. (1994) Psychotherapy and memories of childhood sexual abuse: A cognitive perspective. *Applied Cognitive Psychology*, 8, 281–338.

Lindsey, R. V., Shroyer, J. D., Pashler, H. and Mozer, M. C. (2014) Improving students' long-term knowledge retention through personalized review. *Psychological Science*, 25, 639–47.

Lindsley, O. R., Skinner, B. F. and Solomon, H. C. (1953) *Studies in Behavior Therapy*. Waltham, MA: Metropolitan State Hospital.

Lindstrom, M. (2005) *Brand Sense: How to Build Powerful Brands through Touch, Taste, Smell, Sight and Sound*. London: Kogan Page.

Link, B. G., Phelan, J. C., Bresnahan, M. et al. (1999) Public conceptions of mental illness: Labels, causes, dangerousness, and social distance. *American Journal of Public Health*, 89, 1328–33.

Link, S. W. (1994) Rediscovering the past: Gustav Fechner and signal detection theory. *Psychological Science*, 5, 335–40.

Linszen, D. H., Dingemans, P. M., Nugter, M. A. et al. (1997) Patient attributes and expressed emotion as risk factors for psychotic relapse. *Schizophrenia Bulletin*, 23, 119–30.

Lipps, T. (1907) Das Wissen von fremden Ichen. In T. Lipps (ed.) *Psychologische Untersuchungen* (vol. 1, pp. 694–722). Leipzig: Engelmann.

Lipsitt, L. P. (1977) Taste in human neonates: Its effects on sucking and heart rate. In J. M. Weiffenbach (ed.) *Taste and Development: The Genesis of Sweet Preference* (pp. 125–41). Washington, DC: US Government Printing Office.

Liston, C. and Kagan, J. (2002) Memory enhancement in early childhood. *Nature*, 419, 806.

Liszkowski, U., Carpenter, M., Henning, A. et al. (2004) Twelve-month-olds point to share attention and interest. *Developmental Science*, 7, 297–307.

Little, B. R. (1983) Personal projects: A rationale and method for investigation. *Environment and Behavior*, 15, 273–309.

Livesley, W. J. and Bromley, D. B. (1973) *Person Perception in Childhood and Adolescence*. London: Wiley.

Livingstone, M. and Hubel, D. (1988) Segregation of form, color, movement, and depth: Anatomy, physiology, and perception. *Science*, 240, 740–9.

Lloyd, P., Mann, S. and Peers, I. (1998) The growth of speaker and listener skills from five to eleven years. *First Language*, 18, 81–103.

Locke, J. ([1690]1947) *An Essay Concerning Human Understanding*. New York: E. P. Dutton.

Locksley, A., Ortiz, V. and Hepburn, C. (1980) Social categorization and discriminatory behavior: Extinguishing the minimal intergroup discrimination effect. *Journal of Personality and Social Psychology*, 39, 773–83.

Loeber, R. and Stouthamer-Loeber, M. (1998) Family factors as correlates and predictors of conduct problems and juvenile delinquent. In M. Tonry and N. Morris (eds) *Crime and Justice* (vol. 7, pp. 29–149). Chicago: University of Chicago Press.

Loehlin, J. C. (1992) *Genes and Environment in Personality Development*. Newbury Park, CA: Sage.

Loftus, E. F. (1974) Reconstructing memory: The incredible witness. *Psychology Today*, 8, 116–19.

Loftus, E. F. (1975) Leading questions and eyewitness report. *Cognitive Psychology*, 7, 560–72.

Loftus, E. F. (1993) The reality of repressed memories. *American Psychologist*, 48, 518–37.

Loftus, E. F. (2003) Make-believe memories. *American Psychologist*, 58, 867–73.

Loftus, E. F. and Ketchum, K. (1994) *The Myth of Repressed Memory*. New York: St Martin's Press.

Loftus, E. F. and Pickrell, J. E. (1995) The formation of false memories. *Psychiatric Annals*, 25, 720–5.

Loftus, E. F., Miller, D. G. and Burns, H. J. (1978) Semantic integration of verbal information into a visual memory. *Journal of Experimental Psychology: Human Learning and Memory*, 4, 19–31.

Logan, G. D. (1988) Toward an instance theory of automatization. *Psychological Review*, 95, 492–527.

Logie, R. H. and Della Sala, S. (1999) Repetita (non) luvant. In S. Della Sala (ed.) *Mind Myths: Exploring Popular Assumptions about the Mind and Brain* (pp. 127–37). Chichester: Wiley.

Long, D. L. and Prat, C. S. (2002) Memory for Star Trek: The role of prior knowledge in recognition revisited. *Journal of Experimental Psychology: Learning, Memory and Cognition*, 28, 1073–82.

Longstreth, L. E. (1981) Revisiting Skeels' final study: A critique. *Developmental Psychology*, 17, 620–5.

Lorenz, K. (1943) Die Angebornen Formen mogicher Erfahrung. *Zeitschrift fur Tierpsychologie*, 5, 233–409.

Lorenz, K. (1952) *King Solomon's Ring*. New York: Crowell.

Lorenz, K. (1966) *On Aggression* (trans. M. Kerr Wilson). New York: Harcourt, Brace & World.

Lorenz, K. (1973) *Autobiography*, http://nobelprize.org/nobel_prizes/medicine/laureates/1973/lorenz.html.

Lozano, B. E. and Johnson, S. L. (2001) Can personality traits predict increases in manic and depressive symptoms? *Journal of Affective Disorders*, 63, 103–11.

Lubinski, D., Webb, R. M., Morelock, M. J. and Benbow, C. P. (2001) Top 1 in 10,000: A 10-year follow-up of the profoundly gifted. *Journal of Applied Psychology*, 86, 718–29.

Luborsky, L. and Singer, B. (1975) Comparative studies of psychotherapies: Is it true that 'everywon has one and all must have prizes'? *Archives of General Psychiatry*, 32(8), 995–1008.

Luborsky, L., Rosenthal, R., Diguer, L. et al. (2002) The dodo bird verdict is alive and well – mostly. *Clinical Psychology: Science and Practice*, 9, 2–12.

Lucas, R. E., Clark, A. E., Georgellis, Y. and Diener, E. (2003) Reexamining adaptation and the set point model of happiness: Reactions to changes in marital status. *Journal of Personality and Social Psychology*, 84, 527–39.

Ludwig, A. M. (1966) Altered states of consciousness. *Archives of General Psychiatry*, 15, 225–34.

Luhrmann, T. M., Padmavati, R., Tharoor, H. and Osei, A. (2014) Differences in voice-hearing experiences of people with psychosis in the USA, India and Ghana: Interview-based study. *British Journal of Psychiatry*, doi: 10.1192/bjp.bp.113.139048.

Luria, A. R. (1968) *The Mind of a Mnemonist: A Little Book About a Vast Memory* (trans. L. Solotaroff). New York: Basic Books.

Lustig, C., May, C. P. and Hasler, L. (2001) Working memory span and the role of proactive interference. *Journal of Experimental Psychology: General*, 130, 199–207.

Lustman, P. J., Caudle, M. L. and Clouse, R. E. (2002) Case study: Nondysphoric depression in a man with type 2 diabetes. *Clinical Diabetes*, 20, 122–3.

Lykken, D. T. (1995) *The Antisocial Personalities*. Hillsdale, NJ: Erlbaum.

Lynn, M. and Shurgot, B. A. (1984) Responses to lonely hearts advertisements: Effects of reported physical attractiveness, physique, and coloration. *Personality and Social Psychology Bulletin*, 10, 349–57.

Lynn, R. (1998) In support of the nutrition theory. In U. Neisser (ed.) *The Rising Curve: Long-Term Gains in IQ and Related Measures* (pp. 207–18). Washington, DC: APA.

Lynn, R. (2011) *Dysgenics: Genetic Deterioration in Modern Populations* (rev. edn). London: Ulster Institute for Social Research.

Lynn, R. and Vanhanen, T. (2002) *IQ and the Wealth of Nations.* Westport, CT: Praeger/Greenwood.

Lynn, S. J., Rhue, J. W. and Weekes, J. R. (1990) Hypnotic involuntariness: A social cognitive analysis. *Psychological Review*, 97, 169–84.

Lyon, H., Startup, M. and Bentall, R. P. (1999) Social cognition and the manic defense. *Journal of Abnormal Psychology*, 108(2), 273–82.

Lyons, D. E., Young, A. G. and Keil, F. C. (2007) The hidden structure of overimitation. *Proceedings of the National Academy*, 104, 19751–6.

McAdams, D. (1993) *The Stories We Live By: Personal Myths and the Making of the Self.* New York: Morrow.

McAndrew, F. T. (1986) A cross-cultural study of recognition thresholds for facial expression of emotion. *Journal of Cross-Cultural Psychology*, 17, 211–24.

McClelland, D. C., Atkinson, J. W., Clark, R. A. and Lowell, E. L. (1953) *The Achievement Motive.* New York: Appleton-Century-Crofts.

McClintock, M. K. (1971) Menstrual synchrony and suppression. *Nature*, 299, 244–5.

McCloskey, M. (1983) Intuitive physics. *Scientific American*, 248(4), 122–30.

McCloskey, M. and Zaragoza, M. (1985) Misleading postevent information and memory for events: Arguments and evidence against memory impairment hypotheses. *Journal of Experimental Psychology: General*, 114, 1–16.

Maccoby, E. E. (1980) *Social Development: Psychological Growth and the Parent-child Relationship*. New York: Harcourt Brace Janovich.

Maccoby, E. E. (2002) Gender and group process: A developmental perspective. *Current Directions in Psychological Science*, 11, 54–8.

McConkey, K. M., Barnier, A. J. and Sheehan, P. W. (1998) Hypnosis and pseudomemory: Understanding the findings and their implications. In S. J. Lynn and K. M. McConkey (eds) *Truth in Memory* (pp. 227–59). New York: Guilford Press.

McCrae, R. R. and Costa, P. T. (1990) *Personality in Adulthood*. New York: Guilford Press.

McCrae, R. R. and Costa, P. T. (1999) A five-factor theory of personality. In L. A. Pervin and O. P. John (eds) *Handbook of Personality: Theory and Research* (pp. 139–53). New York: Guilford Press.

McCrea, S. M., Buxbaum, L. J. and Coslett, H. B. (2006) Illusory con-junctions in simultanagnosia: Coarse coding of visual feature location? *Neuropsychologia,* 44, 1724–36.

MacDonald, S., Uesiliana, K. and Hayne, H. (2000) Cross-cultural and gender differences in childhood amnesia. *Memory*, 8, 365–76.

McDougall, W. ([1908]2003) *Introduction to Social Psychology.* Mineola, NY: Dover.

McDougall, W. (1930) The hormic psychology. In C. Murchison (ed.) *Psychologies of 1930* (pp. 3–36). Worcester, MA: Clark University Press.

McEvoy, S. P., Stevenson, M. R., McCartt, A. T. et al. (2005) Role of mobile phones in motor vehicle crashes resulting in hospital attendance: A case-crossover study. *British Medical Journal*, 331, 428–30.

McFall, R. M. and Treat, T. A. (1999) Quantifying the information value of clinical assessments with signal detection theory. *Annual Review of Psychology*, 50, 215–41.

McFarland, C. and Ross, M. (1987) The relation between current impressions and memories of self and dating partners. *Personality and Social Psychology Bulletin*, 13, 228–38.

Macfarlane, A. (1975) Olfaction in the development of social preferences in the human neonate. In A. Macfarlane (ed.) *Parent–Infant Interactions* (pp. 103–17). Amsterdam: Elsevier.

McFarlane, A. H., Norman, G. R., Streiner, D. L. et al. (1980) A longitudinal study of the influence of the psychosocial environment on health status: A preliminary report. *Journal of Health and Social Behavior*, 21, 124–33.

McGarty, C. and Turner, J. C. (1992) The effects of categorization on social judgement. *British Journal of Social Psychology*, 31, 253–68.

McGowan, P. O., Suderman, M., Sasaki, A. et al. (2011) Broad epigenetic signature of maternal care in the brain of adult rats. *PLoS ONE*, 6, e14739.

McGrath, J. E. (1984) *Groups: Interaction and Performance.* Englewood Cliffs, NJ: Prentice Hall.

MacGregor, J. N., Ormerod, T. C. and Chronicle, E. P. (2001) Information processing and insight: A process model of performance on the nine-dot and related problems. *Journal of Experimental Psychology: Learning, Memory and Cognition*, 27, 176–201.

McGue, M. and Bouchard, T. J. (1998) Genetic and environmental influences on human behavioral differences. *Annual Review of Neuroscience*, 21, 1–24.

McGuire, P. K., Shah, G. M. and Murray, R. M. (1993) Increased blood flow in Broca's area during auditory hallucinations in schizophrenia. *Lancet*, 342, 703–6.

McHoskey, J. W. (1999) Machiavellianism, intrinsic versus extrinsic goals, and self-interest: A self-determination theory analysis. *Motivation and Emotion*, 23, 267–83.

McHugh, P. R., Lief, H. I., Freyd, P. P. and Fetkewicz, J. M. (2004) From refusal to recollection: Family relationships after an accusation based on recovered memories. *Journal of Nervous and Mental Disease*, 192, 525–32.

McKetin, R., Ward, P. B., Catts, S. V. et al. (1999) Changes in auditory selective attention and event-related potentials following oral administration of D-amphetamine in humans. *Neuropsychopharmacology*, 380–90.

Mackinnon, A. and Foley, D. (1996) The genetics of anxiety disorders. In H. G. Westenberg, J. A. Den Boer and D. L. Murphy (eds) *Advances in the Neurobiology of Anxiety Disorders* (pp. 39–59). Chichester: Wiley.

Maclean, P. D. (1970) The triune brain, emotion, and scientific bias. In F. O. Schmitt (ed.) *The Neurosciences: A Second Study Program* (pp. 336–49). New York: Rockefeller University Press.

Macmillan, M. (2000) *An Odd Kind of Fame: Stories of Phineas Gage*. Cambridge, MA: MIT Press.

Macmillan, M. (2008) Phineas Gage: Unravelling the myth. *The Psychologist*, 21, 828–31.

Macmillan, N. A. and Creelman, C. D. (2005) *Detection Theory.* Mahwah, NJ: Erlbaum.

McNally, K. (2007) Schizophrenia as split personality/Jekyll and Hyde: The origins of the informal usage in the English language. *Journal of the History of Behavioral Sciences*, 43, 69–79.

McNally, R. J. (2003) *Remembering Trauma*. Cambridge, MA: Belknap Press/Harvard University Press.

McNally, R. J. and Steketee, G. S. (1985) Etiology and maintenance of severe animal phobias. *Behavioral Research and Therapy*, 23, 431–5.

McNamara, B., Ray, J. L., Arthurs, O. J. and Boniface, S. (2001) Trans-cranial magnetic stimulation for depression and other psychiatric disorders. *Psychological Medicine*, 31, 1141–6.

McNamara, T. P. (2005) *Semantic Priming: Perspectives from Memory and Word Recognition*. Hove: Psychology Press.

McNeilly, A. S., Robinson, I. C., Houston, M. J. and Howie, P. W. (1983) Release of oxytocin and prolactin in response to suckling. *British Medical Journal*, 286, 257–9.

MacPherson, S. E., Phillips, L. H. and Sala, S. D. (2002) Age, executive functioning and social decision making: A dorsolateral prefrontal theory of cognitive aging. *Psychology and Aging*, 17, 598–609.

Macrae, C. N., Bodenhausen, G. V., Milne, A. B. and Jetten, J. (1994) Out of mind but back in sight: Stereotypes on the rebound. *Journal of Personality and Social Psychology*, 67, 808–17.

Macrae, C. N., Moran, J. M., Heatherton, T. F. et al. (2004) Medial prefrontal activity predicts memory for self. *Cerebral Cortex*, 14, 647–54.

McWilliams, N. (1994) *Psychoanalytic Diagnosis: Understanding Personality Structure in the Clinical Process*. New York: Guilford Press.

McWilliams, P. (1993) *Ain't Nobody's Business If You Do: The Absurdity of Consensual Crimes in a Free Society*. Los Angeles: Prelude Press.

Madill, A. and Gough, B. (2008) Qualitative research and its place in psychological science. *Psychological Methods*, 13(3), 254–71.

Madsen, K. M., Hviid, A., Vestergaard, M. et al. (2002) A population-based study of measles, mumps, and rubella vaccination and autism. *New England Journal of Medicine*, 347, 1477–82.

Maestripieri, D. (2005) *Primate Psychology*. Cambridge, MA: Harvard University Press.

Magee, W. J., Eaton, W. W., Wittchen, H.-U. et al. (1996) Agoraphobia, simple phobia, and social phobia in the National Comorbidity Survey. *Archives of General Psychiatry*, 53, 159–68.

Maguire, E. A., Woollett, K. and Spiers, H. J. (2006) London taxi drivers and bus drivers: A structural MRI and neuropsychological analysis. *Hippocampus*, 16, 1091–101.

Maguire, E. A., Gadian, D. G., Johnsrude, I. S. et al. (2000) Navigation-related structural change in the hippocampi of taxi drivers. *Proceedings of the National Academy of Science*, 97, 4398–403.

Mah, K. and Binik, Y. M. (2002) Do all orgasms feel alike? Evaluating a two-dimensional model of the orgasm experience across gender and sexual context. *Journal of Sex Research*, 39, 104–13.

Mahajan, N. and Wynn, K. (2012) Origins of 'us' versus 'them': Prelinguistic infants prefer similar others. *Cognition*, 124, 227–33.

Main, M. and Solomon, J. (1986) Discovery of a disorganized/disoriented attachement pattern. In T. B. Brazelton and M. W. Yogman (eds) *Affective Development in Infancy* (pp. 95–124). Norwood, NJ: Ablex.

Makin, J. E., Fried, P. A. and Watkinson, B. (1991) A comparison of active and passive smoking during pregnancy: Long-term effects. *Neurotoxicology and Teratology*, 16, 5–12.

Malatesta, C. Z., Culver, C., Tesman, J. R. and Shepard, B. (1989) The development of emotion expression during the first two years of life. *Monographs of the Society for Research in Child Development*, 54(1–2, serial no. 219).

Maldonado, J. R. and Butler, L. D. (1998) *Treatments for Dissociative Disorders*. New York: OUP.

Malooly, A. M., Genet, J. J. and Siemer, M. (2013) Individual differences in reappraisal effectiveness: The role of affective flexibility. *Emotion*, 13, 302–13.

Mandel, D. R. and Lehman, D. R. (1998) Integration of contingency information in judgments of cause, covariation, and probability. *Journal of Experimental Psychology: General*, 127, 269–85.

Mandela, N. (1995) *Long Walk to Freedom*. London: Little, Brown.

Mandler, G. (1967) Organization and memory. In K. W. Spence and J. T. Spence (eds) *The Psychology of Learning and Motivation* (vol. 1, pp. 327–72). New York: Academic Press.

Mann, J. J., Waternaux, C., Haas, G. L. and Malone, K. M. (1999) Toward a clinical model of suicidal behavior in psychiatric patients. *American Journal of Psychiatry*, 156, 181–9.

Mann, L. (1981) The baiting crowd in episodes of threatened suicide. *Journal of Personality and Social Psychology*, 41, 703–9.

Manning, R., Levine, M. and Collins, A. (2007) The Kitty Genovese murder and the social psychology of helping: The parable of the 38 witnesses. *American Psychologist*, 62, 555–62.

Mäntylä, T. (2003) Assessing absentmindedness: Prospective memory complaint and impairment in middle aged adults. *Memory and Cognition*, 31, 15–25.

Mäntylä, T. (2013) Gender differences in multitasking reflect spatial ability. *Psychological Science*, 24, 514–20.

Marangell, L. B., Martinez, J. M. and Niazi, S. K. (2004) Vagus nerve stimulation as a potential option for treatment-resistant depression. *Clinical Neuroscience Research*, 4, 89–94.

Marangell, L. B., Martinez, J. M., Jurdi, R. A. and Zboyan, H. (2007) Neurostimulation therapies in depression: A review of new modalities. *Acta Psychiatrica Scandinavia*, 116, 174–81.

Marangell, L. B., Silver, J. M., Goff, D. M. and Yudofsky, S. C. (2003) Psychopharmacology and electroconvulsive therapy. In R. E. Hales and S. C. Yudofsky (eds) *The American Psychiatric Publishing Textbook of Clinical Psychiatry* (4th edn, pp. 1047–149). Washington, DC: American Psychiatric Publishing.

Marcel, A. (1983) Conscious and unconscious perception: Experiments on visual masking and word recognition. *Cognitive Psychology*, 15, 197–237.

Marcus, G. B. (1986) Stability and change in political attitudes: Observe, recall, and 'explain.' *Political Behavior*, 8, 21–44.

Marcus, G. F. (2004) *The Birth of the Mind: How a Tiny Number of Genes Creates the Complexities of Human Thought*. New York: Basic Books.

Marcus, J., Hans, S. L., Auerbach, J. G. and Auerbach, A. G. (1993) Children at risk for schizophrenia: The Jerusalem infant development study, II. Neurological deficits at school age. *Archives of General Psychiatry*, 50, 797–809.

Markman, A. B. and Gentner, D. (1993) Structural alignment during similarity comparisons. *Cognitive Psychology*, 25, 431–67.

Markman, E. M. (1990) Constraints children place on word meanings. *Cognitive Science*, 14, 57–77.

Marks, I. M. and Nesse, R. M. (1994) Fear and fitness: An evolutionary analysis of anxiety disorders. *Ethology and Sociobiology*, 15, 247–61.

Markus, H. (1977) Self-schemata and processing information about the self. *Journal of Personality and Social Psychology*, 35, 63–78.

Markus, H. and Kitayama, S. (1991) Culture and the self: Implications for cognition, emotion and motivation. *Psychological Review*, 98, 224–53.

Marlatt, G. A. (ed.) (1998) *Harm Reduction: Pragmatic Strategies for Managing High-risk Behaviors*. New York: Guilford Press.

Marlatt, G. A., Larimer, M. E., Baer, J. S. and Quigley, L. A. (1993) Harm reduction for alcohol problems: Moving beyond the controlled drinking controversy. *Behavior Therapy*, 24, 461–504.

Marmot, M. G., Stansfeld, S., Patel, C. et al. (1991) Health inequalities among British civil servants: The Whitehall II study. *Lancet*, 337, 1387–93.

Marr, D. and Nishihara, H. K. (1978) Representation and recognition of the spatial organization of three-dimensional shapes. *Proceedings of the Royal Society of London B*, 200, 269–94.

Marshall, E. (2004) Forgetting and remembering: A star-studded search for memory-enhancing drugs. *Science*, 304, 36–8.

Marshall, J. C. and Halligan, P. W. (1988) Blind sight and insight in visual-spatial neglect. *Nature*, 336, 766–7.

Marsolek, C. J. (1995) Abstract visual-form representations in the left cerebral hemispheres. *Journal of Experimental Psychology: Human Perception and Performance*, 21, 375–86.

Martens, A., Johns, M., Greenberg, J. and Schimel, J. (2006) Combating stereotype threat: The effect of self-affirmation on women's intellectual performance. *Journal of Experimental Social Psychology*, 42, 236–43.

Martin, A. (2007) The representation of object concepts in the brain. *Annual Review of Psychology*, 58, 25–45.

Martin, A. and Caramazza, A. (2003) Neuropsychological and neuroimaging perspectives on conceptual knowledge: An introduction. *Cognitive Neuropsychology*, 20, 195–212.

Martin, A. and Chao, L. L. (2001) Semantic memory and the brain: Structure and processes. *Current Opinion in Neurobiology*, 11, 194–201.

Martin, G. and Koo, L. (1997) Celebrity suicide: Did the death of Kurt Cobain influence young suicides in Australia? *Archives of Suicide Research*, 3, 187–98.

Martin, N. G., Eaves, L. J., Geath, A. R. et al. (1986) Transmission of social attitudes. *Proceedings of the National Academy of Sciences*, 83, 4364–8.

Martin, R. A. (1989) Techniques for data acquisition and analysis in field investigations of stress. In R. W. Neufeld (ed.) *Advances in the Investigation of Psychological Stress*. New York: Wiley.

Marucha, P. T., Kiecolt-Glaser, J. K. and Favagehi, M. (1998) Mucosal wound healing is impaired by examination stress. *Psychosomatic Medicine*, 60, 362–5.

Maslow, A. H. (1937) Dominance-feeling, behavior, and status. In R. J. Lowry (ed.) *Dominance, Self-esteem, Self-actualization: Germinal Papers by A. H. Maslow* (pp. 177–201). Monterey, CA: Brooks-Cole.

Maslow, A. H. (1954) *Motivation and Personality*. New York: Harper & Row.

Maslow, A. H. (1962) *Toward a Psychology of Being*. New York: Van Nostrand Reinhold.

Maslow, A. H. (1970) *Motivation and Personality* (2nd edn). New York: Harper & Row.

Masters, W. H. and Johnson, V. E. (1966) *Human Sexual Response*. Boston: Little, Brown.

Masuda, T. and Nisbett, R. E. (2001) Attending holistically vs analytically: Comparing the context sensitivity of Japanese and Americans. *Journal of Personality and Social Psychology*, 81, 922–34.

Mather, M. and Carstensen, L. L. (2003) Aging and attentional biases for emotional faces. *Psychological Science*, 14, 409–15.

Mather, M., Canli, T., English, T. et al. (2004) Amygdala responses to emotionally valenced stimuli in older and younger adults. *Psychological Science*, 15, 259–63.

Matthews, G. and Deary, I. J. (1998) *Personality Traits*. Cambridge: CUP.

Matthews, G. and Gilliland, K. (1999) The personality theories of H. J. Eysenck and J. A. Gray: A comparative review. *Personality and Individual Differences*, 26, 583–626.

Matthews, G., Zeidner, M. and Roberts, R. D. (2003) *Emotional Intelligence: Science and Myth*. Cambridge, MA: MIT Press.

Mattingly, J. B. (2009) Attention, automaticity, and awareness in synesthesia. *Annals of the New York Academy of Sciences*, 1156, 141–67.

Maudsley, H. (1886) *Natural Causes and Supernatural Seemings*. London: Kegan Paul, Trench.

Maurer, D. (1997) Neonatal synaesthesia: Implications for the processing of speech and faces. In S. Baron-Cohen and J. E. Harrison (eds) *Synaesthesia: Classic and Contemporary Readings* (pp. 224–42). Oxford: Blackwell.

Maurer, D. and Maurer, C. (1988) *The World of the Newborn*. New York: Basic Books.

Maurer, D. and Mondloch, C. J. (2006) The infant as synesthete? In Y. Munakata and M. H. Johnson (eds) *Processes of Change in Brain and Cognitive Development: Attention and Performance XXI* (pp. 449–71). Oxford: OUP.

Maurer, D., Pathman, T. and Mondloch, C. J. (2006) The shape of boubas: Sound-shape correspondences in toddlers and adults. *Developmental Science*, 9, 316–22.

Maxwell, J. P. and Visek, A. J. (2009) Unsanctioned aggression in rugby union: Relationships amongst aggressiveness, anger, athletic identity and professionalism. *Aggressive Behavior*, 35, 237–43.

May, R. (1983) *The Discovery of Being: Writings in Existential Psychology*. New York: Norton.

Mayer, J. D., Caruso, D. and Salovey, P. (1999) Emotional intelligence meets traditional standards for an intelligence. *Intelligence*, 27, 267–98.

Maynard-Smith, J. (1965) The evolution of alarm calls. *American Naturalist*, 100, 637–50.

Maynard-Smith, J. and Szathmary, E. (1995) *The Major Transitions in Evolution*. Oxford: OUP.

Maziade, M., Caron, C., Coté, R. et al. (1990) Psychiatric status of adolescents who had extreme temperament at age 7. *American Journal of Psychiatry*, 147, 1531–6.

Mead, G. H. (1934) *Mind, Self, and Society*. Chicago: University of Chicago Press.

Mead, M. ([1935]1968) *Sex and Temperament in Three Primitive Societies*. New York: Dell.

Meaney, M. J. (2001) The development of individual differences in behavioral and endocrine responses to stress. *Annual Review of Neuroscience*, 24, 1161–92.

Medin, D. L. and Schaffer, M. M. (1978) Context theory of classification learning. *Psychological Review*, 85, 207–38.

Medvec, V. H., Madey, S. F. and Gilovich, T. (1995) When less is more: Counterfactual thinking and satisfaction among Olympic medalists. *Journal of Personality and Social Psychology*, 69, 603–10.

Mei, J. (1994) The northern Chinese custom of rearing babies in sandbags: Implications for motor and intellectual development. In J. H. van Rossum and J. I. Laszlo (eds) *Motor Development: Aspects of Normal and Delayed Development* (pp. 41–8). Amsterdam: VU Uitgeverij.

Meijer, E. H. and van Koppen, P. J. (2008) Lie detectors and the law: The use of the polygraph in Europe. In D. V. Canter and R. Zukauskiené (eds) *Psychology and Law: Bridging the Gap* (pp. 31–50). Aldershot: Ashgate.

Meins, E. (2003) Emotional development and attachment relationships. In A. Slater and G. Bremner (eds) *An Introduction to Developmental Psychology* (pp. 141–64). Malden, MA: Blackwell.

Meins, E., Fernyhough, C., Fradley, E. and Tuckey, M. (2001) Rethinking maternal sensitivity: Mothers' comments on infants' mental processes predict security of attachment at 12 months. *Journal of Child Psychology & Psychiatry & Allied Disciplines*, 42, 637–48.

Mekel-Bobrov, N., Gilbert, S. L., Evans, P. D. et al. (2005) Ongoing adaptive evolution of ASPM, a brain size determinant in *Homo sapiens*. *Science*, 309, 1720–2.

Melby-Lervåg, M. and Hulme, C. (2012) Is working memory training effective? A meta-analytic review. *Developmental Psychology*, 49, 270–91.

Meltzoff, A. N. (1988a) Imitation in televised models by infants. *Child Development*, 59, 1221–9.

Meltzoff, A. N. (1988b) Infant imitation and memory: Nine-month-olds in immediate and deferred tests. *Child Development*, 59, 217–25.

Meltzoff, A. N. (1995) Apprehending the actions of others: Re-enactment of intended acts by 10-month-old children. *Developmental Psychology*, 31, 838–50.

Meltzoff, A. N. and Moore, M. K. (1977) Imitation of facial and manual gestures by human neonates. *Science*, 198, 75–8.

Meltzoff, A. N., Kuhl, P. K., Movellan, J. and Sejnowski, T. J. (2009) Foundations for a new science of learning, *Science*, 325, 284–88.

Melzack, R. and Wall, P. D. (1965) Pain mechanisms: A new theory. *Science*, 150, 971–9.

Mendes, W. B., Blascovich, J., Lickel, B. and Hunter, S. (2002) Challenge and threat during social interaction with white and black men. *Personality & Social Psychology Bulletin*, 28, 939–52.

Mennella, J. A., Jagnow, C. P. and Beauchamp, G. K. (2001) Prenatal and postnatal flavor learning by human infants. *Pediatrics*, 107(6): E88.

Merikangas, K. R., Wicki, W. and Angst, J. (1994) Heterogeneity of depression: Classification of depressive subtype by longitudinal course. *British Journal of Psychiatry*, 164, 342–8.

Meroni, L., Gualmini, A. and Crain, S. (2007) The strength of the universal quantifier in child language. In A. Belikova, L. Meroni and M. Umeda (eds) *Proceedings of the 2nd Conference on Generative Approaches to Language Acquisition North America (GALANA)* (pp. 277–85). Somerville, MA: Cascadilla Proceedings Project.

Mervis, C. B. and Bertrand, J. (1994) Acquisition of the 'novel name' nameless category (N3C) principle. *Child Development*, 65, 1646–62.

Merzenich, M. M., Recanzone, G. H., Jenkins, W. M. and Grajski, K. A. (1990) Adaptive mechanisms in cortical networks underlying cortical contributions to learning and nondeclarative memory. *Cold Spring Harbor Symposia on Quantitative Biology*, 55, 873–87.

Mesoudi, A. (2009) The cultural dynamics of copycat suicide. *PLoS ONE*, 4(9), e7252.

Messick, D. M. and Cook, K. S. (1983) *Equity Theory: Psychological and Sociological Perspectives.* New York: Praeger.

Metcalfe, J. (2009) Metacognitive judgments and control of study. *Current Directions in Psychological Science*, 18, 159–63.

Metcalfe, J. and Finn, B. (2008) Evidence that judgments of learning are causally related to study choice. *Psychonomic Bulletin and Review*, 15, 174–9.

Metcalfe, J. and Wiebe, D. (1987) Intuition in insight and noninsight problem solving. *Memory & Cognition*, 15, 238–46.

Methven, L., Allen, V. J., Withers, G. A. and Gosney, M. A. (2012) Aging and taste. *Proceedings of the Nutrition Society*, 781, 556–65.

Metzler-Baddeley, C. and Baddeley, R. (2009) Does adaptive training work? *Applied Cognitive Psychology*, 23, 254–66.

Micali, N., Hagberg, K. W., Petersen, I. and Treasure, J. L. (2013) The incidence of eating disorders in the UK in 2000–2009: Findings from the General Practice Research Database. *BMJ Open*, 3, e002646.

Michaels, J. W., Blommel, J. M., Borcato, R. M. et al. (1982) Social facilitation and inhibition in a natural setting. *Replications in Social Psychology*, 2, 21–4.

Michaelson, L., de la Vega, A., Chatham, C. H. and Munakata, Y. (2013) Delaying gratification depends on social trust. *Frontiers in Psychology*, 4, 355.

Michelson, D., Pollack, M., Lydiard, R. D. et al. (1999) Continuing treatment of panic disorder after acute responses: Randomized, placebo-controlled trail with fluoxetine. The Fluoxitine Panic Disorder Study Group. *British Journal of Psychiatry*, 174, 213–18.

Michotte, A. (1963) *The Perception of Causality.* New York: Basic Books.

Middlemast, R., Knowles, E. and Matter, C. (1976) Personal space invasions in the lavatory: Suggestive evidence for arousal. *Journal of Personality and Social Psychology*, 33, 541–6.

Miklowitz, D. J., Goldstein, M. J., Nuechterlein, K. H. et al. (1988) Family factors and the course of bipolar affective disorder. *Archives of General Psychiatry*, 45, 225–31.

Mikulincer, M. (1998) Attachment working models and the sense of trust: An exploration of interaction goals and affect regulation. *Journal of Personality and Social Psychology*, 74, 1209–24.

Milard, M. R. and Quirk, G. J. (2012) Fear extinction as a model for translational neuroscience: Ten years of progress. *Annual Review of Psychology*, 63, 129–51.

Miles, D. R. and Carey, G. (1997) Genetic and environmental architecture of human aggression. *Journal of Personality and Social Psychology*, 72, 207–17.

Milgram, S. (1963) Behavioral study of obedience. *Journal of Abnormal and Social Psychology*, 67, 371–8.

Milgram, S. (1974) *Obedience to Authority.* New York: Harper & Row.

Milgram, S. and Toch, H. (1968) Collective behavior: Crowds and social movements. In G. Lindzey and E. Aronson (eds) *The Handbook of Social Psychology* (2nd edn, vol. 4, pp. 507–610). Reading, MA: Addison-Wesley.

Milgram, S., Bickman, L. and Berkowitz, O. (1969) Note on the drawing power of crowds of different size. *Journal of Personality and Social Psychology*, 13, 79–82.

Miller, A. J. (1986) *The Obedience Experiments: A Case Study of Controversy in Social Science.* New York: Praeger.

Miller, C. F., Martin, C. L., Fabes, R. A. and Hanish, L. D. (2013) Bringing the cognitive and social together. In M. R. Banaji and S. A. Gelman (eds) *Navigating the Social World: What Infants, Children, and Other Species Can Teach Us* (pp. 306–13). New York: OUP.

Miller, D. T. and Prentice, D. A. (1996) The construction of social norms and standards. In E. T. Higgins and A. W. Kruglanski (eds) *Social Psychology: Handbook of Basic Principles* (pp. 799–829). New York: Guilford Press.

Miller, D. T. and Ratner, R. K. (1998) The disparity between the actual and assumed power of self-interest. *Journal of Personality and Social Psychology*, 74, 53–62.

Miller, G. A. (1956) The magical number seven, plus or minus two: Some limits on our capacity for processing information. *Psychological Review*, 63, 81–96.

Miller, J. (1994) On the internal structure of phonetic categories: A progress report. *Cognition*, 50, 271–85.

Miller, J. G. and Bersoff, D. M. (1994) Cultural influences on the moral status of reciprocity and the discounting of endogenous motivation. *Personality and Social Psychology Bulletin*, 20, 592–602.

Miller, K. F. and Stigler, J. (1987) Counting in Chinese: Cultural variations in a basic cognitive skill. *Cognitive Development*, 2, 279–305.

Miller, N. E. (1960) Motivational effects of brain stimulation and drugs. *Federation Proceedings*, 19, 846–54.

Miller, N. E. and Campbell, D. T. (1959) Recency and primacy in persuasion as a function of the timing of speeches and measurements. *Journal of Abnormal & Social Psychology*, 59, 1–9.

Miller, T. Q., Smith, T. W., Turner, C. W. et al. (1996) A meta-analytic review of research on hostility and physical health. *Psychological Bulletin*, 119, 322–48.

Miller, T. W. (ed.) (1996) *Theory and Assessment of Stressful Life Events.* Madison, CT: International Universities Press.

Mills, P. J. and Dimsdale, J. E. (1991) Cardiovascular reactivity to psychosocial stressors. A review of the effects of beta-blockade. *Psychosomatics*, 32, 209–20.

Milne, E. and Grafman, J. (2001) Ventromedial prefrontal cortex lesions in humans eliminate implicit gender stereotyping. *Journal of Neuroscience*, 21, 1–6.

Milner, A. D. and Goodale, M. A. (1995) *The Visual Brain in Action.* Oxford: OUP.

Milner, B. (1962) Laterality effects in audition. In V. B. Mountcastle (ed.) *Interhemispheric Relations and Cerebral Dominance* (pp. 177–95). Baltimore: Johns Hopkins University Press.

Mineka, S. and Cook, M. (1988) Social learning and the acquisition of snake fear in monkeys. In T. Zentall and B. G. Galef Jr (eds) *Social Learning* (pp. 51–73). Hillsdale, NJ: Erlbaum.

Mineka, S. and Öhman, A. (2002) Born to fear: Non-associative vs. associative factors in the etiology of phobia. *Behaviour Research and Therapy*, 40, 173–84.

Minsky, M. (1986) *The Society of Mind.* New York: Simon & Schuster.

Mischel, W. (1968) *Personality and Assessment.* New York: Wiley.

Mischel, W. (1981) Metacognition and the rules of delay. In J. Flavell and L. Ross (eds) *Social Cognitive Development* (pp. 240–71). Cambridge: CUP.

Mischel, W. and Ayduk, O. (2004) Will power in a cognitive-affective processing system: The dynamics of delay of gratification. In R. F. Baumeister and K. D. Vohs (eds) *Handbook of Self-regulation: Research, Theory and Application* (pp. 99–129). New York: Guilford Press.

Mischel, W. and Shoda, Y. (1999) Toward a unified theory of personality: Integrating dispositions and processing dynamics within the cognitive-affective personality system. In L. A. Pervin and O. P. John (eds) *Handbook of Personality: Theory and Research* (pp. 208–41). New York: Guilford Press.

Mischel, W., Shoda, Y. and Rodriguez, M. L. (1989) Delay of gratification in children. *Science*, 244, 933–8.

Mita, T. H., Dermer, M. and Knight, J. (1977) Reversed facial images and the mere-exposure hypothesis. *Journal of Personality and Social Psychology*, 35(8), 597–601.

Mitchell, J. P., Heatherton, T. F. and Macrae, C. N. (2002) Distinct neural systems subserve person and object knowledge. *Proceedings of the National Academy of Sciences*, 99, 15238–43.

Miura, I., Okamoto, Y., Kim, C. et al. (1994) Comparisons of children's cognitive representation of number: China, France, Japan, Korea, Sweden, and the United States. *International Journal of Behavioral Development*, 17, 401–11.

Miyake, A., Friedman, N., Emerson, M. et al. (2000) The unity and diversity of executive functions and their contributions to complex 'frontal lobe' tasks: A latent variable analysis. *Cognitive Psychology*, 41, 49–100.

Miyake, A., Friedman, N. P., Rettinger, D. A. et al. (2001) How are visuospatial working memory, executive functioning and spatial abilities related: A latent-variable analysis. *Journal of Experimental Psychology: General*, 130, 621–40.

Miyake, K., Chen, S. and Campos, J. J. (1985) Infant temperament, mother's mode of interaction, and attachment in Japan. *Monographs of the Society for Research in Child Development*, 50(209), 276–97.

Moghaddam, B. and Bunney, B. S. (1989) Differential effect of cocaine on extracellular dopamine levels in rat medial prefrontal cortex and nucleus accumbens: Comparison to amphetamine. *Synapse*, 4, 156–61.

Mojtabi, R. and Rieder, R. O. (1998) Limitations of the symptom-oriented approach to psychiatric research. *British Journal of Psychiatry*, 173, 198–202.

Monahan, J. L., Murphy, S. T. and Zajonc, R. B. (2000) Subliminal mere exposure: Specific, general, and diffuse effects. *Psychological Science*, 11, 462–6.

Mondschein, E. R., Adolph, K. E. and Tamis-LeMonda, C. S. (2000) Gender bias in mothers' expectations about infant crawling. *Journal of Experimental Child Psychology*, 77, 304–16.

Monti, M. M., Vanhaudenhuyse, A., Coleman, M. R. et al. (2010) Wilful modulation of brain activity in disorders of consciousness. *New England Journal of Medicine*, 362, 579–89.

Monzanil, F. P., Del Guerra, P., Caracciol, N. et al. (1993) Subclinical hypothyroidism: Neurobehavioral features and beneficial effect of l-thyroxine treatment. *The Clinical Investigator*, 5, 367–71.

Mook, D. G. (1983) In defense of external invalidity. *American Psychologist*, 38, 379–87.

Mook, D. G. (1996) *Motivation*. New York: Norton.

Moore, K. L. (1977) *The Developing Human* (2nd edn). Philadelphia: Saunders.

Moray, N. (1959) Attention in dichotic listening: Affective cues and the influence of instructions. *Quarterly Journal of Experimental Psychology*, 11, 56–60.

Morgan, G. A. and Ricciuti, H. N. (1969) Infants' responses to strangers during the first year. In B. M. Foss (ed.) *Determinants of Infant Behaviour* (vol. 4, pp. 253–72). London: Methuen.

Morgan, H. (1990) Dostoevsky's epilepsy: A case report and comparison. *Surgical Neurology*, 33, 413–16.

Morin, A. (2002) Right hemisphere self-awareness: A critical assessment. *Consciousness & Cognition*, 11, 396–401.

Morris, C. D., Bransford, J. D. and Franks, J. J. (1977) Levels of processing versus transfer-appropriate processing. *Journal of Verbal Learning and Verbal Behavior*, 16, 519–33.

Morris, R. G., Anderson, E., Lynch, G. S. and Baudry, M. (1986) Selective impairment of learning and blockade of long-term potentiation by an N-methyl-D-aspartate receptor antagonist, AP5. *Nature*, 319, 774–6.

Morris, R. G., Garrud, P., Rawlins, J. N. and O'Keefe, J. (1982) Place navigation impaired in rats with hippocampal lesions. *Nature*, 182, 681–3.

Morris, T. L. (2001) Social phobia. In M. W. Vasey and M. R. Dadds (eds) *The Developmental Psychopathology of Anxiety* (pp. 435–58). New York: OUP.

Morrison, B. (1997) *As If*. London: Granta Books.

Morrongiello, B. A., Fenwick, K. D., Hillier, L. and Chance, G. (1994) Sound localization in the newborn human infants. *Developmental Psychobiology*, 27, 519–38.

Morrot, G., Brochet, F. and Dubourdieu, D. (2001) The color of odours. *Brain and Language*, 79, 309–50.

Morrow, D., Leirer, V., Altiteri, P. and Fitzsimmons, C. (1994) When expertise reduces age differences in performance. *Psychology and Aging*, 9, 134–48.

Morton, J. and Johnson, M. H. (1991) CONSPEC and CONLERN: A two-process theory of infant face recognition. *Psychological Review*, 98(2), 164–81.

Moruzzi, G. and Magoun, H. W. (1949) Brain stem reticular formation and activation of the EEG. *Electroencephalography and Clinical Neurophysiology*, 1, 455–73.

Moscovici, S. (1980) Toward a theory of conversion behavior. In L. Berkowitiz (ed.) *Advances in Experimental Social Psychology* (13th edn, pp. 209–39). New York: Academic Press.

Moscovici, S. (1981) *L'Age des Foules*. Paris: Fayard.

Moscovici, S., Lage, E. and Naffrechoux, M. (1969) Influence of a consistent minority in a color perception task. *Sociometry*, 32, 365–80.

Moscovitch, M. (1994) Memory and working-with-memory: Evaluation of a component process model and comparisons with other models. In D. L. Schacter and E. Tulving (eds) *Memory Systems* (pp. 269–310). Cambridge, MA: MIT Press.

Moscovitch, M., Nadel, L., Winocur, G. et al. (2006) The cognitive neuroscience of remote episodic, semantic and spatial memory. *Current Opinion in Neurobiology*, 16, 179–90.

Motley, M. T. and Baars, B. J. (1979) Effects of cognitive set upon laboratory induced verbal (Freudian) slips. *Journal of Speech & Hearing Research*, 22, 421–32.

Moulin, C. J., Conway, M. A., Thompson, R. G. et al. (2005) Disordered memory awareness: Recollective confabulation in two cases of persistent déjà vécu experience. *Neuropsycholgica*, 43, 1362–78.

Mroczek, D. K. and Spiro, A. (2005) Change in life satisfaction during adulthood: Findings from the Veterans Affairs Normative Aging Study. *Journal of Personality and Social Psychology*, 88, 189.

Mueller, C. M. and Dweck, C. S. (1998) Intelligence praise can undermine motivation and performance. *Journal of Personality and Social Psychology*, 75, 33–52.

Mueller, E. T. (1990) *Daydreaming in Humans and Machines: A Computer Model of the Stream of Thought*. New York: Ablex.

Mueller, T. I., Leon, A. C., Keller, M. B. et al. (1999) Recurrence after recovery from major depressive disorder during 15 years of observational follow-up. *American Journal of Psychiatry*, 156, 1000–6.

Muenter, M. D. and Tyce, G. M. (1971) L-dopa therapy of Parkinson's disease: Plasma L-dopa concentration, therapeutic response, and side effects. *Mayo Clinic Proceedings*, 46, 231–9.

Muggleton, N., Tsakanikos, E., Walsh, V. and Ward, J. (2007) Disruption of synesthesia following TMS of the right parietal cortex. *Neuropsychologia*, 45, 1582–5.

Muir, D. (1999) Theories and methods in developmental psychology. In A. Slater and D. Muir (eds) *The Blackwell Reader in Developmental Psychology* (pp. 3–16). Oxford: Blackwell.

Mukherjee, S., Sackeim, H. A. and Schnur, D. B. (1994) Electroconvulsive therapy of acute manic episodes: A review of 50 years' experience. *American Journal of Psychiatry*, 151, 169–76.

Mullen, B. (1986) Atrocity as a function of lynch mob composition: A self-attention perspective. *Personality and Social Psychology Bulletin*, 12, 187–97.

Mullen, B. and Cooper, C. (1994) The relation between group cohesiveness and performance: An integration. *Psychological Bulletin*, 115, 210–27.

Mullen, B., Chapman, J. G. and Peaugh, S. (1989) Focus of attention in groups: A self-attention perspective. *Journal of Social Psychology*, 129, 807–17.

Muller, D., Atzeni, T. and Butera, F. (2004) Coaction and upward social comparison reduce the illusory conjunction effect: Support for the distraction-conflict theory. *Journal of Experimental Social Psychology*, 40, 659–65.

Muller, M. N. and Wrangham, R. W. (2004) Dominance, aggression and testosterone in wild chimpanzees: A test of the 'challenge hypothesis'. *Animal Behaviour*, 67, 113–23.

Müller, U., Rowe, J. B., Rittman, T. et al. (2013) Effects of modafinil on non-verbal cognition, task enjoyment and creative thinking in healthy volunteers. *Neuropharmacology*, 64, 490–9.

Multhaup, K. S., Johnson, M. D. and Tetirick, J. C. (2005) The wane of childhood amnesia for autobiographical and public event memories. *Memory*, 13, 161–73.

Mumford, D. B., Whitehouse, A. M. and Platts, M. (1991) Sociocultural correlates of eating disorders among Asian schoolgirls in Bradford. *British Journal of Psychiatry*, 158, 222–8.

Munroe, R. L., Hulefeld, R., Rodgers, J. M. et al. (2000) Aggression among children in four cultures. *Cross-Cultural Research*, 34, 3–25.

Murphy, F. C., Nimmo-Smith, I. and Lawrence, A. D. (2003a) Functional neuroanatomy of emotion: A meta-analysis. *Cognitive, Affective and Behavioural Neuroscience*, 3, 207–33.

Murphy, N. A., Hall, J. A. and Colvin, C. R. (2003b) Accurate intelligence assessments in social interactions: Mediators and gender effects. *Journal of Personality*, 71, 465–93.

Murray, C. J. and Lopez, A. D. (1996) *The Global Burden of Disease: A Comprehensive Assessment of Mortality and Disability from Diseases, Injuries, and Risk Factors in 1990 and Projected to 2020.* Cambridge, MA: Harvard School of Public Health.

Murray, H. A. (1938) *Explorations in Personality.* New York: OUP.

Murray, H. A. and Kluckhohn, C. (1953) Outline of a conception of personality. In C. Kluckhohn, H. A. Murray and D. M. Schneider (eds) *Personality in Nature, Society, and Culture* (2nd edn, pp. 3–52). New York: Knopf.

Murray, L., Fiori-Cowley, A., Hooper, R. and Cooper, P. (1996) The impact of postnatal depression and associated adversity on early mother-infant interactions and later infant outcome. *Child Development*, 67, 2512–26.

Murray, S. L. and Holmes, J. G. (1997) A leap of faith? Positive illusions in romantic relationships. *Personality and Social Psychology Bulletin*, 23, 586–604.

Murray, S. L., Holmes, J. G. and Griffen, D. W. (1996a) The self-fulfilling nature of positive illusions in romantic relationships: Love is not blind, but prescient. *Journal of Personality and Social Psychology*, 71(6), 1155–80.

Murray, S. L., Holmes, J. G. and Griffen, D. W. (1996b) The benefits of positive illusions: Idealization and the construction of satisfaction in close relationship. *Journal of Personality and Social Psychology*, 70(1), 79–98.

Mussen, P. and Eisenberg-Berg, N. (1977) *Roots of Caring, Sharing and Helping*. San Francisco, CA: Freeman.

Myers, D. G. and Diener, E. (1995) Who is happy? *Psychological Science*, 6, 10–19.

Nadasdy, A. (1995) Phonetics, phonology, and applied linguistics. *Annual Review of Applied Linguistics*, 15, 68–77.

Nadel, L. and Zola-Morgan, S. (1984) Infantile amnesia: A neuro-biological perspective. In M. Moscovitch (ed.) *Infant Memory* (pp. 145–72). New York: Plenum Press.

Nagasako, E. M., Oaklander, A. L. and Dworkin, R. H. (2003) Congenital insensitivity to pain: An update. *Pain*, 101, 213–19.

Nagel, T. (1974) What is it like to be a bat? *Philosophical Review*, 83, 433–50.

Nagin, D. S. and Pogarsky, G. (2003) An experimental investigation of deterrence: Cheating, self-serving bias, and impulsivity. *Criminology*, 41, 167–94.

Nahemow, L. and Lawton, M. P. (1975) Similarity and propinquity in friendship formation. *Journal of Personality and Social Psychology*, 32, 205–13.

Nairne, J. S. and Pandeirada, J. N. (2008) Adaptive memory: Remembering with a stone age brain. *Current Directions in Psychological Science,* 17, 239–43.

Nairne, J. S., Pandeirada, J. N. and Thompson, S. R. (2008) Adaptive memory: The comparative value of survival processing. *Psychological Science*, 19, 176–80.

Nairne, J. S., Thompson, S. R. and Pandeirada, J. N. (2007) Adaptive memory: Survival processing enhances retention. *Journal of Experimental Psychology: Learning, Memory, & Cognition,* 33, 263–73.

Nakazato, M., Murakami, N., Date, Y. et al. (2001) A role for ghrelin in the central regulation of feeding. *Nature*, 409, 194–8.

Nash, J. (1951) Non-cooperative games. *Annals of Mathematics,* 54, 286–95.

Nasser, M. (1986) Comparative study of the prevalence of abnormal eating attitudes among Arab female students of both London and Cairo universities. *Psychological Medicine*, 16, 621–5.

Natani, K. and Surley, J. T. (1974) Sociopsychological aspects of a winter vigil at South Pole Station. *American Geophysical Union Antarctic Research Series*, 22, 89–114.

Nathan, P. E. and Lagenbucher, J. W. (1999) Psychopathology: Description and classification. *Annual Review of Psychology*, 50, 79–107.

National Center for Health Statistics (2004) *Health, United States, 2004.* Hyattsville, MD: National Center for Health Statistics.

National Research Council (2003) *The Polygraph and Lie Detection.* Washington, DC: National Academies Press.

Neal, D. T. and Chatrand, T. L. (2011) Embodied emotion perception: Amplifying and dampening facial feedback modulates emotion perception accuracy. *Social Psychological and Personality Science*, 2, 673–8.

Neilson, T. A., Deslauriers, D. and Baylor, G. W. (1991) Emotions in dream and waking event reports. *Dreaming*, 1, 287–300.

Neimark, J. (1996) The diva of disclosure, memory researcher Elizabeth Loftus. *Psychology Today*, 29, 48–80.

Neimeyer, R. A. and Mitchell, K. A. (1988) Similarity and attraction: A longitudinal study. *Journal of Social and Personal Relationships*, 5, 131–48.

Neisser, U. (1967) *Cognitive Psychology.* New York: Appleton-Century-Crofts.

Neisser, U. (ed.) (1998) *The Rising Curve: Long-term Gains in IQ and Related Measures.* Washington, DC: APA.

Neisser, U. and Becklen, R. (1975) Selective looking: Attending to visually significant events. *Cognitive Psychology*, 7, 480–94.

Neisser, U., Boodoo, G., Bouchard, T. J. Jr et al. (1996) Intelligence: Knowns and unknowns. *American Psychologist*, 51, 77–101.

Nejad, L. M., Wertheim, E. H. and Greenwood, K. M. (2005) Comparison of health belief model and the theory of planned behaviour in the prediction of dieting and fasting behaviour. *E-Journal of Applied Psychology, Social Section*, 1, 63–74.

Nelson, C. A. (2002) The ontogeny of human memory: A cognitive neuroscience perspective. In M. H. Johnson, Y. Munakata and R. Glimore (eds) *Brain Development and Cognition: A Reader* (2nd edn, pp. 151–78). Oxford: Blackwell.

Nelson, K. (1986) *Event Knowledge: Structure and Function in Development*. Hillsdale, NJ: Lawrence Erlbaum.

Nelson, K. and Fivush, R. (2004) The emergence of autobiographical memory: A social cultural developmental theory. *Psychological Review*, 111, 486–511.

Nemeth, C. and Chiles, C. (1988) Modelling courage: The role of dissent in fostering independence. *European Journal of Social Psychology*, 18, 275–80.

Neter, E. and Ben-Shakhar, G. (1989) The predictive validity of graphological inferences: a meta-analytic approach. *Personality and Individual Differences*, 10(7), 737–45.

Netherlands Ministry of Justice (1999) *Fact Sheet: Dutch Drugs Policy*. Utrecht: Trimbos Institute, Netherlands Institute of Mental Health and Addiction.

Nettelbeck, T. and Burns, N. R. (2009) Processing speed, working memory and reasoning ability from childhood to old age. *Personality and Individual Differences*, 48, 379–84.

Nettleback, T. and Lally, M. (1976) Inspection time and measured intelligence. *British Journal of Psychology*, 67, 17–22.

Neubauer, A. C. (1997) The mental speed approach to the assessment of intelligence. In J. Kingma and W. Tomic (eds) *Advances in Cognition and Education: Reflections on the Concept of Intelligence* (pp. 149–73). Greenwich, CT: JAI.

Neuberg, S. L. and Newsom, J. T. (1993) Personal need for structure: Individual differences in the desire for simple structure. *Journal of Personality and Social Psychology*, 65, 113–31.

Neugebauer, R., Hoek, H. W. and Susser, E. (1999) Prenatal exposure to wartime famine and development of antisocial personality in early adulthood. *Journal of the American Medical Association*, 282, 455–62.

Newberg, A., Alavi, A., Baime, M. et al. (2001) The measurement of regional cerebral blood flow during the complex cognitive task of meditation: A preliminary SPECT study. *Psychiatry Research: Neuroimaging*, 106, 113–22.

Newcomb, A. F., Bukowski, W. M. and Pattee, L. (1993) Children's peer relations: A meta-analytic review of popular, rejected, neglected, controversial and average sociometric status. *Psychological Bulletin*, 113, 99–128.

Newell, A., Shaw, J. C. and Simon, H. A. (1958) Elements of a theory of human problem solving. *Psychological Review*, 65, 151–66.

Newman, A. J., Bavelier, D., Corina, D. et al. (2002) A critical period for right hemisphere recruitment in American Sign Language processing. *Nature Neuroscience*, 5, 76–80.

Newman, L. S., Baumeister, R. F. and Duff, K. J. (1995) A new look at defensive projection: Thought suppression, accessibility, and biased person perception, *Journal of Personality and Social Psychology*, 72, 980–1001.

Newman, M. L., Pennebaker, J. W., Berry, D. S. and Richards, J. M. (2003) Lying words: Predicting deception from linguistic styles. *Personality and Social Psychology Bulletin*, 29, 665–75.

Newsome, W. T. and Paré, E. B. (1988) A selective impairment of motion perception following lesions of the middle temporal visual area (MT). *Journal of Neuroscience*, 8, 2201–11.

Neylan, T. C., Metzler, T. J., Best, S. R. et al. (2002) Critical incident exposure and sleep quality in police officers. *Psychosomatic Medicine*, 64, 345–52.

Nikles, C. D. II, Brecht, D. L., Klinger, E. and Bursell, A. L. (1998) The effects of current concern- and nonconcern-related waking suggestions on nocturnal dream content. *Journal of Personality and Social Psychology*, 75, 242–55.

Nikula, R., Klinger, E. and Larson-Gutman, M. K. (1993) Current concerns and electrodermal reactivity: Responses to words and thoughts. *Journal of Personality*, 61, 63–84.

NIMH (National Institute of Mental Health) (2003) *In Harm's Way*. Washington, DC: National Institutes of Health, US Department of Health and Human Services.

Ninan, P. T. (1999) The functional anatomy, neurochemistry, and pharmacology of anxiety. *Journal of Clinical Psychiatry*, 60, 12–17.

Nisbett, R. E. (2005) *The Geography of Thought: How Asians and Westerners Think Differently ... and Why*. London: Nicholas Brealey.

Nisbett, R. E. and Cohen, D. (1996) *Culture of Honor: The Psychology of Violence in the South*. Boulder, CO: Westview Press.

Nisbett, R. E. and Wilson, T. D. (1977) Telling more than we can know: Verbal reports on mental processes. *Psychological Review*, 84, 231–59.

Nisbett, R. E., Caputo, C., Legant, P. and Maracek, J. (1973) Behavior as seen by the actor and as seen by the observer. *Journal of Personality and Social Psychology*, 27, 154–64.

Nishino, S., Mignot, E. and Dement, W. C. (1995) Sedative-hypnotics. In A. F. Schatzberg and C. B. Nemeroff (eds) *American Psychiatric Press Textbook of Psychopharmacology* (pp. 405–16). Washington, DC: American Psychiatric Press.

Nissen, M. J. and Bullemer, P. (1987) Attentional requirements of learning: Evidence from performance measures. *Cognitive Psychology*, 19, 1–32.

Nolen-Hoeksema, S. (1987) Sex differences in unipolar depression: Evidence and theory. *Psychological Bulletin*, 101, 259–82.

Nolen-Hoeksema, S. (1990) *Sex Differences in Depression*. Stanford: Stanford University Press.

Noreen, S., Bierman, R. and MacLeod, M. (2014) Forgiving you is hard, but forgetting seems easy: Can forgiveness facilitate forgetting? *Psychological Science*, 25, 1295–302.

Norton, A. J. (1987) Families and children in the year 2000. *Children Today*, July–August, 6–9.

Norton, G. R., Harrison, B., Hauch, J. and Rhodes, L. (1985) Characteristics of people with infrequent panic attacks. *Journal of Abnormal Psychology*, 94, 216–21.

Nosanchuk, T. A. and Lightstone, J. (1974) Canned laughter and public and private conformity. *Journal of Personality and Social Psychology*, 29, 153–6.

Nuffield Council on Bioethics (2002) *Genetics and Human Behaviour*. London: Nuffield Council on Bioethics.

Nunn, J. A., Gregory, L. J. and Brammer, M. (2002) Functional magnetic resonance imaging of synesthesia: Activation of V4/V8 by spoken words. *Nature Neuroscience*, 5, 371–5.

Nutt, D. (2009) Equasy: An overlooked addiction with implications for the current debate on drug harms. *Journal of Psychopharmacology*, 23, 3–5.

Nuttin, J. M. (1985) Narcissism beyond Gestalt and awareness: The name letter effect. *European Journal of Social Psychology*, 15, 353–61.

Nyberg, L., McIntosh, A. R., Houle, S. et al. (1996) Activation of medial temporal structures during episodic memory retrieval. *Nature*, 380, 715–17.

Oakes, L. M. and Cohen, L. B. (1990) Infant perception of a causal event. *Cognitive Development*, 5, 193–207.

Oately, K., Keltner, D. and Jenkins, J. M. (2006) *Understanding Emotions* (2nd edn). Malden, MA: Blackwell.

Ochsner, K. N. (2000) Are affective events richly recollected or simply familiar? The experience and process of recognizing feelings past. *Journal of Experimental Psychology: General*, 129, 242–61.

Ochsner, K. N., Bunge, S. A., Gross, J. J. and Gabrieli, J. D. (2002) Rethinking feelings: An fMRI study of the cognitive regulation of emotion. *Journal of Cognitive Neuroscience*, 14, 1215–29.

O'Connor, T. G., Rutter, M., Beckett, C. et al. (2000) The effects of global severe deprivation on cognitive competence: Extension and longitudinal follow-up. *Child Development*, 71, 376–90.

Ofshe, R. (1992) Inadvertent hypnosis during interrogation: False confession due to dissociative state, misidentified multiple personality, and the satanic cult hypothesis. *International Journal of Clinical and Experimental Hypnosis*, 40, 125–6.

Ofshe, R. and Watters, E. (1994) *Making Monsters: False Memories, Psychotherapy, and Sexual Hysteria*. New York: Scribner/Macmillan.

Öhman, A. and Dimberg, U. (1978) Facial expressions as conditioned stimuli for electrodermal responses: A case of preparedness? *Journal of Personality and Social Psychology*, 36, 1251–8.

Öhman, A. and Mineka, S. (2001) Fears, phobias, and preparedness: Toward an evolved model of fear and fear learning. *Psychological Review*, 108, 483–522.

Öhman, A. and Soares, J. J. (1998) Emotional conditioning to masked stimuli: Expectancies for aversive outcomes following nonrecognized fear-relevant stimuli. *Journal of Experimental Psychology: General*, 127, 69–82.

Öhman, A., Dimberg, U. and Öst, L. G. (1985) Animal and social phobias: Biological constraints on learned fear responses. In S. Reiss and R. Bootzin (eds) *Theoretical Issues in Behavior Therapy* (pp. 123–75). New York: Academic Press.

Okagaki, L. and Sternberg, R. J. (1993) Parental beliefs and children's school performance. *Child Development*, 64, 36–56.

O'Keefe, J. and Nadel, L. (1978) *The Hippocampus as a Cognitive Map*. Oxford: Claredon.

Okuda, J., Fujii, T., Ohtake, H. et al. (2003) Thinking of the future and the past: The roles of the frontal pole and the medial temporal lobes. *Neuroimage*, 19, 1369–80.

O'Laughlin, M. J. and Malle, B. F. (2002) How people explain actions performed by groups and individuals. *Journal of Personality and Social Psychology*, 82, 33–48.

Oldham, J. M., Skodol, A. E. and Bender, D. S. (2005) *The American Psychiatric Publishing Textbook of Personality Disorders*. Washington, DC: American Psychiatric Publishing.

Olds, J. (1956) Pleasure center in the brain. *Scientific American*, 195, 105–16.

Olds, J. and Fobes, J. I. (1981) The central basis of motivation: Intracranial self-stimulation studies. *Annual Review of Psychology*, 32, 523–74.

Olds, J. and Milner, P. (1954) Positive reinforcement produced by electrical stimulation of septal areas and other regions of rat brains. *Journal of Comparative and Physiological Psychology*, 47, 419–27.

Oliner, S. P. and Oliner, P. M. (1988) *The Altruistic Personality*. New York: Free Press.

Ollers, D. K. and Eilers, R. E. (1988) The role of audition in infant babbling. *Child Development*, 59, 441–9.

Olson, K. R. and Shaw, A. (2011) 'No fair, copycat!': What children's response to plagiarism tells us about their understanding of ideas. *Developmental Science*, 14, 431–9.

Oltmanns, T. F. and Turkheimer, E. (2006) Perceptions of self and others regarding pathological personality traits. In R. Kreuger and J. Tackett (eds) *Personality and Psychopathology* (pp. 71–111). New York: Guilford Press.

Oltmanns, T. F., Neale, J. M. and Davison, G. C. (1991) *Case Studies in Abnormal Psychology* (3rd edn). New York: Wiley.

Olton, D. S. and Samuelson, R. J. (1976) Remembrance of places passed: Spatial memory in rats. *Journal of Experimental Psychology: Animal Behavior Processes*, 2, 97–116.

Onishi, K. H. and Baillargeon, R. (2005) Do 15-month-old infants understand false beliefs? *Science*, 308, 255–8.

Ono, K. (1987) Superstitious behavior in humans. *Journal of Experimental Analysis of Behavior*, 47, 261–71.

ONS (Office for National Statistics) (2007) Education: Girls continue to outperform boys, www.statistics.gov.uk/cci/nugget.asp?id=1892.

ONS (2012) Divorces in England and Wales, 2011, www.ons.gov.uk/ons/dcp171778_291750.pdf.

ONS (2014) Living alone in England and Wales, www.ons.gov.uk/ons/rel/census/2011-census-analysis/do-the-demographic-and-socio-economic-characteristics-of-those-living-alone-in-england-and-wales-differ-from-the-general-population-/sty-living-alone-in-the-uk.html.

ONS (2015) Alcohol-related deaths in the United Kingdom, www.ons.gov.uk/ons/rel/subnational-health4/alcohol-related-deaths-in-the-united-kingdom/2013/stb---alcohol-related-deaths-in-the-united-kingdom--registered-in-2013.html.

Orban, G. A., van Essen, D. and Vanduffel, W. (2004) Comparative mapping of higher visual areas in monkeys and humans. *Trends in Cognitive Sciences*, 8, 315–24.

Orne, M. T. and Evans, F. J. (1965) Social control in the psychological experiment: Antisocial behavior and hypnosis. *Journal of Personality and Social Psychology*, 1, 189–200.

Osborn, A. F. (1953) *Applied Imagination: Principles and Procedures of Creative Problem-solving*. New York: Scribner.

Ost, J., Vrij, A., Costall, A. and Bull, R. (2002) Crashing memories and reality monitoring: Distinguishing between perceptions, imaginations and false memories. *Applied Cognitive Psychology*, 16, 125–34.

Öst, L.-G., Lindahl, I.-L., Sterner, U. and Jerremalm, A. (1984) Exposure in vivo vs. applied relaxation in the treatment of blood phobia. *Behaviour Research and Therapy*, 22, 205–16.

O'Sullivan, L. F. and Allegeier, E. R. (1998) Feigning sexual desire: Consenting to unwanted sexual activity in heterosexual dating relationships. *Journal of Sex Research*, 35, 234–43.

Oswald, L., Taylor, A. M. and Triesman, M. (1960) Discriminative responses to stimulation during human sleep. *Brain*, 83, 440–53.

Oviatt, D. P. and Iso-Ahola, S. E. (2008) Social facilitation and motor/athletic performance: A meta-analysis. In J. H. Humphrey (ed.) *Sports and Athletics Development* (pp. 1–28). Hauppauge, NY: Nova Science.

Owen, A. M., Coleman, M. R., Boly, M. et al. (2006) Detecting awareness in the vegetative state. *Science*, 313(5792), 1402.

Owen, A. M., Hampshire, A., Grahn, J. A. et al. (2010) Putting brain training to the test. *Nature*, 465, 775–9.

Owens, W. A. (1966) Age and mental abilities: A second adult follow-up. *Journal of Educational Psychology*, 57, 311–25.

Ozer, D. J. and Benet-Martínez, V. (2006) Personality and the prediction of consequential outcomes. *Annual Review of Psychology*, 57, 401–21.

Page, R. A. and Moss, M. K. (1976) Environmental influences on aggression: The effects of darkness and proximity of victim. *Journal of Applied Social Psychology*, 6, 126–33.

Paivio, A. (1969) Mental imagery in associative learning and memory. *Psychological Review*, 76, 241–63.

Paivio, A. (1971) *Imagery and Verbal Processes*. New York: Holt, Rinehart & Winston.

Paivio, A. (1986) *Mental Representations: A Dual Coding Approach*. New York: OUP.

Palinkas, L. A., Reed, H. L. and Do, N. V. (1997) Association between the Polar T3 Syndrome and the Winter-Over Syndrome in Antarctica. *Antarctic Journal of the United States Review*, 32, 112–14.

Palma, B. D., Gabriel, A. Jr, Colugnati, F. A. and Tufik, S. (2006) Effects of sleep deprivation on the development of autoimmune disease in an experimental model of systemic lupus erythematosus. *American Journal of Physiology: Regulatory Integrative and Comparative Physiology*, 291, 1527–32.

Palmieri, R. M., Ingersoll, C. D. and Stone, M. B. (2002) Center-of-pressure parameters used in the assessment of postural control. *Journal of Sport Rehabilitation*, 11, 51–66.

Papez, J. W. (1937) A proposed mechanism of emotion. *Archives of Neurology and Pathology*, 38, 725–43.

Papp, K. V., Walsh, S. J. and Synder, P. J. (2009) Immediate and delayed effects of cognitive interventions in healthy elderly: A review of current literature and future directions. *Alzheimer's and Dementia*, 5, 50–60.

Parfit, D. (1986) *Reasons and Persons*. Oxford: OUP.

Pariante, C. M. and Miller, A. H. (2001) Glucocorticoidreceptors in major depression: Relevance to pathophysiology and treatment. *Biological Psychiatry*, 49, 391–404.

Park, J. H., Faulkner, J. and Schaller, M. (2003) Evolved disease-avoidance processes and contemporary anti-social behaviour: Prejudicial attitudes and avoidance of people with physical disabilities. *Journal of Nonverbal Behavior*, 27, 65–87.

Parker, D., Manstead, A. S. and Stradling, S. G. (1995) Extending the theory of planned behaviour: The role of personal norm. *British Journal of Social Psychology*, 34, 127–37.

Parker, I. (2004) Criteria for qualitative research in psychology. *Qualitative Research in Psychology*, 1, 95–106.

Parkinson, B. and Totterdell, P. (1999) Classifying affect-regulation strategies. *Cognition and Emotion*, 13, 277–303.

Parrott, W. G. (1993) Beyond hedonism: Motives for inhibiting good moods and for maintaining bad moods. In D. M. Wegner and J. W. Pennebaker (eds) *Handbook of Mental Control* (pp. 278–308). Englewood Cliffs, NJ: Prentice Hall.

Partinen, M. (1994) Epidemiology of sleep disorders. In M. H. Kryger, T. Roth and W. C. Dement (eds) *Principles and Practice of Sleep Medicine* (2nd edn, pp. 437–52). Philadelphia: Saunders.

Pascual-Leone, A., Amedi, A., Fregni, F. and Merabet, L. B. (2005) The plastic human brain cortex. *Annual Review of Neuroscience*, 28, 377–401.

Pascual-Leone, A., Houser, C. M., Reese, K. et al. (1993) Safety of rapid-rate transcranial magnetic stimulation in normal volunteers. *Electroencephalography and Clinical Neurophysiology*, 89, 120–30.

Passini, F. T. and Norman, W. T. (1966) A universal conception of personality structure? *Journal of Personality and Social Psychology*, 4, 44–9.

Passman, R. H. (1987) Attachments to inanimate objects: Are children who have security blankets insecure? *Journal of Consulting and Clinical Psychology*, 55, 825–30.

Pasupathi, M., Staudinger, U. M. and Baltes, P. B. (2001) Seeds of wisdom: Adolescents' knowledge and judgment about difficult life problems. *Developmental Psychology*, 37, 351–61.

Patrick, C. J., Cuthbert, B. N. and Lang, P. J. (1994) Emotion in the criminal psychopath: Fear image processing. *Journal of Abnormal Psychology*, 103, 523–34.

Patterson, M. L. (1983) *Nonverbal Behavior: A Functional Perspective*. New York: Springer.

Patterson, M. M. and Bigler, R. S. (2006) Preschool children's attention to environmental messages about groups: Social categorization and the origins of intergroup bias. *Child Development*, 77, 847–60.

Pattwell, S. S., Casey, B. J. and Lee, F. S. (2013) Altered fear in humans and mice. *Current Directions in Psychological Science*, 22, 146–51.

Pattwell, S. S., Bath, K. G., Casey, B. J. et al. (2011) Selective early-acquired fear memories undergo temporary suppression during adolescence. *Proceedings of the National Academy of Sciences*, 108, 1182–7.

Pattwell, S. S., Duhoux, S., Hartley, C. A. et al. (2012) Altered fear learning across development in both mouse and human. *Proceedings of the National Academy of Sciences*, 109, 16318–23.

Paul, A. M. (2004) *The Cult of Personality Testing.* New York: Free Press.

Pavlidis, I., Eberhardt, N. L. and Levine, J. A. (2002) Human behaviour: Seeing through the face of deception. *Nature*, 415, 35.

Pavlov, I. P. (1923a) New researches on conditioned reflexes. *Science*, 58, 359–61.

Pavlov, I. P. (1923b) Pavloff. *Time*, 1(21), 20–1.

Pavlov, I. P. (1927) *Conditioned Reflexes.* Oxford: OUP.

Pawlowski, B., Dunbar, R. I. and Lipowicz, A. (2000) Tall men have more reproductive success. *Nature*, 362, 156.

Pays, O., Dubout. A. L., Jarman, P. J. et al. (2009) Vigilance and complex synchrony in red-necked pademelon. *Thylogale thesis*. *Behavioral Ecology*, 20, 22–9.

Pearce, J. M. (1987) A model of stimulus generalization for Pavlovian conditioning. *Psychological Review*, 84, 61–73.

Pearce, J. M. (2008) *Animal Learning and Cognition: An Introduction* (3rd edn). Hove: Psychology Press.

Pearce, P. L. (1980) Strangers, travelers and Greyhound terminals: A study of small-scale helping behaviors. *Journal of Personality and Social Psychology*, 38, 935–40.

Peissig, J. J. and Tarr, M. J. (2007) Visual object recognition: Do we know more now than we did 20 years ago? *Annual Review of Psychology*, 58, 75–96.

Pelham, B. W. (1985) Self-investment and self-esteem: Evidence for a Jamesian model of self-worth. *Journal of Personality and Social Psychology*, 69, 1141–50.

Pendergrast, M. (1995) *Victims of Memory: Incest Accusations and Shattered Lives.* Hinesburg, VT: Upper Access.

Pendry, L. F. (2008) Social cognition. In M. R. Hewstone, W. Stroebe and K. Jonas (eds) *Introduction to Social Psychology* (4th edn, pp. 66–87). Oxford: Blackwell.

Penfield, W. and Rasmussen, T. (1950) *The Cerebral Cortex of Man: A Clinical Study of Localization of Function.* New York: Macmillan.

Pennebaker, J. W. (1989) Confession, inhibition, and disease. *Advances in Experimental Social Psychology*, 22, 211–44.

Pennebaker, J. W. and Beall, S. K. (1986) Confronting a traumatic event: Toward an understanding of inhibition and disease. *Journal of Abnormal Psychology*, 95, 274–81.

Pennebaker, J. W., Colder, M. and Sharp, L. K. (1990) Accelerating the coping process. *Journal of Personality and Social Psychology*, 58, 528–37.

Pennebaker, J. W., Francis, M. E. and Booth, R. J. (2001) *Linguistic Inquiry and Word Count: LIWC 2001*. Mahwah, NJ: Lawrence Erlbaum.

Pennebaker, J. W., Kiecolt-Glaser, J. K. and Glaser, R. (1988) Disclosure of traumas and immune function: Health implications for psychotherapy. *Journal of Consulting and Clinical Psychology*, 56, 239–45.

Penton-Voak, I., Rowe, A. C. and Williams, J. (2007) Through rose-tinted glasses: Relationship satisfaction and representations of partners' facial attractiveness. *Journal of Evolutionary Psychology*, 5, 169–81.

Penton-Voak, I., Thomas, J., Gage, S. H. et al. (2013) Increasing recognition of happiness in ambiguous facial expressions reduces anger and aggressive behaviour. *Psychological Science*, 24, 688–97.

Perenin, M.-T. and Vighetto, A. (1988) Optic ataxia: A specific disruption in visuomotor mechanisms, I. Different aspects of the deficit in reaching for objects. *Brain*, 111, 643–74.

Perfect, T. J. (1994) What can Brinley plots tell us about cognitive aging? *Journal of Gerontology: Psychological Sciences*, 49, 60–4.

Perkins, D. N. and Grotzer, T. A. (1997) Teaching intelligence. *American Psychologist*, 52, 1125–33.

Perls, F. S., Hefferkine, R. and Goodman, P. (1951) *Gestalt Therapy: Excitement and Growth in the Human Personality.* New York: Julian Press.

Perner, J. (1991) *Understanding the Representational Mind.* Cambridge, MA: MIT Press.

Perrett, D. I. (2010) *In Your Face: The New Science of Human Attraction*. Basingstoke: Palgrave Macmillan.

Perrett, D. I., Rolls, E. T. and Caan, W. (1982) Visual neurons responsive to faces in the monkey temporal cortex. *Experimental Brain Research*, 47, 329–42.

Perrett, D. I., Burt, D. M., Penton-Voak, I. S. et al. (1999) Symmetry and human facial attractiveness. *Evolution and Human Behavior*, 20, 295–307.

Perrin, J. S., Merz, S., Bennett, D. M. et al. (2012) Electroconvulsive therapy reduces frontal cortical connectivity in severe depressive disorder. *Proceedings of the National Academy of Sciences*, 109, 5464–8.

Perris, C. (1992) *Bipolar-unipolar Distinction* (2nd edn). New York: Guilford Press.

Perry, R. and Sibley, C. G. (2012) Big Five personality prospectively predicts social dominance orientation and right wing authoritarianism. *Personality and Individual Differences*, 52, 3–8.

Persons, J. B. (1986) The advantages of studying psychological phenomena rather than psychiatric diagnoses. *American Psychologist*, 41, 1252–60.

Pesonen, A. K., Räikkönen, K., Feldt, K. et al. (2010) Childhood separation experience predicts HPA axis hormonal responses in late adulthood: A natural experiment of World War II. *Psychoneuroendocrinology*, 35, 758–67.

Peters, E. R., Joseph, S. A. and Garety, P. A. (1999) Measurement of delusional ideation in the normal population: Introducing the PDI (Peters et al. Delusions Inventory). *Schizophrenia Bulletin*, 25(3), 553–76.

Peterson, C. and Siegal, M. (1998) Changing focus on the representational mind: Concepts of false photographs, false drawings and false beliefs in deaf, autistic and normal children. *British Journal of Developmental Psychology*, 16, 301–20.

Peterson, L. R. and Peterson, M. J. (1959) Short-term retention of individual verbal items. *Journal of Experimental Psychology*, 58, 193–8.

Peterson, S. E., Fox, P. T., Posner, M. I. et al. (1989) Positron emission tomographic studies of the processing of single words. *Journal of Cognitive Neuroscience*, 1, 154–70.

Petitto, L. A. and Dunbar, K. N. (2004) New findings from educational neuroscience on bilingual brains, scientific brains, and the educated mind. In K. Fischer and T. Katzir (eds) *Building Usable Knowledge in Mind, Brain and Education*. Cambridge: CUP.

Petitto, L. A. and Marentette, P. F. (1991) Babbling in the manual mode: Evidence for the ontogeny of language. *Science*, 251, 1493–6.

Petrie, K. P., Booth, R. J. and Pennebaker, J. W. (1998) The immunological effects of thought suppression. *Journal of Personality and Social Psychology*, 75, 1264–72.

Pettinati, H. M., Tamburello, B. A., Ruetsch, C. R. and Kaplin, F. N. (1994) Patient attitudes towards electroconvulsive therapy. *Psychopharmocology Bulletin*, 30, 471–5.

Petty, R. E. and Cacioppo, J. T. (1986) The elaboration likelihood model of persuasion. In L. Berkowitz (ed.) *Advances in Experimental Social Psychology* (vol. 19, pp. 123–205). New York: Academic Press.

Petty, R. E. and Wegener, D. T. (1998) Attitude change: Multiple roles for persuasion variables. In D. T. Gilbert, S. T. Fiske and G. Lindzey (eds) *The Handbook of Social Psychology* (4th edn, vol. 1, pp. 323–90). Boston: McGraw-Hill.

Petty, R. E., Cacioppo, J. T. and Goldman, R. (1981) Personal involvement as a determinant of argument-based persuasion. *Journal of Personality & Social Psychology*, 41, 847–55.

Pew Research Center for the People & the Press (1997) *Motherhood Today: A Tougher Job, Less Ably Done*. Washington, DC: Pew Research Center.

PHE (Public Health England) (2014) Laboratory confirmed cases of measles, mumps and rubella, England and Wales: October to December 2013. *HPR*, 8(8).

PHE (n.d.) UK and Ireland prevalence and trends, www.noo.org.uk/NOO_about_obesity/adult_obesity/UK_prevalence_and_trends.

Phelan, J., Link, B., Stueve, A. and Pescosolido, B. (1997) Public conceptions of mental illness in 1950 in 1996: Has sophistication increased? Has stigma declined? Paper presented at the American Sociological Association, Toronto, Ontario.

Phelan, J., Link, B., Stueve, A. and Pescosolido, B. (2000) Public conceptions of mental illness in 1950 and 1996: What is mental illness and is it to be feared? *Journal of Health and Social Behavior*, 41, 188–207.

Phelps, E. A. (2006) Emotion and cognition: Insights from studies of the human amygdala. *Annual Review of Psychology*, 24, 27–53.

Phelps, E. A. and LeDoux, J. L. (2005) Contributions of the amygdala to emotion processing: From animal models to human behavior. *Neuron*, 48, 175–87.

Phelps, E. A., O'Connor, K. J., Cunningham, W. A. et al. (2000) Performance on indirect measures of race evaluation predicts amygdala activation. *Journal of Cognitive Neuroscience*, 12, 729–38.

Phillips, A., Wellman, H. M. and Spelke, E. S. (2002) Infants' ability to connect gaze and emotional expression to intentional action. *Cognition*, 85, 53–78.

Phillips, D. P. (1974) The influence of suggestion on suicide: Substantive and theoretical implications of the Werther effect. *American Sociological Review* 39, 340–54.

Phillips, D. P. and Carstensen, L. L. (1986) Clustering of teenage suicides after television news stories about suicide. *New England Journal of Medicine*, 315, 685–9.

Piaf, E. (2004) *The Wheel of Fortune: The Official Autobiography*. London: Peter Owen.

Piaget, J. ([1932]1965) *The Moral Judgment of the Child*. New York: Free Press.

Piaget, J. (1954a) *The Construction of Reality in the Child*. New York: Basic Books.

Piaget, J. (1954b) *The Child's Concept of Number*. New York: Norton.

Piaget, J. and Inhelder, B. (1956) *The Child's Conception of Space*. London: Routledge & Keegan Paul.

Piaget, J. and Inhelder, B. (1969) *The Psychology of the Child* (trans. H. Weaver). New York: Basic Books.

Pickering, M. J. and Garrod, S. (2004) Toward a mechanistic psychology of dialogue. *Behavioral and Brain Sciences*, 27, 169–226.

Pillemer, D. (1998) *Momentous Events, Vivid Memories*. Cambridge, MA: Harvard University Press.

Pinker, S. (1994) *The Language Instinct*. New York: Morrow.

Pinker, S. (1997a) *How the Mind Works*. New York: Norton.

Pinker, S. (1997b) Evolutionary psychology: An exchange. *New York Review of Books*, 44, 55–8.

Pinker S. (2003) *The Blank Slate: The Modern Denial of Human Nature*. New York: Penguin.

Pinker, S. and Bloom, P. (1990) Natural language and natural selection. *Behavioral & Brain Sciences*, 13, 707–84.

Plato (1956) *Protagoras* (trans. O. Jowett). New York: Prentice Hall.

Platt, J. J., Yaksh, T. and Darby, C. L. (1967) Social facilitation of eating behavior in armadillos. *Psychological Reports*, 20, 1136.

Plomin, R. and Caspi, A. (1999) Behavioral genetics and personality. In L. A. Pervin and O. P. John (eds) *Handbook of Personality: Theory and Research* (vol. 2, pp. 251–76). New York: Guilford Press.

Plomin, R. and Spinath, F. M. (2002) Genetics and general cognitive ability. *Trends in Cognitive Sciences*, 6, 169–76.

Plomin, R. and Spinath, F. M. (2004) Intelligence: Genetics, genes, and genomics. *Journal of Personality and Social Psychology*, 86, 112–29.

Plomin, R., De Fries, J. C., McClearn, G. E. and Rutter, M. (1997) *Behavior Genetics* (3rd edn). New York: Freeman.

Plomin, R., DeFries, J. C., McClearn, G. E. and McGuffin, P. (2001a) *Behavioral Genetics* (4th edn). New York: Freeman.

Plomin, R., Hill, L., Craig, I. W. et al. (2001b) A genome-wide scan of 1842 DNA markers for allelic associations with general cognitive ability: A five-stage design using DNA pooling and extreme selected groups. *Behavior Genetics*, 31, 497–509.

Pomerantz, E. M., Ruble, D. N., Frey, K. S. and Gruelich, F. (1995) Meeting goals and confronting conflict: Children's changing perceptions of social comparison. *Child Development*, 66, 723–38.

Pomerleau, A., Bolduc, D., Malcuit, G. and Cossette, L. (1990) Pink or blue: Environmental gender stereotypes in the first two years of life. *Sex Roles*, 22, 359–67.

Poole, D. A., Lindsay, S. D., Memon, A. and Bull, R. (1995) Psychotherapy and the recovery of memories of childhood sexual abuse: U.S. and British practitioners' opinions, practices, and experiences. *Journal of Consulting and Clinical Psychology*, 63, 426–87.

Pope, A. W. and Bierman, K. L. (1999) Predicting adolescent peer problems and antisocial activities: The relative roles of aggression and dysregulation. *Developmental Psychology*, 35, 335–46.

Porter, R. (2003) *Madness: A Brief History*. Oxford: OUP.

Posey, T. B. and Losch, M. E. (1983) Auditory hallucinations of hearing voices in 375 normal subjects. *Imagination, Cognition and Personality*, 3, 99–113.

Posner, M. I. (1980) Orienting of attention. *Quarterly Journal of Experimental Psychology*, 32, 3–25.

Posner, M. I. and Raichle, M. E. (1994) *Images of Mind*. New York: Freeman.

Posner, M. I., Walker, J. A., Friedrich, F. J. and Rafal, R. D. (1984) Effects of parietal injury on covert orienting of attention. *Journal of Neuroscience*, 4, 1863–74.

Post, R. M. (2004) Differing psychotropic profiles of the anticonvulsants in bipolar and other psychiatric disorders. *Clinical Neuroscience Research*, 4, 9–30.

Posthuma, D. and de Geus, E. J. (2006) Progress in the molecular-genetic study of intelligence. *Current Directions in Psychological Science*, 15, 151–5.

Postman, L. and Underwood, B. J. (1973) Critical issues in interference theory. *Memory & Cognition*, 1, 19–40.

Potmes, T. and Spears, R. (1998) Deindividuation and antinormative behavior: A meta-analysis. *Psychological Bulletin*, 123, 238–59.

Poulin-Dubois, D. (1999) Infants' distinction between animate and inanimate objects: The origins of naïve psychology. In P. Rochat (ed.) *Early Social Cognition: Understanding Others in the First Months of Life* (pp. 257–80). Mahwah, NJ: Erlbaum.

Prasada, S. and Pinker, S. (1993) Generalizations of regular and irregular morphology. *Language and Cognitive Processes*, 8, 1–56.

Pratkanis, A. R. (1992) The cargo-cult science of subliminal persuasion. *Skeptical Inquirer*, 16, 260–72.

Pratkanis, A. R., Greenwald, A. G., Leippe, M. R. and Baumgardner, M. H. (1988) In search of reliable persuasion effects, III. The sleeper effect is dead: Long live the sleeper effect. *Journal of Personality and Social Psychology*, 54, 203–18.

Pratto, F., Sidanius, J., Stallworth, I. M and Malle, B. F. (1994) Social dominance orientation: A personality variable predicting social and political attitudes. *Journal of Personality and Social Psychology*, 67, 741–63.

Premack, D. (1962) Reversibility of the reinforcement relation. *Science*, 136, 255–7.

Premack, D. (1988) Minds without language. In L. Weiskrantz (ed.) *Thought without Language* (pp. 46–65). Oxford: Clarendon Press.

Prentice, D. A. and Miller, D. T. (1993) Pluralistic ignorance and alcohol use on campus: Some consequences of misperceiving the social norm. *Journal of Personality and Social Psychology*, 64, 243–56.

Prentice-Dunn, S. and Rogers, R. W. (1982) Effects of public and private self-awareness on deindividuation and aggression. *Journal of Personality and Social Psychology*, 43, 503–13.

Pressman, S. D., Cohen, S., Miller, G. E. et al. (2005) Loneliness, social network size and immune response to influenza vaccination in college freshman. *Health Psychology*, 24, 297–306.

Preston, C. and Ehrsson, H. H. (2014) Illusory changes in body size modulate body satisfaction in a way that is related to non-clinical eating disorder psychopathology. *PLoS ONE*, 9(1), e85773.

Preston, S. D. and de Waal, F. B. (2002) Empathy: Its ultimate and proximal bases. *Behavioral and Brain Sciences*, 25, 1–72.

Provine, R. R. (1992) Contagious laughter: Laughter is a sufficient stimulus for laughs and smiles. *Bulletin of the Psychonomic Society*, 30, 1–4.

Provine, R. R. (1996) Contagious yawning and laughter: Significance for sensory feature detection, motor pattern generation, imitation, and the evolution of social behavior. In C. M. Heyes and B. G. Galef (eds) *Social Learning in Animals: The Roots of Culture* (pp. 179–208). New York: Academic Press.

Prudic, J., Haskett, R. F., Mulsant, B. et al. (1996) Resistance to antidepressant medications and short-term clinical response to ECT. *American Journal of Psychiatry*, 153, 985–92.

Pruitt, D. G. (1998) Social conflict. In D. T. Gilbert, S. T. Fiske and G. Lindzey (eds) *The Handbook of Social Psychology* (4th edn, vol. 2, pp. 470–503). New York: McGraw-Hill.

Ptacek, J. T. and Dodge, K. L. (1995) Coping strategies and relationship satisfaction in couples. *Personality and Social Psychology Bulletin*, 21, 76–84.

Putnam, F. W., Guroff, J. J., Silberman, E. K. et al. (1986) The clinical phenomenology of multiple personality disorder: Review of 100 recent cases. *Journal of Clinical Psychiatry*, 47, 285–93.

Pyszczynski, T., Holt, J. and Greenberg, J. (1987) Depression, self-focused attention, and expectancy for positive and negative future life events for self and others. *Journal of Personality and Social Psychology*, 52, 994–1001.

Pyszczynski, T., Solomon, S. and Greenberg, J. (2003) *In the Wake of 9/11: The Psychology of Terror.* Washington, DC: APA.

QAA (Quality Assurance Agency for Higher Education) (2007) *Subject Benchmark Statement: Psychology*. London: QAA.

Quattrone, G. A. (1982) Behavioral consequences of attributional bias. *Social Cognition*, 1, 358–78.

Quattrone, G. A. and Jones, E. E. (1980) The perception of variability within in-groups and out-groups: Implications for the law of small numbers. *Journal of Personality and Social Psychology*, 38, 141–52.

Querleu, D., Lefebvre, C., Titran, M. et al. (1984) Reactivite de bouveau-ne de moins de deux heures de vie a la voix maternelle. *Journal de Gynecologie Obstetrique et de Biologie de la Reproduction*, 13, 125–34.

Quiroga, R. Q., Reddy, L., Kreiman, G. et al. (2005) Invariant visual representation by single neurons in the human brain. *Nature*, 435, 1102–7.

Rabin, B. M. and Rabin, J. S. (1984) Acquisition of radiation- and lithium chloride-induced conditioned taste aversions in anesthetized rats. *Animal Learning & Behavior*, 12, 439–41.

Rachman, S. J. and DeSilva, P. (1978) Abnormal and normal obsessions. *Behavioral Research and Therapy*, 16, 223–48.

Radford, E. and Radford, M. A. (1949) *Encyclopedia of Superstitions.* New York: Philosophical Library.

Radvansky, G. (2006) *Human Memory*. Boston, MA: Pearson.

Ragan, C. I., Bard, I. and Singh, I. (2013) What should we do about student use of cognitive enhancers? An analysis of current evidence. *Neuropharmacology*, 64, 588–95.

Rahe, R. H., Meyer, M., Smith, M. et al. (1964) Social stress and illness onset. *Journal of Psychosomatic Research*, 8, 35–44.

Raichle, M. E. and Mintun, M. A. (2006) Brain work and brain imaging. *Annual Review of Neuroscience*, 29, 449–76.

Raichle, M. E., Fiez, J. A., Videen, T. O. et al. (1994) Practice-related changes in human brain functional anatomy during nonmotor learning. *Cerebral Cortex*, 4, 8–26.

Rakic, P. (1995) Corticogenesis in human and nonhuman primates. In M. S. Gazzaniga (ed.) *The Cognitive Neurosciences* (pp. 127–45) Cambridge, MA: MIT Press.

Ralph, P. and Coop, G. (2013) The geography of recent genetic ancestry across Europe. *PLoS Biology,* 11(5), e1001555.

Ramachandran, V. S. and Blakeslee, S. (1998) *Phantoms in the Brain: Probing the Mysteries of the Human Mind.* New York: Morrow.

Ramachandran, V. S. and Hubbard, E. M. (2001) Synaesthesia: A window into perception, thought and language. *Journal of Consciousness Studies,* 8, 3–34.

Ramachandran, V. S. and Hubbard, E. M. (2003) Hearing colors, tasting shapes. *Scientific American*, 288, 52–9.

Ramachandran, V. S., Rodgers-Ramachandran, D. and Stewart, M. (1992) Perceptual correlates of massive cortical reorganization. *Science*, 258, 1159–60.

Rapaport, D. (1946) *Diagnostic Psychological Testing: The Theory, Statistical Evaluation, and Diagnostic Application of a Battery of Tests.* Chicago: Year Book.

Rapport, R. (2005) *Nerve Endings: The Discovery of the Synapse.* New York: Norton.

Raskin, N. J. and Rogers, C. R. (2000) Person-centered therapy. In R. J. Corsini and D. Wedding (eds) *Current Psychotherapies* (6th edn, pp. 133–67). Itasca, IL: F. E. Peacock.

Raz, N. (2000) Aging of the brain and its impact on cognitive performance: Integration of structural and functional findings. In F. I. Craik and T. A. Salthouse (eds) *The Handbook of Aging and Cognition* (pp. 1–90). Mahwah, NJ: Erlbaum.

Read, J. (2005) The bio-bio-bio model of madness. *The Psychologist*, 18, 596–7.

Read, K. E. (1965) *The High Valley.* London: Allen & Unwin.

Reason, J. and Mycielska, K. (1982) *Absent-minded?: The Psychology of Mental Lapses and Everyday Errors.* Englewood Cliffs, NJ: Prentice Hall.

Reber, A. S. (1967) Implicit learning of artificial grammars. *Journal of Verbal Learning and Verbal Behavior*, 6, 855–63.

Reber, A. S. (1996) *Implicit Learning and Tacit Knowledge: An Essay on the Cognitive Unconscious.* New York: OUP.

Reber, A. S. and Allen, R. (2000) Individual differences in implicit learning. In R. G. Kunzendorf and B. Wallace (eds) *Individual Differences in Conscious Experience* (pp. 227–47). Philadelphia: John Benjamins.

Reber, A. S., Walkenfeld, F. F. and Hernstadt, R. (1991) Implicit learning: Individual differences and IQ. *Journal of Experimental Psychology: Learning, Memory, and Cognition*, 17, 888–96.

Reber, P. J., Gitelman, D. R., Parrish, T. B. and Mesulam, M. M. (2003) Dissociating explicit and implicit category knowledge with fMRI. *Journal of Cognitive Neuroscience*, 15, 574–83.

Rechtshaffen, A., Gilliland, M. A., Bergmann, B. M. and Winter, J. B. (1983) Physiological correlates of prolonged sleep deprivation in rats. *Science*, 221, 182–4.

Reddy, V., Markova, G. and Wallot, S. (2013) Anticipatory adjustments to being picked up in infancy. *PLoS ONE*, 8(6), e65289.

Reder, L. M. (1987) Strategy selection in question answering. *Cognitive Psychology*, 19, 90–138.

Redick, T. S., Shipstead, Z., Harrison, T. L. et al. (2013) No evidence of intelligence improvement after working memory training: A randomized, placebo-controlled study. *Journal of Experimental Psychology: General*, 142, 359–79.

Reed, G. (1988) *The Psychology of Anomalous Experience* (rev. edn). Buffalo, NY: Prometheus Books.

Reese, E., Sparks, A. and Leyva, D. (2010) A review of parent interventions for preschool children's language and emergent literacy. *Journal of Early Childhood Literacy*, 10, 97–117.

Regan, D. T., Williams, M. and Sparling, S. (1972) Voluntary expiation of guilt: A field experiment. *Journal of Personality and Social Psychology*, 24, 42–5.

Regan, P. C. (1998) What if you can't get what you want? Willingness to compromise ideal mate selection standards as a function of sex, mate value, and relationship context. *Personality and Social Psychology Bulletin*, 24, 1294–303.

Regier, D. A., Narrow, W. E., Rae, D. S. et al. (1993) The de facto US mental and addictive disorders service system: Epidemiologic Catchment Area prospective 1-year prevalence rates of disorders and services. *Archives of General Psychiatry*, 41, 934–41.

Reicher, S. (2001) The psychology of crowd dynamics. In M. A. Hogg and R. S. Tindale (eds) *Blackwell Handbook of Social Psychology: Group Processes* (pp. 182–208). Oxford: Blackwell.

Reichhardt, T. (2003) Playing with fire? *Nature*, 424, 367–8.

Reidy, D. F., Foster, J. D. and Zeichner, A. (2010) Narcissism and unprovoked aggression. *Aggressive Behavior*, 36, 414–22.

Reinarman, C., Cohen, P. D. and Kaal, H. L. (2004) The limited relevance of drug policy: Cannabis in Amsterdam and San Francisco. *American Journal of Public Health*, 94, 836–42.

Reinstein, D. and Riener, G. (2012) Reputation and influence in charitable giving: An experiment. *Theory and Decision*, 72, 221–43.

Reis, H. T. and Carothers, B. J. (2014) Black and white or shades of grey: Are gender differences categorical or dimensional? *Current Directions in Psychological Science,* 23, 19–26.

Reis, S. M., Neu, T. W. and McGuire, J. M. (1995) *Talents in Two Places: Case Studies of High Ability Students with Learning Disabilities Who Have Achieved.* Storrs, CT: University of Connecticut, National Research Center on the Gifted and Talented.

Reissland, N. (1988) Neonatal imitation in the first hour of life: Observations in rural Nepal. *Developmental Psychology*, 24, 464–9.

Reitz, A. K., Zimmermann, J., Hutteman, R. et al. (2014) How peers make a difference: The role of peer groups and peer relationships in personality development. *European Journal of Personality*, 28, 279–88.

Rensink, R. A., O'Regan, J. K. and Clark, J. J. (1997) To see or not to see: The need for attention to perceive changes in scenes. *Psychological Science,* 8(5), 368–73.

Repacholi, B. M. and Gopnik, A. (1997) Early reasoning about desires: Evidence from 14- and 18-month-olds. *Developmental Psychology*, 33, 12–21.

Rescorla, R. A. (1966) Predictability and number of pairings in Pavlovian fear conditioning. *Psychonomic Science*, 4, 383–4.

Rescorla, R. A. (1968) Probability of shock in the presence and absence of CS in fear. *Journal of Comparative and Physiological Psychology*, 66, 1–5.

Rescorla, R. A. (1988) Classical conditioning: It's not what you think it is. *American Psychologist*, 43, 151–60.

Rescorla, R. A. (2006) Stimulus generalization of excitation and inhibition. *Quarterly Journal of Experimental Psychology*, 59, 53–67.

Rescorla, R. and Wagner, A. R. (1972) A theory of Pavlovian conditioning: Variations in the effectiveness of reinforcement and nonreinforcement. In A. H. Black and W. F. Prokasky (eds) *Classical Conditioning: II Current Research and Theory* (pp. 64–99). New York: Appleton-Century-Crofts.

Ressler, K. J. and Nemeroff, C. B. (1999) Role of norepinephrine in the pathophysiology and treatment of mood disorders. *Biological Psychiatry*, 46, 1219–33.

Ressler, K. J., Rothbaum, B. O., Tannenbaum, L. et al. (2004) Cognitive enhancers as adjuncts to cognitive therapy: Use of D-cycloerine in phobic individuals to facilitate extinction of fear. *Archives of General Psychiatry*, 61, 1136–44.

Rich, A. N., Bradshaw, J. L. and Mattingley, J. B. (2005) A systematic, large-scale study of synaesthesia: Implications for the role of early experience in lexical-colour associations. *Cognition*, 98, 53–84.

Richards, M. H., Crowe, P. A., Larson, R. and Swarr, A. (1998) Developmental patterns and gender differences in the experience of peer companionship during adolescence. *Child Development*, 69, 154–63.

Richardson, A. J. and Montgomery, P. (2005) The Oxford-Durham study: A randomized, controlled trial of dietary supplementation with fatty acids in children with developmental coordination disorder. *Pediatrics*, 115, 1360–6.

Richert, E. S. (1997) Excellence with equity in identification and programming. In N. Colangelo and G. A. Davis (eds) *Handbook of Gifted Education* (2nd edn, pp. 75–88). Boston: Allyn & Bacon.

Richeson, J. A. and Shelton, J. N. (2003) When prejudice does not pay: Effects of interracial contact on executive function. *Psychological Science*, 14, 287–90.

Richland, L. E. and Burchinal, M. R. (2013) Early executive function predicts reasoning development. *Psychological Science*, 24, 87–92.

Richters, J., de Visser, R., Rissel, C. and Smith, A. (2006) Sexual practices at last heterosexual encounter and occurrence of orgasm in a national survey. *Journal of Sex Research*, 43, 217–26.

Riddoch, G. (1917) Dissociation of visual perceptions due to occipital injuries with special appreciation of movement. *Brain*, 40, 15–47.

Rieber, R. W. (ed.) (1980) *Wilhelm Wundt and the Making of Scientific Psychology*. New York: Plenum Press.

Rimm-Kaufman, S. E. and Pianta, R. C. (2000) An ecological perspective on the transition to kindergarten: A theoretical framework to guide empirical research. *Journal of Applied Developmental Psychology*, 21, 491–511.

Ringelmann, M. (1913) Recherches sur les moteurs animés: Travail de l'homme. *Annales de l'Institut National Argonomique*, 2, 1–40.

Rizzolatti, G. (2004) The mirror-neuron system and imitation. In S. Hurley and N. Chater (eds) *Perspectives on Imitation: From Mirror Neurons to Memes* (pp. 55–76). Cambridge, MA: MIT Press.

Rizzolatti, G. and Craighero, L. (2004) The mirror-neuron system. *Annual Review of Neuroscience*, 27, 169–92.

Roberson, D., Davidoff, J., Davies, I. R. and Shapiro, L. R. (2004) The development of color categories in two languages: A longitudinal study. *Journal of Experimental Psychology: General*, 133, 554–71.

Roberts, G. A. (1991) Delusional belief and meaning in life: A preferred reality? *British Journal of Psychiatry*, 159, 20–9.

Roberts, R. (2011) Psychology at the end of the world. *The Psychologist,* 24, 22–5.

Roberts, R. D., Zeidner, M. and Matthews, G. (2001) Does emotional intelligence meet traditional standards for an intelligence? Some new data and conclusions. *Emotion*, 1, 196–231.

Robertson, I. H., Nico, D. and Hood, B. M. (1995) The intention to act improves unilateral left neglect: Two demonstrations. *NeuroReport*, 7, 246–8.

Robertson, L. C. (1999) What can spatial deficits teach us about fea-ture binding and spatial maps? *Visual Cognition,* 6, 409–30.

Robertson, L. C. (2003) Binding, spatial attention and perceptual awareness. *Nature Reviews Neuroscience,* 4, 93–102.

Robins, E. and Guze, S. B. (1972) Classification of affective disorders: The primary-secondary, the endogenous-reactive, and the neurotic-psychotic concepts. In T. A. Williams, M. M. Katz and J. A. Shields (eds) *Recent Advances in the Psychobiology of Depressive Illnesses* (pp. 283–93). Washington, DC: US Government Printing Office.

Robins, L. N. and Regier, D. A. (1991) *Psychiatric Disorders in America.* New York: Free Press.

Robins, L. N., Helzer, J. E., Weissman, M. M. et al. (1984) Lifetime prevalence of specific psychiatric disorders in three sites. *Archives of General Psychiatry*, 41, 949–58.

Robinson, A. and Clinkenbeard, P. R. (1998) Giftedness: An exceptionality examined. *Annual Review of Psychology*, 49, 117–39.

Robinson, D. N. (1995) *An Intellectual History of Psychology.* Madison: University of Wisconsin Press.

Robinson, R. G. and Downhill, J. E. (1995) Lateralization of psychopathology in response to focal brain injury. In R. J. Davidson and K. Hugdahl (eds) *Brain Asymmetry* (pp. 693–711). Cambridge, MA: MIT Press.

Robinson, W. A. (2006) *The Last Man Who Knew Everything: Thomas Young.* London: Pi Press.

Rochat, P. (2009) *Others in Mind: Social Origins of Self-Consciousness.* Cambridge: CUP.

Rochat, P. and Hespos, S. J. (1997) Differential rooting response by neonates: Evidence for an early sense of self. *Early Development & Parenting*, 6(2), 1–8.

Rochat, P. and Striano, T. (2002) Who is in the mirror: Self-other discrimination in specular images by 4- and 9-month-old infants. *Child Development*, 73, 35–46.

Rodgon, M. and Rashman, S. (1976) Expression of owner-owned relationships among holophrastic 14-to 32-month-old children. *Child Development*, 47, 1219–22.

Rodieck, R. W. (1998) *The First Steps in Seeing.* Sunderland, MA: Sinauer.

Rodriguez, M., Mischel, W. and Shoda, Y. (1989) Cognitive person variables in the delay of gratification of older children at-risk. *Journal of Personality and Social Psychology*, 57, 358–67.

Roedell, W. C. and Slaby, R. G. (1977) The role of distal and proximal interaction in infant social preference formation. *Developmental Psychology*, 13, 266–73.

Roediger, H. L. III (2000) Why retrieval is the key process to understanding human memory. In E. Tulving (ed.) *Memory, Consciousness, and the Brain: The Tallinn Conference* (pp. 52–75). Philadelphia: Psychology Press.

Roediger, H. L. III and McDermott, K. B. (1995) Creating false memories: Remembering words not presented in lists. *Journal of Experimental Psychology: Learning, Memory, and Cognition*, 21, 803–14.

Roediger, H. L. III and McDermott, K. B. (2000) Tricks of memory. *Current Directions in Psychological Science*, 9, 123–7.

Roediger, H. L. III, Weldon, M. S. and Challis, B. H. (1989) Explaining dissociations between implicit and explicit measures of retention: A processing account. In H. L. Roediger and F. I. Craik (eds) *Varieties of Memory and Consciousness: Essays in Honor of Endel Tulving* (pp. 3–41). Hillsdale, NJ: Erlbaum.

Roffler, S. K. and Butler, R. A. (1967) Localization of tonal stimuli in the vertical plane. *Journal of the Acoustical Society of America*, 43, 1260–6.

Rogers, C. R. (1951) *Client-centered Therapy: Its Current Practice, Implications, and Theory.* Boston: Houghton Mifflin.

Rogers, C. R. (1957) The necessary and sufficient conditions for therapeutic personality change. *Journal of Consulting Psychology*, 21, 95–103.

Rogers, T. B., Kuiper, N. A. and Kirker, W. S. (1977) Self-reference and the encoding of personal information. *Journal of Personality and Social Psychology*, 35, 677–88.

Rokach, A. (2013) *Longing, Intimacy and Loneliness*. London: Routledge.

Rönnlund, M., Carlstedt, B., Blomstedt, Y. et al. (2013) Secular trends in cognitive test performance: Swedish conscript data 1970–1993. *Intelligence*, 41, 19–24.

Rosch, E. H. (1973) Natural categories. *Cognitive Psychology*, 4, 328–50.

Rosch, E. H. (1975) Cognitive representations of semantic categories. *Journal of Experimental Psychology: General*, 104, 192–233.

Rosch, E. H. and Mervis, C. B. (1975) Family resemblances: Studies in the internal structure of categories. *Cognitive Psychology*, 7, 573–605.

Rose, J. D. (2011) Diverse perspectives on the groupthink theory: A literary review. *Emerging Leadership Journeys*, 4, 37–57.

Rose, S. P. (2002) Smart drugs: Do they work? Are they ethical? Will they be legal? *Nature Reviews Neuroscience* 3, 975–9.

Roseman, I. J. (1984) Cognitive determinants of emotion: A structural theory. *Review of Personality and Social Psychology*, 5, 11–36.

Roseman, I. J. and Smith, C. A. (2001) Appraisal theory: Overview, assumptions, varieties and controversies. In K. R. Scherer, A. Schorr and T. Johnstone (eds) *Appraisal Processes in Emotion: Theory, Methods, Research* (pp. 3–19). New York: OUP.

Rosenberg, M. (1965) *Society and the Adolescent Self-image.* Princeton, NJ: Princeton University Press.

Rosenhan, D. (1973) On being sane in insane places. *Science*, 179, 250–8.

Rosenstein, M. J., Milazzo-Sayre, L. J. and Manderscheid, R. W. (1990) Characteristics of persons using specifically inpatient, outpatient, and partial care programs in 1986. In M. A. Sonnenschein (ed.) *Mental Health in the United States* (pp. 139–72). Washington, DC: US Government Printing Office.

Rosenthal, R. (1994) On being one's own study: Experimenter effects in behavioral research – 30 years later. In W. R. Shadish and S. Fuller (eds) *The Social Psychology of Science* (pp. 214–29). New York: Guilford Press.

Rosenthal, R. and Fode, K. L. (1963) The effect of experimenter bias on the performance of the albino rat. *Behavioral Science*, 8, 183–9.

Rosenzweig, M. R. (1992) Psychological science around the world. *American Psychologist*, 47, 718–22.

Rosip, J. C. and Hall, J. A. (2004) Knowledge of nonverbal cues, gender, and nonverbal decoding accuracy. *Journal of Nonverbal Behavior*, 28, 267–86.

Ross, B. H. (1984) Remindings and their effects in learning a cognitive skill. *Cognitive Psychology*, 16, 371–416.

Ross, H. S. and Lollis, S. (1989) A social relations analysis of toddler peer relations. *Child Development*, 60, 1082–91.

Ross, H., Conant, C. and Vickar, M. (2011) Property rights and the resolution of social conflict. *New Directions for Child and Adolescent Development*, 132, 53–64.

Ross, L. (1977) The intuitive psychologist and his shortcomings: Distortions in the attribution process. *Advances in Experimental Social Psychology*, 10, 173–220.

Ross, L. and Nisbett, R. E. (1991) *The Person and the Situation.* New York: McGraw-Hill.

Ross, L., Amabile, T. M. and Steinmetz, J. L. (1977) Social roles, social control, and biases in social-perception processes. *Journal of Personality and Social Psychology*, 35, 485–94.

Ross, L., Lepper, M. R. and Hubbard, M. (1975) Perseverance in self-perception and social perception: Biased attribution processes in the debriefing paradigm. *Journal of Personality and Social Psychology*, 32, 880–92.

Ross, L., Lepper, M. and Ward, A. (2010) History of social psychology: Insights, challenges, and contributions to theory and application. In S. Fiske, D. T. Gilbert and G. Lindzey (eds) *Handbook of Social Psychology* (5th edn, pp. 3–50). Hoboken, NJ: Wiley.

Ross, S. and Ross, J. G. (1949) Social facilitation of feeding behavior in dogs: I. Group and solitary feeding. *Journal of Genetic Psychology*, 74, 97–108.

Rossano, F., Rakoczy, H. and Tomasello, M. (2011) Young children's understanding of violations of property rights. *Cognition*, 121, 219–27.

Rossi, A. S. (1977) A biosocial perspective on parenting. *Daedalus*, 106, 1–31.

Roth, M. and Mountjoy, C. Q. (1997) The need for the concept of neurotic depression. In G. B. Akiskal (ed.) *Dysthymia and the Spectrum of Chronic Depressions* (pp. 96–129). New York: Guilford Press.

Rothbart, M. K. and Bates, J. E. (1998) Temperament. In W. Damon and N. Eisenberg, *Handbook of Child Psychology*, vol. 3. *Social Emotional and Personality Development* (5th edn, pp. 105–76). New York: Wiley.

Rothermundt, M., Arolt, V. and Bayer, T. A. (2001) Review of immunological and immunopathological findings in schizophrenia. *Brain, Behavior, and Immunity*, 15, 319–39.

Rotten, J. and Kelly, I. W. (1985) Much ado about the full moon: A meta-analysis of lunar-lunacy research. *Psychological Bulletin*, 97, 286–306.

Rotter, J. B. (1966) Generalized expectancies for internal versus external locus of control of reinforcement. *Psychological Monographs: General and Applied*, 80, 1–28.

Rovee, C. and Rovee, D. T. (1969) Conjugate reinforcement of infant exploratory behavior. *Journal of Experimental Child Psychology*, 8, 33–9.

Rovee-Collier, C. (1999) The development of infant memory. *Current Directions in Psychological Science*, 8, 80–5.

Rowland, L. W. (1939) Will hypnotized persons try to harm themselves or others? *Journal of Abnormal and Social Psychology*, 34, 114–17.

Rowley, M. and Delgarno, E. L. (2010) A-level psychology teachers: Who are they and what do they think about psychology as a subject and a discipline? *Psychology Teaching Review*, 16, 54–61.

Royal College of Psychiatrists (2012) *Eating Disorders in the UK*, www.rcpsych.ac.uk/files/pdfversion/CR170.pdf.

Roy-Byrne, P. P. and Cowley, D. (1998) *Pharmacological Treatment of Panic, Generalized Anxiety, and Phobic Disorders.* New York: OUP.

Roy-Byrne, P. P. and Cowley, D. S. (2002) Pharmacological treatments for panic disorder, generalized anxiety disorder, specific phobia, and social anxiety disorder. In P. E. Nathan and J. M. Gorman (eds) *A Guide to Treatments That Work* (2nd edn, pp. 337–65). New York: OUP.

Royzman, E. B., Cassidy, K. W. and Baron, J. (2003) 'I know, you know': Epistemic egocentrism in children and adults. *Review of General Psychology*, 7, 38–65.

Rozin, P. (1968) Are carbohydrate and protein intakes separately regulated? *Journal of Comparative and Physiological Psychology*, 65, 23–9.

Rozin, P. and Fallon, A. E. (1987) A perspective on disgust. *Psychological Review*, 94, 23–41.

Rozin, P. and Kalat, J. W. (1971) Specific hungers and poison avoidance as adaptive specializations of learning. *Psychological Review*, 78, 459–86.

Rozin, P., Bauer, R. and Catanese, D. (2003) Food and life, pleasure and worry, among American college students: Gender differences and regional similarities. *Journal of Personality and Social Psychology*, 85, 132–41.

Rozin, P., Haidt, J. and McCauley, C. R. (1999) Disgust: The body and soul emotion. In T. Dalgleish and M. J. Power (eds) *Handbook of Cognition and Emotion* (pp. 429–45). New York: Wiley.

Rozin, P., Millman, L. and Nemeroff, C. (1986b) Operation of the laws of sympathetic magic in disgust and other domains. *Journal of Personality and Social Psychology*, 50, 703–12.

Rozin, P., Dow, S., Moscovitch, M. and Rajaram, S. (1998) What causes humans to begin and end a meal? A role for memory for what has been eaten, as evidenced by a study of multiple meal eating in amnesic patients. *Psychological Science*, 9, 392–6.

Rozin, P., Hammer, L., Oster, H. et al. (1986a) The child's concept of food: Differentiation of categories of rejected substances in the 1.4 to 5 years range. *Appetite*, 7, 141–51.

Rubin, B. D. and Katz, L. C. (1999) Optical imaging of odorant representations in the mammalian olfactory bulb. *Neuron*, 23, 499–511.

Rubin, K., Coplan, R., Nelson, L. and Cheah, C. (1999) Peer relationships in childhood. In M. Borstein and M. Lamb (eds) *Developmental Psychology: An Advanced Textbook* (4th edn, pp. 451–501). Mahwah, NJ: Erlbaum.

Rubin, Z. (1973) *Liking and Loving.* New York: Holt, Rinehart & Winston.

Rude, S. S., Wenzlaff, R. M., Gibbs, B. et al. (2002) Negative processing biases predict subsequent depressive symptoms. *Cognition and Emotion*, 16, 423–40.

Rudman, L. A., Ashmore, R. D. and Gary, M. L. (2001) 'Unlearning' automatic biases: The malleability of implicit prejudice and stereotypes. *Journal of Personality and Social Psychology*, 81, 856–68.

Rusbult, C. E. (1983) A longitudinal test of the investment model: The development (and deterioration) of satisfaction and commitment in heterosexual involvements. *Journal of Personality and Social Psychology*, 45, 101–17.

Rusbult, C. E. and van Lange, P. A. (2003) Interdependence, interaction and relationships. *Annual Review of Psychology*, 54, 351–75.

Rusbult, C. E., Verette, J., Whitney, G. A. and Slovik, L. F. (1991) Accommodation processes in close relationships: Theory and preliminary empirical evidence. *Journal of Personality and Social Psychology*, 60, 53–78.

Rushton, J. P. (1995) Asian achievement, brain size, and evolution: Comment on A. H. Yee. *Educational Psychology Review*, 7, 373–80.

Russell, J. (1996) *Agency: Its Role in Mental Development*. Hove: Erlbaum.

Russell, J. A. (1980) A circumplex model of affect. *Journal of Personality and Social Psychology*, 39, 1161–78.

Rutter, M. and Silberg, J. (2002) Gene-environment interplay in relation to emotional and behavioral disturbance. *Annual Review of Psychology*, 53, 463–90.

Rutter, M., O'Connor, T. G. and English and Romanian Adoptees (ERA) Study Team (2004) Are there biological programming effects for psychological development? Findings from a study of Romanian adoptees. *Developmental Psychology*, 40, 81–94.

Ryan, R. M. and Deci, E. L. (2000) Self-determination theory and the facilitation of intrinsic motivation, social development, and well-being. *American Psychologist*, 55, 68–78.

Sachs, J., Bard, B. and Johnson, M. L. (1981) Language learning with restricted input: Case studies of two hearing children of deaf parents. *Applied Psycholinguistics*, 2, 33–54.

Sackeim, H. A. and Devanand, D. P. (1991) Dissociative disorders. In M. Hersen and S. M. Turner (eds) *Adult Psychopathology and Diagnosis* (2nd edn, pp. 279–322). New York: Wiley.

Sacks, H., Schegloff, E. A. and Jefferson, G. (1974) A simplest systematics for the organization of turn-taking in conversation. *Language*, 50, 696–735.

Sacks, O. (1985) *The Man Who Mistook His Wife for a Hat, and Other Clinical Tales*. London: Summit Books.

Sacks, O. (1995) *An Anthropologist on Mars*. New York: Knopf.

Sacks, O. (2007) The abyss: Music and amnesia. *The New Yorker*, 24 September.

Sadker, M. and Sadker, D. (1994) *Failing at Fairness: How America's Schools Cheat Girls*. New York: Scribner.

Saffran, J. R., Aslin, R. N. and Newport, E. I. (1996) Statistical learning by 8-month-old infants. *Science*, 274, 1926–8.

Sagiv, N., Heer, J. and Robertson, L. (2006) Does binding of synesthetic color to the evoking grapheme require attention? *Cortex*, 42, 232–42.

Sahakian, B. J. and Morein-Zamir, S. (2011) Neuroethical issues in cognitive enhancement. *Journal of Psychopharmacology*, 25, 197–204.

Saint-Georges, C., Mahdhaoui, A., Chetouani, M. et al. (2011) Do parents recognise autistic deviant behavior long before diagnosis? Taking into account interaction using computational methods. *PloS ONE*, 6(7), e22393.

Saito, S. and Miyake, A. (2004) On the nature of forgetting and processing-storage relationship in reading span performance. *Journal of Memory and Language*, 50, 425–43.

Salamé, P. and Baddeley, A. D. (1989) Effects of background music on phonological short-term memory. *Quarterly Journal of Experimental Psychology*, 41A, 107–22.

Salapatek, P. (1975) Pattern perception in early infancy. In L. B. Cohen and P. Salapatek (eds) *Infant Perception: From Sensation to Cognition*. New York: Academic Press.

Salge, R. A., Beck, J. G. and Logan, A. (1988) A community survey of panic. *Journal of Anxiety Disorder*, 2, 157–67.

Salsburg, D. (2002) *The Lady Tasting Tea: How Statistics Revolutionized Science in the Twentieth Century*. New York: W.H. Freeman/Owl Books.

Salthouse, T. A. (1984) Effects of age and skill in typing. *Journal of Experimental Psychology: General*, 113, 345–71.

Salthouse, T. A. (1987) Age, experience, and compensation. In C. Schooler and K. W. Schaie (eds) *Cognitive Functioning and Social Structure over the Life Course* (pp. 142–50). New York: Ablex.

Salthouse, T. A. (1996a) General and specific mediation of adult age differences in memory. *Journal of Gerontology: Series B: Psychological Sciences and Social Sciences*, 51B, 30–42.

Salthouse, T. A. (1996b) The processing-speed theory of adult age differences in cognition. *Psychological Review*, 103, 403–28.

Salthouse, T. A. (2000) Pressing issues in cognitive aging. In D. Park and N. Schwartz (eds) *Cognitive Aging: A Primer* (pp. 43–54). Philadelphia: Psychology Press.

Salthouse, T. A. (2001) Structural models of the relations between age and measures of cognitive functioning. *Intelligence*, 29, 93–115.

Sampson, E. (1991) *Social Worlds, Personal Lives: An Introduction to Social Psychology* (6th edn). San Diego, CA: Harcourt Brace Jovanovich.

Sapolsky, R. M. and Share, L. J. (2004) A pacific culture among wild baboons: Its emergence and transmission. *PLoS Biology*, 2, e106.

Sarris, V. (1989) Max Wertheimer on seen motion: Theory and evidence. *Psychological Research*, 51, 58–68.

Sarter, M. (2006) Preclinical research into cognition enhancers. *Trends in Pharmacological Sciences*, 27, 602–8.

Savage, C. R., Deckersbach, T., Heckers, S. et al. (2001) Prefrontal regions supporting spontaneous and directed application of verbal learning strategies: Evidence from PET. *Brain*, 124, 219–31.

Savage-Rumbaugh, S. and Lewin, R. (1996) *Kanzi: The Ape on the Brink of the Human Mind*. New York: Wiley.

Savage-Rumbaugh, S., Shanker, S. G. and Taylor, T. J. (1998) *Apes, Language, and the Human Mind*. Oxford: OUP.

Saver, J. L. and Rabin, J. (1997) The neural substrates of religious experience. *Journal of Neuropsychiatry and Clinical Neurosciences*, 9, 498–510.

Savic, I., Berglund, H. and Lindstrom, P. (2005) Brain response to putative pheromones in homosexual men. *Proceedings of the National Academy of Sciences*, 102, 7356–61.

Savitsky, K., Epley, N. and Gilovich, T. (2001) Is it as bad as we fear? Overestimating the extremity of others' judgments. *Journal of Personality and Social Psychology*, 81, 44–56.

Sawa, A. and Snyder, S. H. (2002) Schizophrenia: Diverse approaches to a complex disease. *Science*, 295, 692–5.

Sawyer, K. (2008) *Group Genius: The Creative Power of Collaboration*. New York: Basic Books.

Scaife, M. and Bruner, J. (1975) The capacity for joint visual attention in the infant. *Nature*, 253, 265–6.

Scarborough, E. and Furumoto, L. (1987) *Untold Lives: The First Generation of American Women Psychologists*. New York: Columbia University Press.

Scarr, S. and McCartney, K. (1983) How people make their own environments: A theory of genotype-to-environment factors. *Child Development*, 54, 424–35.

Scazufca, M. and Kuipers, E. (1998) Stability of expressed emotion in relatives of those with schizophrenia and its relationship with burden of care and perception of patients' social functioning. *Psychological Medicine*, 28, 453–61.

Schachter, S. and Singer, J. E. (1962) Cognitive, social, and psychological determinants of emotional state. *Physiological Review*, 69, 379–99.

Schacter, D. L. (1987) Implicit memory: History and current status. *Journal of Experimental Psychology: Learning, Memory, and Cognition*, 13, 501–18.

Schacter, D. L. (1996) *Searching for Memory: The Brain, the Mind, and the Past*. New York: Basic Books.

Schacter, D. L. (1999) The seven sins of memory: Insights from psychology and cognitive neuroscience. *American Psychologist*, 54(3), 182–203.

Schacter, D. L. (2001a) *The Seven Sins of Memory: How the Mind Forgets and Remembers*. Boston: Houghton Mifflin.

Schacter, D. L. (2001b) *Forgotten Ideas, Neglected Pioneers: Richard Semon and the Story of Memory*. Philadelphia: Psychology Press.

Schacter, D. L. and Addis, D. R. (2007) The cognitive neuroscience of constructive memory: Remembering the past and imagining the future. *Philosophical Transactions of the Royal Society of London. Series B: Biological Sciences*, 362, 773–86.

Schacter, D. L. and Buckner, R. L. (1998) Priming and the brain. *Neuron*, 20, 185–95.

Schacter, D. L. and Curran, T. (2000) Memory without remembering and remembering without memory: Implicit and false memories. In M. S. Gazzaniga (ed.) *The New Cognitive Neurosciences* (2nd edn, pp. 343–62). Cambridge, MA: MIT Press.

Schacter, D. L. and Moscovitch, M. (1984) Infants, amnesics, and dissociable memory systems. In M. Moscovitch (ed.) *Infant Memory* (pp. 173–216). New York: Plenum Press.

Schacter, D. L. and Scarry, E. (2001) *Memory, Brain and Belief*. Harvard: Harvard University Press.

Schacter, D. L., Addis, D. R. and Buckner R. L. (2007) Remembering the past to imagine the future: The prospective brain. *Nature Reviews Neuroscience*, 8, 657–61.

Schacter, D. L., Addis, D. R. and Buckner, R. L. (2008) Episodic simulation of future events: Concepts, data, and applications. *Annals of the New York Academy of Sciences*, 1124, 39–60.

Schacter, D. L., Dobbins, I. G. and Schnyer, D. M. (2004) Specificity of priming: A cognitive neuroscience perspective. *Nature Reviews Neuroscience*, 5, 853–62.

Schacter, D. L., Harbluk, J. L. and McLachlan, D. R. (1984) Retrieval without recollection: An experimental analysis of source amnesia. *Journal of Verbal Learning and Verbal Behavior*, 23, 593–611.

Schacter, D. L., Israel, L. and Racine, C. A. (1999) Suppressing false recognition in younger and older adults: The distinctiveness heuristic. *Journal of Memory and Language*, 40, 1–24.

Schacter, D. L., Wang, P. L., Tulving, E. and Freedman, M. (1982) Functional retrograde amnesia: A quantitative case study. *Neuropsychologia*, 20, 523–32.

Schacter, D. L., Alpert, N. M., Savage, C. R. et al. (1996a) Conscious recollection and the human hippocampal formation: Evidence from positron emission tomography. *Proceedings of the National Academy of Sciences*, 93, 321–5.

Schacter, D. L., Reiman, E., Curran, T. et al. (1996b) Neuroanatomical correlates of veridical and illusory recognition memory: Evidence from positron emission tomography. *Neuron*, 17, 267–74.

Schaeffer, M. A., McKinnon, W., Baum, A. et al. (1985) Immune status as a function of chronic stress at Three-Mile Island. *Psychosomatic Medicine*, 47, 85.

Schafer, R. B. and Keith, P. M. (1980) Equity and depression among married couples. *Social Psychology Quarterly*, 43, 430–45.

Schaie, K. W. (1996) *Intellectual Development in Adulthood: The Seattle Longitudinal Study*. New York: CUP.

Schaie, K. W. (2005) *Developmental Influences on Adult Intelligence: The Seattle Longitudinal Study*. New York: OUP.

Schaller, M. and Park, J. (2011) The behavioral immune system (and why it matters). *Current Directions in Psychological Science*, 20, 99–103.

Schanberg, S. M. and Field, T. M. (1987) Sensory deprivation stress and supplemental stimulation in the rat pup and preterm human neonate. *Child Development*, 58, 1431–47.

Schapira, A. H., Emre, M., Jenner, P. and Poewe, W. (2009) Levodopa in the treatment of Parkinson's disease. *European Journal of Neurology*, 16, 982–9.

Schatzberg, A. F., Cole, J. O. and DeBattista, C. (2003) *Manual of Clinical Psychopharmacology* (4th edn.) Washington, DC: American Psychiatric Publishing.

Scheff, T. J. (1984) *Being Mentally Ill: A Sociological Theory*. Chicago: Aldine.

Scherer, K. R. (1999) Appraisal theory. In T. Dalgleish and M. Power (eds) *Handbook of Cognition and Emotion* (pp. 637–63). New York: Wiley.

Scherer, K. R. (2001) The nature and study of appraisal: A review of the issues. In K. R. Scherer, A. Schorr and T. Johnstone (eds) *Appraisal Processes in Emotion: Theory, Methods, Research* (pp. 369–92). New York: OUP.

Schildkraut, J. J. (1965) The catecholamine hypothesis of affective disorders: A review of supporting evidence. *American Journal of Psychiatry*, 122, 509–22.

Schimmack, U., Radhakrishnan, P., Oishi, S. et al. (2002) Culture, personality and subjective well-being: Integrating process models of life-satisfaction. *Journal of Personality and Social Psychology*, 82, 582–93.

Schmechel, R. S., O'Toole, T. P., Easterly, C. and Loftus, E. F. (2006) Beyond the ken? Testing jurors' understanding of eyewitness reliability evidence. *Jurimetrics*, 46, 177–214.

Schmidt, F. and Hunter, J. (2002) Are there benefits from NHST? *American Psychologist*, 57, 65–6.

Schmidt, F. L. and Hunter, J. E. (1998) The validity and utility of selection methods in personnel psychology: Practical and theoretical implications of 85 years of research findings. *Psychological Bulletin*, 124, 262–74.

Schmidt, N. B., Lerew, D. R. and Jackson R. J. (1997) The role of anxiety sensitivity in the pathogenesis of panic: Prospective evaluation of spontaneous panic attacks during acute stress. *Journal of Abnormal Psychology*, 106, 355–65.

Schnapf, J. L., Kraft, T. W. and Baylor, D. A. (1987) Spectral sensitivity of human cone photoreceptors. *Nature*, 325, 439–41.

Schneider, B. H., Atkinson, L. and Tardif, C. (2001) Child-parent attachment and children's peer relations: A quantitative review. *Developmental Psychology*, 37, 86–100.

Schneier, F., Johnson, J., Hornig, C. D. et al. (1992) Social phobia: Comorbidity and morbidity in an epidemiologic sample. *Archives of General Psychiatry*, 49, 282–8.

Schnorr, J. A. and Atkinson, R. C. (1969) Repetition versus imagery instructions in the short- and long-term retention of paired associates. *Psychonomic Science*, 15, 183–4.

Schooler, J. W., Reichle, E. D. and Halpern, D. V. (2001) Zoning-out during reading: Evidence for dissociations between experience and meta-consciousness. Paper presented at the Annual Meeting of the Psychonomic Society, Orlando, FL.

Schouwenburg, H. C. (1995) Academic procrastination: Theoretical notions, measurement, and research. In J. R. Ferrari, J. L. Johnson and W. G. McCown (eds) *Procrastination and Task Avoidance: Theory, Research, and Treatment* (pp. 71–96). New York: Plenum Press.

Schreiner, C. E., Read, H. L. and Sutter, M. L. (2000) Modular organization of frequency integration in primary auditory cortex. *Annual Review of Neuroscience*, 23, 501–29.

Schroeder, D. A., Penner, L. A., Dovidio, J. F. and Piliavin, J. A (1995) *The Psychology of Helping and Altruism: Problems and Puzzles*. New York: McGraw-Hill.

Schultz, D. P. and Schultz, S. E. (1987) *A History of Modern Psychology* (4th edn). San Diego: Harcourt Brace Jovanovich.

Schwartz, C. E., Wright, C. I., Shin, L. M. et al. (2003) Inhibited and uninhibited infants 'grown up': Adult amygdalar response to novelty. *Science*, 300, 1952–3.

Schwartz, J. H. and Westbrook, G. L. (2000) The cytology of neurons. In E. R. Kandel, G. H. Schwartz and T. M. Jessell (eds) *Principles of Neural Science* (pp. 67–104). New York: McGraw-Hill.

Schwartz, S. and Maquet, P. (2002) Sleep imaging and the neuropsychological assessment of dreams. *Trends in Cognitive Sciences*, 6, 23–30.

Schwartzman, A. E., Gold, D. and Andres, D. (1987) Stability of intelligence: A 40-year follow-up. *Canadian Journal of Psychology*, 41, 244–56.

Schwarz, N. and Clore, G. L. (1983) Mood, misattribution, and judgments of well-being: Informative and directive functions of affective states. *Journal of Personality and Social Psychology*, 45, 513–23.

Schwarz, N., Mannheim, Z. and Clore, G. L. (1988) How do I feel about it? The informative function of affective states. In K. Fiedler and J. Forgas (eds) *Affect Cognition and Social Behavior: New Evidence and Integrative Attempts* (pp. 44–62). Toronto: C. J. Hogrefe.

Schwenkreis, P., El Tom, S., Ragert, P. et al. (2007) Assessment of sensorimotor cortical representation asymmetries and motor skills in violin players. *European Journal of Neuroscience*, 26, 3291–302.

Sclafani, A. (1995) How food preferences are learned: laboratory animal models. *Proceedings of the Nutrition Society*, 54, 419–27.

Scoville, W. B. and Milner, B. (1957) Loss of recent memory after bilateral hippocampal lesions. *Journal of Neurology, Neurosurgery, and Psychiatry*, 20, 11–21.

Scribner, S. (1975) Recall of classical syllogisms: A cross-cultural investigation of errors on logical problems. In R. J. Falmagne (ed.) *Reasoning: Representation and Process in Children and Adults* (pp. 153–73). Hillsdale, NJ: Erlbaum.

Scribner, S. (1984) Studying working intelligence. In B. Rogoff and J. Lave (eds) *Everyday Cognition: Its Development in Social Context* (pp. 9–40). Cambridge, MA: Harvard University Press.

Searle, J. R. (1969) *Speech Acts*. Cambridge: CUP.

Segal, M. W. (1974) Alphabet and attraction: An unobtrusive measure of the effect of propinquity in a field setting. *Journal of Personality and Social Psychology*, 30, 654–7.

Segall, M. H., Lonner, W. J. and Berry, J. W. (1998) Cross-cultural psychology as a scholarly discipline: On the flowering of culture in behavioral research. *American Psychologist*, 53(10), 1101–10.

Selfe, L. N. (1977) *A Case of Extraordinary Drawing Ability in Children*. London: Academic Press.

Seligman, M. E. (1971) Phobias and preparedness. *Behavior Therapy*, 2, 307–20.

Seligman, M. E. and Hager, J. L. (1972) Biological boundaries of learning: The sauce-bearnaise syndrome. *Psychology Today*, 6, 59–61, 84–7.

Selikoff, I. J., Robitzek, E. H. and Ornstein, G. G. (1952) Toxicity of hydrazine derivatives of isonicotinic acid in the chemotherapy of human tuberculosis. *Quarterly Bulletin of SeaView Hospital*, 13, 17–26.

Selye, H. and Fortier, C. (1950) Adaptive reaction to stress. *Psychosomatic Medicine*, 12, 149–57.

Semenza, C. and Zettin, M. (1989) Evidence from aphasia from proper names as pure referring expressions. *Nature*, 342, 678–9.

Senghas, A., Kita, S. and Ozyurek, A. (2004) Children create core properties of language: Evidence from an emerging sign language in Nicaragua. *Science*, 305, 1782.

Serpell, R. (1974) Aspects of intelligence in a developing country. *African Social Research*, 17, 578–96.

Seymour, K., Clifford, C. W., Logothetis, N. K. and Bartels, A. (2010) Coding and binding of color and form in visual cortex. *Cerebral Cortex*, 20, 1946–54.

Shackelford, T. K. and Larsen, R. J. (1999) Facial attractiveness and physical health. *Evolution and Human Behavior*, 20, 71–6.

Shafritz, K. M., Gore, J. C. and Marois, R. (2002) The role of the parietal cortex in visual feature binding. *Proceedings of the National Academy of Sciences*, 99, 10917–22.

Shah, J., Higgins, E. T. and Friedman, R. S. (1998) Performance incentives and means: How regulatory focus influences goal attainment. *Journal of Personality and Social Psychology*, 74, 285–93.

Shallice, T. and Warrington, E. K. (1975) Word recognition in a phoneme dyslexic patient. *Quarterly Journal of Experimental Psychology*, 27, 187–99.

Shallice, T., Fletcher, P., Frith, C. D. et al. (1994) Brain regions associated with acquisition and retrieval of verbal episodic memory. *Nature*, 368, 633–5.

Shantz, C. U. (1987) Conflicts between children. *Child Development*, 58, 283–305.

Shatz, M. A. and Best, J. B. (1987) Students' reasons for changing answers on objective tests. *Teaching of Psychology*, 14, 241–2.

Shaver, P. R. and Brennan, K. (1992) Attachment styles and the 'Big Five' personality traits: Their connections with each other and with romantic relationship outcomes. *Personality and Social Psychology Bulletin*, 18, 536–45.

Shedler, J. and Block, J. (1990) Adolescent drug use and psychological health: A longitudinal inquiry. *American Psychologist*, 45, 612–30.

Sheehan, P. (1979) Hypnosis and the process of imagination. In E. Fromm and R. S. Shor (eds) *Hypnosis: Developments in Research and New Perspectives* (pp. 381–411). Chicago: Aldine.

Sheese, B. E. and Graziano, W. G. (2005) Deciding to defect: The effects of video-game violence on cooperative behavior. *Psychological Science*, 16, 354–7.

Sheingold, K. and Tenney, Y. J. (1982) Memory for a salient childhood event. In U. Neisser (ed.) *Memory Observed* (pp. 201–12). New York: Freeman.

Sheldrake, R. (2003) *The Sense of Being Stared At: And Other Aspects of the Extended Mind*. New York: Crown.

Shell, R. M. and Eisenberg, N. (1992) A developmental model of recipients' reaction to aid. *Psychological Bulletin*, 111, 413–33.

Shenton, M. E., Dickey, C. C., Frumin, M. and McCarley, R. W. (2001) A review of MRI findings in schizophrenia. *Schizophrenia Research*, 49, 1–52.

Shepherd, G. M. (1988) *Neurobiology*. New York: OUP.

Sherif, M. (1966) *Group Conflict and Cooperation*. London: Routledge & Keegan Paul.

Sherif, M., Harvey, O. J., White, B. J. et al. (1961) *Intergroup Conflict and Cooperation: The Robbers Cave Experiment*. Norman, OK: University of Oklahoma Book Exchange.

Sherrod, D. (1974) Crowding, perceived control, and behavioral aftereffects. *Journal of Applied Social Psychology*, 4, 171–86.

Sherry, D. F. and Schacter, D. L. (1987) The evolution of multiple memory systems. *Psychological Review*, 94, 439–54.

Shih, M., Pittinsky, T. L. and Ambady, N. (1999) Stereotype susceptibility: Identity salience and shifts in quantitative performance. *Psychological Science*, 10, 80–3.

Shimamura, A. P. and Squire, L. R. (1987) A neuropsychological study of fact memory and source amnesia. *Journal of Experimental Psychology: Learning, Memory, and Cognition*, 13, 464–43.

Shimoda, K., Argyle, M. and Ricci-Bitt, P. E. (1978) The intercultural recognition of emotional expressions by three national racial groups: English, Italian, and Japanese. *European Journal of Social Psychology*, 8, 169–79.

Shiner, R., Masten, A. S. and Tellegen, A. (2002) A developmental perspective on personality in emerging adulthood: Childhood antecedents and concurrent adaptation. *Journal of Personality and Social Psychology*, 83, 1165–77.

Shipstead, Z., Redick, T. S. and Engle, R. W. (2012a) Is working memory training effective? *Psychological Bulletin*, 138, 628–54.

Shipstead, Z., Redick, T. S. and Engle, R. W. (2012b) Cogmed working memory training: Does the evidence support the claims? *Journal of Applied Research in Memory and Cognition*, 1, 185–93.

Shiv, B., Loewenstein, G., Bechara, A. et al. (2005) Investment behavior and the negative side of emotion. *Psychological Science*, 16, 435–9.

Shiwach, R. S., Reid, W. H. and Carmody, T. J. (2001) An analysis of reported deaths following electroconvulsive therapy in Texas, 1993-1998. *Psychiatric Services*, 52, 1095–7.

Shoda, Y., Mischel, W. and Peake, P. K. (1990) Predicting adolescent cognitive and social competence from preschool delay of gratification: Identifying diagnostic conditions. *Developmental Psychology*, 26, 978–86.

Shomstein, S. and Yantis, S. (2004) Control of attention shifts between vision and audition in human cortex. *Journal of Neuroscience*, 24, 10702–6.

Shore, C. (1986) Combinatorial play: Conceptual development and early multiword speech. *Developmental Psychology*, 22, 184–90.
Shors, T. J., Anderson, M. L., Curlik, D. M. and Nokia, M. S. (2012) Use it or lose it: How neurogenesis keeps the brain fit for learning. *Behavioral Brain Research*, 227, 450–8.
Shultz, T. R. and Ravinsky, F. B. (1977) Similarity as a principle of causal inference. *Child Development*, 48, 1552–8.
Shweder, R. A. (1991) *Thinking through Cultures: Expeditions in Cultural Psychology*. Cambridge, MA: Harvard University Press.
Shweder, R. A. and Sullivan, M. A. (1993) Cultural psychology: Who needs it? *Annual Review of Psychology*, 44, 497–523.
Sidanius, J. and Pratto, F. (1999) *Social Dominance: An Intergroup Theory of Social Hierarchy and Oppression*. New York: CUP.
Siegal, M. and Peterson, C. C. (1994) Children's theory of mind and the conversational territory of cognitive development. In C. Lewis and P. Mitchell (eds) *Children's Early Understanding of Mind: Origins and Development* (pp. 427–55). Hillsdale, NJ: Erlbaum.
Siegel, A., Roeling, T. A., Gregg, T. R. and Kruk, M. R. (1999) Neuropharmacology of brain-stimulation-evoked aggression. *Neuroscience and Biobehavioral Reviews*, 23, 359–89.
Siegel, B. (1988) Can evil beget good? Nazi data: A dilemma for science. *Los Angeles Times*, 30 October.
Siegel, S. (1976) Morphine analgesia tolerance: Its situational specificity supports a Pavlovian conditioning model. *Science*, 193, 323–5.
Siegel, S. (1984) Pavlovian conditioning and heroin overdose: Reports by overdose victims. *Bulletin of the Psychonomic Society*, 22, 428–30.
Siegler, R. S. (1996) *Emerging Minds: The Process of Change in Children's Thinking*. New York: OUP.
Siegler, R. S. and McGilly, K. (1989) Strategy choices in children's time-telling. In I. Levin and D. Zakay (eds) *Time and Human Cognition: A Life Span Perspective* (pp. 185–218). Amsterdam: Elsevier Science.
Siffre, M. (1975) Six months alone in a cave. *National Geographic*, 147(3), 426–35.
Signorella, M. L., Bigler, R. S. and Liben, L. S. (1993) Developmental differences in children's gender schemata about others: A meta-analytic review. *Developmental Review*, 13, 147–83.
Silver, R. L., Boon, C. and Stones, M. H. (1983) Searching for meaning in misfortune: Making sense of incest. *Journal of Social Issues*, 39, 81–102.
Silverman, I. W. and Ragusa, D. M. (1990) Child and maternal correlates of impulse control in 24-month-old children. *Genetic, Social, and Psychology Monographs*, 116, 435–73.
Simcock, G. and Hayne, H. (2002) Breaking the barrier? Children fail to translate their preverbal memories into language. *Psychological Science*, 13, 225–31.
Simmons, J. P., Nelson, L. D. and Simonsohn, U. (2013) Life after p-hacking. Paper presented at the meeting of the Society for Personality and Social Psychology, New Orleans, 17–19 January.
Simon, B. and Trötschel, R. (2008) Self and social identity. In M. Hewstone, W. Stroebe and K. Jonas (eds) *Introduction to Social Psychology: A European Perspective* (pp. 88–111). Oxford: Blackwell.
Simons, D. J. and Chabris, C. F. (1999) Gorillas in our midst: Sustained inattentional blindness for dynamic events. *Perception*, 28, 1059–74.
Simons, D. J. and Chabris, C. F. (2011) What people believe about how memory works: A representative survey of the U.S. population. *PLoS ONE*, 6(8), e22757.
Simpson, E. L. (1974) Moral development research: A case study of scientific cultural bias. *Human Development*, 17, 81–106.
Simpson, J. A. (1990) Influence of attachment style on romantic relationships. *Journal of Personality and Social Psychology*, 59, 971–80.
Simpson, J. A., Campbell, B. and Berscheid, E. (1986) The association between romantic love and marriage: Kephart (1967) twice revisited. *Personality and Social Psychology Bulletin*, 12, 363–72.
Simpson, J. A., Rholes, W. S. and Nelligan, J. S. (1992) Support seeking and support giving within couples in an anxiety-provoking situation: The role of attachment styles. *Personality and Social Psychology*, 62, 434–46.
Singer, J. and Singer, D. (2006) Preschoolers' imaginative play as precursor of narrative consciousness. *Imagination, Cognition and Personality*, 25, 97–117.
Singer, T., Seymour, B., O'Doherty, J. et al. (2004) Empathy for pain involves the affective but not sensory components of pain. *Science*, 303, 1157–62.
Singh, D. (1993) Adaptive significance of female physical attractiveness: Role of waist-to-hip ratio. *Journal of Personality and Social Psychology*, 65, 293–307.
Skaggs, W. E. and McNaughton, B. L. (1996) Replay of neuronal firing sequences in rat hippocampus during sleep following spatial experience. *Science*, 271, 1870–3.
Skeels, H. (1966) Adult status of children with contrasting early life experiences. *Monographs of the Society for Research in Child Development*, 31(3).
Skinner, B. F. (1932a) Drive and reflex strength. *Journal of General Psychology*, 6, 22–37.
Skinner, B. F. (1932b) Drive and reflex strength, II. *Journal of General Psychology*, 6, 38–48.
Skinner, B. F. (1938) *The Behavior of Organisms: An Experimental Analysis*. New York: Appleton-Century Crofts.
Skinner, B. F. (1948) 'Superstition' in the pigeon. *Journal of Experimental Psychology*, 38, 168–72.
Skinner, B. F. ([1948]1986) *Walden II*. Englewood Cliffs, NJ: Prentice Hall.
Skinner, B. F. (1950) Are theories of learning necessary? *Psychological Review*, 57, 193–216.
Skinner, B. F. (1953) *Science and Human Behavior*. New York: Macmillan.
Skinner, B. F. (1957) *Verbal Behavior*. New York: Appleton-Century-Crofts.
Skinner, B. F. (1958) Teaching machines. *Science*, 129, 969–77.
Skinner, B. F. (1971) *Beyond Freedom and Dignity*. New York: Bantam Books.
Skinner, B. F. (1979) *The Shaping of a Behaviorist: Part Two of an Autobiography*. New York: Knopf.
Slater, A., Mattock, A. and Brown, E. (1990) Size constancy at birth: Newborn infants' responses to retinal and real size. *Journal of Experimental Child Psychology*, 49, 314–22.
Slater, A., Mattock, A., Brown, E. and Bremner, J. G. (1991) Form perception at birth: Cohen and Younger (1984) revisited. *Journal of Experimental Child Psychology*, 51, 395–406.
Slaughter, V. (1998) Children's understanding of pictorial mental representations. *Child Development*, 69, 321–45.
Slotnick, S. D. and Schacter, D. L. (2004) A sensory signature that distinguished true from false memories. *Nature Neuroscience*, 7, 664–72.
Slovac, P. (2007) 'If I look at the mass I will never act': Psychic numbing and genocide. *Judgment and Decision Making*, 2, 79–95.
Smallwood, J. (2013) Distinguishing how from why the mind wanders: A process–occurrence framework for self-generated mental activity. *Psychological Bulletin*, 139, 519–35.
Smetacek, V. (2002) Balance: Mind-grasping gravity. *Nature*, 415, 481.
Smetana, J. G. (1981) Preschool children's conceptions of moral and social rules. *Child Development*, 52, 1333–6.
Smetana, J. G. and Braeges, J. L. (1990) The development of toddler's moral and conventional judgments. *Merrill-Palmer Quarterly*, 36, 329–46.
Smith, A. D., Gilchrist, I. D., Butler, S. et al. (2007) Non-lateralised deficits of drawing production in hemispatial neglect. *Brain & Cognition*, 64, 150–7.

Smith, E. E. and Jonides, J. (1997) Working memory: A view from neuroimaging. *Cognitive Psychology*, 33, 5–42.

Smith, M. (2011) Failing boys, failing psychology. *The Psychologist*, 24, 390–1.

Smith, N. and Tsimpli, I.-M. (1995) *The Mind of a Savant.* Oxford: OUP.

Smith, P., Fernandes, C. and Strand, S. (2001) *Cognitive Abilities Test 3: Technical Manual.* London: NFERNelson.

Smith, R. H., Webster, J. M., Parrot, W. G. and Eyre, H. L. (2002) The role of public exposure in moral and nonmoral shame and guilt. *Journal of Personality and Social Psychology*, 83, 138–59.

Snedeker, J., Geren, J. and Shafto, C. (2007) Starting over: International adoption as a natural experiment in language development. *Psychological Science*, 18, 79–87.

Snow, C. E., Arlman-Rupp, A., Hassing, Y. et al. (1976) Mothers' speech in three social classes. *Journal of Psycholinguistic Research*, 5, 1–20.

Snyder, K. S., Wallace, C. J., Moe, K. and Liberman, R. P. (1994) EE by residential care operators' and residents' symptoms and quality of life. *Hospital and Community Psychiatry*, 45, 1141–3.

Snyder, M. and Swann, W. B. Jr (1978) Hypothesis testing processes in social interaction. *Journal of Personality and Social Psychology*, 36, 1202–12.

Solomon, J. and George, C. (1999) The measurement of attachment security in infancy and childhood. In J. Cassidy and P. R. Shaver (eds) *Handbook of Attachment: Theory, Research and Clinical Applications* (pp. 287–316). New York: Guilford Press.

Solomon, S., Greenberg, J. and Pyszczynski, T. (1991) A terror management theory of social behavior: The psychological functions of self-esteem and cultural worldviews. In M. P. Zanna (ed.) *Advances in Experimental Social Psychology* (vol. 24, pp. 93–159). New York: Academic Press.

Son, L. K. and Metcalfe, J. (2000) Metacognitive and control strategies in study-time allocation. *Journal of Experimental Psychology: Learning, Memory and Cognition*, 26, 204–21.

Sonnby-Borgstrom, M., Jonsson, P. and Svensson, O. (2003) Emotional empathy as related to mimicry reactions at different levels of information processing. *Journal of Nonverbal Behavior*, 27, 3–23.

Soon, C. S., Brass, M., Heinze, H. J. and Haynes, J. D. (2008) Unconscious determinants of free decisions in the human brain. *Nature Neuroscience*, 11, 543–5.

Sørensen, M. J., Mors, O. and Thomsen, P. H. (2005) DSM-IV or ICD-10-DCR diagnoses in child and adolescent psychiatry: Does it matter? *European Child and Adolescent Psychiatry*, 14, 335–40.

Spanos, N. P. (1994) Multiple identity enactments and multiple personality disorder: A sociocognitive perspective. *Psychological Bulletin*, 116, 143–65.

Spearman, C. (1904) 'General intelligence' objectively determined and measured. *American Journal of Psychology*, 5, 201–93.

Spector, P. E. (2000) *Industrial and Organizational Psychology: Research and Practice* (2nd edn). New York: John Wiley & Sons.

Speisman, J. C., Lazarus, R. S., Moddkoff, A. and Davison, L. (1964) Experimental reduction of stress based on ego-defense theory. *Journal of Abnormal and Social Psychology*, 68, 367–80.

Spelke, E. S. (1976) Infants' intermodal perception of events. *Cognitive Psychology*, 8, 553–60.

Spelke, E. S. (2000) Core knowledge. *American Psychologist*, 55, 1233–43.

Spelke, E. S., Breinlinger, K., Macomber, J. and Jacobson, K. (1992) Origins of knowledge. *Psychological Review*, 99, 605–32.

Spellman, B. A. (1996) Acting as intuitive scientists: Contingency judgments are made while controlling for alternative potential causes. *Psychological Science*, 7, 337–42.

Sperling, G. (1960) The information available in brief visual presentations. *Psychological Monographs*, 74(11), 1–30.

Sperry, R. W. (1964) The great cerebral commissure. *Scientific American*, 210, 42–52.

Spinoza, B. ([1677]1982) *The Ethics and Selected Letters* (ed. S. Feldman and trans. S. Shirley). Indianapolis, IN: Hackett.

Spitz, R. A. (1949) Motherless infants. *Child Development*, 20, 145–55.

Spitzer, R. L. (1976) More on pseudoscience in science and the case for psychiatric diagnosis. *Archives of General Psychiatry*, 33, 459–70.

Spitzer, R. L., Gibbon, M., Skodol, A. E. et al. (1994) *DSM-IV Casebook: A Learning Companion to the Diagnostic & Statistical Manual of Mental Disorders* (4th edn). Washington, DC: American Psychiatric Press.

Sprecher, S. (1999) 'I love you more today than yesterday': Romantic partners' perceptions of changes in love and related affect over time. *Journal of Personality and Social Psychology*, 76, 46–53.

Squire, L. R. (1992) Memory and the hippocampus: A synthesis from findings with rats, monkeys, and humans. *Psychological Review*, 99, 195–231.

Squire, L. R. and Kandel, E. R. (1999) *Memory: From Mind to Molecules.* New York: Scientific American Library.

Squire, L. R. and Knowlton, B. J. (2000) The medial temporal lobe, the hippocampus, and the memory systems of the brain. In M. S. Gazzaniga (ed.) *The Cognitive Neurosciences* (pp. 765–80). Cambridge, MA: MIT Press.

Squire, L. R., Knowlton, B. and Musen, G. (1993) The structure and organization of memory. *Annual Review of Psychology*, 44, 453–95.

Squire, L. R., Ojemann, J. G., Miezin, F. M. et al. (1992) Activation of the hippocampus in normal humans: A functional anatomical study of memory. *Proceedings of the National Academy of Sciences*, 89, 1837–41.

Sroufe, L. A., Egeland, B. and Kruetzer, T. (1990) The fate of early experience following developmental change: Longitudinal approaches to individual adaptation in childhood. *Child Development*, 61, 1363–73.

Stack, S. (2000) Media impacts on suicide: A quantitative review of 293 findings. *Social Science Quarterly*, 81, 957–71.

Staddon, J. E. and Simmelhag, V. L. (1971) The 'superstition' experiment: A reexamination of its implications for the principles of adaptive behavior. *Psychological Review*, 78, 3–43.

Stadler, M. A. and Frensch, P. A. (eds) (1998) *Handbook of Implicit Learning.* Thousand Oaks, CA: Sage.

Stangor, C. and McMillan, D. (1992) Memory for expectancy-congruent and expectancy-incongruent information: A review of the social and social developmental literature. *Psychological Bulletin*, 111, 42–61.

Stanovich, K. E. and West, R. F. (2000) Individual differences in reasoning: Implications for the rationality debate. *Behavioral and Brain Sciences*, 23, 645–65.

Starkey, P., Spelke, E. S. and Gelman, R. (1983) Detection of intermodal numerical correspondences by human infants. *Science*, 222, 179–81.

Starkey, P., Spelke, E. S. and Gelman, R. (1990) Numerical abstraction by human infants. *Cognition*, 36, 97–127.

Stauffer, J. M., Ree, M. J. and Carretta, T. R. (1996) Cognitive-components tests are not much more than *g*: An extension of Kyllonen's analyses. *Journal of General Psychology*, 123, 193–205.

Steadman, H. J., Mulvey, E. P., Monahan, J. et al. (1998) Violence by people discharged from acute psychiatric inpatient facilities and by others in the same neighborhoods. *Archives of General Psychiatry*, 55, 393–401.

Steele, C. M. and Aronson, J. (1995) Stereotype threat and the intellectual test performance of African Americans. *Journal of Personality and Social Psychology*, 69, 797–811.

Steele, H., Steele, M., Croft, C. and Fonagy, P. (1999) Infant-mother attachment at one year predicts children's understanding of mixed emotions at six years. *Social Development*, 8, 161–78.

Stein, B. E. and Meredith, M. A. (1993) *The Merging of the Senses.* Cambridge, MA: MIT Press.

Stein, B. E., Meredith, M. A., Hunneycutt, W. S. and McDade, L. (1989) Behavioral indices of multisensory integration: Orientation to visual cues is affected by auditory stimuli. *Journal of Cognitive Neuroscience*, 1, 12–24.

Stein, M. B., Chavira, D. A. and Jang, K. L. (2001) Bringing up bashful baby: Developmental pathways to social phobia. *Psychiatric Clinics of North America*, 24, 661–75.

Stein, M. B., Chartier, M. J., Kozak, M. V. et al. (1998) Genetic linkage to the serotonin transporter protein and 5HT2A receptor genes excluded in generalized social phobia. *Psychiatry Research*, 81, 283–91.

Stein, Z., Susser, M., Saenger, G. and Marolla, F. (1975) *Famine and Development: The Dutch Hunger Winter of 1944–1945.* Oxford: OUP.

Steinbaum, E. A. and Miller, N. E. (1965) Obesity from eating elicited by daily stimulation of hypothalamus. *American Journal of Physiology*, 208, 1–5.

Steiner, F. (1986) Differentiating smiles. In E. Branniger-Huber and F. Steiner (eds) *FACS in Psychotherapy Research* (pp. 139–48). Zurich: Department of Clinical Psychology, University of Zurich.

Steiner, J. E. (1973) The gustofacial response: Observation on normal and anencephalic newborn infants. In J. F. Bosma (ed.) *Fourth Symposium on Oral Sensation and Perception: Development in the Fetus and Infant* (pp. 254–78). Bethesda, MD: US Department of Heath, Education, and Welfare.

Steiner, J. E. (1979) Human facial expressions in response to taste and smell stimulation. *Advances in Child Development and Behavior*, 13, 257–95.

Steinman, R. B., Pizlo, Z. and Pizlo, F. J. (2000) Phi is not beta, and why Wertheimer's discovery launched the Gestalt revolution. *Vision Research*, 40, 2257–64.

Stel, M., Blascovich, J., McCall, C. et al. (2010) Mimicking disliked others: Effects of a priori liking on the mimicry-liking link. *European Journal of Social Psychology*, 40, 867–80.

Stellar, J. R. and Stellar, E. (1985) *The Neurobiology of Motivation and Reward.* New York: Springer-Verlag.

Stellar, J. R., Kelley, A. E. and Corbett, D. (1983) Effects of peripheral and central dopamine blockade on lateral hypothalamic self-stimulation: Evidence for both reward and motor deficits. *Pharmacology, Biochemistry, and Behavior*, 18, 433–42.

Stelmack, R. M. (1990) Biological bases of extraversion: Psychophysiological evidence. *Journal of Personality*, 58, 293–311.

Stephens, R. S. (1999) Cannabis and hallucinogens. In B. S. McCrady and E. E. Epstein (eds) *Addictions: A Comprehensive Guidebook* (pp. 121–40). New York: OUP.

Sterelny, K. and Griffiths, P. E. (1999) *Sex and Death: An Introduction to Philosophy of Biology.* Chicago, IL: University of Chicago Press.

Stern, J. A., Brown, M., Ulett, A. and Sletten, I. (1977) A comparison of hypnosis, acupuncture, morphine, valium, aspirin, and placebo in the management of experimentally induced pain. In W. E. Edmonston (ed.) *Conceptual and Investigative Approaches to Hypnosis and Hypnotic Phenomena* (vol. 296, pp. 175–93). New York: Annals of the New York Academy of Sciences.

Stern, R. and Marks, I. (1973) Brief and prolonged flooding: A comparison in agoraphobic patients. *Archives of General Psychiatry*, 28, 270–6.

Stern, W. (1914) *The Psychological Methods of Testing Intelligence* (trans. G. M. Whipple). Baltimore: Warwick & York.

Sternberg, R. J. (1986) A triangular theory of love. *Psychological Review*, 93, 119–35.

Sternberg, R. J. (1999) Successful intelligence: Finding a balance. *Trends in Cognitive Sciences*, 3, 436–42.

Sternberg, R. J. (2001) What is the common thread of creativity? Its dialectical relation to intelligence and wisdom. *American Psychologist*, 56, 360–2.

Sternberg, R. J. and Grigorenko, E. L. (2002) *The General Factor of Intelligence: How General Is It?* Mahwah, NJ: Lawrence Erlbaum.

Stevens, J. (1988) An activity approach to practical memory. In M. M. Gruneberg, P. E. Morris and R. N. Sykes (eds) *Practical Aspects of Memory: Current Research and Issues* (vol. 1, pp. 335–41). New York: Wiley.

Stevens, L. A. (1971) *Explorers of the Brain.* New York: Knopf.

Stevenson, R. L. (1886) *Strange Case of Dr. Jekyll and Mr. Hyde.* London: Longmans, Green & Co.

Stewart-Williams, S. (2004) The placebo puzzle: Putting together the pieces. *Health Psychology*, 23, 198–206.

Stickgold, R., James, L. and Hobson, J. A. (2000a) Visual discrimination learning requires post-training sleep. *Nature Neuroscience*, 3, 1237–8.

Stickgold, R., Rittenhouse, C. D. and Hobson, J. A. (1994) Dream splicing: A new technique for assessing thematic coherence in subjective reports of mental activity. *Consciousness and Cognition*, 3, 114–28.

Stickgold, R., Hobson, J. A., Fosse, R. and Fosse, M. (2001) Sleep, learning, and dreams: Off-line memory reprocessing. *Science*, 294, 1052–7.

Stickgold, R., Malia, A., Maguire, D. et al. (2000b) Replaying the game: Hypnagogic images in normals and anmesics. *Science*, 290, 350–3.

Stigler, J. W., Shweder, R. and Herdt, G. (eds) (1990) *Cultural Psychology: Essays on Comparative Human Development.* Cambridge: CUP.

Stipek, D., Galinski, H. and Kopp, C. (1990) Self-concept development in the toddler years. *Developmental Psychology*, 26, 972–7.

Stone, J., Perry, Z. W. and Darley, J. M. (1997) 'White men can't jump': Evidence for the perceptual confirmation of racial stereotypes following a basketball game. *Basic and Applied Social Psychology*, 19, 291–306.

Storms, M. D. (1973) Videotape and the attribution process: Reversing actors' and observers' points of view. *Journal of Personality and Social Psychology*, 27, 165–75.

Stott, C., Adang, O., Livingstone, A. and Schreiber, M. (2008) Tackling football hooliganism: Quantitative study of public order, policing and crowd psychology. *Psychology, Public Policy, and Law*, 14, 115–41.

Strack, F., Martin, L. L. and Stepper, S. (1988a) Inhibiting and facilitating conditions of the human smile: A nonobtrusive test of the facial feedback hypothesis. *Journal of Personality and Social Psychology*, 54, 768–77.

Strack, F., Martin, L. L. and Schwarz, N. (1988b) Priming and communication: Social determinants of information use in judgments of life satisfaction. *European Journal of Social Psychology*, 18, 429–42.

Strahan, E. J., Spencer, S. J. and Zanna, M. P. (2002) Subliminal priming and persuasion: Striking while the iron is hot. *Journal of Experimental Social Psychology*, 38, 556–68.

Strayer, D. L., Drews, F. A. and Johnston, W. A. (2003) Cell phone-induced failures of visual attention during simulated driving. *Journal of Experimental Psychology: Applied*, 9(1), 23–32.

Strayer, D. L., Medeiros-Ward, N. and Watson, J. M. (2013) Gender invariance in multitasking: A comment on Mäntylä. *Psychological Science*, 24, 809–10.

Streissguth, A. P., Barr, H. M., Bookstein, F. L. et al. (1999) The long-term neurocognitive consequences of prenatal alcohol exposure: A 14-year study. *Psychological Science*, 10, 186–90.

Strickland, L. H. (1991) Russian and Soviet social psychology. *Canadian Psychology*, 32, 580–95.

Strohmetz, D. B., Rind, B., Fisher, R. and Lynn, M. (2002) Sweetening the till: The use of candy to increase restaurant tipping. *Journal of Applied Social Psychology*, 32, 300–9.

Stroop, J. R. (1935) Studies of interference in serial verbal reactions. *Journal of Experimental Psychology*, 18, 643–62.

Stuss, D. T. and Benson, D. F. (1986) *The Frontal Lobes.* New York: Raven Press.

Stuss, D. T., Craik, F. I., Sayer, L. et al. (1996) Comparison of older people with frontal lesions: Evidence from word list learning. *Neuropsychologia*, 37, 1005–27.

Subramaniam, K., Kounios, J., Parrish, T. B. and Jung-Beeman, M. (2009) A brain mechanism for facilitation of insight by positive affect. *Journal of Cognitive Neuroscience,* 21, 415–32.

Substance Abuse and Mental Health Services Administration (2005) *Suicide Warning Signs.* Washington, DC: US Department of Health and Human Services.

Suddendorf, T. and Corballis, M. C. (2007) The evolution of foresight: What is mental time travel and is it unique to humans? *Behavioral and Brain Sciences,* 30, 299–313.

Sue, S., Fujino, D. C., Hu, L. et al. (1991) Community mental health services for ethnic minority groups: A test of the cultural responsiveness hypothesis. *Journal of Counseling and Clinical Psychology*, 59, 533–40.

Sugita, Y. (2008) Face perception in monkeys reared with no exposure to faces. *Proceedings of the National Academy of Sciences*, 105, 394–8.

Sullivan, A. (2000) The he hormone. *New York Times Magazine*, 2 April, p. 46.

Sullivan, H. S. (1953) *The Interpersonal Theory of Psychiatry*. New York: Norton.

Sulloway, F. J. (1992) *Freud, Biologist of the Mind.* Cambridge, MA: Harvard University Press.

Suls, J. and Fletcher, B. (1985) The relative efficacy of avoidant and nonavoidant coping strategies: A meta-analysis. *Health Psychology*, 4, 249–88.

Summers, G. and Feldman, N. S. (1984) Blaming the victim versus blaming the perpetrator: An attributional analysis of spouse abuse. *Journal of Applied Social and Clinical Psychology*, 2, 339–47.

Sumner, W. (1906) *Folkways.* New York: Ginn.

Sundet, J. M., Borren, I. and Tambs, K. (2008) The Flynn effect is partly caused by changing fertility patterns. *Intelligence*, 36, 183–91.

Suomi, S. J. and Harlow, H. F. (1972) Social rehabilitation in isolate-reared monkeys. *Developmental Psychology*, 6, 487–96.

Susman, S., Dent, C., McAdams, L. et al. (1994) Group self-identification and adolescent cigarette smoking: A 1-year prospective study. *Journal of Abnormal Psychology*, 103, 576–80.

Susser, E. B., Brown, A. and Matte, T. D. (1999) Prenatal factors and adult mental and physical health. *Canadian Journal of Psychiatry*, 44(4), 326–34.

Sussman, L. K., Robins, L. N. and Earls, F. (1987) Treatment-seeking for depression by black and white Americans. *Social Science and Medicine*, 24, 187–96.

Sutton, R. and Douglas, K. (2013) *Social Psychology*. Basingstoke: Palgrave Macmillan.

Suzuki, L. A. and Valencia, R. R. (1997) Race-ethnicity and measured intelligence: Educational implications. *American Psychologist*, 52, 1103–14.

Svetlova, M., Nichols, S. R. and Brownell, C. A. (2013) Toddlers' prosocial behavior: From instrumental to empathic to altruistic helping. *Child Development*, 81, 1814–27.

Swann, W. B. (1983) Self-verification: Bringing social reality into harmony with the self. In J. M. Suls and A. G. Greenwald (eds) *Psychological Perspectives on the Self* (vol. 2, pp. 33–66). Hillsdale, NJ: Erlbaum.

Swann, W. B., Wenzlaff, R. M. and Tafarodi, R. W. (1992) Depression and the search for negative evaluations: More evidence of the role of self-verification strivings. *Journal of Abnormal Psychology*, 10, 314–17.

Swanson, J. W. (1994) Mental disorder, substance abuse, and community violence: An epidemiological approach. In J. Monahan and H. J. Steadman (eds) *Violence and Mental Disorder: Developments in Risk Assessment* (pp. 101–36). Chicago: University of Chicago Press.

Swayze, V. W. II (1995) Frontal leukotomy and related psychosurgical procedures before antipsychotics (1935–1954): A historical overview. *American Journal of Psychiatry*, 152, 505–15.

Swednsen, J., Hammen, C., Heller, T. and Gitlin, M. (1995) Correlates of stress reactivity in patients with bipolar disorder. *American Journal of Psychiatry*, 152, 795–7.

Swets, J. A., Dawes, R. M. and Monahan, J. (2000) Psychological science can improve diagnostic decisions. *Psychological Science in the Public Interest*, 1, 1–26.

Swinkels, A. (2003) An effective exercise for teaching cognitive heuristics. *Teaching of Psychology*, 30, 120–2.

Szasz, T. (1960) The myth of mental illness. *American Psychologist*, 15, 113–18.

Szechtman, H., Woody, E., Bowers, K. S. and Nahmias, C. (1998) Where the imaginal appears real: A positron emission tomography study of auditory hallucinations. *Proceedings of the National Academy of Sciences*, 95, 1956–60.

Szpunar, K. K., Watson, J. M. and McDermott, K. B. (2007) Neural substrates of envisioning the future. *Proceedings of the National Academy of Sciences*, 104, 642–7.

Tajfel, H. (1970) Experiments in intergroup discrimination. *Scientific American*, 223, 96–102.

Tajfel, H. (1978) Social categorization, social identity and social comparison. In H. Tajfel (ed.) *Differentiation Between Social Groups: Studies in the Social Psychology of Intergroup Relations* (pp. 61–78). London: Academic Press.

Tajfel, H. (1981) *Human Groups and Social Categories: Studies in Social Psychology*. Cambridge: CUP.

Tajfel, H. and Turner, J. C. (1986) The social identity theory of intergroup behavior. In S. Worchel and W. G. Austin (eds) *Psychology of Intergroup Relations* (pp. 7–24). Chicago: Nelson.

Tajfel, H. and Wilkes, A. L. (1963) Classification and quantitative judgement. *British Journal of Psychology*, 54, 101–14.

Tajfel, H., Billig, M. G., Bundy, R. P. and Flament, C. (1971) Social categorization and intergroup behaviour. *European Journal of Social Psychology*, 1, 149–78.

Takahashi, K. (1986) Examining the strange-situation procedure with Japanese mothers and 12-month-old infants. *Developmental Psychlogy*, 22, 265–70.

Tam, E. M., Lam, R. W. and Levitt, A. J. (1995) Treatment of seasonal affective disorder: A review. *Canadian Journal of Psychiatry*, 40, 457–66.

Tamminga, C. A., Nemeroff, C. B., Blakely, R. D. et al. (2002) Developing novel treatments for mood disorders: Accelerating discovery. *Biological Psychiatry*, 52, 589–609.

Tanaka, K. (1996) Inferotemporal cortex and object vision. *Annual Review of Neuroscience*, 19, 109–39.

Tang, Y.-P., Shimizu, E., Dube, G. R. et al. (1999) Genetic enhancement of learning and memory in mice. *Nature*, 401, 63–9.

Tang, Y. Y., Lu, Q., Fan, M. et al. (2012) Mechanisms of white matter changes induced by meditation. *Proceedings of the National Academy of Sciences*, 109, 10570–4.

Tang, Y. Y., Lu, Q., Geng, X. et al. (2010) Short-term meditation induces white matter changes in the anterior cingulate. *Proceedings of the National Academy of Sciences*, 107, 15649–52.

Tarr, M. J. and Vuong, Q. C. (2002) Visual object recognition. In S. Yantis and H. Pashler (eds) *Stevens' Handbook of Experimental Psychology*, vol. 1. *Sensation and Perception* (3rd edn, pp. 287–314). New York: Wiley.

Tarrier, N. and Turpin, G. (1992) Psychosocial factors, arousal and schizophrenic relapse: The physiological data. *British Journal of Psychiatry*, 161, 3–11.

Tart, C. T. (ed.) (1969) *Altered States of Consciousness.* New York: Wiley.

Task Force on Promotion and Dissemination of Psychological Procedures (1995) Training in and dissemination of empirically-validated psychological treatments: Report and recommendations. *Clinical Psychologist*, 48, 3–23.

Tavris, C. (1989) *Anger: The Misunderstood Emotion* (rev. edn). New York: Simon & Schuster.

Taylor, D. W., Berry, P. C. and Block, C. H. (1958) Does group participation when using brainstorming facilitate or inhibit creative thinking? *Administrative Science Quarterly*, 6, 22–47.

Taylor, E. (2001) *William James on Consciousness Beyond the Margin.* Princeton, NJ: Princeton University Press.

Taylor, L. D., Davis-Kean, P. and Malanchuck, O. (2007) Self-esteem, academic self-concept, and aggression at school. *Aggressive Behavior*, 33, 130–6.

Taylor, M. (1999) *Imaginary Companions and the Children Who Create Them*. New York: OUP.

Taylor, M. and Carlson, S. M. (1997) The relation between individual differences in fantasy and theory of mind. *Child Development*, 68, 436–55.

Taylor, M., Carlson, S. M., Maring, B. L. et al. (2004) The characteristics and correlates of fantasy in school-age children: Imaginary companions, impersonation and social understanding. *Developmental Psychology*, 40, 1173–87.

Taylor, S. E. (1989) *Positive Illusions.* New York: Basic Books.

Taylor, S. E. and Brown, J. D. (1988) Illusion and well-being: A social psychological perspective on mental health. *Psychological Bulletin*, 103, 193–210.

Taylor, S. E. and Fiske, S. T. (1975) Point-of-view and perceptions of causality. *Journal of Personality and Social Psychology*, 32, 439–45.

Taylor, S. E. and Fiske, S. T. (1978) Salience, attention, and attribution: Top of the head phenomena. In L. Berkowitz (ed.) *Advances in Experimental Social Psychology* (vol. 11, pp. 249–88). New York: Academic Press.

Teasdale, J. D., Segal, Z. V. and Williams, J. M. (2000) Prevention of relapse/recurrence in major depression by mindfulness-based cognitive therapy. *Journal of Consulting and Clinical Psychology*, 68, 615–23.

Telch, M. J., Lucas, J. A. and Nelson, P. (1989) Non-clinical panic in college students: An investigation of prevalence and symptomology. *Journal of Abnormal Psychology*, 98, 300–6.

Tellegen, A. and Atkinson, G. (1974) Openness to absorbing and self-altering experiences ('absorption'), a trait related to hypnotic susceptibility. *Journal of Abnormal Psychology*, 83, 268–77.

Tellegen, A., Lykken, D. T., Bouchard, T. J. et al. (1988) Personality similarity in twins reared together and apart. *Journal of Personality and Social Psychology*, 54, 1031–9.

Temerlin, M. K. and Trousdale, W. W. (1969) The social psychology of clinical diagnosis. *Psychotherapy: Theory, Research & Practice*, 6, 24–9.

Tempini, M. L., Price, C. J., Josephs, O. et al. (1998) The neural systems sustaining face and proper-name processing. *Brain*, 121, 2103–18.

Terman, L. M. (1916) *The Measurement of Intelligence.* Boston: Houghton Mifflin.

Terman, L. M. and Oden, M. H. (1959) *Genetic Studies of Genius*, vol. 5. *The Gifted Group at Mid-life.* Stanford, CA: Stanford University Press.

Terman, M., Terman, J. S., Quitkin, F. M. et al. (1989) Light therapy for seasonal affective disorder. A review of efficacy. *Neuropsychopharmacology*, 2, 1–22.

Tesser, A. (1991) Emotion in social comparison and reflection processes. In J. Suls and T. A. Wills (eds) *Social Comparison: Contemporary Theory and Research* (pp. 117–48). Hillsdale, NJ: Erlbaum.

Tesser, A. (1993) The importance of heritability in psychological research: The case of attitudes. *Psychological Review*, 100, 129–42.

Teyler, T. J. and DiScenna, P. (1986) The hippocampal memory indexing theory. *Behavioral Neuroscience*, 100, 147–54.

Thaker, G. K. (2002) Current progress in schizophrenia research. Search for genes of schizophrenia: Back to defining valid phenes. *Journal of Nervous and Mental Disease*, 190, 411–12.

Thaler, R. H. (1988) The ultimatum game. *Journal of Economic Perspectives*, 2, 195–206.

Tharp, R. G. (1991) Cultural diversity and treatment of children. *Journal of Counseling and Clinical Psychology*, 59, 799–812.

Thase, M. E. and Howland, R. H. (1995) Biological processes in depression: An updated review and integration. In E. E. Beckham and W. R. Leber (eds) *Handbook of Depression* (2nd edn, pp. 213–79). New York: Guilford Press.

Theophrastus (1929) Xapakthpe (The Characters) in *The Characters of Theophrastus*, (trans. J. M. Edmonds). London: William Heinemann.

Thibaut, J. W. and Kelley, H. H. (1959) *The Social Psychology of Groups.* New Brunswick, NJ: Transaction.

Thoma, S. J., Narvaez, D., Rest, J. and Derryberry, P. (1999) Does moral judgment development reduce to political attitudes or verbal ability? Evidence using the defining issues test. *Educational Psychology Review*, 11(4), 325–41.

Thomas, A. and Chess, S. (1989) Temperament and personality. In G. A. Kohnstamm, J. E. Bates and M. K. Rothbart (eds) *Temperament in Childhood* (pp. 249–61). New York: Wiley.

Thomas, G. V. (1981) Continguity, reinforcement rate and the law of effect. *Quarterly Journal of Experimental Psychology*, 33B, 33–43.

Thompson, C. P., Skowronski, J., Larsen, S. F. and Betz, A. (1996) *Autobiographical Memory: Remembering What and Remembering When.* Mahwah, NJ: Erlbaum.

Thompson, M. M., Naccarato, M. E., Parker, K. C. and Moskowitz, G. (2001a) The Personal Need for Structure (PNS) and Personal Fear of Invalidity (PFI) scales: Historical perspectives, present applications and future directions. In G. Moskowitz (ed.) *Cognitive Social Psychology: The Princeton Symposium on the Legacy and Future of Social Cognition* (pp. 19–39). Mahwah, NJ: Erlbaum.

Thompson, P. M., Giedd, J. N., Woods, R. P. et al. (2000) Growth patterns in the developing brain detected by using continuum mechanical tensor maps. *Nature*, 404, 190–3.

Thompson, P. M., Vidal, C., Giedd, J. N. et al. (2001b) Accelerated gray matter loss in very early-onset schizophrenia. *Proceedings of the National Academy of Science*, 98, 11650–5.

Thompson, R. A. (1998) Early sociopersonality development. In N. Eisenberg (ed.) *Handbook of Child Psychology*, vol. 3, *Social, Emotional and Personality Development* (5th edn, pp. 25–104). New York: Wiley.

Thompson, S. K. (1975) Gender labels and early sex-role development. *Child Development*, 46, 339–47.

Thomson, D. M. (1988) Context and false recognition. In G. M. Davies and D. M. Thomson (eds) *Memory in Context: Context in Memory* (pp. 285–304). Chichester: Wiley.

Thorell, L. B., Lindqvist, S., Nutley, S. B. et al. (2009) Training and transfer effects of executive functions in preschool children. *Developmental Science*, 12, 106–13.

Thorndike, E. L. (1898) Animal intelligence: An experimental study of associative processes in animals. *Psychological Review Monograph Supplements*, 2, 4–160.

Thorndike, E. L. (1920) A constant error in psychological ratings. *Journal of Applied Psychology*, 4, 25–9.

Thornhill, R. and Gangestad, S. W. (1993) Human facial beauty: Averageness, symmetry, and parasite resistance. *Human Nature*, 4, 237–69.

Thornhill, R. and Gangestad, S. W. (1999a) The scent of symmetry: A human sex pheromone that signals fitness? *Evolution and Human Behavior*, 20, 175–201.

Thornhill, R. and Gangestad, S. W. (1999b) Facial attractiveness. *Trends in Cognitive Sciences*, 3, 452–60.

Thornton, S. (2008) *Understanding Human Development*. Basingstoke: Palgrave Macmillan.

Thorpe, G. L. and Olson, S. L. (1997) *Behavior Therapy: Concepts, Procedures, and Applications*. Boston: Allyn & Bacon.

Thurber, J. (1956) *Further Fables of Our Time*. New York: Simon & Schuster.

Thurstone, L. L. (1938) *Primary Mental Abilities*. Chicago, IL: University of Chicago Press.

Tice, D. M. and Baumeister, R. F. (1997) Longitudinal study of procrastination, performance, stress, and health: The costs and benefits of dawdling. *Psychological Science*, 8(6), 454–58.

Tienari, P., Wynne, L. C., Sorri, A. et al. (2004) Genotype-environment interaction in schizophrenia-spectrum disorder: Long-term follow-up study of Finnish adoptees. *British Journal of Psychiatry*, 184, 216–22.

Timberlake, W. and Lucas, G. A. (1985) The basis of superstitious behavior: Chance contingency, stimulus substitution, or appetitive behavior? *Journal of Experimental Analysis of Behavior*, 44, 15–35.

Time (2005) Just how happy are we? *Time*, 17 January, A4.

Titchener, E. B. (1896) *An Outline of Psychology*. New York: Macmillan.

Titchener, E. B. (1898) The feeling of being stared at. *Science*, 8, 895–7.

Todd, J. T. and Morris, E. K. (1992) Case histories in the great power of steady misrepresentation. *American Psychologist*, 47(11), 1441–53.

Tolman, E. C. and Honzik, C. H. (1930a) Introduction and removal of reward and maze performance in rats. *University of California Publications in Psychology*, 4, 257–75.

Tolman, E. C. and Honzik, C. H. (1930b) 'Insight' in rats. *University of California Publications in Psychology*, 4, 215–32.

Tolman, E. C., Ritchie, B. F. and Kalish, D. (1946) Studies in spatial learning, I: Orientation and short cut. *Journal of Experimental Psychology*, 36, 13–24.

Tomarken, A. J., Simien, C. and Garber, J. (1994) Retesting frontal brain asymmetry discriminates adolescent children of depressed mothers from low-risk controls. *Psychophysiology*, 31, 97–8.

Tomkins, S. S. (1981) The role of facial response in the experience of emotion. *Journal of Personality and Social Psychology*, 40, 351–7.

Tooby, J. and Cosmides, L. (1990) The past explains the present: Emotional adaptations and the structure of ancestral environments. *Ethology and Sociobiology*, 11, 375–424.

Tooby, J. and Cosmides, L. (2000) Mapping the evolved functional organization of mind and brain. In M. S. Gazzaniga (ed.) *The Cognitive Neurosciences* (pp. 1185–98). Cambridge, MA: MIT Press.

Tootell, R. B., Reppas, J. B., Dale, A. M. et al. (1995) Visual-motion aftereffect in human cortical area MT revealed by functional magnetic resonance imaging. *Nature*, 375, 139–41.

Torgensen, S. (1983) Genetic factors in anxiety disorders. *Archives of General Psychiatry*, 40, 1085–9.

Torrey, E. F. (1994) Violent behavior by individuals with serious mental illness. *Hospital & Community Psychiatry*, 45, 653–62.

Torrey, E. F., Bower, A. E., Taylor, E. H. and Gottesman, I. I. (1994) *Schizophrenia and Manic-depressive Disorder: The Biological Roots of Mental Illness as Revealed by the Landmark Study of Identical Twins.* New York: Basic Books.

Trebach, A. S. and Zeese, K. B. (eds) (1992) *Friedman and Szasz on Liberty and Drugs: Essays on the Free Market and Prohibition.* Washington, DC: Drug Policy Foundation Press.

Treede, R. D., Kenshalo, D. R., Gracely, R. H. and Jones, A. K. (1999) The cortical representation of pain. *Pain*, 79, 105–11.

Treisman, A. (1964) Selective attention in man. *British Medical Bulletin*, 20, 12–16.

Treisman, A. (1998) Feature binding, attention and object percep-tion. *Philosophical Transactions of the Royal Society (B)*, 353, 1295–306.

Treisman, A. (2006) How the deployment of attention determines what we see. *Visual Cognition,* 14, 411–43.

Treisman, A. and Geffen, G. (1967) Selective attention: Perception or response? *Quarterly Journal of Experimental Psychology*, 19, 1–18.

Treisman, A. and Gelade, G. (1980) A feature integration theory of attention. *Cognitive Psychology,* 12, 97–136.

Treisman, A. and Schmidt, H. (1982) Illusory conjunctions in the perception of objects. *Cognitive Psychology,* 14, 107–41.

Triandis, H. C. (1995) *Individualism and Collectivism*. Boulder, CO: Westview Press.

Trickett, S. B., Trafton, J. G. and Schunn, C. D. (2009) How do scientists respond to anomalies? Different strategies used in basic and applied science. *Topics in Cognitive Science*, 1, 711–29.

Triplett, N. (1898) The dynamogenic factors in pacemaking and competition. *American Journal of Psychology*, 9, 507–33.

Trivers, R. L. (1972a) Parental investment and sexual selection. In B. Campbell (ed.) *Sexual Selection and the Descent of Man, 1871–1971* (pp. 139–79). Chicago: Aldine.

Trivers, R. L. (1972b) The evolution of reciprocal altruism. *The Quarterly Review of Biology*, 46, 35–57.

Trivers, R. L. (2011) *Deceit and Self-Deception: Fooling Yourself the Better to Fool Others*. London: Allen Lane.

Trull, T. J. and Durrett, C. A. (2005) Categorical and dimensional models of personality disorder. *Annual Review of Clinical Psychology*, 1, 355–80.

Trut, L., Oskina, I. and Kharlamova, A. (2009) Animal evolution during domestication: The domesticated fox as a model. *Bioessays*, 31, 349–60.

Tsien, J. (2000) Building a brainier mouse. *Scientific American*, 282, 62–8.

Tucker, E. (2003) Move over, Fido! Chickens are becoming hip suburban pets. *USA Today*, 25 June.

Tuerlinckx, F., de Boeck, P. and Lens, W. (2002) Measuring needs with the Thematic Apperception Test: A psychometric study. *Journal of Personality and Social Psychology*, 82, 448–61.

Tulving, E. (1972) Episodic and semantic memory. In E. Tulving and W. Donaldson (eds) *Organization of Memory* (pp. 381–403). New York: Academic Press.

Tulving, E. (1983) *Elements of Episodic Memory.* Oxford: Clarendon Press.

Tulving, E. (1985) Memory and consciousness. *Canadian Psychology*, 26, 1–12.

Tulving, E. (1998) Neurocognitive processes of human memory. In C. von Euler, I. Lundberg and R. Llins (eds) *Basic Mechanisms in Cognition and Language* (pp. 261–81). Amsterdam: Elsevier.

Tulving, E. and Pearlstone, Z. (1966) Availability versus accessibility of information in memory for words. *Journal of Verbal Learning & Verbal Behavior*, 5, 381–91.

Tulving, E. and Schacter, D. L. (1990) Priming and human memory systems. *Science*, 247, 301–6.

Tulving, E. and Thompson, D. M. (1973) Encoding specificity and retrieval processes in episodic memory. *Psychological Review*, 80, 352–73.

Tulving, E., Schacter, D. L. and Stark, H. (1982) Priming effects in word-fragment completion are independent of recognition memory. *Journal of Experimental Psychology: Learning, Memory, and Cognition*, 8, 336–42.

Tulving, E., Kapur, S., Craik, F. I. et al. (1994) Hemispheric encoding/retrieval asymmetry in episodic memory: Positron emission tomography findings. *Proceedings of the National Academy of Sciences*, 91, 2016–20.

Turkheimer, E. (2000) Three laws of behavior genetics and what they mean. *Current Directions in Psychological Science*, 9, 160–4.

Turkheimer, E. and Waldron, M. (2000) Nonshared environment: A theoretical, methodological, and quantitative review. *Psychological Bulletin*, 126, 78–108.

Turkheimer, E., Haley, A., Waldron, M. et al. (2003) Socioeconomic status modifies heritability of IQ in young children. *Psychological Science*, 14, 623–8.

Turkle, S. (1997) *Life on the Screen: Identity in the Age of the Internet.* New York: Simon & Schuster.

Turner, D. C. and Sahakian, B. J. (2006) Neuroethics of cognitive enhancement. *BioSocieties*, 1, 113–23.

Turner, D. C., Robbins, T. W., Clark, L. et al. (2003) Cognitive enhancing effects of modafinil in healthy volunteers. *Psychopharmacology*, 165, 260–9.

Turner, J. C., Hogg, M. A., Oakes, P. J. et al. (1987) *Rediscovering the Social Group: A Self-categorization Theory*. Oxford: Blackwell.

Turner, M. E. and Pratkanis, A. R. (1998) Twenty-five years of groupthink theory and research: Lessons from the evaluation of a theory. *Organizational Behavior and Human Decision Processes*, 73, 105–15.

Turner, R. H. and Killian, L. M. (1987) *Collective Behavior* (3rd edn). Englewood Cliffs, NJ: Prentice Hall.

Tversky, A. and Kahneman, D. (1973) Availability: A heuristic for judging frequency and probability. *Cognitive Psychology*, 5, 207–32.

Tversky, A. and Kahneman, D. (1974) Judgment under uncertainty: Heuristics and biases. *Science*, 185, 1124–31.

Tversky, A. and Kahneman, D. (1981) The framing of decisions and the psychology of choice. *Science*, 211, 453–8.

Tversky, A. and Kahneman, D. (1983) Extensional versus intuitive reasoning: The conjunction fallacy in probability judgment. *Psychological Review*, 90, 293–315.

Tversky, A. and Kahneman, D. (1992) Advances in prospect theory: Cumulative representation of uncertainty. *Journal of Risk and Uncertainty*, 5, 297–323.

Twenge, J. M., Campbell, W. K. and Foster, C. A. (2003) Parenthood and marital satisfaction: A meta-analytic review. *Journal of Marriage and Family*, 65, 574–83.

Tyler, T. R. (1990) *Why People Obey the Law.* New Haven, CT: Yale University Press.

Uematsu, T. (1970) Social facilitation of feeding behavior in fresh-water fish. I. *rhodeus, acheilognathus* and *rhinogobius*. *Annual of Animal Psychology*, 20, 87–95.

UNDP (United Nations Development Programme) (2009) *Annual Report*. New York: UNDP.

Ungerleider, L. G. and Mishkin, M. (1982) Two cortical visual systems. In D. J. Ingle, M. A. Goodale and R. J. Mansfield (eds) *Analysis of Visual Behavior* (pp. 549–86). Cambridge, MA: MIT Press.

UNODC (United Nations Office on Drugs and Crime) (2011) *World Drug Report 2011.* Vienna: UNODC.

Ursano, R. J. and Silberman, E. K. (2003) Psychoanalysis, psychoanalytic psychotherapy, and supportive psychotherapy. In R. E. Hales and S. C. Yudofsky (eds) *The American Psychiatric Publishing Textbook of Clinical Psychiatry* (4th edn, pp. 1177–203). Washington, DC: American Psychiatric Publishing.

Valenstein, E. S. (1973) *Brain Control: A Critical Examination of Brain Stimulation and Psychosurgery*. New York: Wiley.

Valenstein, E. S. (1986) *Great and Desperate Cures: The Rise and Decline of Psychosurgery and Other Radical Treatments for Mental Illness.* New York: Basic Books.

Valentine, T., Brennen, T. and Brédart, S. (1996) *The Cognitive Psychology of Proper Names: On the Importance of Being Ernest.* London: Routledge.

Valins, S. (1966) Cognitive effects of false heart-rate feedback. *Journal of Personality and Social Psychology*, 4, 400–8.

Vallacher, R. R. and Solodky, M. (1979) Objective self-awareness, standards of evaluation, and moral behavior. *Journal of Experimental Social Psychology*, 15, 254–62.

Vallacher, R. R. and Wegner, D. M. (1985) *A Theory of Action Identification.* Hillsdale, NJ: Erlbaum.

Vallacher, R. R. and Wegner, D. M. (1987) What do people think they're doing? Action identification and human behavior. *Psychological Review*, 94, 3–15.

Van Baaren, R. B., Holland, R. W., Kawakami, K. and van Knippenberg, A. (2004a) Mimicry and pro-social behaviour. *Psychological Science*, 15, 71–4.

Van Baaren, R. B., Holland, R. W., Steenaert, B., and van Knippenberg, A. (2003b) Mimicry for money: Behavioural consequences of imitation. *Journal of Experimental Social Psychology*, 39, 393–8.

Van Baaren, R.B., Horgan, R.W., Chartrand, T.L. and Dijkmans, M. (2004b) The forest, the trees and the chameleon: Context-dependency and mimicry. *Journal of Personality and Social Psychology*, 86, 453–9.

Van Baaren, R. B., Maddux, W. W., Chartrand, T. L. et al. (2003a) It takes two to mimic: Behavioural consequences of self-construals. *Journal of Personality and Social Psychology*, 84, 1093–102.

Vance, E. B. and Wagner, N. N. (1976) Written descriptions of orgasm: A study of sex differences. *Archives of Sexual Behavior*, 5, 87–98.

Van den Boon, D. C. (1994) The influence of temperament and mothering on attachment and exploration: An experimental manipulation of sensitive responsiveness among lower-class mothers with irritable infants. *Child Development*, 65, 1457–77.

Van den Boon, D. C. (1995) Do first year intervention effects endure? Follow-up during toddlerhood of a sample of Dutch irritable infants. *Child Development*, 66, 1798–816.

Vander Wall, S. B. (1982) An experimental analysis of cache recovery in Clark's nutcracker. *Animal Behaviour,* 30, 84–94.

Van Dick, R., Tissington, P. A. and Hertel, G. (2009) Do many hands make light work? How to overcome social loafing and gain motivation in work teams. *European Business Review*, 31, 233–45.

Van Dierendonck, M. C., De Vries, H. and Schilder, M. B. (1995) An analysis of dominance, its behavioural parameters and possible determinants in a herd of Icelandic horses in captivity. *Netherlands Journal of Zoology*, 45, 362–85.

Van Essen, D. C., Anderson, C. H. and Felleman, D. J. (1992) Information processing in the primate visual system: An integrated systems perspective. *Science*, 255, 419–23.

Van Gelder, J.-L., Herschfeld, H. E. and Nordgren, L. F. (2013) Vividness of the future self predicts delinquency. *Psychological Science*, 24, 974–80.

Van IJzendoorn, M. H. (1995) Adult attachment representations, parental responsiveness, and infant attachment: A meta-analysis on the predictive validity of the Adult Attachment Interview. *Psychological Bulletin*, 117, 387–403.

Van IJzendoorn, M. H. and Kroonenberg, P. M. (1988) Cross-cultural patterns of attachment: A meta-analysis of the strange situation. *Child Development*, 59, 147–56.

Van IJzendoorn, M. H. and Sagi, A. (1999) Cross-cultural patterns of attachment: Universal and contextual dimensions. In J. Cassidy and P. R. Shaver (eds) *Handbook of Attachment: Theory, Research and Clinical Applications* (pp. 713–34). New York: Guilford Press.

Van Praag, H. (2009) Exercise and the brain: Something to chew on. *Trends in Neuroscience*, 32, 283–90.

Van Stegeren, A. H., Everaerd, W., Cahill, L. et al. (1998) Memory for emotional events: Differential effects of centrally versus peripherally acting blocking agents. *Psychopharmacology*, 138, 305–10.

Vargha-Khadem, F., Gadian, D. G., Watkins, K. E. et al. (1997) Differential effects of early hippocampal pathology on episodic and semantic memory. *Science*, 277, 376–80.

Veltkamp, M., Aarts, H. and Custers, R. (2008) Perception in the service of goal pursuit: Motivation to attain goals enhances the perceived size of goal-instrument objects. *Social Cognition*, 26, 720–36.

Vendetti, M. S., Wu, A. and Holyoak, K. J. (2014) Far-out thinking: Generating solutions to distant analogies promotes relational thinking. *Psychological Science*, 25, 928–33.

Verona, E., Patrick, C. J. and Joiner, T. E. (2001) Psychopathy, antisocial personality and suicide risk. *Journal of Abnormal Psychology*, 110, 462–70.

Vitkus, J. (1996) *Casebook in Abnormal Psychology* (3rd edn). New York: McGraw-Hill.

Vitkus, J. (1999) *Casebook in Abnormal Psychology* (4th edn). New York: McGraw-Hill.

Vondra, J. I., Shaw, D. S., Swearingen, L., Cohen, M. and Owens, E. B. (2001) Attachment stability and emotional and behavioral regulation from infancy to preschool age. *Development and Psychopathology*, 13, 13–33.

Von Frisch, K. (1974) Decoding the language of the bee. *Science*, 185, 663–8.

Von Hippel, W. and Trivers, R. (2011) The evolution and psychology of self-deception. *Behavioral and Brain Sciences*, 34, 1–56.

Von Hofsten, C. (1979) Development of visually guided reaching: The approach phase. *Journal of Human Movement Studies*, 5, 160–78.

Von Mises, R. (1957) *Probability, Statistics and Truth*. London: Macmillan.

Von Restorff, H. (1933) Analyse von Vörgangen in Spurenfeld. I. Über die Wirkung von Bereichsbildung im Spurenfeld. *Psychologische Forschung*, 18, 299–342.

Von Wright, J. M., Anderson, K. and Stenman, U. (1975) Generalization of conditioned GSRs in dichotic listening. In P. M. Rabbitt and S. Dornic (eds) *Attention and Performance* (vol. 5, pp. 194–204). London: Academic Press.

Vortac, O. U., Edwards, M. B. and Manning, C. A. (1995) Functions of external cues in prospective memory. *Memory*, 3, 201–19.

Waddington, C. H. (1942) Canalization of development and the inheritance of acquired characters. *Nature*, 150, 563–5.

Waddington, C. H. (1957) *The Strategy of Genes*. London: Allen & Unwin.

Wade, N. J. (2005) *Perception and Illusion: Historical Perspectives*. New York: Springer.

Wade, T. D. and Bulik, C. M. (2007) Shared genetic and environmental risk factors between undue influence of body shape and weight on self-evaluation and dimensions of perfectionism. *Psychological Medicine*, 37, 635–44.

Wager, T. D., Rilling, J., K., Smith, E. E. et al. (2004) Placebo-induced changes in fMRI in the anticipation and experience of pain. *Science*, 303, 1162–7.

Wagner, A. D., Schacter, D. L., Rotte, M. et al. (1998) Remembering and forgetting of verbal experiences as predicted by brain activity. *Science*, 281, 1188–90.

Wagner, H. L., MacDonald, C. J. and Manstead, A. S. (1986) Communication of individual emotions by spontaneous facial expressions. *Journal of Personality and Social Psychology*, 50, 737–43.

Wagner, U., Gais, S., Haider, H. et al. (2004) Sleep inspires insight. *Nature*, 427, 352–5.

Wagstaff, G. (1981) *Hypnosis, Compliance and Belief*. London: Macmillan.

Wahba, M. A. and Bridwell, L. G. (1976) Maslow reconsidered: A review of research on the need hierarchy theory. *Organizational Behavior & Human Performance*, 15, 212–40.

Wahl, O. F. (1976) Monozygotic twins discordant for schizophrenia: A review. *Psychological Bulletin*, 83, 91–106.

Waite, L. J. (1995) Does marriage matter? *Demography*, 32, 483–507.

Wakslak, C. J., Nussbaum, S., Liberman, N. and Trope, Y. (2008) Representations of the self in the near and distant future. *Journal of Personality and Social Psychology*, 95, 757–73.

Walden, T. A. and Baxter, A. (1989) The effect on context and age on social referencing. *Child Development*, 60, 1511–18.

Waldmann, M. R. (2000) Competition among causes but not effects in predictive and diagnostic learning. *Journal of Experimental Psychology: Learning, Memory, and Cognition*, 26, 53–76.

Walker, C. M. and Gopnik, A. (2014) Toddlers infer higher-order relational principles in causal learning. *Psychological Science*, 25, 161–9.

Walker, L. J. (1988) The development of moral reasoning. *Annals of Child Development*, 55, 677–91.

Walker, N. P., McConville, P. M., Hunter, D. et al. (2002) Childhood mental ability and lifetime psychiatric contact: A 66-year follow-up study of the 1932 Scottish mental Survey. *Intelligence*, 30, 233–45.

Walker, P. and Smith, S. (1985) Stroop interference based on the multimodal correlates of haptic size and auditory pitch. *Perception*, 14, 729–36.

Walker, P., Bremner, J. G., Mason, U. et al. (2010) Preverbal infants' sensitivity to synaesthetic cross-modality correspondences. *Psychological Science*, 21, 21–5.

Walker, P., Bremner, J. G., Mason, U. et al. (2014) Preverbal infants are sensitive to cross-sensory correspondences: Much ado about the null results of Lewkowicz and Minar (2014). *Psychological Science*, 25, 835–6.

Wallace, J., Schnieder, T. and McGuffin, P. (2002) Genetics of depression. In I. H. Gottlieb and C. L. Hammen (eds) *Handbook of Depression* (pp. 169–91). New York: Guilford Press.

Wallbott, H. G. (1998) Bodily expression of emotion. *European Journal of Social Psychology*, 28, 879–96.

Wallerstein, J. S. and Lewis, J. (1998) The long-term impact of divorce on children: A first report from a 25-year study. *Family and Conciliation Courts Review*, 36, 368–83.

Walster, E., Aronson, V., Abrahams, D. and Rottmann, L. (1966) Importance of physical attractiveness in dating behavior. *Journal of Personality and Social Psychology*, 4, 508–16.

Walster, E., Walster, G. W. and Berscheid, E. (1978) *Equity: Theory and Research*. Boston: Allyn & Bacon.

Walton, D. N. (1990) What is reasoning? What is an argument? *Journal of Philosophy*, 87, 399–419.

Walton, K. E. and Roberts, B. W. (2004) On the relationship between substance use and personality traits: Abstainers are not maladjusted. *Journal of Research in Personality*, 38, 515–35.

Wang, L. H., McCarthy, G., Song, A. W. and LaBar, K. S. (2005) Amygdala activation to sad pictures during high-field (4 tesla) functional magnetic resonance imaging. *Emotion*, 5, 12–22.

Wang, M., Eccles, J. S. and Kenny, S. (2013) Not lack of ability but more choice: Individual and gender differences in choices of careers in science, technology, engineering and mathematics. *Psychological Science*, 24, 770–5.

Wang, Q. (2006) Relations of maternal style and child self-concept to autobiographical memory in Chinese, Chinese-immigrant and European American 3-year-olds. *Child Development*, 77, 1794–809.

Wang, R. F. and Spelke, E. S. (2002) Human spatial representation: Insights from animals. *Trends in Cognitive Science*, 6, 376–82.

Wann, D. L., Carlson, J. D., Holland, L. C. et al. (1999) Beliefs in symbolic catharsis: The importance of involvement in aggressive sports. *Social Behavior and Personality*, 27, 155–64.

Warburton, W. A., Williams, K. D. and Cairns, D. R. (2006) When ostracism leads to aggression: The moderating effects of control deprivation. *Journal of Experimental Social Psychology*, 42, 213–20.

Ward. J. (2008) *The Frog Who Croaked Blue: Synaesthesia and the Mixing of the Senses*. Routledge: Hove.

Ward, J., Parkin, A. J., Powell, G. et al. (1999) False recognition of unfamiliar people: 'Seeing film stars everywhere'. *Cognitive Neuropsychology*, 16, 293–315.

Warneken, F. and Tomasello, M. (2006), Altruistic helping in human infants and young chimpanzees. *Science*, 31, 1301–3.
Warrington, E. K. and McCarthy, R. A. (1983) Category specific access dysphasia. *Brain*, 106, 859–78.
Warrington, E. K. and Shallice, T. (1984) Category specific semantic impairments. *Brain*, 107, 829–54.
Washburn, M. F. (1908) *The Animal Mind: A Textbook of Comparative Psychology*. New York: Macmillan.
Watanabe, S., Sakamoto, J. and Wakita, M. (1995) Pigeons' discrimination of painting by Monet and Picasso. *Journal of the Experimental Analysis of Behavior*, 63, 165–74.
Waters, E. and Cummings, E. M. (2000) A secure base from which to explore close relationships. *Child Development*, 71, 164–73.
Watson, D. and Tellegen, A. (1985) Toward a consensual structure of mood. *Psychological Bulletin*, 98, 219–35.
Watson, J. B. (1913) Psychology as the behaviorist views it. *Psychological Review*, 20, 158–77.
Watson, J. B. (1924a) *Behaviorism.* New York: People's Institute.
Watson, J. B. (1924b) The unverbalized in human behavior. *Psychological Review*, 31, 339–47.
Watson, J. B. (1928) *Psychological Care of Infant and Child.* New York: Norton.
Watson, J. B. (1930) *Behaviorism* (rev. edn). Chicago, IL: University of Chicago Press.
Watson, J. B. and Rayner, R. (1920) Conditioned emotional reactions. *Journal of Experimental Psychology*, 3, 1–14.
Watson, R. I. (1978) *The Great Psychologists.* New York: Lippincott.
Watt, H. J. (1905) Experimentelle Beitraege zu einer Theorie des Denkens (Experimental contributions to a theory of thinking). *Archiv fuer die gesamte Psychologie*, 4, 289–436.
Watzlawick, P., Beavin, J. and Jackson, D. D. (1967) *Pragmatics of Human Communication: A Study of Interactional Patterns, Pathologies, and Paradoxes.* New York: Norton.
Wearing, D. (2005) *Forever Today: A Memoir of Love and Amnesia.* London: Corgi Books.
Weber, D., Skirbekk, V., Freund, I. and Herlitz, A. (2014) The changing face of cognitive gender differences in Europe. *Proceedings of the National Academy of Sciences*, 111(32), 11673–8.
Weber, R. and Crocker, J. (1983) Cognitive processes in the revision of stereotypic beliefs. *Journal of Personality and Social Psychology*, 45, 961–77.
Wegner, D. M. (1989) *White Bears and Other Unwanted Thoughts.* New York: Viking/Penguin.
Wegner, D. M. (1994a) Ironic processes of mental control. *Psychological Review*, 101, 34–52.
Wegner, D. M. (1994b) *White Bears and Other Unwanted Thoughts: Suppression, Obsession, and the Psychology of Mental Control.* New York: Guilford Press.
Wegner, D. M. (1997) Why the mind wanders. In J. D. Cohen and J. W. Schooler (eds) *Scientific Approaches to Consciousness* (pp. 295–315). Mahwah, NJ: Erlbaum.
Wegner, D. M. (2002) *The Illusion of Conscious Will.* Cambridge, MA: MIT Press.
Wegner, D. M. and Gilbert, D. T. (2000) Social psychology: The science of human experience. In H. Bless and J. Forgas (eds) *The Message Within: Subjective Experience in Social Cognition and Behavior* (pp. 1–9). Philadelphia: Psychology Press.
Wegner, D. M. and Pennebaker, J. W. (eds) (1993) *Handbook of Mental Control.* Englewood Cliffs, NJ: Prentice Hall.
Wegner, D. M. and Schaefer, D. (1978) The concentration of responsibility: An objective self-awareness analysis of group size effects in helping situations. *Journal of Personality and Social Psychology*, 36, 147–55.
Wegner, D. M. and Wheatley, T. (1999) Apparent mental causation: Sources of the experience of will. *American Psychologist*, 54, 480–92.
Wegner, D. M., Ansfield, M. and Pilloff, D. (1998) The putt and the pendulum: Ironic effects of the mental control of action. *Psychological Science*, 9, 196–9.
Wegner, D. M., Erber, R. E. and Zanakos, S. (1993) Ironic processes in the mental control of mood and mood-related thought. *Journal of Personality and Social Psychology*, 65, 1093–104.
Wegner, D. M., Wenzlaff, R. M. and Kozak, M. (2004) Dream rebound: The return of suppressed thoughts in dreams. *Psychological Science*, 15, 232–6.
Wegner, D. M., Schneider, D. J., Carter, S. R. and White, T. L. (1987) Paradoxical effects of thought suppression. *Journal of Personality and Social Psychology*, 53, 5–13.
Wegner, D. M., Vallacher, R. R., Macomber, G. et al. (1984) The emergence of action. *Journal of Personality and Social Psychology*, 46, 269–79.
Weinberg, R. A. (1989) Intelligence and IQ: Landmark issues and great debates. *American Psychologist*, 44, 98–104.
Weinberger, D. A., Schwartz, G. E. and Davidson, R. J. (1979) Low-anxious, high-anxious, and repressive coping styles: Psychometric patterns and behavioral and physiological responses to stress. *Journal of Abnormal Psychology*, 88, 369–80.
Weir, C., Toland, C., King, R. A. and Martin, L. M. (2005) Infant contingency/extinction performance after observing partial reinforcement. *Infancy*, 8, 63–80.
Weisfeld, G. (1999) *Evolutionary Principles of Human Adolescence.* New York: Basic Books.
Weiskrantz, L. (1956) Behavioral changes associated with ablation of the amygdaloid complex in monkeys. *Journal of Comparative and Physiological Psychology*, 4, 381–91.
Weiskrantz, L. (1986) *Blindsight: A Case Study and Implications.* Oxford: OUP.
Weiss, P. H., Zilles, K. and Fink, G. R. (2005) When visual perception causes feeling: Enhanced cross-modal processing in grapheme-color synesthesia. *Neuroimage,* 28, 859–68.
Weissenborn, R. (2000) State-dependent effects of alcohol on explicit memory: The role of semantic associations. *Psychopharmacology*, 149, 98–106.
Weissman, M. M., Bland, R. C., Canino, G. J. et al. (1997) The cross-national epidemiology of panic disorder. *Archives of General Psychiatry*, 54, 305–9.
Wellman, H. M. and Gelman, S. A. (1992) Cognitive development: Foundational theories of core domains. *Annual Review of Psychology*, 43, 337–75.
Wellman, H. M. and Woolley, J. D. (1990) From simple desires to ordinary beliefs: The early development of everyday psychology. *Cognition*, 35, 245–75.
Wellman, H. M., Cross, D. and Watson, J. (2001) Meta-analysis of theory-of-mind development: The truth about false belief. *Child Development*, 72, 655–84.
Wenzlaff, R. M. (2005) Seeking solace but finding despair: The persistence of intrusive thoughts in depression. In D. A. Clark (ed.) *Intrusive Thoughts in Clinical Disorders: Theory, Research, and Treatment* (pp. 54–85). New York: Guilford Press.
Wenzlaff, R. M. and Bates, D. E. (1998) Unmasking a cognitive vulnerability to depression: How lapses in mental control reveal depressive thinking. *Journal of Personality and Social Psychology*, 75, 1559–71.
Wenzlaff, R. M. and Eisenberg, A. R. (2001) Mental control after dysphoria: Evidence of a suppressed, depressive bias. *Behavior Therapy*, 32, 27–45.
Wenzlaff, R. M. and Grozier, S. A. (1988) Depression and the magnification of failure. *Journal of Abnormal Psychology*, 97, 90–3.
Wenzlaff, R. M. and Wegner, D. M. (2000) Thought suppression. In S. T. Fiske (ed.) *Annual Review of Psychology* (vol. 51, pp. 51–91). Palo Alto, CA: Annual Reviews.

Werker, J., Pegg, J. E. and McLeod, P. J. (1994) A cross-language investigation of infant preference for infant-directed communication. *Infant Behavior & Development*, 17, 323–33.

Wernicke, K. (1874) *Der Aphasische Symptomenkomplex*. Breslau: Cohn & Weigart.

Wertheimer, M. ([1945]1982) *Productive Thinking*. Chicago: University of Chicago Press.

Westen, D. (1991) Social cognition and object relations. *Psychological Bulletin*, 109, 429–55.

Wexler, K. (1999) Maturation and growth of grammar. In W. C. Ritchie and T. K. Bhatia (eds) *Handbook of Child Language Acquisition* (pp. 55–110). San Diego: Academic Press.

Whalen, P. J., Rauch, S. L., Etcoff, N. L. et al. (1998) Masked presentations of emotional facial expressions modulate amygdala activity without explicit knowledge. *Journal of Neuroscience*, 18, 411–18.

Whalley, L. J. and Deary, I. J. (2001) Longitudinal cohort study of childhood IQ and survival up to age 76. *British Medical Journal*, 322, 1–5.

Wheatley, T. and Haidt, J. (2005) Hypnotic disgust makes moral judgments more severe. *Psychological Science*, 16, 780–4.

Wheeler, M. A., Petersen, S. E. and Buckner, R. L. (2000) Memory's echo: Vivid recollection activates modality-specific cortex. *Proceedings of the National Academy of Sciences*, 97, 11125–9.

White, A. E., Kendrick, D. T. and Neuberg, S. L. (2013) Beauty at the ballot box: Disease threats predict preferences for physically attractive leaders. *Psychological Science*, 24, 2429–36.

White, B. L. (1985) *The First Three Years of Life*. Englewood Cliffs, NJ: Prentice Hall.

White, B. L. and Held, R. (1966) Plasticity of motor development in the human infant. In J. F. Rosenblith and W. Allinsmith (eds) *The Cause of Behavior* (pp. 60–70). Boston: Allyn & Bacon.

White, F. J. (1996) Synaptic regulation of mesocorticolimbic dopamine neurons. *Annual Review of Neuroscience*, 19, 405–36.

White, G. M. and Kirkpatrick, J. (eds) (1985) *Person, Self, and Experience: Exploring Pacific Ethnopsychologies*. Berkeley, CA: University of California Press.

White, N. M. and Milner, P. M. (1992) The psychobiology of reinforcers. *Annual Review of Psychology*, 41, 443–71.

Whitehurst, G. J., Falco, F. L., Lonigan, C. J. et al. (1988) Accelerating language development through picture book reading. *Developmental Psychology*, 24, 552–9.

WHO (World Health Organization) (1992) *ICD-10: The ICD-10 Classification of Mental and Behavioural Disorders: Clinical Descriptions and Diagnostic Guidelines*. Geneva: WHO.

WHO (2002) The ecological framework, www.who.int/violenceprevention/approach/ecology/en/.

WHO (2004) *International Statistical Classification of Diseases and Related Health Problems, 10th Revision*. Geneva: WHO.

WHO (2011) *Background of SUPRE: Prevention of Suicidal Behaviours: A Task for All*, www.who.int/mental_health/prevention/suicide/background/en/.

WHO (2015) Obesity and overweight, fact sheet 311, www.who.int/mediacentre/factsheets/fs311/en.

WHO (n.d.) The top 10 causes of death, www.who.int/mediacentre/factsheets/fs310/en/index2.html.

Whorf, B. (1956) *Language, Thought, and Reality*. Cambridge, MA: MIT Press.

Whybrow, P. C. (1997) *A Mood Apart*. New York: Basic Books.

Wicker, B., Keysers, C., Plailly, J. et al. (2003) Both of us disgusted in *my* insula: The common neural basis of seeing and feeling disgust. *Neuron*, 40, 655–64.

Widiger, T. A. (2001) The best and the worst of us? *Clinical Psychology: Science and Practice*, 8, 374–7.

Widiger, T. A. and Sankis, L. M. (2000) Adult psychopathology: Issues and controversies. *An Annual Review of Psychology*, 51, 377–404.

Wiederman, M. W. (1997) Pretending orgasm during sexual intercourse: Correlates in a sample of young adult women. *Journal of Sex & Marital Therapy*, 23, 131–9.

Wiener, D. N. (1996) *B. F. Skinner: Benign Anarchist*. Boston: Allyn & Bacon.

Wiesenthal, D. L., Austrom, D. and Silverman, I. (1983) Diffusion of responsibility in charitable donations. *Basic and Applied Social Psychology*, 4, 17–27.

Wiggs, C. L. and Martin, A. (1998) Properties and mechanisms of perceptual priming. *Current Opinion in Neurobiology*, 8, 227–33.

Wilcoxon, H. C., Dragoin, W. B. and Kral, P. A. (1971) Illness-induced aversions in rats and quail: Relative salience of visual and gustatory cues. *Science*, 171, 826–8.

Wiley, J. L. (1999) Cannabis: Discrimination of 'internal bliss'? *Pharmacology, Biochemistry and Behavior*, 64, 257–60.

Wilkins, A. J., Nimmo-Smith, M. I., Tait, A. et al. (1984) A neurological basis for visual discomfort. *Brain*, 107, 989–1017.

Will, J. A., Self, P. A. and Datan, N. (1976) Maternal behaviour and perceived sex of infant. *American Journal of Orthopsychiatry*, 46, 135–9.

Willatts, P. (1997) Beyond the 'couch potato' infant: How infants use their knowledge to regulate action, solve problems, and achieve goals. In J. G. Bremner, A. Slater and G. Butterworth (eds) *Infant Development: Recent Advances* (pp. 109–35). Hove: Psychology Press.

Wille, B. and De Fruyt, F. (2014) Vocations as a source of identity: Reciprocal relations between Big Five personality traits and RIASEC characteristics over 15 years. *Journal of Applied Psychology*, 99, 262–81.

Williams, C. M. and Kirkham, T. C. (1999) Anandamide induces overeating: Mediation by central cannabinoid (CB1) receptors. *Psychopharmacology*, 143, 315–17.

Williams, K. D. (2009) Ostracism: A temporal need-threat model. In M. Zanna (ed.) *Advances in Experimental Social Psychology* (vol. 41, pp. 279–314). New York: Academic Press.

Williams, K. D. and Nida, S. A. (2011) Ostracism: Consequences and coping. *Current Directions in Psychology*, 20, 71–5.

Williams, K. D., Cheung, C. K. and Choi, W. (2000) Cyber-ostracism: Effects of being ignored over the internet. *Journal of Personality and Social Psychology*, 79, 748–62.

Williams, S. E. and Horst, J. S. (2014) Goodnight book: Sleep consolidation improves word learning via storybooks. *Frontiers in Psychology*, 5, 184.

Willingham, W. W. and Cole, L. S. (1997) *Gender and Fair Assessment*. Mahwah, NJ: Erlbaum.

Wilson, B. and Smallwood, S. (2008) The proportion of marriages ending in divorce. *Population Trends*, 131, 28–6.

Wilson, M. and Dovidio, J. F. (1985) Effects of perceived attractiveness and feminist orientation on helping behavior. *Journal of Social Psychology*, 125(4), 415–20.

Wilson, T. D. (2002) *Strangers to Ourselves: Discovering the Adaptive Unconscious*. Cambridge, MA: Harvard University Press.

Wilson, T. D. and Gilbert, D. T. (2003) Affective forecasting. In M. P. Zanna (ed.) *Advances in Experimental Social Psychology* (vol. 35, pp. 345–411). New York: Elsevier.

Wilson, T. D. and Lassiter, G. D. (1982) Increasing intrinsic interest with superfluous extrinsic constraints. *Journal of Personality and Social Psychology*, 42, 811–19.

Wilson, T. D. and Schooler, J. W. (1991) Thinking too much: Introspection can reduce the quality of preferences and decisions. *Journal of Personality & Social Psychology*, 60, 181–92.

Wilson, T. D., Lindsey, S. and Schooler, T. Y. (2000b) A model of dual attitudes. *Psychological Review*, 107, 101–26.

Wilson, T. D., Centerbar, D. B., Kermer, D. A. and Gilbert, D. T. (2005) The pleasures of uncertainty: Prolonging positive moods in ways people do not anticipate. *Journal of Personality and Social Psychology*, 88, 5–21.

Wilson, T. D., Wheatley, T., Meyers, J. et al. (2000a) Focalism: A source of durability bias in affective forecasting. *Journal of Personality and Social Psychology*, 78, 821–36.

Wimmer, H. and Perner, J. (1983) Beliefs about beliefs: Representations and constraining function of wrong beliefs in young children's understanding of deception. *Cognition*, 13, 103–28.

Windeler, J. and Kobberling, J. (1986) Empirische Untersuchung zur Einschatzung diagnostischer Verfahren am Beispiel des Haemoccult-Tests (An empirical study of the value of diagnostic procedures using the example of the hemoccult test). *Klinische Wochenscrhrift*, 64, 1106–12.

Windham, G. C., Eaton, A. and Hopkins, B. (1999) Evidence for an association between environmental tobacco smoke exposure and birthweight: A meta-analysis and new data. *Pediatrics and Perinatal Epidemiology*, 13, 35–57.

Winerman, L. (2005) 'Thin slices' of life. APA *Monitor*, 36, 54–9

Winner, E. (1997) Exceptionally high intelligence and schooling. *American Psychologist*, 52, 1070–81.

Winnicott, D. W. (1953) Transitional objects and transitional phenomena: A study of the first not-me possession. *International Journal of Psychoanalysis*, 34, 89–97.

Winter, L. and Uleman, J. S. (1984) When are social judgments made? Evidence for the spontaneousness of trait inferences. *Journal of Personality and Social Psychology*, 47, 237–52.

Winterer, G. and Weinberger, D. R. (2004) Genes, dopamine and cortical signal-to-noise ratio in schizophrenia. *Trends in Neuroscience*, 27, 683–90.

Wise, R. A. (1989) Brain dopamine and reward. *Annual Review of Psychology*, 40, 191–225.

Wise, R. A. (2005) Forebrain substrates of reward and motivation. *Journal of Comparative Neurology*, 493, 115–21.

Wiseman, R. (1995) The Megalab truth test. *Nature*, 373, 391.

Wiseman, R. (2007) *Quirkology*. Basingstoke: Palgrave Macmillan.

Wittchen, H.-U. and Jacobi, F. (2005) Size and burden of mental disorders in Europe: A critical review and appraisal of 27 studies. *European Neuropsychopharmacology*, 15, 357–76.

Wittchen, H.-U., Knauper, B. and Kessler, R. C. (1994) Lifetime risk of depression. *British Journal of Psychiatry*, 165, 16–22.

Wittchen, H.-U., Jacobi, F., Rehm, J. et al. (2011) The size and burden of mental disorders and other disorders of the brain in Europe 2010. *European Neuropsychopharmacology*, 21, 655–79.

Wittgenstein, L. ([1953]1999) *Philosophical Investigations*. Upper Saddle River, NJ: Prentice Hall.

Wixted, J. T. and Ebbesen, E. (1991) On the form of forgetting. *Psychological Science*, 2, 409–15.

Wolff, G., Pathare, S., Craig, T. and Leff, J. (1996) Community knowledge of mental illness and reaction to mentally ill people. *British Journal of Psychiatry*, 168, 191–8.

Wollen, K. A., Weber, A. and Lowry, D. (1972) Bizarreness versus interaction of mental images as determinants of learning. *Cognitive Psychology*, 3, 518–23.

Wolpe, J. (1958) *Psychotherapy by Reciprocal Inhibition*. Stanford, CA: Stanford University Press.

Wong, D. T., Bymaster, F. P. and Engleman, E. A. (1995) Prozac (fluoxetine, Lilly 110140), the first selective serotonin uptake inhibitor and an antidepressant drug: Twenty years since its first publication. *Life Sciences*, 57, 411–41.

Wong, Y. and Tsai, J. L. (2007) Cultural models of shame and guilt. In J. Tracy, R. Robins and J. Tangney (eds) *Handbook of Self-Conscious Emotions* (pp. 210–23). New York: Guilford Press.

Wood, J. M. and Bootzin, R. R. (1990) Prevalence of nightmares and their independence from anxiety. *Journal of Abnormal Psychology*, 99, 64–8.

Wood, J. M., Nezworski, M. T. and Stejskal, W. J. (1996) The comprehensive system for the Rorschach: A critical examination. *Psychological Science*, 7, 3–10.

Wood, J. M., Nezworski, M. T., Lilienfeld, S. O. and Garb, H. N. (2003) *What's Wrong with the Rorschach? Science Confronts the Controversial Inkblot Test*. New York: Wiley.

Wood, J. M., Bootzin, R. R., Rosenhan, D. et al. (1992) Effects of the 1989 San Francisco earthquake on frequency and content of nightmares. *Journal of Abnormal Psychology*, 101, 219–24.

Wood, J. N. (2014) Newly hatched chicks solve the visual binding problem. *Psychological Science*, 25, 1475–81.

Wood, W., Lundgren, S., Ouellette, J. A. et al. (1994) Minority influence: A meta-analytic review of social influences processes. *Psychological Bulletin*, 115, 323–45.

Woodley, M. A., te Nijenhuis, J. and Murphy, R. (2013) Were the Victorians cleverer than us? The decline in general intelligence estimated from a meta-analysis of the slowing of simple reaction time. *Intelligence*, 41, 843–50.

Woodley, M. A., te Nijenhuis, J. and Murphy, R. (2014) Is there a dysgenic secular trend towards slowing simple reaction time? Responding to a quartet of critical commentary. *Intelligence*, 46, 137–47.

Woods, E. R., Lin, Y. G., Middleman, A. et al. (1997) The associations of suicide attempts in adolescents. *Pediatrics*, 99, 791–6.

Woods, S. C., Seeley, R. J., Porte, D. Jr and Schwartz, M. W. (1998) Signals that regulate food intake and energy homeostasis. *Science*, 280, 1378–83.

Woods, S. M., Natterson, J. and Silverman, J. (1966) Medical students' disease: hypochondriasis in medical education. *Journal of Medical Education*, 41, 785–90.

Woodward, A. L. (1998) Infants selectively encode the goal object of an actor's reach. *Cognition*, 69, 1–34.

Woody, S. R. and Sanderson, W. C. (1998) Manuals for empirically supported treatments: 1998 update. *Clinical Psychologist*, 51, 17–21.

Woolfe, T., Want, S. and Seigal, M. (2002) Signposts to development: Theory of mind in deaf children. *Child Development*, 73, 768–78.

Worchel, S., Rothgerber, H., Day, E. A. et al. (1998) Social identity and individual productivity with groups. *British Journal of Social Psychology*, 37, 389–13.

Wrangham, R. and Peterson, D. (1997) *Demonic Males: Apes and the Origin of Human Violence*. New York: Mariner.

Wren, A. M., Seal, L. J., Cohen, M. A. et al. (2001) Ghrelin enhances appetite and increases food intake in humans. *Journal of Clinical Endocrinology and Metabolism*, 86, 5992–5.

Wrenn, C. C., Turchi, J. N., Schlosser, S. et al. (2006) Performance of galanin transgenic mice in the 5-choice serial reaction time attentional task. *Pharmacology Biochemistry and Behavior*, 83, 428–40.

Wright, L. (1994) *Remembering Satan: A Case of Recovered Memory and the Shattering of an American Family*. New York: Knopf.

Wright, P., Takei, N., Rifkin, L. and Murray, R. M. (1995) Maternal influenza, obstetric complications, and schizophrenia. *American Journal of Psychiatry*, 152, 1714–20.

Wundt, W. (1874) *Grundzüge der physiologischen psychologie* (*Principles of Physiological Psychology*). Leipzig: Wilhelm Engelmann.

Wundt, W. (1900–20) *Völkerpsychologie* (*Social Psychology*), 10 vols. Leipzig: Engelmann & Kroner.

Wynn, K. (1992) Addition and subtraction by human infants. *Nature*, 358, 749–50.

Wynn, K. (2009) Constraints on natural altruism. *British Journal of Psychology*, 100, 481–5.

Xiaohe, X. and Whyte, K. J. (1990) Love matches and arranged marriages: A Chinese replication. *Journal of Marriage and the Family*, 52, 709–22.

Yamaguchi, S. (1998) Basic properties of umami and its effects in humans. *Physiology and Behavior*, 49, 833–41.

Yang, S. and Sternberg, R. J. (1997) Conceptions of intelligence in ancient Chinese philosophy. *Journal of Theoretical and Philosophical Psychology*, 17, 101–19.

Yarbus, A. L. (1967) *Eye Movements and Vision* (trans. B. Haigh). New York: Plenum Press.

Yardi, S. and Boyd, D. (2010) Dynamic debates: An analysis of group polarization over time on Twitter. *Bulletin of Science, Technology and Society*, 30, 316–27.

Yaro, C. and Ward, J. (2007) Searching for Shereshevevskii: What is superior about the memory of synaesthetes? *Quarterly Journal of Experimental Psychology*, 60, 682–96.

Yarrow, M. R., Scott, P. M. and Waxler, C. Z. (1973) Learning concern for others. *Developmental Psychology*, 8, 240–60.

Yeh, M., Takeuchi, D. T. and Sue, S. (1994) Asian-American children treated in the mental health system: A comparison of parallel and mainstream outpatient service centers. *Journal of Clinical Child Psychology*, 23, 5–12.

Yelsma, P. and Athappilly, K. (1988) Marital satisfaction and communication practices: Comparisons among Indian and American couples. *Journal of Comparative Family Studies*, 19, 37–53.

Yerkes, R. M. and Dodson, J. D. (1908) The relation of strength of stimulus to rapidity of habit-formation. *Journal of Comparative Neurology and Psychology*, 18, 459–82.

Yewchuk, C. (1985) Gifted/learning disabled children: An overview. *Gifted Education International*, 3, 122–6.

Yin, R. K. (1970) Face recognition by brain-injured patients: A dissociable ability. *Neuropsychologia*, 8, 395–402.

Yoon, G. and Vargas, P. T. (2014) The unintended effect of virtual-self representation on behavior. *Psychological Science*, 25, 1043–5.

Young, P. C. (1948) Antisocial uses of hypnosis. In L. M. LeCron (ed.) *Experimental Hypnosis* (pp. 376–409). New York: Macmillan.

Young, R. M. (1990) *Mind, Brain, and Adaptation in the Nineteenth Century: Cerebral Localization and its Biological Context from Gall to Ferrier.* New York: OUP.

Yuill, N. and Perner, J. (1988) Intentionality and knowledge in children's judgments of actor's responsibility and recipient's emotional reaction. *Developmental Psychology*, 24, 358–65.

Yule, G. (1997) *Referential Communication Tasks*. Mahwah, NJ: Erlbaum.

Zahn-Waxler, C. and Radke-Yarrow, M. (1990) The origins of empathic concern. *Motivation and Emotion*, 14, 107–30.

Zahn-Waxler, C., Radke-Yarrow, M., Wagner, E. and Chapman, M. (1992) Development of concern for others. *Developmental Psychology*, 28, 126–36.

Zaitchik, D. (1990) When representations conflict with reality: The preschooler's problem with false belief and 'false' photographs. *Cognition*, 35, 41–68.

Zajonc, R. B. (1965) Social facilitation. *Science*, 149, 269–74.

Zajonc, R. B. (1968) Attitudinal effects of mere exposure. *Journal of Personality and Social Psychology*, 9, 1–27.

Zajonc, R. B. (1980) Feeling and thinking: Preferences need no inferences. *American Psychologist*, 35, 151–75.

Zajonc, R. B. (1984) On the primacy of affect. In K. R. Scherer and P. Ekman (eds) *Approaches to Emotion* (pp. 259–70). Hillsdale, NJ: Erlbaum.

Zajonc, R. B. (1989) Feeling the facial efference: Implications of the vascular theory of emotion. *Psychological Review*, 96, 395–416.

Zaki, J., Schirmer, J. and Mitchell J. P. (2011) Social influence modulates the neural computation of value. *Psychological Science*, 22, 894–900.

Zampini, M. and Spence, C. (2005) The role of auditory cues in modulating the perceived crispness and staleness of potato chips. *Journal of Sensory Studies*, 19, 347–63.

Zebrowitz, L. A. and Montepare, J. M. (1992) Impressions of babyfaced individuals across the life span. *Developmental Psychology*, 28, 1143–52.

Zebrowitz, L. A., Hall, J. A., Murphy, N. A. and Rhodes, G. (2002) Looking smart and looking good: Facial cues to intelligence and their origins. *Personality and Social Psychology Bulletin*, 28, 238–49.

Zeki, S. (1993) *A Vision of the Brain.* London: Blackwell.

Zeki, S. (2001) Localization and globalization in conscious vision. *Annual Review of Neuroscience*, 24, 57–86.

Zelazo, P. D. and Carlson, S. M. (2012) Hot and cool executive function in childhood and adolescence: Development and plasticity. *Child Development Perspectives*, 6, 354–60.

Zenderland, L. (1998) *Measuring Minds: Henry Herbert Goddard and the Origins of American Intelligence Testing*. New York: CUP.

Zener, K. (1937) The significance of behaviour accompanying conditioned salivary secretion for theories of the conditioned response. *American Journal of Psychology,* 50, 384–403.

Zentall, T. R., Sutton, J. E. and Sherburne, L. M. (1996) True imitative learning in pigeons. *Psychological Science*, 7, 343–6.

Zhong, C., Bohns, V. and Gino, F. (2010) Good lamps are the best police: Darkness increases dishonesty and self-interested behavior. *Psychological Science*, 21, 311–14.

Zihl, J., von Cramon, D. and Mai, N. (1983) Selective disturbance of movement vision after bilateral brain damage. *Brain*, 106, 313–40.

Zillmann, D., Katcher, A. H. and Milavsky, B. (1972) Excitation transfer from physical exercise to subsequent aggressive behavior. *Journal of Experimental Psychology*, 8, 247–59.

Zimbardo, P. G. (1970) The human choice: Individuation, reason and order versus deindividuation, impulse and chaos. In W. J. Arnold and D. Levine (eds) *Nebraska Symposium and Motivation 1969* (vol. 17, pp. 237–307). Lincoln, NE: University of Nebraska Press.

Zimbardo, P. G. (2007) *The Lucifer Effect: How Good People Turn Evil.* London: Random House.

Zimmerman, F. J., Christakis, D. A. and Meltzoff, A. N. (2007) Associations between media viewing and language development in children under age 2 years. *Journal of Pediatrics*, 151, 364–8.

Zimprich, D. and Martin, M. (2002) Can longitudinal changes in processing speed explain longitudinal age changes in fluid intelligence? *Psychology and Aging*, 17, 690–5.

Zuckerman, M. (1975) Belief in a just world and altruistic behavior. *Journal of Personality and Social Psychology*, 31, 972–6.

Zuckerman, M. (2009) Sensation seeking. In M. R. Leary and R. H. Hoyle (eds) *Handbook of Individual Differences in Social Behavior* (pp. 455–65). New York: Guilford Press.

Zuckerman, M. and Driver, R. E. (1985) Telling lies: Verbal and nonverbal correlates of deception. In W. Seigman and S. Feldstein (eds) *Multichannel Integrations of Nonverbal Behavior* (pp. 129–47). Hillsdale, NJ: Erlbaum.

Zuckerman, M., Kolin, E. A., Price, L. and Zoob, I. (1964) Development of a sensation-seeking scale. *Journal of Consulting Psychology*, 28, 477–82.

Zulliger, H. (1941) *The Behn-Rorschach Test*. Bern: Hans Huber.

Name index

Subject index

Page numbers in **bold** refer to tables and in *italic* refer to figures.